ISBN 978-1-5285-3525-0
PIBN 10917240

1 MONTH OF
FREE
READING

at
www.ForgottenBooks.com

By purchasing this book you are eligible for one month membership to ForgottenBooks.com, giving you unlimited access to our entire collection of over 1,000,000 titles via our web site and mobile apps.

To claim your free month visit:
www.forgottenbooks.com/free917240

English
Français
Deutsche
Italiano
Español
Português

www.forgottenbooks.com

Mythology Photography **Fiction**
Fishing Christianity **Art** Cooking
Essays Buddhism Freemasonry
Medicine **Biology** Music **Ancient**
Egypt Evolution Carpentry Physics
Dance Geology **Mathematics** Fitness
Shakespeare **Folklore** Yoga Marketing
Confidence Immortality Biographies
Poetry **Psychology** Witchcraft
Electronics Chemistry History **Law**
Accounting **Philosophy** Anthropology
Alchemy Drama Quantum Mechanics
Atheism Sexual Health **Ancient History**
Entrepreneurship Languages Sport
Paleontology Needlework Islam
Metaphysics Investment Archaeology
Parenting Statistics Criminology
Motivational

APPLETONS'

ANNUAL CYCLOPÆDIA

AND

REGISTER OF IMPORTANT EVENTS

OF THE YEAR

1879.

EMBRACING POLITICAL, CIVIL, MILITARY, AND SOCIAL AFFAIRS; PUBLIC DOCU-
MENTS; BIOGRAPHY, STATISTICS, COMMERCE, FINANCE, LITERATURE,
SCIENCE, AGRICULTURE, AND MECHANICAL INDUSTRY.

NEW SERIES, VOL. IV.

WHOLE SERIES, VOL. XIX.

NEW YORK:
D. APPLETON AND COMPANY,
1, 3 AND 5 BOND STREET.
1883.

PREFACE.

The "Annual Cyclopædia" for 1879 has grown into a larger volume than usual from the multitudinous events of a year unusually prolific in legislative action and political changes, and teeming with vitality in the various fields of scientific progress and mechanical development, religious activity, industrial advancement, and commercial transition, which come within the scope of a work which aims to be a complete record of the current history of the United States and of the world, and a register of every fact or occurrence which forms an influential factor in modern civilization.

The articles on the States are lengthened beyond their usual compass by exceptionally important legislation transacted and pending upon the regulation of railroad, insurance, and other corporations; upon temperance, convict-labor, tramps, Chinese immigration, and the different elements of the labor question; upon the regulation of the ballot and the question of the Federal control of elections; upon the question of paying or not paying State and municipal debts, and other subjects of moment. The Legislatures of the individual States are the arenas in which most of the socio-political questions, which in other countries make the great national issues, are fought out; and as the "Annual Cyclopædia" is the only full and comprehensive chronicle of this most momentous portion of the country's history, it must not allow any important acts of legislation, nor any decision of the courts concerning them, or subjects of political agitation, to pass unrecorded. Full and interesting data are given this year upon the industrial and agricultural condition of many of the States, as well as the usual reports of public affairs, statistical information, and record of party action. In CALIFORNIA a synopsis of the new Constitution is found. In MAINE and in PUBLIC DOCUMENTS the documents relating to the election difficulty are given at length. In TENNESSEE, ALABAMA, and VIRGINIA, the debt questions are unfolded; in MINNESOTA and FLORIDA, the question of railroad land-grants; and in other States, whatever subjects are uppermost in the public mind. In separate articles the EXODUS OF THE COLORED PEOPLE and the YELLOW FEVER are thoroughly discussed. In CONGRESS the debates on the anti-Chinese and election investigation bills, and the conflicts over the army and judicial appropriation bills in their successive phases, are very fully reported, with the entire texts of the President's vetoes. The NATIONAL BOARD OF HEALTH is explained in a timely article.

The high value and authority of the exhaustive monographs on the MARINE HOSPITAL SERVICE, the SIGNAL SERVICE, the RESUMPTION OF SPECIE PAYMENTS, and REFUNDING THE PUBLIC DEBT will be appreciated by every reader. Every word in these articles carries the weight of the authority of men who are best qualified and best entitled to speak upon these important institutions and achieve. ments of the national Government—who themselves were *magna pars* in their development. The historical account of the marine hospitals is from the pen of Surgeon-General Dr. John B. Hamilton, the head of the service. The clear and full exposition of the workings of the Meteorological Division of the Signal Service was prepared under the supervision of General Albert J. Myer, Chief Signal Officer. The succinct but complete expositions of the great fiscal achievements of refunding and resumption have for their author J. K. Upton, the present Assistant Secretary of the Treasury.

The "Cyclopædia" is as full as ever of religious information. In EVANGELICAL ALLIANCE the acts of that association are recounted ; in BRAHMO SOMAJ the reform movement among the Brahmans is explained ; and a review of each Church is given under the name of the denomination.

The political history and statistical survey of the different nations of. the earth are as complete as in former years. The Perry laws in France, the tariff reform in Germany, and the leading questions and legislative results in other countries are amply discussed. The Nihilistic troubles are recounted and explained in RUSSIA and NIHILISM. The origin and events of the war in Zooloo-land are described in CAPE COLONY, and the rise and growth of the Zooloo nation in ZOOLOOS ; the history of the South American war is narrated in BOLIVIA and PERU ; of the Afghan war, in AFGHANISTAN and INDIA ; of the Russian expedition into Turkistan, in RUSSIA ; of the Burmese horrors, in BURMAH. In EGYPT the developments of the debt question and the deposition of the Khedive are related. The visitation of the plague in Russia is given in PLAGUE, and a description of the Isthmus Canal scheme and of the various plans and routes in INTEROCEANIC CANAL. The newly erected autonomous states in Turkey are described in BULGARIA and EASTERN ROUMELIA, and sketches of their rulers under their names. This volume is behind none of its predecessors in the department of biography.

The articles on COMMERCE and the commercial statistics presented under the several countries afford a survey of the trade of all nations, and a mass of information upon commerce and industry which can hardly be found elsewhere.

Besides the customary comprehensive scientific articles, there are special ones on the more prominent subjects of recent research and discovery. The article on GEOGRAPHICAL EXPLORATION is more detailed than usual ; the portion relating to Arctic discovery is a valuable contribution from the pen of Captain Howgate.

With the unusually profuse illustrations of this volume it is hoped that nowhere will be felt the want of a map, a diagram, or a drawing which would make the text clearer. There are steel portraits of President Grévy of the French Republic, Speaker Randall, and Secretary Sherman. A glance through the index will show that the present volume is not merely a larger, but that it is a fuller book than usual. As indicated above, uncommon pains have been taken to render the "Annual Cyclopædia," as far as possible, rounder and more cyclopædic in character.

THE
ANNUAL CYCLOPÆDIA.

A

ABD-EL-KADER (properly Sidi el-Hadji Abd el-Kader Uled Mahiddin), a distinguished Arab chief, and one of the most prominent representatives of Mohammedanism in the nineteenth century; born near Mascara in Algeria about 1807, died in Damascus in November, 1879. By a pilgrimage to Mecca, which he made together with his father, who was a marabout (Arab seer), as well as by his studies at the University of Fez, he gained a reputation for piety and the title el-Hadji, the pilgrim. The conquest of Algeria by the French, however, made of the future priest a warrior. Upon the recommendation of his father the people elected him Ameer of Mascara, and he soon, by his perseverance, indomitable courage, and patriotism, gained the love and confidence of the Kabyles to a high degree. In 1832 and 1833 he was engaged in a war with France, and, although repeatedly defeated, finally compelled the French to conclude the treaty of February 26, 1834, by which his sovereignty was acknowledged, and he was permitted to buy arms in France. He next subjugated the native tribes, extending his authority over the entire provinces of Titeri and Oran. In the following year he again waged war against the French, defeating General Trézel on the Makta, June 28, 1835, and General d'Arlanges on the Tafua, April 25, 1836; and he continued his guerrilla struggle with such success that the French, who were then contemplating the capture of Constantine, in order to gain time for this undertaking, made another treaty with him on May 30, 1837, in which they recognized his authority under the nominal sovereignty of France, and by which he was intrusted with the administration of the provinces of Oran, Titeri, and Algeria, with the exception of the capitals and the Metidja of Algiers. In 1839 he renewed the war against France; but this time the French were more successful, so that in 1842 he was compelled to seek refuge in Morocco. Abd-er-Raham, the Sultan of Morocco, received him; but, be-

fore the Sultan had made up his mind what to do, he had involved Morocco in a war with France, which was short and decisive. In the battle of Isly, August 14, 1844, the Moors were completely defeated, and, fearing Abd-el-Kader's influence in Morocco, the Sultan concluded peace with France, and Abd-el-Kader was again a fugitive. Stirring up revolt in Morocco itself, he defeated the troops of the Sultan in several battles. The power against him was too strong, however, and on December 21, 1847, he was forced to enter French territory, and on the following day surrendered to General Lamoricière. The General promised to send him to Egypt or to Syria, and the Duke d'Aumale confirmed this promise. This pledge was broken by the Government of Louis Philippe, and he was retained in captivity for many years. President Louis Napoleon, however, released him in 1852, after he had sworn on the Koran not to oppose the French rule in Africa. He then took up his abode in Brussa, and afterward in Damascus, where he exerted himself strongly in favor of the Christians at the time of the Syrian massacres of 1860, for which he received the grand cross of the Legion of Honor. Louis Napoleon allowed him a pension of 100,000 francs, which was reduced in 1879. He visited the Paris Exposition and England in 1867, and in 1870 offered his services to France against Germany. In 1871 Abd-el-Kader submitted to the Government of Thiers some suggestions relative to reforms in the administration of Algeria. Since that time but little has been heard of him. He was known to live a retired life in Damascus, devoting his time to religious duties, the education of his children, and literary pursuits. Though one of the boldest, bravest, and most intrepid defenders of decaying Mohammedanism against the victorious advance of Christian nations, Abd-el-Kader was by no means an obstinate opponent of modern civilization, but showed an eagerness to learn from his victors. Ever since 1852 he was on the best terms with

France; he became an advocate of the principle of religious toleration, and joined the order of Freemasonry. He did not renounce polygamy, but in his retirement at Damascus had three wives. Most of his numerous children died before their father, and one of his daughters became a Christian. A religio-philosophical work, which he wrote in Arabic in his retirement, was well received, and translated by Dugat into French under the title "Rappel à l'Intelligent, Avis à l'Indifférent" (Paris, 1858).

Special works on Abd-el-Kader have been published by Laménaire, "Vie, Aventures, Combats et Prise d'Abd-el-Kader" (Paris, 1848), and Bellemare, "Abd-el-Kader Sa Vie Politique et Militaire" (Paris, 1863).

ABYSSINIA,[*] a country of Eastern Africa, the boundaries of which continue to be unsettled. The area of Abyssinia proper, which was formerly said to comprise the three important states of Tigré, Amhara, and Shoa, is estimated by Behm and Wagner ("Bevölkerung der Erde," vol. v.) at about 158,000 square miles; the population is believed to be from 3,000,000 to 5,000,000. The larger portion of this country is governed by King John (formerly known as Prince Kassai), while Shoa is under the government of King Menelek. The son of the late King Theodore, Prince Almayoo, who after the death of his father was sent to England to receive there a careful education, died at Leeds on November 24, 1879.

As the King of Abyssinia lays claim to large territories which have of late been annexed to Egypt, especially the port of Massowa, the two countries have been for years on unfriendly terms. In 1879 the Government of Egypt sent Gordon Pasha on a special mission to King John to settle the pending difficulties peaceably. The King refused to accept the propositions made by Gordon Pasha, and threatened to invade Egypt. (See EGYPT.)

An Egyptian functionary, Zobir Pasha, who was ruler of Darfoor before the annexation of this country to Egypt, gave in September to an American writer the following account of the situation of affairs in Abyssinia:

King John has now reduced to obedience his two vassal kings, Menelek and Wold-Mikail. The King knows well that by order of the Sultan at Constantinople the Egyptian army is reduced to 18,000 men. The King knows also that Gordon Pasha has left Cairo with papers from England and France forbidding Abyssinia to make war with Egypt. But will not England and France also prevent Egypt from going to war with Abyssinia? Munzinger Pasha stole for Egypt the country of the Bogos. King John then took back by force a part of this territory. Ismail Pasha then sent three expeditions against Abyssinia. The first, commanded by Munzinger Pasha and consisting of 2,000 men, was annihilated by King John, and Munzinger himself killed. The second, consisting of 1,800 men, shared a like fate, and its commander, Colonel Arendrup, was killed, together with Count Zichy and Arakel Bey, the son-in-law of Nubar Pasha.

See "Annual Cyclopædia" of 1877, art. ABYSSINIA. On the former history of King John, see "Annual Cyclopædia" of 1873 and 1875.

The third expedition, consisting of over 20,000 men, magnificently equipped and provided with a large European and American staff, was also defeated and driven from the land. Soon after the defeat of this third Egyptian army, Menelek, King of the Shoa country, broke out into revolt in the south, and was aided by King Wold-Mikail in the north. King John hastened to put down these formidable revolts, and in the mean time the Egyptians stole back again the Bogos country. But now Menelek and Wold-Mikail are friends with King John, and have taken wives from his family; and, mark well my words, King John will get back the Bogos country (a fertile district on the north and northwest frontiers of Abyssinia) by fair means or by foul, or he will perish in the attempt. Who will prevent him? Egypt can not, and King John does not believe that England and France will go to war with him to prevent his taking back from Egypt what rightly belongs to him.

King Menelek of Shoa, the southern part of Abyssinia, in August informed the British Anti-Slavery Society that he had abolished the slave-trade throughout his dominions. In December the relations between Menelek and the King of Abyssinia were reported to be critical, because Menelek has failed to pay his annual tribute.

ADULTERATION. The Governments of Germany, Belgium, and other European countries have in recent years taken active steps to suppress adulteration and the use of deleterious substances, more particularly in foods or in articles where a direct noxious effect upon the public health results. In Great Britain the health authorities are empowered to suppress the sale of articles of food containing injurious ingredients. In the different American States special acts have been passed relative to debased or adulterated food articles. In the State of New York dealers in artificial butter are compelled to label it as such, and strict measures have been taken to put a stop to the adulteration or reduction of milk. No general laws have been enacted, however, to suppress the debasement or falsification of commercial commodities, or even of food products, a kind of fraud to which the larger portion of the mercantile community are themselves unwilling parties. This subject has been called to the attention of the public frequently of late by chemists, microscopists, and physicians; but the deadly effects of some of the materials from which articles of daily use are manufactured, and the extent to which the adulteration of foods, beverages, and medicines is carried on, according to the testimony of expert analysts, is hardly conceived of by the general public. Dr. Kedzie, President of the State Board of Health of Michigan, has officially warned the people of that State of two very dangerous sources of disease and death in the reckless employment of poisonous materials in manufactures—arsenic to color wall-papers and to dye clothing materials, and lead in the sheet-tin of which cheap cooking vessels are made. In the report of the Canadian Commissioners of Inland Revenue for 1877 it is stated that out of 180 specimens of groceries 93 were found by analysis to be adulterated.

In the report of the Massachusetts Board of Health for 1874 the most common adulterations were enumerated. George T. Angell, who read a paper on the subject of adulterations and poisonous materials before the Social Science Association at Saratoga, was informed by an eminent physician of Boston that patients frequently die because the prescriptions are made up of adulterated drugs and fail of their effect; and a large wholesale dealer and a retail druggist of the same city stated to him that the adulteration of medicines is so universal that no profits could be made on the sale of pure articles.

Nearly all groceries are adulterated very commonly in the United States. Teas are not only frequently adulterated before they arrive in America, but are colored and faced by the admixture of poisonous substances in the United States, large factories existing for this purpose in New York and Philadelphia: one of the processes involves the use of prussic acid; the commonest coloring materials and adulterants employed are arseniate of copper, verdigris, mineral-green, Prussian blue, talc, clay, and soapstone. In England the sale and even the landing of adulterated teas are now stringently prevented. The exclusion of adulterated China teas from the English market naturally causes their importation into the United States to increase. The Japan teas as they are prepared for the retail trade are said to be quite as frequently adulterated and artificially colored as the others. A great number of substances are used to adulterate the coffee which is purchased in a ground state: pea-flour colored with Venetian red is often used; but the commonest adulterant is chiccory, which is itself almost invariably debased by the admixture of various articles, some of them of a highly injurious character. A machine has been invented and is used for molding spurious coffee-berries out of an artificial paste. The article called essence of coffee is composed of various coloring materials. The adulteration of sirups and sugars with glucose is a practice which has recently spread alarmingly. The extensive use of glucose, or the grape-sugar of commerce, is held to be the main origin of Bright's disease of the kidneys, and the cause of the present prevalence of that fatal malady. The importations of glucose increased tenfold between 1875 and 1877, and at the same time extensive factories were established for its manufacture in the Western States. The article sold as grape-sugar is manufactured by boiling corn-starch with sulphuric acid (oil of vitriol), and mixing the product with lime. A portion of the sulphuric acid, and sometimes copperas, sulphate of lime, and other noxious principles, remain in the glucose. In the analysis of seventeen samples of table sirup by Dr. Kedzie, fifteen were found to be made of glucose, one of them containing 141 grains of oil of vitriol and 724 grains of lime to the gallon, and one from a lot which had sickened a whole family contained 72 grains of vitriol, 28 of sulphate of iron (copperas), and 363 of lime to the gallon. The cheap sugars sold in Michigan are stated on the same authority to be adulterated and colored with poisonous substances. Analyses of the sugar sold in New York reveal the presence not only of glucose with its inherent poisons, but of muriate of tin, a formidable poison which is employed in the bleaching process. Mr. Fuller, a retired importer of sugar, called the attention of the United States Board of Trade, in their meeting held at New York in November, 1878, to the dangerous adulterations practiced with sugar, honey, and molasses. Glucose is largely used also to adulterate maple-sugar, candies, jellies, honey, and other sweet foods. Ground stone is undoubtedly used to adulterate sugar and other groceries. It is said that mills are in operation in various parts of the United States in which white stone is ground into dust of varying fineness, which is classified into the soda grade, the sugar grade, and the flour grade. A practice which is now exceedingly common, and is being rigorously suppressed in Great Britain, is the use of alum in bread. The various baking-powders sold now are said to be largely composed of alum, the price of which is less than 3 cents per pound, while cream of tartar costs 30 cents or more. The effects of alum used in this way are colic, constipation, heart-burn, and dyspepsia. The New York chemist, Dr. Henry Mott, Jr., on analyzing sixteen different powders, found alum a very considerable ingredient in every one; some of them contained also terra alba, insoluble phosphate of lime, and other foreign substances. The cream of tartar sold in the shops is seldom found to contain more than 30 per cent. of genuine cream of tartar. It is principally adulterated with terra alba, which produces destructive effects on the stomach and kidneys. Of the milk sold in the larger American cities, 90 to 95 per cent. is said to be reduced with water. This water is supposed to frequently contain the germs of malarial infection, or to be frequently impregnated with lead-poison, and therefore to be a very common cause of infant mortality. The lactometer and creamometer are said to be entirely inefficient to detect adulteration. Cream is made with gums and white glue; and the consistency, taste, and color of watered milk are restored with flour, starch, gum, sugar, carbonate of soda, and the brains of animals. Oleomargarine, which is now extensively manufactured from animal fats as a substitute for butter, is dreaded as a vehicle for infecting the human system with trichinæ and other internal parasites. The fat is not subjected to a higher temperature than 120° F. John Michels, a New York chemist, states that the refuse fat of one pork-packing establishment is to his knowledge sent to the artificial butter factories; and Professor Church found in oleomargarine horse-fat, fat from bones, and waste fat, such as is ordinarily used in making candles. The precautions against the sale of the meat of diseased animals are declared to be anything but sufficient. The adulterations of wines and liquors have often been exposed to the public: coarse rums, potato spirits, and not infrequently wood alcohol, are used as the foundation of liquors and wines ; sulphuric acid is employed in the manufacture of port, sherry, and madeira wines, and of pale malt. At least half of the vinegar sold in the cities is said to contain active poisons: preparations of lead, copper, and sulphuric acid are used in its manufacture. Confectionery is colored with poisonous materials, to which more than once the attention of the public has been directed : cochineal, red lead, and bichromate of lead are used to produce the red 'and pink colors ; chromate of lead, gamboge, turmeric, and Naples yellow to color yellow ; litmus, indigo, Prussian blue, carbonate of copper, and other colors for the blues ; acetate of copper, arseniate of copper, emerald-green, Scheele's green, and Brunswick green for the green shades ; while weight is imparted by terra alba, chalk, and such substances. Soap is often colored with irritating skin-poisons. Olive oil is one of the most universally adulterated articles, and is most frequently made of oil extracted from hemp, rape, cotton, or mustard seed, or from the peanut. Bright green pickles, colored as they are with acetate of copper, have been the cause of frequent cases of poisoning. Mustard is almost never pure. The different pungent table sauces are often flavored with noxious chemicals. Cayenne pepper is adulterated with cinnabar, vermilion, and sulphuret of copper, and colored with red lead and Venetian red. Cocoa is weighted with sulphate or carbonate of lime, and colored with red lead, vermilion, and ocher.

The most insidious and deadly results of the reckless use of poisons in manufactures probably arise from the extensive use of arsenic for colors and dyes, and the use of lead in food-vessels. The amount of arsenic imported into the United States every year would furnish deadly doses enough to kill six times as many human beings as make up the present population of the earth. It is sold in the market at $1\frac{1}{4}$ to 2 cents a pound, and is handled like coal or stone. This terrible mineral furnishes the color for innumerable articles of every-day use —lamp-shades, fancy wrapping papers, tickets, artificial flowers, dried grasses, eye-shades—so that in nearly every house and every room the fine particles of this poison are floating in the air, finding their way into the human system, and producing their sickening and debilitating effects. Various materials of clothing—dress-goods, veils, sewing-silks, stockings, gentlemen's underwear, gloves, linings of hats and of boots and shoes—are colored with arsenic. Professor Nichols of the Massachusetts Institute of Technology found 8 grains of arsenic in every square foot of a ladies' dress pattern ; 10 grains have been detected in a single artifi-

cial flower. A veil thrown over the crib of an infant recently caused its death ; gentlemen have been severely poisoned by the arsenic contained in their underclothing. Arsenic has been found in toilet powders and in candles, and is used to color all sorts of fabrics. But the most extensive and most injurious application of the destructive agent is to color wall-papers. A great variety of colors—green, blue, red, yellow, and all their shades—are produced and employed on all grades and styles of paper-hangings. A book exhibiting 75 specimens of arsenic-containing wall-papers, to which the impressive title of "Shadows from the Walls of Death" was given, was published and distributed by the Board of Health of Michigan to warn the people against the use of such papers. A great number of deaths and innumerable cases of poisoning are supposed to have resulted from such poisonous wall-hangings. The arsenical papers, it is stated, are for sale in every town and village in the State. The citizens are advised to buy no paper without having it first tested for arsenic, and, in case their walls are already covered with poisonous hangings which can not easily be removed, to coat them with varnish as affording a certain measure of protection.

Lead-poisoning is supposed to have become in the most recent period a still more prevalent, though subtiler and more insidious, cause of suffering and death than arsenical poisoning. Lead is a cumulative poison, and the least particles gathering consecutively in the system retain their baneful powers until quantities have been taken sufficient to produce disease, paralysis, and death. The dangers from drinking water which has been conducted through lead pipes has been often impressed upon the people by medical authors. Pipes of galvanized iron are said to be quite as bad as lead pipes. A still more dangerous source of lead-poisoning has lately been introduced to the attention of the public. The tin vessels which are used in every household to hold milk and other fluids, and often for cooking purposes, are said to be made, not of pure tin, but more frequently of an alloy of tin and lead. The lead is easily decomposed by acids, and salts of lead become mixed with the food or drink. A Michigan physician found that a number of cases which had been taken for chorea were in reality *paralysis agitans* caused by this kind of lead-poisoning. Many cases of the death of children from meningitis, fits, and paralytic affections were traced to the same cause, the children having imbibed the poison in milk which had been kept in cans of this alloy, the acid of the milk having dissolved the lead. Fruit acids will act much quicker upon the alloy. An examination of a large number of tin vessels by the Michigan Board of Health showed that nearly every sample contained lead alloy, and many of them a large proportion of lead. Dr. Emil Querner of Philadelphia, in testing a large number of tin vessels, found lead in every specimen. The use of sheet-iron vessels instead of tin plate is on this account advised. The marbleized iron-ware, which was popular a few years ago, is not so much used since a professor of Harvard University pronounced it to be alive with poison.

ADVENTISTS. SEVENTH-DAY ADVENTISTS. —The following is a summary of the statistics of the Seventh-Day Adventists for the year ending November 7, 1879:

CONFERENCES.	Ministers.	Churches.	Members.
Maine............................	3	18	826
Vermont.........................	8	18	892
New England....................	8	24	508
New York........................	11	33	655
Pennsylvania...................	8	12	800
Ohio..............................	8	23	674
Michigan........................	22	94	3,175
Indiana..........................	4	21	422
Wisconsin.......................	12	52	1,107
Illinois..........................	9	34	676
Minnesota.......................	17	58	968
Iowa.............................	18	55	1,202
Nebraska........................	3	28	298
Dakota...........................	1	10	200
Missouri.........................	2	14	898
Kansas...........................	5	34	700
California.......................	7	31	740
Kentucky........................	1	8	76
Tennessee.......................	1	5	54
Oregon..........................	3	9	225
Texas............................	1	4	250
General Southern Mission......	..	3	68
Nevada Mission.................	..	2	45
European Mission..............	2	16	223
Danish Mission in Europe.......	2	6	141
Ontario Mission.................	1	2	70
Province of Quebec Mission.....	1	3	73
Colorado Mission	..	2	55
Virginia Mission................	1	..	55
Wyoming........................	..	..	70
Total......................	144	599	14,141

The number of ministers was 27; of churches, 50; of members, 1,064, greater than in 1878. The number of licentiates was 151, or 3 less than in 1878. The amount of moneys pledged to the Systematic Benevolence Fund was $51,-714, or $4,076 more than in 1878.

The *General Conference* of the Seventh-Day Adventists met in its eighteenth annual session at Battle Creek, Michigan, November 7th. Twenty conferences and two missions were represented by thirty-nine delegates. The Conference Treasurer reported that his receipts and expenditures for the year had been respectively $8,848. A committee, who had been appointed by the previous General Conference to look after a number of Russian "Sabbath-keepers" who had settled in Dakota, reported that they had been found to be holding fast to their principles, and were anxious to become identified with the denomination. The denomination attaches importance to a gift of prophecy which it believes to be possessed by Mrs. E. G. White, and several sessions of the Conference were devoted to the consideration of the subject. The report which was adopted upon it declared that the past experience of the denomination had fully proved "that our prosperity as a people is always in proportion to the degree of confidence we cherish in the

work of the spirit of prophecy in our midst; that the most bitter opposition it had to meet was aimed against this work, showing that its enemies realized the importance of the same; and that great light had shone upon it through this channel. It also recommended several measures for the publication and more extensive circulation of the writings of Mrs. White, particularly the volumes of the "Spirit of Prophecy" and the "Testimonies of the Church," and declared it to be the duty of the ministers to teach the "Scriptural view of the gift of prophecy" and of the relation it sustains to the work of God. Resolutions were adopted expressing the opinion, as the sense of the Conference, "that none but those who are Scripturally ordained are properly qualified to administer baptism and other ordinances," and that it is "inconsistent for our Conferences to grant credentials to individuals to occupy official positions among our people who have never been ordained or set apart *by* our people." A committee was appointed to consider the subject of the proper qualification of ministers, and report to the next meeting of the Conference. A Mission Board of nine members was constituted, and charged with the special oversight of all the foreign missions of the denomination, which is to report annually to the General Conference. The Conference resolved that it was the duty of all members of the denomination to become members of the American Health and Temperance Association, and to induce others to do the same; that health and temperance clubs ought to be formed in every church; that persons should be encouraged to fit themselves to engage in health and temperance work; that ministers especially should prepare themselves to present these subjects and make it a part of their work; and "that it should not be considered that any minister has fully discharged his duty in any new field where a company of Sabbath-keepers has been raised up, until he has fully advocated, in public and in private, the subjects of health and temperance and spiritual gifts, and organized systematic benevolence; and a failure in this shall be considered worthy of censure."

The twentieth annual meeting of the *Seventh Day Adventist Publishing Association* was held at Battle Creek, Michigan, November 11th. The Treasurer reported that the Association possessed property to the value of $215,237, and that its assets over the amount of indebtedness were $103,712, showing an increase of net assets during the year of $4,599. The receipts for the year had been $284,799. The Association published a general religious newspaper, the "Advent Review and Sabbath Herald," papers in the Danish, Swedish, and German languages, a health journal, a monthly and a weekly paper for youth, lesson-sheets for Sabbath-schools, and books and tracts. The periodicals had in all 23,133 subscribers; the total amount of issues of books and tracts during the year had been 14,274,560 pages.

The fifth annual meeting of the *Seventh-Day Advent Educational Society* was held at Battle Creek, Michigan, November 9th. The Treasurer reported that the property of the Society amounted to $52,758 in value, and that its net assets after all indebtedness was paid would be $46,423. The receipts for the year had been $9,416. The institution at Battle Creek had been attended by 426 students. Three new departments, a normal department, or teacher's institute, commercial, and primary departments had been added. The debt of the institution was continually decreasing, and would be reduced to about $6,000, or one half of what it was in 1875, during the present year.

AFGHANISTAN, a Mohammedan country in Central Asia; area, about 278,000 square miles; population, about 4,000,000. The recent war between this country and England, and the views which both England and Russia are supposed to entertain with regard to the annexation of parts of its territory, have attracted the attention of the entire civilized world to Afghanistan, which has hitherto belonged to the least known parts of Asia. The Government of British India has for years made incessant efforts to obtain accurate information about Afghanistan, not only through its military expeditions and diplomatic missions, but through numerous travelers and explorers whom it has supported. These efforts to explore the unknown country have required many sacrifices. Stoddard, who was the first to cross the mountains from Herat to Bokhara, and Arthur Connolly, who pursued a new way from Cabool, by way of Merv, to Khiva, Khokand, and Bokhara, perished in 1841 in Bokhara. Edward Connolly, the first discoverer of Seistan, was shot from an unknown fort in Kohistan. Dr. Lord, the companion of Wood in the valley of the Oxus, was assassinated about the same time. Dr. Forbes was murdered in 1841 in Seistan. Lieutenant Pattinson, who was the first to explore the middle and lower valley of the Helmund, was killed by the mutinous Jan-bas in Candahar. Colonel Sanders, who had drawn an excellent map of the region between Candahar and the Hasareh Mountains, was slain a few years later at Maharajpoor. Eldred Pottinger, who twice crossed the mountains between Cabool and Herat, escaped the massacre of Cabool and the danger of an imprisonment by the Afghans, but died soon after of yellow fever in Hong Kong. Alexander Burnes, one of the most distinguished geographical explorers, was one of the first victims of the rising in Cabool. The most important of the English explorations in Afghanistan are laid down in the collective work, "Central Asia," compiled for Political and Military Reference." A synopsis of all the recent explorations is given by F. von Stein, in Petermann's "Mittheilungen," 1878, I., and 1879, I. and II.

The boundaries of Afghanistan have never been fixed. The frontier which separates the Afghan territory of Herat from the Persian province of Seistan in the southwest, and from Beloochistan in the south, was regulated in 1872 by an English commission of arbitration. In 1873 Russia and England agreed upon the northern frontier of Afghanistan, which was to embrace Badakshan with the dependent district Wakhan, the districts of Koondooz, Khooloom, and Balkh, and the interior districts of Akhshee, Siripal, Maymene, Shibergan, and Anjai. The eastern frontier, which separates it from British India, is likewise fixed, but the Afghan tribes which live east of it can not be relied upon, and frequently make it insecure. The frontier between Afghanistan and Kafiristan has never been settled, and the English maps generally leave it unmarked.

The administrative division of the country was made by Dost Mohammed, who tried to unite the multitudinous independent tribes in an organic whole, and organized the three provinces of Caboolistan in the northeast, Herat in the west, and Candahar in the southeast. The former contains the capital of the country, with the residence of the Ameer, who is accustomed to appoint his nearest relatives governors of the two other provinces. The provinces north of the Hindoo Koosh and its western continuations are treated as conquered lands, and constitute the four administrative districts of Badakshan, Khooloom, Balkh, and Anjai. The governors of all these provinces are appointed by the Ameer, and the Governor of Balkh is regarded as governor-general, the three other governors being dependent upon him.

Afghanistan has not many cities. The capital, Cabool, is situated about 6,000 feet high, and is strongly fortified by nature, being only accessible from one side. The residence of the Ameer, Shere Ali, was in the fort Bala-Hissar. On October 4, 1874, an earthquake destroyed about a thousand houses, and greatly added to the wretched aspect of the city. The number of inhabitants is estimated at 60,000. The city of Candahar is only a shadow of what it was in former times. About twenty miles from the city are the ruins of the city of Alexandria, which was built by Alexander the Great. The present population of Candahar probably does not exceed 15,000, though according to some it is from 60,000 to 80,000. In May, 1874, a part of the city wall fell down, destroyed four hundred houses, and killed many persons. Herat is the chief station on the great road that leads from India to Persia, and as such has long been an apple of discord between the Persians and Afghans. The English regard Herat as so important that they interfered when it was threatened in 1837 by the Persian Shah Mohammed. In 1856 they even began a war against Persia in order to prevent it from occupying Herat. Ghuznee, northeast of Candahar, was the residence of the first Mohammedan dynasty which ruled in India. It was captured by the English in 1839, and again in 1842, and Shere Ali defeated his brother here in 1868, and secured to himself the rule over Afghanistan.

Their language as well as their physical constitution prove the Afghans to belong to the Aryan race. They are a well-formed, handsome, intelligent people, free from Oriental ignorance and indolence. Almost every village has a mollah, who is at the same time school-teacher and reader in the mosque. The boys quite generally learn to read, to write, and to say the common prayers, and it is believed that about one fourth of the entire population is in possession of an elementary education. The instruction is given in the Afghan language, but the boys also learn Persian, which is the literary language in Cabool, Candahar, and Peshawer, as well as the colloquial language of the higher classes, and is spoken in the western districts almost exclusively. The schools in the towns are very good, and their courses of instruction embrace Persian and Arabic. The high school of Peshawer, which embraced the whole course of Mohammedan science, was celebrated throughout Central Asia. Nearly all the Afghans are Sunnite Mohammedans; the educated classes are tolerant, and, inclining toward Sufism, sometimes exhibit considerable indifference in regard to the Koran.

A full account of the British-Indian campaign against Afghanistan to the end of 1878 was given in the "Annual Cyclopædia" for that year, and mention was made of the ending of the active campaign with the capture of Candahar on the 9th of January. At the end of 1878 the British-Indian forces had marched by three columns into the Afghan country, and had seized the principal passes leading to the important stations of Candahar, Cabool, and Jelalabad. Shere Ali, having become convinced that reliance could not be placed on his troops, had fled after the capture of Fort Ali Musjid and the Peiwan, leaving Yakoob Khan in charge of his capital; and the capture of Jelalabad, December 20th, placed the country substantially at the mercy of the invading force. It was for some time doubtful where Shere Ali had gone, and contradictory reports were in circulation on the subject. It appeared from information which afterward reached the Viceroy of India that, when his military condition had become critical, he held a durbar, at which the chiefs agreed that effective resistance was not practicable, and the Ameer decided to seek the protection of the Russians. Yakoob Khan was released from confinement and placed in control, an oath having been administered to him that he would do as the Ameer might direct; and the Ameer left Cabool on the 13th of December. The Afghan envoys who had been sent to the Russian General Kaufmann at Tashkend held a farewell interview with him about the 1st of January, when the General informed them that the Czar absolutely refused to intervene in the affairs of Afghanis-

tan. Two or three days later General Kaufmann received a letter from General Rasgonoff, the Russian agent at Cabool, stating that he had left Cabool with the Ameer for the Russian frontier. General Kaufmann had telegraphed to Prince Gortchakoff for instructions, and had advised that the Ameer be received if he crossed the Russian frontier. Shere Ali left affairs at Cabool in a disordered state. His authority, according to the accounts received from there, had almost disappeared, and Yakoob Khan had difficulty in securing himself in his new position, and there appeared danger for some time that he would be overthrown before he could adopt any definite attitude with respect to the invasion.

The British advance against Candahar was begun on the 31st of December, 1878, when a large part of General Stewart's division marched through the Ghamaja Pass, and General Biddulph's division crossed the Khojek pass. The two bodies met at Tuk-i-Put, at the junction of the two passes, and on the 6th or 7th of January their advanced cavalry encountered the Afghan cavalry, 600 strong, and easily defeated them, with a loss of 34 killed and prisoners, and 4 wounded on the British side. The enemy fled toward Candahar. On the 8th the advancing force was met by two deputations from Candahar. One deputation, representing the townsfolk, reported that the governor of the town had fled with an escort of troops to Herat, taking with him most of the civil officers and a sum of money, and that the rest of the army had fled on receiving the news of the defeat at Tuk-i-Put; and they stated that the people were prepared to open their gates on the arrival of the columns. The other deputation was from the deputy-governor, tendering a formal surrender of the city. On the next day the British entered the city, the first brigade of General Stewart's division and the first of General Biddulph's moving together. The march proved a difficult one, for the dikes by the roadside had been broken and the road was flooded; but the people were quiet, and the troops were well received. The large Hindoo colony dwelling in the town welcomed them, it was said, with delight. Candahar is described by a special correspondent who was with General Stewart's column as "less a great city than a collection of numerous walled villages lying in an oblong plain, intersected every fifty yards by watercourses, and surrounded by a common wall. It is encircled by abrupt stony hills. It possesses no good streets practicable for wheeled vehicles, and in empty spaces within the walls are many rugged trees, and some large sapling plantations, which assist in destroying its appearance as a great city. The mud walls encircling it are of great height and thickness, and are in a state of fair repair. The bastions and towers described as existing in 1840 have now entirely disappeared." The condition of the citadel indicated that military

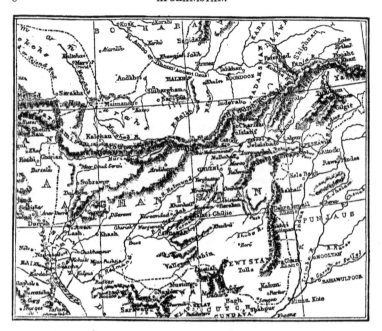

preparations of a rough nature had been made to stand a siege, when the news of the skirmish at Tuk-i-Put caused an entire change of plans.

General Roberts, after annexing the Kuram Valley, advanced into the Khost Valley, in an endeavor to make a new route into Afghanistan. At Bukk, the governor of the province sent in an officer to announce his surrender. At Yakubi, which General Roberts reached January 6th, the deputy-governor of Khost came to pay his respects to the British commander, and transferred to him the forts and records. Notwithstanding these favorable signs, his force was in a critical position. Large numbers of Mangals were hovering around the camps in a threatening manner, and the men were obliged to sleep on their arms. On the 7th, in anticipation of an attack in the night, General Roberts went out against the Mangals, and defeated them after a brisk action. A reconnaissance was made of the southern and western extremities of the valley, and a promise was gained from the people that they would not give the British any trouble. The Mangals, however, continued to maintain a threatening attitude, and a return to the Kuram Valley was decided upon. Before leaving Khost, General Roberts called the chiefs of the valley to a durbar at Matoond

January 22d. Announcing to them his intended withdrawal, he pointed out to them that the British arms had been successful everywhere, that resistance to its progress was hopeless, that neither Shere Ali nor Yakoob Khan could reign at Cabool unless he accepted the British terms, and that it was idle to entertain any hope of Russian assistance. On the next day he marched to Subbery, twelve miles distant, leaving Sultan Jan as the British representative at Matoond. On the following day news arrived that the Mangals were threatening the fort. A force was dispatched back to Matoond, who found the hills swarming with Afghans. General Roberts rescued his representative, stripped the fort, burned the stores, and marched back to his camp, allowing it to be announced that he had abandoued Khost for the present, convinced that similar disturbances would be incessant. Wali Mahomed, a half brother of Shere Ali, tendered his submission, and was received by General Roberts at a durbar held for the purpose.

While these movements were going on, a band of Mazud Waziris, a tribe who did not acknowledge the rule of the Ameer, made an incursion into British territory, and plundered and burned the frontier town of Tank. Reënforcements were sent to the neighborhood to prevent a repetition of the outrage, who made attacks upon the marauders and finally cut them off.

The general demeanor of the inhabitants of Candahar after the occupation of the city was quiet; nevertheless, two attempts were made to assassinate British officers. One was against Major St. John, general political superintendent, who was fired at but not wounded; the other against Lieutenant Willis, of the Royal Artillery, who died a few days afterward from the effects of his wound. Gholah Hussein Khan was appointed civil administrator of Candahar, under the supervision of Major St. John. General Stewart prosecuted a reconnaissance to Khelat-i-Ghilzai, a town eighty-eight miles northeast of Candahar, on the road to Ghuznee and Cabool, and occupied it without resistance January 20th. General Biddulph was dispatched to Girishk, at the ford of the Helmund, on the road to Herat, and reached his destination, also without opposition, on the 29th. General Stewart returned to Candahar, where he made preparations to send his surplus troops back to India, while he retained with him as many men as would be needed. Approaches toward Yakoob Khan with reference to negotiation were repelled by him, he answering in writing that he had orders from Shere Ali to hold Cabool and would do it. He was, however, troubled at home with quarrels with his tribal chieftains. He having occupied a fort of the Ghilzais at Tezeen, hostilities were begun against him by that tribe.

Shere Ali, after his flight from Cabool, made his way toward the Russian frontier. He became ill, and sent to General Kaufmann for a military surgeon. On his arrival at the Russian frontier, his followers were disarmed, he alone being allowed to retain his arms. The Russian authorities endeavored to persuade him not to go to St. Petersburg, but he insisted upon it. He was said to have been astonished at his treatment by the Russians, he having expected to be received as an ally. His illness, which arose from a gangrene of the thigh, increased, and he was obliged to remain at Mazar-i-Shereef, near Balkh, and postpone his journey to Tashkend. He, however, dispatched an embassy to Tashkend, consisting of his nephew, his Grand Vizier, his Minister of Justice, and his Minister of the Interior, which traveled in state and was attended by a numerous suite. General Kaufmann had received instructions from St. Petersburg, in anticipation of the arrival of the embassy, to decline all negotiations. He had previously stated to an American correspondent, in explanation of the attitude of the Russian Government, that there would be no Russian interference between Afghanistan and England unless a European war should break out in which Russia and England should not be on the same side. "Besides," he added, "it is the Emperor alone who can decide the future." All question on this subject was put to rest by the death of Shere Ali,

which took place February 21st. The event was officially announced to the Viceroy of India in a note written to him February 26th by Yakoob Khan, who also, speaking of a previous letter he had sent to the Viceroy, added, "As my father was an old friend of the British Government, I send this information out of friendship." Shere Ali was attended by a Russian doctor, Javorsky, who states that after his death the town was in a state of anarchy for five days. A conflict broke out between the partisans of Yakoob Khan, his brother Ibrahim Khan, and his nephew Ahmed Khan. The partisans of Yakoob Khan were victorious, and appointed a new governor, who released Javorsky from the prison into which the contestants had thrown him, and escorted him to the frontier to secure his personal safety. The ambassadors sent by Shere Ali to General Kaufmann took leave of him March 9th. The Russian General, acting under instructions from the Czar, gave them no message to the new Ameer. The coldness of the Russians toward Shere Ali indicated that they had adopted a different policy in reference to the British in Afghanistan from that which it had been supposed they would pursue. In explanation of the change, it was believed that an understanding had been reached between the British and Russian Governments, involving a toleration by the former of certain features of the Russian policy toward Turkey, in consideration of a similar toleration by the Russians of the British operations in Afghanistan. The diplomatic correspondence on the Central Asian question published in February showed that the withdrawal of the Russian embassy from Cabool had been arranged for in December, 1878.

General Biddulph's rear-guard was attacked on the march from Girishk on the Helmund, February 26th, by from 1,500 to 2,000 Alizai Duranis, who were driven off with an estimated loss of 150 killed. This event rendered necessary a continued occupation of Girishk.

Yakoob Khan was proclaimed Ameer immediately after the death of Shere Ali, and seems to have had no difficulty in retaining the recognition he had already gained at Cabool. Efforts to negotiate with him were continued by the British, with at first but little prospect of success. In the latter days of March Major Cavagnari informed the Viceroy that there were no hopes of coming to peaceful terms with Yakoob Khan, and an immediate advance on Cabool was ordered. The British forces suffered from the guerrilla attacks of the native tribes, in consequence of which expeditions were sent out on the 1st of April to Futtehabad and Lughman, with orders to reduce the tribes holding those places to obedience. A squadron of hussars of the former expedition, in crossing the Cabool River at night, missed the ford, and Lieutenant Harford and fifty men were drowned. The other expedition attacked the Khujianis who were threatening the column, and defeated them.

Early in April the British reconnaissance was pushed forward to Gundamuk, where the forces were placed in a strong position. A messenger was dispatched to Cabool to seek an interview with Yakoob Khan, and was followed on his return to Gundamuk by the Ameer himself, who arrived at the camp on the 8th of May. He was met by Major Cavagnari with an escort, and was received with a parade of troops of all arms, who lined the road to the camp for a distance of two miles and a half, to the point where General Browne and his staff were awaiting him, and with a salute of twenty-one guns. He was much pleased with his reception, and sent a dispatch to the Viceroy expressing the hope that peace would speedily be made and a permanent friendship established between England and Afghanistan. The agreement of the negotiating parties upon the basis of peace was announced in the British Parliament on the 19th of May. The treaty was signed on the 26th, and was ratified at Simla on the 30th of the same month. Its chief provisions were as follows: A British resident was to reside at Cabool, who should have the power to send British agents to the Afghan frontier on special occasions. The foreign affairs of the Ameer were to be conducted under British advice, and Great Britain would undertake to support him against foreign aggression. The British authorities were to have complete control over the Khyber and Michnee Passes, as well as of the relations and independence of the frontier tribes in the district in which the passes are situated. The Afghan territory in British occupation was to be restored to the Ameer, with the exception of the Kuram, Pisheen, and Sibi Valleys, which were assigned to the British for administration, on condition that the Ameer should receive the surplus of revenue after the administrative expenses were paid. The Ameer was to receive an annual subsidy of £60,000, contingent upon his strict execution of the treaty. Yakoob Khan sent a dispatch to the Viceroy expressing his satisfaction at the conclusion of the treaty, and his hope that the friendship now established between England and Afghanistan would be eternal. He said also that he was exceedingly pleased and thankful for the reception accorded to him by the British officers, and purposed, toward the close of the next cold season, to have "a joyful meeting with his Excellency, for the purpose of making firmer the basis of personal friendship, and drawing closer the bonds of affection and amity in a most suitable and appropriate manner." The Viceroy answered the letter in the same spirit. The British troops were ordered back from Jelalabad and the other advanced positions they had occupied, leaving only small detachments to hold the posts temporarily. The Ameer issued a proclamation announcing perpetual peace and friendship between Afghanistan and the British Government, publicly declared a general amnesty, and sent an expedi-

tion in accordance with his agreement, with British officers, to effect the pacification of Badakshan. These proceedings were followed by measures for organizing the financial administration of the country, and introducing good government into the provinces. On the 12th of July the Viceroy of India issued a congratulatory address on the skillful conduct and conclusion of the Afghan war, in which he recognized the gallantry, steadiness, and strict discipline of the troops, and the tact and discretion of the political officers, and acknowledged the loyalty of the native princes. Medals were promised to the British troops who had been engaged in the campaign.

A British mission to Cabool was dispatched from India early in July. It consisted of Major Cavagnari as envoy and minister, Mr. Jenkyns as secretary and first assistant, Lieutenant Hamilton, V. C., as commandant of the escort and assistant, and Dr. Kelly in medical charge, with an escort of twenty-six cavalry and fifty infantry of the corps of the guides. On arriving west of the Shutargardan pass, the embassy was met by an escort of the Ameer's troops to conduct it to the capital. It arrived at Cabool on the 29th of July, and was received with military honors by a considerable body of soldiery of all arms drawn up along the route, and a salute of seventeen guns. A large assembly of people witnessed the entry with orderly and respectful behavior. On the evening of the same day, the British envoy presented his credentials to the Ameer, who gave a friendly answer to his address. The evacuation of the country was begun by the British troops, with the expectation of completing it by the 1st of September. It was considered an evidence of the desire of the Ameer to act up to his treaty engagements that he showed Major Cavagnari three letters which he had received from the Russian General Kaufmann, and consulted him as to the answers he should return to them. Following the advice of the British envoy, he replied courteously to them, and suggested at the same time that all future communications should be sent through the Indian Government.

On the 3d of September the British residency at Bala-Hissar was attacked by mutinous Afghan troops and destroyed, and all of the British officers were murdered. The attack originated in a parade of some of the Ameer's regiments for their pay. They were given one month's pay when they demanded pay for two months. They became violent, stoned their officers, and rushed upon the residency, which was in the neighborhood. Having seized arms from the arsenals and public stores, they kept up a vigorous attack upon the inclosure of the residency, which was gallantly met by the officers and soldiers within. The fight was continued for several hours, during which the disaffected regiments were joined by others and by bodies of the populace. The mob were kept in check by the vigorous resistance of the British till they set fire to the buildings, when the defenders came out, sword in hand, and were all slain. More than two hundred of the mutineers were killed by the British during the conflict. In a letter which he sent with news of the disaster to the British at Ali Khel, the Ameer professed to have been completely surprised at the outbreak, and powerless to control it. Several messengers were dispatched to him from the residency during the attack with requests for help, but they all seem to have been intercepted in going or coming. On one of the letters which reached him he wrote, "If God will, I am just making arrangements," but the answer did not reach the residency. The Ameer sent one of his officers, Daoud Shah, to persuade the mutineers and the mob to desist from the attack; but he was set upon by them and dangerously wounded. He then sent his son, with a similar result. He represented that he was himself besieged, with only five attendants, at the time his letter was sent to Ali Khel, and implored the aid of the British. Thirty-one persons of the residency escaped the massacre, including twenty-two who were out cutting grass, and others who were absent. It has not clearly appeared whether the revolt was a spontaneous outbreak or a premeditated effort to get rid of the British. The enemies of Russia declared that it was the result of Russian intrigue. Some pointed to Ayoob Khan, the Ameer's brother, as its probable instigator. The Ameer was suspected of treachery by many, and believed to be in complicity with it while he pretended to deprecate it; but the Indian authorities appeared, so far as open acts went, still to have confidence in his good faith; and some averred that the event proved the soundness of the position which Shere Ali had maintained, that the temper of the Afghan people was such that he could not safely allow a British embassy to reside with him. The residence of the embassy had not been without warnings of danger several days previous to the outbreak. A street riot took place on the 13th of August between some Afghan soldiers and some members of the envoy's escort, in which the populace took the side of the soldiery, and the residence men were beaten; and on the 16th of August the Ameer advised Major Cavagnari to discontinue the custom of riding about Cabool and its vicinity, as an attempt might be made upon his life. Major Cavagnari is reported to have replied that, if he were killed, there were many more men in India who would be ready to act as his successor.

An outbreak took place at Herat two days after the mutiny at Cabool, when three regiments, which had been ordered to march away to quell disturbances in Turkistan, rose against the Fakir Ahmed Khan, the civil and military governor, killed him, and plundered his house. Another revolt was reported in the district of Kohistan.

On the 11th of September the Ameer wrote to the Viceroy of India: "I am dreadfully distressed and aggrieved at recent events, but there is no fighting against God's will. I hope to inflict such punishment on the evil-doers as will be known world-wide and prove my sincerity. I have twice written on this subject, and the third time by my confidential servant, Shere Mahomed Khan. I had written to say that for these eight days I have preserved myself and family by the good offices of those who were friendly to me, partly by bribes, partly by hoaxing the rebels. Some of the cavalry I have dismissed, and night and day I am considering how to put matters straight. Please God, the mutineers will soon meet with the punishment they deserve, and my affairs will be arranged to the satisfaction of the British Government. Certain persons of high position in these provinces have become rebellious, but I am watching carefully and closely every quarter. I have done all I could to insure Nawab Gholam Hussein's safety. I trust to God for an opportunity of showing my sincere friendship for the British Government and of securing my good name before the world." The Ameer was informed that a strong British force would march speedily on Cabool to his relief, and that he should use all his resources to coöperate and facilitate its march through his country.

Preparations were begun immediately on receiving the news of the massacre of the embassy to dispatch an adequate military force to Cabool to restore order and chastise the rebels. The force was organized in three columns, the first of which, under General Roberts, should consist of three batteries of artillery, one squadron of British cavalry, two and a half regiments of native cavalry, three regiments of British infantry, four regiments of native infantry, and one company of sappers, in all about 6,500 men, and should take the country from Shutargardan to Cabool. A second force, of about 4,000 men, under the command of General J. Gordon, should hold the country from Shutargardan to Thull. The Khyber force—consisting of five batteries of artillery, a body of British cavalry, four regiments of native cavalry, two regiments of British infantry, five regiments of native infantry, and two columns of sappers, in all, about 6,600 men, in addition to the Peshawer garrison and the troops already holding the Khyber Pass, up to Lundi Khotal, the whole placed under the command of Major-General Bright—would protect the road from Peshawer to Gundamuk, garrison the intermediate stations, and provide a movable column to hold Jagdalak and communicate with Cabool. The reserve at Peshawer and Rawul Pindee numbered about 5,000 men. The intention was afterward announced of increasing the Khyber and Kuram forces to the strength of 12,000 men each. The orders which had been issued for the evacuation of positions in Afghanistan were revoked so far as regarded points at which military forces still remained.

A reconnaissance was made from Ali Khel into the Lagar Valley, in which no signs of hostility were observed. The tribes appeared to be friendly, and even to afford assistance to the British. The Governor of Candahar was instructed by the Ameer to be guided by the instructions of the British authorities. The Shutargardan Pass was occupied September 11th, and a strong column was dispatched by General Stewart in the direction of Ghuznee for the purpose of watching, and to maintain order in that part of the country. An attack was made on the camp of the 72d regiment on the night of the 19th, but the assailants had disappeared before the company sent out to clear the ground reached the spot. A treacherous attack was made by Mangals and independent Ghilzais on a convoy of mules on the 22d, and an attack on a tower upon the Tirkai Kotal at the same time. On the 24th General Baker occupied Kushi, a Ghilzai village west of the Shutargardan, on the high-road to Cabool, without resistance. The Afreedees and other tribes in the Khyber Pass guaranteed the safety of their portions of the road to Cabool, and the Shinwarries volunteered to convoy supplies to the front. General Hughes's brigade advanced from Candahar to Khelat-i-Ghilzai on the 23d.

On the 27th General Baker received a letter from the Afghan commander-in-chief, asking whether he would receive him and the Ameer's heir apparent in his camp at Kushi. The General replied in the affirmative. An hour later a message came from the Ameer Yakoob Khan, asking General Baker to receive him. The General responded, saying he would meet the Ameer one mile from the camp. The Ameer, his son and father-in-law, and General Daoud Shah, with a suite of forty-one persons, came to Kushi on the same day, and were received by the British. The visit of the Ameer was regarded with some suspicion, and the fact was pointed out as evidence of his insincerity that he had written to the British after the massacre at Cabool that General Daoud Shah, who accompanied him, had been killed in his efforts to quiet the mob. Nevertheless, it was evident that he had put himself into the hands of the British, and had given in his own person the strongest evidence of his good faith which it was possible for him to offer. He afterward accompanied the British march; but both he and his advisers urged General Roberts to delay his advance, fearing that the Afghan troops, whom he did not trust, would sack the Bala-Hissar on his approach. The General replied that delay was impossible.

In order that the purpose of the British march might be made clear, General Roberts ·was instructed to issue a manifesto to the Afghan people, to the effect that the British army advanced on Cabool to avenge the treachery to the British envoy in that city, that the peaceable inhabitants would not be molested; but, if opposition was offered, those persons with arms in their hands would be treated as enemies. Further, non-combatants, women, and children, were advised to withdraw to a place of safety. The Ghilzais and Mangals were threatening the Shutargardan, and an attack was made on them on the 2d of October, in which forty of them were killed, while two of the British were wounded. On the 6th of October General Roberts was at Charasiab, ten or twelve miles south of Cabool, and separated from it by a single range of hills, the road through which is described as a gorge. Reconnoitering parties were sent out at daybreak on all roads leading to Cabool. They found the enemy advancing in great force from the direction of the city, and soon had to retire. The high range of hills between Charasiab and Cabool was crowded with troops and people from the city, while parties of Ghilzais appeared on the hills running along both flanks of the camp; and reports were received that the road to Zahidabad, along which a convoy of stores and ammunition was expected, was threatened. Warning and assistance were sent to the convoy. General Baker was intrusted with the duty of carrying the heights in front of the camp, and, having with a detachment driven the enemy off the main hills and captured twelve guns, with a loss to his own force of four killed and nine wounded, he with his main force made a turning movement to the left, and in a hot contest carried height after height in gallant style, with a loss of seventy men killed and wounded, while the enemy fled in confusion, having suffered a large loss, including two standards. The enemy's force was said to consist of eleven regiments, with artillery and "immense numbers of hillmen." It was remarked that the Ameer's party, who were still in the camp, watched the result eagerly, and professed great satisfaction with it. The head men of the suburbs of Cabool asked if they might pay their respects to the British commander.

On the 8th General Roberts was before Cabool. Generals Baker and Macpherson were detailed in strength to attack the enemy who had assembled from the hills above Bala-Hissar. The enemy confronting General Baker fled, abandoning twelve guns, were pursued, and scattered. General Massy was sent to cut off the retreat of the Afghans on the road between Bannian and Rochestan, and captured seventy-eight guns in an abandoned cantonment at Shalpoor. At night the citadel and palace of Bala-Hissar had been abandoned by the enemy. On the evening of the next day the British cavalry, returning from the pursuit of flying Afghan bands, rode through Cabool, and found some of the shops open and everything quiet. General Roberts made a public entry into Cabool at noon of October 12th, accompanied by the Ameer and his suite. British troops of all arms lined the road, and the artillery fired a salute when the British standard was hoisted at the entrance to the city. The Bala-Hissar was subsequently occupied by two regiments.

On entering the city, General Roberts made a speech to the effect that it would be necessary to inflict severe punishment. Buildings of the Bala-Hissar and of the city interfering with proper military occupation would be destroyed. A heavy fine would be levied on the citizens. A military governor would be placed over the city and country within a radius of ten miles. All the inhabitants under his jurisdiction would be required to surrender their arms within a week, on pain of death if they failed to do so.

Rewards would be paid for the denunciation and conviction of any person concerned in the massacre of the British embassy. General Hill was appointed military governor of Cabool.

A visit was made soon after the British column had entered Cabool to the place where the massacre of the members of the residency took place. The premises had been plundered of everything valuable, and the embassy building destroyed by fire. The bodies of Major Cavagnari and Surgeon Kelly were found

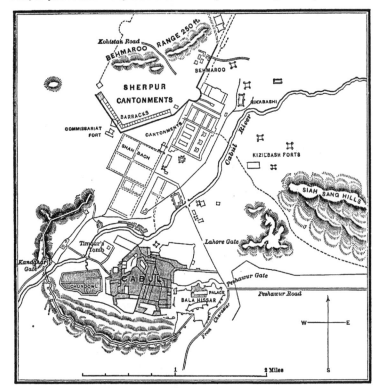

buried under a heap of charred, half-consumed logs of wood, beneath the ruins in front of the embassy. The visiting diary of Major Cavagnari was found in the Ameer's palace. About this time Yakoob Khan announced his intention to abdicate. General Roberts advised him to consider the matter, but he said that he had intended to take that step earlier, but was dissuaded, and would now adhere to his resolution. It accordingly became necessary for General Roberts to make provisional

arrangements for maintaining order and carrying on the internal administration of the country. An investigation was instituted into the cause and circumstances of the outbreak of September 3d. Important papers were discovered tending to implicate one of the Khans, and a court-martial was formed for the trial of persons against whom evidence was found. The father-in-law of the Ameer, the ex-Governor of Cabool, and the Minister of Finance were put under close arrest. Five men were hanged late in October for complicity in the massacre, among whom were the Kotwal of Cabool, the head of the city mollahs, and two generals, one of royal blood; and on the 16th of November forty-nine Afghans had been hanged for complicity in the massacre. A military demonstration was made from Kuram up the Chakmani Valley, which resulted in the dispersion of the hostile bands. In the last days of October, by order of the Viceroy of India, General Roberts issued a proclamation stating that, in consequence of the abdication of the Ameer and the outrage at the British residency, the British Government had been compelled to occupy Cabool and other parts of Afghanistan.

AFRICA. The area, according to Behm and Wagner ("Bevölkerung der Erde," vol. v., Gotha, 1878), is 10,941,000 square miles, and the population 205,219,500. For the area and population of the divisions and subdivisions, see "Annual Cyclopædia" for 1878.

It is believed that about one half of the population of Africa are Mohammedans. After being for many centuries the principal religion of the northern and northeastern coast, Mohammedanism has made more recently great progress in the interior of Africa, and has advanced westward as far as Liberia. The entire Christian population of Africa does not exceed 7,000,000. About one half of these belong to the Abyssinian and Coptic Churches, and are directly descended from the Christian Church of the first centuries. Since the beginning of the maritime discoveries in the fifteenth century, the Portuguese and Spaniards have established their sovereignty over large tracts of land, and the population has gradually become connected with the Roman Catholic Church. In the Portuguese possessions on the continent of Africa, in Congo, Angola, and Mozambique, the carelessness of the Portuguese Government has allowed the missions to fall to ruin, and the connection of the native population with the Catholic Church to become merely nominal, being reduced to the retention of some usages and ceremonies. Large numbers of the natives continue, however, to regard themselves as Catholics, and still figure in the statistical accounts of the Church; and, in view of the greater interest which the Portuguese Government begins to show in its colonies, it is believed that ere long the entire population of the Portuguese colonies, no less than that of the Spanish, will be in real communion with the Catholic Church. The conquest of Algeria in modern times has opened to the same Church a new and large missionary field in Northern Africa, in which already a considerable population of European descent, with a small number of native converts, promise for the future an important addition to its territory. Egypt and Tunis have received large additions to their Catholic population by the immigration of Catholics from Italy and other countries of Southwestern Europe. The Roman Catholics under British rule live chiefly in the island of Mauritius, which formerly belonged to France, and still is predominantly Catholic:

The Protestant missions in Africa are classified as West African, South African, and East African missions. In West Africa, missions are carried on in Gambia, Pongas, Sierra Leone, Mendi, Liberia, the Gold Coast country, Yoruba, Old Calabar, the Cameroons, the Gaboon, Corisco, and the Sherbro country, by seven American, nine English, and three Continental societies. They include, according to the reports for 1878 and 1879, so far as they are completed, 386 missionaries and assistants, and 25,636 members of the Church. The South African missions are planted among the Damaras, in Namaqualand, the Cape Colony, the Transvaal, Caffraria, Natal, and Zoolooland, and are under the control of one American, six British, and nine Continental (including the Moravian, Waldensian, French, German, Finnish, and Scandinavian Lutheran) societies, and the societies of the colonial churches. They embrace, so far as reports are at hand, 637 missionaries and assistants, and 60,000 communicants. The principal East African missions are carried on by the societies of the Church of England and the United Methodist Free Churches. Several societies have established missions in Abyssinia, chiefly among the Jews, and in Algeria; and five societies have begun missions since 1875 in the interior, on the great lakes and the Congo River, employing altogether between thirty and forty laborers, but have not yet made any reports of converts. Denominationally, the working forces and churches of the Western and Southern African missions are related as follows: Baptist, 22 missionaries and assistants, 209 members; Congregational, 26 ministers, 670 members; Episcopal and Anglican, 149 ministers, 6,878 members (including some white colonists in South Africa); American Lutheran, 1 minister, 40 members; Methodist, 190 ministers, 36,751 members; Moravian, 65 ministers, 10,386 adherents; Presbyterian, 33 ministers, 3,732 members; United Brethren, 2 ministers, 70 members; Lady Huntingdon's Connection, 60 preachers, exhorters, and teachers; Continental societies (French, Swiss, German, Finnish, and Scandinavian Lutheran and Reformed), 318 ministers, 31,518 members. The Anglican missions in Sierra Leone have been turned over to the native Episcopal church of the colony, which receives a grant of £500 a year from the Church Missionary Society. This church has 14 clergymen, 4,874 communicants, and 14,000 native Christian adherents, with 4,037 scholars. The Reformed Dutch Church of South Africa includes 50 ministers, 113 congregations, and 220,000 souls. In Madagascar, the London (Congregational) Missionary Society has 414 European and native preachers, with 3,804 other native assistants, 67,729 members, and 233,188 adherents; the Anglican missions have 13 ministers and

800 members; the Norwegian Lutherans have 19 missionaries and 288 members; and the Friends have 100 congregations. Primary schools are taught at all the stations, and are freely attended by pupils of all ages. Higher schools are also connected with the older stations, and most of the missions have normal and training schools for teachers, and theological schools for the education of native preachers. The statistics of those schools of which regular reports are given show that the attendance of scholars generally exceeds the number of members in the churches. Fourah Bay College, of the Church Missionary Society, on the West Coast of Africa, is affiliated with the University of Durham, whence some of its students have received degrees, and provides a full course of collegiate instruction, with comparative philology, theology, and the Hebrew and Arabic languages. The institution of the Free Church of Scotland, at Lovedale, Caffraria, has elementary, literary, and theological classes, of three years each, and is attended by natives and English, most of the native races of South Africa and the stations of all the denominational missions being represented among its pupils. It has furnished trained teachers for the Free Church and other missions, has developed a branch institution at Blythewood in the Transkei, and has contributed to the establishment of the new mission at Livingstonia, on Lake Nyassa. The mission schools of Madagascar have been extensively developed and systematically organized, and have promoted the establishment of a national system of education. Grammars and dictionaries of the languages of the numerous tribes have been prepared by the missionaries, school and religious books have been published in them, and a varied literature has been produced in the Caffre dialects. This literary work gives employment to some respectable printing-houses.

The following table gives an estimate of the population connected, in 1879, with the Protestant, Roman Catholic, and Eastern Churches:

COUNTRIES.	Protestant.	Roman Catholic.	Eastern Churches.
British possessions (inclusive of missions in neighboring native states)....	700,000	182,000	......
French possessions.......	10,000	870,000	......
Portuguese possessions...	....	1,204,000	......
Spanish possessions.......	....	820,000	......
Egypt...................	2,000	28,000	200,000
Abyssinia (including mission among the Gallas)..	.....	10,000	8,000,000
Liberia..................	80,000	.....	......
Morocco.................	....	.....	......
Tunis and Tripoli.........	.....	18,000	......
Madagascar.............	800,000	20,000	......
Orange Free State........	50,000	.....	......
Total.............	1,092,000	2,152,000	8,200,000

The principal event in Africa during 1879 was the deposition of Ismail, Khedive of Egypt, in favor of his oldest son, Prince Tevfik. This was brought about by the pressure of the Western Powers on Turkey, in consequence of the extravagant measures adopted by the Khedive. Several changes of ministry followed, until finally Riaz Pasha, who had been exiled by Ismail and recalled by Tevfik, was appointed President of the Council. The relations of Egypt and Abyssinia were in an unsettled condition. In the latter part of the year Colonel Gordon was sent to Abyssinia to arrange a definite treaty of peace. (See ABYSSINIA, and EGYPT.)

The British had another native war on their hands in South Africa in 1879, and one which eclipsed all of the preceding wars in importance. This year it was the nation of the Zooloo Caffres, under their king Cetywayo, with whom the British came into conflict. The causes that led to it were said by the colonists to be the general insecurity of their frontiers, and the utter disregard which Cetywayo exhibited toward the demands of the governments of Natal and the Cape. On the other hand, the natives who were from time to time captured, as well as Cetywayo himself, stated that at no time had the Zooloo king been anxious for war, and that he had done everything in his power to satisfy his white neighbors. In England, the war was regarded as unnecessary. The British, at first, met with defeat, but on July 4th they gained a complete victory over the Zooloos, which was followed on August 28th by the capture of Cetywayo. The Zooloo land was then subdivided into thirteen districts, and a chief appointed for each, while a British resident at the krall of each chief is to watch over British interests. The question of a South African confederation was again prominently brought forward by Sir M. Hicks-Beach, but received little encouragement from the colonies. (See CAPE COLONY, and ZOOLOOS.)

In Algeria, a complete change of government took place. The supreme civil and military powers, which had been united up to this time in one person, were separated, and a new governor-general and commander-in-chief were appointed. In June an insurrection of Kabyles broke out simultaneously in Tunis, Algeria, and Morocco. A boundary commission which was to settle the disputed boundary between the British colony of Sierra Leone and the Republic of Liberia adjourned *sine die* on April 24th, without settling any one point in the dispute. Agreement between the English and Liberian members was found to be impossible, and the former flatly refused to refer the matter to Commander Shufeldt of the United States Navy, who had been selected as arbitrator.

The Portuguese Government in March sent a man-of-war to Whydaly to blockade the coast of Dahomey, on account of the capture and imprisonment of a Portuguese merchant. The King of Dahomey, on the other hand, ordered all roads leading from the interior to the coast to be blockaded, so that the entire commerce of the country was prostrated.

The French Government in 1879 seized the island of Matagong. The French claimed it from the fact that, being situated between the mouths of the Rio Congo and the Mellacoree, and near a coast undoubtedly French, it ought logically to be French also. In a map, however, of Senegambia, drawn up in 1864 by order of General Faidherbe, then Governor of Senegal, it is depicted as English, as well as the Los Archipelago, more to the north; but this might arise from its being then the private property of a British subject, and the Paris merchant who represents the present proprietors has produced a declaration of 1855 by Sir George Grey, Colonial Secretary, refusing to aid Mr. Isaacs on the ground that Matagong was not British territory.

AGRICULTURE. (See UNITED STATES and the STATES respectively.)

ALABAMA. The regular session of the Alabama Legislature commenced on November 12, 1878, and terminated on February 8, 1879. In the Senate W. G. Little was chosen President; and in the House David Clopton was chosen Speaker.

One of the earliest measures of the session was a joint convention of the two Houses to count the votes for State officers. As there was only one ticket, the results were announced as follows: Total vote for Rufus W. Cobb for Governor, 89,571; total vote for W. W. Screws for Secretary of State, 87,673; total vote for Willis Brewer for Auditor, 87,315; total vote for I. H. Vincent for Treasurer, 88,231; total vote for H. C. Tompkins for Attorney-General, 88,204. The vote for members of Congress, which was canvassed too late for insertion in the "Annual Cyclopædia" of 1878, was as follows:

District.		
I.	T. H. Herndon, Democrat	6,577
	W. Bailey, Opposition	2,941
II.	H. A. Herbert, Democrat	8,364
	J. P. Armstrong, Opposition	6,505
III.	W. J. Sanford, Democrat	6,199
	F. Strange, Opposition	676
IV.	C. M. Shelley, Democrat	8,514
	Jer. Haralson, Republican	6,545
V.	T. Williams, Democrat	6,587
	Theo. Nuron, Opposition	2,734
VI.	B. B. Lewis, Democrat	7,642
	W. R. Smith, Opposition	3,291
VII.	W. H. Forney, Democrat	2,658
	W. W. Garth, Democrat	8,279
VIII.	W. M. Lowe, Opposition	10,324

Of the members of Congress seven were Democrats and one opposition.

The Legislature was divided as follows:

PARTY.	Senate.	House.
Democrats	31	91
Independent Democrats	2	4
Republicans	..	3
Nationals	..	2
Total	33	100

On December 10th the Legislature took a recess until January 15, 1879.

An act was passed requiring the execution of criminals to be in an inclosure which is hidden from public view.

A joint resolution was adopted which declares that the act of Congress imposing a tax of ten per centum on the issues of State banks creates in the national banks an unjust and odious monopoly, and is an unwarrantable abridgment of the power and authority of the State, by appropriate acts of incorporation, to provide its citizens with a lawful currency, suitable to their needs; and the Senators and Representatives of Alabama in Congress were requested to use their untiring efforts to have the same repealed.

A memorial requesting Congress to establish a system for a national quarantine against yellow fever and other infectious diseases was also adopted.

A bill to limit or prohibit the sale of seed-cotton was extensively discussed in relation to its constitutionality. Seed-cotton is the name given to the article as it is in the field. If it is stolen and sold, the owner can not distinguish his property from that of others. The extent of the stealing is such as to be considered a great evil. One member in his remarks said:

There are many roads which lead from the rich farming lands into the city of Montgomery, but to illustrate it I will only refer to one, say the Lime Creek road. During the busy picking season, a gentleman of my acquaintance concluded that he would make some observations; so he posted himself upon the road between midnight and daylight, and not less than thirty vehicles of all descriptions, from a four-horse wagon down to the diminutive cart with the diminutive steer or calf, passed him, and, from the movements of the parties having the cotton-seed and the purchasers of the cotton, there is but little doubt that two thirds of all the cotton on these vehicles, besides that of the innumerable foot-passengers loaded with sacks of all sorts and sizes, were stolen; for all these parties with the cotton so graduate their movements that they reach the city at or before sunrise; and, as soon as the first rays of the golden sunshine touch the dome of this Capitol, the doors of the innumerable shops which before sunrise were closed, and the premises as silent as death, fly open as if by magic. The cotton-sack is hurried upon the scales, hurriedly and many times, perhaps, falsely weighed, then hurriedly spirited away to the back rooms, where at leisure it is carried and sold to the pickeries. Pass over any of the roads leading to the city between the hours of midnight and day, and about the suburbs, and you will find them filled, as I said before, with vehicles of every description, meet hordes of tramps with sacks and baskets, all watching for the first rays of the sun to dispose of their ill-gotten gains. I say ill-gotten, for, if not so, why this unseemly time to bring their wares to market? Why this haste? For this army of wagons, of carts, of tramps with sacks, is soon, like the snow, dissolved by the rising sun; and the 9 or 10 o'clock passer-by has no idea of what had occurred only a few hours before.

In support of the constitutionality of the bill, it was urged that it was based upon the proposition that no man can either use or dispose of his property to the injury of his neighbor; and it is for the Legislature to say how far one citizen may go in the use of his property to prevent injury to his neighbor's. The bill was upon the same principle as the measure which prohibits the sale or giving away of spirituous liquors, or that which provides for the

Th
island
from
moutl
and n
logica
ever, o
der of
Senega
the Lo:
this mi
propert
mercha
tors ha
George
aid Mr
was no
AGR
the Sta
ALA
Alaham
ber 12,
1879.]
Presider
was cho
One o.
was a jo
count the
only one
follows:
Governo
for Secre
Willis Br
for I. H.
vote for I
88,204.
which wa
the " Ann
lows:

District.
I. { T. H
{ W.]
II. { H. A
{ J. P.
III. { W. J
{ F. St,
IV. { C. M.
{ Jer.]
V. { T. W.
{ Theo.
VI. { B. B.
{ W. R.
VII. { W. H.
{ W. W
VIII. W. M.

Of the 1
Democrats .
The Legi:

Democrats .....
Independent De
Republicans....
Nationals.......

Total......

On Decem
recess until J
An act wa:
of criminals
hidden from

PRESIDENT OF THE FRENCH REPUBLIC.

keeping up of fences. All this class of legislation was strictly within the legislative prerogative to enact police regulations for the protection of the public peace and society. It would be quite anomalous to say that an evil may exist to the detriment of the best interests of society, and yet the Legislature had no right to suppress it, or to enact measures for its prevention. The bill does not prohibit the sale of cotton. A bill which proposed absolutely to prohibit the sale of cotton would be unconstitutional, but a bill which simply restricts and limits its sale is no more violative of the Constitution than the bill which restricts the sale of spirituous liquors. It was urged in reply that the sole end of government was to protect the life, liberty, and property of the citizen. Any law that prohibited the sale of property must be in derogation of the right secured to the citizen under the Constitution. It was far more than a police regulation to prohibit the citizen from selling his property in any quantity and manner he pleases. It might possibly be a police regulation to prescribe that the citizen must sell his property at a certain place or within certain specified hours, or that he must pay a license to sell; but to say that he shall not sell at all is in plain derogation of the Constitution. The bill might as well provide that the citizen shall not sell his corn in the ear, his oats in the sheaf, or he must make his timber in certain shapes. The sale of liquor parallel is far-fetched. Spirituous liquors are not necessary for the existence and support of the human family. Cotton is a production upon which the people depend in a measure for their means of support, and to say that they shall not dispose of their means of existence as they see fit, is not only a violation of the Constitution, but it is an assault upon *magna charta* itself—that great fountain from which the whole fabric of free constitutional government is drawn. The bill, however, passed both Houses and became a law.

Subsequently the trial of an indictment against two persons for buying seed-cotton took place before the Circuit Court of Lowndes County. The argument for the defense was that the law violated that clause of the Constitution of the State which provides that "no *ex post facto* law, or any law impairing the obligation of contracts or making any irrevocable grants of special privileges or immunities, shall be passed by the General Assembly," and the further clause which provides that "the sole object and only legitimate end of government is to protect the citizen in the enjoyment of life, liberty, and property; and when the government assumes other functions, it is usurpation and oppressive." The Judge sustained the unconstitutionality of the law, and the case will likely go up to the Supreme Court. The benefit produced by the law is considered very great on the part of the cotton-planters; while the members of the bar with equal unanimity regard it as unconstitutional.

A bill was passed to protect planters and farmers against farmers from Texas who come into the State to obtain colored laborers. A large colored emigration from the State to Texas has caused great inconvenience. The bill as passed applies to the counties of Dallas, Perry, Washington, Barbour; Marengo, Pike, Montgomery, Covington, Monroe, Lowndes, Greene, Elmore, Macon, Talladega, Bibb, Bullock, Lee, Tuscaloosa, and Shelby, and requires a license of $100. It also provides that a person failing to pay such license shall be fined three times the amount of such license, and may also be imprisoned in the county jail, or required to do hard labor for the county for not more than one year.

The reduction of taxation was much discussed, and a resolution passed in the House asking the Governor to furnish all statistics and other information in his possession which would or would not justify the Legislature in reducing the rate of taxation. The Governor in reply stated that the taxable property of the State had diminished in value from $160,000,000 to about $125,000,000, and for the year 1879 the reported assessments indicated a still further diminution amounting to ten millions or more. The amount of interest to be paid on the debt increases as additional bonds are exchanged. This increase will continue until all the bonds covered by the settlement of the debt shall have been exchanged. In 1881 this will be augmented by an increase in the rate of interest from two to three per cent. on one class of bonds, and from two to four upon another, which will amount to an annual increase of one third of the present interest, or about $90,000. The balance in the State Treasury at the close of the session would not exceed $60,000. This would include $40,000 in State obligations and $5,000 in Patton certificates, all of which will be destroyed as provided by law, and thus leave only about $15,000 in cash, which would include all the revenue collected and paid into the Treasury up to that time. If the rate of last year's assessment be maintained for 1879 and 1880, the balance on the 1st of October, 1880, will not exceed $136,000; and as but a small amount of the taxes for the year will go into the Treasury by the 1st of January, 1881, the demands upon the Treasury occasioned by the expense of the session of the General Assembly of 1880, about $40,000, and the January interest in 1881, about $160,000, will exceed the cash in the Treasury $64,000, for the payment of which a loan will have to be negotiated, until a sufficient amount shall be collected from the taxes of that year to pay the same. After a disagreement between the two Houses, the tax rate for 1879 was left unchanged, and for 1880 it was reduced to 65 cents on the $100.

The Committee on Privileges and Elections reported an amendment to the State Code, which directed the form, size, and quality of the paper used as a ballot at elections, and also the inscription on the same. They said that they had had occasion to examine several ballot-boxes, and it would astonish the House if it knew the want of uniformity in the ballots handed in by the electors. They were written on every conceivable kind of paper and in almost every conceivable shape, from a square piece of paper to one more nearly resembling a shoe-string than otherwise, the handling of which, though lightly or carefully done, would endanger it with rents likely to destroy its completeness, if not its expression of the elector's vote.

In consequence of memorials sent to the Legislature, the Committee on Foreign Relations of the House were ordered to investigate the misuse and abuse of power by certain United States officials in the State against citizens of the State, as alleged; which resulted in the adoption of the following joint memorial to Congress:

To the Honorable the Senate and House of Representatives of the United States in Congress assembled:

The joint memorial of the Senate and House of Representatives, composing the General Assembly of Alabama, complaining, respectfully calls the attention of your honorable bodies to the injuries inflicted on the citizens of Alabama by the misuse and abuse, by certain United States officials in this State, of the power intrusted to them. It is apparent to all who see them, that the juries of the United States Courts are not generally a fair representation of the country, but that they are manipulated for a purpose, and for the conviction of petty offenses which are not prosecuted in the true interest of the United States, but to produce fees for those interested in them. It has also been brought to the attention of your memorialists by the representations and petitions of a large number of worthy and reputable citizens, as well as by the statements of many members of this body and of the Senate, that in the Northern and Middle judicial districts of Alabama the internal revenue officers, marshal's deputies and agents, along with traveling United States Commissioner W. H. Hunter, have practiced the grossest abuses under pretense of enforcing the internal revenue laws of the United States. That under this pretense they have raided over the country with large bodies of armed men and, regardless of law and decency, have abused and insulted the people without cause. That they have unlawfully and without pretext broken open storehouses and private trunks, and have either taken the contents or have allowed others to do so. That they have foraged on the country without pay, or upon a tender of the merest pittances for subsistence they have taken. That they have wantonly broken down fences and turned stock in on the growing crops of the people. That they have in mere mischief shot down the cattle and hogs of private citizens. That they have conducted themselves in a riotous and disorderly manner, and in more wantonness have fired into the yards and around the dwellings of defenseless females for the brutal gratification of terrifying them. That they have arrested persons and carried them long distances, when they were at once discharged, without cause; and it has been a common occurrence to arrest and handcuff and carry citizens before United States commissioners at long distances from the homes of such persons, for preliminary investigations, where they have no friends to bail them if bound over, and no means to defray their expenses back in cases of discharge, when there were commissioners of character and standing near to the p a es of arrest. That they have repeatedly refused to take persons so arrested in the near neighborhood of General Joseph W. Burke, a commissioner of the United States residing in Calhoun County, lately of the United States Army, and holding re-

sponsible positions under the courts of the United States, but have taken them to Huntsville for preliminary hearing, in a distant part of the State, and that they have in many other cases traveled circuitous routes to avoid nearer commissioners. And that they have arrested, and without preliminary trial confined one John Jackson in jail for f fty days, during the severe rigor of the late cold weather. Collector Booth, Deputy-Collector Smith, W. H. Hunter, Commissioner, Deputy-Marshals Randolph and G. W. Golson, and others, are charged with these abuses.

The information so laid before your memorialists shows that these officials have not pursued their investigations with any great view to serve the true interests of the United States, nor as agents of a great justice-loving power which was seeking to enforce its laws by necessary but orderly force; but they have acted as if they were the ruthless myrmidons of a power at enmity with its people, and whose laws were enacted, not to shelter and protect, as well as punish, but only to harass and destroy.

As the terms of the courts of the Northern judicial district of Alabama approach, these statements show that the roads and the courtyards are thronged with poverty-stricken witnesses in vast numbers, called term after term, and present a picture which is sad to look upon. The historian Gibbon elegantly but feelingly portrays the vengeance visited by Theodosius upon Antioch, and tells us that "the tribunal of Hellebricus and Cæsarius, encompassed with armed soldiers, was erected in the midst of the forum. The noblest and most wealthy of the citizens of Antioch appeared before them in chains; the examination was assisted by the use of torture, and their sentence was announced or suspended according to the judgment of these extraordinary magistrates. The houses of the citizens were exposed to sale, and their wives and children were suddenly reduced from affluence and luxury to the most absolute distress." The abuses of the United States officials in Alabama, thus brought to the knowledge of your memorialists, show that vengeance of officials has lost nothing in the destructive abuses of power since the days of Theodosius, and that the history of the miseries of Antioch repeats itself in modern times. Your memorialists pray your honorable bodies to relieve our people from a repetition of these disgraceful scenes, and to let them feel more of the protection which will follow from a gentler though it may be a stern administration of the laws of the United States, and so teach them to love, not drive them to hate, its administration.

An act was passed to donate $75 to any resident of the State who, while in the military service of the State or of the Confederate States, lost an arm or a leg.

On the bill to repeal the section of the Code which requires ballots to be numbered at elections, it was urged in its favor as follows:

This is intended to preserve the purity of the ballot-box, whose purity and sanctity are synonymous. Unless the law shuts out every approach to destroy the sanctity of the ballot-box, how shall the weak vote against the strong, the poor against the rich, or the low against the high? The Supreme Courts of eight Northern States have declared by decisions that the violation of the sanctity of the ballot-box in any way is unconstitutional; and the State of Indiana has not only declared this principle by its highest court, but has also cited the numbering of a ballot as a violation of this sanctity, and declared a statute of the State void because it required the ballots to be numbered. It may be asked, Has this decision been acted upon? I can answer, It has. The State of Ohio, one of the greatest Northern States, makes it a violation of law for any one to number, mark, or so designate a vote that it may be known, thereby stamping the numbering of a vote as an infringement and violation of the secrecy of the ballot-box, which is its only safeguard in times of peace, and its only defense in times of trouble. But I am asked, How will you contest the election if the ballot is not numbered? Nothing can be easier. When the votes are counted over and turn out ten more than the number on the poll-list, discard ten votes first taken from the box, and the balance take as good. This rule is adopted by several of the States.

The following resolution relative to changing the manner of choosing Presidential Electors was adopted in the Senate:

Whereas, Interference by officers of the United States in popular elections is justly regarded by the people of this State as an evil of great magnitude; and

Whereas, The manifest purpose of such interference, in part at least, is to influence and control the action of the State in selecting Electors for President and Vice-President of the United States; therefore

Resolved, That the Committee on Foreign Relations be instructed to inquire into the expediency of providing by law for the selection of President and Vice-President by the General Assembly until the acts of Congress authorizing interference by Federal authority are rescinded.

The division of the State into judicial districts was accomplished by making the Congressional districts constitute the circuits, except as to the following counties: Randolph, instead of being in the seventh, is put into the fifth; Olay, instead of being in the fifth, is put into the seventh; Marion and Winston, instead of being in the sixth, are put into the eighth.

The act to organize and regulate the system of public instruction sets apart for the support of the schools and appropriates the following sums, which thus compose the school revenue: The annual interest at 6 per cent. upon all sums of money which have heretofore been received or which may hereafter be received by the State as the proceeds of sales of lands granted or intrusted by the United States to the State, or to the several townships thereof, for school purposes; the annual interest at 4 per cent. on that part of the surplus revenue of the United States deposited with the State under the act of Congress approved June 23, 1836; all the annual rents, incomes, profits, or interests arising from the proceeds of sales of all such lands as may hereafter be given by the United States, or by the State, or by individuals, for the support of the public schools; all such sums as may accrue to the State as escheats, which are to be applied to the support of the public schools during the scholastic year next succeeding their receipt in the State Treasury; also all rents, incomes, and profits received into the State Treasury during the scholastic year, from all lands remaining unsold, which have heretofore been donated by the Congress of the United States for the support of the public schools; all licenses which are by law required to be paid into the school fund of any county, the same to be expended for the benefit of the public schools in such county, and all such license-tax shall be promptly paid by the probate judge, or such person collecting such tax, to the County Superintendent of Education; also the

further sum of $130,000 from any money in the Treasury not otherwise appropriated. The poll-tax of each county shall be retained in the county for the schools thereof. Such poll-tax is fixed at $1.50 on each male inhabitant over twenty-one and less than forty-five years of age. In 1877–'78 it amounted to $109,762.

The public school officers are a State Superintendent of Education, a county and one township superintendent.

The following three sections of this act relate to the schools and the children:

SEC. 48. *Be it further enacted*, That every township and fraction of a township which is divided by a State or county line, or any other insuperable barrier, such as rivers, creeks, or mountains, and every incorporated city or town having three thousand inhabitants, shall constitute separate school districts, and each shall be under the township superintendent of public schools, as to all matters connected with public schools. Each township or other school district, in its corporate capacity as created by law, may hold real and personal property; and the business of such corporations, in relation to public schools and school lands, shall be managed by the township or district superintendents.

SEC. 49. *Be it further enacted*, That every child between the ages of seven and twenty-one years shall be entitled to admission into, and instructed in any public school of its own race or color in the township in which he or she resides, or to any public school of its own race or color, in the State of Alabama, as herein provided.

SEC. 50. *Be it further enacted*, That the scholastic year shall begin on the first day of October of each year, and end on the thirtieth day of September of the following year. Twenty days shall constitute a school month. A school day shall comprise not less than six hours.

According to the report of the Superintendent of Education, the number of school districts in the State in the year 1877–'78 was 1,700; number of schools taught, white 2,696, colored 1,404; number of teachers employed, white 2,722, colored 1,423; grades of schools taught, primary 1,590, intermediate 1,370, grammar 973, high 167; school population, white 214,279, colored 155,168; number enrolled in schools, white 86,485, colored 54,745; average attendance in schools, white 61,584, colored 40,092.

There is a normal school at Florence, upon the most approved plan, for the education of white teachers, male and female. Another, at Marion, is for the education of colored teachers; and a university, connected therewith, for the education of colored students in the higher departments of learning. Another is located at Huntsville in the northern part of the State for the professional education of colored teachers, controlled by a board of three commissioners. Pupils are admitted free of charge, but must bind themselves to teach two years in the public schools of the State. This institution is in successful operation.

In the University of Alabama for the year 1878 there were 38 degrees conferred. The number of students was 178. At the Agricultural and Mechanical College for the same year there were 238 students. The number of students enrolled at the beginning of 1879 was 217, which exceeds the number at the same date the year previous by 46. The advanced classes are larger this year than ever before. Of the 238 students last year, there were in the first class 8, in the second 16, in the third 53, in the fourth 66, in the fifth 95. Of the 217 students in the present year there are in the first class 13, in the second 30, in the third 47, in the fourth 60, in the fifth 65. In college classes proper there were last year, out of 238 students, 143; this year, out of 217 students, there are 150. During the past year improvements were made upon the college building, which give ample accommodations for 300 students. The income of the college is derived mainly from the endowment fund, which consists of $253,500, invested, by act of the General Assembly of the State, in Alabama bonds. These bonds are deposited with the Treasurer of the State. The annual income from this endowment is $20,280.

Two acts were passed by the Legislature which related to the financial affairs of the city of Mobile. The first act repealed the charter of the city, and made provision for the application of the assets of the old corporation in discharge of its debts. Three commissioners were to be appointed by the Governor, with the advice and consent of the Senate, to collect and disburse these assets. Their manner of discharging the duty is to be directed and controlled by the Chancery Court for Mobile. The commissioners are authorized to compromise, compound, and adjust all debts, claims, and demands, including past-due taxes, of every kind which at the date of the passage of the act existed in favor of the city, on such terms and in such manner as, having in view the speedy collection of such outstanding claims and the largest possible reduction of the debt heretofore due from or now asserted against the city, may seem to them best; and for the purpose of so realizing the assets and paying the debt, the commissioners and receivers, with the leave of the Court of Chancery, are authorized and empowered to sell, on the best terms they can obtain, all the real and personal property which may come to their hands as commissioners under the act, and not by existing laws exempt from sale, and so much and such parts or portions of the claims and demands with the collection of which they are charged, as they may be authorized by the order of the Court of Chancery to sell. The commissioners are charged with the duty of opening communication with the holders of the funded debt of the city in relation to the same, with a view to the adjustment thereof, and its settlement; and for that purpose are to conduct negotiations with the creditors to the end that proper legislation may be enacted to secure at the same time and consistently with each other the protection of the life, property, security, and peace of the citizens of the territory of late governed by the municipal organ-

ization of the city of Mobile, and the payment to the utmost extent practicable of the just debt of the city. They are to make report to the Governor of the State, to be laid before the General Assembly at its next term, of the result of their negotiations, together with the draft of such act for their consideration, as in the judgment of said commissioners may be required to carry into effect any scheme of adjustment they may recommend, and secure the objects of the act; and upon the passage of such act they shall apply to the Court of Chancery for such proper orders and decrees as may be necessary to secure the application of the assets under its jurisdiction and control to the uses and purposes which may be agreed upon, and be declared by the act to carry such agreement into operation and effect.

The second act contemplated and provided for the creation of a simple and economical as well as efficient form of local government, to exist provisionally until the next session of the General Assembly, January, 1881. This government, being only for a limited period, is to be intrusted simply with police powers—that is, with power to preserve the public peace, protect the public health, to provide against fires, take care of the streets, and perform such other municipal duties as are necessary for the well-being of the city. This provisional government, however, is to have nothing to do with the settlement of the debt. Eight commissioners are to be elected by the people, one from each ward, to manage the port. There are to be a president of the board, a clerk, and a tax-collector, and such police officers as may be necessary. To defray the expenses of police management, the board is authorized and empowered to lay and collect for each year of its existence, upon all real and personal property and all subjects of State taxation within said port of Mobile, a tax not exceeding six tenths of one per centum of the value of such property or subject of taxation assessed for State taxation during the year preceding that for which said police board may assess and lay the tax above provided for; provided, that where the personal property of any person does not exceed $150, and his real estate does not exceed $200, such property shall be exempt from taxation. The two acts thus passed were first brought forward and approved by the city authorities. The Board of Aldermen considered the bill to repeal the charter first, and recommended it for legislative action by a vote of thirteen to seven. After some debate they adopted the second bill creating a new corporation by a *viva voce* vote, which represented the same majority obtained in favor of the first. The Common Council was unanimous in favor of both bills. These measures were the result of two years of agitation. The objects were to secure an effective adjustment of the debt, to get rid of an expensive system of city government, and to place the property of the citizens beyond the reach of the mandamus writ of the Federal courts.

Among other sources of authority to sustain the action of the Legislature in thus repealing the charter of a public corporation that was in debt, was a reference to the following cases:

But this whole subject, both as to the power of the State and as to the right of the creditors of public corporations, has lately been so clearly defined and settled by the Supreme Court of the United States in the case of Barkeley vs. Levee Commissioners et. al., III Otto, p. 258, that there is now no room for doubt upon the subject. We will set out the head notes of this decision:

"1. A public corporation, charged with specific duties, such as building and repairing levees with in a certain district, being superseded in its functions by a law dividing the district, and creating a new corporation for one portion, and placing the other under charge of the local authorities, ceases to exist except so far as its existence is expressly continued for special objects, such as settling up its indebtedness and the like.

"2. If, within such limited existence, no provision is made for the continuance or new election of the officers of such corporation, the functions of the existing officers will cease when their respective terms expire, and the corporation will be *de facto* extinct.

"3. In such case, if there be a judgment against the corporation, mandamus will not lie to enforce the assessment of taxes for its payment, there being no officers to whom the writ can be directed.

"4. The Court can not by mandamus compel the new corporations to perform the duties of the extinct corporation in the levy of taxes for the payment of its debts, especially where their territorial jurisdiction is not the same, and the law has not authorized them to make such levy.

"5. Nor can the Court order the Marshal to levy taxes in such a case; nor in any case, except where a specific law authorizes such a proceeding.

"6. Under these circumstances, the judgment creditor is, in fact, without remedy, and can only apply to the Legislature for relief."

This opinion was delivered in 1876. It speaks in no uncertain terms; it is the deliberate judgment of an undivided Court, and its authority can not be questioned by any power in this land. It decides that a State has the power to abolish a public corporation, even when it owes debts, and that new corporations may be created over the same territory which are not responsible for the debts of the defunct corporation; and further, that the creditor has no remedy in the courts whatever, but can only apply to the Legislature for relief.

Then, under this decision, the legal right of the creditor only extends to the assets of which the corporation dies possessed, but the creditor has no lien or charge upon the private property of the individuals who resided within the limits of the defunct corporation. (Heine vs. Levee Commissioners, 19 Wall; Barkeley vs. Levee Commissioners, *supra*.) These cases overrule and repudiate the extreme doctrines as to the powers of the Federal courts which Judge Dillon attempted to establish in the cases of Ste. Genevieve vs. Welsh, and Lansing vs. County Treasurer. (Dillon C. C. Reports, 1871, pp. 130, 525.)

The misfortunes of Mobile were ascribed to the decline of its prosperity. For proof of its decline, it is stated that on January 7, 1860, there were in Mobile Bay 74 ships and barks. On that day the cotton receipts for the year had been 490,761 bales, and of this number there had been shipped to New Orleans 17,797 bales. On January 7, 1871, there were in the port only 19 ships and barks, and the receipts

of cotton to that date had been 207,699 bales, of which there had been shipped to New Orleans 37,453 bales. On January 4, 1879, there were in port only 13 ships and barks. The receipts of cotton were 215,521 bales, but of this number there had been shipped to New Orleans for sale and export the enormous sum of 91,005 bales. Nearly half of the receipts have gone to New Orleans. At the time of the passage of the acts the Mayor of the city stated that its bonded indebtedness was $2,-497,856. He was in favor of a refunding of the debt at the rate of 60 cents on the dollar, bearing 5 per cent. interest for ten years, and then 6 per cent. until maturity—running for a period of thirty years. He thought that if this was done the city could pay the interest promptly; he was satisfied that with judicious management the expenses of the city could be reduced to $160,000 per annum. To meet this there was

Three fourths of 1 per cent. on $15,000,-000 taxable valuables	$112,500 00
Licenses, wharves, etc.	70,000 00
Total city expenses	$182,500 00
Surplus over $160,000	$22,500 00

If the city debt were refunded as suggested, the whole tax of the city would be 1¼ per cent. on taxable values. In the opinion of its chief officer, by the lengthy period during which a quarantine was kept in force in 1878, heavy expenses were incurred; but for this the city would have met all its obligations. The statistics of the trade of the city for 1879 have not yet been made up; but, according to the report of the Board of Trade, the business of Mobile for the year ending September 30, 1878, shows a considerable increase. The receipts of cotton were larger than during the previous year, while the value of exports aggregated over $19,000,000, an increase of more than $6,000,-000, and the imports ran up from $648,404 to $1,148,442. The value of the lumber exports increased $50,000, and the importation of all staple articles of merchandise was largely in excess of the previous year. The receipts of cotton advanced from 27,000 bags in 1877 to 51,400 bags in 1878. A second cotton-mill was put in operation in Mobile during the past year. This mill began work with 1,344 spindles, and produced from 900 to 1,000 pounds of yarn, rope, twine, carpet-warp, etc., per day, using from 10 to 12 bales of cotton per week, and employing about 35 operatives. With its present capacity it can use 600 bales annually.

The three commissioners were appointed by the Governor, and they at once proceeded to take the required oath and file their bonds. On February 15th they presented and filed in the Chancery Court their petition to take charge of the city property and assets as provided by the act of the Legislature. This action prevented the appointment of a receiver by a Federal court. The case of Memphis (see

TENNESSEE) was different. A bill was filed in the Federal court and the funds of the city attached under it before the corporation of Memphis was dissolved by act of the Legislature. The corporation of the Port of Mobile was soon organized, and its administration of affairs commenced.

The following resolution relative to the election of Presidential Electors was adopted in the Senate:

Whereas, The interference by officers of the United States in popular elections is justly regarded by the people of this State as an evil of great magnitude; and *Whereas,* Such interference, in part at least, is to influence and control the action of this State in the selection of Electors for President and Vice-President of the United States; therefore, *Resolved,* That the Committee on Federal Relations be instructed to inquire into the expediency of providing for a law for the selection of Electors for President and Vice-President by the General Assembly until the acts of Congress authorizing interference by Federal authority are repealed.

The sum of $3,000 was appropriated to carry into effect the health laws of the State.

An act was passed which provided for the settlement of delinquent taxes. Under its provisions, where lands or real estate of any kind have been sold for taxes and purchased by the State, between the 1st of January, 1866, and 1st of January, 1878, the owner may now redeem the same by paying 50 per cent. of the amount of taxes for which it was sold, together with 50 per cent. of all taxes which have since accrued. When no assessment of taxes has been made of lands or real estate after the first sale thereof for taxes, and purchase thereof by the State, the Judge of Probate of the county in which such land or real estate may be situated shall assess the same for each subsequent year when proposed to be redeemed.

Another act was passed to secure a better payment of taxes in future. It requires the collector to docket the cases of all delinquencies in a book, and hand the book to the Probate Judge by the first day of March. The Probate Judge is to hold court in April, and thirty days thereafter, say about the 1st of May, is to issue to the owner, or his agent or representative, of each parcel of real estate entered in said book, a notice setting forth the parcels of property on which he is reported a delinquent, and notifying him to appear on a given day and show cause why a decree of sale should not be made for the amount due to the State and county. If no defense is made within ten days thereafter, the Judge enters up a decree ordering a sale of the land. At the end of the term of the court the collector advertises the lands for sale, giving thirty days' notice. The Probate Judge attends the sale and makes a record of the result. An appeal lies from the decree of the Probate Judge to the Circuit Court upon giving bonds in twice the amount of the decree. The land thus sold may be redeemed by the owner, his agent or representative, mortgagee or other person having a beneficial interest in such land, at any time before the expiration of two years from the date of sale, by depositing with the Probate Judge of the county in which such real property was sold, the amount of purchase-money, and a penalty of 10 per cent. thereon, damages on the taxes and the costs, and interest on the taxes and costs, at the rate of 8 per cent. per annum from the date of sale, and the costs of the certificates of purchase, all taxes on such land which have accrued subsequently to the sale, unless such taxes have been paid to the collector, as may be shown by his receipt, and also paying the sum of one dollar to the Judge. The tax-collector is compelled by this law to seize any personal property he can find for the collection of taxes; but, before he enters upon his docket any lands of delinquents, he must swear that he has searched diligently for personal property upon which to make the levy, and has not been able to find any.

The Legislature authorized a new loan for the purpose of taking up a million of interest-bearing notes outstanding. The notes were issued at 8 per cent. interest, and were a burden upon the revenue of the State to the amount of $80,000. It was believed that bonds might be sold at par bearing 6 per cent. interest, the proceeds of which could be used to retire the notes. An offer for the whole loan was made to the Governor from Boston at 6 per cent., with a premium of one half of one per cent. This was declined, as another offer had been received, principally from citizens of Alabama, with a premium of 2 per cent. This indication of the healthy condition of the State credit induced the Governor to determine to offer the loan at 5 per cent.

The report of the Auditor in the last of October showed that for the past fiscal year the disbursements of the Treasury were the lowest, all things considered, for any year since the war. The receipts for taxes were $564,722.17; total from licenses and all sources $122,307.58; making a total of $687,029.75. The total disbursements were $685,026.47. The total collections, including school money, amount to $942,998.61; disbursements, including school money, $872,867.48. The receipts are less than last year, but this is mainly due, as the Auditor maintains, to the reduction of the rate of taxation from 7½ to 7 mills. The report shows remarkable diminutions in the amount of assessments in nearly all the counties. Of the 62 counties tabulated in the report, 50 show a decrease as compared with last year's assessment. The Auditor puts it down as the general opinion that, so far from there being depreciation in the value of property throughout the State, there has been just the reverse. He, however, helps the situation somewhat by adding, "Supplemental and collectors' assessments may bring up these counties considerably," though he does not believe the assessment will reach the "total of the present tax year." The State is burdened with real estate, purchased at tax sales, from which it derives no revenue. In one county about 197,000 acres, or nearly one third of the entire county, was bid in by the State for the taxes of 1873.

As the sessions of the Legislature are biennial, the condition of the public institutions is stated for the two years before 1879. In the Deaf, Dumb, and Blind Institute, there were in 1878, mutes 41, blind 13; total, 54. The expense per capita was $224.24. All deaf-mute or blind children residing in the State, whose parents are unable to pay their expenses while at the institute, are entitled to board, tuition, schoolroom expenses, and medicine, free of charge. No provision is made for the payment of traveling expenses, or for clothing. An act of the General Assembly provides that, "in all cases where the parents of pupils sent to the Institution for the Deaf and Dumb and the Blind are too poor to furnish them with good and sufficient clothing, or where pupils are without parents and unable to furnish themselves with such clothing, the Probate Judge of the county shall certify the same to the principal, who shall procure such necessary clothing and charge the same to said county." The total expenses of the institution for the past year footed up $12,453.90.

The total value of railroad property in Alabama, upon which tax assessment is made, is $10,297,033.35. The assessment for 1877 was $10,627,559.90, showing a difference of $330,526.55 in favor of last year.

The number of railroads in the State is 24, and their total length is 1,819 miles. When all the roads are completed which have been projected, there will be a total length of main line of 2,850 miles. The total estimated value of all the railroads, according to the assessors' books, is $10,528,060.

The number of convicts received in the penitentiary from October 1, 1877, to September 30, 1878, was 218, which, added to the number, 655, remaining in the prison October 1, 1877, amounts to 873. The sex of the prisoners is: males, white, 96; females, white, 6; males, colored, 733; females, colored, 38. Of the number, 555 were natives of Alabama; of the previous occupations, 447 were laborers; of the crimes for which they were imprisoned, there were 262 for burglary and 274 for grand larceny. The earnings of the penitentiary, over and above all expenses, for the fiscal year ending September 30, 1878, amounted to $35,649.92. The number of convicts discharged during the past year was 137, and the number pardoned was 30.

The Governor in his efforts to increase the earnings of the penitentiary advertised for proposals to lease the labor. Many bids were made, but before they had been acted upon, with two or three exceptions, those having convicts hired proposed to rescind their contracts on the 1st of January ensuing, and to enter into new contracts for five years from that date at $6 per month for all able-bodied convicts, taking all others at rates to be agreed upon between them and the warden, and receiving all at the jails without cost of transportation. This the Governor agreed to, and rejected all the bids for lease. These new contracts embrace all the convicts in the penitentiary on the 1st of January except the so-called Williams hands, until January 1, 1883, and except about one hundred others under old contracts expiring by March 1, 1881, and all that are sentenced thereto for five years. There are about 650 convicts, of whom about 600 are able-bodied; and this average, maintained for two years, will probably be fully maintained for the five years. Four hundred of these, subject to the new contracts at $6 per month each, will in 1880 earn $28,800. About 100 under old contracts not rescinded, at $5 per month each, will next year earn $6,000. The Williams hands will nominally earn, as heretofore, $6,000 a year until 1883. The gross earnings for 1880, to become larger thereafter as the $5 per month contracts expire, will therefore be $34,400, exclusive of the $6,000 for the penitentiary farm. The dead-heads will cost the State nothing—heretofore an expense of several thousand dollars a year. The transportation of convicts will cost the State nothing—heretofore ranging from $9,000 to $15,000 a year. The State's disbursements will be limited to the payment of the salaries of the officers and inspectors — say $7,000. The net cash receipts, therefore, should be about $27,000 for the calendar year 1880, and greater for each of the succeeding four years. This institution in former years has been a constant drain on the Treasury.

The number of patients in the Insane Hospital on October 1, 1878, was 403, and the daily average 389. The maintenance of these has cost the State a small amount over $64,000. Upon an analysis of the results of the biennial period ending with September 30, 1878, it will appear that the number of patients discharged cured is 40.50 per cent. upon the admissions, and the deaths 3.87 per cent. of the total number under treatment. The report of the officers of the institution thus answers the question, "What is insanity?"—

The fact should be kept prominently in view that insanity is a disease, and a disease of the brain. Too great prominence, indeed, can not be given to these two important considerations. Perception, thought, judgment, memory, imagination, conscience, and, in fact, all the manifestations, are such mysterious forces or results that the average mind turns away in despair from every endeavor to explore their relations or the laws of their origin and normal action. But the states of a diseased organ—how they are brought about, and the precautions necessary to the avoidance of like pathological results under similar conditions—are problems which, in their analogies to those of other organs and functions, invite and encourage investigation. But the definition will be needful in still another aspect. It tends most effectually to controvert, and will ultimately abolish, the absurd notion that insanity is a disgrace. This erroneous view of the disease, born doubtless of the belief, once very prevalent, that insanity implied demoniac possession, does still a vast deal of harm. It causes too often a concealment of the disorder until the curative stage has passed away. It invests it with attributes not only mysterious and forbidding, but alike prejudicial to its proper humane and scientific treatment. It adds greatly, too, to the afflictive burden of those who suffer from its lighter forms, or who have recovered from its more serious attacks.

The report of the physician (Dr. Bryce), after designating alcohol "as the most active of all the exciting causes of insanity," presents the following statement compiled from facts of the total annual expense of alcoholic stimulants in this country :

There are consumed in this country each year 561,-000,000 gallons of alcoholic liquors, which at manufacturers' prices cost the consumers the round sum of $1,841,204,000. It kills 164,062 persons each year, whose days are shortened ten years, making a total of 1,640,620 years of time, which at $50 per year makes $82,031,000. There are 1,523,662 regular or moderate drinkers, who it is estimated lose one third of their time as a consequence of the gratification of this appetite, entailing a pecuniary loss alone of $76,-182,100. The total amount of crime costs the Government annually $32,528,487, three fourths of which, or $24,396,328, is attributable to intemperance. Add the cost of pauperism caused by this evil, $21,375,000, and we find the total annual expense of alcoholic stimulants to the people of the United States to be $2,041,249,428.

Some cases of indictment for election frauds occurred in Dallas County, and were brought up for trial before the United States Court (Judge Bruce), at Montgomery. The counsel for the defense maintained that the jury law in the statute-book was operative and valid, whereas the Court and District Attorney held the reverse, as follows: The counsel for the defense moved to quash the indictments based upon the provisions of section 820 of the Revised Statutes of the United States, Boutwell edition. This section constitutes the pith of the somewhat celebrated ironclad oath. (See CONGRESS, UNITED STATES.) One at least of the members of the recent grand jury of the United States was a Confederate soldier, and consequently could not take this oath. The counsel for the defendants held that so long as the oath was contained in the Revised Statutes it was operative and of full force and effect. Judge Bruce maintained just the reverse. He held that the ironclad oath was effectually repealed prior to the passage of the act adopting the Revised Statutes of the United States by Congress, and that its appearance in the new edition of these statutes did not reënact it. The law which was passed by Congress, accepting the Boutwell edition of the Revised Statutes of the United States, included all laws of a general and permanent character in force on the 1st day of December, 1873. Judge Bruce held that the test-oath act was repealed before December 1, 1873, and consequently, not being one of the acts in force on that date, its appearance in the Revised Statutes did not reënact it. Hence the

motion to quash indictments found by the late grand jury of the United States, because a Confederate soldier was a member thereof (and of course could not take the ironclad oath), was denied. Upon a similar state of circumstances Judge Woods, of the United States Circuit Court, held precisely the opposite of the opinion of Judge Bruce, and quashed several indictments in Louisiana because upon the grand jury which presented them there were members who could not take the ironclad oath. Their decisions were final, because in these cases, which really involve the liberty of the citizen, there is no appeal from the decision of the Federal Judge.

Many revenue cases brought before the Court developed the fact that Commissioners were in the habit of issuing blank affidavits to agents and deputy marshals, to be filled up with the names of such parties as the agent or deputy marshal might be able to charge, on his own oath, with violation of the law, as he had reason to believe. On such warrants many innocent persons have been arrested, and subjected to great expense, injustice, and oppression, and the Commissioners, agents, and marshals have reaped a large amount of unlawful fees. Judge Woods read an able opinion, setting forth these facts, and denounced such proceedings as contrary to the United States Constitution, which declares that "no warrants shall issue but upon probable cause, supported by oath or affirmation, and particularly describing the place to be searched, and the persons or things to be seized." He concluded with an order that no Commissioner shall issue any warrant of search, seizure, or arrest, unless a witness shall first appear before said Commissioner and make the proper affidavit.

The statute of Alabama declares that "all railroad companies in the State . . . may, for the transportation of local freight, demand and receive not exceeding fifty per cent. more than the rate charged for the transportation of the same description of freight over the whole line of the road." The Supreme Court of the State held that, as it is the policy of railroad corporations to so connect their lines as to effect a long continuous connected line of transportation, and under such arrangement the saving of labor and increase of business resulting from such connection enable each road to accept its share of the sum realized from this branch of the business, a sum which would fall much below fair remuneration for receiving, loading, transporting, unloading, and delivering the same quantity and description of freight, whose departure and distribution were each within the limit of the one road, hence the words "over the whole line of its road" mean, and only mean, freight which is taken at one terminus and discharged at the other.

ALASKA. This distant region, belonging by purchase to the United States, has not yet been

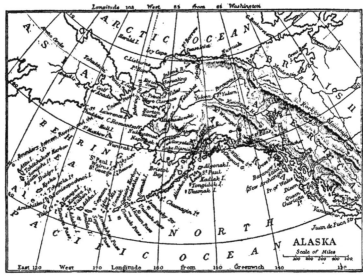

advanced to the dignity of an organized Territory. The relations of the inhabitants to the Federal Government are only such as were obtained for them by the treaty with Russia in March, 1867. The third article provides that the inhabitants of the ceded Territory, with the exception of the uncivilized native tribes, shall be admitted to the enjoyment of all the rights of citizens of the United States, and shall be maintained and protected in the free enjoyment of their liberty of property and religion. The uncivilized tribes are subject to such laws and regulations as the United States may from time to time adopt in regard to the aboriginal tribes of that country. There is no law for the arrest of persons charged with common-law offenses, such as assault, robbery, and murder, and no magistrate authorized to issue or execute process in such cases. Serious difficulties have already arisen from offenses of this character, not only among the original inhabitants, but among citizens of the United States and other countries, who have engaged in mining, fishing, and other business operations there. On July 25th the people at Sitka assembled and resolved upon the organization among themselves of a civil government. This was completed on August 28th. The preamble of the ordinance adopted sets forth the danger to person and property arising under an absence of all civil law; gives the reasons why no previous efforts could be made to form a government; proclaims the intention to secure protection against violence from the Indians, and that they feel able to maintain a

o s ona form until supplanted by a regularly enacted system. A chief magistrate and five selected men, each in separate precincts, were provided and authority given to try civil and criminal cases, to attend to the municipal affairs of Sitka, and to take charge of estates. All citizens entered heartily into the matter, and every one entitled voted, and the government was accepted. The officers elect are: Collector Ball, chief magistrate; selectmen, first precinct, P. Corcoran; second, T. Haltern; third, N. G. Matropolosky; fourth, (omitted); fifth (cannery), Thomas McCauly. There is no test of American citizenship; all white men twenty-one years of age are voters. The officers elect constitute together a provisional council, which regulates and sets in motion the machinery and details of the government, hears appeals from the selectmen's decisions, and tries grave offenses.

In the early part of the year reports were spread respecting apprehended attacks by the Indians; but nothing of the kind has taken place. A letter received at the Navy Department, dated June 23d, from the commander of the United States ship Jamestown, which was ordered there to protect the white settlement from the Indians, represents the state of affairs as very quiet. He says: " I am satisfied that both the local Indians and the Tchilcats have friendly feelings toward the whites, and that there is no danger of any premeditated attack upon the settlement. The whites furnish to the Indians a market for their furs, fish, etc., and supply them with many needed articles. Many of the Indians, both men and women, 'dress up' on Sunday, and cheap dry-goods are in demand. The two settlements have existed in juxtaposition for many years, and it is exceedingly creditable to both that, with no law to govern them, they have both so governed themselves that outrages and disorder are uncommon. There is, however, a terrible danger to which the whites are exposed, and it is far from an imaginary one. When intoxicated with the vile 'hootchenoo,' like all drunken men, the Indians are liable to commit outrages which the whites are powerless to prevent, and to resent which would draw upon them the vengeance of the entire family to which the culprit belonged. It is my belief that in February last the settlement narrowly escaped a massacre. That it did escape is due greatly to the influence of certain friendly Indians of superior intelligence. I do not think that there is any danger while a vessel of war is here, and I hope to be able to so influence the Indians that after we shall have left they will preserve peace."

The revenue derived from the Territory annually is about $300,000, and the supply of fish is destined to equal the demand of the whole country. Coal has been found in abundance, with iron ore of excellent quality. Gold and silver are known to exist, but the mountains are heavily timbered, which interrupts prospecting, especially where there is trouble with the natives. No present inducements warrant the Government in keeping constant military guard over so vast a range. But if there be gold regions and encouragement offered, California would furnish 5,000 miners, who would open the mines and take care of the hostile Indians. With the exception of those that are in the southern section, the Indians and Esquimaux of Alaska are peaceable, friendly, and inclined to trade. The climate, though cloudy and rainy, is not so hard as is supposed. The winters are less severe than in Canada. As timber is plenty, housing is not costly. Alaska is as large as many Californias, and the existence of one gold-field would indicate more. With the furs, fisheries, timber, and coals added to its gold and silver mines, it would soon take rank with California in its productions.

ALEKO PASHA, the Governor-General of Eastern Roumelia, was born about 1830. He is a Bulgarian and a Christian, his Christian name being Prince Alexander Vogorides. His father was the Prince Vogorides who played such an important part during the Crimean war, and who was the first Prince of Samos. He was a native of a small village near the Kazan Pass, and went in early youth to Constantinople, where he was educated in a Greek school. It was mainly owing to his influence that the Greeks during the Crimean war did not openly espouse the cause of Russia. Aleko Pasha, who was his third son, occupied in the beginning of his diplomatic career various subordinate positions at Berlin, London, and

Vienna. During his stay in Germany he devoted himself ardently to study, and he speaks with great fluency French, English, Italian, and German. During the war with Russia he was Turkish Ambassador in Vienna, when his knowledge of Western affairs made him of great value to his Government. When, however, in spite of his repeated assurances that Austria would not permit Servia to take part in the war, the latter country did begin hostilities, he was recalled, particularly as he was a warm friend of Midhat Pasha. Upon the creation of the principality of Eastern Roumelia, he was selected for the position of Prince, as being a Christian and a Bulgarian. He is described as a man of strict integrity, and as possessing a thorough knowledge of the condition of his principality.

ALEXANDER I., first Prince of Bulgaria, was born April 5, 1857. He is the son of Prince Alexander of Hesse, the brother of the Empress of Russia. His mother was the daughter of Count Haucke, who was a Russian general and for a time Minister of War. Upon her marriage with the Prince of Hesse she received the title of Princess of Battenberg. Prince Alexander is the second son of this union, his elder brother being now in the British navy. He served with the Russian army all through the Turkish war, and is well acquainted with Bulgaria and its inhabitants, which could not but recommend him to the Bulgarians. He rode in the ranks of the 8th Uhlans, and was also attached to the staff of Prince Charles of Roumania. At the siege of Plevna he gained unusual experience, was among the first who crossed the Balkans with General Gourko, and accompanied the Grand Duke Nicholas to Constantinople. After the close of the war he was transferred to the Prussian Life Guards, and at the time of his election was doing garrison duty at Potsdam.

ALGERIA, a province of France in Northern Africa. Governor-General in 1879, Albert Grévy. The country is divided into territory under civil administration and territory under military administration. The former is subdivided into departments and the latter into divisions. The area and population, according to the "Statistique Générale de l'Algérie" (1877), are as follows:

DEPARTMENTS AND DIVISIONS.	Square kilometres.	Square miles.	Population.
1. Territory under civil administration:			
Algiers	8,268	3,193	484,711
Oran	15,356	5,929	416,465
Constantine	17,976	6,941	414,714
Total	41,600	16,063	1,315,950
2. Territory under military administration:			
Algiers	96,899	37,418	587,836
Oran	70,747	27,317	236,716
Constantine	109,068	42,121	727,124
Total	276,784	106,851	1,551,676
Total Algeria	318,334	122,914	2,867,626

On March 16th, M. Albert Grévy was appointed Civil Governor of Algeria in place of General Chanzy. General Chanzy, in a farewell address to the inhabitants of Algeria, reviewed his efforts for the gradual assimilation of the colony to the mother-country. Out of 853,000 Europeans, 345,000 are under French common law, as also 1,200,000 natives, military government being confined to 8,000 Europeans settled round advanced posts and 1,267-000 natives inhabiting remote regions. Moderation and justice have been shown toward the natives, and the best relations exist with Tunis and Morocco. The sequestration inflicted on the insurgents of 1871 has been completed, and the law of 1873 on native proprietors is being carried into effect. Educationally, French Algeria figures among the most advanced states, and higher education is being arranged for. Harbor-works, roads, and the reclamation of marshes are in full activity, while 700 kilometres of railways are in working order, 650 under construction, and 1,150 projected. The commerce with Europe amounts to 380,-000,000 francs per annum. Within six years 176 fresh villages have been founded, and the European rural population has increased by nearly 50,000. General Chanzy leaves the country with the satisfaction of seeing it in the path of progress, and with thorough confidence in its future. In a second address to the army, he remarked that, after generously shedding its blood in the conquest of a bravely resisting people, it has been and is still the most powerful instrument of colonization and progress.

M. Grévy on taking possession of his post issued a proclamation to the inhabitants, in which he said that the system which might have been suitable in the early and laborious stages of the colonization of Algeria runs the risk, if prolonged, of compromising the development of the country. The government would, therefore, be essentially civil. The new Governor-General then dwelt on his intention vigorously to carry out the extension of the railways and high-roads and all the reforms feasible to make Algeria for the Europeans and the Frenchmen, whom it attracts more and more, an image of the mother-country. As to the natives, they might count on the kindly disposition of the Government, which, along with the consciousness of its power and rights, is imbued with a sense of its duties toward civilization. By widely diffused education, justice, and order, the tribes will acquire a taste for French institutions.

On June 1st the General-in-Chief telegraphed that unforeseen disturbances had broken out in Aures, in the province of Constantine, among the tribe of the Uled Daud. Several natives and six Spahis accompanying a French officer had been killed, and the latter had escaped with difficulty. To be prepared for any contingency, he had sent three battalions and two sections of artillery from Algiers to Constan-

tine. The revolt was declared suppressed by the middle of the month, after a few engagements. The property of the insurgents was sequestered, and they were required to pay a minimum contribution of 800,000 francs. The leader, however, escaped to the oasis of Zori-bel-el-Wid, from where he could reach Tunisian territory.

In July a commission was appointed by M. de Freycinet, the French Minister of Public Works, to report on the feasibility of a railway from Algeria to Soodan and Senegal. The population of the Soodan, M. Freycinet remarked, is estimated at 100,000,000. The Niger traverses half of it. The inhabitants are industrious. The moving sands, formerly considered universal, are only a local accident, and the soil is everywhere similar to that of European soils. A railway from Algeria to the Niger would not exceed 2,000 kilometres, and would be much less costly than the projected Panama Canal. A preliminary commission had already recommended the scheme, one ground being that it would repress the internal slave-trade; but it enjoined circumspection on account of the imperfect knowledge of certain parts of the Sahara. It therefore suggested a survey of a line of 300 kilometres between Biskra and Wargla, to be connected with the Algiers and Constantine line, and that explorations should be made beyond Wargla toward the Niger. The Budget Committee of the French Chamber and the Senate Committee on Algerian Railways had also pronounced in favor of France taking an active part in the opening up of Central Africa.

ALLEN, WILLIAM, a Governor, Senator, etc., was born at Edenton, Chowan County, North Carolina, in 1806. By the loss of both parents he became an orphan in infancy. As there were no common schools in North Carolina at that time, nor in Virginia, to which he subsequently removed, he had no public opportunities to obtain instruction. By private aid and his own efforts he obtained the rudiments of an education. While at Lynchburg, Virginia, he supported himself by working as a saddler's apprentice. At sixteen years of age, with his bundle in hand, he started on foot for Chillicothe, Ohio, to find a sister whom he had never seen, and who was the mother of Senator Allen G. Thurman. Here he was sent to the town academy, and continued under the supervision of his sister until he became a law student in the office of Edward King, a son of the distinguished Rufus King of Revolutionary fame. He was admitted to practice before he was twenty-one years of age, and soon attained considerable reputation as a criminal lawyer. Public speaking had always presented great attractions to him, and he cultivated the art of addressing juries and assemblies successfully, with more diligence than the learning of cases and the acquisition of pure legal habits of thought and statement. He had a fine figure and a powerful voice, and soon attracted public attention. He shortly after became the Democratic candidate for Congress in a strong opposition district, and had an ex-Governor for a competitor. He was elected by one majority, and was the youngest member in the House of the Twenty-third Congress. At the next election Mr. Allen was defeated by a small majority, but obtained fifteen hundred more votes than the rest of the ticket. In 1837, when only thirty-one years of age, he was elected to the United States Senate and took his seat March 4th, where he became a leader. Just before the expiration of his term he went directly before the people of Ohio as a candidate for reëlection. The result was that the Democrats had a handsome majority in the Legislature, and Mr. Allen was reëlected without opposition. In the Democratic National Convention of 1848, which met in Baltimore, so bitter was the contest between the friends of Cass and Van Buren, the leading candidates, that, to prevent a division, a committee, composed of men from both factions, waited on Senator Allen in Washington and urged him to accept the nomination for the Presidency; but he persistently refused to allow his name to be used, taking the ground that, as he had been an earnest advocate of Cass's nomination, to accept a nomination himself would be a betrayal of his friend. He afterward made a canvass of New York and Pennsylvania in favor of Mr. Cass. Mr. Allen then retired from public life, from which he did not emerge again until 1873, when he ran as the Democratic candidate for Governor of Ohio, and was elected by about 1,000 majority, his associates on the State ticket all suffering defeat. Mr. Allen was again the Democratic nominee for Governor in 1875, but after a vigorous contest was defeated by General Rutherford B. Hayes, who was in the next year the Republican Presidential candidate. Thus closed his political career. He continued in excellent health until the morning of July 10th, when he complained of being unwell, but did not regard his illness of sufficient importance to receive attention until the afternoon. At six o'clock he retired to bed, and was up and down several times during the night. His son-in-law and daughter sat up in an adjoining room. A little before one o'clock she was startled by seeing her father arise from the bed, stagger to a chair, and fall into it. Before they could reach him he was dead. His death was instantaneous.

AMERICA. The prominent change in the administration of affairs in the Dominion of Canada during the year has been the adoption of a system of high protection for home manufactures. It remains to be seen whether this policy, to which the Canadians have committed themselves almost irrevocably, may not prove too burdensome to a people so largely engaged in agricultural and similar pursuits. The general depression of trade had, however, disposed them to welcome any innovation in their commercial policy, and the large increase in imports from the United States during several years, with a decrease from Great Britain, had awakened discontent in all classes. A constitutional question arose out of the dismissal of Lieutenant-General Letellier of Quebec, which became complicated by later events until it involved the Dominion Government, the Governor, and the British Government in a controversy. (See DOMINION OF CANADA.) The extension of railway communications has been one of the prominent Canadian questions of late years, and especially the construction of the Pacific Railroad. During the year a section from Lake Superior to the Province of Manitoba, about 185 miles in length, has been put under contract, and the line has been extended west of the Red River to a point south of Lake Manitoba. The work is also connected at St. Vincent with the system of the Northwestern States.

In the United States, the 1st of January, 1879, was fixed for the resumption of specie payments by the Federal Government at its place of deposits in New York City. This seems to have taken place without producing the slightest unfavorable impression. The enormous exportation and diminished importation of the previous year still continued, and soon enlivened the stagnant trade that had prevailed during the larger part of 1878. The consequence has been a state of remarkable and increasing prosperity during 1879.

The political affairs of the country have been quiet. The only agitation was that produced in Congress by the efforts of the majority to remove from the statutes every appearance of authority for military interference at the elections, while the President vetoed all such bills, although they contained the appropriations necessary for the expenses of the Government. In this conflict between the legislative and the executive departments no conclusion was reached.

The results of the State elections were generally in favor of the Republicans, although the total vote was somewhat reduced. The elections attracted much interest, as they were held in some of the large States, which occupy an important position in a close Presidential election, such as is anticipated in 1880.

Some disturbances occurred with roving bands of Indians on the frontier, by which a few lives were lost on each side. The hostile condition was promptly suppressed, and peace has uniformly prevailed throughout the country.

In Mexico and the Central American States no event of political importance transpired during the year. In the first-named country, demonstrations hostile to the Diaz Administration were for a time apprehended; but, with continued tranquillity, confidence was restored, in the belief that no change would take place in the existing order of things before the elections for a new President in 1880.

Venezuela was the scene of internecine dissensions, though of comparatively little moment, the disturbance having occurred in States far distant from the capital and preserved a purely local character. Guzman Blanco, having resumed his position as Dictator, proposed some notable measures of reform; among others, a new territorial division, reducing the number of States to seven, in order to "limit the central and extend the Federal power of the republic."

The year was marked by more or less agitation in some of the States of Colombia; but the triumph of the Independent party lulled the revolutionary spirit, and was hailed as an earnest of the early return to permanent peace, it being confidently believed that a large proportion of the influential men of all parties would rally round the government of the President-elect, and second his efforts toward the regeneration of the country.

The progress of time can scarcely be said to have improved the condition of affairs in Ecuador. Political arrests and growing discontent of the people with the Government were the almost exclusive burden of such reports as found an echo outside the limits of that distracted country.

A disputed question of boundaries between Chili and Bolivia led to the declaration by the former against the latter of a war, in which Peru, the friend and ally of Bolivia, was afterward involved, and which has proved one of the most disastrous in the annals of South America since the period of independence.

Peace in the remaining countries of the Southern Continent has continued undisturbed, and the efforts of the governments, as well as those of the people, were directed to the development of the various elements of national prosperity.

AMES, EDWARD R., preacher and bishop, was born at Ames township, Ohio, on May 20, 1806, and died at Baltimore, Maryland, on April 25th. His early education was plain and practical. A natural taste for reading was fostered by a local library to which he had access, and when twenty years of age he entered the Ohio University at Athens. There he remained many years, and supported himself mainly by teaching. In 1828 the Ohio Conference of the M. E. Church was in session at Chillicothe, and he attended its meetings. Bishop Roberts, the presiding officer, was so impressed with the young man's ability that he invited him to accompany him to the Illinois Conference, at Madison, Illinois. When there he made the acquaintance of several prominent Methodist clergymen, and opened a school at Lebanon, Illinois, which was the germ of McKendree College. In August, 1830, he entered the itinerant ministry, and was licensed to preach by the Rev. Peter Cartwright. He was sent to the Shoal Creek circuit, which covered an almost unlimited territory, and when the Indiana Conference was organized

in 1832, he, then a young man, went with the new Conference, and was ordained a deacon by Bishop Soule. In 1834 he was ordained an elder by Bishop Roberts, and was employed in several fields of labor, including two years spent in St. Louis, Missouri, until 1840. In that year he was appointed a delegate to the General Conference, held in Baltimore, and that body elected him Corresponding Secretary of the Missionary Society for the South and West. In this office he had the supervision of the Methodist German and Indian missions, and traveled upward of twenty-five thousand miles. He was the first chaplain ever elected by an Indian council, having served the Choctaw General Council in that capacity in 1842. From 1844 to 1852 he traveled as presiding elder on the New Albany, Indianapolis, and Jeffersonville districts of the Indiana Conference. In 1844 the State University of Indiana conferred on him the degree of A. M., and in 1848 he was elected President of the Asbury University, Indiana, but declined the honor. At the General Conference of 1852 he was elected Bishop together with Bishops Scott and Simpson; and he was the first Methodist Bishop who ever visited the Pacific coast. When the question of the separation of the Methodists came up in 1844, he opposed the division, and afterward did all he could to foster a fraternal spirit. When the ecclesiastical property of the M. E. Church South was confiscated for the time being, he was commissioned by President Lincoln and Secretary Stanton to take charge of it. This was a most delicate duty, and in its performance he visited New Orleans and other Southern cities, organizing societies and appointing white and colored preachers. During the twenty-seven years in which Bishop Ames was in the episcopacy his whole public life was marked by a strict adherence to the rules and discipline of Methodism; and even when the most difficult points came up for settlement he displayed a far-seeing judgment and quickness of comprehension which enabled him to grapple successfully with them. He had a happy facility for selecting the right men, and their conduct in the fields to which they were appointed showed the correctness of his judgment. Although grave and dignified in manner, there was a magnetism about him which attracted, and his preaching was always thoroughly enjoyed. He could scarcely be styled an orator, and yet his quiet reasoning, apt aphorisms, pertinent illustrations, and earnestness, impressed more than mere declamation. After a protracted illness from diabetes and pulmonary troubles he gradually sank until released by death. He was married twice, and left a son and two daughters.

ANGLICAN CHURCHES. In 1879 the Church of England contained in England and Wales two ecclesiastical provinces, Canterbury and York. The province of Canterbury comprises the Archbishop of Canterbury and the Bishops of London, Winchester, Oxford, St.

David's, Llandaff, Norwich, Bangor, Worcester, Gloucester and Bristol, Ely, Rochester, Lichfield, Hereford, Peterborough, Lincoln, Salisbury, Bath and Wells, Exeter, Truro (established in 1877), Chichester, St. Albans (established in 1877), and St. Asaph. The province of York comprises the Archbishop of York and the Bishops of Durham, Ripon, Chester, Carlisle, Manchester, and Sodor and Man. The Church of Ireland has the two provinces of Armagh and Dublin, each containing one archbishop and five bishops. The Episcopal Church of Scotland has seven bishops, the Bishop of Moray, Ross, and Caithness being the "Primus." In the British colonies and in missionary territories the Church of England had in 1879 also the following dioceses: 1. In Europe — Gibraltar; 2. In India — Calcutta, Lahore, Rangoon, Madras, Bombay, Labuan, and Colombo, the Bishop of Calcutta bearing the title of Metropolitan in India and Ceylon; 3. In the West Indies — Kingston (Jamaica), Barbadoes, Guiana, Antigua, Nassau, and Trinidad; 4. In China—Victoria and North China; 5. In Africa—Capetown, Graham's Town, Maritzburg, Sierra Leone, St. Helena, St. John's (late Independent Caffraria), Zoolooland, Bloemfontein (Orange Free State), Pretoria, Mauritius, Madagascar, Central Africa, and Niger (mission), the Bishop of Capetown having the title of Metropolitan; 6. In Australasia—Sydney, Melbourne, Ballarat, Adelaide, Newcastle, Bathurst, North Queensland (established in 1878), Grafton and Armidale, Perth, Brisbane, Goulburn, Tasmania, Christ Church (New Zealand), Auckland, Nelson, Wellington, Waiapu, and Dunedin (Otago), the Bishop of Sydney having the title of Metropolitan of Australia, and the Bishop of Christ Church the title of Primus of New Zealand; 7. In North America —Toronto, Newfoundland, Rupert's Land, Saskatchevan, Athabasca, Moosonee, Montreal, Fredericton, Nova Scotia (the first colonial see, founded in 1787), Huron, Columbia, Quebec, Ontario, Algoma, and Niagara; 8. Others —Falkland Islands, Honolulu, Melanesia, and Jerusalem.

The population connected with the Anglican Churches of the British Isles is estimated as follows by E. G. Ravenstein:

England and Wales	17,781,000
Scotland	73,000
Ireland	668,000
Total British Isles	18,522,000

In each of the Australian colonies the Anglican Church is the leading religious denomination. In 1877 the population connected with it in the several colonies was officially reported or estimated as follows:

New South Wales	282,000
Victoria	258,000
South Australia	51,000
Western Australia	15,000
Queensland	44,000
Tasmania	58,000
New Zealand	107,000
Total	760,000

In British North America, the Anglican Church had according to the census of 1871 a population of 494,049 in the provinces of Ontario, Quebec, Nova Scotia, and New Brunswick, 7,220 in Prince Edward Island, and 55,-184 in Newfoundland. Including the districts of British Columbia, Manitoba, and Northwest Territories, the aggregate population connected with the Church of England amounted in 1871 to about 580,000.

The *Convocation of Canterbury* met February 18th. A petition was presented in the Upper House praying the House to take into consideration the repeated applications of the Patriarch, Bishops, and clergy of the descendants and representatives of the Church of Persia and the farther East, whose Catholicos had been recognized at the Council of Nice as ranking next after the three great Patriarchs of the Church. The Archbishop of Canterbury gave some information as to the result of inquiries which had been made into the condition of these people, who constitute the community commonly called the Nestorians. The petition was referred to a committee, who were instructed to consider it and report upon it at the next group of sessions of the Convocation. A committee was appointed to inquire into the sale of next presentations and advowsons. A discussion took place on the character and status of the Reformed Episcopal Church, in the course of which the Archbishop stated that he had received a communication from a person representing himself to be one of the ministers of that body, asking whether he might officiate in any of the churches of his lordship's or any other diocese. To this the Archbishop had replied that as a clergyman of the Reformed Episcopal Church the inquirer was not entitled to officiate in any church of the dioceses of the province; and if he did, the law had provided for the taking of legal proceedings against him for the penalties prescribed in the Act of Parliament. It appeared, from statements made during the discussion, that the Colonial Church Act requires the consent of the bishop to the performance of any service by a person other than a clergyman ordained by a bishop of the Church of England; and that, when an unqualified person is allowed to officiate in the parish church, the incumbent is liable to severe penalties. In the Lower House, a petition was presented from the English Church Union, asking that steps be taken to protect the churches from the desecrations to which they are liable by the celebration therein of the (so-called) marriages of divorced persons whose real husbands or wives are still living. A gravamen was presented which embodied the representations of fellows and other members of the University of Cambridge against the continued use of the so-called damnatory clauses of the Athanasian Creed, and asking for their removal from the Liturgy. It was taken to the Upper House. A report was presented from the Committee on the Sale of Advowsons and Augmentation of Small Livings, containing a scheme for the sale of small advowsons, the patronage of which is vested in public bodies. After discussion, it was referred back. A resolution was adopted expressing the desire of the House that liberty should be given to the deans and chapters of the cathedrals of the new foundation to revise from time to time their statutes, with the consent of competent authority.

The Convocation met again for the dispatch of business on June 24th. Several days were spent in consideration of the revision of rubrics in respect to ornaments, the Athanasian Creed, and the burial service. A synodical declaration was decided upon to be appended to the Athanasian Creed, "for the removal of doubts and to prevent disquietude," which states that the creed "doth not make any addition to the faith as contained in Holy Scripture." A recommendation was adopted to the effect that in the burial service it shall be allowable, under certain circumstances, to read portions of Scripture and prayers from the Prayer-Book not at present included in the service. The following new rubric was agreed upon, to be placed immediately after the "ornaments rubric": "In saying public prayers and administering the sacraments and other rites of the Church, every priest shall wear a surplice with the stole or scarf and the hood of his degree; or, if he thinks fit, the gown, with hood or scarf; and no other vestments shall at any other time be used by him contrary to the monition of the Bishop of the diocese; provided always, that the rubric shall not be understood to repeal the 24th, 25th, and 58th canons of 1604." The schedule of proposed alterations of the rubrics in the Prayer-Book having been completed, a report of the business of revision in which the Convocation had been engaged for several years was ordered to be presented to her Majesty, with an address, in which it was submitted that in approving the accompanying alterations and recommendations, the Houses did not wish to be understood as inviting the sanction of the two Houses of Parliament to what was proposed until the draft bill presented with the report should have become a law.

The *Convocation of York*, at its session in July, declined to take any action on the ornaments rubric, every effort in that direction being defeated by the disagreement of the two houses. A similar result was reached in the propositions which were made to modify the use of the Athanasian Creed. A resolution was offered to the effect that no action of Convocation ought to diminish the frequency of the use of this creed. The Bishop of Durham offered an amendment proposing to change the rubric so as to make the use of the creed optional. Both motions were lost by disagreement. A motion favoring variations in the burial service, similar to those approved in the Convocation of Canterbury, was lost in both

houses. A resolution was passed unanimously, to the effect "that in the opinion of the Convocation it is inexpedient that any legislative sanction be sought for proposed amendments of the rubrics until the 'Bill to provide Facilities,' etc., agreed to by the Convocation of Canterbury July 4, 1879, which was previously in substance agreed to by the Lower House of Convocation of York 19th February, 1879, or some similar measure, had become law."

The Archbishop of Canterbury waited on the Home Secretary August 15th, and placed in his hands the report which had been agreed upon by both houses of the Convocation of Canterbury in answer to her Majesty's letter of business, on the subject of the rubrics of the Book of Common Prayer. The report embodies a bill "to provide facilities for the amendment from time to time of the rites and ceremonies of the Church of England." In principle the bill recognizes that regulations respecting rites and ceremonies require to be revised from time to time, and that, as times, manners, and modes of thought change, old rules and customs must be changed to correspond. It recognizes, too, that in such changes the Church ought to take the initiative, and that the mouthpiece of the Church should be the archbishops and bishops of both provinces and the clergy by representation in the two Convocations. It recognizes, further, the necessity of the assent of the laity through Parliament to any alterations or additions to the Prayer-Book so initiated. The bill consists of eleven clauses, of which three are either explanatory or directive. The remaining eight provide that the archbishops, bishops, and clergy in both Houses of Convocation may prepare from time to time and lay before her Majesty in Council a scheme for making desirable alterations in the Prayer-Book. Any scheme so prepared is to be laid before both Houses of Parliament within twenty-one days of their meeting. Within forty days either House may address the Queen asking her Majesty to withhold her royal consent. If neither House present such address, her Majesty may make an order ratifying the scheme and specifying when it shall take effect.

A memorial from graduates of the universities and persons learned in history and archæology was prepared and addressed to the Home Secretary, asking him to advise her Majesty to take no further judicial action on the ritual reports of the Privy Council until certain historical misstatements, misquotations from, and interpolations in, important documents shall have been examined by learned men appointed by her Majesty for the purpose. Some of the misstatements are specified, such as the assertion that 1549 was the second year of Edward VI.; that the consecration prayer was omitted in 1552; that mixing wine and water apart from the service was unknown to East and West; that there are such documents in existence as the advertisements of

1564; the interpolation of the word "only" in the copies quoted in the reports; the assertion that surplice and alb were not worn "concurrently" according to any known use; the assertion that Bishop Cosin held a visitation in 1687, fifteen years after his death, etc. Decisions based on such statements, they will urge, only bring the law into contempt.

The General Conference of Anglican Bishops which met at Lambeth in July, 1878, appointed a committee "to consider the relations between the Old Catholics and others who have separated themselves from the Roman Communion. To this committee the Archbishop of Canterbury referred a petition which he had received from the dissident French ecclesiastic M. Loyson, praying for official recognition of the Old Catholics by the Anglican Episcopate. Bishop Eden, Primus of Scotland, as chairman of this committee, in the latter part of 1878, addressed a letter to M. Loyson, saying that, in conjunction with the Bishop of Edinburgh, he would so far recognize his mission as to give it a provisional oversight. Under ordinary circumstances, he said, the English Episcopate must have declined the request; but the times were not ordinary, and the conduct of the Church of Rome in issuing the recent Vatican decrees seemed to the bishops to justify a departure from their customary usage, and to authorize them to recognize a principle of yet higher obligation than that of church order. It would be impossible, however, for the bishops to pledge themselves to the administration of episcopal functions in the mission until they had become acquainted with the proposed ritual and order of the Church; and they could then do so only in the event of the ritual "in its language and ceremonies containing nothing inconsistent with the Word of God, with the principles enunciated in our formularies, with the prerogatives of the One Divine head of the Church, or with the One Mediator between God and man, the Man Christ Jesus." (See OLD CATHOLICS.)

The case of the appeals of Lord Penzance, Dean of Arches, and of Mr. James Martin, the promoter of the suit of Martin *vs.* Mackonochie, against a judgment of the Lord Chief Justice making absolute a rule obtained on behalf of the Rev. Alexander H. Mackonochie, restraining all further proceedings in the suit, came before the High Court of Appeal in March. The proceedings against Mr. Mackonochie in the Court of Arches had lasted for four years, when in June, 1878, he was sentenced by Lord Penzance to three years' suspension from his benefice. A rule was obtained in the Queen's Bench for a prohibition, based on the ground that the monition which had been inflicted upon the appellant previous to his suspension was a sentence covering all the penalty awarded, and ended the case; that any further penalty must result from a new trial, and the sentence of suspension to which

the Court appealed against had proceeded could not be imposed without such new trial. In August, 1878, the prohibition was made absolute. The Solicitor-General, who appeared for Lord Penzance, in advocating the appeal, argued that the common-law courts had no authority over the ecclesiastical courts, supporting his position by citations from old writers on the subject when the authority of the spiritual courts was admittedly independent. The case was decided, June 28th, in favor of the appellants, three of the judges giving opinions in favor of reversing, two of sustaining the decision of the Court of Queen's Bench. Lord Chief Justice Coleridge, in giving his judgment, reviewed all the circumstances of the case, and expounded the ecclesiastical laws and usages by which such cases as that before the Court were governed. He held that, both on the ground of reason and on the authorities he had looked into, such a monition as the one in question was perfectly allowable in a Court Christian, and that disobedience to such a monition might subject the offender to some form of punishment. It seemed to him that in this case suspension was warranted by the law and the practices of the ecclesiastical courts. The steps taken in this case were, to his mind, right; but, if he thought they were wrong, his conclusions as to the law and usage would be the same. He could not see the hardship of an officer of the Church being obliged to obey the law of his society, after the law had been declared to him by the highest authority in the country. He thought that Lord Penzance had not done more than he was called upon to do, and no more than what the practice of his Court justified, and he thought that that practice was not contrary to the Church Discipline Act. On the 15th of November Lord Penzance, in the Court of Arches, ordered the enforcement of the writ of prohibition which he had issued against Mr. Mackonochie in June, 1878, the operation of which had been suspended during the pendency of the appeals on the case. The writ involved a suspension of the ecclesiastical functions of Mr. Mackonochie for three years, beginning with the 23d of November. While granting it, Lord Penzance said that he would be willing to hear any application for a relaxation of sentence founded on a promise to obey the law. The Council of the Church Union determined on a policy of resistance to the judgment.

A prosecution was instituted against the Bishop of Oxford in January, requiring him to show cause why he should not institute proceedings of inquiry into charges which had been made under the Church Discipline Act against the Rev. Thomas T. Carter, rector of the parish of Clewer, for adopting ritualistic practices in worship. The Bishop appeared in person, February 27th, in the Court of Queen's Bench, and pleaded that the Church Discipline Act could not intend that he should be deprived of his right of discretion to grant or refuse a commission; and that, if this right were taken away, grave injury would result to the Church from power being given to foolish, frivolous, or vindictive persons to set the law in motion. The Court decided, March 8th, that a mandamus should be issued directing the Bishop to issue a commission of inquiry. The Lord Chief Justice, in giving the judgment of the Court, said that two questions were raised by the proceedings: first, whether the language of the Church Discipline Act imposed a duty on the Bishop which he was bound to fulfill, or merely gave him a discretionary power which he might exercise or not at his option; and, secondly, whether the Church Discipline Act had been superseded by the Public Worship Regulation Act of 1874. In regard to the meaning of the Church Discipline Act, it was a settled canon of construction that, where an act authorized the doing of a thing for the sake of justice and for the public good, the words "it shall be lawful" were to be read in a compulsory sense. The statute in question was passed with the view of enforcing the rights of parishioners to have the service of the parish church performed according to law, and the power given to the Bishop to issue a commission to inquire into the matter was certainly one to be exercised for the sake of justice and the public good. The statute had reference to the administration of justice in ecclesiastical offenses; and the maintenance of the doctrines and ritual of the established religion, for the uniformity of which so many acts have been passed, could not be other than a matter of national interest and concern. Moreover, it was the undoubted right of every inhabitant of every parish in the kingdom, who desired to frequent the parish church, to have the services performed according to the ritual established by law, without having his religious sense shocked and outraged by the introduction of innovations not sanctioned by law nor consistent with usage, and which appeared to him inconsistent with the simplicity of worship of the Church of England. Reading the whole of the act together, and looking at the state of the law previous to its being passed, their lordships were of the opinion that the act imposed a duty upon the Bishop which he might be compelled to exercise. Their lordships were further of opinion that the Church Discipline Act was still in force, and had not been superseded by the later act. The Bishop appealed against this decision to the Supreme Court of Appeal, which decided, May 30th, in his favor, reversing the decision of the Court of Queen's Bench. The decision was given by Lord Justice Bramwell, who held that *prima facie* the words "it shall be lawful," in the third section of the Church Discipline Act, constituted a discretion. In the present case, he thought, the discretion had been erroneously exercised.

The eightieth anniversary meeting of the *Church Missionary Society* was held in Lon-

don, May 5th. The total available income of the Society for the year had been £187,285, and the total expenditure had been £204,186. The total deficit for the last two years, which had to be taken from the Society's working capital, was £24,757. The sum of £35,000 had been deposited with the Society in trust for the development of an evangelistic native agency in connection with the native churches in India, and £10,601 had been given for other special objects, making the whole amount intrusted to the Society during the year £232,-836. Fifteen qualified laborers had been accepted for the work of the Society, and fourteen others had been accepted as suitable to be trained in the missionary college.

The Board of the *Society for the Propagation of the Gospel* in November, 1878, adopted a resolution altering the rule respecting the examination of candidates, so that candidates selected by a colonial bishop or his commissioner need not be required to pass the Board of Examiners. The resolution was regarded as being in the interest of ritualism, since the immediate occasion of its being offered had been the rejection of a candidate by the Board of Examiners on the ground, as was alleged, of his being a member of the Society of the Holy Cross; and dissatisfaction was excited among officers and members of the Society by its passage. The Bishops of Gloucester and Bristol and of Peterborough declared that they would resign their offices as Vice-Presidents of the Society if it were not rescinded; and animated discussions were had over it at the meetings of the Board. At a meeting of the Society held February 2, 1879, the resolution in question was rescinded, and a committee was appointed to consider the by-laws bearing upon the subject and all matters affecting their working.

The annual meeting of the *Society for the Propagation of the Gospel in Foreign Parts* was held in London, April 29th. The Archbishop of Canterbury presided. The receipts of the Society had been £145,223, or about £3,000 less than the receipts of the previous year. There had been employed during the year, in various fields of labor, 567 missionaries, as follows: In Asia, 135; in Africa, 121; in Australia and the Pacific, 61; in America and the West Indies, 248; in Europe, 2. The force of the Society also included about 1,200 catechists and lay teachers, mostly natives in heathen countries, and about 250 students in colleges abroad.

The Rev. Dr. Baring, Bishop of Durham, having resigned his office in consequence of illness, an address was sent him by 531 of the clergy of the diocese, in which it was stated that during his eighteen years' administration of the diocese 119 new churches and 189 parochial schools had been erected, 130 churches and chapels of ease restored, 102 new parishes formed and endowed, and 186 added to the number of the parochial clergy. The Rev.

Joseph Barker Lightfoot, Canon of St. Paul's and Margaret, Professor of Divinity at Cambridge, was nominated to be the new Bishop of the diocese, was duly elected by the Dean and Chapter, and was consecrated Bishop at Westminster Abbey, April 25th. The new Bishop was born in Liverpool, is a little more than fifty years of age, was graduated from the University of Cambridge in 1851, and is one of the most distinguished Biblical scholars in the English Church.

Bishop Samuel Gobat of Jerusalem died May 11th. The Bishop of this diocese is appointed under a joint arrangement of the British and Prussian Governments, by the terms of which he is designated by either alternately. The appointment of the successor of Bishop Gobat falling to the British Government, the Rev. Dr. Joseph Barclay, rector of Stapleton, Herts, was made Bishop. The new Bishop had already spent ten years in Jerusalem as examining chaplain to Bishop Gobat, whereby he had acquired a close acquaintance with the East. He is versed in the Hebrew, Arabic, and German languages, and has translated and prepared commentaries on parts of the Talmud.

The Right Rev. Dr. Reginal Courtney, Bishop of Kingston, Jamaica, having resigned his office, to take effect in April, 1879, the Right Rev. George William Tozer was appointed Bishop of Kingston in August. Bishop Tozer was for several years Anglican Missionary Bishop of Zanzibar, but retired from that position in 1873 on account of his health.

The fourteenth annual report of the Council of the *Church Association* was made in March, 1879. Thirty-three branches had been formed during the year, and the whole number of branches was now 358. Branches of the Association had been established at Edinburgh, Glasgow, and Montrose, in Scotland. In accordance with the object of the Association, which is the maintenance of Protestant principles in the Church of England, organized operations were being made throughout the country to bring the subject of ritualism before candidates for Parliament at the coming election.

The annual meeting of the *English Church Union* was held at Hereford, August 21st. The annual report and the address of the President of the meeting, Major Thomas Palmer of Hereford, represented that the Union and the principles it represented were gaining ground. Thirty years ago, it was claimed, crosses, surpliced choirs, candles, etc., were ruled out; now they had all these. The people in attendance at their churches and the number of communicants had increased, and the observance of the services appertaining to Lent had been more numerous. Resolutions were passed, stating that the Union regarded with surprise and alarm the decision of the Archbishop of Canterbury, and some of the bishops, to displace the Athanasian Creed from its present position in the Prayer-Book, and that it should be left as it is; that the Union disapproved of the action of the Lower House of Convocation in the matter of the ornaments rubric, and they were astonished that the House should accept an addition which contradicts the rubric itself; and that the Union will do all it can to prevent any alteration in the Prayer-Book, as dangerous to the interests of the Church. The holding of a mass meeting in London in November was advised.

The *Confraternity of the Blessed Sacrament* is an association for propagating the doctrine of the real presence in the Lord's Supper, for promoting the administration of that ordinance with a full ritual, the offering of prayers for the dead, the increase of daily celebrations, the receiving of the sacraments for the sick and dying, and auricular confession. According to the report for 1878, 61 priests had been enrolled as members during the year, 53 had withdrawn, and the whole number of priests associate was 933 ; 759 lay associates had been admitted, 47 had withdrawn, and the whole number of lay associates was about 10,563 ; making the total of members in England 11,499. Twenty-one new wards had been formed in England, one in India, one in Canada, and one in South Africa, while six wards had been discontinued ; and there were now 147 English and eight colonial wards. The "Intercession" paper was regularly issued, 10,500 copies being required each month. The income of the Society had been £1,161, and its expenditures £892.

A new society, called the *Church and Stage Guild*, has been established in connection with the Church of England, with the object of promoting religious and social sympathy between the members of the Church and the stage.

The annual meeting of the *Society for the Liberation of Religion from State Patronage and Control* was held in London, April 30th. The expenditures of the Society for the year had been £13,249, after defraying which a balance of £579 was left in the treasury. About eight hundred meetings had been held in England, Scotland, and Wales, and 3,148,000 publications had been circulated. The report dwelt upon the advance which had been made in the cause which the Society was intended to promote, as shown in the movement for the disestablishment of the Scottish Church, in which the Society coöperated ; the agitation on the subject of burials, in the case of which it was claimed that the principles insisted upon by Mr. Osborne Morgan had been acquiesced in in the bill of Mr. Balfour ; and other events. The scheme for the endowment of an Irish Roman Catholic University would meet with strenuous opposition. Resolutions were passed expressing confidence in the success of the movement for disestablishment in Scotland, commending the question of disestablishment to the support of electoral constituencies, and urging preparation to oppose the project to establish a Roman Catholic University in Ireland. Resolutions were passed at the public meeting referring with satisfaction to the tendency of ecclesiastical litigation "to convince the members of the Church that legal coercion is not a fit instrument for the attainment of spiritual ends, and that the advantages of an establishment can not be enjoyed without sacrificing the peace and freedom of the Church," and expressing the hope, in the prospect of the coming general election, "that the friends of religious equality will not fail to press upon the electoral bodies the expediency of putting an end to state interference with religion, and also that in England, no less than in Scotland, there will be a firm determination to secure the early abolition of the Scottish establishment."

The *Church Congress* met at Swansea, October 7th. The Bishop of St. David's, the diocese in which the meeting was held, presided. In his opening address he counseled the avoidance of the danger of making the Congress the battle-ground of different classes of thought in the Church. The subjects discussed on the first day's session were: The missionary work of the Church among the Jews and in India; "The Causes of and Remedy for Dissent"; "Home Reunion"; "Higher and Intermediate Education in Wales"; "How can the Church best gain and retain its Influence over the Young?" and "Church Work among the Seafaring Population." The Bishop of Winchester, President of the Home Reunion Society, opened the discussion on the causes for dissent and its remedy. He traced the history of nonconformity, and sketched the principles on which it should be met. The chief of the remedies which he proposed were: that the Church should not be looked upon as a sect, but as a world-wide society, meant to include in it all who accept Christ as their King; that party spirit and partisan language should be avoided; that mixing of religion with politics should be shunned; that lay work should be increased and lay counsel sought; that a lower order of clergy be enlisted as a permanent diaconate; that what are called irregular devotional services should be encouraged, or at least fully tolerated, and that more missionary and evangelizing labor should be secured, both at home and abroad. The programme of discussions was continued during the succeeding days with papers and addresses on the subjects of "The Maintenance of Voluntary Schools, and the best Means of promoting Religious Education in them and in Board Schools"; "Diocesan Synods and Conferences"; "Church Temperance work"; "Parish Organization," with reference to rich and poor town parishes, and compact and scattered country parishes; "The Church in Wales"; "Ecclesiastical Courts and Final Court of Appeal"; "Religious Benefits from recent Scientific Research." On the subject of religious education in the schools, the opening paper, by Canon Melville, advocated a religious basis in instruction, and mentioned an increase in the number of schools which

had adopted the Lord's Prayer, the Ten Commandments, and the Apostles' Creed as bases of such instruction. In relation to Ecclesiastical Courts, Dr. Phillimore proposed a reform in the organization of the Courts, under which the Church should be given a voice in the appointment of its bishops and archbishops; these officers should sit as judges canonically with the assistance of their clergy, with their chancellors as assessors, and with representatives of the laity to concur; the appeal to be to the synod of the province presided over by the Metropolitan, and, if further appeal be required, to the synod of the whole Anglican Communion. Such a reform, he thought, need not be incompatible with establishment. The discussion of the subject of the Church in Wales bore reference to the difficulties of bilingual parishes and the special education and training of the clergy. The Dean of Bangor showed that, out of a million people speaking the Welsh language, eight hundred thousand are attached more or less closely to the Congregational, Baptist, Wesleyan, Presbyterian, and other chapels. He maintained that the Church had lost its hold on the Welsh people through the indifference it had shown to them; and that, if it would recover them, it must have more earnest and devoted men capable of speaking to them in their own tongue.

Questions concerning the means of securing more friendly relations with nonconformists were considered at the meetings of several of the diocesan synods in October. At the Diocesan Conference of Manchester, a resolution was adopted expressing a desire to promote a friendly recognition of dissenters who would meet Churchmen on the ground of a common Christianity, and an earnest wish to cultivate friendly relations with them and to coöperate with them on any possible platforms of Christian work; further, that "in the opinion of this Conference it is desirable that the Convocation of this province (York) should consider the question of the comprehension of nonconformists with a view to devising the best means of terminating our dissensions and establishing essential unity, and working harmony between all sections of earnest Christian people in the land." The Synod of Peterborough resolved "that in full recognition of the sin and scandal of divisions among Christians, and in humble consciousness that they have been fomented and encouraged by many shortcomings on the part of the English Church, this Conference would hail with the utmost satisfaction any proposals toward home reunion without compromising scriptural truth and apostolic order; and that, while unable to perceive that the time has arrived for formal communications between the authorities of the Church and delegates from nonconformists, it is of opinion that special attention should be directed to a possible concordat with Wesleyan Methodists."

The *Representative Body of the Irish Episcopal Church* had at the beginning of 1879 a

capital sum of upward of £7,000,000, the interest of which forms the yearly endowment
of the Church. The *General Synod* of the
Irish Episcopal Church met at Dublin on April
22d. The most important discussions referred
to the condition and relations of the Divinity School of Trinity College. The friends
of the College moved for a declaration of the
Synod that it is not advisable that it should
cease to teach theology to the members of the
Church of Ireland, or that its control should
pass out of the hands of the provost and fellows. The Bishop of Meath moved a resolution expressing the desire of the Synod that
the bill introduced by Lord Belmore for the
future management of the Divinity School
might speedily become a law, so that the due
maintenance and government of the school in
accordance with the recommendations of the
late University Commission might be secured.
The mover stated that the disposition of this
question was the last special difficulty arising
out of disestablishment. Lord Belmore explained his bill, which, he contended, did not
contemplate any practical separation of the
school from the University. The archbishops
and bishops were requested by the Synod to
confer with the Board of Trinity College, with
a view to promote an arrangement with the
authorities of the University and the Synod.
The Senate of the University having at its meeting on the 1st of May refused to approve the
bill, and having adopted a motion to the effect
that means could be found by which the connection of the Divinity School and the College
can be maintained, and the welfare of the
school, under the conditions as altered by recent legislation, can be better provided for
than under its provisions, the Synod, on the
2d, referred the whole subject with the bill
back to the archbishops and bishops, requesting them to summon the Synod again if an
agreement of terms should be reached. It was
always to be understood that the connection
between the Divinity School and the College
should be as close as possible. Petitions were
presented against a screen which had been
erected in the cathedral. A proposition to
remove the screen was rejected, but leave was
given to introduce a bill declaring that in future
it should not be lawful to erect any screen or
partition separating the officiating clergy from
the congregation. This was lost through a
failure to secure the approval of the clergy,
the vote in the two houses standing—clergy,
yeas 73, nays 78; laity, yeas 130, nays 29. A
scheme was approved for establishing such a
permanent training school for teachers in connection with the Church as may be entitled to
receive support from the state. A special
meeting of the Synod was held in June to consider the questions relating to the Divinity
School of Trinity College, when resolutions
were adopted asserting the right of the bishops
to nominate the professors and lecturers in the
school.

ANIMAL-PLANTS AND PLANT-ANI-
MALS. The singular behavior of the sundew
(*Drosera*) and other plants of its class in prey-
ing upon insects, and the fact that the victims
of these carnivorous plants, which possess various and complex arrangements for attracting and securing their prey, are decomposed
by a fluid which corresponds in its nature and
action to the gastric juice of animals, and are
taken into the system of the plants, awakened
the wonder of the scientific world a few years
ago, when the discovery was made and published by Charles Darwin. The fact that the
nitrogenous matter thus consumed actually
formed a part of the nutriment of this group
of plants still remained to be proved until the
recent experiments of F. Darwin established it
beyond question: he took a large number of
sundew plants and supplied half of them with
nitrogenous food in the form of roast beef; of
the fed plants, 69 per cent. more survived .
than of the unfed; their stems weighed 41
per cent. more; they excelled the starved
plants in the number of their seeds by 141
per cent., and in the aggregate weight of their
seeds by 279 per cent. Equally confirmatory
results were reached in Germany by Keller-
mann, Reiss, and Von Raumer, who fed the
plants with aphides.

Another approach to the animal kingdom in
the physiology of plants has been noticed by
Weyl, and more lately investigated by Sidney Vines in a micro-chemical examination of
the aleurone grains in the seeds of the blue lu-
pine (*Lupinus varius*). These are grains of a
soluble or partly soluble proteinaceous substance which are found in the endosperm or
the cotyledon of the seeds of numerous plants,
and contain the stores of proteid food. The
analysis of Vines revealed the presence of two
proteids belonging to the globuline group,
which have never before been found except
in animals : these were myosine, which occurs
in dead muscular tissue, and vitelline, which is
found in the yolk of eggs. An extract of the
seeds also contained a proteid which possesses
all the properties of peptone, and resembles
very closely the hemi-albuminose of Kühne,
or *a* peptone of Meissner. The peptones,
formed by the action of the gastric or pancre-
atic fluids on proteids in the digestive organs
of animals, are classed by Meissner as the *a*,
b, and *c* peptones, representing three different
stages of decomposition in the digestive process. The presence of these products, which
were supposed to be confined to the physiological economy of animals, has been detected
not only in the higher flowering plants, but is
established by recent researches of Professor
Nägeli in one of the lowest of the protophytes
—the yeast-plant. Nägeli finds by his analysis of the cells of this fungus that, besides the
albuminoids, of which the cells are mainly
composed, they contain about two per cent. of
peptones, and that these exist in all three of
the modifications distinguished by Meissner.

A process completely analogous to the excretion of animals is discovered to take place in this plant. That plants give off carbonic acid as a product of waste tissue, just as animals do, has long been observed. Nitrogenous products of the oxidation were by analogy known to exist, but have never been observed. Nägeli discovered in his analysis of the yeast-fungus, besides the glycerine and succinic acid which were known as extractives of yeast, several of the well-known nitrogenous products of the waste of animal tissue—guanine, xanthine, surkine, and leucine, the last of which is believed to be in animals the urea in one of the stages of its formation.

A no less startling discovery has been made in the animal kingdom by which one of the broadest and plainest marks of distinction between the animal and plant kingdoms has been obliterated. Certain animals are found to exercise a most important physiological process which has been supposed to be the most exclusive and distinctive attribute of vegetable life. The green color of a number of the lower animals, belonging to widely separated groups, is well known to be due to the presence of chlorophyl. This substance is found to exist in certain infusoria, in a species of fresh-water sponge, in the *Hydra viridis*, in a sea-anemone, the *Anthea cereus*, in a tube-worm, the *Chæptopterus Valenciensii*, in the *Bonellia viridis*, in an isopod, the *Idotea viridis*, and in three species of planarians. The green grains contained in these animals were found by the chemical and spectroscopic investigations of Cohn, Ray, Lankester, and others, to be chemically identical with plant-chlorophyl. That they performed the chemico-physiological function of chlorophyl in plants, that they had the power and actually served to decompose carbonic acid, was not established; and that such a process attended and supported the life of these animals seemed quite as incredible as did the fact that the nitrogenous substances dissolved by the gastric fluid of the carnivorous plants actually served as nutriment. An English scientist, Geddes, has now discovered that this process does take place in the planarians at least. Placing a number of specimens in water, and exposing them to the rays of a bright sun, he found that they emitted bubbles of gas which contained from 45 to 55 per cent. of oxygen. In their habitat on the seashore they are always found covered by a few centimetres of water only, and directly exposed to the sun: in an aquarium they seek the fullest exposure to the light, and live much longer when in the light than when kept in the shade. By dissolving out the chlorophyl with alcohol, and subjecting an aqueous extract of the bleached and coagulated substance of their bodies to the delicate and infallible iodine test, he discovered the indisputable presence of starch. The blue coloration, fading out on exposure to heat and reappearing when the solution cooled again, establishes beyond question the existence of this purely vegetable constituent in these animals.

These remarkable discoveries, following closely one upon another, of plants which devour, digest, and are nourished by animal food, of veritable peptones formed by many plants, of plants performing a process of excrementation, and the converse discovery of starch-forming, oxygen-exhaling animals, overturn the broadest, never-questioned generalizations, and obliterate the clearest marks of distinction which have been fixed regarding the demarkation of the animal and vegetable kingdoms. This latest revelation of the infinite complexity and manifold interlinkages of organic nature is accentuated by its discoverer in the following language: "As the *Drosera*, *Dionæa*, etc., which have attracted so much attention of late years, have received the striking name of 'carnivorous plants,' these planarians may not unfairly be called 'vegetating animals,' for the one case is the precise reciprocal of the other. Not only does the *Dionæa* imitate the carnivorous animal, and the *Convoluta* the ordinary green plant, but each tends to lose its own normal character. The tiny root and the half-blanched leaves of *Pinguicula* are paralleled by the absence of a distinct alimentary canal and the abstemious habits of the planarian."

ARGENTINE REPUBLIC (REPÚBLICA ARGENTINA). For detailed statements of the territorial divisions and population, reference may be made to the "Annual Cyclopædia" for 1877 and 1878.

The President of the Republic is Dr. Don Nicolás Avellaneda; the Vice-President, Dr. Don Mariano Acosta; and the Ministers composing the Cabinet, as follows: Interior, Dr. Don Benjamin Zorrilla; Finance, Dr. Don Victorino de La Plaza; Justice, Public Worship, and Public Instruction, Dr. Don Miguel Goyena; War and the Navy, Dr. Don Cárlos Pellegrini. The Argentine Chargé d'Affaires in the United States is Sr. Don Julio Carrié. The Consul-General (at New York) is Sr. Don Cárlos Carranza; and the Vice-Consul, Mr. F. H. Snyder.

The Governors of the several provinces were:

Buenos Ayres	Dr. C. Tejedor (May, 1878).
Minister of the Interior	J. Alcorta.
Minister of Finance	F. L. Barbin.
Catamarca	M. Molina.
Córdoba	Dr. A. del Viso.
Corrientes	
Entre-Rios	Dr. R. Febre.
Jujuy	M. Torino.
La Rioja	V. A. Almonacid.
Mendoza	J. Villanueva.
Salta	J. Solá.
San Juan	R. Doncel.
San Luis	T. Mendoza.
Santa Fé	S. de Iriondo.
Santiago	B. Olachea.
Tucuman	F. Helguera.
Gran Chaco Territory	Lieut.-Col. P. Gómez.

The following tables of the revenue and expenditure of the republic for the year 1878 are taken from the report presented to Congress by the Minister of Finance in 1879:

REVENUE.

Import duties	$12,033,041 13
Export duties	2,299,575 64
Warehouse fees, etc...........................	305,502 24
Stamped paper, patents, etc....................	451,166 17
Post-office and telegraphs..................	891,028 72
Lighthouses, etc............................	85,563 09
Government railways.......................	445,071 01
Interest on national funds loaned to provinces.	20,758 23
Interest and sinking fund, uninvested titles, loan of 1871............................	611,751 92
Interest on shares of Central Argentine Railway.....	74,664 00
Sundries..................................	1,774,775 71
Total.	$18,451,597 86

EXPENDITURE.

Ministry of the Interior..................... .	$1,815,759 55
Ministry of Foreign Affairs..................	156,455 85
Ministry of Finance.........................	8,471,897 22
Ministry of Justice, Public Instruction, etc....	987,247 19
Ministry of War and the Navy...............	3,717,194 59
Expenses extraordinary.........	26,064 00
Total..................	$15,174,618 40

In the report already referred to, the national debt of the republic was set down at $85,589,963.33 on March 31, 1879.

The subjoined tables exhibit the values, sources, and destinations, respectively, of the imports and exports for the year 1878:

IMPORTS.

From.	Values.
Belgium...............................	$2,714,574
Bolivia................................	58,625
Brazil................................	2,103,694
Chili.................................	506,147
France................................	8,695,251
Germany..............................	2,132,778
Great Britain.........................	11,518,011
Holland........	369,583
India.................................	12,379
Italy.................................	2,527,508
Paraguay.............................	571,725
Portugal..............................	58,576
Spain.................................	2,447,404
United States........................	2,778,589
Uruguay..............................	2,000,676
West Indies.......................... ..	94,265
Other countries......................	349,162
In transitu...........................	3,418,228
Total................	$42,347,460

EXPORTS.

Destinations.	Values.
Belgium...............................	$9,264,167
Bolivia................................	221,044
Brazil................................	1,777,045
Chili.................................	2,072,297
France................................	9,390,240
Germany..............................	994,186
Great Britain.........................	3,499,260
Holland...............................	101,831
Italy.................................	804,481
Paraguay.............................	875,707
Peru.................................	18,080
Portugal..............................	21,765
Spain.................................	828,700
United States........................	2,547,187
Uruguay..............................	975,212
West Indies..........................	708,402
Other countries......................	15,870
In transitu...........................	2,707,942
Total................	$26,818,267

The shipping movements at the ports of the republic in 1878 were as follows:

	Sailing vessels.	Tons.	Steamers.	Tons.
Entered.........	1,262	280,323	1,190	616,409
Cleared.........	821	256,469	390	410,120

The foregoing are the only returns of interest published officially since 1878.

The Patagonian question still remains unsettled. In a lengthy memorial, presented to the national Congress in 1879 by the Minister of Foreign Affairs, are found a reassertion of the limits of the portion of Patagonia "belonging to the Argentine Republic," namely, "the Rio Negro on the north, the Atlantic on the east, the Straits of Magellan on the south, and the Andes on the west," and the following mention of a treaty between the two republics: "With a view to decide the pending question of limits between the Argentine Republic and Chili, a treaty was made at Buenos Ayres on January 18, 1878, by the plenipotentiaries of either nation, for the purpose of submitting to arbitrators thereafter to be chosen the question, 'Were the now-disputed territories in the possession of the Viceroyalty of Buenos Ayres or of the Captaincy-General of Chili in 1810?' The treaty, however, was not ratified by Chili, and it was agreed that the arbitration should be conducted in accordance with the treaty of 1856, both governments, to prevent the occurrence of an armed conflict in the mean time, binding themselves to refrain from sending war-vessels on missions of an aggressive character—the Argentines to the Straits of Magellan, or the Chilians to the Atlantic coast of Patagonia." (See "CHILI.")

ARKANSAS. The biennial session of the Legislature of Arkansas began on January 14th, and terminated on March 3d, after the passage of about eighty acts. In the Senate M. M. Duffie was elected President on the forty-third ballot; in the House J. T. Bearden was elected Speaker.

The election of Governor took place on September 7, 1878, and the canvass of the votes by the Legislature showed the following result: William R. Miller, 88,730 votes; Milt Rice, 5; J. N. Cypert, 1; M. L. Bell, 1; B. S. Fox, 1; J. O. McGuire, 5; W. P. Grace, 2; E. N. Conway, 1; Thomas Fletcher, 3; Jeff. Rice, 1; —— Fletcher, 1; S. O. Cloud, 2; Martin Levy, 2; scattering, 15.

A Senator to represent the State in Congress was chosen by the Legislature on the sixth ballot, on February 1st. The vote was as follows: J. D. Walker, 68; United States Senator Robert W. Johnson, 47; scattering, 5. Pending the ballot Representative Davidson of Sharpe County rose and stated that before voting he demanded a promised explanation from Representative Holifield of Clay County. Mr. Holifield had a writing prepared, which he read, to the effect that he had been offered $500 to vote for Johnson. Representative Barnett of Bradley County said he felt authorized in saying the statement was false. Senator Mitchell of Hempstead demanded the name of the offerer of the bribe. Representative Fishback moved to dissolve the convention and investigate. President of the Senate Duffie decided that the motion could not be entertained. Representative Furbush (colored) proposed that members should scatter ballots so as to temporarily prevent election. The roll-call proceeded to the result above stated. Davidson's statement had apparently no effect on the actual ballot, save that Representative Washburne asked and was excused from voting in consequence. No reflections were cast upon Johnson personally.

Under such a charge Colonel Johnson could do no less than demand an investigation; the House could do no less than to order it. It was ordered. Two of the committee were Johnson men, two Walker men, and one a Baxter man. Another was afterward added who had taken no part in the senatorial contest. After some weeks spent in investigation, five of the committee made a majority report, in which they say:

Your committee have failed to find in the testimony before them any evidence whatever reflecting, either directly or indirectly, upon the Hon. R. W. Johnson, or upon his conduct in the senatorial contest; but his record in this, as in all other and previous contests, stands above reproach and above suspicion. Nor do your committee find anything in the testimony which implicates, either directly or indirectly, the Hon. J. D. Walker in any attempt to bribe any member of the General Assembly, while his life-long integrity forbids all idea of such a suggestion. In regard to the members of the House, there is no testimony whatever which shows that any member received a bribe for his vote in the senatorial election, and no satisfactory evidence that any offer of a bribe was made to any member. Nor do your committee find any testimony that any money was on deposit or was used by or for any senatorial candidate in influencing votes for Senator.

One of the committee made a minority report, in which he says:

While a proper discharge of the duty devolved upon them rendered it necessary to admit testimony which could not be justified by the ordinary rules of evidence as applied in courts of justice, yet we fail to see, in the scope we have given the investigation, any infringement of the ordinary rules of propriety. Your minority fully agreed and concur in the majority report in regard to the Hon. R. W. Johnson and the Hon. J. D. Walker, and would add that the same is true of the other senatorial candidates. Your minority are further of the opinion that there is no evidence before this committee indicating that any member of this House received any bribe or valuable consideration to influence his vote in the recent senatorial election, but that the peculiar conflicting and contradictory character of the testimony taken renders it impossible for your committee to say with positive certainty whether or not any such offer was made, and therefore desire to submit the testimony taken for your consideration.

A resolution in accordance with the report of the committee was laid on the table by the House, and another adopted on the last day of the session, and shortly after the report of the committee was made, declaring that an attempt had been made to bribe two of its members, without implicating any of the candidates.

The necessity for an insane asylum in this State has become so pressing that the Governor in strong terms urged upon the Legislature the passage of an act to provide for such an institution. A bill was passed and vetoed by

the Governor. He stated his objections to be that it was located in a wilderness, remote from indispensable conveniences, that the bill made no efficient provision for the erection of an asylum, and that its adoption as a law would probably operate to defeat for the present generation any efficient provision for the object.

A bill was passed to abolish the office of adjutant-general, but this was vetoed by the Governor as an unconstitutional measure.

A proposition to hold the State and Congressional elections on the same day was voted down. This defeat was caused by the existence of Congressional laws authorizing the appointment of supervisors of elections for members of Congress.

A resolution was adopted to appoint a committee of five to prepare an address to the fruit-growers of the State, calling for a convention to meet at Little Rock at as early a day as practicable, for the purpose of organizing a State Horticultural and Fruit-Growers' Association, and requesting such committee to prepare a constitution for the consideration of the Convention.

Exclusive original jurisdiction was given to justices of the peace to try and finally to determine all cases of misdemeanors; the circuit courts, however, have concurrent jurisdiction in cases of false imprisonment and malfeasance and misfeasance in office.

An act for the prevention of cruelty to animals provides that "if any person shall overdrive, overload, torture, torment, deprive of necessary sustenance, or cruelly beat or needlessly mutilate or kill, or cause or procure to be overdriven, overloaded, tortured, tormented, or deprived of necessary sustenance, or to be cruelly beaten or needlessly mutilated or killed as aforesaid, any living creature, every such offender shall, for every such offense, be guilty of a misdemeanor." The details of the act comprise almost every form of cruelty ; and it further provides that "in this act, and in every law of this State passed or which may be passed relating to or affecting animals, the singular shall include the plural; the words 'animal' or 'dumb animal' shall be held to include every living creature; the words 'torture,' 'torment,' or 'cruelty' shall be held to include every act, omission, or neglect whereby unjustifiable physical pain, suffering, or death is caused or permitted; and the words 'owner' and 'person' shall be held to include corporations as well as individuals. But nothing in this act shall be construed as prohibiting the shooting of birds or other game for the purposes of human food."

A bill passed the Senate—yeas 13, nays 6—prohibiting the sale of intoxicating liquor to habitual drunkards.

An act regulating the sale of mortgaged property provides that, at all sales of personal or real property under mortgages and deeds of trust, such property shall not sell for less than two thirds of the appraised value thereof; the act shall not apply to sales of property for the purchase-money thereof; and if the property shall not sell at the first offering for two thirds of the amount of the appraisement, then, in case of personal property, another offering may be made sixty days thereafter, and in case of real property another offering may be made twelve months thereafter, at which offerings the sale shall be to the highest bidder, without reference to the appraisement; and the real property thus sold may be redeemed by the mortgageor at any time within one year from the sale thereof, by payment of the amount for which said property is sold, together with ten per cent. interest thereon and cost of sale.

By another act all lands returned as delinquent to the offices of the county clerks shall there remain for a period of one year, during which time they may be redeemed by the owner or person in whose name the same may be listed. But if the lands are not then redeemed they shall remain in said clerk's office one year longer, during which time the same shall be subject to redemption by any person whatsoever who will pay the tax, penalty, and costs; and upon the payment of the same the clerk shall execute and deliver a proper deed of conveyance. If at the end of this period they are not redeemed, they shall be forfeited to the State.

The following preamble and resolution, intended to respond to the investigation undertaken by the so-called "Teller Committee" (see CONGRESS, U. S.), was passed in the House by yeas 71, nays 15:

Whereas, The purity and absolute freedom of the ballot-box are of the utmost importance in a government by the ballot; and

Whereas, A committee of the United States Senate is now engaged upon an investigation of facts in connection with infractions of the rights of suffrage in the States of the Union, with a professed view to ascertaining a remedy; and

Whereas, The larger the number of facts, the more valuable will be the generalization or conclusion drawn from them; and

Whereas, During the period of reconstruction, there were from 30,000 to 40,000 of the legal Democratic voters of this State who were periodically deprived of a free exercise of their suffrage, either by fraud or intimidation, or both; and

Whereas, Notwithstanding many instances of outrageous fraud upon the ballot were brought in 1874 to the attention of a Republican committee of the national House of Representatives, and by sworn testimony, yet the distinguished presiding officer of the House has recently said upon the floor of the Senate, that he doubted if it be in the power of the most searching investigation to show that in any Southern State, during the period of Republican control, any legal voter was ever debarred from the freest exercise of his suffrage—a statement which would indicate either the very gross inefficiency of such committee, or as very gross ignorance of their findings on the part of those who believe such an assertion; and

Whereas, It is desirable that the committee now engaged in a like investigation make their inquiry searching and complete, lest its labors be obnoxious to the charge of a like inefficiency, or its members to the charge of a like ignorance, and its investigation therefore prove fruitless of beneficial results; and·

Whereas, It is charged by some of the Republican press of the North that the right of suffrage is not fully enjoyed by the colored voters of Arkansas; and

Whereas, It is alleged by members of this body that, in one county of this State, in 1870, a very large number of the legal voters of the county, who were Democrats, were deprived of the free exercise of their suffrage, while at the same time a large number of ballots were fraudulently voted under fictitious names taken from the directory of one of our Northern cities; that in many of the counties of this State, where the white population were largely in the majority, just before the election of 1872 the boards of revision met in secret and scratched from the registration lists names by the hundreds of legal voters who had been legally registered, and for no other known reason except that it had been ascertained "they would not vote the right way."

That, indeed, many of the victims were young men who had just attained to manhood, and not infrequently honorably discharged soldiers of the Federal army, who were so unfortunate as to be Democrats, by these boards, the members of which were generally themselves candidates for lucrative offices at the same election; that on election day armed militia and deputy-marshals surrounded the polling-places, using means calculated and designed to intimidate these illegally "scratched" voters from voting at the polls erected under the enforcement act; that in several instances they actually arrested men for no other offense than that of offering to vote at such polls; that on the day of election printed circulars, purporting to be by order of the Governor, but *having no signatures*, were distributed among the election officers (all of whom were Republicans), directing them to permit no man to vote whose name was either absent or scratched from the registration list, no matter how illegally.

That as an instance and an illustration of their methods, early in the morning of election day in 1872, in the town of Fort Smith, the few negro voters of the precinct were stationed in a line from the door of the polling-place across the street, where they stood until the closing of the polls, preventing all except such as they chose to permit to vote, while in a room just above the polling-place were armed and drilled men, under command of officers, established for the purpose of overcoming any resistance to these so great outrages, and that in the mean time deputy-marshals swarmed about the polls in numbers almost as great as that of the Republican voters. That the better to carry out these outrages, the judges of elections refused to allow the Democratic supervisors, appointed by the United States District Court, to sit with them, ejecting one after another as fast as the Judge appointed them, until he consented to appoint the one whom they themselves designated. That at the same election one of the voting-places of Crawford County was removed by stealth from the usual place to a canebrake, on the farm of the United States Marshal, known to the Republican voters, but unknown to Democrats. That the marshal transferred one of his clerks to this place, and made him a clerk of election. That the same clerk swore before the Poland Committee that he saw the ballot-box stuffed with fraudulent votes. That the Democrats, in the exercise of a commendable patience and forbearance, appealed to the United States District Court for the enforcement of the laws made for their protection, but the guilty Marshal failed to summon the grand jury selected after the usual manner; summoning in their stead a number of his partisans and fellow-conspirators, from whom to make up a grand jury, in the necessary default of the regular panel. That a few Democrats and honest Republicans, who were interested in the punishment of these crimes against the ballot, having an intimation of the marshal's intended default, themselves notified the regular panel to appear, but upon their assembling the regular panel were dismissed, which gave the Marshal his opportunity of making up a new panel of the very men who were more or less implicated, thus preventing the punishment of any guilty party.·

That an address setting forth these facts was drawn up and signed by twenty-one members of the bar of the Western District of Arkansas, and forwarded to the President and Senate of the United States, through the Hon. B. F. Rice, who reported that he handed it in to a committee of the Senate, where it has since slept without a protest, and without even a notice by that honorable body. And

Whereas, Many other devices were resorted to during that unhappy period, by which to "debar" legal voters from a free exercise of their suffrage, and which should be known to the country, and especially to the Senate Committee now engaged with the subject, that they may be the better prepared to draw intelligent conclusions as to the remedy for so great an evil:

Therefore, be it resolved by the House of Representatives of the State of Arkansas, That a committee of nine of its members, selected from different sections of the State, be appointed by the Chair to inquire into and report such facts in connection with the violation of the rights of suffrage in this State as can be established by competent testimony, and in time to be forwarded to our Senators and Representatives in Congress before the adjournment of its present session.

A joint resolution instructing the Representatives of the State and people in Congress to vote for all measures looking to the unlimited coinage and full legal-tender capacity of standard silver dollars, and also for substituting United States Treasury notes for national-bank notes, passed by decisive majorities. In the Senate the vote was—yeas 28, nays 2. The following resolution contains the list of measures in detail:

Resolved, by the General Assembly of the State of Arkansas, That our Senators and Representatives in Congress be, and they are hereby, requested to vote for and support the following measures:

First. The unconditional repeal of the resumption act.

Second. The repeal of the act exempting United States bonds from taxation by the States.

Third. The repeal of all laws exempting greenbacks from taxation.

Fourth. The abolition and prohibition for ever of all bank issues.

Fifth. The free and unlimited coinage of gold and silver.

Sixth. The issue by the Government of *full legal-tender* paper money, receivable for all dues and demands, public and private, in amount sufficient to meet the wants of trade, said amount to be not less than thirty dollars per capita of the whole population of the United States, and provides by law that this paper money shall remain permanently in circulation, and equal before the law with the nation's gold and silver coin.

The following memorial to Congress, relative to the intellectual status of the colored people, also was passed by the Legislature:

To the Honorable Senate and House of Representatives of the United States:
Your memorialists, the General Assembly of the State of Arkansas, would respectfully ask for the passage of the bill now before the lower House of your honorable body, and in the hands of the Committee on Labor and Education, authorizing the appointment of a committee of three colored men to inquire into the intellectual status of the colored people of the Southern States; the expenses of the same, as provided for in the bill, to be paid out of the unclaimed bounty funds of the colored soldiers. Believing that such an action will be productive of great good, not only to an essential element of our society, but to the community in general, and urged so to do by those immediately concerned.

The subject of the finances of the State was the most important before the Legislature. It appears that the amount of warrants drawn on the State Treasury during the fiscal years 1877 and 1878 was $1,296,659.16, of which sum $422,977.57 were expended in payment of the current expenses of the government. To the latter sum should be added $26,792.24, amount of certificates of indebtedness against the State. Total sum expended during the two years, exclusive of interest paid on bonds, $449,769.81; an average of $224,884.90 per annum. The funds in the Treasury at the beginning of the year consisted chiefly of State scrip which had been issued in previous years to pay current expenses, and which was made receivable for all dues except interest. It had been returned to the Treasury in payment of taxes, and at that time there was outstanding $477,729.47. The plan adopted by the Legislature was to stop all further issues of scrip, and to borrow the amount necessary for the expenses of the ensuing two years. By this method the State government would be carried on and the outstanding scrip retired. A State Board of Finance, consisting of the Governor, Auditor, and Treasurer, was created for two years, which was authorized to borrow money for current expenses; and the Governor and Secretary of State are authorized to execute in the name of the State, and the said Board of Finance is authorized to countersign and deliver promissory notes of the State, or rather instruments in writing, as evidence of the indebtedness so incurred. The faith and credit of the State are pledged to the payment of such obligations. For the further security of their payment, the Board was authorized to pledge the bonds of the State authorized to be issued under an act of December 28, 1874; and upon default of payment of the principal sum or interest on said obligations, as the same may become due, a sufficient amount or number of said bonds so hypothecated, to pay off the interest or principal sum then due, may be sold at public sale, at the city of New York or the city of Little Rock, after having given at least thirty days' notice of such sale. The unusual feature of this arrangement is, that to raise a half million for current expenses there are pledged as security for its payment bonds amounting to a million dollars. If the State fails to pay on the day the money borrowed is due, the lender, upon thirty days' notice, can sell the bonds at auction. The credit of these bonds, which have obtained the name of "Loughborough bonds," is based upon the following section of the original act authorizing their issue:

SEC. 10. In order to secure the prompt payment of the interest on said bonds, and to provide a sinking fund for the redemption of the principal thereof, it is further enacted as a part of the contract on which said bonds shall be issued, and as an inviolate condition thereof, that until said bonds, principal and interest, shall have been fully paid off and discharged, there shall be levied an annual tax sufficient to produce the sum of one hundred and fifty thousand dollars for interest, and thirty-eight thousand dollars for sinking fund, which sums are hereby set apart for the purpose aforesaid ; and the first money received in the Treasury annually during the period aforesaid, from any source whatever, is hereby expressly appropriated to said purpose, until the sum of one buudred and eighty-eight thousand dollars aforesaid shall have been applied annually in payment of said interest, and in creating said sinking fund ; and the right of any holder of said bonds to the benefits herein provided, shall be considered as vested and inextinguishable from the time of issuing thereof until the said bonds shall have been fully paid off. All moneys belonging to said sinking fund shall be annually applied by the Treasurer, under the direction of the Governor, in the purchase of any of said bonds which may be outstanding, in the same manner as is provided in section nine of this act, for the purchase of bonds by the trustee or trustees ; and any Judge of the Circuit courts of this State or Chancellor, in term time or vacation, is hereby enjoined and required, upon the application of any holder of any of said bonds, to compel by mandamus or other proper process the authorities of the State to levy, assess, and collect the taxes provided for in this section, and to prevent a misapplication of the moneys set apart for the interest and sinking fund, by injunction or other proper process to compel the proper officers of the State to apply said moneys to the payment of the interest and the purchase of the bonds as herein provided for. And it is provided that all the powers herein conferred upon the Judges of the Circuit Courts of the State and the Chancellors thereof are hereby vested in any Judge of the Circuit or District Courts of the United States, and may be so exercised in the event that any bondholder aforesaid desiring the process of the courts shall be at the time a non-resident of this State, and owning and holding a bond not less than one thousand dollars.

The report of the minority of the Judiciary Committee of the Senate on this measure presents the objections which were considered as sufficient to defeat it, but without avail. The first was, that the issue of bonds to be hypothecated was regarded as a great stretch of power, and only justified as a "military necessity." The original act authorizing the Loughborough bonds was passed after the downfall of the carpet-bag government, which had plundered the Treasury of every dollar and bequeathed to the people a large floating debt ; and its only object was to get money to carry on affairs until the restored government could be established. As that had been accomplished, no more bonds should be issued. Further, the act surrendered to the holders of the bonds issued under its provisions the sovereignty of the State of Arkansas. Section 10 authorizes the State and United States courts, or the judges thereof in vacation, to issue writs of mandamus against the officers of the State, to compel a levy of taxes to pay the principal and interest of said bonds—all of which virtually places the State and her citizens at the mercy and in the power of the bondholders. Again, the act authorized the Board of Finance 'to hypothecate the bonds of the State at one half their par value, with authority given to the holders thereof to sell them for what they may bring, upon default of the State. Also, the act authorized the Governor of the State to mortgage the bonds of the State to secure the payment of said bonds ; and if the necessity

should arise for the sale of the bonds hypothecated, and they should not bring the amount required to pay for the sum borrowed, a trustee is authorized to sell the domain of the sovereign State. Finally, the borrowing of money to defray the current expenses of this State, when it appears that we have $90,000,-000 of taxable property in the State, is an evidence to the world of mismanagement, and a want of confidence in the State by her people, and is sufficient, within itself, to cast a grave reflection upon the honor and dignity of the State.

The acknowledged and undisputed indebtedness of the State amounted at the beginning of the year to $2,969,050, principal and interest, which was then due and unpaid ; and the whole debt was short of five million dollars. All propositions for its arrangement have failed. The Senate at this session passed a resolution from the House providing for a constitutional amendment repudiating certain bonded debts of the State, with a Senate proviso that nothing therein contained shall be construed as a prohibition against paying such part of the State bonds as courts of the State may decide to be just and legal. The resolution was recalled by the House from the committee by a vote of 43 yeas to 41 nays. in the following words :

Whereas, The bonds of this State known as "railroad aid bonds" and "levee bonds" have been decided to be illegal and void by the Supreme Court of the State, and the facts as well as the law upon which these decisions rest are easily accessible ; and

Whereas, The numbers of the bonds known as "Holford bonds" can be ascertained from the books of the Treasurer of State within twenty minutes ; and

Whereas, The character of these bonds has been the subject of discussion and investigation for several years and by several legislative bodies, while they involve twelve millions of the people's money and their settlement involves the future prosperity of the State ; and

Whereas, The Judiciary Committee to whom they have been referred have had them under consideration for nine days ; therefore

Resolved, That the Judiciary Committee be, and they are hereby, directed to report House joint resolution No. 1 (which provides for submitting to the people a constitutional amendment forbidding any Legislature to pay these bonds) back to the House for such action as it may see proper.

This amendment was promptly passed by the House and sent to the Senate.

A resolution was presented in the Senate asking Congress for the early opening of the Indian Territory to white settlement. It was read the third time, and on the question of its adoption considerable discussion ensued, but when put to vote it received 9 yeas to 16 nays. The discussion of the question of the establishment of a territorial government by Congress over the Indian Territory has existed for some time in Arkansas, and is extending to other adjacent States. More than twenty years ago Senator Johnson of Arkansas introduced in the United States Senate a bill for the organization of a territorial form of government over the country ; and from time to time since then bills of a similar character and for a like purpose have been brought to the attention of Congress. At the session of 1878–'79 a bill was introduced in the House of Representatives to establish the Territory of Oklahoma. Its aim was to set up the ordinary territorial government over the Indian country, the same in kind and form as is usually established by Congress when new Territories are created, except where the peculiar condition of affairs there required other provisions to be inserted in the bill. The justice and legality of the measure were discussed, but no final action was taken by the House.

The names of the tribes in the Indian Territory, the area of each reservation in square miles and acres, and the population of each tribe are as follows:

RESERVATION.	Tribes.	Population.	AREA.	
			Square miles.	Acres.
Arapahoe and Cheyenne.	Apache, Southern Arapahoe, and Northern and Southern Cheyenne.	4,766	6,715	4,297,771
Cherokee..............	Cherokee...............................	18,672	7,861	5,031,351
Chickasaw.............	Chickasaw..............................	5,000	7,267	4,650,935
Choctaw...............	Choctaw (Chahta)......................	16,000	10,450	6,688,000
Creek.................	Creek..................................	14,000	5,024	3,215,495
Kansas................	Kansas or Kaw..........................	443	156½	100,141
Kiowa and Comanche....	Apache, Comanche (Komantsu), Delaware, and Kiowa...........	2,985	4,869	2,968,898
Modoc.................	Modoc..................................	117	6	4,040
Osage.................	Great and Little Osage.................	2,679	2,291	1,466,161
Ottawa................	Ottawa of Blanchard's Fork and Roche de Bœuf..........	140	23½	14,860
Pawnee................	Pawnee (Páñi).........................	2,026	443	283,926
Peoria................	Kaskaskia, Miami, Peoria, Piankasha, and Wea.............	202	78½	50,301
Pottawattamie.........	Absentee Shawnee (Shawano), and Pottawattamie...............	778	900	575,877
Quapaw................	Kwapa.................................	235	88½	56,685
Sac and Fox...........	Mexican Kickapoo, Sac (Sauk) and Fox of the Mississippi, including Mokohoko's band....................	929	750	479,667
Seminole..............	Seminole...............................	2,553	312½	200,000
Seneca................	Seneca.................................	240	81	51,953
Shawnee...............	Eastern Shawnee (Shawano).............	97	21	13,048
Wichita...............	Comanche (Komantsu), Delaware, Ionie, Kaddo, Kichaï, and Tawakanay, Wako, and Wichita.................	1,220	1,162	743,610
Wyandotte.............	Wyandotte..............................	258	32½	21,406
....	....	...	3,562	2,279,618
....	....	...	165	105,456
....	....	...	6,184½	3,958,117
....	....	...	1,067	683,189
....	....	...	2,571½	1,645,890
....	....	...	2,362	1,511,576
	Total................................	74,140	64,214	41,097,027

The number of white employees in the service of the above-enumerated tribes is over three thousand, and these are the men who are actually the tillers of the soil in this country. There are about nine thousand other white persons legal residents in this country held by these civilized tribes. Besides this number, there are about three thousand white men without any lawful authority. The area of land devoted to cultivation increases every year, and every agricultural product that is raised in the neighboring States is produced in sufficient abundance to supply the wants of all in the Territory. Live stock of all kinds is reared in excess of domestic demands. There are over two hundred common schools and ten high schools in the Territory. Over six thousand children attend the schools. Nearly all the tribes have abandoned the barbaric religion professed for generations among them. There are more church-houses, a greater number of Sunday-schools, and more children attend them, than in any other Territory of the United States, without regard to population. The traffic in ardent spirits is absolutely forbidden within the limits of this Territory.

After the close of the session of Congress, information was received at Washington of an extensive movement in the Western States with the design of occupying, by unauthorized persons, of certain lands in the Indian Territory, which had been ceded to the Government for the purpose of settlement by other Indian tribes. The President immediately issued the following proclamation:

Whereas, It has become known to me that certain evil-disposed persons have, within the territory and jurisdiction of the United States, begun and set on foot preparations for the organized and forcible possession of, and settlement upon, lands of what is known as Indian Territory, west of the State of Arkansas, which Territory is designated, recognized, and described by treaties and laws of the United States and by the executive authorities, as the Indian country, and as such is only subject to occupation by Indian tribes, the officers of the Indian Department, military posts, and such persons as may be privileged to reside and trade therein under the intercourse laws of the United States; and

Whereas, These laws provide for the removal of all persons residing and trading therein, without express permission of the Indian Department and agents, and also of all persons whom such agents may deem improper persons to reside in the Indian country: Now, therefore, for the purpose of properly protecting the interests of the Indian tribes as well as of the United States in said Territory, and of duly enforcing the laws governing the same;

I, Rutherford B. Hayes, President of the United States, do admonish and warn all such persons so intending or preparing to remove upon said lands or into said Territory without permission of the proper agents of the Indian Department, against any attempt so to remove or settle upon any of the lands in said Territory. I do further warn and notify any and all such persons who may so offend that they will be speedily and immediately removed therefrom by the agent according to the laws made and provided, and if necessary the aid and assistance of the military forces of the United States will be invoked to carry into proper execution the laws of the United States herein referred to.

In testimony whereof, I have hereunto set my hand and caused the seal of state to be affixed.

R. B. HAYES.

By the President:
WILLIAM M. EVARTS, Secretary of State.
WASHINGTON, *April 26*, 1879.

The landed interest of the State of Arkansas is large, and promises, if properly managed, to afford the means of liquidation of a large portion of the indebtedness to the United States, of effective assistance to the cause of education, and of still further, and greatly needed, assistance to the finances.

Immigration societies exist in various parts of the State, and there is also a State society; but they appear to languish for want of adequate support. Nevertheless, the natural attractions of soil and climate steadily induce a certain amount of immigration. The State has now the basis and foundation of a magnificent system of railroads. Two great trunk lines run continuously through it, from north to south and from east to west, and all that is necessary to complete this system and make it efficient in the diffusion of general prosperity, is to multiply feeders to these lines so as to send out their vivifying streams into every quarter and section of the State. Several such subsidiary lines have already been projected, and only await the aid and assistance of the State to become realities. The most prominent of these are the Joplin and Little Rock, connecting the rich and healthy regions of the northwest with the Little Rock and Fort Smith road; the Helena and Iron Mountain road, traversing and opening up that rich section of the Northeast known as the Crowley Ridge country; the Washita Valley road, bringing the great cotton-producing section of the southeast into connection with the Iron Mountain road at Arkadelphia; the Little Rock, Mississippi River, and Texas road, traversing and opening up the still richer cotton-growing regions of the lower Arkansas Valley, and directly connecting the lower Mississippi Valley with the main trunk-lines, with a prospective short-cut from Kansas City and the grain-growing regions of the Northwest, through the State, to New Orleans. All these subsidiary lines can be speedily built with the aid of the State government, without entailing a dollar of expenditure or of debt upon the people. All that they ask of the State is the donation of the public lands lying along their respective routes, and perhaps a little assistance here and there in the way of temporary exemptions or decrease of taxation. The most of these lands are now not only useless and unproductive, but in their present condition are actually hindrances and obstructions to advancement. They present the revolting aspect of deserted farms and silent and forbidding forests, and repel rather than invite immigration. Before the adjournment of the Legislature a bill was passed to aid the railroad from Washington to connect with the Iron Mountain road at Hope. This is the first step in a system that promises sooner or later to redeem all Southwest Arkansas. This road will be extended and branched into all the other counties of that section, and bring their waste lands to the notice of immigrants, and their rich products to market.

Besides the Homestead Act passed by the last Congress authorizing persons desiring to settle on public lands within railroad limits to claim their homesteads out of odd sections in all States except Missouri and Arkansas, there was passed on the last day of the subsequent extra session a bill granting additional rights to homestead settlers on railroad lands in the two above-named States. It authorizes them to claim their homesteads out of odd sections just as they could do in other States. The general law, which is perfected by the new law, gives to every person the right to enter 160 acres instead of 80 acres, as heretofore, on these lands. The new bill provides that odd sections within the limits of any grant of public lands to any railroad company in the States of Missouri and Arkansas, or to these States in aid of any railroad where even sections have been granted, shall be open to settlers under the homestead laws to the extent of 160 acres. It further provides that any person who has, under existing laws, taken a homestead on any section within the limits of any railroad grant in these two States, who has been restricted to 80 acres, may enter an additional 80 acres adjoining the land embraced within his original entry. If the additional land is subject to entry, he may if he wishes surrender his entry to the United States for cancellation, and thereafter can enter lands under the homestead laws the same as if the surrendered entry had not been made. He can do so without payment of fees and commissions. It provides also that the residence of such person upon and the cultivation of land embraced in his original entry shall be considered his residence upon and the cultivation for the same length of time of land embraced in his additional or new entry, and shall be deducted from the five years' residence and cultivation required by law; provided that in no case shall a patent issue upon an additional or new homestead entry under this act, until the person has actually, and in conformity with the homestead laws, occupied, resided upon, and cultivated land embraced therein at least one year.

The public schools of the State are suffering in consequence of the payment of teachers in the depreciated State scrip, which is receivable for all dues and payable for all expenses. A poll-tax appropriated to the support of schools, through imperfect collection, yields about $40,000 instead of $100,000. The Arkansas Industrial University has 300 pupils, which might be increased to 600 under a small additioual outlay by the State. There is a normal branch of this institution located at Pine Bluffs. St. John's College unsuccessfully asked of the Legislature an appropriation of $5,000 per annum, to be expended in the establishment of a department of chemistry, metallurgy, geology, and mining; which department was to accomplish a thorough geological survey of each county, furnish a complete collection of specimens of the mineral productions of the State, and publish the results of its labors. The college engaged further to provide, in consideration of the State aid thus to be received, a free normal school.

It is made the constitutional duty of the General Assembly to provide by law for the support of institutions for the education of the deaf and dumb and of the blind, and also for the treatment of the insane. A beginning has been made for the education of the deaf and dumb and of the blind; but the institutions established for that purpose are imperfect. Owing to the embarrassed financial condition of the State, the appropriations for their support have been insufficient to provide for the education of all of those unfortunate classes residing in it.

In the Blind Institute forty-six pupils have been instructed during the last two years. Through lack of funds the number of pupils was limited and the length of the sessions reduced. The deaf-mute institution requires an appropriation of $8,000 for its maintenance, and for the pupil fund the sum of $180 per pupil. The sum of $50,000 was appropriated in 1873 for the erection of a lunatic asylum. Of this appropriation $21,000 in scrip was drawn by the trustees, and the balance of $29,-000 reverted to the Treasury; $16,000 was expended in purchasing ground for the building, and $5,000 converted into currency, realizing $3,366.61. Out of this amount there has been paid for improvements on the ground, for plans and specifications for buildings, and on other accounts, $1,104.16, leaving in the hands of the trustees $2,262.45. The number of insane persons in the State, as nearly as can be ascertained, is about 300. Many of these are now "confined in loathsome and pestilent jails, unfit for the meanest criminals, without any regard for sex or condition." The trustees estimate that it will require an appropriation of at least $150,000 in current money for the erection of "suitable and substantial buildings for the insane."

An enrollment of the militia of the State has been made, and all irregular organizations disbanded. The State possesses, nominally, 1,162 Springfield breech-loading rifle muskets, 79 muzzle-loading muskets, 61 shot-guns, 1 (62-pounder) Parrott gun, complete, and 1 (64-pounder) siege-gun, with sundry ordnance stores. There is due to the State from the United States, on her quota of arms, $11,977. The number of convicts in the State Penitentiary on December 1, 1878, was 496. There had been released during the year 201. During the years 1877 and 1878 the Governor pardoned 50 convicts out of the penitentiary; released from fines and imprisonment in county jails, 55; commuted the sentence of death passed on three persons to imprisonment for life; and under the provisions of the act of January 31, 1867, granted, for exemplary conduct during their confinement in the penitentiary, commutations of sentence to 177 prisoners.

The investigation by a committee of the House of Congress relative to the failure of the appropriation for the Hot Springs,* showed it to have been the consequence of an oversight and not of a premeditated design. The appropriation was therefore confirmed. The Commissioners were reappointed in December, 1878, for one year. The engineer in charge finished the laying out of the streets in the southern portion of the city. Thirty-nine streets and eight main avenues have been surveyed. The Hot Springs reservation is under the superintendence of General B. F. Kelly of West Virginia. The bath-houses pay an annual rental to the United States of $5 for every bathing-tub in actual use. The money received from this source will be applied toward improving and embellishing the mountain with shady walks, carriage-drives, and summer-houses. Certificates of ownership are granted by the Commissioners, and improvements on an extensive scale are projected.

Considerable excitement was created by the reported discovery of silver ore in Montgomery County, about thirty-five miles from Hot Springs. The locality is at the extension of the Santa Rosa Mountain range into the basin of the Mississippi. The topography and geology of this Arkansas region are similar to that of New Mexico, and may be rich in minerals. Vigorous and successful measures were taken under the direction of the State Board of Health to keep out of the State yellow fever and other infectious diseases.

A colored convention assembled at Little Rock on April 12th to consider the subject of emigration. There was a fair representation from different sections of the State. Fifteen delegates and as many alternates to the conference at Nashville on May 6th were appointed. Resolutions were adopted affirming that, as colored citizens of Arkansas in many localities were not allowed free enjoyment of their constitutional rights, they were desirous of emigrating to some other State or Territory where the elective franchise can be enjoyed unmolested, and recommending the appointment of two colored commissioners under the National Migration Aid Society to select a suitable State or Territory, and a national donation or loan to aid settlers in the territory selected. The convention resolved itself into an auxiliary State Migration Aid Society, and appointed an executive committee.

_____
* See "Annual Cyclopædia," 1878, p. 24.

The embarrassment in many of the counties and towns arising from a failure to pay the bonded indebtedness still continues. In Clark County a vote of the citizens was taken on the question of a dissolution of the county organization on a compromise of the debt. The result was 464 votes for compromise, and 622 for a dissolution of the county organization. The official returns of the election of 1878 were received too late for insertion in the "Annual Cyclopædia" of that year. The vote for Governor, W. R. Miller, to whom there was no opposition, was 88,730. The following State officers were chosen: Secretary of State, John Frolich; Auditor, John Crawford; Attorney-General, William F. Henderson; Land Commissioner, D. W. Lear; Supreme Court Judge, John R. Eakin; Superintendent of Public Instruction, J. L. Denton; Chancellor, D. W. Carroll. The vote for members of Congress was as follows:

DISTRICT.	Democrat.	National and Independent.
I.	8,863	.....
II.	11,226	8,399
III.	7,202	6,808
IV.	4,657	2,637

The State Legislature was divided as follows:

PARTY.	Senate.	House.
Democrats.	29	81
Republicans.	1	6
Nationals.	1	6
Total.	81	98

ARMY OF THE UNITED STATES. The strength of the Army of the United States at present is 2,127 officers, 24,262 men, and 388 retired officers. The enlisted men of the Signal Corps, Engineer and Ordnance Corps, Ordnance Sergeants, Commissary Sergeants, and Hospital Stewards, the prison guard at Fort Leavenworth, and the recruiting detachments, amount in the aggregate to 3,463 men, and are employed in the performance of important duties connected with the military establishments, but these duties bring but few of them into active service in the field. The statute now authorizes a total force of 25,000 men, not including the Signal Corps, which has by law 456 men. The combative force of the army proper consists of 11 generals, 1,559 officers, 20,556 men, and 233 Indian scouts.

The only disturbance of the peace during the year took place on the frontier with the Utes in Colorado and the Apaches in New Mexico. The Indian name "Utee," from which Utah takes its name, was applied to all the nomads west of the Rocky Mountains, as far as Nevada, and south into New Mexico and Arizona. Gradually they have been surrounded by white settlements and broken up into many distinct bands, the four principal of which are located

as follows: The Uintahs, in northeastern Utah, estimated at 430 souls; the "Los Pinos," in the Uncompahgre Valley, Colorado, estimated at 2,000 souls; the "Southern Utes," in southwestern Colorado, with 934 souls; and the "White River Utes," in northwestern Colorado, estimated at 800 souls. These Indians are of the fiercest class, and occupy the roughest parts of our country for farming, grazing, or for military operations. Their management is complicated by the fact that their country is known to possess mineral deposits, which attract a bold and adventurous class of white men. They are very warlike, and have no difficulty in procuring, in exchange for their deer-skins, horses, and sheep, any amount of the best rifles and ammunition. In former years they used to come east of the Rocky Mountains to hunt buffalo, but of late years they have confined their hunting to the bear, elk, and deer of the mountain region. As long as the game lasts they will not work or attempt farming, except in the smallest and most insignificant manner, and that only by compulsion.

A state of irritation, which resulted in a conflict, was produced by the demand of the agent, Mr. Meeker, that the Indians should engage in farming, to which they were uncompromisingly hostile, and, in his endeavor to plow land for farming, Major Thornburgh with a small force announced to the agent his intention of coming to afford him any assistance he might need. The agent in reply stated that the Indians were very much excited, and regarded the approach of troops as a declaration of war; and he suggested to Major Thornburgh to stop at some convenient camping-place, and with five soldiers come into the agency, and a talk and a better understanding could be had. Major Thornburgh accepted the suggestion, and stated that he should move with his entire command within striking distance, and suggested that the agent and some of the chiefs meet him on the road. The former expressed gratification with the plan, and, in a letter dated September 29th, one P. M., said he expected to leave the agency on the next morning, adding: "If you have trouble getting through the cañon to-day, let me know. We have been on guard three nights, and shall be to-night, not because we know there is danger, but because there may be." The Indians lay in wait and made an attack. The result was a loss on the side of the military command of 11 citizens, 2 officers, and 12 soldiers killed and 41 wounded. The Indians admitted a loss of 39. Major Thornburgh was killed in this action, and the agent, Mr. Meeker, at his residence. About the same time some of the Apaches, who belong to the Mescalero Agency, near Fort Stanton, New Mexico, more than 600 miles south of White River, began a raid upon the ranches and settlements in southern New Mexico. Major Morrow, of the Ninth Cavalry, with about 450 men at his command, started in pursuit, but no very serious affair was anticipated. These Apaches have no connection whatever with the Utes. They have always been restless and mischievous, and only resort to agencies to rest, recuperate, and make ready for the next war. As soon as winter comes they are expected to return to their agency and become orderly.

A proposition, often made and recently renewed, to transfer the charge of the Indians from the Department of the Interior to the War Department, has led to such conflicting discussions on the subject of Indian management as to obtain the name of the "Indian problem" for it. The difficulties connected with it have been steadily growing from year to year as the Western country, formerly occupied as hunting-grounds exclusively, is required for agricultural settlement and mining industry. In the same measure as white men and Indians more and more jostled each other, their contact has been apt to result in collision. The Indians are scattered over an immense extent of country, in tribes and bands of different size, with constantly growing and multiplying settlements of whites between them. The game upon which formerly most of them could depend for subsistence is rapidly disappearing. They occupy a number of reservations, some large and some comparatively small; some consisting in great part of fertile lands, some barren; many of which were secured to them for occupancy by treaties in times gone by with them as distinct nations. Many treaty reservations have turned out to be of far greater value in agricultural and mineral resources than they were originally thought to be, and are now equally coveted by the white population surrounding them.

The system of superintendents and agents has continued from an early period; but these officers were few in number and made their reports to the War Office, although neither the Secretary nor any officer of the Department had anything to do with their appointment, nor was the Department charged with the duty of supervising or controlling them. In 1854 an act of Congress was passed by which there was given to the Secretary of War a sort of general superintendency of the agents and sub-agents appointed by the President; and, while by that act the President was authorized to select military men to discharge the duties of Indian agents, a large majority of the agents selected were taken from civil life, and much machinery was employed in the conduct of Indian affairs. Year after year large amounts of money have been expended with a view to civilizing these people, and yet failure has attended the efforts in this direction. The inauguration of the "peace policy" in 1868 by President Grant, in which their management was placed entirely in the hands of civilians, was expected to produce more favorable results. The ends steadily pursued by the Interior Department have been—1. To set the Indians to

work as agriculturists or herders, thus to break up their habits of savage life and to make them self-supporting; 2. To educate their youth of both sexes so as to introduce to the growing generation civilized ideas, wants, and aspirations; 3. To allot parcels of land to Indians in severalty, and to give them individual title to their farms in fee, inalienable for a certain period, thus to foster the pride of individual ownership of property, instead of their former dependence upon the tribe, with its territory held in common; 4. When settlement in severalty with individual title is accomplished, to dispose with their consent of those lands on their reservations which are not settled and used by them, the proceeds to form a fund for their benefit, which will gradually relieve the Government of the expenses at present provided for by annual appropriations; 5. When this is accomplished, to treat the Indians like other inhabitants of the United States under the laws of the land. "This policy," says the Secretary of the Interior, "if adopted and supported by Congress and carried out with wisdom and firmness, will, in my opinion, gradually bring about a solution of the Indian problem,' without injustice to the Indians and also without obstructing the development of the country."

It appears, from the report of the Commissioner of Indian Affairs, that the Indians on reservations have now under cultivation 157,-056 acres, about 24,000 of which were broken by them in 1879, and that the products raised by the reservation Indians during the same twelve months amounted to 328,637 bushels of wheat, 643,286 bushels of corn, 189,654 bushels of oats and barley, 390,698 bushels of potatoes and other vegetables, and 48,353 tons of hay. This exhibit of the products of Indian labor does not include the five civilized tribes of the Indian Territory, who cultivated 237,-000 acres and raised 565,400 bushels of wheat, 2,015,000 bushels of corn, 200,500 bushels of oats and barley, 336,700 bushels of vegetables, and 176,500 tons of hay. At the same time the raising of stock has been encouraged as much as possible. There are owned by reservation Indians 199,700 horses, 2,870 mules, 68,894 head of cattle, 32,537 swine, and 863,-000 sheep, the latter principally by the Navajos. The five civilized tribes in the Indian Territory are reported to have 45,500 horses, 5,500 mules, 272,000 head of cattle, 190,000 swine, and 32,400 sheep. Provision has been made for an additional distribution of 11,300 head of stock cattle among the uncivilized tribes, it being found that the Indians are beginning to take excellent care of their domestic animals, and to be proud of the increase of their stock. Many have commenced raising swine and poultry, and it is thought expedient to encourage such beginnings in every possible way. The cultivation of garden vegetables among them is also rapidly spreading. Preparations have been made to increase the area of cultivated soil very largely in 1880. Considerable quantities of agricultural tools and implements have been distributed, and the demand is constantly growing. So far as regards the solution of the Indian question, the Secretary of the Interior is of the opinion that it "depends upon the civilization of the Indians and their ability to take care of themselves."

The expenditures of the War Department for the fiscal year ending June 30, 1879, were $42,653,723. The appropriations available for the service of the fiscal year ending June 30, 1878, were $45,076,702; those for 1879 were $53,016,040; and those for the fiscal year ending June 30, 1880, were $46,269,821. The estimates for the service of the fiscal year ending June 30, 1881, amount to $40,380,428. The estimates for the civil establishment, which is the War Department proper, amount to $1,159,460. The force of the War Department and its bureaus was reorganized by an act of June 20, 1874, and placed on a basis, as to numbers, grades, and compensation, which seemed to be satisfactory in the transaction of public business, until that basis was materially changed by legislative reduction in 1876, and was thereafter considered by Congress as subject to further decrease. The military establishment is estimated for on the basis of 25,450 enlisted men, the Signal Corps being by law allowed 450 men not to be included in the 25,000. Under this head the estimates for the fiscal year ending June 30, 1880, were $29,335,727.33 ; the appropriations to meet the same were $26,978,847.33 ; and the present estimates are for $29,319,794.78. The principal differences between the estimates and the appropriations are on account of the item for pay, etc., of the army, which is made up of estimates based on arithmetical calculations, and on items for the Ordnance Department which relate to timely provisions for the public defense in any emergency that may arise. The estimates for the public works are $7,557,034.42, which amount is $396,043.34 less than the estimates for 1879, $113,946.88 less than those for 1880, and $3,237,460.19 less than the appropriations for 1880, which were $10,794,464.61. The amounts appropriated for "fortifications and other works of defense" during the last five years have been insufficient to preserve all such Government property from waste. This fact accounts for the annual increase in the amounts suggested for these works by the Chief of Engineers. Under this title the estimates for 1880, which were $3,188,400, were reduced to $1,000,000, and the present estimates, rendered in detail, for $4,028,500, have been reduced in the aggregate to $1,000,000, which amount could be wisely and properly applied to the preservation and care of these works. The estimates for rivers and harbors, rendered by items for $14,326,650, were reduced in the aggregate to $5,015,000, which was the total of the amount appropriated for the fiscal year 1877, and which

seems to have been sufficient for the promotion of the general commerce of the country during that time. The miscellaneous estimates are $2,344,139.73, of which amount about one fourth appertains annually to the departmental collection and diffusion of valuable official data, such as the observation and report of storms through the Signal Service, the compilation and publication of official records of the war of the rebellion, and the like, and the remaining portion (which is over $1,500,000) is made up of items wholly relative to certain moral obligations of the Government, such as the support of the National Home for Disabled Volunteer Soldiers, the furnishing of artificial limbs and other appliances to disabled soldiers, and the care of national cemeteries. The aggregate of the estimates for the next fiscal year is $2,273,294.69 less than the amount of actual expenditures of 1879, $5,889,393.01 less than the appropriations available for the service of the fiscal year 1880, and is $7,289.40 less than the estimates for 1880, which were for a less sum of money than any annual estimates rendered to Congress from the Department for a period of at least eleven years.

The preparation of the Union and Confederate War Records is progressing under the management of Colonel R. N. Scott, of the army. The Secretary of War says: "There is a general disposition on the part of the ex-Confederate officers to contribute material to the official History of the War." The Southern Historical Society has placed its collection at the service of the Department, and valuable documents have been furnished by Generals Johnston, Pemberton, Wheeler, Jones, Ruggles, and others.

The total number of deaths from all causes reported among the white troops was 266, or 12 per 1,000 of mean strength. Of these, 162, or 7 per 1,000 of strength, died of disease, and 104, or 5 per 1,000 of strength, of wounds, accidents, and injuries. The proportion of deaths from all causes to cases treated was 1 to 142. The total number of white soldiers reported to have been discharged the service on "surgeon's certificate of disability" was 677, or 31 per 1,000 of mean strength. The total number of deaths of colored soldiers reported from all causes was 28, or 14 per 1,000 of mean strength. Of these, 15, or 8 per 1,000 of strength, died of disease, and 13, or 6 per 1,000 of strength, of wounds, accidents, and injuries. The proportion of deaths from all causes to cases treated was 1 to 140. The total number of colored soldiers reported to have been discharged on "surgeon's certificate of disability" was 42, or 22 per 1,000 of mean strength.

The survey of the territory west of the 100th meridian has been continued in the States of Colorado, Texas, Nevada, California, and Oregon, and in the Territories of Arizona, New Mexico, Utah, and Washington, and in connection with this work a special survey of Great Salt Lake has been completed. No funds were available for the prosecution of the field-work on this survey after June 30, 1879, and all parties were withdrawn from the field on or before that date. There are eight engineer officers now employed in the Western military divisions and departments in making surveys, and in collecting and mapping the geographical and topographical information obtained in scouts and campaigns against the hostile Indians. Maps prepared in this way are of great value to the War Department and to the army.

The Ordnance Department still continues the test of breech-loading ordnance, especially of the 8-inch rifle converted from a 10-inch smooth-bore gun, and thus far 202 rounds (190 with full battering charges) have been successfully completed. The endurance so far has proved satisfactory, and no evidences of want of endurance in its special construction have been so far afforded; and there are good grounds for the opinion that it will stand its thorough proof, and establish the fact that after this system the original smooth-bore cast-iron guns can be converted into breech-loaders, or original breech-loading cannon of the heaviest construction can be produced. The decided advantages to be derived from the use of breech-loading rifles, especially in casemated works, have been heretofore noticed in these pages. Since then the unfortunate disaster on board of the Thunderer (the bursting of a 38-ton muzzle-loading gun by the accidental insertion of two charges, impossible to occur in breech-loaders), and the unexcelled results (in power, accuracy, and successful manipulation) recently attained at Meppen, by Herr Krupp, in the trials of his breech-loading guns of 70 and 80 tons, have led to the conviction that it is highly probable that the general introduction of breech-loading instead of muzzle-loading cannon in the armaments of Europe, for all heavy ordnance especially, is a mere matter of time. During the last fiscal year there were manufactured at the National Armory 20,005 Springfield rifles, and, under the law authorizing it, 1,000 of the experimental Hotchkiss magazine rifles. The former have been produced at a much less cost than heretofore, owing to the increased number manufactured and the improvement of the plant employed; and, as there is now available a larger appropriation than usual for the present year, it is confidently expected that the cost will be yet further reduced in the future. There were in store on July 1, 1879, only 22,073 rifles and 5,406 carbines at the armory and arsenals. The Hotchkiss arms are now in the hands of the Regular Army for trial in actual service, and upon the reports to be made bimonthly will depend any recommendations for the supply to be hereafter manufactured.

The military board, consisting of Generals J. M. Schofield, A. H. Terry, and George W. Getty, before whom the President ordered a rehearing of the case of General Fitz John Por-

VOL. XIX.—4 A

ter, made a report exonerating him entirely. They state the evidence as presenting itself under several distinct heads: 1. Imperfect and in some respects erroneous statements of facts, due to the partial and incorrect knowledge in the possession of the witnesses at the time of the court-martial, and the extremely inaccurate maps and erroneous locations of troops thereon, by which erroneous statements were made to convey still more erroneous impressions; 2. The opinions and inferences of prominent officers, based upon this imperfect knowledge; 3. Far more complete and accurate statements of facts now made by a large number of eye-witnesses from both the contending forces; 4. Accurate maps of the field of operations and the exact positions of the troops thereon at different periods of time, by which statements otherwise contradictory or irreconcilable are shown to be harmonious, and opposing opinions are shown to be based upon different views of the same military situation; and, 5. The conflicting testimony relative to the plan of operations, the interpretation of orders, the motives of action, and relative degrees of responsibility for the unfortunate results. Concerning the charge of which General Porter was found guilty, of not having moved his command on the night of August 27, 1862, in obedience to an order from General Pope, the Board report that it was a manifest physical impossibility to march over that road that night. They say nothing could have been gained by the attempt, and that it would have been wiser if General Porter had delayed his attempt still longer than he did. They think he exercised the very ordinary discretion of a corps commander, and that it was his plain duty to so express it. The report recites at much length and in detail the important events connected with the military operations of the 29th of August, 1862, and among other important facts it is made clear that Porter's display of troops in the early part of the afternoon of the 29th gave rise to the belief on the Confederate side of an attack about to be made, and that under this belief Longstreet sent his reserves from the extreme left to the extreme right of his army and in front of Porter, thus relieving the Union army under the other commanders from this Confederate force. Porter's duty during the afternoon of that date, the report states, was too plain and simple to admit of discussion, and the Board is unable to find anything in it subject to criticism, much less deserving censure and condemnation. He had made frequent reports to his superiors, stating what he had done and what he had been unable to do; what his situation was in respect to the enemy, and what their strength; what his impressions were from the sounds of action toward his right; how he had failed to get any communications from any commander in the main army, or any orders from General Pope or McDowell as to his designs for the night, sending an aide-de-camp to General Pope for orders and receiving no reply, not even information that the vital 4.30 order had been sent to him; and generally informing his superior officers that if left to himself without orders he would have to retire at night for food and water, which were not accessible where he was. These reports were sent not only frequently but early enough to insure the receipt of orders from General Pope or correct information from McDowell, if they had any to send him.

ASIA. The area of Asia was estimated in 1878 at 17,308,000 square miles, and the total population at about 831,000,000.* (Behm and Wagner, "Bevölkerung der Erde," vol. v., Gotha, 1878.)

In Afghanistan, the British armies having after a series of easy victories gained the important positions of Jelalabad and Candahar, and having secured the passes commanding the approaches to Cabool, the representatives of the Indian Government concluded with the Ameer Yakoob Khan, who succeeded the deceased Shere Ali, the treaty of Gundamuk. In this convention the jurisdiction of the English over the border territories was recognized, perpetual friendship was declared between England and Afghanistan, and the residence of a representative of the British Government at Cabool was stipulated for. The resident appointed in accordance with the treaty was received at Cabool with ceremonial honor; but a few weeks afterward a mutiny broke out among the Afghan soldiers, the residency was destroyed, and its principal members were murdered. Another military expedition was dispatched against Cabool, and occupied that capital October 10th, after which the British officers proceeded to restore order and punish the perpetrators of the outrages against the late residents. In consequence of this occupation, Yakoob Khan declared his abdication as Ameer of Afghanistan, and General Roberts issued a proclamation announcing that for the present the administration of the country would remain with the British authorities. (See AFGHANISTAN.)

Throughout the year the British Government was on the verge of another war with the young King of Burmah. This King, who succeeded his father in October, 1878, proved to be one of the worst tyrants the Asiatic countries have known during the present century, and seemed to be under the influence of a war party which inflamed him against the British. A claim laid by the King to the East Karennee country, which was disputed by England, greatly strained the relations between the two countries, and in October the British Resident at Mandalay left the country. In November the King of Burmah sent a special en$_v$o$_y$ to the Viceroy of India. (See BURMAH.)

While the progress of the British arms in

Afghanistan was watched with great interest and considerable jealousy in Russia, a new Russian expedition against the Tekke Turcomans created some uneasiness in England. The expedition advanced in the direction of Merv, a place which many English statesmen would prevent Russia from occupying even at a risk of war. The Russian Government denied that the direct object of the expedition was the occupation of Merv; it was, however, generally understood that the expedition might ultimately lead to this result. For the present, the utter failure of the Russian army prevented a serious complication between England and Russia; but, as the attempt will be renewed next year, the danger of a collision is by no means averted. This further advance of the Russian armies, and the consolidation under Russian rule of the territories which have of late been annexed or may be hereafter annexed, will be greatly promoted by the building of a Central Asian railroad, which is contemplated for the near future, and by other works of material improvement which are pushed forward by the Russians. (See RUSSIA.)

The rule of the Chinese Government in Kashgaria has been fully reëstablished, and Russia has been prevailed upon to consent to a restoration of Kulja, which was occupied by the Russians eight years ago in consequence of the disorders prevailing among the Mohammedans there. The influence of the Chinese Government in many of the small neighboring countries, like Burmah and Nepaul, seems to be on the increase, but the Government was again harassed in 1879 by several rebellions. (See CHINA.)

The entire incorporation of the Loochoo Islands with the Japanese Empire has strained the relations between Japan and China, as the Government of the latter country has never abandoned its claim to the islands. In discussing the controversy, the native papers of Japan glory in the progress they have made in civilization. (See JAPAN.)

Toward the close of the year the relations between England and Turkey assumed an unfriendly character, because the Government of Turkey, in the opinion of the English Government, had failed to carry out in Asia Minor those reforms which were stipulated for in the Berlin Treaty. In the beginning of November the British Mediterranean fleet was ordered to enter Turkish waters, and Sir A. Layard, in reply to inquiries from the Turkish Government, stated that his Government could not tolerate any further delay in the execution of the reforms promised in Asia Minor. The Turkish Government yielded to these representations, and promised to carry out the reforms. (See TURKEY.)

The religious complexion of Asia appears to be approaching a considerable change. Mohammedanism, which has been in modern times the most progressive of the Asiatic re-

---

* For a detailed account of the area and population of the divisions and subdivisions of Asia see "Annual Cyclopædia" for 1878, article Asia.

ligions in point of territorial extension, is more and more stripped of all political power. (See MOHAMMEDANISM.) The missionary efforts of the Christian Churches, which since the beginning of the present century had not succeeded in adding any large numbers to the Christian population, have begun to be attended with marvelous success, especially in India and China. (See CHINA and INDIA.) In India, moreover, large numbers of the educated classes of natives are connecting themselves with the Brahmo-Somaj, one of the most remarkable reformatory movements of the age, to the rise and progress of which we devote this year a special article. (See BRAHMO-SOMAJ.) The following table exhibits an estimate of the total population connected with the Protestant, Roman Catholic, and Eastern Churches and missions:

COUNTRIES.	Protestant.	Roman Catholic.	Eastern.
Russia.........................	14,000	51,000	5,941,000
Turkey........................	10,030	260,000	3,000,000
Persia........................	8,000	10,000	50,000
China....	50,000	483,000	5,000
Japan.........................	4,000	20,000	5,000
Anam..........................	.....	430,000	.....
Burmah....	.....	5,000	.....
Siam..........................	2,000	25,000	.....
British possessions (including neighboring missions)..........	2,630,000	1,264,000	300,000
French possessions.............	.....	800,000	.....
Spanish possessions.............	.....	4,000,000	.....
Portuguese possessions.........	.....	350,000	.....
Dutch possessions............	170,000	80,000	.....
Total...................	2,858,000	7,828,000	9,301,000

ASTRONOMICAL PHENOMENA AND PROGRESS.

Sun-spots.—The dearth of sun-spots in 1878 and 1879 has been very remarkable. The minimum looked for about 1876 or 1877, and then thought to be at hand, was not reached till 1879, making the last period no less than twelve years. Dr. Schmidt, director of the observatory at Athens, Greece, reports that in 1878 the sun was entirely free from spots on 298 days of observation. At Greenwich, England, during the year ending May 1, 1879, sun-spots were visible but 27 days. It has been remarked, moreover, that throughout this period of quiescence the solar prominences were few and inconsiderable.

Minor Planets.—The search for minor planets during the past year was unusually successful, nineteen having been discovered in about nine months. Of these, eight were detected by Dr. Peters of Hamilton College, New York, and nine by Herr Palisa of Pola. The former has now discovered forty members of the group; the latter, twenty-one. The following names have been recently selected for those discovered, but not named in 1877 and 1878: No. 174, Phædra; 175, Andromache; 179, Clytemnestra; 180, Garumna; 182, Elsbeth; and 183, Istria. The names, together with the principal facts in regard to the discovery, of those detected in 1879 are given in the following table:

NO.	Name.	Date of Disc.	Discoverer.	Place of Disc.	Mag.
192.	Nausikaa..	Feb. 17.....	Palisa....	Pola........	11
193.	Ambrosia..	Feb. 28.....	Coggia...	Marseilles..	12
194.	Prokne....	March 21....	Peters ...	Clinton ...	11
195.	Eurykleia..	April 28....	Palisa....	Pola........	12
196.	Philomela..	May 14.....	Peters ...	Clinton	10
197.	Arete.......	May 21.....	Palisa....	Pola........	12
198.	Ampella ...	June 18.....	Borelly ..	Marseilles..	11
199.	Byblis	July 9.....	Peters ...	Clinton	11
200.	Dynamene .	July 27.....	Peters ...	Clinton	11
201.	Penelope...	Aug. 7.....	Palisa....	Pola........	11
202.	Chryseis ..	Sept. 21....	Peters ...	Clinton	11
203.	Pompeja...	Sept. 27....	Peters ...	Clinton	11
204.	....	Oct. 8.....	Palisa ...	Pola........	12
205.	....	Oct. 18.....	Palisa...	Pola........	12
206.	Hersilia...	Oct. 15.....	Peters ...	Clinton	11
207.	....	Oct. 17.....	Palisa....	Pola........	12
208.	....	Oct. 21.....	Palisa....	Pola........	13
209.	Dido	Oct. 22.....	Peters ...	Pola........	11
210.	....	Nov. 12.....	Palisa....	Pola........	11

Comets.—Brorsen's comet of short period, first discovered in 1846, was detected on its seventh return by M. Tempel of Florence on the 14th of January. It passed its perihelion on the 30th of March. On the 24th of April the same observer found the second comet of 1867 on its third return—its period being nearly six years. Its orbit is the least eccentric known in the cometary system, the perihelion being exterior to the orbit of Mars, the aphelion interior to that of Jupiter. In other words, it is confined to the region of the asteroids. In 1882 it will approach very near to Jupiter, when its orbit may be so changed as to render it invisible on its future returns to perihelion. The third comet of 1879 was discovered on the 16th of June by Dr. Lewis Swift of Rochester, New York. When discovered it was about three minutes in diameter, had a bright central nucleus, and appeared nearly equal to a star of the ninth magnitude. The elements of its orbit have no resemblance to those of any former comet; its motion is retrograde; and its perihelion was passed on the 27th of April. The fourth comet of the year was discovered by Herr Palisa of Pola, August 21st. It had a circular disk nearly three minutes in diameter; its motion was direct; and it passed its perihelion October 4th. On the 24th of August Dr. Hartwig of Strasburg discovered a faint comet—the fifth of 1879—in R. A. 12ʰ 19ᵐ, and decl. N. 61° 2'. Its elements have no marked resemblance to those of any known comet.

Spots on Jupiter.—Observations on Jupiter during the latter part of 1878 and the whole of 1879 have indicated changes of an extraordinary character in the planet's atmosphere. Some of the observers who have given close attention to the phenomena are Dr. Swift of Rochester, New York, Professor Pritchett of Glasgow, Missouri, Dr. Lohse of Potsdam, Mr. Dennett of Southampton, England, and Mr. Gledhill of Halifax. A very large spot, somewhat variable in color, but generally described as red or rose-colored, has been visible seventeen months. This spot when first seen was nearly circular. Gradually, however, it has assumed a more and more elliptical form, its major axis remaining constantly parallel to Jupiter's equator. It seems also, like the solar spots, to have a proper motion upon the surface. Mr. Dennett remarks that "between July 27th and November 15th the longitude of its preceding extremity seems to have increased some twenty-four degrees, which means a proper motion eastward of more than 230 miles per day." In August, 1879, the length of the spot, according to Professor Pritchett, was nearly 25,000 miles, and its greatest breadth about 6,400. Other markings, indicative of unusual atmospheric activity, have been noticed during the year, but this "red spot," by its magnitude, color, permanence, and proper motion, has attracted the special attention of observers.

The Density of Saturn.—In the "Astronomische Nachrichten," No. 2269, Professor Asaph Hall of Washington compares the observed value of Saturn's polar compression with Laplace's formula for the ellipticity of a rotating homogeneous spheroid. The theoretical value of the ratio of the semi-axes is found to be 1·1859. The observed value is 1·1087 according to Bessel, or 1·1223 according to Kaiser. Consequently, as in the cases of the earth and Jupiter, the polar compression is less than it would be if the mass were homogeneous. The density increases, therefore, from the surface to the center of the planet. Moreover, the rate of variation is more rapid in Saturn than in Jupiter, and, as the mean density of the former is considerably less than the density of water, we may conclude that the surface of Saturn is in the condition of vapor.

Meteoric Showers.—The meteors of January 2d were observed at Bristol, England, by Mr. W. F. Denning. The sky was overcast on the night of the 1st, but toward morning the clouds partly cleared away, and in a watch of twenty minutes, commencing at 6ʰ· 14ᵐ· on the morning of the 2d, two thirds of the sky being covered by clouds, fourteen meteors were seen, all belonging to the shower whose radiant is in Quadrans. The shower at this time was evidently very active. Mr. Denning remarks that in a cloudless sky more than one meteor per minute would have been seen by a single observer. The radiant point was at R. A. 230°, decl. N. 51°.

The Meteors of August 8th–12th.—The number of August meteors observed in 1879 was rather less than usual. The weather, however, was unfavorable, not only in our own country but also in England. In the "Science Observer" for September Mr. Edwin F. Sawyer of Cambridge, Massachusetts, gives the results of his watching on the nights of the 10th, 11th, and 12th; a succession of cloudy nights having prevented any previous observations. On the 10th, commencing at 9 o'clock and watching four hours, Mr. Sawyer counted 107 meteors, of which 78 were Perseids. The greatest frequency occurred soon after 11ʰ· 30ᵐ·. "Their persistency to grouping was very noticeable,

and frequently intervals of five minutes and even longer occurred without a single meteor being recorded, and then several being seen almost simultaneously." The radiant was at R. A. 44° 30′ and decl. N. 57°. The number of Perseids observed in 2⅓ hours, beginning at 9 o'clock on the night of the 11th, was 27. On the evening of the 12th the shower had nearly ceased.

The Meteors of November 13th–14th.—A few meteors from this interesting stream were seen at several stations. In a watch of two hours, commencing at 3ʰ· 30ᵐ· on the morning of the 13th, Mr. D. E. Hunter of Washington, Indiana, assisted by several students, counted 190 meteors, the greatest number reported from any one station.

Relative Numbers of Meteors in Different Months.—In order to determine the relative proportion of meteors of all kinds registered by different observers, Mr. W. F. Denning recently summarized the results given in twelve catalogues, which comprise 59,086 meteors, and the following numbers were derived:

January	2,419 meteors.	July	7,869 meteors.
February	1,609 "	August	23,374 "
March	1,449 "	September	2,897 "
April	4,824 "	October	4,827 "
May	1,183 "	November	5,457 "
June	1,825 "	December	2,908 "

Thus August alone contains nearly two fifths of the whole number recorded.

Origin of the November Meteors.—In a lecture recently delivered before the Royal Institution of Great Britain, Mr. G. Johnstone Stoney, after tracing the history of the November meteors, pointing out their connection with the comet of 1866, and indicating the manner in which they were permanently attached to the solar system, presents the following views in regard to their origin:

The question now arises, how the deserts of space which extend from star to star come to be tenanted here and there by a patch of gas or an occasional meteorite? Light has been thrown on this inquiry by discoveries made with the spectroscope in modern times, and by observations during eclipses. These have revealed to us the fact that violent outbursts occur upon the sun, and doubtless on other stars, so swift that the uprush must sometimes carry matter clear away into outer space. Imagine such a mass, consisting in part of fixed gas and in part of condensable vapors, ejected from some star. As it travels forward the vapors cool into meteorites, while the fixed gas spreads abroad like a great net, to entangle other meteors. In some cases both might travel together; in others the gaseous portion would be retarded before it passed the neighborhood of the star, and the denser meteors would get ahead. But even so, in the lapse of ages other meteors would be caught, so that in any event a cluster would at length be formed. Now, the reasonable suspicion that this is the real origin of meteors has received striking confirmation from the discovery of the late Professor Graham, that meteoric iron contains so much hydrogen occluded within it as indicates that the iron had cooled from a high temperature in a dense atmosphere of hydrogen—precisely the conditions about which the vapor of iron would cool down while escaping from a large class of stars, including our sun.

We have now traced an outline of the marvelous history of these Arabs of the sky. We have met with outbursts upon stars sometimes of sufficient violence to shoot off part of their substance. We have found the gaseous portion sweeping through space like a net, and the vapors that accompanied it condensed into spatters that have consolidated into meteorites. We have seen this system traveling through boundless space, with nothing near it except an occasional solitary meteor, and we have seen it in the long lapse of ages slowly augmenting its cluster of these little strangers. As it wandered on, it passed within the far-spreading reach of the sun's attraction, and perhaps has since been millions of years in descending toward him. Its natural course would have been to have glided round him in a curve, and to have then withdrawn to the same vast abyss from which it had come; but, in attempting this, it became entangled with one of the planets, which dragged it out of its course and then flung it aside. Immediately it entered upon the new course assigned to it, which it has been pursuing ever since. After passing the planet the different members of the group found themselves in paths very close to one another, but not absolutely the same. These orbits differed from one another very slightly in all respects, and among others in the time which a body takes to travel round them. Those meteors which got round soonest found themselves, after the first revolution, at the head of the group; those which moved slowest fell into the rear, and the comet was the last of all. Each succeeding revolution lengthened out the column, and the comet soon separated from the rest. Fifty-two revolutions have now taken place, and the little cloud has crept out into an extended stream, stretching a long way round the orbit, while the comet has fallen the greater part of a revolution behind. We can look forward, too, and see that in seventeen centuries more the train will have doubled its length, and that ultimately it will form a complete ring round the whole orbit. When this takes place, a shower of these meteors will fall every year upon the earth, but the swarm will be then so scattered that the display will be far less imposing than it now is.

The Meteor of November 27, 1877.[*]—The number of the "Monthly Notices" of the Royal Astronomical Society for February, 1879, has a brief account of a fire-ball seen in England by Captain Tupman and others on the evening of November 27, 1877, at $10^h 26^m$ Greenwich mean time. A discussion by Captain Tupman of all the observations leads to the remarkable conclusion that the meteor was revolving about the sun in an orbit less eccentric than that of Mercury, and at a mean distance intermediate between those of Mars and the earth. The elements of its orbit are given as follows:

Mean distance	1·1691
Period	462 days.
Eccentricity	0·1568
Longitude of perihelion	70°6′
Longitude of ascending node	245°50′
Inclination	15°0′
Motion direct	....

The radiant point of this meteor was at R. A. 285° and decl. N. 64°. Other meteors near this epoch have had very nearly the same radiant—a fact regarded by Captain Tupman as indicating the probable existence of "a meteoric ring of nearly circular form occupying the position in space defined by the elements given above."

The Meteorite of May 10, 1879.—In the

[*] The accounts of this meteor were received too late for our last volume.

"American Journal of Science" for July, 1879, Professor S. F. Peckham of Minneapolis, Minnesota, gives the principal facts in regard to a meteoric fall at Esterville, Emmet County, Iowa, at 5 o'clock P. M., May 10, 1879. Professor Shepard of Amherst College secured several fragments of this meteorite, and in the September number of the "Journal" he furnishes an interesting description of its structure and composition. The fall was preceded by a terrific explosion, which in a few seconds was followed by others, each succeeding report becoming gradually less violent. The meteoric body was seen to strike the earth at the edge of a ravine, where it penetrated to the depth of fourteen feet. Within a distance of two miles several other fragments were found, one of which, weighing about 170 pounds, was secured for the cabinet of the Minnesota State University. The largest mass weighed 431 pounds, and the third in magnitude, 32. Several small fragments were found after considerable search, making in all about 640 pounds. Professor Shepard characterizes the Esterville aërolite as remarkably unique in its composition. "Judging," he says, "from the specimens in hand, it can not properly be referred to any group of meteoric stones with which we are acquainted."

Meteor of November 24, 1879.—A meteor considerably larger than Jupiter was seen at $8^h 40^m$ on the evening of November 24th, at Bloomington, Indiana, by President Moss of the State University. It became visible nearly in R. A. 67° and decl. N. 13°, and it exploded into four fragments about R. A. 87° and decl. S. 7°. Its motion was slow, but the observer made no estimate of the time of flight. Dr. Moss, who was looking eastward when the meteor appeared, and had a complete view of its track, states that it continued to increase in brightness up to the moment of its explosion. It probably belonged to the group known as Taurids I.

Gold Medal of the Royal Astronomical Society.—The Council of the Royal Astronomical Society of London, at their annual meeting in February, 1879, awarded the Society's gold medal to Professor Asaph Hall of the United States Naval Observatory, Washington, D. C., for his discovery and observations of the satellites of Mars, and for his determination of their orbits. Lord Lindsay, the President of the Society, explained at length the grounds upon which the Council had made their award, gave an interesting sketch of the life and labors of Professor Hall, and closed by delivering the gold medal to the Foreign Secretary, whom he addressed as follows: "And now, Mr. Hind, may I request you, as the Foreign Secretary of the Society, to place this medal in the hands of the Minister of the United States, to be transmitted to Professor Asaph Hall, as the highest mark of esteem in the gift of the Royal Astronomical Society? Assure him at the same time of the deep interest that we in England have ever felt in watching the progress of our beloved science in the hands of our cousins in the Far West."

AUDIPHONE, THE. It has long been known that waves of sound when made to resound on the teeth of deaf persons are appreciable by the auditory nerve, and that, when conveyed by a hard vibratory substance held in close contact to the teeth, the resonance in the mouth affects the nerve independently of the anatomical mechanism by which the waves collected in the aural canal are transmitted. The sonorous vibrations of the teeth and bones of the face are conveyed to the perceptive organism through the Eustachian tube. The sounds thus produced are usually, however, so wanting in clearness and purity that no one until recently has thought it possible to convey by such means any agreeable sounds, much less intelligible speech. At length an American inventor, himself wanting the power of hearing, has perfected an apparatus on this principle, by which the mouth is made to perform the office of the ear, and with which the deaf are made sufficiently sensible to, and able to distinguish and appreciate, all kinds of sounds. The sufferers from this affliction, which deprives them in so great a degree of lively and sympathetic social intercourse, have not found that the ear-trumpet, when they are able to use that clumsy instrument, relieves them much from their social isolation. These trumpets, while they can not convey to the defective ear the language of general conversation or the utterances of public speakers, or enable the wearer to enjoy the impressions of music, have also a tendency to aggravate the infirmity by throwing upon the impaired organ a greater volume of sound than it is able to bear. The inventor of the new instrument called the audiphone, Richard S. Rhodes, of Chicago, is himself deaf, and had his attention first attracted to the subject by the ticking of a watch. By holding the watch between his teeth he perceived that he was able to hear distinctly the clicking of the machinery, while if he held it against his ear no sound was audible. Mr. Rhodes consumed many years in experimenting upon all kinds of materials. He found wood, after trying a hundred different kinds in all possible shapes, too resonant for his purpose. The metals, zinc, silver, steel, brass, etc., gave too hollow a sound. After innumerable failures, he at last tested vulcanized rubber, which yielded most promising results. With another long series of experiments he elaborated the form which bears the sounds to the regained sense most perfectly and distinctly. The instrument, which the inventor proceeded to manufacture after obtaining a patent, has been used with surprising 'results, and promises to bestow the sense of hearing and the power of speech on many who otherwise could only communicate with their fellow beings by signs and gestures. The audiphone is similar in shape to a large fan.

It consists of a sheet of vulcanized rubber firmly attached to a handle of the same material. The sheet is about $\frac{1}{16}$ of an inch in thickness. The first size used was 9 by 9½ inches; but different sizes are now made. When in use, this sheet is bent at the outer end by drawing a cord which passes through holes in the upper rim and down the inner side of the sheet into a slot in the handle. The lower or straight end of the sheet is held against the teeth of the upper jaw. The curve required is a very slight one, usually making an angle of 10° or 12° between the cord and the level surface. The more deaf the person, the tenser must the rubber be drawn. The vibrations imparted by any sound to the tense plate of rubber are communicated to the upper teeth and to the bones of the head, when the rubber is held in contact with the teeth, even if they are artificial teeth well fitted to the jaw; and the impression of the sound is faithfully recorded by the nerve of the ear. The instrument enables a deaf person to hear and enjoy music in a concert-room, as well as to listen to conversation carried on near him in ordinary tones.

AUSTRALASIA AND POLYNESIA. The population of the Australasian colonies of England increases with greater rapidity than that of any other country in the world. While the population of the United States increased during the forty years from 1830 to 1870 from 12,870,000 to 38,560,000, or about 200 per cent., that of Australia and New Zealand has during the same time risen from 300,000 to 2,000,000, or nearly 566 per cent. How rapidly the population has increased from 1871 to 1878 is shown by the following table:

COLONIES.	Population according to census of 1871 (or 1870).	Estimated population in 1878.
New South Wales.......	501,580	675,000
Victoria................	729,568	887,000
South Australia..... ...	188,095	287,000
Queensland.............	120,066	208,000
Western Australia.......	24,785	28,000
Tasmania..............	99,328	107,000
New Zealand...........	294,028	414,000
Natives........	Included in total.	100,000
Total...............	1,958,650	2,651,000

The total increase in seven years was about 692,000, or 35 per cent. The other English possessions in Australasia and Polynesia are:

Feejee Islands—white population.......... 1,569
    "   "   natives ...:................ 118,000
Chatham Islands...................... 172
Lord Howe's Island...................... 40
Fanning Island........................... 150
Malden Island............... 79

    Total................................ 120,010

Adding this total to the population of Australia, Tasmania, and New Zealand, the total population of the British possessions would amount to 2,771,010. The total area, including some small islands which are not inhabited, amounts to 3,084,671 square miles. According to the last official censuses of the several Australasian colonies, taken in 1870 and 1871, the aggregate number of Protestants was 1,382,584, or 74·4 per cent. of the total population; of Roman Catholics, 443,926, or 22·9 per cent.; of Jews, 8,248; of other religions, 12,141; of pagans, 30,905; not declared, 43,931. Among those registered in the last group there were 24,000 who "objected to state their religion from conscientious scruples." The remainder of 20,000 is made up of persons whose declarations could not be verified, and is partly explained by discrepancies which occur in every census. The pagans were chiefly represented by Chinese settlers in the gold districts. Among these Chinese there were no more than about thirty women, and the number of converts to Christianity was only a few dozens. The Jews nowhere exceed one and a half per cent. of the total population. The proportion of Roman Catholics to Protestants did not materially differ in the several colonies in 1871, as will be seen from the following table of percentages:

COLONIES.	Protestant.	Catholic.
New South Wales	67·5	29·8
Victoria	70·9	23·4
South Australia	77·7	15·4
Queensland	68·0	23·4
Western Australia	66·6	26·5
Tasmania	74·7	22·8
New Zealand	70·4	13·9
Total	74·4	22·9

Assuming that the proportion of Protestants and Roman Catholics was in 1878 about the same as in 1871, the aggregate number of Protestants in 1878 was about 1,972,000, that of Roman Catholics, 607,000. Of the 120,000 inhabitants of the other English possessions, about 100,000 may be set down as Protestants, and 10,000 as Roman Catholic, increasing the aggregate Protestant population of the British possessions to 2,072,000, and the Roman Catholic to 617,000. The following table presents an estimate of the total (the Protestant and the Roman Catholic) population of Australia and Polynesia in 1879:

TERRITORIES.	POPULATION IN 1879.		
	Total.	Protestant.	Roman Catholic.
British possessions	2,781,000	2,072,000	617,000
French "	97,000	18,000	89,000
Spanish "	36,000	......	7,000
Hawaiian Islands	57,000	84,000	23,000
All other islands	1,805,000	172,000	16,000
Total	4,776,000	2,296,000	702,000

The Colonial Treasurer of New South Wales, James Watson, made his financial statement in the Legislative Assembly on February 12th. According to his report, the present Government had adopted, with only a few alterations, the estimates prepared by the previous administration. The revenue of 1878 amounted to £5,000,000, which was £76,000 more than was anticipated. The revenue of the present year

would probably be £5,100,000, and the expenditure £4,970,000, leaving a surplus of £130,000. The accumulated surpluses of previous years now amounted to £2,500,000, of which it was proposed to appropriate one half for permanent public works and other important services, leaving the other half for future appropriations. The estimates would contain only services of a reproductive character, such as railways and the water-supply for the metropolis. The railway scheme embraced a line from the present terminus at Redfern, through Sydney, to the waters of Port Jackson, a system of suburban lines, and the projected extension of lines into the interior to a distance of 400 miles. Mr. Watson said that in 1877 the railways paid 4½ per cent. on their capital. The financial prospects of the colony were, he added, so bright that it was unnecessary to change the fiscal system. They had had a splendid season, and an abundant harvest in every district of the colony. A change in the governorship took place during the year. Sir George Robinson, whose time had expired, was succeeded by Lord Augustus Loftus, formerly British Ambassador to St. Petersburg. Lord Loftus arrived at Sydney on August 4th. The budget, after having been passed by the Assembly, was disapproved by the Legislative Council in the latter part of August. It was finally decided to effect a partial remission of the customs duties, and cover the deficit by an increase in the stamp duties to the extent of £70,000. The principal measure of the session, the Government Law Bill, was lost in the Upper House, not by its rejection, but by its withdrawal. The second clause of the bill proposed to reduce from twenty shillings to ten shillings an acre the improvements which free selectors agreed to make on the land they had been allowed to take up. The Council, while willing to make the reduction for the future, objected to an alteration of the bargains already made with the state. The Government declined to go on with the bill unless it was made retrospective. As the Council was inexorable, and refused, in the absence of evidence or petitions, to release free selectors from the contracts they had made, the measure was dropped. The majority in the Assembly then pronounced itself strongly in favor of an elective Council in place of the present system, by which the Council is appointed for life. Nothing was done to secure that object, however, and Parliament was prorogued in the beginning of August.

The International Exhibition at Sydney was opened on September 17th by Lord Loftus, the Governor of New South Wales, in the presence of the Governors of Victoria, South Australia, and Tasmania, and the foreign Commissioners. There was a large display of agricultural implements, machinery in motion, pottery and glassware, and of fine art. There were 800 British industrial exhibitions, and 513 fine-art entries, including photographs.

Germany had 695 entries, including 108 fine-art; Austria, 170; France, 350 industrial and 168 fine-art; Belgium, 236 industrial and 50 paintings; United States, 150 industrial collections. Among the best filled sections were railway apparatus and material, steel and cutlery from Sheffield, guns and miscellaneous manufactures from Birmingham, and Manchester goods.

The term of Sir George Bowen, the Governor of Victoria, expired in 1878, and the Marquis of Normanby was appointed in his place. Lord Normanby had been previously Lieutenant-Governor of Nova Scotia, and Governor of Queensland and New Zealand, and his appointment was welcomed with great satisfaction by the inhabitants of Victoria. The dispute between the Legislative Council and the Assembly terminated in the proposition, made in the latter part of 1878, to send an embassy from the Assembly to the Home Government, to represent to it the state of affairs in the colony, and to ask its intervention. An embassy of three was accordingly sent off, but in February a dispatch from the Colonial Secretary of Great Britain, Sir M. Hicks-Beach, was published in Melbourne, expressing the opinion that no sufficient reason had been shown for the intervention of the Home Parliament. If, however, representatives of both the Council and the Assembly would come to England, every assistance would be rendered them. An act was passed by the Assembly in February, authorizing an International Exhibition, upon a somewhat extensive scale, at Melbourne. The building is to cost £95,000, and the exhibition will be opened on October 1, 1880, and closed on March 31, 1881.

On February 21st the following notice was issued by Sir Bryan O'Loghlen, acting Chief Secretary:

In consequence of the fabrication by, and the publication in, the "Argus" journal of false news, purporting to be genuine and authoritative, concerning the proceedings and discussions of the Cabinet, being continuously persisted in for several weeks past, the public are hereby cautioned against giving any credence to either those statements or any similar kind of news for the future in that journal. The "Argus" journal has been refused any official information of the kind by the Acting Chief Secretary, who feels justified in taking this course, as that journal has for several months unpatriotically attempted to depreciate the financial credit of Victoria.

This action of the Government created considerable excitement, and was severely denounced as aiming at the subversion of the liberty of the press.

On May 3d Sir M. Hicks-Beach sent another dispatch to the Government of Victoria, in which, after referring to the arrival of the Commission, headed by Mr. Berry, and to his former dispatch, he continues as follows:

The request urged by Mr. Berry in his letter of February 26th, that Parliament should, "by a simple alteration of the 60th section of the Constitutional Act of Victoria, enable the Legislative Assembly to enact in two distinct annual sessions, with a general election intervening, any measure for the reform of the Constitution," is, in my opinion, even more open to objection than the proposal I understood him to convey in his memorandum of August 6th. But it is not necessary to discuss the merits of this or any other proposal, for, though fully recognizing the confidence in the mother-country evinced by the reference of so important a question for the counsel and aid of the Imperial Government, I still feel that the circumstances do not justify any Imperial legislation for the amendment of that Constitutional Act by which self-government, in the form which Victoria desired, was conceded to her, and by which the power of amending the Constitution was expressly, and as an essential incident of self-government, vested in the Colonial Legislature with the consent of the Crown. The intervention of the Imperial Parliament would not, in my opinion, be justifiable, except in an extreme emergency, and in compliance with the urgent desire of the people of the colony, when all available efforts on their part had been exhausted. But it would, even if thus justified, be attended with much difficulty and risk, and be in itself a matter for grave regret. It would be held to involve an admission that the great colony of Victoria was compelled to ask the Imperial Parliament to resume a power which, desiring to promote her welfare, and believing in her capacity for self-government, the Imperial Parliament had voluntarily surrendered; and that this request was made because the leaders of political parties, from a general want of the moderation and sagacity essential to the success of constitutional government, had failed to agree upon any compromise for enabling the business of the Colonial Parliament to be carried on.

In speaking of the recent differences, he says they turned upon the ultimate control of the finances. In order to avoid this difficulty, he recommends to the Council and the Assembly to follow the practice of the Imperial Parliament.

Parliament was opened on July 8th. The Governor's speech stated that signs of a revival of trade were apparent, and that agriculture and mining prospects were improving. He expressed regret at the necessity for increased taxation, owing to the loss of revenue. He referred briefly to the recent mission of Mr. Berry to England, which he hoped would result beneficially for the future progress of necessary legislation. The speech announced the introduction of bills for amending the land-tax, and measures of constitutional reform, including the amendment of the electoral law, the abolition of plural voting, and the amendment of the Local Government Act. On July 22d Mr. Berry, the Premier, introduced in the Assembly a bill to amend the Constitution. It gave to the Assembly absolute control over expenditure and taxation, provided for the gradual substitution of a nominee Council in place of the present elective Legislative Council, and provided that bills passed by the Assembly, and twice rejected by the Legislative Council, should be referred by the Governor to a *plébiscite*. On July 30th Mr. Berry presented his financial statement to the Assembly. The revenue for 1878 amounted to £4,807,000, and the expenditure £4,944,000; the estimated revenue for 1879 was £5,088,000, and the expenditure £5,374,000, inclusive of the deficiency of £137,000 from last year's budget. It was proposed to provide for the deficit of the current year by an increase of the land-tax and customs duties. In January a vote of want of confidence in the Ministry was passed by the Legislative Council of Queensland. In consequence, the Ministry resigned, and a new one was formed, composed as follows: Premier and Treasurer, T. Mcllwraith; Colonial Secretary, A. H. Palmer; Minister of Justice, T. M. Thompson; Public Works, J. M. McCrassan; Minister of Lands, T. Perkins; Postmaster - General, C. H. Buzacott. This Ministry met with a vote of want of confidence from the Assembly in the beginning of August. In August the Legislature passed an act declaring that certain islands in Torres Straits, and lying between the continent of Australia and the island of New Guinea, shall, from a day to be fixed by the Governor by proclamation, become part of the colony of Queensland, and subject to the laws in force therein. This territory is described in the act as follows: "All islands included within a line drawn from Sandy Cape northward to the southeastern limit of the Great Barrier Reefs; thence following the line of the Great Barrier Reefs to their northeastern extremity near the latitude nine and a half degrees south; thence in a northwesterly direction, embracing East Anchor and Bramble Cays; thence from Bramble Cay in a line west by south (south 79 degrees west) true, embracing Warrior Reef, Saibai, and Tuan Islands; thence diverging in a northwesterly direction, so as to embrace the group known as the Talbot Islands; thence to and embracing the Deliverance Islands, and onward in a west-by-south direction (true) to the meridian of 138 degrees of east longitude."

The Parliament of New Zealand was opened on July 11th. Among the measures, the introduction of which was promised by the Governor's speech, were manhood suffrage, Parliamentary representation on the basis of population, triennial Parliaments, and the regulation of Chinese immigration into the colony. The revenue of the colony for the preceding year had exceeded the estimates by £190,000; but there had nevertheless been a great falling off in the amount derived from land and from the income-tax, and Parliament would be asked to sanction an additional loan of £5,000,000. A difficulty arose with the Maoris at Taranaki, which at one time seemed to assume serious dimensions. The Maoris had trespassed on lands of white settlers, which had been confiscated from the natives,

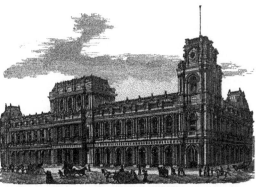

THE POST-OFFICE, MELBOURNE.

and begun plowing on these lands. The settlers applied to the Government for aid, but the Government refused to direct the settlers how to act in the emergency. The settlers thereupon, having first informed the Government of their intention, took the matter into their own hands, and, mustering in considerable numbers, but unarmed, took possession of the plowmen and their teams, and removed them bodily across the Waingogoro River, which forms the boundary of the confiscated lands. No great attempt at resistance was made by the Maoris, and no unnecessary force was used by the settlers; and, after the ejectment had been successfully accomplished, Sir George Grey telegraphed his approval of what had been done. The ejected plowmen were duly warned that in case of their return they would be arrested and sent to prison. But this threat and its subsequent execution did not deter them from their purpose. One party after another renewed the trespass, some of them even coming within the inclosures surrounding the armed constabulary depots with their plows; and party after party was arrested. The imprisoned natives were committed for trial for destruction of property, but they pleaded that their action was simply an assertion of an undefined claim in the confiscated lands, and that they adopted this as the only means of obtaining a hearing. Among the majority of Parliament an evident desire made itself manifest to do justice to the natives, and Sir George Grey, the Premier, who had up to this time enjoyed public confidence to a high degree, was bitterly denounced in Parliament, and charged with maladministration of the native affairs in particular, and public affairs in general. Upon the motion of Sir William Fox, the leader of the opposition, the House declared in August, by a majority of fourteen, that it had ceased to repose confidence in the administration of Sir George Grey. Upon the latter's request the House was dissolved, and a new election ordered within four weeks by the Governor. Upon the assembling of the new House, the Government was defeated by a majority of two, whereupon Sir George Grey resigned, and a new Ministry was formed under Mr. John Hall.

In 1876 New Zealand, previously composed of nine large provinces, was divided into a large number of counties. The census of the colony by counties was taken in March, 1878. The total population of New Zealand, including Chinese, half-castes, and persons on shipboard, but exclusive of Maoris, was 414,412. The North Island had a population of 158,208; Middle Island, 255,757; Stewart Island, 251; and Chatham Island, 196. The provincial districts are still retained for certain purposes, and their population was as follows (exclusive of Chatham Island):

PROVINCES.	Population.
Auckland	82,661
Taranaki	9,463
Wellington	51,069
Hawke's Bay	15,015
Marlborough	7,557
Nelson	25,128
Westland	16,982
Canterbury	91,922
Otago	114,469
Total	414,216

The number of the Chinese was 4,382, of whom only eight were females. The number of the Maoris was 42,819, a decrease since 1874 of 3,197. The males considerably exceeded the females, the former being 23,533, and the latter only 19,286. But the most characteristic feature of these figures was the great disparity

PARLIAMENT BUILDINGS, SYDNEY.

in the proportion of adults and children. Of the total of 42,819 in 1878, no less than 14,533 were males and 11,802 females over fifteen years. In European countries the men usually average one fifth or one sixth of the population, while at present among the Maoris they constitute one third.

The Chinese question, which agitated all of the colonies of the Australian continent, also assumed considerable dimensions in Tahiti, the largest of the Society Islands, and which is under a French protectorate. An order was issued in the beginning of the year that no Chinaman would be permitted to land on the island without a residential permit from the Government. Any Chinese wishing to reside in the country must apply for leave to the authorities, who will make the necessary inquiries as to the character and the ability to work of the applicants; and any Chinaman presenting himself without authority will be sent back by the first ship. If he has not the means to pay his passage, he will be made to work in the Government dockyards until he has earned enough to pay the sum necessary to defray the expenses of his repatriation.

A revolt broke out among the natives on the island of New Caledonia, belonging to France, in the latter part of 1878. It was completely suppressed by February, 1879, and the captured natives were transported to the Isle of Pines and other small islands in the neighborhood.

The later efforts of Protestant missionaries among the aborigines of Australia show that those people have a higher intelligence and a greater capacity for civilization than they had been credited with. The failure of the earlier attempts to instruct them had left an impression that they would hardly receive even a rudimentary civilization. The colonies of natives connected with the Moravian and Episcopal missions have, however, made a respectable intellectual advancement and acquired considerable skill in industrial labor. The Moravians have two stations in Gippsland, to which neat churches are attached, with 125 native Christians living in a civilized manner. The Presbyterian Church of South Australia has a mission at Point Maclay, of which a similar report is made. The Anglican missionaries have schools from which favorable results have been gained, and missions have been established by colonial societies and the German Lutherans. The natives connected with the Moravian mission received a medal at the Vienna Exhibition for arrowroot. The Anglican, Presbyterian, and Wesleyan Churches have also missions among the Chinese immigrants.

Missions are carried on among the Maoris by the Anglican and Wesleyan Missionary So-

cieties and two German societies. The principal mission is that of the Church Missionary
Society, which returns 16 European and 27
native missionaries, with 220 native teachers,
and has about 2,000 members with 10,815 adherents. The Wesleyan missions were nearly
broken up by the wars several years ago. For
1879 they returned live missionaries, two assistants, and 885 members. The Hermannsburg
mission has three stations among the natives.
The Society for the Propagation of the Gospel
and the North German Missionary Society sustain missions to colonists and natives.

Several Protestant missionary societies have
found some of their most fruitful fields of operation in the South Sea islands. This has been
notably the case with the American and British Congregational societies, and the British
Wesleyan societies, whose labors have been
rewarded by the conversion of whole nations.
The condition of these missions, including those
of the Sandwich Islands which have become
a self-supporting Church, is as follows: Congregational churches and missions in the
Sandwich Islands, Micronesia, the Marquesas
Islands, the Society, Loyalty, Samoa, and Hervey Islands, and New Guinea, 36 missionaries,
680 assistants, mostly natives, and 36,580 members; Wesleyan churches and missions in the
Feejee and Friendly Islands, Samoa, Rotumah,
New Britain, New Ireland, and the Duke of
York Islands, 17 missionaries, 572 native assistants, 31,143 members; Presbyterian missions in the New Hebrides, 16 missionaries,
1,150 members; Anglican missions in Melanesia and the Sandwich Islands, 14 missionaries
and assistants, 252 members; French Evangelical missions in the Society Islands, 25 missionaries and assistants, 2,379 members; making a total of 1,360 missionaries and assistants
and 71,471 members. The Rev. S. J. Whitmee,
of the London Missionary Society, estimating
the whole number of converts at 68,101, allots
them among the three races of people thus:
Malayo - Polynesian, 36,079; Melanesian, 30,-
522; Micronesian, 1,500. Taking the number
of church members to be one fifth the number
of nominal Christians, he estimates the whole
number of those who have renounced paganism
and come under the direct influence of missionary teaching to be 340,505. The missionary
churches of the Sandwich Islands and Micronesia are now under the care of the Hawaiian
Evangelical Association, a society organized in
the Sandwich Islands, which is assisted by the
American Board. The Wesleyan South Sea
missions are under the care of the Australasian
Wesleyan Missionary Society, whose office is
at Sydney. The Malayo-Polynesian race have
become almost entirely Christianized, the principal exceptions to the fact being found in the
Marquesas Islands, where the Hawaiian Society has a mission. The Wesleyan missions in
the Friendly Islands are self-supporting and
contribute to the support of the society; the
same is the case to a large extent with those in

the Feejee Islands. Several of the London
Society's missions are largely self-supporting,
the people building their own chapels, buying
their own books, and paying the salaries of
their native pastors and schoolmasters, only
the English missionaries drawing their salaries
from home; but this last item is more than
covered by the amounts which the missions
contribute to the general funds of the Society.
Native pastors and teachers are relied upon in
most of the islands to continue the work, the
white missionaries acting to a large extent as
superintendents and counselors, or, as in the
Sandwich Islands, simply as equals, and tending every year to exercise less authority and
be less necessary. Schools have been established everywhere, and religious books and
school-books have been published in the native
languages, of which those in use at the missions have been reduced to writing by the missionaries. The Wesleyan missions return 47,-
431 scholars. The elementary schools are supplemented by higher schools, training schools
for teachers, colleges, and theological schools.
The colleges of the Sandwich Islands have
been for several years in successful operation.
The Wesleyans have a college at Navuloa, Feejee, where, according to the British Governor,
Sir Arthur Gordon, "a really superior education is given to those who are preparing for
ordination, and to a large number of others of
the best native families." At the Wesleyan
Tubon College, in Nukualofa, Tonga, the pupils are said to have acquitted themselves well
before the Governor when examined in "eu-
clid and algebra, in English, and geography."
In the Anglican Melanesian missions the plan
is adopted of taking youths from their own
islands to a school in Norfolk Island for a few
months in each year, after which they are
returned to their homes with the expectation
that they will exert a favorable influence over
their countrymen. The missionaries in charge
of the school also visit the different islands for
a few weeks or months in the healthy season.

AUSTRO-HUNGARIAN MONARCHY, an
empire in Central Europe. Since the year
1867 the monarchy forms a dual state, consisting of a German or "Cisleithan" monarchy, Austria, and a Magyar or Transleithan
kingdom, Hungary. Each of the two countries has its own Government, while the connecting ties between them consist in the person of the hereditary sovereign, in a common
army, navy, and diplomacy, and a common Parliament, the Delegations. Emperor, Francis
Joseph I., born August 18, 1830; succeeded
his uncle, the Emperor Ferdinand I., December 2, 1848. Heir apparent to the throne,
Archduke Rudolphus, born August 21, 1858.
A member of the imperial family, the Archduchess Maria Christina, was married on November 29th to King Alfonso XII. of Spain.
(See SPAIN.) The following genealogical table shows the relationship between the new
Queen of Spain and the Emperor of Austria:

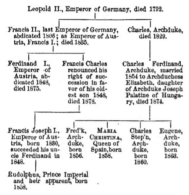

Leopold II., Emperor of Germany, died 1792.

Francis II., last Emperor of Germany, abdicated 1806; as Emperor of Austria, Francis I.; died 1835.

Charles, Archduke, died 1829.

Ferdinand I., Emperor of Austria, abdicated 1848, died 1875.

Francis Charles renounced his right of succession in favor of his oldest son 1848, died 1878.

Charles Ferdinand, Archduke, married 1854 to Archduchess Elizabeth, daughter of Archduke Joseph Palatine of Hungary, died 1874.

Francis Joseph I., Emperor of Austria, born 1830, succeeded his uncle Ferdinand in 1848.

Fred'k, Archduke, born 1856.

MARIA CHRISTINA, Queen of Spain, born 1858.

Charles Step'n, Archduke, born 1860.

Eugene, Archduke, born 1863.

Rudolphus, Prince Imperial and heir apparent, born 1858.

The Ministry for the Common Affairs of the Empire consisted, toward the close of the year 1879, of Karl Heinrich Baron von Haymerle, Minister of Foreign Affairs and of the Imperial House (appointed October 9, 1879); Baron Leopold Friedrich von Hofmann, Minister of the Finances of the Empire (appointed 1876); and Count Arthur Bylandt-Rheidt, Minister of War (appointed 1876).

The Ministry of Cisleithan Austria, at the close of 1879, was composed of Count Eduard Taaffe, President (appointed August 14, 1879); C. von Stremayr, Public Worship and Instruction (November, 1871); General Horst, Defense of the Country (appointed pro tem. November, 1871, definitely in March, 1872); Count Julius von Falkenhayn (August 14, 1879), Agriculture; Baron Karl von Korb-Weidenheim (August 14, 1879), Commerce; Emil Chertek (August 14, 1879), Finance; Florian Ziemialkowski (April, 1873), and Dr. Alois Prazak (August 14, 1879), Minister without portfolio.

Count EDUARD TAAFFE was born February 24, 1833. Having held various administrative offices, he was in March, 1867, appointed Minister of the Interior, and later on in the same year substitute of the Minister-President and Minister of Public Defense; and in 1868 he was appointed temporarily and in 1869 permanently Minister-President. Resigning this post in 1870, he was next called to the office of Governor of the Tyrol, where he showed great administrative talent in reconciling the Italian with the German element. At the beginning of 1879, on the resignation of the Auersperg Cabinet, he was charged with the formation of a new Cabinet, but, having failed in this task on the eve of the expiration of the session of the Reichsrath, and the members of the Auersperg Cabinet being prevailed on to retain their portfolios, the Count joined that body as Minister of the Interior. Under his auspices the Reichsrath was closed and new elections were held. The pro-

gramme of Count Taaffe aimed at the reconciliation of the various nations of Austria, the union of their representatives in the Reichsrath, and the direction of the energies of Parliament to economic and financial questions.

Dr. VON STREMAYR was born October 30, 1823. He was on several occasions Minister of Justice and Worship, until in 1871 he was appointed Minister of Education in the Auersperg Cabinet, which office he held up to the present year.

General Baron HORST, the Minister of Public Defense, has held this position since 1871, and has administered his department with eminent success.

Dr. ZIEMIALKOWSKI, a Pole by birth, had as a youth a very agitated career, and was condemned to death for being compromised in some political affairs. Having been successful as an advocate, he entered Parliament, and was in 1867 elected second Vice-President. In 1873 he was called upon to act as intermediary between the Government and his Polish compatriots.

Count JULIUS FALKENHAYN is the representative in the Parliament of the Clerico-Feudal party, of which he has long been an active partisan. His appointment was regarded as a concession to the rural communes of the Tyrol, Salzburg, Upper Austria, and Styria, where the Clerical party is in the majority.

Baron KORB-WEIDENHEIM, Minister of Commerce, although belonging to the Reichsrath since 1867, was known but very little before his appointment. This was intended to secure to the large landed proprietors of Bohemia a place in the Government.

Dr. A. PRAZAK, born February 21, 1820, was a deputy for Moravia from 1861 to 1863, and again since 1874, and represented in the new Parliament the Czech element. Together with Dr. Ziemialkowski, he was expected to form an instrument of communication between the Government and the new Slav element which had recently entered the Reichsrath.

The area of the Monarchy is 240,348 square miles; population, according to the census of 1869, 35,901,435. The area of Cisleithan Austria (the land represented in the Reichsrath) is 115,908 square miles. The civil population at the end of 1878 was officially estimated at 21,970,649, to which must be added the army, numbering (close of 1876) 177,449 persons; making a total population of 22,148,098. The estimate is based upon the census of December 31, 1869, by adding the average percentage of increase. The civil population was distributed among the different crown lands as follows:

COUNTRIES.	Inhabitants, Dec. 31, 1878.
Austria below the Enns	2,201,428
Austria above the Enns	750,801
Salzburg	154,986
Styria	1,191,782
Carinthia	339,366
Carniola	471,986
Trieste	140,117
Goritz and Gradisca	219,215
Istria	275,798

COUNTRIES.	Inhabitants, Dec. 31, 1876.
Tyrol	796,577
Vorarlberg	108,920
Bohemia	5,486,814
Moravia	2,108,847
Silesia	572,281
Galicia	6,177,998
Bukowina	559,484
Dalmatia	474,854
	21,970,649
At the close of 1877	21,766,887

The movement of population in 1877 was as follows:

COUNTRIES.	Births.	Deaths.	Marriages.
Austria below the Enns	85,389	69,666	16,095
Austria above the Enns	24,109	22,504	5,015
Salzburg	5,822	4,789	912
Styria	36,946	34,920	7,373
Carinthia	10,871	9,909	1,685
Carniola	16,809	14,781	3,012
Trieste	5,218	4,668	1,026
Goritz and Gradisca	5,065	6,897	1,394
Istria	10,961	8,261	2,043
Tyrol	23,604	18,481	4,919
Vorarlberg	3,869	2,635	756
Bohemia	212,382	163,681	41,969
Moravia	82,321	68,202	16,258
Silesia	20,770	18,314	4,195
Galicia	265,644	194,980	49,087
Bukowina	26,441	28,290	4,935
Dalmatia	16,543	13,225	3,614
Army	991	2,757	355
Total	855,743	686,418	164,588

Of the total number of children born, 21,514 were still-born, and of these 17,084 were legitimate and 4,430 illegitimate. Of the live-born children, 717,130 were legitimate and 117,099 illegitimate. Of the total number of children born, 440,830 were males and 414,913 females. Of the total number of deaths, 357,182 were of males and 329,236 of females. In regard to age, 31 males and 45 females were upward of 100 years old at the time of their death. Of the deaths, 69,513 were caused by epidemics (among them, 36 by cholera and 1,274 by small-pox), 607,707 by other diseases, and 9,198 by violence. The latter class includes 2,314 suicides of males and 433 of females.

The number of professors and students (inclusive of non-matriculated hearers) was in the summer semester, 1878, as follows:

UNIVERSITIES.	Professors.	Students.
Czernovitz	89	223
Cracow	82	588
Gratz	112	764
Innspruck	82	887
Lemberg	54	941
Prague	168	1,695
Vienna *	294	3,711
Total	881	8,504

According to the common budget of the whole empire for 1878, the amount required for the ordinary branches of administration was 111,221,662 florins. The receipts for the same branches were estimated at 4,548,196

* Exclusive of the faculty of evangelical theology.

florins, and the receipts from customs 9,000,000 florins, leaving 97,673,466 florins to be distributed in Austria and Hungary. Of this amount, 1,953,469 florins were to come from the Treasury of Hungary, and of the balance Austria contributed 70 per cent. and Hungary 30 per cent. The common debt of the empire on January 1, 1878, amounted to 411,999,868 florins. The budget of Austria Proper for 1878 was as follows (in florins—1 fl. = 48 cents):

RECEIPTS.	Ordinary.	Extraordinary.
1. Ministry of Finance	348,993,836	1,599,107
2. Ministry of Commerce	10,402,840	78,900
3. Council of Ministers	583,000	......
4. Ministry of the Interior	1,071,900	......
5. Ministry of Public Defense	80,000	......
6. Ministry of Worship and Education	5,077,882	1,014,659
7. Ministry of Justice	575,800	......
8. Miscellaneous	60,800	35,306,779
Total	361,795,058	37,999,445
Total receipts	399,795,163	
Net receipts	323,146,471	

Among the receipts of the Ministry of Finance, the direct taxes amounted to 90,000,000 florins (ground-tax 36,000,000, income-tax 20,000,000), and the indirect taxes to 231,632,300 florins (duties 18,634,000, excise 61,481,000, salt monopoly 19,292,000, tobacco monopoly 59,690,000, stamps 17,200,000, judicial fees 32,500,000, state lottery 20,117,700). The expenditures were as follows:

EXPENDITURES.	Ordinary.	Extraordinary.
1. Civil list	4,650,000	......
2. Imperial Cabinet chancery	72,514	......
3. Reichsrath	677,480	300,000
4. Imperial Court	21,000	......
5. Council of Ministers	872,700	16,550
6. Ministry of the Interior	15,800,600	1,405,404
7. Ministry of Public Defense	7,849,100	400,000
8. Ministry of Worship and Education	14,461,945	2,407,708
9. Ministry of Finance	71,800,400	441,192
10. Ministry of Commerce	21,578,900	3,243,900
11. Ministry of Agriculture	9,881,561	984,840
12. Ministry of Justice	19,645,100	1,448,420
13. Board of Control	157,000	1,000
14. Pensions	13,692,000	......
15. Dotations	609,000	28,958,080
16. Public debt	100,170,754	28,281,860
17. Administration of public debt	774,600	......
18. Cisleithan portion of the common expenditure	76,753,146	......
Total	359,067,800	63,888,904
Total expenditure	423,121,704	
Total receipts	399,795,163	
Deficit	23,326,541	

The public debt of Austria Proper on July 1, 1878, was as follows (in florins):

TITLE OF DEBT.	Bearing interest.	Bearing no interest.	Total.
1. Consol. debt, old	589,582	726,697	1,316,279
Consol. debt, new	2,763,268,625	122,612,372	2,885,880,997
2. Floating debt	97,980,029	995,998	98,926,027
3. Rentes for damages	12,555,862	......	12,555,862
4. Rentes to Bavaria	1,750,000	......	1,750,000
Total	2,876,094,098	124,335,067	3,000,429,165

The commerce of Austro-Hungary, comprising imports and exports of merchandise and of bullion, was as follows in each of the years from 1868 to 1876:

YEAR.	AUSTRO-HUNGARIAN CUSTOMS TERRITORY.				CUSTOMS TERRITORY OF DALMATIA.	
	Merchandise.		Bullion.		Imports.	Exports.
	Imports.	Exports.	Imports.	Exports.		
1868...	387,300,000	428,900,000	33,000,000	88,900,000	8,300,000	7,200,000
1869...	420,600,000	438,100,000	39,800,000	26,900,000	8,100,000	7,900,000
1870...	436,000,000	395,400,000	41,000,000	84,100,000	9,200,000	6,600,000
1871...	540,800,000	467,600,000	59,400,000	55,500,000	8,600,000	7,800,000
1872...	613,400,000	384,600,000	36,500,000	66,100,000	9,200,000	6,900,000
1873...	583,100,000	423,600,000	40,900,000	81,100,000	9,700,000	6,100,000
1874...	568,700,000	449,300,000	19,900,000	18,900,000	10,300,000	6,500,000
1875...	552,500,000	504,500,000	15,800,000	18,400,000	13,400,000	10,400,000
1876...	518,000,000	508,600,000	33,600,000	81,300,000	13,800,000	8,200,000

The following statement shows the strength of the commercial marine of Austro-Hungary on the 1st of January, 1878:

	Number of vessels.	Tonnage.	Crews.
Sea-going steamers (15,560 h. p.)...	70	15,883	2,172
Coasting steamers (882 h. p.)......	28	1,576	181
Sailing vessels, including coasters and fishing-smacks............	7,510	273,839	25,298
Total......................	7,608	290,298	27,651

The army of the Austro-Hungarian Monarchy was in August, 1878, composed as follows:

	PEACE FOOTING.		WAR FOOTING.	
	Officers.	Men.	Officers.	Men.
Standing army............	14,710	257,207	28,637	761,929
Imperial Royal Landwehr..	572	2,782	2,916	118,626
Royal Hungarian Landwehr	1,045	9,288	3,028	127,284
Staffs...............	186	90	....	......
Gensdarmes and military police..................	24	1,069	24	1.069
Army studs..............	148	5,095	148	5,095
Total..............	16,685	275,531	29,753	1,018,958

The naval forces at the end of the year 1878 consisted of 14 ironclads and 37 other steamers, the majority of the latter of small dimensions, constructed chiefly for coast defense.

The total length of railways in operation on January 1, 1878, was: In Austria Proper, 11,211 kilometres; in Hungary, 6,773 kilometres; total, 17,984. The length of the telegraph lines and wires, and the number of stations and messages carried were in 1877 as follows:

	Austria.	Hungary.	Total.
Lines...............	34,087 kil.	14,908 kil.	48,995 kil.
Wires...............	87,585 "	49,943 "	137,529 "
Stations.............	2,418	981	3,849
Messages...........	5,358,544	2,667,818	8,025,862

The number of post-offices in 1877 was 4,366 in Austria Proper and 1,960 in Hungary.

The area and population of the occupied districts of Bosnia and Herzegovina, according to the "Neue Freie Presse" of Vienna, were divided as follows: In Bosnia there are 4,499 square miles under agricultural cultivation, 8,659 of forest and woodland, 2,750 of meadow and pasturage, and 530 of sterile soil; altogether, 16,438 square miles. The population includes 325,020 Mussulmans, 390,460 Orthodox Greek Christians, 136,287 Roman Catholics, 2,145 Jews, and 8,290 gypsies; total, 862,202. The occupied portion of the sanjak of Novi-Bazar has 700 square miles under cultivation, 1,592 of forest and woodland, 509 of pastureland, and 721 of mere sterile desert; altogether, 3,522 square miles. The population is set down at 61,150 Mussulmans, 79,948 Oriental Greek Christians, 95 Jews, and 807 gypsies; total, 142,000. The Herzegovina has 806 square miles under cultivation, 849 of forest, 573 of pasturage and meadow, and 2,080 of sterile soil; altogether, 4,308 square miles. The population is composed of 56,000 Mussulmans, 101,348 Orthodox Greeks, 49,217 Roman Catholics, 65 Jews, and 1,340 gypsies; total, 207,970. The entire area of the occupied provinces therefore amounts to 24,277 square miles, and includes a total of 6,005 square miles under cultivation, 11,100 of forest and woodland, 3,841 of meadow and pasture land, and 3,331 of sterile soil, most of which is probably irreclaimable, with a total population of 1,212,172. This population is distributed as follows: 442,170 Mussulmans, or 36·48 per cent. of the whole; 571,756 Orthodox Greeks, or 47·17 per cent.; 185,504 Roman Catholics, or 15·31 per cent.; 2,305 Jews, or 0·18 per cent.; and 10,437 gypsies, or 0·86 per cent.

The Reichsrath reassembled after the Christmas recess on January 15th, and, after the transaction of some minor business, began the discussion of the Treaty of Berlin. There were 28 speakers announced against and 12 for the treaty. In the general debate Pächer moved to reject the treaty and to proceed to the order of the day. Dunajewski denied the right of the Reichsrath to come to a decision on the resolutions of a European Congress, and moved that the House receive the treaty. Deputy Fux of Znaim also spoke against the treaty, and moved the order of the day, or, in case the treaty be accepted, a declaration with regard to the constitutional difficulties in the way of the occupation. The debate was then adjourned. It was continued on the 21st, when the report of the committee was made. Professor Ed. Süss, the reporter of the majority of the committee, confined himself to moving that the constitutional sanction be given to the Treaty of Berlin. He was followed by Dr. Herbst, the reporter of the minority, who stated that the House undoubtedly had the privilege to criticise the events which had come over Austria, and had inflicted on the country and the citizens such heavy burdens. He added that the policy of presenting to the country *faits accomplis*, which had been inaugurated so successfully by the Government, was continued uninterruptedly; that every day new *faits accomplis* were created; and that every day new interrogation marks were placed after the· provisions of the Constitution. He also referred to the address of the Emperor of last November, and declared that since that time no change had taken place to satisfy the people. He closed his address as follows: "This is a difficult time for parliaments, not only in Austria but in all of Europe. The free speech of the individual is to be restricted, but it would be a still greater crime if the Chamber of Deputies was to renounce its free speech." The debate ended on the 25th, in the acceptance of the Treaty of Berlin by 154 votes against 112, together with the resolution proposed by the Left Centre expressing the conviction that in the direction of foreign affairs the Government would henceforth take into due consideration the views expressed by the House in its address to the Crown on November 5, 1878, regarding the serious financial position and constitutional complications to be apprehended from the occupation of Bosnia. Unlike the first debate on this subject, the debate on this occasion grew more and more animated toward the end, attracting universal popular attention. This was due to the circumstance that the internal strife of the different fractions of the Constitutional party, subdued in the earlier debate by a compromise, came this time, after the failure of the compromise, to the front. Added to this, while in the former debate on the address the Government maintained almost a passive attitude, Dr. Unger, its best speaker, came forward in the latter debate, and in a brilliant constitutional *exposé* set forth the anomalies which must needs arise if the paragraph of the Constitution giving the Reichsrath the right of accepting or rejecting international treaties were taken too literally and applied without due discrimination. This brought to the front the constitutional question, in which most of those now in opposition had made their reputation, and afforded them an opportunity to remind their adversaries that they had become faithless to their colors. In the heat of the debate personal attacks and rejoinders became more and more frequent, till toward the end a warm discussion was developed such as had not been heard for years in the House. The effect of all this was, that the schism and decomposition of the Constitutional party, long patent by the

proceedings of the clubs, but hitherto deferred or prevented by a series of compromises from appearing in the House, now came openly to light there, manifesting such an intense revulsion that any further attempts to solder the broken party seemed hopeless. There had been many causes gradually leading to this result, the principal one being that the party had in the course of time lost, so to speak, its right of existence in a country endowed with a parliamentary Government. In face of the combination of Clericals, Federalists, and Nationalists in the time of the Hohenwart Ministry, and of the Czechist fundamental articles threatening destruction to the work of compromise effected in 1867, and aiming to upset the dualistic organization of Austro-Hungary, the gathering together of all the German liberal elements, however antagonistic otherwise, in the one purpose of upholding the present Constitution, insuring the virtual supremacy of the German element in Austria and the consolidation of parliamentary government, was nothing but an act of self-defense. Great, too, had been the results of this combination within the past seven years. By substituting for the deputation of the provincial Diets direct elections to the Reichsrath, the power of particularism had been broken and the supremacy of the Reichsrath fully established; while by the regular working of parliamentary government the vitality of the new liberal institutions had been more and more demonstrated, and the system had recommended itself to the public, more and more gaining the bulk of the population. The more, however, the object for which the party had been formed was attained, the bond hitherto keeping the party together was loosed. The most timid among the defenders of the Constitution ceased to fear a reaction, and even the most obstinate among its opponents, the Czechs, despaired of their cause. The dissimilar elements, therefore, comprising all political shades, being no longer held together by a common object, necessarily began to resolve themselves into their original shape. In the beginning of February the Emperor recalled Count Taaffe, Governor of the Tyrol, and intrusted him with the formation of a new cabinet. On February 4th all the subjects awaiting discussion in the Lower House of the Reichsrath were removed from the order of the day, pending the definitive appointment of a ministry. In the beginning of February the Upper House of the Reichsrath adopted the report of the committee on the Treaty of Berlin, recommending its adoption, unanimously and without debate. On the 11th an imperial decree was published accepting the resignation of the Minister President Prince Auersperg, and of the Minister without portfolio Dr. Unger, and appointing Dr. Stremayr President of the Council, Count Taaffe Minister of the Interior, and reappointing the former Ministers to their posts. Even those most opposed to such a solution saw no alternative after the failure of the attempts to form what might be called a Parliamentary Ministry in the strict sense of the word, supported by a clear and compact majority. Two attempts in the latter direction had been made, the first by Baron Pretis-Cagnodo, which aimed at forming a majority by the fusion of the different fractions of the Constitutional party, and the second by Count Taaffe, who took as the basis of his combination the two more Conservative fractions of the Constitutional party, round which should be grouped some of the fractions outside that political body. Both these schemes, however, failed, and the hope of forming in the present Parliament a compact working majority had to be abandoned. Nothing remained but to tide over the time till the general election, which must be the principal task of the reconstituted Ministry.

The new Ministry met on February 18th in the Reichsrath, and Dr. Stremayr made a declaration, in which he alluded to the attempts made to form a new Cabinet. Besides the difficulties of the general political situation, he said, the circumstance that the duration of the present Parliament would end in the course of the current year proved an insuperable obstacle. This decided the position of the present Cabinet. It had no programme of the future, no new policy to announce; its main office was to guard against any interruption in the constitutional working of Parliament and in the administration. As to the principles directing the Ministry in this province, the House had known them for seven years. In regard to the work to be done, there were, above all, the budget and the bills connected with it. With reference to Eastern affairs, which so deeply affect the interests of the monarchy, a precise and positive basis had been laid down for them by the Treaty of Berlin. Taking its stand on this instrument, the Government would esteem it its duty to execute fully the task assigned it by the Powers. The Government would seek to avoid all constitutional complications and further sacrifices, as far as they regarded it compatible with the honor and security of the monarchy. After voting the budget, the session of the Reichsrath was closed on May 17th by the Emperor. In the speech from the throne he said that the sacrifices which had been made by the country had rendered it possible for the Government, in the interest of the maintenance of peace, to employ all its influence in consolidating the work achieved by Europe in the East, and that the attainment of this object was near at hand.

The elections for the new Reichsrath were held during June and July, and resulted in a loss of seats by the Liberal party. Of the deputies elected, 173 belonged to the different Liberal fractions and 175 to the Conservatives. From these figures it will be seen that the two parties nearly balanced each other, and that if they both were compact parties neither could furnish a working majority. There were,

however, no signs of cohesion on either side. Among the 173 of the so-called Constitutional party, there were the representatives of all the clubs into which the party was divided in the previous session—that is, the Left Center, the Left, and the new and old Fortschritt Clubs. On the other side were reckoned the Clericals, the Czechs, the Poles, and the Slovenes, a conglomeration as mixed as, if not more so, than the other party. A new Cabinet was formed on August 14th under the presidency of Count Eduard Taaffe. (See above.)

An important political conference was held on August 31st at Linz, in which all the newly elected German liberal members of the Reichsrath took part. It was called for the purpose of determining the position of the party toward the new Ministry, which comprised Liberals, Czechs, Clericals, and Feudals. It was unanimously resolved at this meeting that the composition of the present Cabinet did not justify its support by the German Liberal Constitutional party. The leaders of the different groups of the opposition to the Liberal party held a meeting about two weeks later, under the presidency of the Count Hohenwart, and resolved to act as a united Right. In the beginning of October an autograph letter of the Emperor was published, acceding to Prince Carlos Auersperg's repeated request to be relieved, on account of ill health, of the post of President of the Upper House of the Reichsrath. On September 30th the Emperor appointed Count Trautmannsdorf in his place.

The Reichsrath met on October 7th, but the formal opening did not take place till the next day. In his speech from the throne, the Emperor referred with pleasure to the fact that the Bohemian delegates, who formerly had declined to enter Parliament, had taken their seats, and stated that an important step had thus been taken to secure that general reconciliation and agreement which have always been his wish. Among the measures which would probably come before Parliament, he mentioned decrees relating to the military system of the country, laws relating to Bosnia and Herzegovina, and the revision of treaties and trading laws. With regard to foreign affairs he said:

It is with great satisfaction that I record the undisturbed continuation of friendly relations with other Powers. The Berlin Treaty has been carried out in all its essential conditions. The entry into the sanjak of Novi-Bazar has been made upon the basis of that treaty, in friendly accord with the Porte. The Government is now in a position, and it will be its principal task, to devote its earnest and full attention to cherishing with unremitting care its economical relations with the East.

Referring to the finances, he said:

The endeavor to recover an equilibrium in the finances by careful arrangement will above all things concern you, and this also applies to the war budget; so far only, however, as may appear compatible with the position and safety of the empire. A considerable diminution of the expenditure has, through the simplification in the administration of the individual departments of the public service, been arranged, and in respect to this I have ordered the submission of appropriate proposals. The covering of the deficit which the next budget may show should be effected without calling upon the state credit, and without injuring the productive power by increasing the revenue. These proposals will form the subject of your earnest consideration because the contemplated reform in reference to direct taxation undertaken in previous sessions has not been carried out. My Government will submit new proposals, making use of previous preparatory researches, and I hope that the Reichsrath will at last succeed in bringing about the improvements so pressing in our system of taxation in the interests of a more just division of the burdens.

A conference of the Constitutional members of the Upper House was held on October 1st, under the presidency of Herr von Schmerling, and a party club was formally constituted for the first time since the creation of the Upper House. The programme adopted by the conference was as follows: Inviolable adhesion to the fundamental laws of the state, especially those concerning the competency of national representatives; opposition to every attempt at diminishing the rights of the Reichsrath, to the profit of the separate provinces of the Crown. One of the first signatures attached to the programme was that of Cardinal Kutschker.

The Lower House organized by the election as President of Count Coronini, a Constitutionalist, and as Vice-Presidents of Dr. Smolka, a Pole, and Baron Goedel Launay. On the 27th the reply to the address from the Throne was voted by the Lower House, after a short debate. It was on the whole friendly to the Government. On the 28th the Minister of Finance presented the estimates for 1880. The balance closed with a deficit for 1879 of 12,-000,000 florins. This deficit it was proposed to cover without having recourse to any new credit; and for this purpose the Government proposed several alterations in the stamps and special taxes, from which the total increase of revenue expected was 5,800,000 florins; to impose a tax on the consumption of home mineral oils and increase the customs duties on petroleum from 3 to 8 florins, thereby providing an addition to the revenue of 4,800,000 florins; to increase the duty on brandy so as to realize an additional revenue of 1,500,000 florins; and, as temporary measures for 1880 only, to lay a tax of 10 per cent. upon passenger traffic on railroads and steamers, and a supplementary tax on all incomes exceeding 1,400 florins, which were estimated to yield 4,000,-000 florins. The financial statement concluded by saying that reductions in the expense of administration, a thorough reform in the system of taxation, the introduction of a general income-tax, and the taxation of joint-stock companies, would firmly secure a financial equilibrium in the future.

The Delegations met in Pesth on February 27th. The budget was presented by the Government and referred to the Budget Committees. On March 4th the Budget Committee of

the Austrian Delegation, after a long debate, resolved, on motion of Herr Sturm, to give an ulterior sanction to the expenditure of 41,720,-000 florins in excess of the grant of 60,000,000 florins, with the reservation of a final decision being arrived at when the accounts were closed and the results made known. At the same time it was resolved not to approve the additional 5,000,000 florins asked for by the Government for expenses in November and December, 1878. The chief argument urged against granting the credit demanded was that a large sum had already been spent on barracks, roads, and railways, and that in the estimates for 1879 3,000,000 florins were set down for such purposes, which are investments in the provinces which the Delegations had no right to accord. By way of rejoinder, the Minister of War pointed out that all the works undertaken had been determined by purely military considerations, and that the saving they would effect in the cost of transport would in a comparatively short time compensate for the money expended on them. After a similar vote in the Committee of the Hungarian Delegation, the Delegations themselves approved the budget and then adjourned.

In August Count Andrassy resigned his position as Prime Minister of the Common Ministry. Previous to the departure of the Emperor to Ischl in the beginning of August, he had an audience with him. The latter hesitated to comply with Count Andrassy's desire for retirement, and a leave of absence sufficiently long to enable the Minister to recover from the fatigues of office, which had somewhat shaken his health, was at first thought of. The Count, on the other hand, was not disposed to bear the responsibility of the policy of the Government so long as he did not personally direct it. He accordingly renewed his petition on the first opportunity at Ischl, when the Emperor at last granted his request, reserving his formal acceptance of Count Andrassy's resignation to the time when he should have decided on his successor. It was stated officially at the time that the Minister's resignation was entirely spontaneous on his part, and only accorded to his most ardent desire, and that no question of foreign or home policy had brought it about. The change in the Government was completed on October 9th. On that day the "Official Gazette" contained the Imperial letter relieving Count Andrassy of his functions, and also one nominating Baron Haymerle Minister of the Imperial House and of Foreign Affairs, and intrusting him with the Presidency of the Common Ministry. (For a biography of the new Minister, see HAYMERLE.) The letter addressed to Count Andrassy says:

If I, though really with regret and reluctance, grant your request and relieve you of the office of a Minister of my House and of Foreign Affairs, you may take this as a proof of the high value that I set on the preservation of your health. You have for years, during one of the most eventful and memorable periods, and under heavy responsibility, borne the charge with courage, force, and success, and you may quit with well-earned satisfaction your sphere of action, in which you have rendered the most eminent services to the monarchy and to my House. I do not consider, however, your present retreat as the end of your political activity. On the contrary, your loyalty to me and the self-sacrificing devotion with which you have testified this are a pledge to me that you will most readily follow my call whenever and in whatever sphere I may again require your trusty services. You retain my full confidence not less than my grateful recognition.

The administration of Bosnia and Herzegovina was regulated as follows in the beginning of the year: The head of the Government is the Duke of Würtemberg, who is subordinate in questions relating to the civil administration to the Common Ministry only. The latter, in accord with the governments of the two halves of the empire, establishes for the transaction of the current business the Bosnian Commission, composed of three delegates of the Common Ministry and one representative of each of the two Governments of Austria and Hungary. In this Commission the three delegates of the Common Ministry form an executive committee, whose decisions were to be countersigned by Count Andrassy as President of the Common Ministry. As Count Andrassy, however, felt unable to attend to all of this business, it was ordered that these decisions should in future be signed by Baron Hofmann.

After negotiations had continued over nine months, during which they were repeatedly dropped and resumed, a convention was signed on April 21st between Turkey and Austria, concerning Bosnia, Herzegovina, and the sanjak of Novi-Bazar. The convention recognizes the existing condition of affairs in Bosnia. It also recognizes the right of Austria to garrison Novi-Bazar, but it is expressly stipulated that the presence of the Austrian troops shall in no way interfere with the Turkish administration, nor shall any impediment be placed in the way of the Turkish Government if it should desire to send troops to the sanjak. The entry of the Austrian troops into the sanjak of Novi-Bazar was delayed until September. On the 8th, at 6 A. M., a brigade, composed of two regiments of infantry, a battalion of chasseurs, two mountain batteries, and half a squadron of hussars, crossed the frontier of Bosnia close to Svetlo Borje, not far from Cainitza. Every precaution was taken against any unexpected incident, columns being detached from the bulk of the brigade to cover the flanks of the Austrian force—a function which required these detached columns to make their way over almost impassable mountains. The road followed by the bulk of the army was itself sufficiently toilsome, the ground from Cainitza to the frontier rising to the height of 2,100 feet. After a six hours' march, the troops encamped near Han-Kovac. They were well received. The Turkish detachment which held Karakula Gorzd retired at the approach of the Austrian forces. Besides this brigade, which crossed the frontier on the

south side of the sanjak, another entered it on the north side, by way of Visegrad. Crossing the frontier close to Ratcha, the latter portion of the Austrian troops directed their steps to Priboj, where they met with a friendly reception at the hands of the municipality; a superior Turkish officer, the Kaimakam, and the leading men of the place also turning out to welcome the brigade. The southern part of the sanjak occupied by the Albanians was closed by a cordon of twelve Ottoman battalions, extending along Sienitza, Novi-Varosch, and Bielopolje. Previous to the entry of the Austrian troops, Safvet Pasha, the Turkish Minister for Foreign Affairs, declared to the Austrian Ambassador that he considered the Porte had the greatest interest in showing as distinctly as possible the existence of its complete understanding with the Austro-Hungarian Monarchy. With this view, Husni Pasha was expressly ordered to accompany the Austrian troops upon their entry into Novi-Bazar. Fresh orders were also sent from the Sultan to the Turkish authorities in the district to afford every possible facility to the Austrian troops on their advance. The latter met with no resistance whatever, and within a week of their entry those troops not destined for garrison duty began their backward march. As for the remaining troops, a definite agreement was come to by the Duke of Würtemberg and Husni Pasha, as follows: All the important military positions were to be jointly occupied. The line of communication from Priboj to Priepol, as well as that from Cainitza, the most advanced point in Bosnia from the west to Tashlidje, was to be kept open by Austrian detachments posted on the more important points, while the line from Tashlidje to Priepol was to be held jointly by an Austrian detachment occupying the height of Jabunka, which forms the watershed, and a Turkish detachment. The rest of the line was to be held, as hitherto, by the Turks, who would perform likewise the patrolling service.

Spizza was formally taken possession of by the Austrians on May 11th. The Montenegrin commissioner, in an address to the people, called upon them to be loyal to their new sovereign.

On January 20th, a treaty based on the most-favored-nation clause was signed between Austro-Hungary and France. The negotiations had been going on for some time, and, not having been concluded by December 31, 1878, it was feared that the general tariff would have to be applied on both sides, a result which would have almost put an end to commercial intercourse between the two countries. The present general tariff of France is so high that in most cases it would have caused an increase of duty of about 60 per cent. On the other hand, the Austrian tariff, though much lower, permits an addition of 10 per cent. to the duty on all articles coming from countries having no treaty with Austria. This would have told most adversely on articles from France, especially on silks, lace, and wine. The advantages over the general tariff offered by the tariff treaty just concluded, and the disadvantages of the former, were so much felt by the commercial world on both sides that representations were made which contributed to hasten the conclusion of the treaty.

In the beginning of February, a treaty was concluded between Germany and Austro-Hungary, by which the latter renounced its right to enforce Clause V. of the Treaty of Prague, which provided for the retrocession of North Schleswig to Denmark, conditionally upon a popular vote being given to that effect.

Prince Bismarck paid a visit to Vienna, arriving on September 21st, and leaving again on the 24th. His reception by Count Andrassy and the Emperor was of so friendly and cordial a character that it attracted general attention. Although his visit was reported to be entirely of a private character, he had several interviews with the leading Austrian statesmen, at which conclusions of far-reaching importance were supposed to have been arrived at. It was generally assumed that Prince Bismarck and Count Andrassy had concluded a treaty of alliance, and the Emperor William was said to have signed this treaty on October 15th. An article by Dr. Moritz Busch, the author of a book on Prince Bismarck, and who stands in high favor with him, confirmed the general impression. Reviewing the Prince's attitude on the foreign questions, the author glanced at the military activity displayed by Russia since the war, imputing to that power a secret desire, among other things, to achieve yet the conquest of Constantinople, which she knew it was only possible for her to do by marching thither through Berlin and Vienna. To prevent this, and otherwise preserve the peace of Europe, there was no other course for Prince Bismarck than to seek an alliance with Austria.

The Emperors of Germany and Austria met at Gastein on August 9th, and had a long and cordial interview. The Vienna papers declared officially that the meeting had no political significance, but the Hungarian journals apprehended that it implied the subordination of the Austro-Hungarian policy in the East to the views of Prince Bismarck.

The silver wedding of the Emperor and Empress of Austria, the anniversary of which fell on April 24th, was celebrated with great rejoicings throughout the empire, the festivities in Vienna continuing during the entire week. Delegations from all the provinces, including one from Serayevo, the capital of Bosnia, came to Vienna to assure the Emperor of their loyalty. The festivities in the provinces were very limited in consequence of an Imperial letter issued shortly after the catastrophe at Szegedin, which invited those who had such intentions to devote the expenses to the relief of the distressed city.

The erection of a Protestant church in Innspruck, in 1879, attracted considerable attention, as being the first Protestant church in the Tyrol, in which province up to this time the Roman Catholic Church had preserved an exclusive influence. The bishops as well as the Diet sought by the exclusion of Protestants to preserve the unity of faith, and a law to that effect was passed in April, 1866. In October, 1878, an interpellation was introduced in the Diet, signed by thirty-one deputies, together with a protest against the formation of Protestant communities without the consent of the Diet. The Governor, Count Taaffe, referred the members to the Constitution of 1867, by which all recognized religious denominations were granted full liberty in the exercise of their devotions, and by which the law of 1866 had become inoperative. The Catholic General Assembly which met in Innspruck in May, 1878, resolved to use all honorable means to prevent the settlement of Protestants in the country; and that every Catholic Tyrolese not only should not sell any real estate to a member of another faith, but should try to prevent at any cost such a sale in his community.

B

BAPTISTS. I. Regular Baptists in the United States.—The whole number of associations in 1879 was 1,075. The number of baptisms reported during the year was 102,736; number of Sunday-schools, 11,845, with 108,405 officers and teachers, and 872,862 scholars; amount of benevolent contributions, $4,439,-749. The returns of educational institutions are not complete as regards the number of instructors and students, but appear, so far as they are given, as follows: 9 theological institutions, with 37 instructors and 338 students for the ministry; 31 colleges and universities, with 230 men and 93 women as instructors, and 4,897 students, of whom 4,000 were young men and 897 young women, and 584 were students for the ministry; 47 academies, seminaries, institutes, and female colleges, with 293 instructors, of whom 123 were men and 170 women, with 4,956 students, of whom 1,993 were young men and 2,963 young women, and 416 were studying for the ministry. The total value of the property of these institutions was $11,142,904.

The following is a summary of the statistics of the regular Baptist churches in the United States as they are given in the "American Baptist Year-Book" for 1879:

STATES AND TERRITORIES.	Churches.	Ministers.	Members.
Alabama	1,434	662	96,898
Arkansas	1,101	525	48,005
California	90	65	5,885
Colorado	21	10	946
Connecticut	121	183	20,677
Dakota	18	10	597
Delaware	11	14	1,867
District of Columbia	26	21	8,568
Florida	285	195	17,986
Georgia	2,697	1,401	216,962
Idaho	1	1	20
Illinois	938	681	69,225
Indiana	560	352	41,523
Indian Territory	92	88	5,480
Iowa	410	331	24,609
Kansas	349	183	15,767
Kentucky	1,709	998	159,743
Louisiana	713	407	53,122
Maine	261	178	20,954
Maryland	54	38	9,402
Massachusetts	287	331	48,774
Michigan	330	306	27,628
Minnesota	140	100	6,420
Mississippi	1,517	802	115,802
Missouri	1,482	818	88,999
Nebraska	125	67	3,660
Nevada	3	3	52
New Hampshire	86	103	9,210
New Jersey	169	204	31,521
New Mexico	1	1	20
New York	879	815	113,264
North Carolina	1,806	1,012	155,881
Ohio	610	460	47,810
Oregon	61	40	2,433
Pennsylvania	524	458	62,845
Rhode Island	60	72	10,906
South Carolina	1,014	608	130,382
Tennessee	1,298	734	102,951
Texas	1,201	658	71,408
Utah	1	1	16
Vermont	111	90	9,662
Virginia	1,292	635	202,781
Washington	14	14	325
West Virginia	355	187	28,645
Wisconsin	189	125	12,262
Wyoming	3	2	62
Totals	24,499	14,954	2,102,084

The following table shows the number of Baptist churches and members in other American countries:

COUNTRIES.	Associations.	Churches.	Ordained ministers.	Members.
British Columbia	..	1	1	80
Grand Ligne Mission	1	9	5	859
Manitoba	..	8	3	110
Mexico	..	8	3	159
New Brunswick	2	148	78	12,037
Nova Scotia	3	180	102	22,785
Ontario and Quebec	14	351	280	27,020
Prince Edward Island	1	18	12	1,481
West Indies:				
Bahamas	..	28	20	5,285
Hayti	..	6	5	152
Jamaica	..	112	49	19,989
St. Domingo	..	1	1	.....
Trinidad	..	11	12	1,018
Total	21	976	571	90,420
Total in America	1,096	25,475	15,525	2,192,454

The annual meeting of the *American Baptist Publication Society* was held at Saratoga Springs, New York, May 29th. The receipts of the Society in its business and missionary departments for the year had been $335,413, or $30,803 more than those of the previous year. Subscriptions had been secured sufficient to provide for the payment of the entire debt of the Society, about $25,000, of which $19,420 had been paid in. The publications included 57,500 copies of new works, 101,925 copies of works already on the catalogue, and 106,000 copies of tracts. The number of publications on the catalogue was now 1,158. The meeting resolved that particular attention should be paid to the colored men who should emigrate from the Southern to the Northern States. It also decided to confer with the Southern Baptist Convention with reference to publishing catechisms as nearly as possible identical.

The forty-seventh annual meeting of the *American Baptist Home Mission Society* was held at Saratoga Springs, New York, May 29th. The receipts of the Society for the year had been $217,093, and the expenditures $175,209. The debt had been reduced from $45,433 to $30,597. The Society had employed, including teachers, 246 missionaries, or 24 more than in the previous year, who had organized 42 schools, and reported 1,172 baptisms and 19,923 children in Sunday-schools. Nine preaching missionaries had been employed among the Indian tribes in the Indian Territory. Schools were taught among the freedmen in the Indian Territory under a contract between the Government and the Society. The chief work of the Society among the freedmen had been in maintaining the eight schools for teachers and preachers, viz.: Wayland Seminary, Washington, D. C.; Richmond Institute, Richmond, Va.; Shaw University, Raleigh, N. C.; Benedict Institute, Columbia, S. C.; Augusta Institute, Augusta, Ga.; Leland University, New Orleans, La.; Natchez Seminary, Natchez, Miss.; Nashville Institute, Nashville, Tenn.; which together returned 46 teachers and 726 young men and 315 young women—in all 1,041—as pupils. A school had also been established at Selma, Ala., to which designated funds were sent through the Society. The school at Augusta, Ga., was to be removed to Atlanta, Ga.

The *Women's Baptist Home Mission Society* had employed 14 missionaries, of whom 11 had labored among the freedmen, one among the Scandinavians of the Northwestern States, and two among the Indians in the Indian Territory.

The sixty-fifth annual meeting of the *American Baptist Missionary Union* was held at Saratoga Springs, New York, May 27th. The receipts of the Union for the year had been $252,677, of which $17,247 were in the shape of additions to the invested funds. The sum applicable to the payment of current expenses was $235,430. Of the receipts, $46,450 were contributed through three women's societies, $357 from India, $4,242 from Burmah, $1,228 from Assam, and $836 from China. The Rangoon Baptist College had 111 pupils. A new building for this institution, called "Ruggles Hall," was dedicated on the 13th of February, 1879. The theological seminary at Rangoon was in its twentieth year, but had suffered severely from sickness, the 49 pupils with whom the term opened having been reduced by its close to 23. The theological seminary at Ramapatam, Telugu mission, had 152 pupils. A board of councilors for a theological institute for the Baptists of France was organized in connection with the meeting of the Union, and the subject of the appointment of a professor was referred to the Executive Committee of the Society. The following is a summary of the reports of the missions :

ASIATIC MISSIONS.	Missionaries.	Native preachers.	Churches.	Members.
Burmah....................	88	423	440	20,811
Assam.......................	14	48	13	1,207
Telugus, India..............	19	82	11	15,054
Chinese....................	19	43	23	1,829
Japan......................	6	2	2	66
Total.................	141	548	494	38,466
EUROPEAN MISSIONS (carried on by native laborers).				
Sweden....................	..	150	275	16,157
Germany....................	..	270	121	25,000
France	..	12	8	706
Spain......................	..	3	4	140
Greece.....................	..	1	1	6
Total.................	..	436	409	42,009
Grand total............	141	984	903	80,475

The *Women's Baptist Foreign Mission Society* reported that its receipts had been $41,472 during the year, and that it had connected with it 840 circles and 212 mission hands, with 19,500 subscribers to its periodical, the "Helping Hand." It had employed among the Burmans, Telugus, Chinese, Japanese, Shans, and Garas, 83 missionaries and 39 Bible women, under whom 38 schools were conducted.

The twenty-fourth session of the *Southern Baptist Convention* was held at Atlanta, Georgia, beginning May 8th. All the States within the territory of the Convention were represented by about 350 delegates. The Rev. J. P. Boyce, D. D., of Kentucky, was chosen President. The receipts of the Foreign Mission Board for the year had been $54,551, of which $27,479, or more than half, were contributed for the chapel in Rome. The African mission, being near the Zooloo country, had been embarrassed by the war to which that region had been subjected. Three men and six women were employed in connection with the mission in China, with twenty-six native laborers. Regular missions were established in Shanghai, Canton, and Tung-Chow, with outlying stations in several villages. In Italy stations were established at Rome, Venice, Naples, Milan, Modena, Bari, Barietta, Carpi, Cagliari, and Torri Pellice, with more than twenty out-stations. The Board have been invited to open missions in Greece and in the island of Cuba. The "first Baptist Church of Brazil, near Santa Barbara, in the province of San Paolo," a body of forty members in comfortable circumstances, had made several applications to the Board to be received as a self-sustaining mission, and desired to conduct a religious work under its sanction in the surrounding country. The receipts of the Home Mission Board had been $16,200. Thirty-five missionaries had been employed during the year, who reported 400 baptisms. The scheme for holding ministers' institutes for colored preachers, sanctioned by the last meeting of the Convention, had gone into operation under an agreement for coöperation with the American Baptist Home Mission Society. The Rev. S. W. Marston, D. D., had been appointed a superintendent of missions among the colored people, and charged with the organization and conduct of the institutes. The Board had been obliged to withdraw the white missionary appointed to labor among the wild Indian tribes, on account of the prejudices of the Indians against white men, and to appoint in his stead native preachers from the civilized tribes. A missionary had been appointed to labor among the Chinese in California. Provision was made for the preparation of a catechism for children and servants. A committee of five persons was appointed to bear to the Baptists of the Northern States at their approaching anniversaries expressions of the fraternal regard of the Convention, and its assurances that, "while still holding to the wisdom and policy of preserving our separate organizations, we are ready to coöperate cordially with them in promoting the cause of Christ in our own and foreign lands." The resolutions under which this action was taken contained a recommendation for holding a meeting of representative men from all sections to devise and propose plans of coöperation, but this was struck out.

The *Eastern German Baptist Conference* met at Berlin, Ontario, August 27th. Reports from about fifty churches showed that 364 additions had been made by baptism and 30 by letter, with a net gain of 330 members, making the whole present number of members 4,601. The Conference in part supported 20 missionaries during the year. The churches represented in this Conference are situated in the Province of Ontario and in the States of New York, Connecticut, Pennsylvania, Delaware, and Maryland.

The *Western German Baptist Conference* met at Racine, Wisconsin, September 17th. L. H. Donner was elected Moderator. The churches and missions represented by this Conference are situated in a territory which is described as extending from Ohio to Oregon and from Texas to Minnesota. The reports from the churches gave the number of baptisms during the year as 234, and the whole number of members as 3,878. Estimating for the churches whose reports had failed to arrive, the whole number of members was thought to be about 4,000. A new constitution was adopted, in which the name "Conference of German Baptist Churches of the West" was substituted for the old name of "Conference of Ministers, Fellow Laborers, and Delegates of the German Baptist Churches." Steps were taken to incorporate the Conference under the laws of Wisconsin. Contributions of more than $2,100 were reported for missionary work among the German population of the United States. Besides this, the Conference had during the year supported a missionary at Ramapetam, India, and some of the churches had contributed to the missions of the German Baptist Union in Russia.

The *Scandinavian Baptist Churches* in the Northwestern States held their first General Convention at Village Creek, Iowa, in August. The Convention decided that the Scandinavian department should be continued in the theological seminary at Morgan Park, near Chicago, Illinois, and appointed a board to exercise supervision over it. It also determined to form a fund in aid of the publication and diffusion of Scandinavian Baptist literature, and resolved that the officers of the General Convention should, in the interest of Scandinavian missions, communicate directly with the American Baptist Home Mission Society, recommending to it suitable missionaries for new fields and asking aid for such missionaries.

II. FREE-WILL BAPTIST CHURCH.—The following is a summary of the statistics of the Free-Will Baptist Church in 170 quarterly meetings, as they are given in the "Free-Will Baptist Register and Year-Book" for 1880:

YEARLY MEETING.	No. of churches.	Ordained preachers.	Licensed preachers.	No. of communicants.
New Hampshire	117	131	18	9,202
Maine Western	69	62	6	5,007
Maine Central	100	91	6	6,412
Penobscot	112	81	5	4,451
Vermont	60	42	4	3,050
Massachusetts and Rhode Island	58	89	4	3,080
Holland Purchase	35	34	2	2,108
Genesee	22	25	2	1,367
Susquehanna	35	34	1	1,447
New York and Pennsylvania	32	21	4	969
St. Lawrence	14	13	1	694
Union	15	10	7	922
Central New York	39	25	4	2,084
Pennsylvania	5	7	..	333
Ohio and Pennsylvania	36	27	3	1,623
Central Ohio	25	23	3	1,356
Ohio	10	9	..	595
Ohio River	65	55	10	4,050
Indiana	7	5	1	279
Northern Indiana	22	15	1	833
Michigan	99	97	16	4,608
St. Joseph's Valley	25	17	8	1,102
Illinois	34	28	4	1,382
Southern Illinois	33	31	16	1,889
Central Illinois	41	32	9	1,989
Wisconsin	27	53	1	2,304
Minnesota	16	17	2	643
Minnesota Southern	25	15	2	605
Iowa	70	45	5	2,580
Kansas	9	7	..	357
Northern Kansas and Southern Nebraska	17	19	3	319
Virginia Free Baptist Association	13	14	4	946
Kentucky	21	13	5	990
Louisiana	17	35	4	534
Ontario, Canada	15	6	..	467
Bengal and Orissa	5	9	3	478
American Association	6	7	..	275
Union Association	18	13	6	687
Quarterly meetings not connected	21	16	2	581
Churches not connected	12	17	..	239
Total	1,446	1,290	162	77,541

There are several associations of Baptists in North America which in doctrine and polity are in general agreement with the Free-Will Baptists. Among these are the associations of General Baptists in Indiana, Illinois, Kentucky, and some adjoining States, numbering several thousand members. The General Conference of the Original Free-Will Baptists of North Carolina, which met in November, 1878, has 96 churches and 6,000 members. The Southern Baptist Association has 66 churches, 68 ministers, and 3,108 members; it holds correspondence with the Chattahoochee, South Carolina, Tennessee River, and Butts County Conferences, and is represented by the "Baptist Review," La Grange, N. C. The Mount Moriah Free-Will Baptist Association, Alabama, has 21 churches, 24 ministers, and about 1,000 members. The Union Association of General Baptists, Kentucky, has 24 churches, 15 ordained ministers, 4 licensed ministers, and 1,000 members. The Free-Will Baptist Association in Texas numbers 33 ministers. The Texas Free-Will Baptist Association reports 6 churches and 5 ministers. There are other Free-Will Baptist Churches in Tennessee, Mississippi, Arkansas, and Missouri, numbering some thousands of members, that have no organized connection, but are one in doctrine with the Free-Will Baptist Church. The aggregate of these and similar bodies will not fall short of 25,000 members. The Free Baptists of Nova Scotia have 52 churches and 3,368 members. The Free Baptists of New Brunswick number 148 churches and 9,389 members. The General Baptists of Great Britain are in harmony with the Free-Will Baptist Church, and a correspondence by epistles and delegations has long been sustained between them.

The contributions of the churches to the missionary and educational societies of the denomination for the year ending August 1, 1879, were: to the Foreign Mission Society, $19,913; to the Home Mission Society, $7,608; to the Educational Society, $2,131; total, $29,653. Of the contributions to foreign missions, $2,069, and of those to home missions, $1,089 were received through the Woman's Mission Society. *The Home Mission Society* has a permanent fund of $4,745 and a centennial fund of $4,895. Its most important work is among the freedmen, for whom it sustains a school at Harper's Ferry, W. Va. It has also stations at Cairo and neighboring towns in southern Illinois, in Nebraska, and near New Orleans, La. The *Educational Society* has a general fund of $43,826, and a library fund of $2,225. The number of students reported in 1879 as preparing for the ministry in all the schools of the denomination was 88, nine more than the largest number ever given in any former report of the Society. The Foreign Missionary Society supports a mission in Lower Bengal and Orissa, India, which includes 8 missionaries, 4 assistants, 478 members, and 453 scholars in the Sunday-schools.

III. SEVENTH-DAY BAPTIST CHURCH.—The Committee on Statistics of the General Conference of this Church reported in September, 1878, that two churches had been added during the year, making the whole present number of churches 90. Of these churches, 59, or one less than two thirds of the whole, had reported 7,446 members. Presuming the remaining 31 churches to have a proportionate number of members, the total membership of the denomination would be about 11,000. The reports of the contributions of the churches, so far as they were sent to the committee, showed an average of $2.40 per member in the total contributions, and an average of 25 cents per member for denominational work, this head including the tract and missionary enterprises. The Committee on Sabbath-Schools reported that the number of such schools was 88, being larger than ever before, but the number of scholars had decreased three per cent.

The *Seventh-Day Baptist General Conference* met for its sixty-fifth annual session at Brookfield, New York, September 24th. A. B. Prentice was President. A committee which had been appointed by a previous General Conference to present for consideration a denominational exposition of faith made a report embracing eleven articles of belief, viz.: in God; Christ; the Holy Spirit; the Holy Scriptures; Man (affirming his twofold nature, his fall, and the necessity of regeneration); Heirship and Eternal Life; Repentance, Faith, and Baptism; the Lord's Supper; the Sabbath (the seventh day); the Resurrection of the Dead and the Eternal Judgment; and the Resurrection body of the Saints. The report was ordered to be printed and to lie on the table for one year, and the committee was continued. An order of procedure at the sessions of the Conference was adopted, which provides for the previous selection of a list of subjects for discussion, and the appointment for each subject of some person to introduce the discussion in an address or essay, after the reading of which a limited time shall be allowed for general discussion in five-minute speeches. The Conference recommended to young men who contemplate entering the ministry that they endeavor to prepare themselves for that work by a classical education and a full course of theological training; and advised them to study in the schools of the denomination. A policy of engaging the pastors of such churches "as could serve the cause advantageously" to labor in the mission-fields for a month or more at a time, was recommended. The Hon. Horatio Gates Jones, of the State Senate of Pennsylvania, communicated to the Conference the latest results of his efforts to obtain a relaxation of the Sunday laws of that State in favor of those who keep the seventh day as the Sabbath. The bill introduced by him for that purpose had on the 13th of May, 1879, secured a majority of the votes of the members of the Senate present and voting, but had failed to pass for the want of a majority of the whole Senate as required by the Constitution. "From this statement," he said, "you may well suppose that I am not disheartened, for each year has brought fresh accessions to the ranks of those who believe in the great principle of the rights of conscience."

The anniversary meetings of the Educational, Missionary, and Tract Societies were held in connection with the meeting of the General Conference. The Missionary Society sustained home missions at different points in the United States, and a mission at Shanghai, China, which was at present without a missionary superintendent. At Shanghai the Society owned a city chapel to which dwellings were attached, a cottage in the country, and a lot in the missionary burial-ground. The missionary work was in the hands of two or three native preachers or Bible-readers; the Church had eighteen or twenty members, while about the same number of members had died.

IV. THE BRETHREN, OR TUNKERS.—The Annual Council of the Tunkers, or Brethren, met at Broadney, Virginia, June 3d. The sum of $800 being needed for the mission in Denmark during the coming year, a contribution of two dollars was requested from each church. The Council of 1877 had decided that the double mode, viz., that in which one person washes and another wipes the feet of the brother or sister participating in the ceremony, was the proper method of administering the ordinance of feet-washing. A petition was presented asking for a grant of liberty to use the single mode, or that in which the same person washes and wipes. The question was deferred till the next year. The question whether a member who has withdrawn from the Masonic order may or may not answer recognitions from members of the order, was answered in the negative. On the question whether a minority ought to be permitted to prevent a church from establishing a Sunday-school—the customary way of deciding matters in the Brotherhood being by unanimous consent—the Council agreed to ask minorities to yield. Newspapers had been established within the denomination which had indulged in free criticism of some of its peculiar usages. The Council determined that the editors of the papers should be called upon to make acknowledgments of their offenses; that certain elders who were named should be required to give satisfaction for publishing schismatic articles; and that a committee should be appointed to see that the editors of church papers admit no articles assailing the doctrines or principles or practices of the Brotherhood. A request that the wearing of hats by the sisters should not be made a bar to membership was denied. An order was adopted that each brother attending the meetings of the Council should pay one dollar, while payment was left optional with the sisters; and that free board should be given only to brethren and sisters and their special friends.

V. BAPTISTS IN CANADA.—The twenty-first annual meeting of the *Canada Baptist Convention East* was held at Montreal, beginning October 1st. D. Bentley presided. The principal business related to the adoption of a union with the Convention West. A plan for the organization of a Baptist Union of the Provinces of Ontario and Quebec, which had been proposed by the Western Convention, was sanctioned, "subject to such modifications as on further deliberation may be deemed necessary without affecting the main principles of union suggested." To facilitate the formation of the proposed union, it was suggested that committees be appointed by the two Conventions to represent them in considering what modifications should be made, by whose joint action both Conventions should consider themselves bound. In accordance with this action, a committee was appointed by the Convention to represent it. The Canadian Baptists, and the Baptists of the maritime provinces coöperating with them, sustain a mission among the Telugus in India, in which thirteen missionaries including wives and a female teacher are employed. The mission embraces three stations, and returned for 1879 467 "baptized believers."

VI. BAPTISTS IN GREAT BRITAIN AND IRELAND.—The following is a summary of the statistics of the Baptist Churches in Great Britain and Ireland, as they are given in the "Baptist Hand-Book" for 1879 : Number of churches, 2,587; of chapels, 3,451; of sittings, 1,028,-833; of members, 276,348; of Sunday-school teachers, 40,216 ; of Sunday-school scholars, 399,317; of pastors, 1,879 ; of Evangelists, 2,652. Sixty-three new chapels and 28 new schoolrooms were erected during the year ending September 30, 1878. The number of members in the different parts of the United Kingdom was, according to the tables in the "Hand-Book": In England, 199,820; in Wales, 66,043 ; in Scotland, 9,234; in Ireland, 1,251. The Baptists in other countries of Europe returned 452 churches and 367 pastors, and members as follows: Austria, 81 ; Denmark, 2,114; Finland, 400; France (part of whom were in churches aided by the American Baptist Missionary Union), 784; Germany, 15,-287; the Netherlands, 465 ; Italy, 400; Sweden, 15,000; Norway, 615; Poland, 1,747; Russia, 3,686 ; Spain, 244; Switzerland, 403 ; Turkey, 159; total, about 40,000. In Africa (Cape Colony, Port Natal, West Africa, and St. Helena), there were 32 churches, 17 pastors or missionaries, and 1,147 members ; in the Australasian Colonies, 127 churches, 87 pastors, and 7,700 members; in Asia, 514 churches, 213 pastors or missionaries, and 34,006 members. The estimate for the whole world is 28,505 churches, 17,683 pastors or missionaries, and 2,473,088 members. These numbers are made up in part, particularly where churches in foreign lands are concerned, from the reports of two or three years previous to the current year. The real present number of Baptists is not less than 100,000 more than the number given above.

The annual meeting of the *Baptist Union of England and Ireland* was held in London, April 28th. The Rev. George Gould presided. The report of the Secretary showed that 20,000 new sittings had been added to the chapel accommodation during the year, and £145,000 had been spent upon the increase of chapel accommodation and schoolrooms. A resolution was adopted condemning the foreign policy and the expenditure of the Government. The expenditures of the *Society for British and Irish Home Missions* had been £5,571. Three new stations had been opened in England; operations had been extended in some directions and contracted in none. Satisfactory progress had been made in Ireland. The receipts of the *Bible Translation Society* had been £2,244,105. The report gave accounts of the publication and sale of editions of the Bible and New Testament, or of parts of the same, in the Sanskrit, Bengali, Mussulman Bengali, and Hindi languages, the languages of Orissa, Ceylon, and Japan, and one of the languages of Africa. The anniversary of the *Baptist Missionary Society* was held in London, May 1st. The Earl of Northbrook presided. The total receipts of the Society had been £46,092. Favorable reports were made of the condition of the missions in India, where two hundred persons had been baptized ; in Ceylon, in China, where the missionaries had been largely occupied in distributing relief to the sufferers by the famine ; in Brittany, where the missionaries enjoyed greater freedom ; in Africa, where a mission to the Congo had been finally resolved upon ; in Norway, where the "Union of the Norwegian Baptists" had undertaken the general management of the mission; in Italy ; and in Jamaica. The mission in Trinidad had suffered from the loss of many of its members by death. Four missionaries were on their way to the Congo mission in Africa, and would be reënforced by some native helpers from the Cameroons mission. The missions of the Society in India, Ceylon, China, Brittany, Norway, Italy, Africa, the West Indies, and Jamaica were under the care of 88 European missionaries, with 39 native missionaries and 186 evangelists, and returned members as follows : India, 3,653 ; Ceylon, 653 ; China, 108 ; Brittany, 53 ; Norway, 645 ; Italy, 133 ; Africa, 137 ; West India islands, 4,215 ; Jamaica, 21,984; total, 31,581. Number of teachers, 147; of day scholars, 4,269 ; of Sunday scholars, 4,114. The expenditures of the Zenana mission in India had been £3,019. The mission employed about 23 European lady visitors and 42 native teachers and Bible women, who were laboring in Calcutta, Baraset, Delhi, Benares, Allababad, Soorie, Barisaul, Monghyr, and Patona. Nearly 700 women were receiving religious instruction in the Zenanas, and 13 girls' schools, containing about 400 children, were taught by the agents.

The autumnal meeting of the Union was held at Glasgow, beginning October 7th. The fourth report of the annuity fund showed that the total value of its securities in the hands of the Treasurer was £73,882, and that more than £37,000 had been received in redemption of promises amounting to £58,000. Sixty-eight ministers, widows, and children were receiving annuities. The British and Irish Mission reported that new stations had been opened in England and Ireland, and that 611 members had been added in the two kingdoms. The labors of the special evangelists had been successful, but more men were wanted. Ten missionaries had been accepted, and eight sent out during the year to the foreign stations, in pursuance of a resolution which had been adopted in the previous year to raise funds to send out twenty additional missionaries. Mr. Watkins, of Bristol, who had made a gift in the previous year for the African mission, had offered to contribute £700, half the sum required, to send out twelve additional missionaries, if the rest were raised. The required amount was obtained. Discussions were held during the meeting on the subjects of the use and disuse of confessions of faith, the attitude of the Union in relation to religious opinion and belief, politics and the pulpit, and the relations of the Union to other denominations. A resolution was passed declaring that the present condition of the country demanded the serious consideration of the Christian community; expressing the judgment of the assembly that the policy of the Government "has been the cause of needless wars, has involved the nation in grave financial difficulties, and has failed to ameliorate by domestic legislation the social and moral evils under which the country suffers"; and advising the members of the Union to active and united efforts to return members of Parliament pledged to oppose that policy.

GENERAL BAPTISTS.—The one hundred and tenth annual meeting of the *General Baptist Association* was held at Halifax, beginning June 19th. The statistical reports showed that the Association included 179 churches, to which three new ones would be added, the whole containing 24,003 members. The income of the Home Mission Society had been £1,705, the largest amount ever reported in one year. The income for foreign missions had been £8,872, £86 more than that of the previous year. Three additions had been made to the European missionary staff during the year, and a new chapel had been opened in connection with the mission at Rome. During the last twenty years the number of mission churches had increased threefold. Chilnell College had ten students, and had suffered a financial deficiency of £598. Resolutions were passed in favor of the bill for closing the public-houses on Sunday; counseling opposition to the war spirit, and expressing a hope for the termination of the Zooloo war; urging

on the House of Commons not to pass any enactment which would enable particular religious views to be inculcated at the expense of the state; and denouncing the Government Valuation Bill as a measure which, by allowing exemptions in the ratable value of clerical incomes proportioned to the salaries of curates, would virtually give additional endowments to the Anglican Church.

The annual meetings of the *Baptist Union and Home Mission of Scotland* were held in Edinburgh in October. The report of the Secretary showed that the number of Baptist members connected with the Union in Scotland was 8,862, or 513 more than the number reported in 1878. One hundred and forty stations were kept up in the home mission department, in connection with which 28 missionaries had been employed and 214 members had been added during the year.

V. GERMAN BAPTIST UNION.—The German Baptist Union embraces churches in Germany, Austria, Denmark, Holland, Switzerland, Poland, Russia, and Africa. The triennial Conference was held at Hamburg in July, at which 125 delegates were present. The statistical reports showed that an increase of 919 members had taken place during the year, the gains being 76 in Germany, 63 in Austria, 42 in Denmark, 25 in Holland, 56 in Switzerland, 40 in Poland, and 687 in Russia, while there appeared a decrease of 30 in Africa and of 44 in Turkey. The business transacted related to the publishing house, which is hereafter to be under the supervision of Dr. P. W. Bickel, representing the American Baptist Publication Society; to the education of ministers, for which it was resolved to establish and endow a theological seminary; and to the promotion of Sunday-schools.

BARRY, General WILLIAM FARQUHAR, a military officer, born in New York, August 8, 1818, died at Fort McHenry, near Baltimore, July 18th. He entered the United States Military Academy at West Point on September 1, 1834, and graduated on July 1, 1838, with the rank of brevet second lieutenant in the Fourth Artillery. On July 7th of the same year he was appointed second lieutenant, and on the 12th of July was transferred to the Second Artillery. He served first at Carlisle Barracks, Pa., and next at Buffalo, N. Y., during the Canada border disturbances of 1838-'39. After doing garrison duty at a number of different stations, he went with the army to Mexico, remaining there from 1846 to 1848. He was in the battle of Tampico, and served in Major-General Patterson's division, and also as aide-de-camp to Major-General Worth. From 1849 to 1851 he was stationed at Fort McHenry, and was made a captain in the Second Artillery on July 1, 1852. He served in the war against the Seminoles in Florida in 1852-'53, and was in garrison at Baton Rouge, La., in 1855. He did frontier duty at Fort Washington, I. T., in 1855, and at Fort Snelling,

Minn., in 1857. In that year, as also in 1858, he was stationed at Fort Leavenworth, Kansas, during the Kansas disturbances, being transferred afterward to Fort Kearney, Neb. During the year 1858 he was a member of the board to revise the system of light artillery practice, which was adopted on March 6, 1860. The year 1861, the breaking out of the civil war, found him at the arsenal in Washington, D. C. He soon went into active service, assisting the same year in the defense of Fort Pickens, Fla., as major of the Fifth Artillery. He passed through the Manassas campaign as chief of artillery in the army of Brigadier-General McDowell, and was at the first battle of Bull Run, July 21, 1861. He was chief of artillery in the Army of the Potomac from July 27, 1861, to August 27, 1862, and organized its artillery. On August 20, 1861, he was appointed brigadier-general of United States volunteers, and was in the defense of Washington, D. C., until March, 1862. He took a leading part in the Virginia peninsular campaign until August, 1863, being in the siege of Yorktown, at the battle of Gaines's Mill, the skirmish of Mechanicsville, the battle of Charles City Cross Roads, the Malvern Hill contest, and at Harrison's Landing. From the end of that campaign until 1864 he was chief of artillery of the defenses of Washington, D. C., having been appointed lieutenant-colonel of the First Artillery on August 1, 1863. He was assigned to the command at Pittsburgh, Pa., and Wheeling, W. Va., against a threatened cavalry raid in May, 1863, and was next appointed chief of artillery on General Sherman's staff, commanding the military division of the Mississippi from March, 1864, to June, 1866. From May to September, 1864, he was with the invading army in Georgia, and took part in the action of Tunnel Hill. On September 1, 1864, he was made brevet major-general of volunteers and colonel by brevet for gallant conduct at Rocky-Faced Ridge. He was also at Resaca, the battle of Kenesaw Mountain, New Hope Church action, the skirmish of Peach-Tree Creek, and the battle and siege of Atlanta. In the Northern Georgia and Alabama campaigns he passed through the battles of Jonesboro, Lovejoy Station, and the skirmishes of Snake's Creek Gap, Ship's Gap, and Rome. From February to April, 1865, he was in the Carolina campaign at the battles of Averysboro and Bentonville. On March 13, 1865, he was made brevet brigadier-general in the United States army for his services in the campaign ending with the surrender of the army under General J. E. Johnston, and on the same day was made brevet major-general for gallant conduct in the field. On December 11, 1865, he was appointed colonel in the Second Artillery, and was in command of the Northern frontier pending the Fenian raids of 1866. On January 15th of that year he was mustered out of the volunteer service. He served on the Northern frontier to September,

1867, and then commanded the Artillery School of Practice at Fortress Monroe to March 5, 1877, when he was appointed to the command at Fort McHenry. During the labor riots of 1877 he rendered valuable service at Camden Station. He was the author, in conjunction with General J. G. Barnard, of a work published in 1863 entitled "Reports of the Engineer and Artillery Operations of the Army of the Potomac from its Organization to the Close of the Peninsular Campaign."

BATTLE, Judge WILLIAM HORN, a highly honored citizen and jurist, born in Edgecombe County, North Carolina, October 17, 1802, died at Chapel Hill, March 17th. At the age of sixteen years he entered the university at Chapel Hill, and in two years graduated with high honors, with a class some of whose members subsequently manifested distinguished ability. On leaving the university he entered the office of Chief Justice Henderson and prepared himself to practice at the bar. At the end of three years he was admitted, and manifested such proficiency that he was at once advanced to both county and Superior Court practice. He opened his office in Louisburg. The early years of his professional life were not full of promise. But, with pride and pleasure, he was wont to attribute his final success to the encouraging influence and superior character of his wife, a daughter of Kemp Plummer, a distinguished lawyer of Warrenton, with whom he was married in 1827. He represented Franklin County in the House of Commons in 1833-'34, and, associated with Thomas P. Devereux, Esq., reported the Supreme Court decisions from December, 1834, to December, 1839, inclusive. In 1835 he was associated with Governor Iredell and Judge Nash in preparing the Revised Statutes of North Carolina, and personally superintended the printing of that work in Boston. He removed to Raleigh in 1839, and the same year was a delegate to the Convention which nominated William Henry Harrison for President of the United States. In politics he was a Whig, but was never a partisan, and his political career ended with his elevation to the judiciary. In August, 1840, a vacancy occurred on the bench of the Superior Court of the State, and he was appointed by Governor Dudley to fill it, and subsequently elected by the Legislature. In 1843 he removed to Chapel Hill, and in 1845 was elected by the Trustees to the professorship of law in the university, which he continued to hold until the institution went down in 1871, after which he closed his law school and removed to Raleigh. In May, 1848, a vacancy occurred on the bench of the Supreme Court, and he was appointed by the Governor to fill it, but not confirmed by the Legislature, because there were already three judges of the Court residing in the same county; but he was again elected to the Superior Court, where another vacancy occurred, by the same Legislature. This position he accepted, and retained until 1852, when he was called to the bench of the Supreme Court, where he continued to preside as an Associate Justice until the inauguration of the reconstructed State government in 1868. In 1872–'73 he was appointed by the Legislature to revise the statutes of the State; but this revision, the work of his unassisted mind, never attained so high a rank as the joint labors of others. He subsequently removed to Chapel Hill after the death of his wife, and resided with his son until the close of his career. He was a man of much natural excellence of character and extensive learning.

BEET, SUGAR, NEW PRODUCT FROM THE. The chemists have nowhere proved the utility of their science in a more marked and gratifying manner than in extracting so many valuable commercial commodities from the residual products of manufactured materials. The waste products of many an industrial operation, which before the developments of modern chemistry were useless and troublesome to get rid off, cumbering the ground or distaining and poisoning the rivers, have been made to yield the materials for one or more secondary industries, turning out products of valuable properties; so that the residual products now utilized greatly exceed in number those which are still found valueless. In the science of organic chemistry the development has been very recent, and is very imperfect compared with the progress which has been made in analyzing the non-organic mineral constituents of the earth's matter. Every step in this new science, whose threshold has scarcely yet been passed, indicates that the chemistry of life is vastly more complex than the chemical combinations of the mineral world; and nearly every new substance discovered by resolving into their simpler materials, or by recombining organic principles with each other or with non-organic elements, 's found to possess properties of utility, which are sometimes exceedingly novel and remarkable. An important gain to industrial art is likely to result from a process discovered by Camille Vincent of Paris for utilizing another refuse material. In the manufacture of beetroot sugar, the juice of the beet is expressed, and, after filtering, is boiled and allowed to crystallize. A thick molasses is left, which has been used sometimes for sweetening purposes and sometimes for fattening cattle, but is now almost all subjected to fermentation and distillation, yielding a coarse kind of rum. After the alcohol is distilled out there is left in the retort a liquid called *vinasse*, which was formerly thrown away, until Dubrunfaut discovered its value as a source of potash salts. It is evaporated and the dry residuum calcined, yielding an ash which is called *salin*, and is rich in compounds of potassium. In this way 2,000 tons of carbonate of potash are produced annually in the distilleries of France. By this process the products of the beet were appar-

ently all used up. But M. Vincent shows that very valuable principles were allowed to escape. Besides the alkaline matter, the liquor remaining after the distillation of the spirit also contains considerable quantities of organic matter, partly nitrogenous, which is decomposed by the process of calcination, leaving a porous carbonaceous mass containing also the remaining mineral substances. The volatile products of the decomposition may be saved by subjecting the concentrated vinasse to destructive distillation in an iron retort; and, by passing them through condensers, the condensable ones will liquefy, while the permanent gases can be conducted off and utilized as fuel. The portions which admit of condensation consist in bituminous and ammoniacal liquors, which differ in their chemical composition in some important respects from the similar products remaining after the manufacture of illuminating gas from coal. One of the constituents of the ammonia-water thus obtained is the foundation of the new manufacturing process inaugurated by M. Vincent. The liquid is found to contain large quantities of the salts of trimethylamine. Trimethylamine has never before been produced except in very small quantities in the chemical laboratory. It is one of the organic compounds called compound ammonias, the first of which, methylamine, was discovered by M. Würtz in 1848, and the others, dimethylamine and trimethylamine, by Dr. Hofmann, about thirty years ago. In these the organic radical, methyl, performs the part of hydrogen in the gaseous compound of nitrogen and hydrogen, and they were produced by replacing one, two, or all three of the atoms of hydrogen in ammonia by atoms of methyl. The trimethylamine, the hydrochlorate of trimethylamine, yields products of great utility. Upon decomposing the hydrochlorate by heat, it is resolved into free ammonia, which is a valuable product; free trimethylamine, which can be used over again for the same purpose; and chloride of methyl, a compound which has never before been obtained in any quantities, and which possesses some very remarkable properties. The chloride is a combustible gaseous substance, which can be easily condensed into a liquid form in strong wrought-iron cylinders, and transported and handled with safety. One use of chloride of methyl is in the manufacture of the methylated colors, such as Hofmann's violet and aniline green, in which it does the service of the more expensive iodide. It possesses another quality which gives it a far higher and a singular value. It is as a refrigerating agent that it promises to be of the greatest service. By the rapid evaporation of the liquid a reduction of temperature takes place which exceeds that produced by any other means. The liquid is not at all corrosive nor poisonous, and promises to supplant all the other freezing agents. A machine has been constructed by M. Vincent in which a temperature of 55° C. can be produced and maintained by the evaporation of this volatile substance. This temperature is considerably below the freezing-point of quicksilver. The discovery of this new product of the sugar-beet presents an additional inducement for its cultivation in the United States, an object which the Agricultural Bureau has for some time sought to promote. The climatic conditions most favorable to the growth of this useful plant were considered in a paper read before the Association for the Advancement of Science at Saratoga in September, by Dr. William McMurtrie. The best meteorological conditions are a warm, dry spring, and a temperate, moist summer, followed by a cool, dry autumn.

BELGIUM, a kingdom of Europe. Leopold II., King of the Belgians, born April 9, 1835, is the son of King Leopold I., former Duke of Saxe-Coburg, and ascended the throne at his death, December 10, 1865. He was married August 22, 1853, to Marie Henriette, daughter of the late Archduke Joseph of Austria (born August 23, 1836), who has borne him three daughters. The heir apparent to the throne is the brother of the King, Philip, Count of Flanders, born March 24, 1837, lieutenant-general in the service of Belgium, who was married, April 26, 1867, to Princess Marie of Hohenzollern-Sigmaringen (born November 17,

1845), and has two sons, Baldwin, born July 3, 1869, and Albert, born April 8, 1875.

The area of this kingdom is 11,373 square miles. The population according to the census of December 31, 1876, was 5,336,185, and in December, 1877, according to a calculation based upon the movement of population, 5,412,-731. The following table exhibits the population of each province at the close of 1877:

PROVINCES.	Pop. in Dec., 1877.
Antwerp	550,179
Brabant	959,803
Flanders, West	689,395
" East	671,948
Hainault	966,400
Liége	642,264
Limburg	207,204
Luxemburg	206,783
Namur	818,755
Total	5,412,731

The population of the principal cities on December 31, 1877, was as follows: Brussels, 164,598, and including eight adjacent communities, 380,238; Antwerp, 155,820; Ghent, 129,-201; Liége, 118,140; Bruges, 44,950; Malines, 39,776; Verviers, 38,410; Louvain, 34,440; Tournay, 32,180; Courtrai, 26,328; Saint Nicholas, 25,440; Namur, 25,353; Mons, 24,638; Seraing, 24,564; Alost, 21,107.

The movement of population from 1871 to 1877 is shown in the following table:

YEAR.	Marriages.	Births. Inclusive of Still-born.	Deaths.	Still-born Children.	Surplus of Births.	Total Population on December 31.
1871	37,588	166,010	152,996	7,250	13,014	5,118,680
1872	40,084	174,935	127,678	7,558	47,257	5,175,037
1873	40,598	178,491	120,656	7,788	57,835	5,258,821
1874	40,326	181,728	117,345	7,750	64,383	5,336,684
1875	39,050	183,801	130,229	7,749	53,072	5,403,006
1876	38,228	184,845	124,717	7,930	60,128	5,336,185
1877	36,962	183,122	122,314	8,045	60,808	5,412,731

Almost the entire population is connected with the Roman Catholic Church. The number of Protestants is estimated at 15,000; that of Jews at 3,000. The larger portion of both lives in the provinces of Antwerp and Limburg. Of the 5,336,185 inhabitants according to the census of 1876, 2,256,860 spoke French, 2,659,-890 Flemish, 340,770 French and Flemish, 38,-070 German, 22,700 French and German, 1,790 Flemish and German, 5,490 these three languages, 7,650 foreign languages, and 2,070 were deaf and dumb.

According to the census of 1866 the nativity of the inhabitants was as follows:

COUNTRIES.	Population.
Belgium	4,729,787
Netherlands	26,485
Dutch Limbourg	7,419
Dutch Luxembourg	5,625
France	32,021
Germany	20,701
Great Britain	3,008
Other Countries	2,892
Total	4,827,833

The budget for the years 1877 and 1878 esti-

mated receipts and expenditures as follows (in francs):

I. RECEIPTS.	1877.	1878.
1. Direct taxes	43,753,000	44,003,000
2. Indirect taxes	100,790,000	102,985,000
3. From means of communication (railroads, telegraphs, post, etc.)	95,981,400	100,652,500
4. Miscellaneous	9,927,000	9,772,000
5. Reimbursements	1,794,860	2,921,360
Total receipts	252,245,760	260,833,860

II. EXPENDITURES.		
1. Public debt	65,071,815	74,785,815
2. Dotations	4,454,806	4,585,806
3. Ministry of Justice	15,908,889	16,272,849
4. Ministry of Foreign Affairs	1,650,805	1,908,585
5. Ministry of the Interior	19,893,568	20,371,494
6. Ministry of Public Works	81,792,584	81,854,369
7. Ministry of War	41,036,800	41,068,000
Budget of the gens d'armerie	2,883,000	2,920,000
Ministry of Finance	15,174,970	15,274,950
8. Reimbursements and outstanding debt	1,120,000	1,126,000
Total expenditures	248,986,782	259,606,765

The immigration into Belgium has since 1871 always exceeded the emigration from the country, as will be seen from the following table:

	1871.	1872.	1873.	1874.	1875.	1876.	1877.
Immigrants	16,708	15,789	15,792	16,762	15,872	14,446	15,075
Emigrants	13,171	11,040	7,981	8,217	10,157	13,124	11,847
Surplus of immigrants	3,587	4,749	7,811	8,545	5,215	1,322	3,228

The movement of the special commerce of Belgium during the years 1876 and 1877 was as follows, expressed in millions of francs:

COUNTRIES.	IMPORTS.		EXPORTS.	
	1876.	1877.	1876.	1877.
Central Europe:				
France	352·6	354·0	314·1	296·0
Ger'n Customs Union	184·3	197·4	223·0	200·7
Netherlands	185·0	196·8	165·8	165·7
Other countries	11·5	17·4	16·8	22·0
Northern Europe:				
England	248·9	212·6	191·7	220·1
Russia	114·7	82·0	19·3	25·2
Other countries (Sweden, etc.)	32·0	27·8	14·4	18·5
Southern Europe	50·6	62·7	72·6	71·8
America	243·0	250·1	38·8	49·5
Asia	20·9	17·1	1·5	7·8
Africa	5·0	8·3	1·8	2·5
Total	1,448·5	1,426·2	1,063·8	1,074·8

The following table gives in millions of francs the movement of the general and special commerce of Belgium from 1860 to 1877, and compares it with the commerce in 1830:

YEAR.	IMPORTS.		EXPORTS.	
	General.	Special.	General.	Special.
Yearly average, 1860–1864	1,048·9	598·5	966·1	511·3
1865–1870	1,520·3	809·4	1,345·1	638·1
1871–1874	2,240·6	1,288·2	1,983·0	780·6
1875	2,319·8	1,307·1	2,107·6	1,101·8
1876	2,460·4	1,448·5	2,088·4	1,065·8
1877	2,356·6	1,426·2	2,004·2	1,074·3
1880	90·0	90·0	104·6	96·6

The Chambers reassembled in January, and on the 21st the Government introduced a new law on elementary instruction, designed to take the place of the law of 1842. It required every community to establish a school in a proper locality, tuition to be free for poor children. The school-books to be used are to be examined by the school council, and to be approved by the Government. The clerical supervision is to cease. The teachers shall be appointed by the Communal Council, but must be native or naturalized Belgians, and possess a certificate of their ability to teach. The instruction is to comprise morals, reading, writing, arithmetic, object-teaching, the rudiments of the French, Flemish, or German language (according to the locality), geography, Belgian history, drawing, gymnastic exercises, music, and needlework. Article IV. is as follows: "Religious instruction shall be left to the care of the families and of the ministers of the different denominations. A room in the school is to be placed at the disposal of the latter in order to give religious instruction to the school-children before or after school-hours."

A royal decree was published on February 23d, which ordered that, in the state normal schools for the instruction of elementary school-teachers, the principles of constitutional and administrative law shall be taught, embracing a history of the political institutions of the country, a knowledge of the Constitution and the laws relating to it, and the elementary school law. This instruction is to be given by a professor specially appointed for that purpose, who shall if possible be a doctor of laws. In April the Minister of Public Instruction appointed a committee of seventeen to prepare a plan for the improvement of the secondary schools.

The discussion on the new elementary school law in the Chamber of Deputies led to violent scenes and severe recriminations. M. Woeste, one of the leaders of the Clerical party, attempted to show that lay teachers were not fit for their work. For this purpose he cited fifteen cases of teachers who had since 1859 been convicted of improper conduct with their pupils. The Minister of Public Instruction in reply stated that only three of this number had come from state normal schools, which, however, had been under clerical supervision; while the remaining twelve had graduated with high honors from episcopal seminaries. Of 5,393 lay teachers in the public schools, fifteen had committed offenses against morality in twenty years. In the same time, however, of 452 clerical teachers, not less than eighteen had committed similar offenses, who indeed had not all been punished, because some had disappeared.

In May the Minister of Finance submitted a bill abolishing the hearth tax introduced by the laws of 1821 and 1822, and increasing the rent, door, and window taxes. The object of the bill was to put an end to numerous election abuses which had occurred under the old order of things.

The bill on primary education was passed by the Chamber of Deputies on June 6th by a vote of 67 to 60, all but two members being present. In the Senate the bill was passed on June 18th by a vote of 33 to 31, after a bitter speech by the President, Prince de Ligne, who is a member of the Left, in which he denounced the law as an unfortunate law and a war measure. Immediately upon the passage of the school law in the Senate, the bishops of Belgium issued a common pastoral letter condemning it. They declared that the school system which the Government wished to introduce was "dangerous in itself, that it promoted infidelity and indifference, and that it is an attack on the faith, the piety, and the religious rights of the Belgian people." No parents should therefore send their children to a school subject to the new law, if a Catholic school was in their vicinity. No Catholic school should aid in the execution of the new law, should accept a school office, or be a member of the school council.

On June 27th the Minister of Finance presented a financial bill, in which he proposed to tax the cultivation of tobacco, and to increase the import duty on tobacco, as well as the succession and excise duties. The preamble to the bill stated that the proposed augmentations were estimated to yield to the Treasury an additional sum of 7,350,000 francs, whereas the deficit to be covered amounted to 12,000,000 francs. The Government therefore reserved to itself to propose, when expedient, the conversion of the $4\frac{1}{2}$ per cent. rentes. The electoral reform bill was passed in the Lower Chamber in the beginning of July by 69 votes to 60. The discussion on the new financial laws was closed on July 22d, after a speech from M. de Kerwyn urging the necessity of affording protection to the agricultural interests of the country. The Minister for Foreign Affairs replied that there was no occasion to revert to a policy of protection, and the bill was then adopted by 60 to 42 votes. A proposition of the Government to convert the $4\frac{1}{2}$ per cent. rentes to 4 per cents was adopted the same day in the Chamber and the Senate. On July 21st Prince de Ligne, President of the Senate, resigned, and on August 1st the Chambers were closed. In the beginning of September General Liagre was appointed Minister of War in the place of General Renard, who had died shortly before.

The new school laws were considered in a meeting of the Belgian bishops held in Malines in the middle of August, when it was resolved to refuse absolution to the teachers of normal schools; that the religious instruction given in secular schools was schismatic, and all teachers giving such instruction were to be excommunicated. These resolutions were, however, not fully approved by Cardinal Nina, the Papal Secretary of State, in a note to the Papal Nuncio in Brussels, in which Cardinal Nina ordered that the resolutions should not be communicated to the clergy until they had received the sanction of the Holy See.

The bitter feeling existing between the different parties caused the King to address the people at a festival in Tournay, exhorting them to unity and fraternity, particularly in view of the semi-centennial of national independence to be celebrated in 1880.

BIGELOW, Dr. JACOB, an eminent physician, born in Sudbury, Mass., February 27, 1787, died in Boston, January 10th. He was graduated at Harvard College in 1806, and, having prepared himself for the practice of medicine, opened his office in Boston in 1810, and displayed unusual skill. In 1814 he published a work entitled "Florula Bostoniensis," describing the plants of Boston and its envi-

rons, enlarged editions of which were published in 1824 and 1840. He enjoyed the friendship of several noted European botanists, with whom he had an extended correspondence relative to botanical studies and discoveries. Between 1817 and 1821 he published in three volumes the "American Medical Botany," a work that commanded marked attention not only in this country, but also in Europe. He edited with notes Sir J. E. Smith's work on botany in 1814, was one of the committee of five selected in 1820 to form the "American Pharmacopœia," and is to be credited with the principle of the nomenclature of materia medica afterward adopted by the British colleges, which principle substituted a single for a double word whenever practicable. Mount Auburn Cemetery, the first garden cemetery established in the United States, was founded by him, and became the model after which all others in the country have been made. During a term of twenty years Dr. Bigelow was a physician of the Massachusetts General Hospital, and was Professor of Materia Medica and of Clinical Medicine in Harvard University. From 1816 to 1827 he held the Rumford Professorship in the same institution, and delivered lectures on the application of science to the useful arts. These lectures were published in a volume entitled "Elements of Technology," which work, enlarged and improved, was republished some years later with the title "The Useful Arts considered in Connection with the Applications of Science" (1849). At various times he published medical essays and treatises, in the production of which he was industrious and prolific without impairing the value of his work by its quantity. "Nature and Disease," a volume published in 1854, contained several of these essays. Notable among his papers was óne entitled "A Discourse on Self-Limited Disease," which was delivered as an address before the Massachusetts Medical Society in 1835, and had a marked effect in modifying the practice of physicians. He was during many years the President of that Society, and was also President of the American Academy of Arts and Sciences. Retiring from the active practice of his profession some years ago, Dr. Bigelow gave much attention to the subject of education, and especially to the matter of establishing and developing technological schools. In an address "On the Limits of Education," delivered in 1865, before the Massachusetts Institute of Technology, he laid especial emphasis on the necessity of students devoting themselves to special technical branches of knowledge, rather than devoting time and strength to sub ects irrelevant to the particular vocations they are to follow.

BLAINE, JAMES GILLESPIE, an American statesman, born in Washington County, Pennsylvania, January 31, 1830, at Indian Hill Farm, the home of his maternal grandfather, Neal Gillespie. His great-grandfather, Colonel

Ephraim Blaine of Carlisle, Pennsylvania, was Commissary-General of the Revolutionary army from 1778 till the close of the struggle in 1783. Washington attributed the preservation of his troops from actual starvation during that terrible winter at Valley Forge mainly to the heroic and self-sacrificing efforts of Colonel Blaine. Mr. Blaine's father, born and reared in Carlisle, after an extended tour in Europe, South America, and the West Indies, returned and settled in Washington County about 1818, becoming one of the largest landed proprietors in western Pennsylvania. He took special pains to give his son a thorough intellectual training, but died before he was fully grown. At the age of eleven he was sent to school in Lancaster, Ohio, where he lived in the family of his relative, the Hon. Thomas Ewing, at that time Secretary of the Treasury. He graduated from Washington College in 1847, at the age of seventeen. Specially excelling in mathematics and Latin, he shared the first honor of his class with John O. Hervey, now Superintendent of Public Instruction at Wheeling, West Virginia. His college guardian was his uncle, the Hon. John H. Ewing, then a Representative in Congress from the Washington district of Pennsylvania. After graduating, Mr. Blaine taught for a while in Pennsylvania and Kentucky, wrote for the press, and studied law, but never practiced. He married Harriet Stanwood, a teacher from Massachusetts.

In 1853 he went to Maine, where he edited the "Portland Advertiser" and the "Kennebec Journal." He was chosen a member of the Maine Legislature in 1858, where he served four years, the last two as Speaker of the House. The late Governor Kent of Maine, speaking of Mr. Blaine's record in that State, says: "Almost from the day of his assuming editorial charge of the 'Kennebec Journal,' at the early age of twenty-three, Mr. Blaine sprang into a position of great influence in the politics and policy of Maine. At twenty-five he was a leading power in the councils of the Republican party, so recognized by Fessenden, Hamlin, and the two Morrills, and others then and still prominent in the State. Before he was twenty-nine he was chosen chairman of the Executive Committee of the Republican organization in Maine—a position he has held ever since, and from which he has practically shaped and directed every political campaign in the State, always leading his party to brilliant victory."

In 1862 Mr. Blaine was elected a Representative to the Thirty-eighth Congress, and served on the Committee on Post-Offices and Post-Roads. Reëlected to the Thirty-ninth Congress, he served on the Committee on Military Affairs, and the special Committee on the Death of President Lincoln, and as chairman of that on the War Debts of the Loyal States. Reëlected to the Fortieth Congress, he served on the Committees on Appropriations and Rules. Though entering very young, Mr.

Blaine always commanded the attention of the House, and before he had been three years a member he ranked with the highest as a debater. At the period of greatest anxiety and depression in the war, he delivered a speech on "The Ability of the American People to suppress the Rebellion," which has been cited for the great attention and commendation it received. While a member of the Post-Office Committee he took an active part in securing the system of postal cars now in general use. Throughout the period of reconstruction he was active and energetic in influencing legislation, and was especially prominent in shaping some of the most important features of the fourteenth amendment, particularly that relating to the basis of representation. The discussions on this great series of questions, in which Mr. Blaine figured largely, are among the most interesting and valuable in the history of the American Congress.

He was reëlected to the Forty-first Congress, and made Speaker of the House of Representatives, which position he also held during the Forty-second and Forty-third Congresses. It has been said that no man since Clay's speakership presided with such an absolute knowledge of the rules of the House, or with so great a mastery in the rapid, intelligent, and faithful discharge of business. His knowledge of parliamentary law was instinctive and complete, and his administration of it so fair that both sides of the House united at the close of each Congress in cordial thanks for his impartiality. Even more marked than his career as Speaker was Mr. Blaine's course in the House when he returned to the floor at the close of his speakership. His speeches during the debates on the proposition to remove the political disabilities of Jefferson Davis added greatly to his reputation as an orator and parliamentarian.

In June, 1876, Mr. Blaine was appointed by the Governor of Maine to fill the vacancy in the Senate caused by the resignation of Lot M. Morrill, appointed Secretary of the Treasury. On the meeting of the Legislature in January, 1877, he was promptly chosen not only for the remainder of the unexpired term, but for the full term ending March 4, 1883. In the Senate he has taken a prominent part in every important debate. Always a strong party man, he is now one of the recognized leaders on the Republican side.

Mr. Blaine is a man of good temper, with a certain intellectual vehemence that might sometimes be mistaken for anger, of strong physique, with wonderful powers of endurance and recuperation, and of great activity and industry. To these qualities, added to great personal magnetism and a remarkably tenacious memory, he owes his success in public life. In the recent political troubles in Maine his statesmanlike qualities proved sufficient for the emergency, saved the State from threatened violence, and carried the Republican party to success.

BOLIVIA (Repúblics de Bolivia). This republic, so rarely the scene of events of interest to the rest of the world, now emerges from obscurity and claims her share of the attention attracted by a war ranking among the most disastrous in its course, and likely to prove one of the most sterile in useful results, that have ever been waged on the Pacific coast of South America. A brief review of Bolivian statistics, and Bolivia's relations with the neighboring states, for some years past, will suffice to throw into conspicuous relief the true origin of the strife.

With an area (assuming the lowest estimate) of rather more than 500,000 square miles, and a population of 2,325,000,* Bolivia is nearly the equal of Peru in both respects, while she is slightly the superior of Chili in the second and four times her superior in the first respect. But in spite of the vastness of her territory, a large proportion of which comprises cultivable lands of unsurpassed fertility, and notwithstanding the richness and variety of her mineral products, she is commercially and industrially the inferior of both. Possessing but a few miles of seaboard, with two small ports accessible only over a narrow strip of desert wedged between her maritime neighbors, her landlocked position condemns her to the fatal necessity of carrying on through Peruvian territory and Peruvian ports the main bulk of her commerce, which thus becomes a tributary of the Peruvian Treasury. In the official returns last published, for 1875, but which are asserted to give figures far below the truth, the imports and exports were set down as of the total value of $5,750,000 respectively, for the most part exported through Peruvian ports—Arica, etc. The duties on the imports went to the Peruvian custom-houses, and to Bolivia was paid over the sum of $500,000, or little more than one third of the total amount collected, assuming the average rate of duties to have been 25 per cent.! But the official returns, as above suggested, have been pronounced incorrect by some writers, one of whom remarks substantially as follows: The subjoined table, from the "Tableau général du commerce de la France," exhibits the value of the Bolivian, Chilian, and Peruvian trade with the French Republic in 1876:

Bolivia....	Imports...................	$45,956
	Exports...................	635
Chili......	Imports...................	5,528,430
	Exports...................	6,492,008
Peru......	Imports...................	11,906,876
	Exports...................	4,094,908

These figures show a striking disproportion between the Chilian and Peruvian imports and those of Bolivia, although the population and the consumption of foreign commodities are nearly equal in the three republics. The cause of the discrepancy is to be found in the fact that Bolivia's purchases from Valparaiso and

Tacna, which constitute the great bulk of her foreign supplies, do not figure in the list of her imports. Conversely, the full value of her exports is not represented either, as they are transmitted through Peru and Chili, in payment of the merchandise received through these countries. From 1825 to 1840 the value of the silver purchased annually by the Banco Nacional, which was then very generally supposed to monopolize that metal, was from $2,000,000 to $2,500,000; but large quantities have always been exported secretly, the value of which there is no means of determining. Certain it is, however, that all the silver sent out of the country is in payment of imports. Ever since 1850 the yield of the silver mines has steadily increased, and it is now estimated at an annual value of not less than $10,000,000, exclusive of the product of the Caracoles mines. Gold, too, has at all times been exported on an extensive scale, but secretly. Yet, as nowhere in the republic is gold-mining systematically carried on, and as all the gold brought to market is in the shape of *pepitas* or nuggets, laid bare by descending torrents in the rainy season and gathered by the Indians, it is probable there has been no progressive increase of quantity, notwithstanding the increased necessities of the Indian population. Another important article of export is copper from the Corocoro mines, which, in spite of greatly reduced prices, continues to be extracted on account of its superior quality. Tin, though very abundant, is now almost wholly neglected. Merchants who have attentively studied this subject are of opinion that the aggregate value of the gold, copper, and tin at present exported is about $5,000,000 a year; which, with $10,000,000 for silver, constitutes an annual value of $15,000,000 for metal exports alone. The various branches of agricultural industry in Bolivia are for the most part limited by the demand for home consumption. The great Yungas valleys of the east, watered by the snow-covered Cordilleras, extending from the giant peak of Illimani to that of Sorata (a distance of some 300 miles), and with a climate no less favorable than that of tropical Brazil, yield coffee and cacao of excellent quality. Indeed, the cacao is said to be superior to that of Guayaquil; and the *quina* or calisaya-bark of the same region is esteemed for the strength and general superiority of its sulphates. In the absence of necessary data, it would be rash to form an estimate of the quantity exported of these commodities; but it is evidently very much smaller than it might be with improved means of transportation. The sugar-cane is cultivated in the valleys above referred to, and in that of Santa Cruz; but the sugar and molasses manufactured do not exceed the home requirements. Cereals, leguminous plants, and almost every variety of fruits peculiar to the tropical and temperate zones, are abundant and cheap, but, like the products above enumerated, are never sent

---

* For the territorial division, area, population, etc., see "Annual Cyclopædia" for 1872 and 1878.

out of the country, owing to the lack of easy means of communication with the coast. In the event of persistent droughts, such as those of 1877 and 1878, especially that of the latter year, famine spreads desolation over such localities as, by the difficulties of transport, are cut off from immediate relief. Of all Bolivian products, that most assiduously cultivated by the Indians is the coca-shrub (*Erythroxylon coca*), the leaves of which they use as the Asiatics use betel. The annual sales of this article at La Paz, the seat of government of the republic, vary in amount from $4,000,000 to $5,000,000. Cattle, sheep, horses, and mules are abundant, the last being the chief animals of burden on the western slopes of the Andes; while in the elevated regions there are great numbers of llamas, vicuñas, guanacos, and alpacas (varieties of what may be termed the American camel), with the hair of all of which the Indians manufacture hats, fine cloths, etc.

Notwithstanding the absence of positive statistics, as the Bolivian imports are known to consist mainly of manufactured goods, an approximate idea of their *minimum* values may be arrived at thus: Let the population be regarded as made up of—(1), 325,000 Indians in a state of savagery, and not submissive to the laws of the land; (2), 1,000,000 civilized Indians; (3), 500,000 whites, forming the first or upper class; and (4), 500,000 mestizos, constituting the second class. The civilized Indians, the most useful element of Bolivian society, being for the most part land-owners, farmers, cattle-rearers, etc.,—in fine, the factors of the nascent industries of the country—may, in order to avoid possible exaggerations, be excluded from the proposed estimate. Nevertheless, these Indians, besides their usual dress, which is exclusively of home manufacture, make liberal expenditures on gala-dress for their carnival and other feasts, in the regular observance of which they yield to none. If, then, the moderate sum of thirty dollars be assumed as the yearly outlay of the 1,000,000 individuals of the first and second classes (500,000 whites and 500,000 mestizos), for dress and such other necessaries or luxuries as are not produced in the republic—church ornaments, jewelry, watches and clocks, house ornaments, fancy wares, stationery, books, school supplies, musical instruments, hardware, cutlery, wrought and cast iron, agricultural and mining implements, machinery, etc., etc.—the total value of the foreign merchandise annually imported into Bolivia will be $30,000,000. And it may be affirmed, without fear of challenge, that this estimate is far below reality. Now, if the imports amount to $30,000,000, and two millions be assigned as the value of merchandise free of duty, the custom-house duties on the remaining twenty-eight millions should be, according to the Bolivian tariff, from six to seven millions, of which perhaps not one million goes into the Government Treasury! Do the Peruvian cus-

tom-houses and smuggling on the Bolivian coast and frontiers absorb the rest?

The following table shows the national revenue and expenditures as estimated in the budget (voted in 1872) for the fiscal year 1873–'74, since which time no official statement of the finances has been published:

REVENUE.

Customs (duties on imports):		
Arica	$405,000	
Cobija*	250,000	
		$655,000
Mint, export duty on silver		193,696
Guano sales		800,000
Stamped paper		27,268
Import duty on cattle (from the Argentine Republic)		20,880
Colonel Church's loan		650,000
Indian contribution		686,807
Sundries		896,428
Total		$2,929,574

EXPENDITURES.

Ministry of the Interior	$597,458
Ministry of Foreign Affairs	158,940
Ministry of Finance (inclusive of home debt)	2,072,018
Ministry of Justice and Public Worship	399,167
Ministry of War	1,126,916
Expenditures extraordinary	156,010
Total	$4,505,504
Deficit	$1,575,930

This deficit would, of course, be reduced somewhat by the proceeds of the sale of public lands at Mejillones, in the coast region, export duties on silver from the coast mines, and other sources of revenue, the yield of which could not be accurately estimated.

The national debt amounted in June, 1875, to £3,400,000 ($17,000,000), including an item —Colonel Church's loan of £1,700,000, negotiated in London in 1872—which for some years past has been a subject of angry debate in British financial circles, and the details of which are as follows: The loan is designated as the "Bolivian six per cent. of 1872"; the nominal amount was £1,700,000; the issue price, 68; interest and sinking fund, 8 per cent. per annum; and the number of years to run, twenty-four. The net produce† to the borrower was set down at £1,156,000; the annual charge throughout at £136,000; and the total cost to borrower, including capital repaid at redemption, at £3,235,440. The proceeds of the loan were to be applied to the construction of railways.

The regulation strength of the army in time of peace is 3,000, as follows: 8 generals, 1,012 subaltern officers, and 2,000 men! The annual cost of this force is about $2,000,000, or two thirds of the revenue. After the commencement of the war, the number was almost immediately raised to about 20,000 men, neither raw levies nor disciplined soldiers, but men accustomed to fighting and the use of arms.

Bolivia, formerly called the Presidency of Charcas, and afterward Upper Peru, formed from 1767 a part of the viceroyalty of Buenos

---

* Port of entry on the Bolivian coast.
† See "Annual Cyclopædia" for 1875.

Ayres and was erected into an independent state in 1825, taking the name it still bears, in honor of Simon Bolivar.

The signal victory gained over the Spaniards by Bolivar and Sucre at the battle of Ayacucho in December, 1824, proved the death-blow to Spanish sway in America; and the Spanish-American countries, after they had achieved their independence, retained their former boundaries unchanged.

The Chilians urge the point, disputed by the Bolivians, that during the colonial period the Chilian territory extended northward to latitude 23° south, or at least up to the bay of Mejillones, over a portion of the desert of Atacama; and in support of their claim they evoke the testimony of royal letters patent, the jurisdiction exercised by Chili up to the bay just named, the result of a special survey of the coast under the auspices of the Spanish Government, and lastly a clause of a Bolivian President's message to Congress in which Cobija is mentioned as the only port of Bolivia, and in need of improvement. The fact is, Chili remained until 1842 in peaceful possession of the territory which is the prize and in part the scene of the present strife. In that year attention appears to have been for the first time directed, by the President of Chili, to the Atacama Desert as a possible source of national wealth, and then commenced the discussion which has ended in an appeal to arms. Guano discoveries on the barren strip of coast, and the expropriation by the Government of Chili of the deposits whose location had been ascertained by a commission appointed by that Government, brought into the field the Bolivian Government as a claimant for what was supposed to be a rich prize. However, Chili seems to have exercised jurisdiction over the guano deposits at Mejillones, Angama, Santa Maria, and other points on the desert coast, inasmuch as from the year 1842 to 1857, 113 vessels of various nations loaded guano at those places under licenses obtained from the Chilian port ·of Valparaiso. No allusion, it would seem, has been made to any grant of similar licenses from the Bolivian port of Cobija. The discussion as to the proprietorship of the desert was carried on from 1842 until 1864, when the hostile visits of a Spanish fleet to the coast had the effect of uniting the Republics of Chili, Bolivia, and Peru to oppose a common enemy. Under the influence of this feeling the first two republics in 1866 made mutual concessions of their respective rights and privileges, in a treaty of limits establishing the boundary-line at 24° south, but fixing a common zone between latitude 23° and 25° south wherein both countries should share ·equally in customs receipts and export duties on minerals. A transcript of this treaty and of others of more recent date will be found at the end of this article. It is contended on behalf of Chili that Bolivia from the first disregarded the obligations she had contracted; set aside the arrangement for a

partition of revenues; refused permission to the Chilian inspectors to perform their duty; and that the general course she pursued was rather that of a sole than of a joint owner of the territory.

In the mean time it had been discovered that the barren strip of soil was rich, not only in guano, but in metallic and other mineral wealth, and especially in vast deposits of nitrate of soda. The value of this mineral as an agricultural manure is now universally recognized. Almost exclusively through Chilian capital and enterprise, the trade in it soon became important; and Peru, which has rich deposits of her own, was jealous of the menaced competition of the Chilian companies with her nitrate and guano trade. "Accordingly," says an English writer, "the Peruvian Government, which has recently acquired a monopoly of this trade by grievous oppression of the private persons who owned deposits in Peru, and which has been able in consequence to extort enormous prices from foreign customers, is believed to have persuaded Bolivia to follow the same course, in defiance of treaty obligations, against the Chilians." In less than ten years after signing the treaty of 1866, the conduct of Bolivia had become such as to render it necessary for the Government of Chili, in defense of her citizens and their properties, either to negotiate a new treaty or reassert former boundaries. Chili chose the former course, and the treaty of August, 1874, was signed and duly ratified. This treaty abolished the neutral zone, and gave to Bolivia all export and customs dues previously agreed upon except those arising from the sale of guano, freedom from Chilian inspection, etc. The stipulations on behalf of Chili were in protection of her industry. They provided that, for a space of twenty-five years, Chilian capitalists working mines should not be subjected to any increase of export duty, nor in their persons, capital, or industries, to other imposts or any nature whatsoever than those already existing at the time of the treaty. Since then, millions of Chilian capital have been invested in mining and the manufacture of nitrate on this formerly unproductive coast, causing three important towns to be built, nine tenths of the inhabitants of which are Chilians.

The respective rights of the two republics being thus settled by a new treaty (that of 1874), which, while securing the possession of the territory to the Bolivians, protected the interests of the Chilians as capitalists and workers of the mineral wealth of the country, friendly relations were reëstablished; but they did not prove enduring. The Bolivian Government began last year to trench upon these rights, and especially to subject Chilian companies concerned in the nitrate trade to new and heavy burdens (an export duty of 10 cents per quintal, February, 1878), in contravention of express treaty stipulations. It is contended that the influence of the Peruvian Government was the moving power in this "unwise and un-just enterprise." It was believed that Chili, unprepared for military efforts, and afraid of impairing her sound financial position, would submit to any wrongs rather than go to war. Peru had made her guano and nitrate trades a government monopoly, and the Peruvians cal-culated that, if the Chilian competition could be suppressed by the arbitrary measures of the Bolivian Government, the price of commodities for which there was a constant demand among European and American agriculturists might be indefinitely raised. When the Santiago Gov-ernment protested, the crushing export duty was abolished, but the Chilian Company's prop-erty was declared confiscated to the state. If this policy had been successful, the Peruvian and Bolivian Governments would have shared between them a monopoly of guano and nitrate beyond the reach of any rivalry. There was reason to hope at one time that the offer of the Chilian Government to refer the matter to an impartial arbitration might have been accept-ed. But Peruvian influence appears to have been too strong for Bolivia, and this offer was refused. The rejoinder of Chili was swift and decisive. On February 12th, a day celebrated as the anniversary of the Chilian victory over Spanish domination at Chacabuco in 1817, public meetings denounced the act of Bolivia as one of bad faith and spoliation, and de-manded redress by arms. Already, however, the Chilian Government had recalled its Minis-ter and sent forward both ships and troops to the scene. The ironclads Admiral Cochrane and Bernardo O'Higgins hurried to join their mate in Antofogasta harbor, and with them went a small force of Chilian regulars, who on February 14th landed and occupied the town without firing a gun. The next day the O'Hig-gins took possession of the port of Mejillones, while the land forces successively occupied Cara-coles, Cobija, Calama, and Tocapilla. In a word, the entire coast-line was blockaded by Chilian vessels and garrisoned by Chilian troops. Thus Chili's energy had won the first move in the campaign, in a complete mastery of the dis-puted territory. Reenforcements went for-ward, and the Chilian residents and workmen in the nitrate and mining districts were also organized, equipped, and drilled. Chilian pos-tal and customs regulations and general laws were introduced into Antofagasta, two Chilian newspapers were founded, military engineers planned permanent fortifications, and the Chi-lians evidently meant to stay. It would seem as if the Government of Santiago had resolved to accept the nullification of the treaty of 1874 which Bolivia attempted, and to hold by force the territory which Chili originally claimed. A loan of a million and a quarter and an issue of inconvertible paper were sanctioned at once by the Chilian Chambers.

No immediate resistance was offered by Bo-livia, whose government was evidently await-ing the result of a proposed Peruvian media-tion. In the mean time President Daza issued two proclamations: one calling the nation to arms to resist the invader, and the other de-claring an amnesty for all political offenders, since at the present crisis private quarrels should be forgotten in the effort to regain the territory arbitrarily occupied by Chili. Public enthusiasm was intense. The wealthy citizens of La Paz offered to the Government, as a war contribution, 50 per cent. of their revenues; but Daza, declining such a munificent gift, re-stricted his acceptance to 10 per cent. of the sum offered, stating that until it was known whether Bolivian troops would be allowed to pass over Peruvian soil, and to make use of Peruvian railways, he could not estimate the cost of the campaign.

The following decree was issued shortly after the proclamations just referred to:

Hilarion Daza, President of the Republic of Bolivia, considering that the Government of Chili has invaded *de facto* the national territory, without observing the rules of international law or the practice of civilized nations, violently expelling the authorities and Bo-livian citizens resident in the department of Cobija; that the Government of Bolivia finds itself in duty bound to adopt the energetic measures which the grav-ity of the situation demands, without departing, how-ever, from the principles recognized by the rights of nations;

I decree:

ARTICLE I. All trade and communication with the Republic of Chili is prohibited during the continuance of the war undertaken by that republic against Bo-livia.

ART. II. The Chilians resident in Bolivian territory must disoccupy it within the term of ten days from the date of the notification which shall be made them by the local political authority; they being at liberty to take with them their private papers, their baggage, and articles of personal use.

ART. III. The expulsion ordered in the previous ar-ticle can only be suspended for the term which should be strictly indispensable on account of sickness or other serious impediment in the judgment of the au-thorities.

ART. IV. The respective authorities will proceed, as a war measure, to embargo the fixed and movable property belonging to Chilian subjects within the ter-ritory of the repub-ic, wi the exception of the ob-jects designated in Art. IIth Th*e mining property be-longing to Chilians, or in which there should be share-holders of that nationality, may continue to be worked under the charge of an administrator appointed by the authorities, or with the intervention of a representa-tive of the Government, as they may think most de-sirable.

ART. V. The net proceeds of the mining property belonging to Chilians, or of shares belonging to the same, shall be deposited in the national Treasury.

ART. VI. The embargo ordered by this decree will be changed to final confiscation, should the nature of the hostilities engaged in by the Chilian forces require an energetic retaliation on the part of Bolivia.

ART. VII. All transfers of Chilian interests made at a later date than the 8th of November last, on which date the Chilian Government declared the treaty of 1874 annulled, will be ignored; and any contract which should have been agreed upon in this respect will be considered void.

Given in the city of La Paz, the 1st day of March, 1879.

(Signed) H. DAZA.

The mediatory intervention of Peru led only to the discovery by the Santiago Government of a secret treaty of alliance existing between Peru and Bolivia, and the dismissal of the Peruvian Envoy, Don José Antonio de Lavalle, a prominent diplomatist, as set forth in the following note to the latter:

MINISTRY OF FOREIGN AFFAIRS, }
SANTIAGO, *April* 2, 1879. }

SIR: The reply given to the Chilian Envoy in Lima a few days ago, by your Government, that it could not observe neutrality in our present conflict with Bolivia, because there existed a treaty of defensive alliance between them—which is the same that you read to me in the conference held on the 31st ult.—has forced this Government to the conclusion that it is impossible to maintain friendly relations with Peru.

Considering the assurance yo gave me in the first conference we held on the 17th ult., in reply to my interrogation whether such treaty existed or not, that you had no knowledge of it, that you believed it had no existence, and that it could not have been approved by the Peruvian Congress of 1873 (when it was said to have been approved), and much less in the succeeding years, when you formed part of the diplomatic commission—considering this assurance, I repeat, my Government sees that yours, as well as yourself, in denying this treaty, have placed yourselves in an exceedingly irregular position.

My Government is surprised to learn that that of Peru projected and signed that treaty at the time that it professed sentiments of cordial friendship toward Chili.

To this secret transaction, in which the strictest reserve was stipulated, the Government of Chili replies with the fullest frankness, declaring that its relations with that of Peru are broken, and that it considers it belligerent, in virtue of the authority to that effect received to-day from the high authorities of the state.

In forwarding you your passports I have to assure you that the proper orders have been issued in order that you and the *personnel* of the permanent Legation of Peru may receive all due consideration and facility in returning to your country.

With sentiments of distinguished consideration, etc.,
ALEJANDRO FIERRO.

On April 6th Chili declared war against Peru. Owing to the occurrence of untoward events in the course of the month of December, no mention has hitherto been made of the Chief Magistrate or of his Cabinet. Previous to the commencement of hostilities, the President was General Hilarion Daza (installed on May 4, 1876), and the Ministers were: Interior and Foreign affairs, Sr. P. T. de Guerra; War and Finance, Sr. E. D. Medina; Justice, Public Worship, and Public Instruction, Sr. J. Mendez. After the enthusiasm with which the Bolivians had hailed the alliance with Peru as the earnest of prompt vindication of their rights, real or imagined, and the repulse of the invader of their soil, repeated reverses of the allied forces brought a change in the popular sentiment. Reflection and suspicion, according to report, grew in time into the conviction that the people's interests had been jeopardized by an appeal to arms in the interest of a designing few; and the general discontent was ultimately manifested in a revolution. The President, still at the theatre of war, was deposed, and found it necessary to seek safety in flight from the country. General Daza, on setting out at the head of his troops, had left the government in charge of Señor Guerra, the Minister of Foreign Affairs, etc.; but on the death of Guerra, in Sep-

tember, Don Serapio Reyes de Ortiz, secretary to Daza, was sent to form a new Cabinet with the aid of the new Minister of War, General O. D. Tofré. It was rumored, however, that Reyes had placed himself at the head of the revolutionary movement and seized the reins of government.

A narration of the main features and events of the war will be found in the article PERU. "If," says the British writer before quoted, "we accept, as we may at least provisionally, the Chilian version of the events which led to the war, it can hardly be disputed that Chili had a legitimate *casus belli* against Bolivia, if not directly against Peru. But it is another question how far it was wise of her to imperil her merited reputation and her comparative prosperity for the chance of punishing the wrong-doers."

We give below translations of the more important stipulations of the Chilo-Bolivian boundary treaties of 1866 and 1874:

ARTICLE I. The boundary-line between Bolivia and Chili, in the desert of Atacama, shall be the parallel of latitude 24° south, from the Pacific coast to the eastern limits of Chili; so that Chili on the south and Bolivia on the north shall enjoy possession and dominion of the territory extending to said parallel of latitude 24° south, and may exercise over such territory all acts of jurisdiction and sovereignty belonging properly to the "lord of the soil." The exact establishment of the boundary between the two countries shall be made by a commission of competent judges, half of whom shall be appointed by each of the high contracting parties. After the boundary-line shall be determined, it shall be indicated by visible and permanent signals, the expense of which shall be borne pro rata by the Governments of Chili and Bolivia.

ART. II. Notwithstanding the territorial division stipulated in the previous article, the Republics of Chili and Bolivia shall share in equal proportions the products of the guano deposits discovered in Mejillones, and of those which may be discovered in the territories included between the 23d and 25th parallels of south latitude, *as well as the export duties which may be collected on the minerals* extracted from the territory just mentioned.

ART. III. The Republic of Bolivia binds itself to open the bay and port of Mejillones, establishing there a custom-house, with the number of employees necessary to the development of industry and commerce. This custom-house shall be the only fiscal office which shall have the right to receive the products of guano deposits and export duties on metals mentioned in the preceding article. The Government of Chili may appoint one or more fiscal employees, who, invested with full powers of inspection, etc., may examine the records of the receipts at the said custom-house of Mejillones, and receive from the said custom-house directly, and in quarterly installments, or in any other manner which may be stipulated by both states, the share of proceeds pertaining to Chili as expressed in Art. II. The Government of Bolivia shall enjoy the same rights should Chili establish a fiscal office on the territory contained within the parallels of latitude 24° and 25°, for the collection of duties, etc., as stipulated in the foregoing article.

ART. IV. The products from the territory comprised within the 24th and 25th parallels of south latitude, and which may be exported through Mejillones, shall be free of duty. The same exemption shall be extended to the natural products of Chili which may be imported through the same port.

ART. V. The system of working, or the sale of guano, and the export duties on minerals, as indicated in Art. II. of this compact, shall be determined conjointly by the high contracting parties, either by means of special conventions or otherwise, as they may deem most convenient.

ART. VI. The contracting powers bind themselves not to sell or transfer to any other state, company, or individual their rights to possession or dominion over the territory which they share or divide between themselves in consequence of this treaty. In case either of them shall desire to make such sale or transfer, the purchaser can be none but the other contracting party.

ART. VII. In view of the damage accrued, as is well known, from the boundary question between Bolivia and Chili to the parties who, in company, first seriously began the working of the guano deposits of Mejillones, and whose labors were suspended by order of the Chilian authorities, on the 17th of February, 1863, the high contracting parties bind themselves in equity to pay to said parties an indemnity of $80,000,* to be appropriated at the rate of 10 per cent. from the surplus revenues derived from the custom-house at Mejillones.

ART. VIII. The present treaty shall be ratified, and ratifications exchanged at the city of La Paz, in Bolivia, or at Santiago de Chili, within the term of forty days, or sooner if possible.

In testimony of which the undersigned Plenipotentiaries of the Republics of Chili and Bolivia have signed the present treaty, and affixed their respective seals, in Santiago, on the 10th day of the month of August, A. D. 1866.

(L. S.)   ALVARO COVARRUBIAS.
(L. S.)   JUAN R. MUÑOZ CABRERA.

TREATY OF AUGUST 6, 1874.

ARTICLE I. The boundary-line between the Republics of Chili and Bolivia shall be at the parallel of latitude 24° south, from the sea to the Cordillera of the Andes, at the watershed.

ART. II. For the interpretation of this treaty the parallels 23° and 24° fixed by the Commissioners Pissis and Mujia, as recorded in the minutes of February 8, 1870, shall be considered as permanent.

Should any doubts as to the true and exact situation of the Caracoles mining district, or of any other mining region, arise from their being considered beyond the zone comprised between 23° and 24° south latitude, their situation shall be determined by two experts appointed, one by each of the two contracting parties, and the experts shall, in their turn, in case of

discord, appoint a third party; and, should these not be able to agree as to the third party, the appointment shall be made by his Majesty the Emperor of Brazil. So long as no proof shall appear in opposition to this determination, it shall be understood, as heretofore, that that mining district is comprised between the parallels indicated.

ART. III. The guano deposits existing, or which may hereafter be discovered, within the territory mentioned in Art. II., shall be shared in equal proportions by Bolivia and Chili, and the system of working, management, and sale be effected by common arrangement between the Governments of the two republics, as heretofore.

ART. IV. The export duties which may be levied upon minerals worked within the zone mentioned in the preceding article shall not exceed the rates which at present collected, and Chilian residents, their industries and capital shall not be subject to taxes other than now exist. The stipulation contained in this article shall be enforced for the term of twenty-five years.

ART. V. The natural products of Chili, which may be imported through the Bolivian coast comprised between parallels 23° and 24° shall not be subject to any taxes or duties whatever; and reciprocally the same exception is extended to the natural products of Bolivia which may be imported on the Chilian coast between parallels 24° and 25°.

ART. VI. The Republic of Bolivia binds herself to open the ports of Mejillones and Antofagasta, as the chief ports on her seaboard.

ART. VII. The treaty of August 10, 1866, is hereby annulled in all its parts.

(Here follow the signatures of Mariano Baptista, Bolivian Plenipotentiary, and Carlos Walker Martinez, Chilian Plenipotentiary.)

BONAPARTE. The Bonaparte family lost in 1879 two of its prominent members—the Prince Imperial, who was the head of the family and claimant to the throne of France, and Madame Bonaparte-Patterson, the first wife of King Jerome Bonaparte. The following genealogical table shows the relationship of these two members of the family, as well as such others as still occupy a high position:

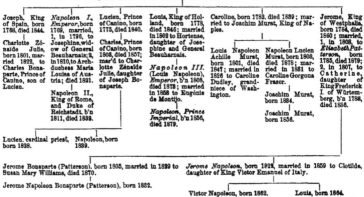

Charles Bonaparte, born 1746, married to Marie Lætitia Ramolino in 1764, died 1785.

Joseph, King of Spain, born 1768, died 1844.	Napoleon I., Emperor, born 1769, married, 1, in 1796, to Josephine, widow of General Beauharnais; 2, in 1810, to Archduchess Maria Louisa of Austria; died 1821.	Lucien, Prince of Canino, born 1775, died 1840.	Louis, King of Holland, born 1778, died 1846; married daughter of Josephine and General Beauharnais.	Caroline, born 1782, died 1839; married to Joachim Murat, King of Naples.	Jerome, King of Westphalia, born 1784, died 1860; married, 1, in 1803, to Elizabeth Patterson, born 1785, died 1879; 2, in 1807, to Catherine, daughter of King Frederick I. of Würtemberg, b'n 1783, died 1836.
Charlotte Zénaïde Julie, born 1801, married 1822, to Charles Bonaparte, Prince of Canino, son of Lucien.		Charles, Prince of Canino, born 1803, died 1857; mar'd to Charlotte Zénaïde Julie, daughter of Joseph Bonaparte.	Napoleon III. (Louis Napoleon), Emperor, b'n 1808, died 1873; married in 1853 to Eugénie de Montijo.	Louis Napoleon Achille Murat, born 1801, died 1847; married in 1826 to Caroline Dudley, grandniece of Washington.	Napoleon Lucien Murat, born 1803, died 1878; married in 1831 to Caroline Gorgona Fraser.
	Napoleon II., King of Rome, and Duke of Reichstadt, b'n 1811, died 1832.		Napoleon, Prince Imperial, b'n 1856, died 1879.	Joachim Murat, born 1834.	Joachim Murat, born 1856.
Lucien, cardinal priest, born 1828.	Napoleon, born 1839.				

Jerome Bonaparte (Patterson), born 1805, married in 1829 to Susan Mary Williams, died 1870.

Jerome Napoleon Bonaparte (Patterson), born 1832.

Jerome Napoleon, born 1829, married in 1859 to Clotilde, daughter of King Victor Emanuel of Italy.

Victor Napoleon, born 1862.   Louis, born 1864.

* That is to say, $40,000 each. Chili's moiety was promptly paid, while that of Bolivia, after various subterfuges and delays, is now repudiated by the Bolivian Government on the plea of non-liability in consequence of the annulment of the treaty by which the indemnity was stipulated.

BONAPARTE, Mrs. ELIZABETH PATTERSON, was born in Baltimore in 1785. She was of Scotch-Irish descent. Her father, William Patterson, emigrated from Ulster to America when quite a lad. He pushed his way steadily upward, became the owner of a line of clipper ships, and, by shrewdness and a steady eye to his own interests, ended by amassing a fortune. He then improved his social position by marriage. His wife was the daughter of a retired officer in the British army, and sister of General Samuel Smith, who served with distinction during the Revolutionary War, and was twenty-three years United States Senator from Maryland. Mr. Patterson writes of himself, that from early life he "believed and practiced that money and merit are the only sure and certain roads to respectability and consequence." Another of his maxims is that "every citizen should contribute more or less to the good of society, when he can do it without too much loss or inconvenience to himself." It is not surprising that he reached the height of his ambition, and was, "Charles Carroll of Carrollton only excepted, the wealthiest citizen of Maryland." His daughter Elizabeth inherited no small share of his characteristics. At the age of ten she is said to have known by heart the maxims of La Rochefoucauld, in addition to those which had been instilled into her by her parent. Her favorite poem was Young's "Night Thoughts." Thus accomplished, Elizabeth Patterson reached womanhood. She is described as tall and graceful, fair of face, with dark hair and eyes. Her contemporaries agree in ascribing to her charms of person and mind of which in later days not a vestige remained. Fully aware of her own advantages, she informs us that she began life with the intention of using them for her own advancement.

In the autumn of 1803 Captain Jerome Bonaparte arrived at New York in command of a French frigate, returning home after a cruise in the West Indies. He journeyed to Baltimore to visit Captain Barney, who had formerly served with him in the French navy. The brother of the First Consul was fêted everywhere. At a ball at the house of Samuel Chase, a signer of the Declaration of Independence, the handsome young officer was introduced to Miss Patterson. She was in the first freshness of her beauty, eighteen years of age. He was a few months her senior. They were mutually pleased. During a dance her long hair became entangled in his chain, which the young couple willingly accepted as prophetic of their fate. Mr. Patterson foresaw that his daughter's marriage with a youth with such brilliant prospects would prove distasteful to the First Consul, and forbade the courtship. Elizabeth proving recalcitrant, he sent her into Virginia. They contrived to correspond, and in a short time she reappeared on the scene of her triumph. They became engaged, and Jerome went so far as to procure a marriage license. Their acquaintance was then only four weeks old. Mr. Patterson represented to his daughter the difficulties before her, but she insisted that she "would rather be the wife of Jerome Bonaparte for an hour than the wife of any other man for life." The match was postponed to December 24, 1803, when Jerome would have passed his nineteenth birthday. All legal formalities were carefully complied with. The contract was drawn up by Alexander Dallas, afterward Secretary of the Treasury. The Vice-Consul of France, the Mayor of Baltimore, and many other dignitaries witnessed the ceremony, which was solemnized with great pomp in the Cathedral by the Most Rev. John Carroll, Archbishop of Baltimore.

In order to impress the First Consul with the respectability of the family and the validity of the marriage, letters were procured from Thomas Jefferson, President of the United States, and from the Secretary of State. The Hon. Robert Livingston, Ambassador to France, agreed to present the affair in its most favorable light. Robert Patterson, brother of the bride, who was then traveling in Europe, was ordered to Paris by his father to advocate his sister's interests. His personal appearance, good manners, and good sense produced a pleasing impression on the Bonaparte family. Lucien, in particular, told him that the marriage was approved by Madame Lætitia, and that he and all his brothers except Napoleon would cordially receive Jerome's wife as a member of their family. Joseph and Lucien advised Jerome to become an American citizen, and took steps to procure him a provision enabling him to live there in accordance with his rank. From first to last Napoleon remained obdurate. The young couple were in New York waiting to embark for France, when the will of their august brother was made clear to them by the following order, transmitted by Dacres, then Minister of State: "Pichon, the French consul-general in New York, is instructed to withhold Jerome's supplies. The commanders of French vessels are prohibited from receiving on board the young person to whom he has attached himself." Accompanying this was an enactment of the French Senate: "By an act of the 11th Ventose prohibition is made to all the civil officers of the Empire to receive on their registers the transcription of the act of celebration of a pretended marriage that Jerome Bonaparte has contracted in a foreign country during his minority, without the consent of his mother, and without previous publication in his native land." At the same time Jerome received a message from his brother to the effect that if he left the "young person" in America, his youthful indiscretion would be forgiven; if he brought her with him, she should not put a foot on French territory. Undismayed, they tried to embark on a French man-of-war, but British cruisers outside detained it in New

York harbor. They next took passage on an American vessel, which was wrecked off the Delaware coast, the passengers narrowly escaping with their lives. "Mme. Bonaparte," says the narrative, "was the first person who jumped into the boat." Finally they sailed in March, 1805, on one of Mr. Patterson's ships. They reached Lisbon, and found a French frigate there to prevent her landing. By the suggestion of Madame Mère, seconded by the advice of Mr. Patterson, Jerome left his young wife, and went to Paris to plead her cause with the Emperor, and be won over by him. This separation proved final. The vessel proceeded to Amsterdam. At the mouth of the Texel two men-of-war awaited her. The Continent was forbidden ground to Elizabeth Bonaparte, and she was forced to seek an asylum in England. Pitt sent a regiment to Dover to prevent mischief, so great was the multitude that thronged thither to witness her landing. A few days later her son, Jerome Napoleon Bonaparte, was born, July 7, 1805, at Camberwell. Here she continued to reside, constantly receiving messages and letters from Jerome, protesting his fidelity and his undying affection for her and his infant son. He was doubtless sincere at that moment, being still hopeful of the Emperor's consent. Napoleon applied to Pius VII. to dissolve the marriage, which the Pontiff steadfastly refused. The decree of divorce was passed by the imperial Council of State. He wrote to Jerome: "Your marriage is null both in a religious and legal point of view. I will never acknowledge it. Write to Miss Patterson that it is not possible to give things another turn. On condition of her going to America, I will allow her a pension during her life of sixty thousand francs a year, provided she does not take the name of my family." Napoleon feigned to consider her residence in England as a special offense. Madame Bonaparte consented to return to America, hoping thus to conciliate her imperial brother-in-law. When Jerome, after vexatious delays, was admitted to Napoleon's presence, he upbraided him rudely for his folly, and concluded: "As for your affair with your little girl, I do not regard it." As a reward for his desertion, Jerome was created a Prince of the Empire, and was promoted Admiral. He received subsequently the rank of general. In 1806 he was made by the Senate successor to the imperial throne in the event of Napoleon leaving no male heir. On the 12th of August, 1807, he married Catherine Frederica, Princess of Würtemburg. By his second marriage he had three children, of whom two survive, the Princess Mathilde Demidoff, and the youngest son, Prince Napoleon, dynastic heir to the Prince Imperial.

Jerome's marriage dispelled the illusions of Elizabeth Patterson. A cynical and disappointed woman, she saw herself condemned to what she termed her "Baltimore obscurity." She loathed her native city so that she says that when residence there seemed the sole alternative she determined to commit suicide, but her courage failed. In 1817 she sailed for Europe, and remained abroad for seven years. Business considerations inducing her to return to Baltimore, she bewailed the time she was forced to spend in a country where "there is. no court, no nobility, no fit associates" for her. Although feeling and expressing an unbounded contempt for the worthless man who abandoned her, she was ever a passionate adherent of Bonapartism. She employed every means to prove the legality of her marriage and the legitimacy of her son. When Napoleon III. mounted the throne a formal trial was granted her. Jerome, the father, was not ashamed to appeal to the Council of State to forbid "Jerome Patterson" to assume the name of Bonaparte. Nevertheless, the Council decreed that the son of Madame Elizabeth Patterson was entitled to the name of Bonaparte, although he could not be recognized as a memfler of the imperial family. After the death of Jerome she again brought suit for a share in his estate. In spite of complete documentary proof and the fact that the validity of her marriage had been sustained by the Church, all the zeal and eloquence of her advocate, Berryer, did not prevent an adverse decision, probably inspired by the Imperial Court. Her son was, however, formally recognized by official decree, that "Jerome Bonaparte was a legitimate child of France."

Ambition, which had been so cruelly nipped in her own case, was equally crushed when she endeavored to advance her son. He was recognized by Madame Mère, and petted by Pauline Borghese, who at one time declared him her heir. Mrs. Patterson bent all her energies to make a fit match for him. Her choice was one of Joseph Bonaparte's daughters. The young man preferred the life of an American citizen, which his mother despised. He chose for himself, and married Miss Williams of Baltimore. His mother wrote to Mr. Patterson on the subject: "I had endeavored to instill into him from the hour of his birth the opinion that he was much too high in birth and connection ever to marry an American woman. . . . I would rather die than marry any one in Baltimore. . . . As the woman has money, I shall not forbid a marriage which I never would have advised. . . . I hope most ardently that she will have no children." She goes on to say that she washes her hands of him and his affairs, that she regrets the economics practiced by her to increase his wealth, and that henceforth she will double her expenditures. But the love of money was too strong for her, and she never carried out this threat. Her letters are full of moans over the expenses of her foreign journeys. She lived and died in a boarding-house, and her expenses did not reach two thousand a year, when her income exceeded one hundred thousand dollars. Her father, with whom she was ever at variance, threatened to disinherit her. In his will he asserts: "The conduct of my daughter Betsey has through life been so disobedient that in no instance has she ever consulted my opinions or feelings." Therefore he refused to give her an equal share in his estate, but he relented so far as to bequeath her for life nine houses in Baltimore. The rapid rise in rents and her penurious habits enabled her to accumulate property estimated at a million and a half. Her jewels were of considerable value. She never parted with her old dresses, and was fond of exhibiting them and descanting on the scenes where she had worn them, and the compliments she had received. She passed many winters in Florence, and counted with infinite pride many royal and distinguished personages among her acquaintance. After their tender parting at Lisbon in 1805, Jerome and Elizabeth saw each other but once. One day in the gallery of the Pitti Palace the ex-King of Westphalia came suddenly upon his ex-wife. He evinced great embarrassment. Whispering to his Würtemburg princess, "There is my American wife," they turned rapidly away. The next morning their ci-devant royalties quitted Florence, leaving Mrs. Patterson in possession of the field. By birth she was a Protestant. She became an avowed free-thinker, but professed always "a great respect for the Roman Catholic belief as the religion of kings and princes."

As a beautiful girl who had married for love, as a wife of youth deserted at the bidding of a despot, there hung about her a certain romance which for a period made her a notability wherever she traveled abroad. It might have retained for her the sympathy of the world. Unfortunately her letters are an unconscious revelation of vanity, selfishness, and niggardliness naïvely displayed. She appears an adroit schemer, quite capable of capturing a thoughtless boy. Jerome almost escapes the scorn which his pitiful conduct merits. It is be regretted that their publication has been permitted. Mr. Patterson evinced a discretion worthy of imitation when he wrote to his daughter Betsey: "I have received your two letters. They have been seen or heard of by no person but myself, and to be candid with you I would have been ashamed to expose them to any one else."

At the downfall of the second empire and the death of Napoleon III., the hopes of this indomitable schemer revived. With the weight of ninety winters heavy upon her, she actively endeavored to put forward the claims of her grandson, Colonel Bonaparte, who had served with distinction in the French army. She prophesied that he would be called to the regency, perhaps to the imperial throne. The American Bonaparte needed only recognition as an "official" member of the family to stand next in succession to the Prince Imperial. This was the last flicker of that restless ambition which was doomed to be ever baffled.

She died in April, 1879, at the age of ninety-four. Mrs. Patterson survived her divorce nearly three quarters of a century. She was already eleven years of age when General Bonaparte first assumed command of the army in Italy. Had she lived a few weeks longer, she would have seen the death-blow of Bonapartism dealt by ignorant savages in Zululand.

BONAPARTE, NAPOLEON EUGÈNE LOUIS JEAN JOSEPH, Prince Imperial of France, born March 16, 1856, died June 1, 1879. The only son of the Emperor Napoleon III., he was born at the time when the Second Empire was at the height of its glory, and his birth was welcomed with the greatest demonstrations of joy. His christening at Notre Dame, on June 5th, was one of the most magnificent spectacles ever witnessed even in France. An English nurse was provided for the Prince, and he remained under her charge until his seventh birthday; so that he could speak English before he could his own tongue, and he always spoke it with remarkable fluency and a pure accent. All through his childhood and boyhood he had an inseparable companion in the young Louis Conneau, son of the Dr. Conneau who aided his father to escape from Ham; and his influence is said to have been highly beneficial to the Prince. The greatest attention was paid to his education, and under General Frossard he made good progress. He was a quiet mannered boy, naturally shy, and disposed to become more so by the diplomatic reserve continually inculcated upon him. He had from his childhood a considerable amount of shrewdness, and frequently said, "I always take off my hat to the Parisians, because they take off one's crown so easily when they are offended." When he was three years old he was placed on the roster of the Imperial Guard. At five he was promoted to a corporalship, was made a sergeant at seven, and wore his sub-lieutenant's epaulet for the first time when he started for the German war with his father. He was not fortunate, however, with his military experience. His appearance on the field brought upon him ridicule; his second military enterprise resulted in death. After the battle of Saarbrücken, the Emperor sent a dispatch to the Empress couched in the most extravagant terms, saying that the Prince had just received his baptism of fire, that the men had wept to see him so calm, and that he had·picked up a spent bullet which had fallen at his feet. After the overthrow of the Empire he accompanied his mother to England. There he entered the Royal Military Academy at Woolwich, where he acquitted himself with considerable distinction. At the final examination in 1875 he stood seventh in a class of thirty-four; and he was always regarded as having inherited, not the personal characteristics, but some of the military instincts of his family. A banquet was given in August, 1875, to a few of the older adherents of the Bonapartes, while the Empress and her son were enjoying a holiday at the castle of Arenenberg in Switzerland, and the young Prince addressed his friends with considerable tact and political ability in the following words: "Should the people some day recall me to power, I will force all honest men to rally round the Empire, by erasing from the French language the words *exile* and *proscription*. If it could only be known what lessons I have learned from the past, what resolutions I have drawn from experience of the events which have passed under my own eyes, it would be seen how well I understand that I must look backward only for instruction and example, but not for objects of vengeance or bitterness. A great people is not to be governed by hatred or revenge." When the British were defeated at the Cape, and reënforcements were sent out, the Prince resolved to join the expedition as a volunteer. His desire was considered and well discussed by those responsible for his actions, and it was decided that he should apply to the War Office for leave to serve in the army to which he had for a time belonged. His request was but partly complied with, and he went out, not as he had asked to do as a soldier, but as a spectator "to see as much as he could of the war." His own reasons he gave in the following letter, dated February 25th:

My dear M. Rouher : I am about to leave Europe, and my absence may continue for some months. I have too many faithful friends in France for me to remain silent as to the reasons for my departure. For eight years I have been England's guest. I completed my education in one of her military schools, and have kept up my connection with the British army by joining it, on several occasions, during its great manœuvres. The war Great Britain is now carrying on at the Cape of Good Hope has lately assumed a much more serious aspect than it had previously. I felt anxious to watch the operations, and I sail in two days.
In France, where, thank Heaven, party spirit has not extinguished the military spirit, people will comprehend that I am anxious to share the fatigues and dangers of those troops united and confident, my comrades. The time I shall devote in assisting in this struggle of civilization against barbarism will not be lost to me.
My thoughts, whether I am near or far, will constantly turn toward France. I shall watch the phases she will gradually pass through with interest and without anxiety, for I am convinced that God protects her!
I trust that during my absence the partisans of the imperial cause will remain united and confident, and will continue to hold before the country the spectacle of a party which, faithful to its doctrines, remains constantly animated by the most ardent patriotism.
Accept, mon cher Monsieur Rouher, the assurance of my sincere friendship.   NAPOLEON.

He set sail on February 27th. Having arrived at the Cape, he was at first prevented from taking part in the military operations through illness, but afterward joined Lord Chelmsford and shared in different skirmishes, distinguishing himself by his courage. On June 1st he set out with Lieutenant Carey, six soldiers, and one friendly Zooloo, for a reconnaissance. An attack was made on the party when about ten miles from camp, in which the Prince was killed. His body when found contained seventeen assegai-wounds, but no bullet-

wound. It was sent to England, where it arrived on July 11th, and on the following day was deposited in the little church of St. Mary at Chiselhurst beside the remains of his father. His funeral was attended not only by his own adherents, but by the royal family of Great Britain and by many other distinguished persons, while his mother received a large number of expressions of sympathy and condolence from all parts of Europe. By a strange coincidence, the surgeon and physician who established the identity of the corpse, Larrey and Corvisart, were the sons of the surgeon and physician of Napoleon I., and the Bishop who accompanied Cardinal Manning to the house at Chiselhurst was Las Cases, the son of the author of the "Memoirs of St. Helena," the most faithful friend of the great Emperor. In his will the Prince constituted his mother his sole legatee, charging her with attending to various legacies amounting to 800,000 francs. At the close of the will he says:

I have no need to recommend to my mother to neglect nothing in order to defend the memory of my great-uncle and of my father. I beg her to remember that as long as there shall be Bonapartists the imperial cause will have representatives. The duties of our house toward the country will not cease with my life. At my death the task of continuing the work of Napoleon I. and Napoleon III. devolves upon the eldest son of Prince Napoleon ; and I hope that my well-beloved mother, in seconding him with all her power, will give us who shall be no more this last and supreme proof of her affection.

A proposition was made, and the sanction of Dean Stanley secured, to erect a monument to the Prince in Westminster Abbey. His reasons for this consent were, that the Prince had died in the service of the country which had received him, and that the country had learned to honor him personally for his blameless and engaging character. This plan was bitterly opposed by the Liberal papers, which had also condemned the public military funeral of the Prince as an insult to the French Republic, and while regarding a monument in Westminster Abbey as the highest honor of its class that could be rendered to the memory of men or women of extraordinary merit, who had done great service to the public, they declared that all these conditions were wanting in the Prince, and that "the English people are heartily sick of the outburst of folly, adulation, and falsehood that has followed the very commonplace incident of an incautious volunteer being surprised and killed."
The death of the Prince Imperial had a very injurious influence upon the prospects of the Bonapartist party, as Prince Jerome Napoleon, who succeeded him as head of the family, was greatly disliked by a considerable portion of the party. (See FRANCE.)
BRAHMO SOMAJ. The Brahmo Somaj of India is the most prominent and active among the sects of high-born Indians which are trying to cultivate a Brahmanism free from the polytheism, superstition, and demonism

with which popular Hindooism has become encumbered. It owes its origin to an effort to restore the pure doctrine of the Vedas; the aim was modified, first in the direction of a religion of theism, then of a religion of nature, in which stage the attitude of the society appeared unfriendly to Christianity, if not antagonistic to it. Within two years, however, the progressive and most active section of the society, as represented by its best known leader, the Baboo Keshub Chunder Sen, has shown a growing friendliness toward Christianity and a disposition to approach it.

The " Brahmo Somaj of India " was formed by a separation from the " Brahmo Somaj," an older society for the reform of the Hindoo worship, which was formed by the Rajah Ram Mohun Roy. This leader, a Brahman who believed fully in the inspiration of the Vedas, was also acquainted with the teachings of the New Testament and esteemed them. He founded a church in Calcutta, published a work called " The Precepts of Jesus," and entered into fraternal relations with the Unitarian Christians who had been established at Madras since 1813. Ram Mohun Roy died in 1813; and, while the influence he had exercised suffered a decline, the society which he had formed was kept up by the accession of students from the religionless Government schools, who had lost their old faith without receiving a new one. A new impulse was given to the movement for religious reform by the accession in 1839 of the Baboo Debendranath Tagore, who soon became the leader of the society. At first he gave a more exclusive adherence to the religious books of the Hindoos than Ram Mohun Roy had done; but the continued study of the Vedas showed that that they did not teach a pure monotheism, and doubts began to be entertained about 1845 of their divine origin. Instead of the whole books, the Brahmists employed collections of isolated texts and sentences from the ancient sages as expressions of their common faith, and at length came to reject the possibility of a written revelation. About the same time the theists became readers of the writings of Francis Newman, and received the ideas of an inward light and a mystical kind of intuition. Soon afterward a movement in the direction of Christianity set in, occasioned, according to the " Indian Mirror," by the secession from the missionary schools of members who became leading men. A new epoch in the history of the society was marked by the accession of Baboo Keshub Chunder Sen in 1857. Mr. Sen was born in 1838, a member of the Vaidya caste. He became dissatisfied with the religion of his fathers while a student at the Presidency College, Calcutta, and turned to the Brahmo Somaj in the hope of finding a better one there. At first he followed the lead of Baboo Debendranath Tagore, but soon became the leader of a progressive party. In 1865 he presented, in the name of his party, three demands as an ultima-

tum, on the rejection of which they would separate and form a new society. They were: 1. That external marks of caste, such as the Brahmanical thread, should no longer be used; 2. That those Brahmists only should be permitted to conduct divine service in the Somaj who were of sufficient ability and bore a good moral character, and whose life accorded with their profession; 3. That nothing should be said in the Somaj which breathed hatred or contempt toward other religions. The conservative party were not ready to give up the use of the Brahmanical thread, and a disruption took place. The progressive party took the name of the Brahmo Somaj of India, while the old party styled itself the Adi (or original) Brahmo Somaj.

The " Brahmo Public Opinion," of India, at the beginning of 1879, in giving a review of the history and development of the Brahmo Somaj from its origin in 1830, divided the history into three epochs—the Vedantic, the Puranic, and the Eclectic. In the first period, which closed with the death of Ram Mohun Roy, there were, it says, strong and earnest protests against idolatry, along with evident indications of a belief in the infallibility of the Vedas. In the hymns and songs there were symptoms of a belief in the transmigration of souls, along with traces of a corresponding faith in the Vedantic doctrine of Unification with the Divine Essence." When the Vedas were given up, Baboo Debendranath Tagore came forward with the doctrine that religion is based on the intuitions of the soul, and directed his attention to the construction of a new form of church service and a new and unidolatrous code of ceremonies. In doing this he did not depart from the Hindoo Shastas, but collected his texts from them alone, and published the book known as the " Brahma Dhurma." This period is styled the Puranic period, because the development of the Puranic idea of separate entity of the Godhead from the human soul, and the development of the Puranic practice of worshiping that Godhead, took place in it. Another leader was growing up in the mean time—Baboo Keshub Chunder Sen, who with his friends " fretted, as it were, under the conventional barriers of the Shastras, and longed to proclaim a broader and more catholic faith to the world, and to inaugurate an era of nobler self-sacrifice." From the day of the separation, the " Public Opinion " continues, dates an unusual expansion of the Brahmo Church. " From that day Brahmoism has been presented to the world as a perfectly broad and catholic faith, eclectic in its principles and universal in its character."

The old party, or Adi Somaj, suffered a loss of religious influence after the disruption, while the Brahmo Somaj has been brought into wide notice by the preaching of Keshub Chunder Sen. Other societies, as the Prarthana Somaj, the Aria Somaj, the Ekimishvarionandali, etc., professing similar principles, are allied with the

Brahmo Somaj. The Prarthana Somaj of Bombay is, however, more conservative than the Brahmo Somaj, and was engaged as late as 1876 in a discussion of the question whether its members should give up the mark on their foreheads, caste, and idolatry.

The "Brahmo Public Opinion" reported concerning the condition of the Church at the beginning of 1879, that there had been in the past year an unprecedented revival in every direction. A separate and powerful organization, the Sadharan Brahmo Somaj—a schism caused by difference concerning the marriage of Mr. Sen's daughter, and the use of idolatrous rites and symbols which were insisted upon by the bridegroom—had been formed. One weekly English and a number of Bengalee papers had come into existence; as many as six marriages according to theistic rites had taken place; two new houses of prayer had been consecrated, and subscriptions had been opened for four or five more; and active and friendly correspondence had been opened with Mofussil Somajes. Furthermore, the Somaj had sent its missionaries to the Punjaub and to the most remote corners of Eastern Bengal. Its executive committee had regularly held meetings every week, had raised and expended money, issued two journals, secured a press, and bought a piece of ground for the purpose of building a house of prayer of their own.

An enumeration of the Somajes in India published in July, 1879, gave the whole number as 149, of which 20 were in Calcutta, 54 in Bengal, 7 in Assam, 3 in Chota Nagpere, 7 in Behar, 2 in Orissa, 8 in the Northwest Provinces, 1 in the Central Provinces, 5 in the Punjaub, 3 in Sinde, 6 in Bombay, and 6 in Madras. Forty-four of them had "mandirs," or places of worship. In connection with the society, 18 periodicals were published, of which 6 were in English, 9 in Bengalee, 1 each in the Hindoo and Oriya languages, and 1 in Anglo-Mahratti. Four schools were kept up by the organization, independently of schools and classes provided by the local Somajes for their own districts.

The Brahmo Somaj and its affiliated societies have accepted the Bible and the fundamental principles of Christianity as entitled to respect along with the sacred books of other religions, but have placed on nearly the same level masterpieces of literature which have not been regarded as religiously inspired; they speak of the Fatherhood of God, and consider Christ as the wisest and best man that ever lived, but superior only in degree to other prophets and great and good men. Gradually the Brahmo Somaj, particularly the section led by Keshub Chunder Sen, has adopted one Christian practice and doctrine after another, has become accustomed to employ Christian terms, and has made the Bible more prominent among its books and Christ among its leaders. Some of their more recent expressions in articles have been very remarkable in this respect. The "In-

dian Mirror," the periodical organ of the Brahmos, frequently publishes contributions in its devotional department in which admiration and reverence for the character and ministrations of Christ are expressed with Oriental warmth. In one of these articles the wish is expressed that Christ had been an Indian instead of a Jew, because, as Rama is endeared to all Hindoos by reason of his sufferings, with no bitter mixture of dogmas, "a prophet like Christ would not have fared worse." Creeds and formulas would not have come to disfigure him, but "he should have devoted an epic to his glory, sung his name through every city and village, comforted the weak in their sorrows and the dying on their death-bed, remembered him in every act of daily life, and died finding consolation and strength in his holy example." In one of the prayers which the "Mirror" publishes regularly are the words: "Unspeakably consoling unto me is the tender ministry of Jesus, and his blessed memory more dear to me than the empty lives of so many who profess his religion. God of love, bind the souls of the ailing and penitent in holy sympathy with the wondrous life; and death of Jesus. Cause us to feel that his glorious ministry is still exercised in the world, and bring us in contact with those men who are truly his ministers."

On April 9, 1879, the Baboo Keshub Chunder Sen delivered a lecture in Calcutta before a large audience of educated Bengalees, in which many Christians were included. His remarks indicated a closer sympathy with Christians than any of the Brahmos had yet shown, and were much commented upon by those who desire to promote the growth of the Christian religion in the country. He opened his address by saying: "I desire to speak of Christ. Christ rules British India, and not the British Government. England has sent us a tremendous moral force in the life and character of that mighty Prophet, to conquer and hold this vast empire. . . . . If, then, India is encompassed on all sides by Christian literature, Christian civilization, and a Christian government, she must naturally endeavor to satisfy herself as to the nature of this great power in the Christian realm, which is doing such wonders in our midst. . . . . She is unconsciously imbibing the spirit of this new civilization, succumbing to its irresistible influence. . . . . If unto any army appertains the honor of holding India for England, that army is the army of Christian missionaries, headed by their invincible captain, Jesus Christ. . . . . They have given us the high code of Christian ethics, and their teachings and examples have directly influenced and won thousands of non-Christian Hindoos. Let England know that, thanks to the noble band of Christ's ambassadors sent by her, she has already succeeded in planting his banners in the heart of the nation." At the close of his address he said: "The Bridegroom is coming; let India be prepared and ready in due season. And you, my friends, rest assured that if there is any truth in Christ, it will overtake and conquer you." The anniversary address of the Baboo for 1879 was devoted to answering in the negative the question whether he pretended to possess prophetic gifts, and to the relation, with much of Oriental imagery and vagueness, of his religious experience. In it he avowed his belief in the omnipresent spirituality of God. "Of what good," he said, "is religion if it does not teach us to believe in a Deity ever near to us? .,.. If he is not found here, then the down-trodden sinner perishes at once, lost in sin. Shall I go to the clouds and seek my God there? Shall I go to the height of the Himalayas to understand and find him? It is impossible for a poor sinner to achieve these impracticable feats. My God must himself come into the sinner's cottage and save him. He goes forth not only to save, but to seek and save the sinner. The omnipresent Lord is here and everywhere, and I have faith in that fact." Further, he said: "The Bible has never of itself animated or inspired any one, nor can it. But the Spirit of God converts its dead letters into living forms. If you wish to see God with your eyes, if you wish to hear him, pray..... Trust that all things shall be revealed unto me and unto you in the fullness of time. The Lord's inspiration shall satisfy our understanding, and remove all our doubts and misgivings." "The spirit of truth," he said near the close of his address, "I have been so long teaching, has silently, quietly, and almost imperceptibly leavened the heart of educated India. It is a wonder and a marvel that, in spite of civilization, there is so much of spirituality growing up in the midst of young Bengal and young India. Take away this Brahmo church, take away this grand theistic organization, and what is left? It is all secular education and material prosperity..... This living faith is not contrary to the spirit of Christianity, or Mohammedanism, or Hindooism. It is religion pure and simple. It is the religion of love, the religion of the living God."

A conference of missionaries of the Somaj, which met in the fall of 1878, issued an address to the societies against sensuality and skepticism, which included the instructions: "The Lord has in all ages rebuked men of little faith, treating the least skepticism on the part of his people as a sin and an abomination. Every believer is bound to believe thoroughly and firmly, never doubting, never wavering. Whoso deliberately harbors doubts in regard to the essentials of faith, or scoffs at the vital truths of religion, is an enemy of God and our church. Who suffers himself to decline in spirituality, devotion, and faith, and boasts of his growing rationalism, is a renegade, whose contact defileth the church to which he belongs..... We humbly request the leading men of all the Brahmo Somajes in India to protect the vital doctrines of our church, namely, the Reality of Divine Presence, Providence, Inspiration,

Daily Prayers, Communion, Immortality, etc., and to promote by every means in their power the highest spirituality and devotion among the Brahmo community. And we beg, too, that our dear church may be kept free from the influence of doubters, materialists, skeptics, and scoffers of all classes."

In the latter part of 1879 the periodicals of the Brahmo Somaj took notice of a new movement in the body, as a tendency toward a more active and definite spiritual life. The "Theistic Quarterly Review" remarked that "such significant words as these—*seeing, hearing, and touching the Spirit of God,*" were becoming quite familiar among advanced Brahmos, and that their devotional literature abounded in striking metaphors and expressions of intense religious emotion. The "Indian Mirror" remarked: "A great change has evidently come over the spirit of the Brahmo Somaj movement. Never was our church so spiritual, so devout, so earnest, or so thoroughly imbued with faith in the realities of the unseen world. .... Imagination and unbelief, unpractical transcendentalism and dreamy sentimentalism are fast dying out, and the vision of faith is extending, both in area and in vividness. The prophets, 'Christ and other masters,' are finding a home in the hearts of our devotees such as they never had before. A strong desire to live in them and with them in God is manifest among our ranks. Formal prayers and stereotyped addresses to an imaginary and abstract deity are giving way to sustained conversation with Heaven's King, and the pleasant flow of deep, unutterable sentiments. The Brahmo's prayer to-day is neither soliloquy nor an unanswered petition, but the soul's spirited dialogue with the indwelling Friend."

BRAZIL (IMPERIO DO BRAZIL). (For territorial divisions, population, etc., see "Annual Cyclopædia" for 1878.) The government of Brazil is a constitutional monarchy. The Emperor is Dom Pedro II., born December 2, 1825; proclaimed April 7, 1831; regency until July 23, 1840; crowned July 18, 1841; married September 4, 1843, to Theresa Christina Maria, daughter of the late King Francis I. of the Two Sicilies. The Cabinet was composed of the following Ministers: Interior, Councilor F. M. Sodré Pereira; Justice, Councilor Lafayette R. Pereira; Foreign Affairs, Councilor A. Moreira de Banos; Finance, Senator Affonso Celso; War, Marquis de Herval, Senator; Navy, J. F. de Mouza; Public Works, Commerce, and Agriculture, J. L. V. Cansansao de Sinimbú, Senator and President of the Council of State. The beginning of the year was marked by a ministerial crisis, Senhor Andrade Pinto resigning the portfolio of the Navy, ostensibly, and perhaps solely, on account of the removal of Viscount de Prados from the presidency of the Province of Rio de Janeiro. The new Cabinet [*] had resolved that no member of the central legislative body

---

[*] See "Annual Cyclopædia" for 1878.

should be president of a province while the Legislature was in session, on the ground that the former system of governing provinces by vice-presidents while the presidents were attending the Legislature at the capital of the empire was prejudicial to the provincial interests. Senhor Andrade Pinto, though not opposed to that measure as a rule, was of opinion that an exception might be admitted in the case of the presidency of Rio de Janeiro, in view of the proximity (twenty-two minutes) of the seat of government of that province to the capital, and the Viscount's continuance in his provincial office being furthermore necessary to the completion of the reforms begun by him. The remainder of the Cabinet, however, insisted on the uniformity of the rule, assigning as a special reason against the advisability of an exception in the present instance, the fact that the Viscount had been elected President of the Chamber of Deputies. This presidency the Viscount resigned on his removal from that of Rio de Janeiro. Senhor Prados is a distinguished astronomer, and was for some years in charge of the Imperial Astronomical Observatory. The new Minister of the Navy is a wealthy planter from Bahia, which province he represents in the Chamber of Deputies, and is reputed a most honorable and active administrator. The Council of State is composed of the following members in ordinary: The Princess Imperial, Donna Isabel; Prince Gaston d'Orleans, Count d'Eu; the Senators Viscounts de Abaeté, do Rio Branco, de Muritiba, de Bom Retiro, de Jaguary, de Nictheroy, and de Araxá; the Duke de Caxias, J. P. Dias de Carvacho, J. J. Teixeira, Vice-Admiral J. R. de Lamare, and Dr. P. J. Soares de Souza; and of six members extraordinary: Senators J. L. C. Paranaguá and M. P. S. Dantas, Viscount de Prados, Councilors Martin Francisco and B. A. de M. Taques, and Dr. J. C. de Andrade. The President of the Senate, which comprises 58 life members, is Viscount de Jaguary; and the Vice-President, Count de Baependy. The Chamber of Deputies is composed of 122 members elected for four years: President, ——; Vice-President, F. de Almeida.

The Presidents of the several provinces were as follows: Alagôas, Dr. C. Pinto da Silva; Amazonas, Baron de Maracajú; Bahia, Dr. Aragão Bulcao; Ceará, Dr. J. J. de Albuquerque Barros; Espirito Santo. Dr. E. S. Martins; Goyaz, Dr. A. S. Spinola; Maranhão, Dr. L. O. Lino de Vasconcellos; Matto Grosso, Dr. J. J. Pedroza; Minas Geraes, Dr. M. J. G. Rebello Horta; Pará, Dr. J. C. da Gama e Abreu; Parahyba, Dr. U. M. Pereira Vianna; Paraná, Dr. M. P. S. Dantas Filho; Pernambuco, Dr. A. de Barros Cavalcante; Piauhy, Dr. J. P. Belfort Vieira; Rio de Jaueiro, Dr. A. M. Marcondes de Andrade; Rio Grande do Norte, Dr. R. L. Marcondes; Rio Grande (or São Pedro) do Sul, Dr. F. Pereira da Silva; Santa Oatharina, Dr. A. A. Oliveira; São Paulo, Dr. L. A. de

Brito; Sergipe, Dr. T. F. dos Santos. The Archbishop of Bahia, J. G. de Azevedo (1875), is Primate of all Brazil; and there are eleven bishops, viz., those of Pará, São Luiz, Fortaleza, Olinda, Rio de Janeiro, São Paulo, Porto Alegre, Marianna, Diamantina, Goyaz, and Cuyabá. The Brazilian Minister to the United States is Councilor A. P. de Carvalho Borges, Envoy Extraordinary and Minister Plenipotentiary, accredited October 9, 1871; and the Brazilian Consul-General (for the Union) at New York is Senhor Salvador de Mendouça.

In pursuance of the law of February 27, 1875, military service is obligatory for all subjects; but there are numerous exceptions admitted, and substitution is allowable. The period of service is six years in the regular army and three in the reserve. The regulation strength of the army in time of peace is 15,000, and in case of war 32,000. The real strength of the army in 1878, however, was 16,806, including 1,753 officers. The arms are distributed as follows: Infantry, 21 battalions, 8 garrison companies, and 1 depot company for the instruction of recruits; cavalry, 5 regiments, 1 squadron, and 5 garrison companies; artillery, 3 regiments of horse and 5 battalions of foot; sappers and miners, 1 battalion; gendarmes, 7,642, of whom 1,070 are at Rio de Janeiro. The National Guard had been disbanded for reorganization on the completion of the new census.

For the most recent naval statistics, reference may be made to the "Annual Cyclopædia" for 1877. In 1878 the Adjutant-General proposed the following classification of the officers of the navy, involving a reduction of their number and a change of denomination for certain ranks: 1 admiral, 2 vice-admirals, 6 rear-admirals, 15 first-class captains (commandantes), 30 second-class and 40 third-class captains, 100 first-class lieutenants, and 120 second-class; total, 314. This modification, if adopted, would reduce the number of officers by 207, and constitute an economy of $103,130 per annum in the pay-lists alone.

The estimated revenue and expenditures for the fiscal year 1879-'80 figured as follows in the budget read by the Minister of Finance at the first session of the Legislature:

REVENUE.

General receipts (ordinary and extraordinary)....	$50,500,000
Slave-liberation fund..........................	450,000
Total..............................	$50,950,000

EXPENDITURES.

Ministry of the Interior........................	$4,411,863
" of Foreign Affairs...................	516,347
" of Finance.........................	25,430,882
" of Justice.........................	3,859,422
" of Agriculture.....................	10,694,892
" of War............................	7,492,114
" of the Navy.......................	5,676,825
Total..............................	$60,559,795
Deficit..............................	$9,609,795

This deficit it was proposed to provide for by further taxation.

Notwithstanding systematic retrenchment in the various ministerial departments (a distinguishing feature of the policy of the new Cabinet), the appropriations demanded are about $7,000,000 in excess of the votes for the same year. Among these appropriations stands an item of $1,800,000 for the redemption of paper money. With regard to assisting planters, the Government asked authorization to apply the necessary sum for guaranteeing the interest and redemption of hypothecated bills to be issued by land-banks of loan. The aggregate amount, from all sources, received into the Treasury during the seven years from 1871–'72 to 1877–'78 inclusive, to be applied for the liberation of slaves, was $4,043,206.

The national debt was as follows April 30, 1879 :

Foreign debt	$79,141,777
Home debt (funded)	186,784,850
Debt before 1827	168,867
Orphans' and other funds	23,706,297
Treasury notes (at 2, 4, and 6 months)	13,637,950
Paper money (Government notes)	94,629,177
Total	$393,058,418

The imports and exports for the year 1876–'77 were of the values of $77,462,000 and $98,389,500 respectively. The values of the chief staples of exports in 1876–'77 were as exhibited below :

COMMODITIES.	Values.
Coffee	$56,055,800
Raw cotton	6,042,800
Sugar	14,996,150
Maté (Paraguay tea)	1,191,700
Skins	4,068,600
Tobacco	3,437,800
India-rubber	5,516,950
Diamonds	520,900

The value of Brazilian exports to the United Kingdom in 1876 was $26,844,675, against $36,053,480 and $47,829,775 in 1874 and 1872 respectively. The striking decrease in this trade from year to year during the decade ending in 1876 is presumed to be attributable, in part at least, to the progressive development of direct relations with some markets which formerly derived their supplies through Great Britain. No marked change has occurred in the quantity of gold and silver (coin and bullion) shipped to the British Isles, the annual value of which varies little from $2,500,000. The mean annual value of the imports from the United Kingdom is about $35,000,000.

The shipping movements at the various ports of the empire in 1876–'77 were as follows :

VESSELS.	Number.	Tonnage.
ENTERED.		
Sea-going vessels { Foreign	2,992	2,226,589
{ Brazilian	312	185,254
Coasting vessels	5,885	1,581,931
CLEARED.		
Sea-going vessels { Foreign	2,978	2,215,534
{ Brazilian	297	141,620
Coasting vessels	4,461	1,507,868

In 1878 there were 1,720 miles of railway in the empire, and 4,250 miles of telegraph, with 106 offices. The number of dispatches for 1875 and 1876 was 119,358. The number of letters transmitted by mail in 1878 was 14,762,144, and the number of post-offices was 1,061.

Statistics relating to public instruction will be found in the "Annual Cyclopædia" for 1877 (p. 78).

The subjoined brief extract contains the more important matters touched upon in the Emperor's speech at the opening of the Legislature on December 15, 1878 :

"It is pleasing to me to have to announce to you that the public tranquillity which this empire has now enjoyed for so many years has remained undisturbed, thus affording an incontestable proof of the progress achieved by the spirit of order through the agency of our institutions. The usual friendly relations have likewise been maintained between Brazil and the foreign Powers. The following diplomatic arrangements have been concluded: a postal convention with the Republic of Chili, an extradition treaty with Germany, an additional extradition treaty with Belgium, a consular convention with Spain, and Brazil's adhesion to the International Telegraph Convention, celebrated at St. Petersburg. Unfavorable markets in Europe, the increase in our expenditures, and a heavy drain upon the revenue to relieve suffering provinces, have embarrassed our finances."

BUDDINGTON, Rev. Dr. WILLIAM IVES, a distinguished clergyman of the Congregational order, was born in New Haven, Connecticut, on April 25, 1815, and graduated at Yale College in 1834. He commenced the study of theology at the school in New Haven, and completed it at Andover Seminary in 1839. In April, 1840, he was installed as pastor of the First Church in Charlestown, Massachusetts, and remained there until 1854, when he removed to Philadelphia. He expected there to enter upon a pastorate, but his plans were changed in consequence of the death of his wife. In December of the same year the Clinton Avenue Congregational Church in Brooklyn invited him to become its pastor, and he accepted the invitation. The church under his charge became one of the prominent ones in the city. He was self-sacrificing, sympathetic, studious, and devoted to the welfare of his people. Decided in his religious convictions, he withstood all innovations, and was warmly supported by his people. Thus he continued in good health and vigor until July, 1877, when a little sore that appeared on his lip developed into a cancer. It was removed, but subsequently reappeared; and thus several operations were performed. Meantime he resigned the active duties of the pastorate, but at the request of the congregation retained the position and emoluments. His disease continued to advance, and a week before his death he began to fail rapidly. The cancer attacked his throat, and it became impossible to give him nourishment. He took to his bed, and for several days suffered intense pain. On

November 26th he gave the last indications of consciousness, and expired on the 28th. Dr. Budington's published literary efforts were confined to the "History of the First Church of Charlestown," his sermon on "Patriotism and the Pulpit," delivered at the anniversary of the American Educational Society of Boston in 1861, and his address on "The Relations of Science to Religion," delivered at Yale College in 1871.

BULGARIA,* a principality of Southeastern Europe, which was created in 1878 by the Treaty of Berlin. Art. I. of this treaty provides that Bulgaria shall be "constituted an autonomous and tributary principality, under the suzerainty of his Imperial Majesty the Sultan. It will have a Christian government and a national militia." Reigning Prince, Alexander I., elected in 1879 (see ALEXANDER I.). Area, about 33,000 square miles; the accurate settlement of the boundaries of the principality was left to a European commission, appointed by the signataries of the Treaty of Berlin. The population is calculated to number 1,859,000, of whom about 600,000 are Mohammedans. Nearly all the others belong to the Bulgarian Church, which agrees in doctrine with the Greek Church of Turkey and Greece, and with the Russian and other branches of the Eastern Orthodox Church, but has had for many years an independent organization.

Bulgaria has one line of railway, from Rustchuk to the port of Varna on the Black Sea, 140 miles in length. It was constructed by a private company for the Turkish Government, and by Article X. of the Treaty of Berlin all the outstanding obligations of the railway fall to the charge of the Government of the principality.

The first Bulgarian Parliament, or Assembly of Notables, as it is called, met at Tirnova on February 22d, after having been previously adjourned from time to time. Prince Dondoukoff-Korsakoff, the Russian Imperial Commissioner, read the opening address to the deputies as follows:

HONORED REPRESENTATIVES OF THE BULGARIAN PRINCIPALITY: By the will and designation of my master, the Emperor of Russia, I congratulate you upon the opening of the first National Assembly of your emancipated country, which is to establish a firm foundation for a state Government of the new principality. In my capacity as Russian Imperial Commissioner, I present to you for approval the project for your organic Constitution, which determines in a general manner the rights of the future Bulgarian Prince and people. With this project I also communicate to you the regulations which will govern you in discussing the proposed Constitution. It is incumbent on you to fully discuss this Constitution in all its bearings, without any partisan feelings, and solely with a view of advancing the social and moral interests of your country. The programme now presented is only a skeleton Constitution, designed to facilitate your labors. This programme should not in any way hamper your convictions as to any changes you may deem necessary.

* For an account of the history of the race, of the progress of education, of newspapers, of industry, and of the Bulgarian Church, see "Annual Cyclopædia" for 1878, art. BULGARIA.

The regulations for your discussions will be read to you. I may remind you that the existing Russian administration has been acting under adverse circumstances, which I hope will justify in your minds my previous orders and regulations, as I have only endeavored to replace disorder by order, thus preparing the population for a higher political life. I hereby appoint M. Loukianoff as my substitute in presiding over your labors. He will give you all needed explanations of matters arising in your discussions and details of your Constitution; but the last and decisive word belongs to you alone. May God assist you in the accomplishment of your sacred task for the good of your country, so dear by blood to the Russians, by the sacrifices Russia has made for you, and by the magnanimous feelings toward you of our Emperor, the liberator of your nation! I announce as opened the first Bulgarian National Assembly. I call upon you now to repair to the Old Cathedral of Tirnova to pray for the successful termination of your important labors, and to offer thanks to the King of kings, who has enabled us to witness the great historical work of the regeneration of your long-oppressed country.

The Bulgarians of Eastern Roumelia and Macedonia had elected deputies, who, however, were admitted as visitors only. The National Assembly consisted of 286 members, who were divided into three groups. The first group comprised: 1. The presidents of the municipal, judicial, and administrative councils of each district, and, as there are 38 districts in Bulgaria, there were 114 members under this class; 2. The presidents of the superior administrative and judicial councils of each sanjak or gubernios. There are five gubernios. The presidents of both the judicial councils being appointed by the Government, there were in the first class 43 members appointed by the Government, while the other 81 members (the presidents of the municipal and administrative councils) were elected by the people. In the second group there were 120 members, who were elected from 120 districts, each with 10,000 inhabitants. Every Bulgarian twenty-two years of age, who possesses real estate or who follows a profession, is a voter. Servants, apprentices, and day-laborers are excluded. To the third group belonged: 1. Nine deputies bishops, and the Greek bishop; 2. The mufti of Widin, and the grand rabbi of Sophia; 3. Thirty members to be appointed by the Governor of Bulgaria. The Assembly adopted a set of rules for its government, of which the following are the most important: The National Assembly now in Tirnova is a *Constituante*, called by special order of the Imperial Russian Commissioner for the examination of the project of the organic Constitution for the government of the Bulgarian Principality. The Assembly consists of members by nomination, election, and *ex officio*, but constitutes a harmonious whole, no distinction between members being made on account of the manner of their appointment; and the deputies not only represent the locality from which they come, but also the whole population of the Bulgarian Principality. The credentials of each deputy can not be canceled until the Assembly has accomplished its high mission. The persons of the national deputies, so long as their credentials remain in force, are inviolable. For crimes committed before or after the opening of the Assembly a deputy can only be prosecuted after the consent of the Constituante has been secured. A deputy can not be prosecuted for opinions expressed in the discussions of the Assembly. There will be three sessions each week—Monday, Wednesday, and Friday; but the sessions may be increased or diminished by a vote of the Assembly. The sessions shall be public, and can only be made secret by the demand of the President, or upon the written request of twenty members, and even then must be sustained by at least one-third of the members present. On March 6th the Assembly elected the former Exarch its President. No work of any importance was done, the Assembly confining itself to speeches on the condition of the Bulgarian race. On March 18th the Assembly adopted the address drawn up by the committee in reply to Prince Dondoukoff-Korsakoff's message. It expressed the gratitude of Bulgaria to the Russian Emperor, and alluded to difficulties placed in the way of the future of the principality by the presence of Turkish troops in the Balkans. On March 19th Prince Dondoukoff-Korsakoff sent a message to the Assembly expressing his regret at hearing that the Assembly had deviated from the line of duty marked out by the Treaty of Berlin, and had been occupying itself with matters entirely outside its jurisdiction. He strongly desired that no more time should be wasted in discussing matters concerning which the Constituante had no power of action or even of suggestion. A motion was then made and carried that the consideration of the Constitution should be immediately proceeded with, and the secretary was ordered to read the draft prepared by Prince Dondoukoff-Korsakoff. A committee of fifteen was appointed to revise the draft, and on April 2d it handed in its report. In regard to religious matters, proselytism should be forbidden. With regard to the Prince, it rejected the clause of the original draft which stated that the relations of the Prince to the Porte should be those of a vassal, and maintained the stipulation that the princely dignity should be hereditary in the direct male line. The civil list was fixed at 600,000 francs per annum. Education was to be compulsory and free. All who paid taxes to the amount of 100 piasters should have a vote; and it proposed to abolish the Great National Assembly, and to constitute a National Assembly and a Senate, partly nominated and partly elected. Of three ecclesiastical senators, one should be the representative of the Mohammedan clergy. The present National Assembly, strengthened by two elected members from each of the 120 districts, should elect the Prince. On April 3d the Assembly began the discussion of the Constitution, and considered the first thirty-five articles, and made several modifications in the original draft. Sophia was selected as the capital of Bulgaria, and the salary of the Prince was fixed at 600,000 instead of 1,000,000 francs. Articles 36 and 37 were passed on the 4th, and Articles 38 to 62 on the 5th. The recommendation of the committee that proselytism be prohibited in the principality was rejected. New articles were added, declaring that slavery should not exist in Bulgaria, that no titles of rank should be instituted, and that only military merit should be rewarded by a decoration, which the Prince alone would have the right to confer. On the 7th the statute for the election of a Prince was considered, and after a short discussion it was decided that the composition of the present Chamber precluded its proceeding with the appointment, and that new elections would be necessary. A resolution was accordingly passed by a large majority requesting Prince Dondoukoff to take steps for the new elections without delay, on the basis of three deputies for each ten thousand of the population. On April 8th the Bishop of Sophia introduced a motion to insert an article in the Constitution requiring all religious publications to be subjected to the censorship of the Holy Synod before being put on sale in Bulgaria. The motion was rejected by an almost unanimous vote. Articles 73 to 78 inclusive were adopted, with the following modifications: Article 73 now reads," Primary education is gratuitous and obligatory." In Article 74 the freedom of the press and of all publications was more emphatically asserted than in the original clause. The discussion over Article 78 became very bitter and personal in its character. A number of members desired to have a Senate as well as a Lower House of Representatives. This was resented by a majority of the deputies as an attempt to establish a privileged class of national legislators, and the motion to establish a Senate was rejected. On the 9th Articles 79 to 117 were assed. Article 79 was entirely remodeled, and it was decided that the ordinary Assembly should be entirely elective, one member representing ten thousand persons of both sexes; the Assembly to sit for three years. Any citizen over twenty-one years of age, enjoying political rights, should be qualified to vote; in order to be eligible to the Assembly, a man must be thirty years of age and able to read and write Bulgarian. On the 19th Articles 118 to 149 were disposed of. Article 137, relating to the composition of the future Constituantes, was changed so as to make these assemblies purely elective by the people, in the same manner as provided for the ordinary Legislative Assembly. Articles 142 to 147 were rejected entirely. These articles provided for the creation of a Council of State, which was regarded as unnecessary. Article 148, defining the duties and jurisdiction of the Council, was thoroughly changed, and the duties of the Council were distributed among the National Assembly, the Court of Cassation, and the Council of Ministers. On the 21st the remainder of the Constitution was disposed of.

The last article, 170, was rejected. It prohibited any change being made in the Constitution in less than five years. The sessions of the 24th and 25th were almost entirely devoted to the reading of the protocols of the sessions in which the Constitution had been discussed. The clause on freedom of association was modified so as to exempt from its privileges all societies aiming at the subversion of good manners, religious observances, or the recognized social decencies of life. A paragraph was added to Article 74, providing that the religious books used in the orthodox churches and schools should be previously examined by the Holy Synod. The former Exarch, the President of the Assembly, and the bishops and their friends, who had withdrawn after the rejection of the intolerance clauses, now took their seats again. On the 28th the session of the Constituent Assembly was closed by Prince Dondoukoff. In his closing speech he alluded to the difficult conditions under which the Assembly had been opened. He congratulated the House upon the accomplishment of their task, and said that the deputies had proved that they possessed qualities hitherto unknown among Bulgarians. The work they had accomplished would be judged by its results; but he was satisfied that the verdict of the future would be a favorable one, and he rejoiced that the labors of the Assembly had been so thoroughly performed.

The Assembly for the election of a Prince of Bulgaria opened on April 29th. Prince Dondoukoff opened the proceedings with a speech, in which he stated that no Russian subject was eligible. The protocol of the Constitution was signed by Prince Dondoukoff and the foreign delegates, with the exception of the Ottoman representative, who refused to sign it. The Assembly then proceeded with closed doors to the election of a Prince. The Archbishop of Tirnova addressed the Assembly, and said that three princes had been prominently put forward as candidates for the throne—Prince Waldemar of Denmark, Prince Reuss, and Prince Alexander of Battenberg. He said that the last was much the best known to them, and was the best choice they could make. The Assembly then elected Prince Battenberg without opposition (see ALEXANDER I.), after which the Assembly adjourned. Immediately upon the election of the Prince, a delegation was appointed to wait upon him. The deputation sent to him the following address:

The representatives of the Bulgarian people, appreciating your noble qualities, and certain that your Highness will not only be imbued with the interests of Bulgaria, but will defend them to the utmost of your power, as you have already defended them during the war of liberation, have confided to your lofty sentiments the future destinies of their country, electing your Highness voluntarily and with unanimity Prince of Bulgaria. A deputation will wait on your Highness with the notification of your election; we having learned through the medium of the present Government of our country that your Highness has honored us with your acceptance. We offer you our

humble congratulations, and assure you of our sincere devotion. We pray God to grant us the happiness of soon seeing you in a country which rejoices at the choice it has made.

Prince Battenberg, after his election, made a tour of the European courts, and on July 5th arrived at Constantinople, where he received the berat of investiture, and on the same day sailed for Varna. His visit to Constantinople was at first opposed by the Turkish Government, as it was feared that it might give rise to excesses; but, upon being informed of the fact by the Turkish Ambassador in Rome, the Prince stated that he would regret it exceedingly if he were not permitted to present himself to his sovereign, and to receive the investiture from his hands. It would be remarked all the more in Europe, as he had visited all the courts; and, in order to avoid any hostile demonstrations, he could make his stay a short one. This proposition was accepted in Constantinople. On July 6th he arrived in Varna, and on the 8th in Tirnova. He was everywhere received with great demonstrations of joy and enthusiasm, his progress through the country being like a triumphal procession. On the 14th he entered Sophia. After he had taken the oath of fidelity to the Constitution in Tirnova, Prince Dondoukoff-Korsakoff immediately departed for Russia. Considerable dissatisfaction made itself felt in Russia with the course of Prince Alexander. Instead of using a proclamation prepared for him by Prince Dondoukoff, in which expression was given to the everlasting gratitude the Bulgarians owed their deliverers, he issued an address of his own, short and having no reference to the Russians—an omission also characterizing his replies to the addresses presented to him. The Russian press bitterly complained that the Prince had not a single word of thanks for the Czar, Russia, or the Slavs in general. On July 18th the Prince appointed the following ministry: M. Bourmof, President and Interior; M. Balabanoff, Foreign Affairs; M. Grecoff, Justice; M. Natchovitch, Finance; and General Baronzoff, War. The ministry belonged to that section of the Bulgarians which is less opposed to foreign (i. e., Russian) influence than the Nationalists, who had been in the majority in the Assembly, and who were led by M. Zancoff, the Governor of Varna. The Russian evacuation of the country was completed on August 3d, when the last Russian troops left Sophia. The transport of war material, however, took some time longer.

Besides the Mohammedans, who continued to disturb the peace of the country, and who proved but unwilling subjects of Prince Alexander, the Greeks, who live in considerable numbers in the large cities, and form the more intelligent and wealthy part of the population, did not take kindly to the new order of things. Thousands of the more wealthy and intelligent at Varna, Shumla, Rustchuk, and other places declared themselves subjects of the King of

Greece, and secured passports from the consuls of that country. The poorer classes of the Greeks, on the other hand, joined the Mohammedans, making common cause with them in disturbing the order and peaceful establishment of the new *régime*. In the middle of August the Bulgarian Cabinet addressed a manifesto to the nation, in which it enjoined the observance of the constitutional laws and the preservation of the peace of the country, and stated its determination to take all possible measures for preventing disturbances in the principality; at the same time it declared its intention to direct its energies without delay to the work of internal organization, and to endeavor to merit the sympathy of the foreign Powers. At a monster meeting held at Tirnova in the first week of September, a vote of want of confidence in the ministry, for what the speakers described as the anti-constitutional acts of the Government, was unanimously passed, and the fact was telegraphed directly to Prince Alexander at Sophia. The session of the Assembly was opened on November 2d by Prince Alexander in person, who in the speech from the throne expressed gratification at the friendly treatment he had met with from the great Powers, who had recognized the principality. He alluded to the warm welcome given him in Servia and Roumania, and expressed the profound gratitude and unlimited veneration felt for the Czar-Liberator by himself, his Government, and his people. He announced that he had inaugurated good and amicable relations with neighboring states. He enumerated several bills to be presented to the Chamber, among others one relative to railways, a plan of which would be submitted for examination; and he also expressed a desire for the establishment of obligatory military service. He then alluded to the brigandage which had made its appearance in the eastern portion of the country after the departure of the Russians, which had necessitated the proclamation of a state of siege; but, he added, the evil had not spread. Speaking of the financial situation, he said that the present revenue was not sufficient, and that he counted upon the patriotism of the Chamber, upon whom the eyes of Europe were fixed, to supply the deficit. After the delivery of the speech, the House proceeded to elect its officers. M. Calaveloff was chosen President, and MM. Stoyandoff and Fischeff Vice-Presidents. As the Liberals were in a large majority, the ministry on the 3d offered its resignation.

Disturbances occurred in the latter part of July in Rasgrad, in which Mohammedans attacked the Bulgarians. They were quelled within a few days, and forty-two of the insurgents being killed, the rest, after a short resistance, took to flight, sheltering themselves in the forests of Osman-Bazar. Other disturbances occurred in various parts of the principality, caused chiefly by bands of robbers; and even Bashi-Bazouks and furloughed

Turkish soldiers took part in them. The Government, therefore, proclaimed a state of siege in the department of Varna, and in some districts of the departments of Tirnova and Rustchuk, and at the same time complained to the Turkish Government.

BURMAH, a kingdom in Farther India; area, 190,000 square miles; population, 4,000,000. The capital is Mandalay, on the Irrawaddy, about 200 miles beyond Thyetmayoo and Tonghoo, two fortified towns of British Burmah, the former situated on the Irrawaddy, the other on the Sitang River, which flows nearly parallel with the Irrawaddy, and is connected with it through the Pegu River and a recently opened navigable canal. Mandalay is separated from the Irrawaddy by two miles of swampy country, cut up by creeks. In July, August, and September, when the river is at its highest, light gunboats could approach the city by some of these creeks. The city itself is about one mile square, surrounded by a wall of sun-burnt brick 20 feet high, which is further protected by an embankment of the same height and by a ditch 90 feet wide and 10 feet deep. The ditch is crossed by five bridges. The palace is in the center of the city, a quarter of a mile square and strongly stockaded. The British residency is between the river and the city. About 350 miles above Mandalay, and near the junction of the Tapeng River with the Irrawaddy, is Bhamo, a town well stockaded. The Tapeng is navigable for 20 miles above Bhamo, by steamer in the rains, and by large boats at other seasons. The Kakhyeng range of hills is reached at 25 miles beyond Bhamo, and 110 miles farther is Momein, an important place, situated in a valley 4,500 feet above the sea, and the occupation of which would probably fall within the scope of operations if the British should ever come again into serious collision with the Burmese Empire.

Burmah is not yet open for travelers, and the official reports of the Government of British India are still our only source of information. The government of the country is a pure despotism. There is no hereditary high nobility of princes and nobles, who in times of danger would rally for the support of the throne; and the Buddhist clergy, however numerous and influential they are in many respects, are not allowed to have any influence upon political and secular affairs. The only kind of aristocracy in the country consists of the numerous princes, princesses, and their families in the palace-city, and to them may be added the highest dignitaries. The numerous state officers of lower rank can in no way be regarded as a support of the throne, because its members may at any moment be removed at the pleasure of the King. Thus the members of the embassy which was sent in 1872 to England, the first sent to any European Court, have been degraded to inspectors in workmen's shops, because their reports on the great power of England were not to the liking of the Bur-

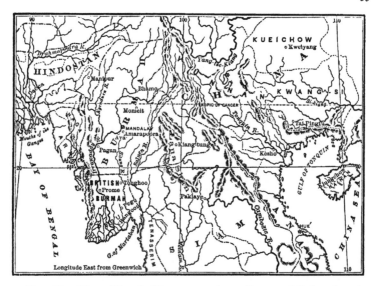

Longitude East from Greenwich

man King. From this condition of affairs results a chronic state of rebellion. People and
officers submit to the permanent rebellion as
an unavoidable evil. The numerous princes
know no other means to realize their wishes
than the usurpation of the supreme power,
and for every rebellion they find friends and
supporters. In 1866 such a plot was almost
successful, and the suppression of the insurrection, which cost the crown prince (brother of
the King) and numerous members of the royal
court their lives, completely paralyzed for a
time all trade and commerce. Still more dangerous was the insurrectionary attempt of 1870,
by which one of the younger sons of the King,
who had been excluded from the palace, aimed
at the throne. His mother and her friends had
sold their jewelry, bought arms, and gained
leaders; but the torture extorted from one
of the conspirators a full confession, and the
prince with forty accomplices was imprisoned.
A royal edict announced that the execution of
the prisoners had been stayed at the request
of a priest, but a year passed before the insurrectionary movements which broke out in all
parts of the kingdom were fully quelled.

The predecessor of the present King, Mendone Meng (also called Mung Long), was raised
by a palace revolution following the humiliating surrender of Pegu in 1853, and died on
October 1, 1878. During the last decade of
his reign he tried to introduce some of the
institutions of civilized countries, expecting to
turn them to his personal advantage. At first
he began to purchase river steamers and some

expensive machines, especially for cotton-spin-
ning and weaving; but for many years the
steamers were exclusively employed for government purposes. These measures exhausted
the royal treasury, and, in order to procure
money, the commerce was monopolized in favor of the King. The importers from British
India, and the leaders of the caravans from
China and Siam, were obliged to sell to and
purchase from the King exclusively. His
agents bought enormous quantities of goods,
especially of Indian cotton goods. In order
to get rid of them, the King forced them, in
payment of salaries, upon all officers of the
kingdom, who in turn disposed of them as
well as they could; and then he found no
longer any purchasers, because the merchants
had bought their supplies at second hand.
As the ships continued to bring new goods,
the King refused to fulfill his contracts, and
compelled the people of his country to take
those already imported. At the same time the
peasants were compelled to sell to the King
their crops; royal steamers carried the rice to
Rangoon, and foreigners were also excluded
from the export trade. These acts of the King
led to many complaints of the Indian merchants, of which even the English Parliament
took notice; but the Government declined to
take any action, because the King had violated
no treaty.

In March, 1872, the first embassy was sent
to England. The preparations were kept secret, but it was known in British India that
the ambassadors had held no influential post,

and the King was notified that they would be received in England at court, but that he must apply to Calcutta if he wanted any new treaty. The embassy visited Rome, as the year before an Italian naval officer had concluded in Mandalay a commercial treaty between Italy and Burmah. In England they visited all the centers of trade and manufactures. On January 24, 1873, a commercial treaty was concluded at Paris between Burmah and France, which if literally carried out would have secured to France a commercial ascendancy in Burmah, at which it had aimed since 1857. It was however found out that the ambassador who had signed the treaty as first plenipotentiary held in Burmah only the rank of secretary, and the whole treaty turned out to be valueless. Other embassies were sent in 1874 to France and Italy, in 1875 to Calcutta, in 1876 to Spain, and in 1877 to Persia. Thus Burmah became better known in Europe, but its internal progress was not promoted. The King did not try, like the ruler of Japan, to secure with the aid of the ambassadors of foreign powers the services of distinguished foreigners; but the foreigners who were appointed were mostly adventurers.

The relations between the English and Burmese Governments began more than a hundred years ago. At that time Burmah extended to the sea; Assam and the valley of the middle Brahmapootra were subjected to its rule, and even from the Ganges tribute was sometimes offered. In 1757 Burmah allowed the establishment of an English factory on the coast; but, though it yielded on this and several other occasions, as a general rule it insulted and even plotted against the life of the ambassadors of British India. Not even the campaign of 1823 to 1826, by which Burmah lost two coast provinces, Aracan in the north and Tenasserim in the south, led to the establishment of regular diplomatic intercourse; and at times the life of the English Resident at Mandalay was endangered to such a degree that the position remained unfilled for years. The campaign of 1852, which was made necessary by continued provocations on the part of Burmah, proved again the superior power of England, cost Burmah its last coast province, Pegu, and led to a change of rulers. The new King, Mendone Meng, continued however to exhibit the same overbearing arrogance toward the British, and even the annexation of Pegu to British India has not been recognized by Burmah up to the present day. The first treaty of commerce and amity between Burmah and Great Britain was concluded in November, 1862. On October 25, 1867, permission was given to Great Britain to appoint a diplomatic agent at Bhamo. It was agreed to appoint, 'for conflicts between English and Burmese subjects, a mixed court in which English agents were to preside. The capital of the country, Mandalay, was connected by electric telegraph with British India. On the other hand, the

traditional mistrust against foreigners continued to manifest itself on many occasions. The Indian steamers were at first altogether forbidden to go up the Irrawaddy beyond Mandalay, and even now a steamer is allowed to ascend as far as Bhamo only once a month. No permission is given to establish a telegraph bureau outside of the royal palace. No concession was made in the "shoe question," or in the demand that an English ambassador shall approach the King barefooted. In 1875 Sir D. Forsyth was reluctantly allowed to step on a carpet instead of the bare floor. Subsequently the late King intended to draw a gauze curtain between himself and the foreigners, in case the latter should insist on not putting off their shoes. In August, 1878, the King is reported to have received the new British Resident, Mr. Shaw, in shoes, but no definite arrangement was made with regard to the subject.

In the last days of his final illness (1878) King Mendone named as his successor one of his oldest sons, the Nyoung Yan Prince, a great favorite in the palace, and much liked by all the British visitors in Mandalay. The daughter of the chief Queen, however, was engaged to be married to Thebaw, the youngest son, about twenty-one years old, and the "Queen of the South" forthwith resolved that her future son-in-law should succeed. She bought over the ministers. The Mendone's death was kept a secret until the plans were matured, and a strong following secured for Thebaw. The Nyoung Yan and his brother, the Nyoung Oke, got wind of what was going on, and, to escape assassination, took refuge at the British Residency. This settled the matter, and Thebaw ascended the throne without bloodshed, a thing unknown in the previous history of Burmah. But all his brothers were thrown into prison, with their wives and children, as a precautionary measure. The young King, with the assistance of the Kin-woon-Mingyee, or Prime Minister, who has twice been to Europe on embassies, then formed a ministry. At first all seemed to be going well. All the monopolies instituted by the late King were abolished; the strict observance of the treaty with the British Government was promised, and hopes of a solution of the "shoe question" were held out. Unfortunately, however, the presence of the Nyoung Yan at the British Residency unsettled the King's mind. The constant suspense in which he had been kept, coupled with the sudden release from the monastic restraint to which he had been accustomed, drove the young King to drink; and he very soon showed signs of the hereditary madness of his family. His fears continued to gain upon him as one after another of the princes pined away and died in the frightful underground prisons of the palace, loathsome with the filth never removed since these dens were constructed years ago. Fear of British intervention alone prevented him from putting them all to death months ago. Suddenly (February, 1879) the news of the disaster in Zoolooland reached Mandalay. That apparently decided him, and a work of cold-blooded butchery began which will hardly find a parallel in history. At first the massacre was carried on according to old Burmese use. The victims were led out of their cells in twos and threes, brought to pay homage to the King, and then disposed of in the ordinary Buddhist fashion. The head of the victim was tied down to his ankles, and a blow on the back of the neck from a heavy club put him out of pain. But this soon proved too mild a spectacle for Thebaw. The Thongzai Prince, on being brought to do reverence to his young brother, professed an utter scorn for what could be done to him, and was flogged to death. The late King's eldest son, the truculent Mekhaya Prince, who used to look on all foreigners as so much dirt under his feet, turned craven, and was taunted and driven to madness before receiving the blow which only half stunned him, when his writhing body was thrown into the gigantic trench dug to receive the victims. The massacre was carried on in a leisurely fashion, extending over several days, fiendish ingenuity being taxed to the utmost to devise fresh horrors. Moung Oke—who was Governor of Rangoon when it was captured by the British in 1856—had his nose and mouth filled with gunpowder, a light was applied, and he was then flung into the trench to be stifled by the bodies of succeeding victims. The daughter of the Nyoung Yan, a young girl of sixteen, was handed over to eight soldiers of the Royal Guard, to be pitched insensible into the same heaving grave when they had gratified their brutal lust. The wife of one prince far advanced in pregnancy was ripped up, and the agonized husband was brought to see his wife and child once more before he died. After some days of this sort of thing, the executioners got weary and hurried through their task. Little children were put in blankets and swung against the palace walls; women were battered over the head, as being less trouble than tying them up so as to get a blow at the neck. Altogether about ninety persons are believed to have been put to death in this way. No one was allowed to leave the palace while the massacre was going on, but it seems certain that Mr. Shaw, the British Resident, was inside the palace walls within a very short time of its commencement. He had been to a concert given by one of the ministers. One object of this *pwai* was to drown the cries of the victims. The remonstrance which Mr. Shaw, at the instance of the British Government, addressed to the King, was received with the utmost contempt. The guard of thirty Sepoys conceded to him arrived a short time afterward, but was not allowed to land for the day, and the detachment for Mr. St. Barbe, at Bhamo, was not allowed to disembark at all,

though the gentleman was in Mandalay. A letter from the special correspondent of the "Daily News," dated Mandalay, April 27, asserted that the King was very much hated by his own people, and that his subjects would murder him were he to leave the Myo or walled town. According to this correspon-

BURMESE LADY AND GENTLEMAN.

dent, "the Nyoung Yan is the man they desire for King. He was always good-natured and jolly, and he is the image of his father, the late King. Moreover, he is not without some claim to military distinction. In the rebellion of 1866 he commanded a division of his father's army, and defeated the rebels in several engagements. Had he been killed with the rest of his brothers, they would have accepted the situation; but now that he is safe in Calcutta, there is always a lingering hope that he may appear and claim the throne his father intended for him."

The Government of the Viceroy of India watched the strange events passing in Mandalay with great anxiety. Reënforcements nearly double the ordinary strength of the garrisons in British Burmah were ordered to the frontier. The Rangoon and Irrawaddy State Railway, 161 miles long, and running three trains daily each way, connects Rangoon with Prome. There is a telegraph from Rangoon to Mandalay, but the line beyond the British frontier, maintained by the Burmese authorities and working irregularly, is now interrupted. The extensive military preparations made by the King caused great anxiety for the safety of British residents and Europeans in Mandalay.

The British Resident at Mandalay, Mr. Shaw, died on June 15, 1879. Notwithstanding the complications existing between England and the Burmese Empire, the Burmese showed considerable regret, and the funeral was attended by most of the King's ministers. Mr. Shaw was a man thoroughly acquainted with Asiatic politics. He originally went to India as a tea-planter, and was first brought into notice by his journey to Yarkand, where he resided for some time at the court of Yakoob Beg.* His knowledge of Central Asian affairs recommended him for political employment, and he was appointed British agent at Ladakh. On the conclusion of the treaty with Yakoob Beg, Mr. Shaw was selected to carry it to Yarkand for signature. Subsequently he was sent to England as officer in charge of the Yarkand envoy. On his return to India he was appointed Resident at Mandalay. He was succeeded in that office by Colonel Horace Browne, who on his arrival at Mandalay was escorted to the Residency by several Burmese officials. On the following day the Premier, the Minister of the Interior, the Judge of the Mixed Court, and others paid official visits to him. Nevertheless, Colonel Browne's gun and sword were detained at the custom-house for a short time, though foreigners are allowed to land these ordinarily without a pass.

The relations between Burmah and the Government of British India became still more strained when Thebaw claimed sovereignty over the East Karennee country. After the close of the Burmese war in 1852, it was first proposed to carry the boundary line between the British province of Pegu and Upper Burmah on to the river Salwen, which forms the western frontier of the Shan States tributary to Siam; but it was ascertained that the Karennee country, lying between the Salwen and Sittang, was independent of the King of Burmah. The British frontier line, therefore, after crossing the latter river, was abruptly turned off to the southeast, so as to avoid Karennee and meet the Salwen at a point considerably lower down its course. The independence of Karennee, thus recognized by the British, was respected by Burmah till the spring of 1875, when the late King laid claim to the western portion of the country, and proceeded to occupy it with troops. The Government of India remonstrated against this movement, and sent Sir Douglas Forsyth on a special mission to Mandalay. For some time war seemed to be imminent, but finally the difficulties were amicably settled. The King of Burmah agreed to recognize the independence of Western Karennee, and the boundaries between that country and Upper Burmah were demarkated by a mixed British and Burmese Commission. The Karennee country has for the Government of British India a strategical importance, as in the case of war it would enable the Burmese to turn the British flank and threaten the British communications between the frontier posts and the seaports.

In July Thebaw again ordered twelve per-

* See "Annual Cyclopædia " for 1874, p. 488.

sons, including several relations of the Nyoung Yan Prince, to be murdered. About the same time a disturbance broke out at Bhamo, due to the King's officials having been sent to collect unusually heavy taxes. They met with armed resistance, and were all killed.

In the beginning of October the British agent and his party left Mandalay, without being in the least molested. The Prime Minister of Burmah wrote to the agent a polite letter, and sent carefully on board the steamer all property left at the Residency. Soon afterward the King dispatched an embassy to the Government of British India. Having arrived at Rangoon, the embassy was not permitted by the British Deputy Commissioner to proceed pending further explanations of the object of his mission.

BURRITT, ELIHU, a scholar and philanthropist, was born at New Britain, Connecticut, on December 8, 1810, and died there on March 9th. In 1828 he became apprentice to a blacksmith, and at the same time devoted all his leisure to obtain an education. So ardent was his desire for knowledge that he wrought mathematical problems while working at the anvil. At the suggestion of his brother, the principal of a small boarding-school, he studied the French, Latin, and Greek languages, and in order to devote more attention to his studies he took a short course in the school. He attempted to perform the duties of a teacher as a means of support, but ill health prevented success. He tried business pursuits, but the financial crisis of 1837 left him destitute. He then went to Worcester, Mass., and resumed work at the anvil and the study of languages. Here he translated all the Icelandic Sagas relating to the discovery of America, and obtained the name of the "Learned Blacksmith." Mr. Burritt made his first public appearance in 1841 as a lecturer, claiming in his addresses that all attainments were the result of persistent study and effort. In 1842 he started the "Christian Citizen" at Worcester, a weekly journal, devoted to antislavery, peace, temperance, and self-culture. Four years later he went to Europe, and during a visit of three years devoted himself to coöperation with the English peace advocates. During this time, also, he developed the basis of an international association known as the League of Universal Brotherhood, which aimed at the abolition of war and the promotion of fraternal relations and feelings between different countries. He was prominent in organizing the first Peace Congress, and took part in two subsequent congresses, in 1849 and 1850. In 1852 he became the editor of the "Citizen of the World" in Philadelphia. In this paper he urged the compensated emancipation of Southern slaves. The John Brown movement, at Harper's Ferry, was the death-blow of this plan, which was rapidly gaining advocates. His disappointment at the failure of his project was great. He had advocated it clearly and forcibly; he saw no other way of removing the evil. To its advancement he had devoted all his time and resources, living at times almost in poverty. Mr. Burritt then retired to a small farm which he owned at New Britain, and gave his attention to farming. He made a brief visit to England in 1863, and during the following two years he published three new books and several volumes of general writings. He was appointed United States Consul at Birmingham in 1865, and held the office until the changes in the English consulates by President Grant. He returned to America in 1870, and spent the remainder of his days in his native village. He had published "Sparks from the Anvil," London, 1848; "Miscellaneous Writings," 1850; "Olive Leaves," 1853; "Thoughts of Things at Home and Abroad," Boston, 1854; "A Walk from John O'Groat's to Land's End," 1865; and "Lectures and Speeches," 1869.

BUTT, ISAAC, an Irish lawyer and statesman, born in 1813, died May 5, 1879. He was educated at Trinity College, Dublin, where he took high classical and mathematical honors and distinguished himself as a speaker in the debates of the College Historical Society. He was elected at an early age to the Professorship of Political Economy there, and was one of the first editors of the "Dublin University Magazine." He was called to the bar in 1838, and practiced on the Munster Circuit with great success. On his first entrance into public life he was a strenuous champion of the Conservative and Protestant party, and was chosen an Alderman of the Corporation of Dublin by that party, in order that he might be opposed to Alderman Daniel O'Connell. His Parliamentary career commenced by his election for Harwich in May, 1852. A general election followed soon after, when he stood at Youghal against Hon. John Fortescue, and was elected by a majority of two. He continued to sit for Youghal until 1865. At that

time Mr. Gavan Duffy and Mr. George Henry Moore were the most conspicuous members of the Irish party. Mr. Butt kept aloof from them, remaining a Liberal-Conservative, and avoiding the tenant-right and other popular causes. Finally he became in the House an assiduous though unattached follower of Lord Palmerston. His speeches at that time were short and devoid of any pretension to oratory. It was only in 1871, after his return for Limerick in the National and Home-Rule party interest, that the position of leader was accorded to him by the Irish Liberal representatives. The dissolution was preceded in 1873 by the Home-Rule conference in Dublin, at which a definite programme was adopted for the Home-Rule movement; and on that programme the constituencies were appealed to in 1874. The general election resulted in the return of fifty-six or -seven followers of Mr. Butt, the Liberal representatives having adopted the programme of the conference, and Mr. Butt thus became in the present Parliament the first Irish Parliamentary leader of a majority of Irish representatives. In 1875 the Irish Parliamentary party assumed a definite organization, and under Mr. Butt's leadership procured considerable modification in the Peace Preservation Acts of the Government. In the next session the Home-Rule question came prominently forward, and Mr. Butt drew up a series of bills for the redress of Irish grievances, which were committed to the charge of various members of the party. Prominent among these were the Irish University measure, the franchise bills, and the land bills. The intermediate education bill of 1878 was suggested by Mr. Butt, and his last appearances in the House were those in which he advocated that measure. When a section of the Home-Rule party adopted the policy known as obstruction, Mr. Butt strenuously opposed that proceeding as unconstitutional, and thereby lost a considerable share of his influence.

C

CALIFORNIA. The great subject of interest in California during the year was the new State Constitution. The Convention adjourned on March 3d, after having been in session one hundred and fifty-seven days, and the document it presented to the people was received probably with more denunciations from the press than had ever before been bestowed upon a similar instrument. These were even accompanied with reproaches against the members of the Convention. This Constitution was submitted to a vote of the people for acceptance and approved, at an election held on May 7th.

The chief feature of the Constitution consists in some new regulations which it introduces in the affairs of society, and which were

supposed by many to be ruinous to present methods, or to the interests involved in them; while others considered that these provisions would tend to remove unjust and unequal privileges which had grown up under the operations of civil affairs. Some of the provisions which are different from those generally incorporated in the State Constitutions are here presented.

In the Bill of Rights it is provided that a trial by jury may be waived in all criminal cases not amounting to felony by consent of parties, and in civil actions by consent of the parties in such manner as may be prescribed by law. In civil actions and misdemeanors the jury may consist of twelve or any less number the parties may agree upon. Three fourths of a jury may render a verdict in civil actions.

The section regulating the right of suffrage closes with the following provision: "No native of China, no idiot, insane person, or person convicted of any infamous crime, and no person hereafter convicted of the embezzlement or misappropriation of public money, shall ever exercise the privileges of an elector in this State."

The sessions of the Legislature after 1880 commence on the first Monday after the first day of January, and are biennial. The election of members of the Legislature after 1879 will be held on the first Tuesday after the first Monday in November. Senators are chosen for four years and Representatives for two years. There are forty of the former and eighty of the latter. In adjusting the representation of districts, no persons who are not eligible to become citizens of the United States, under the naturalization laws, shall be counted as forming a part of the population of any district. No pay shall be allowed to members after sixty days; and no bill shall be introduced in either House after fifty days except on the consent of two thirds of the members. On the final passage of all bills they shall be read at length and receive the vote of a majority of the members of each House to become laws. The Governor may veto some items of appropriation bills and approve of others. No person holding any lucrative office under the United States or any other power shall be eligible to any civil office of profit under the State. Local officers or postmasters with a salary less than five hundred dollars and militia officers are excepted. "No person convicted of the embezzlement or defalcation of the public funds of the United States, or of any State, or of any county or municipality therein, shall ever be eligible to any office of honor, trust, or profit under the State; and the Legislature shall provide by law for the punishment of embezzlement or defalcation as a felony."

"No money shall ever be appropriated or drawn from the State Treasury for the use or benefit of any corporation, association, asylum, hospital, or any other institution not under the exclusive management and control of the State as a State institution; nor shall any grant or donation of property ever be made thereto by the State; provided, that notwithstanding anything contained in any section of the Constitution, the Legislature shall have the power to grant aid to institutions conducted for the support and maintenance of minor orphans or half orphans, or abandoned children, or aged persons in indigent circumstances—such aid to be granted by a uniform rule, and proportioned to the number of inmates of such respective institutions; provided further, that the State shall have at any time the right to inquire into the management of such institutions; provided further, that whenever any county, or city and county, or city,

or town shall provide for the support of minor orphans, or half orphans, or abandoned children, or aged persons in indigent circumstances, such county, city and county, city, or town shall be entitled to receive the same pro rata appropriations as may be granted to such institutions under church or other control. An accurate statement of the receipts and expenditures of public moneys shall be attached to and published with the laws at every regular session of the Legislature."

"Every act shall embrace but one subject, which subject shall be expressed in its title. But if any subject shall be embraced in an act which shall not be expressed in its title, such act shall be void only as to so much thereof as shall not be expressed in its title. No law shall be revised or amended by reference to its title; but in such case the act revised or section amended shall be reënacted and published at length as revised or amended."

"The Legislature shall have no power to authorize lotteries or gift enterprises for any purpose, and shall pass laws to prohibit the sale in this State of lottery or gift-enterprise tickets, or tickets in any scheme in the nature of a lottery. The Legislature shall pass laws to regulate or prohibit the buying and selling of the shares of the capital stock of corporations in any stock board, stock exchange, or stock market under the control of any association. All contracts for the sale of shares of the capital stock of any corporation or association, on margin or to be delivered at a future day, shall be void, and any money paid on such contracts may be recovered by the party paying it by suit in any court of competent jurisdiction."

In all elections by the Legislature the members shall vote viva voce.

"Neither the Legislature, nor any county, city and county, township, school district, or other municipal corporation, shall ever make an appropriation, or pay from any public fund whatever, or grant anything to or in aid of any religious sect, church, creed, or sectarian purpose, or help to support or sustain any school, college, university, hospital, or other institution controlled by any religious creed, church, or sectarian denomination whatever; nor shall any grant or donation of personal property or real estate ever be made by the State, or any city, city and county, town, or other municipal corporation, for any religious creed, church, or sectarian purpose whatever." The Legislature, however, is not to be prevented from granting aid in the manner above mentioned.

"The Legislature shall have no power to give or to lend, or to authorize the giving or lending, of the credit of the State, or of any county, city and county, city, township, or other political corporation or subdivision of the State now existing, or that may be hereafter established, in aid of or to any person, association, or corporation, whether municipal or otherwise, or to pledge the credit thereof, in any manner whatever, for the payment of the liabilities of any individual, association, municipal or other corporation whatever; nor shall it have power to make any gift, or authorize the making of any gift, of any public money or thing of value to any individual, municipal or other corporation whatever; provided, that nothing in this section shall prevent the Legislature granting aid" as above mentioned; "and it shall not have power to authorize the State, or any political subdivision thereof, to subscribe for stock, or to become a stockholder in any corporation whatever."

"The Legislature shall have no power to grant, or authorize any county or municipal authority to grant, any extra compensation or allowance to any public officer, agent, servant, or contractor, after service has been rendered, or a contract has been entered into and performed, in whole or in part, nor to pay, or to authorize the payment of, any claim hereafter created against the State, or any county or municipality of the State, under any agreement or contract made without express authority of law; and all such unauthorized agreements or contracts shall be null and void."

"The Legislature shall pass laws for the regulation and limitation of the charges for services performed and commodities furnished by telegraph and gas corporations, and the charges by corporations or individuals for storage and wharfage, in which there is a public use; and where laws shall provide for the selection of any person or officer to regulate and limit such rates, no such person or officer shall be selected by any corporation or individual interested in the business to be regulated, and no person shall be selected who is an officer or stockholder in any such corporation."

"Any person who seeks to influence the vote of a member of the Legislature by brihery, promise of reward, intimidation, or any other dishonest means, shall be guilty of lobbying, which is hereby declared a felony; and it shall be the duty of the Legislature to provide by law for the punishment of this crime. Any member of the Legislature who shall be influenced in his vote or action upon any matter pending before the Legislature by any reward, or promise of future reward, shall be deemed guilty of a felony, and upon conviction thereof, in addition to such punishment as may be provided by law, shall be disfranchised and for ever disqualified from holding any office or public trust. Any person may be compelled to testify in any lawful investigation or judicial proceeding against any person who may be charged with having committed the offense of bribery or corrupt solicitation, or with having been influenced in his vote or action, as a member of the Legislature, by reward, or promise of future reward, and shall not be permitted to withhold his testimony upon the ground that it may criminate himself or subject him to public infamy; but such testimony shall not afterward be used against him in any judicial proceeding, except for perjury in giving such testimony."

The term of office of the Governor and State officers is four years. The Governor's salary is fixed at $6,000 per annum, and those of the State officers at $3,000 per annum. These salaries may be reduced by the Legislature, but they can not be increased. No fees are allowed to either of these officers. The Governor is made ineligible to the United States Senate during his term of office.

The Chief Justice and the six Associate Justices of the Supreme Court are to be chosen at the State elections, and their term of office is fixed at twelve years. A Superior Court is created for each county. "The salaries of the Justices of the Supreme Court shall be paid by the State. One half of the salary of each Superior Court Judge shall be paid by the State; the other half thereof shall be paid by the county for which he is elected. During the term of the first Judges elected under this Constitution, the annual salaries of the Justices of the Supreme Court shall be $6,000 each. Until otherwise changed by the Legislature, the Superior Court Judges shall receive an annual salary of $3,000 each, payable monthly, except the Judges of the city and county of San Francisco, and the counties of Alameda, San Joaquin, Los Angeles, Santa Clara, Yuba and Sutter combined, Sacramento, Butte, Nevada and Sonoma, who shall receive $4,000 each." "No Judge of a Superior Court nor of the Supreme Court shall, after the first day of July, 1880, be allowed to draw or receive any monthly salary unless he shall take and subscribe an affidavit, before an officer entitled to administer oaths, that no cause in his court remains undecided that has been submitted for decision for the period of ninety days."

"The public-school system shall include primary and grammar schools, and such high schools, evening schools, normal schools, and technical schools as may be established by the Legislature or by municipal or district authority; but the entire revenue derived from the State school fund and the State school tax shall be applied exclusively to the support of primary and grammar schools." As to the use of appropriations, it is provided that "no public money shall ever be appropriated for the support of any sectarian or denominational school, or any school not under the exclusive control of the officers of the public schools; nor shall any sectarian or denominational doctrine be taught, or instruction thereon be permitted, directly or indirectly, in any of the common schools of this State."

Private property shall not be taken or sold for the payment of the corporate debt of any political or municipal corporation. "No county, city, town, township, board of education, or school district shall incur any indebtedness or liability in any manner or for any purpose, exceeding in any year the income and revenue provided for it for such year, without the assent of two thirds of the qualified electors thereof voting at an election to be held for that purpose, nor unless before or at the time of incurring such indebtedness provision shall be made for the collection of an annual tax sufficient to pay the interest on such indebtedness as it falls due, and also to constitute a sinking fund for the payment of the principal thereof within twenty years from the time of contracting the same. Any indebtedness or liability incurred contrary to this provision shall be void." "No public work or improvement of any description whatsoever shall be done or made in any city, in, upon, or about the streets thereof, or otherwise, the cost and expense of which is made chargeable or may be assessed upon private property, by special assessment, unless an estimate of such cost and expense shall be made, and an assessment in proportion to benefits on the property to be affected or benefited shall be levied, collected, and paid into the city treasury before such work or improvement shall be commenced or any contract for letting or doing the same authorized or performed. In any city where there are no public works owned and controlled by the municipality for supplying the same with water or artificial light, any individual or any company duly incorporated for such purpose under and by authority of the laws of this State shall, under the direction of the Superintendent of Streets or other officer in control thereof, and under such general regulations as the municipality may prescribe for damages and indemnity for damages, have the privilege of using the public streets and thoroughfares thereof, and of laying down pipes and conduits therein, and connections therewith, so far as may be necessary for introducing into and supplying such city and its inhabitants either with gaslight or other illuminating light, or with fresh water for domestic and all other purposes, upon the condition that the municipal government shall have the right to regulate the charges thereof."

"Each stockholder of a corporation or joint-stock association shall be individually and personally liable for such proportion of all its debts and liabilities contracted or incurred during the time he was a stockholder, as the amount of stock or shares owned by him bears to the whole of the subscribed capital stock or shares of the corporation or association. The directors or trustees of corporations and joint-stock associations shall be jointly and severally liable to the creditors and stockholders for all moneys embezzled or misappropriated by the officers of such corporation or joint-stock association during the term of office of such director or trustee."

"No railroad or other transportation company shall grant free passes, or passes or tickets at a discount, to any person holding any office of honor, trust, or profit in this State; and the acceptance of any such pass or ticket,

by a member of the Legislature or any public officer, other than Railroad Commissioner, shall work a forfeiture of his office." The State is to be divided into three districts, in each of which a Railroad Commissioner shall be elected by the voters. Some of the duties assigned to these Commissioners are thus stated: "They shall have the power, and it shall be their duty, to establish rates of charges for the transportation of passengers and freight by railroad or other transportation companies, and publish the same from time to time, with such changes as they may make; to examine the books, records, and papers of all railroad and other transportation companies, and for this purpose they shall have power to issue subpœnas and all other necessary process; to hear and determine complaints against railroad and other transportation companies, to send for persons and papers, to administer oaths, take testimony, and punish for contempt of their orders and processes, in the same manner and to the same extent as courts of record, and enforce their decisions and correct abuses through the medium of the courts. Said Commissioners shall prescribe a uniform system of accounts to be kept by all such corporations and companies. Any railroad corporation or transportation company which shall fail or refuse to conform to such rates as shall be established by such Commissioners, or shall charge rates in excess thereof, or shall fail to keep their accounts in accordance with the system prescribed by the Commission, shall be fined not exceeding $20,000 for each offense; and every officer, agent, or employee of any such corporation or company, who shall demand or receive rates in excess thereof, or who shall in any manner violate the provisions of this section, shall be fined not exceeding $5,000 or be imprisoned in the county jail not exceeding one year. In all controversies, civil or criminal, the rates of fares and freights established by said Commission shall be deemed conclusively just and reasonable; and in any action against such corporation or company for damages sustained by charging excessive rates, the plaintiff, in addition to the actual damage, may, in the discretion of the judge or jury, recover exemplary damages. Said Commission shall report to the Governor, annually, their proceedings, and such other facts as may be deemed important."

Land and improvements thereon shall be separately assessed. Cultivated and uncultivated land, of the same quality and similarly situated, shall be assessed at the same value.

"The Legislature shall have the power to provide by law for the payment of all taxes on real property by installments." "The Legislature shall by law require each taxpayer in this State to make and deliver to the county assessor annually a statement under oath setting forth specifically all the real and personal property owned by such taxpayer, or in his possession, or under his control, at 12 o'clock meridian on the first Monday of March." "All property, except as hereinafter provided, shall be assessed in the county, city and county, city, town, township, or district in which it is situated, in the manner prescribed by law. The franchise, roadway, road-bed, rails, and rolling stock of all railroads operated in more than one county in this State shall be assessed by the State Board of Equalization, at their actual value, and the same shall be apportioned to the counties, cities and counties, cities, towns, townships, and districts in which such railroads are located, in proportion to the number of miles of railway laid in such counties, cities and counties, cities, towns, townships, and districts; and all other property of railroads shall be assessed by the counties in which such property is situated."

"Income taxes may be assessed to and collected from persons, corporations, joint-stock associations or companies resident or doing business in this State, or any one or more of them, in such cases and amounts, and in such manner, as shall be prescribed by law." "The Legislature shall provide for the levy and collection of an annual poll-tax of not less than $2 on every male inhabitant of this State, over twenty-one and under sixty years of age, except paupers, idiots, insane persons, and Indians not taxed. Said tax shall be paid into the State School Fund."

"The Legislature shall not, in any manner, create any debt or debts, liability or liabilities, which shall, singly or in the aggregate with any previous debts or liabilities, exceed the sum of three hundred thousand dollars, except in case of war to repel invasion or suppress insurrection, unless the same shall be authorized by law for some single object or work to be distinctly specified therein, which law shall provide ways and means, exclusive of loans, for the payment of the interest of such debt or liability as it falls due, and also to pay and discharge the principal of such debt or liability within twenty years of the time of the contracting thereof, and shall be irrepealable until the principal and interest thereon shall be paid and discharged; but no such law shall take effect until, at a general election, it shall have been submitted to the people and shall have received a majority of all the votes cast for and against it at such election; and all moneys raised by authority of such law shall be applied only to the specific object therein stated, or to the payment of the debt thereby created."

Article XIX. contains the following provisions relative to the Chinese:

SECTION 1. The Legislature shall prescribe all necessary regulations for the protection of the State, and the counties, cities, and towns thereof, from the burdens and evils arising from the presence of aliens who are or may become vagrants, paupers, mendicants, criminals, or invalids afflicted with contagious or infectious diseases, and from aliens otherwise dangerous or detrimental to the well-being or peace of the State, and to impose conditions upon which such persons may reside in the State, and to provide the means and mode of their removal from the State upon failure or refusal to comply with such conditions; provided, that nothing contained in this section shall be construed to impair or limit the power of the Legislature to pass such police laws or other regulations as it may deem necessary.

SEC. 2. No corporation now existing or hereafter formed under the laws of this State shall, after the adoption of this Constitution, employ, directly or indirectly, in any capacity, any Chinese or Mongolian. The Legislature shall pass such laws as may be necessary to enforce this provision.

SEC. 3. No Chinese shall be employed on any State, county, municipal, or other public work, except in punishment for crime.

SEC. 4. The presence of foreigners ineligible to become citizens of the United States is declared to be dangerous to the well-being of the State, and the Legislature shall discourage their immigration by all the means within its power. Asiatic coolyism is a form of human slavery, and is for ever prohibited in this State, and all contracts for cooly labor shall be void. All companies or corporations, whether formed in this country or any foreign country, for the importation of such labor, shall be subject to such penalties as the Legislature may prescribe. The Legislature shall delegate all necessary power to the incorporated cities and towns of this State for the removal of Chinese without the limits of such cities and towns, or for their location within prescribed portions of those limits, and it shall also provide necessary legislation to prohibit the introduction into this State of Chinese after the adoption of this Constitution. This section shall be enforced by appropriate legislation.

Among the miscellaneous provisions of the Constitution are some new ones. Any citizen of the State "who shall, after the adoption of this Constitution, fight a duel with deadly weapons, or send or accept'a challenge to fight a duel with deadly weapons, either within this State or out of it, or who shall act as second, or knowingly aid or assist in any manner those thus offending, shall not be allowed to hold any office of profit, or to enjoy the right of suffrage under this Constitution." "All property, real and personal, owned by either husband or wife before marriage, and that acquired by either of them afterward by gift, devise, or descent, shall be their separate property." "Every person shall be disqualified from holding any office of profit in this State who shall have been convicted of having given or offered a bribe to procure his election or appointment. Laws shall be made to exclude from office, serving on juries, and from the right of suffrage, persons convicted of bribery, perjury, forgery, malfeasance in office, or other high crimes. The privilege of free suffrage shall be supported by laws regulating elections and prohibiting, under adequate penalties, all undue influence thereon from power, bribery, tumult, or other improper practice." "Mechanics, material men, artisans, and laborers of every class shall have a lien upon the property upon which they have bestowed labor or furnished material, for the value of such labor done and material furnished; and the Legislature shall provide by law for the speedy and efficient enforcement of such liens." "Eight hours shall constitute a legal day's work on all public work." "No person shall, on account of sex, be disqualified from entering upon or pursuing any lawful business, vocation, or profession."

The following most ample provisions were made for the election relative to the Constitution:

SEC. 4. The Superintendent of Printing of the State of California shall, at least thirty days before the first Wednesday in May, A. D. 1879, cause to be printed at the State printing-office, in pamphlet form, simply stitched, as many copies of this Constitution as there are registered voters in this State, and mail one copy thereof to the post-office address of each registered voter; provided, any copies not called for ten days after reaching their delivery office shall be subject to general distribution by the several postmasters of the State. The Governor shall issue his proclamation, giving notice of the election for the adoption or rejection of this Constitution, at least thirty days before the said first Wednesday of May, 1879, and the boards of supervisors of the several counties shall cause said proclamation to be made public in their respective counties, and general notice of said election to be given at least fifteen days next before said election.

SEC. 5. The Superintendent of Printing of the State of California shall, at least twenty days before said election, cause to be printed and delivered to the clerk of each county in this State five times the number of properly prepared ballots for said election that there are voters in said respective counties, with the words printed thereon, "For the new Constitution." He shall likewise cause to be so printed and delivered to said clerks five times the number of properly prepared ballots for said election that there are voters in said respective counties, with the words printed thereon, "Against the new Constitution." The Secretary of State is hereby authorized and required to furnish the Superintendent of State Printing a sufficient quantity of legal ballot paper, now on hand, to carry out the provisions of this section.

It was provided that the Constitution should take effect and be of force on and after the 4th of July, 1879, at 12 o'clock meridian, so far as related to the election of all officers and the commencement of their terms of office and the meeting of the Legislature. In all other respects and for all other purposes it should take effect on January 1, 1880, at 12 o'clock meridian.

The Convention adjourned on the 3d of March, about two months previous to the election, and a vehement campaign against it was commenced. It was conducted with so much virulence that it probably in the end produced, as is usual in such cases, a reaction in favor of the instrument. A canvass of the position of the press of the State on the question, including some papers of neighboring States with business interests closely identified with California, showed on April 19th one hundred and fifty papers arrayed against the Constitution, and only forty-seven urging its adoption.

A Republican mass meeting on March 19th, at Sacramento, adopted the following among other resolutions:

Fifth. That, inasmuch as the ruffian king of the sand-lots has ordered his followers to support the new Constitution, and has, through his brutal speeches and his self-appointed and unscrupulous newspaper organ, made support of that instrument the test of membership in his so-called Workingmen's party; and as the proposed new Constitution is dangerous in its tendencies, experimental in its main provisions, lacking in the essential qualities of a Constitution, conspicuous for its sins of omission, and generally unworthy the confidence of the people, we call upon all good citizens to unite in defeating him and his schemes and Constitution, believing that the adoption of the new Constitution under such auspices would work irreparable damage to California; that as Republicans we oppose it, as citizens we oppose it, and we ask the party and people to aid us in defeating Kearney and the new Constitution at one and the same time.

One speaker said: "The election of May 7th for or against the new Constitution was to be the most important one in which the people of California were ever called upon to take part. The Kearney party had made the adoption of the new Constitution a party plank, and the Republican party must declare against it and defeat Kearney and his Constitution also; for a victory for Kearney in May would go far toward giving him victory in September, when Congressmen are to be elected and a Legislature chosen. The people must in May decide whether they will leave the safe retreat in which they have prospered for thirty years, and sail away into experimental seas under a Constitution which the men who made it can't explain and the people who read it can't understand. The Republicans of the State must take position against the instrument, this mongrel Constitution which it is sought to crowd down the throats of the people."

The vote on the Constitution was a very full one. In the counties of the State which were equally settled, the vote cast was nearly as large as that given at the Presidential election in 1876. The following counties serve as an illustration:

COUNTIES.	1876.	1879.
Alameda	8,296	8.221
Colusa	2,235	2,200
Contra Costa	2,022	1,999
Fresno	1,296	1,226
Lake	1,093	1,006
Monterey	2,195	2,100
Napa	2,118	1,984
Sacramento	6,324	6,210
San Benito	1,099	919
San Bernardino	1,281	1,204

The same rule is observable in all the agricultural counties with one or two exceptions. Three counties exhibited an increase over 1876, two agricultural and the third mining, viz.:

COUNTIES.	1876.	1879.
Marin	1,279	1,818
Mono	278	1,120
Mendocino	2,212	2,879

These changes agree with observed facts. Railroad extension has been settling up Marin and Mendocino very rapidly. The recent mineral discoveries in Mono have attracted a large population. But nearly all the other mining counties have been losing, viz.:

COUNTIES.	1876.	1879.
El Dorado..............................	2,773	1,496
Nevada................................	4,205	3,416
Placer................................	2,888	2,031
Sierra................................	1,428	654

The vote in San Francisco was 3,760 behind that of 1876, although three years' growth should be added.

The vote on the Constitution, as canvassed by the Governor and other officers, lacking the returns from Mariposa County, was 77,959 for the Constitution, 67,134 against the Constitution; total vote, 145,212. Majority for the Constitution, 10,825.

Grand demonstrations of the Workingmen in San Francisco and Sacramento were made on the adoption of the Constitution. The resolutions adopted by the former related chiefly to some local grievances. Those adopted by the latter are expressive of the sentiment of the meetings, some of which were as follows:

Whereas, The Workingmen's party is the party of reform, honesty, integrity, and manhood;

Whereas, The new Constitution emanated from the Workingmen's party, and through its instrumentality and by its votes became the law of the land; therefore,

Resolved, That the Workingmen are the men to administer the government of California according to the Constitution we have given her, a right we must and shall enjoy; and be it further

Resolved, That we thank our brothers in New York and Chicago, the Internationalists and Socialists, for the sympathy generously tendered us, and the admiration expressed for our noble and gallant leader, Denis Kearney.

The political divisions of the State have been greatly modified by the new Constitution. There are to be no more judicial districts. Every county in the State is to elect a Superior Judge, with the following exceptions: Yuba and Sutter are to elect one; San Francisco is to elect twelve; and Sacramento, San Joaquin, Los Angeles, Sonoma, Santa Clara, and Alameda, two each. In addition there are three railroad districts, as follows: First Railroad District—Alpine, Amador, Butte, Calaveras, Colusa, Del Norte, El Dorado, Humboldt, Lake, Lassen, Mendocino, Modoc, Napa, Nevada, Placer, Plumas, Sacramento, Shasta, Sierra, Siskiyou, Solano, Sonoma, Sutter, Tehama, Trinity, Yolo, and Yuba. Second Railroad District—San Francisco, Marin, and San Mateo. Third Railroad District—Alameda, Contra Costa, Fresno, Inyo, Kern, Los Angeles, Mariposa, Merced, Mono, Monterey, San Benito, San Bernardino, San Diego, San Joaquin, San Luis Obispo, Santa Barbara, Santa Clara, Santa Cruz, Stanislaus, Tulare, Tuolumne, and Ventura. The Legislature has the power to alter or change in any way that it sees fit these districts. The other district officers to be elected are the members of the Board of Equalization, who are four in number, with the Comptroller as chairman. They are to be chosen from the Congressional Districts, which are as follows: First Congressional District—

San Francisco. Second Congressional District—Contra Costa, Alameda, San Joaquin, Calaveras, Amador, El Dorado, Sacramento, Placer, Nevada, Alpine, and Tuolumne. Third Congressional District—Marin, Sonoma, Napa, Lake, Solano, Yolo, Sutter, Yuba, Sierra, Butte, Plumas, Lassen, Tehama, Colusa, Mendocino, Humboldt, Trinity, Shasta, Siskiyou, Klamath, and Del Norte. Fourth Congressional District—San Diego, Los Angeles, San Bernardino, Santa Barbara, San Luis Obispo, Tulare, Monterey, Fresno, Kern, Merced, Mariposa, Stanislaus, Santa Clara, Santa Cruz, San Mateo, Mono, and Inyo. The members of the Board of Equalization are to be taken from these districts, while the Railroad Commissioners are assigned to larger and different groups of counties. The Third Railroad District takes in more than the Fourth Congressional District. The Second Railroad District is larger by two counties than the First Congressional District, while the First Railroad District very nearly embraces the Second and Third Congressional Districts. These divisions within divisions will require much forming and reforming on the part of the State Conventions. Having made the nominations for State officers, they must separate first into three parts to nominate Railroad Commissioners, and then into four parts to nominate members of the Board of Equalization and members of Congress.

An active campaign preparatory to the State election was immediately commenced. Five distinct parties soon held their conventions to make nominations for State officers and a declaration of their principles.

The State Convention of the Workingmen's party assembled at San Francisco on June 3d for the nomination of candidates for State officers. Denis Kearney, president of the party in California, presided. The following ticket was nominated: For Governor, William F. White; for Lieutenant-Governor, W. R. Andrus; for Secretary of State, A. A. Smith; for State Treasurer, L. B. Clarke; for State Comptroller, Hugh Jones; for Attorney-General, C. W. Cross; for Surveyor-General, H. J. Stevenson; for Superintendent of Public Instruction, H. D. Trout; for Chief Justice of the Supreme Court, R. F. Morrison.

The following platform was reported by the Committee, considered *seriatim*, and adopted with some additions:

The Workingmen of California, in convention assembled, do adopt and proclaim the following as their platform and declaration of principles:

1. That we recognize the Constitution of the United States of America and the Constitution of the State of California as the great charters of our liberties and the paramount law of the land, and California as an inseparable part of the American Union, and the system of government thereby inaugurated as the only wise, free, just, and equal government that has ever existed—the last, best, and only hope of man for self-government.

2. The letter and spirit of the new Constitution must be enforced.

3. We utterly repudiate all spirit of communism or agrarianism.

4. No land or other subsidies shall ever be granted to corporations.

5. Vested rights in property must be respected, but land monopoly must be prohibited.

6. Money, mortgages, and bonds must be taxed.

7. The dignity of labor must be upheld, and labor of male and female, when of equal value, must be equally compensated.

8. Any official who shall violate the pledges given to secure his election should be punished as a felon.

9. The contract system of labor of criminals should be abolished, and criminal labor so regulated as not to conflict with free labor throughout the United States.

10. All public officers shall receive fixed salaries, and all fees must be accounted for as public money.

11. That the honors and legal pay of all officials should be considered equivalent for the best services they can render the State, while official jobbery, bribery, or corruption must be visited by sure and severe punishment.

12. All labor on public works shall be performed by the day at ruling rates, and eight hours must constitute a day's work.

13. A system of compulsory education for children between the ages of eight and fourteen years must be adopted; education free in public schools, and all books paid for by the State. That the State should acquire a copyright for school text-books, which must be the property of the State for ever, and the State print the same at the State printing-office.

14. We pledge this party to maintain in its purity the public-school system authorized by the Constitution, and will, when in our power, establish in connection therewith departments for industrial education.

15. Article XI. of the Constitution must not be construed in favor of the appointment of public officials whenever their election by the people direct is at all practicable.

16. Lobbying having been declared a felony in the new Constitution, we demand that the Legislature shall enforce said provision of the fundamental law by the most stringent enactments.

17. Foreigners ineligible to citizenship shall not be licensed to peddle goods or commodities of any character throughout the State of California.

18. Land monopoly being contrary to the spirit of republican institutions and detrimental to the progress of society, and conducing to the creation of a wealthy class of landholders side by side with a landless multitude, therefore we hereby declare ourselves in favor of adopting every legitimate means to prevent the monopoly of the soil in a few hands.

19. Malfeasance in a public office must be punished as a felony.

20. That the laws now existing for the punishment of buying and selling votes are insufficient, in that, both the buyer and seller being equally guilty, neither can be obliged to give evidence of the guilt of the other. We therefore favor the enactment of laws by which the person bribing or attempting to bribe an elector shall alone be punished.

21. We demand that the fullest investigation be had, under the authority of the ensuing Legislature, into the alleged scandalous character of the opposition to the adoption of the new Constitution; and if the charges prove true, that condign punishment be visited upon the guilty ones.

22. The Legislature should cause to be examined and prosecuted land frauds in the State of California.

23. The same value should not be taxed twice the same year under the same system of taxation.

24. Interest on money should not exceed 6 per cent. per annum.

25. We demand the immediate restoration to preemption and sale of all forfeited railroad lands, and that no further extensions be granted.

26. We condemn the action of our Senators and Representatives in Congress in depriving this State of representation for one year, while her most important interests are at stake, as an unwarrantable perversion of their official duties, made under a false pretense of economy, but really in the hope to gain a political advantage over the W. P. C.

27. That we condemn the inaction of our Senators and Representatives in Congress not attempting to have the withdrawal from preëmption and sale of lands illegally claimed by the defunct Atlantic and Pacific Railroad Company removed, and said lands restored to the people and reopened to preëmption and sale.

28. We condemn the "Desert Land Bill" and all other land-grabs, under whatever name or on whatever pretense.

29. Contracts by debtors for the payment of fees of the attorneys of creditors should be prohibited.

30. Laws should be passed providing for deductions of debts due bona fide residents from unsecured credits in matters of taxation.

31. That notaries public should be elected by the people, one from each county. That the best protection of our frontier will be a population of settlers owning their own lands, and that it will be the part of wisdom for the Government to expend the money now squandered for such protection by settling the people on the unoccupied land.

Whereas, Great apprehension exists in the mining counties that some legislation under the new Constitution might be unfavorable to mining interests, we declare that under the protection of our party their vested rights shall be respected.

That the President and Vice-President of the United States and United States Senators should be elected by direct vote of the people, and that no man should be elected to the office of President or Vice-President of the United States for two consecutive terms.

We are tired of the dreary discussion of dead issues in our National Congress, while great living issues are confronting the country. The people want bread and not stones. We hail the awakening of the oppressed workingmen and impoverished farmers to a sense of their power and the cause of their sufferings as the harbinger of a new revolution in behalf of human rights against vicious systems and dishonest politicians.

That the national bank law should be repealed, and all moneys issued by the United States be a full legal tender for all debts public and private.

Congress ought to pass fare and freight bills and bills to prohibit unjust discriminations and other abuses in the management on the overland routes.

That the Government of the United States should establish throughout the States a system of postal savings banks.

Charges for freights and fares on railroads and for the use of water, gas, etc., must be so regulated that there shall be no discrimination between persons and places, and that capital actually invested in railroad, water, and gas rights should yield no greater net income than capital invested in farming and other productive industries. The Legislature must pass laws to carry into effect the police power of the State in order to prevent the importation of Chinese, and Congress should abrogate all treaties that come in conflict with the nineteenth article of the new Constitution.

We hold that the State and county tickets formed under the auspices of the W. P. C. must be made up of friends of the new Constitution, irrespective of party predilections. To further secure the efficiency of the new organic law, we will attack its opponents with the most effective weapons; but among ourselves, in difference of opinion, we will allow liberal discussion, give considerate attention, and exercise the largest charity. To these ends we invite the coöperation of all the friends of the new Constitution. We must do all in our power as a party to prevent any conflict between the interests of mining and agriculture, by just laws, engineering skill, and public aid.

That the cardinal principles of true reform in politics is that the office shall seek the man and not the man the office, and that honesty, capability, and faithfulness to our republican system of government are the main requirements in the selection of candidates for office.

That the Democratic and Republican parties have signally failed to apply these principles, inasmuch as both have been completely controlled by "rings," seeking office only to betray the people. That we denounce and condemn the efforts of both the old political parties to create a solid North or a solid South, and thereby sectionalize the country; that in the organization of our party we know no North, no South, no East, no West, that we are determined the government of our country shall be so administered as to secure equal rights to all our people, be they high or low, rich or poor, black or white, and that by so doing the Union can and will be perpetuated for ever.

The following are some of the additions made to the platform: "That all lands belonging to the State or to the General Government should be disposed of to actual settlers only, and in limited quantities—not to exceed 320 acres." This declaration was simply added to the original plank. To the resolution relating to the punishment for bribing a voter, leaving the guilt wholly on the one who offers the bribe, Mr. Sweasey offered an additional clause to declare men who attempt to intimidate their employees as guilty of bribery. Adopted. Postmasters were added to the list of public officials to be elected by the people. The clause relating to the suppression of Chinese immigration was amended by the addition of a resolution asking the Workingmen of the East to pledge their candidates for Congress to vote for the abrogation of the Burlingame treaty. A separate resolution was passed condemning President Hayes for his veto of the anti-Chinese bill. The resolution added that cooly labor is a form of slavery, and that the Chinese must go. It was also resolved that "judicial officers shall take no active part in politics"; that "corporations must discharge their Chinese or go out of business. Laws must be passed to purge the communities of the presence of Chinese and to prevent their acquiring any further foothold among us," etc., etc.

The Republican State Convention for the nomination of State officers under the new Constitution assembled at Sacramento on June 18th. Frank Pixley was made chairman. The following nominations were made for State officers: For Governor, George C. Perkins; for Lieutenant-Governor, General John Mansfield; for Secretary of State, D. M. Burns; for Comptroller, D. M. Kenfield; for Treasurer, John Weil; for Attorney-General, A. L. Hart; for Surveyor-General, J. W. Shanklin; for Clerk of Supreme Court, Frank W. Gross; for Superintendent of Public Instruction, F. M. Campbell; for Chief Justice, A. L. Rhodes. The following platform was reported, accompanied by a minority report upon one point:

Resolved, That we reaffirm our allegiance to the principles of the grand national party of free soil, free labor, equal rights of the people, honest money, good public faith, and the integrity of the national Union—the party whose record furnishes some of the grand-

est and most illustrious chapters of our national history.

Resolved, That the attempt by the Democratic majorities in Congress to repeal the laws for the preservation of the purity of the ballot-box at elections for members of Congress, is in keeping with the history of the pa   whose crimes against the ballot in New York City under the Tweed dynasty in 1868 led to the enactment of those laws; that the method by which they seek to accomplish this result, by withholding appropriations for the courts of the United States unless the President will join them in their conspiracy, is revolutionary; and that the denial of the power of Congress to make regulations for the conduct of Congressional elections—a power specifically granted in the Constitution of the United States—is a palpable attempt to revive the baneful doctrine of State supremacy, which was the cause of the great rebellion.

Resolved, That the firm and united opposition of the Republican party in Congress and of the President to this new revolt against the nation should be sustained by all patriotic and law-abiding people throughout the land.

Resolved, That the new Constitution is the organic law of the State, adopted by the people in accordance with our republican form of government. It must and will be sustained by the Republican party in loyalty. It must and will receive honest legislation. It must and will receive a just and generous judicial interpretation. It must and will be enforced by an honest executive administration; and we condemn any effort to evade its provisions as unwise and treasonable to the popular will legally expressed.

Resolved, That an independent and intelligent agricultural population is the chief element of a nation's strength and prosperity, and it should be the policy of the State and General Governments to encourage the acquisition of lands in small holdings for actual use, and to discourage the monopoly by individuals or corporations in large bodies.

The Chinese question is one of national importance, demanding the consideration of the National Congress. Unrestricted Chinese immigration imperils the best interests of our coast, and ultimately that of the whole country. It menaces the labor class with an unequal competition, and is dangerous to our civilization. Not unmindful of its history and our own part therein, regarding the rights of present immigrants acquired, we demand of the General Government such legislation as shall restrict or control Chinese immigration in the future, and the repeal or modification of so much of the Burlingame treaty as interferes with the accomplishment of that object. We will spare no effort within our own State to secure by legislative enactment a judicial enforcement of the same results. Chinese immigration must be restricted and controlled.

Resolved, That it is a paramount duty and interest of the State to provide ample educational opportunities for its youth, and to permit none to be deprived of their enjoyment, and that, so far as the provisions of the new organic law will permit, legislation should facilitate and encourage the adoption of a uniform standard of qualifications for teaching, courses of study, and text-books for the public schools.

Resolved, That the Republican party—always the true friend of labor, in all its varied forms—pledges itself to secure the passage of such laws under the new Constitution as will foster, protect, and promote the development and growth of all the industries of the State.

Resolved, That the Republican party, as a just arbiter of the people, pledges itself to insist upon the passage of such laws as will prevent any conflict between the mining and certain portions of the agricultural districts and interests of the State; and we declare that vested rights of all parties shall be scrupulously respected and protected.

The Republican party, claiming to represent the principles of justice, honesty, and moral sentiment, declares its fidelity to the law and its unalterable opposition to any attempt on the part of any class to disturb the ownership of property; and while it would disfavor the accumulation of great landed estates in the possession of individuals or corporations, it would as firmly protect all the rights of all persons to all the wealth that they may legally and honestly acquire.

Whereas, The regulation of fares and freights upon all inter-State railroad travel and traffic is subject to the action of the Congress of the United States, and the regulation of fares and freights within a State is subject to local legislative jurisdiction and control;

Resolved, As the opinion of this Convention, that the Railroad Commissioners who shall be nominated by the District Conventions should make such reductions in the rates of fares and freights upon all local travel and traffic carried over railroads which have received national or State aid, operated within this State, as will reduce the same by a certain specified percentage upon the rates declared, collected, or charged by published rate-bill in force upon any such road on the first day of June, 1879; and that such Commissioners shall hereafter make such further reductions as may seem to them just and demanded by the interests of the people, but shall in no case authorize or permit any increase thereafter upon such rates so ordered.

Mr. Gorham moved that all the report except that referring to railroad matters be adopted. Carried unanimously.

Mr. Gorham then read the minority report at great length. In substance it sets forth that the figures of the annual reports of the Central Pacific Railroad show it has received $132,000,000 for transportation of freight and passengers, and that the cost therefor has been but $58,000,000, leaving a net profit of $74,000,-000 on property derived through Congressional and State legislation, and valued by the company at $100,000,000. That the people have paid on the average per year to the Central Pacific Railroad $15,522,714. That during six years the average operating expenses of said road have been but $6,856,091 per annum. That the net earnings have thus been $8,666,623 per year. That the condition of the country demands that the power vested in the State to regulate tolls on the roads between points within the State be exercised. That there should be no longer a waiting for voluntary reductions of rates by the road. That to circumvent fraud and corruption, every candidate for Governor, Lieutenant-Governor, the Legislature, or Railroad Commissioner should take a pledge to afford the relief demanded. That the rates between points within the State, for freights and fares on railroads which have received national or State aid, should be one fourth less than the rates actually charged June 1, 1879. That as only experts can make a tariff of equitable rates between various kinds of railroad service, and fairly adjust the discriminations which should be made on account of the difference in kinds of freight, quantities carried, grades, distances, curves, etc., the meaning of the resolution is that for each dollar usually and actually demanded by the railroad companies which have received national or State aid for any service whatever, a reduction shall be made of 25 cents. That until these results are accomplished transpor-

tation is of the most vital importance, and must be settled in advance of all other State questions. That pledges be exacted of the candidates, and that they can not be broken after election without endangering the peace of society.

PLEDGE OF RAILROAD COMMISSIONER.

I do solemnly pledge my word of honor that I will, if elected a Railroad Commissioner, faithfully support, without any modification or change whatever, the following order: Ordered, that the rates of fares and freights on all railroads between all points within this State which have received national or State aid, shall, from and after the 1st day of February, 1880, be fixed at three fourths the usual rates demanded and received on the 1st day of June, 1879, or at any time during the six months prior thereto, and the words usual rates above used shall be deemed to mean the rates usually and actually charged in each case, whether the same be nominally fixed or special rates; and it is further ordered that no change shall be made in the mode of computing charges or in the weight and measurement of freight, or on the classification of service which shall affect the substantial rights of parties under this order, the true object being to reduce all charges for services rendered by railroads, between points within the State over roads which have received national or State aid, one fourth below present rates. And I further solemnly pledge myself that during my term of office I will never vote for any increased rate of charge for any railroad service, but that any charge voted for by me after February 1, 1880, shall be a reduction.

PLEDGES FOR GOVERNOR, LIEUTENANT-GOVERNOR, ASSEMBLYMEN, AND RAILROAD COMMISSIONERS.

I do solemnly pledge myself to the earnest and faithful support of the new Constitution, and that I will exert all the influence I possess to aid in the election of Railroad Commissioners pledged to a reduction of one fourth on all railroad fares and freights on roads which have received national or State aid, and if elected I pledge myself in the performance of my official duties to act in accordance with this pledge.

A delegate of Solano moved to lay the report upon the table. Mr. Gorham claimed that he had not yielded the floor, and moved the adoption of the minority report as a substitute for that part of the majority report referring to railroad matters.

Mr. Gorham then spoke at length in favor of the adoption of his substitute. Afterward Mr. Houghton of Santa Clara offered as a substitute the following resolution, which was adopted:

Resolved, That in the opinion of this Convention justice demands that the present rate of freights and fares upon all lines of railroads in this State that have received State or national aid ought to be reduced at least 25 per cent.

At the same time the subject of Mr. Gorham's remarks and the original railroad resolution were referred to the District Conventions—yeas 205, nays 200.

The State Convention of the New Constitution party was held at Sacramento on June 26th. Marion Biggs of Butler County was chosen President. The following nominations were made: For Governor, Dr. Hugh J. Glenn, by 128 votes to 115 for Jonathan V. Webster; for Lieutenant-Governor, J. P. West; for Secretary of State, Lawrence E. Crane; for Comptroller, H. M. Larue; for State Treasurer, Cyrus Jones; for Attorney-General, C. W. Cross; for Surveyor-General, F. J. Clark; for Clerk of the Supreme Court, Edwin F. Smith; for State Superintendent of Schools, A. L. Mann; for Chief Justice, Nathaniel Bennett.

The following platform was adopted:

Whereas, In the recent election on the adoption of the new Constitution the voters of this State, without regard to party lines, obtained a glorious victory over the combined power of the moneyed rings, banks, and corporations, and have thus shown to all the world that they have sufficient intelligence, honor, and patriotism to preserve, guard, and protect the liberty bequeathed to them by the illustrious fathers of the republic; and whereas, the banded cohorts of capital are now endeavoring by their usual corrupt means to wrest the fruits of the recent victory of the people of this State from them by electing to office those who are inimical to the new Constitution, for the purpose of construing and administering the same in behalf of the moneyed power, and against the rights of the laboring and producing classes; and whereas, the opposition to the new law was unequaled in violence, and the efforts to defeat it were characterized by bribery and coercion theretofore unparalleled; and whereas, a Constitution can not execute itself, but must be vitalized by appropriate legislation, and be enforced by just interpretation and friendly construction; and whereas, a single transportation company is collecting from the people an annual revenue so enormous as to cripple all the industries of the State; and whereas, from the commencement of its existence that company has been operating on capital furnished entirely by the people of the State and nation; and whereas, the Democratic and Republican party organizations, which, openly professing to ignore the subject of the adoption of the new Constitution, did in fact use the machinery of those parties in the interests of the enemies of the new Constitution in order to defeat it; and whereas, the people adopted the new Constitution without the aid of either the Democratic or Republican party organizations; and whereas, the presence of the Chinese in California is an unmitigated evil and an intolerable nuisance; therefore, be it

Resolved, That the new Constitution embodies principles just to all, oppressive to none, dear to ourselves, and of untold benefits to posterity.

Resolved, That the people of the State of California would prove recreant to their own interests, false to their professions of friendship to the new Constitution, and deficient in a proper spirit of manhood, if they were to submit that instrument to the hands of its enemies, and thus permit it to be strangled in its infancy.

Resolved, That the New Constitution party, organized for the purpose of releasing the people from the oppressions and thralldom of capital in the State of California, can not have and is not intended to have any influence whatever on the national politics of any individual.

Resolved, That in a republic, where the people are the source of all political power, and where the avenues to promotion and wealth are open and free to all alike, there is not and can not be any room for agrarianism, socialism, or communism.

Resolved, That the New Constitution party will protect the liberty, labor, and property of every citizen, and that therefore it commends itself to the support of all.

Resolved, That the first Legislature elected under the new Constitution shall put into immediate effect the stringent clauses of that instrument against the Chinese, and that everything that can be done shall be done to make the Chinese census coming and to cause those now here to speedily depart.

Resolved, That the State and County Central Committees of this party be and they are hereby directed to print upon their tickets at the next election, "Against Chinese immigration."

Resolved, That our principles are embodied in the new Constitution; that while we believe in the doctrine that principles and not men should be subserved by party action, we can not safely submit the execution of the instrument that embodies our principles to men who were but yesterday violently opposed to them, and who have shown no better evidence of conversion than a desire to hold office.

Resolved, That the rates of freights and fares of those railroad companies in California which have received Government aid should be reduced at least one third, and that each person receiving a nomination from the New Constitution party for an office in the exercise of which, and whose duty it shall be, to establish rates of charges for the transportation of passengers and freights, shall be deemed and held to be pledged to carry out in good faith the policy enunciated in this resolution, and, as far as possible, relieve the people of California from the extortion and oppression by those great corporations.

Resolved, That laws shall be passed to carry into effect the provisions of the new Constitution, that all property shall be taxed, according to its value, once in each year, strictly avoiding all species of double taxation.

Resolved, That it is the duty of the Legislature to provide for the election by the people of all State and county officers under the Constitution, except in cases where their appointment is specially provided for in the Constitution.

The following additional resolution was adopted:

Whereas, For many years after California became a State mining for gold was the leading industry—even now it is the second; many of her most enterprising citizens, as individuals and as associations under incorporation laws, have invested millions of dollars in developing placers and constructing ditches to enable the miners to work the same; and with the foregoing facts in view,

Resolved, That the New Constitution party pledges itself that it will stand firm as the miners' friend, and in case any attempt shall be made at any time to pass unfriendly legislation the New Constitution party will openly and boldly oppose any and all attempts to infringe upon the vested rights of the miners and ditch-owners.

The following was adopted in lieu of the resolution on Chinese:

Resolved, That, in accordance with a joint resolution passed by the last Legislature, the Governor be urged to submit to the people of the State at the general election in September next the question of Chinese immigration to this State; and that, whether such question be submitted officially or not, we hereby recommend that every ticket of the New Constitution party have printed immediately following the names of the candidates the words "Against Chinese immigration."

The Democratic State Convention assembled at Sacramento on July 2d. Dr. J. B. Shorb was chosen chairman. The following nominations were made: For Governor, Hugh J. Glenn; for Lieutenant-Governor, Levi Chase; for Secretary of State, W. J. Tinnin; for State Treasurer, G. T. Pauli; for Comptroller, W. B. C. Brown; for Attorney-General, Joseph Hamilton; for Surveyor-General, William A. Minnis; for Clerk of Supreme Court, D. B. Woolf; for Superintendent of Public Instruction, Henry C. Gesford; for Chief Justice, R. F. Morrison.

The following platform was adopted:

1. That the Democratic party is the only party which has always observed, obeyed, and maintained

the Federal Constitution, and is therefore the only political party which the people can safely trust to administer the organic law of the State.

2. The Democratic sentiment is an indissoluble union of indestructible States under the paramount authority of the Federal Constitution in all powers which have not been reserved by the States.

3. That as suffrage is a privilege conferred exclusively by the States, each State for itself agreeably to the constitutionally expressed will of the people thereof, any attempt of the General Government to interfere with the elections in the States, or in any of them, is dangerous to the liberties of the people and destructive of the sacredness of the elective franchise; and therefore we condemn as unconstitutional and subversive of the freedom of the ballot the odious laws of Republican origin and adoption, by which Federal supervisors of elections and deputy marshals are empowered to interfere with the registration of voters and at the polls, and United States troops are stationed at polling-places to intimidate or disfranchise citizens, native and naturalized.

4. That in unison with their party brethren throughout the republic, the Democrats of California denounce the repeated abuses of the veto by Rutherford B. Hayes, acting as the executive officer of the Government, in defeating the will of the people, as expressed by Congress, in his rejection of the bills passed by that body to repeal obnoxious and unconstitutional laws during the present special session.

5. That the Democracy of California earnestly approve the conduct of the Democrats in both Houses of Congress for their firm adherence to the just determination to repeal the laws by which the rights of voters are interfered with, at the instance and under the authority of the Republican Administration, to the extremity of depriving citizens of suffrage for the purpose of carrying elections by force and fraud.

6. That the Democracy of California are united and devoted in support of, and obedience to, the new Constitution, and maintain it as a sacred duty to administer the State government in strict and unqualified accordance with the spirit and letter of that instrument.

7. That the Democratic party is pledged by its principles and immemorial usages to reform, retrenchment, and the utmost economy compatible with good government in the administration of public affairs; that it adheres to the cardinal doctrines of its founders that taxation and representation should go together, that the lowest practicable tax-rate commensurate with the expenses of the State should be levied, and taxation should be equally and justly imposed on all property to the end that one class shall not be burdened with the taxes fairly due from another, and that no exemption of tax should be allowed to capital which is withheld from other species of property.

9. That the Democrats of California were the first in the early establishment of the State government to proclaim antagonism to Chinese immigration and cooly cheap labor; that it was under a Republican Administration that the Burlingame treaty was made, by which Chinese were admitted to the rights and privileges accorded to emigrants from Europe; that it was a Republican occupant of the Presidential chair who vetoed the bill passed by a Democratic Congress to prohibit the further immigration of Mongolians, and that the Republican minority in Congress prevented the passage of the bill over the veto; and that therefore it is only to the Democratic party the people can confidently look to secure legislation that shall abate and abolish the evil and curse of cooly importation, which cripples trade and palsies the arm of white labor.

10. That the Democrats of California approve the action of the Democrats in Congress who secured the passage of the Thurman bill, by which the Pacific Railroads are compelled to pay to the Government the just share of interest annually due from them upon the bonds, agreeably to the terms of the charters granted to the respective companies.

11. That the railroad and other transportation corporations in California should be subject to State regulation of rates for passengers and freight, in order that a material reduction should be made, that unjust and discriminating rates shall not be imposed or extorted, and that the enforcement of the reduction should particularly apply to the railroads which have been subsidized.

12. That mining, as the original and still a very important interest of California, is entitled to the fostering care and should be fostered and receive the fullest protection from the State government, and the property and possessions of all engaged in mining enterprises should be guarded by the legislative, judicial, and executive departments of the State and Federal governments.

13. That the large reduction of expenditures in the public service in the administration of the State government during the past four years under Democratic management, at this time of general depression in trade and labor, especially commend to the people of this Commonwealth the election of the candidates of the Democratic party at the coming election to administer the State government for the ensuing constitutional term.

The following was adopted as a substitute for the twelfth resolution:

Resolved, That mining and agriculture, as the overshadowing interests of California, should equally receive the fullest protection from the State government, and the property and possessions of all engaged in either pursuit should be carefully guarded by the legislative, judicial, and executive departments of both the State and Federal governments.

The Prohibition party also put up candidates for State officers, as follows: For Governor, A. G. Clark; for Lieutenant-Governor, —— Reed; for Secretary of State, A. A. Smith; for Treasurer, W. O. Clark; for Comptroller, M. C. Winchester; for Surveyor-General, J. W. Shanklin; for Attorney-General, Charles W. Cross; for Superintendent of Public Instruction, S. N. Burch; for Chief Justice, A. L. Rhoades.

The following nominations were also made for members of Congress: Republican—1. Horace Davis; 2. Horace F. Page; 3. Joseph McKenna; 4. Romualdo Pacheco. Democratic—1. Charles A. Sumner; 2. T. J. Clunie; 3. C. P. Berry; 4. Wallace Leach. Workingmen—1. Clitus Barbour; 2. H. P. Williams; 3. C. P. Berry; 4. James J. Ayres.

The following nominations were made for Associate Justices: Workingmen—S. B. McKee, S. M. Buck, J. R. Sharpstein, W. T. McNealy, C. A. Tuttle, and J. H. Budd. Republican—A. P. Catlin, E. G. Belcher, Garrett T. Richards, D. J. Wheeler, J. E. Hale, H. M. Myrick. Democratic—E. W. McKinstry, S. B. McKee, J. D. Thornton, E. M. Ross, T. B. Stoney, T. B. Reardon.

The following nominations were made for Railroad Commissioners: Republican — 1st dist., Joseph S. Cone; 2d dist., —— dist.; 3d dist., C. H. Philips. Democratic—1st dist., —— Carpenter; 2d dist., —— Thomas; 3d dist., G. H. Stoneman. Workingmen—1st dist., Henry Larkin; 2d Dist., —— Beerstecher; 3d dist., G. H. Stoneman.

The following nominations were made for members of the State Board of Equalization, one from each Congressional district : Republican—1st dist., —— King ; 2d dist., Moses M. Drew ; 3d dist., Warren Dutton ; 4th dist., J. A. Clayton. Democratic—1st dist., —— Bradford ; 2d dist., C. H. Randall; 3d dist., C. E. Wilcoxson ; 4th dist., T. B. Heiskell. Workingmen—1st dist., —— Hoagland ; 2d dist., W. B. Keller ; 3d dist., J. P. Cavanagh; 4th dist., O. T. Chabb. The election was held on the 3d of September. The laws which regulate it, especially in San Francisco, are worthy of notice. The subdivision into precincts is so extensive and minute that it prevents crowding and secures quiet. Every voter is registered and published previously, avoiding delay at the polls. Ballots are of one size, one tint, and one style. It is unlawful to address a voter within one hundred feet of the polls ; the limit is conspicuously marked. The judges can not leave the room that evening till the votes are counted and dispatched to headquarters.

It will be seen that many persons nominated in the conventions were not voted for. They declined the nomination, and others were substituted and received the votes.

FOR GOVERNOR.

Perkins, Democrat 67,970
Glenn, Democrat and New Constitution...... 47,562
White, Workingmen........................... 44,620

FOR LIEUTENANT-GOVERNOR.

Mansfield, Republican....................... 67,301
Chase, Democrat............................. 31,287
Andrus, Workingmen.......................... 42,800
Reed, New Constitution...................... 19,814

FOR SECRETARY OF STATE.

Burns, Republican........................... 67,673
Tinnin, Democrat............................ 81,827
Smith, Workingmen and Prohibition.......... 41,256
Crane, New Constitution............ 19,583

FOR COMPTROLLER.

Kenfield, Republican........................ 67,567
Brown, Democrat........... 32,190
Jones, Workingmen........................... 40,784
Larue, New Constitution..................... 20,347

FOR TREASURER.

Weil, Republican............................ 67,673
Escandon, Democrat.......................... 30,245
Clark, Workingmen........................... 40,785
Jones, New Constitution..................... 19,074

FOR ATTORNEY-GENERAL.

Hunt, Republican 66,971
Hamilton, Democrat.......................... 29,289
Cross, Workingmen........................... 41,838
Terry, New Constitution..................... 28,544

FOR SURVEYOR-GENERAL.

Shanklin, Republican........................ 67,182
Minis, Democrat............................. 82,581
Stevenson, Workingmen....................... 40,961
Clark, New Constitution..................... 20,180

FOR CLERK OF SUPREME COURT.

Gross, Republican........................... 64,808
Woolf, Democrat............................. 85,008
Thornton, Workingmen........................ 40,697
Smith, New Constitution..................... 20,387

FOR SUPERINTENDENT OF PUBLIC INSTRUCTION.

Campbell, Republican,....................... 67,099
Gesford, Democrat........................... 81,673
Barch, Workingmen........................... 40,702
Mann, New Constitution...................... 20,992

FOR CONGRESSMEN.

District		
I.	Davis, Republican..................	20,074
	Sumner, Democrat...................	2,942
	Barbour, Workingmen................	18,460
II.	Page, Republican...................	19,856
	Clunie, Democrat...................	12,547
	Williams, Workingmen...............	5,189
III.	McKenna, Republican................	19,170
	Berry, Democrat and Workingmen.....	20,018
	Pacheco, Republican................	15,171
IV.	Leach, Democrat....................	12,069
	Ayres, Workingmen..................	10,529

FOR CHIEF JUSTICE.

Rhodes, Republican.......................... 68,171
Morrison, Democrat and Workingmen....... 72,689
Bennett, New Constitution.................. 20,242

FOR ASSOCIATE JUSTICES.

Catlin, Republican.......................... 66,856
Belcher   " 67,506
Richards,   " 66,659
Hale,   " 66,194
Myrick,   " 67,987
Wheeler,   " 65,077
McKinstry, Democrat and Workingmen 80,885
Thornton,   "   72,696
Stoney, Democrat............... 81,268
Ross, Democrat and Workingmen.......... 72,161
McKee,   "   76,114
Sharpstein,   "   70,180
Buck, Workingmen...... 41,960
Campbell, New Constitution................. 20,805
Dorsey,   "   20,086
McKune,   "   19,903
Tuttle,   "   20,180
Burch,   "   20,082
Benham,   "   20,202

FOR RAILROAD COMMISSIONERS.

District		
I.	Cone, Republican...................	23,486
	Carpenter, Democrat................	14,586
	Larkin, Workingmen........'........	22,594
II.	Phelps, Republican.................	18,067
	Thomas, Democrat...................	2,522
	Beerstecher, Workingmen............	20,227
III.	Soule, New Constitution...........	8,497
	Philip, Republican................	19,434
	Stoneman, Democrat and Workingmen....	85,518

FOR STATE BOARD OF EQUALIZATION.

District		
I.	King, Republican...................	19,019
	Hoagland, Workingmen...............	18,472
	Bradford, Democrat.................	8,949
II.	Drew, Republican...................	18,811
	Randall, Democrat..................	6,290
	Keller, Workingmen.................	18,848
III.	Dutton, Republican................	16,157
	Wilcoxon, Democrat.................	12,298
	Cavanaugh, Workingmen..............	5,870
IV.	Clayton, Republican...............	18,367
	Heiskell, Democrat................	16,722
	Chubb, Workingmen.................	8,694

The state of parties in the Legislature was such as to give the Republicans a small majority. At the time when the vote was given on the new Constitution, 154,638 votes were cast to prohibit Chinese immigration.

The fiscal year of the State expires on June 30th, and the reports embrace a period of two years, as the sessions of the Legislature are biennial. The amount of the State debt on June 30, 1879, was as follows:

Outstanding bonds of 1857................... $5,000 00
Outstanding bonds of 1860.................... 1,500 00
Outstanding soldiers' relief bonds.......... 95,500 00
Outstanding State Capitol bonds of 1870...... 250,000 00
Outstanding State Capitol bonds of 1872...... 250,000 00
Outstanding funded debt of 1873............. 2,801,000 00

Total bonds outstanding................ $3,406,000 00
Outstanding Comptroller's warrants.......... 58,170 25

Total debt................. $3,466,170 25

The decrease of the debt since 1875 amounts to $356,214.29. The increase of assets during the same period amounts to $1,099,371.57.

Receipts from all sources for the 29th fiscal year $4,071,294 45
Receipts from all sources for the 30th fiscal year   3,709,870 77

Total................................. $7,781,165 22
Balance on hand July 1, 1877.............   1,408,177 43

Grand total.......................... $9,189,382 65

Disbursements for the 29th fiscal year...... $3,878,687 12
Disbursements for the 30th fiscal year......   3,812,144 98

Total................................. $7,690,832 10
Balance in Treasury June 30, 1879..........   1,498,450 55

Grand total.......................... $9,189,282 65

The tax levy for the 30th fiscal year (ending June 30, 1879) was, for the general fund (from which is paid the current expenses of the State government), $1,320,000, or a rate of 25·6 cents on each $100 valuation of property, which was the smallest tax levied for said current expenes since the year 1871; and yet, at the end of said year, June 30, 1879, there was in the general fund a balance of over $384,000. The amount levied for the general fund for the 31st fiscal year, commencing July 1, 1879, is $1,450,000, or a rate of 30 cents on each $100 valuation of property. This is the smallest levy for general purposes since the year 1871, except that of 1878–'79. The rate for said general fund for the 31st fiscal year is 4·4 cents on each $100 greater than it was for the preceding year; the most of this increase is due to the fact that the assessment roll upon which the tax was levied is less by nearly $37,000,000 than in 1879–'80 than it was in 1878–'79. There has been a greater amount of fees of office and commissions paid into the State Treasury by the Harbor Commissioners, Surveyor-General, Secretary of State, and Clerk of the Supreme Court during the last three years and a half than was paid in during the same length of time by their predecessors, and the taxes have been more closely and cheaply collected than ever before. There has been a material reduction in the running expenses of the State government during the past three and a half years, and the financial condition of the State is sound and healthy. The State also holds a claim against the United States Government of $241,625 for sums advanced in the suppression of Indian hostilities.

The progress of the public schools of the State during the last twenty-five years has been very rapid. In 1855 the State had but 227 schools, with an attendance of 13,000, and 26,077 census children. In 1865 it had 947 schools, with an attendance of 50,089, and 95,067 census children. In 1875 it had 2,190 schools, with ·130,930 scholars in attendance, and 171,563 census children. In 1879 it had 2,743 schools, with an attendance of 144,806, and 216,404 census children. In 1855 teachers were paid $181,906; in 1879, $2,285,732.39. Up to the present time the people of California have devoted to the cause of public education for pub-

lic schools $33,743,819.84; for State Normal School, about $566,600; for State University, about $4,150,000. In percentage of average attendance on school population California stands ninth among the States. The following details belong to the year 1879

White boys between 5 and 17.............   108,285
White girls between 5 and 17.............   105,818
Negro boys between 5 and 17.............   647
Negro girls between 5 and 17.............   625
Indian boys between 5 and 17.............   591
Indian girls between 5 and 17.............   493

Total census children between 5 and 17...   216,404
Increase over 1877...................   16,387

White children under five years, 85,870; average number of census children belonging to public schools, 105,837; average daily attendance, 98,468. From July 1, 1878, to June 30, 1879, 144,806 were enrolled in the public schools, while the average number belonging, the actual pupils of the schools, were 105,837, and only 98,468 were in daily attendance during the whole time school was maintained. Census children attending private schools at any time during school year, 15,432; percentage of census children enrolled in public schools, 66·91; percentage in private schools, 7·04; percentage attending no schools, 26·05; per cent. of children of native-born parents, 46·15; per cent. of children who had one foreign parent, 12·68; per cent. of children who are of foreign parents, 41·17; school districts, 1,999; increase over 1877, 171; first-grade schools, 999; increase, 85; second grade, 1,081; increase, 98; third grade, 663; increase, 36. Total number of schools, 2,743; increase, 258. By the first grade are meant high, grammar, and first-grade schools; by second grade are meant intermediate and third grade; and by third grade are meant primary and third-grade schools. Number enrolled in high schools or the advanced grade, 4,871; number enrolled in grammar or first-grade schools, 20,197; number enrolled in intermediate or second-grade schools, 38,693; number enrolled in primary or third-grade schools, 91,788; number of male teachers, 1,236; number of female teachers, 2,217; average monthly salary paid male teachers, $82.18; average paid female teachers, $66.37; decrease in monthly salary paid male teachers, compared with 1877, $1.65; decrease in monthly salary paid female teachers, compared with 1877, $3.31; new schoolhouses erected, 122; institutes held, 34; cost of institutes, $2,988.22. Total receipts of the school department from all sources, State and county apportionments, city and district taxes, etc., for 1878, $3,820,661.26; for 1879, $3,653,798.96; State apportionments per census child—1878, $7.67; 1879, $6.60; decrease since 1877, 77 cents; county apportionments per census child—1878, $3.54; 1879, $3.59; total receipts of all kinds per census child—1878, $18.59; 1879, $16.84; decrease since 1877, $1.20.

The expenditures for teachers' salaries, school libraries, school apparatus, rents, repairs, etc., have been as follows:

	1878.	1879.
Teachers' salaries............	$2,272,551 19	$2,285,782 89
Rents, repairs, fuel, contingents..................	426,707 66	871,902 18
School libraries.............	58,947 85	46,490 50
School apparatus.:..........	12,518 65	13,565 73
Total current expenses...	$2,765,720 85	$2,717,780 75
For sites, buildings, and school furniture.................	890,094 92	298,126 88
Total expenditures......	$8,155,815 27	$8,010,907 13

The valuation of school property is as follows:

	1878.	1879.
Valuation of sites, schoolhouses, and furniture......	$5,990,276 50	$6,477,028 00
School libraries.............	242,676 25	258,045 00
School apparatus...........	110,417 10	122,316 00
Total valuation..........	$6,343,369 85	$6,857,389 00
Increase since 1877	....	$1,289,472 05

The State Superintendent of Schools makes the following recommendations:

Greater attention to the school library system; in favor of free text-books and the abolition of the text-book from the school-room whenever possible; to secure permanency to teachers' positions; that the exaggerated estimate placed upon the supposed virtue of examinations be corrected; that steps be taken to prevent the waste of one half of the school money because of the incapacity and neglect of local officers; the adoption and teaching of the metric system; in favor of the reform or phonetic system of spelling; the encouragement of the kindergarten system in the larger cities by permitting graduates of kindergarten normals to serve for three months without salary as a preparatory course.

The condition of the insurance business in the State on January 1, 1879, is shown in the following statements:

FIRE INSURANCE.

Amount written	$238,689,040 98
Amount of premiums received...........	8,589,522 23
Amount of losses paid..................	981,995 61
Ratio of losses to premiums received........	26.3

MARINE INSURANCE.

Amount written..................	$77,106,770 10
Amount of premiums received..........	1,363,388 64
Amount of losses paid, as far as reported....	551,128 45

TOTAL FIRE AND MARINE.

Amount written......................	$315,745,811 08
Amount of premiums received..........	4,902,855 87
Amount of losses paid, as far as reported.....	1,483,124 06

Apportioned as follows:

To Companies of this State.

FIRE INSURANCE.

Amount written...................	$62,865,487 00
Amount of premiums received..........	695,908 02
Amount of losses paid................	279,399 83

MARINE INSURANCE.

Amount written...................	$16,508,605 00
Amount of premium received..........	415,180 30
Amount of losses paid................	257,495 41

To Companies of other States.

FIRE INSURANCE.

Amount written...................	$54,980,796 04
Amount of premiums received..........	875,881 88
Amount of losses paid................	290,686 60

MARINE INSURANCE.

Amount written...................	$441,450 00
Amount of premiums received..........	7,144 08
Amount of losses paid................	6,055 53

To Companies of Foreign Countries.

FIRE INSURANCE.

Amount written	$190,842,760 89
Amount of premiums received..............	1,765,242 83
Amount of losses paid.....................	421,909 68

MARINE INSURANCE.

Amount written........................	$60,156,715 10
Amount of premiums received.............	941,050 81
Amount of losses paid, as far as reported....	287,577 51

LIFE INSURANCE.

New life policies written (California business), 2,208.

Amount of................................	$7,810,889 00
Premium.................................	201,063 12

Renewed policies, 7,055.

Amount of................................	$24,644,595 20
Premium.................................	8,591 00

Policies in force December 31, 1878, 10,997.

Amount of..............................	$85,855,291 20
Losses and endowments paid..............	1,126,709 99

The railroads of the State have been chiefly constructed during the last ten years, and the larger part of the entire system was either built or subsequently constructed by the Central Pacific Railroad Company. This company was incorporated in 1862, and in 1865 it had only 56 miles of road in operation. This was increased to 187 in 1867. During the ten succeeding years, the miles of road operated were increased from year to year as follows: 1868, 468; 1869, 742; 1870, 900; 1871, 1,094; 1872, 1,222; 1873, 1,222; 1874, 1,219; 1875, 1,309; 1876, 1,425; 1877, 1,783. The figures for the last two years include leased railroads. A long stride was made in 1877, when 868 miles of railroad came under the control of the Company, the largest for any one year in its history up to that time. The Southern Pacific is built to Casa Grande, 182 miles from Yuma and 913 miles from San Francisco. This is a longer single stretch of rail than the northern branch. Commencing at the westerly end of Oakland wharf, the road runs northerly to Martinez, thence easterly to Tracy, thence in a southeasterly direction to its present terminus at Casa Grande in Arizona, passing through such towns as Merced, Fresno, Visalia, Bakersfield, Los Angeles, Colton, Yuma, and Maricopa. At Visalia there is a branch to Halford, and at Los Angeles there are three branches, one running to Santa Monica, one to Wilmington, and one to Santa Ana. Much of this southern road has been built within the past three years. The work of extending it is still in progress, and it will soon reach a point where connections can be made with the roads traversing the Atlantic States, thus giving two roads across the continent.

The gross earnings of the Central Pacific Railroad Company for the year 1877 were $16,000,000, as follows:

Coin receipts....................	$10,687,329
Currency receipts................	5,883,815
Total.......................	$16,471,144
Operating expenses..............	7,774,418
Net receipts of Central Pacific..........	$8,696,726
Net receipts of California Pacific........	506,826
Net receipts of both roads.........	$9,203,552

These net receipts were subject to deduction by some items as follows:

Interest	$3,716,984
Taxes	330,846
Miscellaneous and general expenses	482,559
Legal expenses	146,112
Civil engineering	22,045
Discount on currency	810,898
Land Department expenses	18,610
Leased railroads	2,266,186
Total	$7,288,240

Deducting these items of legitimate expenditures from the net total receipts, we have the following as the net income for that year:

Net receipts for 1877	$9,203,558
Expenditures	7,288,240
Real net income	$1,915,318

This amount was too small to justify the usual April dividend, and so it was passed. This balance is subject to a further deduction of $1,200,000 under an act of Congress known as the Thurman act. Early in 1878 Senator Thurman of Ohio introduced and was instrumental in the passage of a bill by Congress which compels the Union and Central Pacific Railroad Companies to pay 25 per cent. of their annual net earnings, including the whole of the compensation due them for services rendered to the Government, to the Treasurer of the United States, to be by him applied partly in payment of the accrued interest upon the bonds issued by the Government to the two companies, and partly to the establishment of a sinking fund in the United States Treasury for the final payment of the Company's bonded indebtedness. The companies contested the law in the courts, claiming that it was unconstitutional. The decision rendered by the Supreme Court early in 1879 was not unanimous, three judges dissenting from the opinion, but it probably settles the question.

The report of the Central Pacific Railroad Company for 1877 shows the following indebtedness to the United States for bonds:

Central Pacific	$25,885,120
Western Pacific	1,970,560
Total	$27,855,680

The amount of interest paid on these bonds by the Government to May 1, 1879, is $17,-600,000, as follows:

ROADS.	For mails.	In cash.	Total.
Central	$2,561,849	$13,902,224	$16,463,578
Western	9,867	1,126,830	1,136,197
Totals	$2,570,716	$15,029,054	$17,599,770

The annual interest on the bonds held by the Central and Western Pacific is $1,671,341, which hereafter must be annually paid over to the Treasurer of the United States, less the amount reserved for carrying the mails. This decision of the U. S. Supreme Court is noticed above.

The amount of bonds issued by the United States to Pacific Railroads is as follows:

Central Pacific	$25,885,120
Kansas Pacific	6,303,000
Union Pacific	27,236,512
Central Branch Union Pacific	1,600,000
Western Pacific	1,970,560
Sioux City and Pacific	1,628,320
Total	$64,623,512

These bonds were issued under the acts of July 1, 1862, and July 2, 1864. They all bear 6 per cent. interest, and are payable thirty years from date. Part of them are therefore payable July 1, 1892, and the remainder July 2, 1894. The annual interest on these bonds aggregates $3,877,511, and is payable in January and July. Thus far the interest has been paid by the United States. As an offset, the compensation that should have been paid to the companies for carrying the mails has been withheld by the Government.

According to the surveys which have been made, the area of the State is 100,500,000 acres, which is divided as follows:

Agricultural and mineral lands surveyed to June 30, 1879	49,054,114
Agricultural and mineral lands unsurveyed	39,065,654
Private grants surveyed to June 30, 1879	8,459,694
Mission Church property	40,707
Pueblo lands	188,749
Private grants unsurveyed	18,000
Indian and military reservations	818,631
Lakes, islands, bays, and navigable rivers	1,581,700
Swamp and overflowed lands surveyed	1,610,037
Swamp and overflowed lands unsurveyed	110,714
Salt-marsh and tide-lands around San Francisco Bay	100,000
Salt-marsh and tide-lands around Humboldt Bay	5,000
Aggregate area	100,500,000

The exports of wool for the six months ending June 30, 1879, were 23,291,500 lbs. The spring clip was under the average of the previous five years. That for 1871-'73 was from 12,600,000 to 14,600,000 lbs.; in 1874, it was 19,400,000 lbs.; in 1875, 23,600,000 lbs.; in 1876-'77 there was an average of 28,000,000 lbs.; in 1878 the crop fell off to 18,800,000 lbs.; and in 1879 it was 20,651,000 lbs. The export of wheat and flour from San Francisco during the eleven months ending May 31, 1879, was as follows:

MONTHS.	Flour, barrels.	Wheat, centals.
July, 1878	81,600	850,700
August	52,900	1,584,800
September	43,800	1,774,600
October	86,000	1,106,800
November	58,300	964,600
December	82,800	818,900
January, 1879	40,300	516,600
February	44,300	574,500
March	47,100	719,500
April	65,300	795,700
May	85,500	516,900
Totals	487,800	9,671,600

Including flour reduced to wheat, there was cleared over 31,000 tons of wheat in the month of May, making the total for eleven months ending on May 31st, 555,675 tons of 2,000 lbs. The month of June scarcely increased the total to 575,000 tons. More than 270 ships and barks were dispatched loaded with this export.

The climate of the State is most admirable for the success of grain-crops. While farmers in other parts of the world are in constant fear of rain during haying and harvest, and often lose the work of an entire year during one storm, the California farmer has nothing to fear from this source. He has from April to October almost entirely exempt from storms of any kind, in which to secure all his crops. Even the dews do not fall to bleach his hay, and his wheat may lie in the field in the bundle or bunch or stack, or even in the sack, without damage from rain. No time is lost from showers or winds, or other natural causes, but the work begun in May is continuously and constantly pushed without interruption all through that month and June and July, August and September. In the Eastern States it costs much more to cut and secure grain than it does in California, because of the advantages secured by its favorable climate. There they can cut the grain with the header, taking only the heads, which are elevated into an attendant wagon with a capacious box, and deposited directly into the hopper of the machine to be immediately threshed, or into a pile to remain in bulk till a convenient time for threshing it.

The lumber trade of the State has its chief center at San Francisco. The hard woods used for wheelwright purposes, cabinet-work, veneering, and ornamental work are imported, with the exception of California laurel or myrtle, mountain mahogany, maple, and alder. The staple lumber, used for house- and ship-building, street and dock work, fencing, boxing, and the like, is obtained on the coast within the limits of the State and the neighboring forests of Oregon and Washington. The chief varieties of staple lumber obtained on the coast are sugar-pine, white cedar, redwood, spruce, Oregon pine or fir, and yellow pine, named in the order of their commercial value. White or sugar-pine comes from the Sierra; white cedar from Port Orford north to Coos Bay, exclusively; fir or Oregon pine from Puget Sound and many sections of Oregon, or more particularly from Coos Bay north; spruce from Coos Bay, Umpqua, Shoalwater Bay, and the coast of Oregon, generally; redwood, from the great redwood region of the California Coast Range. Oregon pine or fir, known commercially as "Oregon," is used in Pacific coast ship-building almost exclusively, and for the rafters, beams, scantlings, furring, flooring, and stepping of houses, for piles, planking, and side walking, and for nearly all purposes where lateral strain is an *essential*, and comparative inexpensiveness desirable. Redwood is used altogether for the outside construction of frame houses, in the form of rustic siding, batting, and shingles, and in inside finish, as "tongue and groove" for ceiling, wainscoting, and the like, and for cornices and moldings. For all purposes where durability is not affected by friction or strain, redwood is the most durable

of the domestic woods, with the single exception of white cedar, standing exposure to the weather as nothing else can. The receipts, consumption, and stock on hand of lumber in the San Francisco market for ten years ending January 1, 1879, were as follows:

YEAR.	On hand January 1.	Receipt for year.	Consumption.
1869............	15,666,672	244,879,577	226,449,642
1870............	33,596,605	217,477,251	225,121,382
1871............	25,952,524	192,420,840	196,726,971
1872............	21,646,898	231,201,587	220,701,083
1873............	32,146,847	201,831,095	198,969,288
1874............	35,008,654	250,964,826	252,782,280
1875............	33,241,250	303,184,188	287,977,819
1876............	48,447,619	310,185,974	303,227,914
1877............	55,465,679	287,045,228	295,665,580
1878............	46,845,877	264,942,465	266,984,225
1879............	44,858,617	....	....
Totals....	....	2,508,682,981	2,474,506,034

Home consumption—in which are included shipments made to the interior, and from San Francisco to foreign ports—was highest in the centennial year, 1876; falling off in the years 1877 and 1878 about thirty-seven million feet. The shipment of fruit to the Eastern cities has become quite extensive. Its profitableness or unprofitableness has depended chiefly on the carefulness with which the requirements of success have been heeded. This has been seen in those who have selected the kinds of fruit that would hear shipping the best; those who have taken the most pains in assorting the fruit to be shipped; those who have boxed with the most care; those who have packed in the cars so as to secure the greatest circulation of air through and between the boxes; those who have shipped in cars attached to the express and passenger trains, and thus secured the quickest transit. Pears and plums have been found the best fruits to ship, and of pears the Bartlett has proved a good shipper and the most profitable to send to the Eastern market. This pear can be picked in California and placed on the markets in the East before any other kinds of fruit are plentiful there, and consequently is insured a good demand and good prices. Plums are also a profitable kind of fruit to ship. They stand the voyage well, and meet the markets in a good time for good prices. Peanuts are grown largely in the State on sandy river-bottoms, and some years ago they proved a very profitable crop, but the markets are now liable to be overcrowded. Still they yield so well that even at a small price there is room for some profit. It takes from one bushel to a bushel and a half of good seed to plant an acre. The seed must be fresh, plump, and of a good bright color. If the rows are put three feet apart, and the hills eighteen inches in the row, the best satisfaction will be given.

A most important legal case came before the State courts. It related to the injury done to the Sacramento and San Joaquin Valleys by the *débris* from the mines. From surveys made by the State Engineer it has been ascertained that over 18,000 acres of valley-land on the Yuba—land that was once the finest bottom-land in the State—have been utterly destroyed and buried beneath the mining *débris*, so that now this vast area has been transformed into a desert of sand and slickings, alternating with impenetrable jungles of willow swamp. Probably as much if not more of equally good land has been similarly destroyed on Bear River. Although these lands have been exposed to sunshine and rain for years, they produce not a blade of grass—nothing but willows and kindred semi-aquatic plants, that derive their nourishment chiefly from the stratum of water percolating underneath the surface, and not from the soil itself. From the beginning of hydraulic mining to the present time over 150,000,000 cubic yards of solid material have passed the foot-hills, and have been deposited on the bottom-lands of the Yuba and into the waters of the Feather and Sacramento Rivers, the Bays of Suisun and San Pablo, and finally into the Bay of San Francisco. Such a mass deposited on a farm of 160 acres would cover it to a depth of 581 feet; or, if spread evenly, one foot in depth, would cover 93,000 acres, or 145 square miles of land, and absolutely destroy it for agricultural or any other purpose. The bed of the Yuba at Marysville is now filled up to the level of the streets of that city, where prior to the era of hydraulic mining there was a well-defined channel of clear water from 20 to 25 feet in depth. The Feather and Sacramento Rivers have shoaled in a lesser degree, but still sufficiently to almost destroy their usefulness as a highway of commerce. The suit is between farmers and miners, and in the lower court an injunction was obtained against the latter. In the Supreme Court the merits of the case were passed over, and it was decided that there was a misjoining of the defendants. Thus far only has it advanced.

An ordinance of the city and county of San Francisco provided that every male person imprisoned in the county jail, under the judgment of any court, should have "the hair of his head cut or clipped to a uniform length of one inch from the scalp thereof." The case of Ho Ah How *vs.* Matthew Nunan, involving the validity of the ordinance, was decided by Justice Field in the U. S. Circuit Court. The complaint was filed to recover $10,000 damages, and came before the Court on the plaintiff's demurrer to the defendant's plea of justification. Justice Field said:

It appears that in April, 1876, the Legislature of California passed an act "concerning lodging-houses and sleeping-apartments within the limits of incorporated cities," declaring, among other things, that any person found sleeping or lodging in a room or an apartment containing less than 500 cubic feet of space in the clear for each person occupying it, shall be deemed guilty of a misdemeanor, and on conviction thereof be punished by a fine of not less than ten dollars nor more than fifty dollars, or imprisonment in the county jail, or by both such fine and imprisonment. (Laws, sessions of 1875-'76.) Under this act the plain-

tiff in April, 1878, was convicted and sentenced to pay a fine of ten dollars, or in default of such payment to be imprisoned five days in the county jail. Failing to pay the fine, he was imprisoned. The defendant, as sheriff of the city and county, had charge of the jail, and during the imprisonment of the plaintiff cut off his queue as alleged. The complaint avers that it is the custom of Chinamen to shave the hair from the front of the head, and to wear the remainder of it braided into a queue; that the deprivation of the queue is regarded by them as a mark of disgrace, and is attended, according to their religious faith, with misfortune and suffering after death; that the defendant knew of this custom and religious faith of the Chinese, and knew also that the plaintiff venerated the custom and held the faith, yet, in disregard of his rights, inflicted the injury complained of; and that the plaintiff has in consequence of it suffered great mental anguish, been disgraced in the eyes of his friends and relatives, and ostracized from association with his countrymen; and that hence he has been damaged to the amount of $10,000.

Two defenses to the action are set up by the defendant; the second one being a justification of his conduct under an ordinance of the city and county of San Francisco. It is upon the sufficiency of the latter defense that the case is before us. The ordinance referred to was passed on the 14th of June, 1876, and it declared that every male person imprisoned in the county jail, under the judgment of any court having jurisdiction in criminal cases in the city and county, shall immediately upon his arrival at the jail have the hair of his head "cut or clipped to a uniform length of one inch from the scalp thereof," and it is made the duty of the sheriff to have this provision enforced. Under this ordinance the defendant cut off the queue of the plaintiff.

The validity of this ordinance is denied by the plaintiff on two grounds: 1. That it exceeds the authority of the Board of Supervisors, the body in which the legislative power of the city and county is vested; and, 2. That it is special legislation imposing a degrading and cruel punishment upon a class of persons who are entitled, alike with all other persons within the jurisdiction of the United States, to the equal protection of the laws. We are of the opinion that both these positions are well taken. . . .

The cutting off the hair of every male person within an inch of his scalp, on his arrival at the jail, was not intended and can not be maintained as a measure of discipline or as a sanitary regulation. The act has no tendency to promote either discipline or health. The close cutting of the hair which is practiced upon felons at the State Penitentiary, like clothing them in striped pants, is to distinguish them from others, and thus facilitate their capture in case of escape. They are measures of precaution. Nothing of the kind is practiced or would be tolerated with respect to persons confined in a county jail for simple misdemeanors, most of which are not of a very grave character. The plaintiff in this case, who had the option of paying a fine of ten dollars, or of imprisonment for five days, required no such clipping of his hair for the purpose of discipline or detention. It was done designedly to add torture to his confinement.

But even if the proceeding could be regarded as a measure of discipline or as a sanitary regulation, the conclusion would not help the defendant, for the Board of Supervisors had no authority to prescribe the discipline to which persons convicted under the laws of the State should be subjected, or to determine what special sanitary regulations should be enforced with respect to their persons. That is a matter which the Legislature had not seen fit to intrust to the wisdom and judgment of that body. A discipline to which disgrace is attached, and which is not enforced as a means of security against the escape of the prisoner, but merely to give torture to his confinement or to aggravate its severity, can only be regarded as a punishment additional to that imposed by the sentence. If inflicted in consequence of the sentence, it is punishment in addition to that imposed by the Court; if inflicted without regard to the sentence, it is wanton cruelty."

CAPE COLONY AND BRITISH SOUTH AFRICA.

The area and population of the British possessions in South Africa were as follows at the beginning of the year 1879:

COLONIES.	Area.	Population.
1. Colony of Cape of Good Hope:		
a. Cape Colony proper, inclusive of British Caffraria........	199,950	720,984
b. Basuto Land.................	8,450	127,701
c. Griqua Land West...........	16,682	45,277
d. Caffraria, exclusive of Pondo Land......................	12,452	254,500
2. Natal........................	18,750	326,959
3. Transvaal....................	114,840	275,000
Total.....................	370,574	1,750,421

The population of Cape Colony proper was divided as follows according to race:

Europeans or whites......................	236,783
Malays..................................	10,817
Hottentots..............................	98,561
Fingoes.................................	73,506
Caffres and Bechuanas....................	214,183
Half-breeds and others...................	87,184
Total...	720,984

The different denominations were represented as follows:

DENOMINATIONS.	White.	Colored.	Total.
Anglican churches...............	26,548	13,493	40,041
Protestants and Christians not classified.....................	32,522	25,768	58,290
Presbyterians (including Free Church of Scotland, Reformed Presbyterians, Scotch Protestants, and United Presbyterians)........................	3,430	4,243	7,673
Independents (including Congregationalists, London Mission, Dutch Independents, Nonconformists, Union Church, Free Church)....................	2,574	21,173	23,747
Wesleyans and Methodists......	7,960	24,317	32,277
Baptists.......	2,173	218	2,391
Lutherans......................	6,278	11,143	17,421
Dutch Reformed Church........	143,076	28,420	171,496
Moravians......................	125	10,270	10,395
Unitarians.....................	26	40	66
Other Protestants	414	878	1,292
Catholics......................	8,666	1,001	9,667
Other denominations...........	15	8	23
Jews...........................	588	......	588
Mohammedans.................	18	11,196	11,214
Belonging to no church	178	277,377	277,555
Unknown......................	2,242	54,656	56,898
Total..................	236,783	484,201	720,984

The gross revenue of Cape Colony proper in 1877, including loans, was £2,631,602; the expenditure, £3,428,392; and the public debt on December 31, 1877, £5,028,959. The imports during the same year amounted to £5,457,000, and the exports th £3,663,000.

In the course of the year certain portions of the Transkei and Nomans Land, containing about 8,600 square miles, were incorporated with the Cape Colony. Moreover, the war against the Zooloos resulted in making Zoolooland to a large extent a dependency of the British Government. (See ZOOLOOS.)

The conflict with Cetywayo or Ketchwhyo,

King of the Zooloo Caffres, which threatened the colony during 1878, actually broke out in January, 1879. Sir Bartle Frere, the British High Commissioner in South Africa, reviewed in a memorandum the causes which led to it. He stated that during the lifetime of King Panda the Government of Natal had rarely had occasion to complain of any unfriendly act on the part of the Zooloos. When Panda died in 1872, he was succeeded by his son Cetywayo, whose peaceable succession was mainly due to his recognition by the British Government of Natal some years before, when there were many rival candidates for the succession, and to the presence of the British representative at his installation. Cetywayo then made many solemn promises and engagements. None of these had been fulfilled. The cruelties and barbarities which deformed the internal administration of Zoolooland in Panda's reign had been aggravated during the reign of Cetywayo. He had also maintained a formidable military despotism, which had become a standing menace to all his neighbors, and had sought to gain the consent of the British Government to wars of aggression, particularly against the inhabitants of a large tract of land between the Buffalo and Fongolo rivers, which had long been regarded as Transvaal territory. But since his installation the tone of Cetywayo in his communications with the Natal Government had essentially altered, notably in reply to a remonstrance addressed to him by the Lieutenant-Governor of Natal regarding the barbarous massacre of a number of young women by the King's orders. Cetywayo addressed the Government of Natal in terms of unprecedented insolence and defiance, affirming his irresponsibility to the Natal Government for anything he might please to do, denying his solemn promises at his installation, and declaring his intention of shedding blood in future on a much greater scale. These declarations were in 1876 followed by raids upon the missionaries, who were driven from the country, while at least three of the converts were killed. After the annexation of the Transvaal, he sent a military force to the territory between the Buffalo and the Pongolo, and ordered the inhabitants to quit. Sir Theophilus Shepstone, who then governed in the Transvaal, endeavored to come to an amicable arrangement, but his advances were received with very scant courtesy; and in reply to his invitation to discuss the matter, a peremptory demand was made in the King's name for the immediate cession of all that the Zooloos claimed. Cetywayo, however, ultimately accepted the suggestion of the Natal Government that the matter was one for inquiry, and at his request a commission was appointed to inquire into the merits of the dispute, with a view to its settlement by arbitration. This commission decided that the greater portion of the land in dispute, of which the Zooloos had lately taken forcible possession, had never ceased to belong of right to them. This ver-

dict was affirmed by the High Commissioner. Those private rights of *bona fide* settlers which had grown up during the Transvaal occupation, and which could not in justice be abrogated by any change of sovereignty, were reserved and protected under the guarantee of the British Government. All Zooloo claims to sovereignity north of the Pongolo and west of the Blood River were at the same time negatived. The High Commissioner's award was delivered on December 11, 1878. In the interval between the decision of the commissioners and its confirmation by the High Commissioner, several events occurred which materially affected the relations of the British Government with the Zooloos. Repeated notices to quit had continued to be sent in the King's name to European subjects of the Transvaal, long settled north of the Pongolo, within what had for years been recognized as the boundary between the Transvaal and Zoolooland. The notices were enforced by raids into Swaziland, and there was every apparent indication of an intention to repeat north of the Pongolo the same aggressive conduct in occupying territory claimed which had passed unpunished a few months previously between the Blood River and the south bank of the Pongolo. Further encroachment

was only checked by the movement of detachments of British troops from Utrecht to Luneburg on that frontier. In the latter part of July, after the Commissioners had given their verdict, the sons and brother of an influential Zooloo chief, Sirayo, entered British territory with a considerable armed force, and, dragging from the kraals of British subjects two women who had sought refuge there, forcibly carried them into Zoolooland, and there, it is believed, put them to death. Redress for these violations of British territory was promptly demanded by the Lieutenant-Governor of Natal, but the demand was not complied with. These and other complaints and claims for redress were detailed in the message delivered to the envoys of Cetywayo on December 11th, with a final demand that the offenders be given up for trial and a fine for previous non-compliance be paid within twenty days. To this time ten days was afterward added; but, no answer being received up to that time, Lord Chelmsford, on January 11th, crossed the border into Zoolooland.

During the negotiations of 1878, the South African authorities strained every nerve in order to prepare for what was expected would be a serious campaign. The officer commanding the troops, Lord Chelmsford, massed all his available force in Natal and the Transvaal ; the Admiral on the station coöperated by landing a naval brigade ; and by the end of December the British troops lay ready to enter Zoolooland in four columns. The right, under Colonel C. K. Pearson, was concentrated at Fort Williamson, near the mouth of the Tugela River. It numbered about 3,500 men, and, besides native levies and volunteers, comprised the 2d battalion of the 3d Buffs, the 99th Foot, a half battery of Royal Artillery, and the naval brigade. The right center column, under Colonel A. W. Durnford, R. E., consisted of 200 English volunteers, two guns Royal Artillery, some rocket tubes, and the 1st Native Regiment, about 3,000 in all. The left center column, under Colonel Glyn of the 24th Foot, numbered about 4,000 men ; with it were both battalions of the 24th Foot, a battery of the 5th brigade, and the 2d Native Regiment. The northern column, under Colonel Evelyn Wood, comprised the 1st battalion of the 13th Somersetshire Light Infantry, and the 90th Perthshire Light Infantry ; Tremlett's battery of Royal Artillery ; 11th battery, 7th brigade ; some frontier light horse ; and about 1,000 native allies. According to official returns, the total strength of Lord Chelmsford's force was as follows : Royal Artillery, 20 7-pounder guns, 263 men ; infantry, 5,128 men ; cavalry, 1,193 men ; native infantry, 9,035 ; mounted natives, 315 ; total fighting men, 15,934. But of these about 2,000, under Colonel Hugh Rowland, were at Pretoria watching Secocoeni. The force at the command of Cetywayo was estimated at between 40,000 and 50,000 men—in fact, the entire nation capable of bearing arms. Every youth on attaining the age of fifteen is drafted into a regiment, and after a year's service permanently posted to a military kraal, of which there are twelve in the country. There are thirty-three regiments in the Zooloo army, each having its own distinguishing dress and ornaments. The organization of all is alike. They are divided into right and left wings, each commanded by a wing officer, and subdivided again into eight or ten companies, each of which has a captain and three subalterns. Of the thirty-three regiments, eighteen are composed of married, fifteen of unmarried men. The former shave their heads, which are then bound round with a band made of the skin of some beast, leopard and otter predominating; they carry white shields. The unmarried regiments wear their hair naturally and carry black shields. Drill, in our sense of the word, is unknown in the Zooloo army, but they perform a few simple movements with ease and celerity. Their discipline, however, is most severe. When on service, falling out of the ranks is punishable with death, which, indeed, seems to be inflicted for the most trivial offenses. All officers have their proper duties, and the men obey them without hesitation. The system of commissariat and transport is simple in the extreme. Three or four days' provisions, consisting of maize or millet, are carried by a number of boys or women, who also bring up mats, ammunition, and blankets, and help to drive a herd of cattle. The Zooloos invariably attack in a crescent formation, enveloping the flanks of their enemy, on whom they pour a ceaseless fusillade directly he is surrounded; when within 200 or 300 yards they, with loud yells, make a rush, and, after having expended their assegais (spears) in the charge, dash in with their short swords. The Zooloo army, until lately, was armed with the usual Caffre weapons—rifles of divers patterns, Birmingham muskets, and such like. Of late, however, the King, whose power was despotic, insisted on each soldier providing himself with a breech-loading weapon. Thousands of arms in the course of a few months were landed at Delagoa Bay, and then rapidly passed into the hands of the Zooloos. The Portuguese authorities at that port were not powerful enough to stop the traffic. A correspondence on this subject passed between Sir Bartle Frere and the Portuguese Governor, which resulted in the latter official pledging himself to stop the trade, and a gunboat was accordingly dispatched to Delagoa Bay to protect the inhabitants.

The communications in Zoolooland are of the most primitive description, being merely wagon-tracks leading from the principal fords to the capital. Two, crossing the Tugela opposite Fort Williamson, run to Ulundi; a third from Rorke's Drift makes for the same point, and a fourth runs from Utrecht across the Blood River also to the capital. It was by these roads

that the English troops were advancing—Colonel Pearson, with No. 1 column, by the westernmost road; Lord Chelmsford, with columns Nos. 2 and 3, by that from Rorke's Drift; and Colonel Evelyn Wood, from Utrecht. The first column crossed the Lower Tugela Drift at Fort Pearson on January 12th. On the 23d they were attacked by the enemy in force at the Abroi River, five miles from Ekowe. The Zooloos were defeated with a loss of 800, while the loss of the British was but small. The same day Colonel Pearson proceeded on his march to Ekowe, which he reached in safety, and where he intrenched himself and formed a permanent post. The third column crossed the Buffalo River at Rorke's Drift also on the 12th, and on the same day a successful attack was made on Sirayo's place. On the 21st the main body of the British, under Lord Chelmsford, having advanced beyond Rorke's Drift on the Tugela River, left a small force, consisting of five companies of the 24th and about 600 natives, in charge of a valuable convoy, consisting of 102 wagons, 1,400 oxen, two pieces of artillery, 400 shot and shell, 1,200 rifles, 250,000 rounds of ammunition, one rocket trough, and £60,000 worth of commissariat stores. This convoy guard, under Colonel Pulleine, which was left some ten miles beyond Rorke's Drift at a point called Isandula or Isandlana to await the arrival of the column under Colonel Durnford, was attacked by the main body of the Zooloo army, reported to be 20,000 strong, who simply overwhelmed the British force by numbers. The attacking body of the Zooloos, consisting of the flower of Cetywayo's army, swarmed like bees around the British position, upon which they advanced under a heavy fire regardless of consequences, and came at once to hand-to-hand fighting with their short assegais. The result was an almost entire destruction of the British force, the total loss being stated at 30 officers and 500 men of the imperial troops and 70 men of the colonial troops, and the capture of the whole train together with the colors of the 24th by the Zooloos. They remained in possession of the camp until Lord Chelmsford's return at the close of the day, when they retired with the spoils, having previously destroyed everything they could not carry away. The General made his bivouac that day on the battlefield, and proceeded next morning to Rorke's Drift, at which place a company of the 24th Regiment had resisted the attack of a vastly superior body of Zooloos through the entire night, killing 370 of them with the loss of 12 men. The loss of the Zooloos was estimated at 2,000. The battle of Isandlana was regarded as a national calamity in England and the Cape. In order to repair the damages, considerable reënforcements were ordered to the Cape, comprising the 57th, 58th, 91st, and 94th Foot, the 1st Dragoon Guards, the 17th Lancers, two batteries of Royal Artillery, the 30th company of Royal Engineers, the 2d battalion of the 21st Foot, and the 3d battalion of the 60th Foot—in all, nearly 7,500 men and officers. About the same time, on the 24th, Colonel Wood's column, which started from Utrecht in the Transvaal, engaged between 3,000 and 4,000 Zooloos in the Tambua mountains, with little loss on his side; but owing to the disaster at the Isandlana Camp or Rorke's Drift, he took up a defensive position to cover Utrecht, and to be able to move if necessary in the direction of Colonel Glyn's column. After the victory at Isandlana, which Cetywayo failed to improve, most of the Zooloo warriors were dismissed to secure the crops. On February 17th two messengers arrived in Colonel Wood's camp from Obam, half-brother of Cetywayo, stating that he had escaped from the King's kraal, where he had been kept a prisoner since the end of last December. Oham was at this time in his own kraal, about twenty-five miles from the camp. He stated that he was still anxious to come over to the British, and suggested that Colonel Wood should name a place of meeting, where matters might be arranged. Oham had always wavered in his allegiance to his brother, and for this reason Cetywayo ordered him to Ulundi when war became inevitable. He finally surrendered on March 4th, together with his son and 300 men. Another serious reverse befell the British troops on March 12th. At daybreak a convoy of 100 men of the 80th Regiment, under Captain Moriarty, in charge of 20 wagons from Derby to Luneburg, was surprised by a large body of the enemy. Captain Moriarty fell in the action, and 60 of his men were lost, killed and missing. Lieutenant Harward, who escaped with 45 men, said that he was encamped with his men on one side of the river Intombi, and that Captain Moriarty with the remainder of the men was on the other side. Although some previous alarms had been given, they were surprised at daybreak by the irruption of a body of over 4,000 Zooloos. The Zooloo loss was heavy, but seemed to make no impression on them. The wagons with the supplies were removed by the enemy, but some rockets and ammunition were recovered.

In March King Cetywayo sent messages to Bishop Schroeder, of the Norwegian missions, asking for peace. He begged that the Bishop would explain to the Government that he never desired this war; he had never refused the terms proposed by Lower Tugela; he had already collected 1,000 head of cattle to pay the demand made on him. Sirayo's sons had escaped, and he was looking for them when he heard the English armies had crossed the Tugela; they attacked and killed many of Sirayo's people, but even then he did not despair of peace, for he then succeeded in arresting Sirayo's sons. He sent them bound with his army under Mavumgwana's charge, to be delivered up to the General at Rorke's Drift; three men were sent on to try and obtain a hearing, but they were fired at, and returned.

The fighting at Isandlana was brought about accidentally; the English horse attacked outlying parties of Zooloos, who returned their fire; more came up and joined in the fray, till the battle became general. The King protested that he never ordered his army to attack the English column, and Mavumgwana was in disgrace for having permitted it. Cetywayo also said that Colonel Pearson provoked the attack made on him by burning kraals and committing other acts of hostility along the line of march. He now asked that both sides should put aside their arms and resume the negotiations with a view to a permanent settlement of all questions between himself and the Government. The King further stated that he would have sent in a message before, but was afraid; because the last time he sent eight messengers to the Lower Tugela they were detained, and he now begged they might be sent back.

Colonel Pearson, who had advanced as far as Ekowe in February, and had there fortified himself, had been cut off completely from his friends. Communication had, however, been kept up with him by means of the heliograph, an instrument composed of mirrors, which by reflecting the sun's rays transmitted messages to a distance of eighty or a hundred miles. In this way the British were kept advised of the condition of Colonel Pearson's column. In the middle of March Colonel Pearson signaled that his supplies were almost at an end, and that he had a large number of sick persons in his hospital. A relief column was at once fitted out, and on March 29th set out under the personal command of Lord Chelmsford. The column consisted of 2,600 infantry, 640 naval brigade, and 50 mounted Europeans, 150 mounted natives, two 9-pounder guns, four 24-pounder rockets, two Gatlings, and 2,150 native contingent. The plan of relief was to force a passage through to Ekowe with all possible speed; to exchange the garrison and provision the fort for a fresh period of thirty days; to form another post on the Ingingzuni heights, leaving it supplied for a similar period, and perhaps establish a third at the Inyoni. The relieving column formed in *laager* at Ginglelova on the afternoon of April 1st. There were heavy rains throughout the evening, and the Zooloos were hovering about the camp. At 6 in the morning of the 2d the Zooloos attacked the laager on each side in succession, two distinct forces being employed. At 7.30 the attack was repulsed, and the enemy retreated, followed by Barrow's mounted infantry and the native contingent. On the 3d Lord Chelmsford with the greater part of the relief column started for Ekowe, leaving the remainder to guard the baggage. After a successful march of fifteen miles, Colonel Pearson, with a few companies of the 99th and the seamen of the Active, were met. The force reached Ekowe at 9.30 in the evening. On the 4th the garrison marched for the Tugela, and on the 5th Lord Chelmsford's column left for Ginglelova, and Ekowe was completely evacuated. On March 28th Colonel Wood, in order to create a diversion in favor of the relief of Ekowe, made a reconnoissance in force, marching twenty miles to Zlobani Mountain, the stronghold of Umbelini, a disaffected Swazi chief. The mountain was stormed and taken, and a large number of cattle were captured. After four hours' rest, the British, about 400 strong, found themselves surrounded by about 20,000 Zooloos. As the mountain was accessible at only one point, they had to cut their way through. On March 30th Colonel Wood's camp at Kambula was attacked by four Zooloo regiments of Cetywayo's army under Mnyane, who were repulsed with great loss, the British loss also being very heavy. During April and the greater part of May the operations ceased almost entirely, the British being engaged in preparing for a combined advance. This work was considerably delayed owing to a want of facilities for transportation. On May 16th Cetywayo dispatched an envoy to Colonel Crealock, asking him to send a European to discuss terms of peace. John Dunn, who formerly possessed great influence with the Zooloo King, accordingly went to Cetywayo's kraal, but returned within a short time, the negotiations having failed, because the British refused any terms but unconditional surrender, as Cetywayo's good faith was doubted by the military authorities. It was known that Cetywayo had repeatedly sent messengers to sue for peace. Bishop Colenso, of Natal, stated that he had reason to believe that since the battle of Isandlana the King had sent messengers three times to ask for terms of peace. The statement was not contradicted, and it was well known that the Bishop spoke, not from hearsay, but from a knowledge of the efforts which the Zooloos were making. He thought that there was reason to believe that on the first occasion Cetywayo's messengers were informed that their master must make what was equivalent to an unconditional surrender. Cetywayo's second attempt to open negotiations with the military authorities was made at the beginning of April. A party of Zooloos bearing a flag of truce arrived at the Middle Drift, and the flag was fired upon, in order, as was said, "to test its sincerity." The Bishop ascertained that the messengers who made their appearance at the above place were two Zooloos named Infunzi and Nkisimane, who were perfectly well known in Natal as being trustworthy agents of Cetywayo. In the third case it seemed that messengers came down to Ekowe with an offer from the King "to allow Colonel Pearson's force to fall back upon Natal unmolested." These natives were "put in irons," a statement which was confirmed by a native known to Dr. Colenso, who had been shut up at Ekowe with Colonel Pearson's column. It was further known that Cetywayo sent messengers to Colonel Wood's

camp on March 30th, with the message that "he wanted to surrender." Cetywayo's overtures were regarded by the British as of very doubtful sincerity, the British saying that the fact that while the King's messengers were at the English camp, the Zooloos continued their fire upon the outlying parties of the British, did not show any desire to stay the fighting.

A complete change was made in the last week of May in the chief command of the forces, as well as in the civil administration of the colonies of South Africa. Lieutenant-General Sir Garnet Wolseley was appointed to take the supreme military command, and to direct the civil government both of Natal and of the Transvaal, having the authority of High Commissioner to deal with Cetywayo and all other native chiefs and tribes to the northward on the frontier of those eastern provinces. Sir Bartle Frere was to remain Governor of the Cape Colony, but was to act as High Commissioner only for native affairs, such as those of Caffraria, Griqualand, and the Basutos, concerning the western and southern portions of the British dominions. Sir Henry Bulwer, as Lieutenant - Governor of Natal, and Colonel Lanyon, as Administrator of the Transvaal, were to continue in office, but would henceforth be subordinate to Governor Sir Garnet Wolseley. Lord Chelmsford was also to remain, but in a subordinate military command. Sir Garnet Wolseley arrived in Cape Town on June 23d, and proceeded immediately to Natal. A general advance of the British troops was begun in the early part of June. This was made very slowly, so that the British forces under Lord Chelmsford did not reach Ulundi, the King's kraal, and the objective point of the expedition, until early in July. During the march several of the King's military kraals were destroyed. Messengers arrived from the King stating his anxiety for peace. Lord Chelmsford told them Cetywayo must send to headquarters the High Induna, and as an earnest of his sincerity the two small cannon captured at Isandlana. Until these preliminary conditions were complied with, the army would advance in every part of Zoolooland. Cetywayo had power to stop further fighting by agreeing to the terms; but a permanent peace could only be obtained by the Zooloo people themselves agreeing to the conditions dictated to the King. Under these conditions the young men could marry whenever it suited them, and would no longer be liable to be called away from their kraals to assemble in military bodies. On June 30th messengers again came from Cetywayo bearing a sword and a letter. The letter was from Mr. Venn, a Dutch trader, a prisoner with the Zooloos. In it Cetywayo reiterated his desire for peace, but said he had been unable to collect the cattle and arms. Would the great white chief grant a little longer time to do so? On the envelope containing the letter, Mr. Venn, at great risk to himself, had written in pencil: "If you come, be strong. Cetywayo has 20,000 men." The gist of the King's message was verbally conveyed by the two envoys. They declared that Mundala, one of the King's head Indunas, was coming on the following day to meet Lord Chelmsford, bringing with him the two guns and some more cattle taken at Isandlana. On being questioned, they said that the old men were opposed to further hostilities, but the young men would not be guided by them. Cetywayo intended taking his army away, but had not sufficient influence to make a regiment come in and lay down their arms. Lord Chelmsford, in reply, said that if the Zooloos did not fire upon him, he would give orders to cease burning the kraals, and would halt upon the left bank of the White Umvolosi until noon on July 3d. If attacked, he would at once march on Ulundi; and as Cetywayo declared his inability to send in a regiment to lay down arms, he agreed to accept instead a thousand stand of rifles, which must be delivered at once. As Cetywayo failed to comply with Lord Chelmsford's demands, the latter crossed the river early on the morning of the 4th, his movements being watched by a number of the enemy who had collected on the surrounding hills. The British troops were formed into a hollow square on the plain near Ulundi, and while in this formation the Zooloos commenced a desperate attack on all four sides. They advanced repeatedly with great gallantry and determination during about an hour; but being met with a steady fire, they wavered each time and fell back. At length the British cavalry charged them, and a complete rout ensued. After the troops had rested for a short time at Ulundi, detachments were sent out in all directions, who burnt every kraal within a distance of three miles. In the course of the afternoon the British returned to the left bank of the Umvolosi. The loss of the Zooloos was variously estimated at from 800 to 1,500, while the loss of the British was only 10 killed and 53 wounded.

Even before the battle of Ulundi, a large number of chiefs came into the British camp to submit. After the battle the numbers continually increased, so that by July 12th all the principal chiefs except Cetywayo and Sirayo had given in their submission. The King after the battle retreated to the Ngome mountains in the north. Lord Chelmsford after the destruction fell back to Kwamagwasa (afterward called Fort Albert), as his supplies were about giving out. Sir Garnet Wolseley now took the entire management into his own hands, and went to Zoolooland, making his headquarters at Intanjaneni, and arriving at Ulundi on August 10th. On the 8th messengers had arrived from Cetywayo, who said that the King was ready to submit and pay taxes, but the country must be clear of soldiers. They were told that Cetywayo could not be treated with as the King. He was no longer the King, and must surrender unconditionally, except on the guar-

antee that his life would be spared and that he would have fair treatment. Another message was received to the effect that the King had no messengers to call his chiefs together, and could only send the same messenger to each chief in turn. He was told not to trouble himself about the other chiefs, as the Government would communicate with them directly. Cetywayo in his flight was accompanied by his prime minister and by several chiefs of the royal house. The royal cattle were driven with him wherever he sought shelter. These symbols of his royal estate he would never suffer to stray from him. Indeed, the rumor that the herds were being driven to the junction of the Black and White Umvolosi gave to the British the first clew to the King's hiding-place. They started in pursuit of him on August 13th, after burning Ambakage, his new kraal. Though they kept close in his tracks, he always managed to escape them. On the morning of the 15th the cavalry arrived at the kraal where he had spent the night. Lord Gifford was then ordered to continue the pursuit with a party of natives. Then Cetywayo's misfortunes began. His followers left him one by one. His prime minister, two of his sons, and three of his brothers surrendered, with 650 of his cattle; and almost every day arms and cattle were surrendered to the British, so that toward the end of his flight Cetywayo had but very few followers who remained faithful to him. Finally, on August 28th he was captured without resistance by Major Marten. When captured he was utterly prostrated, and his followers were too weak to resist. They were taken to Ulundi, whence Cetywayo was sent to Port Durnford, and then by sea to Cape Town, to be kept there as a state prisoner until the Queen should signify her pleasure in regard to him. The final disposition of Zoolooland was as follows: The country was divided into thirteen districts, over each of which a chief was appointed. A British resident was appointed to each district, while a Governor resident over all was appointed in the person of John Dunn. On September 1st Sir Garnet Wolseley met six of the chiefs at Ulundi, and submitted to them the following treaty, which was signed by them, and shortly after by the remaining chiefs:

1. I will observe and respect whatever boundaries shall be assigned to my territory by the British Government through the Resident of the division in which my territory is situated.

2. I will not permit the existence of the Zooloo military system, or the existence of any military system of organization whatever, in my territory; and I will proclaim and make it a rule that all men shall be allowed to marry when they choose and as they choose, according to the good, ancient customs of my people, known and followed in the days preceding the establishment by Chaka of the system known as the military system; and I will allow and encourage all men living within my territory to go and come freely for peaceful purposes, and to work in Natal and the Transvaal and elsewhere for themselves or for hire.

3. I will not import or allow to be imported into my territory by any person, upon any pretext or for any object whatever, any arms or ammunition from

any part whatsoever, or any goods or merchandise by the sea-coast of Zoolooland, without the express sanction of the Resident of the division in which my territory is situated; and I will not encourage or promote, or take part in, or countenance in any way whatever, the importation into any other part of Zoolooland of arms or ammunition from any part whatever, or goods or merchandise by the sea-coast of Zoolooland without such sanction; and I will confiscate and hand over to the Natal Government all arms and ammunition, and goods and merchandise, so imported into my territory; and I will punish by fine or by other sufficient punishment any person guilty of or concerned in any such unsanctioned importation, and any person found possessing arms or ammunition, or goods or merchandise, knowingly obtained thereby.

4. I will not allow the life of any of my people to be taken for any cause, except after sentence passed in a council of the chief men of my territory, and after fair and impartial trial in my presence and after the hearing of witnesses; and I will not tolerate the employment of witch doctors, or the practice known as smelling out, or any practice of witchcraft.

5. The surrender of persons fugitive in my territory from justice, when demanded by the Government of any British colony, territory, or province, in the interests of justice, shall be readily and promptly made to such Government; and the escape into my territory of persons accused or convicted of offenses against British laws shall be prevented by all possible means, and every exertion shall be made to seize and deliver up such persons to British authority.

6. I will not make war upon any chief or chiefs, or people, without the sanction of the British Government, through the Resident of the division in which my territory is situated.

7. The succession to the chieftainship of my territory shall be according to the ancient laws and customs of my people, and the nomination of each successor shall be subject to the approval of the British Government.

8. I will not sell, or in any way alienate, or permit or countenance any sale or alienation of, any part of the land in my territory.

9. I will permit all people residing in my territory to there remain, upon the condition that they recognize my authority as chief; and any persons not wishing to recognize my authority and desiring to quit my territory I will permit to quit and to pass unmolested elsewhere.

10. In all cases of dispute in which British subjects are involved I will appeal to and abide by the decision of the British Resident of the division in which my territory is situated. In all cases where accusations of offense or crime committed in my territory are brought against British subjects, or against my people in relation to British subjects, I will hold no trial and pass no sentence, except with the approval of such British Resident.

11. In all matters not included within these terms, conditions, and limitations, and in all cases provided for herein, and in all cases when there may be doubt or uncertainty as to the laws, rules, or stipulations applicable to matters to be dealt with, I will govern, order, and decide in accordance with the ancient law and usage of my people.

The duties of the Residents and the policy to be followed in future were set forth in the instructions given them. The principal points of these instructions were as follows:

You will be the eyes and ears of the British Government, and it will be your duty to watch the manner in which the chiefs appointed to rule over the several territories of the country carry out the terms to which they assented as the conditions of their chieftainship. While always ready to give advice to the chiefs of Zoolooland, you will exercise no authority over them or their people. Should you observe in them any departure from the conditions of their chieftainship to

which they have assented, you may remonstrate with them, stating to them that you must report upon their conduct to your Government; but you will be careful to issue no order to them in regard to the matter of complaint. In future no land to the north or west of the Pongolo will be recognized as forming any part of Zoolooland. The western boundary of Zoolooland will start from the Pongolo River, where that river joins the Bevana River, and will run up along the Bevana River to the junction of the Bevana River with the Pemvana River; thence it will run up the Pemvana to the Kambula Mountain, and from the Kambula Mountain down the Lyn or Dabusi River to its junction with the Blood River, whence it will run down the Blood River to the Buffalo River. In dealing with the chiefs you will impress upon them that all the King's cattle now belong to the British Government and must be handed over to you. . . . You will be careful to hold yourself entirely aloof from all missionary or proselytizing enterprises. If any chief desires that a missionary should reside in his territory, there can be no objection to the missionary occupying ground as a site for a mission station and ground to serve for a pastureland and for a garden; but it is to be clearly understood that the chief in no way thereby alienates the land so assigned, and that at any time he may resume the land should he wish to do so. Grants of land by the former King to missionaries can not be recognized by the British Government; but there is no reason why occupation of such land should not be resumed by the now deposed missionaries, provided the chief in whose territory the land in question is situated wishes for the return of the missionaries among his people. You will not prevent any chiefs from corresponding with or visiting the Governor or Lieutenant-Governor of Natal, should they wish to do so.

The settlement with the Zooloos was almost universally condemned in Natal and Cape Colony. The principal objections of the colonists were, that the powers of the Residents were too limited; that the thirteen chiefs possessed as much power for harm as the one King had possessed before, and that consequently the borders would still continue to be in a state of unquietness. The appointment of John Dunn was also severely criticised. He is described as a white man who had lived twenty years or more among the Zooloos, had married Zooloo wives, and had been for many years the right-hand man of King Cetywayo. He was regarded in the colonies as one who had made himself an outcast from all decent society.

An event of the war that for a time created considerable excitement in England and on the continent was the death of the Prince Imperial of France. (See BONAPARTE.) On June 1st he left General Wood's camp on a reconnoissance, accompanied by Lieutenant Carey and a few troopers. The party dismounted in a mealie field near the Ilyotoyozi River. The enemy crept up and assegaied the Prince and two troopers. The English Government was bitterly attacked in the press and in Parliament for accepting the services of the Prince. On June 23d the Duke of Cambridge, the Commander-in-Chief, felt compelled to make the following statement in Parliament:

There is very great doubt as to the circumstances in which the Prince Imperial went to South Africa, and I think it is much to be deplored that that doubt should remain for a moment longer than necessary.

Indeed, it seems to me that I should be neglecting my duty if I did not read to your lordships the two private letters which the unfortunate Prince took out with him as letters of introduction to Sir Bartle Frere and Lord Chelmsford. They are private letters, and are the letters under which the Prince attached himself to the army in Zoolooland:

"*February* 25, 1879.

"MY DEAR CHELMSFORD : This letter will be presented to you by the Prince Imperial, who is going out on his own account to see as much as he can of the coming campaign in Zoolooland. He is extremely anxious to go out, and wanted to be employed in our army; but the Government did not consider that this could be sanctioned, but have sanctioned my writing to you and to Sir Bartle Frere to say that if you can show him kindness and render him assistance to see as much as he can with the columns in the field, I hope you will do so. He is a fine young fellow, full of spirit and pluck, and having many old cadet friends in the Artillery, he will doubtless find no difficulty in getting on; and if you can help him in any other way, pray do so. My only anxiety on his account would be that he is too plucky and go-ahead.

"I remain, my dear Chelmsford, yours most sincerely,
"GEORGE."

That is the letter to Lord Chelmsford, and I should also like to read to your lordships that which was addressed to Sir Bartle Frere, in order that there may be no mistake:

"*February* 25, 1879.

"MY DEAR SIR BARTLE FRERE : I am anxious to make you acquainted with the Prince Imperial, who is about to proceed to Natal by to-morrow's packet to see as much as he can of the coming campaign in Zoolooland in the capacity of a spectator. He was anxious to serve in our army, having been a cadet at Woolwich; but the Government did not think that this could be sanctioned. But no objection is made to his going out on his own account, and I am permitted to introduce him to you and to Lord Chelmsford in the hope and with my personal request that you will give him every help in your power to enable him to see what he can. I have written to Chelmsford to the same effect. He is a charming young man, full of spirit and energy, speaking English admirably, and the more you see of him the more you will like him. He has many young friends in the Artillery, and so I doubt not with your and Chelmsford's kind assistance he will get on well enough.

"I remain, my dear Sir Bartle, yours most sincerely,
"GEORGE."

My lords, having read these letters, all I can say is that I think, so far as the authorities at home are concerned, everybody must feel that nothing has been done by them to place the unfortunate Prince in the position which unhappily resulted in his death. We all deeply regret his loss, and I am sure there is not a man, woman, or child in the country, from her Majesty downward, who does not sensibly deplore what has occurred ; but, certainly, so far as the authorities here are concerned, I feel that we had nothing to do with bringing about such a catastrophe as that which we now all so greatly lament.

Lieutenant Carey, the officer who accompanied the Prince Imperial, was tried by court martial, and at its close was sent home under arrest pending the Queen's decision upon the verdict. In the first days of August the proceedings of the court were quashed on account of an informality. At first Lieutenant Carey was severely censured throughout the United Kingdom ; but as the facts of his case became known, public sentiment completely changed, and upon his arrival in Portsmouth he was to be presented with a numerously signed address, expressive of sympathy for him in his trying position and of confidence in him as a brave officer and a true Englishman. Although this address was not presented in consequence of an intimation from the authorities, the sentiments it contained were expressed to him in other ways, and he was everywhere treated as one who had been unjustly accused.

In the Transvaal the war showed a very bad state of affairs. The Boers, in their hostility to England, went so far as to refuse all assistance against the Zooloos. None of the promises made by Sir Theophilus Shepstone when he annexed the country had been carried out, and the Boers even went so far as to talk of reasserting their independence by force. The news of Isandlana had hardly spread itself throughout the Transvaal before the first threats of displacing the British by force were heard. In order to come to an understanding with the Boers, Sir Bartle Frere set out for Pretoria, and arrived on April 10th. He was received with an address of welcome. In his reply he stated that he had come to see that the existing laws were obeyed, and that the inhabitants enjoyed the same protection as other portions of the Queen's dominions. "I find," he said, "that there are those who think the country may be given up again ; but I think you will see in the promptitude with which the reën-forcements lately asked for were sent a clear proof and guarantee that no territory over which the British flag has once waved will ever be abandoned." On the 12th he entered the camp of 2,000 or 3,000 malcontents who threatened an attack on the seat of government at Pretoria, and succeeded in convincing them that it was best for them to submit quietly. The camp was broken up, and the people quietly dispersed to their homes.

In the Transvaal the Caffres under Secocoeni, who had defeated the Boers in 1877, also became hostile, and Colonel Lanyon was sent in the early part of the year to that province to keep them in check. Several successful patrols were made against them, and Colonel Lanyon had just completed his arrangements for attacking the stronghold of the chief, when in June Sir Garnet Wolseley sent instructions to him to stop and send his men to Derby to protect that part of the border, and prevent Cetywayo from breaking through.

After the pacification of Zoolooland had been accomplished, Sir Garnet Wolseley went to the Transvaal, arriving in Pretoria on September 28th. He was met by a deputation of the people, who presented him an address of welcome. The General read a written answer to the address, which he supplemented with a speech of the same tenor and tone, as to the irrevocable nature of the annexation.

The Zooloo war again brought the question of a South African confederation prominently before the public. On June 12th Sir M. Hicks-Beach addressed a dispatch to Sir Bartle Frere, in which he intimated that "a determined effort" should be made to extend the system of self-government possessed by the Cape to other portions of South Africa, so that the Queen's representative there might be aided by a Union Ministry and Parliament in dealing with the "singularly difficult and intricate problems of government" of the whole country. Setting aside previous suggestions for a conference of delegates from the several colonies to be convened in Cape Town, he called upon the Cape Government, as the principal colony, at once to submit to its Parliament, then assembled, general proposals for the establishment of a South African Union or Confederation on the lines of the South African Act of 1877. In the case of rejection of this demand, it was stated that measures initiated with respect to the lately disturbed territories on the eastern frontier could not be proceeded with; in other words, that the annexation of Galekaland, Tambookieland, and other parts of the Transkei would not be sanctioned. It was further intimated that in future colonists must not rely upon Imperial troops for defense against native attacks or insurrections, and that her Majesty's soldiers would only be permanently placed as a garrison at or near Cape Town for the protection of the neighboring naval station, this station being of great importance to the interests of the whole Empire. In these circumstances, it was suggested that a regular defensive force be organized for maintaining security on the inland borders of the several colonies, toward the maintenance of which force Government would be prepared to contribute from Imperial funds for a period of five years an annual sum equal to that voted by the Union Legislature, provided a pledge was given by the Cape Parliament—to be afterward confirmed by the Union—that no further aid would be required from the mother country for military purposes. The general disapproval of the treaty which had been made by Sir Garnet Wolseley with the Zooloo chiefs caused the proposition for a confederation to be regarded unfavorably, and nothing was done in the colonies with regard to it.

There were also during the year troubles with the Basutos, and with the Caffres in Pondoland. Slight engagements were had in both cases, the British coming out victoriously in the end.

By two proclamations of Sir Bartle Frere, certain portions of the Transkei and No-man's Land were finally incorporated with the Colony of the Cape of Good Hope on October 1st. The area defined in the order includes two distinct districts: First, a three-cornered strip of land bordering the east bank of the river Kei, which may be roughly described as being embraced between that river and its tributary the Geuwa and the Xwexweni Mountains, including Fingoland and the Jantywa Reserve, and containing an area of about 1,600 square miles. This territory is to be known as the territory of the Transkei. The second area, to be known as Griqualand East, includes the territory between the Drakenberg Mountains on the west, the Mataana Mountains on the south, Amapondoland and Alfred County, Natal, on the east, and the Imgwangwane and Umzumkulu rivers on the east. This territory covers about 7,000 square miles.

CAREY, HENRY CHARLES, a writer on political economy, was born in Philadelphia December 15, 1793, and died October 13, 1879. He was the son of Mathew Carey, once a prominent publisher in Philadelphia. He was brought up in the business of his father, and in 1835, having been successful, withdrew to devote himself to the preparation and publication of works on political economy. His discussions of the relations of labor and capital, of finance, and other fundamental questions in that science, soon attracted attention both at home and abroad. His books have been reproduced in Germany, France, Sweden, Italy, Russia, and other European countries. To the close of his life he was the champion of the American protective system, of which his works constitute the most complete exposition. They defend it by a series of facts and an array of figures unsurpassed. He was enthusiastic in his pursuit, and devoted himself to it with great industry and ability. His most important work is his "Past and Present" (3 vols. 8vo, 1848), but his works on the general subject to which he gave his life have been very exhaustive, covering the period from 1835, the date of his "Essay on Wages," to his paper on the "Unity of Law" in 1873. Mr. Carey was fully recognized the world over as a leading and original writer on political economy, and, while his views were not generally accepted, they were always thought to be too important to escape analysis in the leading treatises on the subject. Mr. Carey led a blameless, genial life, full of work; and he was highly respected by a large circle of friends.

CHANDLER, ZACHARIAH, a Senator, member of the Cabinet, and politician, was born in Bedford, New Hampshire, December 10, 1813, and died suddenly in Chicago, November 1, 1879. His education was limited to that of the common schools and an academy in his native State. In 1833 he removed to Detroit and engaged in the dry-goods business, in which he was energetic and successful. In 1851 his public life began by his election as Mayor of Detroit. In 1852 he was nominated for Governor by the Whigs, and, although his success was hopeless, the large vote which he received brought him to public notice. Thenceforward he took an active interest in State and national politics. In the winter of 1856-'57 he was elected to the United States Senate, to succeed General Lewis Cass, who had been a distinguished representative of the State. During this Congress Senator Chandler served as chairman of the Committee on the District of Columbia and of the Committee on Commerce. It was during this term, on February 11, 1861, that he wrote the famous so-called "blood letter," which he acknowledged and defended in one of his latest speeches in the Senate. It can be found in vol. i. (1861) of this work. He was reëlected in 1863, and during that term again served as chairman of the Committee on Commerce, and also on the Committees on Revolutionary Claims and Mines and Mining. He was also a member of the National Committee which accompanied the remains of President Lincoln to Illinois, and was a delegate to the Philadelphia Convention of 1866. In 1869 he was again elected. During the important period of his first term in the United States Senate Mr. Chandler was identified with all the leading measures of Congress. During the term that expired in 1875 he continued chairman of the Committee on Commerce. In October, 1875, President Grant tendered him the post of Secretary of the Interior, to fill the place made vacant by the resignation of Columbus Delano. He served in this position until President Grant's retirement. When Senator I. P. Christiancy resigned his place in the Senate, early in 1879, to accept the post of Minister to Peru, Mr. Chandler was elected by the Legislature of Michigan to fill the unexpired term of the man who had succeeded him in the Senate four years before. His term of service would have expired in 1881. Mr. Chandler took an active part in the exciting Presidential campaign of 1876, being the hard-working president of the Republican National Executive Committee. He was, during the greater portion of his life, engaged in large business enterprises, from which he had realized a handsome fortune. He was a man of commanding appearance, and possessed an excellent practical judgment, great energy, and perseverance.

CHEMISTRY. *Oxygen in the Sun.*—On the 13th of June last Professor Henry Draper laid before the Royal Astronomical Society of London the evidence by which he claims to have demonstrated the existence of oxygen in the sun. From a summary of his paper published in the London "Times" we take the following, which gives a fair idea of the nature of the problem, and of the results of Dr. Draper's investigations. It will be remembered that when in 1859 Kirchhoff showed how the dark lines of the solar spectrum enable us to analyze the vaporous envelope of the sun, the substances the presence of which was recognized belonged with one exception to the family of metallic elements. Iron, zinc, copper, aluminum, sodium, magnesium, cobalt, nickel, calcium, chromium, titanium, and manganese were found to be present; and, besides these metals, hydrogen was also recognized. The absence of all evidence respecting some of the other elements might not have seemed remarkable, because it could well be believed that they were present in quantities relatively so small that our means of analyzing the sun failed to detect them. But that such elements as oxygen, nitrogen, and carbon, all of them important constituents of our earth, should be absent from the sun, or should not be present in quantities large enough to make their detection easy, seemed surprising. In the case of the two latter elements the wonder was increased by the circumstance that Huggins recognized the presence of nitrogen in the

gaseous nebulæ, and that of carbon in certain comets. But, though no spectroscopic evidence of the presence of oxygen in any of the self-luminous celestial bodies had been obtained, so that the absence of any evidence of its presence in the sun was in one sense less remarkable, it was in another sense the most remarkable of all the negative results of solar spectroscopic analysis.

Oxygen is commonly believed to form one third of the mass of our earth's crust, and is known to form eight ninths of the water, where it is combined with hydrogen, and one fifth of the air, where it is mixed with nitrogen. It can not be assumed that the structure of the sun is identical with that of the earth; yet it would be difficult to understand how in the great central mass, in which the denser elements would be the more abundant, the lightest of all, hydrogen, should be present in enormous quantities, while oxygen, so much denser under the same conditions, should be absent, or present only in such small amount as to afford no evidence of its existence. The natural inference would be that oxygen and the other non-metallic elements, though really present in the sun, are situated below that visible surface which is called the photosphere. That at any rate they are not present above that surface in any considerable quantity is clearly shown by what happens during total eclipses of the sun; for whereas, at the moment when the sun is just fully hidden by the moon, the metallic elements usually recognized by the absorptive action of their vapors on the sun's light can be recognized by their emissive action, a rainbow-tinted array of bright lines suddenly replacing the rainbow-tinted streak crossed by a corresponding array of dark lines, the bright lines of oxygen, nitrogen, carbon, and other non-metallic elements have never been recognized, even under these favorable conditions. But if oxygen existed in enormous quantities within the visible globe of the sun, its presence might be recognized in another way. Besides the dark lines in the solar spectrum, there are bright lines certainly at times, and probably always. Some, indeed, have said that as the glowing vapors which produce the rainbow-tinted array of lines just mentioned are at all times present over the sun's surface, there are always bright lines; but as the question is one of relative brightness, and as these particular tints are fainter—corresponding, in fact, to the dark lines—this mode of speaking seems as incorrect as it would be to describe the dull disk of a small red-hot globe, seen projected on a bright background at a white heat, as forming a bright instead of a dark spot on that bright white background. When, however, as sometimes happens, the known lines of some element disappear and presently reappear as bright lines, we perceive that for the time being the spectroscopic evidence respecting that particular element is changed in character. We know that that element is present in the part of the sun examined, but we know this because we see the bright lines, not (as usual) the dark lines of that element.

If oxygen were present in very great quantities in the sun, but always lay below the visible solar surface, and were at a higher temperature than that prevailing at the surface, then oxygen might indicate its presence by its bright lines, and could certainly indicate it in no other way. Now, it is evidence of precisely this kind that Professor Draper seems to have obtained respecting this most important element. He had been engaged since 1863 in obtaining simultaneous photographs of parts of the solar spectrum and of corresponding parts of the spectra of hydrogen, nitrogen, and carbon. In examining a series of such photographs in which the fluted spectrum of nitrogen was in juxtaposition with the solar spectrum, he found reason to suspect that some of the bright lines of nitrogen agreed exactly in position with bright bands in the spectrum of the sun. Pursuing his researches, he found, even at that early stage of his labors, very striking evidence of agreement between the bright lines of oxygen and solar bright bands. It was not, however, till the year 1877 that he was so far satisfied as to announce "the discovery of oxygen in the sun." The paper thus named was illustrated by enlarged views of the negatives he had obtained. In these photographs a part of the spectrum of the sun was seen side by side with the bright-line spectrum of air. The bright lines of iron were shown in company with those of air, in order to indicate the exact agreement of the juxtaposed spectra by the coincidence of the iron bright lines with the corresponding solar dark lines. Every one of the oxygen bright lines was seen to coincide with a bright part of the solar spectrum. In some cases the coincidence was very striking, because the bright line of the air-spectrum not only agreed exactly in position, but very closely in character with a bright band in the solar spectrum. This close resemblance could not in every case be recognized—a circumstance by no means surprising when we remember that if these bright bands in the solar spectrum are really due to the presence of great quantities of oxygen below the visible solar surface, the light of this oxygen can only reach us after passing through the cooler envelope of metallic vapors which produces the dark lines, and must be affected by the absorptive action of those vapors; which, of course, was not the case with the oxygen of the air from which Professor Draper obtained the bright-line comparison spectrum.

Many experienced spectroscopists remained unconvinced by the evidence which Professor Draper thus advanced in 1877; and in the true scientific spirit Professor Draper set to work to apply more searching tests to his result. The scale of his enlarged photographs had been half that of Angstrom's well-known "normal spectrum." Those which he exhibited at the Astronomical Society were on a scale four times greater. The evidence derived from each coincidence was thus increased fourfold in value, the evidence from two coincidences sixteenfold; from three, sixty-fourfold; and from the eighteen recognized coincidences about 68,725,000,000 times. He effected also an improvement likely to have great value in other spectroscopic researches. The electric spark through air which gave the air-spectrum pursued a zigzag course, like a lightning-flash on a small scale. He wanted a straight flash, or at any rate a flat flash, so that seen from one direction it should appear as a straight line. So he invented what he calls the spark-compressor. The terminals between which the spark passes are introduced into a small block of soapstone, and between them a small flat aperture is prepared, between the walls of which the electric flash has to travel. This space is left open on one side, somewhat like the slit of a money-box, and the spark seen from that side necessarily appears as a straight line, though it may have a considerable amount of zigzag play in the plane of the flat space left for its passage. The result of this arrangement is that the spectrum of the air-lines (oxygen and nitrogen), as also of the iron-lines (obtained by having a little iron at one of the poles), is much better defined and more trustworthy than it had been before this plan was adopted.

Most spectroscopists will doubtless admit that Professor Draper does not pass beyond the limits of scientific caution in claiming that the coincidence, shown in his photographs, between the bright lines of oxygen and bright parts of the solar spectrum, establishes the probability of the existence of oxygen in the sun. The burden of proof, or rather of disproof, should now fall on those who consider that the coincidence may, after all, be merely accidental. If such evidence as Professor Draper has obtained is rejected, it would seem as if hardly any spectroscopic evidence can suffice to prove the existence of an element in the sun. The evidence is certainly not stronger in the case of sodium or magnesium, which every physicist regards as present in the sun, than Professor Draper has obtained in the case of oxygen.

A New Explosive.—The discovery of a compound more violent than guncotton or dynamite has recently been announced by M. Nobel, under the name of blasting gelatine, and this again has been endowed with a still greater energy by a modification of its nature effected by Professor Abel, chemist of the British War Department. Nearly all the explosives brought before the public are nitro-compounds or modifications of them. One class owe their origin to guncotton and the other to nitro-glycerine; and these are essentially the same thing, guncotton being made by the nittification of a solid body, and nitro-glycerine by the nitrification of a liquid substance. The methods of manufacture and the agents employed to bring about the nitrification are similar.

In the application of the two explosives, however, there is a wide difference. Guncotton is in a form which makes it conveniently available; but nitro-glycerine, being a liquid, is difficult to use, and this fact led Nobel and others to seek for some suitable vehicle to contain the preparation. A silicious clay, called *Kieselguhr*, which will absorb three times its weight of the liquid, has been found the most favorable vehicle, and dynamite consists of about 75 per cent. of nitro-glycerine and 25 per cent. of this inert substance. In blasting-gelatine the objection to employing an inert material is overcome, the mass being explosive throughout. " Blasting or explosive gelatine is a mixture of nitro-glycerine and guncotton. M. Nobel, to whom is due the credit of having placed the valuable properties of nitro-glycerine at the disposal of mining engineers, has discovered, in pursuing further investigations, that the liquid in question acts as a solvent upon guncotton. Like a mixture of alcohol and ether, nitro-glycerine is found to dissolve nitro-cellulose, and form a description of collodion, or, as M. Nobel terms it, gelatine. It is not, of course, the highly explosive guncotton that will thus dissolve, but that known as photographer's pyroxiline, which does not contain so much nitrogen. Military guncotton, indeed, or tri-nitro-cellulose, to call it by its chemical name, should not be soluble at all, or at any rate only to a slight extent, if properly manufactured, and one of the tests to ascertain if it is of good quality is in fact to treat it with an alcohol-ether mixture to ascertain how far it will dissolve. The soluble guncotton, however, if not so highly nitrified, to coin a term for our purpose, is still a sufficiently explosive body, and this M. Nobel finds he can dissolve to a greater extent in nitro-glycerine than it is possible to do in alcohol and ether. Whereas the latter will dissolve no more than 4 or 5 per cent. of pyroxiline, and frequently less than 2, nitro-glycerine has been found to take up upward of 7 per cent. The operation of dissolving is presumably done when the liquid is warm, and the result is, as we have said, a jellified mass, which has all the attributes of a definite combination. There is no separation of liquid from the mass, and cartridges may be made by simply rolling up the material in paper envelopes. . . . In blasting - gelatine there is no inert body, and the consequence is that, weight for weight, the gelatine is superior in its destructive action to dynamite. The latter, as we have seen, contains 75 per cent. of nitro-glycerine, whereas blasting-gelatine consists of from 90 to 93 per cent. of this liquid, and from 7 to 10 per cent. of soluble guncotton. But there exists another reason still why the detonation of blasting-gelatine should be more energetic, namely, because the combustion of the charge, from more perfect oxidation, is well-nigh complete. . . . By converting the gelatine

into a more solid body by the addition to it of some 10 per cent. of military guncotton, or tri-nitro-cellulose, Mr. Abel appears to have secured a still more vigorous explosive, and one besides that, by reason of its firmness, is more convenient to handle than the soft and pliant jelly. The destructive action of this modified gelatine upon iron plates and heavy masses of lead has been found greater than that of any other form of nitro-glycerine or guncotton; and there is no room for doubt that for torpedoes and military mining, where the object is to secure the greatest degree of violence, regardless of consequences, the compound will find valuable application."

New Aniline Salts.—Messrs. Beamer and Clarke, of the University of Cincinnati, describe in the " American Chemical Journal " several new salts of aniline which they have lately obtained and partially examined. *Aniline chlorate* is formed by cautiously adding chloric acid to an alcoholic solution of aniline, and then evaporating under the receiver of an air-pump. The salt quickly appears in the shape of white, slender prisms about an inch long. This compound is readily soluble in alcohol and ether, but less so in water. On exposure to air or to a gentle heat, its solutions blacken and decompose. It detonates sharply when struck, and explodes when brought in contact with sulphuric acid or when heated to a temperature of 75°. *Aniline perchlorate* is prepared in the same way as the preceding. Its crystals take the form of large rhombic plates, are more stable than the chlorate, and when dry are permanent in the air. They detonate feebly when struck or heated, and are decomposed by sulphuric acid. *Aniline iodate* is obtained by adding aniline to a solution of iodic acid. It is slightly soluble in cold, but more soluble in hot water, and still more so in boiling alcohol. All of its solutions slowly decompose on standing, and even the dry substance becomes discolored by long exposure to the air. When heated slowly to 110° it blackens, but suffers no further change even when the temperature is carried to 150°. By sudden heating, however, it explodes at 125°—130°. On percussion it detonates very feebly, yielding a dense cloud of smoke, which is light-brown by reflected and violet by transmitted light. When thrown upon sulphuric acid, it instantaneously decomposes, yielding the same dense vapors. Specific gravity, 1·48 at 13°. *Aniline fluohydrate* · is formed by the union of aniline and fluohydric acids, appears in beautiful pearly scales, and is very soluble in boiling alcohol. *Aniline phthalate* is formed by the addition of aniline to an alcoholic solution of phthalic acid. Its melting-point is 145° —146°. *Aniline monochloracetate* is deposited in a flocculent mass of white crystals on adding aniline to a solution of monochloracetic acid. *Aniline dichloracetate*, formed like the preceding, crystallizes in long white prisms, which melt at 122°. *Aniline trichloracetate* is prepared by dissolving aniline in an aqueous solution of trichloracetic acid.

The Constitution of the Elements.—In a paper read before the Royal Society, and also in an article published in the "Nineteenth Century," Professor J. N. Lockyer has given an account of the remarkable series of experiments which in his opinion confirm the hypothesis that the so-called elements are really compound bodies. This view, as is well known, was already held by many long before these investigations were begun; indeed, the progress of chemistry has proved several substances to be compound that were previously ranked as elements, and left the list of simple bodies to consist of such only as have hitherto resisted all efforts at decomposition. It was believed that the relations among the atomic numbers furnish strong evidence of the composite nature of many substances now classed as elementary, and spectrum analysis has served greatly to heighten this probability. Writing on the subject several years ago, Herbert Spencer took the ground that the elements are not known to be elementary; that no intelligent chemist holds them to be absolutely so; and that many concurrent considerations compel the inference that they are compounded, and perhaps recompounded, of a few and possibly a single primordial constituent. For his views of the bearings of spectroscopic research on this question, see article "Chemistry" in the "Annual Cyclopædia" for 1878. In a suggestive paper entitled "Evolution and the Spectroscope," published in "The Popular Science Monthly" for January, 1873, Professor F. W. Clarke of Cincinnati expressed similar views. He announced on spectroscopic grounds the hypothesis that the evolution of planets from nebulæ has been accompanied by an evolution of complex from simple forms of matter, basing the idea upon the gradation of chemical complexity in the celestial spectra.

The important facts and fresh illustrations brought forward by Professor Lockyer were published in a summary of his paper before the Royal Society, prepared by a chemist who heard it for the London "Times," and from this the subjoined extracts are taken:

There are many facts and many trains of thought suggested by solar and stellar physics which point to the hypothesis that the elements themselves, or at all events some of them, are compound bodies. Thus it would appear that the hotter a star the more simple is its spectrum; for the brightest, and therefore probably the hottest stars, such as Sirius, furnish spectra showing only very thick hydrogen lines and a few very thin metallic lines, characteristic of elements of low atomic weight, while the cooler stars, such as our sun, are shown by their spectra to contain a much larger number of metallic elements than stars such as Sirius, but no non-metallic elements; and the coolest stars furnish fluted band-spectra characteristic of compounds of metallic with non-metallic elements and of non-metallic elements. These facts appear to meet with a simple explanation if it be supposed that as the temperature increases the compounds are first broken up into their constituent "elements," and that these "elements" then undergo dissociation or decomposition into "elements" of lower atomic weight. Mr. Lockyer next considers what will be the difference in the spectro-

scopic phenomena, supposing that A contains B as an impurity and as a constituent. In both cases A will have a spectrum of its own. B, however, if present as an impurity, will merely add its lines according to the amount present, as we have above explained; whereas, if a constituent of A, it will add its lines according to the extent to which A is decomposed and B is set at liberty; so that as the temperature increases the spectrum of A will fade if A be a compound body, whereas it will not fade if A be a true element. Moreover, if A be a compound body, the longest lines at one temperature will not be the longest at another. The paper chiefly deals with a discussion from this point of view of the spectrum of calcium, iron, hydrogen, and lithium, as observed at various temperatures; and it is shown that precisely the kind of change which is to be expected on the hypothesis of the non-elementary character of the elements has been found to take place. Thus each of the salts of calcium, so long as the temperature is below a certain point, has a definite spectrum of its own; but as the temperature is raised the spectrum of the salt gradually dies out, and very fine lines due to the metal appear in the blue and violet portions of the spectrum. At the temperature of the electric arc the line in the blue is of great intensity, the violet H and K lines, as they are called, being still thin; in the sun the H and K lines are very thick, and the line in the blue is of less intensity than either, and much thinner than in the arc. Lastly, Dr. Huggins's magnificent star photographs show that both the H and K lines are present in the spectrum of α Aquilæ, the latter being, however, only about half the breadth of the former; but that in the spectrum of α Lyræ and Sirius, only the H line of calcium is present. Similar evidence that these different lines may represent different substances appears to be afforded by Professor Young's spectroscopic observations of solar storms, he having seen the H line injected into the chromosphere seventy-five times, the K line fifty times; but the blue line, which is the all-important line of calcium at the arc temperature, was only injected thrice. In the spectrum of iron two sets of three lines occur in the region between H and G, which are highly characteristic of this metal. On comparing photographs of the solar spectrum and of the spark taken between poles of iron, the relative intensity of these triplets is seen to be absolutely reversed; the lines barely visible in the spark-photograph being among the most prominent in that of the solar spectrum, while the triplet, which is prominent in the spark-photograph, is represented by lines not half so thick in the solar spectrum. Professor Young has observed during solar storms two very faint lines in the iron spectrum near G injected thirty times into the chromosphere, while one of the lines of the triplet was only injected twice. These facts, Mr. Lockyer contends, at once meet with a simple explanation if it be admitted that the lines are produced by the vibration of several distinct molecules.

The lithium spectrum exhibits a series of changes with a rise of temperature precisely analogous to those observed in the case of calcium.

In discussing the hydrogen spectrum, Mr. Lockyer adduces a number of most important and interesting facts and speculations. It is pointed out that the most refrangible line of hydrogen in the solar spectrum, h, is only seen in laboratory experiments when a very high temperature is employed, and that it was absent from the solar protuberances during the eclipse of 1875, although the other lines of hydrogen were photographed. This line also is coincident with the strongest line of indium, as already recorded by Thalén, and may be photographed by volatilizing indium in the electric arc; whereas palladium charged with hydrogen furnishes a photograph in which none of the hydrogen lines are visible. By employing a very feeble spark at a very low pressure, the F line of hydrogen in the green is obtained without the blue and red lines which are seen when a stronger spark is used, so that alterations undoubtedly take place in the spectrum of hydrogen similar to those observed in the case of calcium. In concluding this portion of his paper Mr. Lockyer states that he has obtained evidence leading to the conclusion that the substance giving the non-reversed line in the chromosphere, which has been termed *helium*, and not previously identified with any known form of matter, and also the substance giving the 1,474 or coronal line, are really other forms of hydrogen, the one more simple than that which gives the *h* line alone, the other more complex than that which gives the F line alone.

In closing his paper in the "Nineteenth Century" Professor Lockyer thus sums up the results of his investigations:

First, the common lines visible in the spectra of different elements at high identical temperatures point to a common origin. Secondly, the different lines visible in the spectra of the same substance at high and low temperatures indicate that at high temperatures dissociation goes on as continuously as it is generally recognized to do at all lower temperatures.

In my paper I attempt to show that if we grant that the highest temperatures produce common bases—in other words, if the elements are really compounds—all the phenomena so difficult to account for on the received hypothesis find a simple and sufficient explanation. And, with regard to the second count, I discuss the cases of calcium, iron, lithium, and hydrogen. I might have brought, and shall subsequently bring, other cases forward. In all these I show that the lines most strongly developed at the highest temperatures are precisely those which are seen almost alone in the spectra of the hottest stars, and which are most obviously present in the spectrum of our own sun. Now, if it be true that the temperature of the arc breaks up the elements, then the higher temperature of the sun should do this in a still more effective manner.

New Processes for protecting Iron Surfaces. —A new process for protecting iron from rust has been invented by M. Dodé. It consists in coating, either by means of a bath or a brush, any objects in cast or wrought iron (freed from the damp that may adhere to them) with a composition of borate of lead, oxide of copper, and spirits of turpentine. This application soon dries on the surface of the iron, and the objects are then passed through a furnace, heated from 500° to 700° F., according to the thickness of the articles under treatment, so as to bring them to a cherry-red heat when passing through the center of the furnace. At this point the fusion of the metallic pigment takes place; it enters the pores of the iron, and becomes homogeneously adherent thereto, covering the objects with a dark coating, which is not liable to change under the action of the air, gases, alkaline or other vapors, nor to scale off from the surfaces to which it has been applied. When any considerable depth of "inoxidation" is desired, the object may be immersed in the composition for the time requisite to absorb a sufficient quantity of it. This process supersedes painting and varnishing, and iron objects thus treated are impervious to rust. The cost of application is about half a cent per superficial square foot.

A new process for coating iron surfaces with magnetic oxide, for the purpose of preventing rust, has recently been patented in England by Mr. George Bown. The following is the method of procedure: "The articles are first of all heated, and acted on for a certain period by the products of combustion largely mixed with air from a peculiarly constructed furnace (designed by Mr. Anthony Bown), burning slack or small coal. In this way a coating of magnetic oxide is formed close to the surface of the iron, but this is often slightly covered with red oxide, Fe_2O_3. The admission of air to the furnace is then so arranged by a suitable apparatus that a stream of carbonic oxide is passed over the articles for a short time, and the red oxide very speedily reduced to magnetic oxide." The red oxide, first formed, is easily detached from the iron, but the magnetic oxide is hard and perfectly homogeneous. The coating formed by this process has been thoroughly tested, and found to withstand all ordinary oxidizing influences.

The Spectrum of the Sun's Corona. —Before the occurrence of the solar eclipse of 1878, Mr. W. T. Sampson, U. S. N., made elaborate preparations for studying minutely the corona's spectrum, with the sole view of deciding, by the absence or the presence in it of dark lines, whether the light is reflected sunlight, whether it is due to the self-luminous matter of the corona, or whether it is due to both of these causes combined. In the "American Journal of Science and Arts" he describes the instruments used for this research, and the manner in which they were employed. His conclusion is that, inasmuch as he failed to see in the corona spectrum the dark lines of the sun's spectrum, therefore its light of the corona is *not all* reflected light. The following considerations confirm him in this conclusion: "Until this eclipse no observer has ever seen the dark lines in the spectrum of the corona except M. Janssen, who reported dark lines, notably D, in 1871, but much more difficult to see than the bright lines. Several observers during the recent eclipse failed to see the dark lines, though they looked for them carefully. While I do not question the results of observers who report the presence of dark lines, I think all the observations taken together show that the continuous spectrum of the corona is not the spectrum of the sun. Aside from this, Professor Arthur W. Wright made measurements of the polarization of the light of the corona (the first time, I think, it has been attempted), and has found the polarization to be but a small percentage of the whole light emitted. Although all reflected light does not reach us as polarized light, yet I think the small percentage of polarization, taken with the faintness of the dark lines, indicates that the corona is, to a considerable extent, self-luminous. The meteoric dust not only reflects the sun's light, but it is continually showering upon the sun, and in its passage through the atmosphere is rendered incandescent."

A New Base. —From a compound produced by the action of dry chlorine on toluene, and having the formula $C_{21}Cl_{20}$, Mr. Edgar F. Smith has obtained a new base, the properties of which he describes in the "American Chemical Journal." The process of separation was as follows: A quantity of the compound $C_{21}Cl_{16}$, finely divided, was heated in a sealed tube with an excess of aniline for six or eight hours, the temperature during the time not exceeding 180° C. On examination after cooling, a deep-red viscid product was found, which was transferred to a shallow dish, water added, and the whole then heated on a water-bath. Much of the adherent aniline was got rid of in this way, and by repeatedly distilling the residue left after evaporation it was finally obtained in a pure form. The new base thus produced contains chlorine and nitrogen. It forms salts with acids, is easily soluble in water and other solvents, and from concentrated aqueous solutions after long standing it separates in thin, broad scales, that are nearly colorless, refract light strongly, carbonize slightly at 225° C., and fuse at 230° C. It forms a salt with hydrochloric acid, characterized by very long, broad, colorless crystals, that are readily soluble in water and alcohol.

Nitric Acid from the Electric Light.—It is known that when combustion takes place at high temperatures, small quantities of the nitrogen and oxygen of atmospheric air combine, forming several oxides of nitrogen, many of which are strong corrosive acids. This is the case when electric sparks are passed through air, also during combustion in air of hydrogen. It therefore appears probable that, as the temperature of the electric arc is undoubtedly very high, nitric acid or some other oxide of nitrogen might be produced by the electric light. This subject has been investigated experimentally by Mr. T. Wills, with results strongly confirmatory of this theoretical inference. The first experiment was rather surprising. A glass cylinder placed over an electric lamp (Foucault's regulator) for two minutes, and afterward examined, was seen to contain a perceptible amount of red fumes due to peroxide of nitrogen (N_2O_4). The air surrounding the lamp was next drawn through a solution of potash, and the amount of nitric acid estimated; this gave ten to twelve grains of nitric acid produced per hour (it may eventually prove to be more, the difficulty being to collect the whole of it). The next step in the research will be to examine the various forms of electric light, with a view to determine the amount of nitric acid produced by each.

Water Examination as related to Health.—Dr. F. Holdefleiss, in a recent paper on the examination of water in its relation to the health of men and animals, claims that chemical analysis alone is insufficient to determine the character of water. Microscopic examination promises more satisfactory results, in as far as the organisms observed have been found to bear certain relations to the sanitary value of the water. For purposes of examination, only natural, freshly drawn water should be taken, and that from the bottom or sides of the well or tank. Not the number of organisms present, but their nature, must be regarded as indicating the condition of the liquid. In their connection with this subject he classifies organisms as follows: 1. Such as can live only in good, sound water; 2. Organisms free from chlorophyl, nourished solely from putrescent organic matter, and directly promoting the decomposition of organic matter, nitrogenous or non-nitrogenous—organisms which can live only in waters that evince putrefactive processes; 3. An intermediate group, or organisms which can live either in good or bad waters.

Well-water is to be regarded as good when free from all organisms, from ammonia, nitrous acid, and hydrogen sulphide.

Open waters, flowing or standing, are good when they contain living green algæ and diatoms with the contents of the shells normally colored, but no colorless algæ (*Beggiatoa, Leptomitus,* etc.), and none, or but few, *Schizomycetes.*

Drinking-water for human use, in addition to freedom from all organisms, from ammonia, nitrous acid, and sulphuretted hydrogen, should not exceed 18—20° of hardness. If river-water is so purified by filtration that it possesses these properties, and that suspicious organisms do not reappear on standing, it may be used without scruple.

Open waters containing green algæ and living diatoms, and free from ammonia and nitrous acid, may be consumed with safety.

For cattle traces of ammonia and nitrous acid in pond- and river-water may be tolerated if green algæ and living diatoms are present.

Water for fish-ponds should be free from sulphuretted hydrogen, and should be rejected if *Beggiatoa alba* is present in a state of normal vitality. *Leptomitus lacteus* is probably dangerous.

The mere vicinity of waters containing *Beggiatoa* and the *Schizomycetes* is dangerous, as they may infect the atmosphere and communicate germs of a dangerous nature to the ground-water and the wells.

Derivation of Indigo-Blue.— Mr. Edward Schunck has recently published the results of an interesting series of experiments on the leaves of the common woad (*Isatis tinctoria*), undertaken for the purpose of determining whether, as has heretofore been supposed, the indigo-blue obtained from them exists as such in the plant, or is the product of some chemical change occurring to one or more of its constituents during the process of extraction. He finds that the leaves of the plant do not contain either indigo-blue or its hydride ready formed; but that they yield by careful treatment *indican*, a peculiar glucoside, which, when subsequently treated by acids and other reagents, breaks up into indigo-blue and indigo-glucine, the latter resembling glucose. He further ascertained that indican is a highly unstable substance, undergoing when its watery solution is heated for some time, or more rapidly when acted upon by caustic alkalies, an entire change, on the completion of which it no longer yields indigo-blue by decomposition with acids, but in place of the latter gives indigo-red, indifulvine, leucine, and other products. The investigation was afterward extended so as to include *Polygonum tinctorium*,

Blitia Tankesvilliæ, and other indigo-yielding plants, to see if they contained indigo-blue ready formed, or if, like the common woad, the coloring matter exists in the vegetable cells in the form of indican or some other glucoside. The experiments with the *Polygonum tinctorium* led to the conclusion that the leaves of this plant contain a substance not to be distinguished from the indican of *Isatis tinctoria,* which by decomposition with acids yields indigo-blue and glucose, accompanied by some by-products; and that there is no proof of the existence of ready-formed coloring matter in the plant while the latter is living and in a healthy state; and, further, that in all indigo-yielding plants hitherto examined the coloring matter is derived from a glucoside which splits up with great ease into indigo-blue and glucose, and that this glucoside is probably in all cases the same, and identical with the indican of *Isatis tinctoria.*

Solubility of Solids in Gases.—In an investigation undertaken for the purpose of studying the conditions of liquid matter as it approaches and passes the "critical point"—that is, the point at which it changes from the liquid to the gaseous state—Messrs. J. B. Hannay and James Hauston have obtained some very curious and interesting results, which appear to show that solids may be dissolved in gases. The experiments were conducted with such solvents as alcohol, ether, carbon disulphide and tetrachloride, paraffines, and olefines, and such solids as sulphur, chlorides, bromides, and iodides of the metals; and such organic substances as chlorophyl and the aniline dyes were employed. In a preliminary report, the authors explain that, in order to gain some insight into the condition of matter just beyond this critical point, they dissolved in the liquid a solid substance fusing much above the critical point of the liquid, and observed whether, on the latter passing its critical point and assuming the gaseous condition, the solid was precipitated or remained in solution. It was not precipitated, but continued in solution, or rather in diffusion, through the atmosphere of vapor, even when the temperature was raised 130° above the critical point, and the gas was considerably expanded. When the side of a tube containing a strong gaseous solution of a solid is approached by a red-hot iron, the part next the source of heat becomes coated with a crystalline deposit, which slowly redissolves on allowing the local disturbance of temperature to disappear. Rarefaction seems to be the cause of this deposition, because, if the temperature be raised equally, and the volume retained at its original value, no deposition takes place.

An attempt to examine the spectroscopic appearances of solutions of solids, when their liquid menstrua were passing to the gaseous state, was unsuccessful in most cases, owing to the fact that the substances capable of assuming both states gave banded spectra with nebulous edges. At the suggestion of Professor Stokes, the substance obtained by the decomposition of the green coloring matter of leaves by acids was tried, and this, which yields a very fine absorption spectrum, was found to exhibit the phenomenon in a marked manner whether dissolved in alcohol or ether. This compound is easily decomposed by heat under ordinary circumstances, and yet it can be dissolved in gaseous menstrua and raised to a temperature of 350° without suffering any decomposition, showing the same absorption spectrum at that heat as at 15°.

When the solid is precipitated by suddenly reducing the pressure, it is crystalline, and may be brought down as a "snow" in the gas, or as a "frost" on the glass, but it is always easily redissolved by the gas on increasing the pressure. These phenomena are shown to the best advantage in a solution of potassic iodide in absolute alcohol. "We have then," say the authors, "the phenomenon of a solid with no measurable gaseous pressure dissolving in a gas, and not being affected by the passage of its menstruum through the critical point to the liquid state, showing it to be a true case of gaseous solution of a solid."

Determination of the Organic Purity of Potable Waters.—In a long and valuable paper on this subject, read before the London Chemical Society, Mr. C. M. Lidy, after an extended discussion of the various methods which have been proposed for estimating the organic matter in potable waters, gives the preference to a special modification of the permanganate process, to which he has applied the name of "the oxygen process." This consists in adding to a known volume of the water measured quantities first of dilute sulphuric acid, and then of permanganate solution. The author takes two equal portions of the same water, adds equal volumes of permanganate and sulphuric acid to each, and allows the one to stand one and the other three hours. The amount of permanganate remaining is then measured by means of potassic iodide and sodic hyposulphite. The results are expressed in the quantities of oxygen required to oxidize the organic matters in one gallon of water. The relation of the result obtained in one hour's to that in three hours' time permits a conclusion as to the nature of the organic matter, i. e., its susceptibility to oxidation, or of the relation between the readily oxidizable and putrescent, and the less easily oxidizable or non-putrescent, matters. The paper closes with certain important conclusions, which are summed up, as follows:

The ammonia process furnishes results which are marked by singular inconstancy, and are not delicate enough to allow the recognition and classification of the finer grades of purity or impurity. The errors incidental to the process form an array of difficulties which become infinitely serious, seeing that the range (from 0·05 to 0·1 part per million) between pure and dirty waters is comparatively so small. The combustion process has all the evils of evaporation to encounter, but the organic carbon estimation is trustworthy; the organic nitrogen determination, however, scarcely yields absolutely trustworthy evidence on which to found an opinion as to the probable source of the organic matter. The oxygen process avoids the errors incidental to evaporation; its results are constant and extremely delicate; it draws a sharp line between putrescent or probably pernicious and non-putrescent or probably harmless organic matter. By it a bad water would never be passed as good. As far as the three processes are concerned, the oxygen and combustion processes give closely concordant results, while those yielded by the ammonia process are often at direct variance with both.

New Elements.—Toward the end of last year M. Marignac discovered in erbia, which up to that time had been considered as the oxide of a single metal, erbium, the oxide of a new element, which he called ytterbium. On March 24, 1879, M. Nilson announced the discovery of another new element, which he had extracted from ytterbia, and which he named scandium. M. Cléve some weeks later found the same metal in the gadolinite and yttrotitanite of Norway. He has examined its characters, and finds that it occurs only in minute quantities, and forms but one oxide, scandia, which has the formula Sc_2O_3, and is a perfectly white, light, infusible powder, resembling magnesia. The strongest acids attack it with difficulty, though it is more soluble in acids than is alumina. It dissolves more readily in hydrochloric than nitric acid, and is insoluble in an excess of ammonia or of caustic potash. The specific gravity of scandia is given approximately as 3·8. Its hydrate is a white bulky precipitate resembling hydrate of alumina. The atomic weight of scandium is 45·12. M. Cléve also announces the probable existence of two other new metals in erbia, to which he has given the provisional names of *thollium* and *holmium*.

A New Volatile Alkaloid.—In a preliminary note in the "American Chemical Journal," Mr. W. L. Dudley reports the discovery of a volatile alkaloid in *Spigelia marilandica* or pinkroot, the existence of which he was led to suspect by the circumstance that the peculiar medicinal properties of the plant are apt to deteriorate with time. The several steps of the process by which the new alkaloid was isolated are given by the author, together with some of the more important reactions which serve to distinguish it from other volatile alkaloids. The investigation is not yet completed, "but enough was done to distinctly indicate the presence of a new volatile base, to which I naturally apply the name *spigelina*."

CHEVALIER; MICHEL, a French political economist, born January 13, 1806, died November 28, 1879. He was educated at the Polytechnic School and the School of Mines, and shortly before the Revolution of July, 1830, was appointed engineer in the department of Nord. Ardently embracing the doctrines of Fourier and St. Simon, he wrote several articles for the "Organisateur," and then became editor-in-chief of the "Globe," which was the

organ of the St. Simonists. Upon the outbreak of their schism he followed Enfantin, and took a leading part in the preparation of the "Livre Nouveau." The cirular announcing the death of Madame Enfantin, mother of "Notre Père Suprême," was signed by "Michel Chevalier, Apôtre." He was a cardinal in Enfantin's sacred college, and in 1835 was sentenced to twelve months' imprisonment. M. Thiers procured his release at the end of six months, and his dispatch to the United States to study railway and water communications. He wrote a series of letters to the "Journal des Débats," which were afterward collected and published under the title "Lettres sur l'Amérique du Nord" (2 vols., 4th edit., 1842), and attracted much attention. In 1837 he was sent to England to report on the commercial crisis, and upon his return published "Des Intérêts Matériels en France, Travaux Publics, Routes, Canaux, Chemins de Fer" (7th edit., 1843). He was successively appointed Councilor of State in 1838, Professor of Political Economy in the Collége de France in 1840, and Chief Engineer of Mines in 1841; and in 1845 he was elected a deputy from Aveyron. In the Chamber he voted with the Conservative majority, while at the same time he advocated the most liberal industrial ideas in the "Journal des Débats." After the Revolution of 1848, he combated the socialistic theories of Louis Blanc, and in his "Lettres sur l'Organisation du Travail" (1848) defended the old system of political economy, which was then bitterly attacked by the different new schools. He accepted the Empire in 1852, and was appointed an ordinary Councilor of State; but the protectionists prevented his readmission to the Supreme Council of Commerce. He was an ardent free-trader, and took a leading part in negotiating the Anglo-French commercial treaty of 1860, after which he was elevated to the Senate. He presided over the French juries at the South Kensington Exhibition of 1862, and edited the reports on the Paris Exhibition of 1867. After the overthrow of the Empire he took no part in political affairs, which with him were always subordinate to political economy. At the time of the Californian and Australian gold discoveries he advocated a silver standard, but of late years was an opponent of Cernuschi's plan of bimetallism. Among his principal works are : "Cours d'Économie Politique" (3 vols., 1842–'50; new edit. of vol. iii., under the title "La Monnaie," 1866), "Essais de Politique Industrielle" (1843), and "Examen du Système Protecteur" (1851); besides works on the United States, the war in Mexico, ancient and modern Mexico, and on the Isthmus of Panama. Many of his works have been translated into English.

CHILI (REPÚBLICA DE CHILE). The most recent phases of the pending Patagonian question between Chili and her eastern neighbor have been recorded in the article ARGENTINE REPUBLIC in the present volume; but it will

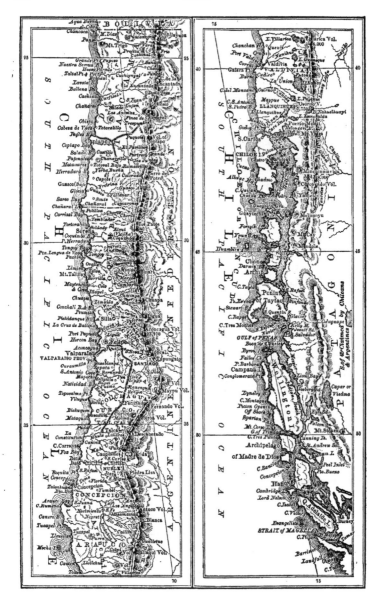

ɔot be uninteresting to insert in this place the following extract from an Argentine publication of undoubted authority, as the genuine expression of popular sentiment in both countries concerning the possible ultimate mode of settlement. The writer says:

We have given considerable thought and attention to the Argentine-Chilian question through its successive phases, and especially to the condition in which it was left at the breaking down of the last two attempts to consummate a treaty. The Fierro-Sarratea treaty provided that arbitrators should settle all questions at issue, the form, nature, and extent of said questions to be arranged by the respective plenipotentiaries of the two republics, provided an arrangement could be reached, in default of which the Court of Arbitrators were to take them in hand and finally dispose of the question from beginning to end. It has puzzled us over since to see any good reason why such a treaty could not have been accepted by both parties. Chili accepted the arrangement, and by so doing has gained a very significant moral advantage over the Argentine Republic, which hailed its acceptance by Chili with great joy, and whose Executive sent the announcement over the world with congratulatory words, the united press of the land calling it a great victory for peace ; but as soon as Chili found itself at war with two nations, the same press and people repudiated it without new light or reason. Subsequent to this a *status quo* arrangement, which involved all elements of danger and trouble, and which afforded no safeguard whatever, was very properly thrown out. This leaves the matter unsettled from first to last. The original dispute remains. Such aggravating instances as the seizure of the Jennie Amelia and the Devonshire remain without adjustment, and therefore liable at any moment to be brought into the case. By the action before mentioned, this republic has declared that it will not arbitrate the pretensions of Chili, so that there are only three alternatives: 1. Chili must yield her pretensions to any part of Patagonia; 2. The Argentine Government must recede from the position which it has deliberately assumed ; or, 3. There must sooner or later be war. Of these alternatives it is exceedingly improbable that the first will occur. Unfortunately, this republic has made no material or vigorous protest to six or seven years of assumed and actual jurisdiction over the disputed territory ; and after Chili has exercised the highest functions of government, in capturing ships of friendly powers in disputed waters because of assumed violation of Chilian edicts, she can not recede without so much as making a case in a Court of Arbitration ; and, in our opinion, when it comes squarely to an issue between this and war, Chili will accept war. It is idle to deceive ourselves on this point. It may and will probably be delayed ; but it will come at last. Chili—we mean the people of Chili—has come to think it has a just claim to the disputed territory. We do not behave it has a just claim, nor do we believe the projectors of the pretension ever thought so ; but they have made public opinion in Chili believe so, and so it comes about that, while cabinets may change, the people will not let go unchallenged this claim. The Argentine Government, at the outset, were grievously remiss in not meeting the first pretension with a most vigorous and decided policy, admitting no such pretension for a moment. This laches, to some extent, gives the case a status at law, and now it is too late to assume that position. It would have been the highest wisdom to have proceeded with an arbitrament; but we have decided otherwise. We have now to decide whether we will insist upon our policy. If so, we should lose no time in preparing for war, for it will come ; and if we are bent on it, we should take advantage of time and circumstances. We are utterly opposed to the policy of our Government at the present juncture. Inaction is our worst possible course. We should lose no time in getting at the question, and keeping at it until it is decided what is to be done. Delays were never more dangerous than in this case, and there should be no further procrastination, but prompt and decided action.

The real interpretation of all this is, that the theory, right or wrong, of a lawful claim to the territory in dispute [*] has, thanks to Argentine supineness, taken possession of the people's minds in Chili ; that Chili's prompt and hitherto successful retort on Bolivian usurpation of her asserted rights may be regarded as premonitory of the course she might, under pressure of popular opinion and flushed with one victory, be led to adopt in pursuit of another ; and consequently that the Argentine Government should, while Chili's hands are full, lose no time in preparing for all issues.

The Republic of Chili is divided for administrative purposes into seventeen provinces and two territories (*de colonizacion*), the former being subdivided into departments, and these into sub-delegations, each of which is apportioned into districts. The provinces, with their population on January 1, 1878, and their capitals, are as follows :

PROVINCES.	Population.	Capitals.
Aconcagua	185,190	San Felipe.
Arauco	58,413	Angol.‡
Atacama	73,405	Copiapó.
Biobio†	79,622	Los Angeles.
Chiloé	67,440	Ancud.
Colchagua	158,657	San Fernando.
Concepcion	156,685	Concepcion.
Coquimbo	161,970	La Serena.
Curicó	96,202	Curicó.
Linares	120,932	Linares.
Llanquihue	50,768	Puerto-Montt.
Maule	119,963	Cauquénes.
Nuble	142,224	Chillan.
Santiago	377,110	SANTIAGO.
Talca	119,857	Talca.
Valdivia	32,578	Valdivia.
Valparaiso	179,858	Valparaiso.
Territories:		
Angol	21,632	
Magallanes	1,213	Punta-Arenas.
Total	2,136,724	

Of this total about 50,000 were Indians.

The foreign population, estimated at 26,635 in 1875, was composed of the following elements approximately :

Argentines	7,183
Germans	4,678
British subjects	4,267
French	3,814
Italians	1,988
Spaniards	1,223
Americans (United States)	931
Peruvians	881
Austrians	388
Portuguese	819
Bolivians	282
Swedes	175
Spanish Americans (not classified)	897
Europeans (not classified)	588
Asiatics	136
Total	26,635

The number of males in the republic, according to estimates of 1878, based on the census returns of 1875, was 1,065,169. The cities of

* See " Annual Cyclopædia " for 1875.
† New province.   ‡ Formerly *Angeles.*

more than 10,000 inhabitants in 1875 were: Santiago (the capital), 129,807 (or 150,367 including suburbs); Valparaiso, 97,737; Cl'il'an, 19,044; Concepcion, 18,277; Talca, 17,496; La Serena, 12,293; Copiapó, 11,432; Quillota, 11,369. The number of marriages registered in the republic in 1877 was 13,576; of births, 82,295; of deaths, 62,349.

The chief magistrates of provinces are Intendants, those of the departments Governors: both are appointed by the President of the Republic, the former for a term of three years, the latter for two years. The salary of the Intendants is $4,000 per annum; that of the Governors, $2,000. The local administration in the departments is vested in municipal corporations elected by the people.

The executive power resides in a President, elected for a term of five years (salary $18,000 per annum), and a Council of State, composed of the Cabinet Ministers (salary $6,-000 each), three members elected by the Senate, three members elected by the Chamber of Deputies, one member of the courts of justice, one ecclesiastical dignitary, one general, the chief of one of the boards of direction of finance, and one ex-minister or ex-intendant, the last five being appointed by the President of the Republic, who is also President of the Council. The legislative power is vested in a Senate, composed of 37 members, whose term of office is six years each, and in a Chamber of Deputies with 109 members elected for three years (at the rate of one deputy for 20,000 inhabitants). The chief of the judicial power is the President of the Supreme Court of Santiago. The President of the Republic is Señor Don Anibal Pinto (September 18, 1876). The Cabinet is composed of the following Ministers: Interior, Don Domingo Santa Maria; Foreign Affairs and Colonization, Don Miguel Luis Amunátegui; Finance, Don Augusto Matte; Justice, Public Worship, and Public Instruction, Don José Antonio Gandarillas; and War and the Navy, Don Rafael Sotomayor.

The Chilian army in 1878 was made up as follows: Regulars—10 generals, 10 colonels, 29 lieutenant-colonels, 57 majors, 134 captains, and 249 lieutenants; 5 battalions of foot (2,000 men), 2 regiments of horse (712 men), 1 regiment of artillery (804); total, rank and file, 3,516. Such was the usual strength, being all that was required for service on the Araucanian frontier and the maintenance of military instruction in the country. When war with Bolivia became imminent, the strength of the regular army was raised to 20,000 (distributed in three divisions: 1st, 10,000; 2d, 8,000; 3d, 2,000), which, with the National Guard, increased to 30,000 at the same time, constituted an aggregate force of 50,000. The National Guard in time of peace is composed of 1,200 horse, 21,200 foot, and 1,900 artillery; total, 24,300.

The navy comprises 22 vessels, classified as follows:

VESSELS.	Horse-power.	Can-non.	Marines.	Crew.
2 iron-clad frigates.......	2,000	19	572	4,064
4 corvettes................	1,140	33	525	4,500
1 monitor*................	...	...	...	...
1 gunboat................	140	8	105	412
1 steamer................	100	..	48	240
8 pontoons..............	...	..	40	3,000
10 transports (5 of which are mounted with guns)	...	..	..	....
Total..............	8,380	55	1,820	12,216

The national revenue amounted in 1878 to $20,443,977, made up as follows: Ordinary receipts, $14,031,868; extraordinary receipts, $4,063,918; balance from 1877, $2,348,191. The expenditures in the same year were as follows: Ordinary, $16,093,981; † extraordinary, $566,308; payment of balances from previous year, $4,715,439; total, $21,375,728, leaving a consequent deficit of $931,751. The chief sources of revenue and their mean annual yield are: Customs, $8,000,000; state railways, $2,800,000; agricultural tax, $2,000,000; tobacco monopoly, $1,500,000. The public debt of Chili stood as follows on December 31, 1878: Foreign debt (exclusively to England), $35,535,000; home debt, $27,647,544; total, $63,182,544. The foreign debt, amounting to rather more than $35,500,000, being guaranteed by mortgage on state railways, the value of which has recently been estimated at $38,329,635, commands at all times a fair price in the London market. The rates of interest on seven loans embodying this debt vary from 3 to 7 per cent. On the home debt, for the most part held by bankers and private capitalists, the Government pays interest at rates varying from 6 to 9 per cent. per annum.

The crisis of 1878, the immediate cause of which was a crushing drain on gold and silver, but which was really determined by the failure of the wheat-crop and the depression in the price of copper, Chili's main staples of export, necessitated the emission by the banks of paper money to the extent of $16,500,000, guaranteed by the state, and redeemable in coin on August 31, 1879, up to which date the banks were authorized by the Government to suspend payments in specie. Before the country had had time to recover from the effects of the crisis, the Government, in the spring of 1879, found it necessary to resort to another emission ($6,000,000) of paper money, but, having failed in the attempt to negotiate therefor with the banks, resolved upon an issue on its own account. Here follows a translation of the decree to that effect:

SANTIAGO, *May* 8, 1879.

Having been unable to make with the banks an arrangement compatible with fiscal interests, in accordance with the power conferred upon me by the law of April 12, 1879, I decree:

ARTICLE I. The Ministers of the General Treasury will proceed to sign bills (*vales*) payable to bearer, for $1,000 each, without interest, and for a term of five

---

* The Huáscar, captured from the Peruvians. (See PERU.)
† Including the expenses of the executive power.

years. The Ministers will open a book, in which they will register these obligations and their number. The Ministry of Finance will decree monthly the quantity to be emitted, up to the sum of six million dollars.

ART. II. The Treasury bills mentioned will serve as legal tender for the payment of all kinds of obligations, whatever be the date thereof and the terms in which they are drawn, in conformity with Art. I. of the law of the 10th of April last.

ART. III. The chief accountant will sign these obligations, and will keep a register of the number corresponding to each.

ART. IV. The Mint will keep an account of the Treasury bills issued under this decree, up to the sum of six million dollars, and the superintendent will sign and seal them with the seal of the Mint.

ART. V. In each successive year, in forming the estimates of the national expenditures, a sum will be set apart for the quantity to be withdrawn from circulation. The Government will propose to Congress in due time that the product of a new tax, or a part of those already existing, shall be devoted to the redemption of said bills.

ART. VI. The Mint will incinerate annually bills to the amount referred to in the preceding article, and will credit the account ordered to be opened by Art. IV. with the sums set down in the estimates for this purpose. The Ministers of the Treasury are ordered to present to the Mint the bills that are to be destroyed. The operation will be witnessed by the chief accountant, the Superintendent of the Mint, and the Ministers of the General Treasury; and a record of the destruction will be drawn up in triplicate, as a voucher for the acquittances to be made by the three offices respectively that intervene in the emission of the bills.

ART. VII. Until these operations are effected, the Ministers of the General Treasury and the chief accountant will sign provisional bills for 100, 50, 20, and 10,000 dollars each, which will possess provisionally the character assigned to the obligations created under Art. V. of this decree. These provisional bills shall be withdrawn when the General Treasury shall have come into possession of the definitive bills.

PINTO,
AUGUSTO MATTE.

The foregoing measure was received with uniform good will. "The bonds," writes an English journalist from Valparaiso, under date of May 24th, "which the Government has begun to float in the market, and which will reach the amount of $6,000,000, are well received by the public, who are ready to make any sacrifice for the safety of the nation. Chili's fiscal resources are amply sufficient to meet the expenses of the war. The most convincing proof of this lies in the fact that, notwithstanding the large expenses incurred by the army, the Government has limited itself merely to the suspension of the sinking fund of the foreign debt, upon due arrangement made with the bondholders, and has continued to pay the interest on her bonds with the usual punctuality. This will strengthen the credit of the republic, and allow her to recover herself rapidly after peace is restored to the Pacific. The capitalists of Santiago and Valparaiso have petitioned Congress to authorize an income-tax to meet the expenses of the war; this idea has been well received, and in a few days longer will become a reality."

The extensive failure of the crops and reduced price of copper, already referred to, produced a decrease of little less than $15,000,000

in the value of the exports for 1877, as compared with those of the year immediately preceding. In this falling off the agricultural products figured to the extent of 8·61 per cent.; minerals, 23·61 per cent.; and manufactures, 15·55 per cent. Comparing the value of the exports with the population of the republic, the following relations are observable: Agricultural products, $3.94 per capita; mining products, $7.23; manufactures, $0.12; miscellaneous, $0.02.

The shipping movements at the various ports of the republic were as follows in 1877:

FOREIGN TRADE.

VESSELS.	Number.	Tonnage.
ENTERED.		
Sailing vessels	949	336,995
Steamers	757	1,002,446
Total	1,506	1,339,441
CLEARED.		
Sailing vessels	718	359,608
Steamers	856	1,060,859
Total	1,574	1,420,467

COASTING TRADE.

VESSELS.	Number.	Tonnage.
ENTERED.		
Sailing vessels	2,003	509,766
Steamers	2,128	1,911,861
Total	4,131	2,421,621
CLEARED.		
Sailing vessels	1,901	480,546
Steamers	2,076	1,842,564
Total	3,977	2,323,110

There are at the present time in Chili 1,015 miles of railway completed and in operation. Of these, 594 miles are the property of the state. The total cost of construction and rolling stock for these lines was $49,857,037, of which $38,329,635 stands for the Government lines. Chief among the latter are those from Santiago to San Felipe, from Santiago to Curicó and Palmilla, from Curicó to Chilian, from Chilian to Concepcion and Talcahuano, and from Los Angeles to Angol on the Araucanian frontier. The principal lines belonging to private companies are those from Caldera to Copiapó and Chañarcillo, from Copiapó to the mines of Púquios, from Coquimbo to La Serena, and from Coquimbo to Ovalle; besides which there is a number of others chiefly engaged in the service of the silver and copper mines. The more densely populated portion of the republic is intersected by a network of telegraphs wires, of an aggregate length of 3,659 miles, with 68 officers, many of which are in charge of female operators. The Transandine telegraph, from Santiago to Buenos Ayres, was constructed by a Chilian company, whose principal office is at the first-named city. The postal service is conducted through 347 post-offices. The number of letters transmitted in 1878 was 14,921,168, and that of money orders, 40,000, for an aggregate amount of $1,014,607.

Article 153.of the present Constitution, promulgated in 1833, contains the following provision: "Public education is one of the chief concerns of the Government." The instruction given in all the public schools, from the *escuelas de párvulos* or infant schools up to the highest university courses, is absolutely free. The amount of national funds expended on this branch in 1878 was little short of a million dollars; in 1876 it reached $1,125,579. Higher instruction is given in the Santiago University and in the professional courses at the lyceums of Copiapó, La Serena, Valparaiso, and Concepcion, comprising the faculties of belles-lettres, jurisprudence, medicine, and mathematics. The number of alumni of the university in 1878 was 1,017. For secondary instruction (*enseñanza secundaria*) there are 16 lyceums distributed through the different provinces, and the National Institute in Santiago, in which last 5,596 received instruction. Primary instruction is given in 1,585 schools, 987 of which are supported by the state; the remaining 598 are private. Of the first mentioned, 23 are designated as *escuelas superiores.* The attendance in 1878 was 122,000. In the same year there were 47 night schools supported by the Government and by private associations, with an aggregate attendance of 3,956 adults of both sexes. There are, besides, the following special educational establishments, all supported by the Government: The Section of Belles-Lettres in the National Institute, comprising schools of design, of painting, of sculpture, and of architecture, with 113 pupils; the Conservatory of Music, with 349 pupils, of whom 249 were females; the National School of Arts and Trades, with 83 pupils; the Agricultural Institute, 43 pupils; the Military Academy, 80; the Naval School, 50; the National School, 120; and the school for deaf-mutes, with an average of 50 pupils. Lastly, there are seminaries supported by the bishoprics in the cities of Santiago, Valparaiso, La Serena, Talca, Concepcion, and Ancud, for the education and preparation of youths intended for the Church, the number of whom in 1878 was 958.

Details relating to the origin and declaration of the war between Chili and Bolivia and Peru are given in the article BOLIVIA, in the present volume; and the military and naval operations of the campaign, etc., will be narrated in the article PERU.

CHINA, an empire in Asia. Emperor, Kwang-Su, formerly called Tsaeteen, born in 1872, a son of Prince Ch'un, and grandson to the Emperor Tau-Kwang, who died in 1850; he succeeded to the throne in 1875. The area of China proper is 1,554,000 square miles; the population is about 405,000,000. The area of the dependencies is estimated at 3,062,000 square miles, with a population of about 29,-580,000; making in all 4,616,000 square miles, with a population of 435,000,000.

A census of the foreign residents taken in 1878 gave the following particulars:

NATIONALITY.	Firms.	Persons.
English.................................	220	1,953
American...............................	85	420
German.................................	49	884
French.................................	9	224
Dutch..................................	1	24
Danish.................................	2	69
Swedes and Norwegians...........	1	85
Spanish................................	1	168
Russians...............................	17	55
Austrians..............................	1	88
Belgians...............................	..	10
Italians................................	..	17
Japanese...............................	9	81
Sundry, uncertain..................	6	841
Total...................	351	8,814

The total population of the treaty ports was estimated at 4,990,000.

The returns of trade at the treaty ports in 1878 were as follows (1 Haikwan tael=$1·346):

Haikwan taels.
Imports.............................. 70,804,027
Exports.............................. 67,172,179

Total.................... 137,976,206

This total is less than in 1877 by 2,702,712 taels. The decrease in 1878 was mainly in the imports. The import of cotton goods declined from 18,800,232 taels in 1877 to 16,029,231 taels in 1878. The customs revenue in 1878 gave a very favorable result, being 12,483,988 taels. Of the new ports, Wu-hu and I-chang show a considerable rise, the trade at the former advancing in 1878 to 3,219,476 taels, or more than double the amount in the preceding year, and I-chang showing a rise from a very small sum to 71,014 taels. The trade at Kiungchow has also increased, though to a small extent; but at Wenchow it has slightly declined, and at Pakhoi no trade at all appears to have been carried in foreign vessels in the year 1878.

The importation of opium into China is gradually increasing, as well as the cultivation of opium in the country itself. The imports from 1871 to 1878 were as follows (1 picul = 133 lbs.):

YEARS.	Piculs.	YEARS.	Piculs.
1871...............	59,670	1875...............	66,461
1872...............	61,198	1876...............	68,042
1873...............	65,797	1877...............	69,052
1874...............	67,408	1878...............	71,492

Most of the opium finds its way into China by Hong-Kong, and the greater portion of it is of the Malwa kind, the remainder being from Patna, Benares, and other parts of India. The trade in opium is gradually passing out of the hands of foreigners into those of natives. The agencies of the large opium-houses in Shanghai, which existed until quite recently, were withdrawn one after the other, and were replaced by guilds of Chinamen, who, instead of entering into a ruinous competition with the large foreign houses, have in several cases paid them a good sum to close their agencies.

The influence of the Chinese Government extends far beyond its own dependencies over other native states of Asia. An embassy from the King of Nepaul to Peking last year called attention to the tributary relation in which the King of Nepaul (or, as the Chinese call him, the King of the Ghoorkas) places himself with regard to the Chinese Emperor. Nepaul is the largest of the so-called Himalaya states which line the northern frontier of British India, and, though entirely independent, are sometimes classed among the tributary states. Its area is about 56,700 square miles, and its population is estimated at 3,300,000. The exact relations between Nepaul and China have hitherto been but imperfectly known. An embassy, it was said, was sent every five years, but no trustworthy accounts of them were published. Early in 1879 the new embassy arrived in the frontier province of Sechuen. They bore a letter from the King of Nepaul dated in July, 1878, and worded as follows: "A dweller in a remote corner of the earth, in a distant and barren land, the King turns with longing toward the civilization of the Middle Kingdom. It has been his practice to gain glory to himself by the dispatch of an envoy, who was admitted to the presence, and he has been entirely dependent upon the rays of his august Majesty's awe-inspiring influence and prosperity for securing peace and tranquillity in his borders." By order of the Chinese Government, the tribute and letter of the ambassador were, on his arrival at Chingtu, the capital of the province, taken charge of by an officer specially appointed for the purpose, and forwarded to Peking.

In Burmah, also, the Chinese influence is a far stronger and more active political power than the British. The King is a submissive vassal to his feudal lord in Peking, and he courts the good will of the Chinese frontier generals and governors with as much assiduity as if he were dependent on it for his existence.

The establishment of the first steam cotton-mill in China is regarded as another stage in the commercial development of the empire. Being one of the projects of the young China party of progress, the first mill is, however, to be a semi-governmental institution, with an imperial edict for a charter and mandarins for foremen. The prospectus of the company is a lengthy document consisting of copies of official correspondence between the promoters and the Governor-General, Li-Hung-Ohang. The prospectus begins by reciting that for China to be powerful and wealthy there are two great requisites: Chinamen should export articles which foreign countries require of China, and they should manufacture themselves those articles which China requires of foreign countries. Scores of millions of taels are sent out of the country to pay for imported cotton piece-goods, and if Chinamen wove these in their own mills this terrible leakage in the resources of the country would be stopped. Accordingly, it is proposed to establish a cotton-weaving company in Shanghai to work the native raw cotton, which the promoters assert to be equal or superior to Indian cotton, into yarn, and to weave it into cotton cloths. For the first three years English workmen will be engaged to teach the Chinese factory-hands, and at the end of that time, if the native workpeople are thoroughly expert, the English teachers will be dismissed. If, however, the Chinese workmen have not learned the art of weaving in that time, the Englishmen are to be fined. On all piece-goods woven by foreign processes in China shall be levied a tax equal in amount to the import tariff on the same class of goods of foreign make. The factory is to have 800 looms, capable of producing from raw cotton 260,000 to 450,000 pieces of finished cloth. There is to be no work done on Sundays. It is estimated that 13,000 piculs (of 133 lbs. each) of raw cotton and 2,000 piculs of starch and clay will be worked yearly. On the lowest scale of production, it is calculated that a profit of 30 per cent. will be made. The capital of the company is £125,000, and the annual charge for the wages of the hands is set down as £2,000.

The mineral wealth of China includes diamonds in the district of Shantung, on which interesting information was published last year by M. Fauvel. The stones are mostly very minute, varying in size from a millet-seed to a piu's head, though occasionally larger ones are found. One as large as a pea was brought to Chefoo and sold to a mandarin there. A peculiar mode has been adopted for collecting the diamonds. Men wearing thick straw shoes walk about in the sands of the valleys and streams of the diamond mountains of Ching-kangling, about fifteen miles southeast of Yichow-foo. The diamonds, which are ragged and pointed, penetrate the straw and remain there. The shoes are then collected in great numbers and burned, the diamonds being searched for in the ashes. As is the case with amethysts and rock-crystal in the Lao-Chan, the priests in the temples of Chingkangling are the principal dealers in these small diamonds. From them they are bought by glaziers at the large fairs held every year at Chuchow, Laichow-foo, and Hwang-hsien. They are not to be found in shops, and are packed in quills.

The insurrection which toward the close of 1878 broke out in the southern province of Kwang-si, under the leadership of Li-Yung-tsai* (see "Annual Cyclopædia" for 1878, p. 101), assumed larger dimensions at the beginning of the new year. Before Li took up arms against the Government, he addressed a letter to the Tartar General of Canton, explaining the nature and reason for the steps he was about to take. He states therein that he was on bad terms with the Governor of Kwang-si, who

---

* In some reports the name is given as Li-Yung-Chol.

treated him like a common fellow and sent him to Canton to be rid of him. He had no money to pay his traveling expenses, could not go to Canton, and, as he had been generally badly used by his official superiors, he intimated his intention of seeking the throne of the kingdom of Anam, to which he claimed to have an hereditary right. He asserted that Anam, under its present government, was a constant menace and danger to China, and this state of things he proposes to put an end to by making himself king. When Anam comes into his hands, he will without the least hesitation pay the tribute which it has been customary for Anam to pay, and freely acknowledge the supremacy of the Ta-Tsing Empire. In October, 1878, Li, along with a famous Anamese rebel, gathered together a number of disaffected and unpaid soldiers, set out to recover the throne of his fathers, and notified the Viceroy of Canton, Liu-Kunyi, that his designs were not treasonable to China. He thereupon proceeded to capture the Chinese city of Tai-Ping-foo, forty miles from the frontier of the Anamese province of Tonquin, and to endear himself to the population by freeing them from all obligation to pay taxes—acts somewhat inconsistent with his manifesto to the Tartar General. The Viceroy at once denounced him as a dangerous character, and, thinking his real aim was to make a descent on the turbulent but impoverished provinces of Kweichow and Yunnan, sent three thousand men under four mandarins after him. Seventy-five per cent. of the expedition and three of the commanding officers at once went over to the rebels; and Li's force, thus augmented, proceeded to capture more Chinese towns. Eventually he moved toward the Tonquin frontier. The Viceroy of Tonquin sent an urgent appeal to the Viceroy of Canton to save him from the rebel, but the Chinese replied that they could do nothing without the imperial sanction. The Imperial Government of Peking merely sent a command that the insurrection be put down at once, and declared that the Viceroy of Canton and the Governor of Kwang-si would be held responsible for letting a turbulent rebel like Li escape. So an expedition by sea, by way of the fort of Haiphong, was determined on, and in the beginning of December, 1878, a fleet of junks, crowded with soldiery and escorted by three gunboats of foreign type, sailed from Canton. As soon as intelligence of this expedition reached Li, who in the mean while had occupied the southwest districts of Kwang-si and the two frontier divisions of Tonquin, he marched toward the province of Yunnan, no opposition being offered to him anywhere. As soon as the government of Hong-Kong was apprised of the outbreak of the insurrection, the Governor, Mr. Pope Hennessy, forbade the export of arms and munitions of war from Hong-Kong to the mainland. The insurrection was reported at an end in September, although Li still remained at large.

His lieutenant, his family, and his entire stores had fallen into the hands of the Government troops.

Simultaneously with the insurrection of Li, another rebellion began toward the close of 1878 in the island of Hainan, which belongs to the province of Canton, has an area of 20,000 square miles, and a population of about 2,000,000. The rebellion seems to be a rising of the Hakkas. They are Chinese settlers in the south of China, whose ancestors emigrated many centuries ago from the populous provinces of Central and Northern China, and have never been absorbed by the local populations among whom they took up their abode. They do not speak the Cantonese dialect of Chinese, but a *patois* of mongrel origin; nor do they, except in rare instances, intermarry with the Chinese of the soil. Some dozen years ago a large number of them, wearied of constant bickerings with their irreconcilable countrymen of the south, migrated to Hainan and settled on government land there. They increased so rapidly that the lands assigned to them are now insufficient for their wants, and this insufficiency of territory and the hostility of the Chinese are said to be the chief causes of their rising. In October, 1878, they took up arms to the number of several thousand, and threatened the capital, Kiungchow, which is one of the treaty ports, and has a population of about 200,000. Hainan is a rich, and on the seaboard districts a fairly prosperous island, which since its opening to foreign trade has developed a most promising trade with Hong-Kong and other ports. They committed horrible atrocities along their line of march, and in January, 1879, defeated the imperial troops within forty miles of Hoihow, the port of Kiungchow. The Taotai himself, four officers, and five hundred soldiers were among the lost. The rebels, however, were repeatedly defeated afterward, and in August finally laid down their arms outside the city of Kiungchow, after mercy had been promised to them. Numbers were deported to Wychow, Hoi-On, and other places, in order to scatter them and prevent their future concentration in force; but none, it is said, were executed. The total number of imperial troops dispatched to Hainan to quell the outbreak was twelve hundred, and of these about one hundred had fallen in different engagements with the insurgents. The latter are said to have lost upward of a thousand men.

The province of Kulja, which for a number of years had been administered by Russia, was restored to China in the latter part of the year. In 1871 the Russian Minister at Peking was instructed by his Government to inform the Chinese authorities that the Russians had been compelled to occupy the province of Kulja by the disorders prevailing among the Mohammedans there, and also by the growing strength of the Atalik Ghazi south of the Thian-Shan, both enemies of the Chinese; but his Government, he said, had no intention of contesting their rights, and whenever a Chinese army should be sent of sufficient strength to maintain order in the province, the Czar would order its restoration to China. During the time that has since passed the province recovered somewhat under Russian rule from the depression into which it had sunk during the Mohammedan rebellion. Very little was heard of the Chinese in this region until the close of 1876. With the campaigns against the Tungani and against Yakoob Beg, they began to reassert their claims to their territory in Central Asia; and after the overthrow of Yakoob Beg's power they claimed the fulfillment of the Czar's promise. But, in spite of the diplomatic representations at St. Petersburg, and the menacing attitude of Tso-Tsung-Tang and his army at Manas and Aksu, the Russian authorities, both at home and in Asia, for eighteen months refused to give the Chinese any satisfaction. A Russian commission was finally appointed to draw up a treaty, and in September it presented its report, containing the draft of a treaty, of which the following are the most important points: First, Russian merchants will be admitted to all the interior markets of China. Secondly, China will pay Russia 5,000,000 rubles. Thirdly, Russia is to receive part of the steppe in the upper regions of the Irtish River beyond the Zaisan Sea. The proposed frontier will begin from the fortress of Saur and be continued past the Bostal and Kanas Seas. On the other side of Kulja the frontier is drawn from a point a little more to the southeast of Kanas to the town of Usuntau, from which it runs eastward to the point where the old frontier is cut by the new one. Thus the Tekes River Valley is to remain Russian territory—that is to say, about a fifth part of Kulja. This valley was once a Chinese possession, and was surrendered by treaty to Russia twenty years ago. The possession of this strip of territory will enable Russia to exert a very material influence upon the progress of events both in Kulja and in Eastern Turkistan. She will continue to hold in her hand the means of reoccupying the province if such a course should in future become necessary. The clauses relating to commerce will undoubtedly place in her grasp much of the trade of Western China; and if the Chinese should place restrictions in the way of Russian merchants, an excuse would be available to revert to the present condition of things. In spite of these disadvantages the treaty was accepted by the Chinese.

In May, Hakim Khan Tufi, the pretender to the Kashgar throne, quitted his exile on Russian territory, and, entering Kashgar with a large number of followers through the Pamir, endeavored to raise a rebellion against the Chinese. This step was taken by Hakim Khan in order to profit by the angry excitement then reigning among the Mussulmans of Kashgar on account of the burning of the remains of Yakoob Beg, their late ruler, by order of the Chinese. In consequence of the rebellious attitude of the Mussulmans of Kashgar, and their openly expressed regrets at the loss of their beloved Yukoob Beg, the Chinese authorities ordered the bodies of Yakoob Beg and of his son, Ishana Beg, to be disinterred and publicly burned to cinders. The ashes of Yakoob were, moreover, sent to Peking. Such a proceeding only served to give new force to the existing discontent, and a conspiracy among the Mohammedans was the result. Hakim Khan endeavored to take advantage of this conspiracy; but the Chinese troops put a speedy end to the troubles.

At the time that Eastern Turkistan again passed into the hands of China, there were taken prisoners four sons, two grandsons, two granddaughters, and four wives of Yakoob Beg. Some of these were executed and others died; but in 1879 there remained in prison at Lanchanfoo, the capital of Kan-suh, Maiti Kuli, aged fourteen; Yima Kuli, aged ten; K'ati Kuli, aged six, sons of Yakoob Beg; and Aisan Ahung, aged five, his grandson. These wretched little boys were treated like state criminals. They arrived in Kan-suh in February, 1879, and were sent on to the provincial capital to be tried and sentenced by the Judicial Commissioner there for the awful crime of being sons of their father. In the course of time the Commissioner made a report of the trial, which he concluded as follows:

In cases of sedition, where the law condemns the malefactors to death by the slow and painful process, the children and grandchildren, if it be shown that they were not privy to the treasonable designs of their parents, shall be delivered, no matter whether they have attained full age or not, into the hands of the imperial household to be made eunuchs of, and shall be forwarded to Turkistan and given over as slaves to the soldiery. If under the age of ten, they shall be confined in prison until they shall have reached the age of eleven, whereupon they shall be handed to the imperial household to be dealt with according to law. In the present case, Yakoob Beg's sons Maiti Kuli, Yima Kuli, and K'ati Kuli, and the rebel chief Beg Kuli's son, Aisan Ahung, are all under age, and were not, it has been proved, privy to the treasonable designs of their parents. They have, therefore, to be handed to the imperial household to be dealt with in accordance with the law, which prescribes that, in cases of sedition, the sons and grandsons of malefactors condemned to death by the slow and painful process, if it be shown that they were not privy to the treasonable designs of their parents, shall, whether they have attained full age or not, be delivered into the hands of the imperial household to be made eunuchs of, and shall be sent to Turkistan to be given as slaves to the soldiery. But, as these are rebels from Turkistan, it is requested that they may, instead, be sent to the Amoor region, to be given as slaves to the soldiery there. As Maiti Kuli is fourteen, it is requested that he may be delivered over to the imperial household as soon as the reply of the Board is received. Yima Kuli is just ten, K'ati Kuli and Aisan Ahung are under ten; they have, therefore, to be confined in prison until they attain the age of eleven, when they will be delivered over to the imperial household to be dealt with according to law.

Kuo-Tung-tao, formerly Chinese Minister in England, returned to China in April, 1879, having been recalled by his Government. He was denounced, it appears, by a member of the body of censors, in a memorial to the throne, which, while accusing him of too great admiration for England, of being on bad terms with his assistant envoy, and of having written an indiscreet account of his voyage to England, based its principal accusations against him on the criticisms of his policy and social demeanor which have from time to time appeared in a Chinese newspaper, called the "Shên-Pao," published at Shanghai, and owned by a British subject. Immediately on his arrival at Shanghai, the Minister set to work to take the opinion of counsel in relation to bringing an action for libel against the "Shên-Pao," and intimated his intention of using every remedy, legal as well as political, against a journal which had done him such wrong. The steps taken by him induced the Shanghai paper to retract all it had said against Kuo, and the latter accepted the apology as sufficient. The Shanghai correspondent of the London "Times" calls Kuo "the most intelligent Chinaman that Englishmen are ever likely to see accredited to England, and the best and rarest type of the Chinese official." Tsêng Howyeh, son of Tsêng Kuo-fan, the famous Viceroy of Nanking, has been appointed, in place of Kuo, Chinese Ambassador to England. He will have two secretaries of legation, one stationed at London and one at Paris, two attachés, several interpreters, and a number of servants—about forty persons in all.

In May and June General Grant paid a visit to China. At Tientsin, on May 20th, a grand

CUSTOM-HOUSE, SHANGHAI.

banquet was given to him by the Chinese authorities in the principal native temple. The Viceroy of Chihli, the Commander-in-Chief and Grand Secretary Li-Hung-Chang, presided. At Peking he received attentions such as had never before been bestowed upon any

foreigner. Calls were exchanged between him and General Kung.

The "Shên-Pao" of Shanghai, the leading native paper in China, published an edict issued by the two Empresses-Regent of China which systematized and reorganized the diplomatic service of the empire in foreign countries. Henceforth China will be represented abroad by ambassadors as well as envoys, and will have consuls-general, consuls, etc. The monthly salaries are fixed as follows: For ambassadors, £350; for envoys extraordinary, £300; for resident ministers, between £200 and £250; chargés d'affaires and consuls-general, £150; consuls, £125; and vice-consuls, £100. The resident medical officer on an embassy will receive a monthly salary of £50. These salaries are to be paid through the custom-house at Shanghai. The Chinese diplomatic representatives will also be repaid all expenses to which they may be put for lodgings, traveling, diplomatic dinners, horses, and carriages. Henceforward every ambassador and envoy will be bound to telegraph direct to the two Empresses in all cases of emergency or pressing importance. But the regulation that no ambassador, envoy, or consul-general should be continued in the same post for longer than three years is still retained as a fundamental principle of Chinese diplomacy.

After the subjugation of the rebels in Yunnan, the Chinese Government set to work to convert the Mohammedan rebels to the state religion. The Yunnanites had hitherto withstood persuasion, theological argument, and torture with stolid resolution; so the mandarins intrusted with the task of weaning them from their dogmatic errors adopted the cunning expedient of making it worth their while to become idolaters. A recent imperial decree ordained that every Mohammedan publicly renouncing his faith should be exempt from taxation, and that this privilege should be extended to his descendants for the period of one hundred years. The actual convert, moreover, should be distinguished by a mark of imperial favor —a peacock's feather or cap-button, according to his condition in life. Meanwhile, the Chinese Government caused five thousand gods, of every orthodox variety, to be manufactured for the especial benefit of the Yunnan metropolis alone. These deities were set up by the police in the porches and courtyards of every house in the town, and the heads of families were compelled to burn incense once a day before their unwelcome Lares, as well as to provide them with new clothes from head to foot at certain stated periods. The Chinese police is instructed to "look up" any householder proving a defaulter in the performance of these obligatory rites, and to stimulate him to the fulfillment of his duties by every convenient inducement.

The desire of the Chinese Government to reëstablish its rule over all territory that had ever been under its dominion, which had been manifested in the past years in the cases of the Tungani, Kashgaria, Kulja, and even in Burmah and Nepaul, also showed itself in the case of the Loochoo Islands, which were claimed and occupied by Japan. Although the authority of China in these islands had long been merely nominal, it resented their occupation by Japan, and serious difficulties between these two countries seemed to be imminent. (See JAPAN.)

A treaty was concluded with Spain relating to the condition of the Chinese in Cuba, and a special embassy was sent to that island. (See SPAIN.)

Twenty-six Protestant missionary societies have agents and churches in China. Ten of them are American, one is Canadian, thirteen are British, and two are Continental societies. The missions have grown very fast within a few years. The most careful estimate that has been made of their aggregate force showed that in 1877 there were connected with them 91 stations, 431 out-stations, 312 churches, 473 missionaries and missionaries' wives, and 13,035 communicants. Later reports from only a part of the societies make the number of missionaries and assistants 16,335, showing an increase of more than 10,500 communicants since 1868, when the number was 5,743, or of about one thousand a year. The principal denominations are represented in the missions, each by two or more societies, as follows: Baptist, 85 missionaries and assistants, 1,819 members; Congregationalist, 53 missionaries and preachers, 2,986 members; Episcopal and Anglican, 173 preaching agents, 1,330 members; Methodist, 149 missionaries and assistants, 2,860 members; Presbyterian (with which is included the Reformed Church in America), 213 preachers, 2,687 members; undenominational missions, 99 agents, 905 members; Continental Lutheran and Reformed missions, 79 missionaries and assistants, 1,748 members. Educational work has not been prosecuted by the missionaries as rapidly as the organization of churches, and appears less prominent than do the educational efforts of missionaries in other fields. The reports to the Shanghai Missionary Conference in 1877 gave 207 boarding and day schools for boys, and 120 for girls, with a total of 5,680 pupils; 20 theological schools, with 231 students; 115 Sunday-schools, with 2,605

scholars and 290 school-teachers. Missionaries have been employed as professors in the Imperial College at Peking, and the Protestant Episcopal Church is endeavoring to establish a missionary college at Shanghai. One thousand and seventy-six religious and more than two hundred secular publications, in the general language and eleven dialects, were issued from the missionary presses between 1810 and 1875. Sixteen missionary hospitals reported 3,730 in-patients treated and 87,505 applications from out-patients in 1876, besides which 41,281 cases were administered to in the same year in 24 missionary dispensaries.

COLLINS, Judge THOMAS WHARTON, born in Louisiana, June 23, 1812, died November 3, 1879. He was admitted to the bar in 1833. Though self-educated, he was a man of great attainments. He was a remarkable linguist. In 1834 he was appointed French and Spanish translator to the State Senate. After this he edited the "True American." He was Chief Deputy Clerk of the United States District and Circuit Court of Louisiana from 1836 to 1838; District Attorney for New Orleans from 1840 to 1842; Judge of the City Court of New Orleans from 1842 to 1846. In 1852 he was a member of the Constitutional Convention. In 1856 he was elected, by a majority of 5,000 votes, Judge of the First District Court of the Parish of Orleans. At the close of the war in 1865 he resumed the practice of the law. In 1867 he was made Judge of the Seventh District Court, which position he retained until that court was abolished. He was the author of "Humanics," "The Eden of Labor," and of various political, scientific, and ethical essays.

COLOMBIA (ESTADOS UNIDOS DE COLOMBIA).* The President of the Republic is General Trujillo (inaugurated April 1, 1878); and the Cabinet is composed of the following Ministers: Interior and Foreign Affairs, Dr. Ancizar (1879); Finance and Public Works, Dr. Wilson (1879); Treasury and National Credit, Señor S. Camacho Roldan; War and Marine, Señor M. Hurtado.

The chief magistrates of the nine States are: Antioquia, General T. Renjifo; Bolivar, Señor B. Noguera; Boyacá, Señor J. E. Otalora; Cauca, Señor M. Garces; Cundinamarca, Señor D. Delgado; Magdalena, Señor L. A. Robles; Panamá, Señor B. Correoso; Santander, Señor M. A. Estrada; Tolima, Dr. J. Manique. There is at present no Colombian Minister accredited to the United States. The Colombian Consul-General in New York is Señor Miguel Salgar. The United States Minister Resident at Bogotá is Hon. E. Deichman. The strength of the Federal army in time of peace is 3,000; in time of war, each of the States is required to furnish a contingent of one per cent. of its population.

The subjoined table exhibits the amount and

---

* For territorial divisions, and detailed statistics concerning area, population, etc., reference may be made to the "Annual Cyclopædia" for 1874 and 1877.

several branches of the Colombian revenue for 1878–'79:

REVENUE.

Customs	$4.025,112
Salt monopoly	1,451,529
Panamá and Sabanilla Railways	384,923
Post-Office	84,524
Telegraphs	29,060
Mint	11,613
National property	9,503
Church property	27,477
Sundries	848,551
Total	$6,872,292

In 1877–'78 the following were the

EXPENDITURES.

Ministry of the Interior ($240,024) and of Foreign Affairs ($63,700)	$303,724
Ministry of Justice	27,892
" of Finance	1,963,607
" of War and Marine	1,138,160
National debt	1,372,994
Ministry of Public Works	2,321,483
Treasury Department	76,084
Public Instruction	331,120
Pensions	116,220
Post-Office	433,986
Total	$8,085,110

It should here be observed that in the expenditure of the Finance Department is included an item of $813,177, amount of the cost of collection of the revenue, or rather more than one eighth of the entire national income! On comparing the revenue for 1878–'79 with that for the year immediately preceding, an increase of $2,033,992 is observable in the former. The year 1877–'78 was marked by a deficit of $2,433,113.

In the budget for 1878–'79, the revenue and expenditures were estimated at $5,998,644.8¼ and $9,622,709.81 respectively; a state of things which, had it become real, would have saddled the country with a deficit almost equal in amount to the revenue itself, and embarrassed the Government beyond all hope of immediate recovery, or indeed of relief otherwise than by resorting to a new loan, which, under existing circumstances, could not have been negotiated without considerable sacrifice. As it is, President Trujillo in his message to Congress frankly stated that the financial situation was not good, and that he saw no probability of improvement before peace should be reëstablished throughout the country, and more serious and united efforts made toward the development of the sources (abundant in themselves) of national wealth. In order to the attainment of this end, "it is indispensable not to damp the public spirit of the people by inaction, or suffer the destruction of the results of labor, but to direct the endeavors of the State authorities and of Colombian capitalists in one common channel with those of the Federal Government." To obviate the serious difficulties attendant upon a deficit, the President found it necessary to avail himself of the powers with which he was invested by the law (No. 60) of 1878 to order, in just such an emergency as the one referred to, the emission of Treasury notes (*pagarés del Tesoro*) to the amount of $2,500,000. Means

were used to effect certain payments which, like those on account of the foreign debt, etc., have to be made in coin; and it was suggested as expedient to unify the various public obligations, at present so confusing from their variety in the market as "not only to prejudice public interests, but also to affect at times the good name of the Government itself." Financially speaking, however, the Trujillo Administration has not proved less successful than those immediately preceding it; bonds payable out of the proceeds of the custom-house and of the salt monopoly have been redeemed to the amount of $1,004,431; and other liabilities, contracted in part by former Administrations, have been liquidated to the amount of $1,586,614; the disbursements in coin on account of the foreign debt having reached $745,388.60, and those for ordinary current expenses, $1,509,691.60, during the same period.

As seen by the foregoing tables, the yield of the customs department for the year 1878–'79 was $4,025,112, or $1,025,112 larger than that for the year 1877–'78; but a considerable falling off is apprehended in this branch of the revenue consequent upon a sensible decrease in the exports, while the imports scarcely experienced any change either in quantity or value—a state of things regarded as bidding fair to continue for one or two years at least. One inconvenience immediately attendant upon such a state would be the necessity for merchants to resort to specie shipments to cover their balances abroad; besides which there would be the possibility of a greater evil, dependent on the first, namely, a monetary crisis which might well assume the proportions of a real disaster if added to the already complicated situation. The attention of the Congress was earnestly called to these matters. A revision of the tariff was suggested, together with the expediency of requesting merchants to communicate to the members of the Legislature their views on that important subject. With a view to the extension of the foreign trade, it was recommended that the Executive should be empowered to make treaties with the different friendly commercial nations for the admission, duty-free or at much lower rates of duty than those now in existence, of such Colombian staples as rice, sugar, coffee, hats, etc., with similar concessions on the part of Colombia regarding imports from those countries.

The national debt in 1878 stood as follows:

Foreign debt	$10,392,500
Home debt	5,606,804
Total	$15,999,304

The imports in 1877–'78 reached a total value of $8,708,797, and the exports, $11,111,197, against $7,328,928 and $14,477,897, respectively, for the year immediately preceding.

The exports in 1877–'78, in regard to destinations, were distributed as follows:

COUNTRIES.	Values.
France	$1,732,708
Germany	3,342,875
Great Britain	3,589,397
United States	1,624,673
Various	871,549
Total	$11,111,197

The more important articles sent out of the country in the same year, and their values, were as follows:

COMMODITIES.	Values.
Gold and silver in bars, dust, or coin	$3,688,246
Cinchona	2,470,246
Coffee	1,504,075
Hides	810,119
Tobacco	564,097
Hats	149,440
India-rubber	175,252
Cotton	139,134

The entries at the various ports of the republic in 1877-'78 comprised 342 steamers, with an aggregate tonnage of 437,044; and 847 sailing vessels, with an aggregate of 42,756 tons.

Coffee culture in the State of Panamá, particularly in the district of Chiriqui, bids fair to prove most satisfactory. The first regular shipment, made in December, 1879, was of 7,140 lbs., being the first crop of an estate the yield of which was expected to reach 300 quintals (of 100 lbs. each). The coffee was represented as of excellent quality, fine color, and delicious aroma, and evidencing careful preparation for market. Indeed, the superior quality and regular fullness of the bean afforded proof of the "entire adaptability of the soil and climate of Chiriqui for the production of a class of coffee second to none on the American Continent."

The article COLOMBIA in the "Annual Cyclopædia" for 1878 contains (page 104) some interesting particulars concerning the export trade of the republic.

Referring to railway matters, President Trujillo, in his message already alluded to, expressed a doubt that Mr. Ross, the contractor of the line which is to place the three northern States of the Union in communication with the Atlantic seaboard, would be able to carry his project into effect. The time fixed upon in the contract for the commencement of the work had expired, and the Executive recommended the raising of a loan of $2,500,000 for the prosecution of the work. Several railways and other enterprises, for which a Mr. F. T. Cisneros is contractor, were spoken of in commendatory terms. The progress in each was satisfactory. Steamers for the navigation of the upper Magdalena were being built at New York, and would be ready for service within a few months. The benefits of cheap and rapid transport thus secured would be shared by an extensive section of country containing, among other natural sources of wealth, important copper and coal mines. The Antioquia and Cauca Railways were progressing satisfactorily, and the intention was announced

of sparing no efforts to push on the work to completion at an early day.*

The Legislature of the State of Bolivar passed a law tending to encourage the navigation of the Dique and Magdalena Rivers, and offering a subvention and a guarantee of 7 per cent. interest on a capital of $200,000 to any company willing to embark in the enterprise.

The President's message contained some brief remarks on new mining interests of considerable promise. Satisfactory reports had been made of a survey of the coal mines of the valley of Dupar and of the Goajira Peninsula. The San Andrés coal mines in the State of Bolivar were represented as of great value, and the assurance given that their development would prove most profitable to the country. A company had been organized for the working of the Samacá iron mines in Boyacá, on which American engineers had reported favorably. General Trujillo suggested the expediency of giving Government aid to the enterprise, either by purchasing stocks or by granting a subvention to the company. The Torrá gold mines were spoken of, on the authority of a competent engineer, as being as rich as any that ever excited the cupidity of the conquistadores. Measures were being adopted for their development.

But more than even the building of new railways or the organization of companies for the working of her mines, the navigation of her rivers, and the extension of her commercial relations abroad, Colombia needs the establishment of peace and order at home and the permanent conciliation of State and Federal interests. The revolutionary era, reopened a few years ago after a lull hitherto unexampled for its duration in the annals of Spanish America, has since been perpetuated by party strife and rebellions aimed, now at one or other of the local governments, now at the Central Government, and causing in some instances considerable effusion of blood. An atrocious episode of one of these outbreaks was reported as follows from Ocaña on September 11, 1879:

Horrible butchery in Bucaramanga! The day before yesterday the Commune was proclaimed in that city, and, headed by the Alcalde, Pedro Collazos, took full possession. The German Consul, Schrader, and Messrs. Obdulio Estevez and Eduardo Mutiz, were assassinated. Another German was seriously wounded. Several stores were destroyed. The greatest consternation prevails among people possessing any means. The Communists are intrenched and hold two cuarteles (military barracks). General Wilches will attack them to-day. Families are fleeing to the mountains for safety. Stores and dwellings are completely sacked and destroyed. It is not known in Barranquilla whether the movement is purely communist, or the beginning of a revolution against the State government. In either case it will no doubt be promptly suppressed and vigorously punished.

The occurrence of election riots in Cundinamarca, the capital of which State is Bogotá, elicited from President Trujillo remarks in his

* For railways and telegraph lines already in operation in Colombia, see "Annual Cyclopædia" for 1877.

message on the absurd position of a Government which, according to the Constitution, is bound to preserve peace, secure its servants in the exercise of their functions, render effective the guarantees for the safety and well-being of its citizens, and the immunities and prerogatives of diplomatic agents resident in the capital, and yet is not permitted to call the sectional government to account for the failure or otherwise of its efforts to restore and maintain order. This anomalous state of affairs has received the attention of each President who has at any time been opposed by the government of Cundinamarca, and various States have petitioned to set apart a section of territory for the use of the national Government; but the evil still continues. Colombia has no capital. Its Federal head is located in a city where the municipality has more absolute authority than the Executive of the nation. A very important paragraph is that relating to the means of conciliation adopted by the Government toward those who were lately in rebellion against its authority. Amnesty is declared, and the banished may return to resume the occupations, associations, and, in many cases, the properties which their own acts destroyed or placed in peril. Sales of confiscated properties have been stopped, and they have, as far as possible, been returned to their owners, who are guaranteed protection under the laws.

"The triumph of the Independent party," writes a Colombian journalist in November, 1879, "in almost all the States of the Union —a party (the Liberal) whose platform is respect for all rights, strict and honest administration of all departments, and individual guarantees to citizens of all political parties—is an evidence that the country is about to enter upon a course which will lead to days more happy and bright with promise for the future than those through which the republic has so lately passed. Peace is necessary to prosperity and progress, and the great natural wealth of the country but awaits a period of prolonged tranquillity for an amazing development. A large proportion of the public men of all parties are disposed to rally around the government of Dr. Núñez, the President-elect, and lend their assistance in the great work of the regeneration of the country. Every friend of Colombia will hope sincerely that such happy auguries may be fully realized."

The candidates for the Presidency were four: Dr. Rafael Núñez, above mentioned, Sr. Tomás Renjifo, Sr. Camargo, and Sr. J. R. Carsola. The last two appear to have obtained but one vote each, so that Núñez (10,-059 votes) and Renjifo (559), the respective representatives of the two recent divisions of the Liberal party, proved the real contestants. (See INTEROCEANIC CANAL.)

COLORADO. The session of the second Legislature of Colorado commenced on January 1st, and closed on Sunday morning, February 9th. In the Senate, James P. Maxwell

was elected President *pro tem.* ; in the House, Rienzi Streeter was chosen Speaker.

One of the first measures after organization was a joint session of the two Houses to canvass the votes given at the election in November previous for State officers. The result was as follows:

FOR GOVERNOR.

F. W. Pitkins, Republican	14,308
W. A. H. Loveland, Democrat	11,585
K. G. Buckingham, National	2,788

FOR LIEUTENANT-GOVERNOR.

H. A. W. Tabor, Republican	13,891
T. M. Field, Democrat	11,968
P. A. Simmons, National	2,641

FOR SECRETARY OF STATE.

N. H. Meldrum, Republican	14,165
John S. Wheeler, Democrat	11,784
J. E. Washburn, National	2,770

FOR TREASURER.

N. S. Culver, Republican	14,141
Nelson Hallock, Democrat	11,843
W. D. Arnott, National	2,685

FOR ATTORNEY-GENERAL.

Charles W. Wright, Republican	14,461
C. Yearnan, Democrat	11,571
Alpheus Wright, National	2,676

FOR AUDITOR.

E. K. Stinson, Republican	14,240
John H. Harrison, Democrat	11,752
G. W. King, National	2,708

FOR SUPERINTENDENT OF SCHOOLS.

J. C. Shattuck, Republican	13,972
O. J. Goldrick, Democrat	11,984
A. J. Chittenden, National	2,604

On January 14th, which was the second Tuesday after the meeting and organization of the Legislature, an election for Senator in Congress was held. In the Senate the vote was as follows: Nathaniel P. Hill, 19; W. A. H. Loveland, 7. In the House the vote was as follows: Hill, 34; Loveland, 12; Richard G. Buckingham, 1. Nathaniel P. Hill was elected.

The following memorial to Congress passed the House without reference to a committee:

To the Honorable the Senate and House of Representatives of the United States of America, in Congress assembled :

Your memorialists, the Senate and House of Representatives of Colorado, most respectfully represent:

That the present Ute reservation, extending along the western boundary of this State, includes an area three times as great as that of the State of Massachusetts, and embraces more than twelve million acres of land, and is occupied and possessed by three thousand Indians, who cultivate no land, pursue no useful occupation, and are supported by the Federal Government.

That said reservation is watered and enriched by many streams and great rivers, and contains many large and fertile valleys and plains.

That it embraces a great area of the best grazing lands within the State of Colorado, and contains nearly one third of the arable land within the entire State.

That it comprises several districts rich in gold and silver and other precious metals.

That the territory embraced within said reservation will support a population of many thousands, and is destined to become one of the most prosperous divisions of our State.

That the only approach by wagon-roads to five extensive and productive mining districts is across said reservation.

That the Indians view with distrust and jealousy all supposed encroachments now necessarily made in communicating with the mining districts aforesaid, and that the transportation of machinery and supplies to said districts, and communication with them, is attended by great risk and danger to life and property.

That by reason of the vast extent of said reservation, the people of the State of Colorado are deprived of the use of a great area of fertile and productive lands, the development of several districts rich in all the precious metals is prevented or impeded, and the growth of the State is hindered by the absence of thousands who will be attracted to the State as soon as the said reservation is opened to exploration and settlement.

That the interest upon a small portion of the moneys which will be derived by the General Government for the sale of lands in said reservation will support its present occupants on another or less extensive reservation.

Your memorialists therefore most respectfully urge and pray your honorable body to take such action as may be necessary for the opening of said reservation to settlement and the removal of the Indians therefrom.

Within the limits of the above-mentioned tract of land are large mountains, from most of which explorers have been excluded by the Indians. Prospectors, however, have explored some portions of the country and found valuable lode and placer claims, and there is reason to believe that it contains great mineral wealth. The number of Indians who occupy this reservation is about three thousand. If the land was divided up between the individual members of the tribe, it would give every man, woman, and child between three and four thousand acres. It has been claimed that the entire tribe have had in cultivation about fifty acres of land. These Indians are fed by the Government, are allowed ponies without number, and, except when engaged in an occasional hunt, their most serious employment is horse-racing. If this reservation could be extinguished and the land thrown open to settlers, it would furnish homes to thousands of the people of the State who desire homes, would furnish grazing for immense herds of cattle, horses, and sheep, and might prove to be exceedingly rich in minerals. It has been necessary already to construct toll-roads over portions of the reservation in order to transport supplies to the population at Ouray, Mount Sneffles, San Miguel, and other prosperous mining camps in that vicinity, for the shipment of ores and the transportation of the mails. The Indians look with jealousy upon any supposed encroachments upon their rights. An accidental quarrel between them and a party of whites would immediately stop all travel across the reservation, would cut off the supplies in these frontier settlements, and involve that whole country in great trouble.

An act was passed to prevent the defacement of natural scenery by advertisements. During its discussion Mr. Walcott of Clear Creek said that in his county "every available rock was already plastered and painted over." Mr. John opposed the bill in its present form, for the reason that "it provides for the deface-

ment of all advertisements by the county commissioners, which would bankrupt every county in the State."

In the Senate, an act was introduced to repeal the code, and extensive debate ensued on the merits of the code system and the common-law practice. One of the speakers asserted that Judge Dillon had said in Denver, when deciding a demurrer in the United States Court (a motion having been made to strike out certain parts of the pleadings demurred to), in substance as follows: "There is no use of that. You are just passing through the experience of other States that have adopted a code. Its adoption has always been followed by a large crop of demurrers and motions and violent opposition. Treat the code fairly. It is the correct system; there is no doubt in my mind about that. Get your cases to issue on the merits. You have adopted and are to have the code. No State has gone back to the common-law practice after adopting the code. You will soon be at work all right under it, and will be surprised after a while that it was the occasion of so much trouble." The code was sustained by a vote of 14 to 10. The question arose in the Senate whether Sunday was included among the legislative days of the session. It was decided that it was, and should be so counted.

An act provides for the appointment of sheep inspectors, and the inspection of every flock brought into the State and its subsequent periodical inspection.

A temperance bill was reported in the House, which provided that "every wife shall have a right of action against the man who makes her husband drunk." A person who rents a building to a saloon-keeper shall be responsible jointly with him for the damages; but the lessor may dispossess the saloon-keeper if he unlawfully sells liquor. There was six majority against the bill, and it was laid aside.

The subject of irrigation received careful consideration, owing to its great importance to the State. The bill provides that the county commissioners of each county shall, at their regular January session, hear all applications from parties desiring the use of the water, with all such details as may be necessary, and proceed to fix the price to be charged for the water from the particular ditch in question. This shall not be changed within two years. Limitations are prescribed to this general grant of authority, and also upon the use of the purchaser. "If at any time any ditch or reservoir from which water is or shall be drawn for irrigation, shall not be entitled to a full supply of water from the natural stream which supplies the same, the water actually received into and carried by such ditch, or held in such reservoir, shall be divided among all the consumers of water from such ditch or reservoir, as well the owners, shareholders, or stockholders thereof, as the parties purchasing water therefrom, and parties taking water partly under and by virtue of holding shares, and partly by purchasing the same, to each his share *pro rata* according to the amount he, she, or they (in cases in which several consume water jointly) shall be then entitled, so that all owners and purchasers shall suffer from the deficiency arising from the cause aforesaid, each in proportion to the amount of water which he, she, or they should have received in case no such deficiency of water had occurred." Restrictions and penalties are prescribed against one causing impurity to the water, as it is the meaning and intent of a portion of the law, "that all the streams, ditches, reservoirs, lakes, and watercourses of every kind in the State shall be kept pure and clean, and fit for household purposes: *provided*, however, that nothing shall be construed to prevent any person from discharging the contents of any sluice, flume, quartz-mill, or other works for mining or saving mineral products into any natural stream." The irrigation districts are defined, and provision is made for the formation of others by the Governor on the application of individuals. In each district water commissioners are to be appointed, whose duty it is "to divide the water in the natural stream or streams of their district among the several ditches taking water from the same according to the prior rights of each respectively; in whole or in part to shut and fasten, or cause to be shut and fastened, by order given to any sworn assistant sheriff or constable of the county in which the head of such ditch is situated, the head-gates of any ditch or ditches heading in any of the natural streams of the district, which, in a time of scarcity of water, shall not be entitled to water, by reason of the priority of the rights of others below them on the same stream." All litigated questions of priority of right, etc., are to be brought before the county district court, to which is given full and exclusive jurisdiction of all cases lying wholly within the county.

The following memorial, prepared and presented in the House, although not passed, probably indicates the manner in which irrigation may hereafter be accomplished:

To the Honorable the Senate and House of Representatives of the United States of America in Congress assembled:

Your memorialists, the Senate and House of Representatives of the State of Colorado, most respectfully represent:

That the portion of this State lying east of the Rocky Mountains, by reason of its extreme aridity, is wholly incapable of successful agriculture without irrigation.

That the soils of this section, when placed under artificial water supply, possess most remarkable qualities of productiveness.

That the agriculture of the State is now confined to the valleys of the water-courses, where the construction of irrigating canals is comparatively inexpensive, and that it will remain so confined unless a more extensive system of irrigation can be established.

That the construction of a system of irrigation which will fully meet the demands of the State in putting these lands into a condition for successful occupancy will be too expensive for either individuals, private corporations, or the State Government without foreign aid.

That immigration to the West is continually increasing; that the public domain subject to the homestead and preëmption laws outside the arid regions is already comparatively exhausted; that the immigrating agriculturist is unable to avail himself of the benefit of these beneficent laws because of his financial inability to construct adequate irrigating canals to render the arid lands inhabitable.

That for the reasons set forth these lands will remain unsold and therefore useless to the General Government unless made available as above indicated.

That also without some aid in the premises the vast mineral resources of the State will of necessity remain in comparative undevelopment.

The policy of the United States has always been one of liberality toward internal improvements. Large tracts of swamp-lands have been generally donated to different Northwestern States, which have been reclaimed to the husbandman through the instrumentality of the State governments. Lands have been donated for the construction of canals, railroads, and other purposes. That the aid here asked is an absolute necessity to the State, that her mining interests may be developed and that her area east of the mountains can be utilized.

Therefore your memorialists would respectfully pray your honorable body to enact a law, under such conditions as may seem just and proper, donating to the State of Colorado all the lands within her boundaries now belonging to the United States (except those designated as mineral) for the purpose of constructing a system of irrigation adequate to reclaim said lands from their present unfruitfulness.

In the Senate a bill was introduced to prescribe an intelligence qualification for voters. The remarks of a few speakers illustrate the manner of its reception. Mr. Rhodes opposed it, and thought it came with poor grace from the Republican side, which had advocated conferring suffrage upon 3,000,000 of blacks who could not read and write. He had known as intelligent men as there are in this body, who knew as much about government and politics as any of them, but who can not read or write a word. Mr. Wolcott of Clear Creek moved to refer the bill to the Educational Committee, but the motion was lost. Mr. Rhodes continued that if the State of Georgia were to pass a bill that no negro who could not read and write could vote, every Republican organ in the land would denounce it as an outrage. Mr. Helm said no Republican organ would complain if the State of Georgia were to pass a bill like this, making it applicable to both whites and blacks; but if they made it applicable only to negroes, it would not be right, and there should and would be a howl. Mr. Barela represented a good many people who can not read and write, and he desired to see them educated; but he would not vote against this bill on general principles. Mr. Webster said in introducing the bill he had no thought but to advance the cause of education, and hoped the bill would meet a ready response in the hearts of every member. Mr. De France said there were universal principles lying at the foundation of our government which are infringed upon by this bill. This is a step in the direction opposite from that which was cherished by the founders of our government. He favored education as much as any man, but believed in an absolute political equality, without any distinctions which would form classes. He said you could provide equally as well that no man should own property until he can read and write. This is an entering wedge, and a step in the direction of an aristocratic and monarchical government. Mr. Webster recognized the right of suffrage as a privilege and not as an inherent right, and that this privilege can be conferred only upon those that the government pleases. Mr. Rhodes said that the question of suffrage was one of inherent right, and quoted from the Constitution of the United States to prove his position. Mr. De France read from the Constitution to prove that the right to acquire property is not considered an inherent right, but one of privilege. There is no more sacred right to the people of this nation than the right of suffrage, and none which could not be touched with less danger to the nation. Mr. John maintained that such a bill would not avoid political corruption. In Ohio, Illinois, or Kansas such a bill as this would be hooted at and ridiculed, and ought not to be received here. The States occupying the most advanced grounds on educational questions have no such laws as this, and do not want them. The bill was referred to the Committee on Elections.

An unsuccessful effort was made in the Senate to repeal the act establishing a school of mines. The objections to the institution were, that it had been organized nine years and has nine pupils in attendance. No part of the mining sections of the State ask for the support of this school, and the State is deriving no benefit from its continuance. The same studies taught in the institution are taught in the State University at Boulder, and the State can not afford to support two institutions of the same nature. Nowhere has such an institution as the School of Mines been a success. In many places they have been tried, and always been abandoned. In reply to these assertions it was urged that the institution was founded in 1870 by an appropriation of about $3,000. In 1872 another appropriation was made to the school, but the Governor pocketed the bill. In 1874 and 1876 appropriations were made, aggregating, with what had before been given, over $12,300. The mill tax has raised the total to $14,572.45. The building and apparatus have cost about $8,000. This shows that the school has been run for about nine years for about $6,500. This accounts for the little that the school has accomplished. The object of the school was to promote and encourage the mining industry. Can any man think that a school can accomplish much on less than $1,000 per annum?

A bill to establish impartial suffrage was introduced in the Senate. When under consideration, one of the Senators (Mr. Haynes) said: "The State Constitution provided that the question of female suffrage should be submitted to a vote at the first general election, and

it was so submitted, and one third of the votes were cast in its favor. Now it is asked, three years later, that the question may again be submitted to vote, and we ought not to be opposed to giving them a chance to convince us that we are wrong in refusing the women an equal chance to vote. How will it appear to the world if we few men here arrogate to ourselves the right to decide that what thousands of the most intelligent and respectable people in the State ask shall not be granted? Common fairness and respect call upon us to give them the chance to educate us as they think they can. The question of the propriety and right of women's suffrage is not what we are now called upon to consider; we are called upon only to give a large class of people a chance that they ought to have, and by right are entitled to." The bill passed the Senate and came up for a second reading in the House, when a motion to indefinitely postpone was made and lost, and it was referred to a special committee appointed to confer with the Senate Committee on the bill.

A bill was passed creating the new county of Carbonate, in which Leadville was situated. On the second day after, a new bill was passed changing the name to Lake, which was the name of the entire district before the division.

Persons practicing confidence games are made liable to indictment, and on conviction are punishable by confinement in the penitentiary from one to ten years.

Any animal injured or killed not having any mark or brand upon it, or having marks or brands unknown, by the trains of any railroad company, said company shall, within thirty days next after such injury or killing, pay the value thereof, according to the schedule of prices as now fixed by law, to the treasurer of the district association of cattle-growers, within the district where such animal is thus injured or killed. All neat stock found running at large in the State without a mother and upon which there is neither ear-mark nor brand, shall be deemed a maverick, and may be taken in charge by the captain or foreman of a legal round-up and sold at such time and place and in such manner as shall be determined by the executive committee of the district association of cattle-growers of the district wherein such maverick shall be taken up. The proceeds arising from such sales shall be paid to the treasurer of such district association; and if any stock so sold shall within the period of six months immediately following such sale be claimed, identified, and proven by the rightful owner, it shall be the duty of such treasurer to forthwith pay the money received for such maverick to such owner. If no owner appears, the money goes to the fund of the association.

A bill for the preservation of fish was passed, which provides that it shall not be lawful to kill, take, or have in possession any trout or other food-fish, taken or killed in any of the public waters of the State, during the months of December, January, February, March, April, May, and June, or in either of the said months in any year ; and the possession of trout or other food-fish during the months above mentioned shall be *prima facie* evidence of the violation of the provisions of the act. A Fish Commissioner is appointed under an act of the previous Legislature.

The act relative to the location and representation of placer-mining claims provides that "the discoverer of a placer claim shall within thirty days from the date of discovery record his claim in the office of the Recorder of the county in which said claim is situated, by a location certificate which shall contain—first, the name of the claim, designating it as a placer claim ; second, the name of the locator ; third, the date of the location ; fourth, the number of acres or feet claimed ; fifth, a description of the claim, by such reference to natural objects or permanent monuments as shall identify the claim. Before filing such location certificate the discoverer shall locate his claim—first, by posting upon such claim a plain sign or notice, containing the name of the claim, the name of the locator, the date of discovery, and the number of feet or acres claimed ; second, by marking the surface boundaries with substantial posts sunk in the ground, to wit, one at each angle of the claim.

" On each placer claim of 160 acres or more, heretofore or hereafter located, and until a patent has been issued therefor, not less than $100 worth of labor shall be performed or improvements made by the first day of August, 1879, and by the first day of August of each year thereafter. On all placer claims containing less than 160 acres the expenditure during each year shall be such proportion of $100 as the number of acres bears to 160. On all placer claims containing less than twenty acres the expenditure during each year shall not be less than twelve dollars ; but when two or more claims lie contiguous and are owned by the same person, the expenditure hereby required for each claim may be made on any one claim ; and upon a failure to comply with these conditions, the claim or claims upon which such failure occurred shall be open to relocation as if the claim had never been made ; *provided,* that the original locators, their heirs, assigns, or legal representatives, have not resumed work upon the claim after failure and before such location ; *provided,* the aforesaid expenditures may be made in building or repairing ditches to conduct water upon such grounds, or in making other mining improvements necessary to the working of such claim. Upon the failure of any one of several coöwners to contribute his share of the expenditures required hereby, the coöwners who have performed the labor or made the improvements may, at the expiration of the year—to wit, the first day of August, 1879—for the locations heretofore made, and one year from the date of locations

hereafter made, give such delinquent coöwner personal notice in writing, or, if he be a non-resident of the State, a notice by publication in the newspaper published nearest the claim, for at least once a week for ninety days, and mailing him a copy of such newspaper, if his address be known ; and if, at the expiration of ninety days after such notice in writing, or after the first publication of such notice, such delinquent should fail or refuse to contribute his proportion of the expenditure required by this action, his interest in the claim shall become the property of his coöwners who have made the required expenditures."

A large number of important acts of a local nature were passed.

The last reports of the Auditor and State Treasurer show the State's indebtedness on November 30, 1878, as follows :

Warrants outstanding	$191,948 99
Certificates of indebtedness issued	29,861 86
Total debt	$221,810 85
Deduct cash in treasury	68,145 59
	$153,164 46
Add interest on warrants	19,886 51
Estimated interest on certificates indebtedness..	1,500 00
Approved penitentiary vouchers outstanding November 30th	12,125 88
Total	$186,616 80

Deduct amount of warrants outstanding which will be met by special taxes now due	$4,565 60	
Estimated amount of fines and penalties, and receipts from sales of laws and fees of Secretary's office	10,000 00	14,565 60
Total outstanding debt		$172,060 70

The amount of revenue due for general purposes, including tax of 1878	$247,619 58
Deduct old delinquent tax	71,090 06
Amount due to meet present debt	$176,529 52

It was estimated that at the close of the fiscal year 1879 the State would be out of debt. The taxes of 1878 were expected to accomplish that result, while those of 1879 would pay the expenses of that year. State warrants at the beginning of 1879 sold at one per cent. above par, although two years previous they sold at seventy-five cents on the dollar.

The assessment of taxes has awakened some consideration in the State, but a change was made in the law at this session. It requires that "all property shall be assessed at its full cash value," and the duty of adjusting the rates of assessment in the different counties according to this standard devolves upon the State Board of Equalization. From the assessors' returns there appear in one county five times as many acres assessed in 1877 as in 1878, and the average value per acre in 1877 one third as much as in 1876 ; in another county one half as much in 1878 as in 1877. Cattle are returned at from $4 to $20 per head, horses from $20 to $90, and other stock in the same manner. The total assessment of all property for 1878 is $43,072,648, nearly $400,000 less than for 1877, while nearly all the items of which it is composed have increased in number. The Governor, alluding to this subject, says: "The present assessment is about one third of what it should be, and the State is therefore placed in a false light abroad, as the rate of taxation is just three times what it should be. The city and county tax of Denver is about 3½ per cent. Under a proper assessment it would be about one."

The public schools of the State are rapidly increasing in number, and those in the city of Denver are particularly commended for their excellence. The State University is located in the vicinity of Boulder. It consists of a new and extensive building, on an eminence, surrounded by finely cultivated and ornamental grounds. In the interior it is arranged for the accommodation of a large number of students of each sex, with their officers and instructors. The number of students is about one hundred, of whom one half are in the preparatory department. There is also a college attached to the State Agricultural Department, in which much interest is manifested. An Institute for the Mute and Blind is not only well established, but it is crowded with pupils. The School of Mines contains twenty-two students, some of whom were attracted from other States to Colorado on account of the special advantages it offers for the study of certain branches of natural science. At the previous session of the Legislature the office of Commissioner of Mines was created, but no appointment has been made. The law directs the appointment of a deputy and also an assistant Commissioner. The aggregate salaries of the three officers would be $4,900, which sum, together with their contingent expenses, is required to be paid out of the fund for the School of Mines. As this fund is less than $4,500, the appointment of these officers would have closed this institution.

The State Penitentiary has been a source of expense to the State. There is a deficiency of $27,463. The appropriation required from the State for the period of two years is $89,425.

Of the public land entered by the State, 29,146·33 acres have been approved by the President of the United States for the public building fund, 25,226·83 acres for the penitentiary, and 44,844·43 for the university. There is a deficiency in the number of acres confirmed to the State, and the number donated by the enabling act, which can be settled only by an act of Congress. The State lands were made subject to sale after March 1, 1879. The arid lands of the State are so extensive that it has been proposed to obtain a donation of them from Congress, offer them for sale for grazing purposes, and devote the proceeds to the irrigation fund.

The prosperity of the State during the past two years has greatly increased. Agriculture has succeeded beyond the most sanguine expectations, so that a part of its products can be exported. The flocks of sheep and herds of cattle show a large increase, with only a slight decrease in their market value. Probably no kind of investment in the country has proved more profitable during the past ten years than that in the stock business in Colorado. During the entire year both cattle and sheep thrive upon the grasses of the valleys and the plains, the former requiring no hay or grain, and the latter only in cases of severe and unusual snow-storms. The losses by death up to the present time have been very small, not usually exceeding two per cent. of cattle, and not a much larger percentage of sheep. As the expenses of herding and caring for the stock are very light, the natural increase in the herds and flocks is mostly profit. No counties in the State are in a more prosperous condition than those which are chiefly devoted to stock-raising. The cattle-herding was in 1878 steadily prosperous. The following winter of 1878-'79 was one of great severity, but the losses were light. The yearly increase was above the average. The increase in the number and value of cattle has been rapid during the past eight years, as shown by the assessor's returns of 1871 and 1878. For the latter year the number of cattle was returned as 483,278, valued at $4,-928,147; for 1871, 145,916, valued at $2,692,-440; the increase in number being 337,362, in value $2,335,707. The figures do not properly represent the number or value of cattle, which are estimated to be about a third more.

New discoveries of rich mines are constantly made, and towns spring up in localities where a few months previous there was scarcely an inhabitant. The increased production of ore creates a demand for the construction of furnaces and smelting and reduction works. The shipments of bullion and ore for 1879 are expected to exceed $12,000,000. The closest estimate for the year ending June 30, 1878, was $8,908,566. The product for the six years ending December 30, 1878, was as follows: 1873, $4,070,000; 1874, $5,362,000; 1875, $5,486,742; 1876, $6,191,908; 1877, $7,365,284; 1878, $9,820,743.

An election was held in the State to fill a vacancy on the bench of the Supreme Court. A Republican Convention to nominate a candidate assembled at Denver on September 19th. J. M. North was elected chairman, and William E. Beck was nominated for Associate Justice. The following resolutions were adopted:

Resolved, That as Republicans we reaffirm the principles upon which the pa   was founded, in support of which it has achieved such victories as have fallen to the lot of no other party, and to the perpetuation of which we once more pledge our best efforts and our every vote.

Resolved, That it is the duty of Congress at its approaching session, by appropriate and judicious legislation, to restore silver as money metal to its equality with gold; and to this end we demand that it enact a law providing for unlimited coinage of the silver dollar on such terms as shall secure to the people the benefits of gold and silver as a circulating medium.

Resolved, That the Republicans of Colorado, in convention assembled, hear with profound gratification of the return of General Grant to the country he saved, and should he conclude to be a candidate for reëlection we pledge now the six votes of the Centennial State.

The Democratic Convention assembled at Denver on September 23d. G. Q. Richmond was chosen chairman, and subsequently he was nominated as the candidate for Associate Justice. The following platform was adopted:

The Democratic party of the State of Colorado, in convention assembled, renewing its pledges of fidelity to the Jeffersonian doctrine that this is a government of the people, where the will of the people should rule, does hereby declare.

That the grave question to be determined by the American people at the election of 1880 is, whether a republican form of government shall remain to the people, or one republican in name but monarchical in fact. That in the arbitrary action of a fraudulent President, by which he and his party defeated the will of a majority in the Senate and House of Representatives of the American Congress, and maintained the right of the Federal Executive to surround the polling places in all the States with troops, and of deputy marshals to arrest citizens at the polls without oath or warrant, can only mean a determination upon their part to use these agencies to maintain themselves continuously in power; and that in clamoring for the nomination of General Grant for a third term as President they are but seeking the man who, as shown by his repeated acts of usurpation while President, and his unlicensed use of Federal troops to control the domestic affairs of sovereign States, has the will to carry out their revolutionary and wicked designs.

That we denounce the combination of crimes by which the country was cheated and robbed of the rightful possession of the offices of President and Vice President of the United States; that it was a plot and fraud unparalleled in free government, and one which should not be condoned, and must never be repeated.

That the action of the Republican party in demonetizing silver was a perfidious breach of the trust reposed in them by the American people; that the action of the Democratic party in securing its remonetization was an act of justice performed in response to the demands of the people, and one which has made resumption not only possible, but a success.

That as the law now exists the Government discriminates against the silver product of the country, in favor of gold and the creditor classes. That, like gold, the coinage of silver bullion into standard dollars of 412¼ grains each should be continued.

The result of the election was the success of William E. Beck, who received 16,920 votes, to 12,702 for G. Q. Richmond, and 1,246 for G. B. Saulsbury. In each of the four judicial districts the Republican candidate for District Attorney was elected.

The returns of the assessors of the various counties of the State, except Arapahoe, to the State Board of Equalization, of the valuation of property of all kinds, give the following summary:

Routt County	$56,665 00
Gilpin	1,904,924 00
San Juan	820,167 00
Boulder	3,269,255 00
Huerfano	998,012 30
Rio Grande	478,036 00
Fremont	1,262,070 00
Summit	257,277 50
Clear Creek	1,819,006 00
Weld	3,380,190 00
Las Animas	2,553,692 83
Bent	2,782,084 00
Jefferson	2,502,346 00
Lake	3,485,087 00

Douglas	1,086,245 00
Grand	60,050 75
Larimer	1,724,820 00
El Paso	3,750,880 00
Ouray	249,507 00
Chaffee	409,944 00
Park	955,458 94
Saguache	724,084 00
Costilla	179,596 00
Elbert	1,558,867 00
Gunnison	185,685 00
La Plata	303,075 38
Pueblo	3,389,400 00
Hinsdale	647,818 00
Custer	716,727 00
Grand total	$41,263,550 70

To this should be added the assessment of Arapahoe County, 16,520,693 00

Following is a summary of the grand totals of stock: Horses, 57,107 heads, valued at $2,136,768; cattle, 424,040 head, valued at $5,640,178; sheep, 664,059 head, valued at $1,075,308; swine, 8,918 head, valued at $35,215.

In the assessment of railroad property the Board made an increase over that of 1878 from $1,200 to $2,000 per mile, in order to bring the railroad property up to an equality with other property in the State. The returns of their work present the following results:

MILEAGE.

Broad-gauge roads	758·16
Narrow-gauge roads	460.44
Total	1,218·60
Total in 1878	1,044·47
Increase during year	174·18

TOTAL ASSESSMENTS.

Broad-gauge	$4,950,747 72
Narrow-gauge	2,736,709 81
Total	$7,687,457 08
Total in 1878	4,975,074 22
Increase	$2,712,382 81

ASSESSMENTS OF ROADS.

Denver and Rio Grande	$2,020,960 00
Pueblo and Arkansas Valley	1,741,080 72
Kansas Pacific	1,484,411 92
Colorado Central	1,227,297 56
Denver Pacific and Boulder Valley	698,478 93
Denver and South Park and Pacific	893,700 00
Union Pacific	84,087 90
Arkansas Valley	55,860 00
Golden, Boulder, and Caribou	28,300 00
Knox's Road	2,600 00
St. Vrain	2,000 00
Longmont and Erie	600 00
Golden and Platte	500 00

Some interesting facts were presented at the meeting of the State Board of Health relative to climatic influences in the State. The instance of Leadville was presented, where two years ago there existed a sage-covered valley whose population scarcely numbered a score, but where there has sprung into existence a city with a present population of over 12,000, and whose increase is at the rate of 2,000 per month. This rapid accumulation of humanity—drawn from almost every portion of the continent, transplanted suddenly to an altitude of over 10,000 feet above sea-level, many of them living under circumstances of comparative discomfort, and ignoring the most important hygienic laws—promises to furnish an opportunity for observing the development of exotic diseases under new conditions; and, although at this time a few facts may be brought in review, they can not, without further and more extended observation, be formulated and made available for purposes of study. By far the larger part of the population live in hastily built houses of wood, unplastered and devoid of most of the concomitants of comfort. In the hotels, boarding-houses, and lodging-houses a system of crowding necessarily prevails, that in many localities would be productive of much disease. In many of the boarding-houses about the mines the conditions are even worse. The bunk-rooms are often arranged to contain two or three times as many occupants as should be lodged in them, often located above the cooking rooms, and receiving through the loose floor or open stairway all the odorous gases from below; beds used both by night and day by alternate occupants, according to their hours of labor, and never subjected to the purifying influence of outdoor air and sunshine; slops, bones, and refuse thrown outside, and remaining near the doors for months. These are the conditions under which many of the miners live—conditions that, under greater degrees of heat and moisture, would breed pestilences from which none could hope to escape. In the city itself the greatest neglect of sanitary precautions may be observed. In the back lots and alleys may be seen heaps of filth and garbage in which are stored the potential germs of manifold disease, only waiting the liberating influence of the spring sun to call them into action and enable them to begin the work of destroying human life, opposed by no disinfection save that which is furnished by the incomparable climate. Thus far the city, notwithstanding its crowded condition and lack of comfort, the irregular hours and hurried unsettled life of the greater portion of the population, and the almost criminal neglect of sanitary measures by the authorities, has not shown an unusual amount of sickness or a large mortality. The total number of deaths occurring in Leadville and the surrounding country during the seven and a half months ending February 15th, as collected from the records of the various undertakers, was 115. The average population for this time by conservative estimates was 9,000. This gives an annual death rate of about 2 per cent. From the above total at least 25 per cent. may be deducted for deaths due to violence, accidental or criminal, and those that may be fairly attributed to intemperance.

Some remarks were made on the subject of clothing. When thermometrical changes are so frequent and sudden and great as in this altitude, the subject of proper clothing becomes at once important and suggestive; and the further fact that nearly two thirds of the present population are to some extent *invalid*, makes it imperative on the medical profession to advise, promptly and positively, as to the changes necessary to protect the bodies and persons of their patients. The fall and most of the winter months the weather is generally very pleasant during the forenoon of each day, but often soon after noon becomes windy and sometimes quite unpleasant. The morning then is inviting. The invalid feels the necessity and the benefit of a ride or open-air exercise. Late rising unfortunately is the rule, and almost invariably the start is made as late as eleven o'clock. The air is balmy; the sunbeams fall warm and pleasant, and, in spite of the kind advice of mother, wife, or friends, the party insists that the present wrappings are quite sufficient. A cold is the consequence, and several days of confinement and doses of medicine follow. From the first of November until the first of May, and sometimes later, the thermometric changes range from 10° to 30° during the twenty-four hours. True, the atmosphere is dry, and this change does not produce the results that an equal change in the lower altitudes does and will; yet, to preserve health, these changes must be met by a corresponding change in clothing. The body must be protected in all such cases—in the robust as well as the debilitated—or harm to some extent will and must be the consequence. Again, this protection of the body is carried to the extreme in the other direction. How many times the physician stands with stethoscope in hand (when a patient presents himself for the first time at the office for a careful examination of the lungs), waiting and watching. Coat and vest are removed, then shirt after shirt, until several great, heavy flannels —enough to tire a common horse to carry— are laid aside, and the "end is not yet." A complete case of chamois skin, buckskin, or perhaps red flannel lined with some of these, and known as "chest protectors," perfectly impervious to air, water, and perhaps lightning, is then removed. In such cases disease is certain—if not from hereditary or acquired cause, most assuredly from abuse in careful protection.

The following plan was proposed at the session, by which pure air may be introduced into any room or building without the least draught, giving free, pure ventilation without exposure or any possible chance of the air striking the patient or sleeping occupants of the chamber, or seated congregation of a public building, until it has passed the entire circuit of the room. It consists of a single flanged piece of zinc, galvanized iron, tin, or sheet-iron, attached to the upper sash of the window, so arranged that, when the windows are lowered two inches (sufficient for pure ventilation), the flange or protector extends half an inch above the casing, leaving a half-inch space. The side-pieces are fastened to the casing on the inner side at a certain distance from the top, so that the flange, when the window is opened the desired distance, will come exactly even with them, thus forming a complete box, compelling the air as it rushes in to ascend to the ceiling. No air can possibly escape from either side, and, when the window is closed, the side-pieces are not in the way, the whole being no incumbrance or inconvenience, not interfering with any kind of curtain, blind, or drapery.

An exciting contest broke out between the Denver and Rio Grande and the Atchison, Topeka, and Santa Fé Railroads, which at one time reached such a pitch of violence as to make it necessary for the Governor to call out a military force to preserve the peace. The editor of the "Denver Tribune" has furnished full details of the grounds of conflict, from which it appears that about 1870 the Rio Grande road commenced from that city with the intention of ultimately reaching the capital of Mexico. At this time the English road-gauge of three feet was introduced and adopted by the Rio Grande. The road soon became popular, and after several years was extended, first to Pueblo and afterward to Cucharas; from Cucharas to El Moro; from Pueblo by a branch line to Cañon City; and afterward from Cucharas to La Veta, and across the Sangre de Cristo range of mountains to Garland, and thence to Alamosa, on the banks of the Rio Grande. At the time when the construction of the Atchison, Topeka, and Santa Fé road reached Pueblo, the Denver and Rio Grande controlled the trade of southern Colorado in every direction, and was in excellent position to make a move in the way of building. It had the advantage of being nearer important passes in all directions than any other line. From El Moro it commanded the Raton Pass and the route via Las Vegas and the trade about Trinidad and southeastern Colorado and New Mexico, except that portion lying along the Rio Grande River. This latter section and the San Juan country was controlled by the branch to Alamosa or into San Luis Valley. Here also the Rio Grande people had the advantage of having a road built over the Sangre de Cristo mountains, a formidable barrier, and an opening line building along down the Rio Grande as far as it might be desirable to go. The Cañon City branch ended almost in the mouth of the Grand Cañon of the Arkansas, almost the only southern opening to the Upper Arkansas and Gunnison centers, and one of the most desirable and feasible routes to the San Juan. Thus fortunately situated, they controlled the trade of the entire south, besides seeming to possess every advantage. An understanding with this line was indispensable to the Santa Fé, whose terminus was at Pueblo. On the other hand, the Santa Fé became of importance to the Rio Grande. The first road was the great trunk channel for the outlet and inlet of the business collected by the Rio Grande. That the two roads should work together in harmony was the most natural thing in the world. In fact, they were regarded as almost an unbroken line from the Missouri River to Denver and other points covered by the Rio Grande. The most perfect harmony prevailed.

But this blissful state of affairs lasted no longer than until the Santa Fé people began to show their ability and desire to be independent. Such a step as this on the part of the Santa Fénians was not for a moment to be thought of. The Rio Grande officers resisted. This led to a strife between the two companies, which has been going forward with occasional remissions since March, 1878. It began on the Raton Mountains, which at the point of crossing constitute the line between Colorado and New Mexico. The Santa Fé began to assert its intention of building into New Mexico and of continuing its line toward the Pacific Ocean, in accordance with its original plans. It was one bright, crisp, frosty morning that the Rio Grande people awoke to the knowledge that the Santa Fé company had decided to run a branch line of their road across the country from La Junta, a station in Colorado some eighty miles east of Pueblo, to Trinidad. Here, the terminus of the Rio Grande road being at El Paso, only four miles distant, the roads would become competitors, and the Santa Fé would have the same chance to command the Raton Pass and the trade of New Mexico as the Rio Grande road. Almost before the parties knew it themselves, each company had a hundred men in the pass asserting its right of way by preparing the way for the road of its line. Intense excitement was the natural consequence, and the wildest rumors were set afloat concerning affairs at the point of contact. It was more than once reported that the employees of the two roads had come together, and that several had been killed. Fortunately, in each instance the report was successfully contradicted. This contest attracted great attention. It soon bounded from a matter of local importance to a place where the entire country looked on with interest. It then became generally understood for the first time that the Santa Fé road had aspirations to cross the continent. The prospect of creating a transcontinental line which should destroy the vast monopoly which was said to be extorting money from the public in all directions was greeted with the heartiest good feeling from every source. Hence the fight on the Raton Pass became a subject widely known and spoken of. The Atchison Company began at the same time to build its line from La Junta. It has now been many months since the road was completed to Trinidad, over the switchback into New Mexico, and it is now striking hard for Las Vegas in the heart of the Territory, with an excellent prospect of opening its line to the Pacific during 1880. It has certainly "scooped" the New Mexico business from the Rio Grande, even if that road should continue in possession of the line which it now holds. It only remains to be said concerning this fight that the Santa Fé people made short work of their opponents, and were soon masters of the entire situation, leaving not even a taste for the Rio Grande.

This affair was followed by another of the same nature, which became even more famous than the one just spoken of. Reference is made to the Grand Cañon war—the fight for the possession of the right of way through the Grand Cañon of the Arkansas—the most sublime and terrible gorge in the eastern slope of the Rocky range. This fight has since figured in one shape or another in nearly all the State and Federal courts, from the police court at Cañon City to the Supreme Court of the United States. It began on the 19th day of April. It was born on the 18th, or perhaps sooner. It is agreed between the parties that there was considerable cipher telegraphing, and it is generally believed that the Rio Grande people possessed themselves of the key to the Santa Fé's cipher; that they sat in their offices at Denver and at Colorado Springs, and became acquainted with the design of the Atchison, Topeka, and Santa Fé company to begin to build a road through the Grand Cañon. While the Raton war was still raging quite furiously, the discovery was made that the Rio Grande people were likely to be attacked at two points at once. Leadville was just then beginning to be an important point for consideration, and the Rio Grande people decided, as between the Grand Cañon and the Raton Pass, to concentrate their efforts on the Cañon. Having ascertained, as above stated, that the Santa Fé people expected to begin operations in that great chasm, the Rio Grande folks attempted to offset them by getting in first, with the idea that if they were the first to obtain possession it would be impossible to oust them. A spirited scramble ensued. Mr. Strong, General Manager of the Atchison, Topeka, and Santa Fé road, was on April 18th at El Moro, where he heard of the preparations which were going forward on the part of the Rio Grande people to cut him out. He at once made application for a special train to carry himself and men from the spot. The Santa Fé Railroad had not then been completed from La Junta. The Rio Grande people refused the train. Thus he was shut up in that little town, without power to get away, when it was so important that he should be elsewhere. Nothing was left to do but to call in the assistance of the telegraph. Engineer Morley of the same road was at La Junta. He was instructed to take a special train to Pueblo and outrun the Rio Grande people for the Cañon. Men came into Pueblo as if on wings, arriving there at 3 o'clock on the morning of the 19th. He asked for a train, but it was refused. At the same time the Rio Grande parties were making preparations to send one hundred men, duly equipped, to the site where the interest centered. Morley was in a corner apparently, but he lost no time. He procured the fastest horse that could be found, threw himself astride his back, and turned his head toward the mountains. He had forty-five miles of road before him and a special train to compete with. It is needless to say that he rode

fast. The horse was killed, but the goal was gained. He rode into Cañon thirty minutes ahead of the train. He did not have a man at his back, but this was an obstacle of very little importance to him. He found Cañon City already in arms against the Rio Grande, and ready to do anything in the world to bring another road into the city. They were sick and disgusted with the Rio Grande and its explorations. Almost to a man the citizens threw off their coats—professional and non-professional men; all laid down the shovel and hoe employed in their usual avocations, to take up the pick. When Engineer McMurtrie of the Rio Grande road arrived on the scene with his hundred followers, he found what was to him a surprising state of affairs. Morley with his one hundred and fifty civilians had taken possession of the mouth of the Cañon and had graded a firm piece of road-bed. Thus began the cañon contest, which was unsettled fourteen months afterward. The attorney for the Santa Fé, Mr. Gast, now applied to the county judge of Fremont County, and obtained an injunction against the Rio Grande parties. The matter was soon brought before the United States Court at Denver. The Atchison, Topeka, and Santa Fé Company then was known technically as the Cañon City and San Juan Company, the name of a local organization. The Rio Grande claimed possession because of a special act of Congress, and the Santa Fé people set forth that they had filed the proper plats of surveys as required by law with the Secretary of the Interior, and that the Cañon City and San Juan Company had not done so. Though often enjoined by Judge Hallett of the U. S. District Court from remaining in the cañon, the Rio Grande men staid there day after day and week after week. Up to this time no one had ever penetrated the Royal Gorge, except in winter when the river was covered with ice, and then but very few went in because of the great danger. Now, however, the Royal Gorge was the home of hundreds of men. They swarmed in there like bees in a hive, climbing about from place to place almost like flies on the wall. There were at one time 1,500 men in the cañon attached to one side or the other. They had no communication with the outside world except that afforded by rope-ladders suspended over perpendicular walls a thousand feet high. During this time the men were armed, and an open outbreak and bloodshed was at all times imminent. It was feared that there would be war on a great scale, and the militia practically lay on their arms for a fortnight. Several parties were arrested for transgressions of the law. Indeed, the excitement ran up almost to the fighting point, and remained there for two weeks. At last a truce was called. The white flag was raised. That happened in this way: The Rio Grande people had become so thoroughly offended with the Santa Fé people that they had long since annulled all traffic contracts with that road, and had sold themselves to the Northern combination, including the Union Pacific, the Kansas Pacific, and the Colorado Central. Thus the Santa Fé was cut out of Denver completely. The Rio Grande would do nothing to accommodate them. This was a disagreeable circumstance, and it was agreed that it must be remedied. The most expeditious way in which to accomplish this end was to build a road from Pueblo to Denver. The road was incorporated and the engineers sent out. They located their line, and the money was at once subscribed to construct it. The Rio Grande people were quick to see that such a line as this would ruin them, and hence they agreed to lease the constructed portion of their road to the Santa Fé Company. This lease was effected on the 19th day of last October. The Rio Grande people took their men out of the cañon, but said that they desired to have the case go forward in the courts as to the right of way. The money was paid over for running stock and implements, and the lease sealed and signed for thirty years.

Soon Leadville began to be a most important point. Emigration poured in and business improved immensely. It was then that the Rio Grande people began to wish that they had their road back. They had no other reason, and their wishes in the matter were the hot-bed out of which have been sprung any number of schemes. As soon as it was determined to make this effort there was a great gathering at Denver. Very soon after a suit was brought in El Paso County, in the name of the people, requiring the Atchison, Topeka, and Santa Fé Company to show cause why it operated roads in Colorado. The case was appealed to the Supreme Court of the State. Subsequently another bill was brought, in Costilla County, requiring that the Atchison, Topeka, and Santa Fé Company should be enjoined from operating railroads in Colorado. Judge Bowen granted the writ, and it was served, and the Rio Grande people took possession by force of arms, killing three men in doing so, and wounding several. The former company then applied to the U. S. District Court for a writ of restriction against the Denver and Rio Grande Company for a return of the property. Judge Hallett, with Mr. Justice Miller concurring, said :

Without going into discussion whether firearms were used, whether any one was killed during the controversy, whether violence was used, it may be assumed, I think, upon all that is stated upon both sides here, that this road was not peaceably surrendered by the Atchison, Topeka, and Santa Fé Company to the Rio Grande Company; that some force was used under this writ to obtain possession; and, if that be true, the result is the same whether the force was much or little. The fact remains that, under a writ which did not authorize any such proceeding, this company obtained possession of this property; and whether the Atchison, Topeka, and Santa Fé Company quietly yielded to the force of the writ as it was interpreted to them, and gave up under protest, or after some show of force was made, or after force was actually used, the result is the same in either case—the possession of the property was unlawfully obtained. It only remains to say upon all that, if these things are true, that process of the Court was used in some way to obtain possession of this property, and unlawfully used. And if so, it appears to me that, before any other proceeding is taken in the cause, the parties are entitled to be restored to the possession in which they were before the writ was issued ; that is to say, the Atchison, Topeka, and Santa Fé Company is entitled to have this property restored to them.

The controversy continued to rage in the courts and out of them with increased bitterness, until it was finally terminated by the action of the U. S. District Court in placing the Rio Grande road in the hands of a receiver.

Meanwhile the Atchison, Topeka, and Santa Fé Company proceeded with the construction of the road through the Grand Cañon, which was a stupendous achievement in railroad engineering. The Grand Cañon of the Arkansas is now known to be eleven miles in length, and the gorge a mile and a half, being the narrow winding way of that river through a converse palisade of granite rock, rising in many places to the height of 2,500 feet. This rock-bound river pathway became known to the Spanish missionaries as early as the year 1642. From that time it was not known that any animal life had ever passed through it successfully until the summer of 1870. The first train passed over the road on May 7th, and the event is thus described by the Denver paper :

On reaching the cañon the engine was placed in the rear, so as to give a better view to the tourists. The approach to the cañon is gradual. The distant hills draw nearer, and the valley of the Arkansas becomes narrower and narrower until the river is shut in closely on both sides by high mountains, sloping gently away, and covered with verdure. Then the slope of the mountains becomes more perpendicular, and the hills become higher, until suddenly the river is completely shut in by mountains with mighty tops. The roar and rattle of the train grows louder, and echoes up and down. The train is fairly in the cañon. It moves slowly. The mountain walls are of a dizzy height, and so close together that, looking ahead, they appear simply to form a crevice—a huge, awful crevice—through which the miserable little train was timidly crawling. The curves of the cañon are superb. They constitute the finishing touch to its grandeur, and fill the mind with a fuller appreciation of this great miracle of nature. But the Royal Gorge ! Imagine two almost perfectly perpendicular walls rising to a height of 2,500 feet, and only thirty feet apart, those walls presenting jagged and irregular masses of rock that on the railroad side hang over the train, all creviced and ready to fall in thousands of tons. The road-bed is cut out of the solid rock, and masses of this hang over it, stretching out a hundred feet. One can not look to the top of this wall on account of these projecting, irregular bluffs ; but the height to the top, even as measured by the eye, disturbs the faculties and brings on vertigo. The cooped-up Arkansas rushes madly by, a narrow thread, made still more so by the rocks thrown into it. There is not room to step from the train without pitching into the river, Not a word is uttered. The engineer whistles occasionally, and timid folks look for the rocks to fall. It is really a strain on the mind to take it in, and this can be only feebly done on a single trip. Two thousand feet above you are the tops of the mountain walls. You are imprisoned in a crack thirty feet wide, and are partially under one mountain wall. You can see on the opposite side the gradations of the verdure, rich below, impoverished above. And the curves become more awful as you look ahead or back. For forty-five minutes the tourists enjoyed this sight. The train stopped at the construction bridge, near the end of the gorge. Salutes were fired, a fifteen-minutes' halt was made, and the engine started the train for Cañon City. There was no sun in the gorge, but it slanted down the opposite mountain wall as the party returned through the cañon, increasing the surpassing beauty of the scene.

Leadville, which has become the most famous spot in the State, was first noticed during the Pike's Peak excitement. At the same time the placer mines of California Gulch, Stray Horse Gulch, and Iowa Gulch were discovered. The population of the region reached 10,000, and in four years about $13,000,000 in gold was gathered. The miners worked only for gold, and the carbonates, which have since become so valuable, were then only dirt and greatly in the way, getting into their sluice-boxes and making a vast amount of trouble. They piled them up anywhere to get them out of the way. In 1874 the placer mines were practically abandoned, and, although since worked at intervals to some extent, they have caused no great excitement. In 1877 they yielded about $70,000 in gold, and can only be worked during the warm weather of the summer. In August, 1877, some twenty shanties comprised the whole town of Leadville. In June, 1878, it had a population of only 400. In October, 1878, it numbered 6,000, and in April, 1879, it had a population of 12,000 to 15,000, with an additional daily floating population of from 1,000 to 3,000, and new-comers flocking in at the rate of 300 to 500 a day and seven days in the week. The cause of this sudden growth was the fact that the carbonates which had been rejected by the gold-miners were found to be very rich in silver. In October, 1878, the first smelting furnace at Leadville was blown in. Since that time, up to August 1, 1879, the several smelting establishments have smelted 48,659 tons of ore, from which have been produced 9,958 tons of bullion, containing 3,401,283 ounces of silver. The value of this silver is stated at $3,725,000, that of lead at $197,420; and there were also produced 211 ounces of gold, worth say $4,000. A large quantity of ore was shipped from Leadville to Denver, Omaha, St. Louis, and other reduction works, both before and since the erection of smelters at Leadville. The value of this ore shipped up to August 1st was about $5,500,000; making a total value of Leadville's production up to August 1, 1879, $9,426,420. Since that date the ore smelted has amounted to about 600 tons a day, yielding an average of perhaps $80 per ton; and there have been shipped per day ten tons, averaging $150 per ton—more than $1,250,000 a month.

COMMERCE, INTERNATIONAL. The intimate and vital bond of international commerce by which the nations of the world are linked together for their mutual weal, but

which, when it is disturbed, causes the hardest sufferings among the inhabitants of the most advanced and prosperous of the sisterhood, is, with its present delicate and all-pervading ramifications, an entirely modern development, dating from the close of the Napoleonic wars. From 1815 to 1872 the commercial and industrial growth of all countries advanced with an even and almost unbroken progress. Production has everywhere increased faster than the population, and consumption in every commercial nation has multiplied. Wars and natural calamities have temporarily and locally interfered with the regular course of the advancement; and at intervals, with an almost astronomical periodicity, in 1837, 1847, 1857, and 1866, general commercial crises occurred, which swept away many mercantile houses who had made a too free use of their credit in a time of unusual speculation, and entailed severe losses on money-lenders. But the effect of these crises was only momentary; the arrest of productive activity has been very brief and transitory in each case, and in a few months at the most commerce and production, purified by the winnowing process, bounded forward again with renewed and heightened activity.

The growth of the system of commercial interdependence, and the slight and transitory effects of former commercial crises, are apparent in the history of the export trade of Great Britain, the pioneer and chief representative of international commerce. The volume of the exports of British products from the United Kingdom to all countries, for each year from 1836 to 1872, were, in millions of pounds sterling, as follows: 1836, 53; '37, 42; '38, 50; '39, 53; '40, 51; '41, 52; '42, 47; '43, 52; '44, 59; '45, 60; '46, 58; '47, 59; '48, 53; '49, 64; '50, 71; '51, 74; '52, 78; '53, 99; '54, 97; '55, 96; '56, 116; '57, 122; '58, 117; '59, 130; '60, 136; '61, 125; '62, 123; '63, 146; '64, 160; '65, 166; '66, 189; '67, 181; '68, 179; '69, 190; '70, 200; '71, 223; '72, 256. The exportation from France, which amounted to 376 million francs in 1810, and had grown to 515 millions in 1837, in the period from 1867 to 1876 averaged 3,407 million francs a year, the single article of silk goods amounting to 437 millions in 1872, and that of woolens to 314 millions. The exports from the United States increased in the same ratio, the domestic exports of merchandise summing up to the following amounts, given in millions of dollars, in the successive years from 1835 to 1872: 1835, 100; '36, 106; '37, 94; '38, 95; '39, 101; '40, 111; '41, 103; '42, 91; '43 (9 months), 77; '44, 99; '45, 98; '46, 101; '47, 150; '48, 130; '49, 131; '50, 134; '51, 178; '52, 154; '53, 189; '54, 213; '55, 192; '56, 266; '57, 278; '58, 251; '59, 278; '60, 316; '61, 204; '62, 179; '63, 186; '64, 143; '65, 136; '66, 337; '67, 279; '68, 269; '69, 275; '70, 376; '71, 428; '72, 428. This gigantic development has been the result of various combined and reciprocally acting causes—

tho application of steam, the perfection of machinery, the development of capitalistic production, and steam transportation over the ocean and across the breast of the continents. One of the main conditions without which this progress would not have been possible has been the removal of restrictions on foreign commerce, first by England, then by France and other countries, and finally by China, Japan, and other remote nations. Another cause, whose importance can not be overestimated, was the increase of the metallic currency of the world, which is the life-blood of trade, by the discovery of the Californian and Australian gold-fields. Before 1848 the stock of metallic money in the world is estimated to have been $5,000,000,000. In 1868 it was $7,000,000,000. This enormous increment did not cause a sudden and abnormal disturbance of values, but was gradually assimilated, producing a slow and even rise of prices, quickening production, and stimulating commerce, allowing it to extend its operations to the remotest parts of the earth.

The present aggregate volume of the world's commerce, according to the computation of Professor Neumann - Spallart of Vienna, is $14,000,000,000. Europe's share is $9,976,000,-000, or 71·26 per cent. of the total international commerce. The aggregate exports of European countries amount to $5,650,000,000; their imports are $4,336,200,000. The American nations have a total foreign commerce of $2,140,-000,000, or 15·30 per cent. of the world's total commerce; their imports amount to $972,-800,000, their exports to $1,167,200,000. The share of Asia and the South Sea Islands in the whole is 8·08 per cent., or $1,131,000,000, with $489,000,000 imports and $641,600,000 exports. Australia and the islands of the Pacific participate to the extent of $462,000,000, or 3·29 per cent., with imports aggregating $237,-800,000 and exports $224,400,000. The aggregate commerce of Africa is $291,000,000, 2·07 per cent. of the whole; its imports are $134,-400,000, its exports $156,600,000. Reckoning the population of Europe at 289,000,000, the amount of commerce per capita is $34·52. America, with a population of 84,840,000, has a commerce of $25·22 per capita. The international trade of Asia, counting its population 806,700,000, is but $1.40 per capita. Australasia's population is given as 1,800,000; its foreign commerce would therefore amount to $256·77 per capita. Africa, with an estimated population of 80,000,000, has a commerce of $3·62 per capita. The total imports of all nations, according to this estimate, sum up $7,-474,400,000, the total exports $6,526,000,000. The disparity between the aggregate values of the imports and exports is partly explainable by the fact that the cost of freight, marine insurance, and other charges, are included in the valuation of imports, whereas exports are assessed at the bare manufacturer's price, understated also in many exports of dutiable articles.

The foreign commerce of each particular country is given in the following tables:

EUROPE.

COUNTRIES.	Imports.	Exports.
Great Britain	$1,876,000,000	$1,284,000,000
Germany	978,000,000	687,000,000
France	797,000,000	715,000,000
Russia	384,000,000	322,000,000
Austro-Hungary	267,000,000	297,000,000
Netherlands	303,000,000	226,000,000
Italy	265,000,000	248,000,000
Belgium	289,000,000	212,000,000
Spain	115,000,000	127,000,000
Turkey	92,000,000	50,000,000
Sweden	79,000,000	62,000,000
Denmark	64,000,000	50,000,000
Norway	49,000,000	29,000,000
Portugal	81,000,000	26,000,000
Roumania	16,000,000	28,000,000
Greece	24,000,000	35,000,000
Servia	6,000,000	8,000,000

AMERICA.

COUNTRIES.	Imports.	Exports.
United States	$485,000,000	$604,000,000
Brazil	100,000,000	107,000,000
Canada	99,000,000	85,000,000
Argentine Republic	86,000,000	49,000,000
Chili	32,000,000	88,000,000
Cuba	30,000,000	85,000,000
Peru	25,000,000	89,000,000
Mexico	30,000,000	38,000,000
English West Indies	23,000,000	20,000,000
French West Indies	12,500,000	15,500,000
Uruguay	14,000,000	18,500,000
Porto Rico	15,500,000	9,000,000
Venezuela	18,200,000	12,000,000
Central America	7,200,000	15,600,000
English Guiana	9,200,000	15,400,000
Colombia	7,200,000	10,600,000
Hayti	9,000,000	8,900,000
Newfoundland	7,600,000	6,800,000
Bolivia	5,800,000	5,000,000
Ecuador	1,200,000	4,000,000
St. Domingo	1,800,000	1,600,000
Dutch Guiana	1,400,000	1,200,000
French Guiana	1,400,000	200,000

ASIA.

COUNTRIES.	Imports.	Exports.
East Indies	$177,000,000	$295,000,000
China	103,500,000	121,000,000
Straits	58,000,000	45,600,000
Java, etc	27,600,000	61,000,000
Japan	27,400,000	26,800,000
Ceylon	26,800,000	30,200,000
Cochin China	13,400,000	17,600,000
Sumatra, etc	14,000,000	16,400,000
Siberia	16,800,000	7,600,000
Siam	7,800,000	9,000,000
Persia	5,400,000	2,800,000
French Indies	1,400,000	3,000,000
Formosa	1,600,000	2,000,000
Labuan	600,000	600,000

AUSTRALASIA, ETC.

COUNTRIES.	Imports.	Exports.
Victoria	$88,400,000	$73,800,000
New South Wales	67,400,000	68,400,000
New Zealand	40,000,000	29,200,000
South Australia	21,000,000	24,200,000
Queensland	16,800,000	19,200,000
Tasmania	6,000,000	5,400,000
Western Australia	1,800,000	2,000,000
Sandwich Islands	1,600,000	2,200,000

AFRICA.

COUNTRIES.	Imports.	Exports.
Egypt	$29,200,000	$66,000,000
Algeria	42,800,000	88,400,000
Cape Colony	25,600,000	20,400,000
Mauritius	11,400,000	18,200,000
Réunion	4,400,000	5,000,000
Natal	5,200,000	3,200,000
Morocco	2,400,000	8,600,000
Tunis	2,400,000	8,400,000
Senegal	2,200,000	2,800,000
Zanzibar	2,200,000	2,000,000
Portuguese colonies	1,800,000	1,200,000
Tripoli	1,400,000	1,400,000
Gambia	600,000	1,000,000

Since 1872 the whole commercial world has been languishing under some depressing influence which has afflicted production and trade with a progressive paralysis, from which there are yet no hopeful signs of recovery. This drooping atrophy and shrinking away is different from any of the sharp and sudden commercial crises that preceded it, which convulsed and disturbed the whole credit system, but which only for a moment checked the advancing march of production and commercial extension. Various causes are assigned for this fatal and protracted depression and gradual collapse of trade. The exhaustive effects of wars must undoubtedly manifest themselves in a succeeding period of privation and severer labor before the wasted capital is replaced and the lost time regained. The extension of productive facilities in all countries beyond the consumptive requirements of the people must result in a sharp struggle for trade, a lowering of prices, a depression of wages, and a diminution of profits. But this process has taken place before repeatedly with the best ultimate results; and to assign it as the cause of the present decline of consumption is not only to deny in a great measure the destruction of capital in wars, but to contradict all historical precedents. The discontent and revolutionary attitude of the productive classes, and their continual strikes and demands, might have the effect to alarm capital and discourage production and enterprise; but there is no evidence that they have produced any such results. Another cause, which has recently been asserted by merchants and bankers practically versed in the phenomena of international trade, may have more to do with the present unprecedented decay of commerce and prostration of industry than any of the others. This is the threatened demonetization of silver by European countries, and the actual fall in its value in consequence of the change of standards and conversion of its currency by the German Empire. Since the first agitation of the question in Germany prices have been declining, and with declining prices in these days of the telegraph and steamship, when mercantile operations are calculated on a minute fractional margin for profits, it is impossible to produce or export without a constant loss. If the disturbance in values caused by the conversion into gold of the silver currency of Germany, and the sale of about $300,000,000 worth of silver, is the cause of the present long and distressing prostration of trade, the action of the other western nations with reference to the 1,500 millions of silver which they still possess is a question of the most vital consequence to civilization. The present prices are based upon the present combined stock of gold and silver in the world, nearly six thirteenths of which consists of silver. Before values can be adjusted to the single standard of gold, the whole fabric of international commerce must fall into ruin, industry and art must decay, population must be thinned out by misery and starvation, and the most advanced races must physically and intellectually deteriorate.

The world's stock of gold and silver money is estimated for 1878 at about 7,850 millions of dollars, of which 4,250 millions is in gold and 3,600 millions in silver coin. The stock of metallic money is distributed in the different countries in the following proportions, given in millions of dollars:

COUNTRIES.	Gold.	Legal-tender silver.	Token silver.
Great Britain	675	....	90
India and British Colonies	225	1,500	35
France and Latin Union	1,550	650	55
Germany	500	95	100
Other European States	350	150	45
American Continent	225	200	120
China, Japan, and other countries	725	560	...
Total	4,250	3,155	445

The statistics of international commerce and domestic production show an absorption, during the ten years from 1866 to 1875 inclusive, of the precious metals in the European countries for which official returns are given to the following amounts in millions of dollars: France, 689; England, 356; Belgium, 230; Russia, 209; Spain, 130; Holland, 50; Portugal, 9; Sweden, 9; Austro-Hungary, 8; Norway, 5; Italy, 1. The total absorption in the above eleven countries is 1,699 million dollars. This sum fails to agree with the statistics of the world's production, given by Soetbeer for the same period as 2,008 million dollars, and of the absorption of Asia, calculated at 562 millions. Deducting the 387 millions produced in Europe, the products of extra-European mines would be 1,621 million dollars. If 1,365 millions of this was absorbed in the above European states, the rest of the world would have but 256 millions to dispose of, or 306 millions less than the amount sent to the East; while the United States during the same period retained 65 millions of the 669 millions produced, and other gold- and silver-producing countries must have kept back a portion of their yield.

The effect of the present depreciation of silver is to most seriously interfere with the intercourse between the gold- and the silver-paying countries, besides its depressing influence on general prices and prosperity. The trade of England with the gold-paying countries showed an actual increase of over 5 per cent. between 1874 and 1878; but in the British trade with most of the bi-metallic countries there was a decline of 32 per cent., and with the countries with the single silver standard of nearly 22 per cent., or of 30 per cent. if India is not counted. Between 1872 and 1878 there was an increase of the exports of British products to countries where the gold standard prevailed of 9 per cent., but a decline of 33⅓ per cent. in the values of the exports to silver-paying countries. The loss to Great Britain in exchange alone in last year's trade with India is computed at 75 millions of dollars, so great is the disturbance caused by the want of a common medium of exchange. If the single gold standard were permanently adopted in Europe and America, intercourse with the Orient would be reduced to barter trade. Even if the single gold standard were safely and successfully adopted all over the world, and values should accommodate themselves to it without destroying the whole progress of the nineteenth century, there would remain another evil connected with it, one from which the world has abundantly suffered in former centuries, and that is a deficient supply of metal to replace the waste of the coin and correspond to the increase in the population.

The general decline of British exports since 1872, the year when they had attained their greatest magnitude, was in the following progression, in millions of pounds sterling: Exports in 1872, nearly 256; 1873, 255; 1874, 239; 1875, 233; 1876, 200; 1877, 198; 1878, 192. The aggregate decline from 1872 to 1878 amounts to 214 million pounds sterling. The exports of British and Irish products in 1879, estimated on the returns for the first half of the year, show a further decline in values of 8 or 10 millions sterling.

The fall in prices within five or six years, when computed for the aggregate production, presents sums of startling magnitude. Of the decline of 42 per cent. in the exports of the leading British manufactures between the years 1872 and 1875, one fourth corresponds to the diminished demand and three fourths to the fall in prices. Of this fall, one half is offset by the corresponding abatement in the prime cost of materials. The decline of 6s. per ton in coal from 1873 to 1878 represents a fall in value for the quantity mined in Great Britain of 200 million dollars a year.

An important consideration regarding the alteration of the existing standards of valuation is the effect which it would have on the solvency of countries which owe large public debts. This specially affects the nations in which the largest amounts of foreign public securities are held. The aggregate public indebtedness of all nations is computed by Ernest Seyd at 22,245 million dollars. Of this amount,

he considers the following state debts, amounting to 9,150 millions of dollars, as almost entirely held in the countries themselves: England, 3,925 millions: France, 3,750 millions; Germany, 825 millions; Holland, 400 millions; Belgium, 180 millions; Denmark, 70 millions. The remaining 13,095 millions he reckons as held principally by other nations, viz.: the debt of the United States, 2,000 millions; Russia, 1,875 millions: Austria, 1,730 millions; Spain, 1,300 millions; Italy, 1,255 millions; Turkey, 1,075 millions: India, 530 millions; Egypt, 475 millions; Mexico, 395 millions; Brazil, 340 millions; Portugal, 330 millions; the British colonies, 315 millions: South American and other small states, 1,475 millions. The amount of the public debt of these nations held in foreign countries is estimated at 10,000 millions, and its present value at 8,500 millions. This aggregate amount is supposed to be held in a few European countries, among which it is distributed in the following proportions: England, the richest nation in foreign state funds and other foreign investmnets, owns 3,750 million dollars, or nearly the amount of her own public debt, in the state securities of other nations, estimating them at their present current values and not at the par of issue; France, 2,250 millions; Germany, 2,000 millions; and Holland, Switzerland, and Belgium together, 500 millions. How nearly the above estimate approximates to the actual European holdings of foreign securities, there are no more accurate data for determining than those at the command of Mr. Seyd. The national debt of the United States, however, must be stricken from the list of public securities held abroad, the main bulk of it has now returned to America. The securities of many of the indebted governments are of very uncertain value under the most favorable commercial conditions. Loud complaints have been heard in Great Britain of late at the swindling foreign loans, public and private, which have been successfully placed in the English market. The losses which have accrued to British investors through worthless foreign investments are immense. A nearer examination of the facts reveals in these operations methods of going to work which well deserve the name of swindling; but the persons who manipulated the loans and deluded the investing public, and who invariably received the lion's share of the plunder, were British bankers and financial agents. The Turkish Government, for instance, can show that it has already paid in interest more than it ever received of its public loan from the English go-betweens. The South American states and a great many financial companies in different parts of the world can relate the same experience.

In France the decline of exports since 1873 has been less marked than with the other great commercial powers of Europe. She is not, however, exempt from the general calamity, but is suffering more and more acutely from a depression in her textile industries and a prostration of her coal and metal trades. The decline of French exports has been in the following progression: 1873, total exports 3,787 million francs; 1874, 3,701 millions; 1875, 3,872 millions; 1876, 3,575 millions; 1877, 3,436 millions. During the same period her imports have increased, having been 3,554 million francs in 1873, 3,507 millions in 1874, 3,536 millions in 1875, 3,988 millions in 1876, and 3,669 millions in 1877. In all articles except the prime necessaries of life, and particularly in all manufactures in which they compete with Great Britain, all the countries of Europe complain of a constantly declining export, or, if an increased export is shown for a single year, of the ruinous prices at which it has been achieved.

While the older settled industrial lands, whose products consist of the luxuries of life or go to satisfy the material requirements of a complex civilization, have been suffering from loss of trade and an industrial stoppage, in certain newer food-producing countries, although they also have had to endure the effects of the general financial derangement, the exports have been steadily growing in value, and have increased in a still more remarkable ratio in quantity, during the present period of depression. The most conspicuous example of this enlargement of trade is America. The extension of manufacturing operations, which preceded the present season of contraction and distress in Great Britain and other industrial lands, was in great measure induced by the demand for extended means of transportation and improved implements of agriculture in the countries which possess a vast area of more fertile and tillable land than Europe; and now these same countries are enabled, with the improved means of transportation, to pay off, even at the present depressed rates of value, the debts incurred for their completion under the inflated prices of a half dozen years ago, by furnishing cheaper food than can be produced in Europe. The United States has thus been in a position, through an excess of exports of merchandise and bullion in the five years from 1874 to 1878, to pay more than $130,000,000 a year of interest and principal of foreign debts. In the magnitude of their export of food-products the United States now greatly surpass all other nations. The development and importance of the trade of the United States in cereals and provisions is shown in the following *résumé* of the international trade in the articles which best reveal the present condition of the world's commerce.

BREADSTUFFS.—In the ante-bellum period the exports of American grain to Europe were for the most part in the form of flour. Since the opening up of railroad communications with the upper Mississippi valley, and the immense extension of the export trade, the exports of wheat-flour have increased but very little, and are principally confined to the supply of the West Indies and South America. Even though the grain could be manufactured into flour more cheaply in the United States than in Europe, the greater facility with which the grain can be handled, stored, and transshipped in its raw state, by the aid of modern machinery and appliances, would preclude the exportation of the manufactured product. The elevators of Chicago in 1876 had storage-room for 19¼ million bushels of grain, and those of Milwaukee for 4½ million bushels.

The imports of wheat into Great Britain during the years 1872-'77, according to Mr. Caird, amounted, in consequence of three bad harvests, to 87 million pounds sterling more in value than in the preceding period of the same number of years. Before 1860 the average annual importations of wheat into Great Britain were 4,500,000 quarters; in the last five years they have been 12,400,000 quarters. Before 1868 the average consumption of wheat for sixteen years was 311 lbs. per capita; since that date it has increased to 335 lbs. per capita, of which 158 lbs. is grown inland and 183 lbs. imported from abroad; whereas between 1852 and 1860, of the same quantity of wheat, 252 lbs. were of domestic growth and 79 lbs. imported. Besides the growing dependence of England on foreign nations for wheat, the main article of food with her people, the importations of other food-products have increased in a similar ratio. The imports of maize from America have increased from 600,000 to 1,300,000 tons; those of potatoes, principally from Germany, from 43,000 to 300,000 tons. The consumption of foreign products in Great Britain has risen in the last twenty years from 128 million pounds sterling in 1857 to 285 millions in 1877. The consumption of foreign meat has increased within the twenty years 360 per cent.; of cheese, butter, and lard, 280 per cent.; of imported wheat, 157 per cent.; of other grains, 176 per cent. The consumption of sugar during the same period has increased 84 per cent.; that of tea, 102 per cent., or from 69 to 149 million lbs., while that of coffee has declined 7 per cent. The consumption of tobacco has grown 41 per cent. Since the conclusion of the commercial treaty with France the use of foreign wines has constantly been increasing, the percentage of the increment during the period under consideration being 170; while the importation of spirits has also risen 140 per cent. The above statements refer to the average annual imports of 1857 and the two following years, compared with the average imports of the three years preceding 1877. In 1867 the consumption of domestic wheat was 40 million cwt., that of foreign wheat 38 million cwt.; in 1876 the consumption of home-grown wheat was 43 and that of imported wheat 50 million cwt. The consumption of domestic meat in the years 1867 and 1877 was about the same, 25 million cwt., but the use of foreign meat developed in the ten years from 2 to 6 million cwt.

The following table gives the average annual exports of wheat, wheat-flour, and maize from the United States, in English cwts. :

YEARS.	Wheat.	Flour.	Maize.
1849.........	818,322	3,689,023	6,628,654
1850.........	326,063	2,424,584	3,297,546
1851-'55.....	1,762,173	4,602,930	2,890,520
1856-'60.....	4,158,061	6,222,393	2,759,790
1861-'65.....	14,818,597	6,915,206	5,261,308
1866-'70.....	8,746,752	4,009,175	4,799,327
1871-'75.....	24,002,058	5,571,474	14,615,291

The exports from the close of the civil war have been for the different years as follows :

YEARS.	Wheat.	Flour.	Maize.
1865.........	5,823,474	4,557,948	1,406,868
1866.........	2,907,573	3,820,387	6,758,825
1867.........	8,292,790	2,375,185	7,444,911
1868.........	8,539,768	3,688,740	5,578,745
1869.........	9,405,576	4,255,773	8,528,598
1870.........	19,587,822	6,060,833	696,057
1871.........	18,377,628	6,394,222	4,913,154
1872.........	14,155,221	4,400,486	17,245,825
1873.........	21,002,207	4,488,650	19,270,965
1874.........	38,057,104	7,164,664	17,217,303
1875.........	26,418,129	6,914,400	14,499,310
1876.........	29,503,453	6,887,146	24,796,786
1877.........	21,603,006	5,851,414	85,480,491
1878.........	38,788,872	6,907,833	42,780,549

Converting the flour into its equivalent in wheat, we find that while the export in the years 1851-'55 averaged 7,515,000 cwts., in the period 1871-'75 it had risen to 31,341,000 cwt. In the course of twenty-five years it had quadrupled. Far the largest proportion of the exports go to England, and they suffice nearly to supply her demand for foreign wheat. As the European demand at present governs the prices of grain in America, so the supply of American wheat since the extension of railroad communications in the western part of the United States has a controlling influence on the prices in Europe, where the crops are never so abundant as to check the constant stream of American exports, as they may be the fitful supplies from Australia, India, and Egypt, and where the farmers everywhere are complaining of the ruinously low prices of American grain with which they must compete. Thirty years ago, from 1846 to 1850, nearly 32 per cent. of the English imports came from Germany, and nearly 20 per cent. from Russia, France furnishing over 9 per cent., and the United States only 6·2 per cent. In the next five years, 1851-'55, the imports from America had risen to 11·6 per cent. of the whole supply, Germany's share being 29 per cent., and Russia's 16 per cent. In the period from 1856 to 1860 America's proportion was 18·8 per cent., Germany's 23½ per cent., and Russia's 19·8 per cent. In the succeeding period, 1861-'65, the imports from the United States advanced to 32·1 per cent., while those from Germany remained at 23 per cent., and those from Russia at 20 per cent. Under the unusual stimulus to exportations furnished by the war, the United States had then driven all the minor

competitors out of the English market, in which they have not been able since to effectually assert themselves. In the following period, 1866-'70, the causes of this abnormally active exportation had ceased to operate, and only 22·8 per cent. of the British imports were derived from America, Russia sending 33 per cent. and Germany 18 per cent. In the next period, 1871-'75, the vast lengths of railroad were completed, which link the pioneer of the prairie more closely to the operative in an English factory than the groaning tenant farmer of the northern shires, and which enabled America to drive Germany out of the field, and even to crowd upon the position of the wretchedly housed and fed and lately enslaved peasantry of Russia. In this last period the imports from the United States into Great Britain were 40·9 per cent. of the whole, those from Russia 27·1 per cent., those from Germany 8·2 per cent. ; while Canada furnished 7·5 per cent., and small supplies first began to arrive from British India and Australia. In 1876 the American imports were 43·5 per cent. of the total, the Russian 19·7 per cent., the Indian 7·4 per cent., and the Australian 6 per cent. In 1877 39·3 per cent. came from the United States, 20 per cent. from Russia, 11·3 per cent. from India. All the maize exported from the United States goes to England, where it has almost entirely supplanted the products of Turkey and Moldo-Wallachia, which between 1860 and 1870 supplied 40 to 50 per cent. of the requirements of Great Britain. This grain is not used in Great Britain as human food except to a very limited extent, but is fed to cattle and consumed in the distillation of spirits.

Germany and France, which could formerly supply England from their surplus products of wheat, have become grain-importing countries, France on account of recent bad harvests, and Germany perhaps permanently. Germany, where rye is used principally for bread, has not imported to any amount directly from the United States, although she has received considerable quantities of late from Holland and Belgium, who have to import largely from America to supply their own wants. France with an average crop is able to supply her own necessities. Her importations are very variable, and are partly dependent on an extensive manufacturing and export trade in flour. The values of the total imports and exports of wheat and flour for the last seven years, given in millions of francs, were as follows: 1872, imports 147, exports 247; 1873, imports 229, exports 175; 1874, imports 330, exports 139 ; 1875, imports 138, exports 202; 1876, imports 239, exports 146 ; 1877, imports 206, exports 190; 1878, imports 577, exports 58. The failure of the crop in the South of France in 1878 obliged the French dealers to seek abroad for supplies to fill up the large deficiency, estimated at 20 million hectolitres. In the first part of the year Russia shipped large quantities, but later the American wheat poured in, driving the prices down to a low figure in spite of the poor harvest.

The production of grain in British India and Australia is rendered uncertain and variable by the severe droughts to which both of those countries are occasionally subject. The English Government aims to encourage the exportation of wheat from the colonies, and to enable them to supply as far as possible the requirements of Great Britain. Since the removal of the export duties the exportation of wheat from India has grown to large proportions. From Bombay, Calcutta, and the other ports the exports of wheat in 1877 were 6,105,-000 cwt., as compared with 4,839,000 cwt. in 1876, 2,498,000 cwt. in 1875, 1,069,000 cwt. in 1874, 1,756,000 cwt. in 1873, and 849,000 cwt. in 1872. In South Australia and New Zealand, as well as in British America, the production of wheat and other cereals has been greatly extended within a few years.

In potatoes there is not much international trade except between the Continent of Europe and England, who imports large quantities of this food, mostly from Germany. The total European production of potatoes is estimated at 1,317 million cwt. per annum, of which 440 million cwt. are raised in Germany, 245 in Great Britain and Ireland, 224 in Russia, 150 in Austria, 130 in France, 40 in Norway and Sweden, 34 in Belgium, 33 in the Netherlands, 14 in Italy, and 7 in Denmark.

PROVISIONS.—The exportation of animal food-products from the United States in the latest period has more than kept pace with the extension of the grain-trade. The war of secession gave the first impulse to this branch of the export trade, which has now developed into gigantic proportions, and occasions no less anxiety to the European farmers than the competition of American grain. Great Britain is by far the largest consumer of this class of American products also. The importations of lard and bacon into England from the United States during the five years from 1856 to 1860 inclusive averaged 197,898 cwt. (1 cwt.=112 lbs.). Within the last ten years they have increased over fivefold, as is shown by the following comparative statement: Imports of American hams and bacon—1868, 428,377 cwt.; 1869, 474,808 cwt.; 1870, 348,819 cwt.; 1871, 823,010 cwt.; 1872, 1,758,068 cwt.; 1873, 2,626,876 cwt.; 1874, 2,096,099 cwt.; 1875, 2,196,203 cwt.; 1876, 2,753,556 cwt.; 1877, 2,506,513 cwt. In the last few years Canada has exported the same articles in variable quantities, ranging from 30,000 to 90,000 cwt. a year. In 1878 the British imports of these commodities were 50 per cent. greater than in the preceding year, amounting to 4,263,901 cwt., nearly the whole of which was furnished by America. The exports of bacon and hams from the United States have increased in the last ten years in the following progression: In 1869 the quantity shipped away was 49 million lbs.; in 1870 it receded to 38 million;

in 1871 it was 71 million; in 1872, 246; in 1873, 395; in 1874, 347; in 1875, 250; in 1876, 327; in 1877, 460; and in 1878, 592. The imports of lard into Great Britain from the United States have also been very considerable for several years past. From 1866 to 1870 they averaged 157,858 cwt.; in 1871 they were 442,545; in 1872, 561,099; in 1873, 557,897; in 1874, 339,932; in 1875, 502,474; in 1876, 505,359; in 1877, 570,429. In 1878, as in the case of hams and bacon, they took a sudden leap forward, exceeding by at least 50 per cent. the imports of 1877: the total imports of lard into Great Britain were 562,174 cwt. in 1876, and 592,264 in 1877; in 1878 they suddenly grew to 908,187 cwt. Germany consumes yearly equally great quantities of American lard; in 1878 her imports from the United States amounted to 820,000 cwt. Many other countries depend largely on America for their supplies of this cheap and important article of food. The exports of lard from the United States have increased with unexampled rapidity in the last ten years. The total lard export in 1869 was 41 million lbs.; in 1870, 35 million; in 1871, 80; in 1872, 199; in 1873, 230; in 1874, 205; in 1875, 166; in 1876, 168; in 1877, 234; and in 1878, 342.

The trade in salt beef and pickled pork between the United States and Great Britain has sunk into a very subsidiary position compared with the other classes of provisions; still, it has undergone a development which, if it has been slow, has also been regular. Of salt beef the imports into England from America averaged 157,000 cwt. from 1856 to 1860, 191,000 from 1861 to 1865, 169,000 from the latter year to 1870, and 198,000 from then till 1875; in 1876 they were 236,277, and in 1877, 204,-507. The average importation of salt pork from the United States was 54,000 cwt. from 1856 to 1860, 69,000 from 1861 to 1865, 60,-000 from 1866 to 1870, 179,000 from 1871 to 1875, 291,604 in 1876, and 243,004 in 1877.

The imports of butter and cheese from America into Great Britain have also assumed enormous dimensions of late years. This branch of trade dates its origin from the impetus given to exports by the necessities of the civil war. The exports of butter to the English market were almost nothing before the war; but during the war they suddenly assumed a magnitude which they have not again attained since, being 180,274 and 142,000 cwt. in 1861, '62, and '63. Between 1866 and 1871 they had receded to only 19,000 cwt. per annum; but during the late depression the cheapness of the American article has enabled it to assert itself again in the English market, the imports having risen to 118,000 cwt. in 1876 and 188,000 in 1877. The exports to England from Canada also are very considerable, amounting to 98,000 cwt. in 1876 and 56,000 in 1877. England is the largest consumer of butter among all the nations of the world, and draws supplies from all the pastoral lands of Europe as well as from

America. The annual consumption per head of population in Great Britain is estimated at not less than 105 lbs. In 1876 France sent 622,000 cwt. into England, Holland 403,000, Germany 234,000, and Denmark 205,000. That these great quantities do not consist exclusively of the natural product of the dairy is evident from the fact that not only in the United States, but in Holland, France, Germany, and Austria, large factories are employed in the manufacture of artificial butter from tallow and fat; in two of the largest of these establishments in Holland 400 cwt. of fat is worked up into this substance every day.

In contrast with the fitful exportations of butter, the trade in American cheese has undergone a more even and natural development, showing a steady increase in almost every successive year during and since the civil war, and advancing at a rate of progression that is unparalleled by any other commodity. Between 1856 and 1859 the annual imports of American cheese into England averaged 56,000 cwt.; in 1860 they rose to 187,000, and the following year to 323,000 cwt. Between 1866 and 1870 they averaged 494,000 cwt.; in 1871 they were 731,000 cwt.; in 1872, 598,000; in 1873, 790,000; in 1874, 849,000; in 1875, 958,000; in 1876, 936,000; and in 1877, 1,082,000. The Canadian exports of cheese to Great Britain, which were only 10,000 cwt. in 1865, increased rapidly until they reached 279,000 in 1875, but receded to 250,000 in 1876, and 214,000 in 1877. Although America has grown thus suddenly to be the largest exporter of this product among all the nations of the world, the cheese-producing countries of Europe have not diminished their exports, the greater quantity of which go likewise to Great Britain. The exports of France in 1876 were 182,000 cwt.; those of Holland, 456,000; and those of Switzerland, 402,000. The imports of cheese into Great Britain in that year amounted to 1,531,000 cwt. About the same quantity is produced annually in the British Islands. The yearly consumption of cheese in the United Kingdom is estimated at 10 lbs. per capita.

The exportation of fresh meat and live animals from America to England is a trade of quite recent origin, which has grown to important dimensions after various fluctuations. After a number of disastrous experiments, the first successful attempt to regularly supply the English market with living cattle transported across the ocean in good condition, on steamers specially constructed to allow the beasts the necessary fresh air and daily exercise, was made by Canadians in 1875. In that year 1,212 head of cattle were exported to England from the Dominion; in the following year, 2,655 live oxen and steers and 2,607 sheep; in 1877, 7,639 live cattle, 6,825 sheep, and 373 hogs; in 1878, 32,115 head of cattle, 62,461 sheep, and 1,798 hogs. The exports of living animals from the United States began to assume considerable proportions in the year 1877,

and in 1878 they far exceeded the Canadian shipments, and began to make a powerful impression on the price of meat in the British market. The imports of living animals from the United States into England are reported as only 299 cattle in 1875 and 392 in 1876; in 1877 they are given as 11,538 cattle, 13,120 sheep, and 226 swine; in 1878, 68,450 cattle, 43,940 sheep, and 16,321 swine. In the report for the latter year a large portion of the Canadian exports are included in the invoices from the United States; the total shipments from the United States and Canada together in that year amounted to 86,439 cattle, 84,072 sheep, and 16,321 hogs. In February, 1879, an unfair blow was dealt to the export trade from the United States by the issue of an order of the Privy Council, on the pretended or supposed discovery of a case of pleuro-pneumonia on one of the vessels, to the effect that all American cattle should be slaughtered on the foreign animals wharves, which are very few in number, and the largest of which is at Deptford, near London. This enabled a small ring of London cattle-dealers to buy up nearly all the United States shipments at their own prices, and occasioned severe losses to shippers. The same discrimination was not made against the Canadian cattle. The influence of the English landholders and of the farmers' interest was at the time brought to bear on the Government to induce it to compel all foreign cattle to be entered and slaughtered at the foreign animals wharves. If this arbitrary application of the Contagious Diseases (Animals) Act is maintained for the protection of British landlords and stock-raisers, this large and promising trade will be nearly destroyed. It will not suffice, however, to keep American meat out of the English markets, since a still more recent improvement in the means of transportation enables American shippers to supply the British consumers with fresh meat in good condition. After many unsuccessful attempts, a method of refrigeration has been perfected, by which butchers' meat is transported across the ocean in large, cold, air-tight chambers, from which all germs of putrefaction have been expelled, and through which is passed a constant current of dried and purified air. Mr. Eastman, a New York cattle-dealer, made the first thoroughly successful attempt to transport fresh meat, with a cooling apparatus constructed by J. J. Bate, in 1876. The same year J. H. Wickes devised another refrigerator, with which a line of steamers sailing between Canada and England were provided. The extension of the fresh-meat trade in consequence of the adoption of the new system of refrigeration commenced in April, 1876. The imports of slaughtered American beef into Great Britain in 1875 amounted to but 3,098 cwt.; in 1876 they had risen to 144,336; in 1877 they were 439,440, and in 1878, 479,118. For the latter year a large part of the Canadian shipments are probably included. In 1876 the direct shipments from Canada were 638 cwt., and in 1877 they had swollen to 19,939.

SUGAR.—The exports of cane-sugar from all the principal sugar-growing countries, according to the latest reports, were as follows, in millions of centals and decimals of millions: Cuba, 10; Java, 4·56; British, Dutch, and Danish West Indies, 5; Brazil, 3·6; Manila, 2·63; Mauritius, 1·8; Martinique and Guadeloupe, 2; Porto Rico, 1·6; China, 1·68; Peru, 1; Egypt, 0·8; Central America and Mexico, 0·8; Réunion, 0·6; British India, 0·56; Australia, 0·43; British Guiana, 0·15; Cape Colonies, 0·15; Sandwich Islands, 0·26; Spain, 0·3. The immense production of India and China has generally only sufficed for their domestic consumption. The exports from India were already large in 1857; but for a long time they were seldom seen in the world's market, and only within a few years have they again begun to compete with the products of other countries. The exportation of sugar from China, which is capable of indefinite extension, is a quite recent phenomenon. The total exports from all countries of cane-sugar amount to perhaps 41 million cwt., of which 22 million is consumed in Europe and 13½ million in the United States. England is the chief consumer of cane-sugar, taking in the year 1877 as much as 15 million cwt.

The Continental peoples depend chiefly upon beet-root sugar. The total sugar-crop of Europe for the season 1874–'75 was 23 million cwt.; 1875–'76, 27 million; 1876–'77, 25 million; 1877–'78, 25 million. Of the crop of 1876–'77, 6·5 million cwt. was produced in France, 5·8 in Germany, 4·1 in Austria, 5 in Russia, 0·9 in Belgium, and 0·5 in Holland.

The total consumption of sugar in the four chief consuming nations in 1877 was approximately as follows: England, 17·6 million cwt.; United States, 13·3; Germany, 5; France, 4·7. The annual consumption per capita in the different European countries is estimated to be at present as follows: England, 26 kilogrammes; Germany, 20; Holland, 11; Belgium, 10; France, 7; Sweden, 7; Austria, 4·75; Switzerland, 4; Italy, 3·75; Spain, 3; Portugal, 2·75; Russia, 2·75; Turkey, 1·5.

The production of beet-root sugar in France, which averaged in the five years from 1838 to 1843 about 30 million kilogrammes, during the period of five years between 1872 and 1877 averaged 392 million kilogrammes per annum. About 500 factories are engaged in this industry. Their annual products during the last five years were reported as follows: for the season 1872–'73, 408 million kilos; 1873–'74, 397; 1874–'75, 451; 1875–'76, 462; 1876–'77, 243. In the year ending August 31, 1879, the exports of beet-root sugar from Germany were 2,796,913 cwt., of which 585,- 629 cwt. was refined. In the preceding year the exports were 1,978,496 cwt., of which the proportion of refined sugar was 437,315 cwt.

WINES.—The commerce in wine is up to the present confined principally to European varieties; yet in these it exceeds in volume the tea and coffee trades taken together. The total wine-production of Europe is estimated at 146,123,000 hectolitres. The average production of the different countries is at present as follows: France, 56,160,000 hectolitres; Italy, 31,500,000; Austro-Hungary, 22,640,000; Spain, 20,000,000; Germany, 6,500,000; Portugal, 5,000,000; Russia and Turkey, 2,134,000; Greece and Cyprus, 1,150,000; Roumania, 662,- 000; Switzerland, 377,000. The consumption of French champagne wines in different countries has been estimated as follows, reckoned in millions of bottles and fractions of millions: United States, 10; England, 5; Russia, 2; France, 2; Germany, 1·5; Holland, 0·6; Italy, 0·5; Belgium, 0·5; Spain, 0·3; Africa, 0·1. The wine-production of France has been subject of late years to enormous variations, as may be seen from a statement of the yearly production: 1873, 35,715,000 hectolitres; 1874, 63,146,000; 1875, 83,837,000; 1876, 41,846,000; 1877, 56,405,000. The loss entailed upon France by the damages of the phylloxera has been estimated up to 1878 at over two milliards of francs, or $400,000,000.

In 1874 the territory devoted to the culture of the vine in France amounted to 2,446,862 hectares, the largest acreage which had ever been attained. Owing to the ravages of the phylloxera, it has steadily contracted since that year; by 1877 the reduction amounted to more than 150,000 hectares, and in 1878 the extent of soil planted was further decreased by 50,000 hectares. The departments of the south have been the principal sufferers, those most affected being Aude, Bouches-du-Rhône, Charente, Lower Charente, Dordogne, Gard, Hérault, Lot, Var, and Vaucluse. In other portions of France there has been an extension in grape-culture, the most signal development being in the departments of the Eastern Pyrenees and Yonne. In 1878 the oidium made its appearance again, and added its devastations to those of the phylloxera. The wine-crop for the year was 48,700,000 hectolitres, 7,705,000 less than the crop of 1877, and 8,093,000 less than the mean crop of the last ten years. While Languedoc, Provence, and Dauphiny were severely scourged, the departments of the east and center showed an increased yield.

Nearly all of Italy's large production of excellent wines is consumed in the country itself, the export not exceeding 1 per cent. of the production, although they increased from 291,- 000 hectolitres in 1873 to 498,000 in 1876. In the Austrian empire about 615,000 hectares of land are devoted to the culture of the vine, two thirds of which is in Hungary. Of the admirable Hungarian wines also the exports are small compared with the domestic consumption. Spain, out of a total of $100,000,000 yearly exports, sends abroad heavy and artificially alcoholized wines of the value of $30,000,-

000, nearly all of which go to England. Although the consumption of the lighter wines of France has been steadily gaining in Great Britain since the conclusion of the reciprocity treaty, it has not yet approached the amount of the heavy Spanish wines consumed, the imports of port and sherry being 10,657,000 gallons in 1877, and those of French wines 6,643,-000 gallons. The British imports of German wines amount to less than half a million gallons, those of Italian wines slightly more. The total consumption of wine in Great Britain 1877 was about 16 million gallons, of the total value of about 37½ million dollars. The production of wine in the United States is slowly but decidedly extending. The culture of the vine at the Cape of Good Hope is declining, the exports of Cape wines having steadily diminished from 319,000 gallons in 1863 to 93,000 in 1866, 88,000 in 1870, 75,000 in 1873, and 55,000 in 1875. These wines are only used to adulterate other sorts.

TOBACCO.—The total world's production of tobacco can not be estimated with any satisfactory degree of accuracy. The tobacco-growing States of the American Union furnish the largest and most productive area devoted to this staple. The total production of the United States is probably at present as much as 400 million lbs. The exports of leaf-tobacco from American ports amounted in 1878 to 283 million lbs., against 282 million in 1877, 218 million in 1876, 223 million in 1875, 318 million in 1874, 213 million in 1873, 234 million in 1872, 215 million in 1871, and 185 million in 1870. From the surplus of the American crop all the European states derive the greater part of their supplies. The Cuban exportation, in consequence of the civil disturbances in the island, fell to 5 million lbs. of tobacco and 139 million cigars in 1876, and 8 million lbs. of tobacco and 88 million cigars in 1877. Large quantities of Central American tobacco are worked up in the Havana factories, and a great number of European-made cigars are shipped there to be reëxported with the Havana brand. Not one half of the cigars dealt in as Havana cigars are supposed to be made from tobacco grown in Cuba. Another Spanish colony, the Philippine Islands, plays an important part in the international tobacco trade: out of 93 million cigars exported from Manila in 1874, 93 million in 1875, and 84 million in 1876, 49 million were taken in China, 142 million went to India and Singapore, and 33 million were sent to Europe; besides which 11 or 12 million lbs. of raw Manila tobacco are annually received in Europe. China, Japan, and the Straits Settlements have a considerable export trade in tobacco, which in the two former countries however has receded since 1873, in which year the Chinese exports were 2 and the Japanese nearly 5 million lbs., those of the Straits Settlements being 212,000 lbs.; in 1876 the Chinese exports were 1,431,000, the Japanese 785,000, and those of the Straits Settlements

435,000 lbs. Holland receives from her colonies enough to supply her own large requirements and leave a considerable surplus for exportation; Java alone produces for export in a propitious year over 30 million lbs., and did export over 40 million in 1874, and 37 million in 1875. All the states of South and Central America produce more or less tobacco to export. Nearly all the European states supply their requirements in part with their own products. The total European crop is supposed to average 260 million lbs. Austria, although the largest tobacco-producer of the European countries, her crop in 1876 being 971,000 centners (1 centner = 50 kilos), is receiving larger and larger quantities each year of foreign-grown tobacco; the imports increased from 106,000 centners in 1869 to 492,-000 in 1875. The 400 or 500 centners produced in Germany do not satisfy a third of her requirements. France produces about 30 million kilos per annum, and imports an equal quantity. Russia's production in 1876 amounted to 40 million kilos; Italy's was 4½ million, Holland's 4 million, and Belgium's not quite 2¼ million kilos. The very considerable production of Asiatic Turkey, Syria, Persia, and Algiers is not to any extent exported except to the bordering lands.

The annual consumption of tobacco per capita in some of the principal tobacco-consuming countries has been estimated as follows: Holland, 4½ lbs. per head of population; Germany, 3₇/₁₀ lbs.; United States, 3 lbs.; Austro-Hungary, 2¼ lbs.; Cuba, 2₃/₁₀ lbs.; Italy, 1¼ lb.; Russia, 1 lb.

The importations of manufactured tobacco into Germany in 1871-'72 were 48 million kilos; in 1872-'73, 76 million; in 1873-'74, 34 million; in 1874-'75, 42 million; in 1875-'76, 46 million; in 1876-'77, 49 million. Almost the whole of the importations are American tobacco through the ports of Bremen and Hamburg. Bremen, in 1876, imported 53 million kilos of tobacco, 48 million of which was from the United States, and exported 45 million, 38 million of which was American tobacco. The consumption of tobacco per capita in Germany is estimated at 1·50 kilo in the seven years preceding 1870, and 1·83 in the succeeding seven years. The culture of tobacco in Germany has shown a tendency to decline within a few years. There was an increase up to the year 1874, when 30,500 hectares were under cultivation, and 54 million kilos were harvested. In 1875 the crop was 42 million kilos; in 1876, 37 million; in 1877, 31 million, the acreage in the mean time having fallen to 21,735 hectares. The cultivation of tobacco is confined almost entirely to the Rhine valley; 31 per cent. of the area devoted to this crop is situated in Baden, 24 per cent. in Prussia, 21 per cent. in Bavaria, and 16 per cent. in Alsace-Lorraine. The production in 1874 and the years immediately preceding was stimulated by the prospect of the restoration of the import duties on tobacco, which question was being agitated at that time.

The monopoly of tobacco in Italy was carried into effect in the year 1869. The manufacture was made the exclusive privilege of the society called the *Régie*, in consideration of a rent paid annually to the state, with a certain share in the profits as an additional royalty. During the first six years of the monopoly the domestic crop of tobacco increased from 3,673,-569 kilos in 1870 to 4,421,418 in 1875; and its value from 1,968,779 to 2,439,948 francs. The consumption of tobacco per capita is 0·708 kilo, of the value of 5·47 francs. The sales increased from 14,252,619 kilos in 1868, the year before the establishment of the monopoly, to 17,658,-347 in 1874; the next year they fell off to 17,-001,000 kilos, and have been gradually increasing again since then. The total receipts from the sales of 1876 were 134,053,132 francs, of which 41,816,795 francs represented the total cost of the materials, manufacture, and sales, and 92,236,337 was net profit. The share of the *Régie* in this profit was 5,093,827 francs; the rent paid in to the Government amounted to 79,484,891 francs; the share of the state in the profits was 5,093,827 francs, besides 2,563,-792 francs which proceeded from supplementary taxes. The home production has not kept pace with the increase in the importations from abroad: in 1871 the domestic growers furnished about 28 per cent. of the total quantity required by the *Régie*, and in 1875 not more than 19 per cent. Italy has therefore become a large consumer of foreign tobacco. The *Régie's* purchases abroad were 9,341,511 kilos in 1871, 14,299,250 in 1872, 12,837,021 in 1873, 15,148,423 in 1874, 19,393,609 in 1875, and 18,-375,031 in 1876. The largest part of the foreign supply is purchased in the United States, whence about 75 per cent. of the imports were derived in 1871, and over 80 per cent. in 1874, 1875, and 1876. The imports of tobacco from the United States for the several years were as follows: 1871, 6,948,145 kilos, value 7,669,511 francs; 1872, 10,549,405 kilos, value 13,902,-493 francs; 1873, 10,470,078 kilos, value 11,-974,690 francs; 1874, 12,865,131 kilos, value 15,544,532 francs; 1875, 15,472,440 kilos, value 25,039,686 francs; 1876, 15,060,020 kilos, value 20,634,298 francs.

COTTON.—In the cotton trade and industry the year 1878 was one of unprecedented depression. The extension of manufacturing facilities in all commercial countries during the period of inflated values and over-stimulated consumption before 1873 necessitated a fierce struggle for trade in the subsequent period of diminished consumption. The short grain-crops in Europe and the famines in India and China lessened the power of consumption, and occasioned a great fall in the prices of the manufactured stock; while no corresponding decline took place in the price of raw material, owing to the short supply of cotton. The deficiency, compared with 1877, amounted at one time to

700,000 bales; while raw cotton declined in average price in Liverpool $\frac{4}{16}d.$ to $\frac{1}{4}d.$ per lb. below the level of 1877;' the prices for yarns in Manchester declined for the twelve months $1\frac{1}{16}d.$ to $1\frac{4}{16}d.$, and manufactured goods $\frac{3}{4}d.$ to $1\frac{1}{16}d.$ per lb. The British imports for 1878 amounte to 3,015,840 bales, an increase of 225,920 bales American, with a decrease of 189,580 bales Brazilian, 109,300 Egyptian, and 90,110 East Indian; the net decrease for the year was 182,250 bales. The average import price in 1878 was $6\frac{4}{16}d.$ per lb., against $6\frac{1}{4}d.$ in 1877, $6\frac{1}{4}d.$ in 1876, $7\frac{1}{16}d.$ in 1875, $9\frac{4}{16}d.$ in 1873, $8d.$ in 1871, and $11\frac{4}{16}d.$ in 1869. The annual consumption of Great Britain for the last ten years, in millions of pounds, was as follows: 1878, 1,176; 1877, 1,237; 1876, 1,274; 1875, 1,230; 1874, 1,266; 1873, 1,246; 1872, 1,175; 1871, 1,205; 1870, 1,071; 1869, 939. The quantities and values of the British exports of cotton manufactures for ten years were as follows, in millions and tenths of millions:

YEARS.	Yarns.		Piece-goods.		Hosiery.	Total value of exports.
	Lbs.	£	Yards.	£	£	£
1878...	250·5	13·0	3,606·0	47·7	5·1	65·9
1877...	227·6	12·2	3,823·0	51·9	4·9	69·7
1876...	232·1	12·7	3,656·6	49·9	4·9	67·6
1875...	215·4	13·1	3,547·8	58·1	5·4	71·7
1874...	220·5	14·5	3,587·1	54·8	5·8	74·2
1873...	214·6	15·8	3,466·5	55·8	5·5	77·3
1872...	212·8	16·6	3,517·5	59·2	5·2	80·1
1871...	198·6	15·0	3,395·1	62·8	4·8	72·8
1870...	186·0	14·6	3,257·4	53·0	3·7	71·4
1869...	169·5	14·1	2,866·1	49·9	3·0	67·1

The following table presents an estimate of the total value of the cotton goods produced in Great Britain and the cost of the raw cotton consumed each year from 1867 to 1878 inclusive, the difference giving the balance left for wages, interest, profits, and all the other expenses of manufacture, the figures representing millions and fractions of millions of pounds sterling:

YEARS.	Total value of goods produced.	Cost of raw cotton.	Balance for wages, profits, etc.
1867.............	90·4	41·2	49·1
1868.............	91·7	40·9	50·7
1869.............	86·1	43·7	42·4
1870.............	93·1	42·1	51·0
1871.............	101·9	40·8	61·1
1872.............	102·2	48·0	54·9
1873.............	104·6	45·4	59·1
1874.............	100·5	40·2	60·3
1875.............	95·4	86·5	55·9
1876.............	88·7	82·9	55·9
1877.............	87·3	82·5	54·7
1878.............	80·7	80·3	50·3

From the above it appears that the labor and capital engaged in the production of the raw material have borne the burden of reduced values in a somewhat greater measure than the capital and labor engaged in its manufacture, and that the cost of the material in the first four years of the twelve was 46·4 per cent. of the manufactured product, in the second four years 42·6 per cent., and in the last four years only 37·5 per cent. During the period of twelve years, while the value of the aggregate manufacture has declined about 10, and the cost of materials about 11 million pounds, the actual production has been increased about 10 per cent. The price of raw cotton has fallen in ten years from 11$\frac{7}{16}$d. to 5$\frac{5}{8}$d. per pound. The price of middling uplands was quoted in the month of October in each of the five years from 1874 to 1878 as follows: 1874, 8d.; 1875, 7$\frac{3}{16}$d.; 1876, 6$\frac{3}{4}$d.; 1877, 6$\frac{11}{16}$d.; 1878, 6$\frac{5}{16}$d. The price of 40-mule yarn at the same dates was 12$\frac{1}{4}$d. per pound in 1874, 10$\frac{3}{4}$d. in 1875, 10$\frac{1}{4}$d. in

1876, 10$\frac{3}{4}$d. in 1877, and 9$\frac{3}{4}$d. in 1878; the price of 39-inch red-end cloth was 11$\frac{1}{4}$d. per pound in 1874, 10$\frac{1}{4}$d. in 1875, 9$\frac{1}{4}$d. in 1876, 9$\frac{3}{4}$d. in 1877, and 8d. in 1878. The margin for the cost and profit of manufacture has been reduced in the five years from 4$\frac{1}{4}$d. to 3$\frac{1}{4}$d., or nearly 24 per cent., on yarn, and from 3$\frac{1}{2}$d. to 1$\frac{3}{4}$d., or over 42 per cent., on long cloth.

The present consumption of cotton in the different countries of the world, both in the form of raw material for manufacture and in imports of cotton fabrics, the latter being the products of British factories, with the consumption per capita in the several countries, is as follows, in millions of pounds:

COUNTRIES.	Population.	Consumption of raw cotton.		Consumption of British goods.		Total consumption.	
		Lbs.	Lbs. per cap.	Lbs.	Lbs. per cap.	Lbs.	Lbs. per cap.
Russia..................	86,260,000	142·5	1·65	2·6	·08	145·1	1·68
Norway and Sweden......	6,291,000	24·8	3·94	8·0	1·27	32·8	5·21
Denmark................	2,023,000	....	....	5·0	2·47	5·0	2·47
Germany...............	42,727,000	249·1	5·88	65·2	1·52	314·8	7·35
Austria.................	37,331,000	101·3	2·71	7·9	·21	109·2	2·92
Holland................	4,130,000	18·8	3·34	48·0	10·41	56·8	13·75
Belgium................	5,336,000	43·2	8·09	17·4	3·26	60·6	11·35
Switzerland.............	2,776,000	42·5	15·30	....	..	42·5	15·80
France.................	86,906,000	230·0	6·23	19·9	·54	249·9	6·77
Spain and Portugal......	21,275,000	79·9	3·75	25·7	1·21	105·6	4·96
Italy and Malta.........	26,948,000	52·8	1·96	51·1	1·59	103·9	3·85
Greece.................	1,450,000	....	....	6·9	4·75	6·9	4·75
Turkey, Roumania, etc...	15,853,000	....	....	87·0	2·40	87·0	2·40
Great Britain....	34,160,000	195·7	5·72	....	....	195·7	5·72
Total Europe.	322,966,000	1,175·6	3·68	289·7	·89	1,465·8	4·52
Turkey, Persia, etc......	24,540,000	....	....	88·0	1·54	88·0	1·54
India..................	250,000,000	295·0	....	330·0	1·32	625·0	2·50
China..................	435,000,000	1,000·0	....	100·0	·23	1,100·0	2·52
Japan..................	33,620,000	65·0	....	20·0	·60	85·0	2·52
Siam, Java, etc....	12,500,000	....	....	80·0	2·40	80·0	2·40
Total Asia........	755,660,000	1,360·0	1·79	518·0	·69	1,878·0	2·48
Egypt and North Africa..	17,000,000	....	....	34·0	2·00	34·0	2·00
Coasts of Africa	13,000,000	....	....	28·0	2·15	28·0	2·15
Interior of Africa........	200,000,000	....	....	....	....	....	....
Total Africa........	230,000,000	....	....	62·0	·26	62·0	·26
United States and Canada..	48,850,000	628·0	12·85	22·0	·45	650·0	13·30
Rest of America.........	43,250,000	....	....	185·0	3·12	185·0	3.12
Total America........	92,100,000	628·0	6·82	157·0	1·70	785·0	8·52
Australia................	2,650,000	....	....	185·0	3·12	185·0	3·12
The World..............	1,403,396,000	3,163·6	2·26	1,141·7	·74	4,205·3	2·98

The following table, showing the average quantities of raw cotton consumed in Great Britain and in the parts of the world whose competition she fears, as well as the percentage of the total supply taken by each for the different years designated, will illustrate the progress that has been made outside of England in cotton manufacturing:

COUNTRIES.	1860.		1870-'71.		1877-'78.	
	Bales of 400 lbs.	Per cent.	Bales of 400 lbs.	Per cent.	Bales of 400 lbs.	Per cent.
Great Britain.....................	2,817	49·4	2,988	47·9	2,988	40·6
Continent	1,794	31·5	1,962	31·4	2,473	33·7
United States	1,088	19·1	1,209	19·3	1,657	22·6
India............................	.....	....	87	1·4	230	3·1
Total........................	5,699	100	6,246	100	7,343	100

WOOL. — The trade in fine colonial wool was moderately satisfactory for the first eight months of 1878. At the close of the September sales a declining demand reduced the level of prices. The subsequent occurrence of several heavy failures caused a panic which drove

prices far below their normal level. In low grades of wool the market was stagnant and depressed during the whole year, and accumulated stocks were piled up without buyers, while prices remained exceptionally low.

The value of the exports of wool to Europe

from the British colonies suddenly increased in the two years 1871 and 1872 from 11 to 17 millions sterling, the average before the year 1871 having been 11 millions, and since that year 18¼ millions per annum. The average value per bale declined from £23¾ in 1865 and £24½ in 1866 to £15¾ in 1869, and then rapidly rose to £26½ in 1872; it has since declined to £18¾, where it has stood for the last three years. The prices in the latter part of 1878 were about 18 per cent. below that figure. The imports into Europe from the chief sheep-grazing countries which export have been for the last eight years as follows, in thousands of bales:

YEARS.	Australasia.	Cape.	River Plate.	Total.
1878	791	164	266	1,222
1877	828	169	277	1,271
1876	771	170	272	1,214
1875	699	175	247	1,123
1874	651	164	245	1,061
1873	551	160	264	976
1872	522	154	237	915
1871	567	148	221	937

The diminution of 49,000 bales in 1878 was occasioned by droughts, but it did not have the effect to raise prices; for, although the quantities absorbed in the European trade were larger than in 1877, the large surplus stocks remaining from the preceding year prevented any deficiency being felt. The decrease in the exports of woolen fabrics from Great Britain has been from 32 millions sterling in 1872 to 17 millions in 1877, two thirds of the diminution being in the quantities exported, and the remaining third in the diminished value of cloth, which was not compensated by any proportionate reduction in the cost of raw wool.

Silk.—Since the silk-crop of Europe has fallen away from 7 down to 3 million kilogrammes per annum, in consequence of the silk-worm disease, the factories of Europe have been obliged to make up the deficiency by increased imports of raw silk from the East. The great factories of Lyons depend almost entirely on Oriental silk. The silk-crop of Europe and Western Asia amounted in 1875 to 4, in 1876 to 1·7, and in 1877 to 2·6 million kilos. Of the product of the last-named year, France furnished half a million, and Italy (mainly raised from cocoons imported from Japan) 1½ million kilos; Spain furnished a small quantity; the rest came from Persia, Syria, and Asia Minor. The total is not as great as it should be, owing to the failure to include the crops of Austria, Greece, Algiers, and other producing lands. The importations of raw silk from Eastern Asia in 1875 were 5·6 million kilos; in 1876, 5·2 million; and in 1877, 5·7 million. In the latter year the proportion furnished by China was 4·1 million, by Japan 0·9 million, and by British India 0·7 million.

The exports from France have diminished at a rapid rate within the past few years. The decline has been from 477 million francs in 1873 to 415, 377, and 270 million, respectively, in the three following years, and illustrates the great decrease in the consumptive capacity of all countries. A part of this shrinkage, however, is to be explained by the loss of the trade of the United States for all except the most expensive silk manufactures, owing to the development of a protected native silk industry. The exports of silks from France to the United States, who used to be one of her best customers, have decreased from 59 million francs in 1871 to 34 million in 1877.

Coal and Iron.—The coal trade of Great Britain exhibits some abnormal and unexpected features, and has passed through an eventful period. In 1872 there was a great activity in the mining industry, owing to the high prices of iron and coal; the output increased 6¼ million tons over that of 1871. In 1873 the wave of prosperity rose still higher, although, owing to labor conflicts, the production surpassed by only 3½ million tons that of 1872. In 1874 the contraction had set in, and there was a decrease of nearly 2 million tons in the production of the mines. Yet in 1875, with an increasing depression in all other branches of industry, the production of coal began again to increase, with a vast stride of 6¾ million tons, and in 1876 a further increase of nearly 1½ million tons occurred. In 1877 the output was still further increased by 1¼ million tons. This augmented volume of trade was only achieved by the gradual reduction of wages to the lowest endurable living rate, and was the result of the great influx of laborers who had been attracted into this branch of industry by the high wages of 1871–'73. But in the last couple of years the aggregate production was increased, while large numbers of men have abandoned the trade; that is, the quantity mined per man has been increasing.

The total production, export, and home consumption of coal in Great Britain for the twelve years 1866–'77 were as follows, in millions of tons:

YEARS.	Exports.	Home consumption.	Total production.
1866	10	91	101
1867	10	93	104
1868	11	91	103
1869	11	96	107
1870	12	98	110
1871	13	104	117
1872	18	110	128
1873	12	114	127
1874	14	110	125
1875	14	117	131
1876	16	116	138
1877	15	118	134

In France, Belgium, and Germany, the coal-mining interest, owing to the contracted consumption of iron, is languishing from the effects of diminishing demand and sinking prices.

The world's production of crude iron approaches the figure of 16 million tons per annum, of which 12 millions are produced in Europe and 6·6 millions in Great Britain alone. The production of the different iron-producing countries advanced between 1868 and 1874 as follows: Great Britain, from 5,050,000 to 6,087,000 tons; German Empire (without counting Alsace-Lorraine), from 1,159,000 to 1,409,000 tons; France (without Alsace), from 1,235,000 to 1,388,000 tons; Belgium, from 436,000 to 533,000; Austrian Empire, from 375,000 to 484,000; Russia, from 325,000 to 326,000; Sweden, from 263,000 to 228,000; United States, from 1,454,000 to 2,439,000. The total manufactures of iron and steel in the different countries are estimated as follows, in thousands of tons: Great Britain, iron 3,500, steel 500; United States, iron 1,602, steel 143; Germany, iron 1,150, steel 200; France, iron 883, steel 138; Belgium, iron 503, steel 15; Austria, iron 300, steel 49; Russia, iron 245, steel 7; Sweden and Norway, iron 191, steel 12; Spain, iron 36; Italy, iron 24; extra-European lands, iron 70. The production of pig iron in the several countries of the world, with the growth in this industry since 1850, is exhibited in the following table, showing the produce of each nation for the years designated in thousands of tons:

YEARS.	Great Britain.	United States.	Germany.	France.	Belgium.	Austro-Hungary.	Russia.	Sweden.	Luxemburg.	Other countries.	Total.
1850....	2,249	564	400	400	141	235	222	139	...	185	4,488
1855....	2,975	697	590	600	288	280	260	184	...	144	5,919
1860....	3,700	818	600	880	313	325	291	181	...	140	7,248
1865....	4,819	829	941	1,179	461	370	310	222	26	140	9,292
1870....	5,963	1,659	1,286	905	558	394	352	294	126	140	11,616
1871....	6,627	1,701	1,392	842	597	416	352	292	139	208	12,565
1872 ...	6,741	2,540	1,771	1,193	642	450	391	382	176	204	14,445
1873....	6,566	2,552	1,943	1,389	595	523	376	388	252	204	14,698
1874....	5,991	2,393	1,627	1,359	522	474	372	321	241	204	13,407
1875....	6,365	2,017	1,743	1,368	529	446	420	343	250	204	13,708
1876....	6,555	1,862	1,582	1,420	559	470	420	345	250	204	13,671
1877....	6,608	2,030	1,535	1,328	416	470	420	343	250	204	13,627

During the period from 1860 to 1876 the number of puddling-furnaces in the United Kingdom was increased from 3,462 to 7,159, augmenting the productive capacity of the country from 2 to 4½ million tons. This increase would have more than sufficed to meet the increased demand for iron, though steel had never supplanted malleable iron in the market as it has done. The extension of blast-furnace facilities was equally enormous and uncalled for; and at the end of 1878 there were 500 blast-furnaces lying idle in Great Britain. A capital of as much as five millions sterling invested in blast-furnaces has remained unproductive for the last two years, while other iron-masters kept their furnaces in blast at a loss until they were completely bankrupted. Now for the first time there are signs of a revival in the market for pig iron, and an upward tendency in prices.

The capital expended in puddling-furnaces is probably lost together. More than half the puddling-furnaces in the north of England, Staffordshire, and Wales have ceased operations probably for ever, and gradually the remaining ones must let their fires go out one by one in the natural course of events. But if England has lost this so lately important industry, she is foremost in pursuing the one which has pushed it to the wall. The production of Bessemer steel has increased within five years from 540,000 to 813,000 tons, while the price has fallen from £14 to £4 10s. per ton. Steel-works have been started on the Mersey and the Tees, at Barrow, Sheffield, and Manchester, and in Wales and Staffordshire. Yet England is not without rivals in the manufacture of the new material. France and the United States early started in the race, and have elaborated their own methods and improvements; and Belgium and Germany compete so well with the British manufacturers that they can frequently cite lower prices.

The competition of English iron manufacturers with foreign manufacturers and with each other has been desperate, and prices have steadily declined. The total exports of iron and steel from the United Kingdom in 1878 were 47,000 tons less than in 1877, but 75,000 tons more than in 1876. The exports in 1878 were only 658,000 tons less than those of 1873; yet the shrinkage in prices made the difference between the two years fully 20 millions sterling. The lowest price was touched in July, 1879, when Scotch pig was quoted at 40s. 3d. per ton. When considerable orders came from the United States a turn in prices resulted, and the trade began to revive. By the middle of September Scotch iron was selling at 49s. 7d., and on the 1st of October at 59s. 6d. Cleveland No. 3 rose between the middle of July and the beginning of October from 32s. 6d. to 44s. 6d., and Cleveland bars from 96s. to 114s.

As the expansion in the iron industry was greater than in any other, and spread over all countries before the crisis of 1873, so now this trade is suffering the most severely from a collapse of prices and a lack of business. In Germany, Belgium, and France the depression is greater than in England, and a long and bitter contest is impending between the new works on the Continent and the capital engaged in the iron and steel industries in England.

PETROLEUM.—The production of petroleum in the oil-fields of western Pennsylvania, in quantities of any commercial importance, began in the year 1859. Only within the last few years has the export trade assumed such dimensions as largely to exceed the home consumption. The production of the wells for the five years from 1859 to 1863, inclusive, was 8,362,-

000 barrels; 1864–'68, 15,140,176; 1869–'73, 30,010,119; and 1874–'78, 57,563,775; total production for the twenty years, 111,082,070 barrels. The exports of petroleum from the United States in the year 1876, in barrels of crude oil or their equivalent, the barrel containing 42 gallons, were 7,497,856 bbls.; the home consumption for the same year, 2,677,-158 bbls.; in 1877, exports 10,175,014 bbls., home consumption 2,761,574 bbls.; in 1878, exports 10,353,774 bbls., home consumption 3,769,226 bbls. Of the production of 1878, 66·4 per cent. was shipped abroad, 24·2 per cent. went into consumption in the United States, and 9·4 per cent. went to increase the surplus stock. The total production in 1878 was 15,165,462 bbls., against 13,135,671 in 1877, and 8,968,906 in 1876. The daily average consumption in 1878 was 38,494 bbls., against 34,351 in 1877, an increase of over 12 per cent. The shipments to New York from the oil regions in 1876 were 24½ per cent. of the total shipments, in 1877 35 per cent., and in 1878 43 per cent. The Cleveland refineries consume 20 to 24 per cent. of the total shipments, and 14 to 19 per cent. goes to Pittsburgh; the Oil Creek refiners, who in 1876 and 1877 took 13 or 14 per cent. of the oil shipped, in 1878 consumed but 2 per cent.

In *England* the evils of declining prices and a contracted trade have made themselves felt with greater severity in each succeeding year. In 1877, as in 1876, the English money market was in a languishing condition. The Bank's mean rate of discount for the year was 2¾ per cent., against 2½ per cent. in 1876; the rate in the open market was about the same as in the preceding year, averaging 2¼ per cent. The financial situation of the country was seriously impaired by a rise in the price of wheat of about 20 per cent.; the advance from 46s. 2d. to 56s. 9d. in this period of stagnation aggravated greatly the general distress. The increase in the cost of living, happening at a time of feeble business and low markets for manufactured goods, excited numerous conflicts between labor and capital: there occurred no less than 161 separate strikes within the year 1877. Pauperism increased 11 per cent. this year, comparing it with the last. Owing to the unusual requirements for food, the importations were largely in excess of those of the preceding year, increasing the total commerce from £698,449,631 to £723,716,620, or 3·6 per cent.; yet the export trade continued in the same downward course which commenced in 1873.

The year 1878 was marked by deepening financial gloom in England, and the appearance of serious distress among the working population. The situation was aggravated by disastrous financial failures. A crisis in the cotton trade occurred, in which the manufacturers, who had been keeping their mills working at a loss for several years, until many of them stood on the brink of bankruptcy, and had kept up the stock of manufactured goods beyond any present demand, and underbid each other till prices were at the lowest ebb, were threatened with a double danger by a dearth in the supply of raw cotton, which kept up the price of the material, while the failure of several manufacturers and the critical situation of others threw their stocks of cotton goods on the market and depressed the prices of manufactures. In the coal and iron industries the situation was equally gloomy, and there can be no doubt that the substitution of steel for iron will cause a gradual decay of those trades, extended as they had been by the sudden and enormous demand for iron before 1873. In the stock market there has been a large unloading of American State securities, which have returned to America, and of Russian securities, which went to Germany and France. The great Glasgow failure caused less distress in the money and loan market than in the industrial districts of the north.

The failure of the City of Glasgow Bank, which closed its payments on the 2d of October, 1878, amounted almost to a national disaster, reducing hundreds and thousands of families in the south of Scotland to beggary. The investigation of the affairs of this gigantic institution after its collapse revealed a degree of willful deceit and criminal recklessness on the part of its managers which set the public to reflecting anew on the justice of the reputation for integrity formerly deserved and long enjoyed by the British merchant. The bank was established in 1839. Its paid-up capital was £1,000,000. It had one hundred and thirty-one branches, distributed all over Scotland. Although its bills had never stood A 1 in Lombard Street, the public had no suspicion of its condition until the day it was closed; on the very preceding day its shares stood at 2·35½ in the market. For years before the published statements of the condition of the bank were made up of a tissue of falsehoods and forgeries. All the books were falsified. The statement published four months before the failure, when a dividend of 12 per cent. was voted, gave the amount of bills receivable over a million pounds too high; the good securities were overstated by nearly the same amount; and a couple of hundred thousand pounds were fictitiously added to the account of cash in the vaults. In the June statement the liabilities to the public were given as ten millions; in October the liquidators found them twelve millions. In June the assets balanced the liabilities and capital account; after the failure they were found to be £7,213,314, leaving a deficit of £6,783,079. The City of Glasgow Bank, like all the Scottish banks of issue except the three oldest, was incorporated under the provision of the unlimited liability of the shareholders. The deluded shareholders, beyond the loss of their investment in the stock, which they had bought mostly at prices far above par, were therefore holden each and all of them, to the extent of every shilling which they possessed, for the outside liabilities of the bank, amounting to £5,190,983. The reckless manner in which credit was extended by the directors, often on purely personal or family grounds, was revealed by the fact that they had loaned over 5¾ millions, the greater part of it to only three persons, on securities which were not worth more than a million and a half. Besides the failure of the City of Glasgow Bank, several other failures in the banking business occurred in Great Britain during the years 1878 and 1879, which affected trade very injuriously. The most formidable of these was the stoppage of the West of England and South Wales Banking Company on the 9th of December, 1878. This large concern had forty or fifty branches; the liabilities were five million pounds and the deficit between one and two millions. In the coal-mining trade numerous bankruptcies occurred; nearly all of the companies started during the period of high prices from 1871 to 1873 have gone into liquidation.

In consequence of the numerous speculative, impracticable, or fraudulent schemes for which joint-stock companies were formed, whose shares were floated without difficulty on the London market prior to the crisis of 1873, a Parliamentary Commission was appointed to inquire into the constitution and usages of the London Stock Exchange, and report on the necessity of legislative interference or supervision. The London Stock Exchange has been in existence over seventy-five years, and counts more than 2,000 members. The Commission exonerated the board of management, which is called the Committee for General Purposes, from all knowledge of or participation in the reckless and fraudulent transactions which gave occasion for the investigation. The premises, business management, and emoluments of the Exchange belong to a body of shareholders, who may or may not be members, and who elect a board of trustees to look after the financial management of the corporation. The yearly dividends amount to 20 or 21 per cent. on the original investment. Among the glaring swindles and disastrous bubble companies which have been launched on the London Stock Exchange of late years, are the Oriental and Australian Navigation Company, the directors of which bought the shares short before the day of issue until they had the sellers at their mercy; the Eupion Gas Company swindle of 1874; Charles Laffitte & Co.; the Marseilles Land Company; the Moscow Gas Company; and the Peruvian Railway Company. The Stock Exchange, before quoting the stock of a new company, subjects it to a certain sort of examination and scrutiny in the interests of the general public, enough to inspire confidence in the public, but not enough to insure it against fraud. The investors can not usually judge of the merits and prospects of a new company, but are guided in their purchases by the quotations of the Stock Ex-

change. When they read in the papers that the stock of a company is quoted at a premium on the Exchange, they conclude that it is in request among the business men best versed in such enterprises. But the premium on the stock before the issue of the shares is of a fictitious character, and is produced purposely to mislead the public. Swindling promoters are thus enabled to dispose of worthless shares at or above par, by first bidding up the price on 'Change before the issue, and after the issue unloading as soon as possible, while the demand thus fraudulently created continues among the gulled and ignorant public. Another common method of fraud is practiced by the founders and directors of new companies on the dealers within the Exchange. The dishonest promoters, through their agents, will buy stock for future delivery at a premium of the speculators, who rely on procuring it in the open market at or about par on the day of issue. But the promoters, who control the issue of the stock, will have put so many shares in the names of themselves, their friends, and abettors, that the dealers can not obtain the stocks to fulfill their contracts except at exorbitant rates. The quotation of shares before the day of issue is a practice which the Commission condemns unqualifiedly, regarding the jobbing in stocks and bonds before the delivery of the shares to subscribers as the means oftenest employed to place fraudulent loans and to float the stock of swindling corporations. They recommend a penal enactment of Parliament against this variety of stock-jobbing. The operations on the Exchange are under the control of the members through their administrative council, the Committee for General Purposes, which is elected annually. A movement is on foot, which is approved of by the Parliamentary Commission, to fuse the two separate societies of shareholders and members into one corporation. Both brokers and dealers are admitted as members on the same footing; but a regulation has recently been adopted forbidding members to act as speculators on their own account and as agents for outsiders at the same time. As the Committee for General Purposes, which consists of seven members, is frequently called upon to decide on questions which affect the interests both of the members of the Stock Exchange and of outside parties, it would be well to insist that each member of the Committee before voting should have listened to the whole of the deliberations, and that he should be compelled to declare that he has no financial interest in the question under consideration.

A comparison of the wholesale prices in London of the leading articles on the 1st of January, 1879, with those of the same date in the years named below, showed the following variations (the sign + signifying the excess over the prices of 1879; —, the increase in 1879 over the prices of the former year; and =, that the prices were the same as those of 1879):

ARTICLES.	1878.	1876.	1870.	1867.
	Per cent.	Per cent.	Per cent.	Per cent.
Wheat	+28	+11	+ 6	+33
Butcher's meat........	+ 6	+17	− 8	− 5
Tea...................	=	−11	− 9	− 8
Sugar	+ 8	−24	=	−26
Coffee	+21	+22	− 9	+ 4
Leather	+ 8	=	−14	−14
Timber...............	+18	+10	−16	−24
Tallow	+ 7	+81	−21	−21
Oils	+ 4	+ 9	+16	+24
Copper...............	+11	+28	+18	+26
Iron.................	+15	+40	+12	+12
Lead.................	+28	+86	+28	+26
Tin..................	+ 9	+22	+44	+22
Cotton	+21	+82	+58	+68
Flax and hemp........	+28	+82	+40	+89
Silk.................	+21	−80	+85	+88
Wool................	+10	+19	−18	+24
Tobacco.............	+17	+40	+ 6	+22
Cotton cloth.........	+20	+87	+40	+58

Between the 1st of January, 1873, and the 1st of January, 1879, the "Gazette" average price for wheat had fallen from 55s. 11d. per quarter to 39s. 7d., or 29 per cent., in London, while the New York price for red spring wheat had fallen from $1.70 to $1.10 per bushel; and flour had fallen from $7.50 to $3.70 per barrel, 51 per cent., in New York, and in London had declined 22 per cent. The London price for Scotch pig iron declined between the two dates from 127s. to 43s. per ton, or 66 per cent.; coals from 30s. to 19s., or 37 per cent.; copper from £91 to £57 per ton, or 37 per cent.; and tin from £142 to £61, or 57 per cent. The fall in inferior beef was 26 per cent., in prime small 10 per cent. Middling upland cotton fell from 10d. to 5¾d. per lb., or 46 per cent.; wool from £23 to £13 per pack, or 43 per cent. The decline in sugar was 26 per cent., in coffee 19 per cent., in black Malabar pepper 39 per cent., and in saltpeter 34 per cent.

The total value of British imports showed a decline in 1878 for the first time since 1872. The fall in the total values imported was from 394 to 366 millions sterling, the total imports for the year amounting to the latter sum. The imports of raw materials, 122 millions, show a decline of 1½ per cent. or 14 millions. In the quantities of food and articles of consumption imported there was an increase of 2 per cent., and in materials for manufactures a decrease of 5 per cent.; in average prices there was a decrease in the first class of about 9 and in the second of nearly 7 per cent. The increase in food imports was confined to animal foods, and chiefly occurred in the articles bacon and hams, much larger quantities of which were imported at reduced prices. Among vegetable foods, there was a decline in quantity and a still greater decline in price in the articles wheat and sugar, and an increase in the article Indian corn. Among the materials for manufactures, the largest falling off was in the textile materials, the decline in prices being considerably greater than that in quantities. In the imports of wood sthere was a remarkable diminution in quantities and a considerable decline in prices. In the total

VOL. XIX.—12 A

imports of all classes there was perhaps a slight increase in quantities, with a decrease in the aggregate value of 8½ per cent. The chief articles of animal food were imported to the amount of 40 millions in value, nearly 4 millions more than in the previous year. In the imports of alcoholic beverages, which amounted to nearly 8¼ millions in value, there was a falling off of about 1¼ million. In petroleum there was a slight falling off in quantity, which was remarkable considering that the value was proportionately much less. In oils and in tallow there was a decline in both quantities and value. In niter there was an advance in quantity at a higher price. In guano and bone fertilizers there was a slightly increased importation. The chief materials for the textile manufactures were imported to the value of 70·43 millions, or 5·84 millions less than in the preceding year—a decrease due in nearly equal measure to lessened quantities and lower cost. On imports of the chief manufactured articles of the value of 6·70 millions, there was a decrease of 0·17 million, principally due to lower prices. Among miscellaneous materials, there was a slight increase in the import of raw hides and tanned leather at a lower cost, and also in rope and linseed. The following table shows the course of trade in the principal articles above mentioned and several others (+, increase; —, decrease):

ARTICLES.	Quantities in millions.		Value, in millions of pounds sterling.	
Wheat.................	57·68 cwt.	− 3·90	34·19	−6·43
Indian corn............	41·68 "	+11·17	12·59	+2·74
Sugar.................	18·21 "	− 1·85	20·58	−6·81
Live oxen.............	28·00 head.	+ 0·06	4·95	+1·26
Sheep	0·89 "	+ 0·09	2·17	+0·06
Bacon and hams.......	4·27 cwt.	+ 1·47	8·69	+1·77
Fresh and preserv'd meat	0·96 "	+ 0·02	2·70	−0·01
Butter................	1·50 "	+ 0·16	9·94	+0·40
Cheese...............	1·97 "	+ 0·82	4·94	+0·18
Wine.................	16·46 galls.	− 8·17	6·00	−1·16
Brandy...............	8·57 "	+ 0·59	1·48	+0·17
Rum..................	....	− 1·80	.....	....
Other spirits..........	....	− 0·76	.....	....
Coffee................	142·62 lbs.	−87·70	6·01	−1·78
Tea..................	205·46 "	+19·23	13·10	+0·69
Tobacco..............	91·88 "	+11·64	3·72	+0·19
Cotton...............	11·98 cwt.	− 0·18	33·52	−1·97
Flax.................	1·55 "	− 0·67	3·48	−1·57
Hemp................	1·22 "	− 0·08	1·92	−0·15
Jute.................	4·25 "	+ 0·64	3·24	+0·84
Silk.................	4·17 lbs.	− 0·27	8·68	−0·77
Wool................	478·90 "	−18·89	24·59	−1·72
Copper...............	0·17 tons.	− 0·02	4·69	−0·60
Iron.................	1·96 "	− 0·04	5·22	−0·19
Timber, hewed........	....	....	4·11	−1·71
" sawed........	....	....	9·01	−4·14

The trade returns for the first nine months of 1879 show a decrease of £23,269,840, or 8·2 per cent., compared with the returns of the same three quarters of 1878, which gave £282,-616,072, against £259,346,232 in 1879. The decrease in the exports was less marked, being £4,761,512, or 3·3 per cent.; the exports in the first nine months of 1878 being £144,926,177, against £140,164,665 in 1879. The imports of raw cotton were about 3 per cent. lighter and about two millions sterling less in value than in the first three quarters of 1878. In the exports of cotton manufactures there was an inappreciable increase in the number of yards of piece-goods, but a decline in the total values of over 4½ per cent. This was partly balanced by an increase in the values of lace, so that the total decline in cotton manufactures was from about 39¾ to 38¼ millions sterling. In cotton yarn there was a reduced exportation to nearly all countries except Russia, and a decline of a million in the values. In raw silk there was a large falling off, which answers to a decline in the exports of silk manufactures. In wool there was an increase in the imports from Australia from 258 to 273 million lbs. The total imports for the nine months were 350,610,036 lbs., against 345,421,768 lbs. in 1878. The exports of raw wool increased from 4,935,278 lbs. to 7,755,100 lbs., the principal increase being made up of shipments to the United States, who had not before bought much at the English sales, and whose purchases for the nine months this year increased from 292,678 lbs. to 3,274,400 lbs. The exports of woolen and worsted yarn remained about the same, being 23,408,000 lbs., those to Germany showing a decline, and those to Russia an increase. In the total values of woolen manufactures exported there was a decline from £12,768,363 to £11,878,871. In woolen cloths there was an increase from 33,637,200 to 33,983,800 yards, the increase being in mixed goods, but a decline in values. In worsted goods, there was an increased exportation of all-wool goods, but a considerable decline in the mixed grades, the total falling off being from 149,228,600 to 142,517,200 yards. To France, the United States, Italy, China, and Japan there was an increased exportation; to all other countries diminished shipments. The imports of flax show a slight falling off in quantity and a considerable decline in value; those of hemp declined over 10 per cent. in quantity and as much as 20 per cent. in value. In jute there was an increased importation, and also an increased exportation of jute and jute manufactures, except bags, which showed a decline. The exports of linen piece-goods declined from 124,733,100 to 120,092,400 yards, and the total value of linen manufactures from £4,337,527 to £4,147,597. The imports of undressed hides fell from 507,000 to 277,000 cwt.; those of tanned and curried hides from 40 to 26 million lbs. The exports of leather showed an increase of nearly 25 per cent. In haberdashery and millinery there was a decline of nearly 10 per cent., in hardware and cutlery of about the same, in pottery an increase, in articles of female apparel and men's ready-made clothing a slight increase in value, and in alkalies an increase in quantity but a slight decline in value. The imports of copper increased, while those of the ore show a decline. The exports of copper declined in value about 4 per cent., while the quantity exported was about 8 per cent. greater than in the preceding year. The importation of nearly all articles of prime neces-

sity was in excess of that of last year. The total imports of wheat for the nine months were 41 million cwt., against 37 million in the corresponding months of 1878; but the total value was only 20 in the place of 21 millions sterling. Of these Russia furnished 5¾ million cwt., instead of 6¼ as in 1878; Germany, 2¾, instead of 3¾ million cwt.; India, only ¼ instead of 1½ million cwt. The importations from Australia increased from 1,144,449 cwt. to 1,860,005 cwt., those from British America from 1,570,638 to 2,662,165 cwt., and those from the United States from 22,562,818 to 25,144,090 cwt.; from the Pacific States the increase was from 4,124,852 to 6,010,863 cwt., and from the Atlantic ports from 18,437,966 to 19,183,227 cwt. There was a large increase in the importation of wheat-flour from the United States. The total importation increased from 5,760,102 to 7,553,383 cwt., that from the United States being 4,890,999 cwt., or nearly double that of the previous year in the same nine months. In the imports of maize there was a decline from 34 to 30 million cwt., or between 8 and 9 per cent. In oil-seed cakes there was also a decline, about 4 per cent. in quantity and 8 per cent. in value. The importation of oats was about the same; that of barley declined nearly one half both in quantity and value.

The foreign commerce of *France* has increased in the last half-century nearly 400 per cent. The average annual trade, import and export together, for the different periods of ten years within the space of fifty years from 1823 to 1876, has been computed as follows, the numbers denoting millions of francs: 1827–'36, general commerce 1,366, special commerce 1,001; 1837–'46, general commerce 2,112, special commerce 1,489; 1847–'56, general commerce 3,175, special commerce 2,301; 1857–'66, general commerce 6,280, special commerce 4,631; 1867–'76, general commerce 8,464, special commerce 6,714. Averaging the returns for the whole fifty years, we find the mean annual volume of the general commerce to be 4,279, of the special 3,227 million francs. The returns for each year of the last decade, 1867–'76, of the total volume of each class of foreign trade, the exports and imports being taken together, were as follows in millions of francs: General commerce—1867, 7,965; 1868, 7,979; 1869, 8,002; 1870, 6,954; 1871, 7,231; 1872, 9,258; 1873, 9,399; 1874, 9,125; 1875, 9,269; 1876, 9,456. Special commerce—1867, 5,852; 1868, 6,094; 1869, 6,228; 1870, 5,670; 1871, 6,439; 1872, 7,332; 1873, 7,342; 1874, 7,209; 1875, 7,409; 1876, 7,564.

The importations into the United States from France in the year 1860, on the eve of the civil war, amounted to about 50 million dollars. In 1864 they were not more than a third as much in amount. During the ten years from 1867 to 1876 the exportations from America to France increased in a steady progression from about 28 million dollars to nearly 53 millions. The exportation of American products to France amounted to nearly 48 millions; but, interrupted by the war, they sank in 1864 to less than 10 millions. In 1876 they were 5 millions more than in 1860. The commodities exported to France from the United States, with the exception of a small amount in machinery, consist of raw materials and articles of food. Of the exportations of American products to France in 1876, 31 millions, or nearly 60 per cent., were in raw cotton; 21 millions, or 8 per cent., lard and tallow; 19 millions, petroleum; and 15 millions, tobacco.

The French customs returns for 1878 give as the values of the imports and exports of that year the following sums (reduced to dollars): Total imports, $892,194,800, viz.: raw materials, $450,355,200; articles of food, $308,661,- 600; manufactures, $89,426,600; other articles, $43,751,400. Total exports, $673,961,- 400, viz.: manufactures, $373,428,400; articles of food and raw materials, $264,173,000; other articles, $36,360,000. Among the imports of food articles, breadstuffs are represented by 116 million dollars, oil-bearing fruits and seeds by 31 millions, sugar by 22 millions, coffee by 22 millions, cattle by 48 millions. Among the chief imports of raw materials are peltries, 82 million dollars; wool, 69 millions; silk, 75 millions; cotton, 39 millions; timber, 33 millions; coal, 33 millions. Among the chief imports of manufactures are cotton yarn, 9 millions; woolen yarn, 4 millions; silk goods, 8 millions; woolen goods, 14 millions; cotton goods, 14 millions; machinery, 8 millions. Of the exports of manufactures, silk goods are the chief item, 66 millions; woolen goods next, 53 millions; then leather manufactures, 30 millions; mercery, buttons, and turned wares, 29 millions; leather, 18 millions; clothing, 17 millions; tools and hardware, 14 millions; jewelry, 12 millions; cotton goods, 12 millions; woolen yarn, 8 millions. The imports of food and crude products exceed the exports by 495 million dollars, while the exports of manufactures are 284 millions in excess of the imports. Compared with 1877, there is an increase in the total imports of 158 million dollars, and a diminution in the exports of 13 millions; the excess of imports, which was 47 millions in 1877, having increased in 1878 to 218 millions.

The French customs returns for the first eight months of 1879, compared with the same period in 1878, show an increase in the imports of alimentary substances from 1,149,527,- 000 to 842,442,000 francs, or 36 per cent. In the imports of natural products and materials for manufacture the slight decrease from 1,430,732,000 to 1,424,457,000 francs is of no statistical significance. The imports of manufactured objects were 289,709,000 francs, compared with 287,501,000 in 1878; those of other merchandise, 142,583,000 francs, compared with 126,699,000. The increase in the imports from 2,687,374,000 to 3,006,276,000

francs, amounting to 818,902,000 francs, or nearly 12 per cent., is therefore attributable to the augmented food importations. In the exports there was an inappreciable diminution in manufactures from 1,116,767,000 to 1,114,- 605,000 francs; a decline of 1 per cent., or from 799,699,000 to 791,121,000 francs, in foods and raw materials, and of 4 per cent., or from 115,495,000 to 110,498,000 francs, in other merchandise. The decline in the total exports was not $\frac{1}{10}$ per cent., being from 2,031,961,000 to 2,016,224,000 francs.

The variations in the ninety principal securities dealt in on the Paris Bourse show a net rise in the aggregate values of securities between the 1st of January, 1878, and the 1st of January, 1879, of 2,996 million francs. The rise in French rentes aggregates 1,000 million francs; in French railway bonds, 548 million francs. Among the few securities which declined in price were Austrian Government bonds, shares of the Bank of France, Suez Canal shares, and certain gas shares, depressed probably, like gas shares in London, by the prospect of the introduction of the electric light. Money was more abundant in Paris during the year 1878 than in any other money market, large amounts flowing out to England during the latter half of the year. The rise in first-class securities is in this case the result of the general depression of industry and commerce, the lowering of the rates of interest, and the diminished demand for capital for productive purposes. Industrial stocks generally declined; the coal stocks of the nineteen principal companies of the north of France depreciated during the year 103 million francs in the aggregate, the fall in shares averaging 47 per cent.

The total volume of the external commerce of *Belgium* in 1877 was 4,360,800,000 francs, about 4 per cent. less than in 1876. The total importations, embracing all the goods received both for consumption and for reëxportation, amounted to 2,356,600,000 francs, a decline of about 4 per cent.; the total exports, including the foreign exports, were 2,004,200,000 francs, showing a falling off of 4 per cent. likewise. Eliminating the transit and reëxport trade, the net amount of the foreign trade of Belgium (the amount of foreign products which entered into consumption and the amount of Belgian produce and manufactures shipped abroad being taken together) was about the same as in the preceding year, the total value being 2,500,- 500,000 francs. The analysis of the total returns shows favorably for Belgium, the value of the imports which went into consumption being 1,426,200,000 francs, a decline of 2 per cent., and the value of the exports of Belgian products being 1,074,300,000 francs, a gain of 1 per cent. over the previous year. There was a diminished importation of grain, of wool and hides, of pig iron, and of coffee and nearly all luxuries and manufactures, and an increase in the importations of iron ore and other mineral products, vegetable fibers, resins and oils, and provisions. Among the exports the articles showing the largest increase were vegetable fibers, machinery, iron products, iron and steel, zinc, the different textiles, and various other manufactures.

The fatal marasmus of contracting commerce and industrial stagnation has afflicted *Germany*, perhaps, more severely and calamitously than any other country. The depression set in very early in the country of the milliards, and was by many attributed to the reaction from the over-speculation excited by the influx of the French gold; now many attribute it to the effect on values of the change to a gold standard which the receipt of the vast sum of indemnity enabled the German Government to accomplish. The Government has recently appointed commissions to inquire into the causes of the continued commercial depression, from whose deliberations projects for its relief and remedy are hopefully awaited.

The German Government has lately abandoned the practice of reporting the value of the imports and exports, and published simply the quantities. The estimated value of the imports and exports of 1878, compared with the values reported in the two preceding years, indicate an intensified prostration of commerce and industry. The total value of the imports of 1876 was 3,913,300,000 marks, and of 1877, 3,877,000,000 marks ; estimated value of the imports of 1878, 3,343,700,000 marks. The total exports in 1876 amounted 2,484,700,000 marks; in 1877, to 2,716,100,000 marks; in 1878 their computed value is 2,360,700,000 marks. The subjoined table exhibits the movement for the three separate years in the chief classes of commodities. The increase made in the importations of the year 1878 under the heads of tobacco and machinery is ascribable to the prospect of tariff reforms. The table gives the complete returns for the first two years, but only the estimates, based on the quantities which passed the borders, for the year 1878. Four marks are approximately equal to one dollar, and a centner is equal to a cwt. of 112 lbs.

ARTICLES.		IMPORTS.		EXPORTS.	
		Quantities.	Value.	Quantities.	Value.
		Centners.	Marks.	Centners.	Marks.
Grain and flour	1876	60,500,000	595,000,000	22,650,000	222,000,000
	1877	78,100,000	716,000,000	39,600,000	878,000,000
	1878	66,400,000	672,200,000	43,680,000	416,600,000
Sugar, coffee, spices, etc	1876	3,168,000	248,000,000	2,210,000	91,000,000
	1877	2,791,000	218,000,000	2,164,000	82,800,000
	1878	2,475,000	210,000,000	3,181,000	115,000,000
Tobacco and manufactures	1876	1,004,019	81,900,000	200,000	23,900,000
	1877	1,043,016	78,500,000	156,400	23,500,000
	1878	1,306,483	103,700,000	86,600	17,700,000
Fuel	1876	106,881,000	73,800,000	118,586,000	98,700,000
	1877	99,925,000	64,600,000	113,926,000	95,100,000
	1878	99,396,000	58,700,000	122,808,000	101,500,000
Raw metals	1876	12,843,000	89,800,000	8,156,000	81,600,000
	1877	11,478,000	72,500,000	9,480,250	77,400,000
	1878	10,366,000	71,600,000	10,712,366	90,400,000
Metals partly manufactured	1876	650,200	10,510,000	4,416,000	48,950,000
	1877	2,982,000	29,600,000	7,640,000	77,300,000
	1878	2,066,000	22,210,000	8,258,000	92,340,000
Hardware	1876	821,000	25,360,000	1,860,000	54,130,000
	1877	1,121,000	30,900,000	2,580,000	66,770,000
	1878	910,000	24,950,000	2,688,000	70,200,000
Textiles	1876	6,490,000	623,000,000	2,214,000	281,000,000
	1877	7,240,000	626,000,000	3,080,000	248,900,000
	1878	7,040,000	613,700,000	2,805,000	286,100,000
Yarns	1876	1,072,000	170,500,000	294,000	45,200,000
	1877	692,000	138,200,000	834,000	50,300,000
	1878	598,000	145,200,000	878,000	58,000,000
Articles of dress and ornament	1876	533,000	171,800,000	896,000	828,500,000
	1877	475,000	142,600,000	898,000	325,900,000
	1878	398,000	126,300,000	734,000	286,900,000
Machines, vessels, and rigging	1876	......	46,100,000	......	59,400,000
	1877	......	48,800,000	......	73,200,000
	1878	......	51,700,000	......	89,700,000

The German Government, impelled on the one hand by the prostration of industry and commerce and the widespread distress among the working people to adopt some extraordinary measure of relief, and actuated on the other hand by its own pressing need of an increased revenue which shall not depend on the doubtful vote of the Parliament, in order to carry out the policy to which it has committed itself, saw fit to abandon its free-trade principles, and drew up a reformed tariff of a highly protective nature, which has lately been accepted by the Parliament. This tariff proposes to raise from 88 to 120 million marks of additional revenue from supplementary duties, which are to be imposed to the amount of 29 to 37 millions on objects already dutiable, and new duties amounting to from 59 to 84 million marks to be levied on imports which have been before exempt. Of the new revenue, 35 to 43 millions is purely fiscal in its character, being imposed on petroleum to the amount of from 20 to 25 millions, and on articles of luxury, with the exception of beer and tobacco, to the amount of from 15 to 17 millions. The remainder of the new revenue is to be levied on imports which compete with native products, with a view to protect home industries from foreign competition. Of this, from 34 to 40 million marks is to be imposed on agricultural and forest products, to wit: 30 to 41 millions on cereals, cattle, cheese, butter, etc., and 4 to 8 millions on products of the forest; and 18 to 28 millions on mechanical products, to wit: 6 to 12 millions on iron and machinery, 9 to 12 millions on textile fabrics, and 3 to 4 millions on other industrial products. In *Italy* the imports declined from 1,327,-187,301 francs in 1876 to 1,148,049,418 francs in 1877; and the exports in a still greater measure, from 1,216,929,416 francs to 967,367,551 francs, thus increasing an adverse balance from 110 to 180 millions and reducing the total volume of trade by 16 per cent. In 1878 the total trade remained about the same as in 1877, but an increase in the exports to 1,040,789,181 francs and a diminution in the imports to 1,-070,802,434 francs reduced the adverse balance to only 30 millions. The principal reduction in the imports took place under the following heads, the values being stated in millions of francs: Spirits, beverages, and oils, 17; colonial products, 24; cottons, 23; metals and minerals, 26. Under the following heads there was an increased importation to the following amounts: Chemical products, 2; hemp and flax and their products, 7; grain and flour, 32. Among the exports there was a diminution of 15 millions in oils and beverages, 2 millions in paper, 3 millions in cereals, flour, and pastes, and 11 millions in animals, etc. The augmentations chiefly arose under the following heads: Colors and tanners' materials, 8; hemp and flax, 14; cottons, 6; wool, 3; silk, 49; wood and straw, 7; stone, earths, and glass, 5.

The trade statistics of Italy for the first half of 1879 show a continued favorable state of commerce. The imports for the six months were of the value of 607,251,075 francs, against 587,956,841 francs in the corresponding part of 1878. The exports were 586,435,744 francs, against 516,082,083 francs in 1878. The increase of 19 millions or 3·28 per cent. in the imports is found under the general head of sugar, tobacco, and other colonial products, which is put down for 106,090,275 francs, against 57,125,043 francs in the first half of 1878. The proposal of the Government to raise the duties on sugar, coffee, and petroleum excited an unusual importation of those articles, particularly of sugar, of which 500,000 quintals more were imported than in the corresponding previous half year. Other articles which show an increased importation are tanning materials, hides, coal, and horses. The stimulated trade in colonial wares produced an increase of over 25 million francs, or about 50 per cent., in the customs receipts. The unusual and anticipated demand for sugar and coffee was nearly set off by a decline in the importation of foreign manufactures. Among the textiles, there was a decrease of 7,000 quintals

in the imports of flax, hemp, and jute materials, 11,000 quintals in cotton yarn, 9,000 quintals in cotton goods, 7,000 quintals in linen and jute manufactures, and 7,000 quintals in woolens. There was a slight decrease among the exports in dried fruit, straw hats, lead, and live stock. There were considerable increases, on the other hand, in the export of wines, olive oil, lime-juice, tanning materials, hemp, raw and thrown silk, paper, dressed skins, sulphur, rice, oranges and lemons, almonds, and dried figs.

The import trade of *Egypt* in 1876 amounted to 162,903,786 francs; the exports were 325,-614,015 francs, an increase of 8,346,099 francs over those of the preceding year. England takes nearly two thirds of the Egyptian exports, France about one quarter, and Italy, the next best customer, not over 6 per cent. In the articles of export, cotton preponderates over all the others, figuring for 213 million francs, and cotton-seed for nearly 38 millions; the export of cereals amounted to 26 millions, that of sugar to 17½ millions. A considerable trade is done in the products of Central Africa, which are exchanged by the natives for English calicoes, copper, and fire-arms, and brought by caravans to Khartoum or the ports of the Red Sea: gums are exported to the value of 8 million francs, ostrich-plumes 3 millions, skins 2½ millions, and ivory 1½ million. The principal trade in these articles is with France, who takes the coffee, the drugs, the skins, the gums, the wax, and the ostrich-feathers, which are brought from the White Nile, Dongola, and Kordofan. The elephant and hippopotamus ivory goes to Austria. The oil of roses and other essences are sent to Turkey and the Levant. The chief imports into Egypt are woods for building purposes from Austria and Turkey; coal and iron from England; fruits and provisions from France, Austria, Greece, and Syria; marbles from Italy and Austria; manufactures and machinery principally from Great Britain; oils, furniture, paper, silks, wines, and liquors from the port of Marseilles; and tobacco from Greece, Turkey, and Syria. England and France are the largest sellers to Egypt. The imports of petroleum from the United States show a diminution of 300,000 francs in 1876. The total imports into Egypt in 1876 were 5,033,142 francs less in value than in the preceding year. This diminution, however, did not affect the leading commercial nations of Europe, as the importations from Great Britain showed an increase of 5 millions for iron, coal, and manufactures; those from Austria showed an increase of 1½ million francs for timber. The importations of breadstuffs from Russia also increased slightly; and those from France were somewhat greater.

The foreign trade returns of *British India* for 1877-'78 show a larger total than in any previous year. This increase, however, is not attributable to the improved prosperity of the people; but, as far as it is affected by the greater importation of grain and pulse, which amounted to 1,250,000 cwt. as compared with 41,000 and 282,000 cwt. in the two preceding years, it is the result of the recent famine. The imports of cotton twist and yarn and of gray piece-goods show a large increase, the former amounting to 36 million lbs., as compared with 33 mill;on lbs. in 1876-'77, and the latter to 992 million yards, as compared with 840 million yards. But this line of trade was unnaturally stimulated by the efforts of English manufacturers to work off their surplus stocks at greatly reduced prices. The imports of salt, which afford a better criterion of the consumptive capacity of the people, have declined from 298,000 tons in 1877, and 365,000 in 1876, to 254,000 tons in 1878. The trade of France and Italy with India through the Suez Canal has greatly increased during the last four years; in 1878 the trade with those countries made 5·3 and 1·8 per cent. respectively of the total commerce. The export trade of India still continues to feel the stimulating effect of the depreciation of silver; the proportion of the exports to the total volume of the merchandise trade, which was 59 per cent. in the years 1867 and 1868, and increased to 67 per cent. in 1871-'72, was 62 per cent. in 1877-'78, against 63 per cent. the previous year, and 61 and 62 per cent. in the second and third years before. The values of the imports and exports of merchandise for the last twelve years were, in lacs of rupees (1 lac=$50,000 approximately), as follows:

YEARS.	Imports.	Exports.	Total trade.
1866-'67	2,901	4,185	7,087
1867-'68	8,566	5,057	8,653
1868-'69	8,598	5,306	8,899
1869-'70	8,287	5,247	8,535
1870-'71	8,834	5,533	8,868
1871-'72	3,081	6,818	9,309
1872-'73	8,047	5,528	8,570
1873-'74	8,162	5,496	8,658
1874-'75	8,464	5,681	9,095
1875-'76	8,711	5,804	9,515
1876-'77	8,586	6,096	9,682
1877-'78	3,982	6,513	10,451

The shipments of silver from England to the East, in millions of pounds sterling and fractions of millions, the silver imports into Great Britain, and the average price of standard silver per ounce in pence, are shown in the following table:

YEARS.	Shipments to the East.	Imports into the United Kingdom.	Average price in London.
1878	5·84	11·45	52$\frac{9}{16}$
1877	17·00	21·62	54$\frac{7}{8}$
1876	10·91	18·56	52$\frac{3}{4}$
1875	8·71	9·50	56$\frac{7}{8}$
1874	7·09	11·80	58$\frac{5}{16}$
1873	2·50	12·30	59$\frac{1}{4}$
1872	6·65	11·14	60$\frac{9}{16}$
1871	8·71	16·52	60$\frac{1}{2}$
1870	1·58	10·65	60$\frac{9}{16}$
1869	2·86	6·73	60$\frac{9}{16}$
1868	1·63	7·71	60
1867	·64	8·02	60
1866	2·36	10·78	61$\frac{1}{2}$

The foreign commerce of the *Dominion of Canada* for each of the ten years from 1868 to 1877 was, according to the official returns, as follows:

YEARS ENDING JUNE 30.	Exports.	Gross imports.	Net imports.
1868	$57,567,888	$73,459,644	$71,985,806
1869	60,474,781	70,415,165	67,402,170
1870	78,573,490	74,814,889	71,287,603
1871	74,173,618	96,092,971	56,947,482
1872	82,639,663	111,480,527	107,709,116
1873	89,789,922	128,011,281	127,514,594
1874	89,351,928	128,213,582	127,404,169
1875	77,886,979	128,070,288	119,618,657
1876	80,966,485	98,210,846	94,783,218
1877	75,875,893	99,327,962	96,800,483

In 1878 the total imports were $91,199,577, and the total exports $79,323,667. The foreign trade of Canada is mainly with Great Britain and the United States. The proportions in which these two countries participate in the aggregate trade has greatly altered in the last few years. In 1873 the imports from Great Britain, $68,522,776, exceeded by nearly 50 per cent. the imports from the United States, $47,735,678, and were more than 75 per cent. in excess of the exports to Great Britain. In 1878 the imports from Great Britain had fallen to $37,431,180, while the imports from the United States, $48,631,739, had not diminished; and the exports to Great Britain had increased to $45,941,539, while the exports to the United States had shrunk to $25,244,898. For the first time in her history Canada has been able to show a favorable balance in her trade with England for the last three years, while her aggregate trade still shows an adverse balance, which is owing now to the United States instead of to Great Britain: in 1873 England supplied Canada with 53 per cent. of her imports, and the United States supplied 37 per cent. ; in 1878 the United States supplied 53 per cent. and Great Britain 41 per cent.

COMMERCE OF THE UNITED STATES. Comparing the latest official statements of the foreign trade of all countries, the commerce of the United States is found to have been less in total volume than that of only three, Great Britain, Germany, and France, and the export trade inferior in magnitude to that of Great Britain and Germany alone. A comparison of the imports and exports of the several countries shows that while the United States in 1877-'78 exported 257 million dollars' worth of merchandise more than they imported, Great Britain imported 690 million dollars' worth in excess of exports, Germany 272, France 45, Netherlands 83, and Belgium 67 millions. The only other countries which show a favorable balance besides the United States are India, whose excess of exports is 115 million dollars; Austria, 37 millions; Japan 2 millions; Siam, 3 millions; and the South American countries —Brazil with 6, the Argentine Republic with 4, and Chili with 2 millions balance on the credit side.

Until 1876 the balance of trade was almost

invariably against the United States. In the period from 1835 to 1850 there was an excess in the imports of merchandise over the exports aggregating 88 million dollars, and an excess in the imports of specie over the exports of 44 millions. From 1851 to 1860 inclusive the importation of merchandise exceeded the exportation by 356 millions; but this was more than balanced by exportation of coin and bullion amounting to 417 millions. During the period of the war there was a small excess of imports. After the war followed a period of unexampled commercial expansion and extension of the facilities of production and transportation, during which the external trade has been nearly doubled. The augmentation in productive facilities was accomplished in part by foreign capital, and to a considerable extent with imported material; so that during the thirteen years from 1861 to 1873, while the exports in the latter part of the period increased in a rapid and steady ratio, a large debt was accumulating abroad against the United States, which is represented in the trade returns by an aggregate excess in the imports of merchandise over exports of 1,155 millions, against which must be offset the net exportation of bullion, amounting to 657 million dollars. In 1874 the merchandise balance turned out in favor of the United States for the first time since the war. It was the first time, indeed, since the discovery of gold in California, save in 1858, when a similar cause worked a sudden reduction of imports, and one year in the beginning of the war, when the exports and imports nearly balanced each other. The excess of exports in 1874 was 18 millions; in 1875 there was again a slight excess in the imports, amounting to 19 millions. In 1876 the balance changed definitively in favor of the United States, the excess of exports in that year amounting to 79 millions, increasing in 1876 to 151 millions, and in 1877 to 257 millions. The aggregate excess of exports for these last three years only more than extinguishes the accumulated debt shown by the aggregate unfavorable balances of the previous period, embracing a destructive war and the multiplication of productive and commercial facilities by means of material imported largely from Europe, and at prices which were fully double those which obtain to-day. The aggregate favorable balance for the five years in the merchandise account is 488 million dollars, which swells by the addition of the net exports of coin and bullion, which were 169 millions, to a total of 657 millions. The imports of merchandise grew from 357 millions in 1868 to 642 millions in 1873, and then declined without a break to 437 millions in 1878. The decline is due in part to the cessation of railroad-building and other improvements with imported material, in part to the diminished power of consumption in the community and the practice of enforced or voluntary economy, and in part to the reduction of values. The exports of domestic products increased steadily

from 281 millions in 1868 to 586 millions in 1874, then fell off to 513 millions in 1875, and increased again with rapid strides to 540 millions in 1876, 602 millions in 1877, and 694 millions in 1878. The decline in 1875 was not due to diminished exportations, but to a large fall in average prices.

The increase in the export trade in merchandise of over one third in value since 1873, in spite of an equal decline in prices, is partly due to the adventitious cause of short crops in Europe; but there is no reason to expect that the recent improvements in the means of production and transportation will not enable the raw products of America to hold their own in the markets of Europe. The export trade in food articles occupies a position of natural rivalry and antagonism to the export trade in manufactures, since the more Europe becomes dependent on America for food, the more sharp will be its competition in its own and neutral markets and in the American market for an outlet for manufactures. If the present extension of agriculture and increase in the exported surplus continues, then the test will be the more severe to which the American manufacturers will be subjected to show in what branches of industry superior skill, knowledge, taste, honesty, cheaper power and cheaper raw material, priority of development, the advantage of accumulated capital, or better commercial communications with the markets, will enable them to sustain the competition of the older industrial nations.

The magnitude of the foreign trade of a country indicates better than any other sign the material progress and social well-being of the people. The average annual value of imports of merchandise into America during the five years from 1835 to 1839 inclusive was 139 million dollars; the average annual exports amounted to 113 millions. The succeeding lustrum, 1840-'44, was a period of retardation, in which the average imports declined to 104 millions and the exports to 92 millions. From 1845 to 1849 the imports averaged 128 and the exports 130 millions. In the succeeding five years, 1850-'54, the imports had increased to 230 and the exports to 187 millions. In the five years from 1855 to 1859 the imports had advanced further to 302 and the exports to 271 millions. After 1850 a new element enters into the account, which is not included in the merchandise returns, viz., the exports of the precious metals. Between 1850 and 1878 the total net exports of gold and silver amounted to about 1,280 million dollars, or some 90 millions more than the total adverse balance in merchandise for the whole period. The war had an unfavorable effect on the external commerce of the United States. In the period from 1860 to 1864, the average imports were 278 million and the exports 221 million dollars. Both the export and import trades were probably greater than in the preceding period, as the commerce of the belligerent Southern

States is not included in the reports. In the next five years, 1865–'69, the annual imports had increased to 368 millions, but the exports, 275 millions, stood about where they did ten years before. Toward the end of this period commenced the rapid development which, judged by the growth of the export trade, is equaled in the commercial history of the country only by the period of similar duration between the discovery of the California gold-fields and the outbreak of the civil war. Then the development was more varied. The American forests afforded the materials for the construction of a vast merchant marine. The possession of the carrying trade was exceedingly favorable to the exportation of manufactures, and numerous industries sprang up for the supply of distant neutral markets with industrial products. The increase in the exports of manufactures of iron and other metals, of cotton manufactures, leather goods, chemical products, and other finished industrial products, was twice as great between 1850 and 1860 as it was between 1860 and 1878. The merchant fleet passed into other bands, and the markets for these manifold industrial productions were rendered less accessible through the civil war. A revolution in naval architecture, whereby iron replaces wood and steam performs more perfectly the service of the wind, confirms the great manufacturing and maritime nation where coal and iron are the cheapest in the possession of the ship-building and carrying trades, where, fortified by an enormous invested capital, they must remain until the new materials can be produced more cheaply elsewhere, since no protective measures not forbidden by the law of nations can suffice to wrest them away. Yet during the late new advance in production the growth of manufacturing interests in the United States has been enormous, as may be seen by comparing the lists of imports for a series of years. Industries of the most vital importance, producing the staple manufactures of prime necessity and universal use, for which America formerly depended largely upon Europe, fostered under the wing of the Government by protective tariffs, are now able to nearly supply the entire needs of the people. Yet the progress seems to have been still more rapid in agriculture, and the population of the country to be more preponderantly engaged in agricultural production and in auxiliary industries, and in the production of crude commodities, than it was twenty years ago. Petroleum, silver, and other new mineral products occupy a similar position with reference to manufactures as agricultural produce. The increase in the exportation of grain and provisions, cotton and tobacco, has been shown in the preceding article. These products of the field form in a greater measure than ever before the main bulk of the exports, and swell the total more and more each year. These four articles, with mineral oil, formed in 1878 about 76½ per cent. of the total exports of domestic

commodities. Whether this extension will stil continue is somewhat problematical, as it has been accelerated by an abnormal demand resulting from recent failures of European crops. It is possible that the present increase of food production may be temporarily or permanently arrested by the return of good harvests abroad. It is more likely that with the increased facilities of transportation the light and fertile soil of the prairies will enable the American farmer to compete with the European, and that on the return of general prosperity the consumptive capacity of Europe will expand sufficiently to absorb all of these and other agricultural products now exported, and still more.

The capacity of the country for agricultural production is indefinitely greater than the crops yet obtained. The total yield of cereal crops in the United States in 1879, according to the reports of the Agricultural Bureau at Washington, was 2,492,169,590 bushels, compared with 2,298,371,150 bushels in 1878. In wheat there was an increase of from 420,122,400 to 448,-750,000 bushels; in corn from 1,388,268,750 to 1,601,151,570 bushels; the other, non-exportable crops showed a slight falling off. The crop of cotton was 4,926,285 bales, against 5,200,000 bales in 1878. The tobacco yield amounted to 384,059,659 lbs. The potato crop was 181,-369,340 bushels, or 57,000,000 bushels more than in 1878. The yield per acre was for wheat 13·7, for corn 30·2, and for potatoes 98·9 bushels; for cotton 176, and for tobacco 779 lbs.

If agricultural production should prove incapable of further development, if it should be fated to relapse and decline, the fortunes of the manufacturing industries will assume greater importance, and then the inquiry will press itself on the public mind whether the protected industries are in position, or will soon be in position, to hold their own in the open market, to produce an exchangeable equivalent for the foreign luxuries demanded by the people, and maintain the position of America among commercial nations. If, on the other hand, the foreign demand for the products of the soil should continue to increase, the same question may be pushed to a speedier solution, as the waxing agricultural interest may demand that the markets should be cleared for the cheapest goods and thrown open to all comers. That there are American manufactures which are able to compete in the neutral markets and in Europe with the products of the older manufacturing nations is seen in the subjoined table of the exports of the articles which are classed as manufactures in the official reports of the Treasury Department, for the years 1850, 1860, 1870, 1872, 1874, 1876, and 1878. This group of articles formed in 1850 11½ per cent. of the total exports of domestic merchandise, in 1860 not quite 13½ per cent., in 1870 something less than 20½ per cent., in 1872 19½ per cent., in 1874 less than 18½ per cent., in 1876 nearly 21 per cent., and in 1878 a little under 20 per cent.:

MANUFACTURES EXPORTED.	1850.	1860.	1870.	1872.	1874.	1876.	1878.
Iron manufactures	$1,914,460	$5,608,547	$13,305,904	$11,265,835	$14,519,681	$15,146,484	$15,742,358
Wood manufactures	4,771,683	8,095,190	11,326,760	12,122,554	15,046,894	12,592,582	13,260,010
Cotton manufactures	4,784,424	10,934,796	8,787,282	2,804,330	8,095,840	7,722,978	11,488,660
Leather and manufactures of.	224,291	1,547,177	678,831	8,684,029	4,756,518	10,008,985	8,950,030
Sugar, etc	322,280	440,210	661,526	1,189,238	1,657,899	6,745,771	4,920,094
Ordnance stores	190,350	467,772	1,228,570	1,165,347	980,877	1,162,589	4,888,070
Tobacco, manufactures of	648,882	8,398,428	1,604,805	2,523,755	2,569,357	2,833,155	3,681,317
Copper, and manufactures of.	105,060	1,664,122	679,061	423,356	868,722	3,732,854	2,921,931
Drugs and chemicals	384,769	1,115,455	2,495,156	2,830,370	2,797,095	3,391,488	2,979,058
Vegetable oils	Not stated.	26,799	312,140	556,016	546,449	418,175	2,864,896
Agricultural implements	Not stated.	Not stated.	1,068,476	1,547,413	8,089,758	2,256,449	2,575,197
Turpentine	229,741	1,916,289	1,357,802	2,521,857	2,758,938	1,672,068	2,383,569
Books, paper, etc	219,171	564,066	912,668	1,257,968	1,399,045	1,608,982	1,955,190
Hemp manufactures	63,188	274,386	586,874	673,108	1,377,281	1,155,141	1,591,756
Cars and carriages	95,722	816,973	976,542	1,419,999	1,693,782	1,147,963	1,511,858
Spirits, distilled, and wine	816,604	1,461,488	767,541	629,212	1,210,150	565,174	1,188,197
Timepieces	Not stated.	Not stated.	589,008	630,587	1,016,077	1,083,575	1,076,797
Toilet articles, etc	28,987	23,552	409,118	704,594	722,097	688,752	1,065,914
Glass and glassware	126,682	277,948	580,654	547,112	681,827	628,121	869,689
Musical instruments	21,634	129,658	267,400	401,194	550,327	815,938	756,477
Soap	664,968	494,405	622,715	606,527	651,282	673,732	621,567
Starch	Not stated.	Not stated.	107,187	165,415	420,809	524,956	605,521
Marble and stone manufact'es	34,510	176,239	188,046	165,811	168,977	236,255	597,356
Wearing apparel	207,682	525,175	424,170	437,799	427,992	579,595	569,762
Wool manufactures	Not stated.	Not stated.	124,159	212,669	124,099	336,380	448,984
Jewelry, plate, and plated ware	49,866	164,846	89,755	139,390	164,174	111,709	423,612
Lead, and manufactures of	85,479	96,527	28,815	48,132	802,044	102,726	814,904
Hats, caps, and bonnets	63,071	211,602	194,505	221,455	199,564	247,855	809,089
India-rubber manufactures		240,843	185,844	241,123	226,260	188,816	405,767
Gas fixtures and lamps	Not stated.	223,809	207,619	281,889	207,048	216,790	304,607
Paints and colors	67,597		109,906	112,572	117,647	179,522	289,075
Refined petroleum			30,429,057	31,709,555	39,008,320	80,502,812	43,564,569
Other articles	186,219	442,887	545,242	713,602	769,701	723,410	980,968
Total	$15,617,730	$42,408,934	$75,916,659	$83,687,761	$104,989,491	$110,208,840	$135,171,921

In the year 1878 the principal classes of merchandise entered in the following proportions into the total value of the exports, which was about 695¾ million dollars: Breadstuffs, 26·12 per cent. of total exports; raw cotton, 25·88; provisions, 17·76; mineral oil, 6·69; tobacco, 4·09; wood and manufactures of wood, 2·41; iron and steel and their manufactures, 2·28; cotton manufactures, 1·64; leather and leather manufactures, 1·16; tallow, 0·96; live animals, 0·84; oil-cake, 0·73; sugar and molasses, 0·70; ordnance stores, 0·69; drugs, chemicals, medicines, and dye-stuffs, 0·41; vegetable oils, 0·41; peltry, 0·38; agricultural implements, 0·37; copper and manufactures of copper, 0·36; naval stores, i. e., rosin, pitch, etc., 0·36; coal, 0·34; spirits of turpentine, 0·34; seeds, 0·33; animal oil, 0·32; hops, 0·31; hemp and its manufactures, 0·23; other metals and their manufactures, 0·22; carriages and cars, 0·22; fruits, 0·20; other unmanufactured articles, 1·04; other manufactured articles, 2·22.

The progress and fluctuations of American trade with the countries with which it has the most extended commercial intercourse are shown in the annexed table, which gives the value of the total imports from and exports to America of each country for the alternate years from 1865 to 1873, and the following successive years to 1877, in millions of dollars:

COUNTRIES.	1865.		1867.		1869.		1871.		1872.		1874.		1875.		1876.		1877.	
	Imp.	Exp.	Imp.	Exp.	Imp.	Exp.	Imp.	Exp.	Imp.	Exp.	Imp.	Exp.	Imp.	Exp.	Imp.	Exp.	Imp.	Exp.
Great Britain	103.4	85.1	225.0	172.3	185.0	153.8	273.2	220.7	316.8	287.2	345.8	180.0	317.1	155.2	386.0	123.8	345.9	118.7
France	11.0	6.6	34.4	29.8	33.1	30.2	26.6	28.0	33.7	89.9	42.9	51.6	33.6	59.7	39.7	50.9	45.1	47.5
Germany	20.8	9.5	22.0	26.5	37.8	25.0	34.9	25.0	61.5	61.4	62.9	48.9	50.4	40.2	50.6	85.8	58.1	33.5
Cuba	18.6	30.0	14.1	33.8	12.4	56.9	14.8	57.5	16.8	77.0	17.1	85.4	15.3	64.5	12.8	56.0	13.8	65.8
Canada	28.8	33.2	21.0	25.0	28.8	29.2	32.2	32.2	32.5	34.5	37.6	43.4	34.8	36.2	28.2	35.0	39.3	24.2
Brazil	6.5	9.7	5.0	19.1	5.8	24.8	6.0	30.5	7.1	38.5	7.7	43.8	7.7	42.0	7.3	45.4	7.5	48.4
Belgium	6.2	1.3	7.1	3.2	6.7	2.9	11.8	4.1	15.7	5.7	20.5	5.7	12.7	6.1	16.7	5.4	18.8	5.0
China	2.6	5.1	3.5	12.1	5.2	18.9	9.0	20.0	9.3	27.1	9.7	13.5	8.5	14.6	4.7	12.8	4.9	12.8
Jamaica, etc.	13.7	9.7	10.0	4.4	9.2	6.5	8.9	7.2	9.3	6.9	9.3	4.9	9.6	7.0	10.2	4.5	9.6	9.7
Netherlands	3.1	0.7	3.0	1.5	4.0	2.6	12.6	2.0	11.2	2.9	18.9	2.5	7.5	2.8	12.2	2.4	70.5	2.5
Italy	6.1	2.1	4.9	5.2	5.7	6.2	6.1	7.4	7.2	7.9	8.3	8.4	7.2	9.1	7.7	7.6	8.4	7.1
British India	0.6	4.6	0.3	8.9	0.4	9.0	0.3	13.7	0.7	16.9	0.4	14.1	0.4	15.5	0.3	12.8	0.3	10.7
Mexico	16.3	6.2	5.3	1.0	4.8	2.8	7.6	8.2	6.2	4.2	5.9	4.8	5.7	5.1	6.2	5.1	5.8	5.9
Russia	0.5	1.8	2.1	1.6	4.3	1.1	6.8	1.4	11.7	2.2	10.8	1.2	11.4	1.8	11.9	1.1	4.4	4.0
Spain	4.0	1.0	5.5	3.0	7.6	8.5	10.2	4.1	10.0	4.9	11.6	4.5	7.5	4.5	10.1	8.8	10.4	8.2
Colombia	4.5	4.1	4.2	1.9	4.2	4.6	4.0	5.5	5.8	6.1	6.2	7.9	4.4	12.2	4.0	5.0	4.0	5.0
Venezuela	1.8	1.3	0.9	1.7	0.8	2.8	0.8	2.9	1.5	5.5	1.9	5.3	1.9	5.9	2.8	5.5	3.8	7.0
Japan	0.0	0.2	0.7	2.6	1.2	3.2	0.4	5.2	1.1	7.9	1.0	6.4	1.6	7.7	1.0	15.4	1.2	18.6
Hayti	6.6	1.5	2.7	1.0	1.4	0.7	2.5	1.0	4.3	2.0	4.7	1.6	5.2	2.4	5.5	3.1	4.5	3.2
Australia	6.6	0.1	5.1	0.2	4.6	0.1	2.4	0.2	3.9	3.1	3.8	1.7	3.5	3.7	3.9	1.4	5.8	1.4
Argentine Republic	1.7	3.5	2.5	5.8	2.4	5.1	1.2	7.0	8.2	7.5	2.6	4.5	1.4	5.8	1.5	3.6	1.2	3.4
Porto Rico	2.8	8.4	1.6	5.8	2.4	7.4	2.5	9.4	7.9	2.0	6.8	2.2	6.9	1.8	4.1	2.0	4.8	3.2
Dutch E. Indies	0.1	1.0	0.2	2.6	0.1	1.9	0.2	8.0	0.2	7.5	0.4	8.8	1.0	6.7	0.6	5.9	2.6	4.5
Hawaiian Isld's	0.6	0.5	0.8	1.0	0.7	1.2	0.8	1.1	0.6	1.2	0.6	1.0	0.6	1.2	0.7	1.3	1.2	2.5

Of the imports of foreign merchandise in 1878, sugar and molasses was the heaviest item, making 18·27 per cent. of the total of $437,051,532; coffee, 11·88; woolens and raw wool, 7·69; silk goods and raw silk, 5·91; chemicals, drugs, dyes, and medicines, 5·66; cottons, 4·47; hides and skins, 3·94; tea, 3·58; linens, 3·57; tin, 2·79; fruits, 2·36; iron and steel and manufactures, 2·07; breadstuffs, 2·02; leather and leather goods, 1·71; tobacco and manufactures, 1·47; wood and manufactures, 1·32; provisions, 1·31; wines and spirits, 1·26; India-rubber, 1·13; and the remaining 14·86 per cent. was about half composed of manufactures.

The countries which take the largest share in the commerce of the United States, according to the returns for 1877–'78, with the total imports from and the total exports of domestic products to each, in millions of dollars, and the percentage of each in the total commerce of the United States, in the total export trade, and the total import trade, are as follows:

COUNTRIES.	Exports to.	Per cent. of total exports.	Imports from	Per cent. of total imports.	Total trade with the U. S.	Per cent. of total commerce.
Great Britain	857·4	54·57	107·3	24·55	494·7	43·14
France	55·8	7·79	43·3	9·92	98·6	8·61
Germany	54·8	7·73	84·7	7·96	89·5	7·81
Cuba and Porto Rico	13·5	1·91	61·7	14·12	75·2	6·56
British America	38·2	5·89	25·3	5·80	63·6	5·55
Brazil	5·6	1·22	42·9	9·88	51·6	4·50
Belgium	23·5	3·32	8·9	0·91	27·5	2·40
China and Hong Kong	0·8	0·97	18·1	4·15	24·9	2·18
Netherlands	13·3	1·58	2·7	0·64	16·0	1·40
Italy	8·7	1·28	6·7	1·54	15·4	1·34
British West Indies and Honduras	7·6	1·08	5·6	1·30	13·2	1·15
British East Indies	0·3	0·13	12·1	2·76	12·2	1·12
Mexico	7·4	1·05	5·2	1·21	12·7	1·11
Russia	11·1	1·57	0·6	0·15	11·7	1·02
Spain	8·2	1·16	8·2	0·75	11·4	1·00
Colombia	4·4	0·63	5·8	1·34	10·3	0·90
Venezuela	2·8	0·89	7·3	1·67	10·1	0·88
Japan	2·2	0·82	7·4	1·70	9·6	0·85
Hayti and San Domingo	4·8	0·68	8·2	0·74	8·0	0·71
Australian Colonies	6·7	0·95	1·1	0·27	7·9	0·69
Argentine Republic	2·1	0·30	4·9	1·13	7·1	0·62
Dutch East Indies	1·4	0·20	4·5	1·05	6·0	0·52
Cape Colony and Gibraltar	4·7	0·66	1·2	0·29	5·9	0·52
Greece	4·8	0·69	0·2	0·05	5·1	0·45
French West Indies and Guiana	1·5	0·28	2·8	0·66	4·4	0·39
Portugal	4·0	0·56	0·4	0·10	4·4	0·39
Hawaiian Islands	1·7	0·25	2·6	0·61	4·4	0·39
Central America	1·2	0·18	2·9	0·68	4·2	0·37
Other countries	21·1	2·95	17·6	4·07	31·2	2·72
Total	709·9	100·00	437·0	100·00	1,146·9	100·00

The proportion in which Mexico, Central America, and the West Indies entered into the total commerce was 10·49 per cent. Intercourse with South America formed 8·03 per cent. of the total trade. The share of British America was 5·55 per cent., making the trade with American countries 24·07 of the total volume. Asia's share, with that of Japan and the East Indian islands, 4·83 per cent.; that of Australasia, 0·70; that of the other islands of the Pacific, 1·08; that of Africa and adjacent islands, 0·57; and that of all other islands and ports, 0·05 per cent. of the total export and import trade.

Of the foreign commerce of 1878, 68·70 per cent. of the total of 1,146 million dollars, or 787 millions, was with the countries of Europe, with all of which there was a heavy balance in favor of the United States. Europe received 583 million dollars' worth, or 82·18 per cent., of the total exports of the United States, and furnished 157 millions worth, or 46·67 per cent., of the total imports into the United States.

Great Britain received 54·57 per cent. of the total exports from the United States, and furnished 24·55 per cent. of the imports. The favorable balance amounted to 280 million dollars, or 2⅗ times the total imports from Great Britain. The value of raw cotton exported to Great Britain was 117 million dollars, or 65·23 per cent. of the total export; the value of breadstuffs, 125 millions, or 69·21 per cent. of the exports, to which may be added a considerable portion of the exports to Canada, making perhaps 75 per cent. in all. The value of the exports of provisions to the United Kingdom was 80 million dollars, or 64·91 per cent. of the total export, and with the Canadian imports added 67·12 per cent. The other principal exports to Great Britain were: tobacco, 9·1 millions; petroleum, 6·8, or 13·97 per cent. of the total export; oil-cake, 4·9; leather and manufactures, 4·7; wood and manufactures, 4·2; live animals and tallow, 3·1 each. Among the other manufactures England took 1 million worth of iron and steel products and 1·4 million worth of cotton fabrics. The values of the principal imports from the United Kingdom were: woolens, 14 millions; linens, 13·1; cottons, 10·3, or 54·17 per cent. of the total imports; tin and manufactures, 9·5; iron and steel and manufactures, 6; soda, 4·4; pottery, 3; hides and skins, 2·9; silk manufactures, 2·7; drugs, etc., 2·7.

The commerce with France formed 8·61 per

cent. of the total foreign trade for the year, amounting to 98 million dollars. France took from the United States 55 million dollars' worth of merchandise, or 7·79 per cent. of the total exports, and furnished 43 million dollars' worth, or 9·92 per cent. of the total imports. The principal exports to France were: raw cotton, 25·9 million dollars, or 14·42 per cent. of the total value exported; provisions, 8·6 millions; breadstuffs, 7·6 millions, 4.21 per cent. of the total export; petroleum, 2·3; leaf-tobacco, 2·2; tallow, 1·5. The principal imports from France were: silk and manufactures, 11·6 million dollars; woolens, 7 millions; leather and manufactures, 3·7; wines and spirits, 3·2; drugs, etc., 2·2; cotton goods, 1·8; fancy articles, 1·5; precious stones, 1·3; and buttons, 1·1.

The trade with Germany amounted to 89 millions, or 7·81 per cent. of the total volume of commerce. The exports to Germany, 54 millions in value, were 7·73 per cent. of the total exports, and the imports from Germany, 34 millions, made 7·96 per cent. of the total imports. Germany received 11·9 million dollars' worth of petroleum, or 25·58 per cent. of the total export, nearly double the export to Great Britain, who was the next largest taker of this commodity. Germany is also the largest consumer of American lard, receiving after England the largest shipments of provisions, amounting to 10·6 million dollars, or 8·62 per cent. of the total exports under this head. Her imports of raw cotton are, next to those of England and France, the most considerable, amounting to 13·3 millions, or 7·41 per cent. of the entire export.

There is an exceedingly heavy balance against the United States in the commerce with the countries which are the sources of the sugar, coffee, and tea supplies, and of certain raw materials, as hides and skins, raw silk, etc. With Cuba and the other Spanish colonies, Brazil, China, and British India, there is an aggregate adverse balance of 112 million dollars, the imports from those countries being of nearly five times the value of the total exports of American commodities to them. These same countries are large consumers of manufactures of the classes in which American manufacturers expect to compete with the industries of England and the other industrial and commercial nations. Some of them are left as much in debt every year to Great Britain for textiles and metal wares as the United States are to them for their agricultural products. There has long been a market in several of these countries for American cured meats and provisions, and for a number of coarse manufactures in which there is no competition with Europe. The use of mineral oil has lately extended to these nations, and the demand is increasing every year. The condition of the trade with other countries occupying a similar position with reference to the United States is not quite so unfavorable as with those mentioned above. The exports to

Venezuela, which furnished 12·46 per cent. of the coffee imported (68·30 per cent. coming from Brazil), amounted to nearly 3 million dollars, against imports of about two and a half times that value. The imports from Japan were 7·4 millions, against exports of the value of 2·2 millions. The Dutch East Indies exported to the United States something over three times as much as they received in exchange, or 4·5 millions against 1·4 million. The exports to the Argentine Republic were 2·1 millions, and the imports 4·9 millions. The balance against the United States in the trade with Central America, with Uruguay, and with the French West Indies was about equal to the exports to those countries; with Peru it was of about half the amount of the exports; with British Guiana there was a very slight adverse balance. In the extensive trade with the United States of Colombia the excess of imports was little over 25 per cent. of the exports, which amounted to 4·4 millions. With the Hawaiian Islands, with whom a special treaty of reciprocity has lately been concluded, the imports into the United States amounted to 2·6 millions, against 1·7 million exports. To Mexico there were exports of the value of 7·4 million dollars, or 2·2 millions in excess of the imports. With Hayti and San Domingo there was a balance of 1·6 million, or one third of the exports, in favor of the United States; with the British West Indies and Honduras the export trade, 7·6 millions, exceeded the imports by 1·9 million; the exports to Chili were of nearly three times the value of the imports. With the other West Indian Islands, with Turkey, Egypt, and the other countries of Africa, and the islands of the ocean, the American exports largely exceeded the imports.

The exports of highly finished manufactures, the industrial products in which the materials are in a large measure modified by human labor and skill, and in which American industry, ingenuity, and commercial enterprise come into direct competition with European work, form thus far but a small portion of the exports of the country. Yet the quality of certain of these products, and the ease and rapidity with which they are making their way in contested markets, have already produced serious misgivings in the minds of the English, who have the most to fear and to lose from American industrial competition. The value of the American exports of this class compared with the exports of Great Britain is very insignificant, and out of all proportion to the feeling which this competition has excited in England. Still it has already had an effect upon sales and prices. The character of the American products, their superior qualities either of ingenuity of design, of honest workmanship, or of cheapness, or frequently of all three combined, and the fact that their sales have increased during the late period of depression, while the exports of British products have greatly shrunk in value, in spite of the higher wages paid in the United States, England's possession of the carrying trade and prestige in the markets, and the power of her accumulated capital, give sufficient cause for fears on one side of the ocean and hopes on the other that the United States will some day share the world's markets with England and become a great industrial nation, receiving substantial rewards from all parts of the earth for the well-directed and energetic application of the acute and laborious practical genius which Americans long ago won the name of possessing. The increase in the exports of the most finished manufactured products has been within the last year or two even greater than in the exports of agricultural produce. This must be looked upon not so much as a vantage actually gained, for a severer struggle with the enormous capital of European manufacturers and labor, compelled to accept lowered wages there while in America it can find other employment, may check for a time the export of staple manufactures; yet it is a certain sign that America will at some not distant date rival the foremost industrial nations in the main branches of mechanical production. The exports of all classes of iron and steel products and of cotton manufactures increased nearly 5 million dollars in 1878. The markets for American manufactures are of two kinds: the old countries whose mechanical arts are of a primitive order, and the new countries whose only products are crude materials, on the one hand (the so-called neutral markets), and the manufacturing countries of Europe on the other. In the neutral markets, owing to the want of direct commercial communications, American manufactures have not gained the footing which they deserve.

The similarity in its natural condition of America to the sparsely populated and undeveloped new countries has led to the invention and manufacture of such implements and other articles as best suit their requirements. In many articles of utility which are adapted to European needs also—especially those in which cheapness, durability, and strength are combined, those in which manual labor has been superseded by mechanical production, and those which embody ingenious mechanical devices—the active spirit of improvement has developed an American product which is superior in form, in the distribution of weight or the selection of material, or in ingenious contrivance. Another important quality for which American wares have thus far been distinguished in foreign markets is their honest genuineness. Even in the style of packing, the wakefulness of the American mind leads to a saving of labor and trouble. When the Sheffield hardware merchants ask the reason of orders which they receive from English and Australian retailers for American small castings, they are informed that it is partly due to the paper boxes in which the goods are packed, from which they can be readily taken out and replaced. All American improvements when once

introduced in foreign markets are soon adopted or imitated by European makers. Even the American trade-mark is copied. When inferior imitations are foisted on any public, the fraud is sure to be detected and the genuine article to come out victorious. It is said that there are more American calicoes made in Manchester than there are imported; yet the export of American piece-goods to England is still increasing. The ordinary qualities of cotton goods of American make, though of lighter weight, wear better than the British, and are always free from the clay and size with which the English goods are often adulterated. If it should prove possible to export cottons from the United States more cheaply or as cheaply as the Manchester product can be exported, the vast markets of the Orient and of all the outlying nations are already opened to American manufactures and alienated from the English by their dishonorable practice of adulteration. The inhabitants of Madagascar, it is said, will take American cottons at any price in preference to others. They are already shipped, mostly in small quantities, to all nations. Of the 11·4 millions of exported cotton goods in 1878, 2·5 went to China and Hong Kong, 1·5 to the United Kingdom, 1·3 to Mexico, 1·2 to British America, 0·8 to Africa and Madagascar, 0·5 each to Chili, Colombia, and Brazil.

The American locomotives and railroad cars are the only kinds adapted to new countries, where railroads must be laid cheaply, with uneven beds and winding curves. The American agricultural machinery goes to all countries where farming on a large scale is practiced, and it has not yet been successfully copied in Europe. The superiority of the simpler tools made in the United States, in material and workmanship, and above all in form and the nice adjustment of weight and parts, is recognized in the British colonies to the consternation of English makers. The form of the American axe is admired as a marvel of ingenious adaptation to the work to be performed; the plow has been subjected to equally important modifications; and in saws, spades, hoes, and mattocks, and all the implements of agriculture and forestry, improvements have been wrought in this country while Europe has contentedly clung to ancient models. In locks and other building hardware, a strong demand has sprung up in England as well as in the colonies, on account of their superiority to the ordinary Birmingham products in strength and finish, and in handy and practical utility of design. All new inventions of remarkable utility are certain to be adopted in Europe, more rapidly usually than European improvements are introduced into America. Thus, the hotel and goods elevators are being introduced in Germany and Holland; and celluloid is already affecting the ivory industry in England and France.

Whether the protective policy has helped or retarded the sound and healthful development of American industry, the truth can not be ignored that a genuine development is taking place in many branches. Not alone in cotton goods and hardware are the American manufacturers proving themselves able to sustain the decisive test of an increasing export of the protected articles. The importations of paper in 1878 were only one tenth in value of the imports of 1873, and were principally confined to fine wall-papers, while the exports have doubled since 1870 and 1871. The fineness and finish of American writing-papers have already gained them a market in China and Japan, and in Holland and other countries. In chemicals the same process of a concurrent decline of imports and increase of exports is taking place. Tartaric acid, of which a short time ago half a million pounds was imported, is now supplied entirely at home. The opening of the borax mines in Nevada has stopped the importation of that article, which England formerly supplied; the price has fallen from 35 to 8 or 9 cents a pound, and England has become a large buyer both of the crude and the refined product. France formerly sent 6 million pounds of cream of tartar to the United States, but now the domestic factories furnish the entire supply. Fruit sirups, which have a large sale in the West Indies and South America, were once supplied by France; but this entire trade is now passing into the hands of American manufacturers, who produce a richer-flavored as well as a cheaper article. Formerly England sent large quantities of doors to Australia and the other colonies poor in forests; now American machine-made joinery—doors, sashes, and Venetian blinds—is being shipped to Australia from California, while in England a demand is arising for the American doors.

There are American industries, it has been seen, which are already able to hold their own in outside markets against European competition. An increasing export at profitable rates for a series of years is a sufficient proof that America is able, with the present development of its natural resources and its existing conditions regarding capital and labor, to enter the field with the industrial and commercial countries in competition for the world's market. That this has taken place in the staple branches of manufacture is an indication that the conditions of production are favorable to that end. Many manufacturers express themselves willing already to see the protective duties removed in their own branches. When the export trade is fairly established, the whole purpose of protection has been gained. Every year new products of American manufacture find a foreign outlet, and there is every indication that the United States have fairly entered upon a career of industrial greatness.

The imports into the United States for the nine months ending September 30, 1879, were: merchandise, $355,736,388; specie, $46,515,595; total imports, $402,251,983. The exports for the same period were: domestic produce, $508,900,787; reëxports, $7,729,847; total merchandise, $516,630,634; specie, $21,033,863; total exports, $537,664,497. The imports for the corresponding nine months of 1878 were: merchandise, $324,611,718; specie, $22,278,788; total imports, $346,890,506. The exports for the same period were: domestic produce, $523,458,842; foreign goods, $10,480,435; total merchandise, $533,639,277; specie, $21,959,384; total exports, $555,898,611. The exports of merchandise for the nine months of 1879 thus show a decrease of 17·3 millions compared with the exports of the same part of 1878, and the imports of merchandise show an increase of 81·1 millions. The favorable balance is decreased from 209·3 to 160·9 million dollars for the three quarters; and including the specie movement, the reduction of the commercial balance is increased by the increased excess in the imports of coin and bullion over the exports, which amounted to 25·5 millions in 1879, against 0·3 million in the nine months of 1878: the total surplus of exports is therefore 135·4 millions, against 209 millions for the three quarters in 1878.

CONGREGATIONALISTS. The following is a summary of the statistics of the Congregational churches of the United States, as they are given in the "Congregational Year-Book" for 1879:

STATES, ETC.	Number of churches.	Number of ministers.	Number of members.	Number in Sunday-schools.
Alabama	15	11	687	1,552
California	79	70	4,447	7,935
Colorado	9	13	410	463
Connecticut	298	874	54,077	52,133
Dakota	20	9	418	560
District of Columbia	1	13	595	1,100
Florida	1	1	74	100
Georgia	11	9	722	1,045
Illinois	241	281	22,787	29,541
Indian Territory	1	1	11	90
Indiana	29	20	1,680	2,010
Iowa	225	208	15,702	18,982
Kansas	152	98	5,207	9,052
Kentucky	8	8	473	786
Louisiana	14	11	863	533
Maine	237	186	21,101	21,285
Maryland	2	1	151	275
Massachusetts	529	673	91,463	100,488
Michigan	225	206	16,935	21,364
Minnesota	123	99	6,223	10,430
Mississippi	4	2	141	275
Missouri	71	47	3,391	4,060
Nebraska	105	66	2,822	3,491
Nevada	1	1	23	40
New Hampshire	186	191	20,317	24,102
New Jersey	23	88	3,293	4,205
New York	296	245	33,115	35,464
North Carolina	5	4	283	615
Ohio	216	168	23,287	28,896
Oregon	9	12	715	1,285
Pennsylvania	76	51	5,194	5,413
Rhode Island	25	34	4,574	5,408
South Carolina	2	1	249	176
Tennessee	7	7	443	465
Texas	7	7	199	357
Utah	2	2	49	180
Vermont	197	209	19,851	22,970
Virginia	3	4	214	405
Washington Territory	11	7	221	882
West Virginia	2	3	67	277
Wisconsin	191	164	18,866	17,586
Wyoming	1	2	45	160
Total	3,690	3,496	375,654	435,741

The whole number of families connected with the churches was 165,842. The baptisms for the year included 10,686 of adults and 5,556 of infants. Of the churches, 2,716 were returned as with pastors and 904 were "vacant," or without regularly installed pastors; of the ministers, 2,360 were in pastoral work, and 1,136 were not in pastoral work. Besides, there were 209 licentiates. Of the members, 48,615 were marked "absent," or thus designated as "persons who live at a place other than that of their church relations, and do not worship with their church." Contributions were reported by 2,760 churches to the amount of $951,890 for benevolent purposes, and of $2,-313,796 for home expenditures. Of the ministers marked as "not in pastoral service," 134 were connected with educational work in colleges, seminaries, and academies, or as superintendents of schools; 60 were connected with the national or other benevolent societies as secretaries, superintendents, etc.; 34 were in missionary or similar work; 22 were editors; 67 were in secular work; and 152 were retired by age or infirmities. The receipts of the *American Home Missionary Society* for the year ending May 1, 1879, were $273,691, and the expenditures were $260,330. The indebtedness of the Society was $50,399, against which it had a balance in the treasury of $13,401. Nine hundred and forty-six ministers were employed during the year in 34 States and Territories, 29 of whom had preached in foreign languages.

The thirty-third annual meeting of the *American Missionary Association* was held at Chicago, Illinois, beginning October 28th. The Hon. E. S. Tobey of Boston, Massachusetts, presided. The Treasurer reported that his receipts for the year had been $314,450, of which $99,019 had been contributed for special institutions. His expenditures had been $213,955, of which $122,665 had been applied to the Southern work (among the freedmen), $6,595 to the work among the Chinese, $347 to that among the Indians, $10,226 to the foreign missions, and $37,390 to the payment of the debt of the Society. The largest work of the Society was among the freedmen in the Southern States, where it had under its care 67 churches, with 4,600 members, and 44 schools, with 190 teachers and 7,207 pupils, classified as follows: primary, 2,739; intermediate, 1,465; grammar, 633; normal, 2,022; collegiate preparatory, 169; collegiate, 63; law, 28; theological, 86. A gift of $150,000 which had been received would be used for the erection of new buildings for the schools at Nashville, Tennessee, Atlanta, Georgia, New Orleans, Louisiana, and Talladega, Alabama. It was estimated that 150,000 pupils had been taught during the year by present and former students of the higher schools of the Association. The Association had now under its care the Indians of four agencies, numbering 13,000 souls. Nine missionaries, teachers, and assistants were employed

among the Indians. The station at Skokomish included a church of 23 members, with three other preaching stations, 128 families, 200 attendants on worship, and 110 children in the Sunday-schools. Seventy-seven Indian boys and nine Indian girls had spent the year at the Hampton Institute, Virginia, where, it was represented, they had been contented and studious, and had made "marked and steady progress." Resolutions were adopted, declaring that the aim of the Association with reference to the Indians should be, "as far as possible, and as rapidly as possible, to secure for them: *a*, a legalized standing in the courts of the United States; *b*, ownership of land in severalty; *c*, the full rights of American citizenship. These three things, we believe, are essential if the Indian is to be, not Christianized or civilized, but saved from extermination." The Association most heartily approved "the plan of the Indian Bureau to secure to as many Indians as possible the advantages of education offered at such distant schools as that at Hampton and Carlisle, at the same time believing that the system of boarding-schools on the reservations, which for many years have been maintained by the Government and the missionaries, is the chief educational agency that must be relied upon for bettering the condition of the Indian." A resolution was also adopted declaring that the Association, "believing that the treaties existing between the United States and China, so far as they relate to the rights of emigration from one country to the other, and the treatment such immigrants should receive from the people and nation among whom and in which they live, are right, just, wise, and Christian, does heartily record its appreciation of the high services which President Hayes, under God, has by his timely veto of the anti-Chinese bill been enabled to render the republic in preserving inviolate its treaty obligations, and also the cause of Christianity, in removing a threatened formidable barrier to the evangelization of the Chinese, not only in America, but also in their native land; and the Association hereby tenders him its profound thanks for the same." The Secretaries were authorized to notify President Hayes of this resolution. Twelve schools were taught among the Chinese of the Pacific coast, which employed 21 teachers, including five Chinese helpers, and returned a total number of 1,489 pupils, with an average attendance of 252 pupils. Eighty-four Chinese had given evidence of conversion, and 137 had renounced idolatry: The Congregational Association of Christian Chinese had 198 members, of whom 44 had been received during the year. The African mission, in the Mendi country, included six missionaries, with the wives of two, and five other assistants, two churches, with 85 members and 190 Sunday-school scholars, and three day-schools, the largest of which, at Good-Hope station, had an enrollment of 245 and an average attendance of 156 scholars. Mr. Robert Arthington of Leeds, England, had a year before offered the Association £3,000 for the establishment of a mission in Eastern Africa, and the officers of the Freedmen's Missions Aid Society of Great Britain had offered to collect other funds for the same object. The Association voted that on receiving the sum offered by Mr. Arthington and a similar sum from the British public, it would appropriate $20,000 to the foundation of the proposed mission, and would undertake to sustain it permanently.

The seventieth annual meeting of the *American Board of Commissioners for Foreign Missions* was held at Syracuse, New York, October 7th. The Rev. Mark Hopkins, D. D., presided. The Treasurer reported that his receipts for the year had been $518,386, and his expenditures $513,817. The year had been marked by retrenchment of all expenses, yet the number of additions on profession of faith in all the fields, given at more than two thousand souls, was larger than in any previous year since the time when an extraordinary number of accessions had taken place in the Sandwich Islands, more than thirty years before. The Turkish missions were recovering from the injurious effects of the late war. The additions to the churches in India—nearly seven hundred—were greater than 'in any former year. In Austria, the missionaries had been embarrassed by official restrictions concerning which representations were to be made to the Government. Nearly fifty additions had been made to the churches in Spain, and the opening of a school for girls was reported. The mission in Mexico had lost ground for the want of men to carry it on. In the Dakota mission, the Indian converts had organized a home missionary society, which had raised more than $800 during the past three years to meet the expenses of native teachers and preachers among the wild tribes. Special reports were also made from the missions in Zoolooland, China, and Japan.

A paper was read on "The Proposed Mission in Central Africa," which, after discussing the various features of the condition of the African Continent, and the missions already established or contemplated in it, recommended the region of Bihé and the Coanza River, in about 12° south latitude and two hundred and fifty miles from the Atlantic Ocean, as the most suitable district in which to found the mission. The paper was approved, and the Prudential Committee was advised to continue the inquiries already set on foot, with the understanding that it was purposed to establish the mission proposed at the earliest practicable day.

CONGREGATIONALISTS IN GREAT BRITAIN.— The following is a summary of the statistics of the Congregational churches in Great Britain and the colonies, as given in the "Congregational Year-Book" for 1879:

England—Churches, 2,071; branch churches, 310; preaching stations, 831; evangelistic stations, 172. Wales—Welsh churches, 546; branch churches, 282;

preaching stations, 83; English churches, 60; preaching stations, 4. Scotland—Churches, 110. Ireland—Churches, 38. Islands of the British seas—Churches 17. Canada and Newfoundland—Churches, 120. Australia—Churches, 116; preaching stations, 112. New Zealand—Churches, 20. Natal—Churches, 2; preaching stations, 10. Cape Colony—Churches independent of the London Missionary Society, 21. Jamaica—Churches independent of the London Missionary Society, 14. British Guiana—Churches independent of the London Missionary Society, 12. India—Churches independent of the London Missionary Society, 6. China—Churches independent of the London Missionary Society, 2. Chapels and schools—New chapels opened, 51; new schools opened, 18.

The annual meeting of the *Congregational Union of England and Wales* was held in London May 12th. The Rev. Professor Newth of New College was elected Chairman of the Union for 1880. The report of the Secretary gave a statement of the recommendations of the committee which had been appointed to inquire into the working of Congregational colleges. It was recommended that the theological course should be separated from that of arts, and that whenever it was practicable advantage should be taken of the teaching afforded by such institutions as Owens College, the Yorkshire College, and the universities of England and Scotland. The committee proposed also a celebration of the jubilee of the Union, to be held in 1880, and to consist in part in the delivery of lectures in London and elsewhere by Congregational clergymen upon certain periods and aspects of church history. The Rev. J. Guinness Rogers had been appointed to deliver the Congregational lecture for the year; his subject would be "Church Systems in England in the Nineteenth Century." The Church-Aid and Home Mission Society, recently organized, reported that £30,000 had been secured for its work during its first year. A resolution was unanimously adopted condemning the foreign policy of the Government, censuring especially the Afghan and Zooloo wars.

The autumnal meeting of the Congregational Union was held at Cardiff, beginning October 14th. The Rev. W. Cuthbertson presided, and delivered an inaugural address on "Independency as a Witness-Bearer," in which, referring to the want of coöperation between the State Church and Nonconformists, he said that no step could much conduce to the social meeting which was desirable until disestablishment came. A paper was read on the position and prospects of Congregationalism in Wales, in which it was stated that there were now in the principality 1,022 chapels, 908 organized churches, 546 ordained ministers, 318 lay preachers, 108,000 communicants, and 108,000 other adherents excluding children under ten years of age, so that in round numbers the Congregationalists included a quarter of a million of people. The assembly resolved to recommend to the county associations to consider the propriety of appointing a confidential committee with which vacant churches and unsettled ministers might confer. The question of special missions was commended to the careful consideration of these associations, with a view of determining whether they should take steps, within their several limits, for the conducting of such missions by competent and certified persons. A long resolution was adopted, condemning the Afghan war, expressing the belief that the policy of which it formed a part ought to be reversed, and urging the members of the churches to employ their votes and influence at the next general election to secure the authoritative condemnation of this policy by the various constituencies. "The Assembly," the resolution continued, "does not in view of the election counsel silence on the part of the Nonconformists in relation to questions touching upon religious equality ; but in the presence of the great political difficulties of the time it feels that this is a crisis in which even these ought not to be allowed to prevent the union of the Liberal party for the purpose of putting an end to the costly and mischievous *régime* which has proved to be so full of menace to our constitutional liberty at home, and to derogate from our good name and our legitimate influence among other nations." Subjects were discussed in papers and addresses relating to collegiate education, business methods and church administration, spiritual life and the consecration of money, and Congregationalism and free thought.

The anniversary of the *London Missionary Society* was held May 16th. Sir William Muir presided. The financial report showed that the total annual receipts of the Society for general and special purposes had been £101,100, which the balance left from the last year increased to £117,813. The expenditures had been £123,-058. There were 153 missionaries employed, of whom 11 were women, with 300 native pastors, evangelists, and assistants, besides 83 native pastors, 500 assistant pastors and evangelists, and 3,400 volunteer preachers in Madagascar. The missions in Madagascar have been enlarged and strengthened by the addition since 1870 of nine country stations, " each provided with its mission-house, its model church, and school." The Central Girls' School, and the Normal School, and the Theological College have been erected at Antananarivo, and a normal school at Fianarantsoa; and the system of primary education has been revised and extended. The churches had been declared to be at liberty to manage their own affairs without any interference from secular or outside authority. A new station had been opened in China, and a new mission in the province of Sze-chuen partly provided for. In South Africa, the beginning of a mission at Lake Ngami and the opening of the Moffat Institution were mentioned. The mission to New Guinea had at the time of making up the report four ordained English missionaries with forty Polynesian missionaries, and had extended its usefulness along the southern coast of eastern New Guinea and to the islands in the neighborhood. The mission to Central Africa had been commenced near Lake Tanganyika, but had met with vicissitudes, and Dr. Mullens, the Secretary of the Society, was to be sent to look after its interests. A woman's mission had been established four years before, which now numbered eleven missionaries. Dr. Mullens was afterward sent to this mission, but he died on the way.

The *Irish Congregational Union* met in Dublin, September 30th. The occasion was marked by the celebration of the jubilee of the Union, it having been founded in 1829, and, though the smallest in numbers, being the second oldest Union in the United Kingdom. The principal business of the session related to efforts to raise the Provident Fund to £5,000.

The *Congregational Union of Scotland* met at Dundee, April 22d. The reports showed that a decrease had taken place in the general contributions. The widows' and ministers' provident funds were in good condition, but the income of the Chapel-Building Society had been only £41 for the year. A chapel-building fund of £10,000 was asked for, toward which £3,000 had been subscribed, and propositions were made for obtaining the rest of the sum by means of subscriptions of £100 each. Thirteen students had attended the Theological Hall.

Congregationalism is represented in France by the *Union of Free Evangelical Churches*, whose basis of union is established on the principle of the freedom of the churches from the support and control of the state, their independence of each other in their own action, and the individual profession of faith. The sixteenth biennial meeting of the Synod was held at Nîmes, beginning October 16th. The opening sermon, by Pastor Hallard of Paris, was devoted to a vindication of the principle of independency, and to showing that freedom from the patronage and interference of the state was essential to the promotion of a real accord of spirit between the churches, as well as to their own internal unity. Pastor George Fisch was chosen President of the Synod. One new church was admitted to the Union; the application of another was postponed on account of insecurity in its financial condition. The question of giving up certain mission stations in the department of Saône-et-Loire, in which success had not been encouraging, was considered, and was finally referred to the Commission of Evangelization for decision. A proposition to form a common fund for all the churches of the Union, similar to the sustentation funds of the Presbyterian churches, excited much discussion. The Synod declined to express any opinion as to whether the institution of such a fund would be agreeable to the principles of the Union, but appointed a committee to examine into the subject and collect facts for the guidance of the next Synod.

Sam. J. Randall

THE SPEAKER OF THE HOUSE OF REPRESENTATIVES.

New York D. Appleton & Co.

the Speaker, Sam-
ania.
ber 3d, the follow-
·y Senator Blaine of

·e on the Judiciary be

n P. Frye, S. D. Lindsey,

·aries B. Roberts, William
nkle, William Walsh.
·po, Benjamin W. Harris,
·, N. P. Banks, George B.
am Claflin, W. W. Rice,
on.
·in Willets, J. H. McGow-
·, Mark S. Brewer, Omar
·y A. Hubbell.
·t. Strait, J. H. Stewart.
·van H. Manning, H. D.
Hooker, J. R. Chalmers,
·han Cole, L. S. Metcalf,
·harles H. Morgan, T. T.
Rea, Henry M. Pollard,
H. Buckner.

James F. Briggs, Henry

J. H. Pugh, Miles Ross,
·homas B. Peddie, A. A.

·Villiam D. Veeder, S. B.
·iholas Muller, S. S. Cox,
·, Fernando Wood, A. S.
·son N. Potter, John H.
·layham, John W. Bailey,
·ams, A. B. James, John
·e A. Bagley, William J.
·Iiscock, John H. Camp,
·ingerford, E. Kirke Hart,
·od, G. W. Patterson.
·a, C. H. Brogden, A. M.
W. L. Steele, William M.

·ioing, Mills Gardner, J. A.
·ox, Henry L. Dickey, J.
·Foster, Henry S. Neal,
·. B. Finley, N. H. Van
·i McKinley, Jr., James
·ownsend.

·in, Charles O'Neill, Samuel
·. Harmer, William Ward,
H. Smith, S. A. Bridges,
·B. Reilly, J. W. Killin-
·ell, J. M. Campbell, W.
·iey, Jacob Turney, Rus-
·S. Shallonberger, Harry
·Vatson.
·ies, L. W. Ballou.
·Richard H. Cain, D. Wy-
·malis.
M. Thornburgh, George
Bright, John F. House,
·i, W. P. Caldwell, Casey

·'ulberson, J. W. Throck-
·ddings, G. Schleicher.
C. Denison, George W.

C. Walker, Joseph Jor-
·:ker, J. T. Harris, Eppa

·n, Benjamin F. Martin.

·, L. B. Caswell, George
·iward S. Bragg, Gabriel
·. C. Pound.

·:GATES.

Sam J Randall

CONGRESS, UNITED STATES. The third session of the Forty-fifth Congress * commenced on December 2, 1878. (For the President's message, see "Public Documents," ANNUAL CYCLOPÆDIA, 1878.) In the Senate the Vice-President, William A. Wheeler, pre-

sided; and in the House, the Speaker, Samuel J. Randall of Pennsylvania.

In the Senate, on December 3d, the following resolution was offered by Senator Blaine of Maine:

Resolved, That the Committee on the Judiciary be

---

* The following is a list of members:

SENATE.

Alabama—George E. Spencer, John T. Morgan.
Arkansas—Stephen W. Dorsey, A. H. Garland.
California—Aaron A. Sargent, Newton Booth.
Colorado—Jerome B. Chaffee, Henry M. Teller.
Connecticut—William H. Barnum, William W. Eaton.
Delaware—Thomas F. Bayard, Eli Saulsbury.
Florida—Simon B. Conover, Charles W. Jones.
Georgia—John B. Gordon, Benjamin H. Hill.
Illinois—Richard J. Oglesby, David Davis.
Indiana—D. W. Voorhees, Joseph E. McDonald.
Iowa—William B. Allison, Samuel J. Kirkwood.
Kansas—John J. Ingalls, P. B. Plumb.
Kentucky—Thomas C. McCreery, James B. Beck.
Louisiana—J. B. Eustis, W. P. Kellogg.
Maine—Hannibal Hamlin, James G. Blaine.
Maryland—George R. Dennis, William Pinckney Whyte.
Massachusetts—Henry L. Dawes, George F. Hoar.
Michigan—Isaac P. Christiancy, Thomas W. Ferry.
Minnesota—S. J. R. McMillan, William Windom.
Mississippi—Blanche K. Bruce, L. Q. C. Lamar.
Missouri—D. H. Armstrong, Francis M. Cockrell.
Nebraska—Algernon S. Paddock, Alvin Saunders.
Nevada—John P. Jones, William Sharon.
New Hampshire—Bainbridge Wadleigh, E. H. Rollins.
New Jersey—Theodore F. Randolph, John R. McPherson.
New York—Roscoe Conkling, Francis Kernan.
North Carolina—Augustus S. Merrimon, Matthew W Ransom.
Ohio—Stanley Matthews, Allen G. Thurman.
Oregon—John H. Mitchell, Lafayette Grover.
Pennsylvania—J. Donald Cameron, William A. Wallace.
Rhode Island—Ambrose E. Burnside, Henry B. Anthony.
South Carolina—John J. Patterson, M. C. Butler.
Tennessee—James E. Bailey, Isham G. Harris.
Texas—Samuel B. Maxey, Richard Coke.
Vermont—Justin S. Morrill, George F. Edmunds.
Virginia—Robert E. Withers, John W. Johnson.
West Virginia—Frank Hereford, Henry G. Davis.
Wisconsin—Timothy O. Howe, Angus Cameron.

HOUSE OF REPRESENTATIVES.

Alabama—James T. Jones, Hilary A. Herbert, Jeremiah N. Williams, Charles M. Shelley, Robert F. Ligon, G. W. Hewitt, William H. Forney, W. W. Garth.
Arkansas—Lucien C. Gause, William F. Slemons, J. E. Cravens, Thomas M. Gunter.
California—Horace Davis, Horace F. Page, John K. Luttrell, R. Pacheco.
Colorado—T. M. Patterson.
Connecticut—George M. Landers, James Phelps, John T. Wait, Levi Warner.
Delaware—James Williams.
Florida—R. H. M. Davidson, Horatio Bisbee, Jr.
Georgia—Julian Hartridge, William E. Smith, Philip Cook, Henry R. Harris, Milton A. Candler, James H. Blount, William H. Felton, Alexander H. Stephens, H. P. Bell.
Illinois—William Aldrich, C. H. Harrison, Lorenzo Brentano, William Lathrop, H. C. Burchard, T. J. Henderson, Philip C. Hayes, G. L. Fort, Thomas A. Boyd, B. F. Marsh, R. M. Knapp, William M. Springer, Thomas F. Tipton, Joseph G. Cannon, John R. Eden, W. A. J. Sparks, William R. Morrison, William Hartzell, R. W. Townshend.
Indiana—B. S Fuller, Thomas R. Cobb, George A. Bicknell, Leonidas Sexton, Thomas M. Browne, M. S. Robinson, John Hanna, M. C. Hunter, M. D. White, W. H. Calkins, James L. Evans, A. H. Hamilton, John H. Baker.
Iowa—J. C. Stone, Hiram Price, Theodore W. Burdick, N. C. Deering, Rush Clark, E. S. Sampson, H. J. B. Cummings, William F. Sapp, Addison Oliver.
Kansas—William A. Phillips, Dudley C. Haskell, Thomas Ryan.
Kentucky—A. R. Boone, James A. McKenzie, John W. Caldwell, J. Proctor Knott, A. S. Willis, John G. Carlisle, J. C. S. Blackburn, M. J. Durham, Thomas Turner, John B. Clarke.
Louisiana—R. L. Gibson, E. John Ellis, Chester B. Darrall, J. B. Elam, J. E. Leonard, E. W. Robertson.

Maine—Thomas B. Reed, William P. Frye, S. D. Lindsey, Llewellyn Powers, Eugene Hale.
Maryland—Daniel M. Henry, Charles B. Roberts, William Kimmell, Thomas Swann, E. J. Henkle, William Walsh.
Massachusetts—William W. Crapo, Benjamin W. Harris, Walbridge A. Field, Leopold Morse, N. P. Banks, George B. Loring, Benjamin F. Butler, William Claflin, W. W. Rice, Amasa Norcross, George D. Robinson.
Michigan—A. S. Williams, Edwin Willets, J. H. McGowan, E. W. Keightley, John W. Stone, Mark S. Brewer, Omar D. Conger, Charles C. Ellsworth, Jay A. Hubbell.
Minnesota—M. H. Dunnell, H. B. Strait, J. H. Stewart.
Mississippi—H. L. Muldrow, Van H. Manning, H. D. Money, O. R. Singleton, Charles E. Hooker, J. R. Chalmers.
Missouri—Anthony Ittner, Nathan Cole, L. S. Metcalf, Robert A. Hatcher, R. P. Bland, Charles H. Morgan, T. T. Crittenden, B. J. Franklin, David Rea, Henry M. Pollard, J. B. Clark, Jr., John M. Glover, A. H. Buckner.
Nebraska—Thomas J. Majors.
Nevada—Thomas Wren.
New Hampshire—Frank Jones, James F. Briggs, Henry W. Blair.
New Jersey—C. H. Sinnickson, J. H. Pugh, Miles Ross, Alvah A. Clark, A. W. Cutler, Thomas B. Peddie, A. A. Hardenburgh.
New York—James W. Covert, William D. Veeder, S. S. Chittenden, Archibald M. Bliss, Nicholas Muller, S. S. Cox, Anthony Eickhoff, A. G. McCook, Fernando Wood, A. S. Hewitt, Benjamin A. Willis, Clarkson N. Potter, John H. Ketcham, George M. Beebe, S. L. Mayham, John W. Bailey, Martin I. Townsend, Andrew Williams, A. B. James, John H. Starin, Solomon Bundy, George A. Bagley, William J. Bacon, William H. Baker, Frank Hiscock, John H. Camp, E. G. Lapham, J. W. Dwight, J. Hungerford, E. Kirke Hart, Charles B. Benedict, D. N. Lockwood, G. W. Patterson.
North Carolina—Jesse J. Yeates, C. H. Brogden, A. M. Waddell, J. J. Davis, A. M. Scales, W. L. Steele, William M. Robbins, Robert B. Vance.
Ohio—Milton Sayler, H. B. Banning, Mills Gardner, J. A. McMahon, A. V. Rice, Jacob D. Cox, Henry L. Dickey, J. W. Keifer, John S. Jones, Charles Foster, Henry S. Neal, Thomas Ewing, M. I. Southard, E. B. Finley, N. H. Van Vorhes, Lorenzo Danford, William McKinley, Jr., James Monroe, James A. Garfield, Amos Townsend.
Oregon—Richard Williams.
Pennsylvania—Chapman Freeman, Charles O'Neill, Samuel J. Randall, William D. Kelley, A. C. Harmer, William Ward, Isaac N. Evans, Hiester Clymer, A. H. Smith, S. A. Bridges, F. D. Collins, H. B. Wright, James B. Reilly, J. W. Killinger, E. Overton, Jr., John I. Mitchell, J. M. Campbell, W. S. Stenger, Levi Maish, L. A. Mackey, Jacob Turney, Russell Errett, Thomas M. Bayne, W. S. Shallenberger, Harry White, J. M. Thompson, Lewis F. Watson.
Rhode Island—Benjamin T. Eames, L. W. Ballou.
South Carolina—J. H. Rainey, Richard H. Cain, D. Wyatt Aiken, John H. Evins, Robert Smalls.
Tennessee—J. H. Randolph, J. M. Thornburgh, George G. Dibrell, H. Y. Riddle, John M. Bright, John F. House, W. C. Whitthorne, J. D. C. Atkins, W. P. Caldwell, Casey Young.
Texas—John H. Reagan, D. B. Culberson, J. W. Throckmorton, Roger Q. Mills, D. W. C. Giddings, G. Schleicher.
Vermont—Charles H. Joyce, D. C. Denison, George W. Hendee.
Virginia—John Goode, Jr., G. C. Walker, Joseph Jorgenson, George C. Cabell, J. R. Tucker, J. T. Harris, Eppa Hunton, A. L. Pridemore.
West Virginia—Benjamin Wilson, Benjamin F. Martin, John E. Kenna.
Wisconsin—Charles G. Williams, L. B. Caswell, George C. Hazleton, William P. Lynde, Edward S. Bragg, Gabriel Bouck, H. L. Humphrey, Thaddeus C. Pound.

TERRITORIAL DELEGATES.

Arizona—H. S. Stevens.
Dakota—J. P. Kidder.
Idaho—S. S. Fenn.
Montana—M. Maginnis.
New Mexico—T. Romero.
Utah—G. Q. Cannon.
Washington—O. Jacobs.
Wyoming—W. W. Corlett.

VOL. XIX.—13 A

instructed to inquire and report to the Senate whether at the recent elections the constitutional rights of American citizens were violated in any of the States of the Union; whether the right of suffrage of citizens of the United States, or of any class of such citizens, was denied or abridged by the action of the election officers of any State, in refusing to receive their votes, in failing to count them, or in receiving and counting fraudulent ballots in pursuance of a conspiracy to make the lawful votes of such citizens of none effect; and whether such citizens were prevented fron exercising the elective franchise, or forced to use it against their wishes by violence or threats, or hostile demonstrations of armed men or other organizations, or by any other unlawful means or practices.

Resolved, That the Committee on the Judiciary be further instructed to inquire and report whether it is within the competency of Congress to provide by additional legislation for the more perfect security of the right of suffrage to citizens of the United States in all the States of the Union.

Resolved, That in prosecuting these inquiries the Committee on the Judiciary shall have the right to send for persons and papers.

Mr. Blaine said : " Mr. President, the pending resolution was offered by me with a twofold purpose in view :

" 1. To place on record, in a definite and authentic form, the frauds and outrages by which some recent elections were carried by the Democratic party in the Southern States ;

" 2. To find if there be any method by which a repetition of these crimes against a free ballot may be prevented.

" The newspaper is the channel through which the people of the United States are informed of current events, and the accounts given in the press represent the elections in some of the Southern States to have been accompanied by violence, in not a few cases reaching the destruction of life ; to have been controlled by threats that awed and intimidated a large class of voters; to have been manipulated by fraud of the most shameless and shameful description. Indeed, in South Carolina there seems to have been no election at all in any proper sense of the term. There was instead a series of skirmishes over the State, in which the polling-places were regarded as forts to be captured by one party and held against the other ; and, where this could not be done with convenience, frauds in the count and tissue-ballot devices were resorted to in order to effectually destroy the voice of the majority. These in brief are the accounts given in the non-partisan press of the disgraceful outrages that attended the recent elections ; and, so far as I have seen, these statements are without serious contradiction. It is but just and fair to all parties, however, that an impartial investigation of the facts shall be made by a committee of the Senate, proceeding under the authority of law and representing the power of the nation. Hence my resolution.

" But we do not need investigation to establish certain facts already of official record. We know that one hundred and six Representatives in Congress were recently chosen in the States formerly slave-holding, and that the

Democrats elected one hundred and one or possibly one hundred and two, and the Republicans four or possibly five. We know that thirty-five of these Representatives were assigned to the Southern States by reason of the colored population, and that the entire political power thus founded on the numbers of the colored people has been seized and appropriated to the aggrandizement of its own strength by the Democratic party of the South.

" The issue thus raised before the country, Mr. President, is not one of mere sentiment for the rights of the negro—though far distant be the day when the rights of any American citizen, however black or however poor, shall form the mere dust of the balance in any controversy ; nor is the issue one that involves the waving of the 'bloody shirt,' to quote the elegant vernacular of Democratic vituperation ; nor still further is the issue as now presented only a question of the equality of the black voter of the South with the white voter of the South. The issue, Mr. President, has taken a far wider range, one of portentous magnitude ; and that is, whether the white voter of the North shall be equal to the white voter of the South in shaping the policy and fixing the destiny of this country ; or whether, to put it still more baldly, the white man who fought in the ranks of the Union army shall have as weighty and influential a vote in the government of the Republic as the white man who fought in the ranks of the rebel army. The one fought to uphold, the other to destroy, the Union of the States ; and to-day he who fought to destroy is a far more important factor in the government of the nation than he who fought to uphold it.

" Let me illustrate my meaning by comparing groups of States of the same representative strength North and South. Take the States of South Carolina, Mississippi, and Louisiana. They send seventeen Representatives to Congress. Their aggregate population is composed of ten hundred and thirty-five thousand whites and twelve hundred and twenty-four thousand colored ; the colored being nearly two hundred thousand in excess of the whites. Of the seventeen Representatives, then, it is evident that nine were apportioned to these States by reason of their colored population, and only eight by reason of their white population ; and yet in the choice of the entire seventeen Representatives the colored voters had no more voice or power than their remote kindred on the shores of Senegambia or on the Gold Coast. The ten hundred and thirty-five thousand white people had the sole and absolute choice of the entire seventeen Representatives. In contrast, take two States in the North, Iowa and Wisconsin, with seventeen Representatives. They have a white population of two million two hundred and forty-seven thousand—considerably more than double the entire white population of the three Southern States I have named. In Iowa and Wisconsin, therefore, it takes one hundred and thirty-two thousand white population to send a Representative to Congress, but in South Carolina, Mississippi, and Louisiana every sixty thousand white people send a Representative. In other words, sixty thousand white people in those Southern States have precisely the same political power in the government of the country that one hundred and thirty-two thousand white people have in Iowa and Wisconsin.

"Take another group of seventeen Representatives from the South and from the North. Georgia and Alabama have a white population of eleven hundred and fifty-eight thousand and a colored population of ten hundred and twenty thousand. They send seventeen Representatives to Congress, of whom nine were apportioned on account of the white population and eight on account of the colored population. But the colored voters are not able to choose a single Representative, the white Democrats choosing the whole seventeen. The four Northern States, Michigan, Minnesota, Nebraska, and California, have seventeen Representatives, based on a white population of two and a quarter millions, or almost double the white population of Georgia and Alabama, so that in these relative groups of States we find the white man South exercises by his vote double the political power of the white man North.

"Let us carry the comparison to a more comprehensive generalization. The eleven States that formed the Confederate Government had by the last census a population of nine and a half millions, of which in round numbers five and a half millions were white and four millions colored. On this aggregate population seventy-three Representatives in Congress were apportioned to those States— forty-two or -three of which were by reason of the white population, and thirty or thirty-one by reason of the colored population. At the recent election the white Democracy of the South seized seventy of the seventy-three districts, and thus secured a Democratic majority in the next House of Representatives. Thus it appears that throughout the South that formed the late Confederate Government sixty-five thousand whites — the very people that rebelled against the Union—are enabled to elect a Representative in Congress, while in the loyal States it requires one hundred and thirty-two thousand of the white people that fought for the Union to elect a Representative. In levying every tax, therefore, in making every appropriation of money, in fixing every line of public policy, in decreeing what shall be the fate and fortune of the Republic, the Confederate soldier South is enabled to cast a vote that is twice as powerful and twice as influential as the vote of the Union soldier North.

"But the white men of the South did not acquire and do not hold this superior power by reason of law or justice, but in disregard and defiance of both. The fourteenth amendment to the Constitution was expected to be and was designed to be a preventive and corrective of all such possible abuses. The reading of the clause applicable to the case is instructive and suggestive. Hear it:

Representatives shall be apportioned among the several States according to their respective numbers, counting the whole number of persons in each State, excluding Indians not taxed. But when the right to vote at any election for the choice of electors for President and Vice-President of the United States, Representatives in Congress, the executive and judicial officers of a State, or the members of the Legislature thereof, is denied to any of the male inhabitants of such State, being twenty-one years of age, and citizens of the United States, or in any way abridged, except for participation in rebellion, or other crime, the basis of representation therein shall be reduced in the proportion which the number of such male citizens shall bear to the whole number of male citizens twenty-one years of age in such State.

"The patent, undeniable intent of this provision was that if any class of voters were denied or in any way abridged in their right of suffrage, then the class so denied or abridged should not be counted in the basis of representation; or, in other words, that no State or class of population not permitted to take part in electing such Representatives. But the construction given to this provision is that before any forfeiture of representation can be enforced the denial or abridgment of suffrage must be the result of a law specifically enacted by the State. Under this construction every negro voter may have his suffrage absolutely denied or fatally abridged by the violence, actual or threatened, of irresponsible mobs, or by frauds and deceptions of State officers from the Governor down to the last election clerk, and then, unless some State law can be shown that authorizes the denial or abridgment, the State escapes all penalty or peril of reduced representation. This construction may be upheld by the courts, ruling on the letter of the law, 'which killeth,' but the spirit of justice cries aloud against the evasive and atrocious conclusion that deals out oppression to the innocent and shields the guilty from the legitimate consequences of willful transgression.

"The colored citizen is thus most unhappily situated; his right of suffrage is but a hollow mockery; it holds to his ear the word of promise, but breaks it always to his hope, and he ends only in being made the unwilling instrument of increasing the political strength of that party from which he received ever-tightening fetters when he was a slave and contemptuous refusal of civil rights since he was made free. He resembles indeed those unhappy captives in the East who, deprived of their birthright, are compelled to yield their strength to the up-building of the monarch from whose tyrannies they have most to fear, and to fight against the power from which alone deliverance might be expected. The franchise intended for the shield and defense of the negro has been turned against him and against his friends, and has vastly increased the power of those from whom he has nothing to hope and everything to dread.

"The political power thus appropriated by Southern Democrats by reason of the negro population amounts to thirty-five Representatives in Congress. It is massed almost solidly, and offsets the great State of New York, or Pennsylvania and New Jersey together, or the whole of New England, or Ohio and Indiana united, or the combined strength of Illinois, Minnesota, Kansas, California, Nevada, Nebraska, Colorado, and Oregon. The seizure of this power is wanton usurpation; it is flagrant outrage; it is violent perversion of the whole theory of republican government. It inures solely to the present advantage and yet, I believe, to the permanent dishonor, of the Democratic party. It is by reason of this trampling down of human rights, this ruthless seizure of unlawful power, that the Democratic party holds the popular branch of Congress to-day, and will in less than ninety days have control of this body also, thus grasping the entire legislative department of the Government through the unlawful capture of the Southern States. If the proscribed vote of the South were cast as its lawful owners desire, the Democratic party could not gain power. Nay, if it were not counted on the other side against the instincts and the interests, against the principles and the prejudices of its lawful owners, Democratic success would be hopeless. It is not enough, then, for modern Democratic tactics that the negro vote shall be silenced; the demand goes further, and insists that it shall be counted on their side, that all the Representatives in Congress and all the Presidential electors apportioned by reason of the negro vote shall be so cast and so governed as to insure Democratic success—regardless of justice, in defiance of law.

"And this injustice is wholly unprovoked. I doubt if it be in the power of the most searching investigation to show that in any Southern State during the period of Republican control any legal voter was ever debarred from the freest exercise of his suffrage. Even the revenges which would have leaped into life with many who despised the negro were buried out of sight with a magnanimity which the 'superior race' fail to follow and seem reluctant to recognize. I know it is said, in retort of such charges against the Southern elections as I am now reviewing, that unfairness of equal gravity prevails in Northern elections. I hear it in many quarters, and read it in the papers, that in the late exciting election in Massachusetts intimidation and bulldozing, if not so rough and rancorous as in the South, were yet as widespread and effective.

"I have read, and yet I refuse to believe, that the distinguished gentleman who made an energetic but unsuccessful canvass for the governorship of that State has endorsed and approved these charges; and I have accordingly made my resolution broad enough to include their thorough investigation. I am not demanding fair elections in the South without demanding fair elections in the North also. But venturing to speak for the New England States, of whose laws and customs I know something, I dare assert that in the late election in Massachusetts, or any of her neighboring commonwealths, it will be impossible to find even one case where a voter was driven from the polls, where a voter did not have the fullest, fairest, freest opportunity to cast the ballot of his choice, and have it honestly and faithfully counted in the returns. Suffrage on this continent was first made universal in New England, and in the administration of their affairs her people have found no other appeal necessary than that which is addressed to their honesty of conviction and to their intelligent self-interest. If there be anything different to disclose, I pray you show it to us, that we may amend our ways."

Mr. Thurman of Ohio: "Mr. President, I offer an amendment, which I send to the Chair."

The Secretary: "It is proposed to add to the resolution the following":

"The committee shall also inquire whether any citizen of any State has been dismissed or threatened with dismissal from employment or the deprivation of any right or privilege by reason of his vote or intention to vote at the recent election, or has been otherwise interfered with; and to inquire whether in the year 1878 money was raised by assessment or otherwise upon Federal officeholders or employees for election purposes, and under what circumstances and by what means; and, if so, what amount was so raised and how the same was expended; and, further, whether such assessments were or not in violation of law; and shall further inquire into the action and conduct of United States supervisors of elections in the several States, and as to the number of marshals, deputy marshals, and others employed to take part in the conduct of the said elections, in what State or city appointed, the amount of money paid or promised to be paid to them, and how or by whom, and under what law or authority."

Mr. Thurman: "Mr. President, I attempted to offer that amendment before the Senator from Maine proceeded with his remarks, but failed to have an opportunity to do so. I intended then to say that, whatever opinion might be entertained on this side of the Chamber as to the propriety of the original resolutions as to the competency of Congress to make all the investigations that those resolutions contemplate, yet we were disposed to waive all scruples of that character and suffer the resolutions to pass without opposition if the amendment now proposed should be added to them. The Senator from Maine, however, having a speech carefully studied and prepared, exercised his right to deliver that speech before my amendment could be offered. I do not complain of that at all, nor do I now rise to make any extended reply to the speech that I have heard just now. Should this debate be protracted, I may exercise my privilege of saying something in reply to the Senator from Maine, but to-day

I shall confine myself to a very few general observations.

" The Senator is frank in one thing. His resolution is broad. It includes all the States; it provides for an investigation whether the rights of American citizens in connection with the elective franchise have been violated or interfered with in any of the States; but he frankly admits in the very outset of his remarks that that was not his purpose, that his purpose was to assail the Democracy of the South. He had two purposes in preparing his carefully elaborated speech ; not to vindicate the right of suffrage throughout this whole Union, but to inquire whether the Democracy of the Southern States had violated the rights of American citizens, and then to find out what could be done with them. Now, Mr. President, that is a very frank, and I have no doubt a very true, statement of the *animus* of this resolution.

" Mr. President, I said that there might be some doubts as to the propriety of this investigation. I repeat it. There may be such doubts, especially to-day. Here is a short session of Congress. We have, excluding the recess that we always take, less perhaps than two months within which to dispose of the appropriation bills and the other measures of legislation that necessarily require the attention of Congress if the business of the session is to be disposed of and no extra session is to be called. And now, sir, the Senator proposes an investigation that I defy any committee that can be formed to make with anything like thoroughness, nay, in any satisfactory manner, with anything like justice either to those who are implicated or to those who may be implicated, within the time that remains of this session of the Senate. It is a simple impossibility. I have therefore wondered why this resolution was introduced, unless it was to be made a string upon which to hang speeches to arouse sectional hatred in one portion of this Union against an almost defenseless people in another portion of the Union.

"Now, Mr. President, this assault of the Senator from Maine is not an assault simply, however, upon the people of the South. I said five months ago in a speech—what I beg pardon for repeating here—that it did seem to me as clear as anything in American politics could be, that there was a deliberately formed purpose, under pretext that there was a solid South, to create a solid North to rule not only the solid South, but to rule one half nearly, if not more, of the people of the North. I thought so then; I think so yet. I thought then, and I think now, that a purpose more unpatriotic, more unjust, more fraught with ruin to this country never entered the brain of man. That is my belief.

" Why, Mr. President, of what is it that the Senator from Maine complains? That there were not enough Republican votes at the South. That is the amount of it; and how does he make that out? He assumes, without one shadow of proof produced here, that the negroes

of the South were prevented from voting, or forced to vote the Democratic ticket. He assumes, therefore, that owing to those causes the negroes of the South are not represented by the members of the House of Representatives who come from that section of the Union, or by the Senators on this floor who represent Southern States. What right has the Senator from Maine to say that the negroes of the South are not represented by the chosen Representatives of the South and the chosen Senators of the South? What right has he to vote those negroes himself on one side, and say that the men who have the credentials of election here do not represent their constituents? Why, Mr. President, it is a bare assumption on his part that he has no right whatever to make.

"But, again, the Senator ought to have thought of this when he was framing his fourteenth and fifteenth amendments, or when he was assisting in framing them. There were men then, men of his own party too, who told him with long foresight that in the end property and intelligence and education will rule the land, and ignorance can not. Mr. President, there were men of his own party who foresaw that those people who have the intelligence, the education, and the property will not be ruled by those who have neither; and in that it is not necessary to separate the community into white people and into colored people. Not at all is it necessary to do that. No, Mr. President, the result of these constitutional amendments was easy enough to be foreseen. I am not here to-day to justify the violation of the rights of any man, however humble he may be, whatever may be the color of his skin, whatever may be the poverty of his situation. I am here for no such purpose as that. If I know my own heart, I am as much in favor of respecting the rights of every man under the Constitution as the Senator from Maine or any other Senator on this floor; but I do know that property, intelligence, education, will assert their influence everywhere on the face of this globe.

"Now, Mr. President, let me say one word more on this subject. Who was it that drew the color line between the whites and the negroes in the South? Let me tell you, sir, that millions of money, of the money of the people of the United States, were expended by your agents, the Freedman's Bureau agents, in getting every colored man in the South into loyal leagues and swearing him never to vote for a Democrat. That is where the color line began to be drawn. That institution, which took charge of the negro at the ballot-box, took charge of him in the cotton-field, took charge of him everywhere, supervised every contract that he made, allowed no contract to be made unless it had the approval of the agents of the Freedman's Bureau, and spent the money and property called ' captured and abandoned property ' that was surrendered to it, and many millions of money directly appropriated out of the Treasury of the United States—it was that Bureau and its agents who first drew the color line. And yet when the white people of the South, when the men owning the property and having the intelligence and the education at the South, saw their very social system menaced with destruction, saw their very households threatened with ruin under an inundation of barbarism directed by the most unscrupulous of men, and when they naturally came together, when they naturally united as people menaced with danger ever will unite, then a cry is raised against 'the solid South!' Ah, Mr. President, it will not do. This system of legislation toward the South that began ten years ago is reaping its fruit; and it is not by additional penal laws that you can better the condition of this country. What does the Senator want more penal laws for? Let him look into the statute-book on this very subject; let him read the statutes in regard to the enforcement of the rights of citizens to vote, and I defy him to find in the statute-books of any civilized country on this globe a body of laws so minute, so searching, and bristling all over with fines and forfeitures as are these laws.

"But that is not all. In addition to that you have a vast machinery of superintendents of election, Federal supervisors, marshals, deputy marshals, paid electioneerers out of the Treasury of the United States, under the guise of being men to preserve the freedom of suffrage and peace at elections. You have a whole army of them provided for by your statutes. What more does the Senator want? I think I see, Mr. President, what is wanted. I think this is a note which is sounded to the people of the North that they must retrace their steps; and this very party which required two amendments to the Constitution to be made in the interest, it was said, of the colored population of the South, is now preparing to face about, retrace its steps, and undo what it did only a few years ago. Either directly or by indirection that is to be done. Indeed, I thought, while the Senator from Maine was making his speech, how much reason this country, and especially the southern part of the country, had to congratulate itself that the next House of Representatives will not have a majority of gentlemen thinking like the Senator from Maine; for if he is right in what he said, if his threats are not mere idle wind—and I certainly do not attribute any such thing to him—if they are deep-seated and permanent thoughts of those with whom he acts, then I should be prepared to see a House of Representatives in which there was a Republican majority exclude Southern members by the score; then I should be prepared to see them decide themselves that the right of suffrage was prohibited down there to the negro, and then to see them in their supreme authority, as they would construe it, vote out the chosen Representatives of the South, not by ones, not by twos, but by the score. It is a fortunate thing for this country,

it is a fortunate thing for our free institutions, that there is not in the present House of Representatives, and will not be in the next, a majority thinking as the Senator from Maine thinks, and willing to act as I fear he is willing to act.

"Mr. President, one word on the amendment I have offered. My own belief is that there is a far greater danger that menaces our institutions and menaces the right of suffrage in this country than that to which the Senator from Maine has alluded. Sir, the most disheartening thing to an American who loves free institutions is to see that year by year the corrupt use of money in the elections is making its way until the time may come, and that within the observation of even the oldest man here, when elections in the United States will be as debauched as ever they were in the worst days of the old borough parliamentary elections in the mother land. Mr. President, there is the great danger. The question is whether this country shall be governed with a view to the rights of every man, the poor man as well as the rich man, or whether the longest purse shall carry the elections and this be a mere plutocracy instead of a democratic republic. That is the danger; and that danger, let me tell my friend, exists far more in the North than it does in the South. Sir, if he wants to preserve the purity of elections, if he wants to have this Government perpetuated as a system that can be honestly administered from the primary election to the signature of a bill by the President of the United States, let him set his face and exercise his great ability in stopping the flood-gates of corruption that threaten to deluge the whole land and bring republican institutions into utter ruin and disgrace.

"Mr. President, there is one thing that made me doubt a little as to the propriety of this resolution, although, as I said, I am going to vote for it; and what the Senator from Maine has said has added to the great doubt which I entertained on that subject; and that is, that I am not quite sure that there are not persons who favor this kind of a resolution, and as much debate upon it as you can have, and as much investigation as you can have, in order to divert public attention from the real questions which ought to engage the Congress of the United States. Questions of economy, questions of finance, questions of currency, all are shoved aside that popular speeches may be made, tending to excite one section of the people against another, and to set their minds mad with passion, instead of appealing to their cool and deliberate reason. I certainly do not charge the Senator from Maine with having got this up for the purpose of putting aside and throwing out of view that which should form the subject of our thoughts and of our legislation; but I fear that such may be in some men's minds one of the things to be effected by such a resolution."

Mr. Lamar of Mississippi: "Mr. President,

when these resolutions are printed and ready for action, I may have something to say upon the question of their adoption. Before the question passes off now, I wish to make one or two remarks, not upon the resolution, but upon one or two points submitted by the Senator from Maine.

"Sir, it is not a surprising thing, nor is it an unnatural one, that that distinguished Senator should feel and manifest a deep interest in the affairs of the Southern States. The people of that section have but recently undergone a vast change, social and political; and it is reasonable, it is eminently fit and proper, that one who here so conspicuous a part in the adoption of the measures which brought about that vast transformation, who occupies so conspicuous a position at the present time, and who perhaps will occupy a still more distinguished position in the future, should scrutinize with anxious solicitude the progress of that people to reconstruction and to their readjustment to the healthy and normal conditions of our national life. Sir, had the Senator come forward with some well-devised scheme of public education by which this newly enfranchised race, who have had such exalted duties imposed upon them without culture and without even the trained intelligence of practical experience, may be fitted to exercise their great duties as freemen and citizens and the participants in the sovereignty of commonwealths, every one would have recognized the propriety and the patriotism of such a movement; for he would have proposed to give to that people what they most need, and what would protect them from every evil and wrong which he now alleges that they labor under.

"There are other evils in that country which might call forth the lofty and enlarged measures of a patriot and of an American statesman; but I must confess to some regret that a Senator so distinguished, in looking upon this recently dislocated member of this great American empire, instead of regarding it with reference to those great interests that affect the whole country through the long track of coming years, should have concentrated his whole attention upon its relation to parties and party contests; that nothing should have struck the Senator's notice or engaged his thoughts except the connection of that people with the ascendancy and defeat of parties and their influence in Federal elections. Party organizations are no part of the Constitution, and they are agencies which work outside of the laws. But, sir, the gentleman's remarks were directed exclusively to the mere party and partisan aspects of this great subject; and with no intent whatever to utter a bitter retort, I can not but feel the regret that one of such resolute energies, of such tenacious purposes, such daring ambition, and such great abilities, should have so narrowed his mind as 'to give to party what was meant for mankind.'

"But, sir, what is the point at last of the gentleman's argument this morning? It was remarkable for its significant omissions. It was directed exclusively to the suppression of the votes of a particular class of suffragans in the South. Mr. President, if I understood the debates at the time of the adoption of the amendment to which he refers, clothing the negroes of the South with the right of suffrage, it was to give them protection for their freedom and for the civil rights which the fourteenth amendment accorded to them. Through the protracted remarks of the Senator he could not utter one word—he could not, because it would not have been the truth if he had—to show that there was a single right of freedom or of citizenship belonging to the black race of the South that was not as secure and as well enjoyed as that of the proudest and freest white man in the land.

"It is also a remarkable fact that in his indictment of the South there is no pretense that there is a single menace in her present attitude to any of the great interests of this country—not an imputation of that character—for 'solid' (according to the usual phrase) as the South may be, she stands in line with a majority of the American people upon nearly every question which is now discussed in this nation or argued here in her council chambers.

"But, sir, to come to the direct point, the Senator asserts that, in consequence of the suppression of the negro vote at the South by means which, he alleges, are illegitimate and irregular, the South has a disproportionate party power in this Government. Sir, before this discussion is over I will show that the negro vote has not been suppressed in the South; I will demonstrate that this political phenomenon, which is the subject of so much discussion and misrepresentation, is a phenomenon that would occur in any free society, and that it has been brought about by the influences which intelligence, and virtue, and sagacity, and the other elements of civilization, always bring to bear upon the classes that are ignorant and debased.

"But, sir, assuming all that the gentleman says to be true, that there are in the House of Representatives one hundred and six Representatives elected of one party complexion, elected by means that are not what he considers legitimate, let us see where we stand in this position. Now, sir, what interest of the North, what interest of this country, is endangered by it? Sir, with a united vote of the South she stands a powerless section in this Government; she is an impotent minority section in any event, unable to protect a single Southern right or to defend a single Southern interest.

"But, says the gentleman, under the operations of these amendments the South have a representation not in proportion to the constituency which elect them, and the States of South Carolina, and Mississippi, and Alabama, have much more power than twice the numbers in some of the Northwestern States which he mentioned. Mr. President, every member of that population in those States entitled to vote ought to be counted. You have no right to draw the line between the black and the white, and assume that the black man, because he did not vote the Republican ticket, is therefore a suppressed voter. Is it to be assumed that in every Southern State the property and population of the State are in such necessary antagonism that no amount of local misrule can teach them the advantage of their natural alliance? What right has he to assume that whites and blacks are never to vote and act together as citizens of a common country? Now, sir, let me call attention to one point in the Senator's argument. If we are to enter upon a system of legislation and political movements in order to adjust representation and political power in this Government according to the number of actually voting constituencies, the principle may operate further than the gentleman thinks. What is the population of the State of Maine? I believe 625,000. It has been diminishing within the last twenty years. I can not now recollect, but perhaps it is 623,000. Vermont, which is also solid, has not more than 350,000. And yet the State of Maine has as much power in this Government with her 600,000 people as the State of New York with her 5,000,000."

A Senator: "You mean in this Chamber."

Mr. Lamar: "No, sir; I mean in this Government. Gentlemen correct me by saying 'in this Chamber'; but I adhere to the phrase. I say, and repeat, that they have the affirmative power of legislation this day; 625,000 in Maine are equal to 5,000,000 in the State of New York. A positive equality of States, whatever be their population, in either Chamber where concurrent legislation is needed, is positive affirmative power in the passage of any law. Why, sir, the whole of New England has not three and a half millions of population; and yet under the operation of the Constitution and laws of the land, of which I make no complaint and which is a legitimate thing, those three and a half millions of population have six times as much power as sovereign commonwealths that have five millions. They have got as much power as twenty millions in the large Northwestern States that the gentleman called attention to. Sir, why is one man in these Eastern States equal to twenty in the Northwest, except by virtue of the Constitution—the Constitution which we are intending to abide by and to maintain?

"But, as the gentleman has vouchsafed advice to Southern men on this floor and outside, in all spirit of fairness and equity I will speak to the people of the New England States and tell them that in my opinion the direst foe they have got on earth is the Representative or Senator, whether from their own section or any other, that will kindle this fire whose subterranean flames will liquefy the very foundations on which these proud and free commonwealths now rear their aspiring heads. Sir, the Senator is fishing in troubled waters upon this subject; and, when you come to agitate questions of this kind, you will find that changes of a more radical and fundamental nature will be necessary in order to adjust representation to numbers in this Government."

Mr. Edmunds of Vermont: "Mr. President, the point of the Senator from Mississippi appears to be, that if a Senator from New England proposes to inquire whether the Constitution has been violated in depriving any part of the people of the States of their right to vote for members of Congress, etc., he thereby incurs the danger of oversetting the Constitution itself, which says that the States in this body shall be equal; and therefore I understand him to put it out as a warning that the people of New England through their Senators and Representatives have no right to stand up for the Constitution as it is in favor of an equal representation by the people of the States in the other House, unless they run the risk of being exposed to the danger of having their senatorial representation overturned. That, then, is the question we are invited to consider, and the peril that we expose ourselves to if we undertake to inquire whether the Constitution of the United States has been violated. In other words, the representatives of the Democratic party of the South say to an inquiry into a violation of the Constitution, 'If you dare to make such an inquiry, you run the risk of overturning the representation of the States and reducing yourselves to a state of servitude.' That is the proposition!"

Mr. Lamar: "I hope the Senator will allow me to explain—"

Mr. Edmunds: "Certainly."

Mr. Lamar: "Or rather to protest against the interpretation which he has put upon my remarks. I made no such suggestion. It was simply in reply to the theory the Senator from Maine had broached, that this investigation was justified in order that the evil which he had disclosed of one hundred thousand white men in the South having a political power and vote in this Government equal to three hundred thousand somewhere else, that I said that the tendency of such a theory would lead to further investigation, and would undermine the principle and the system of government upon which our American fabric rests."

Mr. Edmunds: "I am very glad to know, Mr. President, that the Senator did not mean what his remarks appeared to indicate; and he has misunderstood—"

Mr. Lamar: "I did not mean what the gentleman has attempted to force my remarks into, but which he will never succeed in doing."

Mr. Edmunds: "The Senator is mistaken in that. I have not attempted to force the Senator's remarks into anything. The 'Record' will show exactly what he has said, and I think it will appear that I have not misstated the substance of what he has said; but the Senator has greatly mistaken, with his present explanation, the point of the Senator from Maine. The Senator from Maine did not complain of the inequality of personages in one part of the Union or another. What he complained of was, supposing what he believes to be true turns out to be so when you have an investigation, that a small number of persons in the South, by a gross and outrageous violation of the Constitution, have taken to themselves by that species of usurpation the power of a large number under the Constitution exercised in a rightful way in the Northwest. Is the Senator dissatisfied if that turns out to be true, or would he like to rectify it? The Senator, of course, would like to rectify it. I must assume that he would. What, then, is the use of saying that you are going to overturn the Government if we undertake to find out whether the Constitution has been grossly and flagrantly violated by a denial of equal rights in respect of the elections to the popular branch of the Congress of the United States? And where is the necessity, in such a case, of holding out the terror and kindling the conflagration that the Senator referred to in respect of senatorial representation upon an inquiry of that kind? The people of New England, as far as I may speak for them, believe in justice and in equal rights under the Constitution and according to it, just as the fathers and their successors have made it; and that is, that in the States (and I am surprised to hear a Southern Senator assail the very foundation of State rights) there is and there must be political equality; that in respect of the people represented in the other branch of Congress there shall be the fair equality of fair numbers fairly and freely exercising their rights, and not the subjects of tyranny, and corruption, and fraud anywhere. That makes your Government; nothing more, nothing less."

Mr. Lamar: "Still, Mr. President, I can not accept the position to which the Senator from Vermont assigns me. He says that he is surprised to find a Southern Senator assailing the principle of State rights. He will never find me in that position, sir. I have ever been the defender of that doctrine. But surprises are constantly sprung upon us, and the country will be not a little astonished to find the doctrine of State rights advocated by the distinguished Senator from Vermont."

Mr. Edmunds: "I think not. I have always done it."

Mr. Blaine: "Mr. President, I desire merely to say, in reply to the Senator from Mississippi, that in the little colloquy between him and the Senator from Vermont, I understand this to be about the residuum, that if I move an inquiry into the unconstitutional representation of Mississippi in the other House, he will move one into the constitutional representation of Maine in this branch!"

Mr. Lamar: "That will do pretty well for wit and pretty well for the Senator's peculiar species of perversion; but it will not do for the truth, for, sir, I protested that I not only would move no such inquiry, but that I would oppose and fight against any such purpose. No, sir; the doctrine that I stated was, that if the right of suffrage be invaded anywhere, or any constitutional rights infringed upon, in any quarter or by anybody, it shall be maintained and enforced, if necessary, by all the constitutional power of the Government."

Mr. Edmunds: "Then we are all at one."

Mr. Lamar: "Exactly so, but not upon the ground that States shall be deprived of any of their representatives, because under the operation of the Constitution, either in its original provisions or in its amendments, their political power may be not in exact proportion to their numerical power in this Government. And I repeat the warning against this agitation about sectional power based on numbers; I warn Senators that in throwing their net into this troubled sea they may drag to the shore a vase like that of the fisherman in the 'Arabian Nights,' from which, when the seal was once broken, a demon emerged more potent than his deliverer, and threatening his destruction."

The Vice-President: "The question recurs on the amendment proposed by the Senator from Ohio. Will the Senate agree to the resolutions as amended?"

Mr. Bayard of Delaware: "I propose to amend the first resolution, in line 6, by inserting after 'any State' the words 'or of the United States'; so as to read:

"Whether the right of suffrage of citizens of the United States, or of any class of such citizens, was denied or abridged by the action of the election officers of any State, or of the United States, in refusing to receive their votes.

"This will make the inquiry include both officers of the State and of the United States, who were election officers."

Mr. Blaine: "I have no objection to that. I hope there will be no objection to that amendment."

The Vice-President: "The Chair hears no objection to the amendment suggested by the Senator from Delaware. The resolutions are so modified."

Mr. Conkling of New York: "I suggest that if either branch of this inquiry is to proceed, a special committee should be charged with it. The chairman of the Committee on the Judiciary [Mr. Edmunds] is not here. There are several members of that committee here, and they all know, as I know, that committee is already, I might say, smothered under labor and duties which are put in its charge; and the idea that during this session of Congress either alternative of this inquiry is to be conducted by that committee possibly —my friend before me [Mr. Davis of Illinois] says 'properly' but I say possibly—seems to me so improbable that I venture to call the attention of the Senate to it. Believing as I do that this inquiry ought to be made, and believing further that there is great force in the suggestion that any one single committee will be greatly embarrassed, to say the least, by an attempt to hold all the inquisition here directed, it seems to me that the inquiry ought not to be committed to a standing committee, which committee we know in advance is obstructed already by labors making demands upon its time beyond its possibility to comply. And I will venture to add that there are no seven men, whether they be the members of the Judiciary Committee, or a court, or a commission, who, in the time available between now and the 4th of March to the Judiciary Committee, could by any diligence dispose intelligently, conscientiously, and thoroughly of the matters in charge of that committee without reference to this; and my honorable friend before me [Mr. Davis of Illinois] concurs in and confirms me in that statement. So that, unless I stand in the way of the purpose of those who more especially have charge of the resolution, I will venture to submit an amendment striking out 'the Committee on the Judiciary' and inserting 'a select committee consisting of nine members of the Senate,' to be appointed by the Chair."

Mr. Blaine: "I am entirely willing to have the change made. I would have moved it myself, but for the fact that I do not desire to be chairman or even a member of the committee; and the person who moves a select committee is under some sort of honorable obligation under certain circumstances to accept the chairmanship. I have no objection to the change."

The Vice-President: "The amendment of the Senator from New York is that the subject matters of the pending resolutions be committed to a select committee to consist of nine Senators, instead of the Judiciary Committee. The question is on the amendment of the Senator from New York."

The Secretary proceeded to call the roll, and the result was announced as follows:

YEAS—Allison, Anthony, Barnum, Blaine, Booth, Burnside, Cameron of Pa., Cameron of Wis., Christiancy, Conkling, Davis of Illinois, Dawes, Ferry, Garland, Hamlin, Hoar, Howe, Ingalls, Kellogg, Kirkwood, McDonald, McMillan, Matthews, Maxey, Mitchell, Morrill, Oglesby, Paddock, Patterson, Plumb. Rollins, Saunders, Teller, Voorhees, Wadleigh, Windom—36.

NAYS—Armstrong, Bailey, Bayard, Beck, Butler, Cockrell, Coke, Davis of W. Va., Eustis, Gordon, Grover, Harris, Hereford, Johnston, Jones of Florida, Kernan, Lamar, McCreery, McPherson, Merrimon, Morgan, Randolph, Ransom, Saulsbury, Wallace, Wythe, Withers—27.

ABSENT—Bruce, Chaffee, Conover, Dennis, Dorsey, Eaton, Edmunds, Hill, Jones of Nevada, Sargent, Sharon, Spencer, Thurman—13.

So the amendment was agreed to.

The Vice-President: "As thus amended will the Senate agree to the resolutions?"

Mr. Blaine: "Let the first part of the resolutions be read as amended."

The Vice-President: "The resolutions will be read as amended."

The Secretary read as follows:

Resolved, That a select committee, to consist of nine Senators, be appointed to inquire and report to the Senate—

Mr. Blaine: "Let 'by the Chair' be put in after 'appointed.' Let the portion added by the Senator from Ohio come in after the first resolution. Then the two subsequent clauses follow, and then I move an amendment at the end of the last clause to add these words:

"To take testimony and administer oaths by subcommittees, and to visit any portion of the country when such visit may in their judgment facilitate the object of the inquiry."

Mr. Butler of South Carolina: "May I ask the Senator from Maine to consent to one additional amendment after his, 'that said committee be instructed to sit with open doors?'"

Mr. Blaine: "I think there is a good deal under that suggestion of the Senator from South Carolina. He will pardon me for not inserting it."

Mr. Butler: "I am perfectly earnest in making the suggestion."

Mr. Blaine: "Will the Senator explain the motive of it?"

Mr. Butler: "My motive is to have a perfectly fair, impartial, and open investigation. That is my object."

Mr. Blaine: "The Senator from South Carolina will observe that this committee will undoubtedly have a fair and full representation of the minority of the Senate, or of the other side—I do not know whether it is a minority or not. Both political parties and all shades of political opinion that sit on this floor will be represented on the committee. Now, I can conceive a case, I think I can go a little further and say that I have heard of a good many cases, in which the committee would be embarrassed by having witnesses come before them who did not want to testify openly. There certainly could be no partisan advantage gained if so active and vigilant an eye as that of the Senator from South Carolina was on the minority, and so of many other Senators whom I might name; then no harm could come to the inquiry in that respect. But the Senator is not unaware surely that one of the alleged, if not actual, troubles in the whole investigation of the Southern question has been that the very men who were intimidated at the polls were still more intimidated on the witness-stand; and therefore I would leave that matter altogether to the discretion of the committee. I would neither bind them the one way nor the other. Let them be the judges as to what the propriety of the case demands in this respect."

Mr. Butler: "I understand, then, the Senator to state that he objects to that addition to his amendment upon the ground that there may be in certain parts of this country some witnesses who would not desire to testify openly, but who would be willing to testify secretly. That I understand to be the position of the Senator. I do not know, Mr. President, for one, any part of this country where that state of things exists. The Senator says that it is alleged. Like a great many other allegations, it is entirely without any proof to sustain it. I respectfully submit to the Senator that he has not one particle of proof, and if he desires (and I have no right to question but that he does desire) a free, full, complete, thorough, public investigation of this question, I can not see why he should object to my amendment.

"So far as I am concerned, as a representative in part of South Carolina, I wish to say to the Senator, to the Senate, and to the country, since he has chosen to select and single out my State as the special object for this investigation, that we desire the most complete and the fullest investigation we can get; and I can say to the Senator that any witness who goes before the committee in South Carolina may do so just as safely and may testify as fully as he can in the State of Maine."

Mr. Eustis of Louisiana: "Mr. President, I desire to state to the Senator from Maine, so far as any investigation in Louisiana is concerned, that past investigations prove that Republican witnesses are not intimidated, because Republican witnesses not only testify, but a great many testify on both sides. Therefore I can see no objection to having this investigation a public investigation.

"It was not my intention to reply to the remarks made by the Senator from Maine, because whether or not there has been intimidation is a question of fact and not a question of conjecture or guesswork or partisan statement; and therefore it occurred to me as a very extraordinary position for the honorable Senator from Maine to occupy, that in advance of the examination of a single witness, in the absence of a single inquiry, as the introducer of the resolution asking for an investigation, which implies that there has been so far no sustained fact upon which to base an accusation, the honorable Senator should take the liberty of stating to the Senate and to the people that the colored citizens of the State of Louisiana had no more rights as suffragans and as voters than the inhabitants of Senegambia. I could very easily demonstrate, if this were a proper time, that the election in Louisiana, so far as results are concerned, either as to the general State ticket or as to the Congressional elections, was a fair and a peaceable election, and that there were a great many reasons why the Democratic nominees were elected; and I could also demonstrate that the colored people selected their choice as to Congressional candidates and exercised their choice as to legislative candidates, showing that they exercised a discrimination in the matter."

The Vice-President: "Will the Senate agree to the amendment proposed by the Senator from South Carolina?"

Mr. Blaine: "I have no desire to prolong the debate; but the Senator from South Carolina either possesses or affects great ignorance of past events. He certainly ought to know that one of the primal troubles in every investigation South has been the very one on which I have commented. I used the word 'alleged' because I wanted to put it in as mild a form as possible. I might have used the word 'proved' or 'recorded' in Congressional reports accessible to him as to every other Senator; but in advance of the investigation which the Senate is to order I do not care to go into particulars. I have had as many as two hundred letters from the South giving details of great outrages upon the right of suffrage; many from the State of the Senator who last spoke. I do not adduce them or parade them here. They at least form the basis, in connection with that which has become matter of public notoriety, of a serious and sober investigation; and, if the Senator from Louisiana does not know that a great massacre occurred in one of the parishes of his own State on the last election day, he is probably the only gentleman in the United States who is ignorant of it."

Mr. Butler: "The Senator from Maine says he has two hundred letters from people in the South giving evidence of intimidation and fraud and wrong and riot and murder. Why, Mr. President, I understood the Senator to say the other day, and if I am mistaken I hope he will correct me, that he based his statements upon the newspapers of the country. Well, now, Mr. President, I submit in all frankness and in all kindness to the Senator that, if he based his statements upon the newspaper press alone, he and I should have been hung and quartered long ago. It is not safe for the Senator to base his opinions and his statements and his allegations upon any such authority; not that I mean to say that the newspapers do not communicate the truth, but I do mean to say that when correspondents are sent into a country, as they have been into my country, to make a case, to write down all that is bad about our people and to suppress all that is meritorious, the accounts they send are unreliable. I say to the honorable Senator that with the same feeling and with the same spirit I could go into his State with a corps of detectives and I could make his State a stench in the nostrils of the civilized world."

Mr. Blaine: "You have the authority under these resolutions to do it."

Mr. Butler: "I say I could do that; yet when I propose to open the doors of the committee to permit everybody to go in who has the right to go, whom the committee will permit to go, to allow the witnesses to be cross-examined, the Senator attempts to answer that by saying that witnesses white and colored will be notified that they do that at their peril. I say, Mr. President, that that is not true so far as South Carolina is concerned. I say that it is absolutely untrue. I do not mean this in an offensive sense to the honorable Senator, but I submit and assert upon my responsibility here that a witness may testify before a committee with open doors as freely in my State, and I believe in every other Southern State, as he can in the State of Maine or Massachusetts."

The Secretary proceeded to call the roll on Mr. Butler's amendment, and the result was announced, as follows:

YEAS—Armstrong, Bailey, Bayard. Beck, Cockrell, Coke, Davis of Illinois, Davis of West Va., Eaton, Eustis, Garland, Gordon, Grover, Harris, Hereford, Johnston, Jones of Florida, Kernan, Lamar, McCreery, McPherson, Merrimon, Morgan, Randolph Ransom, Saulsbury, Voorhees, Wallace, Whyte, Withers —30.

NAYS—Allison, Anthony, Blaine, Booth, Burnside, Cameron of Pa., Cameron of Wis., Christiancy, Conkling, Dawes, Ferry, Hamlin, Hoar, Howe Ingalls, Kellogg, Kirkwood, McMillan, Matthews, Mitchell, Morrill, Oglesby, Paddock, Patterson, Plumb, Rollins, Saunders, Teller, Wadleigh, Windom—30.

ABSENT—Barnum, Bruce, Butler, Chaffee, Conover, Dennis, Dorsey, Edmunds, Hill, Jones of Nevada, McDonald, Maxey, Sargent, Sharon, Spencer, Thurman—16.

The Vice-President: "On the amendment proposed by the Senator from South Carolina [Mr. Butler] the yeas are 30 and the nays are 30. The amendment is rejected; and the question recurs on the amendment proposed by the Senator from Maine [Mr. Blaine]. The amendment will be reported."

The Secretary read as follows:

That in prosecuting these inquiries the said committee shall have the right, by itself or by any subcommittee, to send for persons and papers, to take testimony, to administer oaths, and to visit any portion of the country when such visit may in their judgment facilitate the object of the inquiry.

Mr. Davis of West Virginia: "I presume it will be in order to amend the amendment of the Senator from Maine with the words 'shall sit with open doors if any member of the committee desires."

The Vice-President: "The question is upon the amendment just stated, upon which the yeas and nays have been ordered."

Mr. Bayard: "The action of the Senate upon the resolutions and all the amendments has had the mark almost of unanimity. Why shall it not be continued in respect of this proposition? The system of taking testimony in courts of justice is invariably open; and, if there ever was an inquisition as to fact which ought to be public, it surely is that which touches the affairs of a whole community. Ordinarily, in contests as to rights between individuals, issues of fact are created by pleadings, so that some degree of certainty is brought to every mind, and we know the subjects matter and general character of the testimony to be expected. But here is little else than an indictment of communities as a whole, vague, uncertain, and surely there is the spirit of fair play which dictates that, if you strike, you at least shall bear. There is something un-American in secret inquisition, something in the

proposition that is repugnant to a sense of justice. If the charges are true, I hope that exposure will follow, and that punishment may follow exposure. If they be untrue, I hope they may recoil on those who unjustly set them on foot. But the truth is something that no honest man should fear; and, believing that this proposition to try whole communities upon vague and general charges calls especially for open and public investigation of the facts, I do hope that the Senate will unanimously agree that no such thing as a secret inquisition shall be held upon such a state of facts as is alleged by those who have moved this proceeding.

"I have been by the direction of the Senate assigned to duty upon every committee of this public character of inquisition since 1870. The first was in the State of North Carolina; next there followed a joint committee of the two Houses, twenty-one in number, upon all the Southern States; again followed a special committee in respect to the State of Mississippi. All of that testimony was taken in secret; all of that testimony was taken in short-hand and fully published. There was then the same proposition made that we should sit with open doors, that the communities who were to be assailed should hear at least what was said against them that they might reply; but the majority of those who controlled those investigations forbade it, and men came and swore to anything they pleased, assailing men who were absent, uninformed of the time, unprepared to meet it simply from want of knowledge of what had been said. All this testimony was published, published in full, and I have never heard in the succeeding cases, where committees have visited again those States, that the publication of the testimony in full ever produced any breach of the peace whatever."

Mr. Blaine: "May I ask the honorable Senator a question?"

Mr. Bayard: "Certainly."

Mr. Blaine: "Before any of these committees of which he has been a member did he ever know testimony affecting the character of an individual submitted which that individual, through himself or counsel, did not have some opportunity to review and rebut?"

Mr. Bayard: "Yes, sir. I can tell him there was no case except it came through the action of a member of the committee who might choose to summon the man assailed."

Mr. Blaine: "Was he not summoned?"

Mr. Bayard: "Sometimes he was and sometimes he was not."

Mr. Blaine: "What I want to get at is this: Whenever it was regarded as essential to the protection of the reputation of any man, was it not invariably the rule that any one assailed was summoned?"

Mr. Bayard: "I can not say that any such rule prevailed. I mean to say that where a subpœna was asked for I never knew it refused."

Mr. Blaine: "That is what I mean. Now, as the Senator will observe, just as in those committees, so in this, both political parties will be represented, and they will use their discretion; but if you by a rule beforehand say that under no circumstances shall they hold a closed-door meeting, you have taken all proper responsibility from them. You have taken from them any exercise of discretion whatever."

Mr. Bayard: "I do hold that any man, however humble, however poor, has a right to be confronted with the witnesses against him. He has a right to know the charge against him. This proceeding is, as I say, an indictment against a whole people; it is a railing accusation; therefore the more difficult to meet, and therefore the proof in regard to it ought to be open especially. The Senator must see, I submit to his candor, to his sense of fairness, that a man may come in burning with partisan dislike and make false charges against one hundred and fifty men; the Senator or I on that committee have no knowledge of the facts save that which the witness chooses to give us; power of cross-examination we have none, because we have not the knowledge to conduct a cross-examination. There is something in this which strikes my sense of justice and offends it. I would not wish to do by another what I would not have done by me; and I can understand that, if my character were to be assailed in secret without the opportunity of cross-examination, I should feel it exceedingly unjust were I not to be fully informed of it all, and be there at the time that I might defend myself.

"I believe I have already referred to the fact that the most voluminous testimony has been in print for several years, taken at different dates—depositions of witnesses examined and cross-examined in private. They all have been in private; none that I know of, in which there has not been a refusal to allow these matters to be public, although they were subsequently fully published without injury to any one; and yet I believe great injustice was done by that method of taking testimony."

Mr. Hoar of Massachusetts: "Mr. President, I wish simply to call the attention of the Senate to the fact that the proposition made by the Senator from South Carolina [Mr. Butler], and now renewed by the Senator from West Virginia [Mr. Davis], is in opposition to the uniform precedents both of the Senate and the House in all like cases since the foundation of the Government. It is in opposition to the uniform precedents in regard to original investigations wherever criminal or unlawful conduct is charged."

Mr. Bayard: "Will the Senator pardon me?"

Mr. Hoar: "Certainly."

Mr. Bayard: "I was a member of a committee which sat six weeks in the city of New York investigating the custom-house affairs there. That examination was public, and made so by the committee."

Mr. Hoar: "I understood the Senator from Delaware himself to say that, in all the investigations of this character in which he had borne a part, the investigation had been, as proposed by the original resolution, left to the discretion of the committee. I ask the Senator from Delaware whether, in regard to the custom-house investigation, of which he speaks, the question whether the public interest required the session to be secret or open was not left to the discretion of the committee?"

Mr. Bayard: "It was decided by the committee to sit with open doors."

Mr. Hoar: "Certainly."

Mr. Bayard: "There was nothing said about it in the original resolution."

Mr. Hoar: "That is the precise point which I was making."

Mr. Blaine: "That is it exactly."

Mr. Hoar: "In every instance the matter has been left to the discretion of the committee, with the single exception of the famous Crédit Mobilier investigation; and the experience of the House of Representatives in that particular case induced the House, the Democratic House, to return to the old custom, which has never been observed more strictly than during the past two Congresses in the other branch. The reason is obvious. In seeking to discover criminal or unlawful conduct, the tribunal making the investigation must avail itself frequently and very largely of hostile sources of information; and the examination of one witness having put them on the trace of a fact, every other witness who knows that fact, but who desires to keep it secret, is put on his guard if the investigation is open, and flies from the summons of the committee."

Mr. Kernan of New York: "I am in favor of having a full, fair, thorough investigation. I am one of those who, if it be proved that wrongs are perpetrated against the humblest citizen, will endeavor to protect them by corrective legislation, if we can do it. But I wish the investigation to be open and fair, so that the people who are accused may have an opportunity to defend themselves against false charges. The power of this committee reaches all the States. It may be that there are transactions in Northern States to be investigated as to which I may have prejudices against those accused; but I do not know my own heart if I would not resist the proposition that a committee of my political friends should examine witnesses against these parties with closed doors, excluding them from hearing the testimony and cross-examining the witnesses against them. Inasmuch as there have been committees who thought it their right to sit with closed doors taking testimony against individuals and communities charged with offenses, I trust we will now disapprove that practice by at least declaring that, if one of the Senators on this committee believes the doors should be open while witnesses are being examined, this shall be done."

The Vice-President: "The question is on the amendment proposed by the Senator from West Virginia [Mr. Davis]."

The Secretary proceeded to call the roll, and the result was announced, as follows:

YEAS—Armstrong, Bailey, Bayard, Beck, Cockrell, Coke, Davis of Illinois, Davis of West Virginia, Eaton, Eustis, Garland, Gordon, Harris, Hereford, Jones of Florida, Kernan, Lamar, McCreery, McDonald, Mc-Pherson, Merrimon. Morgan, Randolph, Ransom, Voorhees, Wallace, Whyte, Withers—28.

NAYS—Allison, Anthony, Blaine, Booth, Burnside, Cameron of Pennsylvania, Cameron of Wisconsin, Christiancy, Conkling, Dawes, Dorsey, Ferry, Hamlin, Hoar, Howe, Ingalls, Kellogg, Kirkwood, McMillan, Mitchell, Morrill, Oglesby, Paddock, Patterson, Rollins, Saunders, Teller, Wadleigh, Windom—29.

ABSENT—Barnum, Bruce, Butler, Chaffee, Conover, Dennis, Edmunds, Grover, Hill, Johnston, Jones of Nevada, Matthews, Maxey, Plumb, Sargent, Saulsbury, Sharon, Spencer, Thurman—19.

So the amendment was rejected.

The Presiding Officer (Mr. Rollins in the chair): "The question is on the amendment proposed by the Senator from Maine [Mr. Blaine], which will be read for the information of the Senate."

The Secretary: "If amended as proposed the last resolution will read:

"That in prosecuting these inquiries the committee shall have the right, by itself or by any sub-committee, to send for persons and papers, to take testimony, to administer oaths, and to visit any portion of the country when such visit may in their judgment facilitate the object of the inquiry."

The amendment was agreed to.

The Presiding Officer: "The question now is on the passage of the resolutions as amended. The resolutions will be read as they now stand."

The Secretary read as follows:

Resolved, That a select committee, to consist of nine Senators, be appointed by the Chair to inquire and report to the Senate whether at the recent elections the constitutional rights of American citizens were violated in any of the States of the Union; whether the right of suffrage of citizens of the United States, or of any class of such citizens, was denied or abridged by the action of the election officers of any State or of the United States, in refusing to receive their votes, in failing to count them, or in receiving and counting fraudulent ballots in pursuance of a conspiracy to make the lawful votes of such citizens of none effect; and whether such citizens were prevented from exercising the elective franchise, or forced to use it against their wishes, by violence or threats, or hostile demonstrations of armed men or other organizations, or by any other unlawful means or practices. The committee shall also inquire whether any citizen of any State has been dismissed or threatened with dismissal from employment or deprivation of any right or privilege by reason of his vote or intention to vote at the recent elections, or has been otherwise interfered with.

And to inquire whether, in the year 1878, money was raised, by assessment or otherwise, upon Federal office-holders or employees for election purposes, and under what circumstances and by what means; and, if so, what amount was so raised and how the same was expended; and, further, whether such assessments were or not in violation of law.

And shall inquire into the action and conduct of United States supervisors of elections in the several

States; and as to the number of marshals, deputy marshals, and others employed to take part in the conduct of the said elections; in what State or city appointed; the amount of money paid or promised to be paid to them, and how or by whom, and under what law authorized.

Resolved, That the committee be further instructed to inquire and report whether it is within the competency of Congress to provide by additional legislation for the more perfect security of the right of suffrage to citizens of the United States in all the States of the Union.

Resolved, That in prosecuting these inquiries the committee shall have the right, by itself or by any sub-committee, to send for persons and papers, to take testimony, to administer oaths, and to visit any portion of the country when such visit may in their judgment facilitate the object of the inquiry.

Mr. Whyte of Maryland: "Mr. President, I do not rise for the purpose of making any speech, but, inasmuch as I intend to vote against the passage of these resolutions, I desire in a very few words to give my reasons for that course.

"In the first place, I am unalterably opposed to these roving commissions. I am opposed to the system which has grown up since the war of appointing committees upon almost every conceivable subject and sending them at the expense of the country upon roving excursions to see what they can find out. I am opposed to the expense which has been entailed upon the country by the useless commissions that have been ordered by either the one or the other House of Congress within the last few years. We had committees to South Carolina, we had committees to Louisiana, we had committees to Florida anterior to the last presidential count; and, when the evidence gathered by the gentlemen who had gone on these foraging excursions was printed at the public expense and was ready for examination by the parties who were supposed to have charge of the electoral count, we were informed that all of that testimony was *aliunde*. We had a committee sent to Mississippi, and after taking testimony for many days and weeks, and gathering together two volumes as large as this (holding up a book) of Munchausen statements, they made their report to Congress, and I venture to affirm that not ten men in or out of Congress have ever read fifty pages of those volumes. We have had our Potter committee and our Matthews committees, and various other committees. They have all been at work, and the result is absolutely nothing but a large amount of expenditures to be paid out of the public Treasury. I am opposed to it, and I think the time has come when we should set our face against these wandering committees, some of whom I believe, either singly or in twos, have wandered with half a dozen stenographers over the Rocky Mountains during the last summer."

The Vice-President: "Is the Senate ready for the question on the resolution, upon which the yeas and nays have been ordered?"

The Secretary proceeded to call the roll, and the result was announced, as follows:

YEAS—Allison, Anthony, Armstrong, Bailey, Barnum, Bayard, Beck, Blaine, Booth, Burnside, Butler, Cameron of Pennsylvania, Cameron of Wisconsin, Christiancy, Cockrell, Coke, Conkling, Davis of Illinois, Davis of West Virginia, Dawes, Dennis, Eustis, Ferry, Garland, Gordon, Hamlin, Harris, Hereford, Hour, Howe, Ingalls, Jones of Florida, Kellogg, Kernan, Kirkwood, McDonald, McMillan, McPherson, Matthews, Maxey, Merrimon, Mitchell, Morrill, Oglesby, Paddock, Patterson, Randolph, Ransom, Rollins, Saunders, Spencer, Teller, Voorhees, Wadleigh, Windom, Withers—56.

NAYS—Eaton, Hill, McCreery, Morgan, Wallace, Whyte—6.

ABSENT—Bruce, Chaffee, Conover, Dorsey, Edmunds, Grover, Johnston, Jones of Nevada, Lamar, Plumb, Sargent, Saulsbury, Sharon, Thurman—14.

So the resolutions were agreed to.

The Presiding Officer: "The Vice-President has appointed as the seelect committee in relation to the violation of the rights of American citizens at the recent elections, under the resolution of the Senator from Maine [Mr. Blaine], Mr. Teller, Mr. Cameron of Wisconsin, Mr. Kirkwood, Mr. Mitchell, Mr. Plumb, Mr. Bayard, Mr. Wallace, Mr. Bailey, and Mr. Garland."

For the report of the committee, see PUBLIO DOCUMENTS.

In the Senate, on December 10th, Mr. Edmunds of Vermont proceeded to explain the bill from the Committee on the Judiciary to regulate the counting of the votes for President and Vice-President. The bill was read as follows:

A bill to amend sundry provisions of chapter 1, title 3, of the Revised Statutes of the United States, relating to presidential elections, and to provide for and regulate the counting of the votes for President and Vice-President and the decision of questions arising thereon.

Be it enacted by the Senate and House of Representatives of the United States of America in Congress assembled, That the electors of President and Vice-President shall be appointed in each State on the first Tuesday in October in every fourth year succeeding the election of a President and Vice-President, and on the same day in October whenever there shall be a vacancy in both the offices of President and Vice-President declared and certified as hereinafter provided; but no Senator or Representative or person holding an office of trust or profit under the United States shall be appointed an elector.

SECTION 2. Whenever there shall be a vacancy in both the offices of President and Vice-President occurring more than two months next preceding the first Tuesday in any month of October other than that next preceding the expiration of the term of office for which the President and Vice-President last in office were elected, the Secretary of State shall forthwith cause a notification thereof to be made to the executive of every State, and shall also cause the same to be published in at least one of the newspapers printed in each State. The notification shall specify that electors of President and Vice-President of the United States shall be appointed in the several States on the first Tuesday in October then next ensuing.

SEC. 3. The electors of each State shall meet and give their votes on the second Monday in January next following their appointment, at such place in each State as the Legislature of such State shall direct.

SEC. 4. Each State may provide, by law enacted prior to the day in this act named for the appointment of the electors, for the trial and determination of any controversy concerning the appointment of electors,

before the time fixed for the meeting of the electors, in any manner it shall deem expedient. Every such determination made pursuant to such law so enacted before said day, and made prior to the said time of meeting of the electors, shall be conclusive evidence of the lawful title of the electors who shall have been so determined to have been appointed, and shall govern in the counting of the electoral votes, as provided in the Constitution and as hereinafter regulated.

SEC. 5. It shall be the duty of the executive of each State to cause three lists of the names of the electors of such State, duly ascertained to have been chosen, to be made and certified and to be delivered to the electors on or before the day on which they are required by this act to meet.

SEC. 6. Congress shall be in session on the second Monday in February succeeding every meeting of the electors. The Senate and House of Representatives shall meet in the Hall of the House of Representatives at the hour of one o'clock in the afternoon on that day; and the President of the Senate shall be their presiding officer. Two tellers shall be previously appointed on the part of the Senate, and two on the part of the House of Representatives, to whom shall be handed, as they are opened by the President of the Senate, all the certificates, and papers purporting to be certificates, of the electoral votes, which certificates and papers shall be opened, presented, and acted upon in the alphabetical order of the States, beginning with the letter A; and said tellers, having then read the same in the presence and hearing of the two Houses, shall make a list of the votes as they shall appear from the said certificates; and the votes having been ascertained and counted as in this act provided, the result of the same shall be delivered to the President of the Senate, who shall thereupon announce the state of the vote, and the names of the persons, if any, elected, which announcement shall be deemed a sufficient declaration of the persons elected President and Vice-President of the United States, and, together with a list of the votes, be entered on the Journals of the two Houses. Upon such reading of any such certificate or paper the President of the Senate shall call for objections, if any. Every objection shall be made in writing, and shall state clearly and concisely, and without argument, the ground thereof, and shall be signed by at least one Senator and one member of the House of Representatives before the same shall be received. When all objections so made to any vote or paper from a State shall have been received and read the Senate shall thereupon withdraw, and such objections shall be submitted to the Senate for its decision; and the Speaker of the House of Representatives shall in like manner submit such objections to the House of Representatives for its decision; and no electoral vote or votes from any State from which but one return has been received shall be rejected except by the affirmative votes of both Houses. If more than one return or paper purporting to be a return from a State shall have been received by the President of the Senate, those votes, and those only, shall be counted which shall have been regularly given by the electors who are shown by the evidence mentioned in section 4 of this act to have been appointed; but in case there shall arise the question which of two or more of such State tribunals, determining what electors have been appointed, as mentioned in section 4 of this act, is the lawful tribunal of such State, the votes regularly given of those electors, and those only, from such State shall be counted whose title as electors the two Houses, acting separately, shall concurrently decide is supported by the decision of the tribunal of such State so provided for by its Legislature. And in such case of more than one return, or paper purporting to be a return, from a State, if there shall have been no such determination of the question in the State as aforesaid, then those votes and those only shall be counted which the two Houses, acting separately, shall concurrently decide to be the lawful votes of the legally appointed electors of such State. When the two Houses have voted they shall immediately again meet, and the presiding officer shall then announce the decision of the questions submitted. No votes or papers from any other State shall be acted upon until the objections previously made to the votes or papers from any State shall have been finally disposed of.

SEC. 7. That while the two Houses shall be in meeting, as provided in this act, no debate shall be allowed, and no question shall be put by the presiding officer except to either House on a motion to withdraw; and he shall have power to preserve order.

SEC. 8. That when the two Houses separate to decide upon an objection that may have been made to the counting of any electoral vote or votes from any State, or other question arising in the matter, each Senator and Representative may speak to such objection or question five minutes, and not oftener than once; but after such debate shall have lasted two hours it shall be the duty of the presiding officer of each House to put the main question without further debate.

SEC. 9. That at such joint meeting of the two Houses seats shall be provided as follows: For the President of the Senate, the Speaker's chair; for the Speaker, immediately upon his left; the Senators, in the body of the Hall upon the right of the presiding officer; for the Representatives, in the body of the Hall not provided for the Senators; for the tellers, Secretary of the Senate, and Clerk of the House of Representatives, at the Clerk's desk; for the other officers of the two Houses, in front of the Clerk's desk and upon each side of the Speaker's platform. Such joint meeting shall not be dissolved until the count of electoral votes shall be completed and the result declared; and no recess shall be taken unless a question shall have arisen in regard to counting any such votes, or otherwise under this act, in which case it shall be competent for either House, acting separately in the manner hereinbefore provided, to direct a recess of such House not beyond the next day, Sunday excepted, at the hour of ten o'clock in the forenoon. But if the counting of the electoral votes and the declaration of the result shall not have been completed before the fifth calendar day next after such first meeting of the two Houses, no further or other recess shall be taken by either House.

SEC. 10. That section 140 of the Revised Statutes of the United States be, and the same is hereby, so amended that the words "first Wednesday in January then next ensuing" be stricken out and the words "second Monday next after their meeting" be inserted therein.

SEC. 11. That section 141 of the Revised Statutes of the United States be, and the same is hereby, so amended that the words "first Wednesday" be stricken out and the words "on or before the day" inserted therein.

SEC. 12. That sections 131, 135, 136, 142, 147, 148, and 149 be, and the same are hereby, repealed.

Mr. Edmunds: "The first thing, Mr. President, that ought to be considered, undoubtedly, is the state of the Constitution upon this subject, and that is to be found in only two or three places, and in very few and simple words. Article II., section 1, provides, first, that—

"The executive power shall be vested in a President of the United States of America. He shall hold his office during the term of four years, and, together with the Vice-President, chosen for the same term, be elected as follows:

"Each State shall appoint, in such manner as the Legislature thereof may direct, a number of electors, equal to the whole number of Senators and Representatives to which the State may be entitled in the Congress: but no Senator or Representative, or person holding an office of trust or profit under the United States, shall be appointed an elector.

"The electors shall meet in their respective States, etc.

"That is in section 1 of Article II.; but the existing provision of the Constitution as to the mode of election is in the twelfth amendment, which I will read in lieu of that:

"The electors shall meet in their respective States, and vote by ballot for President and Vice-President, one of whom, at least, shall not be an inhabitant of the same State with themselves; they shall name in their ballots the person voted for as President, and in distinct ballots the person voted for as Vice-President, and they shall make distinct lists of all persons voted for as President, and of all persons voted for as Vice-President, and of the number of votes for each, which lists they shall sign and certify, and transmit sealed to the seat of the Government of the United States, directed to the President of the Senate; the President of the Senate shall, in the presence of the Senate and House of Representatives, open all the certificates and the votes shall then be counted; the person having the greatest number of votes for President shall be the President, if such number be a majority of the whole number of electors appointed; and if no person have such majority then from the persons having the highest numbers not exceeding three on the list of those voted for as President, the House of Representatives shall choose immediately, by ballot, the President. But in choosing the President, the votes shall be taken by States, the representation from each State having one vote.

"It is unnecessary to read the rest of that provision, as this bill does not bear upon it. Article I., section 8, of the Constitution, clause 18, provides this in defining and declaring the powers of Congress:

"To make all laws which shall be necessary and proper for carrying into execution the foregoing powers, and all other powers vested by this Constitution in the Government of the United States, or in any department or officer thereof.

"These provisions of the Constitution I believe are all that bear directly upon the question we now have under consideration, the first being in the natural and logical order of the consideration of this question the one that I first read, the first section of the second article to which I now invite the careful scrutiny and consideration of the honorable members of the Senate who do me the honor to listen to me. The very first statement is after the declaration that the executive power shall be vested in the President, 'that each State shall appoint' its electors. This, then, it will be seen, is a duty that is imposed upon the State in language that it appears to me does not admit of doubt or misconstruction. It is the duty of the State in its political and coequal character, with every one of its sisters, to appoint the number of electors to which it is entitled under the Constitution. It is the act of the State, and as Mr. Madison, one of the fathers and constructors of the Constitution, stated in the 'Federalist,' in the time of it and before the Constitution was adopted and as an exposition of the true character of the Constitution in respect of the election of the President, 'it is the political act of each one of the States in its definite and independent character,' which it was to exercise freely for itself in selecting the persons who were to express its voice in the election of President. The particular declaration to which I wish to call the attention of the Senate, although it is hardly necessary, the language of the Constitution is so plain, is that 'the immediate election of the President is to be made by the States in their political characters.' That is to say, it is the political right of the State as a State to select for itself, and without the intervention or decision of any other power, the persons to the number to which it is entitled who are to express its choice in the electoral college for the Chief Magistrate of the Union.

"Then it goes on to provide in this same clause, 'in such manner as the Legislature thereof may direct.' So that taking the whole clause together it reads:

"Each State shall appoint, in such manner as the Legislature thereof may direct, a number of electors equal to the whole number of Senators and Representatives to which the State may be entitled.

"That not only fortifies, but to my mind clinches conclusively the doctrine that the ultimate selection, the actual, the effectual, selection, which is to count in the final expression in this Chamber or in that of the other House where the votes are counted as the voice of the State, is to be made by the State, and it is to be made in the manner that the Legislature of that State may direct. In other words, it is wholly, exclusively, absolutely a matter which the Constitution has remitted to the State and to its authority.

"Now, what does 'manner' include, Mr. President, in respect of what the Legislature is to do? The language is that the State is to appoint its electors who are to give their votes and whose votes are to be counted here as the voice of the State for President. The Constitution says that the manner of doing that, of this selection, shall be such as the legislative power of the State shall direct. Is it not within the manner of this selection for the Legislature of the State to provide that he and he only shall be an elector of that State who in case of a dispute shall have submitted to a certain test of ascertaining whether he is the genuine man the State has appointed or not? If it is not, then there is no value in the delegation to the Legislature of the State of the power to prescribe the manner in which this choice shall be made.

"Can you say that above the State or behind it, or somewhere, there is still a Federal power to enter that State and say, in spite of the declaration of its constituted authorities that those persons and those only who have conformed to certain requisites of the law shall be the electors, that somebody else shall? The Legislature may say that they themselves will appoint the electors. Would it do for the counting power, wherever it may be, in such a case to say: 'Well, this is a provision that is within the Constitution, as everybody knows it is, but we are satisfied that this particular Legislature acted under a mistake; they thought that these

electors were going to vote for the other candidate for President, and we therefore will exercise the full power that belongs to a court of appeal on review to open the whole record and decide for ourselves what that Legislature intended to have done and ought to have done under the circumstances.' That will not do, Mr. President. The two Houses have no power to say that. The form of the action of the State, its most solemn and authentic procedure, which the Constitution says shall be the act of the State, and then in the other clause that the act of the State shall be respected and its votes counted, you will have to change for a decision of Congress, or a Vice-President, or a President of the Senate, or whatever committee or tribunal the law may select or determine upon as the true one to count the votes.

"This fourth section, then, which provides for the conclusiveness of this State determination, is merely saying that the counting authority will recognize as the true act of the State, and give effect to it as such, that body of people that the State itself has finally through its own action determined to be the persons it has chosen. That is all. Can anything be more just if you are to respect the rights of the States under this clause of the Constitution? The very thing, without any law, without any provision, without any rule, that the two Houses meet to do, if it belongs to them to do it, or the very thing that the President of the Senate is to do if it belongs to him to do it, is to count and declare the result of the vote of the State; that is, to ascertain the will of the State, not according to his notion of what he thinks that will ought to have been, but according to his intellectual and judicial or administrative perception of the fact of what that State has done. Therefore this section simply provides that what this bill assumes to be, or confers as, the counting and declaring power shall respect and follow the choice of the State of her electors, and that the evidence of that choice shall be the action of the very machinery that the State itself has provided to determine whom she has chosen.

"This action of the State, Mr. President, you will observe, is not an action of a sovereign and independent body in its original and natural right as a separate and independent body, as between foreign nations such acts of intercourse might take place, because without the Constitution of the United States there would be no such officer as President to be elected; without the Constitution of the United States there would be no such means of the selection of such an officer, if we had one, to be found. The duty of the State, and therefore its power, is one that did not preëxist in itself, to elect a President for itself and for all the others of its sisters; but it is a right and a duty that is imposed upon it by the Federal Constitution, and the Federal Constitution has therefore measured and defined precisely the power that that State shall exert, and precisely the manner in which it shall be exerted. Then this law comes in under the Constitution to declare that when we have this authentic declaration of this exertion by the State of the power that the Constitution has reposed in it and the duty of exercising that power that it has imposed upon it, the national authority will respect the exercise of that power, just as it is bound to respect the exercise of every other power the State may possess.

" So it appeared to the committee that this provision that that body of men shall be taken to be the electors whom the State has appointed in the manner that the Legislature shall have determined that their appointment shall be ascertained, is an inherent part of the right which the State acquires under the Constitution to select its electors for itself and an inherent part of the duty that the Constitution has imposed upon the counting power, let it rest wherever it may, of recognizing and respecting this determination of the State as to the choice and identity of its electors. When you take the next step and have ascertained the body of persons who are to give their votes, then this clause of the Constitution has exhausted itself, the State has no further legal and legitimate concern in the way of control over the action of the electors. The duty and the power that is confided to the State is the duty of choosing a body of men and of choosing them finally, so that that choice shall have its effect in the final aggregate of the votes which are to be counted. That duty being done, then the electors so chosen and determined are officers, under the Constitution, of the United States, whose duties are pointed out by the Constitution, and of course it follows that they in the course of their conduct are subject to the Constitution and the constitutional laws of the United States, and to nothing else.

" This bill, then, in this respect of which I am speaking, simply provides—you may measure and discuss it in what way you will—that the solemn and determinate voice of the State in the selection of the persons whom the Constitution says it shall select and whose votes shall be counted, shall be left where the Constitution leaves it, with the State, and that the counting authority shall respect this act of the State and not undertake upon any notions of its own to overturn it.

" There is something still left; and I say this to those Senators who have sometimes appeared to suppose that if the two Houses of Congress, as this scheme is, have the counting power, the two Houses exercise revisory and judicial powers over whatever questions may legitimately arise. Suppose they do, what then is the true interpretation and the true effect of this bill? It only acts upon that revising and quasi-judicial power, if you call it such—and I assume it for the purpose of this aspect of the argument—in exactly the same way that from the foundation of the Government it has in all sorts of aspects acted upon

the judicial power that the Constitution creates. That is to say, it regulates the mode of procedure, it defines the rules of evidence, and calls upon the court, if you call it a court, to respect the act and deed of the State which is authenticated in a certain way. That is all.

" The Constitution says that the Supreme Court of the United States shall have jurisdiction of all cases that affect public ambassadors. Now, suppose the Congress of the United States immediately after the formation of the Government had decided that the only and conclusive evidence as to who is an ambassador over whom that jurisdiction is to be exercised shall be an appointment of a sovereign under the great seal of state of the foreign country from which he purports to come, and that it should not be competent as a consequence for the Supreme Court to take up, either upon public opinion or upon its own private notions, separate affidavits or what not, to prove the character of the person entitled to appeal to its jurisdiction or upon whom its jurisdiction might rightfully be exercised. Does anybody question that the court would have bowed in obedience to that law and said, ' It is within the legitimate province of the legislative power to provide laws by which this court is to be governed in ascertaining who are and what class are the persons who are entitled to its protection '? Nobody would question it. Other instances as to citizenship, as to the public character of officers, as to the authentication of records from the Departments fill your statutes with regulations that it shall be the duty of the judicial power to receive as authentic, and give effect to them accordingly, copies certified and formalized in a certain way; and when in some instances the courts have been appealed to to disregard these regulations of law, and to say that it is a part of the judicial power to make its own regulations for the government of itself, and that it is by Congress an invasion of the judicial power and a limitation of it to prescribe rules, the court with unanimous voice and for almost a century, whenever the question has arisen, has said, 'No, we can not take that view of it; we can not make regulations for the administration of the very powers that the Constitution has conferred upon us,' not conferred by law, ' against an act of Congress; but it falls within the legislative power to give effect to the jurisdiction that is imposed upon us and to regulate its administration,' just as in all civilized nations it has always been regulated by the national statutes. So that if it were to be established (which I do not at all agree to, but I do not wish to go into that matter now) that the power of the two Houses recognized in this bill, or conferred by it, as the case may be, of exercising a certain canvassing scrutiny over these votes is a plenary and judicial power, there would still be the rightful jurisdiction of the legislative authority of the United States to declare that that jurisdiction and that plenary revising and canvassing power should be exercised in conformity with certain rules in order to give effect to what the Constitution declares to be the root and substance of the whole matter—the independent and untrammeled voice of the State, selecting for itself and by its own instrumentalities the persons whom it has chosen; and there is still left in that view of the case, as with the courts in the other cases I have referred to, the revising power of determining in the case that I have named, first, whether the Legislature of the given State has provided by law for a determination of the dispute; second, whether that dispute has been determined in conformity with the regulations and by the steps that that law prescribes; that is, whether the jurisdiction thus invoked has been followed. Then there only follows the consequence as in the other cases I have named, to illustrate—and I might spend a day in instances, enough certainly to convince the mind of any man, I think—there only follows the consequence that this court (if you call it such) of the two Houses, when it finds that the Legislature of the State has made this provision, when it finds that the provision has been followed, is bound upon the principles and declarations of this act, as it would be without it indeed, on the principles of law, to respect and to follow the determination of the State. I say then that we have not taken away the jurisdiction of the two Houses if it exists; we have not cramped it: we have only provided that in the exercise of that jurisdiction the test of what is the voice of the State shall be found in the declaration of the State itself. That is all.

"I now come, sir, because I wish to be very brief and will take an opportunity hereafter, if it be necessary, to refer to authorities and decisions and precedents for what I have undertaken to uphold—I come to what this function is of counting the votes; and on that I do not wish to provoke a discussion, because it is apparently immaterial, with any gentleman who may differ with me. I know, as I believe I have said, that some have been, and no doubt now are, of the opinion that the function of counting, and as involved in that of determining the identity and validity of a vote to a certain degree, is with the presiding officer of the Senate, whether he happens to be the Vice-President of the United States or the President *pro tempore* of the body. That has been so thoroughly discussed hitherto, and so emphatically decided in an instance where it was largely according to the political wishes of a majority of this body at any rate—and that is the only body I am speaking to—to hold to the authority of the President of the Senate, that I do not think it necessary (certainly it is not on this occasion) to go into any discussion. The Senate held by a very large majority that no such power existed.

"The next question would be whether this power resides in the two Houses, because the scope of this act in the other part of it is either to recognize the existence in the two Houses, as two judges of election, so to speak, of the power to count and decide the necessary questions that are involved in that, and so regulates the exercise of that jurisdiction, or else it is a jurisdiction and an authority that the Constitution has not specifically lodged in any department of the Government, but has only declared that it shall be exercised; and if that be the true construction of the Constitution, of course it follows that it is open to legislative provision, and that Congress may confer upon the two Houses the administrative faculty, with all that it involves, of proceeding with this ceremony of the counting of the votes of the States, and with the decision of all the questions that necessarily arise in every act, whether you call it an executive act, an administrative act, or a judicial act; because it is impossible, as everybody knows, to carry on a government for a day, even in the simplest and the humblest of its executive functions, without recognizing by law in the simplest and humblest executive officer a certain amount of deciding power and a certain amount of responsibility. The judge of a court issues his warrant in conformity to law for the arrest of A B, and it is placed in the hands of the marshal. You say at first sight there is nothing for the marshal to decide, he is to arrest A B; but that very fact implies that the marshal must decide in executing that warrant between A B and the eight hundred million, or whatever it may be, in the world if his jurisdiction extended so far, or between A B and the forty million if his jurisdiction extended over the United States, or the five million as it is in the State of New York, whether A B is one of that five million or whether some other man is the one that he is after. In other words, the marshal must decide for the time being the identity of the man whom he takes into his custody. He decides undoubtedly at his peril. So the President of the United States is authorized by the Constitution to do a great variety of executive acts in certain contingencies, and through his subordinate officers acting under his authority he proceeds to do those acts. In doing them the discretion of the executive power in the application of the law to the subject upon which it speaks must be exercised—judgment, discretion, will, choice. He exercises it at his peril; so do his subordinates where it is administrative. Where it is purely executive, if he makes a mistake the remedy of the citizen is clear and his redress perfect. If it is a matter where the Constitution or the law confides it to him as a judicial discretion, and he exercises it in an ill way rather than a good one, of course it is a perfectly legal act, and it must stand; he is the sole judge, and your only course then is, if he does it corruptly, to impeach him.

"Mr. President, I say this only to call your attention and that of the honorable Senators to the circumstance that whether you say this power is with the two Houses under the Constitution, or whether you say this bill providing for the exertion of it confers it as well, is of no consequence. If it is there, it is the subject of regulation; if it is not there, then it is within the competency of Congress, as everybody will agree, to provide for its being exercised by somebody; and in either case it is, as is the judicial power, to be exercised in conformity to the Constitution and in conformity to the regulations exerted in the spirit of the Constitution to carry the Constitution into effect.

"The Constitution, then, saying that the State shall appoint its electors, and saying that that appointment, which means the creation of some body whose vote is to be counted and nothing else, shall be in the manner that the Legislature shall direct, it is within the competence of Congress, as it appears to us, whether the power of counting be judicial, or wherever it may be lodged, or wherever it may be reposed, either by the Constitution or by the law, to declare that the counting tribunal, whatever it may be, shall obey the Constitution in respecting the act of the State done in conformity with it. It does not take away a deciding power, if one exists; it only regulates the means and the evidence which the court, if you call it a court, shall give effect to.

"Of course, Mr. President, any person who believes that the two Houses of Congress do not under the Constitution possess any power at all to participate, except as witnesses, in the count of these votes, but that that power resides in the President of the Senate alone, would be obliged necessarily to vote against this bill, irrespective of the effect that we give to the voice of the State, because it does provide for the action of the two Houses. He would not be obliged to vote against the fourth section of the bill, if it stood alone, framed to guide the exercise of the jurisdiction of the President of the Senate; because if it were with him, Congress could with equal propriety and with equal validity under the Constitution declare what should be the true authentication of the voice of the State which he should be bound to respect, that authentication being in the direction that the Constitution provides of expressing its voice in the manner that its Legislature directed. But apart from that, of course those who believe that the President of the Senate has this power of counting, be it much or little, as this bill is framed in all its aspects, could not vote for it; but to any gentleman who believes that the power resides in the two Houses, I respectfully submit that this bill does not in its fourth section—nobody claims that it does in any of the others—trench in the least upon the exercise of that power, but it provides regulations in the same manner and of the same nature that the recognized course of the history of this Government shows have always been provided for its judiciary, and which the very letter of the Constitution

as to the appointment of electors and the manner of their appointment declares shall have effect, even if you had not any law, that the authentic voice of the State itself declaring who are her electors shall be recognized and respected."

Mr. Morgan of Alabama: "This bill, as I understand its provisions, is framed upon the proposition that the power to adjudge and to decide upon the validity of the appointment of electors resides in the States, and may be completely and finally exercised through tribunals created by State laws, and regulated in their procedure by State laws. It does not, however, adopt the idea that, if the States decline to adjudge and decide conclusively who are appointed electors, there is no other constitutional authority that can make such a decision. On the contrary, it provides rules to govern in such case the action of the two Houses of Congress as the tribunal which may decide, if the State has failed to decide, the validity of the appointment of the electors. Without stopping at this point to consider more particularly the provisions of this part of the bill with reference to their fitness to accomplish this purpose, I proceed to say that the bill does not by express provision attempt to dispose of the question of the eligibility of the electors that may be appointed by the States. I think that this is the true constitutional course to be observed in this matter. The Constitution expressly declares certain grounds of ineligibility of electors, which operate ex propio vigore so as to annul any appointment of such persons. Other grounds of disqualification of electors may exist, such as age or sex, a want of citizenship, insanity, or corruption through bribery, which the bill does not attempt to provide for. It is a presumption that we must indulge that the States will make provision for such cases in their laws respecting the qualifications of electors; but, if they shall fail to do so, the Houses of Congress are at liberty to act upon such objections. The bill includes the power of the Houses to take such action, by requiring their concurrence in a separate and affirmative vote in counting or refusing to count all votes that have been transmitted to them by the colleges of electors, excepting only the instance in which the States whose returns are questioned have through their own tribunals determined who are lawfully appointed electors of such States upon a controversy instituted for that purpose.

"The leading provisions of this measure may be thus stated with reference to the principles on which they are founded:

"First. The bill secures firmly and broadly that 'each State shall appoint, in such manner as the Legislature thereof may direct, a number of electors equal to the whole number of Senators and Representatives to which the State may be entitled in the Congress.'

"Second. It secures to the State the right

to determine under its own laws what persons have been appointed as electors.

"*Third.* This right the State can enforce fully and conclusively, in reference to all matters that are constitutionally within its jurisdiction, if a contest or controversy arises and is carried before the State tribunals for decision.

"*Fourth.* It asserts the right in Congress to give to the action of a State, so deciding a controversy as to who are appointed electors, a conclusive effect as evidence of the lawful title of electors who shall have been so determined to have been appointed; and that such evidence shall govern in counting the vote, without the necessity of the concurrence of the two Houses in a vote affirming its validity.

"*Fifth.* It secures to the States the right to demand the separate and affirmative concurrent vote of the two Houses in counting the electoral vote, in the following cases:

"1. In rejecting a vote from a State from which but one return has been received;

"2. In deciding which of two tribunals in a State, claiming the right to determine which of the electors have been appointed, is the lawful tribunal; and,

"3. In deciding which of two or more returns from a State shall be counted, where the State tribunals have not determined who are the electors.

"*Sixth.* It secures to a Senator and a member of the House of Representatives the right to join in a demand that the two Houses, met to count the vote, shall consider, separately, any objection in writing that they may submit to the counting of any vote that is offered to be counted.

"The bill does not attempt to define what shall be the character of the objection thus to be submitted; it only provides that in certain named cases or circumstances it shall require the concurrent affirmative vote of the Houses, voting separately, to reject the vote to which objection is made, and in the other cases it requires a vote in like manner concurring and affirmative to admit the vote to be counted. The concurrence of the Houses that is thus required does not depend upon the nature of the objection to the vote, but upon the circumstances attending it when it is offered to be counted. If the State authorities have certified the electors in due form, according to State laws, then the vote is to be counted, unless the Houses concur in an affirmative vote to reject it. If it has been passed upon by the State tribunal duly authorized by State laws to determine its validity upon a contest, then it is to be counted. In these instances the vote is supported by either a presumptive or conclusive intendment in favor of its validity, which is imparted to it by the action of the State authorities. In the absence of such presumption, or where it operates alike in reference to two or more persons claiming a right to cast the same vote, this bill requires the Houses by an affirmative vote to

determine which is the lawful vote. If the States neglect or refuse to make final and conclusive decisions of all matters within their jurisdiction (all matters indeed that relate to the validity of the appointment of electors), it seems but reasonable that when the tribunal that is required to count the vote and declare the election acts upon the subject, it should be provided by law that only one branch of that tribunal should not be permitted finally to determine the matter. It is the better and safer rule that the Houses should concur, even if in such case their non-concurrence should disfranchise the State. Every State can save its vote, if it will do so, against the power of any tribunal lawfully to exclude it for any cause except for the constitutional disability of its electors or for fraud in the action of the State tribunal that determines the validity of the appointment.

"If this bill becomes a law, the States will see the importance of using their rightful authority to provide for the settlement of contested elections or the appointment of electors before the electoral vote is cast. It is within the scope of their authority to compel persons to contest the question whether they are the lawful electors before the State tribunals, and to enact laws which shall annul every pretext of lawful authority to represent the State in the electoral colleges that is claimed by persons who refuse to enter such contests. The distinct enunciation of these rights and powers of the State governments will induce them, as I believe, to settle all questions of contested claims by different persons to the lawful authority to cast electoral votes of the States, and they will thus be excluded as elements of strife from consideration by the Senate and the House when they are met to count the votes.

"I do not like the words 'or paper purporting to be a return' found in several connections in the sixth section of the bill, and especially do I mistrust the effect of these words when they occur in line 53 of the sixth section:

"And in such case of more than one return, or paper purporting to be a return, from a State, if there shall have been no such determination of the question in the State as aforesaid, then those votes and those shall only be counted which the two Houses, acting separately, shall concurrently decide to be the lawful votes of the legally appointed electors of such State.

"I am afraid that their presence in the text of the law would suggest an inducement to some enterprising persons to send to the Vice-President papers purporting to be returns from States, and by means·of such fraud gain the possible advantage of disfranchising a State to get rid of its vote against their favorite. The words signify nothing in the structure of the sentence where they occur beyond a cautious effort to embrace every possible case that could arise upon more than one return from a State, each return having some real ground of good faith to support its claim to recognition. I think this over-caution to prevent the exclusion of a return made in good faith from consideration by the two Houses, on the ground that, in contemplation of law, it is not in fact a return, opens a still wider door to the danger of the introduction of returns that are not made in good faith; that are merely simulated returns, but are drawn up in such form as that they purport to be honest returns. These reflections also suggest the point, upon which the bill is silent, that where a paper purporting to be a return from a State of a vote by electors for President and Vice-President is sent to the President of the Senate, and a question is made whether it is a forged, or false, or simulated paper, that either House should have the right to declare its judgment that such paper is false, or forged, or simulated, and that thereupon it should be rejected; and also that such an objection, when made, should be acted upon separately by each House, and its decision should be announced by the presiding officer in joint meeting, before any other objection should be considered to such vote. These points escaped my attention in the committee, and I now suggest them to the committee, as I should have done at that time, for their consideration. It may be that the bill will be improved by their introduction into it by amendment; at all events it is proper that I should bring these matters to the attention of the committee and of the Senate.

"This bill is an earnest and bold movement to assert the rights of the States in the enjoyment of this important privilege of free constitutional government. It recognizes the right of each State to appoint electors to vote for President and Vice-President, and the right of the Legislature of each State to direct the manner of appointing electors. This is an express grant of constitutional power to the States, and by necessity the power thus granted is supreme in the same sense that the Constitution of the United States is supreme. The power to appoint electors and to direct the manner of their appointment can not be taken away from the States by any law or by the action of any department of the United States Government. This power must be removed from the Constitution before it can be denied to the States, or before any department of the Government can usurp it or participate in its exercise. It is a power that must be fully and completely exercised by the States in conformity to State laws, without their being constrained, directed, or obstructed by any other power whatever."

Mr. Jones of Florida: "Mr. President, I shall consume but very little of the time of the Senate in stating my objections to this bill. The subject it professes to regulate is so full of difficulties that I have no complaint to make of the efforts of the committee, and I freely admit that it is much easier to point out objections to the measure than to supply them by better and wiser provisions.

"The first section of the bill, following the Constitution, requires that all the electors shall be appointed on the second Tuesday in October. The fixing of the time is left to Congress, but the day, whatever it may be, must be the same throughout the United States. This requirement, as we know, was regarded as a most important one; for it is plain that if the appointment of electors could take place in the States on different days, the election of the Chief Magistrate would be controlled by intrigues and influences which would stifle the honest voice of the people. Suppose it was competent for the States to vote on different days, that all but one State voted on the same day, and that the vote of this last State was sufficient to determine the election of President, does any one suppose that after it was ascertained that the election depended upon the vote of a single State it would be possible to have an election there which would be free and tranquil? Is it not clear that every influence of party and power, all that wealth and authority could do, would be done on both sides of the contest to secure that vote? And is it not more than probable that such an immense power concentrated within such narrow bounds would prove too strong for the arm of local authority, and that, with the mind of the whole country excited as we know it would be, an outbreak of violence on such an occasion and in such a State would convulse the entire Union? Every evil which would be likely to result from the appointment of electors on different days might be expected to follow from the operation of this bill.

"The framers of the Constitution guarded the interest not of one State but of every State. The question here is not in regard to the right of a single Commonwealth to select its delegates in the electoral college, but it involves a greater power; it involves the right to select a number of men who, it may be, will hold in their hands the title to the first office in the world.

"What does the Constitution mean when it requires the appointment of the electors to be made on the same day throughout the Union? Does it not mean that on that day, and on that day alone, the rights and powers of every elector shall be fixed and determined, so that the whole country on the night of the day of the election can understand who has been elected President? What, sir, would be our condition it, after the election on the second Tuesday in October and until the 1st of January following, nearly three months, this great country, with its immense interests, should be kept in a state of suspense and excitement? I need not tell grave Senators of the influence which an event like this has upon all the business interests of the country, how much is gained to all classes when it is satisfactorily ended, or how much is lost when uncertainty intervenes to produce alarms and dangers. Under the fourth section of this bill, should it become a law, no one would be able to tell who was elected President until after the contests which it provides for were all settled. The time intervening between the election and the meeting of the electors may be taken up by legal proceedings to determine the title of a sufficient number of electors to control the presidential office. And ought an issue of that kind—one so full of danger to the whole country, involving its peace and happiness, and it may be the liberty of every man within it—be confided to some local magistrate who never had an idea above what was necessary to settle matters of petty jurisdiction? While the Constitution very wisely has left the mode of selecting electors to the States, and is not particular as to how this power is exercised, still it has taken the precaution to guard the interests of the whole Union in two most important particulars connected with such elections. These are, that all the electors must be appointed on the same day, and that they must cast their votes for President and Vice-President on the same day.

"Whatever you may do here, you must not and can not leave open any important question entering into the appointment of electors after the second Tuesday in October. The people of the whole Union have an interest in this matter even greater than any which can belong to any State; for a contest over a single vote in Florida or Oregon, as we well know, might lead to the agitation of the whole country, and endanger the very foundations of the Government. Have we not had some experience of what is likely to result in every case of a close election, when under any system of laws the power of electing a President is placed in the hands of a few men, or an insignificant tribunal? When during the last election it was ascertained that the fate of the Presidency depended upon the decision of two persons unknown beyond the neighborhood in which they lived, and that they carried in their pockets the fortunes of the two great parties of the country, did not these men and the State to which they belonged rise to a height of interest and importance never before dreamt of by any one? Can we ever forget the patriotic pilgrimages of those 'visiting statesmen,' who, laying aside for a time the ease and comforts which surrounded them, rushed into Florida and Louisiana to fawn and cringe before the new-born majesty of McLin and Wells? Is any one weak enough to imagine that, if it should again happen that the fate of the Presidency depended upon the decision of a local court of any kind, a controversy like that could be carried on like other contests? Do we not know that in proportion to the magnitude of the interests involved, the hopes and fears excited by the event, such a tribunal would rise to the highest pitch of importance and power? Would you expect to see the two great parties of the Union, forty millions of people, stand quietly by and await with calmness and composure the result of such a proceeding? Figure to your mind the picture of two local par-

ties, with Smith's Form Book on one corner of their table and a defaced copy of the Holy Bible on the other, sitting in a spare room of a country grocery and hearing with studied patience the great question whom they should make President of the United States.

"Sir, I once witnessed something like this, and I pray to God I shall never behold anything like it again. I saw two men carried by accident to the highest pitch of this great power. I saw the fortunes and destinies of this whole people for a time in the keeping of a returning board in a single State. I saw them surrounded by parasites and flatterers from every quarter of the land. I saw how 'the stormy wave of the multitude retired at their approach.' I witnessed, with sorrow and humiliation and apprehension for the country, the congregation of a large part of the army of the United States to do the bidding of these men, and to put down the strong indignation of the people. After seeing all this, I am well satisfied that nothing could be more unwise or unsafe than to give the sanction of Congressional legislation to a mode of settling electoral contests which has been tried and found wanting. There is nothing in this bill which leads us to conclude that any different processes will be resorted to, in some of the States at least, to determine the Presidency than were resorted to in 1876. The character of the tribunal is not designated; there is nothing definite; it is left absolutely to the decision of the States, and it was boldly claimed in 1876 that, when a State decided through a returning board that one set of electors was elected, the tribunal here must acquiesce. That is the principle of this bill. I must confess that the fourth section of this bill is not at all satisfactory to me. Under this bill any returning board could perpetrate as much fraud as it pleased and certify it here, and there would be no power to look into it.

"I am aware that the late Electoral Commission based its conclusions upon the conclusive character of the State returns. But did this concession to State power and sovereignty, did this following the shadow and disregarding the substance, satisfy the people of the States concerned, or a majority of the voters of the United States?

"But suppose the States do not adopt the suggestion of Congress as contained in this bill, where is your power to enforce it? You say in the fourth section that the States may enact laws looking to the adjustment of all controversies growing out of the election of presidential electors in the State; but you can not enforce that. You admit upon the face of your bill that you have no power to enforce it, that it is a mere suggestion from this Government to the States, that they ought to pass a law providing for the adjustment of all electoral controversies. Suppose the laws of the States remain as they now are after the passage of this bill (and it is very likely that they would in a great measure so remain), what would be the effect of a State return? Would it be *prima facie* or conclusive evidence of its correctness? Or suppose some States decide to provide machinery for the adjustment of electoral contests and others do not. You have no power to enforce your wishes in this matter. You would be compelled to adopt two distinct rules in regard to the same kind of returns. If one State shall follow the suggestion of the law and constitute a tribunal prior to the time fixed for the counting of the electoral votes, and if there should be a trial and a determination to settle that question, I presume when the latter return came here it would be accepted under the provisions of this law as conclusive. But suppose that the State did not, relying upon the law as it now stands —and the laws throughout the Union are generally satisfactory on that subject, and simply comply with the act of 1792—and certified only the title of the electors, what then? In the one case I presume the record would be conclusive evidence that they were the electors, and in the other it would be only *prima facie* evidence. Unless you have the power to enforce this uniform rule and make it applicable to all States, I think you will find great difficulty in carrying out this part of it.

"Notwithstanding all that has been said in favor of this bill as a State-rights measure, it gives to Congress a power over the election of President which in my judgment is most dangerous. It was the observation of a very wise man on this floor that there is very little difference between leaving the presidential election to Congress and leaving Congress to decide that election. The sixth section of this bill gives Congress the power to set aside the vote of any State in this Union if one Senator and one Representative can be found to object to it. This is stating it pretty broadly, but the power is there. I know it is not a legitimate argument to argue against the existence of power from the abuse of it; but on questions of this kind all experience teaches us that whenever Congress is called to act it will act in a party spirit. Unfortunately for the country, unfortunately for all, it will be impossible to obtain any decision by Congress, in my judgment, on a question of this kind, into which party spirit will not enter. That is the great danger in the whole business. Am I to be told that the party majority in Congress will always be wise, moderate, and just, and that there is no danger from usurpation and passion? Give to one Senator and one Representative the power to set in motion this Congressional machinery against the electoral votes of the States, and I believe, sir, that the time is not far distant when it will prove to be the most dangerous delegation of authority ever conferred upon two men.

"There are many other objections that I could make to this bill; but I conceive that it is most important in the view that I take of the meaning of the Constitution, and the practice under it, that there should be no outstanding contest over the electors after election-day if it can be possibly avoided; that the Constitution in requiring the electors to be selected on a given day, and placing that time under the control of the General Government, clearly indicates what the purpose was in regard to it. It was that everything appertaining to or connected with the election of the electors should be settled upon that day. After the first Tuesday in October the election is over, but you have a contest in.Florida, in North Carolina, in Kentucky, it may be in New York; and no living man would be able to say what will be the decision of those local tribunals to whose judgments, under this bill, the main question is submitted. The election has settled nothing; it has brought a controversy into existence, which in its progress, as I said a while ago, may involve the very foundations of the Government, for the reason I have assigned."

Mr. Eaton of Connecticut: "Mr. President, I agree with other Senators who say that this is a grave question. I hope I am second to no man in this body in my desire for peace and good order and love for the Constitution. I am opposed to the passage of this bill. I am opposed to the passage of any such bill. I say, sir, here, that in my judgment there can be constitutionally no legislation upon this subject. There ought not to be any legislation upon this subject. There ought to be no interposition by Congress between the States and the Constitution. If the Constitution of the United States is defective, amend it, not tinker with it by legislation. I am not prepared to say that any amendment is required; but, if it is required, let the people of the country determine what the organic law shall be, and not this Congress of the United States.

"I said, sir, that there could not be, there ought not to be, any interposition between the Constitution and the States. The principle of legislation is vicious, and why? This instrument undertakes to and I believe does determine exactly what the power of the States is in this matter. Is any legislation required? What is necessary to constitute legislation? To legislate successfully requires the assent of the President of the United States, or a two-thirds vote of each House of Congress over his veto. Can this principle be adopted in this case? Is this principle wise? What has the Executive of the United States under the Constitution to do with this matter? Does the Constitution give him over this subject any power? You seek now to pass a bill, and ask the Executive of the United States to sign that bill, and that bill to govern, gentlemen say not the States, but the action of the. States under the organic law of the land. Sir, let us read this clause of the Constitution:

"The electors shall meet in their respective States and vote by ballot for President and Vice-President, one of whom at least shall not be an inhabitant of the same State with themselves; they shall name in their ballots the person voted for as President, and in distinct ballots the persons voted for as Vice-President, and they shall make distinct lists of all persons voted for as President and of all persons voted for as Vice-President, and of the number of votes for each, which lists they shall sign and certify, and transmit sealed to the seat of Government of the United States, directed to the President of the Senate.

"That is plain, clear. The right of the States is well defined. It is absolute. It can not be changed, tinkered with in any way, without destroying the virtue and vitality of the instrument.

"The President of the Senate shall, in the presence of the Senate and House of Representatives, open all the certificates and the votes shall then be counted.

"The Senator from Delaware [Mr. Bayard] urges as one reason why this bill should pass that it admits a great principle for which he has long contended; that is, that the President of the Senate has no right to count the votes, but that that power rests in the two Houses of Congress. Well, sir, a declaration of that sort incorporated in a bill of this character may be true, and yet it furnishes no reason why legislation should be adopted in this case. Further:

"The person having the greatest number of votes for President shall be the President, if such number be a majority of the whole number of electors appointed; and if no person have such majority, then from the persons having the highest number, not exceeding three, on the list of those voted for as President, the House of Representatives shall choose immediately, by ballot, the President.

"It strikes me that this is perfect. It does not require this bill at all in any way or manner.

"Again, the Constitution confers upon a Congress the right to count the electoral votes cast by the several States for President and Vice-President. Is there any doubt about it? 'The President of the Senate shall, in the presence of the Senate and House of Representatives, open all the certificates, and the votes shall then be counted.' Here, I beg to say, is a delegated power to some body. To whom? To what body is this power delegated? There can be no question about it whatever that here is a delegated power by the organic law of the land to Congress. What Congress? Not the Congress of 1800, or 1804, or 1824, or 1878; and we have no control over this delegated power. It is a power delegated to that Congress which has the right under the Constitution to count the votes; and I undertake to say that this Congress can make no law with regard to the counting of the votes that will bind that Congress upon whom that duty devolves. The duty of counting the electoral votes of the States for the next President and Vice-President of the United States will devolve upon the Congress that meets in this building in 1880—not this, but the next; and here we undertake to determine a rule of action for a Congress hereafter in part to be elected, and

upon whom will devolve that duty. The idea, to my mind, is monstrous that a President of the United States has the power in his hands, unless there is a two-thirds vote in each branch of the Federal Assembly to override him, to defeat a bill with regard to the important matter of counting the votes for the next President of the United States! The very statement of it in itself is enough to determine the whole question.

"Now, what is necessary? Is any change in the organic law necessary? If so, are we not competent to advise our fellow countrymen, to advise the different States of the Union, that such an amendment to the organic law would be wise, and prudent, and is necessary? This whole subject with the next Congress will be the simple passage, if anything is necessary, of a joint rule in regard to who shall preside, on which side of the Chamber the Senate shall sit, on which side of the Chamber the House of Representatives shall sit, where the Speaker's chair shall be, and who shall write down the figures. All that is mere matter of a rule to be made by the two Houses and acted upon whenever the count is had.

"Gentlemen speak as though there was great danger. Sir, I am not an alarmist. I do not believe there is any danger in standing by the Constitution of the United States. I did not believe there was any danger two years ago when a bill was passed under which the choice of the people of the United States was defrauded out of an office by the illegal act of an unconstitutional machine. The Constitution is the great charter of the rights of the States and the liberties of the people. I do not propose myself to vote for any law, to be a party to any legislation that interferes in the slightest degree with the rights of each of the sovereign States—I know that term is not liked about these days, but yet I use it—of each of the sovereign States of this confederacy of sovereignties. I have no idea, Mr. President, that this bill is introduced or advocated as a condonation of anything in the past. If I did believe that, I should characterize it with different language than what I now do."

Mr. Hoar of Massachusetts: "Mr. President, I do not propose at this late hour of the afternoon to discuss the pending measure. I propose to vote for it because, after several years' attempt to reconcile conflicting theories, the best minds which the Senate has been able to charge with the duty have reported that this is the best measure which they can devise to remove the present evil. The evil, however, is essential and inevitable after any legislation may have been adopted, which arises from the construction of the Constitution, which I think the correct construction of the Constitution, which was put upon it by the consent of a large majority of both parties at the time of the last presidential election. I could not believe that the framers of our Constitution, jealous as they were of power, jealous as they were of executive power, could have intended to intrust the grave questions which might arise during the count of a presidential vote to the determination of a single officer, who, as the Constitution was originally framed, must have been one of the two last candidates for the Presidency, and in all probability, under their habit of continuing the same men in public service, would be one of the candidates whose election was to be determined by the count. The only other alternative was the construction adopted, which imposed the power and duty of determining these questions upon two equal bodies, who could not therefore act by a majority, who would frequently be of different political parties, and whose difference must of course be expected to occur frequently in practice.

" Now, it does not seem to me that this bill or that any bill has removed the essential difficulty which grows out of that oversight made by the framers of the Constitution. This bill provides that when, in regard to the votes returned from any State by two bodies claiming to have the right to make the return from the State, there is a difference of opinion, neither vote shall be counted. I can not understand, I never could understand, how that could be called a count of the vote for the Presidency, when the counting power simply said they were unable to determine what individuals made up the aggregate which was to be counted. How can you count the number of votes when all you have said is that there are ninety partly for one man and partly for another, and that there are ten which you can not determine whether they belong to the aggregate to be counted or not? That difficulty is untouched by the pending bill, and it can not in the nature of the case be removed except by a constitutional amendment which gives to one authority, and not to the concurrence of two authorities, the power of determining these questions."

Mr. Edmunds: "The objections that have been made to the bill recognize, I think in every instance, the principle upon which it is founded, and that is, the right of each State to determine for itself the choice of its electors. All that follows is the regulative method of going through with the administrative act of counting the votes which the States have sent to the national capital to express their choice for President of the United States."

The Presiding Officer (Mr. Mitchell in the chair): "The question is on the passage of the bill." The Secretary proceeded to call the roll, and the result was then announced—as follows

YEAS—Messrs. Allison, Anthony, Bayard, Blaine, Booth, Burnside, Cameron of Pennsylvania, Cameron of Wisconsin, Christiancy, Conkling, Davis of Illinois, Dawes, Edmunds, Ferry, Hamlin, Hoar, Howe, Ingalls, Kellogg, Kirkwood, McMillan, Matthews, Merrimon, Mitchell, Morgan, Morrill, Oglesby, Paddock, Patterson, Plumb, Rollins, Saunders, Teller, Wadleigh, Windom—35.

NAYS—Messrs. Armstrong, Bailey, Beck, Butler, Coke, Davis of West Virginia, Dennis, Eaton, Eustis, Gordon, Grover, Harris, Hereford, Hill, Jones of Florida, Kernan, Lamar, McCreery, McDonald, Maxey, Randolph, Ransom, Thurman, Voorhees, Wallace, Withers—26.

ABSENT—Messrs. Barnum, Bruce, Chaffee, Cockrell, Conover, Dorsey, Garland, Johnston, Jones of Nevada, McPherson, Sargent, Saulsbury, Sharon, Spencer, Whyte—15.

So the bill was passed. No decisive action on the bill was taken in the House of Representatives.

In the House, on January 29th, the following bill to restrict the emigration of Chinese to the United States, with the amendments of the Committee on Education and Labor, was considered:

Strike out the parts in brackets, and insert the parts in italics.

De it enacted, etc., That no master of any vessel owned in whole or in part by a citizen of the United States, or by a citizen of any foreign country, nor other person, shall take on board such vessel, at any port [of] or place within the Chinese Empire, or at any other foreign port or place whatever, any number exceeding [ten] fifteen Chinese passengers, whether male or female, with the intent to bring such passengers to the United States, or shall bring such passengers to any number exceeding [ten] fifteen on one voyage within the jurisdiction of the United States.

SECTION 2. That whenever the master or other person in charge of any such vessel takes on board the same, at any foreign port or place, any greater number of Chinese passengers than is prescribed in the first section of this act, with intent to bring such passengers to the United States, or bring such passengers to any number exceeding [ten] fifteen on one voyage within the jurisdiction of the United States, he shall be deemed guilty of a misdemeanor, and shall for each passenger so taken on board or brought within the jurisdiction of the United States exceeding the number of [ten] fifteen, be fined $100, and may also be imprisoned for not exceeding six months.

SEC. 3. That the master of any vessel arriving in the United States, or any of the Territories thereof, from any foreign place whatever, at the same time that he delivers a manifest of the cargo, and if there be no cargo, then at the time of making report or entry of the vessel pursuant to law, shall, in addition to the other matters required to be reported by law, deliver and report to the collector of the district in which such vessel shall arrive, a separate list of all Chinese passengers taken on board the vessel at any foreign port or place, and of all such passengers on board the vessel at that time; such list shall be sworn to by the master in the same manner as directed by law in relation to the manifest of the cargo; and the refusal or neglect of the master to comply with the provisions of this section shall receive the same penalties, disabilities, and forfeitures as are provided for a refusal or neglect to report and deliver a manifest of the cargo.

SEC. 4. That the amount of the several penalties imposed by the foregoing provisions shall be liens on the vessel violating those provisions; and such vessel shall be libeled therefor in any circuit or district court of the United States where such vessel shall arrive.

[SEC. 5. That informers shall be entitled to one half of any penalty or fine collected under the provisions of this act upon their information.]

SEC. [6] 5. That nothing herein contained shall be held to repeal or modify any law forbidding the importation of coolies, or of females for immoral purposes, into the United States: Provided, That no consul or consular agent of the United States, residing at any port from which any vessel taking Chinese passengers may take her departure, shall grant the certificate provided for in section 2162 of the Revised Statutes for more than [ten] *fifteen* Chinese passengers on any one vessel.

SEC. [7] 6. That this act shall take effect from and after the first day of [September] *July*, eighteen hundred and seventy-[eight] *nine*.

Mr. Willis of Kentucky, from the Committee on Education and Labor, submitted the following report:

The Committee on Education and Labor, having had under consideration sundry bills in regard to Chinese immigration, beg leave to submit the following report:

Briefly stated, this bill provides that no master of a vessel shall take on board at any point in China, or elsewhere, more than fifteen Chinese passengers with intent to bring them, or shall bring them, within the United States. The violation of this provision is made a misdemeanor, punishable by a fine of $100 for each passenger and imprisonment for six months. The master is required, under like penalties, to report on his arrival a sworn list of all Chinese passengers. The penalty is made a lien upon the vessel. The bill becomes operative on the 1st day of July, 1879.

Waiving for the present any consideration of the merits of the bill, the first question is whether such legislation is within the power of Congress? Can Congress repeal a treaty?

The existing treaty with China gives its subjects an unlimited right of immigration to the United States. The second clause of Article VI. of the Constitution provides that " this Constitution, and the laws of the United States which shall be made in pursuance thereof, and all treaties made under the authority of the United States, shall be the supreme law of the land." It is contended that any law restricting Chinese immigration would contravene this provision of the Constitution, and would therefore be null and void. Such a construction can not be sustained either upon principle or authority. The objects for which the Constitution was formed are higher than any po e granted under it. The general welfare, justice, domestic tranquillity, and the blessings of liberty are of supreme importance, and can not be taken from the people by any treaty however solemnly ratified. The treaty-making power is limited by these objects. Moreover, both in nature and by international law, the first duty is self-preservation. If, therefore, it be true that the presence of the Chinese endangers the peace or prosperity of our people, no mere technical consideration should intervene to prevent an increase of the evil.

The clause of the Constitution above quoted does not, however, admit of the construction contended for. It elevates treaties from the status of mere compacts to the dignity of laws, but does not clothe them with any additional superiority. Laws made in pursuance of the Constitution are equally as binding and authoritative as treaties, and, if last enacted, control any contravening treaty. This conclusion is enforced by numerous decisions, both of the executive and judicial departments of the Government. In 1851, in the case of the Florida claims, an apparent conflict between a treaty and a subsequent act of Congress was decided by Attorney-General Crittenden in these words: " An act of Congress is as much a supreme law of the land as a treaty. They are placed on the same footing, and no preference or superiority is given to the one or the other. The last expression of the law-giving power must prevail, and just for the same reason and on the same principle that a subsequent act must prevail and have effect, though inconsistent with a prior act; so must an act of Congress have effect, though inconsistent with a prior treaty." (" Opinions Attorney-General," volume v., page 345.) To the same effect is the decision of Attorney-General Akerman in the case of the Choctaw Indians: " There is nothing in the Constitution which assigns different ranks to treaties and to statutes; both the one and the other, when not in-

consistent with the Constitution, seem to stand upon the same level and to be of equal validity; and as in the case of all laws emanating from an equal authority, the earlier in date yields to the later." (" Opinions Attorney-General," volume xiii., page 357.)

These decisions of the Executive Department, confirmed as they are by the teachings of Madison, of Hamilton, and of Jefferson, have been followed by the judiciary. In the case of Taylor *vs.* Martin, 2 Curtis, C. C. Rep., 454, the court said: " It is impossible to maintain that under our Constitution the President and Senate exclusively possess the power to modify or repeal a law found in a treaty. If this were true, no change in a treaty could be made without the consent of some foreign government. That the Constitution was designed to place our country in this helpless condition is a supposition wholly inadmissible. It is not only inconsistent with the necessities of a nation, but negatived by the express words of the Constitution. That gives to Congress, in so many words, power to declare war, an act which, *ipso facto*, repeals all treaties inconsistent with a state of war. It can not, therefore, be admitted that the only method of escape from a treaty is by the consent of the other party to it or a declaration of war. To refuse to execute a treaty for reasons which approve themselves to the conscientious judgment of a nation is a matter of the utmost gravity; but the power to do so is a prerogative of which no nation can be deprived without deeply affecting its independence. That the people of the United States have deprived their Government of this power I do not believe. That it must reside somewhere, and be applicable to all cases, I am convinced, and I feel no doubt that it belongs to Congress."

Similar opinions have been delivered in the circuit courts of the country. These decisions were finally reaffirmed by the Supreme Court of the United States in the Cherokee Tobacco Case, reported in 11 Wallace, page 616. The court says: " The effect of treaties and acts of Congress, when in conflict, is not settled by the Constitution. But the question is not involved in any doubt as to its proper solution. A treaty may supersede a prior act of Congress (2 Peters, 314), and an act of Congress may supersede a prior treaty (2 Curtis, 454; 1 Woolworth, 155). In the cases referred to, these principles were applied to treaties with foreign nations. Treaties with Indian nations can not be more obligatory. They have no higher sanctity, and no greater inviolability or immunity from legislative invasion can be claimed for them. The act of Congress must prevail, as if the treaty were not an element to be considered. If a wrong has been done, the power of redress is with Congress, not with the judiciary."

Upon principle, therefore, as well as upon the authority of precedents, judicial and administrative, it would seem clear that Congress has the right, by appropriate legislation, to change or to abrogate any existing treaty. Indeed, Congress has in one instance expressly exercised this power. The act of July 7, 1798, declares that the existing treaties with France are no longer obligatory upon the United States. (1 Statutes at Large, page 578.)

The evils of Chinese immigration have been fully recognized upon the Pacific slope for many years. Welcomed at first as a unique addition to the society and a valuable ally in the development of the material resources of their new home, the Chinese, by their sordid, selfish, immoral, and non-amalgamating habits, within a very short time reversed the judgment in their favor, and came to be regarded as a standing menace to the social and political institutions of the country.

The State laws which had been enacted having been declared unconstitutional by the Supreme Court, and every other means of relief proving ineffectual, it was finally determined to appeal to Congress. Accordingly, as early as the 22d of December, 1869, at the second session of the Forty-first Congress, an effort was made, but without success, to secure restrictive legislation. In the Forty-second Congress, and also in the Forty-third Congress, numerous memorials, resolutions of public meetings, and petitions, one of which numbered over 16,000 signatures, were presented to the same effect and with the same result. At the first session of the Forty-fourth Congress these renewed appeals for relief met for the first time with a favorable response. A joint resolution was introduced and passed calling upon the President of the United States to "open negotiations with the Chinese Government for the purpose of modifying the provisions of the treaty between the two countries, and restricting the same to commercial purposes."

Subsequently, at the same session, another joint resolution was passed, requesting the President to present to the Chinese Government an additional article to the treaty of July 28, 1868, reserving mutually to the two governments the right to regulate, restrict, or prevent immigration to their respective countries. These authoritative requests on the part of Congress failed to secure the desired relief. In the mean while the question had assumed dangerous proportions. The conviction that Chinese immigration was a great evil was so deep-seated and unanimous that mob violence was openly threatened, and in many instances the arm of the law seemed powerless to protect. Recognizing the exigency, the Legislature of California appointed a special committee, whose report, based upon the testimony of witnesses familiar with the subject, ably and graphically sets forth the objections to the Chinese. Subsequently to this a joint committee appointed by the Forty-fourth Congress collected voluminous testimony upon the same subject, and by a majority report urged upon the Executive Department the necessity for an immediate change of the Burlingame treaty, to the end that such immigration might be restricted or prevented. These reports, together with other official documents upon the subject, were laid before the present Congress.

Your committee, in view of the importance and urgency of the question, after a patient hearing of the evidence and argument on both sides, at an early date after its organization presented a resolution which with a slight modification passed both Houses of Congress. This resolution again called attention to the obnoxious features in the Burlingame treaty, and requested prompt action on the part of the Executive Department in securing its change or abrogation. In view of the almost unanimous sentiment of the people of the Pacific slope as to the necessity of such action, it was hoped that these successive resolutions of Congress, together with the various petitions, memorials, and official data in the possession of the Government, would cause negotiations to be opened for that purpose. Such action would have been preferable to the direct interference by Congress, inasmuch as it would have been free from all doubt as to its legality, and would not have jeopardized the friendly feelings and commercial intercourse between the two countries. Moreover, when a change of the treaty was first suggested by Congress, and indeed up to a very recent date, it is believed that the Chinese Government would have made no serious objection, as its policy was opposed to the emigration of its citizens. However desirable such a result, it has thus far not been accomplished. The petitions to secure remedial legislation were presented within a year after the ratification of the Burlingame treaty. These were vigorously renewed at every subsequent session, until finally in the Forty-fourth Congress the resolution already referred to was passed, calling the attention of the Executive Department to the necessity of a change in the treaty. This resolution was again presented and passed in the second session of the present Congress, but has not, as far as your committee is informed, called forth any practical effort at action. So long a period of non-action proves either the unwillingness or the inability of the treaty-making power to cope with the question. In either event your committee consider that further delay would work great injustice to a large portion of our country, provided the evils whereof they complain are well founded.

That these complaints are not without cause can not,

upon the evidence, be doubted. Your committee, in a report accompanying joint resolution H. R. No. 123, at the second session of this Congress, endeavored to present what seemed to them some insuperable objections to Chinese immigration. Further examination of facts only confirms the conclusions therein stated. This whole question is not one of right, but of policy. There is no principle upon which we are compelled to receive into our midst the natives of Asia, Africa, or any other part of the world. The character, source, and extent of immigration should be regulated and controlled with reference to our own wants and welfare. The difficult problems, economic and political, resulting from the presence of the red and black races, would be renewed in a more aggravated and dangerous form by the yellow race. The Mongolian, unlike the Indian, is brought in daily contact with our social and political life; and, unlike the African, does not surrender any of his marked peculiarities by reason of that contact. It is neither possible nor desirable for two races as distinct as the Caucasian and Mongolian to live under the same government without assimilation. The degradation or slavery of one or the other would be the inevitable result. Homogeneity of ideas and of physical and social habits are essential to national harmony and progress. Equally grave objections may be urged against the Chinese from an industrial standpoint. Our laboring people can not and ought not to be subjected to a competition which involves the surrender of the sacred and elevating influences of home and the sacrifice of the ordinary appliances of personal civilization. The question, therefore, is not one of competition, but of a substitution of one kind of labor for another.

No self-governing country can afford to diminish or destroy the dignity, the welfare, and independence of its citizens. Justice to the people of the Pacific slope, the dictates of common humanity and benevolence, as well as the plainest suggestions of practical statesmanship, all demand that the problem of Chinese immigration shall be solved while it is yet within the legislative control.

Governed by these views, your committee present and recommend the passage of the bill accompanying this report.

Mr. Page of California presented the following petition, and said : "As an expression of the views entertained on this subject by the working classes of our State, I submit a memorial presented to Congress, and signed by seventeen thousand of the workingmen of California. I introduce this memorial further to show that this movement is endorsed not by the ignorant and vicious, but by the intelligent and law-abiding citizens of California."

The petition of the undersigned citizens, resident in the State of California, respectfully shows :

That your petitioners view with great alarm the systematic importation and immigration of Chinese laborers into the United States, to be employed at rates of wages ruinous to the free labor of our citizens.

That the vast sums granted by Congress in bonds and public lands to aid in the construction of transcontinental railways are perverted to the employment of this debased Asiatic labor, while thousands of our own citizens in all parts of the Republic are destitute of work.

That your petitioners can not regard such a misdirection of the revenues collected from the industry of the people but as a flagrant abuse of the objects contemplated in these munificent grants of the national resources.

That in all future measures of Congressional aid provision should be embodied against such abuse, and that supplementary legislation to this end should be provided in the exercise of existing grants.

That our recent history shows with what devotion to the great principles of freedom our citizens placed their lives at the command of the Government and poured out their blood and treasure to terminate the blighting influence of slavery in our midst. Yet an equally and, if possible, a more insidious danger must eventuate by the great increase of this servile population.

That this immigration is in no manner homogeneous with us as a people ; that their social wants, habits, and character differ so materially that the standard of labor must be debased to such a degree by their vitiating influence as to repel vast bodies of our most valuable operatives, and not only degrade the social status and moral welfare of our producing classes, but arrest the advancement of our civilization.

That the Asiatic has displaced to a great extent the citizen operatives formerly engaged in the various manufactures of the city of San Francisco, and is rapidly displacing others.

That all occupations giving profitable employment to both male and female have suffered through this cause.

That the aggregate diminution of wages to American citizens can not be less than $9,000,000 annually.

That the expenditure of such vast industrial resources thus withdrawn from circulation has entailed privation among the working classes, taxed the most generous benevolence, and operated most detrimentally against the prosperity of the city.

That the spread and augmentation of the number throughout the State of California have seriously discouraged the increase of the most desirable class of European immigrants, such additions to our industrial population seeking homes where labor is less degraded or in greater demand.

That your petitioners would urge upon your honorable consideration the necessity of an immediate revision of our treaty relations with China to restrain this overwhelming evil.

That all treaty stipulations should be based on the principle of reciprocal advantages, not mutual privileges. The right or privilege for a citizen of the United States to migrate to China and for a subject of China to migrate to the United States are not mutual in advantages, for it is an advantage to the subject while it is disadvantageous to the citizen to migrate. Hence such provision in the treaty is impolitic and unwise.

That the inundation of incompatible races into the various avenues of labor, which are still so inadequate to supply employment to our own producing classes, must evidently lead to the most disastrous consequences.

That your petitioners are actuated by no illiberal feeling inimical to the less advanced races. On the contrary, it is their earnest desire that all the offices of friendly intercourse should be generously fulfilled ; that religious instruction and the advantages of scientific education should be placed at their command ; that instead of permitting the unchristian sordidness of our own race using them to degrade the social condition of our people and to desecrate the noblest hopes of our national destiny, we should render them every service to elevate their civilization.

That a cause which projects and accelerates the concentration of wealth, and thus erects in the very bosom of the nation a power destructive of republican institutions, as evidenced by every record of history, and which draws into conflict the millions whose sole dependence and property consist in labor, and therefore sacred to the interests of their families, impeaches equally the justice and wisdom of such a policy.

That we are but in the first stages of this fatal policy.

That its destructive influence on the industrial condition of California is the inevitable result which must follow its extension into every other State of the Union.

That it now be arrested by the foresight and sagacity essential to the guardianship of a great nation, while the delay or neglect of necessary measures will leave the growing antagonism of interests to gather

force and ultimately consolidate its power in resistance to the most salutary legislation.

That your petitioners earnestly hope that your honorable body, preëminent under the Constitution in its deliberative functions, will not disregard their prayer nor underrate the solemn importance of a subject so grave.

That large numbers of our most valuable operatives have withdrawn from this degrading competition, while others are preparing to abandon a State where a beneficent Providence has spread such immeasurable blessings over its fair villages.

This assuredly demonstrates how limited is governmental knowledge in the administration of Divine bounty, and how much the prosperity of a nation depends on the wisdom of its statesmen.

Mr. Page : " I do not suppose it will be generally claimed by the opponents of this measure that Congress has not full power to legislate on this subject. The right of Congress is unquestionable. The only question that may arise in this connection is that of good faith, and of that I shall speak hereafter. I shall quote only one opinion on this point, which I believe to be conclusive of the question. I send to the Clerk's desk to be read an opinion of Justice Curtis, of the Supreme Court of the United States, Sanford vs. Scott, 19 Howard's Reports, 629 :

" By a treaty with a foreign nation the United States may rightfully stipulate that the Congress will or will not exercise its legislative power in some particular manner on some particular subject. Such promises when made should be voluntarily kept with the most scrupulous good faith. But that a treaty with a foreign nation can deprive the Congress of any part of the legislative power conferred by the people, so that it no longer can legislate as it was empowered by the Constitution to do, I more than doubt.

" The powers of the Government do and must remain unimpaired. The responsibility of the Government to a foreign nation for the exercise of those powers is quite another matter. That responsibility is to be met and justified to the foreign nation according to the requirements of the rules of public law, but never upon the assumption that the United States had parted with or restricted any power of acting according to its own free will governed by its own appreciation of duty.

" The second section of the sixth article is, ' This Constitution and the laws of the United States which shall be made in pursuance thereof, and all treaties made, or which shall be made, under the authority of the United States, shall be the supreme law of the land.' This has made treaties part of our municipal law, but it has not assigned to them any particular degree of authority, nor declared laws so enacted shall be irrepealable. No supremacy is assigned to treaties over acts of Congress. That they are not perpetual, and must be in some way repealable, all will agree. If the President and the Senate alone possess the power to repeal or modify a law found in a treaty, inasmuch as they can change or abrogate one treaty only by making another inconsistent with the first, the Government of the United States could not act at all to that effect without the consent of some foreign government. I do not consider, I am not aware it has ever been considered, that the Constitution has placed our country in this helpless condition. The action of Congress, in repealing the treaties with France by the act of July 7, 1798 (7 Statutes at Large, 578), was in conformity with these views.

" In the case of Taylor vs. Morton (2 Curtis's Circuit Court Reports, 454) I had occasion to consider this subject, and I adhere to the views there expressed.

" This is a dissenting opinion in what was

popularly known as the Dred Scott case. This opinion, however, was endorsed at that time by the people of one section of this country, and is now recognized as being in accordance not only with the principles of liberty, but the dominant sentiments of the country. I regard it as a fortunate circumstance that I am able to refer to a case that involves the question of freedom and free labor in this country, and I invoke the principles announced in that opinion to justify this House in passing a law that involves the present and future happiness of the citizens of this country, as well as the immediate settlement of a question that involves the peace and good order of the Pacific coast.

"The only restriction to the exercise of the power herein claimed under the Constitution and public law, as inherent in the Government of the United States, is in the contingency suggested by Justice Curtis, in which the United States may have for reasons satisfactory to it bound itself not to use its powers in a given direction. There is nothing in the treaty with China that indicates a relinquishment of power on our part, and there can not therefore be a reasonable ground upon which this Congress should decline to take jurisdiction and action upon the subject of discussion."

The amendments were agreed to, and the bill was put on its passage, and the result was as follows:

YEAS—Messrs. Acklen, Aiken, Aldrich, Atkins, Bailey, John H. Baker, William H. Baker, Banning, Bayne, Beebe, Bell, Benedict, Bicknell, Blackburn, Blair, Bliss, Blount, Boone, Brentano, Brewer, Bright, Buckner, Cabell, John W. Caldwell, W. P. Caldwell, Calkins, Campbell, Chalmers, Clarke of Kentucky, Clark of Missouri, Cobb, Cole, Cook, Covert, Jacob D. Cox, Samuel S. Cox, Cravens, Crittenden, Cummings, Davidson, Horace Davis, Deering, Dibrell, Dickey, Durham, Eden, Elam, Ellis, Ellsworth, Errett, James L. Evans, John H. Evins, Ewing, Felton, Finley, Fort, Foster, Freeman, Garth, Gause, Gibson, Giddings, Glover, Gunter, Hale, Hamilton, Hanna, Harmer, Harrison, Hartzell, Hatcher, Hayes, Hazelton, Henkle, Herbert, Abram S. Hewitt, G. W. Hewitt, Hiscock, Hooker, House, Hubbell, Hunton, Ittner, Frank Jones, James T. Jones, Keightley, Kenna, Ketcham, Killinger, Kimmel, Knapp, Landers, Ligon, Lockwood, Luttrell, Mackey, Maish, Majors, Manning, Martin, Mayham, McMahon, Metcalfe, Mills, Money, Morse, Muldrow, Neal, O'Neill, Page, T. M. Patterson, Peddie, Pollard, Potter, Pound, Rea, Reagan, Reilly, Americus V. Rice, Robertson, M. S. Robinson, Ross, Ryan, Sapp, Sayler, Scales, Shallenberger, Singleton, Slemons, William E. Smith, Southard, Sparks, Steele, Stenger, Throckmorton, Amos Townsend, R. W. Townshend, Turner, Turney, Vance, Van Vorhes, Walker, Ward, Michael D. White, Whitthorne, Wigginton, Jere N. Williams, Richard Williams, Albert S. Willis, Willits, Wilson, Wren, Wright, Yeates, and John S. Young—155.

NAYS—Messrs. Bacon, Bagley, Banks, Bisbee, Bouck, Bragg, Briggs, Brogden, Bundy, Burchard, Burdick, Cain, Candler, Cannon, Caswell, Chittenden, Rush Clark, Conger, Crapo, Cutler, Danford, Denison, Dunnell, Dwight, Eames, Hardenbergh, Benjamin W. Harris, Henry R. Harris, Hart, Hendee, Henderson, Humphrey, Hungerford, James, John S. Jones, Joyce, Lathrop, McCook, McGowan, Mitchell, Monroe, Morgan, Norcross, Overton, G.W. Patterson, Phelps, Pridemore, Pugh, Rainey, Randolph, Reed, William W. Rice, Robbins, G. D. Robinson, Sampson,

Sexton, Sinnickson, Smalls, A. Herr Smith, Starin, Stephens, Stewart, Strait, Swann, Thompson, Tipton, M. I. Townsend, Waddell, Warner, Watson, C. G. Williams, James Williams—72.

NOT VOTING—Messrs. Ballou, Bland, Boyd, Bridges, Browne, Butler, Camp, Carlyle, Claflin, Alvah A. Clark, Clymer, Collins, Culberson, Joseph J. Davis, Dean, Eickhoff, I. Newton Evans, Forney, Franklin, Frye, Fuller, Gardner, Garfield, Goode, John T. Harris, Haskell, Henry, Hunter, Jorgensen, Keifer, Kelley, Knott, Lapham, Lindsey, Loring, Lynde, Marsh, McKenzie, McKinley, Morrison, Muller, Oliver, Phillips, Powers, Price, Riddle, Roberts, Shelley, Springer, John W. Stone, Joseph C. Stone, Thornburgh, Tucker, Veeder, Wait, Walsh, Harry White, Andrew Williams, Benjamin A. Willis, Wood, Casey Young —61.

So the bill was passed.

In the Senate, on February 16th, the bill was considered.

The Vice-President : " The pending question is on the amendment of the Senator from New York [Mr. Conkling], which will be read."

The Secretary : " The amendment is to strike out all after the enacting clause, and insert—

" That the President of the United States is hereby requested immediately to give notice to the Emperor of China that so much of the existing treaty between the United States and China as permits the migration of subjects of the Chinese Empire and their domicile in this country is unsatisfactory to the Government of the United States, and, in its judgment, pernicious, and to propose such modifications of said treaty as will correct the evils complained of; said modifications to be made in a new or supplemental treaty to be submitted to the Senate of the United States on or before the 1st day of January, 1880. Should the Government of China refuse or omit to agree by a change of the existing treaty to such modifications, as aforesaid, then the President of the United States is further requested, and he is authorized, to inform the Emperor of China that the United States will proceed by laws of its own to regulate or prevent the migration or importation to its shores of the subjects of China, and after the 1st of January, 1880, to treat the obnoxious stipulations as at an end."

Mr. Hamlin of Maine : " Mr. President, this question has resolved itself into two simple propositions, one of power and the other of expediency. Upon the question of power I have heard no difference of opinion in this body. That we may abrogate our treaties with every foreign power is a doctrine which I maintain ; and when it comes to that point, when we are justified before the civilized and Christianized world in abrogating a treaty, let us do it. But I do not believe in the doctrine, I do not believe in the expediency of seeking to abrogate a treaty upon a single and comparatively unimportant part, expecting that the main features of the treaty shall thereafter remain in force. We have the power ; there can be no doubt upon it in my own mind ; but there is a broad distinction between power and right. We may have the power to do many things that are wrong ; we may have the power to do, and we may do, many things that would not meet the approval of calm and considerate judgment. What we should do, and the rule by which we should be guided, is the rule of right, not of power.

"Oh! it is excellent
To have a giant's strength; but it is tyrannous
To use it hke a giant.

"Now I want to invite the attention of the Senate to the true condition in which this question is presented to us for our consideration and our action. I have no hope of affecting a single vote, but I wish to state the reasons of my own conclusion.

"We negotiated a treaty with a friendly and a foreign power. We, in connection with other governments, forced that treaty upon that power. It is as patent and as true as anything, it is as certain as mathematics, that in securing that treaty there was no section of our country so earnest, so forward, as that which lies upon the Pacific coast. We negotiated the treaty, we battered down a wall of commercial restriction that had surrounded the Chinése Government in the long ages of the past, almost as restrictive as that Chinese wall that preserved that empire from the Tartar hordes of the north. We accomplished, however, the negotiation of a treaty which secured to us the right of trial by jury of our own citizens in that empire, which opened up a given number of ports which should be accessible for the commerce of our country; and we granted in return the immigration of Chinese subjects to our own country. Why, sir, who does not remember with what welcome, with what rejoicing, that treaty was hailed upon the Pacific coast? To say that they honored it, is hardly adequate. That they did homage to the men who negotiated it is nearer the truth. Now, it is affirmed that that treaty is injurious to our friends on that coast, that from its effects they desire to be relieved. We are asked to secure a modification of the treaty thus negotiated, which allows an unlimited immigration from the Chinese Empire to this country. That is the precise question, and it is sought in direct contravention of the fifth article of the treaty to limit that immigration. Is it a desirable thing to do? I will not stop to consider that; but, conceding it to be a desirable thing to do, what is the mode in which it should be done? And that brings us directly to the division which we have here upon this question. I would proceed by the ordinary rules of negotiation; I would treat that empire as I would treat every civilized nation upon the earth, and I believe that there are few Senators on this floor who would be willing to treat a warlike power of Europe in the summary manner in which this bill proposes to treat the Empire of China. I would first make the distinct proposition to that empire to treat. Failing to treat, coming within the scope of the amendment which has been submitted by the Senator from New York, after full and ample notice, I would say then that we might take the matter into our own consideration, and apply the remedy which in our own judgment should be demanded.

"At the last session of this Congress there were a variety of subjects submitted to the consideration of the Committee on Foreign Relations: one a bill almost in the terms of this now presented to us, differing indeed. I believe, only in that but ten citizens of that empire should embark upon any one vessel, this extending it to fifteen. There was another bill proposing to place a capitation tax upon every Chinaman immigrant to this country. There were two or three other propositions. After mature consideration, the Committee on Foreign Relations, believing it just and right and the proper solution of this problem, directed my honorable friend from Wisconsin [Mr. Howe] to report a resolution to this body. Perhaps it is not inappropriate to say that I drew that resolution. It met the approval of the committee, and in my absence the Senator from Wisconsin was kind enough to report it for the consideration of the Senate. It was adopted by the Senate. It has been read; still, you will pardon me for again presenting it, in connection with what I am saying, to the attention of the Senate:

"That the p o is ons of the existing treaty between the Empire of China and the United States, allowing the unrestricted emigration to this country from China, might wisely be modified so as to subserve the best interests of both governments; and the attention of the Executive is respectfully invited to the subject.

"That was a simple invitation on the part of this body, inviting the attention of the Executive to the consideration of this subject, the committee deeming it and believing it to be the precise and best mode in which the result aimed at should be accomplished. It is but a few months since the Senate adopted that resolution. I would leave this question upon that resolution to-day, if I could have my way. I would have no action in this body now. I would leave it there; I would trust it to the Administration in the firm belief—and I do not speak unadvisedly—that if there were not this hot haste to override and to supersede the duties that justly and appropriately belong to the Executive, there would a solution come of this question satisfactory even to our friends upon the Pacific slope."

The Vice-President: "The question is on the amendment of the Senator from New York [Mr. Conkling]."

The result was announced, as follows:

YEAS—Messrs. Anthony, Bruce, Burnside, Butler, Cameron of Wisconsin, Cockrell, Conkling, Conover, Davis of Illinois, Dawes, Edmunds, Ferry, Garland, Hamlin, Hill, Hoar, Howe, Jones of Florida, Kernan, McCreery, McMillan, McPherson, Matthews, Maxey, Merrimon, Morrill, Oglesby, Randolph, Rollins, Saunders, Withers—31.

NAYS—Messrs. Allison, Bailey, Barnum, Bayard, Beck, Blaine, Booth, Cameron of Pennsylvania, Coke, Dennis, Dorsey, Eaton, Eustis, Gordon, Grover, Hereford, Ingalls, Jones of Nevada, Kirkwood, Lamar, McDonald, Mitchell, Morgan, Patterson, Plumb, Ransom, Sargent, Sharon, Spencer, Teller, Thurman, Voorhees, Wallace, Windom—34.

ABSENT—Messrs. Chaffee, Davis of West Virginia, Harris, Johnson, Kellogg, Paddock, Saulsbury, Shields, Wadleigh, Whyte—10.

So the amendment was rejected.

An extended discussion ensued on the bill, and it was put to vote, and resulted as follows:

YEAS—Messrs. Allison, Bailey, Bayard, Beck, Blaine, Booth, Cameron of Pennsylvania, Coke, Dennis, Dorsey, Eaton, Eustis, Garland, Gordon, Grover, Hereford, Jones of Nevada, Kirkwood, Lamar, McDonald, McPherson, Maxey, Mitchell, Morgan, Oglesby, Paddock, Patterson, Plumb, Ransom, Sargent, Saunders, Sharon, Shields, Spencer, Teller, Thurman, Voorhees, Wallace, Windom—39.

NAYS—Messrs. Anthony, Bruce, Burnside, Butler, Cameron of Wisconsin, Conkling, Conover, Davis of Illinois, Davis of West Virginia, Dawes, Edmunds, Ferry, Hamlin, Hill, Hoar, Howe, Ingalls, Jones of Florida, Kellogg, Kernan, McCreery, McMillan, Matthews, Merrimon, Morrill, Randolph, Withers—27.

ABSENT—Messrs. Barnum, Chaffee, Cockrell, Harris, Johnston, Rollins, Saulsbury, Wadleigh, Whyte—9.

So the bill was passed.

In the House, on March 1st, the following veto message from the President was received:

To the House of Representatives:

After a very careful consideration of House bill No. 2423, entitled "An act to restrict the immigration of Chinese to the United States," I herewith return it to the House of Representatives, in which it originated, with my objections to its passage.

The bill, as it was sent to the Senate from the House of Representatives, was confined in its provisions to the object named in its title, which is that of "An act to restrict the immigration of Chinese to the United States." The only means adopted to secure the proposed object was the limitation on the number of Chinese passengers which might be brought to this country by any one vessel to fifteen; and, as this number was not fixed in any proportion to the size or tonnage of the vessel or by any consideration of the safety or accommodation of these passengers, the simple purpose and effect of the enactment were to repress this immigration to an extent falling but little short of its absolute exclusion.

The bill, as amended in the Senate and now presented to me, includes an independent and additional provision which aims at, and in terms requires, the abrogation by this Government of Articles V. and VI. of the treaty with China, commonly called the Burlingame treaty, through the action of the Executive enjoined by this provision of the act.

The Burlingame treaty, of which the ratifications were exchanged at Peking, November 23, 1869, recites as the occasion and motive of its negotiation by the two governments that "since the conclusion of the treaty between the United States of America and the Ta Tsing Empire (China) of the 18th of June, 1858, circumstances have arisen showing the necessity of additional articles thereto," and proceeds to an agreement as to said additional articles. These negotiations, therefore, ending by the signature of the additional articles July 28, 1868, had for their object the completion of our treaty rights and obligations toward the Government of China by the incorporation of these new articles as, thenceforth, parts of the principal treaty to which they are made supplemental. Upon the settled rules of interpretation applicable to such supplemental negotiations the text of the principal treaty and of these "additional articles thereto" constitute one treaty, from the conclusion of the new negotiations, in all parts of equal and concurrent force and obligation between the two governments, and to all intents and purposes as if embraced in one instrument.

The principal treaty, of which the ratifications were exchanged August 16, 1859, recites that "the United States of America and the Ta Tsing Empire, desiring to maintain firm, lasting, and sincere friendship, have resolved to renew, in a manner clear and positive, by means of a treaty or general convention of peace, amity, and commerce, the rules of which shall in future be mutually observed in the intercourse of their respective countries," and proceeds, in its thirty articles, to lay out a careful and comprehensive system for the commercial relations of our people with China. The main substance of all the provisions of this treaty is to define and secure the rights of our people in respect of access to, residence and protection in, and trade with China. The actual provisions in our favor, in these respects, were framed to be, and have been found to be, adequate and appropriate to the interests of our commerce, and by the concluding article we receive the important guarantee, "that should at any time the Ta Tsing Empire grant to any nation, or the merchants or citizens of any nation, any right, privilege, or favor connected either with navigation, commerce, political or other intercourse, which is not conferred by this treaty, such right, privilege, and favor shall at once freely inure to the benefit of the United States, its public officers, merchants, and citizens." Against this body of stipulations in our favor, and this permanent engagement of equality in respect of all future concessions to foreign nations, the general promise of permanent peace and good offices on our part seems to be the only equivalent. For this the first article undertakes as follows: "There shall be, as there have always been, peace and friendship between the United States of America and the Ta Tsing Empire, and between their people respectively. They shall not insult or oppress each other for any trifling cause, so as to produce an estrangement between them; and, if any other nation should act unjustly or oppressively, the United States will exert their good offices, on being informed of the case, to bring about an amicable arrangement of the question, thus showing their friendly feelings."

At the date of the negotiation of this treaty our Pacific possessions had attracted a considerable Chinese emigration, and the advantages and the inconveniences felt or feared therefrom had become more or less manifest, but they dictated no stipulations on the subject to be incorporated in the treaty. The year 1868 was marked by the striking event of a spontaneous embassy from the Chinese Empire, headed by an American citizen, Anson Burlingame, who had relinquished his diplomatic representation of his own country in China to assume that of the Chinese Empire to the United States and the European nations. By this time the facts of the Chinese immigration and its nature and influences, present and prospective, had become more noticeable and were more observed by the population immediately affected and by this Government. The principal feature of the Burlingame treaty was its attention to and its treatment of the Chinese immigration and the Chinese as forming, or as they should form, a part of our population. Up to this time our uncovenanted hospitality to immigration, our fearless liberality of citizenship, our equal and comprehensive justice to all inhabitants, whether they abjured their foreign nationality or not, our civil freedom and our religious toleration, had made all comers welcome, and under these protections the Chinese in considerable numbers had made their lodgment upon our soil.

The Burlingame treaty undertakes to deal with this situation, and its fifth and sixth articles embrace its most important provisions in this regard and the main stipulations in which the Chinese Government has secured an obligatory protection of its subjects within our territory. They read as follows:

"ART. V. The United States of America and the Emperor of China cordially recognize the inherent and inalienable right of man to change his home and allegiance, and also the mutual advantage of the free migration and emigration of their citizens and subjects respectively from the one country to the other for the purpose of curiosity, of trade, or as permanent residents. The high contracting parties, therefore, join in reprobating any other than an entirely voluntary emigration for these purposes. They consequently agree to pass laws making it a penal offense for a citizen of the United States or Chinese subjects to take Chinese subjects either to the United States or to any other foreign country, or for a Chinese subject or citizen of the United States to take citizens of the United States or to China or to any other foreign country, without their free and voluntary consent, respectively.

"ART. VI. Citizens of the United States visiting or residing in China shall enjoy the same privileges, immunities, or exemptions in respect to travel or residence as may there be enjoyed by the citizens or subjects of the most favored nation; and, reciprocally, Chinese subjects visiting or residing in the United States shall enjoy the same privileges, immunities, and exemptions in respect to travel or residence as may there be enjoyed by the citizens or subjects of the most favored nation. But nothing herein contained shall be held to confer naturalization upon citizens of the United States in China, nor upon the subjects of China in the United States."

An examination of these two articles in the light of the experience then influential in suggesting their "necessity" will show that the fifth article was framed in hostility to what seemed the principal mischief to be guarded against, to wit, the introduction of Chinese laborers by methods which should have the character of a forced and servile importation, and not of a voluntary emigration of freemen seeking our shores upon motives and in a manner consonant with the system of our institutions and approved by the experience of the nation. Unquestionably the adhesion of the Government of China to these liberal principles of freedom in emigration, with which we were so familiar and with which we were so well satisfied, was a great advance toward opening that empire to our civilization and religion, and gave promise in the future of greater and greater practical results in the diffusion throughout that great population of our arts and industries, our manufactures, our material improvements, and the sentiments of government and religion which seem to us so important to the welfare of mankind. The first clause of this article secures this acceptance by China of the American doctrines of free migration to and fro among the peoples and races of the earth.

The second clause, however, in its reprobation of "any other than entirely voluntary emigration" by both the high contracting parties, and in the reciprocal obligations whereby we secured the solemn and unqualified engagement on the part of the Government of China "to pass laws making it a penal offense for a citizen of the United States or Chinese subjects to take Chinese subjects either to the United States or to any other foreign country without their free and voluntary consent," constitutes the great force and value of this article. Its importance both in principle and in its practical service toward our protection against servile importation in the guise of immigration can not be over-estimated. It commits the Chinese Government to active and efficient measures to suppress this iniquitous system where those measures are most necessary and can be most effectual. It gives to this Government the footing of a treaty right to such measures, and the means and opportunity of insisting upon their adoption and of complaint and resentment at their neglect. The fifth article, therefore, if it fall short of what the pressure of the later experience of our Pacific States may urge upon the attention of this Government as essential to the public welfare, seems to be in the right direction and to contain important advantages which once relinquished can not be easily recovered.

The second topic which interested the two governments under the actual condition of things which prompted the Burlingame treaty was adequate protection, under the solemn and definite guarantees of a treaty, of the Chinese already in this country and those who should seek our shores. This was the object and forms the subject of the sixth article, by whose reciprocal engagement the citizens and subjects of the two governments, respectively, visiting or re-

siding in the country of the other, are secured the same privileges, immunities, or exemptions there enjoyed by the citizens or subjects of the most favored nations. The treaty of 1858, to which these articles are made supplemental, provides for a great amount of privilege and protection, both of person and property, to American citizens in China, but it is upon this sixth article that the main body of the treaty rights and securities of the Chinese already in this country depends. Its abrogation, were the rest of the treaty left in force, would leave them to such treatment as we should voluntarily accord them by our laws and customs. Any treaty obligation would be wanting to restrain our liberty of action toward them, or to measure or sustain the right of the Chinese Government to complaint or redress in their behalf.

The lapse of ten years since the negotiation of the Burlingame treaty has exhibited to the notice of the Chinese Government, as well as to our own people, the working of this experiment of immigration in great numbers of Chinese laborers to this country, and their maintenance here of all the traits of race, religion, manners and customs, habitations, mode of life, and segregation here, and the keeping up of the ties of their original home, which stamp them as strangers and sojourners, and not as incorporated elements of our national life and growth. This experience may naturally suggest the reconsideration of the subject, as dealt with by the Burlingame treaty, and may properly become the occasion of more direct and circumspect recognition, in renewed negotiations, of the difficulties surrounding this political and social problem. It may well be that to the apprehension of the Chinese Government no less than our own the simple provisions of the Burlingame treaty may need to be replaced by more careful methods, securing the Chinese and ourselves against a larger and more rapid infusion of this foreign race than our system of industry and society can take up and assimilate with ease and safety. This ancient Government, ruling a polite and sensitive people, distinguished by a high sense of national pride, may properly desire an adjustment of their relations with us, which would in all things confirm, and in no degree endanger, the permanent peace and amity and the growing commerce and prosperity which it has been the object and the effect of our existing treaties to cherish and perpetuate.

I regard the very grave discontents of the people of the Pacific States with the present working of the Chinese immigration, and their still graver apprehensions therefrom in the future, as deserving the most serious attention of the people of the whole country and a solicitous interest on the part of Congress and the Executive. If this were not my own judgment, the passage of this bill by both Houses of Congress would impress upon me the seriousness of the situation, when a majority of the representatives of the people of the whole country had thought it to justify so serious a measure of relief.

The authority of Congress to terminate a treaty with a foreign power, by expressing the will of the nation no longer to adhere to it, is as free from controversy under our Constitution as is the further proposition that the power of making new treaties or modifying existing treaties is not lodged by the Constitution in Congress, but in the President, by and with the advice and consent of the Senate, as shown by the concurrence of two thirds of that body. A denunciation of a treaty by any government is, confessedly, justifiable only upon some reason both of the highest justice and of the highest necessity. The action of Congress in the matter of the French treaties in 1798, if it be regarded as an abrogation by this nation of a subsisting treaty, strongly illustrates the character and degree of justification which was then thought suitable to such a proceeding. The preamble of the act recites that "the treaties concluded between the United States and France have been repeatedly violated on the part of the French Government, and the just claims of the United States for reparation of the injuries so committed have been refused, and their attempts to negotiate an amicable adjustment of all complaints between the two nations have been repelled with indignity," and that "under authority of the French Government there is yet pursued against the United States a system of predatory violence, infracting the said treaties, and hostile to the rights of a free and independent nation."

The enactment, as a logical consequence of these recited facts, declares "that the United States are of right freed and exonerated from the stipulations of the treaties and of the consular convention heretofore concluded between the United States and France, and that the same shall not henceforth be regarded as legally obligatory on the Government or citizens of the United States."

The history of the Government shows no other instance of an abrogation of a treaty by Congress. Instances have sometimes occurred where the ordinary legislation of Congress has, by its conflict with some treaty obligation of the Government toward a foreign power, taken effect as an infraction of the treaty, and been judicially declared to be operative to that result. But neither such legislation nor such judicial sanction of the same has been regarded as an abrogation, even for the moment, of the treaty. On the contrary, the treaty in such case still subsists between the governments, and the casual infraction is repaired by appropriate satisfaction in maintenance of the treaty.

The bill before me does not enjoin upon the President the abrogation of the entire Burlingame treaty, much less of the principal treaty of which it is made the supplement. As the power of modifying an existing treaty, whether by adding or striking out provisions, is a part of the treaty-making power under the Constitution, its exercise is not competent for Congress, nor would the assent of China to this partial abrogation of the treaty make the action of Congress, in thus procuring an amendment of a treaty, a competent exercise of authority under the Constitution. The importance, however, of this special consideration seems superseded by the principle that a denunciation of a part of a treaty, not made by the terms of the treaty itself separable from the rest, is a denunciation of the whole treaty. As the other high contracting party has entered into no treaty obligations except such as include the part denounced, the denunciation by one party of the part necessarily liberates the other party from the whole treaty.

I am convinced that, whatever urgency might in any quarter or by any interest be supposed to require an instant suppression of further immigration from China, no reasons can require the immediate withdrawal of our treaty protection of the Chinese already in this country, and no circumstances can tolerate an exposure of our citizens in China, merchants or missionaries, to the consequences of so sudden an abrogation of their treaty protections. Fortunately, however, the actual recession in the flow of the emigration from China to the Pacific coast, shown by trustworthy statistics, relieves us from any apprehension that the treatment of the subject in the proper course of diplomatic negotiations will introduce any new features of discontent or disturbance among the communities directly affected. Were such delay fraught with more inconveniences than have ever been suggested by the interests most earnest in promoting this legislation, I can not but regard the summary disturbance of our existing treaties with China as greatly more inconvenient to much wider and more permanent interests of the country.

I have no occasion to insist upon the more general considerations of interest and duty which sacredly guard the faith of the nation in whatever form of obligation it may have been given. These sentiments animate the deliberations of Congress and pervade the minds of our whole people. Our history gives little occasion for any reproach in this regard, and in asking the renewed attention of Congress to this bill I am persuaded that their action will maintain the public duty and the public honor.

R. B. HAYES.

EXECUTIVE MANSION, *March* 1, 1879.

The Speaker: "The question is, Will the House on reconsideration pass this bill, notwithstanding the objections of the President?"

The question was taken, and resulted as follows:

YEAS—Atkins, Banning, Bayne, Beebe, Bell, Blackburn, Boone, Brentano, Bridges, Butler, Cabell, John W. Caldwell, Carlisle, Chalmers, Clarke of Kentucky, Clark of Missouri, Cobb, Cole, Collins, Cook, Covert, Samuel S. Cox, Cravens, Crittenden, Culberson, Horace Davis, Joseph J. Davis, Deering, Dibrell, Dickey, Durham, Eden, Eickhoff, Elam, Errett, I. Newton Evans, John H. Evins, Ewing, Ebenezer B. Finley, Jesse J. Finley, Forney, Fort, Foster, Garth, Gause, Giddings, Glover, Goode, Günter, Hale, Hamilton, Harmer, Hartzell, Hayes, Hazelton, Henkle, Henry, Herbert, House, Hubbell, Frank Jones, James T. Jones, Jorgensen, Kenna, Kimmel, Knott, Ligon, Luttrell, Maish, Majors, Manning, Marsh, Martin, Mayham, McKenzie, McMahon, Mills, Money, Muldrow, Muller, Neal, Page, T. M. Patterson, Rea, Reagan, Reilly, Americus V. Rice, Robertson, Ross, Sayler, Scales, Shallenberger, Shelley, Singleton, Slemons, Southard, Sparks, Steele, Stenger, R. W. Townshend, Turner, Turney, Walker, Whithorne, Wigginton, Jere N. Williams, Richard Williams, Albert S. Willis, Wright, Yeates—110.

NAYS—Aldrich, Bacon, Bagley, William H. Baker, Ballou, Banks, Blair, Bliss, Boyd, Brewer, Briggs, Browne, Bundy, Burchard, Burdick, Camp, Candler, Cannon, Caswell, Rush Clark, Conger, Crapo, Cummings, Cutler, Danford, Denison, Dunnell, Dwight, Eames, James L. Evans, Frye, Gardner, Garfield, Hardenbergh, Benjamin W. Harris, Henry R. Harris, John T. Harris, Henderson, Abram S. Hewitt, Hunter, Humphrey, Hungerford, Ittner, James, John S. Jones, Keifer, Kelley, Ketcham, Killinger, Landers, Lapham, Lathrop, Lindsey, McCook, Mitchell, Monroe, Morse, Norcross, Oliver, Overton, G. W. Patterson, Peddie, Phelps, Phillips, Price, Pridemore, Pugh, Rainey, Randolph, William W. Rice, G. D. Robinson, M. S. Robinson, Sampson, Sexton, Sinnickson, Smalls, A. Herr Smith, Starin, Stewart, John W. Stone, Joseph C. Stone, Strait, Thompson, Amos Townsend, M. I. Townsend, Waddell, Wait, Ward, Warner, Watson, Harry White, Michael D. White, Andrew Williams, C. G. Williams, James Williams, Benjamin A. Willis—96.

NOT VOTING—Acklen, Aiken, Bailey, John H. Baker, Beale, Benedict, Bicknell, Bland, Blount, Botick, Bragg, Bright, Brogden, Buckner, Cain, W. P. Caldwell, Calkins, Campbell, Chittenden, Claflin, Alvah A. Clark, Clymer, Jacob D. Cox, Davidson, Dean, Ellis, Ellsworth, Felton, Fleming, Franklin, Freeman, Fuller, Gibson, Hanna, Harrison, Hart, Haskell, Hatcher, Hendee, G. W. Hewitt, Hiscock, Hooker, Hunton, Joyce, Keightley, Knapp, Lockwood, Loring, Lynde, Mackey, McGowan, McKinley, Metcalfe, Morgan, Morrison, O'Neill, Pollard, Potter, Pound, Powers, Reed, Riddle, Robbins, Roberts, Ryan, Sapp, William E. Smith, Springer, Stephens, Swann, Thornburgh, Throckmorton, Tipton, Tucker, Vance, Van Vorhes, Veeder, Walsh, Willits, Wilson, Wood, Wren, Casey Young, John S. Young—84.

So the House refused to pass the bill, notwithstanding the objections of the President.

In the House, on February 2d, the bill making appropriations for the support of the army for the fiscal year ending June 30, 1880, was considered.

Mr. Hewitt of New York said: "When I reported the army appropriation bill last year, I undertook to show the House (and I think I succeeded in showing) that the army could be reorganized so as not to impair its efficiency and still save annually about $4,000,000. According to the plan which I then submitted, about half that sum was saved by a reduction in the number of officers, for it is notorious that the army is overloaded with officers; it is top-heavy. The other half was saved by reducing the number of men from 25,000 to 20,500, and by a reorganization of the regiments in such a manner as I believed would make this reduced number of men quite as effective as the number now in the army—25,000. That proposition was adopted in the House, but was rejected in the Senate. The conference committee that had to pass upon this question was placed in one of the most embarrassing positions which could possibly occur in the legislation of the country. The rule of the House is that any general legislation may be incorporated in an appropriation bill, provided it effects a retrenchment of expenditures. The rule of the Senate is that no general legislation can be attached to appropriation bills. As a matter of course, the rule of the Senate could not by any possibility restrict or infringe upon the constitutional right of this House to send to that body a bill in any shape or form it may choose; but, on the other hand, it is quite as impossible for this House to constrain the action of the Senate. If that body thought the general legislation upon an appropriation bill to be inadmissible, we have then presented this alternative—the failure of the bill or the surrender on the part of this House of its claim to legislate upon appropriation bills.

"My own judgment and conviction, the fruit of very considerable study before I had the honor to be a member of this House, and of very much observation since I have been here, lead me to the conclusion that as a rule general legislation upon appropriation bills ought to be avoided. But, Mr. Chairman, the question presents itself whether at any time and under any circumstances this House can be justified in insisting upon legislation in an appropriation bill even to the extent of allowing the bill to fail. That question is answered by a reference to the history of the birth and growth of British liberty. Redress of grievances prior to the passage of appropriation bills, prior to grants of supplies, has been the only instrument by which the British Commons have constructed and maintained the edifice of individual liberty. When the question of personal liberty—the right of the subject as it is called in England, the right of the citizen as we call it—comes in question, then by every lesson of tradition, by every conclusion of statesmanship, this House is not only justified in insisting upon a redress of grievances before agreeing to a supply bill, but to do anything else would be to abdicate its powers and to be treacherous to the memory of that long line of heroes who went before us in building up the fabric of human freedom which we inherited from our British fore-

fathers, and which it is our duty to conserve and protect with the same fidelity as the English people to this hour display through their representatives in the halls of Parliament.

"Now, Mr. Chairman, such an occasion arose in the Forty-fourth Congress. There were two conflicts in that Congress, one of which determined the result of the Presidential election. This House agreed to a method of settlement of the gravest of all political questions which had ever arisen in this country, and it was loyal to its engagements. The second question arose on the army appropriation bill, and it arose in this wise: It was the conviction of a large majority of the members of this House that the result of the Presidential election was not in accordance with the choice of the people, but was governed, influenced, and controlled by the use of the army in the States of Louisiana and South Carolina. There was then presented to the majority of this House one of those crucial tests which try the patriotism and statesmanship of Representatives. True to the lessons of the past, they attached to the army appropriation bill a provision in the exercise of the unquestionable right of Congress directing where, when, and how the army should be used in the States of South Carolina and Louisiana; that the army should not be used to maintain certain State governments which had been created and only kept in existence by the exercise of the military power under the orders of the President. I mean by his 'military power' his control over the military forces of the country, which he exercised under certain statutes passed at the close of the war. The Senate refused to assent to that provision.

"Three several conference committees, composed of different members, met and conferred upon the matter in difference. They failed to come to an agreement, and the result was, the Forty-fourth Congress adjourned without passing any bill for the support of the army. For one, I approved the steps taken by this House. I felt that to have done less would have been a base surrender of the right of a free people to control the army and determine to what use it should be put. I repelled then, and I repel now, the idea that the President of the United States has any other control as Commander-in-Chief of the Army except in accordance with the statutes which Congress may adopt. He is the organ through which the order of the people, expressed by Congress, is to be given to the army; and to surrender the power of regulating and controlling the use of the army would be to be to convert this Government into a centralized despotism.

"Moreover, I was glad the bill failed. It would have been a misfortune to this country if common ground had been found on that occasion by which this question should have been passed by for the moment and put out of sight. The loss of the bill aroused the atten-

tion of the people of this country to the old
story of British liberty, forgotten amid the din
of arms and the conflict of war. It revived to
a youthful generation who knew not the history of those men who from the time of James
I. to that of William III. consecrated their
lives and their fortunes to the cause of human
freedom, and with stern unbending energy
never yielded to the frowns, or the caprices,
or the approaches of power until they had
surrounded the right of the subject with a
bulwark which has never been successfully
attacked in England, and which could never
have been attacked successfully in this country
but for the fact of the civil war. The failure
of that bill brought us back to the old landmark, raised the old question, and brought the
public judgment to a conclusion on that subject which can never again be shattered.

"An extra session was made necessary by
the failure of the army bill. For one, I came
to this House, to the Forty-fifth Congress,
with a determination not to allow any question, public or private, to interfere with the
restoration and the recognition of the right of
Congress to control the army. To me it was
the question of questions. I was placed, to
my own surprise, in charge of the army bill.
The question at once presented itself, Shall we
renew the issue upon this bill which failed, or
shall we reserve it to the bill to come for the
next fiscal year? It seemed to me that to
raise the question upon the bill to take the
place of the one which failed would be a mistake. I did not want to see the Democratic
party arrayed, either by implication or direct
action, against the Administration which had
come into power over their heads and against
their wishes. I felt, and was the first to say,
that the Administration had a title which
could not be successfully attacked; and it
seemed to me it would be a mistake to reopen
the issue as it must necessarily have been reopened on that bill. I thought it was a mistake even to attempt any reorganization or
reduction, and the bill was brought into this
House without any reduction. It was brought
into this House without the reduction of a
man, without an attempt to cut off an officer,
without any provision looking to the assertion
of the right of the people to control the army.
This omission was done purposely, and the bill
passed; and then disappeared, I trust for ever,
the wreck which surrounded the late Presidential campaign.

"When the new bill came along, the bill
under which the army is being maintained for
the present year, then it seemed to me the
question thus passed over ought to be raised
anew. And here I want to make my acknowledgments to the distinguished gentleman from
Kentucky [Mr. Knott], the Chairman of the
Committee on the Judiciary, to whom I applied for help on that occasion, and who, with
the skill of a Somers, drew the clause which is
now known as the *posse comitatus* clause. I

did not think it wise to insert that clause in
the bill as reported by the committee. I preferred that the committee should come in
under the rules of the House with provisions
which should reorganize and reduce the expense of maintaining the army. I preferred
that the fight should be made upon the question of economy, and you, Mr. Chairman [Mr.
Springer in the chair], and other gentlemen
here, will bear witness that whatever power I
had I exerted to the utmost to secure the economy which that bill would have produced; and
it passed the House.

"But I say now that I regarded the question of money involved in that bill, and the
question of reorganization which it presented,
as of utter insignificance compared with the
provision which I had arranged with my
friend from Kentucky [Mr. Knott] to offer in
this House. It was offered; it was ruled in
order; it was passed; and it went to the
Senate, where it and the entire reorganization
scheme were rejected. Then came the conference committee, and an anxious conference
it was. I had a perfect understanding with
my colleague on that committee—I mean my
Democratic colleague—that while we would
secure as much economy and reduction of expenditures as might be possible, yet we would
surrender it all, every jot and tittle of the saving, if we could preserve the *posse comitatus*
clause; and we also had a perfect understanding that, no matter what might be offered in
the way of reduction and economy, it would
be no temptation for us to give up that provision upon which, as he and I believed, the
future liberties of this country depended. I
trust my colleague will pardon me if I say that
this country and this House know not the debt
of gratitude which they owe to him. During
the hours, long and anxious, during which
that provision was under discussion, he exhibited a patience, an acuteness, a breadth of
comprehension, I was almost going to say an
adroitness, which can not be too highly commended; and, if to any man we owe more
than to another the securing of that great
triumph, it is to my friend and colleague from
Illinois [Mr. Sparks].

"But, Mr. Chairman, we secured more than
the *posse comitatus* clause: we secured a clause
providing for the reorganization of the army;
that is to say, creating a commission whose
business it was made to examine into the
whole question and make report by bill or
otherwise to this House; and pending such
report and action thereon by the House, all
appointments and promotions were suspended.

"That provision will secure a reorganization
of the army, whether in this Congress or in
the next I know not, and I frankly say I care
but little.

"But, Mr. Chairman, our work is not done.
The *posse comitatus* clause is objected to by the
Secretary of War in his report. But in his
report he has failed to grasp the magnitude of

this question when he even suggests the idea of a repeal of the *posse comitatus* clause. Repeal, never! Now, sir, I say repeal, never! Definition, yes. The provision may be too broad. It may impede the action, the proper action of the Government. There may be cases wherein the military power might be employed properly and usefully in the execution of civil process. It is not for me who am no lawyer to say what those cases are, but I can understand that on the frontier and in the Territories of the United States there may be occasions when in the absence of police it may be necessary to invoke the aid of the army, and I do not know that even that is prohibited by the clause; but if there be any prohibition which interferes with the security of life, liberty, and property, then let us define and correct it, and I trust it will be the work of the next Congress to define when and where and in what places the military power of the country may be invoked. Now, this work which we have undertaken is not yet completed. I ask the Clerk to read section 2002 of the Revised Statutes."

The Clerk read as follows:

No military or naval officer, or other person engaged in the civil, military, or naval service of the United States, shall order, bring, keep, or have under his authority or control, any troops or armed men at the place where any general or special election is held in any State, unless it be necessary to repel the armed enemies of the United States or to keep the peace at the polls.

Mr. Hewitt: "'Or to keep the peace at the polls.' This statute was enacted in 1865, after the close of the war. It was enacted, as a protection of the citizen in his right of voting against military interference, that 'no military or naval officer or other person engaged in the civil, military, or naval service of the United States, shall order, bring, keep, or have under his authority or control, any troops or armed men at the place where any general or special election is held.' The object was to prohibit the presence of troops at the polls; and then, as if in irony which is almost sublime, the words follow, 'except it may be necessary to repel the armed enemies of the United States or to keep the peace at the polls.' I do not know who wrote that statute, but under favorable conditions he would have developed into a satirist of the highest order. 'To keep peace at the polls!' How easy is it to have a little disturbance at the polls. It can be got up to order, and generally without order, and then the military officer may march up his troops to preserve the peace; but where meanwhile is the voice of the people? *Inter arma silent leges.* On the day of election the people are sovereign. That is the day when the soldier should not be seen. Moreover, it forms no part of the duty of the General Government to 'keep the peace at the polls.' That is the duty of the States; that is a part of the sovereign power which they kept to themselves. Prior to 1865 no one ever suggested that the

Federal Government could enter within the confines of a State and 'keep peace at the polls.' In saying this I do not mean to reflect upon my Republican friends. The close of the war, when this statute was passed, was a martial era. Men still breathed a military atmosphere; passion still reigned supreme—passion upon both sides. The judgment of men was paralyzed. They were in no condition to frame just and wise legislation. But how it happens that this clause has thus far been allowed to remain upon the statute-book passes my comprehension, and I appeal to gentlemen upon the other side of the House with the same confidence that I do to those upon this side, to help us to expunge it from the statute-book as a blot on the charter of American freedom.

"If the gentlemen want to know how monarchical governments protect the liberties of their subjects, let them listen to the wise and solemn words of the British statute. This statute which I will have read was enacted in the reign of Queen Victoria. It was the re-enactment of a statute passed during the reign of George II."

The Clerk read as follows:

Sec. 2. *And be it enacted*, That on every day appointed for the nomination or for the election or for taking the poll for the election of a member or members to serve in the Commons House of Parliament no soldier within two miles of any city, borough, town, or place where such nomination or election shall be declared or poll taken shall be allowed to go out of the barrack or quarters in which he is stationed, unless for the purpose of mounting or relieving guard, or for giving his vote at such election; and that every soldier allowed to go out for any such purpose within the limits aforesaid shall return to his barrack or quarters with all convenient speed as soon as his guard shall have been relieved or vote tendered.

Sec. 3. *And be it enacted*, That when and so often as any election of any member or members to serve in the Commons House of Parliament shall be appointed to be made, the clerk of the Crown in chancery or other officer making out any new writ for such elections shall, with all convenient speed, after making out the same writ, give notice thereof to the Secretary at War, or, in case there shall be no Secretary at War, to the person officiating in his stead, who shall, at some convenient time before the day appointed for such election, give notice thereof in writing to the general officer commanding in each district of Great Britain, who shall thereupon give the necessary orders for enforcing the execution of this act in all places under his command.

Mr. Hewitt: "It will there be seen that whenever an election for members of Parliament takes place the soldier must disappear from the scene. The people are sovereign on that day; and if a riot should break out upon that day the military force could not be used for its suppression. During the hours of election the soldier must be within his barracks. That there may be no mistake about this, the Secretary of State is charged with the duty of making known through the War Office that an election is to take place, in order that the symbol of force may retire and the majesty of the people may reign supreme, at least for one day, when the right of suffrage is exercised in the island of Great Britain.

"Let me here recall the noble preamble of the mutiny act under which the standing army is maintained in Great Britain:

"Whereas the raising or keeping a standing army within the United Kingdom of Great Britain and Ireland in time of peace, unless it be with the consent of Parliament, is against law;

"And whereas no man can be forejudged of life or limb, or subjected in time of peace to any kind of punishment within this realm by martial law, or in any other manner than by judgment of his peers, and according to the known and established laws of this realm.

"Oh, what a proclamation of the rights of the subject is that! No king, no potentate, no power but the law of the land can coerce the subject in time of peace.

"In the forty-first section of that bill is another provision, which until it came under my eye the other day had escaped notice:

"No person who shall be commissioned and in full pay as an officer shall be capable of being nominated or elected to be sheriff of any county, borough, or other p ace, or to be mayor, portreeve, alderman, or to hold any office in any municipal corporation in any city, borough, or place in Great Britain or Ireland.

"So jealous are they of the military power that they will not allow a military officer to hold a civil commission. They are not in England willing to have the power of the army compounded even for a day with the machinery by which civil process is enforced. Yet we, in this country, have solemnly enacted that on an election day, 'if it is necessary to keep the peace,' the army of the United States may be marched to the polls. Such a provision is at war with every principle for which our ancestors contended, and which is embodied in the framework of our Government. Every hour that we allow it to remain on the statute-book is treason to the great men who achieved liberty for us, who founded this Government of ours after fighting for the right of representation, who imbedded this right into the Constitution, who jealously guarded it from the foundation of the Government until 1860, and whose spirits, if they could speak to us in this Hall, would entreat us to remember the sacrifices by which this liberty was secured, and not allow it to be imperiled by the insidious use of the military power.

"Now, I count upon the cordial support of both sides of this House in the attempt to amend the statute which I have just read, by striking out the words 'or to keep the peace at the polls.' At the proper time I shall offer an amendment for that purpose. This provision is not now in the bill as reported to the House, because I think it better that there should be a direct vote of the House taken as to whether it shall come in or not."

Mr. Hale: "The gentleman proposes to move that as an amendment to the army appropriation bill?"

Mr. Hewitt: "Yes, of course, subject to a point of order, which I trust no gentleman will make. I count, indeed, upon the unanimous support of both sides of the House of such an amendment."

Subsequently the bill was amended so as to strike out the words mentioned by Mr. Hewitt in the statute, and it was then passed and sent to the Senate.

In the Senate it was reported back by the appropriate committee with amendments. The bill and report were considered in Committee of the Whole, and the amendment of the House was struck out, as follows:

Sec. 51. That section 2002 of the Revised Statutes be amended so as to read as follows:

"No military or naval officer, or other person engaged in the civil, military, or naval service of the United States, shall order, bring, keep, or have under his authority or control any troops or armed men at the place where any general or special election is held in any State, unless it be necessary to repel the armed enemies of the United States."

And that section 5528 of the Revised Statutes be amended so as to read as follows:

"Every officer of the army or navy, or other person in the civil, military, or naval service of the United States, who orders, brings, keeps, or has under his authority or control any troops or armed men at any place where a general or special election is held in any State, unless such force be necessary to repel armed enemies of the United States, shall be fined not more than $5,000 and suffer imprisonment at hard labor not less than three months nor more than five years."

After the action of the Committee of the Whole was concluded, the bill was reported to the Senate. In the progress of its consideration in the Senate, Mr. Beck of Kentucky asked for a separate vote on striking out section 51 as above. The roll-call having been concluded, the result was announced as follows:

Yeas—Allison, Anthony, Blaine, Booth, Bruce, Burnside, Cameron of Pennsylvania, Cameron of Wisconsin, Chandler, Conkling, Conover, Dawes, Dorsey, Edmunds, Ferry, Hamlin, Hoar, Ingalls, Jones of Nevada, Kellogg, Kirkwood, McMillan, Matthews, Mitchell, Morril, Oglesby, Paddock, Paterson, Plumb, Rollins, Saunders, Teller, Wadleigh, Windom—34.

Nays—Bailey, Barnum, Bayard, Beck, Butler, Cockrell, Coke, Davis of West Virginia, Dennis, Eaton, Garland, Gordon, Grover, Harris, Hereford, Hill, Jones of Florida, Kernan, Lamar, McCreery, McDonald, McPherson, Maxey, Merrimon, Morgan, Ransom, Saulsbury, Shields, Thurman, Voorhees, Wallace, Whyte, Withers—33.

Absent—Chaffee, Davis of Illinois, Eustis, Howe, Johnston, Randolph, Sargent, Sharon, Spencer—9.

The bill was passed by the Senate with other immaterial amendments, and sent to the House for its concurrence in them. The House refused to concur, and asked for a conference. At the conference the House insisted on its position, and the following were the subsequent proceedings on its part:

In the House, on March 3d, Mr. Hewitt of New York said: "Mr. Speaker, the conferees on the part of the Senate and on the part of the House are in no disagreement as to any questions of money involved in this bill. The bill was so carefully matured in the House that but few amendments were offered in the Senate, and the conferees on the part of the Senate were promptly willing to recede from those amendments on hearing the proper explanation: so that I am able to say if other matters could have been arranged this bill could have been reported to the House without the addition of a single dollar, except for a military post which had been recommended subsequently to the passage of the bill by the House.

"There were, however, two points of disagreement in the bill.

"The bill provided for the reorganization of the army in many clauses which were added after full consideration here, as the House will remember. Those clauses were only informally discussed by the conferees. Practically they were passed over in order to see if an agreement could be arrived at on the final provision of the bill in regard to the presence of the troops at the polls. It was very soon apparent that upon this point no agreement was likely to be reached.

"I think I can state without impropriety that there would have been no difficulty in arranging for such a reorganization of the army as would have been satisfactory to this House and to the Senate. Both sides professed their willingness to accommodate themselves to the pressing and admitted necessity which exists for a reorganization of the army. But upon the other point, as to whether it shall continue to be lawful for troops to be present at the polls under any circumstances, the difference seemed to be irreconcilable. The conferees on the part of the Senate declined to assent to the repeal of so much of the two sections of the Revised Statutes as authorize troops to be present at the polls. The issue, therefore, was fairly and clearly defined. On the one side we insisted that the time had come when it should no longer be lawful for a soldier to be at the polling-place on the day of election. Upon the other side it was insisted with equal force that this provision of the statute should be maintained, and the power should remain in the executive to order the troops to the polls on the day of election if in his judgment it was necessary to preserve the peace.

"Mr. Speaker, this presents an issue which involves the very essence of free government. The difference between a despotic government and a free government is this: that in a despotism the military power is superior to the civil; in a free government the civil dominates the military power. And this principle is one which we have fought for; it came to us as an inheritance from our fathers. It was so well recognized that when the Constitution was formed it was not even deemed necessary to insert an article to that effect. But as a protection against military interference provision was made that citizens might bear arms, and that no soldiers should be quartered upon them without their consent. No English-speaking man for two hundred years has questioned the principle that soldiers should never be present at the polls; and the question could never have been raised in this country, the demand could never have been made in our land, but for the unhappy calamity of a civil war. In time of civil war all political rights must be surrendered to the necessities of the conflict. And so it was here. We surrendered the right we had inherited, and which up to that hour we had exercised, that no soldier should show himself at the polls. We surrendered that safeguard as we surrendered many other things that were dear to us. A convertible currency, specie payments, almost every traditional right, disappeared in the presence of the great danger with which we were confronted. Now, for fifteen long years we have been striving to recover that lost ground. We have made gigantic efforts, sacrifices such as the world never saw, to get back to the resumption of specie payments; and yet we have done nothing for the resumption of our political rights, the rights which lie at the very foundation of this government. The time has come to recover this lost ground, and I think it is a reproach to our patriotism that the resumption of specie payments should have preceded the resumption of the rights necessary for the preservation of free government. It is an imputation upon this liberty-loving people and its representatives that they have allowed the time to pass by until now, when the question is finally about to be settled in this bill, and in another bill, the result of the conference on which will soon be reported to this House.

"Now, Mr. Speaker, can we surrender this question? Would we be justified by the people of this country, now that the issue has been raised in conceding the principle in time of profound peace, fifteen years after the close of a civil war, that soldiers may be ordered by the executive power to the polls on the day of election?

"The issue thus made is one that we are ready to accept before the country. Let the people decide whether they are prepared to surrender the sacred right of untrammeled suffrage which this bill seeks to guard, and the provisions which in the legislative bill are designed to maintain unimpaired the trial by jury, which is the great achievement of our race. Unless the blood which courses in our veins has degenerated from the vital fluid which has made the Anglo-Saxon people great and free, I can not doubt the result of the appeal which I now make to the country."

Mr. Foster of Ohio: "The gentleman from New York has been on the conference committee on the army bill alone. Fortunately or unfortunately for me, I have been on the conference committees of both of the bills where these political questions arise, and I can say to the House that so far as my own action is concerned I think I have fully realized the importance of trying to come to an agreement on these bills and save the country the annoyance of an extra session. With this feeling I offered what I thought was a fair basis of compromise, or settlement if you please, which included the question which is now before the House. That basis was something like this: that the Republican side of the House would agree to the proposition that is embraced in this army bill, and would agree further to what is known as the jury clause in the legislative bill; and that the Democrats should recede from what is known as the supervisors and marshals clause in the legislative bill."

Mr. Atkins: "If my friend will allow me, I do not like to interrupt him. He is speaking of the conference on the legislative, executive, and judicial appropriation bill. Does my friend confine his remarks to himself, or does he speak of other members of the conference?"

Mr. Foster: "I am speaking of the proposition that I made."

Mr. Atkins: "For yourself?"

Mr. Foster: "For myself. We were informed in conference by our Democratic friends that they could not yield anything. Now, while I have no right to speak here of what the Senators might have done on this question, yet upon my own responsibility I am willing to say that I believe if this basis of settlement had been agreed to by our Democratic friends an agreement would have been reached.

"For myself, I care but little about this proposition in the army bill. I do not know but that the time has about come when we perhaps ought to agree to it, though I am not quite ready for it yet. The gentleman from New York [Mr. Hewitt] has said a great deal about English-speaking people and the liberty-loving traits of their character. Sir, I think we Republicans are as much in love with liberty as are the English people or as my friend from New York. I have yet to learn from any responsible source that the troops ever prevented any single voter from voting as he pleased. On the contrary, they have assisted hundreds and thousands of poor people to vote, who otherwise could not have voted.

"We Republicans are not quite ready to yield to all these demands. And what is the nature of these demands? Are you going to force us to repeal these laws by provisions on an appropriation bill? I know we have a great deal of discussion about legislation upon appropriation bills. It has been said that Republicans in times past have been in the habit of legislating upon appropriation bills. I agree to that, and for myself I can not see any great harm in legislating upon appropriation bills when both Houses agree to it. But this proposition never was brought into this House as an independent measure. You never sought to have it passed through this House and sent to the Senate as an independent measure. But you come in here with this proposition on an appropriation bill, and you undertake through

the means of an appropriation bill to force the proposition upon the Senate. There, in my judgment, is where the wrong of legislating upon appropriation bills comes in.

"I have been as anxious as my friend from New York or any other gentleman could be to reach a conclusion. I have worked for it steadily. The only propositions that have come from anybody, so far as relate to a basis of settlement, have come from Republicans. But our Democratic friends stood like adamant in refusing to concede one single thing, refusing to dot an *i* or cross a *t;* and that left nothing for us to do but to agree to disagree.

"You gentlemen on the other side will have the next Congress. You can repeal these laws by means of bills passed in the regular form. If the President should see fit to veto them, you can then put them upon appropriation bills and probably force him to take them. There will be no election between now and 1880, except in California, to be affected by these laws; and I want to say to gentlemen on the other side, and I think I speak for my friends on this side, that we are willing to make an exception of California for the purpose of reaching a settlement."

Mr. Garfield: "Mr. Speaker, it is only just that the precise situation of this legislation and the fair relation of all parties to it should be perfectly understood. It has been quite fully stated on both sides, but I desire to enlarge a little upon one or two features of what has been said.

"The gentleman from New York [Mr. Hewitt] has certainly drawn very largely upon what, if I should follow his example, would be my imagination, in his statement that the liberties of this country are now in danger or ever have been in danger from the legislation embraced in the two clauses of the sections of the statutes proposed to be repealed by this legislation. I admit that in a monarchical country like England, especially as England was in the days when their first army law passed, there was danger, great danger, in giving any considerable power to the army. But in a country like ours, where the Legislature controls the purse of the nation, it can freeze the army to death when it chooses. In a country like ours, where the Chief Magistrate is liable to be impeached for any serious violation of law, for any malfeasance or misfeasance on the part of any military officer, where the whole spirit of the government is civil, and the military is completely subordinated, it seems to me that the alarms which my friend from New York raises are wholly imaginary.

"Now, gentlemen ought to bear in mind what these two sections are. They ought to remember in the first place the time when they were passed and the object for which they were passed. It ought to be borne in mind that both the sections sought to be modified in this appropriation bill are restraining sections—sections indeed leveled against the army

—one of them laying heavy penalties upon any soldier, whether enlisted man or officer, who may in any way interfere with the freedom of elections.

"Gentlemen talk as though these sections had been adopted to empower the army to interfere with the freedom of elections. On the contrary, they were in precisely the opposite direction. It should be remembered that these sections were enacted in 1865, when the roar of battle was still in our ears; when our guns were still smoking; when none of the States in rebellion had been reconstructed; when none of them had been restored to their place in the circle of the Union; when all was chaos; when from governor down to the humblest officer in every one of those States there was no one that bore in the new order of things any recognized authority; when even the machinery for the service of ordinary civil process had all to be set up anew; when by the necessity of the case the military occupation of all that part of the country was indispensable even in the view of the most extreme opposers of the Union. It was at the time, when our Government was seeking to restore civil authority in the place of the chaos that the war had left, when it was necessary to have armies all through that portion of the country—it was at such a time that the victorious Government in the interest of liberty put up these muniments and armaments against any aggression of the military upon the right of electors by saying to them, 'You shall obstruct no man in his free right to the suffrage. If you do, imprisonment and fine shall be visited upon the officer or man who may do it.' That is what those laws were for, and that is what they are to-day—laws restrictive of the military power with exception of the single clause which does not prohibit them from keeping the peace at the polls. Is that a wrong, an act of tyranny? Perhaps the law is now as necessary as it was in 1865. I am free to admit for one that these enactments were passed at a period so different from the present that probably we can without serious harm in any direction muster them out, as we mustered out of service the victorious armies when the war was done. For myself, I see no serious practical objection to letting these sections go, though I do not quite see how anybody can say that, while a State may call out its own militia to keep the peace at its own polls (and nobody calls that tyranny, nobody calls that wickedness, injustice, and a menace to civil liberty), so it seems to me that a nation when it has its own elections, which its own Constitution says it may regulate as to the time, place, and manner of holding them, may with great propriety use its own military force to keep the peace at its own national polls. That is all there is in these two sections that any gentleman has complained of. Now, I believe, as a matter of fact, no one will say that any citizen during the thirteen years and more that this law has stood on our statute-book has been denied the full and free exercise of the elective franchise in consequence of the presence of armed soldiers of the United States near the polls. If there has been such a case, I will join with any man of any party in deprecating it, in deploring it, in doing what I can to prevent its recurrence."

Mr. Townshend of Illinois: "The gentleman from New York has uttered a truthful sentiment here, which is creditable to him. He has mentioned the fact that during the late civil war the people of this country did surrender many things, one of which was specie payments. Another surrender of the people of this country was to a large extent their constitutional liberty. He has also announced that we have resumed specie payments, but we have not yet resumed our liberties. I have no more to say upon that point, except to say the time has arrived for a resumption of our liberties. I want now further to call the attention of this House to the spectacle which has been presented to the American people during the past few days.

"Why is it that there is an extra session imminent? It is because gentlemen upon the other side of the House, since last Saturday, have been filibustering and obstructing legislation in order to screen a man holding an exalted position as a representative of the Government abroad from punishment who is charged with high crimes and misdemeanors. There are some other issues before us to which I will refer. Let me call your attention to the fact that an appropriation bill making provision for postal expenses has been in a conference committee and there is a disagreement upon it. Why? Because the Senate, a Republican body, has said to the House, 'Unless you yield to us a scheme for subsidizing the Brazilian steamship line there shall be an extra session.' Another issue is presented before the country upon the army bill, when it is insisted we have reached that period of peace in the country when soldiers should be taken from the polls in order that we may have free elections, a Republican Senate says to us in plain language it will force an extra session before the authority to use troops at the polls shall be repealed. The point, then, that the Senate makes upon us here, as uttered by the gentlemen from Ohio [Mr. Foster and Mr. Garfield] here to-night, is that in reference to the bill providing for the legislative, executive, and judicial expenses of the Government, there shall be no repeal of laws which provide for the appointment of Republican recruiting sergeants at the polls in the shape of deputy marshals and supervisors. I want to state the fact before the House and the country that the Democratic side of this House has not been guilty of resorting to filibustering or any means of obstructing legislation in order to provoke an extra session. If an extra session shall be found necessary, it is because the Republican party is obstructing legislation, and because the Democratic party is standing up here for free elections and against the Brazilian subsidy."

The Speaker: "The question is on the motion of the gentleman from New York that the House further insist upon its disagreement to the Senate amendment to the army appropriation bill."

The motion of Mr. Hewitt of New York was then agreed to.

Mr. Hewitt moved to reconsider the vote just taken; and also moved that the motion to reconsider be laid on the table.

The latter motion was agreed to.

So the bill failed to become a law.

In the House on February 26th the bill making appropriations for the Legislative, Executive, and Judicial departments of the government was considered in Committee of the Whole.

The Chairman: "The question is upon the amendments offered by the gentleman from Ohio [Mr. Southard], which the Clerk will now read."

The Clerk read Mr. Southard's amendments, as follows:

That the several sections of the Revised Statutes of the United States, from and including section 2011 to and including 2031, and all other provisions of law authorizing the appointment of, or the performance of any duty by, any chief or other supervisor of elections, or any special deputy marshal, or other deputy marshal of elections, or the payment of any money to any such supervisor or deputy marshal of elections for any services performed as such, be, and the same are hereby, repealed.

Mr. Hayes of Illinois said: "It is scarcely necessary to remark that I am most decidedly opposed to the amendment offered by the gentleman from Ohio [Mr. Southard], and hope to see it voted down by an overwhelming majority. The reasons upon which I base my opposition are two: first, because I believe it to be bad policy to legislate in regard to general matters in an appropriation bill; and second, because I heartily approve those portions of our law which this amendment proposes to repeal, and am in favor of letting them remain as they now are upon our statute-book. What is this law, let me ask, or rather what are its provisions? The law simply provides that in certain cases the United States court shall appoint persons to act as supervisors of elections, and makes it the duty of United States marshals under certain circumstances to assist these supervisors in the discharge of their duties. The sole object of the law is to prevent fraud at the ballot-box and secure free, fair, and honest elections. This being so, why is it that the gentlemen on the other side are so hostile to it? Are they not in favor of fair and honest elections—of preserving the purity of the ballot-box? It would certainly seem not, if we are to judge from the bitter war they are making against this law. I am free to confess, sir, that I can not see what objec-

tion any honest man can urge against the law as it now stands. I can not see why any one who is anxious to have fair and honest elections in this country should ask for its repeal. The fact is, the war against this law is waged not so much by men who want fair and honest elections, as by mere politicians who hope, by wiping out this law, to advance the interests of the Democratic party, and thus help forward their own ambitious schemes. There is method in what these men are doing, and it will be well for us before we give our votes in favor of this amendment to pause and consider the meaning of the demand for its passage, to pause and consider what peculiar significance attaches to this cry that comes up from a Democratic caucus, asking that this law be repealed. Why, sir, this cry is nothing but a note of alarm, a signal of distress. The Democratic party is in trouble, and this House is called upon to help it out. The future looks dark for that party unless some relief is furnished at once.

"The enforcement of this law by President Hayes has sent terror to Democratic leaders everywhere. As the law goes forth and does its work, they see the immense Democratic majorities in such cities as New York almost entirely wiped out. They see their friends and supporters in South Carolina, Louisiana, Florida, Maryland, and New York arrested, tried, convicted, and sent to the penitentiary. These facts lead them to fear for the future of their party. They know that if this law is suffered to remain upon the statute-book and is enforced, our penitentiaries will soon be filled with Democratic voters. They know, too, that this law, honestly and fearlessly executed, would wipe out the heavy Democratic majorities in many localities, both North and South. They understand fully that while this law is in the interest of honest elections and good government, it is not in the interest of the Democratic party, and hence they have resolved to blot it out.

"Now, sir, I do not blame the Democratic leaders much for being alarmed at the situation. The signs of the times are ominous. This law is cutting down Democratic majorities fearfully. Already hosts of Democratic voters have fallen beneath its unsparing hand. No less than two stalwart Democrats who claim to be elected to the Forty-sixth Congress are already indicted for election frauds, and may be landed in the penitentiary any day. Why, sir, if this thing is allowed to go on much longer, the Democrats may find themselves in a hopeless minority in the next House. But this is only a part of the danger that threatens our Democratic friends. If this law continues in force until 1880, and under its operation we can get a fair and honest election, not only will the Democrats not be able to elect their candidate for President, but many of our Democratic friends on this floor will be retired to the ranks of private life.

"This is the secret of the Democratic hatred of this law. The fact is, the Democratic leaders have determined upon success at the next Presidential election, and as this law stands in their way they have resolved to get rid of it. They propose to repeat in 1880 the frauds and dishonest trickery of their party in 1876, only upon a more extensive scale. They say that in order to carry the State of New York for the democracy the bummers, deadbeats, and plug-uglies of New York City must be allowed to vote half a dozen times apiece instead of only once, as they can do under this law. They say that the white-liners and rifle-club men must be permitted to intimidate Republican voters, drive them from the polls, and vote tissue ballots to their hearts' content, or the Southern States will all go Republican. The repeal of this law will be an act solely in the interest of the Democratic party, and not in the interest of the country. It will simply mean the opening of the flood-gates of iniquity, ballot-box stuffing, intimidation, and fraud in order to make Democratic success certain in 1880. It will only give the Democracy more complete control in those localities where they are in the majority, and thus enable them with impunity to perpetrate such frauds upon the ballot-box as will give them a victory."

Mr. Davis of North Carolina: "The gentleman from Maine [Mr. Powers] said the other day: 'I for one believe that every citizen should have the right to vote, and have that vote honestly counted.' Now, sir, it seems curious to me that gentlemen in the section from which the gentleman from Maine comes, can not discover the fact that in the little State of Rhode Island there are more white men over the age of twenty-one years who are not only not allowed to have their votes honestly counted, but are not allowed to vote at all, than there are negroes disfranchised by intimidation in the States of Louisiana, Florida, and South Carolina combined, even counting all that are alleged to have been intimidated. In the State of Rhode Island free white citizens are excluded unless possessed "of real estate of the value of $134 over and above all incumbrances, . . . or which shall rent for $7 per annum, over and above all rent reserved, or interest of any incumbrance thereon." Yet beam-eyed political saints up there can look over the State of Rhode Island down into the South and find a vast deal to complain of. No man is allowed to vote in the State of Massachusetts unless he can read and write. Apply these tests to the impoverished South, and nine tenths of your Republican brethren would be excluded from the right to vote.

"Now, sir, in regard to Rhode Island, I have only to say that there are free white men who are not allowed to vote. With two Representatives on this floor, she only cast 26,627 votes at the last Presidential election out of a voting population of more than twice that number, and in 1876 there were nearly 6,000 more votes cast in my single district than were cast in the whole State of Rhode Island; that is, less than one half her citizens are allowed to vote, and they may possibly have to resort to another Dorr rebellion to secure their rights as freemen.

"Now, in reply to the gentleman from Ohio. He said the other day: 'Not one man on that side of the House has sought in any way to do anything to purify the ballot-box, but all have favored free fraud in our elections.' Is it possible the gentleman from Ohio meant that? I trust he did not. It is language that can not be reasonably applied to a single gentleman on this side of the House. It is not true, and if applied to any one on this side would be pronounced false and slanderous. Why, sir, this is the old cry of 'Wolf!' 'Stop thief!' this cry of fraud in elections. Why, sir, in 1876 the Democratic majority of all the votes cast was fully a quarter of a million over that cast for the Republican candidate, and counting only the white vote it was nearly or quite one million; and yet the voice of the people was stifled by fraud, by perjuries, by forgeries, by the improper use of the power of Federal officials all over the land, and by the improper use of the army. Having the control of an army of office-holders, with the aid of supervisors and marshals appointed for partisan purposes and paid out of the public funds, by assessments on office-holders, and the improper use of official power, the will of the people was defeated. Sir, this amendment is a protest against fraud and outrages in elections; a protest against the improper use of Federal patronage and Federal power; and it is strange that a charge such as that made by the gentleman from Ohio should come from that side of the House.

"Sir, I may be pardoned for a little feeling when I hear not only my whole party abused, but when I hear statements made in regard to my section and my State which I know to be untrue, and which go all over the land to prejudice and poison the public mind against us. I repeat, the gentleman can not find a man on this side of the House who in any way 'approves of fraud in elections' or in anything else. That, perhaps, belongs rather to the gentleman's own party friends in Louisiana and Florida, all of whom, so far as I know, have been rewarded by his party; known and recognized perjurers have been rewarded by the bestowal of office, I will not say (because I hope it is not true) with the approval of the gentleman from Ohio.

"All this complaint against the Democratic party of the South has its origin in the fact that by the enfranchisement of the colored man, designed to be in the interest of the Republican party, the Democrats have gained power, and our Republican friends have been grievously disappointed. Instead of securing increased power for that party, it has proved, as the late Senator Morton had the good sense to foresee, an element of weakness. Our Republican friends commit a radical mistake when they assume that the colored vote belongs to their party as a matter of right. Their argument, syllogistically put, is this:

"First. The party that gave the colored man the right to vote is entitled to his vote.

"Second. The Republican party gave him the right.

"Therefore, the Republican party is entitled to his vote.

"Colored men are beginning to comprehend this, and to understand that if it is good logic, it may be bad policy; and when they remember how often the men for whom they have voted have cheated and swindled them, it is not strange that they should conclude to change their votes, and regard good policy as better than doubtful logic. They have found by experience—that best of teachers—that the average white radical who came down from the North and professed so much love for them was often a hypocrite, still oftener a swindler, and sometimes a thief. They are beginning to comprehend the situation and to think for themselves and to ask, 'How is it that our good friends who love us so, and who are always whining about our rights and wrongs, especially as election time approaches, how is it that these good friends have never invited us to Maine or Michigan, to Massachusetts or to Minnesota, to Iowa or to Indiana, or to some other northern State where sweet liberty was born and grew for us?' Sir, our Republican friends underrate the colored man if they suppose that he can always be deceived by the cunning arts of the men who first bewildered and then swindled him. It is a mistake to suppose that he will not follow the great law of self-interest which governs other men—especially our Republican friends—and vote in accordance with their interests."

Mr. Hewitt of New York: "Mr. Chairman, the opposition which is expressed against this amendment by the gentlemen on the other side, shows how absolutely impossible it is for them to comprehend the motives which govern the Democracy in their desire and their fixed determination to erase from the statute-books every provision which infringes upon the personal liberty of the citizen. These provisions have all been placed upon the statute-book during and since the close of the late war. For nearly three-quarters of a century the old principles upon which free government had been based were found sufficient for the preservation of the right of suffrage, the most sacred right of the citizen.' Once only in our history was an attempt made to violate the principles upon which George Mason, and Thomas Jefferson, and James Madison, and Alexander Hamilton had firmly planted the structure of free government, and that was when the alien and sedition laws were forced on this country. They were swept from the statute-books in a

burst of popular indignation, which consigned John Adams to private life, and placed Thomas Jefferson, the great expounder of the Democracy, in the Presidential chair. So now the Democracy to-day plant themselves on the old stronghold that there is no safety for civil liberty when power is centralized; that the only security for free institutions lies in the distribution of power among the people, so as to strengthen local self-government. We believe if abuses occur they will be remedied more quickly, more readily, and more effectually than by any central power.

"And when the gentleman from Maine [Mr. Frye] alluded to those corrupt judges who had granted false naturalization papers in 1868, he overlooked the fact that Judges Barnard and McCunn were driven from the bench, not by the Government at Washington, but by the indignant voice of the people of the State of New York. And we say now that these statutes, thus centralizing power in Washington, although they may alleviate temporary difficulty, are sure to produce evils on a scale of infinitely greater magnitude, and to become the parent of abuses which, if tolerated, will imperil, and if permanently tolerated will destroy, the right of suffrage and the inestimable blessings to which it gives birth.

"The gentleman from Maine said it was necessary to repeal these laws in order to carry the State of New York for the Democracy. Does the gentleman not know, did he not himself bear witness to the fact, that the election of 1876 was an honest election in the State of New York; and did not Governor Tilden receive a majority in that State of over thirty thousand? What motive, then, have we to repeal those laws in order that the Democratic party may carry the State of New York? We have carried that State by constantly increasing majorities at every election since their enactment. And we shall do it to the end of time, unless by the abuse of those election laws which we seek to repeal free citizens shall be deterred from exercising the right of suffrage.

"Now, Mr. Davenport has administered this law from the time of its enactment up to the present hour, and found no way honestly to keep Democratic voters from the polls. But in 1876 they taught him a lesson in New Orleans. They issued ten thousand warrants in one day, and upon the strength of that Mr. Davenport, on the night before the election, upon the affidavit of his own clerk, issued warrants which resulted in the arrest of four thousand citizens of the city of New York, and their imprisonment on the day of election in the iron den of the court-house. What occurred on that memorable day has been described with graphic power by General Wingate in his argument before Judge Blatchford against the validity of these arrests, which will be confirmed by my colleague from New York [Mr. Eickhoff], who was present and saw what occurred:

"Such a scene as the room of this court presented on that election day has never before been witnessed in this city or in this country, and it is to be hoped never will again. From early morning until after the polls were closed these rooms were packed and jammed with a mass of prisoners and marshals. Not only were they crowded beyond their capacity, but the halls and corridors were thronged with those who were unable to obtain admission; so that the counsel representing the prisoners and the bondsmen who were to be offered to secure their release had the greatest difficulty and were frequently unsuccessful in obtaining entrance. In addition to all this was this delectable iron 'pen' on the upper floor, in which men were crowded until it resembled the 'black hole of Calcutta,' and where they were kept for hours, hungry, thirsty, and suffering in every way, until their cases could be reached. With scarcely an exception these men had gone to the polls expecting to be absent but a short time. Many of them were thinly clad. Numbers had sick wives or relatives; some were sick themselves. There were carmen who had left their horses standing in the public streets; men whose situations depended upon their speedy return; men who wished to leave the city on certain trains. Every imaginable vexation, inconvenience, injury, and wrong which the mind can conceive existed in their cases, so that it was painful for the counsel who were endeavoring to secure their release to approach sufficiently near the railing to hear their piteous appeals and witness the distress which they had no power to alleviate. And over all this pushing, struggling, complaining crowd, Mr. Commissioner John I. Davenport sat supreme with a sort of oriental magnificence, calmly indifferent to everything but the single fact that no man who was arrested was allowed to vote. And after all this tremendous exhibition of the power of this great Government, after this exhibition of what a United States commissioner and chief supervisor of elections can do if he has a mind to, what was the result? Surely if the offenses which these persons had committed were of so grave a nature as to require these wholesale proceedings, if the morals, the peace, and outraged laws of the community required to be vindicated by the summary arrest of four thousand persons on a single day, it was certainly necessary that the law should be enforced to the end, and that the offenses which were so dangerous as to require this arbitrary action should be punished. But nothing of the kind was done. As these men were brought up before the three commissioners who sat in judgment, they were asked if they had voted. If they had not, they were required to promise that they would not do so. If, to escape the terrors of Ludlow street jail, they surrendered their rights as American citizens and made the promise thus exacted, as the great majority of necessity did, they were released upon their own recognizance. If they did not, they were held to bail. If they had voted, although if not properly naturalized such vote was an additional offense instead of a palliation for the crime charged against them, they were immediately released. After sundown, when the polls were closed and it was too late for any one to vote, the doors appear to have been thrown open and all set at liberty.

"This scene occurred, not in the imperial city of Berlin, where despotism is striving to roll back the tide of time, but in the metropolis of this land of freedom, in the free city of the sovereign State of New York. Fortunately for the cause of liberty, out of these four thousand citizens thus summarily deprived of their freedom and of the sacred right of suffrage, one man alone, so poor that he had no friends to become his bail, and so friendless that he seems not to have known that he might have walked away, was committed to jail, and allowed to lie there until by accident his case was made known in the proper quarter, and proceedings of *habeas corpus* were taken to test the question of the legality of these arrests. The name of that unfortunate citizen was Peter Coleman—a name destined to live in history with that of John Peter Zenger, who, in the colonial days of New York, was so fortunate as to have suffered a similar arrest and to have achieved immortality by vindicating the freedom of the press. Coleman's case was brought before Judge Blatchford, an able and upright Judge of the Federal Court, who never has and never will allow his Republican sympathies to interfere with the stern performance of his duty. The case was elaborately argued, and in a careful opinion he decided that not only was the affidavit whereon the arrest was made insufficient, but that the warrant itself was unlawfully issued. He further decided that the naturalization papers which had been called in question upon the other side had been duly made and issued; and, to quote his own language—

"It therefore appears that Coleman was duly and legally admitted to citizenship, and that the legality of his admission was not invalidated by any act or omission which occurred either prior or subsequently to his admission. As he was legally admitted, it was proper for the Court to give to him the certificate of citizenship which was given to him, and that certificate was not unlawfully issued or made. On this ground he is entitled to his discharge from arrest.

"But there is another ground on which Coleman is entitled to be discharged. Even if there were such a defect in the record of the Superior Court as to make the certificate given to him one that was unlawfully issued or made, he was not guilty of an offense under section 5426, unless when he used the certificate he knew that it was unlawfully issued or made. As it appears that he complied fully with all the conditions imposed on him as prerequisites to his admission, and that the unlawfulness, if any, was in the want of form in the records of the Court, and as he received at the time from the Court a certificate stating that all the statutory requisites had been complied with, and that the Court had ordered that he be admitted to be a citizen, and that he was accordingly admitted by the Court to be a citizen, no court would permit a jury to convict him of using such certificate knowing that it was unlawfully issued. So manifest was this that the moment the facts were brought to the attention of this Court on the hearing on the *habeas corpus*, it announced that Coleman would be discharged immediately on this ground alone. Thereupon the attorney for the United States stated that he did not think the evidence disclosed sufficiently guilty knowledge on the part of Coleman of the defects in the certificate of citizenship, and that he consented that he should go at large. He was immediately released from custody, but no formal decision was made, in order that other questions presented might be argued, considered, and decided.

"An order will be entered discharging Coleman from custody.

"STEWART L. WOODFORD, Dist. Att'y,
"SAMUEL B. CLARKE,
Ass't Dist. Att'y for the United States.
"E. ELLERY ANDERSON,
"GEORGE W. WINGATE,
For Coleman.
"A copy.   JOHN I. DAVENPORT, Clerk.

"Now let me inquire what redress these four thousand citizens thus unlawfully arrested have under the law against Mr. Davenport.

Can they bring suit for damages for false arrest? No; they are met by the conclusive answer that it was an official act done in the performance of a duty required by the statute. Is there any reason why this outrage may not be repeated at the next or any future election? If four thousand men can be arrested in one day upon the affidavit of one man, the entire legal majority of either party might be wiped out in any city of this Union by supervisors bold enough to take the responsibility of such monstrous action.

"My grievance is not that this was done by a Republican official. My objection is that it can be done by any official whatever. I should protest just as earnestly against it if it had been the action of a Democratic supervisor, under a Democratic administration. It simply goes to prove what I have already said, that there is no safety and can be no safety for personal liberty when the fountain of power is not in the people, but resides in a centralized government. The fact that despotism is the inevitable result of centralized power is as old as the story of the human race. The complaints of citizens at a distance from the central power are rarely heard; but where the power to redress grievances resides at home, where men live and move among their fellow-citizens, grievances can not long survive. There is no more striking proof of this fact than the manner in which the Tweed ring, who were the creators of whatever frauds occurred in the years 1868, 1869, and 1870, was utterly broken up and its members consigned to prison and to exile. The very judges who connived at their atrocities were the first to feel the popular indignation, and were driven in disgrace from the bench into obscurity, from which they can never emerge."

Mr. Hazelton of Wisconsin: "Mr. Chairman, there are three propositions, sir, involved in these amendments. The first in order, which provides for the elimination of the restrictions placed upon the jury-box by sections 820 and 821 of the Revised Statues, I support with all my heart. I support it because it opens the jury-box to the intelligence of the South, brings it within that constitutional principle which permits the citizen to be tried by his peers, and places it where it ought to stand in our country, open to every citizen ordinarily eligible to pass upon a question of fact in the courts of the land.

"The next proposition, Mr. Chairman, is one which the American people will repudiate at sight. It is to make the jury-box of our country a political jury-box. It is to select one juror from one political party and the next from another political party, who are to constitute thus made up a jury to try the great questions which shall arise in the administration of justice in the future of our country. It is revolutionary and impracticable. Such a system, sir, will poison the very fountains of justice and undermine and destroy the settled law of ages.

To state the proposition is to condemn it, and I discuss it no further.

"The third proposition strikes down at a blow twenty sections of the statutes, comprising those election laws which constitute to-day the safeguards of the ballot-box and the muniments of liberty. They are all that can protect and keep pure the ballot-box in many States of the Union, and especially in the great city of New York. And I tell the gentleman from New York [Mr. Hewitt] in all fairness that there never has been an instance where any honest voter has been deprived of the exercise of the elective franchise by the enforcement of any one of those laws, and I challenge any man on this floor to show an instance where any man has been deprived of his rights by those great safeguards of our Government."

Mr. Hewitt of New York: "I instance Peter Coleman, by the decision of Judge Blatchford, which I hold in my hand."

Mr. Hazelton: "Now, sir, who asks for this great change; whence comes the demand for these amendments? Do the one million voters of the black race in the South ask for this legislation? Not one of them, sir. Does the demand come from that sentiment that carried the Government through the storm and shock of war and laid its foundations anew in the principles of liberty? No, sir. Where, then, does the voice come from? Louisiana wants it; and her regular political diet has been for the last ten years fraud, intimidation, and blood. Alabama wants it, and upon that declaration of her leading citizens that the exercise of the elective franchise by the black man is a crime against American liberty. South Carolina wants it also; and the gentleman from that State [Mr. Aiken] only the other day boasted on this floor that as a matter of recrimination they were in South Carolina now visiting back upon the Republicans, upon the black men, this whole scheme of the tissue ballot."

Mr. Aiken: "You are sorry the chickens are coming home to roost, are you?"

Mr. Hazelton: "If you tell them a man's right is struck down in South Carolina, they will answer you that the North sent down awhile ago a lot of carpet-baggers. If you say that crimes are committed there against civilization, against humanity, the answer is, 'Why, you sent carpet-baggers down to rule over us.' Now, the gentleman from South Carolina—and no man has a higher respect for that gentleman than I have—says that because, away back, some Republican was elected by tissue ballots, now the thing had come home to roost."

Mr. Whitthorne of Tennessee: "Mr. Chairman, far above party and far above the love I bear the section in which I was born is my attachment to a republican form of government; and whatever else may happen in the future of this country, I trust the inheritance of a free ballot shall be the heritage for all time of the American citizen. Under the Constitution, Article 1, section 4, it is provided that ' That the times, places, and manner of holding elections for Senators and Representatives, shall be prescribed in each State by the Legislature thereof; but the Congress may at any time by law make or alter such regulations, except as to the places of choosing Senators.' Now, it is claimed that under this provision of the Constitution the existing laws in regard to supervisors of election and their aids, deputy marshals, and which are sought to be repealed by the pending amendment, were enacted.

" It is admitted that Congress may rightfully adopt regulations as to the time, place, and manner of the elections of Representatives in Congress, but it is denied that Congress in the exercise of this right to make regulations, either as to time, place, or manner, can determine the question of the sovereignty of the elector or his qualification in this regard. This belongs alone to the States or the people thereof. The people of the States may fix the qualification of the elector as to age, residence, and character, and when so fixed and determined, these electors become and are the supreme sovereignty in and of the Government of the United States. Now, then, any attempt made to impair this sovereignty is an attack upon the fundamental theory upon which our whole popular institutions are based. It is war upon the people and their right of defense and protection. Let me say, Mr. Chairman, that if it be necessary to the preservation of the national life that the existing laws should be enforced, I am in favor of their enforcement. But what is the source of the national life? It is the sovereignty of the people; it is the freedom of the elector.

" The Democratic party of the country believe that the laws sought to be repealed go beyond the rightful authority of Congress to regulate the time, place, and manner of holding the elections for members of Congress; and in the authority given to the supervisors and marshals to arrest and imprison the elector before registering and before voting, as well as in the act of voting, assert a dangerous and unconstitutional exercise of authority upon the part of the Government, and seek to destroy the source of the life of the Government. No more arbitrary, tyrannical, or oppressive power was ever given to any body of men than is lodged in the hands of deputy marshals by section 2022 of the Revised Statutes, which I read:

" Sec. 2022. The marshal and his general deputies, and such special deputies, shall keep the peace, and support and protect the supervisors of election in the discharge of their duties, preserve order at such places of registration and at such polls, prevent fraudulent registration and fraudulent voting thereat, or fraudulent conduct on the part of any officer of election, and immediately, either at the place of registration or polling-place, or elsewhere, and either before or after registering or voting, to arrest and take into custody, with or without process, any person who commits, or attempts or offers to commit, any of the acts or of-

fenses prohibited herein, or who commits any offense against the laws of the United States; but no person shall be arrested without process for any offense not committed in the presence of the marshal or his general or special deputies, or either of them, or of the supervisors of election, or either of them; and for the purposes of arrest or the preservation of the peace, the supervisors of election shall, in the absence of the marshal's deputies, or if required to assist such deputies, have the same duties and powers as deputy marshals; nor shall any person, on the day of such election, be arrested without process for any offense committed on the day of registration.

" It will be seen from this section that an indefinite number of marshals may be appointed. It is a fact that pending the elections of 1876 over eleven thousand were appointed; a body of men in numbers equal to one half of your regular army, and, as I have said, may be multiplied beyond the strength of that army. Remembering that these marshals are paid by the National Government out of the taxes derived from the people, we come to look into the power with which these marshals are vested. They are clothed with the power to decide of their own will, whether ' order ' is observed, either at places of registration or voting; whether there is ' fraudulent registration '; whether there is ' fraudulent voting '; whether there is ' fraudulent conduct ' on the part of any officer of the election; whether the State authorities have rightfully administered their own election laws, and upon their own will to decide and determine whether any attempt to violate the law has been made, and thereupon to arrest and take into custody, with or without process, such parties as they may decide or determine to be guilty of these offenses or any one of them. Thus clothed with new, strange, and extraordinary powers, they are at once judges and executive officers, powers the exercise of which arbitrarily takes from the citizen his liberty and from the elector his sovereignty. Sir, it is simply an invasion of authority upon the freedom of the ballot.

" The genius of tyranny never conceived a more insidious assault upon the rights of a free people than is concealed under this pretense of guarding the purity of the ballot-box. The citizen invested with sovereignty by his State or the people thereof is subordinated to the control and will of a foreign, and it may be antagonistic, tribunal, which, in the assertion of its supremacy by its supple minions, disrobes him of his sovereignty and leaves him the slave of a superior power. The tendency of the law is to prostitute the judiciary to the domination of the executive, and to take away this asylum of the oppressed and make it the castle, if not the bastile, of the oppressor."

Mr. Davidson of Florida: " The amendment proposes to repeal the several sections of the Revised Statutes of the United States from and including section 2011 to and including section 2031. It was introduced by a gentleman whose home is north of the Ohio River, and it is earnestly supported and advocated by members from the North and West as well as from the

South. Yet there are those here who would make it appear that the proposition is a Southern measure only, and they pretend to see in it treason and rebellion. The gentleman from Maine [Mr. Hale] has told us that 'the proposition to repeal all these sections takes hold and violent hold of the whole body of criminal law applicable to the purity of elections in the South and ruthlessly repeals it.' He seems to have forgotten that the sections sought to be repealed apply not only to elections in the South, but throughout the whole country, and at the same time to have misapprehended the purport and scope of the amendment. For it does not propose to repeal the whole body of the criminal law applicable to elections, but only those sections which provide for the appointment of supervisors and deputy marshals. Again, sir, it was very strongly intimated, if not expressly stated, a few days since by the gentleman from New York [Mr. Chittenden], that the object of this amendment was to give to the South absolute control of this Government, and that the proposition to repeal the unwise and iniquitous sections, as I regard them, was an exhibition of audacity which the North would not for a moment tolerate. Sir, the South does not desire absolute control of this Government. It does desire though that the vicious and tyrannical legislation, the enactment of which was the result of bitter feelings engendered during the late great struggle, should no longer remain in force. It does desire that laws which are used as political machines by the political party now in power, and which are manipulated and run altogether in the interest of that party, regardless of the rights of those who are opposed to it, should be repealed. And I fail, Mr. Chairman, to discover in the amendment that audacity which seems to be so apparent to the gentleman from New York. And I could not see it even had the amendment been offered by a Democrat from the South; for in this House the privileges and rights of members are the same whether they come from the North or South, from the East or West.

"And again, sir, it has been argued by the gentleman from Indiana [Mr. Hanna] that the adoption of the pending amendment will sweep away all that legislation which sharply defines, as he expressed it, the difference between loyalty and treason. And it has been said by the gentleman from Indiana [Mr. Baker] that it will undo all the results of the war. Mr. Chairman, I can not appreciate such arguments; neither can I believe that they emanate from sober reflection and sound judgment, but rather do I think that they are the offspring of bitter partisan feeling and uncontrolled prejudice. The members of this House from the South claim no rights here which are not granted to them by the Constitution and laws of their country. And when they assert those rights on this floor, and in a fair and manly manner endeavor to maintain them, that it should be said they are audacious and intimated that they are treasonable is not only unkind, but also most wonderfully presumptuous and arrogant.

"Sir, the proposition on the part of the Democrats to repeal the odious sections mentioned in the amendment is not prompted by a desire to obtain any undue advantage of Republicans. They seek only to take from them that advantage which, owing to partisan legislation, they possess, and which they so harshly, unfairly, and corruptly use at elections in some of the States—use not merely against the interest of the Democratic party, but also in violation of the rights and privileges of the citizens of those States. Mr. Chairman, wrongs, great wrongs, have been and will continue to be perpetrated under the operation of this law so long as it remains in force, and therefore it ought to be repealed."

Mr. Hale: "Mr. Chairman, I rise only for the purpose of stating the position of this question. We may as well understand exactly how this matter now stands before us. The gentleman from Ohio [Mr. Southard], in pressing this amendment, has thrown down the gage of battle. The gentleman from New York [Mr. Hewitt] has asserted this morning that the Democratic party stands here to-day, and will stand, in favor of sweeping from the statute-book all that body of law which he says interferes with the operations of the State governments and State laws with respect to the ballot. Now, there is a plain, distinct challenge; and, Mr. Chairman, I know that, strong as is the feeling on the other side, it is equally strong on this. These laws for the protection of the ballot must not and shall not be repealed. I repeat that this side of the House will never consent to this project of repeal being pushed forward and carried through. Gentlemen on the other side may as well understand that now as hereafter. Thus we are confronted with what the other side must take the responsibility of, an extra session of Congress. Last Tuesday, one week ago to-day, an almost solid vote of this side of the House was given in favor of going into Committee of the Whole upon this appropriation bill. We were voted down by the other side. On Wednesday the bill came up, was discussed, and went over. On Thursday the Republican side again voted solidly to take it up and pass it pure and simple; but we were antagonized with an election case upon which the other side, refusing to consider this bill, unseated a member who had been here within twenty days of his entire term of office. On Friday this bill was antagonized with private bills, and that day was wasted. On Saturday the Republican side again rallied for the purpose of pushing this appropriation bill through; but antagonized as it was by the morning hour and by the bill for the repeal of the tobacco tax, the motion to proceed to the consideration of this bill was, on a vote by tellers, defeated by one vote. I only wish to say that we on this side have done everything to push this bill, and at some stage of this proceeding between now and the final adjournment gentlemen on the other side must yield their position, for these laws can not be and shall not be repealed."

Mr. Southard: "Mr. Chairman, in response to the gentleman from Maine I desire to say for myself, and I think I speak the spontaneous and unanimous sentiment of this side of the House, that these laws, which were enacted for the purpose of controlling the ballot-box and securing the success of the Republican party by bribery, intimidation, and force, must and shall be swept from the statute-books. Let it be distinctly understood that with this side of the House and with the Democratic party rests the responsibility, and they are ready to do, dare, and die, if need be, in defense of the freedom of the ballot and the freedom of the citizen. It is a question of a fair and pure ballot and a question of personal liberty; and the man who yields now in this supreme crisis deserves the condemnation and scorn of a free and independent people.

"These marshals, Mr. Chairman, are appointed by a party, for a party purpose, but they are paid out of the public Treasury. It is idle to say that any Administration will be fair and impartial in the execution of the law against the opposing political party. In addition, these deputy marshals have the power of arresting individuals without affidavit and without warrant upon their own *ipse dixit*, upon their own malice, hatred, interest, or caprice, so that so long as these statutes stand it is utterly impossible that the American citizen can be duly protected in his personal liberty and in his right to vote.

"In St. Louis the special deputy marshals were appointed upon the pledge, and as an indispensable condition, that they would support in the canvass and by their votes the Republican candidates for Congress. One thousand and twenty-eight special deputy marshals were appointed in that city alone, at an expense of over $20,000, and the result was the election of three Republicans in three Democratic districts.

"These supervisors and marshals have in different parts of the country arrested citizens without right and imprisoned them until the hour of voting had passed. In New York last fall, if those who were arrested pledged themselves not to vote they were immediately discharged, but if they insisted on the right to vote they were held in custody; but when the ballot-boxes were closed at six o'clock on election day they were all discharged, and no attempt was made afterward to prosecute them for any crime. The plain inference is that these supervisors and marshals used their authority not to bring to punishment those voting illegally, but simply and solely to secure a victory for the Republican party. This machine is simply one of party for the purpose of perpetuating a party dynasty that has been condemned by the popular judgment of the

country. It is a Northern outrage as well as a Southern outrage. In the North, in 1876, $220,515.64 was paid to these marshals, while in the South but $54,770.96. Four fifths of the money was paid in the North. In 1878 $24,636.74 was paid in the South, while $177,-654·35 was paid in the North, or seven eighths of the entire amount; and Mr. Davenport of New York has still to come in with his bills of thousands more.

"I say again, in response to the taunt from the gentleman from Maine [Mr. Hale], that this side of the House has determined on this measure, not as a question of mere dollars and cents, but as a question of absolute incontestable right, as a question of the freedom and purity of the ballot-box, as a question of freedom from arrest without due process of law. We will no longer permit the control of the ballot-box to remain in the hands of paid and hired agents of one political party for the purpose of carrying elections. It is, as I have already said, a question of personal liberty to the citizen, and we do not mean in this free country that any man shall be arrested and imprisoned until there has been due complaint and warrant of arrest, until there has been due process of law. We mean to protect the citizen in his personal rights and to protect the ballot-box in its freedom and in its purity.

"If the Republican party can beat the Democratic party at the polls, after they have had a free and fair election, we will cheerfully submit, but until that ballot-box is freed we intend to stand as free men to make it free. Let the issue come, and come now. Not a dollar of appropriations should be voted until this most reasonable redress of grievances is conceded."

The Chairman: "The question recurs on the amendment of the gentleman from Ohio [Mr. Southard]."

The committee divided, and the tellers reported—ayes 135, noes 110.

The Chairman: "The amendment is agreed to."

The next amendment from the Committee of the Whole was read, as follows:

After line 16, page 85, add the following:

For defraying the expenses of the Supreme Court, and circuit and district courts of the United States, including the District of Columbia, and also for jurors and witnesses, and expenses of suits in which the United States are concerned, or prosecutions for offenses committed in violation of the laws of the United States, and for the safe-keeping of prisoners, $2,800,000: *Provided*, That the per diem pay of each juror, grand or petit, in any court of the United States shall be $2, and that the last clause of section 800 of the Revised Statutes of the United States, which refers to the State of Pennsylvania, and sections 820 and 821 of the Revised Statutes of the United States are hereby repealed, and that all such jurors, grand and petit, shall be publicly drawn from a box containing the names of not less than three hundred persons possessing the qualifications prescribed in section 800 of the Revised Statutes, which names shall have been placed therein by the clerk of such court and a commissioner to be appointed by the judge thereof, which commissioner shall be a citizen residing in the district in which such court is held, of good standing and a well-known member of the principal political party opposing that to which the clerk may belong, the clerk and said commissioner each to place one name in said box, alternately, until the whole number required shall be placed therein. But nothing herein contained shall be construed to prevent any judge in a district in which such is now the practice from ordering the names of jurors to be drawn from the boxes used by the State authorities in selecting jurors in the highest courts in the State. All general and special laws in conflict herewith are hereby repealed.

The amendment was agreed to.

The next amendment from the Committee of the Whole was as follows:

Insert after the amendment just adopted the following:

That the several sections of the Revised Statutes of the United States from and including section 2011 to and including section 2031, and all other provisions of law authorizing the appointment of or the performance of any duty by any chief or other supervisor of elections, or any special deputy marshal, or other deputy marshal of elections, or the payment of any money to any such supervisor or deputy marshal of elections for any services performed as such, be, and the same are hereby repealed.

The question was taken; and there were—yeas 143, nays 3, not voting 144; as follows:

YEAS—Acklen, Aiken, Atkins, Banning, Beale, Bell, Benedict, Bicknell, Blackburn, Bliss, Blount, Boone, Bouck, Bragg, Bridges, Bright, Buckner, Cabell, John W. Caldwell, W. P. Caldwell, Chandler, Carlisle, Chalmers, Alvah A. Clark, Clarke of Kentucky, Clark of Missouri, Clymer, Cobb, Collins, Cook, Covert, Samuel S. Cox, Cravens, Crittenden, Culberson, Davidson, Joseph J. Davis, Dean, Dibrell, Dickey, Durham, Eden, Eickhoff, Elam, Ellis, John H. Evins, Ewing, Felton, E. B. Finley, Jesse J. Finley, Fleming, Forney, Franklin, Fuller, Garth, Gause, Gibson, Giddings, Glover, Goode, Gunter, Hamilton, Hardenbergh, Henry R. Harris, John T. Harris, Harrison, Hart, Hartzell, Hatcher, Henkle, Henry, Herbert, Abram S. Hewitt, G. W. Hewitt, Hooker, House, Hunton, Frank Jones, James T. Jones, Kenna, Kimmel, Knott, Landers, Ligon, Lockwood, Luttrell, Lynde, Mackey, Maish, Manning, Martin, Mayham, McKenzie, McMahon, Mills, Money, Morgan, Morrison, Morse, Muldrow, Muller, T. M. Patterson, Phelps, Potter, Pridemore, Rea, Reagan, Reilly, Americus V. Rice, Robbins, Roberts, Robertson, Ross, Sayler, Scales, Shelley, Singleton, Slemons, William E. Smith, Southard, Sparks, Springer, Steele, Stenger, Swann, Throckmorton, R. W. Townsend, Turner, Turney, Vance. Veeder, Waddell, Warner, Whitthorne, James Williams, Jere N. Williams, Albert S. Willis, Benjamin A. Willis, Wilson, Wood, Wright, Yeates, John S. Young—143.

NAYS—Chittenden, Fort, Killinger—3.

NOT VOTING—Aldrich, Bacon, Bagley, Bailey, John H. Baker, William H. Baker, Ballou, Banks, Bayne, Beebe, Blair, Bland, Boyd, Brentano, Brewer, Briggs, Brogden, Browne, Bundy, Burchard, Burdick, Butler, Cain, Calkins, Camp, Campbell, Cannon, Caswell, Claflin, Rush Clark, Cole, Conger, Jacob D. Cox, Crapo, Cummings, Cutler, Danford, Horace Davis, Deering, Denison, Dunnell, Dwight, Eames, Ellsworth, Errett, I. Newton Evans, James L. Evans, Foster, Freeman, Frye, Gardner, Garfield, Hale, Hanna, Harmer, Benj. W. Harris, Haskell, Hayes, Hazelton, Hendee, Henderson, Hiscock, Hubbell, Humphrey, Hungerford, Hunter, Ittner, James, John S. Jones, Jorgensen, Joyce, Keifer, Keightley, Kelley, Ketcham, Knapp, Lapham, Lathrop, Lindsey, Loring, Majors, Marsh, McCook, McGowan, McKinley, Metcalfe, Mitchell, Monroe, Neal, Norcross, Oliver, O'Neill, Overton, Page, G. W. Patterson, Peddie, Phillips, Pollard, Pound, Powers, Price, Pugh, Rainey, Randolph, Reed, William W. Rice, Riddle,

G. D. Robinson, M. S. Robinson, Ryan, Sampson, Sapp, Sexton, Snallenberger, Sinnickson, Smalls, A. Herr Smith, Starin, Stephens, Stewart, John W. Stone, Joseph C. Stone, Strait, Thompson, Thornburgh, Tipton, Amos Townsend, M. I. Townsend, Tucker, Van Vorbes, Wait, Walker, Walsh, Ward, Watson, Harry White, Michael D. White, Wigginton, Andrew Williams, C. G. Williams, Richard Williams, Willits, Wren, Casey Young—144.

The Speaker (before announcing the vote): "The Clerk will call my name."

The Clerk called the name of Mr. Randall.

The Speaker: "I vote 'ay.'"

The result of the vote was then announced as above recorded, and the amendment was accordingly agreed to.

The bill was ordered to be engrossed and read a third time. The previous question was demanded and seconded, and the main question ordered. The question was taken, and it was decided as follows:

YEAS—Acklen, Aiken, Atkins, Banning, Beale, Bell, Benedict, Bicknell, Blackburn, Bliss, Blount, Boone, Bouck, Bragg, Bridges, Bright, Buckner, Cabell, John W. Caldwell, W. P. Caldwell, Candler, Chalmers, Alvah A. Clark, Clarke of Kentucky, Clark of Missouri, Clymer, Cobb, Collins, Cook, Covert, Samuel S. Cox, Cravens, Crittenden, Culberson, Cutler, Davidson, Joseph J. Davis, Dibrell, Dickey, Durham, Eden, Eickhoff, Elam, Ellis, John H. Evins, Ewing, Felton, E. B. Finley, Jesse J. Finley, Fleming, Forney, Franklin, Fuller, Garth, Gause, Gibson, Giddings, Glover, Goode, Gunter, Hamilton, Hardenbergh, Henry R. Harris, John T. Harris, Harrison, Hart, Hartzell, Hatcher, Henkle, Henry, Herbert, Abram S. Hewitt, G. W. Hewitt, House, Hunton, Frank Jones, James T. Jones, Kenna, Kimmel, Knott, Landers, Ligon, Lockwood, Luttrell, Lynde, Mackey, Maish, Manning, Martin, Mayham, McKenzie, McMahon, Mills, Money, Morgan, Morrison, Morse, Muldrow, Muller, T. M. Patterson, Phelps, Potter, Pridemore, Rea, Reagan, Reilly, Americus V. Rice, Robbins, Roberts, Robertson, Ross, Sayler, Scales, Shelley, Singleton, Slemons, William E. Smith, Southard, Sparks, Springer, Steele, Stenger, Swann, Throckmorton, R. W. Townsend, Turner, Turney, Vance, Veeder, Waddell, Walker, Whitthorne. James Williams, Jere N. Williams, Albert S. Willis, Benj. A. Willis, Wilson, Wood, Wright, Yeates, John S. Young—142.

NAYS—Aldrich, Bacon, Bagley, John H. Baker, Ballou, Bayne, Blair, Boyd, Brentano, Brewer, Briggs, Brogden, Browne, Bundy, Burchard, Burdick, Cain, Calkins, Camp, Campbell, Caswell, Chittenden, Claflin, Rush Clark, Cole, Conger, Jacob D. Cox, Crapo, Cummings, Danford, Horace Davis, Deering, Denison, Dunnell, Eames, Ellsworth, Errett, I. Newton Evans, Fort, Foster, Frye, Gardner, Hale, Hanna, Harmer, Benj. W. Harris, Haskell, Hayes, Hazelton, Hendee, Henderson, Hiscock, Hubbell, Humphrey, Hungerford, Hunter, Ittner, James, Jorgensen, Joyce, Keifer, Keightley, Kelley, Ketcham, Killinger, Lapham, Lathrop, Lindsey, Majors, Marsh, McCook, McGowan, McKinley, Mitchell, Monroe, Neal, Norcross, Oliver, O'Neill, Overton, Page, G. W. Patterson, Peddie, Phillips, Pollard, Pound, Price, Pugh, Rainey, Randolph, William W. Rice, G. D. Robinson, M. S. Robinson, Ryan, Sampson, Sexton, Shallenberger, Sinnickson, Smalls, A. Herr Smith, Starin, Stewart, John W. Stone, Joseph C. Stone, Strait, Thompson, Amos Townsend, M. I. Townsend, Van Vorbes, Wait, Ward, Watson, Harry White, Andrew Williams, C. G. Williams, Richard Williams, Willits —117.

NOT VOTING—Bailey, William H. Baker, Banks, Beebe, Bland, Butler, Cannon, Carlisle, Dean, Dwight, James L. Evans, Freeman, Garfield, John S.

Jones, Knapp, Loring, Metcalf, Powers, Reed, Riddle, Sapp, Stephens, Thornburgh, Tipton, Tucker, Walsh, Warner, Michael D. White, Wigginton, Wren, Casey Young—31.

So the bill was passed.

In the Senate, on March 1st, the consideration of this appropriation bill and the amendments made by the Senate committee on appropriations was commenced. Among the amendments was the following:

After the word "prisoners," to insert:

And for defraying the expenses which may be incurred in the enforcement of the act approved February 28, 1871, entitled "An act to amend an act approved May 30, 1870, entitled 'An act to enforce the rights of citizens of the United States to vote in the several States of the Union, and for other purposes,' or any acts amendatory thereof or supplementary thereto."

So as to read:

For defraying the expenses of the Supreme Court and circuit and district courts of the United States, including the District of Columbia, and also for jurors and witnesses and expenses of suits in which the United States are concerned, or prosecutions for offenses committed in violation of the laws of the United States, and for the safe-keeping of prisoners, and for defraying the expenses which may be incurred in the enforcement of the act approved February 28, 1871, entitled "An act to amend an act approved May 30, 1870, entitled 'An act to enforce the rights of citizens of the United States to vote in the several States of the United States, and for other purposes,' or any acts amendatory thereof or supplementary thereto," $2,800,000.

The Presiding Officer: "The question is on agreeing to the amendment reported by the Committee on Appropriations. Is the Senate ready for the question?"

The Secretary proceeded to call the roll, and the result was announced as follows:

YEAS—Allison, Anthony, Blaine, Booth, Burnside, Cameron of Pennsylvania, Cameron of Wisconsin, Chandler, Dawes, Dorsey, Edmunds, Ferry, Hamlin, Hoar, Ingalls, Kellogg, Kirkwood, McMillan, Matthews, Mitchell, Morrill, Oglesby, Paddock, Rollins, Saunders, Spencer, Teller, Wadleigh, Windom—29.

NAYS—Bailey, Barnum, Bayard, Beck, Cockrell, Coke, Davis of West Virginia, Dennis, Eaton, Garland, Gordon, Hereford, Hill, Jones of Florida, Kernan, Lamar, McDonald, McPherson, Maxey, Merrimon, Morgan, Saulsbury, Thurman, Wallace, Whyte, Withers—26.

ABSENT—Bruce, Butler, Chaffee, Conkling, Conover, Davis of Illinois, Eustis, Grover, Harris, Howe, Johnston, Jones of Nevada, McCreery, Patterson, Plumb, Randolph, Ransom, Sargent, Sharon, Shields, Voorhees—21.

So the amendment was agreed to.

Mr. Thurman: "Mr. President, I suppose the next amendment is to strike out the proviso on line 2170 and ending in line 2203."

The Presiding Officer: "The Senator is correct. The question now is on agreeing to the amendment, which the Secretary will report."

The Secretary: "The Committee on Appropriations propose to strike out from line 2170 to 2203, in the following words:

"*Provided*, That the per diem pay of each juror, grand or petit, in any court of the United States, shall be $2, and that the last clause of section 800 of the Revised Statutes United States, which refers to the State of Pennsylvania, and sections 801, 820, and 821 of the Revised Statutes of the United States, are hereby repealed: and that all such jurors, grand and petit, shall be publicly drawn from a box containing the names of not less than three hundred persons, possessing the qualifications prescribed in section 800 of the Revised Statutes, which names shall have been placed therein by the clerk of such court, and a commissioner to be appointed by the judge thereof, which commissioner shall be a citizen residing in the district in which such court is held, of good standing and a well-known member of the principal political party opposing that to which the clerk may belong, the clerk and said commissioner each to place one name in said box alternately until the whole number required shall be placed therein. But nothing herein contained shall be construed to prevent any judge in a district in which such is now the practice from ordering the names of jurors to be drawn from the boxes used by the State authorities in selecting jurors in the highest courts of the State. All general and special laws in conflict herewith are hereby repealed. That the several sections of the Revised Statutes of the United States, from and including section 2011 to and including section 2031, and all other provisions of law authorizing the appointment of, or the performance of and duty by, any chief or other supervisor of elections, or any special deputy marshal, or other deputy marshal of elections, or the payment of any money to any such supervisor or deputy marshal of elections for any services performed as such, be, and the same are hereby, repealed."

The Presiding Officer: "The Chair will state the question. The Committee on Appropriations report to strike out the clause which the Secretary has just read. The question is on agreeing to the amendment proposed by the Committee on Appropriations striking out the clause."

Mr. Thurman: "I ask for a division of the amendment, and that the question may first be taken on striking out, beginning at line 2170 and ending with the word 'repealed,' in line 2194. Up to that word the provision moved to be stricken out relates wholly to juries. The subsequent part of the proviso proposed to be stricken out relates to a wholly different subject—to supervisors of elections and marshals. They are wholly distinct subjects, and I ask that the vote may be first taken on the jury proposition, beginning with line 2170 and ending with the word 'repealed,' in line 2194."

The Presiding Officer: "The Chair is of opinion that the question is subject to a division, and will put the question on agreeing to the first branch of the divided proposition. The question, therefore, is on agreeing to strike out from line 2170 to and including the word 'repealed,' in line 2194. Is the Senate ready for the question?"

The Secretary proceeded to call the roll, and the result was announced as follows:

YEAS—Messrs. Allison, Anthony, Blaine, Booth, Burnside, Cameron of Pennsylvania, Cameron of Wisconsin, Chandler, Dawes, Dorsey, Edmunds, Ferry, Hamlin, Hoar, Ingalls, Kellogg, Kirkwood, McMillan, Matthews, Mitchell, Morrill, Oglesby, Paddock, Rollins, Saunders, Spencer, Teller, Wadleigh, Windom—29.

NAYS—Messrs. Bailey, Barnum, Bayard, Beck,

Cockrell, Coke, Davis of West Virginia, Dennis, Eaton, Eustis, Garland, Gordon, Hereford, Hill, Jones of Florida, Kernan, Lamar, McDonald, McPherson, Maxey, Merrimon, Morgan, Saulsbury, Thurman, Wallace, Whyte, Withers—27.

ABSENT—Messrs. Bruce, Butler, Chaffee, Conkling, Conover, Davis of Illinois, Grover, Harris, Howe, Johnston, Jones of Nevada, McCreery, Patterson, Plumb, Randolph, Ransom, Sargent, Sharon, Shields, Voorhees—20.

So the amendment was agreed to.

The Presiding Officer: "The words stated are stricken from the bill. The question now is upon agreeing to the recommendation of the Committee on Appropriations to strike out the remaining words of the clause that was read by the Secretary, namely, beginning with the word 'that' on line 2194, and going to and including the word 'repealed' in line 2203. Is the Senate ready for the question?"

The Secretary proceeded to call the roll, and the result was announced as follows:

YEAS—Messrs. Allison, Anthony, Blaine, Booth, Burnside, Cameron of Pennsylvania, Cameron of Wisconsin, Chandler, Dawes, Dorsey, Edmunds, Ferry, Hamlin, Hoar, Ingalls Kellogg, Kirkwood, McMillan, Matthews, Mitchell, Morrill, Oglesby, Paddock, Rollins, Saunders, Spencer, Teller, Wadleigh, Windom —29.

NAYS—Messrs. Bailey, Barnum, Bayard, Beck, Cockrell, Coke, Davis of West Virginia, Dennis, Eaton, Garland, Gordon, Hereford, Hill, Jones of Florida, Kernan, Lamar, McDonald, McPherson, Maxey, Merrimon, Morgan, Saulsbury, Thurman, Wallace, Whyte, Withers—26.

ABSENT—Messrs. Bruce, Butler, Chaffee, Conkling, Conover, Davis of Illinois, Eustis, Grover, Harris, Howe, Johnston, Jones of Nevada, McCreery, Patterson, Plumb, Randolph, Ransom, Sargent, Sharon, Shields, Voorhees—21.

So the amendment was agreed to, and the bill was subsequently passed.

The House disagreed to the amendments of the Senate, and a committee of conference was appointed in each House. The following is their report to the House of Representatives:

The committee of conference on the disagreeing votes of the two Houses on the amendments of the Senate to the bill (H. R. No. 6240) making appropriations for the legislative, executive, and judicial expenses of the Government, for the fiscal year ending June 30, 1880, and for other purposes, having met, after full and free conference, have been unable to agree.

J. D. C. ATKINS,
M. J. DURHAM, } Managers on the part
CHARLES FOSTER, } of the House.
WILLIAM WINDOM, } Managers on the part
W. B. ALLISON, } of the Senate.
JAMES B. BECK, }

Mr. Atkins: "I move that the House adhere to its disagreement; and upon that motion I call for the previous question."

The previous question was seconded and the main question ordered.

The question being taken on the motion to adhere, it was agreed to.

Mr. Atkins of Tennessee said: "Mr. Speaker, I regret that the conference committee upon this bill, which I regard the most important of the appropriation bills, have utterly failed to agree. We have had three sittings; we have discussed the question in every possible phase of it, and we have found it impossible to come to any agreement. What might have been effected if the whole subject had been left to the conferees themselves, and to themselves alone, it is not necessary for me here to say; nor am I warranted in saying even that they could have come to a conclusion. But they each felt that there was a power behind them which would admit of no agreement. The disagreement between them is radical. As you know, Mr. Speaker, the House has demanded in, I may say, unmistakable terms free elections, untrammeled elections. The House has demanded also intelligent juries, and that jurors should not be subjected to test oaths while members of Congress coming from the Southern States and representing the majesty of the people upon this floor are not subjected to such oaths.

"There were about one hundred amendments to the legislative, executive, and judicial appropriation bill. We were enabled to agree in regard to most of these amendments. We did not agree to the salaries of the officers and employees of the Senate and House of Representatives. I believe it is but candid to say, however, that if we could have agreed upon the other points we might have agreed upon that.

"Mr. Speaker, the deliberate action of this House in attaching the repealing clause to the legislative, executive, and judicial appropriation bill of certain sections of the Revised Statutes has been respected and firmly maintained by the majority members of the House conferees. Upon so grave a question, one not measured by a mere appropriation of money, but involving the rights and liberties of American citizens, the majority of the House conferees did not hesitate a moment to resolutely stand by the injunctions and carry out the action of the body which created our functions. Whatever individual opinions of mere policy in the beginning I or any other Representative may have entertained, and upon which it is usual to exercise the broadest latitude and the most liberal discretion in conference, here is a question involving the most sacred rights and privileges of the citizen, around which this House has thrown the ægis of its protection, and over which this committee has been intrusted a special guardianship, and one which they had no disposition to disregard.

"The committee could not agree upon that feature of the bill which proposes to repeal the test oath now applied to Federal jurors. The importance of selecting juries from among the most intelligent of the people is too plain to admit of argument. The rights of property, the well-being of society, and the safety of the best interests of the State require the abrogation of a law which drives intelligence from the jury-box and installs it with ignorance and prejudice. What public or private harm can result from the repeal of such a law is to my mind inexplicable. Without its repeal the substantial ends of justice will continue to be defeated, and the sanctity of the verdicts and judgments of juries and of courts will sink into ridicule and contempt. Surely, any law which becomes contemptible in its execution and irritates rather than appeases and assuages popular sentiment is radically wrong and ought to be repealed.

"The conference committee were equally unfortunate in not agreeing upon the provisions of the bill which repeal the laws authorizing the appointment of supervisors and deputy marshals. So far as the supervisors are intended to supervise elections and see that a fair count is had, I have heard no complaint. These officers are selected from both political parties, and, if confined to simply supervising elections to prevent fraud, there is not any special objection. But, when these officers are used for police purposes—to make arrests and otherwise interfere with the rights of citizens—there is a vital and fundamental objection. There is no warrant in the Constitution for clothing supervisors with police powers; that power is lodged with the States. But, grant that the Constitution clothes them with police duties and powers, why should they, aided by an army of deputy marshals, turn upon that Constitution and rend it by defeating a fair election? That such has been the unvarying and oft-repeated result for years past is not seriously denied that I am aware of. These deputy marshals are invariably selected on account of their known partisanship and efficiency in manipulating and managing elections; they are appointed by the Administration on account of their facility and readiness to work for the attainment of party ends.

"Realizing that the language of the Constitution (Article I., section 4) only confers the power upon Congress to decide when, where, and how the elections of members of Congress may be held and conducted, but does not extend to the qualifications of voters except such as are made necessary under State constitutions to render a citizen eligible as an elector for members of the most numerous branch of the State Legislature, this House and the country feel that the system of laws which should protect the sanctity of the elective franchise may be and has been converted into an ingenious enginery to deny and even overthrow the purity of the ballot-box, which lies at the base of the very citadel of freedom. All agree that in America a free, unobstructed, and unintimidated ballot is fundamentally essential to free institutions, and any supervision which prevents its voluntary and unfettered exercise is at war with the spirit of the Constitution, no matter though its empty forms may be complied with.

"The practical effect of these laws has been to prevent fair elections, and arouse in the public mind the gravest apprehensions for that purity and legality without which elective government becomes a simple mockery. If intimidation and the fear of arrest drive electors from the polls, or force them to vote against their will, in what does the plebiscit of France which elevated Napoleon to be the supreme ruler of that country differ from our boasted rights of suffrage? No more violent assault was ever made upon the freedom of the elective franchise in France during that period of simulated liberty to which I have just referred, when to have refused to support this mock hero of republicanism was equivalent to incarceration in the Bastile, than was made in the great city of New York and other places on the day of the election in November last, when thousands of American citizens were arrested and imprisoned with the sole view of preventing them from voting. That such acts of tyranny so utterly subversive of liberty may not be repeated, this House has taken its stand in the sacred name of freedom, and demands the repeal of the laws under the cover of which these wrongs were perpetrated.

"The right of the Representatives of the people to withhold supplies is as old as English liberty. History records numerous instances where the common feeling that the people were oppressed by laws that the lords would not consent to repeal by the ordinary methods of legislation obtained redress at last by refusing appropriations unless accompanied by relief measures.

"This is not an ordinary affirmative proposition which is here sought to be ingrafted upon this bill to be carried through by virtue of its momentum, but it is simply a relief measure, a repeal of a bad law. The system of laws so ingeniously blended to obstruct the free exercise of the elective franchise, and against which the majority in this House is now arrayed, grew out of the military ideas which have dominated the legislation of this country since the war. But the time has now come when these measures of injustice and inequality, so long and so patiently endured, must give way to the advancing and well-grounded sentiment of free elections in all the States of this Union, and the equal rights of all men at the ballot-box. As long as these relics of military domination remain upon the statute-book, just so long will the public mind continue to be agitated. As long as statutory contrivances continue to be used to defeat the popular will, so long will the people struggle to wipe them out. As long, too, as these measures encumber the statute-book, economic questions of administration will retire before their presence. For what matters any given line of policy if the people are denied the right of suffrage, or if the chosen Representatives of the people are ejected by arbitrary power from the places to which they have been elected? We therefore submit the general disagreement, and now relegate to the House the trust imposed by the expression of its judgment and action.

"Speaking for myself alone, it seems to me that the majority, having demanded the repeal of these iniquitous laws, have reached a point where retreat is impossible, and where it will be easier to go through than retrace their steps. Whatever responsibility attaches to either House or either party, or the individual members of each, either the one or the other, for the failure of these appropriation bills, the people will fix it where it belongs. That the majority of this House should be blamed for demanding the repeal of statutes which are unjust and unconstitutional, is hardly probable. Believing, therefore, that the repeal is justified by every consideration of fairness and right, the majority can well afford to submit this issue to the verdict of the people."

Mr. Durham of Kentucky: "I shall not detain the House more than a very few moments, and I certainly should not have said anything but for the fact that I have had to hear my share of responsibility in the difficulties of the situation that now surround not only this Congress but the whole of the people of the United States.

"Every member upon this floor, Mr. Speaker, knows what have been my ideas on the subject of putting general legislation upon appropriation bills. Anticipating a result of this kind, it is known to all that in the regular course of legislation a bill repealing all these laws was introduced by myself, referred to the proper committee of this House, and matured by that committee; and the gentleman from Wisconsin, General Bragg, and myself have prepared a report in the regular course of business of this House. That report is now in print. That report gives expression to my sincere and honest sentiments. I believe and have ever believed that the States, and the States alone, have a right to regulate their own elections, and that the Government of the United States has no right to interfere in any election or in any of the domestic affairs of any of the States unless the States prove themselves insufficient to preserve order and carry out and maintain the laws of the country.

"Whenever, Mr. Speaker, insurrection exists, whether it be at the ballot-box, at the polls, or at any other place, and the constituted authorities of that State are insufficient to quell insurrection, to secure every individual that right which is granted to him, not only by the constitution of his State, but the Constitution of the United States, then it may be proper for the Federal Government to interfere; but I do not believe such a state of case has existed anywhere, either North or South. I believe, Mr. Speaker, that these supervisors, these deputy marshals who are employed under the pretext of preserving order at the polls, have been more corrupting to the ballot-box and have thwarted the will of the American people more than would have been done had those officers never been created. I believe it is one of the cardinal principles of the De-

mocratic party—certainly it is one with myself—that the States must regulate these matters for themselves, and, believing so, I had no hesitation in saying from the beginning that all these obnoxious statutes should be wiped and blotted from the statute-book.

"I would have preferred, Mr. Speaker, that these matters should have come in the regular course of legislation, as I said a moment ago; but if that could not be accomplished, then, when it was put on this appropriation bill by the majority of the House, I felt that, as the organ, in part, of the House, I was in honor bound to stand by the instructions given to me; and I should have stood by those instructions until the hands on that dial pointed to the hour of twelve. But if the session had continued one month longer I would have obeyed them. Unless the House had directed me to surrender, I never would have surrendered, but would have stood by the action of the House.

"Only one or two words more. I believe local self-government is the cardinal principle involved in State sovereignty. I believe that it lies at the foundation of all free institutions. Believing, as I said a moment ago, that all these laws in regard to supervisors and marshals corrupt the ballot-box rather than preserve its purity, I am glad that, as I perhaps shall never stand in the American Congress again, that as I shall within a few minutes step out of the position which I have occupied here for the last six years, in the last declaration I shall probably ever utter in the American Congress, the opportunity is presented to me to raise my voice for free elections, free ballots, for State rights, and for unrestricted local self-government."

Mr. Hale of Maine: "Mr. Speaker, I do not think there is a sane man in the country who wants an extra session of Congress. The embarrassments that will follow from it are grave and many. The inflammation of political issues and discussions, the possible conflict between the executive and legislative branches of the Government, above all, the great financial and currency questions, touching nigh the business interests of all the people, which will be disturbed and kept in an uncertain condition, altogether nothing more calamitous could befall the country.

"This side of the House has sat here every day since this session began trying to urge forward the needed legislative business. We have been willing to pass appropriation bills, pure and simple, and to adjourn and let the country have the peace which it needs. The other side of the House has, without need, forced political amendments upon appropriation bills, and the responsibility is theirs. I have faith to believe that there are many moderate, prudent, and patriotic men on the other side, who dread the result of this, who are not satisfied with it. But the spectacle presented is not a rare one in history, where the revolutionary and reactionary elements in a great party, though in a minority as to numbers, have obtained such control of it as to drive the entire force of the party toward revolution. If the people of the North do not appreciate the situation now, they never will appreciate it. If the people of the whole country do not appreciate it now, they never will appreciate it.

"The gentleman from Kentucky [Mr. Durham] has said that it was necessary to put upon the appropriation bills this political legislation. Sir, my comment upon that statement is to say that I hold in my hand a bill passed seventy-four days ago by a Republican Senate repealing the test oath so much insisted on by this Democratic House. That bill is very brief and in these words:

"*Be it enacted, etc.*, That section 820 of the Revised Statutes of the United States be, and the same is hereby, repealed, saving the application of the same to all offenses committed prior to April 20, 1871, and all proceedings for prosecution of offenses pending on the said 20th day of April, 1871.
"Passed the Senate, December 20, 1878.
"Attest: GEO. C. GORHAM, Secretary.
"By WM. E. SPENCER, Chief Clerk.

"Seventy-four days have gone by since that bill came to us from the Senate, and no attempt has been made to take it from the Speaker's table and pass it, so as to give the gentleman from Kentucky [Mr. Durham] and his associates 'an honest and an intelligent jury.' Instead of that, a Democratic caucus has taken this matter into its own hands, has ignored a proper bill passed by a Republican Senate, and has demanded that this and other measures, which they declare to be of vital importance, shall be forced through Congress upon appropriation bills. It has attempted to array this House against a coördinate branch of the National Legislature, the Senate of the United States, as I believe with the intention on the part of some men belonging to the reactionary and revolutionary portion of that party to precipitate an extra session of Congress. That is what I have charged from the beginning, and in proof of the correctness of my assertion is this bill passed by a Republican Senate, but which this Democratic House has persistently refused even to take up and consider."

Mr. Southard of Ohio: "As the mover of a part of these amendments, I desire to say that it was with the highest, the purest, and the most patriotic motives. The positions taken are incontestably right, and will be maintained until these odious laws cease to exist. Laws prescribing test oaths for jurors and those creating marshals and supervisors of elections, clothed with the arbitrary power of arrest without warrant, should cease to exist in this free country, and the polling-places of elections should be free from the presence of the military. As it has been in England since the dawn of her civilization, so shall it be in America. The Democratic party have consid-erately and firmly planted themselves upon these truths. They now appeal to the people of these United States, confidently trusting in their patriotism, their intelligence, and their integrity."

Mr. Atkins: "I believe the gentleman from Maine [Mr. Hale] will remember that there was a motion made to suspend the rules and pass these very measures, and the other side of the House voted against it and defeated it."

Mr. Manning: "Yes, Mr. Speaker, three weeks ago I made a motion to suspend the rules and put upon its passage a bill repealing the test oath and certain election laws. One hundred and twenty-six Democrats voted for the passage of the bill and one hundred and thirteen Republicans voted against it; the Democrats standing solidly for it, and the Republicans solidly against it."

Mr. Hale: "Bring out the record; let us see the record."

Mr. Manning: "It will be seen by reference to the 'Record' of the 11th ultimo, page 20, that I introduced the following bill in the due course of business:

"*Be it enacted, etc.*, That sections 820 and 821 of the Revised Statutes of the United States, and also the sections from 2011 to 2031, both inclusive, and all other sections authorizing the appointment and payment of supervisors of elections and special deputy marshals to aid and assist said supervisors, be, and the same are hereby, repealed.

"All the sections referred to were read to the House. It was my purpose in introducing it to afford a full vindication to the Democratic party in the event of the present threatened emergency that it could not be truthfully said we were undertaking the repeal of these statutes until we had exhausted all ordinary means. So important a fact so recently transpiring could hardly have been forgotten by either the gentleman from Ohio or the gentleman from Maine, as they were both present and voted against the bill."

The Speaker: "Representatives, in a moment this Congress will expire. Its acts, whether for weal or woe, are indelibly inscribed upon the pages of history. In this Hall, party has been arrayed against party and interest against interest in fierce and bitter struggle; but it is due to truth to say that on every side there has been honest ambition to win popular esteem by seeking, each in his own way and according to his best judgment, the general welfare. Whether or not the desired end of the public good has been successfully attained is for time to prove; but that such has been the aim of both sides can not justly be disputed.

"Genuine concord between all the States and the citizens thereof is the corner-stone of our national prosperity. What prostrates or elevates one at the expense of the other inevitably inures to the ultimate injury of all. Although each Representative has championed the wishes of his immediate constituency with earnestness and energy, yet during the whole period of the existence of this House there has not been a single breach of legislative decorum. That noble respect born of generous rivalry in a common good cause has softened all asperities.

"I feel that mere words are inadequate to thank fully this House for its resolution of approval of the manner in which I have discharged the duties of Speaker, always responsible and onerous, and often most delicate and difficult. I have done my best.

"Long service here has taught me that hate or vengeance has never raised any cause to enduring honor, while, on the contrary, justice and mutual regard have often given the weaker side an easy victory. With two great parties dividing the people, each holding an important share in government, with strict accountability on the part of public servants and vigilant eyes watching all, with reviving business and restored confidence, may we not look hopefully to the early dawn of a new era of increased prosperity and greater happiness for the country? Such is my fervent prayer.

"To each and every Representative here I desire to tender my heartfelt acknowledgment for the kindly forbearance extended to me as Presiding Officer of this House, and to say that I shall ever gratefully cherish the honor of which I have been the recipient.

"With the expression of the wish that you all may return safely and in health to your homes, it only remains for me to declare that, in accordance with the Constitution of the United States, this House stands adjourned without day."

In the Senate, on March 3d, the above conclusions of the conference committees were submitted by Mr. Windom of Minnesota, who said: "Mr. President, the conference would have been able to agree on all the items of appropriation in the bill; the point of disagreement was the legislative provisions, those (to state them very briefly) relating to the test oath of jurors and the election laws or the appointment of deputy marshals and supervisors. With reference to these legislative propositions contained in the bill, the conference was unable to agree, the conferees on the part of the House taking the position that the only condition upon which an agreement could be had was that the conferees on the part of the Senate should recede from all of its disagreeing votes on those points. The conferees on the part of the Senate could not accept those conditions.

"I will say, with reference to the condition of the public business so far as the appropriation bills are concerned, that all the bills have now been agreed to and passed by both Houses except the legislative bill, now pending, and the army bill."

Mr. Beck of Kentucky: "Mr. President, I was one of the conferees on the legislative, executive, and judicial appropriation bill when two earnest efforts were made to agree, but

we found it impossible. The Senator from Minnesota has stated correctly that, upon all questions pertaining to the appropriations, the great probability is that we could have agreed, though I believe we did not finally agree even as to them. He is also correct in stating that the House conferees insisted upon retaining that portion of the bill to which he has alluded, but it was also equally certain that the majority of the Senate conferees with equal pertinacity insisted upon the Senate amendments, and maintained that each and all the provisions inserted by the House should be stricken out. There was no attempt at any division of the subjects, and no proposition looking to any modification was considered. Not desiring to revive any political animosities or any discussion at this late hour, I will only state very briefly what seemed to be the condition of things: the House insisted that the armed soldiers of the United States should not be allowed to approach the polls for the mere purpose of keeping the peace, that there should be an honest jury obtained in the courts of the United States in all cases where the rights and liberties of citizens were involved, and that the States should be allowed to conduct their own elections in their own way, free from all Federal interference, and the Democratic conferees on the part of the House seemed determined that unless those rights were secured to the people in the bills sent to the Senate they would refuse, under their constitutional right to make appropriations, to carry on the Government if the dominant majority in the Senate insisted upon the maintenance of these laws *and refused to consent* to their repeal.

"They seemed further to agree, and I agreed with them, that if an extra session must be called, much as it is to be regretted, the very moment it is called the committees of both Houses would be organized and separate bills would be framed and passed as soon as possible asking the President of the United States to agree with the representatives of the States and people in repealing all laws that authorize the soldiers of the Republic to be sent by any authority whatever to the polls at State elections under the pretense of keeping the peace, and in repealing all laws that prevent men who are by intelligence and interest in the public welfare fit and competent to do justice between citizens and between the United States and citizens in the jury-box from exercising that right, thus depriving the courts the benefit of fair jurors, and they will promptly pass another bill declaring that the United States shall not, either through supervisors, marshals, or deputy marshals, interfere with the States in conducting the elections held within the States. We insist that those matters pertain solely to the States and are part of their absolute right, and that they are perfectly competent to attend to them fairly and honestly. When these three laws are submitted to the President for his approval, as they will be, and are approved by him, as they ought to be, the next Congress will in my opinion be ready to pass every appropriation bill, just as it is now, adjourn, and go home without attempting before next December to perfect any further legislation."

The Presiding Officer: "The question is on the motion of the Senator from Ohio [Mr. Thurman] that the Senate recede from its amendment to the legislative, executive, and judicial appropriation bill which has been indicated."

The Secretary proceeded to call the roll, and the result was announced as follows:

YEAS—Bailey, Barnum, Bayard, Beck, Butler, Cockrell, Coke, Davis of West Virginia, Dennis, Eaton, Garland, Gordon, Grover, Harris, Hereford, Hill, Kernan, Lamar, McDonald, McPherson, Maxey, Morgan, Ransom, Saulsbury, Thurman, Whyte—26.

NAYS—Allison, Anthony, Blaine, Booth, Bruce, Burnside, Cameron of Pennsylvania, Cameron of Wisconsin, Chandler, Conkling, Conover, Dorsey, Edmunds, Ferry, Hamlin, Jones of Nevada, Kellogg, Kirkwood, McMillan, Matthews, Oglesby, Paddock, Paterson, Plumb, Rollins, Saunders, Spencer, Teller, Wadleigh, Windom—30.

ABSENT—Chaffee, Davis of Illinois, Dawes, Eustis, Hoar, Howe, Ingalls, Johnston, Jones of Florida, McCreery, Merrimon, Mitchell, Morrill, Randolph, Sargent, Sharon, Shields, Voorhees, Wallace, Withers—20.

So the Senate refused to recede.

The Presiding Officer. "The question recurs on the motion of the Senator from Minnesota [Mr. Windom] that the Senate insist upon its amendments," which was decided in the affirmative, and the bill failed to become a law.

EXTRA SESSION.

On March 4th the President issued the following proclamation as a summons for an extra session of Congress:

Whereas the final adjournment of the Forty-Fifth Congress without making the usual and necessary appropriations for the legislative, executive, and judicial expenses of the Government for the fiscal year ending June 30, 1880, and without making the usual and necessary appropriations for the support of the Army for the same fiscal year, presents an extraordinary occasion, requiring the President to exercise the power vested in him by the Constitution to convene the Houses of Congress in anticipation of the day fixed by law for their next meeting:

Now, therefore, I, Rutherford B. Hayes, President of the United States, do, by virtue of the power to this end in me vested by the Constitution, convene both Houses of Congress at their respective Chambers at twelve o'clock noon on Tuesday the 18th day of March instant, then and there to consider and determine such measures as, in their wisdom, their duty and the welfare of the people may seem to demand.

In witness whereof I have hereunto set my hand and caused the seal of the United States to be affixed.

Done at the city of Washington this 4th day of March, in the year of our Lord 1879, and of the Independence of the United States of America the one hundred and third.

[L. S.]   R. B. HAYES.
By the President
    WM. M. EVARTS, Secretary of State.

This being the first session of the Forty-sixth Congress, the Vice-President took the chair in the Senate, and in the House Samuel J. Randall of Pennsylvania was chosen Speaker. He received 143 votes, James A. Garfield 125, Hendrick B. Wright 13, and William D. Kelley 1.

After the organization the following message from the President to Congress was communicated:

Fellow Citizens of the Senate and House of Representatives:

The failure of the last Congress to make the requisite appropriations for legislative and judicial purposes, for the expenses of the several Executive Departments of the Government, and for the support of the Army, has made it necessary to call a special session of the Forty-sixth Congress.

The estimates of the appropriations needed, which were sent to Congress by the Secretary of the Treasury at the opening of the last session, are renewed, and are herewith transmitted to both the Senate and the House of Representatives.

Regretting the existence of the emergency which requires a special session of Congress at a time when it is the general judgment of the country that permanency in our legislation and by peace and rest, I commend these few necessary measures to your considerate attention.

                        RUTHERFORD B. HAYES.
WASHINGTON, *March* 19, 1879.

SENATE.

Alabama.	*Arkansas.*
1883, John T. Morgan, D.	1883, A. H. Garland, D.
1885, G. S. Houston, D.	1885, James D. Walker, D.
California.	*Colorado.*
1881, Newton Booth, R.	1883, H. M. Teller, R.
1885, James T. Farley, D.	1885, N. P. Hill, R.
Connecticut.	*Delaware.*
1881, W. W. Eaton, D.	1881, Thomas F. Bayard, D
1885, Orville H. Platt, R.	1883, Eli Saulsbury, D.
Florida.	*Georgia.*
1881, C. W. Jones, D.	1883, Benjamin H. Hill, D.
1885, Wilkinson Call, D.	1885, John B. Gordon, D.
Illinois.	*Indiana.*
1883, David Davis, I.	1881, J. E. McDonald, D.
1885, John A. Logan, R.	1885, D. W. Voorhees, D.
Iowa.	*Kansas.*
1883, S. J. Kirkwood, R.	1883, P. B. Plumb, R.
1885, William B. Allison, R.	1885, John J. Ingalls, R.
Kentucky.	*Louisiana.*
1883, James B. Beck, D.	1883, W. P. Kellogg, R.
1885, J. S. Williams, D.	1885, B. F. Jonas, D.
Maine.	*Maryland.*
1881, H. Hamlin, R.	1881, William P. Whyte, D.
1883, James G. Blaine, R.	1885, James B. Groome, D.
Massachusetts.	*Michigan.*
1881, H. L. Dawes, R.	1881, H. P. Baldwin, R.
1883, George F. Hoar, R.	1883, Thomas W. Ferry, R.
Minnesota.	*Mississippi.*
1881, S. J. R. McMillan, R.	1881, B. K. Bruce, D.
1883, William Windom, R.	1883, L. Q. C. Lamar, D.
Missouri.	*Nebraska.*
1881, F. M. Cockrell, D.	1881, A. S. Paddock, R.
1885, George G. Vest, D.	1883, Alvin Saunders, R.
Nevada.	*New Hampshire.*
1881, William Sharon, R.	1883, Edward H. Rollins, R.
1885, John P. Jones, R.	1885, Henry W. Blair, R.
New Jersey.	*New York.*
1881, T. F. Randolph, D.	1881, Francis Kernan, D.
1883, J. R. McPherson, D.	1885, R. Conkling, R.

North Carolina.
1889, M. W. Ransom, D.
1885, Zeb. B. Vance, D.

Oregon.
1883, Lafayette Grover, D.
1885, James H. Slater, D.

Rhode Island.
1881, A. E. Burnside, R.
1883, H. B. Anthony, R.

Tennessee.
1881, James E. Bailey, D.
1883, I. G. Harris, D.

Vermont.
1881, G. F. Edmunds, R.
1885, J. S. Morrill, R.

West Virginia.
1881, F. Hereford, D.
1883, H. G. Davis, D.

Ohio.
1881, A. G. Thurman, D.
1885, G. H. Pendleton, D.

Pennsylvania.
1881, William A. Wallace, D.
1885, J. Don Cameron, R.

South Carolina.
1883, M. C. Butler, D.
1885, Wade Hampton, D.

Texas.
1881, S. B. Maxey, D.
1883, Richard Coke, D.

Virginia.
1881, R. E. Withers, D.
1883, J. W. Johnston, D.

Wisconsin.
1881, Angus Cameron, R.
1885, M. H. Carpenter, R.

Kansas.
1, John A. Anderson, R.
2, Dudley C. Haskell, R.
8, Thomas Ryan, R.

Kentucky.
1, Oscar Turner, D.
2, James A. McKenzie, D.
3, John W. Caldwell, D.
4, J. Proctor Knott, D.
5, Albert S. Willis, D.
6, John G. Carlisle, D.
7, J. C. S. Blackburn, D.
8, P. B. Thompson, Jr., D.
9, Thomas Turner, D.
10, Elijah C. Phister, D.

Louisiana.
1, Randall L. Gibson, D.
2, E. John Ellis, D.
3, Joseph H. Acklen, D.
4, J. B. Elam, D.
5, J. Floyd King, D.
6, E. W. Robertson, D.

Maine.
1, Thomas B. Reed, R.
2, William P. Frye, R.
3, Stephen D. Lindsey, R.
4, George W. Ladd, D.
5, Thompson H. Murch, N.

Maryland.
1, Daniel M. Henry, D.
2, J. F. C. Talbott, D.
3, William Kimmell, D.
4, Robert M. McLane, D.
5, Eli J. Henkle, D.
6, Milton G. Urner, R.

Massachusetts.
1, William W. Crapo, R.
2, Benjamin W. Harris, R.
3, Walbridge A. Field, R.
4, Leopold Morse, D.
5, S. Z. Bowman, R.
6, George B. Loring, R.
7, William A. Russell, R.
8, William Claflin, R.
9, William W. Rice, R.
10, Amasa Norcross, R.
11, George D. Robinson, R.

Michigan.
1, J. S. Newberry, R.
2, Edwin Willits, R.
3, J. H. McGowan, R.
4, J. C. Burrows, R.
5, John W. Stone, R.
6, Mark S. Brewer, R.
7, Omar D. Conger, R.
8, Roswell G. Horr, R.
9, Jay A. Hubbell, R.

Minnesota.
1, M. H. Dunnell, R.
2, Henry Poehler, D.
3, W. D. Washburn, R.

Mississippi.
1, H. L. Muldrow, D.
2, Van H. Manning, D.
3, H. D. Money, D.
4, Otho R. Singleton, D.
5, Charles E. Hooker, D.
6, J. R. Chalmers, D.

Missouri.
1, Martin L. Clardy, D.
2, Erasmus Wells, D.
3, R. G. Frost, D.
4, L. H. Davis, D.
5, Richard P. Bland, D.
6, John R. Waddill, D.
7, Alfred M. Lay, D.
8, Samuel L. Sawyer, D.
9, Nicholas Ford, N.
10, G. F. Rothwell, D.
11, John B. Clark, Jr., D.
12, William H. Hatch, D.
13, A. H. Buckner, D.

Nebraska.
1, Ed. K. Valentine, R.

Nevada.
1, Rollin M. Daggett, R.

New Hampshire.
1, Joshua G. Hall, R.
2, James F. Briggs, R.
3, Evarts W. Farr, R.

New Jersey.
1, George M. Robeson, R.
2, Hezekiah B. Smith, D.
3, Miles Ross, D.
4, Alvah A. Clark, D.
5, C. H. Voorhis, R.
6, John L. Blake, R.
7, L. A. Brigham, R.

New York.
1, James W. Covert, D.
2, Daniel O'Reilly, D.
3, S. B. Chittenden, R.
4, A. M. Bliss, D.
5, Nicholas Muller, D.
6, S. S. Cox, D.
7, Edwin Einstein, R.
8, A. G. McCook, R.
9, Fernando Wood, D.
10, James O'Brien, D.
11, Levi P. Morton, R.
12, Waldo Hutchins, D.
13, J. H. Ketcham, R.
14, John W. Ferdon, R.
15, William Lounsberry, D.
16, John M. Bailey, R.
17, Walter A. Wood, R.
18, J. H. Hammond, R.
19, A. B. James, R.
20, John H. Starin, R.
21, David Wilber, R.
22, Warner Miller, R.
23, Cyrus D. Prescott, R.
24, Joseph Mason, R.
25, Frank Hiscock, R.
26, John H. Camp, R.
27, E. G. Lapham, R.
28, Jere. W. Dwight, R.
29, D. P. Richardson, R.
30, J. Van Voorhis, R.
31, Richard Crowley, R.
32, Ray V. Pierce, R.
33, H. H. Van Aernam, R.

Recapitulation.
Democrats................42 | Independent................1
Republicans..............33 | Democratic majority........8

REPRESENTATIVES.

Alabama.
1, Thomas Herndon, D.
2, Hilary A. Herbert, D.
3, W. J. Samford, D.
4, Charles M. Shelley, D.
5, Thomas Williams, D.
6, Burwell B. Lewis, D.
7, William H. Forney, D.
8, William M. Lowe, N.

Arkansas.
1, Poindexter Dunn, D.
2, William F. Slemons, D.
3, Jordan E. Cravens, D.
4, Thomas M. Gunter, D.

California.
1, Horace Davis, R.
2, Horace F. Page, R.
3, C. P. Berry, D.
4, Romualdo Pacheco, R.

Colorado.
1, James B. Belford, R.

Connecticut.
1, Joseph R. Hawley, R.
2, James Phelps, D.
3, John T. Wait, R.
4, Frederick Miles, R.

Delaware.
1, Edward L. Martin, D.

Florida.
1, R. H. M. Davidson, D.
2, Noble A. Hull, D.

Georgia.
1, John C. Nicholls, D.
2, William E. Smith, D.
3, Philip Cook, D.
4, Henry Persons, D.
5, N. J. Hammond, D.
6, James H. Blount, D.
7, William H. Felton, D.
8, Alexander H. Stephens, D.
9, Emory Speer, D.

Illinois.
1, William Aldrich, R.
2, George R. Davis, R.
3, Hiram Barber, Jr., R.
4, John C. Sherwin, R.
5, R. M. A. Hawk, R.
6, Thomas J. Henderson, R.
7, Philip C. Hayes, R.
8, Greenbury L. Fort, R.
9, Thomas A. Boyd, R.
10, Benjamin F. Marsh, R.
11, James W. Singleton, D.
12, William M. Springer, D.
13, Adlai E. Stevenson, N.
14, Joseph G. Cannon, R.
15, A. P. Forsyth, N.
16, W. A. J. Sparks, D.
17, William R. Morrison, D.
18, J. R. Thomas, R.
19, R. W. Townshend, D.

Indiana.
1, William Heilman, R.
2, Thomas R. Cobb, D.
3, George A. Bicknell, D.
4, Jeptha D. New, D.
5, Thomas M. Browne, R.
6, William R. Myers, D.
7, Gilbert De La Matyr, N.
8, A. J. Hostetler, D.
9, Godlove S. Orth, R.
10, William H. Calkins, R.
11, Calvin Cowgill, R.
12, W. G. Colerick, D.
13, John H. Baker, R.

Iowa.
1, Moses A. McCoid, R.
2, Hiram Price, R.
3, Thomas Updegraff, R.
4, N. C. Deering, R.
5, William G. Thompson, R.
6, J. B. Weaver, N.
7, E. H. Gillette, N.
8, W. F. Sapp, R.
9, Cyrus C. Carpenter, R.

North Carolina.

1, Joseph J. Martin, R.
2, W. H. Kitchin, D.
3, D. L. Russell, N.
4, Joseph J. Davis, D.

5, Alfred M. Scales, D.
6, Walter L. Steele, D.
7, R. F. Armfield, D.
8, Robert B. Vance, D.

Ohio.

1, Benjamin Butterworth, R.
2, Thomas L. Young, R.
3, J. A. McMahon, D.
4, J. Warren Keifer, R.
5, Benjamin Lefevre, D.
6, W. D. Hill, D.
7, Frank Hurd, D.
8, E. B. Finley, D.
9, George L. Converse, D.
10, Thomas Ewing, D.

11, H. L. Dickey, D.
12, Henry S. Neal, R.
13, A. J. Warner, D.
14, Gibson Atherton, D.
15, George W. Geddes, D.
16, Wm. McKinley, Jr., R.
17, James Monroe. R.
18, J. T. Updegraff, R.
19, James A. Garfield, R.
20, Amos Townsend, R.

Oregon.

1, John Whitaker, D.

Pennsylvania.

1, H. H. Bingham, R.
2, Charles O'Neill, R.
3, Samuel J. Randall, D.
4, William D. Kelley, R.
5, A. C. Harmer, R.
6, William Ward, R.
7, William Godshalk, R.
8, Hiester Clymer, D.
9, A. Herr Smith, R.
10, R. K. Bachman, D.
11, Robert Klotz, D.
12, H. B. Wright, D.
13, John W. Ryon, D.
14, John W. Killinger, R.

15, Edward Overton, R.
16, John I. Mitchell, R.
17, A. H. Coffroth, D.
18, Horatio G. Fisher, R.
19, F. E. Beltzhoover, D.
20, Seth H. Yocum, N.
21, Morgan R. Wise, D.
22, Russell Errett, R.
23, Thomas M. Bayne, R.
24, W. S. Shallenberger, R.
25, Harry White, R.
26, S. B. Dick, R.
27, J. H. Hosmer, R.

Rhode Island.

1, N. W. Aldrich, R.

2, Latimer W. Ballou, R.

South Carolina.

1, J. S. Richardson, D.
2, M. P. O'Connor, D.
3, D. Wyatt Aiken, D.

4, John H. Evins, D.
5, G. D. Tillman, D.

Tennessee.

1, Robert L. Taylor, D.
2, L. C. Houk, R.
3, George C. Dibrell, D.
4, Benton McMillan, D.
5, John M. Bright, D.

6, John F. House, D.
7, W. C. Whitthorne, D.
8, John D. C. Atkins, D.
9, C. B. Simonton, D.
10, H. Casey Young, D.

Texas.

1, John H. Reagan, D.
2, D. B. Culberson, D.
3, Olin Wellborn, D.

4, Roger Q. Mills, D.
5, George W. Jones, N.
6, Columbus Upson, D.

Virginia.

1, R. L. T. Beale, D.
2, John Goode, Jr., D.
3, Joseph E. Johnston, D.
4, Joseph Jorgenson, R.
5, George C. Cabell, D.

6, J. R. Tucker, D.
7, John T. Harris, D.
8, Eppa Hunton, D.
9, J. B. Richmond, D.

Vermont.

1, Charles H. Joyce, R.
2, James M. Tyler, R.

3, Bradley Barlow, R.

West Virginia.

1, Benjamin Wilson, D.
2, Benjamin F. Martin, D.

3, John E. Kenna, D.

Wisconsin.

1, Charles G. Williams, R.
2, Lucien B. Caswell, R.
3, George C. Hazleton, R.
4, P. V. Deuster, D.

5, Edward S. Bragg, D.
6, Gabriel Bouck, D.
7, H. L. Humphrey, R.
8, Thaddeus C. Pound, R.

Recapitulation.

Democrats.................150 | Nationals.................11
Republicans.............132 | Democratic maj. over all.. 7

Territorial Delegates.

Arizona—H. S. Stevens.
Dakota—J. P. Kidder.
Idaho—S. S. Fenn.
Montana—M. Maginnis.

New Mexico—T. Romero.
Utah—G. Q. Cannon.
Washington—O. Jacobs.
Wyoming—W. W. Corlett.

In the House, on March 27th, a bill making appropriations for the support of the army for the fiscal year ending June 30, 1880, and for other purposes, was introduced.

Mr. Sparks of Illinois said: "I would say that this is substantially the bill as it passed the House of Representatives of the Forty-fifth Congress at its last session, with the clauses stricken out in relation to the reorganization of the army. It is also substantially the bill as passed by the Senate with the insertion of the clauses repealing the two provisions of the statute relating to the use of the troops at the polls. It is really the bill which was informally agreed upon in the conference committee of the two Houses of the last Congress, excepting the portion relating to the repeal of the provisions of the statutes allowing soldiers at the polls. I now move that the House resolve itself into Committee of the Whole on the state of the Union for the purpose of considering the army appropriation bill."

The motion was agreed to.

Mr. Sparks: "I ask that the Clerk now read section 6."

The Clerk read section 6, as follows:

SECTION 6. That section 2002 of the Revised Statutes be amended so as to read as follows:

"No military or naval officer, or other person engaged in the civil, military, or naval service of the United States, shall order, bring, keep, or have under his authority or control any troops or armed men at the place where any general or special election is held in any State, unless it be necessary to repel the armed enemies of the United States."

And that section 5528 of the Revised Statutes be amended so as to read as follows:

"Every officer of the army or navy, or other person in the civil, military, or naval service of the United States, who orders, brings, keeps, or has under his authority or control any troops or armed men at any place where a general or special election is held in any State, unless such force be necessary to repel armed enemies of the United States, shall be fined not more than $5,000 and suffer imprisonment at hard labor not less than three months nor more than five years."

Mr. Stephens of Georgia said: "One word upon the merits of this question, and that is in regard to the history of the use of the army in civil administration. I will state it that way.

"There seems to be some disagreement and lack of information among members. The calling out of troops to suppress insurrection and violence, referred to by the gentleman from Kentucky [Mr. Carlisle], is a very different provision from the use of the troops in civil administration, totally different. The President, first, by the act of 1795, was authorized, in cases set forth by the Constitution, to call out, not the militia of the State, no; but to put down an insurrection against a State, to preserve the integrity of the State, guaranteeing a republican government under the Constitution, he was authorized to call out the militia of adjoining States. That is the law of 1795. It is not to be presumed that the governor would not call out the militia in his own State, and the militia of adjoining States was to be called out when it was necessary to put down an insurrection in a State. That is the legitimate use of the military power of the country under the act of 1795.

"Now it was not until 1807 that the organized army—the military force and the naval force—was authorized to be called out for a like purpose, to protect the States against domestic violence and insurrection. That law also went further, or some subsequent law—I have not, from indisposition, been able to look up these laws as I expected to do last night, but the provision of the law for the use of the troops in civil cases is entirely a different matter. It is where provision is made for the execution of a mandate or judgment of a court. The generals are not to command the troops in such cases, but the marshals. The civil officers, as the sheriffs in our States, were authorized to call for the use of the troops, and the President was authorized to furnish them to the Legislature or to the governor when the Legislature was not in session or the marshals for the execution of the mandate of a court. That is what I call the execution of process in civil administration of the law. That is a very different thing from the other—the use of troops to suppress insurrection and domestic violence in a State upon the call of a Legislature or the governor as provided by the Constitution.

"Wherever the marshal calls for troops, as was decided by Attorney-General Cushing, it was as a *posse*, not as the army. The United States troops were called upon and they were furnished as a *posse comitatus* to execute the law. They were under the command, not of the United States military officers, but under the command of the marshal who asked for them.

"Now, Mr. Chairman, upon the subject of the use of the troops to keep the peace at elections I have only to repeat what was so well and so often said yesterday. Such a provision never had existence on the statute-book of the United States until after 1860, after the war. This act of 1865 which it is proposed to modify got into existence rather strangely. The law set out by stating that no officer, etc., should order troops, or have them at any election in any State, except for certain purposes, mainly to keep the peace at the polls. It was a negative affirmative. That is, it thus legalized the use of the army. That is the way in which it appeared upon the statute-book. The danger of such a law, I suppose, in this age and in the enlightened condition of public sentiment the world over, need not be argued. The whole of this amendment is simply this: all the new legislation it proposes, or change of legislation, is to repeal that clause which negatively affirms that the troops might be called out and ordered by military commanders to attend at elections under pretense of keeping the peace. That is all of it. The whole thing might have been embodied simply in the expression that all laws that authorize the use of troops to preserve peace at elections should be repealed. That would accomplish the whole object. The use of the other words in the act of 1865 amounts to nothing. The whole of that sec-

tion was to cover that one thing, to preserve the peace at the polls.

"Now, Mr. Chairman, if there is a man on this floor who is in favor of peaceable elections and order throughout the length and breadth of this country, I profess to be equally strong with him in that wish and desire. Purity of elections is the greatest safeguard of liberty. I am for law and order. I have witnessed the presence of soldiers at the polls. I have seen no good from their presence. We had gotten along for three quarters of a century without it. I think the public sentiment is as much against the use of the troops to preserve the peace North as it is South. That the Government of the United States has got a right to control by law, alter, change, and prescribe the rules and manner of holding the election of members of Congress, I am not going to discuss here. It is not pertinent to this question. But we have got along well for many years without this provision; and I think that the future peace and harmony of the whole country, law, order, and prosperity, will be greatly promoted by hereafter adhering to the principles and practice and methods of the fathers of the Republic from the beginning down for more than three quarters of a century. Let the relics and vestiges of the war be buried with the things of the past. I do insist that there will be no harm done, no unsettling of our institutions, no revolution in our matchless system of government, by the repeal of this law. It seems to me, therefore, this amendment being germane, regulating the use and the control of the army, and being also within the purview of a liberal construction of the rule, it is admissible on this bill.

"Now, as to the use of the army, I wish in connection with some remarks which were offered yesterday on both sides upon this subject to state this: Congress has got a right to raise armies. Congress has got a right to designate the use to which the forces, naval or military, may be applied. But the President's right to control and direct the movements of those forces from one part of the country to the other, enlarging the declared function of Congress, is a clear executive right. We have no power to interfere with it, except by impeachment for the abuse of power conferred. But we can say that he shall not use the forces for any particular purposes. We have a right to say this—and I do not think the present Executive would desire it to be otherwise—we have a right to say the forces, land and naval, of the United States shall not be used for the purpose of controlling elections in the States, but that the elections shall be free and fair according to the laws of the land, State and Federal; and if any man violates the law, if there has been any violence at the polls, and a member of Congress has not been duly returned, we are to judge of it here on this floor, and we can set the return aside. Let the land and naval forces of our country be devoted to the objects for which they were raised by Congress. Let the army protect the frontier. Let the navy be afloat on the seas protecting our flag and our commerce everywhere. Let each branch of these forces be kept in that sphere they were created for, and in which in past years they have won such honor and glory to our common country. Let them be performing their duties, and let the civil administration of the Government go on in its own channel. Let members of Congress be returned as heretofore; and if any man has been deprived of his rights to his seat here, then let this high constitutional court, the House of Representatives, decide that question, and not submit it to the decision of bayonets insead of ballots."

Mr. Chalmers of Mississippi: "I desire to say that the Democratic party introduced this law just as it will stand when we make this modification of it. After it was introduced in that form, Mr. Pomeroy, a Senator from Kansas, moved to amend by adding the words 'or to keep the peace at the polls.'

"What did Mr. Powell then say? He was a Kentuckian, whose State had been overrun by armed troops at the polls. He said: 'I object to that, for it will destroy the effect of the bill. The State authorities can keep the peace at the polls.' Upon that question every Democrat voted against putting that amendment upon the bill, and every Republican voted in favor of it. The Democratic party then stood as it stands to-day. After that amendment had been voted upon the bill, the Senator from Kentucky, having failed to secure the law as he introduced it, knowing then his State was ground down by the bayonet at the polls, agreed to accept the law even with that amendment upon it, for it would restrict the use of the troops even as amended. And the Democratic party of the House voted for it for the same reason."

Mr. White of Pennsylvania: "The gentleman from Mississippi has given correctly a part of the history of the passage of the act. It is quite true that Hon. Lazarus Powell introduced the bill originally and made an elaborate speech upon it; and the question was exhaustively discussed in the Senate of the United States. When the question arose upon the passage of the bill, an honorable gentleman, then a Senator from Kansas, moved to amend by adding the words 'to keep the peace at the polls.' Those are the objectionable words now—the bone of contention in this controversy. That motion was the subject of some colloquial debate. Incidentally the misuse of the *posse comitatus* power of marshals in the border-raid troubles in Kansas was brought into the discussion by Mr. Pomeroy. After he had presented the necessity of keeping peace at the polls in order to secure the right of suffrage, the amendment was incorporated upon the bill of Senator Powell. Let me call the attention of the House and the

country to the fact that a most distinguished lawyer, then a Senator, now a private citizen, a man whom the gentleman from Illinois [Mr. Sparks] will recognize as the Magnus Apollo of the Illinois bar, supported that amendment. I allude to Hon. Lyman Trumbull."

Mr. Sparks: "He was then a Republican, was he not?"

Mr. White: "Certainly he was; but he was a good lawyer, I apprehend, then, as he is now. He sanctioned this amendment. Hon. Mr. McDougall then moved to postpone the bill indefinitely. Mr. Powell said, 'No, no'; and upon his request the vote was taken on the passage of the bill, and it was passed. Hon. Mr. Harlan, then a Senator, entered a motion to reconsider, which was subsequently debated; and Hon. Reverdy Johnson (as gentlemen will find if they will follow the debates) made the point, in recognition of the virtue of this amendment, that it was competent to give the President of the United States this power for the purpose of enforcing peace at the polls. The yeas and nays were again called upon the passage of the bill in the Senate, and every Democrat voted for it.

"The bill came to this House and was referred to the Committee on the Judiciary. It was reported to the House, and the honorable gentleman, then a conspicuous member of this body as now, voted for it without making any complaint or criticism about this clause. So did my honorable colleague [Mr. Coffroth], who now represents on this floor a Republican district, and who, I trust, will be consistent with his record in the final vote on this question. So did every other Democrat in this House.

"The point we now make is that the Democratic party having sanctioned the passage of this bill containing this clause 'to keep the peace at the polls,' it is little short of revolutionary for them now to come in and undertake to repeal this legislation upon an appropriation bill. This is the point I make, and the point I for one am willing to stand upon before the country."

Mr. Chalmers: "One word to the gentleman from Pennsylvania [Mr. White]. He said that I had not given a full history of this law; that Reverdy Johnson, the great lawyer of Maryland, had endorsed it in the very words in which it now stands upon the statute-book, and that Mr. Johnson as Senator opposed the reconsideration when it was asked for in the Senate.

"Mr. Chairman, I bow in humble reverence before the name and the memory of Reverdy Johnson. ·I .can never do too much honor to the Spartan firmness, to the more than Roman dignity with which he and Powell and Saulsbury and the little band of Democrats that stood around them then, battled for the Constitution, when an arrogant and intolerant majority banished men from the country for freedom of speech, when they were dragging members from the halls of Congress, and when they were converting a constitutional Union into a military despotism. The gentleman from Pennsylvania has made the charge. Let Reverdy Johnson answer for himself, and, as his words come back to us from the silent echoes of the tomb, let his memory be for ever vindicated. Speaking of these laws, he said : ' The amendments made and which now form a part of this bill go further than I think we have a right to go, but in the name of freedom I implore the Senate not to go a step further. . . . Oh save us ! save us in the name of freedom ; save us in regard to the sacred memory of our ancestors; save us from the rule of military despotism.' Sir, I can now only add to that, may God in his mercy save us from any more political exigencies in which it may seem proper to gentlemen on this floor to misrepresent the dead and blacken the names of such men as Lazarus Powell and Reverdy Johnson by charging that they were ever the advocates of using the United States army to keep the peace at the polls !

" The gentleman from Ohio, and many others on his side of the House, in the last session, admitted that it was repugnant to the very idea of Anglo-Saxon liberty that troops should be used at the polls. He indicated then a willingness that these laws, as he expressed it, might be ' mustered out of service.' Now he has changed his front. His excuse for this change is twofold. First, he says that the Democracy of the Forty-fifth Congress showed no disposition to compromise. Upon this point he is flatly met by the gentleman from Tennessee [Mr. Atkins], chairman of the House conference committee, who states that he was not only willing but offered to compromise, but that no compromise could be made unless he yielded everything which the Republican Senate seriously contended for.

" But the second and the great excuse of the gentleman was that the Democratic party is inaugurating a revolutionary method of legislation by attempting to coerce a coördinate branch of the Government by placing legislation upon an appropriation bill, and this he denounces as revolutionary. If the mere fact that legislation is found upon an appropriation bill be revolutionary, then the history of Republican legislation shows revolution after revolution that has been accomplished by the Republicans during its period of power, and one of these bloodless revolutions has been accomplished by the gentleman from Ohio himself, who, when he was chairman of the Committee on Appropriations, tacked on an appropriation bill one of these objectionable election laws. If it be revolutionary to put upon an appropriation bill a measure which perchance the President may not approve, then the freedom of this House might as well be surrendered, we might as well permit the President to dictate to us what kind of legislation is pleasing to his most excellent highness. If, again, it is rev-

olution to put upon an appropriation bill a measure which we have reason to believe or know will not meet the approval of the President, then a Republican Congress has set that example in its most offensive form. If it be coercion to do what we now propose, then a Republican House in 1856 undertook to coerce both a Democratic Senate and a Democratic President ; and in 1867 they absolutely did coerce Andrew Johnson into a surrender of a portion of his constitutional prerogatives. And all this was done upon an army appropriation bill. Yet the gentleman from Ohio, in a style that the elder Booth might have envied, has attempted to startle the country with the declaration that the Democratic party is entering upon a new and revolutionary method of legislation. The coercion of Andrew Johnson was one of the most iniquitous acts of usurpation ever perpetrated by the Republican party in the long list of its violations of constitutional rights. Andrew Johnson was a President elected by themselves, and yet, because he refused at their dictation to continue the violations of the Constitution which during a state of war were deemed necessary to save the Union, they pursued him with the remorseless fury of hyenas. In the act passed in March, 1867, they not only took from him his constitutional power to command the army, but, as has been well said by my colleague from Mississippi [Mr. Muldrow], they at the same time undertook to deprive ten sovereign States of their constitutional power to protect themselves ; they disbanded their militia, and forbade its reorganization without the consent of Congress. Every man who voted for that iniquitous measure was a Republican. But, as I have just said to gentlemen on the other side, there were some Republicans so shocked at this outrageous violation of constitutional right that they refused to vote with the majority. Andrew Johnson on that trying occasion set an example to his Republican friends which they would do well to remember now. Rather than see the wheels of this Government stopped, he signed that bill; but he signed it under protest, and thus made his appeal to the country.

" If it is deemed necessary to make another appeal to the people on the question now at issue, the Republican President can make his choice. He can either follow the example of Andrew Johnson, or he can, as the gentleman from Ohio said, destroy this Government without firing a single hostile gun. It is for him, not for us, to say which course he will choose.

" Now, Mr. Chairman, legislation upon appropriation bills has been denounced by the Democratic party in the past, and even now we admit that it should never be resorted to except in the most extreme cases like this, where the will of the people has time after time been defeated by factious opposition, and where the resolutions of a Republican caucus that no legislation except appropriation bills shall be acted on, warn us that our act can not be passed in any other mode."

Mr. Hurd: "Mr. Chairman, by the seventh section of the first article of the Constitution it is provided that ' All bills for raising revenue shall originate in the House of Representatives.' In the Forty-fifth Congress the House of Representatives, in the exercise of its unquestioned power, passed the army bill and the legislative bill, appropriating nearly fifty millions of money for the uses of the Government. To those bills they added certain provisions germane to their subject-matter and in the interest of economy, which repealed provisions of the existing statutes, most of which had been incorporated into the law of the land by being in the first instance attached to appropriation bills. These bills, when sent to the Senate, were amended, as that body had the undoubted power to do, by striking out these provisions to which I have referred. They went to committees of conference. Not having been a member of one of the committees of conference, nor familiar with the necessities of legislation at that time pending, I am unable to say what the propositions for settlement and adjustment of the differences between the two Houses were. I have heard it said upon the floor of this House that certain distinguished representatives of the Republican party were willing to concede very much to the wishes of the House, only insisting that there should be one amendment left out. These gentlemen had not power to speak for the body which differed with this House; and I do not know that any proposition was made by the Senate of the United States for a compromise. I do know that as a result of the disagreement of the committees of conference an extra session was called. I will not now discuss the question as to who is to be blamed for the extra session, excepting in the general discussion of the propositions that are involved in this debate. If the House were right in insisting upon these provisions, then the Senate was wrong in compelling an extra session. If the Senate were right in refusing to accept the propositions of the House, then the House was wrong; and I propose, in the few remarks that I shall submit to the consideration of this body to-day, to attempt to show that the House was right in every proposition which it insisted upon in the Forty-fifth Congress and which it insists upon now in the legislation of the Forty-sixth.

" Nor shall I discuss the method by which these amendments or provisions have been attempted to be made parts of the appropriation bills. If anything has been settled by the legislation of the last quarter of a century, it is that even general legislation may be tacked to appropriation bills; and certainly no man at any time in the history of this Government has disputed the proposition that measures in the interest of economy, propositions relating to the revenue, might be incorporated into bills when they were originated by the House under the authority of the section to which I have referred. Who was right? Who is right now? I say, Mr. Chairman, that the House of Representatives was right in insisting that these bills should be repealed. I shall not speak to-day of the test-oath bill. I shall speak only of the two others which relate to elections, because they both are governed by the same principles and both must be settled by the same constitutional doctrine.

" The House of Representatives insisted that the law should be amended so as to strike out that part which authorized the use of troops at the polls; that the law should be amended so that supervisors of elections appointed by Federal authority should no longer possess the power they now have; and that there should be a repeal of all the statutes which conferred upon officers of the United States the power to interfere with or regulate State elections. The House was right and it is right in the demand it makes now, because, first, these provisions are unconstitutional. They interfere with the right of suffrage; they attempt the control of voting in a State in the Union where by the laws of the State the voting power alone is conferred. Have gentlemen who have considered this question read recently section 2, article 1, of the Constitution of the United States, which declares that 'The House of Representatives shall be composed of members chosen every second year by the people of the several States, and the electors in each State shall have the qualifications requisite for electors of the most numerous branch of the State Legislature.' It is the most numerous branch of the State Legislature that determines the qualifications of electors and not the Constitution of the United States. There is no such thing as the right of suffrage for a citizen of the United States. The right of suffrage is possessed and enjoyed by a citizen of a State under the laws created by the State expressly recognized by the fundamental law of the land.

" And if any doubt upon this subject had ever been entertained, I ask you to refer to the decision of the Supreme Court of the United States recently made, in which every doubt is taken away: 'The power of Congress'—I read from 2 Otto, page 215, the syllabus of the case —'The power of Congress to legislate at all upon the subject of voting at State elections rests upon this amendment, and can be exercised by providing a punishment only when the wrongful refusal to receive the vote of a qualified elector at such elections is because of his color, race, or previous condition of servitude.' The highest judicial tribunal of the United States has determined that there is no power in the Congress of the United States to interfere with voting at the State elections excepting in the single instance where the power was conferred upon the General Government by the fifteenth amendment to the Constitution.

" Now, on what theory, I ask you, does this

legislation of which I speak·rest? On what theory does the United States Government send troops to the polls at a State election? On what theory do supervisors of elections stand at the polls to supervise and interfere with State elections? Only upon this: that the right of suffrage is a right guaranteed by the Constitution of the United States, in the exercise of which it is the business of Congress to protect the citizen. But, as I have shown you by the express phraseology of the Constitution and by the decision of the Supreme Court of the United States, no such right does exist to be protected by the Constitution of the United States and by the legislation of Congress. And, therefore, is not the conclusion inevitable and irresistible that any legislation upon the subject is unconstitutional?

"I know that gentlemen undertake to sustain the constitutionality of this legislation by referring to a provision of the Constitution, article 1, section 4: ' The times, places, and manner of holding elections for Senators and Representatives shall be prescribed in each State by the Legislature thereof; but the Congress may at any time by law make or alter such regulations, except as to the places of choosing Senators.' The manifest and true construction of this provision is that in the event of the people of a State failing to make provision on these subjects, Congress in the exercise of its discretion may make regulations on the subject, and that when States make regulations Congress may alter them as to ' the time, places, and manner of holding elections.'

" Who are the voters? They are determined by section 2, which I have already read. They are the persons who can vote under the law of a State and possess the qualifications requisite as voters of the most numerous branch of the State Legislature. The time of holding the election, the place of holding the election, the manner of holding the election, may be provided by Congress in the cases which I have suggested, but when the time and places of holding the elections are fixed, what power remains?

. "The manner of voting may be determined, whether it is to be *viva voce* or by ballot, as Congress may decide, and this view is abundantly justified by the debates in the constitutional convention, and in the various conventions of the States which ratified the Constitution originally, and the speech of Mr. Iredell, of the State of North Carolina, is unanswerable, who said that it never was intended or designed to give the power over the elections in the States to Congress, only the regulation of the time, places, and methods of voting. It has been contended in the progress of this argument that the power over this subject may be derived from that provision of the Constitution which authorizes Congress to guarantee to every State a republican form of government, and to send troops to suppress domestic violence on the call of the executive in the ab-

sence of the Legislature, or of the Legislature of a State.

" There may be such domestic violence at the polls that the Governor of the State, if the Legislature be not in session, would be bound to call upon the President of the United States for assistance, and in such cases as that the power of the Government can be properly exercised; but the ground on which the power is exercised is, that it is at the request of the authorities of the State. The troops of the United States have no business at the polls except for the suppression of violence or for repelling invasion at the request of the State authorities, the State authorities having first indicated to the General Government the desire of assistance. Is not this very clause to which I have referred an additional argument in favor of the position that this law is unconstitutional? The troops of the United States can only be used to suppress domestic violence or repel foreign invasion, and here is a law which proposes to send troops to the polls at any time, at the order of anybody, without any request of the State authorities; and it is the plainest violation of that provision of the Constitution which directs the only way in which the troops of the United States shall be sent to a State. The Constitution thereby prohibited any other way of sending troops to a State. I say, then, that these provisions should be repealed because they are in direct conflict with the fundamental law of the country and in the plainest violation of an expressed adjudication of the highest judicial tribunal of the land.

"In the second place, these laws should be repealed because they introduce a dangerous method and practice into the conducting of elections and the administration of justice. They authorize men to interfere with the election of the local officers of the State. In the State of Ohio, and I believe in most of the States of the Union, the law is that all officers shall be voted for on a general ticket—State officers, county officers, municipal officers, township officers, and members of Congress. In the State of Ohio every man whose name is on the ballot is voted for as an officer of the State, and yet this provision of this law proposes to put United States supervisors to supervise the counting and casting of the votes for county officers and State officers. I submit that no such power was ever intended by the Constitution of the United States to be conferred upon Congress; and I submit that the State can not be shorn of her sovereignty in this way, as is claimed by the Republican party by such a provision as this, without danger to its institutions.

" What arises from the very section to which I have referred? Who are the voters? They are the persons whose qualifications are fixed by the constitution of the State, and under this law the supervisors of election are stationed at the polls, for what? If the law of Congress fixed the qualifications for the electors of a State, then it might be proper that the Federal supervisors should be present to interpret and execute the laws; but under what doctrine of constitutional law, on what principle of government will you say that supervisors appointed by the Federal Government, strangers to the laws of Ohio, shall stand at the polls and interpret our laws and execute them?

"The third objection is that these supervising officers are armed with authority unknown in the history of the common law or State laws. They have authority at the polls on the day of election to arrest, without warrant, any man whom they may suspect of being about to engage in a violation of the laws. There is no principle of common law or State law which can authorize the arrest of citizens on suspicion of an intention to commit an offense. Here are men who honestly believe that they have the right to vote, and who on going to the polls to deposit their ballots are confronted with this extraordinary invasion of the rights of civil liberty and arrested, and, as in the city of New York, incarcerated in many instances for days. What an extraordinary scene was presented for a republican government in the city of New York at the last election! Thousands of men who had failed to get out their naturalization papers in a way that suited the judgment of the supervisor of elections were arrested upon sight. At one time over six hundred men were under arrest who had gone to the polls honestly believing that they had the right to vote. They had committed no breach of the peace; they had committed no felony. They had attempted to exercise what they believed to be their right and their duty. Yet they were incarcerated and prevented from voting. Since that time a judicial tribunal to which the case was referred has determined that these men were not guilty; that they were innocent; that they were entitled to vote at the election. A power so outrageous as that upon the right of suffrage and the exercise of the duties of a freeman, I venture to say, has not within this century been exercised before under any government, monarchical or despotic.

"Another point which I urge against them as a reason for their repeal, and one which so overshadowingly is greater than the others that I have been loath and hesitated to discuss it. It is that these measures in their very nature and essence are dangerous and destructive to civil liberty. All history is full of warnings upon this subject. No republic which has ever perished from the face of the earth has gone to its grave save through military influence. The familiarization of the people through the army with the forms of despotism, the gradual abrogation of the forms of the republic, and the ultimate subversion of all civil government have marked the career of every republic from its birth to its grave, and shall we escape the force and application of

the universal rule? Is power less sweet, are rights more sacred, are liberties more secure in this country, so that we can dare without harm to trifle with a danger that has wrought ruin everywhere before? From lands where republics have died and where monarchies have been erected on their ruins; from lands where the contest for liberty is now going on; from lands where the shadow of despotism darkens every household and compels every citizen to seek shelter upon some foreign shore, helpless to free himself at home, there come the solemn notes of warning against military interference.

"From the presence of troops at the polls to the control of elections by troops is but a single step. In that step free elections are gone; and free elections are the source of free government and the author and originator of its power. Troops at the polls mean intimidation of voters; troops at the polls mean as its result the registration of the will of the commander; troops at the polls mean the substitution of the bayonet for the ballot, the enthronement of the Commander-in-Chief, and the deposition of the President. I have been astounded, as this debate has continued, to hear from gentlemen upon the other side arguments in favor of the use of troops at the polls, the last place in the world where such arguments should be heard; but my regret is lost in joy when I recollect that the party of the army is not in power in this Congress.

"I do not know, Mr. Chairman, even what will be the action of this House upon this bill. I certainly do not know what will be the action of the President of the United States when the bill is submitted to him, if it shall pass; much less can I know what will be the action of the House when the bill may be returned to us with his objections. But this much I do know, that if the power of withholding supplies shall be exercised, then never in all the contests for liberty in English history, never in all the victories which have made that little stormy island the center of civilization of the world, never in all the struggles for the rights of man, was the power of holding supplies exercised more wisely than it will be when we exercise it to preserve the freedom of elections, to subordinate in times of peace the military power to the civil authority, and to preserve pure and uncontaminated the sources of free government."

Mr. Robeson of New Jersey: "It seems to have been assumed on the other side of this Chamber that this is nothing but the repeal of a section of a law enacted in 1865; that it is a negative and not an affirmative provision. Let us see exactly what it is:

"That section 2002 of the Revised Statutes be amended so as to read as follows:

"'No military or naval officer, or other person engaged in the civil, military, or naval service of the United States, shall order, bring, keep, or have under his authority or control any troops or armed men at the place where any general or special election is held in any State, unless it be necessary to repel the armed enemies of the United States.'

"This omits the other exception contained in the original law, 'or to keep the peace at the polls.' This, then, refers to civil officers, and is an affirmative repeal of the right of the civil officers of the Government to keep the peace at the polls. We are not standing here on this side of the House resisting a proposition to take away a real or imaginary power of a standing army to crush the rights of freemen at the polls. We are resisting an affirmative enactment, for the repeal of an exception in a restricting law is itself an affirmative enactment. We are, then, resisting an affirmative enactment which designs to take away the power, not of the officers of the army alone, not of the officers at all, because they under that law as it now stands only have power as they may be ordered or summoned forth by the civil officer to whom the peace of his bailiwick is intrusted. What then is intended by this provision? To restrain the civil officers of the United States Government from keeping the peace at any election in any State, whether it be a United States election or not. By what means? By civil means, not by military means, for the rights of the civil officer, the marshal of the district if you please, to summon the *posse comitatus*, his right to summon any military organizations if they be within the body of his bailiwick, the right to summon armed troops to sustain his civil power, is a civil and not a military right, and is in the interest of the inviolability and the strengthening of the law against, if need be, armed military force. Can that be denied by any lawyer? Can it be controverted by any man?"

Mr. Kimmel: "Will the gentleman describe the bailiwick of United States officers?"

Mr. Robeson: "The jurisdiction of the United States runs into the States whenever it has a United States duty to perform. That is not only good logic but good law."

Mr. Kimmel: "To preserve the peace of an election at a State election?"

Mr. Robeson: "Wherever the United States has guaranteed a right, wherever a right is derived from the Constitution of the United States and is guaranteed or is secured by it, there the United States has the right and must have the power to enforce and carry out that right."

Mr. Kimmel: "What right has it guaranteed in this respect?"

Mr. Robeson: "It has guaranteed the right to every man in the State of Maryland, who has the right to vote for the most numerous branch of the Maryland Legislature, to vote at a peaceable election for members of Congress.

"I know what the decisions of the Supreme Court are upon that subject, and I will meet them fairly. I love the law and its principles, and I shall not shrink from the full effect of the decisions as they are pronounced by the highest tribunals of the country. I know that the Supreme Court of the United States has de-clared that the United States has no voter 'of its own creation' in the States. I know that it has declared that the right of suffrage is not given in the States by the Constitution of the United States. But that does not cover the case. What does the Constitution say? 'The House of Representatives shall be composed of members chosen every second year by the people of the several States; and the electors in each State shall have the qualifications requisite for electors of the most numerous branch of the Legislature.' The right to vote for that most numerous branch of the Legislature is given by the States. The qualifications are made by the States. The United States does not confer the right of suffrage upon these individuals, but it adopts to its right of suffrage and takes as its voters a class which have already the right of suffrage given it by the States. It makes them its voters for the election of its officers, and if it does its duty it is bound to guarantee to them a free and fair election.

"Let me be fully understood. It is technically and verbally true that the Constitution of the United States does not confer the right of suffrage upon the individuals who vote for the most numerous branch of the State Legislature. That right of suffrage and the qualifications necessary to it are prescribed by the State. But the Constitution of the United States does say that every man who does belong to that class, every man who has that qualification, shall be an elector for members of this House. That is the right which it guarantees. It does not give to any individual the right to belong to that class; but when he belongs to that class it gives him the right to vote at an election for a member of Congress.

"What we are resisting here is an attempt to take away the power, not of the officers of the army, not of the commanding general, not of anybody clothed with military authority, but of the civil officers of the Government to keep the peace at the polls if need be by summoning all the power of his bailiwick, including any armed force there may be in it. That is what we are resisting here. We are not here in advocacy of a war measure, but we are here to resist this restraint of civil right.

"My friend, the gentleman from Ohio [Mr. Hurd], the other day said the danger of republics came from military usurpation; that all that had perished had fallen by the sword. Well, sir, and if this be true, how do they fall by the sword? They fall by the sword when the laws are nugatory, when civil rights are denied, when the civil power of the Government can not be enforced. This right which we are now defending is a civil power given to the officers of the law, which should in time of peace be superior to the military power of a country. It is a power which may be exercised in an extreme case to summon the brave hearts and strong arms of the citizen soldiery of any section to put down any attempt of an armed usurping power to interfere with free elections. This is not a fight we are making in behalf of a standing army; it is a fight in behalf of civil process and the power which must lie behind it, if it is to be effective.

"I have no right to speak for the President of the United States, but it has been given out here in debate, it has been given out through channels more or less authorized, it speaks to the common sense of the country when we see these clauses put upon an appropriation bill, that the gentlemen on the other side of the Chamber mean to say to us and to the President, 'Take the whole dose or none'; that they mean to say, 'Pass this affirmative repealing clause taking away the powers of civil officers to keep the peace at the polls, *or do not take the appropriations of the bill.* We do not want peace at the polls; take away the power of the law to enforce peace there, or we shall refuse your supplies.'

"It was argued by my friend from Ohio the other day that this position was right and proper, and he said that, if this should be done, there never was a case where it was more called for. Mr. Chairman, we are here members of a Government under a written Constitution which defines and limits the powers of all branches of the Government. One branch is hardly more popular than another. We have neither King nor Lords nor Commons. We have elements of popular government coördinate under our Constitution; three of them are responsible more or less directly to the people. The President of the United States goes to the people every four years to answer for his conduct and to receive their condemnation or their approval. This House goes every two years. Both are popular, both represent the people within those coördinate spheres and those limits which the Constitution has assigned. There is no analogy with the organization of the English Government, which has a monarch with kingly and royal prerogatives, who represents himself, his family, his royalty, his prerogative, and his inheritance, and a house of peers which represents their property, their dignity, and their peerage, and the House of Commons, which alone is elected by the people and alone is responsible to them. Here all the branches of our popular Government respond to the bidding and are dependent on the votes of the people. Our Constitution provides that when there is a law on the statute-book it shall not be repealed unless that repeal has the assent of both branches of Congress and the approval of the President; and if it fail to receive the approval of the President, then the law shall not be repealed unless two thirds of both Houses concur in that repeal. That is all that the Constitution provides on this subject, and it is all the power under the Constitution which gentlemen on the other side of this chamber and at the other end of this Capitol have. And, if they ask more than that, they ask what the Constitution does not give them, because the Constitution says that when a law is once on the statute-book it shall not be swept away if the President and more than one third of either House object. That is the limit and extent of their constitutional right and power of repeal.

"And when they come here, not waiting for the time which they think they see, when they shall have all the branches of this Government under their own control, and say, 'We will force this repeal, although not constitutionally entitled to it, by withholding supplies,' do they not then do an unconstitutional thing? If they say to another branch of this Government, 'Give us what we have no constitutional right to ask, and if you do not give it we will refuse to do our constitutional duty, refuse to do what the Constitution requires us to do,' is not their action then unconstitutional? If they say to those who deny them, and who have the constitutional right to deny them, 'You shall agree, or we will refuse to discharge our constitutional duties; we will refuse to pay the salary of the President; we will refuse to pay the salaries and expenses of the courts; we will refuse to supply the money necessary to carry on the machinery of this Government,' is not that unconstitutional? And if it be unconstitutional to do that; if their refusal goes to the destruction of the Government itself; if it stops the wheels of Government; if it brings us to a standstill and a destruction, is not that revolutionary."

Mr. Sparks: "I now move the committee rise and report the bill and amendments to the House."

The motion was agreed to.

Mr. Sparks: "I demand the previous question on the bill and amendments."

The amendments of the committee were concurred in. The bill, as amended, was ordered to be engrossed and read a third time.

The question was taken, and it was passed as follows:

YEAS—Aiken, Armfield, Atherton, Atkins, Bachman, Beltzhoover, Bicknell, Blackburn, Bliss, Blount, Bouck, Bragg, Bright, Buckner, Cabell, Caldwell, Carlisle, Chalmers, Clardy, John B. Clark, Jr., Clymer, Cobb, Coffroth, Colerick, Converse, Cook, Covert, Cravens, Culberson, Davidson, Joseph J. Davis, Lowndes H. Davis, De La Matyr, Deuster Dibrell, Dickey, Dunn, Elam, Ellis, Evins, Ewing, Felton, Finley, Ford, Forney, Frost, Geddes, Gibson, Gillette, Goode, Gunter, N. J. Hammond, John T. Harris, Hatch, Henkle, Henry, Herbert, Herndon, Hill, Hooker, Hostetler, House, Hull, Hunton, Hurd, Johnston, Jones, Kenna, Kimmel, King, Kitchin, Klotz, Knott, Ladd, Le Fevre, Lewis, Lounsbery, Lowe, Manning, Benj. F. Martin, Edward L. Martin, McKenzie, McLane, McMahon, McMillin, Mills, Money, Morrison, Morse, Muldrow, Muller, Murch, Myers, New, Nicholls, O'Brien, O'Connor, O'Reilly, Persons, Phelps, Phister, Poehler, Reagan, John S. Richardson, Richmond, Robertson, Ross, Rothwell, John W. Ryon, Samford, Sawyer, Scales, Shelley, Simonton, James W. Singleton, O. R. Singleton, Slemons, Hezekiah B. Smith, William E. Smith, Sparks, Speer, Springer, Steele, Stephens, Stevenson, Talbot, Taylor, Thompson, Tillman, R. W. Townshend, Tucker, Oscar Turner, Thomas Turner, Vance, Waddill,

Warner, Weaver, Wellborn–Whiteaker, Whitthorne, Thomas Williams, Willis, Wilson, Wise, Fernando Wood, Wright, Yocum, Casey Young—148.

NAYS—Nelson W. Aldrich, William Aldrich, Anderson, Bailey, Baker, Ballou, Barber, Barlow, Belford, Bingham, Blake, Bowman, Boyd, Brewer, Briggs, Brigham, Browne, Burrows, Calkins, Camp, Cannon, Carpenter, Caswell, Chittenden, Claflin, Rush Clark, Conger, Cowgill, Crapo, Crowley, Daggett, George R. Davis, Deering, Dunnell, Dwight, Einstein, Errett, Farr, Ferdon, Field, Fisher, Forsythe, Fort, Frye, Garfield, Godshalk, Hall, John Hammond, Benj. W. Harris, Haskell, Hawk, Hawley, Hayes, Hazelton, Hellman, Henderson, Hiscock, Horr, Houk, Humphrey, James, Jorgensen, Joyce, Keifer, Kelley, Ketcham, Killinger, Lapham, Lindsey, Loring, Marsh, Mason, McCoid, McCook, McGowan, McKinley, Miles, Mitchell, Monroe, Morton, Neal, Newberry, Norcross, O'Neill, Orth, Osmer, Overton, Pierce, Pound, Prescott, Price, Reod, Rice, D. P. Richardson, Robeson, Robinson, William A. Russell, Thomas Ryan, Sapp, Shallenberger, Sherwin, A. Herr Smith, Starin, Stone, Thomas, Amos Townsend, Tyler, J. T. Updegraff, Thomas Updegraff, Urner, Valentine, Van Aernam, Van Voorhis, Voorhis, Wait, Ward, Washburn, White, Wilber, C. G. Williams, Willits, Walter A. Wood—122.

NOT VOTING—Acklen, Bayne, Beale, Bland, Butterworth, Alvah A. Clark, Cox, Dick, Harmer, Hubbell, Lay, Joseph J. Martin, Miller, Daniel L. Russell, Wells, Thomas L. Young—16.

In the Senate, on April 15th, the bill from the House was considered.

Mr. Blaine: "I will now offer an amendment to come in at the close of section 6."

The Chief Clerk: "It is proposed to add at the end of section 6 the following:

"And any military, naval, or civil officer, or any other person, who shall, except for the purposes herein named, appear armed with a deadly weapon of any description, either concealed or displayed, within a mile of any polling place where a general or special election for Representative to Congress is being held, shall, on conviction, be punished with a fine not less than five hundred nor more than five thousand dollars, or with imprisonment for a period not less than six months nor more than five years, or with both fine and imprisonment, at the discretion of the court."

Mr. Blaine: "Mr. President, the existing section of the Revised Statutes numbered 2002 reads thus:

"No military or naval officer, or other person engaged in the civil, military, or naval service of the United States, shall order, bring, keep, or have under his authority or control, any troops or armed men at the place where any general or special election is held in any State, unless it be necessary to repel the armed enemies of the United States, or to keep the peace at the polls.

"The object of the proposed section 6 is to get rid of the eight closing words, namely, 'or to keep the peace at the polls,' and therefore the mode of legislation proposed in the army bill now before the Senate is an unusual mode; it is an extraordinary mode. If you want to take off a single sentence at the end of a section in the Revised Statutes, the ordinary way is to strike off those words, but the mode chosen in this bill is to repeat and reenact the whole section, leaving those few words out. While I do not wish to be needlessly suspicious on a small point, I am quite persuaded that this

did not happen by accident, but that it came by design. If I may so speak, it came of cunning, the intent being to create the impression that, whereas the Republicans in the administration of the General Government had been using troops right and left, hither and thither, in every direction, as soon as the Democrats got power they enacted this section. I can imagine Democratic candidates for Congress all over the country reading this section to gaping and listening audiences as one of the first offsprings of Democratic reform, whereas every word of it, every syllable of it, from its first to its last, is the enactment of a Republican Congress.

"I repeat that this unusual form presents a dishonest issue, whether so intended or not. It presents the issue that as soon as the Democrats get possession of the Federal Government they intended to enact the clause which is thus embraced. The law was passed by a Republican Congress in 1865. There were forty-six Senators sitting in this Chamber at the time, of whom only ten or at most eleven were Democrats. The House of Representatives was overwhelmingly Republican. We were in the midst of a war. The Republican Administration had a million or possibly twelve hundred thousand bayonets at its command. Thus circumstanced and thus surrounded, with the amplest possible power to interfere with elections had they so designed, with soldiers in every hamlet and county of the United States, the Republican party themselves placed that provision on the statute-book, and Abraham Lincoln, their President, signed it. I beg you to observe, Mr. President, that this is the first instance in the legislation of the United States in which any restrictive clause whatever was put upon the statute-book in regard to the use of troops at the polls. The Republican party did it with the Senate and the House in their control. Abraham Lincoln signed it when he was Commander-in-Chief of an army larger than ever Napoleon Bonaparte had at his command. So much by way of correcting an ingenious and studied attempt at misrepresentation.

"The alleged object is to strike out the few words that authorize the use of troops to keep peace at the polls. This country has been alarmed, I rather think indeed amused, at the great effort made to create a widespread impression that the Republican party relies for its popular strength upon the use of the bayonet. This Democratic Congress has attempted to give a bad name to this country throughout the civilized world, and to give it on a false issue. They have raised an issue that has no foundation in fact, that is false in whole and detail, false in the charge, false in all the specifications. That impression sought to be created, as I say, not only throughout the North American continent but in Europe to-day, is that elections are attempted in this country to be controlled by the bayonet. I denounce it here as a false issue. I am not at liberty to say that any gentleman making the issue knows it to be false; I hope he does not; but I am going to prove to him that it is false, and that there is not a solitary inch of solid earth on which to rest the foot of any man that makes that issue. I have in my hand an official transcript of the location and the number of all the troops of the United States east of Omaha. By 'east of Omaha,' I mean all the United States east of the Mississippi River and that belt of States that border the Mississippi River on the west, including forty-one million at least out of the forty-five million people that this country is supposed to contain to-day. In that magnificent area, I will not pretend to state its extent, but with forty-one million people, how many troops of the United States are there to-day? Would any Senator on the opposite side like to guess, or would he like to state how many men with muskets in their hands there are in the vast area I have named? There are two thousand seven hundred and ninety-seven! And not one more. From the headwaters of the Mississippi River to the lakes, and down the great chain of lakes, and down the Saint Lawrence and down the valley of the Saint John and down the Saint Oroix striking the Atlantic Ocean and following it down to Key West, around the Gulf, up to the mouth of the Mississippi again, a frontier of eight thousand miles either bordering on the ocean or upon foreign territory is guarded by these troops. Within this domain forty-five fortifications are manned and eleven arsenals protected. There are sixty troops to every million of people. And the entire South has eleven hundred and fifty-five soldiers to intimidate, overrun, oppress, and destroy the liberties of fifteen million people! In the Southern States there are twelve hundred and three counties. If you distribute the soldiers, there is not quite one for each county ; and when I give the counties I give them from the census of 1870. If you distribute them territorially, there is one for every seven hundred square miles of territory, so that if you make a territorial distribution, I would remind the honorable Senator from Delaware, if I saw him in his seat, that the quota for his State would be three, 'one ragged sergeant and two abreast,' as the old song has it. That is the force ready to destroy the liberties of Delaware!

"Mr. President, it was said, as the old maxim has it, that the soothsayers of Rome could not look each other in the face without smiling. There are not two Democratic Senators on that side who can go into the cloak-room and look each other in the face without smiling at this talk, or more appropriately I should say without blushing, the whole thing is such a prodigious and absolute farce, such a miserably manufactured false issue, such a pretense without the slightest foundation in the world, and talked about most and denounced the loudest in States that have not and have not had a sin-

gle Federal soldier. In New England we have three hundred and eighty soldiers. Throughout the South it does not run quite seventy to the million people. In New England we have absolutely one hundred and twenty soldiers to the million. New England is far more overrun to-day by the Federal soldier, immensely more than the whole South is. I never heard anybody complain about it in New England, or express any very great fear of their liberties being endangered by the presence of a handful of troops.

"As I have said, the tendency of this talk is to give us a bad name in Europe. Republican institutions are looked upon there with jealousy. Every misrepresentation, every slander is taken up and exaggerated and talked about to our discredit, and the Democratic party of the country to-day stand indicted, and I here indict them, for public slander of their country, creating the impression in the civilized world that we are governed by a ruthless military despotism. I wonder how amazing it would be to any man in Europe, familiar as Europeans are with great armies, if he were told that over a territory larger than France and Spain and Portugal and Great Britain and Holland and Belgium and the German Empire all combined, there were but eleven hundred and fifty-five soldiers! That is all this Democratic howl, this mad cry, this false issue, this absurd talk is based on—the presence of eleven hundred and fifty-five soldiers on eight hundred and fifty thousand square miles of territory—not double the number of the Democratic police in the city of Baltimore, not a third of the police in the city of New York, not double the Democratic police in the city of New Orleans. I repeat, the number indicts them, it stamps the whole cry as without any foundation, it derides the issue as a false and scandalous and partisan makeshift.

"You simply want to get rid of the supervision by the Federal Government of the election of Representatives to Congress through civil means; and therefore this bill connects itself directly with another bill, and you can not discuss this military bill without discussing a bill which we had before us last winter, known as the legislative, executive, and judicial appropriation bill. I am quite well aware, I profess to be as well aware as any one, that it is not permissible for me to discuss a bill that is pending before the other House. I am quite well aware that propriety and parliamentary rule forbid that I should speak of what is done in the House of Representatives; but I know very well that I am not forbidden to speak of that which is not done in the House of Representatives. I am quite free to speak of the things that are not done there, and therefore I am free to declare that neither this military bill nor the legislative, executive, and judicial appropriation bill ever emanated from any committee of the House of Representatives at all; they are not the work of any committee of the House of Representatives, and, although the present House of Representatives is almost evenly balanced in party division, there has been allowed no solitary suggestion to come from the minority of that House in regard to the shaping of these bills. Where do they come from? We are not left to infer; we are not even left to the Yankee privilege of guessing, because we know. The Senator from Kentucky [Mr. Beck] obligingly told us — I have his exact words here—'that the honorable Senator from Ohio [Mr. Thurman] was the chairman of a committee appointed by the Democratic party to see how it was best to present all these questions before us.' Therefore, when I discuss these two bills together, I am violating no parliamentary law, I am discussing the offspring and the creation of the Democratic caucus of which the Senator from Ohio, whom I do not see in his seat, is the chairman.

"Now, Mr. President, I say this bill connects itself directly with the provisions which are inserted by the Democratic caucus in the legislative, executive, and judicial bill. The two stand together; they can not be separated; because if to-day we enact that no civil officer whatever shall appear under any circumstances with armed men at the polls—I am not speaking of Federal troops or military or naval officers—I should like to know how, if you strike that out to-day in the military bill that is pending, you are going to enforce any provisions of the election laws even if we leave them standing. Take this section of the election law, section 2024 of the Revised Statutes:

"The marshal or his general deputies, or such special deputies as are thereto specially empowered by him, in writing, and under his hand and seal, whenever he or either or any of them is forcibly resisted in executing their duties under this title, or shall, by violence, threats, or menaces, be prevented from executing such duties, or from arresting any person who has committed any offense for which the marshal or his general or his special deputies are authorized to make such arrest, are, and each of them is, empowered to summon and call to his aid the bystanders or *posse comitatus* of his district.

"I should like any one to tell me whether a marshal 'can call together armed men under that if you repeal this section in the military bill. Under heavy penalties you say that no civil officer whatever, no matter what the disturbances, at an election of Representatives to Congress—no civil officer of the United States shall keep order. You do not say that in that same election the State officer may not be there with all the force he chooses, legal or illegal. You say that the United States in an election which specially concerns the Federal Government shall not have anything whatever to do with it. That is what you say, although the Constitution, as broadly as language can express it, gives the Government of the United States, if it chooses to exercise it, the absolute control of the whole subject—

familiar to school-boys, who have even once read the Constitution, in the clause: 'the times, places, and manner of holding elections for Senators and Representatives, shall be prescribed in each State by the Legislature thereof; but the Congress may at any time by law make or alter such regulations, except as to the places of choosing Senators.' And every one knows that the contemporaneous exposition of that part of the Constitution, familiar also to every one in the country, the exposition by Madison and Hamilton, was to the effect that 'every government ought to contain in itself the means of its own preservation,' and according to Mr. Madison, quoting a Southern authority, it was 'more consonant to just theories to intrust the Union with the care of its own existence than to transfer that care to any other hands.'

"There is not the slightest possible denial here that this is a constitutional exercise of power. If there is such a denial, it is a mere individual opinion. There has been no adjudication in the least degree looking to the unconstitutionality of these laws. Your individual opinion is no better than mine; mine is no better than that of any other man who can hear a horn blown from the front steps of the Capitol. No individual opinion is worth anything. We have a department of the Government to pass upon the question. The legislative department has enacted these laws under what is believed to be a clear and explicit grant of power, and you have never had it judicially determined otherwise. But now you propose to assault the election laws, the supervisors, and the marshals in this military bill; and under the pretense of getting rid of troops at the polls you propose that no Federal officer—no civil officer of the Federal Government—shall be there. That is the design; that is the plain, palpable object."

Mr. Withers of Maryland: "Mr. President, as the Senator to whom the charge of this bill has been intrusted by the committee, I propose to make one or two brief statements in response to the rhetorical and highly imaginative utterance to which we have just listened.

"The object of the Committee on Appropriations, or a majority of that committee, in reporting this bill, was simply to provide for the repeal of a law under the operation of which it is possible that the freedom of elections may be utterly destroyed. The fact which has been alluded to by the Senator from Maine so frequently and forcibly that few soldiers were to be found now in any of the States east of the Mississippi, and his futile attempt to divert public attention from the principle which lies at the bottom of this great question to a consideration of that immaterial issue, will not, I am sure, produce much effect upon this Senate or upon the country. It is not a question before this body to decide whether a sufficient number of soldiers are to be found distributed among the States of this Union to dominate and control elections; but the question is, whether under the conditions of the existing law it may not be possible for an Executive who shall so desire to so distribute and so use the soldiery as to destroy the freedom of elections. It is not to confront a present danger which threatens imminently to interfere with elections, but it is to remove from the present or any future Executive the temptation which the possession of this power would offer, should he desire so to do, to destroy the liberties of this people, and erect upon the ruins of the Republic a despotism supported by the arms of a soldiery. Is this a vain and chimerical fear? The Senator from Maine seems so to regard it; and yet, if we look back at the history of every free people who have ever lost their liberties, we shall find that without one solitary exception their liberties have been destroyed through the operation of the military, through the agency of its commander, or under the direction of an ambitious prince or ruler.

"Mr. President, I will state frankly and fully that it is not in the utterances of Senators and Representatives discussing the policy of a party that we are to find those opinions upon which we can most rely in the settlement of so vital a principle as this. I do not profess myself to be above that silent influence which is exerted by political policy in forming opinions upon questions which press upon us for immediate solution; and, whether it be with regard to the use of troops to enforce the fugitive slave law or the various acts which were passed about the time Kansas was erected into a separate State, I am free to state that the parties held positions on those questions which are now precisely reversed. But, sir, I wish to go back to a period antecedent to this; I wish to view the question in the light of the declarations of those Senators who were part and parcel of this Constitution, of those who were contemporaneous with its formation; and I aver on this floor, without the fear of successful contradiction, that in the debates, both in the convention which framed the Constitution and in the State conventions which approved and ratified it, this question of a standing army and its possible use in controlling and dominating elections was, without distinction of party, the point which elicited most interest and most debate, and, whether in Federal Massachusetts or in Republican Virginia, those who stood highest in the councils of each of those States bore united testimony to the dangers to liberty which were involved in the presence of a standing army. It is not, therefore, out of place that I should solicit the attention of the Senate to the discussions which accompanied the adoption of the Constitution as furnishing opinions on which we can best rely as to the dangers that lurk in this feature of the question which we are now discussing.

"I have before me authorities from the debates which were held on this subject in various States, New York, Massachusetts, and Virginia, notably the latter, where the contemporaneous opinion of those men who took an active part in the formation of this instrument, with one consent, declared that the liberties of no people could be regarded as safe in the presence of a military force wielded by the ruler of that country. I will not detain the Senate by reciting them *in extenso*. I simply remark that Hamilton himself, who was the head and front of the Federalists of that day, and who was accused of a strong leaning to monarchical government, admitted the dangers which lurked in the weakness of our Constitution in that regard. But it was George Mason of Virginia who more than any one else was instrumental in framing and shaping this instrument, who gave utterance to that sentiment which has lived from that time to the present, and is now accepted as an axiom among all lovers of civil liberty, that 'the liberty of the people has been destroyed only by those who are military commanders.'

"It is but a puerile effort (if Senators will pardon me for using the term) when a Senator on this floor rises in his place, and, instead of attacking the principles which underlie this great question, devotes himself for half an hour to the attempt to ridicule the arguments of those who oppose him by stating the fact that only one soldier to a county is to be found throughout the States east of the Mississippi. It is an admission on the part of that Senator of the poverty of his case when he can find no stronger argument to use in opposition to the bill which is now before this body. It is not that Senators here fear the presence of one or two or fifty men who may be in their respective States, but it is that a provision of law now exists which renders it possible that not only those who are there, but others, may be brought there if the exigency requires it, and the condition of the public mind or the exigencies of party necessity demand that they should be so used to dominate and control elections. In other words, the presence of the military at the polls is absolutely incompatible with free government; and I announce that as the principle upon which this bill, with this clause of which we hear so much, has been based."

Mr. Voorhees of Indiana: "In the present instance we have vastly more than the mere menace or threat of future subjugation by virtue of the laws under discussion. We are not left to conjecture what will be done hereafter. Already these laws have been executed over the prostrate forms and liberties of American citizens in a manner and to an extent which would arouse any people in Europe to revolt, except, perhaps, the serfs of Russia. I speak not now of the South, which has so long been considered a legitimate prey to the spoiler, but of the great, dominant, and stalwart North. Look to New York, that mighty emporium of the wealth and commerce of the western hemisphere. Scenes have been enacted there within the last few years which bring shame and disgrace to the Republic wherever they are known. John I. Davenport is chief supervisor of elections in the city of New York, appointed by the Circuit Court of the United States. He is also the clerk of the United States Circuit Court, and a United States Commissioner. With all the powers of these manifold official positions combined in his own person, he has indeed been the autocrat of the ballot-box. In the elections of 1876 he had under him one thousand and seventy supervisors, twenty-five hundred deputy marshals, and an indefinite number of commissioners, at an expense for them and for himself of $94,587. In 1878 he employed twelve hundred and twenty - five supervisors, thirteen hundred and fifty deputy marshals, and commissioners in proportion, for all whose pay and expenses he drew upon the money of the people in the Treasury. In June, 1876, as clerk of the United States Circuit Court, he issued warrants for the arrest of twenty-six hundred naturalized voters to be brought before him as United States commissioner and chief supervisor for the purpose of making them surrender their naturalization papers. The Federal courts themselves afterward held that the naturalization papers in question were all legal and valid, but the desired result had been accomplished. The terror inspired by these arrests intimidated thousands from going to the polls. It became well known that there was no personal security in New York in connection with the elections, and the poor, the timid, and the humble staid away. The same course was pursued in 1878. During the summer of that year nine thousand four hundred citizens were notified that they would be arrested unless they surrendered their naturalization papers to the head overseer, John I. Davenport. In the month of October, 1878, thirty-one hundred persons were actually arrested and a reign of terror inaugurated just in advance of the election. The pretense that these persons held fraudulent naturalization papers had already been shown to be false, but it was necessary to party success that an alarm should be raised and a panic created in the minds of foreign-born citizens and of the poor laboring classes generally. The movement was successful, and it has been estimated that ten thousand legal voters remained away from the polls rather than risk the jails and the prison-pens of the chief supervisor and his subordinates. But it was reserved for the day of election itself to give free scope to the frightful powers with which this band of Federal ku-klux is invested. Those who braved the dangers which environed the ballot-box, and approached it as if they were still freemen, soon found their mistake. They quickly ascertained that the previous threats and warnings which they had heard were neither idle nor unmeaning. As a specimen of thousands of similar occurrences on election day, I quote a statement recently made by a member of the other branch of

Congress from New York. Speaking from his place on the floor, he said:

"A neighbor of mine, who had resided in the same district for seventeen years and a soldier of the Union Army at that, was arrested. I was asked to go to the republican headquarters in an adjoining district, whither he had been taken. The street for an entire block was lined with carriages, in which the unfortunate citizens who had fallen into the hands of the Philistines had been or were to be conveyed. When I entered the building I found the front room decorated with the paraphernalia of a political headquarters, and filled with Republican politicians. In the back room a United States commissioner was holding court. The door was closed, watched by a Cerberus. No one was allowed inside but the prisoners and the Republican managers. After about half an hour's waiting I was informed by the doorkeeper that the man I was looking for was no longer there. I asked whither he had been taken. 'Suppose to Fort Davenport,' was the laconic reply.

"Sir, most likely this soldier of the Union Army was with Grant in the Wilderness, at Cold Harbor, and at Petersburg; or perhaps he was with Sherman in his march to the sea, and as a soldier of the Army of the Tennessee took part in the bloody battle of Atlanta. Wherever he was, however, and on whatever field he was baptized with fire, he was assured that he was offering his life for the preservation of the Union under the safeguards of constitutional liberty. He was also assured that human slavery should not survive the triumph of the Union cause, and he rejoiced to believe that his country would in fact soon be the land only of the free. What must have been his reflections, therefore, in November last to find, in attempting to cast his ballot, that he was as very a slave in the hands of a brutal overseer as any negro ever driven in a cotton-field, and that he had no more power under existing laws to protect his personal freedom than an African bondsman on the auction-block before the war. Did he not, most probably, conclude that one of the fruits of the war, under the nurture and cultivation of the Republican party, was the extension of slavery, rather than its overthrow and destruction? Was he not impressed with the fact that the liberation of one race had been followed by the enslavement of another? What were his thoughts, and the thoughts of his fellow victims, who had also been his fellow soldiers, as they lay like felons in prison, in 'Fort Davenport,' for offering to vote? How did their bitter thoughts in that hour of degradation compare with their glorious dreams as they often lay together on the tented field; when their

—" bugles sang truce; for the night-cloud had lowered,
And the sentinel stars set their watch in the sky;
And thousands had sunk on the ground overpowered—
The weary to sleep, and the wounded to die."

The President *pro tempore:* "The question is on the amendment offered by the Senator from Maine [Mr. Blaine], upon which the yeas and nays have been demanded." ·

The Secretary proceeded to call the roll, and the result was announced—yeas 25, nays 35.

The bill was ordered to a third reading, and

was read the third time. The Secretary proceeded to call the roll, and the result was announced as follows:

YEAS—Bailey, Bayard, Beck, Butler, Call, Cockrell, Coke, Davis of Illinois, Eaton, Farley, Garland, Gordon, Groome, Grover, Hampton, Harris, Hereford, Hill of Georgia, Houston, Johnston, Jonas, Jones of Florida, Kernan, Lamar, McDonald, Maxey, Morgan, Pendleton, Randolph, Ransom, Saulsbury, Slater, Thurman, Vance, Vest, Voorhees, Walker, Wallace, Whyte, Williams, Withers—41.

NAYS—Allison, Anthony, Bell, Blaine, Booth, Bruce, Burnside, Cameron of Pennsylvania, Cameron of Wisconsin, Carpenter, Chandler, Conkling, Dawes, Edmunds, Ferry, Hamlin, Hill of Colorado, Ingalls, Jones of Nevada, Kellogg, Kirkwood, Logan, McMillan, Morrill, Paddock, Platt, Plumb, Rollins, Saunders, Teller—30.

ABSENT—Davis of West Virginia, Hoar, McPherson, Sharon, Windom.—5.

So the bill was passed.

In the House on April 30th, the following veto of the bill was received:

To the House of Representatives :
I have maturely considered the important questions presented by the bill entitled "An Act making appropriations for the support of the army for the fiscal year ending June 30, 1880, and for other purposes," and I now return it to the House of Representatives, in which it originated, with my objections to its approval.

The bill provides in the usual form for the appropriations required for the support of the army during the next fiscal year. If it contained no other provisions, it would receive my prompt approval. It includes, however, further legislation, which, attached as it is to appropriations which are requisite for the efficient performance of some of the most necessary duties of the Government, involves questions of the gravest character. The sixth section of the bill is amendatory of the statute now in force in regard to the authority of persons in the civil, military, and naval service of the United States "at the place where any general or special election is held in any State." This statute was adopted February 25, 1865, after a protracted debate in the Senate, and almost without opposition in the House of Representatives, by the concurrent votes of both of the leading political parties of the country, and became a law by the approval of President Lincoln. It was reënacted in 1874 in the Revised Statutes of the United States, sections 2002 and 5528, which are as follows :

SEC. 2002. No military or naval officer, or other person engaged in the civil, military, or naval service of the United States, shall order, bring, keep, or have under his authority or control, any troops or armed men at the place where any general or special election is held in any State, unless it be necessary to repel the armed enemies of the United States, or to keep the peace at the polls.

SEC. 5528. Every officer of the army or navy, or other person in the civil, military, or naval service of the United States, who orders, brings, keeps, or has under his authority or control, any troops or armed men at any place where a general or special election is held in any State, unless such force be necessary to repel armed enemies of the United States or to keep the peace at the polls, shall be fined not more than $5,000, and suffer imprisonment at hard labor not less than three months nor more than five years.

The amendment proposed to this statute, in the bill before me, omits from both of the foregoing sections the words "or to keep the peace at the polls." The effect of the adoption of this amendment may be considered :

First. Upon the right of the United States Government to use military force to keep the peace at the elections for members of Congress ; and,

Second. Upon the right of the Government, by civil authority, to protect these elections from violence and fraud.

In addition to the sections of the statutes above quoted, the following provisions of law relating to the use of the military power at the elections are now in force :

SEC. 2008. No officer of the army or navy of the United States shall prescribe or fix, or attempt to prescribe or fix, by proclamation, order, or otherwise, the qualifications of voters in any State, or in any manner interfere with the freedom of any election in any State, or with the exercise of the free right of suffrage in any State.

SEC. 5529. Every officer or other person in the military or naval service who, by force, threat, intimidation, order, advice, or otherwise, prevents, or attempts to prevent, any qualified voter of any State from freely exercising the right of suffrage at any general or special election in such State, shall be fined not more than $5,000, and imprisoned at hard labor not more than five years.

SEC. 5530. Every officer of the army or navy who prescribes or fixes, or attempts to prescribe or fix, whether by proclamation, order, or otherwise, the qualifications of voters at any election in any State, shall be punished as provided in the preceding section.

SEC. 5531. Every officer or other person in the military or naval service who, by force, threat, intimidation, order, or otherwise, compels, or attempts to compel, any officer holding an election in any State to receive a vote from a person not legally qualified to vote, or who imposes, or attempts to impose, any regulations for conducting any general or special election in a State different from those prescribed by law, or who interferes in any manner with any officer of an election in the discharge of his duty, shall be punished as provided in section 5529.

SEC. 5532. Every person convicted of any of the offenses specified in the five preceding sections, shall, in addition to the punishments therein severally prescribed, be disqualified from holding any office of honor, profit, or trust under the United States; but nothing in those sections shall be construed to prevent any officer, soldier, sailor, or marine from exercising the right of suffrage in any election district to which he may belong, if otherwise qualified according to the laws of the State in which he offers to vote.

The foregoing enactments would seem to be sufficient to prevent military interference with the elections. But the last Congress, to remove all apprehension of such interference, added to this body of law section 15 of an act entitled "An Act making appropriations for the support of the army for the fiscal year ending June 30, 1879, and for other purposes," approved June 18, 1878, which is as follows :

SEC. 15. From and after the passage of this act it shall not be lawful to employ any part of the army of the United States, as a *posse comitatus* or otherwise, for the purpose of executing the laws, except in such cases and under such circumstances as such employment of said force may be expressly authorized by the Constitution or by act of Congress ; and no money appropriated by this act shall be used to pay any of the expenses incurred in the employment of any troops in violation of this section, and any person willfully violating the provisions of this section shall be deemed guilty of a misdemeanor, and on conviction thereof shall be punished by a fine not exceeding $10,000 or imprisonment not exceeding two years, or by both such fine and imprisonment.

This act passed the Senate, after full consideration, without a single vote recorded against it on its final passage, and, by a majority of more than two thirds, it was concurred in by the House of Representatives.

The purpose of the section quoted was stated in the Senate by one of its supporters as follows :

Therefore I hope, without getting into any controversy about the past, but acting wisely for the future, that we shall take away the idea that the army can be used by a general or special deputy marshal, or any marshal, merely for election purposes as a *posse*, ordering them about the polls or ordering them anywhere else, when there is no election going on, to prevent disorders or to suppress disturbances that should be suppressed by the peace officers of the State, or if they must bring others to their aid they should summon the unorganized citizens and not summon the officers and men of the army as a *posse comitatus* to quell disorders and thus get up a feeling which will be disastrous to peace among the people of the country.

In the House of Representatives the object of the act of 1878 was stated by the gentleman who had it in charge in similar terms. He said :

But these are all minor points and insignificant questions compared with the great principle which was incorporated by the House in the bill in reference to the use of the army in time of peace. The Senate had already conceded what they called, and what we might accept, as the principle, but they had stricken out the penalty, and had stricken out the word "expressly," so that the army might be used in all cases where implied authority might be inferred. The House committee planted themselves firmly upon the doctrine that, rather than yield this fundamental principle, for which for three years this House had struggled, they would allow the bill to fail, notwithstanding the reforms which we had secured, regarding these reforms as of but little consequence alongside the great principle that the army of the United States, in time of peace, should be under the control of Congress and obedient to its laws. After a long and protracted negotiation, the Senate committee has conceded that principle in all its length and breadth, including the penalty, which the Senate had stricken out. We bring you back, therefore, a report with the alteration of a single word, which the lawyers assure me is proper to be made, restoring to this bill the principle for which we have contended so long and which is so vital to secure the rights and liberties of the people.

. . . .

Thus have we this day secured to the people of this country the same great protection against a standing army which cost a struggle of two hundred years for the Commons of England to secure for the British people.

From this brief review of the subject, it sufficiently appears that under existing laws there can be no military interference with the elections. No case of such interference has, in fact, occurred since the passage of the act last referred to. No soldier of the United States has appeared under orders at any place of election in any State. No complaint even of the presence of United States troops has been made in any quarter. It may therefore be confidently stated that there is no necessity for the enactment of section 6 of the bill before me to prevent military interference with the elections. The laws already in force are all that is required for that end.

But that part of section 6 of this bill which is significant and vitally important is the clause which, if adopted, will deprive the civil authorities of the United States of all power to keep the peace at the Congressional elections. The Congressional elections in every district, in a very important sense, are justly a matter of political interest and concern throughout the whole country. Each State, every political party, is entitled to its share of power which is conferred by the legal and constitutional suffrage. It is the right of every citizen possessing the qualifications prescribed by law to cast one unintimidated ballot, and to have his ballot honestly counted. So long as the exercise of this power and the enjoyment of this right are common and equal, practically as well as formally, submission to the results of the suffrage will be accorded loyally and cheerfully, and all the departments of Government will feel the true vigor of the popular will thus expressed.

Two provisions of the Constitution authorize legislation by Congress for the regulation of the Congressional elections.

Section 4 of article 1 of the Constitution declares:

The times, places, and manner of holding elections for Senators and Representatives shall be prescribed in each State by the Legislature thereof; but the Congress may at any time by law make or alter such regulations, except as to the places of choosing Senators.

The fifteenth amendment of the Constitution is as follows:

SECTION 1. The right of citizens of the United States to vote shall not be denied or abridged by the United States or by any State on account of race, color, or previous condition of servitude.

SEC. 2. The Congress shall have power to enforce this article by appropriate legislation.

The Supreme Court has held that this amendment invests the citizens of the United States with a new constitutional right which is within the protecting power of Congress. That right the Court declares to be exemption from discrimination in the exercise of the elective franchise on account of race, color, or previous condition of servitude. The power of Congress

to protect this right by appropriate legislation is expressly affirmed by the Court.

National legislation to provide safeguards for free and honest elections is necessary, as experience has shown, not only to secure the right to vote to the enfranchised race at the South, but also to prevent fraudulent voting in the large cities of the North. Congress has, therefore, exercised the power conferred by the Constitution, and has enacted certain laws to prevent discriminations on account of race, color, or previous condition of servitude, and to punish fraud, violence, and intimidation at Federal elections. Attention is called to the following sections of the Revised Statutes of the United States, namely:

Section 2004, which guarantees to all citizens the right to vote without distinction on account of race, color, or previous condition of servitude;

Sections 2005 and 2006, which guarantee to all citizens equal opportunity, without discrimination, to perform all the acts required by law as a prerequisite or qualification for voting;

Section 2022, which authorizes the United States marshal and his deputies to keep the peace and preserve order at the Federal elections;

Section 2024, which expressly authorizes the United States marshal and his deputies to summon a posse comitatus whenever they or any of them are forcibly resisted in the execution of their duties under the law, or are prevented from executing such duties by violence;

Section 5522, which provides for the punishment of the crime of interfering with the supervisors of elections and deputy marshals in the discharge of their duties at the elections of Representatives in Congress.

These are some of the laws on this subject which it is the duty of the executive department of the Government to enforce. The intent and effect of the sixth section of this bill are to prohibit all the civil officers of the United States, under penalty of fine and imprisonment, from employing any adequate civil force for this purpose at the place where their enforcement is most necessary, namely, at the places where the Congressional elections are held. Among the most valuable enactments to which I have referred are those which protect the supervisors of Federal elections in the discharge of their duties at the polls. If the proposed legislation should become the law, there will be no power vested in any officer of the Government to protect from violence the officers of the United States engaged in the discharge of their duties. Their rights and duties under the law will remain, but the National Government will be powerless to enforce its own statutes. The States may employ both military and civil power to keep the peace, and to enforce the laws at State elections. It is now proposed to deny to the United States even the necessary civil authority to protect the national elections. No sufficient reason has been given for this discrimination in favor of the State and against the national authority. If well-founded objections exist against the present national election laws, all good citizens should unite in their amendment. The laws providing the safeguards of the elections should be impartial, just, and efficient. They should, if possible, be so non-partisan and fair in their operation that the minority—the party out of power—will have no just grounds to complain. The present laws have, in practice, unquestionably conduced to the prevention of fraud and violence at the elections. In several of the States members of different political parties have applied for the safeguards which they furnish. It is the right and duty of the National Government to enact and enforce laws which will secure free and fair Congressional elections. The laws now in force should not be repealed, except in connection with the enactment of measures which will better accomplish that important end. Believing that section 6 of the bill before me will weaken, if it does not altogether take away, the power of the National Government to protect the Federal elections by the civil authorities, I am forced to the conclusion that it ought not to receive my approval.

This section is, however, not presented to me as a separate and independent measure, but is, as has been stated, attached to the bill making the usual annual appropriations for the support of the army. It makes a vital change in the election laws of the country, which is in no way connected with the use of the army. It prohibits, under heavy penalties, any person engaged in the civil service of the United States from having any force at the place of any election prepared to preserve order, to make arrests, to keep the peace, or in any manner to enforce the laws. This is altogether foreign to the purpose of an army appropriation bill. The practice of tacking to appropriation bills measures not pertinent to such bills did not prevail until more than forty years after the adoption of the Constitution. It has become a common practice. All parties when in power have adopted it. Many abuses and great waste of public money have in this way crept into appropriation bills. The public opinion of the country is against it. The States which have recently adopted constitutions have generally provided a remedy for the evil by enacting that no law shall contain more than one subject, which shall be plainly expressed in its title. The constitutions of more than half of the States contain substantially this provision. The public welfare will be promoted in many ways by a return to the early practice of the Government, and to the true principle of legislation, which requires that every measure shall stand or fall according to its own merits. If it were understood that to attach to an appropriation bill a measure irrelevant to the general object of the bill would imperil and probably prevent its final passage and approval, a valuable reform in the parliamentary practice of Congress would be accomplished. The best justification that has been offered for attaching irrelevant riders to appropriation bills is that it is done for convenience' sake, to facilitate the passage of measures which are deemed expedient by all the branches of Government which participate in legislation. It can not be claimed that there is any such reason for attaching this amendment of the election laws to the army appropriation bill. The history of the measure contradicts this assumption. A majority of the House of Representatives in the last Congress was in favor of section 6 of this bill. It was known that a majority of the Senate was opposed to it, and that as a separate measure it could not be adopted. It was attached to the army appropriation bill to compel the Senate to assent to it. It was plainly announced to the Senate that the army appropriation bill would not be allowed to pass unless the proposed amendments of the election laws were adopted with it. The Senate refused to assent to the bill on account of this irrelevant section. Congress thereupon adjourned without passing an appropriation bill for the army, and the present extra session of the Forty-sixth Congress became necessary to furnish the means to carry on the Government.

The ground upon which the action of the House of Representatives is defended has been distinctly stated by many of its advocates. A week before the close of the last session of Congress the doctrine in question was stated by one of its ablest defenders as follows:

It is our duty to repeal these laws. It is not worth while to attempt the repeal except upon an appropriation bill. The Republican Senate would not agree to, nor the Republican President sign, a bill for such a repeal. Whatever objection to legislation upon appropriation bills may be made in ordinary cases does not apply where free elections and the liberty of the citizens are concerned. . . . We have the power to vote money; let us annex conditions to it, and insist upon the redress of grievances.

By another distinguished member of the House it was said:

The right of the Representatives of the people to withhold supplies is as old as English liberty. History records numerous instances where the Commons, feeling that the people were oppressed by laws that the Lords would not consent to repeal by the ordinary methods of legislation, obtained redress at last by refusing appropriations unless accompanied by relief measures.

That a question of the gravest magnitude, and new in this country, was raised by this course of proceeding, was fully recognized also by its defenders in the Senate. It was said by a distinguished Senator:

Perhaps no greater question, in the form we are brought to consider it, was ever considered by the American Congress in time of peace; for it involves not merely the merits or demerits of the laws which the House bill proposes to repeal, but involves the rights, the privileges, the powers, the duties of the two branches of Congress, and of the President of the United States. It is a vast question; it is a question whose importance can scarcely be estimated; it is a question that never yet has been brought so sharply before the American Congress and the American people as it may be now. It is a question which, sooner or later, must be decided, and the decision must determine what are the powers of the House of Representatives under the Constitution, and what is the duty of that House in the view of the framers of that Constitution according to its letter and its spirit.

Mr. President, I should approach this question, if I were in the best possible condition to speak and to argue it, with very grave diffidence, and certainly with the utmost anxiety, for no one can think of it as long and as carefully as I have thought of it without seeing that we are at the beginning, perhaps, of a struggle that may last as long in this country as a similar struggle lasted in what we are accustomed to call the mother land. There the struggle lasted for two centuries before it was ultimately decided. It is not likely to last so long here, but it may last until every man in this chamber is in his grave. It is the question whether or no the House of Representatives has a right to say, " We will grant supplies only upon condition that grievances are redressed. We are the representatives of the tax-payers of the Republic; we, the House of Representatives, alone have the right to originate money bills ; we, the House of Representatives, have alone the right to originate bills which grant the money of the people. The Senate represents States: we represent the tax-payers of the Republic; we, therefore, by the very terms of the Constitution, are charged with the duty of originating the bills which grant the money of the people. We claim the right, which the House of Commons in England established after two centuries of contest, to say that we will not grant the money of the people unless there is a redress of grievances.

Upon the assembling of this Congress, in pursuance of a call for an extra session, which was made necessary by the failure of the Forty-fifth Congress to make the needful appropriations for the support of the Government, the question was presented whether the attempt made in the last Congress to ingraft, by construction, a new principle upon the Constitution should be persisted in or not. This Congress has ample opportunity and time to pass the appropriation bills, and also to enact any political measures which may be determined upon in separate bills by the usual and orderly methods of proceeding. But the majority of both Houses have deemed it wise to adhere to the principle asserted and maintained in the last Congress by the majority of the House of Representatives. That principle is that the House of Representatives has the sole right to originate bills for raising revenue, and therefore has the right to withhold appropriations upon which the existence of the Government may depend, unless the Senate and the President shall give their assent to any legislation which the House may see fit to attach to appropriation bills. To establish this principle is to make a radical, dangerous, and unconstitutional change in the character of our institutions. The various departments of the Government, and the army and the navy, are established by the Constitution, or by laws passed in pursuance thereof. Their duties are clearly defined, and their support is carefully provided for by law. The money required for this purpose has been collected from the people, and is now in the Treasury ready to be paid out as soon as the appropriation bills are passed. Whether appropriations are made or not, the collection of the taxes will go on. The public money will accumulate in the Treasury. It was not the intention of the framers of the Constitution that any single branch of the Government should have the power to dictate conditions upon which this treasure should be applied to the purposes for which it was collected. Any such intention, if it had been entertained, would have been plainly expressed in the Constitution.

That a majority of the Senate now concurs in the

claim of the House adds to the gravity of the situation, but does not alter the question at issue. The new doctrine, if maintained, will result in a consolidation of unchecked and despotic power in the House of Representatives. A bare majority of the House will become the Government. The Executive will no longer be what the framers of the Constitution intended, an equal and independent branch of the Government. It is clearly the constitutional duty of the President to exercise his discretion and judgment upon all bills presented to him, without constraint or duress from any other branch of the Government. To say that a majority of either or both of the Houses of Congress may insist upon the approval of a bill under the penalty of stopping all of the operations of the Government for want of the necessary supplies, is to deny to the Executive that share of the legislative power which is plainly conferred by the second section of the seventh article of the Constitution. It strikes from the Constitution the qualified negative of the President. It is said that this should be done because it is the peculiar function of the House of Representatives to represent the will of the people. But no single branch or department of the Government has exclusive authority to speak for the American people. The most authentic and solemn expression of their will is contained in the Constitution of the United States. By that Constitution they have ordained and established a government whose powers are distributed among coördinate branches, which, as far as possible consistently with a harmonious coöperation, are absolutely independent of each other. The people of this country are unwilling to see the supremacy of the Constitution replaced by the omnipotence of any one department of the Government.

The enactment of this bill into a law will establish a precedent which will tend to destroy the equal independence of the several branches of the Government. Its principle places not merely the Senate and the Executive, but the judiciary also, under the coercive dictation of the House. The House alone will be the judge of what constitutes a grievance, and also of the means and measure of redress. An act of Congress to protect elections is now the grievance complained of. But the House may, on the same principle, determine that any other act of Congress, a treaty made by the President with the advice and consent of the Senate, a nomination or appointment to office, or that a decision or opinion of the Supreme Court is a grievance, and that the measure of redress is to withhold the appropriations required for the support of the offending branch of the Government.

Believing that this bill is a dangerous violation of the spirit and meaning of the Constitution, I am compelled to return it to the House in which it originated without my approval. The qualified negative with which the Constitution invests the President is a trust that involves a duty which he can not decline to perform. With a firm and conscientious purpose to do what I can to preserve, unimpaired, the constitutional powers and equal independence, not merely of the Executive, but of every branch of the Government, which will be imperiled by the adoption of the principle of this bill, I desire earnestly to urge upon the House of Representatives a return to the wise and wholesome usage of the earlier days of the Republic, which excluded from appropriation bills all irrelevant legislation. By this course you will inaugurate an important reform in the method of Congressional legislation; your action will be in harmony with the fundamental principles of the Constitution and the patriotic sentiment of nationality which is their firm support; and you will restore to the country that feeling of confidence and security and the repose which are so essential to the prosperity of all of our fellow citizens.

RUTHERFORD B. HAYES.

EXECUTIVE MANSION, *April 29*, 1879.

In the House on May 1st the question on the vetoed bill was considered.

The Speaker: "The question is, Will the House on reconsideration agree to pass the bill? Under the Constitution it is required that this vote shall be taken by yeas and nays." The question was taken, as follows:

YEAS—Acklen, Aiken, Armfield, Atherton, Atkins, Beale, Beltzhoover, Bicknell, Blackburn, Bliss, Bragg, Bright, Buckner, Cabell, Caldwell, Carlisle, Chalmers, Alvah A. Clark, John B. Clark, Jr., Clymer, Cobb, Coffroth, Colerick, Converse, Covert, Cox, Cravens, Culberson, Davidson, Lowndes H. Davis, De La Matyr, Deuster, Dibrell, Dickey, Dunn, Elam, Ellis, Evins, Ewing, Felton, Forney, Frost, Geddes, Gibson, Gunter, N. J. Hammond, John T. Harris, Henkle, Henry, Herbert, Herndon, Hill, Hooker, Hostetler, House, Hurd, Johnston, Kimmel, King, Kitchin, Klotz, Knott, Ladd, Le Fevre, Lewis, Manning, Benjamin F. Martin, McKenzie, McLane, McMillin, Mills, Morrison, Muldrow, Myers, New, O'Brien, O'Connor, O'Reilly, Persons, Phister, Poehler, Reagan, J. S. Richardson, Richmond, Robertson, Ross, Rothwell, Samford, Sawyer, Scales, Shelley, J. W. Singleton, O. R. Singleton, Slemons, Hezekiah B. Smith, William E. Smith, Sparks, Speer, Springer, Steele, Stephens, Stevenson, Talbott, Taylor, Thompson, Tillman, R. W. Townshend. Oscar Turner, Thomas Turner, Vance, Waddill, Warner, Wellborn, Whiteaker, Whitthorne, Thomas Williams, Willis, Wise, Wright, Casey Young—120.

NAYS—Nelson W. Aldrich, William Aldrich, Anderson, Baker, Bayne, Belford, Bingham, Blake, Bowman, Boyd, Brewer, Briggs, Brigham, Browne, Burrows, Butterworth, Cannon, Carpenter, Caswell, Chittenden, Claflin, Conger, Cowgill, Crapo, Daggett, George R. Davis, Deering, Dunnell, Einstein, Errett, Farr, Ferdon, Field, Fisher, Ford, Forsythe, Fort, Frye, Garfield, Gillette, Hall, John Hammond, Harmer, Benjamin W. Harris, Haskell, Hawk, Hawley, Hazelton, Heilman, Hiscock, Horr, Houk, Hubbell, Humphrey, James, Jones, Jorgensen, Joyce, Keifer, Kelley, Lindsey, Lowe, Marsh, Mason, McCoid, McGowan, McKinley, Miles, Mitchell, Monroe, Morton, Murch, Newberry, Norcross, O'Neill, Overton, Pierce, Pound, Prescott, Reed, Rice, D. P. Richardson, Robeson, Robinson, William A. Russell, Thomas Ryan, Shallenberger, Sherwin, A. Herr Smith, Thomas, Amos Townsend, Tyler, J. T. Updegraff, Thomas Updegraff, Urner, Valentine, Van Aernam Voorhis, Van Voorhis, Wait, Ward, Washburn, Weaver, White, Wilber, C. G. Williams, Willits, Walter A. Wood, Yocum, Thomas L. Young—110.

NOT VOTING—Bachman, Bailey, Ballou, Barber, Barlow, Bland, Blount, Bouck, Calkins, Camp, Clardy, Cook, Crowley, Joseph J. Davis, Dick, Dwight, Finley, Godshalk, Goode, Hatch, Hayes, Henderson, Hull, Hunton, Kenna, Ketcham, Killinger, Lapham, Lay, Loring, Lounsbery, Edward L. Martin, Joseph J. Martin, McCook, McMahon, Miller, Money, Morse, Muller, Neal, Nicholls, Orth, Osmer, Phelps, Price, Daniel L. Russell, John W. Ryon, Sapp, Simonton, Starin, Stone, Tucker, Wells, Wilson, Fernando Wood—55.

So the bill failed to pass.

On June 6th another bill making appropriations for the army was reported. The objectionable feature of the previous bills was omitted, and instead thereof the following clause was inserted:

That no money appropriated in this act is appropriated or shall be paid for the subsistence, equipment, transportation, or compensation of any portion of the army of the United States to be used as a police force to keep the peace at the polls at any election held within any State.

In this form the bill passed both Houses and was approved by President Hayes.

In the House, on May 7th, a bill to prohibit military interference at elections came up for consideration. The bill was read, as follows:

Whereas, The presence of troops at the polls is contrary to the spirit of our institutions and the traditions of our people, and tends to destroy the freedom of elections: Therefore,

Be it enacted by the Senate and House of Representatives of the United States of America in Congress assembled, That it shall not be lawful to bring to, or employ at, any place where a general or special election is being held in a State any part of the army or navy of the United States, unless such force be necessary to repel the armed enemies of the United States, or to enforce section 4, article 4, of the Constitution of the United States and the laws made in pursuance thereof, upon the application of the Legislature or the executive of the State where such force is to be used; and so much of all laws as is inconsistent herewith is hereby repealed.

Mr. Knott of Kentucky said: "I have been informed by gentlemen representing the minority of the committee that it is desired to offer a substitute for the bill just reported. When that substitute has been offered, I propose that the previous question be immediately ordered upon the bill and substitute."

Mr. Robeson of New Jersey: "I offer as a substitute what I send to the desk."

The clerk read as follows:

A bill to further protect the freedom of elections.

Whereas, The unnecessary presence of troops at the polls is contrary to the spirit of our institutions and the traditions of our people and would tend to destroy the freedom of elections; and

Whereas, The presence of troops at the polls has heretofore been and may hereafter be necessary and proper for the suppression of illegal and powerful combinations of armed men in military array engaged in obstructing by force the due execution of the laws of the United States and in destroying the freedom and peace of elections; and

Whereas, Experience has shown that the existence of the Republic, the supremacy of its laws, and the liberties of its people can only be maintained against the military and other powerful combinations of their enemies by the exertion of the military power of the Government in subordination to the civil power in the support of the laws; and

Whereas, The injunction of the Constitution that the President "shall take care that the laws be faithfully executed" is equally binding in respect to the laws relating to elections, the course of justice, and all other laws of the United States, without distinction of days, places, or occasions: Therefore,

Be it enacted, etc., That it shall not be lawful to bring to, or employ at, any place where a general or special election is being held in a State, any part of the army or navy of the United States, unless such employment be necessary to carry out the provisions of the Constitution of the United States, or to overcome forcible obstruction to the execution of laws made in pursuance thereof.

SEC. 2. Every person who violates the provisions of this act shall be subject to the penalties named in section 5528 of the Revised Statutes of the United States.

Mr. Knott: "I demand the previous question on the bill and the substitute."

The previous question was seconded, and the main question was ordered to be put. The question first recurred on Mr. Robeson's substitute. The question was taken; and it was decided in the negative, as follows:

YEAS—N. W. Aldrich, William Aldrich, Anderson, Bayne, Belford, Bingham, Blake, Bowman, Boyd, Brewer, Briggs, Brigham, Browne, Burrows, Cannon, Carpenter, Caswell, Chittenden, Claflin, Conger, Cowgill, Crapo, Daggett, George R. Davis, Deering, Dunnell, Farr, Ferdon, Field, Fisher, Fort, Frye, Garfield, Godshalk, Hall, Harmer, Benjamin W. Harris, Haskell, Hawk, Hawley, Hayes, Heilman, Horr, Houk, Hubbell, Humphrey, Joyce, Keifer, Kelley, Killinger, Lindsey, Loring, Marsh, Mason, McCoid, McCook, McGowan, McKinley, Mitchell, Monroe, Morton, Neal, Newberry, Norcross, O'Neill, Overton, Pierce, Pound, Prescott, Reed, Rice, D. P. Richardson, Robeson, William A. Russell, Thomas Ryan, Shallenberger, Sherwin, A. Herr Smith, Stone, Tyler, J. T. Updegraff, Thomas Updegraff, Valentine, Van Aernam, Van Voorhis, Voorhis, Wait, Ward, Washburn, White, Wilber, Walter A. Wood, Thomas L. Young—93.

NAYS—Acklen, Aiken, Armfield, Beltzhoover, Bicknell, Blackburn, Bliss, Blount, Bouck, Bright, Buckner, Caldwell, Carlisle, Chalmers, John B. Clark, Jr., Clymer, Cobb, Coffroth, Colerick, Converse, Covert, Cox, Cravens, Culberson, Davidson, Lowndes H. Davis, De La Matyr, Deuster, Dibrell, Dickey, Dunn, Elam, Ellis, Evins, Ewing, Felton, Ford, Forney, Frost, Geddes, Gibson, Goode, Gunter, N. J. Hammond, John T. Harris, Henkle, Henry, Herbert, Herndon, Hill, Hooker, Hostetler, House, Hurd, Johnston, Jones, Kimmel, King, Kitchin, Knott, Ladd, Le Fevre, Lewis, Lowe, Manning, Benjamin F. Martin, Edward L. Martin, Joseph J. Martin, McKenzie, McLane, McMillan, Mills, Morrison, Muldrow, Murch, Myers, New, O'Reilly, Persons, Phister, Poehler, Reagan, J. S. Richardson, Richmond, Robertson, Ross, Rothwell, John W. Ryon, Samford, Sawyer, Scales, O. R. Singleton, Siemons, Hezekiah B. Smith, William E. Smith, Sparks, Speer, Springer, Steele, Stephens, Stevenson, Taylor, Thompson, Tillman, R. W. Townshend, Oscar Turner, Thomas Turner, Vance, Waddill, Warner, Weaver, Wellborn, Wells, Whiteaker, Whitthorne, Thomas Williams, Willis, Wise, Fernando Wood, Wright, Yocum—120.

NOT VOTING—Atherton, Atkins, Bachman, Bailey, Baker, Ballou, Barber, Barlow, Beale, Bland, Bragg, Butterworth, Cabell, Calkins, Camp, Clardy, Alvah A. Clark, Cook, Crowley, Joseph J. Davis, Dick, Dwight, Einstein, Errett, Finley, Forsythe, Gillette, John Hammond, Hatch, Hazelton, Henderson, Hiscock, Hull, Hunton, James, Jorgensen, Kenna, Ketcham, Klotz, Lapham, Lay, Lounsbery, Joseph J. Martin, McMahon, Miles, Miller, Money, Morse, Muller, Nicholls, O'Brien, O'Connor, Orth, Osmer, Phelps, Price, Robinson, Daniel L. Russell, Sapp, Shelley, Simonton, J. W. Singleton, Starin, Talbott, Thomas, Amos Townsend, Tucker, Urner, C. G. Williams, Willits, Wilson, Casey Young—72.

So the substitute was not agreed to.

The Speaker: "The question is now on the passage of the bill."

The question was taken, as follows:

YEAS—Acklen, Aiken, Armfield, Beltzhoover, Bicknell, Blackburn, Bliss, Blount, Bouck, Bright, Buckner, Cabell, Caldwell, Carlisle, Chalmers, John B. Clark, jr., Clymer, Cobb, Coffroth, Colerick, Converse, Covert, Cox, Cravens, Culberson, Davidson, Lowndes H. Davis, De La Matyr, Deuster, Dibrell, Dickey, Dunn, Elam, Ellis, Evins, Ewing, Felton, Ford, Forney, Forsythe, Frost, Geddes, Gibson, Gillette, Goode, Gunter, N. J. Hammond, John T. Harris, Henkle, Henry, Herbert, Herndon, Hill, Hooker, Hostetler, House, Hurd, Johnston, Jones, Kimmel, King, Kitchin, Klotz, Knott, Ladd, Le Fevre, Lewis, Lowe, Manning, Benjamin F. Martin, Edward L. Martin, Joseph J. Martin, McKenzie, McLane, McMillan, Mills, Morrison, Muldrow, Murch, Myers, New, O'Reilly, Persons, Phister, Poehler, Reagan, J. S.

Richardson, Richmond, Ross, Rothwell, John W. Ryon, Samford, Sawyer, Scales, O. R. Singleton, Slemons, Hezekiah B. Smith, William E. Smith, Sparks, Speer, Springer, Steele, Stephens, Stevenson, Taylor, Thompson, Tillman, R. W. Townshend, Oscar Turner, Thomas Turner, Vance, Waddill, Warner, Weaver, Wellborn, Wells, Whiteaker, Whitthorne, Thomas Williams, Willis, Wise, Fernando Wood, Wright, Yocum—124.

NAYS—N. W. Aldrich, William Aldrich, Anderson, Bayne, Belford, Bingham, Blake, Bowman, Boyd, Brewer, Briggs, Brigham, Browne, Burrows, Cannon, Carpenter, Caswell, Chittenden, Claflin, Conger, Cowgill, Crapo, Daggett, George R. Davis, Deering, Dunnell, Farr, Ferdon, Field, Fisher, Fort, Frye, Garfield, Godshalk, Harmer, Benjamin W. Harris, Haskell, Hawk, Hawley, Hayes, Heilman, Horr, Houk, Hubbell, Humphrey, Joyce, Keifer, Killinger, Lindsey, Marsh, Mason, McCoid, McCook, McGowan, McKinley, Mitchell, Monroe, Morton, Neal, Newberry, Norcross, O'Neill, Overton, Pierce, Pound Prescott, Reed, Rice, D. P. Richardson, Robeson, William A. Russell, Thomas Ryan, Shallenberger, Sherwin, A. Herr Smith, Stone, Tyler, J. T. Updegraff, Thomas Updegraff, Valentine, Van Aernam, Van Voorhis, Voorhis, Wait, Ward, Washburn, White, C. G. Williams, Walter A. Wood, Thomas L. Young—90.

NOT VOTING—Atherton, Atkins, Bachman, Bailey, Baker, Ballou, Barber, Barlow, Beale, Bland, Bragg, Butterworth, Calkins, Camp, Clardy, Alvah A. Clark, Cook, Crowley, Joseph J. Davis, Dick, Dwight, Einstein, Errett, Finley, Hall, John Hammond, Hatch, Hazelton, Henderson, Hiscock, Hull, Hunton, James, Jorgenson, Kelley, Kenna, Ketcham, Lapham, Lay, Loring, Lounsbery, McMahon, Miles, Miller, Money, Morse, Muller, Nicholls, O'Brien, O'Connor, Osmer, Phelps, Price, Robertson, Robinson, Daniel L. Russell, Sapp, Shelley, Simonton, J. W. Singleton, Starin, Talbott, Thomas, Amos Townsend, Tucker, Urner, Wilber, Willits, Wilson, Casey Young—71.

So the bill was passed.

In the Senate, on May 8th, the bill was considered.

Mr. Blaine of Maine said: "I gave notice of an amendment to this bill, which I should be glad to have read and ordered to be printed."

The Chief Clerk read as follows:

SEC. 2. Any person who shall carry a concealed deadly weapon at any place, or within a mile of any place where a general or special election for Representative to Congress is being held, shall, on conviction thereof, be punished with a fine not less than five hundred nor more than five thousand dollars, or with imprisonment for a period not less than six months nor more than five years, or with both fine and imprisonment, at the discretion of the court.

Mr. Blaine: "I withdraw my amendment for the present."

The bill was reported to the Senate without amendment.

The President pro tempore: "If there be no amendment in the Senate the question is, Shall the bill be read the third time?"

Mr. Blaine: "Mr. President, I want to make a single remark on the bill itself, if there is to be a vote upon it. I desire simply to put a punctuation point in the progress of things as they are now going on, and that punctuation point is to mark the high tide which the ancient doctrine of State rights is reaching in this Chamber and in this Congress. That question has engaged the attention of the American people for just about fifty years. It has had

its ups and downs, its victories and its defeats. It was strangled for the time by Jackson; it was dallied with by Van Buren; it rose to full strength under Polk and Pierce and Buchanan; it marshaled itself for a deadly struggle under Breckenridge; and if I mistake not a majority of Senators who sit on that side of the Chamber supported Breckenridge when he embodied that deadly heresy. In whatever there was in the issue between Calhoun and Jackson, that side of the Senate Chamber represents Calhoun. Whatever there was in the contest dividing the Democratic party between Breckenridge and Douglas that side of the Chamber represents all the evil there was in the politics of Breckenridge. And I desire here to affirm and point out that there never was before the rebellion, there never was at any time in the history of the country, any such assertion of State rights, any such assertion of mastery of the State Government over the Federal Government in its own domain, as is here asserted by the heirs lineal of Calhoun and of Breckenridge.

"I shall not debate this bill. It were useless. It has been exhaustively debated. The whole measure is a removal of the Federal Government from its proper domain, and the installation of the States into degrees of power that were not dreamed of by Calhoun and were not asserted by Breckenridge. We thought there had been something gained on this question in a costly war and in amendments to the Constitution. But the tide as it now sweeps is on the ebb, and the power of the Federal Government was never so weak as these laws and these proceedings will make it.

Pass this bill. While warning off all interference or control of the Federal Government, you voted down on the other bill a proposition that armed men should not come to the polls. You voted down on the other bill a proposition that armed men should not come to the polls with the express intent of interfering with the rights of voters, and you did it under the paltry quibble that it was not within the constitutional power of the United States Government to warn bloody-handed ruffians from the polls where the Representatives in the Federal Congress were being chosen.

"Pass this bill. Pass it as the triumph of the reactionary party against the spirit of the Union. Pass it in defiance of all the lessons and all the teachings that have come from a bloody and abortive rebellion. Pass it, and mark it as the high tide of that reaction which were it to rise higher could lead only to another and more formidable rebellion against the legitimate authority of the Union."

Mr. Chandler of Michigan: "History, Mr. President, is repeating itself. It has been said that the old Bourbons learned nothing and forgot nothing. This is more preëminently true with the old Bourbons of Democracy in America. In 1851 the Bourbons had absolute control of this Government, in both Houses of Congress, the White House, and the Supreme Court. The whole of this Government was under your control. You had a majority in this body, a majority in the other House; and you brought up the repeal of the Missouri compromise. You forced your men then, as you are forcing them now, to vote for that repeal, and you did it by caucus dictation. Then, sir, you crowded your Northern allies until you crowded them off the bridge.

"In 1857, when I first took my seat in this body with Mr. Jefferson Davis, there were in this body forty-four Democrats, twenty Republicans, and two Independents. Of those Democrats, twenty-eight were from the Southern States, sixteen from the Northern States. Then, as now, the Independents in this body, upon every question connected with slavery, voted with the South. You in caucus, soon after I entered the Senate, decreed that Stephen A. Douglas, because he asserted that he did not care whether slavery was voted up or voted down, should be degraded from the chairmanship of the Committee on Territories; and there were but three Northern Democrats out of the sixteen on this floor who dared to resist caucus dictation. You did degrade him and put him off from that committee. Ah, sir, then you crowded your men off the bridge, and they sank into the waters of oblivion to rise no more for ever. Then you had from the Northern States on this floor: from California two members; from Illinois one; from Indiana two; from Iowa one; from Michigan one. I am giving the Democratic Senators from the North who obeyed and those who did not obey caucus dictation. From Minnesota you had two; from New Jersey two; from Ohio one; from Oregon two; from Pennsylvania one; from Rhode Island one; which made the sixteen. Of those sixteen members not a solitary man from the North ever came up to the surface of the waters of oblivion. You crowded them off the bridge. You compelled them to vote for measures which the North could not and would not sustain.

"To-day you are doing the self-same thing. To-day you have in this body forty-two Democrats, thirty-three Republicans, and one Independent. To-day, as twenty-two years ago, on all questions connected with State rights, the Independent party as a unit votes with the Democratic party. To-day you have, as I said, forty-three Democrats in this body, forty-two leaving out the Independent party. You have twelve members of this body from the North. There are twelve Democratic Senators from the North, and they are arranged thus: from California one; from Indiana, now as then, you have two; from New Jersey you have two, now as then; from Ohio you have two, you had but one then; from Oregon you have two now and you had two then; from Pennsylvania you have one now, you had one then; from Rhode Island you have none now, but

you have one from Connecticut; and you have one from New York.

"Mr. President, as I said in the beginning, history is to-day repeating itself. You are to-day repeating what you did in 1857 and 1858; you are crowding your men off the bridge, and the men of to-day, as the men of 1857, will sink into the waters of oblivion to rise no more for ever. Look at the elections of this last year. Look at the change that has taken place since the 1st day of March, 1859. Sir, the people are more thoroughly aroused to-day against this heresy of State rights than they were from 1857 to 1861. You proposed to pension Jefferson Davis, and every single one of your Northern allies voted to pension him. You eulogized him as a patriot to be compared side by side with Washington and all the patriots of the Revolution, and every one of your Northern allies voted 'ay.' After the close of the rebellion you claimed that you were poor, that you were suffering; and we found you poor and suffering; we found you ragged and we clothed you. We put upon you the robe of American citizenship which you had forfeited, and we killed for you the fatted calf and invited you to the feast, supposing that, after being clothed, you were in your right mind; and when we have invited you to the feast you say, 'We always owned the calf, and you have no interest in it.'

"But, Mr. President, I did not rise to discuss this question. I rose simply to say to gentlemen upon the other side, You have your day in court; make the most of it; your time is short. The people of the North have taken this question in hand, and from the Atlantic to the Pacific, from one end of this land to the other, the people are aroused and alarmed at the statements that have been made and the action that has been taken in this Senate Chamber and in the other House within the last sixty days. And let me say to you, gentlemen upon the other side of the Chamber, that *mene, mene, tekel, upharsin* is written all over your brows."

The President *pro tempore:* "The question is, Shall the bill be read the third time?"

The Secretary proceeded to call the roll.

The result was announced—yeas 33, nays 23. So the bill was ordered to a third reading, and was read the third time. The Secretary proceeded to call the roll, and the result was announced as follows:

Yeas—Bayard, Beck, Butler, Call, Cockrell, Coke, Davis of West Virginia, Eaton, Garland, Groome, Hampton, Harris, Hereford, Houston, Johnston, Jonas, Jones of Florida, Kernan, Lamar, McDonald, Maxey, Morgan, Pendleton, Randolph, Ransom, Saulsbury, Slater, Thurman, Vance, Vest, Voorhees, Walker, Withers—33.

Nays—Allison, Anthony, Booth, Bruce, Burnside, Cameron of Pennsylvania, Cameron of Wisconsin, Chandler, Conkling, Edmunds, Hill of Colorado, Hoar, Ingalls, Kellogg, Logan, McMillan, Morrill, Platt, Plumb, Rollins, Saunders, Teller, Windom—23.

Absent—Bailey, Bell, Blaine, Carpenter, Davis of Illinois, Dawes, Farley, Ferry, Gordon, Grover, Hamlin, Hill of Georgia, Jones of Nevada, Kirkwood, McPherson, Paddock, Sharon, Wallace, Whyte, Williams—20.

So the bill was passed.

On May 12th, the President sent the following veto of the bill to the House:

To the House of Representatives:

After careful consideration of the bill entitled " An Act to prohibit military interference at elections," I return it to the House of Representatives, in which it originated, with the following objections to its approval:

In the communication sent to the House of Representatives on the 29th of last month, returning to the House without my approval the bill entitled "An Act making appropriations for the support of the army for the fiscal year ending June 30, 1880, and for other purposes," I endeavored to show, by quotations from the statutes of the United States, now in force, and by a brief statement of facts in regard to recent elections in the several States, that no additional legislation was necessary to prevent interference with the elections by the military or naval forces of the United States. The fact was presented in that communication that at the time of the passage of the act of June 18, 1878, in relation to the employment of the army as a *posse comitatus* cr otherwise, it was maintained by its friends that it would establish a vital and fundamental principle which would secure to the people protection against a standing army. The fact was also referred to that, since the passage of this act, Congressional, State, and municipal elections have been held throughout the Union, and that in no instance has complaint been made of the presence of the United States soldiers at the polls.

Holding as I do the opinion that any military interference whatever at the polls is contrary to the spirit of our institutions, and would tend to destroy the freedom of elections, and sincerely desiring to concur with Congress in all of its measures, it is with very great regret that I am forced to the conclusion that the bill before me is not only unnecessary to prevent such interference, but is a dangerous departure from long-settled and important constitutional principles.

The true rule as to the employment of military force at the elections is not doubtful. No intimidation or coercion should be allowed to control or influence citizens in the exercise of their right to vote, whether it appears in the shape of combinations of evil-disposed persons, or of armed bodies of the militia of a State, or of the military force of the United States.

The elections should be free from all forcible interference, and, as far as practicable, from all apprehension of such interference. No soldiers, either of the Union or of the State militia, should be present at the polls to take the place or to perform the duties of the ordinary civil police force. There has been and will be no violation of this rule under orders from me during this administration. But there should be no denial of the right of the National Government to employ its military force on any day and at any place in case such employment is necessary to enforce the Constitution and laws of the United States.

The bill before me is as follows:

Be it enacted, etc., That it shall not be lawful to bring to, or employ at, any place where a general or special election is being held in a State, any part of the army or navy of the United States, unless such force be necessary to repel the armed enemies of the United States, or to enforce section 4, article 4, of the Constitution of the United States, and the laws made in pursuance thereof, on application of the Legislature or executive of the State where such force is to be used; and so much of all laws as is inconsistent herewith is hereby repealed.

It will be observed that the bill exempts from the general prohibition against the employment of military force at the polls two specified cases. These exceptions recognize and concede the soundness of the principle that military force may properly and constitutionally be used at the place of elections, when such use is necessary to enforce the Constitution and the laws. But the excepted cases leave the prohibition so extensive and far-reaching that its adoption will seriously impair the efficiency of the executive department of the Government.

The first act expressly authorizing the use of military power to execute the laws was passed almost as early as the organization of the Government under the Constitution, and was approved by President Washington May 2, 1792. It is as follows:

SEC. 2. *And be it further enacted*, That whenever the laws of the United States shall be opposed, or the execution thereof obstructed, in any State, by combinations too powerful to be suppressed by the ordinary course of judicial proceedings, or by the powers vested in the marshals by this act, the same being notified to the President of the United States by an associate justice of the district judge, it shall be lawful for the President of the United States to call forth the militia of such State to suppress such combinations, and to cause the laws to be duly executed. And if the militia of a State where such combination may happen shall refuse or be insufficient to suppress the same, it shall be lawful for the President, if the Legislature of the United States be not in session, to call forth and employ such numbers of the militia of any other State or States most convenient thereto as may be necessary ; and the use of militia, so to be called forth, may be continued, if necessary, until the expiration of thirty days after the commencement of the ensuing session.

In 1795 this provision was substantially reënacted in a law which repealed the act of 1792. In 1807 the following act became the law by the approval of President Jefferson:

That in all cases of insurrection or obstruction to the laws, either of the United States or of any individual State or Territory, where it is lawful for the President of the United States to call forth the militia for the purpose of suppressing such insurrection, or of causing the laws to be duly executed, it shall be lawful for him to employ, for the same purposes, such part of the land or naval force of the United States as shall be judged necessary, having first observed all the prerequisites of the law in that respect.

By this act it will be seen that the scope of the law of 1795 was extended so as to authorize the National Government to use not only the militia but the army and navy of the United States in "causing the laws to be duly executed."

The important provision of the acts of 1792, 1795, and 1807, modified in its terms from time to time to adapt it to the existing emergency, remained in force until by an act approved by President Lincoln, July 29, 1861, it was reënacted substantially in the same language in which it is now found in the Revised Statutes, viz.:

SEC. 5298. Whenever, by reason of unlawful obstructions, combinations, or assemblages of persons, or rebellion against the authority of the Government of the United States, it shall become impracticable, in the judgment of the President, to enforce, by the ordinary course of judicial proceedings, the laws of the United States within any State or Territory, it shall be lawful for the President to call forth the militia of any or all the States, and to employ such parts of the land and naval forces of the United States as he may deem necessary to enforce the faithful execution of the laws of the United States, or to suppress such rebellion, in whatever State or Territory thereof the laws of the United States may be forcibly opposed, or the execution thereof forcibly obstructed.

This ancient and fundamental law has been in force from the foundation of the Government. It is now proposed to abrogate it on certain days and at certain places. In my judgment no fact has been produced which tends to show that it ought to be repealed or suspended for a single hour at any place in any of the States or Territories of the Union. All the teachings of experience in the course of our history are in favor of sustaining its efficiency unimpaired. On every occasion when the supremacy of the Constitution has been resisted, and the perpetuity of our institutions imperiled, the principle of this statute, enacted by the fathers, has enabled the Government of the Union to maintain its authority and to preserve the integrity of the nation.

At the most critical periods of our history, my predecessors in the executive office have relied on this great principle. It was on this principle that President Washington suppressed the whisky rebellion in Pennsylvania in 1794.

In 1806, on the same principle, President Jefferson broke up the Burr conspiracy by issuing "orders for the employment of such force either of the regulars or of the militia, and by such proceedings of the civil authorities, ... as might enable them to suppress effectually the further progress of the enterprise." And it was under the same authority that President Jackson crushed nullification in South Carolina, and that President Lincoln issued his call for troops to save the Union in 1861. On numerous other occasions of less significance, under probably every administration, and certainly under the present, this power has been usefully exerted to enforce the laws, without objection by any party in the country, and almost without attracting public attention.

The great elementary constitutional principle which was the foundation of the original statute of 1792, and which has been its essence in the various forms it has assumed since its first adoption, is that the Government of the United States possesses under the Constitution, in full measure, the power of self-protection by its own agencies altogether independent of State authority, and, if need be, against the hostility of State governments. It should remain embodied in our statutes unimpaired, as it has been from the very origin of the Government. It should be regarded as hardly less valuable or less sacred than a provision of the Constitution itself.

There are many other important statutes containing provisions that are liable to be suspended or annulled at the times and places of holding elections, if the bill before me should become a law. I do not undertake to furnish a list of them. Many of them—perhaps the most of them—have been set forth in the debates on this measure. They relate to extradition, to crimes against the election laws, to quarantine regulations, to neutrality, to Indian reservations, to the civil rights of citizens, and to other subjects. In regard to them all, it may be safely said that the meaning and effect of this bill is to take from the General Government an important part of its power to enforce the laws.

Another grave objection to the bill is its discrimination in favor of the State and against the national authority. The presence or employment of the army or navy of the United States is lawful, under the terms of this bill, at the place where an election is being held in a State, to uphold the authority of a State government then and there in need of such military intervention, but unlawful to uphold the authority of the Government of the United States then and there in need of such military intervention. Under this bill the presence or employment of the army or navy of the United States would be lawful, and might be necessary to maintain the conduct of a State election against the domestic violence that would overthrow it, but would be unlawful to maintain the conduct of a national election against the same local violence that would overthrow it. This discrimination has never been attempted in any previous legislation by Congress, and is no more compatible with sound principles of the Constitution or the necessary maxims and methods of our system of government on occasions of elections than at other times. In the early legislation of 1792 and of 1795, by which the militia of the States was the only military power resorted to for the execution of the constitutional powers in the support of State or national authority, both functions of the Government were put upon the same footing. By the act of 1807 the employment of the army and navy was authorized for the performance of both constitutional duties in the same terms.

In all later statutes on the same subject-matter the same measure of authority to the Government has been accorded for the performance of both these duties. No precedent has been found in any previous legislation, and no sufficient reason has been given for the discrimination in favor of the State and against the national authority which this bill contains.

Under the sweeping terms of the bill the National Government is effectually shut out from the exercise of the right and from the discharge of the imperative duty to use its whole executive power whenever and wherever required for the enforcement of its laws at the places and times when and where its elections are held. The employment of its organized armed forces for any such purpose would be an offense against the law unless called for by, and therefore upon permission of, the authorities of the State in which the occasion of, the authorities of the State in which the occasion arises. What is this but the substitution of the discretion of the State governments for the discretion of the Government of the United States as to the performance of its own duties? In my judgment this is an abandonment of its obligations by the National Government; a subordination of national authority and an intrusion of State supervision over national duties which amounts, in spirit and tendency, to State supremacy.

Though I believe that the existing statutes are abundantly adequate to completely prevent military interference with the elections in the sense in which the phrase is used in the title of this bill and is employed by the people of this country, I shall find no difficulty in concurring in any additional legislation limited to that object which does not interfere with the indispensable exercise of the powers of the Government under the Constitution and laws.

RUTHERFORD B. HAYES.

Executive Mansion, *May* 12, 1879.

The previous question was seconded and the main question ordered.

The Speaker: "The question is, Will the House on reconsideration pass the bill? On this question the Constitution requires that the vote shall be taken by yeas and nays."

The question was taken as follows:

Yeas—Acklen, Aiken, Armfield, Atherton, Bachman, Beale, Bicknell, Blackburn, Bliss, Bouck, Bright, Buckner, Cabell, Caldwell, Carlisle, Clardy, John B. Clark, jr., Clymer, Cobb, Coffroth, Converse, Cook, Covert, Cox, Cravens, Culberson, Davidson, Joseph J. Davis, Lowndes H. Davis, De La Matyr, Deuster, Dibrell, Dickey, Dunn, Elam, Evins, Ewing, Felton, Ford, Forney, Geddes, Gibson, Gillette, Goode, Gunter, John T. Harris, Hatch, Henkle, Herbert, Herndon, Hooker, Hostetler, House, Hurd, Johnston, Jones, Kenna, Kimmel, King, Kitchin, Klotz, Knott, Ladd, Le Fevre, Lewis, Lounsbery, Lowe, Manning, Benjamin F. Martin, Edward L. Martin, McKenzie, McLane, McMahon, McMillan, Mills, Morrison, Muldrow, Muller, Murch, Myers, New, O'Connor, Persons, Phelps, Phister, Poehler, Reagan, J. S. Richardson, Richmond, Robertson, Ross, Rothwell, Samford, Sawyer, Scales, Shelley, J. W. Singleton, O. R. Singleton, Slemons, Hezekiah B. Smith, William E. Smith, Sparks, Springer, Steele, Stephens, Stevenson, Talbott, Taylor, Thompson, Tillman, R. W. Townshend, Oscar Turner, Thomas Turner, Vance, Waddill, Warner, Weaver, Wellborn, Wells, Whiteaker, Whitthorne, Thomas Williams, Willis, Wilson, Fernando Wood, Wright, Yocum, Casey Young—128.

Nays—N. W. Aldrich, William Aldrich, Anderson, Bailey, Barber, Bayne, Bellord, Blake, Bowman, Boyd, Brewer, Briggs, Brigham, Browne, Burrows, Camp, Cannon, Carpenter, Caswell, Claflin, Conger, Cowgill, Crapo, Crowley, Daggett, George R. Davis, Deering, Dunnell, Einstein, Errett, Farr, Ferdon, Field, Fort, Frye, Garfield, Hall, John Hammond, Haskell, Hawk, Hawley, Hayes, Hazelton, Hellman, Henderson, Horr, Houk, Humphrey, Joyce, Keifer, Kelley, Ketcham, Killinger, Lindsey, Marsh, Mason, McCoid, McCook, McGowan, McKinley, Miles, Monroe, Morton, Neal, Newberry, Norcross, O'Neill, Orth, Osmer, Overton, Pound, Prescott, Price, Reed, Rice, Robeson, Robinson, Thomas Ryan, Sapp, Shallenberger, Sherwin, A. Herr Smith, Starin, Stone, Thomas, Amos Townsend, Tyler, J. T. Updegraff, Thomas Updegraff, Urner, Valentine, Wait, Ward, Washburn, C. G. Williams, Willits, Thomas L. Young—97.

NOT VOTING—Atkins, Baker, Ballou, Barlow, Beltzhoover, Bingham, Bland, Blount, Bragg, Butterworth, Calkins, Chalmers, Chittenden, Alvah A. Clark, Colerick, Dick, Dwight, Ellis, Finley, Fisher, Forsythe, Frost, Godshalk, N. J. Hammond, Harmer, Benjamin W. Harris, Henry, Hill, Hiscock, Hubbell, Hull, Hunton, James, Jorgenson, Lapham, Lay, Loring, Joseph J. Martin, Miller, Mitchell, Money, Morse, Nicholls, O'Brien, O'Reilly, Pierce, D. P. Richardson, Daniel L. Russell, William A. Russell, John W. Ryon, Simonton, Speer, Tucker, Van Aernam, Van Voorhis, Voorhis, White, Wilber, Wise, Walter A. Wood—60.

So, on reconsideration, the bill was rejected, two thirds not having voted in favor thereof.

In the House, on April 8th, the bill making appropriations for the legislative, executive, and judicial departments of the Government was taken up.

Mr. Atkins of Tennessee said: " I desire to state that a good many gentlemen on both sides of the House have requested me to report this bill upon the basis of the conference reports of the two Houses as nearly as possible. I will state to the House that the entire money part of the bill—the appropriations—was agreed to by the conference committees of the two Houses, or very nearly so. There are several subjects, however, upon which we did not agree; and in respect to those and these parts upon which we do not agree, the bill conforms to the bill as it passed the House; but in regard to all other particulars, where the conference did agree, the bill conforms to the conference report."

Mr. Coffroth of Pennsylvania: " Mr. Chairman, I turn to the bill under discussion. In it we propose to repeal certain statutes regulating supervisors of election and the appointing of deputy marshals.

" *First.* The judges of the United States Circuit Court, at the instance of any two citizens of any town or city having upward of twenty thousand inhabitants, or at the instance of any ten citizens in any county or parish, may appoint two citizens resident of the city, town, or voting precinct, being of different political parties, who shall be designated as supervisors of election. These supervisors are required to attend at all times and places fixed for the registration of voters who are entitled to vote for a Representative or Delegate in Congress, to challenge any votes supposed to be improperly offered, to remain with the ballot-box after the voting is over until the votes are entirely counted, and after the votes are counted and tabulated to certify their correctness or append objections, and do and perform other acts and things in the premises.

" *Second.* United States marshals are authorized to appoint deputy marshals, who are authorized ' either at the place of registration or polling-place or elsewhere, and either before or after registering or voting, to arrest and take into custody without process any person who commits or attempts or offers to commit any of the acts or offenses prohibited herein, or who commits any offense against the laws of the United States.'

" Sir, it will be seen that this law authorizes the arrest of a citizen without process on the mere whim or caprice of a deputy marshal. If the most upright citizen in this great nation offers to vote, not having been registered, he is liable to be seized, taken into custody, and imprisoned by a deputy marshal. Sir, where is the boasted liberty of the citizen if he can be arrested and imprisoned without process of law? Why, sir, under the law of my State about one in twenty of all the voters at every Congressional election is subject to arrest under this statute, inasmuch as about that proportion is generally not registered; yet, by the law of the State, non-registered citizens are entitled to vote by making affidavit to their residence if otherwise qualified.

" The Constitution of the United States provides in Article IV. that ' the right of the people to be secure in their persons against unreasonable seizures shall not be violated; that no warrant shall issue but upon probable cause, supported by oath or affirmation.' And in Article V. it declares that no person shall be deprived of 'liberty or property without due process of law.' Thus it will be seen that the power given to deputy marshals is not only dangerous to the dearest rights of the citizen, but is in violation of the Constitution of the United States.

" I beg permission to read from the report of the committee appointed by the last Congress to examine into and report on the laws in regard to the appointment and pay of supervisors of election and deputy marshals:

" The law was enacted professedly to aid in securing a full, free, fair, honest ballot. That it has failed has become a matter of history; for since the enactment of these sections and the exercise of power under them there has been complaint of more and greater fraud than ever existed prior to its passage.

" The power to anticipate an election fraud, real or fanciful, prior to its attempted perpetration, to seize and hold to bail or put in prison a voter as a means of preventing his coming to the poll, or to deter therefrom upon suspicion, is a little more power than should be conferred upon any partisan.

" The experiment to secure an honest vote, by the medium of appointees under this law, we believe has signally failed, and the powers conferred have been too often used to prevent rather than to secure an honest vote. The administration of these laws has not only been productive of no affirmative good, but has cost large sums of money without any good return.

" Mr. Chairman, at the elections held in 1876 there were 4,863 supervisors and 11,610 deputy marshals, at a cost to the United States of $275,296.70. At the elections held in 1878 the number of supervisors was 4,599, and there were 4,467 deputy marshals, at a cost to the United States of the enormous sum of $202,- 291.69. In New York City alone there were

1,494 supervisors and 3,565 deputy marshals in 1876, at a cost to the United States of $155,021.88. This enormous sum of money was taken from the people to hire men to corrupt the voters and pollute the ballot-box in order to carry the State of New York for the Republican party. In Pennsylvania there were 1,592 supervisors and 396 deputy marshals in 1876, at a cost to the United States of $33,590. All the supervisors and deputy marshals were in Philadelphia, except 273, and the amount expended in Philadelphia to coerce the voter and keep that city Republican was $30,860. In 1878 in Pennsylvania there were 1,682 supervisors and 773 deputy marshals, at the enormous cost to the United States of $43,943. All of the deputy marshals and all of the supervisors except 312 were at Philadelphia. The sum spent at Philadelphia at this election was $40,820. The sworn testimony of the marshal of the eastern district of Pennsylvania before the Wallace-Teller investigating committee of the United States Senate shows the most astounding fact that every one of the deputy marshals in Philadelphia was a Republican. Even if they had been reputable persons, which they were not, this would be so unjust that it should meet the condemnation of every fair-minded citizen.

"Now, sir, I will give a summary of part of the sworn testimony before that committee to prove the desperate and depraved character of these deputy marshals. Detective Charles Miller, connected with the district attorney's office of that city, testified that

"He knew Philip Madden, a deputy of the Fourth Ward. He was one of the worst men in Philadelphia, violent and dangerous. He has been out of prison about eight months for highway robbery. Andrew Lamvello, of the First Ward, is a fugitive from justice. Dan Redding is a bad, dangerous character, and has been tried for murder. George Cornelius is a bad reputation. Michael Slater is a notorious repeater and thief. Pitts, of the Seventh Ward, keeps a gambling place; he is colored, and has been arrested. Henry Scott, colored, of Lombard Street, has a bad reputation. Radney F. Springfield, of the Fifteenth Ward, was tried for murder and acquitted. All these men were deputy marshals to the knowledge of the detective.

"Other witnesses testified to the bad and debased character of the deputy marshals; that many of them were drunk; that they insulted and maltreated the voters. From this sworn testimony, and which I am told can not be contradicted, among the deputy marshals in the great city of Philadelphia appointed to protect the purity of the ballot-box and sustain a free and untrammeled election, we find the most debased characters, highway robbers, fugitives from justice, repeaters, thieves, keepers of gambling-houses, murderers, keepers of bawdy-houses, and drunkards.

"Mr. Chairman, this is an astonishing revelation. Think of it, sir! This is the city where ' old Independence bell ' first rang out the joyous peals of liberty. Liberty of the citizen was then the thrilling cry of the patriots of the Revolution; but now, more than one hundred years thereafter, comes up a bitter and shameful complaint that the inestimable right of the citizen to a free ballot, uncontrolled by military or civil Federal power, is trampled under foot by a horde of debased and drunken deputy marshals.

"Mr. Chairman, as a native of the great State of Pennsylvania and one of its Representatives on this floor, I enter my solemn protest against this debasing interference with the elections in my State. Pennsylvania has laws upon its statute-books which secure to every elector his right to vote."

Mr. Robeson of New Jersey: "The real question between the gentlemen on the other side and myself is a difficulty which arises on the main propositions of this case; not a difficulty in logic or in argument, not even in verbal propositions; but we differ about our premises, about the principles from which we start. And, if that were otherwise, I should hesitate myself before I arrived at a different conclusion from the distinguished gentlemen who have so clearly and ably presented the other side of this case. But the difference between us is found in our ideas of the organic principles of our Government, about the design of the men who established it, and the purposes for which it was constituted. These gentlemen seem to argue, and I believe—for such is the influence of early education and habit of thought—they honestly and habitually think that we are living, not under the Constitution of the United States, but under a confederacy of separate sovereignties; whereas I think that we are members of a government established for the government of the people and not of the States, a government which has all the attributes of a government, including sovereignty—a government which acts directly upon the people, upon their rights, and upon their property. It seems to me, if I have read aright the principles and history of our Government, that it was for this very purpose that our fathers abandoned the original idea of the Confederation, and appealing again to the people, not to the States, drew from that rich and natural source the powers with which they endowed the Government under the Constitution. And when they turned to that source and took from that natural well their powers of government, they took them pure and unalloyed by any intervening element which could impair or weaken; they drew them direct and pure, not through the doubtful vehicle of intervening government or State sovereignty. If I have read history aright, sir, our fathers found that a confederation of States, where the central power was dependent upon the several States for the execution of its laws, the enforcement of its decrees, and the protection of its people, was insufficient for the purposes of government; and therefore these men, learned in all the principles of government and law, elevated to a loftier mood by their contact with great principles and the great sacrifices they had made, turned again to the people of the country, and from them sought anew the authority upon which this Government was founded; and, clothed with full powers by the people whom they directly represented, they proceeded to establish and ordain a new government with far different, broader, and better-established duties and powers.

"Let us look at the objects which the founders sought in establishing the Government, as it is expressed in the preamble of the Constitution itself. What did they mean to do? 'To form a more perfect union, establish justice, insure domestic tranquillity'—not by the power of State laws or the interference of State officers, but by the force and action of the Government itself; and to 'secure the blessings of liberty to ourselves and our posterity, we'—who?—'we, the people of the United States'—do what? Do we enter into an agreement between parties? No. Do we join in a league between States? No. Do we make a confederation between governments? No. Is this a compact between sovereignties? No. 'We do *ordain and establish*'—What?—'this Constitution'—for what?—'for the United States of America.'

"This, then, is not a confederation of powers, not a league between States, not an agreement between sovereignties, but a Government established and ordained, constituted by this written Constitution—established and restrained, empowered and restricted by this written Constitution thus ordained. I admit, Mr. Chairman, that all the powers of this Government are and must be found within the written Constitution. Here is the source from which the river of our power must flow or else run dry. Nothing is to be claimed, nothing is to be exercised except what flows from the powers there declared, the rights there guaranteed. And if there be any power in these laws which can not be rationally, legitimately, and logically inferred from the provisions and powers of this written Constitution of the country, it should be swept from the statute-book in disdain and dishonor. But, my friends, if there be powers that are necessary for the maintenance of the Government itself, if there be powers that are necessary for its security and preservation, and if these powers be clearly derivable by right and proper reasoning from the Constitution itself or its proper inferences, it is just as much a violation of the Constitution to misconstrue them or deny their force as if you sought to ingraft some foreign power on the Constitution, to the injury of the people for whose government and protection it was established.

"We come now more directly to the consideration of the authority which is to be found in this Constitution for the enactment of the laws now under consideration; for, as I have said, if they are unconstitutional, let them be swept from the statute-book; but if they be constitutional, although in your wisdom, acting as a majority, you may see fit to repeal them, do not put it on the ground of their unconstitutionality, or else your judgment may remain a false precedent for future action, a landmark and guide-post to error and to wrong.

"The gentleman from Kentucky [Mr. Carlisle], who has so ably presented his side of the case, has said that the power derived from the second section of the first article of this Constitution was a power which I had the honor to discover. I should be proud if that were so, but it is a power which is as old as the Constitution itself, as old as the principles which are there set forth; a power which I do not believe has ever before been denied by any one."

Mr. Carlisle: "Was it ever asserted?"

Mr. Robeson: "It would have been asserted if it had been denied. There are many things which are so self-evident when written upon the face of laws that they assert themselves to the understanding of law-givers; and this has been so plainly written that it needed no reassertion by the feeble language of men like myself, for there it is, written on pages of the Constitution of our country, a self-existing, self-standing, self-asserting proposition which has challenged denial since the Constitution was formed: 'The electors in each State shall have the qualifications requisite for the electors of the most numerous branch of the State Legislature.' Electors for what? For the House of Representatives. The House of Representatives of what? Of the national Legislature, of the Congress of the United States. 'All legislative powers granted shall be vested in a Congress'—what of?—'of the United States, which shall. consist of a Senate and House of Representatives.' Not the Legislature of a State, not a governmental body to make laws for a State, but a legislature of the United States, deriving its powers directly from the people and not from the States; a legislature that makes laws for the United States, the members of which swear to maintain the Constitution of the United States and not the constitution of any State. They may not be civil officers, such as come within the list of those enumerated as subject to impeachment. I know it has been held in the case of Senator Blount that he, for acts which he did as a private citizen or as Governor of Tennessee, was not such an officer, and did not do such acts as made him liable to impeachment as one of the civil officers of the Government under that clause of the Constitution. But the decision of that case goes to this extent, and no more. I care not whether you call Representatives in this House officers or not, I care not whether they are civil officers or not, it is a quarrel about words and names; they hold no commission, but they are members of the United States Government, to whom are committed important legislative functions. They discharge United States duties; they are amenable to the rules and government of this House, call them what you will.

"I have said that this clause which I have read, though it confers no right of suffrage, yet adopts to its suffrage that class of voters which are here described. The doctrine of conveying rights by description is not unknown to any of my friends. I may convey to my friend a lot in this city; if I choose I may describe it by proper metes and bounds, or I may say 'lot numbered 1 in subdivision of square numbered 1, as surveyed and recorded in the clerk's office by the surveyor of the city,' and when my friend takes the title for that lot does he take it from me or does he take it from the surveyor who describes it?

"The fourteenth amendment of the Constitution of the United States declares that all persons born or naturalized in the United States are citizens of the United States and citizens of the State in which they reside. Do they take their title of citizenship from the mothers who bore them or the court which naturalized them, or from the Constitution of the United States which describes and adopts them? The Speaker of this House, under certain contingencies, may become the President of the United States, because he had been elected by the citizens of Philadelphia, and afterward selected by our votes to be Speaker. Does he derive that title from the Constitution of the United States or from the votes of the Fourth Ward of the city of Philadelphia? It seems to me to be too clear for argument. There are some propositions which in their statement are so conclusive that you confuse them by illustration or argument.

"Now, then, if this be a United States election for members of the United States Government, who are to have United States qualifications and to execute United States laws, is it not a right guaranteed to every citizen that that election shall be fair? Gentlemen will say there are no citizens—or would have said in the old time—there are no citizens except the citizens of a State, and therefore it is they who must protect the rights which are guaranteed to citizens. Since the adoption of the fourteenth amendment, as I have said, there are citizens of the United States independent of and above the States; and by that Constitution they are as citizens entitled to every right which is there guaranteed and secured. More than that, this House, this national Legislature, is the judge of the election, qualification, and returns of its own members. Is that a State function or a United States function? And may it not be reasonably said, may it not be irresistibly argued, that the Congress of the United States has the right, if it chooses to exercise it, to make all laws and all rules which are necessary to give them all the information which it is proper and necessary they should have in order to decide upon these questions?

"But it is not necessary to argue from general propositions upon this subject. By the eighth section of the first article of the Constitution it is provided that Congress shall have power 'to make all laws which shall be necessary and proper for carrying into execution the foregoing powers, and all other powers vested by this Constitution in the Government of the United States or in any department or officer thereof.' In the very section of the Constitution which gives this right and declares this qualification and establishes this election, and which also gives the right to Congress, when they choose, to make all needed regulations with regard to the time, place, and manner of holding it—in the very concluding section of that article the power to make these laws is expressly and explicitly given. Now, then, Mr. Chairman, what does that mean? If there is any remark to be made about this Constitution, it is that it was the work of master hands, and that, dealing in general statements and general terms, there is nothing within it which is unnecessary to its operation. Let us see whether it covers the whole of this case. The distinguished gentleman from Alabama [Mr. Lewis], who opened this debate in a speech which seemed to me to be as fair, as compendious, and as logical as any that I have heard, put this proposition on what seemed to me to be its strongest ground, if strong ground it has. He said that this was an alternate power of the United States Government, which resided originally in the States, and could not be exercised by the United States unless the State refused or neglected properly to exercise it. If I have misstated the proposition, I see the gentleman in his seat, and I hope he will correct me. He founded that assertion on the language of some of the writers of that time, and also on the debates on the Constitution in various of the States, and on the protests which some of the States made against its adoption. But it seems to me that the very argument on which he founded it avails for its overthrow. It was an objection made by the States. Why? Because it was not an ultimate power, but because it was an original power. It was an objectionable clause to which they proposed amendments, but those amendments, after consideration, were not adopted, and the original Constitution remained as it was."

Mr. Chalmers of Mississippi: "There are two laws standing upon the statute-book in regard to supervisors of elections, one made for the country, the other made for the city, confessedly made for the city of New York; and John Davenport boasts that they were made at his dictation. The city of New York is Democratic; the country districts are Republican. Hence we find that, through the ingenuity of this matchless trickster in politics, we have one law for the Democrat and another for the Republican. The supervisors who are to watch over the Democratic polls are entrusted with extraordinary power, to supervise registration, in effect to determine the qualifications of voters, and, with or without warrant, to arrest citizens at the polls. In the country districts there is no such power.

"By section 2029 of the Revised Statutes, which remains unchanged, it is expressly provided: 'The supervisors of election appointed for any county or parish in any Congressional district, at the instance of ten citizens, as provided in section 2011, shall have no authority to make arrests, or to perform other duties than to be in the immediate presence of the officers holding the election, and to witness all their proceedings, including the counting of the votes and the making of a return thereof.'

"Now, all that is proposed by this bill is, that we shall equalize the powers of supervisors everywhere in the Union—make their power the same in the cities that it is in the country districts, the same for the Democrat that it is for the Republican, the same for the bond-holding, purse-proud man in the rural districts of New York that it is for the toiling masses in the city of New York, who have been denounced on the floor of Congress as thieves, scoundrels, and the very scum of the earth. That is the full extent of the legislation here proposed—no more. Yet when we have proposed to equalize the power of supervisors it has been suddenly discovered that they are mere 'stool-pigeons with their wings clipped.' If they are stool-pigeons, we did not create them; the Republican party created them, and at. the same time that they made stool-pigeons with clipped wings to nestle gently at Republican polls, they created vultures with fierce beaks and sharpened talons to hover around Democratic precincts and to tear the vitals of Democratic voters. We simply demand that the law shall be equalized. We leave the supervisors as we found them. We do not even change their pay, lest perchance it should be said that we recognized the constitutionality of their appointment, which we utterly deny. We leave them the same in the South that they are to-day, not because it is right, but because we do not desire to demand upon an appropriation bill anything that is not vital and immediately essential for the preservation of civil liberty. That is all there is in this bill as to supervisors of elections."

Mr. Atkins demanded the previous question on the passage of the bill; and the question was taken as follows:

YEAS—Acklen, Aiken, Armfield, Atherton, Atkins, Bachman, Beale, Beltzhoover, Bicknell, Blackburn, Bliss, Bragg, Bright, Buckner, Cabell, Caldwell, Carlisle, Chalmers, Clardy, Alvah A. Clark, John B. Clark, jr., Clymer, Cobb, Coffroth, Colerick, Converse, Cook, Covert, Cravens, Culberson, Davidson, Joseph J. Davis, Lowndes H. Davis, De La Matyr, Deuster, Dibrell, Dickey, Dunn, Elam, Ellis, Evins, Ewing, Felton, Finley, Forney, Frost, Geddes, Gibson, Gillette, Goode, Gunter, N. J. Hammond, Hatch, Henkle, Henry, Herbert, Herndon, Hill, Hostetler, House, Hull, Hunton, Hurd, Johnston, Jones, Kenna, Kimmel, King, Kitchin, Klotz, Knott, Le Fevre, Lewis, Lounsbery, Lowe, Manning, Benjamin F. Martin, Edward L. Martin, McKenzie, McLane, McMillan, Mills, Money, Morrison, Muldrow, Muller, Murch, Myers,

New, Nicholls, O'Connor, O'Reilly, Persons, Phelps, Phister, Poehler, Reagan, John S. Richardson, Richmond, Robertson, Ross, Rothwell, John W. Ryon, Samford, Sawyer, Scales, Shelley, Simonton, James W. Singleton, O. R. Singleton, Slemons, Hezekiah B. Smith, William E. Smith, Sparks, Speer, Springer, Steele, Stephens, Stevenson, Talbott, Thompson, Tillman, R. W. Townshend, Tucker, Oscar Turner, Thomas Turner, Vance, Waddill, Warner, Weaver, Wellborn, Whiteaker, Whitthorne, Thomas Williams, Willis, Wise, Fernando Wood, Wright, Yocum, Casey Young—140.

NAYS—Nelson W. Aldrich, William Aldrich, Anderson, Bailey, Baker, Barber, Barlow, Bayne, Belford, Bingham, Blake, Bowman, Boyd, Brewer, Briggs, Brigham, Browne, Burrows, Butterworth, Calkins, Camp, Cannon, Carpenter, Caswell, Claflin, Rush Clark, Conger, Cowgill, Crapo, Daggett, George R. Davis, Deering, Dunnell, Dwight, Errett, Far, Ferdon, Field, Fisher, Ford, Fort, Frye, Garfield, Godshalk, Hall, John Hammond, Harmer, Benjamin W. Harris, Haskell, Hawk, Hawley, Hayes, Heilman, Henderson, Hiscock, Hubbell, Humphrey, James, Jorgensen, Joyce, Keifer, Kelley, Ketcham, Killinger, Lapham, Lindsey, Loring, Marsh, Joseph J. Martin, Mason, McCoid, McCook, McGowan, McKinley, Miles, Miller, Mitchell, Monroe, Morton, Neal, Newberry, Norcross, O'Neill, Osmer, Overton, Pierce, Pound, Prescott, Price, Reed, Rice, D. P. Richardson, Robinson, William A. Russell, Thomas Ryan, Sapp, Shallenberger, Sherwin, A. Herr Smith, Starin, Thomas, Amos Townsend, Tyler, J. T. Updegraff, Thomas Updegraff, Urner, Valentine, Van Aernam, Van Voorhis, Voorhis, Wait, Ward, Washburn, White, Wilber, C. G. Williams, Willits, Walter A. Wood, Thomas L. Young—119.

In the Senate, on April 24th, the bill was considered.

Mr. Conkling of New York said: "Why now should there be an attempt to block the wheels of government on the eve of an election at which this whole question is triable before the principals and masters of us all? The answer is inevitable. But one truthful explanation can be made of this daring enterprise. It is a political, a partisan manœuvre. It is a strike for party advantage. With a fair election and an honest count, the Democratic party can not carry the country. These laws, if executed, insure some approach to a fair election. Therefore they stand in the way, and therefore they are to be broken down. I reflect upon no man's motives, but I believe that the sentiment which finds expression in the transaction now proceeding in the two Houses of Congress has its origin in the idea I have stated. I believe that the managers and charioteers of the Democratic party think that with a fair election and a fair count they can not carry the State of New York. They know that with unrestrained course, such as existed in 1868, to the ballot-box and count, no matter what majority may be given in that State where the green grass grows, the great cities will overbalance and swamp it. They know that with the ability to give eighty, ninety, one hundred thousand majority in the county of New York and the county of Kings, half of it fraudulently added, it is idle for the three million people living above the Highlands of the Hudson to vote. This is a struggle for power. It is a fight for empire. It is a contrivance to clutch the National Government. That we believe; that I believe.

"The nation has tasted and drunk to the dregs the sway of the Democratic party, organized and dominated by the same influences which dominate it again and still. You want to restore that dominion. We mean to resist you at every step and by every lawful means that opportunity places in our hands. We believe that it is good for the country, good for every man North and South who loves the country now, that the Government should remain in the hands of those who were never against it. We believe that it is not wise or safe to give over our nationality to the dominion of the forces which formerly and now again rule the Democratic party. We do not mean to connive at further conquests, and we tell you that, if you gain further political power, you must gain it by fair means, and not by foul. We believe that these laws are wholesome. We believe that they are necessary barriers against wrongs, necessary defenses for rights; and, so believing, we will keep and defend them even to the uttermost of lawful honest effort.

"The other day, it was Tuesday, I think, it pleased the honorable Senator from Illinois [Mr. Davis] to deliver to the Senate an address, I had rather said an opinion, able and carefully prepared. That honorable Senator knows well the regard not only, but the sincere respect in which I hold him, and he will not misunderstand the freedom with which I shall refer to some of his utterances. Whatever else his sayings fail to prove, they did, I think, prove their author, after Mrs. Winslow, the most copious and inexhaustible fountain of soothing sirup. The honorable Senator seemed like one slumbering in a storm and dreaming of a calm. He said there was no uproar anywhere—one would infer you could hear a pin drop—from center to circumference. Rights, he said, were secure. I have his language here. If I do not seem to give the substance aright I will stop and read it. Rights secure North and South; peace and tranquillity everywhere. The law obeyed, and no need of special provisions or anxiety. It was in this strain that the Senator discoursed.

"Are rights secure, when fresh-done barbarities show that local government in one portion of our land is no better than despotism tempered by assassination! Rights secure, when such things can be as stand proved and recorded by committees of the Senate! Rights secure, when the old and the young fly in terror from their homes and from the graves of their murdered dead! Rights secure, when thousands brave cold, hunger, death, seeking among strangers in a far country a humanity which will remember that

    "'Before man made them citizens,
     Great Nature made them men!'

"Read the memorial signed by Judge Dillon, by the Democratic mayor of Saint Louis, by Mr. Henderson, once a member of the Senate, and by other men known to the nation, detailing what has been done in recent weeks on the southern Mississippi. Read the affidavits accompanying this memorial. Has any one a copy of the memorial here? I have seen the memorial. I have seen the signatures. I hope the honorable Senator from Illinois will read it, and read the affidavits which accompany it. When he does, he will read one of the most sickening recitals of modern times. He will look upon one of the bloodiest and blackest pictures in the book of recent years. Yet the Senator says all is quiet. 'There is not such faith, no, not in Israel.' Verily 'order reigns in Warsaw.' *Solitudinem faciunt, pacem appellant.*

"Mr. President, the Republican party everywhere wants peace and prosperity—peace and prosperity in the South as much and as sincerely as elsewhere. Disguising the truth will not bring peace and prosperity. Soft phrases will not bring peace. 'Fair words butter no parsnips.' We hear a great deal of loose flabby talk about 'fanning dying embers,' 'rekindling smoldering fires,' and so on. Whenever the plain truth is spoken, these unctuous monitions, with a Peter Parley benevolence, fall copiously upon us. This lullaby and hush has been in my belief a mistake from the beginning. It has misled the South and misled the North. In Andrew Johnson's time a convention was worked up at Philadelphia, and men were brought from the North and South for ecstacy and gush. A man from Massachusetts and a man from South Carolina locked arms and walked into the convention arm in arm, and sensation and credulity palpitated and clapped their hands, and thought a universal solvent had been found. Serenades were held at which 'Dixie' was played. Later on, anniversaries of battles fought in the war of Independence were made occasions by men from the North and men from the South for emotional, dramatic, hugging ceremonies. General Sherman, I remember, attended one of them; and I remember also that, with the bluntness of a soldier, and the wisdom and hard sense of a statesman, he plainly cautioned all concerned not to be carried away, and not to be fooled. But many have been fooled, and, being fooled, have helped to swell the Democratic majorities which now display themselves before the public eye. Of all such effusive demonstrations I have this to say: Honest, serious convictions are not ecstatic or emotional. Grave affairs and lasting purposes do not express or vent themselves in honeyed phrase or sickly sentimentality, rhapsody, or profuse professions. This is as true of political as of religious duties. The Divine Master tells us, 'Not every one that saith unto me, Lord, Lord, shall enter into the kingdom of heaven; but he that doeth the will of my Father which is in heaven.' Facts are stubborn things, but the better way to deal with them is to look them squarely in the face.

"The Republican party and the Northern people preach no crusade against the South. I will say nothing of the past beyond a single fact. When the war was over no man who fought against his flag was punished even by imprisonment. No estate was confiscated. Every man was left free to enjoy life, liberty, and the pursuit of happiness. After the Southern States were restored to their relations in the Union no man was ever disfranchised by national authority—not one. If this statement is denied, I invite any Senator to correct me. I repeat it. After the Southern State governments were rebuilded and the States were restored to their relations in the Union by national authority, not one man for one moment was ever denied the right to vote, or hindered in the right. From the time that Mississippi was restored there never has been an hour when Jefferson Davis might not vote as freely as the honorable Senator in his State of Illinois. The North, burdened with taxes, draped in mourning, dotted over with new-made graves tenanted by her bravest and her best, sought to inflict no penalty upon those who had stricken her with the greatest, and, as she believed, the guiltiest rebellion that ever crimsoned the annals of the human race. As an example of generosity and magnanimity, the conduct of the nation in victory was the grandest the world has ever seen. The same spirit prevails now. Yet our ears are larumed with the charge that the Republicans of the North seek to revive and intensify the wounds and pangs and passions of the war, and that the Southern Democrats seek to bury them in oblivion of kind forgetfulness.

"We can test the truth of these assertions right before our eyes. Let us test them. Twenty-seven States adhered to the Union in the dark hour. Those States send to Congress two hundred and sixty-nine Senators and Representatives. Of these two hundred and sixty-nine Senators and Representatives, fifty-four, and only fifty-four, were soldiers in the armies of the Union. The eleven States which were disloyal send ninety-three Senators and Representatives to Congress. Of these, eighty-five were soldiers in the armies of the rebellion, and at least three more held high civil station in the rebellion, making in all eighty-eight out of ninety-three. Let me state the same fact, dividing the Houses. There are but four Senators here who fought in the Union Army. They all sit here now; and there are but four. Twenty Senators sit here who fought in the army of the rebellion, and three more Senators sit here who held high civil command in the Confederacy. In the House there are fifty Union soldiers from twenty-seven States, and sixty-five Confederate soldiers from eleven States. Who, I ask you, Senators, tried by this record, is keeping up party divisions on the issues and hatreds of the war?

"The South is solid. Throughout all its borders it has no seat here save two in which a Republican sits. The Senator from Mississippi [Mr. Bruce] and the Senator from Louisiana [Mr. Kellogg] are still spared, and whisper says that an enterprise is afoot to deprive one of these Senators of his seat. The South is emphatically solid. Can you wonder if the North soon becomes solid too? Do you not see that the doings witnessed now in Congress fill the North with alarm and distrust of the patriotism and good faith of men from the South? Forty-two Democrats have seats on this floor; forty-three if you add the honorable Senator from Illinois [Mr. Davis]. He does not belong to the Democratic party, although I must say, after reading his speech the other day, that a Democrat who asks anything more of him is an insatiate monster. If you count the Senator from Illinois, there are forty-three Democrats in this Chamber. Twenty-three is a clear majority of all, and twenty-three happens to be exactly the number of Senators from the South who were leaders in the late rebellion. Do you anticipate my object in stating these numbers? For fear you do not, let me explain. Forty-two Senators rule the Senate; twenty-three Senators rule the caucus: a majority rules the Senate; a caucus rules the majority; and the twenty-three Southern Senators rule the caucus. The same thing in the same way, governed by the same elements, is true in the House.

"This present assault upon the purity and fairness of elections, upon the Constitution, upon the executive department, and upon the rights of the people—not the rights of a king, not on such rights as we heard the distinguished presiding officer, whom I am glad now to discover in his seat, dilate upon of a morning some weeks ago; not the divine right of kings, but the unborn rights of the people—the present assault upon them could never have been inaugurated without the action of the twenty-three Southern Senators here, and the Southern Representatives there [pointing to the House]. The people of the North know this and see it. They see the lead and control of the Democratic party again where it was before the war, in the hands of the South. 'By their fruits ye shall know them.' The honorable Senator from Alabama [Mr. Morgan], educated no doubt by experience in political appearances and spectacular effects, said the other day that he preferred the Democrats from the North should go first in this debate. I admired his sagacity. It was the skill of an experienced tactician to deploy the Northern levies as the sappers and miners; it was very becoming certainly. It was not from cruelty, or to make them food for powder, that he set them in the fore-front of the battle; he thought it would appear better for the Northern auxiliaries to go first and tunnel the citadel. Good, excellent, as far as it went; but it did not go very far in misleading anybody; putting the tail foremost and the head in the sand only showed the species and habits of the bird.

" We heard the other day that the logic of events had filled the Southern cities with men banded together by a common history and a common purpose. The Senator who made that sage observation perhaps builded better than he knew. The same logic of events, let me tell Democratic Senators and the communities behind them, is destined to bring from the North more united delegations.

" I read in a newspaper that it was proposed the other day in another place to restore to the army of the United States men who, educated at the nation's cost and presented with the nation's sword, drew that sword against the nation's life. In the pending bill is a provision for the retirement of officers now in the army with advanced rank and exaggerated pay. This may be harmless, it may be kind. One sparrow proves not spring; but along with other things suspicion will see in it an attempt to coax officers now in the army to dismount, to empty their saddles, in order that others may get on.

" So hue and cry is raised because courts on motion, for cause shown in open court, have a right to purge juries in certain cases. No man in all the South under thirty-five years of age can be affected by this provision, because every such man was too young, when the armies of the rebellion were recruited, to be subject to the provision complained of. As to the rest, the discretion is a wholesome one. But, even if it were not, let me say in all kindness to Southern Senators, it was not wise to make it a part of this proceeding, and raise this uproar in regard to it.

" Even the purpose, in part already executed, to remove the old and faithful officers of the Senate, even Union soldiers, that their places may be snatched by others, to overturn an order of the Senate which has existed for a quarter of a century, in order to grasp all the petty places here, seems to me unwise. It is not wise, if you want to disarm suspicion that you mean aggrandizing, gormandizing, unreasonable things.

" Viewing all these doings in the light of party advantage—advantage to the party to which I belong, I could not deplore them; far from it; but, wishing the repose of the country, and the real, lasting, ultimate welfare of the South, and wishing it from the bottom of my heart, I believe they are flagrantly unwise, hurtfully injudicious.

" What the South needs is to heal, build, mend, plant, sow. In short, go to work. Invite labor; cherish it; do not drive it out. Quit proscription, both for opinion's sake and for color's sake. Reform it altogether. I know there are difficulties in the way; I know there is natural repugnance in the way; but drop passion, drop sentiment which signifies naught, and let the material prosperity and civilization of your land advance. Do not give so much energy, so much restless, sleepless activity, to an attempt so soon to get possession once more and dominate and rule the country. There is room enough at the national board, and it is not needed, it is not decorous, plainly speaking, that the South should be the MacGregor at the table, and that the head of the table should be wherever he sits. For a good many reasons it is not worth while to insist upon it.

" Mr. President, one of Rome's famous legends stands in these words: Let what each man thinks of the Republic be written on his brow. I have spoken in the spirit of this injunction. Meaning offense to no man, and holding ill will to no man because he comes from the South or because he differs with me in political opinion, I have spoken frankly, but with malice toward none.

" This session, and the bill pending are acts in a partisan and political enterprise. This debate, begun after a caucus had defined and clinched the position of every man in the majority, has not been waged to convince anybody here. It has resounded to fire the democratic heart, to sound a blast to the cohorts of party, to beat the long roll and set the squadrons in the field. This is the object of it, as plainly to be seen as the ultimate object of the attempted overthrow of laws. Political speeches having been thus ordained, I have discussed political themes, and, with ill will to no portion of the country, but good will toward every portion of it, I have with candor spoken somewhat of my thoughts of the duties and dangers of the hour."

Mr. Hill of Georgia: " Mr. President, the speech of the Senator from Vermont ought to be studied by every statesman in this Union, for it shadows, as that distinguished Senator only knows how to shadow, the great distinction that lies at the bottom of all the differences between the two parties that now contend for the mastery in this Government. This whole argument goes upon the idea that there is no protection for the citizens of this country save by the military arm. This whole argument of the honorable Senator from Vermont is replete with the idea that when you withdraw the army, or fail to furnish the military arm for the protection of the citizen, he is without protection; when you fail to give the President the army and the navy to enforce the laws, the President is without power to enforce the laws!

" Well, sir, if we have arrived at that condition of things, our condition is indeed lamentable. We have been taught from our youth to believe that this was a country of self-government, that the people are able to protect themselves, that freemen did not need a standing army and a navy to protect themselves—protect themselves from themselves. It has not been customary to teach our people that they must look to the arms of military power through a Federal centralism for the protection and preservation of their rights; and yet I challenge any gentleman to give this speech a critical reading, and it goes altogether on the assumption that if military protection is withdrawn there is no protection worth having remaining; and the practical result of the Senator's argument is to show that by passing this bill, which simply declares that the army and the navy shall not be used at the polls, we repeal all the acts which authorize the enforcement of the laws previously passed, and leave the President powerless to enforce the laws and the citizens without protection.

"I heard a similar argument from that distinguished Senator on another memorable occasion. I noticed it then, and I call the attention of the country to it now. I heard it on one of those bills during the last Congress before us making appropriations for the army, in which there was a clause prohibiting the army from being used as a *posse comitatus* to execute the law. If Senators will turn to the short speech made by the distinguished Senator on that occasion, they will find that he said broadly that if that clause of the appropriation bill became a law, and a mob should be organized in the city of Washington to rob the Treasury, there would be no power to protect the Treasury from that mob; impressing the country with the idea that its defense, that its safety, that its protection rests in the arm of the military power. Can it be true? If a mob should organize in the city of Washington for the purpose of capturing the Treasury and robbing it, is it true that because there is no army here, because the army can not be used as a *posse comitatus*, therefore the mob has only to go and take possession of the Treasury? In a city of one hundred and fifty thousand inhabitants is there no power to protect the Treasury from a mob save through an army? Sir, that idea is at war with every feature of our Government, and certainly at war with all its fundamental principles. Our Government rests upon the idea that we are capable of self-government, that the people are patriotic, and the defense and protection of the property and liberties of the country rest in that belief—the people and the authority of the courts, which are the same thing, because they come from the body of the people. It rests upon the idea that we do not need a standing army to protect the American people from outrage by the American people as a body. Of course there are exceptions, as in all countries. The people must be protected from mobs, but the people can be protected from mobs without the use of the army.

"What would be the result of this style of argument? Gentlemen strangely have come out here now, and, in opposition to the bill passed yesterday, they have taken the distinct position that it is necessary to keep upon your statute-book the right to use the army and navy for the purpose of keeping the peace at the polls. Well, sir, it is idle, it is worse than idle, to give the President of the United States authority to use your army for any purpose, and not furnish him an army for use. You

say the President must have the right to use the army to control the elections. That is what you say by your opposition to this bill, for that is the only idea that the bill negatives. If it is necessary to have the right to use the army, the right is worthless unless you furnish an army to use. Make the calculation. Let the citizens of this country make the calculation, and see what destiny is in wait for them when the proposition is once established that an army must be supplied for the purpose of keeping the peace at the polls. How many troops will it take? What sized army must you have? You must have an army in every State, in every county, in every town; for, if one portion of the country is entitled to protection, and that protection can only be extended by the army, every other portion of the country is entitled to protection; every other portion of the country must have an army; and America, free America, will present to the world the singular spectacle of standing more in need of an army than any country on the globe, and we must have a larger standing army than Germany or Russia.

"Sir, does not every man see, in the very idea that the people of this country, on that day when they as sovereigns come to exercise the power of a sovereign, that they must have an army to control them, an army to protect them, an army to regulate them, an army to keep the peace among themselves in the exercise of this great power, that even by that very idea they must admit that free self-government is a failure? It is the last idea that an American ought to admit. Of all ideas possible in this day and age of degeneracy, I should have supposed the very last idea an American statesman would have admitted as at all applicable to the condition of things in this country would be that we needed military interference on the days of elections for the purpose of protecting the people at the polls. Whenever the American Congress shall in solemn form tell the world that an army is needed to protect American freemen when American freemen go to the polls, they have admitted that the American popular system of government is at an end.

"I must say that I am loth to believe, and I do not believe, that the distinguished gentleman who made the argument of this kind on yesterday, and which necessarily leads to this result, any more believes the statement he was making than did the Senator from the State of New York believe the statement of figures he made was correct. Neither of them had any purpose to make an incorrect statement, but both of them were after the great purpose of this whole movement—to excite one section of this country against the other, and to avail themselves of any occasion for that purpose. I have been watching during the progress of this discussion not only the character of the speeches that have been made, which have convinced my mind thoroughly of the whole purpose of it, but simultaneously the extraordinary movements that are going on through the country. Take the Republican newspapers of the day, and it seems to me that they are fuller of abuse, misrepresentation, and vituperation of the section of the country from which I have come than they ever were before. I know, from direct communication to myself, that various gentlemen who have been living for a few years in the South are going through the North, some of them as lecturers, some of them in the garb of ministers of the Gospel, and their whole lectures are simply replete with the most extravagant and false statements of wrongs and injuries in the South.

"Designing persons are circulating letters and documents among the poor colored people, telling them that in Kansas they can have forty acres and a mule and money free of cost, and the Government, the great good Government that freed them, will take care of them. For what purpose is this second signal movement among the poor negroes of the South, the effect of which is to dissatisfy them with their condition? That they may, as many of them have been, be deceived and undertake to emigrate to this heavenly region, the new Canaan of the negro—the colored man. Why is that done? Not for the purpose of benefiting the poor colored man—oh, no ; but for the double purpose of making it an occasion to vituperate the Southern people before the Northern people, charging their own duplicity to be the effect of cruelty and wrong by the very men whose advantage it is to be kind to their laborers and to keep them among them in contentment. There is the political purpose. Thus they get thousands of poor creatures away from home, naked and hungry, and then the appeal comes to the philanthropy of Northern people and the plethora of the Treasury to come and take care of them; and the agents who circulate the falsehoods and create the dissatisfaction and produce the mischief come in, of course, as dispensers of the alms. It is a sad fact that these sectional passions are yet used by statesmen, by politicians, by bad men, and by thousands of small men in a hundred shapes and forms—these sectional passions that keep the people of the North and the people of the South distrustful of each other, and which are made commerce of by these people for their own selfish ends without any regard to consequences.

"We are to be told that the military arm is essential to the protection of the country, but that under no circumstances can the North trust one third of the people of this Union. No man can read these remarkable declarations of the leading men of that great party, and not feel that the American Rubicon is in sight, and that Cæsar is ready to cross over.

"But, sir, I should not have perhaps said one word, notwithstanding my convictions, of the purposes of the discussion here, the style of discussion, the manner of the discussion, its perfect consonance with what is going on outside, notwithstanding the conviction on my part that there is this day a concerted movement in this country permeating the whole Republican party, high and low, for the purpose of consolidating one section in this country against the other for no purpose but that of dominion, right or wrong —I perhaps should have said nothing in view of all this but for the fact that in the present case the immediate legislation and the purpose manifested in opposing that legislation would amount to nothing unless they could control the President of the United States. If the President should oppose the bill passed by the majority of Congress, of course that was an end to the contest here ; and distinguished gentlemen who had made such tremendous clamor against the bill would be like Othello—their occupation would be gone. I do not wish to do any one injustice, but it can not be disguised before the country that a persistent, earnest, arbitrary, I almost said dictatorial, purpose has been manifested by that party to get control of the President and influence him to veto the bill. I have never believed it would be done. I do not believe the President will lend himself to the scheme, and I have not believed it. The present Chief Magistrate of this country distinguished his administration in a manner worthy of his best predecessor when he first took charge of it, by signalizing the beginning of that administration by the removal of the troops from the polls of the States and from interference with the States. I can not believe that a President who thus signalized his administration in the beginning would be guilty of the enormous inconsistency of now insisting, against the will of a majority of Congress, that he should have the power to use troops, not only to control the States, but to control all the elections in the country. It would be too manifestly inconsistent.

" There is no clause in the Constitution which says in so many words that Congress shall vote appropriations ; but the preservation of the Government itself requires that appropriations shall be voted. The taxes are paid into the Treasury for the purposes of supporting the Government, and the Congress which willfully refuses to appropriate money to support the Government, in my judgment, is guilty of revolutionary conduct which can not be excused. I suppose I have stated that with sufficient strength for the Senator from New York. Now, what are the facts? Mark what I state : that the refusal to vote the appropriations to support the Government is unconstitutional, that we are bound by the very terms of our oath to take care of this Government, to support it, to maintain it, and to that end to make the necessary appropriations. What are the facts? Take the Forty-fifth Congress. Every Democrat in the House voted for appropriations ; every Democrat in the Senate voted for appropriations ; and every Republican in the House and Senate voted against the appropriations.' Who violated the Constitution? Did the Democrats who voted to make the appropriations violate the Constitution? Did the Republicans who voted not to make the appropriations support the Constitution? The Senator says it is a constitutional duty to make appropriations. I admit it. Why was it that appropriations were not voted by the Forty-fifth Congress to support the army and to carry on the Government? It was because every Republican in this body rallied and defeated the bill making appropriations for that purpose. There is the record. Let us get the facts right, and I will attend to the excuses afterward. The unconstitutional act of voting against appropriations was done by the Republican party. The constitutional duty of voting for appropriations was performed by every Democrat in both Houses. How, then, can it be charged over the country that the Democratic party is responsible for the failure of the appropriations?

"Not only was that true in the Forty-fifth Congress, but it is true of the Forty-sixth. This Congress was called together, and every Democrat in both Houses voted for a bill appropriating money to support the army, all that the departments demand and need. Every Republican in both Houses voted against it. If it is unconstitutional to refuse appropriations, who has refused appropriations? But the Senator is right again. If it is a constitutional duty on the part of Representatives and Senators to vote for appropriations, it is equally a constitutional duty on the part of the Executive to approve the appropriation bill, because under the forms of the Constitution every bill has to go to him for approval or disapproval. The appropriations can not be made by a majority of Congress without the concurrence of the President; and, therefore, it is just as unconstitutional for the President to defeat an appropriation as for Congress to do so. The President has done it in this case, but they say there are excuses for it.

"The first question I wish to put to the Senator is this: What excuse can justify a man in doing an unconstitutional act? The Senator says it is unconstitutional to vote against appropriations. What excuse can justify a man in voting against an appropriation? What excuse can justify the President in vetoing an appropriation bill? I think it must be conceded on all hands that no man can be justified in doing an unconstitutional thing for any reason less than the preservation of the Constitution itself. Now, what are the excuses offered in this case? The excuse is the general legislation that was attached to the appropriation bill. What was the form of that legislation? First, it is admitted to be usual and constitutional. The Senator from New York himself admits that. The Senator from New York goes further, and says that so far as the mere form is concerned any bill which Con-

gress has the power to pass can be attached to an appropriation bill, and, unless the President can find cause on its merits, it is difficult to see how the veto of such a bill could be sustained; and the Senator is right. The form was usual and constitutional. So the President can not be justified in vetoing the bill, nor can the gentlemen on the other side be justified in voting against the bill because of the form, if the form of the bill is usual and constitutional. Mark you, they say to vote against the bill is unconstitutional. To refuse an appropriation (and every man by his vote against an appropriation does refuse it) is unconstitutional. Then you can not plead that you do not like the form for the purpose of justifying the unconstitutional act. Then take the substance of the bill. What is it? It is nothing in the world but to repeal certain legislation. That is constitutional. The Senator from New York would admit that Congress has a right to repeal those acts; that it is constitutional to repeal the acts we seek to repeal.

"Mr. President, I advance to a more significant proposition, one which I consider still more important than any that has been discussed. You can not believe that this great party, led by such intelligent gentlemen, is simply influenced, and influenced alone, by a desire to control an election. There is a greater significance. I will not say the manifest purpose, but I will say the logical tendency of the doctrines which have been advanced, and which are in perfect consonance with the history of the Republican party, is the destruction of the States as an element in the character of this Union. Take the argument of the Senator from New York. Let me read what he said. The Senator from New York said:

"In the city of New York all the thugs and shoulder-hitters and repeaters, all the carriers of slung-shots, dirks, and bludgeons, all the fraternity of the bucket-shops, the rat-pits, the hells, and the slums, all the graduates of the nurseries of modern so-called democracy [laughter], all those who employ and incite them, from King's Bridge to the Battery, are to be told in advance that on the day when the million people around them choose their members of the National Legislature, no matter what God-daring or man-hurting enormities they may commit, no matter what they do, nothing they can do will meet with the slightest resistance from any national soldier or armed man clothed with national authority.

"Now, does the Senator from New York mean to say (and his argument is utterly worthless unless he does mean to say so) that protection from thugs and shoulder-hitters and the various unnamable bad men that he enumerates is impossible in New York except through the national soldiery, except through the arm of the National Government? Is that what the honorable Senator means? Yet that is what he says. He says that every one of these terrible characters is to be told that he may commit any enormity he pleases; he can not be interfered with by any national soldiery. That is all true; but does it therefore follow that they can do these great crimes with impunity? Has New York no power to protect her citizens in the exercise of the right of suffrage? Is New York so given up to thugs and shoulder-hitters—I can not remember those other hard names—but is New York such a hell that New York can not protect her own people; and does the ambassador from New York, in his high place, say that to the country? If New York can protect her people, why does she clamor for the national arm? Is New York unable to protect her citizens? Then let New York petition this Congress and say so, and we will help the poor, feeble, emasculated State of New York! Is New York able to protect her citizens and yet unwilling to protect them? Then New York does not deserve help; then New York does not deserve to be a State. One or the other must be true. If she demands the Federal arm, if she demands the army and the navy, if she demands that the soldiery shall protect her people, it must be because she is either unable to protect them or unwilling to protect them."

Mr. Kernan: "She is neither."

Mr. Hill of Georgia: "Ah, my friend, you are right; she is neither. She is able and she is willing to protect her citizens in this right. But let the argument progress. If the Senator is right, and if in New York the national soldier must protect her citizens in the exercise of the right of suffrage, must we not do the same thing in every other right? If New York can not protect her people in one right, can she protect them in any other right? If New York must have the national arm to help her protect her people in the exercise of one right, I repeat, must not New York demand the national arm to help her protect her people in all other personal rights, and what is the result? The argument comes just to this, that the State of New York is unable to protect her people in any of their rights, and therefore it is necessary for New York to have the protection and the help of the National Government in the protection of all. If New York can not protect her people, what State can? If New York, with her five million people, the largest State in this Union, the wealthiest State in this Union, having the commercial metropolis of this great country, is unable to protect her people from thugs and shoulder-hitters and rat-pitters, what other State is able to protect her people? Does not every man see the necessary logical result of the honorable Senator's argument, that States must be destroyed, that the Government must absorb to itself all the power of protecting the citizens of this country, all their rights, and reduce the States to incompetent provinces? That is the goal of the Republican party. Every hour of their history has been a direct march to the destruction of the States.

"Here is the truth, Mr. President: the whole war was the result of crimination between two extreme ideas. I deny that the Union, as interpreted by Madison and expounded by Web-

ster, was any party to the late war except as a victim, a threatened victim, and a very dangerously threatened one. It is true that the war was the result of a collision of ideas and interests between the extreme nationalists and the extreme federalists. They brought about the war; but the slavery question entering into it sectionalized it, and therefore the North became consolidated on one side, and the South, or a portion of the States of the South, consolidated on the other. After the war arose the Union became involved, and therefore it is that those who fought on the side of the Federal Government fought for the Union, and are entitled to all the benefits that result from that relation, and no man will always give them to them more cheerfully than myself. The war being the result of this collision of extremes, the consolidationists, the centralizationists, the monarchists (for that is what they mean) had the advantage in that they had possession of the Union, possession of its power, possession of its army, and possession of its navy—an advantage which they acquired by secession folly. The collision coming on in this form, secession was crushed out in the conflict, utterly crushed out. I want the country to understand that. It was utterly crushed out. There is no longer any danger to this country by reason of secession. It has no advocate in the South. It is a heresy which has had its day, wrought its wrongs, and gone to its grave, for which there is no resurrection, unless it gets that resurrection in the home of its birth, New England.

"But, sir, that other extreme enemy of the Constitution and Government and Union, as expounded by Madison and Webster, was not crushed out by war. It was the cardinal principle of the Republican party. All good Union men at the North, by reason of the condition of things, being compelled to go into the Federal army, as others in the South of a like character who had no sympathy with secession were compelled to go into secession, it was by the aid of the Democracy of the North, of the conservative men of the North who did not agree to absolute nationalism, who did not agree to the doctrine of consolidation, who did not agree to the absolute theory of a national government in the Federal head—it was by the aid of these Democrats and conservative men that the Federal armies were enabled to triumph and crush out secession. A united North overpowered a divided South. But the men who happened to be the party in power, and who are the representatives of this extreme idea of consolidation, took all the credit to themselves; and one of the dangers now arising to this country is from the fact that the party which represents this central, absolutely national idea—this consolidation idea, this monarchizing idea—that party claims the credit of having saved the Union. It gives no credit to its allies whatever. What would you have done without the Democrats in the war? And yet it was amusing to hear the distinguished Senator from New York the other day in his own way describing the Democratic party as consisting of a Northern tail and a Southern head. What would you have done without that tail in the war? If the conservative Union men North and South could have left the war to be fought out by the advocates of secession on the one hand and the advocates of consolidation on the other, there would have been some other party in control of this country for the last eighteen years.

"But, as I say, the respective sections became involved without regard to the individual opinions of their people. This national party, this party of absolutism, is not only the party in power by reason of its representation that it saved the Union, and taking all the credit of saving the Union, but it claims all the credit of having suppressed the rebellion, and demands that it shall be esteemed as the secessionists shall be hated.

"These two sources of strength to the Republican party are now endangering the States. Why, sir, every step of the Republican party is to the destruction of the States. Take the very measures now under consideration. What are they? In 1862, for purposes which every man can explain, a test oath was prescribed for jurors. In 1865 a clause was put in an army bill authorizing the use of troops to keep the peace at the polls. Neither of these statutes was ever known on our statute-book before; they did not exist in the early days of the Republic; they never existed until they were enacted during the war. In 1870 and 1871 your election laws were passed. They never existed before. Up to that time all parties had agreed that the States were both able and willing to take care of the elections and protect their citizens. Now, I put it to every intelligent man, what stronger indication of a desire to grasp power, what stronger indication of a purpose to crush out the States than the attempt to drive intelligence and virtue and property from the jury-box and use the army at the elections, and to place in the Federal Government power by supervisors and deputy marshals to take absolute control of the States in their elections, things that were never done before?

"If either one of the laws which we now propose to repeal had been proposed for enaction in any administration of this Government from the days of Washington to 1860, it would have ruined the man that made the proposition. No man could have stood before the indignation of the American people who would have proposed to place upon the statute-book a law keeping intelligence and virtue from the jury-box, a law surrounding the polls with the army and the navy, or a law giving to the Federal Government absolute control of the elections, and, as my friend from Kentucky [Mr. Beck] suggests, fixing the Congressional elections to come off on the same day with Presidential elections and State elections, so as to control all.

"I have given this subject careful consideration. I wish to do no man injustice; but, with a full sense of responsibility to my country, I affirm to-day that this heated contest we have had here for six weeks has no meaning, has no purpose, and can have no result but the absolute control of the States by force through the Federal Government to perpetuate the Republican party in power, whether the people will it or not; and if the President shall use the veto power, conferred upon him for a high conservative purpose, to aid these party schemes, and the people shall not rise in their indignation and drive from power these men who thus abuse power and disregard their duty, the Union will be destroyed in the destruction of the States.

"I grant you that the people of the North ought to have solid arguments on this subject. I grant what the Senator from New York intimated, that gush will not do; simply talking about shaking hands and locking arms does not amount to much. That will do for children and Sunday-school teachers. Statesmen want facts; statesmen want arguments; statesmen want reasons why the Southern people are not the enemies of the Government, and therefore ought to be friends and can be safely trusted. I propose to give some of those reasons.

"The laws that are now proposed to be repealed have been made the occasions for all kinds of intimations from the leaders of the Republican party that the South is not worthy to be trusted. How on earth can a proposition to repeal a law which was unknown to the country for the first seventy-five years of the existence of the Government be an evidence of disloyalty? How is it any evidence that we are not to be trusted because we want intelligence and virtue in the jury-box? How is it an evidence that we are not to be trusted because we want the absence of the army from the polls when the army was never known at the polls in the days of our fathers? How is it that we are to be declared disloyal because we are in favor of taking away from the Federal Government the control of the elections through the deputy marshals and the supervisors? United States deputy marshals and supervisors in elections were never known to the history of this country for the first eighty years of its government. Are we disloyal because we want what Washington had, what Jefferson had, what Madison had, what Jackson had? The President in his message says that he invites us back to the good old habits and customs of the country, and he says that the habit of tacking legislation to appropriation bills was unknown in the first forty years of the Government, and invites us back to those good old days. I mean to accept his invitation. I say to the President, 'Come sir, let us go back to the good old days when for not forty but seventy-five years troops were not known at the polls; let us go back to the good old days when for not forty but for eighty years supervisors and deputy marshals in control of the elections were unknown to the Federal statute-book. Now, come, let us go back.' Why not? That is what we are trying to do.

"But I want to give the reasons why the South is trustworthy, and I want to call the attention of the country to them. First, the Southern men went to war for what they believed their self-preservation. They defended their convictions bravely. They have surrendered; they have abandoned their convictions; they have abandoned secession, both as a doctrine and a remedy; and a people who were brave enough to defend their convictions with their blood are honorable enough to keep their pledges. When the Senator from New York points out that eighty-five out of the ninety-three Southern Senators and Representatives —I will not quarrel with the figures—went to the battle-field and shed their blood for their convictions, he stated a strong reason why they are trustworthy; when he shows that twenty Southern Senators on this floor were willing to defend their convictions with their life, and only four on that side of the Chamber, he shows a large proportion of Republicans who were very anxious to get up war, and very few who were willing to fight in the wars.

"But, sir, there is another reason why the South ought to be trusted. I say here that the South did not secede from hostility to the 'Union nor from hostility to the Constitution. That is your assumption. You are always talking about the Southern people as enemies of the Union. Not a word of it is true. As I said, the South was driven into secession by the opposite extreme at the North, who were as inimical to the Constitution as the secessionists themselves. That is the truth, and every intelligent man and every honest man admits it. The aggravations of the slavery question got possession of their respective sections and carried them into war, but do you suppose that every Southern man who stood by his section in a sectional war was hostile to the Union? Not a word of it.

"No, sir; the South seceded because there was a war made upon what she believed to be her constitutional rights by the extreme men of the North. Those extreme men of the North were gaining absolute power in the Federal Government as the machinery by which to destroy Southern property. Then the Northern people said, a large number of the leaders and the Republican party said, that if secession was desired to be accomplished it should be accomplished in peace. Mr. Greeley said that they wanted no union pinned together by bayonets. Here is the condition in which the South was placed: They believed the Northern extremists would use the machinery of the Government to their injury; the people of the South believed that they would protect their property by forming a new union in the South precisely upon the basis of the old. They believed they could do it in peace; and I say here there were thousands upon thousands, yea, hundreds of thousands of the best men of the South who believed that the only way to avoid a war was to secede. They believed the Northern conscience wanted to get rid of the responsibility for slavery; they believed they had a right to protect their slave property, and they thought they would accommodate the Northern conscience by leaving the Union and preserving that property. They believed they could do it in peace; and if they had believed that a war would result they never would have seceded.

"Sir, if the South were solid from any motives of hostility to the Union, from any motives of hostility to the Constitution, from any motives of hostility to the Northern people, the South would be exceedingly reprehensible. We were made solid in defense of our own preservation; we are now solid in defense of our own honor and self-respect. We will be kept solid in defense of the Constitution of our fathers as interpreted by Madison and expounded by Webster. We would be glad, if it could be, to see two national parties in this country, national in organization, national in principles, national in hopes, and consistent with the true interpretation of the Constitution; but the Northern man who after having made the South solid by calumny, by wrongs piled mountain high extending through years, that Northern man who takes advantage of the wrongs he has inflicted upon the South, and thereby made them solid, who now undertakes for that very reason to make the North solid too, having a solid North against a solid South, is a disunionist in fact; for whenever we shall have a solid North and a solid South in this country the Union can not last.

"No, my good Northern Democratic brethren, you saved the country at last: you saved the Union in the hour of its peril; not the Republican party. You who had shown your devotion to your flag saved the Union, and now it is for you to go before your people and tell them that the solid North must never become a fact against the solid South. If so, disunion will be accomplished. It is you that we look to. You saved the Union, and you will save the States. We could not help you save the Union, but we are here with all the power that God has given us to help you preserve and save the States of this country against the only remaining enemy of either the States or the Union."

Mr. Chandler of Michigan: "Mr. President, this is the fourth time since 1861 that allusion has been made to a letter written by me to the Governor of the State of Michigan: first it appeared in a newspaper published in Detroit, a copy of which was sent to me, and a copy was likewise sent to the late Senator Powell. The letter was a private note written to the Governor and no copy retained. Senator Powell approached me with his copy of the letter and asked me if it was a correct copy. I told him I did not know; I had written to the Governor of Michigan a private note and had kept no copy, and could not say whether this was correct or not. He told me that if it was a correct copy he would wish to make use of it; and, if it was not, he did not propose to make use of it. I said, 'Sir, I will adopt it, and you may make any use of it you please.' So to-day that is my letter. If not originally written by me, it is mine by adoption.

"And, Mr. President, what were the circumstances under which that letter was written? I had been in this body then nearly four years, listening to treason day by day and hour by hour. The threat, the universal threat daily, hourly, was, 'Do this, or we will dissolve the Union; if you do not do that, we will dissolve the Union.' Treason was in the White House, treason in the Cabinet, treason in the Senate, and treason in the House of Representatives; bold, outspoken, rampant treason was daily and hourly uttered. The threat was made upon this floor in my presence by a Senator, 'You may give us a blank sheet of paper and let us fill it up as we please, and then we will not live with you.' And another Senator stood here beside that Senator from Texas and said, 'I stand by the Senator from Texas.' Treason was applauded in the galleries of this body, and treason was talked on the streets, in the street-cars, in private circles; everywhere it was treason—treason in your departments, traitors in the White House, traitors around these galleries, traitors everywhere. The flag of rebellion had been raised; the Union was already dissolved, we were told; the rebel Government was already established with its capital in Alabama. 'And now we will negotiate with you,' was said to us. Upon what basis would you negotiate? Upon what basis did you call your peace convention? With rampant rebellion staring us in the face, sir, it was no time to negotiate. The time for negotiation was past. We had offered everything we could in the way of negotiation, everything in the way of compromise, and all our proffers had been indignantly refused.

"Sir, this was the condition of affairs when that letter was written; and, after Mr. Powell had made his assault upon me in this body for it, I instantly responded, relating what I have related here now with regard to the letter, and I said, 'I stand by that letter,' and I stand by it now. What was there in it then, and what is there in it now? The State of Michigan was known to be in favor of the Constitution and the Union and the enforcement of the laws, even to the letting of blood if need be, and that was all there was and all there is in that letter. Make the most of it.

"The Senator from Georgia says that I did not shed any blood. How much blood did he shed? Will somebody inform us the exact quantity of blood that the Senator from Georgia shed?"

Mr. Hill: "The difference between us is, that I was not in favor of shedding anybody's blood."

Mr. Chandler; "Nor I, except to punish treason and traitors. Sir, the Senator is not the man to stand up on this floor and talk about other men saving their own blood. He took mighty good care to put his blood in Fort Lafayette, where he was out of the way of rebel bullets as well as Union bullets. He is the last man to stand up here and talk to me about letting the blood of others be shed.

"Mr. President, I was then, as I am now, in favor of the Government of the United States. Then, as now, I abhorred the idea of State sovereignty over national sovereignty. Then, as now, I was prepared even to shed blood to save this glorious Government. Then, as now, I stood up for the Constitution and the Union. Then, as now, I was in favor of the perpetuity of this glorious Government. But the Senator from Georgia was, as he testified before a committee, 'a Union secessionist.' I have the testimony here before me. Will somebody explain what that means—'a Union secessionist'? Mr. President, I should like to see the dictionary where the definition can be found of 'a Union secessionist'! I do not understand the term.

"He says that they have a right to have a solid South, but a solid North will destroy the Government. Why, Mr. President, the South is no more solid to-day than it was in 1857."

Several Senators: "Eighteen hundred and sixty-one, you mean."

Mr. Chandler: "Well, it was the same in 1857. It was just as solid in 1857 as it is to-day. It has been solid ever since, and it was no quarrel with the North that made it solid. It was solid because it was determined either to 'rule or ruin' this nation. It tried the 'ruin' scheme with arms; and now, having failed to ruin this Government with arms, it comes back to ruin it by withholding supplies to carry on the Government. Sir, the men have changed since 1857. There is now but one member on this floor who stood here with me on the 4th of March, 1857. The men have changed, the measures not at all. You then fought for the overthrow of this Government, and now you vote and talk for the same purpose. You are to-day, as you were then, determined either to rule or ruin this Government, and you can not do either."

Motions were made on the Republican side to strike out all the clauses of the bill repealing the portions of acts relating to jurors, supervisors, and marshals. These were rejected by a strict party vote.

The President pro tempore: "If there are no further amendments, the question is, Shall the bill be read the third time?"

The bill was read the third time.

The President *pro tempore:* "The question now is, Shall the bill pass?"

The roll-call having been concluded, the result was announced as follows:

YEAS—Bailey, Bayard, Beck, Call, Cockrell, Coke, Davis of West Virginia, Eaton, Garland, Gordon, Groome, Grover, Hampton, Harris, Hereford, Houston, Johnston, Jonas, Jones of Florida, Kernan, Lamar, McDonald, McPherson, Maxey, Morgan, Randolph, Ransom, Saulsbury, Slater, Thurman, Vance, Voorhees, Walker, Wallace, Whyte, Williams, Withers—37.

NAYS—Allison, Anthony, Bell, Blaine, Booth, Bruce, Burnside, Cameron of Pennsylvania, Cameron of Wisconsin, Chandler, Conkling, Edmunds, Ferry, Hill of Colorado, Hoar, Ingalls, Kellogg, Kirkwood, Logan, McMillan, Morrill, Paddock, Platt, Rollins, Saunders, Teller, Windom—27.

ABSENT—Butler, Carpenter, Davis of Illinois, Dawes, Farley, Hamlin, Hill of Georgia, Jones of Nevada, Pendleton, Plumb, Sharon, Vest—12.

So the bill was passed.

In the House, on May 29th, the following veto from President Hayes was received and read:

To the House of Representatives:

After mature consideration of the bill entitled "An Act making appropriations for the legislative, executive, and judicial expenses of the Government for the fiscal year ending June 30, 1880, and for other purposes,"I herewith return it to the House of Representatives, in which it originated, with the following objections to its approval:

The main purpose of the bill is to appropriate the money required to support during the next fiscal year the several civil departments of the Government. The amount appropriated exceeds in the aggregate $18,000,000.

This money is needed to keep in operation the essential functions of all the great departments of the Government, legislative, executive, and judicial. It the bill contained no other provisions, no objection to its approval would be made. It embraces, however, a number of clauses relating to subjects of great general interest, which are wholly unconnected with the appropriations which it provides for. The objections to the practice of tacking general legislation to appropriation bills, especially when the object is to deprive a coördinate branch of the Government of its right to the free exercise of its own discretion and judgment touching such general legislation, were set forth in the special message in relation to House bill No. 1, which was returned to the House of Representatives on the 29th of last month. I regret that the objections which were then expressed to this method of legislation have not seemed to Congress of sufficient weight to dissuade from this renewed incorporation of general enactments in an appropriation bill, and that my constitutional duty in respect of the general legislation thus placed before me can not be discharged without seeming to delay, however briefly, the necessary appropriations by Congress for the support of the Government. Without repeating those objections, I respectfully refer to that message for a statement of my views on the principle maintained in debate by the advocates of this bill, namely, that "to withhold appropriations is a constitutional means for the redress" of what the majority of the House of Representatives may regard as "a grievance."

The bill contains the following clauses, namely:

And provided further, That the following sections of the Revised Statutes of the United States, namely, sections 2016, 2018, and 2020, and all of the succeeding sections of said statutes down to and including section 2027, and also section 5522, be, and the same are hereby, repealed ; . . . and that all the other sections of the Revised Statutes, and all laws and parts of laws authorizing the appointment of chief supervisors of elections, special deputy marshals of elections, or general

deputy marshals, having any duties to perform in respect to any election, and prescribing their duties and powers and allowing them compensations, be, and the same are hereby, repealed.

It also contains clauses amending sections 2017, 2019, 2028, and 2031 of the Revised Statutes.

The sections of the Revised Statutes which the bill, if approved, would repeal or amend, are part of an act, approved May 30, 1870, and amended February 28, 1871, entitled "An act to enforce the rights of citizens of the United States to vote in the several States of this Union, and for other purposes." All of the provisions of the above-named acts which it is proposed in this bill to repeal or modify relate to the Congressional elections. The remaining portion of the law, which will continue in force after the enactment of this measure, is that which provides for the appointment, by a judge of the Circuit Court of the United States, of two supervisors of election in each election district, at any Congressional election, on due application of citizens who desire, in the language of the law "to have such election guarded and scrutinized.'l The duties of the supervisors will be to attend at the polls at all Congressional elections, and to remain after the polls are open until every vote cast has been counted, but they will "have no authority to make arrests, or to perform other duties than to be in the immediate presence of the officers holding the election, and to witness all their proceedings, including the counting of the votes, and the making of a return thereof." The part of the election law which will be repealed by the approval of this bill includes those sections which give authority to the supervisors of election "to personally scrutinize, count, and canvass each ballot," and all the sections which confer authority upon the United States marshals and deputy marshals, in connection with the Congressional elections. The enactment of this bill will also repeal section 5522 of the Criminal Statutes of the United States, which was enacted for the protection of United States officers engaged in the discharge of their duties at the Congressional elections. This section protects supervisors and marshals in the performance of their duties by making the obstruction or the assaulting of these officers, or any interference with them by bribery or solicitation, or otherwise, crimes against the United States.

The true meaning and effect of the proposed legislation are plain. The supervisors, with the authority to observe and witness the proceedings at the Congressional elections, will be left ; but there will be no power to protect them, or to prevent interference with their duties, or to punish any violation of the law from which their powers are derived. If this bill is approved, only the shadow of the authority of the United States at the national elections will remain— the substance will be gone. The supervision of the elections will be reduced to a mere inspection, without authority on the part of the supervisors to do any act whatever to make the election a fair one. All that will be left to the supervisors is the permission to have such oversight of the elections as political parties are in the habit of exercising without any authority of law, in order to prevent their opponents from obtaining unfair advantages. The object of the bill is to destroy any control whatever by the United States over the Congressional elections.

The passage of this bill has been urged upon the ground that the election of members of Congress is a matter which concerns the States alone ; that these elections should be controlled exclusively by the States ; that there are and can be no such elections as national elections ; and that the existing law of the United States regulating the Congressional elections is without warrant in the Constitution. It is evident, however, that the framers of the Constitution regarded the election of members of Congress in every State and in every district as, in a very important sense, justly a matter of political interest and concern to the whole country. The original provision of the Constitution on this subject is as follows (section 4, article 1):

The times, places, and manner of holding elections for Senators and Representatives shall be prescribed in each State by the Legislature thereof: but the Congress may at any time by law make or alter such regulations, except as to the places of choosing Senators.

A further provision has been since added, which is embraced in the fifteenth amendment. It is as follows:

SECTION 1. The right of citizens of the United States to vote shall not be denied or abridged by the United States or by any State on account of race, color, or previous condition of servitude.

SEC. 2. The Congress shall have power to enforce this article by appropriate legislation.

Under the general provision of the Constitution (section 4, article 1), Congress in 1866 passed a comprehensive law which prescribed full and detailed regulations for the election of Senators by the Legislatures of the several States. This law had been in force almost thirteen years. In pursuance of it all the members of the present Senate of the United States hold their seats. Its constitutionality is not called in question. It is confidently believed that no sound argument can be made in support of the constitutionality of national regulation of senatorial elections which will not show that the elections of members of the House of Representatives may also be constitutionally regulated by the national authority.

The bill before me itself recognizes the principle that the Congressional elections are not State elections, but national elections. It leaves in full force the existing statute under which supervisors are still to be appointed by national authority, to "observe and witness" the Congressional elections whenever due application is made by citizens who desire said elections to be "guarded and scrutinized." If the power to supervise, in any respect whatever, the Congressional elections exists under section 4, article 1, of the Constitution, it is a power which, like every other power belonging to the government of the United States, is paramount and supreme, and includes the right to employ the necessary means to carry it into effect.

The statutes of the United States which regulate the election of members of the House of Representatives, an essential part of which it is proposed to repeal by this bill, have been in force about eight years. Four Congressional elections have been held under them, two of which were at the Presidential elections of 1872 and 1876.

Numerous prosecutions, trials, and convictions have been had in the courts of the United States in all parts of the Union for violations of these laws. In no reported case has their constitutionality been called in question by any judge of the courts of the United States. The validity of these laws is sustained by the uniform course of judicial action and opinion. If it is urged that the United States election laws are not necessary, an ample reply is furnished by the history of their origin and of their results. They were especially prompted by the investigation and exposure of the frauds committed in the city and State of New York at the elections of 1868. Committees representing both of the leading political parties of the country have submitted reports to the House of Representatives on the extent of those frauds. A committee of the Fortieth Congress, after a full investigation, reached the conclusion that the number of fraudulent votes cast in the city of New York alone in 1868 was not less than 25,000. A committee of the Forty-fourth Congress, in their report submitted in 1877, adopted the opinion that for every 100 actual voters of the city of New York in 1868, 108 votes were cast; when, in fact, the number of lawful votes cast could not have exceeded 88 per cent. of the actual voters of the city. By this statement the number of fraudulent votes at that election, in the city of New York alone, was between thirty and forty thousand. These frauds completely reversed the result of the election in the State of New York, both as to the choice of Governor and State officers, and as to the choice of electors of President and Vice-Presi-

dent of the United States. They attracted the attention of the whole country. It was plain that if they could be continued and repeated with impunity free government was impossible. A distinguished Senator in opposing the passage of the election laws declared that he had "for a long time believed that our form of government was a comparative failure in the larger cities." To meet these evils and to prevent these crimes the United States laws regulating Congressional elections were enacted.

The framers of these laws have not been disappointed in their results. In the large cities, under their provisions, the elections have been comparatively peaceable, orderly and honest. Even the opponents of these laws have borne testimony to their value and efficiency, and to the necessity for their enactment. The committee of the Forty-fourth Congress, composed of members a majority of whom were opposed to these laws, in their report on the New York election of 1876, said:

The committee would commend to other portions of the country and to other cities this remarkable system, developed through the agency of both local and Federal authorities acting in harmony for an honest purpose. In no portion of the world, and in no era of time, where there has been an expression of the popular will through the forms of law, has there been a more complete and thorough illustration of republican institutions. Whatever may have been the previous habit or conduct of elections in those cities, or howsoever they may conduct themselves in the future, this election of 1876 will stand as a monument of what good faith, honest endeavor, legal forms, and just authority may do for the protection of the electoral franchise.

This bill recognizes the authority and duty of the United States to appoint supervisors to guard and scrutinize the Congressional elections, but it denies to the Government of the United States all power to make its supervision effectual. The great body of the people of all parties want free and fair elections. They do not think that a free election means freedom from the wholesome restraints of law, or that the place of an election should be a sanctuary for lawlessness and crime. On the day of an election peace and good order are more necessary than on any other day of the year. On that day the humblest and feeblest citizens, the aged and the infirm, should be, and should have reason to feel that they are, safe in the exercise of their most responsible duty and their most sacred right as members of society, their duty and their right to vote. The constitutional authority to regulate the Congressional elections which belongs to the Government of the United States, and which it is necessary to exert to secure the right to vote to every citizen possessing the requisite qualifications, ought to be enforced by appropriate legislation. So far from public opinion in any part of the country favoring any relaxation of the authority of the Government in the protection of elections from violence and corruption, I believe it demands greater vigor, both in the enactment and in the execution of laws framed for that purpose. Any oppression, any partisan partiality, which experience may have shown in the working of existing laws, may well engage the careful attention both of Congress and of the Executive in their respective spheres of duty for the correction of these mischiefs. As no Congressional elections occur until after the regular session of Congress will have been held, there seems to be no public exigency that would preclude a seasonable consideration at that session of any administrative details that might improve the present methods designed for the protection of all citizens in the complete and equal exercise of the right and power of the suffrage at such elections. But with my views, both of the constitutionality and of the value of the existing laws, I can not approve any measure for their repeal except in connection with the enactment of other legislation which may reasonably be expected to afford wiser and more efficient safeguards for free and honest congressional elections.

RUTHERFORD B. HAYES.

EXECUTIVE MANSION, May 29, 1879.

Mr. Atkins: "I ask that the House now proceed to the reconsideration of the bill as prescribed by the Constitution."

The Speaker: "The question is, Will the House on reconsideration agree to pass this bill, notwithstanding the objections of the President? This question, according to the requirements of the Constitution, must be taken by yeas and nays. The Clerk will call the roll."

The question was taken as follows:

YEAS—Acklen, Aiken, Atherton, Atkins, Bachman, Beale, Beltzhoover, Bicknell, Blackburn, Bliss, Blount, Bright, Cabell, Caldwell, Carlisle, Chalmers, Clardy, John B. Clark, Clymer, Cobb, Coffroth, Colerick, Converse, Cook, Covert, Cox, Cravens, Culberson, Davidson, Joseph J. Davis, Loundes H. Davis, Dibrell, Dickey, Elam, Ellis, Evins, Ewing, Felton, Finley, Forney, Frost, Geddes, Gibson, Goode, Gunter, N. J. Hammond, John T. Harris, Hatch, Henkle, Heury, Herbert, Herndon, House, Hunton, Johnston, Kenna, Kimmel, King, Klotz, Ladd, Le Fevre Lewis, Manning, Benjamin F. Martin, Edward L. Martin, McKenzie, McLane, McMahon, McMillan, Mills, Morrison, New, Nicholls, O'Connor, Persons, Phelps, Phister, Poehler, Reagan, J. S. Richardson, Richmond, Robertson, Ross, John W. Ryon, Samford, Sawyer, Scales, Simonton, O. R. Singleton, Siemons, William E. Smith, Speer, Springer, Steele, Stephens, Stevenson, Talbott, Taylor, Thompson, Tillman, R. W. Townshend, Oscar Turner, Thomas Turner, Vance, Waddill, Wellborn, Whitaker, Whitthorne, Thomas Williams, Willis, Wilson, Wise, Wright, Casey Young —114.

NAYS—N. W. Aldrich, Anderson, Baker, Barber, Barlow, Bayne, Belford, Bingham, Blake, Bowman, Boyd, Brewer, Briggs, Brigham, Browne, Burrows, Calkins, Cannon, Carpenter, Caswell, Conger, Crapo, Daggett, George R. Davis, Deering, Dunnell, Errett, Farr, Ferdon, Fisher, Ford, Fort, Frye, Godshalk, Hall, John Hammond, Harmer, Benjamin W. Harris, Haskell, Hawk, Hawley, Hayes, Hazelton, Heilman, Henderson, Hiscock, Horr, Houk, Hubbell, Humphrey, Joyce, Ketcham, Lindsey, Marsh, McCoid, McGowan, Miller, Mitchell, Monroe, Neal, Newberry, Norcross, O'Neill, Orth, Osmer, Overton, Pound, Prescott, Price, Rice, D. P. Richardson, Robinson, William A. Russell, Thomas Ryan, Sapp, Shallenberger, Sherwin, A. Herr Smith, Starin, Stone, Thomas, Tyler, Thomas Updegraff, Urner, Valentine, Van Aernam, Van Voorhis, Voorhis, Wait, Ward, Wilber, C. G. Williams, Willits—93.

NOT VOTING—William Aldrich, Armfield, Bailey, Ballou, Bland, Bouck, Bragg, Buckner, Butterworth, Camp, Chittenden, Claflin, Alvah A. Clark, Cowgill, Crowley, De La Matyr, Deuster, Dick, Dunn, Dwight, Einstein, Field, Forsythe, Garfield, Gillette, Hill, Hooker, Hostetler, Hull, Hurd, James, Jones, Jorgensen, Keifer, Kelley, Killinger, Kitchin, Knott, Lapham, Lay, Loring, Lounsbery, Lowe, Joseph J. Martin, Mason, McCook, McKinley, Miles, Money, Morse, Morton, Muldrow, Muller, Murch, Myers, O'Brien, O'Reilly, Pierce, Reed, Robeson, Rothwell, Daniel L. Russell, Shelley, J. W. Singleton, Hezekiah B. Smith, Sparks, Amos Townsend, Tucker, J. T. Updegraff, Warner, Washburn, Weaver, Wells, White, Fernando Wood, Walter A. Wood, Yocum, Thomas L. Young—78.

So the bill was not passed, two thirds not voting in favor thereof.

In the House, on June 10th, an amended appropriation bill was considered. Mr. Atkins of Tennessee said: "Mr. Speaker, I am unanimously authorized and directed by the Committee on Appropriations to report a substitute for the bill presented a few days ago

(H. R. No. 2172) making appropriations for defraying the expenses of the legislative, executive, and judicial departments of the Government, and which was recommitted; and I now ask unanimous consent to submit a brief statement, and that the gentleman from Connecticut [Mr. Hawley] may likewise be allowed to make a statement."

There was no objection, and it was ordered accordingly.

Mr. Atkins: "The restriction that was upon the vetoed bill, and which created such a contest upon this floor, is not embraced in this bill. Nor is the appropriation for the contingent expenses of the courts of the country, amounting to $2,600,000 or $2,700,000, embraced in this bill. You will remember, Mr. Speaker, that it was upon that portion of the appropriation bill that the restrictive clauses were placed with regard to the payment of deputy marshals and supervisors of elections. That matter will be embraced in a subsequent bill, a supplemental bill, if I may so style it, a supplemental judicial appropriation bill, which my honorable friend from Ohio [Mr. McMahon] will probably report to-day to the House."

Mr. Hawley: "As the chairman of the Committee on Appropriations has said, this bill aims to do what was aimed at in the more regular legislative, executive, and judicial appropriation bill, omitting what are characterized as the political sections. Now, we of the minority of the committee, and I might say the Republicans in general, are opposed to the present form of the bill—very much opposed to it. The minority would very much have preferred to pass the regular appropriation bill for these branches of the public service which was substantially approved by the last Congress, which went through this House and the Senate, came back from the Senate with certain amendments in which the House concurred, making approval No. 3, and which was again approved by a majority of the House when it was attempted to pass the bill over the veto, which makes approval No. 4. Four times Congress, within four months, has approved the legislative, executive, and judicial bill, which, minus the politics, we should have preferred to take because of its very much better form, because of its clearness in doing the work aimed at. It contains, as has been stated sufficiently, no political matters of the kind ordinarily described as such, and we finally rather consented to its passage than approved of it."

Mr. Atkins: "I now move that the rules be suspended and the bill passed."

So the bill was passed—ayes, 187; noes, 22; not voting, 77.

In the Senate, on June 14th, the bill was considered.

Mr. Beck of Kentucky said: "Mr. President, I am instructed by the Committee on

Appropriations to report back the bill sent to us from the House with the amendments added by the Committee on Appropriations; but I am not authorized by the committee to offer the amendment which I propose to offer as a substitute for it. I desire to say before the bill is read, if the Senate will allow me, that the Committee on Appropriations of the House, instead of pursuing the usual form of presenting a detailed bill, thought it best to send House bill No. 2251, which makes this provision as its principal operative clause :

"That for the purpose of providing for the legislative, executive, and judicial expenses of the Government for the fiscal year ending June 30, 1880, there is hereby appropriated, out of any money in the Treasury not otherwise appropriated, the same sums of money and for the like purposes (and continuing the same provisions relating thereto), as were appropriated for the service of the fiscal year ending June 30, 1879, by the act entitled 'An Act making appropriations for the legislative, executive, and judicial expenses of the Government for the fiscal year ending June 30, 1879, and for other purposes,' approved June 19, 1878 (except as hereinafter declared), subject to all the limitations and conditions in respect to the disbursement of the appropriations hereby made that were imposed by said act, and the other laws of the United States upon or in respect to the appropriations made by said act.

"Then follow first a number of exceptions, from line 20 to line 46 ; then from line 47 to line 57 are provisions affirmatively changing the act of June 19, 1878, saying that no more than the sums stated respectively are appropriated ; and from line 58 down to the close of section 1, on line 121, are amendments to that act. Section 2 provides for the salary of certain offices created by acts of 1879, and for matters provided for in other acts, and for the mints and assay offices, and 'the following additional sums are hereby appropriated'; then follows a list of them running through each of the departments, with two other sections at the end making general provisions.

"Therefore, Mr. President, as I was directed to take charge of this bill and present it to the Senate, I desire to say to Senators, first, that before they can understand the bill intelligently they will have to obtain the act approved June 19, 1878, being public act No. 135 of the second session of the Forty-fifth Congress, which I suppose can be obtained in the document-room ; at least I obtained a few copies there. As that is the act which the House has reënacted in substance, without that act no Senator can very well know what he is doing or what he is voting for in the House bill now before us.

"I have endeavored in the amendment I offered to present the bill of the current year as now amended in a form to be easily understood. Therefore it was that I thought the House bill as amended by the Committee on Appropriations of the Senate ought to be read at length, with my amendment in the hands of Senators, as it differs in its form so essentially from the bills ordinarily presented."

A discussion ensued, during which some amendments were made to the bill, and it was passed.

The House disagreed to the amendments of the Senate. The result of this disagreement was a conference between the two Houses, at which the differences were adjusted and approved by each House, and the bill became a law.

———

In the House, on June 10th, the judicial appropriation bill was considered.

Mr. McMahon said : "I desire to make a privileged report from the Committee on Appropriations. I report back the bill (H. R. No. 2252) making appropriations for certain judicial expenses, and I ask for its consideration now."

The bill was read.

Mr. McMahon : "Mr. Chairman, I desire to make a short statement to the Committee in regard to this bill. The bill which we now present for consideration has heretofore been a part of the sundry civil bill. The amount appropriated by this bill has generally been appropriated in one sum, the sum of $2,500,000, some years, $2,600,000, $2,700,000, and $2,800,000, in other years, and sometimes $3,000,000, but always in one sum and undivided as to its uses. The Committee have thought it proper to have this large sum itemized. We have required the Department of Justice to estimate to the Committee the appropriations needed for the several different purposes, and we have followed the estimates sent to us except as to three different items. We have reduced the appropriation for the pay of district attorneys and their assistants $50,000 below the estimates. We have also reduced the pay of United States marshals and their deputies $50,000. We have reduced the pay of jurors $190,000, because we have incorporated into the bill a provision reducing their compensation from three to two dollars a day, and we have the authority of the Attorney-General himself that such a reduction will enable us to dispense with $200,000 of the appropriations. The fees of witnesses we have left according to the estimate of the Department of Justice ; so also for the support of United States prisoners ; so also for the rent of United States court-rooms, and for certain miscellaneous purposes, such as fuel, lights, stationery, furniture, sweepers, etc., a total appropriation of $280,000, which amount may seem very large, but it covers a very large and uncertain contingent ground. The entire amount appropriated for all purposes is $2,690,-000 for the next fiscal year. I think the appropriations will be found amply sufficient for the purpose.

"In answer to numerous inquiries I desire to call attention to one clause of this bill, and to state that no money is appropriated for the payment of deputy marshals, 'special' deputy marshals as they are sometimes called, for services on the day of election. The last clause of the first section of the bill provides that 'no part of the money hereby appropriated is appropriated to pay any salaries, compensation, fees, or expenses under or in virtue of title 26 of the Revised Statutes or of any provision of said title.' Now, if gentlemen will look at that title of the Revised Statutes they will see that it covers the appointment of deputy marshals, their duties, pay, etc., the subpoenaing of witnesses in certain cases before the supervisors of elections, etc. I will say that the clause in the bill which I have quoted is a very sweeping one, and is intended to prevent the enforcement of the supervisors and deputy-marshals clauses of the Revised Statutes during the next fiscal year, so far as a failure to appropriate money for their compensation will effect the purpose.

" In the second section is a provision that all sums appropriated in this bill shall be in full for the persons and purposes designated for the next fiscal year. And to that we have added a clause by which we slightly modify the existing law, to the effect that 'no department or officer of the Government shall, during said fiscal year, make any contract or incur any liability for the future payment of money, until an appropriation to meet such contract or pay such liability shall have first been made by law.' The present law is that no department of the Government shall involve the Government in any liability for the future payment of money or make any contract until the money shall have been first appropriated. We have added the words 'no officer of the Government,' and have also added the words ' or incur any liability.'

" In section 3 of this bill we have included what is generally known as the jury clause, repealing the juror's test oath, and providing a new method of drawing jurors. In that we have only followed out the frequent recommendations of the Attorneys-General of the United States, and particularly of Mr. Pierrepont in a letter to the first session of the Forty-fourth Congress, that some uniform system was necessary. There is no department of our Government that ought to be purer in its administration, but I am sorry to say that there is none where, in proportion to the amount of money appropriated, greater scandals are involved. I think I can say that upon the authority of some of the Attorneys-General of the United States.

" We have also added a proviso which will not be found in any of the previous bills passed by this House upon the subject, providing that 'no citizen possessing all other qualifications which are or may be prescribed by law shall be disqualified for service as grand or petit juror in any court of the United States on account of race, color, or previous condition of servitude.' The purpose of that amendment will be apparent to every one. It is intended only to demonstrate what was already the fact,

that we did not in any way intend to abridge the rights of our colored citizens as jurors, and that we intended to guarantee them all their rights everywhere, whatever may be the State law upon the subject.

" We have added another clause, section 4. In looking over the reports of the Attorneys-General we discovered a very extraordinary fact. We discovered that the report which the Attorney-General makes to the House of Representatives of his annual expenditures in any one year covers only the amount expended *during* that fiscal year out of the funds appropriated *for* that particular year. To illustrate, if at the end of the fiscal year ending June 30, 1879, there was left an unexpended balance of $500,000, and that amount should be expended for obligations incurred during the year ending June 30, 1880, it would not be found in the next annual report made to this Congress for the expenditures of the fiscal year ending June 30, 1879, nor would it be found in the expenditures for the fiscal year beginning July 1, 1880. Therefore a very large amount of money is and may be expended by the Department in that way which is never accounted for to Congress anywhere. Your committee, therefore, have never been able to ascertain what was annually expended by the Department in any one fiscal year."

The Speaker : " The question recurs on the passage of the bill."

The question was taken, as follows :

YEAS—Acklen, Armfield, Atherton, Atkins, Bachman, Beale, Beltzhoover, Bicknell, Blackburn, Bliss, Bouck, Bright, Cabell, Caldwell, Carlisle, Clardy, John B. Clark, Clymer, Cobb, Coffroth, Colerick, Cook, Covert, Cravens, Culberson, Davidson, Joseph J. Davis, Lowndes H. Davis, Deuster, Dibrell, Dunn, Elam, Felton, Finley, Forney, Frost, Geddes, Gibson, Gunter, N. J. Hammond, John T. Harris, Hatch, Henkle, Henry, Herbert, Herndon, Hill, Hooker, Hostetler, Hull, Hunton, Johnston, Kenna, Kimmel, King Klotz, Manning, Benjamin F. Martin, Edward L. Martin, McMahon, McMillan, New, O'Connor, Persons, Phelps, Phister, Poehler, Reagan, Robertson, Ross, Rothwell, John W. Ryon, Samford, Sawyer. Scales, Simonton, O. R. Singleton, Slemons, Hezekiah B. Smith, William E. Smith, Sparks, Springer, Steele, Stephens, Stevenson, Taylor, Thompson, Tillman, R. W. Townshend, Oscar Turner, Upson, Vance, Waddill, Wellborn, Wells, Whiteaker, Whitthorne, Thomas Williams, Willis, Wilson, Wise, Wright—102.

NAYS—N. W. Aldrich, William Aldrich, Anderson, Bailey, Baker, Barber, Bayne, Bingham, Blake, Bowman, Brewer, Briggs, Brigham, Burrows, Butterworth, Calkins, Camp, Carpenter, Claflin, Conger, Crapo, Crowley, Daggett, George R. Davis, Deering, Dunnell, Errett, Farr, Ferdon, Field, Fisher, Frye, Garfield, Godshalk, Hall, John Hammond, Harmer, Haskell, Hawk, Hawley, Hayes, Hiscock, Horr, Humphrey, Joyce, Keifer, Killinger, Loring, Marsh, Mason, McCoid, McGowan, McKinley, Mitchell, Monroe, Morton, Newberry, Norcross, O'Neill, Osmer, Overton, Pound, Price, Rice, D. P. Richardson, Robinson, W. A. Russell, Thomas Ryan, Sapp, Shallenberger, Sherwin, A. Herr Smith, Stone, Thomas, Tyler, J. T. Updegraff, Urner, Valentine, Van Aernam, Voorhis, Wait, Wilber, C. G. Williams, Willits, Thomas L. Young—85.

NOT VOTING — Aiken, Ballou, Barlow, Belford, Bland, Blount, Boyd, Bragg, Browne, Buckner, Car non, Caswell, Chalmers, Chittenden, Alvah A. Clark, Converse, Cowgill, Cox, De La Matyr, Dick, Dickey, Dwight, Einstein, Ellis, Evins, Ewing, Ford, Forsythe, Fort, Gillette, Goode, Benjamin W. Harris, Hazelton, Hellman, Henderson, Houk, House, Hubbell, Hurd, James, Jones, Jorgensen, Kelley, Ketcham, Kitchin, Knott, Ladd, Lapham, Lay, Le Fevre, Lewis, Lindsey, Lounsbery, Lowe, Joseph J. Martin, McCook, McKenzie, McLane, Miles, Miller, Mills, Money, Morrison, Morse, Muldrow, Muller, Murch, Myers, Neal, Nicholls, O'Brien, O'Reilly, Orth, Pierce, Prescott, Reed, J. S. Richardson, Richmond, Robeson, Daniel L. Russell, Shelley, J. W. Singleton, Speer, Starin, Talbott, Amos Townsend, Tucker, Thomas Turner, Thomas Updegraff, Van Voorhis, Ward, Warner, Washburn, Weaver, White, Fernando Wood, Walter A. Wood, Yocum, Casey Young—99.

So the bill passed.

In the Senate, on June 14th, the bill was considered and amended, and passed by the following vote:

YEAS—Bayard, Call, Cockrell, Coke, Davis of West Virginia, Davis of Illinois, Eaton, Garland, Groome, Hampton, Harris, Hill of Georgia, Houston, Jonas, Jones of Florida, Kernan, Lamar, McDonald, Maxey, Morgan, Pendleton, Ransom, Slater, Vance, Vest, Walker, Wallace—27.

NAYS—Blaine, Bruce Burnside, Cameron of Pennsylvania, Cameron of Wisconsin, Carpenter, Chandler, Conkling, Dawes. Hill of Colorado, Ingalls, Logan, Morrill, Rollins, Windom—15.

ABSENT— Allison, Anthony, Bailey, Beck, Bell, Booth, Butler, Edmunds, Farley, Ferry, Gordon, Grover, Hamlin, Hereford, Hoar, Johnston, Jones of Nevada, Kellogg, Kirkwood, McMillan, McPherson, Paddock, Platt, Plumb, Randolph, Saulsbury, Saunders, Sharon, Teller, Thurman, Voorhees, Whyte, Williams, Withers—34.

The House disagreed to the Senate's amendments, and they were adjusted in a conference and approved, and the bill sent to the President. He returned it with the following veto message:

To the House of Representatives :

After careful examination of the bill entitled " An Act making appropriations for certain judicial expenses," I return it herewith to the House of Representatives, in which it originated, with the following objections to its approval:

The general purpose of the bill is to provide for certain judicial expenses of the Government for the fiscal year ending June 30, 1880, for which the sum of $2,690,000 is appropriated. These appropriations are required to keep in operation the general functions of the judicial department of the Government, and if this part of the bill stood alone there would be no objection to its approval. It contains, however, other provisions, to which I desire respectfully to ask your attention.

At the present session of Congress a majority of both Houses, favoring a repeal of the Congressional election laws embraced in title 26 of the Revised Statutes, passed a measure for that purpose, as part of a bill entitled " An Act making appropriations for the legislative, executive, and judicial expenses of the Government for the fiscal year ending June 30, 1880, and for other purposes." Unable to concur with Congress in that measure, on the 29th of May last I returned the bill to the House of Representatives, in which it originated, without my approval, for that further consideration for which the Constitution provides. On reconsideration the bill was approved by less than two thirds of the House, and failed to become a law. The election laws, therefore, remain valid enactments, and the supreme law of the land, binding not only upon all private citizens, but also alike and equally binding upon all who are charged with the duties and responsibilities of the legislative, the executive, and the judicial departments of the Government.

It is not sought by the bill before me to repeal the election laws. Its object is to defeat their enforcement. The last clause of the first section is as follows:

" And no part of the money hereby appropriated is appropriated to pay any salaries, compensation, fees, or expenses under or in virtue of title 26 of the Revised Statutes, or of any provision of said title."

Title 26 of the Revised Statutes, referred to in the foregoing clause, relates to the elective franchise, and contains the laws now in force regulating the Congressional elections.

The second section of the bill reaches much further. It is as follows:

SEC. 2. That the sums appropriated in this act for the persons and public service embraced in its provisions are in full for such persons and public service for the fiscal year ending June 30, 1880, and no department or officer of the Government shall, during said fiscal year, make any contract or incur any liability for the future payment of money under any of the provisions of title 26 of the Revised Statutes of the United States authorizing the appointment or payment of general or special deputy marshals for service in connection with elections or on election day, until an appropriation sufficient to meet such contract or pay such liability shall have first been made by law.

This section of the bill is intended to make an extensive and essential change in the existing laws. The following are the provisions of the statutes on the same subject which are now in force:

SEC. 3679. No department of the Government shall expend, in any one fiscal year, any sum in excess of appropriations made by Congress for that fiscal year, or involve the Government in any contract for the future payment of money in excess of such appropriations.

SEC. 3732. No contract or purchase on behalf of the United States shall be made unless the same is authorized by law or is under an appropriation adequate to its fulfillment, except in the War and Navy Departments, for clothing, subsistence, forage, fuel, quarters, or transportation, which, however, shall not exceed the necessities of the current year.

The object of these sections of the Revised Statutes is plain. It is, first, to prevent any money from being expended unless appropriations have been made therefor; and, second, to prevent the Government from being bound by any contract not previously authorized by law, except for certain necessary purposes in the War and Navy Departments.

Under the existing laws the failure of Congress to make the appropriations required for the execution of the provisions of the election laws would not prevent their enforcement. The right and duty to appoint the general and special deputy marshals which they provide for would still remain, and the Executive Department of the Government would also be empowered to incur the requisite liability for their compensation. But the second section of this bill contains a prohibition not found in any previous legislation. Its design is to render the election laws inoperative and a dead letter during the next fiscal year. It is sought to accomplish this by omitting to appropriate money for their enforcement and by expressly prohibiting any department or officer of the Government from incurring any liability under any of the provisions of title 26 of the Revised Statutes authorizing the appointment or payment of general or special deputy marshals for service on election days until an appropriation sufficient to pay such liability shall have first been made.

The President is called upon to give his affirmative approval to positive enactments which in effect deprive him of the ordinary and necessary means of executing laws still left in the statute-book, and embraced within his constitutional duty to see that the laws are executed. If he approves the bill and thus gives to such positive enactments the authority of law, he participates in the curtailment of his means of seeing that the law is faithfully executed while the obligation of the law and of his constitutional duty remains unimpaired.

The appointment of special deputy marshals is not

made by the statute a spontaneous act of authority on the part of any executive or judicial officer of the Government, but is accorded as a popular right of the citizens to call into operation this agency for securing the purity and freedom of elections in any city or town having twenty thousand inhabitants or upward. Section 2021 of the Revised Statutes puts it in the power of any two citizens of such city or town to require of the marshal of the district the appointment of these special deputy marshals. Thereupon the duty of the marshal becomes imperative, and its non-performance would expose him to judicial mandate or punishment, or to removal from office by the President, as the circumstances of his conduct might require. The bill now before me neither revokes this popular right of the citizens nor relieves the marshal of the duty imposed by law, nor the President of his duty to see that this law is faithfully executed.

I forbear to enter again upon any general discussion of the wisdom and necessity of the election laws or of the dangerous and unconstitutional principle of this bill, that the power vested in Congress to originate appropriations involves the right to compel the Executive to approve any legislation which Congress may see fit to attach to such bills, under the penalty of refusing the means needed to carry on essential functions of the Government. My views on these subjects have been sufficiently presented in the special messages sent by me to the House of Representatives during their present session. What was said in those messages I regard as conclusive as to my duty in respect to the bill before me. The arguments urged in those communications against the repeal of the election laws and against the right of Congress to deprive the Executive of that separate and independent discretion and judgment which the Constitution confers and requires are equally cogent in opposition to this bill. This measure leaves the powers and duties of the supervisors of elections untouched. The compensation of those officers is provided for under permanent laws, and no liability for which an appropriation is now required would therefore be incurred by their appointment. But the power of the National Government to protect them in the discharge of their duty at the polls would be taken away. The States may employ both civil and military power at the elections, but by this bill even the civil authority to protect Congressional elections is denied to the United States. The object is to prevent any adequate control by the United States over the national elections by forbidding the payment of deputy marshals, the officers who are clothed with authority to enforce the election laws.

The fact that these laws are deemed objectionable by a majority of both Houses of Congress is urged as a sufficient warrant for this legislation.

There are two lawful ways to overturn legislative enactments. One is their repeal; the other is the decision of a competent tribunal against their validity. The effect of this bill is to deprive the executive department of the Government of the means to execute laws which are not repealed, which have not been declared invalid, and which it is, therefore, the duty of the Executive and of every other department of Government to obey and to enforce.

I have in my former message on this subject expressed a willingness to concur in suitable amendments for the improvement of the election laws; but I can not consent to their absolute and entire repeal, and I can not approve legislation which seeks to prevent their enforcement.

　　　　　　　RUTHERFORD B. HAYES.
Executive Mansion, June 28, 1879.

The Speaker: "The question before the House is, Will the House on reconsideration agree to pass the bill? on which the Constitution requires the yeas and nays shall be taken; and, in obedience thereto, the Clerk will now call the roll."

The question was taken; and it was decided in the negative—yeas 102, nays 78, not voting 106.

At this extra session of Congress there were introduced in the Senate 727 bills and 46 joint resolutions, of which 26 bills and 7 joint resolutions became laws. In the House there were introduced 2,395 bills and 119 joint resolutions, of which 36 bills and 17 joint resolutions became laws. The following are of general importance, in addition to those above mentioned:

A bill to prevent the introduction of contagious or infectious diseases into the United States.

A bill to authorize the Secretary of the Treasury to contract for the construction of a refrigerating ship for the disinfection of vessels and cargoes.

A joint resolution relating to the organization of the National Board of Health.

To provide for the appointment of a Mississippi River Commission for the improvement of said river from the head of the passes near its mouth to its head-waters.

To put salts of quinine and sulphate of quinine on the free list.

To provide for the exchange of subsidiary coins for lawful money of the United States under certain circumstances, and to make such coins a legal tender in all sums not exceeding ten dollars, and for other purposes.

In addition to the five bills originating in the House which were disapproved by the President, there was one bill originating in the Senate vetoed—namely, the bill to amend the act of March 3, 1879, for the relief of Joseph B. Collins.'

Both Houses adjourned on July 1st to the regular session commencing in December.

CONKLING, Roscoe, an American statesman, born in Albany, New York, October 30, 1829. His father, Alfred Conkling, was a Representative in the Seventeenth Congress, and was appointed by John Quincy Adams Judge of the United States for the Northern District of New York in 1825, and Minister to Mexico by President Fillmore in 1852. He was the author of several valuable books on law.

His son Roscoe received a common-school and academic education. Removing to Auburn and Geneva with his father, he studied law three years under his tuition. In 1846 he entered the law-office of Spencer and Kernan in Utica, the latter of whom is now his colleague in the Senate. In 1849 he was appointed by Hamilton Fish District Attorney for Oneida County, several months before he attained his majority. On the day he was twenty-one he was admitted to the bar, at which he had already acquired considerable reputation. During the next decade he disclosed rare managing qualities, and was looked to as a leader in local politics. In law he ranked with the first of the profession as an advocate. The triumphs which he achieved at the bar, and which were his passport to public preferment, were gained before he reached the age of twenty-nine. In later years he has accepted only a few cases, but in these his success has been marked. He married Julia Seymour, a sister of ex-Governor Horatio Seymour.

In 1858 he was elected Mayor of Utica. The campaign which followed Mr. Conkling's election as Mayor resulted in a tie vote between J. C. Hoyt and Charles S. Wilson, a circumstance which necessitated Mr. Conkling's holding over for the full year, neither gentleman being qualified to succeed him.

In November, 1858, he was elected a Representative to the Thirty-sixth Congress, and took his seat in that body at the beginning of its first session, in December, 1859—a session noted for its long and bitter contest over the Speakership. He was a member of the Committee on the District of Columbia. He was reëlected in 1860. His brother, Frederick A. Conkling, was elected at the same time from a New York City district. The two brothers entered the Thirty-seventh Congress at the opening of the special session convened by President Lincoln, July 4, 1861. In this Congress, Roscoe Conkling was Chairman of the Committee on the District of Columbia, and also of a special committee to frame a bankrupt law.

A candidate for reëlection to the Thirty-eighth Congress, he was defeated by his old law partner Francis Kernan. At the election in 1864, the same parties being nominated, Mr. Conkling gained the victory, and resumed his seat in the Thirty-ninth Congress, where he served on the Committees on Ways and Means and on Reconstruction. The fame of Mr. Conkling as an orator had preceded him, as had his reputation as a party manager. He startled the nation by a vigorous assault upon the tactics of General McClellan, and gave the keynote for earnestness in all future war legislation at a time when hesitancy and vacillation prevailed. In February, 1862, he opposed Mr. Spaulding's legal-tender act by speech and vote, sustaining, contrary to the prevailing party policy, Mr. Horton's amendment providing for the issue of an interest-bearing note, and against the final passage of the bill as amended by Thaddeus Stevens. In the same session he voted for the payment of interest on the debt in coin. Mr. Conkling was a firm supporter of all legislation tending to uphold the hands of the Administration in prosecuting the war for the suppression of the rebellion.

In the fall of 1866 Mr. Conkling was elected to the Fortieth Congress, but before that Congress met he was chosen to succeed Judge Ira Harris as United States Senator from the State of New York. He took his seat in the Senate March 4, 1867; was reëlected, his second term beginning March 4, 1873; was again elected, and began his third term as Senator March 4, 1879. He was a zealous supporter of General Grant's Administration. The general policy of that Administration toward the South was largely directed by Senator Conkling, who advocated it with all the powers of his eloquence and all the potency of his personal and political influence. He was also largely instrumental in the inception and passage of the civil rights bill. Upon the vital question of hard money

Mr. Conkling was, in harmony with the sentiment of his party, strictly in favor of the resumption of specie payments.

One of the most important acts of Senator Conkling's political career was the prominent part he took in framing the act for an Electoral Commission in 1876. Many of the foremost men of his own and of the other party were the prey of extreme partisan views, which, if insisted on, might have plunged the country into civil strife. It was largely owing to his indefatigable labors, his thorough knowledge of the history of the question and of all the precedents, and the powerful effect of the speech he delivered in the Senate, that the success of the Electoral Commission bill was due. In regard to the powers conferred upon the Commission by this bill, he said: "Mr. President, I had supposed that the Constitution had raised not only a hedge and a fence, but a wall of limit, to the powers it confers. I supposed that, when five of the most largely instructed and trusted members of the Senate, and five of the most largely instructed and trusted members of the House, were authorized to meet five Judges of the highest and most largely instructed judicial tribunal of the land, we might trust to them to settle what a Court of Oyer and Terminer settles whenever it is called upon to determine whether it has jurisdiction to try an indictment for homicide or not. I had supposed that, giving it the instrument by which its jurisdiction is to be measured, we could trust this provisional tribunal of selected men to run a boundary and fix the line marking their jurisdiction."

CONNECTICUT. The Legislature of this State assembled at Hartford on January 8th, and for the first time opened their regular session in the new State House, where they had closed the session of 1878. In the Lower House, Dexter R. Wright of New Haven was elected Speaker. Gilbert W. Phillips of the Fourteenth District was appointed President pro tempore of the Senate.

Upon taking the chair as President, Senator Phillips addressed the Senate as follows:

SENATORS: I thank you very heartily for the kindness which permits me to be your temporary presiding officer, and I can assure you that it will be my aim to serve you in such a manner as shall meet your approval. We meet in obedience to the public voice, and I trust it will be our pleasure, as well as our duty, to so conduct the business intrusted to us as to meet the approbation of our constituents.

Before addressing ourselves to the duties before us, allow me to say a word concerning this proud edifice in which we meet for the first time. It is a cause of sincere congratulation that it has been carried on to completion under management so satisfactory. The commission in charge, it seems to me, for its wisdom, deserves the thanks of the State. In all ages of the world, nations have displayed their characters by the beauty and magnificence of their public buildings. The Greek temple, the Gothic cathedral, the Parliament House at London, our own proud Capitol at Washington, and the hut of the Indian in the American wilderness, each represents, or did represent, somewhat the thought and character of the people who caused their construction. This of ours no less stands as a representative of our people and of our times—having for its primary object the increase of personal conveniences and comfort, yet, whether considered in its architecture or its construction, artistical in all. Commemorative of liberty and civilization, of cultivation and refinement, and of prosperity and happiness, it shadows forth that proper State pride, that high aspiration of thought, which will ever serve to elevate and ennoble the people of this good old Commonwealth.

Senators, in all our acts let us bear in mind the honor of the State, and the upholding of the best government that the world ever beheld. Armed in all the strength of justice, may it stand to the latest day to bless mankind!

In his address to the House of Representatives, before occupying the Speaker's chair, Mr. Wright referred favorably and at some length to the resumption of specie payments, upon which subject the following joint resolution was passed, and concurred in by the Senate:

Resolved, by this Assembly, that we cordially unite with our people and Government in their congratulations over the successful resumption of specie payments, together with the signs of returning prosperity which everywhere accompany it; and we request our Senators and Representatives in Congress to continue to stand firm in their efforts to resist all attempts to debase our currency.

On the first day of the session Governor Hubbard, having been officially notified by a joint committee that the two Houses were organized and ready for business, sent them a written communication dated January 8th, informing them of the appointments to office which, under resolutions passed by the last General Assembly, he had made since its adjournment, and of the action he had taken to fix the weekly rate to be paid in the hospitals of Hartford and New Haven for the admission, medical treatment, and support of invalid soldiers and sailors who served on the quota of the State in the late civil war.

A joint convention was held by the two Houses on January 9th for the purpose of electing a Governor and the other executive State officers, as none of the candidates at the general election in November, 1878, had been elected. The joint committee appointed to canvass the votes cast at the said election reported the two competing candidates who had received the greatest number of votes for the respective offices: For Governor, Charles B. Andrews of Litchfield and Richard D. Hubbard of Hartford; for Lieutenant-Governor, David Gallup of Plainfield and Charles Durand of Derby; for Secretary of State, David Torrance of Derby and Dwight Morris of Bridgeport; for State Treasurer, Talmadge Baker of Norwalk and Edwin A. Buck of Windham; for State Comptroller, Chauncey Howard of Coventry and Charles C. Hubbard of Middletown. These competitors were also balloted for by the joint Assembly, with the result that the first-named one for each office received a majority of votes, and was declared by the President as duly elected "for the term of two years ending on the Wednesday after the first

Monday of January, 1881." The proportional number of votes cast for Republican and Democratic candidates at the said ballots was nearly uniform in all—about 150 to 100. After the joint Assembly had been dissolved, separate resolutions declaring each of the Republican candidates duly elected to his respective office were passed by the House of Representatives, and concurred in by the Senate. Later on the same day the two Houses met again in joint Assembly, and the new Governor was inaugurated.

The Hall of Representatives in the new Capitol is much complained of by members of the Legislature, as being seriously defective on several accounts. Within the first week of the session the following resolution was introduced and adopted:

Resolved, That a committee, consisting of eight members of the House, be appointed to consider and report to the House what changes and alterations are required in the Representatives' Hall to render the hall more convenient and comfortable both to the members of the House and to the citizens of the State who may desire to witness its proceedings.

The author of the resolution pointed out several defects, especially with reference to the acoustic properties, in which respect he characterized the hall as "a complete failure." These defects he laid to the charge of the architect, and also of the Commissioners on the Capitol Building, "whose duty it was to see that the architect constructed a building that would answer all the purposes for which it was intended to be used; but they had, he thought, failed to attend to their duty in the particular named." After the resolution had been passed, other members spoke against the acoustic defect of the new hall, which some said is "not so good" as the Representatives' Hall in the old State House.

The official term of William H. Barnum, a United States Senator from Connecticut, expired on March 3, 1879. The Republican members held a caucus on January 16th, to select their candidates. Out of the 149 votes cast on the thirty-eighth ballot, Orville H. Platt received 76, Joseph R. Hawley 72, and Marshall Jewell 1. The nomination of Mr. Platt was then, on motion, made unanimous. On January 21st Mr. Barnum, the previous incumbent, and Mr. Platt were voted for by the two Houses separately, and the votes stood 13 to 6 in the Senate, and 139 to 91 in the Lower House; so Mr. Platt was elected.

The short experiment of winter sessions seems to have made on the members of the Legislature a decidedly adverse impression. The subject of changing the time from January to May was proposed in the House on January 22d, when several members advocated the change as advantageous and preferable on many accounts, including a saving to the State of some two hundred dollars a day, which she must now expend for heating and matters relating to it. A joint resolution was then offered by a member·and passed by the House unanimously, "instructing the Committee on Constitutional Amendments to prepare and report an amendment providing for spring sessions of the General Assembly." This resolution, by a vote subsequently taken in the House, was "continued to the adjourned session of the ·General Assembly in January, 1880," which the Senate concurred in.

The following joint resolution was passed by the Lower House and concurred in by the Senate respecting the bill on Chinese immigration then under deliberation in Congress:

Resolved, by this General Assembly, that the proposed law now pending in the Congress of the United States, restricting Chinese immigration, is a flagrant violation of a sacred and honorable treaty, and is wholly inconsistent with the principles and traditions of our republic, and with the broad principles of human freedom; and it is our earnest hope that its provisions may not disgrace our statutes.

Governor Andrews, in his message to the Legislature, endorsed and urged the recommendations made by his predecessor at the opening of the session of 1878, more particularly those relating to a reduction of the number of probate districts in the State; to the correction of the joint-stock laws, for the prevention of fraud and other abuses, or their punishment; to the engrossment of bills; and to taking a provisional adjournment before closing the session, its time to be employed in perfecting what had been acted upon during the session, and not for action on any new business. Concerning the two last-named subjects he suggested that the provisional adjournment which in 1878 took place in pursuance of the advice given by his predecessor, should be made obligatory by the enactment of a statute, or by the adoption of a joint rule; and as to the engrossment of bills he recommended a change of the existing statute, so as to permit them to be printed instead of being engrossed in writing. He says: "Such a change would to a great extent relieve the Secretary, would lighten the labors of the Committee on Engrossed Bills, and enable them much more speedily to prepare bills for presentation to the presiding officers of the two Houses for their signatures, and to the Governor for his approval." He recommended that the taxes on property recognized by the laws of 1877 and 1878 as belonging to married women exclusively should be assessed against

NEW LONDON.

the wife, and not set in the lists of the husband, as is now done by statute. A bill to effect that object was acted upon at the session of 1878, but failed to pass. He urged the repeal of all the statutes, whether public or private, under which a large amount of property in the State is claimed by its owners to be exempted from taxation. From this general rule he excepted only "clear cases of exemption by irrepealable grant from the Legislature." Upon this subject of taxation for State purposes, the Governor pointed out the absurdity and injustice now committed in the assessment of property of the same kind, its average valuation at different and not distant localities being so different as to be in one town double what it is "in a town next beside it." In order to secure as much uniformity as possible on this point, he suggested periodical assessments to be made by officers appointed by the State, who should actually visit every town once in five or ten years, and make an appraisal. He says: "An assessment made once in ten years would establish a basis for the Board of Equalization, such as they do not now possess, and enable them to act intelligently in the adjustment of State taxation." The Commissioners appointed under a resolution of the General Assembly of 1878, "to inquire into the feasibility of simplifying the system of legal procedure in the State, and secure a more speedy administration of justice," having submitted a detailed report of their labors, with a bill intended to carry their recommendations into effect, Governor Andrews invites the Legislature to give these documents " a careful and most cautious consideration," and to pass the new procedure act " if it may render the means of access to the tribunals of justice more easy and plain, . . . and free the courts of the State of Connecticut from the reproach of that delay which oftentimes amounts to a practical denial of justice." In this connection he urged them to attend to the matter of " costs in civil cases," and " by all means to do away with continuances, at least after the first term." He suggested the limitation of these costs by the passage of a law enacting that " a certain sum should be payable each time the cause advances one stage, as at the entry of the action, when issue is joined, and at final judgment," concluding with these words: " Let it be fixed so that the costs shall be a spur to diligence, and not a premium to delay." He recommended the submission to the people for adoption or rejection of the constitutional amendment for biennial sessions, and pointed to the advantages that will result to the State from such a measure, especially in regard to economy and the " relief from the growing mischief of over-legislation."

The January session of the Legislature in 1879 was closed by final adjournment on March 28th.

An act was passed to provide for the printing of bills, instead of engrossing them by hand while yet under action of the Legislature, as recommended by the Governor.

The bill entitled " An act to simplify procedure in civil causes, and to unite legal and equitable remedies in the same action," submitted with their report by the Commissioners appointed to inquire into the feasibility of simplifying the system of legal procedure, was favorably reported upon by the Committee on the Judiciary, and passed by both Houses. This act, which alters the method of legal procedure heretofore obtaining in the State, and is now in force, is said to be received with disfavor by the lawyers generally, who object against it especially on the ground that it is calculated to work confusion and increase litigation. At the time of its final passage in the Senate, on March 13th, a Senator moved that "the bill and the report of the Committee be continued to the next session of the General Assembly, and that the bill and the report of the Commission be published with the laws of the present session, and that the Secretary of State be requested to send a copy of the bill and report of the Commission to the President of each County Bar for consideration and action." This motion was lost by a tie vote. In regard to the object of the said act, a joint resolution was also passed by the Lower House and concurred in by the Senate on March 21st, "continuing the Commission appointed to consider the feasibility of simplifying the system of legal procedure."

Two constitutional amendments, separately proposed by the Lower House at the session of 1878, were approved by both Houses at the session of 1879, and submitted to the people's vote for adoption or rejection at the State election, October 6, 1879. One provided for biennial sessions of the General Assembly, and the other that Judges of the Supreme Court of Errors and of the Superior Courts should hold office during good behavior, but not after seventy-five years of age. In the Senate these amendments were approved with but one negative vote.

" An act concerning tramps " was passed, being a substitute for the original bill, to which many amendments were made. It now resembles in several particulars the New Hampshire tramp law in a milder form.

An act was also passed repealing the act of January, 1877, which made a reduction of ten per cent. in salaries and fees paid by the State.

By acts passed in 1879, the catching of salmon is prohibited till May, 1883 ; and the fishing season for shad is fixed between March 1st and June 20th each year.

A joint resolution was adopted "raising a commission to examine and revise the laws relating to joint-stock companies " ; also a joint resolution "continuing to the adjourned session of this Assembly in January, 1880, the joint resolution of the House of Representatives No. 32, instructing the Committee on Constitutional Amendments to report an amendment to the Constitution of this State providing for spring sessions of the General Assembly "; also a joint resolution "appointing a joint standing committee, to consist of one Senator and eight Representatives, on retrenchment, reform, and abuses ; and providing that hereafter such a committee shall be appointed on or before the third day of each session."

A bill "relating to the taxation of the separate property of married women," providing that such property shall be set in the tax-lists in the wife's own name, and not in the lists of the husband, as recommended by the Governor, was introduced in the House of Representatives, reported on adversely by the Committee on the Judiciary, and finally rejected by the House, and by the Senate in concurrence, on March 3d.

The following four bills were also introduced in the Lower House in behalf of women, reported upon unfavorably by the appropriate committees, and after deliberation rejected in the Lower House: An act " providing that all the property, real and personal, owned in her own right by any woman in this State, shall be entirely exempt from taxation "; an act " conferring upon tax-paying women the right to vote in city, borough, and town meetings "; an act " conferring upon women the right to vote in school districts " ; and an act " conferring upon women the right to vote on all questions relating to the sale of intoxicating liquors."

A very large number of bills acted upon at this session were defeated at various stages by either of the two Houses, such as the following: Acts "to regulate railroad fares"; "for cheaper railway travel"; "to secure the representation of minorities in corporations"; "creating the office of Attorney-General," with an annual salary of $5,000; "to establish a Bureau of Labor Statistics"; "regulating the hours of labor in manufacturing establishments," limiting ordinary workmen's labor to ten hours a day; "relating to the laying of pipes through the land of adjoining proprietors, for the purpose of conducting water from springs or streams for domestic uses"; "in alteration of an act concerning crimes and criminal prosecutions," the object of which was the abolition of capital punishment; and "concerning the Sabbath," designed to repeal the laws prohibiting trading, driving, etc., on Sunday.

At the State election held on October 6th, the two constitutional amendments, providing for biennial sessions of the Legislature and for the office-tenure of Judges of the Supreme and Superior Courts till the seventy-fifth year of their age, were both rejected by great majorities; the votes having been, on the Judges' tenure of office, 21,321 for, 45,845 against; and on biennial sessions, 17,843 for, 48,859 against.

The general election of November 4, 1879, was restricted to the choice of members of the Legislature, namely, all the Representatives and eleven of the twenty-one Senators, representing the unevenly numbered districts, and resulted in favor of the Republicans. Of the 11 Senators, the Republicans elected 9, the Democrats 2. Of the 245 Representatives, the Democrats elected 82, the Republicans 163. The political complexion of the Legislature at the January session of 1880 will be as follows: In the Senate—Republicans 16, Democrats 5; in the House of Representatives—Republicans 163, Democrats 82. At the January session of 1879 the proportions were: In the Senate—Republicans 14, Democrats 7; in the House of Representatives—Republicans 143, Democrats 100.

The financial condition of the State continues satisfactory. Her public debt at the close of the last fiscal year was the same as in the previous year—$4,967,650, in bonds payable within different periods hereafter, and all bearing interest. The balance in the State Treasury at the beginning of the fiscal year 1879 was $842,322.11, and the public revenue from all sources during the same year amounted to $1,534,288.48, making a total of $2,376,660.59. The aggregate public expenditures for all purposes in the said year, including $287,626 paid as interest on State bonds, were $1,534,-513.64. Balance in the Treasury for the new year, $842,146.95. The ordinary expenses of the State in 1879 were about the same as in 1878, except the judicial, which were increased more than $41,000. The total public revenue for the fiscal year 1880 is estimated at $1,550,050.

and the expenditure at $1,397,246, leaving an estimated balance of $152,804 in the Treasury at the end of the year. The amount of the grand list for the value of all the taxable property in Connecticut in 1879 fell short of what it was in 1878 by more than ten million dollars.

The savings banks in the State seem to be in a more prosperous condition than heretofore, showing also a tendency to further progress. During the year ended October 1, 1879, their total deposits increased $326,974.86. The increase of interest and surplus for the same time was $11,974.70, and their liabilities decreased $120,832.88.

The education of youth in Connecticut is generally satisfactory. The number of schools during the scholastic year 1879 was 1,638, with an average yearly school-time of 178½ days. The aggregate number of children in the State of school age, between four and sixteen years, was 138,428, of whom 119,382 attended the public schools, and 11,212 other than public schools; the percentage of children in attendance at schools of all kinds having been last year 94·2. The total revenue for school purposes from school fund, State, town, and district taxes, and other sources, amounted to $1,300,-972.54. The aggregate amount expended was $1,375,881.01, showing an excess of expenses over income of $74,908.47. The sum expended for the erection of new school-buildings in 1879 was about $37,000. The same item of expense in 1878 amounted to $125,000. The school expenditures in 1879 were reduced in the aggregate by about $130,000.

In the Connecticut Hospital for the Insane at Middletown, on December 1, 1879, there were 510 patients. Their number during the year was 644. All of these, except three who are paying patients, were supported at the charge of the State. Of the three paying patients, two are themselves paupers, their expenses being paid by relatives who live out of the State. Besides the above-mentioned number of indigent insane at the hospital, there were at the close of the year four hundred more poor insane persons in the State, kept in almshouses or elsewhere, supported wholly or in part by their respective towns.

In the State Prison the number of convicts on November 30, 1879, was 251. During the year 137 prisoners were discharged, and 110 received. The income of the prison within the year has covered all the expenses of board, clothing, and medical care for the prisoners, the salaries of all its officers, and the incidental expenses, and left a cash balance of $602.79. For repairs and other matters of the Penitentiary, the sum of $7,644.95 was expended and paid from the State Treasury.

The militia of Connecticut is now completely organized, as the maximum of the number of companies allowed by the State law has been reached, and no room left for new organizations. The muster held in November, 1879, shows the present military force of the State to consist of 183 commissioned officers and 2,894 enlisted men, which is an increase of 632 over the previous year. The battalion of colored men, which was authorized by act of the Legislature at the January session of 1879, forms part of the said increase, it having actually been organized, and consisting of 274 men. Of the 3,077 men, the present whole number of the National Guard, 2,958 are fully uniformed, armed, and equipped; 2,775 of these, including the colored battalion, have received entirely new uniforms during the year, at a cost of a little less than $25 each. The expense of the National Guard for the year, not including the uniforms, was about $65,000. The commutation tax will amount to $94,000.

The divorces granted in Connecticut within the year ending January 31, 1879, were 401, which is something less than their number in the preceding year. It is observed that, out of every ten divorces, eight at least are granted upon uncontested hearings, husband and wife often colluding with one another to be divorced.

The long-pending dispute between the States of Connecticut and New York, in regard to their boundary-line on the Connecticut western and southern border, appears to have been determined by amicable adjustment. The Governor of the State of New York, under act of its Legislature passed in March, 1879, appointed the Secretary of State, the Attorney-General, and the State Engineer a commission for that purpose; and a similar commission was then appointed by Governor Andrews on the part of the State of Connecticut, consisting of Origen S. Seymour, Lafayette S. Foster, and William T. Minor. The two commissions have met together, and settled the matter by a unanimous agreement upon the entire line between the two States. Their report will be laid before the Legislature in 1880.

CORONINI, Count FRANZ, the President of the Austrian Reichsrath, was born in Göritz in 1833. After having studied philosophy in the University of Vienna, he entered the army in 1850. In the war of 1859 he was at first in Italy, but afterward was stationed in Bohemia. In 1866 he was with the Army of the North, and distinguished himself at the battle of Sadowa. After this war he left the army and went to Göritz, where he was elected to the Provincial Diet in 1870. His general popularity was shown even at this election, the Italians as well as the Slavs voting for him. The Emperor appointed him immediately afterward Landeshauptmann (Governor) of Göritz, which position he held until 1878. In 1871 he was elected by the Diet to the Reichsrath, after having declined the election the year before, and has since belonged uninterruptedly to that body. He voted at first generally with the Constitutional party, and acted with the Club of the Left, and then with the Progress Club. This he left recently on account of his views on the Bosnian question. He was, however,

respected and honored by all parties, and when he was elected President of the Chamber of Deputies he received 338 out of 341 votes. He also belonged to the Delegations after 1872, and at the last session was the President. He is the author of an essay on the nationality question in the "Oestreichischen Revue," and of a book on Aquileja.

COSTA RICA (REPÚBLICA DE COSTA RICA).[*] The President of the Republic is General Tomás Guardia; the first Vice-President, Sr. Pedro Quiroz; and the second Vice-President, Sr. Rafael Barroeta. The Cabinet comprises the following Ministers: Interior, War, and Marine, Sr. Rafael Machado; Foreign Affairs, Justice, Public Instruction, and the Poor-Commission, Dr. José Maria Castro; Commerce and Finance, Sr. Salvador Lara; Public Works, Sr. M. Arguéllo. The Bishop of San José is the Rt. Rev. Luis Bruschetti. The Minister of Costa Rica to the United States is Sr. Manuel M. Peralta (absent), accredited in March, 1878; and the Consul-General at New York, Sr. J. M. Muñoz. The United States Minister (resident in Guatemala and accredited to the five Central American Republics, Costa Rica, Nicaragua, San Salvador, Honduras, and Guatemala) is Dr. Cornelius A. Logan; and the United States Consul at San José is Mr. A. Morrell.

The military force of the republic consists of the militia, comprising all male inhabitants between the ages of eighteen and thirty, numbering 16,370, of whom 900 are usually engaged in active service; and the reserves, made up of men between the ages of thirty and fifty-five.

The revenue for the year ending April 30, 1878 (see "Annual Cyclopædia" for that year), was $3,819,211, and the expenditures were $3,904,657, leaving a deficit of $85,446, of the means to be resorted to for the covering of which no mention was made in the ministerial returns. In the budget for 1878–'79 the revenue and expenditures were estimated at $3,-023,780 and $1,794,767 respectively, the prospective surplus to be devoted to the prosecution of the railways. "It should, however, be noted," says a journalist, "that the revenue, as estimated, would be in excess of the total value of the imports for the year referred to, and would constitute no inconsiderable proportion of the estimated value of the exports." In a semi-official report, published in July, 1879, the so-called actual revenue for 1878–'79 stands at $3,113,631; from which, however, should be deducted $324,365, alluded to as "balance from previous year." Any balance from 1877 –'78, as already seen, could only be accounted for by the non-liquidation of a portion of the liabilities of that year, the more so as those liabilities exceeded the revenue by $85,446. The finances of the republic are, nevertheless, in a much more satisfactory condition now than a decade ago, and quite enough so to jus-

---

* For geographical situation, area, territorial division, population, etc., see previous volumes of "Annual Cyclopædia," and particularly that for 1877.

tify the commendatory remarks of the author of the report just mentioned. "Let it not be supposed," he writes, "that this *enormous revenue* tends to impoverish the people, or is derived from oppressive imposts. In the first place, the people are rich, and the profits of their agricultural industries are such as to enable them to pay their taxes without embarrassment; and, in the second place, if these taxes be compared with those of other countries, it will be seen that the Costaricans have no cause to complain of being overburdened. It has now become so natural to see the Government with ample means at command for the execution of its numerous projects of improvement or reform, that the marvels it has already accomplished have passed almost unnoticed. After the heavy outlays made or contracted for by the Government for thirty miles of rails for the Atlantic and twenty-five for the Pacific division of the railway, locomotives, thirty iron and a number of wooden bridges, the tripling of the number of workers, and other measures necessary for the simultaneous prosecution of the enterprise on both divisions of the line, the Peruvian Minister comes forward to claim the $100,000 (with interest to double the amount) loaned by his Government to that of Costa Rica to enable it to carry on the war against the filibusters in 1857; and the debt was liquidated at once, without bringing any of the Government wheels to a standstill." Another proof of the prosperity of the country is furnished by the fact that the yield of the custom-house in 1869-'70—the first year of the decade above spoken of—was but $278,-595.53, while in 1877-'78 it reached $1,010,787, and in 1878-'79, $1,088,890.30. The total foreign debt of Costa Rica in 1877 was $5,058,-055, all to England, arising from loans negotiated in 1871 and 1872 for the purpose of building the interoceanic railway already referred to, and defraying the expenses to be incurred by other public works.

The most recent statistics of the foreign commerce of the republic are those given in the "Annual Cyclopædia" for 1878. The coffee crop for the year 1878-'79 comprised 400,000 quintals (of 100 lbs. each), of which 287,387 quintals had been exported up to April 12, 1879. The early setting in of the wet season prevented the export of nearly 100,000 quintals, according to good authority, while it is claimed that losses were sustained during the season by the scarcity of coffee-gatherers. All difficulties of transportation will cease with the completion of the railway.

The educational system of the country, under the able administration of Dr. Castro, has of late been greatly improved. The laws divide public instruction into the following grades or classes: Instruction primary-inferior, primary-superior, secondary, university or professional. The primary-inferior establishments, which are mostly situated in small country places, number 145 for males, with 6,949 pupils and 176 teachers; and 91 for females, employing 147 teachers, and with an attendance of 4,742. The cost of this branch of the public-school system for the last year was $101,783. The schools known as primary-superior are situated in the capitals of provinces and of departments. For boys there are 28 schools of this class, employing 68 teachers, the attendance at which averaged during the year 2,991. Twenty-five girls' schools also exist, employing 70 teachers, with an average of 2,176 pupils. The cost of this department for the year was $57,140. To the girls' schools in this department is attached a class in telegraphy, which employed during the year six teachers, the expense incurred being $2,880. Secondary instruction is that which is imparted at the National Institute, and for boys only. A moderate sum is collected from the pupils for board and maintenance, and any deficiency at the end of the year is made up by the Government. During the year 1878 there were 224 students in all, employing 1 director and 20 professors, the total expense being $26,874, to which the fees of students contributed to the amount of $14,-501. Belonging to this same grade of instruction, although including with it the inferior grades previously mentioned, are establishments in the principal cities and towns, which receive $3,600 annually from the Government. The female college at Alajuela, under the management of the Daughters of Sion, is not directly subsidized by the Government, except that the gift of the building, grounds, furnishing, etc., which cost $77,292.20, was borne by the Government. This college numbers 98 students, and the results of its operations are already most satisfactory. In Cartago there is another prosperous seminary for females, under the control of another order of sisterhood. It has at present 66 pupils. A subsidy of $3,000 is annually paid to the College of the Catholic Seminary, which at present numbers 57 regular students. The professional or university course is as complete and varied as will be found in colleges elsewhere, and is under most able management. The number of pupils is small, however (only 22), owing to various causes, among which is the former inferior character of the schools of secondary instruction wherein are prepared the candidates for the university. This evil is fast disappearing. There are, besides, 22 private schools in the republic, with 612 pupils, male and female. The total expenditure for public instruction during the year was $197,803, or $58,721 more than in 1877. It is remarkable that in Costa Rica there are more school-teachers than soldiers in active service —a fact unparalleled in all Spanish America.

"The republic," says the President in his message, "maintains cordial relations with its more immediate brethren, although a marked coldness appears in its relations with Guatemala and Honduras on account of misunderstandings, differences of policy in certain matters, etc., with the Presidents of those countries. In the interior peace reigns undisturbed, and the people have been able to devote themselves to their various industries without molestation or disturbance, and with their well-known industry and zeal."

CUSHING, CALEB, a lawyer, soldier, and statesman, was born at Salisbury, Mass., January 17, 1800, and died at Newburyport, January 2, 1879. He was a member of a family that has been noted in Massachusetts from the early colonial days. He graduated at Harvard College in 1818, and afterward became a student at the college for two years in moral philosophy, mathematics, and law. After continuing the study of law for five years, he was admitted to practice, and settled in Newburyport. While he rose rapidly in the legal profession, he did not neglect literature or abstain from political pursuits. He was a frequent contributor to the "North American Review" and other periodicals. He was soon chosen a member of the Lower House of the State Legislature, and afterward was elected a Senator. In 1829 he visited Europe, and was absent two years. On his return to Massachusetts he published an "Historical and Political Review" of European affairs consequent on the occurrence of the French Revolution of 1830, and also his "Reminiscences of Spain." He was again sent to the Legislature for the years 1833 and 1834, and finally elected to represent the district in the Lower House of Congress. To this position he was three times reëlected, serving regularly until March 4, 1843. In 1840 the Whig party triumphed by the election of William Henry Harrison of Ohio as President and John Tyler of Virginia as Vice-President; while Martin Van Buren, the Democratic candidate, was defeated. After an administration of thirty days President Harrison died, and Vice-President Tyler became President. Henry Clay, Senator from Kentucky, as the leader of the Whigs, attempted to pass through Congress certain measures forming a system of policy. Among these was the charter of a United States Bank. This measure was passed and twice vetoed by President Tyler, who undertook to compromise on a "Fiscal Agency." A break in the party ensued, and Mr. Cushing was one of the very few Northern Whigs who continued to support the President, who nominated him for Secretary of the Treasury. The Senate refused to confirm him. He was subsequently confirmed as Commissioner to China, and made the first treaty between that country and the United States. On his return he was elected a Representative in the Massachusetts Legislature, and in 1847 he raised a regiment for the Mexican war and became its

colonel, and was subsequently made brigadier-general. In 1847, and again in 1848, he was nominated by the Democrats for Governor, but failed of an election. He continued to represent Newburyport in the Legislature until 1852, when he was appointed Associate Justice of the State Supreme Court. In 1853 he was appointed U. S. Attorney-General by President Pierce, and retained the office until 1857. Again he became a member of the Massachusetts Legislature, and coöperated with the Democratic party in its opposition to the anti-slavery aggressions. In April, 1861, he tendered his services to Governor Andrew "in any capacity, however humble, in which it may be possible for me to contribute to the public weal in the present critical emergency." The Governor, an ardent anti-slavery and war champion, did not respond. His services were often employed during the war in the departments at Washington, and in 1866 he was appointed Commissioner to codify the laws of Congress. In 1868 he was sent to Bogotá to arrange a diplomatic difficulty. President Grant appointed him one of the American counsel before the Tribunal of Arbitration that was provided for by the treaty of Washington for the settlement of the Alabama claims, which met at Geneva in 1871 and concluded its labors nine months later. The other counsel were Mr. Waite, now Chief Justice of the Supreme Court of the United States, and Mr. Evarts. In 1873 General Cushing published a volume entitled "The Treaty of Washington," in which a history of the arbitration is given—a work written in his seventy-fourth year, but showing no decline of mental power in the author. The death of Chief Justice Chase, in the spring of 1873, created a vacancy in the highest judicial office in the country. At the close of the year President Grant sought to have the office filled by the appointment of General Cushing, but the Senate evinced so much reluctance to confirming the nomination that he declined it. Soon afterward he was nominated and confirmed as Minister to Spain, our relations with which had become exceedingly critical, owing to circumstances that grew out of the Cuban insurrection. Assuming this arduous post in his seventy-fifth year, General Cushing discharged its duties with ability and fidelity, and to the entire satisfaction of the appointing power, and also of his country. He arrived home in April, 1877. Notwithstanding General Cushing's prominent career and many public services, he was never popular. Neither the Whig nor the Republican party really liked him, and he was still further from being a favorite with the Democrats.

D

DANA, RICHARD HENRY, editor, poet, and essayist, was born in Cambridge, Mass., November 15, 1787, and died in Boston, February 2, 1879. He passed nine years of his early life at Newport, R. I., and in 1804 entered Harvard College, and left in 1807 without graduation. His regular studies were, however, completed at Newport during the next two years. He was admitted to the practice of law in 1811. He still further pursued his legal studies in Baltimore, and after a time returned to Boston, and was elected a member of the Legislature. Being more inclined to literature than to legal practice, he became a member of the Anthology Club, by which the publication of the "North American Review" was commenced in 1815. To that work Mr. Dana contributed his earliest writings — his essay, on "Old Times," an article on Allston's "Sylph of the Seasons," and papers on the Edgeworths, Hazlitt, and Irving. His writings were distinguished not only by their ability, but because of the boldness with which they assailed some received opinions, to question the justice of which was held to be heretical action. In 1820 he withdrew from the "Review," and soon after started a periodical for tales and essays called "The Idle Man," which went through six numbers, and contained some of the best of his pieces. His first poem, "The Dying Raven," was sent to the "New York Review," then (1821) edited by Bryant; the "Husband and Wife's Grave" appeared in the same periodical. In 1827 "The Buccaneer and Other Poems" appeared in a small volume, and in 1833 these poems and his prose articles from "The Idle Man" were published. These poems and prose writings were republished in 1850, in two 12mo volumes. The "United States Review," in 1826–'27, contained articles from his pen on Mrs. Radcliffe and Charles Brockden Brown. In 1839 and the following year he wrote a series of ten critical essays upon Shakespeare's characters, and these were delivered in 1839–'40 in Boston, New York, Philadelphia, and many other cities. They were received with much favor, and are among his most valuable contributions to literature. He was also a contributor to the "Spirit of the Pilgrims," writing for it papers on Pollok's "Course of Time," pamphlets on "Controversy," "Natural History of Enthusiasm," and "Henry Martyn." To the "American Quarterly Observer" he furnished an article on "The Past and the Present," and to the "Biblical Repository" one on "Law as suited to Man." His connection with periodical literature ceased in 1835, just as that literature was beginning to show some signs of becoming a paying pursuit.

The first fifty years of his life Mr. Dana was regarded as an invalid on account of the morbid condition of his nervous system; but after that period his health began to mend, and from the age of sixty-five to within a few weeks of his death he was in excellent bodily condition. Most of his life was passed in retirement and literary pursuits. He had no taste for active affairs, and never sought popularity. His personal appearance at the time of his eighty-fifth year, with his whitened locks and flowing beard, is described as attracting marked attention on the street. In his home, however, he was seen to the best advantage as a gentleman of the old school, with "his mild countenance and soft, beaming eyes of grayish-blue, lighting up his face, otherwise marked by sorrow and deep thought." His forehead was high and broad. His person was slight, and a little below the medium height.

DARGAN, EDMUND SPAWN, a Congressman and Chief Justice, born in Montgomery County, North Carolina, April 15, 1805, died in Mobile, Alabama, about November 22, 1879. He was the son of a Baptist minister of Irish descent, at whose death the son was left without means wherewith to acquire an education; but by his own exertions he obtained a fair knowledge of English, Latin, and Greek. He was engaged on a farm till he was twenty-three years old, and then read law in the office of Joseph Picket at Wadesboro. In 1829 he went to Alabama, and taught school three months at Washington, Autauga County. Here he was elected a justice of the peace, and filled that office for some years, in the mean time practicing law. In 1833 he removed to Montgomery, and there rose rapidly in his profession. In 1840 he was a candidate for the State Legislature, and defeated. A year later he was elected by the General Assembly to the bench of the Circuit Court of the Mobile District, and at once removed to Mobile. He resigned the office of Judge in 1842, and in 1844 was elected to the State Senate from Mobile. He resigned the following year, when he became the nominee of his party for Congress, and was elected. While in Congress the question of the northwestern boundary of Oregon became very important. On this he made an able speech and offered some valuable amendments to the resolution of notice. He declined a renomination; and a vacancy occurring on the bench of the Supreme Court, he was elected by the Legislature, at the session of 1847, to fill the place. In July, 1849, he became Chief Justice by the resignation of Justice Collier. He occupied this position till December, 1852, when he resigned and resumed the practice of law in Mobile. He was not again in public life till 1861, when he was elected a delegate to the State Convention of that year, and voted for the ordinance of secession. At the first election of Representatives in the Confederate Congress, he was returned from the Mobile District and served throughout the term. He declined a reëlection, and afterward remained in private life, successfully engaged in legal practice. He was a man of a very estimable character and an eminent jurist.

DAZA, HILARION, a Bolivian soldier and statesman, of humble parentage, partly Indian, born at Sucre in 1840. The name of his father, who was a Spaniard, was Grosolé; but, owing to domestic dissensions, that gave place to the maternal family name, Daza. While still but eighteen years of age, he began his military experience as a volunteer in the army of the "Liberals," then engaged in a revolutionary movement; and that party having been victorious, he remained in the service and gained rapid advancement. Subsequent successful revolutions lifted him into notoriety, and won for him the patronage and confidence of Melgarejo, whom for a time he faithfully served and supported. Two large Bolivian rivers, the Pilcomayo and Bermejo, crossing the wooded plains of the Gran Chaco, and emptying into the Paraguay, would if navigable afford a ready outlet to the Atlantic Ocean, and favor the development of Bolivian industry and commerce, hitherto paralyzed by the lack of easy means of communication with the Pacific seaboard. To explore the courses of those rivers, numerous fruitless expeditions have been organized; and in one of these, during the brief lull from political strife which marked the dictatorship of Melgarejo, the year 1867 found young Daza second in command, with the rank of lieutenant-colonel. He next became conspicuous in January, 1871, in league with Colonel Juan Granier against his former friend and patron, whose tyranny had brought upon him the odium of all parties. On the deposition of Melgarejo, Daza, at the head of his famous regiment of cuirassiers, held in check the turbulent factions at La Paz, for which service he was rewarded by President Morales with further promotion and the portfolio of War. As minister and general, he again succeeded in maintaining order after the death of Morales, assassinated (1872) by his own nephew, and insured the peaceful accession of the constitutional successor. In the same year he supported the candidature of Ballivian, and on the death of the latter became himself a candidate for the Presidency, against Salinas (civil candidate), Oblitas, and Vásquez (representative of the Corral party). The elections once over, a dispute ensued as to the majority, and Daza, it is contended, apprehensive of undue favor from the Government toward his rival, seized the power as his right, and was inaugurated on May 4, 1876. Notwithstanding this unconstitutional act, his government was as popular and troubled with as few revolutions as that of any of his predecessors. On the outbreak of the war with Chili, he assumed the title of Captain-

General. (For the remainder of his public acts, see BOLIVIA and PERU.)

DE KOVEN, Rev. JAMES, D. D., born at Middletown, Connecticut, about 1832, died at Racine, Wisconsin, March 20, 1879. He graduated at Columbia College in 1850. He then entered the General Theological Seminary of New York, passed through the course of studies, and was ordained. Then he went to Minnesota at the age of twenty-three years, and was in charge of a parish three or four years. In 1859 Racine College (founded in 1852) and St. John's Hall of Neshotah were united, and he was called to take the place of warden of the institution, which is now styled the University of Racine. It is situated in the midst of ninety acres of ground overlooking the lake, and has accommodations for 110 students. Its discipline and methods of study are modeled upon those of Rugby, England. In 1873 he lacked only a few votes of being elected Bishop of Massachusetts. The issue of the election was between the High and Low Church parties of New England, and he was the candidate of the former. It had put him forward as one of the most powerful orators of the Episcopalian pulpit. But a more general attention was attracted to him by an able address which he made in the Convention of 1874. The issue between the High and Low Church parties of the denomination in this country had assumed a bitter antagonism, which threatened a serious dissension if not a final division. The High Church movement had been growing in importance for several years previously, and was regarded with some alarm by a majority of the Episcopal clergy. The address of Dr. De Koven on the question at issue created a profound impression. His party, however, was in a minority. In September, 1875, he was elected Bishop of Illinois. He declined to accept, but continued his efforts to sustain the struggling university at Racine. In 1878 he was called to be assistant rector of Trinity Church, New York, but declined the call. A short time before his death the vestry of St. Mark's Church, Philadelphia, elected him as rector, but he did not live either to accept or decline it. In his social relations, Dr. De Koven was distinguished for genial humor, kindly courtesy of manners, and brilliant conversational powers. As an orator he possessed the rare quality of compactness of composition, combined with a fascinating mellowness of voice, graces of action, and emotional power. A volume of his sermons has been published since his death.

DELANE, JOHN THADDEUS, a British journalist, born in October, 1817, died November 24, 1879. He was educated privately and at Magdalen Hall, Oxford, where he graduated B. A. in 1840, and took his M. A. degree in 1846. His first connection with the "Times," of which his father was financial manager, dates from the year 1839, when he became one of the assistant editors to Mr. Thomas Barnes, on whose death in 1841 he succeeded to the chief post as editor of that journal, when he had barely attained his twenty-fourth year. He retained that post until November, 1877, when he resigned on account of ill health, with a liberal pension, and was succeeded . by the present editor, Mr. Thomas Chenery, late Professor of Arabic at Oxford. He studied law, and was called to the bar at the Middle Temple in 1847, but never practiced that profession. . As an editor he was eminently successful, and under his management the "Times" flourished greatly and wielded an immense influence.

DELAWARE. The biennial session of the Legislature of Delaware commenced on January 7th. The Senate elected Charles J. Harrington as Speaker. In the House, Swithin Chandler was elected to that office.

The most important occurrence in the first part of the session was the inauguration of Governor Hall, which took place on January 21st. It was considered as brilliant and attractive as could be desired, the display eclipsing that of any previous occasion. A large number of prominent men assembled, and the military and people from all parts of the State. It was estimated that there were at least 3,000 persons present. The account proceeds to state that the members of the Legislature, numbering altogether thirty persons, and their officers, formed in line, the Speakers of both Houses in advance, and escorted the Governor elect, who walked with the retiring Governor, to the court-house, on the public square, several hundred yards distant. The court-house is a new red-brick building, three stories high. It was in the second story of this building that the oath was administered. Here, in advance of the all-important arrival, a numerous assemblage of well-dressed people, including many ladies, had gathered to do honor to the occasion. The judges' "bench," a platform, the bar, and the jurors' box had been specially reserved for members of the Legislature, judges, and other official personages, ladies, etc. For these reserved places cards of admission in limited numbers had been issued. Though small, the audience was notable for its fine-looking men and beautiful women. The General Assemblymen sat in the bar. Governor Cochran and Secretary of State Grubb, the Governor elect and Mr. Walcott, the new Secretary of State, judiciary, members of Congress, ex-Governors, etc., sat on the judges' platform, over which was inscribed in letters of evergreen the name of the new Governor. In the jury-box sat Mrs. Hall, the Governor's wife, his daughter, Mrs. Lister, and other members of the family. Among the judges on the bench were Chief Justice Joseph P. Comegys, the State Chancellor, Hon. Willard Saulsbury, who was formerly one of the United States Senators of Delaware, and Associate Justice John W. Houston. Among other prominent men assisting on the occasion were United States Senator Eli Saulsbury, Hon.

James Williams, Representative of the State in Congress, and Hon. E. L. Martin, elected his successor to Congress; ex-Governors James Ponder and Gove Saulsbury, Adjutant-General J. Park Postles, and other State officials. The inauguration ceremony was very brief. Prayer and benediction by legislative chaplains opened and closed the proceedings.

Among the appointments made by the Governor during the year were those of Captain J. Park Postles as Adjutant-General of the State, and George Gray to be Attorney-General for five years from October 3d. James M. Walcott was also selected as Secretary of State by the Governor.

The Legislature consists of three Senators and seven Representatives from each of the three counties of the State. Both Houses are entirely Democratic. In 1875 there was one Republican in the Legislature, and in 1873 there were eight.

An act was passed in relation to tramps. It declares that any person without a home in the town or hundred in which he may be found wandering about, without employment and the regular and visible means of living, shall be deemed and taken to be a tramp, and shall be dealt with accordingly. It is further made the duty of the corporate officers of every city and town in the State to cause every tramp, found within the limits of such town, to be immediately arrested and put to work on the streets, or other public works thereof, or to hire out such tramps to private persons, and for this purpose said officers may employ such overseers as may be necessary. The term of working them on the streets, etc., shall not exceed one month, and they shall receive such wages as the officers may deem just.

A canvass of the votes for Governor by the Legislature showed the following result:

COUNTIES.	Hall.	K. J. Stewart.	Scattering.	Total.
New Castle....	5,080	675	81	5,686
Kent..........	2,208	33	7	2,248
Sussex........	3,492	2,127	0	5,619

Hall's majority over Stewart, 7,507.

A joint resolution reducing the compensation to the Secretary of State from $275 to $200 was adopted.

Some applications for divorce were made to the Legislature, so that a joint resolution was offered in the Senate to the effect that no divorces would be granted during this session for causes cognizant before the Delaware courts. In asking its adoption Senator Sharpley said that it was a stigma on Delaware that people were justly led to remark that "marriage was hard in Delaware and divorce was easy." The conducting of divorce cases in the State was not proper so far as the decision upon them in the Legislature went. If we open the Senate chamber as a divorce court, said the Senator in concluding, we will have no less than fifty cases of divorce upon our hands.

Mr. Denney offered an amendment to the effect that no bills for incorporations cognizable before the courts be taken up.

Mr. Sharpley said that often when divorces were applied for to the Legislature that body overstepped its powers. The causes for which divorces are granted are adultery, desertion for three years, drunkenness, impotency, extreme cruelty, marriage under age, and willful neglect. Over all these the court has sole charge. The Legislature only has the right to decide on cases whenever the cruelty has not been extreme or something like that. The list which had just been recited covered all causes for which husband and wife could be separated. It seemed to the Senator that the Legislature was going too far when those petitions were granted, when the courts were the proper place for them. As to the adoption of the amendment, Mr. Sharpley thought that it should be presented in a separate petition.

The amendment to the resolution was lost.

In speaking on the resolution, Mr. Cooch said that the Legislature was not prepared to hear the cases fully and properly.

Mr. McWhorter: " There is a strong feeling in the courts of justice that many of the divorces granted by the Legislature are illegal, and out of this many questions concerning the illegitimacy of children and the settlement of real estate will arise in after-years and be decided in the courts. The courts have the sole power to grant divorces."

Mr. Sharpley: " There is frequent illegality in the petitions for divorce in which the petitioner makes affidavit that there is no collusion between him and the other party—that is, that there is no mutual agreement to that effect. In nearly every case that comes before the General Assembly there has been an understanding of that kind."

The resolution was adopted, all the members voting in the affirmative.

In the House the resolution was amended so as to provide for summoning one or more responsible witnesses before a joint committee, and thus approved by each House.

An act was passed requiring a stamp on oleomargarine to distinguish it from butter.

An act was passed to regulate the business of insurance companies created by the State. It provided for the establishment of an Insurance Department and an Insurance Commissioner to be appointed by the Governor, who is to be an expert accountant, and to give $2,000 security for the performance of his duties, which are described in the bill as follows: To see that all the insurance laws of the State are enforced, and to demand from all companies doing business in the State certified copies of their charters, with the names and residence of their agents. When he deems it advisable, or upon application of policy-holders to the amount of $10,000, a thorough examination shall be made of the affairs and condition of any company, and the result of such examination published;

and if necessary an expert is to be employed, to be paid by the company so examined, and the books and papers of such company must be submitted to the examination of the Commissioner. When the Commissioner is satisfied that any company is fraudulently conducted, and that its accounts are not sufficient to carry on its business, or upon any non-compliance with the act, the facts are to be certified to the Attorney-General, who is to apply for a rule upon the company to show cause why its business should not be closed; and the Chancellor is authorized in vacation to appoint a receiver, upon sufficient cause shown, to wind up the business of such company. He is to publish annually a statement showing the condition, with the assets and liabilities, of all companies doing business in the State for the preceding year, in at least three papers in the State, the cost of such publication to be borne equally by said companies. He shall, as soon as possible in each year, ascertain the net value on the 31st day of December of the preceding year of all policies in force on that day in each life-insurance company doing business in the State. He may accept the valuations made by the Insurance Commissioner of any other State, if the same have been properly made; and each such company is required to furnish him with a certificate of any valuation of its policies made by the Insurance Commissioner of any other State on or before the first day of March, and if such company fail to comply with this demand he is to revoke its authority to do business in this State; and if he shall find that such company is unsafe, he is to revoke its authority to do business in the State. Upon payment of the proper fine he is to give certified copies of any paper in his office to any one asking for them. He is to make a semi-annual report to the Legislature of his acts during the two years, and exhibit the condition of the insurance companies doing business in the State. All insurance companies doing business in the State are to make a detailed report every year to the Commissioner of the actual condition of such companies, which are to be sworn to by some authorized officer of each company.

An act was also passed to refund the State debt to the amount of $800,000. The debt outstanding consisted of $500,000 in bonds due in 1885, and $800,000 in bonds due in 1890, all at 6 per cent. These it is proposed to refund in bonds due in 1900 at 4½ per cent. The total State debt at the beginning of the year was $953,000, with no floating debt. If the total assets were deducted from the total debt, it would leave the assets in excess of the indebtedness $165,799, with sums due January 1st amounting to $90,858.

The most important subject before the Legislature was the bill to create a Board of Railroad Commissioners. It provided for the appointment of three Railroad Commissioners, one from each county, with a salary each of $500 a year. The Commissioners have general supervision over all railroads in the State, and when they think that any railroad combination is violating the State laws and the provisions of its charter, they shall inform the president or some officer of the company in the State; and if such violation continues, the Attorney-General is to be directed to take such action as is expedient. Whenever repairs upon any railroad are necessary, or any addition to the rolling stock, etc., or any change in the rates of fare, for the transportation of passengers or freight, or other changes are deemed expedient, the Commissioners shall notify the president of such road or some officer in the State, and a report of such proceedings shall be included in the annual report of the Commissioners. All railroad corporations are required to furnish all information sought by the Commissioners concerning the management and operation of the road; and copies of its books, leases, contracts, and agreements are to be furnished upon application, together with all rates, charges, etc.; and any discrimination in freight charges against any individual or corporation shall l» reported to the Governor and to the Attorney-General. Upon refusal to furnish such information and an annual report of the operation of the road sworn to, they shall forfeit $1,000, to be recovered by suit at law in the name of the State. The Commissioners are required to make an annual report, with recommendations, etc. The Commissioners are to draw upon the State Treasurer for $100 per year for expenses of experts, incidentals, etc., and they, with their experts and other agents whom the Commissioners may deem valuable, are to ride over the roads free of charge.

The bill originated from the complaints of the fruit-growers. Petitions were presented in which it was charged that the Philadelphia, Wilmington, and Baltimore Company had discriminated grossly against the fruit-growers, who stated that the charges notwithstanding did not exceed the limit of eight cents allowed in the charter, being only seven and a half cents per mile. One petition from the fruit-growers to the Legislature commences with the statement that, "from Jersey City, the New Jersey Central Railroad has offered to carry car-loads of fruit, ferriage included, at three cents per ton per mile, as against seven and a half cents per ton per mile charged by the Philadelphia, Wilmington, and Baltimore and Pennsylvania Railroads; a difference amounting to a total, since 1868, of over two million dollars, exacted from the now impoverished fruit-growers," etc., etc.

The constitutionality of the bill was the chief point in question. Those who denied its constitutionality urged that one section in the State Constitution provided that the people should be secure in their persons, houses, papers, and possessions from unreasonable searches and seizures; and it was claimed that the essential parts of the bill would be decided to conflict with the prohibition against unreasonable searches so far as the Philadelphia, Wilmington, and Baltimore Company's books were concerned. As they were kept without the jurisdiction of the State, they could not be demanded with any force. Reference was also made to a decision of the highest court showing the power of legislation against chartered railroad corporations. This was a decision of the State Court of Errors and Appeals made in 1873, upon an appeal taken by the aforesaid railroad company. The circumstances of the case were that the company had charged one Bowers for passage from Philadelphia to Wilmington 50 cents, which is at the rate of $0.0189 per mile, and on the same day had charged him $1.85 to Port Deposit, which is at the rate of $0.05 per mile; and had charged for freight at the rate of $0.39.38.37 per mile for 9,000 feet of lumber from Port Deposit to Wilmington, and from Newport to Wilmington had charged for the same quantity of lumber at the rate of $1.82¼ per mile. The Legislature had previously passed an act the fourth section of which was as follows:

That if the said Philadelphia, Wilmington, and Baltimore Railroad Company, or any other railroad company in this State, shall, either as an operator of its own railroad or railroads, or as lessee of other roads within the State, charge and receive a greater rate per mile for the carriage of passengers, or for the carriage or transportation of goods, wares, or merchandise, or other property whatsoever, from place to place within the State, or from a place within the State to a place without the State, than is charged by such company for the carriage of passengers and the transportation of property or freight for like distances, or per mile, from places without the State to places within the State, or from places without the State through the State to other places without the State, the person or persons paying such charges, either as fare or freight, shall be entitled to recover from such company, so charging and receiving the same, a sum of tenfold the amount of money so paid, to be recovered in an action of debt or assumpsit as like amounts are now recovered by law.

The intention of this act was to prevent discrimination in the freight and passenger tariff on the part of the railroads in the State, and Mr. Bowers sought under the act to recover $56.80 before certain justices of the peace, from whose verdict in his favor the company took an appeal as above mentioned. Chancellor Bates announced the unanimous opinion of the Court upon an issue taken as to the constitutionality of the fourth section above cited of the act. The Court decided that the charter of a railroad company was a contract between the State and the company, and under the provisions of the Constitution of the United States, which declared that "no State shall pass any law impairing the obligation of contracts," an act of the Legislature having the effect to abridge or restrict any power or privileges vested by the charter, which were material to the beneficial exercise of the franchise granted—without the reservation of the right to pass such an act, and passed without the consent of the company—impaired the obligation of the contract and was invalid. The other part of the decision had a more direct hearing. The power of the railroad company to charge for passengers and freight was adjudged to be one of the essentials to the enjoyment of the franchise, and a part of the consideration of the contract; "and," proceeded the Chancellor, "the power to adjust its tariffs of charges by its own officers, according to their views of the necessities of business and of justice to the public, without any reservation in the charter of such legislative control or supervision over them, being a part of the franchise as it was granted, an act of the Legislature which assumes for the State the right to regulate what under the charter was granted as an absolute discretion of the corporation, viz., the right to adjust its tariff of charges for the carriage of passengers and freight, undoubtedly impairs the obligations of the contract in the sense of the constitutional prohibition, and is inoperative and void."

These views were enforced by a letter from U. S. Senator Bayard, then at Washington, of which the following is an extract:

I regret the introduction of the bill, because I do not see how the rights and powers and duties of the companies under their charters can be modified or restrained by legislation now. I am disposed to doubt the power of the Legislature to make the inquisition into the business of the companies, and examine their books and papers. I think that it would be resisted, and then not only would angry contest be engendered, but large expenses, which in the end would come out of the people of the State. As we now stand, we receive a full and regular revenue, paid without trouble or expense into our Treasury by the companies, which saves us from laying other taxes on our people. A system of commissionership, which might be needed and be very useful in a large, extensive, and complicated system of railroads in the construction and ownership of which the State was interested, such as in Massachusetts, New York, and other large States, would not apply so well to our little State. We have no men who, for $500 per annum, would be competent to give such counsel to the State as would be safe to rely upon.

There is an unavoidable monopoly in the transportation by every important railroad, and competition is the only sure cure for this, unless in incorporating the companies the State shall reserve power to regulate fares, etc.; and Delaware has omitted to do this.

The reply of the advocates for the Board of Commissioners to this letter consisted in the publication of an extract from the speech of Senator Bayard in the Senate, April 5, 1878, "on the act compelling the Pacific Railroads to pay an amount in opposition to the decision of the Supreme Court, and also enacting a conditional revocation of all the rights, privileges, grants, and franchises derived or obtained by said railroads from the United States." This was accompanied with opinions of other respectable authorities. The bill, however, failed to pass.

A bill was passed making Wilmington the county-seat of New Castle County.

An unsuccessful effort was made to pass a bill for the enrollment of a State militia. Its passage was urged upon the grounds that it was the duty of the State to protect its citizens against violence by its own strong arm, and not to depend upon the dangerous influence of the National Government. Pennsylvania had failed of its duty, and now a bill was pending to take from the State Treasury over $4,000,000 to pay for the ravages of the mob in Philadelphia and Pittsburgh.

A bill to grant "local option" to towns for the sale of liquors was reported by a committee of the House, but failed to pass. An unsuccessful effort was also made to establish a State Board of Health.

The estimate of the receipts of the year ending January 14, 1880, was $147,211, and the expenditures $118,920. The receipts from licenses are estimated at $52,000, and from railroad taxes $40,000. The sum of $81,000 is due to the State on arrears of taxes and interest. The expenses of the executive government are estimated at $9,500. The total expenses of the government during the year 1878 were only $25,781.90. This includes the State expenses only, and not any amount expended in payment of interest and redemption of bonds. The largest item of expenses was for judicial salaries, $12,000. The Executive Department cost $9,775, which includes salaries of Secretary of State, State Treasurer, Auditor, Attorney-General, and School Superintendent. An examination of the sources of revenue shows that there was raised by taxation for State purposes $106,687.39. This does not include revenue from investments, or from box-tax paid by the county treasurers, but only the taxes current during the year and the amounts of fines from the counties, which are for State purposes. Of this amount of taxation, New Castle County paid about $90,-000, Kent about $10,500, and Sussex $6,000. The State revenues are obtained from certain investments, from interest on the Junction and Breakwater and Breakwater and Frankford Railroad bonds, from indirect taxation in the shape of fees and license-tax, and from tax on the railroads and banks. None of the railroads in the two lower counties, except the Maryland and Delaware road, are taxed, nor is the Delaware road. The assessments in New Castle County amount to $40,682,378, and the per cent. of tax paid to the State upon this assessment is 0.002. The assessment of property in Kent is $12,639,255, and the per cent. of taxes paid 0.0008. The assessment of property in Sussex is $8,576,215, and the per cent. of State tax is 0.0007. Although there appear in the State Treasurer's account receipts for State tax from counties amounting to $31,099.19, there is in fact not now any direct tax levied in the counties for State purposes. The counties had not, when the old 18 per cent. real estate law was repealed, paid up their assessments, and are now doing so. New Castle has paid all of her arrears of taxes, but both Kent and Sussex still owe the State Treasury, the former $12,000 and the latter $13,000. In addition to the revenue from the sources mentioned above, the State has the following investments, which pay annually into its Treasury a considerable sum:

Farmers' Bank stock, 1,275 shares, at $50 per share.	$63,750
Stock of the Bank of Delaware, 20 shares, at $465 per share	9,300
Loan to Junction and Breakwater Railroad	400,000
Loan to Breakwater and Frankford Railroad	200,000
Total	$673,050

The receipts and expenses of schools in New Castle County for the year 1877–'78 were: from the district tax, $90,743 ; amount received from the school fund, $8,013.50 ; total, $98,743.39. There was paid for tuition $61,-334.36, and for contingencies $32,288.73 ; total, $93,623.09. The School Commissioners had in their hands an unexpended balance of $11,-344.40. There was a falling off of receipts as compared with the years 1876–'77 of $62,000, and a decrease of expenses of $57,000. In New Castle County there were reported 11,435 scholars, 112 schools, and the average time of operation of each school was nine months and four days. None of these figures take in account the schools of Wilmington. In Kent County, for the same period, the amount received from taxes was $25,589.25 ; from the school fund, $8,124.64 ; total, $33,713.89. Amount paid for tuition, $28,052.75 ; for contingencies, $4,744.-11 ; total, $32,796.36. Balance in hands of Commissioners, $3,989.36. In Kent there were reported 5,325 scholars, 113 schools, and the average time of operation of each school seven months and two days. In Sussex County, during the same period, there was received from taxes $15,937 ; from school fund, $9,048.03 ; total, $24,985.03. Amount expended for tuition, $22,286.24 ; for contingencies, $3,748.33 ; total, $26,034.57 ; amount in hands of Commissioners, $4,095.88. In the year previous there was $25,965.26 received and $26,816 expended ; balance in hands of Commissioners, $5,036.65. In Sussex there were reported 6,422 scholars, 162 schools, and the average time of operation of each school four months and fourteen days. These results show an increase in scholars in New Castle of 1,229 as compared with the previous year, and an increase of 11 schools and a decrease of 12 days in the average operation. In Kent there was an increase of 507 scholars and 5 schools, and a decrease of two months in the average operation. In Sussex there was an increase of 20 scholars, a decrease of 4 schools, and an increase of five days in the average operation of schools. The colored schools are supervised by the Actuary of the "Delaware Association for the Education of Colored People." The number of schools during the year 1878 was 52, being an increase of 6 over the previous year. The number of pupils enrolled was 2,249. The manner of establishing the schools is thus described by the Actuary:

The opening and closing of the schools is governed by no systematic rules. Usually the people interested in the schools assemble in their different localities, and, after an interchange of views as to their financial means, etc., select trustees for the management of the schools, and then address the Actuary, stating how much salary they can pay a teacher, when the school will be ready to open, and asking him to send a suitable and competent teacher. Within a short time the necessary arrangements are completed, the teacher is sent, the school is opened, and continues until the falling off in the attendance or the lack of financial support necessitates its close. I have endeavored to use my best judgment in the selection of teachers. Many of them are graduates of the school for colored youths in Philadelphia, who have been educated especially with the view of teaching ; others come from New England, and still others from our own State. The salaries in our schools are so low that we are deprived of the best and most experienced teachers ; but, taken altogether, I am convinced that the colored schools in Delaware have never had a better educated, more energetic, and ambitious corps of teachers than during the past year.

The State appropriates for the education of the blind, deaf and dumb, and feeble-minded, the sum of $2,971. There are 13 of these pupils.

The subject of the construction of the Delaware and Maryland Ship-Canal was brought before the Lower House of Congress and referred to the Committee on Canals and Railways. A sub-committee of the same was appointed to investigate and determine on the routes. A report was made at the winter session of 1879, based chiefly on surveys and estimates made at the instance of Congress by engineers under the direction of Colonel Churchill and Major Hutton.

It appears that the peninsula is fifty-six miles wide from the mouth of the Choptank River to Cape Henlopen. At the mouth of the Sassafras it is twenty-eight miles wide. There is deep water on the eastern side of the Chesapeake at nearly all points, but the western shore of the Delaware River is marked by wide shoals and by marshes. The watershed of the peninsula is nowhere more than ten to fifteen miles distant from Delaware Bay. Its general surface is flat, the ridge having an elevation increasing from twenty-five feet on the lower routes to eighty feet on the line of the Sassafras. The tides on the Delaware have a range of about four feet, but on the Chesapeake of less than two feet. The facilities for the construction will be considerable. Excavations will be easy to make, and the excavated earth easily handled. The underlying clays afford the basis for good foundations, and the streams are easy to follow or cross without requiring costly safeguards to protect the structure from flood, of tide or freshet. Surveys were made of five routes, omitting the Sassafras route, which had already been fully surveyed. The lengths of the various routes are as follows: Ferry Creek, from Baltimore to the Atlantic Ocean, 149·81 miles ; Wye River, 128·42 ; Queenstown, 109·29 ; Centreville, 106·13 ; Southeast Creek, 115·78 ; Sassafras River, 129·25. The miles of excavation would be: Ferry Creek, 37·67 ; Wye River, 42·99 ; Queenstown, 53·78 ; Centreville, 50·95 ; Southeast

Creek, 38·35; Sassafras River, 14·20. All of the routes will be easy to dredge and keep free from silt and filling up. The various routes are briefly described as follows:

The Queenstown route starts at the mouth of the Chester River, at Queenstown, and proceeds thence in a straight line over a high and generally flat country to Broad Kill Creek, and thence through the marshes to the Delaware Bay, near Lewes, 53¼ miles from Queenstown.

The Centreville route leaves Chesapeake Bay 27½ miles from Baltimore, and passes through a shallow "jut" into Chester River, 3½ miles from its mouth, by this cut gaining 8 miles. It proceeds up the Chester River to Corsica Creek, 5½ miles, thence in nearly a straight line over a flat country ranging from 65 to 75 feet above tide, entering Delaware Bay at the same point as the Ferry Creek and Queenstown line, the distance from Corsica Creek being 51 miles.

The Wye River route enters Wye River from Eastern Bay (the *débouchure* of Miles River), passes up to head of tide at Skipton Creek, thence directly to Milford, Delaware, 37½ miles. The ridge between the bays at these points does not exceed 60 feet.

The Southeast Creek route enters Chester River as by Centreville route, ascends that river 12 miles to Southeast Creek, follows the latter 2½ miles, thence in a straight line 29 miles over a flat country 60 to 70 feet above low water to Little Creek, on the Delaware. It follows this marshy creek for 3½ miles, reaching Delaware Bay at a point 30 miles above Lewes.

The Sassafras route passes from Baltimore 30 miles up the Chesapeake Bay, and up the Sassafras River 14½ miles over a flat country rising to 80 feet at summit. It then crosses the ridge by Blackbird Creek, entering Delaware Bay 14½ miles from the head of tide on Sassafras River and about one mile from a point giving 24 feet water on the bay.

The Ferry Creek route leaves the Choptank River about 25 miles above its mouth, passes through low country and marshy grounds to the Nanticoke River, up the latter for 12 miles in navigable water and 4 miles farther in shoal water, then over a sandy country of height ranging from 7 to 50 feet, to the Delaware Bay, 3 miles above Lewes, following the bed of Broadkill Creek.

The following are the estimates for a ship-canal 26 feet deep at low tide, and 100 feet wide at bottom and 178 feet wide at surface of canal: Ferry Creek route, $16,412,312; Wye River, $26,554,498; Queenstown, $37,-261,235; Centreville, $41,556,000; Southeast Creek, $24,825,350; Sassafras, $8,085,330. The cost will be greatly reduced if the canal be made but 75 feet wide at bottom. The report recommends the Queenstown route, and that it be built under the supervision of the War Department.

The fruit crops of the State were large. The heart of the fruit country is that section of Kent County directly around the State capital, Dover. It is there that the great evaporating and canning establishments cluster thickest, and at the capital itself, which from its position is an admirable center, the greater part of the business between the fruit-growers and their customers from the outer world is transacted. Next to Dover, the district about Milford, on the Junction and Breakwater Railroad, farther south, forms another point of attraction, with its extensive establishments for "putting up" the fruit. The entire fruit district is now estimated at 29,500 acres. At the

same time farming in many sections is very indifferent and unsatisfactory. This has led to the consideration of the culture of beets for the manufacture of sugar. During the year a large factory for its manufacture was erected near Edge Moor, on the Delaware River. About 810 tons of beets were received as the full crop, and some 40,000 pounds of melado had been manufactured.

DENMARK, a kingdom of Northern Europe. The reigning sovereign is Christian IX., fourth son of the late Duke William of Schleswig-Holstein-Sonderburg-Glücksburg, appointed to the succession of the Danish crown by the Treaty of London of May 8, 1852, and by the Danish law of succession of July 31, 1853. He succeeded to the throne on the death of King Frederick VII., November 15, 1863. He was married May 26, 1842, to Louise, Princess of Hesse-Cassel. The heir apparent is Prince Frederick, born June 3, 1843, and married July 28, 1869, to Louisa, only daughter of King Charles XV. of Sweden. Their children are three sons, born in 1870, 1872, and 1876, and a daughter, born in 1875. The King has a civil list of 500,000 rigsdalers, and the heir apparent of 60,000 rigsdalers. The present ministry was formed on June 11, 1875, and at the close of 1879 was composed as follows: President of the Council and Minister of Finance, J. B. S. Estrup; Minister of the Interior, E. V. R. Skeel; Minister of Justice and Minister for Iceland, J. M. V. Nelleman; Minister of Worship and Public Instruction, J. C. H. Fischer; Minister of Foreign Affairs, O. D. Baron Rosenörn-Lehn, appointed October 11, 1875; Minister of War, General Kaufmann, appointed January 4, 1879; and Minister of the Navy, Commodore Ravn, January 4, 1879.

The area of Denmark proper, inclusive of lakes, is 14,753 square miles; of European dependencies (Faroe Islands and Iceland), 40,-268 square miles; of American possessions (Greenland, St. John, St. Thomas, and St. Croix), 759,000 square miles. The population of Denmark proper, according to the census of 1870, was 1,784,781; and in 1878 it was estimated at 1,940,000. The population of the dependencies in 1870 was 127,401, and in 1878, 130,400. The emigration from Denmark in 1878 amounted to 2,972.

The annual financial accounts, called *stats-regnskab*, for the years 1875-'76, 1876-'77, and 1877-'78 (the financial year closes on March 31st), were as follows (in crowns—1 crown = 27 cents):

YEAR.	Revenue.	Expenditure.
1875-'76.............	51,494,068	46,842,244
1876-'77.............	47,016,647	49,529,428
1877-'78.............	46,956,231	43,880,407

In the budget estimates for the financial year ending March 31, 1880, the revenue was estimated at 46,347,086 crowns, the expenditure at 40,909,737 crowns, and the probable surplus at 5,437,349 crowns. The chief sources of revenue and expenditure were as follows:

REVENUE.

		Crowns.
1.	{ Domain, net........................	887,411
	{ Forests, net.......................	607,603
2.	State property.......................	4,078,870
3.	Direct taxes.........................	9,083,400
4.	Indirect taxes.......................	23,183,000
5.	Postal and telegraph department*....	....
6.	Surplus of lottery...................	800,000
7.	{ Revenue from the Faroes............	49,773
	{ Revenue from the Danish West Indies	12,500
8.	Miscellaneous receipts...............	1,196,267
9.	Reimbursements.......................	1,087,910

Total............................	46,486,789
Excess of cost of the posts and telegraphs over receipts................	139,658
Net receipts......................	46,347,086

EXPENDITURES.

	Crowns.
Civil list...............................	1,000,000
Appanages..............................	422,384
Rigsdag................................	200,000
Council of State.......................	106,616
Public debt............................	7,490,300
Pensions, civil........................	2,618,280
" military......................	653,115
Ministry of Foreign Affairs............	878,512
" of Worship and Public Instruction	982,086
" of Justice...................	2,435,385
" of the Interior..............	1,609,697
" of War......................	8,722,842
" of the Navy.................	5,357,670
" of Finance..................	2,950,402
Administration of Iceland..............	109,600
Extraordinary expenditure..............	3,746,721
Public works...........................	1,394,982
Advances..............................	644,145

Total............................	40,909,737

The national debt of Denmark has been in the course of reduction since 1866, and from 1875 to 1878 was as follows:

DEBT.	1875.	1876.	1877.	1878.
Internal debt..	160,355,623	159,655,045	158,959,192	158,974,096
Foreign debt..	26,790,200	22,118,200	17,289,250	15,449,650
Total.....	187,145,823	181,773,245	176,248,442	174,423,746

VESSELS.	SAILING VESSELS.		STEAMERS.		TOTAL.	
	Number.	Tons.	Number.	Tons.	Number.	Tons.
Entered. { Coasting vessels....	14,908	161,805	6,736	159,773	21,644	321,578
{ Ocean vessels......	14,100	778,410	6,203	386,087	20,303	1,164,497
Cleared. { Coasting vessels....	15,599	144,120	6,663	150,824	22,262	294,944
{ Ocean vessels......	13,827	180,506	6,328	229,313	20,155	359,819

The commercial navy was as follows in 1877:

VESSELS.	Number.	Tons.
Sailing vessels..........	8,091	213,201
Steamers...............	183	45,124·5
Total..............	8,279	258,325·5

Several American Protestant churches have established missions in Denmark, the largest of which is that of the Methodist Episcopal Church, with 8 Danish ministers, 618 members, and 121 probationers. Other missions are those

*The cost of administering the posts and telegraphs exceeded the receipts by 139,658 crowns.

The total strength of the Danish army in 1879 was as follows:

ARMS.	REGULAR ARMY.		ARMY OF RESERVE.	
	Officers.	Rank and file.	Officers.	Rank and file.
Infantry..........	774	26,992	245	10,925
Cavalry..........	128	2,180	...	......
Artillery..........	145	4,755	41	2,068
Engineers.........	59	624	...	......
Total.........	1,106	34,551	286	12,993

The staff of the army was composed of 25 commissioned and 21 non-commissioned officers.

The navy in 1878 consisted of 35 steamers, of which 8 were armor-clad ships, and the rest unarmored vessels, mostly of small size. The navy is recruited by conscription from the coast population. It was manned by 2,830 men, and officered by 1 admiral, 15 commanders, 34 captains, and 67 lieutenants.

The following table exhibits the value (in crowns) of Danish commerce in 1877:

COUNTRIES.	Imports.	Exports.
Great Britain	53,559,000	63,688,000
Germany....................	84,888,000	53,930,000
Sweden....................	24,395,000	26,150,000
Norway....................	5,439,600	11,961,000
Russia....................	11,460,000	917,000
Holland....................	5,240,000	574,000
Belgium....................	4,707,000	897,000
France....................	3,351,000	1,106,000
Iceland....................	3,605,000	2,789,000
Greenland....................	888,000	876,000
United States..........	8,055,000	16,000
Danish West Indies........	944,000	617,000
Brazil....................	3,494,000	1,000
Faroe Islands.............	475,000	508,000
Other countries...........	14,876,000	1,911,000
Total...................	225,380,000	164,288,000

The movement of shipping during the year 1877 was as follows:

of the Seventh-Day Adventists, with one missionary, three native laborers, and 80 members; the Disciples of Christ, with one missionary and 70 members; the Brethren (or Tunkers), with one missionary and 8 members. The Friends have one missionary, and the New Jerusalem Church has ministers laboring in the kingdom.

The elections for the Folkething took place on January 3d. In this election the Right gained 10 members, having now 37. The Radicals elected 35, against 30 in the former Parliament; but their former leader, Tauber, was not reëlected. The Moderate party lost 10 seats, electing 28 members only. The opposition, therefore, still disposed of 63 votes. The Folkething met on January 31st, and, after reëlecting its former President, Krabbe, began with the examination of the elections. The Left attempted to declare the elections invalid for those districts which the Right had gained from them. It began with the election of Dahl in Slagelse, which Tauber had formerly represented, and, in spite of the large majority of Dahl, his election was declared invalid by 62 to 32 votes. In February the Folkething demanded of the Government an explanation of Article V. of the Treaty of Prague and its abrogation, as well as of the position of Denmark toward the foreign Powers. (See GER-MANY.) The Government thereupon declared in the Landsthing that it would give to the Rigsdag all explanations with regard to Article V. of the treaty which had now been repealed by Germany and Austria, without being requested to do so by the Rigsdag, and as far as was compatible with the public interest; but that it would not permit a discussion on this subject in the Chambers. In the beginning of March, the Left in the Folkething proposed measures to relieve the distress among the lower classes of the population caused by the prostration of all industries. As the Government holds fast to the principle that the communes and not the state should provide for the poor, and that only if the former were not able to do so should they call upon the Government for help, the Left proposed that 500,000 crowns be set aside by the Government for the purpose of loaning them to communes for the relief of people without work. In 1877 a million crowns were set aside for the same purpose, but only 240,000 crowns were borrowed. As the Folkething did not pass the budget by April 1st, the beginning of the new financial year, the Government as in preceding years submitted a temporary one in which the expenses up to May 15th were estimated on the basis of the budget of the preceding year, which was sanctioned by the Chambers. In the latter part of April the Government submitted a bill giving to those inhabitants of Frederikstad, on the island of St. Croix, who had suffered by the negro rebellion of last year, 55,000 crowns, and loaning to them 50,000 crowns. In May the Folkething passed the budget as reported by the leader of the opposition, Berg, by 68 votes to 6. Six Krupp cannons demanded by the Government for the sea-forts were granted by 53 to 39 votes, while the demand for two new war-vessels, an ironclad and a corvette, was denied by 56 to 30 votes. The provisional financial law, which expired on May 15th, was extended to June 15th; and on June 14th the Chambers adjourned.

The new Chambers were opened on October 6th. In November the Minister of War introduced a bill for the reorganization of the army. His proposal was that the military forces of the country should be divided into

the line, the reserve, and the landwehr, the last named forming two classes. The line is intended for active operations, the reserve and the first section of the landwehr for the defense of fortified places, and the second section of the landwehr for coast defense. The line is to consist of ten regiments, each having three battalions of infantry and the guard, the regiments being formed into brigades by groups of two each. The cavalry of the line is to consist of four regiments, each with four squadrons, a squadron of escort, and cavalry school. The artillery is to be made up of four regiments of field artillery, with three batteries of eight guns and a train company, and of two regiments with four battalions for the defense of fortresses. There are to be ten companies of engineers, sappers, and miners, two companies of telegraph-men, one of railway-men, and one for pontoon-work. The reserve is to be made up of one battalion of the guard; four reserve battalions for Copenhagen, five regiments each, with three battalions for the provinces; four field batteries and four fixed batteries, two of which are to be at Copenhagen. The first section of the landwehr is to comprise old soldiers under forty-two years of age, and the second section those between forty-two and fifty. The field officers in the landwehr are to be nominated by the Crown, and the others elected by the troops. The preamble of the bill gives a sketch of the plan proposed for defending the country from invasion, from which it appears that the Government would not attempt to protect the whole of the territory, but would concentrate their defense upon Copenhagen and the island of Seeland, abandoning Jutland and the rest of the country to the enemy. The whole of the army would be concentrated in Seeland, covered by the fleet; and, in order to facilitate operations, it is proposed to complete the railway system of Seeland, and to fortify the capital both seaward and inland.

On June 16th the Superior Court of Justice gave judgment in a political trial, which in Denmark had become a *cause célèbre*. On June 3, 1877, a manifesto was published in the "Morgenbladet," signed by nine of the leading members of the Radical party in the Lower House, in which, without actually preaching treason, the Cabinet Ministers were, among other things, charged with having, "knowingly and with malice aforethought, kept the King in ignorance of, or wickedly misrepresented to his Majesty, the true political feeling in the country," as well as with having violated the Constitution. The Premier, M. Estrup, on behalf of himself and his colleagues, prosecuted the nine signataries of the manifesto, among whom were M. Berg and Count Holstein-Ledreborg; and the judgment condemned each of the defendants to three months' imprisonment, without the option of a fine.

On June 4th the four hundredth anniversary of the University of Copenhagen was celebrated with great pomp. The university is situated opposite the metropolitan church, called "Frue Kirke," in which stand Thorwaldsen's "Twelve Apostles," hewn in marble. The ceremonies were held in this church. Several members of the royal family, the whole corps diplomatique, delegations from the Universities of Christiania, Upsala, and Lund, the most prominent members of the clergy, and a large number of poets, statesmen, actors, painters, and singers, were present. The principal speaker was Geheimeraad Madvig, Rector Magnificus of the University. Four hundred years ago, he said, the King of Denmark, together with some of the most prominent men of the country and a host of foreign *doctores et magistri*, assembled on the same spot where the anniversary was celebrated to-day, for the purpose of founding, with the permission of the Pope, a Danish university. If we would compare these men with those who stand at the head of the university to-day, we would find a great difference. They would hardly be able to understand that it was their work which was being continued. They would even be astonished to hear that such a solemn ceremony as the present one was carried on in the vernacular instead of in Latin. In the course of his speech Geheimeraad Madvig mentioned several eminent men who had graduated from and taught at the university, and whose genius and vast learning had carried the name of Denmark to the remotest corners of the globe; among others Hans Christian Oersted, whose discovery, he said, is every minute of the day whispered through all the telegraph wires in the world. It was at first intended to send out invitations to all the universities in the world; but on the abrogation of Article V. of the Treaty of Prague, by which North Schleswig was incorporated with Prussia, an influential section of the professors of the university, headed by the Rector Magnificus, M. Madvig, determined not to invite deputations from German universities; and finally, but not without protests from the entire press, it was decided to celebrate the four hundredth anniversary of the creation of the university solely as a national *fête*. This decision was much regretted; but as the only alternative was that of losing the services of M. Madvig, his decision was submitted to.

The Althing, the Parliament of Iceland, which sits every other year, met in 1879 on July 1st, and adjourned on August 27th. This was the third session since the grant of the new Constitution in 1874, and with it closed the first parliamentary period, the elections for the new Parliament occurring in the course of 1880. Both Houses seized the occasion of a general dissolution to vote addresses to the King, congratulating him and the country upon the complete success of the experiment of self-government, and thanking him anew for the gift of a Constitution. Many old laws had been

carefully remodeled, and the new ones had been such as greatly to promote the prosperity of all classes. The biennial budget had been promptly voted, and the taxes had been so liberally levied that each period of two years had shown a surplus of from 50,000 to 100,000 crowns. Of the new laws, the one most nearly concerning foreigners was that completely abolishing the tonnage duty on vessels entering Icelandic ports, which had hitherto amounted to two crowns a ton. To make good the deficiency likely to result from the loss of these imposts, the customs duties on spirituous liquors were largely increased. The postal laws were so amended as to provide for the issue of postal cards and for the increase of the number of trips made by the post-steamers. Several important educational schemes came before the assembly. One of the last bills passed made it the duty of each priest to see that all the children of his parish are taught writing and arithmetic, and authorized him, together with the civil overseer of the parish, to remove any children whose parents are negligent in the matter to another farmstead, where they are to be instructed at the expense of the parents. The laws passed during the previous session establishing a school of law at Reykjavik and a technical school at Mödruvellir, in the north of the island, were greatly modified, both the number of teachers and the amount of the annual appropriation being increased. Some changes were also made in the government of the National College at Reykjavik, rendered necessary by the larger number of students who yearly frequent it. Within a few years the National Library had outgrown its old quarter in the large loft of the cathedral at the capital, while a considerable collection of Icelandic antiquities had grown up, chiefly through the exertions of a single enthusiastic artist and scholar, the late Sigurdur Gudmundsson. To provide for these and for the accumulating collections in natural history, as well as to furnish increased accommodation for its own body and various public departments, the Althing voted 80,000 crowns for the erection of a Capitol, or Althing-house.

DIPLOMATIC CORRESPONDENCE. See UNITED STATES.

DISCIPLES OF CHRIST. The *General Christian Missionary Convention* of the Disciples of Christ met at Bloomington, Ill., October 17th. The Treasurer reported that his total receipts during the year in cash and pledges had been $24,510, and his disbursements had been $5,891. The Society had employed nine men for a greater or less part of their time, who had preached 1,220 sermons, and through whose instrumentality 408 persons had been added to the church. The Board had circulated about 60,000 pages of tracts within the field of its operations. The report of the Board showed the following aggregate results: Whole number of baptisms, 1,803; of other accessions, 983; whole amount of money received for missions, $31,414; whole amount of pledges received, $32,484; making the total amount of money and pledges together, $63,898.

The *Foreign Christian Missionary Society* met at Bloomington, Ill., October 16th. The report of the Board was published in the "Christian Standard" of October 25th. It stated that the "general current of sentiment was that, after fulfilling our present obligations to our missions in Paris, Copenhagen, Constantinople, and in England, any enlargement of our work should look to France, Italy, Japan, Africa, and China; and that at least one new mission should be undertaken, if possible, in some one of the three countries last named during the next year." The receipts of the Treasurer for the year had been $12,547, and his expenses had been $11,577. His report showed that pledges of an estimated value of $25,000 would fall due between the time of the meeting and October, 1884. The operations of the Society in the foreign field embraced stations at Southport, Chester, Southampton, and Tranmere, England; Paris, France; Copenhagen, Denmark; and Constantinople, Turkey; all of which, except those at Southampton and Copenhagen, which were established in 1876, had been established since the beginning of 1878. The stations in England had 464 members and 2,161 attendants; the station at Copenhagen, 99 members and 325 attendants; and that at Paris, 27 members and 250 attendants; making an aggregate of 590 members and 2,740 attendants. The Rev. G. N. Shishmanian, an Armenian, had been appointed a missionary to Constantinople, where there were already two members. A missionary had been dispatched to Acapulco, Mexico, where he had immersed seven members, but had since been obliged to give up his enterprise. The Society adopted a report recommending that new missions should be entered upon at the first possible moment, and mentioning Japan, Africa, and China, among the heathen, and Italy and France (outside of Paris or new quarters in Paris), among civilized nations, as the most suitable fields.

The *Christian Woman's Board of Missions* met at Bloomington, Ill., October 14th. The total receipts of the Treasurer for the year had had been $4,283, and the expenditures $2,130. The Society had an endowment fund of $1,020, of which $1,000 were lent at interest. A report was made from a mission in Jamaica, where a branch society had been organized, and an appropriation was made for the salary of a teacher in the French mission.

DIX, JOHN ADAMS, an eminent public officer, born at Boscawen, New Hampshire, July 24, 1798, died in New York, April 21, 1879. His father, Timothy Dix, was once Lieutenant-Governor of New Hampshire. The son early went to a school in Montreal, where he had the opportunity of learning the rudiments of the French language, which became of much service to him when he was Minister to France

in 1867. In 1812 he was made a cadet in the Military Academy at West Point, and thus, at the age of fourteen years, entered the service of the Federal Government. In the latter part of the year 1813 he surrendered his appointment to become an ensign in the army. In this position he engaged in service on the northern frontier during the war of 1812-'15. In 1814 he was made a third lieutenant; in 1815, a second lieutenant; in the same year he was transferred from the Twenty-first Infantry to the artillery; a year later he became an adjutant. His service in the army continued sixteen years. In 1818 he was made a first lieutenant. In 1819 he was aide-de-camp on the staff of General Jacob Brown, then Commander-in-Chief of the Army. When he left the service in 1828, he was captain of the Third Artillery. His years of staff duty were mostly spent at Washington, during an interesting period of the country's history. On retiring from the army, he made a prolonged visit to Europe. About 1830 he became a lawyer and settled in Cooperstown, New York. He soon became interested in politics, and was an ardent advocate of the measures of President Jackson. In 1831 he received from Governor Throop an appointment as Adjutant-General of the State. Two years later he became Secretary of State, and the office was held by him six years. He then retired to private life for three years, and in 1842 was chosen member of the New York Legislature from Albany County. In 1845 he was chosen to succeed Silas Wright in the Senate of the United States. In 1848 the "Free-Soil" agitation broke out in the Democratic party of New York, and made a division in it. Senator Dix ultimately joined the Free-Soilers, and made one or two important speeches in the Senate sustaining their views, which were summarized in the motto "Free Soil, Free Labor, Free Speech, and Free Men." His most notable speech, however, was on the question of the Oregon boundary. In the same year he was the Free-Soil Democratic candidate for Governor, but Hamilton Fish was elected. In 1849 he was succeeded in the Senate by William H. Seward. In 1852, the Democratic party of the State having become united on the Presidential candidate, Mr. Dix warmly supported Mr. Pierce of New Hampshire for the office, and after his election he received the appointment of Assistant Treasurer of the United States in New York. This office he soon resigned, and devoted himself to his private affairs until 1860, when he was appointed by President Buchanan, Postmaster at New York. In January, 1861, he was appointed Secretary of the Treasury by Mr. Buchanan, and held the office until March 4th, when Mr. Lincoln became President. It was during this short and exciting period that he issued the most famous utterance of his life: "If any man attempts to haul down the American flag, shoot him on the spot!" It was more significant than anything else he ever .said, and meant much for the Union cause. The sentence was the last one of a brief telegram to Treasury Agent W. Hemphill Jones of Delaware, then at New Orleans. It was sent January 29, 1861. In the same year President Lincoln made him a major-general in the army. His commands during the war comprised in succession the departments of Maryland, of Virginia and North Carolina, and of New York. It was while holding the latter command, on May 18, 1864, that he received orders from Washington to place a strong military guard in the newspaper-offices of the New York "Journal of Commerce" and "World," and issued warrants for the arrest of the editors and their imprisonment in Fort Lafayette. At the same time a vessel was lying under steam at one of the wharves to convey them there. The suppression of the papers continued for two days, when the offices were restored to the proprietors. Governor Horatio Seymour caused the arrest of General Dix and his officers, but an order ·came from Washington directing the General "not to relieve himself of his command or be deprived of his liberty for obeying any order of a military nature while the civil war lasts." (See "Annual Cyclopædia," 1864, page 391.) In 1866 General Dix was President of the Philadelphia Union Convention. In the same year he was appointed Minister to France by President Johnson ; in 1869 he resigned that position. In 1872 he received the Republican nomination for Governor of New York, and was elected. On the expiration of his term he was renominated, and defeated by Samuel J. Tilden. He afterward made public addresses in political campaigns, but held no other political office. For a short time he acted as President of the Board of Directors of the Erie Railway. In every sphere of life to which he was called he acquitted himself well. He had many qualities which insure success in public positions. He was careful of details and fond of them. He was punctual, diligent, orderly, and deliberate. This made him a good executive official. Moreover, he had learned the duties of command in the school of obedience, and his career was an ascensive instruction. As a soldier, he was identified with no battles of the civil war. He tempered martial law in loyal or unmenaced posts, and he yielded less to the spirit of arbitrary arrest than others. An officeholder by profession, he was an honest one, as well as a citizen of many virtues, fair talents, and marked and varied cultivation. Industrious, courteous, abstemious, and honorable in his inclinations, his career will be at least as notable for duration as for service, and his service will be more notable for quantity than for any extraordinary results. He was a man of culture and fine literary tastes, and his writings were always models of good English. His works of travel were widely read, and he was the author of a very useful volume on "The Resources of

the City of New York." His miscellaneous speeches and addresses have been collected into two handsome volumes of interesting reading. He remained a scholar throughout his busy life. In manners he was ever the calm and courteous gentleman to all coming into his presence. In person he was erect and soldier-like, with a native dignity of bearing.

DIXON, WILLIAM HEPWORTH, a British author, born in Yorkshire, June 30, 1821, died December 27, 1879. He had no academic training, but was very observing and fond of reading, and when still quite young made his literary *début* by privately printing a five-act tragedy, which has remained unknown to the public. He was an early contributor of verse to Douglas Jerrold's "Illuminated Magazine," and about 1844 became literary editor of a paper at Cheltenham. In 1846 he settled in London as a law student at the Inner Temple, and began contributing to the "Daily News" a series of articles on the "Literature of the Common People" and on "London Prisons," which were well received. His first published book, "John Howard, a Memoir," appeared in 1849. In 1850 he was appointed a deputy commissioner for the organization of the World's Fair of 1851. In 1851 he published a "Life of William Penn," in which he defended the celebrated Quaker from the attacks of Macaulay in his "History of England." In 1852 he made a tour of the Continent, and the following year became chief editor of the "Athenæum," which post he held until 1869. His treatment of American subjects and American authors in this journal, as well as in his books on America, was considered in the United States unjust and incorrect, although he made many friends in his visits to this country. In 1864 he made a long tour in the East, which resulted in a work on "The Holy Land " (2 vols., 1865). He spent a few months in 1866 in travel in the United States, paying especial attention to Mormonism and spiritualism. As a result he published his two best known works, "New America" (1867) and "Spiritual Wives" (1868). The former was translated into most of the languages of Europe. In 1869 he made a tour of Russia, the narrative of which he entitled "Free Russia" (2 vols., 1870). His largest work was entitled "Her Majesty's Tower" (4 vols., 1869-'71), which was supplemented in 1878 by a similar work on "Royal Windsor." He made many other trips to the Continent, and revisited America in 1874-'75. This visit produced his "White Conquest " (2 vols., 1876), which contained some useful information about the condition of the negroes, the Indians, and the Chinese in America, and which was generally regarded as his best book on America. In 1878 he visited Cyprus, and wrote a book on that island. Other of his writings are: "The Lives of the Archbishops of York " (1863); "The Switzers " (1872); "The History of Two Queens—Catharine of Aragon and Anne

Boleyn" (4 vols., 1873-'74); "Diana, Lady Lyle" (3 vols., 1877); and "Ruby Grey" (3 vols., 1878).

DOMINION OF CANADA. The Conservative party, after a seclusion of five years, returned to office upon gaining the general election of September 17, 1878, upon the tariff issue. Sir John A. Macdonald, assuming the Ministry of the Interior, formed the present Cabinet, as follows: Sir Leonard Tilley, Minister of Finance; Sir Charles Tupper, Public Works; J. H. Pope, Agriculture; James Macdonald, Justice; F. R. Masson, Militia; Mackenzie Rowell, Customs; F. G. Baby, Inland Revenue; J. C. Pope, Marine and Fisheries; A. Wilmot, without portfolio; John O'Connor, President of the Council; J. C. Aikins, Secretary of State; Mr. Langevin, Postmaster-General; Alexander Campbell, Receiver-General.

The first session of the Fourth Dominion Parliament was opened on the 14th of February, 1879. The Marquis of Lorne delivered the speech from the throne, amid unusual ceremonial. It pledged the Ministry to the promised alterations in the tariff, and proposed the assumption of the business of insurance by the Government, in view of the success of Government savings banks. J. G. Blanchet was elected Speaker of the new House of Commons. This sitting of Parliament was perhaps the most momentous one since the confederation of the provinces, made so by the adoption of the national policy, which can not but have a serious influence upon the prosperity of the Dominion for many years to come. Whether the policy of protection, to which the Canadian people have committed themselves almost irrevocably, will not prove too burdensome for a people who are engaged to far the greatest extent in agricultural and similar pursuits, will depend in the first place upon the facility with which the industries which are propagated by the new fiscal measures can supply the nation with suitable manufactures, and next upon the willingness of the protected capitalists to forego a portion of the profits which, in a country where competition can not be strong in capitalistic industry, the protective measures will enable them to extort. There will remain, however, a way by which the Canadians can return to their old system without openly recanting their newly avowed principles—that is, by making a new reciprocity treaty with the United States, whose provisions, according to the rules insisted upon by the Imperial Government, would apply to Great Britain as well. In such a treaty any desired compromise between free trade and protection could be effected. One cause of the popularity of the national policy has been the belief that by such a strong course of action Canada would be enabled to exact more favorable terms in her future commercial negotiations with the United States.

The programme of protection which brought the Conservatives into power was heralded as a new departure, which would produce great and striking improvements in the material condition of Canada. The new tariff was elaborated by Mr. Tilley and laid before Parliament on the 14th of March. As was expected by the country, it embodied protective principles of the strongest character. The protective measures were directed chiefly against the import trade from the United States. The general depression of trade had disposed the people to welcome any innovation in the commercial policy of the Dominion, and the large increase in imports from the United States which had taken place during several years, accompanying a diminishing importation from Great Britain, had aroused a feeling of discontent among all classes, and had grated against both the sentiment of Canadian patriotism and of British loyalty. The free-trade Liberal party, which had possessed the popular favor a few years back, had rejoiced in the large imports as a sign of prosperity, and welcomed the commercial bonds which were forming between Canada and the American Republic. The new commercial system, which was proclaimed as the National Policy, was designed in a sense and spirit directly opposed to the objects which had prompted the treaty of reciprocity. The Canadians of the older provinces, whose lands, like those of the Atlantic States of the Union, had become less valuable for agricultural purposes since the development of the resources of the interior, hoped by emulating the protective policy of the Americans to build up flourishing manufacturing industries likewise. The tariff framed with this purpose could not fail to prove exceedingly hostile to the interests of British as well as American manufactures. Besides the general depression which had produced a disposition among the people favorable to an alteration of the fiscal policy, the deficit in the Treasury would in a measure justify the Government in establishing the new tariff even if it failed of attaining the expected objects, if it only produced a larger revenue—furnishing the excuse, in the event of its not affording the promised commercial relief, that at least it produced a revenue. Although protective measures, however beneficial they may prove in the end, can not produce immediate relief in a depressed state of trade, but rather tend on the whole to augment the financial distress, yet if the introduction of the new policy is concurrent in time with a renewed activity in business, even though the improvement is directly due to a commercial revival in the United States, whose intimate commercial relations with the Dominion it would take much more decisive measures of exclusion to break off, it will appear justified, in spite of the continued and able remonstrances of an active free-trade opposition. The inauguration of this bold and experimental course involves also active efforts on the part of the Government to provide an outlet for the fostered manufactures, the encouragement and, if necessary, subvention of lines of communication with promising foreign markets, and the promotion of other facilities of exportation, and particularly the conclusion of special treaties of reciprocity with countries from whom no competition with the infant industries is to be feared. Sir Alexander T. Galt was sent to England, being endowed with the new title of Resident Minister, to look after the commercial interests of Canada in Europe. He entered into negotiations with Spain and France with reference to reciprocal commerce, while the authorities in Canada sought to make special arrangements with the Government of Brazil, which affords a favorable market for Canadian fish, lumber, and agricultural implements and other manufactures.

The new tariff is a protective one of the most pronounced character, and avowedly discriminates against the products of the United States where it is possible. Two of the duties specifically discriminate against American imports—one a duty on tea imported from the States of 2 cts. per lb. and 10 per cent. ad valorem, and the other a duty on all salt not from Great Britain or British dependencies of 8 cts. per cwt. The instructions to Lord Lorne did not contain the clause, then omitted for the first time, stating that any bill imposing differential duties should be submitted for approval to the home authorities. The general ad valorem duties were raised from 17½ to 20 per cent. Numerous classes of imports were additionally subjected to duties of a highly protective character. The duty on cotton fabrics is 2 cts. per square yard or 1 cent per linear yard, and 15 per cent. ad valorem. Silk goods pay 30 per cent. ad valorem. The duty on flannels, blankets, and shawls, woolens, yarns, and knit goods is 7½ cts. per lb. and 20 per cent. ad valorem. Articles of apparel and ready-made clothing pay 10 cts. per lb. and 25 per cent. ad valorem; woolen carpets, 10 cts. per square yard and 20 per cent. ad valorem. The duty on pig iron is $2 per ton; on iron in slabs, etc., 12½ per cent. ad valorem; in bars rolled or hammered, on boiler and plate iron, nails, and spikes, 17½ per cent.; on rolled wire in coils, 10 per cent.; on iron rails, 15 per cent.; on fish-plates, etc., 17½ per cent.; on iron and steel wire, 25 per cent.; on tin plates, 10 per cent. Cabinet furniture must pay 35 per cent.; agricultural implements and wooden ware, 25 per cent. A duty of 15 per cent. is imposed on breadstuffs and barley. Machinery for cotton and woolen milling enters free. Foreign vessels must pay 10 per cent. duty for registration in Canada. The drawbacks allowed by the American Government on manufactured sugar exported are opposed by a duty irrespective of such drawbacks of 35 per cent. ad valorem, in addition to 1 cent per lb. on all above No. 14 by the Dutch color standard; on all below that grade and above No. 9, ¼ ct. per lb. and 30 per cent. ad valorem; and on all under No. 9, ⅛ ct. per lb. and 30 per cent. ad valorem. For the benefit of the coal interests

of Nova Scotia, a duty of 50 cts. per ton of 2,000 lbs. is imposed on coal, both anthracite and bituminous. The average percentage of revenue is 13¾ per cent. of the average value of all imports. On evidence of exportation of manufactures, a drawback is allowed on the materials imported. The cordage used in ships, which pays a duty of 10 per cent., is not released from the duty, but the other portions of all new ships have their duties remitted. The development of the iron-ore deposits which have been discovered, not only in Nova Scotia, but in New Brunswick, in Quebec, in Ontario, and in the Ottawa Valley, was one of the favorite schemes of protection, and with this object the duty of $2 per ton was laid on pig iron. Pamphlets and periodicals are made to pay a duty of 6 cts. per lb.; British copyright publications, 12½ per cent. ad valorem and 6 cts. per lb.; books and periodicals imported through the mail, 1 ct. for every two ounces or fraction thereof; newspapers by mail, free. Advertising pamphlets pay $1 per hundred, and other printed work, as advertising cards, bills, posters, etc., 30 per cent. ad valorem. All printed music pays 6 cts. per lb.

In the new duties on alcoholic beverages an object is aimed at which is independent of considerations both of revenue and protection. The duties are arranged in the interest of temperance, so as to encourage the consumption of malt liquors in comparison with strong drink, and to render spirits less accessible than before. For this purpose the excise duties have been changed as well as the customs duties. The customs duty on brandy has been raised from $1.20 to $1.45 per imperial gallon, and that on other spirits from the same to $1.32 per gallon. The excise duty on spirits has likewise been raised 10 per cent., while that on ales and beers has been decreased. French light wines have to pay a duty of only 25 cts., which is made thus light for the same object of encouraging the consumption of the more harmless beverages. Champagne wines, on the other hand, as a luxury, are taxed $3 per gallon.

The inspiring motive of the new fiscal policy is declared in the following words of Sir John A. Macdonald: "As between English and American manufacturers, we prefer the English; but as between the English and Canadian manufacturers, we prefer the Canadian. We know that we can gain the two objects of giving full protection to all our infant industries against the industries of any other country, including England, at the same time giving a preference to England in our markets; so that if we have to go out of Canada to make purchases, we will go to England rather than elsewhere." The effect of the new tariff was declared by Sir Leonard Tilley, eight months after its going into force, to have been a falling off in the imports of the leading manufactures from England of 9 per cent., and in the imports of the same articles from the United States of 47 per cent. The new tariff was expected to increase the revenue from $21,670,000 to about $24,120,000, and to soon wipe out the deficit in the Treasury accounts, which had been accumulating for four years, and which amounted altogether, to about $7,000,000. The division on the new tariff, or the national policy, was taken in the middle of April, 136 voting in its favor and 53 against it.

A constitutional question, arising from the dismissal by Lieutenant-Governor Letellier, of Quebec, of the De Boucherville Ministry in March, 1878, on account of what he judged to be an infringement on the privileges of his office and an official affront, became more and more complicated by later events. The Province of Quebec, already in a very unhealthy state of political agitation, was wrought up to a condition of feverish passion, and the excitement spread throughout the Dominion, as the Dominion Government, the Governor-General, and finally the British Government, were drawn into the controversy. The election of a Conservative Parliament in September, 1878, was the means of making the question of Letellier's act a Dominion matter. The Macdonald Ministry decided in April, 1879, to remove Letellier, and advised Lord Lorne accordingly. To this the new Governor-General demurred, and applied to the Home Government for instructions, being of opinion that the interference of the Federal Government was a violation of the prerogative of the Crown on the one hand (as the British North America Act of 1867 states that the office of Lieutenant-Governor shall continue "during the good pleasure of the Governor-General"), and on the other hand that it plainly trenched on the autonomy of the provinces, and openly violated the principle of responsible government, since the Joly Cabinet, which had succeeded the De Boucherville Ministry, had received the support of the country in the next provincial election. The Dominion Minister of Public Works, Mr. Langevin, repaired to England to present the case of the Government before the British Cabinet. The position of the Dominion Ministry was upheld by the British Government, and the Marquis of Lorne was informed in dispatches from Sir Michael Hicks-Beach that the advice of his constitutional advisers must be followed. The right of the Federal Government to remove the provincial Governor was thus established as a principle of the Canadian Constitution and a concomitant of responsible government. This decision, which was due partly perhaps to the political exigencies of the moment, and to the unwillingness of the home authorities to incur any responsibility in the direction of colonial affairs, not even so far as regards the interpretation of the Constitution, creates a principle against which the very people who were clamoring for Federal intervention might under ordinary circumstances be the first to rebel; the *habitans* of this same old French colony

will probably be the loudest in their protestations against any further advances in the direction of centralization. The Province of Quebec had been long subjected to a chronic political fermentation on account of the disputes growing out of this situation. This was one of the first questions to which the attention of the Governor-General was called upon his arrival. He was unwilling to accede to the demands of the Conservatives of the French provinces to dismiss the Lieutenant-Governor, and it looked as if the whole country might be plunged through this affair into a constitutional crisis of great peril. It seemed to the Marquis of Lorne to be straining the Federal authority very much to dismiss the Lieutenant-Governor for acts the entire responsibility for which rested with and was assumed by his constitutional advisers, who still retained the confidence of the provincial Legislature and were able to conduct the government of the province. There was no precedent in this case, and the question was settled by Sir John A. Macdonald's insisting that his demands should be acceded to, and by the prompt reply from the Home Government, which complacently interpreted the Constitution in the sense required by the Federal Government.

The transaction of the public business of the province was facilitated through the happy issue of a somewhat dangerous and violent act of the Legislative Council, resulting in the retirement of the Liberal Government and the assumption of the reins of power by a Conservative Ministry. The ministerial crisis was brought about by the refusal of the Legislative Council to vote supplies, and a motion offered by the Minister, Mr. Joly, in the Assembly for indemnity for Government expenditures. Such an application, being for a money grant, should, according to all precedent, have been made in the form of a message from the new Lieutenant-Governor, Robitaille. An amendment presented by Mr. Lynch, which, without upholding the action of the Legislative Council, imputed weakness to the Government, was passed, and was the occasion of the resignation of the Joly Ministry. If the province had not tired of the long rivalries and contentions, the course of the Legislative Council would have aroused the liveliest animosity. As it was, the motion that Mr. Joly had "lost his usefulness" was carried through the votes of several of his former supporters, who now desired tranquillity above all things. Upon receiving the sense of the Parliament thus plainly expressed, Mr. Joly was perfectly free to resign, and Mr. Chapleau to form a new administration.

A late ministerial crisis in Manitoba recalls unpleasantly the old dissensions which long rent Lower Canada, when the people were divided into hostile camps by a strict race and creed line. When a Constitution was given to Manitoba, and an inceptive Constitution to the Northwest Territory, the ultra-Protestant element found much fault with its provisions, declaring that its effect would be to create a second Province of Quebec in the west and insure the ascendancy of the French Canadians. The Premier, Mr. Norquay, was recently confronted with an interpellation from the leader of the French-speaking section of the inhabitants, and another member of the Cabinet, asserting that his government had not the confidence of the majority of the English-speaking population. Mr. Norquay responded that it was on account of the presence in it of these two gentlemen, and requested them to resign. After a considerable search he replaced them with Messrs. Beggs and Taylor, and was sustained in his action by the vote of the Legislature. The Government subsequently published a programme proposing a reapportionment of the electoral districts to secure a larger majority in the Legislature to the English, the adoption of English for the official language, and the appointment of English premiers. Some of these changes are unconstitutional, but, as the tide of immigration into Manitoba is now from English-speaking countries, the Constitution is susceptible of alteration in the sense demanded.

In different provinces a sentiment is growing in favor of the abolition of the Legislative Councils. This reform has already been accomplished with good results in Ontario, the most progressive of the provinces, and is demanded in the others, principally on the score of economy. The power which this branch of the Legislature, which is a relic of the old era of Crown domination, holds to thwart the purposes of responsible government, is exemplified by the action of the Legislative Council of Quebec, which refused to vote the supply bill until the Lieutenant-Governor should change his constitutional advisers, thus forcing the retirement of the Joly Cabinet, and involving the province in the expenses of a new election. In Nova Scotia the Government presented an act for the abolition of the Legislative Council, and in the Quebec Parliament Mr. Joly introduced the same measure.

A legislative union of the maritime provinces has been proposed, and the scheme of legislative union of all the provinces has gained many supporters since the Letellier affair. The simplification of government is demanded, among other reasons, in the interest of retrenchment, a ground which always has great weight in Canada. A reduction in the number of Cabinet officers is agitated on the same ground. The office of Receiver-General has been abolished. Civil-service reform is one of the questions of the day, the permanent civil service, constituted as it is at present, being unpopular. Some advocate the American system of rotation, or the redistribution of all the offices upon a change of administration, while others deem the introduction of the English system of competitive examination sufficient to remove the objections.

The Ontario elections on the 4th of June resulted in the victory of the Ministry by a large majority, notwithstanding the hopes of the Conservative party to supplant the Mowat Government in consequence of their triumph in the Dominion.

In the election of Dr. Medley, the new Metropolitan, the principle was established that the order of seniority should henceforth prevail in the Canadian Church in the appointment of the Metropolitan. The new Primate was born in England in 1804, and came to Canada in 1845 to be consecrated as Bishop of Fredericton, over which see he has since presided.

The alleged discovery of pleuro-pneumonia among cattle arrived at Liverpool on the Dominion steamer Ontario, from Portland, January 27th, led to an order in Council prohibiting the entrance of American cattle into Canada for three months commencing February 1st. The trade in live animals has been cultivated to a greater extent in Canada than in the United States; the exports in 1878 from the Dominion were 32,115 head, against 6,412 in the preceding year.

One of the most prominent questions in Canadian affairs of late years is that of the extension of railway communications, and especially the construction of the Pacific Railway. The plan of the former Conservative Government, before it went out of power in 1873, was to grant to a company a subsidy of 50,000,000 acres of land and $30,000,000 in money for the building of the road. Under the Mackenzie Government it was undertaken as a public work. The present Government determined to return as far as possible to their original plan. The terminus chosen by the late Administration, Burrard Inlet, does not seem to meet the approval of the present Government, who speak of going back to their first choice, Bute Inlet, although it would make the road 57 miles longer and carry it over very difficult grades. The progress reported by the Department of Public Works in the construction of the Pacific Railway is as follows: the Pembroke branch, 84½ miles in length; from Fort William to English River, 102 miles laid with rails, and 60 miles ballasted; from Keewatin to Cross Lake, 36 miles under construction; from Cross Lake to Selkirk, 76 miles graded and bridged, and 75 miles laid with rails. On the extension of the Canada Central, 37 miles were located and 25 being constructed. The line from Pembroke to Lake Nipissing was being built under a subsidy not to exceed $1,404,000, and the line from Nipissing to Cantin's Bay on the French River was contracted for. Under the new Government, the section of Lake Superior and the Province of Manitoba, about 185 miles in length, has been placed under contract, and the line has been extended west of the Red River to a point south of Lake Manitoba. Tenders have also been accepted for the construction of 150 miles from Emory's Bar to Kamloops. In July 50,-000 tons of steel rails were purchased by Sir

Charles Tupper in England, the Government taking advantage of the low range of prices and paying for them $1,212,000, or $1,518,000 less than Mr. Muckenzie had paid for an equal quantity in 1874. The Canada Pacific Telegraph line had been constructed at the time of the report of the Minister of Public Works, in February, 1879, from Selkirk to the longitude of Edmonton, 1,197 miles, and was in operation to Battleford, 967 miles. The line between Selkirk and Fort William, 410 miles, was in use; and the line in British Columbia from Cache Creek eastward to Kamloops, 50 miles, was completed and equipped. There were 642 miles of telegraph in operation in British Columbia.

The North Shore Railway, built under the auspices of the Quebec Government, was completed on the 9th of February, 1879, bringing Quebec and the country north of the St. Lawrence into communication with Montreal.

The junction of the Pembina branch of the Canada Pacific Railway with the St. Paul and Pacific at St. Vincent connects the Canadian road with the system of the Northwestern States. The route was changed under the new political administration from the northern or Narrows course to one running south of Lake Manitoba. Lands lying within twenty miles of the track on both sides have been reserved for the Government, and their sale is expected to pay for the gradual extension of the road. Thus 100,000,000 acres have been set aside for purposes of construction, and invested in a commission, upon which the Imperial Government is represented. The cost of the Pacific Railway for the portions completed or under contract up to 1879 has been $25,396,000, embracing the subsidy of $1,500,000 to the Canada Central, $18,000,000 for the road between Kaministiquia and the Red River, $1,900,000 for the road from Georgian Bay to the mouth of French River, $1,750,000 for the Pembina branch, $1,100,000 for the Pacific Telegraph under contract, 1,300 miles, and $3,861,000 expended on surveys.

A plan of certain American capitalists to increase the international communications by building a bridge over the St. Lawrence at Coteau du Lac, and a line of railroad from Ottawa connecting with the New York and New England system of railroads, awakened the keenest opposition in Canada. It was thought that such a line would divert the traffic of the North Shore and the Intercolonial Railways, and greatly injure the commercial prospects of Montreal, Quebec, St. John, and Halifax. An outcrop of the excitement attending the inauguration of the national policy was the expectation that Halifax might become, or easily be made, the winter port of Canada.

The enlargement of the Lachine Canal gives it a width of 270 feet between gate-quoins and 45 feet at bottom. There are two locks between the harbor of Montreal and Wellington bridge, having a depth of 18 feet on the sills.

The canal between these points will have a depth of 19 feet. The three locks at St. Gabriel, Cote St. Paul, and Lachine will have a depth of 14 feet on the sills. All permanent structures have been so built that the prism of the canal may be eventually deepened to 15 feet without disturbing them. The two lower locks are connected by a basin 540 feet long, with an average width of 260 feet. No. 2 basin has been enlarged at its southwest end. Wellington basin is 1,210 feet long and 225 feet wide. A second basin is projected, of the same length and depth and 250 feet wide, parallel to it. From below Wellington bridge to Cote St. Paul lock the canal will have an average width of 200 feet, and from the lock to Lachine 150 feet. The new locks are located adjoining the old locks as independent structures, and hereafter the canal will be navigable through the double range of locks, with double entrance at Montreal and Lachine.

Government has entered into an examination of a new route for the grain of Manitoba and the fertile but yet uncultivated regions about Lake Winnipeg. It is proposed to convey the grain to Port Nelson, at the mouth of the Nelson River, or some other port on Hudson's Bay, and to ship it on steamships from there to Liverpool. A railroad 800 miles in length would connect Lake Winnipeg with Hudson's Bay. Port Nelson is distant only 2,966 geographical miles from Liverpool by the route proposed, which would cross the ocean from Cape Farewell, the southernmost extremity of Greenland, to the north of Ireland in a direct line. The route from the mouth of the Nelson River would be shorter than the nearest route between Liverpool and New York. Hudson's Bay and Straits are said to be navigable from July to October inclusive. The navigable tributaries of Lake Winnipeg—the Saskatchewan, Qu'Appelle, Assiniboine, and Red Rivers—run far back into the grain countries of Manitoba and the Northwest Territory.

The rush of settlers to the Red River country has been stronger this last year than ever. The province of Manitoba, situated between latitude 49° and 53° 30' north and longitude 96°and 99° west from Greenwich, having the United States boundary-line on the south and Lakes Winnipeg and Manitoba on the north, was purchased from the Hudson's Bay Company by the British Government in 1869, and constituted into a province the following year. It is only within the last three or four years that the tide of emigration has set strongly in that direction. Not only emigrants from Ireland, England, and Scotland, and Canadian farmers, have been attracted, but settlers from Iceland and Russian Mennonites, and even prosperous farmers from the United States, have flocked to this land of promise. In 1876 the sales of land amounted to 153,535 acres to 807 settlers; in 1877 they were 1,392,368 acres, and the takers numbered 8,648. In the month of April, 1878, the Emerson Land-Office alone sold 52,960 acres, and

30,400 acres in the first week of the following month. At the same season in 1879 the arrivals of new settlers ammounted to·as many as 2,000 per week. The wheat-growing region of western British America is said to be more fertile than Minnesota, and, instead of possessing the polar climate which has hitherto been ascribed to it, to be so temperate that melons and cucumbers ripen in August, and stock can be wintered without shelter, and find ample nourishment in the succulent grasses which are kept green by the snow. Manitoba soil yields 20 bushels of remarkably fine flinty wheat to the acre, of 63 to 66 lbs. to the bushel. Oats, barley, rye, potatoes, turnips, beets, flax, and hemp thrive admirably. Wild fruits abound; the forests are full of game, large and small, and the lakes and streams of fish—whitefish abounding in the lakes, pike, catfish, sturgeon, etc., in the rivers, and trout in the brooks. The capital of the province, Winnipeg, formerly Fort Garry, has grown in three years into an intensely active business town of 10,-000 inhabitants. The price of wheat, owing to the want of railway communications, is only 45 cents a bushel. When the Pacific Railway is completed and the country settled, the Canadians expect that Manitoba and the Northwest Territory will be able to undersell the Americans in both breadstuffs and meat and provisions, and supply the entire European demand for imported food materials. The area of their newly discovered wheat-fields is, according to a sanguine estimate accepted in Canada and Great Britain, at least 2,984,000 square miles, or three quarters of the area of entire Europe.

The public accounts of the Dominion show a total indebtedness at the close of the fiscal year 1878 of $174,957,268, with assets of $34,675,834, against $174,675,834 of liabilities and $41,440,525 of assets in 1877. The Treasury receipts for the year were $22,375,011. The total expenditures were $23,503,158, incurred under the following heads: debt and subsidies, $11,659,523; charges on the revenue, $5,301,124; ordinary expenditure, $6,-542,510. There was a decrease in the ordinary expenditure of $293,167, compared with the previous year. The estimates of public expenditures for 1879 were $23,427,882, a decrease of $241,171 compared with the appropriations of the previous year. The Finance Minister went to England about the middle of the year to negotiate a loan of £3,000,000, which he succeeded in placing on favorable terms.

According to the last volume of the census of 1871, the increase of population in the four provinces of Ontario, Quebec, New Brunswick, and Nova Scotia was from 2,312.919 in 1851 to 3,090,561 in 1861, and 3,485,761 in 1871. The area of these provinces is 337,524 square miles, making the population per square mile 6·8 in 1851, 9·2 in 1861, and 10·3 in 1871. Of the inhabitants of Canada in 1871, 20·26 per cent. were of English extraction, 15·77 per cent. of Scotch, and 24·48 per cent. of Irish

descent, while the descendants of the French original settlers comprised 31·07 per cent. The immigration from the United States was found to have been very considerable, the number of those born in the United States numbering more than half as many as the immigrants from Scotland. The inhabitants in the Province of Quebec who had come from the States exceeded in number the English-born settlers in that province. The most populous of the four provinces in proportion to its extent is New Brunswick. Quebec is the least thickly populated.

The religious statistics show that 42·80 per cent. of the population are Catholics, 16·27 per cent. Methodists, 15·63 per cent. Presbyterians, and 14·20 per cent. members of the Church of England. In Quebec the Roman Catholics form an absolute majority; in another province they are relatively the most numerous, and in a third are nearly equal in numbers to the most numerous religious body. In Ontario the Methodists exceed any other denomination in numerical strength, and in Nova Scotia the Presbyterians.

According to the trade and navigation returns, the aggregate import and export trade of the Dominion again shows a falling off, the value of exports having been $79,323,667 in the fiscal year ending June 30, 1878, against $75,-875,393 in 1877, an increase of $3,448,274, while the value of imports was $93,081,787 in 1878, against $99,327,962 in 1877, a decrease of $6,-246,175. The total for 1873 was $217,304,516; for 1877, $172,175,876; for 1878, $170,523,-244. The trade with Great Britain in 1878 was made up as follows: imports, $37,431,-180; exports, $45,941,539. The imports from Great Britain decreased $2,141,059 in 1878, while the exports increased $4,374,070 as compared with the previous year. The trade with the United States decreased $3,211,777 in 1878, the exports showing a reduction of $531,-347, and the imports a reduction of $2,680,930. Trade with the British and Spanish West Indies fell off $700,000: in imports, $210,000; in exports, $490,000. Trade with Australia increased $185,000, which may be attributed to the impetus given to the export of Canadian manufactures by the Sydney Exhibition.

The total number of vessels registered in the Dominion of Canada in 1878 was 7,469, measuring 1,333,015 tons. This gives Canada the fourth largest merchant marine in the world, Great Britain, the United States, and Germany alone leading her. The number of steamers registered was 834, with a gross tonnage of 183,-935 tons. The estimated value of the total shipping is $39,990,000. The number of vessels built during the year was 329, measuring 100,-873 tons. The number of ocean-going ships which visited the port of Montreal during the year was 516—249 iron ships, with an aggregate tonnage of. 311,968, and 267 wooden ships, with a tonnage of 85,298; 482 of the vessels, with a tonnage of 382,056 tons, were British.

The products of the fisheries in 1878 were valued at $13,373,486, against $12,029,957 in 1877. The increase took place in the takings of cod, mackerel, lobster, and salmon. The exports of fish amounted to $6,929,366, an increase of $1,055,006.

The latest report of Canadian railway statistics gives the length of the roads in operation as 6,143 miles, of rails laid in partially constructed roads as 721, and of railways under construction as 1,042; making a total length of 7,906 miles, against 5,594½ miles in operation and 1,996⅔ under construction at the time of the preceding report. The total nominal capital outlay represented is about $360,000,-000: of this, $122,176,000 consists of the ordinary share capital, $69,155,000 of preferred stock, and $83,710,000 of the bonded debt. The amount subscribed and guaranteed by the Government and municipal authorities was $87,-456,000, which was reduced $1,887,000 by paid-up securities. The aid received from the Dominion Government amounted to $65,939,-000, that from the provincial Governments to $14,291,000, that from municipal sources to $7,224,000. The capital investment per mile is $45,995. Steel rails are laid on 3,583 miles. The tonnage of freight handled during the year ending June 30, 1878, was 7,883,472 tons, an increase of 15 per cent. over the business of the preceding year. The total earnings amounted to $20,520,000, an increase of $1,-778,000; the earnings per mile were $3,479, an increase of $61. The net profits were $4,419,000, an increase of 28 per cent. The revenue from the canals has decreased by $42,898, or 11·38 per cent., the decrease on the Welland Canal amounting to $37,959.

DORSEY, Mrs. SARAH A., died in New Orleans on Saturday, July 4th. She was the daughter of Thomas G. Ellis, a planter in Mississippi, and was born in Natchez, February 16, 1829. She received a careful education, and enjoyed the advantage of extended foreign travel. Her mother was the sister of the poetess and novelist Mrs. Catherine Anne Warfield, née Ware, authoress of "Poems by Two Sisters of the West," "The Household of Bouverie," "Beauseincourt," and other romances marked by a certain wild, untutored originality. This lady, who died in 1877, exercised a formative influence on her niece, who became her literary executor, Mrs. Warfield having left in her hands a mass of manuscript, the greater part of which is still unpublished. After her mother's second marriage, Sarah Ellis, on January 19, 1853, married Samuel W. Dorsey of Ellicott's Mills, Maryland. At the time he was practicing law and planting in Tensas Parish, Louisiana. Mr. Dorsey was a man of ability, wealth, and social position, and, despite disparity of years, the union proved a happy one. Mrs. Dorsey was fond of society, travel, and literature. Having no children, she gave herself unreservedly to the indulgence of these tastes. She spoke fluently several modern languages, was a proficient in Greek and Latin, and an ardent student of Sanskrit. She published a biography of Governor Henry W. Allen of Louisiana, and the novels "Athalie," "Lucia Dare," "Agnes Graham," and "Panola." Of these "Panola" is the latest, having appeared in 1877, and "Agnes Graham" is the best known. In addition she wrote a treatise on the Aryan philosophy, and was an industrious contributor to various journals and periodicals. Mrs. Dorsey was at one time an Episcopalian with high ritualistic tendencies. She built a chapel on her plantation, and devoted herself to the religious instruction of her slaves. Her studies of comparative theology and investigations of Eastern systems for a while unsettled her convictions; but these doubts passed away, and during her lingering illness she was sustained by the faith of her childhood. She was widely known in literary circles at home and abroad. She kept up an active interchange of ideas with savants in India, Germany, Italy, France, and England. Among her correspondents were the Rossettis, Dean Stanley, Carlyle, Herbert Spencer, and other celebrities. Mrs. Dorsey was far more distinguished as a conversationalist than as a writer. Her quick intellect and fervent affections gave her a peculiar charm. By temperament she was a hero-worshiper. She was enthusiastic and unchanging in her friendships. Although her means were much diminished after the war, the hospitality of her home was as freely extended as ever. There Mr. Jefferson Davis and his family were frequent and honored guests during the years of poverty and misfortune following the failure of the Confederacy. Mrs. Dorsey made no secret of her intention to constitute Mr. Davis or one of his children her heir, and thus do her part toward repairing his losses. Having given liberally to her own family during her lifetime, and deriving her entire means from her husband, she felt herself entitled to make this disposition of her property, and only regretted the smallness of the legacy. The appraised value of her whole estate is under twenty-five thousand dollars. After the death of Mr. Dorsey in 1875, she removed from her plantation in Tensas Parish, and resided at Beauvoir, a small place on the Gulf-shore. Here she continued to employ herself in literary labors, chiefly acting as amanuensis to Mr. Davis, in the progress of whose autobiography she felt a profound interest. These occupations she never intermitted, although suffering from the ravages of an hereditary malady, an internal cancer, which would have disabled one with less powers of endurance. When it became necessary, she faced the alternatives of life and death with composure. Removing to New Orleans, she submitted calmly to a surgical operation which proved unavailing. She died professing herself at peace with the world and in the Christian faith, and left behind her an unblemished character.

E

EASTERN ROUMELIA, an autonomous province of Turkey; area, 13,664 square miles; population, 751,000. The dissatisfaction in this province with the division of Bulgaria continued in 1879, and led to serious excesses against the International Commission and its agents. Thus, in February the financial director Schmidt was mobbed at Haskioi, Slivno, and other places. Not even the presence of General Stolypine, the Russian Governor, was sufficient to restore order, and it was necessary to send for troops for this purpose. The population elected delegates to the Bulgarian Constituent Assembly, which met in Tirnova on February 22d; but these delegates were not admitted. The disordered state of the country gave rise to a Russian note to the Powers, in which a mixed occupation of the country was suggested. (See RUSSIA.) The Russian note was immediately followed by a Turkish note complaining of the treatment the Mohammedans in Eastern Roumelia received at the hands of the Bulgarians. It was as follows:

The situation of the Mussulman population in Roumelia had never ceased to be precarious, full of dangers and difficulties, but there was reason to believe that with time the exclusive and hostile spirit which animates the Bulgarians would give way to juster and more humane sentiments. This hope has not been realized, and it is with the greatest pain that the Sublime Porte finds itself obliged to observe that the condition of the Mussulman inhabitants of Eastern Roumelia has become almost intolerable in every part of the province, and especially at Bournar, Yamboli, and Sagra. They are constantly subjected to acts of oppression and violence on the part of their Bulgarian fellow countrymen. The latter seem to pursue a system of extermination which the repeated measures of our authorities have not been able to check. The victims, in despair, are leaving their homes and seeking safety in expatriation. The emigration is considerable. Adrianople has already received a great number of emigrants within its walls, and their number, daily increasing, is becoming a source of serious embarrassment for our newly installed authorities there. Please to call the serious attention of the Government to which you are accredited to this situation. We appeal to the humane feelings of the Powers to deliver the Mussulman population of Eastern Roumelia from the persecution to which it is subjected, and to obtain security for their persons and property. You will not fail to point out that the Treaty of Berlin, conforming to the most elementary principles of justice, meant that all sections of the population of Eastern Roumelia, without distinction of race or religion, should be treated on the footing of the most perfect equality. It is therefore impossible that the signatory Powers of that treaty should allow a certain class of inhabitants openly to seek the suppression or systematic exclusion of another class, which has the same rights and which should enjoy the same protection.

The proposal for a mixed occupation at first met with general approval, but was finally abandoned, as no agreement could be reached by the Powers in the settlement of the details. In its stead a plan proposed by the Turkish Government, of prolonging the supervising authority of the European Commission, was adopted. On April 14th the Turkish Government nominated Aleko Pasha, Prince Vogorides, as Governor. (See ALEKO PASHA.) This nomination was confirmed by all the Powers. The time for the withdrawal of the Russian troops from the province fixed by the Treaty of Berlin was May 3d, the evacuation to be completed within three months—by August 3d. In accordance with this provision, the Russians began to withdraw from the province on May 2d. The organic statute for the province was approved by the Porte. It provides that the Governor shall be in full possession of the executive powers in the province. He is to have at his disposal military and gendarmerie, and is to be allowed to call for Turkish troops when necessary, to proclaim a state of siege, to submit financial and other bills to the Provincial Assembly, and to open and close its sessions. The Sultan has the right to occupy the frontiers, to call the Governor-General to account, to nominate his General Secretary, to sanction the laws voted by the Provincial Assembly, and to approve the officers of administration and justice nominated by the Governor-General. In the administration the Governor-General is to be aided by a Senate, consisting of the commander of the militia and gendarmerie, and the heads of the departments of Justice, Finance, Public Education, Agriculture, Commerce, and Public Works. The making of laws is vested in the Provincial Assembly. Besides this, the province has to send deputies to the Turkish Parliament at Constantinople. The Provincial Assembly has besides the right to modify all laws promulgated by the Porte so far as they regard Eastern Roumelia. The province is divided into six circles and twenty-eight districts, the former having each a council. The official language with the Porte is to be the Turkish, but in the circles and districts the language will be that of the majority of the inhabitants, whether Bulgarian, Turkish, or Greek. In respect to the financial obligations of the country, the International Commission estimated the yearly income at 800,000 Turkish pounds. Three tenths of this amount, £240,-000 Turkish, is to be paid to the Porte. Besides this, Eastern Roumelia will share in proportion to her income in Turkey's financial burdens for the maintenance of order and peace, as well as for the expenses of the national administration. The gendarmerie will, when occasion requires, be helped by the country militia. The militia is based on the principle of universal service; that is to say, every man is obliged to serve for four years on active duty. The manner of putting this statute into execution was a question of considerable difficulty. The military and gendarmerie, composed of all sections of the population, and commanded by officers named by the Sultan, as provided for by the statute, had not been created, so that when the Russians began to evacuate the tranquillity of the province would in the interval have to be intrusted to the Bulgarian militia, organized by Prince Dondoukoff-Korsakoff, and officered in a great part by Russians. As the Bulgarians had hitherto shown themselves hostile to the Commission, it seemed doubtful whether this militia could be relied upon to suppress disorders. The Governor-General had by the treaty the right to call in Ottoman troops; but the exercise of this right would inevitably cause serious disturbances. The Porte, also, which at first had insisted upon occupying Burgas and other points, had abandoned this project, and therefore no Turkish troops were in a position to promptly answer such a call. If the extreme party among the agitators should get the upper hand, it might even be impossible for the Commission to remain at Philippopolis. These difficulties were fully recognized both by the Porte and the foreign diplomatists; but, since the abandonment of the scheme of a mixed occupation, no one seemed to know what should be done. This state of uncertainty soon had serious consequences. The Mussulmans, afraid of being left alone with the Bulgarians, emigrated in great numbers from Roumelia, so that in the beginning of May from 50,000 to 60,000 were in Adrianople.

On May 27th Aleko Pasha entered Philippopolis. He wore on this occasion a Bulgarian bonnet, although the Sultan had ordered him to wear the Turkish fez. The question, in spite of its apparent insignificance, had become a warmly debated one. The fez is regarded as the emblem of the old Turkish *régime*, and the hat as that of the new European administration. The Russians had undertaken to use their influence in favor of the hat, and obtained from Aleko Pasha a formal promise that he would not wear the fez. Relying upon this promise, Generals Obrutscheff and Stolypine publicly declared upon several occasions that the new Governor-General would wear the hat, and thus manifest that he did not belong to the old school of Pashas. On May 30th Aleko Pasha was formally installed as Governor-General. After the reading of the two firmans of the Sultan sanctioning the organic statute, and appointing Aleko Pasha, the following manifesto of the new Governor-General was read:

My dear Fellow Countrymen: His Imperial Majesty the Sultan, our august sovereign, desiring to procure a revival of prosperity for your province, which has suffered so much in consequence of recent events, and to insure tranquillity for all the inhabitants without distinction, has appointed me Governor-General of Eastern Roumelia for a period of five years, with a view of carrying into effect the organic statute prepared by the Mixed Commission which was formed for that purpose, and which was composed of Commissioners from the great Powers signataries to the Treaty of Berlin. The reforms which the Porte de-

sires to introduce into the government of Eastern Roumelia are contained in detail in the above-mentioned statute, and I think it is needless to enumerate them here. It is sufficient to add here that the union of all is necessary to insure a faithful and complete application and fulfillment of the statute, as well as the submission and good will of the inhabitants. I earnestly recommend people not to allow themselves to be discouraged by the recollection of past evils, but to endeavor, on the contrary, to profit by the advantages granted them by the Porte, as well as by the principles applied by virtue of the organic statute above mentioned, and to endeavor thereby to repair all past misfortunes. You are not ignorant of the fact that in all situations and in all countries the fruits of skill and of labor, as well as the continued growth of public riches and prosperity, depend mainly upon order and good understanding in general and between individuals. It is the duty of all of you, therefore, to employ your best efforts to maintain public tranquillity while steadily pursuing your own occupations and labors. The entry of Ottoman troops into the interior of Eastern Roumelia being dependent upon the maintenance of public order and upon my own request for that purpose addressed to the Porte—a request which is not to be made except upon my personal appreciation of the circumstances requiring it—I rely with confidence upon those of the inhabitants who are attached to their country that they will abstain from all acts of a character which would justify the entrance of the Ottoman troops. Those who seek to create a belief that the entry of Turkish troops will be carried out, thereby causing alarm to the inhabitants of Eastern Roumelia, completely ignore the real intentions of the Sublime Porte; for whenever the Imperial Government shall deem it necessary to occupy by its troops the frontiers and certain other localities, this will only be done in conformity with the stipulations of the Treaty of Berlin, without giving cause for alarm to the inhabitants. What proves this is the fact of my arrival in the chief town of the province without the presence of any Ottoman troops. Therefore I entreat you not to listen to the malevolent suggestions, but to manifest your gratitude to the Porte for its anxiety for the well-being and interest of your country, and by employing all your efforts in facilitating the literal execution of the organic statute which assures you a free administration. In conclusion, I salute you, and offer up most hearty prayers to the Almighty for your good health and a happy life.

The question of hoisting the Turkish flag had been considered, and for that purpose a flag-staff had been erected at the gate of the kouak. The Prince having been informed that the display of the flag might cause demonstrations and disorder, he consulted the Commissioners, observing that if disorder did occur he should immediately resign and leave for Constantinople. The Commissioners thereupon had a meeting to consider this question. The chief Ottoman Commissioner having explained that it was not customary to hoist a flag before a konak which was not a fortress, the Commission decided that, as the formality of the hoisting or not of the Ottoman flag could have no influence upon the execution of the organic statute, the Commission considered that the Governor-General alone could decide upon the opportuneness of observing this formality. The Prince acted upon this decision, and, wishing to avoid all risks of disturbance, directed that the flag should not be hoisted. The troops then defiled before the Governor-General, and the ceremony ended. On June 3d the Governor made the following nominations, and submitted them to the Sultan for approval: M. Christovitch, Secretary-General and Minister of the Interior; M. Kessakoff, Minister of Justice; M. Vulcovitch, Minister of Public Works; and M. Schmidt, Minister of Finance. The International Commission on the same day unanimously decided to transfer immediately the financial administration of the province to the Governor-General. The action of Aleko Pasha brought upon him the displeasure of the Turkish Government, and it informed the Powers that the refusal of Aleko to wear the fez was a violation of engagements between him and the Porte. The Government would wait until Eastern Roumelia was evacuated, when it would summon Aleko Pasha to wear the fez and hoist the Turkish flag. In fact, if the demand should not be complied with, the Porte would request the Powers to sanction Aleko's removal, and would send a body of Turkish troops to occupy the Balkans. In other respects also Aleko Pasha was charged with acting contrary to the wishes of the Porte, and contrary even to the letter and spirit of the existing enactments. Thus he appointed none but Bulgarian officials, to the utter neglect of the Greek and Turkish elements in the country. Of the Bulgarian Ministers nominated by him, one, M. Kessakoff, the brother of General Kessakoff, late commander of the Eastern Roumelian troops until the arrival of General Obrutscheff, agitated for the reunion of Eastern Roumelia and Bulgaria by main force. The advocate of rebellion a few weeks before Aleko Pasha's arrival, he was at once made Minister of Justice. In the latter part of June the Porte approved the entire Ministry with the exception of M. Kessakoff. To his non-confirmation by the Porte Aleko Pasha replied that the organic statute did not absolutely oblige him to obtain the ratification of his nominees; that he considered M. Kessakoff a fit person, and that he (Aleko), having been elected for five years, should not be interfered with during his term of office.

The Russian evacuation proceeded rapidly, and on July 27th the last Russian troops embarked at Burgas, leaving the country in the hands of the authorities. A tumult occurred in Philippopolis as soon as General Stolypine had left that town. A Bulgarian flag was raised, which Aleko Pasha ordered to be lowered, adding that in the event of non-compliance he would leave the country and return to Constantinople. His demand was complied with. Disorders continued to occur in various parts of the country, caused both by Turks and Bulgarians. In the beginning of September the Mohammedans at Philippopolis presented a petition to the representatives of the European Powers, complaining of the ill treatment they were receiving at the hands of the Bulgarians. They declared that they were insulted, attacked, wounded, and assassinated by Bulgarians. Should any of them repair to the

Government konak to complain of these misdeeds, they were driven away with blows of the whip by the officer on duty. They no longer, they said, demanded restitution of their property, but asked merely that their lives and honor should be protected. They had, however, no hope of obtaining even this small measure of justice so long as all the judges and officials were Bulgarians.

The relations of the Government with the Porte also continued in an unsatisfactory state. The Government of Eastern Roumelia having delayed the restoration of returning Mohammedan refugees, the Turkish Government sent numbers of them back to their homes, where, of course, no provision had been made for them; and they would certainly have starved if they had not been cared for by their co-religionists.

The Provincial Assembly was opened November 3d by Aleko Pasha, who in his speech recommended the impartial enforcement of the organic statute and the strict administration of justice. He further asked the Assembly to devote its attention to the budget, and to discuss the best means of improving the condition of the population.

In November Aleko Pasha paid a visit to Constantinople, after he had repeatedly refused to do so when requested by the Porte. The visit was productive of good results. Most of the differences existing between Philippopolis and Constantinople were removed, and an understanding was come to on the most important point, that of the Mohammedan refugees. All the European Powers had also taken steps to urge upon Aleko Pasha the necessity of something being done to remedy the existing state of affairs. The principal difficulty in the way of the repatriation of the fugitives having been the preparation of the necessary means of subsistence for them, the proposal formerly made by M. Schmidt, of the International Commission, to provide by a loan for these requirements, which had been rejected both by the Porte and the Government of the province, was now seriously entertained by both governments. After the return of Aleko Pasha from Constantinople a gradual change occurred in the public sentiment. The bearing of the Bulgarians became very friendly toward the Mohammedans, and even the Provincial Assembly refrained from touching any question which might disturb the peace.

EATON, Margaret L., widow of General John Henry Eaton, Secretary of War in the Administration of President Jackson, was born in 1796, and died at Washington on November 8, 1879. Her maiden name was O'Neil. In her youth she possessed high personal beauty and a peculiar fascination of manner, which, combined with a persistent will and high ambition, enabled her to attain a prominent position in society. Her first husband, by whom she had several children, was Mr. Timberlake, a purser in the United

States Navy. In 1828, after his death, she became the wife of General Eaton, then a Senator from Tennessee, but who, a few months afterward, was given a seat in the Cabinet of President Jackson. The other members of the Cabinet were Martin Van Buren, Secretary of State; Samuel D. Ingham of Pennsylvania, Secretary of the Treasury; John Branch of North Carolina, Secretary of the Navy; John McPherson Berrien of Georgia, Attorney-General; and William T. Barry of Kentucky, Postmaster-General. This promotion of General Eaton gave to his wife a social position she had long desired. But she had not been able to escape reports so often assailing dazzling characters in the excitable society of a national capital; and so she was refused a reception on equal terms by the families of the other members of the Cabinet. This repulse soon extended to the families of foreign ministers in Washington. The husbands could not resist the influence of their dutiful wives, and a feud sprang up among them which even involved the President. At this time the estrangement between President Jackson and Vice-President Calhoun had begun, and a belief was awakened in the mind of the former that the latter had shrewdly fomented the general excitement, and it was said took an active part in promoting the crisis. Finally, the President demanded of his Secretaries the recognition of the social status of Mrs. Eaton, and was refused by all of them excepting Mr. Van Buren. As a compromise it was suggested that her public status should be conceded, while each lady should act as she chose in regard to private recognition. General Jackson wrote a very plain-spoken note on the subject to Vice-President Calhoun, but only elicited from him the diplomatic reply that it was a "ladies' quarrel," with which men could not successfully interfere, adding that "the laws of the ladies were like the laws of the Medes and Persians, and admitted neither of argument nor of amendment." The President then sent for Mr. Van Buren, the head of his Cabinet, and the only member who had been complaisant to his views (for he was a widower), and requested him as a favor to send in his resignation, which necessarily would be followed by that of the other Secretaries. Mr. Van Buren complied April 7, 1831, and was soon recompensed with the appointment of Minister to England, and proceeded to his post; but in the following winter he was rejected in the Senate by the casting vote of Vice-President Calhoun. He returned home from England as a man who had been wronged in the house of his friends, and was rewarded by a nomination for Vice-President on the same ticket with President Jackson. Both were elected, and on the expiration of the second term of President Jackson, Mr. Van Buren was elected as his successor. Two or three years later General Eaton was appointed Governor of Florida Territory, and in 1838 Minister to Spain. In the Spanish capital Mrs. Eaton is said to have become a social favorite, and to have shone with great brilliancy at the court of the youthful Isabella. She also became a noted belle in London and Paris. Returning to Washington in 1840, she resided there very quietly until the death of her husband in November, 1856. She was left with a large estate and the custody of five grandchildren. A year later she made the acquaintance of a teacher from Italy, and subsequently married him. The marriage was an unhappy one; she lost a large portion of her property; the husband went to Europe, and of late years she lived in retirement at Washington.

ECUADOR (REPÚBLICA DEL ECUADOR). The President of the Republic is General Ignacio de Veintemilla, inaugurated in December, 1876. The Minister of the Interior and of Foreign Affairs is General José Maria Urbina; the Minister of Finance, Dr. Martin Icaza (of Guayaquil); and the Minister of War, Colonel C. F. Boloña. According to the terms of the new Constitution, made at Ambato in 1878, there are two *Designados* or Vice-Presidents to replace the President should circumstances require it: the First Designado is Señor L. Salvador; the Second Designado, Señor J. Novoa. General Urbina and Dr. Icaza were appointed to their respective portfolios in March; but the former did not enter at once upon the duties of his post, the President having determined to send him on a mission southward as peacemaker between Bolivia and Chili. His department during his absence was to be under the direction of the Minister of War. The Governor of Guayaquil is General J. Sanchez Rubio. The Consul for Ecuador at New York is Mr. A. I. Duvale; and the United States Consul at Guayaquil is Mr. Ph. Eder.

The present strength of the Ecuadorian army is reported at 5,000 rank and file.

Of public instruction in the republic little is known, except that it is under the exclusive control of the clergy and the Christian Brothers. The late President Garcia Moreno, in his last message to Congress, in 1875, stated that ninety-three schools had been established, with an average attendance of 32,000.

Almost the only establishment for higher education is the Academy of Ecuador, inaugurated at Quito in May, 1874, in accordance with the decree of the Royal Academy of Madrid. The studies are under the supervision of a director, aided by a censor and a secretary.

In an official report published in 1878, the national revenue for the year ending on August 31, 1877, was stated to have amounted to 2,228,000 pesos;[*] but of the expenditure, which averages about 3,350,000 pesos, no mention was made. The following table will serve to show the various sources of the revenue and the average yield of each:

---

[*] The par value of the Ecuadorian peso is about 77 cents of United States money, but the average exchange value is rarely over 71 cents.

SOURCES.	Amounts in Ecuadorian pesos.
Custom-house	1,700,000
Tobacco tax	19,000
Spirit tax	112,000
Salt monopoly	810,000
Gunpowder monopoly	30,000
Stamped paper	115,000
Income tax	65,000
Tax on sales of lands	215,000
Tithes	870,000
Pawn-Office	1,000
Post-Office	95,000
Government lands	52,000
Sundries	510,000
Total	3,594,000

The total national debt, interesting details concerning which may be found in the "Annual Cyclopædia" for 1874 and 1875, amounted in January, 1877, to 22,938,000 Ecuadorian pesos, viz.: home debt, 10,150,000; foreign debt (accruing from British loan of 1855 = £1,824,000), 12,788,000 pesos.

The foreign trade being for the most part carried on through Guayaquil, by far the larger portion of the customs are collected at that port, as may be seen by the annexed table for the seven years 1870–'76 inclusive:

YEARS.	Receipts in Ecuadorian pesos.
1870	1,360,000
1871	1,371,440
1872	1,591,780
1873	1,672,650
1874	1,442,000
1875	1,047,986
1876	1,174,058

The total value of the imports through Guayaquil for 1878 was reported at 4,734,055 pesos; and that of the exports, inclusive of precious metals, at 4,183,612 pesos. The commodities shipped in largest quantities were cacao, *tagua* or vegetable ivory, India-rubber, *jipijapa* (or so-called Panama hats), etc.

The new cacao crop (1879) was unusually abundant, and commanded an advanced price; the average price per quintal (of 100 pounds) of the crop immediately preceding having been £3 free on board. The shipments of ivory-nuts amounted in 1878 to 10,000 tons, which is a marked increase as compared with previous years. This article was sold in March at £17 10s. free on board.

The following extract from a correspondence dated Guayaquil, August, 1879, will serve at once to show the sentiments inspired by President Veintemilla's "great capacity to rule a free people," and make known the terms of recent railway contracts:

Elevated by treason and the accident of circumstance to the chief magistracy of the country, a position which he [General Veintemilla] has sustained by practices worthy of the middle ages, he does not pay the country he misgoverns even the small compliment of endeavoring to save appearances. His patriotism is self-interest, as will be understood when the fact is known that his willing tools at the convention of Ambato donated him a large increase of salary, and other substantial rewards for services which in a well-organized country would have gained for him imprisonment or banishment. His manner of granting concessions and celebrating contracts is, even in these lands of surprises, unique and striking. A case recited in the issue of the "Nacion" of the 7th inst., a newspaper of Guayaquil, is to the point. In Quito,

in January of the present year, Mr. Herman Gohring effected a contract with the Government of Ecuador, represented at that time by Don Luis Salvador, as the illustrious commander-in-chief of the armies and navies of Ecuador was at that time sojourning temporarily in Guayaquil, for the construction of a railroad from Yaguachi to Quito. The terms of the first contract, which occasioned considerable unfavorable comment in the country at the time, may be briefly stated. The contractor guaranteed within three years and a half from the date of signing the contract to finish the road, binding himself to begin the work within nine months. In return for this service the Government agreed to grant the following favors: the ownership and use of thirty miles of railroad, now existing over the new route to Quito, without any remuneration whatever to the Government; the cession of alternate sections of the public lands through which the road should pass; a subsidy of $150,000 per annum for four years, and of $100,000 for six years following; on the opening of the line for traffic a bonus of $200,000; for the space of fifty years the contractor should enjoy not only the use of the railroad, but no other should be constructed to compete with it; the fifty years expired, the contractor should still enjoy the profits of the road for twenty years longer, but any others might build a road in opposition to the enterprise. This contract was duly ratified, and published in the official paper on the 7th of February. The common sense of the country condemned the contract as soon as its terms were made known, on the ground that the conditions were too favorable to the contractor. Veintemilla's method of placating public opinion was characteristic. He ignored the contract and effected another under terms more favorable still for the contractor. He increased the total subsidy by $600,000, doubled the bonus to be paid at the completion of the work, extended the time allowed by the first contract for that purpose, undertook for account of the Government the construction of certain station buildings, etc., and doubled the number of years in which the contractor was to enjoy the usufruct of the enterprise, after the expiration of the exclusive privilege.

EGYPT, a tributary of Turkey in Northeastern Africa. The ruler of Egypt, who has the title of Khedive, is Mohammed Tevfik, born in 1852, the eldest son of Ismaïl Pasha, who resigned June 26, 1879. The eldest son of the Khedive is Prince Abbas Bey, born July 14, 1874.

The area and population of Egypt were as follows in 1879:

	Area in square miles.	Population.
I. EGYPT PROPER.		
Governments	68,168	569,115
Provinces	826,194	4,948,512
Total Egypt proper	894,362	5,517,627
II. OTHER POSSESSIONS.		
Nubia	333,800	1,000,000
Soodan	323,000	10,800,000
Total other possessions	656,800	11,800,000
Foreigners		68,653
Grand total	1,051,162	17,386,280

For an account of the finances, public debt, and commerce, see "Annual Cyclopædia" for 1878.

In the latter part of 1878 Mr. Rivers Wilson made a tour of inspection through the Delta, visiting the chief towns of every province; and wherever he went he held a kind of small durbar, which all the leading functionaries of the district attended. He began with Shibeen, went on to Damanhour, thence returned south to Tauta, and from Tanta he passed on to Zagazig and Mansoorah. Thus he traversed nearly the whole of Lower Egypt. Crowds came to the stations as he went from place to place, and the people filled the streets to see the English "Monfettish." At each town he inquired into the fiscal administration, and at Tanta he made a short address to the sheiks and officials as follows :

A new era has begun for Egypt. Reforms are already initiated, and if you will only have patience you can count on their completion. If you have grievances, make them known to us and you shall be righted. We wish to establish equality and legality in the country, and the law shall no longer be for the rich alone; it shall work for rich and poor alike.

Hundreds of petitions were presented to the Minister on his circuit, and he received them all personally. The courage to present complaints was quite a novelty in Egypt. Their presentation was regarded as a sign that a belief was growing in the permanence of the changes. In the last days of 1878 the Council of Ministers also adopted a beneficial step toward simplifying the provincial administration. It abolished the office of governors of large cities, and transferred their duties to the prefects of the provinces. The Minister of Finance ordered the appointment of inspectors of finance in the provinces, whose business it should be to watch over the payment of the duties and their rightful application. Three inspectors-in-chief, two for Lower Egypt and one for Upper Egypt, were to be at the head of this important branch of the administration. Mr. Fitzgerald, the new Accountant-General, who had accompanied Mr. Wilson on his tour, and had shown great energy in the adjustment of the questions of taxation, in one of his reports described the confusion existing in this branch of the financial administration as beyond all conception, making the execution of the orders of the Minister of Finance an impossibility; and to do away with these evils the financial inspectors were to be appointed. In February, 1879, the Commissioners of the Public Debt published their report of the financial results of the year 1878. The Commissioners said that they could not admit that one class of creditors should be paid to the prejudice of others, and that, if the resources of the Egyptian Government were not sufficient to enable it to meet all its obligations, the sacrifices to be made should be borne equally by all. It seemed that since 1876 the total indebtedness of the country had only been reduced £655,000, notwithstanding the operations of the sinking fund.

A serious demonstration was made at Cairo on February 18th. After an ordinary Council of Ministers, Nubar Pasha and Mr. Rivers Wilson on leaving in a carriage were stopped by a large throng of armed officers, estimated at 400, clamoring for payment of long arrears

of salary. Both were grossly insulted and forced back, the coachman being wounded. The crowd penetrated into the courtyard, up the staircase, and into the corridor, invading even the Ministers' private room. The passages, however, were eventually cleared, but the crowd remained outside the staircase and completely surrounded the building, preventing all exit. The Khedive ultimately arrived on the scene with a mere handful of soldiers. The crowd thereupon cheered, but called out, "Go back! we must get money from the Ministers." The Khedive, however, though with great difficulty, succeeded in forcing his way into the place, and a regiment of soldiers shortly followed. The Khedive then addressed the mob from the window, promising that justice would be observed toward them. After two hours the Khedive tried to leave the building, but met such resistance that he ordered the soldiers to charge. The Master of Ceremonies and five of the mob were wounded. Many were arrested and the rest dispersed. On the following day Nubar Pasha offered his resignation, which was accepted. This event created considerable excitement in London and Paris, and was regarded in those capitals as an attempt to get rid of Nubar; and it was considered as certain that the Khedive either instigated the attack, or was at least only too ready to profit by it. Ismail Pasha called in Nubar Pasha at a moment when the Governments and public of Europe required to be assured, and when Nubar Pasha's ability and special relations were indispensable to him in promptly forming a Cabinet which should stand as a guarantee to Europe in regard to the Khedive's policy. But it was easy to see that the Khedive would find it difficult to put up with Nubar Pasha's authority; for, well as he knew Nubar's intelligence and ability, the Khedive had a profound aversion for him personally. As soon as the Cabinet was formed, mainly through the efforts of Nubar Pasha, who was supported by England and France, the Khedive's only further thought was to get rid of Nubar, whom he fancied he could henceforth do without. Nubar Pasha knew this himself, and on January 20th wrote to a friend: "The everlasting political comedy or tragedy is being played on the little stage here, just as it is everywhere else: a lost power sought to be regained, persons interested in not letting it be regained, who yet aid it for personal motives or to give themselves importance—and not a sou in the Treasury withal. What a situation for the country, for the interested countries, and for your friend ! "

On February 26th Prince Hassan, son of the Khedive, and commander-in-chief of the Egyptian army, paid an official visit to Mr. Vivian, the English Consul-General, and in the presence of the leading English residents apologized, on behalf of the Khedive, the army, and the country, for the gross insult offered to Mr. Rivers Wilson by officers of the army the preceding week. Mr. Vivian replied that he deeply regretted the incident. It was incumbent on every civilized country to respect the laws of hospitality toward foreigners. It was more especially incumbent on Egypt to respect and protect an Englishman who had been sent by her Majesty's Government, at the express request of the Khedive, to take a prominent part in the government of the country. Mr. Rivers Wilson expressed satisfaction at the apology, and said that the army and the whole country should have remembered that in coming to Egypt he had only the interest of the country at heart. Under great difficulties his sole object was the introduction of order and reform into the administration.

The British Government, immediately upon the resignation of Nubar, proposed to the French Government to take joint action looking to the reinstatement of Nubar. The latter acceded to this proposition, and on March 8th a joint note was dispatched by the two Governments to the Khedive, which contained the conditions for the settlement of the crisis. These conditions included the right of Messrs. Wilson and De Blignières to veto all propositions which were not acceptable to them. The note concluded as follows: "The Khedive will comprehend the great responsibility which he has assumed in taking the initiative in these new arrangements, and the consequences to which he would expose himself if he were not able to secure the complete execution of those arrangements, or if difficulties were placed in the way of the Government, or disturbances of the public peace should take place." A new Ministry was finally formed in the second week of March, with Prince Tevfik as President of the Council, and Zulfikar as Minister for Foreign Affairs. Mr. Wilson remained Minister of Finance, and M. de Blignières Minister of Public Works. Riaz Pasha retained the portfolio of the Interior, and also discharged the duties of Minister of Justice. Ratif Pasha was succeeded in the Ministry of War by Eflatoun Pasha, a man brought up in England, used to English ways, well versed in the English language, and enjoying a high reputation for talent and honesty. The decree of nominations was signed by the Khedive and countersigned by Prince Tevfik. It was accompanied by a document of greater importance than even the decree. This document was a letter from the Khedive to Prince Tevfik containing an authoritative interpretation of the new Constitution published in August, 1878, in a letter from the Khedive to Nubar Pasha. The letter to Prince Tevfik was as follows:

HIGHNESS: At the moment when I intrust to you the presidency of the Council of Ministers, and with it the duty of forming a Cabinet, I wish to remind you that perfect harmony of views must exist among the members of that Cabinet; and I must also communicate to you my ideas concerning the accomplishment of the reforms which were inaugurated by my decree of the 28th of August last, which is the basis of our system of government.

When I established the new order of things I had no intention of separating myself from my Ministers, with whom, on the contrary, I wish to remain in close union. It is, therefore, most important that before the Cabinet comes to any decision concerning any bill or decree proposed by any one of its members, such bill or decree, with the report on which it is based, should be laid before me by the proper Minister. It is also necessary that I should inform the Cabinet of all measures of general importance which I may feel it right to introduce. In either case it is necessary that the Cabinet should meet, if I require it, to consider in concert with me the proposed measures. But, in order to maintain the complete independence of the Cabinet, I will always refrain from assisting in the deliberations.

On the other hand, as the native Ministers now form a majority in the Cabinet, it is right, in order to restore the balance of power and lend to the intervention of our European Ministers all the usefulness possible, that they should be entitled to a veto on all measures they agree in disapproving.

I hope these new plans will insure the working of the new organization, whose success will bring so much good to Egypt. The Cabinet may rest assured that, under all circumstances, it can count on the most complete and loyal assistance from me, just as I count on their devotion to the work we are carrying out in common. ISMAIL.

On April 7th a peaceable revolution occurred. Its origin was as follows: Mr. Wilson, acting with his French colleague, Mr. Baring, and the Debt Commissioners, having found it impossible to meet all the demands on the public debt, elaborated a plan for an equitable reduction of the claims of all classes of creditors, taking as a basis the last two budgets, and submitted the plan to the Khedive, who proposed a counter-project giving better terms, especially to floating-debt holders. A petition was signed in support of the Khedive's scheme by pashas, ulemas, members of the native Parliament, the Coptic Patriarch, the chief Rabbi, and the large land-owners—in fact, an essentially Egyptian opposition to European influence. The projects naturally clashed. Prince Tevfik resigned the presidency of the Council, and the Khedive dismissed Messrs. Wilson and De Blignières. A new Cabinet was then formed under the presidency of Sherif Pasha, composed entirely of native ministers. Mr. Rivers Wilson and M. de Blignières refused to resign their posts unless authorized to that effect by the British and French Governments. An official statement was promulgated explaining the action taken by the Khedive. It declared that the Khedive, complying with the daily growing national feeling, had decided to form a truly Egyptian Cabinet. A new Ministry had therefore been formed under the presidency of Sherif Pasha, the members of which would be responsible to the Council of Delegates. The latter would be invested with full powers, on the model of the European Legislative Chambers. It was added that the national financial scheme communicated by the Khedive to the Consuls-General had been elaborated by the Egyptian notables and dignitaries, and would be scrupulously carried out. A letter was also published from the Khedive, in which he accused the European Ministers.

especially Mr. Rivers Wilson, of wishing to establish laws repugnant to the manners, customs, and religion of the Egyptian population. A striking fact in this rebellion of the Khedive against the influence of the Western Powers was, that the most influential part of the population, and the chief religious and political authorities, were on his side, and resented the intrusion of European influence into Egyptian affairs. The leaders of the nation were with him in the struggle he had commenced for what he deemed independence. He had, in the first place, the support of the ulemas or priests. In Egypt, as in Constantinople, their hatred of European intrusion is intense and unfeigned. The predominance of Islam seems necessary to their very existence, and they abhor any approach to Christian rule. But it was still more significant that the Chamber of Delegates was also on the Khedive's side. This institution in 1879 was thirteen years old, the first meeting of Parliament in Egypt having been held on November 25, 1866. There is only one Chamber, and the number of dele-

gates, which up to 1879 was seventy-five, was in this year increased to one hundred. Every male inhabitant over twenty-five years of age, who is not legally interdicted, has a right to vote. Cairo names three members, Alexandria two, and Damietta one; and the rest of the country is divided into electoral districts, each returning one member. It is very probable that many of the members thus elected were the creatures of the Khedive, but the Parliament nevertheless developed considerable independence. Thus, when the Minister for Foreign Affairs went to close the session, which had come to an end by mere lapse of time, one of the deputies, Abdul Salem Mouchli, declared, on behalf of the Parliament, that they could accept no such dismissal. The Chamber, he said, had as yet done nothing; they had still much to do in the supervision of the Ministry, and they declined to separate. His colleagues supported him, and the Chamber remained in session, claiming that all ministries, whether native or foreign, should be dependent on its will and responsible to it for their conduct of

SUEZ.

affairs. Then there was the influence of the harems, which is subtle and persistent. A strict system of economy under European supervision is fatal to feminine luxury and extravagance. In short, the influential pashas, the religious party, female influence, and the principal land-owners of the provinces, all combined to support the Khedive in a determined resistance to European predominance. The latter, in the beginning of April, offered Messrs. Baring and De Blignières posts as Comptrollers-General of receipts and expenditures. Both gentlemen declined, giving as reasons, first, that the Khedive's plan was not realizable, was beyond the capabilities of the country, and opposed to the interests of Egypt and the creditors; and, secondly, that they could not concur in a *régime* which violated recent engagements with England and France. The new Government took a step on April 15th which met with the disapproval of the Western Powers. It ordered the Post-Office to open pamphlets and detain copies of the second report of the Commission of In-

quiry just published by the *Caisse Publique*. The Postmaster protested against this order, adding that he could no longer urge the European Governments to abolish their independent post-offices in Egypt. The report recommended a reduction of interest, and antedated the Egyptian bankruptcy from April 6, 1876. The *Caisse Publique* prefaced the report as follows: "We were firmly resolved to advise the acceptance of the project if the recent exclusion of European Ministers had not destroyed the only guarantees on which the success of the reforms depended." The first work of the Khedive and the new Ministry was to issue a decree on April 22d, which was virtually a suspension of payment. The decree admitted that Egypt could not for the present pay her way, and declared the necessity of a general reduction. It declared that there should be no further borrowing to pay arrears of interest; and this is what was particularly vexatious to the creditors. The Khedive in this decree, however, while recording the failure of Europeans, said that in the future the

Egyptian estate would be managed by honest and sensible men, and that the creditors might look forward to a respectable liquidation.

This new revolution created a profound sensation in Western Europe, and particularly in England and France, and led to negotiations between these two Powers as to what should be done next. In the first place, the two Governments considered that the bondholders' interests were only a secondary question, and that the principal point was the establishment in Egypt of a good administration, leaving no Power any pretext for intervening in Egyptian affairs on the plea of protecting the interests of its subjects. The consequence of this first principle on which the Cabinets agreed was that a good administration was only possible in Egypt apart from the Egyptian element, or at least with the coöperation of the European element, the exclusion of which seemed to them utterly unacceptable. This conclusion was common to the two Governments. But their views diverged on the question of persons. France would have liked to force back the two dismissed Ministers upon the Khedive. England, on the contrary, had special reasons for not insisting on this point. There had been conflicts between Mr. Vivian, the English Consul - General, and Mr. Wilson, and Mr. Vivian was summoned home to give explanations, while Mr. Wilson was recalled from Egypt and replaced in his English functions. In these circumstances the French Government, of course, had to abandon its wish to make the Khedive receive back his dismissed Ministers, and to content itself with keeping him to the principle of European Ministers coöperating in the administration of Egypt. Another consequence was that, ceasing to exact the restoration of the old Ministers, the French Government could no longer require the Khedive not to change his European Ministers without the consent of the two Governments. The first instructions, therefore, sent to the agents of the two Governments and communicated to the Porte, were that France and England regarded a good administration in Egypt as indispensable to their own interests and to foreign residents, and that such an administration did not seem to them feasible without the presence of two European Ministers in the Egyptian Cabinet. The two Governments, therefore, invited the Khedive to comply as promptly as possible with their demand, and to hand over the portfolios of Finance and Public Works to English and French Ministers. There was no question in these instructions of a threat of coercive measures, nor did the note have a threatening tone. An offer was made by the Sultan in the latter part of April to depose Ismail Pasha, and to appoint Halim Pasha, Ismail's uncle (who according to the Mohammedan law of succession was the rightful heir), his successor. This proposal did not find favor with France, which wished to keep the Egyptian and Eastern questions

separate. The German Government also protested against the action of the Khedive, in a note delivered on May 17th. This note was of the same tenor as that of 1878, containing a reservation of all rights acquired by the international arrangements respecting the international courts of law and the Commission of Control, and a protest against any arbitrary change of system on the part of the Khedive which might prejudice the interests of German subjects. This note, which was aimed mainly against the decree of April 22d, was communicated to the other European Governments, and England, France, Austria, Russia, and Italy all took the same line and protested against the non-execution of the judgments of the tribunals.

The proposal made by the Porte in April to depose Ismail Pasha in favor of his uncle was repeated in June, when the Powers counseled the Khedive to abdicate, voluntarily promising to support his son Tevfik. The Khedive asked for this promise in writing, which was refused. On June 19th the British and French Consuls-General proceeded together to the palace and formally demanded the abdication of the Khedive, who asked to be allowed forty - eight hours in order to communicate with the Porte before giving his reply. To the Khedive's inquiry at Constantinople a reply was received from the Sultan personally to this effect: "Your abdication is not a question that concerns you; you await our further orders. This is the only reply you can give." On June 25th the Consuls waited on the Khedive and informed him that deposition in favor of Halim had been decided upon the day before at Constantinople, and would be proclaimed before the Council there that day. They finally urged abdication, promising a guarantee to Tevfik in writing. The Khedive demanded as conditions of abdication that his family should be provided for, as was done prior to the cession of their lands, and that the abdication should be made into the hands of the Sultan. The Consuls replied that this last condition broke off all negotiations, that they consequently withdrew their offers, and that events must take their course. The Sultan was still undecided in respect to Tevfik's succession, when Sir Austen Layard, the British Ambassador, semi-officially represented to him that if he declined to displace the Khedive the Powers would be compelled to take that step upon themselves, and Turkey would in that case eventually lose Egypt. Sir Austen Layard added that the Powers were firmly determined to establish good administration in Egypt. The Porte advised the Sultan to acquiesce in the course recommended, and accordingly, on June 26th, he signed the firman deposing the Khedive in favor of Prince Mohammed Tevfik. On the same day the Porte addressed a dispatch to the Powers, confirming the Imperial iradé of 1841, and abolishing the iradé of 1873, which authorized the Khedive of Egypt to conclude treaties with foreign powers and to maintain a standing army. The dispatch added that the Porte would exert its influence to restore the finances of Egypt and remove the abuses existing in that country. The change itself took place without any disturbance. Ismail Pasha in the morning received an order from the Sultan requiring him to abdicate in favor of Prince Tevfik, and he at once complied with the demand. In the evening at six o'clock, Prince Tevfik was proclaimed Khedive as Tevfik I. Ismail received an annual allowance of £50,-000; his sons Hassan and Hussein, £20,000 each; and his mother, £30,000. The new Khedive was offered £150,000, but accepted only £50,000. Ismail Pasha left Egypt on June 30th for Naples. Tevfik's first official acts created considerable dissatisfaction with the Powers. He formed a new Ministry under Sherif Pasha composed entirely of natives, and in a decidedly offensive manner prohibited Nubar Pasha from returning to Egypt. This prohibition, however, was revoked in August, through the influence of the Powers. In the beginning of August the firman of investiture was communicated to England and France. Those Powers informed the Porte that some phrases used in it, while giving force to the prerogatives it had been sought to put in question, did not seem explicit enough, appearing to leave certain points in doubt, a state of things they could not agree to. In consequence of these observations, the Porte handed to the Ambassadors of the two Powers an official and identical declaration setting forth that all the rights and prerogatives conferred upon Egypt, and which were not expressly abolished by the firman of investiture, remain in force. This was tantamount to saying that no change had occurred in the situation of Egypt toward the Porte, and that the latter had promptly abandoned the idea of profiting by circumstances to gain a greater sway over Egypt. All the other Powers withdrew after the collective step which led to Ismail's abdication, in order in no way to encumber the joint influence of England and France; and even Germany, after having shown by her decisive intervention that she meant to be listened to even in Egypt, took no further steps apart from the two more especially protective Powers, and hastened to state that she entirely recognized their begemony, and had no intention of interfering with their joint influence. On August 14th the firman was presented to the Khedive. The Ministry of Sherif Pasha was dismissed on the 18th, and a new one was formed, in which the Khedive holds the presidency. The other departments were distributed as follows : Zulticar Pasha, Minister of Justice; Mansour Pasha, Interior; Mustapha Fehmi Pasha, Foreign Affairs; Hardar Pasha, Finance; Osman Reski Pasha, War and Marine; Mehemed Menachli Pasha, Public Works; Ali Ibrahim Pasha, Public Instruction. In September Messrs. Baring and De Blignières were appointed English and

French Comptrollers - General, upon the recommendation of their respective Governments. The Khedive at first desired that their duties should be clearly defined before their definite appointment, but finally yielded to the demands of England and France, and appointed them without such understanding. The Ministry with the Khedive as President was replaced by a new one on September 21st, which was composed as follows: Riaz Pasha, President of the Council, Minister of the Interior, and *ad interim* Minister of Finance; Ali Moubarek Pasha, Minister of Public Works; Mustapha Fehmi Pasha, Foreign Affairs; Osman Pefki Pasha, War and Marine; Fakri Pasha, Justice; and Ibrahim Pasha, Public Instruction. An important circular was issued by the Ministry on October 15th to all governors, tax-collectors, inspectors, and fiscal authorities, which ordered that the pashas and other high officials, who had formerly evaded payment of taxes, should be treated like all other subjects of the Khedive; and, if they did not pay within a certain time, their rents were to be seized or their produce sold. European holders of land and houses were also to pay in future their uncontested taxes, i. e., those sanctioned by the Ministry of Finance. The foreign Consuls-General were informed of this fact.

The relations with Abyssinia were again disturbed in 1879. In July it was stated that the treaty of peace between the two countries had never been signed, and that King John had ordered 15,000 men to take possession of various districts. The Egyptian garrisons at the time consisted of 200 men at Massowah and 200 at Sennite; but Colonel Gordon left Khartoom with 3,000 men and twelve cannons for Sennite, as the bearer of a letter from the Khedive to King John. Gordon Pasha was empowered to offer the King the ports of Aith, Duroro, and Tchilioky on the Red Sea, provided he renounced all other claims and concluded a lasting peace with Egypt. In case the King refused, Gordon was to resume the offensive. In September King John wrote to the mercantile firm representing him in London, stating that he had written to Queen Victoria complaining that the outlets of his territory were closed by the Egyptians. He also stated that the English General Kirkham, in his service, was poisoned at Massowah while on his way to England with letters to the Queen.

Colonel Gordon, on arriving in Abyssinian territory at Abba, was received by one of King John's court officials, who gave several entertainments in his honor and detained him a whole week. At Adowah he was received by the King with great pomp and ceremony, and a villa was placed at his disposal, where he lodged at the King's expense. Four days after his arrival he received notice that the King had left for the province of Amhara, where an insurrection had broken out, and would be absent three weeks. The King not having returned at the end of that time, the Egyptian envoy had no alternative but to follow him to Amhara. After his arrival at Debra Tabor in Amhara, Gordon Pasha had two audiences with the King, which led to no result, as the latter argued that without the high dignitaries of the kingdom he could take no important resolution. A fortnight afterward the King returned with Gordon Pasha to Adowah. A grand council was then assembled, but after several sittings they declared that the question of peace or war concerned the King alone, as he knew best what was good for his people. Thereupon the King put forward the following conditions of peace: 1. Restitution to Abyssinia of the coast territory that had been ceded; 2. Departure from those districts of the Mussulman colonists; 3. Restitution of the taxes collected there during the Egyptian occupation, amounting to 50,000,000 francs; 4. Restitution of the Bogos territory; 5. An extensive rectification of frontier in the direction of the Nile; 6. Recognition of King John as Emperor of Abyssinia; 7. The obligation for Egypt not to supply the Mussulmans living south of Abyssinia with arms and ammunition; 8. Suspension of customs dues between the Egyptian town of Zeilah and Abyssinia. These demands Egypt could not grant, and in consequence Gordon Pasha returned to Egypt, arriving in Massowah on December 10th. Military preparations had been going on since the first arrival of the news of the unfavorable reception of the Egyptian envoy by King John, and the latter also prepared himself for war. On December 11th the Abyssinian chiefs of the army of King John, which had assembled on the Egyptian frontier, made their way into the Khedive's territory, and succeeded in levying tribute from his subjects. In an interview with the Khedive, Gordon Pasha said that the King of Abyssinia hated and was hated by all who came in contact with him. Abyssinia, he said, was surrounded on all sides by discontented tribes and rulers. To the eastward, King Menelek of Shoa was sullenly opposing King John, but was afraid to show open hostility; to the south, Rasadall was in almost open rebellion; and in other quarters six or more chiefs were in actual revolt. Placed in this position, Abyssinia could not attack Egypt. If the Khedive would supply the malcontent tribes with arms, the second son of King Theodore would soon be placed on his father's throne.

Upper Egypt was visited during 1879 by a severe famine. A Famine Commissioner, Mr. Baird, was appointed to visit the afflicted localities, to relieve the distress, and report on the causes of the famine. He presented his report in May, representing the condition of the peasants as heart-rending. The peasants, Mr. Baird says, are without capital, steeped in poverty, and wholly dependent on the Nile both for their daily sustenance and the unfailing demands of the tax-collector. The Nile in 1877 was so low that much arable land was left unwatered, and consequently was not cultivated. This disaster was followed by an excessive Nile, which drowned the maize, the local food-crop, and the peasants were left to beg, steal, or starve. The reason of the complete collapse before this temporary calamity is thus explained:

Even in ordinary circumstances the Egyptian peasant leads a life which has little that is attractive to European eyes. His food consists of coarse maize-bread, with beans, lentils, onions, and various weeds. He wears scanty clothing of cotton or rough homespun woolen cloth, and sleeps in a mud hut or in the open air. . . . The worst feature in his life is his chronic state of indebtedness, either to the Government for arrears of taxation or to the merchant who supplies him on credit with seed-corn and corn for his household, to be repaid with exorbitant interest when his crops are ripe. The merchants for the most part are Europeans, and are always ready to make advances to the needy peasant, provided the interest is high enough. The fellah, called upon to pay his taxes at a moment when his crops are still unripe, is compelled to borrow, and is not in a position to wrangle about the interest. For instance, last year, when great pressure was put upon the Egyptian Government to pay the coupon due in May, the peasants were forced to sell their growing crops, and in some cases, perfectly authenticated, corn was sold to the merchants for 50 piasters per ardeb, which was delivered in one month's time and then fetched 120 piasters. These are no exceptional cases; the same thing was going on over the whole of Upper Egypt. . . . At one place, where the market price of maize was 80 piasters, I found the peasants purchasing what they required for their households at 170 piasters on credit.

The famine was clearly caused by the complete absence of any reserve fund on which the peasants could fall back. The usurer and the tax-collector had brought the fellah to a completely hand-to-mouth life. There was plenty of corn in the country, so much that Mr. Baird was able to buy it under market price; and yet, during the months of September, October, November, and December, 1878, some 700,000 people were starving and 10,000 actually died from starvation. Mr. Baird drew the following conclusion from his inquiry:

The famine was a money famine; nobody who had money need starve. The agricultural population are extremely poor and overtaxed. Those who suffered most were women, children, old men, and professional beggars. The relief was sent some months too late. Owing to the good crops this year the famine is almost at an end. Unless something is done to release the people from their constant state of debt, another failure of the crops would produce equally deplorable results.

The condition of the fellahs, however, was greatly improved by the good crops of 1879, and the policy of moderation adopted by the new Government in the collection of the taxes. Unlike former years, when taxes were generally collected a year or two in advance, the tax-collectors this year confined themselves to collecting the taxes remaining unpaid from the previous year, and they received strict orders from the Khedive not to use harsh means in collecting the taxes from the fellahs.

The agricultural condition of Egypt during 1879 was a decided improvement on that of the preceding year. The cotton crop, which in 1878 was unusually small, promised to be doubled this year, amounting to about 9,000,-000 cantars, of the estimated value of £7,500,-000, while the value of the cotton-seed was estimated at £1,500,000. The success of this year's crops was due mainly to the high Nile and the inundations of 1878. In Upper Egypt, the grain and sugar crops were also in a much better condition than in the previous year.

The receipts of the Suez Canal Company in 1878, according to its annual report, were 32,403,611 francs, or about 500,000 francs less than in the preceding year. The expenses had also decreased 560,221 francs, the amount for 1878 being 16,897,750 francs. After the payment of 5 per cent. interest on the shares, there remained a surplus of 3,627,109 francs, of which 71 per cent. went to the shareholders, 15 per cent. to the Egyptian Government, 10 per cent. to founders of the company, and 2 per cent. each to the Board of Directors and the employees. The number of vessels which passed through the canal in 1878 was 1,593, of 3,291,535 tons, against 1,663, of 3,418,949 tons, in 1877. Of the vessels which passed through in 1878, 1,089 were merchant steamers, 282 postal steamers, 75 transport-vessels, 59 tow-boats, 25 sailing vessels, 9 corvettes, 5 gunboats, 4 frigates, 4 ironclads, 14 avisos, and 27 miscellaneous vessels. Of passengers, there were 58,274 troops, 26,170 private citizens, and 11,919 pilgrims.

In June the Government issued a decree, in the face of Oriental superstition, sanctioning a census every decade, the first to be taken in 1880. The reasons given for this step are noteworthy. It will be of service, said the Minister, for the distribution of taxes, for military conscription, and for the labor due to the state on works of public utility. In a minor decree it was also recommended as useful from a statistical point of view.

The Egyptian Government, in accordance with a resolution made some time ago, on January 1, 1879, opened the kingdom of Darfoor to commerce.

MOHAMMED TEVFIK, the new Khedive, was born November 19, 1852. By the firman of 1866, which changed the law of succession in Egypt, he became the heir apparent to the throne. He took but little part in public affairs prior to his appointment as President of the Ministry in 1879. Mr. Edwin de Leon, author of "The Khedive's Egypt," described him as follows in 1878: "I believe the heir apparent, Prince Mohammed Tevfik, has never enjoyed the advantages of foreign travel nor a foreign curriculum, but has been brought up and educated at home. Yet he does credit to his teachers, both as to mind and manners, being one of the most modest and at the same time one of the best-informed young men to be met with anywhere, universally respected as well as liked both by foreigners and by natives, though he shrinks from rather than

courts observation or society. Whether this proceeds from native modesty or from policy, the position he occupies (1878) being a more difficult and delicate one in the East than elsewhere, I am not sufficiently intimate with him to say; but my impression was that the former cause had as much to do with it as the latter. Yet his retiring manner by no means indicates a lack of will or firmness. On the contrary, I should judge he was naturally obstinate. Less politic and plausible than his father, Prince Tevfik impresses you with belief in his sincerity, a quality very clever men are often deficient in. He does not affect the Western air and habits, as do his two brothers, although he wears the Stambouli costume, and is reputed a conscientious though liberal Mussulman in creed and practice. His private character is above reproach. Prince Tevfik is decidedly Oriental both in face and figure, of the Circassian type, with square head, heavy frame, dark eyes and hair, and with something solid and substantial about him. He is the husband of but one wife, the Princess Emineh, daughter of El Hamy Pasha, and has a son, Prince Abbas, born July 14, 1874."

ELECTRIC LIGHT, EDISON'S. The most attractive field for inventive ability of late years is that of electric illumination, a subject which engrosses the attention of the electricians of all countries, who have already produced so many inventions for this purpose, on so many different principles and systems, that the popular mind is bewildered in the attempt to follow them. The development of the electro-magnetic machine by Niardet, Wilde, Brush, Fuller, and many other inventors, but especially through the improvements of Gramme and Siemens, seemed to place the electric light, if not the electric motor also, almost within reach, so economically can electric currents be produced by the modern mechanical generators. The important discovery of the divisibility of the electric current for the production of the voltaic arc between carbon-points by Jablochkoff made possible for the first time an electric light of real practical value—one which has been applied with the highest degree of success where an exceedingly brilliant, colorless, and steady light is desired; but the cost of production, the attention which the apparatus requires, the consumption of the carbon-candles, and the limitations to the subdivision render it unsuitable for purposes of general illumination. The Jablochkoff candle and the other systems of illumination by the voltaic arc, devised by Carré, Foucault, Serrin and Lontin, Rapieff, and Werdermann, were described in the article ELECTRIC LIGHT in the Annual "Cyclopædia" for the year 1878. In the same place the generation of electrical currents by the magneto-electric battery is described at length, with the most recent improvements in mechanical generators.

When it was known that Edison, whose genius has enriched the world with so many important applications of electricity—with duplex, quadruplex, and quite recently sextuplex telegraphy; with the electric pen; with some of the best forms of the telephone and its various modifications, as the microphone, the microtasimeter, the megaphone, the aërophone, the phonometer; with the phonograph (see biography of THOMAS ALVA EDISON, in "Annual Cyclopædia" for 1878)—when it was reported that this indefatigable experimenter and versatile inventor had turned his attention to the problem of electric illumination, the public expected that his fertile and practical mind would succeed if it were possible in overcoming the minor but stubborn difficulties which yet stood in the way of electrical illumination. The confidence which was felt in his ability is shown by the fact that during the months in which he was engaged in studying this subject, newspaper rumors of the success or non-success of his laboratory studies made the prices of gas-stock rise or fall on the Paris and London Exchanges. He commenced his experiments in September, 1878, and, after fifteen months of research, in the latter part of December, 1879, he published the record of his investigations to the world, and gave a public trial of the elaborated result.

Divining that the practical electric light of moderate illuminating power could not be produced by the voltaic arc, to which recent experiments have been chiefly confined, and with which Jablochkoff, Serrin, Werdermann, and others have obtained remarkable results, but by the incandescence of some resistant material, he confined his attention to the substances of low conducting powers from which the incandescent light can be obtained. These are platinum, iridium, and like metals and alloys, which only fuse at an exceedingly high temperature, and the forms of carbon which possess a high degree of purity and homogeneity. His earlier experiments were expended upon metallic material. Considering that the incandescence of the metal is the greater, the stronger the electrical current to which it is subjected, he directed his thoughts first to the invention of a regulating apparatus which would automatically break off the current when the temperature of the metal approaches the point of fusion. Constructing a lamp with a double platinum spiral as the incandescent conductor, he inserted within the spiral a platinum rod connected with a lever, one end of which is connected with the wire which conducts the current to the platinum spiral, and the other end of which is a circuit-closer, which being lowered closes the circuit with the wire which conducts off the current, causing it to pass through the lever and deflecting it from the incandescent platinum conductor. The expansion of the platinum rod by the heat presses down the end of this lever, forming the necessary continuous metallic connection, and closing the circuit below, but only momentarily, since the lowering of the temperature of the

spiral instantly causes the rod to contract, breaking the new circuit until the heat of the spiral again rises to the dangerous point. This device was, however, found to be untrustworthy after a certain period of use, the pressure of the rod upon the lever after a while bending it out of shape. Among the other circuit-closing regulators which he devised was one by which the heated air pressed a diaphragm outward, closing and breaking the circuit so rapidly that no variation in the intensity of the light was observable. Another was a device by which the expansion of the luminous conductor itself was made to draw a rod upward, which actuated a circuit-closer through an arrangement of levers. Edison developed in the earlier stages of his investigations a novel kind of lamp, from which he obtained a very brilliant light by the incandescence of a piece of zircon to which the heat-rays of the incandescent platinum spiral were transmitted by reflection. The spiral of platinum and iridium was placed in the focus of an elliptic reflector of copper coated with gold, and the heat-rays were focalized upon a thin piece of zircon, which attained a degree of luminosity greatly exceeding that of the incandescent platinum.

Edison's experiments were necessarily directed mainly to the material to be rendered incandescent, and the form in which it will afford the best results. The brilliancy of the light depends upon the resistance which the incandescent conductor offers to the passage of the electric current. Expecting the best results from platinum, he found that the light was intensified by incorporating fine particles of this conducting agent in a non-conducting, incombustible, and non-fusible material, which was itself rendered luminous by the heat. By imbedding finely divided platinum in a non-conducting substance, he obtained a light from currents too weak to render the spiral luminous. A large spiral of platinum whose coils were coated and separated by magnesia produced a good light; it was with this form of lamp that he employed the regulator in which a metallic cup at the top of the coil pulled a rod upward, actuating a circuit-closing apparatus. Among the other materials upon which he experimented were the oxides of different metals. He obtained a fine light from iridosmine, a natural alloy of osmium and iridium, which he inclosed in a powdered state in a tube of zircon. He tried also a combination of platinum and carbon, the latter becoming highly incandescent as the current passed to it from the platinum rod, encountering a greater resistance.

Still considering platinum the most promising material, he was startled after a couple of months of experimentation by the discovery that the platinum degenerated, and that its incandescence was seriously affected through the action of the atmosphere. Plates and wires of platinum, and also of iridium and other metallic conductors whose point of fusion is at a very high temperature, he found, when heated while exposed to the atmosphere to a temperature near their melting-point, by a current of electricity passing through them for a number of hours together, crack and break in innumerable places. These fissures are found under the microscope all over the surface of the metal, running in every direction, and sometimes penetrating to the center of the rod or wire. Holding platinum and alloys of platinum and iridium in the heat of a candle, he observed a loss of weight; and even when they are exposed to heated air there is a diminution of weight. The consumption is sufficient to cause a hydrogen jet to take on a greenish hue. The metal after a while becomes so fractured that it falls to pieces. He thus perceived that the ordinary platinum or platinum and iridium, as sold in the market, is useless for his purpose, and also that the metal can not be employed for illumination by incandescence, as the cracks cause it gradually to deteriorate and eventually destroy it, while they greatly lessen the degree of incandescence of which its surface is capable. The knowledge of the cause of the disintegration of platinum suggested the remedy. Lodyguine, the Russian physicist, invented a carbon-lamp in 1873, in which the cracking and wasting away of the carbon under incandescence, by the action of the oxygen of the atmosphere, was obviated by inclosing the burner in a glass globe from which the air was exhausted. It was necessary to purify the platinum and inclose it in a vacuum to prevent its deterioration when heated to incandescence. Edison devised a method of producing a more perfect vacuum, and at the same time cleansing the platinum burner of all the air and other gases which it contains. A glass globe is connected by an aperture with a mercury air-pump, and the air exhausted. The wires connecting the spiral or other form of burner with the battery pass through holes in the glass which are fused together and hermetically sealed. After the air is exhausted from the glass the current is turned on, heating the platinum to a temperature of about 150° F., at which point it is kept for from ten to fifteen minutes. The gases which issue from the platinum are carried away by the air-pump. The current is then increased until the temperature rises to 300°, at which point it is kept again ten or fifteen minutes. It is thus raised by successive stages until the platinum attains a brilliant incandescence, and the glass about the aperture connecting with the mercury pump melts with the heat and fuses together, hermetically sealing the vacuum. The wires purified by this process are found to have a gloss and brightness greater than that of silver. Their light-giving power is increased in a remarkable ratio. The same burner which will give when new a light of only three candles, emits in the vacuum a light of twenty-five. Testing spirals which had been prepared and sealed in a glass vacuum in this manner by subjecting them to sudden currents of electricity which raised them to incandescence a great number of times, no cracks

or breaks were discoverable, nor the slightest loss of weight. Wires of chemically pure iron and nickel were found to give a light in the vacuum equal to that of platinum exposed to the atmosphere; and carbon-sticks, freed from air and inclosed in a vacuum in the same manner, may be heated until they become soft and plastic, and then regain their former consistency when cool again. Edison next tried the combination of platinum and iridium alloy with magnesia in the vacuum. He found that the oxide will unite with the metal, hardening it and rendering it more refractory to such a degree that a spiral so fine that it would melt without the coating of magnesia could be raised to a dazzling incandescence and remain quite elastic. Such a spiral, with a surface of only three-sixteenths of an inch, will give a light of forty candles. He next turned his attention to securing the greatest possible amount of resistance in the conductor. Instead of using lamps of only one or two ohms of resistance, he reached the conclusion that the light could be more economically produced from conductors having two hundred ohms of resistance or more.

The perfected form of the platinum lamp consists of a long coil of wire coated with magnesia, supported in a glass vacuum tube by a rod of platinum, the tube resting upon a metallic frame containing a regulating apparatus in a chamber within. The conducting wires pass through the bottom of the globe and into this chamber, where the circuit can be instantaneously broken and closed again by the regulator. Around the vacuum tube is a glass globe resting upon the frame, with openings into an aneroid chamber below, whose bottom is a diaphragm which distends sufficiently when the air within the globe is heated to a certain degree to press a pin in its center downward against a straight spring, which rests with an upward pressure upon a metallic block, through which the current is transmitted through the spring to the wire which leads it to the incandescent spiral. When the contact between the spring and the block is broken, the flow of electricity is interrupted, to be restored again by the immediate cooling and contraction of the air in the globe and aneroid chamber, which is so instantaneous that no variation in the intensity of the light is perceptible. While bringing the platinum lamp to this high state of perfection, Edison set on foot inquiries regarding a larger supply of platinum; and the miners of the gold regions, incited by his advertisements, discovered such frequent indications of its presence that this exceedingly valuable metal may be expected to be produced in much larger quantities than the present supplies. The vacuum which Edison's method produced was much nearer perfect than had been before attained. One of the reasons for the want of success of lamps in which the light was produced by the incandescence of carbon in a vacuum was the impossibility of sufficiently exhausting the air in the glass chamber. By the present process it could be reduced to but little over one millionth of an atmosphere.

The inventor thought that he had elaborated a lamp which embodied the best principles, and which was sure to prove a commercial success. He had introduced improvements in the electric machine by which the equivalent of about 90 per cent. of the power expended was returned in electricity. When he was nearly ready to give the lamp in this form to the world, he began, led partly by accident, to experiment with carbon, with results which induced him to alter his whole system and adopt a carbon instead of a metallic burner. A prominent cause for the failure of carbon burners had been the impossibility of obtaining a form of carbon sufficiently pure in substance and homogeneous and even in texture. Edison was encouraged to try new forms from obtaining a remarkably brilliant light in the vacuum by the incandescence of a piece of calcined cotton thread. He placed in the glass a thread of ordinary sewing-cotton, which had been placed in a groove between two blocks of iron and charred by long exposure in a furnace, exhausted the air, and sealed the tube. He then turned on the electrical current, and increased it until the most intense incandescence was obtained before the slight filament broke. Examining then the fragments under the microscope, he found that the fragile substance had hardened under the excessive heat, and that its surface had become smooth and glossy. This led him into a long series of experiments with carbon. After carbonizing and testing a great variety of fibrous substances, he found that paper yielded the most satisfactory results. The burner on which he finally settled was made from Bristol cardboard in the form of a tiny horseshoe. Strips about two inches long and an eighth of an inch wide, curved in the shape of an elongated horseshoe, are struck from a sheet of cardboard, and a number of them laid one upon another, with pieces of tissue-paper between, in an iron mold; this is tightly closed and placed in an oven, which is gradually raised to a temperature of 600°; the mold is next placed in a furnace and allowed to come to a white heat, and then removed and left to cool. The carbonized paper horseshoe (F) is then taken out with the utmost care, mounted in a diminutive glass globe, and connected with the wires. The air is then pumped out and the glass hermetically closed. The form of the lamp is a small bulb-shaped glass vacuum (A), globular above, with an elongated end resting upon a standard (B), through which the wires leading to and from the generator pass, connecting with thin platinum wires (E, E′) which penetrate the thick end of the glass; to these the carbon burner is attached by clasps made from the same metal (G, G′). No regulating apparatus is attached to the lamp, as the current can be regulated at the central station where the electricity is generated.

The inventor has developed a method by which the currents can be cut off from any of the lamps and the lights extinguished, without

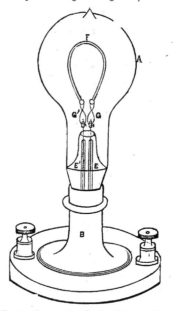

affecting the supply of electricity to those which are left burning. He proposes to supply the electricity in cities for lighting the houses and public places, from stations in which a number of electric machines adequate for supplying an area of about a third of a square mile are driven by one or two powerful steam-engines. Each generator is capable of supplying about fifty burners. The wires conducting the electricity from the central station into the houses can be led through the gas mains and pipes, and the burners attached to ordinary gas-fixtures with little labor and expense. The amount of electricity supplied in each household is measured and recorded by an ingenious but simple device. The electrometer, which like a gas-meter may be placed in any part of a house and connected with any number of burners, consists of an electrolytic cell and a small coil of wire. The passage of electricity causes the deposit on a small plate in the electrolytic cell of particles of copper. The weight of this deposit indicates the amount of electricity which has passed through the meter during any period. The apparatus takes up about half the space of an ordinary gas-meter.

The generating machine devised by Edison consists of a magnet composed of two upright iron columns, three feet and eight inches in height, wound with coarse wire and resting upon blocks, which form the magnetic poles. These are made in such a way as to nearly inclose a wooden armature of cylindrical form, wound lengthwise with coarse wire, which is revolved on its axis with great rapidity between the poles of the magnet, which nearly clasp it about. Springs resting upon a metallic portion of the revolving cylinder convey to the conducting wires the electricity which is generated in the wires, which run around the wooden cylinder parallel to its axis.

The system adopted by Edison dates from an invention patented by Edward A. King of London, for obtaining a light from the incandescence of either platinum or carbon. It had before been observed that a thin wire interposed in an electrical current became heated, and that the heat generated was proportionate to the degree of resistance of the metal. Children showed that an electric current passed through a chain composed of silver and platinum in alternate links, caused the metal of low conductivity to be heated to a bright glow, while the silver links remained dark and cool. King's attempt to utilize this property of substances of high electrical resistance was with a strip of platinum leaf or piece of carbon leaf between conductors, and rendered luminous by a properly regulated current within a glass globe which protected the incandescent substance from air-currents. In 1849 Petrie obtained a fine light from the incandescence of iridium or one of its alloys. In Lodyguine's lamp, in which the light was obtained from carbon rendered incandescent *in vacuo*, one part of the carbon rod was made thinner than the rest; and the thin portion was that which became incandescent, as the electrical resistance was greater here than elsewhere. This renewed attempt to obtain a practical light by incandescence was made long after the labors of King and the other preceding inventors were forgotten, and obtained for Lodyguine the Lomonosoff prize from the St. Petersburg Academy of Sciences. Konn of St. Petersburg devised and patented, in 1875, a lamp in which several carbon rods were held in reserve to replace the incandescent rods automatically as they were consumed. Even in an exhausted chamber it was found that the carbon wasted away: Another Russian inventor, Bouliguine, devised a lamp in which a single rod of carbon was used; it was made of great length, and the lamp was so constructed that this rod was pushed gradually upward through a tubular holder, the portion exposed at the top of the tube alone becoming incandescent, as this part was firmly held between conical jaws of carbon which allowed a free passage to the electricity.

The form of carbon used in Sir Humphry Davy's electric light was ordinary wood-char-coal. In 1844 Léon Foucault substituted that variety of carbonaceous matter which is deposited in the interior of gas-retorts, and which bears the name of gas-graphite. It is produced by the decomposition of dense hydrocarbons at a very high temperature. It is deposited in layers on the walls of the retorts during the manufacture of coal-gas. It is of a very hard texture, and when sawn into rods or pencils is better adapted to electric lighting than the less dense forms of carbon, like wood-charcoal, being much more durable. It has, however, some serious defects. It varies in its compactness and texture, and with the variations in its density the light obtained from it fluctuates in brightness. Many have attempted before Edison to obtain a carbon of a more perfectly homogeneous texture. Carré and Gaudoin in France have attained a tolerable degree of success in producing carbon of greater homogeneity by artificial processes.

ENGELHARD, JOSEPH ADOLPHUS, was born at Monticello, Mississippi, September 27, 1832, and died at Raleigh, North Carolina, February 17, 1879. His school-days were spent in Mississippi and New Albany, Indiana (principally at the latter place), whence he went to Chapel Hill, North Carolina, in 1850, and graduated in 1854. He studied law first at Harvard, then at Chapel Hill, under Judge Battle, afterward with Judge Fowle, and was licensed to practice in the County Courts in 1856, and in the Superior Courts in 1857, locating in Tarboro, where he remained until the breaking out of the war. In May, 1861, he entered the military service of the State as captain and quartermaster of the 33d regiment. In April, 1862, he was promoted to be major and quartermaster of the brigade of General Branch, and in December of that year was transferred to General Pender's brigade as its adjutant-general. In May, 1863, he became the adjutant-general of Pender's division, afterward Wilcox's division, in which capacity he remained until the surrender at Appomattox Court House. In 1865 he became interested in the "Wilmington Journal," and its editor. In recognition of his services in this position his party nominated him for Secretary of State at the last election. He was elected, and in discharge of the duties of the office at the commencement of his fatal sickness.

ENGINEERING. If one half of the great engineering undertakings which are now seriously proposed, and demonstrated by more or less exact calculations to be feasible, were, by a happy unanimity of private and national will and action, to be carried into effect, then for a generation or two to come all the labor and productive energy of civilized nations would find full scope and employment, and changes would be wrought in the face of nature of greater magnitude than all the physical transformations which human skill has accomplished from the beginning of man's life on the planet. There must be a great future for an art whose professors offer in sober earnestness to achieve physical miracles the possibility of which in the nearest past was not yet dreamed of. These schemes aim at nothing less than to alter the form of continents and modify the character of climates; to create navigable channels across the bosom of continents, and to burrow dry paths underneath the surging tide of the sea; to turn parching deserts into watery gulfs, and to join a landlocked sea to the ocean system by a rushing artificial river. It is most likely that none of these ambitious projects will be carried out in the early future.

Captain Roudaire's scheme of flooding a portion of the Desert of Sahara with the waters of the Mediterranean is still advanced as a project which presents no extraordinary engineering difficulties, and which will produce a radical improvement in the climate and soil of the surrounding country. A similar plan is warmly advocated by General Fremont for reclaiming a portion of the desert land of the great West. By making two cuttings leading in from the Gulf of California, it is believed that the depression of the alkali desert will be submerged, giving a sea-coast to Arizona and changing the arid region around into smiling corn-fields. The now almost completed St. Gothard Tunnel does not seem to invite the restless spirit of modern enterprise to repose; for a scheme for a still longer tunnel under the Simplon Pass is being pressed, while some propose to bore a passage directly through the mass of Mont Blanc. The improvements in tunneling processes, and the accomplishment of longer and longer bores through all kinds of rock, render the proposal of a tunnel for the passage of masted vessels under the mountains of Panama only a question of stock subscriptions and profits, and deprive of its extravagant or visionary character the scheme of carrying a railway under the British Channel. The engineers are still groping in the chalk ledges under the Straits of Dover for the shortest and best course for the projected tunnel. The air is so full of schemes for new ship-canals and harbor-excavations that the actual progress from year to year in these most important requisites of commercial development is apt to be lost sight of. The modern engineer can make a harbor where none exists, and, with titanic walls against which the tempestuous ocean-surges boom and beat and are broken, he marks his line and compels the sweeping tide to obey the command of thus far and no farther. He can also hollow deep, long channels in the underlying rock, and float the laden sea-craft on the tidal waters within the walls of inland cities. Paris and St. Petersburg are thus to be made seaports. The long-projected scheme of an American inter-oceanic canal will in a few years be an accomplished fact, unless the still more startling but demonstrably less difficult project of a ship railway approves itself a commercial venture of better promise. Ship-canals are pro-

posed in the United States through the States of Maryland and Delaware, to connect navigable waters. A more important project is being considered in Canada for a ship-canal to connect Lake Huron and Lake Ontario, which would greatly shorten the distance between the northwestern wheat-lands and Liverpool, and reduce the cost of transport. The successful construction of bridges across the broad estuaries of the Tay and the Severn, which are to be followed by one across the Frith of Forth, and the sinking of their massive cylindrical piers in the midst of tremendous tidal currents, encourage the belief that the scheme, recently broached by Vérard de Sainte-Anne, of a colossal viaduct across the English Channel from Cape Grisnez to Folkestone, may some day be realized. The enormous public works projected in France by M. de Freycinet seem to meet with public approval, and will probably receive legislative sanction in their entirety. His schemes for railway and canal extension and harbor improvement involve the labor of many years and the expenditure of thousands of millions. The railway network is to be developed beyond that of any other country. A great number of light or narrow-gauge roads are to be constructed as feeders to the main lines. An improvement which is urgently called for by the French public is a ship-canal through the north of France, from Oreil-sur-Oise to Beauvais, Amiens, and Albert, with two large branches.

The completion of the great Severn railway bridge, over the estuary of the Severn at Lydney, supplies a link whose want has long been felt in the railway communications of England. The only means of intercommunication for the inhabitants of the districts separated by the Severn River, below Gloucester, has been the irregular and dangerous passage by ferry-boats. The new Severn Bridge Railway furnishes the desiderated connection, and affords an outlet for the iron-ore and coal-production of the Forest of Dean and South Wales, allowing of their easy transshipment from the cars to vessels in the Gloucester and Berkeley Canal. The scheme of this bridge and railway was conceived by G. W. Keeling, who while engaged in a survey of the river in 1859 came to the conclusion that the best and most economical site for a bridge was at this point, where the channel never varies, and where firm foundations are found at no great depth. Several other projects for bridges to meet the pressing demand for communication were advanced and subsequently abandoned, two of them after receiving the authorization of Parliament. Mr. Keeling, in conjunction with G. W. Owen, brought forward the project for the present bridge in 1870; but it was not until 1872 that it attracted sufficient financial support and was authorized by Parliament. The plan, as now carried out, consists of a railroad about five miles long connecting with the Severn and

Wye and the Great Western Railways at Lydney, crossing the river on a bridge three quarters of a mile long, and terminating at the Sharpness Docks, where it forms a junction with the Midland Railway. After much delay, owing to conflicting pecuniary interests, the works were commenced in 1875. The construction of the bridge has taken four years. Its total cost was £200,000; the railway and approaches, including a tunnel a quarter of a mile long on the Lydney side, cost an equal amount. The total length of the bridge is 4,162 feet. The width of the river at the crossing is 3,558 feet. The bridge is in 35 spans. On the Lydney shore 13 of the spans are arches of heavy hammer-dressed stone, 12 of them semicircular, and one elliptical with a span of 52 feet. They rest in alluvial deposit on foundations of concrete. In the river the spans are bow-string girders. One of these forms a swing-bridge on the opposite side, hanging half over the canal and half over the shore. The length of the swing-bridge is 197 feet, the depth of its girders 19 feet 4 inches; the bridge weighs 500 tons, and turns on an arrangement of conical rollers called a live ring, being carried upon a circular pier of strong masonry. The motive power is supplied by a steam-engine in an engine-house resting on the top of the girders, which contains also a reserve engine connected with reserve machinery to provide for any accidental stoppage of the regular machinery. The turning and locking are accomplished by friction-gearing so arranged that the turning and locking apparatus can never be in gear at the same time. The locking is accomplished by two large iron wedges at each end of the bridge, which are driven home in opposite directions by rods connected by toggle-joints with great iron bars, which advance longitudinally with the bridge, and, extending beyond the wedges, enter sockets in the piers, thus trimming the rails. An indicator in the engine-house, which shows the engineer the position of the wedges, also serves to break the telegraphic connection, so that the bridgeman can not signal a train to advance unless the bridge is in position and locked. Besides the swing-span, the iron part of the bridge consists of 21 spans. The first span, adjoining the masonry on the Lydney side, is 134 feet long, with girders 16 feet deep. This carries the bridge to the edge of the deep channel of the river. Then the two main spans, 327 feet long, with girders 39 feet deep, carry it over the navigable river at a clear height of 70 feet above high water. The next five spans are 171 feet long, with girders 20 feet 4 inches deep; the last 13, 134 feet long, with girders of 16 feet 9 inches. The elevation gradually decreases from 70 feet over the main channel, near the north side, to 50 feet in the clear over the water at the swing-bridge on the Sharpness side. All the girders are on the bow-string principle; the curved boom has a trough section; the tension-chord is composed of flat

bars riveted together; the vertical compression-joints in the side of the girders are 12 feet apart, and are connected with the cross-gird. ers, to which the strong rail-bearers are also riveted. The floor is composed of wrought-iron plates riveted to the cross-girders and the rail-bearers. The swing-span is 24 feet 6 inches wide in the clear; the other spans of the bridge are adapted only for a single track, being 14 feet 6 inches in width. The piers which support the bridge are composed of cast-iron cylinders, 6 to 10 feet in diameter. They were made in 4-foot sections, and bolted together through flanges on the inside. They were sunk to a solid foundation, penetrating the bottom rock from 4 to 15 feet. The cylinders which compose the piers are of cast iron, 1¼ to 1½ inch thick. The piers which support the two main spans are formed by four cylinders each, 10 feet in diameter below low water and 7 feet in diameter above; the diameter of the cylinders supporting the five 171-foot spans is 9 feet below and 7 feet above low-tide mark; the remaining piers have a uniform diameter of 6 feet. The piers are composed of two cylinders each, except the three supporting the two long spans. The greatest difficulties were encountered in fastening the scaffolding for the piers and the girders. Beginning to sink the piers on the south side, it was possible to excavate from the interior of the cylinders until the twelfth pier was reached, after which compressed air was employed. From this point, after many unsuccessful attempts to sink the scaffold-piles in the shifting sand, with the strong tide bearing down upon them, the problem was finally solved by the use of Brunlees's system of sinking piles in sand; that is, by carrying a gas-pipe down to the foot of the pile, and forcing a stream of water through it strong enough to displace the sand and allow the pile to sink. While placing the fourteenth and fifteenth piers, the staging and cylinders were swept away together by the tide. Equal difficulties were overcome in sinking the remaining piers. In the channel, with the tide 30 feet high and flowing 10 knots an hour, and a depth from high water to bed-rock of 70 feet, the task seemed almost impossible to accomplish. The sand was scoured away here so that only a few feet remained; but fortunately there was a layer of firm gravelly clay over the rock, which gave the piles of the gigantic scaffolding a firm hold. The staging was swept away once or twice ere it could be secured. When in place the 4-foot lengths of the cylinders were lowered by screws and chains, and excavation was carried on inside them by divers. They were then built up to 12 feet above high water, and until they would sink no deeper in the sand. The air-compressing apparatus by which the piers were sunk to their foundations was in the shape of a bell, and was bolted to the top of the cylinders, and provided with air-locks for the entrance of the workmen; the pressure was from 5 to 40 lbs., the latter pressure allowing the deepest piers to be sunk 4 feet into the bed-rock. The piers, when being lowered were loaded with 150 lbs. of ballast, and when in place were filled up solid with concrete. The swiftness of the currents and the great rise of the tide prevented the ordinary method of floating out the girders and hoisting them upon the piers from being employed. They had, therefore, to be fitted together on the spot by the costly and primitive method of working from scaffolds. The engineers were George W. Keeling and George Wells Owen, with the consulting engineer, Thomas K. Harrison. The amount of iron used in the construction of the bridge was 7,000 tons. The formal opening took place on the 17th of October, 1879.

The longest bridge in Europe will be the bridge now building over the Volga River on the Siberian Railroad in the government of Samara, Russia. The river at the point crossed by the bridge is 4 miles wide in the spring of the year, and 4,732 feet wide in the autumn. The part of the bridge which overhangs the permanent channel will rest on 12 piers, 85 feet high, and placed at the distance from each other of 364 feet. The estimated cost of the entire structure is $3,500,000. Each pier is guarded by an ice-cutter faced with granite, 35 feet high. Two thousand men are employed in the construction of this colossal work, which will be completed some time in 1880.

Within the last dozen years American bridge-builders have been carrying into practice bolder and bolder plans, and have erected works which far surpass in magnitude anything attempted formerly. Such are Linville's swing-bridge at Raritan, which turns on a column of masonry, and has a length of 472 feet; the Rock Island swing-bridge, designed by C. Shaler Smith, which weighs 750 tons; and bridges with draw-spans of over 360 feet on the Mississippi. Such are the great channel span over the Ohio in the new Cincinnati bridge, which was also designed by Mr. Linville, and which is 520 feet long, and the main spans of 300 to 400 feet in four other bridges on the Ohio. Besides these extensive works, which adhere to the ordinary types of construction, entirely new forms have been developed for the achievement of engineering tasks of even greater magnitude. Such are the steel-ribbed arches for the St. Louis bridge, whose three spans are each about 500 feet in length; such the stiffened suspension bridge at Pittsburgh; and such the Brooklyn suspension bridge with its steel-wire chords, its masonry anchorage, and clear span of 1,600 feet.

Both in Europe and America steel is coming into favor as a material for bridges. The adaptability of steel for bridge construction is much questioned by some engineers. The sudden breakage of pieces of steel of a warranted high degree of tensile strength, and the fact that different bars of high carbon steel, made from the same materials by the same process, will differ in strength and elasticity, add an element of danger and uncertainty to the employment of steel for bridges which is not encouraging. Other engineers entertain no doubts or fears, and would proceed at once to substitute steel for iron in bridge-making. If there is any such uncertainty in the strength and quality of steel, it can doubtless be removed by improvements in the process of the manufacture. The construction of a bridge built entirely of steel, for the Chicago and Alton Railroad, over the Missouri River at Glasgow, Mo., marks a new departure in American bridge-building. The bridge was designed by D. D. Smith, who carried on experiments for several years in the commission of the United States Government on the relative strength of iron and steel. The project for this bridge is the result of the conclusion, to which his researches led him, that steel bridges equal to iron in durability can be constructed at a smaller cost. The bridge has five spans of 314⅞ feet each. Its elevation is 50 feet above high-water mark. The quantity of steel used in the whole structure was 1,500 tons, equal in strength to nearly double that weight of iron. The girders are of the Howe truss pattern. The structure, held and braced in mid-air by slender steel rods, presents a very frail and slight appearance, yet it is able to bear a load which few iron bridges could support. Three of the spans are above the grade of the road, and two below. The depth of the trusses is 36 feet from center to center of the pins. The length of the steel bridge is 1,573¼ feet. Including an iron trestle 210 feet long, and two deck-spans of iron 140 feet each in the east approach, and an iron trestle 510 feet long and wooden trestle 864 feet long in the west approach, the total length of the bridge is 3,577¼ feet.

In the Soodan Railway, which is to connect Wady Halfa, at the second cataract, with Khartoom, and thus bring the regions of equatorial Africa into railroad communication with the Mediterranean, the most important engineering task, the building of an iron bridge over the Nile at Kohé, will soon be completed. The contractors are Appleby Brothers, of Greenwich, England; the designs have been drawn by the well-known engineer, John Fowler. The point at which the railroad, whose gauge is 3 feet 6 inches, is to be carried over the Nile, is 1,170 miles above Alexandria, and 750 miles below the confluence of the White and Blue Niles. The length of this railroad from Wady Halfa to the terminus, Khartoom, which is the chief emporium for the products of Central Africa, is 560 miles; the distance between the two places by river is 910 miles. The construction of the bridge involves no engineering difficulties except such as result from the distance of the site from civilization. The volume of water passing here is even greater than it is at Kasr-el-Nil, 1,000 miles below, so much is lost by evaporation and absorption, and so much is drawn off for irrigation purposes. Yet, owing to the gentle flow of the river—which at low Nile, with a discharge of 800 cubic metres a second, is seven eighths of a mile, and at high Nile, when the discharge is 14,000 feet a second, becomes 4¾ miles per hour—the works required are very light. Owing to a bend in the river at this point, there is slack water for nearly the whole breadth of the river, where the bottom is sandy; and where the current passes near the left bank a rocky foundation is found. The bridge will consist of 16 spans of 20 metres each, supported on cast-iron piles filled with concrete, 6 spans resting on screw-piles, and a continuous girder-bridge with two central spans of 50 metres and two side spans of 39 metres, resting on four pairs of cylinders filled with concrete. The deep portion of the river is crossed by two continuous girders, which are of the lattice type and single-webbed, with deep trusses for cross-girders. The weight of the superstructure of the four large spans is 236 tons, and that of the twenty-two small spans 254 tons. In the piers 600 tons of iron are used, and in the caissons 200 tons.

A new interoceanic railroad is being constructed in Mexico. Edward Learned of Pittsfield, Massachusetts, has obtained for this purpose a land grant from the Mexican Government, together with the complete control of the harbor at the mouth of the Coatzacoalcos River and of the lakes on the Pacific side. The railroad is pushed forward with energy, laborers and engineers having been sent to the spot immediately, and supplies shipped on from Galveston and other places. The work is expected to be completed in three years. The road starts from the harbor, and will terminate at the Upper Lagoon on the Pacific shore, its length being 90 to 100 miles. The creation of a new harbor at Coatzacoalcos is an important consideration to the Government at Mexico, as the harbor at Vera Cruz is rapidly being sanded and will soon be worthless. The mouth of the Coatzacoalcos River where the railroad commences is 110 miles southeast of Vera Cruz. The company is bound to complete annually, to the satisfaction of the Government, 39 miles of road. . The track, of 4½ feet gauge, may be either single or double. The path of this road across the Isthmus of Tehuantepec has easy grades and contains no serious natural obstacles; the climate is wholesome and temperate, and the country rich in natural productions. The maximum estimate of cost is $5,500,000. This route, it is claimed, has substantial advantages over all other lines of communication between the Atlantic and Pacific seaports.

The Canadian Government proposes to expend $5,000,000 per annum, which is to be raised on bonds, on the Pacific Railway, and to keep the road built after the present year fifty miles in advance of the settlements. For the distance between the head of Lake Superior and Lake Winnipeg the road has been nearly completed; contracts have been awarded

for a stretch of 100 miles beyond Winnipeg; and funds are in hand for 200 miles more. It is expected, therefore, that these 700 miles of railroad beyond Lake Superior will be completed within two years. Fifty or sixty thousand tons of steel rails have lately been purchased in England for this purpose.

The foundation-stone of the new Eddystone Lighthouse, now constructing under the management of John N. Douglass, was laid by the Duke of Edinburgh on the 21st of June, 1879. The plan of the new structure is essentially the same with regard to its general form as that of Smeaton's lighthouse, and is described by the engineer as a concave elliptic frustum, the generating curve of which has a semi-transverse axis of 178 feet and a semi-conjugate axis of 87 feet. While the old tower was built of granite for the outside walls and with blocks of Portland stone for the interior, the new one will be constructed entirely of granite, which is of a quality superior to that used before. The dimensions and illuminating range of the new lighthouse exceed considerably those of the old one: instead of a base of 32 feet and a light 72 feet above high water, with a range of 14 nautical miles, the new tower will have a base 44 feet in diameter, the focal plane of its light will be 130 feet above high water, and its range of illumination 17 nautical miles. The old tower contained four rooms besides the lantern, each 12½ feet in diameter; the new one will have nine rooms, not counting the lantern, the seven uppermost chambers having a diameter of 14 feet. The stone used in the construction of Smeaton's column was 13,343 cubic feet; for the new tower 69,100 feet will be required. Smeaton was the inventor of the process of dovetailing stone, and the ingenuity which he applied to the adapting and fitting of the blocks in the lighthouse was the especial feature which made it the wonder of the age; still he required 636 stone joggles, 1,800 oak treenails, 4,570 pairs of oak wedges, 8 circular floor-chains, and 226 iron clamps, to join and fit the blocks. In the new structure, such improvements have been made upon his system of dovetailing, and such still greater superiority do the modern quick-setting cements possess for hydraulic work over the blue lias and pozzolana lime of Smeaton's day, that no treenailing, joggling, nor other such appliances are used in the new tower, except some composition-metal bolts, slit and wedged at both ends, for anchoring down the foundation - stones. The latest method of dovetailing, invented by Nicholas Douglass, is described as consisting "in having a raised dovetailed band, 3 inches in height, on the top bed and one end-joint of every stone. A corresponding dovetailed recess is cut in the bottom bed and end-joint of the adjoining stones, with just sufficient clearance for the raised band to enter it freely in setting. The work which is cut and fitted in this manner and set in Portland cement is as firm and solid as though it were continuous granite. While

Smeaton had to employ sailing craft to convey his material from Milbray to the rock, which sometimes in unfavorable weather could not approach the rock for days together, the material for the new structure is brought to Eddystone in a twin-screw steamer, whose load is 120 tons, which makes the passage from Oreston in a little more than an hour; the stones are loaded and unloaded by means of a pair of double-barrel steam-winches, and are raised into position by another winch on the rock. The machinery of the steamer also serves to pump out the water from the foundation at every tide. The rock-drill used in excavating the foundations can do as much work in an hour as ten of Smeaton's Cornish tinners with their jumpers. By comparing the time required in completing Smeaton's Eddystone Lighthouse with that spent on the Wolf Lighthouse, built in 1869, it appears that it took Smeaton six and a half times as long to accomplish a given amount of labor as it takes an engineer of the present day. The most important advances, however, which have been made in lighthouse engineering since Smeaton's day, are in the illuminating facilities. The old lantern was of the square type, with heavy sash-bars which intercepted nearly half of the light. Until quite lately this kind of lantern was still in use in the lighthouse service of the United States. Considerable improvements were made from the use of inclined framing and other expedients for obviating the obstruction of the frame, by Stevenson and Walker, and in 1864 the type of lantern now universally adopted in British lighthouses was invented; this is the helically framed lantern, which, besides being optically perfect and possessing a maximum of strength, casts no shadow which is distinguishable at a distance of over a hundred feet. The 24 tallow candles, of 67-candle power, which were first used in Smeaton's tower, are now replaced by the 4-wick Trinity House lamp with an illuminating power of 7,325 standard candles, and in the new tower still stronger illumination can be used.

An iron pier constructed by the Ocean Navigation and Pier Company, of which Jacob Lorillard is president, at West Brighton, Coney Island, near New York, was erected under the superintendence of Messrs. Maclay and Davies. It starts at high-water mark, and extends outward 1,000 feet; it is 50 feet in width, with enlargements 100 feet wide at the shore end, the center, and the bulkhead. It is double-decked, and has an iron substructure. The whole is supported by tubular wrought-iron piles of 9 inches diameter, the wall being half an inch thick. These columns are placed in rows 20 feet apart longitudinally and 16 feet 8 inches apart laterally. A circular cast-iron disk, 2½ feet in diameter, sunk 15 or 20 feet in the sand, affords a base for each pile to rest upon. The jet-water system was used in driving the piles. At the top of the columns iron capitals are bolted on, supporting 15 - inch

wrought-iron beams bolted together. These uphold the superstructure. Heavy horizontal struts are bolted to the beams transversely, and diagonal rods 1½ inch in diameter brace the structure. The entire structure is supported by 260 iron pillars. The landing-stage is on the lower deck, and is guarded by heavy oaken fenders.

A strong iron tubular pier has been erected at Long Branch. At the end of this new pier, which is about 860 feet long, there is a depth of 22 feet at dead low water. The pier is supported by tubular iron piles 6 inches in diameter for the first 150 feet from the shore, and then gradually increasing to 12 inches in diameter at the end. They are driven into the sand to the depth of from 14 to 17 feet. The pier is 25 feet wide in some parts and 50 feet in others. An approach 94 feet in length leads down to it. The pier is floored with ash, which it is proposed to remove at the end of every watering season, to allow the waves to flow freely among the iron supports without damage.

The large blocks of stone with which the lower ends of the Mississippi jetties were capped have proved entirely insufficient to withstand the tremendous force of the waves. Although they weighed one or two tons each, the first gale swept them all away. This has necessitated a supplementary labor, which has been accomplished in a way that will obviate all necessity of repeating it. As there was no available rock for the purpose within five hundred miles, it was decided to cap the jetties with blocks of concrete. Finely broken rock was brought down from the neighborhood of Rose Clare on the Ohio River, and, with the addition of sand, gravel, and Portland cement, was molded into huge blocks of concrete on the jetties. These are the largest blocks of concrete ever used for such a purpose, some of them being nearly double the weight of the largest masses of artificial stone employed in the great Cherbourg breakwater. The proportion of the ingredients was 15 parts of broken stone, 4·38 parts of gravel, 8·28 parts of sand, and 3 parts of cement, which were mixed with 10½ per cent. of water. It was decided to be necessary to cap the last 3,800 feet of the east jetty and the last 2,800 feet of the west jetty with solid blocks of this material weighing from 25 to 75 tons apiece. The materials are mixed by steam in revolving iron boxes, and immediately dumped into the molds and left to harden.

On the 18th of October, 1879, the new floating basin of the Bordeaux docks, which has been three years in construction and has cost three millions of dollars, was formally opened. The basin, fed with water from the Garonne and from a very deep artesian well, is 100,000 square metres in area and 10 metres deep. It was made in a marshy spot, where it was necessary to sink solid blocks of masonry to a depth of 12 metres in order to construct the quay, which is 18 metres broad. The port of Bordeaux has been very deficient in dock facilities, vessels having to wait sometimes a month before they could come alongside the quays. The port has only been able to accommodate 200 vessels. Along the docks which are to be made around the new basin 80 ships of the largest tonnage can lie at the same time. Another basin has been made alongside it for the repairing of men-of-war.

Extensive improvements are in progress in the harbor at Antwerp, under the joint auspices of the Belgian Government and the municipality of the city, designed to unite the purposes of extending the harbor and of obviating the floods which sometimes sweep through the streets of the town. The works, costing according to the estimates $7,655,000, embrace the straightening of the bank of the Scheldt, the deepening of its channel by dredging, and the building of a quay wall of brick faced with stone 47 feet high, 19·6 feet thick at the top, and 28 feet thick at the foundation, and the construction of three basins with locks connecting them, one 874 by 197 feet, and the others 806 and 738 feet respectively in length and 164 feet in width.

For the projected American isthmus canal, see INTEROCEANIC CANAL. A plan for a ship-railway across the Isthmus of Panama attracts much attention. Captain Eads, who has made a thorough study of the possibilities and difficulties of this plan of transportation, has elaborated designs for its construction, according to which it would cost about $50,000,000, or not more than one third of the lowest estimate for a canal. It holds out the promise not only of a perfectly practicable, safe, and economical method of transportation, but also of a very profitable financial investment, which can not be said of any of the proposed canals in the present state of commerce. The railway would have a road-bed not over 40 feet wide, and 8 or 10 rails for the car to run on. This would be composed of several separate sections, each about 100 feet long and running on some 200 wheels, some of them driving-wheels propelled by an engine attached to the outside of the section. The number of these sections (every one of which constitutes a locomotive) to be joined together in making up the car would vary according to the length of the ship. Rubber or steel springs should be placed between the wheels and the frame of these sections. Drawn by five such locomotives, a vessel and cargo weighing 10,000 tons could be transported without giving a pressure on the track under each wheel of more than 12 tons, or a pressure on the road-bed to exceed 1,200 lbs. per square foot; this is about double the pressure under the driving-wheels of an ordinary goods locomotive, and not one half the pressure on the ground under ordinary railroad-ties. The grades would be even and moderate. It would be possible to haul vessels over such a railway at a speed of fifteen or twenty miles an hour,

or at the same rate of speed as is run by freight trains over ordinary railways; although it is not proposed to run at a greater speed than eight miles an hour. The cost of transportation would probably be less for the same tonnage of freight than on an ordinary railway, since all the operations would be performed by machinery. The transfer of the ships from the sea to the cradle could be accomplished in two different ways: the platform holding the cradle might be lowered to receive the vessel by means of a lock or by the aid of hydraulic engines. The lock should be in two compartments, a deep one with sea-gates, into which the ship would be floated, and in which after the gates are closed it would be raised by the admission of water to the level of the upper lift, in which it would be floated upon the car. After the ship rests firmly on the cradle in the upper compartment, which is to be on the level of the railroad track and connected with it by a gate, the water is to be drawn off and the gate opened, leaving the car and its burden high and dry on the continuous track. By the other proposed method an iron frame of great strength and solidity, containing the car and a portion of the track, would be lowered in the basin far enough to allow the ship to be floated into the cradle, and then raised by means of hydrostatic cylinders until the track on this platform meets the main track.

The reward offered by the State of New York in 1871 for an economical method of propelling boats on the Erie Canal has not been the means of evoking the new system which it was hoped might be developed by the active brains of American inventors, although a good number of novel schemes of more or less merit have been offered for consideration. The five thousand or more boats which navigate the artificial waterways of the State are still propelled for the greater part by animals, and the rest of them by objectionable methods of steam propulsion. The problem seems now to have found its best solution in the adoption of the Belgian system of towing. The New York Steam Cable-Towing Company have obtained the exclusive privilege for fifty years of laying a cable for this purpose in the Erie Canal, and have been engaged in propelling boats by this means between Buffalo and Lockport. They have now extended their cables as far as Rochester, and will probably before long have them working over the whole extent of the canal, from Buffalo to Albany. This system of towage is not new, having been in use in Europe for eighteen or twenty years; but the substitution of the lighter and cheaper steel ropes for the ponderous iron chains, and the use of a clip-drum or driving-wheel instead of the indented windlass, are great advancements in respect to economy and expedition. Two cables, made of steel wire with a hemp core, are laid in the bed of the canal on different sides. One is used for towing the boats down the canal and the other the boats going in the opposite direction. The cable is an inch in diameter and weighs four tons to the mile. The tow-boat has an inverted vertical engine. The clip-wheel, which is situated on one side of the boat, is provided with strong clips or jaws, which automatically seize and hold the cable as it goes over and release it as it passes off. The cable passes over a sheave near the forward end of the boat on emerging from the water, and over another one aft on returning. The cable is held taut and firm against the drum by two wheels on either side, under which it passes before and after being drawn over the driving-wheel. The clip-wheel makes one revolution to eight of the engine. The engine has a 14-inch cylinder and a 16-inch stroke. Four or five loaded canal-boats can be towed by one boat at a speed of three miles an hour. The boats are provided with rudders at either end, and a screw for propelling them through the locks. Ten of these tow-boats have been operating, and it is intended to employ about eighty of them on the canal. The boats are 78 feet 6 inches long and 16 feet wide, and draw, when loaded with their supplies of coal, 5 feet of water. The shaft on which the wheel is turned is about on a level with the deck. By the new system the cost of towing is reduced one half and the time consumed two thirds. This method when completed along the whole line will be of great advantage to eastern shippers to the West, as the boats will return fully laden instead of with only part loads as heretofore, and the freights from New York to Buffalo and the West will thus be reduced to merely nominal rates.

A new mode of street-car traction has been successfully employed in San Francisco for some time past. It is said to have proved satisfactory beyond expectations, and to have shown itself well adopted to all kinds of city traffic, and especially where the surface is so uneven that neither horses nor steam-motors can be economically employed. This is the case with many parts of San Francisco, and led to the development of this novel system in that city, where it has already been adopted by three companies. In a tube just below the surface of the ground an endless wire rope is kept in constant motion by a stationary engine. The tube lies in the middle between the two tracks, and has a narrow slot in its upper side through which the gripping attachment that connects the car with the constantly moving rope passes; the rope is kept in position in the tube by means of sheaves. Clay Street, in which the system was first employed, is 5,197 feet long, and has a total rise of 367 feet from Kearny to Jones Street, then an equally sharp descent on the other side of the hill, with a slight incline again from Polk Street to Van Ness Avenue. The steepest grade is 1 in 6·15. As on such a hilly route locomotion by horse-power was very expensive, a more economical motive agency was desired; yet it must be one which did

not involve the use of a motor which would frighten horses or endanger life. A. S. Hallidie's plan of an endless steel-wire rope was finally adopted. In working out such a scheme very serious mechanical difficulties are presented by the conditions that the rope must be worked below the level of the street, and must be safely covered; that the cars shall be started smoothly, and instantly brought to a halt at any point of the road; and that the mechanical apparatus shall be simple and easily controlled. An endless steel-wire rope, 3 inches in circumference, 11,000 feet long, and weighing 16,000 lbs., made of 114 wires hardened and tempered, travels up and down Clay Street in two iron tubes, running on sheaves at the bottom of the tube, placed 39 feet apart, with other sheaves projecting from the top, where an upward incline requires a guard to keep the rope from rubbing on the roof of the tube, and other larger ones around which the rope passes at every change of angle in the road. At the end of the line the rope passes around a sheave 8 feet in diameter, and returns through the other tube. At the engine-house it passes over two angle-sheaves and over the grip-pulleys, also 8 feet in diameter. The patent grip-pulleys by means of which the rope is kept in motion are furnished with jaws at their circumference which automatically grip and release the rope as it passes around them, their action being governed by the pressure of the rope upon them. The whole length of the tubes, on one side of the path of the rope on the sheaves, is a thin slot seven eighths of an inch broad. Through this passes an iron bar, which has at its end the gripping apparatus; this is attached to the dummy which pulls the car, and is fastened to the rope by means of a hand-wheel and screw, by which its jaws are made to close over the rope or to release it again. These operations are accomplished by means of a slide working in a standard and actuated by the hand-wheel. This slide has at its lower end a wedge-shaped block, which moves two jaws horizontally. These operate according to the direction in which the slide moves, closing when it is raised and opening again when it is lowered. When the rope is thus gripped it is raised free from the sheaves into the open center of the tube. The grip is so constructed, and the dummy coupled to the car in such a manner, that the impetus of the car when running on a descending grade is not checked by brakes, except when it is necessary to stop, but the car is held back only by the rope and grip attachment; and so the momentum of the car is utilized to help keep the rope in motion and save power.

A sudden new start has been taken lately in ocean telegraphy, a branch of enterprise which has remained for five or six years at a standstill. Three long ocean-cables have recently been or are being submerged by English companies in the East, and a transatlantic double line by a French association of capitalists. The

Eastern Telegraph Company completed the duplication of their lines from England to Bombay in 1878. The Eastern Extension Telegraph Company also have just duplicated their cables, which extend the connection from Bombay to Australia by way of Madras, to Penang in the Malay Peninsula, and to the East Indian islands. The last year also the Eastern Telegraph Company have been engaged in laying their cable to the Cape of Good Hope. This company entered into an agreement with the British Government to have the line down between Durban and Zanzibar by the end of July, 1879, and to have the whole cable laid and in working order by the end of the year. In consideration of an annual subsidy of $17,500, the company gives the priority to Government messages, and agrees to transmit them over the cable, which shall be capable of telegraphing fourteen words a minute, at half the rate charged the public. The British Government has also stipulated for the right to take possession of the wires and offices, or to allow any of the colonies so to do, in the event of a war, rebellion, or other public emergency, and to keep possession as long as is seen fit, upon the payment of a reasonable compensation. To guard against the teredos and other mischievous insects which have proved so injurious to the older cables by eating into gutta-percha, the Cape cable is covered with a brass wrapping, except in the deep-sea portions, where these pests are not found. The French Pouyer-Quertier scheme includes two cables from Brest to New York. This new line may partly find its motives in the French national pride, but it furnishes, no doubt, a promising investment for French capital, and may press the present lines hard in competition for the whole English and Continental traffic, besides securing the French. The cables were manufactured at Charlton, England, in the workshops of Siemens Brothers. On the 16th of November the American end of the cable was landed at North Eastham, Mass., on Cape Cod, from the steamer Faraday. No ocean-cable had ever been constructed and submerged at so rapid a rate: the line was completed and messages sent from continent to continent seven months after the French Government had granted the concession to the company. The insulation of the wires was found to be remarkably perfect. A new cable has recently been put down between Germany and Norway, at the cost of the German Government. This line was considered diplomatically, since the only telegraphic communication between Germany and Scandinavia has been through Denmark. It is a three-wired line, and extends from Romoe, an island off the coast of Schleswig, to a point near Arendal. All telegraphic traffic between Norway and Germany, and the greater part of the telegraphic correspondence with other countries, except Denmark, England, and France, will pass over the new wires and be taken away from the Danish lines. The cable was manufactured by Siemens & Halske of Berlin. Russia has submerged a short cable across the Caspian Sea. The line is 150 miles long, and extends from Cape Gurgian to Krasnovodsk. By it telegraphic communication is established between Tjikislar and Asterabad; so that messages from Tjikislar can be sent, by way of Teheran, over the Indo-European line to Tiflis.

Among the projects of submarine cables is one which promises to be realized at no distant day, and which when accomplished will complete the telegraphic circuit of the earth. This is a cable to be laid from California to the Sandwich Islands, and thence to China and Japan. Cyrus W. Field has obtained the exclusive concession for such a cable from the Government of the Sandwich Islands, and expects to receive similar privileges from Japan and perhaps China. Japan has long been desirous of electric communications as complete as possible with the outer world, and even China is awakening to the advantages of telegraphic intercourse. A still more ambitious project has been talked of for a new cable between America and Europe. This scheme is for a cable running from New York to Flores, one of the Azores, whence two extensions will be carried to the European Continent—one to France, England, and Holland, and the other to Fayal, San Miguel, and Lisbon. The entire length of cabling required to carry out this plan would be 7,300 miles.

Subterranean telegraph wires have been in use for many years on the Continent of Europe, and are regarded with such favor in Germany that they are being constantly extended. At first employed only for shorter distances, now several long lines are laid underground, which appear to work successfully. In England, however, where there are 10,000 miles of underground wires, they do not seem to be attended with the same success. W. H. Preece, the electrician of the postal service, reported lately that, while their cost was three or four times that of overhead wires, their power of carrying currents is only a third or a quarter as great, and that the gutta-percha covering is attacked by rats and mice, and eaten away by an insect called *Tempeltonia crystallina*, and also injured by a fungus. The British public approves the adoption of this system on account of the danger to passengers from the elevated wires. The lines are carried through the cities below ground. Probably in the open country they would be less liable to destructive attacks.

A novel system of insulation for underground telegraph wires, invented by David Brooks of Philadelphia, is said to be open to none of the difficulties which attend this mode of telegraphy, and which have produced such discouraging results from the subterranean wires laid in Great Britain. If wires can be well insulated and protected from destructive agencies underground, their advantage over the overhead telegraph wires strung on posts is obvious. The substance used as an insulator is a novel one to practically apply to this purpose, although its remarkable properties as a non-conductor are well known. . This is paraffine-oil. The wires are wrapped in cotton and bound together to the number of fifty or more in a tight cover of netting, and then inclosed in a pipe. After the pipe is laid in the ground, it is filled with the oil. Elevated reservoirs connected with the pipe keep it constantly full of the oil under pressure. Short lines insulated in this manner have been in successful operation for a couple of years; one of them is laid under the Schuylkill River in thirty-five feet of water. Such a line of underground telegraph will probably soon be working between Philadelphia and New York.

ESPARTERO, Don BALDOMERO, Duke of Vitoria, a Spanish general and statesman, born October 27, 1793, died January 9, 1879. He was the son of a poor wheelwright, and, being of a weakly constitution, prepared for the priesthood. In 1809 he entered the army to take part in the war against France, and soon rose to the rank of lieutenant. After the retreat of the French in 1814 he joined the expedition of General Morillo to the South American colonies, which at that time were carrying on their war of independence. During the ten years in which he remained there he found many opportunities to distinguish himself, and rose rapidly in rank. In 1824 he was sent to Spain by the Viceroy to report on the state of affairs, and after his return was captured and imprisoned for a whole year by the enemy. In 1832 he openly declared himself in favor of the succession of the daughter of Ferdinand VII., and when after the death of the King the civil war broke out, he was appointed Commandant - General of Biscay. In 1836 he was appointed to the chief command of the Army of the North, Viceroy of Navarre, and Captain-General of the Basque Provinces. When in 1837 Don Carlos appeared before Madrid, he saved the capital, drove the enemy beyond the Ebro, completely defeated them in the battle of Luchana (for which he was created Count of Luchana), and relieved Bilbao. In 1838 he completely defeated the Carlist General Negri at Burgos. In 1839, by making good use of the dissensions existing among the Carlists, he carried on negotiations with the Carlist General Maroto, who finally capitulated at Bergara. After this Don Carlos was compelled to retire to France. As a reward for his services, Espartero was raised to the rank of marshal, and was created Duke of Vitoria and a grandee of the first class. In 1840 the Cortes passed a law restricting the municipal charters. Espartero advised Queen Christina not to sanction the law; but she refused to listen to his advice, and he placed himself at the head of the movement against it, which finally com-

pelled Christina to resign and go to France. In 1841 he was elected Regent of Spain, and as such conducted the Government with great energy. He opposed the demands of the Church, subdued the Republicans who attempted to create disturbances in Valencia and other towns, prevented the abduction of the young Queen, defeated the attempts to bring about an insurrection in the army made by the Generals Diego Leon and Manuel Concha, and kept in entire subjection the Basque Provinces. He now began to turn toward England, and, refusing to dismiss his favorite, the Secretary Linage, was accused of favoring a commercial treaty with England which was unfavorable to Spain. In a very short time the opposition to him culminated in open rebellion, which soon spread over Andalusia, Aragon, Catalonia, and Galicia. On June 13, 1843, a junta formed in Barcelona deposed him, and declared Queen Isabella of age. After Narvaez had taken Madrid on July 22d, he escaped to Cadiz, whence he went to England. While he was received in England with the honors of a regent, he was deprived in Spain of all his honors and titles. After passing five years in England, a decree of Queen Isabella restored to him all his titles, and he returned to Spain, but for a long time kept himself aloof from political life. In 1854 he together with O'Donnell was the leader of the insurrection, and Queen Isabella, in order to save her throne, placed him at the head of the new Ministry, in which O'Donnell became Minister of War. His first act was to banish Queen Christina for the second time. But the union of parties as represented in his Cabinet could not endure, and he was forced by the intrigues of O'Donnell to resign on July 14, 1856. After this he retired completely from public life, but his influence did not cease with his retirement. In 1869, long after he had taken any part at all in public affairs, a proposition was made in the Cortes to elect him King; and even Alfonso XII., upon his accession to the throne, considered it necessary to go to Logroño in order to secure Espartero's good will.

EUROPE. The area of Europe is estimated at 3,824,240 square miles. Leaving out of account the area of the European dependencies, as well as that of the German-coast waters of the Baltic and North Seas, the Lake of Constance, and the Sea of Azov, the European states occupy the following relative position in point of area:

COUNTRIES.	Square miles.
1. Russia..............................	1,983,784
2. Austro-Hungary....................	241,085
3. Germany..................	208,481
France.............................	204,092
Spain..............................	198,229
Sweden............................	170,979
Finland............................	144,228
4. Norway.........;:................	122,860
5. Great Britain and Ireland..........	121,608
10. Italy.............................	114,415
11. Turkey...........................	105,912
12. Roumania........................	49,262

COUNTRIES.	Square miles.
13. Portugal	34,606
14. Bulgaria	24,659
15. Greece	19,353
16. Servia	18,757
17. Switzerland	15,981
18. Denmark	14,789
19. Netherlands	12,731
20. Belgium	11,373
21. Montenegro	3,642
22. Luxemburg	999
23. Andorra	191
24. Liechtenstein	68
25. San Marino	24
26. Monaco	6
Total	3,766,992

With regard to population they hold the following relative position:

COUNTRIES.	Population.
1. Russia (exclusive of Finland)	72,018,381
2. Germany	42,727,360
3. Austro-Hungary	37,712,731
4. France	36,905,788
5. Great Britain and Ireland	34,517,000
6. Italy	28,209,620
7. Spain	16,342,996
8. Turkey	7,008,000
9. Belgium	5,476,668
10. Roumania	5,376,000
11. Sweden	4,531,863
12. Portugal	4,348,551
13. Netherlands	3,981,887
14. Switzerland	2,792,264
15. Finland	1,968,626
16. Denmark	1,940,000
17. Bulgaria	1,859,000
18. Norway	1,808,900
19. Greece	1,679,775
20. Servia	1,576,622
21. Montenegro	236,000
22. Luxemburg	205,158
23. Andorra	18,000
24. Liechtenstein	8,664
25. San Marino	7,816
26. Monaco	7,049
Total	313,312,669

In this table the European dependencies of Great Britain, Portugal, and Denmark are not taken into account. They are as follows:

Great Britain (Malta, Gibraltar, Heligoland).	174,362
Portugal (Azores)	264,352
Denmark (Faroe Islands, Iceland)	83,000
Total	521,714

Adding these figures to the above sum, the total population of the European states, inclusive of their European dependencies, is found to be 313,834,383.

The execution of the provisions of the Treaty of Berlin progressed favorably during 1879. The new principality of Bulgaria elected a Constituent Assembly, which prepared a Constitution, and elected a Prince in the person of Prince Alexander of Battenberg. (See BULGARIA.) In the autonomous province of Eastern Roumelia, the excesses committed by the Bulgarians in the early part of the year caused some doubts to be entertained as to its stability; but toward the close of the year it appeared as if the Bulgarian part of the population had determined to treat their Mohammedan neighbors with more fairness in future. (See EASTERN ROUMELIA.) In Roumania, the emancipation of the Jews proved to be a difficult question to solve. A settlement, however, was finally arrived at by the adoption of

a compromise which, while acceptable to the Roumanians, also gained the approval of the Powers. (See ROUMANIA.) The work of the different commissions on boundaries proceeded favorably with one exception, that of the Greek frontier. Several skirmishes occurred on the Servian border, while in the new districts of Montenegro attempts at resistance were made by the Albanians. In Turkey the greatest distress prevailed in consequence of the disordered state of the finances. The deplorable condition of Asia Minor led Sir Austen Layard, the British Minister at Constantinople, to make demands for the appointment of able officials to administer the Asiatic provinces of Turkey. This demand was in the end complied with. (See TURKEY.) The negotiations with Greece for a new boundary continued during the year, but no progress was made, as the plenipotentiaries could not agree on what should constitute the basis of the negotiation. (See GREECE.) The Porte in 1879, for the first time in some years, took an active part in the administration of Egypt, by the deposition of Ismail Pasha. (See EGYPT.)

An important change was made in the direction of foreign affairs of the Austro-Hungarian Monarchy. Count Andrassy resigned his position as President of the Common Ministry and Minister for Foreign Affairs on account of ill health, and was succeeded by Baron Haymerle. (See HAYMERLE.) The change in persons, however, did not mean a change of policy. In April a convention was concluded with Turkey regarding the sanjak of Novi-Bazar, and this district was then occupied without resistance. In Austria an important change took place in the government. At the elections for the Reichsrath held in June and July, the Constitutional party, which had ruled the country for a number of years, lost some seats, making the strength of the parties about equal. An important feature in the new Reichsrath was the entrance of the Bohemian delegates for the first time since 1867. The Auersperg Ministry had resigned previous to the elections, and was finally succeeded by a fusion Ministry under Count Taaffe. (See AUSTRIA.)

The senatorial elections held in France on January 5th resulted in a Republican victory, thus making both Chambers Republican for the first time in the history of the third republic. The effect of this was felt in all departments of the Government, and in February President MacMahon resigned, as he no longer felt himself able to govern in accordance with the wishes of the majority. In his place the two Chambers in Congress assembled elected Jules Grévy, the veteran President of the Chamber of Deputies. The Ministry formed by M. Waddington introduced two important bills affecting higher education. Both were passed in the Chamber of Deputies, but were laid over in the Senate until 1880. In the latter part of the year the Ministry of M. Waddington, although sustained in the Chamber on several occasions by large majorities, was forced to make way for a Ministry composed of more radical members under M. de Freycinet. (See FRANCE.)

In Belgium, the question of Church and secular schools was solved by the adoption of the Government bill providing for the supervision of all schools by the state. (See BELGIUM.) In Spain the year witnessed a struggle for supremacy between General Campos and Señor Canovas del Castillo. The principal question before the Cortes was the pacification of Cuba. An attempt was made on the life of the King shortly after his marriage to the Archduchess Christina of Austria. (See SPAIN.)

The attention of England in 1879 was chiefly absorbed by the wars in Afghanistan and Zoolooland. In the latter part of the year the distress in Ireland consequent upon the agrarian depression became very great, and led to a serious anti-rent agitation. Disturbances occurred in different parts of the country, and numerous arrests were made. At the same time strong efforts were used to relieve the distress. (See GREAT BRITAIN.)

The after-effects of the war with Turkey were felt very strongly in Russia during 1879. In spite of the most stringent measures adopted by the Government to suppress it, Nihilism was stronger this year than ever, and another unsuccessful attempt on the life of the Czar was made. Another danger resulting from the late war threatened Russia in 1879, in the form of the plague, which appeared in several governments; but, through the efforts of the Government, it was confined to a comparatively small part of the empire. (See PLAGUE.) The advance of Russia in Asia received a check this year by the defeat of the Russian army by the Tekke Turkomans. (See RUSSIA.)

In Germany a complete revolution in the financial policy took place. The session of the Reichstag in the beginning of the year was occupied almost exclusively with the discussion of the new tariff, which was finally passed by a coalition of the Conservatives and the Catholic Center. This alliance was remarkable from the fact that the Catholics, who had for years been Prince Bismarck's most bitter opponents, had now joined hands with him. The reactionary spirit was also felt in the administration of Prussia, where the Liberal Ministers were virtually forced to resign and a Conservative Ministry was put in their place. The elections for the Diet in Prussia resulted in a large gain for the Conservatives, giving them with their new allies, the Catholics, a bare majority over the united Liberals. (See GERMANY and PRUSSIA.)

EVANGELICAL ALLIANCE. This association has for its object to represent the unity of all those churches which collectively are called Evangelical in all the more important articles of faith, notwithstanding their separation by external organization. It has held general assemblies at London in 1846, at Paris in 1855, at Berlin in 1857, at Geneva in 1861, at Amsterdam in 1867, and at New York in 1873.

The seventh *General Conference* of the Evangelical Alliance was held in 1879 at Basel, Switzerland, beginning September 1st. On the evening of the preceding day, Sunday, August 31st, a service of greeting between the delegates from the different countries was held in the Vereinshaus, when fraternal addresses were delivered in the German, French, and English languages. Pastor Ecklin spoke in behalf of the citizens of Basel, and as the representative of the German-speaking countries; Professor Vignet of Berne for French Switzerland and France; and the Rev. Philip Schaff, D. D., of New York, for the English-speaking delegates. M. Charles Sarasin, ex-Councilor of State, was chosen President of the Conference, and delivered the opening address. He dwelt upon the necessity of a liberal and wise judgment in theological thought, even though it might sometimes seem to make too many concessions to the demands of science; at the same time, he held, there must be no compromise of the fundamentals of Christianity. He believed that a reconciliation is possible between faith and science, and that one of the duties of the Evangelical Alliance is to find it. Reports were then made by delegates concerning the religious condition of their respective countries. Pastor Gödet of Basel represented Protestantism in Switzerland as divided into parties and suffering from the growth of rationalism. Dr. Cremer, of the University of Greifswald, described Germany as in a condition of religious unrest, enduring a contest between faith and unbelief. He thought that much advance must be made before the masses could be reached and cured of their indifference and infidelity. Pastor Babut of Nismes represented the French Protestant churches. The Rev. E. V. Bligh spoke, in reference to the religious condition of England, and dwelt especially on the success and progress of the evangelistic meetings which were instituted during the tour of the American evangelists, Messrs. Moody and Sankey, in 1874, and had been continued since. Dr. Van Oosterzee, of the University of Utrecht, described the religious condition of Holland. The Rev. Dr. Philip Schaff described the United States as the land of churches and Christian activity, and ascribed the variety of denominational forms existing there largely to the diverse nationalities from which the people have originated, each tending to transplant the spirit of its own religious life. Dr. Tardy spoke of the growing activity of Protestantism in Austria and Hungary. Dr. Von Scheele gave an encouraging view of the condition of the Scandinavian churches. Among the general addresses was one by the Rev. Dr. Stoughton of London, on "The Connection between Basel and the Early English Protestants." Sectional meetings were held for the reading of papers in the French and English languages. The theme for special discussion on the second day of the session was the "Unchangeableness of the Apostolic Gospel." Papers were read on this subject by Professor Orelli of the University of Basel, and Professor Fr. Godet of Neufchâtel. The address of Professor Orelli attracted an unusual degree of attention, and was considered the most important paper contributed to the meeting. Papers were read in the French section on "Home Evangelization" by the Rev. M. Lelièvre of Nismes, France, the Rev. H. S. Ashton of London, and the Rev. Dr. Fisch of Paris. Pastor Lelièvre represented that France was undergoing a religious awakening, in the development of which it invoked the coöperation of the whole Protestant family, and spoke of Belgium as being in a similar situation and having similar needs. Mr. Ashton described the evangelistic labors of Mr. and Mrs. McAll in Paris, which, having been begun in 1871, had extended till they embraced twenty-three stations regularly attended by more than five thousand hearers. Professor Emilio Comba, of the Waldensian College in Florence, spoke on evangelistic work in Italy. At another sectional meeting papers were read on "Preparation for the Ministry of the Gospel," by Professor Guest of Breslau and Professor Porret of Lausanne. These speakers held that the present system of education for the ministry is defective, and not adapted to the wants of the age; that it should be more comprehensive and less ecclesiastical, and should rely more on ethical and Biblical than on dogmatical forces. The subject of Sunday-schools was discussed in the Anglo-American section, with addresses by the Rev. Dr. T. D. Anderson of New York, the Rev. Dr. Oswald Dykes of London, several speakers from Germany, France, Switzerland, and Italy, and the Rev. Dr. John Hall of New York.

The most important discussion of the third day was held in the Anglo-American section on the subject of religious liberty. The Rev. Dr. James H. Rigg, ex-President of the English Wesleyan Methodist Conference, gave a survey of the position of the different countries of the world in reference to that question, from which he drew the conclusion that the principle of liberty was becoming better understood by the nations of Europe, and would ultimately be generally recognized. The Rev. Eustace Carder of England presented a paper on the functions of conscience in relation to civil and religious liberty. The subject of "Christian Union" was considered in the same section, in a paper by the Rev. T. D. Anderson of New York, and in an address by the Rev. William Arthur of London.

Social questions were considered on the fourth day, when papers were read on the "Relations of Christianity and Modern Society," by Professor Wach of the University of Leipsic; "Our Duty to the Working Classes," by Mr. G. Steinheil, manufacturer, of Alsace, and the President of the Conference; and "Socialism and Communism," by the Rev. Dr.

Washburn of New York. Other papers were on the "Christian Regeneration of the East," by Dr. Fabri of Barmen, Germany, and "The Christian and Anti-Christian Influence of the Press on the Nation," by the Rev. A. Jouelli, editor of the "Allgemeine Schweitzerzeitung," of Basel, the Rev. Dr. E. de Pressensé of France, who spoke of the mission of the Protestant press, and the Rev. L. B. White of London. "The Present State of Religious Liberty" again engaged attention in the consideration of a paper which had been presented on behalf of the Rev. J. P. Thompson, D. D., of Berlin, embodying a memorial of the American Board of Commissioners for Foreign Missions in reference to the interference by the police with persons connected with its missions in Bohemia, and calling attention to restrictions which were imposed on the exercise of religious freedom in Bavaria. The memorial recited that the missionaries of the Board, who had for some years been laboring in Austria, had carefully conformed to the regulations of the Government concerning domestic worship and public religious meetings, and till recently had been allowed to carry on their work of evangelization with only occasional interruption from the police. As teachers of religion they had scrupulously refrained from intermeddling with the domestic concerns of the state. Their converts had taken the precaution to withdraw from the recognized churches to which they had belonged in the manner prescribed by law, and had submitted to the police a statement of their belief and of their desire to worship together as Biblical Christians, not connected with any recognized confession. The police had allowed them to hold religious meetings in a public hall and in their private dwellings, and, after carefully inspecting these assemblies, had found nothing in them contrary to law. Suddenly, however, and without the assignment of any cause, the authorities began to look upon these assemblies with suspicion. "Gendarmes would enter a meeting and take down the names of all present, by way of warning. They would even go into private houses at the hour of family worship and take notice of any strangers present. At length, on the 20th of March, 1879, in place of the customary permission to hold evangelical meetings, Mr. Adams and his assistant Mr. Horky were notified that persons belonging to a confession not legally recognized have only the right to hold domestic worship, and that at domestic worship only the family and members of the household may be present. The right to hold public religious meetings, in accordance with the provisions of the meeting-law, was also denied, and the meetings Messrs. Adams and Horky had announced to the police, both public and private, were forbidden. Mr. Adams and his assistant Mr. Nowak were summoned before the police, and, under a penalty of twenty-five days' imprisonment or a hundred florins' fine, were forbidden to hold in private houses any meeting for religious exercises, or to admit to their family worship any person not strictly a member of their own households. They were even forbidden to attend religious worship in each other's houses, or in any society not recognized by law." These acts were considered to be in direct contravention of the fundamental law of Austria, and were supposed by Dr. Thompson to be unknown to the Emperor and his immediate counselors, and "due to the excessive and mistaken zeal of the provincial authorities." Another statement described the case of the people of two villages in which voluntary assemblies for worship had been similarly interfered with. The case was discussed in the Anglo-American section and in meetings of the several deputations, and the following memorial was agreed upon, to be presented to the Emperor of Austria by an international deputation representing the Alliance as a whole:

The seventh General Conference of the Evangelical Alliance, in Basel (Switzerland) assembled, has received from members of a religious community, not recognized by the state, in Prague and its neighborhood, representations, as shown in the documents hereto attached, respecting infringements of the liberty of faith and conscience in particular, even of the exercise of family worship, which they, in contravention of the guarantees contained in the Constitution, have had to suffer, which sufferers, as they inform us, have made due appeal to the supreme Government of Austria; and this Conference of the Evangelical Alliance, under a sentiment of fraternal sympathy, esteems it a duty to associate itself with those petitioners, and begs to present to his Majesty the Emperor of Austria, with profound respect and due confidence, its petition, praying that as speedily as possible it may grant to the request of our brethren in faith an answer, whereby these questions may be decided in a sense favorable to toleration and religious liberty.

The deputation consisted of the President (ex-Councilor Sarasin) and Vice-Presidents of the Alliance, and included among its members Count Bismarck-Bohlen, a cousin of Prince Bismarck and an aide-de-camp of the Emperor of Germany.

The Conference also considered some cases of the restriction of religious freedom which had occurred in Greek territory, where it was represented that the rights of parents not of the orthodox religion to have their children educated without the interference of the authorities of the Greek Church had been infringed upon. This was regarded as in contravention of the provisions of the Treaty of Berlin. It was stated that Lord Salisbury had ordered remonstrances to be made against these interferences, and that they would probably cease. Cases of persecution said to have occurred in Spain were referred to the British Committee, to be dealt with as should seem fit to them.

The fifth day was given to the discussion of subjects connected with the work of missions. A paper was read on "Missions to the Jews," by M. de le Roi of Breslau and Professor Christlieb of the University of Bonn; and one of the editors of the "Allgemeine

Missions Zeitung" gave a review of the condition of Protestant missions among the heathen, and was followed by addresses on the general subject of missions, on the "Results of Missionary Labor in India and Africa," and on kindred topics, by the Rev. William Arthur of England, the Rev. Dr. Barde of Geneva, the Rev. Dr. Murray Mitchell of England, and the Rev. Dr. Heman. Professor Christlieb's address embodied a condemnation of the British opium-trade as being one of the greatest hindrances to the progress of Christianity in China, and the following resolution proposed by him was adopted unanimously:

Resolved, That this Conference, prompted by the reports laid before it as to the present state of Evangelical missions in China and India, expresses its full sympathy with the efforts for the suppression of the opium-traffic which have been made during many years past, and desires to support the protests against this trade which from time to time have been raised by various Evangelical and Missionary Churches, and by many distinguished friends of Christian missions. The Conference unites with their English brethren in declaring this long-established trade to be a crying injustice against China, a cause of offense which deeply injures the honor of the Christian name, both in Christian and heathen countries, and especially an immense obstacle to the spread of Christian missionary work. The Conference feels constrained to place on record its conviction that a change in the policy of England as regards this traffic is urgently necessary, and it instructs its president to bring this resolution to the knowledge of her Majesty's Secretary of State for India.

On the last day of the session, Saturday, September 6th, topics relating to Christian union were discussed in papers by the Rev. Dr. Plitt, Professor in the Moravian Theological Seminary at Gnadenfeld, Prussia, the Rev. Th. Fallot of Paris, and the Rev. J. F. Hurst, D.D., President of Drew Theological Seminary.

The deputation appointed by the General Conference to present a memorial to the Emperor of Austria in behalf of religious liberty were received by his Majesty at the palace in Buda-Pesth, and presented the petition of the Alliance to him. The Emperor received the memorial very graciously, promised to inquire into the subject of the grievances to which it related, and assured the deputation that justice should be done if the facts as stated in it were substantiated.

The third biennial meeting of the *Evangelical Alliance of the United States* was held at St. Louis, Missouri, beginning October 28th. The meetings were continued through the two succeeding days, during which papers were read as follows: "Christian Scholarship and Christian Unity," Rev. James S. Bush, D. D. (Episcopalian), of New York; "The Sunday Question," ex-President T. D. Woolsey of Yale College; "Christian Truth and the Periodical Press," Rev. W. Craig, D. D. (Presbyterian), of Iowa; "City Missions and our Foreign Population," Rev. W. V. Tudor, D. D. (Methodist), of St. Louis, Missouri; "Harmony in Essential Doctrines promoted by the Alliance," Rev. J. L. Burroughs, D. D. (Baptist), of Louisville, Kentucky; "Christian Morals and the Public Schools," Rev. J. M. King, D. D. (Methodist), of New York City; "The Churches and Social Reforms," Rev. T. M. Post, D. D. (Congregationalist), of St. Louis, Missouri; "The Mohammedan Powers and Christian Missions," Rev. Galusha Anderson, D. D., of Chicago, Illinois; "Union of Churches and Union of Church and State," Rev. Stuart Robinson, D. D. (Presbyterian), of Louisville, Kentucky.

The Annual Conference of the *British Organization of the Evangelical Alliance* was held at Edinburgh, beginning October 28th. An address was made at the opening meeting on "The Recent Conference at Basel," by the Rev. Dr. Stoughton of London, who remarked that the statements which had been made at that Conference in regard to the state of religion in the world had impressed on his mind, among other things, that a decided advance had taken place within a few years throughout Europe in what was called religious toleration. To this was largely due the spread of religious infidelity, for men were now allowed to state just what they thought. While, however, much skepticism and infidelity were shown to be prevalent, a very great amount of Christian work also appeared to be going on, not only in England and Scotland, but all over Europe. The sessions of the Conference were continued through three days, during which addresses were delivered on "The Practical Resolutions of the Alliance," by Canon Battersby and the Rev. W. Robertson; "The State of Religion on the Continent," by the Rev. R. S. Ashton of the Evangelical Continental Society, Rev. Dr. Jessup of Syria, and the Rev. J. C. Burns; "Home Mission Work," by the Rev. J. N. Wilson of Edinburgh, and others; "Missions to the Heathen," by the Rev. Dr. Murray Mitchell and the Rev. Mr. McCarthy of China, etc.

EVANGELICAL ASSOCIATION. The following is a summary of the statistics of the Evangelical Association as given in its "Christian Family Almanac" for 1879:

CONFERENCES.	Itinerant preachers.	Churches.	Members.
East Pennsylvania	87	195½	14,790
Erie	27	87	2,685
Central Pennsylvania	74	108	11,215
New York	88	56	4,101
Pittsburgh	61	131	7,967
Atlantic	19	20	2,020
Iowa	59	56	4,199
Michigan	47	67	5,809
Des Moines	34	28	3,121
Illinois	87	122	10,218
Canada	35	67	4,684
Ohio	56	131	7,526
Indiana	83	98	5,224
Wisconsin	63	121	10,054
Minnesota	45	50	3,975
Southern Indiana	20	32	1,896
Kansas	87	24½	2,046
Pacific	7	6	658
Germany	47	81	7,477
Total	881	1,425	109,762

Number of local preachers, 558; of Sunday-schools, 1,925, with 20,640 officers and teachers, and 118,514 scholars; of parsonages, 416; probable value of the same, $392,364; probable value of the churches, $3,080,027; amount of Conference contributions, $4,718.02; of missionary contributions, $71,419.74; of Sunday-school and Tract Union contributions, $1,949.-13. The principal periodicals published by the Association are one English and one German weekly general religious newspaper, the latter of which, begun in January, 1836, is the oldest German Protestant newspaper in the United States. Several Sunday-school and other religious periodicals are also published in both the English and German languages. The principal educational institutions are the Northwestern College, Napierville, Ill.; Union Biblical Institute, in the same place; Union Seminary, New Berlin, Pa.; and Ebenezer Orphan Institute, Flat Rock, Seneca County, Ohio, at which 54 children were supported and taught in 1879. The statistics reported to the General Conference differ slightly from those published in the "Almanac," and give totals as follows: Number of itinerant preachers, 909; number of local preachers, 636; number of church members, 109,773; number of churches, 1,434; probable value of churches, $3,170,602; number of parsonages, 449; probable value of parsonages, $406,541; number of Sunday-schools, 1,918; number of scholars, 118,640; number of officers and teachers, 20,-553.

The mission in Germany is organized into a Conference, with about 8,000 church members and 14,000 Sunday-school scholars. It has a publishing-house and printing-office at Stuttgart, and a theological school at Reutlingen. A mission is supported in Japan, with two missionaries and three female assistants, having small congregations at Tokio and Osaka.

The quadrennial report of the Book Agent to the General Conference showed that in four years the resources of the publishing establishment had been increased by $92,344; that $51,492 had been added by improvements; that $26,951 had been distributed among the Conferences; and that the total profits had been $92,344.

The annual meeting of the *Missionary Society* was held in Chicago, Ill., during the sessions of the General Conference. A full report was made of the mission in Japan, showing that it included 17 full members, four Sunday-schools with 100 scholars, and a catechetical class with seven scholars. Two adults and seven infants had been baptized during the year, and there were five candidates for baptism. The Board resolved to send another missionary to Japan. It also made an appropriation and arrangements for establishing a mission in Texas.

The quadrennial *General Conference* of the Evangelical Association met at Chicago, Ill., October 2d. Eighty-seven delegates were present, four of whom were from Germany. The four bishops presided in turn. The proceedings were conducted in the English and German languages. The bishops presented a quadrennial address, which dwelt at the opening upon a decrease in the rate of growth of the Church, which had become evident during the last four years. The fact was illustrated by tables giving the rates of growth in different particulars, by quadrenniums, of which the table of members showed that the rate of increase has been as follows: from 1863 to 1867, 18 per cent.; from 1867 to 1871, 23 per cent.; from 1871 to 1875, 20 per cent.; from 1875 to 1879, 13 per cent. The following resolution was adopted in reply to an invitation from the General Conference of the Methodist Episcopal Church to the Association to take part in an Œcumenical Conference of Methodist bodies accepting the Arminian theology:

1. That we duly appreciate and most heartily reciprocate the fraternal spirit which prompted and which pervades said invitation to participate in the deliberations of said Conference.

2. That, although we are not a "Methodist body," but yet are closely allied to Methodism in doctrine and practice, we herewith accept the invitation and make arrangements to be properly represented at said Conference.

The Committee of Ways and Means was instructed to take steps to have the Church properly represented at the Œcumenical Conference. The need of a more appropriate translation into the English language of the original name of the denomination (*Evangelische Gemeinschaft*) was recognized by the Conference, and a resolution was adopted,.to be submitted to the Annual Conferences for approval, ordering that the English name of the Church in the future should be the *Evangelical Church of North America*. A committee was appointed to take in hand the necessary measures to make the contemplated change of name legal. The rule with regard to teaching in theological schools was amended so as to read: "The teachers of the theological branches must be ministers of our Church; for non-theological branches other competent persons may be appointed, whose character and faith are in accordance with the directions of our Church Discipline." The rule concerning the Board of Publication was modified so as to read: "There shall be a Board of Publication consisting of the Bishops and eight other men. The Church shall be divided into eight districts, from each of which one man shall be elected for four years by the General Conference. The Board shall be amenable for its management only to the General Conference." The Committee on Sunday-Schools reported that a gratifying success had been attained in that department of the work of the Church, and that the ministry were manifesting an increasing interest and zeal in carrying it forward. The Conference advised that, in addition to the Conference and district conventions

already often held, Sunday-school institutes be held, as far as possible, at all appointments, under the direction of the pastor, and that normal classes be established, where instructions may be given in the Biblical sciences and the best methods of teaching. A committee was appointed to prepare and publish a course of study for normal classes; and the speedy publication of a catechism for Sunday-schools in the English and German languages, and the preparation and publication of a Biblical geography, in German, were recommended. Articles were approved, to be recommended to the Annual Conferences, providing that the Bishops, except the one who is at the time in the chair, shall be permitted to take part in the deliberations of the General Conference, without having the right to vote, and that such general officers of the Church as were at present members of the General Conference by virtue of their office should have the privilege of choosing the Annual Conferences of which they would be members, or of retaining membership in the Conferences with which they were already connected, while their official membership of the General Conference should cease. The Rev. Jacob J. Esher, the Rev. Rudolph Dubs, D. D., and the Rev. Thomas Bowman, D. D., were reëlected to the office of Bishop.

EXODUS OF COLORED PEOPLE. The attention of the country during the past year has been attracted to movements among the colored population, chiefly in the States bordering on the Mississippi. There was no appearance of organization or system among these persons. Their irregularity and the absence of preparation seemed to indicate spontaneousness and earnestness. Bands moved from the plantations to the Mississippi River, and thence to St. Louis and other cities, with no defined purpose, except to reach some one of the new States west of the Mississippi, where they expected to enjoy a new Canaan. Their movements received the name of the "Exodus." A large number of these estrays were returned to their homes. Others were sent forward to Kansas, where the welcome was not cordial. There has been much suffering and destitution among them. That there should be a restless and migratory spirit exhibited from time to time by this population, that this should impel to inconsiderate and unorganized efforts for change, and result in unsuccessful experiments, is not surprising. The number of this population is large and increasing. Their place in political and social life is ill-defined, and their merely economical and domestic relations are open to disturbance through the interference and influence of persons unconnected with them socially or economically. Their relations as citizens and voters give them an importance in the eyes of those who are indifferent to them in any other of their relations. A brief retrospect of the history of this race, with a view to ascertain their present condition and future destiny, may not be amiss in view of the interest this exodus has awakened.

The slavery of the African race upon the American Continent had one feature which distinguished it from any form of slavery that had prevailed elsewhere. The slaves were not captives of their masters, nor slaves because of crime nor of patriarchal authority, nor because of debt and the power of the creditor. The African slave-trade was conducted purely for commercial profit. It was regarded as a prime source of wealth and strength, and treaties were made to secure a monopoly of its advantages. It had been carried on for two centuries before the conscience of the world was fully aroused to its atrocity. The contest for its abolition lasted for nearly half a century before full success was attained. There was an intimate relation between the origin of the trade and the destination of its subjects. The arguments for the suppression of the trade at the place of its origin applied with much force to its abolition at the place where the slaves were employed. The abolition of the slave-trade in 1808 in the United States was followed in a few years by attempts to determine the territorial bounds to which slavery should be confined within the United States, and into this discussion the distribution of political power in the States and sectional aggrandizement largely entered. A continuous agitation for some half-century, commencing with the attempt to delay the admission of Missouri into the Union till slavery was prohibited; the fixing of the line of 36° 30′, and the territory north as free territory ; the contests over the territories acquired from Mexico, and upon the admission of Oregon, California, and Kansas to the Union; finally, the civil war and the addition of the Thirteenth, Fourteenth, and Fifteenth Amendments to the Constitution, furnish chapters for the same history. During the period from 1775, when the first motion was submitted for the abolition of slavery (and not then noticed or discussed), until the adoption of the Thirteenth Amendment, in December, 1865, the African race had increased in the United States from less than three hundred thousand to the number of five million persons.

The history of slavery on the eastern continent shows that the progression of the slave population to a condition of freedom and equality was gradual, and that the traces of the progress were indistinct and scarcely discernible, and the fact accomplished without any marked change of law or custom. The abolition of African slavery on this continent has obeyed impulses derived from external forces, and not from the concessions of the master or the demand of the slave.

In 1832 the Ministry of England proposed for inquiry : First, whether the slaves, if emancipated, would maintain themselves, be industrious, and disposed to acquire property by labor ? Secondly, whether the dangers of

convulsions are greater from freedom withheld than from freedom granted ? Before answers were made, Lord Stanley announced that the Ministers had determined to make the "frightful experiment" of emancipation, and spoke of it as "an unreasoning necessity." The Parliament adopted a measure of apprenticeship of the slaves of four and six years, and voted to pay four ninths of their appraised value, and appropriated £20,000,000 for compensation. The Government of Louis Philippe of France proposed a delay of ten years and compensation; but before the measure proposed was adopted the revolutionary government of Lamartine, in a decree of a few lines, terminated the discussion and abolished slavery in the French Antilles. In 1861 one branch of the Congress of the United States assented to an amendment of the Constitution to prohibit the Federal Government from passing any act of abolition without the consent of the slaveholding States. In 1865, by an amendment of the Constitution, slavery was for ever prohibited in any place within the jurisdiction of the United States. In none of these last instances were there consultations with masters or with slaves. In none was there provision for any consequences to arise from the abrupt termination of existing relations. There was no thought taken for the support of the inferiors in these relations in the performance of the obligations and responsibilities of their changed state. Under the law and custom of slavery, the slave was in a great measure discharged from these. His home in general was upon the lands of the master. His daily life was confined to this habitation. He could not leave it but for a few hours or a few days, and that only by permission. He did not select his vocation or employment ; these were provided, and all he did was under supervision. He did not buy, sell, or barter. There were no associations in life or business, nor did he bequeath or inherit. He did not hold property nor perform contracts. The conditions in which he was placed led him to habits of industry, abstinence, and obedience. The gross vices of the world did not have an opportunity to grasp him. It is therefore observable that in all the contentions, controversies, and woes resulting from the existence of these relations, the slave scarcely performed any part whatever—in no instance a conspicuous part. During the civil war in the United States the slaves made no quarrel, no insurrection, and while they remained with their owners they were submissive and obedient. The cessation of hostilities in 1865, and the disruption of the ties which had held the two races in connection, were followed by anarchy and by the disorganization of the economical and domestic relations of the two races. The slaves left their habitations and wandered wildly over the land. They deserted the plantations, their homes, and crowded to the towns and villages. There was no definite aim nor apparent object. They congregated in masses, and spent their days in idleness and vacancy. Then there was a necessity for a Freedman's Bureau, in 1865 and for several years, to furnish them with some guardianship, guidance, and maintenance. The restoration of order and repose, that order and repose which consist in steady pursuits and settled conditions, was not fully attained for many years. In many instances, probably in most instances, the plantation slaves returned for a time at least to their former homes and resumed their accustomed work. The transition from a condition of servitude, where all responsibility and care for themselves was superseded by the control and superintendence of others, to a state of freedom, in which these responsibilities and demands were greatly increased, must have been distressing to the greater part of this population. It would be strange if the majority did not find themselves incompetent to the task. Nor is it surprising that there has not been any marked improvement in their moral or physical condition. The habits and affections acquired in the time of servitude we have mentioned. Sobriety, industry, and domestication we may suppose to have retained a hold upon them, and to account for the absence of any disorder or tumult, and for the maintenance of the existing relations. But a new generation is rapidly rising that did not share in any of the results of this training. They have come into life with instincts to separate from all the associations and to banish the recollections of the life of their progenitors. The seclusion of the plantations, the steady and continuous labor required there, and the absence of excitements and amusements which are found in village and town life, must be repulsive to the sensual natures of this generation. The statesmen of the African race in Hayti seem to have observed this disposition. Toussaint l'Ouverture remanded the laborers on the plantations to their former abodes. He required that they should be supplied with a house and a garden, should have the benefit of a Sunday's market, and should share in the productions of the plantation—generally, one fourth of the gross product. They were prohibited from leaving the plantation without the permission of the owner. The rural code of Hayti in 1826 was more detailed and explicit. "The citizens of the agricultural class" could not be withdrawn from their pursuits except in cases provided by law. They were forbidden to leave the country to reside in towns or villages without permission of the magistrate of their domicile and the consent of the town or village they would reside in. They were prohibited from sending their children to school without such permission. They were not allowed to cultivate a plantation for themselves, and were required to make contracts for service as laborers on the plantations, and were not allowed to leave without permission. The hours of labor were determined, and provisions were made for a house and plot of

ground and means of transportation. Whether this system has been carried into effect, and Hayti is possessed of a sober, industrious, and improving population, may be doubted. The fact is certain that there has been no approximation to the wealth and improvements existing a century ago. In the smaller islands of the British Antilles the relations between the blacks and whites have been harmonious. In Jamaica the tendency has been to estrangement, and the probability is that in the course of a few years there will be none other than the descendants of Africans in that island, as in Hayti.

We have not been able to attribute any particular importance to the movements which have been observed during the past year among the colored population. The publications in the newspapers have been much exaggerated, and the motives for it have been misrepresented. It is quite probable that partisans, eager to accomplish a triumph in an election, may have tempted emigrations from the densely populated districts on the Mississippi River, for a transient and mischievous use of them in some contested election. It may be that some speculators may desire to have a population for waste lands in the far West, and they may have circulated prints and descriptions of a region producing milk and honey, where a black man may bask in the sunshine in idleness between his meals. It may be that there have been instances of wrong and injustice in the dealings of the shopkeepers who besiege the plantations and tempt the laborers to improvident and ruinous dealings, subjecting them to penury and want. It may be that fanatical efforts for establishing large bodies together for religious enterprises or excitements have been operative. It must be remembered that here is a population of about five millions who have been suddenly relieved from restraint and discipline, without being furnished with instruction, and who are without accumulated experience or information of the world and its habits of intercourse. The most improved and advanced are barely able to take care of themselves. The larger proportion are imbecile and incapable for that purpose, and need guidance and guardianship. All of the events of the years following the removal of the restraints we have spoken of, tend to separate this population from those who live in the States where they belonged. There is no reason why there should not be migrations from this part of the country to other portions, and these must be expected. This population will number ten millions of persons within half a century. It is not a population which will add to the intellectual wealth of the country for a long period of time. It is of the utmost consequence that the measures to be adopted in respect to them shall not tend to deteriorate their morals, or fit them to be instruments in the hands of wicked and unscrupulous persons. In so far as projects for a spread of this population over the land tend to the amelioration of their condition, the promotion of their well-being, none should object. It is probable that the interests of the Southern States would be advanced if there was a distribution of this people. At present their numbers exclude from those States a better population. But to entice them to remove upon hopes that are delusive is vicious and criminal.

The temporary disorganization of labor in limited portions of the South threatened disaster to the growing crops. The excitement spread rapidly among the colored people. On April 17th a colored convention assembled in a Baptist church in New Orleans. There was a total attendance of about two hundred persons, at least one third of whom were colored pastors. The assemblage was ill-organized and tumultuous. They refused to appoint a committee on credentials, on the ground that all present belonged to the classes designated in the call for this convention, viz., "clergymen, teachers, or social directors." In point of fact, the body was simply a mass meeting, composed chiefly of blacks brought down from the country as witnesses in the recent political trials. After a recapitulation of the threadbare story of violence and intimidation, they proceeded to discuss the migration of the African race to the Northwest. They were far from unanimous in regard to the expediency of this movement. Mr. Pinchback (colored), of New Orleans, spoke in opposition. He stated that he saw people in Madison Parish sacrificing their stock and tools, and asked them why they did so. The answer was that they were starving; that they were swindled; that they were afraid of the Constitutional Convention; that the Indians were coming to occupy the soil and drive them off. If any colored man wanted to go, let him go; but, having met to consider the interests of their race, he was opposed to a general movement, and must warn the convention of its ruinous consequences. Another orator cited the published opinion of Frederick Douglass adverse to the exodus. The name of Douglass brought down a storm of yells and hisses. Finally a resolution was passed that it was the sense of this convention that the colored people of the South should migrate. Much of the time of the convention was given to the discussion of correspondence from abroad. One of these communications was from the "Congress of Humanity" in New York, suggesting that the Government should provide the people with industries, etc. The convention closed with an "appeal for material aid to the official and moral influence of the President of the United States," and to the Republican party and the country at large.

The Mississippi Valley Labor Convention met in Vicksburg on May 5th. Its object was "to adopt such measures as will allay the excitement prevailing, or will enable them to supply the places of those laborers who have gone, or who may hereafter go, to the West. ern States." Colored delegates were invited to present their grievances and assist in their removal. There was a numerous attendance of planters and of representative colored men. The following resolutions embody the results of their deliberations:

Resolved, That the unrestricted credit system prevailing in all the States here represented, based upon liens or mortgage on stock and crops to be grown in the future, followed by short crops, provoked distrust and created unrest, and disturbed the entire laboring population; and all laws authorizing liens on crops for advance constituted of articles other than those of prime necessity at moderate profits, whether such advances are made by the landlord, planter, or merchants, should be discountenanced and repealed.

Resolved, That this Convention call upon the colored people here present to contradict the false reports circulated among and impressed upon the more ignorant and credulous, and to instruct them that no lands, mules, or money await them in Kansas or elsewhere, without labor or price, and report to the civil authorities all persons disseminating such reports.

Resolved, That it is the constitutional right of the colored people to emigrate where they please, to whatever State they may select for residence; but this Convention urges them to proceed in their movements toward emigration as reasonable human beings, providing in advance by economy the means for transportation and settlement, sustaining their reputation for honesty and fair dealing by preserving intact until the completion of contracts for labor-leasing which have already been made. If, when they have done this, they still desire to leave, all obstacles to their departure will be removed and all practicable assistance will be offered them. Their places will be refilled by other contented labor.

The Nashville Colored Convention assembled in that city on May 7th. It was largely attended by delegates from Alabama, Arkansas, Georgia, Indiana, Illinois, Louisiana, Mississippi, Missouri, Nebraska, Ohio, Oregon, Pennsylvania, Tennessee, and South Carolina. The report set forth the various obstructions to the progress of the blacks during the fifteen years since emancipation. These were attributed solely to the prejudices of color and caste. It recounted the services of the colored people to the Union in freely shedding their blood in defense of its flag and thus securing its victory. It demanded social and political equality as a right. It recommended to the various State Legislatures the adoption of a compulsory system of public education. It insisted that separate schools are injurious to the interests of both races, and foster color prejudices, and that where such schools exist colored teachers alone should be employed. It voted to memorialize Congress to place in the hands of colored regents $300,000, the amount of unclaimed bounty of the colored soldiers and sailors in the Union army during the late war, to be used in establishing and maintaining an industrial and technical school for colored youths in the unoccupied buildings of Harper's Ferry, or at some other place easy of access. The Committee on Organization reported the constitution of an "American Protective Society," whose objects are to prevent injustice to the colored people, to improve their civil, political, educational, moral, and sanitary condition, and to solicit contributions everywhere for these objects. The following resolution was adopted: "*Resolved*, That it is the sense of this conference that the colored people should emigrate to those States and Territories where they can enjoy all the rights which are guaranteed by the laws and Constitution of the United States, and enforced by the executive departments of such States and Territories; and we ask of the United States an appropriation of $500,000, to aid in the removal of our people from the South."

The first refugees to Kansas reached Wyandotte in the beginning of April. By the 1st of August over seven thousand needy and starving persons had arrived in that State. A Relief Society was formed, with its headquarters at Topeka. In spite of strenuous efforts to provide employment, the temporary barracks erected for their shelter were overcrowded, and the association had already expended over $7,000 in alms. On the 15th of March the Mayor of St. Louis issued a proclamation advising colored people without means not to come to that city, as it could neither support them nor forward them to their destination. A meeting of delegates from the Kansas Relief Committees published a resolution that, "to prevent want and suffering among our colored immigrants, we hereby express our opinion that proper means should be taken to divert the tide of immigration to other and older States, where accumulated wealth and population afford facilities for their successful settlement." Notwithstanding these discouragements, the exodus has continued intermittently and from various parts of the South. The blacks are an emotional, credulous, and capricious race. Emancipation came to them without preparation or effort on their part. They understood by freedom exemption from labor. Nothing but experience can dispel the delusions and disquiets fostered by their peculiar political education.

In regard to the exodus, public opinion in the South tends to a policy of masterly inactivity.

F

FECHTER, CHARLES ALBERT, a French actor, born in London, October 23, 1824, died at Quakertown, Pa., August 4, 1879. His father, a native of France, was of German lineage; his mother, a native of Flanders, was of Italian lineage; so that in him were united distinct and opposite characteristics of race. In temperament and speech, however, he was decidedly French. He was educated in England and France. His father desired him to become a sculptor, but his tastes were more inclined toward the dramatic profession, and he soon abandoned the *atelier* for the stage. His début occurred in 1840 at the Salle Molière in Paris. After this event he studied several weeks at the Conservatory, and then went to Florence, Italy, with a dramatic company, as leading juvenile. Upon his return to Paris, at his father's request he turned his attention once more to sculpture, becoming a student at the Academy of Fine Arts. Within a short time he was again at the Conservatory, remaining, however, but three weeks, when his name was placed on a list of applicants for a début at the Théâtre Français. While waiting for an opportunity he modeled a piece of sculpture representing "The Seven Capital Sins," for which he received the grand medal of the Academy. In 1844 he made his début as Seide in Voltaire's "Mahomet," and subsequently played Valère in Molière's great comedy. He was next heard of at the Theatre Royal of Berlin, where he acted miscellaneous parts under the management of M. Saint-Aubin. In 1847 he again appeared in Paris, acting in the Vaudeville, and in the same year took a company to London. In 1848 he filled a third engagement in Paris, and from this time to 1860 was a reigning favorite on the French stage. His great success in those days was gained as Armand Duval in "Les Dames aux Camélias," of which he was the original representative. In 1860 he again went to London, this time with the intention of playing in English. On October 27th he made his début in English drama at the Princess's Theatre as Ruy Blas, which was followed by "The Corsican Brothers," "Don César de Bazan," and finally, in March, 1861, by "Hamlet," in which he achieved great success. In 1869 Charles Dickens wrote as follows:

Perhaps no innovation in art was ever accepted with so much favor by so many intellectual persons, precommitted to and preoccupied by another system, as Mr. Fechter's Hamlet. I take this to have been the case (as it unquestionably was in London), not because of its picturesqueness, not because of its novelty, not because of its many scattered beauties, but because of its perfect consistency with itself. As the animal-painter said of his favorite picture of rabbits, that there was more nature about those rabbits than you usually found in rabbits, so it may be said of Mr. Fechter's Hamlet that there was more consistency about that Hamlet than you usually found in Hamlets. Its great and satisfying originality was in its possessing the merit of a distinctly conceived and executed idea. From the first appearance of the broken glass of fashion and mold of form, pale and worn with weeping for his father's death, and remotely suspicious of its cause, to his final struggle with Horatio for the fatal cup, there were cohesion and coherence in Mr. Fechter's view of the character.

In 1863 he leased the Lyceum Theatre, and brought out there "The Duke's Motto," "Bel Demonio," and other successful pieces. In 1870 he came to New York, and then went to Boston, and at both places he met crowded audiences. He next attempted to act as manager of the Globe Theatre in Boston, but failed in the venture. He also on several other occasions essayed management, the principal enterprises being the Lyceum and Park Theatres in New York, but generally met with great financial losses. He was, however, eminently successful otherwise, and he was always well received on his appearances in different cities.

FEVER, YELLOW. The first outbreak of the fever during this year was in an unexpected quarter. The United States ship Plymouth sailed from Santa Cruz to Norfolk on the 7th of November, 1878, with several cases of yellow fever on board. In this infected condition she was ordered to Portsmouth, N. H., where she underwent a rigid quarantine. On the 17th of December she entered Boston Harbor. Taking with them their bedding and personal effects, officers and crew left the vessel on the 8th of January, and did not return to it until February 12th. The official report says: "During this period the temperature of the air was generally below the freezing-point, and ice formed and remained solid in buckets throughout the ship. Hatches and air-pipes were left open. Fumigations with sulphurous acids were several times used, disinfectants applied to the bilges, and lime-water was freely used. In fact, the disinfecting agents of cold, fresh air, and fumigation were freely used." The Plymouth sailed for the Windward Isles on March 15th. At sea, on the 21st, yellow fever broke out on board.

On December 16, 1878, a family who had resided for eight months in Chicago took passage in a Pullman palace-car for New Orleans, and arrived there on the 18th. On the 22d one of the children was taken down with an undoubted attack of yellow fever. No cases of fever had occurred in the house occupied by this family. It was new and freshly painted and whitewashed, had been opened to the frosty air for thorough ventilation previous to their occupancy, and was altogether in admirable sanitary condition. The child's case was regular in all its manifestations. It had black vomit, and recovered. There were in this household several unacclimated persons in close attendance upon the patient, but none of them contracted the disease. The thermometer in the sick-room marked 42°. Outside the weather was bitterly cold.

Throughout the South the winter was one of unusual severity; but the cold proved insufficient to destroy the yellow-fever virus.

Memphis.—Memphis was blighted by a recurrence of the scourge. It is difficult to trace the inception of the disease. It must be remembered that many material interests are destroyed by the announcement of a single case. It is not surprising that, acting in all good faith, physicians hesitate to affix this dreaded name so long as there is the slightest doubt. It is probable that there were several cases in Memphis during the first week of July. There was a death in the Tenth Ward on July 8th, registered as malarial fever. It may be presumed that this was really yellow fever, from the fact that persons residing in the neighborhood, who visited this patient, contracted that disease. On July 8th the first case was reported to the Board of Health. Death occurred on the 10th, and a *post-mortem* examination left no doubt of its genuineness. So soon as this became known, an unparalleled panic broke out. Railroad tickets to the value of over ten thousand dollars were sold in one day. Streets and avenues were blocked, and every available vehicle was pressed into service. On that day a number of suspicious cases were reported, of which five proved to be yellow fever. These six cases appeared simultaneously in widely separated parts of the town. One was in the Sixth Ward, two in the Eighth, and three in the Tenth, at least a mile distant from the other two points. No communication between them has been traced. They were attended by different physicians, who did not meet, and belonged to different social classes not likely to be thrown in contact. It is noticeable that the three houses in which these cases occurred were not inhabited during the previous epidemic. It is said that bedding and clothing used by members of the family who died of yellow fever in 1878 were still preserved in one of these houses, and that in the other second-hand bedding had been purchased. These may have imparted the poison. Strenuous efforts were made by isolation and disinfection to stay the progress of the disease. For a time there was hope of success, but by the 19th of July, thoroughly disheartened, the authorities advised the people to leave. On the 10th of August the pestilence was declared epidemic. No part of the city was then exempt, except the Ninth Ward, an outlying suburb called Chelsea. The condition of Memphis was now gloomy beyond precedent. Yellow flags at every turn betokened the presence of the destroyer. Door after door bore this inscription, "Closed until after the fever." There was no life except on the bluff where the colored troops were encamped. The darkest chapter in the story of this epidemic is the unruly disposition evinced by the negro population. They flocked into the town, attracted by the expectation of free rations, and became not only food for the fever, but a menace to the living. Robbery and incendiarism were of daily occurrence. The white population were insufficient for the care of the sick and the protection of property. The colored companies were called out, and, under the command of Colonel Cameron, aide to the Governor of Tennessee, succeeded in repressing the disturbances. About eight miles from the city refugee camps were prepared for this class of the population. It was very desirable that they should be placed out of risk of starvation and infection, thus freeing the city from riot and pauper sick. It was with much difficulty, and under the promise of government support, that they were induced to remove.

The epidemic of this year did not rouse public attention to the same degree as the last; therefore there was not the same outflow of sympathy and substantial aid. The Howard Association, fully organized, pursued its labor of charity; but the efficiency of its work was cramped by lack of means. Yet the necessity was great. The mortality in proportion to the unacclimated population was greater than during the summer of 1878, and the suffering was unprecedented. The population when the fever showed itself is estimated by the superintendent of camps at 38,400; of these 20,000 were sent into camp outside the town, within a distance of ten miles. This prompt depopulation left within the city limits about 18,500, of whom 14,500 were black. The following table shows the number of cases and deaths as registered by the Board of Health to the middle of November:

CASES.

MONTHS.	White.	Colored.	Total.
July	153	85	188
August	320	363	683
September	240	208	448
October	132	73	205
November	8	..	8
Total	853	679	1,532

DEATHS.

MONTHS.	White.	Per cent.	Colored.	Per cent.	Total.
July	52	88·9	5	14·2	57
August	134	41·9	43	11·8	177
September	116	48·3	43	20·6	159
October	65	49·2	15	20·5	80
November	12	1·5	..	....	12
Total	379	44·4	106	15·6	485

The unsanitary condition of Memphis is admitted, and is in great part attributed to the disorganization occasioned by the plague of 1878. Sickness and death did their work on the *personnel* of the Board of Health itself. Sanitary work, suspended during that epidemic, was not recommenced until the succeeding February. When reorganized, the Board of Health was in a measure paralyzed. The charter of the city of Memphis was abolished by the Legislature in January. The Legislative Council, as the new government was styled, accepted neither the assets nor the liabilities of their predecessors, thus beginning their administration with an empty treasury and without credit. The operations of the Council were further suspended pending a suit to ascertain its legality. Thus for seven months a city claiming a population of 40,000 was without power or means to enforce the most ordinary health ordinance. Its condition needs no description. The necessity for sanitary work was so apparent that, once begun, it was prosecuted with vigor. Much was accomplished

through individual effort. It is said that in July the condition of the city compared favorably with that of the preceding year. Streets and alleys had been cleansed. Proper garbage-carts had for the first time been procured, and they were in daily use. But the evil is beyond the reach of superficial cleanliness. Situated on a bluff, with the current of the mightiest of rivers sweeping below, nature has offered every facility for proper drainage and sewerage. No advantage has been taken of this. The Gayoso Bayou is a fruitful source of miasma. The system of vaults is noisome. The water in wells and underground cisterns is contaminated. The Nicolson pavement is in a state of decay, and a large portion of it had been torn up preparatory to a substitution of stone. The fever has been attributed to the work on this pavement. The uncovered earth and rotting wood may have generated malaria, but the relaying of the pavement can not be the cause of the fever, since it was begun on the 29th of August, after the fever was epidemic, and only on a short portion of a business street leading to the Charleston depot. Much opposition was made to the order prohibiting the traffic in cotton. It is a common opinion that cotton does not carry infection. The French code ranks it also among the second or less dangerous class of fomites, on what scientific grounds is not known. The question was hotly debated, local interests being bound up in the decision.

The yellow fever spread from Memphis to many neighboring points. At Buntyn Station, where it proved severe, there is some doubt as to its importation, a child having died there on June 27th of continued fever ending in black vomit. This case was reported to the Shelby Medical Society on July 2d, but not pronounced yellow fever. Five similar cases among children in Memphis, resulting in recovery, were reported at the same meeting, six days before the first acknowledged case of yellow fever. Near Oak Grove, Miss., thirty miles southeast of Memphis, the outbreak is traced to goods wagoned from that town. A young lady, whose wedding attire was brought in this way, was the first victim. After five days' illness, she died on September 22d. Unfortunately, the disease was not recognized, isolation was not attempted, and it spread rapidly among her relations and friends in this thickly settled section. At Forest City, Ark., out of the first thirteen deaths, nine were females. They attended the funeral of a victim of this unrecognized malady, and probably contracted the disease in the close room where the services were performed. At Vidalia and Concordia the fever ran a short but severe course. In Memphis it gradually declined until October 25th, when pickets and inspectors were disbanded, and the epidemic was declared at an end.

New Orleans.—The year opened with a novel but welcome sight. During several days the pavements were almost impassable. In the gardens and public squares every blade of grass and the broad banaua-leaves were cased in ice, which glittered but did not melt under a brilliant sun. It is conceded that fever does not spread with the temperature below 60°, and it has been the prevalent belief that a cold lower than 32° is destructive of the poison. Houses were thrown open to freely admit this beneficent natural disinfectant. But reliance on refrigeration did not supersede other attempts at sanitation, the lessons of the previous year being too vivid. The city authorities, and the local and the national Boards of Health, were ably seconded by a volunteer organization, the New Orleans Auxiliary Sanitary Association. They collected their own funds by private subscription, coöperated with the municipal authorities, and did much work that the city and Board of Health could not perform. They established a systematic house-to-house inspection. Not satisfied with suggesting disinfection, they undertook it, and it was done efficiently and continually. Pumps, one of which cost $9,000, were presented by the President of this Association and a public-spirited firm of merchants. With their aid the gutters were constantly flowing with fresh water. The potter's-field, a crying evil, was covered with a deep layer of earth, and a new one was opened. Roused by their appeals, public opinion enforced many reforms. The Common Council undertook the work of filling, not with garbage but with pure river-sand, the "fever-holes" which for over twenty-five years have disfigured the Levee, extending for a mile along the river-front. The magnitude of the work accomplished may be better estimated when it is said that they average six feet in depth. The area to be filled was 644,000 square feet, or about fifteen acres, and required 129,000 cubic yards of sand. Much is due to these energetic and patriotic exertions. The exemption from epidemic is doubtless the result of a combination of causes. The weather throughout the summer was unusually and sometimes unseasonably cool. The tables on page 363 show the relative temperature, barometer, and rainfall of the two seasons. The languor and oppression under which sick and well suffered during 1878 belong evidently to atmospheric conditions not yet tabulated. It is to be regretted, in the interests of science, that the Signal Service does not in New Orleans test the degree of electricity. The alkalinity of the air should also be registered.

In the teeth of much heated opposition, a strong quarantine was maintained by the local Board of Health. Notwithstanding this, the first case of this season entered the city on the 27th of March. The steamship Baltimore, from Rio Janeiro, reached quarantine on March 25th. After due fumigation and ventilation, and two days' detention, she was allowed to proceed. The coxswain was taken down with fever on the evening of the 26th. Removed to the Touro Infirmary, he passed through the

disease to recovery. No infection spread from this patient. The next cases occurred eleven weeks later, in a house on Third Street, between Constance and Camp. Constance Street has been for years the spot where the fever comes earliest and lingers latest. Through this section once ran a sluggish bayou, long since filled up. Possibly its marshy surroundings, or its action as a natural drain to the neighborhood, may cause its unhealthiness. There had been several cases and one death in this Third Street house during 1878. It was rented by an unacclimated family, who had never spent a summer in New Orleans. It had been thoroughly renovated and cleansed, except the vault, which had not been emptied for more than a year. This was done on June 8th. On the 16th one of the children showed fever symptoms. On the 17th the second child was taken. The third was attacked on the 22d, and the fourth on the 27th. On the 12th of July the uncle of these children caught the disease. On the 14th the last child was fever-stricken. On the 17th the father, pilot on board a river-steamer, was prostrated by the disease when the boat was twenty miles below Vicksburg. Of these seven cases all recovered. The symptoms were not so marked as to convince the attending physician, a man of experience and integrity, that they were yellow fever, and they were therefore not reported. A servant employed in this household, after nursing the sick children, went to Mississippi City to visit her family, who reside near this seashore resort, situated a short distance from New Orleans on the Gulf coast. Apparently well when she left New Orleans, on the 6th of July she was seized, before she reached her home on the evening of that same day. On the 10th she died. The fever was communicated to her family. On the 18th two were taken, on the 19th two more, and on the 20th the last brother was attacked. Of these six cases, two died. Some two hundred yards distant from them was the residence of a gentleman whose son was taken ill on July 25th. It is believed that this child played with his little neighbors, and thus contracted the disease. Much difference of opinion prevailed among the physicians who examined these cases. Some classed them as bilious, some as malarial hæmorrhagic fever. The question was practically settled when an Italian girl dwelling at the corner of Constance and Second Streets, within a short distance of the house where the seven doubtful cases had previously appeared, died of undoubted yellow fever on July 27th. A washerwoman living in the next yard carried home the clothing of a family in Washington Street, who received the infection. They perceived an odor of carbolic acid, and discovered too late that it was due to disinfectants lavishly used on the adjoining premises.

Within two squares of the first infected house was the mansion of General Hood. Af-

Comparative Statement of Mean Daily Barometer for June, July, August, September, and October, 1878 and 1879, at New Orleans, La.

DATE.	June 1878	June 1879	July 1878	July 1879	August 1878	August 1879	September 1878	September 1879	October 1878	October 1879
1	29·98	30·01	29·94	30·01	30·04	30·06	30·09	29·48	29·98	30·18
2	29·93	30·05	29·85	30·09	30·00	30·11	30·05	29·81	30·00	30·11
3	29·98	30·10	29·82	30·11	29·91	30·08	30·01	29·97	29·98	30·09
4	30·01	30·12	29·89	30·15	29·90	30·04	29·99	30·01	29·98	30·02
5	30·01	30·09	29·96	30·15	29·83	30·04	29·98	30·08	30·01	29·91
6	29·95	30·00	29·99	30·08	29·92	30·03	29·94	30·06	30·03	29·81
7	29·84	29·96	30·00	30·10	29·95	30·00	29·97	30·05	30·05	29·94
8	29·82	29·95	30·02	30·15	29·94	30·01	29·98	30·05	30·04	30·05
9	29·82	29·92	30·03	30·12	29·94	30·08	29·89	30·06	29·97	30·08
10	29·98	29·90	30·01	30·05	29·94	30·04	29·84	30·11	29·89	30·07
11	30·02	29·94	30·07	29·97	29·98	30·06	29·92	30·13	29·98	30·01
12	29·96	29·98	30·06	29·94	29·95	30·04	29·98	30·05	30·06	30·04
13	30·00	29·88	30·07	29·95	29·91	30·00	30·09	30·02	30·09	30·05
14	29·97	29·96	30·02	29·99	29·92	29·91	30·13	30·04	30·10	30·00
15	29·89	29·86	29·92	30·02	29·95	29·90	30·10	30·04	30·05	29·85
16	29·84	29·92	29·88	30·04	30·01	29·90	30·10	30·05	30·00	29·82
17	29·89	29·99	30·00	30·01	30·04	29·91	30·15	30·07	30·08	30·01
18	29·91	29·99	29·98	29·98	30·07	29·98	30·16	30·02	30·14	30·08
19	29·88	29·99	29·98	29·99	30·08	30·02	30·05	29·96	30·15	30·07
20	29·86	30·06	30·01	30·00	29·96	29·98	29·98	29·93	30·06	30·01
21	29·83	30·12	29·96	30·00	29·98	29·88	30·00	29·92	29·98	30·00
22	29·95	30·12	29·95	29·91	29·92	29·64	30·01	29·99	30·08	30·05
23	30·02	30·04	29·99	29·86	29·97	29·66	30·05	30·06	30·18	30·22
24	30·01	30·00	29·96	29·94	30·01	29·81	30·10	30·12	30·19	30·21
25	29·99	30·01	29·88	29·98	29·94	29·92	30·08	30·11	30·22	30·29
26	30·06	30·05	29·84	29·99	29·89	29·90	30·12	30·10	30·20	30·26
27	30·10	30·00	29·91	29·99	29·92	29·86	30·06	30·14	30·19	30·11
28	30·05	29·87	29·93	30·00	29·96	29·98	30·02	30·10	30·10	30·07
29	30·03	29·86	29·95	30·00	29·91	29·94	30·00	30·07	29·90	30·02
30	30·00	29·91	29·99	30·00	29·90	29·90	29·98	30·11	30·18	30·07
31	....	....	30·01	30·01	30·02	29·77	....	....	30·37	30·22
Monthly mean.	29·952	29·987	29·959	30·019	29·956	29·945	30·025	30·025	30·072	30·059

Comparative Statement of Mean Daily Temperature and Rainfall for June, July, August, September, and October, 1878 and 1879, at New Orleans, La.

DATE.	TEMPERATURE.										RAINFALL.									
	June 1878	June 1879	July 1878	July 1879	Aug 1878	Aug 1879	Sep 1878	Sep 1879	Oct 1878	Oct 1879	June 1878	June 1879	July 1878	July 1879	Aug 1878	Aug 1879	Sep 1878	Sep 1879	Oct 1878	Oct 1879
1	83·0	78·0	88·5	83·2	84·7	83·0	80·7	79·2	79·5	79·2	....	·72	·24	·08	·05	·54	·18	·84	·58	....
2	82·7	75·7	81·2	83·0	85·7	82·5	88·7	80·2	81·0	79·5	....	1·52	·24	·66	·01	·05	·01	—	....	·02
3	82·0	73·2	79·2	80·5	88·0	84·0	80·2	80·7	81·2	80·0	·01	....	·65	1·88	1·85	·18	·29	....	....	....
4	81·2	73·7	81·0	81·5	79·7	84·0	79·2	82·0	79·2	80·5	....	....	....	....	....	·09	·08	·97	....	....
5	82·5	76·0	80·0	82·7	83·0	80·5	81·7	80·0	77·0	78·0	·04	·01	·18	....	·01	1·48	....	....	·06	·18
6	82·0	76·7	81·2	83·2	83·7	81·5	82·7	80·7	76·0	74·7	—	·08	·08	....	....	·04	·01	....	....	·05
7	82·7	77·2	85·2	83·0	84·7	82·5	83·2	77·2	76·2	....	—	·26	....	....	....	·86	·08	....	....	·05
8	80·5	80·0	84·5	83·2	85·5	81·5	81·5	83·2	79·2	78·0	—	·14	....	....	....	·82	·95	—	·01	·11
9	79·7	82·0	85·0	85·2	85·7	80·0	84·0	84·0	74·7	79·2	·73	....	....	....	....	1·11	....	....	2·05	....
10	78·7	82·5	85·0	85·2	84·7	79·7	84·2	78·7	74·0	79·2	·71	....	....	....	....	....	....	·09	·20	....
11	77·5	81·7	84·0	85·2	84·0	77·7	74·2	79·5	75·5	79·0	....	—	·14	....	·25	·02	....	·05	....	·02
12	80·5	81·5	82·2	85·5	83·5	78·2	70·7	79·0	74·7	77·2	·34	—	·10	....	·02	·45	....	·77	....	....
13	83·0	82·5	85·5	85·0	82·7	77·5	70·0	73·5	74·2	77·2	—	·10	·84	....	·21	2·54	....	·19	....	....
14	82·7	84·0	85·0	86·0	82·0	79·7	72·5	76·0	75·5	77·2	....	....	....	....	·09	·08	....	....	....	....
15	79·5	82·2	86·7	86·5	84·7	81·0	70·5	76·0	75·2	74·2	·72	·18	....	....	....	....	....	....	....	·17
16	80·2	84·0	86·0	82·7	81·5	80·0	76·5	77·5	76·7	76·7	·08	....	....	....	....	....	....	·08	....	·01
17	83·7	84·2	82·5	82·0	84·0	79·5	78·7	77·7	71·5	77·5	....	....	·28	·19	·01	....	....	....	·66	·01
18	84·2	86·0	84·0	83·7	84·7	79·2	79·0	80·0	67·0	71·0	....	....	·39	·17	·01	....	....	....	....	....
19	96·7	83·2	84·2	84·0	85·0	79·2	78·5	79·5	59·0	67·7	....	....	....	·87	....	—	....	....	....	....
20	85·0	81·5	86·2	82·7	85·5	81·5	77·2	80·0	62·5	65·0	....	....	....	1·38	....	....	....	....	....	....
21	85·5	90·7	82·2	88·0	86·2	81·2	78·7	78·0	62·2	70·2	·02	....	2·74	....	....	·37	·14	....	....	....
22	83·0	82·0	84·7	83·0	86·2	80·5	77·7	74·2	61·2	71·5	....	....	·18	·52	2·11	·10	—	·07	....	....
23	82·0	81·0	86·2	83·2	85·2	82·7	79·7	75·0	73·0	70·5	....	....	....	1·01	·01	·21	·01	....	....	....
24	81·5	80·2	87·7	83·0	84·7	83·7	73·5	77·2	63·5	58·5	....	....	....	·07	....	....	·48	....	....	....
25	81·0	81·7	85·7	82·7	84·7	78·5	75·5	68·0	61·0	....	....	....	....	....	....	....	....	....	....	....
26	81·0	81·7	86·0	82·5	80·7	84·0	80·7	77·2	70·7	60·0	·76	....	·04	·08	·01	....	....	....	....	·25
27	83·7	82·7	85·0	83·0	82·2	81·2	80·2	75·5	65·0	62·0	....	....	·08	....	·01	....	—	....	·01	·54
28	82·0	83·7	85·2	83·2	83·5	80·7	78·5	75·7	60·0	65·0	1·65	....	....	·01	....	....	—	....	·01	....
29	80·2	84·7	85·2	83·0	78·0	82·0	76·2	76·5	66·5	66·5	1·35	....	....	2·05	....	....	....	....	1·48	....
30	81·2	83·0	84·0	81·5	79·5	80·7	78·5	76·0	65·0	67·7	·22	....	·01	·06	·14	....	....	·97	....	....
31	....	....	85·7	81·7	80·7	77·7	....	....	57·0	64·5	....	....	....	·57	....	....	....	....	....	—
Monthly mean	82·0	80·9	84·1	83·0	83·5	80·0	78·7	78·5	70·6	72·4	7·85	2·96	6·21	7·04	5·81	10·44	2·64	3·15	5·07	1·86

Note.—The rainfall is given in inches and hundredths. The dash (—) signifies that the amount of rainfall on that day was too small to measure.

ter three members of the family had fallen victims to the fever, a careful inspection by the physician of the local Board of Health revealed two ill-constructed and unventilated vaults beneath the basement. These were securely sealed, and, whether as a result or as a simple coincidence, no further cases occurred in this numerous and unacclimated household. The deaths in this family gave an unusual notoriety to the existence of fever in New Orleans. Quarantines were maintained with rigor, and the commercial loss to the city was as great as in years of severe epidemic.

A focus of infection was well established, and round it the disease smoldered slowly. The local Board of Health attacked it promptly, and exhausted the resources of science in disinfection. Always menacing, the disease never attained the mastery, until frost, or the power that controls both pestilence and frost, relieved the people from deadly apprehension.

The infected district lay between Tchoupitoulas and Constance, First and Seventh Streets, comprising in all forty-five squares. From these must be excluded six squares in the southwest corner which were exempted. Within this limited area occurred twenty-four out of the forty-one cases of this year. Of the remaining seventeen cases, five were imported. The twelve others were distributed over different parts of the city. These may or may not have been "original cases." It has been found impossible to trace their causes. They evinced no disposition to spread except in the infected district. This dangerous locality was the scene of the sharp autumnal epidemic of 1876, while the rest of the city was spared. It is the field upon which public-spirited sanitarians should expend all their energies. Its redemption from pestilence would silence the opponents sooner than columns of paper argument.

Although there have been cases of doubtful or difficult diagnosis, the faculty have shown a spirit of candor. Suspicious cases have been reported, and due consultation has been held with a single eye to truth. The following table is worthy of acceptance as containing the whole truth and nothing but the truth:

DETAILS.	Males.	Females.	Total.
Total number of cases, diagnosis perfected and recorded as yellow fever...........................	22	19	41
Total deaths.......................	9	10	19
Cases of children ten years of age and under..........................	11	6	17
Deaths of children ten years of age and under........................	4	4	8
Cases of persons over ten years of age	12	12	24
Deaths of persons over ten years of age................................	5	6	11

Of the forty-one cases, all were whites; nineteen were natives of New Orleans, two of the State at large, and twenty were persons from abroad. The five imported cases reached New Orleans, one from Rio Janeiro and four from Morgan City.

Morgan City is a port of entry on Berwick's Bay, about eighty miles from New Orleans. It has a fine harbor, used chiefly by the Texas steamers connecting with Morgan's Texas and Opelousas Railroad. The population is about 3,000. It was scourged in 1878. The fever broke out again early in the season. The house in which the Jewish rabbi and his wife died in 1878 was hurriedly closed. Not even was the last meal removed from the table. In May the house was opened and the effects were sold at auction. From this house and its scattered contents the virus spread. From Morgan City the infection was taken to Berwick and thence to Centreville. Persons from Bayou Bœuf who visited Morgan City before the disease was recognized carried the infection home with them. Thence it spread through Assumption Parish, and in a capricious and sporadic manner visited various small settlements and plantations. It followed the lines of travel rather than those of prevalent winds. At the Patout settlement it was generally disseminated, and was fatal during its brief visitation. A social gathering was held at the house of one of the principal families of the neighborhood, a young lady belonging to which had returned from a visit indisposed, but not ill. The festivities went on until a sudden change for the worse occurred, and before the guests could leave the house she died of pronounced yellow fever. Many of them were soon fever-stricken.

In comparison with 1878, the fever record of 1879 is insignificant. A wide field for study and experiment was opened. The warmth of the discussion provoked proves the earnestness of the inquirers. It is to be hoped that preventives or remedy may be found. The question of quarantine is still an open one. Until disproved, its officers should be upheld by opinion and the press. No commercial interests should weigh against the public health. That the virus is transported in ships is known. Many pronounce it a ship-disease. In 1872 there was in the harbor of Pernambuco a frightful epidemic confined wholly to the shipping, no cases whatever being produced on shore. A new ship, built in 1876, the Niagara, became infected in Havana and underwent scientific disinfection. The day after leaving New York, on the return trip, yellow fever broke out on board. From this it is argued that the vessel itself communicated the infection. It is known that infection clings to decayed wood. The captain attributes it to faulty construction, as two inches of her bilge-water can not be pumped out. These are suggestive instances. Refrigeration has not yet been fairly tested. It ought to be fully tried, although Alpine researches have demonstrated that low-class organisms inclosed in ice for an indefinite period have retained vitality.

The most hopeful signs of the times are the vigorous measures taken to confront the foe.

Public interest is aroused. Scientists are grappling with unsolved but not insoluble problems. Sewerage and drainage are discussed. The country at large is receiving advanced instruction in hygiene. Sanitary associations are prosecuting the work of disinfection and cleanliness. The American Health Association is continuing its labors. Railroad managers have met in convention to secure liberty of traffic and security to health. State boards of health are employing local experience and State powers. The Government has undertaken to be the arbiter of inter-State difficulties, and the guardian of the whole water-line in preventing importation. (See HEALTH, NATIONAL BOARD OF.) We may trust that the year is at hand when the land will be delivered from the noisome pestilence.

FINANCES OF THE UNITED STATES.

The improvement in commercial and financial affairs of the previous year was continued during 1879, although the last six months of it passed under a resumption of specie payments. The refunding of the Government bonds was entirely successful, and even a lower rate of interest was suggested as practicable.

In the annual report of the Secretary of the Treasury made in December, 1878, there was presented a statement of the receipts and expenditures of the Government for the first quarter of the fiscal year ending June 30, 1879, and an estimate of the same for the remaining three quarters, as follows:

RECEIPTS.	For the quarter ending September 30, 1878. Actual.	For the remaining three quarters of the year. Estimated.
From customs.............	$38,868,268 10	$94,181,781 90
From internal revenue.....	28,572,144 46	86,427,855 54
From sales of public lands..	260,765 63	789,234 37
From tax on circulation and deposits of national banks	3,868,519 03	3,381,480 97
From repayment of interest by Pacific Railway Companies.............	897,737 10	952,262 90
From customs fees, fines, penalties, etc...	244,883 93	705,116 07
From fees—consular, letters patent, and lands....	508,890 76	1,491,109 24
From proceeds of sales of Government property ..	41,127 51	208,872 49
From premium on sales of coin....................	5,441 28	44,558 77
From profits on coinage, etc.	71,968 31	1,728,031 69
From miscellaneous sources	1,060,027 87	1,239,972 68
Total receipts........	$73,399,723 48	$191,100,276 57

In the actual receipts for 1878–'79, given below, there was an increase compared with the previous year of between 16 and 17 millions—in customs revenues, 7 millions; in internal revenue, nearly 3 millions; and from interest from Pacific Railroads, coinage profits, and other sources, over 6¼ millions—offset by a decrease in public land sales, profits on sales of coin, bank-taxes, etc., footing up about two thirds of a million.

The expenditures for the same period, actual and estimated, were:

EXPENDITURES.	For the quarter ending September 30, 1878. Actual.	For the remaining three quarters of the year. Estimated.
For civil and miscellaneous expenses, including public buildings, lighthouses, and collecting the revenue	$15,044,519 62	$39,955,480 88
For Indians.................	1,750,517 25	3,049,482 75
For pensions...............	7,802,465 68	21,497,534 37
For military establishment, including fortifications, river and harbor improvements, and arsenals.....	10,258,900 87	28,741,099 13
For naval establishment, including vessels and machinery, and improvements at navy yards......	4,520,742 84	10,479,257 16
For interest on the public debt..................	33,967,427 06	63,032,572 94
Total ordinary expenditures.............	$73,344,573 27	$166,755,426 73

Total receipts, actual and estimated............ $264,500,000
Total expenditures, actual and estimated....... 240,100,000

Leaving a balance of...................... $24,400,000
applicable to the sinking fund, which is estimated for the year at $36,954,607.87.

By this estimate it was expected that the surplus would be $24,400,000. But the ordinary revenues from all sources for the fiscal year ending June 30, 1879, were as follows:

From customs	$137,250,047 70
From internal revenue....................	113,561,610 58
From sales of public lands.................	924,781 06
From tax on circulation and deposits of national banks....................	6,747,500 32
From repayment of interest by Pacific Railway companies..........................	2,707,201 03
From customs fees, fines, penalties, etc......	1,100,871 66
From fees—consular, letters patent, and lands.	2,186,051 79
From proceeds of sales of Government property ..	181,128 81
From premium on sales of coin..............	8,104 88
From premium on loans..................	1,496,943 25
From profits on coinage, etc..............	2,924,988 67
From revenues of the District of Columbia...	1,741,461 16
From miscellaneous sources................	8,046,544 05
Total ordinary receipts...............	$273,827,184 46

The ordinary expenditures for the same period were:

For civil expenses.......................	$16,489,997 17
For foreign intercourse....................	1,333,586 13
For Indians...........................	5,206,109 08
For pensions, including $5,373,000 arrears of pensions.................................	35,121,482 39
For the military establishment, including river and harbor improvements and arsenals,	40,425,660 73
For the naval establishment, including vessels, machinery, and improvements at navy yards..................................	15,125,126 84
For miscellaneous expenditures, including public buildings, lighthouses, and collecting the revenue..........................	33,870,205 78
For expenditures on account of the District of Columbia.............................	3,597,516 41
For interest on the public debt..............	105,327,949 00
For payment of Halifax award...............	5,500,000 00
Total ordinary expenditures........	$266,947,883 53
Leaving a surplus revenue of.............	$6,879,300 93

Which was applied as follows:

To the redemption of United States notes, etc..	$31,617 50
To the redemption of fractional currency....	705,158 66
To the redemption of six per cent. bonds for the sinking fund.........................	18,500 00
To increase of cash balance in the Treasury..	6,124,024 77
Total..............................	$6,879,300 93

The amount due the sinking fund for the year was $36,955,604.63, leaving a deficiency on this account of $30,076,303.70. Compared with the previous fiscal year, the receipts for 1879 have increased $16,711,159.70, in the following items: In customs revenue, $7,079,367.-50; in internal revenue, $2,979,985.84; in premium on loans, $1,496,943.25; in repayment of interest by Pacific Railroad companies, $1,-840,246.67; in profits on coinage, $1,234,176.-84; and in miscellaneous items, $2,580,440.10. There was a decrease of $647,853.94, as follows: In sales of public lands, $154,962.31; in premium on sales of coin, $308,997.92; in semi-annual tax on banks, $115,552.64; and in proceeds of sales of Government property, $68,341.07; making a net increase in the receipts from all sources for the year of $16,063,-305.76.

The expenditures show an increase over the previous year of $32,223,731.26, as follows: In the War Department, $8,271,512.88; in the Interior Department, $8,561,292.11 (Indians $576,828.80, and pensions $7,984,463.31); in the interest on the public debt, $2,827,074.35; and in the civil and miscellaneous, $12,563,-851.92. There was a decrease of $2,240,174.-53 in the Navy Department; making a net increase in the expenditures of $29,983,556.73.

The receipts and expenditures for the first quarter of the fiscal year ending June 30, 1880, and the estimates for the three remaining quarters, were as follows:

RECEIPTS.	For the quarter ending September 30, 1879. Actual.	For the remaining three quarters of the year. Estimated.
From customs.......... ..	$44,088,497 98	$107,916,502 07
From internal revenue.....	29,409,691 81	86,590,308 19
From sales of public lands..	117,388 61	882,616 39
From tax on circulation and deposits of national banks	8,860,569 60	8,889,430 40
From repayment of interest by Pacific Railway companies	252,427 46	1,247,572 54
From customs fees, fines, penalties, etc...........	289,579 26	860,420 74
From fees—consular, letters patent, and lands......	506,864 29	1,698,185 71
From proceeds of sales of Government property....	55,965 33	144,034 67
From profits on coinage, etc.	469,486 09	2,030,513 91
From revenues of the District of Columbia........	288,864 06	1,461,185 94
From miscellaneous sources	1,009,384 17	1,940,665 83
Total receipts........	$79,843,663 61	$206,156,336 39

The estimated expenditures for 1879–'80 show an increase of 24 millions over those of the preceding year. The unusual charge of arrears of pensions makes up this whole excess. There is a decrease of about 3 millions in the interest account, and another of about 4½ millions in the civil and miscellaneous expenses, offset by an increase in military expenses of over 4 millions, and in regular pensions of 2 millions. The expenditures for the first quarter and estimates for the remaining three quarters of the year are as follows:

EXPENDITURES.	For the quarter ending September 30, 1879. Actual.	For the remaining three quarters of the year. Estimated.
For civil and miscellaneous expenses, including public buildings, lighthouses, and collecting the revenue	$12,165,764 84	$89,587,769 66
For Indians..............	2,048,748 09	3,451,251 98
For pensions—regular.....	10,892,742 06	20,480,257 94
For arrears of pensions.....	16,374,249 60	8,252,760 40
For military establishment, including fortifications, river and harbor improvements, and arsenals......	12,104,897 88	81,017,692 62
For naval establishment, including vessels and machinery and improvements at navy yards.....	4,196,569 59	11,808,480 41
For expenditures on account of the District of Columbia	1,163,728 65	2,182,737 85
For interest on the public debt......................	32,786,685 46	61,140,724 54
Total ordinary expenditures............	$91,683,385 10	$172,816,614 90

Total receipts, actual and estimated........ $288,000,000 00
Total expenditures, actual and estimated... 264,000,000 00

Leaving a balance of.... .... $24,000,000 00

After applying the balance of the special deposit of United States notes held in the Treasury for the redemption of fractional currency, amounting to $8,375,934, to the payment of arrears of pensions, as directed in section 8 of the act approved June 21, 1879, the increased revenue derived during the months of July, August, and September of this fiscal year, 1879–'80, was fully absorbed by current expenses, and the payment of $16,374,249.60 arrears of pensions accruing under the act approved January 25, 1879. Notwithstanding these unusual demands, the Department was able to purchase and apply to the sinking fund, out of the surplus revenues for the month of October, $10,050,000 six per centum bonds of 1881, and $676,050 five per centum bonds, act of March 3, 1864, the latter of which is the excess of redemptions of these bonds over issues of four per cents under the refunding acts; and unless unexpected appropriations, available for expenditure within the year, are made by Congress, the surplus revenues, in addition to paying off the balance of arrears of pensions, will probably enable the Department to apply to the sinking-fund account, during the year, the sum of $24,000,000.

It is contemplated in the estimates of revenue that the receipts will be about the ordinary amount, and that the increase in the first quarter was abnormal and not likely to continue. They will therefore be sufficient for the demands of the Government unless Congress should make some unusual appropriations, or repeal or reduce existing taxes. Should this be the case, it will be necessary to provide other sources of revenue to meet the deficiency, and for this purpose a moderate duty on tea and coffee and an internal tax upon manufactures of opium are recommended. Opium particularly is recommended, because large quantities

THE FOLLOWING IS A STATEMENT OF THE OUTSTANDING PRINCIPAL OF THE PUBLIC DEBT OF THE UNITED STATES, JUNE 30, 1879.

TITLE	Length of loan	When redeemable	Rates of interest	Price at which sold	Amount authorized	Amount issued	Amount outstanding
Old debt (up to 1837)	....	On demand	5 and 6 per cent	Par	....	....	$665 00
Treasury notes prior to 1846	1 and 2 years	1 and 2 years from date	1 mill to 6 per cent	Par	....	....	82,505 35
...ary notes of 1846	1 year	1 year from date	1 mill and 5⅖ per cent	Par	$10,000,000 00	$7,687,800 000	6,000 00
Mexican ...	....	April and July, 1849	5 per cent	Par	350,000 00	303,573 92	1,104 91
Treasury notes of 1847	1 and 2 years	After 60 days' notice	5⅖ and 6 per cent	Par	23,000,000 00	*26,122,100 00	950 00
Loan of 1847	20 years	January 1, 1868	6 per cent	.0125 to .02 p.c.pr'm	28,207,000 00	†28,207,000 00	1,320 00
Bounty-land scrip (1847)	Indefinite	July 1, 1849	6 per cent	Par	Indefinite	233,075 00	8,300 00
Texan ... ty stock (1850)	14 years	January 1, 1865	5 per cent	Par	10,000,000 00	5,000,000 00	21,000 00
...ry notes of 1857	1 year	60 days' notice	5 and 5⅖ per cent	Far to .073 pr'm	20,000,000 00	20,000,000 00	1,700 00
Loan of 1858	15 years	January 1, 1874	5 per cent	.0275 to .073 pr'm	20,000,000 00	20,000,000 00	48,000 00
Loan of ...	10 years	January 1, 1871	5 per cent	Par to .0145 pr'm	21,000,000 00	7,022,000 00	10,000 00
Loan of February, 1861 (1881s)	10 or 20 years	January 1, 1881	6 per cent	Par	25,000,000 00	18,415,000 00	18,415,000 00
Treasury ...tes of 1861	2 years	2 years after date	6 per cent	Par	22,468,100 00	33,864,450 00	8,000 00
Oregon war debt (1861)	20 years	July 1, 1881	6 per cent	Par	2,800,000 00	1,090,850 00	945,000 00
Loan of July and August, 1861 (1881s)	20 years	July 1, 1881	6 per cent	Par⅛	250,000,000 00	60,000,000 00	...50 00
Old ...utes (1861-'82)	....	On dmd	No...	Par	60,000,000 00	139,931,830 00	61,470 00
Seven-thirties of 1861	3 years	August 19 and ...ber 1, 1864	7⅖ per cent	Par	140,094,750 00	140,094,750 00	16,600 00
Five-twenties of 1862	5 or 20 years	May 1, 1867	6 per cent	Par	515,000,000 00	514,771,600 00	402,500 00
Legal-tender notes (1862-'63)	....	On demand	None	Par	450,000,000 00	$449,338,902 10	346,681,016 00
Temporary loan (1869)	Not less than 30 days	After 10 days' notice	4, 5, and 6 per cent	Par	150,000,000 00	....	8,060 00
Certificates of indebtedness (1862)	1 year	1 year after date	6 per cent, compd	Par	No limit	561,753,241 65	4,000 00
Fractional currency	....	On presentation	None	Par	50,000,000 00	49,102,660 97	15,842,625 78
One-year notes of 1863	1 year	1 year after date	5 per cent	Par'ge pr'm of 4.18	75,000,000 00	73,500,000 00	75,...
Two-year notes of 1863	2 years	2 yr's after date	5 per cent	Par	400,000,000 00	44,520,000 00	...50 00
Coin-certificates (from 1863)	....	On demand	None	Par	400,000,000 00	166,450,000 00	...00 00
Compound-interest notes (1863-'64)	3 years	June	6 per cent, compd	Par to 7 p.c. pr'm	Indefinite	57,888,400 00	16,418,700 00
Ten-forties of 1864	10 or 40 years	March 1, 1874	5 per cent	Par to ½ p.c. pr'm	400,000,000 00	266,595,440 00	...00 00
Five-twenties of June, 1864	5 or 20 years	...ber 1, 1869	6 per cent	Par	200,000,000 00	196,117,300 00	188,425,100 00
Seven-thirties of 1864 and 1865	3 years	August 15, 1867, June 15, 1868, and July	7⅖ per cent	Par	400,000,000 00	125,561,300 00	71,900 00
Five-twenties of ...ber 1, 1865	5 or 20 years	July 1, 1870	6 per cent	Par	580,000,000 00	830,000,000 00	147,550 00
6s of 1865	....	July 1, 1870	6 per cent	Par	Indefinite	14,000,000 00	...00 00
6s of 1867	5 or 20 years	July 1, 1872	6 per cent	Par	203,327,250 00	203,827,250 00	145,650 00
6s of 1868	5 or 20 years	July 1, 1873	6 per cent	Par	339,998,950 00	332,998,950 00	...00 00
Three per cent. ...	Indefinite	On demand	3 per cent	Par	379,618,000 00	379,618,000 00	41,324,400 00
Five per cent. ...	....	May 1, 1881	4 per cent	Par	42,539,830 00	42,539,830 00	20,108,550 00
Four and a half per cent.	10 years	May 1, 1881	4 per cent	Par	55,155,000 00	55,155,000 00	...00 00
Four per cent. loan of 1891 (refunding)	30 years	September 1, 1891	4 per cent	Par to ⅒ p.c. pr'm	1,500,000,000 00	...60,045,000 00	183,000,000 00
Five per cent. loan of 1881 (for silver)	15 years	September 1, 1907	4 per cent	Par	Indefinite	135,000,000 00	635,...
Four and a half per cent. loan of 1891 (resumption)	15 years	September 1, 1891	4½ per cent	Par	Indefinite	698,029,900 00	65,000,000 00
Four per cent. 4s of 1907	30 years	September 1, 1907	5 per cent	Par	Indefinite	17,494,150 00	17,494,150 00
6s of ...t. loan of 1881 (to pay J. H. Eads)	10 years	May 1, 1881	5 per cent	Par	Indefinite	65,000,000 00	45,000,000 00
...er 6s of ...	Indefinite	On demand	None	Par	No limit	30,500,000 00	500,000 00
Refunding certificates (from 1879)	Indefinite	Convertible into 4 per ct. bonds	4 per cent	Par	No limit	64,750,000 00	30,570,000 00
							2,466,950 00
							12,548,210 00
Total existing debt	....	....	....	....	....	39,396,110 00	$...53 04

* Including reissues.   † Including conversion of Treasury notes.   ‡ $50,000,000 6 per cent. stock issued at a discount of $3,888,763.09, being equivalent to 7 per cent.
§ Highest amount outstanding January 30, 1864.

prepared for smoking are brought into the country, and the article, being of small bulk and great value, is easily smuggled. A similar article is manufactured in this country from the crude opium, and it is difficult to determine whether the product in any given case is of domestic or foreign manufacture. Therefore an internal tax equal to that on the imported article, $6 per pound, is recommended on all prepared in this country for smoking.

The payments into the sinking fund have not been kept up to the requirements of the acts of Congress. Those of February 25, 1862, and July 14, 1870, direct the purchase or payment of one per centum of the entire debt within each fiscal year after July 1, 1862, to be set apart as a sinking fund, and the interest to be applied to the purchase or payment of the debt. The loss of revenue consequent on the general depression of business during the last few years rendered it impossible to comply with these acts and meet the appropriations of Congress.

The resumption of specie payments, as required by act of Congress, took place on January 1, 1879, on United States notes, at the Assistant Treasurer's office in New York. The reserve of coin over and above all matured liabilities at that date was $133,508,804. The operation of the resumption act is thus described by the Secretary of the Treasury in his report to Congress:

Previous to that time, in view of resumption, United States notes and coin were freely received and paid in private business as equivalents. Actual resumption commenced at the time fixed by law, without any material demand for coin and without disturbance to public or private business. No distinction has been made since that time between coin and United States notes in the collection of duties or in the payment of the principal or interest of the public debt. The great body of coin indebtedness has been paid in United States notes at the request of creditors. The total amount of United States notes presented for redemption, from January 1 to November 1, 1879, was $11,256,678. But little coin has been demanded on the coin liabilities of the Government during the same period, though the amount accruing exceeded six hundred million dollars. Meantime coin was freely paid into the Treasury, and gold bullion was deposited in the assay-office and paid for in United States notes. The aggregate gold and silver coin and bullion in the Treasury increased during that period from $167,558,734.19 to $225,133,558.72, and the net balance available for resumption increased from $133,508,804.50 to $152,737,- 155.48.

To meet the local demand for coin in places other than New York City, persons applying have been paid silver coin for United States notes, the coin being delivered to them on established express lines free of expense; and for some time gold and silver coin has been freely paid out at the several sub-treasuries upon current obligations of the Government. There has been, however, but little demand for coin, and United States notes and the circulating notes of national banks have been received and paid out at par with coin in all business transactions, public or private, in all parts of the country.

The specie standard, thus happily secured, has given an impetus to all kinds of business. Many industries, greatly depressed since the panic of 1873, have revived, while increased activity has been shown in all branches of production, trade, and commerce.

In his opinion the provisions of law now existing are ample to enable the Department to maintain the resumption.

The question whether United States notes ought still to be a legal tender in the payment of debts has not escaped the notice of the Secretary. His views are thus expressed:

The power of Congress to make them such was asserted by Congress during the war, and was upheld by the Supreme Court. The power to reissue them in time of peace, after they are once redeemed, is still contested in that Court. Prior to 1862, only gold and silver were a legal tender. Bullion was deposited by private individuals in the mints and coined in convenient forms and designs, indicating weight and fineness. Paper money is a promise to pay such coin. No constitutional objection is raised against the issue of notes not bearing interest to be used as a part of the circulating medium. The chief objection to the emission of paper money by the Government grows out of the legal-tender clause, for without this the United States note would be measured by its convenience in use, its safety, and its prompt redemption. In war, and during a grave public exigency, other considerations may properly prevail; but it would seem that during peace, and especially during times of prosperity and surplus revenue, the promissory note of the United States ought to stand like any other promissory note. It should be current money only by being promptly redeemed in coin on demand. The note of the United States is now received for all public dues, it is carefully limited in amount, it is promptly redeemed on demand, and ample reserves in coin are provided to give confidence in and security for such redemption. With these conditions maintained, the United States note will be readily received and paid on all demands. While they are maintained, the legal-tender clause gives no additional credit or sanction to the notes, but tends to impair confidence and to create fears of over-issue. It would seem, therefore, that now and during the maintenance of resumption it is a useless and objectionable assertion of power, which Congress might now repeal on the ground of expediency alone. When it is considered that its constitutionality is seriously contested, and that from its nature it is subject to grave abuse, it would now appear to be wise to withdraw the exercise of such a power, leaving it in reserve to be again resorted to in such a period of war or grave emergency as existed in 1862. The Government derives an advantage in circulating its notes without interest, and the people prefer such notes to coin, as money, for their convenience in use and their certain redemption in coin on demand. This mutual advantage may be secured without the exercise of questionable power; nor need any inconvenience arise from the repeal of the legal-tender clause as to future contracts. Contracting parties may stipulate for either gold or silver coin or current money. In the absence of an express stipulation for coin, the reasonable presumption would exist that the parties contemplated payment in current money, and such presumption might properly be declared by law and the contract enforced accordingly.

The Secretary therefore respectfully submits to Congress whether the legal-tender clause should not now be repealed as to all future contracts, and parties be left to stipulate the mode of payment.

Since November 23, 1878, there have been refunded of the bonds of the United States $370,848,750 six per cent., and $193,890,250 five per cent., into bonds bearing interest at four per cent., making an annual saving of interest hereafter of $9,355,877.50.

The following table shows the transactions in refunding since March 1, 1877, and the annual saving of interest therefrom:

TITLE OF LOAN.	Rate per ct.	Amount refunded.	Annual Interest charge.
Loan of 1858.........	5	$260,000	$9,707,512 50
Ten-forties of 1864....	5	198,890,250	
Five-twenties of 1865..	6	100,486,050	
Consols of 1865........	6	202,668,100	89,071,742 00
Consols of 1867........	6	810,022,750	
Consols of 1868.......	6	87,478,800	
Total...............	......	$845,345,950	$48,779,254 50

In place of the above bonds there have been issued bonds bearing interest as follows:

TITLE OF LOAN.	Rate per ct.	Amount issued.	Annual Interest charge.
Funded loan of 1891...	4½	$135,000,000	$6,075,000
Funded loan of 1907, including refunding certificates..............	4	710,345,950	28,413,888
Total...............	......	$845,345,950	$34,488,888

making a saving in the annual interest since March 1, 1877, of $14,290,416.50.

These transactions have been accomplished without the loss of a dollar, and without appreciably disturbing the current business of the country.

The entire transactions in refunding since 1870 have been as follows:

TITLE OF LOAN.	Rate per ct.	Amount refunded.	Annual Interest charge.
Loan of 1858.........	5	$14,217,000	$10,405,862 50
Ten-forties of 1864....	5	198,890,250	
Five-twenties of 1862..	6	401,143,750	
Five-twenties of March, 1864...............	6	1,827,100	
Five-twenties of June, 1864...............	6	59,185,450	71,284,322 00
Five-twenties of 1865..	6	160,144,500	
Consols of 1865........	6	211,387,050	
Consols of 1867........	6	316,428,800	
Consols of 1868.......	6	87,677,050	
Total...............	......	$1,395,345,950	$81,689,684 50

In place of the above bonds there have been issued bonds bearing interest as follows:

TITLE OF LOAN.	Rate per ct.	Total issued.	Annual Interest charge.
Funded loan of 1851...	5	$500,000,000	$25,000,000
Funded loan of 1891...	4½	185,000,000	8,325,000
Funded loan of 1907, including refunding certificates.........	4	710,345,950	28,413,888
Total...............	......	$1,395,345,950	$61,738,888

making an annual saving hereafter in the interest charge on account of refunding operations of $19,900,846.50.

The following-described bonds will mature in 1880 and 1881:

AUTHORIZING ACTS.	Rate of Interest.	Date of maturity.	Amount.
February 8, 1861......	6	Dec. 31, 1880	$18,415,000
July 17 and August 5, 1861.............	6	June 30, 1881	182,605,550
March 3, 1863........	6	June 30, 1881	71,787,000
March 3, 1861	6	July 1, 1881	823,800
July 14, 1870, and January 20, 1871.......	5	May 1, 1881	508,440,850
Total.............	......	....	$782,071,700

Of these bonds, the loan of February 8, 1861, maturing December 31, 1880, is payable upon the demand of the holders, and can probably be provided for from the surplus revenues.

Under the refunding acts of July 14, 1870, and January 20, 1871, bonds for refunding purposes were authorized in the amount of $1,500,000,000. Of this amount there have been issued, as above stated, $1,395,345,950, leaving available for future refunding operations $104,654,050.

A distinctive paper has been adopted for printing public securities. It has for its special feature a continuous silken thread and distributed silk fiber of different colors, both of which are incorporated with the pulp in the process of manufacture.

The value of the coinage executed during the year was:

Gold...................................	$40,986,912 00
Standard silver dollars..............	27,227,500 00
Subsidiary silver coin................	882 50
Minor coin.........................	97,798 00
Total..................... ..	$68,312,592 50

Gold and silver were separated in the refineries of the mints and the assay-office at New York in the amount of $20,759,549.97 in gold, and $10,687,526.97 in silver, a total of $31,447,076.94, and fine and unparted bars were made in the amount of $12,976,812.68 of gold, and $9,045,802.11 of silver. The coinage of standard silver dollars has been kept fully up to the requirements of law, notwithstanding the difficulty experienced in procuring silver bullion for the mints at San Francisco and Carson, at market rates. The amount of silver coin of less than a dollar provided for by law having been executed, the coinage of this money has been suspended. The demand for minor coins, particularly for the one-cent piece, has been pressing. The bullion production from the mines of the United States for the last year is estimated by the Director to be nearly $80,000,000, the proportions of gold and silver being about equal. The year's total production is less than that of the preceding year, caused by a diminution in the yield of the mines of Nevada, which was not compensated by increased production in other places. The Director estimates the coin in the country on October 31, 1879, at $305,750,497 of gold, and $121,456,355 of silver. The bullion in the mints and New York assay-office at that date awaiting coinage amounted to $49,931,035 of gold, and $4,553,182 of silver, making the total amount of coin and bullion $481,691,069.

The market value of the bullion in the silver dollar has been during the past year from 10 to 16 per cent. less than the market value of the bullion in the gold dollar. The total amount of silver dollars coined to November 1, 1879, under the act of February 28, 1878, was $45,206,200, of which $13,002,842 was in circulation, and the remainder, $32,203,358, in the Treasury at that time. No effort has been spared to put this coin in circulation.

Owing to its limited coinage it has been kept at par.

The number of banks in operation on October 2, 1879, was 2,048, and the aggregate capital $454,067,365; surplus, $114,786,528; individual deposits, $719,737,568; specie, including United States coin certificates, $42,173,731; legal-tender notes and certificates, $95,973,446; loans, $875,013,107; circulation, $337,181,418.

The monetary transactions of the Government have been conducted through the offices of the United States Treasurer, 9 assistant treasurers, 510 depositaries, and 222 national-bank depositaries.

The receipts of the Government from all sources have amounted during the last year, as shown by warrants, to $1,066,634,827.46, of which $792,807,643 have been received from loans, $137,250,947.70 from customs, $113,561,610.58 from internal revenue, and $23,015,526.18 from sales of land and from miscellaneous sources. These receipts were deposited as follows: In independent-treasury offices, $413,363,508.43; in national-bank depositaries, $653,271,319.03.

The receipts from the several sources of taxation under the internal-revenue laws for the fiscal year ending June 30, 1879, were as follows:

From spirits	$52,570,264 69
From tobacco	40,135,002 65
From fermented liquors	10,729,320 08
From banks and bankers	3,198,888 59
From penalties, etc.	279,497 80
From adhesive stamps	6,706.384 06
From arrears of taxes under repealed laws	299,094 00
Total	$113,918,466 87

The following is a list of subjects of taxation under the internal-revenue law:

Deposits in bank, or with persons, etc., engaged in the business of banking.

Deposits in savings banks. [Savings banks are now exempt from tax on $2,000 of savings deposits made in the name of and belonging to any one person, thus exempting the percentages of all poor persons.]

Capital of banks, etc., and capital employed by any person in the business of banking beyond average amount invested in United States bonds.

Circulation issued by any bank, etc., or person, per month.

Banks, etc., on amount of notes of any person, State bank, or State banking association, used for circulation and paid out.

Banks, bankers, or associations, on amount of notes of any town, city, or municipal corporation, paid out by them.

Every person, firm, association other than national bank associations, and every corporation, State bank, or State banking association, on the amount of their own notes used for circulation and paid out by them.

Every such person, firm, association, corporation, State bank, or State banking association, and also every national banking association, on the amount of notes of any person, firm, association other than a national banking association, or of any corporation, State bank or State banking association or of any town, city, or municipal corporation, used for circulation and paid out by them.

Bank-check, draft, order, or voucher for the payment of any sum of money whatsoever, drawn upon any bank, banker, or trust company.

Medicines or preparations, perfumeries and cosmet-

ics, friction-matches, wax-tapers, cigar-lights, playing-cards.

Spirits distilled from apples, peaches, or grapes.

Spirits distilled from materials other than apples, peaches, and grapes.

Rectifiers of any quantity less than 500 barrels.

Rectifiers of 500 barrels or more.

Wines, liquors, or compounds known or denominated as wine, and made in imitation of sparkling wine or champagne, but not made from grapes grown in the United States, and liquors not made from grapes, currants, rhubarb, or berries grown in the United States, but produced by being rectified or mixed with distilled spirits.

Retail liquor-dealers, wholesale liquor-dealers, manufacturers of stills, stills or worms, manufactured.

Stamps for distilled spirits intended for export; stamps, distillery warehouse; stamps for rectified spirits; stamps, wholesale liquor-dealers; stamps, special bonded warehouse; stamps, special bonded warehouse (rewarehousing); stamps for imported spirits.

Cigars and cheroots; cigarettes; manufacturers of cigars; snuff of all descriptions, domestic or imported, and snuff flour sold or removed for use, per pound; tobacco, chewing and smoking; dealers in leaf tobacco; retail dealers in leaf tobacco; dealers in manufactured tobacco; manufacturers of tobacco; peddlers of tobacco.

Fermented liquors; brewers; retail dealers in malt liquors; wholesale dealers in malt liquors.

The total tonnage of the country on June 30, 1879, was 4,169,600 tons. Of this tonnage 1,491,533 tons represented 2,717 vessels registered for the foreign trade, and 2,678,067 tons represented 22,494 vessels enrolled and licensed and engaged in the coasting or domestic trade. There has been an increase of 94,350 tons employed in domestic trade, and a decrease of 137,514 tons employed in the foreign trade by sea, as compared with the tonnage of 1878. The vessels built during the year are classed as follows:

VESSELS.	Number.	Tonnage.
Sail-vessels	468	66,867
Steam-vessels	335	86,361
Canal-boats enrolled	86	4,069
Barges	293	25,783
Total	1,182	198,080

The total tonnage of vessels entered at the seaboard ports from foreign countries was 11,530,527 tons during the year ended June 30, 1878, and 13,768,137 tons during the last fiscal year, showing an increase of 2,237,610 tons, or about 19 per cent. The American tonnage entered exhibited an increase of only 40,306 tons, or 1 per cent., while the foreign showed an increase of 2,197,304 tons, or nearly 26 per cent. Of the total amount of merchandise brought in at seaboard, lake, and river ports, during the last fiscal year, an amount of the value of $143,599,353 was imported in American vessels, and $310,499,599 in foreign; of the exports, a value of $128,425,339 was shipped in American, and $600.769,638 in foreign vessels. Of the combined imports and exports, 23 per cent. only of the total value was conveyed in American vessels.

The great financial and other events of 1879 —such as the resumption of specie payments;

the negotiation of $540,000,000 of United States four per cent bonds, mostly at home; an excess of exports over imports of $270,000,000 in the fiscal year ending June 30th; a net import of gold amounting to $78,000,000 in five months from August 1st; and crops estimated at 448,755,000 bushels of wheat, 1,544,899,000 bushels of corn, and 5,500,000 bales of cotton—gave rise to extraordinary movements in commercial and financial affairs. The prices of merchandise and all classes of securities rapidly advanced. A state of buoyancy, activity, and speculation at the chief centers of trade ensued, which has never been equaled when the country was on a specie basis. The following summary, from the "Financial and Commercial Chronicle," shows the condition of the New York Clearing-House banks, the premium on gold, rate of foreign exchange, and prices of leading securities and articles of merchandise, on or about the 1st of January in each year, from 1878 to 1880, inclusive:

STATISTICAL SUMMARY ON OR ABOUT JANUARY 1, 1878–1880.

SUBJECTS.	1880.	1879.	1878.
New York City Banks—			
Loans and discounts	$276,706,200	$234,250,000	$289,256,400
Specie	$48,282,100	$20,986,200	$25,207,500
Circulation	$28,748,600	$19,848,800	$19,787,100
Net deposits	$242,087,100	$206,173,000	$201,981,500
Legal tenders	$12,723,500	$41,882,600	$34,612,000
Surplus reserve (over 25 per cent.)	$483,825	$11,275,550	$9,824,125
Money, Gold, Exchange—			
Call loans	6 @ 6 and 1/32 com.	4 @ 7	7–½ p. d.
Prime paper	5½ @ 6	4½ @ 5	5 @ 6½
Gold	100	100	102⅞
Silver in London, per oz	52 7/16	49¼	54
Prime sterling bills, 60 days	4 80½–4 81½	4 82 @ 4 82½	4 82 @ 4 82½
United States Bonds—			
6s, 1881, coupons	104½	106⅝	106⅝
6s, currency, 1898	122	119⅛	118¼
5s, 1881, coupon	108⅝	107	105½
4½s, 1891, coupon	106⅝	104⅞	103⅛
4s of 1907, coupon	108	99½	101½
Railroad Stocks—			
New York Central and Hudson River	129¼	114½	106¾
Erie (N. Y., L. E., and W.)	42½	22⅞	8⅜
Lake Shore and Michigan Southern	103½	69	61⅛
Michigan Central	90	73⅛	62
Chicago, Rock Island, and Pacific	149	120½	100¼
Illinois Central	99½	80½	74
Chicago and Northwestern, common	91	50½	35¼
Chicago, Milwaukee, and St. Paul, common	75⅝	37¼	36¼
Delaware, Lackawanna, and Western	84	48½	51
Central of New Jersey	89¼	33¼	12¼
Merchandise—			
Cotton, middling uplands, per lb	12 9/16	9 7/16	11 5/16
Wool, American XX, per lb	44 @ 53	30 @ 36	38 @ 47
Iron, American pig, No. 1, per ton	33 00 @ 35 00	16 50 @ 18 00	18 00 @ 19 00
Wheat, No. 2 spring, per bushel	1 46 @ 1 48	96 @ 98	1 30 @ 1 33
Corn, Western mixed	60 @ 63	44 @ 48	55 @ 63
Pork, mess	12 75 @ 13 00	7 10 @ 7 20	12 25 @ 12 50

FINOTTI, Joseph M., was born in Italy in 1817, and died at Central, Colorado, January 10, 1879. He was of a distinguished family, and his early and ardent desire for knowledge raised him to a high position as a scholar. His studies were pursued in the best universities in Rome. He became a member of the Society of Jesus, and was ordained a Catholic priest in 1842. He discharged the duties of his office, and was sent to the missions of America with other fathers. But his health failing, he received dispensation of his vows, and for sixteen years occupied, as a secular priest, a very important parish in the diocese of Boston. He was for a short period the principal editor of the "Boston Pilot," and before and since that time wrote several works and contributed largely to different reviews and monthly and weekly Catholic papers. He was at one time a professor in Mount Saint Mary's Seminary of the West, near Cincinnati, and just prior to going to Colorado was appointed to the presidency of the new college at Omaha. But the climate of Nebraska being unfavorable to his health, he offered his services to Bishop Machebœuf of Colorado, who cheerfully accepted them. He remained three or four months as assistant at the cathedral of Denver, and was then sent as pastor to the church at Central, where, by his zeal and piety, he gained the esteem and affection of all.

FISH, Asa I., a distinguished lawyer, born in Philadelphia in February, 1820, died in that city May 5, 1879. He graduated at Harvard College in 1842, studied law at the Harvard Law School, and was admitted to the bar in Philadelphia in 1846, and opened an office for practice. From the year 1853 to 1862, he was one of the editors of the "American Law Register." Among his many contributions to legal and general literature are "Trowbat and Haly's Practice," "Tidd's Practice," "Selwyn's Nisi Prius," and "Williams on Executors and Administrators." As a student of Shakespeare's works he was eminent. For twenty-six years he held the position of Dean of the Skakespeare Society in Philadelphia, and was also a member of the new Shakespeare Society of England. In 1844 he received the degree of LL. B. from Harvard, and in 1852 the same degree from Pennsylvania College. In 1867 Kenyon College conferred on him the degree of LL. D. During the last fifteen years of his life he filled the office of Treasurer of the Philadelphia Law Association, of which he was an active and prominent member.

FLORIDA. The biennial session of the Legislature commenced on January 7th. In the Senate Lieutenant-Governor Hull presided; in the House Charles Dougherty was elected Speaker.

One of the first resolutions adopted in the Senate was the following:

The people of the State of Florida, represented in Senate and Assembly, do resolve as follows: That the recent employment of Federal officials, especially deputy marshals, appointed in great numbers for the purpose of supervising and influencing elections held under State laws, meets our emphatic condemnation as subversive of the foundation of popular government, and tending toward dangerous centralization of power, and that the Senators and Representatives in Congress from Florida are hereby requested to secure all possible legislative safeguards against its recurrence.

In answer to an inquiry of the Senate as to the amount of money received during the previous year by the State from various industrial pursuits for licenses, the following statement was furnished: From merchants selling general merchandise, $8,200; from liquor-dealers, $22,700; from practicing physicians, $1,010; from druggists, $1,040; from keno and pool tables, $155; from public exhibitions. $380; from land agents, $15; from boarding-houses, $400; from eating-houses, $435; from peddlers, $240; from hotels, $1,075; from butchers, $410; from billiard-tables, $510; from practicing lawyers, $290; from livery stables, $350; from insurance agents, $380; from express agents. $120; from banks, $400; from photographers, $60; from dentists, $90; from undertakers, $20; from bakers, $20; from auctioneers, $60; from sewing-machine agents, $30; total, $38,390. To this sum should be added $11,598 unapportioned to the different pursuits.

On January 21st Wilkinson Call was chosen a United States Senator by the Legislature. The vote in the Senate was 23 for Call, 4 for Senator S. B. Conover, and 3 scattering. In the House it was 46 for Call, 18 for Conover, and 7 scattering. Senator Call was born in Kentucky, but went to Florida early in life. He is about fifty years of age, a lawyer by profession, of much political experience, and a fluent speaker. In 1867 he and Judge Marvin, then Provisional Governor of Florida, were elected to the United States Senate, the former drawing the long and the latter the short term, but were never permitted to take their seats in that body in consequence of the subsequent passage of the act of reconstruction.

In the Assembly the following resolution relative to the manner of choosing Presidential electors was adopted:

Whereas, Interference by officers of the United States in popular elections is justly regarded by the people of this State as an evil of great magnitude; and whereas, the manifest purpose of such interference, in part at least, is to influence and control the action of the State in selecting electors for President and Vice-President of the United States for the year 1880; therefore, be it

Resolved, That the Judiciary Committee be instructed to inquire into the expediency of providing by law for the selection of electors for President and Vice-President of the United States in the coming election of the year 1880 by the General Assembly, until the acts of Congress authorizing interference by Federal authority are repealed.

In the Senate a bill was introduced to provide for the appointment of the electors.

On the death of Mrs. Hugh A. Corley, the wife of the Commissioner of Lands and Immigration, who was a member of the Governor's cabinet, both Houses of the Legislature adjourned for the day as a "tribute of respect to the deceased, and an indication of sympathy with the bereaved husband."

To secure a revision of the State Constitution, it is necessary, in the first place, that a resolution to that effect should be adopted by a majority of all the members of two successive Legislatures. Such resolution was adopted by the Legislature of 1877, and again by its successor in 1879. The next step is for the Legislature to recommend to the electors, at the next election for members of the Legislature in 1881, to vote for or against a Convention; and, if it shall appear that a majority of the electors, voting at such election, shall have voted in favor of calling a Convention, the Legislature shall, at its next session, provide by law for a Convention, to be holden within six months after the passage of such law, and such Convention shall consist of a number of members not less than both branches of the Legislature.

In the House a resolution was adopted, which instructed the Finance Committee to inquire into the mode and manner in which the bonds issued in pursuance of the law of 1873 were disposed of; whether the same was in accordance with law; whether the bonds of 1868 and 1869, under hypothecation in New York, were properly chargeable with the amount allowed, and whether any portion of said bonds were exchanged for the bonds of 1873; whether, if it shall be found that the said bonds, or any portion thereof, were disposed of in violation of law, the State is legally bound to pay such bonds. The resolution was subsequently modified so as to require a joint committee of both Houses to make the investigation. On March 7th they reported that in 1868 and 1869 there were issued $500,000 in State bonds bearing interest at 6 per cent., which were authorized to be sold at not less than seventy-five cents on the dollar. Seventy-nine thousand dollars of these were sold or exchanged for former indebtedness. Of the remainder, $413,000 were hypothecated in New York in 1869 for temporary loans amounting in the aggregate to about $100,000.

In 1871, $350,000 of 7 per cent. bonds were issued under a law which was passed over the Governor's veto, and the bonds were absorbed in redeeming the floating debt of the State.

At an extra session of the Legislature, called by Governor Hart for the special purpose, one million dollars more bonds were issued, five hundred thousand of which were directed to be used for the exchange for and redemption of the valid bonds of the State outstanding, "except the bonds of 1871 and the hypothecated bonds of 1868 and 1869."

The remaining five hundred thousand were directed "to be sold by the Governor and Comptroller at New York or elsewhere, as might be deemed best for the interests of the State, at a sum not less than eighty cents net on the dollar, United States currency, but in no case to be hypothecated; and out of the proceeds, to be deposited with the Treasurer, or to his order, the Treasurer shall first pay the amount necessary to redeem the bonds of 1868 and 1869 under hypothecation, and next pay the indebtedness of the State accruing after the first day of July next ensuing." The law also provided that " in no event shall any agent be employed in negotiation and sale of said bonds," and it prohibited the levying of any tax for interest until one fourth of the bonds were sold. In these particulars this law was violated: First, in appointing an agent in New York for the sale of the bonds; second, in not selling the first quarter million bonds for cash and depositing the money with the State Treasurer, or to his order, as required in the law as a condition precedent to a levy of a tax for the interest; and, third, in exchanging the bonds for the hypothecated bonds of 1868 and 1869. The committee said:

We are of the opinion that the passage of the law was procured through the influence of a firm of New York brokers, L. P. Bayne & Co., who were in personal attendance at Tallahassee, with two attorneys; and who, failing to get a bill passed directly authorizing the employment of an agent, at a commission of five per cent., for the sale of the bonds, procured from Governor Hart the calling of an extra session of the Legislature and the passage of the present law, with an understanding afterward carried out that Bayne & Co. were to have enough bonds to pay their claim against the President of the Jacksonville, Pensacola, and Mobile Railroad Company in exchange for the hypothecated bonds of 1868 and 1869, held by them for money advanced, or said to have been advanced, to the said President, and also have the control of the half million of bonds authorized to be sold, for a specific time, which enabled them to obtain the $80,000 from the sale of the Agricultural College scrip which had been negotiated, and thus to carry out the contract to take the quarter million bonds necessary to enable the Comptroller to levy the tax for interest on the bonds. Of the avails of this quarter million bonds, less than $10,000 was paid into the Treasury, the remainder being disposed of in violation of law.

By this conspiracy between the Comptroller and L. P. Bayne & Co., to which the Governor afterward became a party, we find that the State was defrauded of over $100,000 in the bonds of 1873, and we therefore recommend the passage of the accompanying resolution :

Resolved. That the Attorney-General is hereby directed to examine into the circumstances of the origin and disposition of the bonds issued in 1873, and to ascertain whether suits should not be instituted against the late Comptroller, C. A. Cowgill, and L. P. Bayne & Co., for the recovery of the amount of the bonds illegally sold, and also for conspiracy to defraud the State.

The resolution was adopted by the Legislature.

An act was passed fixing the rate of taxation for 1879 and 1880 at seven mills. For ordinary county purposes it was fixed at two mills, with a proviso that it might be raised to four mills if it was proposed by a grand jury of the county.

The State Comptroller estimated the amount required for the expenses of 1879 to be $284,303. In making up this amount he estimated as outstanding jurors' and witnesses' certificates issued between 1867 and 1877, amounting to $44,706. This was receivable for taxes, and it was expected an amount equal to $10,000 would thus come in. Still, as other items of expense outside of his estimate might be added by the Legislature, it was concluded that his estimate was low enough.

The following were the sources of revenue from which it was expected to meet the wants of 1879 : There were first the uncollected taxes of 1878. The gross assessment for that year was $147,356; deducting 10 per cent. for failures to pay, leaves as net $132,621, of which $9,195 was collected and paid in 1878, which left to be collected on the 1st of January, 1879, $123,426. Again in 1878 there was received as back taxes $26,820, and it was anticipated an equal amount would be received in 1879. The licenses collected in 1877 amounted to $59,985.03 ; in 1878 the receipts were $55,804.01, showing a falling off of $4,181.02. A proposed change in the license law was expected to increase the income from this source and make the receipts for 1879 reach $65,000. The change proposed in the liquor law put all those persons who sold liquor by the quart on the same footing with those who sold by the glass, and each class is to be charged $100. In 1877 there were estimated to be 172 retail dealers and 191 wholesale dealers in the State, and this was the number of licenses issued respectively during that year.

The miscellaneous sources of revenue include an auction-tax, tax from commissions, redemption of lands sold for taxes, etc. In 1878 the receipts from this source were $5,162, and the same amount would probably be received in 1879. The tax-box of 1878 returns 43,100 polls, on which there is a tax of one dollar. The State is entitled to one half this tax, and the counties to the other half. But only property-owners pay the tax, so that the amount likely to be received by the State is estimated at $8,000. The only remaining source of income available to meet the expenses of 1879 will be the small amount that may be collected between November and December of the tax assessment of the year. In 1878 there were only $9,195 collected of the assessment of that year, and a like sum may be collected in 1879 from the assessment of 1879. There was a balance in the Treasury on the 1st of January of the present year of $21,149, which will enter into the available means for 1879.

These estimates left a deficiency of $25,000, on a basis of taxation of five mills. But as the Legislature was providing revenue for the two years, 1879 and 1880, similar estimates applied to the latter year showed that there would be a deficiency at its termination of $70,962. No other resource was left but to advance the rate of taxation to seven mills. Of this tax, one mill as provided in the Constitution goes to the schools; three mills are required to pay the interest on the State debt without the sinking fund, which leaves three mills for the State expenses. The valuation of taxable property in the State is about $30,000,000.

A change was also made in the law so as to secure a fairer valuation. It required every person to render to the assessor, between the first days of March and August in each year, a list of the taxable property of every kind owned by him or which he should return for taxation, and such list shall contain a description thereof, and a statement of the value of each parcel of land and of the different kinds of property, and the same shall be made under affidavit that the same is just and correct, which shall be made before the assessor, or any officer authorized to administer oaths. Any person who shall fail to render such list, or when it shall be demanded by the assessor, shall be liable to a double tax, and his property shall be assessed by the assessor at double the usual rates; and any person failing to render such list shall not be permitted to reduce, or have reduced, the valuation made of his property by such assessor.

An extensive system of railroads was devised after the close of the war, and it was contemplated that their construction should be aided by donations of State lands. Some lines have been in part built, public lands have been lost to the State, and many roads sold by the courts. In the Senate the Committee on Railroads were instructed to investigate the cause, manner, and legality of the sales of the roads constructed under the provisions of the Internal Improvement act of January 6, 1855; and all matters connected therewith, and to recommend such action as may be necessary for the interest and protection of the Internal Improvement Fund.

They reported that the sales of the Florida, the Pensacola and Georgia, and the Florida, Atlantic, and Gulf roads were unconstitutional, and recommended the passage of bills by which legal proceedings could be instituted by the present Board of Trustees to recover and reëstablish the rights of the Improvement

Fund in all of these roads. Bills were accordingly passed for this object, but the Governor vetoed them on the ground that the companies had for twelve years acquiesced in the sales, and also that the trustees were not prepared to meet the expenditures they would encounter, and that the measures would prove injurious to the fund and the State.

Three other bills were also vetoed by the Governor, but these were intended to aid in the construction of railroads. One was entitled "An act to grant certain lands to the Tampa, Pease Creek, and St. John's Railway Company"; the second, "An act to grant certain lands to the Gainesville, Ocala, and Charlotte Harbor Railroad Company"; and the third, "An act to incorporate the Chattahoochee and Pensacola Railroad Company." The first proposed to grant to the railroad named the alternate sections of the swamp and overflowed lands granted to the State by the act of Congress of September 28, 1850, lying along and adjacent to its projected line of railway from Tampa to the St. John's River, a distance of about one hundred and ten miles, to the extent or quantity of ten thousand acres per running mile, and further provided that if any of such lands were sold before a survey of the route was filed in the office of the Secretary of State, then that the quantity so sold should be made up from the even-numbered sections of such land or any State lands lying nearest the line. The second proposed to grant to the railroad named the alternate sections of swamp and overflowed lands for fifteen miles on either side of its projected road, including its branches, to the amount or quantity of eight thousand acres per mile. The length of this line, including branches, is at least four hundred miles. The third bill proposed to grant to the railroad named, being two hundred and seventy-five miles in length, the aid provided for in the Internal Improvement act and its amendments, including those which may be passed at this session, and also the swamp and overflowed lands lying along and adjacent to said line, its extension and branches, to the amount of ten thousand acres per lineal mile. The amount of land which these bills proposed to donate is seven millions of acres. The Governor in stating his objections presented a distinct view of the claims on these lands. He says that the lands hereby to be appropriated are those granted to the State by the United States by the act of September 28, 1850, and are commonly known as the "swamp and overflowed lands." These lands, and the five hundred thousand acres of internal improvement lands granted to the State by the act of Congress of September 4, 1841, were, by the act of the Legislature entitled "An act to establish a liberal system of internal improvement in this State," approved January 6, 1855, vested in the Board of Trustees of the Internal Improvement Fund of the State. To this Board was given power to make arrangements for reclaiming swamp and overflowed lands as contemplated by the act of Congress of September 28, 1850, and decided by the Supreme Court in the case of the Trustees of the Internal Improvement Fund *vs.* Gleason (15 Florida), and to manage and sell the lands. The net proceeds of the sales of these lands, over and above the amounts necessary for the purpose of management and reclamation, were, by this act of January 6, 1855, pledged to the payment of the interest on the bonds which might be issued by railroad companies which should undertake the construction of any part of the line of railroad from the St. John's River to Pensacola Bay, with an extension from suitable points on this line to St. Mark's River, or Crooked River at White Bluff on Apalachicola Bay in Middle Florida, and to the waters of St. Andrew's Bay in West Florida, and a line from Amelia Island to Tampa Bay, with an extension to Cedar Key. Certain companies constructed railroads on these lines from Jacksonville, on the St. John's River, to Quincy, in Middle Florida, and from Tallahassee to St. Marks, and from Amelia Island to Cedar Key. To aid in their construction, the accompanies issued bonds, which were endorsed by the trustees of the fund, with an agreement guaranteeing the payment of the interest thereon out of the proceeds of the land. Thus these lands became pledged to the payment of this interest. It was a provision of this act of January 6, 1855, that no bonds issued after the end of eight years from its passage should be so guaranteed.

The reare now outstanding of the past-due coupons representing the interest on these bonds about $367,000; and as these coupons, like other negotiable paper, bear interest themselves, there is now due upon these about $650,000. There are additional coupons. It was the evident intent and purpose of the internal improvement law that these lands or their proceeds should be applied to no purposes of internal improvement other than those named in the fourth section of that act, until the coupons had all been paid, or at least placed on a safe basis of payment. That this was the contract between the coupon-holder and the State, is not only plain from the language of the act, but it has several times been adjudged by the courts, and it is shown by the history contemporaneous with the enactment of the law. Therefore, he concludes that neither the Legislature nor the Trustees can divert the lands from the payment of the interest on the bonds.

The whole quantity of land so far selected in the State as swamp and overflowed lands is about 15,000,000 acres. Of this, about 1,600,000 have been heretofore disposed of, leaving about 13,400,000 acres selected. Only, however, 11,794,000 acres have been confirmed by the United States Government, and taking from this the amount disposed of, there is on hand, under the control of the Board, only

10,200,000 acres. The act of Congress above mentioned granted to the State all the lands within its limits which were swamp and overflowed, and too wet for cultivation without artificial drainage. But, before the lands so granted could be ascertained and set apart to the State, a large quantity claimed as swamp was entered at the United States land-offices. Not wishing to disturb the possession of purchasers under these circumstances, Congress passed the acts of March 2, 1855, and March 3, 1857, which confirmed to such purchasers the lands entered by them between the date of the grant and the passage of the last-named act, agreeing to pay over to the State the purchase-money received from such lands. The amount due the State as indemnity for these sales is about $200,000, and frequent efforts have been made on the part of the State to procure an adjustment, but, thus far, without success. At last, however, the United States authorities have consented to send out three agents to examine the lands for which indemnity is claimed, and they have commenced the investigation. To enable the State to get the purchase-money paid for any tract sold by the United States, proof must be made of the swampy character of the land at the date of the grant (1850), and two witnesses are required for each tract.

The Lieutenant-Governor, Noble A. Hull, was a candidate for Congress at the election on November 5, 1878. After this election it was asserted that frauds were committed in Brevard County, and grave charges were made against Mr. Hull in connection with them, and an indictment was found against him in the United States Court. A committee of five was appointed in the Senate to investigate the charges. The committee reported, on February 27th, that "they had assumed, for the purpose of this inquiry, that such a fraud was committed, and confined themselves to the inquiry whether Lieutenant-Governor Hull was in any way connected with it, or had any knowledge of it."

The report is lengthy, and concludes in the following words: "Your committee respectfully submits that the evidence in this case proves that Lieutenant-Governor N. A. Hull had no connection with the alleged election frauds in Brevard County; that he had no knowledge of them, either before or after their alleged commission; that there is no reason for even a suspicion of any complicity on the part of Governor Hull in them, either directly or indirectly; and that there is no reason for any further action on the subject by the Assembly."

The competitor of Lieutenant-Governor Hull, Mr. Horatio Bisbee, contested the declared result at every point. (For the inspectors' return of votes, see "Annual Cyclopædia," 1878—FLORIDA.) On his application the Supreme Court issued a peremptory mandamus under which the County Canvassers of Alachua County made a canvass embracing returns from all the precincts in the county, which was filed in the Clerk's office of the Supreme Court. The canvassers conclude their certificate with this statement: "We certify that the precinct returns are so irregular, false, and fraudulent that we are unable to determine what the true vote of Alachua County is for Representative in Congress and for members of the Assembly." The returns made by the inspectors were canvassed, and the names for whom the votes purport to have been cast are given precisely as they appeared in the inspectors' certificates for Representatives in Congress: Noble A. Hull, 1,178; Horatio Bisbee, 735; Horatio Bisbee, Jr., 751; Horatio Bisby, Jr., 68; Horache Bisbee, 191.

The decision of the Court, rendered in January, 1879, on a demurrer of the relator to objections of the respondents, embraced the following points:

1. It is not a valid objection to the jurisdiction of State courts in mandamus proceedings, relating to the canvass of election returns, that the office affected is that of Representative in Congress.

2. A return by election inspectors, in which the votes cast for a person are given twice or repeated, constitutes no ground for refusing to include such return in the statement and certificate by the county canvassers, it being on its face a mere verbal repetition, and not an attempt to misstate the votes cast. The fact that the statement sent to the Clerk contained such repetition, while that sent to the County Judge did not contain it, does not create such a variance between them as to authorize their rejection.

3. When the jurat to the oath of inspectors of election is not signed, or when the inspectors have not been sworn, but have acted as such and made proper returns, their acts are valid and their return of election should be counted.

4. A statement in the caption of inspectors' returns forwarded to the Judge that the election was held under an act of 1868, and the amendments thereto (without giving the dates of the amendments), while that sent to the Clerk gave the date of the act and also of the amendments, does not render the returns indefinite, uncertain, contradictory, or in any sense repugnant to each other, but they are regular and conformable to law. The difference is immaterial.

5. County canvassers can not look beyond the inspectors' returns, except to determine their genuineness as being signed by inspectors appointed or elected as such of the precinct. Ballots found in a ballot-box can not be considered by the county canvassers.

6. Where the County Judge and Clerk have called in a Justice of the Peace, who acts with them in canvassing election returns, the Justice becomes a member of the Board of County Canvassers, and is, like the other members, amenable to the writ of mandamus to control or correct their action.

Demurrer sustained. Judgment for relator.

Again, on the application of Mr. H. Bisbee, Jr., the Supreme Court issued another peremptory writ to the Board of State Canvassers, being the Secretary of State, the Comptroller, and the Attorney-General, commanding them to reconvene and canvass and count the true returns, etc., etc. The respondents filed a demurrer to the alternative writ on the ground that the relator did not show that he was twenty-five years of age, and that the writ showed that the return from Madison County

did not represent the true vote cast. The Court overruled the demurrer, and decided the following points:

1. It is not good ground of demurrer to an alternative writ of mandamus directing a canvass of votes for Representative in Congress, that the relator does not show that he is qualified to take the office; the question of eligibility belonging exclusively to Congress to determine.

2. The statute authorizes the Board of State Canvassers to lay aside and not include in their canvass the county returns or papers purporting to be county returns, when it appears to them that such returns are "so irregular, false, or fraudulent" that the Board can not "determine the true vote" for any office, i. e., the vote actually cast. The law requires the county canvassers to canvass the precinct returns received on the sixth day after the election, whether the precinct returns from all the precincts are then in or not; and further requires the County Board to certify the result of this canvass to the State canvassers, to be included in the State canvass, unless they are shown or appear to be of the character above described. The returns from one county were shown to have been complete, except that no return had been made to the County Board of votes cast at one poll, and no vote from that poll was included in the county canvass and return to the State Board; and for this reason the State Board did not include the vote returned from that county, on the ground that it was so irregular or false that it did not show the "true vote." Upon this state of facts, it was held: That the county return was in no wise so irregular or false, within the meaning of the law, that the State canvassers could not determine the "true vote" from such return; that the county return, being genuine, regular, and strictly legal in all respects, and required to be made for the purposes of the State canvass, and included only votes actually cast, could not be condemned as "false," but was a return expressly required by law to be counted.

Mr. Bisbee next applied to the Governor to issue the certificate of election to him. Governor Drew replied that it was impossible, as he had already issued and signed a certificate to another person as member of Congress from the district. Subsequently Mr. Bisbee instituted mandamus proceedings in the Supreme Court against the Governor to compel him to issue the writ as requested. The counsel of the Governor moved to quash the alternative writ, on the ground that the Court had no power to issue it against the Governor. This motion brought squarely before the Court the question of the Governor's independence of the judicial department in the performance of his executive duties. The decision of the Court, delivered by Chief-Justice Crandall, embraced the following points:

1. The courts have no power to control the action of the Governor in the discharge of any duty pertaining to his office under the laws of the State.

2. The issuing of a commission or a certificate of election, required by law to be issued by the Governor, though ministerial in its nature, is yet an executive act pertaining to his office as the Chief Magistrate of the State.

3. Each department of the government of the State is independent of the other in the performance of its own duty, and one can not control the other in such performance without destroying this independence.

4. The person of the Governor is subject to the process of the courts only in reference to private acts and acts not pertaining to executive functions imposed by the Constitution or laws.

5. In respect to his executive duties as Governor,

he alone may judge of the manner in which he will perform them, and the judicial department may determine the effect of acts performed. Alternative writ dismissed.

Whether the issuing of a second certificate by Governor Drew might have operated as a revocation of the first does not appear to be decided; but in the case of a commission issued to a person on a partial canvass of votes, the commission can only be vacated by an appeal to the courts. This was setted in Missouri, where the Secretary of State, in a canvass of votes cast for Judge, had refused to open and count the returns from two counties, and had certified the result to the Governor, who issued the commission on this partial canvass. An application was made by Congressman Bland to the Supreme Court of that State for a mandamus to compel the Secretary to open and canvass the returns from the two counties, whose votes, if counted, would have elected him instead of the other candidate. The Court held that, though the Secretary of State had no right to refuse to open and canvass the returns from the two counties, nevertheless, as the commission had already been issued, it would not direct him to do so. The Court said: "The officer derives his title to the office by virtue of his election, and the commission is *prima facie* evidence only. The case has passed beyond the control of this Court, and the only redress the relator has, if he considers himself aggrieved, is by legal contest made in pursuance of law." This question of a contested seat came up in the House of Representatives in Washington on December 18th, and it was given to Noble A. Hull—yeas 140, nays 136.

Many resolutions were presented in the Legislature to provide for the assembling of a State Constitutional Convention. These were referred to a joint committee of both Houses, who agreed upon a report recommending some less important changes.

Three important bills relating to railroads were presented on the same day in each House. The first would have aided in the construction of new roads, and under the others all necessary steps would be taken to bring the existing roads to account and to enforce the penalties they may have incurred.

A complicated case of railroad litigation was decided in the United States Circuit Court by Justice Bradley. The parties were the Western North Carolina Railroad against the Florida Central, and the Jacksonville, Pensacola, and Mobile Railroad Company, and others; also the case of J. Fred. Shuette and others against the same defendants. The cases were tried together. These suits were founded upon claims against the defendants. The effect of the decision was to award to the parties interested their rank as claimants and the amounts to which they were entitled. The roads were ordered to be sold, and as a result of the sale the formation of a new organization was anticipated.

A requisition from the Governor of North Carolina upon the Governor of Florida for the delivery of a person indicted in the former State for "obtaining money under false pretenses" was not granted by the latter Governor. Upon being arrested, the party sued out a writ of *habeas corpus*. After a hearing, the Judge made an order discharging him from arrest, holding that there was a variance between the charge named in the requisition and warrant and that specified in the indictment; and, also, that he was not a fugitive from justice within the meaning of the Constitution and statutes of the United States.

The power of the judiciary to review the action of the Governor in such cases is recognized by some courts, at least to the extent of deciding whether the party is a fugitive from justice. (Joues *vs.* Leonard, decided in the Supreme Court of Iowa, December term, 1878, page 112 of "Albany Law Journal" of February 18, 1879; in the matter of Manchester, 5 Cal., 237.) In this case there was a judicial determination of the question of his being a fugitive from justice, and the Governor declined to assume that the judicial decision was erroneous.

An action of ejectment brought to recover possession of two lots of land in St. John's County was taken to the United States Supreme Court. It was entitled George Burt, plaintiff in error, against Maria M. Ponjoud. Among the errors assigned was a ruling of the lower Court to the effect that a certain Henry Holmes, called to be a juror in this case, was not obliged to answer any questions touching his qualifications as a juror, under section 820 of the Revised Statutes. Under this ruling Holmes declined to say whether he did or did not participate in the rebellion. He was challenged on the ground that he was disqualified under the aforesaid section of the Revised Statutes, and the Court overruled the challenge. Upon this point the Supreme Court held that a juror was no more obliged than a witness to disclose on oath his guilt of any crime, or of any act which would render him infamous, in order to test his qualifications as a juror. The question asked him, if answered in the affirmative, would have convicted him of the crime of treason. Whether pardoned by a general amnesty or not, the crime was one which, in the opinion of the Court, he could not be required to disclose in this manner. If he were guilty, the challenger had the right to prove it by any other competent testimony. As he did not offer to do this, and as the juror's incompetency was not proved, the Court was not bound to exclude him. As to the ownership of the lots, this Court held that there was sufficient evidence of defendant in error's prior possession, and that she was entitled to them both. Mr. Justice Miller delivered the opinion.

Mr. Justice Field delivered a separate concurring opinion with regard to the test-oath demanded of the juror Holmes, as follows: "I agree with the Court that the juror Holmes in this case can not be required to answer the questions put to him, but I go further. I do not think that the act of Congress which, by requiring a test-oath as to past conduct, excludes a great majority of the citizens of half the country from the jury-box is valid. In my judgment the act is not only oppressive and odious, and repugnant to the spirit of our institutions, but is clearly unconstitutional and void. As a war measure, to be enforced in the insurgent States when dominated by the national forces, the act could be sustained; but after the war was over and the insurgent States were restored to their normal and constitutional relations to the Union, it was as much out of place and as inoperative as would be a law quartering a soldier in every Southern man's house."

In a subsequent case of Atwood *vs.* Weems, from the Circuit Court of the District of Florida, the Supreme Court held on the question of jurors' test-oaths that the right under section 820 of the Revised Statutes to require a panel of jurors called to serve for a term to take the oath therein prescribed, or be discharged, is a right which can be exercised only by the District Attorney; that it does not belong to either of the suitors in the case about to be tried. Justice Field, in concurring in the opinion, reiterated his previously expressed belief that section 820 of the Revised Statutes was unconstitutional and void. He held that Congress might undoubtedly prescribe the qualifications of jurors in the Federal courts, but if any of the causes for disqualification was the commission of an act which the law had pronounced a public offense, it was not competent for the Court to go into an investigation to determine the guilt or innocence of a juror; that is to be ascertained only in one way—by a separate trial of the party upon an indictment for the offense, and the only competent evidence in such a case is the record of his conviction or acquittal.

The products of the State, as shown by the returns of the assessors for 1877, which are somewhat defective, as seven counties made no reports, nevertheless amounted as follows:

Cotton, upland, bales	14,007
" Sea Island, lbs.	5,844,575
Corn, bushels	1,628,988
Oats, "	346,310
Wheat, "	608
Rye, "	11,098
Rice, "	26,382
Sugar-cane, gallons of sirup	601,208
Sugar, lbs.	963,910
Tobacco, lbs.	16,572
Orange-trees in grove	20,481,541
" bearing	18,521
Oranges produced	16,084,558
Lemons "	344,498
Citrons "	23,789
Limes, bushels	8,789
Guavas "	6,917
Bananas, bunches	17,970
Pineapples	886,800
Peaches, bushels	238,250
Apples, "	7,095
Pears, "	117

Grapes, bushels	13,312
Wine, gallons	8,545
Garden-peas, crates	7,497
Beans, crates	7,590
Potatoes, Irish, bushels	28,756
" sweet, "	1,684,704
Melons	2,084,206
Cucumbers, crates	7,207
Tomatoes, "	6,154
Hay, tons	87,570

The number of the convicts in the State Prison at the beginning of the year was 163. Of these 24 were white males, 1 white female, 135 colored males, and 3 colored females.

The expense of the prison for 1877 was $5,962.27, of which $3,159.10 was for conveying prisoners and $927.60 was for repairs of the buildings at Chattahoochee. The expense of 1878 was $6,616.03, of which $4,514.53 was for conveying prisoners to the convict camps. This expense, by the contract since made, is hereafter to be borne by the contractor.

The proposition for a ship-canal across the State was revived again during the year. In 1877 General Q. A. Gillmore, in charge of the river and harbor improvements on that portion of the line of coast which embraces the shores of the States of Florida, Georgia, and South Carolina, submitted a report in answer to a resolution of the Senate directing the Secretary of War "to communicate all information in his possession concerning a water-line of transportation from the mouth of the St. Mary's River, between the States of Georgia and Florida, through Okefenokee Swamp and through the State of Florida to some suitable point on the Gulf of Mexico, embracing the probable nature and character of such a water-line, and the extent of country and population to be benefited by its construction, and an estimate of the cost of the necessary surveys or examinations therefor."

The main purpose sought to be attained by the proposed water-line is assumed to be a cheap means of sending eastward the products of the Mississippi Valley over a route that shall shorten the time and avoid the danger of the trip through the Gulf of Mexico and the Florida Straits.

Two methods of accomplishing these objects have been suggested:

1. By a water-line of barges across the peninsula of Florida, continued westward to the Mississippi River by another inside barge route through the landlocked sounds and bays bordering the Gulf of Mexico in the States of Florida, Alabama, Mississippi, and Louisiana.

2. By a ship-canal across the State of Florida, of dimensions sufficient to pass large ocean-going vessels.

In determining the western terminus for a peninsular barge-canal from St. Mary's River, through Okefenokee Swamp, to the Gulf of Mexico, the advantages offered by the harbor of St. Mark's become at once apparent.

From St. Mark's westward to Lake Borgne or Lake Ponchartrain there exists a nearly continuous natural landlocked water route, by means of tidal sounds, bays, and connecting streams, requiring improvement by dredging in some places, but only a comparatively short aggregate length of solid cutting. The selection of a terminal point to the eastward of St. Mark's would render the connection with this western branch to the Mississippi less direct.

The chief object that would be attained by this canal is barge transportation for the grain and cotton of the Mississippi Valley, and a portion of the cotton, timber, and lumber of the Gulf States, to some suitable harbor on the Atlantic coast for reshipment to foreign and domestic markets.

The needed supply of water for the summit level of the canal and the service of its two locks, and for all the various losses incidental to such works, is expected to be drawn from the Okefenokee Swamp.

A straight line, measured on the map, from the mouth of St. Mary's to St. Mark's, has a length of about one hundred and sixty-five miles. By taking advantage of the natural watercourses in proximity to that line, which are either navigable or can presumably be made so by slack-water dams for the largest class of barges destined to pass the canal, the length will of course be augmented.

The total length of St. Mary's River, from its mouth to Ellicott's Mound, where the head of one of its branches is found, is about one hundred miles.

The feasibility of a ship-canal for large ocean-going vessels, that shall connect the St. Mary's River with the Gulf of Mexico through Okefenokee Swamp, is more uncertain than that of the barge-canal above mentioned. The project must provide for a suitable harbor at each terminus of the line. On the Atlantic this could possibly be accomplished by the enlargement for ships of the existing inside passage between St. Mary's River and Brunswick, making this point the shipping port. On the Gulf side the choice would probably have to be made between St. Mark's and Cedar Keys, as they are the only harbors at all near the direct line possessing sufficient natural depth of water approach to encourage any attempt to enlarge them to the required capacity by the construction of artificial works. On the St. Mark's bar there is a depth of eight feet and on the Cedar Keys bar a depth of nine feet at mean low water. If St. Mark's should be selected for the Gulf terminus, the general location of the route would probably not vary greatly from that of the barge line; while if it should run to Cedar Keys, the Suwanee River, from the western end of the summit-level division to some point near its mouth, would most likely form a part of it. It was estimated that such a work would shorten the navigable distance to Europe and coastwise, in respect to the commerce of the Mississippi and the Gulf of Mexico, nearly eight hundred miles, and that the commercial advantages would be very great. A company sustained by French capital was investigating the work.

The number of Indians in Florida is about 300, divided into four bands or camps. About one third are Creeks, the remainder Seminoles. They avoid all intercourse with the whites, are no expense to the Government, and are opposed to any closer relationship to the inhabitants.

Some discussion on the subject of emigration took place among the colored people of Leon County in October, but no movement followed.

The Florida school system comprises the following officers:

Superintendent of Public Instruction; State Board of Education; County Superintendents; County Boards of Public Instruction; School Trustees. Seminaries: East Florida Seminary, Gainesville; West Florida Seminary, Tallahassee. These institutions were established for the purpose of training persons in the art of teaching. School age, between six and twenty-one; attendance, voluntary.

The Superintendent of Public Instruction is appointed by the Governor for a term of four years; is President of the Board of Education, etc.

The State Board of Education consists of the Superintendent of Public Instruction, the Secretary of State, and the Attorney-General; has charge of all lands and public educational funds belonging to the State, etc.

The County Board of Public Instruction consists of from three to five members, appointed by the State Board of Education, who hold office for four years. They receive, pay out, and account for school moneys; build or otherwise provide schoolhouses, employ teachers, etc.

The County Superintendent of Schools is appointed for two years by the Governor; visits and inspects schools at least once in every three months; is secretary and agent of the Board of Public Instruction; makes annual statistical reports to the State Superintendent, etc.

School trustees are appointed for four years by the County Board of Public Instruction on the recommendation of the patrons. They recommend parties to be employed as teachers to the County Board, and have charge and oversight of the building, grounds, and other property belonging to the school for which they are appointed.

Statistics.—1878. School days in the year, average 106
County Superintendents 83
Schoolhouses 634
Number of teachers 970
Enumeration of children 87,750
Enrollment in schools 31,133
School fund $243,500 00
Addition to fund during the year 8,300 09
Value of school property 116,984 50

REVENUE FOR THE YEAR.

Interest on the common-school fund $17,962 08
State tax 30,889 15
Local tax 119,751 88

FLOYD, SALLY BUCHANAN, born in 1802, died in Abingdon, Va., May 7, 1879. She was the widow of the late General and Governor

John B. Floyd. Her grandmother was Elizabeth Henry, the sister of the famous orator Patrick Henry, and the wife of General William Campbell, who commanded at the battle of King's Mountain in the Revolutionary war. Their only child, a daughter, became the wife of General Frank Preston of Abingdon, who was a member of the first three Congresses. Their children were all more or less distinguished. One son, Mrs. Floyd's brother, was William C. Preston, Senator from South Carolina, of which State he had become a resident. In the Senate, some years before the late war, he was one of the most eloquent speakers. She was a sister of Colonel John S. Preston, the Commissioner of South Carolina to Virginia in 1861. Mrs. Floyd was also the last of a family of distinguished sisters, viz.: Eliza, wife of General Edward C. Carrington of Halifax County, Va.; Susan, wife of Governor James McDowell of Lexington, Va.; Sophonisba, wife of Rev. Robert J. Breckenridge, D. D., of Lexington, Ky.; Maria, wife of John M. Preston of Washington County, Va.; and Margaret, wife of General (now Senator) Wade Hampton of South Carolina. Mrs. Floyd had no children, but early adopted two orphaned relatives of both herself and her husband—John Preston Johnston, afterward a gallant young artillery-officer of the army, who was killed on the field of battle at Contreras in the Mexican war, and his sister, Mrs. Judge Hughes of Norfolk.

FOLEY, THOMAS, D. D., born in Baltimore, Md., March 6, 1822, died in Chicago, Ill., February 19, 1879. His education was obtained at St. Mary's College, Baltimore, and the Theological Seminary of St. Sulpice, where he was ordained a priest on August 16, 1846. Subsequently he was appointed to take charge of the Catholic missions in Montgomery County, Md., officiating there four months. He was made assistant pastor of St. Patrick's in Washington, D. C., his senior being the venerable Father Matthews. In that parish he passed two years, and was then called to the Baltimore Cathedral, where he labored twenty-two years. In 1851 he became secretary to Archbishop Kenrick, and was also Chancellor of the archdiocese of Baltimore; while later he held similar positions under the late Archbishop Spalding. In 1867 he became Vicar-General of the archdiocese of Baltimore. In 1869 he was appointed by Pius IX. coadjutor of the Bishop of Chicago and administrator of that diocese. He was consecrated Bishop of Pergamus *in partibus infidelium* at the Cathedral of Baltimore, February 27, 1870, Bishop Duggan of Chicago having retired on account of infirm health. Bishop Foley was then in the forty-seventh year of his age and the full vigor of life. Of commanding stature, he possessed at the same time benignant and winning manners. Physically he was a splendid type of manhood, and his virtues and piety endeared him to hosts of friends in Baltimore, irrespec-

tive of religious faith or predilection.. He was also a man of great capacity for business, and his enterprise was proverbial. After he become administrator he erected twenty-five churches, schools, etc., and saw various other institutions come into existence under his benign rule. The great work of his life was the rebuilding of the Cathedral of the Holy Name. To raise this edifice from its ashes cost nearly $300,000, and it is one of the finest churches in the country, and the largest and most costly edifice of the kind in Chicago. As an orator he was exceedingly graceful and persuasive, and on this account he was selected to deliver discourses on several occasions of public interest. A severe cold increased to pneumonia, which became typhoid, and was so aggravated by abdominal inflammation that his physical system could not hold out, and he quietly and peacefully passed away. In the Legislature of Illinois, which was in session at the time of his death, a resolution was adopted, stating that the death of this eminent Catholic prelate is learned with deep regret, recognizing that in his death the Catholic citizens of the State have lost an able and dignified executive, and a divine who was beloved by people of all denominations for his sanctity, piety, and true Christian charity, and closing by expressing sympathy with the Catholic people of Chicago and the family of the late Bishop.

FORMATION OF MOUNTAINS. One of the most controverted subjects in dynamical geology has been the problem of the formation of the mountain groups, plateaus, ridges, and sierras which form a prominent feature in every continent, producing some of the meteorological conditions which are most favorable to life, and which vary not less the profile of the submerged portions of the earth's surface, the higher elevations forming the rows and groups of islands which dot the sea. Distinct from these great symmetrical congeries of rocky elevations are the mountains of volcanic origin, formed by the outpouring of molten rock through craters, which are usually of a conical form and stand isolated or in rows without connecting ridges, and also the inferior eminences which have been left after glacial action and denudation have swept away the materials between them. The mountain systems are generally supposed to be corrugations which have resulted from the contraction of the earth's mass. This is now the accepted theory; but there is still some dispute as to the effects of the contraction, some holding that the elevations are produced by forces which draw the intervening mineral masses inward, some that they are upheaved by forces pushing them outward, and a third and more numerous school believing that the direction of the dynamic forces is lateral, and that the elevated masses are the plications produced by horizontal compression attending the secular subsidence of the earth's crust. Professor Alphonse Favre of Geneva has recently terminated a series of experiments on the effects of lateral pressure, in which the conditions of nature were better preserved than in the famous experiments of Sir James Hall with various cloths folded and held down by the superposition of heavy weights, which he made to assume shapes analogous to the disposition of masses of rocks by squeezing them from each side. M. Favre used a homogeneous and plastic material, and left the upper surface free to assume the forms which would result from lateral contraction, and which resembled hills and mountains. He took sheets of India-rubber, 16 millimetres in thickness and 40 by 12 centimetres in area. Stretching them to a length of 60 centimetres, he covered them with a layer of soft potters' clay, which varied in thickness in the different experiments from 25 to 60 millimetres. The contraction of one third which he produced in most of his experiments corresponds to that which has actually taken place in certain parts of Savoy. The strata in the mountains between Dessy and the Col du Grand Barnaud, for instance, are folded and contorted into two thirds the compass which they had before compression when lying horizontal. If the solid crust of the earth rests upon a pasty nucleus whose volume is slowly and constantly diminishing, then the hard, rocky mass will be broken and thrust out of shape as the interior supporting mass contracts.

Such a dislocation of the external strata has taken place at different geological periods and in all parts of the world. In many places the lower strata are distorted, while the more recent overlying formations are unbroken and horizontal. Often the contraction has been much greater than that obtained in the experiments. In some places the folds are very close together and their sides nearly vertical. These disturbances must have occurred with imperceptible slowness, as they follow the contraction by minute degrees of the earth's radius.

Drawing horizontal lines on the side faces of the clay to indicate the position which strata would take after compression, and confining the extremities of the clay band within vertical wooden strips, he allowed the caoutchouc to contract, thus producing lateral compression by the double means of the adhesion of the clay to the caoutchouc and the pressure of the wood supports. The contraction of the caoutchouc alone would produce only slight wrinkles on the surface of the clay, and the action of the wooden ends alone would only cause the clay to bulge at the extremities, producing no effect in the center. The pressure secured in Professor Favre's experiments produced contortions of strata very similar in configuration to the earth's surface. In some places the plane surface of the clay was elevated without being broken or thrown much out of the horizontal position; in others vaults and plications were produced which resemble hills, mountains, and valleys. The ridges some-

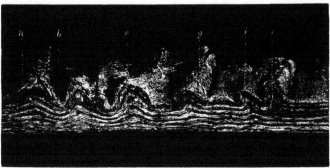

Fig 1.

times approached the perpendicular; at times they were complete folds, at other times they separated at the summit in a longitudinal fracture increasing in width downward, and at the base in a complementary fracture widest at the mouth. The strata are broken in places, producing fissures and caverns below the surface, or are crossed by clefts or faults, sometimes vertical, sometimes inclined. The contortions do not extend perpendicularly across the clay band, but take various directions, the opposite sides showing different deformations.

The experiment shown in Fig. 1 was with a band of clay about 25 millimetres thick, which after compression attained a thickness at the culminating point of 62 millimetres. It reproduces many of the common features of the Jura, the Alps, and the Appalachians. At a is a vault slightly broken at the summit, covering a cavern ; b is a valley open at one end and closed at the other ; e is a vault, nearly straight and of even elevation ; g and h are twisted and slightly broken vaults ; and i is a ruptured fold whose sides are nearly vertical.

In Fig. 2 the clay was 40 millimetres thick originally, and 65 after compression. At a is a very perfect vault. At b, c, d, and e are spots where the pressure found the least resistance, and where the strata were violently broken and their ends often separated. One of these vaults is replaced on the opposite side by a single fault. M. Favre calls these places of extreme pressure *zones de refoulement*.

In Fig. 3 an experiment with a band of va-

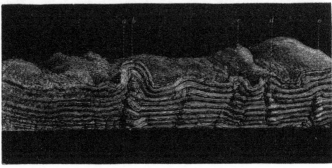

FIG. 2.

riant thickness is represented. The division a was 33 centimetres long and 25 millimetres thick; b was 25 centimetres long and 65 millimetres thick; a gentle slope 35 millimetres thick at b connected them. After compression the mean thickness of a and b was 45 and that of c 75 millimetres. In this experiment he sought to obtain the effect of compression at a point where a mountain meets a plain. The height of the mountain c has been increased; the five or six upper layers have encroached upon the plain; but the resistance of the plain has been sufficient to cause the strata of the mountain to be strongly inflected. The first hill d, at the foot of the mountain, is the result of the struggle between the mountain and the

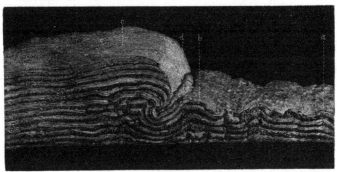

FIG. 3.

plain; as also is the vault b, the elevation of which has caused the strata of the plain to be deflected and depressed at contact with the mountain. Such a phenomenon as the depression of the strata at a lower elevation under the foot of a mountain is often observed in the Alps at the junction of the first calcareous chain and the hills of the *molasse*.

In Fig. 4 the thickness of the clay band was 45 millimetres, and after compression the highest elevation was over 100. The object of the experiment was to reproduce the effect of lateral pressure on moist strata at the bottom of the ocean, near two solidified mountain masses. Two semi-cylinders of wood were inserted under the clay at equal distances from the extremities and the same distance from each other. After pressure a valley c was formed above the semi-cylinder *a* by a deflection of the beds to the right and by a little mountain *d* on the left. On the semi-cylinder *b* an enormous elevation has taken place, attended by a violent rupture in which on one of the sides, *f* and *g*, the strata have been completely reversed, turning over as if on a hinge at the point *h*. On the line between *x* and *z* the strata are found

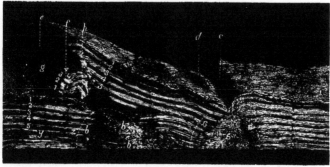

FIG. 4.

to overlie each other in a treble series, once in the natural order, once inverted, and again in their original position. If the disjoined and inverted section were pushed away, the five layers would be found doubled. Such examples of superimposed and inverted stratification are not uncommon geological phenomena.

FRANCE, a republic of Europe. President at the close of 1879, François Paul Jules Grévy, elected January 30, 1879. The French Cabinet was at the close of 1879 composed as follows: M. de Freycinet, President of the Council and Minister of Foreign Affairs (see FREYCINET); M. de Lepère, Minister of the Interior and of Worship; M. Cazot, Minister of Justice; M. Magnin, Minister of Finance; General Farre, Minister of War; Admiral Jauréguiberry. Minister of Marine; M. Jules Ferry, Minister of Public Instruction; M. Varroy, Minister of Public Works; M. Tirard, Minister of Commerce; M. Cochery, Minister of Posts and Telegraphs. The President of the Republic is elected by the Senate and Chamber of Deputies, united in National Assembly. The term of his office is seven years, and he is eligible for reëlection. The Senate is composed of 300 members, of whom 75 hold their seats for life, the vacancies being filled by the votes of the Senators. The remaining 225 seats are divided by lot into three classes of 75 each, one class going out at successive periods of three years. The election of these 225 Senators is by an indirect process. In the first instance, the communes and municipalities of France, 14,200 in number, elect a fixed number of *électeurs sénatoriaux*, who in their turn, after a lapse of two months, meet together to choose the Senators. The Chamber of Deputies is elected by universal suffrage under the *scrutin d'arrondissement* adopted by the Na-

tional Assembly, November 11, 1875. The law orders every arrondissement to elect one deputy, and, if its population is in excess of 100,-000, an additional deputy for each 100,000 or portion thereof.

The area of France, according to the latest official calculations, is 204,092 square miles. The population, according to the census of 1876, was 36,905,788. The table on page 383 exhibits the area of each department, its population according to the censuses of 1872 and 1876, and the movement of population in 1876.

The movement of population from 1867 to 1876 was as follows:

YEARS.	Births.	Deaths.	Surplus of births (B.) or deaths (D.)	Percentage of increase (I.) or decrease (D.) of population.
1867...	1,007,515	886,887	B. 120,628	I. 0·81
1868...	984,140	922,088	B. 62,102	I. 0·16
1869...	948,526	864,820	B. 84,206	I. 0·21
1870...	944,115	1,046,909	D. 91,794	D. 0·28
1871...	826,121	1,271,010	D. 444,889	D. 1·22
1872...	966,000	793,064	B. 172,986	I. 0·48
1873...	940,364	844,588	B. 95,776	I. 0·28
1874...	954,652	781,706	B. 172,946	I. 0·48
1875...	950,975	845,062	B. 105,913	I. 0·28
1876...	966,682	824,074	B. 182,603	I. 0·86

The relation of marriages to the total population from 1870 to 1876 was as follows:

YEARS.	Total population.	Marriages.	Number of marriages to 100 inhabitants.
1870........	36,985,212	228,705	0·60
1871........	36,544,007	262,476	0·72
1872........	36,102,921	352,754	0·98
1873........	36,260,928	321,238	0·89
1874........	36,388,481	308,113	0·83
1875........	36,542,910	300,427	0·82
1876........	36,905,788	291,236	0·79

DEPARTMENTS.	Area in sq. miles.	Population in 1872.	Population in 1876.	Births, 1876.	Deaths, 1876.	Marriages, 1876.
Ain...	2,889	363,290	365,462	8,845	7,830	2,772
Aisne...	2,839	552,439	560,427	18,784	12,205	4,698
Allier...	2,822	390,812	405,783	10,925	7,117	3,328
Alpes (Basses)...	2,685	139,332	136,166	3,671	3,741	1,012
Alpes (Hautes)...	2,158	118,898	119,094	3,680	3,422	906
Alpes (Maritimes)...	1,512	199,087	203,604	6,063	5,408	1,733
Ardèche...	2,184	380,277	384,878	11,356	9,449	3,409
Ardennes...	2,020	320,217	326,782	7,776	6,768	2,555
Ariége...	1,890	246,298	244,795	6,255	6,385	1,814
Aube...	2,317	255,687	255,217	5,155	5,482	2,004
Aude...	2,488	285,927	300,065	7,902	7,009	2,277
Aveyron...	3,376	402,474	413,826	13,569	9,664	3,202
Bouches-du-Rhône...	1,971	554,911	556,379	16,016	14,749	4,150
Calvados...	2,182	454,012	453,220	9,209	10,944	3,197
Cantal...	2,217	231,867	281,086	6,042	4,792	1,809
Charente...	2,294	267,520	378,950	8,656	8,167	3,222
Charente-Inférieure...	2,686	465,658	465,028	10,208	9,124	4,726
Cher...	2,779	383,892	345,018	9,780	6,516	3,080
Corrèze...	2,365	302,746	311,925	9,801	7,448	2,941
Corsica...	3,377	258,507	262,701	8,291	7,198	1,844
Côte-d'Or...	3,363	374,510	377,063	7,611	7,306	2,585
Côtes-du-Nord...	2,652	622,295	630,957	19,724	14,178	4,991
Creuse...	2,150	274,668	278,428	6,926	4,741	2,160
Dordogne...	3,545	480,141	489,848	13,327	10,021	4,788
Doubs...	2,019	291,251	306,094	8,847	7,168	2,444
Drôme...	2,518	320,417	321,756	8,147	7,550	2,648
Eure...	2,300	377,874	378,029	7,250	8,691	2,656
Eure-et-Loire...	2,268	282,022	283,075	6,724	7,129	1,999
Finistère...	2,595	642,963	666,106	23,500	17,111	5,160
Gard...	2,258	420,131	423,804	12,738	11,387	3,286
Garonne...	2,429	479,362	477,780	10,566	9,720	3,424
Gers...	2,425	284,717	283,546	5,871	6,269	2,134
Gironde...	3,761	705,149	785,242	15,121	15,100	6,058
Hérault...	2,398	429,878	445,058	12,111	11,189	3,299
Ille-et-Vilaine...	2,597	589,582	602,712	17,889	14,418	5,006
Indre...	2,624	277,098	281,948	7,425	5,825	2,368
Indre-et-Loire...	3,360	317,027	324,875	6,711	6,013	2,559
Isère...	3,201	575,784	581,099	15,462	13,330	4,987
Jura...	1,928	287,684	298,823	7,192	5,487	2,363
Landes...	3,597	300,598	308,506	8,159	5,602	2,442
Loir-et-Cher...	2,452	268,801	372,684	6,734	5,602	2,241
Loire...	1,888	550,611	590,618	17,782	12,782	4,928
Loire (Haute)...	1,916	308,782	313,721	9,575	6,658	2,412
Loire-Inférieure...	2,654	602,206	612,972	14,180	12,256	5,508
Loiret...	2,614	353,021	360,903	9,548	7,714	2,768
Lot...	2,012	281,404	276,512	6,241	6,047	2,377
Lot-et-Garonne...	2,067	319,289	316,920	5,000	7,120	2,386
Lozère...	1,996	135,190	138,319	4,670	3,166	1,196
Maine-et-Loire...	2,750	518,471	517,258	10,000	10,584	3,524
Manche...	2,259	544,776	539,910	12,070	12,261	4,233
Marne...	3,150	386,157	407,790	10,285	9,160	3,097
Marne (Haute)...	2,402	251,196	252,448	5,830	5,284	1,973
Mayenne...	1,996	350,637	351,933	8,866	8,414	2,864
Meurthe-et-Moselle...	2,020	365,137	404,609	9,999	8,031	3,287
Meuse...	2,405	284,725	294,054	6,526	6,527	2,199
Morbihan...	2,625	490,052	506,578	16,592	11,579	4,202
Nièvre...	2,682	339,017	346,822	8,869	6,240	2,815
Nord...	2,198	1,447,764	1,519,585	50,426	33,926	11,415
Oise...	2,251	396,804	401,618	9,069	9,284	2,996
Orne...	2,854	398,250	392,726	7,172	9,116	2,787
Pas-de-Calais...	2,550	761,158	798,140	24,771	17,075	5,657
Puy-de-Dôme...	3,070	566,468	570,207	13,293	11,909	4,702
Pyrénées (Basses)...	2,945	426,700	481,025	11,354	9,249	8,198
Pyrénées (Hautes)...	1,750	235,156	238,067	5,607	5,288	1,689
Pyrénées-Orientales...	1,592	191,856	197,940	6,704	5,481	1,790
Rhin (Haut)*...	286	56,781	68,600	2,000	1,856	540
Rhône...	1,077	670,247	705,131	17,089	17,088	6,083
Saône (Haute)...	2,062	308,068	304,052	7,581	6,667	2,246
Saône-et-Loire...	3,302	598,344	614,309	17,186	12,882	5,047
Sarthe...	2,397	446,608	446,289	9,242	10,186	3,369
Savoie...	2,224	267,958	268,361	7,684	6,580	1,671
Savoie (Haute)...	1,665	273,027	273,801	6,999	6,148	1,8 4
Seine...	185	2,220,060	2,410,849	65,747	60,806	21,401
Seine-Inférieure...	2,330	790,022	798,414	23,847	21,919	6,142
Seine-et-Marne...	2,215	341,490	347,323	8,045	7,944	2,686
Seine-et-Oise...	2,164	580,190	561,990	12,716	13,544	3,960
Sèvres (Deux)...	2,317	331,248	336,655	8,448	6,178	2,802
Somme...	2,379	557,015	556,641	12,798	12,577	4,018
Tarn...	2,317	352,718	359,282	9,270	7,514	2,694
Tarn-et-Garonne...	1,436	221,610	221,364	4,422	4,795	2,058
Var...	2,327	298,757	295,763	6,678	7,056	1,792
Vaucluse...	1,670	263,451	255,703	6,181	5,857	3,791
Vendée...	2,588	401,446	411,781	11,966	9,680	3,106
Vienne...	2,691	320,595	330,916	8,894	6,530	3,045
Vienne (Haute)...	2,130	322,447	336,061	11,119	7,328	3,208
Vosges...	2,259	392,988	407,082	11,146	9,621	2,768
Yonne...	2,868	363,608	359,070	7,328	7,689	
Total...	204,092	36,102,921	36,905,788	966,082	884,074	291,866

* Formerly called Belfort (territoire de).

Of the 966,682 children born in 1876, 66,-
306 were illegitimate. The relation of births
to the total population from 1870 to 1876, and
the number of still-born children for the same
period, were as follows:

YEARS.	Total population.	Births.	Births for 100 inhabitants.	Still-births.
1870......	36,985,212	943,515	2·55	45,169
1871......	36,544,067	826,121	2·26	40,315
1872......	36,102,921	966,000	2·67	43,967
1873......	36,2:0,928	946,861	2·61	44,457
1874......	36,383,481	954,652	2·62	44,613
1875......	36,542,910	951,975	2·60	48,824
1876......	36,905,788	966,682	2·62	44,680

The proportion of deaths to the total population from 1870 to 1876 was as follows:

YEARS.	Total population.	Deaths.	Number of deaths to 100 inhabitants.
1870.......	36,985,212	1,046,900	2·83
1871.......	36,544,067	1,271,910	3·43
1872.......	36,102,921	793,064	2·19
1873.......	36,260,928	844,588	2·33
1874.......	36,383,481	781,706	2·16
1875.......	36,542,910	845,062	2·31
1876.......	36,905,788	834,074	2·26

The receipts and expenditures in the general
budget for 1880 were estimated as follows (in
francs):

REVENUE.

Direct taxes....................	421,077,160
Stamps and registration..............	628,548,000
Produce of forests	38,102,600
Duties.........................	283,982,000
Indirect taxes......................	1,035,997,600
Produce of posts....................	108,768,000
Telegraphs......	18,592,000
Miscellaneous receipts..............	16?,997,654
Total	2,701,080,014

EXPENDITURES.

Ministry of Justice...................	34,812,000
" of Foreign Affairs	12,919,000
" of the Interior........... ...	80,096,626
" of Finance..................	21,312,882
" of Public Instruction	116,882,354
" of Agriculture and Commerce.	34,059,692
" of Public Works.......... ...	150,819,678
" of War	552,941,362
" of the Navy..................	190,961,498
Administration of colonies........... }	
Public debt......................	1,175,319,656
Dotations	28,262,358
Chambers........................	10,321,000
Expenses of collection..............	269,629,826
Reimbursements....................	17,850,000
Total...........................	2,700,087,792

The interest on the public debt, according to
the budget of 1879, was as follows:

Consolidated debt....................	746,586,867
Capital that may be called in.........	208,093,902
Dette viagère......................	180,689,387
Total.............	1,175,319,656

On January 1, 1873, the new army law of
July 27, 1872, went into operation. Its first
article enacts universal liability to military service. Every Frenchman capable of bearing arms
must serve for 20 years, namely, 5 years in the
standing army, 4 years in the reserve of the
standing army, 5 years in the territorial army
(Landwehr), and 6 years in the reserve of the
territorial army (Landsturm). By a law of

July 24, 1873, on the reorganization of the
army, France is divided into 18 districts, each
of which is occupied by an army corps. One
army corps is also organized in Algeria. Each
of the 18 army corps consists of 2 divisions of
infantry, 1 brigade of cavalry, 1 brigade of artillery, 1 battalion of engineers, 1 squadron of
the train. a general staff, and the subordinate
staffs. The composition of the army in time
of peace will be as follows:

ARMS.	Men.	Horses.
Infantry (156 regiments, 641 battalions, 2,575 companies).................	281,601	2,649
Cavalry.......................	68,617	59,028
Artillery	66,531	32,690
Engineers............................	10,960	788
Train...............................	9,392	7,650
Staff................................	88,782	4,452
Gendarmes...........................	27,014	18,667
Total	502,697	120,894

According to an estimate of the "Journal
des Sciences Militaires" for January, 1879, the
strength of the French army on a war footing
would be as follows:

Infantry:
817½ battalions of the active army............	817,500
449 battalions of the territorial army............	449,000
Total infantry	1,266,500

Cavalry:
892 squadrons of the active army.............	58,800
79 squadrons of the territorial army............	11,850
Total cavalry	70,650

Artillery:
312 field batteries of the active army. }	
57 mounted batteries " "	124,000
88 field batteries of the territorial army........	56,000
407 batteries with 2,442 cannon	180,000

Engineers:
Active army................................	26,000
Territorial army	19,000
Total engineers	45,000
Pontoniers, active army	5,000

This gives a total of 1,031,300 men for the
active army, and 535,850 for the territorial
army; in all, 1,567,150 men. For the train, the
administration, and the sanitary troops, there
would still be necessary 155,000 men for the
active and 58,150 for the territorial army;
which would give the following result:

Active army	1,186,300
Territorial army	594,000
Total.....................	1,780,300

The navy on January 1, 1879, comprised 258
vessels. Of these, 66 were ironclads (32 large
war vessels and 34 for coast defense), 156
steamers (44 cruisers, 29 transport vessels, 40
dispatch-boats, 36 gun-boats, 7 torpedo-boats),
and 36 sailing vessels.

The foreign trade of France is officially divided into "commerce général," which comprises the entire imports and exports, including goods in transit, and "commerce spécial,"
which embraces the imports consumed and the
exports produced within the country. The following table exhibits the movements of French
commerce from 1859 to 1878:

YEARS.	GENERAL COMMERCE.		SPECIAL COMMERCE.		GOLD AND PRECIOUS METALS.	
	Imports.	Exports.	Imports.	Exports.	Imports.	Exports.
1878	....	....	4,461,000,000	3,869,800,000	546,000,000	189,600,000
1877	4,570,000,000	4,371,000,000	3,669,800,000	3,436,800,000	683,100,000	141,200,000
1876	4,908,500,000	4,547,500,000	3,988,400,000	3,575,600,000	804,000,000	234,000,000
1875	4,461,800,000	4,807,000,000	3,536,600,000	3,872,600,000	228,000,000	219,000,000
1874	4,422,500,000	4,702,100,000	3,507,700,000	3,701,100,000	952,000,000	159,000,000
1873	4,576,400,000	4,822,300,000	3,554,800,000	3,787,800,000	565,000,000	402,000,000
1869–1878	4,107,000,000	4,061,800,000	3,342,500,000	3,250,700,000	402,000,000	371,000,000
1864–1868	3,813,800,000	3,988,800,000	2,858,700,000	2,961,800,000	709,000,000	451,000,000
1859–1863	2,846,600,000	3,088,200,000	2,121,100,000	2,271,000,000	607,000,000	513,000,000

The special commerce of France in 1877 was as follows:

COUNTRIES, ETC.	Imports.	Exports.	COUNTRIES, ETC.	Imports.	Exports.
Great Britain	874,800,000	1,059,000,000	Spanish-American colonies	18,900,000	15,800,000
Belgium	408,900,000	446,400,000	Japan	13,600,000	7,600,000
Germany	372,800,000	895,100,000	Venezuela	12,600,000	8,500,000
Italy	841,800,000	185,500,000	Portugal	11,500,000	23,600,000
United States	257,800,000	216,600,000	Senegambia	11,200,000	4,900,000
Russia	202,200,000	15,900,000	British possessions in America	9,000,000	6,500,000
Turkey	157,600,000	86,600,000	British possessions in Africa	8,600,000	8,200,000
British India	149,500,000	8,400,000	United States of Colombia	7,900,000	17,700,000
Algeria	122,100,000	189,100,000	Mexico	5,900,000	18,400,000
Argentine Republic	112,000,000	75,700,000	Africa not enumerated	5,000,000	700,000
Spain	109,200,000	182,500,000	Philippine Islands	4,600,000	1,300,000
Switzerland	96,100,000	287,200,000	Cochin-China	3,500,000	4,400,000
Peru	61,500,000	19,700,000	Greece	3,100,000	15,200,000
Brazil	56,200,000	77,800,000	Oceania	2,400,000	4,800,000
Sweden	55,700,000	11,700,000	Mayotte, Nossi-Bé, etc	2,100,000	800,000
Austria	53,800,000	20,400,000	Malta and Gibraltar	1,800,000	4,000,000
Egypt	53,400,000	24,900,000	French possessions in India	1,400,000	1,100,000
China	36,600,000	3,100,000	Bolivia	1,800,000	300,000
Dutch Indies	35,900,000	3,100,000	Guatemala	1,200,000	2,600,000
West Coast of Africa	34,600,000	8,000,000	Denmark	1,100,000	4,500,000
Netherlands	34,200,000	85,200,000	Ecuador	1,000,000	2,400,000
Uruguay	32,600,000	20,700,000	Siam	700,000	
Hayti	30,800,000	12,000,000	St. Thomas	600,000	10,900,000
Saint Pierre and Miquelon	27,800,000	5,800,000	Goods picked up at sea	600,000	
Norway	27,000,000	12,500,000	French Guiana	300,000	5,400,000
Barbary States	22,600,000	11,700,000	Dutch colonies in America	200,000	1,200,000
Réunion	22,300,000	8,100,000	Australia		1,400,000
Guadeloupe	20,800,000	11,300,000			
Martinique	20,000,000	14,000,000	Total	3,669,800,000	3,436,800,000
Chili	15,100,000	28,800,000			

The principal articles of imports and exports in 1877 and 1878 were as follows:

CLASSES.	IMPORTS.		EXPORTS.	
	1877.	1878.	1877.	1878.
Articles of food	1,456,456,000	1,320,825,000	1,005,507,000	1,543,808,000
Raw materials			2,050,421,000	2,251,776,000
Manufactured goods	1,814,468,000	1,867,142,000	419,487,000	447,188,000
Other merchandise	165,380,000	181,800,000	194,490,000	218,757,000
Total	3,436,304,000	3,369,807,000	3,669,845,000	4,460,974,000

The number of vessels entered and cleared in 1878 was as follows:

NATIONALITY.	TOTAL.	
	Vessels.	Tons.
French	16,859	5,571
Foreign	36,448	10,544
Total	53,807	16,115

The commercial navy in 1878 was as follows:

CLASSES OF VESSELS.	Vessels.	Crews.	Tons.
Sailing vessels	14,884	84,801	758,824
Steamers	565	10,387	230,304
Or—			
Fishing vessels	9,786	53,077	188,721
Coasting vessels	2,529	10,386	111,597
Long voyage	2,180	29,318	702,961
Vessels out of use or probably lost	954	2,507	85,849
Total, 1878	15,449	95,188	989,128
" 1877	15,407	96,164	1,011,128

All the railroads in France are private roads, which are assumed by the Government at the expiration of their charters. The number of kilometres in operation on January 1, 1878, was as follows:

Main roads..................................... 21,228
Local roads..................................... 2,570

Total..................................... 23,798

The statistics of telegraphs were as follows:

Length of lines in 1877, kilometres......... 57,110
Length of wires in 1877, " 150,506
Government stations in 1877......... 2,984
Private and railroad stations in 1877...... 1,477
Inland dispatches in 1877......... 8,584,909
International dispatches in 1877......... 2,877,203
Official dispatches in 1877......... 1,460,000
Total dispatches in 1877......... 12,422,112

On December 31, 1876, there were 534 authorized savings banks. Of these, 162 had 736 branches. The number of books out on December 31, 1876, was 2,625,209, and there was due to depositors 769,034,686 francs. According to a report of the Minister of Commerce on the savings banks in France, the number of depositors in 1870, before the war, was 2,130,000; in 1872, 2,016,000; in 1875, 2,642,000; in 1877, 2,863,000; and in 1878, over 3,000,000. The deposits in this interval rose correspondingly from 711,000,000f. in 1870 to 1,010,000,000f. in 1878. From 1851 to 1870 (18 years) the whole progress made was 1,500,000 in the case of the number of depositors, and 553,000,000f. as regards the deposits.

The French colonies and dependencies had, according to the latest official reports, the following area and population:

COLONIES AND DEPENDENCIES.	Area, sq. m.	Population.
Algeria (1877).......................	258,217	2,867,626
I. Colonies.		
Asia.		
1. India: Pondichéry, Chandernagor, Karikal, Mahé, Yanaon (1876).....................	191·85	285,022
2. French Cochin-China (1876)...	21,716·49	1,523,846
Total possessions in Asia.......	21,912·94	1,818,853
Oceania.		
1. New Caledonia and Loyalty Islands (1876)..................	7,614·51	72,134
2. Marquesas Islands (1875)......	478·86	6,011
8. Clipperton Island..............	2·12	not inhab.
Total Oceania..................	8,094·09	78,145
Africa (exclusive of Algeria)..........		
1. Senegambia (1876)...........	?	197,431
2. Gabun.......................	....	?
8. Réunion (1876)..............	969·70	183,786
4. Mayotte and Nossi-Bé (1876)..	195·17	17,052
5. Ste. Marie (1876)............	67·18	6,948
Total Africa..................	1,232·05	405,217
America.		
St. Bartholomew..............	8	2,874
St. Pierre, Miquelon, etc. (1875)..	81·22	5,121
Martinique (1875)............	381·42	161,995
Guadeloupe and dependencies (1876)...	712·44	175,516
French Guiana (1875)..........	46,879·77	27,082
Total America..................	48,062·85	352,088
Total colonies (except Algeria).	79,302·98	2,669,808
II. Dependencies.		
Asia.—Cambodia (1874).............	82,879·29	890,000
Oceania.		
1. Tahiti, Moorea, Tetuaroa, Maltea (1876)...................	461·78	21,996
2. Tubal, Varitu, and Rapa......	55·80	675
8. Tuamotu Islands (79)........	2,572·54	8,000
4. Gambier Islands (6)..........	11·48	1,500
Total dependencies............	85,481·59	922,100
Colonies and dependencies.....	373,000·00	6,459,000

The resignation of General Borel, the Minister of War, was accepted on January 13th, and General Gresley was appointed in his place. General Gresley was formerly head of the War-Office General Staff, and some of the most important military reforms, particularly the organization of the territorial army, are attributed to him. On February 5th a new Cabinet was formed as follows: M. Waddington, President of the Council and Minister for Foreign Affairs; Léon Say, Finance; M. de Marcère, Interior; M. Leroyer, Justice; Jules Ferry, Public Instruction and Fine Arts; M. Lepère, Agriculture; M. de Freycinet, Public Works; General Gresley, War; and Admiral Jauréguiberry, Marine. On March 3d M. de Marcère resigned, and was replaced by M. Lepère, who was succeeded by M. Tirard in the department of Agriculture. This Cabinet was succeeded on December 28th by that of M. de Freycinet (see above). For a biographical sketch of Freycinet, see FREYCINET.

CAZOT, THÉODORE JULES JOSEPH, Minister of Justice, was born February 11, 1821. In 1870 he was Secretary of the Home Ministry, accompanied the delegation to Tours and Bordeaux, and followed Gambetta in his retreat. He was elected to the Senate from the department of Gard in 1876, and is a member of the Extreme Left.

LEPÈRE, EDME CHARLES PHILIPPE, Minister of the Interior, was born February 1, 1823. He was a member of the National Assembly of 1871, and in 1876 was elected to the Chamber of Deputies from the department of Yonne, and has retained his seat at each succeeding election. He is a member of the Extreme Left, and was for a long time President of the Republican Union. He was also at one time Vice-President of the Chamber, and held the same position he now holds in the Waddington Cabinet.

MAGNIN, JOSEPH, Minister of Finance, was born January 1, 1824. He was chosen Minister of Commerce and Agriculture, September 4, 1870, and rendered valuable services to Paris during the siege. He was elected a Life Senator in 1875, and belongs to the Republican Left. (See "Annual Cyclopædia" for 1875, page 321.)

VARROY, HENRI AUGUSTE, Minister of Public Works, was born March 25, 1826. He is well known as an able engineer, was a member of the National Assembly, and was elected to the Senate from Meurthe-et-Moselle in 1876. He has always voted with the Republican Left.

FARRE, General, Minister of War, was born in 1816. He belongs to neither Chamber. He was selected for the post he now holds in the Dufaure Cabinet when General Borel resigned, and was put forward by M. Gambetta; but Marshal MacMahon refused to appoint him, as he had never held the position of chief of an army corps.

JAURÉGUIBERRY, Admiral, Minister of the Navy, is a member of the Senate, of which he was elected a life-member on May 27, 1879.

TIRARD, PIERRE EMMANUEL, Minister of Commerce, was born September 27, 1827. He was a member of the Commune, but resigned at the first session; was a member of the National Assembly for Paris, and afterward of the Chamber of Deputies; and always acted with the Left, belonging to the Republican Union.

COCHERY, LOUIS ADOLPHE, Minister of Posts

and Telegraphs, was born in 1820. In 1848 he held an office in the Ministry of Justice. He was elected a member of the Corps Législatif in 1869, and was one of the 84 who voted against the war with Germany. In the National Assembly he was one of the best friends of M. Thiers. He has been a member of the Chamber for Loiret since 1876, and acts with the Republican Left.

FERRY, JULES FRANÇOIS CAMILLE, Minister of Public Instruction, was born April 5, 1832. He was a member of the Corps Législatif in 1869, was Prefect of the department of the Seine in 1870, and in 1871 was elected to the National Assembly, and in 1876 to the Chamber of Deputies. He gained considerable celebrity in 1879 by his higher education bill, on account of which he was retained in the Cabinet of M. de Freycinet. He is a member of the Republican Left.

Elections were held on January 5th for one third of the members of the Senate. As indicated by the elections on October 27, 1878, of the delegations who choose the Senators, the result was a complete victory for the Republicans. Of 82 Senators chosen, 66 were Republicans and only 16 belonged to the opposition. The new Senate therefore would contain 177 supporters of the Government, against an opposition of 123.

The Chambers resumed their sittings on January 14th. In the Lower House M. Grévy was reëlected President, the members of the Right abstaining from voting; and in the Senate M. Martel was elected President by a large majority.

M. Senard in the Chamber of Deputies demanded the sacrifice of Procurators-General, District Prosecutors, and some Prefects. A murmur of dissent was raised when he proposed that the Ministers should convene a joint meeting of the Deputies and Senators, to settle in conjunction with the former the dismissals deemed necessary. M. Dufaure, in reply, said that the Ministry regarded the recent elections as finally establishing the republic as the government of the country, and as consolidating republican institutions. Now more than ever they must require from public functionaries a really republican spirit, and this the Government intended to insist upon. Those officials, however, who had conducted themselves under the preceding Government as the docile instruments of their ministerial chiefs, and those, on the contrary, who had resisted their wishes, could not both be treated in the same manner. He enumerated the officials who had already been dismissed, and said that the work had never been considered as at an end. He concluded by expressing the hope that 1880 would pass as peacefully as the previous period of the republic. M. Madier de Montjau, representing the Extreme Left, and M. Floquet, representing the Republican Union, both spoke against the ministerial programme, which they characterized as incomplete and

unsatisfactory; and at the conclusion of M. Floquet's speech the sitting was suspended. During the interval an understanding was arrived at between the Government and the Republican Left and Left Center; and on the resumption of the sitting Jules Ferry proposed the following resolution:

The Chamber of Deputies, confiding in the declarations of the Government, and convinced that the Cabinet, henceforth in possession of its full liberty of action, will not hesitate, after the general vote of January 5th, to give the Republican majority the legitimate satisfactions it has long demanded on behalf of the country, especially as regards the administrative and judicial staff, passes to the order of the day.

This resolution was adopted by a vote of 223 to 121, after a motion of M. Floquet for the order of the day pure and simple had been rejected by a vote of 168 to 222. On January 25th M. Léon Say submitted to the Cabinet Council the list of changes he proposed to make among the Treasurers-General. President MacMahon said nothing, but asked M. Dufaure to remain after his colleagues. When they were alone the President said: "I will not sign those decrees. M. Léon Say is a Minister who gets into a passion. These changes must not be made. There must be no going into a passion." M. Dufaure replied that M. Say was not a Minister who goes into a passion; that the Cabinet at a previous meeting had taken a formal pledge to carry out the changes demanded, and that they were resolved to act up to it. He added that each Minister had his list of dismissals ready, and he hoped the Marshal would sign them; "for by not signing, so far from screening the functionaries, you would perhaps expose them, seeing that what we do not do others will do still more energetically; and if you prefer, as you tell us, to retire, not only will you not save those you wish to protect, but you will jeopardize those whom we are now really protecting." The following day the President signed the financial changes. On the 28th M. Dufaure laid before him the decree affecting six public prosecutors. He examined it, and then turning to M. Dufaure said, "I am going to sign this decree, but I leave the responsibility of it to you." General Gresley in turn submitted his list on the morning of the 29th. It dealt with nine generals, of whom four, including the Duc d'Aumale, were to be transferred, and five generals — Bourbaki, Lastigues, Bataille, Du Barail, and Montaudon — definitely relieved of their command. The Marshal declared he could not sign this decree. "I can not," he said, "sign a decree suspending brave generals, my own friends and companions, whose legal term of command only expires in five or six months. There is no danger in my refusal. I can not consent to stay at such a cost. I blush at the thought of it. I assure you on my honor I will not do it. It will have to be another who does it. Political categories must not be created in the army. I would prefer to resign if I am forced to it. My children would not forgive me for such an act. I can not, where the army is concerned, for which I am responsible before the nation; obey the injunctions of newspapers like these," and the Marshal showed some Republican papers which for some days past had been publishing lists of officials classed in political categories. At a meeting on the same afternoon, the Cabinet determined to maintain their resolution. At 10 o'clock on the morning of the 30th they were individually informed of the Marshal's resolution to resign, and at 1 o'clock, in the Cabinet Council at Versailles, he officially announced it. The Ministers then proposed to hand in their resignations if he thought any other Cabinet could obtain the confidence of the Chambers without obliging him to rigorously observe the engagements accepted at the sitting of the Chamber on January 20th. The Marshal replied, with some emotion, that he deemed such a step useless, and endeavored to show them that he had not been aware of the full bearing of the engagements to which his Government stood pledged by the order of the day voted on that occasion. The Ministers then took their departure, and waited on the Presidents of the Chambers to acquaint them with the letter of resignation, and to concert with them the measures thereby rendered necessary. The Chambers met at 3.20 P. M., and M. Grévy read the letter. It was as follows:

At the opening of this session the Cabinet laid before you a programme of measures which, while satisfying public opinion, could seemingly be voted without danger to the security and good government of the country. Waiving all personal ideas, I had given it my entire approbation, for I was not sacrificing any of the principles to which my conscience bound me to remain faithful. The Cabinet, in the belief of responding to the opinion of the majority in the two Chambers, now proposes to me as regards the great commands general measures which I deem contrary to the interests of the army, and consequently to those of the country. I can not subscribe to them. In view of this refusal the Cabinet resigns. Any other Cabinet taken from the majority of the Chambers would impose the same conditions on me. I accordingly think it my duty to curtail the duration of the trust with which the National Assembly invested me: I resign the Presidency of the Republic. In leaving office, I have the consolation of believing that during the fifty-three years I have devoted to the service of my country as a soldier and as a citizen I have never been guided by other sentiments than those of honor and duty and by perfect devotion to my country. I beg you, sir, to inform the Senate (or Chamber of Deputies) of my decision.

M. Grévy next read to the House the articles of the Constitution providing that the Chambers shall immediately meet in convention in case of a vacancy, to proceed to the election of a new President of the Republic. Pending that appointment, the Cabinet remains charged with the executive power. M. Grévy then announced that the Congress would meet at 4.30 in the Chamber of Deputies, and the session closed. At the stated time, 4.30 P. M., the two Chambers assembled in Congress and proceeded to elect a President. Out of 713 votes, M. Jules Grévy received 563, and

General Chanzy 99. On January 31st M. Gambetta was elected President of the Chamber of Deputies by 314 votes out of 405. Immediately upon the election of President Grévy, the Dufaure Cabinet resigned, and on the 5th of February a new Cabinet was formed under the presidency of M. Waddington. (See above.)

On February 6th President Grévy sent the following message to the Chambers:

The National Assembly, by raising me to the Presidency of the Republic, has imposed great duties on me. I shall unceasingly strive to fulfill them, happy if, with the sympathetic coöperation of the Senate and the Chamber of Deputies, I am able not to fall short of what France has a right to expect from my endeavors and my devotion. Sincerely submissive to the great law of the Parliamentary system, I shall never enter into conflict with the national will expressed by its constitutional organs. In the bills it will present to the Chambers and in the questions raised by Parliamentary initiative the Government will be inspired by the real wants, the indubitable wishes, of the country, and by a spirit of progress and pacification. Its especial anxiety will be the maintenance of tranquillity, security, and confidence, the most ardent of the desires of France, and the most imperative of her requirements. In applying the laws which give the general policy its character and direction, it will be imbued with the ideas which dictated them; it will be liberal and just to all, the protector of all legitimate interests, the resolute defender of those of the state. In its solicitude for the great institutions which are the pillars of the social fabric, it will devote a large share to our army, the honor and interests of which will be the constant object of its dearest preoccupations. Always taking vested rights and services rendered into fair account, now that the two great powers are animated by the same spirit, which is that of France, it will take care that the republic is served by functionaries who are neither its enemies nor its detractors. It will continue to uphold and develop the good relations existing between France and foreign Powers, and thus contribute to the consolidation of general peace. By this liberal and truly conservative policy, the great powers of the republic, ever united, ever animated by the same spirit, ever advancing with prudence, will produce the natural fruits of the government which France, enlightened by her misfortunes, has given herself, as the only one capable of insuring her repose and promoting the development of her prosperity, force, and grandeur.

In the Chambers the reading of the message was preceded by M. Gambetta's inaugural speech. He said:

In taking possession of the post of honor which the Chamber has intrusted to me, I address to you my warm thanks. Allow me to add that the historical circumstances which preceded and determined this mark of your confidence have rendered it at once more precious and more formidable for me. I am, indeed, succeeding the great citizen, the statesman whom the suffrages of the representatives of the country have spontaneously called to the Presidency of the Republic, whither the irresistible adhesion of France, the unalterable fidelity of Parliament, and the esteem of everybody follow him. If he is now the chief of the nation, he is still our instructor and model here. We shall follow his lessons and his example without presuming to replace him, with the steadfast design, however, of reproducing the principal features of his magistracy: vigilant attention to all your discussions, impartiality toward all parties, scrupulous care of our rules, and jealous watchfulness over the liberties of the tribune. Elected by the Republican majority, a resolute guardian of your rights and prerogatives, I know my duties of protection toward minorities. I hope to be able unflinchingly to combine them with the respect every one owes here to the Constitution and powers of the republic. We may, we ought all of us now to feel that governments of combat have lived out their time. Our republic, having at length issued victorious from the strife of parties, must enter the organic and creative period. I beg you, moreover, gentlemen, especially to concentrate your ardor, your intelligence, your talents, your every effort on the great educational, military, financial, industrial, and economic questions before you, the solution of which is legitimately expected by the rising generation, the army, the producers, the whole nation. Twice elected by universal suffrage, you have obeyed the first of its wishes by saving the republic. You will carry out the rest of its wishes by insuring it, in accord with the Government, the benefits of peace, the guarantees of liberty, and the reforms demanded by public opinion and founded on justice.

In the Senate the Presidential message was much applauded. The proposed memorial on the site of the sittings of the National Assembly from May to October, 1789, was then discussed. M. de Gavardie indulged in a tirade against that body and the Revolution in general, and offered to support the proposal if Louis XVI.'s name was inscribed on the memorial as the restorer of French liberty. To this M. Henri Martin replied that Louis XVI. was to be pitied, but he had already a memorial, the Chapelle Expiatoire, which successive revolutions had respected. In the Chamber, after M. Gambetta had read his speech and M. de Marcère the President's message, the Franco-Italian and Franco-Austrian conventions were ratified.

A Cabinet Council was held on February 11th, at which the amnesty bill was definitely adopted, and the decrees appointing new procureurs-générales and new commanders of the army corps were signed. The amnesty bill was presented to the Chamber on the same day. The amnesty was to apply to all persons condemned for acts relating to the insurrection of 1871, who had been or might be liberated or pardoned by the President within three months after the passing of the act. On the 13th the bureaus in the Chamber of Deputies elected the Committee on the Amnesty Bill. Seven of the members were favorable to the Government measure, while four desired a full and complete amnesty. The committee met on the 16th. It subsequently communicated with the Government, who consented to the introduction of a clause extending the amnesty to all political crimes committed before or after the insurrection of March 18, 1871. The bill as amended by the committee and accepted by the Cabinet was as follows:

1. The amnesty is accorded to all those condemned for acts relating to the insurrections of 1871, and to all those condemned for crimes or offenses relating to political acts who have been and shall be liberated, or who have been and shall be pardoned by the President of the Republic within three months after the promulgation of the present law. 2. The punishments pronounced by default for the same acts may be remitted by way of pardon. 3. From the promulgation of the present law the prescription of Article 637 of the Code of Criminal Procedure shall apply to

acts relating to the insurrections of 1871 which shall not yet have been the subject of condemnations by default or otherwise. 4. From the date of the notification of the letters of pardon virtually involving an amnesty, the condemned persons who shall have returned to France shall no longer enjoy the benefit of Article 476 of the Code of Criminal Procedure. 5. The present law shall not be applicable to persons who, independently of the acts which it has in view, shall have been condemned in person or in default for common-law crimes or offenses of the same nature, involving a sentence of more than twelve months' imprisonment.

The debate on the bill began in the Chamber on the 20th. The principal amendment, that of M. Louis Blanc, proposing an unconditional amnesty, was rejected by 363 to 105 votes; and, after some other amendments had been disposed of, the Government bill, as amended by the committee, was passed by 340 to 99 votes. The bill was placed on the table of the Senate on the following day. On the 27th M. Rivière read the committee's report on the bill. It declared that, while indulgence should be shown, measures of defense and protection should be taken, and the committee would not have agreed to a plenary amnesty. Pity should neither in politics nor in morals stifle the voice of justice. On the other hand, they rejected M. Bérenger's counter-scheme, because it did not even contain the word "amnesty," and implied fears which there was nothing to justify. They likewise rejected M. de Gavardie's proposal that the Communist ringleaders should be excluded from the amnesty, and a list of them be published by the Government. They agreed to the bill as it stood. The bill was discussed in the Senate on the 28th, and, notwithstanding a vehement speech from Victor Hugo, was carried by 163 to 86.

In the Chamber M. de Marcère, Minister of the Interior, replied to an attack on his conduct in relation to accusations made against the police. On March 3d M. Clémenceau, after hearing M. de Marcère's explanations, moved an order of the day expressing the regret of the House at the insufficiency of the explanations. The Chamber then suspended its sitting. On reassembling, the order of the day pure and simple was proposed. M. Clémenceau adopted it, as being virtually the same as his own, and it was carried by a large majority. M. Marcère thereupon resigned, and was succeeded by M. Lepère, Minister of Agriculture and Commerce, who in turn was succeeded by M. Tirard.

On March 8th M. Drisson presented to the Chamber the report of a committee appointed to consider the question of the impeachment of the De Broglie Ministry. The report charged the late Government with various unconstitutional acts, and with an intention to bring about a coup d'état. At the request of the Government the debate was postponed until the 13th. Marshal MacMahon wrote a letter to President Grévy, in which he declared that he assumed the responsibility for the acts of his Ministers of May 16th, and if they were to be impeached he declared his intention of placing himself beside them at the bar of the High Court of Justice. The debate began on the 13th, and the bill was defeated by 225 votes of the Left to 187 of the Extreme Left and Right combined. M. Clémenceau then proposed the order of the day pure and simple, seeing that the Chamber, having abandoned the impeachment, had no right to brand the Ministers in question. This proposal was rejected by 225 to 187; and M. Rameau then brought forward a resolution declaring that the Ministers of May 16th and November 23d, by their culpable schemes against the Government of the republic, betrayed the Government which they should have served, and that the Chamber accordingly delivered them over to the judgment of the nation. M. Rameau further proposed that the resolution should be placarded in every commune in France. This was carried by 240 to 157.

On March 15th M. Jules Ferry submitted two important bills to the Chamber, one on higher education, the other on the Supreme Council of Public Instruction. The former abolishes the mixed jury of examiners for degrees instituted by the law of 1875, and confines academic degrees to candidates registered and examined in the state universities. It also precludes free or non-state institutions from assuming the title of university or faculty, which is to be reserved for state establishments. No member of a religious community not recognized by the state may henceforth act as a teacher, and the declaration of public utility which accords the compulsory purchase of sites and other advantages will be conceded only by a bill sanctioned by Parliament, instead, as at present, of being granted by the Council of State on the recommendation of the Supreme Council of Public Instruction. The second bill reorganizes the Supreme Council, the law of 1872 on that subject having just

HAVRE.

expired. It excludes from the new Council the four prelates elected by the episcopate, also the representatives of the other state churches. It likewise excludes the three representatives of the Council of State and those of the Court of Cassation and the Ministries of War and Marine. Fifteen members are to be nominated by the Government from professors and school inspectors; five *ex officio* members will also be appointed; these twenty holding office for life; while twenty-six others are to be elected for six years by various educational bodies, and four representatives of non-state education are to be nominated by the Government. The preface to the higher education bill showed that the intention was to disqualify

from all classes of teaching religious communities not recognized by law. This was justified on the ground that foreigners were not allowed to teach, and that the same exclusion should apply to "an order essentially foreign by the character of its doctrines, the nature and aim of its statutes, the residence and authority of its chiefs." This passage referred to the Jesuits, who, according to the statistics given by the "Temps," have 27 colleges in France, with 848 teachers, viz.: St. Affrique, 25; Marseilles (two colleges), 33; Aix, 41; Dijon, 18; Brest, 25; Toulouse (three colleges), 76; Montpellier, 8; Tours, 20; Dôle, 40; St. Etienne, 21; Vals, Haute-Loire, 101; Rheims, 27; Vannes, 34; Montgré, Rhône, 24; Paray-le-Monial, 8;

Le Mans, 34; Paris, Vaugirard, 44; Paris, Rue Lhomond, 30; Paris, Rue de Madrid, 19; Amiens, 62; Avignon, 48; Poitiers, 65; Algiers, 22; and Oran, 13. The disability would also affect 26 other communities, having 61 establishments and 1,089 teachers. The recognized communities, whose establishments would not be interfered with, but whose members would eventually be subjected to the same examinations as lay teachers, instead of obtaining episcopal certificates, called "letters of obedience," are 28 in number. They have 2,443 schools, 768 colleges, and 22,769 teachers. Most of the clauses of a bill were voted on March 19th, which provided that within four years normal schools for the instruction of primary schoolmasters and schoolmistresses should be established in every department of France.

M. Paul de Cassagnac's election was on the 19th declared valid. On the 23d the Chamber of Deputies decided by 330 to 131 votes in favor of convening both Houses of the Legislature in Congress, with a view of revising that article of the Constitution which fixed the seat of the Legislature at Versailles. On April 1st a motion brought forward by the Government in the Senate was adopted, postponing until after Easter the consideration of the question. The Chambers adjourned on April 5th. The Senate met again on May 8th, but adjourned until the 12th, and again until the 15th, when the Chamber also reassembled. On May 23d the Senate adopted a bill adding eight members to the Council of State. On May 27th Admiral Jauréguiberry and General Gresley were elected life-members of the Senate. In the Chamber, on the same day, M. Clémenceau proposed a resolution for the liberation of Blanqui, to enable him to appear to defend his election; but the Government opposed, and the motion for urgency was rejected by 272 to 171. On June 5th the time expired in which President Grévy had the power of amnesty, without this privilege having been applied to Blanqui, and he was therefore ineligible for the Chamber. The debate on Blanqui's liberation was marked by one of the stormiest meetings of this session. In the course of it M. Le Royer, Minister of Justice, said that M. Clémenceau could not share the Cæsarean doctrine of right *versus* legality, invoked by a man who, violating all the laws of his country and exulting in his crime, dared to say, "I depart from legality to reënter into right." M. Paul de Cassagnac here interrupted the speaker, demanding that he should withdraw the word crime; and when the President attempted to call him to order, a perfect uproar arose. After this had ceased, M. de Cassagnac disclaimed having disputed the authority of the Chair, but complained that M. Le Royer had insulted the Bonapartists by declaring that the Empire had originated in a crime. If the President would condemn that expression, he himself would withdraw anything too strong he had uttered.

He regretted the scene, but hoped the President would censure M. Le Royer's words. The President said he should not have hesitated to condemn any insulting or offensive term such as the word "criminals," but M. Le Royer had simply spoken of an historical event according to his right and his conscience. A censure was then voted on M. de Cassagnac.

On the 14th the Senate took up the discussion of the bill for the return of the Chambers to Paris. M. Waddington, who opened the debate, said: "The Government, after having examined the question under every aspect, and with every means of inquiry at its disposal, declared, without the slightest hesitation, that the return of the Chambers to Paris involved no inconvenience and no kind of danger." The principal speech against the return was made by M. Laboulaye. He summed up the arguments on his side as follows: "When we speak of Paris, the great industrial and commercial Paris must first be taken into consideration. Do you think that commerce and industry derive any advantage from, I will not say revolutions, but from a certain agitation, from orders falling off, from anxiety creeping up on every side, and labor being less in demand? You have not received a single petition on the part of commercial and industrial Paris." He pointed out that the Exhibition did not fail for want of the Chambers; that the Paris of arts and sciences got on as well without as with them; that foreigners flocked thither as usual, and did not ask for their return. Political Paris remained, for he would not assert that there were not certain persons who did desire the return, but even political Paris was far from unanimous. M. de Freycinet answered M. Laboulaye. He concluded as follows: "By making Versailles the seat of government after every preceding *régime* has had Paris for its seat of government, you proclaim that the republic does not seem to you in a position to do what preceding governments have done. In saying that you would consent later to do what does not seem to you prudent just now, you are declaring that the present situation is not satisfactory. Well, the whole Cabinet says the danger which alarms you does not exist. We have thoroughly examined the situation you dread, and we assure you there is nothing that ought to prevent the return to Paris." The bill was finally passed by 149 votes to 130. The majority comprised 143 Republicans, 4 Bonapartists, and 2 members of the Right not inscribed in any particular group. The minority consisted of 108 members of the Right (that is, almost their entire force) and 22 Republicans.

On the 16th the discussion of the Ferry bill was resumed. M. de Cassagnac again became violent and insulted the Government; so that M. Gambetta asked for an exclusion from the Chamber for three days, which was granted by the Chamber, the first instance of the kind under the republic. On June 28th the general debate was brought to a close. On the

30th the Chamber declared urgency for the bill, the effect of this declaration being that a single reading would suffice to procure its definite adoption. The Chamber then proceeded with the discussion, and negatived the counter-project of MM. Langle and Mitchell, Bonapartists, and afterward rejected by 350 votes to 176 the amendment of M. Bardoux, who proposed to restore to the state the right of conferring degrees, but to concede to religious fraternities the liberty to teach under state control. Clause 1 of the bill was adopted on July 3d, clauses 2 to 6 on the 4th, and clause 7 on the 9th, and finally the bill itself by a vote of 362 to 159, after an amendment introduced by M. Madier de Montjau, aiming at the prohibition of all religious orders to teach, had been defeated by 381 to 78. Article 7, which was most bitterly attacked, disqualifies members of religious bodies not recognized by the state from teaching. The principal unauthorized teaching bodies in France since 1820 are enumerated as follows: In 1820 the Jesuits numbered 162; in 1840, 226; in 1850, 565; in 1860, 689; in 1870, 974; and in 1878, 1,502. The number of their establishments rose, from 1820 to 1878, from 5 to 59. The Dominicans numbered 14 in 1820 and 327 in 1878. There are in all 136 establishments belonging to unauthorized bodies, of which 16 are congregations of men and 120 of women. The figures are contained in replies sent in officially under returns ordered by the law of 1876, and are relied upon as nearly accurate. The congregations have between them 555 establishments for the instruction of female students and 81 for men and boys, and there are employed in the educational work no less than 4,857 female and 1,556 male teachers. The pupils amount to about 61,000, the women and girls being about twice as numerous as the men and boys, and of these some 3,500 boys and 6,000 girls are in receipt of pecuniary assistance by way of what we shall call scholarships or exhibitions. The expenses of providing this aid amount to nearly $300,000 a year. M. Spuller, the official reporter of the bill, in his report said: "The invasions of Ultramontanism have reached their term. The Government of the republic severs itself from a policy which has hitherto closed men's eyes to these invasions when it has not favored them. That is the meaning of the bill; that is its aim; that is what France must see in it. And this very considerable event explains the excitement of the reactionary parties, of whom Ultramontanism is the bond of union, and the warm sympathy manifested by republican democracy to measures of reparation long awaited." The Chamber on July 15th, by 363 to 140, passed the bill, which, as Monseigneur Freppel complained in the "Univers," would put a body composed of forty-six representatives of state education and four of Catholic education over the inspection of Catholic schools, over the books used in them, and over the teachers employed. The bill on the return to Paris was adopted in the Chamber on the same day, after it had previously passed the Senate. It had to be returned to the Senate, on account of an amendment empowering the President of either Chamber to make requisition for troops for defense, instead of demanding them of the Minister of War; and on July 19th the Senate concurred in the amendments. The Chambers were prorogued on August 2d.

The new session of the Chambers opened on November 27th. For the first time since 1870 the National Legislature met in Paris. The buildings appropriated for the use of the Chambers are the Luxembourg for the Senate, and the Palais Bourbon for the Chamber of Deputies. M. Gambetta, on taking the chair, addressed the Chamber as follows:

GENTLEMEN: The second National Congress, by bringing back the public powers to Paris, has restored to our incomparable capital the legal title of which it had too long been deprived, without, however, being discredited. The sovereign Assembly by this vote of reparation has drawn closer the tie of national unity. It has placed the seat of government at the only point of the territory whence one governs with authority. It wished at length to show the world that the nation had confidence in the patriotic population of Paris, which is still, after so many ordeals, the head and heart of France. Henceforth, relieved of fatiguing daily journeys, we shall be able to devote in labor to the country the hours thus wasted in locomotion. The great tasks undertaken by you in scholastic, financial, economic, military, and political reforms are about to derive a fresh impulse from your residence in this marvelous laboratory of Paris, where all the intellectual resources accumulate, whither flow all the living forces of society, all the data of internal and external policy, made fruitful by a public spirit, the vivacity of which does not impair its judgment or good sense. You have prepared many materials for reconstruction; you have elaborated many projects. They must be carried out. I adjure your committees to work with redoubled energy to lay before us at the proper moment—which I hope will be soon—the results of their internal discussions. At this great tribune mature and practical reforms will enforce themselves; the country, daily enlightened in regard to its affairs, will at last see its constancy rewarded. As regards my own labors, gentlemen, believe me, I will do my utmost, scrupulously confined to the special duties with which you have charged me, to perform them with all the impartiality, activity, and zeal of which I am capable. Let us, then, all set resolutely to work, let us place ourselves above private interests, let us avoid useless or violent incidents, and concentrate all our faculties and efforts on our great aim—the greatness of our country, the consolidation of the republic.

On December 2d M. Baudry d'Asson, a Legitimist, withdrew a question he had given notice of, which had been looked forward to as likely to afford the Ministers an opportunity of explaining their policy. M. Waddington thereupon complained of the custom which had been introduced of giving notice of a question and afterward withdrawing it. The Ministry was said to be in extremity, but it was not at private conventions, but openly from the tribune, that questions relating to it ought to be brought forward. It was for the House to proclaim whether the Ministers did or did not possess its confidence. If they did not, they were ready to retire.

On the 8th M. Jules Simon in the Senate presented the report of the Committee on the University Bill, but it was not to be discussed until January. On the 12th M. Le Royer, Minister of Justice, resigned; but on the 16th he was interpellated by M. Lockroy regarding the manner in which the partial amnesty law had been executed. M. Lockroy said the law had not been carried out in accordance with the intention of the Chamber, and he accused M. Le Royer of having considered the persons— notably Henri Rochefort —and not their offenses, in drawing up categories of those who should be excluded from the benefits of the bill. M. Le Royer replied that the power of granting amnesty rested with the President of the Republic. He read a number of offensive letters to President Grévy, sent by some of those who had been deported, and also the manifesto of twenty-eight convicts who were excluded from amnesty, in which they assume the responsibility for the assassinations during the Commune. M. Le Royer said the Cabinet would not have fulfilled its duty if it had pardoned such people as the writers of these documents. M. Jules Ferry, Minister of Public Instruction, stated that the whole Ministry shared M. Le Royer's opinion. M. Clémenceau vehemently attacked the Ministers, accusing them of inaction. Premier Waddington having refused to accept the order of the day pure and simple, as implying censure upon the Government, M. Clémenceau fell back on that motion, which was rejected by a vote of 276 to 109. The Chamber then, by a vote of 255 to 57, adopted an order of the day, which was accepted by the Cabinet, declaring that the Chamber adopted the views of the Ministers, and, approving their explanations, passed to the order of the day. A report published by M. Le Royer on November 28th showed that of the 4,311 Communists still unpardoned at the end of last January, 3,113 were admitted to the benefit of the partial amnesty, while 203 had their punishment commuted. Of the remaining 1,198, 368 have been pardoned since the expiration of the amnesty law, and 209 have received a commutation of sentence, thus leaving only 830 excluded from clemency. Of these 830, 554 were tried in person and 276 by default; 65 were members of the Commune, 89 had committed common-law crimes against the person, 104 had com-

mitted common-law crimes against property, 521 had been previously convicted for non-political offenses, and 51 belonged to the class described by M. Le Royer as "persons who, irrespective of all political considerations and for causes of unquestionable unworthiness, ought to be excluded from a measure of clemency, or men who, seriously implicated in the insurrection, evince abroad, according to all the information obtained, such an attitude as to render any measure of clemency toward them impossible."

CHERBOURG.

On December 21st M. Raynal, after having unsuccessfully asked General Gresley, Minister of War, in private, to dismiss from the army M. de Carayon-Latour, lieutenant-colonel in the territorial army, for the part he took at a Chambord banquet on Michaelmas day, publicly demanded it from the tribune, and pointed out that while M. Latour remained unpunished two of his subordinates, who were present on the same occasion, had been removed from their commands. The Minister of War replied: "I in no wise either approve or excuse the conduct of the officers of the territorial army who were present at the Legitimist banquets at Bordeaux or elsewhere. I took with regard to these officers the disciplinary measures within my power: I suspended them. Toward M. de Carayon-Latour I acted differently, because I thought that, he being a superior officer, and deprived of his position as mayor, what I had to obtain was his dismissal as lieutenant-colonel. I handed him over with a view to this to the council of officers; the decision it gave did not permit me to cause his being superseded. I hold myself wholly responsible; but as to reversing my decision as you desire by setting at naught the decision given by the council, I refuse, and will never consent to do so." General Gresley then went direct to the Elysée and offered his resignation, which was followed by that of the entire Cabinet. Messrs. Waddington, Léon Say, and De Freycinet were all called upon to form a new Cabinet. The negotiations continued for several days, until on the 28th a Cabinet under M. de Freycinet (see FREYCINET) was formed, composed entirely of members of the Republican Union and of the Republican Left, and excluding the Left Center. This Cabinet was regarded as a victory of Gambetta over Grévy, as all its members are strong friends of the former, and the majority of them were members of the Government of National Defense at Tours. On the other hand, President Grévy desired to retain Messrs. Waddington and Say, who are members of the Left Center, but finally yielded to M. Gambetta.

The death of the Prince Imperial in South Africa (see BONAPARTE) led to considerable speculation as to who should in future be the recognized leader of the party, and in the event of a restoration of the Empire should become Emperor. Article IV. of Chapter II. of the *senatus consultum* of 1870 declared: "In default of a legitimate or adopted heir, Prince Napoleon Bonaparte and his direct heirs, natural and legitimate, from male to male by order of primogeniture, and to the perpetual exclusion of women and their descendants, are called to the throne." (See "Annual Cyclopædia" for 1870, page 311.) But the Prince Imperial in his last will had designated the oldest son of Prince Napoleon, Prince Victor, as his successor. This caused dissensions to arise in the party, one section looking to Prince Napoleon as the new head of the family, while others, in accordance with the last will of the Prince Imperial, recognized Prince Victor as such. Among those who took the latter view were several of the most influential members of the party, including M. Paul de Cassagnac. Prince Napoleon, who at first was more unconcerned than his own followers, took a decided stand in the beginning of November, and constituted his " pretendential " household with a care denoting a resolution to depart from his previous attitude of indifference.

The anniversary of the Count de Chambord's birth, which took place September 29, 1820, was selected as the occasion of a great Legitimist manifestation. Encouraged by the death of the Prince Imperial, and by the momentary extinction of Bonapartist hopes, the leaders of the party resolved to celebrate the birthday of Henry V. by banquets in twenty arrondissements of Paris, and also at Dijon, capital of the department of Côte-d'Or, where the Princes of Condé had their palace and the earlier of the Bourbon kings their castle; at Marseilles, which has never shown strong allegiance to the family; at Perpignan, in the Pyrénées-Orientales; at Montauban, capital of Tarn-et-Garonne, one of the first towns to embrace the Reformation, and consequently

one of the most subject to royalist persecution: and at Chambord, a village near Blois, from whose castle, presented by Louis XV. to Marshal Saxe, and by Louis XVI. to the family of Polignac, the self-styled Henry V. took his best-known name. The price of tickets to the banquets was fixed at five francs. By setting the price so low, the leaders hoped to attract orators from the working classes and partisans from the disaffected of every stripe. The *menus* of all the banquets were precisely identical, having on one side the subscriber's name, on the other a photograph of Henry V. To avoid the possibility of dissension or disturbance from such troublesome Orleanists as M. Hervé of the "Soleil," it was agreed that no speeches should be delivered, and that the toasts should be replaced by addresses to Chambord, uniform in text, expressing devotion to the Count and his cause, and to be read precisely at the same hour at the banquets, by delegates named beforehand. The most notable of the Parisian banquets were held in the Faubourg St. Germain, the Champs Elysées, the Palais Royal, the Marais, at Montmartre, Belleville, Menilmontant, Passy, and Charenton. Notwithstanding the prohibition, there were personal toasts and speeches at all the celebrations. The Ferry education bill was the principal theme of denunciation. The gatherings comprised, as was intended, all classes, from the workingman to the noble. To the other banquets in the provinces, at Bordeaux and Marseilles, and Perpignan, Poitiers, and the rest, crowds came from all parts of the country. At Chambord service was held at noon in the beautiful village church. The banquet was attended by a large number of Senators and Deputies, and a number of enthusiastic speeches were made.

FREYCINET, CHARLES LOUIS DE SAULCES DE, a French statesman, born in 1828. He was educated at the Polytechnic School, and graduated in 1848, the fourth in his class. In the same year he was appointed Engineer of Mines at Mont-de-Marsan, in 1854 at Chartres, and in 1855 at Bordeaux. In 1856 he was appointed *chef d'exploitation* (manager) by the Railway Company of the South. He held this important office for five years, and left a set of orders and regulations which are in force to the present day, and have to a great extent been adopted by the other railroad companies. It was at this period that he published his works, "Traité de Mécanique rationelle," "Étude sur l'Analyse infinitésimale," and "Théorie Mathématique sur la Défense des Rampes de Chemins de Fer." Having reëntered the service of the Government, he was charged during several years with a series of scientific and industrial missions, the results of which were published in official reports, several of which were awarded premiums by the Institute. In 1870, after the revolution of September 4th, he was appointed by the Government of National Defense Prefect of Tarn-et-

Garonne, and was soon after charged with the supreme direction of the war, with the title of personal delegate of the Minister in the Department of War. His efforts in this sphere, although not attended by success, were marked by great ability; and even his political opponents, like General Borel, attested to the rare talent displayed by him in this position. After the armistice, M. de Freycinet retired from the administration of the War Department, and laid down his experience in "La Guerre en Province pendant le Siége de Paris." In 1876 he was elected to the Senate from the department of the Seine, and he has on several occasions held the post of Minister of Public Works. In December, 1879, he was intrusted with the formation of a Cabinet by President Grévy, after the Waddington Ministry had been compelled to retire. He was selected mainly on account of his intimacy with M. Gambetta, the leader of the French Republicans. The favorite idea of M. de Freycinet's life has been for the Government to take the control of all the railroads. He is now in a position to give effect to the scheme, or at least to bring it fairly before the country.

FRIENDS. A meeting of Friends appointed by some of the American Yearly Meetings was held at Indianapolis, Ind., December 10th and 11th, to consider and act upon a proposal which had been made by the Ohio Yearly Meeting for the formation of an American Board of Friends' Missions. The Ohio, Western, North Carolina, Iowa, Kansas, Indiana, New York, and New England Yearly Meetings were represented by twenty-six delegates. Fifteen of these delegates were from Yearly Meetings which had fully agreed to the proposal of the Ohio Yearly Meeting. A plan of operations agreeable to that proposal was adopted, to be laid before the Yearly Meetings at their annual gatherings for approval by them, of which the principal features are as follows: The Board of Missions, to be constituted after approval by the Yearly Meetings, shall be called the *American Friends' Missionary Society.* Its object shall be "to promote the work of missions and advance the cause of Christ in the earth by effecting a general and more specific coöperation of Friends everywhere." The Board shall consist of two members appointed by each Yearly Meeting of the Association, with a like number from such Association of Friends in Philadelphia as may unite in the scheme, and shall meet annually, and oftener if necessary. Its duties shall be to procure information in regard to the needs of the various missionary fields, and exercise a general supervision over the work and workers under its care; to receive and consider applications from persons who may desire to engage in the work, and recommend them to such fields for labor as may seem to them to be the best, and under such regulations as it may determine; to recommend to the Missionary Committees of such Yearly Meetings as may have committees of this kind suitable fields for their labor and suitable workers for those fields; to correspond with such committees upon the general and particular needs of the work, and report to the Yearly Meetings through their committees all information that may be of interest to them, or may aid them in furthering the interests of the cause; and to keep Friends generally advised, through the press, of the progress of the work, and make such application of the funds intrusted to its care as may seem best, either in the establishment of new missions, or in the assistance of those already established by individual Yearly Meetings. The expenses of the Board are to be borne by means of voluntary contributions. The meeting recommended that a corresponding secretary be appointed by each Yearly Meeting. It also voted that "such Yearly Meetings as are already engaged in missionary work are encouraged to continue in their respective fields; but when they wish to engage in other fields, it is recommended that they do so only with the sanction of the Board, that the work may be properly distributed and the best results obtained by the committee." The committees of the Yearly Meetings were requested to make reports to the Board. Among the fields for missionary work spoken of in the meeting were the American Indians, the colored people, the Chinese, and people of other nationalities that are similarly situated.

The *London Yearly Meeting* of the Society of Friends was opened May 28th. Epistles were read from most of the American Yearly Meetings, giving accounts of the condition of the Society, of its work among the Indians, and of the relations borne by the meetings and the members to the questions of education, temperance, etc. Reports were also read from Friends in Australasia, the south of France, Germany, Mount Lebanon, and Denmark. Mr. Barnabas C. Hobbs of Indiana gave an account of visits which he had made to the Governments of Russia and Germany in the interest of religious liberty and of universal peace. A Friend just returned from South Africa gave an account of his visit, and of the religious labors of Mr. Sharpe and his companion at the Cape of Good Hope. A deputation was appointed to visit the Friends in Ireland. The reports of the Tract Societies showed that the London Society had issued during the year 126,866 tracts and leaflets, making a total of 8,282,663 tracts and leaflets issued by it since its formation.

The thirty-second report of the *Friends'* (English) *First-day School Association* shows that there are connected with the Union 110 schools in 66 places, with 1,300 teachers and 20,713 scholars; and 22 other schools not connected with the Union in 21 places, with 128 teachers and 1,521 scholars. Of the scholars, 12,363 are adults. The returns show an increase of 298 junior and a decrease of 40 adult scholars during the year.

The Friends of England support, at an annual outlay of about £6,000, three missions, viz., one in Madagascar, one in Hoshungabad, India, and one in Syria. The mission in Madagascar includes many schools and about one hundred congregations. The preaching is almost entirely by natives. In India, the work is carried on by three missionaries, and two native converts were reported in 1878. The Syrian mission embraces stations at Ramallah, near Jerusalem, and at Brumana, on Mount Lebanon, with schools. The meeting at Brumana has fourteen members.

The Yearly Meeting of *Friends in Ireland* was begun April 30th. The meeting decided not to adopt the changes which the London

Yearly Meeting had some years before made in the constitution of the Meeting of Ministers and Elders, but determined to retain its Meeting of Ministers and Elders intact, and also to institute an Overseers' Meeting. It advised that the Meeting of Ministers and Elders and the Overseers' Meeting should hold a conference at least once in three months, to consider the care of their flocks. It also decided that elders and overseers should be appointed, not as formerly for life, but once in three years. A minute was approved, recognizing the right as having always existed, under the direction of the Holy Spirit and subject to the judgment of the Church, to use the Bible in worship.

G

GARRISON, WILLIAM LLOYD, an editor and abolitionist, born at Newburyport, Massachusetts, December 12, 1804, died in New York, May 24, 1879. The early loss of his father and the straitened circumstances of his mother made it necessary to place him as an apprentice to a shoemaker at the age of ten years, and subsequently to the publisher of the "Newburyport Herald." At the age of eighteen he began to write some pieces for the paper. After the termination of his apprenticeship he was connected in an editorial capacity with several newspapers, notably the "Journal of the Times," at Bennington, Vermont, in 1828, when he advocated the reëlection of John Quincy Adams to the Presidency, supported Mr. Clay's American system, and took advanced ground on the questions of international peace, total abstinence from intoxicating drinks, and the ultimate abolition of negro slavery. His views on the last-named subject led to his association with Benjamin Lundy, the Quaker philanthropist, in conducting the "Genius of Universal Emancipation" at Baltimore. Mr. Lundy had participated in the memorable struggle of 1820 –'21 against the admission of Missouri to the Union as a slaveholding State. The fire then kindled in his bosom had never gone out. He had started the paper above mentioned seven years previous to his knowledge of Garrison. He favored the gradual emancipation of the colored race, and was a moderate advocate of their colonization in Africa. Garrison was for immediate abolition, and against colonization. He became joint editor of the "Genius" with Lundy in the fall of 1829. In 1830 he was convicted of a libel on Captain Francis Todd, for denouncing as a "domestic piracy" the action of the ship Francis in carrying slaves from Baltimore to New Orleans, and sentenced to pay a fine of $50 and costs. He was unable to pay the costs, and was put into jail. The owner of the ship also obtained judgment of $1,000 damages in a civil suit, but it was never enforced. His arrest and imprisonment created

much excitement. He remained in jail forty-nine days, when he was released by the payment of his fine by Arthur Tappan, who thus anticipated by a few days a like generous purpose on the part of Henry Clay of Kentucky.

Mr. Garrison now commenced a lecturing tour on emancipation, with the hope of obtaining means to establish an abolition journal of his own. He lectured in New York, Philadelphia, New Haven, Hartford, and Boston. His intention was to commence his publication in Washington, but it was finally located in Boston. The intelligent sentiment of the country at this time was antislavery, and such it had been from the close of the war of the Revolution. The constitutional provision that the importation of slaves might cease after 1808; the donation of the immense Northwestern Territory by Virginia to the Union on the express condition that slavery and involuntary servitude, except for crime, should be there unknown; the gradual but complete emancipation which had taken place in all the Northern States above Maryland; the establishment of the Missouri compromise line; the passage of an emancipation bill through one House of the Virginia Legislature, and its bare failure on a second trial in the other; movements in Kentucky looking forward to ultimate liberation of the slaves; the frequent acts of emancipation by individual masters— these were all undeniable facts of history. In 1809 the importation of slaves from Africa ceased, and in the ensuing short period of twenty years all these facts, except the donation of Virginia and some State emancipations, had followed. Such was the sentiment and such the progress of the country. Incident thereto, not a drop of blood had been shed, nor a life lost. On January 1, 1831, Mr. Garrison commenced the publication of the "Liberator." It struggled for existence for some time, but gradually secured kindred instrumentalities by which it was carried along. A weekly paper, advocating simple emancipation, in a State where slavery had been unknown for many years, could not expect to survive expenses unless it introduced and presented some novel features. Such were soon to be found in the columns of the "Liberator." It did not advocate, but it demanded, the immediate emancipation of every slave in the land. There it stopped on that point. It did not advocate or present any system of measures for the support, maintenance, occupation, protection, or education of the slaves thus suddenly to be set free. The intelligence of the country at that time revolted at such a doctrine as barbarous and inhuman. The logic of the "Liberator" was of this sort: Slavery is a sin against Almighty God; therefore it should cease instantly. On this position all was based. If it was pointed out that no provision was made for the emancipated, the answer came that sin against God should cease immediately; and it was further added, in effect, that those who are fighting for the destruction of such a huge and horrible sin have no time to look after consequences. Mercy was not an ingredient of the contest. Whoever poohpoohed the doctrine, as was often done at that time, was a foe to God and man. The manner adopted by Mr. Garrison in which to conduct his cause was that of "moral suasion"; but it was to be used with such a force and vim of invective, such reproach, denunciation, and extravagance of language, as would put his mother-tongue to its utmost tension. After an existence of two or three years, the paper reached the conclusions to which its doctrine led. Therefore every arrangement of society, every institution, organization, or individual, that was socially, politically, or professionally an obstacle unwittingly to the success of this vehement effort for the extermination of the sin of slavery, or was deemed to be such an obstacle, was not spared. The Constitution of the United States, under which the institutions of the States were sheltered from the interference of non-residents, was denounced as "a league with hell"; and the Union which flourished under it was declared to be a "covenant with death." The Christian clergy of the country were branded as "a brotherhood of thieves"; and the American church was stigmatized as "the bulwark of American slavery," and American Christianity as "the forlorn hope of slavery." Sensitive and scrupulous consciences in country parishes, who read these statements, were moved in all parts of the North to manifest their innocence by a call for a public meeting to denounce slavery and slaveholders. This awoke the Union sentiment of the people, and, without distinction of party, they turned out to suppress all such "disunion agitators," as they were called. Antislavery societies were formed, and in 1834 an antislavery lecturer from England, George Thompson, was introduced. This caused scenes of mob violence in Boston and in every other place where meetings were held. A mob of "gentlemen of property and standing" in Boston broke up the meeting there, caught Garrison as he was hiding in the loft of a carpenter's shop, let him down by a rope from the window to the ground, took off most of his clothes, and dragged him through the streets with a rope to the City Hall, where he was rescued by the orders of the Mayor, Harrison Gray Otis, and sent to jail as "a disturber of the peace." Riots broke out in all directions. Portions of 1834, and all of 1835, were a reign of terror. Sober, sensible men lost their heads. Abolitionists, however respectable in church and state, talked they ever so mildly for the negro, were hunted from city to city. Arthur Tappan's house in New York was gutted. Unoffending colored men were shot. Antislavery presses were thrown into the streets. Antislavery assemblies, gentle and orderly, were broken up. The halls wherein they met were stormed and shattered, and even church edifices were burned to the ground. Thompson, in the mean time, fled the country. These scenes resulted from the agitation among the people of the Northern States, not through any hostility to emancipation, not through any sympathy for slavery or the interests of slaveholders as such, but because it assailed the Union sentiment of the people. The issue it presented was immediate abolition or disunion, and separation from all fellowship with those who were guilty of such sin. The epithet "Union-saver" was early manufactured and applied to those who opposed the doctrines of Mr. Garrison. But the violence of the agitation soon ran its course after this manifestation of the decided and irresistible opposition in the heart of the people to whatever threatened to endanger the Union. The activity of Mr. Garrison and his immediate friends, however, did not slacken. Moral suasion was applied to tender consciences with blistering strength, and the number of champions gradually increased. At one of the anniversaries of the Antislavery Society in New York a proposition was made, chiefly by members from that city, to carry the question into politics. This was opposed and condemned by Mr. Garrison. A warm discussion ensued, but the New York members came off successful. Mr. Garrison was the President of a "non-resistant" society, and disposed to eschew politics, and probably had no confidence in an attempt to obtain results by political action. He returned to Boston, and confined himself to his adopted manner of agitation, which he continued until the close of the war. The section of the members who adopted political action commenced simply another method of effort, and based it on another and sympathizing organization. They put forward their candidates for offices and gave them their votes. But their progress was slow. They gave up the cognomen of Abolitionists, and called themselves the "Liberty party"; but what tended more than anything else to increase their numbers was the

avowed purpose to bring their action against
slavery within the limits of the Constitution
and the laws, instead of proceeding in antagonism to that instrument and denouncing the
Union formed under it. They saw the fatal
mistake early made by Mr. Garrison, and avoided it. The Liberty party grew. Some of its
members were seen in legislative bodies. Distinguished editors threw crumbs to it; others
espoused it. Its Senators took seats in Congress. Its candidates appeared for the Presidency, and, though with no hope of an election
for themselves, they decided which one of the
other candidates should be elected. The most
important subsequent events are to be found
in the preceding volumes of this work. Wiser
and shrewder men than Mr. Garrison had
taken the conduct of this crusade into their
hands.

During his life Mr. Garrison made four or
five visits to England for antislavery purposes,
and was received with much distinction. On
one of these occasions the Duchess of Suther-
land, the Mistress of the Robes—a kind of female prime minister—invited him to sit for his
portrait, and subsequently placed it among the
pictures of nobles and statesmen that adorn
the walls of Stafford House. While abroad in
1867 the Duke of Argyll, John Bright, John
Stuart Mill, Earl Russell, and other prominent
persons, gave him a banquet in London; while
the Lord Provost of Edinburgh, in obedience
to a vote of the civil authorities, conferred
upon him the freedom of the metropolis of
Scotland.

In 1843 Mr. Garrison was chosen President
of the American Antislavery Society. He
held the position till the anniversary meeting
in May, 1865, when, the war being over and
the negroes free, he counseled the dissolution
of the Society on the ground that its work was
done, insisting that an American antislavery
society was a misnomer after American slavery
had ceased to exist. He failed to carry his
point, and thereupon he resigned the office of
President. On the same grounds he suspended
the publication of the " Liberator " at the close
of the war. Its work was done.

GEOGRAPHICAL PROGRESS AND DIS-
COVERY. The largest geographical areas yet
unknown which now invite exploration, excepting the regions surrounding the poles, are
found in the central portions of the continent
of Asia and in the interior of Africa. The
greater part of New Guinea, the second largest
island in the world, is also a *terra incognita*,
which still incloses secrets of great probable
importance to commerce and to science alike.
The most important accessions to geographical
science to be chronicled are the fruits of two
national expeditions into the interior of Africa
from the western coast. The advance from this
side is notoriously more arduous than from the
eastern coast; and both the French and Portuguese expeditions have encountered obstacles
and dangers of the most trying description.

The former has settled the question of the
source of the Ogowé, finding its basin to be of
much smaller extent than was supposed. The
latter traversed the continent by a southeasterly route from Angola to the Transvaal,
passing through the regions in which Livingstone took up his abode, and obtained a solution, which, however, can hardly yet be accepted as final, of a hydrographical question of
equal importance, that of the discharge of the
great river Cubango. The geographical data
obtained by the Portuguese explorer are more
complete, and probably more trustworthy, than
those of the other transcontinental travelers.
D'Albertis, the naturalist whose devotion to
science led him to pass many years as a hermit
among the savages of New Guinea, and who
has contributed more than any other traveler
to our knowledge of the interior regions of that
strange tropical island, is able since his return
to Europe to furnish a detailed and most interesting narration of his experiences and observations in geography, natural history, and
ethnology, in all which branches he is an acute
and able investigator. From the new Russian
possessions in Asia a dozen or more expeditions composed of learned and experienced
specialists are now sent out into the unexplored
regions of Central Asia every year, nearly every one of which has something to contribute
on its return to the knowledge of these vast
and interesting regions. The very thorough
geodetic and topographical surveys of the
English approach this same wide domain of
unexplored territory from the south. Great
interest is felt in the lands of Thibet, highly
interesting from geographical, naturalistic, and
ethnographical reasons, and of even greater
importance from a commercial standpoint.
This country, whose peculiar natural products
are of exceeding value, has been completely
closed to the outside world, and is still, by the
jealous and exclusive restrictions of the Chinese
territorial government; but there are indications that these rigid barriers, which can not
possibly be long upheld, will soon give way to
the inevitable progress of civilized commerce.

The achievements of the most striking and
transcendent interest, however, have been
within the last couple of years, and promise to
be in the immediate future, in the domain of
Arctic discovery. The accessions in this fascinating field for research have not been of a
scientific character solely. The icy regions of
the north which have been unlocked to the
world by the efforts of courageous polar navigators yield many products which are highly
prized in the commerce of the world, and which
the labors of these hardy pioneers will have
rendered soon more abundantly accessible.
The vast alluvial lowlands of Northern Asia
possess an excellent soil for cereal crops, and
perhaps in the not distant future the enormous
plains of Siberia and the prairies of the Hudson
Bay Territory, two regions which have been
looked upon as hopeless frozen wildernesses,

will furnish bread for the whole commercial world.

Asia.—In Central Asia the important expedition of Severtzov has brought to light the principal features of the Pamir and revealed its relations to the Thian-shan range. The party started from Osh. While the topographers were taking down the route to the Kara-kul and the outline of its basin, Severtzov studied the geological characters of the Pamir and the Thian-shan at the sources of the Kashgar Darya. Meeting again at the Kara-kul, they started out on an unexplored route, lying between Forsyth's and Kostenko's, following up the northern Ak-baital, and crossing a pass 15,000 feet high to the southern Ak-baital River, which they descended to its confluence with the Ak-su. An excursion into the unexplored Ran-kul Pamir disclosed the true nature of the disputed orography of the east Pamir. It does not consist in a ridge of mountains, as Hayward supposed; there is also no abysmal wall, as Fedschenko reported, but a broad mountain system. The peaks of the Kysyl-yart, from 21,000 to 25,000 feet in altitude, are in separate groups of snow-covered mountains, between which extends the valley of the Little Kara-kul with a diameter of about 50 kilometres, which is formed by a very complex system of lower mountains 14,000 to 15,000 feet in height. After fixing an astronomical point on the Ran-kul, and returning to the Ak-baital, which they followed down to the Ak-su, they sought the unknown region of the Alitshur Pamir by way of the Kara-su and the pass of Naisa-tush, 14,-000 feet high. They crossed the Alitshur to the Jashil-kul River, which intersects it, discovering in its eastern part a group of lakes. Their provisions failing, they were forced to return to the Kara-kul. This lake lies in an expanded portion of a very long valley, whose eastern opening leads into the valley of the Kak-shai River, and which opens at its west end into that of the Ak-su. Both of the outlets which in former ages connected with these rivers are now dried up; although in times of high flood, but not every year, an overflow still takes place by the southwestern outlet into the Kudara, a confluent of the Murgab. The scientific observations and collections made on this expedition were much more extended than those of its predecessors. The region between the Pamir and the Thian-shan was also explored. The geological material collected suffices for working out the whole geology of the Pamir. Many specimens of about 1,000 different species of plants were gathered. The zoölogical collection was particularly complete, increasing the fauna of the Pamir from 10 to 60 species of mammals, from 4 to 20 species of fish, and from 110 to 350 species of birds.

One of the most interesting questions of Asiatic geography has advanced another step toward its final solution through the enterprise of one of the native Indian surveyors employed in the British geodetical operations in South-

ern Asia. The identity of the Sanpoo, or great river of Thibet, with the Brahmapootra, has been accepted by most geographers; yet it has never been established, and the course of the Sanpoo through the mountains, where it makes a curve from an easterly to a southwesterly course as laid down on the maps, is purely conjectural. Klaproth published an hypothesis that the Irrawaddy instead of the Brahmapootra was the continuation of the Sanpoo, and others have sought to identify the latter with the Subansiri. The exploration of the Indian topographer has practically settled this much-debated question, and leaves no room for doubt that the Sanpoo emerges under the name of the Dihong, as the Brahmapootra is called where it issues from the mountains into the Assam Valley. The energetic native explorer was instructed by Lieutenant Harman to go to Chetang, whose position was determined by the pundit Nain Sing in 1875, and explore the Sanpoo downward as far as he could. On the north bank he followed the river a distance of about 30 miles to a point where a small river called the Mikchoo flows into it from the northeast. He was obliged to make a detour up the valley of this stream and over the Lung-la Pass in the range of mountains which forms the eastern boundary of the Lhassa basin, and then down a valley in which he passed two monasteries to the town of Gyatsa-jong, where he again struck the Sanpoo at a distance of 20 miles from where he had left it. Following the left bank for 30 miles, he then crossed near Thak Nong-jong, not far from which a river joins the Sanpoo from the south. This latter, he learned, flows by a town named Tsari, which is probably identical with D'Anville's Chai. Nain Sing saw the course of the river for 30 miles below Chetang, which is to the southeast. A short distance below Gyatsa-jong the course changes to due east. After following it in that direction for about 50 miles, he found that it turned then to the northeast, and flowed 80 miles in a northwesterly course, reaching its northernmost point in about latitude 30° and longitude 94° E., about 12 miles from a town called Chamcar, doubtless the same as the Tchumca of D'Anville. It here takes a sharp and sweeping turn and flows in a southeasterly direction. He followed it for 15 miles to a place called Gya-la Sindong, where he was obliged to discontinue his explorations. He saw its course for a long distance beyond, to an opening in the mountains through which it passed to the west of a high peak called Jung-la. The distance from Gya-la Sindong, according to its position as determined by the explorer, to the highest point on the Dihong attained by Wilcox, is only about 100 miles. The distance to which the present exploration extends east of Chetang is some 200 miles. The altitude of Gya-la Sindong he determined to be 8.000 feet above the level of the sea, showing a fall of 3,500 feet in the 200 miles of its course from Chetang. The fall between Gya-la Sindong and the junction of the Dihong with the Brahmapootra, a distance of 160 miles, must be 7,000 feet. This is equaled by the fall of other rivers of the Himalayas; yet such a descent in a river of such magnitude must present scenes of imposing grandeur. The conjecture that the Sanpoo was the upper course of the Subansiri was based on the supposition that the volume of the Subansiri was greater than that of the Brahmapootra, and on the difficulty of accounting for the size of the Subansiri with the area of drainage to which it seemed confined if it were not identified with the Sanpoo. Harman has proved that the volume of the Dihong is really two or three times as great as that of the Subansiri. The discovery of a considerable area within the great bend of the Sanpoo greatly increases the probable drainage area of the Subansiri.

The English advance into Afghanistan has been productive of valuable geographical results. The route of Colonel Prendergast to Candahar, through the Sulimani Mountains and the Chacar Pass and across the Vatakri Plain (the same route by which General Biddulph returned), was over new ground. Lake Ab-istada, which was supposed to have no outlet, is found to overflow into the northern branch of the Arghasan River, a tributary of the Helmund.

The directors of the trans-Himalayan operations of the Indian Trigonometrical Survey —Ryall, who surveyed the regions about the sources of the Sutlej, and Kinney, whose field was the neighboring region from which the western feeders of the Ganges spring—have given some interesting information upon the character and customs of the people of this part of Chinese Thibet, as well as regarding the hydrography and orography of the country. The western district of Thibet, which borders upon British India and is drained partly by the upper Sutlej and Karnali Rivers, is called Nari-Khorsam, or sometimes Hundes. The snow-line, Ryall supposes, is rarely below 20,000 feet in any part of Hundes. He laid down 38 different peaks covering an extent of country 100 miles in length. The most remarkable of these, besides Leo Pargial, described by Andrew Wilson, were Gurla Mandhata (25,360 feet) and Kailas, which lie on opposite sides of the lakes of Manasarowar, Cho Mapang and Lang Cho. Kailas, although inferior in altitude to Gurla Mandhata, presents probably the most magnificent aspect of any part of the Himalayas excepting Nanga Parbat. It resembles in form a Pandoo temple with the tip of its conical summit broken off, and is therefore invested with a sacred character by the Hindoos of Northern India. Its extraordinarily huge mass overtops by several thousand feet all the other summits for forty miles around. The Hundes Valley, viewed from an elevated position, presented the appearance of a wide plain interrupted at intervals by low ridges in its eastern portion to the west of the

Manasarowar lakes. The plateaus and mountains of this sterile country, which produces no trees except poplars on the borders of streams, are composed of clay, slate, and fossiliferous limestone. Kinney ascended from Nilang to the main watershed of the Himalayas, and sketched the district of Tsaparang, one of the three districts of Hundes, the others being named Daba and Purang. The entrance to the Nilang Valley from Bhairongati is through a terrific gorge, inclosed between snowy peaks over 20,000 feet in height, which seem to directly overhang the river-bed. The Bhotias of Kumaon and Gurhwal are the traders between Thibet and India. The principal exports from Hundes are borax and shawl-wool; trade in the former has suffered much from a fall in price of 70 per cent., and that in the wool, which is called *pashm*, has also greatly fallen off in late years, and numbers of the shawl-goats are sold in India for sacrificial purposes. The shawl-wool is sold at Gartok to Cashmere merchants, who take it to the manufactories of Cashmere and to Amritsar and other markets in the Punjaub. The finest pashm is grown in the neighborhood of the Manasarowar lakes. Gold is found in the gold-fields at Thok Jalung and on the shores of the lakes, but it is not brought in any quantity into India. The wild and tame varieties of the yak furnish a useful kind of soft wool. The inhabitants of the higher plateaus of Hundes are nomads, and those on the arable lands along the Sutlej and its tributaries are partly nomadic in their habits. Their herds are composed of goats, sheep, and yaks. The people of Hundes are of purely Tartar origin, and are very strongly marked with the physical characteristics of that race. They are hideously wrinkled, even the young having furrowed faces. The Hunias, as they are called, are uncleanly in their habits, fond of tea, which they mix with butter, and much addicted to a beer brewed from rye without any bitter ingredient, which is called *chang*. The brick-tea which they use is the monopoly of the Lhassa Government, and is dealt out to the provincial governors at a fixed price, who force the people to take it in quantities regulated by the wealth and standing of each family, at the rate of about one rupee per pound. Salt and borax can be dug up in any quantity near the Thok Jalung gold mines. The inhabitants of the Bhotia Mehals of Kumaon and Gurhwal are of mixed race, the Tartar blood predominating. The Bhotias are enterprising and intelligent, and not infrequently good-looking. The inhabitants of the Nilang Valley differ in no way from the Hunias. The Bashahris of Independent Gurhwal are said to be the only foreign traders allowed to travel without hindrance all over Thibet.

The present state and future prospects of trade between Bengal and Thibet were the subject of a paper read by Lieutenant-Colonel Lewin before the British Association. The present difficulties which are thrown in the way of the entrance to Thibet are due to the interested fears of the Lamas or governing class, who now possess the monopoly of the commerce, that their revenues would be destroyed if the markets were opened to foreign traders. The jealousy of the Chinese authorities has its grounds in political and commercial motives, and is in no way due to religious prejudice, since the people are Buddhists. The principal wealth of Thibet consists in her flocks and herds. From ancient times she has been known as the best wool-growing country in the world, and now produces the wool of the finest quality. The principal exports to India at present are coarse blankets and carpets, wool, yak-tails, borax, musk, and rhubarb. The country abounds in minerals; but they are not worked, except gold, which is made into rude ornaments. The gold-fields run along the base of the southern watershed of the Sanpoo. A still more important export than the others is brick-tea, which is obtained from a coarse-flavored leaf grown in Sze-chuen, which is preferred by the Bengalese, as it is by the inhabitants of the hill countries and the Punjaub, to the bitter-tasted products of the valleys of the Himalayas and Assam. The taxes and profits from the sale of this tea are one of the principal sources of revenue to the Lhassa Government and the official class. A trade route over the Himalayas would not only be an outlet for the valuable products of the Thibetan highlands, but would open up the great province of Sze-chuen also, with its silk, tea, amber, jade, musk, rhubarb, and cinnabar. The Thibetans are a peaceable, well-instructed, and commercially inclined people. The route to Lhassa and China by way of Darjeeling is now the best, and will be so until a railway shall be built up the Assam Valley.

AFRICA.—The French expedition to the Ogowé, under Savergnan de Brazza and Dr. Ballay, has succeeded, by the exercise of courage and perseverance, in making some geographical discoveries of unusual value. This party set out from France in the summer of 1875, and at the commencement of 1876 were ascending the Ogowé River in canoes to Lopé. After exploring the country of the Fans, they advanced to the village of Doumé, about 50 miles south of the equator, where the course of the river is northwestward. Brazza was obliged to return to the coast on account of illness, but rejoined the party in the following spring, and advanced to the Poubara Falls, in latitude 1° 45' south, where the river is an insignificant stream coming from the south. Having thus finished their explorations of the Ogowé, Brazza boldly resolved to penetrate the unknown interior. Journeying to the eastward, they crossed the water-parting, and followed the course of a stream which led them to a large and unknown river called the Alima, which flows eastward and is undoubtedly an affluent of the Congo. Leaving this river, they traveled northward, crossing several streams which flow to the east,

and striking another large river on the equator, which is called the Licona. At a place called Okango, 30 miles farther north, they were obliged to turn back again on the 11th of August, 1878, reaching Gaboon on the 30th of November. The distance between the Ogowé and the Alima is about 50 miles; the country is crossed by ridges of hills with easy passes. This region was devastated by famine. The tribes on the Alima, whose breadth was about 160 yards and its depth 16 feet, were ferocious and predaceous, attacking them from every village. The cupidity and impudent behavior of the blacks gave the travelers constant trouble from the beginning to the end of their three years' explorations. The course of the Ogowé may be divided into three sections—the middle one flowing parallel to the equator, the lower one inclining about a degree and a half to the southward, and the upper one trending northwestward and making about the same angle with the middle course. After Brazza had settled in the negative the question of a connection between the Ogowé and the great lakes, and, in spite of his diminished supplies, had determined to leave the river on an exploring expedition into the interior, he found himself obliged, from the deceitful and thievish character of the hired porters, to purchase forty slaves to carry the baggage. With these they were enabled to traverse the countries of the Oudoumbo, Umbété, and Batéké, and pursue their explorations until shortness of provisions and the reduction of the stock of merchandise obliged Brazza to send Dr. Ballay and Quartermaster Hamon back to the Ogowé, and the approach of the rainy season compelled him for the sake of safety to follow not long after. The new country explored by Brazza extends about 160 geographical miles south of Lopé and 240 miles to the eastward, reaching half way to where the Zaire crosses the equator. The point where he abandoned the Ogowé was as much as 150 miles beyond the farthest point attained by Dr. Lenz, and 75 miles beyond that reached by Marche the year before. When the French and Portuguese expeditions started forth on their explorations, the secrets of the interior, the problems of the Congo and the lower lake region, had not yet been unsealed through the labors of Cameron and Stanley. When Brazza arrived at Lopé in the beginning of 1876, near which place Marche and Compiègue had been obliged to resort to arms to defend themselves against a murderous attack of the natives three years before, he resolved to enter this dangerous region without an escort. This proved the best and safest course. He gained the good will and confidence of the Osyeba, whose incessant feuds with the Adouma and the Okanda are prompted by jealousy of their commercial operations up and down the river, as they themselves possess no skill in navigation. In June, 1876, he was in Doumé, in the country of the Adouma, in company with the Austrian traveler, Dr. Lenz; and here his companions, Marche, Ballay, and Quarter-master Hamon, found him dangerously ill some weeks after. Regaining his health, he advanced with his associates (except Marche, who had returned to Europe broken down, by fever) to the bifurcation of the river formed by the junction with the Passa, which comes from the southwest. The Ogowé above this point, latitude 1° 36' S., flows from the south, and is named the Rebanyi by the natives. Both streams are obstructed by cataracts and rapids a short distance above. The fall at Poubara, about latitude 1° 45' S., longitude 11° 5' E. from Paris, is 30 to 40 metres. Three or four days' march farther up the Ogowé is easily fordable at low water; and the same is true of the Passa. Having thus satisfactorily solved the problem of the source of the Ogowé, they were attracted by the unknown interior to the east. They could find no carriers to accompany them into these dread regions, whose barbarism the blacks depicted in the darkest hues. They therefore felt driven to the purchase of their forty slaves. Leaving the well-wooded banks of the river, they struck out into a sandy and waterless country, intersected by deep ravines, destitute of provisions, and inhabited by what were reported to be quarrelsome and ferocious cannibals. A few miles this side of the village of Obanda, which is in latitude 1° 34' 59" S., longitude 11° 59' 48" E. from Paris, they crossed the water-parting. In the inhospitable region which they now entered, sprinkled with sand-hills, with occasional rocks jutting out, were encountered the Batéké, a tribe which Stanley found living on the Zaire. In the new hydrographic basin in which he found himself, Brazza crossed four different rivers, all easily navigable and varying from 60 to 140 metres in breadth. In descending the Alioa they were stopped by the fierce Apfurus, and only saved themselves by escaping into a marshy jungle. Thirty or forty miles farther north, near the Lebainguco River, the sickness of many of the men induced Brazza to send them all back with Dr. Ballay and Hamon, and to continue his explorations entirely alone, which he pushed to Okanga, 0° 30' north latitude, longitude about 12° 45' E. from Paris, reaching there the the 11th of August, 1878. North of the Lebainguco the desolate country covered with sand-hills ends, and when the Licona River is reached vegetation is abundant. The country of the Ashimbo, north of the equator, is covered with dense forests. The villages of the Batéké and Umbété, who occupy the arid region, are few and wretched. These tribes resort to very singular tactics to ascertain the disposition of strangers approaching their villages. The men conceal themselves behind the village, leaving the women in their houses and sending out the children toward the strange party. If the children are not molested, they lead the strangers into the village, and the men come from their hiding-place and receive them cordially. If, however, they attempt to lay

hands on the children, the latter dexterously elude them, while the warriors wait until the foe has entered the village and scattered in search of plunder, and then, descending from their ambush, have them at their mercy. The houses in these countries are all rectangular in form, built of bamboo, and roofed with the same. A multitude of petty independent chiefs govern these tribes. Cannibalism is universally practiced by the victors in battle. On the upper Ogowé they worship fetiches and the skulls of their ancestors. Elephants and enormous gorillas are found on the upper Ogowé. The dominions of the chiefs were of greater extent down the Alima.

The English are much interested at present in opening up the shortest routes in the lake and Upper Nile regions of Africa, and in establishing communication between their missionary stations. An able and ardent young explorer, Keith Johnston, was commissioned by the Royal Geographical Society to explore a direct route from Dar-es-Salaam, near Zanzibar, to the north end of Lake Nyassa, and then to push across to the southern end of Tanganyika. These are two connections which are of the highest importance for missionary operations in these parts of Africa. The country which he was to have traversed is very interesting as a field for scientific exploration also, and he was instructed to make as complete observations as he could in the zoology, ethnology, botany, geology, and meteorology of these regions, and to study the phenomenon of a sudden rise in the waters of Lake Tanganyika, alleged by Stanley to have taken place in recent times. Keith Johnston reached Zanzibar on the 5th of January, with one companion, Mr. Thomson. He was able to obtain the services of Dr. Livingstone's favorite attendant, Chuma, as head-man. In May the party left Zanzibar: it consisted of the leader and his European companion and 138 native attendants. Before he had accomplished one third of the distance between Dar-es-Salaam and the head of Lake Nyassa the accomplished explorer fell a victim to the deadly climate at Behobeho, in latitude 8° N., longitude 38° E. The expedition proceeded under the command of Mr. Thomson. The country traversed up to the place in which the leader breathed his last was of a monotonous description, consisting of level sandy plains varied by marshes. The route taken was to the Lufigi River, which was found to be quite unnavigable except for canoes, being full of sand-banks, islands, and snags, although in places it is deep and the current is strong. They struck the Lufigi near the village of Mzetusa, from which they marched in a west-north-westerly direction to Behobeho. Here the country began to grow much better. Thomson's plan was to proceed in a westerly direction for seven days to the large Khutu village of Mgunda, and then to march southward for two days through the jungle to the Ruaha, to ford this and reach the Uranga

In two days, and in two days more to arrive in Ubena. The country which this route would take him through was reported to be well peopled and well supplied with food.

The traveler Otto Schütt, who was sent out on an expedition to Central Africa by the German African Society, has made some very interesting discoveries in the basin of the Congo. Between the two known affluents of the Congo, the Quango and the Kasai, he discovered four others, whose names are the Quengo, the Marata, the Cinlu, and the Kwanger. He reconnoitred a portion of the Kasai River which had not before been visited, that between the eighth and ninth parallels. The lake which was called Sankora by the English explorers, and is named Mucaruba by the natives, is situated on the fifth parallel of south latitude. South of this lake there lives a tribe of dwarfs. The tribes dwelling along the banks of the Quengo and the Kasai are cannibals. The traveler, being forbidden by the Muata Janva to cross the Loulona River, returned to Loanda.

Interesting accounts of the political and physical condition of the southeastern interior of Africa, the same countries which were traversed by Serpa Pinto, and which have been studied by one of the most deserving of modern explorers, Dr. Emil Holub, are contained in the papers of the late Captain Patterson, who was sent by Sir Bartle Frere in 1878 to Lobengule, the King of the Matabeli, as an envoy, and who died from drinking the water of a spring which was probably poisoned for the purpose of killing game. There was suspicion that he and his companions were the victims of a murderous conspiracy. Matabeli-land is a large kingdom with a strong and tyrannical political system, containing about 200,000 inhabitants, who are spread over a fertile and well-watered territory of about 150,000 square miles. The boundaries are the Zambesi River on the north, the Shasha on the south, the Sabia on the east, and the Zouga on the west. The population is divided into three classes. The Abazunzi, descended from the Zooloo conquerors of the country, form the aristocracy, and are about one fourth of the population, and the Abeutla, the sons of Bechuana prisoners taken on the march into these regions from the southeast, form another fourth. The Amacholi, the original inhabitants conquered by the late King Masilikatze, composed of different tribes, are now the servants of the conquerors. The people are assigned to their settlements by the King, who collects about him the young men of the country, and, after putting them through a course of military training, settles them over the country, each regiment, after it has passed through its four years' drill, being made the nucleus of a new town. The principal occupation of the men is warfare with the neighboring tribes. The women till the soil, which is very productive. They possess a few cattle, goats, and sheep. They are ruthless and cruel in their wars, slaying all but the children, whom they carry off as slaves. The King rules with a rod of iron, inflicting the punishment of death for the slightest offense. He visits the same dread penalty upon all who threaten to become too powerful by amassing property or advancing in any way. The governors of towns, called indunas, report all offenses to the King, who reserves to himself in all cases the power of passing judgment. The capital, Gubuluwayo, situated near the center of the kingdom, is only occasionally the residence of the King. The greater portion of the year he wanders about the kingdom, living in temporary towns constructed at his pleasure. During the life of Masilikatze, his father, and for some time after he became King, Lobengule affected the society of white people and wore the European dress. Of late years he has adopted the ways and habits of a savage, and does all that he dares openly and secretly to exclude the whites and restrict their influence. The whole country of Bamangwato on the west, as far as Lake Ngami, is claimed by the Matabeli by right of conquest. They are constantly encroaching also on the territory of their neighbors on the east. The Banyaie, a southeastern tribe, who occupy the Mashona Mountains, are able to successfully withstand them. The Mashona can offer no resistance. They are a peaceful and industrious race, skilled in the working of iron, in making excellent baskets, and in weaving a good cloth from the cotton which they grow. They occupy a fertile, well-watered country, with large level plateaus like the Orange Free State. In the Mashona and Tati districts gold is found in quantities and iron is abundant. The vegetation of Matabeli-land is very luxuriant. Mapene, mimosa, and baobab trees attain an enormous size. There are large and fine forests. The breadfruit-tree, palms, cotton, olive, and numerous wild fruits grow prolifically. The people of Bamangwato, ruled by a Christian chief, are rapidly taking on the customs of civilization. The country is comparatively barren, the soil sandy, and covered with stunted bush. The Limpopo, Zambesi, and Zouga traverse the country, as well as the Tati, Shasha, and Makalapogo, which are sand-rivers in which water can only be obtained in the dry season by digging. The inhabitants outside the towns in Bamangwato are of two classes, the Bakala and the Masawa, the latter being slaves without the right to own property. Shoshong, the capital, once contained 30,000 inhabitants; but, owing to the hostile inroads of the Matabeli, its population is reduced to 10,000. The people often emigrate to the other Bechuana nations. The women cultivate gardens near the town and the men follow the chase. They are temperate in their habits. The European dress is common. Khame, the chief, is a wise ruler, sincerely attached to principles of humanity and justice. The country over which Khame claims jurisdiction is an irregular triangle, with the Makarakari salt lake in the center; one of its angles is the junction of the Shasha and Limpopo Rivers, another the junction of the Chobe with the Zambesi, near the Victoria Falls.

Andrew A. Anderson, like Dr. Holub, has spent many years in southern Central Africa, and has collected interesting data regarding the countries of the South African plateaus and their inhabitants. East of the Mashona country, which he counts as belonging to Mata-beli-land, is the Makombe country, about 40,-000 square miles in extent, reaching to the Portuguese possessions. South of this is a territory extending to the Limpopo, with an area estimated at 70,000 square miles. Parts of this are inhabited by a tolerably thick and industrious population, who grow and weave cotton. South of Bamangwato, which has an extent of about 70,000 square miles with a population of about 45,000, is Secheli's country, which extends from the Limpopo on the east to the Kalihari Desert on the west, whose population, exclusive of Bushmen,* is about 45,000; this region has an area of about 30,000 square miles; the capital town is Molopololo. In the same country two independent chiefs rule over about 30,000 people. Immediately south of this country, between the Transvaal and the desert, is Gasietsise's country, 60,000 square miles in extent, with Kanya for its chief town, and a population, exclusive of Bushmen, but including the followers of two chiefs who live there by sufferance, amounting to 35,000; and to the east, bordering on the Transvaal, is the territory of the chief Macasi. South of Gasietsise's dominions Monsiwe rules over about 20,000 square miles of territory, with a population of perhaps 15,000. Below this country and north of Griqualand West is about 30,000 square miles of territory, occupied by several petty tribes, numbering some 20,000. West of Bamangwato, the region about Lake Ngami is governed by a son of the late Lechuatabele, whose kraal is at the foot of the lake, where the Zouga or Botletle issues. His territory has an extent of about 40,000 square miles; the people number about 20,000. The countries west of the Kalibari Desert are Ovampo-land, Damara-land, and Great Namaqua-land. Ovampo-land, on the north, would be an excellent grazing country for cattle and sheep, having plenty of water and very fine veldt; the mountains are reported to be rich in minerals. This country contains about 60,000 square miles, and supports a population of only 30,000; the people are industrious, and raise grain and vegetables. Damara-land lies to the south and west of Ovampo-land and north of Great Namaqua-land, extending in its southern portion from the sea to the desert. It has lately been annexed to Cape Colony. Along the coast the country is a sandy desert, but its eastern portion is mountainous and rich in mineral products. The same is true of Damara-land, running from Great Namaqua-land to Orange River on the south, and from the Atlantic Ocean

to the desert of Kalibari, and containing an area of some 70,000 square miles. In the east, near the Great Fish River, are also good grazing-grounds. The population is very mixed, embracing Namaquas, Hottentots, Bushmen, Griquas, and Damaras, with different varieties of half-breeds called Kurumas, Veldskoendrawers, Bundle-Swaarts, and Africanders, and a good number of Caffres who have run away from the Cape. The latter, numbering about 20,000, live under arms and are given to plunder. The great Kalibari Desert is 900 miles long, and in some places 500 miles broad; it contains 260,000 square miles, besides a tract of 20,000 square miles on the Orange River. Between 1864 and 1872 Mr. Anderson explored and surveyed the desert of Kalibari. He was always accompanied by a large following of Bushmen, who, he says, are the best behaved but the worst treated of all the black races he has met in Africa. The desert is rich in minerals: coal is abundant; copper is found in considerable quantities on the west side; and gold was discovered by him in two mountain ranges. Those parts of the country in which water is always to be found are well adapted for farming. Near the large sand-rivers water is always obtainable. The rainy season is from January to May. Sheep and cattle fatten well on the herbage. The fine grassy pastures are full of large game. There are large forests of bush and timber. The cotton-growing region in the Mashona country is described by Mr. Anderson as embracing an area of 25,000 square miles. Lobengule now bars the way to this rich field for European settlements. Transportation to the coast is everywhere easily to be accomplished by the numerous watercourses. Rice is also cultivated in this district; spices of all varieties thrive exceedingly; and oranges, lemons, citrons, and many vegetables attain the highest degree of perfection. Gold is found in this same country, as well as silver and other minerals. Portions of the Mashona district and other parts of Matabeli-land are absolutely free from fever, which is unknown in the elevated and mountainous regions. West of Lake Ngami, in Kalibari and the Ovampo, Damara, and Namaqua countries, there is no fever. The fever districts of this part of Africa are principally confined to the valley of the Zambesi and the regions east of Lake Ngami, in the low country along the Zouga and Mababe Rivers from the great salt-pan of Makarakari up to Victoria Falls, and along the Chobe or Cuando River. The sickly season begins when the mapane-trees, which grow to a great size and have a frond and flower like those of the orange-tree, send out their young shoots; from May to October the whole country is free from fever.

One of the most important geographical achievements of the year was accomplished in south Central Africa by Major Serpa Pinto, an energetic and accomplished young Portuguese explorer. The expedition was sent out by the Portuguese Government, and had for its object the exploration of the interior of the African Continent, particularly the river systems of the Zambesi and the Congo. The commander of one division of the expedition, Major Albert da Rocha Serpa Pinto, was eminently fitted for his task by his experience in African life, by his knowledge of the languages, and by his scientific attainments. Born in 1846 and educated for the Portuguese military service, he took part in 1869 in the campaign against the rebellious chief Bonga in the region of the Zambesi, and on that occasion ascended that river as far as the Victoria Falls. He then spent a considerable time among the Comore and Seychelle negroes, hunting on the shores of Lake Nyassa, and returned by way of Goa to Europe. The expedition arrived at the mouth of the Congo in August, 1877, where they encountered Stanley just at the completion of his trying march through the dark continent. Stanley's attendants, after their terrible experience, could not be induced to encounter the toils and hardships of another overland journey with Serpa Pinto. The expedition consisted of two others besides Serpa Pinto, Brito Capello and Ivens. Not finding carriers in Loanda, they went to the banks of the Congo in search of some. It was while on this errand that they fell in with Stanley. His exploration of the Congo River obliged them to considerably modify their plans, the ascent of the Congo and determination of its sources having been one of the principal objects for which they were sent out. They started from Benguela for the interior on the 12th of November, 1877, accompanied by an escort of fourteen soldiers and fifty-seven carriers. Traversing the districts of Dombe, Guillenguez, and Caconda, they reached Bihé in March, 1878, after painstaking observations in the little known regions through which they passed. The positions assigned to some of the localities by Sá da Bandeira differ in some cases five or six degrees from the positions determined by Pinto: according to the latter, Benguela is situated in latitude 12° 34' 17" S., longitude 13° 25' 21" E. from Greenwich, and has an elevation above the level of the sea of 7 metres; Dombe Grande is in latitude 12° 55' 12" S., longitude 13° 7' 45", with an absolute elevation of 98 metres; Guillenguez is in latitude 14° 3' 10" S., longitude 14° 5' 3", and is 900 metres above the mean tide-mark; Caconda is in latitude 13° 44', longitude 15° 1' 51", with an elevation of 1,678 metres; and Bihé is in latitude 12° 21' 40", longitude 16° 49' 24", and has an elevation of 1,670 metres. At Bihé the explorers decided to separate, Brito Capello and Ivens journeying to the northward to explore the river Cuanza, while Serpa Pinto was to push on into the interior to the eastward. Senhor Pinto had enjoyed good health until his companions left him; but, after they had parted he fell ill of rheumatic

fever, and was compelled to remain in Bihé for three months, nearly consuming the whole of the share of supplies which had fallen to him on the division. His attendants abandoned him, and he had to organize another party; and in May he made a start, although still suffering extreme weakness and prostration.

On the way from Benguela to Bihé they had already made a geographical discovery of interest, in finding the source of the Cubango to the west of that place, instead of to the east, as has been supposed. They obtained no water until they reached Caconda, except by wringing their tents when they were wet with the cassimba or heavy night-dews. The district of Dombe Grande is the most fertile portion of Angola, and furnished corn for the whole province during three years of drought. At Caconda they fell in with an eminent naturalist, Anchietta, who has preserved, during the twelve years which he has passed among the wilds of Central Africa, the elegant habits of city life, receiving them in evening dress and offering them tea in Sèvres china. He has a library well stocked with modern works, in which he seeks relaxation from his engrossing naturalistic researches and collections. Besides the head-stream of the Cubango, Pinto passed two affluents before arriving at Bihé, and also the river Cuqueima, which is marked on the maps as an affluent of the Cubango, and was supposed to be one by Ladislaus Magyar, but which Pinto was surprised to find running north; it curves afterward toward the southwest, and is a tributary of the Cuanza. This stream forms the boundary-line of the territory of Bihé, the greater part of which country is governed directly by the chief, and the remaining portions by chiefs who are subject to him. Starting from Bihé, he soon entered a most interesting region, the magnificent plain of Cangala, in which within a few miles of each other all the great rivers of South Africa take their rise. This is a plateau about 1,700 metres in altitude. A very remarkable phenomenon is here exhibited. The sources of great rivers flowing in different directions are dovetailed between each other without any perceptible water-partings. On this one spot rivers which soon assume magnificent proportions, and which finally empty thousands of miles away from each other, in the Atlantic, in the Indian Ocean, and in the thirsty sands of the Kalibari Desert, all take their rise within a few miles of each other, flowing in opposite or diverse directions, only separated by short stretches of the same level plain. In some spots only a few paces separate streams which feed the Congo, the Zambesi, and the Cubango. This plateau is the southern limit of the Benguelan highlands. Its climate is exceedingly salubrious; and its remarkable agricultural and commercial capabilities render it one of the most promising regions in Africa for colonization. In this plain, which is transected by the twelfth parallel, rise the Cuito, an important affluent of the Cubango, which flows southward and unites with the main river at a place called Darico; the Cuiba, a tributary of the Cuanza; and the Lungo-e-ungo, an important river flowing eastward, and emptying into the Liba—all close together; and in the neighboring regions other affluents of the Cuanza and the Cubango, and the head-waters of the Cuando, the Quango, and the Cuuene, take their rise. The Cuando rises in latitude 13° S., longitude 19° E., east of the Cuito. This is a large and deep navigable river, receiving several affluents as navigable as itself, watering a great area of fertile and inhabited country. It was this same river which Livingstone called Chobe, and which is the principal affluent of the Zambesi, uniting with the main stream in about latitude 18° S., longitude 25° E., after a navigable course of 500 miles. The standard of size must be taken differently in Africa from that applied to European rivers, as the smaller rivers in Africa exceed those which are usually called great in Europe. The rise of rivers in Africa is a singular and apparently mysterious process. A trickling rill is observed and followed down a short distance, and is seen to wax rapidly, without receiving any visible affluents, into a flowing, navigable river. From the head-waters of the Cuando, Serpa Pinto took a course which would lead him to the Liba or Upper Zambesi. He traversed a region covered with forests, in which the elephant still abounds. Here he came across a singular race of people, whose skins are yellowish-white, paler in fact than the average European, and whose head is covered with a tufted growth of short woolly hair. He observed one day that one of his carriers had a white skin, and upon inquiry he learned of this anomalous people that they were a nomadic race who live upon roots and the products of the chase, wandering in bands of from four to six families in the region between the Cuchi, one of the affluents of the Cubango, and the main river, and eastward as far as the Cuando. They are extraordinarily muscular, burying their arrows entirely in the flesh of the elephant. They are the only African people who devour their food without cooking. They hold no intercourse with the neighboring tribes, except when they are threatened with famine, on which occasions they exchange ivory for the necessaries of life with the Anguellas. They never stay a second night in the same encampment. This tribe are called Cassequeres. Their tufted hair might warrant the conjecture that the Bushmen of the south are descendants of this race intermarried with the blacks. Their faces are very prognathous, and their eyes are set obliquely in their heads like those of the Chinese. As none of the Portuguese traders have ever made mention of this strikingly marked people, it seems not unlikely that Senhor Pinto has permitted himself to be misled by an albino. In one of Petermann's maps, published

in 1858, a tribe of Bushmen named Kassakarie are put down in the region between the Cunene and the Cubango. Another nomadic tribe, called the Mussambas, inhabit this country. Their wanderings extend as far as the country of the Sulatebele. They are a black race, entirely distinct from the Bushmen of the Kalibari Desert, called Massaruas. The regions lying between Bihé and the Zambesi are inhabited by three distinct races, the Kimbaudes, the Luchares, and the Ambuellas; while a fourth, the Kibokwes, are migrating at present from the north to the banks of the Cubango and the Cuando, where they find a soil more productive than that which they have occupied. The whole country is exceedingly fruitful. The people of all these tribes are lively and capable of learning quickly; they show a remarkable fondness for dress. They are governed by chiefs whose power is absolute. Different tribes join together in confederations. They had never seen a European before the arrival of Serpa Pinto, but him they received very cordially. Between the Cuando and the Liambai he encountered no important river. In this eastward journey through the valley of the Lungo-e-ungo the expedition was put to severe straits, going without food at one time for 103 hours, and repeatedly for nearly 48 hours, and then breaking fast only with some *alpista* or canary-seed. The country traversed was very marshy, but contained no trace of game, and not even the turtles which are so abundant in the marshy spots along the Zambesi. Crocodiles, however, were so numerous that bridges had to be constructed over some of the streams to avoid them. After troubles and hardships without number he reached at last the town of Lialui (probably the same as the Katongo of Livingstone), on the Liambai, or Upper Zambesi, in latitude 15° 12′ S., longitude 22° 48′ E.

Serpa Pinto had intended to proceed from here to the northeast. In that direction he hoped to discover the true source of the Lualaba, which, according to a map drawn for him by a Biheau, is not the Luapala connecting the lakes Bangweolo and Moero and the Chambeze, but the true Lualaba, which rises, like the other great African rivers, in about the 12th degree of south latitude, between the Liambai and the Luengwe or Cafuque, the river which was called by Livingstone Cafue. In this same region live the Chuculumbe, a ferocious race of savages, who will not suffer either whites or Arabs to set foot within their territories, but who carry on considerable commerce through the agency of native traders. Although warned by Stanley not to enter the dominions of these relentless barbarians, he intended to push his way in that direction; but the sudden desertion of his followers compelled him to alter his plans. In the night of the 6th of August, while encamped at Lialui, a fire suddenly broke out in the camp, and simultaneously they were attacked by the natives. His men were very active and vigorous in rescuing his instruments and in repulsing the assailants; yet the morning after the victory he found that his carriers had abandoned him in a body, all the Benguelans leaving, and only a handful of Biheaus, seven in number, remaining with their leader. Pinto was forced to turn his course to the southward, into the country which has been made very familiar to the world by the writings of Livingstone. Yet important political changes have taken place since the sojourn of the Scotch traveler with Sebituane, the able King of the Makalolos. That kingdom has been overthrown, and the very nation itself has been completely exterminated. Livingstone foresaw its decay on his second visit to the Makalolos under the second King, Sekeletu. The empire which Sebituane had founded, by conquering the nations around and consolidating them into a strong kingdom, was destroyed by the former possessors of the land, who rose suddenly in the reign of the third King, and put the greater part of their masters to death, subsequently destroying the rest, who fled to Bihé and made from there an incursion in January, 1878. The hardy and brave nation which Sebituane had formed from all the different races of South Africa owed their decay and final destruction to the enervating effects of fevers and to licentiousness and the use of *bang*. On the Zambesi Serpa Pinto met Mechuana, Livingstone's companion, who was then a Luina slave of Sekeletu, but who is now a prominent man in the nation. The banks of the Zambesi were at first covered with woods, and pulse was everywhere plentiful. Soon he reached basaltic formations and uninterrupted cataracts and rapids down to the Victoria Falls. There are 72 of these falls and rapids between the 16th parallel of latitude and the Victoria Falls, a distance of 220 geographical miles. The only affluents of the Zambesi from the west were the Lungo-e-ungo, the Uhengo, and the Cuando, except a small one close to the Victoria Falls. The Uhengo is formed by the junction of three rivers, the Ninda, the Loati, and the Luanginga. The level of the land declines between Bihé and the Zambesi about 1,200 feet; but south of the Cuando the land begins to rise again, and a luxuriant vegetation is met with; yet the country is almost uninhabited. The country south of the Zambesi is not attractive to settlers, although exceedingly fertile, both because of the hostile attitude of the Matabeli, who regard the Zambesi as their natural frontier, and because of the malarial climate. Down to the Victoria Falls, with the exception of the barren region of the rapids, the country is well peopled. East of the river live the fierce and warlike Makalakas, many of whom are taken captive in their constant wars, and serve the surrounding tribes as slaves. At Linyanti, on the Cuando, he expected to find an English mission; but the mission was deserted, the missionaries having fallen victims to the deadly climate,

and he was confronted, ill and exhausted as he was, by hostile natives. Fortunately, he did encounter Europeans at this juncture. The first was an English naturalist, Dr. Bradshaw, whose life and circumstances contrasted strikingly with the elegant hermitage of his Portuguese compeer in Angola; for, inured to wild life, and supporting himself by the chase, he was found pursuing his vocation barefoot and coatless among the ceaseless perils of this wilderness. While in the company of this gentleman the negroes surrounded their habitation one night, prowling about with evil intent while they held a vigilant watch. In the morning the Portuguese traveler found that they had robbed him of the remainder of his baggage. He then went in search of a French missionary who lived with his wife and sister at Guiyama, and, falling very ill on the way, he was tenderly cared for by this brave family. Recovering from the fever, he set out to find the solution of the problem of the discharge of the Cubango. Pastor Coillard and the ladies insisted on bearing him company in the toilsome excursion into the Kalibari Desert. Kalibari is nowhere strictly a desert, as trees and pastures, water and game are found, and people live in all parts of it; yet water in many portions is only to be had at certain seasons of the year, and the inhabitants are obliged to follow a nomadic life, changing their abode as the waters come and go. The explorer did not succeed in reaching the Cubango; but, from what he observed and learned from the natives, he believes that he has settled the question of the discharge of that river, a question of great importance in the hydrography of Southern Africa. The Cubango is laid down variously on recent maps as flowing into the Cunene, to lagoons near Lake Ngami, or to the Chobe. Its upper course has been made known by Portuguese traders, and is traced on Sá da Bandeira's map as far as latitude 170° S. C. J. Andersson struck this river in 1859 in latitude 17° 47' S., longitude 18° 51' E., and navigated it up and down for a distance of 100 miles. It was here called the Okavango, and was 200 to 300 yards broad, very deep, and flowing at the rate of 2½ to 3 miles an hour. Baines and Andersson both supposed that it flowed into the Chobe and formed the principal branch of the Zambesi. At the upper end of the Kalibari Pinto came upon the great Macaricari salt-pan. The Macaricari is connected with Lake Ngami by the Botletle River. The Cubango River, according to Serpa Pinto's reports, has no connection whatever with the Cuando or the Zambesi, but its waters, considerably reduced in volume by evaporation, are entirely absorbed by the Kalibari Desert. It empties into Lake Ngami, which in very rainy seasons overflows into the great salt-pan. The Macaricari and the Botletle both exhibit some very mysterious and complicated phenomena, according to Serpa Pinto's statements. The salt-pan is sometimes a perfectly dry and empty basin, whose bottom is covered with a glittering saline incrustation; but at other times it is filled with water, forming a broad and deep lake. Other similar basins present the same phenomenon; but this one differs from them all in that its changes seem to have no connection with the seasons of rain or drought in the surrounding regions. The behavior of the Botletle is even more surprising and unusual. Livingstone reported it as flowing westward, and Baines represented it as flowing to the east. Serpa Pinto affirms that both statements are true, and that its current at certain seasons is toward Lake Ngami, while at others it carries the waters of that lake into the Macaricari, according as rainfall occurs in the country of the Matabeli or in the valley of the Cubango. If the outlet of the Cubango is into Lake Ngami, and there is no regular connection with the Cuando—which can not yet be accepted as proved, notwithstanding the positive convictions of Serpa Pinto, since the identity of the Okavango, as the middle course of the Cubango which Andersson explored was called, and the Tioghe, which empties into the lake, was established, and neither the Cubango nor the Cuando has been explored over its whole course —there may yet be a periodical overflow into the Ouando from Lake Ngami; as Baines asserts that the Tamalukun, which discharges into the Botletle, and the Mababe, which flows in an opposite direction into the Cuando, are joined in especially wet seasons by a navigable channel.

Serpa Pinto next visited the cataracts to which Livingstone gave the name of Victoria Falls, and which the natives call Mosi-va-tonia. He found the height of the fall to be 180 metres. He then took leave of the Coillard family, and made his way to Shoshong, where the people, among whom the missionaries Mackenzie and Price long resided, are Christians, and use gold currency, and even have a credit system. Thence he was able to send dispatches to Europe on the 2d of January, 1879. A few more weeks brought him to Pretoria, the capital of the Transvaal; and he arrived at Durban on the 14th of April, sixteen months after he had left the opposite coast. Of the four hundred men who formed his escort when he left Benguela, only eight remained faithful to him, and accompanied him throughout the toilsome and perilous journey. These he took with him to Lisbon, to be returned from there to their native country.

Major Serpa Pinto made no extensive collections of the fauna and flora, nor any special naturalistic studies. He observed in the upper Cuando two species of antelopes, whose singular habits make them a curiosity in natural history: although true antelopes, they live altogether in the water like the hippopotamus. He made a particular study of the ethnology of the countries traversed, besides his thorough geographical and meteorological observations.

The Italian naturalist, Signor D'Albertis, who has spent a large portion of the last six years, secluded from civilization and surrounded with dangers, studying in the wilds of New Guinea the wonderful fauna of that island, has contributed more perhaps than any other man to our information of this land of marvels, which has been reserved until the present to be explored, although known to be one of the most interesting regions of the earth. D'Albertis arrived for the first time in New Guinea in 1872, in company with Dr. Beccari. Unable to make a landing at the mouth of the Wamuka River, in longitude 136° 15′ E., latitude 4° 40′ S., and to ascend that river and reach the Charles Louis Mountains, according to their intentions, they landed, after touching at several points along the coast, at Serong, a small island between Salwatti and the mainland, latitude 0° 52′ S. Obliged to depart from here on account of the unwholesomeness of the climate, they proceeded to Dorei, a trading-post on the northwestern peninsula, and established their quarters at the village of Andai, a few miles distant, where there was a Dutch mission. This is the country of which Wallace wrote in his accounts of the birds-of-paradise. D'Albertis explored the regions around in search of specimens of this bird, but only found ordinary and uninteresting varieties. The rare and richly feathered species, which are only known to naturalists from mutilated specimens that have been prepared for commerce by the native hunters, live farther inland, in the Arfak Mountains, to the foot of which the naturalist's earlier explorations extended. He was the first European to ascend into the highlands which are the habitat of this most beautiful creature in the feathered race. Because of the dread in which the coast natives hold the mountain tribes, who are reputed to be cannibals, no attempt (if any had been made) to penetrate this region had yet succeeded. D'Albertis was the first civilized being who studied the bird-of-paradise in its native woods. The Arfak range is of volcanic origin. The highest peak, Mount Arfak, is not far from 9,000 feet in height. From this the range runs in a southerly direction until it joins the central ridge of the interior. Numerous streams roll down the side of the mountain-chain into Port Geelvink and Geelvink Bay. The whole range, even the highest summits, are thickly clad with magnificent forests of lofty trees. To his astonishment he discovered among the vegetation a species of oak and a conifer, identified by Dr. Beccari with the *Araucaria*. In this spot, in 134° E. longitude, and almost upon the equatorial line, the flora of all climates, from that of the torrid to that of the upper temperate zone, is found in a variety nowhere else to be met with. The climate here is humid, but, to judge from the vigorous and well-proportioned frames of the inhabitants, must be exceedingly healthy. These people possess in the most marked degree the characteristics of the Papuan type, and may be taken as the purest examples of this race, which, however, is not in the least entitled, in the opinion of D'Albertis, to be considered a distinct variety of the human species. This fine race of mountaineers held themselves jealously aloof from the outside world until the most recent period. Before D'Albertis visited them they bore universally the reputation of cannibalism. They live in tribes, each under the headship of a chief called Korano. They live in large houses partitioned off to accommodate several families, in which the men and women occupy separate sides. These Papuans are agricultural, cultivating tobacco, yams, sweet potatoes, and bananas, possess savage arts of a superior character, and are tolerably industrious. They have no religious ideas, but are superstitious about death, believing in the continuance of life after death and in the transmigration of souls. They place tobacco and food on the graves of their dead, for them to arise and consume in the nighttime. In spite of the earnest dissuasion of the missionaries, D'Albertis was determined to visit the Arfak Mountains. Attended by an interpreter, under the protection of a friendly Korano, he entered the mountains in the beginning of September, 1872, escorted by eight or ten Papuans from the village of Andai. He passed a month in one of the Papuan houses, exploring the woods in quest of the bird-of-paradise, and ascending the mountains in his excursions to the height of 5,000 feet. The fickle and ferocious character of the savages made this expedition a really dangerous venture. They are extremely jealous and capricious, and the very intimacy which he was able to establish with some tribes was enough to excite the animosity of others. They have a mania for collecting human skulls, and think nothing of taking life; so that the daring scientific enthusiast was in constant peril. His bold adventure terminated fortunately, however, and the tact which he exercised in his intercourse with the natives was the means of rendering the visits of subsequent explorers secure. He was compelled by the premonitions of disease to leave his task uncompleted, but not before he had observed the birds-of-paradise in their native haunts, and made a collection of fine examples of rare and brilliant species. He left New Guinea on the Italian naval vessel which was sent to take them off, with a settled purpose to visit the southern part of the island as soon as his health should be reestablished. This purpose was inspired and strengthened by the discovery of a new and beautiful species of the bird-of-paradise, the *Paradisea raggiana*, and the sight of mountain-peaks far to the east close to the coast.

In the month of March, 1875, D'Albertis was back again in New Guinea, settled this time off the southern coast of the mainland on Yule Island, near Point Moresby. Absolutely

nothing was known of the interior before he came. The natives had never caught sight of a white skin, except on the crew of the Basilisk, with whom they had had no dealings. He chose Yule Island for his residence because it seemed a healthy spot, and was near the mainland and the range of high mountains which runs southeastward from Mount Yule to the high peak called Mount Owen Stanley. Without possessing a word of the language, D'Albertis was left entirely alone. His object was to study the inhabitants, who belong to a different race from the Papuans of the other half of the island, and to ascertain whether this entirely unknown country offered any advantages for colonization or commerce, as well as to collect objects of natural history. Although at first unable to communicate with the natives except by signs, his relations with them were generally most satisfactory. His stay on Yule Island lasted eight months, at the end of which period his failing health, impaired by the climate, notwithstanding its salubrity compared with other parts of New Guinea, obliged him to depart in November.

In the winter of 1875 D'Albertis, notwithstanding his reduced condition of health, joined the missionary expedition up the Fly River in the Ellengowan. Constantly attacked by the hostile natives, they made their way up the river for 150 miles, and then were obliged to put about just as they were entering the most interesting region. D'Albertis determined to make another attempt to explore the Fly River, and, repairing to Sydney, he enlisted the interest of the Government and private citizens in the design. Furnished with a steamboat drawing but 3½ or 4 feet of water, he succeeded in 1876 in ascending the river to its head-waters, 500 miles from its mouth. He was carried too far to the westward by the river, and his crew were suffering too much from disease and privation, for him to strike across the mountains to Yule Island, as was his intention. The Fly River rises in the lofty chain called the Charles Louis range, which traverses the center of the island, and the party had ascended to where the mountainous country begins. After spending three months in making collections, he returned to Sydney, determined to made one more expedition up the Fly River. Obtaining the loan of the same vessel he had used before, the Neva, but paying the expenses of this expedition out of his own pocket, he started on the third expedition to the Fly River in the beginning of May, 1877. The crew of ten persons consisted of the explorer and engineer, the only white members, and five Chinamen and three South-Sea Islanders. Along the lower course of the river the natives, who had attacked the preceding expeditions and had been given exhibitions of the powers of firearms, now kept away or came as friends; but in the upper part of the river, in a country which they had supposed to be totally uninhabited, they were fiercely assailed in the middle of an intensely dark night from the shore and in canoes. The assailants were on the point of boarding the steamer when D'Albertis awoke. He was obliged to fire upon the savages in order to save his life and that of his crew. Continuing to ascend the river, he spent two months in making collections, the few inhabitants whom they encountered fleeing at their approach. The insubordination of the crew now gave the explorer trouble, and finally obliged him to return. The Chinamen deserted, and the three South-Sea Islanders mutinied. Moreover, the drought had greatly reduced the volume of the river, and made it probably impossible to carry out his plans. After chasing the Chinamen down the river, he attempted to ascend again to the point where a bar of pebbles had stopped the passage, and there wait until the rains came. The natives attacked them, and he was reluctantly obliged to use guns to frighten them off. In a tropical thunderstorm the boat was driven upon a sand-bank and left high and dry by the receding tide, while the natives, summoned by horns and drums, assembled from far and near and were dancing their war-dances a few rods away. They did not attack, however, before the next tide carried the boat off. Two of his sailors deserted; and the remaining one and the engineer were both sick, and D'Albertis himself in a low condition, when they made the perilous return voyage across Torres Straits again to Thursday Island. The highest point reached in this third voyage up the Fly River was 475 miles from the mouth, or 45 to 50 miles this side of the farthest point touched in the preceding year's voyage. There are probably other large streams emptying into the delta of the Fly River. This part of New Guinea does not appear promising as a field for colonization, on account of the slight elevation of the vast plain of which it is made up, which is covered with interminable forests and grassy meadow-lands, and is to a large extent submerged during the wet season. Although very fertile, the lowlands at the mouth of the river would probably never do for the abode of white settlers. The depth and length of the Fly River adapt it admirably for navigation, and the mountainous regions toward its source, between 5° and 6° south latitude, are probably wholesome and are rich in many natural products; yet it is questionable whether, unless valuable minerals should be discovered there, it would prove a profitable field for either colonization or commerce. Its products, as far as is known, are vegetable substances, several of them quite valuable. There are numerous commercial woods; the nutmeg grows in abundance, and gums and resins of value are found in the woods. The fauna of New Guinea is yet far from being fully known. Large animals are of course absent.

D'Albertis recommends Yule Island and the neighboring coast as the most favorable spot to plant a colony—the island on account of the salubrity of the climate, its convenient situation, and its harbor; the adjacent mainland on account of its well-watered lands and its intelligent, well-conditioned, and industrious inhabitants. From a hill-top about 1,200 feet high, a level plain sprinkled with lagoons, through the middle of which courses the Amama or Hilda River, which flows from the north into the Nicura a short distance above its mouth, carpeted with succulent grasses, stretches out as far as the eye can reach. The Amama is deep enough for navigation, but is rendered impassable by innumerable snags. The rivers and lagoons abound in fish of many kinds, and some of them of large size. These form the principal nourishment of the inhabitants of the villages on their banks, who also pursue diligently the cultivation of bananas, yams, and taro (*Arum*). Breadfruit-trees are also abundant. The inhabitants of the village of Bioto, containing four or five hundred souls, were the finest-looking and strongest people that he saw in all New Guinea. They were very good-natured, and exceedingly garrulous, chattering the whole night through. A few miles away is another large village, containing forty or fifty houses bordering a long street, in the midst of extensive plantations of bananas. In the middle of the village are two roomy *mareas* facing each other. These are the reception-houses in which the hospitalities of the village are exercised, and belong to the four chiefs, who eat their meals therein. The village bachelors sleep in these large huts; and they also serve as places of reunion, where the talkative villagers gossip away many an hour. Their walls are hung with nets, weapons, and old shields. The toilet of the young men is a long process: their hair is carefully combed, their faces stained with black, red, or yellow colors, and their ornaments carefully arranged. The houses are built on the stumps of trees, with their floors about ten feet above the ground; their walls are of wood, and their roofs of the leaves of the *nipa* palm. They are lower in the rear than in front, and present the appearance of inverted boots cut in two. After dressing, the men spend the cool hours of the morning in twisting cords for their nets, and the women in cleaning the huts and cooking the early meal. Four meals a day are eaten. Their food consists of bananas, yams, taro, sago, and breadfruit, the flesh of the emu and the kangaroo, and fish; but, notwithstanding the abundance of these articles, they eat also snakes, frogs, fresh-water turtles, and the larvæ of different insects. They are very fond of a fresh-water mussel called *ebe*, whose shells furnish a variety of implements; with these they clear their path in the forest, cutting down a thick bamboo-stalk as quickly as with a hatchet; with them they clean the fiber of which they make the cords for their fish-nets; they use them for spoons; and with pieces of them they bore holes in wood, or with great dexterity draw out splinters and thorns. The lower jaw of the kangaroo is also a very useful tool, which is employed in carving and decorating the bones of the emu, of which they make combs, forks, etc. These people are exceedingly vain and fond of their ornaments of feathers, mussel-shells, and grasses, their necklaces and bracelets. .The chiefs wear breast-plates of mother-of-pearl mussel-shells. The beard- and body-hairs are plucked out by the roots, by twisting threads around each hair. They tattoo themselves with care; the chiefs and the women are tattooed all over. Their infants are carried in sacks of netting. They are fond of public discussions, and listen for hours to one of their village orators as he dilates upon the events of the day ; and when his harangue is finished another will rise and respond. They are always in the mood to talk, to laugh, or to dance. When they have had remarkably good luck in the chase, or have made an unusually large catch of fish, it is the custom to invite the people of a neighboring village to a feast, at which they appear in their finest ornaments, the feathers of the bird-of-paradise, necklaces of shells and mother-of-pearl, artificial flowers made of feathers and shell, and the highly treasured tail of the kingfisher. The sons of chiefs drill the boys in hurling the spear. In the same vicinity were three other villages which were almost cities in size. The street in Mou was covered with white sand. The huts and *mareas* were built with a variety of designs and ornamented with wood-carvings and paint: lizards, doves, and human figures with bird-claws were some of the decorative designs. D'Albertis supposes the inhabitants of Yule Island and the coasts to the east and westward, who belong to a race entirely distinct from the Papuans, have invaded the island and driven the latter back into the mountains. They are physically and morally superior to the Papuans of the western peninsula and the mixed races of the interior. Their hair is chestnut-brown, their eyes of a clear brown, and their skins of a chocolate color, which is deeper in the parts exposed to the sun. The height of the men is 5 feet 6 inches to 5 feet 9 inches; of the women, 5 feet 4 inches to 5 feet 6 inches. Their hair is curly, but never woolly like that of the Papuans. The lips are usually well formed; the chins and foreheads recede ; the limbs and body are muscular and symmetrical. The sexual differences are very salient. Each village has three or four chiefs, who exercise a sort of feudal lordship, and who differ from the rest in build and appearance. The temper of these people is kind and peaceable. They are not remarkably courageous. They are very sensitive and quick to take offense, but easily conciliated again. Quarrels between husbands and wives are frequent. In some of the villages the women have the upper hand. The men and women are both industrious, the latter doing the lighter kinds of work. They carry on commerce among each other to

some extent, holding markets for sale and barter at certain seasons. Theft is unknown. To what race these gentle and intelligent savages belong can not be determined with certainty. They have many of the characteristics of the Polynesians, and yet differ from them in important marks.

Raffray, the French naturalist who spent about a year on the northern peninsula of the island of New Guinea, describes the Papuans of the Arfak Mountains as of a very greedy and covetous disposition. He says that they are also cannibals. The same traveler visited the Molucca Islands, where he observed that the fauna differs on each of the islands, the birds and insects on Ternate, Tidor, and Gilolo belonging to completely distinct though allied species.

ARCTIC EXPLORATION.* — The geographical event of the year has been the successful termination of Professor Nordenskjöld's expedition in search of the northeast passage. We begin the narrative at the point where it was left in the " Annual Cyclopædia " for 1878. The Vega arrived September 27, 1878, near the promontory which bounds Koljutchen Bay on the east. During the day the ship passed through several patches of newly formed ice, but the temperature was very little below zero, while the weather was calm and fine. On the 28th the Vega proceeded under steam, intending to take advantage of a narrow open channel, which, on the previous day, had been observed to extend between the shore and the masses of drift-ice which were beginning already to press closely upon the promontory. When little more than a mile to the eastward the water became muddy, nor could deeper water be found among the drift-ice, which during the night had become firmly bound together by newly formed ice. All attempts at further progress were fruitless, until a southerly wind should disperse the ice which barred the way. The position of the Vega was by no means a safe one. She lay frozen in, but not anchored, in a roadstead quite exposed to the north, and only moored to a mass of ground-ice which had stranded in a depth of about thirty feet of water and about three quarters of a mile distant from land. This iceberg was the vessel's only protection against the enormous ice-pressure which winter storms produce in the polar seas. It was about three hundred feet long, eighty feet broad, and its highest point rose twenty feet above the level of the sea. During the fierce storms which assailed the vessel in the autumn and winter, the ship, the ground-ice, and the sheet of newly formed ice in which she was held fast, were all moved together considerably nearer the shore. The spot where the Vega was frozen in is situated in latitude 67° 7′ N., longitude 173° 30′ W. from Greenwich. The neighboring land was a wide, undulating plain, bounded

* The following section on Arctic explorations is from the pen of Captain H. W. Howgate, U. S. A.

on the south by hills which rise gradually in the distance, and attains farther inland a considerable elevation. At the time of the Vega's arrival the ground was frozen and covered with hoar frost, but still free from snow, so that the botanists of the expedition were able to obtain specimens of the flora of this hitherto unknown region. Nearest to the shore they found dense beds of *Elymus*, interspersed with patches of *Helianthus peploides*. A barren gravelly plain farther inland was covered in spots with a black lichen, *Gyrophora proboscida*, and a few flowering plants, among which *Armeria sibirica* was the most common. South of this was a tract covered with lagoons and small lakes, whose shores produced a luxuriant growth of varieties of grass and sage. On the neighboring high ground, where the soil, derived from weather-worn strata of gneiss and dolerite, is richer, the vegetation is more varied. Here were thickets of willows, extensive patches of *Empetoura nigrum* and *Andromeda tetragona*, and large tufts of a species of *Artemisia*. Here were found also the frozen remains of the red whortleberry, the cloudberry, *Taraxacum officinale*, and other plants peculiar to the far north. In the interior it was observed that on the driest portions of the land the most common plants were *Aira alpina* and *Poa alpina;* on the lower places, *Glyceria pedicularis* and *Ledum palustre*. *Petasites frigida* and a species of *Salix* occurred everywhere, the latter growing in large, compact masses, covering spots several hundred square feet in extent, the bushes in some places being three and four feet high.

At the time the ship was frozen in, the water nearest to the shore was covered with thin ice, which would not bear a man's weight; while to seaward the drift-ice was so firmly bound together by newly formed ice that the ship could make no impression upon it. On the 2d of October it was possible, with some precaution, to walk on the ice close to the ship, and on the 3d some of the native Tchuktches came on board on foot. On the 13th Dr. Almqvist started on foot over the ice in a northeasterly direction, following the track of some natives who had gone out walrus-hunting; but after a very laborious journey he was compelled to return without having reached open water. He ascertained that the Vega was hemmed in by a belt of drift-ice about eighteen miles wide, and all hope was abandoned of being released before the following summer. Upon the narrow belts of sand which separated the lagoons from the sea were two Tchuktches' settlements. The one situated nearest to the Vega's winter-quarters was called Pitlekaj, and numbered originally seven tents; but, in consequence of the scarcity of food, the inhabitants in the course of the winter moved to a district near Behring Strait, which offered a more abundant supply of fish. The other settlement, Jinretlen, lay nearer to the promontory. It also contained seven tents, but the inhabitants appeared to be better off than those of Pitlekaj. Four other encampments, named Fidlin, Koljutchin, Ryraitinop, and Irgunnuk, were situated at a greater distance toward the east, yet near enough to enable the inhabitants to make frequent visits to the ship. It was difficult to ascertain the number of persons belonging to each tent, as the Tchuktches were continually going from tent to tent, but the average number was about five or six. In all there were about two hundred natives in the vicinity of the Vega's winter-quarters. Their complete ignorance of the value of money, and the small store at the disposal of the expedition of articles suited to their wants, necessarily increased the price of the latter. To the great disappointment of the natives, the usual articles of commerce in the polar regions, skins and blubber, were not to be had on board the Vega. Partly by giving food in return for small services rendered on board, partly by distributing it as a gift, the Vega was the means of alleviating the famine which usually prevails during the winter. A complete collection of native weapons, garments, and household utensils was secured by the expedition. None of the natives in the vicinity of the vessel were Christians, nor did any of them speak any European language except an occasional English or Russian word. Lieutenant Nordqvist studied their language with so much zeal and success that after a few weeks he could make himself understood. He brings back to Europe a complete vocabulary of the language, and also an outline of its grammatical structure.

The temperature during the winter was recorded as follows, in degrees centigrade:

MONTHS.	Minimum.	Maximum.	Mean.
October.....................	−20·8°	+0·6°	− 5·21°
November...................	−27·2	−6·3	−16·59
December...................	−37·1	+1·2	−22·81
January....................	−45·5	−4·1	−25·05
February...................	−48·8	+0·2	−25·08
March.....................	−39·8	−4·2	−21·65
April.....................	−38·0	−4·6	−18·98
May......................	−26·8	+1·8	− 6·97
June.....................	−14·8	+6·8	− 0·80

The most remarkable observations which the wintering of the Vega has yielded appear to relate to the aurora. During the winter of 1878-'79 it never appeared with the splendid bands or draperies of rays so common in Scandinavia, but always in the form of faint luminous arches, which remained unaltered in position hour after hour and day after day. They were constantly visible when the sky was not clouded nor their feeble light dimmed by the rays of the sun or the full moon. The tidal observations, when compared with other series made in the Arctic seas, give important indications regarding the distribution of land and sea in the polar basin. The greatest range at the Vega's winter-quarters was only eighteen centimetres, which shows that the sea north of Behring Strait forms a marine basin of limited extent, connected with the ocean only by sounds. The variations in the height of the water produced by winds were much greater, amounting nearly to two metres. Still greater irregular changes in the position of land and sea appear to have occurred within the memory of man; for the Tchuktches were at one time afraid that the Swedes would cause inundations along the coast. This appears to show that the sudden changes in the position of the earth, which are well known in the volcanic regions farther south, had extended so far north. As most of the Tchuktches' villages are situated close to the sea, one of the mighty waves which earthquakes give rise to would completely destroy an immense number of them. The magnetical observations made during the winter, in an observatory built of ice and snow, which, being necessarily on land, was at a very inconvenient distance trom the vessel, consisted of (1) absolute determinations whenever opportunity offered; (2) observations of the changes in the strength and direction of the magnetic forces, made along with necessary absolute determinations every hour between November 27th and April 1st; (3) five-minute observations on the 1st and 15th of every month, from and including January 15th.

The natural history of the region in which the Vega wintered is very poor in the higher plants and fungi, but lichens are abundant. The number of insects and other invertebrate land animals was very small. Land and freshwater mollusca were completely wanting. Of coleoptera only twenty species were found, belonging principally to the families *Carabi* and *Staphylini*, with two *Curculiones* and *Chrysomelæ;* and the other orders appeared to be equally poor, with the exception perhaps of the *Diptera* and *Podurida*. On the other hand, the sea-bottom, though covered with a stratum of water always about 2° C. below the freezing-point, swarmed with a large number and a great variety of the lower animal types, of which the dredging-boat almost daily made a rich collection in the channel which opened early in summer in the neighborhood of the vessel. Birds here occur in much smaller number but in a much greater abundance of types than in Nova Zembla, Spitzbergen, and Greenland; and the bird-world in its entirety has thus quite a different stamp. The birds common on Greenland, Spitzbergen, Nova Zembla, and the coast of Northwest Siberia— *Larus glaucus, eburneus,* and *tridactylus, Harelda glacialis, Somateria spectabilis, Plectrophanes nivalis, Phalaropus fulicarius,* and *Tringa maritima,* the common raven and several other species—are found here. But in addition to these the following uncommon birds are met with: The American eider (the common eider, *Somateria mollissima,* being absent); a grayish-brown goose with bushy yellowish-white feathers round the neck; a swan-like goose, white with black wing-feathers; a species of *Fuligula,* marked in white

and green, with a fine black-velvet head; the beautifully marked, uncommon *Larus Rossi;* a little brown snipe with a bill widened spoonlike at the point; several beautiful singers, among them *Sylvia Evermanni,* which for somo days visited the coast in great flocks, probably on their way to breeding-places farther north, or waiting till the bushes in the interior should be free of snow. A portion of the purely Scandinavian species here exhibit some variations in color-marking and size. The most common mammal is the bare. It differs from the common Scandinavian mountain hare by its greater size (its weight often rising to fourteen pounds), and by the nasal bone not diminishing so rapidly in size. The mountain fox (*Vulpes lagopus,* L.) is very common. The common fox (*Vulpes vulgaris,* Gray) appears also to be common. A red fox, shot in October, differs considerably from the common, and approaches the mountain fox in several particulars. The fox's food during winter appears to consist of hares, ptarmigans, and lemmings. Of lemmings three species were met with, *Myodes obensis* (the most numerous), *M. torquatus,* and *Arvicola obscurus.* The Tchuktches state that a little mouse also occurs, which Nordqvist supposes to be a *Sorex.* The two lemmings often showed themselves above the snow during winter, which was not the case with *Arvicola obscurus.* The wolf was seen only twice. The wild reindeer was also uncommon, traces of it having been seen only once. Traces of the land-bear were also seen, and the natives stated that it was not uncommon in summer. The marmot (*Arctomys*) occurs in abundance. An animal described by the natives as living by the banks of streams is supposed to be the common otter. Two weasel-skins were obtained from the natives. It is not certain whether the ermine occurs there. Only two marine mammals were seen during the winter, the polar bear and the ringed seal (*Phoca fætida*). The latter is caught in great numbers, and, along with fish and various vegetables, forms the main food of the natives. Of land-birds, there winter in this region only three species, viz., *Strix myctea, Corvus corax,* and *Lagopus subalpina.* The last mentioned is the most common. On December 14th two large flocks of ptarmigan, one numbering about fifty, were seen about ten miles from the coast. The raven is common at the Tchuktches' villages. Its first egg was obtained on May 31st. The mountain owl was seen for the first time on March 11th, but the natives say that it is to be met with all winter. In open places on the sea there occur during winter, according to the natives, two swimmers, *Uria Brünnichi* and *Uria grylle.* Besides these, there possibly winter on the sea a species of *Mergulus* and one of *Fuligula,* a specimen of the former having been obtained on November 3d and of the latter on March 9th. During the wintering of the Vega large quantities of the bones of the whale were found on the beach. These at first were supposed to be the remains of whales that had been killed by the natives or by American whalers, but on examination it was found that they must be sub-fossil. This was confirmed by the natives, who stated that no whale had driven on land in the memory of man. The remains were found to belong to four or five different species, of which *Balæna mysticetus*, or a nearly allied type, was the most common.

Along the coast, from the White Sea to Behring Strait, no glacier was seen. During autumn the Siberian coast is nearly free of ice and snow. With one exception there were no rocks along the coast precipitous enough to be suitable breeding-places for sea-fowl, but a large number of these birds were seen during spring flying farther to the north. A warm current, as in Europe, was found to flow along the northwestern coast, and to create there a far milder climate than that which prevails on the Asiatic side. The limit of trees, therefore, lies a good way to the north of Behring Strait, while the whole of the Tchuktch Peninsula appears to be devoid of trees.

For the use of future Arctic expeditions Professor Nordenskjöld gives the following description of those parts of their winter equipment which were found to be most serviceable: According to the meteorological observations, the winter was not particularly cold when compared with the winters experienced in the Franklin Archipelago and in the coldest regions of Siberia. On the other hand, the Vega's winter station proved unusually stormy, and day after day and night after night the officers had to walk in a heavy gale of wind to the observatory, nearly a mile distant from the ship, and with the thermometer ranging from −30° to −46° C. In calm weather a temperature of from −40° to −50° was not felt so severely, but even with a slight breeze a temperature of −35° and over became quite dangerous to those who tried to walk against it, or incautiously exposed parts of their faces, hands, or wrists. Without giving warning by any violent pain, frost-bites occurred, which, if not thawed in time by rubbing the injured part with the hands or with melted snow, soon become serious. Most of those who were wintering in the Arctic regions for the first time were more or less frost-bitten as soon as the cold set in; and in several cases large blisters, an inch in diameter, made their appearance, but happily no serious calamity occurred. Nor was there a single accident of frost-bitten feet, owing to the excellent foot-covering used by the expedition, which consisted of large canvas slippers with soles of leather lined with a layer of prepared sedge (*Carex vesicaria*). Each foot was incased in one or two pair of stockings and a covering of felt. This arrangement was a compromise between the foot-covering introduced by Parry for Arctic traveling and the boots filled with hay used by the Laplanders.

All who used it were of the opinion that it left nothing to be desired. On long journeys in the wet snow this foot-covering is preferable to leather, which becomes heavy and soaked, and hardly dries in the open air during the night, while canvas shoes filled with hay dry readily. Even when wet they are light and healthy on account of the air which circulates through the hay. For protecting the hands, gloves were used made of sealskin and chamois, lined inside with sheepskin and with a border of long-haired fur round the wrist. They were generally suspended by a string round the neck, as children are made to carry their gloves. Besides these, for out-of-door work, thin woolen gloves were always worn. The rest of the costume consisted of the ordinary Swedish winter clothing, perhaps a little heavier and warmer than usual. Reindeer coats and reindeer leggings were provided for every man, besides a variety of furs; but they were seldom used, even when the thermometer stood at 45° C., the men preferring a loose canvas suit worn over the ordinary sailor's dress, which afforded a welcome protection against snow and wind. The head was similarly sheltered by a hood worn over the Helsingör cap, a supply of which had been procured from St. Petersburg.

Observations on the weather were taken until the 1st of November every fourth hour; from that date until the 1st of April, every hour; and afterward again, six times a day. Between the 27th of November and the 1st of April the instruments were placed on the land at the magnetic observatory; before and after that time, on board the Vega or in the immediate neighborhood of the ship. During the winter the superintendence was intrusted to Dr. Stuxberg, who, when everything around was covered with ice, had to abandon his own zoölogical researches. The meteorological observations made in the Vega's winter-quarters form the first complete contribution to our knowledge of the climatic conditions which prevail in the peninsula that separates the Frozen Sea of Siberia from the Pacific Ocean; and the information obtained regarding the monsoon-like northwest winds which steadily blow in this part of the world during the winter is of importance, not only as regards the climatology of Siberia in general, but also in connection with the study of the typhoons and monsoons encountered on the coasts of China and Japan. The greatest cold during the several months was observed on the following days: October 24th, −20·8° C.; November 30th, −27·2°; December 23d, −37·1°; January 25th, −45·7°; February 2d, −43·8°; March, 29th, −39.8°. Twice the barometer rose to an unusual height, viz.: December 22d, at 6 A. M., 30·78 in.; February 17th, at 6 A. M., 31·03 in. The lowest barometer up to April 1st was observed December 31st, at 2 A. M., 28·69 in. The weather during the winter was in general very stormy, and the direction of the wind nearest to the earth's surface almost constantly between N. W. and N. N. W. Judging from the direction of the clouds, a similar uninterrupted current, but from S. E., prevailed in the upper strata of the atmosphere, which, when it descended now and then to the surface of the earth, brought with it a warm and comparatively dry air. While the temperature was falling to —40° C., both the mercury and the spirit thermometers were read off, but below —40° C. only the latter was used. None of the mercury thermometers used by the expedition suffered any injury from the alternate freezing and thawing of the mercury. The latter when freezing always contracted into the bulb, although —40° C. on the scale was marked a good way up the tube. It is therefore probable that mercury, like water, requires a greater degree of cold in order to freeze when it is inclosed in a fine tube.

With regard to the possibility of establishing regular navigation in the Polar Sea of Siberia, Professor Nordenskjöld has come to the following conclusions: 1. The voyage from the Atlantic to the Pacific Ocean, along the north coast of Siberia, can be accomplished in a few weeks by a suitable steamer manned by experienced sailors ; but, so far as the conditions of the Siberian Sea are known at present, this route is not likely to be of any practical importance to commerce. 2. It may now be asserted that there is no difficulty in establishing communication by sea between the Obi-Yenisei and Europe for purposes of trade. 3. In all probability the voyage by sea between the Yenisei and the Lena, and between the Lena and Europe, may be utilized for trading purposes; but the journey there and back, between the Lena and Europe, can not be made in the same summer. 4. Further explorations are necessary to decide whether a practicable communication by sea between the mouth of the Lena and the Pacific Ocean can be established. The experience gained up to the present time shows that at all events machinery, heavy tools, and other goods which can not be easily conveyed by sledge or on wheels across Siberia, may be sent round by this new sea-route, from the Pacific Ocean to the estuary of the Lena.

On the morning of July 18, 1879, after having been imprisoned in the ice for 294 days, the Vega weighed anchor, or, more correctly, cast off from the large piece of ground-ice to which she had been moored during the winter, and which had sheltered her from the most violent storms and ice-pressure. Having first steamed a few miles to the northwest in order to clear the ice-fields, she steered her course along the coast toward the most eastern promontory of Asia, the East Cape. Her progress was impeded not so much by the ice as by the misty weather. Now and then the fog lifted, and revealed the same castellated cliff formation which had been already observed in several places on the north coast of Eastern Siberia. As regards beauty of scenery, the north

coast of Siberia is much inferior to Spitzbergen, with its deep fiords surrounded by steep, black, and boldly shaped mountains, and its dazzling white or azure-blue glaciers. Nor has the north coast of Asia been at any time cut up by glaciers into fiords and cliffs like Greenland, Spitzbergen, and Norway. Along the whole of the enormous distance between the White Sea and Behring Strait there is not to be found at present a single glacier reaching down to the sea, and in autumn the north coast of Siberia is almost free from ice and snow. Only in the high mountains on the east side of the Taimyr Peninsula, and between Behring Strait and Cape Jakan, are there some valleys filled with snow during the late autumn ; but it is doubtful whether any of them form the bed of a real glacier, which in any case would be of small extent and terminate at a considerable height above the level of the sea. Nor does one see any snowy summits or mountains covered with snow all the year round, although some of the mountains—for example, those on the western side of Koljutchin Bay—attain a height of 2,000 feet and more. If we may apply the conception of a snow-line derived from the study of mountains in more southerly regions to countries situated in the far north, an assumption which can not be quite taken for granted, the snow-line of the north coast of Asia must lie at a height of over 1,500 feet.

On July 20th, at 11 A. M., the entrance of the Vega into Behring Strait was celebrated by the hoisting of flags and a Swedish salute. From the East Cape her course was shaped toward St. Lawrence Bay, a large fiord which at a distance of about forty miles to the southward of the cape penetrates the Tchuktch Peninsula. Some days after the ship anchored in Konyam Bay, in latitude 64° 49' N., longitude 172° 58' W. Here reindeer-owning Tchuktches were met with. It was Professor Nordenskjöld's intention to penetrate as far as possible into St. Lawrence Bay, in order to give the naturalists an opportunity of completing the study of the physical conditions of the Tchuktch Peninsula, which they had carried on during the autumn of 1878 and the spring of 1879; but the entrance to the bay was found so full of ice that the Vega was obliged to anchor off the settlement of Nunamo, situated immediately north of the mouth of the fiord. Extensive, though quite thin and rotten, ice-fields drifted past the ship in such quantities that it was not deemed advisable to remain in this place longer than necessary, and the Vega only stopped here until the afternoon of July 21st. The encampment of Nunamo is not situated, like other Tchuktch settlements, low down on the beach, but rather high up on a promontory between the sea and a river which empties here, and seems to be full in the season when the snows melt. Immediately above the strand-terrace rises a high mountain, the slopes of which are occupied by immense bowlders, the abode of numerous marmots, and of *Lagomys alpinus*, a species of gnawing animal the size of a large rat, and remarkable for the care with which during the summer it gathers provisions for the winter. The mountain is separated from the sea by a narrow terrace, from fifty to one hundred feet high, on which stood a few tents, and which, as it happened, was adorned with an extraordinary display of flowers. In a very short time and within the space of a few acres Dr. Kjellman here collected a hundred different species of flowers, many of which he had not previously found on the Tchuktch Peninsula. On the sides of the mountains there were still some patches of snow-drift, and from the summits one could see large masses of ice continually drifting backward and forward on the Asiatic side of Behring Strait. Dr. Stuxberg made the ascent of one of the neighboring mountains. On the way he came across the dead body of a native laid out upon a stone grave of the usual Tchuktch form. By the side of the dead lay a broken gun, a spear, arrows, a tinder-box, pipe, snow-screen, *issil* (a tool used for removing the ice-rubbish when cutting an ice-hole), and sundry other things considered necessary for the departed in a better world. The body had been lying here since the previous summer.

From Nunamo the course of the Vega was shaped for Port Clarence, on the American side of Behring Strait, where the ship anchored in the afternoon of July 22d, after a passage across a sea covered with drift-ice on the Asiatic side and quite free from ice on the American side. Port Clarence is a very large but excellent harbor, situated immediately to the southeast of Cape Prince of Wales. It was the first real harbor in which the Vega had anchored since she left Actinia Harbor on Taimyr Island, August 18, 1878. On the 26th the Vega steamed out of Port Clarence, and, favored by good weather, proceeded to recross Behring Strait, her next destination being Senjavine Strait, situated about 115 nautical miles to the southwest of East Cape. During the passage across, soundings were taken, also samples of water for analysis, as well as the temperature at various depths. The dredge or trawl was lowered frequently, with the most satisfactory results. In the course of the 28th the Vega stopped, not, as had been at first intended, in Glasenapp Harbor, which was filled with unbroken ice, but at the entrance of the most northerly fiord, Konyam Bay. The inner part of this bay was also covered with ice, the breaking up of which on the 30th nearly brought the Vega's voyage to an abrupt conclusion by pressing her against the land. Happily the movement was seen in time, and the ship removed to a part of the fiord free from ice. The southeastern shore of Konyam Bay, near which the Vega was anchored for a few days, was a waste bog, the breeding-place of numerous cranes. Farther inland, the low-lying hills were composed of granite, and above them rose several mountain-summits of trachyte for-

mation, about 2,000 feet high. The zoölogists and botanists, finding the harvest on the neighboring strand but scanty, proceeded in the steam-pinnace to the north side of the bay, where they discovered grassy slopes decked with tall shrubs and a great variety of flowers; and Dr. Kjellman increased his collection of the larger plants of northern Asia by more than seventy species. Here also the first land mollusca on the Tchuktch Peninsula were met with. Three reindeer Tchuktch families had set up their summer tents at the outlet of a deep brook on the northwestern shore of Konyam Bay. Their manner of life differed but little from that of the coast Tchuktches near the Vega's winter-station, and their dress was also the same, with the exception of small bells which they wore on their belts. On July 31st the expedition anchored off the northeastern shore of St. Lawrence Island, called by the Tchuktches *Engna.* At some distance from Senjavine Strait the last drift-ice was seen. The island seemed to offer no good harbor; so, after devoting a few days to an exploration which yielded an abundance of zoölogical and botanical specimens, the Vega continued her journey on the 2d of August, and on the 14th dropped anchor in an indifferently sheltered harbor on the northwest coast of Behring Island. Here again the naturalists succeeded in gathering a rich harvest of interesting specimens, among others a large collection of the bones of the supposed extinct sea-cow (*Rhytina Stelleri*). The Vega left Behring Island in the evening of August 19th. During the early part of her cruise toward Japan, and while the ship was sailing with the cold current which flows from the north, the wind was favorable, the weather mild, and the temperature of the sea-surface between 9° and 11° C. But on the 25th, when in latitude 45° 45' N. and longitude 156° E., the temperature of the water began to rise rapidly; and on the 28th, in latitude 40° N., longitude 147° 41' E., the thermometer recorded a surface temperature of 23·4° C. This showed that the Vega had left the Arctic current which had hitherto aided her progress, and had entered what has been called the Gulf Stream of the Pacific Ocean, known as the Kuro-Siwo. The winds now became less favorable, the weather oppressively hot in spite of violent squalls accompanied by thunder and showers of rain, and on the 31st the mainmast of the Vega was struck by lightning. In the evening of September 2d the Vega anchored in the roadstead of Yokohama, and on the 15th the three learned societies of Japan, viz., the Tokio Geographical Society, the Asiatic Society of Japan, and the German Asiatic Society, received Professor Nordenskjöld and his companions at a great banquet given in Tokio, in the large hall of the Koku Dai Gaku, and presided over by H. I. H. Prince Kita-Shirakawa-No-Miya.

The Dutch Arctic Expedition, consisting of the schooner William Barents, commanded by

Captain De Bruyne, sailed from Amsterdam June 3, 1879, on her second attempt to reach Franz-Josef Land. The crew numbered nine men. H. M. Speelman had charge of the magnetic observations. Mr. W. G. A. Grant again accompanied the party as photographer, and Mr. L. De Jeude, student at Utrecht, as zoölogist. Captain De Bruyne was assisted by two officers, Mr. Broeklurjen, Lieutenant first class, and Mr. Kalmeyer, Lieutenant second class. The cruise was successful, as on the 7th of September Mount Brunn on McClintock Island (a part of Franz-Josef Land) was sighted; the first time that the newly discovered continent had been seen from a sailing vessel. The Barents began her return voyage on the same date, and reached Hammerfest on September 18th. A number of scientific observations were made during the cruise.

Captain A. H. Markham, R. N., and Sir Henry Gore Booth made a pleasure excursion to the Barents Sea in the Isbjorn, a sailing vessel of about 43 tons burden. They left Tromsö on the 18th of May, and, passing through the fiords to the southward of North Cape, made the first ice on June 4th, forty miles from the "Goose Coast" of Nova Zembla. The Matoshkin Shar was found to be impassable on the 26th, so they shaped a course northward along the west coast of Nova Zembla until they were stopped by the ice off Cape Nassau. On July 31st they passed through the Matoshkin Shar, but found the Kara Sea full of heavy floes, and therefore returned by the same strait. On August 18th they met the Dutch expeditionary vessel William Barents. The Isbjorn was then steered northward along the west coast once more, and this time succeeded in rounding Cape Nassau, and reaching as far as Cape Mauritius, the extreme northeastern point of Nova Zembla. Finally pushing due northward between Spitzbergen and Nova Zembla, on the meridian of 47°, they met the ice in latitude 78° N., and succeeded in penetrating through loose streams of it as far north as 78° 24', thus reaching within eighty miles of Franz-Josef Land. Returning, they arrived at Tromsö on September 22d. The explorers made a good natural history collection, and did some useful geographical work by adding to our knowledge of the drift and nature of the ice along this important route to the pole.

The steamer Jeannette, fitted out through the liberality of Mr. James Gordon Bennett, sailed from San Francisco on July 8, 1879, via Behring Strait, for the purpose of exploration and discovery. She measures 420 tons, carries thirty-two men, and is provisioned for three years. The officers of the expedition are: Lieutenant George W. De Long, U. S. N., commander; Lieutenant Chipp, U. S. N., executive officer; Lieutenant Danenhower, U. S. N., navigating and ordnance officer; Dr. Ambler, surgeon; chief engineer, Melville; ice-pilot, Dunbar; Mr. Newcomb, collector of specimens of natural history, etc.; and Mr.

Collins, meteorologist and scientific observer, also "Herald" correspondent. The Jeannette reached Oonalaska August 2d, and was last seen in the neighborhood of Herald Island on September 3d. It was expected that she would winter at some harbor on the coast of Wrangell Land.

The Franklin Search Expedition, which sailed from New York on the 19th of June, 1878, went into winter-quarters on the 9th of August of the same year, on the northern shore of Hudson's Bay, in about latitude 64° N. and longitude 90° W. Reports from Lieutenant Schwatka indicate that the information in reference to the missing relics of Sir John Franklin, which formed the basis of the expedition, was untrustworthy. It is probable that the expedition will return to the United States during the year 1880.

GEOLOGY, EXPERIMENTAL. In the article on the FORMATION OF MOUNTAINS an example has been given of the occasional value of experimentation in seeking an understanding of the processes of nature in the geological evolution. Although most of the conditions under which the geological processes have taken place can not be reproduced in the laboratory, yet in individual cases new light can be thrown on geological problems by chemical and physical experiments. When Sir James Hall was able to obtain in his crucible a stony mass, instead of the vitreous substance which had been predicted, from the chemical constituents of basalt, he established Hutton's proposition that the basalts were of volcanic origin. Bischoff in Germany and Sénarmont in France have studied experimentally some of the chemical processes through which the mineral masses of the earth have been formed with considerable success. One of the most enthusiastic students in this field is M. Daubrée, Director of the French School of Mines, who has been engaged for over thirty years in investigating geological phenomena by the application of the experimental method, and has just published a volume containing the results of his work.

One of the most valuable successes obtained by Daubrée was the artificial production of quartz crystals. Like most of his chemical experiments, this one was conducted by subjecting the substance operated upon to extraordinary pressure. This is necessary in order to fulfill the conditions of the chemical changes which take place far down under the earth's surface, under an enormous weight of superincumbent rocks. The operation is, however, attended with much danger, and only after many failures from the rupture of materials of insufficient resistance can a successful result be reached. Heating water in closed glass vessels to a temperature at which the steam would often rend the strongest vessels apart like tinder, he observed the action of the superheated water on those which were able to withstand the pressure for several days. The glass on the inside of the tubes was found to be partly converted into hydrated silicates of the type called zeolites, minerals which occur in the cavities of volcanic rocks and sometimes in mineral veins. Another product found in the walls of the glass was the common constituent of rock formations, the anhydrous silicate which is called augite. But the most interesting result was the occasional production of silica in a crystalline form, with all the characteristics of quartz. The quartz usually obtained in the laboratory is a pasty substance which dries up into an amorphous powder. The silica obtained by Daubrée was perfectly crystallized, and corresponded in every respect to quartz crystals, except that, owing to the short duration of the experiment, the crystals were extremely minute in size.

The pressure and the heat under which many of the geological changes of the earth have occurred can not be repeated artificially in physico-chemical experiments. Another condition which the experimentalist is still less able to compass is the secular duration of the chemical processes of nature: if all the natural conditions could be artificially produced, the mineral transformations could not be observed, as in most instances the chemical action must be prolonged far beyond the life of man. Fortunately, however, this important element has been supplied in certain instances, and we are able to read the results of experiments which, none the less fruitful because accidentally begun, have extended over definite periods of many centuries. Most valuable opportunities for watching mineral changes are offered by the thermal springs used by the Romans, in which various mineral substances have been left exposed to the action of the heated water for sixteen or eighteen centuries. The chemical decompositions and combinations which have resulted afford an invaluable experimental illustration and revelation of the process by which mineral lodes or veins are formed. The richest discoveries of this nature were made in the excavations of the hot springs at Bourbonne-les-Baius, in the department of Haute-Marne in France. In the deposits at the bottom of the old Roman baths nearly five thousand Roman coins, most of them of bronze, but three or four of gold, and a considerable number of silver, were unearthed, and also pins and rings, statuettes, and other objects in bronze, gold, lead, and iron. Underneath the mud containing these metallic relics was a layer of conglomerate formed of sand and fragments of sandstone cemented together by mineral substances which had been produced by the solvent action of the water, heated to a constant temperature of from 58° to 68° C., on the metallic objects during the sixteen centuries that they had been exposed in the spring. These products were identical with the minerals which occur in veins, and in numerous cases they had taken on perfect crystalline forms indistinguishable from those of like substances occurring in natural veins. A great

variety of these products were detected in the agglutinated mass. One of the most common was cuprite, or red oxide of copper, occurring in octahedral crystals, which was one of the products of the bronze. Chalcosite, or sulphide of copper, in well-formed crystals, was also found. The yellow copper ore (copper pyrites, the ordinary ore of the copper-mines), the purple copper ore, in which the crystallization is more perfect, and the gray copper ore, a rare mineral which occurs in beautiful tetrahedric crystals, and is thence called tetrabedrite, were all three present. The leaden pipes of the ancient springs yielded a similar list of products, including the ordinary minerals contained in lead-veins, and also some rare varieties of minerals, among which may be mentioned phosgenite. From the decomposition of the iron resulted pyrites and other ferruginous substances. Even the bricks and concrete of the masonry were wrought upon by the action of the hot water continued through so long a period, and yielded various silicates which are identical with native minerals.

An important but thus far unsolvable problem in geology is that of the formation of the vast quantities of limestone rock in which there is no trace of organic structure, but which are made up of fine granular particles of carbonate of lime. They may be formed of the decomposed substance of shells, but in the absence of structural remains the supposition is equally warrantable that they are merely chemical deposits of grains of carbonate similar to the concretions formed in hot calcareous springs, which are called in Germany *Sprudelstein*, and to the species of limestone rock called oölite. If the rock were formed simply by the precipitation of granular particles of carbonate of lime, the question would remain whether or not the material was derived from the decomposition of older rocks which had been built up of organic remains. The researches of the English geologist Sorby into the nature of limestone rocks belong to the department of experimental geology. It is possible to distinguish by their different density and hardness, and by their different optical properties—one being optically biaxial, or having two directions in which double refraction does not take place, and the other transmitting the ray undivided in one direction only — between the two forms of the dimorphous crystallization of carbonate of lime, even when the external form is hidden. Sorby shows that it is an important consideration regarding the preservation of shells in a fossil form, whether they are composed of carbonate of lime crystallized in the dimorphic form of calcite or in that of aragonite. The latter is an unstable form, whose particles are easily disturbed, and under the action of heat tend to recrystallize in the form of calcite. In a rock composed of shells whose composition was of aragonite the traces of organic forms would entirely disappear. The true corals seem to be principally aragonite. The greater number of the shells of gasteropods are composed of the same ; while the shells of brachiopods are invariably built from calcite. Some shells show no trace originally of organic structure. Such is the case of the tube of the teredos. In all shells composed of aragonite the organic forms would become effaced. The absence of corals or other such shells in limestone formations is therefore no evidence that such organisms did not enter into the original composition of the rock. The preservation of calcite remains, such as the shells of sea-urchins, and the rarity or entire absence of corals and other fossils of aragonite composition, do not prove that the latter did not exist in large numbers, since, their substance being in a state of unstable chemical equilibrium, the latter would have fewer chances to be preserved.

The metal *lithium* was supposed until quite recently to be one of the rarest of all minerals. By the aid of the spectroscope chemists have recently established its presence in a considerable variety of mineral compounds—in feldspars and micas, in the ashes of tobacco and a number of other plants, and quite abundantly in many mineral springs. Dieulafait, a French geologist, has added to the list of substances unexpectedly containing lithium. He finds it in all the primordial rocks, and also in the waters of the ocean and inland seas. It was before detected in sea-water by Bunsen ; but Dieulafait finds it so diffused as to show its presence in a cubic centimetre of water from the Mediterranean, and in the waters of the Atlantic and the Indian Oceans, the Red Sea, the China Sea, and the Arctic and Antarctic Oceans. In certain mineral springs he detects it in a single drop of the water. He concludes that the salt lithia is no less frequent in mineral waters, and in the mineral kingdom generally, than potash, soda, and the other kindred alkalies, though present in smaller quantities.

On the great and mysterious question of the condition of the interior of the earth, the experimental method has been appealed to, and the latest theories are chiefly based upon actual observations of the behavior of substances analogous to the mineral constituents of the earth during solidification. The theory that the central nucleus is a solid and not a molten mass is founded on the experiments of Bunsen, Hopkins, and others, which seemed to prove that silicious substances contracted during solidification. From this fact the deduction would be evident that pressure would counteract the effect of heat to keep them in a liquid state, that their melting-point would be raised by pressure, and that they would be solid under pressure at temperatures where they would fuse when allowed to expand. The question as to the liquid or solid state of the central portions of the globe would then depend on the extent of the contraction of the materials at solidification and the relative degrees of heat and pressure to which they are subjected. Without such con-

traction the solidification of the earth would commence at the surface, the masses which first hardened and sank into the liquid mass fusing again as they descended, until the whole became sufficiently viscous to prevent the solidified portions from sinking; then a solid crust would form over the whole surface, which would become thicker and thicker as the cooling process went on, until the globe parted with all its internal heat, and became entirely refrigerated. But if the melting-point of the materials were elevated under pressure to such a degree that solid portions sinking into the liquid mass would not fuse, the conclusion would be that at the center, where the pressure was greatest, the process of solidification commenced, and extended gradually outward, another solidification taking place at the surface at the same time, perhaps.

The calculations of Sir William Thomson on this subject were based on experiments of Bischoff, which went to show that solid rocks are twenty per cent. denser than the same materials in a molten state. Yet Mallet found that the blast-furnace slags contract only six per cent. Mr. Siemens has recently published a series of experiments made by his brother, which reconcile the discrepancies between these different results, and which, with his arguments based on the phenomena of volcanic eruptions, furnish a strong body of proof in favor of the old doctrine that the interior of the globe is filled with a semi-fluid mass of molten rock. Friedrich Siemens found that when glass fused to a thin liquid was allowed to cool, the contraction was marked and rapid until it approached a plastic, viscous consistence ; but that after that the contraction was slight in amount, and became less and less ; and that at the point of solidification a slight reëxpansion seemed to take place. Mr. Siemens insists on the impossibility, on Sir William Thomson's hypothesis of a solid nucleus, of accounting for the sedimentary strata, many thousand feet in thickness at the earth's surface. The theory of a solid globe fails also to account for the eruptions of volcanoes, since the assumption of pockets of liquefied lava existing at different depths below the surface does not explain the overflow of lava at the surface. Siemens assumes that the hydrous and alkaline lavas which are discharged from volcanoes are less dense than the silicates with which they are associated in the interior of the earth, and than the solid materials of the earth's crust; and that they are forced into the cavities and narrow fissures of the crust by hydrostatic pressure, and, when the channel communicates with the surface, are forced out with a pressure which is increased by the inclosed vapor and gases, unless the height of the column is so great that hydrostatic equilibrium is attained before the lava reaches the surface. In harmony with many other recent thinkers, Siemens supposes the ocean-beds and lower portions of the earth's surface to be composed of a crust of denser materials than the elevated continental areas. The difference in elevation between the Central Asian plateau and the bottom of the Pacific Ocean amounts to 12,000 metres, representing a difference of pressure on the viscous magma of about 1,000 atmospheres, which could not be maintained unless there are adhering to the crust partially solidified masses of sufficient thickness and density to compensate for the difference. The theory of Siemens of a difference in the specific gravity of the rocks which form the continental elevations and those in the depressed portions of the surface of the globe is borne out by some observations made during the measurement of the great arc of a meridian in the Indian Trigonometric Survey. The deviation of the plumb-line in the neighborhood of the Himalayas was found to be greatly less than the computations of Archdeacon Pratt, showing that the density of the rocky mass of the mountains was inferior to that of the plains. It has been ascertained also in geodetical surveys that gravity at the coast is generally greater than at the corresponding stations in the interior of continents. The general tendency among men of science in England, as well as on the Continent, is to return to the old doctrine that the' earth consists of a spheroid of molten, viscous matter, supporting a thin solid crust.

GEORGIA. The recess of the Legislature of this State, which commenced on December 14, 1878, came to an end on July 1, 1879, when that body resumed its labors. The session was then continued until the final adjournment on October 15th. More than 1,000 bills were introduced and read the first time. Of these nearly 600 were discussed. Of those discussed, 320 were passed. Of those passed, the whole 320 received the Governor's signature and thus became laws. Of these there are over 40 that change sections of the Code, and over 100 that are public bills, or bills of general application.

The largest bill that passed was the military bill, and the most important was the railroad bill. The title of this measure, which expresses its object very fully, is " An act to provide for the regulation of railroad freight and passenger tariffs in this State; to prevent unjust discrimination and extortion in the rates charged for transportation of passengers and freight; and to prohibit railroad companies, corporations, and lessees in this State from charging other than just and reasonable rates, and to punish the same, and prescribe a mode of procedure and rules of evidence in relation thereto; and to appoint commissioners, and to prescribe their powers and duties in relation to the same." The State Constitution makes it the duty of the Legislature " to pass laws from time to time to regulate freight and passenger tariffs, to prohibit unjust discriminations on the various railroads of this State, and to prohibit railroads from charging other than just and reasonable rates, and enforce the same by adequate penalties." The act provides for the

appointment of three Commissioners, one of experience in the law and one of experience in railway business, whose terms will ultimately continue six years. Neither of them shall have any interest in any way in any railroad, and shall so continue during the term of office. Any railroad company doing business in the State that shall charge, collect, demand, or receive more than a fair and reasonable rate of toll or compensation for transportation of passengers or freight of any description, or for the use and transportation of any railroad-car upon its track, or any of the branches thereof, or upon any railroad within this State which it has the right, license, or permission to use, operate, or control, the same shall be guilty of extortion, and upon conviction thereof shall be dealt with as hereafter stated. If any railroad corporation shall make any unjust discrimination in its rates or charges of toll or compensation for the transportation of passengers or freights of any description, or for the use and transportation of any railroad-car upon its said road, or upon any of the branches thereof, or upon any railroads connected therewith, which it has the right, license, or permission to operate, control, or use, within the State, the same shall be deemed guilty of having violated the provisions of the act, and upon conviction thereof shall be dealt with as hereafter stated. The fifth section requires that the Commissioners shall make reasonable and just rates of freight and passenger tariffs, to be observed by all railroad companies doing business in the State on the railroads thereof; shall make reasonable and just rules and regulations, to be observed by all railroad companies doing business in the State, as to charges at any and all points for necessary hauling and delivering freights; shall make such just and reasonable rules and regulations as may be necessary for preventing unjust discriminations in the transportation of freight and passengers on the railroads in the State; shall make reasonable and just rates of charges for use of railroad-cars carrying any and all kinds of freight and passengers on said railroads, no matter by whom owned or carried; and shall make just and reasonable rules and regulations, to be observed by said railroad companies, to prevent the giving or paying any rebate or bonus, directly or indirectly, and from misleading or deceiving the public in any manner as to the real rates charged for freight and passengers. Nothing in the act shall be taken as in any manner abridging or controlling the rates for freight charged by any railroad company in the State for carrying freight which comes from or goes beyond the boundaries of the State, and on which freight less than local rates on any railroad carrying the same are charged by such railroad : but said railroad companies shall possess the same power and right to charge such rates for carrying such freights as they possessed before the passage of the act, and the Commissioners shall have full power by rules and regulations to designate and fix the difference in rates of freight and passenger transportation, to be allowed for longer and shorter distances on the same railroad, and to ascertain what shall be the limits of longer and shorter distance. If any railroad company, by its agents or employees, shall be guilty of a violation of the rules and regulations provided and prescribed by the Commissioners, and if, after due notice of such violation given to the principal officer thereof, ample and full recompense for the wrong or injury done thereby to any person or corporation, as may be directed by the Commissioners, shall not be made within thirty days from the time of such notice, such company shall incur a penalty for each offense in the sum of not less than one thousand dollars nor more than five thousand dollars, to be fixed by the Judge presiding. An action for the recovery of such penalty shall lie in any county in the State where such violation has occurred or wrong has been perpetrated, and shall be in the name of the State of Georgia. The Commissioners shall institute such action through the Attorney-General or Solicitor-General, whose fees shall be the same as provided by law. The three Commissioners appointed by the Governor were ex-Governor Smith, Samuel Barnett, and Major Campbell Wallace.

There was a large number of local-option laws passed, and the tendency of the legislation shows that the cause of prohibition is gradually gaining ground. In many counties the prohibition is made absolute, and in many others it is left to the vote of the people. In the northern part of the State the interest is the most decided.

The highest rate of interest that may be exacted in the State is eight per cent., but only in specified cases. When no rate is named in a contract, the legal rate remains at seven per cent. A violation of these conditions brings a forfeiture of the interest and excess of interest charged.

A military bill was passed, which provides for a reorganization of the State volunteer system. There are to be no regiments, but all the companies are to be formed into battalions. The Governor is to enforce such organization. The white and colored battalions are to be kept separate, and are to be organized in different series, so that each series will have its senior officers. A State flag is adopted for the first time. Not a dollar is to be expended on the military except what may arise from the fines and forfeitures of the military courts-martial, which will be nominal. The proposition urged by the Military Commission that a per capita tax of fifty cents be levied for military purposes was rejected by the Judiciary Committee as unconstitutional. The Governor remains the Commander-in-Chief of the army and navy of the State, and the Superintendent of Public Buildings, who is Mr. John B. Baird, was made Adjutant-General of Georgia.

An act was passed appropriating $60 a year for five years to every soldier of the State who lost an arm or a leg in the late war. The appropriation was made for the purpose of allowing the disabled men to buy a leg or arm for themselves. It is estimated that the cost to the State will be between $50,000 and $100,000.

The most important measure relating to education was the passage of an act creating a normal school. The law requires that the State shall furnish an appropriation of $6,000 per annum whenever the agent of the Peabody fund may furnish a like amount. The school shall then be located in the city or town of the State that offers the most liberal inducements to it.

An act was passed to define the crime of lobbying, and to prescribe penalties for the same. It declares two classes of persons to be lobbyists: 1. Persons who misrepresent the nature of their interests in any matter pending in either House; and, 2. Persons who are employed for a consideration, by any person or corporation interested in any measure, to favor or oppose such measure. These two classes are prohibited from any personal solicitation of a member of either House, by private interview, letter, message, or other means and appliances not addressed to the judgment. All others may approach members in any manner, but the above classes are prohibited from doing so under penalty of being guilty of a felony. The man who approaches a member under false colors, or who comes with a fee or other reward, becomes a felon.

Previous to the recess of the Legislature in December, 1878, a committee was appointed to make an investigation into alleged frauds in the disposal of wild lands on the part of the office under the charge of Comptroller-General Goldsmith. These are lands not in cultivation or use, and of course bringing no revenue to their owners. They are scattered throughout the State, and the taxes are scarcely ever paid on them. The law provides that they shall be sold in default of taxes. Hundreds of thousands of acres have been sold within the past year or two, bringing only about enough to pay the taxes. It was found that the fi. fas. for these lands had been transferred by the Comptroller to four men, who, as speculators, bought in thus probably 300,000 acres of land for little more than the taxes, and less than one per cent. of their assessed value. The speculation was a gigantic one, and an investigation was ordered. The Comptroller claimed that he had made the transfers under the written opinion of the Attorney-General, which was true. The committee made their report on July 7th. The majority said they could find no evidence that the Comptroller had any interest in the transactions, except his charge for costs, and added: "In view of the wholesale frauds committed in these transactions, we respectfully recommend that the Legislature do pass an act declaring all these sales had under transferred *fi. fas.* null and void, as some of the courts have already decided, and another to withdraw all protection of any statute of limitation or law of prescription from all such titles, or others founded on them or emanating from them; and this committee beg leave to continue their organization for the purpose of preparing these bills, and reporting them as soon as possible." The minority report opposed such a law as unconstitutional, and said: "But the greatest objection to the course recommended by the majority is, that to pass such act would be to usurp the prerogative of the judiciary, a coördinate branch of the government. This we can not do. The Constitution forbids it, and any such act, if passed, would be *ipso facto* void. It would be far wiser to attempt no retroactive legislation, but leave all these intricate legal questions to be decided by the courts, the tribunals established by the Constitution to interpret and administer the law." The Comptroller then addressed a letter to the committee, in which he said:

I do not propose to discuss the legality of the transfers or the recommendation which you make to declare them void, because these recommendations are concurred in by a majority of your committee, and because, if they are valid, no legislation can make them void, and, if they are void, no legislation can make them valid. The law of 1874 fixes their status, and what that is the courts, I presume, will determine in reference to the law as it then existed. Being doubtful myself as to the transfers, I applied to the Attorney-General, and acted on his opinion. If the transfers are declared void by the courts, I shall have no sympathy with any one except such *bona fide* purchasers as may have been, under the opinion of the Attorney-General, misled in the investment of their money. Beyond this, I shall rejoice with the committee in the defeating of any frauds that may have been perpetrated by any one.

The portion of your report that does not express what I understand to be the views of a majority is the omission to state that it was in evidence that before the appointment of your committee I had taken official action through the Solicitor-General in Dodge and Montgomery Counties to compel the sheriffs by rule to account for the entire sales in those counties, less the legal costs and amount of taxes paid to the State by the transferees; and at the time of your investigation it was in evidence that I had directed rules to be issued against every sheriff who had failed to make proper returns. In doing this I exhausted my power as Comptroller, and if any unnecessary delay has occurred, the fault, if fault there be, is not in my department. These views, I understand, were concurred in by a majority of your committee, and were to be embodied in the report. If these facts were stated, I should have no complaint; but their omission leaves an inference that I had left undone what I ought to have done, in order to compel an accountability by the sheriffs.

I also understand that the committee agreed to report, instead of what was reported, that, "after thorough investigation, nothing could be found to implicate the Comptroller-General, directly or indirectly, in any fraud or speculation whatever." All these facts are borne out by the evidence and my statement before the committee, and I understood were to be covered by the report. They have been omitted, and as the omission subjects the report to misconstruction, I ask you respectfully to indicate by your concurrence in this statement the truth of the facts set forth. I make this request because I feel confident

that it will be your pleasure to do for me this act of justice.   W. L. GOLDSMITH.

The paper exonerating the Comptroller, of which the above is an extract, was presented to members of the committee with a request for them to sign it. Two of them did so, two refused, and the chairman was not approached. A friend of Goldsmith went to the two members who refused to sign the paper and pleaded with them to do so. They still refused. He then offered one of them $250 and the other $100 and a suit of clothes, to sign the paper. They indignantly refused, and reported the attempted bribery to the chairman. The committee made a supplemental report, stating among other matters that an attempt had been made by bribery to induce two of its members to sign a paper prepared by the Comptroller. "This paper had for its object the acknowledgment by the members of the committee that certain things had been omitted in the report which ought to have gone into it, and that certain other things embraced in the report were couched in language different from that in which a majority of the committee had agreed should be employed, thus doing the Comptroller-General unintentional injustice." He reported it to the Legislature, and the whole city was soon greatly excited over it. The House of Representatives ordered the arrest of Hinton Wright, the man who had offered the bribes, and appointed a new committee of investigation. In a few days this committee reported that they had discovered a series of gross frauds in the office of the Comptroller-General, and recommended the impeachment of that officer. The House elected six managers of the impeachment, who presented at the bar of the Senate the following series of charges:

ARTICLE 1. That Washington L. Goldsmith, Comptroller of the State of Georgia, did, on the 1st day of October, 1877, illegally, wrongfully, and corruptly collect fifty cents on all *fi. fas.* against wild lands.

ART. 2. That said Goldsmith, on the 25th day of September, 1877, did, illegally, wrongfully, and corruptly, issue writs of *fi. fa.* against lands in certain counties.

ART. 3. That said Goldsmith extorted from W. P. Anderson $4 on eight *fi. fas.*, although said lots had not been advertised thirty days according to law.

ART. 4. That said Goldsmith did, illegally, wrongfully, and corruptly, refuse to receive from W. P. Anderson taxes on wild lands, compelling said Anderson to pay $4 on eight *fi. fas.*, although said land had not been advertised the requisite thirty days.

ART. 5. That said Goldsmith did, on or before the 31st day of October, 1877, for and in consideration of $100, paid by Daniel Lott, issue *fi. fas.* on the lands of Rondeau & Co.

ART. 6. That said Goldsmith, on divers occasions after October 11, 1877, did illegally pay out to divers parties money aggregating in amount $8,175.73, without the consent or warrant of the Governor.

ART. 7. That said Goldsmith, unmindful of his duties, etc., did illegally issue to the sheriffs of the State circulars delegating to the same certain trusts and duties intrusted to him by the State.

ART. 8. That said Goldsmith, on the 1st day of June, 1879, without the color of right, and in disregard of the duties of his office, did fail to turn over to the Treasurer large sums of money, aggregating $4,-582.50, which had been collected by him as taxes upon wild lands, keeping, holding, and retaining in his possession said money.

ART. 9. That said Goldsmith, between March, 1874, and February, 1875, did make and present to John Jones, Treasurer, fraudulent returns concerning moneys collected by him on account of wild-land taxes.

ART. 10. That said Goldsmith collected as insurance fees the sum of $12,678.06, and paid into the Treasury of this sum only $2,457.60, keeping in his possession the sum of $9,720.46, the law requiring him to pay immediately into the Treasury all sums thus collected.

ART. 11. That said Goldsmith did, in the month of May, 1879, permit to be fraudulently changed and altered certain records used in the Comptroller-General's office.

ART. 12. That said Goldsmith does keep and employ in his office one James M. Goldsmith, after knowing of his unlawful acts in changing records in the Wild-Land Office.

ART. 13. That said Goldsmith did, on the 1st of October, 1878, make and prepare false and incorrect statements and exhibits of money collected by him to the Governor and Legislature.

ART. 14. That said Goldsmith has appropriated to his own use money belonging to the State.

ART. 15. That said Goldsmith did, on the dates of the 10th, 12th, and 15th of July, 1879, collude, combine, and conspire with one Hinton P. Wright to control and influence P. D. Davis, a member of this body.

ART. 16. That said Goldsmith did, on the —— of July, 1879, employ one Hinton P. Wright to bribe the Hon. Lewis Strickland, a member of this body.

ART. 17. That said Goldsmith, by the proceedings and conduct as set forth in preceding sections, for the sake of lucre and self-aggrandizement, has set a miserable precedent to those in high office.

Charges of impeachment against the Comptroller were made by the House to the Senate, and that body organized into a court for the trial of the same, with the Chief Justice of the State in the chair, on August 21st. The trial was, however, postponed to the first Monday in September. Its result is stated in the following sentence read by the Chief Justice:

The House of Representatives and all the people of Georgia vs. Washington L. Goldsmith, Comptroller-General. Impeachment.

Whereas, it appears from the record of the trial had in the above-stated case, now before the Court, that the defendant was guilty of the charges contained in the first, third, fourth, fifth, tenth, thirteenth, fourteenth, and seventeenth articles of impeachment preferred against him by the House of Representatives, and was found not guilty of the charges contained in all the other articles; whereupon it is considered, ordered, and adjudged by the High Court of Impeachment of the State of Georgia, now here, that the defendant, the said W. L. Goldsmith, Comptroller-General of the said State of Georgia, be and he is hereby removed from the said office of Comptroller-General, and that the same be and is hereby declared to be vacant; and that the said W. L. Goldsmith be and is hereby declared to be disqualified to hold and enjoy any office of honor, trust, or profit within the State of Georgia during his natural life.

HIRAM WARNER,
Chief Justice Supreme Court of Georgia.
September 19, 1879.

On August 11th, in the House, four committees of nine members each were appointed to investigate the Treasury Department, the Agricultural Department, the office of the principal keeper of the penitentiary, and the office of the State School Commissioner.

The committee on the investigation of the Treasury Department made majority and minority reports on September 16th. The majority say that they "have found at the very threshold of their investigations such conclusive evidence of malfeasance in office by J. W. Renfroe, Treasurer of the State, that they feel it their imperative duty to lay the same before the House without delay." They then proceed to state instances in which he deposited money in certain banks, under an agreement with his sureties, and received some interest on such deposits for his own use. Then they say:

The testimony shows this to have been the understanding and agreement, but the committee are of the opinion that in this matter the Treasurer has been guilty of a plain, direct, and palpable violation of the law and breach of his official duty. Prior to the adoption of the present Constitution the law controlling this question is contained in the eleventh paragraph of section 12 of the act of the General Assembly approved February 25, 1875, which is in these words: "The Treasurer shall not under any circumstances use himself, or allow others to use, the funds of the State in his hands; and for every violation of this section he is liable to the State for the sum of five hundred dollars as a penalty, or a forfeiture of his salary, if such forfeiture will pay the penalty incurred." While, therefore, it is true that the stipulations already recited were made between the Treasurer, the sureties, and the banks, and were intended to meet the letter of this law, yet the contract between the sureties and the banks for the payment to the sureties of interest on the State deposits, and the receiving by the Treasurer of his portion of those payments, is clearly and unquestionably a violation of the law in its spirit and substance.

Again, more than one half the entire amount received by the Treasurer from this source was paid to him subsequently to the 5th day of December, 1877, on which day the present Constitution was ratified and adopted by the people and became the organic law of this State; and whatever justification or excuse may be set up by the Treasurer under the language of the statute just cited, he certainly could not mistake or misconstrue the plain, positive, and comprehensive provision of the Constitution upon this subject. Paragraph five of section two of article five of that instrument provides that "the Treasurer shall not be allowed, directly or indirectly, to receive any fee, interest, or reward from any person, bank, or corporation for deposit or use in any manner of the public funds; and the General Assembly shall enforce this provision by suitable penalties."

They further reported that the Treasurer, for signing officially the coupons on the bonds of the Northeastern Railroad Company, endorsed by the State, charged said railroad company therefor 1¼ cent per coupon, and did on the 2d of January, 1878, receive from the officers of the company $247 in payment of that claim, which sum of money he converted to his own use and benefit. And they concluded by recommending that he be impeached for high crimes and misdemeanors in office, and that a committee of seven be appointed to announce the matter to the Senate.

The minority of one took an entirely different view of the case, saying that he felt compelled to submit his report "in deference to my views of the true interests of the State, and to my sense of justice to a public officer." In his report he says:

The committee have submitted the Treasury Department to the closest scrutiny, and have ascertained that the condition of the accounts, as shown by the records and books, is satisfactory to the most exacting. The method observed by that officer is calculated to secure correctness, and is at the same time simple and easily understood. The funds of the State have either been expended upon proper vouchers, or have been at all times deposited in banks in conformity to law.

It has been demonstrated that the Treasurer has spared no efforts at all times, and upon all occasions, to protect the public interests confided to him. There are two matters, however, which I deem proper to bring to the attention of the House.

On the day of the assembling of the committee, we received from the Treasurer a communication, requesting the closest scrutiny of his department and of his official conduct, whether the investigations be based "on rumor or otherwise." After we had thoroughly examined his office, his books, his bank accounts, etc., and found everything in admirable condition, we summoned him before us, and found him ready and prompt to answer any and all inquiries. Among other matters, he stated that, at the request of some of the securities on his official bond, he had deposited the public money in certain banks; that these banks were selected by him, with the approval of the Governor, under the requirements of the law; that they were designated by his securities on account of their recognized solvency, and because they would pay to them commissions of from two to five per cent. on the monthly balances of the deposits; that these commissions were received by the securities referred to, and they paid a portion thereof, varying from one third to one half, to him; that he justified his course in this particular under par. 8, sec. 92, of the Code, also under par. 11, sec. 18, of the act of 1876, which is but a reënactment of the section of the Code alluded to; also under the resolution of December 8, 1871, which is as follows:

"*Whereas*, It has not been customary to require the State Treasurer to pay into the Treasury interest on the deposits of the State funds;

"*Be it resolved*, That the Treasurer of the State shall not be held liable for any such interest; and be it further resolved, etc.," directing the dismissal of certain suits for such interest against the then Treasurer.

The statement of the Treasurer, after searching in every quarter in which light might be had, was not materially affected.

I would not be understood as endorsing this course of conduct, but on the contrary believe it to be deserving of censure. It will be observed that sec. 92 of the Code, reënacted in the act of 1876, declares that "the Treasurer shall not, under any circumstances, use himself, or allow others to use, the funds of the State in his hands." In handling such large sums of money as annually pass through the Treasury of Georgia, under the very necessities of the case, large deposits must be made in banks. The law itself, as found in the Code and the act of 1876, contemplate this course. The evidence does not disclose that the Treasurer, in reference to the deposits, did more than this. He deposited in certain banks, with the approval of the Governor, the funds in his hands, precisely as any business man or corporation would deposit.

The law, in providing for such deposits, contemplates necessarily that the banks thus patronized would use the money precisely as they use the funds of other depositors—nothing more, nothing less. Were such not the case, we should soon have no banks in which to deposit. The statement of the Treasurer, together with the evidence taken upon this point, fails to indicate or even to suggest that he

placed the public funds in any of these institutions upon any other terms than those which impliedly attach to all deposits. The fact that he received a commission or percentage on the monthly balances does not of itself add to the character of the deposits any additional attribute of using himself, or permitting others to use, the public funds. If he is in the latter case within the prohibition of the statute, he is equally so though no commission or percentage be paid him. It would seem that, to violate the law as it then stood, there must have been some contract with the banks in reference to the time the money was to remain in their custody, or as to the amount to be deposited, or as to some other feature which destroyed the identity of the transaction with the ordinary deposit. That a commission or percentage was paid *ipso facto* did not vary the terms of the deposit, and more emphatically is this so when the banks expressly agreed with the securities that no such result would follow, but that such deposits were subject to the check of the Treasurer at any and all times.

When we add to this reasoning the resolution of 1871, passed by the first Democratic Legislature which met under the Constitution of 1868, it is, to say the least, a matter of grave doubt whether any law was violated up to the adoption of the Constitution of 1877. That resolution says expressly that the Treasurer shall not be held liable for any interest on deposits. It is a legislative construction of the section of the Code above alluded to. It is true that paragraph five of the second section of the fifth article of the Constitution of 1877 provides that "the Treasurer shall not be allowed, directly or indirectly, to receive any fee, interest, or reward from any person from the deposit, etc., of public funds"; but it will be observed that it is also provided that "the General Assembly shall enforce this provision by suitable penalties." The present General Assembly is proceeding by an appropriate act to enforce this provision, but the Treasurer has long since ceased the receipt of any commission. The evidence disclosed that he promptly discontinued the receipt of such moneys so soon as his attention was called to the constitutional provision, and long in advance of any investigation of his department. The last commission received by him was about November 1, 1878.

The second matter to which I desire to call attention is the payment to the Treasurer by Mr. Childs, the President of the Northeastern Railroad, of $247 for extra work done in endorsing the bonds and coupons of such road. This is in substantially the same condition as the commissions on the deposits. He received 1¼ cent for each bond and coupon signed. This amount had always been allowed by the State to preceding Treasurers, the only difference being that they collected that amount from the State, while the present Treasurer collected it from the railroad. It appears that the railroad authorities pressed him to do this work with the utmost speed, and hence he was compelled to labor late at night and early in the morning, out of office hours. The State has lost nothing, and, if the transaction be objectionable, it can not happen again. There is not a particle of evidence that the Treasurer forced its payment through the power of his office.

I desire to call attention to a few special instances in which the Treasurer has shown great and constant fidelity to the interests of the State, and his ability in the management of her finances:

1. In the change from the Fourth National to the National Park Bank of New York, as the fiscal agent of the State, by which an average of $2,000 per annum is saved in commissions, etc., the latter institution contracting to transact the business of this State for no moneyed consideration whatever.

2. In the gradual reduction of the amount of, and rates of interest on, temporary loans, until this unhealthy branch of the State's finances has been done away with entirely, and the expenditures of the government so managed as to be covered by the regular annual income from taxation.

3. In the negotiation of $542,000 of bonds under the act of 1876, to take up matured coupons on the Macon and Brunswick Railroad bonds, by which a premium of $2,300 was realized to the State, and all of this at an expense of $591.15.

4. In the negotiation of the $2,298,000 of bonds, under the act of 1877, to take up the Macon and Brunswick Railroad bonds, at par, at an expense of $665.45.

5. In the determination, so successfully executed, to pay no commissions for the sale of State bonds.

6. In the economical management of the question of exchange on New York, making the banks sell to him upon nearly every occasion at par.

The excellent management of the Treasurer in the negotiation of bonds can be seen at a glance, by comparing it with the expense of disposing of the $1,200,000 of the Nutting bonds, which cost the State in commissions, etc., $8,000. The present Treasurer negotiated $2,840,000 at an expense to the State of $1,256.65.

I am well aware of the fact that public sentiment is against the reception of any interest, fees, or perquisites by officers beyond their salaries, and this Legislature is taking such measures as will prevent such action in the future. But whatever sums the Treasurer has received came into his hands before November, 1878. It is manifest that the State suffered no injury. Her credit is perfect; her securities rank with the best in every market; her Treasury is in easy condition; her taxes are lower; and no effort has been spared by the Treasurer to bring about these advantageous results.

While the resolution to impeach was pending in the House, the Treasurer sent to that body a communication in which he tendered all the fees he had received, and also appended his resignation of the office, addressed to the Governor. It was now urged against the resolution to impeach, that the effect of impeachment was to vacate the office and disqualify the incumbent for the future. But a resignation had been made, and a tender of the fees; why, therefore, incur the expense of impeachment merely to disqualify the incumbent? It was further urged that the House should express its unqualified condemnation of the acts of the Treasurer, accept the resignation and tender, and instruct the Governor to proceed against him for all moneys improperly used. This last proposition received yeas 43, nays 109. The vote was then taken on the resolution to impeach, and it was adopted—yeas 126, nays 13.

Six articles containing specific charges against the Treasurer were brought forward by the House, and they were tried before the Senate. The first article of the list, and reply of the Treasurer, were as follows:

ARTICLE 1. That on July 3, 1878, respondent received through the hands of V. R. Tommey, from the Georgia Banking and Trust Company of Atlanta, the sum of $250, and did appropriate the same to his own use; the inducement for the payment of this sum by the bank to the sureties upon respondent's official bond being the deposit of funds of the State in that bank. But the respondent denies that in receiving this money he acted corruptly, or was unmindful of the duties of his office or of his oath of office, or knew that such receipt was contrary to the laws or the Constitution of the State, and now pleads not guilty of the charge of high misdemeanor contained in the same.

The vote of the Court on this article was, on the question of guilty, yeas 25, nays 17. A

two-thirds vote being required for conviction, he was declared "Not guilty." The second and third articles contained similar charges with the first, and the result of the vote was the same. The fourth article contained the charge of corruptly collecting fees to the amount of $247 to which he was not legally entitled, for signing the coupons attached to the bonds of the Northeastern Railroad Company. On the question of guilty, the vote was, yeas 24, nays 18. On article five, the vote on the question of guilty, yeas 7, nays 35. On article six the vote was, yeas 18, nays 24. So the Treasurer was acquitted of the respective charges as contained in the several articles.

On the same day on which the verdict of acquittal was given, the Legislature passed a resolution instructing Governor Colquitt to issue a _fi. fa._ against Treasurer Renfroe and his sureties for the amount of interest taken by him for the use of the public funds, and for the fines and forfeitures that had accrued under the law by his course. The resolution requested the Governor to do this as he "is authorized and required by law." The process indicated was that laid down in the act of 1876, in which it is provided that if the Treasurer misapplies any funds in his hands, etc., the Governor need not proceed against him and his sureties by regular process of suit, but executions shall be issued against him and his sureties, and they shall have no more defense against these _fi. fas._ than is allowed to tax-collectors when the _fi. fas._ of the Comptroller-General are issued against them. This means that there is no defense at all. The _fi. fas._ were issued for over $26,000, but resistance was anticipated on the part of the defendant. This is as far as the matter had proceeded at the end of the year.

The committee of nine appointed by the House to investigate the office of the principal keeper of the penitentiary of the State presented three reports, two of which were signed by four members of the committee and one by one member. The first report declared that the keeper had "grossly abused the authority and powers of his office by prostituting the same for his private gain." The second report states that, having discovered what they believe to be the true state of affairs, the undersigned "suggest that the principal keeper is guilty of nothing more than following a reprehensible precedent, and we conclude with expressing the opinion that, beyond censuring such conduct, further action is unnecessary." The third report concluded with recommending the adoption of the following resolution:

Resolved, That the testimony taken by the special committee of nine, appointed by the Speaker, on the office of the principal keeper of the penitentiary, be certified as correct, and by the chairman of the committee laid before his Excellency the Governor; and that his Excellency the Governor be, and is hereby, requested to take such action in the matter as the facts therein justify.

The charge that the keeper used his office to oppress the lessees of the convicts led to the investigation. The reports show that the lessees, being forced by law to bear the expense of carrying the convicts from the county jails to the various camps, have found it best to make a contract with the keeper to deliver the convicts at so much per head. This practice has prevailed for many years. The price charged by the keeper was $12 a head. A certain company of the lessees refused to pay what was demanded, and made the charge.

The committee appointed to investigate the conduct of the State School Commissioner made a long report, in which they presented an itemized account of all the receipts and expenditures of the office; also a statement of the amounts received in the State from the Peabody fund. The report in the highest terms commended the zeal, efficiency, and good management of the State School Commissioner, and showed how skillful and economical had been his administration of the school interests of the State.

The investigation of the Agricultural Bureau was unimportant.

The measures before the Legislature related with few exceptions to local affairs. They were very numerous in consequence of the modifications of the State Constitution.

The financial condition of the State appears to be most satisfactory. During the last two and a half years the expenses have been reduced in every department. The floating debt of $350,000 has been paid, and above $200,000 has been unexpectedly obtained from claims. The funding of high-rate interest bonds in low-rate bonds has been very successful. The public debt is only one twenty-sixth of the property, and under the new Constitution can not be increased, but must be steadily diminished.

At the previous session of the Legislature an act was passed to issue about $3,000,000 in small-sized bonds, some as low as five dollars, at 4 per cent. interest, free from taxes. The cost of the preparation of these bonds was $3,197. The entire issue was sold at the Treasury as fast as they could be signed; and when the last were sold, orders remained that could not be filled. The objection was raised against the bonds that they were bills of credit, and subject to 10 per cent. tax under the internal revenue law. In consequence, one of the Representatives of the State in Congress, Mr. Henry Persons, asked the following questions of the Commissioner of Internal Revenue, Mr. Green B. Raum:

1. Will you kindly inform me if there is any law or ruling which can tax any bank, corporated or private, for paying out a bond of any sovereign State in the United States in payment of checks upon said banks, when the holders of such checks are willing to receive said bonds in payment of said checks?

2. Or is there any law or ruling which can in any manner tax any bank for receiving or paying such bonds in lieu of currency beyond the usual tax on average deposits of any character?

3. Would not State, private, and national banks stand on the same footing as to receiving or paying out such bonds?

The reply of the Commissioner was as follows:

The bonds or obligations particularly in question are, as I understand, of various denominations, some of them as low as five dollars. One of them of the denomination of five dollars has been shown me. It was issued by the State of Georgia under an act of the Georgia Legislature, is payable to the bearer by the State, January 1, 1885, with annual interest represented by coupons at the rate of 4 per cent. per annum, and is signed by the Treasurer and the Governor of the State. In short, it is an interest-bearing obligation of the State of Georgia, payable to bearer at a definite future time.

It has never been considered as within the spirit of the internal revenue laws or the policy of Congress to impose a tax upon the bonds or other similar obligations of a State. In fact, the tenor of the decisions of the United States Supreme Court in analogous cases is that Congress has no authority to impose such a tax. However that may be, I am of the opinion that not only has Congress not imposed any tax upon the obligations in question, but that it has passed no statute which purports to impose them.

The tax imposed upon bank deposits by section 3,408 of the Revised Statutes is upon "deposits of money." I do not regard the bonds in question as "money" within the meaning and intent of that word as used in that portion of the statutes. They are obligations which a bank may buy and sell as it buys and sells all bonds and other similar obligations; but they are not money.

The only other internal revenue tax to which these obligations may be thought liable is the tax of 10 per cent. imposed upon certain notes mentioned in sections 3,412 and 3,413 of the Revised Statutes, and sections 19 and 20 of the act of February 8, 1875 (Abbott's "Statutes at Large," 311). Even assuming the obligations in question to be "notes," they are nevertheless liable to tax neither under said section 3,412 nor said section 19. The tax imposed by those sections is upon the notes of persons, firms, associations, State banks and State banking associations within the meaning and intent of this statute (13 "Opinions of Attorneys-General," 176); and it would hardly be claimed that a State falls within either of the classes enumerated in the section cited.

The tax imposed by said sections 20 and 3,413 is upon the notes of any town, city, or municipal corporation. The expression of one thing implies the exclusion of others. The mention of towns, cities, and municipal corporations implies the exclusion of a State. If it had been the purpose of Congress to impose a tax upon notes issued by a State, States would undoubtedly have been included in the enumeration in the statute.

In reply to your inquiries, therefore, I have to say that there is no ruling of this Bureau, nor in my opinion is there any internal revenue law, which requires a tax from any bank or banker for paying out bonds of the State of Georgia in satisfaction of checks drawn upon such bank, nor is there any internal revenue law which imposes a tax upon any bank or banker for receiving or paying out such bonds in lieu of currency. State banks, private banks, and national banks stand upon the same footing, under internal revenue laws, as to receiving and paying out such bonds.

The returns to the office of the Comptroller show the amount of property held subject to taxation in the State to be $225,000,000. The returns also show that the property now held by the colored people of Georgia aggregates $5,182,398, against $5,124,875 last year, and this, too, when the bulk of property has decreased at least 10 per cent. in value. They have added 39,309 acres to their possessions during the last year, making a total of 341,199 acres owned by them. There are only four colored men in the State worth over $10,000, so that the property of $5,182,398 is divided in small lots among the colored people of all classes and all sections.

The Atlanta University is the college for colored students, and is in a prosperous condition. The School Superintendent of Bibb County states that some of the most efficient and conservative teachers in the county were educated at this university. Of the 51 alumni of the institution, 42 have engaged in teaching as a profession, while three are pastors of churches, two theological students, and one is pursuing the study of law. Of the teachers four only have located beyond the limits of the State. In addition, over 90 of the more advanced pupils employ their time during vacation in teaching. Its students number 240, representing ten different States and forty-seven counties in Georgia. The trustees hold sixty acres of valuable land adjoining the college edifices, which is in itself a splendid endowment. The other revenues cover $8,000 per annum from the State of Georgia, tuition fees (only $2 per month), and donations usually amounting to $2,500 from charitable institutions at the North. The library of the institution comprises 4,000 volumes, with a balance on hand in cash of $700 for further augmentation, derived from the interest on the permanent library endowment, which is $5,000.

The law for the punishment of the crime of murder was amended at a previous session of the Legislature, by providing that, on a recommendation of the guilty to mercy by the jury, the penalty shall be changed from death to imprisonment for life. The effect of this amendment has been virtually to abolish capital punishment in the State. In a recent case, in which a father murdered his son, he was arrested and his guilt was clearly shown; but he was "recommended to the mercy of the Court," and under the law the death-sentence could not be passed on him. Judge Wood, who presided, said: "I am satisfied that we have seen the last of capital punishment in Georgia until this law is repealed. It is impossible to escape the recommendation."

The management of penitentiary convicts in the State is in some respects unusual. They are leased for a period of twenty years. The law to this effect went into operation in the spring of the year. It was passed by the Legislature in February, 1876, to take effect on the expiration of the lease then existing. This act provides for the leasing of the convicts to three companies, who are to pay the State $25,000 per annum for twenty years. This sum is prorated between the three companies according to the number of convicts which each is working. These three companies are as follows: Company No. 1 is composed of J. E. Brown, Julius Brown, John T. Grant, and W. D. Grant. Company No. 2 is composed of B. G. Lockett, W. B. Lowe, John B. Gordon, and C. W. Howard. Company No. 3 is composed of W. W.

Simpson, W. D. Grant, and the heirs of Thomas Alexander. These three companies control and operate all the convict camps in the State. Of these there were under the old act one at Augusta, one at Old Town in Jefferson County, one in Greene, one at Albany, two in Washington County, and one at Dade coal-mines. Under the new lease some of these camps will be abolished, and there will be but three divisions of the convict labor, though there will be several minor camps. Company No. 1 will operate at Dade coal-mines, No. 2 at Albany, and No. 3 in Greene County. The last two companies use the convicts in farming operations, and the first companies use them in the mines. This lease is to a certain extent a speculation on the part of the lessees. If the number of convicts decreases, they lose; if it increases, the profit will increase. There were 1,200 convicts early in the year, the term of many of whom expired before its close. The convicts generally are said to work well. If their number remains as large as it now is, the lessees will probably find their investment well made. The State will get a million clear, and it is doubtful if the old penitentiary system paid so much in any twenty years of its existence. Under the new lease the Dade Coal Company will receive 300 "long-term men," as they are called. The other two companies will receive about 375 each. As soon as the term of a convict expires his place is filled by another, if the State has him on hand; and, if he is not forthcoming, the lessee has to lose the services of one hand until the necessary criminal appears and takes his place. In order to transfer large numbers of them by railroad, they have to be chained in box-cars, which are well ventilated and made as comfortable as possible. Two guards well armed are put in the doors of the cars. Thus any shrewd fellow who should slip his chain would be powerless to do any harm or to help the others loose. All three of the new companies are chartered, and are distinct organizations; and the question has been raised whether this status does not place them beyond the reach of the Legislature. The lessees are acting under the new lease, and their rights have become vested.

A series of questions relating to sheep husbandry in the State was addressed by the Commissioner of Agriculture to men engaged in the business. Their answers presented these results: Of those who have tested crosses in Georgia, 98 per cent. report the cross of the merino and the native most profitable. The average annual profit on the capital invested in sheep in Georgia is 33 per cent. This presents a very marked contrast between the profits of sheep-raising and cotton-growing. The average annual cost per head of keeping sheep is only 54 cents. In answer to a question, the average cost of raising a pound of wool is only 6 cents, while the average price for which the unwashed wool is sold is 33½ cents, or 27½ cents net. An average of 74 lambs are raised for every 100 ewes, notwithstanding the ravages of dogs. The average yield of unwashed wool to the sheep is 3·44 pounds, which, at 27½ cents net, gives an average clear income in wool from each sheep of 94 cents. The average price received for lambs sold to the butcher in Georgia is $1.87. The average price of stock sheep is $2.58 per head. The average price of muttons is reported at $2.75 per head. Ninety per cent. of the correspondents report dogs the principal and generally the only obstacle to sheep husbandry. The United States census of 1870 gives the number of sheep in Georgia as 419,465. Mr. David Ayers, of Camilla, Mitchell County, in southwestern Georgia, where snow never falls and the ground seldom freezes, and where the original pine forest is carpeted with native grass, says his sheep—3,500 in number—cost him annually 14 cents per head, clip 3 pounds of unwashed wool, which sells at 30 cents per pound, giving a clear profit of 90 per cent. on the money and labor invested in sheep. He does not feed his sheep at any time during the year, neither has he introduced the improved breeds, using only what is known as the native sheep. He complains of the ravages of dogs on the sheep, and of hogs and eagles on lambs. Mr. Robert O. Humber, of Putnam County, in middle Georgia, furnishes some interesting facts from his experience in sheep-raising as a factor of mixed husbandry, in which the famous and much-dreaded Bermuda grass is utilized. He keeps 138 sheep of the cross between the merino and the common stock. He says they cost "nothing except the salt they eat," while they pay 100 per cent. on the investment, in mutton, lambs, and wool. They yield an average of 3 pounds of wool per head, which he sells at the very low price of 25 cents—less than the market price. It costs him nothing except the shearing. His sheep range on Bermuda-grass old fields in summer, and the plantation at large, embracing the fields from which the crops have been gathered and the cane-bottoms in winter. They are never fed at any season.

There are thousands of acres of land in the State suitable for the manufacture of turpentine, which can be purchased for one dollar per acre. The following facts embrace the whole subject of its manufacture: Any number of pine-trees tapped are called an orchard. Ten to ten and a half thousand trees tapped are called a crop. One to three boxes are cut into every tree within one or two feet from the ground. Seventy-five trees will usually average 100 boxes. One and a quarter to one and a half cent is paid for cutting each box. One man can scrape in one week the trees of one crop. One man can gather in one week the rosin of two crops. A season lasts seven to seven and a half months. Trees are generally used three successive seasons, though sometimes longer. Where trees are plenty they are by preference used but one season, the virgin turpentine being considered the best. The

first season the rosin is gathered every four weeks; after that every six weeks. Five thousand boxes average daily during the season one barrel of rosin of 280 pounds, including the weight of the barrel, and 6 to 6½ gallons of turpentine of about 6½ pounds each. Eighty men employed in all will produce daily 60 bar, rels rosin and 360 gallons turpentine. Turpentine was worth in 1879 26 cents per gallon in Savannah, and it sold as high as 60 cents per gallon in 1875 and 1876 without having cost any more to produce it. Rosin varied in 1879 from $1.10 to $4 per barrel, the lightest colored and freest from turpentine being the best. Distilling it too long darkens the rosin. Distilling it generally pays all the expenses of manufacture, leaving the spirits of turpentine clear profit. New oak barrels for turpentine cost in New York $1.35, and delivered in Savannah about $1.85 each; old ones are cheaper but less useful, as they sell poorer when filled. Rough pine barrels for rosin are made near the turpentine distilleries. Distillers sometimes buy and sometimes lease pine lands. The establishment of a turpentine still is not very expensive. Laborers about stills get 75 cents per day—often less. Tapping trees retards their growth—often even kills them, and decreases largely the value of lumber made of them.

The progress of gold-mining in the State within the last few years has been rapid. It was somewhat stimulated by the developments of the geological survey. In 1874 there were only four gold-mills in the State, and the total yield was about $40,000. In 1879 there were 46 mills, and the yield was over $500,000. These mills cost $10,000 each, which gives a total of about $500,000 invested in machinery alone, against $40,000 five years ago. The gold-belt has been defined, and it is estimated that the increase in its value has not been less than $40,000,000. The following facts are stated among other results of the geological survey:

The calling of attention to the marl-pits in the eastern part of the State has been of great benefit. These marls are very rich in lime, and many of them contain 3 per cent. of potash, and, used with stable and home-made manures, would almost do away with the buying of fertilizers. The experiments made with these marls have turned out splendidly. Used at the rate of 100 bushels to the acre, they have increased the yield 70 per cent., and at the rate of 200 bushels have increased it 90 per cent. They will in time supplant very largely the costly fertilizers.

One of the most important pieces of work done by the Bureau is the location of the water-powers of the counties in which the survey has been made. Over 600 streams have been carefully measured and explored by Professor Locke, and the water-powers on each, ranging from one-horse powers to 35,000, have been located upon the maps. In a very few years the people and strangers will begin to utilize these water-powers in the manufacture of wagons, furniture, etc., out of the splendid wood with which the forests abound.

The manufacture of ice is becoming quite extensive, and companies are formed for that purpose in many cities. The machine used is thus described: "In the water-machine about fifty pounds of liquid ammonia are stored in a very strong iron cylinder, and this is connected with a coil of pipes immersed in a tank of strong brine; into this brine galvanized iron cans holding pure water are placed, and these cans are of the size of the blocks of ice which are formed. The liquid ammonia is allowed to flow through these coils, and it gradually becomes gaseous, and in becoming so abstracts from the water so much heat that it speedily freezes. A powerful steam-pump forces the gaseous ammonia back into the iron cylinder again, thus liberating great heat, which is disposed of by cold water dropping upon coils of pipes through which the ammonia passes on its way to the condenser. The process is a continuous one, and if the pumps and coils do not leak, there is no loss, and the operation may go on so long as the machinery lasts. The ice is sold for half a cent a pound."

The receipts of cotton at Savannah in the year 1878-'79 amounted to 694,611 bales, an increase over the previous year of 82,639 bales, and of 217,477 bales over 1876-'77. The receipts of rice amounted to 31,357 casks, of which 24,469 casks were exported. In naval stores the statistics embrace portions of the two naval seasons—the latter part of 1878 and the first of 1879. The aggregate receipts were 177,447 barrels rosin and 34,368 barrels spirits turpentine, against 177,104 barrels rosin and 31,138 barrels spirits turpentine in 1878—a small increase. In dry-goods the domestics manufactured in Georgia are said to have driven from the market all other goods of the same class.

At the beginning of the late war the General Government levied a direct tax of $20,-000,000 upon the States for the purpose of conducting the war. The seceded States were regularly charged with their proportion, which in the case of Georgia amounted to $584,000, and about the same for Kentucky, Tennessee, Virginia, etc. Six per cent. interest was charged to this amount for each year from its assessment. After the war special agents were sent into the various States to collect it. These agents took the State tax-books and proceeded directly against the tax-payers. In Georgia $86,500 were collected in one year. In South Carolina the whole amount due was collected, enough lands being sold to have paid five times the amount. The Arlington estate was sold under the operation of this levy, and the tax-payers of every State have been forced to pay something. About ten years ago the collection was suspended, and the State governments have been held liable for the amounts. All claims of these States when allowed by Congress have been credited against this indebtedness. Recently, the ruling of the Treasury has been revised, and the charges against the States have been marked off, which releases Georgia from nearly a million dollars, and the other States from large amounts. The position taken was, that a State could not be as-

sessed or taxed in its sovereign capacity, but that all assessments must be against the individual tax-payers.

GERMANY, an empire in Europe, reëstablished January 18, 1871. The Emperor, William I., was born March 22, 1797, and was married June 11, 1829, to Augusta, daughter of the Grand Duke Charles Frederick of Saxe-Weimar. The heir apparent, Frederick William, born October 18, 1831, has the official titles of Crown Prince of the German Empire and Crown Prince of Prussia. Imperial Chancellor (*Reichskanzler*), Otto, Prince von Bismarck-Schönhausen; President of the Imperial Chancery (*Reichskanzler-Amt*), Karl von Hofmann, Minister of State.

The legislative functions of the empire are vested in the Bundesrath or Federal Council, and the Reichstag or Diet of the Empire. The Bundesrath represents the individual states of Germany, and the Emperor must have its consent to declare war which is not merely defensive. The members of the Bundesrath are appointed by the Governments of the individual states for each session. On January 1, 1880, the German Bundesrath was composed of the following members: *Prussia* — Prince Bismarck, President and Imperial Chancellor; Count zu Stolberg-Wernigerode, Vice-President of the State Ministry; the Ministers Hobrecht, Count Eulenburg, Leonhart, Kameke, and Maybach; Von Bülow, State Minister, and Secretary of State in the Ministry for Foreign Affairs; Von Stosch, chief of the Admiralty; Hofmann, President of the Imperial Chancery; Von Philippsborn, Director in the Foreign Office; Dr. Friedberg, Secretary of State in the Ministry of Justice; Stephan, Postmaster-General; Hasselbach, Director-General of the Indirect Taxes; Burghart, Ministerial Director in the Ministry of Finance; Herzog, Under-Secretary of State for Alsace-Lorraine; Von Möller, Oberpräsident of Alsace-Lorraine. *Bavaria*—The Ministers Von Pfretschner and Dr. von Fäustle; Von Rudhart, Ambassador in Berlin; Ministerial Director von Riedel; Colonel von Xylander. *Saxony*—The Ministers H. von Nostitz-Wallwitz and von Könneritz; O. von Nostitz-Wallwitz, Ambassador in Berlin; Major von der Planitz. *Würtemberg* — Minister von Mittnacht; Hugo von Spitzemberg, Ambassador in Berlin; Major-General von Faber du Faur; Councilor Hess. *Baden*—Turban, President of the Ministry; State Ministers Elstätter and Stöszer. *Hesse*—Freiherr von Stark, President of the Ministry; Ministerial Councilors Neidhart and Schleiermacher. *Mecklenburg-Schwerin*—Von Prollius, Ambassador in Berlin; Oldenburg, Director of Customs. *Saxe-Weimar*—Councilor Dr. Stichling. *Mecklenburg-Strelitz*—Councilor von Prollius. *Oldenburg*—Councilor Seldmann. *Brunswick*—Councilors Schultz and von Liebe. *Saxe-Meiningen*—Minister von Giseke. *Saxe-Altenburg*—vacant. *Saxe-Coburg-Gotha*—Minister von Seebach. *Anhalt*—

Minister Freiherr von Krosigk. *Schwarzburg-Rudolstadt*—Minister von Bertrap. *Schwarzburg - Sondershausen* — Minister Freiherr von Berlepsch. *Waldeck*—Director von Sommerfeld. *Reuss* (elder line)—Faber. *Reuss* (younger line)—Dr. von Beulwitz, State Minister. *Schaumburg-Lippe*—Councilor Höcker. *Lippe-Detmold*—Eschenburg. *Lübeck*—Dr. Krüger, Minister Resident in Berlin. *Bremen*—Dr. Gildemeister, Burgomaster. *Hamburg* — Dr. Kirchenpauer, Burgomaster.

The German Empire consists at present of twenty-six states, of which four are kingdoms, six grand duchies, five duchies, seven principalities, three free cities, and one, Alsace-Lorraine, an imperial province (*Reichsland*). The following table exhibits all the states of the German Empire, the area, the population according to the census of 1875, the number of representatives of every German state in the Federal Council, and the number of deputies who represent each state in the Reichstag:

	STATES.	Area in English square miles.	Population in 1875.	Votes in Federal Council.	Deputies to the Reichstag.
Grand duchies. Kingdoms.	1. Prussia (including Lauenburg)	134,178	25,742,404	17	236
	2. Bavaria	29,291	5,022,390	6	48
	3. Saxony	5,789	2,760,586	4	23
	4. Würtemberg	7,531	1,881,505	4	17
	5. Baden	5,824	1,507,179	3	14
	6. Hesse	2,965	884,218	3	9
	7. Mecklenburg-Schwerin	5,137	553,785	2	6
	8. Saxe-Weimar	1,388	292,933	1	3
	9. Oldenburg	2,471	319,314	1	3
Duchies.	10. Mecklenburg-Strelitz	1,181	95,673	1	1
	11. Brunswick	1,425	327,493	2	3
	12. Saxe-Meiningen	958	194,494	1	2
	13. Saxe-Altenburg	511	145,844	1	1
	14. Saxe-Coburg-Gotha	760	182,599	1	2
	15. Anhalt	906	213,565	1	2
Principalities.	16. Schwarzburg-Rudolstadt	364	76,676	1	1
	17. Schwarzburg-Sondershausen	833	67,480	1	1
	18. Waldeck	433	54,743	1	1
	19. Reuss-Greitz (elder line)	122	46,985	1	1
	20. Reuss-Schleitz (younger line)	320	92,375	1	1
	21. Schaumburg-Lippe	171	33,133	1	1
	22. Lippe-Detmold	459	112,452	1	1
Free cities.	23. Lübeck	109	56,912	1	1
	24. Bremen	99	142,200	1	1
	25. Hamburg	158	388,618	1	3
	26. Alsace-Lorraine (Reichsland)	5,603	1,531,804	..	15
	Total	208,481	42,727,860	58	397

Population of Berlin, December 31, 1877, 1,018,818. For the population of the other principal cities see "Annual Cyclopædia" for 1877.

In the following table will be found the full exhibit of the governments of the particular states, including the names and the titles of all the sovereign princes, their years of birth and accession to the throne, and the names of the heirs apparent:

STATES.	Title.	Name.	When born and when succeeded to the throne.	Heir apparent.
Prussia	King	William I.	Born 1797, succ. 1861...	Frederick William, son.
Bavaria	King	Louis II.	" 1845, " 1864...	Otho, brother.
Saxony	King	Albert	" 1828, " 1873...	George, brother.
Würtemberg	King	Charles	" 1823, " 1864...	William, cousin.
Baden	Grand Duke	Frederick	" 1826, " 1856...	Frederick William, son.
Mecklenburg-Schwerin	Grand Duke	Frederick Francis II.	" 1823, " 1842...	Frederick Francis, son.
Hesse	Grand Duke	Louis IV.	" 1837, " 1877...	Ernest Louis, son.
Oldenburg	Grand Duke	Peter	" 1827, " 1853...	Augustus, son.
Saxe-Weimar	Grand Duke	Charles Alexander	" 1818, " 1853...	Charles Augustus, son.
Mecklenburg-Strelitz	Grand Duke	Frederick William	" 1819, " 1860...	Adolphus Frederick, son.
Brunswick	Duke	William	" 1806, " 1831...	Disputed.
Anhalt	Duke	Frederick	" 1831, " 1871...	Leopold, son.
Saxe-Altenburg	Duke	Ernest	" 1826, " 1853...	Maurice, brother.
Saxe-Coburg-Gotha	Duke	Ernest II.	" 1818, " 1844...	Prince Alfred, cousin.
Saxe-Meiningen	Duke	George	" 1826, " 1866...	Bernard, son.
Lippe-Detmold	Prince	Waldemar	" 1824, " 1875...	Hermann, brother.
Reuss (elder line)	Prince	Henry XXII.	" 1846, " 1859...	Henry XXIV, son.
Reuss (younger line)	Prince	Henry XIV.	" 1832, " 1867...	Henry XXVII., son.
Schaumburg-Lippe	Prince	Adolf	" 1817, " 1860...	George, son.
Schwarzburg-Rudolstadt	Prince	George	" 1838, " 1859...	Günther, second cousin.
Schwarzburg-Sondershausen	Prince	Günther	" 1801, " 1835...	Charles, son.
Waldeck	Prince	George	" 1831, " 1852...	Frederick, son.
Bremen	Burgomaster	F. L. Grave. Dr. O. Gildemeister	1879–1883. 1877–1881.	
Hamburg	Burgomaster	Dr. H. A. O. Weber. Dr. O. Petersen	1879. 1879.	
Lübeck	Burgomaster	Dr. H. T. Behn	1879–1880.	
Alsace-Lorraine	Stadtholder, appointed by the Emperor	Freiherr von Manteuffel.		

The ducal line of Brunswick is likely to become extinct on the death of the reigning Duke. The succession is disputed by the Duke of Cumberland (son of the late King of Hanover) and the Emperor of Germany. The heir apparent is the son of the reigning sovereign in only fourteen of the twenty-two sovereign houses which belong to the German Empire. The movement of emigration from the ports of Bremen and Hamburg was as follows:

FROM	Bremen.	Hamburg.	Total.
Germany................	11,829	11.827	23,156
Other countries...........	10,154	12,976	23,180
Total, 1878............	21,843	24,803	46,286
" 1877............	19,179	22,570	41,749
" 1876............	21,665	28,731	50,896
" 1875............	24,503	31,810	56,313
" 1874............	80,633	48,443	74,076
" 1873............	68,241	69,176	132,417
" 1872............	80,418	74,406	154,824
" 1871............	60,516	42,224	102,740
" 1870............	46,781	82,556	79,887
	(1870-'78......	40,935	41,080	82,015
	1865-'69......	62,098	45,579	107,672
Average	1860-'64......	21,580	20,085	41,665
number.	1855-'59......	32,541	21,892	54,433
	1850-'54......	51,361	25,804	77,165
	1845-'49......	81,290	5,416	86,706
	(1836-'44......	12,949	1,704	14,653
Total since 1832......	1,518,001	986,527	2,454,528

Besides this number, emigrants left Germany as follows: by way of Stettin, 1875-'78, 630; Antwerp, 1872-'78, 13,656; Rotterdam, 1872, 1,486; Havre, 1872-'76, 14,627; Marseilles, 1873 and 1874, 47; Genoa, 1872, 7. The principal points of destination of the emigrants from Bremen, Hamburg, Stettin, and Antwerp in 1878 were as follows: United States, 20,373; Australia, 1,718; Brazil, 1,048; Africa, 394; South American republics, 449; West Indies and Central America, 96. The movement of population in 1877 was as follows:

STATES.	Marriages.	Births. Deaths. Inclusive of still-births.		Still-births.
Prussia................	210,372	1,095,432	717,305	44 496
Bavaria...............	89,372	220,724	162,179	7,513
Saxony...............	24,919	129,876	86,868	4,969
Würtemberg	14,337	87,402	61,865	3,215
Baden...............	11,400	61,957	48,865	2,008
Alsace-Lorraine......	10,187	55,756	42,046	2,814
Hesse...............	6,945	84,740	23,848	1,450
Other states..........	30,228	132,663	55,721	5,192
Total...........	347,310	1,818,550	1,223,692	71,157

According to Brachelli ("Statistische Skizze des Deutschen Reichs," 1878), the population of Germany in 1875 comprised 26,718,823 members of the Evangelical Church, 15,371,-227 Roman and Old Catholics, 100,608 other Christians, 520,575 Jews, and 16,127 others.

Germany has twenty universities, of which nine are in Prussia, three in Bavaria, two in Baden, and one each in Würtemberg, Hesse, Saxony, Saxe-Weimar, Mecklenburg, and Alsace-Lorraine. The number of professors and of students in the German universities in 1878 were as follows:

UNIVERSITIES.	State.	Professors.	STUDENTS. Matriculated.	Total.
Berlin...........	Prussia........	216	8,213	5,187
Bonn............	"	101	848	889
Breslau	"	108	1,329	1,338
Erlangen........	Bavaria........	62	434	484
Freiburg........	Baden.........	56	864	408
Giessen.........	Hesse.........	56	862	372
Göttingen.......	Prussia........	115	990	1,007
Greifswald......	"	60	597	513
Halle...........	"	108	950	984
Heidelberg......	Baden	112	495	551
Jena............	Saxe-Weimar...	82	443	464
Kiel............	Prussia........	70	226	317
Königsberg......	"	91	686	698
Leipsic.........	Saxony.........	158	3,061	3,072
Marburg........	Prussia........	73	471	476
Munich.........	Bavaria.......	181	1,621	1,662
Rostock........	Prussia.......	40	161	161
Strasburg......	Alsace-Lorraine.	96	684	747
Tübingen......	Würtemberg...	91	986	996
Würzburg......	Bavaria.......	72	941	966
Total......	....	1,996	15,672	21,187

Sometimes the academies of Münster and Braunsberg, containing each the two faculties of Catholic theology and philosophy, are counted among the German universities. In 1879 Münster had 32 professors and 279 students. At the following universities outside of the German Empire the German language is exclusively or predominantly used, and in the province of literature they may be counted as German universities:

UNIVERSITIES.	Countries.	Professors.	STUDENTS. Matriculated.	Total.
Basel...........	Switzerland....	69	205	244
Bern	"	67	394	3·1
Czernowitz......	Austria.........	38	186	285
Dorpat	Russia.........	70	988	954
Gratz...........	Austria.........	89	676	773
Innsbruck......	"	73	496	592
Prague.........	"	133	1,460	1,614
Vienna.........	"	263	....	....
Zürich.........	Switzerland....	68	308	352

The budget of the German Empire for 1879 –'80, as declared by the laws of March 30, May 16, and July 6, 1879, estimates the revenue at 546,594,477 marks and the expenditure at 545,894,037 marks (1 mark = 23·8 cents). The revenue was derived from the following sources:

	Marks.
1. Customs and excises of consumption......	251,696,860
2. Stamps on playing-cards................	1,316,000
3. Stamp duty on bills of exchange.........	6,377,900
4. Administration of postal affairs and telegraphs	15,622,988
5. Administration of railroads.............	9,910,000
6. Administration of the imperial printing-office.	1,105,440
7. Imperial Bank and other receipts	2,105,000
8. Receipts of various descriptions..........	7,208,000
9. From the imperial funds for invalids........	88,015,879
10. Surplus of former years................	1,130,000
11. Profit from the coining of imperial money....	100,000
12. Interest from invested capitals..............	6,270,173
13. Extraordinary receipts..................	190,268,974
14. Matricular contributions................	90,371,890
Total....................	546,594,477

The matricular contributions were divided among the particular states as follows:

STATES.	Marks.
Prussia	44,199,812
Bavaria	19,015,557
Saxony	4,739,518
Würtemberg	6,777,330
Baden	4,864,561
Hesse	1,517,657
Mecklenburg-Schwerin	949,119
Saxe-Weimar	502,607
Mecklenburg-Strelitz	168,933
Oldenburg	547,822
Brunswick	561,707
Saxe-Meiningen	333,833
Saxe-Altenburg	250,258
Saxe-Coburg-Gotha	313,555
Anhalt	366,758
Schwarzburg-Rudolstadt.	131,522
Schwarzburg-Sondershausen	115,701
Waldeck	93,754
Reuss (elder line)	80,667
Reuss (younger line)	1.8,572
Schaumburg-Lippe	56,569
Lippe	192,362
Lübeck	97,365
Bremen	245,024
Hamburg	669,344
Alsace-Lorraine	3,425,579
Total	90,371,390

The expenditures of the empire were estimated as follows:

EXPENDITURES.	Ordinary.	Extraordinary.
1. Chancellor of the Empire.	108,780	608,504
2. Imperial Chancery and Bundesrath	2,154,795	260,000
3. Imperial Diet	851,580	
4. Foreign Office	6,385,925	870,000
5. Administration of Posts and Telegraphs		10,128,180
6. Imperial army	321,184,910	43,114,249
7. Navy	28,122,780	20,614,010
8. Administration of Justice.	1.233,540	301,200
9. Imperial Treasury	2,929,216	2,289,247
10. Railroad Office of the empire	260,750	180,000
11. Imperial Chancery for Alsace-Lorraine	171,760	
12. Interest on the debt of the empire	8,482,500	
13. Chamber of Accounts	460,798	35,000
14. Railroads of the empire		16,200,826
15. Mint		22,700,000
16. Reimbursement to Prussia for the government printing-office		4,672,500
17. General pension funds	17,217,736	
18. Expenditures arising from the war with France		5,256,872
19. Imperial invalid funds	33,015,579	
Totals	419,022,949	126,871,088
Grand total	545,894,037	

The public debt of the German Empire consists of three loans, one of 77,731,321 marks (authorized by the law of June 14, 1877), one of 97,484,865 marks (law of June 14, 1878), and one of 68,021,071 marks (law of June 18, 1879). There is also a floating debt consisting of Treasury notes issued for short periods only. In accordance with the law of April 20, 1874, the Imperial Government has issued paper money (*Reichscassenscheine*) to the amount of 120,000,000 marks, which has been distributed among the several states in proportion to their population on December 31, 1871. The same law authorized the issue of paper money to the amount of 54,889,940 marks to facilitate the carrying out of the reform in the coinage. Of this amount, 54,075,860 marks had been issued on April 1, 1879, and 10,977,960 had been withdrawn, leaving the paper money in circulation on that date 163,097,900 marks. The budgets and public debt of the several states in 1879 were as follows (in marks):

STATES.	Gross receipts.	Expenditure.	Debt.
Alsace-Lorraine	39,735,175	39,735,175	
Anhalt	16,184,000	16,151,000	5,118,951
Baden (1878 and 1879)	34,198,435	34,775,685	39,650,751
Bavaria	221,633,348	221,633,348	1,315,810,896
Bremen	18,191,586	15,055,071	88,207,023
Brunswick	7,506,000	7,506,000	86,786,972
Hamburg	27,692,600	30,157,200	106,517,060
Hesse	20,285,247	17,142,497	54,258,111
Lippe	978,697	974,395	1,142,404
Lübeck	2,599,624	2,599,624	28,504,918
Mecklenburg-Schwerin	(?)	(?)	20,791,000
Mecklenburg-Strelitz.	(?)	(?)	6,000,000
Oldenburg	847,500	847,577	37,009,582
Prussia (see PRUSSIA)	711,500,758	711,500,758	1,097,822,279
Reuss (elder line)	49,549	549,840	909,866
Reuss (younger line)	1,117,146	1,115,168	1,891,070
Saxe-Altenburg	2,274,847	2,274,847	1,847,076
Saxe-Coburg-Gotha	5,860,221	4,862,415	8,708,992
Saxe-Meiningen	4,646,565	4,123,100	12,372,972
Saxe-Weimar	6,766,805	6,787,687	7,871,924
Saxony	net 62,491,000	62,481,417	668,270,725
Schaumburg-Lippe	704,522	704,522	360,000
Schwarzburg-Rudolstadt	1,772,270	1,772,270	4,426,704
Schwarzburg-Sondershausen	2,164,742	2,151,846	3,518,825
Waldeck	978,404	978,404	2,492,700
Würtemberg	49,958,400	53,674,593	376,756,196

The following table gives the military forces of the empire in time of war:

I. FIELD ARMY.

DIVISIONS.	Officers.	Men.	Horses.
Higher staff	868	5,170	5,070
Infantry	10,328	463,564	20,060
Jägers	440	20,520	800
Cavalry	2,144	59,814	55,608
Artillery	2,335	82,460	81,702
Pioneers	599	21,720	9,139
Train	668	43,004	46,842
Administration	216	2,826	10,864
Total	17,591	699,078	230,685

II. RESERVES.

DIVISIONS.	Officers.	Men.	Horses.
Substitutes of the staff	875	1,836	320
Infantry	2,886	212,690	1,059
Jägers	80	6,860	20
Cavalry	465	23,994	19,717
Artillery	396	16,422	5,930
Pioneers	89	6,621	24
Train	247	12,287	8,930
Total	4,538	280,210	31,000

III. GARRISON.

DIVISIONS.	Officers.	Men.	Horses.
Staffs, etc.	850	10,00?	1,850
Infantry	7,896	814,483	2,543
Jägers	80	4,020	20
Cavalry	828	22,968	25,380
Artillery	1,370	54,865	8,114
Pioneers	128	6,482	
Total garrison	11,159	412,728	37,877
" reserves	4,538	280,210	31,000
" field army	17,591	699,078	230,685
Grand total	33,281	1,392,011	299,562

The military forces of the empire in time of peace are as follows:

DIVISIONS.	Officers.	Men.	Horses.
1. Staff......................	1,094	4	....
Infantry of the line.........	8,879	259,018	....
Chasseurs....................	424	11,148	....
Landwehr	348	4,622	....
2. Infantry..................	9,651	274,788	....
3. Cavalry....................	2,358	64,709	62,591
Field artillery............	1,629	30,737	14,845
Foot artillery...............	683	15,159	....
4. Artillery.................	2,312	45,896	14,845
5. Pioneers.................	394	10,824	....
6. Train....................	200	5,000	2,457
7. Particular formations......	811	948	....
Total..................	17,220	401,659	79,893

The number of recruits in 1877–'78 was 142,-937, against 140,197 in 1876–'77 and 139,855 in 1875–'76. Of the recruits in 1877–'78, 134,-189 had received an education in the German language, and 6,292 in other languages, making a total of 140,181, and leaving 2,406, or 1·73 per cent. of the total number of recruits, without a schooling. In 1876–'77 the number of recruits without an education was 2,975, or 2·12 per cent., and in 1875–'76, 3,311, or 2·37 per cent.

The German navy was composed as follows in 1879:

VESSELS.	Number.	Guns.	Tons.	Horse-power.
1. Steamers—Ironclads:				
Frigates.............	7	85	30,754	43,100
Corvettes...........	4	26	17,474	19,800
Batteries...........	1	4	1,280	1,200
Gunboats...........	7	7	5,438	4,900
Total ironclads......	19	122	54,946	69,000
Frigates...........	1	168	24,194	27,600
Corvettes...........	7	62	9,821	10,800
Dispatch-boats........	3	4	1,768	2,150
Artillery ship........	1	23	3,318	8,000
Imperial yachts......	2	5	1,993	3,650
Gunboats............	14	45	4,465	4,710
Torpedo vessels......	11	..	2,122	8,780
Transport steamers ...	2	..	425	320
2. Sailing vessels:				
Frigates............	1	10	1,052	....
Brigs..............	3	18	1,708	....
Total..............	74	452	105,812	125,010

The German Customs Union includes the entire German Empire, with the exception of the free ports of Bremen, Hamburg, Bremerhaven, Geestemünde, Brake, and a small part of Baden, in all 150 square miles, with 594,576 inhabitants. It also includes the grand duchy of Luxemburg, with an area of 999 square miles and 205,158 inhabitants, and the Austrian community of Jungholz, having an area of 2·2 square miles and a population of 206. The imports for 1878 and exports for 1877 in the customs territory of Germany were estimated as follows (value in marks—1 mark = $0·238):

VOL. XIX.—28 A

CLASSES OF GOODS.	Imports, 1878.	Exports, 1877.
Grain.......................	612,900,000	876,900,000
Malt and other liquors..........	58,700,000	64,2–0,000
Colonial produce	202,900,000	52,400,000
Tobacco and cigars............	106,600,000	28,600,000
Seeds and fruits...............	138,900,000	79,100,000
Animals and animal provisions...	396,600,000	216,800,000
1. Articles of food.........	1,513,900,000	908,000,000
Fuel........................	59,500,000	95,000,000
Minerals and ores.............	76,700,000	88,100,000
Raw metals.................	65,400,000	77,400,000
Hair, hides, and leather.........	176,360,000	89,900,000
Spinning material.............	557,000,000	244,100,000
Wood and timber..............	199,300,000	74,800,000
2. Raw material.........	1,164,200,000	669,800,000
Pottery and glassware..........	12,900,000	31,500,000
Metal manufactures...........	46,200,000	155,700,000
Machines and vessels..........	54,700,000	72,100,000
Leather, etc..................	18,000,000	63,900,000
Yarn.......................	141,700,000	51,800,000
Cordage, woven goods, and cloth'g	123,200,000	418,600,000
Caoutchouc and wax goods	6,500,000	14,200,000
Paper......................	6,400,000	28,500,000
Wood and carvings...........	16,700,000	89,000,000
Jewelry and art goods.........	13,900,000	49,200,000
Manuscripts, articles for printing.	10,200,000	20,900,000
3. Manufactured goods....	450,400,000	944,200,000
4. Miscellaneous goods.....	401,400,000	192,600,000
Total merchandise..........	3,529,900,000	2,709,100,000
Precious metals............	209,000,000	66,200,000
Total	3,738,900,000	2,775,300,000

The movements of shipping in the German ports in 1877 were as follows:

STATES	TOTAL VESSELS.		STEAMERS.	
	Number.	Tons.	Number.	Tons.
Entered.				
Prussia...........	34,698	3,498,889	6,525	1,803,268
Hamburg	4,985	2,187,813	2,953	1,780,788
Bremen	2,081	717,091	455	891,660
Lübeck...........	2,302	801,910	981	191,930
Oldenburg........	2,361	145,068	50	18,270
Mecklenburg	1,112	116,018	159	84,102
Total..........	47,829	6,970,779	11,123	4,164,272
Cleared.				
Prussia...........	33,971	3,448,556	6,491	1,785,518
Hamburg	5,269	2,222,108	2,961	1,787,581
Bremen	2,216	732,882	474	408,226
Lübeck...........	2,332	801,557	979	191,868
Oldenburg........	2,464	145,468	51	18,728
Mecklenburg	1,124	119,036	162	85,051
Total	47,376	6,979,952	11,118	4,171,422

The commercial navy in 1878 was as follows:

STATES.	TOTAL VESSELS.		STEAMERS.		
	Number.	Tons.	Number.	Tons.	Horse-power.
Prussia.........	3,271	496,050	138	31,578	10,828
Hamburg......	459	221,474	101	54,127	18,487
Bremen........	274	216,054	60	57,877	19,297
Oldenburg...	405	112,373	9	3,612	952
Oldenburg......	850	61,801	1	27	40
Lübeck........	46	10,923	27	6,468	1,504
North Sea fleet..	2,742	659,588	182	144,650	89,459
Baltic fleet......	2,063	458,987	154	88,699	11,144
Total, 1878..	4,805	1,117,985	336	158,379	50,608
" 1877..	4,509	1,108,650	318	180,946	49,675
" 1876..	4,745	1,084,882	319	188,569	50,755
" 1875..	4,602	1,068,888	299	189,998	48,422
" 1874..	4,495	1,033,725	253	167,633	41,755

The total length of railroads in Germany, open for traffic, was as follows on January 1, 1879 (in kilometres—1 kilometre = 0·62 mile):

STATES.	State roads.	Private roads under state administration.	Private roads.	Total.
Prussia....................	4,950·2	8,621·4	8,861·1	17,432·7
Bavaria.........................	3,885·3	......	563·2	4,448·5
Saxony.........................	1,786·3	92·3	......	1,878·6
Würtemberg.....................	1,385·3	.....	16·7	1,402·0
Alsace-Lorraine.................	1,028·4	88.5	.....	1,106·9
Baden...........................	1,073·6	128·2	.....	1,201·8
Hesse...........................	290·4	.....	131·2	321·6
Oldenburg.......	278·8	.....	33·0	311·8
Schaumburg-Lippe...............	24·4	.....	.....	24·4
Saxe-Meiningen.................	20·3	.....	170·9	191·2
Hamburg........................	19·0	.....	.....	19·0
Bremen.........................	104·9	.....	.....	104·9
Saxe-Weimar....................	.....	.....	176·7	176·7
Brunswick......................	.....	.....	339·6	339·6
Mecklenburg....................	.....	.....	326·6	326·6
Saxe-Coburg-Gotha.............	.....	.....	17·3	17·8
Main roads....................	14,841·9	8,925·4	11,036·3	29,803·6
Local roads	782·4	237·1	813·2	1,832·7
Total......................	15,024·3	4.162·5	11,849·5	31,636·3

The postal statistics of the empire, according to the latest official publications, were as follows:

ITEMS.	Imperial mail, 1878.	Bavaria, 1877.	Wurtemberg, 1877.	Total.
Total number of articles sent......................	1.224,381,151	170,710,090	68,671,507	1,463.800,000
(a.) Letter mail..................................	1,159,966,251	155,473,618	64,295,375	1,379,700,000
Letters..................................	537,934,310	56,411,725	25,169,684	621,500,000
Postal cards..............................	108,093,840	4,687,872	3,428,208	116,200,000
Printed matter............................	117,301,420	4,544,086	4,456,044	126,300,000
Samples of goods..........................	9,668,370	1,094,760	308,750	11,100,000
Postauftragsbriefe.........................	3,161,204	240,050	107,461	3,500,000
Money orders.............................	86,608,042	4,509,851	1,814,106	42,900,000
Postnachuahmebriefe (C. O. D. letters).......	3,374,700	895,420	469,862	4,700,000
Newspapers..............................	830,383,303 } 13,441,062 }	81,140,309	28,546,210	453,500,000
Supplements to newspapers.................				
(b.) Parcel and money mail....................	64,414,900	15,286,477	4,876,232	84,000,000
Parcels without declaration of value...........	54,507,780	7,765,724	3,506,238	65,800,000
Parcels with declaration of value..............	2,598,120 } 7,309,000 }	5,350,568 } 2,120,185 }	869,994	18,200,000
Letters with declaration of value..............				
Total value of money letters (in marks).............	13,672,818,190	963,792,325	527,649,920	15,169,800,000
Total weight of parcels sent (in kilogrammes)........	245,207,440	26,885,377	13,688,577	285,800,000

The extent of electric telegraphs (in kilometres), and the amount of their business, are shown in the following table:

LINES AND DISPATCHES.	Imperial telegraph, 1878.	Bavaria, 1877.	Wurtemberg, 1877.	Total.
Lines..................................	49,876·52	7,947·7	2,591	59,915
Wires..................................	173,817·06	33,465·0	6,858	219,140
No. of state stations....	4,396 } 2,699 } 7,095	998	870	8,458
No. of railway stations..................				
L Private dispatches......................	7,539,186	810,640	289,081	8,638,907
2. Official dispatches	297,523	89,648	119,054	506,225
3. International dispatches :				
Sent...............................	1,668,792 }			
Received...........................	1,886,596 }	1,076,170	521,887	5,443,669
4. Transit dispatches.....................	340,274 }			
Total, 1878.........................	11,682,371	....	.... }	14,588,801
Total, 1877.........................	11,391,846	1,976,458	929,972 }	

The second session [*] of the Reichstag was opened on February 12th by the Emperor William in person. In his speech from the throne, the Emperor thanked the House for the assistance it had rendered him in arresting the Socialist agitation, and said bills would be introduced for removing the evils afflicting com-

[*] The first session was opened on September 9, 1878, and closed in October. For an account of the proceedings, see " Annual Cyclopædia " for 1878, p. 380.

merce. "I consider it my duty," added the Emperor, "to strive at least to preserve the German market for articles of national production as far as that course is consistent with our interests, and also to cause the customs legislation to be once more assimilated to those well-tried principles which, in our commercial policy since 1865, have in some essential points been abandoned." After mentioning the abrogation of clause 5 of the Treaty of Prague, by a special convention with Austria, the Emperor referred to the fulfillment of the hopes he had expressed for the termination of the war in the East, and said that tranquillity in Turkey and the maintenance of peace in Europe might be expected to result from the arrangements made at the Congress. On February 13th Herr von Forckenbeck was reëlected President by 151 votes, against 67 received by Herr von Seydewitz; the candidate of the Conservative party, Herr von Stauffenberg, was reëlected first Vice-President, and Prince von Hohenlohe-Langenburg second Vice-President. As the latter declined, Herr Lucius was elected second Vice-President. On the 19th the Reichstag, after a brilliant defense of Parliamentary reform by Dr. Lasker, almost unanimously resolved to refuse the Government permission to imprison and criminally prosecute two Socialist deputies, Fritzsche and Hasselmann, who had returned to Berlin in obedience to the Emperor's general convocation of Parliament, and in defiance of the police decree against their further residence in the capital. On motion of Herr Rickert, it was furthermore declared, with all votes against those of the two Conservative parties, that the Reichstag, in framing the law of October, never meant that a member might be prevented by a police decree of expulsion from taking his due share in the proceedings of Parliament.

The discussion of the new commercial treaty with Austria began on the 20th. Although there was hardly any opposition to the approval of the treaty, the discussion became at once very animated, as it turned on the radical change in the financial policy of the empire which the speech from the throne had announced. The most remarkable speeches were made by Herr Delbrück, formerly President of the Imperial Chancery, and Prince Bismarck. The lines between the Free-Trade and Protectionist parties were distinctly drawn. Delbrück is looked upon as the leader of the Free-Trade party. He defended, in two elaborate speeches, the traditions of the commercial policy of Prussia, tracing the history of the reformatory movement, which he said began with the customs legislation of 1818, was continued in the Customs Union, and quietly and steadily kept on developing, with only a short interruption, until recently. By a long array of commercial statistics he attempted to refute the assertion made in the speech from the throne, that the commercial policy followed since 1865 had been unsuccessful. Prince Bismarck made a characteristic speech, in which he explained the reasons why the Government proposed to return to the path they had followed between 1823 and 1865. He stated that until a year ago he had confided the supreme management of the commercial policy of the empire to Herr Delbrück, whom he regarded as the highest authority in all questions of commercial legislation; and though he had not fully agreed with the views of Herr Delbrück,

he had been satisfied that the commercial interests were intrusted to the best hands which could be found in Germany. Gradually, however, the conviction had grown upon him that a radical change was required; and, much as he regretted that he could no longer have the coöperation of Herr Delbrück, he believed a change in the commercial policy necessary for the salvation of Germany.

The great debate on the reorganization of the customs and commercial polity of the empire began soon after the Easter recess, which had lasted from the 3d to the 28th of April. During this recess the Bundesrath had completed the draft of the Government's bills, which had been communicated to all the members of the Reichstag by mail. The discussion was opened on May 2d by Prince Bismarck, who in a speech lasting about an hour said that Prussia had not taken the initiative in any tax reform since 1824—a fact to be explained by the relation of the various states to the Zollverein. That union, possessing the power to impose indirect taxes, had not a pliant character, a circumstance which logically justified the fact that the development of such imposts in Germany lagged behind that of all other countries. The possibility of a reform in this respect first appeared with the creation of the North German Confederation and of the empire; and if he did not then undertake financial reform, this was because, apart from his defective health and multitudinous duties, he did not primarily regard that as the duty of the Imperial Chancellor. But now the case was different, the present cohesive relations between the empire and the various states being of such a nature as to demand the most prompt and pressing remedy. The first motive for reform was the need of financial independence for the empire, a principle willingly recognized on the settlement of its constitution. The contributions of the various states to the general exchequer were unequal, and he desired to see the necessary income raised in the least burdensome form. At present there were too many direct and too few indirect taxes, and he aimed at reversing this order. The Prince contended that civil servants should not have to pay the income-tax. Another mistake was the distinction made between movable and immovable property. No branch of industry was so highly taxed as agriculture, and the present indirect taxation did not give native labor the protection which it ought to have. He would not enter into the question of free trade versus protection, but one thing was clear, that, through the widely opened doors of its import trade, the German market had become the mere storage-space for the over-production of other countries. They must, therefore, shut their gates, and take care that the German market, which was now being monopolized by foreign wares, should be reserved for native industry. Countries which were inclosed had become great, and those which remained open had fallen behind. Were the perils of protectionism really so great as sometimes painted, France would long ago have been ruined, instead of which she was more prosperous after paying the five milliards than Germany is today. And protectionist Russia, too—look at her marvelous prosperity! Manufacturers there had lately been able to save from 30 to 35 per cent., and all at the cost of the German market. The question before them was not a political but a financial one, and they should put all personal sensibility aside. Nor should they forget the maxim, "Bis dat qui cito dat"; and whichever of them would not quickly give would do detriment to the economic interests of the realm. Dr. Delbrück warned the House to beware of approving the proposed taxes on cotton yarns, as thereby certain branches of export industry would in the highest degree be imperiled. Dr. Delbrück then contrasted France and Germany in this respect, proving by statistics that in the former the customs on cotton yarns are very high as compared with those in the latter, and that, though the imports are thrice as great as in Germany, the export is only a third. On the 3d Herr Bamberger, of the National Liberal party, a great financial authority and an ardent free-trader, undertook to refute the speech made by Prince Bismarck the day before, which, he urged, contained nothing but the assurance of future prosperity sure to result from the acceptance of his scheme, and raised hopes which in the long run could not be realized. Whether such a course was judicious in view of the efforts and expectations of social democracy seemed to him highly questionable. The strength of Prince Bismarck lay in the domain of foreign policy, but his intervention in matters of finance was at variance with his Highness's activity in the past. The Prince's pillar of support was the Center, and the tendency of the Ultramontanes was invariably retrograde. Nor had the Federal Council shown much independence in their discussion of the bill. Herr Bamberger proceeded to consider the probable effects of the new tariff from all general points of view, ending with the assurance that if it were accepted German industry would most assuredly suffer euthanasia, or die a calm and gradual death. On the 4th Herr Richter, Progressist, and a financier of no mean order, chained the attention of the House for nearly three hours, and drew a gloomy picture of the evils sure to result to the empire from the adoption of Prince Bismarck's bill. The Fortschritt (Progressist) party were unanimously opposed to the proposed taxes on tobacco and beer, petroleum, and the most indispensable articles of daily consumption, and they would listen to no compromise. They looked upon the question of customs and taxes as one of might. Money was power, and this Prince Bismarck was evidently bent on gaining for the empire at all risks. In proportion as direct taxation was lessened, the parliamentary influence of pro-

vincial assemblies, and even that of the various states, would be weakened. The proposals before them aimed at absolutism. He reminded all who loved freedom that it was never sent down direct from heaven, but had to be fought for and won. He bade them hold fast together, for liberty and the future of the German Empire were at stake. On the 5th Freiherr von Varnbühler, President of the Tariff Commission, combated the arguments advanced during the last few days by such champions of free trade as Herren Bamberger and Richter. On the 8th Deputy Lasker called the attention of the House to a letter written by Prince Bismarck to the Bavarian Herr von Thüngen, the chief of the so-called Agrarian party, as revealing plans still more reactionary than those indicated by the new tariff. Herr von Thüngen, in his letter to Bismarck, had complained that the interests of German agriculture were not sufficiently protected in the new tariff, at all events not in due proportion to commerce and industry. A number of agricultural products continued to be imported free of duty. The agricultural middle class was on the point of disappearing. Rich capitalists buy real estates for small sums; the peasant becomes again what he was a thousand years ago, a shepherd; some emigrate, the others become Social Democrats, and the social revolution which ends in imperialism is completed. The Imperial Chancellor in his reply expressed his concurrence in the opinion of Herr von Thüngen that the corn duties were insufficient as a protection of agriculture in proportion to the burdens which it bears; but, in his negotiations with the Governments of the other German states and the Tariff Commission, he had been unable to obtain greater concessions, and had found it even difficult to retain the concession that had been made. In view of this correspondence, Lasker laid a special stress on the corn duties proposed in the new tariff, and with great vehemence denounced the intention of the Chancellor. The reply of Prince Bismarck admitted that in his opinion the agricultural interests of the empire deserved a more energetic protection than they received at present. Herr Windthorst, the leader of the Ultramontane Center, declared that his party would support the new protective policy of the Chancellor. A few days before, Herr Windthorst ("the Pearl of Meppen"), who is not only the leader of the Center, but also the trusted adviser of the ex-royal family of Hanover, and who for long years had been the uncompromising foe of the Prince, had for the first time had an interview with Bismarck, and on May 4th he had attended the parliamentary soirée of the Prince, who was observed to receive him with warm and prominent hospitality. It was therefore inferred from the speech of Deputy Windthorst, that Prince Bismarck must have secured some kind of agreement with the Center. On the 11th the tobacco-tax bill was defended by Deputy von Schmid of Würtemberg, who contended that taxation of tobacco was preferable to a Government monopoly in it, and there were many reasons why it should be taxed by weight. Herr Meyer of Bremen described the unsatisfactory result of the French monopoly system, which he implored the House not to think of. The tax on manufactured goods was most preferable, as having to be paid whenever a sale was made, and as being a real consumption-tax. He hoped the license-tax, moreover, would be rejected as being inquisitorial and vexatious. Herr Fritzsche (Social Democrat) energetically opposed the measure, from the acceptance of which he ventured to prophesy would accrue the most baneful results to the tobacco trade in Germany.

The debate on the tariff bills was finished on May 12th. In accordance with the motion of Deputy Löwe (Progressist), the Reichstag resolved to refer part of the new tariff and the tobacco-tax bill to a special committee, but to let the second reading of the other part of the tariff take place in the Reichstag itself. On the 16th the Reichstag rejected, by 192 against 125 votes, a motion to reduce by a half the proposed tax of one mark on pig and scrap iron. A motion of Count Stolberg-Wernigerode, to admit duty-free between Memel and the Vistula all pig and scrap iron, on written certification of its destination for foundries, etc., was also rejected, though most of the members from Posen and the Prussian provinces supported this. On the 17th, on motion of Dr. Delbrück, the duty on Swedish bar-iron destined for the manufacture of certain kinds of wire was reduced to 50 pfennigs (about 12 cents). On the 19th the House passed to the first reading the so-called *Sperrgesetz* or frontier-closing measure, for immediately and provisionally putting in force the stipulations of the new tariff bill under consideration, with a view of frustrating the tactics of those who were importing large quantities of goods to escape the heavy protective duties threatened thereafter. The House unanimously approved the proposed immunity from customs of bronze and ores, and after some discussion also supported the Government in its intention to make flax and raw material for spinning, with the exception of cotton, free. On the 20th the House began the discussion of the tariff under the head of grain and agricultural produce, the new duties proposed thereon being one mark per 100 kilos on wheat, oats, and husked fruit; 50 pfennigs (half a mark) on rye, barley, maize, and buckwheat; 20 pfennigs on malt; 3 marks on anise-seed and caraway-seed; other products being free. On the 21st Prince Bismarck made a long speech on the subject, in which he tried to show that the imposition of the duties proposed, by bettering the fortunes of the agricultural class, would in reality give an impetus to industrial activity. England, France, Belgium, and the Netherlands were cited in proof. The Prince disclaimed all intention of seeking to increase the Impe-

rial Exchequer by a corn-tax; all he desired was merely to do justice to the long-suffering countryman by removing to the frontier, in the form of a consumption duty, part of a direct tax pressing on him. On the 23d the proposals of the Tariff Commission in regard to the duties on grain were carried by 226 against 109. On the 27th the House carried the motion of Deputies Windthorst and Hammacher, Ultramontane and National Liberal respectively, to extend the *Sperrgesetz*, or provisional customs bill, to iron, groceries, and petroleum, in addition to wine and tobacco, as recommended by the Tariff Commission. This protective and preventive ordinance would lapse as soon as the various tariff bills now under consideration should become law, or at the latest fifteen days after the close of the present session of Parliament. On the 28th the House passed the *Sperrgesetz*. A majority of 172 against 88 also approved the proposed tax of 10 pfennigs per 100 kilos on building timber, raw or rough-hewn, as also of 25 pfennigs on sawn wood or planed boards, and other manufactures of wood. On June 16th the proposed duty of 50 pfennigs per kilo on beams and blocks of hard wood was approved by 140 votes against 86. Those on carpenters' goods, wood for parquets and furniture, and wood combined with metal and glass, 3, 4, and 10 marks respectively, were also approved. The duty of 10 pfennigs on building timber, raw or rough-hewn, was carried by 140 votes to 86. On the 17th the House approved the proposed duties of 20 marks per kilo on all fine-wood and carved goods, 30 marks on uncovered upholstered furniture, and 40 marks on covered. The tax of 20 marks on every hundred kilos of hops was also finally accepted. On the 24th the proposed duties on oil and grease were approved by large majorities, although the free-traders made a strenuous endeavor to reduce the duty of 10 marks per 100 kilos on lard, as being the butter of poor men. The House also granted the proposed duties on candles and furs, and the clauses on soap and perfumery, playing-cards, stones, and stonewares.

The second reading of the tariff bill was completed on July 5th, when the House by a considerable majority voted the so-called financial duties proposed by the Government on tobacco, coffee, petroleum, etc. The Liberals and Socialists made a desperate stand against the duties on coffee and petroleum, Herr Bebel declaring that they would breed very bad blood among the people and furnish fresh stimulus for social-democratic agitation. On the 8th the Reichstag passed by a majority of 163 against 148 that section of the law which provides that goods coming from countries which treat German vessels or wares of German origin more unfavorably than those of other states may be taxed with an addition of 50 per cent. over the rate of the imposed tariff. On the 9th, after a long and lively debate, in which Prince Bismarck took a prominent part, the Reichstag, by a majority of 211 against 122, adopted the motion of Herr Frankenstein with reference to the so-called constitutional guarantees, with an amendment of Herr Varnbühler in harmony therewith. This section of the tariff law now provides that the surplus in any year over 130,000,000 marks, arising from the receipts of customs and the tobacco duties, shall be distributed among the various states of the empire in proportion to their population and the rate of their annual contributions to the general exchequer. This stipulation is to take effect from the 1st of April, 1880; and any surplus over 52,651,815 marks accruing between the 1st of October, 1879, and the 31st of March, 1880, will be subtracted under similar conditions *pro rata* from the matricular contribution of the states for that period. On July 12th the debate on the new tariff and the

tariff law, after lasting for nearly three months came to an end. The House passed it in its entirety by a majority of exactly 100, the numbers being 217 against 117. Before the vote was taken, Dr. Delbrück once more strove to show that the bill would grievously injure export industries, and oppressively raise the price of the commonest necessaries of life, that the corn duties would change the whole financial policy of the empire, and promised nothing but discontent and confusion. Dr. Lasker prophesied perpetual conflicts between the Federal Council and the Finance Ministers of the various states; and he looked upon the law as the beginning not of peace, but of strife.

On March 4th the Reichstag began the discussion of the bill introduced by the Government concerning the coercive power of the Reichstag over its members. The bill found

HAMBURG.

hardly any friends among the deputies. Professor Hänel, of the Law Faculty in Kiel (Progressist and formerly second Vice-President of the Reichstag), attacked the measure in an eloquent and learned speech, and defended full freedom of speech and its corollary, the right to publish the proceedings. He sought to show that the adoption of such a law would make the Reichstag unlike any other Parliament, and declared himself opposed to any change in the standing orders of the House, especially at the present time, when they might appear to act under pressure. Herr Bebel, the well-known leader of the Social Democrats, maintained that the bill was intended to gag the Social Democrats, and suggested that it would be better to modify the law granting the franchise to all Germans over twenty-five to the extent of excepting those whom the police have cause

to suspect of revolutionary tendencies. Such a measure was possible in no other country but Germany. On the 7th the bill of the Government was rejected by a large majority. On the other hand, on motion of Herr von Stauffenberg (first Vice-President), it was resolved to ask the Standing Order Committee to consider whether any changes are necessary in the manner of conducting business, and, if so, to formulate and lay regular proposals before the House.

Among the most important measures adopted by the Reichstag is the final regulation of the government of Alsace-Lorraine. In the early part of the session the deputies Schneegans, North, Rack, and Lorette, belonging to the party of the so-called Autonomists, introduced a motion to request the Chancellor of the Empire to prepare for Alsace-Lorraine an independent government residing in the country itself. The motion was supported by a large portion of the National Liberal party, as Bennigsen, Lasker, and Stauffenberg, and was approved in its essential parts by the Chancellor himself. The discussion began on March 21st. Deputy Schneegans, the leader of the party of Alsatian Autonomists, referred to the fact that the obstacles which formerly prevented the establishment of an independent administration of Alsace-Lorraine, in place of the central Government located in Berlin, had now disappeared. The Chancellor had himself repeatedly promised the establishment of an independent government. Herr Schneegans expected from the adoption of his motion a revival throughout Alsace and Lorraine of the old attachment to the German Fatherland. Deputy Kablé read, in the name of the Alsatian Protest party (who demand reannexation of Alsace and Lorraine to France), a declaration in which the party express their concurrence in the wish for the establishment of an independent government. They, however, are convinced that no permanent institutions can be created in Alsace and Lorraine, and no real independence secured, without the concurrence of a legislative assembly elected by a general vote. While willing to vote for the motion of Deputy Schneegans, the party do not mean to prejudice their future movements. Prince Bismarck explained to what extent he was willing to accept the motion. He was, in particular, willing to grant to the imperial province a resident Stadtholder, surrounded with administrative officers having the rank of ministers, and also some kind of representation in the Federal Council. On May 15th the Chancellor submitted to the Reichstag a bill concerning the constitution and administration of Alsace and Lorraine. During the discussion of the bill only a few insignificant changes were proposed and adopted, and on June 23d the bill was passed by a unanimous vote of all parties, except that of the French Protest party, which left the House before the vote was taken. It was signed by the Emperor on July 4th, and an imperial decree of July 23d provided that the law should go into operation on October 1st. According to the new law, Alsace-Lorraine remains an imperial possession, and becomes virtually a federal state, of which the Emperor of Germany as such, not in his capacity as King of Prussia, is the ruler. The Emperor appoints a Stadtholder, who resides in Strasburg, and may at any time be recalled. The Stadtholder does not exercise the functions of the sovereign, but merely those which were hitherto exercised with regard to the Reichsland by the Imperial Chancellor and by the Oberpräsident (Lord-Lieutenant) of Alsace-Lorraine. The section of the Imperial Chancery for the Reichsland and the bureau of the Oberpräsident will be replaced by a ministry for Alsace-Lorraine, under the presidency of a Secretary of State, which will be divided into a number of sections, at the

head of each of which will be an Under-Secretary of State. In the Federal Council the country will be represented by a delegate elected by the Landesausschuss (Provincial Assembly). The delegate will take part in the discussions of the Federal Council, but will have no right of voting. For the examination of bills prepared by the Government a State Council is formed, consisting of the Stadtholder as president, the Secretary of State, the commanding general of the 15th army corps, the Under-Secretaries of State, the Chief Justice of the Supreme Court, the Attorney-General, and seven members appointed by the Emperor, of whom three are proposed by the Landesausschuss, one must be a judge, and one an ordinary professor of the University of Strasburg. The Landesausschuss will hereafter consist of fifty-eight members, who will be elected by indirect vote for a term of three years. On July 23d, the same day when the new Constitution for Alsace-Lorraine was promulgated, the Emperor appointed General Edwin Freiherr von Manteuffel Stadtholder of the Reichsland. At the same time Dr. Herzog, heretofore Under-Secretary of State in the section of the Imperial Chancery for Alsace-Lorraine, was appointed Secretary of State.

Some important information, not known heretofore, on the history of the unification of Germany, was given on July 7th during the discussion of the new German tariff law by the Reichstag, in a speech of Herr von Varnbühler, member of the Federal Council for Würtemberg, and the virtual author of the new tariff. In reply to imputations launched against him by Dr. Boretius, in connection with the attitude of Würtemberg toward Prussia in 1866, Herr von Varnbühler stated that he did all he could at that time, and though the vae victis which he had uttered with regard to Prussia came unfortunately to apply to Würtemberg instead, the very mild form in which this happened was due to the great statesman now at the helm of German affairs, and he could never forget the debt of gratitude thus incurred by his country. After peace was concluded it was from his (Herr von Varnbühler's) initiative that the federal treaties arose. He strove too for the preservation of the Zollverein; and when Prussia sought to withdraw from it, it was he who was instrumental in convening the Customs Parliaments, so that the chief bond of cohesion in Germany should not break. All these statements were willingly confirmed by Prince Bismarck, who was present at the discussion.

On May 20th Herr von Forckenbeck, President of the Reichstag, sent in his resignation, in a letter in which he declared that the fact of his being at variance with the majority of the House on important questions before it, together with imperious considerations of health, had rendered it incumbent upon him, in the interest of public business, no longer to retain the office. On the next day the Reichstag, in which now the alliance between the Conserva-

tive parties and the Catholic Center controlled
a majority of votes, elected Herr von Seydewitz, Conservative, as President. The Liberals did not vote, and of 204 valid tickets 195
were found to be in favor of the Conservative
candidate. On May 23d Freiherr von Stauffenberg resigned his post as first Vice-President of
the House, and on May 24th Baron von Frankenstein, one of the leaders of the Catholic Center, was elected in his place. As this was
the first time that an Ultramontane had been
elected to this high office, the Catholic press of
Germany characterized the event as a great
victory of its party. It is a noteworthy fact
that previous to the election of Herr von Seydewitz both the President of the Reichstag,
Herr von Forckenbeck, and the two Vice-
Presidents, Freiherr von Stauffenberg and Dr.
Lucius, were Catholics ; but none of the three
sympathized with the Ultramontane Center,
and, though belonging to different political
parties, all of them, in the conflict between the
German Government and the Catholic Church,
sided with the former.

The Socialists of the Reichstag repeatedly
produced scenes of great commotion. On
March 17th, when the report of the Government, stating the reasons which had induced
them to place Berlin in a minor stage of siege,
was under discussion, Herr Liebknecht, the
Socialist Deputy for Dresden, severely attacked
the Prussian Administration. He denied that
the Socialists ever advised resistance to the law,
that they were connected with the Russian Nihilists, or that they were responsible for the attempts to murder some of the European princes.
The spirit of murder was an epidemic, as
might be seen from the rapidly succeeding attempts in the earlier part of the reign of Queen
Victoria, than whom a more blameless and
constitutional ruler could not exist. When the
speaker finally sought to defend himself from
the charge of willfully insulting the Emperor
by remaining once seated when the Chancellor
proposed three cheers for the Emperor, his
words produced a general uproar, and the
President declared that the speaker in acting
as he did had wounded the feelings of the
Reichstag and the whole German people in a
way which nothing else could have equaled,
and that, having warned the speaker twice already, he must put it to the House whether the
speaker should be permitted to proceed. Herr
Liebknecht did not wait for the vote, but left
the tribune. On March 31st the only Socialist
member present in the House again ostenta-
tiously kept his seat when the House respectfully rose to its feet to express its sympathy
with a recent affliction of the imperial family
(death of Prince Waldemar, grandson of the
Emperor). On May 14th the Reichstag was
informed that a communication from Washington to the Postmaster-General of Prussia denied the assertion made some time ago by the
Social Democrat, Herr Liebknecht, that the
United States authorities had complained of

letters from Germany being broken open or
tampered with before crossing the sea.

On March 11th Herr von Bühler of Würtemberg, moderate Progressist, moved that Prince
Bismarck be requested to call a congress of the
Powers, with the view of bringing about an
effective general disarmament, to the extent at
least of half their present peace strength, for a
probationary period of from ten to fifteen years.
All thinking men, the speaker said, agreed that
the continued competition among European
states as to which should spend most on armies
must necessarily lead them to bankruptcy, if it
had not partly done so already. The motion
received the support of only about a dozen
men, including Socialists, Alsatian Particular-
ists, and Poles.

On June 19th Herr Delbrück presented an
interpellation in regard to the Government's
discontinuing the coinage of silver. He said it
was necessary to clearly define the situation,
especially as in the debates of the British Parliament the question whether Germany intended to modify the law fixing upon a gold standard had been treated as an open one. Prince
Bismarck replied that he did not know the
views of the federal governments, but he himself did not think it expedient unnecessarily to
commit himself to an expression of opinion
upon a question of such moment. He thought
the interpellation had not been well considered,
but, treating the matter from a business point
of view, he could assure the House that neither
the Federal Council nor the Prussian Ministry
had mooted the question of a modification of
the gold-standard law. Suspension of the silver sales was a measure of expediency, adopted
pending an increase of value. Any doubt respecting the stability of German coinage legislation was wholly unwarranted. He had never
discussed the question with the Minister of Finance. The gentleman from whom Lord Odo
Russell, the British Ambassador, had derived
his information that " the German Government is preparing to introduce and adopt a
double standard, as in France," must have been
better informed than the Imperial Government.
The President of the Imperial Bank, addressing the House, said the Government had already lost by its sales of silver 96,500,000 marks.
Herr Bamberger stated that the deputies who
introduced the interpellation (he was one) had
done so because of the report of Lord Odo
Russell, who had been informed by the British Consul-General, who was also a member of
the Bank Committee. The President of the
Bank observed that the British Consul-General,
though a member of the Bank Committee, was
not informed of the intentions of the Government.

The Reichstag was closed on July 13th by
Prince Bismarck, in the name of the Emperor.

The special convention with Austria concerning the northern part of Schleswig, to
which the imperial speech from the throne referred, was concluded at Vienna on October

11, 1878, by Prince Reuss, the German Ambassador in Vienna, and Count Andrassy, and it was ratified on January 11, 1879. In consequence of this convention, Article V. of the Treaty of Prague reads now: "His Majesty the Emperor of Austria transfers to his Majesty the King of Prussia all his rights to the duchies Holstein and Schleswig acquired by the Peace of Vienna of October 30, 1864." The provision which was formerly added to this article, that the northern districts of Schleswig, in case the people thereof should indicate by a free vote their desire to be united with Denmark, should be ceded to Denmark, has been abolished. As the Emperor stated in his speech, his Government had failed in repeated attempts to settle the question with Denmark, and meanwhile the people affected by the promise were kept in uncertainty.

On July 14th, the day after the close of the Reichstag, the "Official Gazette" of the Government published a decree by the Emperor, dated the 27th of May, ordaining, in accordance with the previous recommendation of Prince Bismarck, a department for the management and control of imperial railways. Herr Maybach, Prussian Minister of Public Works, was appointed chief of the new department. A decree published on the 16th empowered Prince Bismarck to create an Imperial Treasury Department immediately, under the authority of the Prince, in lieu of the financial department hitherto attached to the office of the Imperial Chancellor. Another imperial decree, addressed to the Chief of the Admiralty, ordained the formation of an Engineer Torpedo Corps, to be especially intrusted with the study and handling of the latest instruments of destruction in naval warfare.

In July the court-martial appointed to inquire into the cause of the disaster which in 1878 befell the ironclad Grosser Kurfürst sentenced Rear-Admiral Batsch to imprisonment in a fortress for six months, Captain Klauser to a similar imprisonment for one month, while Captain Kühne was acquitted. It is a noteworthy fact in connection with this trial that the tribunal which passed this sentence was for the most part composed of military men, and that the chief of the Imperial Admiralty at this time, Herr von Stosch, was also a soldier.

Herr Windthorst, the leader of the Catholic party, and formerly Minister in the kingdom of Hanover, successfully negotiated the pension or annuity claimed by him for Queen Mary of Hanover. The Queen, through the Duke of Altenburg, thanked the Prussian Government for the readiness with which it had responded to her wishes.

On May 18th the German Imperial Consul for Egypt, Baron von Saurma, delivered to the Khedive in the name of his Government the following protest: "The Imperial Government, regarding the decree of the 22d of April, by which the Egyptian Government on its part only seeks to arrange its debt relations in a way involving the suspension of existing recognized rights, as an open and direct infringement of the international obligations assumed by it along with judicial reforms, must deny to the said decree all legally binding operation with reference to the competence of the mixed tribunals and the rights of the Imperial German subjects, and holds the Viceroy responsible for all the consequences of his illegal conduct."

On June 11th the Emperor and Empress celebrated their golden wedding, which was attended by representatives of all the European Courts. Public rejoicings were general throughout the empire, and large sums of money were collected for the endowment of charitable institutions in commemoration of the festival. A few weeks before, on May 13th, the Emperor had become a great-grandfather by the birth of the first child of the heir apparent to the duchy of Saxe-Meiningen, who last year was married to the oldest daughter of the Crown Prince of Prussia.

On May 17th a *Städtetag* (convention of cities) was held at Berlin, which was attended by the representatives of seventy-two cities and municipalities. The object of the meeting was to register their protest once more against the proposed new duties on cattle and corn, and to point out the wrongs and disadvantages which the laboring and industrial populations of large towns would thereby suffer. A resolution was passed setting forth that a tax on beef and bread would prevent workingmen from enjoying the necessary means of sustenance, would thereby lessen the power of labor, and thus impede the commercial activity of German towns. Only four of the seventy-two municipalities represented voted against the resolution.

The Supreme Court of Germany was opened at Leipsic on October 1st, in accordance with the laws finally passed on December 21, 1876. Dr. Friedberg, Secretary of State, in his inaugural speech, referred to the successful activity at Leipsic of the Supreme Imperial Court of Commerce, which was now absorbed and superseded by the new institutions, and lauded the legal unity now introduced into all Germany of which it was the crown and symbol. After the various members had been sworn in, Dr. Simson, the President of the Court and ex-President of the Reichstag, proposed three cheers for the German Emperor, which were given with great enthusiasm. The judiciary reforms which came into operation all over the empire on this day primarily affect the organization of the various courts and the forms of procedure. All previous upper courts are declared dissolved on the 30th of September, and in their place comes the Supreme Imperial Court, with its seat in Leipsic. Tribunals of first instance are formed by the Landesgerichte, or provincial courts, with their various dependent branches, while appeals will first go to the Oberlandesgerichte, or upper district courts, and afterward to the supreme tribunal, of which Dr. Simson is the head.

On January 24, 1879, a treaty of friendship was concluded between Germany and the chiefs of the Samoan Islands, which secures to the German merchants great advantages. The treaty was sanctioned by the German Reichstag on June 16th.

German trade in the South Pacific received a severe blow in 1879 by the failure of the house of J. C. Goddefroy & Son of Hamburg. This house had for two centuries been one of the largest of the German shipping-houses, and had established numerous stations in the South Sea Islands, notably in the Samoan Islands, which were virtually owned by them. In 1878 they transferred their property on these islands to the "German Commercial and Plantation Association of the South Seas," which was formed for that purpose. In order to protect the German interests at stake, it was proposed to reconstruct the company, which should pass under the immediate protection of the German Government. The coöperation of Prince Bismarck was secured, and a proposal to the above effect was to be submitted to the Reichstag upon its meeting in 1880.

During the year 1879 there were fifteen cases of cremation at Gotha. The time occupied in each case varied from one and a half to two and a half hours. The first case of cremation occurred in Gotha on December 10, 1878.

GERM THEORY OF DISEASE. The doctrine of *contagium vivum* is constantly being strengthened by new and substantial evidence derived from laborious investigations, undertaken by many scientists in different countries. If it can be shown that many of the epidemic and zymotic diseases are due to the invasion of the animal system by microscopic parasitic organisms, which increase with enormous rapidity, covering the tissues of the body or disturbing functional action, then the ways will soon be found for preventing some of the most mysterious, incurable, and destructive maladies which befall mankind, sweeping off the vigorous and the enfeebled with an equal fatality. Those classes of diseases which decimate the ranks of society have their generic representatives in many maladies to which the higher orders of animals are subject, to some of which the domestic animals fall a frequent prey, and from which they also may be preserved when the true source and nature of the disease is discovered. The fact that animals are also attacked by contagious diseases enables investigators to study closely and experimentally the theory of *contagium vivum* by subjecting them to infection and watching the symptoms, and subsequently examining the tissue and fluids of their bodies under the microscope to detect the expected parasitic destroyers.

The discovery that splenic fever is caused by the presence of a bacillus is followed by the detection, by the minute investigations of Dr. Klein, of another bacillus as the cause of a second disease to which one of the higher animals is subject — the infectious pneumoenteritis or typhoid fever of the pig. Cultivating the bacillus in such a way as to obtain it free from the presence of any other organism, he inoculated healthy swine with the fluid containing the bacteria. In due time the disease appeared, and followed its course with the usual train of symptoms. From the dried blood of horses which had died in India of the "Loodiana fever," which has committed fearful devastations in the East, a crop of *Bacillus anthracis* was raised in the Brown Institution in England, with which other animals were infected. Experiments proved that the exhausted malt from breweries upon which cattle are often fed affords a soil in which these bacteria thrive remarkably well. Cattle were infected with the anthrax by feeding them with such grain in which the bacillus had been cultivated. The practice of feeding stock with brewery refuse is therefore a constant source of danger; only recently the disorder broke out in a previously uninfected district in England, and inquiry showed that the cattle which suffered had all been fed upon grains procured at one particular brewery.

Dr. Koch, who a couple of years ago established the fact that splenic fever was always accompanied by a multiplication of the bacterial organism known as *Bacillus anthracis*, has turned his attention lately to infectious traumatic diseases, or those infectious disorders which originate in the introduction of poisonous matter through a wound. The presence of bacteria in the blood and tissues in these diseases has long been observed. In order to establish the doctrine of *contagium vivum*, it is necessary to prove not only that the bacteria are not merely incidental or resultant concomitants of the morbid symptoms, but that they are not introduced into the wound along with the poison or otherwise, and multiply because the tissue affords them nourishment, while the toxic effects are produced by a specific poisonous substance. To prove this, it is enough to show that each disease is attended by a distinct and well-characterized bacterial form, which coëxists with the particular symptoms, and is present in sufficient quantities to produce the morbid derangement, while on the other hand the different bacteria are never present in the tissue without being accompanied by the same particular symptoms. Koch's experiments for this purpose were very extensive. His method was to inoculate mice or rabbits with decomposing animal matter, and notice if any morbid symptoms resulted, and then to subject the tissues of the infected animal to a microscopic examination for the same form of microphyte which was contained in the injected fluid. In a series of experiments for producing septicæmia in mice, he found that putrid blood injected under their skin produced death in a few hours, but that the blood appeared to be free from bacterial life on microscopic examination, and was incapable of producing symptoms of disease in other animals inoculated with it. The bacteria introduced were found still confined in the subcutaneous cellular tissue of the dead subjects. He further found that a certain amount of the fluid required to be injected before the disease was produced. He therefore concluded that these symptoms were not due at all to living germs, but to a soluble poison—septin or sepsin—contained along with the bacteria in the putrid fluid. Another disease, however, was produced in about one third of the cases, no matter how small the quantity of the injected fluid. This disease ran through a certain order of characteristic symptoms, and was followed after a definite period by death. Taking the blood of one animal to infect another, he produced this form of traumatic septicæmia in seventeen successive subjects. He found that only house-mice were susceptible of the contagion, while on rabbits, and even on field-mice, the infected blood would have no effect. In the blood of the infected animals be detected swarms of bacteria of a definite form and size, bacillus-like in structure, which were evidently the contagion of this peculiar disease.

No other bacteria injected with these bacilli were able to live and multiply in the living tissue; but occasionally a form of micrococcus was observed which multiplied with great rapidity, forming chains in the subcutaneous tissue, while the bacillus lived and spread in the blood. This micrococcus when injected into the ear of the mouse produced a distinct disease—necrosis of the tissues of that organ. It found here so congenial a medium to propagate in, that it spread through and through the tissues until they were completely destroyed. This disease could never be produced in the house-mouse unless its blood was simultaneously infected with the septicæmia bacillus; but the field-mouse, which is not liable to septicæmia at all, could be infected from the house-mouse with the micrococcus, and the house-mouse when inoculated from an infected field-mouse then harbored the parasite, which spread in its chain-like forms with the same rapidity and produced the same symptoms of progressive necrosis as in the field-mouse, or in the house-mouse accompanied by septicæmia.

Injection of putrid blood into rabbits produced an entirely different effect. Abscesses were formed in the subcutaneous tissue, which increased gradually in size, causing death in a few days. These abscesses were found on examination to be surrounded by a thin layer of micrococci in the zooglœa state. The cheesy, granular contents of the abscesses were probably derived from the zooglœa and the dead tissues invested by them. A little of the matter of the abscess diffused in water invariably produced the disease in healthy subjects; but

the injection of the blood of the diseased rabbits produced no effect. The artificial production of pyæmia in rabbits revealed the presence of micrococci, but they were neither in chains nor in zooglœa films, and differed in size from those attending the other diseases. They occurred either singly or in pairs in the blood-vessels, surrounding the corpuscles, and formed accumulations which sometimes caused a stoppage in the vessels. By the injection of putrescent infusions both septicæmia and erysipelas were produced in rabbits. Septicæmia was accompanied by a distinct form of micrococcus, and could be transmitted from one animal to another. Erysipelas showed the presence of small bacilli, but could not be transmitted.

Pasteur believes that he has discovered in recent researches the microscopical organisms which produce puerperal fever and malignant pustule. The parasite which causes puerperal fever he describes as an entozoön containing two, four, or six cells united together. The cells have an average diameter each of two thousandths of a millimetre. His researches into the cause of malignant pustule have convinced Pasteur that this disease is engendered by the bacterium which Davaine discovered in 1860. The method of investigation was by obtaining the organisms to be observed by cultivation. This method, which he first employed in 1857, is the only means of obtaining specimens in a state of purity. He took a minute drop of blood from a case of malignant pustule, and sowed it in a liquid propitious for the development of the organisms—the froth of beer-yeast. By repeatedly infecting fresh yeast-froth with a drop of that which he had before infected, he could keep on hand for years a constant supply of the organisms. By introducing this liquid into the blood of guinea-pigs, sheep, and certain other animals, malignant pustules were reproduced in them. If he filtered the liquid through a plaster filter, the germs remained on the filtering substance, with which the disease could be inoculated, but not with the filtered fluid. The poultry cholera can be cultivated and fowls infected in the same manner. Puerperal septicæmia could probably also be preserved by culture and inoculated from the medium of cultivation. Thus the evidence in favor of the germ theory is rapidly accumulating.

The facts that the above diseases can be communicated from one animal to another by the injection of infinitesimal quantities of the diseased blood or tissue, that each disease has its own characteristic form of bacterium, and that they multiply at a sufficient rate to account for the symptoms, seem to prove the parasitic origin of these diseases. There is conflicting evidence which leaves the question of a living contagium still in doubt, even in regard to some of the diseases in which the presence of a characteristic microphyte has been established. Panum, Richardson, and others, for instance, have discovered that a septiferous fluid can not be deprived of its virulent properties by either filtering, boiling, evaporation, or combination with acids in the form of salts. As no life could survive such operations, it must be inferred that the toxic agent is not the zoöphytes themselves, but a specific poison produced by them by a process of fermentation in the putrescent fluid.

Professors Klebs of Prague and Tommasi of Rome spent several weeks in the spring season in the Agro Romano, a part of the Roman Campagna, notorious for the prevalence of marsh or intermittent fever, in investigating into the physical cause or specific poison of this disease. This they believe that they have discovered in a minute fungus which abounds in the soil and the lower strata of the air in that region. This microscopic fungus is a bacillus, growing in rod-shaped forms. It consists of numerous movable, shining spores of elongated oval form. They cultivated the germs artificially in different kinds of soil. The residual solids of this bacterium, after the soluble matter had been repeatedly filtered and washed out, were cupable, when injected under the skin of a dog, of bringing on all the symptoms of the disease in their regular order. To this newly discovered epizoötic parasite the name of *Bacillus malariæ* has been given.

Besides the diseases in which the presence of a characteristic microscopic parasite has been actually observed, the number of which is already considerable, as has been seen, and those in which there are strong indications of a similar origin, and those others which by analogy may be ascribed to such a cause, there is a tendency to attribute to morbific bacteria certain diseases which are not classed as epidemic, as contagious, nor scarcely as endemic, so great a hold has the germ theory lately acquired upon scientific minds. In Germany it is now held, on almost purely theoretical grounds, that tuberculosis is caused by a specific bacterial germ. Even Professor Klebs of Prague, who stands high as a medical authority, is committed to this theory. The effects of a novel cure for phthisis, which is producing an unusual stir in German medical circles, are ascribed to its destroying the living germs. The new remedy is sodium benzoate. The method of taking it is described as follows: *Natrium benzoicum* (sodium benzoate)—1 per mille of the bodily weight, diluted to a solution of 5 per cent.—is inhaled twice a day, in the morning and evening, by means of a Siegel's pulverizator (an atomizing inhaler), for seven weeks uninterruptedly. The appetite, which is said to be soon excited by this treatment, should be fully satisfied by a meat diet, plenty of fresh air taken, and all enervating influences avoided. The proportion of the salt to be inhaled—$\frac{1}{1000}$ of the bodily weight of the patient at each inhalation, or about $2\frac{1}{4}$ ounces for a person weighing 140 pounds—is strictly adhered to: the inhaler must be care-

fully adjusted to permit such a large amount to enter the air-passages; and still a portion will escape, so that the patient should remain in the room an hour at least after each inhalation. This treatment is said to have produced remarkable cures in the hospital at Innspruck and elsewhere. It might be expected to prevent the formation of pus in the morbid cavities; but it is said to attack the true seat of the disease, and put an end to the tuberculizing process—and this, as is boldly held, by destroying the characteristic bacteria to which the degeneration of the tissue is solely due. Rabbits confined in an atmosphere of these benzoic vapors can not be infected with tuberculosis, although the disease can otherwise be readily induced in these animals. The benzoate of soda is extremely irritating to the air-passages, and many patients would find difficulty in breathing such large quantities of the fumes.

GODON, SYLVANUS W., a naval officer, born in Pennsylvania, died in France, May 20, 1879. He entered the navy as a midshipman in 1819, and reached the rank of lieutenant in 1836. In 1847 he took part in the siege of Vera Cruz as an officer of the bomb-brig Vesuvius. After the breaking out of the civil war in 1861 he was commissioned as captain, and took command of the sloop of war Powhatan, one of the vessels employed in Du Pont's expedition to Port Royal. In 1863 he was promoted to be commodore, and commanded the steamer Susquehanna and the fourth division of Admiral Porter's squadron at the two battles of Fort Fisher, December, 1864, and January, 1865. Commissioned as rear-admiral July 25, 1866, he commanded the South Atlantic squadron on the coast of Brazil during that year and 1867. From 1868 to 1870 he was commandant at the Brooklyn Navy Yard, and was subsequently placed on the retired list.

GOLDTHWAITE, GEORGE, a jurist and Senator, born in Boston, Massachusetts, December 10, 1809, died at Montgomery, Alabama, March 18, 1879. He received his early education in Boston, at a grammar-school then attended by Charles Sumner, R. C. Winthrop, and George S. Hillard. In his fourteenth year he was appointed a cadet at West Point, and was there at the time when ex-President Davis, Generals Lee and Joe Johnston, and Bishop Polk were students in the Academy. In 1826 he left West Point and went to Montgomery, where he began the study of law in the office of his brother, and was admitted to the bar in his eighteenth year. He located at Monticello, Pike County, where he remained many years. He then returned to Montgomery, where he practiced with increasing reputation till December, 1843, when he was elected to the Circuit Court bench. He held this post till January, 1852, when he was elected a Justice of the Supreme Court. By the resignation of Judge Chilton in January, 1856, Judge Goldthwaite became Chief Justice, a dignity he held only thirteen days. Resigning, he returned to practice. When hostilities began between the States, he was appointed by Governor Moore Adjutant-General of the State, and held the place about three years. In 1866 he was elected Judge of the Circuit Court, but he was ejected from office by an act of Congress in 1868. In 1870 he was elected to the Senate of the United States. His term expired on March 3, 1877, and he was succeeded by John T. Morgan. His career on the bench established his reputation as a calm and profound jurist. He was warm in his attachments, exceedingly kind, charitable, and just in his transactions, and was esteemed as a useful citizen and prudent public servant.

GRANT, ULYSSES S. The second term of General Grant as President of the United States expired on March 4, 1877. He soon left Washington for Philadelphia, with the design of making a tour of the world. This he began on May 17th, with his wife and elder son, by embarking on board the steamship Indiana at that port. He arrived in Liverpool on the 28th, having made the passage in eleven days. From Liverpool he went to London, and dined with the Duke of Wellington on the 2d of June. During his stay in England the General was honored with an invitation to dine with Queen Victoria at Windsor Castle. The invitation having been given and accepted in due form, at half-past eight on the 26th of June the Queen, surrounded by her court, received him in the magnificent corridor leading to her private apartments in the Quadrangle. The dinner was served in the Oak Room. Among those present were Prince Leopold, Prince Christian, Princess Beatrice, Lord and Lady Derby, the Duchess of Wellington, General Badeau, and others. After dinner the Queen entered into conversation with the party, and about 10 o'clock took her leave, followed by her suite. The next morning the General and party returned to London, and for some days afterward received the most flattering attentions from the nobility and the statesmen of the kingdom. On the 26th of July the ex-President and his party arrived in Geneva, Switzerland. He afterward crossed the Simplon Pass, made the tour of the northern part of Italy, and returned to Ragatz by the 14th of August. Thence he made a flying trip through Alsace and Lorraine. Returning to England, he left London on the 5th of July for Ostend, where King Leopold tendered the party the use of the royal car to Brussels. On their way they stopped and examined the principal places of interest at Ghent. On the 7th of July King Leopold of Belgium called on General Grant at his hotel, and had a long conversation with him. The visit was returned the next day at the palace. The party arrived in Palermo, Italy, on the 23d of December. Here they spent Christmas, and dined on board the United States ship Vandalia. On the morning of January 19, 1878, the ex-President and his com-

panions entered Siout, Egypt, and were welcomed by the American Vice-Consul and his son. From Egypt he proceeded to Jaffa on the Mediterranean, and thence made the tour of the Holy Land. After a trip full of pleasant and complimentary incidents, he embarked from Beyrout, in Syria, for Constantinople, and arrived there immediately after the treaty of San Stefano, which ended the late Russo-Turkish war. Thence he proceeded to European Turkey, and returned to Stamboul on the 5th of March, where he was received by the diplomatic representatives of the United States. In the latter part of March the ex-President sailed for Italy, arriving in Rome soon after the election of Leo XIII. to the Pontificate. Having visited the principal cities of Italy, the party left for France and arrived in Paris on the 7th of May, and thence soon after went to Holland. From Holland they went to Germany, arriving in Berlin on the 26th of June, when they were met by the late Minister, Bayard Taylor. They reached Hamburg by rail on July 2d, and made a tour through Denmark, Sweden, and Norway. On the last of the month the party crossed the Baltic from Stockholm to St. Petersburg. After a visit to the principal cities of Russia and to Poland, the ex-President reached Vienna, Austria, on the 18th of August; thence he proceeded to Switzerland, and thence through southern France, and finally to Spain. The ex-President arrived at Vitoria on the 16th of October, having entered Spain from France via Bayonne, and was received by Señor Castelar, ex-President of the Spanish Republic, and subsequently by King Alfonso. In December the party was still in Spain and Portugal. In January, 1879, the General and party visited Ireland, and returned thence to Paris. On the 24th he embarked at Marseilles for Bombay, India, where he arrived on the 12th of February. The ex-President's visit to India was marked by the attention and respect shown him everywhere by the native officers and English rulers. In Calcutta, where he arrived on the 10th of March, he was received by a guard of honor and an aide-de camp of the Viceroy. At a state dinner given in the evening, Lord Lytton, in an eloquent speech, proposed a toast to their distinguished guest. All the notables of India were present. After dinner the General received many native gentlemen and princes. On the 17th he proceeded to Burmah, and thence to China. At Bangkok he received a letter from the King of Siam inviting him to visit that kingdom as the guest of the Government. The letter was encased in royal purple satin. The party arrived at Hong Kong on the evening of April 30th. The ship was boarded by United States Consuls Mosby of Hong-Kong and Lincoln of Canton, Chargé d'Affaires Holcombe, and deputations of citizens of various countries, including Japan. The party was received at Canton on May 6th by the consular officials and conducted to the Viceroy's residence. They left Hong Kong for

the north of China on May 11th. There were
receptions and entertainments by European and
Chinese parties, and a public garden gathering.
The ex-President and his party reached Yokohama, Japan, about the 1st of July, and on the
4th the distinguished tourist, accompanied by
Mrs. Grant, was admitted to an audience with
the Emperor and Empress. The Mikado welcomed his guest in a cordial speech, highly eulogistic of the ex-President and of the country
which he represented. It gave him, he said,
especial pleasure to greet the ex-President on
the anniversary ef the independence of the
United States. On the 7th there was a brilliant review in honor of the General, and on
the 8th a gorgeous festival was arranged for
him in the great hall of the Kobu Dai Gaku.
No effort was spared by the Japanese authorities to make his stay in that country agreeable
and varied in all its phases. A special and
highly complimentary feature of his visit to
China was his conversation with Li-Hung-
Chang, Viceroy of the Province of Tientsin, in which the General was invited to become the mediator between that Government
and Japan concerning the Loo-choo difficulty,
the Viceroy's proposition being authorized by
Prince Kung. The party left Yokohama on
the 25th of August, and had a pleasant passage
to San Francisco, where they arrived on September 20th. During this tour he was received
with distinguished honors by the following
persons, besides many others: Queen Victoria
of England; King Leopold of Belgium; the
Khedive of Egypt; the Sultan of Turkey;
King Humbert of Italy; Pope Leo XIII.;
President MacMahon of France; the King
of Holland; Emperor William of Germany;
Prince Bismarck; King Oscar of Sweden; the
Emperor Alexander of Russia; the Emperor
Francis Joseph of Austria; King Alfonso of
Spain; President Grévy of France; M. Gambetta; Viceroy Lytton of India; King Thebaw
of Burmah; Prince Kung of China; the Emperor of Siam; the Mikado of Japan. His reception in San Francisco was very flattering.
He visited several towns in this State, also
Oregon and the adjoining States, and returned
slowly to his home in Illinois, and thence to
Philadelphia. At the close of the year he left
for a tour in the West India Islands and Mexico. (See preceding volumes of "Annual Cyclopædia.")

GREAT BRITAIN AND IRELAND, a kingdom of western Europe. The Queen, Victoria,
was born May 24, 1819. She is a daughter of
Prince Edward, Duke of Kent, the fourth son
of George III.; succeeded her uncle, William
IV., in 1837; and married in 1840 Prince Albert of Saxe-Coburg-Gotha.

Children of the Queen.—1. Princess Victoria, born November 21, 1840; married in 1858
to the present Crown Prince of Germany. 2.
Prince Albert Edward, heir apparent, born
November 9, 1841; married in 1863 to Princess Alexandra, daughter of King Christian IX.

of Denmark. Issue, two sons and three daughters; eldest son, Albert Victor, born January
8, 1864. 3. Princess Alice, born April 25,
1843; married in 1862 to Louis IV., Grand
Duke of Hesse; died December 14, 1878. .4.
Prince Alfred, Duke of Edinburgh, born August 6, 1844; married in 1874 to the Grand
Duchess Maria of Russia. He is heir apparent
to the Duke of Saxe-Coburg-Gotha. He has
issue one son and three daughters. 5. Princess
Helena, born May 25, 1846; married in 1866
to Prince Christian of Schleswig-Holstein-Son-
derburg-Augustenburg. 6. Princess Louise,
born March 18, 1848; married in 1871 to the
Marquis of Lorne. 7. Prince Arthur, Duke of
Connaught and Strathearne, born May 1, 1850;
married March 13, 1879, to Princess Louise
Margaretha, daughter of Prince Frederick
Charles of Prussia. 8. Prince Leopold, born
April 7, 1853. 9. Princess Beatrice, born
April 14, 1857. .

The Cabinet was composed as follows at the
close of 1879: First Lord of the Treasury,
Right Hon. Benjamin Disraeli, Earl of Beacons-
field; Lord High Chancellor, Lord Cairns;
Lord President of the Council, Duke of Rich-
mond and Gordon; Lord Privy Seal, Duke of
Northumberland; Chancellor of the Exchequer,
Sir S. H. Northcote, Bart., M. P.; Secretaries
of State: 1. Home Department, Right Hon. R.
A. Cross; 2. Foreign Affairs, Marquis of Salis
bury; 3. Colonies, Sir Michael Hicks-Beach;
4. War, Colonel Frederick Stanley, M. P.; 5.
India, Viscount Cranbrook; First Lord of the
Admiralty, Right Hon. W. H. Smith, M. P.;
Postmaster-General, Right Hon. Lord John J.
R. Manners, M. P.; President of the Ministry
of Commerce, Lord Sandon.

Parliament is composed of two Houses, the
House of Lords and the House of Commons.
The number of peers in 1879 was 494. Of
these, 5 were peers of the royal blood, 2 archbishops, 21 dukes, 19 marquises, 115 earls, 24
bishops, 25 viscounts, and 247 barons. In addition to these there are 16 Scotch and 28 Irish
representative peers, making in all 502 members. The Speaker of the House of Lords was
Lord Cairns, the Lord High Chancellor, and
the Chairman of Committees Lord Redesdale.
The Speaker of the House of Commons was
Henry Bouverie William Brand, and the Chairman of Committees Henry Cecil Raikes. The
members of the House of Commons are elected
by the counties, boroughs, and universities.

The area and population of the British Empire in 1879 were as follows:

COUNTRIES.	Area in square miles.	Population.
United Kingdom.............	121,608	34,517,118
India and Ceylon.............	924,043	198,851,002
Colonies and possessions.......	7,208,322	11,812,894
Total British Empire......	8,253,973	240,281,009
Tributary states in India.......	557,903	49,203,053
Total empire and tributary states................	8,811,876	289,484,062

The following table gives a complete list of the colonies and possessions:

COUNTRIES.	Square miles.	Population.	Year.	COUNTRIES.	Square miles.	Population.	Year.
I. EUROPE:				**IV. AUSTRALASIA:**			
Heligoland	0·21	1,918	1871	Queensland	668,259	208,000	1878
Gibraltar	1·98	25,143	1873	New South Wales	308,560	675,000	1878
Malta	142·73	147,306	1876	Norfolk Island	16·8	451	1871
				Victoria	88,451	887,000	1878
Total Europe	144·87	174,862	....	South Australia	380,602 }	287,000	1878
II. ASIA:				Northern Territory	523,581 }		
Cyprus	3,708	185,000	....	Western Australia	975,824	28,000	1878
British India	899,341	191,095,445	1872	Natives in Australia	.....	100,000	1878
Ceylon	24,702	2,755,557	1877	Tasmania	26,215	107,000	1878
Straits Settlements	1,445	308,097	1871	New Zealand	104,272	414,216	1878
Hong-Kong	32	139,144	1876	Maoris in New Zealand	.....	48,219	1878
Labuan	30	4,898	1871	Chatham Islands	628	196	1878
Nicobar Islands	725	5,900	1857	Auckland Islands	196·7	.....	....
Andaman Islands	2,551	13,500	1874	Lord Howe's Island	3·2	25	1878
Laccadive Islands	744	6,800	?	Feejee Islands	8,033·8	4,555	1877
Ouria-Muria Islands	21	.....	....	Natives of the Feejee			
Aden	7·71	22,707	1872	Islands	.....	118,000	1876
Perim	4·55	?	....	Fanning Island	21	150	1858
Mosha	0·4	?	....	Starbuck Island	?	.....	....
Kamaran	64	500	....	Caroline Island	25·5	.....	....
Keeling Islands	8·5	400	1853	Malden Island	32	79	1876
Total Asia	933,384	194,487,048	....	Total Australasia	3,048,671	2,872,951	....
III. AFRICA:				**V. AMERICA:**			
Cape Colony, inclusive of British Caffraria	199,950	720,984	1875	Dominion of Canada	3,872,290	3,666,596	1871
Basuto Land	8,450	127,701	1875	Newfoundland	40,200	161,374	1874
West Griqua Land	16,632	45,277	1877	Bermuda	40·8	18,601	1877
Transkei Territory	12,452	254,500	....	British Honduras	7,562	24,710	1871
Natal	18,750	325,512	1877	Bahama Islands	5,390	39,162	1871
Transvaal	114,340	40,000	....	Turks Islands	9·7	2,845	1871
Natives in Transvaal	.....	275,000	....	Caicos Islands	213	1,878	1871
Namaqua Land	99,927	16,850	....	Jamaica	4,193	506,154	1871
Damara Land	99,965	121,150	....	Caymans Islands	225	2,400	1871
Gambia	69	14,190	1871	Leeward Islands	650·6	118,018	....
Sierra Leone	468	38,936	1871	Windward Islands	530	292,985	....
Gold Coast	16,626	520,070	1871	Trinidad	1.754	109,688	1871
Lagos	73	60,221	1871	British Guiana	85,425	218,909	1874
St. Helena	47	6,241	1871	Indians and garrison in			
Ascension	84	27	1871	Guiana	.....	21,600	....
Tristan da Cunha	45	85	1875	Falkland Islands	6,500	1,320	1877
Mauritius	739	348,265	1877	Staten Island	?	.....	....
Dependencies of Mauritius	286·5	18,891	1871	Total America	3,525,283	5,201,135	....
New Amsterdam	25·5	.....	....				
St. Paul	2·8	.....	....	Total British colonies			
Total Africa	583,882	2,928,400	....	and possessions	8,182,365	205,663,896	....

The following table gives the area and population of the United Kingdom according to the census of 1871, as well as the estimates of the Registrar-General (who does not include the islands in the British waters, nor the soldiers and sailors abroad) for 1877, 1878, and 1879:

COUNTRIES.	Acres.	Pop. in 1871.	Pop. in 1877.	Pop. in 1878.	Pop. in 1879.
England and Wales	37,319,221	22,712,266	24,547,309	24,854,987	25,165,836
Scotland	19,495,132	3,360,018	3,560,715	3,593,989	3,627,458
Ireland	20,819,903	5,412,377	5,388,906	5,351,060	5,368,824
Islands in the British waters	193,647	144,638	145,000	145,000	145,000
Soldiers and sailors abroad	....	216,080	216,000	216,000	216,000
Total	77,828,903	31,845,879	33,607,930	34,160,386	34,517,118

The British colonies are grouped in forty administrative divisions, some of them embracing a number of formerly separate colonies. Of these four are in Europe, eleven in America, ten in Africa, seven in Asia, and eight in Australasia. According to the form of government the colonies are divided into three classes, viz.: 1. Crown colonies, in which the Crown has entire control of legislation, while the administration is carried on by public officers under the control of the Home Government; 2. Colonies possessing representative institutions, in which the Crown has no more than a veto on legislation, but the Home Government retains the control of public officers; 3. Colonies possessing responsible governments, in which the Home Government has no control over any public officer except its own representative. The first class embraces twenty-four colonies, the second class seven, and the third class nine. The latter comprise Canada, Newfoundland, Cape Colony, and the colonies of the Australian continent, with the exception of Western Australia.

The movement of population from 1871 to 1878, according to the "Statistical Abstract of the United Kingdom," No. 26, 1864–1878 (London, 1879), was as follows: ·

YEARS.	Marriages.	Births.	Deaths.	Excess of births.
ENGLAND AND WALES.				
1871................	190,112	797,428	514,879	282,549
1872................	201,267	825,907	492,265	333,642
1873................	205,615	829,778	492,520	387,258
1874................	202,010	854,956	526,682	328,324
1875................	201,212	850,607	546,453	304,154
1876................	201,874	887,968	510,815	377,653
1877................	194,859	888,200	500,496	387,704
1878................	180,657	891,418	539,574	351,844
SCOTLAND.				
1871................	28,966	116,127	74,644	41,483
1872................	25,580	118,873	75,741	43,182
1873................	26,780	119,733	76,857	42,876
1874................	26,247	123,795	80,676	43,119
1875................	25,921	123,693	81,785	41,908
1876................	26,563	126,749	74,122	52,627
1877................	25,790	126,824	73,946	52,878
1878................	24,833	126,707	76,715	49,982
IRELAND.				
1871................	28,960	151,665	88,720	62,945
1872................	27,114	149,292	97,577	51,715
1873................	26,270	144,877	97,587	46,840
1874................	24,481	141,288	91,961	49,327
1875................	24,037	138,820	98,114	40,206
1876................	26,888	140,469	92,324	48,145
1877................	24,722	139,659	98,543	46,116
1878................	25,368	134,370	99,839	34,531

The sum raised by poor-rates in England and Wales in 1878 was £12,585,677; the receipts in aid amounted to £904,035, forming a total receipt of £13,489,712. The gross rental during the same period amounted to £150,980,-679. The number of paupers was 805,080. In Scotland the number of paupers on May 14, 1879, was 97,676, and in Ireland in 1878, 324,046.

The following table gives the population of the principal cities in July, 1879, according to the estimates of the Registrar-General:

1. London........ 3,620,863
2. Glasgow...... 578,156
3. Liverpool.... 588,838
4. { Manchester.. 361,819 / { Salford 177,849
5. Birmingham .. 388,884
6. Dublin........ 314,666
7. Leeds........ 311,860
8. Sheffield 297,188
9. Edinburgh.... 226,075
10. Bristol........ 209,947
11. Bradford...... 191,046

12. Nottingham.... 169,896
13. Newcastle - on - Tyne.......... 146,948
14. Hull.......... 146,347
15. Portsmouth.... 131,831
16. Leicester...... 125,622
17. Sunderland..... 114,515
18. Oldham........ 111,318
19. Brighton...... 105,008
20. Norwich...... 85,222
21. Wolverhampton 75,100
22. Plymouth...... 74,293

The number of emigrants from the United Kingdom during the years 1853-1878 was as follows:

NATIONALITIES.	To United States.	To British North America.	To Australia and New Zealand.	To other countries.	Total.
English........................	989,071	195,094	519,408	110,464	1,814,082
Scotch.........................	175,982	73,651	128,582	16,279	394,504
Irish	1,602,165	124,095	222,904	18,925	1,968,079
Foreigners	618,221	89,785	21,290	23,218	752,514
Not specified.........	167,689	52,796	20,898	53,522	304,855
1853-1878..................	3,548,078	535,421	923,077	222,408	5,228,984
1815-1878..................	5,612,659	1,572,185	1,233,913	273,869	8,692,576

The number of emigrants from the United Kingdom in 1878 was as follows:

NATIONALITIES.	To United States.	To British North America.	To Australia and New Zealand.	To other countries.	Total.
English.......	32,099	7,957	23,055	9,212	72,323
Scotch.......	3,998	1,155	4,871	1,068	11,087
Irish	18,602	1,540	8,553	797	29,492
Foreign.......	25,659	3,127	723	2,183	31,697
Not specified .	1,204	57	7	1,796	3,064
1878......	81,557	13,830	37,214	15,056	147,663

The receipts and expenditures from 1872 to 1879 were as follows:

YEARS.	Receipts.	Expenditures.	Surplus (S.) or Deficit (D.).
1872-'73....	£76,608,770	£70,714,448	S. £5,894,322
1873-'74...........	77,385,657	76,466,510	S. 869,147
1874-'75...........	74,921,873	74,328,040	S. 593,888
1875-'76...........	77,181,693	76,621,773	S. 509,920
1876-'77...........	78,565,086	78,125,227	S. 489,809
1877-'78...........	79,763,298	82,403,495	D. 2,640,197
1878-'79...........	83,115,972	85,407,789	D. 2,291,817

The revenue for the year ending March 31, 1879, was as follows, showing a slight increase in customs receipts, a large falling off in the income-tax, and a slight decrease in stamp-duties and some of the other items:

SOURCES.	Gross receipts.	Delivered to the Exchequer.
1. Customs.................	£20,499,253	£20,816,000
2. Excise..................	27,875,164	27,400,000
3. Stamps	10,844,397	10,670,000
4. Land-tax and house-duty.	2,703,800	2,720,000
5. Property and income-tax.	8,952,068	8,710,000
6. Post-Office	6,277,682	6,240,000
7. Telegraph service......	1,590,422	1,325,000
8. Crown lands	489,449	410,000
9. Interest of sums advanced for local works and the purchase of Suez Canal shares.................	1,091,752	1,091,752
10. Miscellaneous...........	4,216,707	4,223,220
Total..............	£35,540,194	£83,115,972

The expenditures were as follows:

Payments out of the Exchequer for services charged on the consolidated fund:

Interest and management of debt......	£21,516,872
Terminable annuities....................	5,711,818
Interest of exchequer bills................	188,484
New sinking fund.......................	633,876
Interest on loans by Bank of England......	314,932
Interest and principal of Exchequer bonds (Suez)...............	329,251

Other charges on the consolidated fund:

Civil list..........	407,108
Annuities............	156,621
Pensions	157,045
Salaries......	94,459
Courts of justice......	687,806
Miscellaneous expenses	171,389
Civil service..........	14,974,761

Voted-supply services:

Army services.................	17,658,473
" " charged on account of troops in India......	1,080,000

Expedition to Abyssinia	17,865
War in South Africa	1,500,000
Navy services	11,962,816

Charges on the revenue:

Customs	962,722
Inland revenue	1,594,447
Post-office	8,273,000
Telegraph service	1,109,000
Post-office packet service	777,600
Total ordinary expenditure	£85,407,789
Localization of the military forces	450,000
Greenwich Hospital and School	145,120
Exchequer bonds paid off	4,250,000
Other expenses	38,468,956
Total	£128,721,565

The public debt of Great Britain was as follows at each of the periods mentioned:

MARCH 31.	Funded debt.	Terminable annuities.	Not funded debt.	Total.
1874...	£723,514,005	£51,289,640	£4,479,600	£779,283,245
1875...	714,797,715	55,811,671	5,239,800	775,848,686
1876...	718,657,517	51,911,227	10,701,800	776,270,544
1877...	712,621,355	49,808,558	13,948,800	775,878,713
1878...	710,543,008	46,835,589	20,603,000	777,781,597
1879...	709,430,558	42,778,147	25,870,100	778,078,840

The British army is filled up exclusively by recruiting. The term of service is twelve years, after which a soldier can serve for nine years more. At the end of three years he can also enter the reserve, one year in the regular army being counted as three in the reserve. By the reorganization of 1872, the United Kingdom is divided into 68 military districts. In each district there is one brigade depot of 182 men, two battalions of the regular army, which alternately serve abroad, two battalions of militia, and the volunteers of the district. Besides these there are the following organizations: In Ireland there is a police force under military discipline, consisting of 13,000 men and 4,000 horses; the Channel Islands have a militia of 300 officers and 7,000 men, subsidized by the British Government; India has a police force, under military discipline, of 190,000 men, the officers of which are Europeans; the colonies all have a militia and a volunteer corps of their own. In 1878 the army, excepting the last-mentioned forces, was composed as follows:

TROOPS.	Officers.	Soldiers.	Total.	Animals.*
I. REGULAR ARMY.				
1. Cavalry	854	16,446	17,300	13,525
2. Artillery	1,400	83,850	85,250	14,660
3. Engineers	840	4,810	5,650	450
4. Infantry	4,850	121,150	126,000	1,250
5. Colonial corps	122	2,368	2,490	12
6. Administrative corps	1,734	5,746	7,480	1,950
7. Reserve	1,500	58,500	60,000	......
Total	11,300	242,870	254,170	42,147
II. TERRITORIAL ARMY.				
1. Yeomanry and militia	4,600	126,790	131,390	15,800
2. Volunteers	7,700	186,510	194,210	1,770
Total	12,300	313,300	325,600	17,570
III. IMPERIAL ARMY OF NATIVES IN INDIA.				
1. Gardes du corps	2	170	172	70
2. Cavalry	310	18,500	18,810	20,100
3. Artillery	20	800	820	600
4. Engineers	40	3,200	3,240	200
5. Infantry	1,100	101,200	102,300	2,220
6. Staffs	1,528	......	1,528	1,000
Total	3,300†	123,870‡	127,170	24,190
Grand Total	26,900	680,040	706,940	78,907

In 1878 the army was distributed as follows:

TROOPS.	Great Britain.	Colonies.	India.	Total.
I. Regular army	151,400	40,120	62,650	254,170
II. Territorial army	325,600	......	......	325,600
III. Native Indian army	......	......	127,170	127,170
Total	477,000	40,120	189,820	706,940

The navy consists of 68 ironclads, about 360 steamers, and 120 sailing vessels. Of this number 254 were in commission on September 1, 1879, 122 being at home, and 132 abroad. The navy is manned by 45,800 seamen, 13,000 marines, and 21,420 men belonging to the Royal Navy reserve.

The imports and exports of merchandise from 1874 to 1878 were as follows:

YEARS.	IMPORTS.	EXPORTS.		
		British goods.	Foreign and colonial goods.	Total.
1878	£368,771,000	£192,849,000	£52,635,000	£245,484,000
1877	394,420,000	198,893,000	53,453,000	252,346,000
1876	375,155,000	200,680,000	56,137,000	256,776,000
1875	373,940,000	223,466,000	58,140,000	281,612,000
1874	370,083,000	239,558,000	58,092,000	297,650,000
1869-'73 (average)	331,143,000	224,806,000	53,247,000	278,053,000

The declared value of the imports and exports of precious metals, coined and in bars, in the same period, was as follows:

YEARS.	GOLD.		SILVER.		TOTAL.	
	Imports.	Exports.	Imports.	Exports.	Imports.	Exports.
1878	£20,871,000	£14,969,000	£11,552,000	£11,718,000	£32,423,000	£26,687,000
1877	15,442,000	20,361,000	21,711,000	19,437,000	37,153,000	39,798,000
1876	28,476,000	16,514,000	13,578,000	12,948,000	37,054,000	29,464,000
1875	23,141,000	18,048,000	10,124,000	8,980,000	33,265,000	27,628,000
1874	18,081,000	10,462,000	12,298,000	12,212,000	30,379,000	22,554,000

* Horses, elephants, and steers.   † English officers.   ‡ Native officers and soldiers.

The value of imports and exports in the years 1877 and 1878 was as follows:

COUNTRIES.	IMPORTS.		EXPORTS.	
	1877.	1878.	1877.	1878.
I. FOREIGN COUNTRIES.				
Russia..............................	£22,142,000	£17,804,000	£4,179,000	£6,559,000
Sweden and Norway..............	10,455,000	9,127,000	4,181,000	2,799,000
Denmark and Iceland............	3,950,000	4,585,000	1,828,000	1,526,000
Germany........	26,270,000	23,571,000	19,642,000	19,457,000
Netherlands.......................	12,861,000	21,466,000	9,614,000	9,808,000
Belgium...........................	12,889,000	12,387,000	5,804,000	5,526,000
France.............................	45,823,000	41,379,000	14,283,000	14,595,000
Spain..............................	10,842,000	9,115,000	8,687,000	8,211,000
Portugal, with the Azores........	4,089,000	3,516,000	2,425,000	2,226,000
Italy...............................	4,101,000	3,252,000	6,219,000	5,364,000
Austria-Hungary..................	1,541,000	1,866,000	1,042,000	763,000
Greece, with the Ionian Islands..	2,454,000	1,763,000	867,000	982,000
European and Asiatic Turkey.....	6,852,000	4,779,000	5,625,000	7,742,000
Roumania..........................	247,000	971,000	197,000	887,000
Egypt..............................	11,302,000	6,145,000	2,273,000	2,194,000
Europe and Mediterranean countries....	£182,618,000	£161,626,000	£81,266,000	£83,870,000
United States of North America...........	£77,826,000	£89,146,000	£16,877,000	£14,552,000
Mexico............	799,000	507,000	996,000	778,000
Central America	1,850,000	968,000	980,000	782,000
Cuba and Porto Rico..............	1,505,000	1,805,000	2,244,000	1,890,000
Other West Indian Islands.	262,000	247,000	628,000	572,000
Venezuela.........................	64,000	98,000	620,000	478,000
Colombia..........................	472,000	938,000	912,000	1,082,000
Ecuador...........................	186,000	800,000	252,000	200,000
Brazil.............................	6,345,000	4,651,000	5,959,000	5,518,000
Argentine Republic and Uruguay..........	2,434,000	1,744,000	3,170,000	3,316,000
Chili...............................	3,280,000	2,199,000	1,501,000	1,191,000
Peru...............................	4,697,000	5,232,000	1,266,000	1,870,000
America............	£99,250,000	£107,820,000	£34,850,000	£31,679,000
China, without Hong-Kong..............	£13,421,000	£18,601,000	£24,405,000	£23,788,000
Japan...............................	784,000	629,000	2,203,000	2,616,000
Dutch East Indies..................	1,956,000	1,851,000	2,061,000	1,668,000
Philippine Islands..................	1,756,000	1,258,000	1,292,000	835,000
Algeria............................	562,000	857,000	211,000	169,000
Morocco............................	812,000	891,000	398,000	191,000
Canary Islands	297,000	828,000	172,000	170,000
West Coast of Africa................	1,626,000	1,286,000	1,178,000	1,140,000
Other countries....................	1,834,000	1,678,000	879,000	1,040,000
Asia and Africa....................	£22,998,000	£21,879,000	£12,854,000	£11,562,000
Total foreign countries..............	£304,866,000	£290,835,000	£128,970,000	£126,611,000
II. BRITISH POSSESSIONS.				
Channel Islands....................	£724,000	£726,000	£555,000	£586,000
Gibraltar.... ....:....	70,000	85,000	869,000	710,000
Malta..............................	286,000	177,000	819,000	1,161,000
Colonies in North America..........	12,036,000	9,531,000	7,614,000	6,487,000
West Indies, Honduras, and Guinea........	7,129,000	6,838,000	3,007,000	2,780,000
Australia and New Zealand..............	21,782,000	20,855,000	19,286,000	19,578,000
East Indies........................	31,225,000	27,470,000	25,888,000	28,277,000
Singapore.........................	2,722,000	2,587,000	2,276,000	1,776,000
Ceylon............................	4,499,000	2,922,000	1,045,000	808,000
Hong-Kong.........................	1,895,000	1,674,000	3,508,000	2,871,000
Mauritius..........................	1,891,000	887,000	403,000	409,000
Colonies in South Africa............	4,275,000	4,381,000	4,116,000	4,913,000
British West Africa, and islands...........	768,000	622,000	810,000	873,000
Other possessions..................	302,000	286,000	187,000	189,000
Total British possessions..............	£89,554,000	£77,986,000	£69,923,000	£66,288,000
Total imports and exports..............	£394,420,000	£368,771,000	£198,893,000	£192,849,000

The commercial navy was as follows in 1877 and 1878:

PARTICULARS.	SAILING VESSELS.		STEAMSHIPS.		TOTAL.	
	Vessels.	Tons.	Vessels.	Tons.	Vessels.	Tons.
Number of ships registered :						
United Kingdom.... { 1877....................	21,169	4,261,000	4,564	2,139,000	25,733	6,400,000
1878.	21,058	4,239,000	4,826	2,316,000	25,884	6,555,000
Number of vessels used in 1878 (exclusive of river steamers) :						
Coasting.....	10,516	696,000	1,324	243,000	11,840	939,000
Coasting and long-voyage	953	144,000	246	106,000	1,199	250,000
Long-voyage	5,235	3,236,000	1,820	1,811,000	7,055	5,047,000
Total, 1878	16,704	4,076,000	3,390	2,160,000	20,094	6,236,000
Ships registered in British colonies, 1878..................	11,451	1,598,000	1,281	176,000	12,732	1,774,000

The value of the principal articles of import and export was as follows in 1878:

CLASSES OF GOODS.	Imports.	Exports.	CLASSES OF GOODS.	Imports.	Exports.
Grain	£64,652,000	£688,000	Pottery and glassware	£2,050,000	£2,550,000
Malt and other liquors	8,779,000	2,156,000	Metal manufactures	1,242,000	9,052,000
Colonial produce	42,367,000	1,861,000	Machines and vessels	1,074,000	8,561,000
Tobacco and cigars	8,586,000	....	Leather, etc	1,301,000	2,544,000
Seeds and fruits	14,121,000	2,816,000	Yarn	1,569,000	18,884,000
Animals and animal provisions	40,888,000	1,795,000	Cordage and twine, woven goods		
			clothing	21,362,000	87,703,000
1. Articles of food	£174,438,000	£9,311,000	Paper	551,000	924,000
			Wood carvings	....	1,688,000
			Manuscripts, articles for printing	....	891,000
Fuel		£7,830,000			
Minerals and ores	£4,152,000	573,000	3. Manufactured goods	£29,149,000	£182,750,000
Raw metals	8,082,000	18,702,000			
Hair, hides, and leather	10,137,000	1,177,000	4. Miscellaneous goods	£57,386,000	£22,452,000
Spinning material	70,196,000	547,000			
Wood and timber	15,281,000	....	Total merchandise	£368,771,000	£192,849,000
			Precious metals	32,423,000	26,687,000
2. Raw material	£107,798,000	£28,336,000	Total	£401,194,000	£219,536,000

The movement of shipping in the foreign and colonial trade was as follows (in tons):

YEARS.	ENTERED.			CLEARED.		
	British.	Foreign.	Total.	British.	Foreign.	Total.
Total entrances and clearances:						
1860	6,889,009	5,283,776	12,172,785	7,025,914	5,490,593	12,516,507
1877	17,281,384	8,889,839	25,621,173	17,484,573	8,425,331	25,909,904
1878	17,327,733	7,965,988	25,298,721	17,963,750	8,837,608	26,801,358
Laden vessels entered and cleared:						
1860	5,760,587	4,294,444	10,054,981	6,358,917	4,424,020	10,782,987
1877	14,894,448	7,237,176	22,131,624	15,358,083	5,887,323	21,195,836
1878	14,513,688	6,804,558	21,318,246	15,783,486	5,798,200	21,581,688
Steamers entered and cleared:						
1860	2,145,000	404,000	2,549,000	2,042,000	877,000	2,419,000
1877	11,560,288	2,277,360	14,137,648	11,921,166	2,896,255	14,817,424
1878	12,528,657	2,499,127	15,027,784	12,912,543	2,616,387	15,528,930

The following table gives the postal statistics for the year ending March 31, 1879:

ARTICLES.	England and Wales.	Scotland.	Ireland.	Total.
Letters	922,000,000	99,000,000	76,000,000	1,097,000,000
Postal cards	....	....	....	111,000,000
Newspapers and printed matter	265,000,000	36,000,000	27,000,000	328,000,000
Money orders:				
1. To United Kingdom	£14,900,000	£1,500,000	£1,100,000	£17,400,000
2. To foreign countries and colonies	....	....	....	100,000
3. From foreign countries and colonies	....	....	....	300,000
Amount of money orders:				
1. To United Kingdom	22,259,000	2,401,000	1,584,000	26,244,000
2. To foreign countries and colonies	....	....	....	422,000
3. From foreign countries and colonies	....	....	....	933,000

The railroad statistics for 1878 were as follows:

COUNTRIES.	Miles in operation.	Capital.	Gross receipts.	Net receipts.
England	12,230	£581,097,000	£51,098,000	£25,055,000
Scotland	2,845	87,189,000	6,618,000	3,842,000
Ireland	2,260	32,276,000	2,770,000	1,284,000
Total, 1878.	17,335	£700,562,000	£60,486,000	£29,681,000
" 1877.	17,077	674,059,000	60,544,000	29,115,000

The number of telegraph offices in 1878 was 5,816, of which 1,555 were private and railway stations. The length of the government lines was 25,040 miles, of wires 108,110 miles. The number of dispatches sent, exclusive of press and official dispatches, was 22,477,921.

The table on page 452 shows the finances, commerce, and movement of shipping of the British colonies in 1877, according to the "Statistical Abstract for the Colonial and other Possessions of the United Kingdom in 1863–'77" (London, 1879).

The session of Parliament was resumed on February 13th. In the Lords, Lord Beaconsfield stated the measures to be proposed by the Government, which included, among others, the substitution of a permanent act consolidating the whole body of military law for the annual Mutiny Bill, a Bankruptcy Bill, a Criminal Code Bill, a County Boards Bill, a Workman and Employers Bill, and a Public Works Bill. The leader of the Opposition, Lord Hartington, had previously, while addressing a meeting of Liberals at Liverpool on February 7th, intimated the programme of the party in the ensuing session, specifying support of the Burial Bill, extension of the suffrage in counties, elec-

COLONIAL STATISTICS.

COLONIES.	Income.	Expenditures.	Debt.	Imports.	Exports.	Movement of shipping, tons.
Gibraltar*	£32,000	£41,000	....	£778,000	£34,685	4,772,000
Malta	172,000	170,000	....	6,991,000	6,809,000	4,863,000
Dominion of Canada	4,535,000	6,433,000	£27,751,000	20,093,000	15,807,000	6,645,000
Newfoundland	130,000	202,000	273,000	1,584,000	1,425,000	571,000
Bermuda	80,000	27,000	11,000	283,000	73,000	168,000
British Honduras	42,000	40,000	5,000	166,000	125,000	74,000
Bahamas	5,000	51,000	61,000	154,000	111,000	148,000
Turk's Islands	8,000	6,000	....	22,000	22,000	94,000
Jamaica	538,000	536,000	684,000	1,552,000	1,459,000	708,000
Virgin Islands	1,000	1,000	....	4,000	18,000	11,000
St. Christopher	24,000	27,000	5,000	134,000	147,000	57,000
Nevis	10,000	9,000	2,000	35,000	49,000	21,000
Antigua	34,000	35,000	59,000	176,000	210,000	51,000
Montserrat	7,000	6,000	....	25,000	32,000	17,000
Dominica	19,000	19,000	8,000	59,000	78,000	26,000
Santa Lucia	28,000	28,000	44,000	111,000	179,000	34,000
St. Vincent	28,000	29,000	....	143,000	175,000	42,000
Barbadoes	129,000	120,000	23,000	1,144,000	1,098,000	832,000
Grenada	23,000	30,000	7,000	127,000	146,000	168,000
Tobago	13,000	13,000	....	59,000	63,000	18,000
Trinidad	310,000	318,000	173,000	1,709,000	2,034,000	612,000
West Indies (total)	1,218,000	1,223,000	1,023,000	5,450,000	5,887,000	2,369,000
British Guiana	390,000	381,000	324,000	2,283,000	3,049,000	520,000
Falkland Islands	7,000	7,000	....	33,000	63,000	22,000
British India	55,996,000	58,179,000	188,985,000	48,577,000	65,044,000	5,634,000
Straits Settlements	336,000	349,000	....	13,119,000	12,204,000	3,072,000
Ceylon	1,536,000	1,437,000	774,000	5,383,000	5,780,000	2,538,000
Hong-Kong* (1879)	193,000	182,000	....	4,677,000	1,174,000	4,360,000
Labuan*	7,450	7,200	....	157,000	156,000	....
Australia	17,793,000	16,170,000	68,603,000	48,303,000	45,834,000	7,008,000
Cape Colony	2,932,000	3,423,000	5,023,000	5,457,000	3,663,000	925,000
Natal	272,000	234,000	1,232,000	1,167,000	630,000	190,000
Sierra Leone (1875)	83,000	87,000	....	336,000	350,000	284,000
Gold Coast	93,000	88,000	....	837,000	387,000	147,000
Gambia (1876)	20,000	21,000	....	86,000	86,000	110,000
St. Helena	18,000	18,000	....	154,000	85,000	111,000
Lagos	59,000	42,000	....	614,000	735,000	820,000
Mauritius	718,000	704,000	1,000,000	2,359,000	4,201,000	566,000
Feejee (1876)	87,000	72,000	....	118,000	83,000	27,000

* The commerce of Gibraltar, Hong-Kong, and Labuan is with the United Kingdom only.

toral rearrangement in large towns, and a fair consideration of fresh claims. By common consent, subjects likely to agitate or divide public opinion were set aside, to be dealt with after the general election, when the judgment of the country on conflicting principles and schemes may be ascertained.

The Army Discipline Bill will hold a prominent place in the Parliamentary annals of 1879. It was introduced on the 27th of February, and read a second time on the 7th of April, without any indication of serious opposition. It got into committee on the 1st of May, and during the whole of May and June, and the early part of July, the discussion of the details of the measure absorbed the attention of the House of Commons. The greatest excitement was aroused by the controversy touching corporal punishment. At first the Government took up a strong position, in which they were supported by the leaders of the Opposition. They contended that flogging was, in the opinion of the highest military authorities, indispensable to the maintenance of discipline in the army. When the bill had been seven weeks in committee, Colonel Stanley was apparently worried by the persistency of the opponents of the "cat" into a series of concessions. While the Secretary for War was considering in what form and limits his concessions should be couched, the opposition to the bill increased

and became more violent. The progress of the bill was considerably obstructed by amendments proposed by Mr. Parnell and some of his Irish colleagues, so that when it passed the third reading, on the 18th of July, it was almost too late. The Mutiny Continuance Act was to expire on the 25th, and the House of Lords was compelled to run the measure without debate through all its stages, in order that it might receive the royal assent in time. In the House of Commons the measure spread discord in the ranks of the Liberals. Lord Hartington reproved Mr. Chamberlain and the Radical opponents of flogging, and cautiously supported the Secretary for War; and Mr. Chamberlain revenged himself for this dissension by calling Lord Hartington the late leader of the Opposition. A week later, however, Lord Hartington came round to the conviction of Mr. Chamberlain. On July 14th, in committee upon the Army Discipline Bill, he announced that, having reconsidered the whole question, he was prepared to support the total abolition of flogging in the army except as a substitute for the penalty of death. On July 17th Lord Hartington moved a resolution for the abolition of flogging in the army, which he justified by the indecision of the Government in respect of the military necessity for that punishment. Mr. Gladstone supported the resolution, which was opposed by Colonel Stanley and Lord Sandon. The resolution was negatived by 289 to 183. The "Times" called the Army Bill "a measure of which the great importance and the great value are acknowledged on all hands." It introduces a system of free enlistment, and abolishes many of the snares with which recruiting has hitherto been surrounded. It constitutes enlistment really a free contract, which men will be more at liberty to abrogate than at any previous time, if they dislike its conditions. It takes away or greatly modifies the absolute power of the provost marshal, who will only exercise his authority under the control of the statute, and will carry out what is simply the record of a summary court martial; while punishments have in several respects been mitigated.

Considerable attention was devoted to educational matters. The Government originally did not intend to deal with the complicated subject of university education in Ireland, but the O'Conor Don introduced a measure professing to follow the lines of the Intermediate Education Act, and appropriating a large part of the Irish Church surplus to the maintenance of a new university. It was objected to this bill that in reality it differed widely in its application from its presumed model, and that it would in substance endow a number of sectarian colleges in Ireland. The debate on the second reading, which began before Whitsuntide, was resumed on the 25th of June, when Mr. Forster supported the Irish demand for denominational teaching, and Mr. Cross, remarking incidentally that Mr. Forster's argument would justify Home Rule, surprised the House with the statement that the Government, recognizing the existence of a substantial grievance, would attempt to carry a remedial measure. The O'Conor Don's bill was accordingly abandoned, and a few days afterward the Lord Chancellor brought forward the ministerial proposals in the Upper House. The main feature of the ministerial scheme was the dissolution of the Queen's University and the transference of graduates and matriculated students of the Queen's Colleges to the new university to be established. The new university was to consist of a Chancellor and a Senate, the Senate to be appointed by charter of the Crown. The number of the Senate was not to exceed thirty-six, and the Convocation, which was to be composed of the graduates of the new university and of the graduates of other universities who might be transferred to it, might fill up vacancies to the number of six as they occurred in the Senate. The Senate would elect a Vice-Chancellor, and the university as thus constituted would appoint examiners for matriculation and degrees, and would confer degrees in all the faculties except theology, and this without evidence of education at any particular college or other place. The exhibitions attached to the Queen's Colleges which had been provided for by the money of private individuals would not be interfered with, but the vote of Parliament for the Queen's University would, if the bill passed, be transferred to the new university. The bill was brought down to the Lower House on the 17th of July, and on the second reading Mr. Lowther stated that provision would be made for university prizes. Mr. Shaw, the Home Rule leader, moved an amendment that no measure could be accepted which did not assist collegiate education in Ireland as well as throw open degree examinations. Mr. Gladstone and a considerable number of Liberals, including several ex-Ministers, voted with Mr. Shaw; but the Government was supported by a strong contingent of independent members of the Opposition, and the amendment was defeated by a majority of 257 against 90. The resistance of the Home Rulers, however, was not persevered in. A proposal by Mr. P. J. Smyth to refer the question to a Royal Commission was not entertained. The measure passed rapidly through its remaining stages, the Government refusing to admit any important modifications. On August 13th the House of Lords agreed to the amendments of the Commons that had so completely transformed the bill, and it received the royal assent.

Besides Ireland, the principality of Wales also put forth a claim for an enlargement of its educational institutions. On July 1st, in the House of Commons, Mr. H. Vivian moved a resolution calling upon the Government to take steps to assist in extending the means of higher education in Wales. He described to the House the existing means of higher education open to the Welsh people at Jesus College, Oxford, at Aberystwith, and at Lampeter, and contrasted the expenditure on Scotch and Irish universities with the total neglect of the claims of Wales. If grants were made to the principality on the same scale as to these two kingdoms, she would receive from £8,000 to £10,000 for university education, where now she received nothing. Mr. Vivian insisted on the separate nationality of the Welsh people, and mentioned among other contemporaneous facts that out of 686,000 religious worshipers, 36,000 only worshiped in the English language. The bill was supported by Mr. Gladstone. Mr. B. Williams was of opinion that what the Welsh people desired was a subsidy for the college at Aberystwith which they had themselves established. Lord G. Hamilton and the Chancellor of the Exchequer recognized the claim of Wales to consideration, but said that measures were in progress which it was hoped would contribute toward the end desired. Upon a division the resolution was negatived by 105 to 54.

On June 30th the Duke of Richmond and Gordon said the Government had determined to advise the Crown to grant a charter for a university for the North of England, to be called the Victoria University.

On June 10th Mr. R. Yorke called attention to the increasing expenditure of the London School Board, and condemned the unnecessarily high standard of education maintained at public expense. Mr. W. E. Forster defended the Board from the charge of extravagance, and contended that results would amply compensate for the expense. Lord G. Hamilton, on behalf of the Government, admitted that the expenditure was very large, and indicated several points on which it was considered that limitations might be imposed.

On May 5th, in the House of Lords, Lord Houghton moved the second reading of a bill to legalize marriage with a deceased wife's sister, of which the Prince of Wales, in presenting a petition from Norfolk, signified his approval. The Bishop of London and Lord Cranbrook opposed the second reading, which upon a division was rejected by 101 to 81. The Prince of Wales, the Duke of Edinburgh, and the Bishop of Ripon voted for, and fourteen bishops against the second reading.

The suffrage question was repeatedly the subject of discussion. On March 4th Mr. Trevel-

yan moved resolutions favoring the extension of household suffrage to the counties and a redistribution of representation. One reason why he pressed the question was that household franchise was the only mode of correcting the abuse of fagot votes. He dwelt on the "sin and the shame" of depriving large classes of all voice in legislation and all control over the administration of the country. Sir C. Dilke, in seconding the motion, asserted that manufacturing of fictitious votes was carried on to a large extent in the southern counties, and that the anomalies of the present system were as great as any which existed before 1832. Lord C. Hamilton moved as an amendment, "that it is inexpedient to reopen the question of Parliamentary reform at the present time." The "abstract right" and "representation of classes" arguments, if insisted on, would sweep away the old Parliamentary system, and Eng-

GREAT SEAL OF ENGLAND.

land would come in the end to equal electoral districts and universal (including female) suffrage. He denied that a class was necessarily unrepresented because it did not possess votes, and contended that of the small boroughs at least seventy-five would disappear under this law. In Ireland the proposal would place entire power in the hands of the ignorant and bigoted Roman Catholic peasant, and certainly end in the return of ninety obstructionists. The composition of the House of Commons had deteriorated under household suffrage. Sir C. Legard, who seconded the amendment, predicted that the proposed change would lead to universal suffrage and to the ultimate establishment of a democratic House of Commons as the sole power in the state. Mr. Lowe repeated his well-known objections to further reductions of the franchise, insisting that it must be considered not from the philanthropic point of view, but solely with regard to the permanent interests of the country. Each further change in this

direction would alter the structure of the House of Commons, in which now all power was centered, and the result must be the establishment of an unchecked democracy, which all history showed was devoid of stability. Mr. Knowles and Mr. Courtney argued earnestly in favor of the representation of minorities. The Chancellor of the Exchequer remarked that it was not desirable to reopen the suffrage question, which was settled in 1867 with the assent of the Liberal party. The Marquis of Hartington avowed himself as averse as any one could be to reopening the question of reform, but objected strongly to the attitude of the Government. Mr. Trevelyan's resolution was negatived on a division by 291 to 226. Lord Hamilton's amendment was then unanimously agreed to, after (on motion of Mr. Lowe) the words "at the present time" had been omitted. The suffrage question came up again for discussion in the House of Commons on March 7th, when Mr. Courtney moved a resolution in favor of extending the Parliamentary franchise to women possessing the statutory qualifications which entitle them to vote in municipal, parochial, and school-board elections. Experience of female suffrage, he contended, both in the United Kingdom and the United States, was uniformly favorable to it; and he advocated it strictly from a utilitarian point of view, on account of the benefit which it would confer both on the state and on the women themselves. The Chancellor of the Exchequer objected to the form of the motion, which he thought would commit the House to the reopening of the reform question. Although he believed the elevating influences of female suffrage had been exaggerated, and did not admit that women were treated unjustly because they had no votes, he was not indisposed, at a proper time and under proper circumstances, to consider the claim for equal treatment. Mr. Blennerhasset contended that the Parliamentary franchise ought to follow as a matter of right from the concessions already made; and Mr. Beresford-Hope read extracts from the writings of leading advocates of women's rights, contained in what was described as the "Ladies' Green Book," to illustrate the real character of their claims. Mr. Bristowe thought that if the vote were given, the right to be elected must also follow. Sir H. James commented on Mr. Courtney's inconsistency in proposing to enfranchise some 900,-000 women while he stoutly opposed the admission of the agricultural laborer. He denied woman's fitness for the franchise; she could not obtain the necessary experience, for a woman's only profession was marriage. What injustice, he said, to women to deprive them of a vote as soon as they became successful in their profession, and to give it only to failures! A quotation from the Queen's diary, telling against the measure, provoked a solemn objection from Mr. Sullivan to "the introduction of the sovereign's name to influence debate," which the Speaker held was not tenable. Sir Henry finally appealed to the Liberal party not to sanction the enfranchisement of a class of all others most subject to influence. Mr. W. E. Forster opposed the motion, not because he doubted the fitness of women, but because he regarded electioneering as man's work, and not woman's. Moreover, he objected to giving a vote without accompanying it with the capacity of being elected. He denied that a majority of the women wished for the vote, and predicted that the motion could never be carried. After some remarks from Sir H. Jackson, who asserted that the franchise was desired by considerable numbers of the most distinguished women, the resolution was negatived by 217 to 103. A resolution, moved by an Irish member, Mr. Meldon, on February 14th, in favor of the assimilation of the Irish borough franchise to the system existing in England and Wales, was supported by Mr. W. E. Forster and the Marquis of Hartington, but opposed by Mr. Lowther and the Chancellor of the Exchequer, upon the

ground that there was no necessity for a change in the electoral system so lately settled. Upon a division, the resolution was rejected by 256 to 187.

On March 12th the Clerical Disabilities Bill, proposed by Mr. Goldney, to enable clergymen of the Church of England without cure of souls to sit in Parliament, was rejected by 135 to 66, Mr. Cross having pointed out that if clergymen wanted to come into Parliament, all' they had to do was to take advantage of the act of 1870, which allowed clergymen to lay aside their orders.

On April 2d Mr. Mundella's bill, repealing the property qualifications for serving on municipal corporations, boards of guardians, local boards, etc., was discussed. Mr. Burt, in supporting the bill, mentioned that, though he was capable of sitting in Parliament, he had lived fourteen years in the borough which he represented without being eligible for a municipal office. The bill was thrown out by 173 to 167.

The House of Lords adjourned on April 4th, and the House of Commons on April 7th, for the Easter vacation.

The continuance of foreign complications frequently gave an opportunity to the Opposition to attack the Government. In the House of Commons, the largest share of attention was bestowed on the Greek claims. Mr. Cartwright about the middle of April moved a resolution, supported by Mr. Gladstone, Sir William Harcourt, and other leading Liberals, demanding the settlement of the question in accordance with the Berlin protocol. He was defeated by a majority of 16. More than three months later Sir Charles Dilke reopened the question in a more elaborate manner, but the debate was adjourned without a decisive division. Some signs of restlessness and suspicion with respect to the Afghan policy of the Government were visible early in the year, which died out rapidly after the announcement, on the 19th of May, that bases of peace with Yakoob Khan had been settled. On the 4th of August a vote of thanks was carried in both Houses to the troops engaged in the Afghan campaign. The resistance was slight.

The war in South Africa, which, when Parliament met in December, 1878, had been looked upon as a matter of minor importance, rose into prominence in February, 1879. A discussion of the whole subject was brought on, when, on the 25th of March, the Marquis of Lansdowne moved a resolution in the House of Lords, censuring Sir Bartle Frere for provoking Cetywayo to war "without authority from the responsible advisers of the Crown," condemning the inception of an offensive war "without imperative and pressing necessity or adequate preparation," and regretting the maintenance of the High Commissioner in power after the censure passed upon him in the Colonial Secretary's dispatch. The resolution was rejected by a majority of 156 against 61. On

the 27th of March a debate on a similar resolution, proposed by Sir Charles Dilke, began
in the House of Commons. After a discussion
lasting three nights the resolution was negatived by 306 against 246 votes, a smaller majority than that obtained by Ministers in the
division on the Eastern Question. The official
announcement of the end of the war caused
great rejoicing, not only on the Ministerial,
but on the Opposition benches.

The Government was very reticent in regard
to Egyptian affairs, but repeatedly gave a
pledge that no engagement involving a guarantee would be entered into without the
knowledge of Parliament. At the close of
the session Sir Julian Goldsmid animadverted
upon the interference of the Government in
the internal affairs of Egypt, but the Government was not attacked by any formal resolutions. (See EGYPT.)

Indian affairs, except in relation to the Afghan war and the frontier question, were not
prominent in Parliament. (See INDIA.)

The estimated revenue of 1878–'79 was £83,-
230,000, and the actual receipts, in spite of an
apparent decrease in the consuming power of
the country, fell short of this calculation by no
more than £114,000. But there was a wider
discrepancy between the estimated and the actual expenditure. Sir Stafford Northcote had
reckoned in 1878 upon an outlay of £81,000,-
000, or nearly two millions and a quarter less
than the estimated income. The actual outgoes
were £85,400,000, due to the accumulation of
the extraordinary charges, those for the Zooloo war being added to the Exchequer bonds
representing the unpaid balance of the six millions vote of credit. The result was that in
April the Chancellor of the Exchequer had to
deal, not, as he had anticipated, with a surplus
of a million or thereabouts, but with a deficit
of £2,291,000, and with not less than £4,750,-
000 of unpaid Exchequer bonds. For 1879–'80
he estimated a revenue of £83,055,000 and an
expenditure of £81,153,000, not including extraordinary charges. The surplus, he believed,
would be adequate to defray the current expenses for the Zooloo war. With respect to
the outstanding Exchequer bonds, Sir Stafford
Northcote proposed that payment be postponed, on the understanding that two millions
were to be paid off next year and the balance
in the following year. The policy of the Government was attacked by Mr. Gladstone, Mr.
Rylands, Mr. Baxter, Mr. Goschen, and others;
but on a division the Government were supported by a majority of 303 against 230.

Frequent allusions were made to the distress
prevailing throughout the country, and particularly to the complaints of the agricultural interest. In both Houses the doctrine was pro-
'pounded that free trade was at the root of all
difficulties; but this view failed to obtain any
Parliamentary support, and the Prime Minister emphatically repudiated the protectionist
system in any shape or form. The representa-

tives of the sugar industry, however, complaining that Continental countries have crushed
them by an unfair bounty system, induced the
Government to assent to an investigation of
the subject by a select committee. The London tradesmen obtained the appointment of
another select committee to inquire into the
working of the coöperative stores, which they
allege have injured their business. An inquiry
into the wine duties was initiated, mainly with
a view to procuring such modification of the
alcoholic scale as might induce foreign countries, and especially Spain, to deal more reasonably with British trade in their tariff arrangements. The same uneasy feeling which
prompted these inquiries inspired the demand
for the establishment of a Ministry of Commerce. This was proposed by Mr. Sampson
Lloyd, and the Government were willing to accept the proposal, if the proviso that the Minister of Commerce shall be a member of the
Cabinet were omitted. An amendment to this
effect was, however, rejected by the House,
and Mr. Lloyd's resolution adopted by a majority of 20.

On March 11th Sir W. Lawson moved a resolution favoring the transfer of the power of
granting licenses for the sale of intoxicating
drinks from magistrates to inhabitants of localities. He set forth, in language borrowed
from a resolution of Convocation, that, as the
ancient and avowed object of licenses was to
supply a public want without detriment to the
public welfare, the legal power of restraining
the issue of them should be placed in the
hands of those most likely to be injured; and
he based its necessity on the notorious increase
of drunkenness, arising, as he contended, from
the unlimited facilities for the opening of
public houses. The words of the resolution,
though wide enough to include the Permissive
Bill, Licensing Board, the Gothenburg system,
etc., did not commit anybody to details. All
the religious bodies of the country had decided
in favor of it, and there was no organized opposition to it except from the publicans. Mr.
Wheelhouse moved a counter-resolution, ob-
jecting to any change in the present licensing
arrangements. He denied that drunkenness
was on the increase, and attributed its mischief not so much to the legitimate licenses as
to the grocers and other "off" licenses. Sir
M. Ridley, on behalf of the Government, opposed the original resolution, the fatal defect
of which was its subordination of the privileges of the sober to the reformation of the
drunkards. The House ought not to deal with
a question of this kind by passing a vague resolution, which merely meant that something
must be done. He did not see in local option
the elements of a satisfactory licensing tribunal, which ought to be judicial, consistent,
and independent. The Government held that
further legislation of some kind was necessary,
whether by increased police supervision or enlarged magisterial discretion, or by increas-

ing the rent necessary for licenses; and they, therefore, though they opposed the resolution, could not accept the amendment which merely meant *Non possumus.* Mr. W. E. Forster said, though he had always opposed the Permissive Bill, believing it to be oppressive and impracticable, he intended to support this resolution, because it embodied the principle of local control. The evil of drunkenness, he believed, could most effectually be checked by those who had the local knowledge; and he also held that the wishes of the inhabitants of a district should be consulted. Lord Hartington declined to vote for the resolution, to which different meanings were attached by its supporters. The resolution was rejected by 252 to 164. Mr. Wheelhouse's amendment was negatived without a division; and Lord T. Hervey's proposition, to defer legislation on the subject until the report of the Lords' Committee on Intemperance had been received, was defeated by 169 to 121.

On June 13th, in the House of Lords, Lord Truro moved the second reading of a bill to prohibit vivisection. On evidence given before the Royal Commission on the subject, Lord Truro denied that great medical and surgical discoveries had been made through vivisection, and he told the House that the opponents of vivisection would persevere until they should secure its prohibition. Lord Shaftesbury, who supported the bill, argued that the restrictions imposed by the bill of 1877 had not had the effect of preventing cruelty. Some anæsthetics inflicted more pain than the operation itself. The question was taking a prominent position in Europe, even in Russsia. The system had a tendency to brutalize the human heart. He repudiated the doctrine that the Almighty sanctioned the infliction of these refined tortures on any of his creatures. The Bishop of Peterborough deprecated the abolition of vivisection in the interest of humanity, though he would guard the practice by any conditions which might be thought necessary. He had heard from the lips of one of the greatest surgeons that an operation which had been discovered in our own times, and by which thousands of human lives had been saved, was owing to observations made on twelve rabbits which had been subjected to vivisection. Lord Aberdare, as one who had filled the office of President of the Society for the Prevention of Cruelty to Animals, opposed the bill on the ground that it would prohibit vaccination and many useful operations. The motion was negatived by 97 to 16.

On August 15th Parliament was prorogued. Immediately after the prorogation Great Britain was the scene of a determined and passionate political campaign, which was opened by Mr. Gladstone at Chester and Sir Charles Dilke at Chelsea. Meetings addressed in the latter part of October at Manchester by Lord Salisbury, Mr. Cross, and Colonel Stanley, were remarkable for their enthusiasm, as well as the meetings addressed the following week in the same city by Lord Hartington and Mr. Bright, on which occasion the Liberal champions were welcomed by equally large crowds and with as much enthusiasm as had greeted the representatives of the Government the week before. Hardly any new arguments were presented in these oratorical displays, which seemed mainly to have been intended to rouse the political spirit of the constituencies. The Prime Minister's speech at the Guildhall on Lord Mayor's day had been expected with general curiosity, as likely to contain some interesting references to the Ministerial policy and the relations of the empire. But Lord Beaconsfield was more than usually reserved. He spoke with ominous mystery of the state of Europe, "covered with millions of armed men," and would only express a qualified hope of the maintenance of peace. He enjoined Englishmen to hold fast by the motto, *Imperium et Libertas,* and pointed out the manifold perils of an "insular policy." He, as well as the Chancellor of the Exchequer, rejoiced in the improvement of trade, and was hopeful that financial embarrassments would soon disappear. The most remarkable and crowning episode of party warfare was Mr. Gladstone's extraordinary campaign in Scotland, which began in the last week of November and lasted almost without interruption for fully two weeks. In the beginning of the year Mr. Gladstone had been invited to contest the liberal candidate for Mid-Lothian, a constituency traditionally subservient to the Conservative influence of the ducal house of Buccleugh. During the first week of the campaign he reviewed for the Mid-Lothian electors the whole field of politics, domestic, foreign, financial, ecclesiastical, and local, in a series of elaborate speeches. Quitting Edinburgh, he went north into Perthshire, and, again returning to the southwest, delivered his rectorial address before the University of Glasgow, instantly resuming the political controversy and sustaining it all the way home through Scotland and the north of England as far as Chester. During this campaign he attracted the general attention of the country, and it was described as having never been surpassed as a succession of grand oratorical displays.

Ireland during the year was the scene of a violent agitation, and in some localities of severe distress. In consequence of the poor harvests and the general decline in the prices of farmers' produce, the tenants of Ireland demanded a proportionate reduction of rents. The first public demonstration occurred on June 8th, when an open-air meeting was held at Westport in County Mayo, which was attended by from four to five thousand men. The sentiments of the meeting were expressed by the inscriptions on the banners, such as "The land for the people," "Down with jobbing landlords," and others of a similar character. The principal speaker on the occasion was Mr. Parnell. In the course of his speech he said: "You must show the landlords that you intend to hold a firm grip on your homesteads and land. You must not allow yourselves to be dispossessed as you were dispossessed in 1847. You must not allow your small holdings to be turned into large ones. If rents are not reduced on those properties on which the rents are out of all proportion to the times, you must help yourselves, and public opinion of the world will stand by you and support you in your struggle to defend your homesteads." A resolution was also carried without a dissentient voice, "That the occupiers being unable to pay the current rents, owing to bad harvests and other depreciations of farmers' produce, any landlord who evicts a tenant for non-payment of an unfair rent is an enemy to the human race, and we pledge ourselves to protect by every means in our power the victims of such oppression." It was remarked that the clergy had taken no part in the meeting. Indeed, Archbishop McHale had put his veto upon it in advance in a letter published in the "Freeman's Journal," in which he condemned the meeting as "a combination, organized by a few designing men, who, instead of the well-being of the community, seek only to promote their personal interests; and the faithful clergy will not fail to raise their warning voices, and to point out to the people that unhallowed combinations lead invariably to disaster and the firmer riveting of the chains by which we are unhappily bound as a subordinate people to a dominant race." The Government at once acted promptly in the matter. A deputy inspector-general of the constabulary was dispatched on a special mission to the districts concerned, to consult with the magistrates and local constabulary, and report what additional police were required in order to insure full protection to all persons in the exercise of their legal rights. Considerable reënforcements were drafted into the districts concerned, and notice was given that in the event of any outrage the cost of these measures would be levied upon the district where it occurred. Another meeting was held on June 15th at Milltown, County Galway, at which the language used by the speakers was even more violent than at Westport. No further meetings were held during the summer, but occasional murders were committed in the disaffected counties. After the close of Parliament, Mr. Parnell made a tour through Ireland in favor of the tenant-right agitation, and meetings were addressed by him at Limerick, Tipperary, Tuam, Ennis, and other places. Large crowds attended these meetings, and the spirit manifested by the people was very violent. In his addresses to the meetings Mr. Parnell dwelt upon the necessity for a revision of the relations between landlord and tenant, and declared that if the tenants would refuse to pay any rent until a satisfactory reduction was made, the landlords would be unable to resist.

Resolutions were passed calling upon Parliament to consider the depressed condition of Irish farmers, and pledging those present not to occupy any farm from which a tenant had been evicted for non-payment of a rack-rent. At Tullow Mr. Parnell, while denouncing the landlords as rapacious, insisted that the Government should appoint a tribunal to determine what are fair rents, and asserted that the land question could never be satisfactorily settled until the occupiers were the owners of the soil.

An attempt was made by Mr. Parnell to call a national convention, in which he intended to reconstruct the Home Rule party. The attempt failed, however, through the opposition of the more conservative members of the party. On the other hand, Mr. Parnell in October organized a National Irish Land League, of which he was chosen president. The objects of the League were clearly indicated in the speeches made at the different meetings—a reduction of rents, and refusal to pay if such a reduction were refused, and, finally, an entire change in the land laws, peasant proprietors to be substituted for the landlord. While Mr. Parnell in his speeches avoided a direct breach of the law, other speakers were not so careful; and the consequence was that on November 19th three of the speakers at a meeting held on the 2d at Gurteen, County Sligo, were arrested on a charge of having used seditious language. These three were Mr. James Bryce Killen, a barrister, Mr. Michael Davitt, a liberated Fenian convict, and Mr. James Daly, proprietor of the "Mayo Telegraph." The prisoners after a preliminary hearing were admitted to bail. Large meetings were subsequently held at Balla, Dublin, Liverpool, and in Hyde Park, London. The last was the largest ever held there, being attended by over 100,000 persons, to protest against the arrest of Davitt, Daly, and Killen. Resolutions to that effect, as well as calling for a revision of the land laws in Ireland, were passed. On December 5th one of the secretaries of the Irish National Land League, Mr. Thomas Brennan, was arrested on a charge of seditious language at the Balla meeting on November 22d. He also was admitted to bail.

The distress in the west of Ireland was described as very great indeed, and to relieve the suffering the Duchess of Marlborough, wife of the Viceroy of Ireland, addressed an appeal to the benevolence of the British public. In her address she said: "In the counties of Kerry, Galway, Sligo, Mayo, Roscommon, Donegal, and the south of the county of Cork—in fact, in most of the western districts of Ireland—there will be extreme misery among the poor, owing to want of employment, loss of turf, loss of cattle, and failure of potatoes, unless a vigorous effort of private charity is got up to supplement the ordinary system of Poor-Law relief."

In England, the agricultural outlook was very poor. Continued rains had seriously damaged the crops, while the competition of American produce interfered with the sale of the remainder of the crops. In this state of affairs a large number of farmers organized for emigration, or turned their attention to other pursuits, so that many farms remained unlet in spite of the reductions made on numerous estates by the landlords.

GREECE, a kingdom of southeastern Europe. Reigning King, George I., born December 24, 1845, second son of the reigning King of Denmark; elected King of the Hellenes by the National Assembly at Athens, March 18 (30), 1863; accepted the crown June 6, 1863; declared of age by a decree of the National Assembly, June 27, 1863; married October 27, 1867, to Olga, daughter of the Grand Duke Constantine of Russia, born August 22, 1851. Their children are: Constantinos, Duke of Sparta, born August 2, 1868; George, born June 24, 1869; Alexandra, born August 30, 1870; Nicholas, born January 21, 1872; Maria, born March 3, 1876.

The area is 19,353 square miles: the population, according to the census of 1879, 1,679,775. The following table shows the area and population of each of the nomarchies into which the kingdom is divided:

NOMARCHIES.	Square miles.	POPULATION IN 1879.		
		Male.	Female.	Total.
Attica and Bœotia........	2,481	99,640	85,724	185,864
Eubœa...............	1,574	49,543	45,593	95,136
Phthiotis and Phocis	2,053	65,381	63,059	128,440
Acarnania and Ætolia....	3,024	71,647	66,797	138,444
Achaia and Elis..........	1,908	95,908	85,724	181,632
Arcadia................	2,028	78,130	70,775	148,905
Laconia	1,678	60,842	60,274	121,116
Messenia..............	1,226	81,855	73,905	155,760
Argolis and Corinthia....	1,448	68,679	67,402	136,081
Cyclades................	926	65,112	66,908	132,020
Corcyra (Corfu).........	437	55,126	50,983	106,109
Cephallenia (Cephalonia).	302	89,579	40,964	80,543
Zacynthus (Zante)	278	28,985	20,587	44,522
Soldiers and marines....	....	20,523	......	20,523
Sailors out of the country.	....	5,180	......	5,180
Total...............	19,353	881,080	798,695	1,679,775

The movement of population has been as follows:

YEARS.	Marriages.	Births, exclusive of still births.	Deaths.	Excess of Births.
1874..........	9,529	45,212	29,863	15,349
1875..........	10,250	44,386	30,936	13,450
1876..........	9,773	47,248	31,083	16,165
1877..........	9,472	46,355	31,280	15,075

In the budget for 1879 the receipts were estimated at 45,808,000 drachmas, and the expenditures at 60,078,760 drachmas (1 drachma = 19.3 cents).

The foreign debt at the close of 1878 amounted to 395,513,422 drachmas, and the home debt to 147,569,480 drachmas; in all, 543,082,902 drachmas.

The strength of the army on a peace footing is as follows:

Infantry....................................	16,136
Chasseurs..................................	4,082
Cavalry....................................	845
Artillery...................................	1,959
Engineers..................................	1,104
Sanitary troops.............................	800
Total.................................	24,876

There is in addition a corps of gendarmes comprising 2,508 men.

According to an estimate of the Minister of War, the army in time of war will comprise 200,000 men, of whom 120,000 belong to the active army and its reserves, 50,000 to the landwehr, and 30,000 to its reserve. The general staff consists of 19 officers. The fleet in 1877 consisted of 1 ironclad, 1 monitor, 1 royal yacht, 8 screw-steamers, and 10 sailing vessels.

The Turco-Greek Commission appointed under the Treaty of Berlin to rectify the frontier between Turkey and Greece assembled in January. On February 13th it was recorded in the protocols that the Commission was unable to come to an understanding as to the basis on which the negotiations were to be carried on. The standpoint taken by Mukhtar Pasha, the principal Turkish commissioner, was that the delimitation indicated in the 13th protocol of the Congress was never intended to be binding on the Porte, as was clear from the 18th protocal, in which, in reply to the demand of Caratheodori Pasha to adjourn the decision on the 24th article of the treaty, it is stated that, in the event of Turkey being unable to come to an understanding with Greece on the subject of the frontier regulation suggested in the 13th protocol, the Powers reserved to themselves to offer their mediation. The President of the Congress, Mukhtar Pasha represented, declared distinctly that the paragraph in question expressed not a resolution, but only a wish on the part of the Congress, to which the Porte was asked to accede. The Powers but expressed their desire to see the negotiations succeed, and there seemed no occasion then either for the Porte giving its opinion on the subject or for the Congress taking any resolution, seeing that, according to the precise statement of the President, there was no resolution taken by the Congress with regard to the extent of the frontier delimitation, much less any consent on the part of Turkey to any such resolution. The line indicated in the 13th protocol as embodying the wish of the Powers in this respect might, and indeed would, be taken into consideration, but could scarcely be accepted by the Porte as the unalterable basis on which these negotiations must be carried on. Mukhtar Pasha, while maintaining this view, expressed his readiness to take into consideration any positive line of delimitation which the Greek Commissioners might propose, discussing it fairly on its own merits. According to Mukhtar Pasha, in judging of any line to be proposed by the Greek Commissioners, the ethnographical conditions of the territory claimed would demand the first and foremost consideration. On the Turkish side of the present frontier line the population was a mixed one of Greeks, Albanians, and Wallachs, Mohammedans and Christians. Not the Greeks alone, but all of these, had a right to be considered in any eventual cession of territory to Greece. In reply to all this, the Greek Commissioners said that they could propose no other line but that indicated in the 13th protocol, their instructions forbidding their entering into negotiations on any other basis, and much less themselves proposing another. Minister Delyannis, on receiving the report of the Greek Commissioners, had recourse to M. Waddington, informing him of the state of the case; whereupon the latter sent a note to the Porte, expressing the regret of the French Government at the slow progress of the negotiations, and supporting the view of the Greek Government that the basis of negotiations could only be that laid down in the 13th protocol. The negotiations were again taken up, and in the beginning of April a new frontier line was proposed by the Porte. On the side of Thessaly, the line followed nearly that indicated in the protocol, including Volo, Larissa, and Agrafa. In Epirus it included the valley of the Arta, together with the town of that name—Janina and Preveso, however, remaining in the hands of the Turks. On April 6th a deputation of Epirotes presented an address to the King praying him not to consent to the abandonment of the demand of the cession of Janina to Greece, as such a course would seriously affect Greek interests. The King in reply said that the question was one of vital importance to Greece, and expressed a hope that the Great Powers would never commit the injustice of refusing the claim of Greece to Janina. On June 22d the dragomans of the British, French, German, Italian, and Russian embassies presented to Caratheodori Pasha, the Turkish Minister of Foreign Affairs, identical notes urging the Porte to appoint commissioners for the settlement of the question of the Greek frontier. In the beginning of July the Turkish Government officially notified the Powers of its readiness to appoint the commissioners, and soon after appointed Aarifi, Munif, and Nedjib Pashas. Upon the change in the Turkish Ministry, however, these names were recalled, and on August 16th Safvet, Sawas, and Ali Said Pashas appointed in their places. In August the Turkish Government concentrated large numbers of troops on the frontier, under the command of Edhem Pasha, who hastened to take up good positions in front of the town of Larissa. Still more remarkable than these movements of troops was the distribution of arms which had been ordered by the Turkish Minister of War among the Albanian Mohammedans, amounting to 6,400 Snider guns and 5,000 percussion guns, with a considerable quantity of ammunition. The Mohammedans on receiving these arms were instructed not to leave their homes, but to hold themselves in readiness for marching. This distribution among fanatical Mohammedans created considerable uneasiness among the Christian population of Epirus and Thessaly.

The first meeting of the new Turco-Greek Commission was held on August 22d, when the Commissioners exchanged credentials and discussed the course of procedure. Safvet Pasha declared to the Greeks that the Sublime Porte was ready to accept the frontier suggested by the Treaty of Berlin as the basis of negotiations, but at the same time repeated all the reserves and protests it had formerly urged in this respect. He also declared that the Porte contested the obligatory character of the protocol. The discussion on this question of the obligatory or non-obligatory character of the protocol was continued in the following sessions. In the fourth session, held on September 11th, the Greek delegates, while maintaining their view of the question, suggested that, as neither party wished to impose its view on the other, the general question as to the obligatory or non-obligatory character of the protocol might be for the moment left in abeyance, and the more practical question as to the new line of frontier might be discussed. Safvet Pasha thereupon prepared and read a short memorandum, in which he expressed satisfaction that the Hellenic plenipotentiaries had somewhat approached the point of view of the Ottoman Government, and declared that he and his colleagues were ready to enter upon the practical question, taking the 13th protocol as the basis of the negotiations. Another session, held on October 5th, brought out a declaration from the Greek delegates, which had been approved by the Powers, that the 13th protocol of the Berlin Congress should be taken as a starting-point in the negotiations. The Turkish delegates, however, insisted that the indications in the protocol must be susceptible of modifications. The meeting then adjourned to allow the Greek delegates to communicate with their Government. Another meeting was held on October 24th, when the Turkish delegates declared that the part of Thessaly and Epirus which was left to Turkey by the line of frontier indicated in the 13th protocol would be in an isolated position and without a port, and that it was therefore impossible to accept it. The Greek members of the Commission stated their demands, and Sawas Pasha, Turkish Minister for Foreign Affairs, addressed a note to the Powers, pointing out that these demands exceeded the frontier line indicated in the 13th protocol. At a meeting of the Commission held on November 17th, the line of frontier proposed by the Porte was indicated, giving Greece an extension of frontier to the west, but leaving Turkey almost the whole of Epirus.

Elections for the Chambers were held on October 5th. All the Ministers were returned except those of Marine and Justice, and a majority for the Ministry was secured. The

Chambers were opened on November 1st by the King, who said in his speech that the negotiations with Turkey were shortly expected to have a favorable issue. It was necessary, however, that the forces of the country should be maintained in an effective condition, and military preparations must continue, because strength greatly regulated the relations between nations.

GREEK CHURCH. The following table gives an estimate of the population connected with the Greek or Orthodox Eastern Church at the end of 1879, and compares it with the entire population of the several countries:

COUNTRIES.	Total population.	Population connected with Greek Church.	Percentage of Greek Church to total population.
Russia, inclusive of Finland	88,823,000	60,600,000	68·6
Austria-Hungary	37,712,000	3,205,000	8·5
Bosnia and Herzegovina...	1,212,000	571,000	47·2
Roumania	5,376,000	4,700,000	87·4
Servia	1,577,000	1,487,000	94·5
Montenegro	236,000	236,000	82·5
Greece	1,680,000	1,662,000	98·9
Bulgaria	1,860,000	1,260,000	67·7
Eastern Roumelia	875,000	751,000	50·0
Turkey (except Bosnia, Herzegovina, Bulgaria, and Eastern Roumelia)	43,000,000	3,425,000	7·9
China	....	5,000	....
Japan	....	5,000	....

Adding to the above figures a population of about 10,000 scattered through all other countries, especially in North America, the aggregate population connected with the Greek Church may be estimated at about 77,912,000. It will be seen that the Greek Church in 1879 controlled the majority of population in seven countries, in the following order: Greece, 98·9 per cent.; Servia, 94·5; Roumania, 87·4; Montenegro, 82·5; Russia, 68·6; Bulgaria, 67·7; Eastern Roumelia, 50. Besides, a large minority (47·2 per cent.) belongs to this Church in Bosnia and Herzegovina, where the remainder is divided between the Roman Catholic Church and Mohammedanism.

The most prominent bishop of the entire Church is still the Patriarch of Constantinople, but the churches of Russia, Austria, Greece, Servia, Roumania, Montenegro, Bulgaria, and the churches of Bulgarian nationality in Eastern Roumelia, are independent of his jurisdiction. The Patriarch has formally recognized the entire independence of the churches of Servia and Roumania. Therefore, although the honorary preëminence of the see of Constantineple continues, the direct jurisdiction of the Patriarch has become limited to the Greeks living in the Turkish Empire. The progressing consolidation of the Bulgarian nationality, and the prospective annexation of large districts of the European part of Turkey to Greece, are likely soon to reduce this jurisdiction of the Patriarch to still narrower limits.

As the Greek Church in Bosnia and Herzegovina is of the same (Servian) nationality as a large portion of that in Austria-Hungary, the Austrian Government has given special attention to the establishment of a closer union between the two churches. It is estimated that in Austria-Hungary about 3,100,000 inhabitants belong to the Servian nationality. Adding to these the population of Bosnia and Herzegovina, Austria now rules over more than 4,300,000 people of that race, considerably exceeding in number all Servians living outside of Austria. The establishment of a strong ecclesiastical center in Austria for all Servians appears therefore to many Austrian statesmen as a matter of great political importance. Up to the time when the Treaty of Berlin was concluded, the church of Bosnia and Herzegovina was under the direct jurisdiction of the Patriarchate of Constantinople. The Patriarch appointed the bishops, who generally were Greeks and did not understand the language of the natives. This rule of Greeks over Servian churches has long called forth considerable dissatisfaction, which in late years greatly increased as the national feeling among the different branches of the Servian people grew stronger. When the Treaty of Berlin in 1878 placed Bosnia under the administration of Austria, the Servians of Austria fostered this feeling of dissatisfaction. The history of the past relations between Constantinople and the Servian nation was appealed to as a proof that the jurisdiction claimed by Constantinople over the Servians is in fact a usurpation, and that the latter are therefore fully justified in shaking it off as soon as they have the power. At the time when Servia was a powerful kingdom it had its own Patriarch at Ipek, whose independence the Patriarchs of Constantinople were prevailed upon to recognize. The Patriarchs of Ipek maintained their supremacy even after the subjection of the country by the Turks in 1389. In 1690, when the attempted rising of the Servians against Turkish rule had failed, the Patriarch Arsenius of Ipek, with 30,000 Servian families, settled in Hungary. This Patriarch was recognized by the Austrian Government as metropolitan, and the Servian emigrants were authorized to elect thereafter a Vayvode and a Patriarch. After the death of Patriarch Arsenius, however, the Servians of Hungary elected only metropolitans, who remained dependent upon the Patriarch who had been elected at Ipek as successor of Arsenius. This dependence was greatly disliked by the Court of Austria, which entered into negotiations with the Patriarch of Ipek in regard to the transfer of the Patriarchate to Austrian territory. In consequence of these negotiations, Patriarch Arsenius Yoranovitch Shakobent, who felt aggrieved by the Turkish rule, emigrated with several thousand families to Hungary, bringing with him all the documents and church utensils of the Patriarchate of Ipek. After the death of the Austrian Metropolitan he was confirmed by the Empress Maria Theresa, in 1741, as Patriarch, Archbishop, and Metropolitan of the entire Servian Church. After his death the title Patriarch fell into disuse, but the metropolitan and archbishop, who was elected by the Servians of Hungary and who took up his residence at Carlovitz, was considered as the head of the national church of Servia and the legitimate successor of the Patriarch of Ipek. The see of Ipek existed nominally until 1765 (according to others until 1769), when it was united with the see of Constantinople. In Hungary the title Patriarch was revived in 1848, and the Patriarch Archbishop of Carlovitz therefore appears now more than ever as the legitimate heir of the national Patriarchate of Ipek. In view of these facts, it has been proposed by prominent leaders of the Servians in Hungary to place the Greek Church of Bosnia and Herzegovina under the Patriarch of Carlovitz. A measure of this kind would of course tend to promote a permanent political union of these countries with Austria-Hungary. At the end of November the Patriarch of Carlovitz and the Bishops of Ofen and Neusatz were called to Vienna and to Pesth, to be consulted on the subject by the Governments of Austria and Hungary.

In view of the proposed consolidation of the churches in Bosnia and Herzegovina with the Servian Church of Hungary, the proceedings of the Servian Church Congress of Hungary in 1879 were of more than ordinary importance. This Congress consists of the Patriarch, the bishops, and a number of clerical and lay deputies. Before the meeting of this Congress, which took place in October, it had been feared that serious differences of opinion would show themselves between the bishops on the one hand and the majority of deputies on the other. The deputies were desirous of using the influence of the Church for promoting the political aims of the Servian nationalists, while the bishops did not conceal their dissatisfaction with the liberal organization of the Church and the proposed legal organization of the parishes. After the opening of the Congress, however, a mutual understanding was attained, and the proceedings were harmonious. The law of organization was adopted almost unanimously. It provides that the parish priests shall not be *ex officio* presidents of the parochial meetings, but that the presidents shall be elected. The Congress was in session six weeks, and at its close, November 9th, the royal commissary announced that the Government intended to convoke the Congress again early in 1880 to complete its labors.

The Synod of the Church of Roumania was opened on November 26th, and was closed about the middle of December. In Roumania, as in Austria and in the new states of the Balkan peninsula generally, the coöperation of elective church synods in the affairs of the Church is now fully secured.

In Russia, the Holy Synod is contemplating a reform of the monasteries and nunneries under its jurisdiction. It is especially intended to deprive the lower grades of the religious orders of the privilege of holding and acquiring private property. The annual revenue of the religious orders of Russia is understood to exceed 3,000,000 roubles. They are holders of dividend-bearing stocks of various kinds to the amount of 29,000,000 roubles.

GRÉVY, JULES, President of France. (For biography, see "Annual Cyclopædia" for 1878.)

GUATEMALA (REPÚBLICA DE GUATEMALA). To the details heretofore given concerning area, territorial division, population,* etc., it is only necessary here to add that the number of departments into which the republic is divided has been increased to twenty-two, these being, in order of importance, as follows: Guatemala, Sacatepéquez, Escuintla, Amatitlan, Chimaltenango, Sololá, Suchitepéquez, Quezaltenango, Retalhulen (formerly a part of Suchitepéquez), Totonicapan, Quiché, Huehuetenango, San Márcos, Alta Verapaz, Baja Verapaz, Peten, Izabal, Zacapa, Chiquimula, Jutiapa, Jalapa, and Santa Rosa.

By the terms of a new convention † signed in March in the city of Mexico, and exchanged and ratified in Guatemala on the 1st of August, the time allowed for the surveys and other operations necessary to the determination of the first section of the boundary-line between the two republics was extended to the end of 1879, and a still longer time granted for the final ascertainment and adjustment of the "precise frontier." The extension of time thus granted was regarded as important, as many circumstances had concurred to retard the commencement of the engineers' work, and as it is to be desired that such an accurate survey be made as shall render diplomatic discussion of the subject needless.

The President of the Republic is General Rufino Barrios, elected May 7, 1873. The Cabinet is composed of the following Ministers: Interior and Justice, Sr. Don A. Ubico; War, Finance, and Public Credit, Sr. Don J. M. Barrundia; Public Works and (*ad interim*) Foreign Affairs, Sr. Don Manuel Herrera; Public Instruction, Sr. Don Delfino Sanchez. In the course of the year an important change took place in the Cabinet by the retirement of Sr. Salazar, the previous Minister of State (Interior), and the appointment in his stead of Sr. Ubico, who had already given proof of zeal and activity as *Jefe Político* (Governor) of several of the departments, and also as Under-Secretary of War for more than two years. He is, besides, familiar with the duties of his new post, having filled it temporarily in 1877 during the absence of the Minister. Sr. Don Ramon Uriarte, Minister to Mexico since 1872, was recalled for his unsatisfactory conduct of the recent questions with that republic. His successor is Sr. Don Manuel Herrera, Jr.

The regular army is 3,200 strong, and the militia 13,000.

---

* See "Annual Cyclopædia" for 1875.
† See "Annual Cyclopædia" for 1878, p. 415.

The educational movement, which owes its origin to the Barrios Administration, continues to elicit the admiration of all interested in its progress. According to the report of the Minister of Public Instruction, there are at present in the republic, besides the University, the Normal School, the *Instituto Nacional* (the largest school in Central America), and other institutions for higher branches of study, about 600 primary schools (165 of which are for females), with an average daily attendance of 26,822 scholars. The monthly expenditure in teachers' salaries for these schools amounts to $12,375, of which $7,807 is paid by the central Government and the remainder by the municipalities. Unprecedented numbers of applications were made for admission to the various schools, and unusual energy displayed in the formation of new classes. The attendance at the Military School, which had for a few years considerably fallen off, has again risen to its wonted average; the Normal School, with a thorough reorganization under the auspices of a new director, began the year with an increase of nearly 50 per cent. in the number of pupils; and at the *Instituto Nacional* the new applicants were so numerous as to necessitate the enlargement of the already extensive edifice devoted to that highly creditable college. The Government had resolved upon the adoption of measures for educating the Indian population.

Judging from the report of the Minister of Finance, the condition of that department is no less flattering than it was in 1877, since which year no full returns have been published, and for which the revenue and expenditures were set down at $4,503,523 and $4,428,298 respectively, leaving a surplus of $75,225. In the volume of the "Annual Cyclopædia" for 1878, however, it is remarked that, "in the course of the year (1877), the Government made proposals for a new loan of $1,000,000 to meet current expenses and for the amortization of the convertible debt"; and as for 1879, the Government, it is understood, to provide for "immediate and pressing necessities, has issued a new internal loan, in bonds bearing interest at one per cent. per month; offered to the public at 80, and regarded so favorably that they are marketable at 78." This loan is to be paid out of the proceeds of the custom-house.

The total amount of the national debt was reported at $5,369,529 on January 1, 1879. A committee appointed by Congress to consider and report on the British debt, suggested that a special tax of 5 or 6 per cent. be levied on all taxable commodities in the republic, until such time as the accumulated interest is paid off, and that the first claim on the revenue of the state be for the payment of the sums annually due the bondholders. The suggestions were favorably received by Congress, and the urgency of their adoption unanimously sustained.

As complementary to the remarks in our volume for 1878 on the International Bank, we transcribe the subjoined extract from a report dated December, 1879:

Among the most successful and useful enterprises which have been inaugurated in Guatemala during late years must be reckoned the International Bank. Although but a little over a year in existence, this bank has not only just paid a second dividend of $700 per share, but has also laid the basis of a powerful reserve fund. Its capital consists of one hundred shares at $10,000 each. Up to the present, only $7,000 per share has been called in, with the results given above, which, of course, are highly satisfactory to the bondholders. All over the republic the notes issued by the bank are received at par.

The condition of commerce had not materially improved. The total values of the exports and imports for 1878 were $3,918,912 and $3,238,000 respectively, against $3,773,180 and $3,133,000 in 1877. Coffee was exported of the value of $3,349,740; cochineal, $220,000; muscovado sugar, $110,600; hides, $79,000; specie, $320,000; indigo, $1,300. The proportion of these articles taken by Great Britain represented a value of $1,130,000; the United States, $1,486,000 (New York, $149,126); France, $492,000; Germany, $490,000. The values of the imports from the countries just named were as follows: Great Britain, $994,-000; United States, $461,000; France, $513,-000; Germany, $407,000. Duties were increased 25 per cent., payable in cash. Ten days' notice of this change was given to Central American ports; thirty days' to Mexico, California, and the republics of the south coast; two months' to New York and the West Indies; and four or six months' to European ports, according to the class of vessels in which goods are embarked. The duties now charged on merchandise may be estimated when it is stated that entries at the custom-house during the month ending June 26th amounted to $140,405, on which the duties paid were $98,353, or over 70 per cent.! "The late change in the tariff is an added burden to commerce, which looks hopefully forward to good crops and a continuance of peace for an improvement in the situation."

The work on the Central Railway was progressing with unremitting activity, and an official report published in the Government journal under date of December 20, 1879, speaks of the completion of two or three miles of the line at the San José (Pacific coast) end of the line; the arrival of some rolling-stock; the expected early arrival of more; and the presence of a locomotive in operation to aid in the transport of materials, etc. Indeed, it is understood that the entire necessary material had been purchased early in the autumn: the woodwork, etc., in San Francisco; the locomotives and other rolling-stock in Philadelphia; and the rails in London. This railway is essentially an American enterprise, the company having been organized at San Francisco, and the shareholders and directors of the works

(Colonel Schlessinger and Mr. Nanne) being citizens of the United States. In the contract which the Government signed with Mr. Nanne, it is stipulated that, at various times during the progress of the work, sums of money shall be paid to him by the Government, such sums to amount altogether to $210,000, to be paid, as understood, in seven installments. Owing to various causes, the Government not being (February, 1879) very well off as regards ready money, and Mr. Nanne being naturally anxious to arrange these payments upon a secure basis, so that there might be no trouble or indecision as to his receiving them when they fell due, all doubt in that respect was completely set at rest by the spontaneous offer of a number of the largest capitalists in Guatemala City to guarantee the whole amount promised by the Government; and not that alone, but also any further sums which the Government might contract to pay in a like manner for similar enterprises.

Of telegraph lines (the property of the Government) there were over 1,150 miles, with 52 officers; * and the Minister of Public Works reports that, on February 20th, telegraphic communication was formally opened with the republics of Honduras, San Salvador, and Nicaragua. A treaty has lately been made in New York by Mr. J. Baiz, Consul-General, on the part of the Guatemala Government, with the Central and South American Cable Company (a branch of the Western Union Telegraph Company), to connect with the United States on the Gulf coast near to the Mexican frontier. The tariff will be 75 cents per word for dispatches, against $2.28 per word via Panama. Cheapness will not be the only advantage offered by the direct cable: there will likewise be a very material economy of time, since the minimum loss of time via Panama is five days, as dispatches have to be transmitted thence northward or vice versa by steamer.

By the terms of a new Constitution, promulgated on December 12, 1879, with upward of a hundred articles, all of a liberal and progressive tendency, and consequently the reverse of those of the rejected Constitutions of 1873 and 1874, the term of office of the President of the Republic is extended to six years, from four; the duties of the executive and the legislative powers are clearly defined; the law of habeas corpus is introduced, and complete liberty of conscience guaranteed; the conferring of military rank above that of colonel is an attribute of the legislative power, the promotion to be proposed by the executive; the legislative power declares war and makes peace; primary instruction is compulsory, and that given under the auspices of the Government is secular and gratuitous; perfect freedom in matters of religion is established, etc., etc. Agreeably to one of the articles of the new Constitution, the Presidential term of

office begins on March 1, 1880; consequently elections were to be held before that time. Several candidates were already in the field, but none with any apparent element of popularity. The general desire seemed to be for the reëlection of General Barrios, or, if he should not consent, to elect Sr. Martin Barrundia as his successor.

A new immigration law was promulgated in February, in which liberal inducements are offered to foreigners to settle in the republic, with the guarantee of protection of all their rights and interests.

GUEST, John, a naval officer, born in Missouri in 1821, died at Portsmouth, New Hampshire, January 12, 1879. He entered the navy as a midshipman in 1837, and in 1843 became a passed midshipman, in 1853 a lieutenant, in 1866 a captain, and in 1873 a commodore. He served with distinction on the eastern coast of Mexico in the Mexican war, and took part on shore in several sharp engagements. In 1854 he was second in command of the seamen and marines of the United States steamer Plymouth in a severe and victorious fight with the Chinese rebels of Shanghai, who endeavored to plunder the foreign residents of that city. Captain Guest commanded the Owasco, of Admiral Porter's mortar flotilla, in the bombardment of Forts Jackson and St. Philip prior to and during the passage of Farragut's fleet by the forts on its way to New Orleans, April 24, 1862. He also commanded the same vessel at the bombardment of Vicksburg in the summer of the same year, and received the highest praise from his superiors. He was in command of the Itasca at both of the Fort Fisher fights, in which engagements he added to his previous enviable reputation as a gallant and discreet officer.

GURNEY, William, an army officer, born in Flushing, Long Island, August 21, 1821, died in New York, February 3, 1879. He was in business in New York at the outbreak of the civil war, and was a lieutenant in the Seventh city regiment. In April, 1861, he entered the United States service with that regiment for the three months' term. Returning from that, he accepted a commission as captain in the Sixty-fifth New York regiment (the Fighting Chasseurs), and served with that regiment through the early campaigns of the war. In 1862 he was appointed an assistant inspector-general and examining officer on the staff of Governor Morgan. In July, 1862, he received authority to raise a regiment of his own, and in thirty days he recruited the 127th New York regiment, at the head of which he returned to the field, joining the Twenty-third Army Corps. He was assigned to the command of the Second Brigade of General Abercrombie's division in October, 1862, and in 1864 he went with his brigade to join General Gillmore's command, on the South Carolina coast. In December, 1864, he was severely wounded in the arm in an engagement at De-

* See "Annual Cyclopædia" for 1878.

voe's Neck, and was sent North for treatment. When convalescing he was assigned to the command of the Charleston post. While in command of Charleston he was promoted for gallantry in action to the rank of brigadier-general of United States volunteers; but he returned to New York with his regiment, and was mustered out in July, 1865. He returned to Charleston in October, 1865, and established himself in business. In October, 1870, he accepted the position of Treasurer of Charleston County, which he held for six years. He was Presidential Elector for South Carolina in 1872, and in 1874 was appointed by President Grant a Centennial Commissioner, being elected a vice-president of the Commission.

H

HALE, Mrs. SARAH JOSEPHA (BURL), was born in Newport, New Hampshire, in 1795, and died in Philadelphia on April 30, 1879. This amiable lady was married in 1814 to David Hale, and left a widow with five children in 1822. She resorted to the pen as a means of support, publishing in 1823 "The Genius of Oblivion, and other Original Poems." In 1827 she published "Northwood, a Tale of New England," and during the same year was invited to take charge of a ladies' magazine which was about to be established in Boston. After some hesitation she decided to accept, and in 1828 she removed to that city. In 1837, the "Ladies' Magazine" having been united with "Godey's Lady's Book," published in Philadelphia by Mr. Louis A. Godey, Mrs. Hale became editress of the consolidated periodical, remaining in Boston, however, until 1841, when she removed to Philadelphia. In this position she advocated woman's advancement, urging that teachers of girls should always be of the female sex. She suggested the observance of a national thanksgiving in 1846. The idea of educating women for medical and missionary service in heathen lands was another thought of Mrs. Hale, and she devoted much labor to the securing of its practical adoption. In 1850 the first medical college for women ever founded was established in Philadelphia, and thus the opportunity was presented. The Ladies' Medical Missionary Society was formed, and under its auspices two ladies prepared for the work of treating the diseased bodies and undeveloped minds of women in heathen nations. In 1860 the Woman's Union Missionary Society for Heathen Lands was formed. Mrs. Doremus was the first President of this Society, Mrs. Hale succeeding her and holding the office nine years. In 1877 she retired from editorial labor. Among her published volumes are: "Sketches of American Character," "Traits of American Life," several tales, a manual for housekeepers, and "Woman's Record from the Creation to A. D. 1854." She wrote pleasing poetry, and was respected and esteemed by all who knew her.

HARTRIDGE, JULIAN, a lawyer and member of Congress, born in Savannah, Georgia, about 1831, died in Washington, D. C., January 8, 1879. He received a collegiate education at Brown University, Rhode Island, graduated at the Harvard Law School, and com-

meneed the practice of law in his native city. After having held various public positions in the State of Georgia, and serving as a member of the Charleston Convention in 1860, he bore arms in the Confederate army during the first year of the war, and was subsequently a member of the Confederate Congress. In 1871 he was chairman of the Executive Committee of the Democratic party in Georgia, and in 1872 was delegate-at-large from that State to the Democratic National Convention, and elector-at-large on the Democratic ticket. He was elected to Congress as a Democrat in 1876 from the First Georgia District, and was reëlected in 1878.

HAYMERLE, KARL, Freiherr von, an Austrian statesman, born December 7, 1828. He is descended from an old German family of Bohemia, one of the members of which was knighted by the Empress Maria Theresa. He was educated at the Oriental Academy of Vienna. Together with other students of this institution, he took part in the revolutionary movements of 1848. He was made prisoner, and was sentenced to death by Prince Windischgrätz, but was saved by the intercession of an old friend of the family. He completed his studies in 1850, and in the same year went to Constantinople as assistant interpreter to the Austrian embassy. During the Crimean war he was intrusted with a difficult and important mission to Omer Pasha, regarding the protection of Austrian subjects, which he carried out to the full satisfaction of his Government. In 1857 he went to Athens as secretary of legation, and in 1861 in the same capacity to Dresden, and in the following year remained attached to the Bundestag in Frankfort, where he also remained during the Congress of German Princes. In 1864 he was appointed chargé d'affaires in Copenhagen, where he brought about a good understanding between the Austrian and Danish courts. After the war with Prussia he was appointed chargé d'affaires in Berlin, and here also through his ability restored good relations with his Government. In 1868 he was recalled to Vienna, where he was employed for a short time in the Ministry of Foreign Affairs, and then went to Constantinople as chargé d'affaires. In 1869 he was appointed Ambassador to Greece, and in 1872 to the Netherlands. In 1876 he was created a Baron (Freiherr), was appointed Ambassador to Italy in 1877, and in 1878 was one of the Austrian delegates to the Congress of Berlin. When Count Andrassy retired from his office, it was thought desirable that one of the delegates to the Congress of Berlin should succeed him. As Count Karolyi, the second delegate, declined, Freiherr von Haymerle was appointed. He is regarded as one of the ablest men of the empire, and is described as very pleasant in company. He is the first Austrian who has held the office of Minister for Foreign Affairs since the establishment of the dual monarchy, Count Beust being a Saxon and Count Andrassy a Hungarian.

HAYS, ISAAC, a scientist and eminent physician, born in Philadelphia in 1796, died there, April 13, 1879. He graduated from the department of arts in the Pennsylvania University in 1817, and from that of medicine in 1821. His literary labors were very extensive and valuable. He edited Hall's edition of Wilson's "American Ornithology" (Philadelphia, 1828); Hoblyn's "Dictionary of Medical Terms," etc. (1846); a new edition of the same, from the last London edition (1855); Lawrence's "Treatise on Diseases of the Eye" (1847), and successive editions; and Arnott's "Elements of Physics" (1848). He was the editor of the "American Journal of the Medical Sciences," which is still published. It was originally started in 1820 as the "Philadelphia Journal of the Medical and Physical Sciences," and was edited by the late Professor Nathaniel Chapman. In 1826 Dr. Hays joined the editorial staff, and in 1827 it was converted into the "American Journal of the Medical Sciences," of which he was thenceforth sole editor until 1869, when his son was associated with him. He was elected a member of the Academy of Natural Sciences of Philadelphia in 1818, and was its president from 1865 to 1869. He was an active member of the American Philosophical Society, and for a number of years a member of its Council. He was one of the founders of the Franklin Institute, and in early years its secretary, and at the time of his death was the oldest living member. He was one of the oldest members of the College of Physicians of Philadelphia, and for a number of years one of the censors. He was one of the founders of the American Medical Association, and author of its code of ethics, which has since been adopted by every State and county medical society in the Union. Many other honorary positions were held by him in scientific bodies in this country and abroad.

HEALTH, NATIONAL BOARD OF. The evil results of quarantines, established at every country town or even cross-roads by irresponsible boards, wholly inefficient to protect the public health, but destructive of trade and prosperity, plainly pointed out the necessity for a National Board of Health. The Constitution gives no specific power to the General Government to make sanitary regulations. The "power to regulate commerce with foreign nations," however, implies the control of that which interferes most materially with it. Epidemics destroy commerce; it may be conceded, then, that their prevention should be intrusted to the long purse and strong arm of the central Government, which alone can enforce obedience to its mandates. The act constituting the National Board of Health was approved on March 3d. The Board consists of eleven members, viz., seven civilian physicians, one army surgeon, one navy surgeon, one medical officer of the Marine Hospital service, and one officer from the Department of Justice. The duties prescribed are, that they should obtain information upon all matters affecting the public health, and advise the several departments of the Government, the executives of the several States, and the Commissioners of the District of Columbia, on all questions submitted by them, whenever in the opinion of the Board such advice may tend to the preservation and improvement of the public health. They are to coöperate with the Academy of Sciences, and to collect the views of leading sanitary organizations and scientists in order to perfect a plan, to be submitted to Congress at its next session, for a permanent health organization. This is explicit, and the Board has clearly understood and complied with these injunctions.

On June 3d the national quarantine law was passed. This is vague in terms, and gives little or no authority to do any specific work. The Board may request the President to appoint medical officers to assist consuls in foreign ports from which infection may be imported. To prevent the introduction of infectious diseases from foreign ports, or from one State to another, the National Board is to coöperate with State and municipal boards. The extent of this coöperation and the means by which it is to be carried out are not provided for. Should local provisions appear inadequate, the National Board is to report to the President, who may order it to make rules and regulations to meet the case. If the President approve these, the Board is to promulgate and the State authorities to enforce them. Should the State authorities fail in this duty, it is discretionary with the President to detail an officer to see to their enforcement.

In regard to the rules and regulations to be observed by vessels coming from infected ports, the Board has no more definite authority. It has power to obtain from consuls, and medical officers assisting them, weekly bulletins of the sanitary condition of foreign ports from which danger is apprehended. These warnings are invaluable. It is authorized to collect and publish weekly reports of the health of towns and cities throughout the United States. It is expected to procure information relating to the climatic and other conditions affecting the public health. It is to supply information and suggest rules and regulations concerning vessels, railroad trains, and other modes of interior communication. In compliance with law the National Board publishes weekly bulletins, thus distributing gratuitously to those who are most interested in such matters a record of all important work done by the Board, or information gathered. Still further disseminated by the daily press, it thus furnishes to the working minds of the country the data most important for them to obtain, and which would be extremely costly in time and money if only to be accumulated by private endeavor. In one of its circulars it proffers aid, in means and information, to leading professional or scientific men who are willing to devote their labors to the objects in view. Being in complete communication with local boards and associations, it is in a position to mass and sift facts and to compare results, so as to reduce to a system all tentative efforts.

Beyond a doubt the most important function of the Board is the fashioning of a permanent organization. The deliberative wisdom of Congress will rarely be employed on a more important work than the framing of the act which will place the permanent National Board of Health on a solid basis, far above sectional or party considerations. It should become a great national educator, collecting facts and distributing knowledge, unadulterated by individual theories or prejudices. It must apply science to the stamping out of disease, and erect barriers against its importation, at the same time that it must render impossible all selfish or senseless quarantines suggested by other interests than the public health. The act must clearly determine the means and regulate the mode. Local rights and customs should be respected so far as they are not inimical to the interests of the general public. Suitable officers must be selected to carry out the provisions of the act with the greatest possible advantage to health and the least possible disturbance to trade. These delicate functions may be so exercised as to insure the barring out of all preventable diseases.

Other diseases have been ignored by the public mind, and in point of fact the National Board is judged by its yellow-fever work. It is difficult to say just how much effect upon the spread of this infection has been due to the labors of the National Board. The original bill contained a clause authorizing the Board to pay half the expenses of local boards, organized on the plan proposed by the National Board. This clause was altered. Doubtless it would have increased the efficiency of local boards, which have at least experience and interest to lead them to use such funds properly. By subordinating the local boards to the National Board uniformity of action is obtained. If the National Board is accused of halting and vacillating, it may be answered that its powers are ill-defined, its labors are in a new field, there are no precedents to guide, and there are many subtle questions of State and inter-State and national

rights involved. With the desire on all sides to waive other considerations than the public good, these causes account for hesitation and other sins of omission and commission. The *personnel* of the Board has also been the subject of much criticism. Physicians with lucrative practices and scientists with life-pursuits, if found, are not easily induced to surrender them and devote their entire energies to such purposes. It is conceded that some at least of the leading men of the country are members of the Board. The only proper inquiry is not who are they, but what are they doing? Here the people and the press have a proper topic for discussion. Early in the summer the Board issued a well-considered circular. If its terms seem too cautious, let it be remembered that the whole question is still an open one. Not only do physicians of all ranks differ in regard to diagnosis and treatment, but men of equal pretensions to science dispute rancorously whether yellow fever is contagious or infectious, preventable or non-preventable, exotic or indigenous. Hence the non-committal tone of the following official utterance of July 12th:

Whatever opinions may be held as to the causes of yellow fever and the recent appearance of that disease in Tennessee and Mississippi, it is best to act as if it were a disease due to a specific particular cause, which is capable of growth and reproduction, transportable, and may be destroyed by exposure to a temperature above 240° F., or by chemical disinfectants of sufficient strength if brought into immediate contact with it. It is also prudent to assume that the growth and reproduction of this cause are connected with the presence of filth, in the sanitary sense of that word, including decaying organic matters and defective ventilation as well as high temperature.

The cases of yellow fever recently observed should be considered as due to causes surviving from last year's epidemic, and not to recent importation from other countries. . . . The object of the present circular is to advise that all cities and towns be made clean, in a sanitary point of view. . . . The results of a careful sanitary inspection of almost any city or town will show the existence of collections of decaying and offensive matters previously unknown. . . . Such inspections, to be of value, must be thorough, and made by persons competent to recognize foul soils, water, and air, as well as the grosser and more palpable forms of nuisance. They should also be made by persons who will report fully and frankly the results of their observations, without reference to the wishes of persons or corporations. . . . The remedy is usually self-evident.

The weekly reports contain, besides other valuable information, the mortality from specific diseases of the chief cities of the world. The Board has also issued six bulletins, which contain rules and regulations "for securing the best sanitary condition of vessels, cargoes, passengers, and crews coming from infected foreign ports"; "for quarantined ports, with special reference to yellow fever"; "concerning the sanitary condition of vessels, cargoes, passengers, and crews going from an infected port of the United States to another port in the United States"; "for securing the best sanitary condition of railroads, station-houses, road-beds, and of cars, freights, passengers, and employees coming from a point where yellow fever exists"; "to be observed by the health authorities of a place free from infection, having communication with an infected place"; "concerning the course to be adopted in a place already infected with yellow fever." These publications carefully embody the best sanitary and medical views of the day, and give plain and sensible directions for practical use. Reading them produces a conviction that, well followed, they would not only stay the progress of yellow fever, but increase the average of human health and life by eradicating the cause of half the ills which flesh is heir to. Inspectors and other employees of the Board may have erred through too much zeal; they may have been too inquisitorial; they may have been rash in telegraphing cases which were disproved by later diagnosis. In these ways they may have produced panics and injured the material interests of some communities, which have already suffered too much. These are the difficulties to be expected in the working of a new and untried scheme. But they are errors on the right side. The public has not heretofore been satiated with too much truth. In the end it will work out good. Nothing is more calming to apprehension than the certainty that there is no concealment. The publications of the Board have had a wholesome effect on public opinion in regard to sanitation. The people have learned the difference between dirt and filth, and, instead of resting satisfied with superficial cleanliness, they are seeking to eradicate the hidden evil.

In the diversity of opinions, the weight of testimony inclines to the view that yellow fever is a specific disease not originating in this country, but chiefly from the West Indies, where it has its habitat. In order to make a scientific examination of these important questions, the National Board organized a commission, composed of three physicians and a civil engineer, to visit the island of Cuba, called "the Havana Yellow Fever Commission of the National Board of Health of the United States." The Board instructed this Commission—1st, to ascertain the sanitary condition of the chief ports of Cuba, and to determine how to prevent the introduction of the cause of yellow fever into the shipping; 2d, to investigate the pathology of yellow fever and the changes and results which it produces in the human body; 3d, to obtain all information in regard to the endemicity of yellow fever in Cuba. In addition the Board enjoined them to attack other unsolved and perhaps insoluble problems in regard to the nature and natural history of yellow fever. They were to experiment on animals, and to seek to discover the immediate cause of yellow fever other than the production of the disease in man. Amply supplied with apparatus, photographic, microscopic, and chemical, for the prosecution of these researches, the Commission sailed from New York on the 3d of July, and arrived in Havana on the 7th. The Captain-General

furthered their aims in every way, and appointed twelve eminent physicians and *savants* as an auxiliary commission to coöperate with the American Commission during their stay, and to continue the study of yellow fever after their departure. Much valuable information collected is due to the zeal with which these learned and courteous gentlemen seconded their American *confrères*. A circular containing questions was distributed over the entire island. The responses from Spanish commissioners, American consuls, physicians, and scientists furnished the Commission with reports, the most extensive yet amassed touching yellow fever.

The subjects proposed by the Board were treated in the following order:

I. *The principal ports of Cuba from which shipments are made to the United States.* The "ports of entry" of Cuba are fifteen in number, of which eight are on the northern and seven on the southern side. The island has also two hundred minor ports on its coast-line of 2,200 miles. Twenty-five hundred vessels, carrying thirty thousand sailors, pass annually from Cuba to the United States. More than two fifths of these enter the port of New York. In 1875 only 571 out of 2,236 sailed to the eighteen ports south of Norfolk, which alone are liable to yellow fever. The intercourse with Cuba is largest during May and June, and decreases during the summer months. The people of the United States may well ask themselves whether their welfare would not be promoted by suspension of intercourse during the dangerous months. In January, 1879, it was stated before the Congressional committee investigating the epidemic, that the restriction on the West India trade of New Orleans injured that city to the extent of $100,000,000. This statement passed unchallenged. The total exports of Cuba in 1878 were $70,881,552. Imports into New Orleans from Cuba amounted to $2,043,697. The United States is an indispensable market to Cuba, and any loss arising from the restriction of commerce to certain months would fall chiefly on the shipping interest. Sanitary hindrances to this trade do not and will not cause loss to any great amount.

II. *The endemicity of yellow fever in Cuba.* Though it may be suspected that the sickness which prevailed in Santo Domingo in 1493–'94, and in succeeding years in various countries bordering on the Caribbean Sea, was yellow fever, the first unquestionable epidemic of this fever occurred in 1640, in Guadeloupe. Its first recorded appearance in Havana was in 1761. The next year Havana was captured and held by English soldiers, and was ravaged by another epidemic. Before 1761 Cuba was noted for its salubrity. Yellow fever could not have prevailed, if at all, to any great extent. Since 1761 it has been present every year, and it is therefore said to be endemic. Some authorities aver that yellow fever was imported from Africa in the slave-ships. Several thousand slaves were entered in 1763. In 1774 there were 75,180 blacks. Diligent inquiry was made for some spot on the island exempt from visitation. Reports from more than forty towns prove that wherever there is food for it in unacclimated population, it prevails, though with varying and erratic intensity. At Puerto Principe, an inland and elevated city, hospital records show its prevalence every year but one since 1850. In Havana the fever is usually epidemic from June to October, and endemic during the rest of the year. From 1870 to 1879, in no month have there been fewer than 4 deaths, nor more than 675. During this decade the minimum of deaths was 515 in 1872; the maximum, 1,619 in 1876. From one fourth to one half of these deaths occur in the military hospital. This disproves the assertion that yellow fever is specially severe in the shipping and harbor.

III. *The causation of this endemicity.* The geography, geology, and meteorology have not altered since 1761. Endemicity must be caused by differing conditions. Previous to the English invasion in 1762, Cuba had no commerce. The introduction of steam navigation in 1819, and of railroads in 1836, contributed to the rapid spread of the disease. Spanish medical authorities, official and unofficial, class yellow fever among contagious diseases. Though some may deny its contagiousness, none dispute its portability and importability. Yet in the military hospital, where yellow fever is rarely absent, the lower story is used to store blankets, clothing, and other hospital supplies for general distribution over the island. The paper currency of Cuba is noisome and filthy to a degree. On October 4th clean bills of health were furnished by Havana officials. During that week there were eighty cases and twenty deaths of yellow fever, and nine infected vessels in the harbor. The Commission procured the meteorological records of Havana for twenty years. The annual mean temperature of the island varies from 77° to 79° F. The only record of a frost is on the 24th and 25th of December, 1856. The average rainfall is about 50 inches; number of rainy days, 102. Violent winds and hurricanes are injurious to the sick, but they affect the poison and lessen the number of new cases. Investigations of electricity, magnetism, and ozone have so far yielded no satisfactory results.

IV. *The actual sanitary condition of Havana, Matanzas, and other Cuban ports.* The unsanitary condition of Cuba is demonstrated by the death-rate. In different parts of the island and in different years the annual mortality varied from 39·5 to 67·05 per thousand. Among destructive diseases yellow fever ranks third. Phthisis stands foremost. This malady makes frightful havoc among residents, yet consumptives are still ordered to Havana. Statistics confirm Bowditch's law concerning the pernicious influence on consumption of foul air combined with subsoil moisture. Under

whatever name registered, swamp-poison or malaria is the deadliest agent in Cuban mortality. The water-supply flows, partly through an aqueduct, partly through a ditch, from the Almandares River, four miles distant. Water is scarce and costly. A large part of the population purchase it from street venders. Personal and household cleanliness is rendered difficult. That part of the supply which comes through the Zanga, an open earth-ditch, is impure as well as inadequate. A half-finished aqueduct, which has already cost $3,000,000, may obviate this difficulty if it is carried to completion. The sewerage is grossly defective. The surface-soil is shallow. The substratum rock is porous and friable, admitting a high degree of saturation. A moisture-mark may be observed high on walls of houses, even on those built a hundred feet above the sea-level. The water and soil being in such plight, the air is necessarily foul. Ventilation in the old town is obstructed. The streets are so narrow that vehicles are only allowed to travel in one direction. The paved streets of the modern town are kept clean. Even there, however, repulsive odors greet the nostrils, teaching the presence of fecal and kitchen refuse reeking within the courts of even the better class of houses. These are usually built low. The floors, of wood or brick, are on the ground, if not below it. The interior arrangements are unwholesome. Kitchens, cabinets, and stables are close to sleeping apartments and intolerably offensive. Buzzards resting on the roofs show the call of nature for scavengering. *Mamposteria*, or rubble masonry, is the ordinary building material. The walls testify to its porous and absorbing qualities. Rents are high and houses overcrowded. Since 1806 burial in churches has ceased. In 1871 the intramural cemetery of Espada was closed upon its 300,000 dead. The new cemetery is well located, beyond the reach of evil influence. No abatement of fever has been observed.

The picturesque harbor of Havana suffers under a bad reputation. English naval vessels are forbidden to use the harbor-water for any purpose. The anchorage-ground for large vessels is contracted. An average of 100 vessels, sometimes as many as 227, lie close to each other and to the shore. It is the receptacle of a vast surplus of filth. Very little clean water finds its way into it. The tide has a rise and fall of about two feet. The remarkable phosphorescence of its waters has been considered connected with yellow fever. In 1879 the fever made its appearance, and not the phosphorescence. On its southern edge lie five piles of ballast. This ballast, which freely absorbs fluids and gases, should be treated as dangerous yellow-fever fomites, at least until this theory is disproved. Hygienic laws are thus violated in all the Cuban ports, and that where the conditions most favorable to yellow fever exist, viz., hot climate and dense population.

V. *The means by which the sanitary condition of Havana, Matanzas, and other Cuban ports can be best made satisfactory.* Cuba does not lack scientific engineers, who see what is required for its sanitation. Here, as elsewhere, two factors are needed for the elimination of disease, hygiénic education for the people and financial power in the Government. There are persons who pronounce yellow fever a nautical disease. The weight of evidence collected by this Commission goes to prove that the more communication between the crew and the town, and the closer the vessel lies to the shore, the more liable it is to become infected. While ships are known to carry this poison from port to port, in the opinion of this Commission they receive it from the land and not from the harbor. There is no proof of its spontaneous origin on ships.

VI. *What can and should be done to prevent the introduction of the cause of yellow fever into the shipping in Cuban ports?* The United States can protect itself by prohibiting entrance into its ports of vessels from infected ports. The eradication of the evil in Cuba depends solely upon the Spanish authorities. The following preventive measures are recommended: Clean, dry, and less porous ballast should be procured, and this should be thoroughly disinfected in the ship. Vessels should lie as far as possible from shore and other vessels, and well to windward of infected localities or ships. On leaving port every part of the ship should be cleansed, fumigated, and ventilated. The order to the Spanish navy requires strict precautions at all seasons. This is equally incumbent whether there are or are not fever cases on board, as the virus is known to lie long dormant. The need for stringent sanitary measures is self-evident; the execution of them is difficult. Right methods must be enforced by right men. In the act of June 2d Congress essays to regulate this important affair. An older law requires captains to pay three months' extra wages to sick seamen discharged in a foreign port. To avoid this mulct, masters of small vessels often prefer to sail with their fever-smitten sailors. This should be amended. Legal enactments should secure the prompt report to the United States Consul of suspicious cases on shipboard, and the non-intercourse of persons on board with the shore.

The quarantine act of June 2d was denounced by the Cuban press. Permission to promulgate it was not granted by the authorities. Inspectors were appointed under the act, but the Spanish Government refused to allow other bills of health to be issued than those given by their own officials. The loose construction under which they give clean bills of health has been shown. During this imbroglio vessels left Cuba and were admitted into the United States, not being provided with the required certificate, and in contravention of the act for preventing the importation of disease. This part of that law is thus in abeyance, and the public

health imperiled, until these important points are decided. The consent and aid of Spain in the enforcement of the statute should be sought. An international sanitary code, modeled on the French code of 1853 and providing uniform regulations, is a great desideratum.

VII. *Examination of the blood in yellow fever.* Micro-photographs were taken with powerful instruments. The only peculiarity observed is certain granules in the white corpuscles. These may or may not be symptomatic of this disease, or causative of it. The Commission were able to deduce no new facts from their examinations. They hold that these photographs reveal all that there is in the blood. No organism is shown in any preparation photographed immediately after collection. No chemical examination was attempted.

VIII. *Experiments upon animals.* Animals of various species imported from the United States were exposed to infection in the holds of vessels; they were fed upon the excretions of yellow-fever patients; the blood of such patients, in different stages of the disease, was injected into their veins; they were made to sleep in infected bedding and clothing. Ingenuity exhausted modes of injection. In no instance was yellow fever developed in an animal. One suspicious case turned out to be a well-known fever, called *romadiza*, common in dogs imported into Cuba.

IX. *Culture experiments.* In verification of the hypothesis that the essential cause of yellow fever is a living germ or organism, capable under certain circumstances of indefinite multiplication, the Commission made experiments in germ-culture. A certain fungus was developed, but whether distinctive of yellow fever only no one on the Commission, unluckily, had sufficiently precise knowledge of the lower forms of vegetable life to determine. Careful micro-photographs were obtained, which should be submitted to expert mycologists. The *aqua coco* (cocoanut-milk) from the unripe nut, being transparent and inclosed in a germ-proof receptacle, was found a convenient fluid for detecting bacteria. Exposed to infected air, it soon developed a pellicle containing cells of a fungus, and turned milky white. Portions of the same fluid, protected by a bell-glass, retained their purity and transparency.

X. *Examination of the water of the harbor.* The harbor-water has the same specific gravity as that of the gulf outside. After heavy rains its gravity falls, especially in the vicinity of sewers. Kept in an open vessel, it developed no putridity recognizable by the senses. That taken near the sewer-mouths contained infusoria, but they showed no activity, being probably fresh-water species destroyed by salt water.

XI. *Examination of the air.* Microscopic examinations of air from hospital wards, and other infected localities, revealed certain slender, glistening, acicular crystals in great abundance, unknown to the Commissioners, and undescribed in the standard works on the subject.

Subsequent observations, made in Washington, showed the same crystals deposited on glasses brought from infected spots, such as Morgan City, Bayou Bœuf, and the New Orleans Charity Hospital, while none were found in those from Bellevue Hospital, New York.

Finally, twenty-two autopsies were performed in Havana. Preparations of tissues were made and brought to the United States. The statements in the preliminary report, of which the above is a brief synopsis, are to be regarded, the Commissioners say, as suggestions rather than conclusions. The value of the work done by the Commission can only be estimated by the amount of pabulum it furnishes to the scientific minds of the country.

In addition, they publish an interesting report on the alkalinity of the atmosphere, by Dr. Charles Finlay of the Spanish Commission. Observations dating from 1858 have convinced him of the excessive alkalinity of the Cuban atmosphere. To show the alkalinity resulting from free ammonia in other atmospheres, he instances the ventilation experiments in St. Mary's Hospital, Paddington. The maximum value obtained in these hospital wards in July, 1875, was 2,000 times smaller than the Havana maximum of 1879, and 228 times smaller than the Havana maximum in October, 1864. This alkalinity increases and diminishes in intensity *pari passu* with yellow fever. The blood, breath, and excretions during certain stages of yellow fever are markedly alkaline. The most recommended disinfectants are just the agents that would destroy a volatile alkali. Empirical treatments by non-professionals in the West Indies have oily and acid substances for their basis, just as if the object were to saponify or neutralize some alkaline poison. Scientific investigations may verify his proposition that some volatile alkali of the compound ammonia type, disseminated in the atmosphere surrounding centers of infection, is the material cause of yellow fever.

The National Board has completed a sanitary survey of Memphis, with a view to removing causes which might bring about a recurrence of yellow fever.

Twenty State boards are now working in subordination to the National Board. The American Health Association, in its convention at Nashville, commended and endorsed the National Board, and recommended its continuance with increased powers. Whatever the discrepancy between public expectation and the results gained by the Board, it must be admitted that during its brief existence its labors have been neither few nor small. With more definite powers it must have a field of ever-widening usefulness. The creation of this bureau was an imperatively needed act of legislation.

HELIOGRAPH, THE. The Mance heliograph, an instrument for signaling by means of reflected solar rays, was made use of among the British forces in Afghanistan, and in the latter part of the war in South Africa. The signals made by the Mance heliograph are visible, under favorable conditions of position and atmosphere, to very great distances, and have been read as far as eighty and a hundred miles. It consists of a specially prepared mirror, with mechanism for reflecting the sun's rays with absolute precision to any required spot, notwithstanding the sun's apparent motion. By pressure on a finger-key the flashes are made of short or long duration, thus adapting the instrument to the Morse code of telegraphy. A second mirror is provided to permit of signaling being carried on irrespective of the sun's position. The instrument intended for field service weighs from six to eight pounds, and is mounted on a light tripod stand. The working parts are protected from injury during transit, and the complete apparatus admits of being easily carried, as it is also efficiently worked, by one man. By working different adjusting screws the sun's rays may be made to strike any desired point on the mirror. The groupings and duration of the flashes admit of sufficient variety to give a different signal for every sign and letter, so that verbal messages can be transmitted. Different forms of this instrument have occasionally been used for various purposes a long time. It never, however, so recommended itself to military use as when General Roberts, beleaguered in Khost, employed it to signal for reënforcements to Baunee, sixty miles away. In the present improved form it is capable of being used with great advantage in the signal service or for other purposes between points which have no telegraphic communication by electric wires.

HILL, BENJAMIN HARVEY, an American statesman, born in Jasper County, Georgia, September 14, 1823. He is of Irish lineage on his father's side, and of English on his mother's. He graduated with the first honors from the University of Georgia in 1844, studied law, was admitted to the bar, and began the practice of his profession at La Grange, Georgia, in 1845. In November of that year he married Caroline E. Holt, daughter of Cicero Holt, a prominent lawyer of Athens, Georgia. He soon acquired a high standing as an advocate and orator, and now ranks as the foremost lawyer at the Georgia bar.

In 1851 he was elected to the State Legislature. Without being fully in sympathy with the American or Know-Nothing party, he was chosen an elector at large on that ticket in 1856. His speeches during this Presidential campaign enhanced his reputation as an orator and popular speaker. In 1859 he was elected to the State Senate as a Union man. In 1860 his name was on the Bell and Everett electoral ticket. He was a member of the Secession Convention held at Milledgeville, January 16, 1861. Georgia did not secede without considerable hesitation on the part of a large proportion of her people, nor without solemn warning and earnest remonstrance from her most eminent citizen, Alexander H. Stephens, who was a member of this Convention. On the third day of the sessions of the Convention, Mr. Stephens made a speech endorsing his celebrated speech of November and deprecating the dissolution of the Federal Union. Mr. Hill also spoke with characteristic zeal and earnestness in favor of the Union ; but, when he found that the passage of the ordinance of secession was inevitable, he finally voted for it, believing with many of his friends that it was his duty to follow the fortunes of his State. He was a member of the provisional Confederate Congress which assembled at Montgomery, Alabama, February 4, 1861. The State Legislature in the fall of that year elected him a member of the Confederate Senate, in which body he served during the continuance of the war. After its close, in May, 1865, he was arrested and confined in Fort Lafayette, New York Harbor. In July he was released on parole, and returned to his home at La Grange.

During the next ten years Mr. Hill held no official position, but was active in the political affairs of his native State, speaking and writing against the reconstruction acts of Congress. He was a zealous supporter of the Greeley movement in 1872. Elected a representative to the Forty-fourth Congress, he took his seat December 6, 1875, and was appointed a member of the Committee of Ways and Means. The debate on the "Amnesty bill" brought him into prominence at the beginning of his Congressional career. In his speech on January 11, 1876, he said : "Is the bosom of the country always to be torn with this miserable sectional debate, whenever a Presidential election is pending? The victory of the North was absolute, and God knows the submission of the South was complete! But, sir, we have recovered from the humiliation of defeat, and we come here among you and ask you to give us the greetings accorded to brothers by brothers. We propose to join you in every patriotic endeavor and to unite with you in every patriotic aspiration that looks to the benefit, the advancement, and the honor of every part of our common country. Let us, gentlemen of all parties, in this centennial year, indeed have a jubilee of freedom. We divide with you the glories of the Revolution and of the succeeding years of our national life, before that unhappy division—that four years' night of gloom and despair; and so shall we divide with you the glories of all the future. We are here; we are in the house of our fathers, our brothers are our companions, and we are at home to stay, thank God! We come charging upon the Union no wrongs to us. The Union never wronged us. The Union has been an unmixed blessing to every section, to every State, and to every man of every color in America. We charge all our wrongs upon that 'higher-law' fanaticism that never kept a pledge nor obeyed a law. Brave Union men of the North—you who fought for the Union

for the sake of the Union, you who ceased to fight .when the battle ended and the sword was sheathed—we have no quarrel with you, whether Republicans or Democrats. We felt your heavy arm in the carnage of battle; but above the roar of the cannon we heard your voice of kindness, calling, ' Brothers, come back!' and we bear witness to you this day that that voice of kindness did more to thin the Confederate ranks and weaken the Confederate arm than did all the artillery employed in the struggle."

He made a speech January 17, 1877, in .favor of the Electoral Commission, characterizing it as a measure wholly constitutional, wise in every provision, and patriotic in every purpose.

He was reëlected to the Forty-fifth Congress, but resigned to enter the United States Senate, March 5, 1877, where he served on the Committees on Privileges and Elections, Revolutionary Claims, and Mines and Mining. In addition to these, in the extra session in March, when the Democrats came into power, he was made a member of the Committee on Foreign Relations and chairman of the Committee on the Contingent Expenses of the Senate. His most important speeches in the Senate have been on the silver bill, delivered February 8, 1878, in which he favored the recoinage and remonetizing of silver, but opposed the unlimited free coinage of the silver dollar; on the Thurman Pacific Railroad Funding bill, May 20, 1878; on "The Union and its Enemies," May 10, 1879; and in defense of his Union record during the war of secession, in reply to Senator Blaine, June 10, 1879.

HILL, Sir ROWLAND, K. C. B., D. C. L., F. R. S., born at Kidderminster, December 3, 1795, died in London, September 2, 1879. He was brother to Matthew Davenport Hill, Q. C., who fifty years ago had reached distinction as a Reform member of Parliament. These brothers were sons of Mr. Thomas W. Hill, schoolmaster in Birmingham. Rowland Hill was educated in his father's school, and for seventeen years lived the uneventful life of a teacher in that institution. In 1835 he entered the public service as Secretary to the Commissioners for the Colonization of South Australia. His mind was turned to the subject of postoffice reform, which became his life-work, by the following incident: Coleridge, on a tour through the Lake district, arrived at a wayside inn as a postman delivered a letter to the waiting-maid. She examined it carefully and returned it to the postman, saying she could not afford the shilling. Finding that the letter was from her brother, the poet insisted on paying the postage. Afterward, in explanation of her reluctance to accept his kind offices, the girl showed him that the letter was blank. On the outside were certain marks which conveyed to her the knowledge that her brother was well. Thus by a prearranged system they managed to correspond with each other and defraud the Government. Mr. Hill was much impressed by this narrative, and henceforth dedicated his energies to an amelioration of the law. . He lived to see the complete success of his system in Great Britain, and its adoption throughout the civilized world. Postage before his day, except to the easy classes, was prohibitive. News was smuggled through the mails in many ingenious ways. He met with much official opposition. When Mr. Hill proposed his plan to the Postmaster-General, it was unceremoniously rejected. In 1837 he published a book on " Post-Office Reform." By a convincing array of facts and figures.he proved that, despite increase of business and growth of population, the post-office revenue had decreased from 1815 to 1835, so universal was the custom of sending letters through private channels. He argued, in favor of cheap postage, that a greater number of letters at reduced rates would increase the total revenue. The public were quick to perceive the merit of his plan. In 1838 the House of Commons appointed a committee to investigate the subject, which recommended its adoption. During 1839 more than two thousand petitions in its favor were addressed to Parliament. In spite of official obstructions, early in 1840 the penny post was established. Mr. Hill was appointed to a place in the Treasury to superintend its inauguration. Results have more than justified his prophecies. In 1838, the last complete year of the old system, 76,000,000 chargeable letters were delivered in the United Kingdom. This number was more than doubled during the first year of the cheap system. In 1854 it reached 443,000,000. In 1878 the aggregate amounted to 1,900,000,000. Within ten years the postal receipts equaled the greatest highpostage revenue. Since that period the increase has continued without fluctuation. In 1842, on a change of ministry, Mr. Hill was removed from office on the score that his services, though successful, were no longer needed. This did not meet the general approbation. A subscription for a public testimonial was begun, which rapidly brought in £13,360. In 1843 he was · manager of the London and Brighton Railway. Subsequently· he became its chairman. He was afterward appointed a member of a Royal Commission on Railways. His dissenting views were published in a separate report from those of his fellow commissioners. In 1846 he was made Secretary to the Postmaster-General. In 1854 he received the appointment for which he was eminently fitted, that of Chief Secretary This post he filled with honor to himself and benefit to the nation until declining health forced him to resign it in 1864. The Treasury, after a handsome acknowledgment, continued to him for life his full salary of £10,000. Parliament voted him also a grant of £20,000. In 1860, in recognition of his services in the Post-Office, he was created a Knight Commander of the Bath, Civil Division. In 1864 the University of Ox-

ford conferred on him the degree of D. C. L. In that year he received the first Albert gold medal of the Society of Arts. In 1877 a subscription for a statue (no contribution over sixpence allowed) resulted in £1,600 from over 100,000 persons raised in a short time. A few months before his death the freedom of the city of London was conferred upon him. The ceremony was performed at his house, where he was confined by ill health, and where soon after, full of years and honors, he died.

HILLARD, GEORGE STILLMAN, an editor and author, born at Machias, Maine, in September, 1808, died in Boston, January 21, 1879. He graduated at Harvard College in 1828, and in 1833 was admitted to the bar in Boston. In the same year he became editorially connected with the " Christian Register," a Unitarian weekly newspaper. Subsequently he became associated with Charles Sumner in the publication of " The Jurist." In 1856 he bought an interest in the " Boston Courier," and took the position of associate editor, but retired at the beginning of the civil war. He was most successful in his contributions to magazines and reviews, among which were the "Atlantic Monthly" and the " North American Review." His articles were chiefly reviews of books and essays on subjects of art. In 1845-'47 he was a member of the Boston Common Council. He then visited Europe, and on his return published " Six Months in Italy," which was successful here and republished in England. In 1850 he was a member of the State Senate; in 1853 a member of the State Constitutional Convention; in 1854-'56 Boston City Solicitor; and in 1866-'70 United States District Attorney for Massachusetts. He was a pleasing speaker, and delivered many public addresses. He published in 1856 a series of school readers which were very successful. In 1889 he published, in five volumes, "The Poetical Works of Edmund Spenser, with a Critical Introduction." His "Selections from the Writings of Walter Savage Landor," published in 1856, was well done. Several translations were also made by him, one of which was Guizot's "Essay on the Character and Influence of Washington." In 1864 he published the " Life and Campaigns of George B. McClellan." He began to prepare for publication the life and letters of George Ticknor, but was unable to finish the work, which was completed by Miss Ticknor.

HOOD, JOHN B., Lieutenant-General in the Confederate Army, born at Owenville, Bath County, Kentucky, June 1, 1831, died of yellow fever in New Orleans, August 30, 1879. His preparatory education was received at Mount Sterling. In 1849 he entered the Military Academy at West Point. He graduated in 1853 in the same class with Chambliss, Bowen, McPherson, Rich, Schofield, Sheridan, Terrill, and other distinguished military leaders. Assigned to duty in the 4th Infantry, he served two years in California. In July, 1855, he was transferred to the 2d Cavalry, of which Albert Sidney Johnston was colonel, and Robert E. Lee lieutenant-colonel. This regiment, which gave so many officers of note to both Northern and Southern armies, was then guarding the northern and western frontiers of Texas. Hood won his first laurels in a desperate fight at Devil's Run in July, 1856. With twenty-five men of his company he charged a numerous band of Comanches and Lipans, and captured them. But in a hand-to-hand encounter with an Indian warrior he received an arrow-wound, from which he was laid up for two years. At the outbreak of the civil war he was cavalry instructor at West Point. On the 16th of April, 1861, he resigned his commission in the United States Army, returned to the South, and in May reported to General Lee with the rank of first lieutenant. Appointed to the captaincy of an irregular squadron of mounted volunteers, he was ordered to the Peninsula, and under General Magruder took part in the fight at Big Bethel. He was called to Richmond to organize a body of Texans, partly recruited by Van Dorn, partly individual volunteers who had hurried to Richmond at the first call. He was elected colonel of the 5th Infantry, which with the 1st Texas was brigaded under General Wigfall. In March, 1862, Wigfall having been elected to the Confederate Congress, Hood was appointed to the vacant brigadiership. This was the famous Texas Brigade, to which Hood was so strongly attached, and of which he spoke with his dying breath. Its valor was native, its efficiency was due to the drill of its commander. The brigade was ordered to the Peninsula, and formed part of the 11,000 troops who, under Magruder and Johnston, opposed the advance of McClellan. Its first fight was near West Point on York River, where Hood's Texans attacked Franklin's command; and the brigade bore a fair part in the seven days' battle around Richmond. Perhaps the proudest day in its annals was the desperate fight at Gaines's Mill. Hill's assault having been repulsed, Pickett's brigade attacked the formidable works and was foiled. Whiting's division, to which Hood was attached, was ordered to attempt the difficult task. Hood's Texans charged at a double-quick across a ravine open to the enemy's fire, and up the hillside, carrying the triple line of intrenchment. They lost more than half their numbers, yet on the summit they re-formed their broken line and repelled a sudden onset of cavalry. The following day, when Stonewall Jackson surveyed the battle-ground, he exclaimed, "These were soldiers indeed." This utterance of the silent hero was the stamp of fame to the Texas Brigade. Hood led them, afoot and sword in hand, and was shot in the body. He was made a major-general.

With Longstreet's corps, Hood's command shared the varied fortunes of the two Maryland campaigns. At the second battle of Manassas, Hood led the charge which resulted disastrous-

ly for Pope. At Boonesboro, with D. H. Hill, he held that pass against all opposition until Lee returned with a corps and checked McClellan. At Fredericksburg his command supported Jackson's left. At Antietam, on the Confederate left, his men were in the thickest of the fight. At Gettysburg the Texans confronted Meade's left. At one time they fought their way to a rocky eminence commanding the Union lines. Too few to hold it, they fell back after their leader had been wounded in the left arm. A painful surgical operation, two resections of the bone, preserved the shattered limb, but it was ever after useless.

Two months later, with this still unhealed arm buckled to his side, he rejoined his command, which, with the rest of Longstreet's corps, was ordered to Tennessee to reënforce Bragg. In the battle of Chickamauga Hood's division was stationed on the left of the Confederate line. In the second day's fight, perceiving that the line wavered where his own Texans were posted, he rode up to them, saying, "Give me the colors." "Against my orders, General," the young color-bearer answered, "but I'll carry them wherever you command." Just then a ball struck Hood. The Texans rallied and charged. He was borne off the field, but not before he heard and joined in the shout of success. Amputation of the right leg was the consequence of this wound. While still in hospital he was offered a bureau place. He refused, saying: "No bomb-proof for me. I purpose to see this fight out in the field." Within six months the mutilated soldier returned to the post of duty.

During the spring of 1864, at the head of his corps, he fought through the memorable retreat of Johnston from Dalton to Atlanta. When the Confederate Administration decided on the perilous move of changing commanders in face of an advancing enemy, their choice fell upon Hood, whose record was preëminently that of a "fighting general." Aware of the deep dissatisfaction of the army at the change, "reluctantly and only in obedience to orders," he assumed command on the 18th of July. Within two days he acted on the offensive. On several successive days there were stubborn engagements where he claimed the victory. Finally, with one division of his army in Atlanta, and the other under Hardee twenty miles away, near Jonesboro, he found himself completely outflanked by Sherman. Hardee's attack on the Union lines having failed, Hood's position became untenable. He evacuated Atlanta. This left Sherman in his rear, and enabled him to make that "march to the sea" which proved the death-blow of the Confederacy. Hood began his counter-movement into Tennessee. This whole campaign is said to have been planned in Richmond by General Bragg, with the approval of President Davis. Hood executed it with vigor, if not with success. In September the Army of Tennessee was on its northward march. In November they drove the Union force out of Decatur and crossed the Tennessee at Florence, confronted by General Thomas, a foeman worthy of their steel. Thomas retired slowly toward Nashville. On the 30th of November occurred the battle of Franklin. Hood's army drove the Union front to their second line of intrenchments and captured many prisoners and stands of colors. Their dead and wounded were left in his hands. The carnage on the Confederate side was frightful, especially in officers. General Cleburne fell mortally wounded as his horse was leaping the breastworks. The veteran soldiers, though they fought as well as ever, felt that their real enemy was far behind them, and that their desperate valor was futile. When reproached for the costly losses of this campaign, Hood defended himself with this reply : " I did my duty as commander of the forlorn hope of the Confederacy. I was put there to fight, and fight means kill and be killed."

Immediately after the battle of Franklin Nashville was closely invested. On the 16th of December the Union army, having received reënforcements, attacked the Confederates along their entire line. After a fierce fight Hood's center suddenly gave way. His retreat was covered by General Forrest, yet supplies, ammunition, and ordnance that could ill be spared had to be abandoned as he fell back. After a weary march, during the severest winter weather, the broken remnant of this once splendid army recrossed the Tennessee.

At his own request General Hood was relieved of his command. At Tupelo, Mississippi, he parted from his soldiers. In his farewell address, after paying tribute to the men who had borne defeat and hardship without a murmur, he took upon himself the whole responsibility of the campaign, saying, "I strove hard to do my duty in its execution." At the close of the war he carried with him into civil life the esteem of his countrymen, friend and foe. After a sojourn in Texas, the State to which he was bound by so many associations, he removed to Louisiana to enter into business as a factor and commission merchant. He was the agent of the Texans, who confided their financial interests to him. He was also appointed President of the Louisiana branch of the Life Association of America. At one time he had acquired a competent fortune, but subsequently, by some sudden fluctuation, he lost all. These reverses he bore with equanimity. With a due regard for his military reputation, he employed his leisure hours in writing the story of his campaigns, which he completed. Intended as his vindication, it must prove valuable to the future historian of the war, emanating as it does from a man of such marked simplicity and truth. Much adverse criticism has been bestowed upon the strategy which resulted in failure. Whether fitted or not for the greatness which was thrust upon him, no one denies Hood's fighting qualities.

General Hood had a fine physique and dignified bearing. He was a devout member of the Protestant Episcopal Church. He was most happy in his domestic relations. In 1868 he married Miss Anna Marie Hennen, a native of New Orleans. She died suddenly on the 22d of August. This was the first blow of fate which Hood could not summon fortitude to sustain. Prostrated by grief, the fever found in him an unresisting victim. The General and his eldest daughter were laid in the same tomb, which had reopened thrice within ten days. Ten little orphans survived him. Death being near, he was questioned in regard to his dependent family. He expressed a willingness to live for their protection, but repeated emphatically, " What God does is right." Then he talked of his old brigade, and added, " The Southern soldiers will never let my children want." Thus trusting in God, and, under Him, to his stanch comrades, he died as he had lived, without fear and without reproach.

HOOKER, Major-General JOSEPH, born at Hadley, Massachusetts, in 1815, died at Garden City, Long Island, October 31, 1879. He graduated from the Military Academy at West Point in 1837, and served in the Mexican war, rising to the rank of captain of artillery, and the brevet of lieutenant-colonel in the staff. From 1859 to 1861 he was a colonel in the California militia. When the civil war broke out in 1861, he was made brigadier-general of volunteers and put in command of the defenses of Washington, August 12, 1861 ; but his commission was dated back to May 17, 1861. When General McClellan moved to the Peninsula General Hooker's brigade was added to the command, and for gallant service at Williamsburg he was promoted to be major-general of volunteers, May 5, 1862. During General Pope's operations before Washington General Hooker was very active, and at Antietam, September 17, 1862, was wounded, and was soon after promoted to the rank of brigadier-general of the regular army. At the disastrous repulse of Burnside at Fredericksburg in December, 1862, he commanded the center of the army. In January, 1863, he was appointed to the command of the Army of the Potomac, and on May 2d–4th fought and lost the battle of Chancellorsville. The Army of Northern Virginia, under command of General Lee, soon after attempted to carry the war into Pennsylvania, but General Hooker followed closely. He resigned his command on the 28th of June, and General Meade, his successor, commanded at the battle of Gettysburg, July 1–3, 1863. General Hooker remained in Baltimore waiting orders till September 24th, when he was put in command of the 20th army corps (consolidated from the 11th and 12th), and sent to Chattanooga, Tennessee. He distinguished himself at Lookout Valley, Lookout Mountain, Missionary Ridge, and Ringgold, October 27 to November 27, 1863 ; was actively engaged in the march to Atlanta ; again relieved of command, July 30, 1864; in command successively of the Northern, Eastern, and Lake Departments, and of the Retiring Board till September 1, 1866. He was brevetted Major-General of the United States Army in March, 1865, and in consequence of disability put upon the retired list, with the full rank of major-general, in 1868.

HUNGARY, a kingdom of Europe, and one of the two principal divisions of the Austro-Hungarian Monarchy. (See AUSTRO-HUNGARY.) The Hungarian Ministry at the close of 1879 was composed as follows: President of the Ministry and Minister of the Interior, Koloman Tisza de Borosjenö; Minister near the King's Person (ad Latus), Freiherr von Orczy; Minister of Education and Worship, A. von Trefort; Minister for the Defense of the Country, Colonel B. Szende von Keresztes; Minister of Public Works, Thomas Péchy von Péch-Ujfalu; Minister for Croatia and Slavonia, Koloman Bedekovitch de Komor; Minister of Justice, Dr. Theodor Pauler; Minister of Finance, Count Szapary; Minister of Agriculture, Commerce, and Industry, Freiherr Kemény.

The area and population of the countries of the Hungarian Crown are as follows, according to the "Statistiche Handbuch der österreich.-ungarischen Monarchie":

COUNTRIES.	Square miles.	Population in 1876.
Hungary and Transylvania.........	108,263	13,724,442
Fiume (free city).....	8	18,178
Croatia and Slavonia.....	8,852	1,218,180
Military Frontier...................	7,303	693,783
Total........................	124,426	15,654,583

The movement of population was as follows in 1876:

Marriages............................... 154,305
Births.. } inclusive of still-births. } 713,156
Deaths . } 561,279
Excess of births...................... 151,877

The budget for the countries belonging to the Hungarian Crown for 1879 was voted by the Lower House on February 28th by a majority of 227 against 174. It was as follows (1 florin = 48 cents):

RECEIPTS.

Florins.
1. Direct taxes.............................. 82,635,500
2. Indirect taxes........................... 84,677,857
3. Receipts from Government property and state institutions 25,155,195
4. Extraordinary receipts of the Ministry of Finance 8,046,173
5. Receipts of the other Ministries............ 19,868,445
6. Other receipts......................... 4,308,000

Total ordinary receipts.................. 219,691,170
Extraordinary receipts.................. 2,517,482

Total................................ 222,208,602

EXPENDITURES.

1. Royal household. 4,650,000
2. Royal cabinet chancery.................... 69,669
3. Diet....................................... 1,809,960
4. Council of Ministers.... 808,690
5. Ministry ad Latus......................... 50,843
6. " for Croatia and Slavonia............ 35,580
7. " of the Interior..................... 7,492,469

Florins.
8. Ministry of Public Defense............,.......... 6,398,015
9. " of Education and Worship.......... 4,228,410
10. " of Justice..................... 9,914,869
11. " of Agriculture and Commerce...... 10,512,874
12. " of Communications 12,470,887
13. " of Finance....................... 89,487,859
14. Administration of Croatia and Slavonia...... 5,882,709
15. " of Fiume................ 84,140
16. Pensions.;....................... 4,043,898
17. Public debt......................... 43,852,907
18. Contributions to the common expenditure of the empire.... 38,757,899
19. Contribution to the Austrian debt........... 30,478,430
20. Guaranteed interest to private railroads..... 10,200,000
21. Miscellaneous....................... 18,944,844

Total ordinary expenditures............ 248,167,645
Extraordinary expenditures............ 8,268,735

Total............................. 256,486,880

Deficit...................... 34,227,778

In the budget for Croatia and Slavonia for 1878 the receipts were estimated at 3,312,234 florins, and the expenditures at 3,310,234 florins.

The public debt of Hungary at the close of 1877 amounted to 660,176,966 florins, exclusive of the common debt of the empire. Hungary also has a share in the public debt of Austria proper, about 30 per cent. of its amount previous to 1868. This debt is regarded as exclusively Austrian, but Hungary pays annually a fixed sum for interest and for amortization. The assets of the state were estimated in 1876 at 762,500,000 florins. The Diet on February 15th authorized a gold-rente loan of 100,000,-000 florins (to bear interest in gold), intended to provide the means for defraying the costs of the occupation of Bosnia and Herzegovina and to cover the deficit of the year. If it should turn out that a gold rente can not be negotiated, the Minister is empowered to arrange for a temporary advance; and if sufficient can not be obtained in that way, then he may borrow on the security of the state domains. Lastly, if he finds it more convenient, he may have recourse to all three plans.

In the estimates for 1880, the expenditure was calculated at 253,669,662 florins, the revenue at 236,350,294 fl., making a deficit of 17,-319,368 fl. If the Legislature should accept the proposed increase of the duty on petroleum, expected to yield 1,800,000 fl., this deficit would be reduced to 15,529,368 fl., against 28,829,591 fl., the figure for 1879. In this estimate the expenses of the occupation were not comprised. They had been fixed under 8,000,000 fl. This would entail a charge for Hungary of 2,512,000 fl., so that the total deficit for 1880 was set down in round numbers at 18,000,000 fl., for which, however, no new credit would be asked.

The aggregate length of railways open for traffic on January 1, 1879, was 7,002 kilometres (1 kilometre = 0·62 mile). The number of post-offices in 1877 was 1,980; the number of letters, newspapers, postal cards, samples, etc., 114,327,000; and the value of letters and packages, 838,700,000 florins. The length of telegraph lines in 1878 was 14,328·9 kilometres, and of wires 50,072·2 kilometres. The number of telegraph stations was 900, and the number of dispatches sent and received was 2,-832,259.

On March 12th the city of Szegedin was completely inundated by the river Theiss. It is situated at the confluence of the Theiss and its chief tributary the Maros, lies almost entirely on low alluvial ground, and, with the exception of the suburb New Szegedin, on the right bank of the Theiss. In order to protect it from the Theiss, a large high dike was carried along the river, and, in connection with other parties interested, the people had taken measures to protect the rear of the town by carrying several transverse dikes from the higher land and isolated hillocks to the river. The first of these is about twelve miles north of the town, where the river turns almost at right angles to the east. This, which might be called the outwork of the lines of defense, gave way as early as March 4th, the waters sweeping in and flooding the whole space to the second line, which runs from the higher land in the west in a southerly direction, being intersected by the embankment of the Alföld Railway, which runs southwest. In the night of the 7th the northern frontier of this second line was broken through, leaving as a last defense the southern portion of the Bakto dike and of the railway embankment, on which, therefore, all efforts were concentrated. Besides the military dispatched thither to work under the superintendence of the engineers, the population were called upon to give their assistance. In spite of the most heroic efforts, this dike had to be abandoned between one and two in the morning of the 12th, and before the people could secure places of safety the waters were upon them. Out of 10,000 buildings, 8,200 were destroyed, 4,800 being dwelling-houses. The number of persons who lost their lives was estimated as high as 2,000, and even according to the lowest estimate was deplorably large. All available means were employed in the work of saving those in the town, several thousands being removed by railroad and distributed among the different villages between Szegedin and Temesvar. The event was considered a national disaster, and the Emperor went in person to the afflicted city to cheer by his presence the unfortunate people. All parts of the empire joined in contributing to the relief of the sufferers. The Lower House of the Diet adopted a resolution empowering the Minister of Justice to carry into effect by decrees such extraordinary judicial measures as might be rendered necessary by the catastrophe. A motion was also made to send a committee of the Diet to Szegedin to see what could be done for the unfortunate city. M. Tisza opposed it on the ground that the necessary relief must be provided without delay, and added that the Government, after examining the recommendations of the scientific and practical men who had been called in, would submit proposals for retrieving the dis-

aster. In the ministerial programme submitted to the Diet on October 8th, M. Tisza stated that the plans for rebuilding the town had been made and were under examination, and that the dikes which were to protect it from similar catastrophes would be completed before winter set in. He also stated that the total sum received in aid of the city amounted to about 2,750,000 florins.

The foreign relations of the country occupied the attention of the Diet. The abrogation of Article V. of the Treaty of Prague (see GERMANY) was the subject of an interpellation on February 15th in the Lower House. Herr Tisza replied that it was more to the interest of Austria-Hungary to renounce all claims to the realization of that clause than to allow it to be used at a future time as a snare by which other interested Powers might involve the country in an unpleasant position. Germany, the Minister said, never expected any return for the service rendered by her to Austria-Hungary with regard to the occupation of Bosnia and Herzegovina. On March 1st the Government presented to the Lower House a bill expressive of its assent to the Treaty of Berlin. The discussion began on the 24th. M. Tisza, in opposing a motion on the part of the opposition to reject the treaty, maintained the view that international treaties concluded by the Crown did not depend for their validity upon the assent of Parliament. The controlling power of Parliament did not begin until the Government submitted estimates for the purpose of carrying out a provision of the treaty. The bill was finally adopted by a large majority in the Lower House on March 27th, and in the Upper House without a debate on the 29th.

The desire of the Hungarians to Magyarize the different nationalities inhabiting the lands of the Hungarian Crown was again shown by the passage of a bill in May ordering the Magyar language to be taught in all the non-Magyar primary schools.

Minister Tisza, upon the reassembling of the Diet in October, called the attention of the House to the failure of the crops in many parts of the country. He said the Government had taken the necessary measures to ascertain the real state of things, and had come to the conclusion that, in consequence of this failure, it might well be incumbent upon them in some districts to make a provision either by loans or else by giving work to relieve the distress that might ensue in the course of the winter and in early spring. In many places the crops had not yielded the seed necessary for the next year, or else of such inferior quality that it would be dangerous to use it. The Government thought it, therefore, imperative to take measures, in concert with the local authorities, to grant under proper security loans for the purchase of seed. It did not mean to ask now for any grant of money from Parliament for this purpose, chiefly because, according to its opinion, the grant of a sum of money by Parliament might lead to unjustifiable and exaggerated demands.

In November the Chamber of Deputies adopted a bill declaring that any native of the country who voluntarily resides abroad for an uninterrupted period of ten years shall lose his civil status. The Extreme Left violently opposed this measure, accusing the Government of leveling it directly at Louis Kossuth, but it was finally carried by 141 votes to 52.

HUNT, WILLIAM MORRIS, an artist, born in Brattleboro, Vermont, March 31, 1824, died at Isles of Shoals, New Hampshire, September 8, 1879. He entered Harvard College, but withdrew before completing his course and went to Europe. In 1846 he began the study of sculpture at Düsseldorf, but soon went to Paris, and in the studio of Couture began his career as a painter. Such was his skill that for four years from 1852 he was an exhibitor in the Salon of that city. In 1855 he returned to this country, and established a studio in Boston, where he was one of the first to introduce French art. Among his best known paintings may be mentioned his "Morning Star," "Bugle-Call," "The Lost Kid," "The Choristers," "Girl at Fountain," and "Girl selling Violets," nearly all of which have been engraved. Visitors to the Metropolitan Museum of Art in New York will recall with pleasure his "Marguerite" and "Boy chasing a Butterfly." A more splendid monument of the powers of this remarkable man is in the Assembly Chamber of the State Capitol at Albany. His mural paintings, "The Flight of Night" and "The Discoverer," far excel anything of the kind ever before attempted in this country. In portraiture Mr. Hunt also excelled, and some of his portraits are reckoned among the masterpieces of American art. An admirable head, "A Portrait of a Gentleman," in the last exhibition of the American Society of Artists, was an excellent likeness of himself. While Mr. Hunt excelled in drawing and modeling, his forte was in color. His touch was firm yet tender, and his hues were at once vivid and deep. Solidity and richness were the most striking characteristics of his work.

I

ILLINOIS. The biennial session of the Legislature commenced on Wednesday, January 8th, and ended on May 31st. In the Senate Lieutenant-Governor Sherman presided, and Senator Hamilton, Republican, was chosen President pro tem. by a vote of 27 to 22 for Senator Archer. In the House the custom prevails of making a temporary organization, which continues until the members have taken the oath of office and have affixed their names to their affidavits. Then the permanent organization is made by the usual election. On the next day, William A. James, Republican, was elected Speaker, by a vote of 81 to 60 for James Herrington, Democrat, with 9 scattering and 2 not voting.

One of the first measures of the Legislature was the election of United States Senator. In the Senate, John A. Logan received 26 votes, John C. Black 24, and John McAuliffe 1. In the House, Logan received 80 votes, Black 60, Alexander Campbell 10, and McAuliffe 3. In the House a young miss twelve years of age was appointed as one of the pages. A proposition to dispense with the services of a chaplain, and to call on members who may volunteer to offer prayers for the House, received 29 yeas to 74 nays, after a report by the Committee on Retrenchment recommending its rejection.

The sum of $80,000 was appropriated to pay the military for services in suppressing the riots of 1877, and for other expenses connected therewith.

A Board of Fish Commissioners was established, to increase the product of fish by artificial propagation and cultivation.

An act was passed declaring all saloons or places where intoxicating liquors are sold, in which minors are allowed to play with cards, dice, etc., disorderly houses, and prescribing penalties for keeping such places.

Another act reduced the rate of interest which may be paid or collected on written contracts to eight per cent.

Another act required the polls to be kept open from 8 A. M. to 7 P. M. in all city, town, or village elections.

The amount of taxes that might be levied and collected by cities was limited to two per cent. on their assessed valuation.

Counties were authorized to issue bonds with the amount as low as $25, and interest payable semi-annually.

Grave-robbery is made a felony, and punishable by imprisonment in the penitentiary from one to ten years.

The following resolutions relative to the coinage of silver were adopted in the Senate—yeas 40, nays 7:

Whereas, There is a world-wide effort on the part of certain special interests to demonetize silver, and thus destroy as money one half of the coin of the world, thereby causing a shrinkage of values, prolonged through a series of years, deranging business, and paralyzing industry and enterprise; therefore,

Resolved, by the Senate, the House concurring, That the silver dollar coming to us from colonial times, as it existed under the republic for nearly a hundred years, should be restored as the unit of value, with unlimited coinage, with the issue of bullion certificates, and all other privileges accorded to gold.

Resolved, That if experience shall prove that there needs to be a readjustment of weights as between gold and silver coin, gold should be the adjusting coin, as it has been heretofore.

Resolved, That the Secretary of State is hereby requested to send attested copies of these resolutions to our Senators and Representatives in Congress, with a request that they present them to their respective Houses as the voice of the people of the State of Illinois represented in the General Assembly, and that our Senators are hereby instructed and our Representatives requested to labor zealously to so change the laws as to secure these results full and complete.

The receipts of the State government during the past two fiscal years (ending October 1, 1878) had been $8,650,052.14, and the expenditures for the same period $6,538,628.18, leaving a balance of $2,012,223.96. The total State indebtedness two years ago was $1,478,-600.27, of which only $652,742.06 is outstanding. Of this last sum $357,442.06 is payable at the pleasure of the State, leaving a remainder of $195,300, the aggregate of the State debt which is not subject to immediate payment. The State is thus practically out of debt, and after January 1, 1881, will be really so.

The following is an official statement of the appropriations made by the Legislature for the State institutions under the charge of the State Board of Charities:

NORTHERN HOSPITAL FOR THE INSANE.

For ordinary expenses	$200,000	
For special expenses	22,080	
		$222,080

CENTRAL HOSPITAL FOR THE INSANE.

For ordinary expenses	$220,000	
For special expenses	85,496	
		255,496

SOUTHERN HOSPITAL FOR THE INSANE.

For ordinary expenses	$180,000	
For special expenses	18,000	
		198,000

EASTERN HOSPITAL FOR THE INSANE.

For ordinary expenses	$90,000	
For special expenses	167,500	
		257,500

INSTITUTION FOR THE DEAF AND DUMB.

For ordinary expenses	$156,000	
For special expenses	20,979	
		176,979

INSTITUTION FOR THE BLIND.

For ordinary expenses	$46,000	
For special expenses	6,634	
		52,634

ASYLUM FOR FEEBLE-MINDED CHILDREN.

For ordinary expenses	$100,000	
For special expenses	17,255	
		117,255

SOLDIERS' ORPHANS' HOME.

For ordinary expenses	$75,500	
For special expenses	8,500	
		88,000

EYE AND EAR INFIRMARY.

For ordinary expenses	$34,000	
For special expenses	4,000	
		88,000

STATE REFORM SCHOOL.

For ordinary expenses	$50,000	
For special expenses	5,600	
		55,600

| Total | | $1,456,494 |

The appropriations made for their benefit, with the exception of the State Reform School, by the last four General Assemblies, have been as follows:

By the Twenty-seventh General Assembly	$1,807,520 41
By the Twenty-eighth General Assembly	1,481,418 78
By the Twenty-ninth General Assembly	1,876,880 00
By the Thirtieth General Assembly	1,333,276 80

The reports of the Commissioners are made biennially, and the term ends on September 30th. At that date in 1878 there were in the nine institutions 2,038 inmates. The total number of beneficiaries of the State in the charitable institutions during the past two years was 7,549. The number remaining and actually present in the institutions, September 30, 1878, was:

Northern Hospital for the Insane	525
Central Hospital for the Insane	584
Southern Hospital for the Insane	458
Institution for the Deaf and Dumb	403
Institution for the Blind (in vacation)	7
Asylum for Feeble-Minded Children	200
Soldiers' Orphans' Home	290
Eye and Ear Infirmary	65
State Reform School	192
Total	2,674

This is an increase of 27½ per cent. over the number present at the close of the year 1876. The average number for the two years in all the institutions, in 1875–'76, was 1,940; in 1877–'78 it was 2,280, an increase of nearly 20 per cent. The average for the next two years, it was estimated, would be still greater. Two causes operate to bring about this increase —the natural growth of the population of the State, and the enlargement of the institutions, of which the former is primary and the latter an inevitable consequence. The increase in cost does not keep pace with the increase in numbers, and the per capita cost is steadily diminishing.

The subject of commitments to insane hospitals was extensively discussed by the Commissioners. The law of the State, as modified, makes it a crime, not simply to receive or detain an insane person "against the wishes of such person," but to receive him at all without a jury trial. But it was not framed for the protection of the insane. Its obvious intent is to protect sane persons from false imprisonment. The defect in the law, which is fundamental, is that it distinguishes between the sane and the insane, recognizes a possible peril to the former, overlooks the real danger which everywhere and always threatens the insane class, and extends the ægis of its protection to that one of the two classes which least needs it, because it is in the least danger and is the best able to protect itself. The Commissioners then proceed to say:

There is something almost ludicrous in the idea of "accusing" a man of insanity, as if insanity were not a disease but a crime; and his "prosecution" and "defense" by opposing attorneys, who, from want of experience or of discretion, sometimes take this opportunity to display their legal acquirements and forensic talent to an admiring world, is singularly inappropriate in a medical inquest, especially where the sincerity of the patient's friends and even the fact of his insanity is doubted by nobody. In one instance, in this State, to avoid the irritation of the patient, who was aged and infirm, by the ordinary forms of court procedure, the court, including judge, jury, attorneys, and witnesses, organized as a croquet-party, solemnly played a game of croquet in his presence, observed him, conversed with him, and then with equal solemnity retired and found a verdict of insanity, which was entered upon the record of the court, but never communicated to the "accused" himself.

The law to be adopted, in their view, is one which should provide for the determination of the sanity or insanity of a person alleged to be insane, first, by an exhaustive personal examination of the case by competent medical men, and second, by the submission of the evidence in the case to the Judge of the Circuit or Probate Court for his approval; and which should also provide that the order of a Court shall be an indispensable prerequisite to the admission of any insane person into any hospital or asylum; and which should make the superintendent of the hospital or asylum fully and primarily responsible for the subsequent detention of the patient, and for his discharge when recovered, or if he is found not to be insane. Such a law meets all the fundamental requirements of a good law upon this subject. All else is matter of detail. The details of such a law are nevertheless worthy of careful study. They are very important. Various questions arise at once. For instance: Shall the medical examiners in each county be selected by the patient or by the Court? and if by the Court, shall special examiners be appointed for each case? or shall a permanent board of examiners be created in each county, and if permanent boards are established, shall they be appointed by the courts or by the Governor? and if by the courts, by which courts—the Circuit or the County Courts? Again, what shall be the necessary qualifications of a medical examiner in a lunacy case? Although permanent boards would accumulate experience by practice, yet the Commissioners think it to be more advisable to appoint special examiners in each instance, both on account of their greater nearness to the patient, and because there may be special reasons for the employment of a particular physician in a particular case. They would not allow the family of a patient to select their own examiners, because the Judge to whom an application is made for an order of commitment would be likely in many cases to make a wiser choice, uninfluenced by considerations which might affect them. The Judge would feel a greater sense of responsibility for the selection of the most competent men, and a report made to him by men in whose judgment he had confidence would afford him a more solid basis for his own action. Applications might be addressed to judges either of the Circuit or County Courts, and the Judge in all cases should appoint as examiners only registered, competent physicians, of good repute for intelligence and integrity. Provision should also be made for a brief report in writing, by the examining physicians, of the reasons which satisfied them as to the insanity of the party examined, and this report

or a copy of it should be transmitted by the clerk of the court, with the order of commitment, to the superintendent of the hospital or asylum, at the time when application is made for the patient's admission.

The question of the disposal of the criminal insane was not overlooked. The number of insane convicts in the State is twenty-eight. The most feasible plan of disposing of them properly, in the opinion of the Commissioners, would be to build, in one or both of the penitentiaries, an insane ward within the prison walls. The erection of such wards would relieve the hospitals and make room for as many more insane who are not convicts.

A general interest pervaded the State on the subject of taxation, which led to some modifications of the existing laws by the Legislature. The assessment of the capital stock of all companies and associations organized under special or general laws of the State was by the revenue law of 1872 assigned to the State Board of Equalization. In the interest of manufacturing corporations, the Twenty-ninth General Assembly amended the general act by providing "that, in assessing companies and associations organized for purely manufacturing purposes, or for printing, or for publishing of newspapers, or for the improving and trecding of stock, the assessment shall be so made that such companies and associations so organized shall only be assessed as individuals under like circumstances would be assessed, and no more; and such companies and associations shall be allowed the same deductions as allowed to individuals." The courts held that this clause did not change or modify the law, for the reason that such companies were *not* assessed at any greater rate than individuals were under like circumstances.

An act of this Legislature. which took effect on July 1st, takes from the Board of Equalization the right to assess the classes of corporations named in the amendment quoted above, and relegates the valuation of their property for taxation entirely to local assessors. Gas companies (manufacturers of gas), brewing companies (manufacturers of beer), and packing companies (manufacturers of provisions) all loudly declare that the Board has no longer anything to do with *their* property. Should it be so held, that branch of the Equalizers' duties will be considerably lessened. Out of the forty-six companies against which a capital stock assessment was made in 1878, twenty-seven will be exempt under this amendment. It was provided that in 1880 and every fourth year thereafter there shall be a general assessment of real property. It is to have an annual examination by the assessor for the noting of additions to and destruction of improvements. Equalizations are to be made, and personal property is to be assessed, annually. The intent of the framers and promoters of this act was that there should be but one book, which should start with the original assessment of the realty, contain the four years' taxes based thereon, and be the record of payments, judgments, sales, forfeitures, and redemptions for each of said years.

In making assessments of personal property, the act requires the "numbers, amounts, quantity, and quality to be scheduled by the taxpayer under oath." The statute does not require the *valuation* of the property to be stated in the schedule. This is left entirely to the assessor, as in the old law. The same act increases the penalty for allowing forfeiture of property for taxes to 25 per cent., and makes all delinquent taxes bear interest at the rate of one per cent. per month after the first day of May until paid or forfeited.

The third change under this law consists in making a judgment for the sale of real estate for delinquent taxes conclusive as to all objections which existed at or before the rendition thereof, and which might have been presented as a defense to the application for such judgment.

In amending one of the sections to conform to the provision for increased penalties on forfeitures, a clause of the old law is reënacted which has been passed upon adversely by the courts repeatedly. The county clerk is authorized to sell property after forfeiture to any applicant who may offer to pay the tax, penalty, and costs due thereon. Thus the sale may be made without notice to the owner and without public competition.

The matter of the taxation of railroads was one of the most important subjects of the session. The present methods of assessment and valuation show the following results: The net earnings of all the roads in the State, as officially reported to the Board of Warehouse Commissioners for the year ending June 30, 1878, were $17,368,502. If it be supposed that the net earnings are 10 per cent. of the value of the roads, then these earnings indicate a value of $173,685,020. Fifty per cent. on one half of this indicated or cash value is $86,842,510. Now the equalized valuation made by the State Board of Equalization was $40,461,865. Thus it appears that, while one half of the indicated or cash value, which is generally considered a fair basis of taxation, was $86,842,510, the sum of $40,461,865 was the valuation on which the taxes were laid. Many of the shorter roads were assessed within a small margin of their net earnings, and the stronger roads paid proportionally a much less tax. A call upon the Auditor by the Legislature for the amount of railroad taxes charged on his books of 1878 brought out the following: tax of 1878, $987,704; back tax, $1,112,276; total, $2,099,980.

The State Constitution provides that "every person and corporation shall pay a tax in proportion to the value of his, her, or its property." The revenue law also declares that the State Board of Equalization, in assessing the capital stock of railroads, "shall adopt such rules and principles for ascertaining the fair

cash value of such capital stock as to it may seem to be equitable and just." Under these provisions the State Board of Equalization in 1873 proceeded to assess the capital stock of the railroads. Their total assessment of all the railroad property, including capital stock, amounted to $133,520,633, of which the capital stock amounted to $64,611,071. In 1874 another assessment was made, amounting in all to $81,707,594, of which $31,314,175 was capital stock. In 1875 the total assessment of railroad property in the State was $60,486,343, of which $22,649,222 was capital stock. In 1876 the total valuation of railroad property for taxation was $44,329,489, of which $10,106,258 was capital stock. In 1877 the total was $41,637,243, and, on oath, the Board said the whole capital stocks of the railroads of the State were not worth one cent, and so repudiated them and the law altogether. In 1878 the Equalizing Board assessed for taxes the whole railroad property of the State at the sum of $40,461,865, and again the capital stocks were without value, notwithstanding more than $50,000,000 of stocks of the Illinois railroad companies were selling every day for more than par. For the last three years the average net income of all the roads in the State (excluding the Illinois Central, which pays a constitutional tax of seven per cent. on its gross earnings) has averaged about the sum of $16,000,000 each year; which sum has been paid out to bond- and shareholders or invested in new forms connected with the various roads. In other words, the roads of the State have earned between 35 and 40 per cent. net on their taxed values.

These facts excited the attention of the Legislature, and an effort was made to correct them, which, although not quite successful, was too important to pass unnoticed. Its object was to furnish the State Board with a rule by which they should be compelled to honestly value, for taxation, the capital stocks and franchises of the railroads. A bill was introduced into the Lower House proposing certain amendments to the existing revenue law, as follows: The substitution of the Governor, Secretary of State, Auditor, and Attorney-General for the present State Board of Equalization. In addition to the existing schedules of returns to be made to the Auditor, sworn statements are required, showing—

1. The total gross earnings or income of the road within the State of Illinois for the year ending on the 31st day of December then next preceding; 2. All the expenses incurred in operating and maintaining the road and the equipment thereof in the State of Illinois during the same time, including amounts paid for salaries of officers and agents, and wages of employees, amounts paid for repairs and renewal of track, fences, bridges and buildings, locomotives and cars, shop machinery and tools, office, shop, and train supplies, attorneys' fees, costs of suits, taxes, injuries to passengers and other persons, damages to and losses of freight and baggage, injuries to cattle and stock, injuries to property by fire, and all other operating expenses necessary to be shown in order to determine the net

earnings or income of the road; 3. The amount of net earnings or income; 4. The amount expended in this State during the same time in purchase of real estate, lands and lots, and for improvements and betterments thereon, for construction of depots, shops, and other buildings, principal and interest on bonds and indebtedness, dividends on stock, purchase of other lines of roads, construction of new track, and all other expenses not properly chargeable as operating expenses.

Part of this information is required of the roads by the existing law, but the bill proposes to make the requirements much more searching. The particular object aimed at in these provisions was to prevent the frauds extensively practiced by charging up to operating expenses expenditures for purposes mentioned in the above section. This section was regarded as of the utmost importance for securing accurate information as to the actual net earnings of any one of the great railroads. Without such facts, it was impossible to determine how much of the earnings had been buried up in improvements of various kinds and other expenditures, which were actually paid for out of the net earnings just as much as were dividends, and which were as properly chargeable to the income account and as justly subject to taxation.

But the principal feature of the bill was the new method which it proposed for arriving at the taxable value of the capital stock and franchises of the railroad corporations. It was contained in this section:

The valuation and assessment of the capital stock and franchise of railroad companies shall be determined by said Board in the manner following, viz.: The net annual earnings or income of each railroad company shall be taken as being a certain percentage on the actual value of the property and franchises represented by the capital stock thereof; the actual rate of such percentage shall be fixed upon, and the principal sum which would produce the amount of such net earnings or income at such rate per cent. shall be held to be the true cash value of such capital stock: Provided, that the same rate per cent. shall apply to each and every railroad company for the same year's valuation and assessment. The valuation so found shall be taken as the assessed valuation of the capital stock, and the same shall be equalized by the Board and distributed to the several counties, towns, cities, villages, and districts, in the same manner now provided by law.

The purpose of this rule was to secure the equitable taxation of all the roads. Without interfering in any way with the method of taxing the tangible property, it proposed only to change the method of ascertaining the taxable value of the capital stock and franchise. Under it the Board have no discretion, except in determining the rate per cent. upon which the taxable value of the capital stock depends. The lower this percentage, the higher would ·be the tax. It was believed by the advocates of the bill that, as the value of money and of all property fluctuated from year to year, it would not be just to fix this percentage to rigid limits. It was estimated that on an average the industrial and agricultural interests of the State realized 5 per cent. per annum, net, on

the amounts invested and expended. But, in order that no injustice should be done, it was assumed that the railroads of the State ought to be allowed 10 per cent. on their investments, which obviously gave them a decided advantage over any other business or industry.

To illustrate the operation of the bill, it was then supposed, as an instance, that a railroad company was reported by the local assessors of the counties through which its line runs to possess $500,000 worth of tangible property. The sworn returns made by its officers show its actual net earnings last year to have been $200,000. Ten per cent. having been agreed upon as the rate, "the true cash value" of the capital stock and franchise of the company is found to be $2,000,000. The State rate for purposes of taxation is 50 per cent. of this, which would give $1,000,000. Now, deduct therefrom the value of the "tangible property," and the assessed valuation of the capital stock and franchise is fixed at $500,000, the taxes upon which are to be distributed among the several counties, etc., in proportion to the mileage of the road in each. The value of the tangible property is deducted, because the taxes thereon belong to counties in which it is assessed. The theory of the law is that the assessed value of the tangible property represents its intrinsic value, what it would sell for whether the road was running or torn up. A large proportion of the $500,000, in the case supposed, might be represented by the machine-shops, located in one county, while the adjoining county perhaps would not be justly entitled to any taxes except upon the track and its share of the capital stock. This explains why the value of the tangible property is deducted in the calculation. The application of the rule to three or four of the railroads in the State showed the following results: The Chicago and Alton under the rule would be taxed on $16,536,685. The equalized value of the State Board was $5,078,627. The company actually earned 41·5 per cent. upon the amount on which it was taxed. The Chicago and Northwestern under the rule should have been taxed on $11,323,635, but the amount on which it was taxed was $3,225,955. On this amount it realized the enormous income of 70·1 per cent. The results were similar in other cases. The bill, however, failed to become a law.

On an early day of the session the House requested the Governor to inform them of the expense to the State of the Board of Railroad and Warehouse Commissioners, together with such information as he might have regarding the benefit (if any) of the Commission to the people of Illinois. The cost of the Commission from July 1, 1871, to September 30, 1878, has been $118,682; of which $46,159 have been used for expenses, and chiefly in the prosecution of suits against railroad companies for violation of law. His answer relative to the benefit of the Commission is full of interesting and important facts bearing upon the relations of the railroads to the State and the people, and their subjection to civil authority. Some points are thus stated:

Since the passage of the law creating the Railroad and Warehouse Commission in 1871, Illinois has made very important advances toward the solution of the railroad problem. The questions involved in this problem have not only been before the people in this State, but in other States and countries. In England, after the railroad was a fact, it was recognized as a public highway. The right of Parliament to fix rates for the transportation of passengers and freights was therefore asserted, and schedules of rates were put into their charters. Those familiar with the subject need not be told that the attempt to establish rates in this manner was a failure. Then it was asserted that competition, if encouraged by the Government, would prove a remedy for the abuses with which railroads were charged. The suggestion was acted upon; the Government encouraged the construction of competing lines. As a result, rates fell. Competition, however, finally began to entail disaster upon the competitors, and, compelled to become allies to escape destruction, the competitors combined. Railroads were consolidated, rival lines were united, and competition was thus destroyed. The danger of great combinations of this kind, not only to the business interests of the country, but also to the State, was at once suggested and occasioned alarm. This alarm resulted in a public opinion that the Government should own the railroads. But consolidation, to the surprise of the prophets of evil, did not result in higher rates; on the contrary, lower rates and higher dividends resulted. Thus, by a logical process of attempt and failure to control railroad corporations, the conclusion was reached that wise policy required permission to such corporations to operate their railroads in their own way, upon ordinary business principles. But at the same time a Board of Commissioners was wisely created and authorized to hear and determine complaints against railroad corporations and exercise other important powers. This Board in England was created about five years ago, and the most noticeable feature in its career, says Charles Francis Adams, Jr., "is the very trifling call which seems to have been made upon it. So far as can be judged from its annual reports, the cases which come before it are neither numerous nor of great importance. It would, however, be wholly unsafe to concede the fact that such a tribunal is unnecessary. On the contrary, it may be confidently asserted that no competent Board of Railroad Commissioners, clothed with the peculiar powers of the English Board, will either there or anywhere else have many cases to dispose of. The mere fact that a tribunal is there—that a machinery does exist for the prompt and final decision of that class of questions—puts an end to them. They no longer arise."

The process through which the public mind of America has passed on the railroad question is not dissimilar to that through which the public mind of England passed. But here competition was relied on from the first. To all who asked for them railroad charters were granted. The result has been the construction of railroads in every part of the country—many of them through districts of country without business or even population, as well as between all the business centers, and through populous, fertile, and well-cultivated regions. Free trade in railroad-building and the too liberal use of municipal credit in their aid have induced the building of some lines which are wholly unnecessary, and which crowd, duplicate, and embarrass lines previously built, which were fully adequate to the needs of the community. In Illinois railroad enterprises have been particularly numerous, and have made the State renowned for having the most miles of railroad track, the chief railroad State. Competition did not result according to public anticipation. The competing corporations worked without sufficient remuneration at the competing points, and, to make good the losses resulting there, were often guilty of

extortion at the non-competing points. They discriminated against persons and places. Citizens protested against these abuses in vain. The railroad corporations, when threatened with the power of the Government, indulged in the language of defiance, and attempted to control legislation to their own advantage. At last, public indignation became excited against them. They did not heed it; they believed that the courts would be their refuge from popular fury.

In Illinois the feeling of the people expressed itself in many ways, and finally found utterance in the Constitution of 1870. In this Constitution may be found all the phases of opinion on the railroad question through which the English mind has run. The railway is declared to be a public highway. The establishment of reasonable maximum rates of charges is recognized as necessary to the public welfare, and the General Assembly is required to pass laws to correct abuses and prevent unjust discriminations and extortion in the rates of foreign passenger tariffs on the different railroads in the State, and enforce such laws by adequate penalties, to the extent, if necessary for that purpose, of forfeiture of their property and franchises. The Constitution did more than this. To correct abuses of the interests of the farmers, from whose fields warehousemen, in combination with corporate common carriers, had been drawing riches, it declared all elevators or structures where grain or other property was stored for a compensation, public warehouses, and expressly directed the General Assembly to pass laws for the government of warehouses, for the inspection of grain, and for the protection of producers, shippers, and receivers of grain and produce.

Promptly after the adoption of the Constitution containing these affirmative provisions in 1871, the Legislature attempted to give them vitality by the enactment of laws to carry them out. One of these created the Railroad and Warehouse Commission, and imposed upon it certain important duties. Another was an act to regulate public warehouses and warehousemen and the inspection of grain, and to give effect to Article XIII. of the Constitution. By this act other important duties were imposed upon the Railroad and Warehouse Commissioners. A grain-inspection department was created and placed under their charge. Another statute divided the railroads of the State into classes and fixed maximum passenger rates. Another prohibited unjust discrimination and extortion in freight rates, and fixed severe penalties for disobedience of law. Under the warehouse laws the Commissioners commenced a suit against Ira Y. Munn and George T. Scott, warehousemen, to compel them to recognize the right of the General Assembly to regulate their business in the interest of the people. The case was made a test one. It was decided by both the State and Federal Supreme Courts in favor of the people, and in its decision the Supreme Court of the United States declared a doctrine of the greatest importance to the people of the whole country—the doctrine that, under the powers inherent in every sovereignty, a government may regulate the conduct of its citizens toward each other, and, when necessary for the public good, the manner in which each shall use his own property. The value of this decision to the farmers and grain-consumers of the country can not be wholly estimated in money.

Under the law to establish reasonable passenger rates on railroads, a suit was commenced and taken to the Supreme Court. The Court decided that it was necessary to prove that the rate charged by a railroad in excess of the maximum rate fixed by law was unreasonable.

The law against unjust discrimination and extortion by railroad corporations was passed upon by the Supreme Court in the effort of the Commissioners to enforce its provisions; and the Supreme Court decided that the act could not be enforced until so amended as to make the charging of a greater compensation for a less distance, or for the same distance, merely *prima facie* evidence of unjust discrimination, instead of conclusive evidence, and in dictum expressed the opinion that " what is a reasonable rate of freight over a railroad is at best a mere matter of opinion depending on a great variety of complicated facts, which but few persons could intelligently investigate, and which it would be wholly in the power of the company to furnish or withhold."

In 1873 the present law to prevent extortion and unjust discrimination in rates charged for transportation of passengers and freight on railroads in this State was passed. It was prepared and passed with the decision of the Supreme Court in the case of The People *vs.* the Chicago and Alton Railroad Company fresh in the minds of the members of the General Assembly, and every suggestion made by the Court was observed. The Commission since its establishment has brought many important suits against railroad corporations for alleged violation of law, and obtained judgments in the lower courts. In one of these, against the Illinois Central Railroad Company, for unjust discrimination in the matter of delivery of grain upon the track and to elevators, a judgment of $1,000 and costs was obtained. The judgment was paid by the company, and the unjust discrimination discontinued. At that time the railroads charged six dollars per carload more for delivering grain on the track than to an elevator. Since then the railroads have discontinued this practice. The action of the Commissioners in stopping this abuse has resulted in an annual saving to the grain-raisers of Illinois of vast sums of money. Other cases won by the people were appealed to the Supreme Court. The judgment in one of these was reversed, but in the opinion delivered by the Court, as two of the dissenting Justices assert, the constitutionality of the act is assumed, and an intimation is given that it will be sustained when its merits are discussed; but the law has not yet been passed upon by the Court, and the fact must therefore be apparent that the Commissioners can not act under the existing condition of things with the confidence they would possess if the law had been decided by the highest tribunal in the State to be constitutional.

Notwithstanding the difficulties experienced by the Commissioners, there has been rapid progress made in Illinois toward a settlement of the railroad question through their agency.

In 1871 the Railroad and Warehouse Commission was established. Its creation was resisted both by railroad corporations and public warehousemen, and after its organization they treated it with little consideration. They refused to recognize its authority. But after the decision by the Supreme Court of the United States declaring the doctrine that the Government may regulate the conduct of the citizens to each other, and, when necessary for the public good, the manner in which each shall use his own property, the railroad corporations and public warehousemen began to grow less determined in their opposition to the attempts to control them, until now there is very little opposition. They now give prompt attention to requests of the Commissioners for the correction of abuses called to its notice by their patrons, and thus the Commissioners not only settle questions arising between railroad corporations and their patrons, but it may as truthfully be said of this as of the English and Massachusetts Commissions, that the very fact of its existence has put an end to many of the abuses formerly practiced by such corporations which were angrily complained of by the people. The Commission has also, in some instances, shown to complainants that the hardships complained of were not the fault of the railroad companies, but resulted from causes affecting the markets outside of railroad control and interference.

It is a curious fact that the conclusion reached by the English statesmen in 1874 was reached in Illinois in 1873—the conclusion that railroad companies ought to have the right to control their own affairs, fix their own rates of transportation, be free from meddlesome legislation, and, as it has been expressed, work out their own destiny in their own way, just so long as they show a reasonable regard for the requirements of the community. An analysis of the railroad law will prove this. It recognizes the right of a railroad company to establish its own rates for the transportation of passengers and freight over its railroad, provided that in doing so it neither extorts from nor unjustly discriminates against any of its patrons; and that questions of unjust discrimination may be determined, it declares what shall be unjust discrimination *prima facie;* and that complaints of extortion may be determined, the law provides a way to make the corporation complained about produce the facts on which is based the opinion of what is a reasonable rate on its road. This is done by requiring the Railroad and Warehouse Commissioners to prepare schedules of reasonable maximum rates for the transportation of freights and passengers on each of the railroads of the State, and in every suit against a railroad corporation are made *prima facie* evidence that the rates fixed by the Commission are reasonable maximum rates. By this process a corporation that has made a rate that is complained about as extortionate is compelled to prove that the rate is reasonable. In this way the law says to the railroad company, You may charge what you please if you can show, when your charges are questioned, that they are reasonable. In other words, the General Assembly has attempted to take the burden of proof from the shoulders of the complainants in a suit against a railroad company for extortion, and put it on the shoulders of the defendant; and it has done this because the Supreme Court has said that " what is a reasonable rate of freight over a railroad is at best a mere matter of opinion, depending on a great variety of complicated facts, possessed only by the railroad company, and which it may furnish or withhold."

The Legislature has attempted to make the possessors of the facts furnish them for the use of courts and juries. It is true the Supreme Court has said that the schedules of rates are something more than evidence, that they are facts upon which actions against railroads must be based. But the Legislature did not intend to absolutely fix maximum rates. The Legislature intended to establish a standard of what is fair and reasonable in the charges made in the transactions of railroad business; it was intended to allow the roads to charge all they ought to, and devise a method by which a determination could be reached, when any one should complain that they were charging more than in fairness they ought to charge.

In conclusion he said:

In my judgment, if the Commission were dispensed with by the Legislature, difficulties would soon arise, agitation would commence again, and controversies would run riot. New legislation would follow, another board of some kind would soon be created, and the track we have just passed over would be again traveled by the people's representatives. The Board should be sustained in the interest of all the people. Instead of being destroyed, it should be strengthened. It should not only have the authority with which it is now vested, but more; it should be made a legal arbitrator in all matters of controversy between railroad companies and warehouses and their patrons, and should be required to make examination of roads, and be invested with authority to compel reparation of unsafe or defective bridges, culverts, track, and rolling stock.   S. M. CULLOM, Governor.

The railroads of the State which reported to the Commissioners, counting double and single tracks, etc., own 18,477 miles, of which 12,934 are laid with iron. During 1878 920 miles of steel and 293 of iron were laid. Forty-three corporations with 14,475·02 miles of road report $364,145,683.95 capital stock. Of this, $59,684,277.56 is preferred, and is reported by fourteen companies. Eight roads make no capital stock returns. Six of these are in the hands of receivers. During 1878 dividends were declared aggregating $11,058,030.06, or an average of 5·19 per cent. on the entire amount of common and preferred stock reported as paying dividends. Forty-two roads, with 14,885·12 miles of track, report bonded indebtedness of $328,799,590.68, an average of $21,531 per mile. Thirty-three companies report floating debts aggregating $11,838,802.79. The aggregate of bonded and floating debt reported in 1879 is $340,638,399.47, an increase of $65,680,859.34 over last year—$60,635,366.26 of bonded and $5,045,493.08 of floating. This increase may be accounted for in some measure by the fact that some of the roads have added to their debts, but much the larger portion of it is due to the more perfect returns made by the companies. The ordinary operating expenses of 1878 compared with those of 1877 show a decrease of $423,179.81, while the expenses called extraordinary have been increased over those of that year $7,862,621.26. The total number of passengers carried during 1878 was 21,535,-487. The number carried one mile was 830,-817,698. The average receipts per passenger per mile were 3·18 cents. The total tons of freight carried were 30,233,308. The total tons carried one mile were 5,937,068,254. The average number of tons carried per train, twenty-one reporting, was 107. The highest average number of tons carried per train was 320; the lowest average was 28 tons. The average number of tons carried per car was 7·54. The increase in tonnage of 1878 over that of 1877 is 3,758,172, or 12·4 per cent.

The Committee on Railroads in the Lower House of the Legislature instructed its chairman to inquire of the State Attorney-General " whether corporations operating sleeping-cars in the State were subject to legislative control." His reply was as follows:

The same question was submitted to me by the House Committee on Railroads two years ago. The conclusion then reached was that persons or corporations operating sleeping-cars upon railroads, as that business is now generally conducted, were subject to legislative control in like manner as common carriers. (9, " Chicago Legal News," p. 221.) Subsequent reflection has confirmed me in that opinion. The recent decisions of the Supreme Court of this State and of the United States recognize the following as a sound legal principle: Whenever any person pursues a public employment, and sustains such relations to the public that the people must of necessity deal with him, and are under a moral duress to submit to his terms if he is unrestrained by law; then, in order to prevent extortion and abuse of his position, the price he may charge for his service may be regulated by law. (Scott & Munn vs. The People, 69 Ills., 80; Munn & Scott vs. The People, 40 Ills. (94 U. S.), 113 ; C. B. and Q. R. R. Co. vs. Iowa, 4 Ills., 155 ; Peck vs. C. and N. W. Ry. Co., id., 164; Stone vs. Wisconsin, id., 181.) Persons or corporations operating sleeping-cars upon railroads may not, in a strict sense, be common carriers, yet they participate in the carriage of passengers for hire, and perform in part, at least, the duties which would otherwise devolve upon the common carriers. Upon the line of railroads upon which they operate, they furnish all the sleeping-cars used. All competition, so far as that mode of travel is concerned, is wholly excluded. They pursue a "public employment" in the same sense that the vocation of common

carriers, warehousemen, or ferrymen is held to be a public employment, as distinguished from ordinary business pursuits, and in my opinion are equally subject to legislative control as common carriers.

A sub-committee then proceeded to Chicago to consider the propriety of legislating for the reduction of sleeping-car rates. Ample facilities were offered to them by the President of the Pullman Palace Car Company (Mr. George M. Pullman), who likewise made a statement of the expenses and earnings of the company. He read the contract with the Chicago and Alton Railroad, in accordance with which the Pullman Company runs it scars on the line of that road, and then submitted statements drawn from the books showing that the investment account of the Pullman Company with the Chicago and Alton road was $175,090 in eleven sleepers, the number on that road. The gross earnings for 1878 of these eleven cars were $55,-023, and the Pullman Company received $7,080 mileage from the Alton Company, making the gross revenue $60,104. The operating expenses, on the other hand, for conductors, porters, etc., were $12,940; repairs on cars were $18,287; and the taxes and insurance on the eleven cars were $1,210, making the net earnings $22,-664.33, from which was to be deducted 5 per cent. for annual depreciation on the cars. This showed, as the result of the figures, that out of about $60,000 gross earnings the company realized $13,999.83, which were divided among the stockholders. Similar statements were submitted, showing the state of affairs with regard to the Illinois Central, the Chicago, Burlington, and Quincy, the Northwestern, and other roads. It was next shown from statements before the committee that on the Chicago and Alton road, taken as an example, the year's earnings per car per trip were $21.34, and the expenses $16.40, leaving the net earnings of each trip at $4.94 a car; further, that the gross earnings per passenger were $1.73 and expenses $1.33, leaving the net earnings at 40 cents per passenger. Mr. Pullman explained that the reason the gross earnings per passenger were $1.73 instead of $2, the price per berth, was that many of the passengers were not berth but merely seat passengers.

A most important military question was raised by the action of the Legislature. The Military Committee of the House were instructed to report " on the present necessity for a State military organization." They reported that, in the light of the events of the last two years, and with that experience so fresh in the minds of every member, they were compelled to recognize the wisdom which provided the State with a citizen soldiery in that hour of urgent need (referring to the railroad riots). Therefore they concluded that "it was an absolute necessity which the representatives of the people could not safely ignore." A bill was accordingly reported. The object of this measure was brought out in the following remarks by one of the members (Mr. Trusdell) in the debate on the bill :

He denied Mr. Erhardt's statement that, because the Constitution gave one man the right to carry arms, any number had the same right. There was such a thing as constitutional authority which must be obeyed. No body of men in the State had the right to drill and carry arms in defiance of constituted authority. He knew the people were able to suppress riots, but it was not fair to require them to meet sudden dangers without sufficient preparation, and these dangers must arise unless these men are compelled to lay down their arms. Such defiance of law can not be tolerated for a moment. He knew that an armed body of men existed in Chicago who were a menace to the peace and order of that city. He cared not what they were called, but was in favor of compelling them with shotted guns to lay down their arms, and preventing the bloody contests that will inevitably come if they are not disbanded. If they had grievances, they must redress them at the ballot-box. No other remedy can be allowed them. He was in sympathy with them and knew their grievances. Their condition was pitiful and painful, but it was not the law that made it so. Their condition was vastly better than it was in Europe. Their homes were protected, and no execution officer can enter there to strip them of their home comforts. In every way, Democrats and Republicans alike had emulated each other to elevate the condition of the workingmen.

The bill passed the House by a vote of 100 yeas to 37 nays. Of those voting for the bill, 71 were Republicans, 23 were Democrats, and 6 were Greenbackers. Of the 37 voting no, 3 were Socialists, 2 Greenbackers, 2 Republicans, and 30 Democrats. It provided substantially that the entire male population shall be enrolled in the militia, and that only a portion consisting of 8,000 men shall be organized and armed; and the parade and drill of all other military organizations, except under certain stated circumstances, is prohibited unless licensed by the Governor. This law when enforced would oblige the armed companies reputed to be Socialists in Chicago to disband. A test case under the law was therefore made up by one of these companies, which drilled without a license. One of its members was arrested and convicted, but subsequently released on a *habeas corpus* writ by the Circuit Court. It declared the law to be unconstitutional on two grounds: first, that the right to bear arms is an inalienable one, of which a man can not be deprived except under due process of law; and, second, that Congress by its act of 1792 has enrolled every able-bodied citizen in the ranks of the militia, and no State law can provide for drilling and organizing only a part of this militia force. This decision is based nominally on the amendment of the Constitution of the United States which declares that " a well-regulated militia being necessary to the security of a free State, the right of the people to keep and bear arms shall not be infringed." The case will be taken to the highest Court for final decision.

A compulsory education bill, requiring the attendance of children between the ages of eight and fourteen for at least twelve weeks in each school year, unless the child is excused

by the Board of Education or School Directors when it is shown that its bodily or mental condition, or application to study for the required period, prevents its attendance, or for any other sufficient cause, passed the House by a vote of 87 yeas to 49 nays, and became a law.

A " store-pay " bill, as it is usually called, to prevent the payment of any laborer, miner, or mechanic, as wages, with goods or supplies, or any order, check, device, etc., after passing the Legislature, was vetoed by the Governor. His objection was based on the hardship which would ensue to the laborer without money, to be thus cut off from the credit he requires to obtain goods or supplies.

The number of prisoners in the penitentiaries of the State at the beginning of the year was 1,893, of whom 29 were females. A proposition to change the law relative to life-sentences was again presented to the Legislature by the Committee on Penitentiaries. It was urged in its favor that the tables of Joliet Prison, as well as other prisons, show that a man sentenced for life rarely lives more than ten years. After that time the terrible strain upon his mind, with no hope of ever again being permitted to see his friends in this world, causes him to give up in despair and die, or he becomes a maniac and is sent to an asylum to spend the remaining years of his life. If the law was so amended that a convict should not be sentenced for a longer term than thirty-three years—the average life of man—he might, under the present good-time law, shorten his time one year and three months in the first five years and one half after that; so that if a man is sentenced for thirty-three years, he can, by obeying all the rules of the prison, end his sentence in a little less than twenty years. The committee say they are of the opinion that, if a man can not be reformed in that time and safely returned to society, he ought to have been hung in the first place.

An act was passed to create a Bureau of Labor Statistics, with five Commissioners, three of whom shall be manual laborers. Its duties are to collect, assort, systematize, and present in biennial report to the General Assembly, statistical details relating to all departments of labor in the State, especially in its relations to the commercial, industrial, social, educational, and sanitary conditions of the laboring classes, and to the permanent prosperity of the mechanical, manufacturing, and productive industry of the State. The compensation of the Commissioners is limited to $150 per year, and of the secretary to $1,200.

The returns of the local assessors of the State made in August show the valuation for the year in all but five counties. The following are the returns since 1872: 1873, $1,194,-221,550; 1874, $1,194,456,451; 1875, $1,025,-428,289; 1876, $958,405,808; 1877, $892,380,-972; 1878, $818,987,409; 1879, $752,239,937. In addition the Board of Equalization assesses annually about $40,000,000. These figures show that in this period there has been a decrease in the local assessment of about 37 per cent. It is believed that for 1879 the actual assessment does not exceed 40 per cent. of the actual cash value of the property. The number of cattle assessed in the counties of the State in June, 1878, was 1,775,101; in 1879, 1,722,057; of fat cattle for market in 1879, 376,573. The number of sheep assessed in like manner for 1878 was 775,757; for 1879, 762,788; number of fat sheep for market in 1879, 155,532. The number of horses assessed in 1877 was 915,995; in 1878, 904,948; in 1879, 927,117. The number of mules and asses assessed in 1877 was 127,117; in 1878, 125,875; in 1879, 122,348.

The crop of wheat for 1879 was the largest ever produced in the State. Its amount, as likewise the amount, price, value, etc., for the last twenty years, may be seen in the following table:

YEARS.	Number of acres.	Average yield per acre, bushels.	Bushels produced.	Price per bushel.	Total value.
1860...	2,109,471	11·3	23,837,029	$0 85	$20,261,469
1861...	2,109,471	11·8	23,887,020	0 71	16,994,384
1862...	2,300,964	14·0	32,213,500	0 76	24,492,262
1863...	2,617,847	12·0	31,403,163	1 05	32,978,571
1864...	2,328,763	14·3	33,371,173	1 55	51,725,318
1865...	2,396,977	11·0	25,266,745	1 09	27,541,732
1866...	2,196,263	13·0	28,551,421	1 93	55,104,243
1867...	2,456,140	11·4	28,000,000	1 97	52,160,000
1868...	2,483,478	11·5	28,560,000	1 20	34,272,000
1869...	2,607,142	11·2	28,200,000	0 76	22,192,000
1870...	2,259,583	12·0	27,115,000	0 94	25,488,100
1871...	2,059,081	12·8	25,216,000	1 18	29,754,880
1872...	2,042,231	12·1	24,711,000	1 23	30,394,580
1873...	2,104,963	13·5	28,417,000	1 10	31,258,700
1874...	2,619,304	11·5	30,122,000	0 86	25,904,920
1875...	2,600,000	10·5	27,300,000	0 91	24,343,000
1876...	2,520,430	9·3	23,440,000	0 93	21,799,200
1877...	1,977,745	16·4	32,490,556	1 15	38,002,032
1878...	2,324,755	14·6	33,983,396	0 80	27,059,460
1879...	2,440,809	18·0½	45,417,661	0 87	39,930,039

It will be seen that the acreage of 2,440,809 for 1879 has been exceeded by the wheat acreage of 1863, 1867, 1868, 1869, 1874, and 1875. The average yield per acre, 18½ bushels, for 1879, is the largest on record. The exceptionally large average yields reported generally consist of new varieties of wheat recently introduced. The 1879 crop is over forty-five million bushels (45,417,661), or over eleven million (11,534,263) bushels more than any preceding crop. The value of this crop is nearly forty million dollars ($39,930,639), which, owing to the low average price (87 cts.) per bushel when compared with former years, will not yield the producer as large returns as the 1864, 1866, and 1867 crops. The 1864 wheat crop of 33,371,173 bushels, at $1.55 per bushel, returned the producer over fifty-one million dollars ($51,725,318). The 1866 crop of 28,-551,421 bushels, valued at $1.93 per bushel, brought $55,104,243; and the following crop, 1867, of twenty-eight million bushels, at $1.97, was valued at $55,160,000. The price per bushel was lower than that of 1879 in 1860, 85 cts.; 1861, 71 cts.; 1862, 76 cts.; 1869, 76 cts.; 1874, 86 cts.; and 1878, 80 cts. The

spring wheat crop of 1878 was 3,870,251 bushels; the crop of 1879 was 3,376,409, a decrease of nearly half a million bushels (493,-842). The 1878 crop was valued at $3,189,203, while that of 1879 is valued at $2,663,882, a decrease in one year of over half a million dollars ($525,321).

The product of hay shows a falling off in acreage, as against 1873, of 185,793 acres, the total acreage in 1878 being 2,347,553, and in 1879, 2,161,760. The average yield per acre in 1879 was one and a fifth ton, and the average price per ton $6.37, making the total value of the crop $16,428,012.

The rye crop ranks fourth in the extent of area of the cultivated crops grown in the State. The area of rye reported for 1879 was 235,073 acres; the area for the previous year was 252,-768, showing a decrease for 1879 of 17,695 acres. The 1879 acreage, with one exception (1878), is the largest reported, and the average yield per acre has not been equaled except in 1872. The 1879 crop of 4,238,824 bushels was the largest ever produced in the State, and the quality was good. The crop was valued at $1,991,404, and has only been exceeded by the crop of 1877, which was estimated at $2,103,-800.

The crop of oats was of medium good quality. The area for 1879 was 1,631,139 acres; the 1878 acreage of oats was 1,757,953—a decrease of 126,814 acres in 1879. The average yield per acre of oats was 33½ bushels—an increase of three bushels per acre over that of the previous year.

The corn crop of 54,664,569 bushels exceeded the 1878 yield of 53,424,555 bushels by 1,240,014 bushels. The average price per bushel of 22 cts. was two cents in advance of the price of 1878 at corresponding date. The 1879 crop, valued at $12,059,162, exceeds that of 1878, valued at $10,684,911, by $1,374,251.

The report of the Chicago, Burlington, and Quincy Railroad, which with its branch and leased roads has 1,856 miles of track in Illinois and Iowa, gives as the gross earnings for 1879 $14,812,105, and as the net earnings $7,260,038. There was an increase of 61,673 over 1878 in the passengers carried, and of 711,343 tons in the freight traffic.

The number of fire, marine, and inland insurance companies complying with the laws of the State, and authorized to do business for 1879, was 171. These companies may be classified as follows: Joint-stock companies of Illinois, 8; mutual companies of Illinois, 3; joint-stock companies of other States, 136; mutual companies of other States, 6; foreign companies, 18. Total, 171. The number of district, county, and township mutual fire-insurance companies organized in the State, and authorized to do business during 1879, was 129, being an increase of 10 during the past year. The following table gives a comparison of the aggregate business of last year with that of former years since 1869:

YEARS.	Number of companies.	Losses.	Expenses, estimated at 30 per cent. of receipts.	Premiums received.
1869.......	109	$2,450,824	$1,210,899	$4,576,986
1870.......	108	8,765,667	1,455,338	4,710,769
1871.......	94	25,763,728	1,008,075	8,854,798
1872.......	118	1,477,017	1,711,458	5,704,861
1873.......	146	1,737,100	1,876,969	6,259,887
1874.......	157	4,435,650	1,970,579	6,568,597
1875.......	187	1,587,792	1,856,788	6,245,354
1876.......	200	1,491,478	1,588,698	5,296,051
1877.......	181	1,976,719	1,472,706	4,908,353
1878.......	171	1,407,559	1,373,757	4,571,710

Some decisions relating to schools in the State have been made. No board can employ a teacher legally for a period extending beyond their term of office. The teacher must have a legal certificate when he makes his contract with the directors.

A minority report from a committee on optional studies made to the School Board in Chicago objects to the higher branches, as German, music, and drawing, introduced in the lower grades of schools to the exclusion of English studies. The minority say that Chicago has school-rooms large enough to hold at any one time but 40,000 of the 125,000 children of a school age. On the average, children in Chicago attend a school but 410 days before leaving the public schools altogether, and one fourth of the children in school, it was found on inquiry, had averaged but 100 days of schooling. Of this limited time, which must of necessity include all the instruction received in public schools in reading, writing, and arithmetic, one sixth goes to learning to read music. Taking the entire number of children collectively, and the exclusion of music and drawing would add one month a year to the instruction of 43,000 children in common-school studies; and three fourths of these children do not stay more than long enough to receive a rudimentary drill in those studies under the most favorable training. The Chicago school authorities decided, however, to continue the present course of music and drawing, a course arranged for twelve years, although not one child in a hundred completes it.

The question, "Are school boards authorized to make such regulations as will allow teachers and principals to require written excuses from the parents of pupils when the pupils are absent from school?" was asked of State Superintendent Slade, to which he replied:

In the 48th section of the school law are these words: "They (the directors) shall adopt and enforce all necessary rules and regulations for the management and government of the schools." These necessary rules and regulations certainly include those that tend to secure prompt and regular attendance, and to prevent truancy, tardiness, and absenteeism; and I can think of no more reasonable regulation for securing regularity and punctuality of attendance than that of requiring pupils to show, by means of a written excuse from parent or guardian, that they are not absent from school without good cause. I fully concur in the opinion given on this subject by Dr. Bateman when he was Superintendent. He says: "The right and duty of directors to make and enforce such regulations as will secure regularity and punctuality of attendance (those prime requisites of a good school) have been affirmed by several of our Circuit Courts, and by the Supreme Courts of many States, notably and recently that of Iowa."

The right of directors to prescribe a course of study was decided by the Supreme Court during the previous year. It said:

It is an indispensable element to the validity of all by-laws (and such are, in effect, the rules and regulations here authorized) that they be reasonable; and whenever they appear not to be so, the courts must, as a matter of law, declare them void. To render them reasonable, they should tend in some degree to the accomplishment of the objects for which the corporation was created and its powers conferred. It is unquestionably reasonable that pupils shall be classified with respect to the several branches of study pursued, and with respect to proficiency or degree of advancement in the same branch; that there shall be prompt attendance, diligence in study, and proper deportment. All regulations or rules to these ends are for the benefit of all, and presumptively promotive of the interests of all.

By a decision of the Supreme Court, about three million dollars of the obligations of the city of Chicago, issued in excess of the constitutional provision, were invalidated. It was held that municipal bodies can exercise only such powers as are conferred upon-them by their charter; and all persons dealing with them are supposed to see that they have power to perform the proposed act. Such corporations are created for governmental and not for commercial purposes. Hence no power to borrow money is incident to the performance of the duties which their charters impose, and it is by a grant of power only that they can create debts. No one has the right to presume the existence of such power, and persons proposing to loan money to a city should see that there is such power; and if the holders of certificates omitted to do so when they loaned the money, it was their own fault. In the case of the Northwestern University vs. The People, etc., the Supreme Court of the United States thus speak of the term "for school purposes," which was material to the case:

The distinction is, we think, very broad between property contributing to the purpose of a school, made to aid in the education of persons in that school, and that which is directly or immediately subjected to use in the school. The purposes of the school and the school are not identical. The purpose of a school or university is to give youth an education. The money which comes from the sale or rent of land dedicated to that object aids this purpose. Land so held or leased is held for school purposes, in the fullest and clearest sense. A devise of a hundred acres of land "to the President of the University, for the purposes of the school," would be not only a valid conveyance, but, if the President failed to do so, a court of chancery would compel him to execute the trust; but if he leased it all for fair rent and paid the proceeds into the treasury of the corporation to aid in the support of the school, he would be supported as executing the trust.

What is known as "minority representation," or the cumulative method, prevails in the election of members to tho State Legislature. (See "Annual Cyclopædia" for 1871, page 678.) The State is divided into fifty representative districts, and each elects three members of the Lower House of the Legislature, thus making the total number 153. Each voter has three votes for Assemblymen, and can cast them for whomsoever he pleases, or can divide them up into fractions of not less than one half and distribute them among the candidates; or can cast one vote only in whole or in halves, two votes only in wholes or in halves, or not vote at all. The working of the system will be illustrated by comparing the votes for Secretary of State and for Assemblymen in several districts.

In the 11th district the relative strength of the three parties, and the aggregate number of voters, are shown by the return for Secretary of State at the election in November, 1878, as follows:

COUNTIES.	Rep.	Dem.	Nat.
Carroll	1,475	397	841
Whiteside	2,494	902	1,576
Totals	3,969	1,299	1,917
Whole number			7,185

Republican majority over all, 753. The vote for members of the House was as follows:

COUNTIES.	Allen, Rep.	Shaw, Rep.	Pratt, Nat.	Green, Dem.
Carroll	2,185½	2,241	1,007	1,139½
Whiteside	3,921½	3,367	4,322	2,611½
Totals	6,107	5,608	5,329	3,850

Two Republicans and one National were elected, the latter representing the stronger minority. One Republican received more votes than the other, for various reasons. The whole number of Republican votes was 11,715; of National votes, 5,829; of Democratic votes, 3,850. Dividing these aggregates by three will give, approximately, the number of voters of each party, viz.: Republican, 3,905; National, 1,609 and 2 votes over; Democratic, 1,283 and 1 vote over; an aggregate of 6,798, which was 377 votes less than the number cast for Secretary of State.

The 13th district is composed of the counties of De Kalb, Kendall, and Grundy, and gave for Secretary of State the following vote:

COUNTIES.	Rep.	Dem.	Nat.
De Kalb	2,377	651	698
Kendall	1,513	153	653
Grundy	1,596	193	1,155
Totals	5,486	997	2,506
Whole number of votes			8,989

The number of candidates for the Legislature was the same as in the 11th district, and the votes were as follows:

COUNTIES.	Byers, Rep.	Brigham, Rep.	Smith, Nat.	Clover, Dem.
De Kalb	3,774½	3,768½	2,737½	1,014½
Kendall	2,324½	2,280½	2,306	807½
Grundy	2,358	2,250½	279	3,510½
Totals	8,357	8,258½	5,372½	5,132½

The result was the election of the two Republicans and one National as before, although the change of Grundy to Clover, the Democrat, nearly secured his election.

The 16th district, composed of Kankakee and Iroquois Counties, gave the following vote for Secretary of State:

COUNTIES.	Rep.	Dem.	Nat.
Kankakee	1,729	800	888
Iroquois	2,443	695	2,042
Totals	4,172	1,495	2,480
Whole number of votes			8,097

The vote for members of the House was as follows in the district: Buck, Rep., 6,241½; Secrest, Rep., 5,808½; Taylor, Dem., 4,313; Peters, Nat., 7,955. Two Republicans and one National were elected. By dividing the aggregate vote of each party by three, it will be observed that each party cast about the same proportionate vote for members of the House as for Secretary of State.

The 17th district is composed of La Salle County, and gave the following vote for Secretary of State: Republican, 4,357; Democratic, 2,617; National, 2,637. The National vote was only 20 in excess of the Democratic, but the Democrats had two candidates and the Nationals one. The result was as follows: Crooker, Rep., 6,799; Bowen, Rep., 6,118; Armstrong, Dem., 4,234; Miller, Dem., 3,732½; Richey, Nat., 7,532½. The two Republicans and the National were elected.

The vote for Secretary of State in the 36th district was as follows:

COUNTIES.	Rep.	Dem.	Nat.
Mason	989	1,273	450
Brown	516	1,026	661
Cass	834	1,280	589
Menard	701	1,049	787
Totals	3,040	4,628	2,387

The candidates and vote for members of the House were as follows: Wheeler, Rep., 8,376; Snyder, Dem., 7,623; Masters, Dem., 6,446½; Savage, Nat., 7,914½. The result was that one of each party was elected.

In the 46th district the vote for Secretary of State was as follows:

COUNTIES.	Rep.	Dem.	Nat.
Jefferson	616	1,277	672
Hamilton	265	1,034	826
White	1,000	1,764	296
Totals	2,081	4,075	1,794

The vote for members of the House in this district was as follows: Green, Dem., 6,522; Campbell, Dem., 5,075½; Taylor, Rep., 5,936; Moss, Nat., 5,830. One of each party was elected.

With regard to the whole State, the following statement shows the number of votes of each party, the number of members to which each was entitled, and the number which each obtained:

PARTIES.	Voters.	Members entitled to.	Members elect.
Republican	206,468	71	79
Democratic	170,085	59	61
National	65,689	22	10
Socialists	2,228	1	3
Total	444,470	153	153

Where there are but two parties, and each district elects three members, the cumulative system enables a minority to be represented where the minority has more than one third as many votes as the majority party, but not otherwise.

The election for members of the judiciary was held on June 2d. The Supreme Court was unchanged, all the old incumbents being reelected. Of the forty-four Circuit Judges chosen in the thirteen circuits of the State and Cook County, twenty-nine were reëlected, and fifteen were new men. Politically, the Supreme Judges stand 5 Democrats to 2 Republicans, and the Circuit Judges, 26 Republicans to 18 Democrats; but party lines were not drawn in the election of the former, and in only a few circuits in the choice of the latter.

INDIA,* a British viceroyalty in Asia. Viceroy and Governor-General of Bengal, Lord Lytton, appointed in 1876; Commander-in-Chief of the Army, Sir Frederick P. Haines. The Executive and Legislative Council is composed as follows: The Viceroy, the Commander-in-Chief, Major-General Sir E. Johnson, Sir John Strachey, Whitley Stokes, A. Rivers Thompson, Sir Andrew Clarke, and Sir Alexander J. Arbuthnot. The lieutenant-governors of the provinces are honorary members of the Council when it meets in their respec-

tive provinces. Government Secretaries: For the Interior, Sir S. C. Bayley; for the Finances, R. B. Chapman; for Agriculture and Commerce, A. O. Hume; for Foreign Affairs, A. C. Lyall; for Military Affairs, Colonel A. Johnson; for Public Works, Colonel A. Fraser; for Legislative Affairs, D. Fitzpatrick. The governors of the different provinces are as follows: Bengal, Lieutenant-Governor, Sir A. Eden; Northwest Provinces, Lieutenant-Governor, Sir G. E. W. Couper, Bart.; Punjaub, Lieutenant-Governor, R. E. Egerton; Central Provinces, Chief Commissioner, J. H. Morris; British Burmah, Chief Commissioner, C. Atchison; Madras, Governor-General, Duke of Buckingham and Chandos; Bombay, Governor-General, Sir R. Temple, Bart.

The area and population of British India, according to the census of 1872, were as follows:

PRESIDENCIES AND PROVINCES.	Square miles.	Population.
Presidency of Bengal:		
Lower Bengal	156,200	60,502,897
Assam	45,302	4,162,019
Northwest Provinces	105,895	42,001,486
Punjaub	104,975	17,611,498
Central Provinces	84,208	8,201,519
British Burmah	88,556	2,747,148
Ajmeer and Mairwara	2,711	896,889
Berar	17,711	2,226,496
Mysore	29,825	5,055,412
Coorg	2,000	168,312
Presidency of Madras	188,856	31,672,613
" of Bombay	124,102	16,849,306
Under British administration.	809,841	191,095,445
Feudatory states	557,908	49,208,053
Total	1,457,224	240,298,500

The emigration of coolies has been as follows:

YEARS.	From Madras.	From Calcutta.	From French ports.	Total.
1873	1,554	17,171	1,812	20,087
1874	2,569	24,569	2,105	29,243
1875	1,886	20,280	3,209	25,325
1876	294	9,251	1,944	11,489
1877	....	7,734	2,826	10,560
1878	8,890	18,448	2,804	25,182

The receipts and expenditures for the years 1875-'78 were as follows:

YEARS.	Gross receipts.	EXPENDITURES.			Surplus (+) or Deficit (—).
		In India.	In England.	Total.	
1875-'76	£51,801,063	£40,486,068	£9,155,050	£49,641,118	+ 1,668,945
1876-'77	55,995,785	44,710,800	18,467,763	58,178,563	— 2,182,778
1877-'78	58,969,801	48,464,038	14,048,850	62,512,888	— 8,548,087

The new coinage for the year ending March 31, 1878, was as follows: Gold, £15,636; silver, £16,180,326; copper, £148,591; total, £16,-344,593, against £6,394,553 in 1877.

The public debt of India on March 31, 1878, was as follows:

I. Consolidated Debt.
1. Payable in India:
Bearing interest £74,906,450
Not bearing interest ... 48,070 } £74,954,520
2. Payable in England:
Bearing interest 59,656,116
Not bearing interest ... 20,917 } 59,677,033

Total consolidated debt £134,631,553
II. Not consolidated debt 12,058,217

Total, March 31, 1878 .... £146,684,770
"   "   " 1877 138,986,029

* For a full account of the area and population of the different provinces, the distribution of the population according to religion and sex, and the population of cities, see "Annual Cyclopædia" for 1876.

The values of the principal articles of import and export for the years 1877–'78 were as follows (according to the "Statistical Abstract relating to British India," No. 13, London, 1879):

ARTICLES.	Imports.	Exports.
Grain, particularly rice and paddy............................	....	£10,184,000
Seeds and fruits............ ...		
Colonial goods, particularly tea and coffee............	£289,000	7,360,000
Wines, spirits, and malt and other liquors.....................	1,560,000	5,601,000
Coal.............................	1,402,000	....
Metals..........................	1,008,000	....
Cotton, silk. and wool............	280,000	524,000
Woods, timber, and carving material.............................	8,604,000	....
Hides and skins.................	737,000	14,684,000
Drugs, chemicals, oils, and resin.	1,432,000	9,123,000
Opium...........................	....	12,374,000
Yarns and woven goods of all kinds...........................	20,781,000	8,487,000
Other manufactures.............	5,282,000	485,000
Miscellaneous goods	3,251,000	1,490,000
Total goods	£39,326,000	£65,186,000
Total precious metals........	17,355,000	2,155,000
Grand total..................	£56,681,000	£67,341,000

The movement of shipping for 1877–'78 was as follows:

NATIONALITY.	ENTERED.		CLEARED.	
	Vessels.	Tons.	Vessels.	Tons.
British.............	1,881	2,157,155	1,972	2,193,225
British Indian......	1,573	219,786	1,445	198,938
Foreign	777	893,913	740	878,081
Native.............	2,123	106,795	2,027	104,486
Total, 1877–'78.	6,358	2,377,649	6,184	2,876,780
Total, 1876–'77.	6,376	2,791,884	6,388	2,842,153

On March 31, 1878, there were 8,215 miles of railroad in operation, of which 2,171 miles are government roads, and 6,044 miles private roads. The number of post-offices was 4,107. The number of letters sent in the year preceding was 115,089,336, and the number of papers 10,999,758. The length of the telegraph lines on March 31, 1878, was 18,210 miles, and of wires 42,687 miles; number of stations, 239. In the year 1877–'78 the number of dispatches sent was 1,431,452; the receipts were £306,-089, and the expenditures £352,186.

The most important event in the history of British India during the year 1879 was the war against Afghanistan. The history of this war until the reoccupation of Cabool by the British has been given in the article AFGHANISTAN. A proclamation was issued by General Roberts after he reoccupied Cabool, offering an annuity to those Afghans (provided they had not been concerned in the attack on the embassy) who had taken up arms under the belief that Yakoob Khan was a prisoner in the British camp, on condition of their surrendering their arms. Sir Richard Temple arrived at Candahar November 13th, and held a brilliant levee, which was attended by the Afghan Governor and all the chiefs of the city and the surrounding districts. The Governor of Ghuz-

nee arrived at Cabool on the 15th, having been summoned there by General Roberts for an inquiry into his loyalty, and reported that his district was very unsettled. The mollahs had been preaching against the British occupation, and malcontents had assembled there in considerable numbers. General Baker was dispatched with a small body of troops to settle the country and procure supplies. On the 20th General Roberts received the first convoy from Peshawer by the new route of the Lataband Pass, the crest of which is 8,000 feet above the sea. Skirmishing continued with the natives. Some cavalry who were sent out to arrest participators in the massacre of the British embassy were attacked by the Afghans from the hills, and retired. A larger force, which was sent out at daybreak the next day to attack the enemy, found that they had fled, whereupon it burned nine villages containing only a few inhabitants, who were first driven out.

On the 1st day of December the Ameer Yakoob Khan started secretly, under the care of a British guard, for Peshawer, whither he had been summoned by the Viceroy. It was now apparent that the Ameer was really held a prisoner by the British. He still, however, asseverated his innocence of any connection with the massacre, having told the correspondent of the London "Times" the day before he left the camp that he had never had one moment's disagreement with Sir Louis Cavagnari, and that the outbreak was an unpremeditated act of the rebellious soldiery, which he was utterly unable to control, and which he deeply deplored.

Mohammed Hussein, a son of the great Ameer Dost Mohammed, was appointed Governor of the Maidan, a district thirty miles from Cabool, but was murdered a few days afterward by the Afghan regulars and hill-men. The newly appointed governors of Kohistan and the Logar Valley were threatened with the same fate. The Afghans who had collected at Ghuznee, now numbering 7,000 men, started from that place in the first week of December, with the intention of joining a body of 3,000 men who were marching from Kohistan upon Cabool. On the 10th General MacPherson occupied Sarkh-Kotal just in time to prevent the junction of the two bodies, attacked the Kohistanis who occupied a position near by, and dislodged them. General Baker was to move by the way of Charasiab to take them in the rear, while General Massey was to join General MacPherson by the way of the Chardeh Valley for a combined movement, with the object of driving the enemy upon General Baker's command. The latter movement miscarried, and General Massey was met by the force from Ghuznee under Mohammed Jan, considerably outnumbering his own. He charged upon them without apparent effect upon their body. The enemy then, having been checked in an attempt to reach the Cabool gorge, turned and occupied the heights south of the Bala Hissar. An attempt was made by the British on the 13th to capture the ridge above the Bala Hissar, but it was not carried out with success, and the fighting of the 14th and 15th did not result in any material improvement of their position. · General Roberts then collected his troops in the Shirpoor cantonments, northeast of Cabool, where he waited for reënforcements, while the Afghans were left in possession of Cabool. The cantonment of Shirpoor was considered well enough fortified to withstand any attack that was likely to be made upon it, and was supplied with provisions to last several months. A few days afterward the Indian Government published an explanation of the military situation, stating that General Roberts had ample transport and ammunition; that, besides the 23 cannon belonging to his force, he had 214 captured cannon, many of which were rifled. His intrenchments could easily be held by 2,500 men, leaving 6,000 free for offensive operations. General Bright had 12,000 men between Jumrood and Jagdalak, with 30 cannon, two months' supplies, and sufficient transport. Including the forces at Candahar and in the Kooram Valley, the total field force was 45,000 men, with 160 guns, and was considered ample for present requirements.

On the 17th of December General Gough left Jagdalak with reënforcements for Shirpoor and Cabool. By the 18th the defenses of the Shirpoor cantonments had been completed. The enemy at that time occupied the heights over the city, but did not descend into the plains, which were patrolled by the British cavalry. General Roberts was awaiting the arrival of General Gough to make an attack, but intended to begin the offensive before he came up if a suitable opportunity should offer. The enemy's force was diminishing. One of their prominent leaders had been killed in a skirmish which took place on the 17th. Mohammed Jan Mardak, the real Afghan leader, was reported to have proclaimed Yakoob Khan's eldest son Ameer. On the 22d General Gough reported that he had been obliged to engage the Ghilzais all along his line in order to repress their desultory attacks, had driven them off, and hoped that they were dispersing. Reenforcements continued to advance, but General Roberts did not find it necessary to wait for them. Desultory attacks were kept up all the day of the 22d; and information was received during the day that an attack would be made by the enemy at daybreak on the 23d. Bodies of the enemy were seen occupying the distant villages and approaching nearer ·as it became dark. At 6 o'clock the next morning a fire was lighted on the Asmi Heights as a signal, and immediately afterward the attack was begun on three sides. The British were already prepared for it. The strongest demonstrations were made on the northeast, where, as soon as the enemy's intention was fully developed, a counter-attack with cavalry and ar-

tillery was ordered. A fire was accordingly opened on the enemy's flanks, which speedily dislodged them. The cavalry pursued and sabered numbers of the enemy, who retired from all points and hastily entered the city. Some near villages were occupied by the British, particularly those on the Butkak road. The success of the British proved to be complete. The enemy's loss was severe, one report saying that the ground around Shirpoor was thick with the bodies of the slain. Those of the enemy who lived in Cabool went straight to their houses after their defeat. The Kohistanis and Logaris remained in Cabool for a few hours, but all fled during the night. Two of the enemy's leaders, Mushki Alim (a priest) and Mohammed Jan, fled early in the day, and another prominent leader was reputed to have fled toward Wardak, with Yakoob Khan's eldest son. Yakoob Khan's wife and mother, and a daughter of the late Akbar Khan (who was the principal opponent of the British in 1841), were captured. The Bala Hissar and the city of Cabool were reoccupied, and by the 29th of December the country around Cabool and the line of communications were reported clear. An attack was afterward made by a khan with 2,000 followers on Colonel Norman at Gundamuk, but the enemy was driven off. General Baker was dispatched on the 27th with 1,700 infantry, a regiment of cavalry, and four guns, to Kohistan. He there destroyed the fort of the hostile chief Mirbatcha, which he found abandoned, and received the submission of several Kohistani and Logari chiefs. Mohammed Jan sent propositions for peace, in which he demanded, among other conditions, that the British forces should return to India, and that a promise should be given to send back the Ameer, while two British officers should remain at Cabool as hostages for the fulfillment of the promise. No notice had been taken of these propositions at the end of the year.

A fresh body of reënforcements from England left Portsmouth on the morning of the 1st of January, 1880. At that time 10,000 men were on their way through the Afghan defiles to the relief of General Roberts; about one fourth were British and the rest natives. Two thousand men held the fort of Lundi Kotal, and a similar number that of Ali Musjid. There were 500 Sepoys at Jumrood and 5,000 at Peshawer, and bodies were marching forward from Jelalabad and Gundamuk, whose places were to be supplied by troops from Agra, Meerut, and Bombay.

The annual financial statement, published by the Indian Government in March, produced an unfavorable impression. In view of the fact that the actual deficit of 1877–'78 and the estimated deficit of 1878–'79 amounted to over 16½ millions, and that the public debt within the same time increased by about 15 millions, a strong dissatisfaction was felt with the resolution of the Government to exempt from import duty all cotton goods containing no yarn of a higher number than 30's, a measure which was expected to have the effect of diminishing the revenue by £200,000. The Indian press and public were almost unanimous in condemning that step, and many went so far as to assert that the interests of India were being sacrificed to those of Manchester. Tenders for a new 4½ per cent. loan of 50 millions of rupees having been called for by the Government, a total amount of over 67 millions was tendered in May, of which 40 millions allotted to the lowest tender were accepted at 94 per cent., and the loan was issued at an average rate of 94⅜, making the actual amount to be received by the Government about 38 millions of rupees. On May 3d a Government order was issued on the subject of the reduction of public expenditure. All departments were directed to retrench expenses, but it was in the public works that the greatest retrenchment was contemplated. No new works, even if already sanctioned, were to be commenced without special orders, and the outlay on reproductive works was to be largely cut down. Military charges were left untouched for the present, but the duty was declared of reducing them to the lowest point compatible with safety.

A memorial addressed by the Madras Chamber of Commerce to the British House of Commons was especially severe in its criticism upon the financial administration of the Government. It charged Sir John Strachey with direct breach of faith in having applied the famine taxation to the general purposes of the country, and affirmed that any bank or public company, which ignored the solemn pledges it had given to the shareholders in the same way as the Government of India had broken faith with the taxpayers, would forfeit all claim to public confidence. Equally severe was an address delivered in May by Mr. Yule, President of the Bengal Chamber of Commerce. Speaking of the trades' license tax instituted last year for the purpose of raising a famine-insurance fund, he asserted that this tax had been levied and collected in such a way as to lead large numbers to conclude that, if there were a choice between famine and tax, they would certainly prefer famine.

In the latter part of May the Government issued a circular to the local administrations directing that in future no person, not being a member of the Covenanted Civil Service or of the Staff Corps, or a native of India, shall be appointed to any office carrying a salary of 200 rupees per month or upward without the previous sanction of the Governor-General in Council. Exceptions, however, are made in favor of persons appointed by the Secretary of State to the financial, educational, and forest departments; and the circular is to be held not to apply to the appointments to the departments of opium, salt, customs, survey, mint, public works, and police.

On June 16th the Supreme Government issued a financial circular to all the local governments, giving a sketch of the actual financial position of the Indian Government. It pointed out that orders had already been issued for reducing the expenditure the next year; that altogether in the civil department alone a saving of £1,000,000 was hoped for; and that an inquiry was even then proceeding with a view to the reduction of the military expenditure. A policy of rigid economy and retrenchment was to be followed in every branch of the public service. The first step taken by the Supreme Government toward reducing the central establishments was the abolition of the separate departments of revenue, agriculture, and commerce, established by Lord Mayo in 1871. The business of these departments was divided between the home and financial offices, the former to be henceforth called the Home, Revenue, and Agricultural, the latter the Finance and Commerce Department. The business connected with ports and navigation, which had hitherto been transacted in the Revenue, went to the Military Department. The immediate saving would be only the salaries of the secretary and the registrar, amounting to 50,000 rupees per annum; but it was expected that a further saving of 40,000 rupees would be ultimately effected.

In July Mr. Hope introduced a bill in the Supreme Council for the relief of the indebted ryots of the Deccan. Its main points are as follows: All loans are to be registered before village registrars; imprisonment for debt is abolished; courts of conciliation and arbitration—in other words, the old system of village punchayets—are recommended; receipts are to be furnished to borrowers, as well as an annual statement of accounts. By these means the ryot, invariably an uneducated man, is virtually protected from fraud. It was referred to a select committee, and was passed by the Supreme Council on October 24th.

On November 14th Sir John Strachey introduced a bill in the Legislative Council for amending the license-tax acts, and extending taxation to the official and professional classes. The ostensible object of the measure was to relieve the poorer commercial classes at the expense of the richer professional and salaried classes. The passage of this bill was postponed until 1880, but it was opposed by the Chambers of Commerce of Madras, Bombay, and Calcutta, which bodies pointed out, in memorials addressed to the Council, that the proposed tax was but an income-tax under another name, and earnestly protested against the reversal of the policy deliberately adopted after an exhaustive inquiry six years ago. The memorial of the Calcutta Chamber further pointed out that the state finances were in a much better condition than was anticipated when the budget was prepared, and that there was a good prospect of further improvement. These prospects should not be clouded by vexatious changes of the law, which would have the effect of adding to the public burdens at a time when the people were ill able to bear them.

The great khoomb, or duodecennial festival, at Hurdwar proved, like that of 1867, disastrous in its consequences. From 750,000 to 1,000,000 pilgrims assembled, and, despite the precautions taken by the authorities, cholera in a severe form broke out a few days before the close of the fair. The streams of returning pilgrims carried the disease in various directions toward their homes, and soon after the close of the fair outbreaks were reported from Delhi, Umritsur, Rawul Pindee, and other places of northern India. Great mortality among the pilgrims was reported from several districts; thus it was asserted that of 80,000 who went to the fair from a single district of Kumaon, one fourth were missing.

A severe famine prevailed in the tributary state of Cashmere, and excited the serious attention of the Indian Government, which impressed upon the Maharajah the duty of adopting effective measures of relief. A British officer was sent to assist the local authorities, and large quantities of grain were dispatched to the distressed districts.

On May 22d, in the English House of Commons, Mr. C. Stanhope made a statement of the finances of India, showing an estimated deficit of £1,400,000 for the coming year, which it was proposed to meet by a reduction of outlay upon public works and upon other branches of expenditure. Mr. Fawcett, accepting the statement as a vindication of his views, changed his announced resolution diminishing expenditure into one of approval of the Government's recommendations. On May 23d Mr. O'Donnell moved a vote of censure upon Lord Lytton for his reply to a deputation of the British Indian Association, but it was rejected by 215 to 36. On June 12th Mr. Gladstone spoke in strong terms of some of the recent acts of the Indian Government, and urged the establishment of a permanent control over Indian expenditure. On July 1st the House of Commons discussed the bill to enable the Government of India to purchase the East Indian Railway, and a resolution of Mr. Fawcett that the measure should not be regarded as a precedent was agreed to. On the 2d the bill was passed.

In order to lay some of the grievances of the people of India before the British public, the Indian Association sent a barrister to Calcutta, Mr. Lai Mohun Ghose, to England. On July 23d a crowded meeting was held in London, under the presidency of John Bright, to hear his address and "consider certain questions affecting the interests of the people of India." The Indian barrister severely attacked the English Government in India. Questions concerning education and taxation had alike been decided in such a way that the Indian subjects of the Queen had no voice in their consideration, although they had to pay the taxes which were necessary to defray the expenses. The people of India protested against the war in Afghanistan, a war in which politics had been divorced from morals; and contended that in the circumstances they ought not to be called upon to pay any part of the cost, or that, if any payment was to be made, England should bear an adequate part of the cost. The main grievance which the natives felt was that they had no voice in the government of the country, and this they thought ought to be remedied. Mr. Bright also made a long speech in which he dwelt on the burdensome character of the military expenditure in England, and said, if there was no possible escape from it, he thought it would be almost better to surrender, to confess the failure of English rule, and to say that the government of a great empire in Asia by persons sent out as rulers from the small island of Great Britain was impossible, and should never have existed. He complained of the high salaries paid to civil servants in India, and of the non-fulfillment by successive governments of the pledges made to the people of India with respect to the facilities to be afforded for their admission to the civil service.

An attempt on the life of the Viceroy was made on December 12th. He had just arrived in Calcutta, and as his cortége was driving to the Government house, and after crossing the Hoogly bridge, a Eurasian in the street fired two shots from a revolver at Lord Lytton's carriage, and then a third shot at the next carriage, in which Colonel and Lady Colley were seated. Colonel Colley jumped from the carriage, and with Captain Rose arrested the assassin without difficulty. They found on him a revolver with two chambers loaded and three recently discharged. The man, whose name is Deesa, was described as being intoxicated at the time, and as having been in a lunatic asylum. He was in Government employ in a subordinate capacity, but was dismissed owing to his weakness of intellect, and was said on that occasion to have threatened to kill the head of his department.

A fresh trouble arose in October for the Indian Government in the Naga Hills. On October 14th the Naga tribe, which murdered an English officer nearly five years ago, attacked and killed Mr. G. H. Damant, deputy commissioner and political agent for the Naga Hills. The tribes which cause the British the most trouble are those which inhabit the country south of Assam. They occupy the districts stretching into Burmah past Cachar, Chittagong, and Aracan. Some of the Nagas have settled down to a peaceful mode of existence. Those of the Lebsagur district may be classed among these. Whenever (and it has been very seldom indeed) an outrage has occurred among them, they have at once made ample atonement to the British officials, resorting to the simple expedient of closing the neighboring market to the offenders. With many other sections this remedy has proved efficacious, and very often offenders have been handed over to the British to exact justice from their persons for the murder of the police or for similar crimes. But it is from the Augami Nagas that most trouble has come. These hold a portion of the hills which stretch between Assam and Munnipoor. The Rajah of Munnipoor, at whose court the British have an agent, originally sought their protection from the tyranny of the Burmese ruler. The Rajah, acting under the advice of the British representative, has governed his little state to their entire satisfaction; but he has himself been beset by frontier difficulties with those very Augami Nagas who had given the British so much trouble for over fifty years, and who were again the aggressors. The attack took place at Konoma, in the heart of the Augami country. Immediately after the murder of Mr. Damant, together with some seventy of his followers, at Konoma, the Nagas of that village marched upon Kohima, and were joined by thousands of their tribesmen. The little garrison then consisted of Lieutenant Reid and a small detachment of the 43d regiment; Mr. Chorley, of the police, with his wife and his children; Mr. Hinde, of the police, and Mrs. Damant, who, with all the terrible affliction that had just fallen upon her, had now to go through the miseries and privations of a siege. At the most there were only 150 men whose loyalty could be depended upon, in a hostile village of 1,200 houses, while they were, in addition, completely hemmed in by a horde of savages, who were wrought up to the highest pitch of excitement. Mr. Hinde with 100 police was the first of several relief parties to reach the garrison, but was not strong enough to assail the Nagas. Colonel Johnstone, the political agent of Munnipoor, with 50 regulars, 50 police, and 2,000 tribesmen, reached Kohima on October 27th. He was only just in time. The Nagas were besieging in regular form behind intrenchments. The garrison, after thirteen days of defense, was reduced to the last extremity. Major Evans, with 200 men, arrived later, and the whole party fell back on Samagating. A force under General Nation was assembled at Golaghat, and in the early part of November set out to punish the Nagas. Several villages were occupied and burned, and on the 26th the village of Konoma was attacked by the British. After a severe struggle the natives retreated to some neighboring heights, and the village was burned on the following day. This virtually put an end to the hostilities.

Christianity has of late begun to make considerable progress. According to the latest attainable statistics of the Protestant missionary societies, their total force in India was represented in 1879 by 1,833 ordained and assistant missionaries, and 88,149 communicant members. This statement is based only in part on the reports for 1878–'79, since several of the societies have not recently published

detailed reports, and it does not include the very large accessions of 1877 and 1878 to the two Anglican societies. The growth of the missions is indicated by the fact that a careful census taken by the Rev. M. A. Sherring in 1871 gave the number of communicants in India, Ceylon, and Burmah at 78,494, and the number of persons connected with the Christian community as 318,363, while the figures given in the above statement for 1878–'79 are for India alone. The present number of the Christian communities in India, Ceylon, and Burmah is reckoned by Mr. Sherring at 460,000 souls. An unprecedented accession of adherents took place in 1877 and 1878 to the Anglican and Baptist missions in southern India, amounting in all to about 45,000 persons. The most rapid progress has been made hitherto among the aboriginal and Dravidian races and the lower castes. The higher castes have been until recently nearly inaccessible. Conversions have, however, lately begun to take place among the Brahmans, but are still so rare as to be generally deemed worthy of especial mention. The Methodist, Presbyterian, and Anglican missions in the Northwest Provinces and the Punjaub are among a Mohammedan population, who are represented as becoming gradually more amenable to their influence. The Anglican mission at Peshawer has outposts among the Afghans, and records several persons of that nation among its converts. The most extended and successful operations of the women's missionary societies are among the zenanas of the Hindoo women, through which and the schools connected with them the families of the higher castes, otherwise inaccessible, are brought under missionary influence. The missionary schools are elementary or vernacular, middle or high vernacular, and Anglo-vernacular schools, and colleges in which the course prescribed by the University is followed and instruction is given in English. The number of pupils in these schools in 1872 was 122,372, and is now estimated at 140,000, of whom about 20 per cent. are girls. Secular education has been greatly encouraged by the introduction of competitive examinations for civil appointments, but the same influence has been found to work detrimentally to the religious side of education. Eight colleges are connected with the Protestant missions, all of which are affiliated with one or another of the Indian universities.

INDIANA. The biennial session of the Legislature of Indiana commenced on January 9th. Lieutenant-Governor Gray presided in the Senate; in the House Henry S. Cawthorne was elected Speaker. At the end of sixty days the regular session expired; a special session then followed, and the final adjournment took place on March 31st. More than twice as many bills were passed at the special session as during the regular one.

A Senator of the United States was elected on January 24th. In the House Daniel W.

Voorhees, Democrat, received 57 votes; Benjamin Harrison, 38; —— Buchanan, 2. In the Senate Voorhees received 26 and Harrison 22 votes. For the short term caused by the death of the late Senator Morton, and which Mr. Voorhees had been appointed by the Governor to fill until the meeting of the Legislature, Mr. Voorhees received in the House 57 votes and Godlove S. Orth 37. In the Senate Voorhees received 26 and Orth 22. Mr. Voorhees was elected in each instance.

An act was passed relating to foreign corporations doing business in the State, which provides that any such corporation which shall transfer to the United States Court any suit commenced by or against it in a State Court, on a contract made in the State, shall thereby forfeit all right to transact business in the State, or hold real estate, or liens thereon. The object of the law is to limit outside corporations to the courts of the State in all suits founded on contracts made under State laws, and prevent the harassing and expensive practice of forcing citizens engaged in litigation with such corporations to appear, with their witnesses, before the United States Court at Indianapolis.

A Department of Statistics and Geology was created, of which the chief officer is required to be an expert in the sciences of geology and chemistry. His duties are to collect, systematize, tabulate, and present in annual reports, statistical information and details relating to agriculture, manufacturing, mining, commerce, education, labor, social and sanitary condition, vital statistics, marriages and deaths, and to the permanent prosperity of the productive industry of the people of the State. The several city, incorporated town, county, and township assessors, trustees, officers of school boards, and boards of health, in their respective cities, towns, counties, and townships, the agents or superintendents of all manufacturing, mining, and mechanical establishments, the managers and superintendents of all corporations, manufacturing, mechanical, and transportation companies and associations, and county superintendents of schools, are required to make reports and answer such questions as the bureau may require from them. The chief officer is further required to take charge of the geological cabinet, museum, chemical laboratory, apparatus, and library, and from time to time, as may be practicable, to add specimens to the cabinet of minerals, organic remains, and other objects of natural history peculiar to the State and to other States and countries.

Another act requires locomotive engineers to open the steam-whistle when approaching a turnpike or highway crossing at least eighty rods distant therefrom, " and to sound the same continuously until the crossing is passed."

In the House, resolutions relating to the following subjects were voted upon, with the results stated: To indefinitely postpone a resolution congratulating the country on the resumption of specie payments—yeas 50, nays 33. For a reduction of the salaries of Federal officers—yeas 90, nays 2. The unconditional repeal of the specie resumption act—yeas 50, nays 40. The repeal of the act exempting United States bonds from taxation—yeas 57, nays 34. The repeal of the law exempting greenbacks from taxation—yeas 76, nays 12. The abolition of all bank issues—yeas 59, nays 32. The free and unlimited coinage of gold and silver—yeas 85, nays 5. The issue by the General Government of full legal-tender paper money, receivable for all dues, public and private, in amounts sufficient to meet the wants of trade, or at least $30 per capita—yeas 50, nays 40. To prohibit the further issue of interest-bearing Government bonds; lost—yeas 43, nays 45. That Congress take immediate steps whereby the bonded indebtedness of the Government shall be paid off as fast as it shall become due, according to agreement—yeas 84, nays 4.

An act was passed providing that the rate of interest, in cases in which the parties do not agree, shall be six per cent., but may be taken yearly or for a shorter period or in advance; and no agreement to pay a higher rate shall be valid, unless the same be in writing signed by the party to be charged therein. By and in such cases it shall not be lawful to contract for more than eight per cent. per annum. When a higher rate of interest than six per cent. is contracted for, the contract will be void as to the usurious interest contracted for; and in an action on such contract, if it appear that interest at a higher rate than six per cent., or in case of a written contract a higher rate than eight per cent., has been directly or indirectly contracted for, the excess of interest over six per cent. will be deemed usurious and illegal; and in an action on a contract affected by such usury, the excess over the legal interest may be recovered by the debtor whenever it has been reserved or paid before the bringing of the suit.

An act was passed to protect the miners of Indiana from the many accidents incident to coal-mining. It provides for better ventilation and other means of safety. A mine-inspector will be appointed by the Governor, and he must be a practical miner of twelve years' experience. Also an act abolishing coroners' juries was passed.

Seven important amendments to the State Constitution were agreed to in 1877, by a majority of the members elected to each of the two Houses of the Legislature. The Legislature at this session, by a similar majority, agreed to the same amendments. An act was also passed providing that these amendments should be submitted to the electors of the State for ratification or rejection, at an election to be held on the first Monday in April, 1880. The law providing for the submission of these amendments to the electors of the State enacts that "the Secretary of State shall procure ballots of blue paper, on each of which shall be printed the proposed amendments, and below each amendment shall be printed the word 'Yes' in one line, and in another line the word 'No'; that any qualified elector may vote for or against any amendment by depositing one of said ballots in the ballot-box. If he intends to vote for any amendment, he shall leave thereunder the word 'Yes' and erase the word 'No' by drawing a line across it, or otherwise. If he intends to vote against any amendment, the word 'Yes' shall in like manner be stricken out and the word 'No' left; and if both words are allowed to remain without either of them being so erased, the vote shall not be counted either way." These amendments are designated by numbers, and are numbered 1, 2, 3, 4, 5, 6, and 9, numbers 7 and 8 having failed to receive a majority of the votes of both branches at this session.

These amendments relate chiefly to the matters of economy and honest elections. The first proposes to amend section 2 of Article II. so as to read as follows:

SECTION 2. In all elections not otherwise provided for by this Constitution, every male citizen of the United States of the age of twenty-one years and upward, who shall have resided in the State during the six months, and in the township sixty days, and in the ward or precinct thirty days immediately preceding such election, and every male of foreign birth, of the age of twenty-one years and upward, who shall have resided in the United States one year, and shall have resided in the State during the six months, and in the township sixty days, and in the ward or precinct thirty days immediately preceding said election, and shall have declared his intention to become a citizen of the United States, conformably to the laws of the United States on the subject of naturalization, shall be entitled to vote in the township or precinct where he may reside, if he shall have been duly registered according to law.

As the Constitution now stands, no fixed period of residence is required in a township or ward before voting, and no barriers against fraudulent voting can be maintained. When this amendment is adopted, one whose vote is challenged will have to swear that he has been a resident of the township sixty days, and of the ward or precinct thirty days, and thus the importation of votes and frauds upon the ballot-box may be measurably prevented.

The second amendment simply provides for striking out the words, "No negro or mulatto shall have the right of suffrage," contained in section 5 of the second article of the Constitution. The State Constitution is thereby made to conform to the Constitution of the United States. The prohibition in the former has become a dead letter.

The third proposes to amend section 14 of Article II. so as to read as follows:

SECTION 14. All general elections shall be held on the first Tuesday after the first Monday in November, but township elections may be held at such time as may be provided by law; *provided*, that the General Assembly may provide by law for the election of all judges of courts of general and appellate jurisdiction by an election to be held for such officers only, at which time no other officers shall be voted for; and

VOL. XIX.—32 A

shall also provide for the registration of all persons entitled to vote.

The reasons for this amendment are, that the cost of holding a general election in Indiana is about $1,000 to the county, or nearly $100,000 to the State. By this amendment the State is saved the expense of double elections in Presidential-election years. But this is not all. The other States of the Union having nearly all changed the time of their elections to November, as long as Indiana continues to vote in October she assumes the burden of the Presidential day. In 1876, counting money expended and time devoted to it, the October election cost the people of Indiana over $1,000,000, which expense was avoided by the States which did not vote until November.

The fourth amendment provides for striking out the word "white" from sections 4 and 5 of Article IV. of the Constitution, and thereby making it conform to the Constitution of the United States.

The fifth proposes to amend the fourteenth clause of section 22 of Article IV. so as to read as follows:

In relation to fees or salaries, except the laws may be so made as to grade the compensation of officers in proportion to the population and the necessary services required.

This provision will enable the Legislature to grade the compensation of county officers, and pay them in proportion to the population of the county and the services actually required. It will take away from that body the excuse urged for paying exorbitant fees and salaries to these officers, such as are out of all proportion to the compensation given for similar services in other avocations.

The sixth proposes to amend section 1 of Article VII. so as to read as follows:

SECTION 1. The judicial power of the State shall be vested in a Supreme Court, Circuit Courts, and such other courts as the General Assembly may establish.

The words "such other courts" are substituted for the words "such inferior courts," enabling the Legislature to establish other courts not inferior in jurisdiction to the Circuit Court, and to establish a perfect system of jurisprudence, which will greatly reduce expenses and at the same time facilitate business.

The next and last amendment proposed is as follows:

No political or municipal corporation in this State shall ever become indebted, in any manner or for any purpose, to an amount in the aggregate exceeding two per centum on the value of the taxable property within said corporation, to be ascertained by the last assessment for State and county taxes previous to the incurring of such indebtedness, and all bonds or obligations in excess of such amount given by such corporations shall be void; *provided*, that in time of war, foreign invasion, or other great public calamity, on petition of a majority of the property-owners, in number and value, within the limits of such corporation, the public authorities, in their discretion, may incur obligations necessary for the public protection and defense, to such amount as may be requested in such petition.

This provision is designed to protect the tax payers and limit the amount that may be assessed against them, and to which these municipalities may be burdened with debt.

The question was asked of the State Attorney-General whether, if the first and third amendments were adopted, it would be obligatory on the Legislature to pass a registry law, or only directory. He replied:

In the event of these amendments being adopted, it would undoubtedly be the duty of the Legislature to provide for a registration of voters, but the failure to do so, in my opinion, would not operate to disfranchise the electors otherwise qualified to vote. In other words, the central idea that the elections shall be held as provided for in the Constitution and laws can not be defeated by the failure of the Legislature to pass the registration law. So if the amendments are adopted, and there should be no session of the Legislature before the next election, persons otherwise qualified will be entitled to vote, although they have not been "duly registered according to law."

An act was passed to provide for the organization and support of an asylum for feeble-minded children. The number in the State is estimated at five hundred. It is intended by the act to gather up the children from the county poor-houses, and provide a home for them where they may be improved. Parents of such children who were able to pay their expenses would be required to do so, or if they could not pay all, then one half of them. It was stated that there were eleven such institutions in the United States, and the statistics obtained show that 70 per cent. of the feeble-minded children gathered into such homes were taught to read, and 43 per cent. to read and write, while all of them were very much improved. An instance was given of a patient, persevering philanthropist of Philadelphia, engaged in the work, who took a child so feeble-minded as not to observe for two years a red ball rolled daily backward and forward before its eyes; at the end of that time it noticed the ball, and at the end of two years more he had taught the child to read.

An act was passed which takes the power of appointing the boards of trustees of the asylums from the Legislature, in whose hands it has always been, and gives it to the Governor.

The Woman Suffrage Association of Indiana, desiring to be heard upon the matter of bestowing the elective franchise upon the fair sex of the State, the House resolved by a unanimous vote to grant them an audience on February 25th, and to invite the Senate to be present on the occasion. The report upon the audience concludes by saying: "Whatever may have been the feeling awakened in the minds of the members, they certainly could not have failed to be impressed with the earnestness and seriousness which characterized the papers read before them."

A bill passed the House which provided that all juries should be composed of six instead of twelve men.

Grave charges having been made that the plan of the new State House was decided upon unjustly, and that the contract for the construction of the said building was let against the interests of the State, a committee of seven was appointed in the House to investigate them. All of the committee save one made a majority report in detail. It sets out the charges preferred before them, and the answer thereto, and states that the whole action of the board, from its organization forward, was inquired into by the committee. They find that not one of the charges has been sustained or is true in point of fact; that no corruption, dishonesty, collusion, conspiracy, failure to perform duty, or improper discharge of duty upon the part of the board or any member thereof, is shown or found to exist. This report was adopted by the House—yeas 71, nays 24.

The propositions to divide the State into Senatorial and Representative districts, and also into Congressional districts, awakened much interest. The voting population, as shown by an official enumeration recently taken, is 451,025; consequently the average number of voting population requisite for a State Senator would be 9,020, for a State Representative 4,510, and Representative in Congress 34,694. A separate bill forming the districts for members of the Legislature was passed. In the Senate the Congressional apportionment bill was referred to a committee, which made a majority and a minority report. The minority considered the measure impolitic: 1. Because a new census would be taken by the Government in 1880, under which Indiana will be entitled to additional representation in Congress, and a new apportionment will be required; 2. It would violate a hitherto unbroken practice, and tend to a struggle every two years for a change; 3. The bill proposes to give 194,770 Democrats in this State nine Representatives in Congress, while 220,072 voters will have three or four. Amendments were made in this bill, and the Congressional districts as finally adopted are as follows:

First—Posey, Gibson, Vanderburgh, Warrick, Pike, Spencer, and Perry. Vote, 34,350. Democratic majority in 1876, 1,909; in 1878, 1,729.

Second—Knox, Sullivan, Greene, Lawrence, Martin, Daviess, Orange, and Dubois. Vote, 32,877. Democratic majority in 1876, 4,388; in 1878, 4,546.

Third — Jackson, Jennings, Washington, Scott, Clark, Floyd, Harrison, and Crawford. Vote, 32,381. Democratic majority in 1876, 4,474; in 1878, 5,943.

Fourth—Union, Franklin, Decatur, Ripley, Dearborn, Ohio, Switzerland, and Jefferson. Vote, 33,731. Democratic majority in 1876, 1,435; in 1878, 2,020.

Fifth—Putnam, Hendricks, Morgan, Owen, Monroe, Brown, Johnson, and Bartholomew. Vote, 32,488. Democratic majority in 1876, 2,183; in 1878, 2,525.

Sixth—Rush, Fayette, Henry, Wayne, Randolph, and Delaware. Vote, 33,348. Republican majority in 1876, 7,854; in 1878, 6,832.

Seventh—Marion, Hancock, and Shelby. Vote, 35,191. Republican majority in 1876, 241; Democratic majority in 1878, 502.

Eighth—Warren, Fountain, Montgomery, Vermilion, Parke, Vigo, and Clay. Vote, 36,810. Republican majority in 1876, 1,360; Democratic majority in 1878, 257.

Ninth—Tippecanoe, Clinton, Boone, Tipton, Hamilton, and Madison. Vote, 84,828. Republican majority in 1876, 853; Democratic majority in 1878, 422.

Tenth—Lake, Porter, Newton, Jasper, Pulaski, White, Carroll, Cass, Fulton, and Benton. Vote, 84,804. Republican majority in 1876, 1,045; in 1878, 1,680.

Eleventh—Miami, Howard, Wabash, Grant, Huntington, Wells, Adams, Blackford, and Jay. Vote, 89,863. Republican majority in 1876, 400; Democratic majority in 1878, 840.

Twelfth—La Grange, Steuben, Noble, De Kalb, Whitley, and Allen. Vote, 84,957. Democratic majority in 1876, 1,864; in 1878, 3,113.

Thirteenth—Laporte, Starke, St. Joseph, Marshall, Elkhart, and Kosciusko. Vote, 85,291. Democratic majority in 1876, 151; in 1878, 682.

In the Senate the bill was passed by a vote of 26 to 23, and in the House by a vote of 57 to 37.

On March 9th the regular session expired by limitation, and on the same day the Governor issued his proclamation convening the Legislature in an extra session. The members again took the oath of office, and the officers of the previous session were by resolution continued.

A resolution was adopted to appoint a committee of five to investigate the affairs of ex-Attorney-General Buskirk, the previous incumbent, during his term, and ascertain what amount of money has been collected by said Attorney-General from any and all sources; what amount thereof has been accounted for and paid over, and what amount, if any, has not been accounted for. The charges related to money collected for the State from counties and county officers. The term of office of James C. Denny was subsequently included in the investigation. The whole matter turned upon an interpretation of the statutes of the State, whether the Attorney-General was entitled to fees on the amount collected in addition to his regular salary. According to an act passed in 1855, providing for the election of an Attorney-General, fixing his compensation, and prescribing his duties, it is said to be clear that the statute as it then stood provided that the only compensation was the salary named in the act. Whether Messrs. Denny and Buskirk have accounted to the State for all moneys collected by them depends in part upon the construction to be given to the supplementary act relating to the duties and compensation of the Attorney-General, approved March 10, 1873. Section 2 of that act makes it the duty of the Attorney-General to collect all fines and forfeitures where the prosecuting attorney has failed to collect and pay the same into the proper Treasury for one year after such fine is assessed or recognizance forfeited, and no additional compensation beyond the $3,000 salary is provided. The main difficulty arises under section 9 of the act, which provides for additional services and allows therefor additional compensation in the way of commissions on moneys collected. By applying to this section the familiar rule of construction that requires us if possible to ascertain the legislative intent and give it effect, it is clear that the section contains two, and but two, separate and distinct propositions, which, although they are somewhat confounded as they stand in the sections, may be readily separated. The first part of the section is a distinct proposition and complete in itself. It authorizes no suits and provides for no fees or commissions for the performance of the services required, but simply requires the Attorney-General to ascertain what money belonging to the State has been collected by such officeholder, and requires the officer, under penalties, to furnish him with the necessary information. It does not even require the officer to pay it over to the Attorney-General, but seems to presume that, if it has been collected, it has reached or will reach the Treasury through the proper channels as provided by law. The other proposition in section 9 is equally independent. It seems very clear that the purpose of the first proposition is to aid the Attorney-General in enforcing the second, because, having ascertained what money belonging to the State has been collected, it is an easy matter to ascertain what is uncollected. It then becomes his duty, if the proper officer has refused or neglected to take the proper legal steps to collect the moneys of the State for twelve months or more, to step in and institute suit, or such legal proceedings as may be necessary. Under the first proposition the Attorney-General is not entitled to any fees or commissions for merely ascertaining what moneys belonging to the State the officer has collected, but his commissions must be alone on that which the officer refused or neglected to collect, and the Attorney-General did collect. The committee report the facts in part, and leave them to the House to determine what action shall be taken.

Ex-Attorney General Denny held that the ninth section authorized him to take the proper steps to collect any money due to the State in the hands of any officer in default. This was the construction given to the act by the judges of the courts in all the counties where the question had been raised. He also said:

The first portion of section 9 makes it the duty of the Attorney-General to ascertain from time to time the amounts paid to any public officer, etc., and to aid him in doing so the latter clause was added. It reads as follows: "And for the purpose of enabling the Attorney-General to ascertain the facts herein contemplated, it is hereby made the duty of the officer having the custody of any such moneys to report the same to said Attorney-General," etc. Now, the question raised by the committee is fully settled by the Supreme Court in the case of Moore, administrator, vs. the State, ex rel. Denny, Attorney-General, 55th Indiana, p. 360. In that case the Court say that the ninth section of the Attorney-General's act repeals the sixth and seventh clauses of section 2 (1 Davis's Statutes, p. 157). The sixth subdivision of the above act reads as follows: "The Auditor of the State shall, sixth, institute and prosecute, in the name of the State, all proper suits for the recovery of any debts, moneys, or property of the State, or for the ascertainment of any right or liability concerning the same; seventh, direct and superintend the collection of all moneys due the State, and employ counsel to prosecute suits instituted at his instance, on behalf of the State." That the said ninth section repeals. The seventh section of the act of March 8, 1873, as to county superintendents, provides that the county superintendent may examine "the official dockets, records, and books of account of the clerks of the courts, county auditors, county commissioners, justices of the peace, prosecuting attorneys, mayors of cities, and township and school trustees. . . . shall be open at all times to the inspection of the county superintendent, and whenever he shall find that any of said officers have neglected or refused to collect and pay over interest, fines, forfeitures, license, or other claims due the school funds or revenues in their possession, he shall be required to institute suit in the name of the State of Indiana for the recovery of the same, for the benefit of the school fund or revenues, and make report of the same to the board of county commissioners and to the State Superintendent." These two sections cover all the funds that have been collected by the Attorney-General, and the Supreme Court in the case referred to holds that the ninth section of the act of March 10, 1873, repealed the sections above referred to, and took the place of said sections.

Ex-Attorney-General Buskirk, after reading the report, sent a letter to the chairman of the committee, of which the following is an extract:

So far as your report shows small discrepancies to exist in certain counties, I hope to be able to explain them when I can personally examine the accounts; but your report, so far as it relates to me, seems devoted mainly to certain fees retained by my assistants and myself. On that subject, the law being loosely and awkwardly drawn, I took the opinion in writing of one of our best lawyers in the State—then Governor—and I think such fees were retained in accordance with it. I desire that the courts may decide the question. If they hold I am liable for what was retained by my assistants and myself, it would probably amount to more than my bond. My situation for paying is just this: I have mortgaged all I have to my surety, hardly sufficient to indemnify. I have nothing else, having come back here poorer by about $4,000 than when I went to Indianapolis four years ago. I then left a law practice worth over $5,000 a year, and so far since my return have had an equally good business, probably better. If the courts decide I owe anything, I am willing to devote the balance of my life to work to pay it off, to show that I did not wish to steal anything from the State. It may be proper for me to add that while you will see I could have done so to large amounts, I actually had to borrow money to pay in part the freight on my household furniture to get back here. Do not understand me as finding fault with the committee; only I beg respectfully to dissent from its views of the law upon the subject of the fees of the assistants and myself. Please submit this to the House.

Another case, involving the State Auditor Henderson, came before the House of Representatives. The point in this case was a question of fees. A committee of investigation was appointed, which made a majority and a minority report. The gentlemen making the minority report construed the law against the Auditor, and recommended that suit be brought against Mr. Henderson for the recovery of $13,000 alleged to have been illegally collected by him while Auditor and retained. The majority report construed the law differently. It justifies the Auditor at every step; it finds that he had a right to collect and hold fees from the Land Department on private contract; it holds that the act of 1877 was amen-

datory of and supplemental to the act of 1865, and separate and distinct from the acts of 1873 and 1875; "that nothing whatever can be found in the law of 1865, or in the act of 1877, compelling or authorizing any of the money derived from such fees and charges to be paid over into the Treasury"; and that the Auditor was not bound to turn any of the fees collected under these acts over into the Treasury. It further said: "We recognize the fact that the question as to whether Mr. Henderson ought to account to the State for any portion of the moneys received by him from the additional fees and charges authorized by the law af 1877 is one wholly of the proper construction of the statute, which is by no means plain or free from ambiguity, and about which men and courts may, and very likely honestly, differ in opinion." The minority and majority agree that Mr. Henderson never, at any time, disguised or attempted in any way to conceal the fact that he charged and retained all of said fees, claiming that he was entitled to do so by a fair construction of statute; and that Mr. Henderson upon request furnished the committee with all the facts desired. The minority report was adopted—yeas 58, nays 30.

A bill providing for the codification of the school laws of the State was also adopted. The amendments made to these laws were, that the levy for special school purposes be reduced from 50 to 25 cents on the $100, with a provision that, in case the school officers in any district have created a debt, they may make an additional levy of 15 cents to pay such indebtedness; that the levy for local tuition purposes be reduced from 25 to 20 cents on the $100; that county superintendents shall hereafter be appointed by the board of county commissioners instead of by the township trustees, and that their per diem shall be fixed by the county commissioners, provided, however, that it shall not be less than $3 per day; that teachers shall pay a fee of $1 for examination, such fee to be the only compensation of the superintendent for holding examinations; also, that county superintendents shall be authorized to hold township institutes or joint township institutes, and that teachers shall be required to attend such institutes not less than two nor more than three days during each year; that but one six months' license shall be issued to the same person in the same county, but that persons who have received a six months' license shall not be again licensed unless they have reached a grade sufficient to obtain a twelve months' license; and that the county commissioners may fix the number of days on which superintendents shall visit schools, provided that the number so fixed shall not be less than three fourths as many days as there are schools in the county over which the superintendent presides.

The number of persons in the State between the ages of six and twenty-one years is 707,-

845. The average daily attendance in the schools during the year was 312,143. The total number of white pupils admitted into the schools during the year was 496,066; of colored pupils, 7,826. Teachers to the number of 13,490 were employed, the average compensation of men in the townships being $1.86 per day; of women, $1.64. In cities the male teachers were paid $3.64, female teachers $2.10. The total school revenue was $4,902,-163.77; the total expenditures were $3,002,-517.94. The school fund consists of assets valued at $9,000,000. The value of permanent school property is $12,000,000. An investigation of the high schools in some twenty cities of the State showed the following average results:

Per cent. of patrons who pay no property tax............ 18
Per cent. paying on less than $500...................... 36
Per cent. paying on less than $1,000.................... 50
Per cent. paying on less than $5,000.................... 83
Per cent. paying on more than $10,000................... 8
Per cent. of children of widows or parentless........... 16
Per cent. of children of manual laborers................ 40
Per cent. of children of agents, clerks, and others on salary 20
Per cent. of children of professional men............... 11

The debt of the State on October 31, 1879, was as follows:

FOREIGN DEBT.

Five per cent. certificates, State
 stock.................................. $14,469 99
Two and one half per cent. certifi-
 cates, State stock..................... 2,925 13
War loan bonds, 6 per cent......... 189,000 00
Temporary loan bonds, 5 per cent.,
 due April 1, 1884................... 510,000 00
Temporary loan bonds, registered 6
 per cent., due December 1, 1879. 200,000 00
Temporary loan bonds held by Pur-
 due University, 5 per cent., due
 April 1, 1831........................ 200,000 00
Internal improvement bonds...... 27,000 00
                                          ———— $1,093,395 12

DOMESTIC DEBT.

School fund bond No. 1, January 1,
 1867................................ $709,024 85
School fund bond No. 2, January
 20, 1867............................ 2,653,057 30
School fund bond No. 3, May 1,
 1868................................ 184,284 00
School fund bond No. 4, January
 20, 1871............................ 177,700 00
School fund bond No. 5, May 3,
 1878................................ 175,767 07
                                          ———— $3,904,783 22

 Total debt.......................... $4,998,178 34

The receipts and expenditures of the State during the year were as follows:

Net cash receipts during year................. $3,187,221 37
Deduct net cash disbursements during year... 3,127,825 91
                                                ————
Leaves excess of receipts over disburse-
 ments....................................... $59,395 46
Add balance cash in Treasury October 81, 1878. 524,356 46
                                                ————
Makes cash balance chargeable against
 Treasury October 31, 1879............. $583,751 92

An investigation was made by a committee of the Legislature of charges made against the President of the Board of Benevolent Institutions and the Superintendent of the Hospital of the Insane Asylum. The majority reported charges made for extra services, and the minority reported the application of some funds contrary to the meaning and intent of the statute. Both found that the charges of cruelty and neglect of the inmates in general were

not sustained. No action was taken by the Legislature.

The office of State Geologist was abolished by the Legislature. Some of the results of the geological survey have been very valuable. Before the survey, the coal lands of the State were worth from $2 to $10 per acre. They now sell readily at from $50 to $200 per acre, while Indiana coal is used to a very large extent by railroads and manufacturing establishments, and also for fuel, and still more extensively abroad. The reports issued showing the good quality of the coal have either suggested or aided the construction of four or five important railroads, and prepared the way for others. Placing the average extent of counties included in the coal regions at 250,000 acres, the increased value of previously unproductive land would exceed $30,000,000; and adding the benefits derived from the setting up of forges, furnaces, factories, and mills, and the building of railways, it is estimated within the mark to state that the aggregate increase in values resulting from the development of the coal-fields has reached $100,000,000. This great benefit to the State has been brought about to a very great extent, if not altogether, by the labors of the geological survey. The money invested in operating the coal-fields is largely foreign capital, which has been brought within reach for the purposes of taxation. The increased shipments from the town of Brazil, in Clay County, represent annually more money than the entire cost of the survey. Ten years ago a few car-loads per annum constituted the entire export trade; and the same statement holds equally true in regard to the Washington mines, in Daviess County. The annual shipments are now from 250,000 to 300,000 tons, and the proprietors of mines are glad to arm themselves with analyses and letters from the State Geologist showing the purity and excellence of Indiana coal, by means of which they have built up an extensive shipping trade, while the cannel coal of Daviess County, by reason of its superiority as a grate fuel and for its illuminating qualities, now commands a full market in all directions outside of the State.

The quarries of building-stone in the State are estimated to cover a surface of more than 200 square miles. This stone has been found in great variety of color and grade, and the tests applied have shown it to be of such enduring strength as to create a large demand. The product of the quarries, which a few years ago did not exceed $30,000 per annum, during 1879 amounted to at least $500,000. The citizens of Owen, Monroe, Lawrence, Washington, Harrison, and other counties consider that in the near future the increase of Indiana's wealth from her stone-quarries will be equal to that resulting from the successful working of her coal-mines.

An officer to be known as a Mine Inspector was created by the Legislature. Among beneficial results anticipated from the administration of such an officer, one is that it will have a good effect in setting at rest existing troubles between mine-owners and operatives. The law requires that the officer shall be a resident of the State, a practical miner of not less than twelve years' experience, two of which shall have been spent in digging and mining coal in the State; and he is not to be at the time of his appointment pecuniarily interested in any coal-mine within the State, directly or indirectly. On entering upon his duties he is to execute a bond of $10,000, to be filed with the Secretary of State, and take an oath of office. The Mine Inspector is to have his office in some central part of the mining district, is to be paid a fee of $5 for each semi-annual inspection of a mine, and is to have power to enter, examine, and inspect coal-mines, machinery, etc., the owner or agent being required to furnish facilities for such inspection, failure or refusal to do so being declared a misdemeanor punishable by a fine of $100. The Mine Inspector is to devote his whole time and attention to the duties of his office, and to collect and make tabulated statements of certain facts in relation to the yearly production of coal, methods of operating mines, amount of capital and number of men employed, and such other information as he may deem necessary, together with his opinion in regard to the condition of the mines as to safety and ventilation, all of which is to be set forth in an annual report to the Governor.

The wheat crop of the State for 1879 was computed at 55,000,000 bushels; of this it was estimated that about 43,000,000 could be exported, leaving the remainder for home consumption.

The number of hogs packed at various points in the State from November 1st to March 1st, for two seasons, was: 1878–'79, 682,321; 1877–'78, 496,025. The following statement shows the result in detail for Indianapolis alone:

DETAILS.	Years.	
Winter Season.		
November 1st to March 1st.	1878–'79.	1877–'78.
Number of hogs packed...	472,455	270,150
Average gross weight. lbs........	225·69	244·28
Average net weight, lbs....	180·55	195·48
Aggregate net weight, lbs........	85,305,172	52,975.480
Average yield of lard, lbs........	26·59	32·05
Aggregate pounds of lard	12,521,365	8,657,517
Average cost of hogs, gross......	$2 86	$3 94
Average cost, net, 100 lbs........	$3 58	$4 93
Barrels of pork made............	1,080	778
Mess-pork	.....	228
Extra prime....................	.....	50
Clear..........................	.....	50
Rump..........................	1,080	130
Other kinds....................	.....	820
Tierces of lard made, 880 lbs.....	37,948	26,285
Summer Season.		
March 1st to November 1st.	1878.	1877.
Number of hogs packed..........	312,224	204,264
Average gross weight, lbs........	204·67	220·00
Twelve Months.		
March 1st to March 1st.	1878–'79.	1877–'78.
Number of hogs packed..........	784,679	474,414

The Supreme Court of the State has decided that the 28th and 29th days of February must be counted in legal and commercial affairs as one day. The decision is in these words:

It must be regarded as settled in this State that the 28th and 29th days of February in every bissextile year must be computed and considered in law as one day. It has been held by this Court that the English statute—21 Henry III.—is in force in this State. This statute, speaking of the 29th day of February, in leap-year, provides, " *Computitur dies ille et dies proxime præcedens pro unico die.*" (And that day as well as the day next preceding shall be computed as one day.) This English statute is recognized as a part of the law governing this State. The service of the summons was not sufficient in law to justify either the default entered or the judgment rendered.

In the case of the Chicago, Danville, and Vincennes Railroad Company, the Supreme Court of the United States decided "that the Court may, as condition of appointing receiver, provide for claims for back pay, materials, etc., and that when money which the Court may apply for back dues is used for the betterments, the Court may, in proper cases, provide for such debts out of proceeds of sale to extent of such diversion. Title to cars remains in conditional vendor as between him and mortgagees."

INDUCTION-BALANCE, HUGHES'S. By arranging two primary coils of equal size near each other, each with a secondary coil beside it, the induction-current induced in the one secondary coil by the passage of a current of electricity through the adjacent primary coil may be made to exactly neutralize and balance a similar current induced in the other secondary coil. An instrument of the most delicate sensitiveness has been constructed by Professor E. D. Hughes, the English electrician, on this principle. A microphone is placed in the primary circuit, and a telephonic receiver is connected with the secondary coil. To this instrument he gives the name of the induction-balance. One of its modifications is the sonometer, an instrument which promises to be of considerable practical value. The sonometer is constructed by placing two primary coils in a horizontal position at a distance of forty centimetres apart. A secondary coil midway between them is so arranged that it can be moved to one side or the other along a graduated bar divided into millimetres. The primary coils have similar poles facing each other, so that a secondary current induced in the movable coil by one of them would take the opposite direction from the induction-current produced by the other, and in a certain position of the secondary coil the two forces would exactly counterbalance each other; no current would pass, and the telephone could not be made to emit the slightest sound. When the two primary currents are equal in intensity, the neutral position for the secondary is exactly half way between them. When the coil is slid the least distance to either side of the neutral point, a sound is produced which increases as the coil is pushed farther to the side. The sonometer is capable, therefore, of measuring the intensity of sound, as the sound increases in the exact ratio of the distance from the neutral point, which distance is indicated on the graduated rod.

When the secondary currents are in equilibrium, if a piece of metal is placed in either of the primary coils of an induction-balance, the balance is disturbed, and a sound can be immediately heard on the telephone. Bringing then a sonometer connected with the induction-balance into circuit by means of a circuit-changing key, and moving the sliding coil from the neutral position to such a distance that the same degree of sound is heard as on the telephone of the induction-balance, so that by moving the key up or down and connecting either telephone with the circuit, no difference in the intensity of the sound can be detected; then the exact amount of the disturbance caused by the piece of metal is measured on the graduated scale of the sonometer. Experiments show that the sounds produced by the same piece of metal remain constant, but that different metals and different masses of the same metal produce different sounds, as also the same piece of metal in different molecular conditions. As every metal has its own sound-measure, which is always the same for equal weights and coincides with that of no other metal, the sonometer may be employed in detecting the nature of samples of metals of unknown character. Standard gold gives a different degree of sound from any of the alloys used in imitating coin, so that counterfeit pieces can be instantly detected by the aid of the sonometer. When two genuine coins are placed one in each primary coil, the equilibrium is maintained; but with a debased coin in one and a standard coin in the other of the coils, the telephone will give forth a sound. The sensitiveness of the instrument is so keen that when a freshly coined shilling is balanced against one which is the least worn, or even rubbed in the hand, a sound is produced by the microphone. Experiments made upon various alloys with the induction-balance and sonometer in the British Mint, by Chandler Roberts, proved the instrument to be so extremely sensitive that it may be of practical use to the assayer. The slightest alloy of silver in gold or of gold in silver was indicated by the sonometer.

The sound-measuring part of the instrument has been employed successfully by Dr. B. W. Richardson in testing the hearing powers. When employed for this purpose, the sonometer is called the audiometer. The graduated bar is divided into two hundred parts. It was found that a person who hears the sound perfectly well when the coil is in a certain position may not be able to detect the slightest trace of sound when it is reduced by moving the coil only two degrees toward the center. Right-handed people hear best with the right ear, and left-handed people with the left ear.

When the barometer stood at thirty inches Dr. Richardson was able to detect sounds when the coil was removed the minutest distance from the zero, but could not hear within two degrees of the zero when the mercury was lower. Deaf persons can decide through the audiometer upon the value of different kinds of artificial drums. Dr. Richardson concludes that the best material for artificial drums is fine gold. In one case, where the natural tympanum had been destroyed, the introduction of a gold drum had the effect to improve the hearing by fifty of the two hundred degrees on the measured scale. The audiometer enables the aurist to decide, also, whether a case of partial deafness is caused by a defect in the ear itself, or whether it is throat-deafness caused by a closure of the Eustachian tube. The audiometer can not fail to prove of high value in determining the qualifications of persons for positions on railways, for example, where great acuteness of hearing is required.

INTEROCEANIC CANAL, THE. The International Congress for the study of the Interoceanic Canal met at Paris, in the rooms of the Geographical Society, May 15, 1879. The Congress was opened by Baron de la Roncière de Noury. Count Ferdinand de Lesseps was elected President; Commodores Ammen, of the United States Navy, and Likhatscheff, of the Russian Navy, Colonel of Engineers Sir John Stokes, of the British Army, and Cristoforo Negri, Italian Minister Plenipotentiary, were chosen Vice-Presidents; Henri Bionne, General Secretary; and Boissevin, H. Capitaine, J. Jackson, and Charles Wiener, Secretaries. Five committees were appointed: one on statistics, to estimate the probable traffic of the canal and the tonnage which would pass through it, as well as the probable share of each nation in the traffic; the second on economical and commercial questions, which should consider the advantages and saving in the costs of transportation which would accrue to each nation from the use of the canal, and the influence which it would exercise upon the commerce of each country through opening new markets and increasing trade and industry; the third on navigation, to consider the class of vessels which would be likely to frequent the canal and the adaptation of the canal to the requirements of navigation and commerce, the influence which the canal would have on naval architecture, the influence of the prevailing winds and ocean-currents on the frequentation of the canal, the meteorological and climatic conditions of the Isthmus, and the influence of these conditions upon the conservation of the canal; a fourth on technical questions, for the technical examination of the different routes, the estimation of the cost of construction, the annual cost of working, the annual cost of maintenance and repairs, the facility and security of navigation in the canal and harbor approaches; the fifth on ways and means, to estimate from the probable traffic the probable gross revenue, and to study the sum which should reasonably be applied to the construction and maintenance of the canal in view of the possible traffic.

The Committee on Statistics, in its report, recommended a canal cut down to the level of the sea, and without locks, as the only profitable plan, as no canal with locks would be able to accommodate a traffic sufficiently great to yield a revenue which would return an ordinary rate of dividends to the stockholders. The minimum paying traffic at the toll-tariff proposed of 15 francs per ton was estimated at 6,000,000 tons per annum, or an average traffic of 8 ships of 2,050 tons per diem. This traffic would not be distributed evenly over the year. A traffic of 6,000,000 tons per annum would correspond to one of perhaps 16 ships a day during the commercial season, which during the busiest season, that succeeding the Californian wheat-harvest, would increase probably to an average of 24 ships daily. The only profitable kind of a canal, therefore, would be one which could allow of the passage of at least 50 vessels a day for many days together. The passage of an ocean-vessel through a lock would occupy probably two hours—at the least calculation one hour— allowing from half an hour to an hour for the filling and emptying of the lock-chamber, and as much time for the slowing of speed when approaching the lock and the time required in getting under way again after leaving it. A single lock would therefore limit the number of ships which could pass through in a day of 24 hours to from 12 to 24. The amount of traffic which would naturally have passed through the canal in 1876, had it been completed, was 4,830,000 tons, 3,500,000 tons from one side and 1,330,000 tons from the other. The increase in the commerce of the countries to whose ports the canal would be the avenue has been 6 per cent. per annum for the past fifteen years. Calculating the future annual increase at only 5 per cent., the probable traffic of the canal in the year 1887, the date at which the canal might reasonably be expected to be opened, would amount to 7,250,000 tons, 5,250,000 tons from one side and 2,000,000 tons from the other.

The Committee on Economical and Commercial Questions dwelt in its report on the shortening of the distance between the ports of the Atlantic and those on the western side of the American Continent, and between the Atlantic seaboard of the United States and the countries of the Orient and islands of the Pacific. The distance from Liverpool, Havre, or New York to San Francisco by sea is now 18,000 miles. Not only would the cocoa, the guano, the copper, the niter, and the wool of South America, and the wheat and other products of California, reach their markets by a much shorter voyage, but the storms of Cape Horn and the calms of the equinox would be avoided. The countries which would most profit by the canal would be the Pacific states of South America

and the republics of Central America, and their commerce in the above-cited products, as well as in vegetable ivory, cotton, alpaca-fleeces, sugar, cinchona and other barks, and vegetable essences, metals, and tropical food-products. Central America, particularly, would find for the first time a vent for its rich productions —a region which is not only the natural home of the most valuable vegetable products, such as cotton and other fibrous materials, coffee, cocoa, sugar, indigo, cochineal, rice, maize, caoutchouc, the finest cabinet and dye woods, and a thousand other choice products, but which contains a great variety of undeveloped mineral resources, iron, copper, lead, gold, silver, sulphur, and precious stones, and the other valuable minerals which are known to exist there. The nation, however, which would derive the most immediate benefit from the interoceanic canal would be the United States. As 79 per cent. of the commerce which passes through the Suez Canal is in the hands of the English, so the Americans would monopolize the navigation of the new gateway between the oceans.

The Committee on Navigation recommended that the canal should have a minimum depth of 8·3 metres, a breadth of 25 metres at the bottom and of 70 metres at the surface, which could be lessened to 30 metres in rocky parts. If a canal with locks should be decided upon, these should have a width at the gates of 22 metres and a length of 150 metres. The locks should be so limited in number and so disposed as to allow of the passage through the canal of 50 vessels per diem. If the canal at sea-level should be chosen, the same width should be adopted, as it would be necessary to accommodate sailing vessels as well as steamers.

The Technical Committee, to which the examination of the various schemes was confided, reported in favor of the route between the Gulf of Limon and the Bay of Panama, and recommended the construction of a canal without locks at the tide-level.

The Committee on Ways and Means, calculating on the basis of a prime cost of 600,000,000 francs, to be expended during a period of construction of eight years, and upon a gross revenue of 90,000,000 francs per annum from an average traffic of 6,000,000 tons at the rate of 15 francs per ton, estimated that there would remain an annual surplus of 42,000,000 francs after deducting 37,500,000 francs, interest on the total invested capital of 750,000,000 francs at 5 per cent., 6,000,000 for the annual cost of maintenance and operation, and 4,500,000 for the royalty to be paid to the state granting the right of way, taken at 5 per cent. of the gross revenue. It advised the employment of the negroes of the West Indies and Louisiana in building the canal. It recommended that the rate of toll should not exceed a maximum of 15 francs per ton, which is 50 per cent. greater than the tariff of the Suez Canal, and corresponds to the greater cost of the present undertaking. The sentiment was approved that the canal should be declared absolutely neutral and free to all, notwithstanding any existing state of war.

At the closing session, on the 19th of May, the Congress voted in favor of the route recommended by the Technical Committee. The terms of the conclusion adopted were: "The Congress considers that the cutting of an interoceanic canal at the tide-water level, so desirable in the interest of commerce and navigation, is possible; and that this ship-canal, in order to secure the facilities of access and passage which such a channel ought indispensably to afford, should take the course from the Gulf of Limon to the Bay of Panama." The plan recommended by Henri Bionne was adopted with greater unanimity than was expected. In the division, out of 98 voters, 74 voted in favor of it, and 8 against, while 16 members abstained from voting.

The routes which were submitted to the consideration of the Congress were five in number: 1. The route across the Isthmus of Te-huantepec, 148 miles long, and requiring 120 locks, taking a vessel 12 days to make the passage; 2. The Nicaragua route, 180 miles in length, requiring 17 locks, and taking 4½ days for the passage; for which route two projects were submitted, the American plan elaborated by Lull and Menocal, and one by the French engineers Wyse and Reclus; 8. The route across the Isthmus of Panama, length 45 miles, for which the same American engineers proposed a canal with locks, but the French engineers a deep tide-level cutting, with a tunnel 5½ miles long, the plan which was adopted by the Congress; 4. The route by the Isthmus of San Blas, another project of a tide-level canal, 33 miles in length, and time of passage 1 day; 5. The Atrato-Napipi route, with a length of 179 miles, requiring 3 locks, and 2 days for the passage. The number of projects from which the Congress had to choose was seven, or with the alternate Panama plan of Wyse-Reclus, eight, of which the following tabular statement gives the main features of character, cost, and construction:

ROUTES.	Length of canal.	Number of locks.	Length of tunnels.	Cost of construction.	Working expenses capitalized.	Total capital required.	Time of passage.
	Kilometres.		Kilomet's.	Million fr.	Million fr.	Million fr.	Days.
Tehuantepec	240	120	..	?	?	?	12
Nicaragua. { Lull and Menocal's project	290	20	..	880	180	460	4½
{ Blanchet's project	292	14	..	770	180	900	4½
Panama... { Wyse and Reclus's project, á niveau..	73	1 sea-lock.	9	1,070	180	1,200	2
{ Lull and Menocal's project, with locks.	73	25	..	870	180	1,000	2½
{ Wyse and Reclus's project modified, with locks	73	18	..	580	180	700	2
San Blas. Kelley's project, á niveau	58	1 sea-lock.	16	1,270	180	1,400	1
Atrato-Napipi, Selfridge's project	290	8	8	1,000	180	1,180	3

The Tehuantepec route lies in Mexican territory, running from the Bay of Vera Cruz in the Gulf of Mexico to the Gulf of Tehuantepec on the Pacific side. The isthmus through which this route runs is extremely level and low for the greater part of its breadth. The mountainous mass of the Cordillera occupies only a narrow strip on the Pacific coast. The Atlantic slope is drained by the Coatzacoalcos River, whose course is very sinuous, but which is navigable as far as Miuatitlan, having a depth of not less than 6 or 7 metres for that distance, after the bar at its mouth is passed. The Pacific slope is not more than 50 kilometres in breadth, and is drained by numerous small streams, which flow into a series of large lagoons that extend down to the coast. Both slopes are composed of alluvial soil, and are easy to excavate. The mountain mass is composed of schist and calcareous rock. At the mouth of the Coatzacoalcos there is a sandy shore on a substratum of stiff clay. Over the bar of the river there is a depth of water of 4½ metres, which does not sensibly vary in the different seasons of the year. The engineer Fuertes and Captain Shufeldt, commissioned by the United States Government, explored this route in 1871. The plan which they worked out was to make the highest level of the canal at the Pass of Tarifa, 223 metres above tide-water, where the canal could be fed from the upper course of the Coatzacoalcos with a cutting 7 metres deep in the pass, descending to the ocean on both sides by means of 130 locks divided between the two slopes. An aqueduct 43 kilometres long would be necessary to conduct the water from the upper Coatzacoalcos which is here called the Corte, to the canal, for which 5 kilometres of tunneling would be required. The canal on the Atlantic slope follows the valley of the Tarifa, then that of the Chichihua to its junction with the Coatzacoalcos, and, continuing along the right bank of this river in the mountainous region, departs from it afterward to rejoin it again north of the Island of Tacamichapa, 50 kilometres from its mouth, thence utilizing its bed down to the sea. The length of the canal would be 280 kilometres, though the distance to be executed would only be 230 kilometres. The breadth proposed was 49 metres at the surface and 18 metres at the bottom, the depth 6·6 metres. These dimensions, although not adapted to the largest ocean-going craft, were sufficient for the American coasting vessels and for nine tenths of the other ships which would use the canal. M. de Garay, who presented this scheme to the Congress, suggested that it

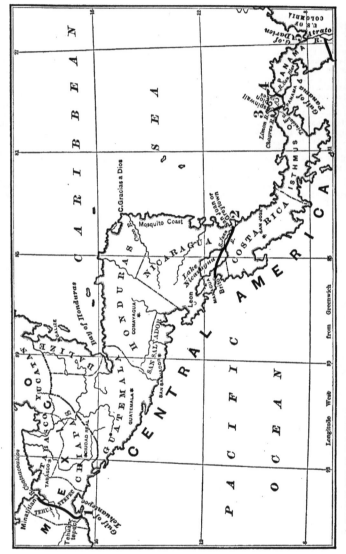

A GENERAL MAP OF THE ISTHMUS OF CENTRAL AMERICA, SHOWING THE VARIOUS PROJECTED ROUTES FOR THE INTEROCEANIC CANAL.

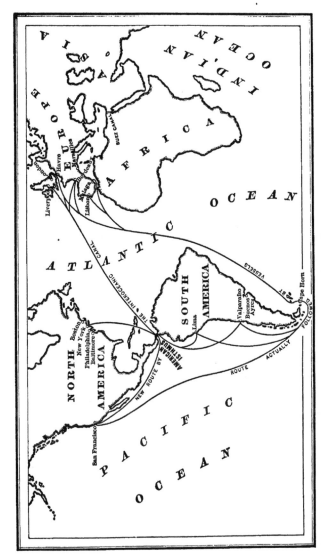

A MAP OF THE WORLD, SHOWING THE GREAT COMMERCIAL ROUTES TRIBUTARY TO THE PROPOSED CANAL.

might be modified by deepening the cut in the Pass of Tarifa, thus reducing the number of locks to 120, by carrying the canal nearly to Minatitlan before uniting it with the Coatzacoalcos, and by directing it straight across the lagoons to the sea instead of carrying it obliquely by the way of certain torrents to the Bay of Salina Cruz. The country was declared to be more healthy, and the facility and rapidity with which the canal could be constructed greater, than by way of Nicaragua or Darien. The objections to this route were not based solely on the number of locks which would be required and the length of time which the passage would take, but also on the frequency of volcanic disturbances of the soil, which would possibly necessitate extensive repairs at times in the locks, stopping for the time being all traffic.

Nicaragua, the second contraction in the long neck which connects the two Americas, was the site specially favored by the American engineers present at the Congress and by the American public for the prospective canal. This isthmus seems destined by nature for an interoceanic canal—notwithstanding that its minimum breadth, 208 kilometres, exceeds that of Tehuantepec or Darien—owing to the presence of the Lake of Nicaragua, lying in the center of a valley which extends across the isthmus from northwest to southeast, with the port of Greytown or San Juan del Norte at one end, and that of Fonseca, on the Pacific, at the other. The lake is 176 kilometres (107 miles) long and 56 kilometres (34 miles) broad. The elevation of the lake at mean high water is 32.6 metres above the sea-level; its variations of level are 1½ to 2 metres. The lake is 40 metres deep in the middle, and has a depth of 8 metres close to its western shore; but in its eastern portion the alluvial deposits of the river Frio have created shoals for a distance of 10 kilometres. The outlet of the lake is not far from the mouth of the Frio by the river San Juan, whose length in a straight line is 125 kilometres. This river down to the débouchure of the San Carlos winds in a very tortuous course between two mountain-chains, and is broken in five places by rapids. The San Carlos and the Serapiqui affluents wash down large quantities of alluvium. Its valley broadens below the mouth of the San Carlos. Its lower course is through a low plain; and its mouth is a delta with two principal branches, the San Juan proper, which discharges at Greytown, and the Rio Colorado, which empties farther south and carries off the greater part of its waters. It was not proposed to carry the canal up the valley in the northwest by way of Lake Managua to Fonseca, but to find a passage to the Pacific from the western shore through the mountains, a distance of only 16 kilometres (10 miles), by passes whose elevation hardly exceeds that of the yoke of Managua. Five different passages proposed vary from 23 to 38 kilometres in length, and

the elevation of their highest ground from 46 to 800 metres above the sea. The character of the region west of the lake is essentially volcanic, the surface rocks of trap and basalt being 15 metres thick in places. The calcareous rocks on which they rest are exposed in various places. Conglomerates which are disintegrated by the action of the air are also common. In the hollows and places of low elevation there is an alluvial deposit 12 or 15 metres in depth. The mountains which incase the San Juan River are likewise the cones of extinct craters, and their sides are covered with feldspar which glitters with iron pyrites. The harbor at Greytown was still good in 1860, but is now nearly blockaded by a bar of sand, and is only accessible through a long and winding channel. On the Pacific side the different routes terminate in harbors such as the Bay of Salinas, the port of San Juan del Sur, and the Bay of Nacascoba, which are or could easily be made accessible for vessels of the deepest draught; the Bay of Brito, at the mouth of the Rio Grande, is a little too open, but could be made into a large and quiet haven by the construction of a jetty. The climate of the elevated portions of the Nicaragua route is extremely healthy; but in the lowlands on the Atlantic side, where there is a fall of rain almost every day in the year, fevers are common and easily contracted; yet, owing to the frequent breezes from the northwest, which carry off the miasma, they are generally of a mild type. The configuration of the Isthmus of Nicaragua, like that of the Tehuantepec route, forbids the idea of a canal without locks. The plans of Lull and Menocal are the result of extensive surveys of this region in 1872 and 1873. The Lake of Nicaragua forms the natural reservoir of the canal. The surface of the lake at mean high water is 32.6 metres above the sea-level. To descend to the two oceans, 20 locks would be constructed, 10 on each side. It would follow the bed of the San Juan, on the Atlantic slope, as far as the mouth of the San Carlos, a distance of 102 kilometres, and would then be carried on the left bank of the river a distance of 70 kilometres, to terminate at Greytown. Lateral canals, dams, and locks would have to be constructed at the rapids— the lock at the Castillo rapids with a lift of 5.7 metres, others at the rapids of Balas and Machuca with lifts of 5.8 and 6.8 metres, a fourth at the head of the artificial canal with a dam extending across the river. The canal to be carried across the plain from the mouth of the San Carlos to Greytown would be partly excavated and partly banked up, the work being so calculated, and the six locks so disposed, that the excavated soil would be just sufficient for the embankments, and that the deepest cut would not be over 3 metres above the surface of the water in the canal. The descent to the Pacific from the western side of the lake offers no excessive difficulties. The engineers chose the passage by the Rivas Pass, although its elevation is 28 metres higher than the Pass of Guyscoyol. The route follows the course of the Rio del Medio to the Rio Grande. The canal leaves the lake near the mouth of the Rio del Medio, receiving the waters of this small stream at the distance from the lake of 8 kilometres. After crossing the Rivas Pass, it receives another creek, the Chicolata, beyond which the first lock is located, 17 kilometres from the lake, joins the valley of the Rio Grande at the place where it broadens, and terminates at a point near the mouth of that river. The total length of the canal would be 290 kilometres, the distance requiring artificial canalization 100 kilometres. The principal excavations to be made in the western section would be the excavation of a channel into the lake for 360 metres by blasting, and a cutting through the Rivas Pass 41 metres high above the surface of the water in its deepest spot, and averaging 8 metres for the whole distance to the first locks. In the eastern section, besides the inland canal, partly excavated and partly diked in, and the dams and locks to produce slackwater navigation in the Rio San Juan, the rocks in the rapids of Toro will have to be cleared away, and the bed of the river to be deepened by an average of 1½ metre down to those rapids, and also for 1½ kilometre above the lock at Balas; the deposits of the Frio River will also have to be dredged out to a mean depth of 2½ metres below the present bottom of the lake for 10 kilometres. The sands would have to be removed to make a harbor at Greytown, and a breakwater must be constructed at Brito. The proposed depth of the canal is a uniform one of 8 metres throughout its course; in the diked-in portions of the canal, and generally in the excavations in earth, the breadth at bottom is to be 22 metres, at the water-level 46 metres, at 3 metres above 55 metres, the banks having an incline of over 45 degrees, the increase in breadth being to the increase in elevation as 3 to 2. In the deep cuts in earth the same relative profile is preserved, but the breadth is lessened to 15·2 metres at the bottom and 37 metres at the water-line. In the rocky excavations the incline of the banks is increased to over 45 degrees, and the breadth at the bottom is diminished to 18·2 metres, that at the water-line being 27·4 and at 3 metres above 32·3 metres. The harbor at Greytown would be preserved from the deposits which are washed down by the San Juan, by damming that river and turning its course into the Colorado. A second jetty at Brito would shut off the harbor in like manner from the Rio Grande and protect it on that side. Besides the 10 locks on the Pacific side, a sea-lock would be constructed at Port Brito. The total excavations necessary would amount to 48,000,000 cubic metres of excavation in the canal, blasting on the west side of the lake and in the Toro rapids, and the rest of it dredging. The cost of the different portions of the work was estimated as

follows: For the western division, from the mouth of the Rio del Medio to the Brito harbor, $21,680,777; for subaqueous excavations in the lake, $715,658; for the eastern division, from Fort San Juan to Greytown, embracing the establishment of 63 miles of slackwater navigation in the San Carlos and the construction of 45 miles of canal, $25,020,914; for works in the harbor of Brito, $2,333,739; for harbor-works at Greytown, $2,822,630. This makes a total cost of $52,577,718, which by adding 25 per cent. for errors and contingencies is augmented to $65,722,147.

A second project for a lock-canal across Nicaragua was presented by M. Blanchet, materially different from the plan of the American engineers. Its principal feature was a scheme for preserving the level of the lake in the canal for the greater part of the length of the San Juan River, as far as the San Francisco, an affluent which joins the San Juan from the north between the mouths of the San Carlos and Sarapiqui. As in this project also it is necessary to shut out from the canal the waters of the Rio San Carlos, heavily charged with detritus, the valley of the San Juan, whose whole breadth is occupied by the canal down to this point, is dammed, and the canal is carried into a channel which runs close to the heights on the left bank, the necessary excavations furnishing the material for embankments on the southern side of the canal. Besides these cuttings, the only other labors necessary from the lake to the San Francisco will be the blasting of the rocks in the rapids of Castillo and Toro to a depth of 1½ and 6 metres respectively, which operations will enable the current to carry away the accumulations above Toro. A long wall in the lake will protect the channel from new deposits of the Frio. Two or three locks near the Rio San Francisco bring the canal down to the second level, which extends down as far as the San Juanillo branch of the delta. Here, as above, it is led along the cliffs of the left bank, and shut off from the transverse valleys on the right by embankments thrown across their mouths. The canal is lowered to the sea-level by means of four or five locks, placed at the head of the San Juanillo, and carried across to Greytown by excavations in the low flat. On the Pacific side a channel is to be made through the valley of the Lajas, by blasting 1,200 metres into the lake, and by a cut in the Guyscoyol Pass, into the valley of the Rio Grande, which is to be made into a lake, like the San Juan Valley, by a dam at La Flor; from which point the canal would descend to the sea at Brito by 7 locks. The dam at La Flor must be 400 metres long, and must support 20 metres of water. The locks are to be 200 metres each in length and 24 metres broad, able to accommodate two large ships at a time; their average lift would be 4½ metres. In order to avoid delay from a pressure of traffic or during repairs, there should be a complete double system of locks at each change of level. The summit-level of the canal would by Blanchet's plan take up 237 of the 292 kilometres of the total length of the canal, and would consist of two artificial lakes and Lake Nicaragua, with which they would be connected by two narrow channels, one at the head of the San Juan and one through the Guyscoyol Pass. These lakes, filling the valleys of the rivers, would be broad sheets on which ships could ride abreast or pass each other under full headway. The depth of 9½ metres would be maintained through the whole length of the canal. The material to be excavated is estimated at 30,000,000 cubic metres, of which it was hoped that the action of the water would remove about half. The estimated cost of this project is 362,000,000 francs.

A project submitted by M. Mainfroy proposed to excavate the canal in the clay of the left bank of the San Juan, leaving the bed of the river 12 kilometres below the lake, and descend to the sea by 6 double locks; and on the Pacific side to carry the canal through the valley of the Sapoa River, and make the terminus the Bay of Salinas.

M. Belly presented a theoretical scheme according to which the San Juan River could be restored to the navigable state in which it is reported to have been in the seventeenth century from the Caribbean Sea to the Lake of Nicaragua, by clearing away the rocks in the rapids and turning the waters of the Colorado branch into the San Juan outlet.

The American isthmus contracts in the region of Panama to its narrowest dimensions. The rocky barrier between the two oceans at the Isthmus of Panama is only 55 kilometres as the crow flies, and at the Isthmus of San Blas only 50 kilometres. The pass at Culebra, through which the Panama Railroad finds its way, is only 87 metres above the mean tide-level, the lowest pass of the whole isthmus after that of Guyscoyol. The survey of this region by Lull, with Menocal as engineer-in-chief, in 1875, commanded by the United States Government, led them to the conclusion that a tide-water canal was commercially impracticable; and they therefore confined their studies to a project of a lock-canal. The bays of Colon and Panama being settled upon as the most convenient termini, the route must necessarily cross the course of the Chagres River; and in order to avoid the dangers with which the excessive floods in that river would threaten the canal, it was decided to carry the canal across by a high aqueduct at Matachin, whose bottom would have to be 30 metres above the sea-level. The depth of 8 metres chosen for the canal would make the water-line here 38 metres above tide-water, which elevation would be the summit-level of the canal. The daily outflow through the 80 locks, 40 on each side, by which the descent to the two oceans is effected, would amount to about 950,000 cubic metres, which would be

supplied from the Chagres River by means of a dam between two rocky walls through which the river flows a few kilometres above, and conducted by the aid of a subterranean duct 4,000 metres long into a broad basin through which the canal passes. The canal would go through the Culebra Pass, crossing the divide a little to the east of the railroad, descending into the valley of the Rio Grande, and leaving it on the right to enter the harbor 400 metres to the east of the railroad quays. No streams except insignificant brooks would be allowed to discharge into the canal. The Rio Grande would have to be deflected into a new channel, and an outlet canal constructed to receive its affluents from the east. On the Pacific side 11 alignments would be necessary, with curves of not less than 1,500 metres radius; on the Atlantic slope there would have to be 28 alignments and curves, with radii as short as 760 metres. The displacement of earth necessary for the execution of this project would amount to 37,000,000 cubic metres, and the total cost to about 480,000,000 francs. In presenting this plan to the Congress, Menocal declared it decidedly less desirable than the Nicaragua project.

When, at the instigation of Ferdinand de Lesseps, the French naval officers Wyse and Reclus, accompanied by M. de Célier, engineer of the Bureau of Roads and Bridges in France, and other explorers and engineers, examined the American isthmus, it was with reference solely to cutting a canal through it at the tide-level, through which the largest ocean steamships could pass without stoppage. It was supposed at first that the most favorable line for such a canal was across the Isthmus of Darien, connecting the two large rivers, the Atrato, which flows into the Caribbean, and the Tuyra, which discharges into the Pacific, and running between the parallel and separate mountain-chains of the Andes and the Cordilleras. A thorough examination of this region revealed the impossibility of digging a tide-level canal here. The same engineers undertook a second expedition at the solicitation of De Lesseps, and under the auspices of the Society of Exploration, constituted with General Türr as its president, and this time located a route for a tide-water canal across the Isthmus of Panama, in nearly the same line as that followed by the Panama Railroad. Satisfied by their survey that the piercing of the American isthmus by a tide-level canal which would accommodate the higher marine, the great iron steamships whose keels are 140 metres long and whose tonnage ranges up to 5,000 tons, is technically feasible, De Lesseps invited, in concert with Henri Bionne, of the Geographical Society, delegations from the different chambers of commerce and societies of engineers and statistics to meet in a Congress to discuss the question of an American canal. The Wyse and Reclus project was the one adopted by the Congress. The object of the

French explorers was essentially different from that of the various American surveys. Having in view the development of the higher transmarine commerce in enormous iron vessels, rather than the commercial profitableness of the canal itself, and being unwilling to depart from the model of the Suez Canal, they were not dismayed at a prospective cost entirely disproportionate to any immediate commercial needs. The material interests of the American public, on the other hand, seemed more identified with the construction of a canal which would be more hopeful as a commercial venture, and promised to return the usual profits to investors, and which would accommodate the smaller classes of vessels which now form the bulk of their marine.

The Wyse-Reclus route runs from the Bay of Limon, with its terminus at the town of Colon or Aspinwall, to the Gulf of Panama. The canal starts from the natural harbor at Aspinwall, at a point where its depth is 8½ metres, crosses the marsh of Mindi, and attains the Chagres after two alignments in the vicinity of Gatun. It keeps close to the river, crossing its bed in several places, as far as Matachin, changing its direction seven times in the interval, and crossing the line of the railroad at Barbacoas, where a swing-bridge will have to be constructed. Beyond Matachin the canal occupies the valley of the Obispo, which descends from the pass of Culebra, at a point where the ground is 40 metres above the mean tide-level. From this point it is necessary to cut a tunnel 7,700 metres in length through the mountain. The canal emerges at a point where the ground has the same elevation as at the entrance to the tunnel; and, occupying the valley of the Rio Grande, after three more curves it terminates in the Gulf of Panama next to the islands of Naos and Flamenco, at a spot where the depth is 7·3 metres at the lowest tides. The line has a total length of 75 kilometres. The curves, 13 in number, are none of them of a shorter radius than 3,000 metres. It borrows the course of the streams throughout its entire length, and would receive the whole of the drainage of the two valleys which it follows. Where it encounters the Chagres at Matachin, a cataract of 15 metres fall would necessitate a lateral cutting to conduct the river into it by a longer course; and similar labors would have to be performed in other places to protect it from streams which become formidable torrents in the rainy season. The depth of the canal is 8·5 metres below the mean tide at its terminus in the Bay of Limon, and by an incline which is distributed over the entire line it is lowered about 2 metres, or to 10·55 metres below the mean tide-mark, at its Pacific terminus, in order to have at that point a depth at the lowest neap-tide of 7·3 metres. The width at bottom is 20 metres throughout its course, and in the harbors this is gradually widened to 100 metres just before the points where the natural depth

is sufficient. The incline of the banks is 1 in 2 in the submerged portions at the termini; 8½ in 15 in the alluvial soil on the Atlantic side, which extends about 20 kilometres; and in the earthy portion on the Pacific side, about 10 kilometres in extent, 10 in 15; and in the rocky portions which occupy the whole central part of the route, 6¼ of elevation to 3 of base, which sharper incline leaves the width of the surface at mean tide-level only 32 metres. In the tunnel the width at water-line is further reduced to 24 metres at mean tide, and the incline of the sides is increased to 2 of lateral extension to 9¼ or 10 of elevation. Above the water the cross-section profile of the tunnel has the form of a Gothic arch terminating in an arc with a radius of 4 metres, whose summit is 34 metres above the mean tide-level. The cross-section of the tunnel, above and below the surface of the water, is an average area of 780 square metres. These dimensions do not permit vessels to cross each other while under way. At distances averaging 9 kilometres there will be stations where the width is expanded, in which vessels going in one direction will wait while those going in the opposite direction pass by. The flow of the water in the canal, it was calculated, would not exceed 1·7 metre per second. The rise of level in the tunnel during the period of freshets would never, it was hoped, be greater than 6 metres. To avoid the danger of a sudden rush of water into the canal after a rain-storm, it was proposed to build dams at different points in the upper valley of the Chagres, where the rocky banks approach each other, by which the waters would be retained in large natural reservoirs, and the discharge of the river in times of flood be reduced to the maximum of 200 or 300 metres a second. The Bay of Limon, which would serve as the port on the Atlantic side, is generally calm, being protected from the northeasterly winds, which blow with considerable violence in the dry season, by the island of Manzanillo: for the sake of additional security a sea-wall was proposed in the project, which would have a length of 850 metres. The entrance channel on the Pacific side, where stormy weather is of rare occurrence, would be sufficiently protected by walls on each side constructed from the rock excavated in the cuttings.

The plan for executing the work was to commence by leveling the line on the Pacific side down to the mean level of the Chagres and the Rio Grande, and to excavate the tunnel down to 10 or 12 metres above the final level; then to turn the Chagres into this new channel, and make it empty into the Pacific while its old bed is being lowered to the required level of the canal; and then, after the Atlantic division has been completed, to make it again the channel of the Chagres, and complete the excavations in the tunnel and on the Pacific side. In this way all would be dry excavation above the tide-level, and no blasting under water would be necessary. The excavation of the earthy portions near the shore on both sides can be easily accomplished by dredging. The total material to be excavated was estimated at 47,000,000 cubic metres, of which 28,000,000 metres would be rock excavation, including 6,000,000 metres in the tunnel. The total expense was calculated by the projectors at 475,000,000 francs. Messrs. Wyse and Reclus presented alternative plans by which the tunnel could be shortened, or even done without, but only by considerably increasing the quantity of material to be excavated. To avoid having a tunnel, it would be necessary to make a cutting 87 metres deep in the pass of Culebra.

A project for a canal with locks was worked out by the same engineers during the sittings of the Congress, and was favored by some of the members on account of the difficulties, climatic as well as financial, which they thought would attend the execution of a tide-level canal. This modified scheme was similar in character to Blanchet's project for a Nicaragua canal. It was proposed to construct a dam at a spot in the course of the Chagres where it passes through a ravine, and one at a similar spot in the valley of the Rio Grande, thus creating two lakes, which could be connected by a cutting 72 metres deep at the deepest place. These lakes would extend to within 22 kilometres of Colon and 12 kilometres of Panama, and would be broad enough for ships to pass each other anywhere without stoppage, and deep enough to give 10 metres of natural depth at all points. Their plane would be 24 metres above the sea, which would be reached by a series of 5 locks on each side. The excavations would amount to only 12,000,000 cubic metres; the total expense was estimated at 428,000,000 francs.

The San Blas route was first explored by MacDougal in 1864 at the private cost of Mr. Kelley of Philadelphia, and subsequently by Selfridge. Wyse and Reclus also examined the Isthmus of San Blas, and especially the Pacific watershed. The indentation in the northern coast formed by the magnificent Bay of San Blas makes this the narrowest portion of the Panama Isthmus, only 30 kilometres broad. The water-parting here is near the Atlantic coast, instead of close to the Pacific as at Nicaragua and Panama. The height of the Cordilleras and the disposition of the water-courses in this region preclude the notion of a tide-level canal. The canal by this route, according to the surveys of Wyse and Reclus, would have a total length of 53 kilometres; but the excavations would only extend over 40 kilometres, of which 16 kilometres would have to be traversed in a tunnel. The excavations would amount to 34,000,000 cubic metres; the estimated cost is 475,000,000 francs. The surveys instituted by Kelley make the length of the tunnel only 12 kilometres.

The examination of the portion of the Isthmus of Darien where the sources of the Tuyra and the Atrato Rivers are not far apart, by Wyse and Célier, led to the elaboration by the latter of a scheme for a canal with locks, whose summit-level would be 50 metres above the sea. It would be necessary to cut a passage between the valley of the Coquirri, which the canal would follow down to the Atrato, and the valley of the Cué, which it would occupy down to the Tuyra, through a pass whose elevation is 146 metres above the sea. To reduce the excavations in this pass, a tunnel 1 kilometre in length would be bored. The descent to the ocean-level would be made by 10 locks on the Atlantic side and 10 on the Pacific side. The length of the line would be 220 kilometres, but the excavations would extend over only 100 kilometres. The excavations would amount to 65,000,000 cubic metres. The total cost was estimated at 650,000,000 francs.

A project for a canal without locks across the Isthmus of Darien, from the Gulf of Acanti to the Tuyra, was sketched by Wyse and Reclus. The most favorable route which they could find for a tide-level canal was by way of the valley of the Tupisa, an affluent of the Tuyra, and its arm the Tiati; but it would be necessary to cross the Cordillera where the elevation is 1,000 metres, by a tunnel about 17 kilometres in length. The excavations necessary for such a canal would amount to 70,-000,000 cubic metres. The estimate of the cost is 600,000,000 francs.

Another project for a canal à niveau was presented by M. de Puydt, who stated that he had found a passage in the Cordillera, whose greatest elevation was only 46 metres, between the Tuyra and Porto Escondido.

The Atrato-Napipi route, which has been very thoroughly explored by Selfridge and Collins, follows up the Atrato River, which always has a depth of at least 7·8 metres, for 240 kilometres, to the mouth of the Napipi affluent. The canal proper commences here. The distance from the mouth of the Napipi to the Bay of Chiri-Chiri is only 45 kilometres in a straight line. The direction of the route is nearly east and west. The highest point is at an elevation of 233 metres, and is found about 2 kilometres from the shore of the Pacific. Two projects for a canal by this route were submitted by Commander Selfridge, one for a canal with 22 locks, and one, for a tide-level canal, with a double lock at the Pacific entrance. In the former the summit-level would have an elevation above the sea of 42·7 metres. The descent from the highest level, situated at the confluence of the Doguado and the Napipi, about 30 kilometres above the junction of the latter with the Atrato, would be effected by means of 12 locks through 7 levels, one of the lifts requiring a series of 4 locks. The total lift of the 12 locks from the Atrato at low water would be 37 metres. The total descent on the Pacific side is made by means of a connected series of 10 locks. The summit-level would have a length of 16·5 kilometres, of which 5·5 kilometres would be in tunnel.

The second plan, which was more seriously proposed and warmly advocated by the projector, was for a tide-level canal by nearly the same route. The level of the canal would be lowered to that of the Atrato. Above the Doguado the canal would pass under the Napipi in a tunnel, which must be 30 metres high, and which would necessitate a change in the route, which must pass farther up the valley of the Napipi. From the Atrato, for 9 kilometres up the valley of the Napipi, the excavations can be done with dredges. The project proposes a constant free connection with the Atrato, but a lock may be necessary for security in time of high water. The depth of the cutting increases gradually from the 9th to the 37th kilometre, to 50 metres; at the 37th kilometre the tunnel, 9 kilometres in length, commences; at the end of the tunnel will be a basin and two locks to bring the vessels down to the level of the ocean, which in the Bay of Chiri-Chiri is at mean tide 5·7 metres below the level of the canal; the variations of the tide are 1·8 metre above and below the mean tide-level. The length of the tunnel can be reduced to 5,600 or even to 4,000 metres, by making the cuts on each side more than 50 metres deep. The mouth of the Atrato chosen for the Atlantic outlet of the canal is that arm of the delta called the Uraba mouth. A bar must be cut through for about 1,000 metres, and the passage lined with walls of masonry. In the Bay of Chiri-Chiri the port will be protected by two jetties. The expense of the canal is estimated at 491,000,000 francs.

IOWA. The election for township officers in this State takes place in April. The question which was extensively agitated was the prohibition of licenses for the sale of liquors. There was cast a considerable vote on the question by women. In Des Moines central precinct they cast 480 votes, of which 477 were for prohibition. In almost every town where a prohibition ticket was nominated it was defeated.

A petition was addressed to the United States Secretary of War by Mrs. Elizabeth Upright, of Butler County, requesting the discharge of her eleventh son from the army. The Secretary, under date of February 11th, replied as follows:

The discharge of this soldier is asked by the petitioner, who says she is seventy-two years old, on the ground that she had ten sons in the Union army during the rebellion, including one employed as a teamster, and that the one above named, her eleventh and youngest son, has served for over five years in the regular army. She furnishes the names of her sons and a statement of the organizations in which they served.

The papers having been referred to the Adjutant-General for an examination of the records with a view to verifying her statements, that officer reports that they are true in every particular.

1. G. W. Merchant was a private in Company C, Seventy-fourth Illinois Volunteers, afterward a lieu-

tenant, and was honorably discharged September 26, 1865.

2. Abel L. Merchant was a private in Company C, Fifteenth Illinois Volunteers, and died in service.

3. De Witt C. Merchant was a private in the last-named company, and was killed in action July 22, 1864.

4. Enoch Merchant was corporal in Company F, One Hundred and Fifty-Sixth Illinois Volunteers, and honorably discharged September 20, 1865.

5. David O. Merchant was a private in Company C, Seventy-fourth Illinois Volunteers, and honorably discharged June 10, 1865.

6. Silas B. Merchant was a private in Company C, Forty-fourth Illinois Volunteers, promoted to first lieutenant, and resigned September 25, 1864.

7. Ario J. Merchant was a private in the last-named company, and honorably discharged September 25, 1865.

8. Lewis A. Merchant was a private in Company G, Forty-fifth Illinois Volunteers, and honorably discharged September 26, 1864.

9. Aaron Merchant was a private in Company G, Fifteenth Wisconsin Volunteers, and was killed at Island No. 10, December 26, 1862, by the accidental discharge of a cannon.

10. James B. Merchant, teamster, in the employ of the Quartermaster's Department.

11. Thomas M. Merchant enlisted March 3, 1873, as a private in Company B, Sixth United States Cavalry (regulars), and was discharged March 11, 1878, by reason of expiration of term of service. He again enlisted May 4, 1878, and was assigned to Battery B, Fourth Artillery, and is now in the service. The discharge of this soldier will be ordered in accordance with his mother's request. Discharges from the army as a matter of favor are not granted except in extraordinary cases, but this is, in my opinion, such a case. Indeed, I doubt whether another like it can be found upon record. But if another mother can be found who gave ten sons to the service of our country during the war, she may confidently ask, and expect to receive, similar favorable consideration. I have the honor to remain, very respectfully, your obedient servant,

GEORGE W. McCRARY,
Secretary of War.

The result of the operation of the law to secure the planting of trees throughout the State, by allowing a certain sum to be deducted from the tax for the number of trees planted by each person, has been most successful. The amount of property returned by the assessors for the years 1879 and 1880, and thus made exempt for five or ten years, was $5,949,730.

The State assessment is two mills on the dollar, or two fifths of one per cent., and thus the annual cost of the tree-planting law to the State in the loss of taxes is $11,899. The entire amount of tax-levy, including State and county, averages about three per cent., and thus those who have taken advantage of the law saved just about $178,492 per annum in taxes.

The following statement shows the amount of live stock assessed in the State for the year 1878; cattle, horses and mules under one year, and swine under six months, are not included in the assessment: Cattle, 1,530,056; horses, 672,808; mules, 42,566; sheep, 301,743; swine, 2,324,116. The average assessment of animals varies greatly; cattle in some counties are valued at $8, while in others they run all the way along to $14 and $15; hogs and sheep are valued at from 50 cents to $2 and $3; horses from $20 to $40, just as the estimates of the different assessors varied.

The following shows the equalized valuation of the cities of Iowa for 1879, as determined by the State Board of Equalization: Burlington, $2,661,171; Cedar Rapids, $1,417,239; Clinton, $1,111,848; Council Bluffs, $1,527,-636; Davenport, $2,819,970; Des Moines, $3,242,203; Dubuque, $3,886,634; Iowa City, $1,118,769; Keokuk, $2,046,582; Marshalltown, $1,039,532; Muscatine, $970,408; Oskaloosa, $581,029; Ottumwa, $1,385,485; Sioux City, $628,405; Waterloo, $781,401. The number of acres of land assessed in 1879 was 34,-570,638. The value of these lands and the town lots, as equalized by the State Board of Equalization, was $303,715,646. The equalized total value, including personalty and railroad property, was $405,763,581. The assessment of property for taxes was the subject of considerable discussion in the State. The law requires the assessment to be made on the cash values, and many believed that all the inequality arose from a disregard of the law, and that the taxes of individuals would be less if it was strictly obeyed. The State Auditor in a letter on the subject expresses these views:

I am clearly of opinion that if we could have a just valuation of all the property of the State, and a consequent reduction in the rate of levies, the disposition to concealment of property would practically disappear, and the great majority of taxpayers have a less amount of taxes to pay than has hitherto been experienced.

It should be understood, and we have a right to expect, that upon a just assessment the rate of tax must be lessened, and I apprehend that in most cases the officers who determine our tax-levies would have regard to this fact, and by proper reductions do their whole duty to the people, whose representatives they are. We know that taxation is often heavy, but we also know that those taxes are heaviest which we individually and voluntarily vote upon ourselves, and we fully realize their necessity. Therefore, ceasing to inveigh against taxes and taxation which we know are an absolute necessity in our government, we should endeavor to have the law so administered that every species of property shall contribute its rightful and proportionate share. The law declares that property shall be assessed at its "true cash value." It is not always easy to ascertain with exact precision this value, but the assessor must exercise his best judgment, based upon all the information he is able to obtain. But it is quite as easy to determine what is cash value as to fix upon third or half value, or even a less proportion, as is frequently done.

The Board of Supervisors of Jefferson County, who are likewise a County Board of Equalization, prepared tables of the classification of property for the use of the local assessors, and addressed a circular to them, saying:

Inasmuch as the laws of the State require all property to be assessed at its true cash value, and the arbitrary departure from that standard or basis of taxation in different portions of the State, according to the whims of each particular locality, causes the grossest inequality and injustice in the distribution of the taxation, the Auditor of State is endeavoring to secure the assessment of all property at one common value—the true one. Upon you is placed the original and entire right and duty to adjust, level up, increase, diminish, and equalize the valuations of your townships;

and you are expected to see that all property pays its share, and its share only, of the burden of taxation.

Land should be classed in the class which fixes its true value; moneys and credits may be valued at par or less, as may be judged their cash market value. The Board has no power over this matter, and it is to be desired that you assume the responsibility of seeing that the township values are justly proportioned and brought to a cash value.

The Board further call your attention to the fact that no fears need be entertained that an increase of valuation of individual property will, in the end, perceptibly increase the aggregate taxation. It will not. The estimated amount of taxation to carry on the machinery of State government and to meet the appropriations of the Legislature has been made and distributed to the counties, and the levy will meet it.

Who shall regulate the rates of railroad freights was shown by the action of the State Board of Railroad Commissioners. In the latter months of 1878 three of the principal lines crossing the State advanced their rates on coal transportation variably from 5 to 25 per cent. Immediate complaints were addressed by the shippers to the Commissioners, who at once instituted an inquiry into them. Finding them supported by the new tariff tables, they addressed the companies, requiring them to forward copies of the schedules for examination. On their receipt they were scrutinized and compared, and it was found that an equal advance had been made by all three of the companies. The Commissioners then addressed a letter to the companies, setting forth that complaints were made, and protesting against the increase. The companies were asked to modify their increased tariff unless they could show good cause for refusal. Correspondence took place between the Board and companies which resulted in an agreed conference. This meeting was held on the 26th of March, and the presidents, general managers, or general superintendents, together with the general freight agents of the railway companies, were present. The entire subject was elaborately discussed, and the result was a modified tariff which went into effect on all three of the roads in April. A table of the modifications showed considerable reduction of the rates on merchandise, a reduction on grain, still more on stock, while the reduction on flour and meal, salt, lime and stucco, and coal was very marked and lower than the Granger-law rates. The rates on coal were the same as those of the Granger act; those on lumber were but slightly higher. There is also a new class created, with a very low rate, for which the Granger law made no provision. The readjustment of classification and the addition of the new class bring the reductions down to an average approximating to the charges of the Granger law. For long hauls in the State less than Granger rates are charged; and as the through or inter-State rates have been from time to time reduced since the enactment of the law of 1874, it is evident that the new tariff is a close approximation in the average to the repealed Granger rates. It was estimated that the reduction which the Commissioners had succeeded in accomplishing would save to the producers and shippers of the State hundreds of thousands of dollars annually.

The railroads of the State are assessed by the Executive Council. Their aggregate assessed value for the year 1879 amounted to $22,540,904. This is nearly a million dollars above the assessment of 1878. The amount of the tax to be paid by them is nearly $150 per mile.

The capital stock of the railroads in Iowa amounts to $90,612,451, being an increase of one million and three quarters since last year. The aggregate debt of all the railroads in the State is estimated at $70,243,795, an increase of over three millions. Altogether fifteen roads have increased their indebtedness, while six have reduced. The stock and debt aggregate $160,856,246, or $36,612 per mile. The entire earnings of the roads for the year are:

Passengers, mail, and express........	$5,335,177 36
Freight and miscellaneous............	16,005,583 08
Total, year ending June 30, 1879.	$21,840,700 44
Total last year..................	20,714,496 07
Increase of present year.........	$626,213 37

The total operating expenses as returned are $12,904,420, leaving $8,436,288.52 to represent the net earnings, an increase over last year of $287,742.78. The lines which charge the lowest average rates earn the most money, owing to the large business done. The railroads of the State paid last year in taxes $584,169.79, or 11 per cent. of their net earnings after deducting operating expenses, interest, and taxes. Of the roads in the State 3,399 miles are owned by the companies operating them; 997 miles are leased by foreign corporations. There are 1,219 miles of steel rail in the State, or 27½ per cent. of the whole trackage. There are 743 stations, or one to every six miles of road. The total number of locomotives in use is 1,036, of which 660 weigh 30 tons and upward each. There are 578 passenger cars, 275 express and baggage cars, 17,940 box freight cars, 2,512 stock cars, 7,693 platform cars, 561 cabooses, and 1,682 other cars—31,584 in all. Besides these a large number of fast freight-line cars are in use in the busier seasons, and at these times the roads are frequently unable to supply all the cars that are needed. The report shows the classification of tonnage, the total being 8,650,881, and the percentage as follows: Grain, 31 per cent.; flour, 4 per cent.; provisions, 3 per cent.; animals, 10 per cent.; other agricultural products, 1 per cent.; lumber and forest products, 15 per cent.; coal, 11 per cent; salt, lime, and plaster, 1 per cent.; iron and steel, 3 per cent.; stone and brick, 3 per cent.;

manufactures, 2 per cent.; merchandise, etc., 16 per cent.

At the biennial session of the Legislature in 1877 a law was passed creating a Board of Railroad Commissioners. In their report the Commissioners thus describe the operation of the law:

Before this system was enacted suits at law were the sole remedy for unjust charges upon shippers. These suits, conducted at vast expense in the aggregate, were the source alike of exasperating delays and serious annoyance to both complainants and defendants. Oftener than otherwise these suits were contested through all the grades of our courts, and when at last the end was reached, it was an end of each several case only, others of like character and involving like principles following upon its heels. It might be an interesting, as it certainly would be a startling exhibit, could the aggregate annual expenditure from both public treasury and private purse, on account of these suits, be spread before the public. To the Commissioners any and all persons aggrieved apply for redress, no matter how small the amount involved, confident of prompt hearing and without expense to themselves. The Commissioners are simply a court of arbitration, its expenses being borne by assessments upon the railroads. Not one suit at law, arising from alleged unjust or discriminative charges, so far as the Commissioners have knowledge, has been prosecuted against any railroad company in Iowa since the Commissioner system was adopted. All grievances of this character have been referred to this Board, and by it investigated and adjudged, the result in every case, with perhaps a single exception, being accepted as final. Moreover, the Commissioners are not aware of an instance where any railroad company has persisted in charges that have been complained of after such rates have been held to be unjust or discriminative by the Board. . . . It seems to vastly simplify the relations between the railroads and the public, and to cheapen the cost of adjusting whatever differences or grievances may from time to time be complained of.

In a case brought to recover damages for injury to a valuable cow while in transportation, caused by the collision of a car in switching it, the Burlington Railroad denied any negligence on their part, and showed that in the contract of shipment it was stipulated that they "were released from all liability above the value of common stock." They also pleaded that it was the universal custom of defendant, as well as all other roads, to receive fancy or blooded stock only on these conditions; that such practice was general and uniform, and well known to stock-shippers generally. They also pleaded that the plaintiff was guilty of negligence in shipping a cow in the condition of that one. The Judges in Johnson County held that the release in the shipping contract was void, as against public policy. As to the second ground of defense, the Court ruled that it was the duty of the company to receive and ship blooded as well as other stock, and that no custom could be shown authorizing the making of any contract which would exempt common carriers from liability for gross negligence. It was urged with much earnestness that the defendant was not a common carrier of blooded or fancy stock, though it was of common stock; but the Court held otherwise. The Judge instructed the jury that the measure of damages was the difference between the value of the cow immediately before and immediately after the injury; and they were to take into consideration the enhanced value of such a cow with calf, as well as the blood of the cow.

In a case decided by the Supreme Court in June, raised notes were declared a forgery, and therefore the maker was released from liability. The State has for some years been overrun with agents and peddlers of every kind, who would get a note from a farmer for a small sum, raise it a hundred dollars, sell it to a bank, and the farmer would be obliged to pay it. The lower courts held that there were no defenses of fraud as between the innocent purchaser of a fraudulent note and the maker; and in several cases it was held that where the maker of a note left the blanks unfilled, so that it could be raised by writing in a larger amount, it was negligence of the maker, whereby the fraud was permitted to be made, and he could not take advantage of his own laches. Usually the decision of the lower courts was sufficient, and the maker paid the note rather than contest it further. In one county alone $20,000 was paid over last year by the victims on the advice of their own lawyers. In the case above referred to, the Knoxville National Bank vs. John Clark, appellant, the appellant gave a note for ten dollars, leaving the blank uncanceled, and the name of the bank at which it was payable entirely blank, because the person to whom he gave it said an agent would be around to collect it when due. The payee then wrote in "one hundred dollars" before the "ten," and inserted "Knoxville National Bank, Knoxville, Iowa," in the blank, and sold it to that bank. Several other like notes were also sold. When due, the bank brought an action to recover, and under the general rule of negotiable paper the lower Court gave judgment for the bank. The Supreme Court, however, reversed the decision, holding that the case did not come within the rule that where the blanks are left unfilled in a note the presumption of law is that the payee has authority to fill the blanks, and if he exceeds the amount agreed upon with the maker, it is simply a breach of trust, and does not release the maker from liability. In the case at bar, the alteration of the amount was a forgery, and the law would not make a person civilly liable for the criminal acts of another, or perform a contract he did not make.

In a case for "civil damages," Mary J. Loan vs. Peter Hiney, the Supreme Court held that in an action at law for damages against the person who has caused the intoxication, the plaintiff may, if he chooses, join the property-owner by proper averments, and pray for a decree for a lien; and if a judgment for damages shall be rendered, the Court may transfer the action as to lien to the equity docket.

The criminal returns for the State, compiled by the Secretary of State, show that in 1878 there were 1,491 convictions, on which the aggregate imprisonment adjudged was 728 years

in the penitentiary and 17 in the county jail. Of the 1,491 persons sentenced, 1,304 could read and write, 37 could not, and the educational advancements of 142 were unknown; 690 of them were native-born citizens of the United States, 597 were foreign-born, and the nativity of the remainder was unknown; 440 were classed as "moral," 754 as "immoral," and 289 as "unknown." The total amount of fines unpaid was $52,966.68; fines collected, $24,839.97. The total cost of criminal prosecutions was $325,933.48. The cost to the counties of the State for criminal prosecutions during the last four years has been as follows: in 1874, $188,846.38; in 1875, $180,890.03; in 1876, $235,187.42; in 1877, $318,322.70; in 1878, $303,668.13; in 1879, $401,659.39. The District Attorneys' fees in 1874 were $18,-368.19; in 1875, $18,890.03; in 1876, $22,-071.87; in 1877, $25,996.70; in 1878, $23,260.-35; in 1879, $24,891.73. Total cost, $1,762,-052.92, being nearly $1,000 per day for each working day. The Governor, in the discussion of this subject, thus alludes to grand juries: "The judiciary of the State are, almost without exception, of the opinion that it is desirable to do away with the grand jury system. This can only be done by amendment to the Constitution. The number of the grand jury is now fixed at fifteen, costing the counties thirty dollars per day during its session. Could not the work of this jury be as well done if it were reduced to five? This would save twenty dollars a day and the mileage of ten jurors to the respective counties during the time of session."

The lawlessness of tramps in the State during the last two years has been so great that the Governor determined to prevent it. As the time approached for their appearance, he issued orders to the military clearly defining their duties when called upon, and also the following to the sheriffs of counties:

The season of the year is approaching in which, judging from the experience of the past few years, it may be expected the State will be visited by numbers of lawless characters commonly called "tramps." It is believed that by prompt and efficient measures taken early, much of the evil arising from this cause may be averted. You are therefore required to use all due diligence in arresting tramps and vagrants, and bringing them before the proper authorities to be dealt with according to Chapter 69 of the acts of the Sixteenth General Assembly. If they visit your county in bands, as they have heretofore many of the counties of the State, and commit depredations either on the property of private citizens, or by taking possession of railway trains, you will use all the power vested in you by the laws of the State for the dispersion of such riotous gatherings, and the apprehension of the individuals concerned therein.

Chapter 6, Title XXV. of the Code, to which chapter your attention is specially invited, empowers you, whenever necessary, to summon a posse to aid you, and also to call out any military company in the county, to whom will be given instructions promptly to respond to any call made on them by the civil authorities.

The time for the election of members of Congress has been a subject of dispute in the

State. In 1878 it was ordered by the Governor to be held in October. (See "Annual Cyclopædia" for 1878, page 453.) It was claimed that this election was invalid, and another was held in November. At this second election the Republicans refused to run any candidates, relying upon the October election. The Democratic candidates were accordingly voted for without opposition, and at the commencement of the Congressional session they appeared and claimed their seats. The subject was referred to the Committee on Elections, which became divided and presented three reports. Eleven members of the Committee—Messrs. Manning of Mississippi, Armfield of North Carolina, Beltzhoover of Pennsylvania, Sawyer of Missouri, Phister of Kentucky, Keifer of Ohio, Camp of New York, Calkins of Indiana, Field of Massachusetts, Overton of Pennsylvania, and Weaver of Iowa—agreed that the law having been construed by the State authorities to require the holding of the Congressional election in October, that election should be considered legal, and the present incumbents—Messrs. Sapp and Carpenter, from the Eighth and Ninth Districts respectively—retained in their seats. Representative Springer of Illinois, Chairman of the Committee, in an elaborate and extended opinion, took the ground that, as the State laws of Iowa did not prescribe places for holding elections in November, and as Congress has prescribed that to be the legal month, and that elections held at any other time "shall be void," hence neither of the Iowa elections was held according to law, and should both be declared illegal. Representative Calkins of Indiana contended that the Iowa election held in November was the legal election, that the October election was contrary to the requirements of law, and that the contestants who were elected in November were entitled to their seats in the House. These several views were submitted to the House of Representatives, which permitted Messrs. Sapp and Carpenter to retain their seats.

The receipts and expenditures of the State for the biennial period, embracing general revenue, temporary school fund, swamp-land indemnity fund, agricultural college endowment, and miscellaneous in gross from these sources, amounted to $2,260,360.61, which, with the balance of $73,737.39 on hand September 30, 1877, makes a total of $2,334,098. The disbursements for all purposes for the biennial period have been $2,259,910.63, leaving balance in the hands of the State Treasurer of $74,187.37. Of the balance on hand, $2,226.65 belongs to the permanent school fund, $217.85 to the coupon fund, and the remainder, $71,742 87, is in interest-bearing bonds, being trust funds held by the State for the benefit of the Agricultural College. The amount of warrants outstanding on September 30, 1877, was $267,776.31, and on September 30, 1879, only $96,993.54, being a decrease of $170,782.77. Since the close of the fiscal term, the amount

of outstanding warrants has increased until, on January 5, 1880, it reached $130,361.42. Two years ago, at the same date, it was $340,826.56; decrease in the two years, $210,465.14. The State funds in the hands of the respective county treasurers of the State on September 30, 1879, amounted to $116,817.09, more than sufficient, when paid in, to meet the outstanding warrants at that date.

The debt of the State is $545,435.19. Of this amount, $245,435.19 is due to the permanent school fund, part of it being made irredeemable by article seven, section three, of the Constitution. The remaining debt, $300,000, was created under the acts of the special war session of the Eighth General Assembly in 1861, for purposes of war and defense. This debt matures July 1, 1881.

The number of persons between the ages of five and twenty-one in the State by the last returns is placed at 577,353; the number enrolled is 431,317; and the number attending school is 264,702, showing that a large percentage does not attend school. Of this percentage a small number should be deducted for attendance in private schools. The financial part of the school system is in some disorder. It appears that there are 4,279 treasurers of school districts in the State, who have in their hands the sum of $2,672,304.49. These treasurers received as compensation during the past year the sum of $48,834, and are delinquent to the school fund for the year 1879 in the sum of $45,652.49; and the startling fact is shown that the deficiencies and defalcations of this class of officers from 1873 to 1879, inclusive, aggregate the enormous sum of $491,518.51. Of this large amount of money in the hands of school treasurers, $1,770,213 belongs to the teachers' fund.

The receipts of the State University from all sources for general and specific purposes, up to June 15, 1879, have been $125,126.36, of which there has been expended $121,511.58, leaving balance in the hands of the treasurer of the University of $3,614.78. The University is in a flourishing condition. The collegiate and professional departments have already increased to a degree that about compensates for the loss of students occasioned by abolishing the preparatory classes.

The number of pupils in the Normal School is large and constantly increasing. The receipts of the institution were $14,626, and the expenditures $14,453.

The Agricultural College of the State is quite flourishing, and rapidly outgrowing its accommodations. The departments of botany and zoölogy are steadily advancing. A creamery is under construction to supply the college boarding-hall with butter. The course in domestic economy has been considerably enlarged. This College is said to be the only institution in the West which endeavors practically to teach the household arts. A small kitchen was opened two years ago, wherein the girls of the junior class were taught plain cooking. Its success has demonstrated so clearly the practicability of making this branch of domestic economy a part of the college curriculum, that the trustees have been encouraged to take another step forward in developing the department. During 1879 the course was to be extended from one term to the entire year. The girls of the sophomore class were to be taught during the first term to wash, iron, and sew, including the cutting and fitting of dresses, etc., and the juniors were to go into the kitchen to cook the second term. This improvement was received with much satisfaction. The receipts of the College for the biennial period, including the sales of lands, the proceeds of which have been paid into the State Treasury, have been $133,533.81. The disbursements have been $127,768.42, and the balance on hand of all funds is $5,765.39. The Seventeenth General Assembly appropriated for laboratory and sewer $3,972.25, which has been drawn and expended. The United States donated to the State 204,206 acres of public domain for its foundation. Of these lands, 30,962 acres have been sold, and the proceeds thereof, amounting to $71,742.87, have been paid into the State Treasury. Of the remainder, 147,735 acres are under lease, and 25,580 acres are unleased. The College has in addition 15,013 acres of land, which were purchased in 1868 with surplus interest funds at a cost of $15,000, of which 12,213 acres are leased, and 1,200 are unleased, the remainder having been sold. The purchase of this land has been a most advantageous one, the College having already received over $22,000 in interest, and the remaining lands are constantly increasing in value.

The following are the general statistics of the schools:

DETAILS.	1878.	1879.
Township districts...................	1,119	1,140
Independent districts...............	8,117	8,189
Sub-districts......................	7,266	7,548
Ungraded schools...................	10,218	10,457
Rooms in graded schools...........	2,008	2,083
Average duration in months........	7·81	7·85
Number of teachers employed, male	7,561	7,578
Number of teachers employed, female......	18,023	18,579
Average monthly compensation, males......................	$33 98	$31 71
Average monthly compensation, females......................	$27 84	$26 40
Pupils between the ages of 5 and 21 years....................	575,474	577,858
Enrollment in public schools......	428,363	431,317
Total average attendance..........	256,913	264,702
Frame school-houses..............	9,506	9,783
Brick "	650	684
Stone "	244	250
Log "	76	72
Value..................	$9,161,101	$9,066,145
Value of apparatus..............	$178,841	$170,468
Number of volumes in library.....	20,587	22,581

The grand total of the school fund reaches the sum of $3,484,411.18, all of which, save the sum of $8,561.65, is interest-bearing. The amount held in the counties, subject to loan, is $3,221,402.93, having been increased within

the two years. The interest upon this sum at 8 per cent. is semi-annually apportioned to all the school districts in the State, in proportion to the number of persons therein between the ages of five and twenty-one years, and during the fiscal term of 1877–'79 amounted to $560,-281.88, inclusive of interest on State and Eads's loans, being an annual average of fifty cents to each individual.

The Institution of the Deaf and Dumb expended $50,516 during the biennial period. Its receipts were $61,568. The College for the Blind received $52,708 and expended $47,428. The receipts of the Institution for Feeble-minded Children were $29,249, and the expenses $28,708. The receipts of the Mt. Pleasant Hospital for the Insane were $224,152, and the expenses $211,248; those of the institution at Independence were $139,096, and the expenses $129,771. The receipts of the State Prison from all sources were $73,448, and the expenditures $62,456. The surplus from the convicts' earnings paid into the State Treasury amounts to $17,144. The amount allowed by law for the support of the convicts is seven dollars per month. During the time of the present warden's incumbency, he has by rigid economy supported the convicts, exclusive of salaries of officers and guards, at a cost of about $6.40 per month; quite a contrast with the monthly expenditure of his predecessor, which was, as is shown by the report of the Investigating Committee of the Seventeenth General Assembly, during his first term, exclusive of salaries of officers and guards, $11.35¼, during his second term $17.35¼, and during his third term $15.26, being an average, during his six years' term of ofhee, of over $14 per convict per month. The convicts are well fed and clothed; the discipline and sanitary conditions of the prison are good.

From the following table it will be seen that there are nine boards of trustees in charge of the State institutions, and a board of regents in charge of the University, composed in all of fifty-one persons, and that their per diem and mileage for the biennial period has been as follows:

Agricultural College..................	$1,858 60
Asylum for Feeble-Minded.............	1,056 40
Hospital for Insane at Independence.....	1,369 50
Hospital for Insane at Mt. Pleasant.....	1,508 05
Soldiers' Orphans' Home...............	818 60
Reform School......................	1,580 40
Normal School.....................	769 70
State University....................	2,196 70
Institution of the Deaf and Dumb......	1,836 60
College for the Blind.................	1,468 20
Total..................	$13,448 65

How best to manage educational, charitable, and penal institutions has attracted the attention and engaged the thoughts of many philanthropists. The result has been, in most cases, to create additional supervisory boards, such as "boards of charities," "commissioners," etc., all of which are expensive, and impose additional burdens on the tax-payers. On this subject the Governor of Iowa says: "On examination of the workings of the system, I am clear in the opinion that, instead of increasing supervising boards, the best thing to do, in the interest of good government and economy, would be to reduce the number of boards."

The following shows the debt of the counties, cities, and school districts on January 1, 1879, so far as returns have been made:

90 counties........................	$2,876,586 02
15 cities........................	2,598,630 43
858 school districts..................	1,197,158 00
Total..........................	$6,167,374 45

—equal to about 1½ per cent. of the assessed value of the State. The above is $1,000,000 less than in 1869, and $2,500,000 less than the same debts amounted to in 1873.

The amount of risks written during the last insurance year in Iowa, ending February 1st, was as follows:

Risks written by Iowa companies..........	$22,664,856 00
Risks written by non-State companies......	89,174,354 00
Total fire insurance written in 1878.....	$111,888,788 00
The total premium receipts for the year, by seven Iowa companies, were.............	$549,988 86
Of the non-State companies................	1,066,871 64
Amount paid for insurance.............	$1,616,809 93

The losses for the year foot up the sum of $590,875, divided as follows:

State companies........................	$137,688 83
Other companies........................	453,191 78
Total........................	$590,875 11

The figures above given have no reference to the county and township mutual fire associations in the State, of which there are quite a large number.

Coal is abundant in the State. It lies on three measures or strata, the upper, middle, and lower, with a dip to the southwest. The coal-field may be outlined on the map by beginning at the southwest corner of Van Buren County, where Des Moines River leaves the county, going north near the county line to the northeast corner of Jefferson County; thence north and diagonally across Keokuk County, following a course parallel to the course of the Des Moines River, cutting off the southwest corner of Poweshiek and northeast corner of Jasper; thence north through the west half of Marshall to Eldora, in Hardin; thence westward across the north part of Hamilton and Webster above Fort Dodge; thence a little south direct to the Missouri River. The south line is the State line from the Des Moines River. This will give the coal-fields of Iowa, embracing over three thousand square miles, or an area larger than the whole State of Massachusetts. This embraces the lower coal-formation. The middle and upper coal-measures are thinner and not so profitable. At this point the lower coal-measures are reached at a depth of 125 to 135 feet, where the measure is from four to five feet thick. As you go southward it is deeper from the surface, the dip being in that direction. This

measure crops out at the northern line of the field. It thickens as you go southward. The entire thickness of the carboniferous strata in Iowa is estimated at 1,150 feet. It is estimated that a shaft 1,000 feet deep will pass through all the coal-measures in Iowa at any point. This would be in the south and west extremes of the State. Practically the supply of coal is inexhaustible. Its quality is good, and improves as you follow the dip southward.

The Democratic State Convention assembled at Council Bluffs on May 21st. General A. C. Dodge was chosen President. The following nominations were made: For Governor, H. H. Trimble; for Lieutenant-Governor, J. O. Yeoman; for Supreme Judge, Ruben E. Noble; for Superintendent of Schools, Irwin Baker.

The following resolutions were adopted:

Resolved, That the Democratic party now, as in the past, insists that our liberties depend upon the strict construction and observance of the Constitution of the United States and all its amendments.

Resolved, That the State and the General Governments should be sternly restrained to their respective spheres, and to the exercise only of the powers granted and reserved by the Constitution.

Resolved, That the policy of the Republican party, by which it inflates the importance of the States when necessary to cover the theft of the Presidency, and in turn magnifies the functions of the General Government to cover the coercion of the States into endorsement of the partisan will of the fraudulent Executive, is a policy full of evil and fruitful of danger.

Resolved, That such policy is intended to array section against section, the States against the General Government, and it against the States in turn, for the purpose of destroying the freedom of both, and teaching the people to look to a stronger Government as shelter from the anarchy its advocates have planned.

Resolved, That the evidence of these nefarious purposes is furnished by the present attitude of the Republican party, which is arrayed against a free ballot, on which depend all the liberties secured to us by the Constitution.

Resolved, That we view with alarm the determination of the Republican party, through its fraudulent Executive, to deprive this Republic of its army, so necessary to the defense of its frontier and its protection from foreign and domestic enemies, by vetoing appropriations for the pay and support of our soldiers, unless they can be used to force voters to record the mere will of the Executive.

Resolved, That we hail the Democratic Senators and Representatives in Congress as worthy the heroic lineage of American citizens in standing firmly for the American idea in government, as against the despotic theory from which our revolutionary fathers revolted; and we ask all lovers of liberty to join us and them in protest against the change in the form of our government proposed by the Republican party, which will substitute the will of one man for that of the majority of all the people.

Resolved, That we are in favor of the substitution of United States Treasury notes for national-bank notes, and of the abolition of national banks as banks of issue; that the Government of the United States issue the money for the people; and, further, that we favor a reduction of the bonded debt of the United States as fast as practicable, and the application of the idle money in the Treasury to that purpose.

Resolved, That we favor the free and unlimited coinage of the silver dollar of 412½ grains, and providing certificates for silver bullion which may be deposited in the United States Treasury, the same to be legal tenders for all purposes.

Resolved, That we favor a tariff for revenue only.

Resolved, That we are in favor of economy in public expenditures, including the reduction of salaries, local and general, whenever they may be deemed excessive, and also a reduction in the number of the officials.

Resolved, That the Democratic party of Iowa is desirous of promoting temperance, and, being opposed to free whiskey, it is in favor of a Judicious license law.

Resolved, That we favor the holding of all public servants to a strict accountability, and their prompt and severe punishment for all thefts of public moneys and maladministration of public office.

The Nationals met in Convention at Des Moines on May 28th. John Porter was chosen President. The following nominations were made: For Governor, Daniel Campbell; for Lieutenant-Governor, H. H. Moore; for Supreme Judge, M. H. Jones; for Superintendent of Schools, J. A. Nash. The following preamble and resolutions were adopted:

Whereas, The sovereign and supreme power of the American Union is vested in the free will of the citizens thereof, who have an equal and unquestionable right to express that will as to them may seem best adapted to secure the peace, perpetuate the liberty, and promote the prosperity of each individual, as well as to enhance and protect the common welfare of our country; and,

Whereas, This power has been delegated to unworthy servants, who have diverted it from its original purpose, whereby grievous wrongs have been perpetrated on the masses of the people, subjecting them to gross injustice and widespread poverty, untold privations, and business paralyzation; and,

Whereas, These grievances have been greatly augmented by limiting the legal-tender quality of the greenbacks; by loaning the credit of the Government to national-bank corporations; by changing Government bonds into coin bonds, and making the same exclusively payable in gold; by the conversion of a non-interest-bearing circulating medium into an interest-bearing Government debt; by defrauding labor of employment; by the ruinous shrinkage in the value of property; by the depression of business; by the willful restrictions placed upon the remonetization of the silver dollar; by the exemption of capital from its just share of the burden of taxation; by the contraction of the greenback currency; by the forced resumption of specie payments; by the increase in the purchasing power of money, and its attendant hardships on the debtor class; by declaring poverty a crime, and providing punishments therefor; by the criminal waste of the public domain, through enormous grants of land to railroad corporations; by an oppressive taxation; by high rates of interest for the use of money; by exorbitant salaries and fees to public officers; by official corruption in the administration of public affairs; and,

Whereas, A moneyed despotism has grown up in our land out of this state of affairs, which controls the law-making power of our country, dictates judicial decisions, wields an undue influence over the chief executive of the nation in the consideration of laws passed for the benefit of the people, thus enabling the money power to carry on its schemes of public plunder, under and by which colossal fortunes have been gathered in the hands of the ambitious and unscrupulous men whose interests are at war with the interests of the people, hostile to popular government, and deaf to the demands of honest toil:

Therefore, We, the representatives of the Union Greenback-Labor party of Iowa, adopt the following as our platform of principles:

1. The General Government alone to issue money; the amount in circulation to be fixed by a constitutional amendment upon a per capita basis; calling in of all United States bonds, and the payment of them in full legal-tender money.

2. That the national banks, as banks of issue, must be abolished by law, and that legal-tender greenback money of the Government of the United States shall be substituted for their circulation.

3. That we demand the unlimited coinage of the silver dollar of the present standard weight and fineness.

4. That the American people owes a debt of gratitude to the Union soldiers that can never be fully paid, and in recognition of their patriotic services we endorse the arrearages of pensions, and favor the passage of a bill providing for the equalization of bounties similar to the one vetoed by ex-President Grant.

5. That we view with grave apprehension the continued oppression of the people by corporate powers, and while we execrate the inhuman treatment of Union soldiers in the prison-pens of the South during the late rebellion, we condemn the violence of partisan spirit in the legislative halls of Congress, which seeks to revive the dead issues of the past, while conspiring against and deliberately refusing to provide measures of relief adequate to the living necessities of the present.

6. That it is the right and duty of all qualified electors of any State in the Union to vote according to their conscientious convictions, and to have that vote honestly and fairly counted; and that any attempt to interfere with that right either by threats or bands of armed men, or the use of troops at the polls, or by fraud in conducting the election, or bribery in making out the returns, or by threats to dismiss from service, or any other means by which that right is abridged, is a crime that should be severely punished.

7. That the officeholders of our country are the servants and not the masters of the people, and that these officers should be removed and punished to the full extent of law whenever they betray the public trust confided to them; and we demand that all official fees and salaries, commencing with the President, should be reduced from 25 to 50 per cent.; and we further demand the strictest economy in the administration of our courts of justice, and in all other Federal and State offices.

8. That we highly commend the moral reform of men and the elevation of families by the agency of the temperance cause, and demand the use of all just and legal means for the suppression of the evils of intemperance.

9. That all real estate be assessed to the owner, and the tax thereon be paid by him; provided, that in case there is a mortgage or vendor's lien upon the land, and he pays the whole tax, that he may deduct as a payment on said lien the *pro rata* share of the tax.

10. That the revenue law of the State shall be amended so that the penalty or interest on the sale of delinquent taxes should not exceed the sum of ten per cent. per annum, and that the time of redemption shall be extended to a term of five years.

11. We favor the repeal of the present Railroad Commissioners' law, and the adoption of a suitable legislative action to reduce and equalize freight.

12. That the prison-convict labor shall never come in competition with free labor, by the contract system, under any name.

Resolved, That we approve the bold and independent stand taken by our Greenback Representatives in Congress: and we especially endorse the conduct of Messrs. Weaver and Gillette in their contest with the combined opposition of both old parties.

The Republican State Convention assembled at Des Moines on June 11th. Ex-United States Senator James Harlan was chosen President. The following nominations were made: For Governor, John H. Gear, renominated; for Lieutenant-Governor, F. T. Campbell, renominated; for Supreme Judge, J. M. Beck; for Superintendent of Schools, C. W. von Coelln. The following resolutions were adopted

The Republican party of Iowa, in convention assembled, declares:

1. The United States of America is a nation, not a league. This is the doctrine of the Constitution, confirmed by the result of the war of the rebellion. The

Democratic party denies this, and opposes to it the doctrine of States' rights, which includes the power of a State to dissolve its connection with the Union. Therefore it is dangerous to the national life to intrust it to the Democratic party.

2. Upon the foregoing doctrine of nationality depends the power of the Republic to protect its citizens in all their rights, both at home and abroad; and from its denial by the Democratic party have resulted the barbarous outrages perpetrated on citizens in all of the disturbed section of the Southern States; and redress can be had alone through the administration of public affairs in the several departments of the Government by the Republican party.

3. We denounce the attempt of the Democratic party in Congress to render the Federal elections insecure by the repeal of the election laws of the United States, as dangerous to a free and pure expression of the will of the people through the ballot-box, and as tending to subject said elections to the domination of the bulldozing elements of the Southern States, and of the repeaters and promoters of fraud in the city of New York and elsewhere; and the resistance made to the accomplishment of this result by the Republican Senators and Representatives in Congress, and President Hayes for his veto messages, are accorded our profound commendations.

4. That the Democratic threat of "not a dollar for the army" unless the appropriations can be limited for partisan ends, is but the echo of the cry heard during the rebellion from the same quarter of "not another man nor another dollar" for the purposes of the war. The end will be the same. The Government of the Union could not be beaten to death then, and it can not be starved to death now.

5. That we approve the financial policy of the Republican party, and refer with pride to its results. Southern Democratic rebellion, for the perpetuation of slavery and the enforcement of State rights, forced an enormous interest-bearing debt on the people, which, in August, 1865, reached its highest point, and then amounted to $2,381,530,294.96, requiring an annual interest payment of $150,977,697.87. On the first of August next, when the Republican refunding operations will be completed, this Democratic debt will be reduced to $1,797,643,900, with an annual interest charge of but $83,773,778.50; showing a reduction in the principal of $583,886,594.96, and of annual interest charge of $67,203,919.37; and we declare that this debt shall be honestly paid in honest money; and to this end we are in favor of keeping our coin circulation at its largest practicable volume, and of maintaining our paper currency where the Republican policy has placed it, at par with coin; and to the further end that the dollar earned by labor shall be worth as much as the dollar earned by capital.

6. Concerning further financial legislation we say, "Let us have peace," undisturbed by Congressional tinkering, that our business interests may revive, investments of more idle capital be encouraged, commercial interests fostered, and the general welfare promoted.

7. The profit arising from the coinage of gold and silver should inure to the benefit of the Government, and not to the advantage of the private owners of the bullion, as this tends to diminish the burdens of the tax-payers; and no part of the taxpaying currency of the country should be converted into the non-taxpaying list.

8. That we favor a wisely adjusted tariff for revenue.

9. We demand a strict economy in the imposition of public taxes and the expenditure of public moneys, and such a just reduction and equalization of the salaries and fees of public officers as shall place them on an equality with like positions in private employment.

10. That we renew our expressions of profound gratitude to the soldiers and sailors of the Union, and denounce the removal of employees of this class by the Democrats in Congress and the appointment in their stead of members of the Confederate army.

11. That we reaffirm the position of the Republican party heretofore expressed upon the subject of temperance and prohibition, and we hail with pleasure the beneficent work of reform clubs and other organizations in promoting personal temperance; and in order that the entire question of prohibition may be settled in a non-partisan manner, we favor the submission to the people, at a special election, of a constitutional amendment prohibiting the manufacture and sale of all intoxicating liquors as a beverage within the State.

The Prohibitionist Convention assembled at Cedar Rapids on July 16th. J. Pinkham was chosen President. The following resolutions were adopted:

Resolved—1. We recognize the traffic in intoxicating liquors as the great moral, financial, social, and political evil of the present age; that it is one of the worst relics of barbarianism; that it has always been the moving cause of crime, and is, therefore, subversive of our republican form of government, and should be overthrown.

2. We believe that the prohibition of the traffic in intoxicating liquors is the only sound legislative theory upon which this vexed question can be solved and the nation saved from bankruptcy and demoralization. Therefore we insist upon the maintenance and enforcement of our prohibitory liquor law, and upon such amendments by the next Legislature of Iowa as will place ale, wine, and beer under the same condemnation as other intoxicating liquors.

3. We believe that in the security of home rests the security of the state; that woman is by her very nature the acknowledged guardian of this sacred shrine, and that intemperance is its greatest enemy; therefore we claim that the daughters of this commonwealth, as well as her sons, be allowed to say, by their vote, what laws should be made for the suppression of this evil and what persons shall execute the same.

4. That the present movement inaugurated by the temperance organizations of the State to so amend the Constitution of the State as to prohibit the manufacture and sale of alcoholic liquors except for medicinal and medicinal purposes, including malt and wine liquors, meets our active support.

5. We are in favor of the election of honest pronounced Prohibitionists to enact and to administer the laws, and that we, at this convention, put in nomination a State Prohibitory ticket, and that we recommend the election of Prohibitionists only for the Legislature.

The following was offered as a substitute for the fifth resolution and adopted—yeas 41, nays 32:

Resolved, That we, as the Prohibitionists of the State of Iowa, in view of the great questions of public interest affecting the perpetuity of our General Government which are now absorbing the thought and action of all our people, deem it inexpedient and unwise to nominate a State Prohibitory ticket at the present time.

The following additional resolutions were adopted, and the Convention adjourned:

Resolved, That we are in favor of the amendment of the Constitution of the United States so as to forbid the manufacture, importation, and sale of all alcoholic liquors except for medical and mechanical purposes.

Resolved, That we believe that the cause of temperance can be best subserved at the present time in our State by devoting all our energies and labors to the election of Prohibitionists to the next session of the Legislature.

Immediately after the adjournment, another convention was held by nearly forty of the delegates, and the following ticket nominated:

For Governor, Professor G. T. Carpenter ; for Lieutenant-Governor, Frank T. Campbell; for Supreme Judge, J. M. Beck; for Superintendent of Public Instruction, J. A. Nash. After which resolutions were adopted and a State Central Committee appointed. Professor Carpenter, when notified, declined the nomination. The activity and energy of the temperance advocates became so great, that representatives of the interests of the dealers in liquors assembled in convention at Des Moines on July 30th. The Convention was called to order by M. McTighe, who in some remarks referred to the reasons which had brought them together. It was to inaugurate a contest of protection against fanaticism, and to notify all prohibitionists that the liquor-sellers had determined to stand up for their rights. They were assembled together not for the purpose of making or influencing nominations for office, and for no party purpose. J. F. Daugherty was elected President, and the following resolutions were adopted:

Whereas, We have made the sad experience as a class of business men, that the prohibitory liquor law of this State does not in any degree promote the cause of temperance or morality for which it is intended, and consequently does not afford the people of this State the desired protection, but on the other hand it is used as a lever to throttle us and to constantly hurl against us an army of dead-beats, blackmailers, and spies, who have in no wise the welfare of the people of the great State of Iowa in view, but who seek to destroy what it has taken years to build up, only to satisfy either their malice, personal greed, or ambition ; and

Whereas, It is furthermore a universally recognized principle, that wherever there is a demand for any commodity in life, there will always be a supply of the same, and as this supply should always be controlled and regulated in the interest and true wants of the people ; therefore, be it

Resolved, By the saloon-keepers, brewers, and liquor-dealers of the State of Iowa, in convention assembled in Des Moines on this, the 30th day of July, 1879, that we claim, as a class of business men, the same rights and protection under the Constitution and fundamental laws of this country as any other class of business men enjoy.

Resolved, That it is our firm belief that a well-regulated and judicious license-law in this State, giving the necessary protection to the dealer and manufacturer, and at the same time placing them under all reasonable restrictions, would greatly tend to decrease the evils of intemperance, and be in fact a better temperance law than we have at the present day in our statute-books.

Resolved, That in order to bring about the repeal of the present vicious liquor law at the earliest moment, and enact in its stead a just and equitable license law, we hereby firmly and unqualifiedly declare that we will not vote for nor support any candidate for the next Legislature, no matter what his political creed may be, who does not unmistakably pledge himself to use the utmost endeavors, when elected, to attain such result.

Resolved, That while the members of this convention belong to all political parties, and are therefore strictly non-partisan, we are not unmindful of who is our friend and who our foe; and we therefore pledge ourselves not to support any candidate for any office within the gift of the people of the State who is an enemy to the interest which we represent, or who will not pledge himself in favor of a judicious license law.

Resolved, That we recommend to the friends of personal liberty and license the organization of clubs in every township where practicable, for the purpose of

securing a greater unity of action, and to enable the people to become acquainted with the losses the farmer and business man sustains through the pernicious operation of. the existing prohibitory liquor law of this State.

The result of the election, which was held on the second Tuesday in October, was as follows :

FOR GOVERNOR.

John H. Gear, Republican.................. 157,571
H. H. Trimble, Democrat................... 85,056
Daniel Campbell, National................. 45,429

FOR LIEUTENANT-GOVERNOR.

F. T. Campbell, Republican............... 161,708
J. A. O. Yeomans, Democrat.............. 86,400
M. H. Moore, National.................... 45,750

FOR JUDGE OF SUPREME COURT.

J. M. Beck, Republican................... 160,604
Reuben Noble, Democrat................... 85,788
M. H. Jones, National.................... 45,719

FOR SUPERINTENDENT OF SCHOOLS. .

C. W. von Coelln, Republican............. 159,904
Edwin Baker. Democrat................... 84,945
G. A. Nash, National r.................. 47,848

The members of the Legislature were divided as follows:

PARTIES.	Senate.	House.
Republican..........................	41	81
Democratic..........................	7	14
National............................	2	4
Independent.........................	..	1
Total...............................	50	100

ITALY, a kingdom of southern Europe. King in 1879, Humbert I., born March 14, 1844. He succeeded his father, Victor Emanuel II., January 9, 1878. He married, April 22, 1868, Margaretha, daughter of Prince Ferdinand of Savoy, Duke of Genoa. Heir apparent, Victor Emanuel, Prince of Naples, born November 11, 1869.

The following table gives the area of the larger territorial divisions (*compartimenti*), with the population, male and female, of each, according to the census of 1871, and the total population at the close of 1878, according to an official calculation :

TERRITORIAL DIVISIONS.	Square miles.	INHABITANTS, 1871.		Inhabitants at the close of 1878.
		Male.	Female.	
Piedmont.....	11,806	1,450,357	1,449.207	3,077,200
Liguria.......	2,056	419,919	428,593	886,885
Lombardy.....	9,085	1,755,545	1,705.279	3,653,941
Venetia......	9,060	1,384,364	1,308,448	2,812,022
Emilia........	7.921	1,078,686	1,085,142	2,193,445
Umbria.......	3.720	262,574	267,027	578,405
The Marches..	3,746	449,548	465,871	948,284
Tuscany......	9,287	1,096,652	1,045,573	2,219,422
Rome........	4,601	449,346	387,808	849,125
The Abruzzi and Molise ..	6,677	625,547	657,485	1,388,056
Campania....	6,942	1,366,557	1,388,085	2,879,717
Apulia........	8,539	708,514	712,878	1,522,782
Basilicata.....	4,122	249,220	261,828	532,927
Calabria......	6,663	593,829	612,473	1,261,810
Sicily	11,291	1,284,531	1,299,568	2,798,672
Sardinia.....	3,899	327,073	309,587	667,427
Total	114,415	13,472,262	13,323,892	28,209,620

The movement of population was as follows in 1878 :

Marriages.................................... 199,885
Births.. {inclusive of still-births. { 1,012,475
Deaths. {   { 818,550
Still-births 81,805
Excess of births............................ 198,925

The number of emigrants in 1878 was 96,-268. Of these, the largest number, 33,552, went to France, 18,391 to Austria-Hungary, 10,782 to Switzerland, 10,105 to Brazil, Venezuela, Mexico, and Central America, 1,993 to the United States, and the remainder to other countries.

The receipts in the budget for 1878 were as follows (in lire; 1 lira = 19·3 cents):

1. Income from Government property........		85,680,410
2. Direct taxes:		
Ground-tax..................	128,820,000	
Building-tax.................	61,325,000	
Other taxes..................	178,583,581	
		858,728,581
3. Indirect taxes:		
Registration.................	53,000,000	
Stamp-tax...................	89,500,000	
Customs.....................	116,500,000	
Grist-tax....................	81,000,000	
Tobacco and salt monopoly...	198,500,000	
Others......................	140,052,057	
		628,582,057
4. Miscellaneous receipts:		
Lottery.....................	70,000,000	
Post, railroads, and telegraphs	71,690,550	
Returns of payments..... ...	18,115,218	
Miscellaneous...............	85,624,000	
		195,429,768
Total ordinary revenue...............		1,218,420,816

The extraordinary receipts amounted to 109,-968,310 lire, and special revenue from various sources to 112,439,443 lire, making the total revenue 1,435,828,569 lire.

The expenditures were as follows:

DEPARTMENTS.	Ordinary.	Extraordinary.
Ministry of the Treasury......	774,227,771	19,289,962
" of Finance...........	117,435,272	1,846,583
" of Justice and Worship	27,655,398	195,000
" of Foreign Affairs.....	6,092,261	151,000
" of Public Instruction...	26,535,747	1,471,557
" of the Interior	52,581,757	3,948,358
" of Public Works......	55,816,119	82,353,748
" of War...............	177,264,205	9,966,000
" of the Navy...........	42,252,842	2,071,546
" of Agriculture	7,774,685	463,140
	1,287,656,055	120,556,894
Total....................	1,408,212,949	

The public debt at the close of 1878 was as follows:

	Lire.
Funded debt...............................	7,091,929,661
Redeemable debt in the "Rentes" of 8 and 5 per cent.......	1,642,773,107
Treasury bonds............................	183,010,500
Paper currency............................ ..	840,000,000
Total....................	9,757,618,267

The strength of the Italian army on September 30, 1878, was as follows:

Infantry of the line......................	256,403
Military districts......................	239,074
Companies of the Alps..................	8,688
Bersaglieri............................	44,471
Cavalry...............................	81,424
Artillery..............................	60,417
Engineers.............................	11,981
Gendarmes (carbineers)...........	18,923
Military schools.......................	4,497
Sanitary companies....................	3,979
Veterans..............................	1,070
Stud depots...........................	225
Disciplinary companies.................	1,153
Penal institutions.....................	1,776
Officers in service.....................	11,573
Other officers.........................	2,161
1. Standing army.....................	698,095
2. Provincial militia..................	251,819
3. Officers of reserve.................	2,403
4. Territorial militia..................	423,191
Total...........................	1,375,508

The navy was composed as follows in 1877:

VESSELS.	Number.	Guns.	Tons.	Horse-power.
Men-of-war:				
Ironclads............	20	242	105,460	13,890
Screw-steamers......	18	143	24,280	4,610
Paddle-steamers....	6	41	7,960	2,050
Total men-of-war..	44	426	137,700	20,550
Transports:				
Screw-steamers......	20	40	17,703	2,914
Paddle-steamers......	9	12	2,244	725
Total transports...	29	52	19,947	3,639
Total navy........	73	478	157,647	24,189

At the end of 1879 the navy contained 86 steamers, including 16 ironclads finished or building, and armed with 676 guns.

The movement of shipping in 1877 is exhibited by the following table:

VOYAGES.	TOTAL.		LADEN.		STEAMERS.	
	Vessels.	Tons.	Vessels.	Tons.	Vessels.	Tons.
ENTERED.						
1. Long voyage:						
Italian......................	10,316	1,419,408	8,556	1,247,299	927	587,384
Foreign.....................	5,428	2,262,116	4,746	2,099,725	2,581	1,804,017
Total long voyage........	15,739	3,681,519	13,302	3,347,024	3,508	2,341,401
2. Short voyage:						
Italian......................	81,404	6,516,416	62,890	5,724,828	11,294	4,340,198
Foreign.....................	3,603	2,299,855	2,989	2,103,164	2,859	2,189,942
Total short voyage.......	85,007	8,816,271	65,879	7,927,492	14,158	6,380,065
Total....................	100,746	12,497,790	79,181	11,174,516	17,661	8,721,466
CLEARED.						
1. Long voyage....................	16,411	4,150,270	12,472	3,326,184	3,959	2,647,588
2. Short voyage...................	84,098	8,409,232	65,815	7,558,658	13,685	6,079,971
Total....................	100,509	12,559,502	78,287	10,879,842	17,644	8,727,559

The commercial navy in 1878 comprised 8,590 vessels of 1,029,157 tons, of which 152 of 63,020 tons were steamers.

The movement of the special foreign trade from 1871 to 1878 was as follows (in lire):

YEARS.	OFFICIAL VALUE.		COMMERCIAL VALUE.	
	Imports.	Exports.	Imports.	Exports.
1871	880,100,000	756,600,000	968,700,000	1,085,500,000
1872	1,139,200,000	1,108,800,000	1,186,600,000	1,167,200,000
1873	1,184,500,000	1,083,500,000	1,286,700,000	1,188,200,000
1874	1,281,700,000	1,088,400,000	1,305,000,000	985,500,000
1875	1,280,000,000	1,158,800,000	1,215,400,000	1,084,000,000
1876	1,864,800,000	1,228,000,000	1,327,200,000	1,216,800,000
1877	1,280,700,000	1,044,900,000	1,156,800,000	967,400,000
1878	....	....	1,070,800,000	1,045,800,000

The commercial value of the imports from and exports to the different countries in 1877 and 1878 was as follows:

COUNTRIES.	Imports, 1877.	Imports, 1878.	Exports, 1877.	Exports, 1878.
France	332,100,000	272,900,000	418,900,000	489,800,000
England	296,500,000	237,100,000	125,700,000	96,900,000
Austria-Hungary	237,500,000	196,600,000	185,000,000	178,400,000
Switzerland	28,000,000	83,500,000	181,500,000	99,000,000
Russia	28,400,000	53,500,000	20,000,000	17,700,000
United States	89,900,000	54,200,000	27,200,000	86,500,000
Germany	25,200,000	39,500,000	16,600,000	20,800,000
South America	50,800,000	28,000,000	48,500,000	27,800,000
Turkey	55,600,000	40,400,000	8,500,000	14,800,000
Other countries	60,800,000	115,100,000	89,600,000	69,500,000
Total	1,154,800,000	1,070,800,000	966,500,000	1,045,800,000

The value of the different articles of import and export in 1878 was as follows, the transit trade being included in both the imports and exports:

ARTICLES.	Imports.	Exports.
Grain	128,200,000	60,800,000
Seeds and fruit	17,200,000	58,800,000
Colonial goods	92,100,000	6,000,000
Tobacco	18,900,000	....
Wine, beer, ale, etc	7,500,000	18,200,000
Animals and food for animals	58,500,000	122,900,000
1. Articles of food	817,700,000	261,700,000
Fuel	42,800,000	3,500,000
Ores, etc	8,500,000	25,200,000
Metals, raw	44,000,000	1,800,000
Hair, hides, and leather	41,200,000	19,500,000
Spinning materials	143,300,000	816,200,000
Wood and carving materials	29,700,000	13,000,000
2. Raw materials	309,500,000	878,700,000
Glass and pottery ware	12,200,000	5,400,000
Yarns	47,400,000	6,800,000
Woven goods and articles of clothing	163,600,000	80,400,000
Manufactures of different kinds	84,000,000	111,100,000
Paper, books, etc	2,200,000	1,800,000
3. Manufactured goods	309,400,000	160,500,000
Manure	700,000	500,000
Drugs and chemical products	84,800,000	86,700,000
Resin, fats, and oils	61,500,000	92,500,000
Goods not specified	25,500,000	18,500,000
4. Miscellaneous goods	122,500,000	198,200,000
5. Precious metals	11,700,000	46,700,000
Total	1,070,800,000	1,045,800,000

At the close of 1877 there were 8,046 kilometres of railroad in operation, 486 in process of building, and 654 projected. The length of telegraph lines in 1877 was 24,088 kilometres; of wires, 80,596; of submarine cables, 178. The number of stations was 1,977; of dispatches, 5,609,298, of which 5,057,789 were private, 235,148 official, 105,837 service, and 210,524 transit dispatches.

The number of post-offices in 1877 was 3,-126; of letters and postal cards, 170,848,672; of packages of printed matter and samples, 61,713,852; and of newspapers, 83,314,302.

The principal question before the country in 1879 was the abolition of the grist-tax, and in connection with this the general question of finance. On March 10th the report of the Commission on the provisional estimates for 1879 was submitted to the deputies. These estimates were originally prepared by the former Minister of Finance, Signor Seismit Doda, whose anticipation of a surplus of 60,000,000 lire, and his intention of repealing the grist-tax, were denounced in unmeasured terms during the struggle for the overthrow of the Cairoli Cabinet. The new Minister of Finance, Signor Magliani, though calculating that the revenue would yield 11,000,000 less and the expenditure amount to 7,000,000 more than Signor Seismit Doda had estimated, nevertheless expressed confidence in obtaining a surplus of not less than 42,000,000; and the majority of the Commission endorsed his anticipations to the extent of 40,000,000. The minority of the Commission, however, who were more directly antagonistic to Signor Seismit Doda, considered the income announced by Signor Magliani as over-estimated to the extent of 18,000,000, and therefore predicted that the surplus would not exceed 22,000,000. The debate on the budget of revenue closed on March 28th. The Government accepted an order of the day proposed by Signor Cairoli, upholding the abolition of the grist-tax and the adoption of the reforms forming the programme of the Left. Signor Depretis appealed to his political friends to aid in a reconstruction of the Left, and the Chamber, having by 255 votes against 99 rejected a motion made by Signor Minghetti, approved by 241 votes against 88 the order of the day moved by Signor Cairoli. This vote was generally considered as the sign of an understanding between the different groups of the Left and the Ministry. On May 4th the Minister of Finance laid a financial statement before the Chamber. Speaking of 1878, he stated that the receipts for that year had been 9,500,000 less than the amount estimated, and the expenditures 5,000,000 less. Taking these differences into account, together with the increased expenditure sanctioned by the Chambers after the estimates were voted, the expected surplus of 11,000,000 became reduced to something less than 500,000. The surplus for 1879, which in the provisional budget was estimated at 41,-000,000, was reduced to 12,000,000. He further expected surpluses of 10,000,000 in 1880, 2,000,000 in 1881, 28,500,000 in 1882, and 38,-000,000 in 1883. These surpluses would, however, be insufficient to fulfill the vote of July 7, 1878, of gradually abolishing the grist-tax, which would involve a decrease of income of 18,000,000 in 1879, of 36,500,000 in 1880, 1881, and 1882, and of 75,500,000 on its total abolition in 1883. In order to meet this decrease, he proposed to increase the taxes on sugar, alcohol, coffee, petroleum, and other colonial goods, the registration and stamp taxes, and the octroi. He estimated the total increase of the revenue from these sources at 30,000,000 lire. If these taxes were not granted, he considered it impossible to proceed with the abolition of the grist-tax and prevent a deficit. The Senate on June 24th, by a vote of 136 to 50, approved the abolition of the grist-tax so far only as regarded maize and grain of an inferior quality. This decision was of great political importance, as it was contrary to the wishes of the Ministry, who demanded the entire abolition of the tax. The bill as originally presented, and as it had passed the Chamber of Deputies in 1878, proposed that the tax on inferior grains should be entirely remitted from July 1, 1879, that the tax on corn should be reduced one fourth from the same date, and that the tax should altogether cease on January 1, 1883. The Senate was willing to agree to the remission of the tax on inferior grains, and to the prospective repeal of the whole tax in 1883; but it objected to the reduction on corn until an equivalent impost was voted. The Ministers, by the attitude which they took during the debate, converted the question into one of serious constitutional import. They denied the right of the Senate to alter or modify a money bill passed by the Chamber. It might accept or reject such a bill *en bloc*, but it had no right to do anything else. The Senate, however, maintained the other side of the question. The law for the abolition of the grist-tax, after its modification in the Senate, again came up in the Chamber. But, before a vote on it was reached, a vote of want of confidence in the Ministry was passed on July 3d, by 250 to 170 votes, in consequence of which the Cabinet resigned. This result was brought about by a most heterogeneous combination between various factions of the Conservatives and Radicals under the leadership of Signors Sella, Nicotera, and Baccarini. Signor Cairoli was intrusted with the formation of a new Ministry, which was completed on July 13th, and was composed as follows: Signor Cairoli, Presidency and Foreign Affairs; Signor Villa, Interior; Signor Grimaldi, Finance; Signor Baccarini, Public Works; Signor Vare, Worship and Justice; Signor Perez, Public Instruction; General Bonelli, War. On the 17th Signor Cairoli, in presenting the new Cabinet to the Chamber, said that the country needed a long period of peace and industry; that the Ministers would devote themselves exclusively to questions of internal interest, in conformity with which their foreign policy would be framed. At the same time he asked the Chambers to come to an agreement on the grist-tax. This was finally effected, as follows: The tax on the cheaper grains was to be abolished entirely, that on the better qualities reduced one fourth after July 1, 1880, and all taxes abolished after January 1, 1884. In this form it passed the Chamber on July 19th, and the Senate on the 24th.

The Chamber adjourned on July 23d, and the Senate on the 29th.

On September 15th Signor Grimaldi sent the details of his provisional budget for 1880 to the President of the Chamber, in conformity with the Parliamentary regulation, hitherto neglected, which requires its presentation on that date. The revenue was estimated at 1,402,000 000 lire, and the expenditures at 1,395,000,000 lire, leaving a surplus of 7,000,000. The report accompanying the budget, however, stated that, taking into account the expenditures already submitted to Parliament, there would be a deficit of 6,000,000 lire. Differences of opinion as to the budget led Signor Cairoli to resign on November 18th. The Chambers reassembled on the 19th, when Signor Cairoli announced that the Ministry had felt themselves under the necessity of placing their resignation in the hands of the King, and that his Majesty had intrusted him with the charge of forming a new Administration. The negotiations to that effect were proceeding regularly; but, in the mean time, he requested that the Chambers would adjourn until the 27th. The Chambers adjourned accordingly. The new Ministry was completed by the 27th, and was composed as follows: Cairoli, Presidency and Foreign Affairs; Depretis, Interior; Magliani, Finance; Villa, Justice; Baccarini, Public Works; De

Sanetis, Education; General Bonelli, War; Admiral Acton, Navy; Micelli, Agriculture and Commerce. On the same day Signor Cairoli presented the new Ministry to the Chambers and made a statement of the questions with which they had undertaken to deal. A cold reception was given to the Ministry, and leave was asked to interpellate the Government relative to the late Ministerial crisis. On the following day Signor Sella introduced his interpellation. Signor Cairoli in reply stated that the difference which arose between the members of the last Cabinet concerned the course to be pursued in regard to the grist-tax question. On December 5th Signor Magliani presented his modifications in the budget for 1880. These modifications showed an increase of 13,000,000 lire over the original estimates, 8,000,000 lire of which were due to retrenchments, mainly in the army, and 5,000,000 lire to the surplus of the revenue. An understanding was reached by the Ministry with Signor Crispi, and the latter was elected President of the Budget Committee.

The relations of Italy to foreign countries were discussed by the Chambers on several occasions. On January 20th Signor Vitelleschi in the Senate said that Italy ought to join with Austria, England, and France in assisting the populations of the East to set up constitutions for themselves, apart from the predominating influence of any foreign power. Signor Depretis, replying on the following day, said that the Government considered that the Berlin Treaty formed part of the public law of Europe, and they would loyally coöperate to secure its execution. The Government, he added, had not yet undertaken mediation between Turkey and Greece. In Tunis and Egypt the Cabinet desired to maintain the legitimate influence of Italy, and nothing more. On January 22d an order of the day was accepted by the Minister and adopted by the Chamber, stating that "it is necessary not only that treaties be loyally executed, but that the internal policy of the country shall not disturb the financial equilibrium or the organization of the military forces." On July 28th the new Cabinet was interpellated with regard to its foreign policy relating to Greece, Egypt, and Roumania. Signor Cairoli in reply said that it was impossible fully to discuss so delicate a subject, more particularly as the Government had only recently taken office, and had yet to make a complete examination of the documents and the acts of its predecessors. Regarding Greece, he might declare that the Government would faithfully maintain the Treaty of Berlin, and he was glad that the part in which the plenipotentiaries of Italy and France had agreed in taking an initiative at the Congress was in accord with the principles of nationality Italy had always professed. Italy had close relations with Greece and felt profound sympathy for her, and she would not be untrue either to the one or the other. In Egypt Italy had never failed in pro-

tecting her subjects, and had sustained her rights in order that other Powers might not have exclusive influence.

A provisional treaty of commerce with France was signed on January 15th, and ratified by the Chambers in February. It was to be in force for one year, and secured to the two countries the treatment of the most favored nations. A treaty of commerce with Austria was sanctioned by the Chambers in January.

On May 19th the civil-marriage act, providing that the civil act shall in all cases precede the religious ceremony, was passed by the Chamber of Deputies, by a vote of 163 to 101, after inserting amendments to the effect that penal action instituted against married persons who have gone through the religious ceremony shall be stayed on their registering their marriage before the civil authorities. The bill was strongly opposed by the clerical deputies, while the Minister of Justice declared that civil marriage as regarded by the law contained nothing detrimental to the privileges of the Church, but only protected those of the state.

The Chamber of Deputies on June 30th approved, after a debate extending over two months, by a vote of 257 to 96, the Ministerial railroad bill, which provides for the construction of 6,020 kilometres of railroad within twenty-one years, at an annual expenditure on this account of 60,000,000 lire.

The seizure of a Republican flag at Milan, on which occasion several arrests were made and a number of persons wounded, was made the subject of an interpellation. Signor Cavallotti, of the Extreme Left, attacked the Government, declaring that the Ministries of the Right, and even the Austrian Government, had not been as intolerant as the present Ministry. Signor Depretis, the Minister President, declared that the prefects had only done their duty; that the country desired peace and order, which only a strong government could give. Signor Tajani, the Minister of the Interior, in speaking of the Republican Associations, said that they numbered over 20,000 members, and that, wherever the Government had come in contact with them, it had been found that they were preparing to overthrow the existing order of things, and no Government could tolerate such a state of affairs. The debate terminated on April 4th in a vote of confidence, which was carried by 273 to 37 votes. All parties of the Right, Center, and Left voted in favor of the Government, excepting the 37 members of the Extreme Left headed by Signors Cavallotti and Bertani.

In the beginning of April General Garibaldi arrived in Rome, and called a meeting of the leaders of the Republican party for the 21st. In his letter convoking the meeting he said that he considered it to be the duty of the Republican party to rally all its forces in the field of legal agitation, in order progressively to secure that liberty which is their undoubted right, but which now depended on the whim of a Minister or the programme of a Ministry. Universal suffrage is the fundamental basis of reform. Those who obey the laws ought to make them. Those who are obliged to fight in defense of their country should also have the right to elect their syndics and their representatives in Parliament. This, he said, is the basis of social justice. He told those who impugn this that the people to whom the *toga virilis* is denied were considered capable of first founding with their arms and afterward confirming by their vote the unity of Italy; and he said that the dreaded phalanx of the Clericals is also desirable in Parliament, seeing that the establishment of two conflicting principles will dispel the languor which now renders it impotent and arouse all the energies of which Italy is capable to vital discussions. The meeting organized under the presidency of General Garibaldi. A resolution was adopted for the establishment of a central committee in Rome, with sub-committees in the provinces, to agitate for universal suffrage and other reforms. The meeting also sent a greeting to "our brethren of Italy unredeemed." Garibaldi made a speech, in which he said that the Constitution must be reconsidered, and Italy must be armed to be ready to claim the unredeemed provinces.

Considerable attention was aroused by a pamphlet entitled "Italicæ Res," which appeared in Vienna in August. The author was Aloys Ritter von Haymerle, brother of the new Austrian Minister of Foreign Affairs, colonel in the Austrian general staff, and for five years military attaché to the Austrian embassy in Rome. In this pamphlet he spoke of the Italia Irredenta party as a powerful agent, likely sooner or later to imperil the peace between Italy and Austria. He described this party as one "which, under the banner of the nationality principle and the theory of natural boundaries, did not permit the country to obtain peace, and in order to bring about new complications attempted to impress upon the mind of the nation the facts that the honor of Italy would remain sullied and its political existence doubtful as long as the smallest part of the Italian-speaking people remained subject to a foreign Government." At the same time he pointed out that the agitation of the party was directed only toward those portions of Italy under Austrian rule. On the other hand, he declared most decidedly that the policy of the Italian Government, as well as the sentiments of the large majority of the Italian population, were hostile to these aggressive demonstrations. In September both Count Andrassy and Baron Haymerle assured the Italian Ambassador at Vienna that they regretted the publication of the pamphlet, and disapproved the political comments contained in it. In Italy the pamphlet was very generally denounced, even by the Conservatives, who oppose the Government wherever they have an opportunity. The pamphlet was answered by the Italia Irredenta Association in another

pamphlet, entitled "Pro Patria," which was very bitter in its tone against Austria, and declared that no friendship between the two countries was possible until the Austrians had left Italy. It defined as unredeemed Italy the government of Innspruck, including the districts of Roveredo, Trent, Botzen, Brunnecken and the Giudicaria di Glovenza, the districts of Trieste, Gorizia, Pisina, and Adelsberg in Illyria, the Hungarian Littoral districts, and a part of the county of Agram in Croatia.

An eruption of Mount Etna took place at six o'clock on the evening of Sunday, May 25th. The sight was described as being very grand at Taormina. An opening occurred on Monday on the northern side, from which issued dense volumes of smoke and flames. Showers of ashes fell on Messina, where a severe undulatory shock of earthquake was felt on the 27th. Reggio in Calabria was covered with a lurid cloud, and large quantities of ashes also fell in that city. Three new craters opened, distant from each other about twelve miles, in the form of a triangle. A number of brilliant balls of fire were thrown to a great height on the night of the 28th, and burst like rockets, emitting a fiery shower. The stream of lava was estimated at seventy metres in width. The eruption increased on the night of June 2d. The Government on June 4th appointed a commission to visit Mount Etna and report on the volcanic phenomena. The most serious of the openings was that between the Monte Frumento and Monte Nero, an equal distance between Randazzo and Linguaglossa. At this spot the land was highly cultivated, and here the flow of lava was very great indeed. Here stood the bridge of the Pisciaro, which carried the national road over the river of that name as it descended from the mountain to the Alcantara River. This bridge was carried away by the avalanche of lava, and the road was overflowed for about 100 metres. The other two points of outbreak were—one between Bronte and Aderno, on the western slope, the other between Giarre and Aci Reale, on the southern. The former at one time seemed to threaten the town of Aderno, but all three craters gradually subsided in the beginning of June. The eruption was accompanied by a loud, rumbling noise and by earthquakes, and caused consternation and panic among the neighboring population. The loss of property and life was very great.

The destruction of Pompeii eighteen centuries ago was celebrated in the ruins of that city on September 26th, in the presence of a large number of scientific men and other spectators. From a pavilion erected in the ancient Basilica Professor Ruggieri, the director of the excavations, delivered an address explaining the newest mode of prosecuting discoveries, and giving an account of some of the more important discoveries that have been made since the excavations were commenced. He attempted to describe to the guests assembled the city as it must have appeared eighteen hundred years ago, and referred to the account of the destruction of the city and Herculaneum given by the younger Pliny in his famous letter to Tacitus narrating the death of his uncle, the elder Pliny. Count Guanciali and Mgr. Mirabelli then declaimed Latin verses commemorative of the event. After a visit to the ruins, excavations were begun under Signor Ruggieri's superintendence. A large number of vases, articles of jewelry, kitchen utensils, and coins were found, which were presented to the museums of Naples and Pompeii.

Giovanni Passanante, the man who attempted to assassinate King Humbert in 1878, was sentenced to death. At the instance of the King, however, a decree was signed by the Ministry commuting the sentence of death to one of penal servitude for life, and Passanante was then sent to the Island of Elba.

J

JAPAN, an empire in eastern Asia. The sovereign bears the title of "Tenno" or "Mikado." The reigning Mikado, Muts-Hito, was born at Tokio, September 22, 1852, and succeeded his father, Komei-Tenno, in 1867. He was married on December 28, 1868, to Princess Haruko, born April 17, 1850, daughter of Prince Idchidgo. There is no regular law of succession, and, in case of the death or abdication of the Mikado, the crown does not generally devolve upon his son, but upon either the eldest or most distinguished member of the Shi Shinnô, the four imperial families of Japan. These families are the Katzura, Arisugawa, Fushimi, and Kannin. The power of the Mikado is unlimited in temporal as well as spiritual affairs. He acts through an executive ministry divided into nine departments, viz., of the Imperial House, Foreign Affairs, War, Navy, Finance, Interior, Public Instruction, and Ecclestiastical Affairs. At the side of the Ministry stand the "Sain" or Senate, composed of thirty members, and the "Shoûi" or Council of State, of an unlimited number of members, both nominated by the Mikado, and consulted by him at his pleasure.

The area, according to an official publication in 1877, is 146,613 square miles. The population on January 1, 1876, was 34,338,404, of whom 17,419,785 were males and 16,918,619 females. The population of the principal cities was as follows: Tokio (1872), 595,905; Tokio with suburbs (1876), 1,036,171; Kumamoto, 300,000; Kioto or Miako (1872), 238,663; Osaka (1877), 281,119; Kajosima, 200,000; Yokohama (1872), 61,553; Kanasawa, 60,000; Nagasaki (1876), 47,412; Niigata (1872), 33,772. The budget for 1879–'80 was as follows (in yens—1 yen = 99·7 cents):

REVENUE.

1. Customs	2,181,310
2. Ground-tax	41,000,950
3. Mining dues	11,587
4. Tax on the salaries of officials	81,992
5. Taxes on the products of the northern provinces	363,971
6. Tax on alcoholic liquors	4,507,272
7. Tobacco-tax	348,674
8. Stamp dues, patent dues, etc	2,787,123
9. Receipts from mines	218,960
10. Railroads	391,100
11. Mint	506,000
12. Other receipts from public works	78,880
13. Public lands	712,560
14. Miscellaneous receipts	1,647,746
15. Reimbursements	813,304
Total	55,651,879

EXPENDITURES.

1. Public debt	21,200,281
2. Civil list and appanages	877,000
3. Pensions	1,059,404
4. Council of State	800,860
5. Senate	142,480
6. Ministry of Foreign Affairs	170,960
7. " of the Interior	1,275,500
8. " of Finance	1,505,800
9. " of War	7,190,100
10. " of the Navy	2,636,800
11. " of Public Instruction	1,189,970
12. " of Public Works	591,800
13. " of Justice	1,314,800
14. " of the Imperial House	308,700
15. Colonization	1,518,174
16. Land-tax reform	970,000
17. Provincial administration	3,786,700
18. Postal administration	1,050,000
19. Funds to promote industry	1,005,084
20. Police	2,486,452
21. Priests, temples	185,000
22. Public buildings, canals, etc	1,987,200
23. Ambassadors and consuls	500,000
24. Miscellaneous	1,877,814
25. Unforeseen expenses	1,500,000
Total	55,651,879

The public debt on July 1, 1879, was as follows:

1. Home debt:

Bearing interest at 4 per cent.	11,327,675	
" " 5 "	46,412,555	
" " 6 "	89,425,290	228,631,180
" " 7 "	107,997,015	
" " 8 "	14,592,225	
" " 10 "	8,876,870	
Bearing no interest	9,439,792	
Paper money	113,427,992	
	351,498,854	

2. Foreign debt:

Bearing interest at 7 per cent.	10,865,120	11,829,120
" " 9 "	1,464,000	
Total	363,327,974	

From this amount should be deducted:

Reserve fund	50,898,872
Outstanding loans	7,495,220
Total	58,394,092
Debt not provided for	304,933,882

The Japanese army in 1878 was composed as follows:

ARMS.	Peace footing.	War footing.
Infantry (46 battalions)	29,568	48,008
Cavalry (8 squadrons)	390	450
Artillery (10 divisions or 20 batteries)	2,420	2,960
Engineers and train (17 companies)	1,670	2,060
Coast artillery (9 companies)	720	900
Officers	2,009	2,843
Total	86,777	51,721

The navy in 1879 comprised 10 steam-vessels, of an aggregate of 2,930 horse-power, and with 49 guns. Three of the vessels are ironclads. The fleet is manned by 3,500 men, inclusive of 200 officers.

The foreign commerce in the years 1868 and 1874–'79 was as follows (in yens):

YEARS.	Imports.	Exports.	EXCESS OF	
			Imports.	Exports.
1879...	29,815,353	24,614,700	5,200,653	....
1878...	32,563,864	25,524,570	7,039,294	....
1877...	25,900,541	22,866,708	3,088,833	....
1876...	24,087,515	27,669,466	....	3,581,951
1875...	29,975,627	18,611,110	11,364,517	....
1874...	23,461,814	19,315,064	4,146,750	....
1868...	10,693,071	15,553,472	....	4,860,401

The countries principally concerned in the commerce of 1879 were as follows:

COUNTRIES.	Imports.	Exports.
Great Britain.....................	16,190,233	3,486,941
China.........................	4,667,434	5,733,925
United States.....................	3,437,985	7,435,627
France.........................	3,295,704	6,000,238
Germany.........................	1,017,111	84,363
East Indies and Siam...........	998,494	433,910
Belgium.........................	179,090	35
Australia.........................	93,644	177,670
Italy...........................	65,860	703,312

The imports of precious metals in 1879 amounted to 11,052,556 yens, and the exports to 2,791,405.

The movement of shipping in the ports open to foreign commerce was as follows in 1878:

NATIONALITY.	Vessels.	Tons.
British...........	336	285,430
American......	124	167,434
German........................	57	24,805
French.........................	33	45,307
Japanese.......................	64	108,936
Others.........................	50	34,608
Total.......................	664	661,520

There were besides 29 French mail-steamers of 48,264 tons, 27 American mail-steamers of 124,968 tons, and 26 British mail-steamers of 25,519 tons.

The aggregate length of railroads in operation is 105 kilometres. Eight lines of telegraph have an aggregate length of 2,934 kilometres.

The postal administration of Japan has been rapidly improving since the country, on June 1, 1877, joined the World's Postal Union. According to the annual report of the Postmaster-General, the total number of postal stations on June 30, 1878, was 8,792. The number of letters sent was 47 millions, an increase of 23·1 per cent. over the preceding year. The number of postal cards was 10 millions. The number of money-orders has increased 21·1 per cent.; of letters and parcels sent to foreign countries, 10·4 per cent.; of letters, etc., received, 16·7 per cent. The postal savings banks, which the Government has introduced but recently, are meeting with great favor, and have attained the number of 292; the ag-

gregate number of the deposits has increased 88·3 per cent., and the aggregate value 270 per cent. The financial year 1877–'78 was the first in which the receipts of the department exceeded the expenditures (5·9 per cent.).

A new educational law was promulgated on September 29, 1879. All educational establishments, including public and private schools and libraries, are to be under the care of the Minister of Education. The schools are divided, into primary schools, higher schools, colleges, and normal and technical schools. Primary schools are to be established in all cities and villages, but this provision need not be carried out wherever there is a good private school. The school age comprises the sixth to the fourteenth year, and during this period all children are to attend school for at least sixteen months. Corporal punishment is not permitted.

An important change in the monetary affairs of the empire was made in September. According to an official decree of the Government, the silver yen of 416 grains, and 900 fine, is to be accepted in future at par with the Mexican dollar, not only by the Government, but also by the subjects of Japan in all their private transactions. At the same time the two foreign banks in Yokohama, the Oriental Bank and the Hong-Kong and Shanghai Bank, gave notice that in future they would accept the yen at par with the Mexican dollar, and would keep their accounts in dollars.

The number of foreign residents in 1879 was 2,475, or 17 less than in 1877. They were divided among the different nationalities as follows: British, 1,067; Americans, 479; Germans, 300; French, 230; Dutch, 105; Portuguese, 95; others, 209. The number of Chinese in the same year was 3,028.

The silk season which closed in June, 1879, was not a successful one. The principal features of the season had been the increasing importance of the trade with America, and the falling off of the English trade. Up to June 19th the export had reached 19,070 bales, as against 21,975 bales in the previous year. The whole production of the silk season of 1878–'79 was 63,210 Japanese bales, of about 75 pounds each.

The remaining local autonomy possessed by the Loochoo Islands was suppressed in 1879, and the administrative system which prevails throughout Japan Proper has been extended to these islands. The Loochoo (or Liu Kin) Islands have an area of 808 square miles, and 167,000 inhabitants. They formerly paid a tribute to Japan, but they retained a sort of relative independence until 1609, in which year the Daimio of Satsuma, the southwest corner of Japan, obtained permission from the Shogoon to set out on an expedition for the final conquest of the islands. He succeeded, and from 1609 to 1868 they formed part of the territory of the Princes of Satsuma, being governed by them under the Shogoon. A nominal king was allowed to continue to exist in

Loochoo. When, eleven years ago, the feudal system was swept away in Japan, and all the domains of the Daimios were absorbed in the empire, the so-called King of the Loochoo Islands became simply an ordinary subject of the Japanese Gavernment, like all the other local princes who were then mediatized; but he received from the Mikado a title of consolation, which placed him foremost among the nobility of the land. The political sovereignty of Japan was regularly applied to his country, though a certain local autonomy was still left to it on administrative questions. A proof of the application of the sovereignty of Japan to the islands was given in 1874, when the Mikado sent a force to Formosa to avenge the murder of some shipwrecked Loochooans, nearly involving Japan in a war with China, which claimed to be the suzerain of Loochoo; but China finally recognized the right of the Mikado to protect his Loochooan subjects, and paid an indemnity. As China had never abandoned her claims to the islands, the Chinese Ambassador in Tokio has protested against the annexation.

Early in the year the Mikado issued the following decree on the subject of economy:

Order and economy in all things form the basis of all good government. It is essential to avoid unnecessary expense, and, to ameliorate the conditions of existence of the people by all practicable means, every one must conscientiously and strictly do his duty. I desire that henceforth the greatest possible economy be enforced in the construction of the ministries and other public buildings. The prefects of the different fus and kens of the empire will all of them, so far as they are concerned, act in strict accordance with the spirit which leads me to issue this decree. They will seek to reduce expenses as much as possible, so as not to exceed the credits allowed to them by the budget. Above all things, they will constantly bear in mind that they are not to impoverish the people.

The following notification from the Minister of the Imperial Household, published in the Yokohama papers in March, shows how practically the Mikado is applying his decree to his own house:

Of his gracious will, his Majesty the Mikado has notified the necessity of practicing the greatest economy. It is therefore ordered by his Majesty that the expenses of food and all other household matters must be reduced.

Considerable excitement was produced in July in consequence of the British Minister's interference with the Japanese quarantine regulations. As cholera prevailed in the southern parts of the empire, a strict quarantine was ordered for Yokohama. The United States Minister issued immediate instructions for the compliance of Americans with the quarantine regulations. The British Minister denied the right of the Japanese Government on account of extra-territorial jurisdiction, and declared that any English ship should break quarantine and be protected in doing so by British men-of-war. Owing to indignant remonstrances from influential quarters, especially from Governor Hennessy of Hong-Kong, who was at that time visiting Japan, the British Minister

modified his attitude and consented to coöperate with the Japanese Government; but he still asserted his right to break quarantine at that place. The German Minister supported the British Minister. All the other diplomatic representatives were indifferent, except the Russian Minister, who sided with the United States Minister.

General Grant arrived at Nagasaki June 21st. By imperial decree his reception was to be in all respects identical with what would be accorded the reigning monarch of any European country. On his arrival at Nagasaki he received an address of welcome by a committee of thirteen, chosen to represent all alien nationalities there.

JEWS. The sixth Council of the *Union of American Hebrew Congregations* was held in New York, beginning July 8th. More than two hundred delegates were present, representing twenty-five States. Mr. William B. Hackenburgh of Philadelphia was chosen President. The report of the Executive Board represented that the feeling in favor of a union of the Hebrew people had grown, and recommended for the consideration of the Council the topics of a stricter observance of the Sabbath, the establishment of a young ladies' seminary, the encouragement of agricultural pursuits, and further legislation respecting civil and religious rights. The Board, to whom the subject had been referred at the previous meeting of the Council, had decided that it was inexpedient for the present to introduce the system of circuit preaching; but, as the decision had been unfavorably commented upon by the small communities which felt the want of Sabbath-schools and able sermons, the subject was again recommended to consideration. A report was adopted favoring the erection of a new building for the Hebrew College in Cincinnati. A clause opposing the opening of a branch of the college in New York was objected to, and was referred back for modification. A report on the observance of the Sabbath was adopted, to the effect that "the religious welfare of the Jewish community depends greatly on the preservation of the Sabbath. It is necessary for us, as for all religious bodies, to have certain ideas in common, and to have certain outward symbols to express them. The means for obtaining a better observance of the Sabbath are, however, not within the reach of the Council. Persuasion, example, and education alone can produce a proper sentiment on the subject; no legislation by us can influence the matter." Some of the speakers on this report desired to have a specific mention made of the seventh day as the Sabbath that was intended; but their views did not prevail, a general agreement being manifest that no other day could be regarded as the Jewish Sabbath. A report on circuit preaching recommended the practice, and gave the names of a number of ministers who had volunteered to engage in that work. The sum of $1,000 was appropriated to put into execution a plan to provide volunteer visiting preachers for such communities as are not able to support a minister. The duties of the circuit preachers will be to organize congregations, awaken the religious spirit, and establish religious schools. Each minister will have a salary fixed by the Executive Board, and his expenses, not more than $500 a year, will be paid, except when the community visited can furnish the money. A report on the subject of a young ladies' seminary admitted that the establishment of such an institution would be desirable, but remarked upon the lack of funds for the purpose. A committee was appointed to consider the advisability and feasibility of establishing two self-sustaining seminaries, one for boys and one for girls, and report at the next session of the Council.

A committee of the Board of Delegates to whom the subject had been referred in the previous year presented a report in favor of the encouragement of agricultural colonies and the training of youth to agricultural pursuits, and the following recommendations were adopted on the subject : " That a tract of land should be purchased large enough to accommodate at least fifty families and support a model-farm school ; that managers of Jewish schools and charitable institutions should introduce into the institutions elementary instruction on the subject; that the opportunity now opens for a good investment of money by capitalists; and that the Executive Board of the Council be empowered to select from their number a committee of five on agriculture, to solicit donations of land, farming implements, and money ; to allot to each family in the colony from fifty to eighty acres of land that shall be rent-free for seven years, after which the land taken up shall be offered to the incumbent for a reasonable price, the money received to be applied to the purchase of other land, and so on ; to purchase such additional tracts of land as may from time to time in the colonial life be expedient, and as the funds on hand may allow ; and that the Board's committee should consult with kindred organizations as to the best means of accomplishing the project of the colony."

The Committee on Statistics reported that they had made no further progress. It appeared, however, that 115 congregations were now joined to the Union ; that for the last fiscal year the sum of $4,374 had been received for the college from congregations, with yearly contributions of $957, $3,837 as gifts to the sinking fund, and $1,821 for the support of indigent students. The miscellaneous receipts had been $2,647, and the total disbursements $11,619. The college had a balance on hand of $3,055, and $2,453 in the sinking fund. Expressions of fellowship were exchanged with the Alliance Israélite Universelle of Paris, the Anglo-Jewish Association of London,

the Alliance of Vienna, and the Deutsche Gemeinde Bund of Leipsic.

The first instance of the interchange of fraternal courtesies between Jews and a Christian church in the United States took place in St. Louis on June 29th. The Second Baptist Church in that city having been burned, the congregation were given the use of the Synagogue Shaari Emeth for purposes of worship until they could provide themselves with a new building. At the close of the period, when the Baptists were about to go to their own church, a joint religious service of the two congregations was held in the synagogue, with prayer, hymns from the Jewish and Baptist hymn-books, Scriptural lessons, and addresses by the Baptist pastor and the Jewish rabbi.

A plan has been under consideration in England·for the reorganization of Jews' College, which contemplates a division into junior and senior classes. Candidates for admission into the junior class must have passed the matriculation examination of the University of London, and be between sixteen and twenty years of age. The course of study in this class is arranged for three years, during which the students shall attend classes at the University College. Candidates for the senior class shall have passed the second B. A. examination of the University of London, and shall occasionally have opportunities of practicing the arts of preaching, reading, and teaching, and of being instructed in the theory and practice of *Shechitah* and *Milah*. The Council shall grant certificates of competency to students who have qualified themselves for the offices of minister, preacher, reader, and teacher of religion. An elementary class is also to be established. In Germany societies have been formed among the rabbis and teachers of various provinces to promote a new methodical system of instruction, and the German Board of Delegates is working with the same object. In Austria a sharp impetus has been given to education by the efforts of the Vienna Alliance and the Lemberg " Shomer Israel."

The *Alliance Israélite Universelle* of Paris has branches in every prominent European capital ; its agents are in active communication with the most distant Jewish communities in India, China, Abyssinia, etc. ; and its schools in Palestine, Turkey, Morocco, and other countries are making rapid progress. Its political influence was exhibited at the Congress of Berlin, and its schools in the East attest the efficacy of its educational influence.

An *International Jewish Convention*, under the auspices of the Alliance Israélite, met in Paris on August 12th, and was attended by about two hundred delegates, among whom were some of the most distinguished representatives of the race in Europe and America. M. Crémieux, President of the Alliance, presided. The opening addresses dwelt chiefly upon the stipulation for the emancipation of the Jews in Roumania in the Treaty of Berlin as marking an event of great importance and an occasion of joy. The Rev. H. S. Jacobs of New York spoke of the great influence which America was destined to exercise in Jewish affairs, and of the interest which was felt in the United States in Jewish progress. A vote of thanks was given to the American delegates. The subject of education was prominent among the matters considered by the Convention, and whatever related to the establishment and improvement of schools in the East was received with favor. A proposition was adopted to commemorate Jewish emancipation in the East by means of a medal. Propositions concerning the organization of the Alliance and modifications of its constitution were much debated, and a final decision upon them was postponed till the next year.

JULIO, E. D. B., a painter, born on the island of St. Helena, near the spot where the great Emperor lingered out his years of captivity, in 1843, died in Georgia, September 15, 1879. He was the son of an Italian father and a Scotch mother, and inherited his poetic and artistic tendencies from one and his indomitable perseverance from the other. At an early age he was sent to Paris, where he received a careful education. During the war he removed to America and settled at the North. The fragility of his constitution and his natural sympathies induced him to move South. He established himself in New Orleans, and was successful as a portrait painter. Ambitious and like every true artist, dissatisfied with his own powers of execution, he abandoned his career and went back to Paris to become a pupil of Bonnat. On his return to this country he began in New Orleans a school of art. His best known painting, engravings of which are widespread, is "The Last Meeting of Lee and Stonewall Jackson." It is a composition of considerable merit. The faces of the two Southern leaders are admirable likenesses. Though essentially a portrait-painter, Julio was ambitious of excelling in landscape. He painted many Louisiana scenes, but his work does not compare with that of the lamented Clague, who alone has caught the very trick of the indolent waving moss pendent from the wide-spreading branches of the live-oaks, the sharply defined shadows of the leaves, the transparent atmosphere, and the dark untroubled waters. Though Clague had no rival and left no successor, Julio bore some impress of his genius, and paid him the homage of sincere admiration. Unfortunately his career was untimely nipped. To try change of air, he went to Georgia, but consumption was too far advanced. He left many unfinished works. His "Diana" is a striking and graceful figure. The coloring is defective, but the drawing is fine. He was a rapid and skillful draughtsman. His crayon sketches are meritorious. One of his pictures was exhibited at the Centennial and favorably criticised. It was entitled "Harvest Scene," and represented cane-cutting on a Louisiana sugar plantation.

K

KANSAS. The biennial session of the Legislature of Kansas commenced on January 13th. Lieutenant-Governor L. U. Humphrey presided in the Senate; and in the House Sidney Clarke was chosen permanent Speaker.

An election of a Senator in Congress, to fill the vacancy caused by the expiration of the term of John James Ingalls, was concluded on January 31st. Mr. Ingalls was reëlected. The vote on each ballot was as follows:

CANDIDATES.	Tuesday.	Wednesday.	Thursday.	Friday.
Ingalls	60	63	72	86
Anthony	26	26	25	0
Simpson	17	17	17	0
Phillips	11	14	13	0
Campbell	6	4	0	0
Horton	8	2	2	80
Pomeroy	2	2	3	0
Goodin (Dem.)	20	22	17	1
Mitchell (Green.)	19	18	18	2

Charges of bribery in the election were immediately made, and the following resolution was adopted by the House:

Whereas, It is charged that during the progress of the late Senatorial election acts of bribery and corruption were resorted to, to influence the votes of members of this House for United States Senator; and,

Whereas, It is also charged that offers were made to pay large sums of money for votes for Senator, and that in some cases these corrupt offers were made by members of this House; and,

Whereas, The honor of the State, the integrity of this House, and the character of the Senate of the United States demand that a full and impartial investigation should be had of all the facts and circumstances connected with the aforesaid charges; therefore,

Resolved, That a committee of five members be appointed, whose duty it shall be to investigate all charges of bribery and corruption connected with the late Senatorial election, and all charges of corruption in office made against the recently elected Senator, to the end that the innocent may be vindicated, and all acts of bribery and corruption, if any, shall be found, exposed, and punished.

A similar resolution was adopted in the Senate, and for the sake of economy it was proposed to change the committee into a joint one, but the House refused to concur.

The committee of the House submitted three reports, one a majority and two minority. The chairman reported that the charge that acts of bribery and corruption were resorted to with intent to influence the votes of members of the House was sustained; but no acts of bribery and corruption were proven against Senator Ingalls.

Another member of the committee reported

that the evidence submitted fully convinced him that Mr. James S. Merrett was a general manager in the interest of Senator Ingalls at Topeka during the pending of the late Senatorial election, and had general charge of his rooms and the direction of his affairs; that he was aided and assisted in his plans to reëlect Senator Ingalls, among others, by Mr. J. S. Danford and Mr. Calvin Hood; that Senator Ingalls and those parties employed corrupt and illegal means to secure the election of said J. J. Ingalls to the United States Senate, and but for said improper influences his election would not have been obtained.

The majority of the committee reported that they had examined about forty-five witnesses, and that they find from the testimony that John J. Ingalls, the recently elected United States Senator, used no corrupt means to secure his election to the United States Senate, and that neither of the late Senatorial candidates was guilty of bribery or corruption in the late Senatorial election; and they further said that Ingalls, the recently elected United States Senator, had not been guilty of any corruption in office; and that there was no evidence against any member or members of the House which would warrant or justify their expulsion.

The House adopted the report of the majority by a vote of yeas 60, nays 44.

The following resolution was also adopted by the House:

Whereas, The testimony taken by the Investigation Committee discloses the fact that certain members of this House did, during the late Senatorial contest, take especial pains to place themselves in position to be offered money to influence their votes, and did, in some instances, actually receive money, though not from either of the Senatorial candidates; therefore, be it

Resolved, That the conduct of all such members is deserving of, and this House does administer upon them, its severest censure, committing them to their constituents for their ultimate condemnation, which they so justly deserve.

The vote was—yeas 51, nays 48.

A committee of the Senators in Congress subsequently investigated the charges against Senator Ingalls, and made a report entirely exonerating him, but condemning many of the proceedings at the election.

During this investigation a question was raised which is of far more importance than the matter then at issue. The committee summoned the telegraph operator to appear before them, and bring any original messages in his possession. The operator sent to them a communication stating that he was ready to appear, but that he had been instructed by the management of the Western Union Telegraph Company to decline to produce any original telegrams in his possession, as the custodian thereof for the company; and further, that the company had forwarded by mail a communication inclosing the answer which it desired him to make in its behalf in support of its right to withhold from any tribunal original messages, or the contents of original messages, intrusted

to it for transmission from one person to another. The operator by order of the House was arrested by the Sergeant-at-Arms, on an attachment "for a contempt in refusing or neglecting obedience to the summons (*sub pœna duces tecum*) before the investigating committee of the House of Representatives of the State of Kansas," and was imprisoned. Meantime the answer of the company was received. It presents their view of the legal aspect of the question of the inviolability of telegraphic messages of individuals, and is one step toward the final decision of the question which must ultimately be made. The points embraced in their answer were as follows:

The Telegraph Company distinctly disavows all partisan feeling or interest in the investigation ordered by the House, and which is being prosecuted before the committee appointed for that purpose. The company has no desire to hinder, defeat, or delay any investigation ordered or conducted by any tribunal for the discovery of any illegal act against the State, or against the rights of an individual. Their objection is, that the company ought not to violate the confidence of its patrons, and that to compel it to do so would be against public policy, and most dangerous to public and private security. The senders of twenty-five millions of messages a year, intrusted to the confidence of the Telegraph Company, representing as they do the capital, the enterprise, and the intelligence of the country in every department of human affairs, have a peculiar claim upon all departments or branches of Government for protection from the seizure of their private communications, and especially from any use of them which would be liable to intensify political excitement. The Telegraph Company has therefore adopted, as a rule for the guidance of all its officers, agents, and employees, that no messages, whether original or copy, in any office of such company, shall be taken or removed from the actual possession or control of the company without the consent or direction of the company's Executive Committee, or of its Board of Directors. The sacredness of this confidence is recognized in some States by statutes prescribing penalties for a voluntary betrayal—a security which the law has not given to those ordinary communications between private parties from which analogies are drawn supposed to justify the application of the *sub pœna duces tecum* to telegrams. During the period in which the law affecting them has been in process of adaptation from the law of evidence upon analogous topics, a disposition has been shown to apply to telegrams some of the considerations of public policy which impute sanctity to a letter confided to the post-office, and to demand the same protection to the same communication when confided to this *quasi* public agency, which holds a power over men's affairs through its possession of their secrets exceeding that which any Government obtains through the mere physical custody of sealed letters. Telegraph companies naturally desire to enhance the public confidence in the safety of communications intrusted to them, and they have strenuously endeavored to establish some ground, either of entire exemption from, or of regulation of, the control over the contents of their files asserted by courts and legislative bodies. These ideas find support in some respectable places where neither the interest nor feelings of the telegrapher can be supposed to have influence.

Judge Cooley, in the last edition of his work on "Constitutional Limitations," under the head of "Constitutional Protection of the Citizen against unreasonable Searches and Seizures," declares his solemn judgment that the agents of the telegraph can not be lawfully compelled to produce the messages confided to them for transmission over their wires under a *sub pœna duces tecum*, and clearly and emphatically expresses his opinion that certain decisions of some of the State courts, affirming their power to require the production of such messages, are founded upon erroneous doctrines and unsound reasoning.

The Telegraph Company is aware that in several instances decisions have been made adverse to the position herein contended for. These cases, or the principal ones, are the case of E. W. Barnes, before the lower House of Congress in January, 1877; the case of The State vs. Litchfield, 58 Maine, 267; the case of Henister vs. Freedman, 2 Parsons's "Selected Cases," 274: and the case of National Bank vs. National Bank, 7 West Virginia, 544.

In the case of Barnes, a local telegraph manager at New Orleans, the witness was subpœnaed to produce telegrams before a committee appointed in December, 1876, by the lower House of Congress, to investigate the alleged frauds in the Presidential election in Louisiana. Barnes declined to produce the messages. His answer was referred to the Judiciary Committee, and that committee, on the strength of the cases The State vs. Litchfield and Henister vs. Freedman, above cited, decided that the witness must produce the messages. It is believed, however, that the opinion of Judge Cooley, already quoted, and which was written as a direct reply to the arguments presented in the case from Maine, far outweighs the reasoning of the Court. The cases of Henister vs. Freedman and National Bank vs. National Bank are no stronger than the case from Maine, and are therefore fully met and answered by the convincing reasoning of Judge Cooley.

As against the decision of the Judiciary Committee of the House of Representatives in the Barnes case, we may cite the opinions of Senators Conkling and Sherman in the case of Turner, a telegraph operator who was subpœnaed before a committee appointed by the United States Senate to investigate certain alleged frauds in Oregon shortly after the Presidential election of 1876. In the discussion before the Senate, as to the power and authority of the Senate to compel the witness to produce certain telegraph messages, Mr. Conkling, although interested politically in supporting the investigation then on foot, believed that an abuse of power was involved, and that a precedent dangerous to private rights would result; and Mr. Sherman said he thought there ought to be a statute defining the nature of the testimony which may be brought out in such cases, the limits within which it can be called for, and the circumstances or foundation which should be laid, before telegrams should be produced. The opinions of these eminent statesmen, and eminent lawyers as well, ought to have great weight in determining a question so momentous as that involved in the question of the power of this House to compel the Telegraph Company to open up to the whole world the secret affairs of every citizen, whether personal, business, or political.

The case of Babcock, before Judge Dillon (3 Dil. Ct. Ct. R., 566), has also been quoted as adverse to the claim of inviolability for telegraph messages. But this question was not raised in that case, as will appear in the opinion of Judge Dillon, page 569, where he says: "No objection is made on the ground that these messages are privileged, confidential communications; that is, the Telegraph Company does not insist that they stand in any different relation from what private persons would if they had custody of the same papers." The only question decided was whether the sub pœna duces tecum sufficiently described the messages. The case was decided in 1876, before the Presidential election of that year. The question of the inviolability of the confidence existing between the sender or receiver of a message and the Telegraph Company had not then been much discussed nor much considered. Since that time the question, by reason of the momentous interests involved in its decision, has challenged the attention of the reading public throughout Europe and America, and it is not too much to say that careful, thoughtful, prudent men everywhere are fast reaching the conclusion that the best interests of the government and the people demand that the seal of confidence reposed in the telegraph companies by their patrons shall not be violated.

The operator was released in this instance without the production of the messages.

The following resolution was adopted in the Senate—yeas 22, nays 12:

That the Senators of the State of Kansas are hereby instructed, and the Representatives in Congress are requested, to make all reasonable efforts to secure such a change in the Federal judiciary system as will take from the United States courts all civil jurisdiction, whether by original action or removal from State courts, except by appeal or writ of error from State courts of final resort in cases as now authorized.

An act was passed to repeal the annual levy of one mill on the dollar for school purposes. This was an important tax for the welfare of the schools, and the constitutionality of the act was finally sustained by the State Supreme Court. Section 3 of Article VI. of the Constitution, among other things, provides that the interest on the sale of public lands "and such other means as the Legislature may provide by tax or otherwise shall be inviolably appropriated to the support of common schools." In pursuance of this provision of the Constitution, the Legislature in 1861 passed a law (section 5, chapter 76) declaring, "There is hereby levied and assessed annually one mill on the dollar for the support of the common schools of the State." This law was reënacted in section 76, chapter 92, general statutes of 1868. The proceeds of this tax were distributed semi-annually, in March and July, by the State Superintendent, to the several school districts in the State, in proportion to the number of school children therein. In the year 1878 the one-mill tax amounted to $138,698, or sixty cents to each child of school age in the State. For the year 1879 the amount would have been about the same per capita. For years the constitutionality of this law has been questioned, it being held that an annual levy, year after year, is in violation of section 24, Article II., of the Constitution, which reads, "No money shall be drawn from the Treasury except in pursuance of a specific appropriation made by law, and no appropriation shall be for a longer time than two years" (under the old provision, one year). Because of the uncertainty of the levy under the Constitution, and because it was claimed by many that the eastern portion of the State, with the greater part of the taxable property of the State, was paying for the education of the children of the west, the Legislature attempted to repeal the law. This bill for the repeal of the school-tax levy was first introduced in the House. After its passage there it was discovered that the law of 1868 had been reënacted in 1876, and that in the opinion of many of the members, if the bill should become a law, it would be of no effect. Consequently, the bill never reached the Senate; but the same provisions were inserted in the revenue act and became a law. Its effect is to strike off about one month's salary of teachers in each city or school district in the State.

Another act was passed relating to school-books. It requires the school-district boards of officers to designate a particular series of school-books, and then to make no change for the ensuing five years. Another act was passed to regulate the sale of school lands. It provides that all new sales shall be made on twenty years' time and seven per cent. interest. All renewals of purchasers who have never been in default shall be on twenty years' time and at seven per cent. interest. All renewals of those in default shall remain on ten years' time and ten per cent. interest. Such renewal to be made prior to October 1, 1879.

During the year ending on July 31, 1879, the whole number of school districts was 5,575; increase for the year, 439. The whole number of persons between the ages of five and twenty-one years, as reported, was: males, .160,542; females, 150,768; total, 311,310. The increase in school population was by far the greatest of any year in the history of the State. It represented an immigration to the State of not less than 160,000 persons, and was as follows: males, 23,140; females, 21,595; total, 44,735. Thirteen counties report an increased school population of more than 1,000 each. The number of persons enrolled in public schools some portions of the year was: males, 107,095; females, 101,314; total, 208,409; increase for the year, 30,603. The average daily attendance on public schools was: males, 62,120; females, 61,876; total, 123,996; increase for the year, 17,064. The reports show an increase in the length of the school-term. In 1878 the average for the State was 22·6 weeks, and in 1879 it was 24·6 weeks, the increase for the year being two weeks. The number of different teachers employed in the common schools of the State for the year was: males, 3,128; females, 3,579; total, 6,707.

The sources from which the common-school fund was derived were:

Balances from preceding year..................	$261,467 72
State annual school fund.....................	362,506 50
Sale of bonds for building purposes..........	272,110 04
District taxes...............................	918,835 24
All other sources............................	53,643 52
Total receipts........................	$1,578,563 02

The school expenses were as follows:

For teachers' wages..........................	$1,012,699 16
To superintendents of graded schools.........	10,958 42
For rents, fuel, and incidentals..............	274,260 15
For text-books...............................	10,772 91
For district libraries.......................	4,026 82
For maps and apparatus.......................	19,999 45
For sites, buildings, and furniture..........	258,082 80
Total..................................	$1,590,794 80

At the close of the last fiscal year, June 30, 1879, the permanent common-school fund of the State, deposited with the State Treasurer, amounted to $1,601,631.92, $1,523,226.03 of which was invested as follows: United States bonds, $140,000; Kansas State bonds, $607,-925; Lawrence city bonds, $100,000; school-district bonds, $675,301. Sixty-six normal institutes were held during the year, at an ex-

pense of $18,357.17, $15,941.33 of which was for instruction, and $2,405.84 for incidentals. These institutes were in session from four to six weeks each, and in them 6,050 teachers received instruction.

An act was passed defining the term of duration and existence of certain railroads. The act extended for seventy-nine years the charters of all railroads granted by the Territorial Legislature, together with some five others. The charters of the former were for twenty years, and expired on February 11th.

The regulation of freights and fares was regarded as one of the most important subjects before the Legislature. There are about 2,500 miles of railroads in operation in the State. Their assessed value is $15,525,033. The law of the State prohibits the railroad corporations from charging over six cents per mile for transporting passengers. Other sections of the law relating to the classification of and charges for carrying freight are still less restrictive. A bill to create a Board of Railroad Commissioners was proposed, but not passed. Another to regulate, control, and establish rates of fare and freight on railroads, establish rules to regulate the same, and provide for the punishment of a violation of the provisions thereof, was brought forward in the House, but failed to become a law.

The taxation of the railroads is secured by the laws of the State, which require that all property shall be assessed at its value in money. Property other than railroad property is assessed by local assessors. Railroad property is assessed by a "State Board of Railroad Assessors," consisting of the Lieutenant-Governor, Secretary of State, Auditor of State, Treasurer of State, and the Attorney-General. The assessment of all classes of property in the State does not exceed sixty per centum of its "value in money." All the real estate of railroad companies connected with the right of way and used in the daily operation of the road is assessed with the track, ties, iron, etc. All other real estate is assessed by the local assessor of the township or city in which the real estate is situated. Personal property, as rolling-stock, ties, iron, timbers, material, tools, moneys, etc., are assessed to the railroad corporation the same as to individuals. The franchises of railroad companies are not taxed. The *property* of the railroad corporations being taxed, the stock is not taxed. The receipts are not taxed, except that portion of receipts over expenditures which is found to be surplus on March 1st each year. All moneys and all credits in excess of debts on hand March 1st are taxed. The total value of all classes of rolling-stock is ascertained from a sworn inventory by the company, and the valuation apportioned equally to each mile of road. Local taxes are levied by the local authorities upon the railroad property in the several counties, cities, townships, and school districts, as returned by the State Board of Assessors. State taxes are apportioned by the State Board and collected by the County Treasurer of the counties through which the roads run. The annual taxes are divided so that they can be paid in semi-annual payments on December 20th and June 20th. All taxes unpaid at those dates have a penalty of five per centum added. All taxes on personal property (for the purposes of taxation all railroad property is held to be personal property), after the dates above mentioned, shall be collected by the sheriffs of the several counties by seizure and sale of property. This law has been in force for three years, and is giving satisfaction to the people and the corporations. Under its provisions the assessment of railroad property has increased three millions of dollars over the assessments made by local assessors. The taxes assessed on the right of way, track, road-bed, rolling-stock, tools and materials, telegraph lines, etc., for 1879, amounted to $490,323.

A joint resolution was passed by the Legislature recommending that a State constitutional convention should be called.

The estimated assessment of property for 1879 was $140,000,000, and for 1880, $145,000,000. These estimates would require, to meet expenditures, a tax-levy of four mills, distributed as follows: for general revenue, three mills; for Capitol extension, one half mill; for sinking fund, one tenth mill; for interest, four tenths mill. The following items are from the statement of the assessment of personal property for 1879:

PROPERTY.	Number.	Total assessed value.	Average assessed value.
Horses	240,250	$7,768,463 94	$32 84
Neat cattle........	802,014	8,533,020 02	10 63
Mules and asses....	36,287	1,467,720 05	40 04
Sheep.............	243,842	280,077 25	1 14
Hogs.............	574,733	875,577 86	1 52
Wagons	65,951	1,842,257 70	20 85
Carriages	11,695	376,979 20	32 23
Pianofortes........	1,883	173,753 00	92 27

The agricultural products of the State show annually an increase in amount and value. The values of these in 1878 are thus reported by the Secretary of the Board of Agriculture:

Field products.......................... $49,914,484 88
Increase in total value of farm animals 6,401,871 30
Products of live stock.................... 10,415,389 89
Products of market garden................. 247,510 29
Apiarian products....................... 55,141 15
Horticultural products.................... 2,642,770 87

Total valuation of farm products for 1878. $69,677,067 81

Acres in organized counties, 33,599,600; in unorganized counties, 18,443,920; acres under cultivation, 6,538,727.85; increase of cultivated acres during the last six years, 3.567,120.85; increase from 1877 to 1878, 943,422.86. The acreage of wheat in 1879 in the State was greater than in the previous year by 223,104 acres, making the aggregate for winter wheat amount to 1,297,525 acres. During the last three years the area in winter wheat has increased over 100 per cent. The area in spring wheat was over 412,139 acres. The area in

corn was 2,925,070 acres, an increase of 589,588 acres over 1878, and of 60 per cent. during the past three years. The area in oats was 573,928 acres; in potatoes, 65,000 acres; in flax, 69,383 acres; in castor beans, 68,179 acres. The area in tame grasses, clover, millet, timothy, and blue-grass, aggregated 139,976 acres, and in prairie, meadow, and pasture, 484,019 acres. The total area in all farm crops aggregated 7,757,130 acres, an increase during the past year of 1,218,403 acres. The winter wheat was unusually fine. The corn promised the largest yield ever known in the State. The live-stock reports show an increase during the past three years of 51 per cent. in horses, 97 per cent. in mules, 46 per cent in milch cows, 44 per cent. in other cattle, 116 per cent. in sheep, and 283 per cent. in hogs. The farm dwellings erected during the year number 15,952, valued at nearly $3,000,000. The population of Kansas on the 1st of March, 1879, was 839,978, an increase of 141,481 during the previous year. At the same date there were 2,444 miles of railway in the State, and 528 miles were built during 1879.

There were 8,025 sheep reported killed by dogs for the year ending March 1, 1879. The number that died by other causes was 19,021. There were 1,059,640 pounds of cheese made in the State during the year, and 14,506,494 pounds of butter. The value of poultry and eggs was $393,070.48, while the value of animals slaughtered or sold for slaughter was $8,665,143. The produce of market gardens footed up $307,292.48. Chickens and eggs foot up more than gardens. There are but 31,190 stands of bees in the State, and they made 370,398 pounds of honey, and 10,949 pounds of wax. There are in the State 1,867,192 apple-trees in bearing, 58,482 pear-trees, 4,784,076 peach-trees, 169,940 plum-trees, 443,726 cherry-trees. Those not in bearing are: apple, 3,978,062; pear, 154,265; peach, 4,049,801; plum, 254,968; cherry, 678,426. Fruits of all kinds, except grapes, were a very short crop. Most of the counties reported an average crop of grapes, but in a few the crop was light. The number of acres in vineyards was 3,418, and 84,079 gallons of wine were made.

The charitable institutions of the State are in a prosperous condition. They are controlled by twenty-five persons, divided into five boards, as follows: Regents of the Normal School, five; Regents of the State University, six; Regents of Agricultural College, six; Trustees of Charitable Institutions, five; and Directors of the Penitentiary, three. The total amount paid to the members of the Boards for the fiscal year ending January 30, 1879, amounted to $5,626.60. The consolidation of the control of the several charitable institutions, which placed them all in the hands of one board, was made in 1876, and has worked well.

The debt of Leavenworth county and city, in bonds issued to aid in railroad construction, exceeded at the beginning of the year $2,000,-

000, which was 30 per cent. of the taxable property of the county and 40 per cent. of that of the city respectively. The interest remained unpaid so long that the creditors became wearied with waiting, and brought suit on their bonds. The United States Court gave judgment in their favor, and ordered the County Commissioners to levy a tax to pay the judgments. This order the Commissioners declined to obey, and they were cited before the Court to answer why they should not be punished for contempt. Popular meetings were then held both at Leavenworth and Lawrence, at which the Commissioners were exhorted to persist in their refusal, even if they had to go to prison. The resolutions declare that they were elected on this very issue, with the understanding that under no circumstances would they levy a tax to pay the interest, and it was expected that they would keep their pledge. Some of them publicly declared that they would not obey the order of the Court. The following resolution manifests the defiant attitude of the people:

Resolved, That the tax-payers of Leavenworth County will stand by the Board of County Commissioners in its efforts to compromise the railroad indebtedness as long as they are governed by the wish of the tax-payers as expressed in this motion, and will protect them from personal loss and pay all expenses that are necessary to be incurred in an effort to bring about a compromise of this indebtedness; and in fighting it to the end, if the members have to be sent to Jail, the county will compensate them for their time while detained from their business, and if they are compelled to pay any fines, the county will fully indemnify them.

These proceedings, as in all other cases, led to an arrangement.

The decline in the amount of life-insurance policies in the State during the year was $1,-180,584, although there was an increase in the number of policies.

The movement, or " exodus " as it was called, of colored families from the States on the lower part of the Mississippi River to Kansas is treated elsewhere in these pages. It is sufficient to show here the manner in which they were received by the people and their condition on arrival. This is briefly done in the following appeal to the friends of the colored people:

TOPEKA, KANSAS, *June* 26, 1879.

To THE FRIENDS OF THE COLORED PEOPLE :—The directors of the Kansas Freedman's Relief Association, in view of the present situation, deem it proper to make public this address, and ask the friends of the colored people for further aid in caring for the helpless and destitute refugees.

This is a matter not local to our State, but is one of national concern. It involves the solution of a great question, important alike to the people of the whole country, and if properly met will go very far to work a cure of the ills of the freedmen of the South. If we prove equal to the occasion, and can assist these people who are seeking homes in the North will discover a kindlier feeling and better treatment in the South.

In organizing this association we were moved by two controlling motives. The first was one of humanity. Many of them were old and decrepit, and many young and helpless, and with few exceptions were

destitute. They were landed on the river banks by hundreds, in the chilly days of early spring, after a long and tedious journey, fraught with hardships and privations. Many were sick and dying from exposure, and many were suffering for food, clothing, and medical assistance. The simplest dictates of humanity demand immediate and organized effort for their relief.

Another incentive to meet this emergency was to maintain the honored traditions of our State, which had its conception and birth in a struggle for freedom and equal rights for the colored man. She has shed too much blood for this cause to now turn back from her soil these defenseless people fleeing from the land of oppression.

We have not sought to stimulate or encourage their migration hither. We have always endeavored to place before the colored people of the South the plain facts, hoping thus to properly restrain an improvident hegira, based upon delusive hopes and expectations. We have also sought to impress upon them that other Western and Northern States possess equal advantages for homes for the laboring man. In brief, we have undertaken, so far as lies in our power, to provide for the destitute of these people, who come voluntarily among us, the common necessities of life, and to assist them in obtaining situations where they can earn a livelihood.

We have made an effort to establish a colony about fifty miles west of this city in Wabaunsee County. Finding that good land could be bought for $2.65 per acre, we are locating about thirty families on forty acres each. This is university land, one tenth to be paid down and the balance in nineteen years at 7 per cent. interest. We have furnished for their use teams and some agricultural implements, built barracks to be used in common, and furnished rations. We also agreed to make the first payment for them. Some ground has been broken and planting done, but it was too late to realize much this season. This is an experiment, and so far seems successful, but it requires more money than we anticipated. The ultimate success of this colony must depend on future contributions. The refugees have established three other colonies, one in Graham, one in Hodgeman, and one in Morris County. The association is not responsible for these, but they will need assistance.

This association has taken charge of, and aided more or less, about three thousand of these people, and there are still here and on the way from St. Louis about four hundred more. We have received money from all sources, $5,819.70. We have expended and incurred obligations for the whole of this fund. A large quantity of clothing and blankets have been received, and we have a large lot of clothing now on hand. What we need is money with which to obtain shelter, medical assistance, and furnish transportation to such places as will give them employment. This we must have or else relinquish all further efforts at organized assistance to these refugees.

The good people who have already so generously contributed to the cause have our sincere thanks.

All contributions should be sent to Governor John P. St. John.

JOHN P. ST. JOHN, President.
JNO. FRANCIS, Treasurer.
P. I. BONEBRAKE, Auditor.
ALBERT H. HORTON, Chief Justice.
C. G. FOSTER, U. S. District Judge.
JAMES SMITH, Secretary of State.
J. C. HEBBARD, Secretary.
WILLARD DAVIS, Attorney-General.
Board of Directors—N. C. McFarland, T. W. Henderson, and J. B. Jetmore.

KENTUCKY. The question of a revision of the Constitution of Kentucky was submitted by the Legislature to the voters at the election in August, 1879. A majority vote against revision determines the question until it may be again submitted by the Legislature. It is regarded as one of the defects of the existing Constitution that some of its provisions operate against the progress of internal improvements. The Legislature is not expressly empowered to levy taxes, contract debts, or make appropriations for internal improvements. The consequence has been that a local system of taxation has been adopted for internal improvements, and such numbers of counties and towns in the wealthier sections of the State have levied taxes and contracted debt to make their own improvements that, if they are not absolutely unable, they are at least unwilling to submit to further taxation, should it be proposed under this general provision of the Constitution, to construct internal improvements in those counties in other sections of the State unable to provide the means by local taxation. By reason of this the Legislature has become powerless to levy taxes and contract debt on behalf of the State for improvements in those counties and parts of the State where they are necessary to develop their resources, or elsewhere for the general benefit of the State. That this local system of taxation has reduced the State to this helpless condition is evidenced by the failure of the last Legislature to vote a dollar to repair river improvements. This has led to unavailing petitions to Congress for aid. Another defect is the present mode of organizing the judiciary department.

The receipts of the State Treasury for the fiscal year ending on October 10, 1879, were, with the balance on hand of the previous year, $2,166,192 ; the expenditures were $2,095,321. Although this presents an apparent balance of $70,870, there was really a deficiency, owing to the amount of outstanding claims unpaid. This was ascribed by the Auditor to a reduction of the revenue tax from twenty to fifteen cents on the hundred dollars, the increase of litigation and crime, the multiplication of courts and asylums for the relief and protection of the unfortunate, etc.

The total amount of the bonded indebtedness of the State, exclusive of the school fund, which is a permanent loan, is $180,394. The ample resources of the sinking fund to pay this indebtedness are as follows:

Net proceeds of the redemption of the 5-20 gold-
  bearing interest bonds of the United States,
  purchased under the act of March 19, 1873, by
  the Commissioners of the Sinking Fund........ $296,671 72
406 shares of stock in the Bank of Louisville...   82,480 00
Stock in turnpike roads (estimated) worth 500,000 00
                                                  _____
    Total resources.................... $768,151 72

The amount of bonds due and unpaid, to wit, $6,394, it is supposed will never be presented for payment, judging from the length of time they have been due, and from the additional fact that the interest ceased on them after maturity. It is supposed they have been lost or destroyed.

The condition of the schools and school system of the State is rather unfavorable. The resources of the school fund are: a bond of the Commonwealth held by the Board of Education, $1,327,000 ; bank stock, 735 shares in Bank of Kentucky, valued at $73,500 ; total, $1,400,500 ; besides dividends on Bank of Kentucky stock, tax on capital stock of the Bank of Shelbyville, Farmers' Bank of Kentucky, Farmers' and Drovers' Bank, fines and forfeitures for gambling, tax on every $100 worth of taxable property in the State, tax on dogs over six months old (one dollar on each dog in excess of two owned or kept by any bona fide housekeeper, and on each dog in excess of one owned or kept by any person not a housekeeper), and the non-transferable bond for the surplus bearing interest at six per cent. per annum, the whole bond aggregating $345,447.30. The total receipts from all these sources at the end of the fiscal year were $826,426.67, and the warrants paid amounted to $819,887.25. Of the collections, the dog tax amounted only to $965.70, and the tax on billiards to $2,605.57. The total collections only give about $135 to each of the six thousand school districts into which the State is divided, and this is not enough to keep a school in operation three months out of the year.

The number of children of school age in the State is placed at 400,000 whites and 50,000 colored. The per capita has fallen to $1.60 for white and 52 cents for colored children. At the same time about 200,000 white and 25,000 colored children do not attend the schools. The negro tax collected by the sheriffs amounted only to $25,716. Nevertheless, 1,800 schoolhouses have been built during the last eight years, while there are 7,000 school districts in the State. The Superintendent says: "The school-buildings of Louisville alone are worth nearly as much as all the school-houses in the rural districts. Louisville, with a population of about 175,000, expends $250,000 annually on her system, almost one third the whole cost of education to the State. If our people, in the same proportion with those of Louisville, would patronize education, we would expend annually $3,750,000 on our common schools, which would be about seven dollars to the pupil child included in the census, and almost seventeen dollars to every one in attendance at any time during the scholastic year."

At a State Convention of colored teachers held in Louisville on August 27th, a memorial to the Legislature was adopted, in which they say:

We, the colored teachers of this Commonwealth, in convention assembled, do, after having given the subject our most careful study and attention for the past two years, most respectfully represent: First, that the present colored school fund is wholly inadequate for the purpose of securing to the colored children of the Commonwealth general elementary instruction; that in a great many school districts schools are not held at all, and in many others the pro rata of the school fund is not sufficient to allow trustees to obtain any but incompetent teachers, who squander, as it were, the public money without securing to the children those educational advantages designed by the creation of the colored common-school system. In this connection we respectfully call your attention to the fact that the average salary of colored teachers in this State is only about $50 per annum, or about one third the average salaries of colored teachers in the other ex-slave States; and furthermore, the *per capita* which our fund yields is only about one fourth that given a white child, with a difference of four years in the limit of school age in favor of the white child, while in other States the *per capita* and limit of school age are the same for the colored as for the white child. Believing that, while this great difference remains, our common-school system will not only not accomplish the object for which it was intended, but will in time be entirely abrogated on account of its inefficiency, we do most respectfully ask at the hands of your honorable body an equalization of the *per capita* and limit of school age for all the children of this Commonwealth, as the only true means of securing to every child the necessary educational facilities.

Second, that the majority of the colored teachers of this State, by reason of the failure on the part of the State to make provision for normal instruction, are wholly incompetent as instructors. While the other ex-slave States have found it especially necessary to organize and foster, in many instances by State appropriations, normal schools for the education of colored teachers, which amount to twenty chartered colleges and twenty-nine normal schools, we have not a single normal school organized by aid of Kentucky for the same purpose; and while nearly or quite $20,000,000 have been expended on the colored people of the South for educational purposes since the close of the war, a very small proportion of this vast amount has found its way into Kentucky.

The acreage of wheat was larger than in 1878, but there are no means by which to determine its extent. The crop was estimated between 8,000,000 and 9,000,000 bushels. The corn-crop was fair, but suffered in consequence of the damage to the seed, which is left in the field, from the severe winter and the heavy rains late in the season. Tobacco was subject to the same drawbacks and casualties as the corn-crop. Much of it was damaged by wind, hail, and rain. The extent of the damage could be stated only approximately. The crop was much below the previous year. The hemp-crop, although it grew out better than was anticipated, was very short compared with any previous crop, and of light fiber and inferior quality. Much of it was caught by the heavy rains after being cut, and consequently considerable of the gluten washed off. In addition, it was discolored by the rains instead of being bright and lively, as Kentucky hemp usually is. The fall crop of grass was finer than any in a score of years, and it compensated for the short spring crop and half crop of hay. The crop of Irish potatoes was short, yet sufficient was raised for home use, and of medium quality. The season was unusually favorable to the growth of sweet potatoes, and the crop was large and of extra quality. The same may be said of the other great garden staple, cabbage. Live stock of all kinds was reported in good and thrifty condition, and unusually exempt from disease. In fact, not a single disease was mentioned in any locality in the State; on the contrary, there was a remarkable exemption from those pests, hog and chicken cholera. The bees had a hard time, and many stands perished during the winter.

The drought ran through the entire honey-making season, and they were unable to lay in their usual store. There had not been one swarm this year where there are usually fifty.

The number of idiots in the State is 758. These are supported by the State at an expense of $75 each, making a total of $56,850. An examination as to the localities of the State to which they belong shows the following results: Jefferson County, embracing the city of Louisville, with a population of over 200,000, has only sixteen idiots; while Wayne County in the mountains, with a population of 10,602, has thirty idiots. Again, Kenton County, embracing the city of Covington, has a population of about 40,000 inhabitants and four idiots, while Whitely County in the mountains, with a population of 8,278, furnishes twenty-three idiots. Fayette County, with a population of 26,656, has one idiot, while Morgan County in the mountains, with a population of 5,975, has twenty-one idiots. Daviess County, with a population of 20,714, has seven idiots, while Wolf County in the mountains, with a population of 3,603, has thirteen idiots. Henderson County, with a population of 18,-457, has four idiots, while Harlan County in the mountains, with a population of 4,415, has eighteen idiots. Campbell County, with a population of 27,406, has one idiot, while Clay County in the mountains, with a population of 8,297, has twenty-three idiots. At least three fourths of the idiots generally drawing pay from the Treasury are in the sparsely settled counties in Eastern Kentucky, familiarly known as the mountain counties.

The condition of the State Prison of Kentucky, according to the representations of Governor Blackburn, is truly horrible. The number of convicts at the close of the year was 969, with only 780 cells for their reception. The Governor says:

This terrible state of affairs required, as a necessity, that 378 of those wretched men should be thrust and immured two in a cell, although these cells were but 3 feet 9½ inches wide, 6 feet 3½ inches high, and 6 feet 8 inches long. These small, dark, ill-ventilated cells did not even contain sufficient air to support one man, and the death-record gives us abundant proof of this fact. From the 1st of January last up to the present time, there have died 74. This is a fearful mortality. To show the terrible torments some of these convicts must endure, we quote from the testimony of Dr. William Rodman, an eminent physician of Frankfort, upon this subject. In a suit of the State against Jerry South, the present lessee of the Penitentiary, to recover money due the State, the defendant South introduced as a witness Dr. Rodman, who, being duly sworn, testified as follows: "That he had been a physician to the penitentiary for about eight years, and is well acquainted with the cell-houses and work-shops. The cell-houses have been as bad as they well could be. Each man ought to have in his cell 840 feet of air; they get there 170 feet to two men. This has affected the health of the men in the prison, and very materially their working capacity." The Black Hole of Calcutta, so abhorred in history, was not much worse than this. Only think of it: two human beings crowded together in these dark, unwholesome little dens. To what beastliness may it not lead; yea, to what beastliness has it not already led! Ask those who have kept you prison, and they will tell you; but shuddering delicacy will turn away and avert its head at the disgusting recital. The revelations would remind you of Sodom and Gomorrah. Let not such things be even under the very shadow of our Capitol. Remember, our Constitution says cruel punishment shall not be inflicted. If this is not cruel, the English language has lost all meaning.

There are in the State three asylums for the insane, but these are overcrowded, because of various counties thrusting into them a class of incurable epileptics and idiots. Many of this class of unfortunates are entirely harmless and quite rational, except when in epileptic convulsions, which occur at intervals of weeks or more, and last but a few hours. There is also an Asylum for the Blind at Louisville, a Deaf and Dumb Asylum at Danville, and the Feeble-Minded Institute at Frankfort. The condition of these institutions is represented as very favorable. The number of children in the last-named institution is 131. The receipts of the year were $32,579, and the disbursements were $28,045. Of the operation of the institution the superintendent thus speaks:

Less than one year ago a carpenter shop was erected, and a practical mechanic employed to teach them, and several boys put to that trade. They have progressed so satisfactorily, that they can now be sent to any part of the premises to do the most intricate work. Some months afterward a shoe-shop was furnished with necessary tools and leather, a teacher, also a practical mechanic, employed, and several boys put to that trade. So that now we are doing all the work required about the institution in carpentry, and also making and mending all the shoes used in the institution, saving largely in annual expenditures in this direction, teaching the boys valuable trades, and enabling the management, in the course of a few years, to send out annually a class of competent workmen. It is believed that the number of self-sustaining boys thus leaving every year will be at least equal to the number desiring admittance, and in this way we shall be able to provide for all the children of this class in the State; for as these boys improve, and get from under the immediate care of their instructors, others will take their places, until all who are old enough will be engaged in some industry.

The geological survey of the State is nearly completed. Four volumes have been published and two are ready for publication. The most considerable part of the work that yet remains to be done is the topographical surveying necessary to complete the State map. This work has already so far advanced that a relatively small expenditure will secure as complete and accurate representation of the geography and geology of the State as has yet been given of any State in the Union.

The success of fish-culture has been very encouraging. Many millions of young fish have been placed in the waters of the State, and abundant results are anticipated.

The number of insurance companies now regularly authorized to transact business in Kentucky is ninety-six, of which nine are life and eighty-seven are fire companies. One of the life and nine of the fire companies are organized and operated under the laws of Ken-

tucky; eight of the life and sixty-three of the fire companies are organized under the laws of other States; and fifteen fire companies are of foreign countries. The amount of insurance upon lives and property of citizens of this State, December 31, 1878, was $116,567,851. The premiums received during that year from this State were $1,860,591, and the losses paid amounted to $1,028,397. Of these amounts, $22,655,687 were issued by Kentucky companies, $93,912,164 by companies of other States and foreign countries. Kentucky companies collected in the State, for 1878, $335,545, and companies of other States and foreign countries collected $1,525,046. Companies of the State paid for losses $120,528, and companies of other States and foreign countries paid $907,869. Not included in the above statement is the business of two accident and three mutual fire companies, the three latter being companies whose operations are confined to this State alone.

The number of the colored population of the State is 250,000. According to the assessment returns in the Auditor's office, the following results are shown

WHITES.

Total value of property for taxation, 1879....	$341,949,321 00
Total tax on same, at 40 cents per $100.....	1,367,797 28

BLACKS.

Total value of property for taxation, 1879....	$3,088,554 00
Total tax on same, at 45 cents per $100......	18,898 49

Total valuation for 1878....................	$354,019,676 00
Total tax for 1878........................	1,416,078 70
Total valuation for 1877...................	353,012,786 00
Total tax for 1877........	1,532,050 94
Total valuation for 1876.............	396,584,486 00
Total tax for 1876........................	1,586,187 94
Total valuation for 1875...................	417,602,688 00
Total tax for 1875........................	1,879,212 09

The value of the railroads, as made by the State Board of Equalization for taxation, is as follows:

	Valuation.
St. Louis and Southeastern..................	$610,784 00
Memphis, Paducah, and Northern..........	306,425 00
Paducah and Elizabethtown.................	585,498 20
Mobile and Ohio	199,825 00
Chicago, St. Louis, and New Orleans.......	392,261 75
St. Louis, Iron Mountain, and Southern....	12,868 18
Nashville, Chattanooga, and St. Louis........	63,000 00
Owensboro and Nashville...................	105,000 00
Louisville and Nashville and Great Southern..	5,677,571 00
Louisville, Cincinnati, and Lexington........	2,287,444 00
Louisville Railway Transfer.................	20,650 00
Elizabethtown, Lexington, and Big Sandy....	256,978 00
Lexington and Big Sandy, Eastern Division..	176,800 00
Eastern Kentucky Railway Company.......	125,771 00
Southwestern Railroad.....................	20,852 27
Louisville and Harrod's Creek Narrow-gauge.	55,400 00
Mt. Sterling Coal Road....................	42,000 00
Kentucky Central.........................	1,273,925 00
Maysville and Lexington Railroad, Northern Division...............................	451,700 00
Maysville and Lexington Railroad, Southern Division................................	286,700 00
Cincinnati Southern Railroad...............	2,600,950 00
Shelby Railroad Company..................	140,675 00
Total.................................	**$15,644,684 40**

The increase is $703,000 over the assessment for 1878.

The State guards who were sent to quell disturbances in Breathitt County in December,

1878, returned in March with thirteen of the principal actors. It was generally considered that the disorders there had not grown out of barbarism, or any relapse from the social status. An imperfect organization has resulted from the practical isolation of the people, the unlettered authorities, and the absence of schools and moral example. They need the contact of more advanced communities.

A great excitement was produced in the State by the killing of John M. Elliott, one of the Judges of the State Court of Appeals, by Thomas Buford. The tragedy occurred on the steps of the Capital Hotel in Frankfort on March 26th. Buford had embarked all the property that he owned, together with the whole estate of his sister, since deceased, in a tract of land in Henry County, and, the parties from whom he purchased failing to make a title to the land, a suit was pending before the Court of Appeals for the rescission of the trade, and the repayment to Buford of the twenty or thirty thousand dollars which he had paid on the property. A little more than a year previous, under a decision of the Circuit Court, the farm was sold for the deferred payments still due from Buford—some twelve thousand dollars—and the parties from whom he had purchased became the buyers, bidding in the property for the sum of twelve thousand dollars, thus taking from him, without recourse, the twenty odd thousand dollars already paid, and leaving him a pauper. This decision and sale were appealed to the highest Court in the State, and the decision was rendered on March 21st sustaining the sale, and leaving him to brood over his entire loss of everything. Buford was convicted of the murder and sentenced to hard labor in the State Prison during his life. The case was brought to the Court of Appeals for revision, and on filing the record, a paper in the nature of a protest against any action in the case by the present members of the Court was presented. To this the Court acceded, and the Governor appointed special judges to try the case.

The election of State officers was held on August 1st. In preparation for the same, the Democratic Convention assembled at Louisville on May 2d. John W. Stevenson was chosen permanent chairman. The following nominations were made for State officers: For Governor, Luke P. Blackburn; for Lieutenant-Governor, James E. Cantrill; for Attorney-General, P. W. Hardin; for Auditor, Fayette Hewitt; for Treasurer, James W. Tate; for Superintendent of Schools, J. Desha Pickett; for Register of Land-Office, Ralph Sheldon.

The following resolutions were adopted:

The Democracy of Kentucky, in convention assembled, reaffirm their attachment to the Constitution of the United States and the Union of the States, as the best guarantee for the liberties of the people and their prosperity and happiness.

They rejoice in the fact that it is in their power to recognize that all the States are restored to their political autonomy.

They hereby record their solemn protest that a popular verdict at the polls has been reversed by the action of an Electoral Commission, and they declare that, while in the interest of peace that result was acquiesced in, yet it shall not be held as a precedent for future violations of right and justice. Though thus deprived of control of the executive power in the administration of the Federal Government, they congratulate the people of the country at large that the popular will, expressed at the polls, has secured the supremacy of a Democratic majority in both Houses of Congress.

In further expression of our views, we resolve that we have viewed with intense interest the issue between the Congress of the United States and the President, and contemplate with unfeigned anxiety and condemnation the unprecedented attitude assumed by the Executive in his message rejecting the supplies tendered by the people for the support of their army, upon the wholesome condition that no military force should be used at their elections.

Resolved, That we heartily endorse the position taken by our Senators and Representatives in Congress in coupling with the appropriation bills now pending a demand for redress of grievances by the repeal of existing laws which tolerate the presence of soldiers at the polls, the continuance of test-oaths as a condition for jury service, and the employment of supervisors and deputy marshals to control elections.

Resolved, That in this great issue between the people and a partisan Executive we have implicit confidence in our Senators and Representatives, and, endorsing their action up to the present, hereby assure them of our hearty support in whatever action they may take to maintain the fundamental principle that the military power shall be kept subordinate to the civil, and that elections shall be free from executive interference.

Resolved, That we approve the action of the General Assembly in submitting to the people the question of calling a convention for the purpose of forming a State Constitution, and we hereby commend the call to this favorable consideration of the Democratic voters of the State.

Resolved, That we approve the measures heretofore adopted to create a general and efficient system of common-school education, and pledge the Democratic party to take such steps as from time to time experience may demonstrate to be wise to so perfect the system as to furnish every child in the State the means of a fair English education.

The Republican Convention for the nomination of State officers assembled at Louisville on April 10th. John D. White was elected chairman. Walter Evans received the nomination for Governor; for Lieutenant-Governor, O. S. Deming; for Attorney-General, A. H. Clark; for Auditor, J. Williamson; for Treasurer, R. P. Stoll; for Superintendent of Schools, M. McIntire; for Register of Land-Office, John H. Wilson.

The following resolutions were adopted:

The Republicans of Kentucky contemplate with pride the history and achievements of the Republican party of the United States. We hold up to the world the record it has made, both in war and in peace. We do not ask that any of it be forgotten; on the contrary, we point to its great deeds, and recall them to remembrance: the suppression of armed rebellion, its unparalleled magnanimity to the overthrown enemies of the Union, the emancipation and enfranchisement of an enslaved race, its determined purpose to honestly pay the national debt, its further stand on the side of honest money, the skill and prudence of its financial management, and its steadfast purpose that justice and right shall be done to all citizens of the United States under the laws, without distinction of race or color or previous condition of servitude.

We firmly adhere to the principles declared by the Republican party in the platform adopted at Cincinnati in 1876. The education of the people of all classes is a matter of the first necessity to the welfare of the State, and it is a wise and most economical use of public resources to advance to the highest efficiency our common-school system, and we pledge our hearty support to any system of public schools that will advance that end. A convention should be called at the earliest practicable time to revise our State Constitution, and we urge upon all the people of the State the duty of voting on all proper occasions in favor of calling such convention.

We condemn in the strongest terms the gross mismanagement of public affairs in this State by the Democratic party, which has had entire control of the State for the past fourteen years. It has failed to foster a common-school system worthy of the name, and has robbed the children of the State. It has sacrificed the important interests of State internal improvements, and, while it makes a boast that the State has no debt, we have the mortifying spectacle of a State with no public works or enterprise, and meager, antiquated, and inadequate police institutions. By useless and reckless extravagance, the current expenses of the State are nearly three times as great as before the war, while there is no reason or excuse for their being any greater.

By continuous appeals to the lower passions of the people, and by the constant laudation and encouragement of that spirit of contempt for constituted authority lately rampant in the rebellion, the people of the State have been educated into a disregard of law and order, until the good name of Kentucky has been blasted in the estimation of our sister States. The frequent necessity for using the militia to suppress disorder, and the lawless spirit which stops short of no crime, from the lynching of obscure white and colored persons to the assassination of judges on the bench, is the natural outgrowth of the pernicious teachings of the Democratic party.

The Republican party demands such a change in the conduct of our State affairs as will encourage our own people to remain in the State, instead of going from us, and induce immigration into our borders that our soil may be tilled and our resources developed.

While we favor economy, we demand that it be practical in cutting off useless extravagances, and we favor a more generous and liberal expenditure of the public money for the purpose of fostering our internal welfare, and aiding and encouraging our citizens in the general betterment of the condition of the State.

It is a cardinal principle of the Republican party that the currency of the country shall be sound and uniform in value, regulated by the authority of the nation, and convertible into coin at the will of the holders. The national debt should be paid in the most scrupulous good faith. We are proud that the Republican party has already been able to pay off a large portion thereof, and fund the remainder at a low rate of interest. We are proud that the Republican party, in the face of bitter Democratic opposition, has been able to resume specie payment; that it has established a currency that circulates with equal readiness in all parts of the country; and that it has made such a record upon financial questions that the whole world has an abiding faith that, so long as it remains in power, our national credit will remain unimpaired.

The Federal and State governments are part of one system, alike necessary for the common prosperity, peace, and security, and ought to be regarded alike with cordial, habitual, and immovable attachment. Respect for the authority of each, and acquiescence in the just constitutional measures of each, are duties required by the plainest considerations of national, State, and individual welfare; but the Constitution of the United States and the laws made in pursuance thereof are the supreme laws, anything in the Constitution or laws of

any State to the contrary notwithstanding. The legislative and judicial departments of the government are independent of each other, and each should be left to exercise its own duties under the Constitution.

The right of the President to veto a measure is as clear as the right of Congress to pass it. We therefore witness with indignation the present lawless attempt on the part of the Democratic Congress to coerce the President into subserviency to its views by the threat of withholding appropriations. In the trying position in which the President is thus placed, he is entitled to the encouragement and support of all good citizens. The declared purpose on the part of the Democratic members in Congress, to refuse appropriations until he yields to their demand, is revolutionary in its spirit; and as in 1861 secession was resorted to by those who could not control the Government in their own way, so now this declared determination to rule or starve the Government is another exhibition of rebellion, and every consideration of duty to the country demands that the President shall resist, by every constitutional means in his power, this spirit of lawlessness.

The Republican party is committed to the doctrine that every voter is entitled to one vote, and but one. Holding this doctrine, it stands in no terror of those wise and timely laws enacted by Congress to secure honest elections.

We have seen with pride and pleasure the distinguished honors paid to ex-President Grant by all classes in Europe. His services in war, and his patriotism and ability in the discharge of the high civil duties to which the confidence of his countrymen respectively called him, his wisdom, prudence, moderation, and integrity of character, entitle him to this striking and remarkable exhibition of courtesy and respect abroad, and to the lasting gratitude of his own people. His name and fame are inseparably linked with the most important events in our country's history. It is our pleasure thus to declare our admiration and esteem for him, our gratitude to and our confidence in him.

There was also a National ticket nominated, as follows: For Governor, C. W. Cook; for Lieutenant-Governor, D. B. Lewis; for Attorney-General, I. H. Trabue; for Auditor, Henry Potter; for Treasurer, W. T. Hardin; for Superintendent of Schools, K. C. McBeath; for Register of Land-Office, Gano Henry.

The result of the election was as follows: For Governor—Blackburn, Democrat, 125,799; Evans, Republican, 81,882; Cook, National, 18,954. For Lieutenant-Governor—Cantrill, Democrat, 124,368; Deming, Republican, 81,-201; Lewis, National, 18,487. For Attorney-General—Hardin, Democrat, 224,495; Clark, Republican, 78,819; Trabue, National, 18,380. For Auditor—Hewitt, Democrat, 124,424; Williamson, Republican, 80,749; Potter, National, 18,364. For Treasurer—Tate, Democrat, 124,173; Stoll, Republican, 81,067; Hardin, National, 18,334. For Superintendent of Schools—Pickett, Democrat, 124,430; McIntire, Republican, 80,858; McBeath, National, 18,342. For Register—Sheldon, Democrat, 123,688; Wilson, Republican; 46,298, O'Dogherty, Republican, 26,739; Henry, National, 18,192. In the Legislature the Democrats had a large majority.

The proposition for a Constitutional Convention was defeated.

L

LAWRENCE, John Laird Mair, Baron, a British statesman, born March 4, 1811, died June 27, 1879. His education was directed with a view to civil service under the East India Company, and in 1829 he received his first appointment as writer to the Company. He held in the succeeding years various posts, and on all occasions discharged his duties with such ability that in 1848 he was appointed Commissioner of the Trans-Sutlej Provinces. For short periods at about the same time he acted as Resident at Lahore. The second Sikh war, which broke out in 1848, resulted in the annexation of the Punjaub. A Board of Administration was appointed for the government of the new province, consisting of Mr. John Lawrence, his brother Henry, and Mr. Mansel; and in 1852 John Lawrence was made Chief Commissioner. Under this government the Punjaub was ruled so wisely and so satisfactorily to the native population that, although newly annexed, the province stood almost alone in its adherence to the English when neighboring and distant districts broke out in open mutiny against foreign rule. The new administrative system had greatly ameliorated the condition of the people of the Punjaub, and order and peace had taken the place of lawlessness. Upon the outbreak of the mutiny, the vigilance and energy of John Lawrence contributed materially to the work of upholding English supremacy in India. Skillfully turning to account the natural configuration of the province, he isolated it from the mutineers by stopping all means of communication. In 1858–'59 he was the first Lieutenant-Governor of the province. In 1856 he was made a K. C. B., and in 1857 G. C. B. He was created a baronet in 1858, sworn a member of the Privy Council, and on the creation of the order of the Star of India was made K. S. I. The Court of Directors of the East India Company granted him a life pension of £2,000, which, under a special act of Parliament, he continued to enjoy, together with his full salary, when he became Viceroy of India. He succeeded Lord Elgin in that post in December, 1863, and held it for the usual period of five years. In April, 1869, he was created Baron Lawrence. After his final return from India, he took a prominent part in philanthropic and educational movements in England. On the formation of the London School Board in 1870 he was chosen its chairman, and he held that post until 1873, when he resigned. In questions of Indian politics he continued to take an active interest, and during 1878 and 1879 he frequently wrote letters to the "Times," in which he warmly opposed the Afghan policy of the Government —a policy which was a distinct departure from that which he had carried out, and which had

been described by the phrase of "masterly inactivity." In India the news of his death called forth expressions of grief and sympathy from all classes of the people, and the Viceroy in Council ordered that on July 1st, at all the seats of government throughout India, the flags should be lowered to half-mast, that thirty-one minute-guns should be fired at sunset, and that the last gun should be fired and the flag dropped at the same time.

LINDERMAN, Dr. Henry R., Superintendent of the United States Mint, born in Lehman township, Pike County, Pennsylvania, December 26, 1825, died in Washington, January 28, 1879. He studied medicine with his father, and completed his course at the University of New York. He returned home, and practiced his profession till 1853, when he was appointed chief clerk in the office of the Director of the Mint at Philadelphia, in which position he continued for twelve years, when he resigned to engage in private business. He was appointed Director of the Mint in 1867, and held that office for two years. On account of his great experience and thorough knowledge of such subjects, he was appointed by Secretary Boutwell to examine the mints on the Pacific coast and adjust some intricate bullion questions. He made many valuable reports to the Treasury Department upon various subjects connected with the mint service. In 1869–'70 he was associated with Comptroller Knox in the preparation of the coinage act of 1873, which was a codification of all the mint and coinage laws of the United States, with important amendments, and established the mint and assay offices of the United States as a bureau of the Treasury Department at Washington. When this act took effect, on April 1, 1873, he was appointed by President Grant Superintendent of the Mint, and organized the Mint Bureau in the Treasury Department, and from that time had the general supervision of all the mints and assay offices in the United States. His reports as Superintendent of the Mint are exceedingly valuable documents. The one for 1877 contained an elaborate and able argument in favor of the gold standard. He was the author of a volume on "Money and Legal Tender," published in June, 1877, which has received the highest praise. Dr. Linderman was socially a genial and kind-hearted gentleman, and accustomed to the practice of a liberal hospitality.

LITERATURE, AMERICAN, IN 1879. Contemporaneous American literature is not less distinctively national in character than that of former epochs, nor comparatively less prolific and nationally complete. Yet it has lost its more salient and effective national characteristics. The attention to literary correctness and æsthetic refinement, and the repugnance to

any kind of excess, which séem at present to
be the dominant principles in American letters,
can only be cultivated at the expense of spontaneous force and originality. The present movement is a true characteristic phase in the national literary development, not a factitious
effort to correct national shortcomings upon
foreign models. In accurate æsthetic percep-
tions and true artistic impulses the bellelettristic
writers in America are now distinguished above
those of any other nation. An analogous sagacity and balance of mind, a self-critical power, and the perception of the true aims of investigation and limits of speculation, characterize the scientific workers and authors and
the scholars and historians of America. Although few publishers can say that it has been
a satisfactory year, owing to the peculiar condition of the trade, the press has been unusually busy, and the public has consumed a large
amount of literature this last year. Judging
the state of the national intelligence by the
quality of the books provided for its requirements which meet with the strongest demand,
an encouraging elevation of the standard of
literary taste is noticeable. A still more satisfactory phenomenon is the lively and widespread interest taken in science and in art.
Science and the arts have come under the influence of the democratic spirit. Through cheap
popular treatises, written in language which is
universally understood, and by the auxiliary
means of improved processes of pictorial reproduction, a knowledge of the elementary
principles and leading facts in the sciences,
and some acquaintance with the æsthetic purposes of art-production and familiarity with
the best examples of art, have become a part
of popular education.

In the departments of *Religion and Philosophy* the publications have not been numerous,
but include some works of exceptionally high
character. Religious literature has certainly
fallen off in bulk, compared with other classes
of books, of late years; but, when examined in
all its aspects, the phenomenon does not prove
discouraging to the friends of religion. The
volumes of crude sermons, meditations, and
rhapsodies, with which the press formerly
teemed, are replaced by other popular reading, some of it more intellectually edifying.
The sectarian controversies on minor dogmas
have been silenced by the nobler warfare with
anti-theological thought. The scientific assailants of religion are confronted by champions
of the faith who are quite their equals in mental culture and dialectical skill. The tone and
substance of the religious and popular theological books which now issue from the press
betoken an advancement in intellectual comprehension and refinement in the religious community. The character of the more serious doctrinal and exegetical works of the day shows a
corresponding elevation of standard in scholarship and mental training among professional
theologians. The learning of foreign scholars,

notably the German, has been made use of, but
not without subjecting it to the more alert
and thorough critical methods of American
thought and assimilating it to the national type
of mentality. In speculative metaphysics there
is no vitality, the theologians and their scientific antagonists occupying the whole arena of
philosophical literature. Professor George D.
Fisher's "Faith and Rationalism" is a temperate and philosophical defence of evangelical
truths, written with considerable dialectical
power (New York, Charles Scribner's Sons).
"Practical Theology" is a manual of homi-
letics by Professor J. J. van Oosterzee (Boston,
Houghton, Osgood & Co.). The late Rev. Dr.
Charles Hodge's "Conference Papers" contain an able exposition of Christian doctrines.
"Society the Redeemed Form of Man" (Houghton, Osgood & Co.) is a thoughtful expression
of liberal religion by Henry James. A popular
book by Professor Swing is "Motives of Life"
(Chicago, Jansen, McClurg & Co.). "Studies
in the Model Prayer" is an analysis of the
Lord's Prayer by the Rev. Dr. George D. Board-
man (New York, D. Appleton & Co.). "The
Epiphanies of the Risen Lord," by the same author, is an elegant illustrated volume in which
the appearances of Christ after the Resurrection are recounted. Dr. G. Uhlhorn's "Conflict of Christianity with Heathenism" (Charles
Scribner's Sons) is a translation of a learned
work on the rise of Christianity, vividly presenting the forces, intellectual and physical,
which combined to crush the infant Church.
The Rev. Dr. Joseph A. Seiss, in "A Miracle
in Stone" (Philadelphia, Porter & Coates), gives
a clear and popular account of the Great Pyra-
mid of Gizeh, and insists on the miraculous
nature of the coincidences detected by Piazzi
Smyth and others between its proportions and
various astronomical measurements and other
physical facts. "Voices from Babylon," by
the same author, is a volume of speculations on
the fulfillment of prophecy. The American
translation of Lange's Commentary on the
Bible is completed by the issue of the volume
on Numbers and Deuteronomy (Charles Scribner's Sons). A "Commentary on Paul's Epis-
tle to the Romans," by Professor W. G. T.
Shedd, is published by Charles Scribner's Sons.
"The Book of Job: Essays and a Metrical Paraphrase" (D. Appleton & Co.), by Rossiter
W. Raymond, contains besides the paraphrase
thoughtful and scholarly comments and eluci-
dations. "Sacred Cities," by the Rev. Dr.
John S. Lee, is a popular description of Biblical places, of which a second edition has appeared (Cincinnati, Williamson & Cantwell).
"Apostolic Fathers and Apologists of the Second Century," by the Rev. G. A. Jackson, is
the first number of a series of "Early Christian
Literature Primers" (D. Appleton & Co.).

The interest felt in the recent developments
of *Science* is as keen in the United Sates as in
any country; but the original investigators in
science are yet comparatively few in America,

and the instructors upon whom the public relies for scientific information are most frequently the writers and scientists of other lands, particularly the English popularizers of science. Professor Ernst Haeckel's "The Evolution of Man," published by D. Appleton & Co., is the great text-book on Darwinism, the accepted and authoritative exposition of the theory of descent. Professor Haeckel in preparing this work had the double object in view of presenting and elucidating in one orderly whole his doctrine of evolution, and collecting and coördinating the evidence in its support, and that of instructing and convincing the general public. The task of rendering popularly intelligible a scientific exposition of new theories is most difficult to accomplish in any language, and is rarely attempted in German; but Haeckel, although as a pioneer of science obliged to invent many new terms, expounds his subject with remarkable lucidity, which is well preserved in the translation. "The Human Species," by Quatrefages, the distinguished French anthropologist and geographer, forms the twenty-seventh volume of the "International Scientific Series," published by D. Appleton & Co. of New York; this volume not only bears the impress of the author's unrivaled learning and profound grasp of his subject, but, with the exercise of a rare degree of literary skill, the theme has been enveloped in a most attractive garb and rendered exceedingly fascinating. Professor Rood's contribution to the "International Scientific Series," "Modern Chromatics," is more than a handbook of instruction; it is a work of original research in this difficult and inchoate branch of science, and a guide as well to the artistic use of color. Dr. B. Jay Jeffries's "Color-Blindness, its Dangers and its Detection" (Houghton, Osgood & Co.), is a systematic treatise on this defect, which has been the subject of much investigation of late in different countries, the results of which are digested in this volume. "The Multitudinous Seas" (D. Appleton & Co.) is a picturesque and scientific account of the ocean and its phenomena, by S. G. W. Benjamin. Elliott Coues's "Birds of the Colorado Valley," printed at the Government Printing-Office in Washington, is the first part of a great work on American ornithology, entitled "Passeres to Laniidæ." The eminent naturalist who has undertaken this task has wisely sought to render the work intelligible to non-scientific readers by discarding the scientific nomenclature in his account of the life-history of the birds. Charles Pickering's "Chronological History of Plants" (Boston, Little, Brown & Co.) is a posthumous work containing a vast amount of recondite information, but which is imperfectly digested and faultily arranged, being published without revision in the unfinished form in which it was left by its author.

In *Mechanics* and the applications of science to the practical uses of life, the American nation is not behind the others, nor its literature

poorer or less extensive. A description of late electrical inventions is given in George S. Prescott's "The Speaking Telephone" (D. Appleton & Co.). A valuable practical treatise on surveying and locating railroads has been written by William F. Shunk, entitled "The Field Engineer" (New York, D. Van Nostrand). "Railroad Accidents," by Charles Francis Adams, Jr. (New York, G. P. Putnam's Sons), is an account of the more noteworthy catastrophes on railroads and a practical inquiry into the causes and the means of preventing such accidents. Other works on mechanical subjects are William M. Burr's manual on fuel combustion, published by Yohn Brothers of Indianapolis; Emory Edwards's "Marine Steam-Engine" (Philadelphia, H. C. Baird & Co.); W. Kent on the "Strength of Materials" (New York, D. Van Nostrand); "Manual of Power for Machines, Shafts, and Belts," and "History of Cotton Manufacture in the United States," by S. Webber (D. Appleton & Co.). A systematic and exhaustive treatise on breeding domestic animals to develop desired points and qualities, by Dr. Manly Miles, is entitled "Stock-Breeding" (D. Appleton & Co.).

The medical profession of America is distinguished for its progressive activity. A very extensive special literature is published embodying the latest researches in *Medical Science*, American and European. A popular literature for the spread of medical and hygienic knowledge has lately appeared, which is more satisfactory in its character and more effective in its form than anything of the kind which has preceded it. Besides the excellent "Health Primers" published by D. Appleton & Co. (see LITERATURE, BRITISH, IN 1879), a similar series of "American Health Primers" has been issued by the Philadelphia publishers, Lindsay & Blakiston, the contributors to which are American physicians exclusively: it includes "Summer and its Diseases," by Dr. James C. Wilson; "Winter and its Dangers," by Dr. Hamilton Osgood; "The Throat and the Voice," by Dr. J. Solis Cohen; "Eyesight, and How to Care for it," by Dr. G. C. Harlan; "The Mouth and the Teeth," by Dr. J. W. White; and "Hearing, and How to Keep it," by Dr. Charles H. Burnett. Dr. Richard McSherry's "Health, and How to Promote it" (D. Appleton & Co.), is an excellent work of the same class, as is also "Emergencies, and How to Meet them" (G. P. Putnam's Sons), by Professor Burt C. Wilder. "The National Dispensatory" (Philadelphia, Henry C. Lea), by Drs. Alfred Stillé and John M. Maisch, is a much-needed comprehensive, critical digest of the material contained in the last edition of the "United States Pharmacopœia," presenting the present condition and reflecting the latest accepted principles of materia medica. A presentation of the homœopathic views on the action of medicinal remedies is given by Dr. Carrol Dunham in "Lectures on Materia Medica" (New York, Francis Hart & Co.). Among the new works on special medical subjects may be mentioned the translation by J. O. Green of Hermann Schwarze's treatise on the pathological anatomy of the ear (Houghton, Osgood & Co.); F. Mortimer Granville's "Common Mind-Troubles" and "The Secret of a Clear Head" (Salem, S. E. Cassino); a translation of Hoffmann and Ultzmann's treatise on urine examination (D. Appleton & Co.); Galabin's text-book of female diseases (Lindsay & Blakiston); and J. Gamgee's treatise on yellow fever (D. Appleton & Co.), which he thinks originates on ships.

A few books have been published during the year upon subjects connected with the *Law*, which, from their character or the form in which they are presented, are of interest to the lay public. A contribution to the question of international copyright, treating of the theories of ownership in literary property which guide legislation and judicial decisions in both Great Britain and America, and arguing in favor of an international guarantee of authors' rights, is Eaton S. Drone's "Treatise on the Law of Property in Intellectual Productions" (Boston, Little, Brown & Co). G. H. Putnam and Appleton Morgan have published opinions on the same subject, the former in one of G. P. Putnam's Sons "Economic Monographs," and the latter in an open letter to Secretary Evarts, published by Aug. Brentano, Jr., of New York. E. M. Gallaudet's "Manual of International Law" (New York, A. S. Barnes and Co.) is based on Calvo's French treatise. A revised and final edition of Professor Woolsey's standard work on this subject has been issued. A popular treatise on a legal subject of much interest to the investing community is "A Treatise on the Law of Railroad and other Corporate Securities," by Leonard A. Jones (Houghton, Osgood & Co.). "The Law of the Road," by R. Vashon Rogers, Jr. (San Francisco, Sumner, Whitney & Co.), aims to instruct the general public in legal principles; and to render the study attractive, the book is interspersed and enlivened with wit and anecdote. It is one of a series of such books, another of which, by the same author, is "The Law of Hotel Life." A manual of the laws relating to shipping and admiralty according to British and American decisions has been compiled by Robert Desty (Sumner, Whitney & Co.); and the same subject is treated in Theodore M. Etting's essay on "Admiralty Jurisdiction in America" (Philadelphia, Rees, Welsh & Co.). In the series of "Economic Monographs," published by G. P. Putnam's Sons of New York, is an interesting tract by E. R. Squibb on the subject of the adulteration of food and its legislative prevention. The law of extradition is set forth in a special treatise by S. T. Spear (Albany, Weed & Parsons). Other new works are G. W. Brandt's treatise on "The Law of Suretyship and Guaranty," and M. T. Cooley's "Treatise upon Wrongs and their Remedies" (Chicago, Callahan & Co.); a "Treatise upon the Law of

Principal and Agent," by W. Evans (Chicago Legal News Co.); a compilation of the insolvent statutes actually in force in the different States and Canada, by Raphael J. Moses, Jr. (New York, Baker, Voorhis & Co.); "Commentaries on Lunacy Laws," by James Ordronaux (Albany, J. D. Parsons, Jr.); a treatise on the "Law of Eminent Domain," by H. E. Mills, and one of Seymour D. Thompson on the "Liability of Stockholders" (St. Louis, F. H. Thomas & Co.).

In *Philology* America produces her share of books. The completest dictionary of the English tongue is the product of American scholarship; and the enterprise of its publishers and the learning and industry of American scholars are sufficient to prevent this great work from becoming antiquated. The new edition of Webster's "Unabridged Dictionary," edited by Chauncey A. Goodrich and Professor Noah Porter (Springfield, G. & C. Merriam), contains an appended biographical pronouncing dictionary, and a vocabulary of five thousand new words which have gained currency since the last edition was issued. Andrews's edition of Freund's Latin lexicon had been for a generation the instrument with which American students have obtained their knowledge of Roman literature. In Harper's "Latin Dictionary" the old work has been thoroughly worked over and considerably augmented by Charlton T. Lewis and Charles Short. Professor W. Dwight Whitney has published an improved grammar of classical Sanskrit and the older dialects (New York, B. Westermann & Co.). "The English Language: its Grammatical and Logical Principles," by Harris R. Greene (Houghton, Osgood & Co.), is an elementary theoretical treatise on English grammar. R. Morris's "Elementary Lessons in Historical Grammar" deals with accidence and word-formation (D. Appleton & Co.). Brother Azarias's "Development of English Literature" is an excellent text-book (D. Appleton & Co.), as also J. H. Gilmore's "The English Language and its Early Literature." Rasmus B. Anderson has published an English translation of the "Younger Edda" (Chicago, S. C. Griggs & Co.).

An improvement can be remarked year by year in the methods and quality of the instruction in American schools, and a system of pedagogics adapted to the national needs is slowly and quietly developing. Among the works treating of the methods of *Education* may be mentioned the study of James H. Hoose "On the Promise of Methods of Teaching," the tract of Fitch on the art of questioning, and that of Bennett on national education in different countries (Syracuse, Davis, Baldwin & Co.); also the essays of Hamerton, McCosh, and others on the higher education (New York, A. S. Barnes & Co.). A hand-book of the requirements for admission into the different colleges, by A. F. Nightingale, is published by D. Appleton & Co. The lectures delivered at their summer's meeting have been published in Boston by the American Institute of Instruction. C. F. Adams, Jr., has published essays on "The Public Library and the Common Schools" (Boston, Estes & Lauriat). The theory of tuition according to the laws of the mind is discussed in "Education as a Science," by Alexander Bain (D. Appleton & Co.), reprinted for the "International Science Series." Ernst Haeckel's "Freedom in Science and Teaching" (D. Appleton & Co.) is his famous assertion of the rights of science insured by the German Constitution, in reply to the warnings of Virchow. The text-books for school use are improving in range and quality. Several publishing houses vie with each other in producing excellent books of this class; and educators and writers of ability are devoting their talents more and more to the preparation of school-books. Nevertheless a movement has commenced in some of the States in favor of official text-books. Many of the popular scientific manuals of small size which are issuing in series and singly from the press are well adapted for text-books, and are often used for the purpose.

In the field of *Literary History and Criticism*, Professor Moses Coit Tyler's important work on the "History of American Literature" (G. P. Putnam's Sons) is the most notable production of the year. The first two volumes only bring the subject down to the year 1765. The author endues the literature of the American colonies with a charm and interest which as literature purely it lacks entirely, by tracing through it the germination and development of American ideas. Only in the highest reaches, and as the latest product of the most modern mental methods and discipline, has it been possible to write the intellectual history of an age or race; and the effort of Professor Tyler to deal with the evolution of American social and political thought, animated as it is all through with a contagious enthusiasm, can not fail of an elevating and broadening influence on national education. "Some Newspaper Tendencies," by Whitelaw Reid (New York, Henry Holt & Co.), is a clear and practical explanation of the practice and purposes of American journalism. "Studies in German Literature" (G. P. Putnam's Sons) consists of a course of lectures by the late Bayard Taylor on the classical authors of Germany and the early periods of her literature. Hosmer's "Short History of German Literature" (St. Louis, G. I. Jones & Co.) is a well-written and comprehensive survey of the chief currents of German thought and literature.

The growing interest of the public in *Æsthetics* is satisfied by a number of books of high character. "Conversations on Art Methods," by Thomas Couture (G. P. Putnam's Sons), is a translation by S. E. Stuart of a book which has exerted considerable influence on contemporary art. Another book which marks a great development in art thought and method is "Ruskin on Painting," containing the pith of his "Modern Painters," published in D. Appleton & Co's "Handy-Volume Series." Eugène Véron's "Æsthetics" (Philadelphia, J. B. Lippincott & Co.), translated by W. H. Armstrong, is an exposition of the principles of reform in art and of revolt against the rigid rules of French classicism, and an appeal in favor of the liberal catholicity advocated by Viollet-le-Duc. Anthony's American edition of Jacob von Falke's "Art in the House," with notes by Charles C. Perkins (Boston, L. Prang & Co.), is an illustrated work on decorative art, which, as might be expected from its German source, suggests a wider range of decorative conceptions, derived from the more comprehensive study of the history of ornament in all times and countries, than the numerous treatises which have their source in the late movement in decorative art in England, which has also spread to America; the work of the German professor is also interesting as a history of domestic architecture and ornament from ancient times down to the present. Seemann's "Illustrations of the History of Art," an extensive German pictorial work, has been reproduced by L. Prang & Co. of Boston. Among the literary outcroppings of the recent popular interest in the ornamental arts is an illustrated volume by Jennie J. Young on "The Ceramic Art" (New York, Harper & Brothers); it is a book of peculiar interest, in that it shows the history and condition of the American production in the potter's art. A technical work on the same subject, entitled "A Practical Treatise on China-Painting in America" (New York, John Wiley & Sons), has for its author Camille Piton of the National Art-Training School in Philadelphia. "Bibelots and Curios" (D. Appleton & Co.) is a manual for collectors by Frederic Vors. S. G. W. Benjamin's "Art in America" (Harper & Brothers) is a critical and historical sketch of the development of the fine arts in the United States. Helmholtz's discoveries in acoustics and their hearing on musical art are ably discussed in William Pole's "The Philosophy of Music" (Houghton, Osgood & Co.).

The present activity of thought upon subjects relating to *Politics and National Economy* manifests itself in numerous productions by the pen. "A True Republic," by Albert Stickney (Harper & Brothers), is a treatise on American politics, and an appeal for certain constitutional changes for the purpose of avoiding the evils resulting from party conflicts and the spoils system. "A Proposal for a Reform in the Federal Executive," by Mortimer G. Tibbits, favors a responsible executive chosen by Congress (New York, Brentano's Literary Emporium). Sir George Campbell's "White and Black" gives the opinions of a member of the British Parliament on the negro question formed during a visit to America (New York, R. Worthington). The question of civil-service reform, viewed in the light of British example, is presented by Dorman B. Eaton in a book entitled "Civil Service in Great Britain" (Harper & Brothers). "The Currency Question" (G. P. Putnam's Sons) is an argument against inflation and against State banks, by Judge Robert W. Hughes of Virginia. Secretary John Sherman's principal writings on subjects connected with finance and taxation are given in a volume of "Selected Speeches and Reports" (D. Appleton & Co.). Charles Francis Adams, Jr., deals with the political questions connected with railroading in a volume on "Railroads, their Origin and Problems" (G. P. Putnam's Sons). Boscher's standard German treatise on political economy has been translated by John J. Lalor and published by Henry Holt of New York. Professor Francis A. Walker's "Money, Trade, and Industry" (Henry Holt & Co.) is a valuable contribution to political economy, discussing the relations of money to commerce and production, and defining the true nature of money from the standpoint of the political economists with great clearness and force; a branch of economical science which has a peculiar present interest to the American public, being involved in some of the living questions of politics. Professor Roswell D. Hitchcock, in "Socialism," while deprecating the theories of the socialistic teachers of Europe, appeals to Christian sentiment to supply the links of sympathy and fellowship whose absence embitters and antagonizes the different classes of society. "Labor and Capital Allies, not Enemies" (Harper & Brothers), contains the substance of an argument presented before the Hewitt Congressional Committee by Edward Atkinson. The Rev. Joseph P. Thompson discusses socialism and the labor question in "The Workman: his False Friends and his True Friends" (American Tract Society). Henry Ammon James's essay on "Communism in America" (Henry Holt & Co.) received the Yale Porter prize in 1878. A series of "Economic Monographs" (G. P. Putnam's Sons) includes "Honest Money and Labor," by Carl Schurz; "National Banking," by M. L. Scudder; "Bimetallism," by Hugh McCulloch; "Labor-making Machinery," by F. Perry Powers; and "Andrew Jackson and the Bank of the United States," by William M. Royall. The "Industrial History of the United States," by Albert S. Bolles (Norwich, Conn.), is a work on an important subject, compiled with considerable labor. The "American Almanac and Treasury of Facts" for 1879 is a compilation of well-selected statistics, by A. R. Spofford (New York, American News Company). The "Primer on the Natural Resources of the United States" (D. Appleton & Co.) is a useful compendium by J. H. Patton. "The Commercial Products of the Sea," by P. L. Simmonds (D. Appleton & Co.), is the first general treatise yet written on this interesting subject. Holyoake's "History of Coöperation in England" (J. B. Lippincott & Co.) is a work of exhaustive research, a faithful and comprehen-

sive account of an important economical development.

A moderate number of books of *Travel and Geography* of a light and popular character have been produced, and some with more studious and thoughtful contents. "Four Months in a Sneak-Box" is a narrative of a voyage in a small hunting-boat on Western rivers, by Nathaniel H. Bishop (Boston, Lee & Shepard). Updegraff's "Bodines" is a narrative of the experiences of two amateur fishermen upon their excursions in the woods of Pennsylvania (J. B. Lippincott & Co.). "The Witchery of Archery" (Charles Scribner's Sons), by Maurice Thompson, is an entertaining book of descriptions of nature by one fond of roving the woods with a long-bow in his hand, and a manual of the sport of bow-shooting. "A Fool's Errand, by one of the Fools," is a caustic account of the social condition of the South by an officer of the Federal army who lived there for several years after the war (New York, Fords, Howard & Hulbert). Mrs. H. W. Beecher's "Letters from Florida" (D. Appleton & Co.) are descriptions of that subtropical State, presenting its advantages as a sanitarium. J. Codman's "The Round Trip by Way of Panama" is an excellent descriptive and statistical account of the Pacific and Rocky Mountain States and Territories (G. P. Putnam's Sons). William H. Rideing's "A-Saddle in the Wild West" (D. Appleton & Co.) is a remarkably entertaining book of travel in the Western country, relating experiences passed through in the Wheeler Expedition, and graphically describing the scenes and objects encountered. "The Great Fur Land" is an illustrated volume descriptive of the Hudson's Bay Territory, by H. M. Robinson (G. P. Putnam's Sons). "Brazil, the Amazons, and the Coast," by Herbert H. Smith (Charles Scribner's Sons), is an account of travels and explorations in Brazil by a naturalist who is at the same time an intelligent observer of social and economical conditions. "Around the World with General Grant," by John Russell Young, is published by the American News Company in the form, growing in favor, of a subscription part book. An account of the ex-President's tour has also been written by J. M. Keating, "With General Grant in the East" (J. B. Lippincott & Co.). "The World's Paradises" is a readable account of the most noted sanitaria, by S. G. W. Benjamin, published in Appleton's Handy-Volume Series, which includes also "The Alpenstock," an agreeable description of Alpine scenes and explorations, by W. H. Rideing. Horatio King's "Sketches of Travel" is a narrative of European travel by ex-Postmaster King (Washington, J. Bradley Adams). William Winter's "Trip to England" (Boston, Lee & Shepard) is filled with the sentiments inspired in a mind of tender sensibilities on visiting the scenes of historic memories. "Spain in Profile," by James Albert Harrison (Houghton, Osgood & Co.), is a volume of impressions and descriptions of travel. "Tyrol and the Skirt of the Alps," by George E. Waring, Jr. (Harper & Brothers), is a pleasant and instructive work of travel, handsomely illustrated. One of the finest subscription books produced in recent times is the great geographical work of Élisée Reclus, "The Earth and its Inhabitants," issued in parts by D. Appleton & Co. The Rev. Dr. S. C. Bartlett's "From Egypt to Palestine" (Harper & Brothers) is a historical study of the exodus of the Hebrews from Egypt, as well as a narrative of travels through the scenes of their wanderings; the theories of rationalistic commentators are critically examined, and the supernatural character of the recorded miracles is strenuously maintained. The book is most valuable as a collated digest of hypotheses and discoveries of Biblical antiquities; but the Biblical learning of which it is full is animated and brought much nearer to the reader by the graphic descriptions of the scenes and objects from actual observation, and by the narrative of personal experiences in the Wilderness, written with the sympathy and feeling of an ardent student of the Bible and believer in its literal interpretation. H. Ballantine's "Midnight Marches through Persia" (Lee & Shepard) is an account of a horseback journey full of adventures, containing interesting information on the life and manners of the people and the commercial resources of the country. "Progressive Japan," by General Le Gendre (San Francisco, A. L. Bancroft & Co.), contains well-considered opinions on social and political reforms in Japan. The author writes with a knowlege of and a sympathy for Japanese traditions and culture, and protests against violent innovations foreign to the national spirit. "The Sunrise Kingdom," by Mrs. Julia D. Carrothers (Philadelphia, Presbyterian Board of Publication), is a record of missionary life in Japan. "China and Japan," by the Rev. J. D. Wiley (Cincinnati, Hitchcock & Walden), is an account of travels and residence in those countries.

Although no special impulse toward historical studies has manifested itself, several works of *History* of unusual ability and scholarship, and of enduring value, have first seen the light during the past year. An account of the prehistoric remains in the burial mounds and caves of Kentucky, Missouri, and Mississippi, with speculations as to the aboriginal American people, is given by A. J. Conant in "Footprints of Vanished Races in the Mississippi Valley" (St. Louis, C. R. Barnes). John T. Short's "The North Americans of Antiquity" (Harper & Brothers) is a popular manual of the discoveries and theories of antiquarian research on the early inhabitants of America. J. A. Farrer, in "Primitive Manners and Customs" (Henry Holt & Co.), discusses the problems connected with the savage stage of development. M. D. Conway, in "Demonology and Devil-Lere" (Henry Holt & Co.), gives the fruits of many years' study of a subject

which, notwithstanding its historical importance, might be soon lost and hidden in the lumber-room of antiquarianism had not the present author allowed his mind to become fascinated and so thoroughly saturated with this theme that he bestowed upon it the thought and research which many historians devote to a much wider field of investigation. A series of "Essays in Anglo-Saxon Law," by Henry Adams, H. Cabot Lodge, Ernest Young, and J. Laurence Laughlin (Little, Brown & Co.), is a work of comparative jurisprudence in which the authors have expended on their different subjects the long and deep research, enlightened by the newer school of historical jurisprudence, which the originals of our legal institutions demand. As one of the first products of American study in a field of investigation that has only been cultivated in countries which afford literary leisure or support a literary class, it is a hopeful and gratifying phenomenon. "A Popular History of the United States" (Charles Scribner's Sons), commenced under the nominal editorship of the late William Cullen Bryant, is a hasty compilation by several hands, bearing few marks of serious research, and carelessly edited, but popular in its literary form and choice of materials, and rendered still more attractive by numerous woodcuts. The "History of New York during the Revolutionary War," by Judge Thomas Jones, is a document of great historical value, containing a record of the events of the Revolution and trenchant reflections on men and politics by an ardent Tory; having been kept until now out of the reach of historians even, its publication in full by the New York Historical Society is well justified by the graphic and lively style in which it is written, as well as by the historical materials which it contains. "The Constitutional and Political History of the United States" (Chicago, Callaghan & Co.), translated from the German of H. von Holst, is the most studious analytical work which has appeared on the political development of the American Republic. Written by a foreigner after a searching critical examination, it gives a more complete, objective, and judicial criticism of American political institutions than a native historian could present, but not without a bias, derived from his own nationality, in favor of a strong and supreme centralized government. Alexander Johnston's "History of American Politics" is a record of parties and political questions conveniently summarized, and a useful book for American students. General George W. Cullum has ably recounted the military history of the second war of the United States with England in "Campaigns of the War of 1812–'15" (New York, James Miller), in which many valuable historical facts have been gleaned and admirably digested from inaccessible and scattered documents.

The republication of the classics of American oratory serves the double purpose of preserving models of the grand, impressive, and full-flavored national style of rhetoric, which has since too often degenerated into empty bombast, and of keeping before the minds of the people the inherent and ever-recurring problems of the American form of government. The "Addresses and Orations" of Rufus Choate (Little, Brown & Co.) preserve and exemplify those characteristics of poetry and imagination and harmonious flow, which at one time, together with a high moral inspiration, distinguished American oratory, and of which the speeches of Rufus Choate furnish some of the purest, if not the most brilliant examples. Webster's more famous speeches have also been published, accompanied with a critical essay by E. P. Whipple (Little, Brown & Co.).

Several of the *Biographies and Memoirs* published during the year are chiefly valuable through the light they shed upon history. "Petrus Martyr" is an account of the earliest historian of discoveries in America, the fruit of researches in American libraries, written by H. A. Schumacher, German Consul-General, and issued by the German publisher E. Steiger of New York. The Diary of Judge Sewell, which presents a vivid picture of life and manners in Boston at the end of the seventeenth and the beginning of the eighteenth century, has been often used by colonial historians, but has been recently published in its entirety for the first time by the Massachusetts Historical Society. "The New Puritan," by James S. Pike (Harper & Brothers), is an account of Robert Pike, a man ahead of his age who lived in the days of Salem witchcraft. J. N. Arnold's "Life of Benedict Arnold " (Chicago, Jansen, McClurg & Co.) contains new facts, and is an attempt to rescue the name of the impetuous and selfish officer from the obloquy which has attached to it. "The Life of Albert Gallatin," by Henry Adams, and the "Writings of Albert Gallatin" (J. B. Lippincott & Co.), contain, though in an excessively voluminous form, a valuable store of information upon an eventful formative epoch in American history, and introduce to the reader a man who, from his high character and the important part he played in politics, deserves not to be forgotten. "The Life and Epoch of Hamilton," by Judge George Shea (Houghton, Osgood & Co.), is a panegyrical essay upon the life and works of that statesman, containing much biographical information that is new concerning the earlier portion of his career. "The Life of David Glasgow Farragut," by his son Loyall Farragut (D. Appleton & Co.), is a book of deep and varied interest; the great naval commander is made to tell the story of his own life, as far as possible, by extracts from his diaries, clear and vigorous in style, manly and elevated in tone, and full of individuality, containing life-like sketches of the principal officers in the American navy, and spirited accounts of the sea-engagements from the war of 1812 down to the close of the civil war; it is a valuable contribution to American history, as well as a biog-

raphy of a man of rare force and purity of character. "John Lothrop Motley," by Dr. Oliver Wendell Holmes (Houghton, Osgood & Co.), is a generous tribute of praise to a dead friend, and a vindication of Motley's character and conduct as a diplomatist. "Destruction and Reconstruction" is a book of personal reminiscences of the war of secession by General Richard Taylor, of the Confederate Army (D. Appleton & Co.). The "Memoir of S. S. Prentiss" (Charles Scribner's Sons) preserves the memory of a once famous wit and orator, and reveals the social condition of the Southwest in the ante-bellum times. The "Personal Memoirs " of E. D. Mansfield is a volume of interesting reminiscences by a vetern Western journalist (Cincinnati, Robert Clarke & Co.). A most interesting volume of reminiscences relating to the history of the Napoleonic era is the "Memoirs of Madame de Rémusat," containing remarkable revelations concerning Napoleon, and novel details of the secret history of the First Empire, and interesting pictures of court life (D. Appleton & Co.). "Bismarck in the Franco-German War, 1871 " (Charles Scribner's Sons), is a translation of a diary kept by the Chancellor's secretary, Dr. Moritz Busch, the Boswellian minuteness and unreserve of which has aided in rendering the personality of the German statesman much more familiar to the world than it was before the publication of this curious work. Two French works on the late President Thiers and the events in which he was a prominent actor have been published in translations: "The Government of M. Thiers, from the 8th of February, 1871, to the 24th of May, 1873," by Jules Simon (Charles Scribner's Sons), and "The Life of Louis Adolphe Thiers," by François le Goff (G. P. Putnam's Sons).

A few of the biographical publications of the year, of literary, artistic, or personal interest, are equally worthy of note. "Hector Berlioz" is a collection of the letters and musical criticisms of an erratic and impetuous man of genius, who did much for the development of musical art both as a critic and as a composer; these interesting memoirs are translated by William F. Apthorp, and published by Henry Holt & Co. Mrs. Frances Anne Kemble's "Records of a Girlhood " (Henry Holt & Co.) is a pleasant volume of reminiscences of intellectual society in England and America fifty years ago, recalling the very life and atmosphere of the past generation. An agreeable volume of literary biography by Professor Hjalmar H. Boyesen, published by Charles Scribner's Sons, deals with the lives and works of Goethe and Schiller, reflecting the spirit and tenor of German criticism; it is a work which bears the impress of sincere and sympathetic labor, written in a clear and masterly style. A series of biographies of "American Authors " is published by Sheldon & Co. of New York. "A Life Worth Living," by Leonard Woolsey Bacon (New York, Anson D. F. Randolph &

Co.), is a memoir of Mrs. Emily Bliss Gould, an American Protestant lady who devoted herself to labors of reform and education among the poor of Rome. The "Life of Mrs. Eliza A. Seton," by the Rev. Dr. Charles J. White (Baltimore, Kelly, Piet & Co.), is a biography of a lady whose memory is held in high reverence by the Roman Catholics of America, the foundress of the order of the Sisters of Charity in the United States.

There is no lack of writers of *Essays* in the United States; yet, owing to the facilities afforded by the periodical press for the publication, and the preservation also, of their productions, they are seldom reproduced in book form. "Locusts and Wild Honey," by John Burroughs (Houghton, Osgood & Co.), is a collection of essays written in the best vein of this consummate literary artist and lover of nature, whose works appeal with singular force to the admiration of the American public as being instinct with poetry, but with a poetry which accepts and allies itself with science and common sense. Some of the earlier articles in the "North American Review," by famous American authors, have been collected into a volume by the editor, Allen Thorndike Rice (D. Appleton & Co.). Judge J. D. Caton's "Miscellanies" are essays on a variety of subjects, social and scientific (Houghton, Osgood & Co.).

A considerable number of books of *Poetry* have been published during the past year. The younger poets seem to lack the true inspiration, the flavor of the soil, and the vigorous and natural powers of expression, with which the older generation stirred and enchanted the popular mind. An edition of Longfellow, published by Houghton, Osgood & Co., is one of the most ambitious and elaborately illustrated publications ever attempted in America; about half of the pictures are actual views and portraits of places and persons mentioned by the poet. The "Poems" of Sarah Helen Whitman (Houghton, Osgood & Co.) were inspired more perhaps by association with poets and admiration for their works than by an original poetic instinct; yet they must find admirers for their own sake, as not only true to the models chosen, but delivering the sentiments of a high-toned and thoughtful mind. The sonnets of George McKnight, "Life and Death" (Henry Holt & Co.), have nothing of the nature of the modern sensuous and picturesque poetry; they deal with moral truths, and carry more weight and dignity in that they have no garnish whatever derived from poetical figures and imagery of either the present or a past manner, while still remaining strictly poetical in form and substance. J. J. Piatt's "Poems of House and Home" (Houghton, Osgood & Co.), containing many pieces which have not appeared in former collections, is marked by a unity of spirit and theme, the subjects being such as have given the poet some of his best inspirations. Nora Perry's "Her Lover's Friend, and other Poems" (Houghton,

Osgood & Co.), are poems with dramatic subjects, depicting the experiences of different imaginary characters in a variety of situations, some of them serious studies of the passions and some of a lighter nature. A new volume of poetry by Mrs. S. M. B. Piatt, "Dramatic Persons and Moods" (Houghton, Osgood & Co.), contains more subtle psychological studies, presented in a more elaborate but less lucid poetical form. "Along the Way," by Mary Mapes Dodge (Charles Scribner's Sons), is a volume of pleasant and simple lyric poetry. "In Berkshire with the Wild Flowers," by Elaine and Dora Goodale (G. P. Putnam's Sons), is a second series of poems by two young New England girls, whose subjects are supplied by the native flora of the district. "A Masque of Poets" is a volume of the "No Name Series" (Roberts Brothers), containing anonymous contributions from the poets, which present the variety of theme and manner that might have been expected, and are generally marked by a freshness and excellence which could not have been expected in a collection of invited poems. "Briefs of a Barrister" is the title of a volume of society verses by E. R. Johns (G. P. Putnam's Sons). The first collection of the ballads of Thomas Dunn English is published by Harper & Brothers. Robert D. Joyce's "Blanid" is a historical poem based on old Irish legends, written by the author of "Deirdré" (Roberts Brothers' "No Name Series"). Henry Abbey's "Poems" (D. Appleton & Co.) relate to historical subjects; they have already been published and well received in England. "All Quiet along the Potomac, and other Poems," is a collection of short pieces of verse on domestic and pathetic subjects by Ethel Lynn Beers (Philadelphia, Porter & Coates). "The Historical Poetry of the Ancient Hebrews," by Michael Heilprin (D. Appleton & Co.), is a scholarly critical disquisition, with new translations of the poetical books of the Bible.

Novels stream from the press in an increasing flood. Those who deprecate the influence of this kind of literature should remember that an increase in the novels which figure in the lists of the booksellers means a decrease in a pernicious class of fiction with which they come into competition, which spreads false views of society, false principles of morality, and all kinds of misinformation. In many novels of the better kind much serious thought and much genuine information are interwoven in the web of the story. A fair general education is often attained from the reading of novels alone. Moreover, the realistic novel of the day is not open to the strictures usually passed upon fiction. Although not altogether free from adventitious allurements and tricks of art, its purpose, to hold the mirror up to society, to embody sociological facts, makes it a genuine study of history of the highest character. For the first time in the history of American literature there has arisen a school of American novelists, who draw their inspiration from the well-spring of nature and model their dramatic personages after social types actually observed. In a new edition of "Uncle Tom's Cabin," containing also a bibliographical account of the work and its translations in all the literary languages of the world, Mrs. Stowe gives a simple and touching recital of the genesis of this epochal book in her mind. "The Lady of Aroostook," by W. D. Howells (Houghton, Osgood & Co.), is one of the most noteworthy novels which have been produced in the United States; it is more rounded and more artistically complete than the preceding works of the author, and is characterized in a fuller measure by the fine qualities which distinguish his style, refined humor, well conceived and finely sustained characters, bright, incisive strokes of characterization, shrewd observation of life and manners, and a fine appreciation of æsthetic propriety. In two novels by Henry James, Jr., "The Europeans" and "Daisy Miller," his favorite study of contrasted types of character, developed under the variant social conditions of Europe and America, is still his theme, handled with the dramatic consequence in character-drawing, the gleaming wit, and the finished neatness of style which make his sketchy stories finished products of novelistic art despite their scanty and poor materials. "An International Episode" is another recent study in the same limited field of observation, even slighter in dramatic construction and thinner in substance than its predecessors. Frances Hodgson Burnett, who in a former work has depicted life among the humble classes in Lancashire with great force, originality, and naturalness, now appears with a fresh novel of similar character, and not behind her former writings in truthful character-drawing and dramatic force. Three of Mrs. Burnett's earlier stories, "Kathleen Mavourneen," "Theo," "Pretty Polly Pemberton" (J. B. Lippincott), it was an injustice to reprint after her riper and better work. "Airy Fairy Lilian" (J. B. Lippincott) is an exhilarating novel of the lightest kind. George W. Cable's "Old Creole Days" contains several novelettes by a new author, which are saturated with the local color of scenes fruitful of materials for romance; the creole life is treated with artistic instinct and affords a fascinating story. "Signor Monaldini's Niece" (Roberts Brothers), one of the numerous class of cosmopolitan novels, written by an American resident in Rome [Miss M. A. Tincker], is still one of the best constructed and most workmanlike stories in the "No Name Series." "As it may Happen" (Porter & Coates) is a novel of American scenes containing some strong realistic touches. "The Colonel's Opera Cloak," a number in the second "No Name Series" (Roberts Brothers), is a lively and laughable story. "Detmold, a Romance," by W. H. Bishop (Houghton, Osgood & Co.), belongs to the better class of American novels; the characters are clearly outlined and

well developed, the dramatic theme original but not extravagant nor unpleasant, and the style refined and correct. "Modern Fishers of Men" (D. Appleton & Co.) is a faithful study of life in a small American town. "A Gentle Belle," by Christian Reid [Francis S. Fisher], is one of Appleton's "Handy-Volume" books. "Colonel Dunwoddie, Millionaire" (Harper & Brothers), is a realistic picture of life in the Southern States. Charles Scribner's Sons have published Frank R. Stockton's laughable stories of "Rudder Grange." "Tales of Table Mountain" (Houghton, Osgood & Co.) are some of Bret Harte's later short stories. "Gordon Baldwin; The Philosopher's Pendulum; Liquidated; The Seer" (D. Appleton & Co.), are four international stories whose scenes and characters are taken from the various countries where the author has resided; they are well conceived and possess strong and good qualities. Hjalmar H. Boyesen's "Falconberg" is an idealized story, whose characters are Norwegian emigrants, in which the virtues of the Scandinavian character and the sentiments of American liberty are gracefully and eloquently depicted. A romance by F. Hassaurek, "The Secret of the Andes" (Cincinnati, Robert Clarke & Co.), presents with historical fidelity the condition of the Peruvians after the conquest and their longings and struggles for liberty. Another historical romance, "The Puritan and the Quaker" (G. P. Putnam's Sons), is a well-written picture of life in old New England. "Captain Nelson" (Harper & Brothers) is a tale of colonial times by the well-known antiquary and historian, Samuel Adams Drake. The following may be mentioned among the other successful novels of the year: "The Unknown City," by W. F. Washburne (Jesse Haney & Co.); "The Felmeres," by Sada Elliott (D. Appleton & Co.); "Di Cary," by M. Jacqueline Thornton (D. Appleton & Co.); Bertha M. Clay's "Lady Damar's Secret" (G. W. Carleton & Co.); Miss Susan Warner's "My Desire," a story of the present (Robert Carter & Brothers); "The Breton Mills," by Charles J. Bellamy (G. P. Putnam's Sons); "An Earnest Trifler" (Houghton, Osgood & Co.); "His Majesty, Myself" (Roberts Brothers' "No Name Series").

Translations and adaptations from the leading Continental novelists, as well as all the more popular novels which the numerous novel-writing profession in the British Isles produce, are required to satisfy the large capacity of the American public for this class of literature. The more important translated novels offered to the public during the year are as follows: "The Maid of Stralsund," by the masterly Dutch novelist De Liefde (New York, Dodd, Mead & Co.); "A Thorough Bohémienne," by Mme. Charles Reybaud, one of the "New Handy-Volume Series" (D. Appleton & Co.); Henry Gréville's [Mme. Durand's] "Bonne-Marie" and "Philomène's Marriages" (Philadelphia, T. B. Peterson & Co.), the scenes of which are laid in the native land of the author, which she lately occupied as a new and fruitful field for her delicious social pictures; "The Diary of a Woman," by the refined and admired Octave Feuillet (D. Appleton & Co.); "Raymonde," by André Theuriet (D. Appleton & Co.); "Jean Téterol's Idea," by the popular Cherbuliez (D. Appleton & Co.); "L'Assommoir," "Nana," and other works by Emile Zola, the leader of the French realists (T. B. Peterson & Brothers); "At a High Price," by E. Werner [E. Bürstenbinder], published in the "Cobweb Series" of Estes & Lauriat; "Young Maugars," by André Theuriet (D. Appleton & Co.); "Castle Hohenwald," by Adolph Streckfuss, translated by Mrs. Wister. (J. B. Lippincott & Co.); E. Marlitt's [Eugenie John's] "In the Schillingscourt," translated by Mrs. Wister (J. B. Lippincott & Co.); "Markof, the Russian Violinist," another bright novel from the French of Henry Gréville (T. B. Peterson & Brothers); and "Tales from the German of Paul Heyse" (D. Appleton & Co.), which acquaint the reader with the most agreeable modern writer of short stories.

LITERATURE, BRITISH, IN 1879. Not more than a moiety of the literature required for the intellectual nourishment of the people of the United States is the product of American pens. A nation of readers, the Americans avail themselves of the labors of the numerous profession of well-trained writers in England to such an extent that the enumeration of the products of American literature proper gives a very incomplete idea of the literature actually required and consumed. The widely separated and politically divided English-speaking nations are becoming reunited in taste, thought, and feeling through reading the same literature. They form more truly than formerly a single reading public. The successful English author is sure of an American public, and American authors are read and admired in Great Britain. The use of a common literature in these two distant, populous, and progressive countries is most salutary in preserving in its purity and power a noble and expressive language, in correcting false and erratic tendencies, and in infusing new thought and stimulating intellectual activity, now in the one nation, now in the other.

Herbert Spencer's "Data of Ethics" (New York, D. Appleton & Co.) is the first part of the final and most important of the series of works in which the author's system of philosophy is unfolded. The profoundest expositor of the synthetic principles and method which form the groundwork of present science, Spencer has already attained a commanding position as a guide and philosopher. If the evolution doctrines are to become the belief of the future, this may prove a supremely epoch-making book; for the establishment of a basis of morality, a settled faith, though founded on science, must lead to a revival of conscience, must erect a fundamental sanction, and reawaken the springs and principles of moral action which

are relaxed in an age of drifting skepticism. The "Problems of Life and Mind" of the versatile and skillful author, George Henry Lewes, are his maturest and most thoughtful work. The first one of the third series, "The Study of Psychology, its Object, Scope, and Method" (Boston, Houghton, Osgood & Co.), was left unfinished at his death, and is given to the world by his widow, who supplied the necessary work of editing and revision. "The Realistic Assumptions of Modern Science Examined" is a controversial treatise by Thomas M. Herbert (New York, Macmillan & Co.). William Hurrell Mallock's "Is Life Worth Living?" is one of the cleverest of that author's volumes of satirical, trifling, airy reflections on the intellectual conflicts of the age, written with the levity of a mind which seems neither to possess a serious faith nor to be troubled by serious doubts (New York, G. P. Putnam's Sons). Maudsley's "Pathology of the Mind" (D. Appleton & Co.) is a valuable addition to physiological psychology. An admirable series of elementary works on special scientific subjects, "Text-Books of Science" (D. Appleton & Co.), includes "The Elements of Mechanics," by Professor T. M. Goodeve; "Metals," by C. L. Bloxam; "Introduction to the Study of Inorganic Chemistry," by Dr. W. A. Miller; "Theory of Heat," by the late Professor J. C. Maxwell; "The Strength of Materials and Structures," by J. Anderson; "Electricity and Magnetism," by Professor F. Jenkins; "Workshop Appliances," by C. P. B. Shelley; "Principles of Mechanics," by Professor Goodeve; "Introduction to the Study of Organic Chemistry," by Professor H. E. Armstrong; "The Qualitative Chemical Analysis and Laboratory Practice," by Professor T. E. Thorpe; "Telegraphy," by W. H. Preece and J. Sivewright; "Railway Appliances," by J. W. Barry; "The Art of Electrometallurgy," by J. Gore; "Introduction to the Study of Chemical Philosophy," by W. A. Tilden; "The Elements of Machine Design," by Professor W. C. Unwin; "Treatise on Photography," by De W. Abney; and "The Study of Rocks," by Frank Rutly. Professor Grant Allen, in "The Color Sense" (Houghton, Osgood & Co.), combats the theory of Magnus and Gladstone that the perception of colors is a faculty developed in man through civilization. Of Roscoe and Schorlemmer's "Treatise on Chemistry" (D. Appleton & Co.), the second volume deals with the metals in a very complete and comprehensive manner. Gegenbauer's "Elements of Comparative Anatomy" (Macmillan & Co.) is the standard work on zoölogy treated from the standpoint of the evolutionist school, now for the first time placed within the reach of English readers.

Among the small, readable manuals for popular instruction, which have multiplied so greatly within the last few years, none will serve a better purpose than the series of "Health Primers" (D. Appleton & Co.), prepared by several eminent medical and scientific men in London, including "Exercise and Training," "Alcohol," "The House and its Surroundings," "Premature Death,"."Personal Appearances in Health and Disease," "Baths and Bathing," and "The Skin." Benjamin Ward Richardson's "A Ministry of Health," and other addresses, are earnest appeals in the interest of sanitary progress.

A number of books of *Travel* of unusual interest have been published. The Rev. R. W. Dale's "Impressions of America" (D. Appleton & Co.'s "Handy-Volume Series") is a highly appreciative account of American institutions and society. "Our Autumn Holidays on French Rivers," by J. L. Molloy, is a lively narrative of a boating excursion, recounted in a refreshing tone of youthful frolic and enjoyment of outdoor life (Boston, Roberts Brothers). "Through Asiatic Turkey," by Grattan Geary (London, Sampson Low, Marston & Co.), contains the views of an intelligent and judicious observer of the Turkish question, formed no the spot by the aid of a knowledge of the language and customs of the country. A more studious and systematic work on Asiatic Turkey is McCoan's "Our New Protectorate" (London, Chapman & Hall), in which is gathered a mass of economical, geographical, social, ethnic, political, and religious information upon the Turkish provinces. "Six Months in Ascension," by Mrs. Gill, is a most interesting record of experiences and observations of an English lady who accompanied her husband to the lonely island in the middle of the South Atlantic Ocean on the expedition for the determination of the sun's parallax. Mosely's "Notes by a Naturalist on the Challenger" is an agreeable recital of experiences and observations on the famous scientific voyage, a popular narrative which touches on the scientific purposes and results of the expedition only where they are of interest to the reading public (Macmillan & Co.). "Wanderings in Patagonia," by Julius Beerbohm, is one of Henry Holt & Co.'s "Leisure - Hour Series." "A Few Months in New Guinea" is an account of a residence in that little-known land by Octavius C. Stone (Harper & Brothers).

In the department of *History*, several important works have appeared in the branch of historical sociology which deals with the origin of civilization, in which such fruitful results have been obtained through the application of the methods inaugurated by the comparative philologists. Pezzi's "Aryan Philology," translated by E. S. Roberts (London, Trübner & Co.), is a compendium of the science of comparative philology itself in its present condition. Professor W. E. Hearn of Melbourne, in "The Aryan Household" (London, Longmans, Green & Co.), groups together the researches into the constitution of early society for the purpose of constructing a picture of the life of the primitive Indo-European race. A translation of Duncker's "History of An-

tiquity," by Evelyn Abbot, is being published by R. Bentley & Son of London; it is from a revised edition, and gives the latest results of Biblical research and hieroglyphic and cuneiform interpretations. A compendium of the researches in Aryan antiquities and the prehistoric condition of society, under the title of "The Dawn of History" (Charles Scribner's Sons), has been compiled in a form adapted for easy popular reading by C. F. Keary. The subject of comparative mythology is ably and exhaustively treated by the Rev. Sir George W. Cox in "The Mythology of the Aryan Nations" (London, C. Keegan Paul & Co.); he goes farther than his predecessors in tracing affiliations between the legends of the different nations, and affirms that all the Aryan national epics had their source and groundwork in the same original pantheistic interpretation of the phenomena of nature. "Fairy Tales, their Origin and Meaning," is a popular account of the historical origin of legends by John Thackray Bunce, forming the twenty - fifth volume of Appletons' "New Handy-Volume Series." In "Lectures on the Origin and Growth of Religion" (Charles Scribner's Sons), Max Müller has at last broached a subject in which he is no longer a mere popularizer of other men's discoveries and retailer of others' thoughts. In his life-long philological studies the subject of comparative religion was so attractive to his cast of mind that in this he has hammered out ideas of his own. Spencer Walpole has executed his contemporary history of England, "A History of England from the Conclusion of the Great War in 1815" (London, Longmans, Green & Co.), with a bold and steady hand; it is a sagacious inspection into the politics and a luminous review of the social and literary development of England in the recent period. Justin McCarthy's "History of Our Own Times" (Charles Scribner's Sons) is an extremely graphic and entertaining as well as a judicious and impartial survey of recent British history, commencing at the accession of Queen Victoria. "The French Revolutionary Epoch" (D. Appleton & Co.) is a history of France from the French Revolution to the close of the German war by the able translator of Taine, Henri Van Laun. In "The Renaissance in Italy" (New York, Henry Holt & Co.) John Addington Symonds has given a philosophical study of one of the most interesting revolutions of ideas and manners in the history of European civilization. The able history of the luxuriant development of art and the attendant revolution in thought and manners in France under the invigorating influence of the humanistic and classical revival, entitled "The Renaissance of Art in France," by Mrs. Mark Pattison (London, C. Keegan Paul & Co.), is a fitting supplement to the exhaustive study of the movement at its fountain-head by Mr. Symonds. George Finlay's "History of Greece," revised by H. F. Tozer (Oxford, Clarendon Press), is the ripe and learned work of a sagacious historian, embracing the history of the whole Hellenic race and extending down to the most recent times: the present edition is almost a new work, every paragraph showing the marks of revision, and a large amount of new matter having been added. "New Greece," by Lewis Sergeant (Cassell, Petter & Galpin), records the remarkable material and political progress of the Greeks during the present century, and defends their aims and claims in relation to the Eastern question. A contribution of considerable value to the history of the last century is the Duc de Broglie's "The King's Secret" (Cassell, Petter & Galpin), containing the secret correspondence of Louis XV. "Selection from the Correspondence of the late Macvey Napier, Esq." (Macmillan & Co.), is a book which initiates the reader into the secret councils of the "Edinburgh Review," and reveals the literary privacy, the jealousies and ambitions of the leaders of the great Whig party. "The Letters of Charles Dickens" (Charles Scribner's Sons) is a book which acquaints the reader more thoroughly with the character of the great novelist than any of the lives and reminiscences of him which have appeared. Philip Gilbert Hamerton, in "The Life of J. M. W. Turner, R. A." (Roberts Brothers), rescues the memory of the great English painter from the cloudy regions to which the extravagant panegyrics of Ruskin had consigned it, dealing with the artist and his work with judicial calmness, and with the subtle discrimination which has given the author note as an appreciative and well-balanced art-critic. A biographical dictionary of "Artists of the Nineteenth Century" (Houghton, Osgood & Co.) contains the name of every recent artist of the least note, and is made up of original information obtained by extensive correspondence and painstaking inquiry by Mrs. Clement and Lawrence Hutton. James Anthony Froude's "Cæsar" is a historical sketch, written in the author's brilliant and elegant style, in which the action of history is presented with vivid picturesqueness (Charles Scribner's Sons). Two books of biography by Professor J. R. Seeley, "The Life and Adventures of Ernst Moritz Arndt," and "The Life and Times of Stein" (Roberts Brothers), illustrate the condition of Germany in the Napoleonic era. Dr. Samuel Smiles never took up a subject for biographical preaching better adapted to awaken the sympathies of his readers than the modest and enthusiastic student of nature, "Robert Dick, Baker, of Thurso, Geologist and Botanist" (Harper & Brothers). The biographical monographs on "English Men of Letters" (Harper & Brothers) are short studies on the representative men of English literature by representative English critics of the most modern stamp and tendencies—Leslie Stephen writing on the character and works of Samuel Johnson, Richard H. Hutton on Walter Scott, James H. Morrison on Gibbon,

John A. Symonds on Percy Bysshe Shelley, William Black on Oliver Goldsmith, Mark Pattison on Milton, Dean Church on Spenser, William Minto on Daniel Defoe, and Professor Shairp on Robert Burns. The most important of the series from its philosophical and tendential character is Professor Huxley's study of Hume; another of the volumes, which must have considerable influence on political thought, is the study of Burke, by the editor of the series, John Morley. The series contains a sketch of Thackeray by his brother-novelist Anthony Trollope, which, if it does not give a thoroughly adequate estimate of the subject, is a frank discussion of the scope and mission of the English novel from the point of view of one who has won distinction in composing them.

Among the recently published collections of *Essays*, the first volume of the series "Gleanings of Past Years, 1844-'78," of William E. Gladstone (Charles Scribner's Sons), is a book as replete with thought and scholarship as the former productions of the literary statesman; the first of the seven contains the essay on America, "Kin beyond Sea," which aroused considerable feeling against the author on its first publication. In Matthew Arnold's new volume of "Mixed Essays" (Macmillan & Co.) the philosophical critic makes a strenuous appeal, notably in the lecture on "Equality" here reproduced, in favor of a more invigorating and humaner culture for the middle ranks of society. A volume of "Essays Historical and Theological" has been published (London, Rivingtons), written by the thoughtful and learned late Canon Mozley, and showing great intellectual grasp, acute historical criticism, originality of thought, and unusual powers of literary expression. "Essays in Romance, and Studies from Life," by John Skelton (Edinburgh, W. Blackwood & Sons), is a new volume by the essayist whose graceful and poetic thoughts and observations have been hitherto published under the pseudonym *Shirley*. A. Hayward's "Selected Essays" (Scribner & Welford) are most entertaining sketches on historical and social subjects, filled with pointed illustrations and anecdotes. "The Gamekeeper at Home," "The Amateur Poacher," and "Wild Life in a Southern County" (Roberts Brothers), are three pleasant books on nature and rural scenes in England. "Literary Studies" (Longmans, Green & Co.) is a volume of essays by the late Walter Bagehot, in which the same ripe judgment and sagacious insight that rendered him preëminent among financial writers is brought to bear on various subjects of literary criticism which a broad culture and fine æsthetic sensibilities made his own. Two books have been published on the father of modern German literature, "Lessing," by James Sime (London, Trübner & Co.), and "Gotthold Ephraim Lessing," by Helen Zimmern (Longmans, Green & Co.). Of the three great masters in German literature Lessing, the most comprehensible to English readers, has remained comparatively unknown and unstudied; an interest in this poet and leader of thought is now first awakened in England. A translation of his "Dramatic Works" has also been published by George Bell & Sons of London, five of the comedies and two tragedies, one of which is "Miss Sarah Sampson," appearing for the first time in English versions. "Studies in the Literature of Northern Europe," by Edmund W. Gosse, the English poet (C. Keegan Paul & Co.), is a scholarly work in literary history, in which Milton's indebtedness to the contemporary Dutch poet Vondel for a part of the plan of his epic is pointed out for the first time, and in which the characteristics of Scandinavian literature are unfolded with unusual critical acumen and appreciation. G. B. Selkirk, the author of "Ethics and Æsthetics of Modern Poetry" (London, Smith, Elder & Co.), is a thoughtful critic with original ideas who has lately come before the public.

The present is an era in which the poetical form is little cultivated. Among the few works of *Poetry* published during the year, there is none which seems a genuine product of the age except the poems of Robert Browning. "The Lover's Tale" is a poem which was written by Alfred Tennyson at the age of nineteen: published first without his consent, he, conscious of its inferiority to his later works, concluded to give it to the world in a better and revised form (Houghton, Osgood & Co.). Robert Browning's new volume of poems, "Dramatic Idyls" (Smith, Elder & Co.), is not freer than his former works from his faults and mannerisms, capricious involutions of language, vague fancies, and obscure phraseology; neither is it lacking in his noble traits of genius, dramatic force, intense human sympathy, and deep insight into the human soul. Edwin Arnold, editor of the London "Telegraph," has written an epic poem on the life of Buddha, entitled "The Light of Asia" (Roberts Brothers), in which a profound knowledge of the spirit of Buddhism and of Oriental life, thought, manners, and history is worked up into a poem of unusual power and grandeur. "The Sonnets of Michael Angelo Buonarotti and Tommaso Campanella" have been produced by J. A. Symonds with excellent notes and explanations (Smith, Elder & Co.). Roberts Ffrench Duff's translation of the "Lusiad" is reprinted by J. B. Lippincott & Co.

The English novel also seems to have entered upon a period, not of degeneration, but of abeyance. There are more good novels produced now than ever before; but since the death of the two great masters of English fiction, and since George Eliot has retired from the field, no great work can be found in their number. George Eliot's "The Impressions of Theophrastus Such" is a group of character-sketches, which are marked by the fine powers of psychological analysis and deep philosophy

of life which characterize the author's novels; William Black in "Macleod of Dare" attempted a high but too difficult task—to characterize the savage passions which at times possess members of society—the same fierce passions which are the burden of many romances, idealized, and made to appertain to civilized society, but here correctly distinguished as a lurking taint inherited from a wild, undisciplined ancestry. "The Return of the Native," by Thomas Hardy, is a powerful novel of a high dramatic character, the actors in which are English country-people, from whose humble life the author has woven a web of deep tragic interest.

LITERATURE, CONTINENTAL, IN 1879.

FRANCE.—In France there is considerable attention paid to philosophical speculations by the opposite schools of theological and positive thinkers. In the essays on "Philosophes Modernes Étrangers et Français," A. Franck assumes an original position. Funck-Brentano has written a severe criticism of Stuart Mill, Herbert Spencer, and the Utilitarian group of thinkers ("Les Sophistes Grecs et les Sophistes Contemporains"). From the positive point of view, the most important book of the season is Schutzenberger's "Traité de Chimie Générale." M. Buisson's "Dictionnaire de Pédagogie et d'Instruction Primaire" is exhaustive and accurate. Compayré, in a historical review of education in France, treating of the theories of the Jansenists, the Jesuits, and the eighteenth-century philosophers on this subject, and Félix Pécaut in "Études au Jour le Jour sur l'Éducation Nationale," both advocate reforms in educational methods proposed by Michel Bréal and Jules Simon.

Several learned historical works have appeared. Lenormant's "La Monnaie dans l'Antiquité" has reached the third volume. Boidit has published an exhaustive study of Demosthenes and his epoch. Renan's large work on the origins of Christianity is approaching its conclusion ("L'Église Chrétienne"). M. Guiraud endeavors to show, in opposition to Professor Mommsen's view, that right was on the side of the Senate in the contest it carried on with Julius Cæsar. An interesting work is Demay's study of costume in the middle ages as illustrated by seals, in which the illustrations add much to the value of the book; as they do also in Duruy's volumes on Roman history.

The illustrated books are increasing in number and in excellence. Among these may be noticed the history of Tobit, illustrated by Bida and published by Hachette; M. Duplessis's "Histoire de la Gravure"; and another of the pictorial books by Paul Lacroix, published by Didot, "Le XVII' Siècle, Institutions, Usages, Costumes." The fifth volume of the "Géographie Universelle" is devoted by Élisée Reclus to a description of Russia and Scandinavian Europe. Vivien de Saint-Martin's geographical dictionary has reached the end of its first tome. M. de Valroger publishes useful researches on the origin and character of Celtic civilization ("Les Celtes et la Gaule Celtique"). M. Gebhardt, in "Les Origines de la Renaissance en Italie," treats of the various causes which led to the outburst of the intellectual revolution to which the name of Renaissance has been given. The publication of the famous *recueil* of satirical songs collected by Gaignières and Clairambault will do much toward making us acquainted with the secret history of the eighteenth century. M. de Loménie's work on the Mirabeaus, the memoirs of Mme. de Rémusat, Mme. de Bloqueville's biography of Marshal Davout, and the life of General Dessaix, are useful contributions to the history of the Revolution and of the Empire. M. Dareste has completed his popular history of France by two volumes on the Restoration. Henri Martin's large work is continued down to the Treaty of Campo Formio. The furor which exists at present for productions of the last century, such as the poems of Dorat and of Bernis, the tales of Crébillon the younger, and even the very free novelettes of La Morlière, lies at the door of Arsène Houssaye and MM. de Goncourt, who have made the eighteenth century their favorite theme for historical and biographical sketches. The authors of "Henriette Maréchal" and "Germinie Lacerteux" especially enjoy the talent of making the most of *inédits* documents, and their history of the Duchesse de Châteauroux and her sisters is the natural accompaniment of the previous volumes on Mme. Dubarry and Mme. de Pompadour. Coming to our own times, we find a memoir of the caricaturist Gavarni, and one of Théophile Gautier, both interesting, but with such an abundance of details never meant for publication that, if the fashion sets in for biographizing great men after that style, the lives of our future great men will be as unreadable as the novels of MM. Zola ("Nana"), Huysmans ("Les Sœurs Vatard,"), or Ernest Daudet ("Les Rois en Exil"). M. Pons is still more to be blamed for his exposure of the worst side of his hero's character in "Sainte-Beuve et ses Inconnues." Alphonse Karr's *log-book* ("Le Livre de Bord") is extremely amusing, and full of noteworthy particulars about the history of French literature during the last fifty years. The same praise can be bestowed upon the reminiscences of M. Werdet.

Victor Hugo's "Pitié Suprême" is the only poetical composition of importance.

Besides the outrageous productions of the realistic novelists mentioned above, Bélot of the same school has produced the "Femme de Glace," in which he outdoes his master. The novelists of the more refined class, such as Henry Gréville, Mme. de Chandeneux, and Mme. Th. Bentzon, seem to lack the vigor and originality of these dissectors of morbid morality.

GERMANY.—Although the materialistic teachings of Haeckel and his school, or the less positive materialistic skepticism of Dubois-Reymond, have taken possession of the minds of a large number of thinkers, yet the philosophy which occupies the strongest position to-day in Germany is a revival of the Kantian doctrines. A school of thinkers have assumed the designation of Neo-Kantian, and occupy themselves with logic and the problems of the mind. An important treatise on inductive logic has been written by W. Wundt. Kehrbach is at work upon a commentary on Kant's "Critique of Pure Reason." The history of philosophy is being treated by W. Windelband.

Valuable materials are placed at the disposal of the new school of history by the issue, undertaken at the expense of the German Emperor, of an accurate edition of the correspondence of Frederick the Great, as well as by the memoirs of Prince Metternich, which his son promises. The liberal opening of the Record Offices at Berlin and Vienna, so long jealously closed, will make possible in the future an impartial history of the ancient rivals. To impartiality H. von Treitschke's "German History in the Nineteenth Century" makes no pretense. A band of historians, at the head of which stands W. Oncken, has undertaken a comprehensive "Universalgeschichte in Einzeldarstellungen," which is designed to fill forty volumes. The first installments, "Egyptian History," by Johannes Dümmichen, and the "Ancient Persian History to the Extinction of the Kingdom of the Sassanidæ," by Ferdinand Justi, are all that could be wished. Carl Hillebrand is writing a history of France from Louis Philippe to Napoleon III. Following upon the magnificent illustrated work on "Egypt" by George Ebers, has appeared a similar book on "Hellas and Rome," by Falke, the art-historian.

Gottfried Semper's great work on "Style in the Fine Arts" is being reissued. Hermann Hettner has treated of art and literature in Italy in his "Italian Studies."

Oscar Lenz and Hübbe-Schleiden have both produced "Studies of West Africa," the one from Senegal, the other from Ethiopia. The "Wanderbuch" of Field-Marshal Moltke would attract attention on account of its authorship, even were its contents less valuable.

The autobiographical sketches with which Franz Dingelstedt, under the title of "Münchener Bilderbogen," has supplemented his "Bilderbuch" of last year, closely resemble a novel. The daughter of Dingelstedt's former associate, the powerful minister of the literary King Maximilian, has published from her retirement in America a revelation of her relations to the agitator Lassalle, which has had a remarkable run. The "Bismarck Letters" are letters of the Prince to his wife, his friends, and his sister and confidante Malwina. The political life and activity of Bismarck is revealed in L. Hahn's collection of his speeches, his dispatches, and diplomatic acts arranged in chronological order, without note or comment. "Die

Familie Mendelssohn" is the title of a pleasant book compiled from family papers by Sebastian Hensel, the nephew of the composer Mendelssohn, and the son of his darling sister Fanny.

The mystic poetry of Siegfried Lipiner, a Galician Jew by origin, marks a reaction from the pessimistic atheism which has been the tone of German poetry since Heine. Lipiner's latest poem, entitled "Renatus," is intended to describe those who have been reborn in the light of a new faith. Paul Heyse's "Verse aus Italien " is distinguished by classic smoothness.

Wilbrandt—whose "Maler," together with G. Freytag's "Journalisten," may be considered the best among recent German comedies—has been less successful with his last two productions, the comedy "Der Thurm in der Stadtmauer" and his "Natalie," a piece written in Iffland's style. A comedy entitled " Rosenkranz und Güldenstern," by Klapp, has gone the round of all the theatres in Germany.

Berthold Auerbach has published an instructive novel in the style of "Waldfried," under the title of "Forstmeister." Friedrich Spielhagen has, since the publication of his romance "Sturmflut," appeared with a three-volume novel entitled "Plattland." "Eekenhof," by Theodor Storm, may be considered one of the chief works of the year. Almost as much power is exhibited in the romantic tale " Der Schelm von Bergen," by Julius von der Traun (Alexander Schindler). Gustav Freytag has brought his historical pictures, given in the continued romance "Die Ahnen," down to the period of the Thirty Years' War. Louise von François has produced another admirable historical novel, " Die Katzenjunker."

BELGIUM.—In Belgium many pens are busied with subjects connected with the national history. "Le Siècle des Artevelde," by Léon Vanderkindere, is an exhaustive study of the foreign politics, the aristocracy, the democratic revolution, the economical movement, political centralization, the artisans, agricultural laborers, religion, clergy, thoughts, ideas, and morals of Flanders and Brabant during the fourteenth century. " L'Histoire Politique Interne de la Belgique," by Edm. Poullet, professor at the University of Louvain, is a powerful sketch. J. Künziger has published a short but interesting history of the Netherlands in the sixteenth century, under the title of "Nos Luttes contre l'Intolérance et le Despotisme." The late Minard van Hoorebeke's "Description de Méreaux et de Jetons de Présence, etc., des Gildes et Corps de Métiers des Pays-Bas " gives an account of the societies of artisans of Ghent and other places. Eug. van Bemmel edits "La Belgique Illustrée," which supplies a pictorial and historical description of the principal towns and districts. Ferdinand Vanderhaeghen is preparing a general bibliography of the Netherlands, in which he proposes carefully to describe all the books printed in the Low Countries during the fifteenth and sixteenth centuries, and also the principal works that have been published since.

Godefroid Kurth, professor at the University of Liége, in his voluminous work entitled "Sitting Bull," examines the question of the Redskins of the United States from a point of view strictly Catholic. J. Dauby has devoted an interesting book to the question of "Grèves Ouvrières," and J. Stevens one to that of "Prisons Cellulaires en Belgique." Georges de Laveleye has treated a subject which is the question of the day, "Les Bilans et les Inventaires."

Paul Voituron, in his work "Le Libéralisme et les Idées Religieuses," extols a new religion. Aristide Astruc, chief Rabbi of Belgium, has published a broad and original study entitled "Entretiens sur le Judaïsme, son Dogme et sa Morale." "La Philosophie Scientifique," by Captain H. Girard, is a bold attempt to prescribe a general method for all sciences.

Max Rooses has finished his magnificent work on the Antwerp school of painters.

Chief among the writers in Flemish, Hendrik Conscience continues his artless and simple narratives of Flemish habits and customs. A remarkable production is a work entitled "Drie Novellen," by Miss Virginie Loveling.

The most noteworthy drama is a little play from the pen of Emiel van Goethem, entitled "Tony en Belleken."

HOLLAND.—Holland is prolific in novelists who delight in portraying with more or less idealization the simple lives of the poor. Israël is exceedingly successful in depicting the hopes and sorrows, the joys and hardships of the Dutch fishermen, and Cremer in his pictures of the comfortable and good-natured Dutch farmers and their families. Three younger writers have appeared, MM. Otto, Martin Kalff, and Justus van Maurik, who paint their Dutch interiors from the home-life of the humbler classes of townsfolk. MM. Ten Brink and Wolters, among a number of other popular story-writers, have produced good novels.

Two new poets have arisen who give good promise of future excellence—Gosler, author of "Licht en Schaduw," and Waalner. Emants has written a poem, in three cantos, entitled "Lilith."

Under the inappropriate title of " Causeriën," Berckenhoff has published a readable volume of letters to a supposed lady friend on art and criticism. The Rev. J. Craandijk has just issued the fourth volume of the "Wandelingen door Nederland," beautifully illustrated by Schipperus's drawings. Van Assendelft de Coningh has written a pleasant book, recounting his forty years' experience as a sailor, called "Ontmoetingen ter Zee en te Land." Busken Huët has published another volume of "Literarische Fantasiën," containing essays on Victor Hugo, Paul de Kock, Lord Lytton, etc. Another valuable book of this fascinating but often paradoxical author is "Het Land van Rubens."

DENMARK.—After a rather long period of

stagnation, signs of vigorous progress are apparent, mainly the result of the efforts made by the able critic Georg Brandes. His last work is "Benjamin Disraeli, Earl of Beaconsfield." The author of "Jason with the Golden Fleece" has followed his first production with others equally lifelike, clear, and free from false decoration. Another pseudonymous writer, "Diodoros," has produced under a general title, "The Eternal Strife," three poems demanding notice for their graphic style, earnest feeling, and graceful humor. A. Skram has published a boldly realistic romance called "Gertrude Colbjörnson." K. Gjellerup tells in "The Idealist" the story of an enthusiast with "humanitarian" views of life. In Schandorph's story in verse called "Youthful Days" the hero is a young man of our times whose will is energetic, while his practical aims are not clear. Erslev, in his historical sketch "King and Vassal in the Sixteenth Century," gives able descriptions of old institutions and their relations. "Insignificant People" is a collection of stories by Carit Etlar. In "Religion and Politics," given in the shape of the last will and testament left by a Socialist, the writer, whose pseudonym is "Theodorus," assumes an independent ideal position.

SWEDEN.—The work which has caused the greatest excitement in Sweden of late, "Röda Rummet" ("The Red Chamber"), contains accounts of the artistic and literary life of Stockholm. The young author, August Strindberg, is acknowledged by every one to be most gifted, but he belongs to the school of Zola. The volume is of special interest as being the first of its kind in Sweden. The author is also eager to show not only that this world is the worst of all possible worlds, but that the artistic-literary world of Stockholm is especially bad. An admirable collection of novelties is "Gamla Kort" ("Old Bard"), by Claes Lundin. Richard Gustafsson calls his latest work "Metropolitan Types." Another group of tales, "Svart pa Hvitt" ("Black upon White"), is by Frans Hedberg. The popular novels published under the signature "H." are by the wife of a professor in the principal university.

A promising new poet bears the name of Baath. Oestergren has produced a new volume of poems. The splendid collection of popular Swedish ballads has been republished with notes by R. Bergström and J. L. Höijer.

Professor G. Retzius, the famous anthropologist, has published a work on Finnish craniums.

A Positivist disciple, Dr. A. Nyström, has written a studious essay on Comte and his doctrines.

NORWAY.—In Norway the fermentation of religious thought has impregnated the entire literature. The dramas of Ibsen and Björnstjerne Björnson are saturated with religious speculations. The new dramas of the latter, "Leonarda" and "Det nye System" ("The New System"), are indignant protests against the hypocrisy and Philistinism of modern society. Ibsen's latest work, "Et Dukkehjem" ("The Doll's House"), is a masterly tragedy of domestic life.

There is no lack of novelists in Norway. Their favorite subject hitherto, peasant life, has at last been abandoned for more fruitful fields. The sketchy novelettes of Alexander Kjelland, a young author of genius, are the best productions of the year.

The new theory of Professor S. Bugge and Dr. A. Chr. Bang, that Scandinavian mythology is derived from Greek and Roman sources or based upon Christian legends, is creating a good deal of excitement in intellectual circles.

POLAND.—Historical research has the most attractions for Polish scholarship. A number of collections of historical materials, such as the "Diplomatic Codex of Great Poland," the "Monumenta Poloniæ Historica," etc., are being published. "The Ancient History of Poland," a posthumous work by Julian Bartoszewicz, and Professor Bobrzynski's "Outlines of Polish History," are remarkable books. The latter has created much stir owing to the gloomy views the author takes of the events and actors in Polish history. Several works upon subjects connected with the literary history of Poland have appeared.

Poetical literature has degenerated in Poland as well as in other countries. The few volumes of verse published are of indifferent quality.

In theatrical literature, the most noteworthy productions are "Article 264," a broad comedy, by Kas. Zalewski, and "Dama Treflowa," a comedy of unusual excellence, by the same writer.

The most prolific of authors, Joseph J. Kraszewski, has produced no less than ten new novels during the year. Mme. Elise Orzesko, in "Meir Ezofowicz," depicts the life of the Polish Jews with remarkable power and fidelity. Other new novels are by "T. T. Jez" (Sig. Milkowski) and Sig. Kaczkowski, the historical novelist.

BOHEMIA.—Literary activity was greater in 1879 in Bohemia than in any preceding year. More and more interest seems to be taken in the national literature, and more ambitious works are written and published than formerly.

In poetical literature may be mentioned Verchlicky's translation of the "Divina Commedia" and his "Myths," and particularly Heyduk's "Grandfather's Bequest," a charming love-tale, and at the same time an allegorical eulogy of popular song. Pokorny's "Under the Bohemian Sky" and "Unerotic Songs" are written in a pleasant vein of satire.

In drama the most conspicuous productions of the year are the comedy entitled "The Literary Tilt-Yard," by Vesely, and J. Fric's tragedy "Svatupluk and Rostislav."

There is an increased abundance of novels, by Steankovsky, Jirasek, Berta Mühlstein, and others.

Sobotka's work on "Plants and their Significance in the Songs, Stories, Myths, etc., of the Slavonian Race," is a valuable contribution to primitive Slavic history. Sembera's "Middle Ages " is a still more interesting study of Slavic history. Other important works on history have been published. The travels of Dr. Emil Holub are awakening much interest.

HUNGARY.—An important event has been the completion of the greatest poetical work of the chief of Hungarian poets. John Arany, under the title of "Toldy Szenelme" ("The Love of Toldy "), an epic poem, has concluded his famous Toldy trilogy, of which the first part, a description of the youth of the hero, was published in 1846, while the third part, in which the fall and the death of Toldy are related, came out in 1854.

"Rab Ráby," a new novel by Maurice Jókai, is a story of the time of Joseph II. It is founded on a memoir published in Strasburg in 1797.

Francis Pulszky's memoirs make a valuable contribution to history from the light they throw on the Revolution of 1848. A delightful volume of memoirs, by a deceased actress, Mme. Déry, has been published. The posthumous works of Count Stephen Széchenyi, a distinguished patriot, have attracted much attention.

Some most interesting works on comparative philology have appeared, such as Professor Budenz's "Comparative Dictionary," which has reached the division of words commencing with vowels; those in the Finn-Ugrian as well as in the Tatar-Turkish languages are few compared with those commencing with consonants. Vambéry has edited the poems of the Turkoman bard Makdumkuli. Professor Genetz has published some Lapponian texts. The Codex of Festus, a part of the literary treasure presented to Hungary by the Sultan, has been edited by Professor Tewrewk. A systematic grammar of the Magyar language in its relations to cognate tongues has been written by Professor Simonyi. Salomon's "History of Buda-Pesth in Antiquity " and Baron Radranszky's "Mediæval Households in Hungary " are both valuable accessions to the national history.

ITALY.—The study of the national literature draws the attention of Italian authors more than any other subject at present. Signor Bartoli continues the publication of his "Storia della Letteratura Italiana." He has also prepared a catalogue of the National Library in Florence. Professor Del Lungo devotes two thick volumes to proving the authenticity of the Chronicle of Dino Compagni. Dr. Attilio Hortis has published an able study on the Latin works of Boccaccio.

Senator Marco Tabarrini has written an interesting account of the life and studies of Gino Capponi. A biography of Manzoni contains some interesting letters of his. P. G. Molmenti has written a good critique on Goldoni; and a volume of the poet's inedited letters has been published. An intensely interesting book is the autobiography of the famous living sculptor, Giovanni Dupré.

The novels of Zola and the poetry of Lorenzo Stecchetti find many admirers and imitators. "Giacinta " is a novel by a brilliant author, Capuana, which has the full flavor of French naturalism. Two more novels of the ultra-realistic school are "Candaule," by R. Sacchetti, and "Cesare," by Bruno Sperani (pseudonym of a lady). Among others are a beautiful story by Barrili, "Il Tesoro di Golconda," and a historical novel, the scene of which is laid in Rome in the seventh century, "Saturnino," by R. Giovagnoli; finally, the spirited sketches of Matilde Serao, a young Greek lady settled at Naples, and of Giovanni Faldella. Edmondo de Amicis and Salvatore Farina are each of them busy with a novel.

An interesting revelation of Nihilistic thought is given in a volume by G. B. Arnando. In protest and in contrast to the realistic productions is the "Grido " of the poet Rizzi, and the "Anticaglie " of Felice Cavallotti. "Lachrymæ," a volume of elegiac verse by Giuseppi Chiarini, " L' Acqua," by Giuseppi Regaldi, and Rapisardi's translation of Lucretius, are poems of merit and beauty.

Senator Tullo Massarani has written a volume of admirable art criticism, "L' Arte a Parigi."

Vittorio Bersezio describes in an attractive manner the reign of Victor Emanuel, giving importance to the literary movement under that monarch. Signor Ruggiero Bonghi sums up in a single volume of lectures, conceived in a large fashion and in broad outlines, the whole of the ancient history of the East and of Greece.

Count Terenzio Mamiani, the venerable patriot and philosopher, has just brought out a remarkable volume entitled "La Religione dell' Avvenir." Count Mamiani is a Neo-Platonist who has studied St. Augustine and St. Thomas, a poet and a dreamer, whose instincts and sympathies are those of an artist, and whose religion of the future is the apotheosis of art-feeling.

SPAIN.—There is at present considerable literary activity in Spain. A work of unusual value is the life of Las Casas by Don Antonio Fahié. Of the "Documentos inéditos para la Historia de las Indias " twenty volumes have already appeared. Several other books on the history of discoveries in America have been published by the Government, among them a large collection of early maps; also the reprint "Tres Relaciones de Antigüedadas Peruanas." Professor Costa has written a learned and valuable essay upon the Celts in Spain.

An astonishing amount of poetry is published in Spain annually, but of little value. The considerable array of novels are most of them after French models. Plays and playwrights abound, but most of the dramas are of an ephemeral character. Rubi, Echegaray, and Selgas have produced new theatrical pieces.

Several valuable works on scientific subjects of a practical bearing have appeared, such as "La Vid Comun," by Rojas Clemente, reprinted at the expense of the Government, Maffei's work on mining, and an able treatise on forestry by Don Luis de la Escosura.

PORTUGAL.—Among the few works published in Portugal may be mentioned the studies of Oliveira Martin on the early historical developments in the Iberian Peninsula; a good satirical poem by a poet of the last century, Antonio Diniz da Cruz e Silva, now printed for the first time; "Os Noivos," an excellent realistic novel, by Teixeira de Queiroz; "O Senhor Ministro," a portrayal of Lisbon society, by the same author; and a book of travels containing acute and brilliant notes on French society, by Ramalho Ortigão. In a series of novels published under the title of "Phototypias do Minho," José Augusto Vieira has discovered in the interesting customs of the Minho a new and fertile subject for fiction.

In works of philosophy and politics radical and positivistic notions are gaining ground.

LOUISIANA. The regular session of the Legislature commenced on January 6th and closed on February 1st. The Senate was called to order by Lieutenant-Governor Wiltz. In his brief address reference was made to the pestilence of the previous summer, which visited many localities of the State and destroyed thousands of lives, and the great philanthropy displayed by the people of the North, East, and West to the sufferers. He suggested that the representatives of the people "should record these facts in monumental resolutions upon their statute-books, coupled with a vote of thanks in suitable terms, so that the world may know that we are not ungrateful, and so that our children's children may remember the great calamity that fell upon their ancestors, and the noble generosity with which the women and children of distant lands came to their rescue."

In the House, J. C. Moncure was chosen Speaker. He believed that the Legislature should do little else than consider the expediency of holding a Constitutional Convention, and passing the laws necessary for that object.

One of the earliest measures adopted by the Legislature was the act providing for the session of a State Constitutional Convention. The election of delegates was directed to take place on March 18th, and the assembling of the Convention on April 21st.

The following joint resolutions, offered in the Senate, passed both Houses:

Whereas, During many months of the past year an epidemic pestilence of the most virulent character prevailed at the capital and throughout a large portion of the State of Louisiana, carrying sorrow, distress, and death into thousands of homes; and

Whereas, In the days of our mourning and sore trouble, magnanimous strangers in all sections of the United States and in many foreign lands voluntarily came to the relief of our afflicted people, with contributions aggregating $1,100,000; therefore, be it

VOL. XIX.—36 A

Resolved by the Senate and House of Representatives of the State of Louisiana in General Assembly convened, That the earnest, heartfelt thanks of the people of this Commonwealth be and are hereby tendered to all those large-hearted philanthropists who contributed so spontaneously and munificently to the relief of the Louisiana sufferers by the yellow-fever epidemic of 1878.

Be it further resolved, etc., That we, the representatives of the people of Louisiana, deem it right and proper thus to acknowledge and commend this unsurpassed philanthropy, and to place upon our statute-books this testimonial of gratitude, so that, in all time to come, those who follow us, while remembering the calamity that fell upon their ancestors, may be reminded of the noble generosity of the men, women, and children of other States of the Union, and of distant lands, who came to their relief in the days of their affliction.

In the Senate the following joint resolution was offered:

Resolved by the Senate and House of Representatives of the State of Louisiana in General Assembly convened, That the State Government is fully equal to the discharge of the duties for which governments are organized, the protection of life, liberty, and property. That the interference of the General Government in our internal affairs is a reflection upon our civilization, a reproach to republican governments, and calculated to engender bitterness and strife by intermeddling with domestic affairs which can well be adjusted by the people interested, before the constituted authorities of the State.

On its second reading the following amendment was offered and accepted:

Whereas, The Constitution of the United States has not conferred the right of suffrage upon any one, and the United States have no voters of their own creation in the States, but the matter of suffrage is left entirely with the States themselves, with the reservation of the provisions of the fifteenth amendment, which has invested the citizens of the United States with a new constitutional right, to wit, the exemption from discrimination in the exercise of the elective franchise on account of race or color or previous condition;

Whereas, The functions of Congress under this constitutional amendment are limited to prevent, by proper legislation, the denial or abridgment by a State of the right of a citizen to vote, on account of race, color, or previous condition of servitude of the voter:

Resolved, That sections 5506, 5507, 5508, and 5509 of the Revised Statutes of the United States are in derogation of the Constitution of the United States and of the amendments thereof, in this, that the Federal Government, by these sections, assumes plenary jurisdiction of the matter of suffrage, without reference to the action of the States as such, and without interference on their part to deny or abridge the right of suffrage as indicated in the said constitutional amendment.

Resolved, That the proceedings in the United States Circuit Court at New Orleans against citizens of various parts of the State of Louisiana, and the subjecting of numerous citizens thereof to the hardships of arrest from distant homes, and their removal to New Orleans to be tried for alleged offenses against the above-stated sections of the Revised Statutes, are pregnant with the gravest consequences; and the people of this State can not but protest energetically against such harsh and unwarrantable prosecutions.

Resolved, That this protest of the State of Louisiana, which, by her laws and in her courts, does make no discrimination between her citizens on account of race, color, or previous condition of servitude, be respectfully laid before the President of these United States and the Senate and House of Representatives of these United States.

Subsequently the resolutions were made concurrent instead of joint, and passed the Senate by yeas 21, nays 9. They also passed the House. The Governor transmitted a copy to the President of the United States with the following letter:

EXECUTIVE DEPARTMENT, STATE OF LOUISIANA, }
NEW ORLEANS, *February* 13, 1879. }
To His Excellency R. B. Hayes, President of the United States:

I have the honor of transmitting herewith to your Excellency (in accordance with the provisions thereof) a duly certified copy of "concurrent resolutions" passed by the General Assembly of the State of Louisiana at its last session.

In doing so, I desire, as Governor of Louisiana, to express, in reference to the prosecutions now pending in the Circuit Court of the United States against citizens of Louisiana, under the sections of the Revised Statutes alluded to in the resolution, my profound regret that, in a matter of such importance as to call forth the legislative action of a State, a Judge of the Supreme Court of the United States should not be present to participate in the decision of the vital questions which those cases involve, so as to afford the amplest opportunity of having them passed upon by the highest tribunal of the land, the Supreme Court of the United States.

Any decision which might be rendered in those cases, resting upon a mere concurrence of opinion of two Judges of inferior jurisdiction (the effect of which concurrence would be to bar the presentation of the legal questions involved to the Supreme Court of the United States), would not carry with it the weight and authority which the importance of the issues raised and the sense of justice and right of the American people absolutely and imperatively require.

I have the honor to sign myself, with great respect, your Excellency's obedient servant,
FRANCIS T. NICHOLLS,
Governor of Louisiana.

The election of a Senator in Congress was accomplished only after a large number of joint meetings. At the last one there were 33 Senators and 88 Representatives present. The nominations were H. C. Warmoth and B. F. Jonas. Mr. Jonas received 98 votes and Mr. Warmoth 28. The former was declared to be elected. His term commenced on March 4, 1879. He was a lawyer of distinction in New Orleans. He has held many positions of trust and honor, and has filled them well. He has been a member of the House, a member of the State Senate, and Attorney of the city of New Orleans. In the canvass of 1872 he was nominated for Lieutenant-Governor on the Democratic ticket, but, in order to consolidate the anti-Republican vote, he gave way to Mr. Penn. In 1877 he lacked three votes of the nomination for Senator, which was conferred on Senator Spofford. (See "Annual Cyclopædia," 1878, page 497.)

The following act for the prevention of cruelty to animals was passed:

SEC. 1. *Be it enacted, etc.,* That section 816 of the Revised Statutes of the State shall be amended and reënacted so as to read as follows:

"SEC. 816. Whoever shall wantonly or maliciously cruelly beat, maim, disable, starve, or otherwise ill-treat any domesticated animal, including those specified in the fo egoing section, shall, upon conviction, be fined not exceeding $100, or imprisoned not exceeding three months, or both, at the discretion of the court."

There was a failure to pay the interest falling due on the State debt on January 1st. The subject was brought before the Legislature. By the Auditor's report the tax system of the State seems to be greatly defective in regard to the payment or non-payment of taxes and the inequality of assessments. The practice of non-payment by many owners of taxable property is most persistent. The evil has grown to so great a magnitude that there is a class of non-taxpayers, whose interests are so large and influence so extensive that it is almost impossible to deal with them effectively. The compulsory collection of their past-due taxes would amount to practical confiscation. By the imperfect system of assessment, the property of others is largely undervalued and almost entirely escapes taxation. Some striking illustrations of inequality of valuation are presented in the Auditor's report. For instance, the whole State of Louisiana appears to own household goods, jewelry, silver plate, mechanics' tools, and other such personal property to the value of $1,716,530, of which only $22,340 worth appears to be owned in the country. What is still more remarkable is, that only ten country parishes own any of these articles, and forty-seven parishes are entirely destitute of them. It appears, further, that while the city of New Orleans has 25 per cent. of the population of the State, the assessments of real estate for New Orleans are 61 per cent. of the assessments of the State. That is to say, New Orleans appears to be between two and three times as rich as the rest of the State. The real estate of New Orleans is valued at $104,000,000, and the real estate of the country parishes at $73,000,000, so that all the land in the State of Louisiana, with its houses, fences, cotton-gins, sugar-houses, steam-engines, etc., is worth only three dollars an acre, according to the official assessments. The rate of taxation previous to the session of the Constitutional Convention had been fixed at 5½ mills on the dollar to meet the interest on the outstanding State bonds, which yielded a gross amount of $973,500 upon a total assessment of about $117,000,000. Allowing 25 per cent. for deductions on assessments, compensation to assessors, and commissions for collection, it would net $780,125 to meet a debt of $821,105.15, leaving a deficiency of $90,980.15 at the end of the year. The debt at that time was estimated at $13,000,000, and the interest (at 7 per cent.) at $910,000; and the net amount of taxes at $730,125, which left a deficit of $180,075. This deficit, the Auditor said to the Legislature, "can only be met by an increase of the interest-tax, or by a compromise with the bondholders, thereby reducing the interest to such a rate as will enable the State hereafter to meet its obligations promptly. Whether a compromise can be effected I am unable to say; but is it not better for the bondholders to receive their interest punctually, at a lower rate than now fixed by law, than to wait for an indefinite period?

It should be recollected that the funding act was passed at a time when the *bona fide* owners of the soil of this country had no say-so in the affairs of this government; and, poverty-stricken to-day, they are unable to come forward. No one seems to be benefited by this state of things; and while the taxpayers have to apply for relief at the hands of the Legislature, I merely caution those who hold the obligations of the State, and are pressing their claims, not to do so to the injury of the people. That the interest now due will eventually be paid, I have no doubt. The only question to be settled is, when can it be paid, and what time will be granted to do so? Not invested with any power in the premises, I am compelled to refer the whole subject to your honorable body, and trust that, by wise legislation, the State may be relieved from its present financial difficulties."

The exceptional causes which operated to produce financial embarrassments in New Orleans during 1878 were such that even the teachers of the public schools of the city received no pay after the middle of August to the close of the year. In a report to the Legislature the State Superintendent suggested, as the only remedy to be found, the withholding of the contributions of the city to outside parishes. By the State law New Orleans is required to keep open the public schools for ten months in the year, and to pay annual salaries to the teachers. During a course of years the city has been contributing out of the State school-tax collected from her property-owners at least $120,000 annually toward the education of the children of several poor parishes in Middle and Southeast Louisiana. While during periods of prosperity this generosity was possible and proper, the Superintendent was of the opinion that it was only justice that, during the utter inability of the city authorities to discharge the obligations imposed upon them by law, owing to the profound financial distress which crippled every branch of industry in the community, so recently afflicted by a dread pestilence, this annual contribution should, for the present year at least, be voluntarily declined by the usual beneficiaries, and returned to New Orleans, to enable the directors of the schools to rescue their teachers from embarrassments and destitution. He urged, therefore, that a special act should be passed by the Legislature authorizing him to apportion back to the city of New Orleans such an amount of State school-taxes, paid by her citizens into the State Treasury for the years 1877 and 1878, as will enable the City Board of School Directors to discharge, as far as practicable, all outstanding obligations for the month of December, 1877, and the last four months of the year 1878. A bill for this object failed to pass.

The public school fund of the State includes, first, the "current school fund," or State tax of two mills on the dollar value of property in the respective parishes of the State, collected and paid into the State Treasury. The amount of this tax levied for collection in the year 1878 was $345,000, or about $1.20 per child of school age in the State; but the amount collected and rendered apportionable to the parish boards was only $208,159.69, or about 76½ cents per child. This is but a small fraction of the $500,000 deemed necessary in the general appropriation act of March 22, 1878, as the State's contribution toward the support of good free schools in every locality of the State where such schools were needed. Second, the poll-tax of one dollar imposed upon all adult male inhabitants of the State, for school and charitable purposes. The amount of this tax paid into the State Treasury during the year 1878 aggregated only $14,620.60, showing conclusively that only a few of the "all male inhabitants of the State" have been required to contribute this tax; and of this amount the free public schools have been allowed to receive only one fourth. The State Constitution has required all taxation to be equal and uniform throughout the State, and imposed on the General Assembly the obligation to "levy a poll-tax on all male inhabitants of the State over twenty-one years old"—authorizing it, at the same time, to raise this capitation tax to one dollar and fifty cents per annum. Legislation was therefore needed in obedience to the mandate of the Constitution to enforce payment of the poll-tax by every male inhabitant, so that it might not continue to be paid by property-owners alone, who are required to pay other taxes also for the support of the government and the schools.

The system of schools in operation in New Orleans is known as that of separate schools, one set being for white children and another set for colored children. The right of the directors to establish these separate schools was brought to a judicial test in the case of Bertonneau *vs.* the Board of Directors of the city schools of New Orleans and others, in equity. The decision was rendered by Judge W. B. Woods of the United States Circuit Court in February. The Judge said:

The grievance, and the sole grievance, set out in the bill, is that complainant's children, being of African descent, are not allowed to attend the same public schools as those in which children of white parents are educated. Is this a deprivation of a right granted by the Constitution of the United States? The complainant says that the action of the defendants deprives him and his children of the equal protection of the laws, and therefore impairs a right secured to him and them by the fourteenth amendment to the Constitution of the United States. Is there any denial of equal rights in the resolution of the Board of Directors of the city schools, or in the action of the subordinate officers of the schools, as set out in the bill? Both races are treated precisely alike. White children and colored children are compelled to attend different schools. That is all. The State, while conceding equal privileges and advantages to both races, has the right to manage its schools in the manner which in its judgment will best promote the interest of all. The State may be of opinion that it is better to educate the sexes separately, and therefore establish schools in which the children of different sexes are educated apart. By such a policy can it be said that the equal rights of either sex are invaded? Equality of right does not involve the necessity of educating children of both sexes, or children without regard to their attainments or age, in the same school. Any classification which provides substantially equal school advantages does not impair any rights, and is not prohibited by the Constitution of the United States. Equality of rights does not necessarily imply identity of rights.

These views have been held by the Supreme Court of Ohio in respect to a law under which colored children were not admitted as a matter of right into the schools for white children. State *vs.* McCann et al., 21 Ohio State, 198. See also State *vs.* Duffy, 7 Nevada, 342, and People *vs.* Gaston, 13 Abb. (New York), 160, where substantially the same doctrine is held. See also the able concurring opinion of Mr. Justice Clifford in Hall *vs.* De Cuir, 95 U. S., 491. In the State of Georgia there is a law forbidding the intermarriage of white persons and persons of African descent. It was held by Mr. Justice Erskine, of the United States Court, that this law was not obnoxious to the fourteenth amendment to the Constitution. (*Ex rel.* Hobbs and Johnson, 1 Woods, 537.) The argument in support of this decision is that the law applies with equal force to persons of both races. Its prohibition applies alike to black and white, and the penalty for disobedience falls with equal severity on both. These authorities, it seems to me, fully sustain the views above announced by this Court.

The last point was that the establishment of separate schools was contrary to the Constitution of the State. The Court said: "Whether the directors of the New Orleans schools are the State, or so represent the State that their acts are to be considered the acts of the State, it is unnecessary to decide. The Court has no power, and it does not sit, to supervise the conduct of State officers, unless such conduct impairs some rights confered by the Constitution of the United States, or unless the citizenship of the parties gives it jurisdiction. Otherwise the Court will not and can not take cognizance of violations of State law or State constitutions, by the officers of a State."

A bill was introduced to repeal the charter of the Louisiana State Lottery. This charter was granted in 1868 for a term of twenty years, and the company paid an annual license fee of $10,000. As this had been in part paid for the year 1879, the point discussed turned on the legality of an immediate repeal. The Senate adopted March 31st as the date for the repeal to take effect, and passed the bill. In the House the vote was 63 yeas to 20 nays. The repeal, however, failed to become effective, the law being regarded as violating a regular contract.

The elections for delegates to the seventh State Constitutional Convention was held on March 18th. The vote was much less than had been anticipated, being under 70,000, which was smaller than at any election during the twelve previous years. The delegates elected from senatorial districts were divided politically as follows: Democrats 29, Republicans 5, National 1, Independent 1; total, 36. The delegates from parishes were divided as follows: Democrats 69, Republicans 27, National

1, Independent 1; total, 98. The total was: Democrats 98, Republicans 32, Nationals 2, Independents 2. Mr. L. A. Wiltz was chosen President of the Convention, having received 102 votes, and Pierre Landry 27. One of the first resolutions adopted by the Convention was the following—yeas 76, nays 49:

Resolved, That there is no intention whatever entertained by this body of impairing or restricting the political, civil, or religious rights of any class of citizens of this State on account of race, color, or previous condition of servitude, but on the contrary the intention is to defend and maintain the rights of the colored citizens as guaranteed by the Constitution of the United States and of this State, under the new Constitution about to be formed.

There were two or three seats of delegates contested. In a case from East Carroll Parish, the question turned on the citizenship of the sitting delegate. The majority report was in his favor, while the minority recommended that he be ousted. Mr. Girard moved the rejection of the majority report, saying: "It has been said there are no laws requiring qualifications for members of the Convention. This was true, because no laws could be framed to govern the duties of a Constitutional Convention. Consequently the Convention would naturally follow the rules of other general assemblies. It was repugnant to every sentiment of Americans to allow foreigners and aliens to represent them. He could not recognize any one as a true son of Louisiana who would favor allowing aliens to make an organic law for this State. It was admitted that no man could be a citizen of two States; the party in question could not be a citizen of both Louisiana and Ohio." Mr. Warmoth said "he did not believe a man had to be a Louisianian to occupy a seat in the Convention. This is an assemblage of the people's representatives in their primary capacity. The Convention has no laws or regulations governing its proceedings. There is no law of any kind to limit the power of the people to send a representative to this Convention. A parish might send a woman or any one else, and it would be a piece of impertinence to say such a representative should be turned out." The motion to reject the majority report was lost—yeas 28, nays 83.

The question relating to the powers of a Constitutional Convention was incidentally discussed. It came up in connection with the majority and minority reports on an ordinance making appeals to the Supreme Court from certain parishes returnable in New Orleans in 1880. The majority report advised the rejection of the ordinance, principally because it partook of a legislative character and had nothing to do with the preparation of an organic law. The minority report favored the ordinance, and claimed that unless some such provision was made the appeals could never be taken, which would be an act of injustice. Judge Land moved to reject the majority report, and touched on the powers of the Convention. He said:

The powers of the Convention were only limited by the Constitution of the United States. He contended, in discussing the power of the Convention, that they had the supreme power to frame a Constitution without submitting it to the people. In support of this proposition he cited a list of constitutions which had never been submitted, as follows: The constitutions of Virginia, 1776; Ohio, 1802; Pennsylvania, 1776 and 1790; South Carolina, 1776 and 1790; Tennessee, 1796; Vermont, 1777, 1786, and 1793; Missouri, 1820; New Hampshire, 1776; New Jersey, 1776; New York, 1777, and amendments adopted by the Convention of 1801; North Carolina, 1776; Kentucky, 1792; Illinois, 1818; Indiana, 1816; Delaware, 1776, 1792, and 1831; Florida, 1865; Connecticut, 1776; Alabama, 1819 and 1867; Arkansas, 1836; Georgia, 1777, 1789, amendments adopted 1795 and 1798, and amendments to Constitution of 1780 adopted in 1812, 1818, 1824, 1835, 1840, 1841, 1843, 1847, and 1849. The question of whether the Convention was bound by the call of the Legislature had long since been decided in the negative. The Convention of 1845, which was composed of the ablest jurists of Louisiana, had, by a vote of 66 to 6, decided that the Legislature had no right to prescribe its limits. From these facts he concluded the Convention had power to make a Constitution without submitting it. In the Convention of 1812, after the Constitution had been passed and signed by the President, the Convention passed a separate and distinct ordinance, having no connection with the Constitution.

Mr. George disagreed with Judge Land on the question of the Convention's power to frame a Constitution without submitting it to the people. It was true the Convention was the representative of the people, but only to the extent of performing those duties for which they had been called. He attached but little importance to the precedents read by Judge Land, but he thought the opinions of Judge Cooley, the great constitutional lawyer, were entitled to greater weight. This was a progressive age. The rights of the people were better understood and maintained to-day than a hundred years ago. It would be found that, in the majority of cases, the Constitutions not submitted had been framed in the early days of the States, and when everything was crude and unsettled.

Mr. Caffrey declared that the sovereignty of the people could not be alienated or transferred. It is true they might delegate certain powers to representatives, such as in the case of the Convention. He did not hesitate to say that if the Convention attempted to frame a Constitution without submitting it to the people, it would surely be defeated. When the Convention was called by one branch of the government, and when it was expressly stipulated in that call that the Constitution should be submitted to the people, he felt it his duty, as a dutiful citizen, to obey the dictates of the call. If this Convention did not submit the Constitution, the people would call another Convention, and this would be the remedy to defeat the Convention. Referring to the argument used by those supporting the other side of the question, that the Georgia Convention passed an original law in appropriating $25,000 to pay its expenses, Mr. Caffrey said this proved nothing as to the power of the Convention. When the people of Georgia called the Convention they implied that nothing should be done to prevent its meeting; and, as no provision had been made to pay the expenses of the Convention, it was only natural that the Convention itself should make the appropriation. It was right, because in doing so the Convention only followed the implied wish of the people that they should meet. In following out this idea the speaker asserted that this Convention could sit longer than sixty days, or could appropriate an extra amount, because these actions would be in compliance with the wish of the people that the Convention should frame an organic law, and it might be necessary to sit longer, or to have more funds, to frame this law.

Mr. Pardee took the ground that the Convention had no power to legislate, as the Constitution of the United States declared that every member of a Legislature should take an oath to support the Constitution of the United States, and the Convention had passed a resolution declaring it was not necessary for its members to take such an oath.

The most important subject that came before the Convention was that of the State debt. It was referred to a committee of seventeen members to examine and report upon. Two sub-committees were appointed, one consisting of four members, and the other of two members. The sub-committee of four made a report which embraced the facts relative to each class of original bonds as set forth in the report of the State Auditor to the Convention. They also examined all the acts of the Legislature pledging the faith of the State to the payment of her obligations, and to ascertain whether or not adequate provisions for their redemption at maturity and the payment of interest had been made under the requirements of the Constitution. The questions before them were: 1. Whether the Legislature of 1874 was competent to bind the people of a free State? 2. Whether any evidence exists in the office of the Secretary of State showing the adoption by the people of the constitutional amendments of 1874? A report of three of the sub-committee held that the Legislature that passed the act of 1874 was not chosen by the people, but was upheld by the military arm of the Federal Government; the funding act was therefore invalid. With regard to the second question, it held that the constitutional amendments of 1874 were not ratified by the people, the returns having been counted by the Returning Board in violation of the facts.

One member of the sub-committee submitted a minority report, saying that the Legislature of 1874 was recognized by the Government of the United States, and therefore it was a competent body. With regard to the second question, Mr. Caffrey urged "that public officers are presumed to do their duty. The amendments have been duly promulgated and acted on; under them millions of bonds have been funded, and the question of whether there is sufficient evidence in the office of the Secretary of State of their adoption has been swallowed, as it were, by the great fact that the amendments have been acted on and acquiesced in by the people, and by every department of government."

A recapitulation of the details embraced in the majority report of the sub-committee presented the following results:

BONDS RECOMMENDED TO BE PAID.

Relief of State Treasurer	$698,500
New Orleans and Nashville Railroad	458,000
Floating debt	500,000
State Penitentiary	500,000
Free School Fund	1,198,500
Seminary Fund	186,000
Total	$3,486,000

This amount was subsequently increased to $4,000,000 by additions for interest.

New Orleans, Jackson, and Great Northern Railroad	$619,000
New Orleans, Opelousas, and Great Western Railroad	586,000
Vicksburg, Shreveport, and Texas	248,000
Baton Rouge, Gross Tete, and Orleans Railroad	130,000
New Orleans, Mobile, and Texas Railroad, first issue	875,000
New Orleans, Mobile, and Chattanooga Railroad, second issue	750,000
New Orleans, Mobile, and Texas Railroad, third issue	2,500,000
North Louisiana and Texas Railroad Company	1,122,000
Bœuf and Crocodile Navigation Company	80,000
Floating debt	2,450,000
Purpose paying certain debts	978,000
Relief of P. J. Kennedy	184,000
Mississippi and Mexican Gulf Ship Canal Company	480,000
Certificates of indebtedness	250,000
Levee bonds, first issue	1,000,000
" " second issue	4,000,000
" " third issue	2,960,000
Planters' Consolidated Association	581,447
Total	**$19,693,447**

The other sub-committee, consisting of two members, was instructed to inquire and report whether or not the body or assembly of men who passed the so-called "funding act of 1874" was a constitutional Legislature, competent to bind the people of a free State, and whether or not there was any legal evidence in the office of the Secretary of State to show that the so-called "constitutional amendments of 1874" were ratified by the people. They reported that it was a matter of public history, established and proven by the testimony taken in 1873 before the committee of the United States Senate on Privileges and Elections, that in December, 1872, and January, 1873, the State-House was seized by a regiment of soldiers of the United States army, and the legally elected Legislature was, by overpowering force and illegally, prevented from assembling and choosing its own officers, and judging of the elections and qualifications of its members, according to the Constitution of the State. Therefore the body of men alleged to have passed the "so-called funding act" of 1874 was not a constitutional Legislature competent to bind the people of a free State. They also reported that there was no evidence in the archives of the State that the "so-called" constitutional amendments of 1874 were ever ratified or adopted by the people. The returns of the election were not to be found in the archives of the State, nor was there in the office of the Secretary of State any compilation, or certificate, or proclamation showing, certifying, or proclaiming that said "so-called amendments" to the Constitution had been ratified or adopted by the people. There was in said office a mutilated copy of the newspaper called the "New Orleans Republican," of December 24, 1874, in which were printed what purported to be the certificates of J. Madison Wells, Thomas C. Anderson, J. M. Kenner, and Casanave, purporting to certify the vote of a portion of the people of the State on the constitutional amendments. This publication on its face omits entirely the vote of four large and

populous parishes, and the sub-committee were assured by the fifth member of the Returning Board that it falsified and altered the actual vote in many of those parishes which it purported to state. These men had no constitutional authority to determine whether or not the constitutional amendments had been adopted; and if they had, their certificate and finding was not on file or on record in the office of the Secretary of State.

The main Debt Committee, upon the reception of these reports, appointed a sub-committee to draft an ordinance to be submitted to the Convention based on the reports of the sub-committees, and recommending the payment of about $4,000,000 of the debt. This ordinance was prepared and endorsed by a majority of the main committee, and presented with a report to the Convention. At the same time a report from the dissenting minority of seven was also presented. The majority say in their report that they considered it to be their first duty to inquire into the validity of constitutional amendments claimed to have been adopted in 1874, and that they were unable to find any legal evidence in the office of the Secretary of State to indicate that the amendments were ever adopted by the people. They then investigated the acts of the Legislature pledging the faith of the State, with the results contained in the ordinance of $4,082,358 of valid claims. They then say: "The theory or principle upon which your committee have prosecuted their inquiry and based their recommendation is, that no invalid nor fraudulent debt should be paid by the people of the State, and that the valid and honest debt should be paid." The fact that a part of this debt had subsequent to its creation been scaled and funded they thus meet and answer: "They are unable to concede that the funding of any portion of the debt has given it any greater validity than it originally possessed; and, on the other hand, they do not admit that the absolute repudiation of forty per cent. of debt detracts in the least from the validity of that which was legal and honest." They then proceed to say that if the State was in a condition to be generous, they probably would not have regarded it as so necessary to invoke a strict construction of the law and the Constitution; that their sympathy for a small class of creditors should not induce them to do injury to a far greater number of persons equally entitled to all the sympathy that human nature can bestow. After expressing their exceeding regrets that any recommendation of theirs "should necessarily affect deleteriously the interests of any other than their own citizens," and that they would "greatly prefer that all the ills that may arise from the final settlement of this long-questioned debt should be borne by our own people alone," they conclude the whole matter of the non-payment of the debt by a reference to "the eternal fitness of things," thus:

But may it not be in the order of the eternal fitness of things that those who directly or indirectly (unwittingly, it may be) aided to tear down the basis of our former great prosperity should share some of the ills that have so long and so powerfully borne upon the once proud and wealthy people of Louisiana?

E. E. KIDD,
Chairman of the Committee.

The following members of the committee concur in this report: H. R. Lott, G. W. Munday, Joseph Henry, B. R. Forman, David John Reid, J. M. Moore, J. C. Vance, B. F. Jenkins, H. M. Favrot.

Those who signed this majority report were estimated to represent an assessed valuation of $25,295,750.

The minority of the committee made a very able report, in which they gave the reasons for their dissent. They say:

The startling results of the report of the committee necessarily induce hesitation and reluctance in accepting the principles which have guided the committee in reaching its conclusions. The mind is dazed by the annulment of nearly twelve millions of bonds by a stroke of the pen; and, although in times of revolution, when the imagination is superheated by political excitement, such an extraordinary act may be accepted as the necessity of the occasion, one can not witness it in the midst of profound peace without grave apprehensions of its justice and propriety. Doubtless, some who approve the measure are amazed at the moderation of the committee, but the undersigned do not believe a majority of this Convention are in accord with the views expressed by the committee, or after due consideration will sustain its report.

The committee have found that of all the bonds issued by the State, outstanding on January 1, 1874, and which, according to the committee's report, amounted to $27,987,500, only a fraction thereof—to wit, $3,486,-000—is legal; and they reject $19,693,447.50 as of no force, legal or moral. Of the amount of the debt found by the committee to be legal, to wit, $3,486,000, the State is entitled to $1,329,500 to be carried to the credit of the free-school fund and the seminary fund, leaving outstanding in the hands of third parties $2,156,500. To whom this $2,156,500 is to be paid can not be ascertained, as the bonds considered valid by the committee have been exchanged at 60 cents on the dollar for consols, issued under the act of 1874, and the particular consols thus issued in exchange for these bonds can not be identified. The result is that the State owes itself $1,329,500 as trustee for the purposes of education, and it also owes to a nameless creditor $2,156,500. How this unknown creditor is to be ferreted out puts the imagination at fault, and hence all that the Legislature can do is to advertise for him as is done in the case of unknown heirs of vacant successions, and retain the amount of the debt in the Treasury until he appears; for it is impossible to make the exchanges proposed in the ordinance reported by the committee, since the bonds recognized by the ordinance as valid and exchangeable have been surrendered and canceled by the owners, who have accepted consols in lieu thereof.

What strikes the mind in contemplating the plan of the committee is, that the State is held bound to pay bonds when purchased by itself as an investment of the school funds, while the State is considered discharged from responsibility for the same kind of bonds when purchased by individuals. For instance, the free-school fund was partially invested in railroad bonds issued by the State prior to the war; the amount of railroad bonds thus purchased was $401,000, including $18,000 of the bonds issued to the Nashville Railroad Company. If third persons who invested in the same kind of bonds are to be deprived of their rights for the reasons set forth by the committee, it seems to be just that the State and its school fund should be subjected to the same heroic treatment.

The committee in its report completely disregards all moral and legal obligations on the part of the State to refund the consideration received by it for any of the bonds declared to be illegal. The difference between a fraudulent bond and a bond void for want of power to issue it is well known, and important consequences flow from it. If a debt be contracted in fraud, and the debtor receive no consideration for it, then there is no legal or moral obligation on the part of the debtor to respect his contract. But if a State or corporation issues a bond in a manner not authorized by the Constitution of the State or the law creating the corporation, though the bond may be void, the obligation to restore the consideration received for it subsists in law and in equity.

In the case of McCracken vs. San Francisco, 16 California Reports, p. 629, Chief Justice Field as the organ of the Court held that, although the ordinance passed by the Common Council authorizing the sale of the real estate belonging to the city of San Francisco was void, yet the obligation to restore what was unjustly received was independent of the restraining clauses of the city charter. The obligation to restore the price of the sale made, and which had been received by the city, it was held, arose from the obligation to do justice, to restore what belongs to others, which rests upon all persons, natural or artificial; and, in the language of the Court, "it may well be doubted whether it would be competent for the Legislature to exempt the city, any more than private individuals, from liability under circumstances of this character." The same doctrine is announced by the Court of Appeals of New York, in the case of the Oneida Bank vs. Ontario Bank, 21 New York, 490. In that case, a bank issued an illegal certificate prohibited by the banking laws of New York; yet the holder of the certificate was allowed to recover back the consideration paid to the bank, and the endorsee of the void certificate was held entitled to recover the consideration received by the bank from the payee of the certificate; the endorsee of the void certificate was regarded as equitable assignee of the consideration given for it.

In the light of these suggestions, it is not enough to show that the bonds issued by the State are void for non-compliance with constitutional provisions. It is necessary to go a step further, and establish that the State received no consideration for the bonds issued by it. Every sentiment of honor and justice demands that he who receives what does not belong to him should restore it. If the bonds are void, the State has received something for nothing. Law and justice concur in the enforcement of the duty on the part of the State to surrender that something to its true owner.

A statement is then made in the report of the amount of money received on each class of bonds which it was proposed to repudiate. From this it appears that since the war the State received in cash $6,893,507 for $12,141,240 of bonds and State notes, reduced by funding to $7,294,744. Yet it was proposed, with the exception of $500,000, to reject as void these $7,294,744 of consols, for which the State has received in cash $6,893,507.31, or within $401,256.69 of the face value of the bonds. The circumstances connected with other issues of bonds are then stated, and the minority further say:

The undersigned have entered into this discussion merely to remove the impression which seems to have taken possession of the minds of some, that the eleven and a half millions of consols now constituting the debt of the State represent no legal obligations of the State, and are based on no valid consideration. But the funding act of 1874, and the contemporaneous constitutional amendment, created a tribunal to determine the validity of the obligations tendered in exchange for consols, and authorized the creditor to appeal to the courts, in case the Funding Board rejected his claim. Subsequently the authority of the Funding Board was restricted by the supplemental funding act of 1875, which prohibited the funding of certain classes of bonds until their validity was established by a decree of the Supreme Court. The bonds mentioned in said supplemental act constituted about one half of the State debt.. Hence the outstanding consols represent bonds adjudicated by the Funding Board or the Supreme Court to be valid obligations of the State. This adjudication is conclusive on the State. Hence the Supreme Court, through Chief Justice Manning as its organ, in May, 1878, said : " We regard the faith of the State as irrevocably pledged to the payment of her consolidated bonds issued under the authority of that act (1874), and to the payment of such other bonds as may be issued under the sanction of the decree we shall make herein. The contract with the holders of these bonds is one which, in the language of the constitutional amendment, the State can by no means and in no wise impair." (State ex rel. Pacific Railroad vs. Nicholls, Governor, 30 A., 986. In the same case, page 981, the Court say the funding act was approved January 24, 1874, and on the same day an amendment to the Constitution was approved. " This amendment has become a part of the Constitution by its subsequent ratification by the voters at the polls." The Supreme Court of the State had already decided in July, 1875, that " this amendment was adopted, and it now forms part of the organic law of the State." (27 A., 579, Forstall's case.)

The Supreme Court of the United States, in the case of McComb vs. Board of Liquidation, say : " On the day of passing this act [speaking of the funding act of 1874] the General Assembly passed another act, proposing to the people of the State an amendment to the Constitution of the State, which was adopted at the ensuing election." This case was decided in October term, 1875 (2 Otto, 531). The Nicholls General Assembly on the 12th of March, 1877, passed an act the title of which is as follows : " An act to enforce effectually the constitutional amendments proposed January 24, 1874, ratified at the general election held on November 2, 1874, relative to the State debt and the funding thereof; to protect the interests of the State and the holders of the bonds issued by virtue of said amendments ; for that purpose to amend and reënact an act, . . . No. 3, approved January 24, 1874," etc. This act is No. 58 of the regular session of 1877, approved by Governor Nicholls, the first section of which provides "that act No. 3, approved January 24, 1874, pages 39 to 42 inclusive, statutes of 1874, commonly known as the funding bill, entitled ' An act,' etc. . . . be and the same is hereby amended and reënacted as follows," etc.

Under these circumstances, the undersigned never conceived it possible that any one would undertake to assail the validity of the bonds issued in pursuance of the provisions of the act of 1874 and the constitutional amendment of that year, on the grounds stated by the committee. All departments of the State Government had recognized the binding force of the funding act and the constitutional amendment enforcing it. The Supreme Court of the State on two occasions, and the Supreme Court of the United States on one occasion, expressly declared that the amendment was ratified by the people of the State. The funding act has been accepted by the Supreme Court of the State as one of the statutes of the State from the day of its passage to the present moment. The creditors of the State were invited to surrender the bonds held by them at a discount of forty per cent., and accept in lieu thereof the consols authorized by the legislation of 1874 ; the process of funding the entire debt of the State under that legislation has been going on undisturbed for five years, and it may be said the funding is almost complete. The Nicholls General Assembly, on the 12th of March, 1877, so far from repudiating the legislation of 1874, passed a law to amend and reënact the funding bill and enforce the constitutional amendment. Who now has the constitutional power to say that

the act of 1874, with its contemporaneous constitutional amendment, is not the law of the land so as to affect contracts entered into under it ; or that it shall not remain so until those contracts are satisfied ? Any contrary declaration by this Convention will be disregarded by judicial tribunals. The undersigned are not prepared to announce to the world that the State of Louisiana refuses to recognize a contract which all of its courts, as well as all the courts of the United States if called on to enforce it, would not hesitate to use the judicial power of the State or nation to enforce. When a man refuses to pay debts recognized by the courts of the country as legal, and to enforce which they will exert their judicial power, it is said that he repudiates his debts. There is no reason why the same terms should not be predicated of similar conduct on the part of the State, except the desire to use diplomatic and euphuistic language when speaking of a sovereign. The fact is, whether a Legislature be a Legislature is a political question, and therefore it is a question of force. The Legislature that is, and exerts its authority to legislate, and which can enforce its enactments, is the Legislature of the State. In this country the Legislature of a State is that Legislature whose laws the President of the United States will enforce, if called on so to do by the Legislature if in session, or the Governor of the State when the Legislature can not be convened. This has been adjudged many years ago, if adjudication were necessary. (Luther vs. Borden, 7 Howard, p. 42.) It is matter of history that the President of the United States recognized the Legislature of 1874, and would have enforced its enactments if resisted.

The report was signed by the following members of the committee : Thomas J. Semmes, D. Caffrey, Hugh Breen, H. C. Warmoth, M. Cahen, G. Legardeur, Jr. One absent member, McConnell, approved. These members were stated to represent an assessed valuation of $102,075,769. The report closed with the recommendation that a special committee of nine should be appointed to ascertain whether or not an equitable adjustment of the consolidated debt of the State contracted under the legislation of the year 1874 can be effected.

These reports were subsequently considered by the Convention, and a debate ensued which continued through several daily sessions. A motion was then made that, for the purpose of ascertaining definitely and making arrangements to pay the trust fund due the Agricultural and Mechanical College, the matter of the State debt be recommitted to the special committee of eighteen on that subject, and that said committee have full power to reconsider the whole subject of the State debt. On a subsequent day the chairman reported back the majority report, with an additional ordinance to pay the trust fund of the Agricultural and Mechanical College, amounting to $185,000. A minority report was also presented, advising that the principal of the debt be paid, with interest at three per cent. for five years and four per cent. afterward. A second minority report was presented which advised that the debt should be scaled to an amount just between its highest and lowest market value since the funding act, and to pay four per cent. interest.

On the next day (June 30th) a motion was made to adopt the majority report. Then a motion was made to substitute the minority report. While this motion was before the Convention, a motion was made to amend the minority report by extending the three per cent. interest to ten years instead of five years. This was lost—yeas 49, nays 80. The minority report was then lost—yeas 47, nays 82. The majority report was then put to vote and lost —yeas 40, nays 89. A motion was then made to reconsider the vote by which the minority report was lost. This was agreed to. A substitute for the minority report was then offered, to scale the debt to seventy-five cents on the dollar with four per cent. interest. An amendment to this was offered, that the debt should be scaled to fifty cents on the dollar, with four per cent. interest. Another amendment to the substitute was offered, that the debt should remain intact, and that interest be paid at the rate of two per cent. for five years, three per cent. for ten, and four per cent. afterward. An amendment was offered to this last proposition, that it be three per cent. interest for ten years, and four per cent. afterward. This was lost— yeas 51, nays 63. Another amendment to this proposition, that the debt bear two per cent. interest till maturity, was lost—yeas 23, nays 99. On the question to give the bondholders their choice between seventy-five cents at four per cent. and the face of the bond at two per cent. for five years, three per cent. for ten years, and four per cent. afterward, the vote was— yeas 25, nays 91. To amend the minority report by allowing three per cent. interest for fifteen years and four per cent. afterward, the vote was—yeas 67, nays 59. Finally, all the proposed amendments were lost, especially those for scaling the debt below seventy-five cents on the dollar. After much subsequent discussion, the whole subject was disposed of by the adoption (yeas 71, nays 41) of the following ordinance, to be submitted to a popular vote:

ART. 1. *Be it ordained*, That the interest to be paid on the consolidated bonds by the State of Louisiana be and is hereby fixed at two per cent. for five years from the 1st of January, 1880, three per cent. for fifteen years, and four per cent. thereafter; and there shall be levied an annual tax sufficient for the full payment of said interest, not exceeding three mills, the limit of all State tax being hereby fixed at six mills. Provided, the holders of consolidated bonds may, at their option, demand in exchange for the bonds held by them bonds of the denomination of five dollars, one hundred dollars, five hundred dollars, one thousand dollars, to be issued at the rate of seventy-five cents on the dollar of bonds held and to be surrendered by such holders, the said new issue to bear interest at the rate of four per cent. per annum, payable semi-annually.

ART. 2. The holders of the consolidated bonds may at any time present their bonds to the Treasurer of the State, or to an agent to be appointed by the Governor —one in the city of New York and the other in the city of London; and the said Treasurer or agent, as the case may be, shall endorse or stamp thereon the words, "Interest reduced to two per cent. for five years from January 1, 1880, three per cent. for fifteen years, and four per cent. thereafter"; provided, the holder or holders of said bonds may apply to the Treasurer for an exchange of bonds, as provided in the preceding article.

ART. 3. *Be it further ordained*, That the cou-

pons of said consolidated bonds falling due the 1st of January in the year 1880 be and the same are hereby remitted, and any interest tax collected to meet such coupons are hereby transferred to defray the expenses of the State Government.

Be it further ordained, and it is hereby ordained by this Constitutional Convention, That the foregoing provisions and articles relative to the consolidated debt shall not form a part of this Constitution, except as hereinafter provided, as follows:

At the election held for the ratification or rejection of this Constitution, it shall be lawful for each voter to have written or printed on his ballot the words, "For ordinance relative to State debt," or the words "Against ordinance relative to State debt"; and in the event that a majority of the ballots so cast have on them the words, "For ordinance relative to State debt," then the said foregoing provisions and articles of this ordinance shall form a part of the Constitution submitted if the same is ratified; and if a majority of the votes so cast shall have endorsed on them the words, "Against ordinance relative to State debt," then said provisions and articles shall form no part of this Constitution.

This ordinance was to be submitted to the vote of the people on the same day with the Constitution.

The reason advanced for scaling the debt by those who sustained it was that the question of ability or inability of the people to pay was the one on which the action of the Convention turned.

The provision of the Constitution for the relief of the delinquent taxpayers declared all interests, penalties, costs, fees, and charges whatever on taxes and licenses due to the State or any political corporation, prior to January 1, 1879, and still unpaid, to be remitted. All property forfeited to the State or any political corporation for non-payment of taxes shall be redeemable by paying the principal due at any time previous to January 1, 1881, with eight per cent. interest subsequent to January 1, 1880.

The preamble to the Bill of Rights was as follows:

We, the people of the State of Louisiana, in order to establish justice, insure domestic tranquillity, promote the general welfare, and secure the blessings of liberty to ourselves and our posterity, acknowledging and invoking the guidance of Almighty God, the Author of all good government, do ordain and establish this Constitution.

Article 6 of the Bill of Rights was as follows:

ART. 6. There shall be neither slavery nor involuntary servitude in this State otherwise than for the punishment of crime, whereof the party shall have been duly convicted.

The General Assembly is authorized to create a Bureau of Agriculture. The State tax on property is not to exceed six mills on the dollar, or five mills if the State debt ordinance is not adopted. No parish or municipal tax, for all purposes whatsoever, shall exceed ten mills on the dollar; and for bridges and other special objects there shall be no increase of tax unless first submitted to a vote of the property-owners and approved.

Among the other provisions of the Constitution are the following:

No qualification of any kind for suffrage or office, nor any restraint upon the same, on account of race, color, or previous condition, shall be made by law.

The General Assembly shall establish in the city of New Orleans a university for the education of persons of color, provide for its proper government, and make an annual appropriation of not less than five thousand dollars for its maintenance and support, nor more than ten thousand dollars.

Women twenty-one years of age and upward shall be eligible to any office of control or management under the school laws of this State.

The school funds of this State shall consist of:
1. The proceeds of taxation for school purposes, as provided in this Constitution;
2. The interest on the proceeds of all public lands heretofore granted by the United States for the use and support of the public schools;
3. Of lands and other property which may hereafter be bequeathed, granted, or donated to the State, or generally for school purposes;
4. All funds or property, other than unimproved lands, bequeathed or granted to the State, not designated for other purposes;
5. The proceeds of vacant estates falling under the law to the State of Louisiana.

The Legislature may appropriate to the same fund the proceeds, in whole or in part, of public lands not designated for any other purpose, and shall provide that every parish may levy a tax for the public schools therein, which shall not exceed the State tax; provided, that with such tax the whole amount of parish taxes shall not exceed the limits of parish taxation fixed by this Constitution.

The General Assembly may provide for the organization or establishment of a State Board of Education, and of Parish Boards of Education; provided, that the members of said Boards shall serve without compensation.

The general exercises in the public schools shall be conducted in the English language and the elementary branches taught therein; provided, that these elementary branches may also be taught in the French language in those parishes in the State or localities in said parishes where the French language predominates, without incurring additional expense.

The term of the State offices is four years. The State capital is to be removed to Baton Rouge.

The general features of this Constitution are similar to those of others. It was provided that the election should be held on the first Tuesday in December, and at the same time there should be chosen all the State officers and members of the General Assembly. The term of all such officers shall commence on the second Monday in January, 1880. The final adjournment took place on July 23d, it being the eighty-first day of the session.

The subject of the resources of the State was alluded to in the Convention. Although the amount of the staples produced is large, they are subject to a very serious discount for the expense of the necessaries of life, which are largely imported for consumption. Thus it may prove that a free State in which the agriculture is devoted to such staples as cotton, sugar, and tobacco is not so rich as one in which the cereals and kindred crops are cultivated. From a statement made in the Convention it appears that the State assessment in 1877-'78 was about $177,000,000, of which the parish of Orleans represents $109,000,000,

sugar parishes (sixteen in number) $26,700,-000, thirty-six cotton parishes $33,400,000, and five parishes (part cotton and part sugar) $8,-250,000. The cotton parishes represent a production of about $29,000,000; sugar parishes, $19,000,000. The position of the State in 1860 was: Assessed values, $420,000,000; liabilities, outside of property banks, $4,700,000. After the war, December 31, 1865: Assessed values reduced to $200,000,000; liabilities, outside of property banks, $5,780,000. Levees all destroyed, plantations wrecked, everything to be replaced and repaired. There is no record of the cotton crop prior to 1872-'73; but estimating on the basis of the total cotton crop of the country, the pro rata of Louisiana can not be put down in the year 1867-'68 at over 300,000 bales; crop of sugar same year, 37,645 hogsheads. Beginning in 1872-'73, the records show the following productions: Cotton, 434,000 bales; sugar, 108,520 hogsheads; gradually increasing year by year until in 1877-'78 Louisiana occupied the third rank as a cotton-producing State, the crop of cotton being 645,000 bales; sugar, 208,841 hogsheads —within 50,000 hogsheads of her average crop before the war, and only surpassed by ten crops in all her history as a sugar-producer. During the same period her rice productions increased from 52,206 barrels in 1872-'73 to 140,785 in 1877-'78, and 157,770 in 1878-'79. Of the fruit crop, which has become an important item in the exports, 30,000 barrels of oranges passed over one route alone. In 1865 there were two small oil factories; now there are six, consuming 100,000 tons of seed, exporting in 1877-'78 3,280,650 gallons of oil and about 60,000 tons of cake, representing a value, together, of over $3,000,000. There are now two cotton factories, five sugar refineries, soap and ice factories, representing $2,000,000—all sprung up since the war. The imports from the interior in 1877-'78 were $143,000,000, against $135,000,000 in 1876-'77. The exports during the same period were $69,000,000 in 1876-'77, against $84,000,000 in 1877-'78. In 1877-'78 Louisiana produced quite $50,000,000 in cotton, sugar, molasses, rice, and manufactures.

The following summary shows the relative proportion of direct taxes on real and personal estate from the levy of 1877 (collected in 1878) paid by the city of New Orleans and that paid by the country during 1878 and the first quarter of 1879, as shown by the Auditor's report:

Parish of Orleans in 1878	$908,550 70
Parish of Orleans, first quarter of 1879	106,875 95
Total parish of Orleans	$1,015,425 95
Country parishes in 1878	189,790 15
Country parishes, first quarter of 1879	454,822 85
Total country parishes	$594,043 00
Total for the State	1,609,468 95

In addition to the above, the licenses paid in during 1878 were:

Parish of Orleans.............................	$155,414 50
Other parishes..............................	107,494 44
Total present assessed value of property......	177,279,294 00
Total present assessed value of parish of Orleans property.........................	111,184,064 00
Total present assessed value of property of country parishes.........................	66,185,234 00
Total amount of taxes levied in parish of Orleans...................................	1,322,479 00
Total amount of taxes levied in country parishes...................................	727,487 00
Percentage of taxation in Orleans............	68
Percentage of taxation in country parishes....	37

In addition to the above taxes for State purposes, the parish of Orleans was called upon to expend, on account of city government during 1878, the sum of $2,318,620, of which $1,-667,018 consisted of tax on real and personal estate. The total direct tax burden, city and State taxes, upon property in New Orleans last year was, therefore, $2,889,497. The average rate of taxation for local purposes in the country, as shown by returns to the Auditor, is less than one per cent. The rural parishes, therefore, bear a total tax for parish and State purposes of about 20 or 21 mills, aggregating $1,388,839.

The consolidated 7 per cent. bonds were quoted at 60 to 67 in January, but were 20 per cent. lower at the end of the year.

The Democratic State Convention to make nominations assembled in New Orleans on October 6th, and was organized by the election of F. B. Peche as chairman. The nominations were as follows: For Governor, Louis A. Wiltz; for Lieutenant-Governor, S. D. McEnery; for Attorney-General, J. C. Egan; for Secretary of State, W. S. Strong; for Auditor, Allen Jumel; for Superintendent of Schools, E. H. Fay. The platform adopted was as follows:

Resolved, as heretofore declared, That our designation of Democratic party of Louisiana is significant of the power of the whole body of the people, and is used to express our determination to secure every citizen of the State the equal rights guaranteed to him by the Constitution of the United States and its amendments, and the laws made in pursuance thereof, and to promote reform in every department of the State Government.

Resolved, That the Democratic party of Louisiana has no other object in view than to preserve for the present generation and for posterity the national Government according to the spirit of the framers; to protect and guard the rights of the States as determined by the Constitution and the decisions of the courts of justice; to promote and advance popular education, enforce a proper subordination of the military power to civil authority, protect the purity of elections, and encourage and develop the material resources of our people.

Resolved, That the improvement of the Mississippi River, the building of levees on the bank, so as to afford ease and safety for commerce, and a channel for navigation, as well as to protect the valley from inundation, and the keeping open of the mouth of the river, is a work of national importance, evidently warranted by a just construction of article I., section 8, of the Constitution of the United States, which confers upon Congress the power to regulate commerce.

Resolved, That the union and coöperation of all citizens of Louisiana is earnestly invited, in order to secure the adoption of the Constitution now offered for their consideration, and to prove by a great and overwhelming popular vote that the people of the State have exercised their rightful power to ordain and establish for themselves an organic instrument of government, and to do away with for ever and consign to

oblivion the Constitution of 1866 as a relic of wrong and military oppression.

Resolved, That the counting of the electoral vote of Louisiana in favor of Rutherford B. Hayes for President of the United States, and William A. Wheeler for Vice-President, was notoriously a fraud on popular rights, effected by evil machinations, the plots and conspiracies of the late odious Radical State administration and their aiders and abettors at home and abroad; and that the Democratic party of Louisiana, appealing to the evidence of the case as now published by authority, arraign the authors of this great crime against liberty and the Constitution for the just condemnation of their fellow citizens.

Resolved, That the Democrats of the Senate and House of Representatives of the Congress of the United States are entitled to the grateful acknowledgments of the country, for the zeal and fidelity and courage shown by them in securing the passage of laws by which the interference of the military at the polls has been prohibited and the trial by jury in the Federal courts made impartial.

Resolved, That the rights, the liberties, the interests and honor of Louisiana demand that her rightfully chosen Senator in Congress, Henry M. Spofford, be at last recognized and duly seated.

Resolved, That Francis T. Nicholls, now Governor of Louisiana, is entitled to the grateful acknowledgments of his fellow citizens for his patriotism and public services, his devotion to Louisiana, and his success in effecting the redemption of her liberties.

The Republican State Convention assembled in New Orleans on October 21st, and nominated for Governor, Taylor Beattie; for Lieutenant-Governor, James M. Gillespie; for Attorney-General, Don A. Pardee; for Auditor, Clodius Mayo; for Secretary of State, James D. Kennedy (colored); for Superintendent of Schools, M. F. Bonzeno. The following is a synopsis of the resolutions:

First—We hold that our government is national in its character and composed of States free in their separate spheres, but subordinate to the national Government. Second—It is the privilege, right, and duty of the national Government to guarantee a free republican form of government to each State. Third—No government of, for, and by the people can exist when the ballot is not free, nor when the result of the ballot is changed by fraudulent and corrupt returns. Fourth—We favor a protective tariff. Fifth—That it is the duty of the national Government to improve the rivers and harbors of the nation, especially the Mississippi River and its tributaries. Sixth—Favors national aid for the southern route to the Pacific coast, and advocates striking from all treaties of clauses therein which place one and all upon the basis of the most favored. Eighth—Favors the encouragement of American shipping by subsidies. Ninth—Holds it to be the duty of the national Government to secure by all means the construction of a canal or other system of transportation across the isthmus of Darien, and insist that no non-American nation or native shall have a predominating influence in the management thereof. Tenth—Asserts that the honor of the State and its citizens as well as their national interests are pledged to an attempt in good faith to pay the State debt represented by consolidated bonds issued under the constitutional amendments approved and ratified by the people in 1874, that ordinance constituting a valid contract which is guaranteed by the State. Eleventh—That if misfortune should prevent a full compliance with the letter and spirit of our bonds, their settlement should be sought after consultation with our creditors as our equal, which shall at the same time be just to them and commensurate with our resources. Twelfth—Avers that good faith with the creditors demands that the vote of the party should as a unit be cast against the State debt ordinance of the proposed Constitution, but the question of adoption or rejection of the Constitution is left to the individual conviction of the voters. Thirteenth—Holds that the judicial department of the government should be kept free and unpolluted by the political turmoil, recognizing honest differences of opinion as to the proper construction of the constitutional and statutory laws, and recommends therefore that each of the great political parties be represented upon the bench.

A resolution was adopted, setting forth that if colored people are allowed to vote and have their votes counted, they will remain in the State; if not, they will be forced to emigrate. A resolution was also adopted declaring General Grant their unalterable choice for President in 1880. The election of Dumont, who is an out-and-out Sherman man, as permanent president of the Convention, is considered an endorsement of the Administration.

At the election on December 8th, the vote given for the Constitution was 86,494; against it, 27,346. The vote for the ordinance relative to the State debt was 59,932; against it, 49,445. The vote for State officers was as follows: For Governor—Wiltz, Democrat, 74,769; Beattie, Republican, 40,760. For Lieutenant-Governer—McEnery, Democrat, 76,003; Gillespie, Republican, 39,961. The other Democratic candidates were elected by about the same majorities. The division in the Legislature was: in the Senate, 31 Democrats, 25 Republicans; in the House, 76 Democrats, 17 Republicans, 2 Independents, 1 National. The vote for members of Congress was in favor of the Democratic candidates: First District, Gibson; Second, Ellis; Third, Acklen; Fourth, Elam; Fifth, King; Sixth, Robertson.

The domestic exports from New Orleans for the year ending July 31, 1879, amounted to $63,624,797; the imports for the same period amounted to $7,141,989. The steady increase of depth in the water at the mouths of the Mississippi has attracted the attention of shipowners. Two new lines of steamers have been added to the foreign trade, and another will come in a few months. The Morgan New Orleans and Texas Railroad is completed to Vermillionville, where it connects with the Louisiana Western, affording a through line to Houston. The New Orleans Pacific is rapidly extending. The cotton trade shows a decline of 200,000 bales, which is ascribed to the epidemic and the low stage of water. The yield of sugar was the largest since the war. The receipts of grain were 10,678,306 bushels.

The power of the judicial department to order a tax-levy came up before the Supreme Court of the United States, in the case of Morris Ranger vs. The city of New Orleans. The litigation arose out of an application for a writ of mandamus to compel the authorities of that city to levy a tax to pay certain judgments rendered against it upon bonds issued to the New Orleans, Jackson, and Great Northern Railroad Company. The city set up as a defense that there was no legislative authority for the levy of such a tax. The petitioner demurred to this answer, but the

Circuit Court overruled the demurrer and denied the writ, whereupon the petitioner took an appeal. The Court below proceeded on the principle that the power of taxation belongs exclusively to the legislative branch of the government, and that the judiciary can not direct a tax to be levied when none is authorized by the Legislature. The Supreme Court held, however, in a careful opinion delivered by Justice Field, that, although the power of taxation is a legislative prerogative, it may be delegated to a municipal corporation, and that when such a corporation is created the power of taxation is vested in it as an essential attribute for all the purposes of its existence, unless its exercise is in express terms prohibited. When, therefore, authority to borrow money or incur an obligation to carry out any public object is conferred upon a municipal corporation, the power to levy a tax for its payment or the discharge of the obligation accompanies it, and this, too, without any special mention that such power is granted. It is always to be assumed, in the absence of clear restrictive provisions, that when the Legislature grants to a city the power to create a debt it intends that the city shall pay it, and that its payments shall not be left to its caprice or pleasure. Whenever a power to contract a debt is conferred, it must be held that a corresponding power of providing for its payment is also conferred. The latter is implied in the grant of the former, and such implication can not be overcome except by express words of limitation. In the present case the indebtedness of the city of New Orleans is conclusively established by the judgments recovered. Owing the debt, the city had the power to levy a tax for its payment, and it was clearly its duty so to do. The payment was not a matter resting on its pleasure, but a duty to the creditors; and having neglected that duty, a mandamus should have been issued to enforce its observance. The judgment of the lower Court must therefore be reversed and the cause remanded, with directions to issue the writ in compliance with the petition.

There were apprehensions that a repetition of the negro exodus would take place in the winter of 1879–'80; but the condition of the colored laboring people seemed to have much bettered itself, and no large number of them seemed disposed to emigrate. The share system was still the mode of payment in use, none being paid wages except in the sugar districts. The cotton crop on the bottom lands was excellent, and most of the laborers had money saved up at the end of the year. On the hills the yield was poor, and a part of the population moved to the low lands. Contracts were readily entered into for the next season, even in Tensas and Madison parishes, where the most fears were felt.

LUTHERANS. The following is a summary of the statistics of the Evangelical Lutheran Church in the United States, as they are given in the " Church Almanac " for 1880:

SYNODS.	Minis-ters.	Congre-gations.	Members.
I. GENERAL COUNCIL.			
Ministerium of Pennsylvania	199	883	79,888
Ministerium of New York	69	65	25,309
Pittsburgh Synod	72	145	11,994
Texas Synod	29	25	4,550
District Synod of Ohio	32	72	7,000
Augustana Synod (Swedish)	130	313	40,154
Michigan Synod	25	43	4,600
Canada Synod	25	45	5,711
Indiana Synod	15	45	2,104
Holston Synod	13	27	1,800
Synod of Iowa (German)	135	230	17,700
Augustana Synod (Norwegian)	18	70	7,000
Total	**762**	**1,467**	**207,205**
II. SYNODICAL CONFERENCE.			
Joint Synod of Ohio (6 districts)	185	303	90,467
Joint Synod of Missouri (8 districts)	659	883	229,771
Wisconsin Synod	83	149	35,825
Norwegian Synod	166	500	64,200
Minnesota Synod	31	50	10,000
Illinois Synod	25	85	5,752
Total	**1,149**	**1,875**	**436,015**
III. GENERAL SYNOD, SOUTH.			
Synod of South Carolina	32	47	5,344
Synod of Virginia	31	53	4,048
Synod of Southwest Virginia	21	43	2,750
Mississippi Synod	7	9	865
Georgia Synod	8	12	761
Total	**99**	**174**	**13,268**
IV. GENERAL SYNOD, NORTH.			
Maryland	70	86	11,629
West Pennsylvania	65	110	16,994
Hartwick	80	32	4,092
East Ohio	41	87	6,090
Franckean	23	84	2,938
Allegheny	49	183	11,474
East Pennsylvania	76	98	13,719
Miami	38	85	8,419
Wittenberg Synod	43	64	5,679
Olive Branch	18	81	9,235
Northern Illinois	31	44	1,934
Central Pennsylvania	23	74	7,421
Iowa	26	23	1,188
Northern Indiana	40	73	3,507
Southern Illinois	11	24	1,473
Central Illinois	22	25	1,817
New York and New Jersey	46	87	6,901
Susquehanna	39	40	6,683
Pittsburgh	26	55	4,410
Kansas	24	26	734
Ansgari	25	20	1,300
Nebraska	18	23	1,300
Wartburg	36	23	4,057
Middle Tennessee	18	31	1,778
India Mission	4	..	2,036
Total	**840**	**1,217**	**124,792**
V. INDEPENDENT SYNODS.			
Synod of North Carolina	23	43	4,508
Tennessee Synod	21	65	7,500
Buffalo Synod	13	24	3,200
Hauge's Nor. Evan. Luth. Synod	31	58	5,860
Conference of Nor. Dan. Luth. Ch'rch	64	279	18,564
Synod of Maryland (German)	8	9	2,710
Augsburg Synod	10	13	1,203
Total	**165**	**491**	**43,545**

Total for the Church, 58 Synods, 3,015 ministers, 5,224 congregations, 824,825 members. The German "Almanac" of Messrs. Brobst and Diehl (Allentown, Pa.) gives the following: General Council—761 ministers, 1,455 congregations, 210,170 communicants; Synodical Conference—1,169 ministers, 1,875 congregations, 291,444 communicants; General Synod,

North—838 ministers, 1,290 congregations, 122,573 communicants; General Synod, South—98 ministers, 175 congregations, 13,436 communicants; Synods standing alone—221 ministers, 581 congregations, 51,572 communicants; total, 58 Synods, 3,087 ministers, 5,376 congregations, 689,195 communicants. The compiler of the statistics for this work says that the number of ministers may be regarded as correct, but that the number of congregations and communicants assigned to some of the Synods is taken from the reports of the previous year.

The "Church Almanac" gives a list of 17 theological seminaries, four of which are connected with the General Council, four with the General Synod, North, five with the Synodical Conference, one with the General Synod, South, one with the North Carolina Synod; the remaining two Scandinavian. The literary institutions include 18 universities and colleges, 12 classical schools, and 7 seminaries for young women. There are 30 institutions of mercy, including orphans' homes and schools, hospitals, infirmaries, and immigrant and negro missions. The list of periodicals includes 12 weekly publications, of which 6 are English, 3 German, and 3 Norwegian; 13 semi-monthly, of which 10 are German and 3 Norwegian and Danish; 39 monthly, of which 14 are English, 13 German, 5 Swedish, and 7 Norwegian and Danish; one German bi-monthly, one English and one Norwegian quarterly publications, and six annual calendars in the English and German languages. Most of the monthly publications are intended for the use of Sunday-school teachers and scholars.

The *General Synod* met in its twenty-ninth Convention at Wooster, Ohio, June 11th. The Rev. W. D. Strobel, D. D., of Rhinebeck, N. Y., was chosen President. Reports were made of the operations of the boards and benevolent societies of the Synod during the past two years. The receipts of the Pastor's Fund Society had been $1,250, and its disbursements $1,050. The assets of the Publication Society above all its liabilities were $33,239. The circulation of the periodicals issued by the Board was as follows "Lutheran Sunday-School Herald," 36,000; "Augsburg Teacher," 5,500; "Augsburg Lesson Leaf," 26,500; "Primary Lesson Leaf," 12,000; and 22,000 "Lesson Books," containing the lessons from January to July, 1879. The receipts of the Board of Home Missions for two years, some of which were from bequests, had been $25,686, and its expenditures $23,973. The Board had sustained 51 missions, of which 11 were new ones, while 5 had become self-sustaining; and it had now 47 missions under its care, with 63 congregations, 4,183 members, and 50 Sunday-schools with 5,433 scholars. The amount of $20,000 a year was appropriated for the work of this Board. The receipts of the Board of Foreign Missions for two years had been $38,938, and its expenditures $37,056.

Debts resting against the Board of $7,000 in the United States and $2,000 in India had been paid, and the current expenses of the two missions had been promptly met. The India mission (at Goontoor) returned 4,731 baptized natives, of whom 2,086 were adults and regular communicants, with 813 candidates for baptism, and reported a net gain in one year of 1,191. Several Sunday-schools had been organized. The mission was conducted at an average cost of nearly $11,000 a year. The African mission, conducted at an average cost of about $3,750 a year, had forty Christian families residing in its neighborhood, and more than sixty children in its school. A project for forming a second station in Africa, if it be found expedient, was approved. The pledge of the Synod of $10,000 a year for Church extension was continued for two years. The Committee on Sunday-Schools reported that about 10,000 scholars had been added to the rolls of these schools during the past year. The committee had secured a representation on the International Lesson Committee and the International Executive Committee. The reports of the literary and theological institutions showed them to be prosperous. A resolution was passed declaring it to be the judgment of the General Synod that the policy of the Church should be, for the present, "rather to strengthen and enlarge the colleges and theological seminaries we have than to found new ones; and that the organization of new institutions of these grades, when needed, should take place, not under an irresponsible individualism, but only under the direction of responsible Synods or the General Synod, except in cases where generous men may found and permanently endow them by their own large gifts and legacies." The District Synods were advised to permit the contributions of German churches for education to be appropriated for the theological training of young men for work among German Lutherans. A committee of German ministers was appointed to prepare a plan for promoting German theological training. A Scandinavian Secretary was appointed to lay the work of the Synod before the people of that nationality.

The eighth annual meeting of the *Synodical Conference* was held at Columbus, Ohio, in July. About fifty delegates were in attendance, representing the Synods of Illinois, Minnesota, Missouri, Ohio, Wisconsin, and the Norwegian Synod. The Rev. W. F. Lehman was reëlected President. The discussion of doctrinal questions was continued, and the 14th and 15th theses on Church Fellowship were adopted as follows:

·· 14. It is in decided. conflict with the Confession when, in an ecclesiastical body calling itself Lutheran, the doctrinal discipline which God's Word requires is not exercised, and the popular theory of open questions is accepted.

15. It is not in accord with the Confession when a Synod or larger ecclesiastical body makes no efforts to have the discipline in doctrine and life which Christ requires, and which is more particularly defined in Matthew xviii. 15–17, gradually brought into exercise in its congregations.

The mission among the negroes was represented as in a flourishing condition, and the opening for extending the work as promising. A German and an English periodical are published in the interest of this mission. A plan for the establishment of an English theological quarterly review at Columbus, Ohio, was adopted, dependent on its approval by the Synods, and Professor M. Long of Columbus and the Rev. F. A. Schmidt were designated to be its editors. A plan was adopted for the formation of State Synods, the chief features of which are as follows: The German Synods connected with the Conference are to form State Synods; these State Synods are again to form two or three joint Synods, one east of Indiana, one to embrace the northwestern, another to embrace the southwestern States and Territories; the Norwegian Synod not to be affected by these boundaries, and English Synods to belong to the joint Synods in whose territory they lie. The Synods thus formed are to establish a joint theological seminary at Milwaukee, Wisconsin, with three faculties, German, English, and Norwegian; or with two faculties, if the Norwegians prefer to have a separate seminary. The Conference recommended that the celebration of the three hundredth anniversary of the adoption of the Augsburg Confession be celebrated on the 25th of June, 1880. Hereafter, the Conference will meet biennially.

The *General Council* met at Zanesville, Ohio, October 9th. The Rev. C. P. Krauth, D. D., presided. Reports were presented from the institutions and enterprises of the Council, as follows: The income of the Immigrant Mission in New York from October 1, 1877, to October 1, 1879, had been $1,806, and the expenditures $1,799. The income of the Emigrant Home Association for the two years ending April 1, 1879, had been $13,544, and the expenditures $13,174. A favorable report was made of the working of these institutions, which are for the care and comfort of Lutheran immigrants on their arrival at New York, and they were commended for greater liberality of support by members of the Church. The total receipts of the Foreign Mission Committee for the two years had been $11,473, and its expenditures had been $11,291.

The most prominent business before the Council consisted in the discussion of the theses which had been prepared by the Rev. Dr. Krauth by order of a previous General Council on "Pulpit and Altar Fellowship," and the continued consideration of the proposed new "Constitution for Congregations." The theses on "Pulpit and Altar Fellowship" were designed more fully to establish and explain the position of the Council on the so-called Galesburg rule, adopted in 1875, which declared in substance that Lutheran pulpits were for Lutheran ministers, and Lutheran altars for Lutheran members only. This rule, the resolution of adoption asserted, "accords with the Word of God and with the Confessions of our Church," but admitted that there might be exceptions, to be judged according to particular circumstances. Upon the question arising the Council decided that the present consideration of the theses was for dicussion, to bring out more fully the views of the Church, with the object of arriving at a uniform understanding of the rule. Of the "Constitution for Congregations," section 4 of Article IV., relative to the duties of the pastor, was adopted. It provides that the pastor "shall conduct the public service of God's house on the Sundays and other festival days of the Church year; shall permit no one to occupy the pulpit of whose soundness in the faith confessed by the Lutheran Church there is reason to doubt; shall carefully give instruction to the young and all others needing it; shall watch over the Sunday-school and other schools of the Church; shall confirm those who, having been duly instructed, give satisfactory evidence that they are desirous of being faithful followers of Christ. He shall baptize publicly, except in special cases, and all private baptisms shall be publicly announced. He shall administer the Lord's Supper to all those who desire to come to it, if he has been notified, and of whose fitness, both as to faith and life, he is satisfied, as also, if he shall judge best, to members unable, from age or sickness, to come to the house of God. He shall be active in the work of a pastor, most of all among the poor, the sick, the sorrowing, and among all those whose spiritual estate es-

pecially demands his care. He shall perform the marriage ceremony in strict accordance with the laws of the State and of God; shall use the burial service for the dead who die in the fellowship of the Church; shall earnestly urge and carry out the discipline of the Church; shall promote all wise plans of Christian beneficence and effort, and shall labor to prevent all deadness and fanaticism, all schism, heresy, separation, and alienation in the congregation."

The committee having the subject in charge reported that a seal for the General Council had been prepared. The custody of the seal was given to the President. A committee was appointed to prepare for the next meeting of the General Council a paper setting forth the true relation of confirmation to adult baptism, and the principles involved in the determination of the proper liturgical forms for those ministerial acts. The attention of the Church was directed to the former action of the Council adverse to secret societies, and the Synods were urged to prevent pastors connected with them from being members of any society disapproved in that action. A report of the work of the district Synods mentioned much that had been accomplished in the work of education and missions by those bodies, and showed that many new points had been occupied by the churches of the Council. A committee was appointed to arrange for the tercentenary anniversary of the adoption of the "Formula of Concord." The further consideration of the theses on "Pulpit and Altar Fellowship" was recommended to the next Convention of the General Council.

M

MAINE. The regular session of the State Legislature commenced on January 1st. J. Manchester Haynes was elected President of the Senate, and Melvin P. Frank Speaker of the House. The session closed on March 5th. It had been confined almost wholly to local affairs and questions.

Among the resolves passed was one submitting to the people constitutional amendments providing for biennial elections and biennial sessions of the Legislature, and changing the term of office of Governor, Senators, Representatives, and other State officials, from one to two years. These amendments were to be passed upon by the people at the September election, and if a majority of the votes cast were in favor of them they were to become a part of the Constitution.

The act relating to the Industrial School for Girls was so amended as to allow inmates to be received between the ages of seven and fifteen years.

Another act was passed providing that the fact that the defendant in a criminal prosecu-

tion did not testify in his own behalf should not be taken as evidence of his guilt.

An act to prevent the adulteration of sugar and molasses provides that no person shall knowingly, willfully, or maliciously sell or offer, or expose for sale, within this State, any sugar, refined or not, or any molasses, which has been adulterated with salts of tin, terra alba, glucose, dextrine, starch sugar, corn sirup, or other preparations from starch, under the penalty of a fine not exceeding $500, or imprisonment not exceeding one year.

Deaf-mutes who are fit persons for instruction are to be sent to the Asylum in Hartford, Connecticut, or to the Portland school.

The salaries of the State officers were fixed as follows: Governor, $1,500; Secretary of State, $1,200; Treasurer, $1,600; Adjutant-General, $900; Judges of the Supreme Court, each $2,000; Attorney-General, $1,000.

The operation of the act creating free high schools in cities, towns, and plantations was suspended for one year.

Towns are authorized to loan money, not exceeding five per cent. on the regular valuation, to aid in the construction of railroads, upon the approval of the same by a two-thirds vote of the citizens.

The sum of $1,800 was appropriated to the support of the three normal schools in the State.

No change whatever was made in the prohibitory law. An attempt was made to declare native wine, etc., not intoxicating within the meaning of the law, and an attempt to repeal the act relating to the duties of sheriffs and county attorneys, known as the "Enforcement Act," but both were unsuccessful.

An act was passed providing that freight and passage over all railroads in the State should be at equitable rates; that shippers of freight should have a right to elect which read, south or west of Portland, their freight should be shipped over, and all agents of roads shall follow directions explicitly, and there shall be no discrimination by connecting roads against any road in regard to passengers.

Certain cities and towns that loaned their credit to the Knox and Lincoln Railroad Company, finding that it would be inconvenient for them to raise money to pay their bonds coming due within two years, obtained authority to issue new bonds and sell them to raise money for that purpose.

The act relating to the State College of Agriculture and Mechanic Arts was amended so as to allow a reasonable charge to students for tuition, to be determined by the trustees. No appropriation was made for the college.

The act allowing the employment of detectives by the State was repealed.

The Farmers' Bank at Bangor was granted a charter as a State bank, but without power to issue bills to be used as currency. This was formerly a national bank, and surrendered its charter as such.

The publication of the reports of the Board of Agriculture is to be omitted, and the salary of the Secretary is reduced to $100 per annum.

The use of weirs was limited to one eighth of the channel of any river. The annual close-time of lobsters for canning purposes was fixed from August 1st to April 1st, and no lobsters less than 10½ inches shall be sold or exposed for sale between those dates, under penalty of $5 for each lobster. Fishing for porgies with steamboats and seines was further restricted by prohibiting such fishing in bays and harbors the entrance to which is two miles wide or less. Plover is omitted from the·list of birds protected.

The amount of appropriations was $1,329,-028, of which $353,000 was for interest on the public debt. The State tax was four mills on the dollar, the same as in the preceding year. It amounts to $899,712.

The Land Agent was authorized to convey by deed all lands held by settlers under contract, without the performance of further settling duties. In 1826 all of the wild lands, af-

ter they had been surveyed, were divided between Maine and Massachusetts. Aroostook County being thus opened, and its value becoming known, it was necessary for roads to be built. To bring about any action relative to the lands, concurrent resolves of the two States were necessary. But a large portion of the State, which belonged both to Maine and Massachusetts, was not laid out into townships, and from 1843 to 1850 surveys were made. Then it was thought best for the State to purchase Massachusetts's share of the property, and it was done in 1853, the State paying $362,-500. Then the State gave it away to railroads, but with the provision that if any tract was found suitable and was wanted by settlers it should be surveyed, roads built, and put into the market at not more than one dollar per acre. This land has all been sold by the State, and it now only owns the fees from 72,000 acres, which the settlers hold not by deed but by certificate. The Treasury of the State does not derive one cent from this arrangement. The chief condition which was to benefit the State was the performance of the road labor.

The following resolutions relative to the resumption of specie payments passed the Senate, but failed in the House:

Resolved, That the resumption of specie payments by the United States on the 1st day of January, A. D. 1879, after a suspension of seventeen years, is greeted with satisfaction and approval by the Legislature of Maine.

Resolved, That the attainment of coin resumption puts an end to the myriad evils inseparable from an irredeemable, depreciated, and fluctuating currency, gives to labor a sure reward, places our commercial exchanges upon the only stable foundation, renders a healthy and permanent revival of business possible, and, best of all, preserves the faith of the nation inviolate.

Resolved, That national honor, public credit, and private interest alike demand that specie resumption, now happily achieved, shall be maintained honestly and uninterruptedly at every hazard; and to this end our Senators and Representatives in Congress are requested to use their best endeavors.

Resolved, That a copy of these resolutions be sent to each Senator and Representative from Maine in the Congress of the United States.

An act was passed for a valuation of all property in the State based upon "the full, fair cash value thereof." The reductions in the annual expenditure made by the Legislature amounted to $91,850.

The census of the Penobscot tribe of Indians taken in January, 1878, amounts to 450 persons. Their annual election was held on Wednesday, November 6, 1878, at which Stephen Stanislaus was elected Governor, Saul Neptune Lieutenant-Governor, and Sabattis Dana delegate to the Legislature of 1879. Public schools were taught during 1878 at all the places designated in the act making appropriations for their support. In some of them the money had been fully expended at the end of that year; others consumed the entire amount some months later. The day-school on Oldtown Island averaged about fifty scholars. The moral and social condition of that portion of the tribe residing at Oldtown was notably improved in 1878, through the special efforts of Father O'Brien, one hundred and twenty-five having signed the pledge. Bishop Healey of Portland last summer established a community of Sisters of Mercy on Oldtown Island, and they inculcated principles of morality, industry, and economy. An evening school had been established there. Low wages, continued depreciation in the price of baskets and other wares usually made by the tribe, and decreasing demand for their labor, prevailed during 1878; yet many of the Indians made improvements in their dwellings, and they have erected several new buildings, and generally have devoted more labor and attention to agricultural pursuits. More land than usual had been cultivated. The Legislature at this session made the following appropriations for this tribe: Interest on trust funds, $4,429.70; annuity, $1,800; agricultural purposes, $700; bounty on crops, $450; agent's salary, $200; instructor in agriculture, $100; schools, $385; repairs on schoolhouse, $30; salary of priest, $100; salary of Governor, $50; salary of Lieutenant-Governor, $30; repairs on chapel, $150.

The whole number of the Passamaquoddy tribe at the time of taking the census was 513, of whom 268 were males and 245 females. The whole number of deaths during 1878 was 26, 20 being of children under ten years of age. The principal causes of the deaths among the children were whooping-cough and scarlet fever. Included in the number of deaths among the adults were Governor Newell Neptune and wife. He had held the office of Governor for many years, and was much respected by the tribe. The portion of the tribe residing at Pleasant Point had taken much more interest than usual in farming, and it was their intention to persevere in that direction in the future. The following appropriations were made by the Legislature for this tribe: May dividend, $400; November dividend, $300; poor, $2,000; agricultural purposes, $600; crops and plowing, $450; salaries of Governor and Lieutenant-Governor, $140; wood, $200; road repairs, $50; contingent expenses, $100; educational purposes, $300; salary of priest, $100; dressing for land, $100; salary of agent, $200; contingent fund, $500.

A report of the schools during the preceding year was made by the State Superintendent to the Legislature at this session, containing the following details: Whole number of scholars between four and twenty-one, 214,797; decrease from the previous year, 2,620. Average attendance in summer schools, 102,805; increase, 1,823. Average attendance in winter schools, 108,940; increase, 1,287. Whole number of different scholars registered in schools during the year, 155,150; decrease, 378. Number of districts in State, 4,005; decrease, 34. Number of parts of districts, 344; decrease, 10. Number of schoolhouses, 4,215; decrease, 7;

number built during the year, 82, costing $92,-746. Estimated value of all school property, $3,063,418. Number of male teachers employed in summer, 274; in winter, 2,280. Number of female teachers employed in summer, 4,540; in winter, 2,389. Average wages of male teachers per month, excluding board, $32.63; average wages of female teachers per week, excluding board, $3.98. Amount of money expended for common schools, $936,-648; decrease from the last year, $15,229. Balance unexpended, $90,205. Among the needs of the schools, the Superintendent says, "Another is better teachers. The times demand a higher grade of culture than formerly, and that the schools shall be, more than ever before, nurseries of purity, morality, and uprightness of thought and action. Again, the times demand better supervision, and a revolution in our system of employing, examining, and certificating teachers."

At the State Educational Association held at Brunswick a short time previous to this report, numerous papers were read. One of them urged the necessity of a change in the system of examination of teachers and schools, and advocated the appointment of a board of examiners in each county. It said:

One of the reasons for examining boards as proposed is that many persons too young are permitted to teach. At the examination of fifty teachers at one of our normal schools, it was found that 12 per cent. began teaching before fifteen years of age. Persons of too poor attainments are employed. Many teachers are employed who have no fitness for the work, knowing nothing of plans and methods, and the great mass of the twelve hundred committeemen employed in the different towns in the State are as ignorant as the teachers of the best ways and means of school management. The importance and responsibility of the teachers' work is not felt by very many teachers or committeemen. What importance can be attached to any work which any boy or girl of fifteen or eighteen years of age may undertake with a week's or a day's preparation, as their friends or themselves may take a notion that it would be a good thing to do? In some communities, so far is the idea of teachers' qualifications from the right one, that ignorant agents, falling in with the vulgar prejudice of the ignorant against the learned, refuse to employ well-educated and trained teachers, and prefer the more ignorant and less skillful. The cause of these deficiencies is not in agents, but in the examining committees, whose duty by law is to examine all applicants, and certificate those qualified and reject those who are not. Often these boards are made up of lazy, good-natured men, who do not wish to reject those whose fathers and mothers they know, and often as ignorant of the best methods of school requirements as of calculating an eclipse.

The number of deaf and dumb in the State is nearly 350, of whom 125 are between the ages of four and twenty-one years. Fifty of these are at the asylum in Hartford. To this institution, on account of this class of persons, the State has paid the sum of $216,000, and to other institutions outside of the State enough more to make the total amount $298.251.

A statement of the Secretary of State says that the cost paid by the State to persons defending criminals in 1871 was $600; in 1872, $200; in 1873, $1,075; in 1874, $2,647.50; in

1875, $1,250; in 1876, $677; in 1877, $280; in 1878, $725; total cost from 1871 to 1878, $7,454.

The returns made by the inspectors for cities and towns show the number of barrels of pickled fish inspected by them during the year ending November 30, 1878, to have been as follows: Mackerel, 23,434; herring, 4,081; cod, 15; shad, 67; alewives, 6; swordfish, 14; total, 27,611.

At the close of the year 1878 there were forty-two fire, fire-marine, and marine insurance companies organized under the laws of the State, and authorized to do business therein, of which one was stock fire-marine, two were stock marine, one was mutual fire-marine, one was mutual marine, and thirty-seven were mutual fire insurance companies. During the previous six years the risks written in Maine amount to $466,383,678.73, and the premiums paid to $6,758,383.61. The companies have paid for losses the sum of $4,495,969.07. At the close of the year 1878 there were ninety-five fire, fire-marine, and marine insurance companies of other States and countries authorized to transact business in Maine, of which ninety-one were stock and four mutual companies. The aggregate amount of tax on premium receipts paid by the several companies was $8,241.20. The domestic stock companies received premiums on marine risks amounting to $228,844.24, and paid losses on the same amounting to $182,558.07, or 80 per cent. of losses to premiums. The companies of other States and countries received premiums amounting to $736,634.71, and paid losses amounting to $665,935.20, or 90 per cent. of premiums received. The assets of the mutual companies that made returns amounted to $753,079.08, of which amount $639,184.64 consisted of premium notes.

The statement of the Treasurer of the Maine Beet-Sugar Company represents that industry as improving. The pulp produced from the beet is one of the great benefits arising from its culture. Twenty-three tons of beets per acre is the average in Europe; one ton of beets makes 400 pounds of pulp, which is worth more than the beets themselves for feeding purposes. When dry the beet has 13 per cent. of sugar. If kept until spring, the sugar is reduced to 8 per cent. Pulp is sold at $1 per ton, the railroad transports it for 80 cents, and this is equal to hay at $4 per ton. Twenty pounds of pulp, ten pounds of straw, and one pound of meal is the feed per day of a cow in Europe. The farmers in the vicinity of Portland raised from 14 to 40 tons of beets per acre; average amount of sugar, 11 per cent. In 1878 fifty acres of beets were raised in that section, and as many more in Aroostook. A capital of $150,000 is required for the manufacture of the sugar. No one can raise beets at a profit but a farmer, and no one can manufacture but a refiner. Deep plowing, early planting, and early thinning out are essential.

Forty tons per acre is not a large yield with good cultivation. In France the beet-producers receive $3.50 per ton; the company paid $4.

A statement of the amount of ship-building on the Kennebec River has been prepared, which shows the number and tonnage of vessels built there from 1781 to 1879, classified according to rig, to have been as follows:

VESSELS.	Number.	Tons.
Steamers	43	7,649·85
Ships	846	658,930·80
Barks	236	118,789·85
Brigs	669	126,857·61
Schooners	1,018	117,716·29
Sloops	129	7,840·87
Scows	8	529·49
Barges	8	736·96
Total	2,947	1,088,551·22

During this time vessels have been built in Augusta, Hallowell, Gardiner, Farmingdale, Richmond, Bowdoinham, Pittston, Vassalboro', Waterville, Sidney, and Chelsea.

A National Home for disabled volunteer soldiers is located at Togus, near Augusta. The number of soldiers and sailors aided by the institution during 1878 was 1,351; admitted, 267; readmitted, 121; honorably discharged, 92; dishonorably discharged, 6; transferred to other branches, 45; deserted, 47; average number present during the year, 836; belonging to regular army, 17; volunteer service, 1,330; navy, 4; disabled during the war of rebellion, 1,340; Mexican war, 2; war of 1812, 9; one colored man. Of the whole number, 216 came from Maine, 521 from Massachusetts, 296 from New York, 95 from New Hampshire, and the remainder from several other States in the Union; 568 were native-born, and 783 foreign-born; 573 were married and had children; 627 were common laborers, the remainder having trades; 917 could read and write; 434 could do neither; one had lost both arms, 60 one arm, 70 one leg; 4 were totally blind, 18 partially blind; 11 partially insane, one totally insane. Pensions have been paid to 664, to the amount of $70,272.98; of this sum $10,023.23 was retained for the purposes of the Home, $27,296.75 used for the benefit of relatives, and $4,185 retained in trust for pensioners. The boot and shoe manufactory has been carried on, employing 55 of the men, with a total product of $12,819.20 and a net profit of $4,255.21. Total value of farm products, $7,756.38, including 275 tons of hay. Total number of inmates employed for pay, 257; paid out for labor the past year, $22,385.98. There are 4,326 volumes in the library, 22 daily newspapers, 115 weeklies, and other periodicals and publications. Protestant and Catholic religious services are held weekly, and temperance organizations sustained. The total amount paid for expenses of the Home during the year was $103,647.12; average cost of keeping each man—with clothing, $134.25; without, $119.37. Many of the men have brought their families there, and live in cottages near the Home, receiving their ration in kind and carrying it home.

The Industrial School for Girls contained at the last report 84 inmates, and 36 in homes. The proportion of older girls is unusually large. Some are grown to more than ordinary woman's size, and are capable of efficient service.

The Agricultural College asked of the Legislature an appropriation of $6,000, in addition to $8,200 received as interest, to meet its necessities, as follows: To pay for instruction, $4,000; for apparatus, $1,000; for current expenses, $1,000. For 1879 the catalogue shows an attendance of 101 students 'who have entered for the full course of four years, besides those who are pursuing a special course. One hundred have graduated, and most of them entered upon active and useful pursuits. The instruction in shop-work, on the Russian plan, although the means were inadequate, was very satisfactory.

The vexatious question of mileage which troubled the members of the Legislature was decided against them. The Constitution says, "The expenses of the House of Representatives in traveling to the Legislature and returning therefrom once in each session, and no more, shall be paid by the State," etc. The Revised Statutes say, "Each member of the Senate and House of Representatives shall be paid an annual salary of one hundred and fifty dollars for the regular annual session of the Legislature, and two dollars for every ten miles travel from his place of abode, once in each session." The members voted themselves mileage both ways, viz., going and returning. The Governor refused to approve of the act, and with the Council referred the question to the Justices of the Supreme Court. The Justices, looking at the statute alone, said: "The limitation of once in each session excludes the idea of more than once. The member is entitled to mileage on the first day of the session, and this mileage is all to which he is entitled."

A case involving the meaning of the words "tippling purposes" came before the courts. The liquor law forbids the sale of cider for "tippling purposes." The defendant admitted that he had sold cider to be carried away from his premises, and such was the proof; but it also appeared that the persons who bought the cider took it out by the roadside and into the neighboring fields, and there got drunk upon it. The defense contended that the words "tippling purposes" meant drinking upon the premises. But the Judge presiding, after fully explaining to the jury the meaning of the word tipple, charged them that "a man may as well tipple in the street as in a building—in his own house as in the shop where the liquor is sold." And he gave them further instruction to the same effect. Upon exceptions taken to the charge of the Judge, the full Court decided that the exceptions must be sustained, holding in effect that, in order to

convict a person of selling cider for "tippling purposes," the Government must prove that the tippling was done in the shop or building kept by the defendant.

A convention was held at Augusta on June 2d of the surviving members of the Senate and House of Representatives of 1851, who voted for the passage of the original Maine Liquor Law, as well as other friends of prohibition, the occasion being the twenty-eighth anniversary of the signing of the bill by Governor Hubbard. One of the members stated the action of the Legislature on the subject. He said:

The bill had been twice passed before, but failed to receive the Governor's signature. The search and seizure act was perfected in 1853, which takes right hold of the critter himself. This law was remodeled in 1855, improved, and made very stringent, so that our friends who were opposed to it thought it almost unendurable. In 1856 a new Governor arose "who knew not Joseph," and the Maine Law was swept from our statutes. To one Phinehas Barnes of Portland was assigned the task of drafting a license law, which passed, and which contained no local option. This law amounted to about the same as free rum. This law remained until 1858, and then was reënacted the Maine Liquor Law, which, with its amendments, has since remained. This law has given Maine a world-wide reputation, and this is something to be thankful for.

An address to "the temperance people of the world," reported by Neal Dow, thus describes the Maine legislation on the subject:

To show conclusively the position which this policy now holds in the public opinion of Maine, it is only necessary to mention the facts that since 1851 several acts additional to the Maine Law, all in the direction of greater stringency, have been passed, except that in 1856 there was a general breaking up of political parties, and one came into power by which the law was repealed, and a license law substituted for it. But at the next election that party was ignominiously defeated by a tremendous majority, and the Maine Law was reënacted in a more stringent form, and was submitted to a popular vote, by which it was approved by more than four to one, and since that day there has been no attempt at repeal. In 1871 an act additional, of greater stringency than any which had preceded it, was adopted without a dissenting voice in either House; and at the session of 1879 a question came up for the modification and the amelioration of the penalties and the requirements of the law, which was promptly defeated by the emphatic vote of 127 to 17. This latter vote may be fairly considered as marking the present condition of public opinion of this State upon the whole principle and policy of prohibition, and the determination of the people to suppress the liquor-traffic.

In the same address the following results are ascribed to the operation of this law:

It is not too much to say that the quantity of liquor now smuggled into the State and sold in violation of law is not one tenth so large as it was before the law. This great change in the habits of the people procures an enormous saving in the wages of labor and in the resources of the State, which were formerly so largely squandered and wasted in strong drink. By some slight additions to the law, the absolute extirpation of the traffic may be easily effected. This saving in the money and morals of the people by the suppression of the liquor-shops has produced most important results, which may be seen everywhere throughout the State. Better houses and buildings, public and private, better farms, better ways of life, and increased prosperity, mark very emphatically the result of prohibition. No one who knows what Maine was before the law, and what it has been since, and is now, can fail to see the wonderful change for the better in all its interests, public and private.

On the other hand, a writer who has visited Maine, and claims to have obtained some knowledge of the operation of the law in the State, says:

It is so strictly enforced that you can not get a bottle of sherry or brandy at a drug-store, except upon the prescription of a physician, and then the quantity sold is limited to a pint in every instance. No wine is sold to be drunk at dinner in hotels. A person's private supply must be replenished outside of the State. The only authorized liquor-dealer is the State government. A "State Liquor Agent" is appointed by the Governor, who opens a warehouse. Twenty citizens of any town may petition to have a town agency opened, and the Governor makes an investigation of the case. If he is favorably disposed, a town agent is appointed, who rents a building and is supplied with liquors from the State agency. When a person wants a pint of brandy he applies to the local agent, but he can not have it unless he is known to be a reputable citizen, or can find some "reputable citizen" to identify him as such. The brandy is sold only for "medicinal or mechanical" purposes, the mechanical largely predominating. When the applicant receives his liquor, he registers his name in a book that is open for the inspection of the public. Great care is supposed to be taken against allowing this transaction to be repeated too frequently. So much for the manner in which the law is enforced. Now as to the manner in which the law is not enforced. The city of Portland has a population of 35,000, and one local agent suffices to accommodate all the demands made in the legal way; but it is not to be supposed that nearly all of those 35,000 people abstain from the use of intoxicating liquors. Five per cent. of them drink as much as they would if there were a saloon on every corner. A system of social clubs prevails, by means of which the law is successfully evaded. An ordinary club is organized, procures and furnishes rooms. A sideboard is one of the articles of furniture, and it is well laden. A member of the club drops in, helps himself, and extends the courtesy of the club to a friend. The waiter in attendance registers the amount and quality of the liquor drunk, and at the end of the month the treasurer of the club "assesses" the individual "club dues" to a corresponding amount. The popularity of these clubs throughout the State is marvelous.

A mass State Temperance Convention was held at Augusta on January 22d. Governor Garcelon presided. A series of resolutions was adopted, which return sincere thanks to God for the progress made in the cause; express a firm conviction of the righteousness of the principle of prohibition; declare that scientific investigation has proved that alcohol is not essential even as a medicine; recognize the evil of liquor agencies and call for a more strict supervision; assert that while many druggists are honorable men, they should not have special privileges in the sale of intoxicating liquors; express opposition to the wholesale transportation of liquors into the State by public carriers, railroads, etc.; call for legislative enactment on the same; urge temperance organizations to action; call for the education in temperance principles of the children and youth, and ask parents, guardians, and teachers to do their duty in this respect; demand the use of temperance text-books in our schools; and request Congress, by constitutional amendment, to for ever prohibit the importation, manufacture, and sale of alcoholic drinks.

The National or Greenback-Labor Convention assembled at Portland on June 3d. There were 910 delegates. William M. Rust was selected for President of the Convention. Joseph L. Smith was nominated for Governor, and the following resolutions were adopted:

This Convention reaffirms the cardinal principles enunciated in the platform of the National Greenback Convention of Maine, holden at Lewiston June 5, 1878, and looks with pride and satisfaction at the endorsement of the same by the people at the September election, and the rapid growth of the party in the country at large, the vote at the latest elections showing the unprecedented increase from 82,000 in 1876 to 130,000 in 1878.

That the increase of coin bonded indebtedness of the Government in a time of profound peace, from $1,100,000,000 in 1865 to $2,000,000,000 in 1879, is a fact so startling as to alarm every friend of the country.

That the reduction of the rate of coin interest, and at the same time increasing the principal to such an amount as to vastly increase the coin interest continually, under the pretext of economy by the reduction of the rate of interest, is such a deception and fraud upon the people as to merit the most severe condemnation.

1. *Resolved*, That we favor the unlimited coinage of gold and silver, to be supplemented by full legal-tender paper money, sufficient to transact the business of the country.

2. *Resolved*, That we favor the immediate use of the coin in the Treasury for the reduction of the bonded debt.

3. *Resolved*, That we favor the substitution of greenbacks for national-bank notes.

4. *Resolved*, That the volume of our money should not vary with the chance production of the precious metals or the caprice of corporations.

5. *Resolved*, That a graduated tax on incomes is imperatively demanded, to the end that the capital of the country may equally bear its burdens.

6. *Resolved*, That we oppose all subsidies or legalized monopolies, and denounce as one of the highest crimes corruption at the ballot-box. We favor few and simple laws, and those vigorously enforced.

7. *Resolved*, That we hereby denounce communism in all its forms and phases.

This Convention also congratulates the people of Maine upon the reforms inaugurated by the Nationals and carried forward by the last Legislature of Maine, whereby the expenses of the State and counties have been greatly reduced, while the efficiency of the public service has in no way been impaired; and we demand a continuance of the policy of retrenchment and all true reform and the practice of the most rigid economy in all departments of the public service.

The decay of American shipping is a subject that justly causes anxiety and alarm, and its revival should enlist the closest attention of our entire people; and we demand such legislation as shall cause its early restoration.

The Republican State Convention assembled at Bangor on June 26th. The number of delegates present was 1,238. F. A. Pike was selected for temporary and permanent President. On the third ballot Daniel F. Davis was nominated for Governor. The following resolutions were then adopted:

The Republican party of Maine presents to the people of the State the following statement of its aims and principles: It believes that this is a "nation" and not a "confederacy" of States, and that the national Government is supreme on all subjects lodged with it by the Constitution. It recognizes as one of these subjects the right and duty of the national Government to protect the citizen in the exercise of all his constitutional and legal rights, none of which are more important than a free, fair ballot, uninfluenced by fraud or violence. It believes that existing laws for the protection of the American citizen should not be repealed, and it condemns as revolutionary the attempts of the Democratic party in Congress to force the Executive to consent to such repeal by aid of refusal of appropriations necessary for the existence of the Government. It appreciates the noble and patriotic position taken by the President and the Republican members of both Houses of Congress, in sustaining wise and just laws against the treasonable and revolutionary course of the Democratic party in Congress; and it hereby pledges them its hearty support in their efforts to uphold the financial credit of the Government and to insist upon free elections and the rights of the United States to enforce its own laws.

It protests against the reopening by the Democratic leaders of exciting and sectional issues, which had been settled by the victory of the national arms over the rebellion, and calls upon loyal men everywhere to sustain by their votes the fruits of that victory.

It believes now, as always, in good honest money for the people, and it opposes an irredeemable paper currency as the worst curse that can be inflicted upon a nation. It rejoices that the Government's promises to pay are now kept, and that the paper currency of the country is redeemable on demand in coin; so that now the dollar of the laborer is as good as that of the capitalist. It condemns all schemes to tamper with the currency of the people and thereby again unsettle public confidence, now happily fast being restored.

It recognizes temperance as a cause which has conferred the greatest benefit on the State, and it sustains the principle of prohibition, which in its opinion has so largely suppressed liquor-selling and added incalculably to the sum of virtue and prosperity among the people. It believes that every interest of the State and its people urges the thorough and impartial enforcement of all the laws.

It believes that State affairs should be conducted economically and prudently, and that the expenses of administration should be kept as low as consistent with the efficient operation of its several departments.

The Democratic State Convention assembled at Bangor on July 1st. Abram Sanborn was selected for temporary and permanent President. Governor Alonzo Garcelon was renominated, and the following resolutions were adopted:

Resolved, That the partisan acts of a Congress that withdraws the control of elections from honest electors and places them in the custody of the tools of the Executive, are not designed to secure an honest vote, but to enable a fraudulent Administration to perpetuate its power.

Resolved, That the power to buy up the refuse of every city, under the name of deputy marshals, without limit as to their number and price, and at the expense of the public Treasury, and the power in a single minion of the Executive to arrest and imprison, with or without warrant, any and as many of the peaceable electors as he may choose to keep from voting, are powers that can not be trusted to any administration.

Resolved, That we approve the efforts of the Democratic members of Congress to secure the repeal of these outrageous laws. So contrary are they to all the traditions of the builders of our republican system, that we do not hesitate to declare no further appropriation should be made by Congress to carry them into effect.

Resolved, That we condemn the action of Republican leaders in keeping alive sectional issues and the hatreds engendered by war, and we call upon true men and patriotic citizens everywhere to recognize no North, no South, no East, no West, but one whole country, composed of equal States in one inseparable Union.

Resolved, That we are in favor of a currency of gold, silver, and paper, the paper to be kept at par with coin at all times, and are in favor of free, unlimited coinage of silver.

Resolved, That we approve the measures of economy and the reduction of State expenditures inaugurated by the union of the Democrats and Greenbackers of the last Legislature, and insist upon their continuance in the future, as the only salvation from ruinous taxation or hopeless bankruptcy.

Resolved, That the Democrats of Maine take pride in again presenting to the people of the State the name of Hon. Alonzo Garcelon of Lewiston as a candidate for reëlection as Governor, believing him to be a worthy, true, and honest exponent of the principles this day enunciated. The cautious, dignified, and faithful manner in which he has discharged his responsible duties in the past is an ample guarantee that he has the character and ability successfully to maintain and carry forward all the great and varied interests of the State.

The election was held on September 8th, and the vote for Governor was as follows: Davis, Republican, 68,766; Garcelon, Democrat, 21,-688; Smith, National, 47,590. The returns of the election of members of the Legislature, as made up by the Republican press, after the election, made the Senate to consist of 19 Republicans and 12 Democrats, with a Republican majority of 7; and the House to contain 89 Republicans and 61 Democrats, with one Republican vacancy by death. This gave a clear Republican majority of 28, and when the vacancy was filled, 29.

The State Constitution provides that at the town meetings for the choice of Representatives, the selectmen shall "receive the votes of all the qualified electors present; sort, count, and declare them in open town meeting and in the presence of the town clerk, who shall form a list of the persons voted for, with the number of votes for each person against his name; shall make a fair record thereof in the presence of the selectmen and in open town meeting. . . . And fair copies of the lists of votes shall be attested by the selectmen and town clerks of towns and the assessors of plantations, and sealed up in open town and plantation meeting; and the town and plantation clerks respectively shall cause the same to be delivered into the Secretary's office [at Augusta] thirty days at least before the first Wednesday of January annually. And the Governor and Council shall examine the returned copies of such lists, . . . and twenty days before the said first day of January annually shall issue a summons to such persons as shall appear to be elected by a plurality of all the votes returned, to attend and take their seats. But all such lists shall be laid before the House of Representatives on the first Wednesday of January annually, and they shall finally determine who are elected." In section 4 of the second part of the same article, the same provision in regard to the duty of the Governor and Council is made applicable to Senators. Section 32 of chapter 4 of the Revised Statutes provides that the whole number of separate ballots given shall be counted and "distinctly stated, recorded, and returned," and, as amended by chapter 213, acts of 1877, after directing the counting of votes for ineligible persons, declares that the person having the highest number of votes shall be declared to be elected, "and the Governor shall issue a certificate thereof." In 1878 this section was amended by the addition of a proviso that it should not be construed to give the Governor and Council any authority to determine questions of eligibility in cases of Senators and Representatives. The statutes contain many and minute regulations respecting the manner in which Senators and Representatives shall be elected, but, the Republicans claimed, "whether these regulations are or are not observed in an election, whether the votes deposited and counted did or did not conform to the statute requirement, whether the check-lists were tampered with, or whether voters were bribed, are questions into which the Governor and Council have no authority to inquire. Their only duty is to examine the returned copies of the lists of votes, and to issue a summons to such persons as appear to be elected by a plurality of the votes returned."

About the middle of November a great excitement began to prevail among the Republicans, which was caused by rumors that the Governor and Council would endeavor to count out the Republican majority in the Legislature and count in a Fusion (Democrats and Nationals) majority. The Governor and Council arrived at Augusta on Monday, November 17th, and assembled at the State House in the afternoon, where they were visited by a sub-committee of distinguished Republicans gathered from all parts of the State. The report says:

The conference between the sub-committee and the Governor lasted some time, and resulted in the Governor giving the following specific assurance: That the returns should not be considered open in the sense of allowing any amendments or corrections under the statutes, until the Committee of the Council on Elections should report the result of their canvass to the Governor and Council, and that there would be twenty days from that time for any corrections allowed by law, and for any hearings that might be desired. He further gave the assurance that this understanding should be adopted by the Council and made a matter of record, and public notice given thereof.

In addition to the foregoing, Governor Garcelon gave the following concluding assurance: "Ample opportunity will be given to correct any errors in the returns which can be corrected under the statutes. If any returns are fatally defective, you must take the consequences." The Council immediately after went into session, when the Committee on Elections reported that they had canvassed a part of the returns and opened the whole, and that twenty days from this date would be allowed for corrections under the statutes.

Numerous unsuccessful applications were made to the Council for a hearing by persons who conceived their interests to be in danger. The words of the statute on this point are as follows:

The Governor and Council, on or before the first day of December, in each year, shall open and compare the votes so returned, and may receive testimony on oath to prove that the return from any town does not agree with the record of the vote of such town, in the number of votes or the names of persons voted for, and to prove which of them is correct; and the return when found to be erroneous may be corrected by the record. No such correction can be made without application within twenty days after the returns are opened, stating the error alleged, and reasonable notice thereof given to the person to be affected by such correction.

On Saturday, November 22d, the following order of the Governor and Council was issued:

Ordered, That the Secretary give public notice that the Governor and Council will be in session from December 1st to the 13th, for the purpose of examining the returns of votes for candidates for Senators, Representatives, and county officers.

Candidates claiming irregularities or other causes presumed to vitiate their election, will have reasonable opportunity to be heard either personally or by duly authorized counsel.

Applications to the Supreme Court were made for a mandamus to the Secretary of State commanding him to exhibit the returns in the cases specified. The petition and response and arguments of counsel were heard, but the Judge concluded to dismiss the application. At the same time, on December 9th, access was given to the returns by the Governor and Council. It appears by the statement of Governor Garcelon that the returns of the election were placed in the hands of a sub-committee of the Council, to examine in detail and report upon the same to the Council. On the basis of this report the Council acted. In a speech at Lewiston on December 27th the Governor says:

If there has been any act of my life which I am proud of, it is of the performance of my duty in tabulating and counting those returns. We have simply followed the Constitution and laws as interpreted by the Supreme Court, time and time again. The Constitution prescribes certain things for cities and towns to do at an election. If the requirements of the Constitution are not complied with, there is no legal election. These provisions were made for the purpose of securing an honest election. It turns out sometimes that there are informalities in returns. The Legislature undertook to provide by law for correcting this. That correction must be made by the record. If there is no record, what can returns be corrected by? If the record is like the returns, where can a correction come in? Now, when this avalanche of Republican statesmen came in on me at Augusta, it popped into my head that their very object was to see the returns and then go home and see that their records were made all right. In the case of Portland the returns were illegal, and the records were sent for. Lo! the record was found to be just like the returns. Republicans say the intention of the voters must be regarded, and not the Constitution and law. The Selectmen of the town of Danforth had the presumption to go to the clerk and demand that he change and correct the records. I have a letter from Mr. Berry, town clerk, saying he was threatened with fine and imprisonment unless he complied. That is what comes of this amending the records. Amend your records three months after election, and where is the result of an election? The tabulations were made upon the basis of the Constitution as explained by the Court, as far as possible. The circumstances that have surrounded me have been unfavorable. I have in reality had to face a frowning world on account of the foul lies of the Associated Press, and the vituperation and slander heaped upon me for over a quarter of a century.

Again, in a published defense of his proceedings, after stating the provisions of the Constitution, he speaks of the statutes, and the action of himself and the Council under them, thus:

So much for the Constitution. Supplementary to this the statutes provide (chapter 4, section 32) that in order to determine the result of any election by ballot, the number of persons voted for shall first be ascertained by counting the whole number of separate ballots given in, which shall be distinctly stated, recorded, and returned. Blanks are not to be counted as votes, and votes for persons not eligible to the office shall not be counted as votes; but the number of such blanks and the number and names on ballots for persons not eligible shall be recorded and return made thereof. These provisions of the Constitution and the laws apply to cities as well as towns and plantations, and impose upon them—that is, the municipal officers—the duty of examining and comparing the lists of votes given in the several wards, of which the city clerk shall make a record, and return thereof shall be made in the same manner as selectmen of towns are required to do.

Such are the plain and unmistakable provisions of the Constitution of this State, and in the discharge of their duty of examining the returns and issuing certificates of summons to the parties appearing to be elected, the Governor and Council have not only endeavored to follow both the letter and spirit of the Constitution, and laws made in accordance therewith, as indicated by their own judgment, but the advice of their duly appointed legal officer, aided by the best legal talent in the State.

And here let it be remembered that the decision of the Governor and Council is not final. The Constitution makes the Senate and House of Representatives, respectively, the final arbiters of the election of their own members. All the lists or returns which have been confided to the Council are to be laid before the Senate and House of Representatives on the first Wednesday in January annually, and they shall finally determine who are elected.

With these directions and requirements before them, what are the Governor and Council required to do? To examine these returns, ascertain their validity, and compare them with the provisions of the Constitution and the law. And, first, they must have been sealed in open town meeting and in presence of the selectmen, and by necessary implication must come into the hands of the Governor and Council in that condition. Secondly, they must be genuine returns, coming from bona fide towns or plantations, legally constituted and organized. Thirdly, they must be signed by the legal officers of the towns—that is, as decided by the courts, by a majority of the municipal officers of a town or city—and certified by the clerk. Fourthly, they must contain a statement of the whole number of ballots cast for the officers voted for, and the office for which he was voted to fill. Fifthly, the name of each person voted for, with the number of votes against his name that were thrown for him. Sixthly, the names of the officers signing the returns must be written with their own hands (as per judicial decision, 68 Maine, page 587). Applying these rules to the various returns, a tabulation of the persons voted for the different offices, with the votes each has received, determines the result.

In the inspection of returns and tabulation of the same, which has just been completed by myself and Council, it has been our purpose to apply to every return the same rule, to wit: Compliance with the requirements of the Constitution and the law, without fear or favor; and if the result as to the political complexion of the Legislature is different from what was claimed by politicians interested in influencing the elections in other States, it is owing in part to the fact

that the claim was unfounded, and in part to the carelessness of municipal officers in making their returns. The truth is, the popular vote was against the Republican party, and in the Representative and Senatorial districts the vote was extremely close. In addition to the fact that several persons fail to receive their certificates in consequence of "fatal defects" in the returns from their towns or cities, there are others who would have been presumably elected but for the carelessness of the voters themselves or the ignorance of the candidates or those who provided ballots at the elections. The Judges of our Supreme Court have decided that ballots cast for William H. Smith and W. H. Smith are ballots to be counted separately. Several changes have resulted from this condition of affairs. In one county persons with as many as four different combinations in initials received the Republican vote and two the Democratic. That county was entitled to only one Senator, and there was no alternative but to give the certificate to the person having the highest number of votes. In the Danforth district, already notorious, the name of the Republican candidate was Charles A. Rolfe. The town of Danforth voted for Chas. Rolfe. The result was that his competitor received the certificate, and from like causes other changes have occurred.

The great hue and cry about "conspiracy," "fraud," etc., arises from the fact that we have taken the Constitution for our guide, fortified by the opinions of the Supreme Court of the State and the advice of several of the foremost legal gentlemen of the forum, and have not permitted substitution, alteration, or unauthorized amendments of the returns transmitted to us for examination, and by us to be transmitted to the Legislature for their final action.

The sub-committee of the Council to whom the returns were submitted made public on December 26th their report to the Council of their proceedings, as follows:

Your committee, in submitting this report, deem it necessary to state specifically certain facts connected with the returns from many of the towns, cities, and plantations which have materially affected the result of the canvassing of the votes returned. There are many returns which, owing to fatal defect, can not be counted, but we shall specify only those which have affected the result. Article 4, part 1, section 5, of the Constitution, regulates the manner of electing Senators and Representatives of the Legislature, and also the process of transmitting to the Governor and Council the evidence by which they are to determine who have been elected. This section provides, in case of towns and plantations, that municipal officers shall, in open town and plantation meetings, at the close of election day, sort, count, and declare the votes cast, and form a list of all persons voted for, and after the name of each person thus voted for shall write the number of votes received by him. This list shall be recorded in open meeting by the clerk, and a copy of this recorded list shall be signed by the selectmen and attested by the clerk and sealed up in open meeting. This copy of the recorded list, thus attested, is to be deposited in the office of the Secretary of State within thirty days thereafter. Section —— of the Revised Statutes requires that, in addition to the foregoing specific mandatory provisions of the Constitution, the returns shall state the whole number of ballots cast at the election. The same section of the Constitution requires that the Governor and Council shall open and compare the returns thus transmitted, and from them determine who appears to be elected, and the Governor is to issue to such persons as thus appear to be elected a summons to take seats in the Legislature. Of course, the first requirement is that the returns shall be made and sealed up in open town or plantation meetings. We understand that this is required in order that electors may be present and see that the returns are made in accordance with the facts; and we are of the opinion that the returns not made up in open meeting are illegal and can not be counted, and we have acted upon this belief in making our tabulations. Several protests, accompanied with affidavits to support them, against counting the returns specified therein, have been considered by us. These protests allege that the said returns should not be counted, because they were not made up in open town meeting, but after the meeting was closed, in some private office or store, when no one but a portion of the municipal officers were present, and in some cases only the clerk. This condition of things in several cases has been proved to our entire satisfaction, and we rejected the returns thus defective in our tabulations. In the case of the town of Stoneham, an affidavit was signed by two selectmen, who established the fact that they signed the returns in blank, and the town clerk took them home and filled them up, and the selectmen have no knowledge of what the returns contain. For the foregoing reasons we rejected, in our tabulation, the representative returns from the towns of Jay, Stoneham, Lisbon, Webster, and Farmington. The returns from the town of Seaport have also been rejected because they were not sealed up in open town meeting. By means of these rejections, five persons will receive seats in the Legislature who would not have been seated had the returns from the aforesaid towns been made up as the Constitution requires. They are James White, of Jay district; Louis Voter, of Farmington district; N. Bradbury, of Stoneham district; Joshua Jourdan, of Searsport district; Leonard Beal, of Durham district. The Supreme Court have held that municipal officers shall sign the returns with their own hands, or make their mark, otherwise the returns can not be counted. We found several returns fatally defective in this particular, and accordingly rejected them by this rule laid down by the Court. New Sharon has also been rejected by us. This rejection upsets the election of one representative. We found several returns fatally defective because the seal is attested by the town clerk. The Supreme Court held that such returns are not legal, and we rejected them. They are quite numerous, but we shall specify only such as affect the result of the election. The representative returned from the town of Lebanon is one of them. Its rejection affects the election of one representative, viz., Stephen Lord. Vanceboro and Albany are like cases, and the rejection of the returns from these towns affects the election of two representatives. The representative districts in most cases are composed of several towns. In some towns the full Christian names of candidates seem to have been used, and in others only the initials, and we hesitated as to whether we could count the initial names with the full names. On examination of the law we find the Supreme Court held that the Governor and Council must count them as distinct and separate persons. By adopting this rule laid down by the Court, the election of five representatives seemed to be affected, viz.: F. W. Hill, of Exeter; Aaron Woodcock, of Danforth district; James Clark, of Newcastle; John Brown, of Hodgdon district; and James Leighton, of Blank district. The Revised Statutes require in the case of plantations, in addition to the forms required by the towns, that the list of voters of plantations be sent to the Secretary of State, otherwise the returns from such plantations shall not be counted. We found the returns from several plantations irregular in this particular, and we specified them in our tabulations. It will then appear the rejection of those returns affects the election of two representatives. The statute requirement of setting forth in the returns the whole number of ballots in many cases was not complied with. We found it had been the practice of the Governor and Council for many years to reject such returns, and we have not deemed it safe to deviate from this long-established interpretation of the law, so fully recognized by our predecessors, and in making our tabulations have omitted all such returns. It will be perceived that this rejection affects several representatives in the county of Washington. One candidate

for the Senate seems to have been voted for in some towns by the name of John F. Wallace, Jr., and in others by the name of Jno. T. Wallace; but we tabulated the votes as thrown for two different men, as we have no legal knowledge that the same person is meant. Two sets of returns were sent in to the Secretary of State from the town of Fairfield, each of which contradicts the other; and as it was impossible from the conflicting character of the returns to determine the result of the election, we rejected the returns from that town in our tabulations. The rejection affects the election of one representative. Accompanying and attached to the representative return from the town of Skowhegan there was a statement signed by the selectmen that a certain number of ballots were protested as being illegal, under section 29, chapter 4, Revised Statutes. One of the ballots objected to was attached to the returns. The selectmen allege how many such ballots were thrown, and in this certificate they inform the Governor and Council that they make the return subject to the legality or illegality of that kind of ballot. The ballot was in the form of an ordinary sheet of paper, folded to make two leaves. On one of the pages half of the candidates' names are printed, and on the next page the balance of the names of candidates appear. We are fully satisfied that this kind of ballot is clearly in violation of the letter and spirit of the foregoing-named statute, and we accordingly rejected a number of ballots in making our tabulations. A protest was filed against counting the returns from the town of Cherryfield, on the ground that the officers who attested the returns were not legal officers. Affidavits were presented with the protest to establish the fact that not one of the legal selectmen presided at the making out of the returns and the receiving of the votes. One selectman was a foreigner, and could not legally hold office. The Superior Court have held that a board of town officers consisting of less than three is not a legal board. Acting upon this opinion, we rejected the returns from Cherryfield. This affects the election of one representative. Several protests and affidavits to support them were referred to us, asking the rejection on account of bribery and intimidation of voters, and on account of legal defects in calling the town meeting, also on account of improper check-lists. The copy of the record presented to us from the town of Skowhegan shows that for the election in that town only one copy of the warrant was posted, and the record does not show that one was posted in the town. Objection to the counting of the votes of the city of Auburn was made because voters' names were added to the check-lists in three of the wards, in violation of the law, while voting was going on election day. The affidavits filed fully establish the fact, and other affidavits show a similar condition of things in other cities. We consider these facts as not legally cognizable by the Governor and Council as a canvassing board, and we disregarded them in our tabulations. We recommend the reference of all such papers to the Legislature. The returns from Portland are defective because they do not comply with the constitutional requirement which provides that the names of all persons receiving votes shall be stated in the returns. A large number of votes were returned from said city as scattering, and there was no possible means afforded by the returns to determine for whom such votes were thrown. The returns from the cities of Saco, Lewiston, Bath, and Rockland are fatally defective, because they were not signed by a majority of the aldermen. Under the statutes and by decisions of the courts, such returns can not be counted, and we have been obliged to reject them. It will devolve on the House of Representatives to determine in the first instance, and finally, who have been elected to the House from these cities, as we have no legal evidence before us to determine that question.

A correspondence ensued between ex-Governor Morrill and Governor Garcelon, in which the former proposed that the disputed points should be submitted to the Supreme Court for adjudication. To this Governor Garcelon replied on December 27th, saying:

You intimate that it is in my power to restore peace, tranquillity, and good feeling to the State and all its inhabitants by asking the opinion of the Supreme Judges on each law-point involved in the variations of the count from the returns. Nothing would give me greater pleasure than an authoritative opinion upon the points involved in the present condition of affairs, and also upon such as might be likely to arise. Please to indicate the points that occur to you which have not already been adjudicated upon, and I doubt not that we may be able to secure a satisfactory solution of the doubtful complications, or, if not satisfactory, at least such as may be deemed authoritative.

On December 28th ex-Governor Morrill again wrote, and submitted a series of fourteen questions for opinions of the Supreme Court; but Governor Garcelon declined to approve of them, and they were not submitted. Subsequently the Governor and Council submitted the following series of questions to the Court:

1. When the Governor and Council decide that there is no return from a city on which representatives can be summoned to attend and take their seats in the Legislature, is it their duty to order a new election, or is it competent for the House of Representatives, if it shall appear that there was an election of such representatives, to admit them to seats, though no return thereof was made and delivered to the office of Secretary of State?

2. Is it competent for the Governor and Council to allow the substitution of other evidence in place of the returned copies of such lists as are provided for in article 4, part 1, section 5, of the Constitution, to enable them to determine what persons appear to be elected as representatives to the Legislature by a plurality of all the votes returned?

3. Is a return signed by a minority of the selectmen of a town, or the aldermen of a city, valid within the requirements of the same section?

4. Is a return by the aldermen of a city which does not give the number of votes cast for each person voted for as a member of the Legislature, and does not show what persons were voted for as such member in any one of the several wards of such city, a valid return within the requirements of the same section?

5. Are returns from towns or cities which are not attested by the town or city clerk valid within the same section?

6. Have the Governor and Council a right to reject returns of the election of members of the Legislature, required by the same section from the officers of towns, which were not made, signed, and sealed up in open town meeting?

7. Is the return of two persons purporting to be the selectmen of a town valid and sufficient evidence of the vote of the town, when it appears that there were at the time of the meeting at which the election was had but two selectmen of that town?

8. Can a person who is not a citizen of the United States at the time be legally elected or constituted a selectman of the town?

9. If a ballot has a distinguishing mark in the judgment of the Governor and Council, such as would make it illegal under the statute, have they authority to disregard it in their ascertainment of what persons appear to be elected, where it appears by the official return of the officers of the town that such vote was received by the selectmen subject to the objection, and its legality referred to the Governor and Council for decision?

10. If the names of any persons appear in the return without any number of votes being stated or carried out against them, either in words or figures, is it the duty of the Governor and Council to treat those persons as having the same number of votes as another

person received for the same office, and whose name is placed first in the return, if they find dots under the figures or words set against such other person's name?

11. Have the Governor and Council the legal right to decide what kind of evidence they will receive, and what the mode of proceeding before them shall be, to enable them to determine the genuineness of returns required by the article and section of the Constitution above mentioned?

12. If the Governor and Council have before them two lists of votes returned from the same town, differing materially from each other in the number of votes returned as cast for the same persons, but identical in all other respects, both having been duly received at the Secretary's office, and they have no evidence to enable them to determine which is the true and genuine return, are they required to treat either of them as valid, and if so, which?

On January 3, 1880, the Court unanimously made an answer to the questions, which was entirely in opposition to the views of the Governor and Council. The answer of the Court is not inserted here, because it was unheeded by the Governor, and on account of its length.

Meantime the certificates of election had been sent out to the members of the Legislature, and that body convened on January 7th. Seventy-eight Democrats and Nationals had received certificates of membership in the House of Representatives. That body assembled and proceeded to organize under the assistant clerk as presiding officer. A committee introduced Governor Garcelon, who administered the necessary oath to each member who presented himself, and then stated that seventy-six had been qualified. Only one Republican (Eugene Hale) was qualified, but during the session of the day another appeared and was qualified. Seventy-six votes constitute a quorum of the whole House of 150 members, and during all the preliminary measures the objection was raised by the single Republican member that there was no quorum voting. This was overruled by the chairman. John C. Talbot was chosen Speaker by 72 votes, and the Clerk was then chosen by 74. The objection of no quorum voting was overruled by the Speaker, who said that he had the highest authority for ruling that a majority of the whole number elected constitutes a quorum, and 70 was that number.

The Senate was called to order by the Secretary of the previous year. The Governor came in and administered the oaths of office. When it came to the election of officers the Republicans did not vote, and the candidates of the Fusion (Democrats and Nationals), Mr. Lamson of Waldo County and Mr. Andrews of Augusta, were respectively chosen President and Secretary.

The term of office of Governor Garcelon expired at midnight on the 7th, and the President of the Senate became ex officio Governor until a successor should be elected by the Legislature.

Thus far, nothing of an official authority had appeared, except the documents inserted above and the unheeded answer of the Supreme Court to Governor Garcelon. On the Republican side there was no official to speak, and whatever was attempted was merely the action of private individuals, and of no avail. They were, in fact, entirely powerless.

On January 12th the following order was issued:

HEADQUARTERS FIRST DIVISION, M. M., }
AUGUSTA, *January* 12, 1880. }

General Orders No 3.

First. The attention of all military organizations now in the service of the State, and of all men liable to military duty in this State, is directed to the following orders:

STATE OF MAINE, ADJUTANT-GENERAL'S OFFICE, }
AUGUSTA, *January* 5, 1880. }

General Order No. 12.—1. The several counties of this State are constituted into the First Division of the Militia of Maine. 2. Major-General Joshua L. Chamberlain is assigned to the command of the First Division. 3. The commanding officers of all military organizations accepted into the service of the State are required to report to him. He will be obeyed and respected accordingly.

By order of the Governor and Commander-in-Chief:
S. D. LEAVITT, Adjutant-General.

STATE OF MAINE, ADJUTANT-GENERAL'S OFFICE, }
AUGUSTA, *January* 5, 1880. }

Special Orders No. 45.—Major-General Joshua L. Chamberlain is hereby authorized and directed to protect the public property and institutions of the State until my successor is duly qualified.

(Signed) ALONZO GARCELON,
Governor.

Second. I am now discharging the duties thus devolved on me in protecting the public property and institutions of the State until a Governor is legally elected and duly qualified.

Third. Particular attention is called to the law rendering it unlawful tor any body of men other than the regularly organized corps of the militia, without authority expressly given, to associate themselves together as a military company or organization, or to parade in public with arms.

Fourth. All persons and organizations will take notice accordingly, and all authorized military organizations will understand that they are to report to me for orders until they are otherwise ordered by or through me.

(Signed) JOSHUA L. CHAMBERLAIN,
Major-General.

Official:
(Signed) FRANK E. NYE,
Major and A. A. G.

About half-past 5 o'clock on the afternoon of the 12th, the Republicans, both those who had certificates of election and those without certificates who claimed to have been elected, quietly proceeded in detached numbers to the State House and took possession of the Legislative chambers. The Senate was called to order by Senator Dingley of Androscoggin, and Senator Harris of Washington was called to the chair. Prayer was offered by the Rev. Dr. Butler, member of the House from Vassalboro'. Charles W. Tilden, Assistant Secretary of the last Senate, called the roll of Senators who appeared by the face of the returns to be elected, and the eighteen Republicans answered to their names, and made a quorum. They were then sworn in by William R. Stratton, Clerk of the Courts for Kennebec County. The following officers were then elected, each receiving nineteen votes: President, Joseph A. Locke of Cumberland; Secretary, General C. W. Tilden of Castine; Assistant, George E. Brackett of

Belfast; Messenger, Charles H. Lovejoy of Sidney. The following order was then passed:

Ordered : That a committee, consisting of three members of the Senate, be appointed by the President to report to the Senate for its action whether the Senate shall call upon the Justices of the Supreme Court for their opinion touching the legal organization of the Senate for the Fifty-ninth Legislature, and to report for the action of the Senate such questions as the law and facts require in the premises.

The members of the House were called to order by Eugene Hale. Prayer was offered by the Rev. Mr. Crane, member from Winthrop. Colonel Mark Wentworth of Kittery was made temporary Chairman. Oramandel Smith of Litchfield was made Clerk *pro tem.* He called the roll of members who appeared to be elected on the face of the returns, and eighty-five Republicans so elected answered to their names, and were qualified by W. M. Stratton, an officer empowered to qualify civil officers. Mr. Strout of Portland offered an order admitting six other Republicans who were elected, but who were counted out on slight defects in the returns, all of which were amendable under the law of 1877. The Hon. George E. Weeks of Augusta was elected Speaker; Oramandel Smith of Litchfield, Clerk; and Edwin C. Burleigh of Linneus, Assistant Clerk.

Mr. Hale then offered a resolution similar to the one above passed in the Senate, which was adopted. In presenting it, Mr. Hale referred in flattering terms to General Chamberlain's judicious management, by which irresponsible men armed with muskets were removed from the State House, and the safety of the people's representatives was secured.

On January 12th Mr. Lamson, who had been elected the President of the Fusion Senate, addressed the following note to General Chamberlain:

STATE OF MAINE, EXECUTIVE DEPARTMENT, }
AUGUSTA, *January* 12, 1880. }

Joshua L. Chamberlain, Major-General, commanding.

DEAR SIR: Having entered on the duties of Governor of Maine, under critical circumstances, it is important for me to understand whether you are prepared to recognize my authority as such. Respectfully, r
(Signed) JAMES D. LAMSON,
Governor.

To this General Chamberlain replied as follows:

STATE OF MAINE, }
AUGUSTA, *January* 18, 1880. }

To the Hon. James D. Lamson.

SIR: I have the honor to acknowledge the receipt of your communication informing me that you have entered upon the duties of Governor, and desiring to know if I am prepared to recognize your authority as such. The gravity of the situation and the importance of my answer to your question demand that I should give to it the most earnest attention. I am acting under authority devolved on me by virtue of the following order [given above].

In the attitude which things have now taken, the responsibility resting on me under this order involves the liberties of the people, their most sacred property, and the stability of constitutional government, their highest institution. I am thankful that you feel and understand this, and realize equally with myself the importance of our proceeding with caution. Your inquiry virtually calls upon me to decide a question of constitutional law, which is a matter falling not at all within the province of my department.

In my military authority I have not the privilege of submitting such questions to the only tribunal competent to decide them. The Constitution declares that the Justices of the Supreme Judicial Court shall be obliged to give their opinion upon important questions of law and upon solemn occasions when required by the civil branches of the Government, but that privilege is not accorded to the military department. Supported by the decision of the Court, I should obey without a moment's hesitation ; but solemnly believing that if, at this juncture, I abandon my trust, there will be no barrier against anarchy and bloodshed, I can not, under the present circumstances, recognize your authority as Governor of Maine.

There are only two ways to settle the questions now at issue and agitating the public mind—by following strictly the Constitution and the laws, or by revolution and blood. In this alternative, and standing where I must be judged by God and man, I can only hold fast in my place, and implore those who have the power to decide these questions by appeal to the peaceful course of law. . Believing that this answer must commend itself to your judgment as the only one possible for me to give, and with the highest respect and esteem, I have the honor to be your obedient servant,

(Signed)   J. L. CHAMBERLAIN,
                         Major-General.

The Republicans proceeded with their legislative action, and submitted a statement of facts and a series of questions to the Supreme Court, which gave a decision sustaining their action as legal. This statement, with the legal points of the questions and the answers thereto, will be found under the title PUBLIC DOCUMENTS. Daniel Davis was chosen Governor by a majority of the members sitting in the Republican organization. General Chamberlain gracefully surrendered his sword to him ; the Fusionists became demoralized; some went over to the other body, and some retired.

MARYLAND. The condition of the State Treasury for the last biennial period has been as follows :

Balance in the Treasury September 80, 1877...	$397,981 13
Receipts for the fiscal year ending September 30, 1878...................................	2,295,263 79
Total amount...........................	$2,693,244 92
Disbursements..........................	2,489,079 14
Balance in the Treasury.................	$204,165 78
Receipts for fiscal year ending September 30, 1879,...................................	2,126,326 87
Total................................	$2,330,492 25
Total disbursements for same time............	1,774,283 26
Balance in the Treasury........	$556,208 99

The debt of the State is as follows :

Sterling debt bearing interest at 5 per cent....	$4,482.222 24
Currency debt bearing 5 per cent............	186,684 88
Debt bearing 3 per cent....................	269,000 00
Debt bearing 6 per cent....................	6,371,700 23
Total................................	$11,259,607 35

As an offset to this debt the State holds stocks and bonds, upon which interest is promptly paid, amounting to $3,585,327.17, leaving as the net debt upon which interest has to be provided, $7,674,280.18. The following stocks and bonds held by the State, which heretofore have been classed as productive, are now put down

as unproductive, the payment of interest having ceased :

Stock in Bohemia Bridge Company...........	$15,576 99
Chesapeake and Delaware Canal Company.....	81,250 00
Bonds of Columbia and Port Deposit Railroad Company..............................	60,000 00
Susquehanna and Tidewater Canal Company mortgage................................	1,000,000 00
Total....................................	$1,157,126 99

The large amount of unproductive assets owned by the State, amounting in the aggregate to $25,000,000, would if sold be more than sufficient to provide for the entire indebtedness.

The valuation of the property of the State for 1879 was $466,470,995 ; adding to this the stock and assets of corporations, valued by the Tax Commissioner at $42,742,896, the total assessment for taxation amounts to $509,13,891. The increase of valuation over 1878 amounts to $37,358,577.

A number of disputed questions relating to the liability of property to taxation were carried by the State to the Court of Appeals, and some important decisions were obtained. The Court decided—1. That the stock, franchises, and property of the Annapolis and Elkridge Railroad Company are not exempted from taxation. 2. That the stock, property, franchises, and gross receipts represented or earned by the entire line of the Baltimore and Ohio Railroad Company between Baltimore and the Ohio River, and all buildings and works necessary for the operation of the railroad company within the meaning of its charter, are exempted from taxation ; but that buildings owned by the company which were used in the business of warehousing were liable to taxation ; that hotels belonging to the company used as places of summer resort, and interests acquired by the company in connecting roads, were liable to taxation ; that interests in steamships and other interests owned by the company, and all its interests in lines of railway built by it under franchises acquired subsequent to the date of its original charter, were subject to taxation. 3. Shares in building associations owned by residents of this State have been declared to be subject to valuation and assessment, although the whole capital of such association is invested in mortgages. 4. All bonds of other States, and of municipal and other corporations, owned by residents of Maryland, have been decided to be completely within the taxing powers of the State. 5. The bonds of all railroad and other corporations which are secured by a mortgage or mortgages upon property which is not wholly within the State, are, when owned by residents of Maryland, subject to valuation and assessment in the State. 6. All shares of stocks in corporations incorporated by other States are subject to valuation and assessment in the State, whether such shares of stock were exempt from taxation by the State creating such corporation or not.

The State has five warehouses for the reception and inspection of tobacco, which have become a losing investment, and their transfer to private individuals is proposed. The average amount of tobacco received and shipped for seven years, ending September, 1878, has been 52,758 hogsheads per annum, or an aggregate of 369,306 hogsheads. The money expended for labor alone to handle and inspect this tobacco has amounted during this time to $532,532, or an annual average of about $76,000.

The number of insane patients in the hospital at the end of the year was 329. The increase for the last two years has been 18 per cent. per annum. There has been a marked improvement in the condition of most of the almshouses and jails in the counties, which were so severely criticised two years ago.

The total number of committals to the House of Correction up to the end of the year was 493, of whom 310 were males and 188 females. The cost of maintaining the institution to the end of the fiscal year was $17,918. The male prisoners have been employed principally in grading the land around the building, and the females in making up the uniforms and other suitable clothing. A large number have also been engaged in sewing upon contract work, from which the sum of $791.60 has been realized. During the year the section of the law which authorizes justices of the peace to commit "habitually disorderly" persons to the House of Correction was called into question, and the claim was set up that it was unconstitutional. Several persons were brought out upon writs of *habeas corpus*, and some were released. A test case was finally made, and argued by the Attorney-General before the Chief Justice of the State, who gave a formal opinion sustaining the validity of the law.

In the State Penitentiary the highest number of prisoners during the year was 929, and the average number 813, of whom 693 were kept constantly employed on contract work. There were only 18 deaths during the year, about two per cent. of the inmates, and the loss of time from sickness was two and a half days in the year for each man. The total cost of the support of the penitentiary for the year ending December 1st was $85,541.40, and the receipts from all sources for the same time amounted to $98,543.25, showing a balance to the credit of the prison and due to the Treasury of $13,001.85. In addition to this, there has been earned by the prisoners for overwork the sum of $8,280.62, of which they will get the benefit as they serve out their time.

The whole force of the State militia consists of one full regiment in the city of Baltimore, and a number of companies in the various counties, aggregating 1,400 men. This organization is thoroughly armed, equipped, and disciplined. The cost of the force has been reduced to $15,000 a year.

The estimated production of the Clearfield coal region for 1879 was about 1,600,000 tons,

as against 1,270,262 tons for 1878, showing an increase of about 330,000 tons. The Cumberland region shipped 1,702,993 tons, an increase for 1879 of about 52,000 tons.

The latest published report of the condition of the public schools made by the Board of Education is for the year ending July 31, 1878. As compared with the school year 1877, the number of schools in the State shows an increase of 33, numbering in all 1,989, and the pupils an increase of 5,998, an aggregate of 156,274 for the year. The highest enrollment in any term was 127,455, or 7,169 more than in 1877, and the average attendance was 81,829, an increase of 6,103. The teachers numbered 3,071, an increase of 175. In the city of Baltimore the schools were open ten months in the year, in the counties 8·7, giving an average of 9·1 months for the whole State. The total expenditures for school purposes for city and counties during the fiscal year amounted to $1,593,259.66, an increase of $48,744.12 over 1877. The total expenses for county schools in 1878 were $915,283.64, showing a decrease from those of 1877 of $12,941.40. The Secretary of the Board states that of 69,303 children between the ages of six and eighteen years, as shown by the school census of the city of Baltimore for 1876, only 44·5 per cent. were in public schools, 12 per cent. in private schools, and 34·5 per cent. in neither. He admits that a compulsory law for school attendance has been tried elsewhere and failed, and then proceeds to suggest a different class of schools for the "neglected," based on the idea of pecuniary advantage to such as the incentive. He is firmly persuaded that the judicious expenditure of $15 a year *per capita* would bring a majority of the neglected children within the reach of instruction, and proposes the following plan for such schools:

As to hours: Two hours a day instead of six at first. As to attendance: Irregularity no cause for loss of privileges at first. As to dress: Rags no objection; even dirt tolerated at first. As to methods of teaching: Oral and objective as far as possible. As to studies: Hand-work made prominent; memory-work diminished; music and drawing in large doses. As to other occupations: Callisthenic exercises; gymnastics and military drill; also some form of industrial occupation leading finally to the acquisition of a trade. As to rewards: A pair of shoes to the shoeless when they are earned, and not sooner; no charity given, but payment made on a given scale for work done.

Technical education has many strong advocates in the State, but nothing has yet been devised to secure it. In Baltimore the colored voters held a series of meetings for the purpose of agitation on the subject of colored teachers for colored schools. One speaker said: "If the white teachers who have been teaching our children all this time have not been able to turn out one teacher among them all, what kind of teachers must they be? It is not reasonable to suppose that a white teacher will try as hard to push a colored child as one of his own race. They will not throw their hearts into it. The white people are not very deeply interested in seeing the negro race exalted. Then the parents get discouraged in sending their children to school. Colored people have as much right to say that colored people shall teach their children as white people have to say that colored people shall not teach their children. We have also as tax-payers a right to have some teachers." Dr. J. H. Brówn, a representative colored man of Baltimore, said:

The colored teachers have been a success everywhere, in Washington, St. Louis, Charleston, and other places. In Washington there are 92 colored teachers in the colored schools; here there are 80 white teachers over the colored children. In Washington, which is the best place for a comparison, Mr. George T. Cook, a colored man, is the principal of all the colored schools. On the school board of 19 members five are colored men, and legislate alike for white and colored schools. Mr. Cook has a salary of $2,250 per annum, and a secretary at $650 per annum. In Baltimore there are 13 schools, one of which is a grammar and the others are primary schools. The pupils on the rolls during the year were 5,433, with an average attendance of 3,066. In Washington there are 5,954 colored scholars, 4,803 in primary schools and 1,053 in grammar schools. The average attendance is 98·1 per cent.; in Baltimore it is but 79·98 per cent. Why is this? The only explanation is that there is no sympathy between the white teacher and the colored pupil. In Washington the average of promotions was 79·8 per cent. of the scholars, and still they say here the colored teacher is incompetent. The following is a statement of salaries paid to colored teachers: Six get $1,000 per annum each; one, $800; 8 get $900; 12 receive $550; 16 get $650; 2 get $750; 36 receive $700; one principal of a high school is paid $1,200; the principal of the normal school receives $1,350; one music teacher has a salary of $800, and a drawing teacher $1,000. These are all colored people, and all this money is paid out by the Washington authorities to what our School Commissioners are pleased to call "incompetent" teachers.

The insurance statistics of the State for the previous year show that there were 13 Maryland fire insurance companies located in Baltimore, their premiums in Maryland amounting to $439,577.29, and their losses paid in Maryland to $78,064.19; there is one Maryland marine insurance company in Baltimore, premiums $24,019.51, losses $10,267.43; 15 Maryland mutual insurance companies in the counties, premiums $122,755.34, losses $91,101.56; 101 fire and marine insurance companies of other States, premiums $848,839, losses $430,937.83; 19 foreign fire insurance companies, premiums $153,197.14, losses $55,588.86. Total premiums, $1,588,348.28; total losses, $666,959.87. There are two Maryland life insurance companies, premiums $104,048.80, payments to policyholders $84,733.71, and 26 life insurance companies of other States, premiums $1,082,473.65, payments $1,033,330.40; total premiums, $1,186,522.45; total losses, $1,118,064.11. The joint-stock insurance companies of Maryland are all located in the city of Baltimore. Their aggregate capital is $2,728,855; assets, $5,446,996.31; liabilities, $3,816,843.85; premiums received, $642,776.69; losses paid, $184,664.90; total amount at risk, $132,121,263.90; premiums received in Maryland, $463,596.70; losses

paid in Maryland, $88,331.02. The fifteen mutual fire insurance companies of Maryland have assets amounting to $3,820,219.66; liabilities, $166,668.22; income, $162,538.16; expenditures, $141,601.37; amount at risk, $49,755,821. There were 104 outside companies admitted to do business in the State. Their capital is $39,139,274; assets, 104,216,036.96; liabilities, $31,152,468.10; amount written in Maryland, $112,259,395.96. The assets of the foreign companies are $19,730,203.74; liabilities, $9,322,273.33; amount written in Maryland, $28,980,589.11.

Much has been said both in Delaware and Maryland relative to a ship-canal across the peninsula. At the session of the State Legislature in 1878 resolutions were adopted requesting Congress to provide for the necessary surveys of the several lines across the peninsula, in order to determine upon the best route for the canal. The sum of $5,000 was appropriated, which was increased to $15,000 in the allotment of Government surveys. The work was commenced in August ensuing, and the report of the result was made in February. It appears that the surveys embraced several routes. (See DELAWARE.) The advocates of the work say: "Such a canal would shorten the distance to Europe and the eastern seaboard States some two hundred miles, and avoid the dangerous coasting to the capes. Such a canal would put Chicago via Baltimore as near to Europe in point of time as by way of New York, with lesser charges for inland transportation; while the advantages such a cut-off would present to the Western and Southwestern States are almost incalculable. It is this consideration that gives to the project for a ship-canal across the Maryland and Delaware peninsula to the sea a national character, and entitles it, above all merely local river and harbor improvements, to Government consideration and assistance." A bill was also introduced in Congress which provides for an endorsement by the Government of the bonds of the ship-canal company, bearing five per cent. interest per annum, to the extent of four millions of dollars; one million to be endorsed when it has been officially certified that one fourth of the excavation and dredging has been completed, and the remaining three millions to be endorsed from time to time in like manner. It is further provided that, in consideration of such endorsement, the United States shall have the right of navigation through the canal free of tolls for all time for all vessels in the United States service, and also be secured by a mortgage on all the rights and property of the company—ten per cent. or $400,000 of the amount of bonds endorsed being retained by the Secretary of the Treasury "for the formation of a sinking fund for the redemption of the principal and interest of said bonds."

The business of the port of Baltimore for the fiscal year from July 1, 1878, to July 1, 1879, as compared with the preceding year, was as follows:

VESSELS.	1878.	1879.
ENTRANCES.		
Sea-going vessels	1,408	1,773
Coastwise "	1,437	1,468
Total	2,845	3,241
CLEARANCES.		
Sea-going vessels	1,475	1,729
Coastwise "	1,794	1,871
Total	3,269	3,600

This shows a gain in 1879 of 396 entrances and 331 clearances; total, 727. The tonnage dues collected in 1878 were $107,450.80, and in 1879, $130,153.30; increase, $22,702.50. Of the arrivals in the foreign trade in 1879, 330 were American vessels, tonnage 108,102, and 1,448 foreign vessels, tonnage 1,234,184, against 329 American, tonnage 119,284, and 1,146 foreign, tonnage 885,905, for 1878. Of the clearances for foreign countries in 1879, 320 were American, tonnage 109,814, and 1,409 foreign, tonnage 1,227,321, as against 329 American and 1,146 foreign for 1878. The value of imports for the same period was: 1877-'78, $16,-938,628; 1878-'79, $14,147,155. Value of exports for 1877-'78, $45,633,501; 1878-'79, $57,563,905. The statement of custom-house receipts from all sources is as follows:

YEARS.	Duties.	Currency.	Fees.
1877-'78	$2,848,350 13	$165,459 26	$21,318 89
1878-'79	1,899,053 04	186,961 18	24,689 77

The decline in the amount of the duties collected in 1879 is thus explained by the Collector of the Port:

The decrease is due to the non-importation of sugar, the decline in the revenue from which, as compared with last year, was $1,078,253. If our imports of sugar had been maintained, the revenue collected at the port would show a gain of $128,980.91 over last year. The destruction of the sugar business of Baltimore, which has been so complete as to cause the suspension of four large sugar refineries and two molasses refineries, is due to the prosecutions of Baltimore importers by the Treasury Department. This has lost us the Demerara and Cuba raw-sugar trade, now transferred to Boston, New York, and Philadelphia, while the revenue of the Government has not been increased by it at all. It has increased the apparent cost of collecting revenue at this port, and has thrown many laborers out of work, the actual cost being reduced $5,272.92 as compared with 1878. The general trade of the port, aside from sugar, shows a sensible improvement. There was a large increase in transportation in bond and in transit. The gains on salt, soda ash, and tin-plate amounted to $168,779. The increase in warehouse and exportation entries during 1879 over 1878 was $283,619.27, an increase of 7·88 per cent. The importation of coffee for the year 1879 comprised 535,117 bags, against 413,585 bags in 1878, an increase of nearly 30 per cent.

An attempt to import beet-sugar from Europe was made at Baltimore, but it was found to be without profit. Several samples were procured from Germany with the hope of making

a market for it which would compete with importations from the West Indies and other places. The merchant found that the cost in Germany would be 4⅝ cents a pound, and hoped to be able to have the customs duty levied on that basis of valuation. Upon taking the samples to the appraisers, however, they rated it at 6¼ cents a pound, an advance of 2¼ cents a pound on the German valuation. The brokerage, freight, insurance, commission for buying, loss in weight, and contingencies, it was calculated, would still further increase the price, until the lowest figure at which it could be landed in Baltimore would be 7·65 cents a pound, which was so high as to preclude all possibility of making any profit by the transaction.

The operations by the United States Government and by the State for the hatching of shad at Spesutia Island, at the mouth of the Susquehanna, and near Havre de Grace, were very successful during the fore part of the year. Since the commencement of the works there in 1871, over 48,000,000 shad-eggs have been hatched, and the fish distributed in rivers in different parts of the country. Some have been sent as far as California, and many of the tributaries of the Mississippi have been stocked, also the rivers of some of the Eastern States. The labor incident to the hatching is done on a scow, which is anchored in the river in the vicinity of the fishermen who are drawing their nets. The works are also provided with a steam-launch and several small boats. These boats are used every night in gathering the supply of eggs from the fishermen. The eggs must be taken from the fish when she is just about to spawn, and it is a comparatively small portion of those which are caught that are in exactly the right condition. A fisherman, when he discovers a female shad from which the eggs may be taken, signals one of the small boats from the scow, and the man therein takes the fish, presses the eggs from her, deposits them in a suitable vessel, takes the milt from a male shad, which he places on the eggs, and returns both fish to the fisherman. In this way the night is spent, and immense numbers of eggs are procured, a female shad ordinarily yielding from 20,000 to 30,000 eggs. An average night's work secures from 350,000 to 400,000 eggs. The fisherman who procures the female shad receives in return a ticket or order which is good for fifty cents, and which is redeemed at the end of the season by the Government. The eggs, having been procured, are at once taken to the scow and placed in tin cans, which are about three feet high and a foot and a half in diameter. The bottom of the can is covered with a fine gauze netting, through which it is impossible for the smallest fish to escape. The cans are hung on wooden arms over the side of the scow, and the arms kept constantly moving up and down by steam, thus lowering the cans in the water and hoisting them part way out again. The object of this is to keep the eggs constantly in a current of fresh pure water, and to prevent them from forming in a solid mass, which would destroy the chances of hatching them out. In from four to six days the little fish appear; they are lively, and swim around their can as if desirous to get out into the large body of water. In ten days or two weeks they are large enough to be shipped to distant points or to be cast back into the river.

One of the most important works·done by the State Fish Commission consisted in the investigations conducted in the lower (or Chesapeake) bay, which resulted in the initiation of the artificial cultivation of the oyster. The statement was made early in June that Professor Brooks of the Johns Hopkins University had succeeded in artificially impregnating the eggs of the oyster; that the process of segmentation occupied four hours, and in six hours free-swimming ciliated embryos were produced. The process was explained by Professor Brooks to a visitor to his residence, who thus describes it:

Half a dozen on the half shell served on a plate, a few watch-crystals, a small glass jar, a little water, and the microscope constitute the laboratory. The oysters had been taken fresh from their beds, and opened carefully. They will live in this way for a day or two if kept in a cool place, and all the while the heart may be seen to pulsate in its little cleft next to the muscle. Close to this beating heart lay what is commonly called the "fat of the oyster," but which is really the reproductive organs. These are wrapped all around the stomach, liver, and digestive organs, the latter being the "black" or "dark part of the oyster." The flaps which extend from the opening point of the shells around the whole of one side of the oyster are his gills, through which he breathes and separates his food. His mouth is at the butt end of the shells, where the hinge joins them.

The oyster's food is microscopic organisms—plants and animals. The gills take in these with water when the shells are opened, making the sucking noise so familiar when the oyster is "feeding." The water is sifted through the gills, leaving the microscopic food on the interior surface. The food is carried by a fringe of cilia, perpetually in motion, down and between two mustachios into the mouth at the opposite end of the mollusk. These hairs or cilia on the edge of the gills vibrate continuously, and the motion which they make is like rowing. A very pretty test showing the passage of substances along the gills has been made with carmine on the fresh-water mussel under water.

Experienced oyster-shuckers at the raw box and oystermen nearly all claim to be able to distinguish the sex of the oyster by simple inspection, but there is no difference apparent to sight. Male and female oysters on the half shell can not be told apart, and indeed one in fifty is believed to be hermaphrodite. It is asserted that oysters are females when young and males when they become older and larger. Snails are known to be of different sexes at different times. But in regard to oysters the fact of sex has not been established with certainty, nor is it of importance.

To produce free-swimming ciliated embryos by artificial process, the operator pinched away with tweezers a particle of the fatty or generative part of the oyster, not knowing in advance whether it was male or female. The fragment was put into a few drops of water in a watch-crystal and stirred until the eggs were well shaken out. Useless tissue was then thrown away, leaving the water milky from the number of eggs. The microscope determined the sex.

In the present experiment the first oyster proved to be of the masculine gender. His heart was regularly beating when the generative part was taken from him. Under the microscope the male cells appeared to be the very finest dots, perpetually in active motion. Myriads of them appeared in a single drop of water, each one being sufficient for impregnation, properly lodged. On the other hand, the female eggs are 100,-000 times larger than the male cells, and are discernible by the naked eye. Female eggs remain perfectly passive when separated. Under the microscope they look to be of the size of a pea, while the male cells are no larger than a grain of the finest kind of writing-sand, if indeed they are so large.

Having been washed out into separate watch-crystals and viewed under the microscope, the eggs are mixed with the male cells. Then viewed under magnifying power, what is going on is revealed. It is a perpetual and wonderful succession of changes, every stage of which the patient scientist has noted and drawn at intervals varying from a minute to fifteen minutes. By the aid of these drawings the changes under the microscope may be anticipated, and the succession is invariably as laid down and noted by the discoverer. The male cells vigorously attack themselves to the egg in eager crowds, but one only of the many is supposed to impregnate. The first change apparent is the disappearance of the germinating vesicle, which is the round transparent center of the egg. This is accomplished in a very few minutes. The egg then becomes perfectly spherical, and remains quiet for one or two hours, when a kneading process becomes apparent. A polar globule appears on the surface of the egg, and this is the beginning of segmentation. By degrees and by regular stages, observed over and over again in the same succession, the egg becomes divided into smaller and smaller sphericles. This process of division occupies two hours, and at the end of it a small, transparent, swimming embryo is formed, which is the oyster in its infantile state. The whole process occupies from four to six hours, according to the temperature. The present experiment was brought to a successful development in four hours. Professor Brooks in his previous experiments raised oysters till they had the cilia which propel the microscopic oys o, but they died without further revelation of the mystery of life. Cilia have life of their own, independent of the animal, and a nervous organization. Word was sent to me four days after the beginning of the last experiment that the embryos were still alive and doing well. Professor Brooks has had the satisfaction of developing them until he could clearly trace their digestive organs, and is inspired with the hope that continued watchfulness will enable him soon to see the infants begin to take on their armor of shells.

As in many other cities and States, so in Baltimore there was an extensive effort made to enforce a Sunday law. So stringent was its application that excursion parties by steamboat and railroad were stopped, including in one instance an excursion of religious people destined to a camp-meeting. This led to the formation of a Liberal League by those opposed to the law. Their views were expressed in the following resolutions:

Whereas, The Constitution of the United States, from beginning to end, in spirit and in letter, is framed in accordance with the principle of the total separation of church and state, and the treaty with Tripoli, signed by George Washington, as a part of the supreme law of the land, declares emphatically that "the Government of the United States is not in any sense founded on the Christian religion";

And whereas, Notwithstanding these facts, the administration of the national Government and the administrations and constitutions of the several State governments maintain numerous practical connections of the state with the church, thereby violating the spirit of the United States Constitution and the glorious traditions which dedicate this country exclusively to the natural rights of man ;

And whereas, The welfare and peace of the republic, the equal religious rights of its citizens, and the most precious interests of civilization, alike require that all the political and educational institutions of the nation which are supported by taxation should be more faithfully conformed to the spirit of its fundamental law ; therefore,

Be it resolved, That, as a means to the accomplishment of this object, we urge the adoption of such a " religious freedom amendment " of the United States Constitution as shall effect the complete secularization of the Government in all its departments and institutions, State and national, and shall secure to every American citizen the full enjoyment of his opinions on the subject of religion, without molestation, disability, or deprivation of any civil or political right.

Resolved, That we advocate the equitable taxation of church property ; the total discontinuance of religious instruction and worship in the public schools ; the repeal of all laws enforcing the observance of Sunday as the Sabbath ; the cessation of all appropriations of public funds for religious institutions or purposes of any kind ; the abolition of state-paid chaplaincies ; the non-appointment of religious fasts, festivals, and holidays by public authority ; and whatever other measures or principles may be necessary to the total separation of church and state.

Resolved, That we promote by all peaceable and orderly means active agitation and propagandism of the great principles of religious liberty and equal rights, and in all other proper and practical ways promote the final emancipation of the state from the control of the church, and to foster the development of that natural intelligence and morality which constitute the necessary and all-sufficient basis of secular government.

One of the Baltimore City Judges, in his charge to the grand jury, argued in favor of the law as a police measure. He is thus reported :

While disavowing all puritanical notions or prejudices in regard to the manner in which the Christian day of rest should be observed, the Judge bore testimony as a magistrate to the value and necessity of a Sunday law restricting and regulating the sale of liquor as a measure of police, and as a security for the preservation of public order and tranquillity on a day of idleness and compulsory abstention from work. Judge Pinkney cited the docket of his Court as a witness in this respect to the beneficial results of the Sunday law. That the law itself was adopted and is maintained absolutely as a measure of police, and not upon merely temperance or moral grounds, the Judge is historically correct in saying.

The occasion of these remarks was supposed to have been furnished by the multiplication of incorporated societies or clubs for avowedly literary, benevolent, or " social " purposes, but with the real purpose, as supposed, of evading the stringent provisions of the Sunday law. In the case of two or three of the well-known social clubs of Baltimore, one of the Judges (Gilmor), when presiding in the Criminal Court, had decided that the law prohibiting the selling or giving away, or otherwise disposing of certain commodities on Sunday, wines and liquors included, had no application. The clubs in question kept no bar in the ordinary sense of the word, did not keep or sell wines, liquors, etc., for profit, and the use of such articles by members or privileged guests was no more inhibited by the law than the use of the same

articles by the guests or boarders of a hotel or members of a private family. The incorporated institutions in question were shown by the evidence at the trial to be in the nature of co-operative housekeeping establishments, and the use and consumption of liquors, etc., merely incidental to the main object of their formation, and in no sense, therefore, to be regarded as an evasion, practical or designed, of the Sunday law.

The question of the power of justices of the peace to commit to jail in default of payment of fine and costs, and in default of security to keep the peace, was thus decided in the Court of Common Pleas :

Since the establishment of the Board of Police the preservation of the public peace and order has been committed to that body, and arrests for the violation of peace and order are now made by the police force under its control, and not by constables. There is no law making it an offense to be drunk in the presence of an officer of the police force, and therefore it is not an offense for the prisoner in this case to be drunk in the presence of the officer who arrested her and who made the charge. It has been suggested that if a man is found drunk on the street and is arrested and brought before a justice, this is drunkenness " in the presence of a justice," which authorizes him to impose a fine. Such a construction of the law would, I think, be unwarrantable, because the accused would be taken against his will into the presence of the justice, and the law could not have been intended to punish him for a compulsory appearance. The justice, therefore, had no right on either ground to impose a fine upon the petitioner, and her imprisonment for the non-payment of the fine and costs is illegal.

The views of the Court on the question whether drunkenness on the public streets is an offense at common law were thus stated :

I now proceed to consider the question whether drunkenness on the public streets is an offense at common law. It is conceded that private drunkenness is an offense against morality, of which the common law takes no cognizance. Open drunkenness on the public streets of towns and cities has unhappily been always a thing of frequent occurrence in England and in this country, and, if it be a criminal offense, it is hardly possible to believe that it would not have been so decided in numerous cases. Few authorities are cited in support of the doctrine. The strongest case is that of Smith *vs.* the State, decided in Tennessee, 1 Humph., 396 ; and yet the Court in that case, while it admitted that open drunkenness was a criminal offense, held that the charge that an individual was " unlawfully, openly, publicly, and notoriously drunk," was an insufficient description of the offense, so as to put the party on his defense and satisfy him of the facts to be proved ; and the Court advised that the charge should always be that the accused was " openly and notoriously drunk upon the day stated, and upon divers other days before that time." In the case in North Carolina of the State *vs.* Waller, 3 Murphy, 229, also relied on by the State, the Court held that private drunkenness is no offense ; that it becomes so by being open and exposed to public view so as to become a nuisance ; that it must be so charged, and that the jury must so find it before the Court can render judgment. The charge in that case was that the defendant was " a common, gross, and notorious drunkard, and that he on divers days and times got grossly drunk." No case has been cited, and I suppose none can be found, where a party has been found guilty at common law on a charge of drunkenness upon a single occasion, and I am satisfied that such a conviction could not be sustained in Maryland. The doctrine of the common law on the subject of drunkenness and disorder is, I think, this: A man who is drunk may walk the streets without being arrested, provided he does so in an orderly manner. If when he is drunk he commits a breach of the peace, or what is called a common nuisance—that is, an offense against the public order and common regimen of the State—he may be punished, not for being drunk, but for breaking the peace or committing the nuisance; but he can not be punished, nor can he be held to bail to answer for the offense, unless the breach of the peace or act of nuisance of which he is accused is described with some particularity. If, for instance, he breaks the peace by assaulting A, he should be charged with so doing; or if he commits a common nuisance by using obscene language publicly, he should be charged with that particular act. Before he can be convicted he may demand that an indictment by the grand jury be had, and that he be tried before a petit Jury.

A young woman, by name Lillie Duer, committed the most extraordinary and incomprehensible act of shooting her young female friend. Both were cultivated and intelligent, and held very respectable positions. She was indicted, tried, and convicted of manslaughter. In view of the prisoner's previous good character and the recommendation of the jury to mercy, the Court remitted imprisonment, and simply sentenced her to pay the maximum fine prescribed by law, namely, $500.

The Democratic party assembled in Convention at Baltimore on August 7th. Herman Stump was chosen President. The following nominations were made: For Governor, William T. Hamilton; for Comptroller, Thomas J. Keating; for Clerk of the Court of Appeals, Spencer C. Jones; for Attorney-General, Charles J. M. Gwinn. The following resolutions were adopted:

The Democratic Conservative party of Maryland, in State Convention assembled, resolves as follows:

1. Our acknowledgments are due to the Governor and other executive officers of this State for the firmness, ability, and discretion with which they have discharged the duties of their respective offices.

2. It will be the duty of the next General Assembly to lighten the burden of taxation in this State by abolishing all offices not necessary for the public service; by reducing all salaries and fees subject to its control to the limit of the compensation of persons engaged in similar employment in private life; by compelling the practice of economy in every detail of State, county, and municipal expenditures; and by enforcing the observance of the constitutional rule that every person in the State, or person holding property therein, ought to contribute his proportion of public taxes for the support of the government, according to his actual worth in real or personal property.

3. Public offices were not created for the benefit of individuals nor for the purpose of rewarding political services, but were intended solely for the public advantage. The perversion of their use to any other purpose is injurious to good morals and to good government.

4. The General Assembly ought, at its next session, to make such further reforms in our civil and criminal codes as are needed for the more speedy and economical administration of justice, so that every man in this State may be enabled to obtain quick and sufficient remedy for any injury done to him in his person or property, and that all offenses against the laws may be promptly and speedily prosecuted and punished, and public order be rigidly maintained.

5. The maintenance of free institutions in this State and the essential interests of its people require that all

elections should be free and pure. The General Assembly ought at its next session to provide further security for fairness in such elections by providing for a correct and accurate registration of the names of all persons entitled to vote in this State, to be made by competent officers at certain fixed successive periods of time, and by directing the first of said new registrations to be made at the earliest practicable period.

6. The obligations and credit of the United States and of the State of Maryland ought to be sacredly maintained. Neither the Federal nor the State debt ought to be increased, but provision ought to be made, as soon as practicable, for funding the debts of each at a lower rate of interest and for the gradual payment of such debts. While they continue to exist, every proper means of legislation should be adopted which may be necessary to give effect to these public obligations and to confirm confidence in their complete security.

7. When the Democratic Conservative party regained power in the Congress of the United States it enforced an economical administration of public affairs, and made the resumption of specie payments a possible event. It will be its duty to maintain the advantage thus gained by firmly establishing the credit of the country upon the basis of coin exchangeable in all the markets of the world.

8. The Democratic Conservative party of the country was deprived by fraud of all the fruits of victory in the Presidential contest of 1876. The reprobation of history will fall upon those who committed this crime against a whole people. It is the duty of that people, acting in their respective States, to protect themselves and their posterity against the recurrence of the offense, by enacting laws which will afford no future opportunity for such fraudulent practices.

9. The Democratic Conservative party of this State, faithful to the supremacy of the Constitution of the United States, rests its construction of that instrument upon the express words of the tenth amendment, adopted in 1791. The powers not delegated to the United States by the Constitution nor prohibited by it to the States are reserved to the States respectively, or to the people.

10. The Republican party in its conduct of national affairs has violated this fundamental article. It has provided by law for Federal interference in State elections. It has assumed the right to confer upon Federal courts, supervisors, marshals, and special deputy marshals the unconstitutional power of enforcing State laws. It has deliberately sanctioned the unconstitutional use of the troops of the United States at the polls in the several States. These are measures of centralization which show a determined purpose to change the organic character of the government bequeathed to us by our fathers, and such measures ought to be resisted by every means within our power.

11. We return our hearty thanks to the members of the Democratic Conservative party in Congress for their endeavors to secure impartial trials by jury in the Federal courts by the abolition of test-oaths, and for the manly steadfastness with which they have resisted Republican encroachments upon the limitations imposed by the Constitution of the United States.

12. The Democratic Conservative party of Maryland, having no other purpose to fulfill except to secure the good government of this State and to aid in the reform of the administration of Federal affairs, expects all citizens of this State who share its opinions to unite cordially in the attainment of these great objects. We therefore ask for the candidates of that party an undivided support of all its members, and we commend them to the approval of all other good citizens of this State.

A Tax-payers' Convention assembled at Baltimore on August 12th. Nine of the largest tax-paying counties were represented. William M. Merrick was chosen President of the Convention. He explained that the Convention was without partisan purpose, and did not design to favor a new party nor to combine for or against either of those existing. Their object was to redress their grievances and secure relief from the burdens of taxation. Both parties were to understand, however, that, whatever politicians might do, the people would not fear to fall out of line whenever they fail of strict fidelity to duty, and that they could not command their allegiance with empty promises nor retain it with broken pledges. Local or county taxation is enormous and burdensome, but local taxes were in their control, and it was their right to say how they should be appropriated. The greatest burdens were at their own doors, but the remedy, which was in their hands, was to give more attention to self-government, and put aside the delusion that they had done their whole duty to society by taking part in national and State politics. They must put good men into the local offices. "If we would build up our State, we shall best do it by building up the counties. Your county commissioner, like the judge, should know no man in administering the finances in which men of all parties have an equal interest and equal rights. All local affairs should be separated, as far as possible, from State and national politics."

The following resolutions were adopted:

Resolved—1. That local self-government being the germinal principle out of which free institutions of the Anglo-Saxon type have grown, its spirit should be fostered, and laws should be so framed as to vest as much as possible of administrative duty in the counties, and whenever practicable in the yet smaller divisions in the body politic.

2. That it is the duty of all good citizens to excite a generous pride in our respective counties, and to use all means to elevate the standard of our local offices, so that no man, however exalted, shall feel it beneath his dignity to share in the obligations of watching over and taking counsel with his fellow citizens about the public affairs of his county.

3. All unnecessary and superfluous offices should be abolished, and the salaries and fees of others be reduced and restricted by law. In view of the present high purchasing power of money, this may be effected without injustice or hardship to officials and with great advantage to the State.

4. The next Legislature of Maryland should, in deference to that spirit of economy which so thoroughly pervades the popular mind and which the times so urgently demand, institute such legislation as will secure necessary reforms, and reduce the expenditures of the public money to such a degree that the outlay shall be commensurate with the services rendered therefor.

5. That, so far as the reform and retrenchment of purely local expenditures in the respective counties is concerned, this Convention remits them to the judgment of the citizens of the several counties, believing that they can be best considered and regulated, and as we think very materially reduced, in every county in the State. In many counties we are satisfied that more than ten per cent. of the annual expenses can be saved if more efficient and impartial officers are selected.

6. That the Legislature has it in its power to save a large sum of money every year from the current revenue of the State by the passage of laws to enforce a more rigid compliance with the requirements of section 1, Article XV., of the Constitution of Maryland, relating to clerks of courts, registers of wills, and all other officers whose pay or compensation is derived from fees or moneys coming into their hands for the

discharge of their official duties, or in any way growing out of or connected with their offices; and also a more rigid observance of the provisions of sections 35 and 45, Article III., of the Constitution, and that the Legislature be called upon to repeal chapter 151, acts of 1865.

7. That the laws relating to the inspection of tobacco should be repealed, to relieve the producers and the State of what has become a burden to the producers and a reproach to the State.

8. That the public-school laws of Maryland are capable of great improvement, and should be amended.

9. That proper legislation should be instituted to reduce the expenses of the courts throughout the State, which have increased in the last few years to such large proportions as to add materially to a burdensome taxation.

10. That provision ought to be made by law for the speedy trial of petty offenders before justices of the peace, with the right of appeal to the Circuit Court.

11. That a committee of one from each county here represented (the President of the Convention to be the chairman) be appointed by the Chair to prepare and present to the Legislature a statement of such offices as ought to be abolished, of such expenditures as ought to be curtailed, of such salaries as ought to be reduced, and of such amendments by law as will insure a greater vigilance in those who have the supervision of public expenditures.

A resolution relating to temperance and the election of favorable candidates to the State Legislature was also adopted.

A Convention of Nationals assembled in Baltimore on September 10th. John Henley was chosen permanent President. In an address to the Convention the chairman of the National Executive Committee said: "The same question is before the people now as existed between the American colonies and their mother country. It is, Shall the government be for the few or for the people? Shall it be a government for a favored class, or for the rich and poor alike? The money power and the would-be aristocracy is making the same fight now it made under Alexander Hamilton, and when Andrew Jackson crushed it. It was defeated then, and will be now. The purchase and control of old party leaders and the manipulation of conventions by the money power created the necessity for the new party."

A preamble and resolutions were adopted, as follows:

The Greenback-Labor party of the State of Maryland, in Convention assembled, in the city of Baltimore, September 10, 1879, reiterating the grand principles of financial reform heretofore promulgated by us to the people of this State, and for the advancement of such other reforms as experience is daily proving and demonstrating the vital necessity of in all industrial pursuits, based upon such remedies as have been persistently, uniformly, heedlessly, and grossly neglected by the dominant political parties in this State and nation, namely, the so-called Democratic and Republican parties, does, in the interest of our long-suffering and law-abiding citizens, again solemnly declare, as absolutely essential to the peace, safety, and welfare of society, that the following principles should be immediately adopted and enforced as national measures:

1. The greenback dollar must be a legal tender for the payment of all debts, public as well as private, and by the Government solely issued, and protected and received as absolute money.

2. That the national Government shall issue no more interest-bearing bonds or obligations, and that

all outstanding bonds shall be redeemed in the full legal-tender money of the United States.

3. That all present issues of national-bank notes be withdrawn, and all future issues of such currency be abolished, the absolute money of the Government being substituted therefor.

4. There should be a graduated income-tax.

5. That postmasters be elected by the people.

6. That Congress provide for the establishment of a labor bureau of statistics in every State.

7. That no more pub ic lands shall be disposed of except to actual settlers.l

8. That there should be land limitation, and lands granted to corporations that have not fulfilled their contracts shall revert to the Government.

9. That eight hours shall constitute a legal day's work.

10. That no species of property, whether in stocks, bonds, or otherwise, shall be exempt from taxation.

11. That the Government should faithfully perform its pledges made to the Union soldiers at time of enlistment, especially that they receive 160 acres of land in fee-simple on being discharged, and an equitable payment per month of each soldier, according to the value of the legal-tender dollar at the time of service.

12. That no man shall be eligible to the office of President of the United States for two consecutive terms.

As State measures, we hold: 1. That such laws should be enacted by the Legislature as will secure proper ventilation and other necessary sanitary regulations of all inclosures wherein manual labor is performed.

2. That the employing of children under twelve years of age in any manufactory where manual labor is required be prohibited.

3. That prison convict labor shall never come in competition with free labor by the contract system under any means.

4. That all unnecessary offices be abolished.

5. That the Legislature shall pass a law giving to mortgagors of real estate the right of redemption five years after sale.

6. That debts due for labor performed shall be entitled to equally as stringent remedy for enforcement as any remedy tolerated by. the State for the enforcement of any other debt.

7. That distress for rent be abolished.

8. That malfeasance in office shall be classed with crimes amounting to felony and punished as such.

9. That any person who offers to buy or does purchase a vote, or any person who shall intimidate a voter, shall be disfranchised.

10. That the laborer is worthy of his hire; therefore equal payment should be made for like labor performed whether by males or females.

11. In no case shall the homestead of a family to the value of $2,000 ever be liable to sale for debt.

12. We demand a new registration law.

13. We demand that such election laws be enacted as will give to each and every contesting party one judge and one clerk at each and every voting precinct, and said judges and clerks shall be acceptable to the candidates in whose interest they are appointed.

Howard Meeks was nominated for Governor, and further nominations were left to the judgment of the Executive Committee.

The Republican State Convention assembled in Baltimore on September 12th. Milton G. Urner was chosen permanent President. The following nominations were made: For Governor, James A. Garey; for Comptroller, Samuel Mallalieu; for Attorney-General, Frank M. Darby; for Clerk of Court of Appeals, J. T. McCulloch. The following resolutions were adopted:

The Republicans of Maryland, in State Convention assembled, resolve as follows:

1. The Republic of the United States is a nation and not a league. Allegiance of the citizen is due primarily to the nation, which within its constitutional sphere is supreme, and is clothed with full power to guard its own life, protect its own citizens, regulate its own elections, and execute its own laws. The opposite doctrine of State sovereignty is the baleful mother of nullification, secession, and anarchy. Republicanism stands for national supremacy in national affairs, and State's rights in State concerns. Democracy stands for State sovereignty, with its twin heresy that the Union is a mere confederacy of States.

2. To refuse necessary supplies for the Government with the design of compelling the unwilling consent of a coördinate and independent branch to odious measures, is revolution; to refuse appropriations for the execution of existing and binding law is nullification. We arraign the Democratic Representatives in Congress as guilty both of revolutionary attempts and nullifying schemes, and we reprobate their action as calculated to subvert the Constitution and to strike at the existence of the Government itself.

3. The safety of the republic demands free and pure elections, but the Democratic party in this State and throughout the country has persistently and systematically sought to overthrow all safeguards of free suffrage. For years past in this State Democratic ruffians and repeaters have, by violence and fraud, reversed the verdict of the people expressed at the polls; juries have been packed in the interests of these criminals; and when, in rare instances, convictions have been secured, the Executive has interposed to shield them from the punishment which was richly deserved, and the infliction of which was demanded by the highest public interests. When Democratic administration of our State laws had thus made a mockery of justice, we invoked the national election laws for the protection of the voter at national elections, and immediately the whole Democratic party, through its Representatives in Congress, engaged in a determined effort to break down those laws by unconstitutional and revolutionary means. And this attempt was only prevented by. the opposition of the Republican Representatives and Senators in Congress, and the vetoes of President Hayes, for which they deserve and receive our hearty approval. We pledge ourselves to spare no effort to prevent the repeal of the national election laws, and to secure from our next Legislature the best system of laws for popular elections that can be suggested or devised.

4. The people of this State can never condone the fraud that was perpetrated by the Democratic party in the election of 1875; and this being the first occasion which they have had to express their sentiments, it is now their duty, and we call upon all good citizens, to rebuke and condemn that fraud at the coming elections.

5. The Republican party neither justifies nor tolerates military interference with elections. It seeks only to protect the ballot-box from the interference of force and fraud. It repels the false charges and denounces the false pretenses of conspirators, who, while professing to favor free elections everywhere, sustain mob-law in the South; while inveighing against troops at the polls to protect citizens, refuse to prohibit armed clubs from surrounding the ballot-box to intimidate them; and, while affecting that the soldiers' bayonets will overawe free electors, remain silent when the assassin's bullet seals the fate of political independence.

6. We call upon the people to remember that the Democratic party forced the extra session of Congress without warrant or excuse; that it prosecuted its partisan purposes by revolutionary methods; that it persistently obstructed resumption, and still constantly presses disturbing measures.

7. That we heartily approve the financial achievements of the present national Administration. The successful resumption of specie payments, despite Democratic prediction and hostility, is the crowning achieve-

ment of the Republican financial policy. Followed by the returning national prosperity, improved credit, a refunded debt, and reduced interest, it adds another to the triumphs which prove that the Republican party is equal to the highest demands. Our whole currency should be kept at par with the monetary standard of the commercial world, and any attempt to debase the standard, to depreciate the paper, or deteriorate the coin, should be firmly resisted.

8. All unnecessary and superfluous offices should be abolished, and the salaries and fees of others be reduced and restricted by law. In view of the present high purchasing power of money, this may be effected without injustice or hardship to officials, and with great advantage to the State.

9. The next Legislature of Maryland should, in deference to that spirit of economy which so thoroughly pervades the popular mind, and which the times so urgently demand, institute such legislation as will secure necessary reforms, and reduce the expenditures of the public money to such a degree that the outlay shall be commensurable with the services rendered.

10. That the Legislature has it in its power to save a large sum of money every year by the passage of laws to enforce a more rigid compliance with the requirements of section 1, Article XV., of the Constitution of Maryland, relating to clerks of courts, registers of wills, and all other officials whose pay or compensation is derived from fees or moneys coming into their hands from the discharge of their official duties, or in any way growing out of or connected with their offices, and to require a rigid compliance with the provisions of the Constitution and laws of the State by the payment of all excess of their receipts into the Treasury of the State.

11. The laws relating to the inspection of tobacco should be repealed, to relieve the producers and the State of what has become a burden to the producers and a reproach to the State.

12. The public-school and jury laws of Maryland are capable of great improvement, and should be amended. All political considerations and influence ought to be rigidly excluded.

13. Proper legislation should be instituted to reduce the expenses of the courts throughout the State, which have increased in the last few years to such large proportions as to add materially to a burdensome taxation.

14. That we demand that Democratic juggling with the registration of voters shall cease, and that the next Legislature of this State shall in good faith pass such laws as will secure an honest registry, a free vote, and a fair count.

A census of the voters in the city of Baltimore was taken by the police in August, with the following result: White, 61,133; colored, 10,368; total, 71,501; total in 1877, 66,525.

The Independent Democrats of the city organized and held a convention, which they said " was called into existence by the urgent demand of the people for the redress of grievances consequent upon the corruption of party politics and the frauds practiced in the nomination and election of unworthy officials." It recognized "the great necessity of purification and reform in the State and city government, and of lessening the heavy burden of taxation which oppressed every branch of industry and all classes of the community."

A convention of dissatisfied Republicans was also held to protest against the management of the party in the city.

The election was held on November 4th, and resulted as follows: For Governor—Hamilton, Democrat, 90,771; Garey, Republican, 68,609.

The Legislature was divided as follows: Senate—Democrats, 19; Republicans, 5; Independents, 2; total, 26. House—Democrats, 63; Republicans, 21; total, 84.

MASSACHUSETTS. The State Legislature assembled on January 1st, and adjourned on April 30th. It had been in session 120 days, a period equal to that of the session of 1849 and also of 1862, but shorter than any other since the latter date except that of 1876, which continued 115 days. There were 306 bills and 53 resolutions passed, all of which were approved by the Governor, except one which he allowed to become a law without his signature and one which he vetoed.

One of the subjects first considered by the Legislature was that of retrenchment. A joint committee was appointed which investigated every department of the government, and the reduction of salaries and fees which it recommended and which were adopted amounted to $269,632.

An act was passed to establish a Board of Health, Charity, and Lunacy, to consist of nine persons, who should serve without compensation, and have charge of all matters previously under the care of the Board of Health and State charities, and also perform the duties required in the management of the hospitals for the insane and prescribed in the laws relating to the commitment of the insane. (See "Annual Cyclopædia" for 1878—MASSACHUSETTS.) This act abolished the State Board of Health, the Board of State Charities, the Board of Trustees of the State Reform School and the State Industrial School, the Advisory Board of Women, the Inspectors of the State Almshouse and those of the State Primary School, the Trustees of the State Reform School, and the Visiting Agency. The duties thus imposed on the new organization are immense. One branch of the duties of the Visiting Agency alone was during the last three years the visitation and care of more than 6,000 children, and the placing of them in private families. So far as known, in after life about 70 per cent. of offenders of all classes do well, and nearly 95 per cent. of the dependent children. The statistics show that from July 17, 1869, to October 1, 1878, there were before the courts 17,136 complaints against juvenile offenders, of which the Agency had notice, the hearings of which it attended, and of which it has records. The hearings on the complaints resulted in the commitment of 205 to the State Nautical School, 774 to the Board of State Charities, 1,088 to the Reform School, 290 to the Industrial School, 660 to the local institutions of Boston, 415 to local and private institutions in the various parts of the State, 121 to the houses of correction; 5,340 paid money penalties; 4,392 were placed on probation; 2,945 were discharged; 67 were committed to common jails, 4 to the Reformatory Prison for Women; and 885 cases were disposed of by placing them on file, indefinitely continuing

MASSACHUSETTS. 597

them, or returning the offenders to the institutions where they had once been, etc.

The number of children in the State schools was 126 less October 1, 1878, than at the corresponding date in 1869 ; and the number of offenders therein was 253 less in 1878 than in 1869. The expenses of the State on account of its minor wards, for the years since this Agency began its work, arè as follows: 1869, $191,400.26; 1870, $189,853.73; 1871, $171,-284.40; 1872, $146,684.92; 1873, $137,733.64; 1874, $133,013.28; 1875, 142,448.52; 1876, $137,607.06; 1877, $134,234.18; 1878, $154,-789.43. The number of minor wards in the State in families subject to the visitation and care of the Agency exceeded the number in the Reform, Industrial, and Primary Schools by 128 ; and the number of visits made to them during the year 1878 was 1,788, and the per cent. of them found doing well was 85. There were 1,374 to be visited during the same year, and there remained 1,029 to be visited in 283 towns in 1879. In summarizing the work of the year 1878 it appears that 2,222 complaints against juvenile offenders before the courts were looked after ; 458 investigations made upon applications for children, for the release of them from institutions or from places and for special causes. The work of finding places for children was carried on. The Agency had to do with more than 4,000 different children in a year, and with as many other persons in some way related to them.

A further consolidation was made by the Legislature in uniting the Harbor and Land Commissions. The office of the Inspector-General was consolidated with that of the Adjutant-General, and the Surgeon-General's bureau was abolished. A Prison Commission of nine persons, two of whom should be women, was established, and vested with all the rights hitherto exercised by the numerous boards connected with the State penal institutions.

An article in amendment of the State Constitution was adopted, providing that the Legislature shall assemble biennially on the first Wednesday of January, and State officers and members of the Legislature shall hold office two years, the same person to be eligible for the office of Treasurer and Receiver-General for six years successively and no more. The first election shall be on the Tuesday next after the first Monday of November, 1880, and the first session of the Legislature shall commence on the first Wednesday of January, 1881. To become of force, it is necessary that this resolution shall be adopted also by the Legislature which assembled in January, 1880, and then submitted to the people and approved by them.

A bill was presented to extend to public charitable and reformatory institutions the provisions of an act of 1875, which provides that no inmate of any prison, jail, or house of correction shall be denied the free exercise of his religious belief and liberty of worshiping God according to the dictates of his conscience, within the place where such inmate may be kept or confined; and it shall be the duty of the officers and boards of officers having the management and direction of any such institutions to make such rules and regulations as may be necessary to carry out the intent and provisions of this act. Nothing contained in the law shall be so construed as to impair the discipline of any prison so far as may be needful for the good government and safe custody of its inmates. It was objected to the bill in the Senate, that it proposed to give to hundreds of young children the right to decide what religious ministration they should have at a time when they were at too tender a period of life to so determine; and further, that the committee reporting the bill had not heard a single superintendent or trustee of one of these institutions on the subject. In reply to this objection, one of the members of the committee said that "the committee had not summoned witnesses for the reason that the proposition seemed to be so fair and just as not to require outside evidence. He approved the bill because of the great right to religious liberty, because he believed in giving religious instruction to the young, and because the poor children of the State, the juvenile offenders, should have the same right as that enjoyed by thieves, burglars, and murderers. He showed that there were a great many Catholic children or children of Catholic parents, in the State institutions, and declared that they could not be made good Protestants, though they might be made bad Catholics. He denied that children were incapable of judging for themselves, pointing to those innocents who, in ages past, had given their lives for their faith, even though they might not have been entirely familiar with its tenets." An amendment providing that the law should not apply to children under fourteen years of age was rejected. A proviso that "nothing in this act shall be so construed as to prevent the assembling of all the inmates of any State or other public charitable institution in the chapel thereof for general religious instruction, including the reading of the Bible, as the board having charge of the institution may deem wise and expedient," was adopted. The bill was ordered to be engrossed in the House, by a vote of yeas 80, nays 45 ; it passed, and became a law.

The subject of taxation was extensively discussed, and the State tax was reduced to half a million dollars. The actual reduction, however, exceeded $300,000. The poll-tax due to the State and county of one dollar each, which must be paid before an elector can cast his vote at any election, was modified by an act providing that "assessors shall in each year assess upon the polls the State and county tax authorized or required by law; provided, however, that in case either of said taxes shall exceed in amount the sum of one dollar upon each poll, the excess above said amount shall then be apportioned upon property." The act also provides that there shall be no division of the poll-tax unless the person assessed shall make application for such division.

Attempts were also made to modify the general system of taxation, among which the question of the taxation of mortgaged property was conspicuous. A bill relative to this matter was passed in the House, but rejected in the Senate. Some of the features of the bill were, that loans on mortgage of real estate should be exempt from taxation as personal property; that the mortgagee's interest shall be assessed in the city or town where the land lies; that the mortgageor shall be assessed only for the value of the real estate over and above the amount of the mortgage. Mortgageors and mortgagees are treated as joint owners until the mortgagee takes possession. All taxes assessed constitute a lien upon the property, and in case either party fails of payment within a specified time, the other party may pay both taxes; but it is provided that if the mortgagee pays the tax assessed on the mortgageor, such tax, with interest and costs, shall be added to the principal of the mortgage; also that if the mortgageor pays the tax assessed on the mortgagee, he shall have the right to deduct the amount so paid, with interest and costs, from the principal of the mortgage. Finally, it is provided that "loans on mortgage of real estate within the Commonwealth, and assessed as real estate as hereinbefore provided, shall be exempt from taxation as personal property to the amount they are assessed as real estate, and any excess above such amount shall be taxed as now provided by law." A bill was also passed which reduces the maximum rate of interest on unpaid taxes from twelve to seven per cent.

The place of women in political affairs was extensively discussed at this session. Four distinct propositions were considered. The first was that a constitutional amendment should be submitted to the people, giving to women equal political rights with men. On this proposition the Committee of the Senate held a session to hear the petitioners. Mr. T. W. Higginson attempted to refute the argument that women should not be allowed to vote because they were not able to fight. He showed that if that ability were to be made the test, a large proportion of men, especially of professional men, would be disfranchised. The report of the Surgeon-General of the United States showed that of the thousand clergymen who volunteered or were drafted during the war, 945 were declared to be physically unfit for service. Of the lawyers who volunteered or were drafted, 650 were rejected, and of the physicians, 745. You must go down to the mechanics and laborers before you can find a class of men a majority of whom will fulfill this requirement. Of the clergymen who preach that woman suffrage is wrong because women can not do military duty, only one twentieth would themselves

be accepted for such service. There is but one class of men better fitted than mechanics for military service, and that is the prize-fighting class, and therefore the constituency which sent John Morrissey to Congress was the only constituency which ever carried out this idea to the end. Mrs. Margaret W. Campbell insisted that under existing laws women were oppressed and classed with men who were weak-minded or criminal. She said that men were allowed to vote when they reached the age of twenty-one, and she asked that some age might be fixed when women could vote—thirty-one, fifty-one, one hundred and one—and some of them would try to reach that age. Mr. William Lloyd Garrison expressed his sorrow that women should be disfranchised and classed with paupers, idiots, and criminals. Senator Hayes asked him if there were not some difference between a person who was disfranchised and one who had never had the franchise. Mr. Garrison replied that the difference was slight. Senator Hayes then said that he could see no argument for woman suffrage in the proposition that paupers, idiots, and criminals could not vote. Mr. Garrison then showed the improvement which forty years had made in the condition of women in this country—how in that period they had been admitted to the pulpit, the bar, the platform, the practice of medicine, and the public service. He declared that until women were given their rights this country would be divided and corrupt. Mrs. Lucy Stone closed the case for the petitioners by asking that the committee might decide that not a part, but all of the people of mature age, sound mind, and unconvicted of crime, might have the right to vote. In answer to a question from a member of the committee as to whether or not the granting of the franchise would give too much power to ministers of religion because of their greater influence over women than over men, she said that undoubtedly there were more women church members than men, but that as women got into the pulpit the number of male church members increased, just as the female membership of churches increased under male preaching. A resolve providing for a constitutional amendment was reported by the committee, and rejected.

The second proposition considered in the Legislature was that women should be allowed by statute to vote in all municipal elections. A bill to secure this right to women was reported in the House. When it came up in the orders of the day, it was rejected without discussion or a count.

The third proposition was that women should be allowed to vote for members of school committees. A bill giving this suffrage to women was reported in the Senate, and on the question of ordering it to a third reading Mr. Gardner of Hampden County advocated the bill as a measure of expediency, and as an experiment which will demonstrate the wisdom or unwisdom of conferring the broader right of general suffrage upon women. Mr. Winn of Franklin spoke in opposition, reviewing the history of suffrage, and urging the dependent position of women, and their physical inequality with men, as arguments against allowing the former to vote. He gave statistics to prove that since the agitation of women's rights began there has been a decrease in the number of births among the native population, and an increase in the number of divorces and of illegitimate births, and that consequently the conferring of the right of suffrage upon women would be a dangerous experiment, regarded either from a moral point of view or as a question in political economy. Mr. Burrage of Suffolk said that if the Senator's arguments were sound, society would evidently be benefited by a return to that condition of things under which women were held as slaves. He favored the bill on the ground that the State should be no respecter of persons, and that every person meeting the requirements of the Constitution in regard to the qualifications of voters should be allowed to vote, irrespective of color or sex. Mr. Ely of Norfolk advocated the bill, and contended that to give women the right to vote is simply a matter of justice. The bill finally pass the Senate—yeas 24, nays 11. In the Houed it was passed by a vote of 129 yeas to 69 nays. The following is the act:

Be it enacted, etc., as follows:

SECTION 1. Every woman who is a citizen of this Commonwealth, of twenty-one years of age and upward, and has the educational qualifications required by the twentieth article of the amendments to the Constitution, excepting paupers and persons under guardianship, who shall have resided within this Commonwealth one year, and within the city or town in which she claims the right to vote six months next preceding any meeting of citizens, either in wards or in general meeting, for municipal purposes, and who shall have paid by herself, or her parent or guardian, a State or county tax, which within two years next preceding such meeting has been assessed upon her in any city or town, shall have a right to vote, at such town or city meeting, for members of school committees.

SEC. 2. Any female citizen of this Commonwealth may, on or before the fifteenth day of September in any year, give notice in writing to the assessors of any city or town, accompanied by satisfactory evidence, that she was on the first day of May of that year an inhabitant thereof, and that she desires to pay a poll-tax, and furnish under oath a true list of her estate, both real and personal, and she shall thereupon be assessed for her poll and estate, and the assessors shall, on or before the first day of October in each year, return her name to the clerk of the city or town in the list of the persons so assessed. The taxes so assessed shall be entered in the tax-list of the collector of the city or town, and the collector shall collect and pay over the same in the manner specified in his warrant.

SEC. 3. All laws in relation to the registration of voters shall apply to women upon whom the right to vote is herein conferred; provided, that the names of such women shall be placed on a separate list.

SEC. 4. The mayor and aldermen of cities and the selectmen of towns may, in their discretion, appoint and notify a separate day for the election of school committees; provided, that such meeting shall be held in the same month in which the annual town meeting of the municipal election occurs.

This is the first decided triumph of the wo-

man-suffragists in the State, and it gives an opportunity to subject their demands to the test of experiment.

The fourth proposition was the passage of a law to give women the right to vote on all matters relating to the sale of intoxicating liquors. The report of the committee in the Senate was unfavorable, but the Senate substituted a bill providing for special elections in cities and towns to determine whether or not liquors should be sold therein, and providing further that women might vote thereat upon the usual conditions. When the bill reached the House, a great deal of objection was made to the special election provisions which it contained, and it was quite as much upon that consideration as on account of opposition to women voting that the bill was rejected by a very large vote.

The following bill was substituted for an unfavorable report in the House; it is known as the "civil-damage bill":

SEC. 1. Every husband, wife, child, parent, guardian, employer, or other person, who shall be injured in person or property, or means of support, by any intoxicated person, or in consequence of the intoxication, habitual or otherwise, of any person, shall have a right of action in his or her own name, severally or jointly, against any person or persons who shall, by selling or giving intoxicating liquors, have caused the intoxication, in whole or in part, of such person or persons; and any person or persons owning, renting, leasing, or permitting the occupation of any building or premises, and having knowledge that intoxicating liquors are to be sold therein, or who, having leased the same for other purposes, shall knowingly permit therein the sale of any intoxicating liquors, shall, if any such liquors sold or given therein have caused, in whole or in part, the intoxication of any person, be liable, severally or jointly with the person or persons selling or giving intoxicating liquors as aforesaid, for all damages sustained, and for exemplary damages, and the same may be recovered in an action of tort. A married woman may bring such action in her own name, and all damages recovered by her shall inure to her separate use. In case of the death of either party, the action and right of action shall survive to or against his executor or administrator.

SEC. 2. This act shall take effect upon its passage.

The bill is similar to the one previously passed by the New York Legislature. It was amended by adding a section as follows: "Any owner or lessor of real estate, who shall pay any money on account of his liability incurred under this act for any act of his tenant, may in an action of contract recover of said tenant the money so paid." The clause concerning exemplary damages was stricken out; owners and lessees of buildings who should rent them for liquor-selling were made jointly responsible; and no license for the sale of liquor should be granted unless the application therefor had the signature of such owner or lessee. In the Senate the bill was ordered to a third reading by yeas 26, nays 8. In the House the vote to substitute was—yeas 105, nays 54.

The State Detective Force was abolished, and the Governor was authorized to appoint not more than two district police for each judicial district and two for the inspection of factories.

The contract system as it prevails in the penal and reformatory institutions of the State was considered, and numerous measures were proposed. A special committee reported on the subject. There are three systems adopted in the employment of convicts: The contract system, which exists in Massachusetts and nearly all the Northern prisons; the lessee system, which prevails in Georgia and other Southern States; and the public account system below described. Those who make the most complaint in the State are engaged in the boot and shoe trade; and they complain chiefly of two hundred men employed at Concord. The relative cost of labor to the value of the product in the manufacture of boots and shoes is as 1 to 3; that is, of every dollar's value of product, 33⅓ per cent. goes to labor, while the ratio of labor to product in prison-work is 31¼ per cent., showing that the advantage of the prison contractor is really about 2 per cent. in the production of goods on the average. The product of each person employed in the manufacture of boots and shoes in Massachusetts is $1,858 per year; that is, 48,090 operatives— the number of persons so employed in 1875— produced $89,375,792 worth of goods. The product of prison-work per man is $1,142 per annum. The 200 men employed on boots and shoes at Concord produce $228,575 worth of goods per year, on an average; the same number outside would make $371,600 worth of goods. No contractor will object to the abolition of the contract system on personal grounds. The contractor pays for the men he contracts for through the whole year, whether the demand is good or bad, and in some cases they have allowed them to remain idle for the reason that it was less loss to pay wages than to make goods. With rare exceptions all classes agree that productive industry should and must be carried on in the prisons, and it is self-evident that competition can not be avoided so long as two men labor or are employed. While it can not be proved that any great evil growing out of convict labor exists, it must be admitted that there is a seeming, and may be at times a positive, evil existing under the present contract system. After a full discussion of the several substitutes offered, the committee conclude:

1. That convict labor should not be abolished.
2. That legislation to restrain officials in penal institutions from contracting out the labor of convicts at lower rates than the average of outside labor, without allowing contractors to employ or not the men contracted for, simply abolishes labor in such institutions.
3. The reduction of the hours of labor in prison to six per day, with the old rates of contract per day, simply abolishes labor in penal institutions.
4. The general introduction of the public account system, as a rule, simply aggravates the grievances arising from whatever competition may result from the contract system.
5. The increased diversity of employment in penal institutions tends not only to lessen whatever com-

petition now exists, but has an excellent reformatory effect upon the prisoners.
6. The employment of convicts upon public works, when it can be done, is a feature of prison labor commendable, not only from the standpoint of the labor and prison reformers, but from that also of the manufacturers and workingmen.
7. The employment of convicts in breaking and dressing stone, and kindred work, while it palliates the evils of competition, induces to a large degree other conditions far more injurious to the body politic; and that work which requires the most expenditure of muscle and the least expenditure of capital is, if it can be had, the best for a large class of convicts, all things considered.

The Labor Bureau was instructed by the Legislature at its session in 1878 to make a full investigation of the question of convict labor. The annual report of the Bureau, made in February to the Legislature, contains the results of the investigation. The whole number of convicts in the United States in 1878 was 29,197; of these, there were under contract or employed in mechanical industries 13,186. The number of inmates of the penal institutions of Massachusetts November 1, 1878, was 5,048— 4,097 males and 951 females; of these, 2,962 males and 748 females, 3,710 in all, were at work. There were 1,642 males and 16 females employed on contract work, the contract price ranging all the way from 5 to 45 cents per day. The earnings of these institutions for the year were $156,959.18, and the expenses $724,883.43. There were employed in the different industries the following: Manufacture of hats, 200; picture-moldings, 150; boots and shoes, 584; brushes, 211; cotton-ties, 26; harnesses, 70; stone-yards, 100; slippers, 165; cane-seating chairs, 270; clothing 356; crocheting, knitting, etc., 65; corset-making, 100; laundry, 65; leather, 41; prison duties, 1,307; and the location and character of the work are given in detail. At New Bedford 179 prisoners were employed on boots and shoes on public account; that is, the officers of the prison purchased raw materials, manufactured the goods, and sold them in the market, in the same manner as any manufacturing establishment. At East Cambridge 181 are so employed making brushes, and at Deer Island 100 on stone-work. In all, 745 are working on public account and 1,658 on contract work—a total of 2,403 engaged in industrial labor; and there are 1,338 prisoners in the State without employment. The 13,186 convicts employed in mechanical industries in the State Prisons of the United States earn an average of 40 cents per day, which gives $1,624,518.90 as their gross earnings for the year. At $2 per day—the average price for labor outside of prisons—these men would earn $8,122,576. The whole injury done to labor, if any, in the country, by convict labor in the State Prisons, thus appears to be represented by $8,122,576, while the annual products of the mechanical industries of the United States amount to *five thousand million dollars*. The wages paid for prison labor, as shown by the statistics, represents a product of $9,747,090, or less than one fifth of one per cent. of the products of the United States.

An act was passed "to preserve the purity of elections," which provides that in future only plain white paper similar to the ordinary printing paper may be used for tickets. The ballots must be uniform in size, each one bearing the names of more than three candidates to be four and a half inches in width, or within a quarter of an inch of it, and twelve inches long, or within half an inch of that length. No distinguishing marks or devices are allowable, but the head of the ticket, with the names of the candidates for the several offices, must be printed in plain type with black ink. The names are required to be of uniform size, or so nearly so that no one name shall be in letters less than one half the size of those in which the majority of the names are printed. The printing or writing for distribution, or the distribution at the polls, of any ballot printed or written contrary to these provisions, is punishable by a fine not exceeding $100, and by imprisonment in the county jail for a term not exceeding sixty days. The act does not forbid the erasure, correction, or insertion of any name by pencil-mark or otherwise upon the face of the printed ballot, nor authorize the rejection of any ballot, after it has been received into the ballot-box, for any want of conformity with the provisions above specified. But in the counting of the ballots, all names printed in type less than half the size of those generally used on the ticket will be passed over and not counted, each ballot being otherwise good.

The efforts to prevent cruelty to animals are well organized in the State. A society was formed eleven years ago. At that time there were three societies for the prevention of cruelty to animals on the continent; now there are ninety-three in the United States and three in the British Provinces. The Massachusetts Society had then a single prosecuting agent in Boston and about twenty others throughout the State. It now employs three prosecuting agents constantly in and about Boston, and has 465 others representing its interests throughout the State. Its officers had then prosecuted a few violators of the law, and investigated something over 100 cases of cruelty. They have now prosecuted 2,073 persons, and investigated and, so far as possible, remedied 21,756 cases of cruelty. Drinking-fountains are placed in the streets; birds and deer on the Common; check-rein signs at the foot of the hills; thousands of the horses driven without check-reins or blinders; extra horses to aid in drawing the horse-cars; horse-car horses worked only six days in the week, where they used to be worked seven. The great dog-fighter of the State has been driven out, one of his principal survivors fined $250, and others smaller amounts, and dog-fighting and cock-fighting have been substantially stopped in the State. Men are now employed to kill the old and disabled animals in a merciful manner, and prizes have been dis-

tributed by the Governor to pupils of the public schools who had written the best compositions on kindness to animals. There are now five papers published which are devoted to the protection of animals. The humane literature published by the Society is to be found in Oregon and California; France, Spain, Germany, and other European countries; also in Algiers, Calcutta, and Australia. The annual expenditure has been only one half of one per cent. of the amount annually expended by the organized charitable societies of the State; that is, 99½ per cent. is paid directly for the benefit of human beings, and about one half of one per cent. for the welfare of animals.

The Board of Railroad Commissioners, which has been in existence for ten years, is stated to be the only one of all that have been established in the various States that has proved in any great degree a success. The duties of the Board are, first, those of a supervisory character as respects the railroads themselves; second, those which are both supervisory and judicial as between the railroads and the public; and, third, judicial duties as between the different railroad corporations. The supervisory duties include the care of accounts and responsibility for returns, the examination of tracks, bridges, and appliances, and the investigation of accidents; the supervising and judicial duties, so far as the public is concerned, are most extensive in everything relative to the formation, construction, and operation of the roads, and the whole general State legislation of the last ten years is built up on the Board as a foundation. The jurisdiction of the Board between the railroad corporations is both large and final. It is compelled to receive all complaints against the railroads, to investigate them, and find out a remedy. It has no power except to recommend and report, but in practical experience the recommendations of the Board have seldom been disregarded, and they have covered almost all sorts of questions. It is thought that this principle may be developed so as to work a solution of the railroad problem. At present it is an experiment. No small portion of credit is ascribed to the Board for the marked improvement in the tone and character of the railroad management. The material interest which the Board supervises is the largest in the State. It is the interest upon which the whole industrial system hinges, and the tolls and charges the corporations annually levy amount to more than the entire taxation, State, county, and municipal. During the ten years this Board has been in existence its entire cost has in round numbers been $162,000. During the same time the gross receipts of the corporations have amounted to $322,000,000. The cost of supervision, therefore, has been almost exactly the twentieth part of one per cent. of the gross receipts. The Commissioners have brought about a uniform system of keeping the accounts of the railroads, which

was done for the first time during the year
1878, with the certainty that the books, papers, and accounts of the railroad corporations
are to be as open to public scrutiny as those of
the State or any city government.

The business of the Hoosac Tunnel may be
considered as having really commenced in 1876.
The amount of it and the rapidity of its increase are shown by the following statement:

PARTICULARS.	1876.	1877.	1878.
Total receipts	$83,625	$158,141	$209,410
Total expenses	45,779	60,285	80,679
Net receipts............	$37,845	$97,905	$128,731
Number of passengers....	68,715	120,879	154,460
Number of tons of freight.	242,266	325,997	539,488

In 1878 the State received $41,000 as a
small contribution toward the interest account.
During the last year the " constant-circuit rail
system " was tested on the Fitchburg road. It
differs from any other system by using the rails
instead of wire for conducting the electric current. The signals have been found to be reliable
and to do the work expected of them. The
track is divided into sections of a mile, more or
less, according to curves and other contingencies. At one end of the section is placed a battery consisting of one cell, and one pole attached to either rail, and at the other end is
placed the magnet, one electrode attached to
each rail. Thus a constant metallic circuit is
established through the rails and magnet. At
either end of the section is the standard bearing
the signal, which is connected with the circuit.
When a train or pair of wheels enters upon the
circuit, the wheels and axle instantly short-cir-
cuit the current, the magnet is demagnetized,
and on leaving its armature the signal is mechanically thrown to danger, where it remains
as long as the wheels are on the section.
When they pass off, the signal goes back to
safety. Thus it will be seen that the rear of a
train on a road equipped with the signals will
always be safely guarded. It has been found
by actual experience that the rails are vastly
superior as conductors to any surrounding
media, and that the electricity will adhere to
them in preference to passing off to earth, even
during heavy rain and snow.

The course of instruction in Harvard College has been so far modified in favor of female education, that women who can stand
the examinations can be entitled to a course of
study under the faculty for the full term of
four years, apart from the times and classes of
the men.

An important change was made in the public schools of Boston. This consisted in an entire separation of the primary and grammar
schools, and the former are made entirely independent of the principals of the districts as
regards instruction. The superintendent stated
that " he had repeatedly found scholars in the
upper classes of the primary schools who belonged in the lower classes, and the reason for

this was that the upper classes of the primary
schools were depleted to fill grammar classes,
and to fill the classes thus depleted it was necessary to fill them up with pupils from the
lower classes. It was in this system of promotion that he found the greatest cause of discontent between the primary and grammar
schools. From every point of view this system was an abuse of every sound educational
principle, and so precipitated the instruction of
the younger pupils as to drag them through
it half breathless and wholly unprepared to
meet it."

For the details of the State institutions see
the volume of last year.

The National Labor party held a State Convention in Boston on September 12th. Horace
Binney Sargent was chosen President. The
nominations for State officers resulted as follows: For Governor, Benjamin F. Butler; for
Lieutenant-Governor, Albert C. Woodworth;
for Secretary of State, Michael T. Donohoe;
for Treasurer, George Dutton; for Auditor,
Davis J. King; for Attorney-General, Horace
B. Sargent. The following resolutions were
adopted:

Whereas, This government was intended to be a
government of the people by the people and for the
people, of whom 95 per cent. are interested in enterprise and labor; and,

Whereas, It has, by insidious, usurping, and corruptly selfish legislation, been perverted to be a government of the money power by the money power and
for the money power, which has so manipulated the
currency and repudiated printed contracts as to enrich
5 per cent. of the people by the robbery of 95 per cent.:

Resolved, That stability in prices can only be secured
by maintaining a uniform relation between the volume
and the uses of money, and this can be secured only
by a full legal-tender paper money, issued by the Government; a volume that shall not decrease while the
population is increasing, and thus acquire an increased
purchasing power over labor.

Resolved, That legal-tender greenbacks should be
substituted for the national-bank notes in circulation,
as the issue of money is an essential function of national sovereignty and not a pa of legitimate banking.

Resolved, That we favor the immediate use of the
coin in the Treasury for the reduction of the bonded
debt.

Resolved, That the soldier and sailor should receive
a dollar as good as the bondholder; and if, in defiance
of the contract, honesty, equity, and national honor
require the payment of 100 cents in gold for 40 cents
loaned, it is alike demanded by honesty, equity, and
honor that the same measure be meted to those who
shed their blood in the cause of their country's salvation and received a depreciated money.

Resolved, That the truth of the Greenback philosophy has been grandly vindicated by the adoption of
two Greenback measures, viz.: The stoppage of contraction in 1878, thus arresting the further shrinkage
of values, and raising of the greenback to par by receiving it at the Custom-House—measures which, if adopted in season, might have averted six years of unexampled distress, and the opposition to which by the
money power is the greatest impediment to returning
prosperity to-day.

Resolved, That a graduated and progressive tax on
incomes exceeding $1,000, from every source, with a
total exemption of small homesteads, is right, and in
accordance with the constitutional rule that taxes
should be " equal and proportional"; that the ability
to bear should govern, rather than a rule of uniform

percentages, which may leave a vast surplus over all taxes in the hands of one citizen, while another must go hungry to pay a poll-tax, after having paid enormous taxes and duties upon his consumption.

Resolved, That the coin resumption of the Republican party is a sham and a delusion, by making paper bank-notes redeemable in paper United States legal-tender notes, and those notes exchangeable for coin over only one counter in the United States in sums of not less than $50.

Resolved, That the hours of labor shall be shortened, and the employment of young children in exhausting factory labor be prevented; that labor-saving machinery is a boon of God to the sons and daughters of toil, rather than an engine of torture to.wring out larger profits for capital by bringing the laborer into heart-breaking competition with the muscles that never tire. The vast powers of nature are not harnessed by invention to secure even six per cent. dividends, but to relieve the human slaves; not hours of toil, but the product of the new partnership of man with natural forces, should be the rule of compensation, and demands a new system of dividing the profits of capital and labor.

Resolved, That free school-books are an important part of the system of free schools. To spend millions in buildings and teachers, and refuse a few dollars in school-books except by enforcing a humiliating confession of poverty upon parent and child, is inconsistent and unwise.

Resolved, That the contract system of convict labor should be abolished, and that the employment of such labor shall be on the account of the Commonwealth alone, which shall be prohibited from selling the production at a price that shall underbid honest labor.

Resolved, That the National Greenback-Labor party will support no candidate for the State Legislature unless he be pledged to vote for a compulsory secret ballot.

Resolved, That we cordially endorse the amendment to the homestead act presented to Congress by Hendrick B. Wright of Pennsylvania, and for his noble devotion to the cause of labor we extend to him the warm sympathies and hearty thanks of the Greenback-Labor party of Massachusetts.

Resolved, That the shameless legislation of the poll-tax bill, passed at the last session of the General Court, impels us to reaffirm our protest against the outrage on the right of the ballot which that legislation attempts to perpetuate; and we demand that this relic of a property qualification be wiped from the organic laws.

The Republican State Convention assembled at Worcester on September 16th. The nominations for State officers resulted as follows: For Governor, John D. Long; for Lieutenant-Governor, Byron Weston; for Secretary of State, Henry B. Peirce; for Treasurer and Receiver-General, Charles Endicott; for Auditor, Charles R. Ladd; for Attorney-General, George Marston. The following resolutions were adopted:

The Republican party of Massachusetts, at the close of the first quarter of a century of its history, pledging itself anew to the continued performance of the duties in which it originated, and to the defense and maintenance of those principles upon which it was founded, and which are still essential to the peace, security, and prosperity of the republic, makes these declarations:

1. We affirm the doctrine heretofore proclaimed and maintained, that the United States of America is a nation; that, while local self-government in all matters which belong to the States must be fully recognized, the national Government should secure to the citizens from whom it claims allegiance complete liberty and exact equality in the exercise of their civil and political rights; that, whether assailed by political persecution at home or menaced by tyranny abroad, all citizens of the United States, without distinction of origin, race, creed, or color, must be protected by the national Government in all the rights granted to them by the Constitution and laws; that our institutions rest upon the equality of all men before the law, and that a free ballot, uninfluenced by fraud, intimidation, or force, and honestly counted, is the right of every qualified voter; and we demand that elections shall be free from all interference by unlawful bodies of armed men, and shall also be free from the interference of the national or State military forces except when employed as a part of a *posse comitatus*. We denounce that fierce partisan intolerance which prevents a free ballot, denies freedom of political opinion and action, and takes from any of the people the right to choose their homes and to control and enjoy the fruits of their labor.

2. We deprecate the course of the members of the Democratic party who have undertaken to revive sectional animosity for the purpose of securing political ascendancy in the Southern States, and who have revived the memories of sectional strife by the defiant declaration of the purpose to repeal laws made necessary by war and enacted to secure the results of the war; and we condemn their attempts to secure by legislation what was not accomplished by arms, namely, the establishment under the name of State sovereignty of those pernicious doctrines which destroy national supremacy, and which in the past have led to secession and civil war.

3. The pledges of the Republican party to maintain the national honor and to preserve the national credit have been redeemed in the face of bitter opposition, by the prompt resumption of specie payments and a reduction both of the principal and the interest of the public debt; and we congratulate our fellow citizens upon the restoration of confidence and revival of business which followed the honest, prudent, and wise management of public affairs under a Republican administration. We are opposed to repudiation in all its forms, either by a "scaling" of debts or a debasement of the legal-tender circulation. We insist that the paper and the coin circulation of the country shall at all times be maintained at par with the gold standard of the commercial world.

4. We applaud the firm and patriotic course of President Hayes in maintaining the constitutional prerogatives of the Executive, and in courageously and successfully resisting all efforts of a Democratic Congress to cripple the functions of the Government. We recognize the earnestness and sincerity with which he has labored to restore harmony and "good feeling" to all sections of the country, to secure purity, efficiency, and frugality in every branch of the public service, and to divorce the civil service from the management of partisan politics, to sustain the financial credit of the Government, and to insist upon free and honest elections; and we will support the President in the responsibility of making nominations to office without dictation from other departments of the Government, and in persistently carrying out the principles relating to the civil service declared in the Cincinnati platform and letter of acceptance.

5. While the Republican party is practically united in demanding a suppression of intemperance by the wisest legislation, it recognizes an honest difference of opinion among its members as to which form of law will best accomplish that end; and the question is therefore referred to the people, to be settled by them in the Legislature organized for the protection of the weak, the relief of the oppressed, and the elevation of all. The Republican party pledges itself anew to these primary objects, and, believing an effectual means of promoting them is the diffusion of full and accurate information of the condition of the people, it heartily sustains our State Bureau of Statistics of Labor, and endorses the establishment of a national bureau of like character. We again demand that our system of taxation shall be so modified that each person shall contribute only in proportion to what he is worth, to the end that there shall be substantial relief from the existing burdens of taxation. In our opinion,

the time has come when the executive officers of the Commonwealth and members of the Legislature should be elected for a longer time than one year, and the adoption of the constitutional amendment providing for biennial elections and biennial sessions of the Legislature would tend to give steadiness to legislation and to the administration of the laws, and add to the importance of the offices and the care of voters in filling them, and would relieve the people from that frequency of elections which is believed to be no longer conducive to the welfare of the Commonwealth.

6. The administration of the State government during the past year has been able, just, and efficient. The pledges made by the Republican party have been redeemed, in that reforms have been initiated and accomplished, the State tax and expenses have been reduced, commissions have been consolidated, and offices now become unnecessary have been abolished. We appreciate the eminent services of the present Chief Magistrate of the Commonwealth, whose prudence, sound judgment, and integrity of character have largely contributed to this result. In the continuation of its work the Republican party will insist, in the words of Governor Talbot, "on a judicious but not penurious economy in State administration, on a discontinuance of the State tax at the earliest date, on increasing no further the State indebtedness, and a speedy liquidation of existing liabilities, and on shutting the door of the Treasury against all attempts to secure public means for private ends."

7. We commend to the voters of the Commonwealth the nominees of this Convention, whose high character, commanding ability, and large experience in public service are guarantees of official rectitude and a wise administration of our State affairs.

The Independent Democrats assembled at Worcester on September 17th in State Convention. Albert Palmer was chosen President. The nominations for State officers resulted as follows: For Governor, Benjamin F. Butler; for Lieutenant-Governor, Albert C. Woodworth; for Secretary of State, Michael T. Donohoe; for Treasurer and Receiver-General, David W. Skillings; for Auditor, Davis J. King; for Attorney-General, William D. Northend. The following resolutions were adopted:

Resolved, That we recognize the fact that differences of opinion exist regarding certain principles of national administration; that while we may differ as to the true policy to be pursued concerning the adjustment of vexed national questions, we are all united upon the common platform of our great leader—equal rights, equal duties, equal powers, equal privileges, and equal protection by the laws to every man everywhere under the Government, State and national.

Resolved, That we are unalterably opposed to the rule of the ring which has fastened itself upon the Commonwealth; that we put the seal of condemnation upon that growing spirit of "Bourbonism" and "caste," which conceals itself under the pretentious title of the "better element," which sets itself upon a high pedestal of preëminent right to dictate and to control the people because of its alleged superior public virtue; that we denounce these pretenders, and in behalf of the great common people of the State arraign the hypocrisy, the arrogance, the much-vaunted self-purity, and the spirit of unwarrantable abuse which characterize the modern political Pharisees who have so long misrepresented the people of the Commonwealth.

Resolved, That we demand that reform in the State government shall be thorough, impartial, and complete; that all useless offices shall be abolished, incompetent officials discharged, economy take the place of extravagance, thrift supplant waste, watchfulness succeed negligence, energy uproot sloth, system re-

place confusion, and honesty prevail everywhere, to the end that our noble old Commonwealth may resume her place among the best governed communities of the civilized world.

Resolved, That the rights of labor, the creator of all values, should be respected, and to this end we commend the establishment of a National Bureau of Labor Statistics; advocate the rigid enforcement of all laws in the State and nation fixing the hours of labor, as well as those for the protection of life and limb, and for the regulation of child-labor in mills and factories; and oppose any system of convict labor in our prisons by which its products are brought into unjust competition with honest labor outside of prison walls.

Resolved, That we denounce the intimidation of voters, whether by force of arms, the more civilized method of social ostracism, of proscription of employees, or of the withdrawal of business patronage, as opposed to the spirit of our free institutions and deserving the condemnation of every true American citizen.

Resolved, That the evils which now afflict the State, morally and financially, may be and should be cured by unflinching firmness and impartiality on the part of the Governor in the administration of the laws.

Resolved, That the creation of commissions to perform the duties of the Executive is dangerous and extravagant, and should be wholly discontinued.

Resolved, That we are opposed to the system of double taxation which now prevails in this State.

Resolved, That all promises made to our patriotic soldiers and sailors should be kept.

Resolved, That a pure suffrage is the life-blood of the republic. No ballot can be pure which is not free. The way to the ballot-box should be direct, easy, unimpeded, and secure from espionage. We demand, therefore, that the laws be so framed as to insure the one without impairing the others, and that the right to vote should not depend upon its purchase by the payment of a tax.

Resolved, That the office of Governor is one requiring the highest executive ability; that General Benjamin F. Butler will fill it with complete success; and we believe the multitude will applaud in General Butler the citizen soldier who abandoned a lucrative position in private life at the first call of his country, who has served her with untiring industry and unflagging zeal, and who has suffered no associations of party or predilections or political pride to blind him to the true character of the struggle in which the nation was engaged. That we recommend the other nominations of the Convention as the representatives of State reform worthy to be associated with our illustrious leader.

The State Convention of the Prohibitionists assembled in Boston on September 24th. A. A. Miner was chosen President. The nominations for State officers resulted as follows: For Governor, Rev. Dr. D. C. Eddy; for Lieutenant-Governor, Timothy K. Earle; for Secretary of State, Charles Almy; for Treasurer and Receiver-General, David N. Skillings; for Auditor, Jonathan H. Orne; for Attorney-General, Samuel M. Fairfield. The following resolutions were adopted:

Resolved, That we are assembled not to support or to defeat a man, but to maintain principles that lie at the foundation of the welfare of our Commonwealth.

Resolved, That we renew our protest against a liquor policy which makes the State an ally of the traffic, which wastes its wealth, enslaves its labor, begets its paupers and its criminals, and destroys its homes.

Resolved, That for the State to merely tolerate such a traffic is dangerous, while to license it is infamous.

Resolved, That to overthrow the dram-shop, which in all its branches and disguises stands as the enemy of the schoolhouse and the Church, is the highest interest of civilization and the most immediate duty imposed upon the people of Massachusetts.

Resolved, That this can be done by nothing else except by votes.

Resolved, That reason and experience teach that nothing is to be hoped in this warfare from men or from parties who compete for the liquor vote, or who fear a manly utterance upon this great issue; and that the traffic can neither be suppressed nor effectually checked except by a party avowing that object and by men elected to do it.

Resolved, That to this end we again present to our fellow citizens the names of men whose election would proclaim that public condemnation of the liquor-traffic which must necessarily precede its destruction. The task before us is hard, the way may lengthen out, but there is no other path for us to follow. We commend our cause and our course to the considerate judgment of good citizens, and invoke the prayers of Christian men and women.

Resolved, That, as intemperance is an enemy to the home and deals its heaviest blows at the heart of woman, we therefore invite her earnest prayers and efficient work in behalf of our cause; and we look forward with eager hope for the day when sex shall be no longer a condition of suffrage, and woman may be permitted to use the ballot, as she surely will, for her own protection, and for the protection of society, against the cruel wrongs of the liquor-traffic.

The Democratic State Convention was held in Boston on October 7th. The nominations for State officers resulted as follows: For Governor, John Quincy Adams; for Lieutenant-Governor, William R. Plunkett; for Secretary of State, Michael T. Donohoe; for Treasurer and Receiver-General, David N. Skillings; for Auditor, Charles R. Field; for Attorney-General, Richard Olney. The following resolutions were adopted:

The Democrats of Massachusetts, in Convention assembled, reaffirm the national Democratic platform of 1876 as an authoritative exposition of the principles of our party, and congratulate our political brethren of the whole country that these principles were endorsed in the national canvass by the suffrages of a decided majority of the American people and of the Electoral College.

We denounce upon the guilty Republican party stern retribution for the great public crime by which the people were defrauded of their right to be governed by a ruler of their choice, and by which the elective principle was wounded in its most vital part.

Our thanks are due to the Democrats in Congress for their efforts to enforce economy in public expenses, to abolish useless offices, and to correct manifold abuses in public affairs, not least of which are the exclusion of intelligent citizens from the jury-box and the levying and maintaining of an army of official hirelings around the polls for partisan purposes.

We believe in self-government by the people, and desire that the polls shall be free from the interference of Federal bayonets directed by the intrigues of a Federal partisan Executive.

We believe the purity of the ballot-box can be better preserved through State authority than by Federal interference.

We protest against laws which authorize the arrest of citizens at the polls without warrant or hearing, and the suppression of their votes by imprisoning their persons until after the election, as upturning the foundation of free government; and we call on Congress to aid the people and rescue the freedom of the elections, undeterred by Republican clamors or Presidential vetoes.

The Democratic party has always denied that any constitutional power existed in the Federal Government to make anything a legal tender in the payment of debts except gold and silver.

We affirm the obligation of public and private contracts, and demand that public money ought to be kept in the Treasury of the United States, free from control or use by speculators or favorite bankers.

We rejoice with the country at the large and renewed prosperity that attends agricultural and manufacturing pursuits, but we deprecate that Republican policy which, having destroyed our ship-building, placed the carrying trade of the products of our soil in the control of foreign flags, and almost banished our flag from the seas, and imperiled the pursuit of the fisheries among our hardy population, has rewarded Great Britain with spoils she never could have conquered, and abandoned the trident of the seas to her hands.

The election, held on November 4th, resulted in the choice of Long, Republican, as Governor, by 122,751 votes, against 9,989 for Adams, Democrat, 109,149 for Butler, Democrat and National, and 1,645 for Eddy, Prohibitionist. The other Republican candidates were elected by votes ranging from 126,252 for Lieutenant-Governor to 129,024 for Secretary of State.

The state of parties in the Legislature was as follows:

PARTIES.	Senate.	House.
Republicans.....	32	185
Democrats.................	8	59
Nationals...................	..	8
Total...................	40	240

METHODISTS.

I. METHODIST EPISCOPAL CHURCH.—The following is a summary of the statistics of the Methodist Episcopal Church as given in the volumes containing the "Minutes of the Annual Conferences" for 1879:

SPRING CONFERENCES.	Traveling preachers.	Local preachers.	Members.	Probationers.
Arkansas.............	87	66	3,025	467
Baltimore..............	196	176	32,025	4,960
Central Pennsylvania..	217	123	34,274	4,877
East German..........	40	38	3,205	487
East Maine............	113	70	9,485	3,287
Florida..............	85	66	2,356	719
Kansas..............	150	169	12,455	2,602
Kentucky.............	100	153	15,074	3,356
Lexington.............	77	105	5,826	923
Little Rock...........	30	49	1,448	810
Louisiana............	87	249	8,824	1,807
Maine...............	186	78	11,624	1,905
Mississippi...........	96	881	26,101	2,499
Missouri.............	124	158	16,020	2,785
Newark....	207	144	35,494	8,106
New England..........	247	147	27,968	2,547
New Hampshire.......	133	51	13,001	1,443
New Jersey...........	178	196	33,714	4,535
New York...........	273	139	48,608	4,901
New York East........	261	220	40,508	4,727
North Carolina........	48	124	8,762	1,096
Northern New York...	231	116	24,616	3,849
North India..	36	61	1,468	1,058
North Indiana.........	181	228	27,584	5,329
Philadelphia..........	246	296	41,010	5,058
Providence...........	176	97	20,407	2,844
St. Louis.............	121	184	18,280	1,810
South Carolina........	82	841	26,026	5,275
South Kansas.........	137	142	15,686	3,001
Troy................	277	132	34,004	8,980
Vermont.............	131	72	11,676	1,874
Virginia..............	98	52	5,902	1,842
Washington...........	118	286	27,113	8,124
Wilmington...........	183	147	25,819	4,170
Wyoming.............	218	204	26,985	8,905
Total..............	4,925	5,438	687,808	100,128

FALL CONFERENCES.	Traveling preachers.	Local preachers.	Members.	Probationers.
Alabama	85	118	4,512	518
Austin	25	25	947	263
California	184	116	8,195	759
Central Alabama	52	156	6,901	986
Central German	122	97	11,860	984
Central Illinois	210	169	23,757	1,500
Central New York	182	100	21,166	1,953
Central Ohio	138	151	24,281	1,931
Central Tennessee	58	77	4,613	844
Chicago German	67	54	5,262	911
Cincinnati	190	178	84,486	2,143
Colorado	53	42	2,623	392
Columbia River	34	35	1,983	430
Delaware	74	219	18,112	1,874
Des Moines	163	227	22,493	1,897
Detroit	250	196	25,436	2,246
East Ohio	261	225	42,322	1,819
Erie	190	156	28,296	1,915
Foochow (China)	57	80	1,384	647
Genesee	825	152	30,552	2,569
Georgia	84	42	2,514	318
Germany and Switzerland	91	50	9,191	2,099
Holston	117	263	92,594	2,899
Illinois	269	289	87,798	2,222
Indiana	144	189	80,582	2,549
Iowa	135	185	19,761	1,901
Liberia	18	47	1,944	166
Michigan	245	228	28,849	2,979
Minnesota	177	121	14,257	1,791
Montana	6	7	827	37
Nebraska	111	142	10,082	1,348
Nevada	18	29	710	86
North Ohio	165	184	23,449	1,255
Northwest German	82	67	5,889	1,079
Northwest Indiana	150	185	23,264	1,277
Northwest Iowa	72	49	6,184	1,314
Northwest Swedish	42	32	4,180	410
Norway	81	16	2,823	488
Ohio	186	207	42,005	2,004
Oregon	60	77	4,018	729
Pittsburgh	167	110	32,242	1,840
Rock River	230	180	25,381	1,437
St. Louis German	103	112	7,564	680
Savannah	73	215	9,985	3,052
Southeast Indiana	123	184	25,488	1,802
Southern California	30	27	1,674	194
Southern German	27	14	1,985	185
Southern Illinois	158	243	23,771	2,831
Sweden	54	77	5,546	8,451
Tennessee	45	136	6,921	1,101
Texas	98	195	7,256	1,619
Upper Iowa	197	162	21,201	1,469
Utah	6	4	159	44
Western German	46	42	8,015	857
West Texas	78	74	5,705	631
West Virginia	155	226	29,451	2,706
West Wisconsin	142	142	11,812	1,168
Wisconsin	196	107	18,965	1,049
Total Fall Conferences	6,711	7,087	886,703	76,173
Add Spring Conferences	4,925	5,438	687,308	100,123
Total numbers for the year	11,636	12,475	1,524,006	176,296

Whole number of members and probationers, 1,700,302 ; number of baptisms during the year, 56,565 of children. 63,218 of adults ; number of churches, 19,955, of the probable value of $62,520,417; number of parsonages, 5,689, of the probable value of $8,445,092; number of Sunday-schools, 20,359, with 217,- 967 officers and teachers, and 1,549,315 scholars. Amount of benevolent contributions: for Conference claimants, $127,002 ; for the Missionary Society, $481,199 ; for the Woman's Foreign Missionary Society, $62,243 ; for church extension, $62,094 ; for the Tract Society, $12,070 ; for the Sunday-School Union,

$12,575 ; for the Freedmen's Aid Society, $34,546 ; for education, $27,074 ; for the American Bible Society, $25,950. A comparison of the statistics of the Church by decades since 1777 shows that a large increase of members has taken place in every decade, except in the one from 1837 to 1847, when the Methodist Episcopal Church, South, with 462,428 members, was separated, causing an apparent decrease of 22,103 members. The increase of members from 1867 to 1877 was 525,527. The list of educational institutions of the Church includes 34 universities and colleges, 11 theological institutions, and 90 seminaries, academies, and colleges for young women, which return altogether about 21,000 students, and property (including buildings, grounds, furniture, apparatus, libraries, and endowment funds) valued at about $11,500,000.

The twelfth anniversary of the *Freedmen's Aid Society* was held at Jersey City, N. J., November 11th. The receipts of the Society for the year ending July 1, 1879, had been $75,260, and the Society closed the year with a debt of $9,326. The whole amount which had been collected and disbursed for the purposes of the Society in twelve years was given at $788,- 892. Sixty thousand pupils had been taught during the last twelve years, and pupils trained in the schools of the Society had taught at least three hundred thousand of the colored race scattered over the South. A quarter of a million dollars had been invested in permanent school property. Of the special work of the year, the report stated that seventy teachers had been sustained, and a missionary movement had been started in behalf of women in New Orleans. Additions and improvements had been made to the property of Wiley University, Claflin University, Cookman Institute at Jacksonville, Fla., and Meharry Medical College. The last institution had graduated three classes of young men, several of whom had distinguished themselves in work among yellow-fever patients.

The annual meeting of the *General Missionary Committee* of the Methodist Episcopal Church was held in the city of New York in November. The report of the treasurer showed that the receipts of the Missionary Society for the year ending October 31st had been $551,- 859, or $494 more than those for the preceding year. Appropriations were made for the ensuing year to the amount of $678,869.

The tenth annual meeting of the Executive Committee of the *Woman's Foreign Missionary Society* was held in Chicago, Ill., May 23d. The receipts of the Society for the year had been $67,028. The whole number of auxiliary local societies was 2,172, and the number of contributing members 55,560. "The Heathen Woman's Friend," the periodical organ of the Society, had a subscription list of 13,461 names. Eleven missionaries had been sent out during the year.

The committee which had been appointed

by the General Conference in 1876 to further the design of calling an *Œcumenical Confer- ence of Methodism*, reported on November 6th that it had laid the matter of the proposed Conference before the representative bodies of the Methodist Protestant Church, the Methodist Episcopal Church, South, the American Wesleyan Church, and the Evangelical Association, in the United States; also before the representative bodies of the Methodist Church and the Methodist Episcopal Church in Canada, and the Wesleyan Methodist Connection in Great Britain. Every one of these representative bodies had taken action in favor of the Conference, and had appointed a committee, or provided for its appointment, to act in the business and for the furtherance of the objects of the Conference. The committee now judged it to be necessary that a joint meeting of the committees of these bodies, or of their chairmen, or of some persons authorized to act in their stead, should be held to prepare the call for an Œcumenical Conference, determine the time and place of its meeting, suggest a basis of representation, and provide for essential preliminary details, and proposed that it be held in Cincinnati, Ohio, May 6, 1880. It also expressed the desire that the meeting might be attended, not only by the representatives of the several Methodist bodies which had taken action in favor of the Œcumenical Conference, but also, so far as practicable, by authorized representatives of all other Methodist organizations in every part of the world.

II. METHODIST EPISCOPAL CHURCH, SOUTH.— The following is a summary of the statistics of the Methodist Episcopal Church, South, as they were published in May, 1879 : Number of traveling preachers, 3,457 ; of superannuated preachers, 306 ; of local preachers, 5,762 ; of white members, 783,211 ; of colored members, 1,428 ; of Indian members, 4,698 ; whole number of ministers and members, 798,862, showing an increase in one year of 24,120. Number of Sunday - schools, 7,262, with 54,667 teachers and 391,293 scholars. Amount of collections for Conference claimants, $60,425 ; for foreign and domestic missions, $110,551.

The present Book Committee of this Church after their entrance into office in 1878 found that the indebtedness of the Publishing House amounted to $300,000, of which $100,000 were in ten per cent. bonds, and the rest consisted of the vender's lien on the real estate and the floating debt. The committee undertook to pay the interest on the bonds as it accrued, and obtained from the other creditors an indulgence until July 1, 1879. On May 1, 1879, the House under this arrangement had paid $10,500 of interest on its first-mortgage bonds, and had a few thousand dollars in hand, an increased stock in trade, and a constantly growing business; and the committee was convinced of the ability of the House to pay four per cent. on its entire indebtedness, meet all current expenses, and provide an annual fund

for the gradual reduction of the debt. The committee had obtained subscriptions of $221,- 000 on its four per cent. bonds, conditioned on the whole amount of $300,000 being subscribed.

The *Missionary Board* of the Church, at its annual meeting in May, made appropriations of $79,946 to the support of the foreign and domestic missions, of which $15,606 were allotted to China, $27,715 to Mexico and the Mexican Border mission, $5,800 to Brazil, and $9,000 to the Indian Mission Conference.

The first annual convention of the *Woman's Missionary Society* was held in Louisville, Ky., in May. The sum of $3,719 had been collected for the use of the Society.

III. AMERICAN WESLEYAN CONNECTION.— The numerical strength of this denomination was estimated at the General Conference of 1879 to be about 18,000 members. A publishing house has recently been completed in Syracuse, N. Y., at a cost of $40,000, free of debt. The Connection has a seminary at Wasiogy, Minn., with about $20,000 of real estate, $10,000 in scholarships, and $4,000 in endowments. The "American Wesleyan," a general weekly religious newspaper, the "Children's Banner," semi-monthly, and the "Bible Standard," a monthly periodical, are published by the denomination at Syracuse. The agent of the Publishing House reported to the General Conference that the establishment had property to the amount of $37,392, and $3,000 to the credit of the missionary fund.

The tenth quadrennial *General Conference* of the Connection met at Pittsford, Mich., October 15th. The Rev. N. Warduer was chosen President. The Conference was occupied during the principal part of its session with the revision of the Discipline, and made a large number of changes, one effect of which will be to reduce considerably the size of the book. The denomination being strongly opposed to secret societies on grounds of principle, a resolution was passed that no minister should be introduced to the Conference who was an adhering member of such a society, particularly of the Masonic order. The Rev. T. H. Lynch presented his credentials as a fraternal delegate from the General Conference of the Methodist Episcopal Church ; but, as it was understood that he was a member of the Masonic order, his introduction was deferred. A report was made of the vote which had been taken on an amendment to the rule in the Discipline in reference to secret societies, showing that it had been carried ; and the amendment was made a law excluding the members of all secret societies from membership in the churches. An invitation was presented from the General Conference of the Methodist Episcopal Church to the Wesleyan denomination to take part in the proposed Œcumenical Council of Methodism. The vote on accepting the invitation resulted in a tie, and the question was decided in the affirmative by the casting vote of the President.

Two delegates were appointed to attend the Council. A minister was elected to serve as a general connectional evangelist for the ensuing four years, and have charge of the evangelistic and missionary work of the Connection. A committee was appointed to take measures for the incorporation of an Educational Association at Syracuse, for the purpose of receiving pledges, funds, and bequests for educational purposes in the Wesleyan denomination. A report accepting the principles of the so-called national reform movement was adopted, in pursuance of which the following article was added to the Discipline of the Church:

It shall be the duty of the ministers and members of the Wesleyan Methodist Connection to use their influence, in every feasible manner, in favor of a more complete recognition of the authority of Almighty God in the secular and civil relations both of society and of government. We therefore require—
1. That all our ministers and members shall favor the use of the Bible in our public schools.
2. That chaplaincies in the army and navy, and in the State and national Congress, be not abolished.
3. That the Sabbath day be observed by cessation of all labor and the permission of no excursions on the Lord's day.
4. That the name of Almighty God as the basis of authority in civil government shall be considered as one of the fundamental principles of the Wesleyan Methodist Connection of America, and that it is the bounden duty of our ministers and members to use all feasible means to secure such amendments in the national and State Constitutions, as that the name of God shall be inserted in these instruments, which lie at the foundation of civil government; as it is Christ by whom kings reign and princes decree justice.

A committee was appointed to take measures for the establishment and endowment of an institution of learning in the West. Three new Conferences, the North Carolina, Western Iowa, and Nebraska, were admitted; and authority was given for the organization of a Conference in Dakota.

IV. THE METHODIST CHURCH.—A new denomination has been formed within the year, which has taken the name of the Methodist Church. The churches and members of the body are as yet mostly at or near Philadelphia. It is not a secession or an offshoot from any Methodist body, although many of its members have been members of the Methodist Episcopal Church, and it holds to many of the usages of that Church. The doctrines of the new body are the same as those of the Methodist Episcopal Church, but its system is different in many respects. It recognizes but one order of ministers, that of elders, to which women are eligible as well as men. It has no presiding elders and no bishops, but the President of the Annual Conference exercises the powers of a superintendent. It is like the majority of the other Methodist bodies in having class-meetings, attendance on which is made a test of membership, quarterly meetings, local preachers, and exhorters. It encourages plainness, opposes display and raising money by church fairs, and attaches importance to the promotion of holiness. It had at the end of

1879 eleven preaching appointments and nine churches.

V. METHODIST CHURCH OF CANADA.—The following is a summary of the statistical reports of this Church, as returned to the several Annual Conferences of 1879:

CONFERENCES.	Ministers.	Circuits and missions.	Members.
Toronto	859	255	36,081
London	881	224	88,767
Montreal	225	165	22,873
Nova Scotia	119	81	9,540
New Brunswick	98	76	8,187
Newfoundland	50	41	8,165
Total	1,172	842	123,018

The figures show an increase of 408 over the number returned in 1878. Of the whole number of members, 8,317 are classed as "on trial." Number of Sunday-schools, 1,762, with 16,145 teachers and 123,609 scholars.

The *Missionary Society* reported that its receipts for the year had been $135,234, and its expenditures $140,089. It supports missions among the Indians and among the half-breeds in British America, among the French in Quebec and the Germans of the Dominion, domestic missions in the several Conferences, and a mission in Japan, with a total of 414 stations, 400 missionaries, 75 native assistants and teachers, and 36,538 members. Of the members, 3,149 are Indians, 1,412 in the missions to settlers and half-breeds, 488 in the French-Canadian, 199 in the German, and 200 in the Japanese mission.

VI. WESLEYAN METHODIST CONNECTION.— The following is a summary of the statistics of the Wesleyan Methodist Connection, embracing the British and affiliated Conferences, given in the minutes of the Conference for 1879:

COUNTRIES.	Members.	On trial.	Ministers.	Minis. trial.	On trial.	Super-num's.
Great Britain	377,612	28,984	1,467	175	245	
Ireland	25,487	719	187	28	89	
Foreign missions	85,601	10,313	324	185	12	
French Conference	1,853	75	25	1	2	
Total	490,553	35,091	2,008	334	298	

The itinerant preaching work of the Conference is divided into thirty-four districts, with 712 circuits in Great Britain, 135 circuits in Ireland, and 426 circuits abroad.

The annual meeting of the *Wesleyan Missionary Society* was held in London, May 5th. Mr. Richard Haworth of Manchester presided. The receipts of the Society, as shown by the report, had been £124,359, of which £8,974 were contributed from the mission districts; the expenditures had been £157,217. The Ladies' Central Committee for female education in foreign countries and other benevolent purposes had furthermore expended £2,261, besides furnishing school materials, clothing, etc., to many parts of the mission-field. The numerical returns show an increase of 1,531 church members, with 10,315 on trial, and 1,693 children in the schools above the number reported in 1878. A mission had been begun within the year among the Telugus at Madras, India. The mission on the Gambia had suffered from the effects of the climate upon the missionaries. The operations of a mission at Lagos, Africa, had been suspended in consequence of the death of the missionary. The *Wesleyan Conference* met in its 136th session at Birmingham, July 22d. The Rev. Benjamin Gregory was chosen President. The previous Conference had appointed a committee to consider financial interests, with the view to providing means for paying the debts of the several funds and preventing the accumulation of debts in the future. This committee had matured a scheme for raising a fund to be called the Wesleyan Methodist Thanksgiving Fund, to be divided among the educational, missionary, and benevolent enterprises, and had organized a series of circuit and district meetings to be held in behalf of the same. The committee reported to the Conference what they had done, and that £175,000 had been subscribed to the fund, of which £50,000 had been paid in, enabling the treasurers to discharge half the connectional debt and pay £12,-000 into the hands of the treasurers of the new theological institution. There still remained twelve districts in which central, and 504 circuits in which circuit meetings had not been held. The Conference approved the scheme which the committee had prepared, and advised that the remaining circuit and district meetings be held, and as many local meetings besides as should be practicable. The income of the Home Mission for the year had been £27,011, of which amount the home mission stations had contributed £2,090. The Conference approved of regulations for the employment of district missionaries under the direction of the chairmen of the districts, and for a more general and systematic employment of lay agents. The Sustentation Fund was established in 1874, for the purpose of securing a clear income of £150 per annum to each married minister, and of £80 to each unmarried minister. During the five years of its existence a total increase of £24,477, or an average of £4,-895 a year, had taken place in the allowances to ministers. The fund was now established in thirty out of the thirty-three districts, and the number of circuits paying less than the minimum had been reduced from 372 to 217. The Committee for the Extension of Methodism in Great Britain had appropriated during the year £9,538 to 133 chapels. The Committee of the Theological Institute reported that the expenditures of the institution had exceeded its income by upward of £3,000. Measures were adopted to retrench expenses and secure more frequent and larger contributions from the churches for the support of the institution. The new college to be established will be called

" the Birmingham Branch of the Theological Institution." The promises made to the Auxiliary Fund amounted to £100,000, of which £76,000 were paid in. The Schools Fund reported a deficiency averaging £5,000 a year. The foreign missions were prospering in every aspect but the financial one, in which a course of retrenchments had had to be decided upon. The Conference decided to give notice to the Australasian Conference of the termination of the arrangement under which the Australasian and South Sea missions are supplemented by grants from the Wesleyan Missionary Society. In the Pastoral Conference, a proposition made by the General Conference of the Methodist Episcopal Church in the United States for holding an Œcumenical Conference of Methodist Churches was approved. The report on this subject stated, however, that the scheme is on such a large scale, that considerable time must yet elapse before it can be fully carried into effect. A legal question arose during the discussion of the report on the revision of the Liturgy and Book of Offices, on which the discussion was suspended until the next Conference, in order that the opinion of counsel might be taken on the point in doubt. The numerical report showed that the whole number of members within the immediate jurisdiction of the Conference was 377,612, showing a decrease of 3,264 from the previous year, notwithstanding a 61,137 persons had been received on trialth t

VII. OTHER METHODIST CHURCHES.—The following is a summary of the statistics of the *Primitive Methodist Church* of Great Britain, as they were reported to the Conference in June, 1879: Number of members, 182,877; of ministers, 1,135; of local preachers, 15,6834; of class-leaders, 10,454; of connectional chapels, 4,257; of other places of worship, 2,053; of Sunday-schools, 4,022, with 58,275 teachers, 365,004 scholars, and 4,579 catechumens; present value of chapels, £2,238,787; number of chapels built in 1878, 118, at a cost of £129,-389.

The sixtieth annual *Primitive Methodist Conference* met at Leeds, June 11th. The Rev. Thomas Newell was chosen President. Attention was given to the case of the mission in the island of Fernando Po, Africa, which had been broken up through the expulsion of one missionary by the Spanish Government and the death of another. The Conference made a representation of the matter to the British Government, and in answer to its petition a letter was received from the Foreign Office stating that her Majesty's Minister at Madrid would be instructed to ask permission for Mr. Holland, the expelled missionary, to return to the island. The Conference resolved to continue the mission and give it additional force.

The statistical reports of the *United Methodist Free Churches*, presented to the Annual Assembly in July, 1879, showed that the whole number of members was 72,309, of whom 65,-

137 were in Great Britain, and 7,172 at the foreign stations. The number in Great Britain had diminished 477, and the number at the foreign stations had increased 72, during the year. The number of persons on trial was 6,350, and the number of ministers 429.

The following is a summary of the statistics of the *Methodist New Connection*, as they were presented to the Conference in June, 1879: Number of chapels, 478; of societies, 451; of circuit preachers, 180; of local preachers, 1,-138; of members, 26,688; of probationers, 4,131; of Sunday-schools, 449, with 10,961 teachers and 77,250 scholars.

The statistics of the *Bible Christians*, as reported to the Conference in July, 1879, were: Number of itinerant preachers, 276; of local preachers, 1,874; of chapels, 938; of preaching-places, 182; of full members, 30,165; on trial, 904; of teachers, 9,758; of scholars, 50,-690. The returns showed a decrease of 523 full members, 440 on trial, and 215 teachers, which had taken place chiefly in the Cornwall districts.

The *Wesleyan Reform Union* reported in August, 1879, as follows: Number of chapels and preaching-places, 227; of preachers, 532, with 79 preachers on trial, 17 "ministers," and 434 leaders; of members, 7,240; of Sunday-schools, 180, with 2,896 teachers and 18,521 scholars; of day-schools, 2, with 486 scholars. The statistical returns showed that a decrease of 50 members had occurred during the year.

The annual meeting of the *Free Gospel or Independent Methodist Churches* was held at Ashton-under-Lyne, June 23d and 24th. Mr. W. Oxley of Manchester was elected President. An increase of 385 members had taken place.

MEXICO (ESTADOS UNIDOS DE MÉXICO). The territorial division, area, and population * of the republic are stated in detail in the "Annual Cyclopædia" for 1874 and 1875; and reference may be made to the article GUATEMALA, in the present volume, for measures recently proposed or adopted for the settlement of the boundary question with that country.

The President of the Republic is General Porfirio Diaz, inaugurated in November, 1876; and the Cabinet Ministers are as follows, in order of precedence: Foreign Affairs, M. Ruelas; Interior (*Gobernacion*), Felipe Berriozabal; Finance, Manuel Toro; Justice, Ignacio Mariscal; Public Works (*vacant*); War, General Cárlos Pacheco.

The President of the Supreme Court of Justice (and hence, by the terms of the Constitution, Vice-President of the Republic) is Licentiate Luis M. Vallarta; and the magistrates are Pedro Ogazon, J. de Mata Vásquez, M. Alas, A. Martinez de Castro, M. Blanco, Ignacio Altamirano, E. Montes, S. Guzman, J. M. Bautista, M. Saldaña, E. Avila; with J. E. Muñoz, Attorney-General, and D. de la Garza y Garza, Procurator-General.

The Governors of the several States are: Aguas Calientes, F. G. Hornedo; Campeachy, M. Castillo, Chiapas, S. Escóbar; Chihuahua, A. Frias; Coahuila, H. Charles; Colima, D. Lope; Durango, J. M. Flores; Guanajuato, F. Mena; Guerrero, M. Cuéllar; Hidalgo, N. Cravioto; Jalisco, F. Riestra; Mexico, — Mirafuentes; Michoacan, R. Fernandez; Morelos, C. Pacheco; Nuevo Leon, ——; Oajaca, F. Meigneiro; Puebla, I. J. C. Bonilla; Querétaro, A. Gayon; San Luis Potosi, C. Diaz Gutierrez; Sinaloa, L. Cañedo; Sonora, L. Torres; Tabasco, S. Sarlat; Tamaulipas, J. Gójon; Tlaxcala, — Lira y Ortega; Vera Cruz, — Mier y Teran; Yucatan, M. R. Ancona; Zacatecas, T. G. de la Cadena; Lower California (Territory), A. L. Tapia.

The Mexican Minister to the United States is M. de Zamacona; and the Mexican Consul-General in New York is Dr. Juan N. Navarro. The United States Minister to Mexico is P. H. Morgan, appointed toward the end of the year, *vice* John W. Foster, transferred to St. Petersburg; and the United States Consul-General at the capital is Mr. Lennox.

The army is composed approximately as follows: 20 battalions of foot, 14,640 men and 765 officers; 10 corps of horse, 4,840 men and 290 officers; 4 brigades (of 4 batteries each) of artillery, 1,815 men and 148 officers; coast-guards, 71 men and 22 officers; and Invalids, 265 men and 19 officers; total, 22,375.* In March, 1879, were published the names of 17 generals of division, with a salary of $6,000 each, and 45 generals of brigade, with $4,800 each; and the opposition press made political capital of "such an excessive peace establishment of the army," and of the fact that many of these generals held civil offices. A report was current that the army would be reduced so as to save $4,000,000 annually. The ordinary expenditures of the Department of War and Marine have for several years past averaged over $8,000,000, with a navy comprising only four gunboats.

The Archbishop of Mexico is the Rt. Reverend P. A. de Labastida (1863). The predominant faith is the Roman Catholic; but there is no recognized state religion in Mexico. The Protestant denominations (Episcopalian and Methodist) introduced into the republic some years ago have made numerous proselytes, and their services are attended by considerable congregations. It is reported that the Roman Catholic authorities have sanctioned the printing and distribution of the New Testament in Spanish; and a Mexican correspondent regards it as probable that the Bible without notes will before long find its way into the hands of the people. The translation already admitted contains many chapters free of comment, and presents no essential departure from the version commonly used by Protestants. The Mexican

---

* In a report published during the year by the Minister of the Interior, the population is given at 9,686,777.

* The Government organ states that, according to the laws of the country, foreigners serving the Government in any official capacity become thereby Mexican citizens.

Protestant Episcopal Church, while it is the offspring and *protégé* of the Church of the same name in the United States, is neither dependent upon nor an exact counterpart of the latter, nor is the Bishop controlled by the House of Bishops, although created by that body. It is called the "Church of Jesus," and dates from 1865. The first steps toward its establishment were taken by a former Roman Catholic priest named Aguilar, and one Hernandez, a layman of the same faith, who adopted as their model the Protestant Episcopal Church of the United States; Benito Juarez, then President of the Republic, a man of liberal views and undoubted religious tolerance, affording them such aid and protection as he had in his power. In 1868 the Rev. Dr. Henry Chauncey Riley, a native of Chili, but of American parentage and educated and ordained in New York, and some time rector of a New York Protestant Episcopal church exclusively devoted to service in the Spanish language, was invited to Mexico "to help the new congregation in their labors," he having become known to them as the author of a volume on the right and duty of all men to search the Scriptures, which, with pamphlets discussing the same and other kindred subjects, were widely circulated in the republic. In 1871 Manuel Aguas, a Dominican friar, who had been appointed to resist from the pulpit the diffusion of the reformed creed, became himself a proselyte and joined Dr. Riley. They obtained from the Government a grant of two recently sequestrated churches in the capital, and extended their missionary labors to various other cities. Aguas was elected to the bishopric in the same year, but died in 1872, before he was consecrated. In 1874 the House of Bishops of the Protestant Episcopal Church of the United States was petitioned to superintend the affairs of the Mexican Church, and seven members of that body were appointed to the charge, from which they were relieved by the election, as second Bishop of the Diocese of the Valley of Mexico, of Dr. Riley, who was consecrated at Pittsburgh, Pennsylvania, in June, 1879. This Church had, according to a report published in the same year, 57 congregations in its charge, with 3,500 communicants and a large number of unconfirmed attendants; 9 day-schools, where over 200 children were taught; and an extensive publication depot.

A Catholic convent and monastery, surreptitiously established at Querétaro, was closed by the State authorities.

In the budget for the fiscal year 1879–'80, the national revenue was estimated at $16,-550,000, exclusive of the yield of the Post-Office Department, the proceeds of sales of national property, and of the branch of public instruction (old fund), etc., which in 1878–'79 aggregated rather more than $500,000. In the foregoing estimate is included an item of $500,-000 representing the proceeds of a tax on cotton and woolen stuffs of home manufacture. The estimated expenditures for the same year

were set down at $18,895,198. In general about two thirds of the entire revenue are derived from the custom-house; and the outlook for the yield of that branch in 1879–'80 has been spoken of as rather encouraging, with the mention that the receipts at the port of Vera Cruz, the most important port of the republic, amounted in July, the season at which imports are usually at their lowest ebb, to $700,000, against $230,000 for the corresponding month in 1878. A large proportion of that increase might perhaps be accounted for by the stringent measures adopted by the authorities for the prevention of smuggling. Señor Romero, while Minister of Finance, incurred the enmity of the contrabandists by his indefatigable labors to suppress the chronic system of corruption so long deplored in the Mexican customs service; and it was calculated that his internal revenue law would add $5,000,000 annually to the national revenue. Smuggling and contraband trade occupied the attention of the Congress in the spring session, when an act was passed making evasions of the revenue laws a penal offense. This measure was adopted experimentally, and the question was to be reconsidered at the autumn session, opening in September.

The Supreme Court has decided the existence of custom-houses in the interior to be unconstitutional. With their removal, if it be effected, many grave hindrances to commerce and travel will cease.

As stated in the "Annual Cyclopædia" for 1878, the national debt of Mexico has been estimated by a British writer at $395,500,000;¡ but these figures include the claims referring to the Maximilian empire, which have never been recognized by the republican Government. We transcribe the subjoined table and remarks from Minister Foster's dispatch to the Department of State at Washington under date of October 8, 1878:

TOTAL RECOGNIZED NATIONAL DEBT OF MEXICO.

British :	
London loan of 1831....	$51,208,250
Convention claims, etc......................	4,871,614
Interest due in 1862........................	18,231,793
Total British debt.......	$69,311,657
Total Spanish debt............................	9,460,986
Total French debt.............................	2,859,917
Sixteen years' interest to date, at $2,760,022 per annum	44,160,352
Total European debt......................	$125,792,912
Carbajal-Corlies bonds, 1865...................	2,746,630
American claims awards, balance..............	3,375,123
Total foreign debt..................... ...	$131,914,665

In 1861, by a decree of Congress, the payment of interest on all the foreign debt was suspended for two years, although very little interest has been paid since 1854; and since 1861 the Mexican Government has paid no interest on any of its foreign debt up to the present, the transactions under the Maximilian empire not being taken into account. It is a question of interest to the holders of Mexican bonds, a part of whom are American citizens, to form some estimate of the ability and probability of the payment by Mexico of its foreign debt, or at least of the resumption of its interest. A debt of $130,000,000 is not an excessive burden for nine millions of people, even if it had to be paid in full; but there is reason to believe that it might be reduced from 25 to 50 per cent. by agreement with the creditors, if any reliable assurance could be given of certain and regular payments of interest in the future. But it may safely be predicted that if the country is to be afflicted by a revolution every few years, as has been its past history, there is little or no probability that either principal or interest will be paid. With peace and good government, prosperity and competence would gradually return, and the marvelous natural resources of the country could be developed in such measure as to afford the Government the means, in time, of reëstablishing its foreign credit. But justice to Mexico requires that it should be stated that at present the Government is in no condition to resume the full weight of its foreign obligations. The incessant march of revolutions, as Señor Payno expresses it, has consumed the wealth which the colonial order accumulated, paralyzed business and public enterprises, disorganized the economic regulations of the Government, corrupted the revenue collection, and left the country impoverished to an extent hardly equaled in any other Spanish-American country. The national Treasury is just now in no condition to assume obligations additional to the ordinary and necessary current expenses of Government. It has recently been compelled to suspend temporarily the payment of the salaries of the executive and judicial officials on account of the absence of receipts to pay them. It is now owing the United States over $3,000,000 * under the late claims convention, and to the Mexican Railway Company, say, $2,000,000; and as it appears to act upon the principle of paying the debts last contracted in preference to the old ones, these two are likely to receive attention first; and in the present and prospective state of public affairs and of the Treasury, it is a serious question whether it will not be thought necessary to continue its default on the payment of the last-named of these two. The prospect, therefore, for an early resumption of the payment of interest on the foreign debt does not appear to be very flattering. I have not taken into consideration in this dispatch the large interior debt of the country, which, in addition to the funded part, is made up of a large amount of unadjusted claims, which increase enormously with each succeeding revolution.

According to official statistics, the total value of the exports varies from $25,000,000 to $35,000,000 annually, and that of the imports from $27,000,000 to $30,000,000; but habitual smuggling renders it impossible to regard these figures as even an approximation to truth. In the opinion of the best informed concerning the foreign trade of Mexico, it would not be rash to estimate the value of the imports at double the amount officially reported; and the same may be said of the value of the bullion sent out of the country. Less than one third of the trade is with the United States, and rather more than one third with Great Britain. Of the exports of 1876, declared at $25,435,000, silver amounted to about $15,000,000, copper ore, cochineal, indigo, etc., being among the other leading articles.

The annexed table exhibits the total values of the exports (excluding shipments *in transitu*) to the United Kingdom, and of the imports of British and Irish commodities, during the decade from 1869 to 1878:

* The annual installments ($300,000) of this award have up to the present time been punctually paid. A great portion of the 1879 installment was made up of voluntary contributions from citizens throughout the country.

YEARS.	Exports.	Imports.
1869	$1,752,850	$3,158,620
1870	1,499,065	4,554,410
1871	1,986,670	5,245,065
1872	2,217,620	4,215,980
1873	2,497,660	5,970,620
1874	2,788,250	5,628,065
1875	3,609,555	4,424,555
1876	3,310,660	2,511,120
1877	3,994,285	4,977,550
1878	2,585,410	8,866,650

The chief articles exported to the United Kingdom in 1878 were mahogany of the value of $1,203,865, and unrefined sugar, $160,450; while the chief imports therefrom were cotton fabrics of the value of $2,011,785; linens, $357,660; and iron, wrought and unwrought, $428,315. The declared value of the silver ore exported to Great Britain in 1869 was $400; 1870, $16,750; 1871, $148,870; 1872, $128,215; 1873, $80,095; 1874, $11,270; 1875, $89,595; 1876, $72,760; 1877, $72,690; 1878, $25,330.

The exports from the port of Vera Cruz to the United States in the years ending September 30, 1876, 1877, and 1878, were as follows:

ARTICLES.	1876.	1877.	1878.
Ashes, volcanic..		$17 94	
Beans............	$725 16	285 10	$569 29
Bird-seed........	2,590 12		
Books...........	1,654 48	328 00	
Cider...........	17,578 06	10,883 86	45,000 84
Chicle..........	46 77		
Chocolate.......	26 00		
Cochineal.......	17,606 39	80,681 98	82,569 68
Coffee..........	529,916 80	1,419,679 42	895,602 84
Copper..........			898 95
Dyestuff........	772 74		
Esparto-grass...	24 00		
Feathers........	268 01	361 88	566 85
Figures, wax....	2,741 80		502 50
Fish, dry.......			155 25
Fruits..........	298 85	194 44	
Fustic..........	11,149 85		
Garlic..........	99 94	460 75	
Hair, horse.....		176 87	489 92
Herbs, medicinal	1,229 78	782 42	459 49
Hemp...........	275 87	682 48	
Hides and skins.	386,696 90	888,414 59	494,979 79
Honey..........	81 32		
Indigo..........	1,750 83	1,409 08	755 88
Jalap...........	815 80	1,120 07	8,188 68
Leather.........	43 56	89 00	
Luggage.........	5,708 88		911 62
Marble..........	816 47	1,287 29	845 06
Metals..........	109 43	878 78	654 86
Miscellaneous ...	10,313 89	1,459 85	4,921 64
Onyx...........		1,718 53	
Opals..........		150 00	
Paintings	620 00		
Paper..........	80 00		
Pepper..........		87 43	6 22
Plants.........	120 25	148 00	806 68
Returned goods..	2,714 41	502 24	2,795 55
Rubber.........	2,619 48	2,711 75	5,660 28
Rum...........		86 00	
Saffron.........		64 25	855 57
Samples and curiosities........	817 51		2,200 65
Silver, old......	330 80		
Sirup..........	45 00		
Sugar..........	84,789 79	106,226 55	71,586 81
Tobacco........	16,887 09	23,530 16	8,114 49
Tripoli.........		99 22	
Vanilla.........	302,013 29	113,257 00	99,751 88
Woods..........	2,996 85	5,129 10	909 00
Totals	$1,877,916 77	$2,109,506 67	$1,587,916 29

The imports at the port of Matamoros from the United States in the years ending September 30, 1877 and 1878, were:

ARTICLES.	1877.	1878.
Agricultural implements............	$290	$1,311
Ale and beer......................	9,896	18,686
Books............................	343	642
Manufactures of brass.............	385	371
Broad and breadstuffs.............	115,019	106,065
Candles	14,086	11,452
Carriages.........................	1,343	2,029
Cotton goods, colored..............	215,181	190,267
Cotton, bleached and unbleached....	200,367	106,185
Cartridges and arms	9,439	6,788
Chemicals	14,114	16,010
Earthenware	4,769	660
Fancy articles....................	8,069	6,148
Manufactures of glass.............	5,548	11,484
Manufactures of rubber............	2,823	542
Bar-iron and nails................	4,205	5,870
Machinery........................	23,955	26,584
Manufactures of iron and steel.....	4,444	4,170
Boots and shoes...................	39,836	37,291
Manufactures of leather...........	658	1,256
Lime and cement..................	191	414
Matches..........................	547	1,026
Illuminating oils.................	40,792	31,412
Linseed and all other oils.........	225	527
Gunpowder.......................	4,711	1,153
Paint and varnish.................	1,811	1,545
Paper............................	5,584	9,219
Perfumery........................	213	862
Bacon, butter, cheese, and lard....	43,265	43,153
Potatoes and other vegetables......	2,654	8,914
Rice.............................	2,432	1,119
Salt..............................	266	332
Scales............................	1,028	897
Sewing-machines	29,207	31,730
Starch............................	7,671	6,981
Soap.............................	14,472	22,064
Sugar............................	36,946	39,610
Tobacco, loaf.....................	14,900	60,271
Wearing apparel..................	5,304	7,147
Manufactures of wood.............	20,826	39,023
Manufactures of wool.............	3,966	2,432
Total.......................	$905,326	$865,011

The commodities most largely imported in the same years from other countries were coffee of the values of $126,166 in 1877 and $100,763 in 1878; cotton fabrics, $319,211 in 1877 and $287,277 in 1878; linen fabrics, $22,878 in 1877 and $37,532 in 1878; machinery, $14,322 in 1877 and $248,013 in 1878; manufactured clothing, $12,435 in 1877 and $28,762 in 1878; bar and sheet iron, chains, etc., $7,826 in 1877 and $9,828 in 1878; woolen fabrics, $21,401 in 1877 and $20,102 in 1878; and wine and spirits, $28,569 in 1877 and $82,451 in 1878.

The subjoined tables exhibit the exports from Matamoros (all to the United States, the copper and lead *in transitu* for England) for the same years:

EXPORTS IN 1877.

ARTICLES.	Quantities.	Value, including charges.
Hides, skins, hair		$538,487
Wool.........................	186,618 lbs.	17,785
Istle-fiber....................	1,310,577 "	58,485
Live animals..................		21,685
Crude sarsaparilla.............	1,010 lbs.	169
Crude cotton.................	110,000 "	2,255
Copper, in pigs...............	40,864 "	4,215
Lead, in pigs.................	39,326 "	1,640
Corn		984
Sugar.........................	7,080 lbs.	268
Horns........................		272
Miscellaneous................		7,175
Total......................		$658,285

EXPORTS IN 1878.

ARTICLES.	Quantities.	Value, including charges.
Hides, skins, hair...............		$438,163
Wool.........................	191,588 lbs.	17,555
Istle-fiber....................	247,143 "	10,426
Live animals.................	2,727 head	5,695
Crude sarsaparilla............	3,592 lbs.	220
Copper, in pigs...............	31,485 "	3,249
Horns........................		450
Miscellaneous................		1,073
Total.......................		$476,831

The exports from Merida, Yucatan (through the small port of Progreso), for the year ending September 30, 1878, were of the value of $1,194,277; of which $907,239 were to the United States, including *henequen* or Sisal hemp of the value of $843,123; deerskins, $11,195; hammocks, $14,053; hides, $15,478, etc. The value of the imports was considerably under $1,000,000.

The aggregate value of the exports from Mazatlan, on the Gulf of California, for the year ending June 30, 1878, was $3,689,702. The trade of Mazatlan with the United States for that year is shown in the annexed table:

ARTICLES.	Imports.	Exports.
Corn (540 tons)...............	$74,987 00	....
Dry goods...................	713,000 00	....
Flour (800 tons)..............	120,000 00	....
Miscellaneous...............	152,000 00	....
Machinery...................	123,000 00	....
Brazil-wood.................	....	$27,682 00
Specie and bullion...........	....	2,341,000 00
Fruit........................	....	8,500 00
Hides	....	16,829 00
Miscellaneous...............	....	8,800 00
Orchilla.....................	....	5,721 00
Tobacco.....................	....	161 00
Total....................	$1,182,987 00	$2,398,493 00

This table is particularly interesting as showing the exchange of articles of American and of Mexican production which constitute the rapidly increasing trade between this port and the United States, mainly through San Francisco. Until very lately Yucatan was the Mexican State which carried on the most extensive trade with this country; but the foregoing table shows that Sinaloa has now taken the lead.

The year 1879 was marked by the continuance of the depression which began to be felt in commercial circles in the second half of 1878, and which was mainly attributable to the decline in silver in the London market. No better explanation of this phenomenon can be given than the following, extracted from the United States Minister's report to the State Department at Washington, under date of October 29, 1878:

The basis of all monetary transactions in this country is silver. Although the double standard of gold and silver is provided by law, and the Government is constantly minting coins of both metals, for a number of years past the gold coinage has commanded a considerable premium over silver, and during the past two or three years gold has not only ceased to be a circulating medium, but has almost entirely left the country. It is now very difficult to purchase on short notice in this city only a few thousand dollars in gold, and it commands a premium of from 14 to 18 per cent., according to the fluctuations of the London silver market. Silver is by law an unlimited legal tender for all debts, public and private. As indicating the injurious effects on business affairs of the depreciation in the value of silver, I inclose herewith a communication which the Minister of Finance has addressed to Congress, conveying to that body the recommendation tations of the London market, which have resulted in placing foreign exchange at a premium of 22 per cent.* For some weeks previous to the recent decline, exchange on New York ruled at 18 per cent. The main object of the Minister's communication was to bring again to the attention of Congress the recommendation of the Executive, submitted to the last Congress, for a repeal of the export duty of 5 per cent. which is now charged by the Government on all silver, coined and uncoined, shipped abroad, which repeal would reduce the price of exchange to that extent. Mr. Romero, the Minister of Finance, has for many years been a strong advocate of this wise measure of the repeal of all duties on the exportation of silver and other natural products; but thus far the necessities of the national and State Treasuries have defeated it. Besides the export duty collected by the Federal Government, there are heavy export taxes by the States, coinage duties and other charges, all tending to the depressing influence of the London market. A careful estimate of the taxes, duties, and various charges on silver shows that it costs from 13½ to 15½ per cent. to place the silver produced in the Mexican mines in London or in New York. When it is remembered that silver constitutes four fifths of the entire value of export products of Mexico, the effect of these heavy internal taxes and the decline in value in London upon the general trade and business of this country can be easily estimated. In the present depressed condition of all industries in Mexico, the late decline in silver must be regarded for this country as a great national calamity.

The American industrial deputation, referred to heretofore,† was cordially received at the Mexican capital, and the exhibition of United States manufactures inaugurated by President Diaz, who said:

It is a source of great satisfaction to me to accept the invitation you have tendered me to inaugurate your diminutive exhibit of North American merchandise brought to this country for the purpose of augmenting the commercial relations existing between our two republics. This testimony, rendered to peace, to labor, and to progress, highly honors the Association of Manufacturers of the United States. Far from your having to thank the Government of Mexico for having coöperated in the better discharge of your commission, by offering you those attentions and facilities which were due to you, the Mexican nation is thankful to you for having come on this noble mission with the olive of peace in one hand and the torch of civilization in the other. Ever since she conquered her independence, Mexico has maintained her ports open to the trade of the world. Following up the great maxim of the great father of your independence, that honesty is the best policy, I must state to you that, although the fiscal legislation of this country still labors in part from the colonial system, and can not be considered as the most liberal in the world, it has continued and is continuing a progressive march of liberality, with the view of stimulating the development of commerce, the fountain of the wealth and prosperity of nations. Our Constitution ordains that there should be no prohibitions. The list of articles free of all duties, which has

been increasing day by day, comprises various objects, such as machinery of all classes, in regard to which the remarkable mechanical improvements in the United States are such that very few countries can compete with them. Although Mexico and the United States are neighboring nations, they are, unfortunately, very little known to each other, and in each of them errors and prejudices prevail in regard to the other. The step that has been taken by the Manufacturers' Association of the Northwest of your country, by sending you on this mission, will doubtless produce, among other good results, that of dispelling some of the many errors that are entertained in the United States respecting Mexico. As regards Mexico, you will always find her disposed to coöperate in this work of civilization. The generosity and nobleness of sentiments of her citizens are proverbial, and she instinctively accepts all that is good. As regards her Government, it suffices to say that all the administrations which have succeeded each other since the triumph of the republic over the foreign intervention of 1867, whatever may have been the points of internal policy on which they differed, have strenuously endeavored to establish permanent commercial relations with the United States. Nine lines of foreign steamers trade to the Mexican ports; of these, four come from European ports and are supported by subsidies from their respective governments, or by the profits of their traffic; the other five come from ports of the United States, and are supported by a liberal subsidy paid to them by the Mexican Treasury, which, notwithstanding its impoverishment, devotes a not very inconsiderable part of its revenue to sustain these lines of steamers. Without this aid you would not have been able to come from your country to ours by the route and with the rapidity you have done. Thanks to these lines of steamers, the trade between the two countries has somewhat increased, as instead of $2,000,000, to which the commerce between the United States and Mexico reached before the war of the intervention, it now exceeds $10,000,000.

At the end of the year there were 372 miles of railroad in operation in the republic, the principal line being that from Vera Cruz to the capital.* Tidings were received in September, 1879, of the commencement of work on a new line of railroad to cross the Isthmus of Tehuantepec, from the mouth of the Coatzacoalcos River, 110 miles S. E. from Vera Cruz, to the Upper Lagoon, an inland lake on the Pacific coast. The length of the main line will be nearly 150 miles. The grant for the line was made by the Government of Mexico in June last to Edward Learned, of Pittsfield, Massachusetts. It required that the company undertaking the work should deposit with the Government, within six months of the date of the law, $100,000 as a forfeit, and that it should have imported upon the isthmus, prior to the expiration of that period, railroad material of the value of $200,000, or have made harbor improvements of the same value, in which case the deposit might be substituted by mortgage bonds of the company. The road is to have a single or double track four and a half feet in width, and is required to be completed within three years from the date of the approval of the contract; the company being required to construct yearly, to the satisfaction of the Government, a section thirty-nine miles in length. The right of way is 229·64 feet along the entire route, and the Government gives the com-

---

* Exchange on London and on New York was more than once quoted at 23 per cent. premium in the course of 1879.
† See "Annual Cyclopædia" for 1878.

* For details concerning this line see "Annual Cyclopædia" for 1873.

pany such a strip of unoccupied public lands as may be required for the line, and in addition one half of the unoccupied public lands that may be found within one league from each side of the railroad. Lands are also granted for the sites of wharves, docks, and other improvements required in the harbor of Coatzacoalcos and the Upper Lagoon, at which point the company is bound to construct and maintain two lighthouses of the first class, which shall, however, be the exclusive property of the Government. The privilege of erecting a line of telegraph is also accorded by the grant. To aid in the construction of these improvements, the Government, in addition to other stipulations, binds itself to give to the company a subsidy of $12,070.50 for each mile of railroad built, and agrees not to grant a subsidy to any other enterprise of a similar character on the same line for a period of twenty years, although the right is reserved to authorize the construction of a canal. The subsidy is to be paid on each section of five kilometres upon its completion and its approval by the Department of Public Works, 10 per cent. interest to be allowed in cases of any delay in such payments. The grant is limited to ninety-nine years, and at the expiration of that time the railroad and telegraph, with stations, depots, and other works, and the proper complement of rolling-stock, are to be turned over to the Government in good order, upon the basis of a careful appraisement and inventory of the property. The enterprise under the terms of the grant is to remain exclusively Mexican, and the company, though formed abroad, is to be regarded as if created in the Mexican Republic and organized in accordance with Mexican laws; and those engaged in the enterprise in no case will be entitled to plead the rights accorded to aliens, and will have no power to enforce their rights otherwise than before Mexican tribunals. Such of the work as can be conveniently done in this country will be executed here, in order to avoid the expense of more costly labor in Mexico. It is stated that the cost of the entire work will not exceed $5,500,000, which estimate is believed to be considerably in excess of the actual amount necessary to open the road, well supplied with the requisite appliances for the performance of its business. The climate is represented as salubrious, the thermometer ranging throughout the year between 60° and 80°; the country is productive, has easy grades, and presents no unusual or serious obstacles. The route, it would appear, will materially shorten all lines of communication and facilitate the transmission of traffic between the principal ports of the Atlantic and Pacific Oceans.

A contract was signed on December 2, 1879, between the Governor of the State of Yucatan and Messrs. R. G. and O. G. Canton of Merida, for the construction of a railway from that city to Peto, passing through Ticul and Tekax.

President Diaz, in his message to Congress at its spring session, which opened on April 1st, alluded to the signing of a contract by the Minister of Public Works for the laying of a submarine and overland telegraph from a Gulf port of the United States, along the Mexican coast, touching at the various intermediate Mexican ports, and crossing the Isthmus of Tehuantepec to the Pacific coast.*

Referring to the United States, General Diaz complained that the instructions to General Ord, to pursue raiders across the border, were still in force, in violation of the treaty of 1848; and expressed the hope that the United States, "in obedience to the dictates of justice and in the interest of commerce," would revoke said instructions, which were at variance with the spirit of international law.

A few symptoms of and one or two overt attempts at revolution occurred in the course of the year. The leader of one of the latter was General Negrete, commander-in-chief of the Mexican army. General Diaz, on learning of the movement, set out at the head of 3,000 men in pursuit of Negrete; and in this, as in all other instances of the kind, Diaz manifested his capacity to quell disturbances as fast as they arise.

The all-important question at issue in political circles was that of the fast-approaching election for President of the Republic. The principal candidates were Sr. Vallarta, President of the Supreme Court of Justice, whose term of office expires two years later than that of Diaz; Senator Bonitez; General Treviño; Gonzales, Minister of War immediately preceding Pacheco, and the Government candidate; Sr. Riva Palacio; Sr. T. G. de la Cadena; and lastly, though unavowedly, General Diaz himself.

Mexico has entered into the Postal Union.

MICHIGAN. The Legislature met in regular biennial session January 1st, and continued in session until May 31st. The number of public acts passed was 268; of local acts, 408; of joint resolutions, 34; of concurrent resolutions, 19.

The laws regulating the liquor-traffic were revised. The new legislation leaves every dealer to assess himself, instead of, as before, imposing that duty upon the regular assessing officers of cities, townships, and villages.

An act to establish a State Reform School for Girls appropriates $30,000 for grounds and buildings, and to pay the current expenses. It is to be governed by a board of control consisting of four women and two men. Girls between seven and twenty years of age can be committed to it till the age of twenty-one, who have been convicted of disorderly conduct, or of any offense not punishable with imprisonment for life, and apprenticed to suitable persons on giving evidence of reformation.

An act was also passed to establish a separate school for the blind, appropriating $35,000 for the year 1879, and $10,000 for the year

* For other telegraph statistics, see "Annual Cyclopædia" for 1876.

1880. The blind wards of the State are now cared for in connection with the deaf and dumb, and the early separation of the two classes is considered better for both.

Three joint resolutions propose amendments to the Constitution. The first so amends section 12 of Article XIII. as to permit the diversion of fines imposed for breaches of the penal laws from the city, township, or district library fund to the general school fund, as the local school authorities may determine. The second empowers the Legislature to authorize the city of Detroit "to aid in the construction and maintenance of a tunnel or bridge across the Detroit River at or near said city, to an amount not to exceed one per centum of the assessed value of the taxable property in said city." The third increases the annual salary of the Governor from $1,000 to $3,000. The second amendment is to be voted upon at the general election to be held November 2, 1880, and the first and third at the election to be held April 5, 1880.

Appropriations were made for the fiscal years 1879 and 1880, to be levied upon the tax-rolls of those years, as follows:

For State officers and State government.......	$1,161,000 00
" Capitol grounds and sewer...............	22,000 00
" University...........................	95,000 00
" Normal School........................	48,373 00
" Agricultural College....................	83,080 24
" State Public School....................	87,000 00
" Institution for Deaf, Dumb, and Blind.....	$6,800 00
" Michigan Asylum for Insane.............	26,588 00
" Eastern " "	83,209 00
" State Reform School...................	86,937 51
" School for Blind (new).................	45,000 00
" Reform School for Girls (new)...........	30,000 00
" State Prison.........................	20,080 00
" State House of Correction..............	8,600 00
" Fish Commission......................	10,000 00
To reimburse military fund..	25,000 00
Total appropriations...............	$1,908,667 75

On February 10th Governor Croswell communicated to the Legislature the resignation of United States Senator Isaac P. Christiancy, whose term of office would have expired March 4, 1881. The election of his successor took place on the 18th, and Zachariah Chandler was elected by 88 votes on joint ballot, against 22 for Orlando M. Barnes, Democrat, and 3 for Henry Chamberlain, National. In 1875 Mr. Chandler was the caucus Republican candidate for Senator, his third term of continuous service being about to expire, but was defeated by Judge Christiancy, who received the Democratic vote and six Republican votes, giving him one majority. Senator Chandler died suddenly at Chicago, November 1st, and Governor Croswell appointed as his successor ex-Governor Henry P. Baldwin of Detroit.

The biennial election for a Justice of the Supreme Court and two Regents of the University (each for the term of eight years), held on the first Monday in April, assumed unusual importance because of a fusion or coalition of the Democratic and National parties, whose united vote for Governor the preceding November exceeded the Republican vote by 24,-536. The two parties met in separate con-

ventions at Lansing on February 28th, and the Democratic Convention appointed a committee to confer with a committee from the National Convention. The joint committee united in reporting to each convention the following resolutions or platform, two members of the Democratic Committee dissenting on these grounds: "First, it is not germane to the issues involved in the pending election; second, it includes financial doctrines and policies which, in the opinion of a minority of your committee, are neither right nor wise":

1. We deprecate the tendency in our national affairs toward centralization of power and its corrupt use.

2. We believe in the strict equality of all the States and all classes of citizens before the law, and that our government should be in truth and in fact a government of the people by the people and for the people.

3. We are opposed to all further allowance of war claims.

4. We demand that all money, whether paper or metallic, shall be issued by the General Government only, and made a full legal tender for all debts, public and private, except as to such contracts heretofore made as were originally payable in coin.

5. We are opposed to all banks of issue, and demand that greenbacks shall be substituted in place of national-bank bills; and that the coinage of gold and silver shall be placed in all respects upon the same footing.

6. We believe that money should be issued in sufficient volume to meet the requisites of business; that the Government should regulate the value of money by preserving a uniform ratio between the supply and demand; and that this delicate and important power should never be delegated to banks, corporations, or individuals.

7. We are opposed to all monopolies, and demand that the public domain be reserved to the tillers of the soil, and not squandered upon railroad or other corporations.

8. We cordially invite all men, without regard to past political affiliations, who favor the principles herein set forth, and who love their country and its prospects more than party, to unite and work with us to save the people from the bankruptcy and ruin to which the policy of the dominant party is speedily and surely tending.

In the Democratic Convention, after a sharp discussion and a failure, by a vote of 140 yeas to 174 nays, to so amend the sixth resolution as to declare that "all paper money should be convertible into coin at the will of the holder," it was adopted by a vote of 188 to 120; and the other resolutions were also adopted with greater or less unanimity. The National-Greenback Convention adopted them unanimously. The committee reported as candidates: For Justice of the Supreme Court, John B. Shipman of Coldwater, Democratic and National; for Regents of the University, George P. Sanford of Lansing, National-Democrat, and Henry Whiting of St. Clair, National-Republican. Pending their nomination by the Democratic Convention, several delegations withdrew from the Convention. The affiliating Convention accepted the ticket by acclamation.

The Republican Convention was held at Lansing on March 6th. The following candidates were nominated: For Justice of the Supreme Court, James V. Campbell of Detroit; for

Regents of the University, James Shearer of Bay City, and Ebenezer O. Grosvenor of Jonesville. The following platform was unanimously adopted:

Resolved, That the Republican party having fulfilled their pledge to make the greenback dollar worth one hundred cents in gold or silver, and having given to the country a safe and flexible currency, well adapted to the industrial needs of the people, we therefore oppose any radical change in our present financial system, and congratulate the country on the successful resumption of specie payments, and the signs of returning prosperity in all branches of business.

Resolved, That we invite in this election the coöperation of all men of whatever former party affiliation who are in favor of financial honesty and a safe and sound basis for the business of the country.

The election resulted as follows:

FOR JUSTICE OF THE SUPREME COURT.

James V. Campbell, Republican............ 132,313
John B. Shipman, Fusion.................... 126,270

FOR REGENTS OF THE UNIVERSITY.

Ebenezer O. Grosvenor, Republican........ 131,350
James Shearer, Republican................. 131,794
George P. Sanford, Fusion................. 126,614
Henry Whiting, Fusion..................... 126,333

At the same election judges were chosen for two new judicial circuits. In the Twenty-second Circuit, composed of the counties of Monroe and Washtenaw, the vote was: For Gouverneur Morris, Democrat, 5,887; for Ira R. Grosvenor, Republican, 4,987; for Robert E. Frazer, National, 2,741. In the Twenty-fourth Circuit, composed of the counties of Huron, Sanilac, and Tuscola: For Cyrenius P. Black, Fusion, 4,633; for Levi L. Wixson, Republican, 4,987.

The annual report of the State Treasurer makes the following statement for the fiscal year ending September 30, 1879:

Cash balance, September 30, 1878..... $400,340 35
Cash receipts for the year............ 2,225,812 77

Total resources for the year....... $2,626,153 12
Cash payments for the year........... 2,019,885 59

Balance September 30, 1879...... $606,267 58

Of this balance $604,020.18 belongs to the sinking fund.

The receipts for the year may be classified as follows: For delinquent taxes, sales of State-tax lands, redemptions, State-tax deeds, and tax histories and statements, $392,276.79; from trust lands and funds, principal and interest, $234,306.86; from deposit accounts, $2,009.23; from counties—State taxes of 1878, State-tax land sales, general account, and taxes and redemptions—$906,130.35; St. Mary's Canal tolls, $21,000; earnings of convicts in State Prison, $67,974.56; United States, 5 per cent. on sales of lands in State, $606.91; specific taxes, $640.74; specific taxes—from railroad companies(including street-railway and car companies), $430,-739.42; fire-insurance companies, $50,415.83; life-insurance companies, $19,770.65; mining companies, $26,678.72; other corporations, $4,-135; interest on surplus funds, specific taxes, tax sales, and United States 4½ per cent. bonds,

$44,845; sales of Michigan reports, statutes, and old furniture, $9,562.88 fees from State officers and commissions of commissioners of deeds and notaries public, $5,202.15; trespasses on State lands, $7,920; rents, licenses, and refunded items, $596.41. Total, $2,225,812.77.

Classified expenditures: On bonded debt—principal $46,000, interest $59,140; to counties, $524,357.04; on appropriations, $589,817.52; specific tax-fund transfers, $67,815.57; awards by Board of State Auditors, $167,003.39; salaries of State and judicial officers, etc., $177,-222.10; swamp-land warrants, $68,431.74; taxes, etc., refunded, $55,698.38; St. Mary's Canal expenses, $2,335.58; State House of Correction expenses, $28,000; State Prison expenses, $80,702.94; tax sales (advertising and county treasurers' fees), $42,970.48; expenses of Legislature, $98,537.47; miscellaneous items, $9,537.16; special deposits, $2,170.87. Total, $2,019,885.59.

The bonded debt of the State on September 30, 1879, was:

Two-million loan, 6's, due January 1, 1883...... $591,000 00
War-bounty loan, 7's, due May 1, 1890......... 299,000 00
Non-interest-bearing bonds.................... 23,149 77

Total bonded debt............ .... $913,149 77

There was on hand applicable to the payment of this debt:

United States bonds (with Fund Commissioners) $300,000 00
Canal fund (total amount of bonds)............. 8,000 00
Sinking fund................................. 604,000 00

Total....................... .... $912,000 00

The indebtedness of the State to the several trust funds is as follows:

Primary-school fund......................... $2,441,734 79
Five per cent. primary-school fund........... 320,427 44
University fund............................. 458,655 96
Agricultural College fund.................... 139,375 42
Normal School fund.......................... 55,915 32
Railroad and other deposits.................. 3,136 08

Total................................. $3,419,145 01

On the Normal School fund the State pays 6 per cent. interest, and on the other educational funds 7 per cent.

The annual report of the Commissioner of the State Land-Office for the fiscal year ending September 30, 1879, shows that during the year 6,535·18 acres were forfeited to the State, and 69,044·58 acres sold. The number of acres held by the State September 30, 1879, was 2,801,-679·41, of which 2,198,476·39 were swamp-land, 442,510·83 primary school land, and 155,525·68 Agricultural College land. About three fifths of this land, or 1,697,356·43 acres, are not in market — 115,358·88 acres being licensed to homesteaders, 52,415·84 reserved on road and ditch contracts, 1,326,965·34 reserved to the Marquette, Sault Ste. Marie, and Mackinaw Railroad Company, 111,752·80 withdrawn for Menominee Iron Range Railroad, 69,745·97 to aid in the construction of a railroad from L'Anse to Houghton, and 20,406·39 acres to aid in the construction of the Days River and Bay de Nor State road. The number of acres subject to sale September 30, 1879, was 1,104,-302·98. The 69,044·58 acres disposed of during the year were sold for $125,508.32, of which $95,876.81 was paid and $29,631.51 is due. The entire receipts of the office during the year were $246,257.28. The collections for trespass, including those for conveyance, amounted to $15,878.89. The expense incurred was $12,-803.58. Homestead licenses to the number of 897, covering 27,326·82 acres of land, were issued. The sales of land have been mostly in small parcels, and to parties who will in most instances become actual settlers. The sales of Agricultural College land show a great increase over former years. There is now a large inquiry for State lands from the older portions of the State, from the Middle States, and from Canada.

The two following tables from the annual report of the Auditor-General are of more than ordinary interest. By classes of institutions the receipts and expenditures of the year were:

RECEIPTS.

INSTITUTIONS.	From State Treasury.	From other sources.	Total.
Educational......	$228,802 32	$98,129 52	$326,981 84
Asylums.........	170,689 29	153,383 86	823,972 65
Reformatory....	194,904 84	105,770 42	300,674 76
Miscellaneous...	49,500 00	48,189 42	98,689 42
Totals.......	$643,845 95	$400,872 72	$1,044,218 67

DISBURSEMENTS.

INSTITUTIONS.	Current expenses.	Building and special.	Total.
Educational......	$222,658 51	$68,388 19	$291,041 70
Asylums.........	254,432 06	68,685 70	318,117 76
Reformatory....	234,799 48	39,948 03	274,747 51
Miscellaneous...	66,606 30	28,000 00	69,606 30
Totals.......	$778,496 35	$195,016 92	$973,513 27

The disbursements from the State Treasury since the organization of the State, for the support of educational and reformatory institutions and asylums, have been as follows:

INSTITUTIONS.	FROM INTEREST PAID BY STATE.		On account of appropriations.	Total to each institution.	Total by classes.
	On trust funds.	From receipts from holders of part-paid certificates.			
Educational:					
Primary schools.................	$2,743,519 11	$1,710,811 17	....	$4,454,380 28	
University.................	671,074 49	428,788 42	$559,671 60	1,659,529 51	
Normal School.................	54,455 18	58,456 68	331,068 22	443,980 08	
Agricultural College............	62,062 61	58,171 61	508,312 20	628,546 42	
State Public School..............	....	....	335,066 00	335,066 00	$7,516,452 24
Reformatory:					
Reform School.................	....	....	724,531 18	724,531 18	
State House of Correction........	....	....	366,964 60	366,964 60	
State Prison.................	....	....	926,680 68	926,680 68	2,018,176 46
Asylums:					
For Insane—Eastern.............	....	....	510,569 70	510,569 70	
" " Michigan.............	....	....	1,142,919 71	1,142,919 71	
" Deaf, Dumb, and Blind, at Flint......................	....	....	1,017,752 82	1,017,752 82	2,671,241 73
Totals....................	$3,531,111 39	$2,251,222 83	$6,428,586 91	$12,205,870 43	$12,205,870 43

The State taxes for the current year, levied under legislative acts of 1879 and former years, were apportioned to the counties by the Auditor-General on the 4th of October, and were for the following purposes:

University, buildings and aid.................	$93,750 00
Normal School, buildings and support..........	31,178 00
Agricultural College, building, etc..........	21,040 12
State Public School, maintenance.............	43,950 00
State Reform School, building and expenses...	48,815 00
Institution for Deaf, Dumb, and Blind.......	46,700 00
Michigan Asylum for the Insane.............	26,588 00
Eastern Michigan Asylum for Insane..........	33,209 00
New School for the Blind (building).........	35,000 00
Reform School for Girls (new)...............	20,000 00
State House of Correction...................	8,600 00
State Prison, buildings, etc.................	20,080 00
New State Capitol grounds..................	4,500 00
Military purposes..........................	71,691 09
Fish Commission...........................	5,000 00
General purposes..........................	643,000 00
Total State taxes..................	$1,153,096 21
Add for indebtedness of counties..............	264,594 69
Aggregate apportionment.................	$1,417,690 90

The State taxes are apportioned on an aggregate equalized valuation of real and personal estate (made in 1876) of $630,000.000. The per cent. is a fraction less than $1\frac{9}{10}$ mill, or a fraction over 18 cents on each $100.

The fourth annual reports of the County Treasurers, made under the liquor-tax laws of 1875–'77, show 41 wholesale and 2,281 retail dealers in distilled liquors, and 122 manufacturers, 25 wholesale, and 1,734 retail dealers in malt liquors; total, 4,203. Taxes paid:

By manufacturers.........................	$7,822 26
" wholesale dealers.....................	13,783 51
" retail dealers........................	351,810 83
Interest paid on overdue taxes.............	1,072 98
Total..............................	$374,489 18

Uncollected taxes, $35,545.61. These taxes do not go into the State Treasury, but belong to the municipalities in which they are collected, and are generally used for the support of the poor.

The preliminary report of the Commissioner of Insurance for the year ending December 31, 1879, shows the financial condition at that date of each of the stock fire and marine insurance companies doing business in the State.

The entire capital stock is given as $44,487,-200; admitted assets, $116,582,137; surplus as regards policy-holders, $76,773,743; over capital and all other liabilities, $32,383,333.44. In the above aggregates the capital stock of all foreign companies is rated (under the construction of a law of 1879) at $200,000 each, and their financial condition estimated on the basis of their assets and liabilities in the United States. In stating assets and liabilities of both home and foreign companies, all deposits of funds made in States for the exclusive benefit of policy-holders in such States have been deducted, and also the liabilities in such States —the deposits, the Commissioner says, being in most cases largely in excess of the liabilities. The risks, premiums, and losses of the year (in Michigan) were:

COMPANIES.	Risks written.	Premiums received.	Losses incurred.	Losses paid.
2 Michigan companies........................	$12,262,679 38	$115,449 50	$49,621 29	$49,026 58
109 companies of other States...................	126,321,680 27	1,350,913 18	702,012 87	780,191 42
2 Canadian companies, United States branches..	4,484,765 00	52,388 50	40,249 51	83,467 99
16 foreign companies, United States branches....	20,015,148 82	270,828 84	139,990 74	160,511 08
129 Aggregates...............................	$163,584,268 42	$1,789,724 82	$991,874 41	$1,028,196 97

Michigan has but one life-insurance company, the receipts of which for 1879 were: from premiums, $226.015.62; interest, $73,669.02; deposits by policy-holders, $318.14; total, $300,002.78. Paid policy-holders (including surrender value, dividends, etc.), $158,547.21; dividends to stockholders, $25,000; expenses, $66,646.74. Assets, December 31st, $980,396.-

44; liabilities, $664,966.94; surplus over liabilities, $315,429.50.

The seventh annual report of the Commissioner of Railroads bears date October 10, 1879, but only covers the calendar year 1878. The following table .comprises the leading items of interest, with the same items for the year 1877:

PARTICULARS.	1877.	1878.	Increase.	Decrease.
MILEAGE.	Miles.	Miles.	Miles.	
Length of railroads and branches..................	5,436·28	5,619·93	183·65	
" " in Michigan..................	3,455·20	3,564·26	109·06	
" double track........................	308·15	313·48	5·33	
" sidings...................,.........	1,147·69	1,207·43	59·74	
" track computed as single track........	6,900·12	7,188·19	238·07	
FINANCES.				
Capital stock paid in......................	$145,527,661 76	$148,152,011 16	$2,624,849 40	
" " per mile of road...........	28,371 11	28,127 38	....	$243 73
Total debt...............................	167,271,421 65	161,373,748 26	....	5,897,673 39
" " per mile of road...........	32,610 13	30,678 91	....	1,931 22
" stock and debt per mile of road...........	60,981 24	58,802 50	....	2,178 74
" cost of roads and equipment............	292,696,859 18	290,090,195 73	....	2,606,663 40
" " " per mile	57,062 25	55,149 38	....	1,912 87
Proportion of cost for Michigan..................	158,463,713 48	154,256,078 61	....	4,207,634 82
RECEIPTS.				
From passengers...............................	$10,255,865 86	$10,447,268 88	$191,908 02	
" malls.................................	974,663 79	1,013,811 56	88,547 77	
" express.................................	715,656 49	732,106 37	16,449 88	
" freight.................................	27,226,280 80	30,121,618 70	2,895,888 40	
" other sources...........................	874,014 12	401,834 04	27,519 92	
Total earnings...............................	$39,545,930 06	$42,716,139 05	$3,170,208 99	
Receipts in addition to earnings..................	206,971 84	320,107 62	113,136 28	
Total receipts..............................	$39,752,901 40	$43,036,246 67	$3,283,345 27	
OPERATING EXPENSES.				
Maintenance of way and buildings..............	$6,630,173 84	$6,196,622 99	....	$433,450 85
Motive power and cars.......................	3,683,741 25	3,642,503 80	$8,762 05	
Conducting transportation.....................	12,989,088 76	13,134,089 71	145,035 95	
General expenses............................	2,686,806 89	2,645,125 17	5,318 28	
Total operating expenses....................	$25,601,833 04	$25,683,784 67	$81,881 63	
Interest and rental........................	12,351,908 64	12,288,042 10	....	68,866 54
Total expenses, interest, and rental..........	$37,953,761 68	$37,291,776 77	....	$661,984 91
Total net receipts.......................	$1,799,139 72	$5,114,469 90	$3,315,330 18	
BUSINESS.				
Total number of passengers carried..............	9,944,848	10,615,504	670,656	
" tons of freight carried....................	16,489,211	19,980,642	3,491,431	
" " carried one mile....................	2,292,655,424	2,858,981,229*	566,275,805	
" number of miles run by trains..............	28,374,492	30,093,408	1,818,971	

* The average freight-rate per ton per mile was 1·053 cent, an increase of 0·21 of a mill over 1877, but bringing on the aggregate tonnage an increase of $600,375.55 in the freight-earnings.

The railroad interests are represented by 41 distinct corporations, but the business control and management of these roads is vested in 27 companies. Two new corporations report —the Menominee River Railroad Company, mileage 27·4, and the Toledo and Ann Arbor Railroad Company, mileage 45·7. Total increase of mileage in the State during the year, 109·16.

The freight tonnage was classified as follows:

	Tons.
Grain	8,881,297
Flour	1,019,659
Provisions (beef, pork, etc.)	628,668
Animals	950,001
Other agricultural products	467,801
Plaster	74,083
Salt	186,594
Manufactures	386,723
Lumber and forest products	2,711,983
Pig and bloom iron	108,811
Iron and steel rails	84,092
Other iron and castings	170,085
Ores	1,029,983
Stone and brick	167,134
Coal	817,144
Petroleum	572,692
Merchandise and other articles	2,658,080

But five roads paid dividends: the Chicago and Northwestern, 7 per cent. on preferred and 5 per cent. on common stock; Detroit, Lansing, and Northern, 2 per cent. on common; Lake Shore and Michigan Southern, 10 per cent. on preferred and 4 per cent. on common; Michigan Central, 4 per cent. on common; and Mineral Range, 10 per cent. on common. Of the 11,552 stockholders, 4,550 reside in Michigan, holding $4,685,819 of the $147,841,368.37 stock

issued. There were 76 employees and other persons (no passengers) killed during the year, and 159 persons (including 42 passengers) injured. In 1879, 58½ miles of road were constructed.

There are 14 State and 14 savings banks operating under State laws. The State Treasurer, in his annual report, gives the condition of each of the former on July 7, 1879, and of each of the latter on October 6, 1879. The following is a condensation of his tables:

RESOURCES AND LIABILITIES.	State banks.	Savings banks.
Loans and discounts	$2,125,195 60	$4,519,616 81
Bonds and mortgages	187,860 52	1,544,022 92
Cash and cash items	898,833 82	726,902 25
Real estate and fixtures	90,469 56	289,002 00
Due from banks and bankers	478,717 65	809,081 80
Expenses	9,421 86	65,816 43
Overdrafts	80,140 04	4,283 84
Total resources	$3,265,138 75	$7,958,675 55
Capital	$874,400 00	$1,100,000 00
Surplus	151,559 89	165,198 37
Due banks	16,114 81	223,848 04
Due depositors	2,107,140 71	6,360,580 08
Profit and loss	74,852 64	64,633 83
Re-discounts	41,071 20	......
Interest, premium, and exchange	......	38,820 23
Total liabilities	$3,265,138 75	$7,958,675 55

The following statistics of the lumber product of the State for 1879 are from the "Annual Review" prepared by Messrs. Lewis and Cowles for the "Saginawian" and East Saginaw "Courier":

LOCATION OF MILLS.	Number of mills.	Men employed.	Lumber cut in 1879.	Lath cut in 1879.	Lumber on hand December 31, 1879.	Logs in mill-booms.
Saginaw River Mills:						
Saginaw City	8	575	85,691,832	7,480,600	26,166,887	2,200,000
Florence	2	135	23,700,000	3,264,400	9,600,000	2,600,000
East Saginaw	12	567	112,265,482	9,541,000	52,491,000	8,300,000
Carrollton	4	200	26,300,000	700,000	6,500,000	750,000
Milwaukee	4	860	50,265,000	1,706,650	20,286,000	9,600,000
West Bay City	18	643	126,789,708	16,900,000	89,737,758	8,600,000
Essexville	8	110	81,675,000	......	7,285,000	500,000
Bay City	19	1,813	264,568,483	28,866,350	59,818,000	11,850,000
	64	4,003	717,461,455	67,969,000	221,864,595*	81,700,000
Lake Huron Shore	..	....	803,893,229	51,258,000	72,480,000	49,480,000
Railroad and interior mills	..	....	214,504,025	19,112,600	....	....
Inland mills, Saginaw County	..	....	5,615,500	1,023,000	....	....
The West Shore:						
Ludington	..	....	125,812,735	....	....	....
White Hall and Montague	..	....	58,150,000	...·	....	....
Manistee	..	....	212,552,000	...·	....	....
Muskegon	..	....	514,554,675	....	....	....
Grand Rapids	..	....	82,023,185	....	....	....
Other points	..	....	80,000,000	....	....	....
Total	..	....	2,289,066,855	189,357,600	294,294,595	81,180,000

The cut is greatly in excess of any previous year. The cut of shingles has also been unusually large, the reporting mills giving an aggregate of 685,619,150. The reviewers say that the pine forests of the State are rapidly being denuded, and that large areas of heretofore productive territory are already worked

out. During the latter half of the year there was great activity in the lumber market, "greater than during any season of the previous seven years, the closing prices being $6.50, $13, and $28, with $7, $14, and $30 for exceptionally fine lots."

The State Salt Inspector, in his annual report, gives the following comparative table, showing the total amount of salt inspected for the last three years in barrels:

* Of this amount, 85,647,537 feet is reported as already sold.

QUALITY.	1877.	1878.	1879.
Fine..............	1,590,841	1,770,361	1,997,850
Packers'...........	20,389	98,367	13,641
Solar..............	22,940	33,541	18,020
Second quality......	26,818	82,615	29,027
Total..........	1,660,997	1,883,884	2,058,040

In bushels the product of 1879 is 10,290,200, an increase of 1,010,771 bushels over that of 1878. The price averaged $1.03 per barrel, against an average of 85 cents for each of the years 1877–'78. The shipments for the year were 1,777,020 barrels, the larger quantity going to Chicago, and Milwaukee coming second.

The iron statistics of 1879 are condensed from tables prepared for the Marquette "Mining Journal": Ore output of 51 mines, 1,414,-182 tons, valued at $6,423,539.50. Add 39,583 tons of pig metal, and there was an aggregate product of 1,453,765 tons, and an aggregate value of $7,413,114.59. The product is larger than that of any previous year by 215,879 tons (the increase being over 1873), while the valuation is less than that of 1873 by $3,982,772.41. Of the output of 1879, 1,145,093 tons came from the mines of Marquette County, and 269,089 from the Menominee range.

The following crop statistics for 1878–'79 were compiled for the Lansing "Republican," from the returns made to the Secretary of State in June, 1878, by the supervisors of 981 of the 1,041 townships of the State, the non-returning townships being estimated on the basis of their preceding year's reports:

STATISTICS OF 1878.

Wheat, acres harvested.........................	1,576,560
" bushels raised......................	29,511,889
" average number of bushels per acre......	18·71
Corn, acres harvested..........................	761,123
" bushels raised......................	36,663,299
" average number of bushels per acre......	48·17
Oats, acres harvested..........................	453,685
" bushels raised......................	13,454,517
" average number of bushels per acre......	29·62
Clover-seed, acres harvested....................	122,043·41
" bushels raised..................	166,465
" average number of bushels per acre.	1·36
Barley, acres harvested........................	40,168·54
" bushels raised......................	806,463
" average number of bushels per acre......	20·14
Peas, acres harvested..........................	39,772·44
" bushels raised......................	641,061
" average number of bushels per acre.......	16·18
Potatoes, acres harvested.......................	75,825·54
" bushels raised......................	6,190,406
" average number of bushels per acre....	104·63
Hay, acres harvested...........................	856,586
" tons raised............................	1,124,981
" average number of tons per acre..........	1·81
Sheep, number sheared..........................	1,670,790
" pounds of wool sheared.................	6,666,467
" average number of pounds of wool per head	5·19
Apples, bushels sold...........................	8,944,206
Peaches, bushels sold..........................	107,244
Grapes, pounds sold...........................	1,014,950
Cherries, currants, plums, and berries, bush. sold	100,493

STATISTICS OF 1879.

Farms, number of..............................	111,822
" acres of improved land in..............	5,785,102
" acres of unimproved land in...........	4,530,486
" total number of acres in..............	10,315,588
" average number of acres in each.........	92·68
Wheat on the ground in May....................	1,642,709
Horses, number of.............................	272,603
Milch cows, number of.........................	291,243

Cattle, other than milch cows, number of........ 835,910
Hogs, number of................................ 493,109
Sheep, number of............................... 1,772,312
Apples, number of acres in orchards............ 229,262·65
Peaches, number of acres in orchards........... 10,771·16

The yield of wheat per acre in 1879 was fully equal to that of 1878, while the quality was greatly superior. At Detroit, the principal market point of the State, wheat was 93¼ cents a bushel on January 1, 1879, and on December 31, $1.36¼. The receipts of wheat at Detroit by rail for the year were 11,995,961 bushels, and of flour 309,215 barrels.

For the year ending June 30, 1879, the annual report of President Angell to the Regents of the University of Michigan shows : Students in department of literature, science, and the arts, 445 ; in department of medicine and surgery, 329 ; in department of law, 406 ; in school of pharmacy, 71 ; in Homœopathic Medical College, 63 ; in College of Dental Surgery, 62 ; total, 1,376, an increase of 143 over the preceding collegiate year. Number of women in attendance, 134, an increase of 41. Women students are registered in each and every department. Of the whole number of students, 49 per cent. were residents of the State. There were 483 degrees conferred on examination. The receipts of the year (including $10,111.89 on hand July 1, 1878) were $171,113 ; expenditures, $142,402.51 ; balance in treasury June 30, 1879, $28,710.49. Of the receipts, $58,-256.82 came from students, $39,226.68 from interest on land-endowment fund, $765.75 from interest on treasurer's deposit balances, $1.86 from sale of a book, and $62,750 from the State Treasury, on account of general or special appropriations.

The President of the Agricultural College furnishes the following summary of the work of the year : Number of students, 232 ; of graduates at commencement held November 18th (including the pioneer lady), 19 ; total number of graduates, 205. Income from Congressional land-grant, $16,602 ; from all sources, $45,082.61. Expenditures within the income. Inventory, $267,617.70. Legislative appropriations for 1879, $21,040.12 ; for 1880, $12,-040.12.

The State Normal School was opened in April, 1853, and has produced 800 students. The teaching force numbers 12. Attendance in 1878–'79, 543 ; graduates, 84. There are four courses : Common school, full English, ancient languages, and modern languages. "The sole aim of this school is to qualify teachers for their work, to increase their teaching power, and send them forth filled with the spirit of their profession." "Graduation from the higher courses entitles those holding diplomas to legal certificates of qualification to teach in any of the public schools of the State (not under special law) without a renewal."

The Superintendent of Public Instruction furnishes (in advance of his official report) the following primary-school statistics for the fiscal school year ending September 1, 1879 :

GENERAL.

Whole number of school districts.............	6,243
Whole number of children between five and twenty years.......................	486,933
Whole number of children attending public school................................	342,018
Percentage of attendance....................	70·2
Whole number of teachers employed.........	13,616
Total wages of teachers....................	$1,880,945 24
Average wages of male teachers per month....	$38 69
Average wages of female teachers per month..	$23 48
Whole number of schoolhouses...............	6,825
Whole number of sittings in schoolhouses.....	441,291
Estimated value of school property...........	$9,011,454 00
Whole number of volumes in libraries........	254,188

FINANCIAL.

Amount of moneys brought over from preceding year...................................	$729,744 96
Received from two-mill tax..................	494,011 88
" from primary-school fund...........	229,384 98
" from non-resident scholars...........	34,487 94
" from district taxes.................	2,049,755 29
" from all other sources..............	806,406 81
Total resources for the year..............	$3,843,790 86
Amount paid male teachers.................	$712,504 79
" " female teachers..............	1,160,865 26
" " for building and repairs.........	364,185 83
" " on bonded indebtedness.........	329,466 96
" " for all other purposes...........	497,576 49
Carried over to succeeding school year........	779,151 93
Total expenditures, including amount carried over..............................	$3,843,790 86
Bonded indebtedness of the districts.........	$1,289,700 80
Total indebtedness of the districts...........	1,366,641 52
Amount due the districts....................	279,416 02

The following statistics given by Dr. George C. Palmer, Superintendent of the Michigan Asylum for the Insane, are for the fiscal year closing September 30, 1879 :

Number of patients under treatment October 1, 1878....	497
" " received during the year...........	220
Whole number treated during the year..................	717
Number discharged................................	136
Number remaining in asylum September 30, 1879......	581

Those discharged are classified as follows: Recovered, 40 ; improved, 72 ; unimproved, 3 ; died, 21. The cost per week per capita was $4.58. The institution will accommodate 550 patients. The number under treatment at the end of the fiscal year was 31 more than could be comfortably provided for.

Dr. Henry M. Hurd, Medical Superintendent of the Eastern Michigan Asylum, reports as follows: The asylum was authorized in 1873 by act of the Legislature, located at Pontiac in 1874, and the construction of its buildings commenced in 1875. It was completed for the admission of patients and formally opened August 1, 1878, since which time 549 patients have been admitted. The cost of the asylum buildings, grounds, furniture, fixtures, etc., has been $467,000. The capacity of the institution is 400. Statistics for the fiscal year :

PARTICULARS.	Male.	Female.	Total.
Patients October 1, 1878..............	160	146	306
Patients admitted during year.........	103	81	184
Whole number of patients treated......	263	227	490
Discharged, recovered.................	14	8	22
" improved.................	23	19	42
" unimproved...............	5	7	12
" died......................	16	8	24

Total discharged, 100 ; remaining under treatment September 30, 1879, 390 ; average number under treatment, 348½ ; average cost per week per patient, $4.05.

The number of insane in the two asylums at the close of the fiscal year was 971 ; number treated during the year, 1,207 ; estimated number of insane in the State, 1,700.

The statistics for the fiscal year of the Institution for the Deaf and the Blind at Flint are : tution for the Deaf and the Blind at Flint are : Number of pupils, 251—137 males and 114 females, 204 deaf-mutes and 47 blind ; graduated, 11, all deaf-mutes. Number of instructors in educational department, 13 ; in industrial department, 9. Printing is taught to the deaf-mute girls and boys, cabinet-making and shoe-making to the deaf-mute boys, basket- and broom-making to the blind boys, and sewing, knitting, and fancy work to both deaf-mute and blind girls, who are also instructed in domestic work. These industries are carried on similar to school-work, to teach the pupils trades and not as a financial investment, though they are nearly self-supporting (except the printing-office and the blind industries). Pupils in the industries alternate with school-work, three hours in each daily, in two divisions. The younger pupils have daily six hours of school-work. Value of buildings, $375,000 ; volumes in library, 1,000. Disbursements for the year : Current expenses, $44,046.68 ; special purposes, $4,528.89. Earnings (including those from industries, farm, garden, etc.), $3,130.70. The institution is an educational one, and in no sense an asylum.

The State Public School for Dependent Children, located at Coldwater, is designed "to provide for all the dependent children of the State, whether in or out of the county poorhouses, who are sound in body and mind, over three and under twelve years of age ; to maintain and educate them while temporarily in the school, and as soon as satisfactory homes are found to place them there, under contracts securing good treatment as members of the family, and an elementary education, thus fitting them for good citizenship." The accommodations are for 300 children, with their homes in separate cottages, accommodating from 25 to 30 each, and "presided over by cultivated women, who care for the children as mothers of a smaller family." In the table below the second column gives the statistics for the fiscal year closing September 30, 1879, and the third from May 25, 1874, to that date :

PARTICULARS.	1878-'79.	Total.
Number in school October 1, 1878.....	314	...
" received during year.......	106	776
" indentured during year.....	115	307
" returned to counties........	18	51
" absconded...............	1	5
" died....................	1	88
" sent to Reform School.......	..	4

Average number during the year, 305⅔ ; cost of their maintenance, $34,035.27, or $111:34 per capita.

The twenty-third annual report of the State Reform School at Lansing shows : Number committed since opening of school, September 2, 1856, 2,135; in school September 30, 1878, 327; received during the fiscal year, 139; released during the year, 159; remaining in school September 30, 1879, 307; net current expenses of the year, $31,654.86. The commitments for the year were for the following offenses: Grand larceny, 1; burglary, 6; assault and battery, 11; larceny, 86; attempt to murder, 1; rape, 2, malicious trespass, 4; vagrancy and disorderly, 21; arson, 1; returned, 3. Their ages were from 10 to 16 years, averaging 13½ years. Their social status was as follows: 31 had lost a father, 38 a mother, and 9 both parents; 21 had relatives who had been arrested for crime, 37 had used intoxicating drinks, and 58 had been in jail one or more times; 14 did not know the alphabet, and 67 could not write. Of those leaving the school, 116 were discharged reformed, 7 to go out of the State to reside with parents, 19 given one year's leave of absence, 14 sent to live with farmers, 1 escaped, and 2 died.

The annual report of the State House of Correction at Ionia furnishes the following:

Number of prisoners October 1, 1878............	233
" transferred from State Prison................	18
" received on sentence during 1879........	311
" returned by order of court...............	2
" discharged during year................	271
" pardoned...............................	8
" escaped........	2
" in institutions September 30, 1879......	257
Receipts from all sources.......................	$62,573 90
Expenditures...................................	$61,436 60
Gross earnings.................................	$15,363 57
Average net cost of supporting inmates in 1879...	$153 53
" daily cost of supporting each inmate....	$0 43·43

The State Prison statistics for the fiscal year are as follows:

Number of prisoners October 1, 1878.............	804
" received during the year...............	270
" transferred to State House of Correction.	18
" transferred to Detroit House of Correction	2
" discharged.............................	247
" died...................................	6
" pardoned..............................	17
" in prison September 30, 1879...........	777
" of life convicts received during the year..	2
Average length of sentence of prisoners received	
(omitting life-prisoners)................... 3 y. 10 m. 23 d.	
Expenses of prison (net).......................	$34,095 91
Income from convict labor (net) :..............	85,420 65
Total net earnings.............................	58,255 25

The State Board for the general supervision of charitable, penal, pauper, and reformatory institutions report only biennially. For information as to jails, poor-houses, etc., see the "Annual Cyclopædia" for 1878.

MINNESOTA. The Legislature of Minnesota assembled in its twenty-first session at St. Paul on January 8th. In the Senate Lieutenant-Governor Wakefield presided, and in the House Charles A. Gilman was elected by a unanimous vote.

One of the earliest measures was the appointment of a joint committee to investigate certain charges of cruelty made against the officers of the State Prison. The report of the committee subsequently made entirely exonerated the officers of the charges. It also rec-

ommended that the Governor should appoint some one, unknown to the prison authorities, to visit the prison at any time, talk with the convicts, look at the food, or, in other words, constitute himself a detective, and report upon each occasion to the Governor the result of his trip.

An act was passed to regulate the rate of interest, which provides that "interest on any legal indebtedness shall be at the rate of seven dollars upon one hundred dollars for a year, unless a different rate is contracted for in writing; and no person, company, or corporation shall directly or indirectly take or receive, in money, goods, or other things in action, or in any other way, any greater sum or any greater value for the loan or forbearance of money, goods, or things in action, than ten dollars on one hundred dollars for one year; and in the computation of interest upon any bond, note, or other instrument or agreement, interest shall not be compounded. But any contract to pay interest not usurious upon interest overdue shall not be construed to be usury."

The weighing and inspection of wheat were provided for in an act which makes the half-bushel measure the lawful standard. The act also provides that, "if the parties to the sale of any wheat shall consent, it may be lawful to use a two-quart measure to determine the grade of wheat, provided said two-quart measure shall be sealed as herein provided, and so arranged as to easily demonstrate that it is truly balanced with any means of weighing the same, and that such measure is filled in such manner and by such method and device as may be prescribed and approved by the Farmers' Board of Trade of the State." It is then made the duty of the Farmers' Board of Trade, or, previous to its organization, of three men appointed by the Governor, on whom its powers are devolved, to designate what shall be the manner of filling the measures to be used in testing the grade of wheat, and to prescribe such methods as shall best secure uniformity in determining them. The act then goes on to require the Farmers' Board of Trade of the State to designate what shall be the manner of filling the measures to be used under its provisions, in testing the grade of wheat, and to prescribe such methods as shall best secure uniformity in determining the grades of wheat; and they shall require all measures used and means of weighing employed in grading wheat to be sealed and stamped by the lawful sealer of weights and measures. The Board of Trade shall fix and designate the several grades of wheat to be in force each year, after their annual meeting in September, and cause to be published a circular for the use of grain-dealers in the State, defining the rules and regulations to be observed in the grades of wheat, and testing the same, and naming such methods and devices therein to be used in the manner of filling the half-bushel and the two-quart measure, if its use shall be authorized. This last provision, "to fix and designate the several grades of wheat to be in force each year," it has been suggested, is clearly beyond the legitimate scope of legislative power. If the Board should attempt so to do, it would still find that wheat would continue to be bought and sold by the market grades, and any edicts establishing arbitrary grades different from those of the general markets of the world would be a dead letter from the necessity of the case. But it is entirely within the competency of legislation to create an authority to prescribe the methods by which wheat shall be measured and weighed. The author of the act devised a contrivance attached to the two-quart tester for filling it, which, it was said, obviated all the objections to that instrument of measurement or weighing, by securing absolute uniformity in the pressure of the wheat; and that the contrivance was so simple a one that it expedites instead of retarding the process of inspection.

The Farmers' Board of Trade above mentioned was created by another act. This made it the duty of the judge of each judicial district within the State to appoint one of the most able farmers residing therein, who should be well versed in the theory and practice of agriculture, and who was not an incumbent of any public office of the State, and who was not a stockholder, officer, trustee, assignee, or employee of any banking, moneyed, or savings institution or corporation created under the laws thereof, and one that was not directly or indirectly connected with any association which has for its object the buying and selling of produce. The persons so appointed constitute the members of the Board of Trade for two and four years. It is made their duty to assume and exercise a constant supervision over the agricultural interests of the State, and to make a report to the Legislature presenting such facts, statistics, and suggestions as in their judgment may be necessary to induce legislation for the protection and welfare of the entire agricultural interest.

The sum of $7,500 was appropriated to aid the owners of drive-wells to test the validity of the patents under which a royalty is claimed. The owners of these wells, against whom the claim of infringement is made, number about thirty thousand in the State.

Another act authorizes the Governor to appoint a commission of three doctors to visit the insane asylums at least once in every six months, and report upon their sanitary condition and general management, the condition and treatment of the patients, and in detail the results of their observations, with recommendations upon the same. If they find any patients that are not insane, the commission is authorized to remove them to the counties from which they came. All idiotic and feeble-minded are to be transferred to the Deaf and Dumb Asylum, after which, in case they can not be benefited, they are to be returned to their par-

ents, or to the county commissioners of their respective counties.

Nineteen towns, cities, and villages, and nineteen counties were authorized to issue bonds for various purposes. An amendment of the Constitution was also adopted, which proposed to prohibit the Legislature from authorizing any county, township, or city to issue bonds for the construction of railroads to any amount that shall exceed five per cent. of its taxable property.

A State tax was ordered to be levied, not to exceed a mill and five tenths.

Persons found guilty of body-snatching were made subject to a penalty of four years in the State Prison.

The subject of temperance received some notice. A bill to prohibit the sale of intoxicating liquor to be used as a beverage was presented in the House, accompanied by twenty petitions having 10,000 signatures. It failed to pass the House by a vote of 22 yeas to 74 nays. The following amendment to the State Constitution was also presented in the Senate without avail:

SECTION 31. The Legislature shall never authorize or license the sale of any kind of intoxicating liquor as a beverage, nor authorize or license houses of prostitution, nor gambling of any kind, nor any lottery or the sale of lottery tickets ; and all persons are prohibited from manufacturing, selling, giving, furnishing, having, or in any manner dealing in spirituous, vinous, malt, fermented, mixed, drugged, or intoxicating liquors of any kind, to be used for other than medicinal, mechanical, chemical, and scientific purposes, and for use in the arts. The Legislature shall have power by law to license and control the manufacture and sale of such pure liquors for medicinal, mechanical, chemical, and scientific purposes, and for use in the arts, but not otherwise, and shall have power to enact laws for the punishment of persons engaged in any illicit traffic in such liquors, and for the confiscation, sale, or destruction of contraband liquors, and the vessels and buildings connected therewith.

Some favor was shown to a bill for woman's suffrage in the Senate; and a bill to devote the internal improvement lands to the settlement of the old railroad bonds was received and laid on the table. In the Senate a resolution to print the Governor's message in the German, Norwegian, Swedish, French, and Bohemian languages was passed. A bill was also reported by the Committee on Retrenchment and Reform to reduce the salaries of the State officers and their clerks about twenty-five per cent. It received some attention in Committee of the Whole, but it transpired upon discussion that most of the salaries are low enough for capable men ; and, as the capacity of the officials was not questioned, retrenchment among them was suspended. The Senate, however, passed a bill for reducing the mileage of members at future sessions of the Legislature to five cents a mile.

The session was closed about March 12th. Very few general and important laws were passed, although nearly six hundred bills were presented to the Governor for his approval.

A report was presented to the Legislature by the Public Examiner, who was created by an act of the previous session. The duties imposed upon him by the act are very comprehensive and very onerous. He is required to examine the accounts of all State and county officers and of all State institutions, and to enforce uniform and safe methods of book-keeping, and to investigate the affairs of all banking or savings institutions, and is a general supervising as well as examining officer. In the discharge of his duties the Examiner (Mr. Knox) had officially visited twenty-seven counties during the seven months since his appointment, and made fifty-eight more or less exhaustive examinations, including the investigation of the Insane Hospital accounts for twelve years, which occupied nearly a month. He found in a considerable number of counties that the treasurers and auditors were excellent and conscientious officers, skilled and experienced accountants, and to them he was indebted for much valuable aid. But in the majority of counties the systems of keeping the public accounts were so wretchedly loose and defective as to be absolutely no check whatever on the misappropriation of the public funds. As the law stands, when a tax is paid the treasurer fills out a blank receipt and a duplicate—parts of the same leaf bound in a book. When the receipt is torn off and delivered to the tax-payer, the duplicate or stub remains as evidence that the tax is paid; and this is the only evidence, if the treasurer permits it to exist, except that he is required to write the word "Paid" against the tax in his books. But he can easily destroy the stub, or write a receipt from another book of blank receipts, not that exhibited as his record of tax receipts, and may entirely neglect or forget to write the word "Paid" against the paid tax in his books. Nor is there any possible way to trace any little fraud or theft of that sort, unless some tax-payer, published as delinquent, presents his receipt—which experience shows he rarely does till the treasurer has retired from office. It was estimated that tens, perhaps hundreds, of thousands of dollars had been lost to the people of the State by this loose system of accounting for tax receipts.

The proposition to use the swamp-lands of the State to aid one or more railroad enterprises served to call attention to the title to those lands and the purposes for which they were devoted by Congress, and the manner in which the State had disposed of them. It thus appeared that all the State grants of these lands were illegal and might be considered void. More or less of these lands were in each of the Western States along the Mississippi River. In 1826 a Senator in Congress from Missouri unsuccessfully sought to obtain a cession to Missouri and Illinois of the swamps within those States respectively. Other efforts of a similar character were made at intervals, but no definite action was had until the passage of the act of March 2, 1849, which was applicable exclusively to Louisiana. This act was the basis of all other acts

relative to swamp-lands, and its language was as follows:

That to aid the State of Louisiana in constructing the necessary levees and drains to reclaim the swamp and overflowed lands therein, the whole of those swamp and overflowed lands shall be, and the same are hereby, granted to that State.

The next section provides for the manner of selecting such lands, and concludes by saying that the fee simple of such lands shall then vest in the State—

Provided, however, that the proceeds of said lands shall be applied exclusively, as far as necessary, to the construction of the levees and drains aforesaid.

The reasons assigned in debate for this munificent donation were the alleged worthless character of the lands in their natural condition, the great sanitary improvement to be derived from the reclamation of districts notoriously malarial, and the enhanced value of adjoining government property. This legislation contemplated providing a land fund wherewith to enable the beneficiaries, as grantees of the United States, to construct levees to check devastating floods; and further, to make great drains, in swampy regions, for reclamation of lands; and incidentally, although unexpressed except in the debates, to relieve the country from pestilential malaria. The end proposed in the original grant has been attained only to a limited extent. Imperfect works were constructed to limit the waters of the Mississippi to their proper channels; even these were neglected during the war.

The act of 1849 was followed by the general act of September 28, 1850, which act, as expressed by its title, was "to enable the State of Arkansas and other States to reclaim the swamp-lands within their limits." And the language of the act, like its title, says that the lands shall be appropriated for "the necessary levees and drains to reclaim the swamp and overflowed lands therein." The last section of this act extends its provisions to each of the other States of the Union "in which such swamp and overflowed lands may be situated." Minnesota was not then a State; but after she was admitted into the Union March 12, 1860, an act was passed to extend the provisions of the act of 1850 to the States of Minnesota and Oregon. Both in its title and in the body of the law it recites that it is an act to enable these States, as Arkansas, "to reclaim the swamp-lands within their limits." These are the only acts affecting this question. Subsequent acts only refer to and define the manner in which indemnity shall be made. The total amount of such lands selected to the close of 1878 was 69,000,000 acres, an area larger than Great Britain. Surveyor-General Baker of Minnesota, treating of this question, calls attention to the fact that Congress in its statutes has never deviated, in spirit or letter, from the purposes of the original act. The statutory concessions are not couched in indefinite terms. The States themselves, acting upon an implied

sovereignty after the title had been passed to
them by the General Government, have assumed a wide latitude in the disposition of
these lands. But any disposition of such lands
not in accordance with the letter and spirit of
the acts donating them must be null and void.
It has been held that they were available for
purposes of general internal improvements,
and it has been the practice of the States having such lands to so appropriate them. Minnesota, however, is perhaps the only State that
has sought to appropriate these lands to objects
other than those of internal improvement.
The report of the State Auditor shows the several grants of swamp-lands made by the State
Legislature as follows:

YEARS.	Grantees.	Number of acres in grant.
1861	Lake Sup. and Mississippi R. R. Co..	604,400·00
1861	Lake Sup. and Mississippi Branch...	100,000·00
1861	McLeod Co. Agricultural College.....	4,684·17
1862	Madelia and Sioux Falls Railroad....	10,000·00
1863	St. Paul and Chicago Railway Co....	461,440·00
1865	Insane Asylum.......................	100,000·00
1865	Deaf, Dumb, and Blind Asylum.....	100,000·00
1865	State Prison........................	100,000·00
1865	Winona Normal School.............	75,000·00
1865	Mankato Normal School............	75,000·00
1865	St. Cloud Normal School...........	75,000·00
1865	Southern Minnesota Railroad Co.....	85,242·29
1865	Cannon River Improvement Co......	800,000·00
1865	Soldiers' Orphan Asylum...........	Residuary.
1875	Duluth and Iron Range Railroad Co..	422,400·00
1878	Minnesota Northern Railroad Co.....	98,000·00
	Total...............................	2,651,166·46

After the above grants are satisfied, all the
residue under the law was to go to the Soldiers'
Orphans' Asylum. But this institution is in
fact defunct, all the soldiers' orphans having
been cared for that desired to avail themselves
of its benefits. The Surveyor - General says:
"I estimate that from 11,000,000 acres yet to
survey, we will receive not far from 3,300,000
more acres of swamp-land, because the percentage of swamp-lands increases as we advance
into the unsurveyed areas. Out of these lands
already conveyed to the State there have been
actually conveyed to various railroad companies by the State 1,037,180 acres. Most of
these lands, in the older portions of the State,
have already been sold by these companies to
actual settlers, and title passed." In his opinion the grants above mentioned do not pretend
to be in sympathy with, or in any manner
kindred to, the objects of the grant. However meritorious the purposes of such legislation, these acts simply express a betrayal of a
trust, a breach of trusteeship. They should be
promptly repealed, and the statutes cleared of
such worthless rubbish. On the other hand, it
is urged in the State that the grants of swamp-
lands made by the State are secure from any
attempt to shake the title of the grantees by
legal proceedings, notwithstanding the grants
were made in violation of the trust imposed on
the State by an act of Congress, and that the
only danger lies in a possible declaration of

forfeiture by Congress. To support this opinion, reference is made to a decision of the United States Supreme Court rendered in 1868 in
the case of Baker vs. McGee. A grant of lands
had been made by Congress to Missouri to aid
in building railroads from Hannibal to St. Joseph, and it required that the lands thus given
should be disposed of by the State for the purposes contemplated and "no other." The State
granted the lands to a railroad company, but
gave a preëmption right to settlers in actual
occupancy and who had improved the land
prior to the date of the Congressional act.
Suit was brought against a preëmptor who
claimed land under this provision by a man
who had purchased the same land from the
railroad company. The latter claimed, among
other things, that the State had no right to divert the lands to any purpose not contemplated
by the act of Congress granting them to the
State, and was expressly prohibited from doing
so. Upon this the Court said: "It is contended that the Legislature of Missouri had no
power to grant the privilege of preëmption.
If this was a contest between the United States
and the State of Missouri, the question of power would be a proper subject of examination.
But the United States are not complaining, and
no other party has the right to complain."
A still later decision of the same Court, filed
in October, 1878, is decisive of the illegality of
these grants. The case arose in Iowa under an
act of the Legislature of March 22, 1858, which
authorized counties to devote the swamp-lands
to the erection of bridges, roadways, railroads,
or other public improvements, provided no such
transfer should be made unless the person and
company expressly released the State and county from all liability for reclaiming said lands as
provided by the act of Congress. Under this
statute Adams County sold its swamp-lands to
the American Emigrant Company, the company agreeing to erect such public buildings as
the county might request. The county brought
suit in equity to rescind the contract on the
ground of fraud by the company. The case
went to the Supreme Court of the United States.
The opinion there filed held that the act of the
Legislature authorizing counties owning swamp-
lands to devote the same to the erection of public buildings and making railroads through the
county is contrary to the act of Congress granting such lands to the State, and therefore unauthorized and void; that the provision of the
act of Congress that the proceeds of such lands
shall be applied exclusively to the purpose of
reclaiming said lands by drains and levees was
an express trust imposed upon the State to apply the proceeds to the particular purpose for
which they were granted; that trust was sacredly binding upon the State, to be carried
out and not to be abandoned or repudiated.
The transfer by the State of these lands to
counties, subject to the act of Congress, and reserving legislative control over them, involved
no breach of trust, counties being subordinate

political departments of the State, to facilitate the object for which the State government is instituted; but the act of the Legislature of 1858 authorized the devoting of the lands to widely different purposes than what the original grant was intended to secure. It endeavored to throw off all responsibility of the trust. The purchasers were to relieve the State and county from all liability for reclaiming the lands —that is, release them from their responsibility as trustees of these lands; and this absurd form was adopted in the contracts and conveyances that were made. How could the purchaser release the State and county from an obligation imposed by an act of Congress? It is probable, however, that the Legislature meant that the purchaser should indemnify the State and county for their liability; but how does that better the matter? Can the public officers of Iowa throw off their trusteeship in this easy manner, by taking the indemnity of private parties against the consequences of their breach of trust? The State or county could most certainly sell the lands to purchasers out and out, freed from any lien or trust in relation to the improvements which they were intended to secure; but the State or county would hold the proceeds of such sales as a fund devoted to the purposes of the grant, although the purchasers would not be bound to look to the application of the purchase-money. The public authorities might even waste or misapply the fund without any legal remedy to prevent; but that does not prevent the stamp of illegality from being impressed upon a deliberate scheme of spoliation of the trust fund, conceived in the form of law and carried out with an entire disregard of public obligations.

The valuation of property in the several counties of the State in 1879, according to the local boards of equalization, amounted to $229,791,042. The returns of personal property by the same boards amounted to $57,193,455 for 1879 and $53,665,943 for 1878, showing an increase of $3,527,512.

The extent of railroad construction in 1878 was 375 miles. This was more miles of new road than were opened by any other State during that year. The number of miles in operation in the State at the close of that year was 2,608, all of which has been constructed within seventeen years. A narrow-gauge road of three feet was opened from Wabasha to Zumbrota, a distance of 60 miles, during the year, which is the only one in the State. The following table shows the comparative business for five years of all the railroads doing business in the State:

YEARS.	Gross earnings.	Earnings over operating expenses.	Passengers carried.	Tons freight.	State revenue from railroads.
1874....	$6,194,669	$1,894,800	1,012,506	1,434,913	$103,825
1875....	4,952,152	1,026,580	996,218	1,350,177	131,559
1876....	6,000,967	1,798,424	1,169,072	2,079,568	145,393
1877....	5,408,089	1,542,586	1,239,428	1,717,923	165,000
1878....	7,431,199	2,953,871	1,590,649	2,496,559	180,000

The sales of railroad lands in 1878 were unprecedentedly large, as shown in the following table compared with preceding years:

YEARS.	Acres.	Receipts.
1875...................	179,250	$1,317,779
1876...................	808,266	2,155,224
1877...................	242,487	1,809,874
1878 (to December)......	485,629	1,514,900

Total sold to December 1, 1878, 2,144,215 acres. Total receipts to December 1, 1878, $9,762,258. There was no serious railroad accident on any of the roads during the year. Minnesota railroads have had a remarkable exemption from railroad disasters, the Brainerd bridge accident, by which five lives were lost, in 1875, being the only serious one in the history of the State.

A bill was brought before Congress at its early session during the year for the construction of a sluiceway over St. Anthony's Falls in the Mississippi River, and to regulate and provide for the same. It was not enacted.

An act was passed which grants additional rights to homestead settlers on public lands within railroad limits, not only in Minnesota but in other States. It declares that the even sections within the limits of any grant of public lands to any railroad company, or to any military road company, or to any State in aid of any railroad or military road, shall be open to settlers under the homestead laws to the extent of 160 acres to each settler; and any person who has, under existing laws, taken a homestead on any even section within the limits of any railroad or military road land-grant, and who by existing laws shall have been restricted to eighty acres, may enter under the homestead laws an additional eighty acres adjoining the land embraced in his original entry, if such additional land be subject to entry; or if such person so elect, he may surrender his entry to the United States for cancellation, and thereupon be entitled to enter lands under the homestead laws the same as if the surrendered entry had not been made; and the residence and cultivation of such person upon and of the land embraced in his original entry shall be considered residence and cultivation for the same length of time upon and of the land embraced in his additional or new entry, and shall be deducted from the five years' residence and cultivation required by law.

Suits were instituted against about seventy-five persons for trespass upon the Government pine-lands of Minnesota, and about twenty-five other cases were in process of examination by the agents of the Interior Department. The seventy-five cases alluded to were ready for trial at the June term of the United States Court, but the trespassers succeeded in getting a stay of proceedings, which carried over all suits not otherwise disposed of to the December term. Ten of these cases involved an aggregate stumpage of about $75,000, mostly if not entirely against the Minneapolis lumbermen. A commission consisting of the District Attorney and the Surveyor-General of Minnesota was formed by the Secretary of the Interior (Schurz) to investigate and classify the cases of trespass upon the public lands, and to report the facts and suggestions. This undertaking involves a considerable amount of labor, but from the outlook it will enable the trespassers to compromise upon better terms than they would receive at the hands of a jury, and at the same time save the costs of trial, which would be considerable.

An act of the Legislature at a former session required the State Geologist, Professor Winchell, to give an account and accurate chemical analysis of the waters of Minnesota. Soon after a sanitary examination of the wells in the section of Red River Valley extending from Breckenridge to Winnipeg, Manitoba, and also of other wells and springs outside the valley, was made. As reported by him, the wells of the Red River country very generally become offensive after a time from foul gases engendered in them, and when in this condition they originate stubborn intestinal difficulties eventuating in dysentery and various forms of fever. These diseases being identical with those existing in southwestern counties, it has been inferred that the illness incidental to the northern and southern health districts may very probably be induced by the same cause, namely, the use of impure water for domestic purposes.

The effects of the severe cold that prevailed over the middle and northern sections of the country during two or three of the first days in January, 1879, were thus reported by the "Press" at St. Paul:

It is within the limits of candid moderation to say that no region north of Memphis, and between New York and the Rocky Mountains, has suffered so little from the late visitation of cold as that embraced by a radius of one hundred miles from St. Paul and Minneapolis as a center. In this section the thermometer has ranged for a week or more between five and twenty-five degrees below zero; but no individual, enterprise, or corporation has suffered the least pain or inconvenience from the weather. The clear, dry air of our favored prairies has rendered harmless a degree of cold which would make the damp winds of the lower lakes or seacoast messengers of icy death. We have simply exchanged fall for winter overcoats, kid gloves for fur mittens, and gone on hauling wheat and cutting wood in the country, trading and manufacturing in town, without a thought of complaint of the weather. Not a single case of freezing has been reported in St. Paul or Minneapolis. Only one case has been noted in the country, and that was a new-born babe abandoned upon a door-step. Not a single business enterprise has been hindered or suspended. Travel in city and country is facilitated rather than checked by frozen roads, smoother and easier than the most costly Nicolson. Not a railroad train has been stopped or delayed from one end of the State to the other. So far as information goes, not a locomotive has been frozen or a brakeman frost-bitten. This is but a repetition of the experience of last winter, when, from November to March, not a train was delayed an hour by weather in any part of the State, or upon the whole line of the Northern Pacific. While this has been our experience, not for a week, nor a month, but for a term long enough to establish a rule, the condition of the so-called milder latitutes in extreme seasons is vividly reflected in

the telegraphic dispatches of the last few days. From the Atlantic to the Mississippi the wail of frost-bitten humanity goes up, where it is not smothered in avalanches of snow. A degree of cold indicated by the zero point of the thermometer is more fatal to New England, New York, Michigan, the Ohio Valley, Illinois, and southern Wisconsin, all the States indeed which are swept by moisure-bearing winds from fresh or salt water, than one of thirty degrees below to Minnesota. While not an ear has been nipped here, Chicago, Buffalo, Philadelphia, and New York hospitals are filled with frozen subjects. While not a train has been delayed in Minnesota, there is no continuous travel between Chicago and the seaboard; central New York cities are shut off from the world; thirteen locomotives can not bring a train into Buffalo; it is almost fatal to some for a car-load of passengers to be caught out of a depot; and freight helplessly piles up in warehouses.

The remarkable mildness of the climate in the extreme northwestern region has often been noticed. Mr. J. W. Taylor, the United States Consul at Winnipeg, shows by comparative tables of temperature that during the months of February and March it was seven degrees warmer at Battleford, on the North Saskatchewan, 700 miles northwest of Winnipeg, than at the latter place. He also gives thermometrical records of Battleford, Winnipeg, and St. Paul, for the month of April. From St. Paul, in latitude 45°, to Winnipeg, in latitude 50°, is about 500 miles, and from Winnipeg to Battleford, a little below latitude 53°, is 700 miles—a distance of 1,200 miles between the extreme points, and a difference of nearly eight degrees of latitude. Mr. Taylor gives a table of daily April temperatures for each of these three points, and they disclose the fact that while at Winnipeg it was on the average over ten degrees colder than at St. Paul, it was only three degrees colder at Battleford. In other words, the April weather at Battleford was seven degrees warmer than at Winnipeg, nearly three degrees farther south. The summaries of these tables of daily temperatures for April show the following means: Battleford, 46·70°; Winnipeg, 39·10°; St. Paul, 49·70°. Mr. Taylor has no doubt that the districts 500 miles northwest of Battleford—the valley of the Peace River—are warmer than Manitoba. The experience of a single month or of two or three months would be a slight foundation for any general inference as to the climate of the Saskatchewan Valley; but these thermometrical data are simply confirmatory of the generalizations of the climatologists, based on the observations which have been carried on for many years at the posts of the Hudson's Bay Company, that the line of equal mean temperatures, especially for the season of vegetation between March and October, instead of following lines of latitude, bends from the Mississippi Valley far to the north, carrying the zone of wheat from Minnesota away up to the sixtieth parallel in the valley of the Peace River, and reproducing the summer heats of New Jersey and southern Pennsylvania in Minnesota and Dakota, and those of northern Pennsylvania and Ohio in the valley of the Saskatchewan. A recent traveler in the Territory of Dakota, and down the Red River of the North into Manitoba, says that, commencing at the Red River and stretching for hundreds, almost thousands of miles in a northwesterly direction, including the fertile valleys of the system of rivers drained by Lakes Winnipeg and Manitoba, is a tract of country so large that States the size of Ohio might be cut out of it almost by the dozen, and which, until within the last few years, has been thought of as a bleak, uninhabitable waste, valuable only for its fur-bearing animals. But the reports of travelers, and now the test of experience, have proven that no quarter of the country excels this region in the quality and yield of its small grain; and instead of its being confined to the valley of the Red, there is every reason for believing that it embraces the valleys of the Assiniboine, Saskatchewan, and other rivers far to the north. It is stated by an officer of the Hudson's Bay Company, who had traveled extensively over the territory controlled by that company, that, beginning fifty or sixty miles west of the city of Winnipeg, and continuing about 900 miles until it disappeared in the deserts that lie next east of the mountains, and extending an indefinite distance to the north, is a rolling plain, in richness of soil the counterpart of the prairies of Illinois and Iowa.

The statistics of public schools in the State show a considerable advance during the year. The total enrollment for 1878 was 167,825; for 1879, 171,945; increase, 4,120 children. Number of common-school districts, 3,922; of schoolhouses, 3,416. Value of school property, $3,384,026.

An act of the Legislature regulating elections in incorporated cities of over 12,000 inhabitants, required that the ballots should be numbered at the time when they were offered. The question of the constitutionality of this provision came before the Supreme Court, and it was decided to be unconstitutional on the ground that it interfered with and violated the voter's privilege of secrecy.

The National Greenback State Convention assembled at St. Paul on June 10th. Ignatius Donnelly was chosen President, and the following ticket for State officers was nominated: For Governor, Ana Barton; for Lieutenant-Governor, William McGhen; for Treasurer, Andrew Nelson; for Secretary of State, A. P. Lane; for Attorney-General, William L. Kelley; for Railroad Commissioner, Ebenezer Ayers. The following platform was adopted by the Convention:

We, the delegates assembled, pursuant to call, at a State National Greenback-Labor Convention, held in the city of St. Paul, on Tuesday, the 10th day of June, A. D. 1879, do adopt the following declaration of principles and policy:

1. We are in favor of the immediate and unconditional repeal of the act of 1869, falsely entitled "An act to strengthen the public credit," believing that it was an unnecessary, dishonest, and radical change of the original contract between the debtor and creditor classes, an act of robbery of hundreds of millions of dollars from the people, for the benefit of American and European bondholders, and one that was intended to perpetuate the national debt for all time. We therefore demand that all the bonds due by the Government be paid in strict accordance with the letter and spirit of the original terms on which they were issued; and that all the four and four and a half per cent., and all other bonds issued since the passage of that act on long time, subject, as understood, to all the contingencies of subsequent legislation, be immediately paid in non-interest-bearing, full legal-tender currency.

2. We are in favor of the free and unrestricted coinage of silver, upon the same terms and conditions as gold, and its retention as a full legal tender for all debts, public and private.

3. We demand the immediate repeal of the resumption law, believing that its passage at the time was an infamous sin and crime against the debtor classes, whose obligations, contracted in good faith and on a currency basis, were thus more than doubled, while all property was reduced nearly one half. We denounce the whole scheme of locking up in the Treasury-vaults $400,000,000 or $500,000,000 of currency subject to redemption, and coin held for the purpose of redemption, while but little more than $4,000,000 has been redeemed or offered for redemption, as wholly in the interest of a few moneyed men, and suicidal, unjust, and oppressive to the great body of the American people.

4. We regard the whole system of the contraction of the currency, from April, 1866, to the present time, as an act of gross fraud and injustice, subversive of the best interests of the nation, leading to tens of thousands of bankruptcies, the concentration of a large part of the wealth of the people in the hands of a few bullionists and money-holders, and the stagnation and paralysis of almost every industry.

5. After having replaced the entire bonded debt of the nation with legal-tender currency (except where the faith of the Government was originally and specifically pledged to coin payment), we believe that thereafter the circulation should be steadily and gradually increased in exact proportion to the growth of population and wealth and business of the country—the circulation per capita being maintained as nearly as possible the same, so as not to disturb the relative value of money and property.

6. We believe that all private property, and everything that has value, owned or held by individuals or corporations, and all industries and interests in the nation, should bear their equal and legitimate share of taxation for the support of the Government and the protection of the people.

7. We regard the declaration of the Republican party at its last convention in this State, in 1878, that "no constitutional right reposes in the Government to protect the people against monopolies by the powerful, arbitrary, and rapacious," as a most reckless and dangerous heresy, as heartless as it is untrue and anti-republican in sentiment.

8. We are opposed to all unjust and discriminating class-legislation, and in favor of a fair field and open competition for all.

9. We are earnestly opposed to all large landed monopolies, either by railroads, corporations, or private individuals, and believe that the public domain should be held exclusively for actual settlers, in moderate and reasonable quantities. We are opposed to the present or any other national banking system, and in favor of the Government alone issuing all that circulates as money. We are in favor of a graduated and equitable income tax; but one term of office for President and Vice-President; the election of President, Vice-President, postmasters, and, as far as practicable all other officers, by the direct vote of the people; the severe punishment by fine or imprisonment, or both, and by disfranchisement and ineligibility to office, of any person who offers to buy or sell a vote, or is guilty of any fraud or intimidation or threats of violence at a ballot-box or election, with a view to prevent the free and

independent vote of any person or persons whatsoever or whomsoever.

10. We regard the old Minnesota railroad bonds as dishonest and illegal in their whole origin and history; a measure conceived in sin and brought forth in iniquity, and one that is not morally binding on the people of this State.

11. We are in favor of the equalization of the soldiers' bounties.

12. We desire to enter our protest as American citizens against the custom which has been followed almost exclusively by the leaders of both the old parties —and especially the Republicans—since the close of the late war of the rebellion, of fostering local prejudices and sectional strife and hatred, whether between the North and South or the East and West, regarding it as unpatriotic, narrow-minded, illiberal, and fratricidal, and one that can not be too earnestly condemned by all good citizens of the Union; indicating the demagogue and partisan, rather than the statesman or patriot, and obviously intended to divert the attention of the people from grave and more important subjects of a practical character.

13. We denounce the boisterous and vindictive discussion for weeks together by the present Congress of an insignificant and inoperative election law, that has not existed at all until within the last few years, at the same time that they adjourned over Monday week after week, to prevent the introduction of any measures of relief in the interest of the people, as wicked and puerile, and beneath the dignity of any honest and reputable body of American citizens.

14. We are opposed to all land-grabs by wealthy corporations in this State, either of swamp-lands, internal improvement lands, or the public domain, in any form whatever. We believe that the swamp-lands ought to be appraised and sold, the same as the school lands and internal improvement lands now are, and the proceeds funded, and the interest, together with that accruing from the internal improvement land, devoted to school purposes and other general current expenses of the State in such a way that all may participate in the benefits, and the burdens and taxes of the people be correspondingly lightened. We are opposed to all useless and unnecessary offices and sinecures, and all favoritism and fraud, or the retention in office of persons guilty of dishonesty or extravagance in the use of public moneys; and in favor of the most rigid economy and fidelity in the administration of all State and Federal matters.

15. We commend the public speakers and press of our National Greenback-Labor party throughout the State for avoiding all low, vulgar personalities and slang, and confining themselves closely to the measures and principles before the country, rather than striving to traduce and vilify and misrepresent those who differ from them in opinion; believing that a calm, earnest, dispassionate, courteous, and gentlemanly course will be appreciated by our best citizens of all parties. We also desire to express our admiration and appreciation of our Greenback members in Congress for their noble, earnest, and able advocacy of the rights and interests of the people.

16. We are satisfied that there is an imperative necessity for a weekly central or State organ, in the interests of our party, under the editorial management and control of an able and uncompromising man, and will do all in our power to encourage and sustain such a journal, if started.

17. That we are in favor of the soldiers' and sailors' homestead law being so amended as to remove all unfair and obnoxious restrictions, so as to enable the late brave defenders of the Union, their widows and orphans, to become the actual owners of a homestead without price and without cost other than the district land-office fees, thus placing the poor and indigent ex-soldier and sailor upon an equality with his rich and affluent neighbor. And also we are in favor of all lands belonging to the General Government being placed in the market subject to entry or settlement by actual settlers, including pine-lands.

18. That the labor of convicts shall not be let out by contract to any person, copartnership company, or corporation, and the Legislature shall by law provide for the working of convicts for the benefit of the State, thus preventing convict labor from coming in competition with honest labor.

19. The prohibition of the employment of children under fourteen years of age in manufactories and industrial establishments, inasmuch as their employment in such places tends to public demoralization by enfeebling them physically, mentally, and morally, and deprives them of that education in youth on which so necessarily rests the enlightenment of the masses, which we hold to be the sheet-anchor of republican institutions. We demand the enactment of laws making such employment a criminal offense, and punishable as felony.

The State Convention of the Prohibitionists was held at Minneapolis on June 10th. The following ticket for State officers was nominated: For Governor, Rev. W. W. Satterlee; for Lieutenant-Governor, A. B. Williams; for Secretary of State, I. C. Stearns; for Treasurer, H. H. Brown; for Attorney-General, A. W. Bangs. The following platform was adopted:

Whereas, The old political parties are opposed by resolutions in party conventions passed, and by every public act of their representatives in the halls of legislation, to the prohibition of the traffic in intoxicating liquors, and in favor of the policy of license; and,

Whereas, We, as prohibitionists, are opposed to this policy, believing it to be wrong in principle and a failure in practice; we can not, therefore, cast our votes with these parties without violating our conscience and stultifying our manhood; therefore,

Resolved, That we will follow the policy already marked out by the Prohibition Reform party, and, declaring ourselves free from the old party yoke, nominate true men for office, and, standing by them to the last, turn not either to the right nor the left until we win the victory.

Resolved, further, That we do invite and urge upon our fellow citizens to join in this movement, without regard to past party affiliations.

The Republican State Convention assembled at St. Paul on September 3d. J. V. Daniels was chosen permanent President, and the following ticket for State officers was nominated: For Governor, John S. Pillsbury; for Lieutenant-Governor, C. A. Gilman; for Secretary of State, Fred. von Baumbach; for State Treasurer, George Kittleson; for Attorney-General, Charles M. Start; for Railroad Commissioner, W. R. Marshall. The following platform was adopted:

The Republicans of Minnesota, in convention assembled, make the following declarations:

1. We adhere to the platform of principles adopted by the last Convention of the Republican party of the United States at Cincinnati. The eminent success which has attended the resumption of specie payments and the refunding of the public debt at a more favorable rate of interest than has ever before been attained by the Government, indicates the safe and enlightened financial policy which has steadily been adhered to by the Republican party. We cheerfully acknowledge the fidelity and ability with which the finances have been conducted by the present Administration, and we especially commend the course of the President in firmly exercising the veto power to uphold the safeguards of the ballot-box.

2. We desire to cultivate feelings of good neighborhood with our fellow citizens of the Southern States, and rely much upon conciliatory treatment and mutually friendly intercourse to produce those good rela-

tions which in all respects would prove beneficial. At the same time we demand that every constitutional means be exerted to maintain that liberty and security throughout the South which all citizens are entitled to under the Government.

3. We adhere to the advanced position heretofore taken by the Republican party in favor of civil-service reform. A true reform of the civil service should among other benefits lead to a reduction in the number of offices and promote economy. Any important measure of civil-service reform in order to be effective should be put into the form of law, and not be left subject to annulment by mere executive authority.

4. We demand retrenchment wherever practicable, and the strictest economy consistent with wise administration in every department of the national and State governments. Without abandoning a just policy of protection, we nevertheless believe the time has come when some reduction should be made in the tariff, especially in the duties on clothing, on books, and on such other articles as enter into industrial and household economy.

5. The Republican party sets its face absolutely against everything that savors of monopoly, and it will always use every possible constitutional means to protect the people against unjust discriminations and combinations by railroad or other corporations.

6. Whereas the duty on wheat-flour exported from the United States into Cuba is at the enormous rate of six dollars and twelve cents a barrel, and the restrictions both in the ports of Cuba and Mexico bear very heavily on the products of the Mississippi Valley, we would therefore request our Senators and Representatives in Congress to use their best efforts to procure an amelioration of our commercial relations with Cuba and Mexico.

7. Our thanks are hereby tendered to the Senators and Representatives of Minnesota for their successful efforts in obtaining appropriations for improving our lake and river navigation.

8. We will generously coöperate with our fellow citizens, without distinction of party, in securing the shortest and cheapest route for transportation to the seaboard.

9. The prudence, efficiency, and practical sagacity in the management of State affairs by the administration of Governor John S. Pillsbury deserve the continued confidence of the people.

The Democratic State Convention assembled at St. Paul on September 26th. John B. Brisbin was chosen chairman, and the following nominations were made: For Governor, Edmund Rice, Sr.; for Lieutenant-Governor, E. P. Barnum; for Secretary of State, Felix A. Borer; for State Treasurer, Lyman E. Cowdery; for Attorney-General, P. M. Babcock; for Railroad Commissioner, William Colville. The following platform was adopted:

We, the Democracy of Minnesota, in convention assembled, pledge ourselves to the support of the following principles of public policy:

1. The United States is an indissoluble union of indestructible States; the Federal Government is supreme within the limits defined by the Constitution and its amendments; the powers not thereby conferred upon it nor prohibited to the States are reserved to the States respectively or to the people; the preservation in their separate integrity of the just powers of the Union and of the States as part of an harmonious whole; the maintenance of national authority and of local self-government as well as essential to the perpetuity of our free institutions; and we shall resist all attempts to dismember the Union by nullification or secession, or to extinguish the States by centralization or usurpation, as alike unconstitutional, revolutionary, and treasonable.

2. The enormous tribute which the producers of the West are compelled to pay to the monopolists of the East by the present system of protection, is an intolerable burden and a gross injustice. We demand as a right that our people shall be allowed to buy and sell in the markets of the world untrammeled by vexatious and oppressive tariffs. We favor the speedy establishment of free trade as the permanent commercial policy of this country.

3. We demand the thorough revision of our patent laws, to the end that the innocent purchasers of manufactured articles, using the same in good faith, shall be protected from harassing and oppressive suits for the infringement of patent rights.

4. We hold that gold and silver coin is the money of the Constitution; that all paper currency should at all times be redeemable in coin at the option of the holder, and the volume thereof should be regulated by the business wants of the country; that we favor the unlimited coinage of silver coin and its immediate restoration to its original place as money, the same as gold.

5. We favor a genuine reform in the civil service of the country to the end that honesty and efficiency shall alone be the tests of public employment. Such a reform, to be permanent, should not only be put into the form of law, but should also include the abolishment of superfluous offices, and such a wholesome reduction of salaries that the expenses of partisan campaigns can not be paid out of the public funds by the indirect method of political assessments upon official incomes.

6. We hold to the old Democratic maxim, that that government is best which governs least—which bestows upon the citizen the greatest personal liberty consistent with the public peace and welfare, and, while it affords full protection to life and property, leaves the creeds, habits, customs, and business of the people unfettered by sumptuary laws, class-legislation, or extortionate monopolies.

7. We demand a free ballot and an honest count of the votes cast at an election as the inalienable right of American citizens. The presence of armed troops at the polls upon election day, and of partisan officials clothed with arbitrary power to intimidate, arrest, and imprison voters without legal process, is intolerable in a free country, a direct blow to the rights of all adopted citizens, and suited only to the schemes of a desperate party determined to maintain its political power at all hazards. Never again by fraud or force shall the will of the people constitutionally expressed be nullified by treasonable conspiracy of unscrupulous partisans.

Resolved, That the enormous expense attending the administration of the State government by the Republican party demands the most serious consideration of all thoughtful citizens and patriotic men, and that the policy established by that party which has rendered it necessary, in the administration of the State government and the maintenance of the public credit, to wring from the hands of the struggling settlers and producers of our frontier State more than one million of dollars annually, for the purpose of governing less than one million of the most orderly and law-abiding people on earth, is unsound and cruel, and should receive at the ballot-box such a rebuke as will prevent all political parties hereafter from any attempt to repeat the outrage.

We demand that the railroads which the people have chartered and endowed with vast and profitable privileges, shall be operated for their benefit and not for their ruin. And we affirm it to be of the first importance, that the office of Railroad Commissioner in this State should no longer be a political sinecure, but should be intrusted to a man of unchallenged capacity, who is allied to the interests of the people. That while we fully recognize and respect all the rights and privileges legally pertaining to the railroad and elevator corporations of this State, and would discourage any causeless or unnecessary agitation thereof, we nevertheless believe the time has come when the doctrine of the sovereignty of the people over corporations, as expounded by the Supreme Court of the

United States, should find expression in such just and appropriate legislation as will fully protect individuals and localities from extortionate tariffs and injurious discriminations, and that the Legislature of Minnesota should take such action in this behalf as will effectually relieve the producing interest of the crushing burden now imposed upon it.

Resolved, That we condemn the management of our public institutions, and especially the manner in which the public funds were squandered by the trustees and officers of the Insane Asylum at St. Peter, as well as the cowardice of Governor Pillsbury in declining to remove those officers, when their incapacity and mismanagement were reported to him. And we also condemn the action of a partisan Legislature in refusing to pass a bill for their removal. We further condemn the action of a partisan committee of the Legislature, in recommending a settlement of the deficiency of $4,000, reported by the Senate Committee, on the payment of $300.

After the nominations made by the Republican Convention, a question was raised respecting the eligibility of W. C. Gilman for the office of Lieutenant-Governor, as he was at the time a member of the House of Representatives of the Legislature. A clause of the State Constitution declares as follows: "No Senator or Representative shall, *during the term for which he is elected*, hold any office under the authority of the United States or the State of Minnesota, except that of postmaster." It was urged that this constitutional provision had been frequently disregarded. The reply was that "it had lain dormant in practice because no occasion has heretofore presented itself where those who understood its effect felt disposed to invoke these latent powers of the Constitution. But a thousand inadvertent violations of the law do not, in the slightest degree, impair its force or effect whenever the occasion comes for its operation"; and a writ of *quo warranto* was threatened if the candidate took office.

The result of the election, on November 4th, was as follows:

FOR GOVERNOR.

John A. Pillsbury, Republican	55,918
Edmund Rice, Democrat	41,583
W. W. Satterlee, Prohibitionist	2,863
—— Meighen, National	4,264

FOR LIEUTENANT-GOVERNOR.

C. A. Gilman, Republican	59,075
E. P. Barnum, Democrat	33,554
A. B. Williams, Prohibitionist	3,615
J. M. Westfall, National	4,148

FOR SECRETARY OF STATE.

F. von Baumbach, Republican	59,780
Felix A. Borer, Democrat	39,240
I. C. Stearns, Prohibitionist	2,507
A. P. Lane, National	4,139

FOR TREASURER.

Charles Kittelson, Republican	59,950
L. E. Cowdery, Democrat	38,988
—— Dunham, Prohibitionist	2,551
Joseph Gear, National	8,964

FOR ATTORNEY-GENERAL.

C. M. Start, Republican	60,153
P. M. Babcock, Democrat	38,381
A. W. Bangs, Prohibitionist	2,588
O. Stephenson, National	4,064

FOR RAILROAD COMMISSIONER.

W. E. Marshall, Republican	59,995
William Colville, Democrat	39,009
——, Prohibitionist	2,589
Ebenezer Ayers, National	4,048

A constitutional amendment, prohibiting county and municipal corporations from creating debt in aid of railroads in excess of five per cent. of taxable property in them, was adopted—yeas, 55,143; nays, 1,702.

MISSISSIPPI. The Constitution of this State was adopted in 1869, while military rule prevailed. It is the only one of the constitutions adopted at that period in the Southern States which has thus far remained unchanged. The question of holding a Constitutional Convention has of late been often presented. Among the reasons urged in favor of such Convention, it is said that the present Constitution was written and enacted by alien enemies, and the true people of the State had no voice in its formation; the basis of representation in the Legislature is very unequal and unjust; it provides that indictments for penal offenses may be found in any county other than that in which the offense was committed; the judiciary system should be remodeled; the Judges should hold their term of office for four years, and should be elected by the people; the Circuit Courts should be vested with equity jurisdiction; the system of registration should be abolished; the Legislature should have a supervisory power over railroad corporations, savings banks, and insurance companies, by which the people could be protected from their frauds and oppressions; all supernumerary offices, such as chancellors, registrars, and county superintendents of public education, should be abolished, and the duties of the latter devolve upon the Probate Judge; elections should be held only every two and four years (political elections every two years, judicial and ministerial every four years); all special legislation should be prohibited; and any county or city or town forbidden to vote aid to any railroad or corporation, upon the well-recognized doctrine that the majority have no right to tax the minority except for the legitimate expenses of government.

The assessment of real estate was ordered in 1879, and the returns made the valuation amount to $95,937,398. The State tax for a series of years has been as follows: in 1874, 14 mills on the dollar; $14 on $1,000; in 1875, 9½ mills on the dollar, $9.25 on $1,000; in 1876, 6½ mills on the dollar, $6.50 on $1,000; in 1877, 5 mills on the dollar, $5 on $1,000; in 1878, 3½ mills on the dollar, $3.50 on $1,000. The tax of 5 mills in 1877 amounted to $497,686; the 3½ mills in 1878 yielded $335,789. The decrease in the State tax of 1878 over 1877 on account of realty was $143,906.10, and on account of personalty $44,134.05, making a total decrease in State tax of 1878 over 1877 of $188,040.15.

The statistics of public schools in 1878, made up and reported by the State Superintendent in 1879, show the following results:

Number of educable children in the State:

White males	85,528	
White females	72,628	
		158,156
Colored males	97,549	
Colored females	92,539	
		190,088
Total		848,244

Number in school during the year:

White males	51,828	
White females	48,858	
		100,676
Colored males	52,780	
Colored females	51,990	
		104,779
Total		205,455

Average monthly enrollment:

White males	41,876	
White females	40,690	
		82,566
Colored males	43,876	
Colored females	44,784	
		68,660
Total		171,226

Average daily attendance:

White males	83,128	
White females	81,190	
		64,318
Colored males	84,979	
Colored females	86,679	
		71,658
Total		185,976

Teachers employed during the year:

White teachers	2,948
Colored teachers	1,813
Total	4,761

Average number of days taught:

In the country	79
In the cities	154

Average monthly salary paid teachers:

White teachers	$28 02
Colored teachers	26 92½

Expenditures:

Per capita of school population	$1 70
Per capita in school	2 93
Per capita in average daily attendance	8 42
Total receipts for 1878	$626,268 81
Total expenditures	592,805 18

The spirit of enterprise appears to be rapidly increasing among the people, and measures to promote success are on foot in various parts of the State. At Vicksburg, the central point of the greatest cotton-growing region of the South, there has been organized the Mississippi Valley Cotton-Planters' Association. Some of its objects are: "to develop all the material interests of the landlord and laborer by the more scientific and economic cultivation of the soil; to urge on all classes interested the absolute importance of a diversity of crops, to the end that we may be a self-sustaining country, and consequently that cotton shall become a surplus instead of as now the only crop; to encourage the introduction of all improved and labor-saving machinery and farming implements for the drainage of land and handling of crops, by competitive trials of the same before competent committees; to promote the selection and improvement of all kinds of planting-seeds; to foster the introduction of the best classes of live stock for breeding purposes; to enter into correspondence at once with various countries for the introduction of additional labor, and to keep prominently before the States

of Tennessee, Mississippi, Arkansas, and Louisiana, embraced in this Association, the absolute necessity of some united, practical plan of immigration in which this Association will coöperate; to be the medium through which parties interested may obtain information in regard to plantations, timber- or cane-lands for sale or rent; and in general, to harmonize and concentrate for the above purposes the efforts of all those engaged in the cultivation and sale of cotton, as well as those engaged in the manufacture of implements and machinery therefor, and for such other purposes as may hereafter be determined." Measures have been likewise taken for the formation of sub-associations in every neighborhood of every county and parish in the Mississippi Valley.

The following estimate of this great industry of the country has been made by the New York "Financial Chronicle" of a crop of about 5,000,000 bales; all crops and land are left out of the question save cotton and the lands cultivated in cotton:

A crop of 5,000,000 bales, averaging three acres to produce a bale, would give 15,000,000 acres, at $8 per acre, $120,000,000; one mule or horse to twenty-five acres, 800,000 mules, at $90, $72,000,000; implements, harness, etc., and machinery, $50,000,000; showing permanent investment of $242,000,000. Averaging three bales per hand would require1, 666,666 laborers, to feed and clothe whom for a year with their dependents would average $50 each, $82,666,667. To feed team at $40 per mule, 800,000 mules, $32,000,000. Cost of bagging and ties at $1.40 per bale, $7,000,000. Cost of marketing crop, at 1½ cent per pound, would give $25,000,000. Working capital, $146,777,777. Average price expected for present crop, 11 cents for 2,000,000,000 pounds, $220,000,000.

Recapitulation.—Permanent investment of planters, $242,000,000; working capital, $145,777,777; total capital invested exclusively in cotton cultivation, this estimate being made for the share system and not wages, $388,777,777.

Amount received for total crop, $220,000,000, which is divided equally between the planters and laborers. Planters therefore receive $110,000,000—from which deduct cost for team chargeable to planter, $32,000,-000; half cost bagging and ties chargeable to planter, $3,500,000; half marketing crop, chargeable to planter, $12,500,000; 20 per cent. in loss and decreased value of stock, $14,500,000; 20 per cent. in loss and decreased value of implements and machinery, $10,-000,000; total, $72,500,000. Repairing fences, houses, etc., at 10 per cent. on permanent investment, $12,000,-000. Taxes on permanent investment, 3 per cent., $7,260,000. Deduct these amounts from planters' share of crop, $110,000,000, which shows planters' profit on total investment for cotton alone is about 4½ per cent., provided they get 11 cents for cotton, make 5,000,000 bales, and the laborer pays his accounts in full.

Laborers' share of crop, $110,000,000; amount chargeable for food and clothes, $82,666,667; showing a profit for the laborer of $27,333,333. It will thus be observed that the laborer receives $27,000,000 on investment in nothing but his muscle, while the planter receives $18,000,000 on an investment of $388,-000,000 and his services.

Suppose the crop has reached the factory, simply saying that about $25,000,000 more has been added thereby to the price to be paid by the manufacturer since it landed at the seaport from the planter. The 5,000,000 bales now begin to assume some importance, for they run 12,500,000 spindles, which require say $1,000,000,000 in buildings, machinery, and working capital, and employ nearly 800,000 operatives and employees. The manufactured goods are sent to every part of the known world, creating a trade reciprocal business that can hardly be estimated, but without doing which, as can easily be seen, it will reach into the billions.

Early in the year a convention was called at Vicksburg to assemble on May 5th. The object as expressed in the call was "to take into consideration the present agitation of the labor question." The proceedings of this convention are noticed elsewhere (see EXODUS). The signers believed that, by united action, "they might be able to adopt such measures as would allay the excitement prevailing, or which at least would enable them to supply the places of those laborers who had gone, or who might hereafter go, to the Western States."

For a short time previous considerable numbers of the colored population had been selling their effects and emigrating to Kansas, under the ostensible anticipation of improving their condition. An emigration so unusual and so extensive had attracted the attention of the people in all parts of the country, and excited some apprehensions of a scarcity or loss of laborers among the producers of cotton and sugar. For full details, see EXODUS, and KANSAS.

The views entertained in Mississippi relative to the effects of this emigration on the planting interest are very calmly and fully set forth in the following extract from a memorial to the people of the Northern States by the cotton-planters of Washington County, assembled in convention at Greenville on May 28th:

Contracts with the laborers are almost universally of three kinds : 1. Leases for rent payable in cotton or in money ; 2. Contracts for work on shares, the landlord supplying land, team, tools, and forage, the laborer supplying his own subsistence and the labor only, with an equal division of the crop to be made ; 3. For wages to the laborer. In all cases a free election was given to the laborer as to the class of contract under which he would work. In no known instance was he put under compulsion as to contracting, or as to change from one plantation to another, or as to migration in any direction whatever. Whether the laborer elects to rent ground or work upon shares, he always demands and receives from his landlord or his merchant such supplies as he may require during the year. At this season of the year the laborer has generally obtained nearly his year's supply, and the planters are dependent wholly upon the completion of the crop, both for the rents or shares and payment for supplies advanced. It will thus be seen that the loss of even one crop would in all cases seriously injure, and probably in a majority of instances wholly ruin, the sugar and cotton planters, and bankrupt the commercial and business interests of the entire country that are dependent upon the prosperity of those planters. Thus much is embarked upon the faith of the negro's fidelity to his contract, which it is idle and preposterous to assert the planter would impair by unkindly treatment.

In this condition of our planting interests comes this last fearful menace. We do not fear so much the loss of the few hundreds or thousands of negroes who may be carried away by the boats of your benevolent societies, but we know and fear the consequences of the appearance of a single boat dispatched for such purposes. The great body of the colored people have been led to believe by secret emissaries that the United States Government would now make good the hope which they indulged soon after their emancipation, that they would each be provided with permanent homes upon well-improved farms, equipped with the necessary stock and material, and they would be transported to them in the State of Kansas free of charge; placards and chromos have been freely but secretly distributed among the negroes, designed to influence their imagination and seduce them from their contracts by immediate migration. So successful have such efforts been that in a great many instances negroes who were well established for planting, owning their teams, material, etc., and with their crops in fine condition, and others who were owners of lands nearly paid for, seized with the belief thus impressed upon them that the present opportunity to emigrate might be their only one, have sold their horses and mules for $8 or $10 per head, sacrificed their other property, abandoned their lands and crops, and congregated upon the river-bank to await the coming of the Government boat.

Many, and we fear most of the emigrants, exhibit the delusion of a religious mind, and, either of their own conceit or under the machinations of the emissary, believe that the Almighty has called them to go to a "land of Canaan." Added to this the wonderful credulity of the negro—ever ready, as he is, to listen to the marvelous, and hopeful to an absurd degree— it is not surprising that he should be demoralized, enticed from his contracts and crop, and crazed with the fever of emigration. The fact that our crops for several years past have brought low prices, and would not justify the accustomed prodigality of the negro, has, it is true, furnished a pretense to the emissary to assist in discouraging and unsettling the laborers. At this season the loss of ten days' labor would irretrievably injure, if it did not wholly destroy the crop. No substituted labor could be procured.

In view of these facts, we now further state that, if a single boat should make its appearance along our borders and proclaim a free passage to but one load of emigrants, it would confirm the negroes in their delusion, and depopulate every plantation accessible to the river. The Northern philanthropists, whose large-hearted generosity we have had such recent cause to appreciate, can hardly estimate the effect upon the emotional, excitable, and credulous negro of the appearance on the Mississippi River of a single boat whose mission would be to give transportation to the negro Kansasward. While such a steamer could, at the utmost, carry off only a few hundred, the whole country on both sides of the river would become instantaneously aflame with excitement, growing crops would be abandoned, houses left tenantless, the comforts of the laboring man's life would be spurned, the small gatherings of years of labor in the shape of stock and poultry sold for a trifle or thrown away, and the entire negro population would collect on the river-banks, destitute of provisions, means, or the commonest necessaries of life, firmly convinced that the promised day had arrived at last ; that the Government was at length coming up to its promises, and that a life of ease and plenty was to be theirs in the future. A fleet of transports and months of time would be necessary to effect their removal. In the mean time the loss of the bulk of the cotton-crop and bankruptcy of all dependent on it would result. The final destruction, pilfering, and violence that would ensue can better be imagined than described.

No true friend of the negro could desire such a fearful result, and hence we invoke the true philanthropist to pause and investigate and consider well the effect of this effort before adopting the proposed remedy for an unreal, fanciful wrong ; and we invoke the fair-minded, honest people of the North and West, whence this danger emanates, to interpose their condemnation and power to prevent the destruction of the industrial interests of the white and black alike of the Mississippi Valley. It is not true that the negro in the valley of the Lower Mississippi is subjected to the prejudice of race, any personal abuse, any extortion, any denial of political, legal, or social rights, any personal discomforts or want, to which he would not in his condition bo subjected in a greater degree at any other place on the American Continent. At the expiration of the current year, when our crops will have been secured and expenditure and advances repaid, and our business affairs adjusted to so momentous a change, the general migration of the negro would be less injurious and would be based upon more definite information and better preparations upon his part. Any obstacles that may have heretofore been interposed to his free migration have been only in exceptional cases, and have been because of his migration being a violation of his contract, and no such obstacles have been accompanied by anything like violence. It must be borne in mind, in palliation of any such efforts that may have been made, that large amounts have been advanced on the faith of these contracts, which were entered into fairly and honestly at a time when the present exodus was not in any way foreshadowed. The emigration of the negro since the war has been toward this vast, fertile valley, instead of from it; and this exodus has been a surprise to the whole country, neither agitated nor thought of before these contracts for this year were made, and large expenses and advances made upon them.

We believe that the danger of the contemplated movement is not appreciated by the Northern people, and we know that the benevolent are there imposed upon by deception; and we make this, our memorial and remonstrance, not as politicians (for we represent all parties), but as business men and law-abiding people, hoping that it may arouse the friends of peace and order, justice and true philanthropy, to interpose and arrest the threatened invasion of our rights and destruction of our property.

The new industry of growing fruit and vegetables for the Northwestern market advanced rapidly. The central point of this interest is known as Crystal Springs, which is located in the middle of that first pleiocene stratum that crops out at Canton and extends to Woodville, and on which fruits flourish and attain a perfection not found elsewhere in the State. At that point alone there was an acreage of 2,000 in peach-trees, 500 in apples, 250 in plums, 35 in strawberries, and 25 in raspberries. The net receipts from Chicago for the strawberry-crop amounted to $10,000, averaging nearly $300 to the acre. A still larger traffic has been growing up in vegetables, and it has been shown that peas and beans with high cultivation will net $300 to $400 per acre.

The work of most importance to the prosperity of the State is the protection of its alluvial lands from inundation by the Mississippi River, by the construction of levees, and incidentally therewith the improvement of the stream itself. During the administration of President Taylor in 1849–'50 (himself a Louisiana planter and deeply interested in the question), the first resolutions were passed in the Senate of the United States directing a survey of the Mississippi River, expressly to ascertain the best method of reclaiming the alluvial lands of the Mississippi Valley. This, after many years, resulted in the able and exhaustive report of Humphreys and Abbott, Chief Engineers of the United States Army, who emphatically declare that the levee system is the best method of accomplishing this purpose. In furtherance of this object the United States donated the swamp-lands lying in Arkansas,

Mississippi, and Louisiana, which were of no value without protection from overflow, to these respective States to assist in building up their levees. The funds arising from these lands were small and soon exhausted, and millions of their own money were expended by these States in the creation of levees under State legislation. The levees thus constructed were just being tested, and were more or less successful in different places, when the war came on and large portions of them were destroyed ; some by the attrition of wagons and horses, when they were used as a road-bed ; some by the erosion of the water, aided by the paddle-wheels of steamers in high tide; and some directly by the army and navy of the United States. Mississippi and Louisiana have expended large sums of money since the war to repair their levees, but experience has shown that they have not the pecuniary strength to accomplish this great work as individual States, and that they are prohibited by the Constitution of the United States from forming combinations with each other or other States to create a uniform system of levees, which is essential to their protection.

The improvement of the stream of the river is incident to this repair of its banks. It is the greatest artery of internal commerce in the world, and yet it is filled with snags and sand-bars that are the deposit of its annual overflows, which not only destroy vessels, but tax the whole commerce of the West with an increase of insurance that is destructive to property. It is claimed by scientific men that when the water of the Mississippi is permitted to spread over a large surface the velocity of its current is checked, it makes deposits of sediment and snags, creates sand-bars, and obstructs navigation ; and that, on the other hand, the concentration of the water into a narrow stream will increase the velocity so that it will remove the sand-bars, clean out the snags, deepen the channel, and improve navigation. If this be true, as the reports of scientific engineers declare and as the action of the jetties seems to demonstrate, then the construction of the levees, which would confine into a stream one mile wide water that would spread over forty miles without them, must conduce to the benefit of navigation. The system of rivers of which the Mississippi is the grand trunk comprises 35 rivers and 15,000 miles of waterway, floating the largest inland commerce on the face of the globe. Upon these waters float more than 3,000 vessels, with a carrying capacity of about 500,000 tons. This vast fleet is largely increasing year by year, and pushing its pioneers into rivers of the far West and Northwest that were unknown half a century ago. Over thirty steamers more than a year ago were plying upon the Upper Missouri and the Yellowstone. The Mississippi is the outlet for the enormous agricultural productions of the fruitful West. The exportation of grain and of meat and other products of the farm has gained each year an enormous increase. Transportation by railroad when agricultural products are cheap, becomes an item disproportionate to the price received in the market. Commerce then reverts to its old waterways, and demands every facility. The means of water transportation have changed. A single tug carries down a fleet of barges whose cargoes would load a train of 500 cars. One tug carried a tow of barges into New Orleans with 600,000 bushels of coal, a freight for 1,800 cars. The export of corn increased from 20 to 70 million bushels in the three years 1875–'77. In 1876 there were exported 550 million pounds of pork, worth about $70,000,000, 34 million pounds of beef, and millions of bushels of wheat.

This question has been often presented to Congress, and committees of each House have reported bills recommending appropriations for the purpose of protecting the alluvial lands from inundation. In these reports they have been unanimous, but none of them have ever received a favorable consideration until this year. At its late session Congress passed a bill for the creation of a permanent commission for the improvement of the river. It provides for the appointment of a commission consisting of seven members, a majority of whom shall be army engineers, and one of whom shall be an experienced river steamboatman, whose duty it shall be to prosecute and report upon such steps as shall be needed for the greater improvement of navigation on the river. For this commission the following nominations were made by the President: Benjamin Harrison, of Indiana; James B. Eads, civil engineer, Missouri; B. Morgan Harrod, civil engineer, Louisiana; Lieutenant-Colonel Q. A. Gillmore, Major O. B. Comstock, Major C. R. Suter, from the Engineer Corps of the Army; and Henry Mitchell, from the Coast and Geodetic Survey.

The law creating a Board of Health for the State, and authorizing similar bodies in counties and towns, gave to the latter the power to establish local quarantine. This operated so disadvantageously that, upon the creation of the National Board of Health and the publication of its rules and regulations, they were immediately adopted by the State Board and recommended to the local boards.

The provisions of the insurance laws of the State in respect to foreign companies were defined by Judge Hill of the United States Circuit Court, in the case of the Firemen's Insurance Company vs. W. L. Hemingway et al. After having given a full recital of the statutory provisions, as designed to give to insurance companies chartered and doing business in other States an opportunity to establish agencies in Mississippi, he proceeded to say:

But as a protection to our citizens from fictitious or insolvent companies created and doing business in other States, and to give our citizens an opportunity to examine the law of their creation, and their condition every way, the sworn statement of their condition by their principal officers, with a copy of their charter, is required to be filed with the Auditor, and also in the office of the Chancery Clerk, in each county in which

the companies by their agents may desire to do business; and where liabilities may be incurred upon policies issued through such agents, that the companies may be sued, judgment obtained, and satisfaction had, without the policy-holder having to go out of the State to obtain it; hence, the agreement for service of process and the deposit to be made with the Treasurer, and the mode of reaching the funds so deposited with him; and that those taking risks may know the amount of the risks for which the deposit is liable. In other words, it is to give us as far as possible these foreign insurance companies the privileges coupled with the liabilities of companies chartered by this State. Such being the case, the deposit is intended only for those who may obtain their policies through the agents appointed, and doing business in the State and under the provisions of our statutes. No assignment or transfer of the fund so deposited can be made so as to defeat the claims upon it for satisfaction of losses or unearned premiums upon the policies issued by such agents as provided by these statutes. Nor can such company revoke the powers of their agents so as to defeat the remedies provided by the statute, although it may for any other purpose. So that in case such company shall cease to do business in this State, either by withdrawal of agencies or insolvency, any person holding a policy issued through such agent or agents, which has not expired, may cancel the policy or surrender it to the agent, and demand the unearned premiums, which I understand to be the amount of premium due for the unexpired term of the policy. The agent is required to estimate and certify the amount due, and that the policy has been canceled or returned, which has the same effect. This certificate is by law made evidence of the cancellation or return, and the amount of the unearned premiums; but if the agent should refuse to do this duty, the policy-holder, I have no doubt, may cancel or tender the return of the policy and make proof of its value; his redress can not be defeated either by the failure of the agent to do his duty or by the want of such agent. After, however, all these demands have been satisfied, the funds in the hands of the Treasurer are to be returned to the depositor or its assignee. It is the company and not the agent that makes the deposit, although the company acts through its agent, being incapable of any other action. After those are satisfied who have this special lien on this fund, I incline to the opinion that it is liable to other creditors of the depositor or its assignee; but, under my view of the right of the parties to this suit, the decision of this question is unnecessary.

By an act of the Legislature, women were authorized to hold the office of notary public. The question of its constitutionality was submitted to the State Attorney-General. He gave his judgment that the law was constitutional, on the ground that the office of notary public was not such a public office as was contemplated in Section 4, Article XV., of the Constitution of the State.

In another case appealed to the United States Circuit Court from the Southern District of Mississippi, it was decided on March 7th that, under the code of Mississippi, in order to authorize a judgment against a married woman, her liability must be established by showing that she has a separate estate chargeable with the obligation sued on; that a married woman is incapable of being bound either by a contract or judgment except in special cases authorized by law; and that if a suit is against her and her husband, no judgment will be rendered against her unless the liability of her separate property be first established.

An act of the Legislature passed March 5th,

1878, which appropriated a portion of the school fund to certain high schools, was declared by the Supreme Court of the State to be unconstitutional. The Court said that "no portion of the school fund can be diverted to the support of schools which in their organization and conduct contravene the general scheme prescribed. That is to say, the fund must be applied to such schools only as come within the uniform system devised; are under the general supervision of the State Superintendent, and the local supervision of the County Superintendent; are free from all sectarian religious control, and are open to all children within the ages of five and twenty-one years, though this freedom of admission to all will not preclude the classification of the schools according to the ages, sex, race, or mental acquirements of the pupils, provided only they remain free to all who come within the class to which the particular school is set apart."

The Faculty of the University of Mississippi appointed a committee of the professors "to consider the propriety of uniting with other educational bodies in a memorial to Congress for the appointment of a commission whose duty it shall be to inquire into and report upon the desirability of attempting to simplify the English spelling." In a report made on February 11th, the committee state the origin of the proposed reform agitation, the changes contemplated, and the present strength of its friends. So much as relates to the changes contemplated is briefly set forth in these words:

1. There are eighteen Roman letters which commonly represent in English nearly the same elementary sounds which they represented in Latin: a (father), b, c (k, q), d, e (met), f, g (go), h, i (pick), l, m, n, o (go), p, r, s (so), t, u (full).

2. The consonant sounds represented in Latin by i and u are now represented by y and w, and the sonants corresponding to f and s are now represented by v and z.

3. There are three short vowels unknown to the early Romans which are without proper representatives in English, those in fat, not, but.

4. There are five elementary consonants represented by digraphs: th (thin), th-dh (thine, then), sh (she), zh (azure), ng (sing); to which may be added ch (church), g (j).

It seems best to follow the Latin and other languages written in Roman letters, in the use of a single sign for a short vowel and its long, distinguishing these, where great exactness is required, by a diacritical mark. The alphabet would then have thirty-two letters. Twenty-two of these have their common form and power described in 1 and 2. The three vowels in fat, not, but, need new letters. For the consonants now represented by digraphs new letters would be desirable.

The changes recommended are substantially these:
1. Thirty-two letters instead of twenty-six. 2. Of these twenty-three are old ones, viz.: a, b, c, d, e, f, g, h, i, j, l, m, n, o, p, r, s (so), t, u (full), v, w, y, z. 3. Three new vowel-letters for à, ŏ, û. 4. That k, q, and x be dropped. 5. That the digraphs now representing single consonants be for the present named and treated as single letters, viz.: th, dh, sh, zh, ng, ch. 6. That e and i be distinguished by diacritical marks. This is the substance as to the new alphabet proposed; but the committee of the Philological Association in 1878, at Saratoga, made the following suggestions as to spelling:

1. Drop all silent letters, especially silent e after a short vowel, as in have, give; and a in ea when pronounced e short, as in head, health. 2. Write f for ph in such words as alphabet, philosopher. 3. When a word ends in a double letter, omit the last, as in shall, cliff. 4. Change ed final to t where it has the sound of t, as in lashed, impressed.

The alphabet recommended above by the Philological Association was adopted by the Spelling Reform Association in 1877; and the rules for spelling have been since adopted.

The advocates of spelling reform argue thus: 1. The alphabet is redundant, defective, and inconsistent. 2. The spelling hinders our people from becoming readers, (1) by the length of time it takes to learn, and (2) by the dislike of reading it induces. An average German learns, they say, in about one third the time. 3. Civilization and Christianity are both hindered by the difficultness. 4. Vast annual expense is incurred by printing silent letters. 5. In most languages changes in written words rapidly correspond to changes in pronunciation. Why not in ours? 6. The language was made for men, and not men for the language. 7. This system will make it easier for all to read English who read French, German, Latin, Greek, or Anglo-Saxon. 8. It will make the learning of foreign tongues easy. 9. It will settle the school pronunciation of Latin and Greek. 10. Several modern languages have had their spelling reformed by the influence of learned academies, or by government; and surely no language needs reform more than ours, and no race are more ready reformers.

The report to the Faculty concludes with this resolution:

Resolved, That the irregular spelling of the English language is a serious hindrance in learning to read and write, and is one cause of the alarming illiteracy in our country; that it occupies much time in our schools which is needed for other branches of study; and that it is desirable to request our Legislatures, State and national, to appoint commissioners to investigate this matter, and report what measures, if any, can be taken to simplify our spelling.

The elections to be held in the State in 1879 were for approval or rejection of a constitutional amendment, and for the choice of members of the Legislature, district attorneys, sheriffs, Chancery and Circuit Court clerks, and county and municipal officers. The constitutional amendment proposed was as follows:

SECTION 6. The political year shall begin on the first Monday in January; the Legislature shall meet at the seat of government on the first Tuesday after the first Monday in January, A. D. 1882, also on the first Tuesday after the first Monday in January, 1883, and biennially thereafter, unless sooner convened by the Governor. The time and place of meeting may be altered by law.

SEC. 7. A general election, by ballot, shall be held on the first Tuesday after the first Monday in November, A. D. 1880, and biennially thereafter. All officers who go into office on the first Monday in January, 1882, shall be elected at the general election in 1880. All officers who go into office on the first Monday in January, 1880, and all officers who go into office on the first Monday in January, 1882, shall hold their respective offices for three years; but the constitutional terms of their successors shall not be hereby affected. Electors, in all cases, except in cases of treason, felony, and breach of the peace, shall be privileged from arrest during their attendance at elections, and the going to and returning therefrom.

The objection urged against this amendment was, that it would require the State election to be held on the same day with the Congressional elections. If, therefore, the rule of mili-

---

tary supervision of Congressional elections was to be continued, the State elections would be exposed to foreign interference.

At the commencement of the election campaign some attempts were made to arouse and organize those who had formerly been known as Radicals. The tendency of these efforts seems to have been considered on the part of the whites as likely to array against them the blacks. In their apprehensions they were led to demand the withdrawal from the county of Yazoo of the principal or white candidate for sheriff.. This was refused, but the candidate promised to decline the nomination, which was accepted. Subsequently, in the heat of the campaign, personal remarks led to personal encounters, and in some instances a loss of life. There were two cases attended with unusual excitement.

The election was confined to the choice of county officers and a State Legislature. The result of the latter was: in the Senate, 33 Democrats, 2 Nationals, and 1 Republican; in the House, 96 Democrats, 13 Nationals, 5 Republicans, 3 Independents, and 3 vacancies; total, 120.

In addition to the expenditure for public schools, the State has expended during the last nine years for Alcorn (colored) University, $216,250; the colored State normal school at HollySprings, $51,450; that at Tugaloo, $23,-000.

An important invention for the conversion of seed-cotton into yarn was made by L. T. Clements of Smyrna in Tennessee, who died two years ago, without accomplishing anything by his invention. It was taken up by a citizen of Mississippi and improved; new patents were obtained, and it was brought into use in many of the mills in the Carolinas, Tennessee, Georgia, Alabama, and Mississippi, under the name of "the Clements attachment." It is a combination of the gin and the card for converting seed-cotton by one operation into slivers. The machine is thus described:

It consists of a thirty-six inch top-flat, self-stripping card; the attachment (which is a diminutive gin 18 × 18 × 36 inches) is substituted for the licker-in and feed-rollers of the card; its saws are seven inches in diameter, with fourteen teeth to the inch, and revolve from 100 to 200 times per minute. The brush connected with the saws is a cylinder covered with bristles; its periphery revolves little faster than the saws, and has also a traverse or horizontal motion. The periphery of the card travels a little faster than the brush; a feed-table is placed above the card and connected with the attachment by a chute, and gives a regular supply of seed-cotton to the attachment. A stop-motion is used to save waste in case of accident. These, with a small drawing roller between the doffer and calender rollers, to reduce the sliver to the ordinary working size, and a cam-motion to receive said sliver, are all the changes and additions made to the card, and there are none made elsewhere. The seed-cotton is spread upon the endless apron of the feed-table, and passes thence through the chute into the attachment, where the lint is removed from the seed, and while on the fine saw-teeth (after passing the ribs) passes through a set of combing-plates, which removes all extraneous matter, and delivers the filaments to the brush, which delivers

them to the card, and thence, through the doffer, small drawing and calendar rollers, they are delivered as perfect sliver into a revolving can. By this process only four machines are necessary to convert any given amount of seed-cotton into perfect yarns, viz., card, as changed, drawing-frame, speeder, and spinning-frame. It is true a cleanser of seed-cotton is used as a preparatory machine. Its size is 22 × 28 × 44 inches; cost, $75; capacity, 6,000 pounds of seed-cotton per day; power necessary to drive, one half of one horse.

The new process dispenses with fully one half the building, machinery, motive power, and operatives hitherto necessary to convert any given amount of seed-cotton into yarns; causes the card, with the same amount of motive power, to do five times as much work; saves one half the usual waste, and produces baled cotton, which, on account of their extra strength, seldom break or let down, thereby enabling operatives to attend more machinery and each machine to do more work. The thread is equal in every respect to that made of baled cotton, fifty per cent. stronger, and more sheeny. The attachment supersedes the gin, press, and compress, because they are intended and only used to render cotton transportable; the willower, lopper, double lopper, breaker, and four fifths of the cards, because they are only used to try to remedy the injury done by the gin, press, and compress; it supersedes the railway, railway drawing-head, also all jack-frames, slubbers, mules, twisters, eveners, etc., etc., simply because they are costly and unnecessary machines, and perfect thread can be made without them.

The reason why the card will do five times as much, using seed-cotton and the same amount of motive power, as it did by the old process, using baled cotton, is because the filaments are not permitted to leave the machinery, fly, or become tangled, but are kept straight and parallel, and carding is but the straightening of the cotton filaments. The saving of one half the usual waste is because fresh, live cotton is used, and half the usual machinery dispensed with. The extra strength of the thread and skein is owing to the working of the cotton fresh from the seed, the oil of which has kept it alive, light, elastic, and flexible, with all its attenuating qualities perfect; and the fact that it has never been nap-cut or tangled by the gin, pressed, compressed, or permitted to become dry, seasoned, and brittle in this tangled condition, nor has it been injured by the willower, lopper, double lopper, breaker, and cards, where the damage done by the gin, press, and compress is sought to be remedied. But these advantages, great as they are, are not half that are claimed for the "new process." The ginning, baling, bagging, and ties are saved; the seed inures to the manufacturers; no loss from falsely packed cotton; no strikes from operatives, for it is the poor man's factory, and his daughters are the operatives. The entire capital necessary for the smallest-sized new-process mills, including building and motive power, is only $3,500, and will pay a net profit of 30 to 50 per cent. per annum. It saves all expense, loss, waste, dryage, perquisities, general average accounts, stealage and speculation, etc., on cotton in transit from the field to the factory, be that distance 15 or 15,000 miles, as from India to Manchester, England.

MISSOURI. The Legislature of this State assembled on January 8th. In the Senate Lieutenant-Governor Brockmeyer presided, and in the House Mr. Belch of Cole County was chosen Speaker. After a session of 132 days, and the passage of 208 bills, it adjourned on May 20th.

In the House, the following resolution was adopted:

Whereas, There is great financial stringency among the people of the whole country, and especially among the people of Missouri; and,

Whereas, The burdens of taxation are greatly due to our bonded indebtedness, which knows no shrinkage and must be provided for by law; and as the amount of our annual taxation is greatly in disproportion to the value of all agricultural, manufacturing, and other products of labor; and,

Whereas, Coming fresh from the people as we do, to whom we pledged ourselves to be in favor of and aid in all legislation that will tend to lessen the burdens of taxation; therefore, be it

Resolved, That this House is in favor of such retrenchment in all the departments of government as will reduce the burdens of taxation, and in all our legislation we will ever keep before our minds the interests of the great laboring classes of our State.

An election of Senators in Congress took place on January 21st. For the short term, expiring on March 4th, the vote in the Senate was: for General James Shields, Democrat, 26; Charles G. Burton, Republican, 5; T. Z. C. Fogg, National, 2. In the House the vote was: Shields, 102; Fogg, 22; Burton, 12. For the full term ensuing, the vote in the Senate was: for George G. Vest, Democrat, 26; Gustavus A. Finkelnburg, Republican, 5; Henry Eshhaugh, National, 2. In the House the vote was: Vest, 99; Eshbaugh, 25; Finkelnburg, 12.

On January 25th the State Lunatic Asylum, located at St. Joseph, was burned. The fire commenced in the afternoon in the extreme eastern portion of the building, and, the wind being from the east, the flames spread rapidly to the main building, and in half an hour the entire structure was hopelessly destroyed. There were 218 patients in the asylum, and the efforts of the superintendent and officers were immediately directed to the removal of the inmates. Fortunately, their work in this respect was speedily and effectually done. Not a life was lost. An appropriation of $75,000 was passed at this session to rebuild the asylum.

A constitutional amendment to remove the State capital from Jefferson City to Sedalia was rejected. The Legislature concluded that, with an annually recurring deficiency in the revenues and a serious difficulty in meeting it, it was no time for removals that would call for large extra expenditures.

A bill providing for a trial of the bell-punch in Missouri passed the House by a vote of yeas 83, nays 26, but was lost in the Senate by a vote of yeas 8, nays 15.

An effort was made to repeal the rat-bounty law, but failed. This law, passed in 1877, authorized county courts to offer a reward of five cents each for rat-scalps, delivered in round lots of not less than fifty. It was put in practice in a few counties, and found to work too well for the county exchequer. Rat-hunting became a flourishing business, and the revenues of some counties were severely taxed to pay for the scalps. In Bates County as much as $1,700 has been paid out, and in Andrew $3,200. These payments show a slaughter of 34,000 rats in Bates and 68,000 in Andrew; but, as the member from Bates said, it had "nearly bankrupted the treasury," and, as the member from Andrew stated, "if it had not been stopped, the treasury would have been completely drained."

A bill was introduced into the House to make the whipping-post one of the penal institutions of the State. It provided for the use of the lash in cases of petty larceny, wife-beating, and cruelty to children. Mr. Anderson, chairman of the Committee on Retrenchment and Reform, was in favor of the bill as an economical measure in the matter of criminal costs. Mr. Gwynne said the way to whip a man was to destroy his manhood. He was opposed to the bill on principles of humanity. Mr. McIntyre of Audrain said the way of the transgressor was hard, and if men didn't want to be flogged they must not violate the law. Mr. Campbell thought the bill would increase rather than diminish criminal costs; hence he opposed it. Mr. Mudd of Lincoln offered an amendment making the bill apply to embezzlers and those who refuse to return their property to the assessor for purposes of taxation. It was finally lost by a vote of yeas 44, nays 75.

A compulsory education bill introduced in the Senate required all children between the ages of seven and fifteen years to attend the public schools twelve weeks in each year, excepting in cases where it would be obviously improper to compel such attendance. It however failed to become a law.

A delegation of women appeared before the Committee on Constitutional Amendments of the House, to urge upon its members the propriety of reporting a constitutional amendment conferring the right of suffrage upon women. Mrs. Hazard said that if women were permitted to vote, the political pool would not be as muddy as it is. Mrs. Dickinson said that she believed that some of the opposition came from men who feared that women would seek office. Mrs. Starrett said that by mingling with the world and transacting her own business she had come to believe in woman's rights. She did not believe that physical strength was the basis of government. Mrs. Hazard said that in six States women were allowed to vote on school matters. Mrs. Starrett read a communication from the Speaker of the Wyoming House of Representatives, referring in glowing terms to the excellent effects of woman's suffrage in that Territory. Mr. Lackland of St. Charles asked, in case of woman's suffrage, if the husband would not control the vote of the wife? Judge Dryden said that from experience he thought not. Mrs. Hazard said they would be glad to hear the views of the committee, so that they could answer any objections. Judge Dryden said that in behalf of the committee he would be compelled to decline the unequal combat. The committee reported the constitutional amendment to the House, and that body indefinitely postponed its consideration by a vote of yeas 64, nays 61.

A white earth called "tiff" or baryta is an important product of Missouri. It is found in large quantities in Washington, Jefferson, and Franklin Counties, and the other regions where lead abounds. When ground in oil and mixed with a small proportion of white lead, it makes a cheap paint very useful for many purposes. Much of the so-called white lead in the markets contains more tiff than lead, for large quantities of it are exported from the State. A bill was passed not to forbid the mixture of tiff with white lead, but requiring that the proportion of the cheaper material in the mixture shall be marked on every package sold in the State, whether manufactured there or brought from other States, so that purchasers might know what they were buying. The bill peremptorily forbids the mixture of the earth in bread, confections, and other articles of food, under severe penalties.

A resolution designed partly to secure fair voting, and partly to thwart the Federal supervision of State elections, was offered in the House, directing the Judiciary Committee to inquire into the expediency of changing the present method of voting by ballot for the living-voice method, in which every voter announces the name of each candidate he votes for. This was the fashion that prevailed many years ago, and is still in vogue in the old States of Virginia and Kentucky. In all the other States it has yielded to the system of ballots, the object of which is to prevent any one from knowing how the voter votes except himself. The resolution also directed the committee to inquire into the expediency of holding the State election on a different day from that on which the Congressional election is held.

For five years the State revenues have been falling short of the amount needed to defray the expenses of the State government and provide for contingencies. The public expenditures in some departments have been reduced, but still a deficiency annually occurred, which had to be met with a short loan in the shape of revenue bonds. The explanation of this deficiency is to be found in the increase of the number of recipients of public charity—insane, deaf and dumb, and blind—and the consequent increased cost of the charitable institutions; the large sum necessary to defray the cost of criminal trials; and the decrease of the State valuation of property from which taxes were derived. The State rates of taxation are limited by the Constitution to 40 cents on the $100—one half for revenue and one half for interest and principal of the State debt. The interest-tax yields enough for payment of the annual interest on the debt, and something more; but the revenue-tax does not yield enough for the demands on that fund. One fourth of the State revenue has to be paid over for the support of the public schools, and this leaves only 15 cents on the $100 for all other expenses. If it were increased to 20 cents, there would be no deficiency; the revenues would be ample to meet the expenditures, and the Treasury

would be in an easy condition. But as the Legislature has no authority to increase the tax-rates on property, the needed additional revenue must be sought for in special taxes and licenses. Among the schemes devised was the bell-punch tax, the failure of which is mentioned above. A bill for a poll-tax of $1 was introduced, but failed to become a law. A bill was also passed by the House, authorizing the issue of $8,000,000 four per cent. State bonds of small denominations, in imitation, except in one respect, of the Georgia law. (See· "Annual Cyclopædia" for 1878, GEORGIA.) The intent was to gradually replace the six per cent. State bonds as they fell due with four per cents, and thus save two per cent. in the annual interest. The new bonds were to be 5s, 10s, 20s, 50s, 100s, 500s, and 1,000s, a little larger than greenback bills, with small annual interest-coupons attached. They were to be payable at the pleasure of the State after five years from date, but not due till twenty years, and with the coupons were to be receivable for State interest-taxes. They were to be sold or disposed of at not less than their par value, and to be liable to taxation. Only five votes were cast against the bill. Another bill, to issue $250,000 small funding State bonds of the denominations of $5 and $10, was voted down by the Houses after which the vote was reconsidered and the bill referred to a special committee.

There was quite a difference between the views presented to the Legislature by the State Treasurer and the State Auditor. According to the latter, the State assessment, exclusive of the railroads, for the present year, was $523,982,773—a decrease of $32,586,051 from the assessment, and of $60,736,402 from the equalized valuation, of 1877. Estimating that the State Board would increase the assessment $10,000,000, the reduction from 1877 would be $50,000,000. In other words, there would be $50,000,000 less taxable valuation in the State to raise taxes from during the two years 1879–'80 than there was in the previous two. The tax-rate (40 cents on the $100) is fixed by law and can not be changed, so that the Auditor estimated that the decrease in the valuation would cause a reduction in the revenues of $200,000 a year, or $400,000 for the two years. On the other hand, the State Treasurer submitted to the House, in answer to a resolution adopted on May 6th, an official statement for the four months ending April 30th. It stated that the receipts of the Treasury from January 1st to May 1st were $1,677,-455.02, and the disbursements $1,213,872.08. The total balance on hand at the latter date was $936,045.86, of which $704,383.98 was credited to the interest fund, $201,372.16 to the school fund, and $11,502.02 to the revenue fund. He estimated the amounts to be drawn against the revenue and interest funds for 1879–'80 at $5,100,000, or $100,000 less than probable receipts. This opinion was finally adopted by the

Legislature, and the measures of relief above mentioned failed of a final passage.

There were, however, modifications made in some of the tax-laws. Thus the revised revenue law of the State as agreed upon by the Legislature, while leaving the general text of the old law undisturbed, made a few changes. In the first place, it extended the exemption from State taxes which certain kinds of property enjoyed to all other taxes, and made such property free from county, city, and school taxes also. The new provision concerning the return of notes and bonds is very rigorous. The old law merely required the tax-payer to return the gross amount of such notes and bonds owned by him or hér, and this requirement was easily evaded. To make it more effective, the new provision requires the return to give a detailed statement of all notes and bonds owned—the amount and date of each separate note and bond, and the name of the maker. The tax-payer is to make oath to this list, and to state the value of the notes and bonds so returned; but his valuation is not final, as it is subject to review by the County Board of Equalization. It was thought this provision would secure the return of a large amount of notes and bonds held in the State which the owners have habitually refused to give in for taxation. Another law was also passed which more explicitly regulated the assessment and taxation of railroads.

The matter of the late State Treasurer Gates (see "Annual Cyclopædia" for 1878, MISSOURI) was before the Legislature during the entire session. A committee of the House reported on the subject. Resolutions were adopted to appoint a committee to propose articles of impeachment, which were reported, and in the end failed to pass. The whole case is summed up in the following statement:

There is no one in the State who wants to wreak vengeance on the State Treasurer. On the contrary, there is among those who believe he ought to be impeached an almost universal sympathy for his misfortunes, and a keen regret that the scheming authors and beneficiaries of his misconduct can not be reached, instead of himself. It is known that he was entrapped into the official malfeasance that constitutes the ground of complaint by others, who sought to pervert him and his public trust to their own advantage, and it would be a relief to the public if these could be punished and he permitted to escape. It is because he is the official agent of the wrong done, and the only figure that disciplinary measures must take hold of, that the demand for proceedings against him is made. It is absurd to deny that the State Treasurer has done anything wrong. He has admitted the very wrongs charged: first, that he refused to obey the constitutional requirement about depositing the State moneys, because there was no penalty for the offense—though this absence of penalty did not prevent him from obeying the requirement after the moneys had been lost; second, that he took $5,000 out of the Treasury and gave it to persons in Jackson County as indemnity against loss in going bail for him in his individual lawsuit; third, that he deposited $300,000 in the Mastin Bank, after the owners thereof had virtually confessed to him that it was insolvent—thus using the State's money to keep up a failing bank. There is no disputing these facts. They stand admitted; and

VOL. XIX.—41 A

though the State may, after a protracted lawsuit, recover the $286,000 due from the Mastin Bank, it is for the people's Representatives and Senators to decide whether they can afford to permit a conspicuous malfeasance to pass unrebuked.

Although the Legislature did not make any special provision for bringing suit against the Treasurer, yet there is a general law regulating official bonds, recently passed, which reaches the case. It makes it "the duty of the Governor, whenever, in his judgment, the interest of the State would be promoted thereby, to direct the Attorney-General, in the name of the State, to bring and prosecute any suit or suits, upon any official bond or bonds executed to the State, as to him may seem proper"; and it further empowers the Governor to inspect the books, minutes, papers, and vouchers, or direct the same to be done by the Attorney-General, in any of the State offices, so that he may have a thorough understanding of the affairs of the State office inquired into.

A bill was passed to provide for the establishment of a Bureau of Labor Statistics, appropriating $5,000 biennially for its support. The Commissioner, appointed by the Governor every two years, is to be some suitable person identified with the labor interests of the State. His duty will be to collect, assort, classify, and publish in annual reports, statistical details relating to all the industries in the State—giving the number of persons employed in the various industries, the rate of wages paid, the amount of raw material used, and the value of the finished product.

A bill was also passed to provide for the establishment of an Immigration Bureau, with three Commissioners. It makes an annual appropriation of $5,000 for the object, and assigns to the Bureau as a part of its duty to collect and compile, from all available sources, correct statistics and descriptions of the material resources and social condition of the State, and from time to time to prepare and publish pamphlets, with maps of the State, essays, and articles correctly describing its developed and undeveloped agricultural and mineral resources and manufacturing interests, and such other local information as may be of interest to immigrants. It is urged in favor of the State as a desirable location for immigrants, that its land is very cheap; that it has a well-arranged and nearly complete system of railroads penetrating to all sections of the State, while in the newer States the cheap lands lie in regions remote from the few railway lines built; that it possesses both timber and prairie lands, its forests yielding valuable woods for which there is a constant market, and at the same time furnishing a protection against the droughts that afflict unwooded regions. To these may be added an abundance of good water, supplied by both flowing springs and running streams. Missouri is a very large State, more than a third larger than New York, and a considerable proportion of its area has never been brought into service for any purpose whatever. In the southern and western counties game is more abundant than in Kansas and Texas, and three fourths of the area has never been brought under cultivation.

A revision of the law relative to insurance was adopted. It provides that a life policy shall not be wholly forfeited and the holder lose all he has paid on it by his failure to keep the premiums paid up, but that, in case of such failure, he shall be entitled to that proportion of the original amount assured indicated by the payments he has made—the amount to be payable at his death. As to fire policies, the law provides that the amount insured "shall be taken conclusively to be the true value of the property when insured, and the true amount of loss and measure of damages when destroyed"; but it allows the company the choice of either paying this amount in cash or rebuilding and restoring the building to its original condition as to value, size, plan, and general finish. If the building is partially destroyed or injured, the company must pay a sum of money equal to the damage done, or repair the same to the extent of the damage, at the option of the insured. Heretofore this option has been exercised by the company, but the new law gives it to the insured party.

A fish bill was also passed by the Legislature, which places the matter of stocking the streams of Missouri with choice food-fishes under the supervision of three Commissioners, who are not to receive any compensation for their labors, but are to have their actual expenses paid. An appropriation of $3,000 is made for a hatching-house, and a suitable agent to have charge of it, the spawn and fry from this establishment to be distributed in the waters of the State. The act contains severe prohibitions against the wanton killing of fish, and the taking of fish by wholesale by means of nets and traps. A Commissioner, who had been acting during the previous year, obtained from Iowa two hundred thousand salmon-eggs, and with the assistance of gentlemen in various parts of the State, distributed them in the Missouri and its tributaries, Spring River and its tributaries, the Lamine and other streams of Cooper County, the streams that head in the neighborhood of Pierce City, and the lakes and streams of St. Louis County.

The temperance movement received more than usual attention in the Legislature, which seemed disposed to assist it by increasing the difficulties in the way of obtaining a license to sell liquors. A bill passed for the government of cities of the fourth class provides that "no license shall be granted to keep a dram-shop or tippling-house until a majority of the tax-paying citizens shall sign a petition for such license to be granted, which petition shall be filed with the city clerk." Cities of the fourth class are those having a population between 500 and 5,000; they embrace the greater number of considerable towns in the State. In the opin-

ion of the Attorney-General, the term "tax-paying citizen" in the statutes means every person, male or female, who owns property in the block, square, city, or township in which the dram-shop is sought to be located, which is subject to taxation. Whether the taxes on the property have been paid or not is a question that has no pertinence. Persons who pay only a poll-tax are not such "tax-paying citizens." So that the County Court which grants the licenses has no authority to grant such license unless the petition therefor is signed by a majority of the owners of taxable property in the block, square, city, or township in which the dram-shop is desired. Neither, in his opinion, can the Court make an order for the renewal of a license in anticipation of its expiration. For "the sale of intoxicating liquors is by law illegal; it is not a privilege of the citizen. The right to sell can only be acquired by complying with the law. One who does not possess the qualifications prescribed by the statute can not acquire that right. (Austin vs. Bate, 10 Mo., 591; State ex rel. Kyger vs. Holt Co. Ct., 39 Mo., 521.) The qualifications which an applicant for license must possess are, that he has not heretofore sold intoxicating liquors on Sunday or been convicted of any of the violations of chapter 58, or that he has not sold intoxicating liquors to a minor without proper permission, etc. How can the County Court know in December that a person who then has a license to keep a dram-shop will possess them on the first day of February following?"

Several bills were introduced to regulate the sale of liquor by druggists. They had their origin in the complaint that in many towns the suppression of regular drinking-saloons has converted the drug-stores into tippling-places. The withholding of dram-shop licenses by a county court or a town council does not mean any material decrease of liquor-drinking, for the unlicensed drug-stores supply drinkers all the spirits they want. The State Auditor suggested the propriety of requiring the proprietors of drug-stores to take out a dram-shop license. He stated in his report that many drug-stores were "unlicensed tippling-houses." Mr. Anderson of Marion asserted that "drug-stores were doing more to promote intemperance over the State than the saloons." Mr. Riley of Buchanan declared that "the drinking of the greater number of young men begins in drug-stores." It was urged in favor of requiring the license that the sale of spirits by druggists deprived the State of a considerable portion of the revenue that it had a right to exact from the sale of spirits; and that it was unjust to dram-shop proprietors who pay for a license to subject them to the competition of druggists who sell without. On the other hand, it was said in reply that it was only a small minority of the drug-stores in the State that were obnoxious to the charge of being unlicensed tippling-houses, and it would be unfair to make all the others bear the penalty of the offense of these few. Nevertheless, a license bill relating to druggists passed the House by the decisive vote of 93 yeas to 13 nays; but it failed to become a law.

But the most surprising measure acted upon was the proposition to amend the State Constitution by making the well-known "Maine Law" a part of it. A concurrent resolution was reported, which provided for the submission to the vote of the people in November, 1880, of the following amendment to the State Constitution:

That Article XIV. of the Constitution of the State of Missouri be and the same is hereby amended by adding four new sections thereto, which shall read as follows:

"Section 13. The manufacture and sale of intoxicating liquors in this State, except for medicinal, mechanical, and sacramental purposes, is prohibited.

"Section 14. Every person who shall manufacture or expose for sale or sell any intoxicating liquors, except for medicinal, mechanical, and sacramental purposes, shall, upon conviction, be deemed guilty of a misdemeanor, and shall be fined not less than fifty nor more than five hundred dollars, and by imprisonment for not less than one nor more than six months, for each offense.

"Section 15. The Legislature shall regulate such manufacture and sale for medicinal, mechanical, and sacramental purposes, and shall have power to make such other provisions for the enforcement of this article as may be deemed necessary.

"Section 16. The judges of all courts having criminal jurisdiction shall give sections 13, 14, and 15 of this article in charge to the grand jury at each term of court."

This resolution passed the House by a large majority. In the Senate it was reported favorably by the Committee on Constitutional Amendments, but was finally lost by a vote of 12 nays to 10 yeas.

The defaulting of counties, cities, and towns in the payment of their bonds, or in the payment of interest, was undoubtedly greater in Missouri than any other State. The litigation that ensued was immense, and almost every form of question came up in the State and Federal courts. In this state of affairs the Legislature was not inactive. A principal object before it in its action was to prevent or avert the interference of the Federal courts in the financial affairs of the municipalities. One of its earliest measures was the adoption of the following protest, which passed the House by a vote of yeas 94, nays 5:

It being our privilege, as the representatives of all the people of this State, to declare their will, it becomes our duty to do so when, in our judgment, the cause of good government may be thereby advanced; and whereas, as has been truly said, "the jurisdiction now claimed and exercised by the circuit courts of the United States over questions of corporate and individual rights, arising under the laws of the States, tends to oppress and burden litigants to such an extent as to amount to a practical denial of justice in many cases": now, therefore, and to the end that relief may be obtained,

Be it resolved by the House of Representatives of the Thirtieth General Assembly of the State of Missouri, the Senate concurring therein:

That we do earnestly protest against the further ex-

ercise by the Federal courts of such jurisdiction and powers, and demand—

1. The repeal of the existing laws of Congress concerning the "removal of causes" from the State courts to the circuit courts of the United States, known as acts amendatory or supplemental to the "Judiciary Act" of September 24, 1789, and more particularly described as the several acts of Congress, approved, respectively, July 27, 1866, March 2, 1867, and March 3, 1875.

2. The enactment of such laws as will, in all cases not expressly provided for by said judiciary act of 1789, confine the jurisdiction of the Federal courts to such causes as involve the construction, interpretation, or enforcement of some provision of the national Constitution, or of some treaty or law enacted in pursuance thereto, and which will secure to the individual citizen, or to any corporation, private or municipal, an adjudication of all matters of contract, or of other legal rights, and the redress of all legal wrongs, where such Constitution, treaties, or laws are not called in question, in the courts of the State where such contracts were made or wrong inflicted, if made or done by any municipal corporation, and if made or done by an individual citizen or private corporation, then in the courts of the State which may be the domicile of such person, or where such person may be found, or where such corporation may be found to exist.

And further be it resolved, That our Representatives in Congress are hereby requested and our Senators instructed to use their efforts and their influence to the speedy effectuation of the measures aforesaid; and that they may be informed hereof and of our desires in the premises, the Secretary of State is requested to transmit to each of our Senators and Representatives a duly authenticated copy of these resolutions.

An act was also passed providing that the resignation of county officers should take effect from the date of filing in the office of the County Clerk. The previous law required county officers to continue to serve, even after resignation, until their successors were qualified, so that there should be no lapse of the office. The only reason for the act was that it gave county judges an opportunity to evade the process of courts in suits against the county by a sudden resignation, to take effect the moment it was filed. This act was finally vetoed by the Governor.

Another act was passed entitled "An act for the better protection of the county revenue funds of the State." It provides that every county court shall at the May term of every year appropriate "all the revenues collected and to be collected, and moneys received and to be received, for county purposes," in the following order: First, to the pauper fund; second, to the road and bridge fund; third, to the salary fund; fourth, to the jury, witness, and election fund; fifth, to the contingent fund for the other ordinary current expenses of the county not specially provided for, which shall not exceed one fifth of the total revenue. These five funds are to be carefully maintained, separate and distinct; the money in one fund shall in no case be used for any purpose other than its own; and any county officer who shall fail or refuse to perform the duties required of him under the act shall be liable to a fine of one hundred to five hundred dollars, and forfeiture of his office. The real point of the act was considered to be the omission of an interest fund.

A still more important act was approved on March 8th. It is entitled "An act concerning the assessment, levy, and collection of taxes, and the disbursement thereof." Its object is to intrude the judiciary of the State into the dispute between the indebted counties and their creditors, and thwart the judicial collection of these debts by the United States courts. It provides that county courts shall levy only these four taxes, viz., the State revenue-tax, the State interest-tax, the tax for current county expenses, and the school-tax; and that no other tax shall be levied unless ordered by the circuit court for the county, or by the judge thereof in chambers. Any county judge, or other officer, who shall assess, levy, or collect, or attempt to assess, levy, or collect, any other tax without an order from the circuit court, and any county officer "who shall order the payment of any money, draw any warrant, or pay over any money, for any other purpose than the specific purpose for which the same was assessed, levied, and collected, or shall in any way or manner attempt so to do," shall be liable to a fine of five hundred dollars and the forfeiture of his office. This act is known as the "Cottey law," after its author, and was passed with the "emergency clause," and therefore took effect immediately. There existed at this time a sharp and emphatic difference between the Supreme Court of the State and the Supreme Court of the United States on the validity of what are called the township railroad bonds, and also on points involving the validity of some county railroad bonds. If these bonds were invalid, as held by the State court, the county authorities would have no power, under this new measure, to levy a tax to pay them, and the State Circuit Courts, which follow the decisions of the State Supreme Court, would not make orders for the levy of such taxes. And in cases where the United States Court orders the County Court to give a judgment creditor an order on the general fund of the county for the interest on such bonds, this law forbids the County Court to obey, and it also forbids the County Treasurer to make payment of judgments or interest on such bonds out of the general county fund. In short, the measure forbids county courts to pay any bonded debt, or the interest thereon, without an order from the Circuit Court; and it virtually prohibits the payment of all those railroad debts which the Supreme Court of the State has decided invalid, and the United States Supreme Court has decided valid and binding.

The constitutionality of the act was immediately called in question before the courts. The most important case of this kind was discussed before the United States Circuit Court in Jefferson City in March. As the same questions arose in cases pending in the Circuit Court for the Western District of Missouri, the Judge of that Court also sat with the Judges of the Eastern District to hear the arguments. There

were six cases of *mandamus* on judgments against Johnson County on account of bonds issued. Tuesday was the day set for the County Court to make a return to the *mandamus.* It accidentally happened that the "Cottey bill," as it is called, was signed by the Governor on the previous Saturday, and with an emergency clause it went into immediate operation. The returns to the *mandamus,* which were filed on Tuesday by the counsel for the county, set up the Cottey act for a defense.

In the argument on the constitutionality, ex-Governor Reynolds explained the operation of the act, and contended that it was not at all an infringement of Federal jurisdiction, and that, properly construed and with a proper disposition on the part of both the State and United States courts, it would lead to a settlement of the vexed question of the validity of township bonds. The argument against the constitutionality of the act was presented by Mr. Shields of St. Louis, and the points he urged were: 1. That the law was unconstitutional because it impaired the obligation of contracts. 2. That the law under which the bonds in controversy were issued provided for the levy of a special tax by the County Court, in the same manner as taxes are levied for county purposes; that the law was a part of the contract, and the Legislature can not change it by giving the power to the Circuit Court to levy the tax, because it imposed an additional cost and expense on the bondholder and postponed his remedy. 3. That the Cottey law virtually provided that the Circuit Court should levy and assess the tax, thereby conferring on the judicial branch of the government the taxing power, which is essentially a legislative power, and therefore can not be delegated under the Constitution to the judiciary. 4. That the Constitution provides (Article X., section 1) that the taxing power may be exercised by the General Assembly for State purposes, and by counties or other municipal corporations for county and other corporate purposes; therefore the General Assembly can not delegate the taxing power to the Circuit Court. 5. That by section 10 of Article X. of the Constitution the General Assembly shall not impose taxes upon counties, cities, towns, or other municipal corporations, or upon the inhabitants and property thereof, for county, city, town, or other municipal purposes, but may by general law vest in the corporate authorities thereof the power to collect or assess taxes for such purposes. The Circuit Court being in no sense a corporate authority of the county, it necessarily follows that the Legislature has no right to delegate to it authority to levy such taxes. 6. That the Constitution of the United States gives to the Federal Circuit Court jurisdiction to determine controversies between citizens of different States; and that Court having rendered a verdict for plaintiff in the pending case, the Legislature has no authority to provide for a review of such judgment by the Circuit Courts of the State. 7. The judgment in this case was rendered before the passage of the Cottey bill, and the plaintiff is entitled to all remedies under the law which then existed. All the judges agreed in deciding the law to be unconstitutional.

But a directly contrary decision was given in Cass County. The Circuit Court of that county was asked to give an order for a levy of taxes to pay judgments obtained in the Federal Court on township bonds issued under the act for the levy of a special tax. The Court refused the order, on the ground that the township aid act was unconstitutional, and the bonds issued under it is invalid. This the Supreme Court of Missouri had decided, and the Judge held that the decision was binding, not only on the inferior courts of the State, but also on the United States courts, since it was a rule laid down and long recognized by the United States Supreme Court that interpretations of a State law given by the Supreme Court of the State must be accepted and adopted by other tribunals. The Judge of Cass County referred to the opinions given in the United States Circuit Court above mentioned, declaring the Cottey bill unconstitutional because it impaired the obligation of contracts, and emphatically dissented from them. The Supreme Court had declared the township aid act unconstitutional; the bonds issued under it, therefore, were void contracts, and it was absurd, he asserted, to say that the Cottey bill was unconstitutional because it impaired the obligation of void contracts.

A judicial order was issued by the same Judge (Givan) in a case from Johnson County which nearly destroyed the force of the "Cottey law." Under the provisions of the law the Johnson County Court made application to Judge Givan for an order for a special tax-levy to pay the interest on the Normal School bonds issued to secure the location of the Normal School át Warrensburg, and to pay certain judgments of the United States Circuit Court against the county on its township bonds. Judge Givan considered the subject of the Normal School bonds first. He held that they were valid, having been decided to be so by every court that had adjudicated them, and the county was bound to pay the interest on them. As to township bonds issued to railroads, he thought they were invalid and void, because the township aid act of 1868, under which they were issued, was unconstitutional. The Supreme Court of the State has positively decided them to be void, which is conclusive in the State's lower courts. The United States Supreme Court had reached a different decision, but this, he thought, was because it misunderstood the ruling of the State Court, which it attempted to follow. If this was an application for a levy to pay the *bonds*, or the interest on them, he would be bound to refuse it. But it was a very different thing: it was an application for an order to make a levy of taxes to

pay a *judgment*, and he had no right, in such a proceeding, to go behind the judgment, and inquire whether it was lawful or not. The judgment of a court of competent jurisdiction can not be brought up for review in a collateral proceeding; it can be set aside only upon appeal; an unappealed judgment by a United States Circuit Court was binding and must be obeyed. It was a thing adjudicated. If the county thinks the judgment of the United States Circuit Court in favor of the township bonds wrong, its proper remedy was to appeal to the United States Supreme Court. Having waived this right, it was bound by the judgment. The county was bound to pay both the Normal School bonds and the judgments on the township bonds; and, therefore, he granted the order for the special tax-levy asked for. The distinction made between an unconstitutionally contracted debt and a judgment for that debt obtained from a court of competent jurisdiction was not expected.

Two or three instances will serve to show the proceedings in these numerous defaulting cases. A peremptory *mandamus* was issued by the United States Court against the Judges of the County Court of Knox County, demanding of the Court warrants on the general revenue of the county. In the mean time the "Cottey bill" was passed by the Legislature. The County Judges now found themselves standing between two fires, being threatened by the new State law with fine and imprisonment if they issued the warrants, and by the United States Court with like penalties if they did not. A citizens' meeting demanded that they should refuse obedience to the mandate; but the Judges, after weighing the matter carefully, decided otherwise, and issued the warrants required of them and returned a formal certificate of obedience. The failure of the Judges to rely on the "Cottey law" was significant, as its author lived in their county.

In the matter of Buchanan County, judgments were obtained against the county in the United States Court on its bonds issued to the St. Louis and St. Joseph Railroad, and the county officers were ordered to pay them; but the Treasurer used the money in the Treasury for another purpose, and so the judgments were left unpaid. This the Court held to be an act of contempt, and, as a punishment, fined the Treasurer $1,000 and ordered him to be imprisoned till the judgments should be paid. Under the "Cottey law" the conduct of the Treasurer was right: a county officer is forbidden to pay judgments against the county, or any other debt, without an order from the Circuit Court of the county; and to obey the order of the United States Court at Jefferson City would have incurred the penalties of the Cottey law for such cases made and provided. The following remark was publicly made on this case: "The imprisonment of Mr. Hull (the Treasurer) does not secure to the Buchanan County bondholders their money, it is true;

and if all county officers in the State should make up their minds to go to prison rather than obey the orders of the United States courts, these courts would be put to some trouble. But the ready obedience of the Knox County Judges, alluded to, shows that voluntarily going to prison can not be relied on to become epidemic in the State." The Treasurer's bondsmen paid the judgment after three months of his imprisonment.

In Scotland County, the County Court, in obedience to an order from the United States Court, levied a special tax to pay the judgments against the county on their railroad bonds. The tax-payers by common agreement refused to pay this tax, and the collector levied upon and seized some sixty or eighty horses and advertised them for sale. The sale came off in Memphis; but, although the town was full of people, there were no bidders for the horses except the owners thereof, each man bidding for and buying in his own animals at five to ten cents a head. The proceeds of the sale at this rate amounted to next to nothing—not enough to pay the collector's fees—and so the judgments remained unsatisfied. The people had agreed among themselves on this course of action, and it was successfully carried out, there being no outside bidders for the property sold. Recognizing that another seizure of property would have a similar result, the county creditors have abandoned this method, and now bring suit against sixteen substantial citizens of the county who were members of the "Taxpayers' Association," to recover from them the judgment and $3,000 damages besides, on the ground that they, by intimidation and threats, prevented persons from bidding at the sale and thus defeated the process.

The amount of this indebtedness of counties, cities, and townships in the State outside of St. Louis is estimated at $30,000,000.

A difference has long prevailed in the counties of the State relative to the assessment of crops. In some counties they have been assessed and taxed; in others no account has been made of them. This has led to confusion in the minds of assessors and complaints of injustice on the part of the farmers. To secure uniformity in the assessment, the State Auditor on August 2d issued a letter of instructions in explanation of the provisions of the Constitution and the revenue law. By the law all property, real and personal, is to be taxed, except such as belongs to the State, counties, cities, towns, cemeteries, churches, schoolhouses, and agricultural societies. The term "property," wherever used in the law, is declared by it to mean and include "every tangible or intangible thing being the subject of ownership, whether animate or inanimate, real or personal." Even crops, whether growing or secured, are not exempt; they are to be assessed and taxed, but with this important difference, that growing crops are part of the land, and are to be valued with it. Thus, if the naked land is

worth $5 per acre, and the growing but immature corn or tobacco crop on it on the first of August is worth as it stands $1.50 per acre, then the land with the crop is to be valued at $6.50 per acre. Crops that have been secured from the ground are no longer to be regarded as part of it, but are to be treated as personal property and assessed accordingly, due allowance being made for the unmarketable condition they may be in. Thus, wheat, oats, and other grain, threshed and in shock or stack, must be valued lower than grain in marketable condition at the mill. All assessments are to be made on the first of August of each year, and the condition crops are in on that day must determine their values respectively. As a general thing in Missouri small grain and hay are severed from the land on the first of August, and would therefore be taxed as personal property for what they are worth; while corn and tobacco, the other considerable staples, together with cotton in the southeastern counties, are immature growing crops, still attached to the land, and therefore to be assessed with it.

The railroad assessment made by the State Board of Equalization includes buildings, rolling-stock, and other materials of the roads, and amounts to $26,270,096. The bridge assessment amounts to $27,852,350.

The number of pupils in the Deaf and Dumb Asylum is 177. The average cost per pupil for the two years 1877–'79 was $196.85; number of teachers, 9; average salary paid, $714.28. Sales of articles manufactured in the institution foot up $927.02. Total value of the buildings, personal property, etc., $138,342.50.

The receipts of the Missouri Penitentiary for the first quarter of the year were $40,346, and the expenditures $33,889. The number of convicts was 1,332, and the cost of each was $26.86.

The sum of $39,000 was appropriated to the State University, which has between 300 and 400 students, representing from 60 to 70 counties and 13 States. They are of both sexes.

Some attention was attracted to silver-mining in Madison County by its favorable prospects.

The latest agricultural statistics of the State yet compiled are for 1878, and are as follows:

ANIMALS.	Number.	Value.
Mules........................	191,900	$8,824,622
Oxen and cattle.............	1,632,400	24,382,060
Hogs........................	2,817,600	6,226,896
Horses......................	627,300	25,022,997
Cows........................	516,200	9,188,360
Sheep......................	1,296,400	2,061,276
Total value............	....	$75,208,231

Missouri stands first of all the States in number and value of her mules, second in oxen and cattle, third in hogs, seventh in horses, and eighth in sheep. Its chief agricultural products were as follows: corn, 93,062,400 bushels; wheat, 20,196,000 bushels; oats, 19,584,000 bushels; potatoes, 5,415,000 bushels; hay, 1,-

620,000 tons; tobacco, 23,023,000 pounds. In the production of both corn and tobacco, Missouri ranks as the fifth State; in hay, the seventh; in oats and potatoes, the eighth; and in wheat, the eleventh.

MOHAMMEDANISM. While Mohammedanism as a political power is rapidly declining, it is steadily increasing in the number of its adherents. Dr. Döllinger, in an address delivered before the Bavarian Academy of Science on March 28, 1879, estimated the total number of Mohammedans as about one fifth of the population of the earth. According to this, the Mohammedans would number about 288,000,000, a figure considerably higher than any other estimate, and probably too high. The progress of Mohammedanism is especially noted in Africa and India. The following is an approximate statement of its statistics at the close of 1879:

I. In Europe:

Turkey Proper	2,650,000
Bulgaria	600,000
Eastern Roumelia	350,000
Bosnia and Herzegovina	442,000
Roumania	120,000
Servia	75,000
Montenegro	25,000
Russia	2,365,000
Total	6,637,000

II. In Asia:

Russia	5,064,000
Turkey	13,000,000
Persia	6,900,000
Arabia	3,700,000
India	50,000,000
China	5,000,000
Afghanistan and Beloochistan	4,680,000
States of Central Asia	3,000,000
Indian Archipelago	23,000,000
Anam	50,000
Total	115,144,000
III. In Africa	110,000,000
Grand total	231,771,000

Dr. Döllinger, in the address above referred to, treated very fully of the recent history of Mohammedanism. The following extracts supplement the article given in last year's "Annual Cyclopædia": The religion of the Arabian Prophet exhibits at present a singular phenomenon. On the one hand it develops throughout Asia and Africa a power of expansion, a fertility of proselytism, in which it surpasses by far the Christian churches; and, on the other hand, there appear symptoms of inner decay, especially a disease which is common to all Mohammedan states and threatens them with dissolution, incompetency to govern. The sultanate is now on the point of dying out, as formerly the caliphate. The old hierarchical state system of Arabia is extinct. The subsequent hermaphroditic creation of the semi-hierarchical, semi-military state system, which has its type in the Osmanie Empire, is now likewise approaching dissolution, and a new third form is not well conceivable so long as the Koran remains the source of all law; for the primitive and loose tribal association which is found among the Bedouins is not well suited for a larger state system. If, on the other hand,

we look at the marvelous power of expansion by which the Arabian religion peaceably, by means of conversion, achieves at present the most rapid and extensive conquest, we stand before an historical enigma. It is becoming a powerful current in Africa; entire nations in the interior of that continent, who but recently were pagans or worshipers of fetiches, have now become believers in the Koran. In China the Moslems have become so numerous that they could risk an insurrection. In Tongking they already number fifty thousand. Among the Malays of the Indian Archipelago they have made even in our days hosts of proselytes. From Sumatra the Islam has spread over Java, and since the establishment of the Dutch rule the entire population of Java (about eighteen millions) has become Mohammedan. The larger portion of Sumatra, and at least one half of Borneo and Celebes, have been gained for the Islam. Wherever in the Indian Archipelago a population hitherto pagan stands under Dutch dominion, the Islam makes rapid progress, while Christianity, on the other hand, in spite of missionaries and missionary societies, either is advancing very slowly or even retrogrades. Pilgrimages to Mecca, which are so greatly facilitated by the introduction of steamships, are said to be one of the principal causes of this rapid progress of Mohammedanism, because the numerous pilgrims or hadjis after their return generally become zealous missionaries of the Prophet of Mecca. The Islam in eastern Asia and Africa derives a great advantage from the fact that the propagation of the faith is not regarded as the work of any particular class or society, but that every Moslem considers himself obliged to take part in the conversion of the infidels. In British India, especially in the Northwestern Provinces, the conversions to Mohammedanism are likewise numerous, and they take place all the more easily because many Brahman ideas and customs have crept into Indian Mohammedanism. Thus the fifty million Mohammedans may become for the British dominion a great support or a great danger. In a conflict between Russia and England they would undoubtedly side with England, for Russia is regarded throughout the East as the hereditary foe of the Islam. Russia threatens Persia, dismembers Turkey, and subjugates the khanates of Central Asia. The Russian people look upon every war with Mohammedans as a religious war, and the number of the Mohammedan subjects of Russia in Siberia has considerably decreased under the influence of the Russian authorities. On the other hand, the Mohammedan faith leaves to the Mohammedan inhabitants of a country ruled over by infidels only the choice of emigrating or establishing by force of arms an orthodox government. This doctrine is especially diffused in India by the itinerant preachers of the Wahabee sect, the puritans of the Islam. Destruction of the English rule and reëstablishment of the caliphate are the aims of these dangerous fanatics, and there is reason to believe that the bulk of their Indian coreligionists openly or tacitly agree with them. The Mohammedan newspapers have therefore of late undisguisedly discussed the question whether rebellion is a duty. Some years ago an assembly of Mohammedan doctors of Lucknow and Delhi, which was held at Rampoor, decided that India with its English government was not *dar ul Islam*, land of the Islam, but *dar ul harab*, land of war; it ought therefore to be reconquered for the Islam, but since a war against the powerful Englishman was for the present without any prospect of success, and a defeat of the Islam would be discreditable in the eyes of the world, it was necessary to remain quiet for the present. The boldness of this declaration frightened the Mohammedan society of Calcutta, which declared through its doctors of law that India was still a land of the faithful, and an insurrection was unlawful. The disquieted Moslems have now procured an opinion of the doctors of Mecca, who likewise declare India, in spite of the English rule, to be a land of the Islam; intimating, however, in a significant manner, that every Moslem is obliged to do everything that is in his power to reëstablish the recognition of orthodox regulation and laws, and that anything that a foreign government does or introduces contrary to these laws is invalid. The English have done much of this kind. They have replaced Moslem governors by English; they have removed Mohammedan judges; their entire legislation is more or less opposed to the Koran. Hitherto those who regarded it as a sacred duty in such a situation to emigrate have settled on Afghan territory, and this cloud collecting on the northwestern frontier has been one of the causes that drew English armies to the Afghan territory. A small minority of the Indian Moslems try to explain away, by an artificial interpretation of the plain passages of the Koran, the duty of rebellion and of a sacred war against the infidels; but there can hardly be any doubt as to what is thought and believed by the majority of them. The Moslem can never forget that his Indian empire was overthrown by the English. The entire Koran is based on the view that the Moslems are a people who either govern or aim at the government. Moreover, the Mohammedans of India are, though through their own fault excluded from nearly all public offices and positions, most of which are in the hands of Brahmanists.

MONTENEGRO, a principality of southeastern Europe. Reigning Prince, Nicholas I., born October 7, 1841; declared Prince on August 14, 1860, upon the death of Prince Danilo I. He was married, November 8, 1860, to Milena, daughter of Petar Vukotitch. The children of this marriage are two sons, Danilo Alexander, born June 30, 1871, and Mirko, born in 1879, and six daughters. The area of the country in 1878 comprised 3,642 square miles. Of this, 1,814 square miles was the

area before the war, while the Treaty of Berlin had added 1,167 square miles from Herzegovina and 661 square miles from Albania. The population before the war was estimated at 180,000; to this number were added 54,000 in Herzegovina and 52,000 in Albania, making a total population of 286,000.

For an account of the finances, army, and commerce, see "Annual Cyclopædia" for 1878.

In the beginning of March, Prince Nicholas made a number of reforms which he had for some time considered. He established a ministry, and adopted the principle of ministerial responsibility, while preserving for himself all the rights and privileges of a constitutional monarch. The first Montenegrin Ministry was composed as follows: Bozo Petrovitch, Minister President and Minister of the Princely House; Masha Webitza, Interior, Commerce, and Communications; Stanko Radovitch, Foreign Affairs; Ilija Plamenatch, War; Gjura Tchernovitch, Finances; Ljubomir Wenadovitch, Worship and Education. The principality is to be divided into twenty-three districts, which are each to have a district chief. There are to be twelve lower courts, a court of appeals, and a court of cassation. Elementary instruction is to be gratuitous and obligatory. Every child between eight and fourteen years of age must attend school. Three teachers' seminaries and an agricultural school are to be established. Although it seemed desirable to establish representatives at various courts, especially at Vienna, it was deemed advisable, under the present condition of the treasury, to restrict the foreign representation to an ambassador at Belgrade and an agent at Constantinople.

The negotiations with the Porte for the surrender of the districts ceded to Montenegro by the Treaty of Berlin continued throughout January. Considerable opposition made itself manifest among the Albanians who were in future to belong to Montenegro, but it eventually subsided. On February 7th Podgoritza, and on the 8th Spuz and Zabliac, were surrendered by the Porte to the Montenegrins without any resistance on the part of the inhabitants. The Montenegrins on their part evacuated the places they still occupied in Turkish territory. The mixed commission for the definite settlement of the boundary soon after met. A slight difference came to light in the latter part of May between the Turkish Commissioners and their colleagues regarding the delimitation on the western side of the Lake of Scutari—a difference caused by a certain indistinctness in the text of Article 28 of the Treaty of Berlin fixing the limits of Montenegro. The article stated that from Plavnitza, on the eastern shore of the lake, the new frontier should cross the lake near the Island of Gorica-Topal, and, starting thence, ascend in a direct line to the crest of the hills, and thence, following the watershed, descend to the Adriatic at Kruci. The Turks, taking their stand on the words of the treaty specifying Gorica-Topal both for the line across the lake and the land line starting from the shore, maintained that the latter should begin opposite the island. All the other Commissioners, however, interpreted the article as meaning that the island only fixed the direction of the line across the lake, while the watershed formed by the Topal Mountain, a few miles farther south, was evidently intended to be the line of frontier running from the lake to the Adriatic. The difference in point of substance was quite insignificant, but the decision might be of considerable importance as being the first application of the principle of majority in the commissions of delimitation now in operation.

In the latter part of October, the Montenegrins advanced to take possession of Plava and Gusinje. The Porte instructed the Governors of Scutari, Kassovo, and Monastir to proceed to Gusinje and Plava, and take on the spot all necessary measures for the transfer of those districts to Montenegro. The Porte issued instructions at the same time to the local authorities that they should do all in their power to assist the three Governors in order that the cession of territory to Montenegro might be effected as speedily as possible. Without waiting for the voluntary cession which was about to be made, a strong force of Montenegrins marched on Gusinje, pillaging and burning everything in the neighborhood. In a battle which followed large numbers of Albanians were slaughtered, and even women and children did not escape. The Turkish Governors who had been ordered to Gusinje were prevented by Albanians from entering the town. Fifteen battalions of Turkish troops were then sent to the Montenegrin frontier under the command of Mukhtar Pasha, who at one time was reported massacred by the Albanians. His position was very critical, and he was compelled to ask for reënforcements, when twenty battalions were sent to his relief. In December Russia proposed to the Powers a united effort at Constantinople to accelerate the surrender of Gusinje to Montenegro. The Porte then sent a circular to its representatives abroad reciting the measures taken to secure that object, and expressing the hope that the Montenegrins would not precipitate matters, as some delay was necessary if bloodshed was to be avoided. In view of these explanations Russia withdrew her proposal.

MORAVIANS. The following is a statement of the membership in the three provinces of the Brethren's Unity for 1878, as they were published in July, 1879:

The German Province	7,778
Bethel in Australia	90
The Russian Baltic Provinces	65
Prangins	19
Ministers of the Diaspora and their families	100
	— 8,052
The Bohemian Congregations	226
The British Province	5,705
The American Province, Northern District	14,256
The American Province, Southern District	1,980
	— 16,236

Brought forward	30,219
Missionaries in 17 Mission Provinces, and their children	400
Total	30,619

The *General Synod* of the Moravian Church met at Herrnhut, Saxony, May 28th. This is the representative body of the Church throughout the world, and is unique among Protestant assemblies as being the only body which exercises legislative authority over all the branches of its communion wherever found. The affairs of the Church in the several nations are cared for by the legislative bodies in each province, besides which the Unity's Elders' Conference, the executive body for the whole Unity, located at Herrnhut, has the charge of the general administration during the intervals between the meetings of the General Synod. The General Synod consists of 54 members, allotted as follows: Members of the Unity's Elders' Conference, 12; bishops, besides 2 in the Unity's Elders' Conference, 5; delegates from the German, British, and American Provinces, 9 each; missionary delegates, 5; members *ex officio*, 5. Its functions are to enact all legislation in reference to the general concerns of the Unity; to examine, correct, and lay down anew the principles on which the Unity is based; to keep watch of the state and condition of the Unity as a whole and of its parts; to make such arrangements as may be needed for its well-being; and to serve as the occasion for the interchange of views between the different parts of the Church. It has power to determine subjects of doctrine, ritual, and discipline; to appoint or provide for the appointment of bishops; to direct all matters pertaining to the foreign missions; to control such educational institutions as belong to the whole Unity; to direct and superintend all financial affairs of the Church; to elect the Unity's Elders' Conference, regulate the formation and times of meeting of the General Synod, and direct all matters which belong to the general constitution of the Church.

Bishop Edmund von Schweinitz, of the American Province, was elected President of the Synod. The business of the body consisted principally of the consideration of the proposals submitted by the Provincial Synods for amendment of the "Synodal Results," as the digest of acts of the Synod is called, or for new legislation. A recognition of the Apostles' Creed was adopted, to be expressed in the words: "The Brethren's Unity of ancient and modern times, though by its constitution and episcopal ordination a separate church, has nevertheless at all times professed to be but a part of the one universal Church of which Christ is the Head, and more especially of the Evangelical or Protestant Church, whose doctrine is derived from the Holy Scriptures and from them alone. It adheres, with all Christendom, to the doctrines contained in the Apostles' Creed," etc. The section entitled "Our Leading Doctrines" was amended so as to read:

Our view of the leading doctrines is set forth more especially in the Confession of Faith, which has been annually declared by the whole Church on Easter morning for more than a hundred years.

We hold that every truth revealed to us by the Word of God is a priceless treasure, and heartily believe that the gain or loss of everything, even of life itself, can be brought into no comparison with a denial of any one of these truths. And we here especially refer to that truth which the Renewed Church of the Brethren has ever regarded as its most important doctrine, and to which, by God's grace, it has hitherto steadfastly adhered, regarding it as a precious jewel: that Jesus Christ is the propitiation for our sins; and not for ours only, but also for the sins of the whole world.

With this our leading doctrine, the following facts and truths, clearly attested by Holy Scripture, are linked in essential connection, and therefore constitute, with this leading doctrine, the main features in our view and proclamation of the way of salvation:

a. The doctrine of the total depravity of human nature: that there is no health in man, and that, since the fall, he has no strength left to help himself.

b. The doctrine of the love of God the Father, who "hath chosen us in Christ before the foundation of the world," and "so loved the world that he gave his only begotten Son, that whosoever believeth in him should not perish, but have everlasting life."

c. The doctrine of the real Godhead and the real Humanity of Jesus Christ: that the only begotten Son of God, of whom all things in heaven and earth were created, forsook the glory which He had with the Father before the world was, and took upon Him our flesh and blood, that He might be made like unto His brethren in all things, yet without sin.

d. The doctrine of our reconciliation with God and our justification before Him through the sacrifice of Jesus Christ: that He "was delivered for our offenses, and was raised again for our justification," and that we obtain forgiveness of sin, and freedom from the bondage of sin, by faith in His blood alone.

e. The doctrine of the Holy Ghost and the operations of His grace: that without Him we are unable to know the truth, that it is He who works in us the knowledge of sin, faith in Jesus, and the witness that we are children of God.

f. The doctrine of good works as the fruit of the Spirit: by which faith manifests itself as a living, active principle, in a willing obedience to the commandments of God, out of love and gratitude to Him who died for us.

g. The doctrine of the fellowship of believers with one another in Christ Jesus: that they are all one in Him, who is the Head of the body, and all members one of another.

h. The doctrine of the coming of our Lord in glory, and of the resurrection of the dead unto life or unto judgment.

The section on "The Public Ministry" was amended by inserting the clauses:

To the Brethren's Church it must be a matter of serious, heartfelt concern, that, as she herself firmly adheres to her declared view of the mystery of Christ, so also in the proclamation of the Word within her borders, and in the Christian instruction of the young, there may be no departure from this foundation. She considers it for herself neither necessary nor salutary, by framing a creed formulated in every single point of doctrine, to bind consciences and quench the Spirit; nor does she expect to see the well-being of the Church promoted by the pledging of her servants to any such creed, inasmuch as she looks, for the attainment of this object, to the revival and establishment of the true spirit of the Church through the grace of God. At the same time, she can not tolerate that within her borders any one teach and preach contrary to the Holy Scriptures, and, specially, to the declarations

which we, according to our view, regard as the leading doctrines of Holy Writ.

Sunday-schools were recognized as constituting a proper sphere of exertion in the Church, and were commended to the coöperation and intercessions of members, and to the guiding supervision of ministers and elders as a part of their official labor. On the subject of missions, resolutions were adopted discouraging the attempt to educate in Europe native youth from the mission-fields; approving the action of the mission department in declining, principally on account of the lack of funds, seventeen invitations to begin new missions; sanctioning the organization of a new mission in Demerara and additions to the missions in South Africa; and recommending the continuance and, if possible, the extension of the work in the West Himalaya district. The archivist of the Unity reported that the archives contained a collection of historical manuscripts, a library including pamphlets, and a collection of paintings and curiosities referring to the history of the Church. A number of valuable manuscripts had been secured within the last ten years. The Synod made provision for the appointment of a theologically educated person who should qualify himself for the work of thoroughly examining and compiling the existing sources of the history of the ancient Brethren's Church, particularly between the years 1620 and 1722, and who, it was understood, should qualify himself to study the original documents of the Bohemian Church. Measures were decided upon to obtain contributions for the erection of a new and suitable building as a depository for the archives. Three new bishops were chosen: H. L. Reichel, Henry Müller, and T. Wunderling. A new department was added to the Unity's Elders' Conference, to be called the Unity's department, to consist of six members, and be charged with the duty of maintaining and strengthening the bonds of union between the three provinces of the Unity. The year 1889 was fixed upon as the time for the next meeting of the Synod at Herrnhut.

MURCHISON, CHARLES, M. D., F. R. S., was born in Jamaica in 1830. His father was a physician, a descendant of an old Aberdeenshire family. In 1845 Charles Murchison matriculated at the University of Aberdeen. The first year he bore off the prize in Greek, although his tastes were scientific rather than classical. He was an ardent botanist, winning the Balfour gold medal for plant dissection, and the Thompson prize. In 1848, while studying medicine, he lectured before the Botanical Society of Edinburgh on the "Glandular Structures found on the Leaves of Various Plants." In 1851 he graduated with the highest honors, and was appointed physician to the embassy at Turin. In 1852 he returned to Edinburgh as resident clinical physician at the Infirmary. After this he studied both in Dublin and in Paris, until he was appointed Professor of Chemistry to the Medical College of

Calcutta. Later he was placed on the medical staff of the army of Burmah, where he studied the climate and diseases of that country, on which he wrote a valuable treatise. On his return in 1855 he passed his examination for membership of the Royal College of Physicians, London. He worked indefatigably as physician to the Westminster General Dispensary, as demonstrator of anatomy at St. Mary's Hospital, lecturer on botany, assistant physician to King's College Hospital, and physician to the Middlesex Hospital and to the London Fever Hospital. After six years' service in the last-named hospital he wrote his great work on the "Continued Fevers of Great Britain," which has passed through numerous editions and reached the rank of a classic. His experience in Middlesex Hospital is embodied in his work on the "Diseases of the Liver." A second edition of this volume was published in 1877. His practice was enormous and ever increasing, yet he never pretermitted his studies or literary labors, as attested by his contributions to the "Lancet" and the "Edinburgh Medical Journal," and his numerous treatises on scientific as well as professional subjects. Like his distinguished relative, Sir Roderick Murchison, he was passionately fond of geology, and he undertook and accomplished the Herculean task of editing the geological works of Dr. Falconer. It was as a teacher that he reached the highest expression of his powers. In 1871 he was appointed Professor of the Principles and Practice of Medicine. His singular brilliancy and clearness proved a powerful attraction to students. In 1877 he was made President of the Pathological Society. His inaugural is a model exposition of the method and limits of such researches.

In 1872, while in the midst of this life of toil and usefulness, with the honors and rewards of his profession pouring thick upon him, he discovered that he was the subject of serious heart-disease, induced by an attack of typhus contracted in the Fever Hospital. He was advised that cessation of labor would probably delay a fatal termination. After mature deliberation he decided that to him a life of idleness would be the greater evil. Having made the minutest preparations for impending death, he resumed the arduous career of a London physician in full practice, and died in the harness. A patient had just left his consulting-room. He leaned forward to note on a diagram a fact concerning this case when the fatal stroke fell. On the 26th of April he was buried in Norwood Cemetery. Dying thus in the forty-ninth year of his age, in the prime of his powers, he was a loss to science and to the world. He was especially beloved by the students and junior members of his profession. He never spared himself when their interests could be advanced. The sympathy and aid they were sure to evoke were all the more valuable because they came from a man of few words and of a cold and reserved demeanor, who had himself passed unblemished through the ordeals they must undergo.

N

NEBRASKA. The Legislature of this State opened its regular session on January 7th, and closed it on the 27th of February in the morning, after a protracted sitting from the previous day.

A joint resolution was adopted instructing the Nebraska delegation in Congress "to procure legislation to prohibit for ever the payment of the Southern war claims."

An act creating a Reform School at Kearney was passed.

A game law was enacted, fixing the days on which expires the time allowed for the killing of certain species of animals, as follows: of quail and wild turkeys, the first day of December; of wild buffalo, elk, mountain-sheep, deer, or antelope, the first day of January; of wild grouse, the first day of February. It prohibits the transportation of the various classes after the above-mentioned dates respectively; and provides that "it shall be unlawful for any person, agent, or employee of any association, corporation, railroad company, or express company, to receive, carry, transport, or ship away any such animal or bird at any other time of the year."

An act was passed appropriating the sum of $75,000 for the erection of an additional wing in the State-House building. This appropriation, for which the sum originally asked in the bill was $100,000, was greatly opposed in the Legislature, and by the people generally, as unnecessary.

The prohibition bill, so called, forbidding the manufacture and sale of all drinks that may inebriate, failed to pass. This measure, while it was acted upon by the Legislature, engrossed the interest of the people generally in a high degree, a great number advocating and a greater opposing it on several accounts. Two mass meetings, the one for and the other against the passage of the bill, were held at Omaha on February 2d and 3d respectively.

During this session of the Legislature strong efforts were made by a large number of its members to secure after its final adjournment an extraordinary session. Democratic and Republican members met in caucus jointly for that purpose on February 17th, when, after a lengthy discussion, it was resolved, by a vote of 36 to 27, "that the best interests of the State demand an immediate called session to complete the revision laws." No special session, however, was convened within the year.

The general election in November was limited to the choice of an Associate Justice of the Supreme Court, Judges of District Courts, and two Regents of the State University. The Democrats held their State Convention at Lincoln on September 10th. The nominations made were as follows: For Associate Justice of the Supreme Court, Eleazar Wakely; for Regents of the State University, Andrew J. Sawyer and Alexander J. Bear; for Judges of the District Courts: First District, Warren P. Conner; Third District, James W. Savage; Fourth District, William H. Munger; Sixth District, James W. Crawford. For the Second and Fifth Judicial Districts no nominations were made. The following platform was adopted:

The Democratic party of Nebraska, in convention assembled, reposing its trust in the intelligence, patriotism, and discriminating justice of the people, and standing upon the Constitution with all the amendments thereto, on the foundation and limitation of all the powers of government and the guarantee of the liberties of the citizens, do resolve:

1. That we reaffirm all the old time-honored principles of the party, and take no steps backward.

2. That we deprecate the action of Republicans in making treaties with the various tribes of Indians, and then violating the same, and driving them from the lands conveyed to them, and thereby turning loose upon our frontier organized bands of outraged savages, seeking revenge on our inhabitants for the wrongs perpetrated upon them by Republican administrations.

3. The Democratic party maintains, as it has ever maintained, that the military is and ought to be in strict subordination to the civil power in all things. It denies, as it ever has denied, the right of the Federal Administration to keep on foot at the general expense a standing army to invade the States for political purposes, to control the people at the polls, to protect and encourage a fraudulent count of votes, or to fraudulently under the form of law inaugurate a candidate who has been defeated at the polls by a lawful majority both of the people and the Electoral College as provided by the Constitution.

4. That the right of free ballot is the great right of the American people, the right whereof of all other rights—the only means of redressing grievances and reforming abuses. The presence of the military at the polls, and of a host of hireling officials claiming the power to arrest and imprison voters without warrant or hearing, destroys all freedom of election and overturns the very foundation of self-government. We call upon all good citizens to aid us in preserving our institutions from destruction by these imperious methods of supervising the right of suffrage and coercing the popular will, and in keeping the way to the ballot-box open and free as it was to our fathers.

5. We demand the strictest economy in the management of the affairs of government, national, State, and county. We arraign the Republican party of the State for its extravagance in the management of the affairs of the State; for wasteful and corrupt appropriations of the public funds of the State, whereby certain partisans have been enriched at the expense of the tax-paying public of the State. We demand that the system of abuse and misappropriation of the public funds should cease, and we call upon all good citizens, without regard to former party affiliations, to aid us in hurling from power the party that have so long abused the trust reposed in them.

The Republicans held their State Convention at Omaha on October 1st, and nominated the following ticket: For Associate Justice of the Supreme Court, Amasa Cobb; for Regents of

the State University, Joseph W. Gannett and John L. Carson; for Judges of the six District Courts: First District, Andrew J. Weaver; Second District, S. B. Pound; Third District, Charles A. Baldwin; Fourth District, George W. Post; Fifth District, William Gaslin, Jr.; Sixth District, John B. Barnes. The platform adopted was as follows:

We, the Republicans of the State of Nebraska, again renew our pledges of fidelity to the principles of freedom and right for which we have ever contended; and now in convention assembled it is resolved:

1. These United States are a nation, and not simply a league of States.

2. We watch with apprehension the arrogance and treasonable utterances of the rebel brigadiers now in Congress, as a threatening danger to this nation. And, further, the Republican party of Nebraska proclaim that we have no concessions to make to unrepentant rebels; that we still adhere to the principles for which our brave soldiers have fought.

3. That we again offer the principle of freedom of the ballot-box, and demand at the hands of the Executive of this nation protection for the voters of the South, such as is accorded to all political parties in the North.

4. As the same issues are again being presented for decision at the ballot-box for which our armies contended so long and faithfully, with confidence we call upon the soldiers to vote as they fought, for the preservation of the life and purity of the Government.

5. That we welcome with much pleasure the signs of returning prosperity, as evinced by the increased activity of every department of industry, the general revival of manufacturing interests, and the additional confidence exhibited by all departments of business.

6. That we congratulate the country upon the successful resumption of specie payments, ever pledging the support of the Republicans of Nebraska to all efforts of the Republican party in the nation's counsels to protect the credit of the nation, and make the promises as good as gold.

7. That we demand at the hands of all Republican officials the utmost economy in the administration of all affairs of the Government; and that we pledge ourselves as a party to a careful supervision of the expenditures in all the departments of our State.

8. That we as Republicans of the State of Nebraska welcome back to the shores of America the champion of our Union, the protector of our nation's honor, and the hero of the great rebellion—General Ulysses Grant.

The election resulted in the choice by the Republicans of the Associate Justice of the Supreme Court, the two Regents of the State University, and five out of the six Judges of the District Courts. The aggregate number of votes polled by all parties in Nebraska at this election was 84,514; and the highest number cast by the adherents to either party was for one of the two Regents of the State University, as follows: Republicans, 46,376; Democrats, 23,127; Greenbackers, 5,011.

The whole amount of the taxable property in the State is estimated at about $80,000,000. The collection of State taxes for two years will produce, under existing laws, $360,000 for 1879, at four mills on the dollar, and $120,000 for 1880, at two mills. To meet the current and incidental expenses of all the departments of the State government for the said two years, including $122,200 for the erection of public buildings and $112,625.33 for the payment of claims, the Legislature appropriated the aggregate sum of $760,619.33, or $280,629.39 more than the amount to be raised by taxation during the same two years.

Among the appropriations for educational purposes and the support of charitable institutions are the following: For the State University, $50,000; State Normal School, $25,800; State Hospital for the Insane, $67,700; Institute for the Deaf and Dumb, $11,280; Institute for the Blind, $15,000; State Reform School, $10,000.

The Hospital for the Insane is located about three miles from Lincoln. The average number of patients in the institution for the year ending November 30, 1878, was 111; and the whole number treated during that year was 182.

In the Deaf and Dumb Asylum at Omaha, the pupils under instruction at the end of the year 1879 numbered 64, 12 more than in the preceding year. Of the boys, 8 are learning the art of printing and 12 the carpenter's trade. In the female department, 22 girls receive instruction in needlework.

The Nebraska State Prison, situated about the same distance from Lincoln as the Hospital for the Insane, in a different direction, is under excellent management in all respects. The prisoners are kept steadily employed in manual work of various kinds, their labor being under contract for a long term, and the contractor personally superintending the convicts at work in the prison. He furnishes them with clothing and supplies, and pays all the current expenses of the prison, and a stipulated yearly sum to the State for each prisoner. This method seems to have been found of mutual advantage to the State and the contractor. By act of the Legislature, the contract for the convicts' labor has been renewed for ten years, till 1889. During the year 1879 the number of convicts in the penitentiary was gradually increasing. On March 15th it was 207; at the end of November, 266; and on Christmas day, 271. Of the 207 confined there in March, 145 were residents of the State of Nebraska, and 50 of Wyoming Territory; 7 were United States prisoners, and 5 were county prisoners, detained in the penitentiary for safe-keeping. The classes of gravest crimes for which they had been respectively sentenced, and their proportional numbers, were as follows: Murder, 25; manslaughter, 3; malicious cutting, 6; arson, 2; grand larceny, 43; burglary, 18; robbery, 6; horse-stealing, 23.

The grain-crops in Nebraska for 1879 were plentiful and of fine quality. In many counties north and south of Platte River, out to the Republican Valley, the yield for the several crops in bushels per acre ranged as follows: Wheat, 12 to 18; oats, 30, 40, 45, and 50; barley, 25, 30, and 40. The crop of corn, which had been very extensively planted, appears to have been better than that of other grain; the average being 40, 50, and 60 bushels per acre,

according to localities. In Otoe County alone there were 110,000 acres planted, the average yield being reckoned at 60 bushels per acre; and the same was the case with Hall County.

Nebraska seems to be more subject to devastation from grasshoppers than some other Western States. Active measures have been taken to exterminate them. The Legislature has authorized road supervisors throughout the State to order out all voters in their respective precincts to do twelve days' work each in killing grasshoppers, for which each person is to be paid at the rate of two dollars a day in county warrants. Grasshopper clubs, so called, have also been organized everywhere in the State for their destruction.

The cattle-drives which pass through the State are a growing source of material prosperity. The drive of 1879 from Texas and the southwestern ranges is reckoned at 250,000 head, and that from Montana and Oregon at 100,000. Kansas used to be the northern limit of the drive, which gave to Kansas City a considerable advantage as a market. For several years before 1879 the proportion of the stock remaining in Kansas has been steadily diminishing, while that remaining in Nebraska and Wyoming has been increasing. The great rendezvous of cattle-drovers, which formerly ended at Abilene on the Kansas Pacific road, is now to be found at Ogallala on the Union Pacific road in Nebraska, which point, it is predicted, will soon become the greatest stock thoroughfare on the continent.

The internal revenue collections for Nebraska during the year 1879 amounted to $980,105.52, of which sum the Willow Springs distillery at Omaha paid nine tenths.

The most noteworthy event of the year 1879 in Nebraska relates to the writ of habeas corpus issued in behalf of Indians by the Judge of the United States District Court for Nebraska, and by him decided in their favor against the United States Government. It was the first case of that kind ever brought before a judicial tribunal in this country. The Ponca Indians, a peaceful tribe and most friendly to the white man, said also to be to a great extent civilized in their habits, and Christianized, were in the possession and occupancy of their own domain in southern Dakota, when, by a treaty dated March 12, 1858, they ceded to the United States Government all of their lands, excepting a certain tract whose limits are accurately described in the treaty, which they reserved for their own use and the permanent place of their homes. In consideration of this cession the United States Government agreed "to protect the Poncas in the possession of the tract of land reserved for their future homes, and their persons and property thereon, during good behavior on their part." Annuities were to be paid them for thirty years, houses to be built, schools to be established, and other things were to be done for them by the Government, in consideration of the cession. On this reserved tract the Poncas were peaceably living three years ago, when the United States Government determined to remove them to a place eleven hundred miles distant in the Indian Territory. In the general Indian appropriation bill passed by Congress on August 15, 1876, there is a provision authorizing the Secretary of the Interior to use $25,000 for the removal of the Poncas to the Indian Territory, and providing them a home therein, with the consent of the tribe. This consent they persistently refused to give; whereupon the Government removed them from their homes by force, and, under guard of United States troops, they were transported to the Indian Territory. During the long march a great number of the Poncas died, and were buried along the route. The new place also proved so malarious and unhealthy that out of 581 Indians whom the Government had taken away from their reservation in Dakota, 158 died within about a year, i. e., at the rate of one in every three and a half. A large proportion of the survivors also were sick and disabled. It was probably on account of this unexampled mortality that in 1878 the Government took measures to remove the Poncas from that place and locate them elsewhere; as in the Indian appropriation bill passed by Congress on May 27, 1878, a provision authorizes the Secretary of the Interior to expend the sum of $30,000 for the purpose of removing and locating the Ponca Indians on a new reservation near the Kaw River. This second reservation is said to be no less unhealthy than the first. Under these circumstances one of the Ponca chiefs, Standing Bear by name, "to save himself and the survivors of his family, and the remnant of his little band of followers, determined to leave the Indian Territory and return to his old home in Dakota, where he might live and die in peace and be buried with his fathers." He informed the agent of their fixed purpose to leave, never to return, and that he and his followers had finally, fully, and for ever severed his and their connection with the Ponca tribe of Indians, and resolved to cut loose from the Government, go to work, become self-sustaining, and adopt the habits and customs of a higher civilization. In execution of this determination, Standing Bear with his family and followers left the reservation in the Indian Territory at the beginning of January, 1879, and, after sixty days' travel across strange lands for fifteen hundred miles in midwinter, reached the reservation of the Omaha Indians in Nebraska. The Omahas, who speak the same language and have long connected with the Poncas by intermarriage, welcomed the wayfarers and bade them remain, offering them land at their choice to cultivate for their support. While thus staying at the Omaha reservation, Standing Bear and his followers were arrested by Brigadier-General Crook, commander of the military department of the Platte, and detained under his

charge, for the purpose of being taken back to the reservation in the Indian Territory, which they were alleged to have left without permission of the Government. General Crook acted in this matter upon express orders issued to him by his superior officer, the General of the Army, at the request of the Secretary of the Interior.

On April 8, 1879, when these prisoners were on the point of being marched back to the reservation in the Indian Territory, Mr. H. Tibbles, assistant editor of the "Omaha Herald," applied to the Judge of the United States District Court, then in session at Lincoln, for a writ of *habeas corpus* in their behalf, to be served on General Crook. The writ was issued the same day, and made returnable on the 18th. It was duly returned, and an answer filed by General Crook as respondent, stating the authority on which he acted in the arrest and detention of the relators. The case was argued on the first two days of May, G. M. Lambertson, United States District Attorney, appearing for the Government, and A. J. Poppleton and Jonathan L. Webster, two eminent lawyers of Omaha, for the prisoners, whose defense they assumed gratuitously. The main point in question before the Court was not the justice or injustice of the treatment met with by these Indians at the hand of the United States Government concerning their forcible removal from their lands in Dakota to the Indian Territory, but whether the United States District Court had the power to issue the writ of *habeas corpus* in behalf of the prisoners, and hear and determine the case made therein. The District Attorney maintained the negative on the grounds, among others, that an Indian can not appear in Court, is not entitled to the writ of *habeas corpus*, and is not a citizen, and that Indian tribes are not independent, but dependent communities. The prisoners' counsel showed, on the contrary, that the petition of their clients, besides being just, was perfectly legal; that, whether they were considered as still belonging to the Ponca tribe of Indians, an independent community, or as Indians individually, severed from all former connection with that tribe, as they claimed to be, they were legally entitled to the writ of *habeas corpus*, and the Court had the inherent power both to issue such writ and hear and determine the case made therein. They showed also that the Omaha Indians had a perfect right to give the relators part of the land in their reservation, it being their own, as they could give it to an alien coming to them from any nation or government on earth; the United States Government having no legal power to interfere with either. After the argument had been closed on the second day of the hearing, Standing Bear, by an express permission of the Judge, personally addressed the Court in a short speech, stating in plain terms some of the hardships and the mortality of his tribe and family since their compulsory removal from their homes in Dakota, whither he expressed his wish to return. Judge Dundy, in his decision, on May 12th, answered the reasons and objections set forth by the District Attorney against the Indians' right to the writ of *habeas corpus*, and the jurisdiction of the Court in the case; established the principles on which he rested the determination of the matter; and concluded with the decision of the following points, and the appropriate order:

1. That an Indian is a person within the meaning of the laws of the United States, and has therefore the right to sue out a writ of *habeas corpus* in a Federal court and before a Federal judge, in all cases where he may be confined or in custody under color of the authority of the United States, or where he is restrained of liberty in violation of the Constitution or laws.

2. That General Crook, the respondent, being commander of the military department of the Platte, has custody of the relators under color of the authority of the United States, and in violation of the laws thereof.

3. That no rightful authority exists for removing by force any of these Poncas to the Indian Territory, as General Crook has been directed to do.

4. Indians possess the inherent right of expatriation as well as the more fortunate white race, and have the inalienable right to life and liberty and the pursuit of happiness so long as they obey laws and do not trespass on forbidden ground.

5. Being restrained of liberty under color of the authority of the United States and in violation of the laws thereof, the relators must be discharged from custody, and it is so ordered.

In consequence of this decision, and in execution of its mandate, the Secretary of War at Washington issued immediate orders, on May 13th, that Standing Bear and his followers, twenty-five in number, should be released; upon which they were set at liberty.

This case has excited great sympathy for the Poncas among the people of the country generally, and a strong inclination to assist them in the recovery of their own land and homes in Dakota, by bringing the matter before the Supreme Court for adjudication. Well-known lawyers of Omaha and Chicago have offered their gratuitous services in defending the Poncas' rights; and efforts are being made for the purpose of raising a fund sufficient to cover the other expenses of the suit. To this end, public meetings have been held in the principal cities of the Union, which have been addressed, among others, by Standing Bear and an educated Ponca girl called Bright Eyes.

NETHERLANDS, THE, a kingdom of Europe. King, William III., born February 19, 1817; succeeded his father March 17, 1849. He was married first to Sophie, daughter of King William I. of Würtemberg (died June 3, 1877), and secondly to Emma, Princess of Waldeck-Pyrmont. He has but one son living, Alexander, Prince of Orange, born August 25, 1851.

The area of the kingdom is 12,731 square miles. The population in December, 1878, was estimated at 3,981,887. The area and population of each of the provinces were as follows:

PROVINCES.	Area.	Population.
Brabant	1,980	408,667
Gelderland	1,965	468,840
South Holland	1,167	796,109
North Holland	1,053	667.946
Zealand	687	180,866
Utrecht	534	191,370
Friesland	1,282	823,872
Overyssel	1,292	273,770
Groningen	887	248,124
Drenthe	1,028	117,026
Limburg	851	240,497
Total	12,731	8,981,587

The movement of population in 1878 was as follows: Marriages, 30,710; births, 150,493; deaths, 98,486. (The births and deaths include the still-births, numbering 7,747.)

In the budget for 1879, the expenditures and revenue are estimated as follows:

EXPENDITURES.

	Dutch florins.
1. Royal house	750,000
2. Cabinet, supreme state authorities	615,489
3. Ministry of Foreign Affairs	685,990
4. Ministry of Justice	4,488,778
5. Ministry of the Interior	6,891,615
6. Ministry of the Navy	13,186,662
7. Ministry of War	21,644,900
8. Public debt	28,435,920
9. Ministry of Finance	17,892,639
10. Colonies	1,696,086
11. Public works, commerce, and industry	22,544,392
12. Unforeseen	50,000
Total	118,781,491

REVENUE.

1. Direct taxes		24,306,057
Land-tax	10,618,657	
Poll-tax	9,750,000	
Patent-tax	3,942,400	
2. Excise		38,595,000
On spirits	22,400,000	
On other liquors	16,195,000	
3. Taxes on stamps, registration, inheritances		23,460,000
4. Customs		4,611,040
5. Taxes on gold and silver wares		360,200
6. Domains		1,695,000
7. Post		3,600,000
8. Telegraphs		500,000
9. Lottery		480,000
10. Taxes on game and fisheries		148,000
11. Pilotages		900,000
12. Taxes on mines		2,265
13. State railroads		1,626,000
14. Miscellaneous		11,290,135
Total		111,824,897
Deficit		6,956,000

The financial estimates are always framed with great moderation, mostly exhibiting a deficit, which in the final account becomes a surplus.

In 1879 the national debt was represented by a capital of 964,004,052 florins, divided as follows:

DIVISION OF DEBT.	Capital.	Interest.
Debt bearing interest at 2½ per cent.	632,092,902	15,802,323
Debt bearing interest at 3 per cent.	91,322,750	2,739,682
Debt bearing interest at 3½ per cent.	11,157,000	882,620
Debt bearing interest at 4 per cent.	219,481,400	8,777,256
Miscellaneous		58,489
Total	954,004,052	27,760,819
Bearing no interest	10,000,000	
Amortization		675,600
Total 1879	964,004,052	28,435,919
Total 1878	921,721,852	26,718,678

The army of the Netherlands in Europe in 1879 consisted of 2,039 officers and 61,486 men; the East Indian army numbered 1,458 officers and 38,905 men.

The navy on July 1, 1879, consisted of 100 steamers, with 398 guns, and 14 sailing vessels, with 102 guns; total, 114 vessels, with 500 guns.

The merchant navy on January 1, 1879, consisted of 1,100 sailing vessels, of 806,279 metric tons, and 79 steamers, of 160,114 metric tons; total, 1,179 vessels, of 966,393 metric tons.

The aggregate length of railroads in operation on January 1, 1879, was 1,967 kilometres

(1 kilometre = 0·62 English mile), of which 1,089 were state railroads.

The aggregate length of the state telegraph lines on January 1, 1878, was 3,519 kilometres; aggregate length of wires, 12,882 kilometres; number of offices, 346; number of telegrams carried in 1878, 2,452,725; revenue, 791,000 florins; expenditures, 1,181,160 florins.

The number of post-offices in 1878 was 1,209. The number of inland letters was 40,704,846; of foreign letters, 11,698,212; of postal cards, 12,672,744; and of newspapers, etc., 82,797,742.

The movement of shipping in 1878 was as follows:

ENTRANCES AND CLEARANCES.	LADEN.		IN BALLAST.		TOTAL.	
	Vessels.	Tons.	Vessels.	Tons.	Vessels.	Tons.
SAILING VESSELS:						
Entered..........	3,354	2,581,210	236	8,755	3,590	2,618,765
Cleared..........	1,295	699,803	2,276	1,935,206	3,571	2,635,009
STEAMERS:						
Entered..........	4,358	6,041,488	104	141,973	4,462	6,183,461
Cleared..........	3,283	4,233,600	1,216	1,951,441	4,449	6,185,041

The imports and exports in 1877 were as follows (in florins):

COUNTRIES.	Imports.	Exports.
Great Britain..	205,779,000	131,512,000
Zollverein..................	186,108,000	246,672,000
Hanse towns..............	7,586,000	12,868,000
Austria-Hungary...........	157,000	25,000
Belgium..................	106,611,000	90,293,000
Russia...................	66,575,000	7,526,000
Denmark.................	474,000	2,847,000
Sweden and Norway........	11,925,000	7,550,000
France...................	16,623,000	7,014,000
Italy....................	2,357,000	7,823,000
Spain....................	5,334,000	223,000
Portugal..................	1,502,000	727,000
Other countries............	4,438,000	1,340,000
1. EUROPE..............	605,234,000	486,024,000
United States.............	89,039,000	3,976,000
Cuba and Porto Rico......	323,000	402,000
Brazil....................	433,000	......
Rio de la Plata............	1,539,000	570,000
Peru....................	6,322,000	......
Other American countries....	1,914,000	1,197,000
2. AMERICA..............	49,670,000	6,145,000
British East Indies..........	14,749,000	251,000
China....................	87,000	......
Japan	1,397,000	......
3. ASIA..................	16,233,000	251,000
4. AFRICA	4,622,000	1,014,000
5. OTHER COUNTRIES	538,000	16,000
Total foreign countries.	676,297,000	493,450,000
DUTCH COLONIES:		
Java......	74,169,000	117,720,000
Dutch West Indies.......	469,000	217,000
Total Dutch colonies...	74,638,000	47,937,000
Grand total..........	750,935,000	541,387,000

The colonies of the Netherlands are considerably larger and more populous than the country itself. Their area is estimated at 661,400 square miles. In the East Indies, Java and Madura have a population of 18,515,414. The

native population of the other colonies is not known. The foreign population was as follows in 1876: Europeans, 54,230; Chinese, 319,137; Arabians, 14,983; Hindoos and others, 9,853. In America, Surinam, or Dutch Guiana, had in 1877 a population of 68,531; and the island of Curaçao, 41,870.

The budget estimates of the Dutch colonies for the year 1879 were as follows:

COLONIES.	Revenue.	Expenditures.	Deficit.
	Florins.	Florins.	Florins.
East Indies..........	141,489,166	150,145,758	8,706,587
Surinam	1,284,600	1,682,293	447,693
West Indies..........	867,896	640,025	272,129

The commerce of the East Indian colonies in 1876 was as follows: Imports, 121,511,000 florins; exports, 213,519,000. The movement of shipping in the East Indian ports in 1876 was as follows: Entered, 7,363 vessels, of 1,-529,458 tons; cleared, 7,550 vessels, of 1,596,-083 tons. The commercial navy in the same year consisted of 1,384 vessels, of 130,266 tons. Java had 371 kilometres of railroad in 1879. The length of telegraph wires in operation on Java and Sumatra in 1877 was 6,953 kilometres, and of lines 5,654 kilometres. The total number of dispatches sent in 1877 was 860,322; number of stations, 67. The number of letters sent through the East Indian mails was 3,550,-401; number of papers, etc., sent to the different islands, 1,777,389; weight of the papers sent abroad, 48,784 kilogrammes (1 kilogramme = 2·2 pounds); number of postal cards sold, 295,263.

M. de Roo van Andewerelt, the Minister of War, died on December 30, 1878, and in February, 1879, Lieutenant-Colonel den Beer Poortugael was appointed in his place. M. van Bosse, Minister of the Colonies, who died on February 21st, was replaced in March by Otto van Rees, the former President of the Council for India. In July the entire Ministry resigned. The reason for this step was that serious differences had arisen between the Ministry and the King on an important constitutional question. The Ministry desired to increase the number of members of each Chamber, and also to change the qualification of voters, and resigned because the King did not favor the plan. On August 18th a new Ministry was formed, as follows: Lynden van Sandenberg, President and Minister of Foreign affairs; Six, Interior; Modderman, Justice; S. Vissering, Finance; Taelman Kip, Navy; Colonel Reuther, War; Van Golstein, Colonies; Klerek, Commerce and Industry.

The budget of the Ministry of War, which occupied the attention of the Chambers during the spring session, was passed on May 28th by 59 to 14 votes. It proposed extensive fortifications on the coast.

In opening the Chambers on September 15th, the King dwelt upon the distress under which industry, commerce, and navigation were laboring, and upon the poor harvest. These causes, it was to be feared, would result in a decline in the yield of some of the imposts, and a necessity for strengthening the resources of the Treasury. He announced that, for the purpose of promoting the prosperity of the country, the Government would maintain the salutary principles of free trade, and would propose measures for the improvement of the means of communication.

The fall session of the Chambers was occupied with the discussion of the budgets of the kingdom and of the East Indian colonies for 1880, which were both voted by the Chambers. The former showed a deficit of 8,000,000 florins, and the latter of 6,000,000 florins, which was, however, reduced to 2,500,000 florins by the increased sale of tobacco. The duty on sugar was slightly increased.

On January 7th the King was married to Princess Emma of Waldeck-Pyrmont, at Arolsen in the principality of Waldeck. She is the third daughter of Prince George of Waldeck, and was born August 2, 1858.

The war in Acheen was declared by the Government to be virtually at an end at the close of the year, but the Batavian journals described the condition of the country as being far from satisfactory.

NEVADA. The Legislature of this State opened its session of 1879 in the first week of January, and closed it by adjourning *sine die* on March 6th, when the time of its duration expired by constitutional limitation.

On January 14th the two Houses separately voted for the election of a United States Senator, the official term of the present incumbent, John P. Jones, expiring on March 3d. Mr. Jones was reëlected, the vote being as follows: In the Senate—Jones 19, A. M. Hillhouse 6; in the House—Jones 41, Hillhouse 8.

On January 21st W. W. Bishop, T. N. Stone, and J. S. Mayhugh were elected Regents of

the State University by joint ballot of the two Houses.

The most important of the numerous acts of a public character passed at this session were the following: To pay the State debt proper, and to purchase Territorial bonds; fixing the State tax at fifty-five cents on every hundred dollars; exempting from taxation widows' property to the amount of one thousand dollars; to create a State Board of Equalization; to redistrict the State; to encourage the growing of trees; appropriating ten thousand dollars for the relief of the sufferers of Reno. Among the joint resolutions were the following: Instructing the State Representatives in Congress "to support the bill limiting the number of Chinese to be brought to the United States to fifteen for each vessel and voyage," and others tending to discourage the employment of Chinese in the State, and give white men a better chance; asking of Congress an extension of time (ten years) in which to comply with the provisions of the act respecting the use of lands granted the State for educational purposes.

In order to give uniformity to the legislative action relative to railroads, a resolution was adopted by the Lower House appointing a select committee of one member from each county "to prepare a bill to regulate fare and freight rates on railroads"; and a concurrent resolution was adopted by both Houses on February 6th, "referring all railroad bills to a joint select committee of fourteen." On February 25th the committee presented a majority report against the railroad bills, which was sustained. A bill to prevent discrimination in fares and freights on railroads operated wholly or in part within the State passed the House of Representatives on January 30th by an almost unanimous vote; it passed also the Senate on February 4th, with an amendment, which applies the provisions of the act to the local roads of the State, considered as independent and having no connection in the sense of their being a continuous line with the Central Pacific. It provides that their fares and freights shall be regulated directly by the laws of the State, and not indirectly by "schedules, rates, agreements, or contracts" of any outside railroad company whose line operates also within the State. The charges of transportation, especially for merchandise, have been thereby greatly reduced. The reduction on the Virginia and Truckee road, as appears from a detailed statement made by its freight agent in March, 1879, ranges from one fifth to 28 per cent., running through almost all the intermediate numbers between these two extremes, according to the various classes of goods transported, and the distances between the several points on the line. The company estimates the decrease in its gross earnings at 12½ to 15 per cent., which is considered equivalent to a diminution of over 30 per cent. in the net proceeds.

The mines of precious ores, which form the most important among the material resources of Nevada, seem to be increasing in number as well as extent of operations, they being generally under able and energetic management.

The following official abstract statement, relating to mines in Storey County for the quarter ending June 30, 1879, will give an idea of their yield, expense, proceeds, and of the taxes collected on them by the State:

NAME OF MINE OR OWNERS.	ORE EXTRACTED. Tons.	Gross yield or value.	Total cost.	Net yield or value on which taxes are levied.	Total amount of tax.
California Mining Company	19,099	$903,005 51	$376,787 64	$526,217 87	$18,680 74
Consolidated Virginia Mining Company	14,388	620,428 13	365,197 48	255,260 65	9,061 75
Chollar Mining Company.	8		124 27	124 27	4 41
Justice Mining Company	124	795 48	992 00	79 55	2 08
Consolidated Imperial Mining Co. (C. C. Stevenson).	2,350	81,925 50	34,518 20	6,885 10	162 82
Ophir Mining Company	4,427	269,086 26	257,073 55	107,634 51	3,821 02
Potosi Mining Company	8	124 27		124 27	4 41
Silver Hill Mining Company	552	4,507 92	6,272 00	450 80	11 50
Sierra Nevada Mining Company	1,800	110,412 67	211,415 79	44,165 07	1,567 86
Trojan Mining Company	1,297	12,838 55	21,723 45	1,283 86	33 74
TAILINGS.					
Thomas Hully, Bossell Brothers' Mill	407	4,480 00	4,080 00	448 00	11 42
Mariposa Mill	2,296	29,477 97	15,968 84	13,509 12	479 57
Omega Mill	12,613	126,846 71	77,381 45	49,465 26	1,261 86

The value of gold and silver bullion yielded by the Consolidated Virginia and California mines, respectively, during the first six months of 1879, was as follows:

MINES.	Gold.	Silver.	Total.
CONSOLIDATED VIRGINIA.			
January	$65,500	$74,200	$139,700
February	131,000	165,100	296,100
March	193,600	244,800	438,400
April	132,800	207,300	340,100
May	83,000	70,800	153,800
June	66,300	60,700	127,300
Totals	$672,200	$822,400	$1,494,600
CALIFORNIA.			
January	$174,900	$150,900	$325,800
February	83,300	82,600	165,900
March	214,400	246,900	461,300
April	204,400	287,700	487,100
May	131,900	98,300	230,200
June	92,400	98,300	186,000
Totals	$946,300	$910,000	$1,856,300
Consolidated Virginia.	672,300	822,400	1,494,600
Totals	$1,618,500	$1,732,400	$3,350,900

On June 30th the Sutro Tunnel was actually opened to discharge the water of the flooded mines, and the day was celebrated with extraordinary festivities. The following particulars of the opening were written by a newspaper correspondent on the same day:

The final completion of the Sutro Tunnel, for the reception of the water from the Comstock mines, was celebrated in the Carson Valley to-night. After ten years of ceaseless labor day and night, and the expenditure of $6,000,000, the powerful engine of the combination shaft of the Hale and Norcross and Savage mines was started up this morning at precisely 6 o'clock, discharging the water into the Sutro Tunnel, at the mouth of which it made its appearance in one hour and twenty minutes, showing a temperature at first of 101°, which gradually increased to 118° in eight hours. The water in the long-drowned-out mines was lowered one hundred feet. Everything worked well. The wooden boxes, constructed of three-inch tongued and grooved Sierra Nevada pine, did not show a leak. No steam escaped from them, so that the tunnel showed barely an increase of temperature after the hot water was turned on.

Among the natural resources of Nevada, the great forests which cover a large proportion of her surface appear conspicuous; and, of all trees that grow on her soil, the most noteworthy is the nut-pine, for its utility on account both of the wood, which may be put to a great variety of uses, and of the fruit, which is of exquisite taste. The following is an account of it:

It furnishes fuel, charcoal, and timber for the mines, and together with the enduring juniper, so generally associated with it, supplies the ranches with abundance of firewood and fencing. Many a square mile has already been denuded in supplying these demands, but, so great is the area covered by it, no appreciable loss has as yet been sustained. Besides its general uses, this tree yields edible nuts, which are excellent as food, and in fruitful seasons the pine-nut crop of Nevada is perhaps greater than the entire wheat-crop of California. The Indians alone appreciate this portion of nature's bounty, and celebrate the harvest-home with dancing and feasting. The cones, which are a bright grass-green in color, and about two inches long by one and a half in diameter, are beaten off with poles just before the scales open, gathered in heaps of several bushels, and lightly scorched by burning a thin covering of brushwood over them. The resin with which the cones are bedraggled is thus burned off, the nuts slightly roasted, and the scales made to open. Then they are allowed to dry in the sun, after which the nuts are easily threshed out and are ready to be stored away. They are about half an inch long by a quarter of an inch in diameter, pointed at the upper end, rounded at the base, light brown in general color, and handsomely dotted with purple, like birds' eggs. The shells are thin, and may be crushed between the thumb and finger. The kernels are white and waxy-looking, becoming brown by roasting, sweet and delicious to every palate, and are eaten by birds, squirrels, dogs, horses, and men. When the crop is abundant the Indians bring in large quantities for sale; then they are eaten around every fireside in the State, and oftentimes fed to horses instead of barley. Long before the harvest-time, which is in September and October, the Indians closely examine the trees, and as the cones require two years to mature from the first appearance of the little red rosettes of the fertile flowers, the scarcity or abundance of the crop may be predicted more than a year in advance. When the harvest season arrives, the Indians abandon all other pursuits, and, assembling at some central point, scatter in all directions to gather the nuts. Old and young are busy, and in a few weeks they obtain enough to last them all winter. These nuts are their main dependence, their staff of life, their bread.

NEW HAMPSHIRE. The official term of Bainbridge Wadleigh, one of the United States Senators from New Hampshire, having expired on March 3, 1879, and the election of his successor by the State Legislature being necessarily delayed till its meeting for the regular session in June, Governor Prescott appointed Charles H. Bell of Exeter to fill the vacancy in the mean time. The Governor's letters having been duly presented in the United States Senate, that body referred the matter to its Committee on Privileges and Elections, which reported against Mr. Bell's admission, by a vote of 6 to 3. The Senate, however, admitted Mr. Bell—yeas 35, nays 28.

The regular June session of the Legislature, the first of the biennial sessions, commenced on June 4th. Jacob H. Gallinger was elected President of the Senate, and Henry H. Huse Speaker of the House of Representatives. Both were Republicans. The votes stood 15 to 3 in the Senate, and 163 to 101 in the Lower House.

A ballot was taken by the two Houses for the election of United States Senator on June 17th; the candidates were Henry W. Blair of Plymouth, Republican, and Harry Bingham of Littleton, Democrat. The votes were 20 for Blair and 4 for Bingham in the Senate, and 161 and 98 respectively in the House of Representatives.

On June 18th, in joint convention, the Legislature elected the following State officers for the term of two years by ballot: Secretary of State, Ai B. Thompson; State Treasurer, Solon A. Carter; Commissary-General, Benjamin F. Rackley; State Printer, John B. Clarke.

On June 20th the following joint resolution was introduced in the Senate, and made a special order:

Resolved, by the Senate and House of Representatives in General Court convened:

1. That in all cases and at all times the military ought to be under strict subordination to and governed by the civil power.

2. That we approve the several vetoes by the President of the United States wherein he has firmly upheld his constitutional power against the threat and attempt to withhold necessary supplies to the Government, unless he should approve legislation that he does not approve; and we pledge him our continued support in maintaining the rights of the Executive and the national supremacy.

3. That we approve the action of the Republican Senators and Representatives in Congress in exposing and resisting the scheme of the majority to deprive the national authority of all power to keep the peace and secure free and honest voting at national elections; and we pledge them our continued support in resisting all such disorganizing and revolutionary designs.

4. That we condemn as unpatriotic, destructive, and revolutionary all attempts of the majority in Congress to revive the dogma of State supremacy, to rekindle the flames of sectional animosity, and to stop and

starve the Government by withholding necessary supplies, because the President will not approve of legislation that he is constitutionally bound to veto if he does not approve of it. "A refusal to vote the appropriations is revolutionary; it is worse, it is revolution."

5. That a copy of these resolutions be promptly forwarded to the President and to each of our own delegation in Congress.

The June session was closed on July 17th.

Two acts were passed in the interest of children, entitled "An act prohibiting the employment of children under ten years of age by manufacturing corporations," and "An act to provide for the better protection of destitute and abused children."

"An act to protect the rights of citizens of this State, holding claims against other States," has been commented upon by the press of the country generally, being regarded as leveled against the so-called repudiating States, to make them pay any bond once issued by them, though afterward repudiated; the State of New Hampshire assuming, under certain conditions, to personate any private holder of such bonds among her citizens, and in his interest to sue any other State in the Union before the Supreme Court of the United States for that purpose. The main provisions of the act are as follows:

SECTION 1. Whenever any citizen of this State shall be the owner of any claim against any of the United States of America, arising upon a written obligation to pay money issued by such State, which obligation shall be past due and unpaid, such citizen so holding such claim may assign the same to the State of New Hampshire, and deposit the assignment thereof, duly executed and acknowledged, together with all the evidence necessary to substantiate such claim, with the Attorney-General of the State.

SEC. 2. Upon such deposit being made, it shall be the duty of the Attorney-General to examine such claim and the evidence thereof, and if, in his opinion, there is a valid claim which shall be just and equitable to enforce, vested by such assignment in the State of New Hampshire, he, the Attorney-General, shall, upon the assignor of such claim depositing with him such sum as he, the said Attorney-General, shall deem necessary to cover the expenses and disbursements incident to, or which may become incident to, the collection of said claim, bring such suits, actions, or proceedings in the name of the State of New Hampshire, in the Supreme Court of the United States, as he, the said Attorney-General, shall deem necessary for the recovery of the money due upon such claim; and it shall be the duty of the said Attorney-General to prosecute such action or actions to final judgment, and to take such other steps as may be necessary after judgment for the collection of said claim, and to carry such judgment into effect, or, with the consent of the assignor, to compromise, adjust, and settle said claim before or after judgment.

A bill to abolish capital punishment was long and warmly debated, and at last indefinitely postponed by the House of Representatives at the sitting of July 17th, by a vote of 166 yeas to 86 nays.

The measure asking relief of the people from the exorbitant rates and unjust discriminations in the conveyance of passengers and merchandise, practiced by the railway companies operating in New Hampshire, was considered as the most important of the session. The act failed to pass, because of the strong opposition of a large number of members in both Houses; and its failure is reckoned a discredit to the General Assembly.

The Commissioners appointed under an act of the Legislature of 1877 to compile the public statutes of the State then in force, including those of that year's session, and to make such changes and alterations in the existing laws as they might deem necessary on account of the constitutional amendments shortly before adopted, and also on account of any change that might be made in the time of holding the election of town officers, or in the tenure of office of such officers, reported the result of their labors to the Legislature at this session. Their report, after examination and slight modification, was approved by both Houses, and on their order published before the end of the year as the Revised Statutes of New Hampshire. In this new body of State laws Governor Head, in his message to the Legislature of 1879, avers not only that " numerous verbal mistakes occur," but also that " certain statutes have been left incomplete, ambiguous, or in seeming conflict with each other," requesting them to correct its many imperfections, of which he mentions some particular instances. A law was accordingly enacted for that purpose.

The State income and expenditures during the fiscal year ended May 31, 1879, were as follows:

Receipts from all sources, including $18,337.09 cash on hand at the beginning of the year, June 1. 1878................... .... $1,173,104 10
Disbursements on all accounts................ 1,109,847 20

Cash on hand June 1, 1879.................... $63,756 90

The revenue from State tax, railroad and insurance taxes, and other sources, for the same year, was $525,884.43. The expenses were:

Ordinary..................................... $222,898 65
Extraordinary................................. 138,336 77
Interest paid.................................. 208,069 84

Total...................................... $569,205 26

Excess of expenses over revenue.......... $43,360 83

Among the items of extraordinary expenses last year was the sum of $94,704.40 paid on account of the new State-Prison building.

The valuation of property and apportionment of State tax in the various counties, as made by the State Board of Equalization, are as follows:

COUNTIES.	Valuation.	Apportionment.
Rockingham	$28,771,269	$139 04
Strafford..................	22,404,603	108 26
Belknap...................	8,607,196	41 58
Carroll...................	7,058,061	84 10
Merrimack.................	31,788,642	184 84
Hillsborough..............	51,535,017	249 06
Cheshire..................	21,240,939	102 62
Sullivan	10,407,670	50 28
Grafton..................	18,667,670	90 20
Coos.....................	6,527,636	81 52
Total...............	$206,959,017	$1,000 00

Number of ratable polls, 86,704. The valuation in 1876 was $198,660,359, showing an increase of $7,298,696. This increase in the value of property within the State is considered to be wholly or mostly the result of the inventory law enacted in 1878, for assessment purposes.

The public debt of New Hampshire on June 1, 1879, was as follows:

Liabilities............................ $3,638,603 20
Assets................................. 65,052 80

Net indebtedness................ $3,573,550 90

On June 1, 1878, it was:

Liabilities........................... $3,544,508 24
Assets................................. 14,318 17

Net indebtedness................ $3,530,190 07

Increase of debt during the year 1879......................... $43,360 83

On the principal of the State debt the sum of $183,400 was paid in 1878, namely : State bonds, $101,000 ; State notes, $82,400.

" An act to amend the existing law in relation to the annual invoice of polls and taxable property " was passed. The substance of its chief provisions is as follows: Every person or corporation liable to taxation is required to return under oath an inventory of his or their taxable property, and its value, by filling blanks distributed by the Secretary of State for that purpose. The oath required of the tax-payer is to the effect that the inventory returned by him contains a true statement of all his property liable to taxation. If this sworn inventory is found by the assessors, on examination, to be honestly made and exact according to law, they shall assess the tax-payer's property upon the basis of the value set down for it by himself; but "if any such person or corporation shall willfully omit to make such inventory or to answer any interrogatory therein, as required, or shall make any false answer or statement therein, or in relation to the estate or property for which he is taxable, or if such selectmen or assessors shall be of opinion that such inventory so returned does not contain a full, true, and correct statement of the estate and property for which such person or corporation is taxable, according to the requirement of such interrogatories, and that there has been such willful omission or false answer or statement on the part of said person or corporation, the selectmen or assessors shall ascertain as nearly as may be, and in such way and manner as they may be able, the amount and value of the property and estate for which, in their opinion, he is liable to be taxed, and shall then set down to such person or corporation, by way of doomage, four times as much as such estate and property, if honestly inventoried and returned, would be legally taxable."

The condition of the savings banks, in regard to the amount of deposits, number of depositors, and other particulars, for the last year, is as follows:

NEW HAMPSHIRE. 661

Whole number of savings banks in New Hampshire.. 66
Number of depositors............................ 87,387
Decrease in the number of depositors the past year.. 4,294

LIABILITIES.

Total amount of deposits.....................	$26,282,136 09
Decrease in the amount of deposits during the past year...............................	2,507,412 91
Surplus, 1879.............................	1,145,567 91
Guarantee fund, 1879......................	704,284 27
Temporary loans, 1879.....................	20,973 04
Total liabilities, 1879...................	**$28,152,961 81**

RESOURCES.

Loans by note on real, personal, and collateral security...............................	$14,521,719 46
Investments in bonds and stocks...........	11,578,746 45
Real estate, bank fixtures, and miscellaneous items...............................	1,222,051 86
Cash on hand.............................	830,444 04
Total assets.......................	**$28,152,961 81**

The operations of insurance companies of various descriptions doing business in the State appear to be exceedingly large. The gross amount of premiums paid to fire-insurance companies in 1878 was nearly $445,000, of which $417,764.92 was paid to stock companies of other States and countries licensed in New Hampshire, and the remainder to mutual companies in the State. The following is a summary of the operations of the stock companies for 1878 : Total risks written in 1878, $33,-816,838 ; risks in force on December 31, 1878, $50,646,552 ; amount of premiums received, $417,764 ; amount of losses paid, $366,848 ; proportion of losses to premiums, 86 per cent. The receipts of life and accident insurance companies upon their policies in New Hampshire were $260,383.77, and the amount paid by them to representatives of insured persons was $219,484.28. These sums do not include the receipts and payments of the "mutual relief associations" organized among the members of secret societies and others in the State.

The education of youth in the State appears to continue in its healthy condition. The State Normal School at Plymouth is said to be in a more satisfactory condition than ever before.

The State Asylum for the Insane, at the beginning of June, 1879, contained 275 patients. Besides these there are a great number of that unfortunate class in the State, a large proportion of whom are kept by their respective families at home, because they can not afford to pay the weekly rate for board and attendance at the asylum.

The indigent deaf-mutes, blind, and feeble-minded of New Hampshire are kept at the charge of the State in institutions or schools in Connecticut and Massachusetts. Their number in New Hampshire is increasing rather than diminishing. For their support, clothing, and education, the Legislature of 1879 appropriated the annual sums of five thousand, four thousand, and one thousand dollars respectively.

The State Penitentiary continues under excellent management in all respects, the convicts being constantly employed in profitable work, which is the making of bedsteads. There were 68,000 bedsteads manufactured

there last year, 15,000 of which were sold to the New England States, 20,000 to New York, New Jersey, and Pennsylvania, and 33,000 to Maryland, Virginia, and other Southern States and California. The earnings of the prison for the year were $23,618.05 ; the expenses, $17,-492.51 ; leaving $6,126.54 as net earnings. This seems to be a remarkably large sum, considering that the price received for prison-labor is now 46¼ cents a day per man, whereas the rate obtained for it a few years ago was 95 cents. The number of convicts in August, 1879, was 190, or 14 less than were reported in 1878.

The State militia, under the appellation of "National Guard," as ordained by the Legislature of 1878, is composed of thirty companies of infantry, four sections of artillery, and two troops of cavalry ; all of these being organized into three regiments. Three new companies were organized last year.

The members of the New Hampshire Temperance Association met in State Convention at Manchester on February 19th, and adopted the following resolutions :

Resolved—1. That moral suasion is one of the great instrumentalities for promoting the advancement of the cause of temperance to be constantly used and never abandoned.

2. That to the end that there may be any complete triumph of the temperance cause, the places of temptation must be closed, the principles of prohibition must be recognized, and the prohibitory law now on our statute-books must be rigidly enforced.

3. That we do most heartily approve of the detective system in enforcing the law, and recommend the organization of legal-suasion clubs in all parts of the State, and their coöperation in the detective system of enforcing the law, until such time as it shall be enforced by the regularly constituted authorities.

4. That the interests of the temperance cause imperatively demand that the local-option clause of the lager-bier law, passed at the last session of our Legislature, should be repealed.

5. That we condemn the practice of prosecuting officers in "hanging cases up" over the violators of the prohibitory law, and earnestly request the full execution of the law in these as in all criminal cases.

6. That we believe the temperance movement can not complete its work till the manufacture as well as the sale of intoxicants is prohibited by law.

7. That a general mass convention of all who believe in the p omp and rigid enforcement of the law be held, and that a committee of seven be appointed to make all necessary arrangements for the same.

With regard to the main object of the Convention, which was the adoption of some method to secure the enforcement of the existing liquor laws, arrangements were made for the holding of another meeting, in which better-matured plans of action might be presented and decided upon. In accordance with this determination, they assembled again at Concord on March 27th, when they formed themselves into a "State Temperance League." A constitution was adopted, which provides for the formation of a "State Temperance League," in which every church and temperance organization is entitled to seven members ; and for a board of prosecuting officers, whose duty it shall be to prosecute all violations of the liquor law. The resolutions previously adopted at the Manches-ter meeting were reaffirmed. A resolution was also adopted, "that officers seeking reëlection in 1880 shall give pledges that the law regarding the sale of liquors shall be rigidly enforced."

Among the industries pursued by the people of New Hampshire, the manufacture of "leather-board," or artificial leather, holds no inconsiderable place. A visitor thus describes the process of manufacture:

Passing down into the manufacturing room and threading our way through machinery and piles of leather-board, we first stand before an immense tub, filled with a dirty-looking, pulpy mass, which is flowing slowly around it. This shows the first step of the manufacture, which consists in grinding the stock, mixed with water, between eight and twelve hours, until it attains the proper consistency. At this stage may be perceived the fact that leather has as distinct a fiber as cotton or flax, one very much resembling that of wool. Taking up a piece of the half-digested leather, this can be seen very plainly. The best stock for leather-board is technically known as "pancake," from the fact that it consists of the cuttings of sole-leather, which is made by gluing layers together. From the tub the pulp is pumped into an ordinary paper-machine, such as is used in making the coarser kinds of paper, and after passing through this is wound upon a metal drum with a groove running lengthwise. While watching this, suddenly the man in charge touches a handle, runs a sharp knife along the groove, and takes off a sheet of leather-board in much quicker time than I can write it. After this there is nothing to be done but dry and pack; and from here we go into a well-lighted room, having in the middle a large stand which looks very much like a gigantic egg-hatcher. Investigation, however, shows that the tiers of broad shallow drawers contain leather-board. Under each drawer is placed a steam-coil, and in this particular drier there are in all five miles of piping. Straw-board is made in very much the same way, but the straw is treated with lime before grinding; the manufacture takes less time and the board is much softer.

It is undoubtedly true that the use of leather-board in making boots and shoes is a form of adulteration, and especially is this the case when employed in making soles; for, as soon as wet, it comes to pieces. This, however, is not wholly the fault of the manufacturer, since he is obliged to produce a softer article by mixing the stock with other and inferior material, in order to meet the demand of the shoemaker, as leather-board made wholly of leather injures the dies used in cutting it. On the other hand, it may be said in its favor that by means of it a cheaper shoe is produced, of a better material than would otherwise be used, and it consumes a waste which was before of little value. Like all others, the business has suffered from competition and over-production; but some idea may be conveyed of its importance when I say that in this State there are five mills, in Maine ten, and in Massachusetts four.

NEW JERSEY. The sessions of the Legislature of New Jersey are held annually. The one hundred and third commenced on January 14th and closed on March 14th. In the Senate, William J. Sewell was chosen President, receiving 11 votes, to 10 given to George C. Ludlow. In the House, Schuyler B. Jackson received 33 votes for Speaker and was elected, and George S. Duryee 26.

An "act to provide for the election of delegates to a Constitutional Convention" was reported upon adversely in the House, and the report adopted. A motion to reconsider was lost—yeas 16, nays 34.

An adverse report was made to the passage of an act to equalize assessments and establish a uniform system for the valuation of real estate in this State. The report was adopted and the bill indefinitely postponed.

An act was passed authorizing the appointment by the Governor of a special Tax Commission. This Commission is required to make a full and thorough investigation of the manner in which the different kinds of property and the various industries and occupations of the people of the State are affected by existing laws relating to taxation, together with any defects, discrepancies, or irregularities in such laws. It is also required to advise such changes and improvements in the laws relating to taxation as to them shall seem most likely to promote the agricultural, commercial, manufacturing, and other interests of the people of the State.

In the Senate, George Dayton of Bergen, G. W. Atkinson of Middlesex, N. T. Stratton of Gloucester, John Hopper of Passaic, and John P. Jackson of Essex were appointed in executive session as Commissioners. In order that the investigations of the Commission might be as thorough and comprehensive as possible, they invited information or suggestions from every person who was willing to offer either in writing. The points to which they called special attention, as indicated in the law authorizing their appointment, were the following: 1. The manner in which different kinds or forms of property are affected by existing tax-laws. 2. The manner in which different industries or occupations are affected by existing tax-laws. 3. Any defects, discrepancies, or irregularities in such laws. 4. What changes in the tax-laws are needed—as respects, for example (a), the things to be taxed or exempted from taxation; (b), the rate of taxation; (c), the time or mode of assessment or collection.

Another act was passed authorizing the appointment by the Governor and Senate of five judicious persons to prepare a system of general laws for the government of cities now or hereafter to be incorporated. The persons appointed were John Clement of Haddonfield, Barker Gummere of Trenton, William J. Magie of Elizabeth, Frederick H. Tesse of Newark, and Leon Abbett of Jersey City. They determined to visit various portions of the State, for the purpose of securing the views of citizens in regard to the subject generally, and formulated the following queries, which they addressed to the public and to prominent men: 1. The general subject of legislation necessary or proper in respect to counties. 2. The general subject of legislation necessary or proper in respect to townships, including boroughs and incorporated towns. 3. The general subject of legislation necessary or proper in respect to cities. 4. The expediency of passing a general law adapted to all municipalities, leaving to each the option of making use of the whole or portions of the powers granted, or of passing different laws adapted to different classes of municipalities. 5. The best mode of limiting expenditures for municipal purposes within proper bounds, and of securing a proper accountability on the part of all officials. 6. The expediency of prohibiting municipalities from incurring debts or obligations not immediately provided for by tax. 7. The best mode of dealing with the existing debts of municipalities. The propriety of providing for the payment of existing debts by establishing a sinking fund under the control of the State. The propriety of creating a State Commission for the adjustment of debts between defaulting cities and their creditors. 8. The propriety of prohibiting assessments for improvements based on the special benefit derived therefrom. If the system of assessments for special benefits be considered desirable, how to provide for the payment of the expenses of improvements and the collection of assessments. 9. The best mode of providing for the collection of taxes within municipalities. 10. The best mode of providing for the control of public schools within municipalities. 11. The proper extent of municipal regulations respecting matters of public health.

An act to provide for the establishment of schools for industrial education passed the Senate by yeas 34, nays 3. It had previously passed the House. The act provides that the State Board of Education may in their discretion establish schools for industrial education upon the application of not less than ten citizens of the State, who shall agree to pay part of the cost of maintaining any such schools ; and the Board of Education shall have power to prescribe and cause to be enforced all rules and regulations necessary for carrying into effect the provisions of the act. That such schools, when organized, shall be for the training and education of pupils in any industrial pursuits now established in the State, including agriculture, so as to enable them to perfect themselves in the several branches of industry which require technical instruction. That there shall be a board of trustees of each of such schools, to consist of five members, who shall have control of the buildings and grounds, and the power to prescribe the studies and exercises of the school and rules for its management, and to grant certificates of graduation; they shall report annually to the State Board of Education their own doings and the progress and condition of the schools. That any city, town, township, or county shall have the power to appropriate for the support of any such school such amount as they may deem expedient and just. That the said school shall be supported (1) by the amount received from tuition fees; (2) by the money contributed by the petitioning citizens; (3) by the amount appropriated by the city, town, township, or county;

and (4) by the amount contributed by the State Board of Education; provided, however, that the sum annually contributed by the said Board for any one school shall not exceed the sum of five hundred dollars; and the Treasurer is authorized to pay upon the warrant of the Comptroller, approved by the Governor, such sum, not exceeding the amount above specified, as may be called for by the trustees.

An act relative to tramps was passed. It provides that any person going from place to place begging, asking or subsisting on charity, and for the purpose of acquiring money or a living, and having no fixed residence or lawful occupation in the county or city in which arrested, shall be deemed a tramp and guilty of misdemeanor, and on conviction sentenced to imprisonment at solitary confinement at hard labor in the county jail or workhouse for a term not exceeding one year. It also provides that one who enters a dwelling, or kindles a fire on the highway or on the land of another, without first having obtained permission, or who is found carrying firearms, shall be liable to arrest and imprisonment at hard labor not exceeding three years.

An act providing for the summary investigation of county and municipal expenditures was also passed. By its provisions, on the petition of twenty-five freeholders of any municipality to a Justice of the Supreme Court, setting forth that they have reason to believe that the public moneys are being unlawfully or corruptly expended, such Justice may appoint experts to investigate such expenditures. The public officers shall facilitate such investigation, and the expenses shall be paid by the municipality.

After the Federal census was taken in 1870, it became the duty of the Legislature to redistrict the State for members of the House. In 1871 the Legislature, in which the Republicans had a majority, passed an act which the Democratic minority asserted to be unfair in its award of representation. In the session of 1878 the Democrats repealed the act, and passed another in accordance with their views of fairness. At this session the Republicans, being again in a majority, suspended the rules and repealed the districting act of the previous session and re-enacted that of 1871. The vote in the House was—yeas 32, nays 27.

By an amendment of the State Constitution the Judges of the Courts of Common Pleas, both law and lay Judges, are nominated by the Governor and approved by the Senate. Governor McClellan, in the exercise of this duty imposed upon him by the Constitution, nominated certain gentlemen as law Judges for the counties of Essex, Mercer, Middlesex, and Monmouth, and as lay Judges for the counties of Burlington, Camden, Hudson, Hunterdon, Warren, Union, Bergen, Morris, Cape May, Cumberland, and Gloucester. At the same time he sent to the Senate with these names the following letter:

STATE OF NEW JERSEY, EXECUTIVE DEPARTMENT, }
TRENTON, *January* 27, 1879. }

To the Senate:

The amendment to the Constitution which removed the appointment of the lay Judges of the Inferior Courts of Common Pleas from the joint meeting of the Legislature, and committed their selection to the Governor, with the advice and consent of the Senate, was intended to elevate the character of those courts, and to remove the appointment as far as possible from merely partisan influences. The feeling of the great mass of the people of this State is, I believe, strongly against a strictly partisan composition of the courts. Our Supreme Court and that of Errors and Appeals have long, if not always, been non-partisan in their character, and it is not unreasonable to suppose that the high reputation they so justly enjoy is in no small degree due to this fact. It is my firm conviction that one of the greatest evils which can befall a community, especially in a republic, is a strictly partisan judiciary. Something more is necessary than that the judiciary should be really pure, impartial, and just: it is also requisite that the people should believe them to be so, and that they should be convinced that no unintentional or unconscious party prejudice should work injury to any seeking Justice. I believe that, if the judiciary of any nation or state is entirely composed of any one political party, it will often be difficult to convince members of the adverse party that they can always obtain even-handed justice.

The Inferior Courts of the Common Pleas are now composed of two members of one political party and of one member of the other, and it happens that it now for the first time falls to the lot of a Governor of this State to decide whether this condition of affairs shall continue, or whether only one party shall be represented in these courts. With a deep sense of my duty as the Chief Executive of this Commonwealth, whose province it is to render exact and equal justice to all its people, I have determined to preserve the non-partisan character of the judiciary. I do this with the confident hope and expectation that both political parties will maintain this policy in the future, and that the precedent will be approved and followed. by my successors in office, to whatever political party they may belong.

Very respectfully,
GEORGE B. McCLELLAN, Governor.

The nominations and letter were referred to the Judiciary Committee of the Senate, a majority of whom subsequently presented a report to the Senate, approving in strong terms the views of the Governor. They then proceed to say:

Agreeing so fully as we do with the sound public policy expressed by the Governor in his admirable message, your committee feel constrained, in order to fully carry out his views, to recommend that his Excellency's nominations for law Judges of the Courts of Common Pleas in the counties of Essex, Monmouth, Middlesex, and Mercer be not confirmed by the advice or consent of the Senate.

The Governor may have overlooked the fact that by an act of 1878 the number of lay Judges was reduced in all counties having not more than 50,000 inhabitants, and that reduction takes effect in the three counties last named during the present year; and were the nominations confirmed for these counties, the bench in each would be unanimously of one political party, and must so remain for some time to come. Such a result his Excellency the Governor would doubtless deplore, for the reasons given in his message that "one (of the greatest evils that can befall a community is a strictly partisan judiciary, and that in such cases it would be difficult to convince members of the adverse party that they could always obtain even-handed justice." Your committee believe that the courts, whose administration so directly affects the personal interests

of the people as the Courts of Common Pleas, Quarter Sessions, and Orphans' Courts, should be especially free from the slightest suspicion that any unintentional or unconscious party prejudice shall work injury to any one seeking justice therein. We believe earnestly in the principle of a non-partisan judiciary, and in its fair and practical application to the counties named and to all others.

The judiciary at the present time in said counties of Monmouth, Middlesex, and Mercer is non-partisan, and your committee have failed to see or learn any reason why that condition of affairs should be changed by appointments which set the principle of a non-partisan judiciary at defiance upon the very moment of its promulgation.

The nomination for law Judge of Essex County is largely open to the same objections already stated. The administration of justice in that largely populated county, at least in criminal matters, devolves almost entirely upon the Court of Quarter Sessions, which would become, by the appointment made by the Governor, entirely of one party, were this nomination confirmed.

While your committee, therefore, have deemed it wise to adopt the expressed views of the Governor and to coöperate with him in whatever proper appointments he may make in accordance therewith, they are constrained, for the foregoing and other satisfactory reasons, to advise the rejection of the nominations made for law Judges of said counties of Essex, Monmouth, Middlesex, and Mercer, as inconsistent with the letter and principles of the message.

The nominations of the Governor for lay Judges in the counties of Burlington, Camden, Cape May, Cumberland, Gloucester, Hudson, Hunterdon, Warren, Union, Bergen, and Morris, making a minority Republican representation in each of said counties respectively, and being entirely in accord with the principles enunciated in his message, it is recommended that they be confirmed.

The minority of the committee at the same time presented a report on the subject to the Senate, of which the following is an extract:

By usage and of right, the nomination of persons to hold these several judicial offices belongs to the Governor, the Senate having only the power to reject or confirm his nominations. The Governor, together with his message communicating these nominations, also presented a special message, laying down certain principles which he considered should govern the Executive in making judicial appointments, which were an enlargement upon the policy adopted by previous Democratic Governors, looking toward a non-partisan judiciary in this State. This fact is alluded to simply because the majority of the Judiciary Committee, to whom were referred as well the special message as the nominations, have seen fit to use words carefully culled from that message, as the basis of their report advising the rejection of the nominations of the four Democrats for law Judges and the confirmation of the eleven Republicans for lay Judges. If the dominant party in the Senate are willing to accept the principles laid down by the Governor as the correct one, and by which they hereafter intend to be guided, they should at least be fair and accept it as he has announced it.

Governor McClellan, in his special message to this Senate, refers *solely* to the lay Judges of the Common Pleas, and his language is so plain that none can be deceived, save willingly. He says, "The Inferior Courts of the Common Pleas are *now composed of two members of one political party, and of one member of the other*, and it happens that it now for the first time falls to the lot of a Governor of this State to decide whether this condition of affairs shall continue, or whether only one party shall be represented in these courts." To what can this language, which is the keynote of the message, be construed to apply, save to the lay Judges? Of whom can it be said that two members are now of one political party, and one of the other, except the lay Judges of the Common Pleas, and of them alone? The message of the Governor speaks for itself, and having by it enunciated a policy by which he proposes to govern his action, it will be admitted by all fair-thinking men that he should be allowed to develop and perfect that policy at such time and in such manner as he may consider best for the interests of the people; and if, at this time, at the very outset of his undertaking, he does not find it in his power to bring it at once to completion, his message most clearly commits him to its consummation whenever and as the opportunity affords.

I respectfully insist that if the policy of the Governor, as expressed by his nominations, is to be adopted by the Senate, it should be adopted as a whole; and it remains for the representatives in the Senate of the party in power to say whether the principle of a nonpartisan Judiciary shall fall still-born, or whether it shall go on broadening and extending itself until it includes all classes of the judicial branch of the government.

But, aside from all this, despite all factious criticism that may be made upon the message of the Governor, the fact remains that, in the exercise of an undisputed right, the Governor of this State has sent to this Senate nominations which, with the advice and consent of that Senate, will become appointments. It matters not what impelled the Governor to make those political nominations; that is beyond the question or cavil of the Senate. The only question properly before it is, Are the persons named proper persons to hold the offices for which they are named? The majority of the committee do not even pretend otherwise. For these reasons I respectfully dissent from the report of the majority of the committee, and recommend that the nominations for law Judges and for lay Judges of the Courts of Common Pleas, now before the Senate, be confirmed in their entirety.

The Senate concurred in the views of the majority report, and voted against the law Judges nominated. The Governor made no more nominations previous to the adjournment of the Legislature. Subsequently the same persons were commissioned to fill vacancies in the four counties, under the following provision of the State Constitution: "When a vacancy happens during the recess of the Legislature in any office which is to be filled by the Governor and Senate, or by the Legislature in joint meeting, the Governor shall fill such vacancy; and the commission shall expire at the end of the next session of the next Legislature, unless a successor shall be sooner appointed."

A bill was introduced to the House requiring the Governor to withhold commissions from justices of the peace chosen by the people until they have passed an examination and obtained certificates as to their capacity and moral character. A question arose as to the constitutionality of the bill, and it was submitted to the State Attorney-General (Stockton), who said:

The Constitution imparts to the legislative, executive, or judicial department of government no power to annex any other qualificaton to this office than those already prescribed by the Constitution itself as a prerequisite to the exercise thereof. Such a course would be inconsistent with the fundamental principle upon which is founded the whole structure of our political institutions, viz., all political power, not otherwise delegated, is inherent in the people.

Eligibility to public trusts is a constitutional right, which can not be abridged or impaired. The Constitution establishes and defines the right of suffrage, and gives to the electors as well as to other departments of government the power to confer public trust. It prescribes in respect to certain officers particular circumstances, without which a person is not eligible; and provides that persons holding certain offices shall hold no other public trust. Excepting particular exclusions thus established, the electors and the appointing authorities are by the Constitution wholly free to confer public stations upon any person according to their pleasure. The Constitution giving the right of election and the right of appointment, these rights consisting essentially in the freedom of choice, and the Constitution also declaring that certain persons are not eligible to office, it follows from these powers and provisions that all other persons are eligible.

The right to office is not declared as a right or principle by any express terms of the Constitution; but it results, as a just deduction, from the express powers and provisions of the system. The basis of the principle is the absolute liberty of the electors and the appointing authorities to choose and to appoint any person who is not made ineligible by the Constitution.

Eligibility to office, therefore, belongs not exclusively or specially to electors enjoying the right of suffrage. It belongs equally to all persons whomsoever not excluded by the Constitution.

I am of the opinion that this bill is unconstitutional: 1. Because it attempts to limit the body from which the officer may be chosen, thereby excluding from this office a class of persons constitutionally eligible, and establishing a qualification which the State Constitution does not require. 2. Because it attempts to control the Governor in the exercise of a duty confided to him exclusively, and enjoined upon him by the Constitution.

A bill was passed in the House to prohibit the manufacture of shoes in the State Prison, by a vote of yeas 36, nays 19. A motion to reconsider the vote was lost—yeas 14, nays 44. The Committee of the Senate to whom the bill was referred when it reached that body reported that they had deemed it their duty, in examining the question, to take an enlarged view of the subject, and not merely to see what its effect might be upon a single class; and they therefore endeavored to ascertain what action, if any, was necessary to promote the general welfare of the people of the State, and also to inquire what effect the abolition of the system would have upon the prisoners themselves. The cause of the depression in the shoe business as well as in other branches of trade is ascribed to the introduction of machinery into the manufacture of shoes, which has within a few years almost revolutionized the business; and constant improvement shave been made, until the perfection of machine-made work and the rapidity of its construction are marvelous. This of itself must tend to throw upon the market a vast amount of work; and, when the market becomes overstocked, the machines must stop and the employees for a time cease to labor. That this is a true reason is proved by the fact that more than two thirds of the convicts themselves have, since the termination of old contracts, been in a condition of enforced idleness. It is assumed by those who desire the abolition of prison labor, that the price paid by the contractors for the labor employed greatly injures similar business by unfair competition. If it be true that an inadequate price is paid for this labor, it would result in making these contracts so profitable that the former contractors, who are supposed to have been filling their coffers, would not only have gladly renewed their contracts, but the present contractors would find employment for every idle man in the prison. And yet the fact is, that during the past year all the old contracts were terminated without renewal, and new contracts have only been made for about one third of the whole number of convicts. Then, again, the quantity of work made in the New Jersey State Prison, and thrown upon the market, when compared with the vast amount demanded by forty millions of people, can be scarcely sufficient to create a ripple in the current rate of prices. Basing the calculations upon the assertions of the different parties who have appeared, it is estimated that not less than 10,000 persons are employed in New Jersey alone in the manufacture of boots and shoes, while the whole number of convicts employed at the present time is 270—not quite 2¾ per cent. Complaint has also been made that a greater amount of work was secured from the prisoners, because of severe punishments which were inflicted in case of failure to perform their allotted tasks. A synopsis of the record of prison-shop number three, which is a fair sample of all the others, shows that from the 1st day of August, 1878, to the 21st day of February, 1879, a period of six and two thirds months, the daily average of men employed in this shop has been 41. During that period the whole number reported to General Mott on account of work was *seven*, and for other causes *eight*, which is an average of one man in 28½ days on account of work, and of one man in 25 days for other causes. For all causes, this is less than one fourth of one per cent. for the whole number of days' work done, and of itself refutes the idea that the competition of prison-labor is unfair because of the amount of work forced from men by punishments. If the change now demanded is sanctioned, it must result in depriving the State of all the revenue which of late years has been received from the labor of the prisoners. The earnings of the prison-for the past nine years, ending October 31, 1878, have reached the sum of $685,721.68, being a yearly average of $76,191.30. The earnings for the past year have been $63,258.-25, or about $9,000 more than sufficient to meet the current expenses of the maintenance of the prisoners.

Looking at the other aspect of the case, which is the effect upon the prisoners if labor ceases in the prison, it appears from a schedule prepared by the hospital steward of the New Jersey State Prison, showing the number of cases requiring treatment when the prisoners have been fully employed, partially employed, and entirely idle, that on the 31st of May, when all the prisoners were employed, only 21 were unfit for work out of 664; on the 1st day of December, 1875, after six months of idleness, there were 50 unfit for work out of

717; on the 31st day of December, 1877, when 500 convicts were working, there were 38 unfit for work out of 835; and during the month of January, 1879, when only 270 men were employed, 107 men had been under treatment. The record of insane persons in the prison on the 31st day of May, 1875, was *five*, while on the 31st day of December, same year, after six months of idleness, the number was increased to *eighteen!* The number of deaths year by year tells the same story. The number of deaths during 1874, when all were employed, was 3; in 1875, when the convicts were idle six months, the deaths were increased to 13; in 1876, when a small number only were employed, the deaths were 20; in 1877, when 500 were employed, the deaths were only 8; while in 1878, when only 200 were employed, the deaths were increased to 19.

From such considerations the committee reported adversely to the bill. A debate sprung up in the Senate on a motion to place the bill on the calendar. Senator Marsh attempted to show that the amount of work done in the prison had no appreciable influence upon the market, and to this end brought forward the following statistics of the extent of the manufacture in this country:

Neither do I believe that the quantity of work made by prison-labor, and especially that made in the New Jersey State Prison, does to any appreciable extent affect the market injuriously to the outside manufacturer. A writer in the "Shoe and Leather Reporter," after enumerating the firms throughout the country who have contracts for prison-labor, thus proceeds: " This completes the list of contracts for convict-labor in the United States, and shows the total number employed to be 5,325 hands. There are some small jail contracts and some boys employed in houses of refuge, protectories, etc., through the country, but the entire amount would make the number about 5,500 hands. Allowing 310 days' labor a year, and an average of three pairs a day made by each man, would give 5,115,000 pairs made yearly by prison-labor. The average value of the boots and shoes will be about $1.25 a pair for large and small, which will give the total value of such manufacture at $6,393,750 for the year. There are *four* manufacturers in New England (three in Massachusetts and one in Maine) who make more pairs and goods in money value than are made in all the prisons of the United States. Now, when it is understood that the total value of boots and shoes made in the United States in 1876 is estimated by competent authority to reach the sum of $189,974,-922, it will be seen that all the prison-labor of the country combined is less than 3½ per cent. of the whole. I compare with 1876 because I have not been able to get later figures, but have no doubt that the combined production for 1878 is even greater than in 1876. It is an easy matter to ascertain with accuracy the number of boots and shoes made in the United States by machines. Each pair has a stamp, which must be purchased of the patentee, and the statistics for 1876 show that 67,500,000 pairs were made during that year. Add to this the quantity of such work made by hand-labor, and it is estimated that the whole product of the United States in that year was 82,962,-461 pairs, without estimating custom-work at all. And this estimate only gives an average of two pairs yearly to each man, woman, and child in the country, which is certainly not an over-estimate. Of this vast quantity there were made in Massachusetts 52,687,461 pairs, in New York 9,060,009 pairs, and in Pennsylvania 5,000,000 pairs. The city of Philadelphia alone is credlted with having 106 factories, making of all varieties about 4,500,000 pairs. The city of Baltimore produced 1,400,000 pairs, Cincinnati 2,000,000 pairs, and Chicago 9,000,000 pairs. It is needless to enumerate more. Sufficient has already been done to convince this Senate of the vastness of the boot and shoe interest in this great country of ours.

But the legislation now proposed would not decrease the number of boots and shoes made except in New Jersey, and it is important, therefore, to know how many shoes are made in the New Jersey State Prison, and to compare this production with that of the whole country. There are at present employed in the New Jersey State Prison 270 convicts, and I am informed that they average four pairs per man each day, a total of 1,080 pairs per day, and for a year (allowing 300 working days as before) 334,800 pairs. Estimating the average value of this work at $1.50 per pair, this production would reach the sum of $502,200, an amount utterly insignificant when compared with $200,000,-000, the production of the whole country! Whether prison-labor ceases utterly or continues, it can have no perceptible effect upon the vast market of this country, or upon the price paid for labor. As well might you expect to affect the supply of the city of Trenton by taking from or adding to its reservoir a hogshead of water!

Although the bill failed to pass, yet its discussion probably led to the adoption by the Legislature of a joint resolution providing for the appointment of a Commission of seven by the Governor, three of whom may be citizens of other States, to make careful inquiry into the question of prison-labor, as to whether it comes into competition with free labor; to state the best means to prevent such competition, and at the same time to supply employment to the convicts. The Commission will receive no compensation, but may employ a clerk at $300, and must make a report to the Governor before the next session of the Legislature. The Commission appointed by the Governor consisted of the following persons: Edward Bettle of Camden, William R. Murphy of Burlington, A. S. Meyrick of Middlesex, Schuyler B. Jackson of Essex, and Orestes Cleveland of Hudson.

The efforts made to secure a better religious observance of Sunday by the enforcement of laws enacted at a former period caused more active opposition in Newark than in any other part of the country. Early in the year the Law and Order Association began to prosecute the dealers who sold liquor on Sunday. As an offset to the action of the Society, the Germans began to insist on the enforcement of the old Sunday law, which for years had been considered as obsolete. On the first Sunday when the German Protective Association attempted to enforce this law, all the liquor-saloons were closed, and ordinary business was suspended. The object was to make the Sunday laws offensive to the citizens, but the result was to create a public sentiment against the liquor-dealers. The question of repealing the law against the selling of lager-beer on Sunday, which was first agitated in Newark, gradually spread all over the State, and from the Citizens' Protective Association of Newark sprang the Liberal League of New Jersey. This body held a State Convention in Newark in September, and adopted the following resolutions:

Whereas, The founders of our government invited the oppressed of all nations to come here and to participate in a free government for free men; and,

Whereas, In compliance with this invitation people from every land have flocked to our shores, and, blending their nationalities together have formed a mighty nation; and,

Whereas, Of late there has been manifested in certain quarters, and among certain religious bodies, a disposition to exercise extraordinary powers and to prostitute the forms of law for the furtherance of their peculiar views, and to the manifest injury of the civil rights and personal liberties guaranteed to all of our people, and to the contrary of the well-being of the State ; therefore, we, a part of the people of the State of New Jersey, in mass-meeting assembled, do resolve :

1. That every man has an indisputable claim to life, liberty, and the pursuit of happiness.

2. That the liberty of action in the pursuit of happiness gives to every man the right to carve his life in his own way, so far as that way is consistent with the same rights of others.

3. That we proclaim ourselves law-abiding citizens, but that we renounce the spirit of reaction and of bigotry as opposed to the genius of our free institutions, and as contrary to the progressive spirit of the age.

4. That we denounce the attempts recently made by some of the officers of the law in this State, through the instigation of a few fanatics, to revive and enforce obsolete laws, repealed by the consent of three generations, as wrong in principle and vicious in practice, tending to weaken popular respect for all law and to bring the administration of justice into disrepute.

5. That we call upon the Legislature of New Jersey to so modify existing laws as to secure enlightened liberty of action to all classes of our citizens ; and we ask that the Legislature shall see to it that New Jersey shall no longer be the laughing-stock of the civilization of the nineteenth century.

6. And we do hereby pledge ourselves to vote only for such men for the Legislature as will guarantee to us their adherence to the above principles.

This was followed on the same day by an immense procession, the line of which embraced in its different sections not only the representatives of the brewers, and all the trades which contribute to the lager-beer business, but delegations from almost every branch of business which is carried on in the State of New Jersey. At the charter election in Newark in October, the Protectionists were successful by a large majority. This success was not regarded as expressing objections to the Sunday laws as a whole, but as asserting that they needed modification.

At the opening of the Oyer and Terminer in that city in March, Judge Depue thus defined a "disorderly house" under the law of the State:

A disorderly house is defined in law to be a place where the law is habitually violated ; and if in the course of investigation of this subject you find any place in which the law is in either of the respects mentioned habitually violated, such places are disorderly houses within the meaning of the law.

At the last and preceding term of Court indictments were found for keeping disorderly houses, based on the habitual sale of liquor without any license, and at times when the public authorities were forbidden to grant licenses for the sale of liquors. A question having arisen, one of them was made a test case and taken to the Supreme Court, and the indictment was there sustained. So, with regard to that subject, it has been adjudged by the Supreme Court, and there now remains no doubt as to the law on this subject.

Under an act of the Legislature to prevent the spread of contagious or infectious pneumonia among cattle in the State, the Governor appointed William H. Sterling to carry out its provisions. At the time of his appointment the disease, so far as known, existed only in the northern and eastern portions of the State. Wherever it was known to exist, veterinary surgeons were sent to make a correct diagnosis, and the cattle were preserved in all cases where it could be done, and none destroyed except it was absolutely necessary in order to save the herd, or to prevent the spread of the contagion. In all cases a strict quarantine was maintained. All cattle entering or leaving the State were also inspected.

A plan was adopted by Governor McClellan, the object of which was to so improve the efficiency of the militia of the State as to secure a body of troops that would in many respects bear comparison with the regular army. The estimate of the number of reserve militia of the State, based on the census returns of 1875, is 248,127. The number organized in regiments, companies, and battalions is 3,180. These compose two brigades, divided into one battery of artillery, two Gatling-gun companies, and seven regiments and one battalion of infantry. A school for commissioned officers and another for non-commissioned officers were instituted, and attendance was stimulated. Very soon a commendable increase in promptness of attendance of the enlisted men at the drill-rooms began to be noticed. An effort was then made, although hitherto without success, to obtain from Congress a larger appropriation ⁴ of arms, etc., for the militia. Meantime much attention has been given to rifle-practice, in order to improve the marksmanship of the troops. An officer was sent through the State to instruct the National Guardsmen in the use of the rifle in their armories preparatory to practice on the ranges, of which there are two in the State. In order that he should do this successfully, it had been necessary previously to devise a way of making armory practice essentially similar to that on the range. It was necessary that the same rifles, with the same sights, should be used in both instances; yet 75 feet was as long a range as could be constructed in most of the armories. The targets were easily reduced to a size that would make it as difficult to hit them at 75 feet as it would be to hit a target on a range at 200 yards. To prevent accidents in the armories from the premature pulling of triggers, screens that could not be perforated by a rifle-bullet were set up at a distance of about 25 feet from the firing-point. These had holes cut in the center, just large enough to give to the marksman a full view of the target. Lest the continual crack of the rifles should prove a nuisance to persons residing in the neighborhood, it was found necessary to reduce the charge of powder in the cartridges from 70 grains, the ordinary range-charge. to 6 grains. This was found sufficient to drive the bullet—reduced from 420 to 230 grains—to its work. The same

cartridge-shell was used, but it was filled nearly to its mouth with a brass cylinder perforated from end to end to allow a train of powder to extend back to the percussion-powder at the base of the cartridge. In this way practice in the armories was made to take the place of range-practice. After this style of shooting was introduced it became popular. Officers and privates were eager to practice. The practice in the armories, however, had two defects. The reduced charge of powder reduced the force of the recoil, and the rifle was the more easily held to the bull's-eye, and nothing had to be allowed for windage. A marksmen's badge was established, which any National Guardsman could win by making 25 out of a possible 50. Reckoning by the number of marksmen's badges won, there has been an increase in marksmanship this year over last year of more than 300 per cent. This has encouraged the General Inspector (Sterling) to institute a contest at long ranges, the distances to be from 800 to 1,200 yards. He has also in view, should this long-range contest give favorable results, to attempt shooting at 1,500 yards. This distance would lack only 260 yards of a mile, yet he is of opinion that the effect on the men would be beneficial, because it would aid in teaching them to judge of distances, and because it would be properly preparatory to another object he has in view. This is to teach them to shoot at objects they can not see, as, for example (in actual warfare), at soldiers behind a battery, when the elevation of the rifle must be such that the bullet, having passed over the intervening object, will descend toward the objects to be hit.

The work done by the Fish Commissioners during the year previous to April consists of 58,000 landlocked salmon hatched and liberated in lakes in the northern part of the State; 2,500 black bass distributed to lakes and ponds; 1,665,000 shad hatched and liberated in the Delaware River; 225,000 California salmon distributed early in 1878; 500,000 California salmon hatched and partly distributed; 43,500 brook-trout purchased and distributed; 200,-000 brook-trout hatched and nearly ready for distribution; 100,000 whitefish in the hatching-house. The Commissioners deem the introduction of black bass into the State an event of the utmost importance. Their presence in the Delaware has aroused some opposition from those who feared that they would seriously diminish the number of young shad. Bass live mainly above tide-water, and the young shad, after being hatched in the headwaters of the rivers, must, in making their way to the sea, pass through the regions inhabited by the bass. It is not now generally believed, however, that any considerable number of infant shad are sacrificed to the voracious appetite of the bass. It is true that bass prey upon other fish, and it is equally true that they will eat young shad; but it is the opinion of close observers that they will not

NEW JERSEY.   669

eat young shad if they can get any other kind of small fish. The Commissioners have frequently seen a black bass in full chase after a fleeing minnow, while the water was fairly alive with young shad with which he could have gorged himself had he been so disposed; and they have repeatedly found the stomachs of bass filled with other kinds of food, when the fish has just been taken from water in which young shad could be seen in thousands. The brook-trout and California salmon have been placed in the waters of Somerset, Camden, Passaic, Morris, Sussex, Hunterdon, Warren, and Essex Counties. In accordance with the recommendation of Professor Baird, the United States Commissioner of Fisheries, who says that California salmon will thrive in waters where there is no access to the sea, but will be smaller, a large number of young salmon have been introduced into the deep, cold lakes in Morris, Sussex, and Warren Counties.

Nine cases for violation of the "act for the preservation of fish" were argued on *certiorari* before Judge Reed of the Atlantic County Circuit Court. The convictions were of two classes—the first class for the violation of the first section, and the second class for the violation of the second section of the act. The first section of the act provides generally that it shall not be lawful for any persons to fish with a net in any of the waters of this State (except as hereinafter provided) between May 15th and July 15th. The second section provides that it shall not be lawful for any person to fish with a net, etc., in the counties of Atlantic and Burlington, between June 1st and September 1st. It was contended that the second section was local as to its character, and that, being within the body of a general law, it is, first, void in itself, and second, its presence occasions the invalidity of the first section, because it is in contravention of the 4th paragraph of section 7 of the amended Constitution, which provides, "No general law shall embrace any provision of a private, special, or local character." The Judge said that he did not know of a similar provision ingrafted into the Constitution of any other State; that the distinction between those acts which may be considered general or public and special or local acts, as used in the Constitution, has received no direct judicial consideration. The question has been considered in the courts of New York, under the constitutional provision that "no private or local bill which may be passed by the Legislature shall embrace more than one object, and that shall be expressed in its title." There it was held that an act is local, within the meaning of the Constitution, which in its subject relates but to a portion of the people of the State or to their property, and may not, either in its subject, operation, or immediate and necessary results, affect the people of the State or their property in general (43 N. Y., 11). "The test is not whether it applies to acts to be done in a particular lo-

cality, but whether the operation of the act is restricted to the people of that locality. This act does not impose a specific and exclusive penalty for the punishment of the people of Atlantic County, but upon all the people of the State who fish in that locality within a restricted time. I think the statute is constitutional." The other objections raised were to the formality of the proceedings and the right of a trial by jury. The Judge held that the defendants were not entitled to a jury trial, and that the statement of the facts charged brought the defendants within the operation of the statute. The convictions were affirmed with costs.

Two of the cities of the State, Elizabeth and Rahway, are in a condition of bankruptcy. Both have been crippled by the depreciation of values. In the former the debt has been increased by decisions of the Supreme Court which reversed a former decision with regard to assessments for improvements, and thus threw on the city a large amount of obligations of private citizens. The people do not say they will repudiate, but assert that they are unable to pay. There is no authority for compromising the claims against the city, and both the citizens and the bondholders are at a loss what to do.

In 1869 the township of Bernards, in the county of Somerset, issued $128,000 worth of bonds to aid in the construction of the New Jersey West Line Railroad. Eleven miles of the road was built, from Summit to Bernardsville, at a cost of $5,000,000. The road went into the hands of a receiver, and was sold under foreclosure to the Delaware, Lackawanna, and Western Company. Suit was brought on the bonds of the township. They were signed, but not sealed, and were issued in that condition. A plea that the bonds were not valid by reason of such omission was set up in defense. But Judge Nixon, of the United States District Court, granted a perpetual injunction restraining the township from making use of this defense. The principal and interest amount to $200,000.

The great railroad question, as regarded in New Jersey, was briefly and summarily presented on a festive occasion at Long Branch, by the Vice-President (Smith) of the Pennsylvania Railroad, in these words:

The system has to-day outgrown the limits of State sovereignty, and the iron band holding this country together reaches from the shores of the Atlantic to those of the Pacific. Has not the time arrived when the General Government should enact general laws that would be applicable to all the interstate railways of this country, which, among other things, should provide for full reports to be made of their organization, working, and financial condition, as often as might be required, with a power of verifying reports of examiners, which would regulate the proportion of stock to bonds, make the forms of mortgages uniform, forbid the contraction of floating debts by railways · for other than supplies, and provide that the railways shall publish their rates of freight, based on certain principles, and make any evasion of such rates an indictable offense? The rates should be fixed for each class of goods, the classification to be made by the companies per hundred pounds per mile, and when determined might be published as a tariff by which all transportation on each line of railroad should be regulated. These lists of rates should be accessible to every person, and should not be permitted to be changed without reasonable notice. The effect of such provisions as to a fixed basis of rates, with a prohibition for any railroad officer to charge less than the public rates under a severe penalty, would do much toward making the business of the country more stable, the traffic on the railroads more remunerative, and lessen burdens now placed on the public through the agency of secret discriminating rates. The great cardinal principle which should pervade this question of rates is, that the rate on the same class of goods for the same quantity for the same distance should be the same to every one.

The public press, or the number of daily, weekly, and monthly publications in the State, is as follows: Daily, 22; tri-weekly, 1; semi-weekly, 2; weekly, 146; bi-weekly, 1; monthly, 1; total, 178. These are classified politically, etc., as follows: Democratic—daily, 7; tri-weekly, 1; weekly, 41; total, 49. Republican—daily, 9; weekly, 44; total, 53. Greenback—daily, 1; weekly, 3; total, 4. Independent—daily, 5; semi-weekly, 2; weekly, 56; total, 63. Temperance—weekly, 1; monthly, 1; total, 2. Mechanical—weekly, 1. Literary—monthly, 1. Law—monthly, 1. College —bi-weekly, 1; monthly, 2; total, 3. Of the above journals, 1 daily, 9 weekly, 2 semi-weekly, and 1 tri-weekly are published in the German language—all of the others in the English language.

By the report of the Insurance Commissioner it appears that there are fifty-seven insurance companies authorized to do business in New Jersey, other than accident and life insurance companies. Twenty-six of these are joint-stock fire and marine, thirty are purely mutual companies, one is a plate-glass company; and eighteen are companies of foreign countries. The total capital stock of all the stock companies is as follows: New Jersey companies, $4,897,-070; of other States, $28,317,979. Total assets: New Jersey companies, $9,445,260.74; of other States, $74,432,160.87; foreign companies, $20,560,484.04. Total liabilities: New Jersey companies, $6,651,163.78; of other States, $53.-386,905.02; foreign companies, $8,886,803.91. Total net surplus: New Jersey stock companies, $2,795,406.23; of other States, $21,054,-583.19; foreign companies, $11,673,680.13. There are twenty-seven life companies operating in New Jersey, of which twenty-five are from other States, and one is a friendly society. The number of policies in force in New Jersey increased from 28,545 at the close of 1877 to 39,512 at the close of 1878; but this increase was entirely due to the numerous small contracts of the friendly society, 10,627 in 1877 and 22,303 in 1878.

The condition of the savings banks in the early part of the year showed the following results: Resources—Real estate, total value, $841,979.93; loans on bond and mortgage,

$7,991,543.63; United States bonds, $3,622,-221.33; other stocks and bonds, $1,840,632.79; call loans on collaterals, $653,181.92; other assets, $1,640,339.90. Total resources, $16,589,-899.50. Liabilities—Due depositors, $15,749,-319.76; other liabilities, $62,098.80. Surplus over liabilities, $778,480.94. Number of open accounts January 1, 1878, 53,254; number of open accounts January 1, 1879, 62,990; number of accounts opened or reopened during the year 1878, 29,127; number of accounts closed during the year 1878, 19,391.

Cranberries are an important product of the State. The crop in 1878 was estimated at 300,-000 bushels.

The geological survey of the State has brought into notice the oak and pine lands in its southern part. The area of the district southeast of the marl-belt is 1,580,000 acres, or two fifths of the area of the State. The survey has classified the soils of this district in two great general divisions. One is the gravelly loams, upon which oak and pine grow; the other is the more sandy soils, whereon pine alone thrives; and from these trees the groups are designated as oak-lands and pine-lands. There is another division, but of limited extent, and generally found along the sea-border, which is more loamy and supports a more mixed growth of timber. The best of the oak-lands are more commonly known as "white-oak bottoms." All travelers through that part of the State have observed these "bottom-lands." The wastes of white sand, with their fire-scarred and stunted yellow pine, are familiar. An extract from the report of the survey briefly sets forth the advantages of this portion of the State:

The climate is salubrious, and has been especially noted for its entire freedom from malarial influences. It is specially liked by those who suffer from asthmatic and pulmonary diseases; and many come here for the relief they obtain for such ailments. The seaside resorts are continually increasing in number and enlarging in size, and throngs of visitors come to enjoy the delightful air.

The water of this country is pure and soft. It is drained by many large rivers, which are chiefly remarkable for their full and equable flow, being very little affected by storms or by droughts. They furnish excellent water-power for manufacturers' purposes. Those at Mays Landing, Weymouth, Batsto, Atsion, Millville, Bricksburg, Manchester, and Toms River are of this kind, and there are a great many other good ones.

The soil is light but easily cultivated, and when well managed is productive. Mr. Hay's farm, at Winslow, is a model of productiveness for all South Jersey. The improved lands at Vineland, Hammonton, and Egg Harbor City are yielding large crops and promise well for the future. The staple productions are wheat, rye, oats, Indian corn, hay, potatoes, and sweet potatoes. Melons are raised in abundance. Apples, pears, peaches, grapes, blackberries, raspberries, strawberries, and currants grow remarkably well.

The means of communication are good. There is an abundance of gravel for road-making, and the benefits of good roads are highly appreciated. Cumberland County claims to have more good roads than any other county in the State. The West Jersey Railroad, the Glassboro and Millville, the Millville and Cape May, the New Jersey Southern, the Camden and Atlantic, the Philadelphia and Atlantic City, the Mays Landing branch, the Pemberton and Manchester, the Tuckerton, the Toms River branch, the Toms River and Waretown, and the Freehold and Squankum branch to Squan, are all railroads in this district; and every point in it is within an easy drive of railway communication, and, by this, is within three or four hours' ride of the best markets on the continent.

The various public institutions of the State are in a prosperous condition. Their details may be found in the volume for 1878.

NEW YORK. The annual session of the Legislature commenced on January 7th and closed with the month of May. In the Senate the Republican vote was about 20 out of 33, and in the Assembly about 100 out of 128. The Senate was called to order by the Lieutenant-Governor. In the Assembly Thomas G. Alvord was elected Speaker by 95 votes, against 24 for Erastus Brooks.

This session of the Legislature was held in the new Capitol. An effort was made on the evening of February 12th to signalize the change both historically and officially. The two Houses assembled in joint convention; the Judges of the Court of Appeals and the State officers were present by invitation; and speeches were made by the President of the Senate, Lieutenant-Governor William Dorsheimer, the Speaker of the House, Thomas G. Alvord, and one of the distinguished members of the Assembly, Mr. Erastus Brooks. The report of the New Capitol Commissioners was made to the Legislature on January 23d. The amount expended in 1878 on the building was $1,026,463. The finished portion was about one quarter of the area of the whole building; but it contains two of the three great rooms, one of three staircases, one half of the heating apparatus, five of the seven elevators, one third of the furniture, one half of the plumbing, the entire water-supply, the whole exterior drainage, and one half of the basement; also, the walls of the court and the south center section have been built up to the roof-line. The amount of additional appropriation required for the completion of the building and the payment of existing liabilities was estimated by the Commissioners at $4,200,000, in a period of two years. Being asked by the Legislature how much it would cost to administer the new Capitol after it was completed, the Commissioners replied that it could be kept clean, lighted, and warmed "for a moderate sum"; but to accomplish this result it is necessary that its administration should be kept free from partisan influence. They then proceed to say: "A force of forty-three men has been organized, to serve during the session of the Legislature, who take care of the machinery, attend the fires, run the elevators, and do all the work of cleaning the building, and also perform all police duty. The appointments to this force have been equally divided between the political parties, and it is proposed that the men shall serve during good behavior. We believe that upon a system like this the cost of maintaining the new Capitol, when the same

shall be completed, may be brought within $75,000 a year, and our estimate for maintenance during the year 1879 is $25,000."

The election of a Senator in Congress, to fill the vacancy arising by the expiration of the term of Mr. Roscoe Conkling, was made on January 20th. Mr. Conkling received in the Senate 19 votes, and Mr. Dorsheimer 12. In the Assembly Mr. Conkling received 95 votes, Mr. Dorsheimer 23, and Mr. Peter Cooper 2. Mr. Conkling was chosen. A caucus of the Democratic members of the Legislature was held, in which it was proposed to make a protest against the granting of any certificate, or the making of any declaration, that Roscoe Conkling had been duly elected Senator. The grounds for this protest were, that the Constitution of the State requires that, at the next session after every State census, the Senatorial districts shall be altered so as to contain as nearly as may be an equal number of inhabitants, and that the members of Assembly shall be apportioned according to population; that a census was duly taken in 1875, but no alteration of the Senate districts and no reapportionment of the members of Assembly has been made by the Legislature since the said enumeration; that the effect of such neglect has been that large numbers of the people of the State have been and are misrepresented in the Legislature; that its political complexion has been thereby changed from one party to another, the legal result whereof is that the present Legislature is a Legislature de facto and not de jure. This protest the caucus refused to adopt, but they resolved upon an address to the people. The complaints of the address rest upon the grounds set forth above. As an evidence of the justice of the complaints, the following statements were set forth as facts taken from the census returns of 1875:

Under a just apportionment in the Senate, New York City, with Richmond County, is entitled to seven Senators, while but five represent that city. Kings County is entitled to three members, but allowed only two, and this with a surplus population of 46,000. New York City, by the lawful count, is entitled to twenty-seven members of Assembly, instead of twenty-two; Kings County is entitled to fourteen members instead of nine; Monroe County to four members instead of three. These additional members, all belonging to Democratic districts, are now awarded to the following counties, and entirely represented, except one district, by Republican members of the Legislature, viz.: Madison, Delaware, Ontario, Cattaraugus, Columbia, Washington, Niagara, Wayne, Oswego, Oneida, St. Lawrence.

The Assembly representative population also gives the following unequal record:

COUNTIES.	Districts.	Population.
Kings............	Ninth	85,029
New York	Twentieth	78,656
Monroe	Second	65,558
New York	Twenty-first............	64,556
"	Seventeenth............	64,896
"	Eighth	60,054
Kings..........	Fourth.................	63,975
"	Eighth	58,112
"	Sixth..................	54,485
New York	Fifteenth..............	50,920

And this with the following in contrast to the above in single districts:

COUNTIES.	Representatives.	Population.
Delaware	2	41,526
Madison	2	41,114
Oswego	3	75,720
St. Lawrence	3	78,082
Ontario	2	45,403
Cattaraugus	2	45,771
Columbia	2	46,318
Washington	2	46,314
Wayne	2	47,628
Niagara	2	47,691
Otsego	2	49,034

SENATORIAL DISTRICTS.

DISTRICTS.	Counties.	Representative population.
Twentieth	Herkimer and Otsego	89,338
Eighteenth	Jefferson and Lewis	90,596
Twenty-sixth	Ontario, Yates, and Seneca	91,064
Sixteenth	Clinton, Essex, and Warren	101,327
Twenty-sixth	Cayuga and Wayne	106,120

With the following districts showing a most unjust contrast:

DISTRICTS.	Counties.	Representative population.
Third	Kings	292,258
Eighth	New York	235,432
Seventh	New York	173,225
Second	Kings	172,725
Ninth	New York	167,580

These large districts have but one Senator each, and the record given is not the gross, but upon the representative population.

Subsequently an apportionment bill was passed by the Legislature, which gave to New York City twenty-four members of Assembly, a gain of three, and to Kings County twelve members, a gain of three. The following counties lost each a member: Columbia, Delaware, Madison, Oneida, Ontario, and Oswego; and the other counties remained as under the previous apportionment. The bill was sent to the Governor, who allowed it to become a law without his signature. In a message of explanation to the Legislature he said:

As I peruse its provisions, I find that a proper regard for my own official duty forbids me to approve it. For not less explicit than the command to apportion is that other provision that the apportionment shall be made as nearly as may be according to the number of the respective inhabitants of the different localities.

The Senate districts are to be so apportioned that they shall consist of contiguous territory and contain, as nearly as may be, an equal number of inhabitants; and the members of Assembly are to be allotted to the several counties, as nearly as may be, according to the number of their respective inhabitants. This bill does not comply with these provisions of the Constitution. The first Senate district contains 128,267 inhabitants; the second, 160,000. The nineteenth district contains 101,693; the fourteenth, 150,204. The thirty-second district contains 106,522; the adjacent thirty-first district, 180,000. Some slight inequalities of population were doubtless necessary in the arrangement of the districts from contiguous territory, but a glance at the map will show that the rank injustice done in almost every district west of the Hudson River had some other cause than a desire for geographic fitness. For instance, the twenty-sixth district stretches from

the Pennsylvania line to Lake Ontario, and others are scarcely less incongruous. To specify the localities which are wronged either in the location or in the population of the Senate districts, would be to call the roll of half the counties in the State. That these wrongs were in nearly every case unnecessary is the common testimony of all who are familiar with the subject.

In the distribution of members of Assembly the bill is still further from meeting the requirements of the Constitution. I find that Cattaraugus County, with 45,737 inhabitants, has two members; while Suffolk, with 50,330, is given but one. Orange, with 82,225 inhabitants, has but two members, while St. Lawrence, with only 78,014, gets three. Nor can I understand the philosophy which gives to the latter county, with 78,000 inhabitants, the same representation as Monroe, which exceeds it in population by nearly 50,000.

These discrepancies are not to be explained. They admit of no apology or excuse. They are of the same class as the so-called necessity which entirely deprives 150,000 inhabitants in New York and Kings of their proper representation.

While for the reasons stated I am not willing to sign the bill, it is permitted to pass into a law by lapse of time, as a lesser evil than a continued neglect of the entire constitutional direction on the subject.

The following act to regulate the rate of interest was also passed, receiving in the Assembly only seventeen negative votes:

SECTION 1. The rate of interest upon the loan or forbearance of any money, goods, or things in action shall be six dollars upon one hundred dollars for one year, and after that rate for a greater or less sum, or for a longer or shorter time. But nothing herein contained shall be so construed as to in any way affect any contract or obligation made before the passage of this act.

SEC. 2. All acts or parts of acts inconsistent with the provisions of this act are hereby repealed.

SEC. 3. This act shall take effect the first day of January, 1880.

The vexatious question of the taxation of mortgages was brought forward, but no final action was taken upon it. The form in which it was presented is expressed in two sections of the bill for the equalization of taxation, as follows:

SECTION 1. When any debt due or owing by any owner of land is secured by mortgage thereof, the amount of the debt shall be assessed upon the owner of the land as trustee for the creditor; and such amount shall be deducted from the value of such real estate, and the residue of such value only shall be assessed upon the owner of the real estate. The sum paid by such owner as trustee for taxes on such debt shall be a legal set-off against such debt.

SEC. 2. When, for any reason, real estate be not assessed at its full valuation, such part of the value of real estate as is assessable to the owner of the land as trustee, according to the preceding section, shall be assessed at the same percentage upon said full valuation as is assessed upon the part of the value of the said land assessable to the owner of the lands.

Resolutions for biennial sessions of the Legislature were adopted. They will be presented to the next Legislature, and if adopted will then be submitted to a vote of the people.

Some important questions touching the vast subject of the State charities, and facts respecting the institutions, were brought out in reports to the Legislature. There is a State Board of Charities, one of whose duties is to visit charities with a State foundation, those of counties and cities, and those of benevolent organizations. The aggregate financial statistics of these institutions for the year are as follows:

VALUATION.

In real property	$29,415,509 28
In personal property	5,561,253 60
Total	$33,976,762 28

RECEIPTS.

Cash balance from last year	$448,809 94
Received from State	1,047,969 36
Received from cities	3,510,217 16
Voluntary donations	793,337 02
From all other sources	2,109,457 74
Total	$7,909,791 22

EXPENDITURES.

For buildings and improvements	820,778 67
For supervision and maintenance	6,587,975 04
Total	$7,408,753 71
Leaving balance of	$501,037 51

The Board sent an urgent appeal to the Legislature for further provision for the chronic insane poor. They say, "The tide of insanity has swollen beyond the proportions of former years, and unexpected numbers of chronic cases are now on our hands, overflowing the supposed liberal provision heretofore made for them." This increase is shown in the report of the Commissioner of Lunacy for the same period, made during the session to the Legislature. It embraces the previous year, and is summarily as follows:

SUBJECTS.	Males.	Females.	Total.
INSANE.			
In State asylums	1,284	1,315	2,599
In county asylums and poor-houses	2,135	2,923	5,058
In private asylums	191	264	455
Total	3,610	4,502	8,112
IDIOTS.			
In State asylums	173	119	292
In county asylums and poor-houses	298	222	520
In private asylums	...	1	1
Total	471	342	813
EPILEPTICS.			
In State asylums	89	64	153
In county asylums and poor-houses	192	207	399
In private asylums	9	15	24
Total	290	286	576
Total of all classes	...	...	9,501

The mortality statistics for the same period are:

INSANE, IDIOTS, AND EPILEPTICS.	Males.	Females.	Total.
In State asylums	118	91	476
In county asylums and poor-houses	288	188	209
In private asylums	11	10	21
Total	417	289	706

The total number of insane, idiots, and epileptics for 1877 was 7,982; for 1878, 9,501; being an increase of 1,519, or a fraction over 19 per cent. The total mortality for 1877 was 685; for 1878, 706.

An examiner was sent out by the Comptroller to make an investigation of the affairs of the charitable institutions. His report showed the necessity of a responsible supervision over the charities maintained by the State. To accomplish this object, the Comptroller suggested to the Legislature the adoption of the following plan as certain to be efficient:

First. Require all the receipts of the institution to be paid into the State Treasury. Provide appropriations sufficiently large to cover all their expenses, the appropriations to be advanced by the Comptroller upon monthly estimates.

Second. Require the appropriations asked for annually to be estimated for and submitted to the State Board of Charities on October 1st of each year. Make it the duty of said Board to examine said estimates, and certify the amount needed by each institution to the Legislature. No appropriations to be made for any purpose, except they are so certified.

Third. Make it the duty of the State Board of Charities to require of the institutions an annual report classified as to the items of expense and receipt, covering such details as the Board may deem wise. Also, a statement of the quantity and price of the various articles used.

These three simple requirements are intended to place all the elements of a complete supervision in the hands of the proper State officers.

The State Examiner, Mr. E. P. Apgar, recommends a uniform method of accounts in all the institutions as likely to lead to its adoption by the cities and counties. "A common method of keeping and verifying public accounts throughout the State would tend to prevent fraud, facilitate its detection, and protect the fiscal agents of the public against unjust accusation and suspicion." In his opinion there should be an inventory of all property on hand at the end of each fiscal year. The annual report of each institution should contain: First, a statement of receipts and disbursements during the year, classified under such general heads as salaries and wages, labor, provisions, household stores, clothing, fuel, lights, medical stores, ordinary repairs, miscellaneous. Second, a statement in detail of the expenditures under each head; as, for example, under salaries, the name of each officer and his salary, number of attendants of various grades and the pay of each grade, the pay of engineers, watchmen, etc. Under the head of provisions should be stated the quantity and cost of various articles consumed; for example, the number of barrels of flour consumed during the year and the total cost, the number of pounds of sugar and total cost, and so on. Such a statement could be compressed into two or three printed pages, and would thus not materially add to the length of the report. Its advantages are many and obvious. Each superintendent would thus have the benefit of the experience, as to quantities and cost, not only of his own institution, but of all the others.

The expense of the Home of Inebriates at Binghamton has been $10,000 per capita, and in 1878 the cost per capita was $13,087. A comparison of the expense per capita of several of the State institutions with that of similar ones in other States, for the year 1877, gives the following results:

NAME OF INSTITUTION.	Aver'ge number of patients.	Annual cost per capita.
1. Asylum for the Insane, Toronto, Canada.	651	$183 39
2. Asylum for the Insane, Brattleboro, Vt..	472	150 77
3. Asylum for the Insane, London, Ontario.	604	140 20
4. Hospital for the Insane, Halifax, N. S...	847	154 27
5. State Lunatic Asylum, Jackson, Miss....	350	167 58
6. Hospital for the Insane, Dayton, Ohio....	571	166 00
7. State Lunatic Hospital, Taunton, Mass...	727	194 90
8. State Lun'tic Hosp'l, Northampton, Mass.	476	183 72
9. Hospital for the Insane, Cleveland, Ohio.	577	177 19
10. Hospital for the Insane, St. Peters, Minn.	568	180 60
11. Central Insane Asylum, Jacksonville, Ill.	487	217 81
12. Government Hospital for the Insane, Washington, D. C.................	770	213 64
13. Hospital for the Insane, Oshkosh, Wis....	542	216 92
14. Maine Insane Hospital, Augusta, Me	411	219 45
15. State Lunatic Asylum, Harrisburg, Pa....	434	231 59
16. Hosp'l for the Insane, Middletown, Conn.	363	240 84
17. Hospital for the Insane, Catonsville, Md.	245	246 01
18. State Lunatic Asylum, Utica, N. Y......	608	362 58
19. Hudson River State Hospital, Poughkeepsie, N. Y.................	219	855 59
20. State Homœopathic Asylum, Middletown, N. Y.......................	109	431 14

A consideration of the real estate, grounds, and architecture of the State institutions is presented, with the recommendation of much greater economy.

In accordance with the views of the lady-members of the Board of State Charities, a bill was introduced in the Assembly to establish a State Reformatory for Women. To show the necessity for such an institution, Mr. E. Brooks, who reported the bill, cited the following facts from the report of the Board of State Charities:

Let me read from the report of the Board of State Charities some facts as to the present condition of the poor-houses of this State. I will not say the jails of this State, for they are, as a whole, bad beyond contemplation or statement; and yet, as bad as they are, they also are capable of immense improvements in their administration. In regard to the poor-houses of the State and the jails of the State where women are sent, let me present to this House, not to arouse its sympathy but to excite its attention, with a view of securing the reform contemplated in the proposed law, what are some of the facts in some of the counties of this State as presented by the Board of State Charities. I will begin with the county where we are sitting as a legislative body. In the Albany County poor-house is, or was, a single woman, forty years old, of foreign birth, and nine years in the United States, who is the mother of seven illegitimate children; the woman most degraded and debased, and soon again to become a mother. And this county is no worse than the rest, with perhaps here and there an exception. These women are sentenced to jail for a short time or sent for a short period to the poor-house. They are soon discharged, commit the same crimes over and over again, and are sentenced again to the poor-house or jail and discharged, to become again and again a charge upon the county or State. So that this mother, and not the mother alone, but all her illegitimate children, become a tax upon the county. Then there is Chautauqua County. In the poor-house is a woman, as I read, fifty-five years old, admitted at the age of twenty-two as a vagrant, said to have been married, but the whereabouts of her husband is unknown. She too has been discharged from the poor-house and returned immediately for the past thirty-three years, during which time she has had six illegitimate children, all becoming a charge upon the county. Then there is

Cortland County, with an unmarried woman twenty-seven years old, with an infant child, who has been the mother of four illegitimate children; and four of her sisters are also in the same dependent condition and with the same number of illegitimate children, all becoming a charge upon the county. My friends, I see some of you looking at this and that county, to this member and that member, as if their own constituents were not here. They need not make any exceptions; for if they will examine their own poor-house records, they will find about each and every one of them very much in the same condition. Here is the Essex County poor-house, with a black woman, a widow, aged forty-five years, with a daughter, single, aged twenty-four years, and her grandson four years old, illegitimate and born in the house. The first has been the mother of ten children, seven of them illegitimate; the second has had three illegitimate children; and both mother and daughter are unmarried, and both year after year are returned to this poor-house to be supported, over and over again, by the county. In Greene County a vagrant unmarried woman, forty years old, became an inmate when twenty-one years of age; that is, this woman has been for nineteen years off and on and returned to this poor-house, and without any hope of reform, and, perhaps, because there was no place for reform; she goes out like the rest from time to time, but soon returns, and will doubtless continue a public burden for life; and this woman, too, is the mother of five illegitimate children. In the Herkimer County poor-house a single woman, aged sixty-four years, twenty of which have been spent in the poor-house, has six of these same unfortunate children. In the Montgomery County poor-house a woman twenty years old, illegitimate, uneducated, and vagrant, has two illegitimate children; and she, to make wretchedness more intolerable, recently married an intemperate, dissolute man, formerly a pauper, and husband, wife, and child have all become a charge upon the county. In the Rockland County poor-house is an unmarried woman, forty-two years of age; for eleven years she has been an inmate, and she has four illegitimate children, and the mother is unmarried and a vagrant. These, Mr. Chairman, are specimens of the respective county poor-houses of the State relating to females alone.

The bill passed the Assembly by 80 yeas to 7 nays, but failed to become a law.

The first two years of prison management under the reformed system terminated on March 1, 1879. The results of that period, as compared with the results of the last two years under the inspector system, were as follows:

MARCH 1, 1875, TO MARCH 1, 1877, LAST TWO YEARS UNDER INSPECTOR SYSTEM.

PRISONS.	Expenses.	Earnings.
Sing Sing..............	$659,303 47	$257,563 71
Auburn...............	383,718 11	152,770 61
Clinton...............	518,395 38	193,241 29
Total.....	$1,561,416 96	$603,595 61
Deficiency in two years under the old system..	....	$957,821 35

MARCH 1, 1877, TO MARCH 1, 1879, FIRST TWO YEARS UNDER SUPERINTENDENT SYSTEM.

PRISONS.	Expenses.	Earnings.
Sing Sing..............	$400,362 91	$418,908 79
Auburn...............	303,109 60	224,948 18
Clinton	231,446 38	97,681 90
Total...............	$934,858 88	$741,488 57
Deficiency in two Years under the reform system...............	....	$193,370 26

This shows a decrease in expenditures of $626,558.13 in two years, and an increase in earnings of $137,892.96, or a total gain to the State Treasury of $764,451.09. The average number of convicts during the two years ending March 1, 1877, was 3,455, and during the two years ending March 1, 1879, 3,572. The first year of the management of the State canals by a Superintendent instead of Canal Commissioners terminated on February 1, 1879. The results were as follows:

1878—BY SUPERINTENDENT.

Extraordinary repairs	$2,817 00	
General expenditures	10,470 49	
Salaries and travel	16,632 04	
Eastern Division	176,436 15	
Middle Division	140,818 17	
Western Division	121,894 16	
		$468,068 01
Days of navigation, 1878	237	
Tolls received, 1878		$993,848 00

1877—BY CANAL COMMISSIONERS.

Extraordinary repairs	$77,182 25	
Salaries and travel	9,933 41	
Eastern Division	424,978 36	
Middle Division	167,040 72	
Western Division	213,962 87	
		$893,097 51
Days of navigation, 1877	214	
Tolls received, 1877		$880,896 00

RESULTS.

Reduction in expenses for year ending February 1, 1879, over year ending February 1, 1878	$425,029 50	
Increase in tolls (1878)	112,452 00	

These returns include the Erie, Champlain, Oswego, Cayuga and Seneca, Black River, Genesee Valley, Chenango, and Chemung Canals. The success of the new system, which consisted in placing them under one responsible head, was admitted by all parties. The Superintendent in his report makes the following suggestions to the cities of Buffalo and New York for the improvement of the commerce of the Erie Canal. To Buffalo he says: "Provide a low fixed rate of harbor and commission charges on all incoming and outgoing canal freight." And to New York: "Increase your terminal facilities to a capacity whereby the cargoes of canal-boats can be unloaded more quickly and cheaply in your harbor, and ocean-going vessels receive their grain cargoes with greater convenience and dispatch."

A bill was before the Assembly to provide for the tunneling of the Hudson River from Jersey City to New York, and for a grand central underground depot in New York to which all the railroads entering the city would be compelled to run.

Another bill which passed the Legislature defined tramps to be "all transient persons who rove about from place to place, and all vagrants living without labor or visible means of support, who stroll over the country without lawful occasion." The law further says that any act of vagrancy, by any person not a resident of the State, shall be evidence that the person committing the same is a tramp within the meaning of the act, and any person who shall be deemed to be a tramp shall be liable to punishment of not more than one

year's confinement at hard labor in a county jail or a penitentiary.

Charges were transmitted to the Senate by the Governor against John F. Smyth, Superintendent of Insurance. They related to mal-administration in reference to the Atlantic Mutual Life and Globe Mutual Life Insurance Companies. When the subject came before the Senate, the charges were not sustained.

A bill to amend the charter of Brooklyn, which the Governor designated as pluralism, and defined as "a plan by which a man can draw the salaries of two offices and neglect the duties of one," was vetoed by him. Daniel O'Reilly, an Alderman of Brooklyn, was elected a member of Congress. His friends desired that he should hold both offices; a general act was presented and passed both Houses without a dissentient vote to change the organic law of the city, having half a million population, for the convenience of one of them. Such was the bill.

A bill was passed appropriating $8,000, being the award made by the Board of Audit to Terence O'Neil Donnelly for damages sustained by false imprisonment. The case is too peculiar to be passed. Mr. Donnelly was a builder of houses in South Brooklyn. He purchased lots, built houses upon them, and sold them. He was regarded as an honest and industrious man, a public-spirited citizen, and a kind husband and father. His occupation required some outlay and more credit, with diligence and foresight. He owned one of the houses in a block he built. It was worth $9,000, and had a $4,-500 mortgage on it. He maintained his family in plain comfort, in a house of that quality. As inmates of his house were two persons considerably his junior in years. Their relations with him were casual and on a slight business understanding only. The perpetration of a forgery was traced home to them. On being apprehended, it was schemed out for them to exhibit themselves as tools rather than principals. They were instructed to swear that Mr. Donnelly was the instigator and procurer of their crime, and the one who profited by it. They did so. Mr. Donnelly was arraigned, was very hurriedly tried, lost several advantages which defendants generally have, and, against his own protestations of innocence and the proof of his theretofore exemplary character, he was convicted and sentenced to a term of imprisonment. The men who swore the crime on him received the minor degree of punishment they sought. What happened to Mr. Donnelly is summed up in the fact that he went to prison. To his family this happened: They had to move from their homestead into a tenement, and were there in want. They had to withdraw the children from school, as their fellow pupils taunted them with their father's degradation. The man who had the mortgage on the house foreclosed it, and bought the house in for $200 under the face of the mortgage, and the mortgage was only one half

the cost of the property. After this had be-
fallen him, the persistent effort of Mr. Donnelly to prove the innocence he had always declared had this result: The two offenders were,
unknown to each other, carefully examined.
Their object having been accomplished, each,
unknown to the other, told the same story.
They said they had lied on the stand, on legal
advice, being told if they would swear they were
merely accessories their punishment would be
lightened and their victim would get the main
punishment. They swore the offense on Mr.
Donnelly, though he was wholly innocent.
The further evidence of handwriting confirmed
this confession, outside of their statements.
They also showed where the money that remained could be had. It was found there.
On this state of facts, Governor Robinson pardoned Mr. Donnelly. The moral, social, and
business injury done him gave much interest
to his case. After consideration, the Legislature, on April 18, 1879, passed an act authorizing Mr. Donnelly to present a claim to the
State Board of Audit for the damages sustained
by him by reason of his improper conviction
and imprisonment on false testimony, for the
alleged crime of forgery. By the same act,
the Board of Audit was authorized to hear and
pass on said claim, and to award such compensation for the damages sustained by Mr. Donnelly, in consequence of such conviction and
imprisonment, as should appear to be just and
reasonable. The Governor signed the bill. The
Board of Audit, by ample testimony, established the facts above stated. Mr. Donnelly
proved by twenty witnesses his good character, after having shown the injustice done him
and his. He then proved completely a direct
loss of $8,000 in property and loss of time,
etc., as if the case had been a technical one
between him and another man, before a jury,
and a consequential loss of $22,000 more. The
Board of Audit allowed only the direct legal
loss of $8,000. The Legislature voted the
money. The allowance was opposed by the
First Deputy Attorney-General as dangerous
as a precedent; he declared it was untenable
except under the special act on which the Board
was acting; that that act made the allowance
of any award discretionary and not mandatory;
that the act itself was a circumvention of the
general prohibition that the Legislature should
not audit or allow private claims against the
State; that the allowance of any damages
would open an infinitely wide door of expense
and abuse.

The question, Is a State bound to pay prospective profits under the form of damages on
the change of a contract? was decided by the
Governor in the negative by his refusal to approve an item of $65,000 in the general appro-
priation bill. After some progress had been
made on the State Reformatory at Elmira, the
Legislature, dissatisfied with the manner in
which it was being carried on and the unexpectedly large expenditures incurred and likely

to be incurred, passed an act in effect putting
an end to the progress of the work under the
contract which had been entered into by the
commissioners, and adopting a new and more
satisfactory method of completing it. The contractors were fully paid for all that they had
done and all the materials that they had furnished, and suffered no loss whatever at the
hands of the State. The claim made by the
assignee of the contractor was not for any actual loss, but solely for the prospective and uncertain profits he might have made if permitted
to go on with the work. In vetoing the item the
Governor said: "I hold that a sovereign State,
in the discharge of its powers and duties as an
independent government, is at all times at full
liberty to change its policy in regard to any
public building in which the whole State has
an interest; and that if, upon such change by
a public law, it takes care to prevent any actual loss to a contractor and keeps him entirely
whole, it does all which it is in good faith bound
to do. Parties who contract with the government know full well when they do so that it
has, and must have, the right to exercise the
power of changing its policy and its course of
procedure in public affairs. It is not reduced
to the level of an individual engaged in private
business in this respect, and can not be held
liable as such. This inherent right of the government becomes, therefore, in fact a part of
the contract." The opinion of the Attorney-
General was also taken, who maintained the
same view, and enforced it by reference to the
state of the law relative to public officers removed from office. He said:

In constructing public works the State acts as a sovereign. It exercises for that purpose its sovereign powers of taxation and of eminent domain. It acts for the
whole public and not for private benefit. It employs
agencies for such purposes as it creates, and provides
and abolishes compensation for official agencies for the
administration of public affairs; and, except where
restrained by constitutional provisions, the will of the
people, as expressed through the Legislature and the
forms of law, is supreme. It has been accordingly
held by the Court of Appeals that the act of 1874 was
a legitimate exercise of legislative power. It was an
expression of the will of the sovereign that the public
interests required changes in the construction of the
Reformatory and the superintendence and method of
the work. In the case of public officers (in the absence of constitutional restrictions), the State may employ and dismiss them at pleasure, may increase or
diminish their compensation, or abridge their terms of
office. Although a public office is in the nature of a
contract between the incumbent and the public, the
incumbent has no vested title and no legal claim for
damages by reason of the abrogation of his office or
diminution of his compensation. Upon this question
the Supreme Court of the United States has said;
"The promised compensation for services actually
performed and accepted, during the continuance of the
particular agency, may undoubtedly be claimed, both
upon principles of compact and of equity; but to insist beyond this on the perpetuation of a public policy
either useless or detrimental, and upon a reward for
acts neither desired nor performed, would appear to
be reconcilable with neither common justice nor common sense. The establishment of such a principle
would arrest necessarily everything like progress or
improvement in government. . . . It follows, then,

upon principle, that, in every perfect or competent government, there must exist a general power to enact and to repeal laws, and to create and change or discontinue the agents designated for the execution of those laws." (10 Howard, U. S., 416.)

The same principle has been sustained by the Court of Appeals of this State. (1 Selden, 285.) This principle applies with equal force to public works by the State and to the agencies employed in their construction, whether by contract or otherwise.

The right of the State to continue or discontinue public works, to change or abrogate the methods for their construction, and to employ and dismiss agents necessary for that purpose, must exist, or its power to act as a sovereign is ineffectual. If this power exists, there can be no breach of a contract entered into by the State for the construction of a public work, for the right of the State to suspend work and to make any desired change is implied in every such undertaking. No claim for future profits can therefore arise. The State performs its obligation by making full compensation. The Court of Claims at Washington rejects claims of this character against the United States Government, and the Supreme Court of the United States in a recent case (decided October, 1877) has applied the same principle. (McKee vs. United States.)

The question of the respective merits of the district or the township system of common schools was raised before the Legislature by the State Superintendent. The common-school system of the State, which has been in force for many years, is considered as hardly surpassed, if equaled, in excellence elsewhere. Under this system, the territory of the State is divided into school districts of convenient size, so that children of school age can get to school without subjecting them to inconvenience in walking too far. It is a system in the country that reaches more children than any other. The people of every school district have a right to elect their own trustee or trustees, and they have a right to build their own schoolhouses to suit their taste and convenience. In favor of this system, it was urged that the people of each district had a right to control their own schools, and that the further the schools were removed from the control of the people, the less interest they would take in them; and, if the people lose all interest in the schools, they will retrograde. If the township system was adopted, the control would be placed in the hands of a town board elected at the annual town meetings. The consequence might be that the management of the schools would be carried into politics and made a political question. Soon the Legislature would be urged, under this system, to pass a law to establish a central high school in every town at the expense of the tax-payers. Those living near the high school, it was urged, would receive the most benefit of that school, while it would lower the standard of the other schools in the town, etc. The State Superintendent thus explains his proposition: "I recommend that the Legislature abolish the present system of school districts, and in its place establish the township system. Let all the schools of the town be under the care and direction of a board of education to be elected at the annual town meeting; the amount of tax necessary to be raised for the support thereof, after the application of the public money thereto, be levied as a town tax; the powers now vested in the trustees of school districts given to town boards of education, with such additions as wisdom and necessity may dictate; and that the powers now vested in the inhabitants at district meetings be transferred to voters at town meetings, with such modifications and extensions as they may deem expedient. With such a system properly organized and in thorough working order, I predict that the cause of education in the State of New York will be greatly advanced." No change has yet been made.

The report of the State Engineer on railroads for the year 1878 was sent to the Legislature in March. During the year twenty-six corporations were formed, and twenty became extinct. Of 862 railroads organized under the laws of the State, but 275 remain in existence. At the time required by law (December 1st) 109 companies failed to report, and thereby rendered themselves liable to a penalty of $250, and $25 dollars per day until the report was received. The capital stock of the steam-railroads reporting in the State was $392,164,754.-25, and the proportion for the State of pro-rating the roads lying partly in the State and adjoining States was $287,826,957.05, being an increase in the total aggregate of $7,255,616.49. There have been built 107 miles of steam and 8 miles of horse railroads during the year. The number of passengers carried during the year by the steam roads was 48,769,084, an increase of 8,756,863, and each passenger traveled an average of 20·84 miles. The horse-railroads carried 244,290,364 passengers, an increase of 5,748,628. The number of tons of freight carried by the steam roads was 38,320,-573, an increase of 3,335,792. The records of accidents upon the steam roads for the year show 322 persons killed and 567 injured, a total of 887. Of those killed, 11 were passengers, 88 employees, and 223 others. The total horse-railroad accidents were 155, of which 44 were fatal; 5 of those killed were passengers, 9 employees, and 30 others.

The State tax-levy for 1879 was less by 0·37 of a mill than that of the previous year. The total reduction was $263,193.

A code of procedure and a code of substantive law were both passed by the Legislature and vetoed by the Governor.

The policy of the statute of the State relating to savings banks, as explained by the Attorney-General, is to exclude from the management of the bank trust all persons who have any pecuniary relations with a bank or with a borrower from a bank which might induce a lack of vigilance as trustee, or antagonize duty by private interest. He says: "The only rule of safety, therefore, for all cases, in the different forms in which they may arise, is to adhere rigidly to the policy indicated by the statute, to deem as ineligible for the position of trustee or officer of a savings bank all persons who have any pecuniary interest, whether as owner of property subject to mortgage held by the bank or as borrower, guarantor, or partner of a debtor to a bank, which may influence in any degree the performance of official duty. Strict enforcement of this rule may occasionally exclude a good man from such a trust, but like results are incident to all general rules of public policy, and the number of improper men excluded will be much greater."

The number of joint-stock fire and fire and marine insurance companies organized under the laws of the State on January 1, 1879, was 49, against 95 in the previous year. Total unobjectionable assets, $56,585,455.55, an increase of $81,656.92 over the previous year; capital stock, $25,057,020, a decrease of $900,-000; total liabilities, including capital, $37,-984,693.73, a decrease of $1,363,965,20; net surplus beyond capital, $18,616,387.99; total income for the year, $21,097,468.04, a decrease of $1,315,503.45. The fire loss was $7,923,-684.54, a decrease of $1,724,004.67; the marine and inland loss, $848,172.97, an increase of $345,957.81; dividends to stockholders, $3,-019,243.73; all other items of expenditures, $7,799,860.82; and the total amount of expenditures was $19,590,962.06.

Charges were made by the New York Chamber of Commerce against the New York Central and Erie Railroads relative to unjust discriminations in freight expenses against New York City. A committee was appointed by the Legislature to investigate the charges, consisting of A. B. Hepburn, chairman, of St. Lawrence County, and eight other members of the Assembly. The position taken by the president or chief officer of each company was one of public interest. In a joint letter to the committee they substantially declare that the annual reports contain about all the information that can justly be demanded by the public. This position is based on the theory that the rights vested in a railway regarded as a private concern so far overshadow its character as a public corporation that the rights of the public in the latter virtually cease to exist. To the railway the State has granted a part of its sovereignty, to be exercised with due regard to the rights of the grantors—the people; and this endowment of sovereignty has passed beyond the control of the grantor. The committee was clothed by the Legislature with power to send for persons and papers, to investigate the abuses alleged to exist, and to report to the Legislature what legislation, if any, is necessary to protect and extend the commercial and industrial interests of the State. Their first session was held in New York City on June 12th.

, The town-bond repudiation sentiment received a severe blow early in the year by the action of the courts. The town of Lyons, Wayne County, was bonded to aid in the construction of the proposed Corning and Sodus Bay Railroad, which was never built. The

town authorities refused to pay coupon interest, alleging that the bonds were invalid. A suit at law was instituted, and a decision adverse to the town reached in the United States Supreme Court in the last week of April; it held that the recital in the bonds was an estoppel, and that the bona fide holder was not bound to look further, and the obligator could not go behind it. The town of Thompson, Sullivan County, was one of the first to contest its bonds. These were issued in aid of the Port Jervis and Monticello Railroad Company. They were recognized as valid and the interest promptly met until 1872, when further payment was denied on the ground that the obligation was illegal. Two suits to compel the payment of interest due and refused were decided adversely to the town in the United States Circuit Court, and were appealed to the Supreme Court of the United States. On the other hand (and this precedent has led to many other contests), the Court of Appeals of the State, before which the matter was brought in other suits, decided that the controverted bonds were issued without power or authority, and ordered that they should be delivered up and canceled. The bonds were, however, transferred to New Jersey holders, in order that suit might be brought in the Federal Court. The Court overruled the Court of Appeals decision, and ordered a verdict of $28,-220.87 to be entered against the town. The result in these two cases was watched by a number of towns.

The State Convention of Nationals to nominate State officers assembled at Utica on August 29th. William Voorhees was elected chairman. The following nominations were made: For Governor, Harris Lewis; for Lieutenant-Governor, John Wieting; for Secretary of State, P. K. McCann; for Comptroller, John A. Shannon; for Treasurer, Julian Winnie; for Attorney-General, George H. Wright. The following resolutions were adopted:

1. That the national-bank currency shall be withdrawn, and that all money used by the people, whether gold, silver, or paper, shall be issued by the General Government, and be made a legal tender for all debts and dues, public and private. The volume of such money to be about $50 per capita, or sufficient to meet all the requirements of trade.

2. That the established volume of currency shall be increased from time to time in direct ratio with the increase in business and population of the country, so as to maintain for a dollar, or as nearly as possible, uniform purchasing power.

3. That all new issues of paper money shall be used to cancel the interest-bearing debt of the nation, to promote needed public improvements, and to pay the current expenses.

4. That the surplus of money now in the Treasury of the nation shall be used to cancel the interest-bearing debt.

5. That the national Government shall issue no more interest-bearing obligations, and that the outstanding bonds shall be paid and canceled at once.

6. That postal savings banks shall be established.

7. The equal taxation of all property.

8. That the salaries paid to the public officers shall be reduced to the basis of a just compensation for

services rendered; and all unnecessary offices abolished.

9. That there shall be proper legislation for the purpose of collecting and preserving reliable statistics to form a basis of intelligent action on all labor questions, to the end that labor may be fully and constantly employed and justly compensated.

10. The establishment of just and equitable rates for railroad fare and transportation.

11. That the Legislature at the earliest moment possible shall pass a law giving to mortgagees of real estate a right of redemption after five years of the sale.

12. That reasonable land limitation laws shall be enacted to prevent land monopolies.

13. The abolition of the State Prison contract system.

14. That no political assessments of candidates for office or officeholders shall be permitted in this party.

15. A reduction of legal rates of interest.

16. That debt due for labor performed shall take the precedence of all other claims.

17. That no more public lands be voted to corporations, but that they be held for actual settlers.

18. That we favor a tariff which shall protect American industry and manufactures.

19. That the Government should faithfully perform its pledge made to the Union soldiers at the time of enlistment, to wit: That they receive 160 acres of land on being discharged. Fee simple and equitable payment per month of each soldier according to the value of full legal-tender dollar.

The Republican State Convention for the nomination of State officers was held at Saratoga on September 3d. William A. Wheeler was chosen President, and the following State officers were nominated: For Governor, A. B. Cornell; for Lieutenant-Governor, George G. Hoskins; for Comptroller, James W. Wadsworth; for Secretary of State, Joseph B. Carr; for State Treasurer, Nathan D. Wendell; for Attorney-General, Hamilton Ward; for State Engineer, Howard Soule. The following platform was adopted:

The Republicans of New York, pledging ourselves anew to national supremacy, equal rights, free elections, and honest money, declare these principles:

1. The Republic of the United States is a nation and not a league. The nation is supreme within its own constitutional sphere. It is endowed with power to guard its own life, to protect its own citizens, to regulate its own elections, and to execute its own laws. The opposite doctrine of State sovereignty is the haleful mother of nullification, secession, and anarchy. Republicanism stands for national supremacy in national affairs and State rights in State concerns. Democracy stands for State sovereignty, with its own twin heresy that the Union is a mere confederacy of States.

2. To refuse necessary supplies for the Government with the design of compelling the unwilling consent of a coördinate and independent branch to odious measures is revolution. To refuse appropriations for the execution of existing and binding laws is nullification. We arraign the Democratic Representatives in Congress as guilty both of revolutionary attempts and nullifying schemes, and we reprobate their action as calculated to subvert the Constitution and to strike at the existence of the Government itself.

3. The safety of the republic demands free and pure elections. The Democratic Congress has attempted dictation by caucus, by threats of starving the Government, and by months of disturbing agitation, to break down the national election laws. We denounce this effort as a conspiracy to overthrow the safeguards of free suffrage and to open the ballot-box to the unchecked domination of the rifle clubs of the South and the repeaters of New York. We declare our uncompromising opposition to any repeal of these just protective laws, and the Republican Senators and Representatives in Congress, for their resistance to this attempt, and President Hayes for his veto messages, deserve and receive our hearty approval.

4. The Republican party neither justifies nor tolerates military interference with elections. It seeks only to protect the ballot-box from the interference of force and fraud. It repels the false charges and denounces the false pretenses of conspirators, who, while professing free elections everywhere, sustain mob law in the South; while inveighing against troops at the polls to protect citizens, refuse to prohibit armed clubs from surrounding the ballot-box to intimidate them; and, while affecting that the soldier's bayonet will overawe free electors, remain silent when the assassin's bullet seals the fate of political independence.

5. We call upon the people to remember that the Democratic party forced the extra session of Congress without warrant or excuse; that it prosecuted its partisan purposes by revolutionary methods; that it persistently obstructed resumption and still constantly presses disturbing measures; that it reopens sectional questions closed by the national triumph, and threatens to repeal the war legislation; that its Southern element answers conciliation only with violence; that its hope of success rests alone on a solid South, and that its triumph would make the South the ruling force of the nation. We recognize that the great body of the people who defended the Union, of whatever party name, are equally patriotic and equally interested in good government; and we earnestly invoke them to unite in resisting the dangerous designs of a party organization under the sway of those who were lately in rebellion, and seek to regain in the halls of legislation what they lost on the field of battle.

6. The successful resumption of specie payments, despite Democratic prediction and hostility, is the crowning element of the Republican financial policy. Followed by returning national prosperity, improved credit, a refunded debt, and reduced interest, it adds another to the triumphs which prove that the Republican party is equal to the highest demands. Our whole currency should be kept at par with the monetary standard of the commercial world, and any attempt to debase the standard, to depreciate the paper, or deteriorate the coin, should be firmly resisted.

7. The claims of the living and the memories of the dead defenders of the nation conjure us to protest against the partisan and unpatriotic greed which expels old Union soldiers from their well-deserved rewards and advances Confederate soldiers to their places.

8. As the pledge and proof of its economy in State administration, the Republican party, in spite of prolonged Democratic resistance, proposed and passed the constitutional amendments which restrict the expenses of the canals to their receipts, and reform the whole system of canal and prison management, and, by extinguishing the public indebtedness and relieving the people from any further tax, effected a great saving in State taxation. These fruits of Republican measures the Democrats have brazenly attempted to appropriate as their own. Appealing to the records in support of our declaration, we pronounce their claims unfounded, and hold up their authors as public impostors.

9. The inequalities of taxation, which press most upon those least able to bear them, should be remedied. To this end the Republican Legislature created a commission to revise the assessment and tax laws and to reach a class of property which now largely escapes; and we remind the people that this salutary reform was unwarrantably defeated by the present Democratic Executive.

10. Moneyed and transportation corporations are not alone the works of private enterprise, but are created for public use and with due regard to vested rights. It is the clear province and the plain duty of the State to supervise and regulate such corporations so as to secure the just and impartial treatment of all interested; to foster the industrial and agricultural welfare of the people, and with a liberal policy favor the public waterways and maintain the commercial supremacy of

the State. We look to the inquiry now in progress, under the direction of the Legislature, to develop the facts which will guide to all needed action.

The Democratic State Convention assembled at Syracuse on September 11th. J. C. Jacobs was chosen President, and the following platform was adopted:

The Democratic party of the State of New York in convention assembled, profoundly sensible of the important consequences depending upon the immediate result of their deliberations, do declare and reassert the principles of popular liberty and rights laid down by Washington, Jefferson, and other founders of the republic. We hold to the Constitution with all its amendments, sacredly maintained and enforced, and to the rights of the States under the Constitution. The tendencies of the Republican party to centralization and consolidation are contrary to the principles of our institutions. The United States form a nation in the sense, to the extent, and for the purposes defined in the Federal Constitution, and we resist every attempt to transform it into an empire. We insist on unity, fraternity, and concord, and that the issues settled by the war shall not be revived. We deprecate the efforts of the Republican managers to revive sectional feuds and to rekindle the passions of the past. We demand honest elections, and an honest count of votes. Never again, by fraud or force, shall the popular will be set aside to gratify unscrupulous partisans. The Democracy oppose all favoritism. No single interest or class of persons should be protected at the expense of others. Democracy means the government of the whole people for the whole people and by the whole people; but if any class is to receive special consideration, it should be the working people, whom all other governments oppose and crush. The rights of the people should be scrupulously protected from the encroachments of capital and the despotic greed of corporations. The Democracy believe now, as they have always believed, in gold and silver as the constitutional money of the country. We condemn the speculative methods of the present Secretary of the Treasury, the questionable favoritism he has shown to particular monetary institutions or so-called "syndicates," and the extravagance he has permitted in his department in connection with his refunding schemes. We look with shame and sorrow on the disgraceful repudiation of all their professions of civil-service reform by the Executive and his supporters. Federal offices have been freely given for despicable partisan services; leading officers of the Government are making partisan speeches, managing political campaigns, and requiring their subordinates to contribute to campaign funds, in derogation of every principle and promise of an honest civil service. The 104,000 Federal officers constitute an army, moving under a single direction, to keep the Republican party in power, and this vast patronage is now used as a corruption fund against the people. We congratulate the people of New York on the results of Democratic administration in the payment of the State debt, the reduction of expenses, and the diminished burden of taxation. We condemn the efforts of demagogues to create jealousy and antagonism between the city of New York and the rest of the State, when their interests are identical and the growth of the one is the prosperity of the other. The Democratic officers of the State of New York, by the ability and fidelity with which they have discharged their duty during the past three years, by their conscientious application of constitutional tests to the acts of every department of the State government, by their successful resistance to private and partial legislation, and by their economical conduct of the finances and reduction of expenses of the State government, have entitled themselves to the gratitude of their fellow citizens of all parties. The people of New York—farmers, manufacturers, and merchants alike—demand that they shall have all the advantages which accrue to them from their favorable position, and that the railroads they have

chartered and endowed with vast and profitable privileges shall be operated for their benefit and not for their ruin. We therefore endorse as our expression of the foregoing principles the following:

1. Honesty, efficiency, and economy in every department of the government.
2. All property should bear its just proportion of taxation, and we pledge the Democratic party to reform the laws of assessments to that end.
3. Lessening the burdens and increasing the advantages of the working people.
4. The equal protection of the rights of labor and capital under just laws.
5. The railroads prohibited by law from unjust discrimination and from favoring localities or individuals.
6. The tolls upon the canals to be kept at the lowest rates possible, consistent with economical and efficient management.
7. The maintenance of the public schools, the pride and hope of a free State.
8. Prisons for the punishment and reformation of criminals, and not for the injury of honest labor, which should be protected as far as possible from such competition.
9. Municipal self-government in local affairs.
10. That the successful efforts of our Democratic Representatives in Congress, in restoring a fair and intelligent jury system and in protecting the freedom of the ballot, and preventing the unconstitutional interference of the Federal Administration with the State elections, are approved; and the action of the Executive in vetoing the legislation designed to prevent the presence of armed soldiers and the employment of paid Federal supervisors and marshals at the polls, and the use of the public funds for this purpose, is denounced by the Democracy of the State of New York. And as the foundation of all liberty and prosperity, privileges and rights under our government, we shall continue to uphold a system of untrammeled suffrage, absolutely free from Federal force or supervision.
11. It is the duty of the State, alike in the interest of taxation, temperance, and equal and exact justice to the community, to make such revision of the excise laws as will better secure the rights of the citizens to life, liberty, property, and public order.

After the adoption of the platform, nominations for Governor were called for and made. The call of the roll was then commenced, but had not proceeded far when Mr. Augustus Schell of New York rose and said:

MR. CHAIRMAN: The delegation to which I have the honor to belong represents a large portion of the Democratic party. It is one which in past times has been ever ready, ever willing to support all the regular nominations of the Democratic party. I myself, for years, and many gentlemen who are with me, for years and years past, ever have been ready in storm and in sunshine to sustain and support that great party. We find ourselves now in a position which has been communicated to the people of this State, which has been communicated to its representatives on the floor of this Convention, that under no circumstances will the Democracy of the city of New York support the nomination of Lucius Robinson. (Great applause, groans, and hisses.) They, however, in making this announcement, desired to convey to our friends and Democrats in New York, that we were ready and willing to support any other name that they might place at the head of the ticket; but our suggestion has been unheeded, and from appearances in this Convention it has been determined that Lucius Robinson shall be nominated as Governor. I desire to further state, in behalf of my friends from New York, and in behalf of the great and noble constituency whose representatives are now present, that the rest of the ticket which shall be nominated by this Convention will receive its warm and hearty support. I desire now to announce to this Convention that the delegation from New York will retire from the hall.

The New York City delegation then left their seats and retired from the hall amid much excitement. The call of the roll of members was then concluded, with the following result: Lucius Robinson, 243; Henry W. Slocum, 56; Clarkson N. Potter, 1; Horatio Seymour, 1. Governor Robinson was thus renominated. The other nominations were: For Lieutenant-Governor, Clarkson N. Potter; for Secretary of State, Allen C. Beach; for Comptroller, Frederick P. Olcott; for State Treasurer, James Mackin; for Attorney-General, A. Schoonmaker, Jr.; for State Engineer, Horatio Seymour, Jr.

Mr. Reeves of Suffolk County moved the following resolution, which was adopted:

Resolved, That the Democratic organizations of the city and county of New York are hereby requested and authorized by this Convention to organize the Democratic voters of that city in support of the nominees of the Democratic party of the State of New York.

Mr. Tabor of Queens County offered the following, which was adopted:

Whereas, The delegates of the organization in the Democratic party in the city and county of New York, known as the Tammany Hall organization, after having been admitted to seats in this Convention, and having participated on terms of exact equality with the representatives of all other county and district organizations in the proceedings of this Convention until the time had arrived for making the nominations to the various offices to be voted for at the next general election in this State; and,

Whereas, The delegates representing such organization did, before any nomination was made and without just cause or provocation, and on the mere pretext and suspicion that the Convention was about to proceed to the nomination of a candidate for the office of Governor; and,

Whereas, Such delegates did declare that they would oppose and defeat, if it lay in their power so to do, the nominee of this Convention for the office of Governor, in the event that the choice should result in the renomination of the present able and efficient Governor, thereby bidding defiance to the will of the State organization and its representatives in convention assembled; and,

Whereas, Such voluntary withdrawal and setting at defiance the will of the Democratic party, as represented by its delegates in convention assembled, is deemed to sever all connection between said organization and the regular State organization of the Democratic party in this State: therefore, be it

Resolved, That the Democratic party of this State will not hereafter acknowledge or grant to such organization any prestige or preference over any other Democratic organization in said city and county of New York, but will hear and decide upon the merits of all claims to representation in future State Conventions as the same may arise and be presented by those claiming admission from the respective Assembly districts in said county.

Those who had retired from the Convention assembled elsewhere in the evening, and organized by the appointment of D. D. Field as President. A committee was appointed to report a plan of proceedings, who through Lieutenant-Governor Dorsheimer reported the following:

1. That the Convention now proceed to nominate a candidate for Governor.
2. That a committee of fifteen be appointed by the Chair and announced in the future, which shall be constituted with power, with reference to the remainder of the ticket, as may seem to them proper.

He then said that in nominating a candidate to be supported for Governor it became proper that he should speak of his qualifications for the office. He nominated John Kelly of New York, and went on to eulogize him as a public official. He closed by proposing that John Kelly be nominated by acclamation. The Chair put the question, and Mr. Kelly was nominated by acclamation. He then made a speech accepting the nomination.

The election was held on November 4th, and resulted as follows:

FOR GOVERNOR.

Alonzo B. Cornell, Republican	418,567
Lucius Robinson, Democrat	375,790
John Kelly, Independent Democrat	77,566
Harris Lewis, National	20,286
John W. Mears, Prohibition	4,487

FOR LIEUTENANT-GOVERNOR.

George G. Hoskins, Republican	435,804
Clarkson N. Potter, Democrat	485,014
John M. Wieting, National and Workingman	23,067
James H. Bronson, Prohibition	8,902

FOR SECRETARY OF STATE.

Joseph B. Carr, Republican	436,012
Allen C Beach, Democrat	434,188
Peter K. McCann, National and Workingman	22,558
Alphonso A. Hopkins, Prohibition	4,226

FOR COMPTROLLER.

James W. Wadsworth, Republican	433,258
Frederick P. Olcott, Democrat	432,325
John A. Shannon, National and Workingman	22,572
Caleb W. Allis, Prohibition	4,192

FOR TREASURER.

Nathan D. Wendell, Republican	436,800
James Mackin, Democrat	433,485
Julian Winnie, National and Workingman	21,646
Stephen Merritt, Prohibition	4,149

FOR ATTORNEY-GENERAL.

Hamilton Ward, Republican	437,382
Augustus Schoonmaker, Democrat	433,238
James Wright, National and Workingman	21,961
Walter Farrington, Prohibition	4,073

FOR STATE ENGINEER AND SURVEYOR.

Howard Soule, Republican	427,940
Horatio Seymour, Jr., Democrat	439,681
Garrett Nagle, National and Workingman	22,779
John J. Hooker, Prohibition	4,048

The vote on the proposed amendment to section 6, Article VI., of the Constitution, to authorize an additional Judge of the Second Judicial District, was as follows: For the amendment, 95,331; against the amendment, 25,578. The Legislature was divided as follows:

PARTIES.	Senate.	House.
Republicans	25	92
Democrats	8	85
National	..	1
Total	33	128

NIHILISTS. This is the term commonly used to designate the active members of the revolutionary party in Russia. It is often applied to any persons who are implicated in the social and political disturbances with which the empire is afflicted, and is even sometimes made to embrace all who participate in the agitation for a change in the system of government of the country; but in its proper sense it belongs only to those who are supposed to be acting under the direction of a secret revolutionary committee, of which nothing is known beyond what it directs or permits to be published of itself. The names Nihilists and Nihilism did not originate with the party, but were given to express contempt of the latter, because they sought the destruction of the existing order without proposing or seeming to contemplate the substitution of any defined scheme of organization in its place. So far as is known, they were first employed by the novelist Ivan Turgenieff in his stories of Russian society. Russia has been peculiarly exposed to conspiracies and insurrections. The despotic policy of the Government toward the people of annexed or non-Russian provinces has provoked frequent outbreaks. Among its own people, an autocratic administration permeating every department of public life has left no room for the legitimate discussion of political and social questions, in which the active minds of freer countries find healthful exercise; and such minds in Russia, for the want of a better field of activity, have busied themselves with inventing religious heresies and in secret plottings.

The first notable manifestation of the secret political societies was the insurrection of December, 1825, at the beginning of the reign of Nicholas I., which aimed at overthrowing the Czardom and establishing a constitutional form of government. Though the insurrection was suppressed, those engaged in it continued to disseminate their views, and their party quietly gathered strength. One of their leaders, Alexander Hertzen, achieved considerable fame by the energy and boldness with which he spread his revolutionary writings in Russia. He died in 1870. (See "Annual Cyclopædia" for 1870, article HERTZEN.) The earliest advocate of the present doctrines of Nihilism was Michael Bakunin, a member of a rich family of high rank, and a near relative of men prominent at the court and in the army. He was born in 1814, advocated a Russian republic in 1847, and in 1868 founded the "International Alliance of the European Revolution." He died at Geneva in 1876. (See "Annual Cyclopædia" for 1876, article BAKUNIN.) Societies were formed in Russia for the advocacy of the views taught by Hertzen, as the Young Russia, Land and Freedom, etc., whose newspaper organs, the "Sovremiennik" and the "Ruskoie Slowo," enjoyed considerable freedom of circulation under the relaxed press restrictions which prevailed from 1858 to 1872, but were finally suppressed.

In consequence of the general dissatisfaction which prevailed after the Crimean war, the new Emperor Alexander entered upon a more liberal policy of government than had prevailed. The abolition of serfdom was resolved upon as a measure that would improve the condition of the people and conciliate a large mass of them, while it would not infringe upon the absolute sovereignty exercised by the Czar. Representative assemblies began to be talked of, and the nobility were authorized to choose committees to discuss the subject of emancipation. Demands were made in connection with the meeting of some of these committees for a general assembly, for chartered provincial assemblies, for the responsibility of officers to the law, and other features of constitutional and representative government. The Government refused to entertain any of these demands, but manifested its displeasure toward those committees. The deputies of the committees, when they went to the capital with their reports, were not permitted to meet for discussion, or to present objections or propose amendments to the plan which had been laid before them, but were confined to a list of printed questions which they were requested to answer in writing. Thus every attempt to obtain a representative body, or to secure liberty to discuss administrative questions, was put down. Persons of the higher and more intelligent classes who had become interested in such questions were driven to associate with those who sought to accomplish by revolutionary methods what they had found it impracticable to bring about by legal means. The Nihilist party is largely made up of persons of this class. To these are added those who are dissatisfied with the measures of the Government from the act of emancipation down to the war with Turkey, or are disgusted with the corruption which prevails; unruly students; and such uneasy spirits as are called socialists, communists, or red republicans in other countries. The existence of a revolutionary conspiracy was established in 1877, when, after a great trial lasting eighteen months, 135 persons out of 183 who had been arrested were found guilty of belonging to such an organization. The Nihilists began to attract attention as a really formidable organization soon after the trial of Vera Sassulitch in 1878 for shooting at General Trepoff, chief of the secret police. (See "Annual Cyclopædia" for 1878, article RUSSIA.) Her acquittal by a jury of presumed responsibility and conservatism, after she had avowed the offense, and in the face of the evidence and the law, seemed to excite them to activity. A season of uprisings, assassinations, and terror ensued, the disorders of which were only partially arrested after the Government had applied measures of extreme severity for several months. The assassination of General Mezentzoff, who succeeded General Trepoff, was avowed by the Nihilists as their work. Their journal, "Land and Liberty," published an account of the offenses for which he had been adjudged to deserve death, in which it said that he had trampled right under foot, tortured his prisoners, persecuted the innocent, and in his official capacity murdered by brutal ill-treatment, by hunger, thirst, and the rod, a number of persons whose names were given. The assassination of Prince Krapotch-kin, Governor of Kharkov, who was shot February 22, 1879, was explained in a Nihilist circular as having been on account of certain inhuman acts which he had committed against prisoners under his charge. "Death for death, execution for execution, terror for terror," said the circular; "this is our answer to the threats, the persecutions, and the oppressions of the Government. Should the latter persevere in its old course, the bodies of Heyking [commander of gendarmerie at Kiev, who was also killed by Nihilists] and Mezentzoff will not have turned into dust before the Government will hear from us again." General Drenteln, chief of the gendarmerie, was shot at, March 25th, and was warned that he could not escape. In reference to this act, "Land and Liberty" said: "It is not necessary to recapitulate Drenteln's crimes. He deserves death for this alone—that he has been chief of gendarmes during this period of repression." Leon Mirsky, the perpetrator of this act, when tried for it in November, acknowledged what he had done, and only pleaded that he had acted not as a common murderer, but for public reasons and under the orders of a committee which he was bound to obey. The number and character of the victims who were assassinated or attacked under the orders of this mysterious committee was so great in the several towns of the empire as to give a color of foundation to the opinion that a settled purpose existed to spread terror and deter any one from serving the Government in a capacity involving functions of police. The period of murders was followed by one of arson, when whole towns were burned with an enormous destruction of property, the excess of which beyond the average amount of destruction by ordinary incendiarism was ascribed to the instigation of the Nihilists.

Nihilist societies began to be formed in 1859, among the students of the Agricultural College of Petrovski, near Moscow, who had adopted the materialistic views taught by Büchner in his "Force and Matter," and the socialistic views expounded by the German writer Max Stirner, in his "Property and the Individual." Both these books were prohibited by the Government, but that only caused them to be more in demand, and a lithographed translation of the "Force and Matter" was passed around from hand to hand. Other works of similar tendency were read by these students, among them Buckle's "History of Civilization." The first political murder took place at this institution, when one of the students was killed by Netchayeff. The Government, alarmed by this event, treated the students with severity, keeping many of them in prison for years without trial. Among the persons who suffered was Vera Sassulitch, who was a friend of Netchayeff's sister. These persecutions caused the Nihilists to gain many adherents among the people and among literary men. One of the latter class who joined them was Tcherny-

tchevsky, whose novel, "What is to be Done?" is regarded as a kind of text-book of Nihilism. After the Franco-German war the Nihilists adopted the Panslavist cause, but the acquittal of Vera Sassulitch again directed their attention to home affairs. In their later operations they have been drawn further away from Panslavism, the influence of which is rather on the side of imperial ambition, and they now represent the reverse tendency in its extreme.

The fact has been brought to light in the course of the trials of Nihilists that a very large proportion of the party is composed of graduates, students, and persons who have not been able to complete their studies. This circumstance is accounted for as the effect of changes which have been made by the Government in the regulation of university studies. These regulations were greatly relaxed, and the facilities for entering the universities were enlarged at one time, so that the halls of the schools were crowded with students of moderate means. Afterward the standards of examination were made more rigorous, so that the students who had been drawn to the colleges, finding they would not be able to enter the civil service, suddenly dropped their studies, and, being without position or prospects, yielded to the persuasions of political agitators.

The doctrines and objects of the Nihilists must be gathered from the expressions of their leaders and their own declarations of purpose. Michael Bakunin, who is regarded as the founder of the doctrines of the party, in a speech at Geneva in 1868, announced himself the bearer of a new gospel, the mission of which was to destroy the Lie, the beginning of which was God. Having got rid of this belief, the next lie to be destroyed was Right, a fiction invented by Might in order to insure and strengthen her reign. Might formed the sole groundwork of society, made and unmade laws; therefore, our first work, he said, "must be destruction and annihilation of everything as it now exists," the good with the bad; "for if but an atom of this old world remains, the new will never be created." He detested communism, advocated the abolition of marriage and inheritance, and taught that conscience was a mere matter of education. Another Nihilist, in a speech, sought to justify the deeds of political assassins and incendiaries, on the ground of the necessity of rooting out from men's minds the habitual respect for the powers that be. In March, 1876, several Nihilist proclamations were seized in Prussia while on their way to Russia, in one of which were these instructions: "You should only allow yourself to be influenced in the selection of your victims by the relative use which the Revolution would derive from the death of any particular person. In the foremost rank of such cases stand those people who are most dangerous and injurious to our organization, and whose sudden and violent death would have the effect of terrifying the Government and shaking its power by robbing it of energetic and intelligent servants. The only revolution which can remedy the ills of the people is that which will tear up every notion of government by its very roots, and which will upset all ranks of the Russian Empire with all their traditions. Having this object in view, the Revolutionary Committee does not propose subjecting the people to any directing organization. The future order of things will doubtless originate with the people themselves; but we must leave that to future generations. Our mission is only one of universal, relentless, and terror-striking destruction. The object of our organization and of our conspiracy is to concentrate all the forces of this world into an invincible and all-destroying power." It is believed that the number of persons who hold to these principles and act upon them is in reality comparatively small, and that they owe their power to the neutral attitude of the Russians of the middle and upper classes, who, while they will not help them, refuse at the same time to lend any support to the present system of government.

The Nihilists seem to act under the direction of a secret executive, whose authority is exercised in the most positive and direct manner, and whose orders are implicitly obeyed by the individual members of the party. Their government is also said to be divided into sections, each of which acts independently of the others, and the members of which and the place of meeting are changed often, so as to avoid discovery and preserve an effective organization of all the members in case one of the boards should be captured. Each section has the right of pronouncing sentence of death upon dangerous or suspected persons, and is instructed to enter into as close relations as possible with members of high society. For this purpose, a plan has been adopted of placing women belonging to the conspiracy, whenever it can be done, as governesses in the families of high functionaries; and under their machinations and influence numerous women of that class have been imbued with Nihilistic doctrines and drawn into connection with plots, so that the heads of their families have been embarrassed and rendered unable to act against the movement. The Nihilists have carried on their operations with great boldness, and have kept themselves prominent before the public everywhere in the empire; yet they have preserved their secrecy with marvelous success. The whole country has been flooded with their proclamations and handbills; their warnings and notices have been posted on the walls of public places in defiance of the vigilance of the police, and posted up again just after they were taken down, and have been deposited in the public offices; yet the agents by whom these things were done could seldom be detected. Some wildly exaggerated stories and many that had no foundation have been circulated on this subject. Newspapers are published in the interests of the Nihilists in Lon-

don and Geneva, and in Russia. They are said to be sustained mainly from the proceeds of a bequest producing 60,000 rubles a year, which a friend of the cause left for that purpose. The principal journal is the "Zerulia i Svaboda" ("Land and Liberty"), which is published at St. Petersburg once or twice a month, and is said to have regular subscribers, although the police have not been able to find its office. It is an official organ of the Executive Committee, and is the chief medium through which the principles of the organization are promulgated, its warnings given out, and the reasons for its acts explained after they have been committed.

The purposes of a part of the Nihilists have gradually acquired shape, and they are understood to embrace now the establishment of a constitutional representative government, with all the forms of political life as they are enjoyed in other countries, and such as Russia has herself caused to be given to Bulgaria. In 1878 publications appeared in all the cities of the empire denouncing the highest officers for malfeasance, and demanding a constitution, the suppression of the Emperor's private chancellery or secret police, the abolition of corporal punishment in prisons, and reforms in the procedure and administration of justice. The removal of about two hundred officers was demanded by name; and the proclamations continued: "Since we are unable to obtain any redress in a legal way, and that because in Russia not the Czar, but those about the Czar, really govern the country, we shall, unless attention is paid to our wishes, enter upon the illegal way, and we shall shoot, stab, and murder until our demands are satisfied and the Camarilla is swept from the face of the earth." At first they declared that they did not intend any injury to the Czar, and no threat was made against him till a short time before the attempt upon his life by Solovieff in April, 1879, when a proclamation was posted in St. Petersburg telling "Alexander Nicolaievitch" that the warnings and sentences which "the invisible delegates of the murderously oppressed Russian people have sent to the various dignitaries of the present despotic government in Russia belong, as a rule, to the preparative work," and that for that reason neither the Czar nor any member of his family had as yet been threatened, but cautioning him "against upholding the tyranny which the revolutionaries are combating," and warning him that he was "getting into dangerously deep waters." The newspaper "Land and Liberty" declared that Solovieff had no connection with the Executive Committee, but belonged to a distinct band of revolutionists; but it threatened death to any persons who should be concerned in torturing him, if, to obtain information, that process should be resorted to. It also reviewed the condition of affairs which had produced the present situation, and alienated from the Czar the sympathy and affection of his people. Seat.

ing himself on the blood-stained throne of his late father, it said, the Emperor Alexander II. had pledged himself to beneficial reforms, and raised great expectations; but the only result had been bitter disappointment. There was not a section of the Russian world which did not revolt at the prevailing system of administrative corruption and grinding tyranny. The peasantry suffered more than ever, were distressed for arrears of taxes, had been robbed of the lands which they had cultivated for themselves as serfs, were plundered by those who had the management of affairs, were reduced to absolute wretchedness, suffered from chronic famine, were drafted in larger numbers into the army, and now found consolation only in drink. In place of free institutions, which Russian society had been led to expect at the beginning of the present reign, there was nothing but administrative tyranny and outrageous injustice. All individual rights and the rights of humanity were denied or trampled down with pitiless cruelty. The courts of justice were a mockery, while the press subserved an odious system of government. Education was reduced to an absurdity; the elementary schools had been diminished in number, and learning had become almost impossible, while Russia had been drained of all her money and resources, her population had declined, thousands of men had been put into bonds, and generals conspicuously incapable, from the Commander-in-Chief downward, had led the Russian army to the shambles.

A few weeks later the Revolutionary Committee issued a new address to the Russian people. It began with the assertion that the object of the party was to effect a radical change in the social and political conditions of Russia, and to awaken in the nation a consciousness of its rights. To attain this end, it continued, the people must be instructed as to the " criminal intentions " of the ruling classes. When Russians recognize the true cause of their melancholy position, they will soon find the means of fighting for their liberation; they will also learn that their business is not to "drive the Turks from Europe and to uphold the Slavs because they are of the same race and faith," but to improve their own circumstances, and to cease " placing their blood and possessions at the service of a clique which thinks of nothing but its personal advantage." " We have lost many brothers," it concluded; " over their beloved graves let us clasp hands in fraternal union, and let us appeal to the people when the destined hour shall have struck." A pamphlet containing Nihilist poetry was published about the same time, and a posthumous poem by the Nihilist Nekrassoff was announced.

By the aid of minute and severe police regulations instituted in all the large towns, the Government succeeded in suppressing seditious publications for several months, and there seemed to be an intermission in the attacks upon public officers. Almost the only signs that the conspiracy continued to live were observed in the conflagrations, and even these were less numerous than they had been. The revolutionists, however, still nursed their plans, but prosecuted them in such a manner as should not for the time afford any clew to their movements. The first number of a new revolutionary paper, entitled " The Will of the People," appeared in the latter part of October. It was very violent in its tone. The attempt at Moscow on the 2d of December to blow up the train on which the Czar was traveling was followed by the appearance of a manifesto from the Revolutionary Committee, in which attention was directed to Alexander II. as the personification of a despicable despotism.

NORTH CAROLINA. The Legislature of North Carolina commenced its biennial session at Raleigh on January 8th. In the Senate Lieutenant-Governor Jarvis presided; and in the House John M. Moring was chosen Speaker by 68 votes to 27 for R. M. Norment. The Speaker is a native of Chatham County, and represented it in the Legislature at three previous sessions.

Among the measures of the session was an act to abolish private seals and to prescribe a short form of deed for the conveyance of real estate, which is important, as follows:

Whereas, The necessity for the use of the word " heirs " to carry a fee-simple estate is a relic of feudalism and an unnecessary technicality ; and,

Whereas, The reason for using private seals has long since ceased, and the present forms of deeds is [are] complex and lengthy, thereby unduly increasing the cost of registration ; therefore,

The General Assembly of North Carolina do enact :

SECTION 1. That all instruments hitherto requiring a private seal shall be as good and available in law for all purposes as if sealed. And all instruments not requiring an official seal shall be as valid to all intents and purposes in law as if the same had been sealed.

SEC. 2. That in every conveyance of real property, a fee simple shall be presumed to be transferred, unless the instrument shall expressly confer in terms a less estate.

SEC. 3. That the following form shall be sufficient as a deed for real property within the meaning of this act.

Received (of the buyer) ——— $———, in full for (describe the property).
(Dated.)
                                    (Signed by seller.)

SEC. 4. That such deed shall, without express words, import a general warranty, but any other covenants may be inscribed by the parties, or it may operate as a quitclaim if it shall be so expressed.

SEC. 5. That the fee of the clerk for acknowledgment and probate of deeds, including the privy examination of wife (if any), shall be ten cents ; and the fee of the Register of Deeds shall be for registering the same, twenty cents.

By another act it was provided that when real estate shall be conveyed to any person, the same shall be held and construed to be a conveyance in fee, whether the word " heirs " shall be used or not, unless such conveyance shall, in plain and express words, show, or it shall be plainly intended by the conveyance, or some part thereof, that the grantor meant to convey an estate of less dignity.

A tramp is defined to be any person going about from place to place begging and asking or subsisting on charity, and such shall be punished by imprisonment in the county prison not more than six months; but any person who shall furnish satisfactory evidence of good character shall be discharged without cost. Any act of begging or vagrancy by any person, unless such are well-known objects of charity, shall be evidence that the person committing the same is a tramp within the meaning of the act. The blind and minors under fourteen years are exempted from the provisions of the law.

The act to raise revenue reduced the poll-tax from 89 to 72 cents. The tax on real and personal property, moneys, credits, investments in bonds, stocks, joint-stock companies, or otherwise, was reduced from 29⅜ to 24 cents, to be applied as follows: 12 instead of 14⅜ cents to the general fund; 6 in place of 9 cents to the Insane and Deaf and Dumb and Blind Asylums; 6 cents as heretofore to the Penitentiary. The tax on billiard-saloons is $20 on each table, but hereafter every place where liquor is sold is considered a billiard-saloon. Retail liquor-dealers are to pay a monthly license-tax of $5 instead of $3 as before; and retailers of malt liquors only $3, instead of $1.50, as before. "Any grocer, druggist, dealer, or other person who shall sell spiritous or malt liquors, wines, or cordials, in any quantity, if the same or any portion thereof shall at any time be drunk upon the premises where such liquors, wines, or cordials are sold, shall be considered to be a retail dealer within the meaning of the act." Every person or company running sleeping-cars upon any railroad in the State is to pay $50 yearly for every car so run, and shall make returns and pay to the State Treasurer. Penalty for non-compliance, $2,000. Tobacco-warehousemen, instead of a license-tax of $50, are to pay $15 and 1 per cent. on gross amount of their commissions on all sales of tobacco in excess of 300,000 pounds. Any merchant, dealer, or agent selling sewing-machines shall pay a tax of $10 in each county, but the payment of a license-tax of $200 to the State Treasurer will enable any person, company, or manufacturer of sewing-machines to peddle them in any county, employing any number of agents, free of county or municipal tax. A peddlers' license-tax of $10 is hereafter good for a year instead of six months. Itinerant lightning-rod men are to pay $50 instead of $10 for each county. Drummers are to pay $100 annually instead of $50. The liquor-dealers' drummers are to pay $200. Marriage licenses are reduced from $1 to 50 cents.

Children of colored parents born at any time before the first day of January, 1868, of persons living together as man and wife, are legitimate children of such parents or either one of them, with all the rights of heirs at law and next of kin, with respect to the estate or estates of any such parents, or either one of them.

Another act provides that the clerk of a court of record in any other State may act as a commissioner of affidavits and deeds, exercising the same powers as heretofore granted to regularly appointed commissioners for the State.

The debt of the State, as reported to the Legislature by the State Treasurer, was as follows:

1. Bonds issued before the war, known as "old" bonds	$8,871,400	00
Interest due on same	5,007,580	50
Total	$13,878,980	50
2. Bonds issued since the war by authority of acts before the war	$1,774,000	00
Interest due on same	1,015,890	00
Total	$2,789,890	00
3. Bonds issued since the war, by authority of ordinances of Convention, and acts of the General Assembly, passed since the war	$2,012,045	00
Interest due on same	1,160,778	35
Total	$3,172,818	35

4. Bonds issued under funding acts of March 10, 1866, and August 20, 1868:

Funding act of 1868	$2,231,000		
Interest due on same	1,810,262		
		3,541,262	00
Funding act of 1862	$1,657,600		
Interest due on same	990,987		
		2,648,587	00
Total		$6,189,849	00

5. Bonds issued during the war, by authority of acts passed before the war, for internal improvement purposes, to which are added $215,000 issued for Chatham Railroad under ordinance of Convention of January 30, 1862:

	914,000	00
Interest due on same	674,690	00
Total	$1,588,690	00
Total principal of debt, exclusive of special tax bonds	$16,960,045	00
Total amount of interest due	10,160,182	85
Total amount of principal and interest	$27,120,227	85

The principal of the "old" or ante-war debt, as shown in the foregoing classification, is $8,371,400. Of this amount, $2,794,000 were issued for the construction of the North Carolina Railroad. Deducting this amount, there remains as principal $5,577,400. The interest on this class, which is reported at $5,007,580.50, is subject to a deduction of the amount paid by the receiver of the dividends from the North Carolina Railroad Company.

On March 4th the Legislature passed an act "to compromise, commute, and settle the State debt." On the bonds issued before the war (except for the North Carolina Railroad) it proposed to pay 40 per cent. of the principal. The principal of this old debt, less the North Carolina Railroad bonds ($2,794,000), is $5,577,400. These bonds were given for:

Fayette and Western Plankroad	$50,500
Gaston and Weldon Railroad	25,000
Fayette and Center Plankroad	45,000
Fayette and Warsaw Plankroad	10,000
Tar River	15,000
Insane Asylum	70,000
A. and N. C. Railroad	1,351,500
A. and C. Canal	324,000
Western Railroad	856,000
Western N. C. Railroad	1,136,000
W. C. and R. Railroad	1,012,000
"Certain purposes"	1,009,400
C., F. and D. R. Navigation Company	148,000
Total	$5,577,400
Amount payable at 40 per cent.	2,230,960

Some bonds are made redeemable at 25 per cent., as follows:

Western N. C. Railroad	$1,907,000
W. C. and R. Railroad	887,000
Western Railroad	134,000
Literary Board certificates	838,045
Total	$3,261,045
Amount payable at 25 per cent	$815,261.25

Bonds on which it is proposed to pay 15 per cent. of the principal are:

Funding State debt	$2,331,000
" " interest	1,657,600
Total	$3,988,600
Amount payable at 15 per cent	598,290
Total proposed payment	$8,644,511.25

The settlement is to be made by giving in exchange for outstanding bonds, as above, new thirty-year coupon bonds, dated July 1, 1880, bearing 4 per cent. interest, payable at the Treasurer's office on the first day of January and July of each year thereafter. The new bonds are to be of $50, $100, and $1,000 each, are exempt from all State, county, or corporate taxation, and the coupons are to be received for all State taxes. To the payment of interest on them are to be applied all State taxes collected from professions, trades, incomes, merchants, dealers in cigars, and three fourths of all taxes collected from wholesale and retail dealers in spirituous, vinous, and malt liquors. If these taxes are in excess of interest to be paid, the surplus is to be invested in the purchase of the new bonds; if insufficient, the Treasurer is authorized to use any funds he may have, not otherwise appropriated; if still short, forty-year $500 bonds may be issued to the amount of $300,000. It is made "lawful for any executor, administrator, guardian, trustee, director of any corporation, and any and all other persons acting in a fiduciary capacity, holding bonds of the State, to make the exchange provided for in the act, and they shall be absolved from all liability on account of said exchange." The Treasurer is authorized to expend $5,000 for bonds, etc., and to advertise the law in such papers as he may select.

The bonds not provided for in this law are:

N. C. Railroad construction	$2,794,000
Chatham Railroad	1,030,000
Williamston and Tarboro Railroad	150,000
Penitentiary	44,000
Chatham Railroad	215,000
Western N. C. Railroad, special tax	7,960,000
W. C. and R. Railroad, special tax	3,000,000
Williamston and Tarboro Railroad, special tax	300,000
A. T. and O. Railroad, special tax	106,000
Total	$15,599,000

Of this amount the North Carolina Railroad bonds, secured by mortgage of the State stock, are provided for in the following act, as is the item of $150,000 for the Williamston and Tarboro road, leaving $12,655,000 of debt that the State does not acknowledge as debt. In the debt provided for by the act is an item of $324,000 for bonds issued for the Albemarle and Chesapeake Canal, which is also provided for by separate act authorizing their redemption by exchange for the State's stock in the canal.

This act of the Legislature was so acceptable to the bondholders that by August 1st about $4,000,000 of the old debt had been retired, and was represented by only $1,120,000 in the new bonds.

On March 14th the Legislature passed another act "to adjust and renew a portion of the State debt"; that is, to provide for the redemption of the North Carolina Railroad construction bonds, secured by a lien on the State's stock of $3,000,000 in that road. These bonds amount to $2,794,000, of which $496,000 is due on January 1, 1883; $481,000 on July 1, 1883; $455,000 on January 1, 1884; $118,000 on July 1, 1884; $305,000 on January 1, 1885; and $939,000 on April 1st of the same year. Unpaid interest, accrued before the North Carolina Railroad fell into the hands of the courts, amounts to some $600,000 more. Under this act, the Governor of the State is authorized to appoint three commissioners, who are to negotiate with the bondholders terms of renewal with new bonds, subject to approval by the Governor and Treasurer. They are to give well-secured $50,000 bonds, and are to receive from the bondholders for their services one half of one per cent. commission on all the bonds redeemed. For the redemption of the outstanding bonds, new $50, $100, $500, $1,000 forty-year coupon bonds, bearing not greater than six per cent. interest, are to be issued. The new may be exchanged for the old, or may be sold at not less than par and proceeds invested in old bonds at rates not greater than are allowed in the exchange. The new bonds are to be exempt from any and all taxation, and are to be secured as the old by the lien on the State's stock in the North Carolina Railroad, the dividends on which are to be applied to the payment of the coupons, which are also receivable in payment of all taxes, debts, dues, licenses, fines, and demands due the State of every kind whatsoever. All persons acting in a fiduciary character, holding any of the construction bonds, are authorized to exchange them for the new, and all such persons are also authorized to invest funds in the purchase of the new. The commissioners are to hold all the bonds and coupons delivered to or purchased by them "in trust for the payment of the principal and interest on the said new bonds, and shall collect and receive all payments and dividends paid and made on said old bonds and coupons so held by them from any person authorized to pay the same; and shall pay the amounts thus received to the Public Treasurer, to be applied by him to the payment of the interest on the new bonds. The old bonds shall not be canceled, but shall remain in force until the Governor shall direct the same to be delivered to the Public Treasurer for cancellation."

Another act for the settlement of the State debt was passed on March 14th. It authorizes the State Treasurer to exchange with the Albemarle and Chesapeake Canal Company the stock of the State in said company for the bonds of North Carolina issued before the 20th day of May, 1861; the exchange to be at par, and no interest to be allowed upon the bonds. The exchange must be made, if at all, by January 1, 1880.

By another act convicts are to be apportioned among the works of internal improvement authorized to receive them, but in no case are there to be less than five hundred on the Western North Carolina Railroad, nor less than three hundred on the Cape Fear and Yadkin Valley road; and all convicts are to be kept at work on State roads until called for by those authorized to have them.

A fine or imprisonment at the discretion of the Court, or fifteen years in the penitentiary, has been made the penalty for abducting or inducing to leave, or conspiring with another to abduct or induce to leave, any child under fourteen years residing with father, or mother, or uncle, or aunt, or brother, or elder sister, or at school, or with a guardian. The only exemption is to the abductor or inducer who may be of nearer kin to the abducted than the abductee.

The probate judge, sheriff, and county commissioners of each county are "a committee for the relief of the blind and maimed." It is made the duty of the probate judge to notify all persons in his county who lost sight, or both hands, or both feet in the Confederate service, that on proof of the fact before the committee they are entitled to receive from him $5 monthly for life.

It was made unlawful for any fire-insurance company, unless investing all its assets within the State, to transact any business or receive any premium against loss by fire unless and until it has deposited with the Public Treasurer $10,000 in United States bonds. On this deposit, in case of a company's failure to satisfy a final judgment against it, the Treasurer is to raise money enough to pay judgment, interest, and costs; and thereafter the company must make its margin good or cease to do business. This law applies to existing judgments.

Any person who habitually, whether continuously or periodically, indulges in the use of intoxicating liquors to such an extent as to stupefy his mind and to render him incompetent to transact ordinary business with safety to his estate, shall be deemed an inebriate within the meaning of the statute, provided the habit of so indulging has continued a year.

Tar shall be hereafter sold by weight, at the rate of 280 pounds to the barrel, under the same rules that apply to turpentine as to excess of weight.

A bill to revise and consolidate the school law was introduced in the House on the 27th of February, passed its three readings, and was ordered to be engrossed and sent to the Senate for concurrence. It was accordingly transmitted to the Senate, passed its three readings in that House, was enrolled, subjected to the examination of the Committee on Enrolled Bills, and

reported by them as correctly enrolled. The journals further show that it was duly ratified and transmitted to the office of the Secretary of State on the last day of the session, together with a large number of other acts. Upon ascertaining after the adjournment of the Legislature that the signatures of the presiding officers were wanting, the Secretary did not feel authorized to receive it as a law. This question was presented by the facts: Is it the duty of the presiding officers to sign the bill after the adjournment of the General Assembly, they still being members and presiding officers, with a term of office of two years, commencing from the time of their election as members? The presiding officers declined to sign the bill because the Legislature had adjourned, and stated that they supposed they then had no power to do it. The Secretary of State declined to receive it, as it was not signed. The Superintendent of Public Instruction applied to the State Attorney-General for his opinion. He said:

The Constitution commands them to sign all bills which have passed three readings in each House; and while it is usual and proper that this should be done during the session, yet the law does not prohibit them from signing after adjournment in a case where the facts and circumstances, such as the above, so fully show the necessity for it, and so clearly justify it. The evidence in this case is plenary that the bill passed. The part taken by the two Houses has satisfied the requirement of the Constitution so far as they are concerned. Their presiding officers should now perform the part which the same instrument requires of them—affix their signatures that the law may be valid and operative. Even although the bill has "passed into a law" by the concurrence of the Houses, yet it amounts to nothing without the signatures of the presiding officers; and their signatures to a bill which has not passed amount to nothing if it affirmatively appears from the journals that it did not pass. The Constitution requires both the passage and the signatures to give life to the enactment. The signatures are an additional means and constitutional method of authentication, and can not be dispensed with, because the Constitution says, "and shall be signed by the presiding officers of the two Houses."

Suppose the bill to raise and collect revenue had passed under the facts and circumstances attending the school bill, and had not been signed; would the Governor incur the expense to the public of convening the Legislature in extraordinary session, that it may be again considered in order to get funds to carry on the government? or would the Speakers sign after adjournment? or would the necessity arise to institute an action to compel them by mandamus to perform the ministerial act of writing their names? I take it they have no discretion about signing a bill, whether they approve the wisdom of the legislation or not; and it seems to be clear, therefore, that a mandamus would lie in case of refusal. (Cotten vs. Ellis, 7 Jones, 545; Bailey vs. Caldwell, 68 N. C., 472.) And furthermore, if this law remains inoperative by reason of the failure to sign as aforesaid, it amounts to the exercise of a power not granted to any officer of our State government. It would be in effect a veto, and brought about by non-action.

Legal proceedings were commenced to compel the President of the Senate and the Speaker of the House to sign the school bill. On the relation of the Superintendent of Public Instruction, in his official capacity and as a tax-payer, and of the Attorney-General, an application for a writ of *mandamus* was made, and the action thus instituted. The case was called before Judge Earl of the Circuit Court. Both plaintiffs and defendants were ably and fully represented. This being the first time that defendants had been called to answer, they moved for leave to withdraw their answer and substitute a demurrer. Objected to by plaintiffs, but afterward admitted by the Judge. The demurrer objected that the complaint did not state that the signing by the defendants was essential to the validity of the act. The Judge ruled that expressions in the complaint, such as "required by law to authenticate," etc., were sufficient to express the same or a sufficiently equivalent answer, and overruled the demurrer. Exception by defendants. The answer was then filed. In the settlement of the issues the Judge ruled that he could not take the admissions of defendants as conclusively settling the facts on which a public statute might depend, and ruled that the plaintiffs must produce proof. It was agreed that the Judge should try all questions of fact, a jury being waived. The plaintiffs disclaimed charging any intentional wrong-doing by the President of the Senate or the Speaker of the House, and the testimony established the fact that the announcement that the presiding officers had signed the bill was made during the absence of those officers while engaged in the library signing the various bills handed to them by the Committee on Enrolled Bills in the last hours of the session; and the defendants stated that the absence of their signatures to the bill was not called to their attention until after the adjournment of the Legislature, and based their refusal to sign afterward upon the ground that the Legislature had adjourned; that they could not sign except in the presence of the two Houses; that it was a legislative act, and their signing would be a departure from the uniform custom of the General Assembly. The Judge decided that the *mandamus* issue to compel the President of the Senate and the Speaker of the House to sign the bill known as the school bill. An appeal was taken to the Supreme Court. A similar *mandamus* was demanded by the Superintendent against the Secretary of State commanding him to receive the bill. But the Court decided that the Secretary could not be compelled to receive the bill until it was signed.

In September the Supreme Court rendered its decision in the case, holding: 1. That the presiding officers of the General Assembly should sign a bill before it becomes a law, and should do so during the session of the General Assembly; and, 2. That affixing their signature by the Speakers to a bill is the finishing act of legislation, and is not under the control of the Court. This decision was based on two general principles: first, that the executive, judicial, and legislative departments are ever to be kept separate; and, secondly, that the sign-

VOL. XIX.—44 A

ing by the Speakers is a legislative act. Until this legislative act is complete, the legislation remains unfinished; and if the legislation be unfinished, the bill is not finally passed so as to be a law. The bill not having been passed into a law, neither the Speakers nor the Court, nor any other person or power, can make it a law after the adjournment of the Assembly. The decision is a complete vindication of the conduct of the Speakers in withholding their signatures when the fact was made known to them that the bill remained unsigned after the Legislature had adjourned. Had they, subsequent to the adjournment of the Assembly, gone on and set their names to the unpassed bill, it would not have helped matters; the bill would still have been in its old category of an incomplete legislative enactment.

The number of public schools taught during the school year of 1878 was 3,354 for white and 1,707 for colored people. Number of white pupils in attendance, 145,155; colored, 81,290. The average length of school terms was nine weeks, and the average monthly salary of teachers amounted to $23.24¼. During the year, among the whites, 745 certificates of the first grade, 1,295 of the second, and 446 of the third were issued. With the colored people it stood 169 of the first, 415 of the second, and 652 of the third. The following were the receipts of the school fund for the year: From State Treasurer, $808.94; poll-tax, $168,-566.92; property-tax, $122,990.89; fines, forfeitures, and penalties, $13,189.65; liquor licenses, $21,159.34; auctioneers' tax, $102.52; other sources, $15,945.35. Balance on hand at the close of last school year, $108,050.06. Total, including balance on hand, $450,818.61. The following shows the disbursements for the same year: Paid for white schools, $187,390.-81; colored, $104,026.21; for school-houses and sites, for whites, $8,887.57; colored, $3,-976.47; to county examiners, $1,200.80; treasurers' commissions, $9,994.26; clerks of county boards of education, $2,260.78; insolvent taxes refunded, $1,242.49; other purposes, $3,760.-57. Total disbursements, $322,711.96. Balance on hand September 1, 1878, $129,362.82. The University Normal School was opened on June 18th for a session of about six weeks, with 12 instructors and 500 students.

In an amendment to an act relating to railroads, it was enacted that it shall be unlawful for railroad companies operating in the State to pool freights, or to allow rebates on freights; and all persons, whether railroad officials or others, who shall be concerned in the pooling of freights, or who shall directly or indirectly allow or accept rebates on freights, shall be guilty of a misdemeanor, and on conviction shall be fined not less than one thousand dollars and imprisoned not less than twelve months.

On January 21st an election of a Senator in Congress was made by the Legislature. In the Senate, Governor Vance received 33 votes to 12 for R. P. Buxton and 1 for A. G. Merrimon. In the House, he received 77 votes to 39 for Buxton and 2 scattering. On the 28th he tendered his resignation of the office of Governor, and on February 5th was succeeded by Lieutenant-Governor Thomas J. Jarvis. Mr. Jarvis is a native of the State, born in 1836, and the son of a Methodist minister. His early education was achieved under many disadvantages, owing to the straitened circumstances of his father, but he managed to take a full course at Randolph-Macon College, and graduated with honor in 1860. Soon afterward he entered the Confederate service, and remained in the field until May 17, 1864, when he was badly wounded near Drury's Bluff, Va., and compelled to retire from the army. Subsequently he studied law, and began to practice in 1866; was member of several Legislatures, an elector from his district on the Seymour ticket in 1868, also elector at large on the Greeley ticket, and a member of the Constitutional Convention of 1875. James Lowrie Robinson, Lieutenant-Governor, is also a native of the State, served through the war with more than ordinary gallantry, and has since occupied various positions of public trust.

It was enacted for the benefit of land-owners whose land had been sold for taxes before January 1, 1879, that any person who shall within one year from date of this law pay to the Public Treasurer the taxes due at time of sale and ten per cent. upon that amount, all subsequent taxes, and costs and expenses, shall be entitled to a deed of reconveyance. This the Secretary of State will issue upon exhibition to him of the necessary tax-receipts and the payment to him of $1 for the deed. Another act makes provision for land-owners who have inadvertently failed to redeem their lands until the day of grace has expired or is about to expire. In such cases the law extends the time to January 1, 1881. For redemption of any such land (provided the title is yet in the State), it is necessary for the dispossessed owner to pay the taxes due at time of sale and the percentage required by law, all costs of advertising and executing a deed, and all taxes that would have been due had not the land passed into the State's possession.

It is alleged in the preamble to an act to regulate marriageable kinship that "many persons in this State, in estimating what degree of kinship is nearer than first cousins, compute kinship by the half blood as being only half so near as the same degree of kinship by the whole blood." Wherefore, on February 27, 1879, it was enacted that "hereafter, in this State, whenever the degree of kinship shall be estimated with the view to ascertain the right of kinspeople to marry, the half blood shall be counted as the whole blood."

The session closed on March 18th. It consisted of sixty-six working days, during which some nine hundred bills and resolutions were introduced and considered—an average of nearly fourteen per day. Of the whole number,

about four hundred and fifty—one half—were ratified and became laws, an average of seven per day. This amount of work was believed to be unparalleled in the history of legislative sessions in the State.

By the public records it appears that 1,973 pieces of real estate have been sold for taxes amounting to $17,404, and bid in by the State The time allowed for their redemption has expired.

The United States Fish Commission has commenced operations in the State. About six million young shad were hatched in the spring by the Commission in the Albemarle Sound, all but a sixth of which were placed in the waters of the State. The total number released since the beginning of their introduction is about eight million. Of these the Roanoke and Neuse have received seven hundred thousand each; the Cape Fear and Tar half a million each; the Meherrin, Nottoway, and Blackwater over two hundred thousand each, with several millions released at their mouths; the Yadkin and Catawba two hundred thousand each above Salisbury. In the latter streams the General Government and the State of South Carolina, which has now an established commission, have placed between two and four hundred thousand.

An election for three Judges of the Supreme Court and for those for some circuits occurred during the year. For the Supreme Court, a Democratic Convention nominated William Nathan Harwell Smith for Chief Justice, and Thomas S. Ashe and John Henry Dillond for Associate Justices. They were all elected.

The crops of the State were much retarded by the cold weather of the spring. The area of corn was equal to the average, and the yield was ample for the home supply. The acreage of cotton was increased in fifteen counties and diminished in two, yet there was a full crop. The crop of tobacco was a fair average yield and unexcelled in quantity. The area devoted to grasses has been increased within the past three years not less than 50 per cent. Clover, lucerne, orchard, timothy, and red-top are being introduced and tested in all sections of the State with encouraging results.

The desire for improvement in agriculture has brought out very full information of the condition of the State. Over 60 per cent. of her entire area is in woodland, one county, Brunswick, having over 90 per cent., and no less than eleven others between 80 and 90. Some of these are near the seacoast and others among the mountains, with a difference of altitude of more than 6,000 feet, which, with a difference of latitude, surface, and soil, renders the State remarkable for the variety of its flora, ranging from the palmetto to the pine, from tropical or semi-tropical forms to those purely Alpine in character. Eastern North Carolina has furnished the world with nearly all the pitch, tar, turpentine, and rosin that have been consumed as naval stores for the last century. Within the last ten years factories have been built in various portions of Central Carolina for the manufacture of wagon-spokes, hubs, and axe-handles, that require a tough hard wood, using for this purpose the oak and hickory that are the peculiar growth of that section. Considerable quantities of locust pins, used in ship-building, have been shipped from depots on the Western North Carolina Railroad. The yellow locust is found abundantly along the eastern slope of the Blue Ridge and in the mountain gorges, in the entire western district of the State. Within the last two years large quantities of black-walnut lumber—or rather trees, for it is shipped in the log—have been sent to the Eastern markets, and even to France, to be manufactured into furniture, pianos, organs, etc. These are but a very small portion of the useful trees that are to be found in the forests of the State. The white walnut or butternut is largely used as trimming for black walnut. The white ash is another wood that is used in the manufacture of light-colored furniture, or combined with dark woods for decorative purposes. The wild cherry is found in the mountains in great abundance and of fine quality, and is susceptible of a higher polish than the same variety that grows in the lowlands. In addition to these are the maples, the birch or mountain mahogany, suitable for articles that require a fine-grained wood susceptible of a high polish, the poplars and the different varieties of oaks for the ordinary uses of lumber, and the white pine found in the mountains, that is only equaled by the forests of Maine and the Northwest. In the arts where a wood of a soft character and fine grain is needed, the *Magnolia acuminata* or wild cucumber-tree is all that could be desired, and grows abundantly in the mountains west of the Blue Ridge.

There are no great valleys in the State comparable to the Valley of Virginia or the Valley of East Tennessee. But each of the numerous rivers has hewn out a narrow valley for itself, in the bottom of which lies its present channel. The most considerable and best defined of these are found in the mountain regions. The most notable and the largest among them is the valley of the French Broad, which is about fifty miles long, and has a varying breadth of from nineteen to twenty-five miles, having in Transylvania County a great extent of level and very productive bottom-land; but for the most part it is traversed by many spurs or ridges and secondary chains of mountains, from whose intervening valleys and gorges come the numerous tributaries of the French Broad River. The other mountain valleys are of the same description, but are generally narrower and basin- or trough-like, and have been excavated in the same manner by the rivers which drain the successive areas between the transverse chains, and are flanked by numerous projecting spurs and ridges of the surrounding mountains, between which a multitude of subordinate tributary streams ramify. Eastward of the Blue Ridge, in the Piedmont region, are the valleys of the upper Catawba and Yadkin, which may in a general way be considered as consisting of the entire basins or troughs between the parallel chains which inclose them, and so are fifteen or twenty miles wide; but the level lands along these streams are interjected between the mountain spurs, often quite to the foot of the Blue Ridge.

The State embraces an area of 54,000 square miles, over which are distributed 1,300,000 souls. The length from east to west is 500 miles, and the average breadth of the State is a little over 100 miles. Nearly 4,000 square miles' surface of the territory is covered by the water of the rivers, bays, and sounds of the east. The water-transportation facilities of that section, improved and unimproved, are not surpassed in any State. No State possesses greater manufacturing facilities; her agricultural resources are unlimited; her products as varied as they are valuable; soil rich and inexhaustible; climatic advantages not approached by the neighboring States; while in mineral wealth North Carolina stands without a rival. The mountain region embraces an area of 5,400 square miles, of an average elevation of 2,600 feet; the Piedmont region, 6,000 square miles, elevation 1,000 feet; the middle section, 12,000 square miles, 650 feet elevation; the sub-eastern region, 9,000 square miles, 200 feet elevation; the coast region, 15,000 square miles, with an average elevation of 50 feet. Almost if not quite every crop produced in the United States is grown in one region or another of the State, so that the widest diversification is practicable. Corn, cotton, and tobacco claim the first attention of the people, three fourths of all classes of whom are engaged in agriculture; but fruits, grasses, stock, and grapes are largely cultivated, returning a rich and satisfactory yield to the industrious husbandman. Mining and manufacturing are beginning to attain a magnitude of no small importance, and the work of general development of all the varied industries and resources is progressing with advancing spirit. The annual value of farm products is sixty millions, and of manufacturing twenty millions of dollars. The cash products of those engaged in mining, other labor than that engaged in agriculture and manufacturing, the professions, together with those employed in trade, transportation, and commerce, should, it is estimated, swell the annual product of North Carolina to as much as a hundred million dollars.

There are seven large rivers east of the Blue Ridge, and seven west of it, the former navigable more than 1,000 miles, and one of the latter (the Tennessee) 1,000 miles to the Mississippi. The Cape Fear is navigable to within 115 miles, in a straight line, of the Blue Ridge. Some sixty years ago the tributaries of the Yadkin and Catawba were navigated almost to the foot of the Blue Ridge. The water-power of the State aggregates more than three millions of horse-power, exceeding that of all the steam-engines of Great Britain or the United States. More than 1,200 miles of railroad are already built, and several hundred more projected. The climate corresponds with that of northern and middle Italy and southern and middle France—ranging, between its eastern and western borders, as that from the Gulf of Mexico to Canada. Its natural and agricultural productions are consequently of extraordinary variety.

O

OBITUARIES, AMERICAN. ALBERT, WILLIAM J., born in Baltimore, August 4, 1816, died in that city, March 29th. He was educated at Mount St. Mary's College, Maryland, and became a merchant, but retired from business in 1856. In 1864 he was president of the Maryland Electoral College, which voted for President Lincoln. He was one of the founders of the First National Bank of Maryland, and a director in insurance companies, savings banks, and manufacturing companies. He was a Republican member of the Forty-third Congress from the Fifth Maryland District, serving from December, 1873, to March, 1875.

ANDERSON, RICHARD H., a lieutenant-general of the Confederate army, born in South Carolina in 1816, died in Beaufort, June 26th. He entered West Point in 1838, and graduated in 1842. On entering the army, his promotion was rapid until he reached the grade of captain of dragoons, which position he held until 1861, when he resigned and joined the Confederate army. He was at first commissioned colonel of infantry. Owing to his bravery and valuable services in many of the great battles of that memorable period, he was promoted step by step until he reached the grade of lieutenant-general. Since the close of the war, General Anderson led a life of retirement.

AVERY, Judge DANIEL DUDLEY, born at Baton Rouge, Louisiana, April 12, 1810, died at his residence on Petite Anse Island, June 8th. He entered Yale College in 1826. On his return to Baton Rouge he studied law, and was admitted to the bar in 1832. The same year he was elected to the General Assembly of the State, and served for four years. He was joint commissioner with Mr. Maunsel White in superintending the erection of the State House in Baton Rouge. He was afterward thrown out of politics by the breaking up of the Whig party. In 1860 he became Judge of the Florida parishes. After the capture of New Orleans in 1862 he resigned his judgeship and lived on his Petite Anse plantation. The necessity of destroying the salt-works on that island drew General Banks thither in 1863, and Judge Avery went to Texas and remained there until the close of the war.

BRADY, ALEXANDER, a printer, born in 1795, died in Brooklyn, New York, July 26th. He was believed to be the oldest printer in the country at the time of his death. He had been a member of the New York Typographical Society more than sixty years, and connected with the Methodist Book Concern for forty-five years.

BRINSMADE, HORATIO N., D. D, born at New Hartford, Connecticut, December 28, 1798, died at Roseville, New Jersey, January 19th. He graduated at the College of New Jersey, Princeton, in 1822. For nine years he was an instructor in the Asylum for the Deaf and Dumb at Hartford. In 1828 he was ordained by the North Congregational Association, and preached one year at Hartford. In 1831 he went to Collinsville and established a church, where he remained until 1834, when he went to Pittsfield, Massachusetts, where he was pastor until 1841. In that year he was called to the pastorate of the Third Presbyterian Church of Newark, New Jersey. In 1853 he resigned on account of his wife's health, and went to Beloit, Wisconsin, where he was pastor of the First Congregational Church for seven years. In 1860 he returned to Newark to take charge of Wickliffe Chapel, and remained in charge until his death.

CRAVEN, ALFRED W., a civil engineer, born in New York, where he died on March 29th. Early in life he entered the profession of civil engineer, and in 1837 he was engaged, in connection with General George S. Greene, in the construction of an important public work near Charleston, South Carolina. In 1849, when the law was passed organizing the old Croton Water Board, Mr. Craven was made Engineer Commissioner, which position he held until 1868, at which time he resigned for the purpose of going to Europe. Among the many important works projected and carried out by Mr. Craven during his connection with the Croton Water Board were the building of the large reservoir in Central Park, which was completed in 1867, the enlargement of the pipes across High Bridge, and the construction of the reservoir at Boyd's Corners, Putnam County. He also caused to be made an accurate survey of Croton Valley, with a view of ascertaining its capacity for furnishing an adequate water-supply, and was largely instrumental in securing the passage of the first law passed by the Legislature establishing a general sewerage system for New York. He was one of the original projectors and the first President of the American Society of Civil Engineers, organized in 1852, and was also a commissioner, with Allan Campbell, in the work of building the underground railroad through Fourth Avenue.

ELMORE, Colonel HENRY M., son of Judge John A. Elmore of South Carolina, born in that State January 28, 1816, died in Waverley, Texas, February 21st. Early in life he moved with his father to Autauga (now Elmore) County, Alabama. He lived in Tuskegee, and for two years was Probate Judge of Macon County. He married the niece of Governor Fitzpatrick of Alabama. In 1854 he removed to Texas, and settled in Walker County, where he resided until his death. He was elected to the State Senate in 1859 and served two years. At the outset of the war he enlisted as a private in Captain Lewis's company. He was elected colonel of the 20th Texas Infantry, and no man left the army with a better record or retaining more of the confidence of his men. After the war he resumed the practice of the law. His influence was widely felt; he was a man of great firmness and depth of conviction, and to the close of his life he took an active interest in all affairs of government.

FOOTE, Major R. E., a lawyer of distinction, born in Mississippi in 1842, died in Aurora, Nevada, May 23d. He was a son of Henry S. Foote, once Governor and United States Senator of Mississippi. Major Foote entered a regiment of the State at the commencement of the late war, and served with distinction until its close. In 1866 he settled in Idaho, where he remained until 1875. He practiced law in Idaho City, Placerville, Centerville, and other places in the Basin, and was District Attorney for several years. Subsequently he resided in Salt Lake City, Eureka, and Virginia City, finally settling in Aurora and Bodie. He had been engaged in the defense of a person charged with murder, and the verdict was guilty in the second degree. In this result he was considerably disappointed, hoping for a less serious issue. He was in one of the small rooms off the main portion of the hotel, sitting somewhat low in an arm-chair, with his feet resting on the rounds of another chair, and his hands clasped over his head, as if in deep thought, or possibly dozing. People were constantly passing through the room, and noticed nothing peculiar in his position. Upon some one speaking to him, however, and no response coming, it was discovered that he was dead. How long he had been dead was not known, but it was believed to have been half an hour before the fact was discovered.

FORD, BUDD G., born in Salem, New Jersey, March 2, 1840, was drowned at Ocean City, Maryland, July 20th. At an early age he was taken from school and engaged in the pursuits of business, in which he became quite successful. He was elected to the House of Delegates in the Maryland Legislature in 1872 for the term of two years, and in 1875 he was elected State Senator for four years.

GARRARD, KENNER, born in Kentucky, died in Cincinnati, May 15th. He was appointed a cadet at West Point in 1847, and graduated in 1851. He continued in service till 1861, when as lieutenant of cavalry he was captured by Texans and exchanged in 1862. Subsequently in 1862 he was appointed colonel of the 146th New York Volunteers, and was in several engagements, and rose to the rank of brigadier-general of volunteers in 1863. His gallantry was several times recognized by promotions in the regular army, and in 1865 he was made brevet major-general. He resigned in 1866.

GARRETTSON, MARY RUTHERFORD, died near Rhinebeck, on the Hudson River, March 7th, in the eighty-seventh year of her age. She was the daughter of Freeborn Garrettson of Maryland, a prominent Methodist clergyman, who died in 1827. Her mother was Catherine Livingston, the daughter of Robert Livingston of Clermont, and sister of Robert R. Livingston, Chancellor of New York State, and of Edward Livingston, author of the Code of Louisiana, and at one time Minister to France. She was a lady of marked intellectual ability, and was well known for her benevolence.

HAMPTON, Major WADE, Jr., son of Governor Hampton of South Carolina, born in that State in 1838, died December 23d. His mother was Margaret Preston. Young Hampton served through the war with distinction. His brother, Preston Hampton, was killed before Fredericksburg, and almost at the same moment Wade was severely wounded. Their father was on the field. Apprised of their fate, he rode up to the ambulance, and after one look at his sons, one dead and the other apparently dying, without dismounting or delay, he returned to his post of duty at the head of his cavalry division. Major Hampton recovered, and received his promotion. After the war he became a cotton-planter in Mississippi. In the summer of 1879 he married.

IZARD, J. ALLEN SMITH, a military officer, born in Pennsylvania in 1810, died at Richfield Springs, New York, July 27th. He graduated at West Point Military Academy, in 1829 under the name of J. Allen Smith, and was commissioned as second lieutenant of the 3d Artillery. From August 30, 1829, to June 27, 1835, he was Assistant Professor of Geography, History, and Ethics at the Military Academy. His next service was in the Florida war, 1836–'37. Resigning his commission April 30, 1837, he married a daughter of Judge Huger of Charleston, South Carolina, and became a successful rice-planter near Savannah, Georgia.

JOHNSTON, AMOS R., was born in Tennessee in 1812. He began life as a printer, and in partnership with General Zollicoffer edited a newspaper in Tennessee. He removed to Mississippi in 1830. He settled first at Clinton, and then in Jackson, continuing his career as editor. He was an ardent adherent of the Whig party. In 1836 he represented Hinds County in the State Legislature. In 1839 he became Clerk of the Circuit Court of Hinds, and in 1845 was elected Judge. He was a delegate to the State Convention of 1861, and was on the Union side. In the Convention of 1865, which repealed the secession ordinance, he was an influential member. He lived withdrawn from public life until 1875, when he was elected State Senator by the Conservatives and Democrats. He served until 1877, when declining health forced him to resign. He did much to promote improvements in Raymond and in Jackson. He went north in search of health, but died in Cincinnati, and on the 28th of June was buried in Jackson, Mississippi.

MEAD, WILLIAM COOPER, D. D., LL. D., born in Greenwich, Connecticut, died July 17th. He received a systematic education, entered the ministry in the Protestant Episcopal Church, and in 1836 became rector of St. Paul's Church, Norwalk, where he remained till his death, a period of more than forty-three years. He was a Freemason, and took great interest in the order. At different times he was Grand Chaplain of the Grand Lodges of Connecticut and Pennsylvania, and of the Grand Chapter of Connecticut. He was made a Mason in 1824, in Westchester Lodge, No. 46, of White Plains, New York. He was elected an honorary member of St. John's Lodge, No. 6, of Norwalk, in 1849, and was chaplain a trustee for many years. He was one of the four Episcopal clergymen in the United States who have been rector of one parish for a period of forty years. The cane which he held at the time of his death on account of having been longest in a parish of any rector in the State, went to the Rev. B. M. Yarrington of Greenwich, who has been rector there for forty years. Dr. Mead received the degree of LL. D. from Trinity College. He died suddenly, soon after returning from a ride.

MOYNAHAN, Rev. CORNELIUS, born and educated in Ireland, died in New Orleans, February 13th. He emigrated to America in company with his brother, the Rev. J. Moynahan, completed his theological course in New Orleans, was ordained priest by Archbishop Blanc in 1848, and received the Third District as his field. At that time it had no Catholic organization. Father Moynahan built a wooden church for the use of the English-speaking residents. This was afterward converted into a parochial school, and replaced by a large and beautiful brick structure called St. Peter's church. He was a man of ardent, impulsive eloquence, and his influence extended far beyond his own denomination. Like his elder brother, he was canon and counselor of his Grace the Archbishop.

NEW, Major JOHN H., born in Louisville, Kentucky, in 1827, died in New Orleans, January 17th. He procured an education by his own labor, graduated at Oakland College, Mississippi, continued his studies while acting as private tutor, and afterward entered the Cambridge Law School. His first intention was to pursue literature as a profession, and he wrote many graceful minor poems; but after com-

mencing the study of law he devoted himself to it exclusively. He was already in successful practice at Baton Rouge when the war broke out, in which he volunteered as a junior lieutenant, and reached the rank of adjutant-general and inspector-general of division under Stonewall Jackson. After its close he settled in New Orleans with broken health and ruined fortune, forming a law partnership with his companion in arms General Henry Hays. The health of the latter soon gave way, but the talent and energy of the junior partner insured to the firm a rapid and brilliant success. He was able and eloquent, and these qualities won him the professional success he coveted. Just as its highest distinctions lay within his grasp he was attacked by consumption, and he traveled for several years in Japan, through Greece and Spain, and the less frequented parts of Europe and Asia. He was fond of art, and delighted in collecting objects of virtu and curiosities from every country. All the while his disease was making slow but unrelenting progress, and he reached home only to die.

PECK, ASAHEL, born in Royalston, Massachusetts, in September, 1803, died at Jericho, Vermont, May 18th. His father removed to Vermont in 1804, and the son, after fair diligence in youth as a student, was admitted to practice law in 1832. In 1850 he was made a Judge of the Circuit Court, which position he held until the Court was abolished. In 1860 he was one of the State Senators from Chittenden County, and was elected Judge of the Supreme Court, which office he held until 1874, when he was elected Governor. He was simple in manner and habits, and some said grandly so in thought. His memory was very tenacious, and through a long life he applied his mind to the law, and thus was regarded as having a knowledge of it unsurpassed by that of any other man. He was never married, and it has been observed that this was perhaps because he knew the law was a jealous mistress. A man of strong convictions and will, with a temper that could occasionally burst forth, he was yet tender and gentle to the weak; so much so that it was said his one failing as a Judge was "riding" a case for the weaker party. "With a corporation on one side and a woman on the other, the law generally seemed to the jury pretty clear for the woman after the Judge's charge; and what made it bad for the corporation was that it was good law too." Being honest and straightforward withal, he had the respect and confidence of the people beyond any other man in the State.

PELHAM, General WILLIAM, died at his residence near Menchaca Springs, Travis County, Texas, June 8th. He was born in Maysville, Kentucky, April 10, 1803. He moved to Arkansas early in life, and married the sister of Governor Conway. In 1841 he was appointed Surveyor-General of Arkansas by President Harrison, and in 1845 reappointed by Polk. He filled this important office for eight years.

to the entire satisfaction of the people and Government. In 1853 President Pierce appointed him Surveyor-General of New Mexico. It is worthy of note that this appointment was urged by all the Senators, Whig and Democratic, from the States of Missouri, Arkansas, Louisiana, and Texas. New Mexico had then been recently acquired by the Government. To the ordinary duties of the surveyorship was added the delicate task of adjudicating private land-claims. Their adjustment in a manner just at once to the Government and the claimants was a severe test of character. Distrustful as the Mexicans were of American tribunals, they never once impugned his integrity. He was reappointed to his office by President Buchanan. Shortly before the outbreak of the war he resigned it, and returned to his home in one of the loveliest valleys of Texas. His only son was killed on the field of battle.

PIERCE, Dr. LOVICK, born in Halifax County, North Carolina, March 17, 1785, died at Sparta, Georgia, November 9th. In 1804 he entered the Methodist ministry. He afterward studied medicine in Philadelphia and practiced for a time, but soon returned to the pulpit. Dr. Pierce was chaplain in the army in the war of 1812. He was a delegate to the General Conference of 1836, 1840, and 1844, and after the organization of the Southern Church, in 1846, sat regularly in its highest court. He took part in the proceedings of the Louisville Conference of May, 1874, where he had a son and a grandson, three generations being thus represented in the same body. The son referred to, George Foster Pierce, had then been a bishop twenty years. Dr. Pierce, notwithstanding his advanced age, continued to preach occasionally up to within a few months of his death. In the previous year he published a series of theological essays in one of the Methodist periodicals, showing that his intellectual vigor and his interest in the Church were undiminished. On the occasion of his ninety-third birthday, in 1877, he held a family reunion, when it was made known that he had seventy-two descendants.

SCHLEICHER, Hon. GUSTAVE, born in Darmstadt, Germany, November 19, 1823, died in Washington, D. C., January 11th. He was educated in the University of Giessen, became a civil engineer, and was employed in the construction of various European railroads. In 1847 he emigrated to Texas, and in 1850 settled in San Antonio. He was elected to the State Legislature in 1853, and was State Senator in 1855 and 1856. He was elected to Congress in 1874, and reëlected by large majorities in 1876 and 1878. He was a man of splendid physique, weighing 425 pounds. The doors of the House of Representatives had to be taken from the hinges to permit his coffin to be carried into the hall. He was one of the ablest opponents of paper money.

SCRIBNER, JOHN BLAIR, died in New York, January 22d. He was the eldest son of the late Charles Scribner, and was named after his grandfather, John I. Blair, a wealthy contractor in New Jersey. He entered Princeton College, but was not graduated, as he preferred to leave college to assist his father in business. When the latter died, Mr. Scribner became a partner in the new publishing house of Scribner, Armstrong & Co., which was merged in the firm of Charles Scribner's Sons on the death of Edward Seymour and the withdrawal of Mr. Armstrong. He was thoroughly familiar with his business, ambitious and industrious, and was highly esteemed by his associates.

SEVIER, ROBERT, born in Greenville, Tennessee, October 30, 1807, died in Richmond, Missouri, May 16th. He entered West Point Military Academy in 1824, was a classmate of Jefferson Davis and a schoolmate of Robert E. Lee and Albert Sidney Johnston, and graduated with the highest honors of the institution. During the Florida Indian war he was in active service, and afterward on the Texas frontier. He resigned his commission in October, 1837, removed to Ray County, Missouri, in 1840, and was appointed Clerk of the Circuit Court in 1845. This position he continued to hold by election for twenty years, but was removed by the ousting ordinance at the commencement of the late war, although a strong Union man. He was a strict Presbyterian. His first wife was a sister of General Sibley, and his second a sister of the late Austin A. King, ex-Governor of Missouri.

SHERMAN, General THOMAS W., died in Newport, Rhode Island, March 16th. He entered the Military Academy in 1832, distinguished himself in the Creek, Florida, and Mexican wars, and was commissioned captain May 28, 1846. He also did good service in the Indian troubles in Minnesota and in the Lecompton troubles in Kansas. He was made lieutenant-colonel of the 5th Artillery May 14, 1861; brigadier-general of volunteers May 17, 1861; and colonel of the 3d Artillery June 1, 1863. In October, 1861, he commanded an expedition to the Southern coast. He lost a leg at Port Hudson in 1863, being at that time commander of a division under Banks. He was made brevet major-general of the army in 1870, when he retired.

SHERMAN, Mrs., the wife of General Thomas W. Sherman, died in Newport, Rhode Island, March 12th. She was the daughter of the late Wilson Shannon, formerly Governor of Ohio, and about forty-five years of age. She went with her father to Kansas when he was appointed Governor of that Territory. She there met General Sherman, and was married at Lawrence. A few months previous to her death she had submitted to a painful surgical operation, from which she failed to rally, dying four days before her husband. They leave one son, a youth of sixteen years. She was a very estimable lady.

SLAUGHTER, WILLIAM B., born in Culpepper County, Virginia, April 10, 1798, died in Madison, Wisconsin, July 21st. He was educated at William and Mary College, and in 1827 went to Bardstown, Kentucky, where he practiced law for two years, and then removed to Bedford, Indiana. In 1832 he was elected a member of the Indiana Legislature, and introduced into that body a set of resolutions strongly sustaining President Andrew Jackson's proclamation to the South Carolina nullifiers. He was appointed Register of the Land-Office at Indianapolis in 1833, and in 1835 at Green Bay. The same year he was elected a member of the Legislative Council of Michigan, and in that body introduced a memorial to Congress asking that the territory lying west of Lake Michigan be set off from Michigan and organized into a new Territory to be named Wisconsin. In 1837 he went to Wisconsin, and resided on a farm until 1845, when he returned to his birthplace in Virginia. In 1861 he removed to Middleton, Wisconsin, and in 1862 was a commissary of subsistence and quartermaster, which office he held for one year. He was an extensive writer for periodicals, made some contributions to encyclopædias, and published a work entitled "Reminiscences of Distinguished Men I have seen." He was much respected and esteemed.

SOMERBY, GUSTAVUS A., an advocate, died in Boston, July 24th. He was one of the oldest members of the bar in that city, having few or no superiors as an advocate before a jury. His name was made conspicuous by his success in the case of Leavitt Abbey, who was charged with the murder of Abijah Ellis in Boston.

SOULE, GIDEON L., a teacher, born at Freeport, Maine, July 25, 1796, died at Exeter, New Hampshire, May 28th. He was connected with Phillips Exeter Academy over fifty years, and was the principal of the institution from 1838 to 1873. His predecessor, Dr. Benjamin Abbot, was principal of the institution from its foundation in 1788 to 1838, and Dr. Soule was his associate during seventeen years. The great success of the Academy is largely due to the efforts of the latter.

STILLE, Hon. R. B., born in New Jersey in 1804, died in New Orleans July 9th. At the age of twenty-six he removed to Louisiana and engaged in mercantile pursuits. He received from President Taylor in 1849 the appointment of Surveyor of the Port of New Orleans. He was a member of the Legislature in 1866. At the time of his death he was in attendance on the Constitutional Convention as delegate from Sabine Parish.

THOMPSON, JOSEPH P., D. D., born in Philadelphia, August 7, 1819, died in Berlin, Germany, September 21st. He graduated at Yale College in 1838, studied theology at Andover and at New Haven, and was first settled over the Chapel Street Church in the latter city in November, 1840. From 1845 to 1872 he was pastor of the Broadway Tabernacle, New York, and during this extended ministry attained a high rank among scholars, churchmen, and literati. During this period Dr. Thompson, with others, founded "The New-Englander,"

the well-known quarterly, and also assisted at the birth of "The Independent." He was a manager of the American Congregational Union and the Home Missionary Society, and in 1852 originated the plan of the Albany Congregational Convention. In 1852–'53 he visited Egypt, Palestine, and other Oriental countries, and afterward devoted much time and research to Egyptology and other Oriental subjects. Among Dr. Thompson's most permanent literary works are : "Memoir of Timothy Dwight" (1844); "Lectures to Young Men" (1846); "Egypt Past and Present" (1856); "The Believer's Refuge" (1857) ; "Christianity and Emancipation" (1863); "Man in Genesis and Geology" (1869); "Theology of Christ from His Own Words" (1870); "Church and State in the United States" (1874); and a "Life of Christ," published in 1875.

THRASHER, JOHN S., born in Portland, Maine, in 1817, died in Galveston, Texas, November 10th. While yet a youth his parents removed to Havana, Cuba. He became a partner of the wealthy firm of Tyng & Co., but his tastes led him to journalism. In 1849 he purchased the "Faro Industrial," a daily Havana paper, the only organ of the Liberal party. He continued its editor until September 1, 1851, when General Concha suppressed it. On that day Lopez, the famous filibuster, was executed. Thrasher's sympathies and good offices were freely given to his four hundred unfortunate followers. He was court-martialed and condemned to ten years' imprisonment at hard labor in Ceuta, and perpetual banishment from Cuba. He was released after several months, through the intervention of the United States Minister at Madrid, Mr. Barringer of North Carolina, whose wife appealed successfully to Queen Isabella. He afterward established in New Orleans a Sunday paper called the "Beacon of Cuba." From 1853 to 1855 he was an active member of the filibustering associations which organized the expedition under General Quitman. When the United States Government prevented its departure, the Cuban Junta dissolved and Thrasher went to New York. He found a position on the staff of the "Herald," and as a special correspondent traveled extensively through Mexico and South America. In 1856 he published an essay on Humboldt's "Personal Narrative," which he had previously translated into English. He also published various treatises on the social, financial, and political condition of Cuba, one of which, "Cuba and Louisiana," addressed to Samuel J. Peters, was received with marked attention. While still connected with the "Herald," he edited the "Noticioso de Nuevo York," a paper devoted to the interests of the Spanish-American countries. He married a Southern woman whose property was in Texas. During the civil war he remained at the South, and was the agent of the Associated Press at Atlanta. After the war he resumed his editorship, and had charge of Frank Leslie's "Ilustracion Americana" in New York. Latterly he resided in Galveston, Texas.

TILGHMAN, RICHARD COOKE, born in 1807, died of pneumonia in Baltimore, March 14th. He graduated at the West Point Military Academy in 1828, and was appointed second lieutenant of the 1st Artillery, and first lieutenant in 1834. In 1836 he resigned his commission and served as civil engineer for the State of Maryland until the following year, and during the next nine years was employed by the Government in surveying sites for fortifications on Lake Champlain, locating and constructing roads in the Indian reservation in Iowa, making military reconnaissances of the approaches to New Orleans, and superintending harbor improvements on Lakes Erie and Michigan. In 1846 he took possession of his father's place, "The Hermitage," one of the finest estates in Maryland, and from that time devoted his mind much to agriculture. From 1857 to 1867 he was a colonel of Maryland militia, and subsequently Quartermaster-General of the State. One of the incidents of Judge Tilghman's life was acting as groomsman at the marriage of General Robert E. Lee.

VANATTA, JACOB, a lawyer of distinction, born near Hackettstown, New Jersey, in 1825, died in Morristown, April 30th. His father was a poor farmer, and in early life the son was taught the trade of a tailor. Having finished his apprenticeship, he started for the West; but happening to lose his trunk on the first day, by which misfortune he was made destitute, he returned. Subsequently he went to Licking County, Ohio, where he taught school and became a clerk in the post-office. After a year he returned to Morristown, and by the assistance of friends read law and was admitted to practice in 1843, became counselor in 1853, and soon occupied a prominent position in the front ranks of his profession. He held only two important political posts during his life— one as a member of the State Legislature, and the other as Attorney-General of the State from 1875 to 1877. In his pleadings in court he was slow, deliberate, and cautious, seeking to carry his point by a purely legal argument. An illness, the result of overwork, after two weeks terminated in his death. His career is remarkable as indicating what energy and ability can accomplish. Few probably started from a humbler position and gained greater political and legal prominence.

WOODS, JACOB A., a physician, born in Hancock, New Hampshire, in May, 1810, died in New York, March 22d. He had resided in New York about twenty-one years. His specialty was the treatment of spinal diseases.

WOODWARD, Judge WARREN J., born in Wayne County, Pennsylvania, in 1820, died at Hampton, New York, September 23d. He was admitted to the bar in August, 1842, and began his career as a lawyer in Columbia County. In 1856 he was elected Judge of the new Twenty-sixth District, composed of the counties of

Columbia, Sullivan, and Wyoming, and was subsequently commissioned President Judge for ten years. In 1861 Judge Woodward was elected to the bench in Berks County, composing the Twenty-third Judicial District, and at the end of his term was reëlected for the ensuing term of ten years. In August, 1874, he was nominated by the Democratic State Convention for Associate Justice of the Supreme Court, and was elected under the minority clause in the new Constitution. Judge Woodward, during all his career on the bench, bore out the reputation gained in the early days of his judicial career as painstaking and careful, possessing the judicial quality in a remarkable degree, and as giving decisions rarely overruled in the court of last resort.

WOODWORTH, Dr. JOHN M., born in Chemung County, New York, August 15, 1837, died in Washington, D. C., March 14th. Studying medicine, he acquired prominence in his profession, devoting himself especially to contagious diseases. He served in the Union army during the war, and was Medical Director during Sherman's march to the sea. In 1871 he was appointed Supervising Surgeon-General of the Marine Hospital service, which he elevated and made very efficient. In 1878 he organized a commission to examine into the yellow fever then raging at the South, and its report was made the basis for sanitary legislation by Congress. Under a law passed a few weeks before his death a National Board of Health was organized, of which he was a member, and he was preparing for the press a report on the yellow-fever epidemic which would, had he completed it, have been of great value.

WYMAN, LUTHER BOYNTON, born in Woburn, Massachusetts, in 1805, died in Brooklyn, New York, July 27th. He became well known in Boston as a singer previous to his removal to Brooklyn in 1840. There he became prominent in music, and in 1857 with others organized the Brooklyn Philharmonic Society, of which he was president until his death. He was one of the chief movers in building the Academy of Music. During the war he was active in organizing regiments, and gave a number of brilliant concerts, the proceeds of which were devoted to patriotic purposes. He was also one of the organizers of the Mercantile Library in Brooklyn. Four years ago he was stricken with paralysis, which resulted in his death.

OBITUARIES, FOREIGN. ANTONUCCI, ANTONIO BENEDETTO, an Italian cardinal, born September 17, 1798, died January 28th. He received his early training for the priesthood from the Benedictine monks of his native town Subiaco, and afterward went to the Roman College to complete his studies. In 1833 he was sent as chargé d'affaires and vice-superior of the Catholic missions to Holland. His mission proving successful, he was rewarded in 1840 with the bishopric of Montefeltre, whence he was translated two years later to the see of Ferentino. In 1844 he was created Archbishop of Tarsus *in partibus infidelium*, and sent as nuncio to Turin, where he remained until 1851, when he became Bishop of Ancona and Umana, which latter see confers on its holder the title of count. In 1851 he was created cardinal. He remained at his post during the war of unification, and the Italian attack on and occupation of Ancona; but while attending to the duties of his see, he refused to recognize the new rulers, and constantly protested against their acts directed against the property of the Church.

BASTIDE, JULES, a French writer, born November 22, 1800, died March 3d. Having finished his studies, he took an active part in the agitation against the Restoration, and in 1830 was one of the first to plant the tricolor on the Tuileries. During the reign of Louis Philippe he was prosecuted on different occasions, and in 1832 he was even condemned to death after the riot at the funeral of General Lamarque, but escaped to England, where he lived two years. In the Revolution of 1848 he played a prominent part, and was for a time Minister for Foreign Affairs. He was the author of a number of political and historical works, the best known of which are "La République Française et l'Italie en 1848" (1858), and "Guerres de Religion en France" (2 vols., 1859).

BLACKWOOD, JOHN, a British publisher, born December 7, 1818, died October 9th. He was a son of William Blackwood, the founder of "Blackwood's Magazine." After the completion of his studies at the University of Edinburgh and several years of foreign travel, he established a branch office of the Edinburgh house in London. In 1845, upon the death of his brother Alexander, he returned to Edinburgh, and from 1846 up to his death continued to edit the magazine, in which he was eminently successful.

BREWER, JOHN SHERREN, an English historian, born in 1810, died February 16th. He graduated at Queen's College, Oxford, in 1833, and in 1841 was appointed Professor of English Literature in King's College, which position he held until 1876. He edited a large number of valuable works, among them "Fuller's Church History," an edition of the "Nicomachean Ethics," and the "Calendars of State Papers relating to the Reign of Henry VIII." Together with William Bullen, he edited the "Calendar of the Carew Manuscripts."

CHAM, the *nom de plume* of Amédée de Noé, a French caricaturist, born January 2, 1819, died September 6th. He supplied for many years the journals "Charivari" and "Journal Amusant" with illustrations, and was the most popular caricaturist of France. He contributed to these journals a large number of comic drawings, scenes, and reviews, which were afterward published in the shape of albums.

CHENU, JEAN CHARLES, a French naturalist, born August 30, 1808, died November 16th. He studied medicine in Paris, entered the army

as assistant surgeon in 1829, took part in the Crimean war, and during the siege of Paris, 1870–'71, was director-general of ambulances. His principal works are "Illustrations Conchyliologiques" (1842–'47), and "Encyclopédie d'Histoire Naturelle" (31 vols., 1850–'61); and he wrote numerous treatises on medical history and natural history.

COX, EDWARD WILLIAM, a British lawyer, born in 1809, died November 24th. He was called to the bar at the Middle Temple in 1843, attained the rank of sergeant-at-law in 1868, was appointed the same year Recorder of Portsmouth, in 1870 Deputy Assistant Judge of Middlesex, and subsequently Deputy Lieutenant for the same county. He edited for some years the "Law Times," and was the author of several law-books, including "The Advocate," "A Treatise on the Law of Joint-Stock Companies," "A Treatise on the Law of Registrations and Elections," and "A Treatise on the Principles of Punishments." He also published "What am I? a Popular Introduction to Mental Philosophy and Physiology" (2 vols., 1874).

DELIGEORGIS, a Greek statesman, died May 25th. He was President of the Ministry from July to December, 1870, and again from 1872 to 1874, and at the time of his death was Minister of Finance. His second administration was particularly noted for the settlement of the Laurium question. (See GREECE, in "Annual Cyclopædia" for 1872 and 1873.)

DIESTEL, LUDWIG VON, a German theologian, born September 28, 1825, died May 15th. He studied theology in the Universities of Königsberg, Berlin, and Bonn. In 1851 he went to the University of Bonn as lecturer on the Old Testament, was appointed in 1858 inspector of the newly established Evangelical Theological Seminary, and extraordinary professor, went in 1862 to Greifswald as ordinary professor, in 1867 to Jena, and in 1872 to Tübingen, where he remained till his death. His principal work is "Geschichte des Alten Testaments in der Christlichen Kirche" (1868).

DOVE, HEINRICH WILHELM, a German scientist, born October 6, 1803, died April 5th. He was educated at the Universities of Breslau and Berlin, where he devoted himself chiefly to mathematics and physics. In 1826 he was appointed a *privatdocent*, and in 1828 extraordinary professor in the University of Königsberg, in 1829 extraordinary and in 1845 ordinary professor in that of Berlin. In 1837 he was elected a member of the Academy of Sciences. He was among the first who reduced meteorology to the rank of a natural science, and his researches upon the laws of storms and hurricanes will always remain among the most valuable contributions to that department of knowledge. His reports and isothermal maps afforded the first representation of the isothermal lines of the whole globe. He was also the first to announce the presence of a secondary electric current in a metallic wire, and thus claims high rank among the founders of modern electrical science. Many of his discoveries and experiments he described in the publications of the Berlin Academy, Poggendorf's "Annalen," the "Zeitschrift für Erdkunde," the "Zeitschrift" of the Prussian Statistical Bureau, and many other periodicals. Among his principal works are: "Meteorologische Untersuchungen" (1857); "Ueber die nichtperiodischen Aenderungen der Temperaturvertheilung auf der Oberfläche der Erde" (6 parts, 1840–'59); "Ueber den Zusammenhang der Wärmeveränderungen der Atmosphäre mit der Entwickelung der Pflanzen" (1846); "Temperaturtafeln" (1848); "Monatsisothermen" (1850); "Das Gesetz der Stürme" (1857; 4th edit., 1874), which was translated into English and French; and "Klimatologische Beiträge" (2 parts, 1857–'69). His sons Richard Wilhelm and Alfred have both attained considerable prominence, the former in the departments of civil and ecclesiastical law, the latter as an historian.

DUBS, JAKOB, a Swiss statesman, born in the Canton of Zürich in 1822, died January 15th. He studied law in the Universities of Berne, Heidelberg, and Zürich. After having filled several offices in the cantonal courts, he was appointed in 1849 a judge of the new Federal Court, and shortly after President of the Court. His political career began in 1847, when he was elected to the Great Council of his canton. From 1855 to 1861 he was President of the cantonal government, Director of Education, and a member of the Church Council. In 1849 he was also elected a member of the National Council, of which body he was elected President in 1854. In 1861 he was elected into the Federal Council, and in 1864 was President of the Republic. He resigned his position in the Federal Council in 1872, but was elected to the National Council from the Canton of Vaud. In 1875 he was also appointed a judge of the reorganized Federal Court of Lausanne.

FANFANI, FIETRO, an Italian philologist, born April 21, 1815, died March 4th. He studied at first medicine, but afterward devoted himself entirely to philology and *belles-lettres*. He made extensive researches in ancient and mediæval literature, and in 1847 established at Florence the journal "Ricordi Filologici," which at once met with great success. He took part in the campaign against Austria in 1848, was taken prisoner, and confined in Theresienstadt. He returned to Tuscany in September, 1848, and was afterward employed in the Ministry of Public Instruction at Turin under Gioberti, and at Florence under Franchini. In 1859, after the annexation of Tuscany to Italy, he was appointed director of the Marucellian Library. Among his works are dictionaries of the Italian language, of the words peculiar to Tuscany, and of Tuscan pronunciation.

FICHTE, IMMANUEL HERMANN, a German philosopher, son of the celebrated Johann Gottlieb Fichte, born July 18, 1796, died August 8th.

He studied philosophy and philology in the University of Berlin, filled between 1822 and 1842 professorships at the gymnasia of Saarbrücken and Düsseldorf and the University of Bonn, and in 1842 was appointed professor in the University of Tübingen. In 1867 he was pensioned at his own request. His doctrine was that of an ideal theism. Among his principal works are: "System der Ethik" (2 vols., 1850–'53); "Die Seelenfortdauer und die Weltstellung des Menschen" (1867); "Die theistische Weltansicht und ihre Berechtigung" (1873); and "Fragen und Bedenken über die nächste Fortbildung deutscher Spekulation" (1876). In the latter years of his life Fichte expressed great interest in and sympathy with American spiritualism.

GARBETT, JAMES, an English scholar and clergyman, born in 1802, died March 25th. He was educated at Brasenose College, Oxford, where he graduated B. A., taking first-class honors, in 1822. He was elected Michel Fellow of Queen's College, and afterward fellow and tutor of Brasenose and Hulme Lecturer of Divinity; became public examiner of the university in 1829, filling that post for two years with great distinction; was appointed prebendary of Chichester in 1843, and archdeacon in 1851. He delivered the Bampton lectures before the University of Oxford in 1842, and was Professor of Poetry there from 1842 to 1852. Besides his "Bampton Lectures" (2 vols., 1842), he published a volume of "Prælectiones Academicæ," one of "Archidiaconal Charges," five volumes of sermons, and numerous pamphlets on the theological and academical questions of the day.

GISKRA, KARL, an Austrian statesman, born January 29, 1820, died June 1st. He studied law and political economy in the University of Vienna. In 1848 he was chosen a delegate to the German Parliament at Frankfort, and achieved a national reputation for eloquence in debate. He became subsequently a lawyer at Vienna and at Brünn, and gained celebrity as counsel in criminal cases. He was soon elected to the Reichsrath; became Mayor of Brünn in 1866, as which he developed great executive ability; and in 1867 was elected President of the Chamber of Deputies. He was Minister of the Interior from 1867 to 1870 under Prince Carlos Auersperg, and afterward under Count Taafe, and did excellent service in the reconstruction of the Austrian state. After his retirement from the Ministry he took a prominent part in the disreputable "Gründer" operations of that period, and in consequence lost much of his popularity.

GUIDI, FILIPPO MARIA, an Italian cardinal, born July 18, 1815, died February 28th. He entered the Dominican order, became Bishop of Frascati in 1872, was created cardinal priest March 16, 1863, Archbishop of Bologna December 21, 1863, and was shortly before his death raised to the rank of cardinal bishop.

HEER, I., a Swiss statesman, born in 1825,

died March 1st. He attended the Universities of Zürich, Heidelberg, Berlin, and Paris. In 1857 he was elected Landamman (Governor) of the Canton of Glarus, and a member of the National Council. For eighteen years he retained his position as Landamman, and was respected and honored by the entire people. Upon the creation of the North German Confederation, he was appointed Minister at the different German courts, but returned within seven months. In December, 1875, he was elected a member of the Federal Council, and in 1877 its President. Owing to sickness he was compelled to resign in December, 1878. He was one of the ablest as well as the purest statesmen of Switzerland, and his loss is mourned by all parties.

HOWITT, WILLIAM, a British author, born in 1795, died March 3d. He traveled extensively on the Continent and in Australia, and wrote, partly alone and partly with his wife, a large number of works on various subjects. Among his works are : " Book of the Seasons " (1831) ; " History of Priestcraft " (1833) ; " The Rural and Domestic Life of Germany " (1842) ; " Haunts and Homes of British Poets " (1847) ; " History of Scandinavian Literature " (1852) ; " Madame Darrington of the Dene " (1851) ; " Talangetta, or the Squatter's Home " ; " The Man of the People " (1860) ; " Illustrated History of England " (8 vols., 1861) ; " History of the Supernatural in all Ages and Nations " (1863) ; " Discoveries in Australia " (1865) ; and " The Mad War Planet, and other Poems " (1871).

HUBER, JOHANNES, a German scholar, born August 18, 1830, died March 20th. He studied theology and afterward philosophy in the University of Munich, established himself as privatdocent there in 1854, became extraordinary Professor of Philosophy in 1859, and ordinary Professor in 1864. Among his earlier works are: " Idee der Unsterblichkeit " (1864 ; 2d edit., 1865) ; " Johannes Scotus Erigena " (1861) ; and " Die Philosophie der Kirchenväter " (1859), which was placed on the Index Expurgatorius. He was one of the most prominent champions of the Old Catholic movement in Bavaria, and wrote in its support many pamphlets, including " Das Papstthum und der Staat " (1871). He wrote an elaborate work on the history of the Jesuits (1873), and also works criticising Darwin, Strauss, Hartmann, and Haeckel.

JOHNSTON, ALEXANDER KEITH, a British explorer and geographer, born November 24, 1841, died June 28th. He pursued his studies under his father, the celebrated geographer of the same name, and afterward in Leipsic under A. Petermann. In 1874 he went to Paraguay upon an exploring expedition, of which he gave an account to the Royal Geographical Society. Besides frequent contributions to the " Geographical Magazine," he wrote the article on Africa for the new edition of the " Encyclopædia Britannica," and edited, with consid-

erable additions, the volume devoted to Africa in Stanford's " Compendium of Geography and Travel." In November, 1878, he was sent out in charge of the English expedition to explore the head of Lake Nyassa. He was attacked by dysentery, and died after a short illness.

LANDSEER, CHARLES, a British painter, born August 12, 1799, died July 22d. He was the second of the three sons of Mr. Landseer, an engraver of very considerable ability, his younger brother being the famous Sir Edwin Landseer. He was instructed in art by his father and by B. R. Haydon, entered the school of the Royal Academy in 1816, and accompanied Lord Stuart de Rothesay on his mission to Portugal and Brazil about 1820, collecting the materials utilized in many subsequent pictures. He was elected an associate of the Royal Academy in 1837, and Academician in 1845, and was keeper of the Academy from 1851 to May, 1873, when the Council voted him a pension equivalent to his former salary. Among his best paintings are " Pillaging of a Jew's House," " The Temptation of Andrew Marvell," " The Departure of Charles II. from Bentley," and " The Eve of the Battle of Edgehill."

LUBBOCK, Lady ELLEN FRANCES, wife of Sir John Lubbock, born in 1835, died October 20th. She shared the scientific tastes and tasks of her husband, and contributed numerous articles to scientific and literary journals, especially the " Academy " and " Nature." In 1862–'63 she published " Vacation Tourists," containing a description of her researches among the shell-mounds of Denmark.

MARTIN, KONRAD, a German bishop, born May 18, 1812, died July 16th. He was educated at the Universities of Halle, Munich, and Würzburg, was ordained as priest in 1836, and in 1856 became Bishop of Paderborn. He attended the Vatican Council, and after his return to Germany gained considerable celebrity as one of the most bitter opponents of the May laws, which he denounced as the " most atrocious ever launched against the Church of Christ since the era of Diocletian." He was arrested, tried, and deposed from his office in 1875, and shortly after escaped to Holland, whence he was expelled. After that he lived in retirement in Belgium. He was the author of a series of works on the Œcumenical Council, among them " Das unfehlbare Lehramt der Papstes " (1870), " Die Arbeiten des Vaticanischen Concils " (1873), and " Omnium Concilii Vaticani quæ ad Doctrinam et Disciplinam pertinent Documentorum Collectio " (1873). He also published a number of text-books on religion, including " Lehrbuch der Katholischen Religion " (1844 ; 15th edit., 1873), which was translated into many foreign languages, and " Lehrbuch der Katholischen Moral " (1850 ; 5th edit., 1865).

MIERS, JOHN, a British botanist, born August 25, 1789, died October 17th. Early in the present century he went to South America, where he remained many years, traveling and exploring. He published "Travels in Chili and La Plata," "Illustrations of South American Plants," and "Contributions to Botany." He was a member of the Linnæan and Royal Societies.

MURAT, Princess CAROLINE GEORGINE, born April 13, 1810, died February 10th. She was the daughter of Thomas Frazer of Bordentown, New Jersey, and in 1827 married Prince Lucien, the second son of King Joachim Murat. The family for a time was in very straitened circumstances, their only support being a school for girls kept by Mrs. Murat. The establishment of the Second Empire restored to them wealth and titles. Her husband died May 10, 1878.

OGILVIE, ROBERT ANNESLEY, a British statesman, born in 1807, died May 16th. He was educated at Eton, and entered the customs service in 1828. On account of his extensive knowledge of British and continental commerce, he was appointed to take part in the different commercial conferences between Great Britain and the continental powers held since 1860, and for many years he was consulted by the different Chancellors of the Exchequer on the alteration and arrangement of the customs tariffs. In 1863 he was appointed Surveyor-General of Customs, and retired from the service in 1876 on account of ill health.

OMER PASHA, a Turkish general, died February 19th. He was a native of Mitau in Courland, emigrated to Hungary in his youth, took part in the revolutionary movements of 1848-'49, and was compelled to seek refuge in Turkey, where he entered the army and served with distinction in various parts of the empire. In June, 1877, he was made general of division and appointed to a command in Armenia. At the battle of the Aladja Dagh he was taken prisoner, and was sent to Kiev, whence he returned in 1878. Immediately upon his return he was placed under trial by court martial, but the proceedings were spun out to suppress some damaging information. He was seized with an apoplectic fit while in attendance upon the court, and died within a few hours.

PALLADIUS, Archimandrite, the head of the Russian ecclesiastical mission in China, died in February at an advanced age. During his long residence in Peking he was an assiduous student of Chinese literature, and gained a thorough knowledge of the history, philosophy, and religions of China. Though he never published any independent work, he was a large contributor to the Russian periodical published by his mission establishment at Peking (4 vols., 1852 -'66), in which appeared from his pen "A Life of Buddha" (vol. i.), "Historical Studies in Ancient Buddhism" (vol. ii.), "The Navigation between Tientsin and Peking" (vol. iii.), "An Ancient Mongol Account of the Life of Genghis Khan," and "The Mohammedans in China" (vol. iv.). He was also a contributor to the "Recueil Oriental" and the "Proceedings" of the Geographical Societies of Siberia and St.

Petersburg. At the time of his death he had completed and was about to publish a Chinese-Russian dictionary.

ROTHSCHILD, Baron LIONEL DE, a British financier, the first representative of the Jewish race in the English Parliament, born November 22, 1808, died June 3d. He was the oldest son of Nathan Meyer de Rothschild, who in 1822 was created a baron of the Austrian Empire. Baron Lionel de Rothschild, whose great monetary transactions indicate the financial history of the last fifty years, was in political life chiefly known for the part he took in the emancipation of the Jews, and for his consistent advocacy of Liberal principles. He was elected a member of Parliament for the City of London in the Liberal interest in 1847, 1849, 1852, and 1857, but was not permitted to take his seat until 1858, when the Jews' Disabilities Bill was passed. He kept his seat until 1874. He was munificent in his charities, benefiting not only people of his own faith but of all classes. He was married in 1836 to Charlotte, daughter of Baron Charles de Rothschild, and had three sons and two daughters. His oldest son, Sir Nathan Meyer de Rothschild, Bart., M. P. for Aylesbury, was born in 1840, and succeeded to the baronetcy of his uncle Sir Anthony Rothschild in 1876.

STÄMPFLI, JACOB, a Swiss statesman, died May 14th. He was one of the leaders of the Radical party, and was President of the Republic in 1861. He was one of the members of the Geneva Court of Arbitration on the Alabama claims.

WALDEGRAVE, Countess FRANCES ELIZABETH ANNE, an English lady, born in 1821, died July 5th. She was the daughter of John Braham, the famous opera-singer, and was married four times: to John James Waldegrave; then to his relative George Edward, seventh Earl of Waldegrave; thirdly, to George Granville Harcourt; and, fourthly, to Chichester Parkinson Fortescue, created Lord Carlingford in 1874. For a number of years she was one of the most prominent and popular leaders of London society, and her receptions brought together the chief members of the Liberal party, to which she was strongly attached.

WARD, EDWARD MATTHEW, a British painter, born in 1816, died January 15th. He became a student at the Academy in 1834, and was assisted in his studies by Wilkie. In 1836 he went to Rome, remaining nearly three years; and before returning to England he spent a few months in Munich, studying fresco-painting under Cornelius. His picture of "Dr. Johnson reading the Manuscript of the Vicar of Wakefield" (1843) was favorably received, and may be considered as the first of a long series of popular works in which Mr. Ward made for himself a kind of specialty that has been described as "historical genre." In these works, generally minor historical, biographical, and literary episodes or anecdotes are treated, not after the manner of the old historical style of high art, but from more familiar or domestic points of view, with careful attention to costume and all picturesque surroundings and accessories. The most attractive specimens of the paintings of his maturer years are: "Queen Victoria visiting the Tomb of Napoleon in the Hospital of les Invalides in Paris," "Louis Napoleon receiving the Order of the Garter from her Majesty at Windsor," "Jeannie Deans," "The Duke of Argyll," "Dr. Johnson and John Wilkes," "Queen Anne Boleyn at the Tower Stairs," "The Earl of Leicester and Amy Robsart," and "Caught on both Sides."

ZSEDENYI, EDUARD· VON, a Hungarian statesman, born March 18, 1803, died February 20th. He played for many years an important part in the political history of his country, having been first elected a deputy in 1833. From 1865 he was one of the most prominent members of the Deák and afterward of the Liberal party. He was one of the ablest financiers of his country, a privy councilor, and from 1875 General Director of the Evangelical Church of Hungary.

OHIO. The debt of the State on November 15, 1879, was as follows:

Foreign debt, payable in New York:
Loan payable July 1, 1868, not bearing interest.................................... $2,500 00
Loan payable June 30, 1881, six per cent..interest................................ 4,072,640 80
Loan payable December 31, 1886, six per cent. interest........................... 2,400,000 00

Total foreign debt................... $6,475,140 80
Domestic debt, payable at Columbus:
Canal loan, not bearing interest... .... 1,665 00

Total funded debt................... $6,476,805 80
Local indebtedness of the State on September 1, 1879:
Net debt of counties...................... $2,872,834 49
Net debt of townships, including debts created by boards of education other than for separate school districts............... 161,821 10
Net debt of cities (first and second class)... 36,086,069 77
Net debt of incorporated villages............ 969,151 85
Net debt of school districts (special or separate)................................ 1,451,197 82

Total local debts.................... $41,490,574 53
Amount of the reimbursable debt:
State........................... $6,476,805 80
Local........................... 41,490,574 53

Total debt redeemable........... $47,967,379 88
Irreducible debt, composed of school and other trust funds, upon which the State pays interest at six per cent. per annum........... 4,289,718 52

Aggregate public debts in the State.. $52,257,098 35

The revenue and expenditures for the year were as follows:

Balance in the State Treasury November 15, 1878, belonging to various funds.......... $918,694 97
Receipts from all sources.................... 5,730,170 10

Total amount of funds in the Treasury.. $6,648,865 07
Disbursements during the year.............. 5,653,752 83

Cash balance in the Treasury November 15, 1879............................. $995,112 74

Total estimated receipts for 1880, including balance on hand.......................... $5,863,699 28
Total estimated disbursements for 1880....... 4,936,902 03

Estimated balance in the Treasury November 15, 1880.................... $951,797 25

The taxes levied in 1878, collectible in 1879, were:

State taxes.................................. $4,496,876 01
County and local taxes...................... 21,828,069 29
Delinquencies and forfeitures 2,235,820 56

Total for 1879.·.................. $28,559,765 86

The taxes levied in 1879, collectible in 1880, are as follows:

State taxes.................................. $4,450,841 66
County and other local taxes................ 21,806,828 05
Delinquencies and forfeitures............... 2,804,596 55

Total for 1880...................... $28,061,262 16

The value of all the taxable real estate and personal property in Ohio, according to the consolidated tax duplicate for 1879, is as follows:

Real estate in cities, towns, and villages.... $877,657,467 00
Real estate not in cities, towns, and villages   716,111,487 00
Chattel property......................... 442,979,885 00

Total taxable Values for 1879......... $1,586,748,789 00

On personal property there was a decrease in valuation, as compared with 1878, of $18,-480,667; on real estate in cities and towns of $4,285,500; total decrease, $22,716,167. There was an increase on lands not in cities and towns of $6,887,452, making the total net decrease $15,828,715.

At the close of the fiscal year 1878 (November 15th) there was a balance in the Treasury to the credit of the public works of $26,641.66; gross earnings from tolls, fines, and water rents for the current year ending November 15, 1879, $213,350.22, a total of $239,991.88. Received at State Treasury since November 15th, of collections during current year, $5,790.79. Total, $245,782.67. Total expenditures for the year, $187,116.32. Balance to credit of canal fund, $58,666.35; add amount in hands of receivers, $23,466.66, making the real balance to public works, $82,133.01, since their abandonment by the late lessees, over and above all expenses chargeable to them.

The statistics of the principal agricultural products of the State, as reported by township assessors in May, 1879, are as follows: Wheat, 2,123,958 acres, 85,218,773 bushels; corn, 3,037,380 acres, 114,839,127 bushels· oats, 935,315 acres, 29,671,231 bushels; potatoes, 116,513 acres, 7,580,118 bushels; rye, 58,041 acres, 756,502 bushels; barley, 38,461 acres, 1,265,299 bushels; timothy, 1,586,778 acres, 1,951,488 tons; clover, 388,219 acres, 338,985 tons; tobacco, 28,075,140 pounds; butter, 50,332,023 pounds; cheese, 36,401,386 pounds; wool, 16,390,505 pounds; flax, 48,-986 acres, 474,669 bushels seed, 12,036,083 pounds fiber; sorghum, 16,305 acres, 11,909 pounds sugar, 1,273,048 gallons sirup; maple sugar, 2,987,288 pounds; maple sirup, 510,117 gallons; bees, 169,755 hives; honey, 2,521,293 pounds; apples, 30,669,404 bushels; peaches, 1,476,159 bushels; pears, 110,419 bushels.

The number and valuation of animals in the State, as returned by the assessors for the year 1879, were as follows:

ANIMALS.	Number.	Value.
Horses	780,642	$34,705,410
Cattle	1,630,004	24,765,607
Mules	26,793	1,851,001
Sheep	4,267,261	9,311,972
Hogs	2,041,649	4,849,445
Dogs	272,084	878,624

The General Assembly, at its adjourned session, adopted a codification of the statutes, passed a very stringent law to prevent bribery or intimidation at elections, and submitted to the vote of the people proposed amendments to the Constitution as follows:

ARTICLE II.

SECTION 2. Senators and Representatives shall be elected biennially by the electors in the respective counties or districts, at a time prescribed by law; their terms of office shall commence on the Tuesday next after the first Monday of January thereafter, and continue two years.

ARTICLE III.

SECTION 1. The Executive Department shall consist of a Governor, Lieutenant-Governor, Secretary of State, Auditor, Treasurer, and Attorney-General, who shall be chosen by the electors of the State, at the place of voting for members of the General Assembly, and at a time prescribed by law.

ARTICLE X.

SECTION 4. Township officers shall be elected on the first Monday of April, annually, by the qualified electors of their respective townships, and shall hold their offices for one year from the next succeeding their election, and until their successors are qualified; except township trustees, who shall be elected by the qualified electors in the several townships of the State on the first Monday of April, A. D. 1880, one to serve for the term of one year, one for two years, and one for three years; and on the first Monday of April in each year thereafter, one trustee shall be elected to hold the office for three years from the Monday next succeeding his election, and until his successor is qualified.

JUDICIAL ARTICLE.

SECTION 3. The State shall be divided into nine common pleas districts, of which the county of Hamilton shall constitute one, which districts shall be of compact territory, bounded by county lines, and said districts, other than said county of Hamilton, shall, without division of counties, be further divided into subdivisions, in each of which, and in said county of Hamilton, there shall be elected by the electors thereof, respectively, at least one judge of the court of common pleas for the district, and residing therein. Courts of common pleas shall be held by one or more of these judges in every county of the district, as often as may be provided by law, and more than one court or sitting thereof may be held at the same time in each district.

SEC. 5. In each district there shall be elected, by the electors at large of such district, one judge of the district court, by whom the district courts in such district shall be held, and he shall receive such compensation as may be provided by law. District courts shall be held in each county at least once every year. The General Assembly may increase the number of district court judges to three in any district or districts, and may provide for having a judge *pro tempore*, to hold any court whenever necessary by reason of the failure, disqualification, absence, or sickness of any judge; and the amount of pay allowed a judge *pro tempore* may be deducted from the salary of any judge whose default causes the necessity of having the *pro tempore* judge. The times of holding common pleas and district courts shall be fixed by law, but the General Assembly may authorize the judges of said courts, respectively, to fix the times of the holding of said courts.

All the proposed amendments were overwhelmingly rejected at the October election.

The Republican State Convention was held at Cincinnati, May 28th. The following ticket was nominated: For Governor, Charles Foster; for Lieutenant-Governor, Andrew H. Hickenlooper; for Auditor of State, John H. Oglevee; for Treasurer of State, Joseph Turney; for Judge of Supreme Court, W. W. Johnson; for Attorney-General, George K. Nash; for member of Board of Public Works, James Fullington. The platform adopted was as follows:

Resolved, That the Republican party of Ohio, reaffirming the cardinal doctrines of its adopted faith as heretofore proclaimed, especially pledges itself anew to the maintenance of free suffrage, equal rights, the unity of the nation, and the supremacy of the national Government in all matters placed by the Constitution under its control.

Resolv'd, That we earnestly appeal to the people in the exercise of their power through the ballot-box to arrest the mad career of the party now controlling both branches of Congress, under the domination of a majority of men lately in arms against the Government, and now plotting to regain through the power of legislation the cause which they lost in the field, namely, the establishment of State sovereignty by the overthrow of national supremacy.

Resolved, That the Democratic party, having committed itself to an attempt to break up the Government by refusing to appropriate to their legitimate objects the public moneys already collected from the people unless the Executive shall give his official signature to measures which he conscientiously disapproves—measures plainly intended to allow a free course to fraud, violence, and corruption in the national elections, and to impair the constitutional supremacy of the nation—deserves the condemnation of every honest and law-abiding citizen.

Resolved, That the present extra session of Congress, thus compelled by Democratic conspirators, has been prolonged beyond all possible excuse, not only to the depletion of the Treasury, but also to the grave detriment of every industrial and commercial interest of the country, by uncalled-for agitation of the several questions, by persistent efforts in hostility to the resumption of specie payments already happily accomplished, by constantly tampering with a currency system unsurpassed in the world, by reopening and stimulating sectional controversy, especially through the avowed determination to repeal all war legislation, and by seeking to inaugurate a reactionary revolution designed to restore full power to a solid South in the affairs of the Government.

Resolved, That the financial administration of the Government by the Republican party, in accomplishing the great work of the resumption of specie payments, in restoring our currency to par value, in greatly reducing the burden of the national debt, in refunding a large proportion of the same at a rate of interest one third less than the former rate, thereby alone saving to the Treasury $13,000,000 a year, and in enhancing the national credit to a standing never before attained, is a source of just pride to the Republicans of Ohio, and deserves the warm approbation of the American people.

Resolved, That this perpetual disturbance of the country in response to the conciliatory course of the Administration should by the judgment of the people be thoroughly condemned.

Resolved, That the Democratic Legislature of Ohio, going on from bad to worse, from O'Connor reforms of our public institutions resulting in scandals unnumbered and mischiefs unmeasured, to outrageous attempts to reverse the will of the people as declared by their suffrages, and foisting upon them legislative usurpation, defeated candidates for local offices in place of those duly elected by the lawful and unquestioned ballots cast in the interest of honest and decent home government, merits the most indignant rebuke of every intelligent voter of the State.

Resolved, That the memories of our dead heroes who gave their lives to save the nation from destruction protest against the expulsion of their living comrades from public offices to gratify the partisan purposes of the dominant party in Congress.

Resolved, That we send greeting to the President of the United States and our Republican members of Congress, and we cordially thank and honor them for the firm and patriotic stand they have taken in opposition to the designs of the majority of the present Congress, and we hereby pledge them our earnest and undivided support.

The Democratic State Convention met at Columbus, June 4th, and nominated the following ticket: For Governor, Thomas Ewing; for Lieutenant-Governor, A. V. Rice; for Treasurer, Anthony Howells; for Auditor, Charles Reemelin; for Judge of Supreme Court, W. J. Gilmore; for Attorney-General, Isaiah Pillars; for member of Board of Public Works, Patrick O'Marah. The following platform was adopted:

Resolved, That the Democracy of Ohio demand free and fair elections, and to that end denounce all interference with elections by the military power; that the experience of this and other countries has abundantly proved that the presence of troops at the polls is destructive of the freedom of the elections, and is incompatible with the existence of free institutions; that the laws enacted by Congress which, under the pretense of regulating the manner of Congressional elections, interfere with the election of State officers and overthrow the laws of the State governing the choice of such officers, are unconstitutional, and for that reason ought to be repealed; that they are instrumentalities of fraud, force, and corruption, by which the party in power uses the money of the people to corrupt, and thousands of irresponsible officers to harass and coerce the voters, and especially by force and fraud to deprive our naturalized citizens of the right to vote; and for these reasons also, said laws ought to be immediately repealed.

Resolved, That impartial juries are essential to the administration of justice, and thereby to the preservation of liberty; that no man can be secure in his person or property when the juries are "packed" and controlled by the Government for despotic and partisan purposes; that under the Federal jury laws, now in existence, juries have been so "packed" and controlled, and that the highest interests of justice and free government require that these laws be changed so as to secure fair, impartial, and independent juries in the Federal courts.

Resolved, That the Republican minority in Congress, by refusing to vote supplies to maintain the Government unless the majority would agree to the use of troops at the polls, and also to the maintenance of the unconstitutional, corrupting, violent, and unjust election laws aforesaid; and the President of the United States, by his unprecedented use of the veto power, in order to perpetuate said laws and the use of armed men at the polls, have shown a spirit of faction and a devotion to party success instead of the welfare of the country and the preservation of its Constitution and liberties, that demand the condemnation of the whole American people.

Resolved, That President Hayes, by his frequent interposition of the veto in order to defeat legislation that was plainly constitutional, that in no way interfered with the independence of any other department of the Government, and had received the most mature con-

sideration of Congress, has shown an utter disregard of the considerations and principles that induced the insertion of the veto power in the Constitution, and a like disregard of the wishes and welfare of the people.

Resolved, That we declare it as the sense of the Democracy of Ohio that not a dollar should be appropriated by Congress to pay soldiers, marshals, deputy marshals, or supervisors of election, to interfere with or control the elections.

Resolved, That the efforts of the Republican party to open and keep alive the war feeling between the North and South are to be condemned by every lover of his country.

Resolved, That we reaffirm the financial principles heretofore advocated by the Democratic party of Ohio, that the issue of money in any form, and the regulation thereof, belong to the General Government alone, and ought not to be delegated or intrusted to individuals or corporations; that we therefore oppose the perpetuation of the present national banking system, as a means of control over the currency of the country, and demand the gradual substitution of Treasury notes for national-bank currency, to be made receivable for all dues and a legal tender equally with coin, such Government issues to be regulated upon principles established by legislation or organic law, so as to secure the greatest possible stability of value.

Resolved, That after changing the valuation of all property from the scale of paper money, by which the heavy burdens of debt now resting upon the people were created, to the former level of gold and silver, the change then made in the metallic standard itself, by the demonetization of silver, was a monstrous fraud upon the people, cunningly devised in the interests of the holders of bonds, that should be condemned as in violation of every principle of honest dealing, and a covert assault upon the fundamental rights of property; and we therefore demand the full restoration of silver to its original place as a money metal, the same as gold.

Resolved, That the rapid increase of the interest-bearing debt of the Government under the present Administration ought to excite the serious apprehension of the people. We demand that the further increase of the bonded debt in time of peace be stopped, and it be put in process of extinction.

Resolved, That the attack made upon the State Legislature in the Republican platform is wholly undeserved, and that the Legislature, in its arduous work of codifying the laws of the State, in the reduction of fees and salaries of county officers, and the passage of a law to protect the ballot-box and prevent bribery at elections, deserves the commendation of the people of the State.

Resolved, That it is the duty of our Government to maintain to its fullest extent the doctrine that a man may, in good faith, change his habitation and become a citizen of any other country. We should protect in every part of the world all our naturalized citizens as we would our native-born, and should resist all improper claims upon them by the governments to which they no longer owe allegiance. We demand that existing treaties with all foreign governments be rigidly enforced, and that early steps be taken to obtain from the German Empire a fuller recognition of the right of expatriation, and of the right of our naturalized citizens returning or having property there, by a modification of the treaty existing between us.

The minority of the Committee on Resolutions submitted the following additional resolution:

Resolved, That we request the Democratic members of Congress not to vote any appropriation to any army until a provision shall have been made that such army shall not be employed to influence or intimidate people at the polls.

This resolution was defeated by a heavy vote. The National (Greenback-Labor) State Convention was held at Columbus June 4th, while the Democratic State Convention was in session. The proceedings were inharmonious, but the following ticket was finally nominated: For Governor, General A. Saunders Piatt; for Lieutenant-Governor, Hugo Preyer; for Auditor, Andrew Roy; for Treasurer, Charles Jenkins; for Supreme Judge, A. M. Jackson; for Attorney-General, James R. Groghan; for member of Board of Public Works, George A. Platt. The following platform was adopted:

The National-Greenback-Labor party of Ohio, in convention assembled, adopt the following declaration of principles as our platform, and go before the people thereon with the consciousness of thereby performing a sacred duty to our fellow American citizens, as sovereigns of a free republic:

In the recognition and distribution of civil and political rights and privileges there should be no favoritism on account of birth, color, creed, or financial condition.

The General Government should issue an ample volume of full legal-tender currency to meet the needs of the country and to promptly pay all of its debts.

We recognize the deplorable commercial and industrial condition of our country as something appalling to contemplate, and we unhesitatingly hold the old parties responsible for the nefarious and ruinous policy pursued, and point to their record as full and complete evidence to the people that it is folly to hope for relief from either; and we unhesitatingly charge this suffering and degradation as the result of the legislation of the last quarter of a century, being solely in the interest of the moneyed aristocracy and corrupt corporations.

The funding of the national debt into long-time bonds, to be paid over and over in the form of interest, absorbing the wealth of the nation, making business prosperity an impossibility, reducing the laborer to a condition of semi-slavery, and rendering the welfare of the nation subservient to the interests of the bond-holding class, is an outrage so monstrous that any political party that sanctions it is unworthy the support of intelligent and honest men. We are inflexibly opposed to the issue by the Government of interest-bearing bonds of any description for any purpose whatever.

The national banking system should be immediately abolished.

A tariff amply sufficient for the protection of American industries should be maintained till a free financial system may have shown it to be unnecessary to tax labor for the support of capital.

All internal revenue taxes should be dispensed with, and a graduated income tax substituted.

We demand the immediate calling in and payment of all United States bonds in full legal-tender money.

We demand an equalization of bounties for soldiers.

We denounce all references to our late civil war of a malicious and insulting nature as revolutionary and wholly inconsistent with the principles of free government, and antagonistic to the restoration of the old motto: "United we stand, divided we fall."

A platform reported by the minority of the Committee on Resolutions called out bitter discussion, and when it was voted down a number of delegates left the Convention. They issued a circular repudiating its action, and calling a meeting for conference in Toledo on the 24th of June. At that meeting the action of the Columbus Convention was repudiated, and a number of resolutions were adopted, but no attempt to nominate a State ticket was made.

The Prohibitionists had a full ticket in the field.

The election was held October 14th, and re-

sulted in the election of all the Republican candidates, the vote being as follows:

FOR GOVERNOR.

Charles Foster, Republican	336,261
Thomas Ewing, Democrat	319,132
A. S. Piatt, Greenback	9,129
G. T. Stewart, Prohibition	4,145

FOR LIEUTENANT-GOVERNOR.

Andrew H. Hickenlooper, Republican	335,140
A. V. Rice, Democrat	319,462
Hugo Preyer, Greenback	9,566
J. W. Sharp, Prohibition	4,334

FOR AUDITOR.

J. H. Oglevee, Republican	335,184
C. Reemelin, Democrat	317,442
Andrew Roy, Greenback	11,621
M. J. Fanning, Prohibition	4,387

FOR TREASURER.

Joseph Turney, Republican	335,670
A. Howells, Democrat	317,184
C. Jenkins, Greenback	11,222
Elias Blair, Prohibition	4,343

FOR JUDGE OF SUPREME COURT.

W. W. Johnson, Republican	336,009
W. J. Gilmore, Democrat	316,994
A. M. Jackson, Greenback	11,331
J. Harding, Prohibition	4,382

FOR ATTORNEY-GENERAL.

G. K. Nash, Republican	336,100
Isaiah Pillars, Democrat	316,773
J. R. Groghan, Greenback	11,165
S. B. Foster, Prohibition	4,319

FOR BOARD OF PUBLIC WORKS.

J. Fullington, Republican	336,591
P. O'Marah, Democrat	315,968
George A. Platt, Greenback	11,103
J. H. Horton, Prohibition	4,380

OLD CATHOLICS. Both in Germany and Switzerland the Old Catholic movement appears to have lost ground during the year 1879, while in Austria some progress was made in the organization of the Church by the convocation of the first Synod.

In Germany, the Synod was held as in former years at Bonn, where the Bishop of the Church, Dr. Reinkens, resides. It was less attended than any of the five previous Synods, only 16 priests and 42 laymen being present. The usual statistical report on the condition of the Church was not presented this year. The Bishop in his opening address admitted that there had been during the past year no increase of number, but stated that there had not been either a retrogression. He was still very hopeful respecting the future prospects of the Church. It was resolved to establish a pension fund for invalided priests. Next year no Synod will be held, but a Church Congress, either at Heidelberg or Mannheim. The Synodal Council, which remains in power until the meeting of the next Synod, will consist of the Bishop, Professor Schulte (Vice-President), Professors Knoodl, Weber, and Michelis, one parish priest, and four other laymen. The Church suffers considerably from want of funds, and the Bishop stated that several offers from excellent priests had therefore to be declined. Two students were studying theology in the theological faculty of Bonn. The three

Old Catholic professors of this faculty, who last year withdrew from the Synod because they disapproved the abolition of priestly celibacy, had continued to keep aloof from active coöperation in the work of the Church. For the same reason, most of the priests and congregations of Bavaria have suspended their relations with the Bishop and the Synod. Dr. Döllinger, who has never sympathized with the organization of an independent Church, contents himself with protesting against the Vatican Council, and takes no active part in the building up of an Old Catholic Church. He resisted, however, the efforts made by an Austrian prelate, at the special request of the Pope, and by Archbishop Steichele of Munich, his former pupil, to induce him to rejoin the communion of Rome. The Old Catholic Church lost in 1879 some of its most distinguished members, as Professor Huber (see OBITUARIES, FOREIGN) and Classen Kappelmann.

The Synod of the "Christian Catholics" of Switzerland held its fifth annual session on June 5th at Solothurn, the capital of the canton of the same name. The Church has begun and will continue to suffer great losses in property and power in the Canton of Berne, in consequence of the determination of the Roman Catholics (those who adhere to the resolutions of the Vatican Council) to accept the church law of the canton, which provides for an election of all priests by popular suffrage, and subjects them to a reëlection every six years. At the first election which took place in the Catholic parishes, the Roman Catholics refused to take part, and thus nearly all the parishes passed into the hands of the Old Catholics. The latter, though in power, constitute only a minority in most of the parishes, and must be prepared to lose most of them whenever the Roman Catholics conclude to exercise their right of voting. In this way some parishes have already been lost, and others will follow. Bishop Herzog reported this year the number of parishes as 56 (against 61 in 1878), and the number of priests as 72 (against 75 in 1878). The number of students of theology in the Old Catholic theological faculty of Berne was 11. Communion in both kinds, which by the Synod of 1878 was declared permissible, has since been introduced in the cantons of Geneva and Neufchâtel; the parishes of the other cantons have thus far retained communion in one kind. A lively discussion took place this year on the subject of a revised French missal. It has been approved by M. Michaud, the most prominent man of the Church in French Switzerland, who strongly leans toward a union with the Greek Church; but Bishop Herzog condemned the attempt, and only conceded that the manual was not un-Catholic, and recommended the Synod to refer it back to the Genevese for better consideration. The Synod desired to enter into a closer union with the Anglican Churches of England and America, and passed a series of resolutions to that effect. The President of the Synodal Council, Landamman Keller of Aargau, resigned his post on account of old age. He was succeeded by Herr Philippi of Basle.

The Old Catholics of Austria had at the beginning of 1879 three congregations, organized according to law and therefore recognized by the state, at Vienna, Ried, and Warnsdorf. Being as yet without a bishop, they were doubtful whether they had the right to call a Synod; but their legal adviser, Professor Schulte of Bonn, accorded to them the right of constituting themselves "an extraordinary Synod." This Synod met at Vienna on July 5th, simultaneously with the Synods of Germany and Switzerland. A provisional Synodal Council was constituted, with Dr. Linder, a member of the Vienna Town Council, as President, and the three priests of the Church and three other laymen as members. Subject to ratification by a future Synod, the Synodal Council adopted for Austria the reforms thus far introduced by the German and Swiss Synods. These reforms are classified under eight heads: 1. The participation of the laity in the outer government of the Church, popular election of the clergy, etc.; 2. Confession to be voluntary, not compulsory; 3. Freedom of the clergy to marry; 4. Use of the national tongue in the liturgy and all ecclesiastical offices; 5. Fasting and abstinence to be no longer a matter of obligation; 6. Reduction of superfluous festivals; 7. Reforms in the matter of indulgences, the veneration of pictures and relics, religious processions, etc.; 8. Abolition of mass-stipends and all payments for spiritual functions. The Synodal Council was instructed to take the necessary steps to obtain from the Reichsrath an appropriation for the support of the Old Catholic Church, and further to make the necessary preparation for the future election of a bishop.

In France, the first Old Catholic congregation has at last been organized in Paris by Father Hyacinthe (M. Loyson). As long as the French Church has no bishops of her own, it has been arranged between M. Loyson on the one hand, and the Anglican bishops of England, Scotland, and Ireland, who take a special interest in the Old Catholic movement in France, on the other, that the Primus of Scotland shall exercise episcopal jurisdiction. As delegate of the Primus, Bishop Herzog of Switzerland in July administered the sacrament of confirmation to seven persons. Over six hundred names were inscribed in Paris as adherents to the programme of Catholic reform issued by M. Loyson in February, 1879. He was assisted in Paris by two priests.

OREGON. The progress of Oregon by the gradual increase of population and the patient development of its material resources, during the last ten years, presents some remarkable results. The population of the State in 1868 was 80,161; and that of some of the towns was: Portland, 6,717; Salem, 1,200; Albany, 856; Astoria, 556. In eastern Oregon there were then scarcely 10,000 persons. Two years later, on January 1, 1870, the State's population was 90,983, while the number of inhabitants in Portland, owing to the building of the east and west side railroads, had increased to 11,103 on January 1, 1872. From that time to the end of 1874 very little increase was made in the population of Portland or of the State. Portland had on January 1, 1874, 12,-459 inhabitants, while the State's population aggregated 95,673 persons that year. From 1875 to 1878 both the population of the State, Portland, and Astoria had increased wonderfully. Oregon was then estimated to contain 160,000 persons, Portland very nearly 20,000, and Astoria 1,800. But the most rapid stride in population was in eastern Oregon. In 1874 the entire number of white persons therein amounted to only 12,000, and official statistics show that there are now in eastern Oregon and eastern Washington Territory close upon 50,-000 persons.

The tables of grain exports, prepared from the statistics of the Portland Board of Trade by its Secretary, William Reid, show that during the year ending January 1, 1868, Oregon exported 120,980 barrels of flour, and only 45,-810 centals of wheat, none of which was sent to foreign countries. This was considered a remarkable increase over the year ending January 1, 1867, when only 29,811 barrels of flour were exported. In 1869 the total values of wheat and flour exports amounted to $589,872. In 1870 Oregon began to do a direct foreign trade with Europe, and dispatched from the Columbia River 12 vessels with 189,892 centals of wheat, of the value of $379,618. The united exports of wheat and flour to all countries in that year amounted to $1,050,522. In the succeeding year, 1871-'72, there were dispatched to Europe 12 ships of larger tonnage, with 242,759 centals of wheat, of the value of $531,689. So successful had these ventures become that in the next year the foreign exports of wheat were more than doubled, as in 1872-'73 there were dispatched to Europe 24 vessels with 509,430 centals of wheat. The next year, 1873 -'74, Oregon tried the export of flour to Europe, and shipped 97,600 barrels and 999,382 centals of wheat to the United Kingdom in 54 vessels, receiving in return therefor $2,435,794. The total receipts from wheat and flour exports in that year amounted to $4,037,008—an increase in two years unparalleled in the history of any other State. In 1874-'75 there were dispatched to Europe, China, and Australia 73 vessels, with 1,299,318 centals of wheat and 116,000 barrels of flour, in addition to 826,322 centals of wheat exported to California and other countries—the total exports, reducing flour to wheat, that year, 1875-'76, being 2,563,539 centals. The year ending August 1, 1877, did not show any increase of exports in quantity over the preceding year, but the values were

considerably higher. In the last harvest year, ending August 1, 1878, there were exported to all countries, including San Francisco, British Columbia, and Puget Sound, 352,161 centals of wheat, including flour, of the aggregate value of $5,635,156. Estimated by tons, there were exported to Great Britain alone in 1873-'74 49,469 tons of wheat, increased next year to 64,939 tons; the year ending August 1, 1876, 79,911 tons; 1877, 112,697 tons; while to all countries for the year ending August 1, 1878, there were exported 176,000 tons of wheat, including flour. A corresponding increase during the next ten years will make Oregon take rank among the greatest wheat-producing States in the Union.

The tonnage in like manner has been increasing each year since 1868. In that year the gross tonnage of vessels which arrived in Columbia River was 19,966, and of those departing 16,022, including steamers to and from San Francisco; whereas in 1876 the arrivals amounted to 56,882 tons register, and the departures to 76,617, an increase of 300 per cent. on arrivals and nearly 400 per cent. on departures during a period of eight years. In 1868 47 vessels went to sea over the bar of the Columbia River; 106 in 1874, carrying 71,012 tons; 108 in 1875, carrying 134,500 tons; 231 in 1876, carrying 154,459 tons; and 256 in 1877, carrying 232,897 tons; while in 1868 the total tonnage carried to sea by all classes of vessels was 23,367. The river tonnage shows equal development. In 1868 there were received at Portland by river-steamers 418,968 sacks of flour and 55,368 sacks of wheat, and there were, then only nine steamers engaged in the carrying trade on the rivers, with a registered tonnage of 2,179. In 1875 the Oregon Steam Navigation Company, Oregon Steamship Company, and Willamette Transportation Company had together 32 steamers and barges, with an aggregate tonnage of 18,698 alone; in addition to which other individuals then owned 12 smaller steamers, of the aggregate tonnage of 2,473. In 1878 the river-steamers plying on the Columbia and Willamette Rivers, including three steam-tugs on the Columbia bar, numbered 72, with an aggregate registered tonnage of 25,089; in addition to which there were 20 river-barges, of the united tonnage of 5,661. The productions raised by the farming population required greater facilities of transportation and new steamers each year. To these have been added two railroads, 250 miles in length, which bring to Portland daily large quantities of wheat, flour, and other produce. Up to January, 1868, the whole of the export trade, except to Puget Sound and Honolulu, was with San Francisco. According to the manifests of the cargoes of all the steamers and coasters from Oregon to the Golden Gate, the value of merchandise then exported was $1,-678,793; while the shipments by Wells, Fargo & Co., from Oregon mines, of gold dust, bars, coin, and treasure, a record of which was then accurately kept, amounted to $1,001,000. In 1869 and 1870 these gold shipments fell off, and in their place there were shipped increased quantities of produce and merchandise, until for the year ending August 1, 1875, the produce exports to San Francisco amounted in value to $4,105,025; 1877, to $5,329,192; and 1878, to $6,134,491. In 1873 and 1874 the passenger traffic by the ocean-steamers between San Francisco and Portland had fallen off considerably, and at the end of each of these years Oregon had not gained more than 800 to 1,000 per year of arrivals over departures. From August 1, 1875, to August 1, 1876, a manifest increase had taken place in the passenger travel. During that year the State Board of Immigration reported to the Legislature a gain of 11,213 persons in population for the twenty months preceding August 1, 1876, of which it was ascertained that 9,563 had come by the ocean-steamers via San Francisco. From August 1, 1876, to August 1, 1877, the total number of persons who arrived by ocean-steamers at Portland, excluding soldiers, Chinamen, and children under three years, numbered 12,843; and during the year 1878 the estimated gain in population to the State of Oregon was upward of 20,000, the most of whom arrived per Oregon steamers via San Francisco.

The commerce of the State has shown equal improvement. Before 1868 the shipments of gold dust, bars, and treasure formed in value three fourths of all the exports of Oregon; but these gold shipments gradually declined until 1872, when the amount was quite small. In 1868 the total exports of merchandise from the Columbia River amounted to $1,780,408; in 1870 there was very little increase, but in 1873 the gross exports of merchandise amounted to $4,124,606, excluding treasure. The dutiable imports from foreign countries rose from $90,500 in 1860 to $809,540 in 1872, while the foreign exports during the like period kept in the same proportion until 1872, when the *foreign* exports only amounted to $778,376, so that the balance of foreign trade was in that year against Oregon. She rapidly, however, recovered this loss, for the direct imports from foreign countries fell away from $808,540 in 1872 to $475,508 in 1877, while the foreign exports in the same period (five years) rose from $779,376 in 1872 to $1,498,722 in 1874, and to $3,990,191 in 1877; showing a vast gain annually of exports over imports from 1871 to 1877. For the year ending August 1, 1875, the gross exports of produce and merchandise from Oregon amounted to $10,176,251, or deducting shipments of treasure per Wells, Fargo & Co., of $2,278,250 (which properly are not exports), the net total exports for the year ending August 1, 1875, amounted to $9,175,087; 1877, to $11,571,355; and 1878, to $14,644,973. The details of these exports during the years just mentioned are made up from the annual reports of the Board of Trade, and are therefore authentic. As regards the imports since 1872,

only one third of the foreign imports come direct to Portland—the other two thirds coming via San Francisco, where the duties are paid. It is therefore impossible to give a correct detail of the import trade and contrast the same with the exports. The export trade with China and Australia has fallen off, and the cargoes of lumber formerly shipped to those countries are now dispatched from Puget Sound. One vast gain to the commerce of Oregon has been the dissemination of information during the last five years as to the safety of the Columbia bar.

The advance in the value of lands has been no less remarkable. In 1868 prairie and fair improved farming lands in Linn, Lane, and Yamhill Counties, and generally over the Willamette Valley, could easily be obtained at from $15 to $20 per acre, while distant brush-land, or what is now called oak-grub land, was selling at $3 to $4 per acre. When the Oregon and California and Oregon Central Railroads were built, farm-lands were sold at what were then considered speculative prices, $25 to $30 per acre; and afterward, in 1872 and 1873, a reaction took place, and prices of fair farming lands fell to $20 per acre. This did not long continue, however; and in 1875, 1876, 1877, and 1878, prices kept gradually advancing, and instead of large tracts, as was common in 1872 and 1873, being in the hands of a few individuals, unable, as they were then, to cultivate the same, now a majority of the best farming lands in the Willamette Valley are held in tracts of 160 to 320 acres, and at firm prices of $30 to $40, and occasionally, as around Albany and Salem, at $50 to $60 per acre. High oak-lands, which in 1870 commanded $5 per acre, can not so easily now be obtained in advantageous localities at less than $12 to $15 per acre; while hill cleared lands, which were then regarded as fit for pasture merely, and were selling at $10 per acre, now command $20 to $25 per acre, dependent on the location and county. An instance of how little was formerly known as to the value and productiveness of these hill lands is seen in the case of the Waldo Hills around Salem, which are of a red color, highly productive, easily workable, and rich in soil. There, although contiguous to Salem, to good roads, to railroads and steamboats, it was difficult to obtain more than $7 to $8 per acre for these lands when cleared, whereas to-day they sell readily (the cleared portions) at $30 per acre, exclusive of improvements. The best samples of wheat exhibited at the Centennial and Paris Expositions of 1876 and 1878 were raised from these hill lands. In farm-buildings there has been great improvement, and also in fences. The immense tracts of brush-land in Yamhill, Marion, Polk, and Clackamas Counties have been converted since 1874 into wheat-lands. So extensively has this improvement taken place that the aspect and appearance of several districts have been so changed as to be scarcely recognized. In the Waldo Hills clearing operations, both east and west, have put into cultivation large tracts of land which hitherto were unproductive and worthless. So also in the Polk and Benton Hills. The present value of Willamette Valley farms is bound to be maintained, and, although not desirable, the indications are that they will go very much higher—especially in the eastern portion of Lane, Linn, and Marion, where a narrow-gauge railroad is projected from Springfield, in Lane County, to Salem. At present, the value of lands in this stretch of country, 75 miles in length, is 35 to 50 per cent. less than in the western portions of the same counties. A greater progress in value, however, has taken place in the Walla Walla Valley and districts around the same. In 1868 improved land, which now sells there at $20 to $25 per acre, was sold for $2.50 per acre, and in 1873 the same land was selling at $8 per acre. All along eastern Oregon and eastern Washington Territory, up as far as Lewiston, an advance in values of farm-lands has been maintained, although not to the same extent as in the Walla Walla Valley. Improved agricultural lands sell in the Lewiston and Palouse Valley districts for $6 to $10 per acre. In the Umpqua Valley, in southwestern Oregon, good farming lands prior to the opening of the railroad to Roseburg were selling at $5 to $6 per acre; they now find purchasers at $15 to $16, and frequently $20 per acre. In southern Oregon there has been little advance during the past ten years. In some cases, owing to local circumstances, they have advanced slightly; but as a general rule the want of transportation facilities has retarded both the settlement and development of southern Oregon.

In 1868 Oregon and Washington Territory had not commenced the export of salmon, which industry has only progressed during the last seven years. The year 1871 was the first in which canned salmon were exported; 30,-000 cases realized $150,000. In 1873 91,000 cases realized $501,000. At that time salmon was so plentiful and cheap that the enterprise was very profitable, and the foreign demand had so increased that the people were wild with excitement; and as a necessary consequence canneries were erected on both sides of the Columbia River, even as far up as the Cascades. These canneries increased the production and gradually drained the river, and the salmon fisheries, regarded as for ever practically inexhaustible, became endangered through want of proper legislation. In 1875 there were 335,000 cases exported, which realized $1,650,000. In 1876 the capacity of all old canneries was increased, and new canneries were still erected. So greatly had this industry extended that in the end of 1876 there were thirty canneries in operation, with a united capacity for canning 795,000 cases of salmon. In that year, however, the maximum production was reached, 479,000 cases being then exported, which realized $2,598,000. In 1877 there were exported

389,508 cases, yielding $2,338,000. But the catch of that year and of 1878—which latter was only 345,000 cases—conclusively proved that without legislation and the necessary protection to the salmon this valuable commercial product would soon be lost to the State. Accordingly both the Legislatures of Oregon and Washington Territory passed joint laws, which took effect in January, 1879, for the protection of these fisheries, and to raise a revenue each year to propagate and still more develop and increase the artificial production of salmon. This legislation has placed the canneries on a firmer basis, and given those engaged in the industry greater confidence. The foreign demand has become a settled fact, and Oregon canned salmon is now used in nearly all civilized countries as a daily article of diet.

The various agricultural products of the State also show a rapid increase. In 1868 the total wheat-crop raised in Oregon was 1,535,000 bushels; in 1870, 2,270,000 bushels; in 1873, 3,127,000 bushels; in 1875, 5,251,102 bushels; and in 1877, 7,896,676 bushels. These figures indicate a rapid progress, and considering that the State's population in 1877 was about 120,-000 persons, including cities and towns, it will thus be seen that the quantity of wheat raised was made to every man, woman, and child in the State, or an average of 19 bushels per acre; and the price obtained that year was $1.75 to $2.10 per cental. In 1869 the quantity of wool produced all over the State was 1,066,-435 pounds, of which there was exported to San Francisco 3,190 bales, of the value of $134,-749. In 1871 there was 1,750,600 pounds of wool produced; in 1873, 2,036,000 pounds; in 1875, 2,638,050 pounds; while in 1877 there was raised 5,736,650 pounds, of which there was exported to San Francisco alone, as admitted by the Chamber of Commerce of that city, 4,929,-675 pounds. The value of the wool exports had increased from $134,749 in 1869 to $756,-000 in 1876, and $998,305 in 1877; and 1878 returns show it to be $1,267,373, an increase of 750 per cent. in eight years. The quality of the wool each year has so much improved that Oregon wool now commands (like its wheat) the highest prices in the Boston market, and received medals and diplomas at the Centennial of 1876 for (using the words of the commissioners) "merino wool, very fine specimens of fine fiber and good staple, very much resembling Australian wool, and giving evidence that Oregon can produce wool of very great value." The woolen-mills in the State consume a considerable portion of the crop each year, and their consumption is always increasing. The market for the oat-crop is in the State, Puget Sound, British Columbia, and California. In 1868 there was raised 2,029,909 bushels of oats; in 1875, 2,983,086 bushels, which realized $1,657,563; and in 1877, 4,127,663 bushels, averaging 35 bushels to the acre, from which there was exported to San Francisco 135,153 sacks. But this article of commerce fluctuates more than any other agricultural product raised in Oregon on account of the wide difference in prices between one year and another, caused by there being a large or small crop of oats for the time being in California. In the lesser agricultural productions, such as barley, hay, potatoes, and corn, during the last ten years, equally favorable progress has been made. For instance, in 1860, there was raised 26,254 bushels of barley; in 1870, 210,736, averaging 29 bushels per acre. Of rye there was raised, in 1870, 3,820 bushels, and in 1875, 17,263 bushels. In 1860 there was raised only 27,386 tons of hay, and in 1875, 161,433 tons, which realized $1,937,196. Oregon has always been famed as a good potato country. In 1870 Oregon raised 303,319 bushels of potatoes, and in 1875, 527,829 bushels. Of Indian corn or maize there was raised only 72,133 bushels, and in 1875, 96,720 bushels; but Oregon is no corn country, owing to the cool nights of summer. It may be noticed that the average per acre of each product raised is small compared with the amount raised in Great Britain. This is quite true, but in Oregon the low average is due to a very superficial knowledge—often no knowledge at all—of farming, and to volunteer crops. But while this is so, the United States Commissioner of Agriculture at Washington, D. C., in his annual report to Congress for 1876, says *that in all crops* (except Indian corn) which have been raised in the United States, Oregon far exceeded the average of every other State in the Union, and has continued to do so year after year. The same officer estimated the value of farm products in Oregon annually per head of farming population to be $539, and per head of the entire population of the State, $78.06; while he estimated the value of farm property owned by persons engaged in agriculture to be $2,300 per head. The amount of exports is $100 to every person in the State. The increase in stock is to be found chiefly in eastern Oregon. There are in that part of the State 57,416 square miles of land, which, with the exception of a very limited portion, is all fit either for grazing or agriculture. In 1870 there were 318,123 sheep in the State, one fourth of which were located in eastern Oregon, one half in the Willamette Valley, and the remainder in Douglas County and southern Oregon. These flocks kept increasing very materially in eastern Oregon, until there were in 1877 about 1,963,556 sheep in the State, of which eastern Oregon possessed nearly two thirds, and the remainder were in western or southern Oregon. These figures are tested by the wool product of 1878, which realized upward of 6,000,000 pounds of wool; and as the average yield is but three pounds of wool per sheep, the figures above given are thus below the correct number of sheep. This industry promises to develop itself enormously during the next ten years, as evinced by what has taken place in California. That State twenty years ago only produced 1,000,000 pounds of

wool, or less than one fifth of what Oregon now produces, and it was then stated of California, as is frequently said now of Oregon, that she could not produce much more; yet in 1876 California produced the enormous quantity of 56,550,970 pounds of wool, as shown by the statistics of the Chamber of Commerce of San Francisco. The vast public domain in eastern Oregon and eastern Washington, containing together upward of 100,000 square miles of land preëminently suited for sheep-pasturage, may therefore be, as in California, eventually occupied by sheep-ranches; and if, as statistics have shown, Oregon wool increased 750 per cent. the last eight years, it is reasonable to suppose the same increase may follow in the next ten years, in which case the production of wool would then amount to 58,960,000 pounds. In 1870 there were 120,197 cattle in the State; in 1875, 276,466; the number in 1878 is estimated at 425,000. The prices realized in 1874 and 1875 were poor, but now that cattle from the eastern ranges are transported to the Union and Central Pacific Railroads for shipment to the Western States, prices have advanced considerably and given cattle and stock men greater encouragement to increase their herds. In 1870 there were raised 119,455 hogs; in 1875, 181,500. Wheat had attained such a high figure during these five years that farmers, instead of putting it into hogs, sold it, and no inducement was thus afforded to cultivate or increase the production of hogs. A noticeable feature is the increase of milch cows. In 1870 there were 62,400 milch cows; in 1875, 80,900; and in 1878 (estimated), 93,000. The United States Commissioner of Agriculture points out that since 1872 Oregon has given more attention to dairying, and shows, compared with other States, the largest increase in numbers (per population) of cattle and milch cows. The raising of horses has become another favorite industry, developing gradually. In 1870 there were 52,802 horses in the State; in 1875, 75,966; and (estimated) in 1878, 106,-350.

Beyond a very large number of flour and saw mills, four woolen-mills, a number of furniture and sash and door factories, eight or ten foundries and machine-shops, one iron-smelting works, one oil-works, one flax and one paper mill, a shoe factory, and a few other lesser factories, there are no great manufacturing enterprises, except ship-building at Coos Bay, where 43 vessels, including two large ships, the latter of the value of $80,000 each, have been built. At Portland the majority of the river-steamers (there are 72 in number) have been built, and a United States steamer; the cutter Tom Corwin was also built in 1877. The flour manufactured in the State is of the finest quality, and finds a good increasing market in San Francisco, British Columbia, and Great Britain, the exports of flour having increased since 1872. The several coal-mines on the coast of Oregon export annually about 55,-

000 tons of coal to San Francisco, while the lumber exports from Coos Bay alone are 24,-000,000 feet annually. The total number of feet of lumber produced in the year 1875, according to the State census returns, was 98,-285,684 feet. There are owned at Portland five ocean-steamers, of the value of $700,000; nine sailing vessels, of the value of $210,000. The extent of railroads in the State is as yet limited. The Oregon and California and the Oregon Central in 1870 opened up and developed western Oregon, making what was considered prior thereto a wilderness one of the most favored valleys in the United States. Since 1871 no new railroad has been constructed in the State, except the Dayton and Grande Ronde narrow-gauge road, which has opened up to Portland a fine farming country, and which is now advancing to Dallas, in Polk County, a distance of 36 miles. The intention of the owners of the west side railroad is to continue that road to Corvallis from St. Joseph during 1879, a distance of 55 miles, while on the east side of the Willamette Valley a new road is projected on the narrow-gauge system, to extend from Springfield in Lane County along the foot-hills of the Cascades on to Salem, a distance of 75 miles, opening up a country which has suffered hitherto for want of transportation facilities, and which railroad will eventually be continued to Portland *via* Oregon City and the west side. A ten-mile railroad is also expected from Corvallis to Philomath this year, which will become a feeder to the Oregon Central (broad gauge) Railroad when constructed to Corvallis. A railroad (narrow gauge) is also projected from Umatilla to Grande Ronde Valley, Union County, 120 miles, which is much needed to open up one of the finest agricultural sections of the State. Various other narrow-gauge railroads are proposed.

The financial progress has been steady, so that the State and the city of Portland possess all the banking and money-loaning capital necessary to carry on business for some years to come. Outside of the capital owned and employed by the various banks and financial institutions, there are large sums of money loaned out by private capitalists seeking investment, which have been and are being invested in various productive enterprises, while rates of interest on loans and discounts are reduced to 10 per cent. per annum, and money can now be obtained on good security whenever required.

Prior to 1868 large shipments of gold and silver were made from Oregon, the gold product alone of the State between the years 1851 and 1866 amounting to $22,000,000. From that year until 1874 the product fell off, and has not since averaged $1,500,000 per year.

Since 1868 the locks at Oregon City, the State Capitol at Salem, the University of Oregon at Eugene, the penitentiary at Salem, the post-office at Portland, the county court-houses at Albany, Salem, and Portland, and various lesser public buildings have been erected, at an aggregate cost of $2,050,000; while the United States have spent in the improvement of the rivers and in the locks building at the Cascades close on $1,000,000 in the last ten years.

In 1879 the spring crop of wheat from the Willamette Valley proved below the average. At the same time the fall wheat seeded in the autumn of 1878 was double that of any preceding year, but the spring was backward and the rains continued unusually late. The receipts were therefore estimated at 45,000 to 48,000 tons of wheat from eastern Oregon and eastern Washington, and 85,000 to 90,000 tons of winter or fall-sown wheat, and from 40,000 to 45,000 tons of spring-sown grain, from western Oregon, aggregating about 180,000 tons. Deducting therefrom what is necessary to sustain the population of 160,000 souls, and seed for next year's crop, the probable surplus of wheat for export would certainly not exceed 140,000 tons—a deficiency of 10 to 12 per cent. compared with last year. Oats and barley yielded an average crop all over the State; also potatoes. Fruits, especially the plum, peach-plum, cherry, and smaller fruits, suffered much, and fell far short of previous years, while the apple and pear crops are slightly deficient. The hay-crop shows an increase of 50 per cent. over previous years, while pastures never were in finer condition in the fall; and feed for cattle and sheep, both in eastern and western Oregon, has been most abundant and exceedingly above the average. Flaxseed was a profitable and prolific crop; and hops have advanced considerably in price, and the quality was very good.

The exports of salmon for the year from August 1, 1878, to August 1, 1879, aggregated 412,924 cases, yielding $1,863,069, of which 271,139 cases were exported *via* San Francisco, and 141,785 cases to Great Britain direct from the Columbia River, showing a decrease of 79,323 cases in direct shipments to Great Britain, and an increase of 99,812 cases in shipments by way of San Francisco over the preceding year. The total exports for the year ending July 30, 1879, amounted to $12,282,047; for 1878, $14,644,973; for 1877, $11,571,355.

The religious statistics of Oregon show the following results: Baptists — 6 associations, 77 churches, 3,454 members; Catholics—18 churches and numerous stations, 20,000 members; Congregationalists — 28 churches and 996 members; preaching stations, 996 members; Jews—1 synagogue; Methodist Episcopal — 3 conferences, 5,500 members; Presbyterians—2 presbyteries, 27 churches, 1,564 members; Protestant Episcopal, 34 churches, 883 members; Seventh-Day Adventists—7 churches; Unitarians—2 churches; Universalists—5 churches.

The number of children in the public schools in 1879 was 56,458; in 1878, 53,462. The amount of money apportioned for 1879 was $36,137. A portion of the press of the State has constantly urged the necessity of maintaining the public schools simply as common schools, and arresting the growth of the high school as subversive of the intent and ends of the public-school system. It is stated that "one result of the discussion in Oregon has been the creation of a public sentiment which will prevent any further direct appropriations from the Treasury like those so long made in favor of the college at Corvallis." The points presented against high schools in the discussion may be seen in the following extract from the "Oregonian":

We hold that, for the most part, the useless instruction in the primary schools consists of the features required for admission into the higher departments. This is emphatically true as regards schools in the cities, and it will hold good for the provincial schools, so far as they imitate the town customs. The useless, if not directly injurious, features of the primary schools are those which are thrust upon them in order to complete the machinery of the so-called system. The remedy is not far to seek. It is to withdraw the energy now wasted in developing systems, and direct it entirely toward improving the methods of primary instruction. Sufficient mental and material force is now expended on the schools, but it is not exerted in the right direction. The remedy is to give less attention to the ornamental high schools and more to the *alma mater* of the people—the common schools. Children are bewildered and energy is wasted by too rigorous adherence to "method" and "system." Some development of intellectual powers beyond what young children in our schools can be expected to have attained is necessary before formulas and definitions which are pressed upon them can be comprehended. These can be understood only through their application. The process first, and then the "rule." Bright children will often commit to memory rules and definitions fast enough, but after all will not know a syllable of their meaning till they go back and learn what they should have learned at first—namely, the processes out of which the rules and definitions are evolved. Then, after the process is comprehended, the precise manner in which it is formulated makes little difference.

The number of convicts in the penitentiary is 200. The increase has been over fifty in ten months.

An investigation was made by a committee of the Legislature with regard to expenditures under the previous State administration. A lengthy report accompanied with much testimony was made and published.

The Oregon Woman's Association held its sixth annual convention on February 11th. The results secured by the Association are thus summed up in the address of the President:

Never until last September were we honored with other than a brief, spasmodic, and strongly contested hearing, which was in its results unsatisfactory. True, we had prevailed upon our legislators, prior to that time, to give us the "woman's sole-trader bill" and the "married woman's property bill," both of which, however, must remain comparatively null until we can be empowered with the political freedom necessary to make such bills available to any class. Never until the last session has woman's right to a place in the government received a tacit endorsement from a vast majority of its legislators as a body. During that session every bill for the promotion of woman's interests which was brought up for consideration was passed almost without objection. Women were made voters on all school questions and road interests; and their individual property rights were just as nearly secured to them by law as legislative action can secure them to any class which is denied personal representation.

But, though I remained at the capital, as your executive, during two thirds of the entire session, I failed to get a bill before either House for amending the Constitution by striking out the word "male" from its code of rights, the failure resulting from the desire of our friends to pass the other bills above mentioned before reaching this one.

An act of the city of Portland forbade the employment of Chinese laborers on the streets of the city. The contractor applied to the United States Circuit Court to enjoin the city from enforcing the act. Judge Deady granted the injunction, and said that the treaty recognized the right of the Chinese to make this country their home, and this necessarily implied the right to live and to labor for a living. If the State may prevent the Chinese or the subjects of Great Britain from working upon street improvements and public works, it is not apparent why it may not prevent them from engaging in any kind of employment or working at any kind of labor. This view was confirmed by Justice Field, who said that the treaty with China gives Chinese the right to domiciliation in the United States "for purposes of curiosity, for trade, and for permanent residence."

P

PACKER, ASA, born at Groton, Connecticut, December 20, 1806, died in Philadelphia, May 17th. He began to learn the tannery business, but on the death of his employer in 1822 went to a relative in Susquehanna County, Pennsylvania, and learned the trade of a carpenter. He then went to New York and worked at his trade, but, meeting with little success, returned to Susquehanna County. A year later he married the daughter of a poor farmer of Springfield. The fiftieth anniversary of this wedding was celebrated in 1878.

He continued for four years farming and jobbing until the opening of the Lehigh Valley Canal, when he removed to Mauch Chunk to become a boatman on the canal. His was one of the first boats dispatched, and being once engaged in the business, his natural abilities began to manifest themselves. Not contented with the profits from his own boat, he contracted for the mastership of a second, which he put in charge of his brother-in-law. From that time his prosperity grew steadily. He saved his earnings, and invested them judiciously. His penetration of mind now enabled him to see what the circumstances demanded, and in 1831 he opened a small store on the bank of the Lehigh, giving up his charge as a boatman, although retaining a money interest in several boats. Combining the knowledge he had gained with his experiences as a carpenter and builder, he opened a boat-yard and began to build boats, and contracted for building locks on the upper Lehigh, which he completed in 1837. He became well known as a contractor in all the Lehigh country, and in 1838 he engaged to build boats at Pottsville for the transportation of coal to New York City. This work caused a change in the route of transportation to the new canal from that by the way of Philadelphia. He was now fully embarked in the mining and transportation of coal, and had entered upon the career of prosperity and fame in which he achieved great success. In 1851 he succeeded in awakening public interest in his plan for the Lehigh Valley Railroad, and having obtained the necessary subscriptions he submitted his plan for the construction of the road from Mauch Chunk to Easton. In 1855 the work was opened for business, with its connecting branches above Mauch Chunk to Hazleton and Mahanoy City. After this success, Mr. Packer proposed to the company to extend their road north and connect with the Erie Railroad near or on the New York State line. This carried the new road along the windings of the Lehigh River, through the narrow gorge in the mountains, across the Wyoming Valley, and up the Susquehanna River to Towanda, thus opening up the entire anthracite region of Pennsylvania. As he had foreseen, this gave at once an enormous impetus to the coal-mining business, and developed other interests and industries in a proportionate degree, adding greatly to the wealth of the State and its active prosperity. Under Mr. Packer's charge as president, the road became an immense success, and speedily made its projector known and popular not only in the coal regions, but throughout the State. But all this was not accomplished without vast struggles under difficulties. He was really swamped financially, but friends came to his aid and carried him through; and ere long he was rewarded by returning millions, and by a substantial hold upon the vast resources of the Lehigh Valley, which ultimately made him the richest man in Pennsylvania.

Early in his career he became interested in political affairs. In 1844 he was elected to the State Legislature. His object was to secure the creation of a new county, of which Mauch Chunk should be the county seat. He succeeded in obtaining the formation of the present county of Carbon. He then held for five years the position of Judge of the County Court. Afterward he was twice elected a member of Congress, serving from 1853 to 1857 with honor to himself and to the satisfaction of his constituents. He became a prom-

inent Presidential candidate, and received in the Democratic Convention held in New York in 1868 the vote of Pennsylvania through fourteen ballots, and was withdrawn in favor of General W. S. Hancock. In 1869 he was nominated by the Democrats of Pennsylvania as their candidate for Governor, and such was his popularity that he failed of an election by only 4,500 votes. In the previous year General Grant, the Republican candidate for the Presidency, carried the State by a majority of 25,000 votes.

He solved the labor question in his district by founding the Lehigh University. A strike occurred among the boatmen on the Lehigh Canal, and they collected with their boats on the pool of the river, above the dam at Easton, with all the uncontrolled passions and disorderly excesses that accompany such excitements in the coal regions. Mr. Packer, having been himself a boatman a few years previous, and in the full confidence of his kindly feelings and his knowledge of their thoughts and needs, went to them for a friendly talk on the situation. He had no fear of his life in meeting this excited crowd, although from personal experience he knew the temper of these turbulent men. However, they would not listen to him, but seized him and flung him into the river. Without exasperation, and without accounting this outrage an additional reason for severity in pursuing the leaders of the mob to punishment, he viewed it as an outburst of passionate ignorance, and his answer to the outrage was a great free school. It would take a generation to disperse the ignorance, but the rising generation should have the benefit of all that free tuition and the wise disposal of his wealth could give it. The foundation and endowment of this university was the crowning act of his benevolence. The immediate object is to furnish free of cost to young men of talent and ambition a place for a collegiate education of a practical character, such as can be turned to account in the more important walks of professional and business life at the present day. The endowment of the university reached a million and a half before his death. In 1878 a library building was erected at a cost of $70,000, having a shelf capacity for 60,000 volumes. Other buildings for public use were erected by him, among which was an Episcopal church in Mauch Chunk. He was a man at once gentle and firm; amiable in discussion and inflexible after decision. He was greatly esteemed and beloved by those who knew him, and his most honorable monument will be the memory of the noble qualities and virtues with which he adorned the character of the workingman and most useful private citizen.

PENNSYLVANIA. The annual session of the Legislature commenced on January 7th. In the Senate A. J. Herr of Dauphin County, Republican, was elected President pro tem. by a vote of 32 to 17, which was about the relation of parties in that body. In the House Henry M. Long, Republican, was elected Speaker by a vote of 111 to 76. The National vote was 3 in the Senate and 10 in the House, in each for a third candidate.

In discussing the affairs of the State in his message, the Governor alluded to the most important subject of difficulties between workmen and their employers, and brought forward the English system of arbitration, of which he said:

In England, the system of arbitration and conciliation originated with the manufacturers and operators, and has changed, wherever fairly tried, the old feeling of bitter hostility between the employer and the employed into one of mutual respect and confidence. With the same class in Pennsylvania lies the responsibility of the initiative; with the Legislature the responsibility of education. Deeply impressed with the importance of bringing about, if possible, a mutual understanding of the two classes, and creating an arrangement for the amicable and rational settlement of all disputes and controversies, I gladly availed myself in the early part of the year of the services of a gentleman, a student of industrial questions, who visited England to investigate the form, practical workings, and results of the various systems of arbitration in operation there, and commissioned him a special agent, under the seal of the State, to examine and report the same on behalf of the Commonwealth. His report I have the honor to transmit. I have refrained from any discussion of the system, which is elaborately presented in the report, and shall close simply by summing its results. Wherever established, an intelligent co-operation between employers and employed has been effected, and steady employment secured at those rates of wages which the industrial conditions of a competitive market enabled capital to pay and maintain a steady production. Strikes, riots, out ages, and trades-union murders have become things of the past. In prosperous times labor has shared in the increased profits of capital, and in periods of depression each has mutually supported the other with the minimum of loss and suffering.

On January 21st, J. Donald Cameron was elected Senator in Congress by a vote of 28 in the Senate to 16 for Heister Clymer; in the House, Cameron had 107 votes, Clymer 76, and 16 scattering.

An act to encourage the planting of trees along roadsides was passed. It provides that any person liable to road-tax who shall transplant to the side of the public highway on his own premises any fruit, shade, or forest trees of suitable size, shall be allowed by the supervisor of roads where roads run through or adjoin cultivated fields, in abatement of his road-tax, one dollar for every four trees set out; but no row of elms shall be placed nearer than seventy feet, no row of maples or other forest trees nearer than fifty feet, except locust, which may be set thirty feet apart; and no allowance as before mentioned shall be made, unless such trees shall have been set out the year previous to the demand for such abatement of the tax, and are living and well protected from animals at the time of such demand. Trees transplanted in the place of dead trees are to be paid for in the same manner.

A uniform system of municipal government for the various cities of the State was contemplated in a bill placed on the House calendar by a vote of 115 to 38, although it failed to become a law. It proposed to forbid cities to borrow money; the councils should raise and appropriate all moneys; poor-boards, school-boards, highway and street commissioners, etc., were abolished; contracts should be made only to the extent of yearly appropriations; select councils should be composed of tax-payers who had held real estate for at least three years before their election, and should have paid taxes thereon; they were to be elected by the cities at large, in order to obviate a centralization of any single interest. The bill assimilated the office of mayor to that of president or governor; created a permanent and non-political police force; consolidated the various departments, and provided that the expenses for local improvements should be borne by the property immediately benefited and not by the city at large. The preparation of the bill had cost the State $20,000.

An act limiting a day's work to eight hours was indefinitely postponed in the House by a vote of 102 to 57.

A new temperance movement appeared in the Senate under the form of a bill to prevent the sale of any spirituous, vinous, malt, or brewed liquors, which are in any manner adulterated, mixed, drugged, diluted, or compounded with drugs or other deleterious or poisonous matter. It was reported favorably by the Committee on Vice and Immorality. It provided, among other things, for the appointment of inspectors by the courts, the confiscation of liquors, fine and imprisonment of offenders against the law upon conviction after trial by jury, etc. A bill to secure a reformation in the same direction was introduced in the House. It provided for the appointment of a State chemist, who should have a laboratory in connection with the Agricultural Department; that people should send specimens of spirituous liquors, canned fruits, ground spices, pepper, etc., to be analyzed; and that they should not sell anything without being tested, under severe penalties, a fine of $1,000 and imprisonment for from one to five years. Neither of these bills became a law.

An act was passed authorizing councils of cities of the second class of the Commonwealth to make an amicable settlement of municipal liens for grading, paving, and curbing, or otherwise improving streets or avenues in said cities, either under general or special laws.

As the future sessions of the Legislature will be biennial, a bill was passed to provide for the receiving, opening, and publishing of the returns for the election of State Treasurer and Auditor-General, when elected at the same election. It provides for the appointment of a committee from the Senate and House to act in conjunction with the Speaker *pro tem.* of the Senate and Speaker of the House. As the Constitution says, "No senator or representative shall, during the time for which he shall have been elected, be appointed to any civil office under this Commonwealth," the objection was raised to the bill that this was a civil office in order to settle the matter for the future. The Speaker decided the point not well taken, as this was not a civil office, but an additional duty imposed upon certain members of the Legislature, and was clearly constitutional — as much so as the serving upon an inaugural committee or any other committee.

A bill was reported favorably to reëstablish a local-option law in the State. An unfavorable report was made on the bell-punch bill. It was urged that the contrivance in Virginia had proved to be a fraud. Neither passed.

A bill to protect religious liberty and to provide for the relief of persons who observe the seventh day of the week as the Sabbath, and to exempt them from the penalties of the act of Assembly passed April 22, 1794, was discussed in the Senate and failed to pass—yeas 21, nays 17, which was five less than the majority required by the Constitution. The bill has thus been defeated for four sessions, gaining, however, five votes on the last occasion.

The women gained a point at this session by the passage of a bill to remove the disability or disqualification of married women from acting as corporators or officers of any association incorporated heretofore, or that may be incorporated hereafter, for purposes of learning, benevolence, charity, or religion. Another bill, to authorize the appointment of women as prison inspectors, passed the House. In the Senate it was reported negatively; but a motion to place it on the calendar was passed—yeas 37, nays 7. It failed to become a law.

A vagrant act was passed, which declares that any person going about from place to place begging shall be deemed to be a tramp and guilty of a misdemeanor, and on conviction shall be sentenced to solitary confinement at labor, or in the county jail or workhouse, for not less than six months nor over eighteen; provided, that if he can prove that he does not make a practice of going about begging he shall be discharged; also, that any tramp who shall enter a dwelling-house against the will of the occupant, or kindle a fire in the highway or on the land of another, or be found carrying any dangerous weapon, or do or threaten any injury not amounting to a felony, shall upon conviction be sentenced to solitary confinement at labor for not over two years.

A bill called the "store-order" bill was passed. An amendment on its passage in the Senate provided that it should be a misdemeanor or for an employer to sell to an employee any merchandise at a higher price than the cost price of said article in the same neighborhood, and declaring that any person convicted of such misdemeanor should be punished by fine or imprisonment, or both. The object of the bill was to secure to operators and laborers in mines and manufactories of iron and steel the payment of their wages at regular intervals in lawful United States money. When it reached the Governor,

it was vetoed. His objections were, that the bill was special and within the constitutional prohibition. The Governor urged that if the act was general, it would be open to valid objection as being contrary to the genius of our free government, and as based upon a theory subversive of the true principles of the State Constitution, in that it denies the laborer the right to sell his labor to whom he pleases and for such prices and on such terms as seem good to him, without molestation, hindrance, or restriction. Another objection urged was that the bill interfered with the free employment of capital, arbitrarily controlled trade, substituted legislation for the laws of supply and demand, and was the beginning of a system of paternal government at variance with our political institutions, which always proved when tried injurious alike to the employed as well as the employer.

The subject of the State receipts and expenditures was one of the most important before the Legislature. A special communication from the Treasurer stated that the fiscal year beginning on December 1, 1879, would open with a deficiency of $2,219,036. This deficiency he ascribed to decreased revenues and the extraordinary expenses of the riot of 1877. In consequence, a considerable amount was due to the schools, and also to the charitable institutions under an appropriation of which only a small amount had been paid.

A most important revenue measure adopted was the act to tax corporations, which makes some special additions to the existing law. Every corporation is compelled to register in the office of the Auditor-General its name, date of organization, place of business, offices, and the amount of capital authorized and paid in. Every corporation doing business in the State, except banks, savings institutions, and foreign insurance companies, is required to file a report with the Auditor-General in November of each year, showing the amount of stock authorized, number of shares issued and amount paid on each share, amount of capital paid in, and the date, amount, and rate of every dividend paid during the year. When a company fails to declare a dividend of less than six per cent. upon the par value of its stock, the treasurer and secretary of the company shall make a sworn estimate of the actual cash value of the stock, not less, however, than the average price for which such stock sold during the year, and not less than the value as measured by the dividends paid. If the Auditor-General or State Treasurer is not satisfied with this valuation, he is authorized to make a valuation for the purpose of assessment, and the company is allowed an appeal as provided by existing law. In case of failure to furnish the report and appraisement, a penalty of ten per cent. is to be added to the tax of the company for each year such failure occurs. In case a company shall intentionally fail to make report for three successive years, the Governor of the

State may declare its charter forfeited. All companies doing business in the State, with the exceptions mentioned above, are subject to taxation as follows: If dividends have been declared during the year amounting to six per cent. of the par value of the capital stock, or over, the rate will be one half mill upon the capital stock for each one per cent. dividend declared. If no dividend has been declared, or if the dividends amount to less than six per cent. of the capital stock, the tax will be at the rate of three mills upon each dollar of valuation of the capital stock. If there shall be more than one kind of stock, and on one a dividend of six per cent. or over shall have been declared, and on the other no dividend or a dividend of less than six per cent. shall have been declared, the rate shall be one half mill on the capital stock for each one per cent. dividend declared in the first case, and three mills on each dollar of valuation in the second case. When a company has made a profit and added it to its sinking fund without dividing it among its stockholders, such profit will be taxed accordingly. All limited partnerships engaged in business in the State, no matter where organized, are made subject to the provisions of the act. For the purpose of taxation, the interests in limited partnerships are to be deemed capital stock, and any division of the profits among the owners of such interests are to be taxed as dividends. The provisions governing limited partnerships, however, are not made to apply to those organized for manufacturing or mercantile purposes. All companies and limited partnerships engaged in the business of transporting freight or passengers, and all the telegraph, express, and palace- and sleeping-car companies, incorporated and unincorporated, doing business in the State, are required to pay a tax of eight tenths of one per cent. upon the gross receipts of their business on July 31st and January 31st in each year. Where such companies are engaged in mining, purchasing, and selling coal, the receipts derived from the sale of such coal are not to be taxed, but an account of the coal so dealt in must be kept, and the company must charge itself with the transportation thereof at the same rates which are or would have been charged to other companies or individuals for transportation of similar freight; and the sums so charged for transportation are to be taxed as a part of the gross receipts. Insurance companies—excepting those based upon the purely mutual plan—are required to make semi-annual reports, sworn to by the proper officers, and showing the amount of premiums received during the previous six months, whether in cash notes or other substitute for money, and they shall pay a tax of eight tenths of one per cent. upon the gross amount of such premium. All companies owning and operating coal-lands are required to report every six months the amount of coal mined by them, or by other companies or individuals under a lease or other contract from such companies, and also the amount of coal not mined which shall have been purchased by such companies. The act further provides that such coal companies shall pay a tax of three cents upon each ton of coal of 2,240 pounds, mined or purchased, until July 1, 1880, and one cent upon each ton until July 1, 1881, after which time the tax on coal shall cease. The coal consumed by the company producing it is not to be taxed. All private bankers and brokers, unincorporated banking institutions, etc., and all incorporated companies except those liable to a tax on their capital stock or gross receipts, are to make annual statements of their net earnings from all sources. A tax of three per cent. upon such net earnings is to be imposed in addition to the taxes otherwise imposed by the act. All taxes which remain unpaid after the time provided for their payment will bear interest at the rate of twelve per cent. per annum until their settlement. The taxes are made a lien on all the property, real and personal, of the corporations or limited partnerships taxed, and are to take precedence of all claims, incumbrances, or liens arising after the passage of the act. No corporation or limited partnership liable to taxation under the act can be dissolved by decree of court until all taxes have been paid and a certificate of that fact filed in the proper court. All foreign corporations, except insurance companies, are required to obtain an annual license from the Auditor-General to have an office in the State, for which they shall pay one fourth of a mill on each dollar of capital stock which they are authorized to have. For a failure to pay such tax a penalty of fifty per cent. is to be imposed. No license, however, will be required for corporations paying a tax under other provisions of the act, or whose capital stock or a majority thereof is owned or controlled by a corporation of the State which does pay a tax under other provisions of the act., All mortgages, debts due from solvent debtors, except notes or bills for work or labor done, all obligations given to banks for money loaned and bank-notes, all shares of stock in any bank or savings institution incorporated in the State, all public loans or stocks except those of the State or of the United States, all money loaned or invested on interest in any other State, and all moneyed capital in the hands of individual citizens of the State, are to be taxed for State purposes, at the rate of four mills on every dollar of the value thereof, annually. All mortgages, judgments, and moneys due on agreement to sell real estate are exempted from taxation except for State purposes; and all corporations paying interest on loans taxed for State purposes only shall deduct the tax from such interest, and pay the same into the State Treasury. Where a bank elects to collect annually from its stockholders a tax of six tenths of one per cent. of the value of the shares of such bank and pay it over to the State Treasury, the shares, capital, and profits of such banks shall be exempt from all other taxation.

The expectation that ex-President Grant would during the summer arrive at San Francisco on his return from an extensive tour in Europe and Asia, led to the adoption of a resolution for the appointment of a joint committee of ten Senators and fifteen Representatives to act in conjunction with the Governor, Lieutenant-Governor, and Speakers of the Senate and House of Representatives, for the purpose of welcoming him upon his arrival in this country, in the name of the Commonwealth of Pennsylvania, provided that there should be no expense to the State. It was passed in the House by a strict party vote, 79 yeas and 73 nays; also in the Senate by yeas 26, nays 12.

A bill was introduced in the House to appoint a commission to ascertain and adjust the losses caused by the riots of July, 1877, and to provide for their payment. It was referred to the Committee of Ways and Means, and reported back with amendments which were adopted. The bill thus amended appropriated $4,000,000, or as much thereof as might be required to pay the losses. One fourth of the amount of the loss was to be paid into the State Treasury by the county of Allegheny. The Governor was authorized to appoint three commissioners to ascertain the value of the property lost by the respective claimants, and the method was prescribed in which the requisite proofs should be presented. After all claimants were heard the commissioners were required to file with the State Treasurer their report, which should contain the names of all the claimants whose property was destroyed or injured, and the amount of loss suffered by each. If the county of Allegheny failed to pay the twenty-five per cent. of the losses within a certain time after the assessment, claimants were to receive out of the appropriation by the State but seventy-five per cent. of the amount of their claims, and the county should remain liable to the claimants for the balance. When the report of the commissioners was filed in the office of the State Treasurer, that official was to issue to each claimant a certificate setting forth the amount adjudicated in his favor. Upon presentation of this certificate to the Governor he should issue a warrant for the amount payable to the holder or his assignee, who should immediately present it to the State Treasurer. If there were no funds in the Treasury for payment, the State Treasurer should mark the date of presentation, and by publication inform the holder when funds were in the Treasury for payment. The members of the commission were each to receive ten dollars a day for every day occupied in their duties, with their necessary expenses, including clerk-hire.

This bill caused more excitement than any other subject which was brought forward. The question of the liability of the State for

damages caused by riots and the violence of a mob was extensively discussed. The advocates of the bill urged that Allegheny County was not liable for the losses under the laws of 1841 and 1849, which make cities and counties liable for riotous losses, on the ground that these disturbances of 1877 were general and not local, and that the State was constitutionally liable for the restitution of property lost through general riot and mob violence. A decision was cited, proving that any property damaged or destroyed while being used as a barracks or while in possession of State or national authorities, and destroyed by the enemy, should be paid for by the State or nation. The Pittsburgh round-house was an exactly parallel case. It was further urged that it was no riot, but an insurrection, brought about by suffering from depression occasioned by the panic. As soon as the proclamation of the Governor was issued calling out the troops to suppress the insurrection, the State assumed control and responsibility, and this was done before a shot was fired or a torch was lighted. The State was therefore liable in equity, and was morally bound to pay for the damage occasioned by the mob at that time. In 1864 a law was passed commanding the State militia to suppress any invasion or insurrection that might occur within its borders. This was carried into effect by the military acting under the command embodied in the Governor's message. This proved clearly the responsibility of the State for the losses occasioned by said insurrection.

In reply it was said that the Government did not become a general insurance company for the restitution of property destroyed by incendiarism or lawlessness; it was only responsible for the punishment of the incendiary or rioter. The Government only protected property; it did not pay for it when destroyed. The State is not responsible in any case. Riots are always local in their character. New York, New Jersey, Maryland, Missouri, California, and Wisconsin place the responsibility on cities and counties. Maine, Massachusetts, New Hampshire, Kansas, and South Carolina place the responsibility on cities and towns. Local disturbances, as a general thing, are always the cause of riots. No county should seek to evade the law which makes it responsible for these damages. The law making Allegheny County responsible for damages occasioned through riots was asked for by the members from Allegheny County, backed up with petitions from the citizens of that county, in 1849. The people of Allegheny County were now endeavoring to be freed from the liability imposed by a law for which they had asked. The advocates of the bill then strengthened their position by urging that there was involved a principle of equity in the case. It was asserted that the State, which draws five sevenths of her revenues from the taxation of private corporations, should afford them protection and indemnity when assailed by lawless violence; also, that common sagacity would suggest that the State, instead of sturdily refusing indemnity, should be ready and willing to afford the amplest protection and indemnity to corporations which pay into her Treasury the largest part of the revenues for the support of her government, her charitable institutions, and her schools. The railroad company which is the principal loser in the Pittsburgh riots pays into the State Treasury little less than a million dollars a year. Under the present system of taxation, with the receipts of the company increasing, the amount will soon be considerably over a million. It seems, therefore, that obligations and duties should be reciprocal. When a State levies this amount of revenue from a corporation, it should receive indemnity when its property is destroyed through the failure, or neglect, or inability of the authorities of the State to give protection. The obligations should not be all on one side. .

A motion to indefinitely postpone the bill was carried by a vote of 103 to 96. The question on the motion to reconsider this vote was first temporarily and then decisively postponed.

Meantime, during the debate on the bill, one of the members of the House asserted positively that "at least two members of the House of Representatives had been approached in a corruptive manner and had been subjected to corruptive powers." This led to the adoption of a resolution for the appointment of a committee to investigate the charges, "and any other improper influences brought to bear upon members in connection with the bill." One of the first witnesses examined by the investigating committee was Mr. W. H. Kemble of Philadelphia. He stated his occupation to be "president of a bank and of a railroad company." The following is an extract from a report of the investigation, and contains a definition of legislative log-rolling:

Q.—Have you, directly or indirectly, offered any money or thing of value, testimonial, privilege, or personal advantage to any member of the General Assembly to influence him in his official action on House bill No. 103, commonly known as the riot bill? *A.*—No, sir; unless you interpret the common aid that one man gives to another in legislation as "personal advantage."

Q.—Will you please state what you mean by the common aid which one man gives to another? *A.*—I mean this, that if you mean to ask me whether I ever promised to help A in legislation in return for A helping me in legislation, without any money consideration or thing of value, I can't say that I never have; but if it is a money consideration or anything of the kind which the world regards as bribery, I say no. I mean by that this: that I have never offered any man a bribe, directly or indirectly; but the language of the Constitution goes far beyond what any man that ever came to Harrisburg ever lived up to or ever will live up to. I was a friend of the bill, and did all I could for it in an honorable way.

To the next question, as to whether he had personal knowledge of any member having solicited any money, etc., with a view to his official action being influenced thereby, Mr. Kemble said, "No, always excepting the

exceptions which I make." "By what you call log-rolling?" said Mr. Wolfe. "Yes," was the reply, "that's it; always excepting that." Being asked to define "log-rolling," he said: "It is what I regard as higher than all constitutions, that one good turn deserves another; that is all there is of it in passing bills, which, if a man don't do, he may as well stay away from Harrisburg, and yet the strict interpretation of the Constitution prohibits it."

To the question, also, as to personal knowledge of any member having demanded or received, or consented to receive, etc., he answered: "None whatever, except common log-rolling. I tried to log-roll with everybody, so far as that is concerned. I don't deny that."

The report of the committee was made on May 29th. After reciting the resolution directing the investigation, the committee state that the rules which guided them in their conclusions as far as practicable were the same as those which govern the courts. Irrelevant testimony was submitted, but it did no harm to any one. Conflicting testimony was also taken, but they were guided by the reasonable and consistent circumstances. No attempt was made to impeach any witness. In making up the report the committee endeavored to rid their minds of prejudice and passion. They report W. F. Rumberger of Armstrong County, E. J. Petroff of Philadelphia Fifth District, and George F. Smith of Philadelphia Twenty-fifth District, guilty of a violation of section 30, Article III., of the State Constitution, and of the act of Assembly of 1874 defining corrupt solicitations of members, etc. William H. Kemble, ex-member Charles B. Salter of Philadelphia, Jesse R. Crawford of Blair, A. W. Leisenring of Carbon, and Christian Long of Cumberland are found guilty of the same. The committee say there is a considerable mass of evidence showing attempts at improper combinations upon other legislation pending before the House or to be brought before it, in order to further the passage of the riot bill. While these combinations or attempted combinations may not have been such as would render the parties concerned therein criminally liable, yet they have been of such a character as to be antagonistic to pure and wise legislation, to the spirit if not the letter of the Constitution, and to the best interests of the Commonwealth. They find that the public press was not subsidized, but that attempts were made to influence public opinion through the insertion of paid articles in the papers.

Without waiting to accept the report of the committee, separate resolutions were offered in the House to expel each of the members against whom charges were made in the report. Each resolution failed to pass by the constitutional majority of two thirds. The votes for expulsion were as follows: on Petroff —yeas 98, nays 88; on Smith—yeas 88, nays 79; on Rumberger—yeas 104, nays 69. A resolution was also adopted to appoint a committee on the part of the House to commence criminal proceedings against William H. Kemble, Charles B. Salter of Philadelphia, Isaac R.

Crawford, assistant superintendent of public grounds, of Blair County, A. M. Leisenring of Mauch Chunk, and Christian Long of Cumberland County, or such of them against whom they may be satisfied there is sufficient evidence, in the Court of Quarter Sessions of Dauphin County, and that the Attorney-General is requested to lend them such aid as they need in conducting said prosecution. This ended the action of the House relative to the report of the committee.

The following preamble and resolution relating to special schools of instruction were offered in the Senate and adopted:

Whereas, It is the opinion of this body that it is the duty of the State to adopt such measures as will promote the variety and value of her productions, and to foster the establishment of industrial and technical schools having for their object the practical education and training of the boys and young men of this Commonwealth in the mechanic arts and sciences, believing, as we do, that the practical result of our present system of education is to direct the attention of boys and young men too much in the direction of the learned professions, to the great neglect and detriment of the mechanic arts and skilled industries; and,

Whereas, It is believed that the enormous magnitude of the production of iron in the State demands the establishment of a limited number of schools wherein shall be taught theoretically and practically the manufacture of all kinds of articles made from iron and from iron steel: therefore, be it

Resolved by the Senate, That a committee of ten be appointed, consisting of five Senators to be appointed by the President *pro tem.* and five mechanical and scientific mechanics to be appointed by the Governor, whose duty it shall be to examine the matters in the foregoing preamble, and report to the next Legislature such facts as they may deem necessary, together with their opinion as to the advisability and policy of establishing such institutions as are therein mentioned.

A supposed over-issue of $5,000,000 State bonds in 1852 and 1853 was found upon investigation not to be correct.

The committee of the House appointed to investigate the affairs of the State Agricultural College reported that the institution had been very badly managed; that its location was a very undesirable one; that the building was entirely unsuited for the purpose for which it was erected; that the agricultural department, which was intended to be the leading object of the institution, had never been a success; and that the State had never received and is not now receiving benefits at all commensurate with the amount of money which had been appropriated to said institution by the United States and the State. The Congress of the United States granted to the State 780,000 acres of land, which by bad management netted the State only $439,000. The act of Congress granting this vast amount of land required that the proceeds thereof should be used by the State mainly in the interest of agriculture and the mechanical arts. The interest accruing from this fund, in addition to some $400,000 appropriated by the State Legislature, was used and controlled by the trustees

of said Agricultural College. In addition the trustees aforesaid hold the bond of the State bearing six per cent. interest, dated February 2, 1872, calling for $500,000, and falling due fifty years from date, from which they derive a revenue of $30,000 annually. The evidence disclosed the further fact that the deeds for all the freehold belonging to the Pennsylvania State College, including the experimental farms, were held by the trustees, not in trust for the Commonwealth but for themselves and their successors. The committee also found that the experimental farms owned by the trustees, which were to be conducted solely in the interest of the agricultural class of the Commonwealth, have utterly failed to accomplish the object intended. This is notably so in the case of the western farm located in Indiana County, which is not now a third-class farm nor in as good condition as when purchased. At the present session of the college but forty-six students are in attendance, many of whom are non-residents of the State, and there are now in the employ of the college eleven professors, which is out of all proportion with the number of students in attendance. The committee is of the opinion that the trustees have signally failed to carry out the object for which the magnificent land-grant was given by the United States, and which was further sought to be accomplished by most liberal appropriations on the part of the State. The report was received, and a resolution adopted instructing the Treasurer to pay no more money to the college until it was shown that the laws under which it existed were faithfully executed.

A vast amount of local business was transacted, and the Legislature adjourned on June 4th.

The railroad question has perhaps greater prominence in Pennsylvania than in other States. Complaints were formally made to the Governor in 1878 of undue and unreasonable discrimination in charges and in facilities for transportation of freight over the lines of certain transportation companies. Under his directions such legal proceedings were instituted to redress any such wrongs to shippers as were within the reach of judicial remedy. The transportation of oil was the chief cause of complaint. One company aimed at the purchase and refining of the whole product of the State, and had reached such a point of success as to dictate its own price in the purchase of the oil, and to secure from railroads its own terms of transportation. The greatest relief from the oppression of this monopoly was, however, obtained by the producers of oil, by the construction of a line of pipe along the surface of the ground through which the oil might flow from the wells to an independent line of transportation. This line was constructed from Bradford to Williamsport, a distance of 233 miles. (See "Annual Cyclopædia" for 1878, page 682.) The work of construction was commenced in February and completed in May. The line starts at Williamsport and runs slightly north of west over the mountains into Potter County, and on to Coryville, or Frisbie, the initial point, in Me-Kean. It passes over a high range of mountains near the little village of Waterville, at the forks of Pine Creek, and it was found very difficult to lay the line at this point. In several places the sides of the mountains were so steep that the pipe had to be let down with ropes to be placed in position. The distance, according to the figures of the chief engineer, is just 100 miles; and as the pipe is six inches in diameter, it requires nearly 28,000 barrels of oil to fill it, reckoning 41 gallons to the barrel. There are tanks at Coryville and a pumping station. The next pumping station is at a point about four miles from Coudersport. The distance from Coryville to pump-station No. 2 is 22½ miles; from there to Williamsport is 77½, and the oil, when raised 1,200 feet at the summit, runs down to Williamsport of its own gravity, as the fall is 2,100 feet. The pumping-engines are forty-horse power each, and each has an equal share of the lifting to do in the way of the application of power. The last joint of pipe having been laid, and everything in readiness, the engine at Coryville was started on the 28th of May, at four o'clock in the afternoon, and the first oil was forced through the pipe in the direction of the pump-station in Potter County, 22½ miles distant. The pipe is of such a flexible character that it readily adjusts itself to the formation of the ground, except where very sharp turns had to be made, and then short joints, sharply curved, were used. The engineer says that the flexibility of the pipe allows it to deflect at least fifteen feet in one hundred. Every joint has been carefully tested by subjecting it to hydraulic pressure, and but little trouble is apprehended. Joints are liable to burst, however, in which case the pumps would have to be stopped, and considerable oil would be lost before the break could be repaired by putting in a new joint. At Williamsport tanks had been constructed to hold 60,000 barrels, and trains prepared for its constant transportation to tide-water. The capacity of the pipe was 250 barrels per hour, or about 6,000 barrels per day. The first shipment by cars was made on June 7th. Over sixty iron tank-cars were filled. These cars carry 100 barrels each, and about 6,000 barrels were loaded. The siding which has been laid by the Reading Railroad Company for the oil-cars is 2,700 feet in length, and thirty cars can be filled in a very few minutes, so complete are the arrangements. The pipe conducting the oil from the tanks is eight inches in diameter and about one mile in length. At the siding another pipe of the same size runs parallel with it for a sufficient distance to cover fully thirty cars, and there is a stand-pipe opposite each car, which is so curved that the oil flows into the dome in a steady stream. As the tanks are more than 200 feet above the level of the siding, the oil flows with great force. It is thus seen that the facilities for shipping are excellent, and comparatively little time is lost in filling a whole train.

The reports of thirty-eight of the railroad companies of the State for the year 1878 represent the aggregate earnings at $132,168,389, against $127,936,695 in 1877. The increase is about 3·3 per cent. Twenty-four roads have reported their earnings for four years, and show in 1876 an increase of 3·1 per cent. over 1875; in 1877, 0·8 per cent. over 1876; and in 1878, 4·1 per cent. over 1877. The increase in 1878 was larger than in the preceding years. From 1875 to 1878 the increase was about 8·2 per cent. A general decrease in expenses is also shown.

The druggists of the State, although exempted as regular apothecaries from license-fees, have been held by the decisions of several local courts to be liable as venders of patent medicines to pay such fee.

Many questions respecting the legal liabilities of municipal corporations have arisen out of the failure of the city of Williamsport to pay the interest on its bonds. The city was authorized by express grant of the Legislature to issue bonds to the amount of $200,000. The total of bonds issued, however, amounted to $645,000. It was urged on behalf of the city that all of these bonds in excess of $200,000 authorized by the Legislature were illegal and void, inasmuch as no power existed for such action on the part of the municipal authorities. On this point the Supreme Court held, by a majority of one (Justices Agnew, Woodward, and Sterrett dissenting), that when a municipality has lawfully created a debt it has the implied power, unless restrained by its charter or a statute, to evidence the same by bill, bond, note, or other instrument. The Court held that the act of the Legislature did not limit the implied authority of the city of Williamsport to issue bonds for municipal improvements. This decision has been disputed as unsound in other States, and as throwing the door wide open for a wholesale issue of bonds. On the part of the city it was shown that a portion of the bonds issued in excess of the $200,000 expressly permitted by the Legislature ($123,339) were not authorized by Councils; that 67 of the $1,000 bonds were issued for "unknown purposes," and that 183 were to "persons unknown" and for "purposes unknown." The opinion of the Court did not notice or distinguish that the validity of a portion of the bonds in dispute rested on evidence going to show that they were issued fraudulently. At the close of the argument, however, the Court stated that it was not meant "to deprive the city of any special defense to any particular bond or bonds." In dissenting from the majority of the Court, Judge Agnew said: "The citizens of Williamsport find themselves involved in a debt of $645,000, none of which can be contested, when they find their way into the hands of *bona fide* holders for value, if the power to issue this amount be sustained, whether they be legitimate or illegitimate. Here it is that the doctrine of the opinion does a great wrong. It sustains the illegitimate as well as the legitimate issues, on the ground that the implied power to issue them exists, and with this aegis covers the entire sum." Has a municipal bond the attributes of commercial paper? is a question which did not entirely escape notice. Judge Agnew says, in his dissenting opinion: "That logic is false which deduces from the power of a mere municipal corporation . . . a power on the part of such a corporation, created by law for governmental purposes, to issue commercial paper . . . negotiable according to the law merchant or general usage. . . . This is not a municipal power. It flows from no relation of the citizens to the corporation. They are not stockholders, nor partners, nor associates, but are a portion of the people, living under a local government for certain local purposes. *The officers of a municipal corporation are not the agents of the people.*"

A case involving the liability of a municipality for the condition of its thoroughfares came before the Supreme Court. The action grew out of injuries sustained at Pittston. The plaintiff's son was driving his horse and wagon through the main street, which is sixty feet in width, but narrows at a mill which it passes. At this narrowing a perpendicular wall descends to the tracks of a railroad, but there is no abutment or guard of any kind at the edge of the road. The horses of the plaintiff took fright as a train approached, and they, with the wagon, were precipitated to the track below. The boy was hurt, one horse was killed, another injured, and the wagon destroyed. The Court said:

It is true that, without the frightening of the horses, there would have been no accident; but the horse is naturally a timid animal, and is so liable to fright that those having charge of the public highways ought to make reasonable provisions for a matter so common and so likely to happen at any time. Horses abound, but horses that never frighten or are never fractious are exceedingly rare; and, if roads were to be constructed only for such animals, there must need be but little traveling upon them. We think it was well said, in the case of Lower Macungie Township *vs.* Merkhoffer (21 P. F. S., 276), that it was no defense that by careful driving the accident might have been avoided, since that would fall far short of the purpose of a public highway. In the case of Newlin township *vs.* Davis (27 P. T. S., 317), the accident occurred through the fright of a horse upon a bridge unprotected by side-railings; but it was not, in that case, pretended that the omission of such railing was not *per se* neglect, nor that the fright of the horse relieved the township of liability. Now, it is hard to understand why a precipice at the side of a narrow street does not require fencing quite as much as the sides of a bridge. We can readily understand and excuse the want of precautions of this kind in wild and sparsely settled portions of the State, for the finances of the townships are exhausted in the making of roads even of an inferior character; but we can neither understand nor

excuse the motive of a borough of ten thousand inhabitants in refusing to properly guard a place on its main thoroughfare so dangerous as that now under consideration, especially when the expense of so doing would be but trifling. In the present case there is certainly, then, but little, if any, doubt but that the negligence of the borough authorities was the direct cause of the accident complained of, with its resulting damages.

Criminal proceedings were commenced against the persons reported as having attempted to bribe members of the Legislature. Bills of indictment were found against them, but the trial was postponed.

By another decision of the Supreme Court, the liability to taxation of sectarian and other asylums was affirmed. A Protestant Episcopal church had established an orphan asylum. The law of Pennsylvania exempts from taxation public charitable and educational institutions. The Supreme Court held that this orphan asylum, being generally limited to the reception of the orphan children of Episcopalian parents, is not a "public" charitable institution within the proper meaning of the statute, and hence is liable to taxation. The Court also held that, though the asylum sometimes received orphans not of Episcopalian parentage, yet the main object of the asylum was not a "public" charity, but to advance the particular interests of one religious denomination; hence it was not a "public" charitable institution within the meaning of the statute, and is liable to taxation. In illustration of the decision, the opinion of the Court intimates that if Girard College should open its doors only to one denomination or class of persons, it would not be a "public" educational institution, and would be liable to taxation; or if the Pennsylvania Hospital should refuse to receive any but Protestants, or any but Roman Catholics, it would cease to be a "public" charitable institution, and would be liable to taxation.

An election was held on November 4th for the choice of a State Treasurer and the State Legislature.

The State Temperance Convention assembled at Harrisburg on April 24th, attended by 346 delegates from 39 counties and 7 cities. Felix R. Brunot of Pittsburgh was chosen President. A series of resolutions was adopted, which requested the Legislature to change the policy of the State from that of license and regulation to that of prohibiting the manufacture and sale of intoxicating liquors for public drinking purposes; that all males and females over twenty-one years old be clothed with legal power to vote on a duly framed law for prohibiting the traffic in liquors; that each candidate for office be interrogated before and after nomination as to his view of a temperance law, and, if unfavorable, that he be regarded as unfit to represent the people; that the Legislature authorize the appointment of a commission to investigate the alcoholic liquor traffic. A law was framed prohibiting the sale and manufacture of liquors, which will be submitted to the Legislature when in session.

The National Greenback-Labor party assembled in State Convention at Altoona on July 15th. In the permanent organization Samuel R. Mason was made President. For State Treasurer, Henry C. Baird was nominated and declined; Peter Sutton of Indiana County was then nominated. The following series of resolutions was then adopted:

The National Greenback-Labor party of Pennsylvania, in convention assembled, declare:

1. That it is in favor of the payment of the national debt strictly in accordance with the stipulations of the contract under which it was created, and that no more interest-bearing bonds of the Federal Government be issued.

2. That the Federal Government only shall issue money; that such money shall be a full legal tender, and that full legal-tender greenbacks shall be substituted for national-bank notes.

3. We demand, for the sake of economy and convenience, that the trade-dollar and fractional silver coin be replaced by fractional paper currency.

4. We demand the repeal of all laws that foster inequality in condition and opportunity, as they are in violation of universal justice.

5. We demand the enactment of an income-tax law, with heavy penalties for perjury in its violation, and that said tax be graduated in proportion to income.

6. That all debts due for labor performed take precedence of all other claims.

7. That we demand the passage and approval of an act abolishing the store-order or truck system, and compelling the payment of all wages due laborers at regular stated rates, and in the lawful money of the United States.

8. That we demand the passage and enforcement of such laws as will prevent all combinations, discrimination, or the granting of rebates by transportation companies, and compel common carriers to furnish the service for the same price to all men.

9. We demand that no more public lands be voted to corporations, but that they be held for actual settlers.

10. We demand that education shall be free and industrial, and no child shall be allowed to grow up in ignorance.

11. We demand that there shall be a contraction in official fees and salaries to correspond with the reductions of incomes in other directions; that there shall be a specific tariff placed on all raw materials produced here for the protection of American industry; that the hours of labor shall be reduced to eight hours per day; that the contract system of labor in our prisons and reformatory institutions shall be abolished.

12. We denounce any attempt at coalition with any other party; we favor the establishment of national and State labor bureaus.

The Democratic State Convention assembled at Harrisburg on July 16th. A. H. Coffroth was appointed permanent chairman. D. O. Barr of Pittsburgh was nominated for State Treasurer. The following resolutions were reported by the Committee on Resolutions:

1. That we, the Democratic party of Pennsylvania in convention assembled, renew our vows of fidelity to the fundamental principles proclaimed and practiced by the illustrious men who settled our free institutions and founded the Democratic party to protect and preserve them.

2. That the just powers of the Federal Union, the rights of the States, and the liberties of the people are vital parts of one harmonious system; and to save each part in its whole constitutional vigor is to "save the life of the nation."

3. That the Democratic party maintains, as it ever has maintained, that the military are, and ought to be, in all things subordinate to the civil authorities. It denies, as it ever has denied, the right of the Federal Administration to keep on foot at the general expense a standing army to invade the States for political purposes without regard to constitutional restrictions, to control the people at the polls, to protect and encourage fraudulent counts of the votes, or to inaugurate candidates rejected by the majority.

4. That the right to a free ballot is the right preservative of all rights, the only means of peacefully redressing grievances and reforming abuses. The presence at the polls of a regular military force and of a host of hireling officials, claiming the power to arrest and imprison citizens without warrant or hearing, destroys all freedom of elections and upturns the very foundation of self-government. We call upon all good citizens to aid us in preserving our institutions from destruction by these imperial methods of supervising the right of suffrage and coercing the popular will; in keeping the way to the ballot-box open and free, as it was to our fathers; in removing the army to a safe distance when the people assemble to express their sovereign pleasure at the polls; and in securing obedience to their will when legally expressed by their votes.

5. That Rutherford B. Hayes, having been placed in power against the well-known and legally expressed will of the people, is the representative of a conspiracy only; and his claim of right to surround the ballot-boxes with troops and deputy marshals to intimidate and obstruct the electors, and his unprecedented use of the veto to maintain this unconstitutional and despotic power, are an insult and a menace to the country.

6. That the Democratic party, as of old, favors a constitutional currency of gold and silver, and of paper convertible into coin.

7. That we are opposed to the system of subsidies by the General Government under which, during the period of Republican ascendancy, political rings and corporations profited at the people's expense, and to any appropriation of the public moneys or the public credit to any object but the public service. The reforms and economies enforced by the Democratic party since its advent to power in the Lower House of Congress have saved the people many millions of dollars, and we believe that a like result would follow its restoration to power in the State of Pennsylvania.

8. That the Democratic party, being the natural friend of the workingman and having throughout its history stood between him and oppression, renews its expression of sympathy for labor and its promise of protection to its rights.

9. That we look with alarm and apprehension upon the pretensions of the great transportation companies to be above the fundamental law of this Commonwealth which governs all else within our borders; and until they accept the Constitution of 1873 in good faith, they should remain objects of the utmost vigilance and jealousy by both Legislature and people.

10. That the recent attempt, under the personal direction of ruling Republican leaders, to debauch the Legislature by wholesale bribery and corruption, and take from the Commonwealth four millions of dollars for which its liability had never been ascertained, is a fresh and alarming evidence of the aggressiveness of corporate power in collusion with political rings, and should receive the signal condemnation of the people at the polls.

11. That the present condition of the State Treasury, a bankrupt general fund, and even schools and charities unable to get the money long since appropriated to their support, is a sufficient illustration of the reckless financial mismanagement of the Republican party.

From the minority of the committee the following resolutions were then offered as a substitute for the resolution relating to the national finances:

That the power to issue paper money as well as coin is the exclusive right of the General Government, and as the charters of the national banks expire the Government should substitute for their circulation legal-tender Treasury notes, redeemable in coin, and receivable by the Government for all dues at their par face value.

That the coinage of silver should be on the same terms and conditions as gold, and all coins of the same denomination should be of equal value; that the restoration of silver to a perfect equality with gold, both as coin and bullion, is by the dictates of justice and wise statesmanship immediately demanded.

This motion was lost, and the platform was then adopted.

The Republican State Convention assembled at Harrisburg on July 23d. Galusha A. Grow was made permanent Chairman. Samuel Butler of Chester County was nominated for State Treasurer. The following resolutions were then adopted:

1. That the Republican party, again forced to stand forward for the defense of human rights, after a struggle lasting through a generation, finds itself confronted by the same foes of Federal unity, political freedom, and national honor, which it has so often overthrown in civil contests and in armed conflict.

2. That we appeal to the Union-loving people of Pennsylvania to arrest, by their votes, the mad career of the Democratic party, which insists upon placing the national Government under the domination of men who but lately fought to destroy it, and who are now plotting to give triumph to the doctrine they failed to establish in the field—the establishment of State sovereignty by the overthrow of national supremacy.

3. We declare our implacable hostility to the repeal of the national laws which protect the purity of the ballot-box and secure fair elections. The election of Congressmen and Presidential electors being clearly subject to national control, any attempt to throw off that control is simply an effort to establish fraud at national elections. Honest suffrage, equal rights, the unity of the nation, and the supremacy of the national Government in all matters placed by the Constitution under its control, can be maintained only by the Republican party, which is alone committed to their defense.

4. That the Democratic party, having committed itself to an attempt to break up the Government by refusing to appropriate moneys already collected from the people to sustain the Government, unless the Executive shall sanction measures intended to foster fraud, violence, and corruption in the national elections, and to impair the constitutional supremacy of the nation, deserves and invites the signal condemnation of every law-abiding and honest citizen.

5. That we are in favor of the discharge of the national debt in coin according to the understanding between the Government and the lender; of a paper currency redeemable in coin; and of the existing national banking system. We congratulate the country upon returning national prosperity, and upon the accomplishment, under a Republican national Administration, of the successful resumption of specie payments. Our currency, the best ever afforded the country, is restored to its par value; the national credit has been maintained and strengthened, and the burden of the national debt largely reduced. To complete what has been so well done, we demand that our present financial system remain undisturbed.

6. That to the policy and practice of protection to home industry and home production, inaugurated and sustained by the Republican party, we are indebted for the growth and development of our domestic and foreign commerce, and for the prosperous condition and

strength of the national finances; and that to the continuance of that policy must we look in the future for assured prosperity and peace throughout our whole country. In fostering the same we desire to insure constant employment to labor at remunerative wages.

7. That the firm stand of the President in vindicating the prerogatives of the coördinate departments of the Government meets the hearty approval of the Republican party of Pennsylvania.

8. We call on the veteran soldiers of the war for the Union to join us in resenting the unjust expulsion of their wounded comrades from offices by the Democratic Congress, and the transfer of their places to rebel soldiers, whose chief recommendation seems to be unrepentant treason and unending hate of the nation.

9. That we earnestly sympathize with our Southern Republican brethren, who are now passing under the harrow of political persecution. We bid them be of good cheer. Fraud and force can not always triumph, even in a region where fraud and force find a congenial home. If a solid South now deprives them of their just rights, a solid North will not fail, in due time, to secure them that perfect freedom which is the birthright and inheritance of every American citizen.

10. That the United States of America is a nation, not a league; its Constitution and all laws made in pursuance thereof are the supreme law of the land, anything in the Constitution or laws of a State to the contrary notwithstanding.

11. That the tribunal established by the Constitution to determine whether the laws are made in pursuance thereof is the Supreme Court of the United States. All laws once enacted, unless repealed by the law-making power or declared void by said Court, neither law-maker, citizen, nor State has a right to nullify.

12. That the success of the administration of the State under the management of the Republican party, the steady reduction of the State debt, and the enforced compliment of the present Democratic Treasurer that not one dollar of the public funds had been lost or misplaced during the seventeen years of Republican custody of the funds, prove that official integrity and financial skill have been the benefits conferred by our party on the tax-payers of the State, and merit the approval of the people of Pennsylvania.

13. That we pledge ourselves in favor of such legislation as will prevent unlawful and unconstitutional discrimination in freights by the carrying companies of the country.

The result of the election was as follows:

FOR TREASURER.

Butler, Republican	280,158
Barr, Democrat	231,715
Sutton, National	27,207
Richardson, Prohibition	8,219

The Legislature was divided as follows:

PARTIES.	Senate.	House.
Republicans	82	107
Democrats	16	77
Nationals	1	17
Prohibitionist	1	..
Total	50	201

PERKINS, SAMUEL E., Chief Justice of the Supreme Court of Indiana, died at Indianapolis, December 17th. Born in Brattleborough, Vermont, December 6, 1811, he passed his youth on the farm of his adopted father, William Baker, in Conway, Massachusetts, attending the winter schools and devoting his spare hours to study. After reaching his majority he made efforts to complete his general education, and then took up the study of the law, reading in the office of Thomas J. Nevans of Penn Yan, New York, and also with Henry Willis, afterward a Judge of the New York Supreme Court. At the age of twenty-five he proceeded to the newly opened West, intending to establish himself there. Starting for Indianapolis on foot, he found himself without money in Richmond, Indiana, where he remained, reading in the office of Judge Borden and passing his examintion for the bar in the spring of 1837. Opening an office in Richmond, he supplemented his legal practice with writing for "The Jeffersonian," a recently established Democratic paper, of which he afterward became editor and proprietor, conducting it during the campaign of 1840, but not neglecting his practice in the mean time. In 1843 he was appointed prosecuting attorney for the Wayne Circuit. He was a Presidential elector on the Democratic ticket in 1844. In the winter of the same year he was appointed a Judge of the Supreme Court by Governor Whitcomb, but was not confirmed by the Legislature. After the adjournment of the Legislature, however, he was placed on the bench for the term of one year by the Governor. He made Indianapolis his residence from this period. He was continued on the bench until 1864, when the Democratic ticket was defeated. Besides his judicial labors, he compiled while serving as judge a digest of the Indiana reports, and wrote a standard textbook, "Perkins's Practice." He also taught as Professor of Law in the Northwestern Christian University. After his retirement from the Supreme bench he followed the practice of his profession until 1873, when he was appointed Judge of the Superior Court of Marion County, to fill the unexpired term of Judge Rand. He continued in this position, to which he was elected by the people the following year, until 1876, when he was again placed by the popular vote upon the Supreme Court bench, of which he was Chief Justice at the time of his death.

PERSIA, a country of Asia. Reigning sovereign, the Shah Nasr-ed-Din, who was born in 1831, and succeeded his father, Shah Mohammed, September 10, 1848. The heir apparent to the throne, Muzaffer-ed-Din, was born in 1854, and has two sons.

By the Treaty of Berlin Persia received from Turkey the town and territory of Khotoor, containing about 8,000 inhabitants. The total area of Persia is about 637,000 square miles, with a population of 7,000,000. At the end of July, 1878, Persia had 2,490 miles of telegraph lines and 4,782 miles of telegraph wire in operation. The number of telegraph offices was 56, the number of dispatches 665,000. The first regular postal service was opened in January, 1877.

The affairs of Persia begin to attract greater attention, not only on account of the reforms which it has of late begun to introduce, but especially on account of its relation to the Eastern question. Schemes of an alliance between England and Persia, involving proposals for an annexation of western Afghanistan to Persia, were eagerly discussed in England, and warmly advocated by several statesmen. An important lecture on the subject was delivered in London on March 7th by General Sir F. Goldsmid. The lecturer maintained that Persia, with all her misgovernment and short-comings, had great resources for a powerful army. Her army, numbering in bygone times 200,000, and now estimated to consist of 100,000 men, had been formed by British officers on the European model, and was now in the hands of an Austrian officer, a Russian colonel being also there. Persia, as an ally of England, had the elements of material usefulness, and it surely came within the province of Englishmen to impart to so old a kingdom, and one so replete with classical interest, some of the better things of modern civilization. The lecturer dwelt at length upon the importance of an alliance between Persia and England, in case of new difficulties between England and Russia. Sir Henry Rawlinson, who presided, bore testimony to the capacity for discipline which the Persians displayed, and spoke warmly of their powers of endurance and of their virtues of temperance and courage. He thought that a real, honest, and cordial alliance might be formed with Persia by England.

The reorganization of the Persian army under the direction of Austrian officers is proceeding satisfactorily. With the exception of the head-dress, the uniform of the troops is very similar to that of the Austrian army. The infantry wear blue coats or blouses with red facings, and gray trousers; the rifles, gray coats with green facings; while the dress of the artillery and cavalry is exactly like that of the same arms of the service in Austria. The Shah in 1879 visited and inspected some of the barracks—the first time such an event has taken place in the history of Persia—and afterward reviewed the troops.

The British Consul-General Abbott, in a report on the trade of Tabreez in the year 1877 –'78, gives an unfavorable account of the commercial situation of Persia. The war between Russia and Turkey arrested the trade between Tabreez and Trebizond, and rendered the route from the Persian frontier of the Aras to the Caucasus impracticable for the transit of merchandise; and, besides the great difficulties thus thrown in the way of importers of English manufactured goods, the exchanges were very much against them. The rates of transport between Trebizond and Persia rose to more than double what they had been before the declaration of war. The consul observes that the excess of imports over exports, involving a continual drain of specie outward, threatens to produce most serious consequences. The Caspian provinces appear to yield less silk every year; and when it is considered that the prosperity of the foreign commerce of the country chiefly depends upon that of the silk-trade to furnish returns for imports of merchandise from Europe, the conclusion is that Persia is drifting into a state of bankruptcy, which the effects of the late war must tend to accelerate.

PERU (República del Perú). For territorial division, area, population, etc., reference may be made to the "Annual Cyclopædia" for 1873, 1875, and 1878, and to the article Bolivia in the present volume.

The President of the Republic, until December 18, 1879, was General Mariano Ignacio Prado, installed in office on August 2, 1876. The Vice-President was General La Puerta. The Cabinet, in May, 1879, was composed of the following Ministers: Interior, Señor Rafael Velarde; Justice and Public Worship, Señor Mariano Felipe Paz Soldan; Foreign Affairs, Señor M. Irigoyen; War and Marine, General M. Mendiburu (President of the Council); Finance, Señor J. M. Quimper.

In November General La Puerta, in charge of the Government during the absence of the President, who had taken command of the army in the south, formed a new Cabinet composed of his personal friends and political co-operators, as follows: Interior, Señor Buenaventura Elguera; Justice and Public Worship, Señor Adolfo Quiroga; Foreign Affairs, Señor Rafael Velarde; War and Marine, General La Cotera (President of the Council); Finance, Señor J. M. Quimper. After the departure of General Prado from the country, which occurred on December 18, 1879, Colonel Nicolas de Piérola assumed the dictatorship. The President of the Supreme Court was Señor T. A. Ribeyro; the Postmaster-General, Señor F. de P. Muñoz; the Inspector-General of the Army, General M. Rivarola; and the Commandant-General of the Navy, Rear-Admiral A. de la Haza. The Peruvian Consul-General in New York is Mr. J. O. Tracy. The Archbishop of Lima is the Rt. Rev. Orueta y Castrillon.

For particulars concerning the peace strength of the Peruvian army, see the "Annual Cyclopædia" for 1878. In May last, after the outbreak of hostilities with Chili, the number of men under arms was raised to 40,000. The following statement concerning the Peruvian navy was published in December last: "The Peruvian fleet may be said to exist only in name since the combat of Punta Gruesa, in which the Chilian gunboat Covadonga occasioned the loss of the Peruvian ironclad Independencia, and the surrender of the monitor Huáscar and the gunboat Pilcomayo to the Chilian naval forces. Peru's only remaining effective war-vessel is the corvette Union, the old monitors Manco Capac and Atahualpa, built in the United States in 1863, being no longer fit for service otherwise than as floating batteries at anchor. Add the four steam transports, Limeña, Oroya, Chalaco, and Rimac (the only Chilian naval loss by capture in the present war), and we have enumerated the entire Peruvian sea-force now in existence."

In the absence of official reports concerning the national finances, it can only be stated that the average revenue and expenditures are usually estimated at about $60,000,000 and $50,000,000 respectively. The revenue,* derived in part from the custom-house receipts, but chiefly from the sale of guano and nitrate of soda, having for many years past been insufficient to cover the expenditures (a large proportion of which has been for the construction of railroads and other useful public works), formidable annual deficits have become the invariable rule.

Peru has an immense national debt, the home branch of which is estimated at $20,000,000, exclusive of a floating debt of unknown amount, greatly increased by extensive issues of paper money made in 1879 to carry on the war against Chili. In regard to the foreign debt, the following statement, from the pen of a Spanish-American writer, will be found interesting:

The foreign debt of Peru, according to the latest data obtainable, including the unpaid coupons from January, 1876, to July, 1879, amounts to £45,268,103 4s., or $226,340,516, in coin, at five soles to the pound sterling. Since January, 1876, no interest has been paid, nor have any sums been provided for the amortization of this tremendous debt. At the commencement of the present year the interest on the consolidated debt —that is to say, the 6 per cent. loan of 1870, and the 5 per cent. loan of 1872 †—was reduced to 3 per cent. per annum, which reduced the half-yearly interest from £1,690,369 16s. to £659,244 4s. Notwithstanding this large reduction, no interest has been paid during the present year. A remarkable proposition has lately been made to the Government by the French section of the foreign bondholders. The character, advantages, and disadvantages of this proposition are briefly as follows: The principal of the foreign debt shall be reduced to 100,000,000 soles, coin, a gain to the state of $69,036,980. No payment shall be exacted for interest now overdue, which represents another gain to the republic of $57,300,536; these items providing for the extinguishment of a total claim against Peru amounting to the immense sum of $126,340,516. The bondholders will pay the Government for the guano delivered alongside their ships, at the rate of 210s. per ton in coin, or in bills on London at ninety days, on presentation of the receipt of the captain countersigned by the general agent of the society. On the delivery of the guano at the port of destination a further sum of 210s. per ton will be paid in bonds of Peru at their nominal value; or in other words, the Government accepts payment of a certain portion of the value of the guano in its own bonds, and provides to that extent for the amortization of its debt. The Government will be at no expense on account of interests or commissions, and will receive on the acceptance of the terms of the proposition certain advances in the character of a further loan. The society of bondholders will have the sole right to fix the price of the guano, and to sell the same in its native state, or mixed or manipulated, in the markets of Europe. The Government will transfer to the bondholders its rights of proprietorship in the deposits of guano existing in the republic of Peru, and on that account the bondholders are the only parties who have the right to extract guano, and to sell it in the markets of Europe. In virtue of these

---

* See "Annual Cyclopædia" for 1878, p. 687.
† The 1870 and 1872 loans are secured on the guano deposits principally.

ights the bondholders may embargo and sequestrate all guano imported or sold in Europe without their anthorization or consent. In case the deposits of guano should be exhausted before the complete amortization of the debt as at present constituted, or the quality become so inferior as to leave a loss by its manipulation and sale, the Government shall cede its rights to all its nitrate properties, to be handled in the same way and for the same purposes by the bondholders, always understanding that the latter will respect any obligations which the Government may have previously incurred on their account. The Government is also prohibited from paying any debt of the state whatever by means of deliveries of guano or nitrates, which is not in accordance with the terms of this convention. The bondholders will syndicate their claims, and will form themselves into a civil society for the development of the guano interests of Peru, according to the laws of France or England. By this instrument the Government is to recognize the jurisdiction of European tribunals, simply and exclusively, in everything relative to the interpretation and execution of the present contract, and the Government resigns all pretensions or claims which may be contrary or prejudicial to the enjoyment or exercise of the rights and privileges inherent to the transfer of titles to the proprietorship of the guano deposits or nitrate industries of the country; so that in effect, by the acceptance of the terms of the present proposition, the Government may enjoy a revenue of £750,000 per annum, and provide for the amortization of their debt at the rate of £375,000 per annum, with certain advances promised instead of those which the Government now enjoys under its present contract, and an amazing discount on the entire debt, with the sole obligation of losing the proprietorship of their fast-failing guano deposits, and possibly their nitrate-works, and all right of claim before their own courts in case of disagreement with the contractors.

The exports are estimated at the average annual value of $50,000,000, and the imports at considerably less. Of the three chief articles of export, guano, cubic nitre, and sugar, the two former are Government monopolies. The exports of sugar have more than doubled within four years. The value of the exports to the United Kingdom in 1878 was $26,161,525, against $23,482,510 in the year immediately preceding; and that of the imports from the same at $6,849,155 in 1878, against $6,331,970 in 1877. The subjoined tables, from the report of the United States Consul at the port of Callao, show the amount of trade between that port and the United States in the year ending October 1, 1878:

EXPORTS FROM CALLAO TO THE UNITED STATES.

Guano	$961,840
Nitrate of soda	69,300
Cochineal	10,185
Hides and skins	5,309
Wines, liquors, etc	537
Firearms, etc	500
Sugar	132,648
Coca	1,864
Coffee	919
Old iron	6,069
Rags	107
Wool	848
Quicksilver flasks	698
Opium	3,060
Spices	20
Tea	4,000
Salt	4,677
Oil	1,109
Salmon	570
Bark	498
Personal effects	115
Total	**$1,203,602**

IMPORTS FROM THE UNITED STATES THROUGH THE PORT OF CALLAO.

Lumber:	
Oregon pine	$180,000
White pine	90,000
Redwood	40,000
Oak	50,000
Pitch pine	50,000
General merchandise per sail, as per manifest	986,000
General mechandise per steamers (estimated)	480,000
	$1,876,000
Deduct the following, included with cargoes of general merchandise:	
White pine	$90,000
Pitch pine	50,000
Oak	50,000
	190,000
Total	**$1,686,000**

The difference between the totals of the two foregoing tables, $672,398 constitutes the balance of trade in favor of the United States.

The total exports from the republic to all destinations, in the year just mentioned, were as follows:

Guano, 450,000 tons	$18,000,000
Nitrate of soda, 250,000 tons	12,000,000
Sugar, 200,000 tons	15,000,000
Hides and skins	1,000,000
Wool	500,000
Cotton	200,000
Metals other than precious	300,000
Silver	2,225,000
Rice	150,000
Miscellaneous	100,000
Total	**$49,475,000**

We subjoin the latest official statement accessible regarding the nitrate-trade in the most important district, the province of Tarapacá:

SHIPMENTS.	Sacks.	Quintals.
Nitrate of soda shipped to Europe for Government account:		
From Iquique	733,248	2,192,763·62
" Pisagua	361,004	1,088,194·60
" Mejillones	58,819	155,225·78
" Mollendo	20,991	64,631·80
" Tocopilla	4,366	14,060·28
	1,174,428	3,514,875·58
To the United States, from Iquique.	173,669	540,579·41
	1,348,097	4,055,454·99
Nitrate of potash for Government ac't	40,307	113,668·44
Total for Government account..	1,388,404	4,169,123·43
Nitrate of soda shipped for private account, for orders:		
From Iquique	385,295	1,015,205·52
" Pisagua	205,885	608,733·46
" Mejillones	36,716	106,589·74
" Mollendo	8,577	25,527·89
Total for private account	586,423	1,756,067·61
Total shipments:		
Nitrate of soda	1,934,520	5,811,522·60
Nitrate of potash	40,307	113,668·44
Grand total	1,974,827	5,925,191·04

These resources of immense wealth, however, gave rise to incessant disputes between the Governments interested, and led to the disastrous war now being waged between Bolivia, Chili, and Peru. (For the motives and origin of the war, see BOLIVIA and CHILI.) A Chilian company founded at Valparaiso were working the guano deposits on a grand scale, when the

Bolivian Government imposed a tax on the export of saltpeter. The company refused to pay it, invoking the treaty of 1874; but the Bolivian Government answered Chili's protest by ordering the sale by auction of the property of the company on the 13th of February, 1879. The Chilian Government sent at once a man-of-war to Antofagasta and seized the port. The news of the occupation of Antofagasta created a great sensation in Peru. This republic had in 1873 entered into a secret offensive and defensive alliance with Bolivia against Chili; and the latter republic, having demanded in vain the neutrality of Peru, declared war against her on the 5th of April. Presidents Prado of Peru and Diaz of Bolivia occupied with their troops Taena and the neighboring port of Arica. A strong force under General Bundia was ordered to defend the port of Iquique, and a reserve army of 10,000 men was formed at Lima, the capital of Peru. Two Chilian men-of-war, the Esmeralda and Covadonga, having appeared before Iquique, blockading the port, the Peruvian Government dispatched against them from Arica the frigate Independencia and the monitor Huáscar. After a desperate combat between the Huáscar and Esmeralda, the latter having been attacked both by the heavy cannon of the Huáscar and the troops on shore, the Chilian vessel was sunk.

The war assuming grave dimensions, the Peruvian Government, constrained to raise additional revenue, established a stamp-tax on tobacco, opium, cigars, wine, and liquors, and authorized the Executive to sell by public auction all immovable property belonging to the nation not used in the service of the public.

Chilian men-of-war appeared off Pisagua, which was defended by about 900 Bolivians under General Bundia. Two Parrott rifles, mounted on the bluff overlooking the town, afforded inadequate protection to the port. The fight was heavy and the loss of life great; and in spite of the spirited resistance of the shore batteries, Pisagua was captured, and Bundia retired toward San Bernardo, and thence to Agua Santa, fifty miles from Pisagua, being gradually strengthened by other forces. The lack of generalship and concerted action was soon painfully felt, in spite of the bravery of the troops. On the 18th of November Bundia retraced his steps with a force of over 8,000 men, and on the 19th arrived in front of a hill called San Francisco, which commands the valley through which the railroad runs. The Chilians were intrenched on the hill. The allied forces attempted to dislodge them, but failed, losing more than a thousand men, while the Chilians also suffered very heavily. The men were hurled against the impregnable position of the Chilians, stationed on the top of the high hill with precipitous sides, covered with artillery and mitrailleuses. The attacking party behaved nobly, the heights being gained once by two Peruvian regiments; but the fresh troops of their enemy, instantly brought for-

ward, drove the attacking column back, killing and wounding a large number, after a hand-to-hand fight lasting three hours. The next morning Bundia, having again been attacked by the Chilians under cover of a heavy fog, retired with one body toward Tarapacá, while Bustamante with the cavalry took the road for Arica. General Villegas, commanding the Bolivian division, was wounded and made prisoner by the Chilians. The movement commenced by Bundia, and terminating so disastrously at San Francisco, was to be seconded by an attack on the Chilians by 4,000 Bolivians under General Diaz, who, hard pressed by want of provisions, on learning of the defeat at San Francisco determined to return to Arica. The Chilians took possession of the position which their enemy had occupied. About the same time the Blanco met Peruvian vessels off Arica and captured the Pilcomayo. By the 26th of November 3,000 of the allies routed at San Francisco reached the town of Tarapacá, where they were joined by the body of 800 Bolivians and Peruvians who had been in garrison at Iquique. On the 27th the Chilians surrounded the allied troops. Three times the Chilians were driven out of the position they had selected during the night, and as many times did they re-form and charge the Peruvians. After prolonged fighting the Chilians were driven up the heights and retired, making another assault a league from their first position; but they were again attacked, and had again to retire.

After the disastrous defeat at San Francisco, followed by the hardly less costly victory at Tarapacá, President Prado proceeded to Lima, where he resumed the government. He was universally charged with incompetency, and the ruin of the army in the field was attributed to him. His position became untenable, and he fled to Panama, leaving the government to the constitutional Vice-President, who retained the same Cabinet.

One of the greatest disasters to the Peruvians, and also one of the most memorable actions of naval warfare in modern times, had occurred on the 8th of October, when the Chilian men-of-war Cochrane and Blanco attacked the Peruvian monitor Huáscar. The commander of the latter, Admiral Grau, opened fire on the enemy with his turret-guns (two 300-pounder Armstrong rifles); the Cochrane, carrying six guns, instantly replied. From the decks and tops of the two vessels the fire of musketry and Gatling guns was incessant. The other Chilian ironclads arrived soon on the scene, and opened fire on the Huáscar with terrible effect. A solid 300-pound shot from the Blanco struck the ram in the stem, destroyed the steering gear, and, passing directly through the ship, killed the brave admiral and many others. The Huáscar became unmanageable, and the two Chilian vessels concentrated their fire upon the doomed vessel, which was soon at their mercy. Out of her 216 men, only 86 were alive. The combat took place north of Point Mejillones.

The Prefect Lopez Lavalle having turned Iquique over to the care of the foreign consuls, the Chilians sent marines on shore and hoisted their flag. By decree of the Peruvian President, the port was closed to commerce, and the exportation from all the ports of Tarapacá prohibited. The blockade was now extended by the Chilians to Arica. The Peruvians had only one man-of-war left, the Union, the remaining vessels being merely wooden transports badly armed and unable to leave Callao, while the Chilian fleet was reënforced by the thoroughly repaired Huáscar.

After the departure of General Prado, the popular dissatisfaction with the government ot La Puerta became very great. As time was lacking for a regular Presidential election, Nicolas de Piérola assumed the dictatorship after the armed resistance of the governmental troops at Lima had been overcome. Being received at Callao with a warm welcome, Piérola was permitted to take the helm of the state. The people of Lima resolved on the 23d of December to raise him to the "supreme magistrature of the nation, with full powers." Lima was declared under martial law; all citizens capable of bearing arms were enrolled in the line of National Guard regiments. The ports of Iquique and Pisagua were declared closed, and all Peruvian commercial relations suspended during the occupation of the province of Tarapacá by the Chilians. General Bundia was suspended from the command of the southern forces, Rear-Admiral Montero being his successor. The ports of Arica, Ilo, Mollendo, and Islay were blockaded by the Chilian squadron.

PLAGUE, THE. The government of Astrakhan, in Russia, was afflicted for several months in 1878 and 1879 by an epidemic which after investigation was decided to be the genuine Eastern plague. The attention of the countries of eastern Europe was directed to the danger of the disease spreading and becoming general, and renewed interest was awakened respecting a scourge once of the most fearful character, concerning which the Western nations had almost ceased to have any apprehensions. During the present century the plague has appeared to only a limited extent in Europe, and has hardly risen to be an epidemic in any civilized state. The references made to it in history, from the time ot Thucydides down, show that it has been in the past one of the most dangerous diseases that have ever afflicted the human race. The accounts which are given of the number of persons who have fallen victims to it in the different countries and cities it has ravaged from time to time seem hardly credible; and, inasmuch as they are not based on any exact enumeration, but only on estimate, they may be exaggerated. Nevertheless, it is an authenticated fact that extensive districts and flourishing towns have been more than once depopulated by it. Such was the case under the epidemic of the "Black Death" in the fourteenth century, when 25,000,000 persons are said to have perished in Europe. The disease has never since been so universally destructive, but it prevailed several times in succeeding centuries in more limited areas with nearly equal malignancy. During the eighteenth century 300,000 persons are said to have died of it in East Prussia, from 1703 to 1709; Marseilles was visited by it in 1720; 30,000 people of Messina died of it in forty days in 1743; and 52,000 died in Moscow in 1770. During the present century the plague has appeared in only a few places in western Europe: in Malta in 1813; in Bari, in Lower Italy, in 1815; in Majorca, where it became a considerable epidemic, in 1820. It has appeared several times in the Turkish Empire, but not since 1843 in its European dominions. It was an epidemic in Mesopotamia in 1857; it has prevailed in Persia at different times since 1863. An outbreak occurred at Bagdad in 1876, and another at Reshd in 1876-'77. Another variety of the disease, called the Indian plague, which is characterized by bleeding from the lungs, prevailed in different parts of India from 1815 to 1821, in 1836, 1846-'47, 1859-'60, and 1863. In Russia, during the present century and previous to the last visitation, the plague prevailed in the Caucasus in 1806-'7, appearing in Mordok, Astrakhan, and Zarov, and in Saratov in 1808; then drew back in 1810 to the region south of the Caucasus. It broke out at Odessa in 1812, and never wholly disappeared from the country till 1820. At some places attacked during these visitations, all the inhabitants are said to have died.

The removal of Europe from the liability to the attacks of this disease, which it once suffered in common with Eastern countries, is attributed to the general adoption of sanitary precautions and the improved condition of the life of the people. The plague has always originated in the East, generally in Turkish and Persian lands. It is now largely confined there. In these districts, and particularly in the plains of Mesopotamia, every condition is favorable to the generation of disease. The lands, neglected for ages, are exposed to the overflows of the rivers, and are swampy and miasmatic, so that intermittent fevers are always prevailing. The people live in damp, unventilated huts, are filthy and surrounded by filth, and know nothing of the simplest rules of health. Offal is allowed to remain and accumulate where it falls, and extreme carelessness exists in the burial of the dead, whose bodies are seldom perfectly covered. To these is added the Persian custom of bringing their dead to be buried in the ground which is sanctified by the neighborhood of the tombs of Ali and Hussein, in which considerable caravans are often engaged, generating, with the corpses, noxious emanations. Here a plague prevailed in 1876, and hence, it is supposed by some, its germs were carried by returning Russian soldiers to the province of Astrakhan, where the disease broke out in the fall of 1878. The story is that it was conveyed in a Turkish shawl which a Cossack took home and gave to his betrothed. It has been suggested that it may have been transmitted more directly from the Russian army, where an extraordinary mortality was acknowledged from typhus, under which name a worse disease might have been disguised. Against this it is urged that the impartial correspondents of neutral nations who were with the Russian armies say nothing of plague, although they would not have failed to mention it had there been a suspicion of its existence. A simpler theory is that it was communicated from Reshd, where it raged in 1877 and 1878, and whence there was a regular trade by vessels to Zaritzin on the Volga. At Astrakhan, the disease fell under similar conditions to those which favor its propagation in the East. The country is subject to inundations; the people are poor, badly housed, and filthy in their habits; and the principal business of the district, the curing of fish, is one which peculiarly favors the accumulation of offal and the generation of a poisonous atmosphere.

A few cases of disease similar to plague were noticed in Astrakhan in May, 1877, but according to the Russian accounts they soon disappeared. The first cases in numbers occurred at the *stanitza* or village of Wetlianka in the beginning of October, 1878. Wetlianka is situated in the circle of Jenotavsk, 149 versts (about 98 miles) from the city of Astrakhan, and 20 versts (13 miles) from the town of Nicolskov. It lies on the right bank of the Volga, in a tolerably high, level, and exposed situation, with a loamy soil supporting a scanty vegetation. The town is about a hundred years old, and had one thousand inhabitants, with three hundred houses, all of wood, small and not clean. The only occupation of the people was fishing, in connection with which was a considerable curing establishment. The place was considered unhealthly and subject to fevers, and had suffered much from the common epidemics, cholera, and syphilis. From November till the 25th of December, 1878, the weather was moist, cloudy, mild, with only occasional winds, which, blowing lightly from the southwest, brought with them a fine rain. A snow fell on the 12th of December, which soon melted away. According to the official reports, the cases at first appeared of a mild form. At the beginning of November they were represented as progressing favorably after a duration of from ten to twelve days, although purulent swellings were already observed in the armpits of the sick. Dr. Depner, of the Cossack corps, visited the place on the 18th of November, and after some days of observation declared the disease to be typhus. Hardly had he gone away when it changed its type, with a great increase of mortality, so that by the 27th of November the reports obscurely

mentioned that 43 per cent. of those attacked died and 14 per cent recovered, without accounting for the others. Dr. Depner visited the cases again on December 17th, and gave the opinion that the disease was a very malignant typhus, or a new form of disease partaking of the characters of typhus and the Indian plague. The marks of the disease were, according to his account, a palpitation of the heart coming suddenly upon a condition of general good health, irregular pulse, nausea, giddiness, pressure on the breast, spitting blood, thin vomitings, stagnation of the blood, paleness of the face, apathetic expression, and dull, sunken eyes, with enlarged pupils. After three or four hours the patient would suffer an extreme exhaustion, which was followed by dry heats, lethargy, some delirium, suppression of urine, and costiveness. To these were added in some cases after the 22d of December spots on the body from the size of a millet-seed up, and a peculiar honey-like odor known as the "plague-smell"; and death came on during a state of unconsciousness through the rapid decay of the vital forces. The corpses did not become stiff, but began to decay in two or three hours. By the 26th of December 100 per cent., or all who were attacked by the disease, died after a sickness of from twelve hours to three days. Among the victims were Dr. Koch, six surgeons, and a number of priests and Cossacks who took care of the sick. Notwithstanding this malignity of the epidemic, and although the symptoms agreed with those of the true plague, the Government took the utmost care to conceal its real nature, and, contradicting all reports to the contrary, declared that it was a typhoid fever. A second physician sent to visit the infected district, Dr. Krassoffski, declared that the disease was without doubt a true plague. By the 14th of January, 1879, the mortality had reached 368 persons, 85 per cent. of those who had been attacked, and 40 per cent. of the population of the villages of Wetlianka and Prischiba.

Measures were first taken by the Government in January to prevent the further spread of the epidemic. Saratov was put under quarantine, and a medical inspection of the conveniences for it was ordered, under the direction of the sanitary chief of the district. Pains were still taken to conceal the nature and extent of the infection, but the reports of its spread could not be wholly suppressed. Its outbreak was reported at Zaritzin, Nicolaskov, Kereselitzev (100 versts outside of the limits), Selitrena, Udatschnov, Michaelovskov, and toward the end of January in St. Petersburg itself. The identity of the reputed cases in St. Petersburg was stoutly denied, and is in doubt, but they produced genuine consternation. The efforts of the Government to conceal the real condition were not acquiesced in by the physicians. Dr. Botkin, physician to the imperial family, declared unequivocally, at a meeting held January 23d in the rooms of the Society of Practical Physicians, that there could be no question that Russia was again attacked by its old enemy the *tchuma*, or Eastern plague, which seemed to be so closely akin to the "Black Death" of the middle ages, and that the symptoms were just the same as they were of old. The Government had by this time declared that it was ready to allow an international commission to proceed to the seat of the epidemic, and would do everything to assist its labors. Toward the end of January the "Journal de St. Pétersbourg" stated that the timely and energetic measures adopted by the Government, and the promptitude with which information regarding the epidemic was communicated to the public, were proofs that the time was past for bureaucratic mystery concerning the truth in a matter affecting the public health; and the official telegrams announced that there were no persons ill with the epidemic in Wetlianka, and there was only a little of it in the other villages. Commissioners of the Austrian and German Governments visited the infected districts to investigate the disease, but failed to gain satisfactory information. They were treated with politeness, but were not assisted by the officers in the object of their errand.

General Loris-Melikoff was appointed at the beginning of February to go to Astrakhan and take charge of the necessary measures for stamping out the plague. He took with him a commission of experts and assistants, and had authority to use whatever means might be required. Committees were formed in the principal towns for promoting cleanliness among the poorer classes, and lectures on the plague were delivered at many of the medical schools. An imperial decree of February 17th authorized General Loris-Melikoff to try by court-martial all civilians violating the quarantine regulations in those parts of Astrakhan which were to be placed by him under martial law. It was decided to burn Wetlianka and the houses in other villages in which cases of the plague had occurred, with provision for recompensing the people for the losses which they might suffer. These measures were carried into effect, and at the end of February General Loris-Melikoff reported that there was not a case of epidemic illness in the district under his jurisdiction, the last case having been registered on the 9th of the month.

Stringent measures of quarantine were put in force by the Governments of neighboring states as soon as it seemed definitely established that an epidemic existed in Russia. The German and Austrian Governments ordered a detention of passengers and goods, and gave notice that if the epidemic spread to a threatening extent the frontiers should be closed altogether; the Italian Government ordered a quarantine against all vessels arriving from the Black Sea; similar measures were adopted at the ports of other nations visited by Russian vessels; and the Roumanian Government

made the prevalence of the plague a ground for raising fresh objections to the passage of Russian troops through its territory. These precautions were objected to by the Russian Government, which chose to regard them as restrictions inflicted upon its commerce for which the condition of the country did not afford a sufficient justification.

The form in which the plague manifests itself is subject to modifications according to the degree of violence which the disease assumes. In the most violent attacks, illness can hardly be spoken of, for they run their course in about two hours. The French physicians who observed the disease in Egypt called this form *peste foudroyante*. In the next most violent form, the patient after the earlier symptoms falls into a delirious state, with stammering speech. The pulse is hardly perceptible. The only other marked change is an effusion of blood in the skin. The tongue continues moist, but the skin is quite dry, and death ensues after twenty-four or at most forty-eight hours, so that there is no time for the buboes to form, or more than begin. In somewhat less malignant cases, in which recovery occasionally takes place, the buboes or boils are formed in the soft parts, in the armpits, and on the neck, and cause great pain. They are swellings from the size of a pigeon's egg to that of a goose-egg, hard, yielding at first, afterward fixed and painful to the touch when the skin has become red around them, and finally, if the patient has not succumbed to the disease, suppurate in the second or third week. Suppuration is considered a good symptom. In other cases the buboes dry up, and this denotes increased danger. Generally, however, the patients on whom the boils appear die on the fourth or fifth day, before suppuration can take place. The general symptoms are similar to those described as characterizing the disease at Wetlianka, of which extreme exhaustion, vomiting, spitting blood, and the honey-like "plague-smell" are among the marked features. If the person attacked lives through the earlier stages, he is afflicted with offensive sweats, and dies unconscious or in convulsions. In cases which result favorably, a warm sweat comes on, sleep follows, the buboes open, the appetite returns, etc.; but the process of recovery requires weeks and often months. Milder forms of the disease occur, in which the symptoms are mitigated and a favorable result is more frequent. The disease prevails at all seasons, but has been generally found to diminish greatly or disappear in very hot and very cold weather.

PORTUGAL, a kingdom in southwestern Europe. King Luiz I., born October 31, 1838; succeeded his brother, King Pedro V., November 11, 1861; married, October 6, 1862, to Pia, youngest daughter of King Victor Emanuel of Italy. Issue of the union are two sons: Carlos, born September 28, 1863, and Alfonso, born July 31, 1865.

The area is 35,843 square miles; the population, according to the census of January 1,1878, was 4,745,124. The area and population of the several provinces were as follows:

PROVINCES.	Area in square miles.	POPULATION IN 1878.		
		Males.	Females.	Total.
Minho................................	2,821	467,819	547,575	1,015,394
Tras os Montes........................	4,292	204,826	205,635	410,461
Beira.................................	9,258	669,206	721,541	1,390,747
Estremadura..........................	6,934	486,892	464,653	951,545
Alemtejo.............................	9,425	197,169	177,334	374,503
Algarve..............................	1,876	104,399	101,502	205,901
Total continental..............	34,606	2,130,811	2,218,240	4,849,551
Azores............................	922	120,420	143,982	264,352
Madeira...........................	815	68,592	68,329	182,221
Total kingdom................	35,843	2,314,623	2,480,501	4,745,124

The area of the Portuguese possessions in Asia and Africa is 704,132 square miles; the population 3,247,634.

The following were the gross sums of the budget estimates for the financial year 1879–'80, in contos and milreis (1 conto = 1,000 milreis; 1 milreis = $1.08; 5,603 : 876 means 5,603 contos and 876 milreis) :

REVENUE.

1. Direct taxes..................................	5,603 : 876
2. Register....................................	2,746 : 800
3. Indirect taxes..............................	14,290 : 689
4. National domain	2,425 : 556
5. Other receipts.............................	1,357 : 921
Total..................................	26,424 : 842

EXPENDITURES.

1. Interest on home and foreign debt...........	11,716 : 810
2. Ministry of Finance.......................	5,495 : 267
3. Ministry of Foreign Affairs...............	287 : 589
4. Ministry of the Interior...................	2,301 : 393
5. Ministry of Worship and Justice..........	601 : 755
6. Ministry of War...........................	4,336 : 137
7. Ministry of the Navy and Colonies........	1,627 : 364
8. Ministry of Public Works..................	3,538 : 483
9. Extraordinary expenditures................	3,739 : 341
Total..................................	33,544 : 079

The public debt on June 30, 1878, amounted to 374,122 contos.

The actual strength of the army on August 15, 1879, was 1,744 officers and 25,833 men, of whom 11,360 were out on furlough.

The navy in 1879 consisted of 28 steamers, of 4,441 horse-power and 118 guns, and 9 sailing vessels, of 31 guns.

The trade of Portugal in 1876 was as follows (in contos):

COUNTRIES.	Imports.	Exports.
Great Britain	17,541	11,885
France	5,460	2,172
Spain.........................	2,180	1,321
Sweden and Norway...........	924	152
Germany......................	682	919
Russia........................	500	188
Belgium.......................	545	171
Netherlands...................	298	191
United States.................	2,841	400
Brazil........................	1,984	3,736
Portuguese colonies...........	801	1,024
Other countries..............	888	690
Total.	34,558	22.674

The movement of shipping in 1876 was as follows :

FLAG.	ENTERED.		CLEARED.	
	Sailing vessels.	Steamers.	Sailing vessels.	Steamers.
Portuguese :				
Sea-going vessels....	668	98	815	88
Coast	4,961	606	4,783	626
Foreign	2,619	1,715	2,684	1,787
Total..............	8,243	2,419	8,282	2,446

The commercial navy in 1878 consisted of 588 vessels, of which 42 were steamers. The total length of railways in operation in September, 1879, was 1,151·5 kilometres. The length of telegraph lines in September, 1878, was 3,711 kilometres; of wires, 8,042 kilometres; the number of stations, 185; the number of dispatches in 1877, 686,518. The number of post-offices in September, 1879, was 686, of which 38 were on the islands. The number of inland letters in 1877–'78 was 12,342,183; of newspapers, 7,315,915; of printed matter, of postal cards and samples of goods, 1,415,-646; and of foreign letters, newspapers, etc., 3,372,456.

Parliament was opened on January 2d by the King in person, who said in his speech from the throne that a treaty had been made with England for a railway between Goa and British India, and also for a railway uniting the Transvaal to Lourenço Marques. The state of the finances required serious attention. On January 14th Senhor d'Andrade Corvo, Minister for Foreign Affairs, speaking in the Chamber of Peers in reference to a concession granted to a Portuguese subject for farming the forests, mines, and land for agricultural purposes in the Zambesi district in Mozambique, said that Portugal, which for a long time past had in Europe been in close alliance with England, should accept the coöperation of that power for mutually upholding and developing their colonial interests; a coöperation which would be based upon mutual respect for each other's territories, and upon the firm assurance of the loyalty and sincerity of the intentions of each Government toward the other. The Chamber of Deputies organized on January 21st, when the Government candidate was elected president by 82 votes, the opposition abstaining from voting. In the Chamber of Peers, an order of the day favorable to the Government was adopted by 36 to 21 votes. The Minister of Marine subsequently read a telegram from St. Vincent announcing an attack by natives on the Portuguese fort at Bolama on the Guinea coast, in which several persons were killed. He added that the Government intended to send reënforcements to the scene of the disturbance without delay. In the middle of March the Chamber adopted, by 91 votes to 32, an order of the day approving the conduct of the Government in preventing arms and ammunition from reaching the Zooloos by way of the Zambesi. Owing to differences in the Cabinet, the Ministere resigned in June, and a new Ministry was formed under the presidency of Senhor Braancamp. The last official act of the outgoing Ministry was the signature of a treaty of commerce, navigation, extradition, and suppression of the slave-trade, between Portugal and Great Britain, in respect to their dominions in South Africa. General elections for the Chamber of Deputies were held on October 19th, and resulted in favor of the Government.

PRADO, General MARIANO IGNACIO, was born at Huánuco, in northern Peru, in 1826. He took a leading part in the revolution of 1854, which overthrew the conservative government of General Echenique. In 1865 he again took the lead in the revolution against President Pezet, accused of cowardice in having made peace with Spain after the capture of the Chincha Islands. He entered Lima with an army of 12,000 men, and in November of the same year was proclaimed Dictator (Supreme Chief) of the nation. The war with Spain was renewed, and an alliance effected with Bolivia, Chili, and Ecuador. Prado repelled the Spanish squadron from Callao in May, 1866. Chosen constitutional President in the same year for the term of six years, he was overthrown in the following year by a revolution which resulted in the election of Balta to the Presidency in 1868. Prado was received in Chili with great honor, and appointed a general of division in the Chilian army, and afterward Peruvian Minister in Chili. A revulsion of popular sentiment led to Prado's elevation to the Presidency for a term of four years in 1876. At the outbreak of the present war with Chili he proceeded to Arica as "Supreme Director of the War." The reverses of October and November caused his great unpopularity, which induced him to leave the responsibility of the situation to the popular Nicolas Piérola, and to embark on the 18th of December for Panama and Europe.

PRESBYTERIANS. I. PRESBYTERIAN CHURCH IN THE UNITED STATES OF AMERICA.— The following is a summary of the statistics of this Church, giving the number of churches, pastors, and church-members in the several synods, according to the official reports in the Minutes of the General Assembly for 1879:

SYNODS.	Ministers.	Churches.	Communicants.
Albany.................	155	182	19,105
Atlantic.................	69	189	9,658
Baltimore...............	184	189	15,889
Central New York.......	172	162	21,081
China....................	45	89	2,806
Cincinnati..............	151	157	20,885
Cleveland..............	143	165	20,669
Colorado..............	52	60	2,161
Columbia..............	84	48	2,215
Columbus..............	118	177	17,805
Erie..................	187	249	32,097
Geneva...............	122	101	14,185
Harrisburg...........	155	176	22,058
Illinois, Central.......	189	180	10,112
Illinois, North........	166	148	17,566
Illinois, South........	102	157	9,625
India.................	41	22	709
Indiana, North........	82	146	11,998
Indiana, South........	111	162	16,616
Iowa, North...........	109	141	8,468
Iowa, South...........	125	187	11,906
Kansas...............	162	256	10,817
Kentucky.............	64	88	6,188
Long Island..........	98	68	15,928
Michigan.............	149	168	15,900
Minnesota............	108	126	6,650
Missouri.............	181	210	11,148
Nebraska.............	60	101	3,578
New Jersey...........	361	267	46,201
New York.............	320	166	36,688
Pacific...............	118	121	6,845
Philadelphia..........	366	294	51,709
Pittsburgh............	163	195	26,728
Tennessee............	40	57	3,841
Texas................	21	33	900
Toledo...............	82	110	10,098
Western New York.....	180	159	21,231
Wisconsin............	110	181	8,096
Total.................	4,938	5,415	574,486

A committee which was appointed in 1878 to investigate the state of the trust funds held by the various boards of the Church, reported to the General Assembly of 1879 that the amounts of the same were as follows:

1. Presbyterian Board of Publication.......... $63,000 00
2. Board of Trustees of the Presbyterian House. 84,058 00
3. Presbyterian Board of Relief.............. 41,000 00
4. Trustees of the General Assembly of the Presbyterian Church...................... 251,868 58
5. Presbyterian Board of Education.......... 41,950 0
6. Presbyterian Board of Foreign Missions..... 60,560 00
   Railroad bonds held as a special trust........ 12,000 00
7. Board of Home Missions................... 149,670 00
   Township railroad bonds held as a special trust, no income derived...................... 25,000 00
8. Presbyterian Board of Church Erection...... 212,083 69

Total.............................. $941,160 22

The following is a summary statement of the investments of the eight boards:

Bonds and mortgages.................. $357,506 58
Stocks, notes, iron, city, and railroad bonds..... 390,220 87
United States Government bonds 193,433 22

Total.............................. $941,160 22

The General Assembly of the Presbyterian Church in the United States of America met at Saratoga, New York, May 15th. The Rev. Henry H. Jessup, D. D., of Syria, was chosen Moderator. Efforts have been made for several successive years to readjust the basis of representation so as to reduce the number of members of the Assembly, but no measure had been so far devised which could be made satisfactory to the presbyteries, and the overture submitted by the Assembly at its last meeting had been rejected. The effort was renewed at the present Assembly, and a special committee of one minister and one elder from each Synod was appointed to take charge of the subject. This committee reported a proposition to change the ratio of representation from one commissioner of each order for every 24 to one for every 48 members of the Presbytery. The effect of this measure would have been to reduce the representation of the larger presbyteries one half, while it would leave that of the smaller presbyteries unchanged. This proposition was rejected by a vote of 203 to 241.

The following rules were adopted in reference to the formation of synods and presbyteries in foreign missionary fields: 1. That in regions occupied by the Presbyterian Board of Foreign Missions only, presbyteries, and eventually synods, may be organized at discretion, if not already organized, under whose care the native churches in the missions shall be placed; that each presbytery shall consist of all the ministers, foreign and native, not less than five in number, and a ruling elder from each church; and that the synods shall regularly send certified copies of their minutes and reports to the General Assembly. 2. That in regions occupied both by the Board and by the missions of other Presbyterian denominations, missionary churches, presbyteries, and synods should be encouraged to enter into organic relations with each other for joint work in the common field; but for purposes of representation, the foreign and native ministers connected with the Board, if sufficient in number, shall, with an elder from each of the churches, be regarded as a distinct Presbytery, entitled to appoint commissioners to the General Assembly. Provision having been made for the appointment of delegates to attend the meeting of the Presbyterian Alliance to be held in Philadelphia, the Assembly decided that that proceeding would furnish sufficient opportunities for intercourse with other Presbyterian bodies, and that it would not appoint special delegates to visit their courts. Delegates were, however, appointed to the non-Presbyterian bodies with which the Assembly holds correspondence. The Assembly having been invited to rescind or reaffirm the deliverance of the Assembly of 1835, declaring that the Roman Catholic Church "has essentially apostatized from the religion of our Lord and Saviour Jesus Christ, and therefore can not be recognized as a Christian church," and also to reverse the action of the Assembly of 1875 touching the validity of Roman Catholic baptism, the following minute was adopted on the subject:

Renewing with emphasis and in the terms of the Westminster Symbols their protest against the errors of the Roman Catholic Church, the Assembly are, notwithstanding, unwilling to reaffirm the deliverance of the Assembly of 1835, which declares that that body can not be recognized as a branch of the Church of Christ; and they distinctly disavow their belief in the inferences respecting the invalidity of Roman Catholic baptisms which follow from that deliverance, and in support of which the said deliverance has been cited.

Furthermore, while it is true, as our standards teach, that baptism is to be administered but once, yet this is not to be so construed as to foster a superstitious sacramentarianism, nor so as to sacrifice the conscientious convictions of either the applicant for baptism or the pastors and sessions to whom application is made. Respecting the rebaptism of converts from the Roman Catholic Church this Assembly, therefore, reaffirm the deliverance of the Assembly of 1875.

Resolutions were passed discountenancing the attendance of church members at theatres and operas, and the reading of secular newspapers on Sunday.

II. PRESBYTERIAN CHURCH IN THE UNITED STATES.—The following is a summary of the statistics of this Church for 1879, compared with those for 1877 and 1878:

DETAILS.	1877.	1878.	1879.
Synods..................	12	12	12
Presbyteries.............	68	65	66
Ministers and licentiates..	1,115	1,117	1,123
Candidates.	176	145	165
Churches................	1,880	1,873	1,592
Licensures..............	52	41	88
Ordinations.............	41	55	34
Installations............	54	71	67
Pastoral relations dissolv'd	51	49	47
Churches organized.......	48	47	88
Churches dissolved.......	12	24	10
Churches received from other denominations....	5	2	0
Churches dismissed to other denominations.......	8	8	0
Ministers received from other denominations....	1	7	3
Ministers dismissed to other denominations......	1	5	6
Number of ruling elders...	5,122	5,428	5,901
Number of deacons.......	8,388	8,452	8,770
Members added, examination.	6,802	6,875	6,351
Members added, certificate	8,066	8,471	8,209
Whole number of communicants...	112,750	114,578	116,735
Adults baptized..........	1,947	2,185	2,001
Infants baptized.........	4,565	4,561	4,829
Number of baptized non-communicants.........	22,582	24,968	25,470
Children in Sunday-schools and Bible-classes.......	66,624	68,121	70,224
CONTRIBUTIONS.			
Sustentation.............	$39,195	$27,327	$26,864
Evangelistic fund........	12,786	12,689	14,859
Invalid fund.............	9,470	9,042	8,876
Foreign missions.........	89,453	84,939	86,061
Education................	80,088	84,078	29,611
Publication..............	10,495	14,226	7,730
Presbyterial.............	11,528	12,146	12,306
Pastors' salaries.........	512,580	582,502	505,957
Congregational...........	392,093	803,814	320,178
Miscellaneous............	58,208	50,258	58,161
Total................	$1,110,971	$1,080,971	$1,015,851

The *General Assembly* of the Presbyterian Church in the United States met at Louisville, Kentucky, May 15th. The Rev. Joseph R. Wilson, D. D., of Wilmington, North Carolina, was chosen Moderator. The return of the votes of the presbyteries upon a revised "Book of Church Order" which had been submitted to them for their approval, showed that the book had been accepted by a large majority of them, and it was therefore declared to have been adopted. The question of the nature of the proceedings to be taken in the case of members who indulge in worldly amusements not countenanced by the Church was raised by some general inquiries made by the Presbytery of Atlanta, where a member had been excluded for dancing. The Assembly decided that its deliverances on this subject were not necessarily to be enforced by judicial process, but according to the discretion of the different church courts of original jurisdiction, acting under the checks and restraints of the Church. "The perplexity about the nature of the deliverances in question," the Assembly said, "has arisen from confounding two senses in which the word discipline is used in our constitution. One is that of 'judicial process,' the other is that of inspection, inquest, remonstrance, rebuke, and private admonition. . . . The distinction here asserted is recognized in the Word of God, and in our constitution, for substance at least, in the directions given for the conduct of church members in the case of personal and private injuries. If scandal can be removed or prevented in such cases more effectually oftentimes by faithful dealing in private with offenders than by judicial process, it does not appear why similar good results may not follow from the like dealing in the matter of worldly amusements." A report on Sabbath observance was adopted, which recommended among other things the appointment of presbyterial committees to secure the proper agitation of the Sabbath question in their several presbyteries, and to coöperate with the committee of the Assembly. A proposition was made to merge the Colored Evangelistic Fund in the Evangelistic Fund, but it was defeated. It was shown in the course of the debate on this subject that more was done by the Church in behalf of the colored people than appeared in the reports, inasmuch as considerable evangelistie labors conducted under the authority of the presbyteries were not brought to the attention of the Assembly's committee. The presbyteries were requested hereafter to send up annually to the Committee of Home Missions accounts of the work done within their bounds in addition to the work of the Committee for the Colored People, and of the amounts contributed therefor. A full list of delegates (twenty-eight in number) was appointed to attend the meeting of the Presbyterian Alliance to be held in Philadelpia in 1880.

III. UNITED PRESBYTERIAN CHURCH OF NORTH AMERICA.—The following is a summary of the statistics of this Church as they were reported to the General Assembly in May, 1879: Number of synods, 9; of presbyteries, 58; of ministers, 683; of licentiates, 56; of students of theology, 64; of congregations, 798; of mission stations, 65; of members, 80,692; of baptisms during the year, 4,176; of Sunday-schools, 726, with 7,647 officers and teachers and 65,-467 scholars. Amount of contributions: for salaries of ministers, $435,961; for congrega-

tional expenses, $207,678; to the boards, $106,-765; general contributions, $37,126; total contributions, $787,580, being an average of $10.85 per member. The contributions by Sunday-schools were $25,037. The average salary of the pastors was $893. Out of 176 missionary societies, 160 reported 5,650 members, and contributions of $13,363.

The twenty-first *General Assembly* of .the United Presbyterian Church of North America met at New Wilmington, Pennsylvania, May 28th. The Rev. William Bruce, D. D., of Xenia, Ohio, was chosen Moderater. In answer to a question if the imposition of hands by ruling elders in the ordination of ministers is required or permitted in the "Book of Government," the Assembly decided by a small majority that "ordination is an act of government, and is valid in the case of ministers only as authorized by the Presbytery in its constituted capacity. When so authorized, its administration by the imposition of hands is technically the act of Presbytery if performed only by the presiding officer in the name of and as the exponent of the Presbytery. In view of the direct recognition of the power of ordination in teaching elders, and no such direct acknowledgment of it being given to ruling elders, the imposition of the hands of the elders is not required, and therefore is technically to be regarded as not permitted." To the question, "Is the mingling of the sexes in the dance in a private house, where only the moral and respectable are permitted to participate, a violation of the law of the U. P. Church, when the parties engaged in the dance are members of her communion?" answer was returned that promiscuous dancing is one of the vain and ensnaring recreations of the men of the world, and for members of the Church to engage in such amusement, even with one another, is to have fellowship with the world in its sinful recreations, of which the Assembly distinctly and unequivocally disapproves. An important question arose upon the action of the Presbytery of Sealkote, India, which had admitted te church membership persons having more than one wife, who did not see their way clear to disown wives with whom they had lived for several years, and expose them and their children to poverty and contempt. No official report had been made from the Presbytery on the subject. The Presbytery was directed to report to the next General Assembly its official action in the matter, and the ground on which it was based. The Assembly recommended, in reference to the instruction of elders before they are ordained, that pastors must instruct their own elders; hence, first, that the professors in theological seminaries be directed to give their students full instruction on the duties and office of the eldership; second, that pastors instruct their elders in some systematic way, in order to obtain the highest efficiency of session; third, that the faculties of the seminaries be asked to prepare a manual for the instruction of elders as to their duties. Presbyteries were directed to adopt some plan by which contributions to all the boards may be secured at least once a quarter; and the Assembly expressed its judgment that "there should be a careful avoidance of all indirect and questionable means of raising money for the Lord's cause." The report of the Committee on Statistics recommended a careful oversight of all members personally by the sessions, and the erasure of the names, after they have been admonished, of all who continue out of the communion for one year without giving a satisfactory reason for their neglect, and of all who leave their congregation without applying for the usual testimonials and remain away for two years without reporting themselves.

IV. CUMBERLAND PRESBYTERIAN CHURCH.—The following is a summary of the statistics of this Church for the year ending April 30, 1879: Number of presbyteries, 112; of ministers, 1,335; of licentiates, 256; of candidates, 180; of congregations, 2,351; of elders, 8,060; of deacons, 2,335; of baptisms during the year, 4,431; of communicants, 104,994; of officers and teachers in Sunday-schools, 5,988; of scholars in the same, 51,690.

The *General Assembly* of the Cumberland Presbyterian Church met at Memphis, Tennessee, May 15th. The Rev. J. S. Grider of Kentucky was chosen Moderator. The report of the Board of Missions showed that its receipts for the year had been $20,674, and its disbursements $20,211. In accordance with the instructions of the previous General Assembly, a new charter, of a more liberal character than the former one, had been procured. A more systematic and energetic effort than ever before had been made to raise money through the pastors, and had been attended with a large degree of success. The only foreign mission of the Church was at Ozaka, Japan, to which two additional missionaries had been sent, and in connection with which attention was called to the value of women as helpers. The educational reports showed that the literary and theological institutions were in successful operation, but needed larger endowments and better apparatus and libraries. The most important institutions are Waynesburg College, Pennsylvania; Lincoln University, Illinois; Trinity University, Texas; and Cumberland University, Tennessee. The last has a full theological faculty, and theological departments are established or being established in connection with the others.

V. PRESBYTERIAN CHURCH IN CANADA.—The following is a summary of the statistics of this Church, as they were reported in June, 1879: Number of synods, 4; number of presbyteries, 35; total number of ministers, 750; of pastoral charges, 857; of congregations (exclusive of Manitoba), 1,027; of families, 73,116; of communicants, 107,715; of Sunday-school teachers, 8,208; of scholars in Sunday-schools and Bible-classes, 78,628.

VI. PRESBYTERIAN CHURCH OF ENGLAND.—The statistical reports of this Church, presented to the Synod at its annual meeting in May, showed that there were 270 congregations connected with the Synod, having in their chapels and mission-halls 131,496 available sittings, of which 61,272 were let. The number of communicants returned was 53,031, showing an increase of 2,192; number of Sunday-school teachers, 5,768, with 53,855 scholars; number of students, 20; of district visitors, 1,746; of Dorcas societies, 2,329; of young men's societies, 3,425; of members of Bible-classes, 6,643. The entire income of the Church had been £182,719, against £228,727 in 1877.

The *Synod* met in London April 28th, and consisted of 540 members. The Rev. Dr. William Graham of Liverpool was chosen Moderator. The Assembly of the Welsh Calvinistic Methodists having appointed a committee to correspond with this Church, with the object of bringing about practical coöperation between the two denominations, the Synod instructed its Intercourse Committee to take steps toward this end. It was pointed out that it was expedient to form English congregations in Wales, because the English language was forcing itself upon the people of the Principality. A proposition declaring eligible to ministerial charges in the Church "the ministers holding pastoral charges and probationers of all Presbyterian churches, whose center of operations is within the British Empire, and whose doctrinal standard is the Westminster Confession of Faith," was discussed and passed.

VII. ESTABLISHED CHURCH OF SCOTLAND.—A Parliamentary return, giving the number of communicants in the Church of Scotland, was published in May, 1879. It shows that out of a total population of 3,360,018 in the kingdom, 515,786 are communicants in the Kirk, of whom 218,411 are males and 297,375 are females. The returns show an increase of 55,000 communicants since the abolition of patronage.

The *General Assembly* of the Established Church of Scotland met in Edinburgh May 22d, and was opened in the usual manner by the Lord High Commissioner as the representative of the Queen. The Rev. Dr. James Chrystal of Auchinleck was chosen Moderator. The Committee on Union with other Churches reported concerning its correspondence with other bodies with whom negotiations had been entered into, which showed that these bodies were averse to considering the question of union on the basis of the Establishment. The United Presbyterian Church had expressly given in its connection with the state as a reason for declining to consider the question of union. The Reformed Presbyterian Church, it was said, had raised in its answer "an insuperable barrier" in requiring "the recognition of the descending obligation of the National Covenant of Scotland and of the Solemn League and Covenant of the three kingdoms." The United Secession Synod maintained "it to be the duty and privilege of nations, like individuals, to recognize and support the Church of Christ," but that the covenants were of perpetual obligation. The Free Church had expressed the conviction that, "in present circumstances, a reunion of the churches in connection with state endowments can not be accomplished in a satisfactory manner." The committee was discharged. The discontinuance of the official religious inspection of schools was directed.

VIII. FREE CHURCH OF SCOTLAND.—The reports on the proceeds of the collections appointed by the General Assembly of the Free Church of Scotland to be made in the different churches under its charge showed a diminution in the amount of more than £3,365 as compared with the amount raised in the previous years. The whole income of the Church had fallen off £24,901. The Committee on Missions to the Jews made a favorable report of its operations at Pesth, Hungary, its principal station. Seven persons had been baptized. The report on Sunday-schools showed that they employed 17,492 teachers and were attended by 189,759 pupils.

The *General Assembly* of the Free Church of Scotland met in Edinburgh May 22d. The Rev. J. C. Burns of Kirkliston was chosen Moderator. The most important business transacted related to the case of Professor W. Robertson Smith, who was charged with having uttered heretical teachings in the article on the Bible which he had prepared for the ninth edition of the "Encyclopædia Britannica." The case had already engaged the attention of the Assembly for two years, and had been sent back by the Assembly of 1878 to the Presbytery of Aberdeen, with which it originated, for a retrial on an amended libel. (The points in the case as thus sent down are given in the article PRESBYTERIANS in the "Annual Cyclopædia" for 1878.) The action of the Presbytery on this order now came before the General Assembly for revision and further disposition. All the other points having been disposed of, the substance of the charge against Professor Smith lay in the specification that he had published the opinion that "the book of inspired Scripture called Deuteronomy, which is professedly an historical record, does not possess that character, but was made to assume it by a writer of a much later age, who therein, in the name of God, presented in dramatic form instructions and laws as proceeding from the mouth of Moses, though these never were and never could have been uttered by him"; an opinion which, the libel declared, "contradicts or is opposed to the doctrine of the immediate inspiration, infallible truth, and divine authority of the Holy Scriptures, as set forth in the Scriptures themselves, and in the Confession of Faith." The action of the previous Assembly with reference to Professor Smith was reaffirmed. Two motions were made for the disposition of the charges. One by Professor Andrew Bonar was to the effect that the Presbytery of Aber-

deen should be directed to try Professor Smith on the single point to which the libel was reduced, and, on finding it proved, to suspend him from his professional, ministerial, and judicial functions until the next Assembly. The other motion, by Principal Rainy, was that, in consideration of the novelty and perplexity of the case, the Assembly, before proceeding further with the libel, should appoint a committee representative of both parties, to consider the case in all its bearings, and. confer with Professor Smith with the view of ascertaining the best means of arriving at a result securing the truth of God without disturbing the unity of the Church. The motion of Professor Bonar prevailed, by a vote of 321 to 320 for the motion of Principal Rainy. After the vote was announced, Principal Rainy read a protest against the action contemplated by the successful motion being taken on the strength of so small a majority. The resolution of the previous Assembly in favor of the separation of Church and state was reaffirmed, and the committee was reappointed, to take such action as it might see fit. A resolution was adopted expressing decided opposition to the proposed bill for legalizing marriage with a deceased wife's sister. In answer to a number of overtures from presbyteries against lotteries at bazaars, a resolution was passed exhorting the ministers and people "to discountenance the raising of money for ecclesiastical or other religious objects by what is known as raffles."

The Presbytery of Aberdeen met July 1st, to deal with the case of Professor Smith according to the instructions of the General Assembly. Professor Smith was allowed to make a plea to the relevancy of the libel as amended, after which he filed his answer to it. In this answer he stated that he upheld the canonicity and inspiration of the Book of Deuteronomy, and that he did not regard it as a fraud, as had been imputed to him. In denying that Moses was the author of it, he stood within the liberty granted to every office-bearer of the Church, for the book nowhere said that Moses was its author. What he had done was not in the interests of rationalism, but in those of the faith; for he had designed to take the facts which the rationalists had built upon, and reconcile them with a full recognition of the supernatural in the old dispensation and the inspiration of the Old Testament records. The amended libel was served. The Presbytery met again to consider the case in September, when it resolved simply to report the case again to the General Assembly. An appeal was taken to the Synod of Aberdeen against this action, and the Synod, after giving a hearing to both sides, resolved to sustain the Presbytery.

IX. UNITED PRESBYTERIAN CHURCH OF SCOTLAND.—The following is a summary of the statistics of this Church as presented to the Synod by the Home Committee in May, 1879:·

Number of congregations, 544; of ministers, 583; of elders, 4,612; of preachers, 63; of students of divinity, 74; of members,175,066; amount of income for congregational purposes, £239,754; congregational income for missions and benevolence, £86,390; income from voluntary contributions and other sources of revenue, £41,242; total income, £367,388.

The *Synod* of the United Presbyterian Church met in Edinburgh May 5th. The Rev. George Jeffrey, D. D., was chosen Moderator. The report on the statistics of the Church showed that the number of congregations was ten more than in 1878, and that there had been an increase of about 1,500 members during the year. The income of the Church was £11,690 less than in 1877. The Synod proceeded to the discussion of the "Declaratory Statement on the Subordinate Standards" which had been provisionally adopted by the preceding Synod (for the text of which see the "Annual Cyclopedia" for 1878, article PRESBYTERIANS). The statement was adopted finally, after which the Rev. David Macrae of Gourock moved an additional declaration that "in regard to the ultimate penalty of sin the Church does not hold herself bound to the interpretation of the Westminster Confession as to what the Scriptures say on this subject." An earnest debate followed upon the motion, in the course of which the attention of the Synod was brought to the fact that Mr. Macrae, in a speech before the Presbytery to which he was attached, had said that the Church had had recourse to "Jesuitical devices" in the preparation of the declaratory act. The epithet employed by Mr. Macrae was regarded as offensive, and he was requested to withdraw it. He refused to do so, whereupon the Synod passed a resolution of censure upon him for applying the word "Jesuitical" to the proceedings of the court, and the censure was administered to him by the Moderator. Mr. Macrae's motion failed to receive attention. A committee was appointed to confer with Mr. Macrae upon the views expressed by him in his motion and his speech. The committee reported, after having held conferences with Mr. Macrae, that they had unanimously found that his views were irreconcilable with the teaching of Scripture as exhibited in the standards of the Church, and with any reasonable amount of liberty that could be allowed to ministers in relation to the standards, and recommended that he be suspended from the exercise of his ministry, and that a commission be appointed to deal with him and report at the next meeting of the Synod. Among the questions and answers which were quoted in the report as indicating his position were: 1. "Do the lost in hell exist for ever?" "No, if in the state described in the Westminster Confession." 2. "Will they exist for ever in any state?" "We do not know. The Bible speaks explicitly of everlasting life for the good, nowhere of everlasting existence for the bad." Mr. Macrae made an explanatory statement of his belief.

It was decided to leave the question of suspension to the commission, which was appointed to consist of twenty ministers and ten elders, to have presbyterial powers to proceed in the case as they should see cause, the right of appeal to be reserved for both the accused and the members of the commission to an *in hunc effectum* Synod, or, failing this, to a regular meeting of the Synod. The returns of the views of the presbyteries and sessions on the question of marriage with a deceased wife's sister showed that a majority of those bodies were in favor of a relaxation of the law of the Church which excluded from membership persons who contracted such marriages. A committee was appointed to consider the subject and report upon it to the next meeting of the Synod.

The committee appointed by the Synod to deal with the Rev. David Macrae in reference to his views on future punishment held a conference with him after the adjournment of the Synod. The committee found that "the conduct of Mr. Macrae in the premises warrants and requires his separation from his ministerial charge and suspension *sine die* from all ministerial functions." This decision was communicated to the parish church of Gourock on the following Sunday, upon which a protest on the part of the session against the procedure of the committee was read from the pulpit. Mr. Macrae had demanded to be tried by libel, so that the points in which he differed in doctrine from the Church might be specified; but the committee decided that, inasmuch as there was no doubt respecting his views, this was unnecessary. Mr. Macrae then took an appeal to the Synod on three points: 1. The decision not to try him for libel; 2. The suspension from the ministry; 3. The final action of the committee. A special session of the Synod to review the case was called, to meet July 22d. At this meeting the appeal from the preliminary act of the committee in suspending Mr. Macrae was first called up. This was dismissed, and the committee was sustained by a large majority. On the appeal against the refusal of the committee to proceed by libel, a motion to grant a libel was rejected, and a motion to reject the appeal was carried by 277 votes against 47 for a motion that the appeal be sustained. On the third point of appeal, against the final action of the committee that Mr. Macrae's conduct warranted his suspension *sine die* from all ministerial functions, a motion that, "Inasmuch as certain questions addressed by the committee to Mr. Macrae were not based either on Scripture or the Confession, and inasmuch as the divergence between Mr. Macrae and the Church on doctrinal points does not require suspension *sine die*, but may be dealt with by censure or prohibition, the final decision of the committee be not sustained," was rejected; and a motion to "dismiss the protest and appeal and affirm the finding of the committee, and, on the ground of its finding, declare Mr. Macrae no longer a minister of this Church," was carried by a vote of 288 to 29. The decision was formally communicated to Mr. Macrae, after which he was permitted to make a short address to the Synod. Mr. Macrae's congregation afterward seceded from the United Presbyterian Church.

X. IRISH PRESBYTERIAN CHURCH.—The following is a summary of the statistics of the Irish Presbyterian Church, as they were published in connection with the report of the proceedings of the General Assembly of 1879: Number of sittings provided, 228,239; total number of families, 79,632; of communicants, 106,776; of communicants added, 6,282, against 4,728 communicants left; of baptisms, 9,068; of elders, 2,145; of deacons, 6,746; of contributors to the Sustentation Fund, 39,392; of stipend-payers, 68,238. The number of national schools reported as under Presbyterian management was 712, and of Sunday-schools 1,053, with 8,579 teachers and an average attendance of 72,288 scholars.

The *General Assembly* of the Irish Presbyterian Church met in Belfast June 2d. The Rev. Professor Watts, D. D., of Belfast, was chosen Moderator. Statistical reports were presented, showing that the entire income of the Church for the year had been £154,377, or £575 less than the income for the previous year; that the entire indebtedness of the Church was £72,000; that about 228,000 sittings were provided in the churches; and that the number of families connected with the Church had increased 478. Exciting discussions took place on the subject of church music. Petitions were presented, asking that, as hymns and paraphrases of the Psalms were now in use in many of the congregations, the Assembly appoint a committee to prepare a selection of such hymns and paraphrases. These petitions were rejected by a vote of 157 to 225; the ministers giving a majority of one in favor of them, and the elders a majority of 69 against them. The committee appointed by the previous Assembly on the course to be pursued toward congregations which persist in using musical instruments in the service, presented a report advising that, while the authorized mode of celebrating praise in the Church was purely vocal, yet no discipline should be exercised on ministers or congregations using instruments. An amendment was offered to the effect that, as the Assembly had pronounced against instrumental music in 1873, that decision should be reaffirmed, and the presbyteries should be instructed to bring the law before transgressing congregations, and report to the next Assembly; which was adopted by a vote of 313 to 278.

PROTESTANT EPISCOPAL CHURCH. The following is a summary of the statistics of the Protestant Episcopal Church in the United States, divided into 48 dioceses and 14 missionary jurisdictions, as they are given in Whittaker's "Protestant Episcopal Almanac and Directory" for 1880:

DIOCESES AND MISSIONS.	Clergy.	Parishes.	Communicants.	Sunday-school scholars.
Alabama	31	40	3,668	1,788
Albany	117	110	11,877	9,897
Arkansas	11	17	872	846
California	59	31	2,860	3,256
Central New York	96	105	12,088	8,469
Central Pennsylvania	87	89	7,018	11,689
Connecticut	191	147	20,211	14,646
Delaware	26	31	1,919	3,012
Easton	35	34	2,426	1,719
Florida	16	19	1,354	1,854
Fond du Lac	28	37	2,168	1,900
Georgia	38	37	4,171	2,702
Illinois	57	68	5,100	5,695
Indiana	32	39	3,651	3,483
Iowa	42	51	3,829	3,304
Kansas	22	23	1,949	989
Kentucky	36	35	4,142	3,781
Long Island	94	64	14,942	15,000
Louisiana	33	45	2,983	2,383
Maine	23	31	2,086	1,588
Maryland	159	184	19,596	14,251
Massachusetts	182	100	16,522	14,484
Michigan	60	64	6,502	6,045
Minnesota	68	58	4,584	4,275
Mississippi	27	52	1,542	596
Missouri	48	46	5,167	3,681
Nebraska	29	26	1,850	1,858
New Hampshire	29	25	1,881	1,819
New Jersey	88	70	7,140	7,801
New York	299	195	35,000	29,607
North Carolina	66	82	5,294	3,254
Northern New Jersey	76	66	7,786	7,788
Ohio	64	70	6,573	7,542
Pennsylvania	201	124	28,387	32,196
Pittsburgh	46	57	5,507	5,570
Quincy	24	29	1,500	1,006
Rhode Island	45	41	6,396	6,874
South Carolina	44	55	4,455	1,941
Southern Ohio	46	46	4,616	4,947
Springfield	20	21	1,523	1,507
Tennessee	35	44	3,126	2,371
Texas	26	29	2,118	1,508
Vermont	31	49	2,825	1,661
Virginia	128	160	13,800	11,952
Western Michigan	32	29	3,081	2,312
Western New York	102	97	12,404	8,648
West Virginia	16	26	1,643	1,417
Wisconsin	62	89	4,206	2,688
MISSIONARY JURISDICTIONS.				
Oregon and Washington	28	24	888	1,199
Dakota	8	28	450	312
Colorado and Wyoming	32	20	1,091	1,155
Montana, Idaho, and Utah	14	17	722	1,058
Nevada	7	9	323	1,125
Niobrara	16	13	534	....
Northern Texas	18	10	988	598
Western Texas	8	22	684	558
Northern California	16	15	541	924
New Mexico and Arizona	1	2	..	...
African missions	11	21	811	819
China missions	9	8	272	980
Japan missions	7	4	54	164
Europe	6	6	..	...
Total	8,258	2,991	324,995	282,988

Number of baptisms during the year, 45,476; of confirmations, 26,903; of candidates for orders, 369; of Sunday-school teachers, 34,000; amount of contributions, $6,582,979. The churches in Europe included in the table are: the Church of the Holy Trinity, Paris, France; St. Paul's Church, Rome, Italy; American Episcopal Church, Florence, Italy; St. John's Church, Dresden, Germany; Emmanuel Church, Geneva, Switzerland; the Church of the Holy Spirit, Nice, France. The "Church Almanac" gives the number of communicants reported in 48 dioceses and 10 missionary districts as 322,713.

The Rev. Samuel Smith Harris, D. D., of Chicago, was elected by the Diocesan Convention of Michigan, June 4th, to be Bishop of Michigan, in the place of Bishop McCoskry, deposed in 1878. He was consecrated in St. Paul's Church, Detroit, September 17th. The Right Rev. William Henry Odenheimer, Bishop of Northern New Jersey, died August 14th. A special meeting of the Diocesan Convention to elect a new Bishop was held in Newark, October 29th. Seven ballots were taken, when, on the second day of the session, the Rev. Thomas A. Starkey, D. D., rector of St. Paul's Church, Paterson, received a majority of the votes of both orders and was elected. The Rev. Henry Chauncey Riley, D. D., Bishop elect of the Mexican branch of the Church, was consecrated to that office in Trinity Church, Pittsburgh, June 24th. The Rev. John N. Galleher, D. D., has been elected Bishop of Louisiana, to succeed Bishop J. P. B. Wilmer, who died December 2, 1878.

The thirteenth annual meeting of the *Evangelical Education Society* was held in Baltimore, Maryland, November 6th. The Treasurer reported that he had had funds in his hands for distribution during the year to the amount of $18,848, and had expended $14,846. The permanent fund amounted to $59,000.

The annual meeting of the *Board of Managers of the Domestic and Foreign Missionary Society* was held in the city of New York in October. The Domestic Committee, having charge of the domestic, colored people's, and Indian departments, reported that its total receipts had been $141,683, of which $97,635 had been for domestic missions proper, $13,215 designated by the givers for missions among the colored people of the South, and $30,832 similarly designated for missions among the Indians. Besides these, $13,162 had been given in special contributions not under the control of the committee. Three hundred and thirty missionaries had been wholly or partially supported by the committee. The receipts of the American Church Missionary Society (which has become an auxiliary to the Board of Missions) for the year ending September 1, 1879, were $20,529. The Society had commissioned 39 missionaries, and had 34 missionaries in the field at the time its report was made. The enterprises of this Society are mostly of the character of domestic missions. The total receipts of the Foreign Committee had been $148,692, of which, however, only $112,555 were within the control of the Board and Committee. The foreign missions are in Greece, western Africa, China, Japan, Hayti, and Mexico, and return in all 4,499 members and 2,561 day and boarding scholars. An estate known as the "Jessfield Farm," near Shanghai, China, had been bought by Bishop Schereschewsky, as the site for the College of St. John and other educational institutions and missionary residences, and the corner-stone of the college had been laid on Easter Monday of the current year.

The Woman's Auxiliary Society had contributed during the year $35,363 in cash and $65,888 in boxes to supply the wants of the various missions.

A general Missionary Conference was held during the meeting of the Board of Managers, October 14th–17th, when the following topics were discussed: "Association in Mission Work, one of the Securities of the Church's Peace and Order"; "What are the Elements which constitute any Branch of the Church a Power?" "What is wanting to the Successful Evangelization of the Colored People of this Country?" "The Christian Solution of the Indian Problem"; "The Indebtedness of the World to Foreign Missionary Enterprise"; "Diversities of Operation in carrying on the Work of the Church consistent with Christian Unity"; "The Claims of the Mining, Manufacturing, and Agricultural Classes"; "The Policy of Concentration or Diffusion in Missionary Work"; "The Peculiar Aptitude of the Protestant Episcopal Church to meet the American Mind and the Demands of the Age"; and "Medical Missions in China."

The sixth annual *Church Congress* met in Albany on October 21st. The inaugural address was delivered by the Bishop of Albany, who presided. The first topic for discussion, "The Relation of Social Science to Christian Ethics," was considered in papers by Charles J. Stille, LL. D., Provost of the University of Pennsylvania; the Rev. Wilbur F. Watkins, D. D., of Christ Church, Baltimore; the Rev. John Steinfort Kidney, D. D., of the Divinity School, Faribault, Minn.; the Rev. O. Maurice Wines, of St. Paul's, Yonkers, N. Y.; and the Rev. J. F. Garrison, M. D., of St. Paul's, Camden, N. J. The other topics discussed, and the authors of papers and addresses upon them, were as follows: "Positive Christian Education"—papers by the Rt. Rev. F. D. Huntington, D. D., Bishop of Central New York, and the Rev. E. T. Bartlett of Matteawan, N. Y.; "Communism in its Relations to Republican Institutions"—papers by the Rev. J. H. Rylance, D. D., of St. Mark's Church, New York, the Rev. R. Heber Newton of New York, and Joseph Packard, Jr., of Baltimore, Md.; "The Authority of Dogma"—papers by the Rt. Rev. W. E. McLaren, D. D., Bishop of Illinois, the Rt. Rev. Thomas M. Clark, D. D., Bishop of Rhode Island, the Rt. Rev. G. T. Bedell, Bishop of Ohio, and the Rev. John Cotton Smith, D. D., Church of the Ascension, New York; "Non-Attendance at Church: its Causes and Remedies"—papers by George B. Keese of Cooperstown, N. Y., Francis Wells of Philadelphia, and J. Astley Atkins of New York; "Memorial Art"—papers by the Rev. H. N. Powers, D. D., Christ Church, Bridgeport, Conn., the Rev. C. A. L. Richards, St. John's, Providence, R. I., and President E. N. Potter, D. D., LL. D., of Union College, Schenectady, N. Y., and an address by the Rev. Frank L. Norton, St. John's, Troy, N. Y.; "The Personal Work of the Holy Spirit"—paper by the Rev. Samuel Osgood, D. D., LL. D., of New York, and an address by the Rev. James Haughton of Yonkers.

PRUSSIA, a kingdom of Europe, forming part of the German Empire. King, William I., German Emperor and King of Prussia. (For an account of the royal family, see GERMANY.) The Prussian Ministry was composed at the end of 1879 as follows: President, Prince Bismarck, Minister of Foreign Affairs and Chancellor of the German Empire; Vice-President, Count Otto zu Stolberg-Wernigerode (appointed May 29, 1878); Hofmann, President of the Imperial Chancery (June 6, 1876) and Minister of Commerce (July 13, 1879); Count zu Eulenburg, Minister of the Interior (March 30, 1878); Maybach, Minister of Public Works (March 30, 1878); Bitter, Minister of Finance (July 13, 1879); Von Puttkammer, Minister of Worship and Education (July 13, 1879); Dr. Lucius, Minister of Agriculture (July 13, 1879); Dr. Friedberg, Minister of Justice (October, 1879).

In consequence of the termination of the alliance which for many years had existed between Prince Bismarck and the National Liberal party (see GERMANY), the three chief representatives of Liberal views in the Prussian Cabinet—Herr Hobrecht, Minister of Finance, formerly Burgomaster of Berlin, Dr. Falk, Minister of Public Worship, and Dr. Friedenthal, Minister of Agriculture — resigned in July. Their resignation was accepted by the King, who appointed as their successors Herr K. H. Bitter, Under-Secretary of State in the Ministry of the Interior, as Minister of Finance; Robert Victor von Puttkammer, President of the province of Silesia, as Minister of Public Instruction and Worship; and Dr. Robert Lucius, Minister of Agriculture. All the three new Ministers are prominent members of the Conservative party. Herr von Puttkammer was born May 5, 1828, at Frankfort-on-the-Oder, and has been in the service of the Prussian Government since 1852. In the war between Prussia and Austria, in 1866, he was appointed Civil Commissary for Moravia. In 1871 he became *Regierungspräsident* (president of an administrative district, of which most of the Prussian provinces have two or three) at Gumbinnen, in 1874 President of the government of Lorraine, and in 1877 *Oberpräsident* of the province of Silesia. He has been a member of the German Reichstag since 1873. In 1879 he was one of the thirty members whom the King of Prussia appointed members of the General Synod of the United Evangelical Church of Prussia. He is a brother-in-law of Prince Bismarck, his wife being a sister of the Princess Bismarck. Dr. Lucius was born December 20, 1834, at Erfurt in the province of Saxony, and is a very wealthy land-owner. He studied medicine at two German universities, took part in 1860 in the Spanish expedition against Morocco, accompanied from 1860 to 1862 the Prus-

sian embassy to eastern Asia as a physician, and served in the campaigns against Denmark, Austria, and France as officer of the Landwehr cavalry. He has been a member of the German Reichstag and the Prussian Landtag since 1870, and has always been one of the leaders of the German Imperial party (*Deutsche Reichspartei*), or, as it subsequently called itself, the Free Conservative party. He is an intimate friend of Prince Bismarck, and has often acted as his agent in arranging compromises between the Parliamentary parties. In 1879 the German Reichstag elected him second Vice-President. Though he belongs by birth to the Roman Catholic Church, he has always supported the Prussian Government in its conflict with the Church. Herr Bitter, the new Minister of Finance, was born February 27, 1813, at Schwedt, and has been in the state service since 1833. He was from 1856 to 1860 Prussian plenipotentiary in the European Commission of the Danube at Galatz, was appointed in 1860 chief inspector of the Rhine navigation at Mannheim, and in 1869 President of the financial section of the provincial government of Posen. During the war with France he was appointed Prefect of the department of the Vosges, subsequently Civil Commissary at Nancy, in 1872 *Regierungspräsident* in Schleswig, in 1876 in Düsseldorf, and in 1877 he became Under-Secretary of State in the Ministry of the Interior. He has achieved considerable literary reputation as a musical writer, being the author of works on Johann Sebastian Bach (1865), Karl Ph. E. and Wilhelm Friedrich Bach (1868), Gervinus, Handel, and Shakespeare (1869), of "Contributions to a History of the Oratorio" (1872), and of a revised translation of "Don Juan" (1872). Immediately after the opening of the Supreme Court of Germany (see GERMANY), on October 1st, Herr Leonhardt, the Minister of Justice, resigned on account of ill health. He was the last of the Ministers who had since 1867 aided Prince Bismarck in his plans for promoting German unity. He was succeeded by Dr. Friedberg, Secretary of State in the Imperial Office of Justice. Dr. Heinrich Friedberg was born January 27, 1813, studied law in the University of Berlin, was appointed Under-Secretary of State for Justice in Prussia in 1873, and in 1876 Secretary of State in the Imperial Office of Justice. As member of the Federal Council he has taken a prominent part in legislation, having been the author of the German penal code, the military penal code, the law on civil marriage, etc.

The area of Prussia is 134,180 square miles, and the population, according to the census of 1875, 25,742,404. (For the area and population of the different provinces, see "Annual Cyclopædia" for 1878.)

In the budget for 1879-'80, the receipts and expenditures were estimated at 711,500,758 marks (1 mark = 23·8 cents). The sources of revenue were as follows:

SOURCES OF REVENUE.

	Marks.
1. Ministry of Finance............................	301,425,393
2. Ministry of Agriculture, Domains, and Forests	82,218,954
3. Ministry of Public Works....................	270,844,904
4. Ministry of Commerce........................	292,425
5. Ministry of State............................	528,480
6. Ministry of Justice..........................	49,104,900
7. Ministry of the Interior.....................	8,701,895
8. Ministry of Worship and Education.........	2,894,857
9. Ministry of Foreign Affairs................	4,500
10. Ministry of War............................	1,000,000
Total....................	711,500,758

The expenditures are divided into permanent (*fortdauernde*), transitory (*einmalige*), and extraordinary (*ausserordentliche*) disbursements. The permanent are subdivided into current expenditures (*Betriebsausgaben*), administrative expenditures (*Staatsverwaltungsausgaben*), and charges on the consolidated fund (*Dotationen*). The different branches of expenditure were as follows:

CURRENT EXPENDITURES.

	Marks.
1. Ministry of Finance.........................	81,617,970
2. Ministry of Agriculture, etc..................	35,475,880
3. Ministry of Public Works....................	196,422,582
4. Ministry of State............................	494,200
5. Ministry of Worship and Education	583,000
Total current expenditures	264,593,037

CHARGES ON THE CONSOLIDATED FUND.

	Marks.
1. Additions to the crown dotations of the King.	4,500,000
2. Interest on public debt......................	54,779,809
3. Rentes.	1,876,917
4. Sinking fund of debt.........................	18,402,524
5. Management................................	440,690
6. Herrenhaus (House of Lords).................	164,610
7. Chamber of Deputies........................	1,199,520
Total charges on the consolidated fund......	80,864,180

ADMINISTRATIVE EXPENDITURES.

	Marks.
1. Ministry of State............................	2,286,000
2. Ministry of Finance	119,862,443
3. Ministry of Foreign Affairs..................	410,400
4. Ministry of Public Works....................	16,294,072
5. Ministry of Commerce.......................	1,437,605
6. Ministry of the Interior......................	39,170,216
7. Ministry of Justice...........................	69,728,425
8. Ministry of Agriculture, etc	10,483,302
9. Ministry of Worship and Education.........	47,970,381
10. Ministry of War............................	13,055
Total administrative expenditures.........	307,159,899
Total ordinary expenditures................	652,622,066
Transitory and extraordinary expenditures..	58,878,692
Grand total.............................	711,500,758

The public debt of the kingdom according to the budget of 1878-'79 was as follows:

	Marks.
1. Consolidated debt of May 2, 1842 (*Staats-schuldscheine*)..........................	134,964,800
2. Consolidated debt at 4½ per cent............	506,988,150
3. Consolidated debt at 4 per cent............	150,000,000
4. Non-consolidated loans of various dates.....	108,357,000
5. Preference loan of 1855.....................	25,590,000
6. War debt of the Kurmark and Neumark....	2,588,745
7. State railway debt..........................	45,776,941
8. Floating debt, called *Schatzanweisungen*	80,000,000
9. Debt of the provinces annexed in 1866......	93,107,043
Total..................................	1,097,322,379

The principal subject before the Diet at its spring session, commencing on January 8th, was the budget for 1879, which was passed on February 11th. The debate on the appropriation for the Ministry of Worship led to a dis-

cussion of the supposed desire of the Center or Catholic party to negotiate a compromise with the state, when Herr von Schorlemer-Alst (Center), on January 11th, argued that the fact of Prince Bismarck having entered into negotiations with the Pope as to the position of the Catholics in Prussia proved the co-ordination of Church and state. He further stated that the Catholic religion was being forcibly stamped out, and its defenders, to the shame of all Europe, were being hunted out of the land. Having been called to order by the President for the violence of his expressions, he yielded to two other members of the Center, who complained of the excessive favor shown the Old Catholics in Bonn, which gave occasion to a sharp reply from Dr. Falk. On January 29th the House discussed a motion of Herr Windthorst to restore the three articles of the Constitution having reference to the relations of the Church toward the state, and which were annulled when the May laws were passed. Professor Aegidi moved as an amendment that the House should pass to an order of the day, and this motion was adopted, being supported by deputies of all parties except the Center, Polish, and Old Conservative deputies. The Diet was closed on February 21st.

Elections were held throughout Prussia for members of the Diet on October 7th, which resulted in a complete overthrow of the Liberal parties. The strength of each party in the new Diet, as compared with that elected in 1876, was as follows: Conservatives of all shades, 174 (in 1876, 73); Center, 97 (90); National Liberals, 99 (178); unattached Liberals, 5 (8); Progressists, 36 (67); Democrats, 1 (0); Poles, 19 (15); Danes, 2 (2). The result showed a gain for the Conservative parties, and a corresponding loss for the National Liberals in every province except Hanover, where the National Liberals held their own, while the Conservatives gained one seat from the Center. The largest gains of the Conservatives are found in East Prussia (15), Brandenburg (17), Pomerania (9), Silesia (18), Saxony (16), and Hesse-Nassau (9).

The new Diet was opened on October 28th by the King in person. In his speech from the throne he declared the financial condition to be unsatisfactory, and a new loan would be necessary to cover the expected deficit. A bill was announced providing for the application of the revenue falling to the royal coffers from the surplus imperial imposts toward abating the class and income taxes of the monarchy. The most important passage of the speech referred to the railroads. The King said: "Penetrated by the conviction that the resolute achievement of a state railway system was the only way in which the national lines could be made to serve the public welfare, demanded with increasing emphasis by the interests of the country, his Majesty's Government had concluded several agreements having for their object the transfer to the state of important railways.

By means of such steps the Government was enabled to propose the construction of new lines by or with the assistance of the state, intended to open up new and important districts and connect them with the national network of railroads." The strength of the Conservatives was shown by the election of their candidate, Herr von Köller, as President. Dr. Bender, National Liberal, and Herr Heeremann, Center, were chosen First and Second Vice-Presidents. In the Upper House the Duke of Ratibor was chosen President, and Count Arnim von Boitzenburg and Herr Hasselbach First and Second Vice-Presidents.

On October 31st Herr Bitter, the Minister of Finance, submitted the budget for 1880. The deficit was estimated at 47,000,000 marks, which amount was to be covered by means of a loan. He also introduced bills authorizing the purchase of four lines of railroad. For the entire amount of the capital and the debt of these roads, in all 1,116,633,570 marks, consols were to be issued. Several new lines were also to be built, for which purpose another sum of 59,000,000 marks is to be issued in consols. The debate on the railroad bill was opened on November 11th. It was remarkable that the most incongruous elements joined both in support and in opposition to the measure. While it was opposed by members of the Progress and Center parties, the Conservatives and National Liberals spoke in favor of it. Professor Virchow, of the Progress party, argued at length that if the system of state railroads ever came into force in Germany and in all other countries, it would be the greatest calamity that ever visited the world. From a financial point of view even the state was sure to suffer, and great would be the detriment accruing to the working of such a system under a protective ministry. The whole railroad question was not one of political economy, but of political power. Minister Maybach defended the principle of government railroads. He pointed out the disadvantage arising to commerce from the omnipotent companies of England and the six great companies of France, and laid especial stress upon the fact that in France, in a commission of thirty members, there was a unanimous sentiment in favor of the purchase of the entire French roads. In the course of his speech he made some remarks which created considerable excitement at the Bourse, and called forth numerous protests. The Bourse, he said, was deeply interested in the further existence of private railways, for something was always to be earned there in manipulating them. Nevertheless, he would look upon himself as having done a good work could he help in limiting the activity of the Exchange in this respect. He believed the Bourse to be a poisonous tree which flung its shadow over the life of the people, and he would hold it to be a meritorious thing could it be plucked up by the roots. The debate was continued on November 15th.

Herr Miquel (National Liberal), speaking in the name of the great majority of his party, declared in favor of the views of the Government on the subject. The bill was brought up for the third reading on December 11th, and on the 12th was passed by a large majority, the minority being composed of the Progressists, the Center, and the Poles. It was passed in the Upper House on the 17th. The only noteworthy incident in the debate in the Herrenhaus was a speech by Count von Moltke, who pointed out the military advantages of government railroads.

General Synod of Prussia.—The meeting of the General Synod of Prussia which was held at Berlin in October, 1879, was the most important event in the history of the United Evangelical Church in that kingdom since its constitution on the basis of the union of the two leading Protestant denominations in 1817. It marked the completion of the synodal organization, under which the Church had been reconstituted during the last ten years on a basis which allows a representation of the congregational element in all stages of administration. Under the constitution thus formed, beginning with the parish, the congregational bodies, composed of lay representatives freely elected, regulate the temporalities. Above the congregations, each diocese or circuit, and each province, has its specially elected synod. The highest representative body in the Church is the General Synod, which has the right of meeting every six years, and which met for the first time in 1879. The General Synod is not entirely free in its action, for it has to divide its authority with the Superior Church Council, or Board of Royal Administration, as a coördinate body. The sessions of the General Synod continued during three weeks. One of its most important acts was the settling of a liturgical form for marriage in the church to follow the civil ceremony, which the state makes obligatory. A form of service was agreed upon which permits the minister, without appearing to dispute the validity of the contract already entered into, to pronounce the blessing of the Church upon the marriage. A bill was passed for enforcing discipline against those persons who neglect baptism, confirmation, and religious marriage. It provides that such persons shall lose their rights as electors for church officers, and shall in extreme cases be refused the Lord's Supper. Other questions considered were the revision of the Liturgy, for which the present time was decided not to be opportune, Sunday rest, the prevalence of drunkenness, a day of national humiliation, the rights of the congregations in the election of ministers, and the rights of pastors in elections. A general collection was ordered to be taken throughout the kingdom every two years for the support of city missionaries in Berlin. The orthodox party was largely in the ascendant in the Synod. Those called Confessionals and Positive Unionists numbered nearly two thirds, while only nine of the members enrolled themselves as Liberals.

PUBLIC DOCUMENTS. *Questions submitted to the Supreme Judicial Court of the State of Maine by the Republican members of the Legislature, and the answers thereto.*

STATE OF MAINE, IN SENATE, }
January 12, 1880. }

Ordered, That the following statement of facts be submitted to the Justices of the Supreme Judicial Court, and they be required to give their opinions on the questions appended thereto.
Read and passed.   C. W. TILDEN, Secretary.
A true copy.
Attest: C. W. TILDEN, Secretary.

STATE OF MAINE, IN HOUSE OF REPRESENTATIVES, }
January 12, 1880. }

Ordered, That the following statement of facts be submitted to the Justices of the Supreme Judicial Court, and they be required to give their opinions on the questions appended thereto.
Read and passed.
ORAMANDEL SMITH, Clerk.
A true copy.
Attest: ORAMANDEL SMITH, Clerk.
GEORGE E. WEEKS, Speaker.

STATEMENT OF FACTS.

Immediately after the annual election of September 8, 1879, copies of the lists of votes cast in the several towns and plantations for various State and county officers, duly attested by the selectmen of towns and assessors of plantations, and by either the town clerk, deputy clerk, or clerk *pro tem.*, and like copies of lists of votes given in the several wards of the cities, duly attested by the mayor and city clerk and a majority of a legal quorum of the aldermen present, were duly returned and delivered into the office of the Secretary of State, thirty days after the first Wednesday of January, 1880. The Governor and Council opened these returns November 17, 1879.

Application in proper form was made by parties interested for inspection of said returns, for the purpose of discovering and correcting any defects or errors therein; but in a large majority of cases such inspection was refused by the Governor and Council, or granted so late and in such a manner as to be of no avail for the correction of errors.

Senators and representatives elect made application to the Governor and Council within twenty days after the returns were opened, stating the errors alleged, and gave due notice thereof to persons to be affected by such corrections, or requested the same to be given, and offered to correct any errors found therein by the record, or by substituting for such returns, if defective, duly attested copies of the record in each case as provided by the statutes, and by offering such other evidence as is authorized by chap. 212 of the laws of 1877. But the Governor and Council refused to receive such evidence or to correct any errors in said returns, or to receive a duly attested copy of the record to be substituted for any defection by reason of any informality. Under these circumstances the Governor and Council proceeded to examine the returns, with the following results:

The return from the city of Portland was duly signed, and showed upon its face all the facts necessary to constitute a legal election. It showed the whole number of ballots given, and that Moses M. Butler, Almon A. Strout, Ruel G. Maxey, Samuel A. True, and Nathan E. Redlon each received over six hundred and forty votes plurality over each of the candidates opposed to them. The only defect alleged to exist in said return was that it contained the words and figures "Scattering, one hundred and forty-three (143)"; but this number, if added or subtracted or disregarded, would still leave each of the candidates above named a large majority of all the votes cast as above stated. The Governor and Council rejected said return, and refused

to summon the five representatives above named, who were elected and appeared to be elected by a plurality of all the votes returned, to attend and take their seats, and refused to report their names and residence to the Secretary of State to be included in the certified roll to be furnished by him to the Clerk of the preceding House of Representatives, as required by law. Subsequently to the making of said return, Moses M. Butler, one of said representatives elect, died, and in pursuance of the provisions of chap. 4, secs. 38, 44, and 47, of the Revised Statutes, a new election was ordered by the municipal officers of the city of Portland. At such election Byron D. Verrill was elected by a majority of over one thousand votes over all others, and a proper return was made to the office of the Secretary of State; but no summons was ever issued to said Verrill, and the Governor and Council refused to report his name to the Secretary of State for the purpose above stated. In the city of Lewiston, Liberty H. Hutchinson, Isaac N. Parker, and Silas W. Cook were elected by a clear majority of all the votes cast. In the city of Saco, George Parcher; in the city of Rockland, Jonathan S. Willoughby and Theodore E. Simonton; in the city of Bath, Guy C. Goss, were in like manner duly elected representatives. In each of these four cases the returns were in due form and signed by the mayor, city clerk, and three aldermen. The Governor and Council in each of the above cases refused to issue summonses and to report the names and residences of the said elected representatives to the Secretary of State, to be included in the certified roll. In the Webster, Lisbon, and Durham class, William H. Thomas appeared by the returns to be elected by a majority of eighty-three votes. The returns from said towns were without defect, and were duly signed by all the selectmen of each town. Upon rumor that the Governor and Council refused to issue a summons to the persons elected because it was alleged that the names of the selectmen signed upon the returns from the towns of Lisbon and Webster were signed by one person in each town, all of said selectmen appeared before the Governor and Council and made oath that the signatures were genuine. In this district another ground was taken, that it appeared from extrinsic and *ex parte* evidence that either the return was not signed and sealed, or the record not made up, in open town meeting. The Governor and Council refused to issue a summons to said William H. Thomas, or report his name to be entered on said certified roll, but did issue a summons to Leonard H. Beal, a person who was not elected and did not appear to be elected by said returns.

The following is that portion of the statement which recites the facts connected with the organization of the Legislatures:

On the 31st day of December, A. D. 1879, the Governor requested the opinion of the Justices of the Supreme Judicial Court upon certain questions submitted by him; and by the opinion of said Justices, in reply thereto, it appeared that the objections and alleged defects in the returns hereinbefore stated were without foundation in law. The Governor and Council were required in all those cases to recall the summons which by the opinion of the Court appeared to have been improperly issued, and to report the names and places of residence of the persons legally elected to both branches of the Legislature to the Secretary of State to be entered upon the certified rolls as required by law; but this they refused to do. A certified roll was furnished by the Secretary of State to the Clerk of the preceding House of Representatives, containing the names of one hundred and twenty-two persons properly summoned as representatives elect and seventeen persons heretofore enumerated, viz.: Lewis Voter, Daniel Snow, Alfred Cushman, James O. White, Leonard H. Beal, Osgood N. Bradbury, George W. Johnson, Lincoln H. Leighton, Aaron H. Woodcock, Harper Allen, Joshua E. Jordan, F. W. Hill, James W. Clark, James Flye, John H. Brown, James M. Leighton, and Stephen D. Lord, and no more, no names of representatives for the five cities above enumerated appearing on said roll. On the first Wednesday of January the Assistant Clerk of the preceding House of Representatives (the Clerk of said preceding House being present) proceeded to call the names on the certified roll above described, whereupon one hundred and thirty-five persons answered to their names. Attention was then called by one of the persons so responding to the vacancies appearing upon the reading of said roll.

A motion was then made that the representatives from said five cities, appearing by the returns from said cities to have been actually elected, should be permitted to participate in the organization of the House. The Assistant Clerk refused to put the motion, and refused to entertain an appeal. Motion was then made that a committee be raised to inform the Governor and Council that a quorum was present and ready to take the oath. Upon that question a call of the yeas and nays was demanded, and it was so taken, and there were seventy-three votes in the affirmative and none in the negative. Attention was then called to the fact that no quorum was present. Motion was then made to adjourn, which said Assistant Clerk refused to entertain or put, and the same was put by the mover and declared carried. Thereupon a number of the members left the hall. The Governor and Council appeared to administer the oath. One of the members summoned called the attention of the Governor to the fact that no quorum had voted to qualify; but the Governor declined to notice this act on the part of the members summoned. Thereupon the Governor proceeded to administer the oath. After the rolls containing the oath was signed, the Governor announced that seventy-six persons summoned had subscribed the oath; among whom were the persons previously enumerated by name as appearing on said roll, except Lewis Voter and Daniel Snow. The announcement of the Governor that seventy-six persons had subscribed the oath was doubted by a member who had subscribed the oath, and a repeated demand was made that this announcement should be verified by reading the names of those who had subscribed; but the Assistant Clerk declined so to do. Protest was made against the administration of the oath before it was administered. Thereupon an election of Speaker was attempted, and John C. Talbot received seventy-two votes, no other votes being thrown.

On the next day sixty members summoned and whose names appeared on the certified roll applied to James D. Lamson, who claimed to be President of the Senate, to be qualified, and he refused in writing to administer to them the oaths required by law.

The facts connected with the alleged organization of the Senate on the first Wednesday of January, 1880, are as follows: A certified roll was furnished by the Secretary of State to the Secretary of the preceding Senate, on which were the names of twenty-three persons properly summoned and who appeared to be elected as shown on the face of the returns, together with the names of Daniel W. True, Edward A. Gibbs, and William R. Field, of Cumberland County; Rudolphus P. Thompson, of Franklin County; James R. Talbot, of Washington County; Isaac T. Hobson, of Lincoln County; Ira S. Libbey and John Q. Dennett, of York County; and at ten o'clock in the forenoon on said day said Secretary of the preceding Senate called the names on the roll, and each one responded.

Thereupon one of the members properly summoned called attention to the fact that the names above enumerated on the roll had been substituted for the names of Andrew Hawes, Henry C. Brewer, and David Duran, of Cumberland County; George R. Fernald, of Franklin County; Alden Bradford, of Washington County; Andrew R. G. Smith, of Lincoln County; Jeremiah W. Dearborn and George H. Wakefield, of York County, who appeared by the returns to be elected, and moved that their names be substituted on the roll for those first above enumerated. The Secretary refused to entertain the motion. The oath was then administered by the Governor and Council.

The motion was immediately thereafter renewed, and the Secretary again refused to entertain the motion. An appeal was then taken to the Senate; the Secretary refused to put the question. Protest was then made that unless the substitution moved was made, eleven members properly summoned and having a plurality of the Senatorial votes in their respective counties would refuse to participate in the organization of the Senate. No attention having been paid to this protest, said eleven members did not participate in the further proceedings. The remaining twenty persons proceeded to vote for President of the Senate, and James D. Lamson received twenty ballots, which were cast by twelve members properly summoned and by the eight persons first above enumerated. Public protest was immediately made by a member duly summoned against the election of James D. Lamson as President of the Senate, because he had received the votes of but twelve persons lawfully summoned. The remainder of the officers of the Senate were elected in the same manner and by the same persons as the President.

On the twelfth day of January, 1880, the persons claiming to be legally elected members of the Legislature, but having present less than seventy-six in number, attempted to meet in joint convention for the purpose of witnessing the administration of the oaths to James D. Lamson, to qualify him to exercise the office of Governor, together with twenty members of the Senate, only twelve of whom appeared to be elected by the returns. On the same day sixty-two members of the House to whom James D. Lamson, claiming to be President of the Senate, had refused to administer the oath, and who were properly summoned, together with John R. Eaton, William H. Thomas, A. F. Andrews, David N. Norton, Henry C. Baker, Charles A. Rolf, A. B. Cole, Robert French, Cyrus A. Thomas, Hiram A. Stewart, and John Burnham, previously mentioned, together with the representatives of the cities of Portland, Lewiston, Saco, Rockland, and Bath, met in the Hall of Representatives, and organized by the choice of Speaker, Clerk, and the other officers, after being qualified by taking the oaths prescribed by the Constitution before William M. Stratton, a Clerk of Courts for Kennebec County, and authorized by *dedimus potestatem* to administer oaths according to law. The Speaker received eighty-two votes; the Clerk received eighty votes; the Assistant Clerk received eighty-one votes. After organizing, the following members, Isaac Hanscom of Lebanon, Edward K. Hall of Newcastle, Robert W. Loring of Robbinston district, George S. Hill of Exeter, Frank C. Micherson of Linneus, and Oliver P. Bragdon of Gouldsboro district, were admitted by resolution to act as members *prima facie* of said House of Representatives.

On the same day, in the Senate Chamber, eleven members properly summoned, together with Andrew Hawes, David Duran, Henry C. Brewer, of Cumberland County; Jeremiah W. Dearborn, George H. Wakefield, of York County; George R. Fernald, of Franklin County; Alden Bradford, of Washington County, the facts concerning whose election have been hereinbefore stated, met together and were called to order by Jeremiah Dingley, a Senator elect from Androscoggin County, on whose motion Austin Harris, Senator elect from Washington County, was chosen to preside as Chairman, and Charles W. Tilden was chosen Secretary *pro tem.* upon resolution. Andrew R. G. Smith, of Lincoln County, was admitted *prima facie* to a seat.

Upon motion the members elect present proceeded to make a permanent organization by the election of President, Secretary, and other officers. Joseph A. Locke of Cumberland was chosen President, receiving eighteen votes, and Charles W. Tilden was chosen Secretary, receiving nineteen votes.

The members were qualified before election of officers by taking the oaths prescribed by the Constitution before William M. Stratton, Clerk of Courts for Kennebec County, and authorized by *dedimus potes-*

tatem to administer oaths. In the organization of both branches of the Legislature the names of all the members elect, who appear by the uncorrected returns to be elected, were placed upon a roll and were called before proceeding to organize the same as herein last mentioned.

Twenty-seven questions, covering the points comprised in the foregoing statement, were submitted to the Court, to which answers were returned as follows (the answer in some instances, as given below, embodying the terms of the question, and in others sufficiently indicating its nature):

An election has been had by the electors of this State. The rights of the several persons voted for depend upon the votes cast. The result should be truly determined in accordance with the Constitution and laws of the State. It was the duty of the Governor and Council thus to declare it. Any declaration of the vote not thus ascertained and declared is unauthorized and void.

The Governor and Council examined the returns, and undertook to declare the result as appeared by the returns. Various questions involving the true construction of the Constitution and statutes relating thereto arose, and the Governor, by virtue of his constitutional prerogative, called upon this Court for its opinion upon the questions propounded. By the provisions of the Constitution the Court was required to expound and construe the provisions of the Constitution and statutes involved. It gave full answers to those questions. The opinion of the Court was thus obtained in one of the modes provided in the Constitution for an authoritative determination of "important questions of law." The law thus determined is the conclusive guide of the Governor and Council in the performance of their ministerial duties. Any action on their part in determining the vote as it appears by the returns in violation of the provision of the Constitution and laws, thus declared, is a usurpation of authority, and must be held void. It only remains to apply those principles to the subjects embraced in the questions propounded.

The Governor and Council have no right to summon a person to attend and take his seat in the Senate or House of Representatives who by the returns before them was not voted for, or being voted for was defeated. To summon one for whom no votes had been cast would be a deliberate violation of official duty. To summon those whom the returns show were not elected would be equally such violation. Either would be intruders without right into a legislative body. The summons thus given would be void as in excess of any powers conferred by the Constitution. Grant this power, and the right of the people to elect their officers is at an end.

Holders of summonses which are void, for the reason that the Governor and Council have failed to correctly perform the constitutional obligations resting upon them, have no right to take a part in the organization, or in any subsequent proceedings of the House to which they are wrongfully certificated. They are not in fact members; but the members rightfully elected, as shown by the official returns, and the opinion of the Court upon the propositions heretofore by the Governor presented to the Court, are entitled to appear and act in the organization of the Houses to which they belong, unless the House and Senate, in judging of the election and qualification of members, shall determine to the contrary.

A member without a summons who appears to claim his seat is *prima facie* entitled to equal consideration with a member who has a summons. He is not to be deprived of the position belonging to him on account of the dereliction of those whose duty it was to have given him the usual summons. The absence of that evidence may be supplied by other evidence of membership.

The House and Senate have the same right to consider and determine whether in the first instance such persons appear to have been elected, and finally whether they were in fact elected, as they have of any and all the persons who appear for the purpose of composing their respective bodies. Under the facts recited in the statement submitted to us, we are of the opinion that Lewis Voter and associates first named in question three were not entitled to act, and that Cyrus A. Thomas and associates lastly named in the question were entitled to act in the House as members; and that Daniel W. True and those first named in question four were not entitled to act, and that Andrew Hawes and others with him named were entitled to act as members of the Senate. In neither case did the Senate or House itself act upon the question of their membership. Both the Senate and House, "meaning the bodies assembled to be organized as such," were debarred from any action thereon by the conduct of the presiding Secretary and Clerk. The assumption of such officers that no questions should be entertained relative to the rights of persons whose names were not upon the rolls furnished by the Secretary of State, but who were claimants of seats, was unwarrantable. The statute of 1869, embodied in the Revised Statutes, chap. 2, sec. 25, can not preclude either the Senate or House from amending and completing the rolls of membership according to the facts.

Each House has the constitutional right to organize itself. The form provided for aid and convenience in effecting the organization does not confer upon a temporarily presiding officer such conclusive power. We have not failed to carefully consider the act of 1869, chap. 67, incorporated into the Revised Statutes, chap. 2, sec. 25, and so far as it declares that "no person shall be allowed to vote or take part in the organization of either branch of the Legislature as a member, unless his name appears upon the certified roll of that branch of the Legislature in which he claims to act," we think it clearly repugnant to the Constitution, which declares that each House shall be the judge of the election and qualification of its own members. It aims to control the action of each within its constitutional powers, till after a full organization with a majority determined and fixed by the Governor and Council. By their action in granting certificates to men not appearing to be elected, or refusing to grant certificates to men clearly elected, they may constitute each House with a majority to suit their own purposes, thus strangling and overthrowing the popular will, as honestly expressed by the ballot. The doctrine of that act gives to the executive department the power to rob the people of the Legislature they have chosen, and force upon them one to serve its own purpose. It poisons the very fountain of legislation, and tends to corrupt the legislative department of the government. It strikes a death-blow at the heart of popular government, and renders its foundation and great bulwark, the will of the people as expressed by the ballot, a farce. Each House has the same power, and is charged with the same duty, to declare the election of its own members, and organize in any legitimate way, as before the passage of that act.

When the member summoned appears by the returns to be elected only because of some error in the name or initial of the candidate not summoned, when such error is correctable by law under the decision of the Court, and the official record states the name and initials correctly, or when the member summoned appears by the returns to be elected only by rejecting the returns of one town because unsigned by the town clerk, though a duly attested copy of the record of said town is seasonably offered as a substitute, it is the duty of the Governor and Council to hear evidence and determine whether the record or return is correct, and, if they determine the record to be correct, to receive it, or a duly certified copy of it, to correct the return, as is provided in chap. 212 of the acts of 1877. But in such case they are required to determine an issue of fact whether the record or return is correct; and so far as their action is concerned in determining that fact, we think their determination is conclusive, subject, of course, to be reversed by the House. If, however, they should refuse to hear evidence and determine the question, and should by reason of such refusal issue the summons to the candidate not elected, the case would fall under the rule above stated.

If objection was made to the admissibility of the illegally summoned persons as set forth in the statement presented to us, and the Houses took no action thereon, then an organization of House or Senate with less than a quorum would be illegal and void. The Court expressed the opinion on a former occasion that the Senate could organize with less than a quorum of members (35 Maine, 563) where less than a quorum were elected—a condition of things that might happen when it required a majority of votes to elect Senators. That decision met the necessities of that occasion, but the doctrine of that case can not apply when a quorum is in fact elected.

Without a legal organization formed and legal officers chosen by seventy-six members present and voting in the House of Representatives, and by sixteen members present and voting in the Senate, upon the given measure, no officers can be chosen or law passed, nor business done, except to adjourn. No less than seventy-six members can constitute a quorum of the House of Representatives, nor can less than sixteen members, now that a plurality elects, constitute a quorum of the Senate. Nor can either House, without a legal organization formed and without legal officers chosen, compel the attendance of absent members. It is the House or Senate, when formed and organized, that has the power to compel such attendance, and it is not within the power of persons who are merely members elect to do so.

Attendance of members may, under our Constitution, be compelled by such penalties as each House may provide. Until a legal organization has been effected, there is no House to provide penalties for such purpose; until a legal organization is completed, there is no officer in either House to issue a warrant against the absent members. No such power was committed or intended to be committed into the hands of persons not composing and acting as an organized and completed House. It has frequently happened in our history, that legislative bodies have been delayed days, and sometimes weeks, without being able to complete an organization for the want of a quorum.

The vote of no person can be counted to make up a legal quorum who, though summoned, does not appear to be elected by the official returns under the Constitution and the decision of the Court, if the attention of the House is called to the fact that such persons are illegally summoned, and objection is seasonably made to the counting of such persons for the purpose of making up a quorum, and the House does not act upon the question of their admissibility. By the Constitution, Art. IV., sec. 5, "the Senate shall, on the first Wednesday of January annually, determine who are elected by a plurality of votes to be Senators in each district."

By the Constitution, the oath is to be taken and subscribed in the presence of the Governor and Council. By the statute (Revised Statutes, chap. 2, section 23) the Clerk of the preceding House shall preside until the representatives elect "shall be qualified and elect a Speaker; and if no quorum appear, he shall preside, and the representatives elect present shall adjourn from day to day until a quorum appears and are qualified, and a Speaker is elected." Thus it will be seen that while by the statute the Clerk is to preside until a quorum shall appear and be qualified, it is not provided, either in the Constitution or the statute, that a less number than a quorum shall not be qualified, nor can the yea and nay vote on the motion to request the attendance of the Governor and Council for the purpose of administering the oath be deemed of any importance. If the Governor and Council had appeared without a motion or a vote, their authority would have been the same. The qualifying oaths under the Constitution or statute may be administered to the mem-

bers elect of either branch, in any numbers, though a quorum must appear and be qualified before proceeding to an election of Speaker; and if the whole number of votes for Speaker is less than a quorum, and there is nothing upon the record to show that a quorum was present and acting, there would be no election.

In the general provisions of the Constitution, Art. IX., certain oaths or affirmations are prescribed for persons elected, appointed, or commissioned to the offices therein mentioned. It appears that those before whom the prescribed oaths were to be administered refused to act, and that now there is no existing Governor and Council before whom they can be administered. The oath is prescribed. The terms are the essential. Its binding force depends upon its terms, not on the magistrate by whom it is administered. If there is no Governor and Council, or, there being a Governor and Council, they refuse to administer the oath to one representative or to all (for there can be a refusal to all equally as to one), what is the result? Is anarchy to triumph? Can the government be destroyed, or its action paralyzed, because there is no Governor and Council before whom the prescribed oath is to be taken? We think not. The prescribed oath, from the necessity of the case, may be taken before a magistrate authorized to administer oaths. The members must be sworn before they can act It is by their action that a Governor and Council thereafter are to be elected and the government continued. It can not be presumed that the framers of the Constitution had in contemplation that the oath had better not be administered at all than administered by any other officer than the one designated therein. This is one of the most reliable tests by which to distinguish a directory from a mandatory provision (State vs. Smith, 67 Maine, 328).

One whose only title to the Presidency of the Senate is by virtue of an election at which twenty votes only are cast for and against him, and those twenty votes are made up as described, can not become the acting Governor, because he is not a legal President of the Senate. If, of the twenty voting at such choice of President of the Senate, eight did not appear to be elected by the official returns under the Constitution and the decision of the Court, and were not in fact elected; there was then no legal quorum, and could be no valid election of permanent officers, notwithstanding the eight had been summoned by the Governor and Council. Without a legal quorum, and with these eig participating in the proceedings, to the exclusion of those rightfully elected in their places, there could be no valid election of President of the Senate. To proceed with the organization of the Senate without first determining and declaring its own membership, when attention was properly called to the fact that persons were present and acting without right, and that members were excluded, the Secretary refusing to entertain a motion for the correction of the roll and refusing to allow an appeal from his ruling, and the Senate taking no action although protest was made, was illegal and void.

Under the letter of the Constitution, it is at least doubtful whether the President of the Senate is required to take a new oath before exercising the office of Governor, when that office has become vacant in the manner specified therein. The practice since the organization of the State has, we believe, been uniform against requiring such new oaths, and to such practical interpretations of the Constitution, in the absence of express provisions or manifest intention to the contrary, we think effect should be given. A legally chosen President of the Senate may become acting Governor without the administration of any other qualifying oath than that which he has taken in his office of Senator.

It appears from the statement of facts that the members from the five cities of Portland, Lewiston, Rockland, Bath, and Saco were duly elected, as well as by the returns before the Governor and Council; that by law a summons should of right have been issued to them;

that in fact no summons was issued, and that their names were not borne on the roll certified to the House as provided by R. S. M., chap. 2, sec. 25. A motion was seasonably made that these members appearing by the returns beforehand to have been duly elected, should be permitted to participate in its organization; but the Assistant Clerk refused to put the motion and to entertain an appeal. By the Constitution the returns were before the House. By those returns the representatives above named appeared to be elected. Their seats were not contested. The Governor and Council could not, without a violation of their constitutional duty, neglect to issue to them a summons, nor the Secretary of State to place their names on the certified roll which it was his duty to furnish. The Governor and Council could not legally withhold their summonses from those appearing to be elected. They could not order a summons to issue to some appearing to be elected and withhold it from others. If they could, it would be in their power to select from the members appearing to be elected those who should and those who should not take part in the organization of the House.

Sec. 25, chap. 2, Revised Statutes, restricts the vote to those whose names are borne on the certified roll. The restricting the vote to those only whose names are thus borne is at variance with the Constitution in so far as it restricts and limits the action of the House to those whom the Governor and Council may select, and not to those appearing to be chosen and to those the House may determine to be members. The twelve members had a right to act in the organization of the House. Their election was patent on inspection of the returns. The House in no way denied their right. The question whether their names should be added to the roll was not submitted to its determination. Upon the facts set forth they appeared to be and were elected, and it is not to be presumed that the House, knowing such facts, would have prohibited this action if the Clerk had permitted the question to be put. These members had a right to take part in the organization of the House until it should otherwise determine. The House can not legally organize or act under a certified roll of one hundred and thirty-nine names only, and giving no representation to the five cities named, provided the representatives from the cities appeared and claimed their seats, and the House took no action whatever upon the question of their right to participate in the organization, the Clerk refusing to entertain a motion made for that purpose, and refusing to entertain an appeal from his ruling thereon.

When persons are legally elected members of the House from the representative districts of Skowhegan and Farmington, and that fact unmistakably appears on the official returns, and by the decision of the Court on the facts recited in the statement submitted, for those districts, those members elect have a right to take part in the organization and all subsequent proceedings of the House without a summons, the persons summoned having returned their summonses and declined to serve as representatives on the ground that they were not elected, unless the House has acted upon the question of their right to act as members, and determined to the contrary.

Eleven members duly elected and summoned, and seven other members not summoned, but appearing to be elected by a plurality of all the votes returned, under the requirements of the Constitution and the decision of the Court, can constitute and organize a legal Senate, provided said eighteen members each received for Senator a plurality of all the votes cast, and the official records as well as the official returns show that fact; and sixty-two duly summoned members elect of the House of Representatives, together with twelve members elect not summoned from the cities of Portland, Lewiston, Bath, Saco, and Rockland, and two members elect not summoned from the towns of Farmington and Skowhegan, can constitute and organize a legal House of Representatives, when the fourteen members above enumerated were in fact elected, and that fact appears by the official returns and by the decision of the Court, no other persons holding summonses for the same seats. Circumstances may exist which will justify and render legal such an organization of the Senate and such an organization of the House. We think such organizations would be justified and rendered legal by the existence of such circumstances as are recited in the statement of facts submitted to us, and that such organizations effected under such circumstances would constitute a legal Legislature, competent to perform all the functions constitutionally belonging to that department of our government. Tumult and violence are not requisites to the due assertion of legal rights. They should be avoided whenever it is possible to do so. They can never be justified except in cases of the extremest necessity. Such peaceful modes of organization are far preferable to a resort to violence. No rights should be lost by those who seasonably assert them and appeal to the constitutional tribunals instead of resorting to force.

The seventy-six members elect enumerated can constitute and organize a legal House of Representatives, together with nine other members elect who were in fact elected, and appear by the official returns and by the decision of the Court to be elected, though the nine seats aforesaid are claimed by other candidates who were summoned by the Governor and Council, but were not in fact elected, and do not appear to be elected by said official returns under the decision of the Court.

When a person receives a summons as a member of the House of Representatives, and returns the same to the Governor before the assembling of the Legislature and resigns his seat, it makes a vacancy in the House which is to assemble, which vacancy " may be filled by a new election," under the provisions of Art. XII., part 1, sec. 6 of the Constitution. That the proper steps may be taken by the municipal officers to that end, it is necessary to regard such resignation as irrevocable. If, when once made, it could be recalled at will, the municipal officers could never know that the seat was vacant by resignation. One who has thus resigned can not be compelled to attend as a member. He is no longer a member. The language of the Court, in regard to using the power of the Houses to compel the attendance of these members, in the constitutional opinion given in 35 Me., 563, applies only to those who, without vacating their seats, absent themselves from the sessions of the body to which they were elected. It would be alike contrary to the spirit of our institutions and detrimental to public policy to hold that a man might be compelled to accept an office of such a character.

In our recent answer to questions presented by the Governor, we said in substance that one of the objects of the constitutional requirement of a record of the vote to be made at the same time and authenticated in like manner with the return was to guard against the possible result of mistake, accident, or fraud in the official returns of votes. When such returns of the vote for Governor are lost, concealed, or inaccessible by accident or fraud, the result of the election may still be ascertained by using certified copies of the official records mentioned in the question. Neither the carelessness nor the turpitude of the officers charged with the making or the custody of the returns can be suffered to defeat the will of the people as expressed in the election, so long as the Legislature can ascertain it from the records thus made. True, the Constitution provides that the Secretary of State shall, on the first Wednesday of January, lay the lists before the Senate and House of Representatives; but this portion is directory, and a failure to comply with it can not defeat the right of the Legislature to ascertain and declare the result of the election. When the framers of our Constitution and our legislators have taken such pains to perpetuate the evidence of the votes cast, and to guard that evidence against the effect not only of accident, but of human fallibility or perfidy, it is not to be thrown away because the Secretary of State fails or is unable to comply with this direction. The Constitution is to be construed, when practicable, in all its

748 RANDALL, SAMUEL J.

parts, not so as to thwart, but so as to advance its main object—the continuance and orderly conduct of government by the people.

The questions before us are attested in the usual mode, and purport to come from organized bodies. They are of the utmost importance. Our answers are entirely based on the assumption of the existence of the facts as therein set forth. We can not decline an answer if we would. In a case like the present the remarks of Chief-Justice Marshall, in Cohens *vs.* Virginia, are peculiarly applicable. "It is true," he says, "that this Court will not take jurisdiction if it should not, but it is equally true that it must take jurisdiction if it should. The judiciary can not, as the Legisla-

ture may, avoid a measure because it approaches the confines of the Constitution. We can not pass it by because it is doubtful with whatever difficulties a case may be attended. We must decide it if it is brought before us. We have no more right to decline the exercise of jurisdiction which is given than to usurp that which is not given; the one or the other would be treason to the Constitution. Questions may occur which we would gladly avoid; but we can not avoid them."

JOHN APPLETON,   CHARLES DANFORTH,
CHARLES W. WALTON,   JOHN A. PETERS,
WILLIAM G. BARROWS,   ARTEMAS LIBBY,
         JOSEPH W. SYMONDS.

R

RANDALL, SAMUEL JACKSON, an American statesman, born in Philadelphia, October 10, 1828. His father was Josiah Randall, a lawyer of high standing in that city; his mother, Ann Worrall, a daughter of General Joseph Worrall, a Democratic leader in the days of Jefferson. Receiving an academic education, he engaged in mercantile pursuits. He married Fanny, a daughter of General Aaron Ward of Sing Sing, New York. He served four years in the City Councils of Philadelphia and one term in the State Senate of Pennsylvania.

Mr. Randall was a member of the "First Troop Philadelphia City Cavalry," a volunteer military company organized in 1774. It was then known as the "Light Horse of Philadelphia," and acted as body-guard to General Washington, crossing the Delaware with him and participating in the battles of Trenton and Princeton. Immediately after the fall of Fort Sumter the troop tendered its services to the Government, and was mustered into the service of the United States, May 13, 1861, for the term of ninety days, attached to the Second U. S. Cavalry commanded by Colonel (afterward the distinguished General) George H. Thomas, and assigned to the command of General Robert Patterson, who says of the troop: "It was with me in the valley of the Shenandoah in the summer of 1861. It was in the advance at the battle of Falling Waters, when, for the first and only time, that gallant soldier 'Stonewall' Jackson was defeated and driven back." Sergeant S. J. Randall acted as quartermaster to the company, and was afterward promoted to the rank of cornet (a rank corresponding to that of captain in the regular army).

On the first intimation of the advance of the Confederate army north of the Potomac in June, 1863, Cornet Randall proceeded to Harrisburg to make arrangements by which the troop could go into service if it was found necessary. General Couch, on announcing to Cornet Randall, commanding, that Governor Curtin would accept the troop without swearing its members into the service, said, "I know we can trust to the honor of the corps without an oath." On June 24th Mr. Randall with his command made an important reconnoissance,

capturing several of the enemy and establishing their presence in large force between Chambersburg and Williamsport. Retiring from Gettysburg as the Confederate army entered, the troop had a skirmish with an advancing force under General J. B. Gordon near the Susquehanna. During the battle of Gettysburg Mr. Randall was provost-marshal of Columbia. Being released from duty after the retreat of the invading army, letters were received by "Cornet S. J. Randall, commanding First City Troop," from the Governor of the State and from the War Department through General Cadwalader, thanking the company for its efficient services.

At the convening of the Thirty-eighth Congress, December 4, 1863, Mr. Randall took his seat in the House of Representatives, and has been reëlected to every succeeding Congress, covering a period of seventeen years. In the Thirty-eighth Congress he served on the Committee on Public Buildings and Grounds; in the Thirty-ninth, on the Committees on Banking and Currency, Retrenchment, and Expenditures in the State Department; in the Fortieth, on Banking and Currency, Retrenchment, and the Assassination of President Lincoln. Elected as a Democrat, he has constantly acted with his party in Congress. Without occupying the attention of the House with long speeches, he indicated his interest in pending legislation by frequently participating briefly and pointedly in its discussions. In the Forty-first Congress he was a member of the Committees on Privileges and Elections and on Expenditures in the Treasury Department, and of the Joint Committee on Retrenchment. He spoke against repudiation December 16, 1869, in reply to Mr. Munger, saying: "In the time allowed me, it is hardly possible that I should follow the gentleman from Ohio in all his sayings, or what I might mildly term his political heresies; but for myself—and I think I can speak for my constituents—I am utterly opposed to repudiation. But the moment allowed me gives me the opportunity to remonstrate against the enunciation of any scheme of legislation which I believe would place my country in a dishonest attitude before the world. Not only do I believe that we should pay the debt, but I believe, what is of vastly more importance, that the country has the ability, the disposition, and the resources to pay it." In the Forty-second and Forty-third Congresses he served on the Committees on Banking and Currency, Post-Offices and Post-Roads, and Rules, and was one of the most influential members of the minority. His triumphant leadership in the two days' and all night's contest to prevent the "Force bill" from going to the Senate in time for action on it, brought him first into great prominence. When the Democrats came into power at the opening of the Forty-fourth Congress, in December, 1875, Mr. Randall was made chairman of the Committee on Appropriations. He devoted himself to the work of retrenchment, and succeeded in cutting down the appropriations many millions. In giving a summary of what he had accomplished in the way of retrenching, August 14, 1876, he closed with these words: "I believe the real, natural, safe, and permanent way to resumption of specie payments is in the reduction of the expenditures of the Government to what is needed by an economical administration. Human foresight, in my judgment, can not fix the exact hour or day when it shall take place."

On December 4, 1876, Mr. Randall was elected to fill the vacancy in the office of Speaker occasioned by the death of Michael C. Kerr. On taking the chair at that critical time, he said: "We stand in the presence of events which strain and test to the last degree our form of government. Our liberties, consecrated by so many sacrifices in the past, and preserved amid the rejoicings of an exultant people at our centennial anniversary as one among the nations of the earth, must be maintained at all hazard. The people look confidently to your moderation, to your wisdom, in this time fraught with so much peril. Let us not, I beseech you, disappoint their just expectations and their keen sense of right; but by unceasing vigilance let us prevent even the slightest departure from the Constitution and the laws, forgetting in the moment of difficulty that we are the adherents of party, and only remembering that we are American citizens with a country to save." It was greatly owing to his brave and determined spirit in maintaining such sentiments, that the turbulent factions in the House were held in check, and the results of the Electoral Commission quietly acquiesced in. As he expressed it in his valedictory at the close of this Congress, "The Democratic party yielded temporary possession of the administration, rather than entail upon the people civil war with all its attendant horrors."

At the called session of the Forty-fifth Congress, October 15, 1877, he was reëlected Speaker. The two years of this Congress were a period of general financial distress and of labor depressed by heavy burdens. He urged that no backward step should be taken in the work of retrenchment, saying, "When the iron rule of hard necessity darkens every household in the land, extravagance on the part of the people's servants is an unpardonable crime."

At the extra session in March, 1879, he was again elected Speaker of the Forty-sixth Congress.

REFORMED CHURCHES. I. REFORMED CHURCH IN AMERICA (formerly *Reformed Dutch Church*).—The following is a summary of the statistics of the Reformed Church in America as they were reported to the General Synod of 1879: Number of Classes, 32; of churches, 505; of ministers, 546; of communicants, 80,228. One of the Classes, Arcot, with 21 churches, 6 ministers, and 1,106 communicants, is in Asia; the others are in the United States. Number of Sunday-schools, 695, with 79,250 scholars. Amount of contributions for religious and benevolent purposes, $175,424; for congregational purposes, $745,502. The Board of Foreign Missions received during the year $58,443, and paid out $78,798.

The *General Synod* of the Reformed Church in America met in its seventy-third session at Newark, New Jersey, June 4th. The Rev. A. R. Van Nest, D. D., of Philadelphia, was chosen Moderator. The committee appointed at the previous session on the consolidation of boards presented majority and minority reports. The minority report was adopted. It declared it inexpedient to make any changes in the corporate organizations of the benevolent boards, and recommended continued attention by them to means of reducing expenses as far as may be compatible with the best interests of the objects of their care. Since the constitution of the Church recognizes all baptized persons as members, provision was made to secure the full recognition of baptized children, for the insertion in the statistical tables of the Classes of an additional column of "Total of baptized members," to include such children.

II. REFORMED CHURCH IN THE UNITED STATES. —The following is a summary of the statistics of this Church as they are given in its "Almanac" for 1880:

SYNODS.	Ministers.	Congregations.	Members.	Members unconfirmed.
Synod of the United States.	204	433	65,607	37,764
Synod of Ohio*	162	340	24,560	11,307
Synod of the Northwest*	132	202	16,459	18,048
Synod of Pittsburgh*	52	114	9,722	7,836
Synod of the Potomac*	122	247	26,230	16,223
German Synod of the East.	42	88	9,183	5,759
Total, six synods	714	1,374	151,761	91,637

Number of Classes, 45; of baptisms during the year, 12,336 of infants, 1,005 of adults; of additions by confirmation, 8,426; of Sunday-schools, 1,364, with 94,346 scholars. Amount of contributions for benevolent purposes, $57,975; for local objects, $528,506. A foreign mission has been established under the direction of the General Synod in Japan, and was

* Report of 1878.

opened in May, 1879, with one missionary, and his wife as an assistant.

The most important event in the history of this Church during 1879 was the preparation of a declaration of faith designed as a full and final settlement of all differences hitherto existing within its borders. The commission which had been appointed for this purpose (see "Annual Cyclopædia" for 1878, page 720) met at Pittsburgh in November, 1879, and adopted as a basis of harmony a declaration the essential points of which are as follows:

The Reformed Church in the United States unites in the confession of her adherence to the doctrines of the Holy Scriptures, as set forth in the Heidelberg Catechism, taking the same in its historical (or original) sense; and declares that any departure from the same is unauthorized by the Church; and renewedly directs all her ministers, editors, and teachers of theology "faithfully to preach and defend the same." This action is not to be so construed as to forbid or interfere with that [degree of] freedom in scriptural and theological investigation which has always been enjoyed in the Reformed Church.

They agreed further upon the following articles:

I. We recognize in Jesus Christ and his sacrifice for fallen man the foundation and source of our whole salvation.

II. We hold that the Christian life is begotten in us by the Word of God, which is ever living and carries in itself the power to quicken faith and love in the heart, through the Holy Ghost.

III. We do not regard the visible Church as commensurate and identical with the invisible Church, according to the Roman theory, nor do we think that in this world the invisible Church can be separated from the visible, according to the theory of pietism and false spiritualism; but, while we do not identify them, we do not in our views separate them.

IV. We hold that in the use of the holy sacraments the grace signified by the outward signs is imparted to those who truly believe; but that those who come to these holy sacraments without faith receive only the outward elements and condemnation.

V. We have come to a clear apprehension of the fact that the Christian life is something broader and deeper than its manifestations in conscious experience.

VI. We hold the doctrine of justification through true faith in Jesus Christ, according to which only the satisfaction, holiness, and righteousness of Christ is our righteousness before God, and that we can not receive and apply the same to ourselves in any other way than by faith only.

VII. We hold the doctrine of the ministerial office according to which the ministers of the Church are not lords of faith, but servants, messengers, heralds, watchmen of Christ, co-workers with God, preachers of the Word, and stewards of the mysteries of God.

VIII. We hold the doctrine of the universal priesthood of believers, over against all Romanizing tendencies to priestly power; while we also assert the proper recognition of the ministerial office in the Church of Christ.

IX. We affirm our confidence in the truth of Protestantism, over against the errors of Rome on the one hand, and against the errors of rationalism and infidelity on the other.

X. All philosophical and theological speculations [in the Church] should be held in humble submission to the Word of God, which with its heavenly light should illumine and guide the operations and researches of reason.

The commission also resolved to recommend to the next General Synod to take steps for the appointment of a committee representative of all the Synods and tendencies in the Church, whose duty it shall be to prepare an order of worship, while, until this shall be regularly adopted, the use of the existing liturgies shall be permitted. It also recommended that the Synod adopt at the proper time measures for the revision of the constitution and the completion of the ecclesiastical system.

III. REFORMED CHURCH OF FRANCE. — An unofficial Synod of the Reformed Church of France was held in Paris from November 25th to December 5th, for the purpose of considering the condition of the Church, and of organizing the orthodox party as a free confederation within the Church recognized by the state. M. J. Pédézert was chosen Moderator. Two parties appeared in the assembly. One, led by M. Bersier, favored a course of conciliation toward the Liberals, and proposed that the Synod hasten and facilitate the convocation of a General Synod, and labor to induce the churches in general to demand it. The other party favored the organization of a regular unofficial Synod without regard to the Liberal party, but without surrendering the hope of securing an official Synod. The latter course was resolved upon, and resolutions were adopted "that, in two years, unless the Reformed Church of France has been placed under its regular synodal régime, a new unofficial Synod be called"; and "that the permanent commission shall convoke a new session of the present Synod before the lapse of two years, if it shall judge that circumstances render it necessary." Regulations were adopted for the formation of particular unofficial Synods in the several conscriptions, and for the choice of delegates to the General Synod. Adhesion to the Confession of 1872 was made an indispensable condition of participation in these acts; but unofficial minorities of churches which have separated from official churches because of their rationalism, and their pastors, as well as official orthodox churches and their pastors, were recognized as constituents of the Synods. The consideration of propositions in reference to measures for bringing on the operation of the regular synodal régime was deferred, and the local unofficial Synods were requested at their next sessions to take the subject into consideration and transmit their wishes to the permanent commission, to be communicated by it to the next Synod. A permanent commission of nine members was appointed, and charged with the duty of executing the decisions of the General Synod, and of convoking its next meeting.

REFORMED EPISCOPAL CHURCH. The following report of the statistics of this Church was presented to the General Council at its meeting in May and June, 1879: Number of parishes reporting, 70; connected with the same, 10,459 persons; Sunday-school scholars, 8,025; Sunday-school teachers, 787; baptisms, 609; confirmations, 399; received otherwise than by confirmation, 935; total increase,

1,334; communicants, 5,842. Amount reported for current expenses, $102,068; General and Missionary Fund, $7,938; Sunday-school offerings, $4,237; for other benevolent purposes, $13,585; total, $127,828. Present value of church property, $940,536. During the year new congregations have been formed in Wilmington, Del., Detroit, Mich., Indianapolis, Ind., and Cincinnati, O. Six church buildings have been opened and four begun during the year, and 27 ministers have been added to the clergy list, which now numbers—bishops, 6; presbyters, 70; deacons, 24; total, 100.

The seventh *General Council* of the Reformed Episcopal Church met in Chicago, May 28th. Bishop W. R. Nicholson was elected Presiding Bishop for the ensuing year. Differences had prevailed during the year between Bishop Gregg and his associates in Great Britain, threatening to divide the Church in that country. In consequence of them, Bishop Gregg had asked for letters of dismission, but the General Committee had declined to grant them. The action of the General Committee was approved, and the members of the Church in England were advised to meet together in General Synod and "retrace steps"; for the better success of which the Council advised "that all correspondence be mutually surrendered for destruction which bears on the existing differences; that the said Synod be presided over by a temporary presiding officer; that the brethren do then choose a Bishop to preside over their deliberations, and then proceed to organize their Synod and declare abrogated all canons, rules, and regulations which are plainly inconsistent with the principles of this Church, and substitute therefor such others as in the wisdom of the assembled brethren may be determined on as constitutional." The Synod under Bishop Sugden was recognized as the true Synod of the Church in Great Britain. Several alterations in the Prayer-Book, which were chiefly of a verbal character, or intended to make the position of the Church in respect to ritual more clear, were approved for final submission to the next General Council. Two reports from a committee respecting the episcopate came to this meeting from the previous meeting of the General Council. The majority report recommended that the Synods be authorized to nominate their bishops for approval and confirmation by the General Council; the minority report recommended that the right to appoint the bishops be vested in the General Council. The nomination of the Rev. A. S. Richardson by the Synod of Great Britain was confirmed. The Rev. P. F. Stevens was elected Bishop for the special, and the Rev. J. A. Latane for the general, missionary jurisdiction of the South.

The General Synod of the Reformed Episcopal Church in the United Kingdom (under Bishop Gregg), at its meeting held in Sidcup, Kent, in July, 1879, condemned the action of the General Council in America in confirming the election of Bishop Richardson; declared his election, confirmation, and consecration void and not to be recognized; resolved that the course of the General Council in this matter had created an unexpected and insurmountable "obstacle" to carrying into effect its own recommendation for a compromise between the two branches of the Reformed Episcopal Church in Great Britain; and approved the course which had been pursued by Bishop Gregg as justified by the necessities of the case.

In June, 1879, the Rev. Dr. B. B. Ussher, of St. Bartholomew's Church, Montreal, with the congregation of the church, withdrew from connection with the General Council and took steps for uniting with the Reformed Episcopal Church of the United Kingdom under Bishop Gregg. The cause of this action was dissatisfaction with the action of the General Council and the bishops with reference to the Church in Canada. The Presiding Bishop, after examining into the trouble, declaring that a crisis had arisen in the interests of the Church in the Dominion, issued a pastoral letter calling a representative convention of the churches in Canada to meet at Ottawa, July 30th, for the purpose of organizing a Synod and nominating a Bishop. The Convention was attended by the delegates of eleven churches in Nova Scotia, New Brunswick, Ontario, and Quebec. Bishop Latane was chosen to preside. A committee of three presbyters and three laymen was appointed to frame a constitution for a Synod to be submitted to the next meeting of the Convention for approval. The Presiding Bishop and the General Committee were requested "to take steps to have a Bishop elected, or make provision that one of the present bishops be assigned to the special charge and care of the Reformed Episcopal churches in the Dominion of Canada until the proposed Synod for Canada be organized and nominate its own Bishop." A resolution was adopted declaring that the Convention were satisfied to remain in the present position of the Canadian churches with regard to the General Council, and deprecating any separation from the Reformed Episcopal Church as it was originally organized by the late Bishop Cummins. An annual convention of the Canadian churches was decided upon, the next one to be held in the city of Montreal on the last Wednesday of May, 1880, and to be composed of all the clergy of the Church in the Dominion, including deacons who are engaged in church work, and one lay delegate from each parish, with one additional delegate for every fifty communicants in each parish.

REFUNDING THE NATIONAL DEBT.

The refunding of the national debt for the purpose of securing a lower rate of interest or extending the period of payment has from time to time engaged the attention of Congress ever since the organization of the Government under the Constitution in 1789.

The Confederation of States which preceded

that organization felt severely its lack of power to levy taxes for the support of the General Government. The Congress of the Confederation on the 18th of April, 1783, urgently recommended to the States the establishment of permanent funds for the liquidation of its debt, or, at least, for the payment of the interest thereon. The scheme recommended was that of clothing "the United States in Congress assembled" with power to levy duties on imported goods, but it was not adopted by the States so as to make it operative. Recourse was then had to requisitions on the States, but, no response being made thereto, both the principal and interest of the debt were left wholly unprovided for.

The debt outstanding in 1789 was made up of foreign and domestic loans contracted under the Confederation, and of the debts of the several States incurred in their individual capacities, on all of which large arrearages of interest had accrued. The unpaid foreign debt contracted by the Confederation consisted of the following loans (all at 5 per cent. except the French loan of 1779, which was at 4):

French loan of 1776	$153,688 89
" " of 1777	8,267,000 00
" " of 1779	1,815,000 00
" " of 1782	1,089,000 00
Spanish loan of 1781	174,017 18
Holland loan of 1782	2,000,000 00
" " of 1784	800,000 00
" " of 1787	400,000 00
" " of 1788	400,000 00

Total principal	$10,098,706 02
On this there were due arrearages of interest to January 1, 1790, amounting to	1,760,277 58
Making a total foreign debt at that date of	$11,858,988 60
There was also a debt due foreign officers who had served in the war of the Revolution, for which certificates had been issued amounting to	186,988 78
On these latter there were arrearages of interest to January, 1790, amounting to	11,319 32
In all	$198,208 10
The estimated principal of the domestic debt at that time amounted to	$28,858,180 65
On this the arrearages of interest amounted, as nearly as can be estimated, to	11,899,621 80
Total domestic debt	$40,256,802 45
There were also several arrears and claims against the late Government, outstanding and subsequently discharged, amounting to	$450,395 52
All these different sums made the entire debt of the United States on January 1, 1790	$52,764,889 67

In addition to this debt there were the individual debts of the several States, which had been incurred in the common defense of the country, the precise amount and character of which could not be then ascertained. It was estimated by Hamilton at that time to be in the aggregate about $25,000,000.

On the 21st of September, 1789, the House of Representatives resolved as follows: "That the House considers an adequate provision for the support of the public credit as a matter of high importance to the national honor and prosperity." The Secretary of the Treasury was accordingly directed to prepare a plan for such provision and report it to the House at the next session. In obedience to the resolution, on the 9th of January, 1790, Alexander Hamilton, then Secretary of the Treasury, transmitted to the House the first of his famous reports on the public credit, in which he recommended that the entire indebtedness, both State and general, be consolidated into a new loan of such character and upon such conditions as would maintain unquestioned the good faith of the nation, and make no change in the rights of the creditors without their consent. The adoption of the new Constitution, coupled with the belief at home and abroad that some satisfactory provision would be made for the several debts, had already caused a great advance in their market value, to the advantage of the holders, many of whom had paid therefor a less sum than the arrearages of interest amounted to. Notwithstanding this advance in value, there was but little opposition to providing for the domestic debt, and there had been none to paying the foreign; but the proposed assumption by the Union of the State debts met with bitter criticism and created much angry feeling, as some of the States were largely indebted to the General Government, while others had balances due therefrom, and no plan was proposed for an equitable adjustment of these differences. The recommendations of the Secretary, though once rejected by the House, were finally adopted, and were embodied in the act approved August 4, 1790, which provided for the refunding of the debts in the following manner.

For the payment of the foreign debt and the interest thereon, the President was authorized to borrow a sum not exceeding $12,000,000, the right to reimburse the amount within fifteen years being reserved; and under this authority the following loans were issued:

Loan of 1790, Holland	$1,200,000
" of March, 1791, Holland	1,000,000
" of September, 1791, Holland	2,400,000
" of November, 1791, Antwerp	820,000
" of December, 1791, Holland	1,200,000
" of August, 1792, Holland	1,180,000
" of 1793, Holland	400,000
" of 1794, Holland	1,200,000
Total	$9,400,000

These loans bore interest at various rates, some 4, some 4½, and some 5 per cent., and were made payable by installments in from ten to fifteen years from the date of their issue. The net rates realized on them varied from 94½ to 96½ per cent.

For the payment of the domestic debt a loan to its full amount was authorized, payable in the different certificates and bills of credit which had theretofore been issued by the General Government in settlement of the principal and interest of the indebtedness which had been incurred for the expenses of the war of independence. The stock issued upon this loan was of three kinds: 1. Stock in an unspecified amount bearing interest at 6 per cent. per annum, and subject to redemption by payments not exceeding in one year, on account of principal and interest, the proportion of eight dollars upon a hundred of the sums mentioned in the certificates of stock issued. This part of the loan was commonly known as the "six per cent. stock of 1790." 2. Stock in an unspecified amount bearing interest after the year 1800 at 6 per cent. per annum, and subject to redemption in the same manner and at the same rates as the preceding class. This stock was known as the "deferred six per cents." 3. Stock also in an unspecified amount bearing interest at 3 per cent. per annum, subject to redemption whenever provision should be made by law for that purpose. This was known as the "three per cent. stock." It will be seen that the six per cent. stock and the deferred stock were each in fact an annuity of eight dollars for a period of twenty-three years and some months. Of such sums as were subscribed to the loan, and paid in government certificates and bills of credit representing the principal of the domestic debt, subscribers were to receive two thirds in the "six per cent. stock of 1790," and one third in the "deferred six per cents." For such sums as were subscribed to the loan and paid in the interest of the domestic debt computed to December 31, 1790, or in indents of interest, subscribers were to receive "three per cent. stock" in the full amount so subscribed and paid. For the payment of the assumed State debts a loan of $21,500,000 was authorized, payable by the subscribers in the principal and interest of the State certificates to the amounts set forth in the table below, which shows the amount authorized to be issued in the redemption of the debt of each State, and the amounts actually issued. Of sums subscribed to the last-mentioned loan and paid in the principal and interest of the State certificates, the subscribers were to receive four ninths in "six per cent. stock of 1790," two ninths in "deferred six per cents," and three ninths in "three per cent. stock." The law also provided that books for subscriptions to the stock issued for the redemption of the domestic and assumed debt should be open for one year from October 1, 1790, and fixed a limit (stated in the table below) to which the assumed debt of each State would be received for the new stock issued.

The conversions authorized were rapidly made, and thus were completed the first funding operations of the Government; and while perhaps in the assumption of the State debts exact justice was not done in every instance, the plan is generally conceded to have been as equitable as any proposed. The honorable and satisfactory adjustment of these debts raised the credit of the country at home and abroad, and gave the young republic an enviable reputation for a far-seeing and honest public policy.

Under this authority there were issued of the several stocks amounts as follows:

Of six per cents..............................$30,068,897 75
Of deferred six per cents...................... 14,649,828 76
Of three per cents............................. 19,718,751 01

Total...................................$64,456,477 52

The following table shows the amount authorized to be assumed in the redemption of the debt of each State, and the amount assumed:

STATES.	Amount authorized.	Amount assumed.
New Hampshire	$300,000 00	$282,595 51
Massachusetts...........	4,000,000 00	3,981,733 05
Rhode Island	200,000 00	200,000 00
Connecticut...	1,600,000 00	1,600,000 00
New York...	1,200,000 00	1,183,716 69
New Jersey.............	800,000 00	695,302 70
Pennsylvania............	2,200,000 00	777,983 48
Delaware	200,000 00	59,161 65
Maryland...............	800,000 00	517,491 08
Virginia and Kentucky..	3,500,000 00	2,934,416 00
North Carolina..........	2,400,000 00	1,793,803 85
South Carolina	4,000,000 00	3,999,651 78
Georgia.................	300,000 00	246,030 78
Total...............	$21,500,000 00	$18,271,787 47

While the stock issued under this act was exchanged at par for the several issues mentioned, the holders of the domestic debt and debts of the States did not in fact obtain par in coin for the stocks converted by them into the new issue, as the market value of the latter did not at once reach par. From the purchases which were made from time to time by the Sinking Fund Commissioners, the following table has been prepared, showing the approximate market value of $100 of these issues from 1790 to 1795 inclusive:

DATE.	Six per cents.	Six per cents deferred.	Three per cents.
December, 1790.....	$70 00	$30 00	$31 00
December, 1791.....	90 00	45 00	45 00
April, 1792.........	100 00	53 00	60 00
April, 1793.........	87 50	53 00	50 00
December, 1793.....	95 00	57 50	51 00
May, 1794..........	90 00	56 00	50 00
April, 1795.........	100 00	69 00	60 00

It will be noticed that of the amount of $12,000,000 of foreign loan authorized to be issued, only $9,400,000 was sold, and that was sold at a discount, as has been stated, of from 3 to 5½ per cent. As a considerable portion of the proceeds was necessarily applied to the extinguishment of accumulated interest, they were not sufficient to complete the redemption of the amount outstanding; and on January 20, 1795, the entire foreign debt was found to be $13,745,379.53 —an increase since 1790 of $1,837,221.51. Mr. Hamilton, therefore, asked authority to issue an additional loan for the purpose of funding that amount, which authority was given by Congress in an act approved March 3, 1795. This act authorized the issue of a loan receivable by way of exchange in equal sums of the principal of the foreign debt, and provided that any sum so subscribed and paid should bear interest equal to the rate of interest which was then payable on the principal of the foreign debt so exchanged, together with an addition of one half per centum per annum, this extra interest being added for the purpose of inducing parties to surrender the certificates of indebtedness which they then held.

It appears that no arrangement could be effected for refunding the portion of the debt held in Holland; but for that held in France a new loan was issued as follows: five and a half per cent. stock, $1,848,900; four and a half per cent. stock, $176,000; in all, $2,024,900. The issue of this stock closed the account of the French debt, which by these transactions became merged in the domestic debt of the United States. Redemptions of the remainder of the foreign debt began in the year 1807, and were completed in 1815.

The next refunding operation of the Government was in 1807.

On January 1, 1806, there remained outstanding of the old six per cent. and deferred stocks about $31,800,000, and of the three per cents (nominal value) about $19,050,000; total, $50,850,000. Of these stocks the six per cent. and deferred were redeemable at the annual rate of eight dollars per hundred of principal and interest, as before stated. Under this arrangement these stocks sold in England, where a very large proportion of them was held, at about 95 per cent. on the unredeemed amount of each certificate, while the three per cents, which were redeemable at the pleasure of the Government, had a market value of about 60 per cent. of their nominal value. Secretary Gallatin in 1807 proposed that in exchange for all these stocks a common six per cent. stock should be offered to the public creditors; the old six per cent. and deferred stocks to be received at the par value of the unredeemed amount, and the three per cents at about 60 per cent. He thought the exchange would be advantageous to creditors, because, instead of receiving as they did quarter-yearly a small reimbursement of their capital, which was in effect a long annuity, they would by the exchange receive the whole amount within a much shorter time; and because an annuity for a term of years was always worth less in market than its intrinsic value, as exemplified by the market-rate of every lease or estate less than an absolute fee. He thought the exchange would also be advantageous to the United States, because the Government would thereby be enabled to reimburse the whole in less than nine years, instead of eighteen; and also because, if circumstances should render a resort to new loans necessary, the terms on which these could be obtained would in a considerable degree depend on the price of existing stocks. It was therefore desirable that that species the price of which had a tendency to regulate that of all others should be as high as circumstances would admit, and, as has been stated, the six per cent. and deferred stocks sold at less than their intrinsic value. A conversion of the three per cent. stocks, however, could not be so easily effected, they being worth more in market than a six per cent. stock producing the same annual amount; and it would therefore be necessary for the United States in converting this stock to make some sacrifices.

A law for the purpose mentioned was approved February 13, 1807. It provided that a subscription should be opened in the United States and at London and Amsterdam, to the full amount of the old six per cent. deferred and three per cent. stocks. For subscriptions in the old sixes or deferred stocks, a new six per cent. stock was to be issued for the par value of the unredeemed amount of each certificate. The interest on the new stock was to be payable quarterly, and the stock was to be subject to redemption at the pleasure of the United States. No partial reimbursement was to be made on any certificate, and six months' public notice was to be given of any intended reimbursement. For subscriptions in three per cent. stock, certificates equal to 65 per cent. of its principal were to be issued, bearing an interest of 6 per cent. payable quarterly, and reimbursable only with the assent of the holder, and after all the eight and four and a half per cent. stocks, as well as the stock to be issued by virtue of the act in exchange for the old six per cent. and deferred stocks, had been redeemed. It will be observed that the act created two kinds of stocks, one reimbursable at the pleasure of the United States, the other only after a certain period and with the assent of the holder. To distinguish these stocks, the first were called "exchanged," the other "converted" six per cents. There was issued of the "exchanged" sixes, $6,294,051.12; of the "converted," $1,859,850.70; total, $8,153,-901.82. It would appear that the great majority of the holders of the old stocks preferred them to the new, and the plan to refund was a partial failure.

The next refunding took place in 1812.

It seems that by an act approved March 14, 1812, Congress had authorized the issue of a loan of $11,000,000 at not less than par, the certificates therefor to bear interest at 6 per cent., and the proceeds to be applied to defraying current expenses. On June 24, 1812, Secretary Gallatin reported that of this loan but $6,460,000 had then been subscribed, including $200,000 offered on special contract, but not up to that time accepted. He said that the result of the loan was more than doubtful. "The old six per cent. and deferred stocks," he said, "are two or three per cent. under par, and any depression in the public funds would seriously affect the sales of the residue of the new loan. Nor does it appear eligible without an absolute necessity to give a premium or additional interest in order to obtain subscriptions for that residue. For, as it would be just in that case to place the first subscribers on the same footing, the charge to the public would be more than double the premium actually wanted to obtain the four and a half millions which are not yet subscribed." He therefore suggested a conversion of the old six per cent. and deferred stocks into a new six per cent. stock not materially different from that created by virtue of the act authorizing the loan of eleven millions. This he thought would have a favorable effect on the price of those stocks, and thereby facilitate the loan of that year, and prevent the necessity of applying in that and subsequent years the large sums which must otherwise be expended in the reimbursement and purchase of the public debt.

An act for the purpose of effecting a conversion of the old six per cent. and deferred stocks, as recommended by the Secretary, was approved July 6, 1812. It provided that a subscription to the full amount of the old six per cent. and deferred stocks should be proposed to the proprietors thereof, for which purpose books were to be opened at the Treasury and the offices of the Commissioners of Loans on the 1st day of October next ensuing, to continue open until March 17, 1813, the fourteen last days of each quarter excepted. For such part of the amount of the old six per cent. and deferred stocks subscribed and surrendered as should remain unredeemed on the day of subscription the subscribers were to receive certificates of United States stocks, bearing interest of 6 per cent. per annum, payable quarterly, from the first day of the quarter in which the subscription was made. The certificates were to be reimbursable at the pleasure of the United States at any time after December 31, 1824; but no reimbursement was to be made except for the whole amount of stock standing at the time to the credit of any one proprietor, nor until after at least six months' public notice of the intended reimbursement. Nothing in the act was to be construed to alter, abridge, or impair the rights of those creditors of the United States who did not subscribe for the exchanged stock. Under this act $2,984,-746.72 were subscribed in old six per cent. and deferred stocks, and exchanged for certificates of the new stock.

The next effort in refunding was an abortive attempt in 1822 to exchange a stock bearing an interest of 5 per cent. for a part of the six and seven per cents due in the years 1825 and 1826. The stocks due and redeemable in those years amounted altogether to the sum of $39,-819,700, a sum far beyond the capacity of the surplus revenues to meet; and the Secretary of the Treasury, W. H. Crawford, therefore proposed, in his report of December 21, 1821, to offer in exchange for $24,000,000 in these stocks a stock bearing a lower rate of interest and having a longer time to run. He said: "As the current value of the five per cent. stock created during the last and present years exceeds that of the seven per cent. stock, and of the six per cent. stocks of 1812 and 1813, it is presumed that the holders of these stocks will be disposed to exchange them for an equal amount of five per cent. stock, redeemable at such periods as to give full operation to the sinking fund as at present constituted. According to this view of the subject, twenty-four millions of the stocks which will be redeemable in the years 1825 and 1826 may be exchanged for five per cent. stock, redeemable, one third on the 1st of January, 1831, and one third on the same days of 1832 and 1833. This ex-

change of six per cent. stock, if effected on the 1st of January, 1823, will produce an annual reduction of the interest of the public debt, from that time to the first-mentioned period, of $240,000, and an aggregate saving through the whole period of $2,160,000. If the whole of the seven per cent. stock should be exchanged, the saving will be considerably increased."

An act to authorize the issue of a five per cent. stock to be exchanged for those bearing an interest of 6 and 7 per cent. was approved April 20, 1822. It authorized the opening of a subscription to the amount of twelve millions of dollars of the seven per cent. stock and of the six per cent. of 1812, and for fourteen millions of six per cent. stocks of the years 1813, 1814, and 1815. For the six per cent. stocks of the years 1812, 1813, 1814, and 1815, subscribed and transferred to the United States, the subscribers were to receive certificates of United States stock bearing an interest of 5 per cent. payable quarterly, reimbursable one third at any time after December 31, 1830, one third at any time after December 31, 1831, and the remainder at any time after December 31, 1832. For the sums subscribed in the seven per cent. stock, certificates were to be issued bearing an interest of 5 per cent. payable quarterly, redeemable at the pleasure of the United States at any time after December 31, 1833. The funds pledged by law for the payment of the interest and principal of the stocks which might be subscribed or exchanged were to remain pledged to pay the interest and redeem the principal of the stock to be created under this act. The Commissioners of the Sinking Fund were to pay out of the said fund the interest which might become due on the stock, and to purchase the certificates from time to time as they purchased other evidences of the public debt; and so much of the fund as might be necessary was appropriated for the redemption, and was to continue appropriated until the whole of the stock created was reimbursed. Nothing in the act was to be construed to alter, abridge, or impair the rights of such public creditors as did not subscribe.

This attempt to effect an exchange of stocks almost entirely failed, as only a very small sum was subscribed and exchanged for the five per cent. stock. The Secretary, in his report on the state of the finances for 1823, said that the entire amount exchanged under the act had been $56,704.77, as follows:

Six per cent. stock of 1813 (first loan)..... $23,317 82
Six per cent. stock of 1813 (second loan)..   23,386 95
Six per cent. stock of 1814 (first loan)....   3,000 00
Six per cent. stock of 1814 (second loan)..   7,000 00

       In all.................. . ... $56,704 77

The next refunding transactions occurred in 1824.

The Secretary of the Treasury, W. H. Crawford, in his report to the Senate December 31, 1823, gave a very favorable view of the public finances, estimating the revenue of 1824 at $18,550,000, and the balance which would be in the Treasury January 1, 1825, at $9,792,716.- 41. . He said : " Under existing laws there is no probability that any portion of the balance remaining in the Treasury on the 1st of January, 1824, or of the surplus which may accrue during that year, can be applied to the discharge of the public debt until the 1st of January, 1825 ; yet it is not deemed conducive to the general prosperity of the nation that so large an amount should be drawn from the hands of individuals and suffered to lie inactive in the vaults of the banks. On the other hand, the high rate of interest of the great amount of debt which becomes redeemable on the 1st of January, 1825, renders it inexpedient for the Government to apply to other objects any portions of the means which it may possess of making so advantageous a reimbursement. It is believed, however, that every inconvenience may be obviated if authority be given for the purchase of the seven per cent. stock, amounting to $8,610,000, during the year 1824, at such rates as may be consistent with the public interest. As it is now certain that the Government will possess ample means to redeem that stock on the 1st of January, 1825, it is presumed that the holders will be willing to dispose of it during the interval at a fair price ; and as a gradual conversion of it into money, at such times and in such portions as would be most favorable to its reinvestment, would be most advantageous to the moneyed transactions of the community, it is presumed that it would be most acceptable to the holders." He therefore recommended that the Commissioners of the Sinking Fund should be authorized to purchase the seven per cent. stock during the ensuing year at the following rates above the principal of the sum purchased : 1. For all stock purchased before the 1st of April following, at a rate not exceeding $1.25 on every $100, in addition to the interest due on such stock on that day. 2. For all stock purchased between the first of April and the last of July, at a rate not exceeding 75 cents on every $100, in addition to the interest due on the last-mentioned day. He stated that of the $10,331,000 of six per cent. stock redeemable in 1825, about $5,000,000 would probably be redeemed in that year, and there would remain unredeemed, after the application of all the means at the disposal of the Commissioners of the Sinking Fund, about $5,331,000. This sum he thought might be readily exchanged for five per cent. stock redeemable in 1833, and he recommended that provision should be made by law for such an exchange of so much of the six per cent. stock as should not be redeemed during the year 1825.

An act to authorize the exchange of certain stocks was approved May 26, 1824. It authorized the President to borrow on the credit of the United States, on or before April 1, 1825, a sum not exceeding five millions of dollars at a rate of interest not exceeding 4½ per cent., and reimbursable at the pleasure of the

Government at any time after December 81, 1831 ; the money borrowed to be applied, together with the money in the Treasury, to pay off and discharge such part of the six per cent. stock of the year 1812 as was redeemable after January 1, 1825. The Bank of the United States was to be allowed to lend the money or any part thereof, and the Secretary of the Treasury was authorized to raise the money by selling certificates of stock, not under par. Section 3 proposed a subscription to the amount of fifteen millions of dollars in the six per cent. stock of the year 1813, for which purpose books were to be opened at the Treasury and the several loan offices respectively, the subscription to be effected by a transfer to the United States of the credits standing to the subscribers on the books, and by a surrender of the certificates of stock subscribed. For the whole or any part of the sum so subscribed and transferred, certificates of stock were to be issued bearing an interest of 4½ per cent., and reimbursable at the pleasure of the United States, one half at any time after December 31, 1832, and the remainder at any time after December 31, 1833. The same funds already pledged by law for the payment of the interest and the reimbursement of the principal of the six per cent. stocks of 1812 and 1813 was to remain pledged for the payment of the principal and interest of the stocks to be created under this act ; and it was made the duty of the Commissioners of the Sinking Fund to cause to be applied annually such sums as might be necessary to discharge the interest. Nothing contained in the act was to be construed to impair the rights of such creditors of the United States as did not choose to subscribe to the loans. Under this act $5,000,000 were borrowed at par, and under section 3 of the act the sum of $4,454,727.94 was subscribed in six per cent. stock, and exchanged for stock bearing an interest of 4½ per cent.

Another attempt at refunding was made in 1825.

Upon the convening of Congress in December, 1825, the amount of the public debt was stated to be $88,545,003.38, redeemable as follows :

In 1825, of six per cents......................	$7,654,570 98
In 1826, of six per cents of 1813...............	19,002,856 62
In 1827, of six per cents of 1814...............	18,001,437 68
In 1828, of six per cents......................	9,490,099 10
In 1831, of five per cents.....................	18,901 59
In 1832, of four and a half per cents.........	5,000,000 00
In 1832, of five per cents.	1,018,000 72
In 1833, of four and a half per cents.........	6,654,153 72
In 1833, of five per cents.....................	18,901 59
In 1834, of four and a half per cents.........	1,654,153 72
In 1835, of five per cents.....................	4,785,296 80
At pleasure, five per cents...................	7,000,000 00
At pleasure, three per cents..................	18,296,281 45

By this statement it appears that, in the years 1829 and 1830, no part of the public debt was reimbursable excepting $7,000,000 five per cents and the three per cents ; but, as these bore a less interest than that portion of the six per cents of 1813 which was redeemable on the 1st of January, 1826, and which, for the want of means, it was thought could not be reimbursed before the years 1829 and 1830, the Committee of Ways and Means believed it advisable to provide for that portion by a new stock, at a reduced rate of interest and payable at those periods. The committee therefore recommended a new loan, or an exchange to the amount of $12,000,000, at a rate of interest not exceeding 4½ per cent., reimbursable in equal portions in the years 1829 and 1830.

An act for this purpose was approved March 3, 1825. The first section authorized the President to borrow on the credit of the United States a sum not exceeding $12,000,000, at not exceeding 4½ per cent. interest, $6,000,000 of the principal to be reimbursable at the pleasure of the Government at any time after December 31, 1828, and $6,000,000 at any time after December 31, 1829, the money borrowed to be applied to redeeming such part of the six per cent. stock as was reimbursable after January 1, 1826. The Bank of the United States was to be permitted to lend the sum or any part thereof, and the Secretary of the Treasury was authorized to raise the money by selling certificates of stock, not under par. Section 3 proposed a subscription to the amount of $12,000,000 of the six per cent. stock of the year 1813, all subscriptions in this stock to be counted as a part of the $12,000,000 authorized by the act to be borrowed. For the whole or any part of the sum subscribed in money or six per cents, certificates of stock were to be issued at not exceeding 4½ per cent. interest, payable quarterly, and reimbursable as provided for in the first section. The same funds already pledged by law for the payment of the interest and the reimbursement of the principal of the stock which might be redeemed or exchanged, were to remain pledged for payment of the interest and the reimbursement of the principal of the stock created under this act.

The low rate of interest offered made this loan a failure, as far as borrowing money was concerned, and the amount of stock exchanged under the act was comparatively small. The Secretary of the Treasury, in his report of December 22, 1825, says: "The proper measures were taken to execute this act, but have prevailed only to a limited extent. The operation of exchange, which was first resorted to, took effect to the amount of $1,585,138.88, and this sum, divided into equal parts, forms the two sums that now stand in the general table of the debt as redeemable in the years 1829 and 1830, while they have also served to diminish by so much the six per cent. stock of 1813. Proposals for the residue of the sum wanted were next issued, but no offers were received. The causes of the failure, it may be presumed, were the low rate of interest and short periods of redemption held out by the act, in conjunction with an activity in the commercial and manufacturing operations of the country affording higher inducements to the investment of capital."

Under this act stock was issued in the amount of only $1,539,336.16.

With these transactions the refunding operations of the Government closed, not to be renewed again for many years. The outstanding debt continued to be reduced by redemptions from the surplus revenues, until in 1836 it was practically extinguished. Subsequently, however, owing to insufficient revenues and the extraordinary expenses caused by the Mexican war, a new debt was incurred, amounting on June 30, 1861, to $90,580,873.72.

The unprecedented expenses incurred in the war of secession, during the four years from 1861 to 1865, were partly met by the imposition of heavy taxes, but largely by the issue of loans bearing various rates of interest and having different periods to run. Some of the earlier loans were redeemed from the proceeds of loans subsequently issued.

On August 31, 1865, when the debt reached its highest point, the interest-bearing debt was made up of loans bearing interest as follows:

Four per cents....................	$618,127 98
Five per cents....................	269,175,727 65
Six per cents....................	1,281,736,489 33
Seven and three tenths per cents..	830,000,000 00
Total interest-bearing debt....	$2,381,530,294 96

Some of these bonds were paid off, and others were converted into the five-twenty consols of 1865, 1867, and 1868, bearing 6 per cent. interest.

On March 18, 1869, Congress passed an act to strengthen the public credit, in which it is declared that "the faith of the United States is solemnly pledged to payment in coin or its equivalent of all its interest-bearing obligations, except in cases where the law authorizing their issue has expressly provided that the same may be paid in lawful money or other currency than gold and silver; but none of such interest-bearing obligations not already due should be redeemed or paid before maturity, unless at such, time United States notes should be convertible into coin at the option of the holder, or unless at such time bonds of the United States bearing a lower rate of interest than the bonds to be redeemed could be sold at par in coin." This act had the effect of improving the credit of the country, and, as it was believed that the outstanding debt might be refunded into bonds bearing a lower rate of interest, the matter was thoroughly discussed in the succeeding Congress, and an act for the purpose was approved July 14, 1870, entitled "An act to authorize the refunding of the national debt," of which the following is a copy:

Be it enacted by the Senate and House of Representatives of the United States of America in Congress assembled, That the Secretary of the Treasury is hereby authorized to issue, in a sum or sums not exceeding in the aggregate two hundred million dollars, coupon or registered bonds of the United States, in such form as he may prescribe, and of denominations of fifty dollars, or some multiple of that sum, redeemable in coin of the present standard value, at the pleasure of the United States, after ten years from the date of their issue, and bearing interest, payable semi-annually in such coin at the rate of five per cent. per annum; also a sum or sums not exceeding in the aggregate three hundred million dollars of like bonds, the same in all respects, but payable at the pleasure of the United States after fifteen years from the date of their issue, and bearing interest at the rate of four and a half per cent. per annum; also a sum or sums not exceeding in the aggregate one thousand million dollars of like bonds, the same in all respects, but payable at the pleasure of the United States after thirty years from the date of their issue, and bearing interest at the rate of four per cent. per annum; all of which said several classes of bonds and the interest thereon shall be exempt from the payment of all taxes or duties of the United States, as well as from taxation in any form by or under State, municipal, or local authority; and the said bonds shall have set forth and expressed upon their face the above specified conditions, and shall, with their coupons, be made payable at the Treasury of the United States. But nothing in this act, or in any other law now in force, shall be construed to authorize any increase whatever of the bonded debt of the United States.

SECTION 2. *And be it further enacted,* That the Secretary of the Treasury is hereby authorized to sell and dispose of any of the bonds issued under this act, at not less than their par value for coin, and to apply the proceeds thereof to the redemption of any of the bonds of the United States outstanding, and known as five-twenty bonds, at their par value, or he may exchange the same for such five-twenty bonds, par for par; but the bonds hereby authorized shall be used for no other purpose whatsoever. And a sum not exceeding one half of one per cent. of the bonds herein authorized is hereby appropriated to pay the expense of preparing, issuing, advertising, and disposing of the same.

SEC. 3. *And be it further enacted,* That the payment of any of the bonds hereby authorized after the expiration of the said several terms of ten, fifteen, and thirty years, shall be made in amounts to be determined from time to time by the Secretary of the Treasury, at his discretion, the bonds so to be paid to be distinguished and described by the dates and numbers, beginning for each successive payment with the bonds of each class last dated and numbered; of the time of which intended payment or redemption the Secretary of the Treasury shall give public notice, and the interest on

the particular bonds so selected at any time to be paid shall cease at the expiration of three months from the date of such notice.

SEC. 4. *And be it further enacted,* That the Secretary of the Treasury is hereby authorized, with any coin of the Treasury of the United States which he may lawfully apply to such purpose, or which may be derived from the sale of any of the bonds, the issue of which is provided for in this act, to pay at par and cancel any six per cent. bonds of the United States of the kind known as five-twenty bonds, which have become or shall hereafter become redeemable by the terms of their issue. But the particular bonds so to be paid and canceled shall in all cases be indicated and specified by class, date, and number, in the order of their numbers and issue, beginning with the first numbered and issued, in public notice to be given by the Secretary of the Treasury; and in three months after the date of such public notice the interest on the bonds so selected and advertised to be paid shall cease.

On January 20, 1871, an act was approved amending the above, as follows:

Be it enacted by the Senate and House of Representatives of the United States of America in Congress assembled, That the amount of bonds authorized by the act approved July fourteen, eighteen hundred and seventy, entitled " An act to authorize the refunding of the national debt," to be issued bearing five per centum interest per annum, be, and the same is, increased to five hundred millions of dollars, and the interest of any portion of the bonds issued under said act, or this act, may, at the discretion of the Secretary of the Treasury, be made payable quarter-yearly: *Provided, however,* That this act shall not be construed to authorize any increase of the total amount of bonds provided for by the act to which this act is an amendment.

At that time there was considerable doubt as to the ability of the Government to sell any of the bonds on the terms fixed by the law, as the six per cent. bonds which bore interest in coin were still selling in the market at considerably below par.

On February 28, 1871, the interest-bearing debt of the Government consisted of the following:

Statement showing the condition of the interest-bearing debt of the United States, as shown by the books of the Treasury Department, on the close of business, February 28, 1871.

TITLE OF LOAN.	Authorizing act.	Rate per cent.	When redeemable.	When payable.	Amount.
Loan of 1858	June 14, 1858	5		Jan. 1, 1874	$20,000,000
Loan of Feb., 1861 ('81's)	Feb. 8, 1861	6		Dec. 31, 1880	18,415,000
Oregon War Debt	March 2, 1861	6		June 1, 1881	945,000
Loan of July and Aug., 1861 ('81's)	July 17 and Aug. 5, 1861	6		June 30, 1881	189,318,100
Five-twenties of 1862	Feb. 25, 1862	6	After May 1, 1867	May 1, 1882	498,788,850
Loan of 1863 ('81's)	March 3, 1863	6		June 30, 1881	75,000,000
Ten-forties of 1864	March 3, 1864	5	After March 1, 1874	March 1, 1904	194,567,300
Five-twenties of March, 1864	March 3, 1864	6	After Nov. 1, 1869	Nov. 1, 1884	3,102,600
Five-twenties of June, 1864	June 30, 1864	6	After Nov. 1, 1869	Nov. 1, 1884	102,026,900
Five-twenties of 1865	March 3, 1865	6	After Nov. 1, 1870	Nov. 1, 1885	182,112,450
Consols of 1865	March 3, 1865	6	After July 1, 1870	July 1, 1885	264,619,700
Consols of 1867	March 3, 1865	6	After July 1, 1872	July 1, 1887	888,682,550
Consols of 1868	March 3, 1865	6	After July 1, 1873	July 1, 1888	39,668,750
Total		..	....	......	$1,922,843,700

The table on page 759 shows the market price in coin, less accrued interest, of the various securities of the United States Government from 1869 to January 1, 1879, inclusive, and is instructive as showing the state of the public credit at the dates specified. It will be seen that at the time of the passage of

the refunding act, July, 1870, the five-twenty bonds of 1862, which had been redeemable longer than any other class of bonds, and which would naturally be called in first, were worth in the market only $93.30 for each $100. The refunding act authorized the sale of the five per cents at not less than par, and it was

Statement showing the market price, less accrued interest, if any, of the various securities of the United States Government for January and July of each year from 1869 to 1879, inclusive.

DESCRIPTION OF SECURITY.

NAME.	Date of authorization.	Rate per cent.	When payable.	When redeemable.	Coin price of $100, excluding accrued interest—mean of highest and lowest in each month specified.					
					1869.		1870.		1871.	
					Jan.	July.	Jan.	July.	Jan.	July.
Sixes of 1881	Feb. 8, July 17, and Aug. 5, 1861, and March 8, 1868	6	May 1, 1862	Dec. 31, 1880, and June 30, 1881	82·12	88·10	96·25	97·19	100·70	102·56
Five-twenties of 1862	Feb. 25, 1862	6		May 1, 1867	81·62	89·26	98·56	93·80	97·72	100·62
Five-twenties of 1864	March 3 and June 20, 1864	6	Nov. 1, 1864	Nov. 1, 1869	78·90	87·15	98·14	98·20	97·10	100·28
Ten-forties of 1864	March 3, 1864	5	March 1, 1904	March 1, 1874	77·17	79·72	89·99	89·20	96·85	97·87
Five-twenties of 1865	March 8, 1865	6	Nov. 1, 1885	Nov. 1, 1870	79·27	87·61	98·14	98·20	96·87	99·95
Consols of 1865	"	6	July 1, 1885	July 1, 1870	79·11	87·31	98·05	98·27	97·18	99·98
Consols of 1867	"	6	July 1, 1887	July 1, 1872	79·34	87·18	98·20	98·38	97·86	100·10
Consols of 1868	"	6	July 1, 1888	July 1, 1873	79·76	87·18	98·05	98·14	97·81	100·88
Funded loan of 1881	July 14, 1870, and Jan. 20, 1871	5		May 1, 1881						
Funded loan of 1891	"	4½		Sept. 1, 1891						
Funded loan of 1907	"	4		July 1, 1907						
Currency sixes (P. R. R.)	July 1, 1862, and July 2, 1864	6	30 years from date.		73·7	73·5	90·32	90·35	99·87	100·61
Legal-tender notes*	Feb. 25, 1862						89·6	85·6	90·3	89·0

DESCRIPTION OF SECURITY.

NAME.	Date of authorization.	Coin price of $100, excluding accrued interest—mean of highest and lowest in each month specified.														
		1872.		1873.		1874.		1875.		1876.		1877.		1878.		1879.
		Jan.	July.	Jan.	July.	Jan.	July.	Jan.	July.	Jan.	July.	Jan.	July.	Jan.	July.	Jan.	July.
Sixes of 1881	Feb. 8, July 17, and Aug. 5, 1861, and March 8, 1868	103·27	108·50	108·80	109·92	105·83	106·62	105·86	105·88	107·61	107·74	107·25	107·05	106·07	104·86	106·53	106·90	104·25
Five-twenties of 1862	Feb. 25, 1862	99·90	99·68	99·73	99·40	99·66	101·14	101·02	100·86	99·74	(called)						
Five-twenties of 1864	March 3 and June 20, 1864	99·06	99·75	99·46	99·87	99·09	100·33	98·93	101·05	(called)							
Ten-forties of 1864	March 3, 1864	90·06	99·71	89·71	97·03	98·85	100·13	100·34	101·01	108·27	104·23	104·77	105·38	106·65	106·58	104·61	(called)
Five-twenties of 1865	March 8, 1865	100·67	100·07	100·68	101·06	99·88	105·80	101·19	102·53	102·73	101·17	(called)					
6s of 1885	"	103·05	99·88	100·78	100·91	108·93	105·65	104·46	103·13	104·74	106·06	105·06	106·83	101·06	100·58	101·60	(called)
6s of 1867	"	102·11	100·79	101·89	101·94	104·43	105·10	105·24	104·70	106·84	106·73	106·10	108·08	108·07	104·70	104·70	101·80 (called)
Consols of 1868	"	102·57	100·52	101·83	101·56	104·15	106·89	105·80	104·70	107·45	108·19	108·74	108·05	108·64	105·46	107·01	103·49 (called)
Fun ed loan of 1881	July 14, 1870, and Jan. 20, 1871	99·66	96·25	99·83	98·34		101·62	100·89	100·70	108·28	104·50	104·18	104·65	108·53	108·59	105·67	105·38 102·58
Funded loan of 1891	"					99·60	101·42					100·19	108·48	109·92	108·41	104·82	105·56
Funded loan of 1907	"														99·25	99·64	99·52 101·88
Currency sixes (P. R. R.)	July 1, 1862, and July 2, 1864	104·59	99·52	100·87	98·20	101·89	105·34	104·67	106·05	108·29	111·86	114·28	117·20	115·88	119·92	119·50	120·12
Legal-tender notes*	Feb. 25, 1862	91·7	87·5	88·7	86·4	89·7	91·0	88·9	87·2	88·6	89·4	94·0	94·9	97·9	99·5	100·0	100·00

* By the act of January 14, 1875, these notes were made redeemable January 1, 1879.

evident that until the credit of the country could be considerably advanced no successful steps toward refunding under this law could be taken. It will also be seen by that table that, after the passage of the act of March 18, 1869, the market value of United States securities uniformly and rapidly increased. So rapid was this advance that, in February, 1871, it was believed that sales of five per cents could be made; and, accordingly, on the 28th of that month Secretary Boutwell gave public notice that on and after the 6th of the following March books would be opened in this country and in Europe for subscriptions to the bonds issued under the refunding act. All the national banks in this country, and a large number of bankers both here and in Europe, were authorized to receive subscriptions. On the 1st of August following, the subscriptions to the new five per cent. loan amounted to $65,775,550, mainly made by national banks, and a like amount of six per cent. bonds was retired.

Early in that month an agreement was entered into with certain bankers in Europe and in the United States, by the terms of which the parties subscribing had a right to subscribe for the remainder of $200,000,000 of said bonds, by giving notice thereof at any time previous to the 1st of April next succeeding, and by subscribing for $10,000,000 at once, and an average of at least $5,000,000 of bonds per month during the intervening time, subject to the right of the national banks to subscribe for $50,000,000 within sixty days from the 25th day of August. It was also agreed that the subscriptions should be made through national banks, and that certificates of deposit therefor might be issued by said banks to the Secretary of the Treasury; that the bonds should be lodged with the Treasurer of the United States to the amount of the deposit; and that the banks should be made depositaries for this purpose under the provisions of the national banking act. Under this arrangement was initiated the plan by which the Government paid interest on the bonds called in and interest on the bonds issued for a return not exceeding three months in any one case. Secretary Boutwell, in his annual report to Congress for 1871, explained the transaction as follows:

By the act establishing the national banking system the Secretary of the Treasury was authorized to make them depositaries of any public money, except receipts from customs; and the act authorizing the refunding of the national debt directed the Secretary of the Treasury to give three months' notice of the payment of any bonds which, in such notice, might be specified and called for payment. In the same act it was provided that the money received for the new bonds should be used only in payment of bonds outstanding, known as five-twenty bonds. The statute proceeded upon the idea that the holders of five-twenty bonds should receive three months' interest upon their bonds after notice should be given by the Government. As this notice could be given safely only upon subscriptions already made or secured, the general necessary result, even in case the money were paid into and held

in the Treasury of the United States, would be a loss of interest for three months.

It was further agreed that the subscribers should receive as commissions whatever might remain of the half of one per cent. allowed by law upon the $200,000,000 after paying the cost of preparing and issuing the bonds. Under this contract the remainder of the $200,000,000 offered was sold, and the transactions were completed before the 1st of April, 1872.

On January 23, 1873, Secretary Boutwell made another contract with certain bankers, in which they agreed to take at least $10,000,000 of the five per cent. bonds, with a right to subscribe for the remaining $300,000,000. The other conditions of the contract were substantially the same as those of the agreement above mentioned.

Under the contract there were sold by Secretary Boutwell $50,000,000 of the five per cent bonds.

This arrangement appears to have been continued by Secretary Richardson, Mr. Boutwell's successor, who during his term of office sold under its provisions $51,494,700 of the five per cents, and also sold in June, 1874, to other parties, by special agreement, for one fourth of one per cent. commission, an additional $6,000,000 of the five per cent. bonds, the subscribers to pay the accrued interest to date of the maturity of the bonds called against their subscriptions, for all of which six per cent. bonds were retired. He also, under the act of December 17, 1873, issued of the five per cents $13,957,000 in exchange for an equal amount of the five per cent. loan of June 14, 1858.

On the 2d of July, 1874, Secretary Bristow, successor to Secretary Richardson, invited sealed proposals for the balance of the five per cents which remained unsold, $178,548,300, and in response thereto received various bids aggregating in amount $75,933,550. Of these bids there were accepted $10,113,550, at par and above. The proposition of an association of bankers was also accepted for the negotiation of $45,000,000 of the bonds, with an option for the balance of the loan; the subscribers to pay par and interest accrued to *date of maturity of each call*, the calls to be of even date with the subscription, and a commission of one fourth of one per cent. to be allowed upon the amount taken, the parties subscribing to pay all expenses incurred in preparing and issuing the bonds. The bonds were taken in accordance with the contract. The contract was renewed January 29, 1875, with conditions slightly modified, so that the contracting parties were allowed a commission of one half of one per cent. instead of one fourth of one per cent.; and under its terms the balance of five per cents was sold, and for the entire sales a like amount of six per cents was retired.

The entire amount of five per cents authorized by the refunding act having been thus disposed of by Secretary Bristow, Secretary

Morrill, his successor, on the 24th of August, 1876, entered into a contract with certain bankers for the sale of the $300,000,000 of four and a half per cents for refunding purposes, the parties to be allowed one half of one per cent. commission upon the amount they might take, they to assume and defray all expenses incurred in the preparation and issue of the bonds. Under this arrangement there were sold up to March 4, 1877, when Mr. Morrill's term of office expired, about $90,000,000, for which an equal amount of six per cent. bonds was called.

The credit of the country now rapidly advanced, and on April 6th Secretary Sherman, who had succeeded Mr. Morrill, addressed a letter to the associated bankers who had the contract for four and a half per cent. bonds, in which he announced that when the sales reached $200,000,000 he proposed to withdraw the bonds from the market. At that time the four and a half per cents were somewhat below par in Europe, and but little above par in this country. They continued, however, to appreciate, and before the 1st of July the whole $200,000,000 were taken, of which $185,000,000 were applied to refunding, and $15,000,000, by the consent of the contracting parties given on the 11th of May, to resumption purposes.

On the 9th of June, 1877, a contract was made with certain bankers for the sale of four per cent. bonds, with a proviso that the loan should be open to public subscription for a period of one month. This loan and the method of selling it proved very popular, and before the close of the thirty days during which subscriptions were open to the public at large, $75,496,550 of the bonds were sold, of which $25,000,000 were reserved for resumption and the remainder applied to refunding purposes.

The agitation by Congress of such measures as a repeal of the resumption act, and the reestablishing in the currency of the country of the silver dollar, the issue of which had been discontinued by the coinage act of 1873, somewhat alarmed investors, and retarded the further sale of four per cent. bonds. The opponents of resumption, however, were not able to repeal the resumption act, and the advocates of remonetizing the silver dollar succeeded only in having the coin reissued in amounts of not less than $2,000,000 nor more than $4,000,000 per month on Government account, the profit in its coinage to accrue to the Government instead of to the holders of bullion. On the 16th of January, 1878, Secretary Sherman, having concluded all contracts for the sale of four per cents, gave notice that he would receive subscriptions from the public at large for the sale of these bonds, and efforts were again made to popularize them and to facilitate their sale. The purchasers were to be allowed a commission of one fourth of one per cent. on the amount purchased in

excess of $1,000, and all national banks were invited to become depositaries for the purpose of aiding in placing the loan.

The process of refunding continued during the calendar year 1878 with more or less success, and at the close of the year there had been sold of four per cents for this purpose $173,085,450. The resumption act of January 14, 1875, provided for a return to specie payments on January 1, 1879. As resumption would remove the difference in value between the coin and paper currency of the country, the banks belonging to the Clearing-House Association of New York agreed with the Treasury Department that on and after that date they would take legal-tender notes in payment of all obligations of the Government. Under this arrangement payments for interest on the public debt and for bonds called in for redemption, which were theretofore made by the check of the United States Treasurer issued payable in New York, could be made after the 1st of January in legal-tender notes. The necessity for disbursing coin having thus been practically removed, there was no longer any need of requiring payments due the Government to be made in coin. So on the 1st of January, 1879, announcement was made that payments for bonds issued might thereafter be made in legal-tender notes; and a system of graded commissions was established, with a view of encouraging banks to make their subscriptions as large as possible. Under this new arrangement subscriptions came in very rapidly, and there was throughout the country unprecedented activity in the public stocks, which greatly advanced in market value from day to day. As many of the bonds called were held in Europe, the payment of them necessarily caused a drain of gold from the country, and this was beginning to cause a tight money market and embarrassment to the financial operations of the country. To avoid such embarrassment, Secretary Sherman on January 21, 1879, made a contract with certain prominent foreign bankers, by which $5,000,000 a month of the four per cent. consols were to be taken in England, that amount being deemed sufficient to prevent the shipment of gold from this country to pay for called bonds. The plan resulted successfully.

Meanwhile Congress, by an act approved January 25, 1879, authorized the exchange of the four per cent. consols of 1907 for an equal amount of any outstanding uncalled six per cent. five-twenty bonds of the United States, the Department to pay the holders of the bonds exchanged the accrued interest and additional interest for a period of three months. Under this authority there were exchanged for five-twenty six per cent. bonds $806,000. To further facilitate the refunding operations of the Government, Congress, by an act approved February 26, 1879, authorized the issue of refunding certificates in sums of $10, bearing interest at the rate of 4 per cent. per annum, and convertible at any time, with accrued interest, into the four per cent. bonds described in the refunding act—the money received to be applied only in the payment of bonds bearing interest at a rate not less than 5 per cent.

Apprehensions that there would be difficulty in settlements on the 1st of April, 1879, for the large amount of bonds which had been subscribed for in January, caused a temporary depreciation in the price of the bonds and certificates. It was believed, however, that this depreciation was but temporary, and that, when it was found that the settlements could be made without difficulty, the bonds and certificates would again appreciate in value. To secure to the Government the advantage of the appreciation, Secretary Sherman on March 4, 1879, gave notice that when the outstanding five-twenty six per cent. bonds of the United States should be covered by subscriptions to the four per cent. consols of 1907, the latter would be withdrawn from sale under the terms proposed in the Department's circular of January 1, 1879, and the terms stated in the contract of January 21, 1879.

As soon as the 1st of April passed, and without embarrassment in the settlement of balances, subscriptions poured in rapidly. On the 4th of that month one subscription was received for $40,000,000. This was followed by a subscription of $10,000,000, another of $2,000,000, two more of $25,000,000 each, and another of $30,000,000, together with others of less amounts. Of these, $59,565,700 were accepted, and $60,919,800, which came too late, were rejected, and further sales ceased.

The policy of withdrawing further sales of the bonds under the offer of January 1st proved to be a wise one; and immediately after the suspension of sales of certificates and bonds on April 4th, as above stated, steps were taken with a view of again offering them at an advance upon their previous price. On April 16th there were offered to the public $150,000,000 of the four per cents at a premium of one half of one per cent., and in addition thereto about $45,000,000 of refunding certificates, the proceeds of the whole being sufficient to redeem the outstanding ten-forty bonds, which were all the bonds redeemable at that time. The four per cents were also offered in exchange for the ten-forties, as authorized by the act of January 25, 1879. Before the close of the day subscriptions under the new terms for $2,000,000 of the bonds offered were received. The next day came one for $10,000,000, followed by others of $1,000,000, $2,000,000, and $4,000,000 respectively, and others for smaller amounts; and just before the close of business on that day, a subscription was received from one bank, representing a large number of private bankers in New York, for the entire amount of bonds offered and $40,000,000 of the refunding certificates. Subscriptions were received and accepted for $149,389,650, and received and declined for $34,755,000. Exchanges were also

made to the amount of $2,089,500. The subscription of $40,000,000 for the refunding certificates was also declined, the evident intent of the law being that they should be distributed as far as practicable among the people. To bring the certificates within the reach of small investors, on and after April 18th their sale was restricted to Independent Treasury officers and public officers bonded for that purpose, and to sums not exceeding $100 at one time. In response to the invitation to become depositaries for the sale of these certificates, 509 public officers and 76 national banks were designated for the purpose, and engaged in the sale.

The sale of the certificates was completed in June, 1879, and the proceeds were applied to the redemption of the ten-forty bonds. The certificates were sold as follows:

By public officers designated as depositaries..... $28,569,200
By national banks............................... 1,197,670
By Independent Treasury officers................. 10,245,880

In all.................................... $40,012,750

Thus was accomplished the refunding of all the bonds which were then redeemable, without the loss of a dollar, and to the great advantage of the country.

The entire amount of four and a half per cent. bonds issued by Secretary Sherman for refunding purposes has been $135,000,000; of four per cent. bonds and refunding certificates, $710,345,950; making a total of $845,345,950; for which were redeemed of six per cent. bonds $651,195,700, and of five per cent. bonds $194,150,250, resulting in an annual saving in the interest charge of $14,290,416.50.

The following table shows all the transactions under the refunding acts since 1870, with the amount of annual interest charge saved thereon:

TITLE OF LOAN.	Rate per cent.	Amount refunded.	Annual interest charge.
Loan of 1858	5	$14,217,000	
Ten-forties of 1864 ...	5	193,890,250	$10,405,862 50
Five-twenties of 1862.	6	401,148,750	
Five-twenties of Mar., 1864	6	1,327,100	
Five-twenties of June, 1864	6	59,185,450	
Five-twenties of 1865.	6	160,144,500	71,234,822 00
Consols of 1865.......	6	211,837,050	
Consols of 1867.......	6	316,423,800	
Consols of 1868.......	6	87,677,050	
Total	..	$1,395,345,950	$81,639,684 50

In place of the above bonds there have been issued bonds bearing interest as follows:

TITLE OF LOAN.	Rate per cent.	Amount issued.	Annual interest charge.
Funded loan of 1881......	5	$500,000,000	$25,000,000
Funded loan of 1891......	4½	185,000,000	8,325,000
Funded loan of 1907, including refunding certificates.................	4	710,345,950	28,413,583
Total.................	..	$1,395,345,950	$61,738,583

It thus appears that the annual saving hereafter in the interest charge by means of the refunding operations will be $19,900,846.50.

J. K. UPTON,
Assistant Secretary of the Treasury.

RESUMPTION OF SPECIE PAYMENTS.

The resumption of specie payments by the Government took place on January 1, 1879, as provided by law.

No precise date can be fixed when the suspension of specie payments thus resumed occurred, the suspension not having been authorized or sanctioned by law. The banks in the city of New York suspended coin payments on the 30th of December, 1861. Their example was necessarily followed by most of the banks throughout the country, and the Government soon yielded to the same necessity in respect to the United States notes then outstanding and matured. Gold commanded a nominal premium throughout the year 1861, but the first recorded quotation of it was at 103 on January 13, 1862. Of the $50,000,000 of notes which had been authorized by the acts of July 17 and August 5, 1861, there were outstanding at the time of the suspension $33,460,000. After the suspension, on February 12, 1862, an additional emission of $10,000,000 was authorized, making in all $60,000,000. These notes bore no interest, were payable on demand, and receivable in payment of public dues, and could be reissued. They were not intended, however, for general circulation as money, but the practical demonetization of coin as a circulating medium left only the depreciated issues of the banks to supply the entire circulation of the country; and these proving insufficient to meet the extraordinary demands for circulation consequent upon the war, the Treasury notes were drafted into the service as substitutes for the coin which had fled the country.

The balance in the Treasury on December 30, 1860, subject to the warrant of the Secretary, was $2,078,257. During the calendar year 1861 the net receipts of the Treasury from all sources were $218,224,077.64 as against $59,217,030.19 for the previous year; but the expenditures had increased in a still greater ratio, and in January, 1862, the Treasury was unable to answer the requisitions upon it for disbursements. Additional resources to carry on the Government became imperative, but no coin was left in the country for which to sell a loan. Of the depreciated bank currency there was believed to be then in existence only about $150,000,000, and this with the $60,000,000 of Treasury notes made the entire circulation of the country only $210,000,000; and to collect these notes together for public disbursement, scattered as they were throughout the country, would be almost as hopeless a task as to issue a loan for coin and bring back to the country the metallic currency which had gone abroad to pay foreign indebtedness. To meet this emergency, and with a view of utilizing all the resources of the country, Congress, by act approved February 25, 1862, authorized the issue of $150,000,000 of notes not bearing interest, payable at the Treasury of the United States, and of such denominations as the Secretary of the Treasury might deem expedient, not less than five dollars each. Of this amount $60,000,000 were for the redemption of the notes of July 17 and August 5, 1861. The authorizing act further provided as follows:

That the amount of the two kinds of notes together shall at no time exceed the sum of one hundred and fifty millions of dollars, and such notes herein authorized shall be receivable in payment of all taxes, internal duties, excises, debts, and demands of every kind due to the United States, except duties on imports, and of all claims and demands against the United States of every kind whatsoever, except for interest upon bonds and notes, which shall be paid in coin, and shall also be lawful money and a legal tender in payment of all debts public and private, within the United States, except duties on imports and interest as aforesaid. And any holders of said United States notes depositing any sum not less than fifty dollars, or some multiple of fifty dollars, with the Treasurer of the United States, or either of the Assistant Treasurers, shall receive in exchange therefor duplicate certificates of deposit, one of which may be transmitted to the Secretary of the Treasury, who shall thereupon issue to the holder an equal amount of bonds of the United States, coupon or registered, as may by said holder be desired, bearing interest at the rate of six per centum per annum, payable semi-annually, and redeemable at the pleasure of the United States after five years, and payable twenty years from the date thereof. And such United States notes shall be received the same as coin, at their par value, in payment for any loans that may be hereafter sold or negotiated by the Secretary of the Treasury, and may be reissued from time to time as the exigencies of the public interest shall require.

Later in the same session, by act approved March 17, 1862, Congress declared the outstanding notes of July 17 and February 12, 1862, to be a legal tender in like manner, for the same purposes and to the same extent, as the notes authorized by the act of February 25, 1862. Still later, by act of July 11, 1862, Congress authorized an additional issue of $150,000,000 of notes of similar character, and, like those already issued, exchangeable for bonds; and also provided that the Secretary might receive and cancel any notes heretofore issued, and in lieu thereof issue an equal amount of notes authorized by this act. The act also provided that not less than $50,000,000 of these notes should be reserved for the payment of certain deposits, to be used only when, in the judgment of the Secretary of the Treasury, the same or any part thereof might be needed for that purpose. By act of July 17th following Congress authorized the issue of postage and revenue stamps for use as fractional currency, preferring this expedient to metallic coins or tokens reduced in value below the existing standard, making them receivable in payment of all dues to the United States under five dollars, and exchangeable for United States notes when presented in sums of not less than five dollars.

Under these several acts a total circulation of $250,000,000 could be issued, and in an improbable contingency $50,000,000 more; also a supply of fractional currency. These issues, together with the issues of bonds, relieved the Treasury from its embarrassment, and on the 1st of July, 1862, not a requisition upon the Treasury from any department remained unhonored. The military reverses of June, July, and August of that year, however, injuriously affected the financial condition of the country, and Congress, by act of March 3, 1863, authorized, among other measures, an additional issue of $150,000,000 of notes having substantially the same qualities and restrictions as those theretofore issued, and provided that in lieu of any other United States notes returned to the Treasury and destroyed there might be issued an equal amount of notes authorized by this act. It also provided that holders of United States notes, issued under and by virtue of the several acts heretofore cited, must present them for the purpose of exchanging them for bonds on or before the 1st day of July, 1863, and that thereafter the right to thus exchange them should cease and determine. The same act also provided that in lieu of the postage and revenue stamps authorized for use as fractional currency, commonly called postal currency, there might be issued fractional notes of like amounts and in such form as might be deemed expedient; the whole amount of fractional currency issued, including postage and revenue stamps, not to exceed $50,000,000. Under these several acts there could be issued of legal-tender notes $450,000,000, and of fractional currency $50,000,000. No additional issue of notes was thereafter authorized.

The issue of Treasury notes by the Government was no new departure, but the notes issued under the several acts above stated bore certain qualities not given to any issued prior to 1861. They were declared by law to be lawful money and a legal tender for all debts, public and private, except for duties on imports and interest on the public debt, and they were convertible into interest-bearing bonds. Their convertible property, however, ceased to exist on the first of July, 1863, and since that date the Government has had for the first time in its history a national currency of its own notes—notes not convertible into other obligations and not redeemable at any specified time or place. These notes were both a loan to the Government and a national currency. The only justification attempted for their issue was that it was a war measure, one of necessity, not choice; and the notes were not expected to survive the exigencies which caused their issue. It proved, however, a most important measure. For, right or wrong, the employment of these notes as a legal-tender currency has exerted a most powerful and decisive influence over the property and material interests of every individual in the United States, and has become a tremendous factor in every problem, political, social, or economical. The notes were first issued April 1, 1862, and their issue gradually increased in amount un-

til January 30, 1864, on which day there were outstanding $449,338,902, the highest point reached. By act approved June 30, 1864, Congress directed that the total amount of United States notes issued or to be issued should never exceed $400,000,000, and such additional sum, not exceeding $50,000,000, as might be temporarily required for the redemption of temporary loans. Despite this restriction as to the amount of the notes which could be issued, and the extraordinary properties with which they were endowed, their value depreciated until on July 11, 1864, they were worth but 35 cents on a dollar, and their value fluctuated from day to day, unsettling prices of commodities, stimulating speculation, and creating distrust and apprehension in all business circles. A retirement of the amount in excess of four hundred millions was gradually made, in conformity with the law and a generally approved policy of retiring the notes as rapidly as practicable.

Secretary McCulloch, in his annual report for 1865, expressed his opinion that the legal-tender acts were war measures passed in a great emergency; that they should be regarded only as temporary; that they ought not to remain in force a day longer than was necessary to enable the people to prepare for a return to the gold standard; and that the work of retiring the notes which had been issued should be commenced without delay, and carefully and persistently continued until all were retired. The House of Representatives on December 18, 1865, under a suspension of the rules by a vote of 144 yeas to 6 nays, resolved, "That this House cordially concurs in the views of the Secretary in relation to the necessity of a contraction of the currency, with a view to as early a resumption of specie payments as the business interests of the country will permit; and we hereby pledge coöperative action to this end as speedily as possible." To carry out this policy, Congress, by an act approved April 12, 1866, directed that, of United States notes outstanding, not more than ten millions might be retired and canceled within six months from the passage of this act, and thereafter not more than four millions in any one month. Under the authority of that act notes were retired until the amount outstanding December 31, 1867, had been reduced to $356,000,000; but a stringent money market, a decline in values, and the remonstrances of business men somewhat alarmed the country, and no further withdrawals were made. On February 4, 1868, the authority to reduce the volume of legal-tender notes below $356,000,000 was suspended by Congress, leaving that amount of notes outstanding.

There was, however, a general feeling throughout the country that specie resumption should be kept in view, and on March 18, 1869, an act of Congress "to strengthen the public credit" was approved. In this act the faith of the United States was solemnly pledged to make provision at the earliest practicable period for the redemption of the notes in coin. Some doubt arose thereafter as to whether the notes which had been retired and canceled under the act of April 12, 1866, could be reissued up to the limit in the aggregate of four hundred millions. Secretary Boutwell, believing that such authority existed, reissued of them in 1872 $4,637,256, but afterward retired $3,481,541. In the autumn of 1873, however, owing to the monetary panic, there was much distress in business and a great demand for money. To relieve the stringency of the money market, and to prevent if possible any further commercial disasters, Secretary Richardson reissued of the notes retired $24,844,255, making the amount outstanding $382,979,815, of which he subsequently retired $979,815, leaving outstanding $382,000,000; and Congress, by an act approved June 20, 1874, established that amount as the maximum limit to which the notes could be issued.

No further change was made in the amount of outstanding notes, nor any further legislation had in regard to them, until January 14, 1875, on which date was approved the following act:

AN ACT TO PROVIDE FOR THE RESUMPTION OF SPECIE PAYMENTS.

Be it enacted by the Senate and House of Representatives of the United States of America in Congress assembled, That the Secretary of the Treasury is hereby authorized and required, as rapidly as practicable, to cause to be coined, at the mints of the United States, silver coins of the denominations of ten, twenty-five, and fifty cents, of standard value, and to issue them in redemption of an equal number and amount of fractional currency of similar denominations, or, at his discretion, he may issue such silver coins through the mints, the sub-treasuries, public depositaries, and post-offices of the United States; and, upon such issue, he is hereby authorized and required to redeem an equal amount of such fractional currency, until the whole amount of such fractional currency outstanding shall be redeemed.

SEC. 2. That so much of section three thousand five hundred and twenty-four of the Revised Statutes of the United States as provides for a charge of one fifth of one per centum for converting standard gold bullion into coin is hereby repealed; and hereafter no charge shall be made for that service.

SEC. 3. That section five thousand one hundred and seventy-seven of the Revised Statutes, limiting the aggregate amount of circulating notes of national banking associations, be, and is hereby, repealed; and each existing banking association may increase its circulating notes in accordance with existing law without respect to said aggregate limit; and new banking associations may be organized in accordance with existing law without respect to said aggregate limit; and the provisions of law for the withdrawal and redistribution of national-bank currency among the several States and Territories are hereby repealed. And whenever, and so often, as circulating notes shall be issued to any such banking association, so increasing its capital or circulating notes, or so newly organized as aforesaid, it shall be the duty of the Secretary of the Treasury to redeem the legal-tender United States notes in excess only of three hundred millions of dollars, to the amount of eighty per centum of the sum of national-bank notes so issued to any such banking association as aforesaid, and to continue such redemption as such circulating notes are issued until there shall be outstanding the sum of three hundred million dollars of such legal-tender United States notes, and no more.

And on and after the first day of January, anno Domini eighteen hundred and seventy-nine, the Secretary of the Treasury shall redeem in coin the United States legal-tender notes then outstanding, on their presentation for redemption at the office of the Assistant Treasurer of the United States in the city of New York, in sums of not less than fifty dollars. And to enable the Secretary of the Treasury to prepare and provide for the redemption in this act authorized or required, he is authorized to use any surplus revenues from time to time in the Treasury not otherwise appropriated, and to issue, sell, and dispose of, at not less than par in coin, either of the descriptions of bonds of the United States described in the act of Congress approved July fourteenth, eighteen hundred and seventy, entitled "An act to authorize the refunding of the national debt," with like qualities, privileges, and exemptions, to the extent necessary to carry this act into full effect, and to use the proceeds thereof for the purposes aforesaid. And all provisions of law inconsistent with the provisions of this act are hereby repealed.

It will be seen that the above act provided —first, for the manufacture and issue of subsidiary silver coins in redemption of the outstanding fractional paper notes; second, for an unlimited issue of national-bank notes, with a provision for the retirement of legal-tender notes to the extent of 80 per cent. of such issue, until the amount of legal-tender notes outstanding should be reduced to three hundred millions; and, third, for the redemption in coin of the legal-tender notes, on presentation in sums of fifty dollars and upward at the Sub-Treasury in New York on and after January 1, 1879. To carry out the purposes of this act, ample authority was given the Secretary of the Treasury to apply all surplus revenues in coin and also to issue at par an unlimited amount of bonds of the description authorized by the refunding act.

At the time of the passage of this act there were in the Treasury about two million ounces of fine silver bullion. The fractional notes had been gradually approaching par in coin, while the gold price of silver had been gradually falling, and no doubt was entertained as to the possibility of putting and keeping the silver in circulation unless its relative value increased. In this connection the following quotation from the report of the Superintendent of the Mint for 1875 is of interest:

The depreciation of United States legal-tender notes, which commenced soon after their issue took place, caused the silver coins to be exported, and rendered the employment of a substitute necessary. The issue of fractional notes was undoubtedly preferable to the debasement of the silver coins, but their permanent use is neither desirable nor practicable. The annual issue, being about $36,000,000 on a circulation of from $40,000,000 to $45,000,000, shows the average life of these notes to be, say, fifteen months. The estimates of the Treasury officers having charge of the business show the necessary expense of maintaining this currency, during the last fiscal year, to have been $1,410,740. This does not include the expense attending the handling of the fractional notes at the different sub-treasuries and depositaries, all of which receive them for redemption, and which, if added to the expenses incurred at the Department, would probably show the total cost of maintaining the fractional currency to be equal to about 5 per cent. on the annual issue, and corresponding with the interest on the amount of bonds which may have to be sold to procure, say, $36,000,-

000 (gold value) in silver bullion for coinage, and which would give silver coins of the nominal value of $45,000,000.

Notwithstanding the expense incurred, and the care which has been exercised by the Government, to renovate and keep the fractional currency in good condition, it is well known that a large percentage of the notes in circulation, particularly in localities not convenient to banks, are deteriorated to an extent rendering them quite unfit for use. It has also been counterfeited to a much greater extent than coin, and the detection of the spurious notes is infinitely more difficult than of counterfeit coins. The loss to the public from this source must ultimately be very considerable. The "wastage," as the small percentage of these notes worn out or destroyed while in circulation may be properly termed, falls mostly upon a class of people the least able to bear it. It is no satisfaction to a man who suffers the loss of a tenth of his day's wages by receiving a 25-cent note which no one will accept from him in payment, to be told that it reduces to that extent the expenses of the issue of such money by the Government of the United States.

The expense of manufacturing the subsidiary silver coins is estimated by the mint officers at from 1½ to 2 per cent., the rate being less when the mints are worked to their maximum capacity. The total expense attending the manufacture of the coinage of the last fiscal year ($43,854,708) was $889,370, or about 50 per cent. of the expense of maintaining the fractional currency. In this estimate the seigniorage realized on the silver and minor coinage ($436,105.81) has not been considered as reducing the cost of coinage, the same being regarded as a gain to the Government, and not an earning by the mints.

The rule of the principal countries is to redeem in kind the subsidiary silver coins when worn to an extent rendering the inscriptions illegible. A long period, probably fifty years, would elapse before any considerable portion of a new issue of silver coins would diminish in weight by abrasion to an extent sufficient to require their withdrawal. The advantage in this respect of silver coins over paper fractional currency is so great as not to admit of comparison. Moreover, their bullion-value, when presented for exchange for new pieces, would of course be the same, or nearly so, as when issued, less the loss by wear. The seigniorage or gain to the Treasury on the subsidiary silver coins will be from 10 to 12 per cent., and more than sufficient to defray the necessary expenses of coining, distribution, and maintenance in good condition.

The purchase of bullion and the manufacture of subsidiary coins were commenced as soon as practicable, and were continued until February 28, 1878, at which time there had been purchased 31,603,905.87 fine ounces of silver bullion, for which there had been paid the sum of $37,571,148.04 in gold coin—an average of 118·881 cents per ounce. There were coined of these fractional coins $42,974,931. Had the entire amount of fine silver purchased been coined, there would have resulted therefrom $43,689,519. Although the resumption act appeared to give ample authority for the manufacture and issue of these coins in redemption of the fractional notes, the Treasury hesitated about using the power, owing to the value of the notes and the coins to be issued being so nearly equal as to create apprehensions that the latter might be exported, and leave the country without fractional money of any kind; but Congress, by the act of April 17, 1876, directed the Secretary of the Treasury to issue the coins, and on the following day a circular was published

in accordance therewith. Silver, however, continued to depreciate, while the notes continued to appreciate, and consequently none of the apprehensions were realized. The notes were rapidly presented for redemption, compelling the Government to run its mints over business hours, and to use every exertion to supply the demand for the new coins.

There still remaining an apparent scarcity of fractional coin, Congress, by a joint resolution approved July 22, 1876, authorized the Secretary of the Treasury to issue subsidiary coin to an amount not exceeding ten million dollars, in exchange for an equal amount of legal-tender notes, such notes to be kept apart as a special fund, and to be reissued only upon the retirement and destruction of a like sum of fractional currency received at the Treasury in payment of dues to the United States, the fractional currency so destroyed to be counted as part of the sinking fund. The amount of fractional notes retired under this act up to January 1, 1880, was $25,834,429.37, and the amount still outstanding on that day was $15,674,303.78. The balance of the note-reserve fund for the redemption of fractional currency was, however, by the act approved June 21, 1879, directed to be reissued in payment of arrears of pensions, leaving the future redemptions of such fractional notes to be made from the current funds in the Treasury. To reimburse the Treasury for the depletion in its cash consequent upon the redemption of these notes, there was issued of five per cent. bonds of the description authorized by the refunding acts (funded loan of 1881) $17,494,150, and the surplus revenues of the Government supplied the balance.

Soon after the issue of these silver coins commenced, it became apparent that old issues of a like character were returning to the country and coming into circulation. The amount of coins thus returning continued to increase, and, as there was no authority for their redemption or exchange by the Government, the volume of subsidiary coins became so large as to cause inconvenience to the general business of the country. To correct this evil, Congress, by an act approved June 9, 1879, provided for the exchange of subsidiary coins for lawful money of the United States at all Sub-Treasury offices; and under the operations of this act these coins came in so rapidly that on January 1, 1880, the Government held of them $18,881,629.15.

Under the clause of the resumption act of January 14, 1875, authorizing the redemption of legal-tender notes in the amount of 80 per cent. of national-bank notes thereafter issued, the Treasury began to redeem notes in March, 1875, and continued to do so until May 31, 1878, on which date an act was approved forbidding their further redemption. There was thus redeemed of these notes an amount of $35,318,984, leaving outstanding to be redeemed in coin under other provisions of the resumption act $346,681,016. The cash in the Treasury was of course lessened in the amount of this redemption, and the loss was made up by the surplus revenues, which would otherwise have been applicable to the redemption of some other kind of indebtedness.

Toward the redemption of the notes in coin on the 1st of January, 1879, as further provided in the resumption act, no steps were taken before the administration of President Hayes, commencing March 4, 1877. On April 6, 1877, Secretary Sherman addressed a letter to a prominent banking firm, in which he announced his purpose to sell bonds to secure coin with which to meet the redemptions required, provided the surplus revenues proved insufficient to enable him to redeem the notes as required by law. He also announced that whenever the sales of 4½ per cent. bonds (funded loan of 1891) then being made for refunding purposes reached two hundred millions, he proposed to withdraw from the market the remaining one hundred millions authorized to be issued for refunding purposes, and to issue thereafter only four per cents (funded loan of 1907). Before the 1st of July ensuing the limit of two hundred millions was reached, and of the amount sold fifteen millions were applied to resumption purposes. On the 9th of June a contract was made by the Secretary for the sale of said 4 per cent. bonds, under which also twenty-five millions were reserved for resumption purposes.

This amount of forty millions was received in gold coin before October, 1877. In that month Congress convened in special session. Among its first measures was the introduction on one day of thirteen bills for the repeal of the resumption act. One of these bills passed the House on the 23d of the following month. This extraordinary change of sentiment had been brought about by various causes. The depression in business, which had existed since 1873, was attributed by many to the effects of the resumption act. A continually increasing value of the dollar in use rendered it more difficult for debtors to meet their obligations, and the passage of this bill in the House reflected with considerable truthfulness the feeling throughout the country. The bill was amended by the Senate, but in its amended form failed to receive the concurrence of the House. In this session was also agitated the policy of restoring to the currency of the country the old silver dollar of 412½ grains, the coinage of which was discontinued under the coinage act of 1873. The price of silver had so depreciated that, as compared with gold, a dollar of this kind was worth only about 85 cents; and if authority had been given for its unlimited coinage upon the deposit of bullion at the mints by private parties, as in the case of gold, the parties depositing it would, for a while at least, have profited to the extent of about 15 per cent. in the transaction. To prevent this advantage accruing to the holders

of silver bullion, and at the same time to restore the old silver dollar to its place in the currency of the country, Congress passed an act, which was approved February 28, 1878, directing the dollar to be coined at the rate of not less than two million dollars nor more than four million dollars per month, the bullion for such coinage to be purchased by the Treasury at current market rates, and the profit arising in the coinage to be retained by the Government. The act further provided that any holder of this coin might deposit it with the Treasurer in sums of not less than ten dollars, and receive therefor certificates corresponding to the denominations of United States notes, the coin representing such certificates to be retained in the Treasury for their payment on demand, and the certificates to be received for customs, taxes, and all public dues, and when so received to be reissued.

During the winter of 1877–'78 no further action was taken by the executive officers of the Government concerning resumption. On April 1, 1878, in an interview with the House Committee on Banking and Currency, Secretary Sherman announced his purpose to increase the coin reserve by the sale of bonds to the amount of fifty. millions. With this additional amount the total coin reserve in the Treasury applicable to resumption would be about forty per centum of the amount of legal-tender notes outstanding; and with this reserve the Secretary thought it would be practicable and prudent to commence the redemption of the notes on the appointed day as required by law. Four days later negotiations were begun in New York between the Treasury Department and the banks for the sale of 4½ per cent. bonds (funded loan of 1891) for this purpose; and after a little delay a sale was effected to the amount of $50,000,000 at a premium of 1½ per cent. The ability of the contracting parties to place the coin in the Treasury as proposed could not be doubted, and from that date there was but little fear of the success of resumption. Further efforts to repeal the law were abandoned, and the business of the country began to adjust itself to the basis of the approaching resumption of specie payments. The payments for the fifty millions of bonds were promptly met, and in addition thereto the Treasury reserved of the proceeds of sales of 4 per cent. bonds (funded loan of 1907), then being made, an additional amount of $5,500,000 in gold coin necessary for the extraordinary payment of that amount on account of the so-called "Halifax award."

In addition to providing the necessary coin reserve, every step was taken by the Treasury which the law would permit to maintain the reserve intact. On the 1st of January, 1879, about twenty-five millions of interest on the public debt, payable in coin, was to fall due; and, as the law required the redemption-reserve fund to be kept in New York, Secretary Sherman determined that the payment of coin on account of interest should thereafter be made only in that city, but gave permission to other Sub-Treasury officers to pay interest to all persons who might be willing to accept legal-tender notes. Arrangements were also made with the several assay offices by which gold could be purchased for legal-tender notes, whereby the Treasury was replenished to that extent for the probable coin payments in redemption of notes. Steps were also taken by which the Government, to a certain extent and for certain purposes, became a member of the Clearing-House Association of New York. Under this arrangement, in consideration of the Government's receiving and collecting its checks through the Clearing-House, that body agreed to receive all balances due it upon such checks at the counter of the Sub-Treasury in that city, and to accept legal-tender notes in payment of Government checks and drafts of all descriptions. As all interest-checks as well as checks issued in payment of called bonds were by law payable in coin, this agreement on the part of the Clearing-House, through which institution nearly all of the checks passed, relieved the Treasury almost entirely from the necessity of making actual coin payments after resumption took place. This necessity being removed, there was no longer any reason for requiring duties on imports to be paid in coin as provided by law; and the Secretary of the Treasury, in his annual report of December 2, 1878, announced to Congress his purpose to receive notes in payment of such duties. Congress adjourned for the holidays without expressing any opinion as to the legality or advisability of the action proposed, whereupon instructions were given to the Government officers to receive such notes in payment of duties, the notes to be redeemed in coin at New York on Government account whenever it became necessary. Instructions were also given to the Treasurer and other officers of the Department to close up in their accounts all distinctions between coin and currency, and after January 1, 1879, to recognize, in the accounts as well as in the money, that the Government had resumed specie payments, and that the several kinds of money in circulation were of equal value.

The preparations were so complete that on January 1, 1879, the date when resumption took effect, the Treasurer held of gold coin and bullion $135,382,639.42; of standard silver dollars coined under the act of February 28, 1878, $16,704,829; and of fractional silver coin, including silver bullion, $15,471,265.27. The amount of coin held by the Treasury as available for resumption purposes on that day, after deducting all matured coin liabilities, was about $135,000,000, or about 40 per cent. of the amount of notes to be redeemed. The thoroughness of preparation for resumption had quieted all apprehensions as to the success of the policy, and on the first day of resump-

tion only straggling demands for coin were made, the amount aggregating less than the amount of notes preferred by the holders of coin obligations. And during the entire year there were redeemed of the legal-tender notes only the amount of $11,456,536; while for the same period there were paid out of such notes on account of coin obligations more than $250,000,000. There were also received of such notes in payment of customs-dues in the year ending December 31, 1879, $109,467,456.

Thus, after much labor and sacrifice, the country was lifted out of the financial bog of depreciated paper currency, and with the resumption thus happily secured came a revival of business, an extraordinary demand for labor of all kinds, and a confirmation of that confidence which was so necessary for all business enterprises, and which had grown step by step with every movement made toward a specie basis.

The following table shows the market price, in coin, of $100 of the legal-tender notes of the United States for January and July of each year from 1862 to 1879 inclusive — mean of highest and lowest in each month specified:

YEARS.	MONTH.		YEARS.	MONTH.	
	January.	July.		January.	July.
1862......	97·6	86·6	1871......	90·3	89·0
1863......	68·9	76·6	1872......	91·7	87·5
1864......	64·8	88·7	1873......	88·7	86·4
1865......	46·8	79·4	1874......	89·7	91·0
1866......	71·4	66·0	1875......	88·9	87·2
1867......	74·8	71·7	1876......	88·6	89·4
1868......	72·2	70·1	1877......	94·0	94·9
1869......	73·7	73·5	1878.....	97·9	99·5
1870......	82·4	85·6	1879......	100·0	100·0

During the year 1879 coin flowed into the Treasury, while but little demand was made for its payment therefrom; so little, indeed, that the Treasury became drained of its notes, and in December it was obliged to require its creditors to receive in part payment of their dues 20 per cent. in coin—one half in gold coin, the other half in the new silver dollars.

Though resumption has been thus far firmly maintained, and there appears to be ample power, as far as human foresight can divine, to continue its maintenance, yet the question of continuing these notes in circulation, especially with their present legal-tender quality, is likely to be a vexed one in future politics.

A case involving the constitutionality of the legal-tender clause, as relating to contracts made prior to its adoption, was decided in the Supreme Court of the United States, December term, 1869, Chief Justice Chase presiding. The question presented for determination was whether the payee or assignee of a note made before the 25th of February, 1862, the date of the approval of the legal-tender act, should be obliged by law to accept in payment United States notes equal in nominal amount to the sum due according to its terms, when tendered by the maker or other party bound to pay it. The Court held that the defendant in error was not bound to receive from the plaintiffs such currency tendered to him in payment of their note made before the passage of the act mentioned. When this decision was made, the Court consisted of eight Judges, there being one vacancy caused by the death of Associate Justice Wayne. The five concurring in the decision were Chief Justice Chase and Associate Justices Nelson, Clifford, Field, and Grier. Of these, the first three were understood to hold the legal-tender clause to be unconstitutional for all purposes, and the latter two unconstitutional as to prior contracts only. Mr. Justice Miller dissented, and Justices Swayne and Davis concurred in his opinion. This decision was subsequently reversed, as below stated.

In the Supreme Court of the United States, December term, 1870, several cases came up similar in character, the controlling questions of which were: 1. Are the acts of Congress, known as the legal-tender acts, constitutional when applied to contracts made before their passage? 2. Are they valid as applicable to debts contracted since their enactment? The cases were considered by a full bench, and by a vote of five to four the Court held such acts of Congress constitutional as applied to contracts made either before or after the passage of the acts; thus overruling the previous decision in the matter. The opinion was rendered by Mr. Justice Strong, and concurred in by Justices Bradley, Miller, Davis, and Swayne. Chief Justice Chase delivered a dissenting opinion, as did also Justices Nelson, Clifford, and Field.

In this matter Secretary Sherman, in his annual report for 1879, submitted to Congress the following:

The Secretary is, therefore, of opinion that the provisions of existing law are ample to enable the Department to maintain resumption even upon the present volume of the United States notes. In view, however, of the large inflow of gold into the country and the high price of public securities, it would seem to be a favorable time to invest a portion of the sinking fund in United States notes, to be retired and canceled, and in this way gradually to reduce the maximum of such notes to the sum of $300,000,000, the amount fixed by the resumption act.

The Secretary respectfully calls the attention of Congress to the question whether United States notes ought still to be a legal tender in the payment of debts. [The reader is referred to page 367 of this volume for the remainder of the Secretary's remarks on the legal tender of the notes.—ED.]

J. K. UPTON,
Assistant Secretary of the Treasury.

RHODE ISLAND. The Legislature met at the usual time for the January session. An act defining the liability of towns and cities for property destroyed in times of riot was passed in the Senate, January 29th, providing that the owners of such property should be indemnified to the amount of three fourths of its value, and fixing six persons as the minimum number to constitute a mob. An act to rectify the boundary of the two Congressional districts of the State placed the whole of Providence in

the first district and the whole of Pawtucket in the second. By an act passed March 19th a bailor is enabled to release himself from his bond by producing his principal in court during the pendency of the action. A compulsory education bill was brought forward, and elicited considerable debate. It provided that every child between seven and fifteen years of age who should absent himself from school three times within three consecutive months without the consent of his parent, guardian, or teacher should be treated as an habitual truant, and every child who should not attend school for at least three months out of the twelve should be adjudged an absentee, the penalty in either case to be a fine of not more than ten dollars or detention in a reformatory institute of from six months to ten years; and that truant officers should be appointed in every town to enforce the law. A bill was passed prohibiting trap-fishing for two days in each week, between the 1st of May and the 1st of August. The three bills upon which most of the work and time of the January session were expended—a bill for the regulation of savings-banks, one reducing the State tax, and the compulsory education bill—all failed to pass. The General Assembly adjourned on the 11th of April.

The May session of the General Assembly began on the 26th and ended on the 30th of May. The savings-bank bill, postponed from the January session, was passed on the last day. It provides that the Supreme Court, upon application by petition in equity, may order the trustees of an institution under injunction, and unable to pay its depositors in full, to divide their assets into two classes, one class to be denominated the quick assets, and the other the reserved assets; that the Court may permit the institution to go on in business with the quick assets, and may order the deficiencies in the reserved assets to be apportioned among the depositors; that depositors shall give ninety days' notice of an intention to withdraw their funds; and that receivers shall receive not to exceed $2,500 per annum for services in winding up a savings-bank, and not more than $5,000 in all. The fees for jurors were raised from fifty cents to two dollars per diem by an act passed May 30th. Another act allows guardians or executors to whom letters have been granted by a court of probate to manage the estate of a ward or testator during the pendency of an appeal from the decree of the Probate Court to the Supreme Court.

The Prohibitory State Convention met at Providence February 25th. The existing State officers were renominated. The following resolutions were adopted by the Convention:

Resolved, That while we do not ignore other questions of principle and policy that pertain to the interests of the State of Rhode Island, we hereby express our firm belief that the questions of temperance, license, and the prohibition of the liquor-traffic outweigh them all in importance; and we reiterate our unalterable opposition to making that traffic respectable by legal licensing it, and again proclaim our entire confidence in the principle of the prohibition of the liquor-traffic by authority of law, as the best means of ridding our State of crime, pauperism, and an excessive taxation, and of promoting the virtue, prosperity, and happiness of all our citizens.

Resolved, That a prohibitory law, as well as every other criminal law, needs an efficient police force for its execution, and we therefore demand, in connection with the enactment of a law prohibiting the liquor traffic, an efficient force for its enforcement.

Whereas, The prohibition of the traffic in alcoholic liquors in the State of Maine, also in other parts of our land, and in other countries of the world, has proved a success; therefore,

Resolved, That it is the duty of all the members of our close temperance organizations, and of our open societies, to rally around the standard of prohibition, and unite their efforts and action to prohibit the traffic in ardent spirits.

Resolved, That this great success is a source of congratulation among ourselves, and of thanksgiving to Almighty God.

The Democratic State Convention was held in the State House in Providence, March 18th. The Hon. A. B. Lewis was elected Chairman. The following resolutions were adopted:

Resolved, That the Democratic party of the State of Rhode Island, in convention assembled, hails with joy the return of national legislation to the control of the Democratic party—the party which in the past has earned the well-merited reputation of being the party of the Constitution as bequeathed to us by the founders of the republic, and the party of the people; and that we deeply regret that the people of the United States are deprived, through the most unblushing fraud, bribery, and perjury that has ever disgraced the annals of our history, of having in charge of the executive branch of the country Samuel J. Tilden and Thomas A. Hendricks, who were on the 4th day of 'November, A. D. 1876, elected by an overwhelming majority to the offices of President and Vice-President of the United States; and further do we deplore that all of the persons who have been proved to have participated in this great wrong have been rewarded by being appointed to offices of great trust and honor at home or to represent the country in important positions abroad.

Resolved, That the Democratic party of this State, in regard to the internal affairs of the State, pledges itself and its members to a reform in the existing system of taxation in the State, and assures the citizens of the State that its influence will be exerted to establish such laws as will equally distribute the burdens of the State among all of its citizens, and to abolish all forms of double taxation; to such changes in the laws regulating institutions for savings as will restore them to the position of being institutions for the benefit of the laboring classes, from which they have in a large measure been diverted; and to so govern them as to restore such confidence in them as will again make them the favorite institutions of the frugal, in which they can be assured that their small savings will be faithfully, judiciously, and honestly administered and protected; to a change in the laws in regard to the registration of voters, so that all the citizens of this State may have a fair and equal opportunity to qualify themselves to vote at all elections, and for the enactment of a law which will not have the effect, as the present, of disqualifying nearly one half of the voters of this State who are not possessed of real estate; to a most thorough retrenchment in all expenditures by the State and towns, in order that the present burden in the form of taxation may be relieved from our now heavily laden industries; to the enactment of a law disqualifying any person from holding any office to which he may be elected by fraud, bribery, or intimidation, to which he may be a party; to such amendments of the Constitution of the State as will insure to all citizens of this State the right of suffrage without discrimination on account of race, nativity, creed, color, or previous condition of servitude—and particularly to have such change made in behalf of those who fought in the Union army in the late civil war, so that it may some day be said that our State has recognized their services in as generous a manner as the General Government has condoned the offenses of those who bore arms against the Government by rewarding them with the right to participate in the government of the country which they helped to save.

The nominations were as follows: For Governor, Thomas W. Segar; for Lieutenant-Governor, Dr. J. M. Bailey; for Secretary of State, David S. Baker, Jr.; for Attorney-General, Charles H. Page; for General Treasurer, Patrick Farrell.

The Republican State Convention for the nomination of State officers was held in Providence, March 19th. The existing officers were renominated unanimously by acclamation. No resolutions were adopted.

The State election took place on the first day of April. The Republican ticket, supported also by the Prohibitive party, was carried by a majority of 3,826 for the Governor and 4,225 for the Lieutenant-Governor, electing the same officers who had held the offices the previous year: Charles C. Van Zandt, Governor; Albert C. Howard, Lieutenant-Governor; Joshua M. Addeman, Secretary of State; Willard Sayles, Attorney-General; and Samuel Clark, General Treasurer. There was a Greenback ticket also in the field, for which only a trifling vote was polled. The nominee for Governor was Samuel Hill; for Lieutenant-Governor, David A McKay. The total vote was 15,610, or 4,099 less than in 1878. The falling off was 1,736 votes in the Republican party, 2,124 Democratic, and 334 Greenback votes.

In the Senate the election gave the Republicans 29 and the Democrats 8 members. The Republican Representatives elected numbered 54, the Democratic 18.

The Senatorial Committee of Congress empowered to investigate alleged violations of sections 1,754 and 1,755 of the Revised Statutes of the United States, regarding the preference to be given to discharged soldiers and sailors in appointments to offices in the United States civil service, met at Newport on August 15th. It was the standing Committee of the Senate on Civil Service and Retrenchment, and was composed of Senator M. C. Butler, chairman, and Senators Rollins of New Hampshire, Whyte of Maryland, and Beck of Kentucky. The committee was instructed to investigate this matter upon the occasion of a petition being presented to the Senate, signed by three hundred former soldiers and sailors, praying Congress to require the execution of the statutes above mentioned in the assignment of offices in the Providence Custom-House. This petition was accompanied by a memorial of Dr. J. B. Greene of Providence, alleging that several honorably discharged soldiers and sailors had recently been dismissed from that

Custom-House, and their places filled by civilians. The memorial and petition were presented to the Senate by Senator McDonald of Indiana on the 27th of May, and were the subject of a long and animated debate. Among the removals complained of were the displacement of General Shaw, the Collector, who was succeeded by Cyrus Harris, a relative of Senator Anthony, and the dismissal or enforced resignation of Majors Joyce and Bucklin, Mr. Frankland, and Captain Greene, a brother of the memorialist, who was replaced by Major Pomroy, a soldier who was wounded during the war of secession. On the strength of a couple of the new appointments the memorial stated that the dismissed soldiers had been succeeded mainly by relatives of the senior Senator for the State, Mr. Anthony. The committee listened to testimony from Dr. Greene, Major Pomroy, Major Joyce, and others. It had been alleged also that appointments were bestowed in the Custom-House and in the Post-Office as a reward for political services, and that Federal officers used their influence to affect the vote in the State elections, in violation of the rules for civil-service reform. The committee continued its sessions several days, taking down an extensive amount of evidence relating to the removals and appointments in the Custom-House, and also in the Providence Post-Office.

At the time when Senator McDonald presented Dr. Greene's memorial and the petition which it accompanied of the Rev. Augustus Woodbury and others, discharged soldiers and sailors, an investigation into the nature and effect of the property qualification for suffrage required by the Constitution of the State of Rhode Island was also demanded by the Senator. By these laws the franchise is withheld from foreign-born citizens of the United States who are not the possessors of a freehold of the minimum value of $134, or who do not pay a rental of the amount of $7 or over per annum, as well as from native American citizens who do not possess one of these qualifications and who do not pay a tax of at least $1 a year. It was held that if the property qualification was not a violation of the fourteenth amendment of the United States Constitution, it would be necessary to reduce the representation of the State in the Lower House of Congress from two members to one, since the maximum vote polled in the State had not exceeded 24,000, and the total number of the voting population could not be much more. It was estimated that 10,000 or more citizens of foreign birth were excluded from the franchise by the above restrictions. This committee had also to inquire into the alleged employment of money in Rhode Island elections, and intimidation or undue influence exercised by managers of manufactories over their employees to control their votes.

These latter subjects were referred by the Senate to the select committee to inquire into alleged frauds in the late elections, of which Senator Wallace was chairman. At the same time that the Butler Committee met in Newport the Wallace Committee held its sessions in the United States Court - House in Providence. From the testimony taken regarding the effects of the property qualification established by the Constitution of 1842, it appeared that several citizens of respectability were debarred from voting on account of being of foreign origin and possessing no real estate. The Hon. Thomas Davis, who had been a member of Congress, was disfranchised through losing his property by business reverses. A citizen, Colonel James Moran, who as an officer in the army had received and forwarded 'the ballots of the soldiers during the war, was excluded from voting by his foreign birth, while a negro whom he had brought with him was allowed as a native to vote. Several citizens whose property had been expropriated for public improvements were disfranchised during the two or three years which elapsed before the city paid the appraisal to them. It was stated that the failure of the amendment to remove the disqualification in 1871, when only 3,236 votes were cast for it and 6,960 against it, was due partly to an agitation against the Roman Catholics, who were supposed at the time to be striving to secure public moneys to support their schools. The amendment submitted to the people in 1876 to allow soldiers and sailors to vote was stated to have been overshadowed by the issue of the national election. The sentiment of the native population voting with the Republican party and of a part of the native Democrats, as elicited in the evidence, was strongly in favor of retaining the property qualifications; several naturalized voters also expressed the same views.

The receipts of the Treasury during the year ending December 31, 1879, were $970,072, and the disbursements $703,211; the balance in the Treasury amounted to $164,635; the sum of $102,225 was owing to the Rhode Island Hospital Trust Company. The bonded debt of the State amounted to $2,534,500, or, with the deduction of the available sinking fund, to $1,832,462. The total amount of the sinking fund was $733,764, which was invested principally in securities of the city of Providence and of the United States Government.

The number of children in the State between five and fifteen years of age was 49,562. The number of children reported as attending the public schools was 32,793; as attending Catholic schools, 4,374; as attending private schools, 1,782; as not attending any school, 10,549. There were 41,810 pupils enrolled in the day-schools, and 30,001 attended school, the average attendance being 26,939. There were 819 schools altogether. The average school-year lasted nine months and two days. There were 888 teachers regularly employed, the male teachers drawing $98,619 in salaries, and the female teachers $309,780. In the evening schools, with an average duration of fourteen weeks, 2,677 pupils attended, the average attendance being 1,796; the schools were 33 in number, employing 154 teachers. The public schools received an appropriation of $92,923 from the State and $340,237 from the towns, as well as $83,034 for land and buildings, $31,785 from district taxation, and $52,227 from registry taxes and other sources; making a total revenue of $600,208. The cost of instruction per capita of the pupils enrolled in the day-schools was $11.02; of the average number of pupils attending, $17.11. The number of schoolhouses was 446, and the estimated value of school property was $2,654,148.

The appropriation of 1878 for the support of the State Farm, at Cranston, was $28,814; for the State Prison, $16,821. The appropriation made for the support of the State institutions in 1879 was $71,350; the total payments from the Treasury for this purpose and for new works, $91,988. During the year $40,515 was collected for labor, sales of produce, etc., making the net cost of the institutions for the year $51,463, of which $43,000 represented the net cost of maintenance, which would give, assuming the average number of inmates to have been 800, a net cost to the State for each inmate per week of $1.04. In the Asylum for the Insane the number of inmates had increased from 218 in 1878, and from 148 in 1873, to 283.

The new State Prison lately finished and occupied, upon the State Farm, is well built of stone quarried on the spot. The building is 453 feet long, 60 feet wide, and 45 feet high, with a dome over the chapel in the center whose top is 110 feet above the ground. The prison contains 252 cells of three sizes, the smallest of which are 5 feet by 8, and the largest 8 feet square.

For the year 1877 the number of births was 6,235, of marriages 2,282, of deaths 4,450; the first showing a slight decrease, the second an insignificant decrease, and the last a somewhat larger decrease. For the period of twenty-four years the total number of children born was 115,131, of which 4,429 were still-born; the total number of marriages recorded was 47,344, and of deaths 75,492. The proportion of children born of American parentage is slightly less than those of foreign parentage. The divorces granted during the year were 534, of which number 157 were for neglect, 155 for desertion, 68 for cruelty, 61 for drunkenness, and 52 for adultery. The deaths from consumption were 661, from diphtheria 492, the latter being an increase from 159 in 1876.

The Narragansett Indians held a meeting in Charlestown on July 30th to discuss the question of giving up their tribal constitution and acquiring the rights of citizenship. Little interest was shown by the Indians in the proposed change, and the decision was postponed. The question of abolishing the tribal authority of the Narragansett Indians was brought up in the Legislature, and is still pending.

In a suit for an injunction brought by certain tax-payers of the city of Newport to restrain the City Treasurer from paying the expenses of a banquet given by the City Council to officers from British naval ships, Chief Justice Durfee of the Supreme Court decided that the expenditure was unauthorized, and granted the injunction, refusing to entertain the plea that the suitors were estopped from applying for an injunction because their application was not made in advance.

ROEBUCK, JOHN ARTHUR, an English politician, was born December 29, 1802, and died November 30, 1879. He studied law in London, was called to the bar in 1831, and in the following year was elected to Parliament from Bath. He was soon known in the House as the "Objector-General," and, in the words of one of his biographers, "he faced every sort of fact in politics, analyzed all kinds of men, opposed and lectured Whigs and Tories, headed the rest of the Radicals in plain speaking; and, being still a young man, of no definite position and with no obvious aims, he created, inside and outside Parliament, a mingled feeling of detestation, wonder, admiration, and amusement." He was defeated in 1837 by Lord Powerscourt, but was reëlected in 1841. It was during this Parliament—1841-'47—that Mr. Roebuck exhibited the most feverish activity of his life. In 1849 he was returned for Sheffield, and he sat for that constituency until 1868, when he was defeated, and was again returned in 1874. His most memorable appearance in public life was in January, 1855, when he brought forward in the House of Commons a motion for inquiry into the conduct of the Crimean war, which was resisted by the Government of Earl Aberdeen, but carried by a majority of 157, when that Government was forced to resign. In 1857 he made himself conspicuous by his opposition to a projected war with China, and his attitude upon this subject was influential in effecting a dissolution of that Parliament. His course on some important questions, notably his advocacy of the cause of the Confederate States, and his denunciations of trades-unions, led to his defeat in 1868. In 1877-'78 he vigorously supported the policy of the Earl of Beaconsfield, and he was sworn a Privy Councilor in 1878. Early in life he spent some years in Canada, and he was ever afterward one of the stanchest supporters of the rights of that colony and imperial pretensions. Besides numerous articles in the "Westminster" and the "Edinburgh Review," he wrote "Plan for Government of our English Colonies" (1849), and "History of the Whig Ministry of 1830" (1852).

ROMAN CATHOLIC CHURCH. The affairs of the Roman Catholic Church attracted less general interest in 1879 than has been usual in late years. On February 1st Pope Leo XIII. issued Letters Apostolic announcing a general jubilee. He also issued an Encyclical against the doctrines aimed by the Socialists, Communists, and Nihilists at all human authority and all rights of property, urging the bishops and clergy to labor to instill into the young respect for parental and state authority. The Encyclical, by order of the Czar, was read in all the Catholic churches in Russia. The reception of a large deputation of Catholic journalists on February 22d was a recognition of the power of the press.

Some of the Oriental churches had been rent by schisms, and on February 28th he addressed an allocution to the Cardinals on the extinction of the schism among the Chaldeans, and his confirmation of the election of a new Patriarch of Babylon belonging to that rite. Soon after (March 10th) Kupelian, the schismatic Patriarch of the Armenians, notified the Grand Vizier at Constantinople of his renunciation of all claims, and his submission to the Patriarch Hassoun, to whom the Porte restored the church property, an act which the Pope acknowledged in a letter to the Sultan. Kupelian proceeded to Rome and made his submission to the Pope also. His course was imitated by the Bishop of Zaka, and the Chaldean schism ended. On March 24th, by authority of Pope Leo XIII., the ancient order of the Knights of St. John of Jerusalem proceeded to the election of a Grand Master, a position which had been vacant during the century.

The condition of affairs in Rome, the capital of the Christian world, where every insult to the Catholic religion was encouraged and abetted, induced Leo XIII. to address Cardinal la Valletta, Cardinal Vicar of Rome, March 25th, and establish a commission of prelates and members of the Roman Patriciate to direct and supervise all elementary Catholic schools in Rome.

On May 12th the Pope made his first creation of Cardinals, admitting to the Sacred College Julian Florian Deprez, Archbishop of Toulouse; Louis Francis Desiderius Edward Pie, Bishop of Poitiers; Cajetan Alimonda, Bishop of Albenga; Frederick, Landgrave of Fürstenberg, Archbishop of Olmütz; Louis Haynald, Archbishop of Kolocz; Joseph Pecci and John Henry Newman, priests of the Oratory; Americus Ferreira dos Santos Silva, Bishop of Porto; Joseph Hergenrother, a German theologian; and Thomas Zigliara, priest of the order of St. Dominic.

On June 1st he addressed a letter to the archbishops and bishops of the provinces of Turin, Vercelli, and Genoa on the Italian law of civil marriage, which made the conferring of a sacrament a crime, and those who conferred and who received it subject to punishment.

On August 4th he issued an Encyclical Letter on the restoration of Christian philosophy in Catholic schools according to the spirit of the Angelic Doctor St. Thomas Aquinas, in which, after reviewing the whole history of philosophical teaching, he concludes: "We exhort you, Venerable Brethren, most urgently to restore in full vigor and to propagate as far as possible the priceless wisdom of St. Thomas, for the

defense and ornament of the Catholic faith, for the welfare of society, and for the advancement of all sciences. We say 'the wisdom of St. Thomas.' Let teachers, designated by enlightened choice, devote themselves to instilling into the minds of their disciples the teaching of St. Thomas Aquinas, and let them be careful to demonstrate how far it surpasses all others in solidity and excellence. Let the academies you have instituted, or that you shall institute in future, explain and defend this doctrine, and use it in refuting prevailing errors." This Encyclical met a cordial response from bishops in all parts of the world, and caused a general tendency to lay aside all philosophical textbooks which had abandoned the exact system of St. Thomas. Leo XIII. also encouraged the publication of a new and careful edition of the complete works of St. Thomas Aquinas, and, to promote more severe and accurate studies, presided at several disputations on philosophical topics.

On September 19th, in a second promotion of Cardinals, Pope Leo XIII. elevated to that rank Monsignore Peter F. Meglia, James Cattani, Louis Jacobini, and Dominic Sanguigni, the Nuncios at Paris, Madrid, Vienna, and Lisbon.

The twenty-fifth anniversary of the definition of the Immaculate Conception was celebrated with pomp, and the Pope issued an Encyclical on the occasion.

In France a bill introduced into the Chambers by Jules Ferry, entitled "A project of law relating to the freedom of higher education," aimed in its seventh article at the suppression of all schools and academies directed by religious. The Catholic bishops from all parts, beginning with Cardinal Guibert and his suffragans, protested against such an act, and the Pope encouraged the bishops in a letter. The subject was the topic of discussion in the journals, in pamphlets, and in public debate. The objectionable section was finally rejected by the Chambers early in 1880.

In Germany the Government enforced the Falk laws with iron severity, so that more than half the dioceses were without bishops (Dr. Martin, Bishop of Paderborn, dying in exile in July), and a vast number of churches deprived of pastors. The negotiations, formal and informal, between the Government and the Holy See, continued at intervals, but no definite point was reached, although Falk was compelled to retire from his office. The Government in the same spirit began a series of prosecutions of the clergy and others at Marpingen, who had expressed belief in an apparition of the Blessed Virgin Mary. The course of the Government was so arbitrary and oppressive toward the witnesses that the accused were all acquitted.

In Italy the Government commenced a prosecution against the Archbishop of Chieti for acting without its recognition, but, after much vacillation, was finally defeated. A law making civil marriage compulsory, and punishing

Catholic clergy who married persons unless already married, drew forth a letter from the Pope and remonstrances from the bishops in all parts of the peninsula. During the year a Catholic Congress at Modena, encouraged by the Pope, showed a resolution to abandon the policy of abstention from the polls.

In Belgium, as in France, the Catholics were aroused by propositions to fetter their freedom in the education of their children, and the position of the Church was embodied in the pastoral letter of Cardinal Deschamps and his suffragans (September 1st), containing practical instructions for the use of confessors. Attempts were made to show that the bishops were not acting in harmony with the Holy See, but the Pope and the episcopate disavowed at once any difference of opinion.

The confraternities question in Brazil arose in a new form, and the claim of these associations (originally organizations of pious devotees, but recently made up of men having no sympathy with the doctrines or worship of the Catholic Church) to control the churches and the performance of divine worship was a peculiar state of affairs. Bishop Macedo protested against the seizure of a church at Nazareth, and religious services conducted there without the presence of the clergy.

In the United States, the dedication of the Cathedral of New York on May 25th, by Cardinal McCloskey and a vast array of archbishops and bishops, was an event which interested all, the cathedral being the finest and largest ecclesiastical edifice yet erected in the republic.

Among Catholics of note who died during the year 1879 were Augustine Bonetty, founder and editor for many years of the "Annales de la Philosophie Chrétienne," May 26th; Mother Mary Thomas Peacock, an American lady, foundress of the Sisters of the Holy Child Jesus, who died in the mother-house of her order in England, April 18th; Sister Marie de la Croix (Jeanne Jurgan), one of the foundresses of the Little Sisters of the Poor, August 20th; and Mgr. Gaume, author of the "Catechism of Perseverance " and other works, and an active advocate of the abandonment of the classics and the adoption of the writings of the Fathers.

ROON, ALBRECHT THEODOR EMIL, Count von, a German field-marshal, born April 30, 1803, died February 23, 1879. In 1813 he joined the corps of cadets at Culm, and two years later that at Berlin. He entered the 14th infantry as an officer in 1821, and studied at the Military Academy from 1824 to 1827, where he devoted himself particularly to military and geographical studies. In 1827 he became instructor in the Cadet School, in which position he published "Anfangsgründe der Erdkunde" (1834; 12th edit., 1868), and "Grundzüge der Erd-, Völker- und Staatenkunde" (3 vols., 1837 -'40; 3d edit., 1847-'55), both of which soon attained a very large sale. He was employed

from 1833 to 1835 in the Topographical Bureau, was appointed in 1835 a teacher in the War School, and in 1836 was ordered to the general staff with the rank of captain, and at the same time was made a member of the chief military examination committee. At that time he wrote "Militärische Länderbeschreibung von Europa" (1837), and the first part of a military monograph entitled "Die Iberische Halbinsel " (1839). In 1842 he was attached to the staff of the 7th army corps with the rank of major. In 1843 he was ordered back to Berlin and intrusted with the military instruction of Prince Frederick Charles, whom he accompanied to the University of Bonn and on his travels in Italy and France. In 1848 he was appointed chief of the general staff of the 8th army corps, in which capacity he took part in the campaign in Baden in 1849. In 1856 he was appointed to the command of the 20th infantry brigade, and in 1858 of the 14th division. In the latter year he handed a memorial to the Prince Regent (the present Emperor) on the defects of the army, which was received favorably; and in 1859 he was appointed a member of the commission on the reorganization of the army, after having been previously raised to the rank of lieutenant-general. In December of the same year he was appointed Minister of War, and two years later Minister of Marine. The King had boundless faith in his military measures. His leading idea was to base the army on universal service for three years, in order to be ready for all contingencies, the Landwehr to be called out for the defense of the country whenever the line should take the field. On February 10, 1860, the new Minister of War laid his plans before both Houses of the Diet, declaring that there was no intention of breaking with the past, but the Prussian army must thenceforth be the people in arms. During the next few years stormy sittings were of frequent occurrence in the Chambers. As the originator of the new military law, General von Roon was the best-hated man in Prussia; but he clung with great tenacity to his plans, and a powerful ally soon joined him in Otto von Bismarck. The brilliant successes of the Prussian arms in the wars with Denmark and Austria, and particularly the rapidity with which the latter campaign was brought to a close, occasioned a complete revulsion of feeling in favor of Von Roon and Bismarck. His system was again put to the test in 1870, and the rapidity and perfect order with which the German troops entered France and overthrew the French Empire gained for Von Roon again the admiration of the people. On January 19, 1871, he celebrated at Versailles the fiftieth anniversary of his military life, when the Emperor expressed his gratitude for the great services he had rendered him and his house. On June 16th he was created a Count, and was otherwise richly rewarded. In December, 1871, he resigned the Ministry of Marine; but on January 1, 1873, he was appointed President of the Prussian

Ministry, an office which Prince Bismarck had temporarily resigned, while General Kameke was appointed his substitute in the Ministry of War. At the same time he was raised to the rank of field-marshal. But his health was unequal to the duties of his post, and in November he received permission from the Emperor to retire from public life. From that time he lived in complete retirement.

RUSSIA (EMPIRE OF ALL THE RUSSIAS), an empire in Europe and Asia. The Emperor, Alexander II., born April 29, 1818, succeeded his father, Nicholas I., March 2, 1855. The heir apparent is the Grand Duke Alexander, born March 10, 1845.[*]

The area and population of the great divisions of Russia were estimated as follows in 1879 ("Almanach de Gotha," 1880):

DIVISIONS.	Square miles.	Population.
1. European Russia.......	1,895,514	65,864,910 (1870)
Poland	49,159	6,528,017 (1872)
Bessarabia..............	8,274	127,000
2. Grand duchy of Finland.	144,228	1,968,626 (1877)
3. Caucasia	169,578	5,391,744 (1873-'76)
Government of Kars....	9,950	600,000
4. Siberia	4,824,564	3,440,362 (1878)
5. Central Asia	1,288,486	4,401,876
Total..............	8,379,753	88,822,585

For religious and other statistics of the empire see "Annual Cyclopædia" for 1877 and 1878.

The foreign commerce of Russia in 1876 and 1877 was as follows (values in rubles):

COMMERCE.	IMPORTS.		EXPORTS.	
	1876.	1877.	1876.	1877.
Baltic ports..	177,583,000	188,815,000	151,365,000	249,821,000
Overland..	201,708,000	186,007,000	111,332,000	211,221,000
Southern ports	62,541,000	15,927,000	107,012,000	85,185,000
White Sea ports..	962,000	712,000	9,548,000	12,015,000
1. Commerce with Europe..................................	442,789,000	291,461,000	879,257,000	508,292,000
2. Commerce with Finland..................................	10,328,000	9,080,000	12,028,000	12,752,000
3. Commerce with Asia.....................................	24,464,000	20,446,000	9,415,000	6,902,000
Total...	477,581,000	321,087,000	400,700,000	527,986,000

On January 1, 1879, there were 21,840 kilometres of railroad in operation in Russia, exclusive of Finland. In the latter country there were 873 kilometres. The number of post-offices in 1877 was 3,678; of letters sent in 1878, 93,692,546; of wrappers, 6,689,953; of registered letters, 4,676,711; of money-letters, 7,692,640 (value, 2,494,115,000 rubles); of packages, 2,468,573 (value, 82,938,000 rubles); of newspapers, 63,350,064.

The definite treaty of peace with Turkey was signed on February 8th (see TURKEY), and on March 5th the Russians began to evacuate her territory. The condition of affairs in Eastern Roumelia gave occasion to Russia to address in March a note to the Powers, in which the suggestion was made whether it might not be advisable—nay, necessary—in the interest of the execution of the stipulations relative to that country, to make some temporary provisions calculated to tide over the transition between the cessation of the present provisional *régime* and the definitive organization of the province. The quartering in the province for one year of a mixed corps, in which every one of the signatory Powers would be at liberty to participate, would seem to Russia the best means to insure the execution of the provisions of the treaty respecting Eastern Roumelia. Supported by this force, the International Commission, after finishing the statute and having it sanctioned by the Porte in Constantinople, might return to Philippopolis, and, in concert with the Governor appointed by Turkey, introduce the instrument it had elaborated. This proposition was not accepted by the Powers, and in May the Czar assured the Sultan in an autograph letter that he would see to it that the provisions of the Treaty of Berlin with regard to Bulgaria and Eastern Roumelia were carried out. (See BULGARIA and EASTERN ROUMELIA.)

One of the most important events in the history of Russia in 1879 was a new war in Asia. Officially it was announced as being directed against the Turkomans on the southeastern frontier of the empire, but it was commonly believed that its chief object was to capture Merv, the capital of the Tekke Turkomans. This city was in former centuries one of the most populous and important of Central Asia, and both Russians and English look upon it as a point of considerable strategic importance. The Russians have often been suspected of an intention to seize it, and the English have uniformly on such occasions violently protested against it. In 1875, when a Russian force had left the mouth of the Attrek, on the southeastern shore of the Caspian, also for the alleged purpose of occupying Merv, Sir Henry Rawlinson, in his work "The British in India," expressed the opinion that England should rather declare war against Russia than consent to the occupation.[*] The Russian Government not only made no mention of Merv in its official announcements of the objects of this expedition, but expressly denied that it had any intention of taking that city. In the English Parliament, on July 13th, Mr. Bourke, in the

---

[*] For a fuller account of the imperial family, see "Annual Cyclopædia" for 1877, article RUSSIA.

[*] For a full statement of the views of Sir H. Rawlinson and a brief historical sketch of Merv, see "Annual Cyclopædia" for 1875, pages 698-'9.

name of the English Government, said the Russian Government had formally assured Lord Salisbury that there was no intention of advancing upon Merv. One of the leading Russian newspapers, the "Golos," had, however, previously shown that the expedition could carry out its ostensible aim of chastising the Turkomans only by capturing and destroying their chief place of refuge; and a St. Petersburg correspondent to the "Norddeutsche Allgemeine Zeitung" of Berlin (July 8th), the organ of Prince Bismarck, explicitly stated that General Lazareff had been commissioned to capture and destroy Merv.

Before the expedition was ready to start, a severe blow was struck by the Turkomans. General Lomakin had collected 3,000 camels near the wells of Burnak, Kabil, and Sulmen, about 27 miles northeast of Krasnovodsk, where they were to await the beginning of the expedition. The Tekke Turkomans, having closely watched the proceedings of their enemy, on April 15th attacked Burnak, defeated the Russian guard, consisting of 2,000 men, and captured a large number of camels, which they carried away with them. Pursuit being made by reënforcements immediately sent from Krasnovodsk, the Tekke, whose march was impeded by the captured animals, were overtaken, and forced to confront the Russians. And now happened an event which forms a period in the history of Central Asiatic warfare. Instead of having recourse to their usual tactics of dispersing the camels and attacking the Russians in loose order, the Tekke dismounted, occupied a strong position half-way up a hillside, and, making the camels kneel down in front, fired from behind this living wall with the steadiness and rapidity of European sharpshooters. The encounter lasted till night, when the Tekke as well as the Russians retreated in opposite directions. The Tekke, leaving a dozen dead and some forty camels on the spot, marched east, carrying the rest of their booty with them; the Russians, having buried their dead, retraced their steps to the west, finding it too dangerous to follow an enemy whose strength had suddenly so very much increased.

The expedition did not get fairly under way until August. Owing to the glare of the sun and the sand, which was continually being blown about in the desert, large numbers of the troops suffered with diseases of the eyes, while the unwholesome water which they had to use also caused a great deal of sickness. On August 12th General Lazareff, the commander-in-chief of the expedition, died, and was replaced in September by General Tergukasoff.

The news received from the seat of war was very meager, owing to the strict censorship exercised by the Russian military officials. Enough was known, however, to prove that the ultimate object of the expedition was the oasis which was the center of the operations of the Akhal Tekke Turkomans. In the first engagements the Turkomans were everywhere defeated, and disappeared in the desert. The Russians, commanded by General Lomakin (who temporarily succeeded General Lazareff after the sudden death of the latter), pursued them, and penetrated to the oasis, where they found signs of comparative prosperity and peace. Following the enemy from one deserted village to another, threatened only by guerrilla troops of horsemen, the expeditionary force proceeded to attack the fortified position of Dengel Tepe, which appeared to be held by a strong body of Turkomans. No sooner did they do so than the surrounding hills began to swarm with hostile cavalry, and, though the assailants were repeatedly repulsed, the Tekke horsemen suffering losses after every charge and flying before the Russian fire, they were not discomfited. They retired upon a strong position, which General Lomakin attacked. The Russian forces were too weak for the task, and after vainly wasting their powers on the capture of some outworks, a combined assault was defeated by the Turkomans. During the retreat the latter fell furiously upon the retiring Russians, who barely escaped a terrible disaster.

A fact which was closely connected with the opening of the Turkoman expedition, and is of great importance in itself, is the turning of the Attrek River into its old bed, which took place in June. In former times this river fell into the Caspian not far from the bay of Hassan-Kullin, about twelve versts from Tchikislav, the starting-point of the expedition; but nine years ago, in consequence of the Russians having taken possession of Krasnovodsk, the Turkomans, with enormous efforts, constructed a dike or dam near Bent, at a distance of about sixty versts from the mouth of the Attrek, and by this means diverted it through the region of their winter quarters.

The internal condition of the empire continued to be one of revolutionary discontent. The Nihilists were as bold and aggressive as in any former year. Another great shock to public feeling was given on April 14th, when Alexander Solovieff attempted to shoot the Czar in front of the house of the military staff in St. Petersburg. The assassin was arrested, and was found to have capsules containing poison, which he could break in an instant, in his mouth. When asked why he had made the attempt, he answered that the task had fallen on him by lot, and he had no alternative.

This plot led to the adoption of some new extraordinary measures. Generals Todleben, Loris-Melikoff, and Gourko were appointed Governors-General with exceptional powers at Odessa, Kharkov, and St. Petersburg, and similar powers were conferred on the Governors-General of Moscow, Kiev, and Warsaw. These officers were authorized to remove from their districts all persons whose presence they considered pernicious; to subject civilians to martial law; to arrest on their own responsibility any person of whatever rank; to suppress newspapers and periodicals; and generally to adopt whatever measures should appear necessary for the maintenance of public order. At St. Petersburg, Governor-General Gourko gave orders that a porter should be stationed day and night at the door of every house, whose duty it should be to watch that no unauthorized placards were posted up anywhere, and that no objects of a dangerous nature should be placed in the streets. Gunsmiths were ordered to furnish full lists of the goods in their warehouses to the commandant of the city, and were forbidden to sell except to purchasers who could present letters of authorization from that officer. Private persons possessing firearms must make the police acquainted with the fact, and must obtain a permit from the commandant of the city as a condition of their keeping them. The order commanding guards to be stationed before all the houses was found to be impracticable, and was finally not insisted upon. Regulations of a similar character, differing only in details, were made for all the principal towns of the empire.

Several weeks elapsed before the disorders appeared to be at all quieted, even under the most rigorous enforcement of these regulations. Bold attacks were made on officers of the Government and obnoxious persons in broad daylight; residences and offices of the police in some of the towns, as at Rostov, were plundered. The best parts of the towns of Irbit and Orenburg, places to which the Government was accustomed to consign political offenders, were burned down; fires were set at Uralsk, Petropolovski, Irkutsk, and other places; and many of the large towns were thrown into a panic by notices that they would be burned. During May 1,730 conflagrations occurred in the empire, occasioning damage to the amount of more than two million rubles; and the loss which had been inflicted on the country during the past six months was estimated on the 1st of June at 30,000,000 rubles. June was likewise prolific of fires. The number occurring during the month is given as 3,500, causing damage to the amount of 12,000,-000 rubles. Only 900 of these were accounted for; the other 2,600 were attributed to public disturbers. Courts-martial were instituted at Kiev for the trial of the revolutionists, and a plot is said to have been discovered to blow up the court-room during the trial. The first group of persons tried included three noblemen, the daughter of a privy councilor, and a Prussian subject. A part of the number were found guilty of armed resistance to the police, and sentenced to death; others, who were convicted of conspiring against the state and social order, were sentenced to terms of penal servitude. Explosions which were attributed to the revolutionists took place in the police office at Omsk, at Nizhni-Novgorod, and in a powder-magazine near St. Petersburg. Numerous persons were arrested throughout the empire for having explosives or forbidden arms,

or for being engaged in manufacturing explosives. On the night between the 26th and 27th of June more than four hundred persons were arrested at Kiev, large stores of dangerous materials were found, and a secret press and revolutionary documents were discovered in near connection with the ecclesiastical seminary. Michael Solovieff, who attempted to assassinate the Czar in April, was tried in June, found guilty of belonging to a criminal association, the object of which was to overthrow by violence the institutions of the state, and was hanged on the 7th of the month. Several of his relatives were arrested and imprisoned. An imperial order was issued in July empowering the Governors-General to exercise their discretion in the cases of political offenders, whether to send them for trial before the military courts or the ordinary tribunals. The number of persons who had been convicted or were held under arrest exceeded anything that was before known in the history of the present reign, and reports became rife that the prisons were greatly overcrowded. On June 19th six hundred convicts were dispatched from Odessa in the ship Nizhni-Novgorod for the island of Saghalien, off Japan, where they were to serve their terms of punishment. The friends of the Government represented that they were for the most part persons who were guilty of common crimes, but others asserted that by far the larger part of them were revolutionists. The vessel sailed by the way of the Suez Canal and the Red Sea, and arrived at Nagasaki on August 1st. Reports of their frightful sufferings were officially contradicted. In November the Minister of the Interior sent out a circular to the governors of provinces, instructing them to order the rural police not to interfere with the public dances and amusements in the villages, as such interference had produced discontent among the rural population. The trial of Leon Mirsky, with seven persons charged with being his accomplices, for the attempted assassination of General Drenteln, chief of the gendarmerie, began in the military court at St. Petersburg on November 27th. All the prisoners were accused of belonging to a secret society whose object was to overturn the existing Government and to enforce a change of the social order of the empire. Mirsky was also accused specifically of the attempt to assassinate General Drenteln, of resisting the officers who came to arrest him, of fabricating false passports, and of inciting his fellow prisoners after they were arrested to revolt. The chief accusation against the other prisoners was that of concealing Mirsky after his attempt against General Drenteln. Mirsky acknowledged the commission of the offenses for which he was arraigned, and only pleaded that he had committed them for public, not for personal reasons, and asked not to be hanged as a common murderer. A sentence to death by hanging was imposed upon him, but was afterward commuted to one of hard labor in the mines. Tury Tarkhoff, his principal accomplice, was sentenced to labor in a fortress for ten years.

Another attempt upon the life of the Czar was made on December 2d, when a mine was exploded under the railroad with the intention of blowing up the train on which he was entering Moscow. His Majesty, however, was not in the train which was blown up, and escaped. The mine which exploded had been dug out from a house near the line of the railroad which had been bought by the young man who occupied it about three months before, and was worked from the house by galvanic wires. The Czar, it was said, had been warned that an attempt would be made upon him, and changed the arrangement of the trains so as to mislead his assailants.

Minister Valuieff prepared in the earlier part of the year and submitted to the Ozar a draft for a constitution, containing provisions for the formation of a central Assembly at the capital, to be composed of a certain number of state functionaries sitting *ex officio*, and of deputies elected by the provincial and district Assemblies already in existence. The scheme did not contemplate that this Assembly should enjoy the right of proposing new laws; but it would be empowered to discuss projects of laws submitted to it from above, and its members would be entitled to question high officers having seats in the Chamber, and to criticise generally the action of the Government. In November Prince Gortchakoff decided to retire from the office of Chancellor of the Empire, and Mr. Valuieff was designated to succeed him. It was believed that the Czar had at last determined to institute the reforms which had been demanded for so long a time, and that he had given favorable consideration to the plans of Mr. Valuieff. Before there was time to take definite action on the subject, however, the attempt was made to blow up the Czar's train at Moscow. The Czar's mood was immediately changed; he rejected Mr. Valuieff's schemes, saying that he wanted the plans of men of action, not of sentimentalists, and dismissed his newly appointed Minister.

S

SERVICE, UNITED STATES MARINE HOSPITAL. The Marine Hospital Service of the United States was established by an act of Congress passed July 16, 1798, for the relief of sick and disabled seamen. This act was passed after the subject had been before Congress for several years; and while it appears to have originated in a memorial of the Boston Marine Society, yet "hospital money" had been collected in the colonies since 1730, and the system must have been more or less familiar to Congress. The first building known to have been set apart as a hospital exclusively for seamen, among English-speaking peoples, was the palace commenced by Charles II. at Greenwich, which after the battle of La Hogue (1692) was ordered by Queen Mary to be completed "as a retreat for seamen disabled in the service of their country." (Macaulay.) After the death of the Queen, King William caused to be erected, under the superintendence of Sir Christopher Wren, the magnificent "Royal Hospital for Seamen at Greenwich," which Macaulay has alluded to as "the noblest of European hospitals." The seamen of the American colonies were taxed to support this hospital by an act of Parliament passed in the second year of the reign of George III. Instructions given to Patrick Gordon, Esq., Deputy Governor of the Province of Pennsylvania, February 2, 1729–'30, show that the sum of sixpence per month was required to be deducted from the wages of all seamen, English subjects, sailing in and out of American ports. Four receivers were appointed for Pennsylvania: Richard Fitzwilliam and John Moore, Philadelphia; Alexander Keith, Newcastle; and Henry Brooke, Lewes. ("Pennsylvania Archives," vol. i., p. 251.)

This lesson was not lost on the colonies, for as early as October, 1780, the Commonwealth of Virginia enacted that the sum of ninepence per month should be collected as "hospital money" from the pay of all seamen and marines in the State. The naval officers were constituted the collectors of the tax, and a commission of five per centum was allowed on the moneys collected. In October, 1782, a law was passed changing the amount of the tax from ninepence to a shilling per month. On December 20, 1787, a law was passed establishing a marine hospital, and authorizing the appointment of a commission by the Governor to select a site in the town of Washington, county of Norfolk, Virginia. (Hening's "Statutes at Large," vol. xii., p. 494.) The State of North Carolina enacted a law providing for the creation of a hospital fund in 1789, and by a subsequent act (1790) the commissioners of the poor at the different ports of entry were empowered to act as collectors. (Haywood's "Manual of the Laws of North Carolina," Raleigh, 1801, p. 350.) The tax was a capitation tax. Captains on arrival from a foreign voyage were required to pay 5s., mates 2s. 6d., and each member of the crew 1s. 6d.

On August 28, 1789, a bill was introduced into Congress providing for the establishment of hospitals and the adoption of harbor regulations, but was indefinitely postponed. To the Boston Marine Society is due the credit of presenting the first memorial to Congress on this subject.

The Society record shows that at a regular meeting held at the Bunch of Grapes tavern, Boston, October 12, 1790, Captain Mackey presiding, it was " *Voted*, That a committee be appointed to consider what spot of ground may be the most convenient for the erecting a marine hospital, the kind of building that will be the most convenient, and its expense, also to make a calculation of the annual income that will arise from a small tax on seamen for the support of the said hospital, and report at the next meeting." The committee consisted of Captain Mackey, Mr. Tudor, Mr. Russell, Mr. Hodgdon, Dr. Dexter, Dr. Scollay, and Captain Deblois. At the annual meeting of the Society, held at the Bunch of Grapes tavern November 2, 1790, the committee reported, "That from a variety of considerations they are of the opinion that some spot of the heights of Charlestown east of the town is the most eligible situation for such a building"; and it was then voted, "That the committee be further instructed to draw a petition to Congress setting forth the utility of a marine hospital, and pointing out the means of supporting one." On January 4, 1791, the petition was approved by the Society and ordered to be sent forward. This petition is not now extant, but we learn that it was presented in the House January 27, 1791, and that it prayed the establishment of three marine hospitals in the United States for the care and support of aged and disabled seamen, one for the Southern, one for the Middle, and one for the Eastern States. The petition was tabled, but finally referred to the Secretary of the Treasury. A short time previously the Commonwealth of Virginia had passed an act authorizing the sale to the United States of the marine hospital at Washington, Va.; and on April 17, 1792, the Speaker laid before the House the letter of the Secretary of the Treasury, accompanying his report on sundry papers referred to him, concerning a marine hospital at the town of Washington, and on the memorial of the Marine Society of Boston on the subject of marine hospitals, which was read and ordered to be referred to Mr. Ames, Mr. Sterret, and Mr. Parker. (House Journal.) On April 28, 1792, Mr. Ames reported, but his report was tabled. On November 19, 1792, the House took action on the subject by appointing a committee "to prepare and bring in a bill or bills for the relief of sick and infirm seamen." Mr. Laurence, Mr. Goodhue, Mr. Benjamin Bourne, and Mr. Barnwell were the committee. It was further "ordered that the report of the Secretary of the Treasury which was made on the 17th of April last, together with the report of the committee thereon, . . . be referred to the same committee." On January 21, 1793, Mr. Williamson reported a bill, which was read and ordered to be committed to the Committee of the Whole. No further action was taken at this time, but at the next session an act was passed providing for the aid of seamen in foreign countries, and two agents were appointed, one to reside in Great Britain and the other in the West Indies. The President in his message of December 7, 1794, informed Congress that the agent for Great Britain had declined the appointment, and the duty of carrying out the law had devolved on the United States Minister. On February 28, 1797, a committee appointed to inquire into the operation of the act for the relief and protection of American seamen, reported that "the committee find that numbers of seamen, as well foreigners as natives, arrive at the different ports of the United States in such a disabled situation that they either become a great burden to the public hospitals, where any such are established, or are left to perish for want of proper attention. They are of the opinion that a sufficient fund might be raised for the support and relief of sick and disabled American seamen, as well in foreign ports as in the United States, either by an additional tonnage duty on all vessels entering the ports of the United States, or by a charge on the wages of all seamen shipped within the United States, proportioned to the length of the voyage, to be paid or secured by the master and deducted from the wages of his crew." The committee recommended the passage of the following resolutions: "*Resolved*, That provision ought to be made by law for collecting the sum of — cents per month from the wages of every seaman sailing from any port of the United States, to be appropriated—1. To the temporary support and relief of sick or disabled seamen of the United States; 2. To the foundation of hospitals for the relief of such sick and disabled seamen (when a sufficient fund shall be collected)." But the law was not passed until July of the following year. This law provided for the collection of twenty cents per month from the wages of all seamen, and that any surplus remaining after defraying the expenses should be invested in stock of the United States; and the President was authorized to receive donations of land or buildings, and when necessary to erect hospitals. The President was further empowered to appoint directors of the marine hospitals, under whose direction the fund assigned to each port was to be expended, and persons so appointed were allowed no compensation except actual expenses. An additional act passed March 2, 1799, authorized the money collected within any one State to be expended within such State, except the States of New Hampshire, Massachusetts, Rhode Island, and Connecticut (which it was evidently intended to consolidate for the support of the hospital at Charlestown), and authorized the Secretary of the Navy to deduct from the pay of the officers, seamen, and marines of the navy the hospital tax of twenty cents per month, and declared them entitled to the same benefits and advantages of the hospital fund as merchant seamen. It appears that the law did not go into into effect immediately, for Secretary Oliver Wolcott wrote to General Benjamin Lincoln, Collector at Boston, David Austin, New Haven, and Allen McLane, Wilmington, Del., under date of July 20, 1799, as follows :

Sir : Having received no returns for the quarter ending 31st March last of the hospital money collected in your district, for the use of sick and disabled seamen as indicated by law, I will thank you to immediately forward to this office returns of the moneys collected by you during that period for the purpose aforesaid. I will also thank you to conform to the instructions of the Comptroller of the Treasury on that head, by transmitting quarterly returns for the time to come.

I am with consideration, Sir,
Your obedient Servant,
OLIVER WOLCOTT.

The instructions to which he refers were as follows :

TREASURY DEPARTMENT, May 24th, 1799.
BENJAMIN LINCOLN, Esq., Collector of Boston.

Sir : I herewith transmit a Copy of an Act of Congress passed on the second of March last entitled " An Act in addition to an Act for the relief of sick and disabled seamen."

It was hoped that an arrangement could have been formed before this time for the establishment of permanent Hospitals.

It appears, however, that this subject has been placed by the Act of the last session " to regulate the Medical Establishment" under the immediate superintendence of the Physician General ; the object of this communication is therefore confined to a provision for the *temporary relief* and support of sick and disabled seamen in public and private service.

For the present, and until experience shall have shown the expediency of a different arrangement, the moneys collected in the State of Massachusetts will be expended under your directions at or near Boston, and accordingly the sums collected at the outports of the State will from time to time be placed in your hands in pursuance of special directions, of which you will be advised.

The persons entitled to relief from the fund are Officers, Seamen, and Marines of the Navy of the United States, and Masters, Marines, and Seamen employed in private or Merchant Vessels. I think proper to mention, that there may be some danger of a diversion of the fund for the maintenance of persons who ought to be relieved as paupers under municipal regulations. As abuses of this kind, if practised to any considerable extent, will defeat the humane intentions of Congress in the establishment of permanent Hospitals for the support of disabled seamen, they ought to be carefully prevented.

It is, however, the object of the Law that the expenditures of the fund for temporary relief should be made at the Hospital or other proper institutions now established in the Ports of the United States. You will of course endeavor to fix by precise agreements the conditions upon which sick and disabled seamen shall be received and supplied with whatever their necessities may require, and will transmit the Copies of the Contracts which may be formed to this Office. In cases where arrangements can not be made you will pursue established usages respecting similar expenditures, observing all possible economy.

It is not expected that you should personally superintend the details of expenditure ; an agreement therefore with some individual or corporation, that the fund shall be properly applied, appears to be indispensable. The accounts must be rendered to you at least quarterly, supported by such vouchers as are usual, and as circumstances will admit of being taken, which after examination will be paid out of the moneys in your hands.

You will be pleased to keep all your accounts of receipts and expenditures for this Fund distinct from your other accounts. The quarterly abstracts of the

Fund are to be rendered agreeably to the form prescribed by the letter of the Comptroller of the Treasury dated the 19th of September, 1798. The quarterly accounts of expenditure are to be rendered agreeably to the subjoined form, and the whole regularly introduced into an account current which is to be transmitted every quarter.

I am with respect, Sir,
Your obdt Servant,
(Signed)   OLIVER WOLCOTT.

Abstract of moneys paid for the relief of sick and disabled seamen by _____, *Collector of the Customs for the District of* _____, *in the State of* _____, *from* _____ *to* _____.

Date of payment.	Number of voucher.	To whom paid.	NO. OF PERSONS SUPPLIED.		TIME SUPPLIED.		AMOUNT PAID.
			Of the navy.	In private service.	Months.	Days.	

A similar letter was written to John Davis, Collector of New Berne, N. C., and George Latimer, Esq., Collector, Philadelphia.

A letter was written to General Benjamin Lincoln, October 4, 1799, stating that, in order to condense the moneys collected in neighboring districts, collectors will be notified to send the same to him ; * also stating : " The collection of the duty on seamen's wages will be attended with some trouble, for which no compensation is established by the existing law. The object being humane and benevolent will, I presume, interest your attention. If a commission shall be hereafter allowed, I will authorize deductions from the future returns." (Similar letter of same date to Collector at New Berne, N. C.)

(FORM.)

I hereby acknowledge to have received of ——, Collector of the Customs for the District of ——, the sum of ——, being the amount of moneys collected by him for the support of the Marine Hospitals of the United States from —— until ——, agreeably to a letter of advice from the Secretary of the Treasury, dated ——, for which I have signed duplicate receipts.

A few days later a letter was written to General Benjamin Lincoln, regarding the establishment of the hospital :

TREASURY DEPARTMENT, May 29, 1799.
BENJAMIN LINCOLN, Esq., Collector of Boston.

Sir : You will receive by this mail a letter on the subject of a marine hospital for sick and disabled seamen. Without meaning to decide absolutely upon the point, I think proper to point your attention to Castle Island as being a proper place for the establishment. If on reflection you think any other place preferable, you will be pleased to mention it.†

* Letters similar to the above were written to the following Collectors : William Tuck, Gloucester ; Dudley A. Tyng, Newburyport ; Joseph Helder, Salem ; Samuel R. Gerry, Marblehead ; William Watson. Plymouth ; Joseph Otis. Barnstable ; Stephen Hussey, Nantucket ; John Pears, Edgartown ; Edward Pope, New Bedford ; H. Bayliss, Dighton ; Asa Adams, Ipswich.

† Castle Island had formerly been used as a quarantine station. "The General Court enacted in 1788 that the com-

Doctor Thos. Welsh has been particularly recommended as a gentleman well qualified for the appointment of Physician to the Hospital. I take the liberty to mention his name and to request you to ascertain the conditions upon which he will serve, and to arrange the terms of compensation.

I am, with consideration, Sir,
Your m° obdt. Servant,
OLIVER WOLCOTT.

At this time Dr. Thomas Welsh had a contract with the Secretary of War for attending the sick of the troops on that island, and of the recruits then raising in Boston. Dr. Welsh had served with distinction in the Revolutionary war, and was appointed Physician to the Marine Hospital in June, 1799. On the 21st of February, 1800, Dr. Welsh submitted his regulations, and they were approved by the President March 11, 1800.

The purchase of the Washington Point Hospital, Virginia, was completed in 1801, but the building was not immediately repaired or occupied.

The following letter to the Collector at Alexandria shows how far the fund was from being a general fund, and shows the application of the rule that all money should be expended within the collection district where it was collected:

TREASURY DEPARTMENT,
December 12, 1801.

CHARLES SIMMS, Esq.,
Collector of Alexandria.

SIR: The President has directed that the Hospital moneys collected in the Columbia District, since the assumption of jurisdiction by Congress, may be expended if necessary within the district.

You may therefore apply any moneys received by you on that account since the last day of March, 1801, toward the relief of sick seamen in Alexandria; but there being no other funds provided for that object, you must be careful not to exceed that sum.

I have the honor to be, very respectfully, Sir,
Your obedient Servant,
ALBERT GALLATIN.

The port of New Orleans, although at this time under Spanish rule, had a large and increasing traffic with the United States, which resulted in the employment of a considerable number of sailors. The following extract of a letter from Evan Jones, Esq., and E. M. Bay, Esq., of Charleston, to the Secretary of State, describes the situation at that time:

NEW ORLEANS, August 10, 1801.

A great number of American citizens, especially seamen and boatmen from the Ohio, die here yearly, for want of a hospital into which they might be put and taken care of—not that they are refused admittance into the Spanish Poor Hospital, but that building is by much too small for the purpose. No public house of any reputation will take them in, and consequently they lie in their ships or boats, or get into wretched cabins, in which they die miserably, after frequently subjecting the humane among their countrymen to much trouble and expense.

Will not this be an object, Sir, worthy the attention

manding officer at Castle William, and the Keeper of the Light House, shall notify and direct the masters of all vessels coming near them, wherein any infectious sickness is, or hath lately been, at their coming in, to come to anchor as near the before-mentioned house as may be." (Drake's "Boston," p. 604.) Secretary Wolcott, being a physician and a native of New England, was doubtless aware of this circumstance.

of the Government of the United States? And might not a fund be easily established for the preservation of those poor people, by imposing a light tax upon every vessel and boat that comes in, as well as upon every seaman and boatman?

About two hundred vessels have entered here from sea during a twelvemonth past, and allowing eight men only to each, it makes 1,600. Perhaps from 350 to 400 boats have come down from the Ohio, etc., during the same time, and allowing four men to each, it would make about an equal number of men. A small sum from each, added to something from every vessel and boat, would probably produce a capital equal to the exigency.

("American State Papers," vol. vii., "Commerce and Navigation," p. 493.)

Extract of a letter from E. M. Bay, Esq., to the Secretary of State, dated at Charleston, November 4, 1802:

It will readily occur to you, Sir, that thousands of our fellow citizens must soon be employed in navigating the ships and boats which must ever be used as the means of transporting these commodities [those of the Western country] from one place to another. Now, Sir, when we take into consideration the climate and season of the year when this commerce must be carried on, the risk to our citizens must be multiplied in a high degree. It is well known that the Western rivers can not be conveniently navigated into the Mississippi until the breaking up of the frost in the spring of the year. It is then that that great river begins to rise, and it generally remains up until July. The great distance and unavoidable impediments naturally in the way will always carry over these commercial transactions to so late a period as to leave the great bulk of those employed in them at or about New Orleans in the sickly season of the year; which, in that low, flat, unhealthy Southern climate, is fatal in the extreme to the strong, robust constitutions of our Western brethren; hence many of them fall victims to climate and disease, leaving families and friends at a great distance from them.

The want of proper accommodations for poor and infirm seamen and boatmen at New Orleans is another very serious inconvenience our poorer class of fellow citizens are much subjected to in that place. It is really pitiable to see such numbers of distressed objects as sometimes present themselves to view in the sickly months, who have been left to shift for themselves, after their employers have made their markets. Something like an hospital establishment, to be superintended by American physicians, would go a great way to alleviate the distresses of these useful men. I mentioned American physicians because our people are strongly prejudiced against those of the Spanish faculty; and generally not understanding the language, they derive little or no benefit from them.

("American State Papers," vol. vii., "Commerce and Navigation," p. 493.)

The following general report was made by Secretary Gallatin on the condition of the service:

TREASURY DEPARTMENT,
February 16, 1802.

. . . . The only ports where hospitals have been established, or temporary relief afforded to the seamen, are:

1st. Boston, Newport, Norfolk, and Charleston, South Carolina, where marine hospitals have been altogether established under the laws of Congress, exclusively appropriated to the use of seamen, and solely supported out of the funds raised under the authority of the United States. The hospital at Newport has lately been discontinued.

2d. Baltimore, where the hospital is in the same situation as to its funds, but is placed under the control of the Board of Health.

3d. New York and Philadelphia, where sick seamen

are received in the city hospital at a fixed rate per week, paid out of the marine hospital fund.

4th. Portland, New London, Wilmington, North Carolina, Newbern, Edenton, and Alexandria, where temporary relief is afforded in private boarding houses.

5th. Savannah, from which no returns have been received.

By the statement B it appears that the whole sum received from seamen, either in private or in public service, amounts to 147,875 dollars and 53 cents, of which 6,185 dollars and 33 cents have been applied to the purchase of the hospital at Gosport, near Norfolk, and 74,636 dollars and 51 cents have been expended for the relief of sick seamen; that 73,761 dollars and 61 cents remain unexpended in the hands of sundry collectors and agents, and that 6,707 dollars and 87 cents are due to certain agents who have expended more than has been received by them.

This last circumstance has taken place in Newport, Norfolk, and Charleston, namely, in three of the four marine hospitals which have been established; and it will be perceived, by a recurrence to the same statement, that to those three places the navy fund has been exclusively applied; but this last fund being nearly exhausted, it is impracticable to continue any longer the established hospitals at Norfolk and Charleston, unless Congress shall think proper to grant them some aid, or to make such alterations in the law as will permit a more general application of the fund.

Under existing circumstances, if no alteration shall be made, it will be necessary to write to the collectors of both places to discontinue in toto the hospitals after the 31st of March next. For the advances made by them must, by this time, exceed twelve thousand dollars; these have been paid out of the proceeds of the duties on import and tonnage, and cannot be admitted to their credit in their accounts as collectors. It will be necessary for them to continue to collect the seamen money until they shall have been fully reimbursed for their advances.

If it be asked why the funds have proven insufficient in those two places, the following reasons, it is believed, may be assigned: 1st. The establishment of an hospital, instead of having had recourse to city or State institutions, as in Philadelphia and New York, which has drawn with it all the expenses of superintendence, attending physicians, etc. For what reason the Gosport hospital was purchased from the State of Virginia, I am at a loss to know; but if it was intended for the navy, it should be supported out of the funds appropriated for that department and p aced under its control. The building is much too large, and in an unfinished state, and wants immediate and expensive repairs. 2d. Those two seaports are more expensive, and generally, so far especially as relates to non-residents, more sickly than the more northern ports. 3d. The provision of the law which makes seamen on board coasting vessels pay only in the port to which they belong, is unjust in its operation, and bears more particularly on the Southern ports.

It is necessary to state that complaints are frequently received from those ports where no relief has yet been granted; the seamen complaining that they pay without deriving any benefit from it. This may be the case in some instances; but it is doubtful whether the application of the funds in such manner that they might find relief in all the important ports of the Union, may not be more beneficial to them than a provision in the ports where they reside, and where they want it least.

Whilst the expenditure of the money is restricted to the port or State where it is collected, it cannot be considered in any other light than as a municipal establishment, and would more conveniently be placed under the control of the State itself.

I have the honor to be, very respectfully, Sir,
Your obdt. Servt.,
(Signed)   ALBERT GALLATIN.
The President of the United States.
("American State Papers," vol. vii., "Commerce and Navigation.")

On May 3, 1802, an act was passed amending the act of 1798, by which the moneys collected on account of the hospital tax were constituted a general fund; the sum of $15,000 was appropriated for the erection of a hospital at Boston; the President was authorized to take the necessary measures for providing relief at New Orleans; masters of every kind of river-craft entering the port of New Orleans were required to pay the hospital money at Fort Adams; the President was authorized to appoint a director for the hospital at New Orleans; sick and disabled seamen from foreign vessels were authorized to be admitted into the marine hospitals on the application of their respective commanding officers; and it was further enacted that the directors of the marine hospitals should be held accountable in the same manner as other receivers of public moneys, and they were allowed a commission of one per centum on the money disbursed.

On May 6th the Collector at Boston was requested to designate a site for the hospital; but on the 21st of June the following letter was written him:

TREASURY DEPARTMENT,
21st June, 1802.

BENJN. LINCOLN, Esq.,
        Collector of Customs, Boston.

SIR: I have the honor to enclose a letter from the Secretary of the Navy to Samuel Brown, Esq., directing him to designate the ground, not exceeding five acres, which, out of that purchased for a Navy Yard, is to be appropriated for a Marine Hospital.

In order to obtain an eligible plan, it appears proper and I request you to insert in one of the newspapers an advertisement offering a premium of 50 Dollars for the most approved plan of an hospital of 4,000 square feet area, two stories of 10 and 8 feet high, with cellars below; the rooms for the sick to be well aired, and of varied sizes from 12 to 20 feet square; the convenient distribution of the rooms and economy of space and construction will be principally regarded in the decision.

A ground plan, elevation, and section will be expected to be transmitted to the office of the Secretary of the Treasury, on or before the 15th day of August next.

Plans not approved shall be returned.

I have the honor to be, respectfully, Sir,
Your obedient Servant,
ALBERT GALLATIN.

The hospital received from the State of Virginia was in a dilapidated condition. On August 6, 1802, $600 were ordered to be expended in the construction of a new wing, and the entire roof, which was rotten and insecure, was ordered repaired at a total expense of $1,500.

A letter was written to Collector Robert Purviance at Baltimore, in regard to the expenses of that port, as follows:

TREASURY DEPARTMENT,
August 8th, 1802.

ROBERT PURVIANCE, Esq.,
        Agent Marine Hospital, Baltimore.

SIR: Your letter of the 8th ult. was duly received. It is expected that the expenses attending the Baltimore Marine Hospital may exceed the collections made on that account in that port, but, at all events, they should not exceed the total amount collected in the State. The rule adopted in other ports, and which I would recommend in yours, is to confine the admission to seamen in actual service belonging to a vessel *then* in port.

I have the honor to be, respectfully, Sir,
Your obedient Servant,
ALBERT GALLATIN.

A reward of $50 having been offered for the best plan for the hospital at Boston, and only one having been received, that one was adjudged the best, and the author received the money, although the Secretary considered it necessary to make certain alterations, as the following letter shows:

TREASURY DEPARTMENT,
October 11th, 1802.

SIR: I enclose the only plan which has been received for a Marine Hospital at Boston, in consequence of the public advertisement inserted in your newspaper for that purpose. It was transmitted by Asher Benjamin, and although it is not possessed of any great merit, yet, unless you have received some other, we should use it with a few trifling alterations. Mr. Benjamin will in that case be entitled to the reward, but he should give some explanation concerning the thickness of walls and partitions, and the precise absolute dimensions of the building. If you shall have received any other plan, I will thank you to transmit the same to this Department; but if none has been received, the enclosed, with the following alterations in the second floor, may be considered as adopted. Alterations of the second floor, marked with a pencil on the plan: Let the corner rooms be on the same plan as in the first floor; that is to say, that at each end of the building, instead of a room 18 by 19, two 9 by 18 each, and a passage between; there will be a room 18 by 20, and one 16 by 18. Let the four rooms 9 by 16 in the original plan be converted into two rooms 18 by 16. Upon a supposition, then, that no other plan has been received by you, I have to request that you will take the necessary measures to form a contract for the erection of the Marine Hospital in conformity to the enclosed. I presume that the mode adopted for light-houses, that of a public advertisement, will be the most eligible. The building should be brick, the cellar stone; the whole not to exceed the sum appropriated, and to be completed within the course of next summer, at farthest by 1st December, 1803. You will be able to judge of the details necessary to be inserted in the contract in order to secure the best materials, good workmanship, and a compliance with the intended plan. Whenever you shall have received proposals, I will thank you to compare them and transmit the same, with your opinion thereon, to this office.

I have the honor to be with respect, Sir,
Your obedient Servant,
ALBERT GALLATIN.

The "Columbian Centinel" of October 30, 1802, contained the advertisement for the erection of the new building. The advertisement is very lengthy; the following is extracted:

A MARINE HOSPITAL Is to be erected by the United States in Charlestown, on the North Easterly part of the Land purchased to accommodate the Navy Yard, on such part thereof as shall be hereafter directed. In general, the HOSPITAL is to be one hundred and fourteen feet long and thirty-nine feet wide, to be built with brick, two stories high, and a well stoned cellar under the whole. [Very complete details follow, and the advertisement concludes as follows:] In a transaction of this kind, it is difficult to give a minute detail of all the particulars, which must be embraced by a full execution of the plan. In order therefore to avoid any mistakes or painful questions relative to this business, the plat of the building may

be seen at the *Collector's Office* in Boston at all times, prior to the first day of December next, as also the paper on which the dimensions of the timbers [are stated]. The public attention is invited to this benevolent and important object. Those who shall wish to contract for the erection and completion of the hospital, with the appendages, will send their terms in writing, sealed, to the subscriber.

(Signed) B. LINCOLN.

On November 10, 1802, Secretary Gallatin addressed a letter to Collector Lincoln approving the advertisement and the general arrangement of the building, but "presumes that until the establishment may be fixed on a more extensive scale than is at present contemplated, the nurses may and would be better accommodated on the first or second floor than in the cellar." The President, December 20, 1802, appointed Dr. Charles Jarvis physician of the Charlestown hospital, at a salary of $1,000 per annum, to take effect when the sick should be removed to the new hospital. During the year 1803 it was found that the fund was insufficient to meet the demands upon it, and the sick arriving at the smaller ports were furnished transportation to the large seaports whenever able to bear the journey. In this year the President appointed a physician to the hospital in New Orleans, as the following shows, which also gives in detail the general principles on which the service was administered:

TREASURY DEPARTMENT,
April 14, 1804.

H. B. TRIST, Esq.,
Collector, New Orleans.

SIR: The laws respecting sick and disabled seamen being extended to the port of New Orleans, you are appointed, as other Collectors are, in their respective ports, the Agent for that purpose.

No instructions as to the mode of collecting the 20 cents per month from seamen, and accounting for the moneys thus received, appear to be necessary, in addition to those you have already received as Collector of Fort Adams, unless it be to remind you that all seamen belonging to vessels of the United States, including of course those owned in Louisiana, are subject to this tax, those engaged in foreign trade being required to pay it at the time of making entry from each foreign voyage, and those engaged in the coasting trade at the time of taking out the enrollment or license; and to observe that, as some doubts may exist whether the Act of May 3d, 1802, still continues operative so far as to make it necessary for the masters of boats, rafts, and flats going down the Mississippi to New Orleans to make report to the Collector of Natchez of the number of persons employed on board, and to pay to him the amount of the tax on persons thus employed, it will be proper that you should require such report and payment from the masters of boats, etc., coming down the Mississippi in all cases where it shall not appear satisfactorily to you that the tax has been paid previously at Natchez.

The tax cannot be demanded of seamen belonging to foreign vessels; but if application is made for the admission into the Hospital of such seamen, they are to be admitted on the master's paying seventy-five cents per day for each seaman, as provided in the fifth section of the Act of May 3d, 1802.

The fund produced by the tax of 20 cents per month on seamen being much less than would be necessary to afford relief in all cases, it becomes requisite to provide only for the most urgent and to economize in the expenditures as much as possible. With this view it has been prescribed to the agents in the several ports of the United States, and you will consider it as a rule for your government, not to afford relief from the Marine Hospital fund to any person claiming to be a seaman, who shall not, at the time of application for assistance, belong to some vessel or boat then actually in port. This rule, together with the limitation of the sum of five thousand dollars, including the salary of the Physician of the Hospital, beyond which the whole annual expenditure must not be permitted to extend, is all that can be prescribed in a general way as to the mode of granting relief or the extent to which it may be carried. Dr. William Barnwell of Philadelphia has been appointed by the President Physician to the Hospital, with a salary of one thousand dollars per annum, which sum you will pay to him in quarterly payments, at the expiration of each quarter, from the time when he shall leave Philadelphia for New Orleans, which will be shortly, and of which you will be advised. Until he shall arrive you will please provide such medical attendance for the sick seamen as shall appear proper.

The sick seamen have been provided for heretofore under the direction of Mr. Clark, in the "Hospital of Charity," they being charged by the managers of that institution with the bread, meat, etc., consumed by them and their attendants, and a proportionable part of the general expenses of the Hospital. This mode may be still pursued if it shall be deemed the most economical and best calculated for the convenience and comfort of the sick, or they may be attended in any other public building fit for the purpose which the governor may assign or which can be obtained with his permission; or if it shall be more advisable, the sick may be placed out and attended in private houses, as is practiced in some of the ports of the United States; though, from my present view of the subject, this appears to be the least eligible mode.

A quarterly account of the payments made by you for this object, supported with the proper vouchers, is to be rendered to the Comptroller of the Treasury, in which you are authorized (by the Act of May 3d, 1802) to charge a commission of one per cent. on your expenditures. You will be regularly advised by the Comptroller of the settlement of this account, which after such advice you will charge in your general account current as a debit to the United States, and which will be so admitted on your transmitting a receipt of the form and in the manner which will be prescribed by the Comptroller.

I am very respectfully, Sir,
Your obedient Servant,
ALBERT GALLATIN.

An editorial in the "Medical Repository," vol. vi., New York, 1803, says of the establishment of the hospital at New Orleans:

On account of the increasing transportation of produce on the Mississippi, an additional number of American seamen and boatmen find a rendezvous at New Orleans. Many of these from the Ohio and upper country, as well as from the Atlantic ports and the ocean, have died annually in the most forlorn condition at that place. These considerations moved the Government, by a wise and humane proposition, to adopt measures for the support of a hospital in that city for their relief, and to ask permission of the Spanish Government to establish the same.

On March 5, 1804, a memorial was presented in the House from citizens and mariners of Baltimore, protesting against the ruling of the Department that seamen should be excluded from relief who were not actually employed on board a vessel at the time of their application; declaring also that the passage of the law creating a general fund was a public misfortune, and that this alone prevented the accumulation in Boston, New York, Philadelphia, and Baltimore of a handsome surplus which might be

devoted to provide a "fund for the permanent relief of decrepit or superannuated seamen exhausted in the service, though not proper objects of a sick infirmary." ("American State Papers," vol. vii., p. 572.)

In this year a committee was appointed "to inquire into the expediency of exempting pilots from paying hospital money for their apprentices." The committee, considering that the apprentices "receive in professional skill an equivalent for wages, and that they are in fact seamen, it would seem to be a liberal construction of the statute to make it include those persons, and thereby extend the advantages to them"; and the committee submit their opinion that it is inexpedient for Congress to make any declaration concerning the payment of hospital money by pilots for their apprentices. ("American State Papers," vol. iii., "Commerce and Navigation," p. 571.)

Dr. Barnwell was directed, May 3, 1804, to purchase in Philadelphia the necessary medicines for the equipment of the New Orleans hospital, and the Collector, Peter Muhlenberg, Esq., to pay the bills therefor and advance one quarter's salary. On June 18, 1804, the President directed that the "temporary provision" for sick seamen should extend to New Haven, Conn., Wilmington, Del., and Providence, R. I.

On August 30, 1805, the ruling of the Department was defined regarding fishing vessels as follows:

TREASURY DEPARTMENT,
30th August, 1805.

DANIEL COFFIN, Esq.,
Collector, Nantucket.

SIR: Your letter of the 17th inst. was duly received. Seamen employed in fisheries are not expressly excepted from the payment of hospital money; but that payment is confined to vessels licensed for the coasting trade, and to vessels arriving from foreign ports. It results that a vessel exclusively employed in the fisheries, and which has not been during her voyage in a foreign [port], is exempted, but she is not so exempted as a fishing vessel, but merely as being neither a coasting vessel, nor arrived from a foreign port.

It follows that every vessel arriving from a foreign port is equally liable to pay the hospital money, and must pay it on the principle fixed by the words of the law, viz.: for the time which has expired since the vessel was last entered at any port in the United States. No exemption is made in favor of vessels which may have been during a part of that period employed in fisheries, nor can any deduction be made on that account by the Collector.

I have the honor to be respectfully, Sir,
Your obedient Servant,
ALBERT GALLATIN.

The expenses at Philadelphia having largely exceeded the receipts, the Collector at that port was requested to devise a plan for the exclusion of certain beneficiaries; which he did, but at the same time transmitted a communication from a magistrate of that city, which was resented by the President, as the following letter indicates:

TREASURY DEPARTMENT,
December 20th, 1806.

PETER MUHLENBERG, Esq.,
Collector, Philadelphia.

SIR: Your letter of the 11th instant respecting the Marine Hospital was laid before the President of the

United States, who approves the regulations you propose for the reduction of the expenses of that establishment to a level with the receipts of the fund. He adds that no civil magistrate can dictate to the United States who shall be the object of their charity.

I am very respectfully, Sir,
Your obedient Servant,
ALBERT GALLATIN.

A letter to the same Collector, under date of February 28, 1807, informs him that "maniacs and chronic" cases should not be cared for at the expense of the fund.

The Legislative Council and House of Representatives of Mississippi Territory memorialized Congress to provide for the erection of a marine hospital at Natchez; and the committee to whom it was referred, through its chairman, Hon. Thomas Randolph, March 26, 1806, reported favorably on the memorial, and recommended that twenty-four sections (15,360 acres) of land be granted the hospital establishment of Natchez, to be located by the Governor of the Territory. ("American State Papers," vol. vii., p. 66.)

On April 15, 1807, Dr. William Barnwell having absented himself from the hospital at New Orleans without leave, Dr. Blanquet was appointed to fill the temporary vacancy. On May 3, 1807, the east wing of the hospital at Norfolk was destroyed by fire.

The following letter from General Lincoln is characteristic of his extreme caution in contracting expenditures. The record shows the authorization asked for to have been granted:

BOSTON, June 26, 1807.

The keeper of the Marine Hospital informs me that the cellar at the west end of the Hospital is a place where he deposits his wood; the ground is very springy, and at times very muddy, and dangerous for the invalids to enter for wood; he wishes a floor might be laid to prevent the evils experienced, which will cost about one hundred dollars. I do not think myself authorized to do the business. I shall want your directions before I enter upon it.

I have the honor to be, most respectfully,
Your obedient servant,
BENJAMIN LINCOLN.
ALBERT GALLATIN, Esq.,
Secretary of the Treasury.

The following letter shows the contract system at Baltimore to have been far from satisfactory, even at that date. The Dr. Watkins referred to was Dr. Tobias Watkins, afterward Assistant Surgeon-General of the Army, 1818 –'21:

TREASURY DEPARTMENT,
May 10, 1808.

JAMES H. McCOLLOCH, Esq.,
Collector, Baltimore.

SIR: Your letter of the 29th ulto. has been duly received. You are authorized to make the necessary arrangements for the support of sick seamen for one year from the expiration of the contract with Dr. Watkins. From the stipulation made with him by the former Collector, I am inclined to the opinion that he has an equitable claim for another year's contract; provided that his terms be as low as those offered by others, and provided, above all, that there may be a reliance on equally good attendance on the sick. I leave, however, the subject wholly to your discretion, only observing that the complaint made against Dr. Watkins relates to the locality of the house used by

VOL. XIX.—50 A

him as an hospital, and which is stated to be in the vicinity of ale-houses or dram-shops, to which the seamen are improperly permitted (as it is said) to have access. . . .   ALBERT GALLATIN.

Dr. Charles Jarvis, the physician to the hospital at Charlestown, died November 15, 1807. From the "Independent Chronicle," Boston, of the next day, which publishes a somewhat lengthy obituary, it is seen that he died at the comparatively early age of fifty-nine, universally respected by his contemporaries as a man of worth and spotless character. He was succeeded by the appointment of Dr. Benjamin Waterhouse. Then as now, when an officer is first assigned to a new station, improvements and changes were apt to follow, as the following letter from Collector Lincoln to Secretary Gallatin will indicate:

BOSTON, June 16, 1808.

N. B.—The physician of the hospital reports to me that he is in want of a building, I think about twenty five feet square, two stories high, as a barn, in which he can place his hay and straw, and a place in which he can stow away old bunks. Besides, he wants some small room wherein he can cleanse the people who are lousy, and who have the itch, etc.

BENJAMIN LINCOLN.

The Secretary of the Treasury in 1809 recommended an additional appropriation to meet the expenses of the service, as the dues collected were entirely inadequate. Much difficulty was experienced in keeping paupers from being furnished relief at the expense of the fund, owing to the general want of money. The Town Council of Providence, R. I., having made a claim against the Department for the services of a physician, medicines, and subsistence furnished seamen, the Secretary denied the claim, but authorized the Collector to employ a physician at an annual salary of $200. From the report of Secretary Gallatin made at this time we learn that physicians were employed under contract at Newport, New London, and Baltimore—the only marine hospitals in operation at this period being at Boston and Norfolk. Several insane seamen were under continuous treatment, and the sick were furnished hospital relief in the town almshouses at Portsmouth, N. H., Portland, Me., Newport, R. I., and Alexandria, Va. At New York, Philadelphia, and New Orleans, seamen were sent to local hospitals. The following extract from a letter from Secretary Gallatin to General Dearborn, then Collector at Boston, defines the status of the physicians:

April 19, 1809.

. . . . No Directors of the Marine Hospital have been appointed by the President, nor that part of the law ever carried into effect. The whole is still considered as being on the original footing of affording temporary relief to the seamen, and the whole is under your exclusive superintendence, subject only to such general instructions respecting the annual expenses as have been transmitted from this Department. The President has reserved to himself the appointment of the Physician, but all the other officers or servants of the institution are considered as appointed by you. The Physician is only Physician and not director. You are also authorized to prescribe every necessary rule for admission as well as for the government of the house; and with you rests the admission or rejection of charges in their amount, and therefore the regulation of the expenses and the checking of abuses. I presume that in practice it will always be found eligible to give to the Physician such share of the control over the house, its subordinate affairs, and other details, as will secure obedience to his directions and is the usage in other hospitals. But I am apt to think that General Lincoln delegated more than was necessary to the attending Physician. If so, it is in your power to correct the evils whenever you please.

I am, respectfully,
Your obedient servant,
ALBERT GALLATIN.

Shortly after this letter was written, Dr. Benjamin Waterhouse was removed on account of certain irregularities in his accounts, and Dr. David Townsend appointed physician to the marine hospital at Charlestown, which office he retained for a period of twenty years.

In the year 1811 a committee was appointed in the House to consider the propriety of creating a separate hospital establishment for the sick among the officers, seamen, and marines of the navy; and the Secretary of the Navy (Paul Hamilton), in a report dated February 22, 1811, stated that, although the sum of $55,649.29 had been paid into the Treasury on account of hospital money since the enactment of the law, yet "no navy officer, and but very few seamen, had received any benefit from it"; that, among the few seamen sent to the hospitals, "three out of five deserted as soon as they got in a convalescent state." He recommended that the sum collected from the navy be separated from that collected from the merchant service, and stated that if this were made law, "six capacious hospitals would soon be established, in which all the sick of the navy might be comfortably nursed; all the wives of seamen killed in action might be supported; all the children supported and educated; and young men just entering the service as midshipmen might acquire the invaluable knowledge of the theory of navigation, lunar observations, and naval tactics, without costing the public a single cent." He also recommended that the balances due to deserters and deceased seamen, and mulcts of pay by sentences of courts-martial and stoppages of grog, be credited to the naval hospital fund; and that the subordinate officers of the hospital be appointed "from among those disabled seamen in the service who would gladly serve without any addition to their pensions, excepting merely their board, the cost of which to the establishment would be very inconsiderable." The commandants of the navy-yards he recommended to be governors of the hospitals, the wives of seamen killed in battle to be nurses, attendants, and laundresses, and their children, together with the pensioners and convalescents, to work in the gardens; the person in charge of the hospital to be acquainted with navigation, and act as teacher to the children and midshipmen; the latter class to have $10 per month deducted from their pay while studying navigation.

This report, which is more remarkable for its spirit of philanthropy than for anything else, was, we are assured by Surgeon William P. C. Barton, entirely due to the data furnished the Secretary by himself, and was chiefly "written during a tempestuous voyage from Norfolk to New York in the sloop of war Hornet, then commanded by Captain Lawrence." (Barton, "Plans for Marine Hospitals," Philadelphia, 1814, p. x.) The idea of schools was evidently borrowed from the Greenwich Hospital, and the asylum plan from the Chelsea Hospital (England) for the support of aged and decrepit pensioners. On the receipt of this report, a law was passed (February 26, 1811) creating the naval hospital establishment, and separating the naval fund, which was to be disbursed under the direction of the Secretaries of the Treasury, Navy, and War, who were appointed commissioners for naval hospitals.

During the war with Great Britain, the hospitals at Boston and Norfolk were crowded to their utmost capacity. The records of the former are still extant, and show that large numbers were admitted from returned ships affected with inveterate scurvy. The prisoners from the captured British frigate Guerriere, and the exchanged men of the Chesapeake returned from captivity, were treated at that hospital. The following table shows by years the number of American seamen registered as having received "protections" from 1796 to 1812:

YEARS.	Number.	YEARS.	Number.
1796	4,849	1805	10,722
1797	9,021	1806	9,900
1798	7,081	1807	7,987
1799	6,514	1808	1,121
1800	8,390	1809	9,170
1801	6,917	1810	8,668
1802	891	1811	4,828
1803	10,724	1812	8,259
1804	6,822		

No naval hospital having been built, a resolution of inquiry was adopted by the House of Representatives, December 22, 1817; and, in reply thereto, the Secretary of the Navy (B. W. Crowninshield) reported on January 15, 1818, that the commissioners "met in the early part of the year 1812 and had surveys made of several sites in Washington City, but that the subsequent events of the war stopped all further proceedings, until after the peace." He also presented the report of the commissioners, W. H. Crawford, J. C. Calhoun, and B. W. Crowninshield, dated January 14, 1818, which advocated the repeal of the separation act.

On February 28, 1818, part of the marine hospital at Boston was destroyed by fire, the southwest wing and part of the center or main building being burned from basement to roof. The cause was reported officially to have been a defective chimney. In this year Secretary Crawford recommended an addition of 100 per cent. to the fund. A controversy arose be-

* "American State Papers," Class IV., "Commerce and Navigation," vol. ii.

tween the Collector of Customs at New York and the Governors of the New York Hospital, relative to the class of sailors for whose treatment payment should be made; and the latter, taking exception to the ruling of the Collector, memorialized Congress. In the memorial it is stated that the Collector limited the number of sailors to be paid for at any one time to seventy-five, on account of the inadequacy of the fund to meet the demands upon it; and the memorialists pertinently inquire "whether it is consistent with justice or humanity that, such numbers of distressed seamen, who have all contributed equally to the fund, should be abandoned to want and misery." They suggest an addition of ten cents a month to the hospital tax as both reasonable and necessary. The claim of the memorialists was rejected by the House, upon an adverse report of Secretary Crawford. The records show that the claim had been pending more than four years. Much difficulty was experienced by the Collectors in convincing the different hospitals that seamen discharged from the navy were not entitled to relief from the marine hospital fund; but the matter was authoritatively settled in a letter of Secretary Crawford dated August 20, 1821. On January 14, 1822, a memorial was presented to the House of Representatives from the Chamber of Commerce of New York, protesting against the ruling of the Department that "only *sixty* men should be paid for at any one time in the New York Hospital"; that "no relief should be extended to insane seamen, or those suffering from chronic affections"; and that "no patient should be paid for, for a longer period than four months." The memorialists state that much suffering results from carrying out the rules; that the sick sailors, "having no domicile in the city, are not entitled to admission into the almshouse, and must therefore perish unless relieved by the hand of charity." They recommend an increase of the tax to thirty cents per month. On January 28th a memorial was received from the seamen of the port of New York, protesting against the rules vigorously, and also recommending an increase of the dues tax to thirty cents per month. Secretary Crawford reported to Congress that "for three years past I have urged the propriety of doubling the fund. My importunity has been without effect. The state of the Treasury forbids the expectation that inattention to the excessive expenditure of money for the relief of sick and disabled seamen will be considered excusable by those who hold the purse-strings of the nation." The Secretary acknowledges that "maniacs and incurably diseased persons" were discharged, as they were fit subjects for the operation of the poor-laws of the States of which they were citizens or inhabitants. "Had they been retained, the whole fund would in a short time have been expended on maniacs and incurables, instead of being applied to those whose usefulness

might be restored by such application." Notwithstanding these memorials, and the declaration of the Secretary, Congress took no further action in the matter.

Mr. Holmes of Mississippi presented in the Senate, April 26, 1822, a letter from Dr. A. Perlee in relation to the hospital at Natchez, by which it appears that the Legislature of Mississippi had laid a tonnage tax on boats for the support of that hospital, which had been unoccupied from 1819 until August, 1821, when it was again opened. The funds, however, were inadequate for its support, and it was again closed in February, 1822.

It having been decided by the Treasury Department to erect a new hospital at Boston, the Collector was, on December 29, 1824, instructed to turn over the marine hospital, which was in the navy-yard, to the commandant, and a building was rented in Charlestown for the reception of the sailors of the merchant marine. Dr. David Townsend, in reply to a letter of the Collector, recommended Charlestown as a site for a new hospital; the steward, Colonel Charles Turner, recommended Chelsea; and the venerable Dr. Thomas Welsh recommended Dorchester Heights. Some difficulty was experienced in procuring the usual authority from the Massachusetts Legislature, relinquishing jurisdiction over the reservation, as the following letters show:

20th June, 1825.

DEAR SIR: You will be surprised to find that the bill for liberty to the U. S. to purchase a site for a marine hospital did not pass the Legislature.

The fact is, it passed the Senate the first of any bills which were there considered, and was sent to the House, and on the last day but one of the session came back with an amendment providing for a conditional cession only; that is, that certain novel regulations concerning voters living on the premises and paupers which might be carried there should be added. These the Senate disagreed to; the House insisted; a conference was ordered, but failed by limitation of time. The project of the House was instituted by Judge Dana, who alone can explain why he chose to interfere in the strange manner which has caused the loss of the bill.

Yours truly,   J. T. AUSTIN.
General DEARBORN, Collector.

9th February, 1826.

DR. SIR: I have heretofore informed you that Mr. Dana caused the H. of R. to put a rider on the Hospital bill, and that Mr. King and myself are unable to get it changed. Now, if you or Col. Turner after inspecting this bill are willing to accept it, I will have it passed immediately. If you think as I do, that the U. S. ought to have a better bill, the only thing to be done is to wait until the next session. As soon as you give me the result of your judgement on such examination, I will see it carried into effect.

Very truly,   J. T. AUSTIN.

On March 6, 1826, the citizens of Charleston, S. C., presented a memorial setting forth that "some time in the year 1804 they entered into a contract with the then Secretary of the Treasury, Mr. Gallatin, to relieve the United States from the charge of the marine hospital at Charleston, stipulating that $15,000 should be appropriated by the United States for building the hospital, and that the hospital money collected in the port should be paid to them to defray the expenses of the establishment, . . . and to make up the deficiency a tonnage duty should be imposed by the State Legislature, to which the assent of Congress should be asked and granted, not to exceed ten cents per ton." But the memorialists affirmed that they had not had the benefit of the contract; the lot was paid for by the Secretary, but no building erected; and they further stated that they had expended since 1804 $50,000 more than they received. They therefore asked that they be released from the contract, or that an appropriation be made for $15,000, with interest thereon from 1804 to the date of the petition, for the erection of a marine hospital. The site procured was purchased November 14, 1816, of Mrs. Drayton of Hempstead, for $5,500. The committee to whom the petition was referred reported favorably upon this claim, and a bill was introduced authorizing the erection of a hospital; but the act was not finally passed until May 20, 1830.

The report of Secretary Richard Rush, January 29, 1827, shows his adherence to the rules laid down by his predecessor, but he made no recommendations. The new Boston marine hospital was finally located at Chelsea in 1827, and ten acres of ground were purchased of Dr. Shurtleff. The building was finished in October, 1827, at a cost of $25,000. It was a rough stone building, 150 by 50 feet, two stories above the basement, with wings for physician's and steward's quarters. Like the majority of the buildings constructed at that time, no provision was made for ventilation except at the doors and windows, and it had no bath-room. Dr. David Townsend, whose appointment in 1809 as physician to the Charlestown hospital we have noticed, died in April, 1829, and was succeeded by Dr. Charles H. Stedman. Dr. Townsend was born in 1753, had seen extensive service in the Revolutionary army, in which he served continuously from the commencement of the war, and always with distinction, and at the time of his death had spent fifty-five consecutive years in the active practice of his profession. In his declining years, his son, Dr. Solomon D. Townsend, who had served in the navy during the war of 1812, was on duty with him as assistant surgeon.

In a report to Congress made February 27, 1830, by Secretary S. D. Ingham, it is stated that no tax had been collected from seamen in the lake-ports up to that time, but that instructions had been given to insure its collection from that time forward.

On June 8, 1834, Mr. Harper, chairman of the Committee on Commerce, reported a bill for the establishment of a marine hospital at Portland, Me., but action was postponed. On January 18, 1836, a memorial was presented from the physicians of Portland, warmly urging the passage of the bill for the erection of a marine hospital, and they state that the accommodation then provided for the use of seamen at that place was "in connection with the almshouse, infirmary, and house of correction."

On February 13, 1836, Secretary Levi Woodbury reported to Congress the inadequacy of the hospital fund to meet the necessities of the helpless and improvident class for whose benefit the law was designed. There were at this time only three marine hospitals, viz., Chelsea, Norfolk, and Charleston, S. C. The last was managed under a contract with the city authorities, and the general condition of the service was far from satisfactory; it could scarcely be otherwise when so large a proportion of the beneficiaries of the fund were furnished accommodations in the almshouses, to which they might have been admitted without any payment of dues whatever.

An editorial in the Boston "Medical and Surgical Journal," July 20, 1836, speaks of the hospital dues of twenty cents per month as "disgraceful to the Government of the United States," and says that "even in this unrighteous, oppressive mode of sustaining marine hospitals there are not half enough of them." The same writer also says of the new marine hospital at Chelsea, that it is "a libel on modern architecture; six wards are obviously required where there is but one"; and says the medical officer should be given a house by himself; that he is "boxed up in one end of the hospital; his family must not only be annoyed, but the patients are under restraints to which they ought not to be subjected." It also suggests constructing extensive piazzas "entirely round the building," and protests against the low compensation of the surgeon. Nevertheless, it strongly recommends students to avail themselves of the privileges of the institution. The Secretary of the Treasury recognized the crying evils of the service, and reports, in answer to a Senate resolution, a recommendation for a hospital at Holmes's Hole, Mass. He recommends that the customs officers be made by law the directors of the hospital.

On April 1, 1836, a resolution was received in the House of Representatives which had been passed by the General Assembly of the State of Ohio, February 26, 1835, "That the establishment of Western commercial hospitals be recommended to the favorable consideration of Congress; and that his Excellency the Governor be requested to forward a copy of the report of the Medical Convention of Ohio upon this subject, together with this resolution, to each of our Senators and Representatives in Congress." The report transmitted was written by Dr. Drake of Cincinnati, and gave the credit for the origination of the movement to Dr. Cornelius Campbell of St. Louis. The number of steamboats engaged in the navigation of the Mississippi River was estimated at 250, and the number of flatboats at 6,000; the number of steamboats on the lakes at 35;

schooners, sloops, and brigs on the same waters at 250; and the total number of employees on the various classes of these vessels at 43,000. The report alludes to the frequency of steamboat explosions, and states that many lives have been lost for the want of timely aid. The report indicates, as places in need of hospitals, New Orleans, Natchez, Memphis, St. Louis, Louisville, Cincinnati, Pittsburgh, Buffalo, Cleveland, and Detroit, and "some point near the mouth of the Arkansas, Trinity, or a spot near the junction of the Ohio and Mississippi; Evansville, and Parkersburg or Guyandotte." This report was extensively circulated among the various State and national officials, and it is noticeable that hospitals were subsequently built at all the above points, with three exceptions only. An act was passed March 3, 1837, appropriating $70,000 for the erection of a marine hospital at New Orleans; $15,000 for three sites upon the Mississippi and one on Lake Erie, in the selection of which the President was authorized to detail three medical officers of the army; and $10,000 for the erection of a hospital at Mobile; and from the first day of April following, the laws whereby twenty cents per month were deducted from the wages of seamen were suspended for one year, and the sum of $150,000 was appropriated for their benefit. The Secretary of War detailed for this duty Surgeon B. F. Harney, Assistant Surgeons H. F. Heiskell and John M. Cuyler (of whom only the last named is now living). The Board assembled at Baton Rouge, La., June 18th, and received instructions from Surgeon-General Thomas Lawson, authorizing them to select and purchase sites for the marine hospitals on the shores of the Western waters, and to execute contracts for deeds subject to the approval of the Secretary of War. On November 30, 1837, architect Robert Mills submitted his plans for the new marine hospitals to the Secretary of War, and they were transmitted to Congress. The plans, although superior to those on which the hospitals had previously been constructed, were still very defective in the essential particulars of drainage and ventilation. (They may be seen in print in H. R. Ex. Doc. No. 3, Twenty-fifth Congress, second session.)

On January 12, 1838, Mr. Smith of Maine, chairman of the Committee on Commerce, speaks of the prevailing distress among sailors owing to the inadequate fund; he cites the reports of several collectors, calls attention to the report of the Army Medical Board, and opposes extending the benefits of the fund to "farmers," but favors extending the tax and the benefits to fishermen.

The Senate passed a resolution, March 2, 1839, directing the Secretary of the Treasury to "report to the Senate at the next session of Congress whether any change in the system of marine hospitals is expedient, and if so, what; especially if any new hospitals are necessary, and in what manner they ought to be erected,

if deemed expedient, and how supported." The Hon. Levi Woodbury, in answer to this resolution, reported December 19, 1839. In this report he recommends a "change in the system," and gives his reasons. He states that the fund is inadequate to meet all ordinary demands upon it, and that a large class of seamen, not contributors to the fund, are debarred, and occasionally subjected to severe suffering from a want of "change in the system." He suggests that the tax be extended to all seafaring people, and to extend assistance to many cases of a chronic character. He also recommends that hospitals, "besides those now erecting at Mobile and New Orleans," should be built, one at Detroit or Buffalo, and another at Louisville or Cincinnati. He thereupon refers to the report of an Army Medical Board detailed to select sites for marine hospitals upon the Western waters. The Board recommended the construction of hospitals at Cleveland, Wheeling, Louisville, Paducah, Napoleon, Natchez, and St. Louis. The inhabitants of Pittsburgh being desirous that the hospital on the upper Ohio should be at their city instead of Wheeling, a second Board was appointed, composed of Surgeons Mower and Heiskell and Assistant Surgeon Day. This Board reported in favor of the Pittsburgh site, and Congress was compelled to give attention to a running fire of memorials for a period of several months from the advocates of the rival claims of the two cities.

The report of the Hon. William Wilkins, Secretary of War, in answer to a House resolution at the session of 1844-'45, stated that titles had been perfected for three sites, viz., Cleveland, Pittsburgh, and Louisville. He doubted that titles could be perfected at Paducah, Napoleon, and Natchez, and stated that the site at St. Louis "can not now be obtained." He inclosed plans and estimates for hospitals, but thought that the plans might be improved, and the estimates reduced fifty per cent. Accompanying this report was a report from Surgeon-General Thomas Lawson, which stated that deeds subject to the approval of the Secretary of War were executed by the proprietors of the hospital sites, and that appropriations had been asked for, but that five years had elapsed before these appropriations were made. (See act of August 29, 1842.) In consequence of this delay the vender at St. Louis canceled the deed, and otherwise disposed of the property. Sites were actually paid for at Louisville, Pittsburgh, and Cleveland; but no money having been appropriated for the construction of these hospitals, no progress had been made toward erecting them.

The following resolutions were passed by the Legislature of the State of Ohio, in relation to the erection of the Cleveland hospital:

Whereas, In the fall of 1837 the Board of Army Engineers, under the authority of the United States, located at Cleveland, in this State, the site of a marine hospital, and no appropriation has as yet been made by Congress for the erection and organization thereof; and whereas there is no such institution on the whole extent of the lakes, navigated by more than 400 steamboats and other vessels, and in the navigation of which there are employed more than 4,000 men; and the necessity of a hospital for the reception of sick and disabled seamen is urgent, and, in the opinion of this General Assembly, such as demands the immediate attention of Congress; therefore,

Resolved by the General Assembly of the State of Ohio, That our Senators in Congress be instructed, and our Representatives requested, to use their exertions to procure an appropriation by that body, at its present session, of such sum as shall be needful for the erection and efficient organization of such hospital in the said city of Cleveland.

Resolved, That the Governor be requested to forward a copy of the foregoing preamble and resolution, to each of our Senators and Representatives in Congress.

RUFUS P. SPAULDING,
Speaker of the House of Representatives.
JAMES J. FARAN,
Speaker of the Senate.

January 27, 1842.

An amusing example of circumlocution occurred in relation to the hospital at Ocracoke, N. C. The act establishing it was approved August 29, 1842. The site for the location was selected in January, 1843; the purchase was sanctioned by the Secretary of the Treasury in April, 1844; the title was examined and made good by the Attorney-General in May, 1844; and in January, 1845, the Department was officially advised of the transfer of the title to the United States by the State of North Carolina. The proposals for the building were received in March, 1845; and the Department attended to the subject May 7, 1845, and referred the papers to the Collector of Customs at Ocracoke. The Collector expressed his dissatisfaction with the previous proceedings, and recommended that the proposals to construct the building should be renewed; and the Hon. R. J. Walker reported to the House that the building would be completed in September, 1845, at a cost of $5,497.

An act was passed March 1, 1843, extending the provisions and penalties of the act of July 16, 1798, to the masters, owners, and seamen of registered vessels employed in the carrying and the coasting trade, and authorizing the issue of such instructions from the Secretary of the Treasury as would insure the collection of the hospital money. This was simply a re-enactment, the section of the original act including coasting vessels having been suspended by construction since the year 1831.

Secretary of the Treasury John C. Spencer states in a communication to Congress that the act of March 1, 1843, extended the tax to owners of vessels, and he asks that the tax be still further extended, and that monthly or yearly assessments be made in proportion to the tonnage of the vessel.

On Febuary 21, 1843, the General Assembly of Indiana passed a resolution setting forth the necessity of a system of marine hospitals for boatmen, and approving the plan adopted in 1837; but the resolution expressed the opinion that such hospitals should be placed upon a footing separate and distinct from the general marine hospital system of the United States, and their Senators and Representatives in Congress were instructed to use their exertions to obtain an appropriation sufficient to carry out "these views."

The Committee on Commerce, April 2, 1844, reported favorably upon the establishment of a hospital at Key West, Florida, and asked practically that it should be used as a quarantine. Accompanying this report was a presentment of the grand jury of the city of Key West, county of Monroe and Dade, soliciting aid from the General Government on account of yellow-fever cases treated by the city among the sailors. A letter from Dr. James Davis to the Collector of the port sets forth the smallness of his compensation: $3 per week for board and nursing, and 37½ cents for medical attendance, and the last for twenty-five days only.

A bill was introduced by Mr. John P. Kennedy, of the Committee on Commerce, in 1844, making appropriations for the erection of marine hospitals on the Western waters, and to provide for the purchase of a site at the city of Baltimore. In 1848 a petition was presented in the House praying the sale of the marine hospital and grounds in Chelsea, in order that the lands might be given up to the city for taxation.

In compliance with an act of Congress passed March 3, 1849, Dr. Thomas O. Edwards of Lancaster, Ohio, and Dr. George B. Loring of the marine hospital at Chelsea, made a report, October 1, 1849, in relation to marine hospitals and the marine hospital fund. These gentlemen made an inspection of the hospitals then in operation and in process of construction. The report recites the various enactments of Congress in relation to the service, and then proceeds to speak of the several hospitals. The commissioners state that the "condition, internal arrangement, and expense of the hospitals already in operation vary with their number and location," and "neither in form nor in character has any uniformity in their arrangement been observed." They also state that "it is impossible at this date to give in general detail any sketch of a system that could be understood as being applicable to the hospitals collectively; but both in the mode of construction, and in all after-management, each district presents its own individual picture." They then proceed to the consideration of individual hospitals, and recommend that the hospital grounds and building at Chelsea be sold, and a part of the naval tract purchased, and a new building, adequate to the needs of the service, be built thereon. They speak in highly eulogistic terms of the hospital at Norfolk and its able management. They recommend the discontinuance of the hospital at Ocracoke, and erecting one instead at Wilmington. At the latter place they speak of the great necessity for a hospital, and recommend that a building already erected at the private expense of a few individuals, at a cost of $4,000, be purchased by the Government. They make favorable mention of the Charleston hospital, then operated under a contract with the city authorities. At Mobile, they state that they could not find the surgeon of the institution; that "he pursues his own private business in the circuit of the city, and an assistant represents him for months in the wards of his hospital." The name of the surgeon is not stated. They consider it questionable whether a hospital is necessary at Paducah, and think that one hospital above New Orleans, at Natchez, with the one at St. Louis, will be sufficient. The one at Napoleon, they are of the opinion, would be of no use. They speak favorably of the marine hospital at Louisville, then near its completion, also of the hospital at Pittsburgh; and they recommend hospitals at Detroit, Buffalo, Cincinnati, and at one or more ports in Maine. They favor a tonnage duty on all vessels, including fishing vessels. In conclusion, they speak of the tedious way in which the hospitals have been constructed. They review the various regulations that have been issued from time to time, and say that the greatest defect which exists "is that no method of government and internal regulation has been entered upon which would render them parts of a uniform whole"; and they propose to place the hospitals under the control of a "chief surgeon, who shall have his bureau attached to the Treasury Department." The "regulations which are to govern the hospitals should emanate from him." The surgeons employed in the several hospitals should be responsible to him for the proper management of the institutions.

On January 25, 1849, a resolution of the House directed the Secretary of the Treasury to "inquire and ascertain the most favorable terms on which suitable sites can be obtained for marine hospitals at Buffalo, Oswego, Galveston, Detroit, Wilmington, N. C., Newport, R. I., Erie, Pa., and Appalachicola; and that he report the same, with his opinion upon the expediency of erecting hospitals at those places, to Congress at the next session." The Secretary (W. M. Meredith) reported, March 20, 1850, that, "looking only to the comforts and advantages of hospital treatment and accommodation over the existing system of relief at places indicated in the resolution, public hospitals would undoubtedly be desirable in them all. But judging of the wants and claims of other districts, and the insufficiency of the fund for their maintenance, and the consequent dependence of the fund on appropriations to be made by Congress, . . . I can not recommend so large an addition at one time, nor indeed any addition." The reports of the various collectors are transmitted, all warmly recommending the establishment of hospitals at their respective ports.

In a report to Congress for 1850, the Hon. Thomas Corwin, Secretary of the Treasury, states that "means have been taken for the conversion of a building at San Francisco, known as the Presidio, into a hospital, to be used until a suitable structure shall be erected for that purpose." No action having been taken by Congress to secure uniformity in the marine hospitals, or to provide for a medical corps, as recommended in the Edwards-Loring report, we are not surprised that the Secretary, becoming disgusted with their management, prefers a return to the "farming-out" method as the lesser of the two evils. The Secretary (Thomas Corwin), in a report dated June 30, 1852, says he does not "advise the erection of more marine hospitals. The experience of the Department induces me to believe that it is in every way preferable to make an arrangement for the care of sick seamen with local hospitals of high standing, which are under the immediate and vigilant supervision of citizens of the highest respectability at the respective places." He also states that "there is probably no instance where so much relief is granted, and so generally distributed, and with so much advantage to the parties, as that by the marine hospital fund under the present regulations." In conclusion, he requests an additional appropriation for the Evansville hospital. Much difficulty was experienced in procuring a site for the marine hospital at San Francisco; and a contract having been made with Charles Homer to construct the hospital, he was kept waiting for a period of thirteen months before he could begin upon his work. Mr. Homer claimed damages to the extent of $45,182.47, which Congress declined to allow.

The hospital at Chelsea having been in use nearly thirty years, and the land in its vicinity having become valuable, the Secretary of the Treasury (James Guthrie) recommended (December 17, 1854) that the ground be parceled into lots and sold, and that the proceeds be devoted to the construction of a new hospital. He also recommended that ten acres of the navy-hospital grounds be appropriated for the site of the new building.

Whatever may have been alleged against Secretary Cobb, he at least exercised a watchful care against unnecessary expenditures in the marine hospitals, and showed great severity in his rulings. Indeed, he desired the abolition of the entire system, as shown in his report of June 30, 1858, which states that small necessity existed for the many appropriations that had been made for costly marine hospitals, and at the same time showed the "glaring discrepancy between the amount appropriated and the necessities of the case." Thus, "At Natchez, Miss., where a marine hospital had been erected at a cost of $53,250, there have been no returns of patients admitted during the past year. At Portland, Me., a building has been constructed costing over $100,000, and it is estimated it will cost over $4.000 to finish it. The returns for the past year are for only 61 patients relieved, at an average cost of three dollars per week, and a total cost of $4,377.43. At Pensacola but 17 patients have been reported to be relieved, at an average cost of $3.50 per week, and a total of $156. . . . There is a necessity for a different system of legislation for such objects."

In this report a comparison is made between the cost of maintaining the patients under the contract system and in regular marine hospitals, as follows: " *Cost by contract*, each man, per week: Bridgeton, N. J., $1.50; Cincinnati, $5; New York, $4; Portsmouth, $2; Middletown, $2; and at Machias, Waldoboro, Kennebunk, Belfast, Presque Isle, and Sackett's Harbor, each $2.50. *Cost in marine hospitals*, each man, per week: Cleveland, $4.84; Norfolk, $5.09; Chicago, $5.77; Chelsea, $6.11; New Orleans, $6.31; San Francisco, $6.62; Louisville, $7.21; Mobile, $8.19; Key West, $8.47; Pittsburgh, $10.71; Paducah, $16.10; Ocracoke, $18.20; Napoleon, $25.41; Natchez, $70.70." This comparison, besides giving only partial data, was obviously unfair, as those hospitals showing the highest average cost were altogether unnecessary, as is shown by Mr. Oobh himself. He states of the Burlington marine hospital, that there was small necessity for it in the first place. It was originally built at a cost of $39,111.27, which the Collector of that port characterizes as a useless and extravagant expenditure. He estimates $250 per annum as a reasonable estimate for future disbursements; and even this estimate has proved excessive, as the report for the fiscal year 1873 showed an expenditure of $147.25; for 1874, $104.41; and for 1875, $129.28. The great advantage of regular hospitals over those conducted by contract could not be seen when there was but a single hospital with a resident surgeon, when the hospitals were never inspected except at long intervals, when there was but little if any accountability on the part of the persons having them in charge, and when there were no statistics showing the duration of treatment. Wherever seamen are cared for at a per-diem rate, and their discharge from hospital not under control, the duration of treatment will be great, and the expense necessarily large.

At the breaking out of the war of secession, there were marine hospitals belonging to the United States at the following ports: Burlington, Vt.; Burlington, Iowa; Chelsea, Mass.; Cincinnati, Ohio; Charleston, S. C.; Chicago, Ill.; Cleveland, Ohio; Detroit, Mich.; Evansville, Ind.; Galena, Ill.; Key West, Fla.; Louisville, Ky.; Mobile, Ala.; Natchez, Miss.; Napoleon, Ark.; Norfolk, Va.; Ocracoke, N. C.; Paducah, Ky.; Pittsburgh. Pa.; Portland, Me.; St. Louis, Mo.; St. Marks, Fla.; San Francisco, Cal.; and Wilmington, N. C. All of these in the seceded States, with the exception of those at St. Marks and Key West, were taken possession of by the Confederate forces, and held until reoccupied by the national authorities.

On March 1, 1862, Congress, in appropriating $200,000 for the marine hospital fund, authorized the Secretary of the Treasury to rent either of the several marine hospitals to the proper authorities of the cities or towns where they were located, and to contract with the authorities for the relief of the sick and disabled seamen; and further authorized the Secretary to sell the hospital at Burlington, Iowa, or to retain the title and use it for the relief of sick and wounded soldiers of the United States, or to discharge all the officers and servants of the Government connected with it, and to close the hospital, should he deem it more expedient.

Owing to the damages inflicted on American shipping during the war, many American vessels were transferred and sold abroad. This affected the receipts from the marine hospital tax to a considerable extent. In order to guard against this loss, it was enacted by Congress, April 29, 1864, that, in case of the sale or transfer of any vessel of the United States in a foreign port, the consul or other agent of the United States should collect from the master or owner of the vessel all hospital money that had become due at the time of the sale; and, in default of payment of such dues, the sale or transfer of the vessel was declared void.

On June 20, 1864, the Secretary was authorized to sell the marine hospital and grounds at Chicago, and purchase a site and erect a new hospital at that place. The report of the Supervising Architect for 1864 recommends that Congress be asked for authority to sell the marine hospital property at Burlington, Vt., "as there never was any demand for a hospital at that point." The hospitals at Cincinnati, Burlington, Vt., and Charleston, S. C., were sold by public auction during the year 1866. Attempts were also made to dispose of the marine hospital at Ocracoke, N. C., and Napoleon, Ark., but without success, the prices offered having been merely nominal. The marine hospital at Cincinnati, which cost $216,833, and which was completed in 1860, had been used during the war for the reception of wounded soldiers. Although it was nearly new, and in a most eligible situation, it was sold for $70,500. The marine hospital at Charleston, S. C., which had been nearly destroyed during the siege of that city, was sold to the Commissioners for the relief of freedmen for $9,500. Its original cost was $49,235. During the year 1867 the hospitals at Burlington, Iowa, and Evansville, Ind., and the hospital grounds at Paducah, Ky. (the building having been destroyed by fire during the war), were sold. The marine hospital at St. Marks, Fla., was transferred to the War Department. The site for the new marine hospital at Chicago was purchased at a cost of $10,000. The building now stands on the site then purchased, six miles from the custom-house, on a barren sand-bank, exposed to the violent winds which prevail in that region in winter. In 1868 the hospital at Napoleon,

Ark., was swept away by the river, which the Supervising Architect stated in his annual report for that year was the most favorable disposition that could have been suggested, as the property was entirely unsalable, and the building had never been needed for hospital purposes. Some of the materials of the building, however, were rescued and sold for $30. In this year the hospital at San Francisco was partially destroyed by an earthquake.

The Supervising Architect, in his report to the Secretary for the year ending June 30, 1869, says: "So remarkable has been the selection hitherto of locations, that it is difficult to imagine any other motive for the erection of the buildings, in many cases, than a desire to expend money in the locality in which the buildings were located."

In this year Dr. W. D. Stewart, who had served during the war as a surgeon of volunteers, was appointed an Inspector of Marine Hospitals for the Treasury Department; and later Dr. Billings of the army was associated with him in this work, in which he subsequently succeeded him. In accordance with the report of these officers, the Secretary of the Treasury recommended the sale of the marine hospital building and grounds at New Orleans, and the purchase from the War Department of the Sedgwick Military Hospital. Mr. Mullett says of the hospital at New Orleans:

The plans were prepared in 1855 and 1856, and contemplated the erection of a brick structure; but parties interested in the iron trade were permitted to prepare plans for an iron building, which were adopted. During the progress of construction it was thought necessary that the iron walls should be backed with some non-conducting material, and a large amount of money was expended in backing them with unburned clay or adobe. The experiment proved a total failure, and it was finally decided to back the exterior of the walls with brick, as well as make the interior partition of the same material. This portion of the work was not completed. The roof is of galvanized iron, in bad condition, and practically worthless. . . . The building consists of a central structure 130 feet by 62, three stories high, with two wings, 183 by 63 feet, two stories high, the three being connected by verandas.

This building was occupied as a barracks during the war, and was temporarily transferred to the Freedmen's Bureau for a hospital in 1865. One wing is now occupied as a hospital for the pauper insane of Louisiana, by permission of the Department, it having never been used as a marine hospital.

The following letter from Mr. N. B. Devereaux, Chief of the Office of the Revenue, Marine Division, to the Hon. William B. Kelsey, of the Committee on Appropriations, shows the condition of the marine hospital fund on April 20, 1870:

The hospital expenses are about $40,000 per month, say the sum in a year of $475,000; to meet which we have a revenue from seamen of $175,000, leaving a deficit of $300,000. We had an appropriation last session of $100,000, leaving the sum of $200,000 to be met by another appropriation, which we now require to carry us through the present fiscal year ending June

30, 1870. We need at this moment $120,000 to pay bills already due, and claims in office; and $80,000 more will meet the expenses for the next two months, May and June. This is the exact state of the case.

In 1870 the Secretary of the Treasury reported, in answer to a resolution of the House, that the hospital at Mobile was going to ruin; that it would cost $15,000 to $20,000 to repair it; and he recommends discontinuing the hospital, and sending the patients to New Orleans.

In this year Secretary Boutwell renewed the recommendation which had been made in 1836 by the Hon. Levi Woodbury, then Secretary, for the establishment of a marine hospital at New York, as follows:

TREASURY DEPARTMENT, *January* 17, 1870.

SIR: The Department, regarding it highly essential that the port of New York should be provided with a marine hospital, has made a request of the War Department that the buildings on David's Island, East River, formerly an army hospital, but not now required, be purchased by the Treasury Department for marine hospital purposes. It is desired that David's Island be transferred to this Department, and the sanction of Congress is requested, together with an appropriation of $10,000, to purchase the building at the appraised valuation of $6,000, and the balance of $4,000 to put the hospital in proper condition for service. The locality of David's Island is a very superior one for the purposes named, and the Department will be afforded an excellent opportunity of establishing a hospital at this great commercial point, for a moderate expenditure.

David's Island being twelve miles from the city, this recommendation was opposed by the shipping interests, and was never carried into effect.

In this year, January 31, 1870, a bill for the reorganization of the service was transmitted by Secretary Boutwell to the House. The essential changes proposed by this bill had been already foreshadowed in the Edwards-Loring report, heretofore alluded to. This bill for the first time provided for a systematic national service, and the regulations which were subsequently made in accordance with it provided for the examination of medical officers. Prior to the adoption of these regulations there was no limit to the number of employees that might be borne on the pay-rolls of the hospitals, and in many instances the number of attendants far exceeded that of patients. The act, approved June 29, 1870, provided in section 1 that the hospital dues should be increased to the sum of 40 cents per month. Sections 2, 3, 4, and 5 were simply reënactments of previous laws which had fallen into disuse from lack of enforcement. Section 6 authorized the Secretary of the Treasury to appoint a surgeon to act as Supervising Surgeon of the Marine Hospital Service, whose duty it was, under the direction of the Secretary, to supervise all matters connected with that service, and with the disbursement of the fund. It also provided that the word "vessel" should be held to include every description of water-craft, raft, vehicle, and contrivance used, or capable of being used, as a means or auxiliary on or by water. Dr. John M. Woodworth of Illinois, who had served with distinction during the war, was appointed to the office of Supervising Surgeon, March 23, 1871.

By the act of June 10, 1872, Congress placed its disapprobation on the "contract system," by providing that no part of the sum then appropriated should be used for the support of seamen in contract hospitals.

The act of March 3, 1873, directed the Secretary of the Treasury to collect the tax by a schedule based on the difference in rig, tonnage, and kind of traffic; and by an act of the same date, the title of the "Supervising Surgeon" was changed to Supervising Surgeon-General, and the appointment was directed to be made by the President, by and with the advice and consent of the Senate.

The operations of the service since 1871 have been published in the reports for the years 1872, 1873, 1874, 1875, 1876–'77, and 1878–'79. The first board for the examination of medical officers was convened in accordance with the regulations of 1873, since which time no appointments have been made to the service except such as have passed a thorough and rigid examination into their professional qualifications. Since the reorganization of the service all useless hospitals have been discontinued; the hospitals at San Francisco and Chicago have been completed; a system of dispensary or out-patient relief has been inaugurated; and all medicines are purchased in bulk by the Medical Purveyor, who makes such purchases only after a thorough examination into their quality, and they are then distributed to the various hospitals.

The number of seamen in the United States contributing to this service is estimated at 170,-000. The number of patients actually treated during the year ended June 30, 1879, was 20,-922. The offices of the hospitals are, whenever practicable, at the custom-houses at the different ports, and seamen requiring prescriptions only, who are not sick enough to require being sent to hospital, are furnished medicines at these offices as "out-patients." Nearly 10,-000 seamen were treated as out-patients in 1879. Ambulances are furnished at all the principal ports.

In June, 1879, the subject of physical examination of seamen, which had been agitated for several years by Dr. King of Staten Island, and Drs. Woodworth and Bailhache of the Marine Hospital Service, was taken up, and a circular was issued by the writer, with the approval of Secretary Sherman, which provided that on the application of the master, owner, or agent of any vessel of the United States the marine hospital surgeons were required to examine physically any person desiring to ship on board any such vessel, in order to determine his seaworthiness. Although the subject had been under discussion for some time, yet the idea that such examinations could be made popular without a compulsory law seems not to have occurred to any one previously; but the leading daily papers of the country republished the circular with general approbation. This has lately been extended by the action of the Board of Supervising Inspectors of the Steamboat Inspection Service, in adopting new pilot rules, which require that no pilot shall be allowed to take out a license until he shall produce a certificate of examination from a medical officer of the Marine Hospital Service that he suffers from no defect of vision.

In August, 1879, the hospital was opened on Bedloe's Island, New York Harbor, the military having evacuated it; and while this volume is in press (1880), a steam ambulance is being constructed, to ply between the Battery and the island, and elsewhere about the harbor, on receiving the proper signal from any American vessel in port.

The officers of this service consist of a Supervising Surgeon-General, Medical Purveyor, surgeons, passed assistant surgeons, and assistant surgeons. These are designated medical officers. At ports where the service is not large enough to warrant the assignment of a regular medical officer, a private physician is designated as acting assistant surgeon, to act instead of a medical officer. Dr. Woodworth, the first Supervising Surgeon-General, having died March 14, 1879, the writer, at that time a surgeon, was promoted to fill the vacancy.

It is gratifying to add that the growing importance of this service is meeting with the attention its object and character demand at the hands of Congress and commercial interests throughout the country.

JOHN B. HAMILTON,
Supervising Surgeon-General.

SHERMAN, JOHN, Secretary of the Treasury, born in Lancaster, Ohio, May 10, 1823. His paternal ancestors came from Essex, England, in the early days of the colonies, and settled in Massachusetts and Connecticut. His grandfather, Taylor Sherman, was born in Connecticut. An accomplished scholar and able jurist, he received a seat on the bench. He married Elizabeth Stoddard, a lineal descendant of Anthony Stoddard, who emigrated from England to Boston in 1639. Charles Robert, their son (the father of John Sherman), was born in Norwalk, studied law in the office of his father, and was admitted to the bar in 1810. The same year he married Mary Hoyt of Norwalk, and removed to Lancaster, Ohio. In 1823 he was elected Judge of the Supreme Court of that State. His written opinions, published in Hammond's "Reports of the Supreme Court of Ohio," have since been respected by the bar and courts of Ohio and other States as of the highest authority. He died suddenly, June 24, 1829, leaving a widow with eleven children. Her means being limited, friends came to her assistance, and took charge of the oldest children. Thomas Ewing, a neighbor and friend, adopted the third son, William

of Illino'
during tl
Supervis'
By the
its disap
by provic
propriate
seamen it
The act
retary of
a schedul,
nage, and
the same
Surgeon"
General, *
be made b
vice and c
The ope
been pub.
1872, 187i
The first t
officers w*
regulation.
pointment·
cept such *
examinatic
tions. Sir
all useless
the hospit
have been
or out-pati
all medicii
Medical P*
only after .
quality, an*
various hos
The num
contributin
000. The ,
during the .
922. The
ever practic
different po
tions only, *
being sent to
at these offic
000 seamen
1879. Am .
principal po
. In June,
amination o
for several :
and Drs. W
Marine Hos;
circular wa-
approval of
vided that *
owner, or a,*
States the n
quired to exe
ing to ship o.
to determine
subject had '
time, yet the
be made po
seems not t*

Tecumseh, and procured his appointment as a cadet at West Point, where he was trained for his great services in upholding the Union and bearing its flag in triumph "from the mountains to the sea."

John was the eighth child. His recollections are of the gradual scattering of the family, till but three children were left with their mother. In 1831 a cousin of his father, named John Sherman, took him to his home in Mount Vernon, where he remained four years attending school. At the age of twelve he returned to Lancaster, and entered the academy to prepare himself for college. At the end of two years he was far enough advanced to enter the sophomore class. Want of means and a strong desire to be self-supporting changed the current of his life. He obtained the position of junior rod-man in the corps of engineers engaged on the Muskingum improvement. In the spring of 1838, when only fifteen, he was placed in charge of the section of that work at Beverly, and so continued till the summer of 1839, when he was removed because he was a Whig. The responsibility attending the measurement of excavations and embankments, the leveling for a lock to the canal, and the construction of a dam, proved a better education than could have been obtained elsewhere in the same time. He studied law in the office of his brother Charles T. Sherman, afterward Judge of the United States District Court. He was admitted to the bar in 1844, and at once entered into partnership with this brother at Mansfield, where, during the ten years preceding his entrance into Congress, his ability and indefatigable industry gained for him distinction and pecuniary success.

In 1848 Mr. Sherman was a delegate to the Whig Convention at Philadelphia which nominated General Taylor for President. In August of the same year he married Cecilia, only daughter of Judge Stewart of Mansfield. In 1852 he was a Senatorial delegate to the Baltimore Convention, which nominated General Scott. His position as a conservative Whig, in the alarm and excitement consequent upon the attempt to repeal the Missouri Compromise, secured his election to the Thirty-fourth Congress, taking his seat December 3, 1855. A ready and forcible speaker, his thorough acquaintance with public affairs made him an acknowledged power in the House from the first. He rose rapidly in reputation as a debater on all the great questions agitating the public mind during that eventful period: the repeal of the Missouri Compromise, the Dred Scott decision, the imposition of slavery upon Kansas, the fugitive slave law, the national finances, and other measures involving the very existence of the republic. His appointment by Speaker Banks as a member of the committee to inquire into and collect evidence in regard to the "border-ruffian" troubles in Kansas was a turning-point in his political career. On account of the illness of the chairman, Mr. Howard of

Michigan, the duty of preparing the report devolved upon Mr. Sherman. Every statement was verified by the clearest testimony, and has never been controverted by any one. This report, when presented to the House, created a good deal of feeling, and intensified greatly the antagonisms in Congress, being made the basis of the campaign of 1856. He acted with the Republican party in supporting John C. Fremont for the Presidency, because that party resisted the extension of slavery, but did not seek its abolition. In the debate on the submarine telegraph he showed his opposition to monopolies by saying: "I can not agree that our Government should be bound by any contract with any private incorporated company for fifty years; and the amendment I desire to offer will reserve the power to Congress to determine the proposed contract after ten years." All bills appropriating money for public expenditures were closely scrutinized, and the then prevalent system of making contracts in advance of appropriations was denounced by him as illegal. At the close of his second Congressional term he was recognized as the foremost man in the House of Representatives. He had, from deep and unchanged conviction, adopted the political faith of the Republican party, but without any partisan rancor or malignity toward the South. He was reëlected to the Thirty-sixth Congress, which began its first session amid the excitement caused by the bold raid of John Brown. Helper's "Impending Crisis," a book then recently published, was the cause of the protracted struggle which ensued for the Speakership. At the end of eight weeks, Mr. Sherman, who needed but three votes to secure his election, retired from the contest, and Mr. Pennington of New Jersey was elected Speaker. He was then made Chairman of the Committee of Ways and Means. He took a decided stand against ingrafting new legislation upon appropriation bills, saying: "This is a practice which has grown up within the last few years, and the Committee of Ways and Means deem it their duty at once to put a stop to it; and we have determined, so far as we can, to resist the adoption of all propositions looking to a change in existing law by amendments upon appropriation bills. The theory of appropriation bills is that they shall provide money to carry on the government, to execute existing laws, and not to change existing laws or provide new ones."

In 1860 he was again elected to Congress, and when that body convened in December the seceding members of both Houses were outspoken and defiant. The message of President Buchanan showed that he was perplexed and overwhelmed by events which he had not the courage to control. At the beginning of Buchanan's administration the public indebtedness was less than $20,000,000. At this time it had been increased to nearly $100,000,000, and in such a crippled condition were its finances that the Government had not been able for more than a week to pay the salaries of members of Congress and many other demands. Mr. Sherman proved equal to the occasion in providing the means for the future support of the Government. His first step in this direction was securing the passage of a bill authorizing the issue of what have since been known as the Treasury notes of 1860.

In March, 1861, he was elected to fill the vacancy in the Senate caused by the resignation of Salmon P. Chase. He was reëlected Senator in 1867 and in 1873. During the greater part of his Senatorial career he was Chairman of the Committee on Finance, and served also on the Committees on Agriculture, the Pacific Railroad, the Judiciary, and the Patent Office. After the fall of Fort Sumter, under the call of President Lincoln for 75,000 troops, he tendered his services to General Patterson, was appointed his aide-de-camp without pay, and remained with the Ohio regiments in his command till the meeting of Congress in July. After the close of this extra session he returned to Ohio, and received authority from Governor Denison to raise a brigade. Largely at his own expense, he recruited two regiments of infantry, a squadron of cavalry, and a battery of artillery, comprising over 2,300 men. This force served during the whole war, and was known as the "Sherman Brigade." The most valuable services rendered by him to the Union cause were his efforts in the Senate to maintain and strengthen the public credit and to provide for the support of the armies in the field. On the suspension of specie payments, about the first of January, 1862, the issue of United States notes became a necessity. The question of making them a legal tender was not at first received with favor. Mainly through the efforts of Senator Sherman and Secretary Chase, this feature of the bill authorizing their issue was carried through the House and Senate. They justified the legal-tender clause of the bill on the ground of necessity. In the debates on this question Mr. Sherman said: "I do believe there is a pressing necessity that these demand-notes should be made legal tender, if we want to avoid the evils of a depreciated and dishonored paper currency. I do believe we have the constitutional power to pass such a provision, and that the public safety now demands its exercise." The records of the debate show that he made the only speech in the Senate in favor of the national-bank bill. Its final passage was secured only by the personal appeals of Secretary Chase to the Senators who opposed it. Mr. Sherman's speeches on State and national banks are the most important that he made during the war. He introduced a refunding act in 1867, which was adopted in 1870, but without the resumption clause. In 1874 a committee of nine, of which he was chairman, was appointed by a Republican caucus to secure a concurrence of action. They agreed upon a bill fixing the time for the

resumption of specie payments at January 1, 1879. This bill was reported to the caucus and the Senate with the distinct understanding that there should be no debate on the side of the Republicans, and that Mr. Sherman should be left to manage it according to his own discretion. The bill was passed, leaving its execution dependent upon the will of the Secretary of the Treasury for the time being.

President Hayes appointed Mr. Sherman Secretary of the Treasury in March, 1877. His transfer from the Finance Committee of the Senate to the Treasury Department was regarded with great satisfaction by all who were in favor of refunding the public debt into bonds bearing a low rate of interest, and who desired the success of specie resumption in 1879. What has been accomplished, during his administration, relating to these important measures, is fully given in this volume under the titles RESUMPTION OF SPECIE PAYMENTS, and REFUNDING THE NATIONAL DEBT.

SHIELDS, General JAMES, born at Dungannon, Tyrone County, Ireland, in 1810, died at Ottumwa, Iowa, June 1st. He emigrated to the United States in 1826, studied law, and commenced the practice of his profession in Kaskaskia, Illinois, in 1832. He was a man of fine personal presence, and possessed a rich, sonorous voice, which he knew how to use to advantage. His manners were pleasing and cultivated, and there was an attraction about him which made it an easy matter for him to become a leader in anything in which he took a part. Much of the success of his life resulted from this gift. In 1836 he was elected to the Legislature from Randolph County, and while at the capital made the acquaintance of Stephen A. Douglas, Abraham Lincoln, John J. Hardin, and others of subsequent distinction. In 1839 he was elected State Auditor, in 1843 was appointed a Judge of the State Supreme Court, and in 1845 Commissioner of the General Land-Office. When the war with Mexico broke out he was appointed a brigadier-general by President Polk, and was assigned to the command of the Illinois Volunteers. He served under General Taylor on the Rio Grande, under General Wool at Chihuahua, and under General Scott at the capture of the city of Mexico. At the battle of Cerro Gordo he was dangerously wounded by a ball passing through his right lung and barely missing his spine. After his recovery he was engaged in the battles around the city of Mexico. At Chapultepec he was more seriously wounded by a ball in his stomach, and in recognition of his services he was brevetted major-general. In 1848 he was appointed by the President Governor of Oregon Territory, which office he resigned to accept that of United States Senator from Illinois. He served until 1855, and shortly afterward took up his residence in Minnesota, and upon its admission as a State in 1858 was elected Senator for the term of two years. He then removed to California, where he remained two years, and married the wife who survives him. In 1861 he was commissioned a brigadier-general and joined the right wing of the Army of the Potomac. At Kernstown and Port Republic he came nearer defeating General "Stonewall" Jackson than any other Federal general ever did. He resigned his commission in 1863 and settled in Wisconsin, but soon after removed to Carrollton, Missouri, where he resumed the practice of his profession, and served as a Railroad Commissioner. In 1874 he represented Carroll County in the Legislature, and in January, 1879, he was elected by the Legislature to serve out the unexpired term (six weeks) of the deceased Senator Bogg. On his return he was tendered a reception at Jefferson City, which took place in the hall of the House of Representatives. He made a lengthy and very successful address. With the exception of an occasional lecture or address to assemblages of private citizens, he afterward remained in retirement.

SIGNAL SERVICE, METEOROLOGICAL DIVISION OF THE UNITED STATES. In the field, in time of war, the Signal Service of the United States Army is equipped to maintain communication by signals, by telegraph, or by semaphores between different portions of an army or armies, or between armies and fleets. In war or peace it communicates to proper authority information of danger of any description. The field-telegraph trains of the Signal Service are organized for use with armies. They are managed by soldiers who are drilled to march with, manœuvre, work, and protect them. The train carries light or field telegraph lines, which can be very quickly erected or run out at the rate of two or three miles per hour. They can be put in use for any distance, and be as rapidly taken down, repacked, and marched off with the detachment to be used elsewhere.

The Signal Service also transmits intelligence in reference to storms or approaching weather-changes by the display of signals of warnings and by reports posted in the different cities and ports of the United States. Maps showing the state of the weather over the United States are exhibited at Board of Trade rooms, Chambers of Commerce, and other places of public resort. Bulletins of data for all the stations are also prominently displayed and distributed without expense to the leading newspapers.

Signal-stations are also established in connection with the life-saving stations. These stations are connected by telegraph, and, in addition to displaying storm-warning signals and making the usual meteorological reports, make special reports upon the temperature of the water, tempests at sea, the sea-swells, etc. They also summon assistance to vessels in distress from the nearest life-saving stations or from the nearest port.

Stations for river-reports, to give notice of the conditions of the rivers affecting navigation and floods, are also established on the principal interior rivers and their tributaries.

The officers and men of the Signal Service are instructed for the different branches of the service at Fort Whipple, Virginia, and at the Central Office in Washington, D. C. They are taught signaling in all its branches, telegraphy, the use of the various meteorological instruments, the modes of observing, and the forms and duties required at stations of observation; the force is also drilled with arms, with the field-telegraph train, the construction of permanent telegraph lines, and in the usual duties of soldiers. For the duties of the observation of storms and for the display of warning signals, all stations communicate directly with the Signal Office in Washington over telegraphic circuits arranged with the different telegraph companies, and connecting with the office at fixed hours, each day and night. Each station is equipped with the following instruments: barometer, thermometer, maximum thermometer, minimum thermometer, anemometer with electrical attachment and self-registering apparatus, hygrometer, wind-vane, rain-gauge, and, at stations located on rivers, lakes, or seacoasts, thermometers for taking the temperature of water at different depths.

The readings of these instruments, made three times a day at fixed hours, are reported to the central office in cipher.

These reports from the stations of observation extending over territory reaching from the Atlantic to the Pacific Oceans, and from the capes of Florida into British America, are not unfrequently concentrated at the central office in the space of forty-five minutes. The stations at which cautionary signals are displayed are equipped with flags and apparatus for exhibiting the cautionary day or night signals, and also for communicating with vessels of any nationality.

The meteorological division of the United States Signal Service was established in 1870. It was the natural outgrowth of the service of the Signal Corps during the ten preceding years, and was an additional duty imposed upon it. The progress of modern inquiry into the changes taking place in the weather, and especially into the phenomena of storms, had for many years previous strengthened the conviction that they are not capricious, but follow certain laws. To provide, therefore, for taking meteorological observations, with a view to " giving notice by telegraph and signals of the approach and force of storms," was the end originally contemplated by the joint resolution of Congress, which passed February 9th of that year, authorizing the Secretary of War to carry this scheme into effect. The organization of a meteorological bureau adequate to the investigation of American storms, and to their preannouncement along the northern lakes and the seacoast, was, under the auspices of the War Department, immediately intrusted to the Chief Signal Officer of the Army, Brigadier-General Albert J. Myer; and the division thus created in his office was designated as the "Division of Telegrams and Reports for the Benefit of Commerce and Agriculture."

This was the first attempt of the United States Government to inaugurate a national weather service. The peculiar geographical extension of the country, stretching over fifty-seven degrees of longitude and twenty-two of latitude, afforded exceptional advantages for investigating and predicting the storms which cross its broad area; for experience and observation had shown that they generally move from west to east, and not frequently along the meridians. But the vast extent of the storm-field, coupled with the fact that the "law of storms" was then but roughly outlined, made the execution of this task a very difficult and tedious work, calling for great caution and the most accurate observations. Redfield had demonstrated from ship-reports that on the sea cyclonic disturbances in the northern hemisphere rotate from right to left—in a direction contrary to the hands of a watch. Ferrel and others had demonstrated that, mathematically or mechanically, this law should in theory hold good for both land and sea. The Dutch investigator Buys-Ballot, from actual weather-observations, had shown that the law held good for Holland. But its demonstration on the wider continental field of America, as well as the discovery of many details affecting its practical application to weather-prediction, awaited further, more extensive, and more exact research. It was not until November 1, 1870, that the Chief Signal Officer was able to issue weather-bulletins. On that day, from twenty-four stations, the first systematized *simultaneous* reports of the weather ever taken in the United States were read from their instruments by the Signal Service observers, and telegraphed to the Central Signal Office at Washington. The same day the bulletins made up from these reports were prepared and telegraphed by the Chief Signal Officer to more than twenty cities. The first storm-warning was bulletined along the lakes a week later, for the benefit of the large commercial and marine interests exposed to the furious gales which sweep, especially in autumn, over their waters. These tentative attempts to introduce the novel system of practical weather-telegraphy were vigorously followed up, and the success realized so early in the operations of the service was as gratifying to the public as to the office itself. This success was due in large measure to the system of observation and reports being in the strictest sense *simultaneous*.

Weather-Maps.—To arrive at any result, it was found necessary almost from the first to chart weather-maps from the reports thus received by telegraph. The Signal Service weather-map is a map of the United States on which all the Signal Service stations are entered in their appropriate geographical places, and having annexed to each station the figures expressing the readings of the barometer and thermometer, the velocity of the wind, the amount of rainfall within the previous twenty-four or eight hours, etc.; and also symbols indicating the direction of the wind, and the form and amount of cloud, at the given time of observation. The observations taken at each station are all put down on the map, and the relations between them are thus made sensible to the eye of the Signal Officer, by the figures and symbols, and also by lines drawn to group the geographical areas over which like conditions prevail. The weather-map is, therefore, to the meteorologist what the telescope is to the astronomer—an indispensable means of obtaining a survey, and prosecuting a careful and connected study of the phenomena he seeks to understand. The accompanying "War Department Weather-Map," prepared by the Signal Service, illustrates the method of charting the map graphically. This specimen map is about three eighths the size of those from which the Signal Office works. It represents the atmospheric conditions as they were simultaneously observed at 7 A. M. mean Washington time, December 23, 1879: the area marked "LOW" defining a storm or cyclonic area in Texas with low pressure, and that marked "HIGH" defining the limits of an anticyclonic area, in which the barometer is high. Around the latter the winds are seen to draw in the direction of the hands of a clock; but around the former, in a contrary direction.

Simultaneous Weather-Observations.—In organizing this service, the first problem that presented itself was to devise a system of observations which would when mapped accuratel represent the aërial phenomena in their *actua* relations to each other, and thus enable the in vestigator to discover the laws of storms an their rates of movement over the earth's sur face. "The history of science," says one o its foremost representatives, "proves that un connected, unsystematic, inaccurate observa tions are worth nothing." Certainly, in th domain of meteorology, no solid foundation fo the science of the weather could have been lai in 1870 upon any of the then existing observa tional systems. The European weather-station at that date, and long after, were engaged i making non-simultaneous reports; no two o them, unless they happened to be on the sam meridian, read off their instruments at the sam time; and consequently their records, valuabl as they were for purposes of *local* meteorology were inadequate and untrustworthy for pur poses of rigidly scientific comparison, or fo giving accurate numerical data of changes i the ever-restless and fickle atmospheric ocean In this state of the research, which had mad meteorology a proverb for inexactness, Genera Myer proposed a new, independent, and origi nal system of investigation — the system o SIMULTANEOUS METEOROLOGY — on the result of which the weather-predictions and storm warnings of the Signal Service have been base from the beginning of its work until now.

This novel, yet perfectly simple, schem aimed at the rescue of weather-research fro the chaos in which for ages it had lain. Its cardinal principle of observation is to gain a daily or tri-daily view of the atmospheric conditions and movements over the country as they *actually* are, and as they would be seen could they, so to speak, be photographed. In all previous systems this was far from attainable, for lack of simultaneous reports. As formerly observers had read off their barometers and other instruments at the given hours of local time, and not at the same moment of actual time, the reports from stations at widely separated meridians necessarily yielded unnatural and distorted representations of the phenomena to be studied. The Chief Signal Officer's plan reversed this vicious arrangement, and inaugurated one by which all the weather-observers over the entire field of inquiry, from the Atlantic to the Pacific coast, were to observe and read off their instruments "*at the same moment of actual* (not local) *time.*" Under the new method, introduced by General Myer in 1870, all the members of the Signal Corps registered and reported the weather of the United States, as it were, by given strokes of a single clock—the same moments of *physical* time—corresponding to certain fixed moments of Washington mean time.

Simple as this innovation appears, it is vital to all successful research in an aërial sea whose currents and waves rush with great rapidity, and perform some of their evolutions while the sun in his daily march is passing from one meridian to another. The old methods, without exception, though called "synchronous," were not truly so,* since each one of the observers reported at the local time of his own special station. When, therefore, the stations were extended over thousands of miles in an *east and west* direction (as was necessarily the case in the United States, owing to its geographical shape), their data were misleading. Columbus on his first voyage to America discovered that within the tropics the waters of the ocean move from east to west; but in the extra-tropical belt they move from west to east. As with the waters of the sea, so with the winds: from the equator nearly to the polar circles the great perennial air-currents (in which cyclones lie imbedded and in which they move forward as eddies in a stream) move on the surface of the earth along the parallels of latitude, and but seldom along the

---

* By "synchronous" weather-reports meteorologists only mean reports taken *nominally* at the same hour. Thus, if a London observer reported the weather at 7 A. M. Greenwich time, and a Berlin observer reported it at 7 A. M. Berlin time, the two reports would be called "synchronous"; but, in reality, they would not be synchronous, for the difference between 7 A. M. at one and the other point is about 54 minutes. But 54 minutes makes a great difference in the flight of a storm and the shiftings of atmospheric masses, which can not therefore be represented on weather-maps based upon "synchronous" reports. A weather-map prepared from such "synchronous" reports reflects the aërial elements untruly, as a telescopic lens having many irregular faces, and not a single focus, would reflect the surface of the moon. "Simultaneous" reports, on the contrary, when entered on a weather-map, form a true mirror of the atmospheric masses and movements as they are in nature.

meridians of longitude. For this physical reason, it was found to be of the utmost importance to observe these great movements at many points over long portions of the parallels of latitude *simultaneously*. In no other way can the bearings of the various storm-winds and their connected phenomena be detected, or the rates of their transition determined. All the predictions and deductions of the Signal Office, therefore, have from its beginning until now been based on reports taken simultaneously.

Early Developments.—As the early developments of the Signal Service were necessarily pioneer work, it being the first attempt to institute a system of "simultaneous" weather-telegraphy, and finding many of the laws of storms now defined then scarcely formulated or entirely unknown, its advance in 1871 was cautious and slow. But, when once it had established the fact that at any hour of the day or night it could almost instantly call for reports from all parts of the country, and receive them from all its stations, taken at the same moment of time and revealing the actual status of the atmosphere over its whole field of inquiry, the sense of security in its scientific processes, and the confidence that the results were built upon "the solid ground of nature," gave it a powerful forward impulse. The new method of simultaneous reports, it was felt, was a sure road to the desired goal. In a short time additional stations were established within the United States, making sixty-six in

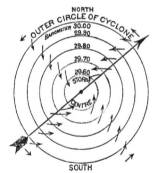

HORIZONTAL MOVEMENTS OF AIR AROUND CENTER OF CYCLONE IN NORTHERN HEMISPHERE.

(Large arrow shows path of storm; smaller arrows show the course of the winds increasing in velocity as they approach the centre.)

all. A comparison of the tri-daily forecasts, or "probabilities," as they were styled, with the weather-conditions following and reported as actually observed, so far as verified up to November 1, 1871, had given an average of 69 per cent. From that date to October 1, 1872, the average of verification rose to 76·8 per cent.; and during the year ending June 30, 1872, 354 cautionary signals were issued, with an estimated percentage of correctness amounting to 70. These results also afforded the best elucidation and the most complete demonstration of the law of storms and the movements of cyclones that had ever been obtained in any country.

By act of Congress approved June 10, 1872, the Signal Service was charged with the duty of providing such stations, signals, and reports as might be found necessary for extending its research in the interests of *agriculture*. The agricultural societies over the land earnestly entered into and coöperated with the Service in this new development of its inquiries and reports. Eighty-nine such societies, thirty-eight boards of trade or chambers of commerce, numerous scientific institutions, colleges, and leading professional men put themselves in communication with the Chief Signal Officer, with a view to facilitate this branch of his work. The scientific societies at home and abroad began to take the liveliest interest in the general labors of the Office, and to express the highest approval of the results attained. And, beyond the limits of the United States, numerous marine observations, which General Myer had previously desired, with the purpose of studying the atmosphere as a unit both on the ocean and the land, were forwarded regularly to his office.

The expansion of the work in 1873, under the stimulus of a world-wide favorable notice, was even more rapid than in the previous year. On March 3d Congress authorized the establishment of Signal Service stations at the lighthouses and life-saving stations on the lakes and seacoast, and made provision for connecting the same with telegraph-lines or cables "to be constructed, maintained, and worked under the direction of the Chief Signal Officer of the Army, or the Secretary of War, and the Secretary of the Treasury." Early in this year the Office also began the regular publication of a "Monthly Weather Review," summarizing all its data and showing the results of its investigations, as well as presenting these in graphic weather-charts adapted to the comprehension of the unscientific part of the communities it was destined to reach. The library of the Signal Office was increased to some 2,500 volumes bearing on the special scientific duties imposed upon it. The tests of meteorological instruments previously instituted enabled it to greatly improve and simplify its entire instrumental apparatus at all stations. The percentage of verification of its predictions for the year ending June 30, 1873, was for each geographical division as follows:

New England	81·50
Middle States	81·17
South Atlantic States	79·92
Lower Lake region	78·90
Upper Lake region	75·25
Eastern Gulf States	77·16
Western Gulf States	74·40
Northwest	74·00

It was in September of this year also that, at the proposal of the Chief Signal Officer in the International Congress of Meteorologists convened at Vienna, the system of world-wide coöperative weather-research, since then so extensively developed, was inaugurated, and began to contribute its observational data to the Signal Office records. Thus, in his report for 1873, the Chief Signal Officer was able to say of its labors, "Their utility is no longer questioned, and effort at home and abroad turns only toward their development." The Service was now no longer an experiment, but an assured success.

The operations of this division of the Signal Service, popularly known as the "Weather Bureau," have been, every year since its creation, somewhat enlarged by Congress, until they have become numerous and varied. The first to be specially mentioned is the daily work of weather-prediction, including storm-warnings. These are issued from the office of the Chief Signal Officer three times every day, under the title of "Indications" and "Cautionary Signals," and are based upon three series of simultaneous weather-reports telegraphed to Washington from all parts of the United States and Canada. The observations are taken simultaneously at all stations at 7 A. M., 3 P. M., and 11 P. M., and at once put upon the wires. The number of stations from which tri-daily telegraphic reports are received at the central office is 133. Telegraphic reports have been also regularly received from one West India station, and during the hurricane season from five. The total number from which such reports are received daily is 159; but, including those sent by mail, it is much larger; while the total of reporting stations within the United States territory, including the special river and sunset stations, on the 30th of June,

SIGNAL SERVICE STATION ON THE SUMMIT OF MOUNT WASHINGTON.

1879, was 229. The vertical range of the observations extends from sea-level to the summits of Mount Washington (6,286 feet) and Pike's Peak (14,151 feet).

Form 106 B.

From the telegraphic data, of course, the tri-daily "Indications" are prepared. The general process is this: Having taken their instrumental and other observations at either of the hours specified, the observers prepare their reports in *cipher*, by which expense for the telegrams and time in their transmission are saved, as well as greater accuracy secured. The observations include the actual and the corrected readings of the barometer and thermometer, and their changes since previous report; the direction and velocity of the wind, as well as its pressure; the relative humidity of the air; the amount of rain or snow fallen since last report; the amount and form of clouds, auroras, haze, fog, smokiness, frost, etc.; and to these data the river stations add the changes or oscillations in the rivers, and the seacoast stations the direction and degree of the ocean-swell. The maximum and minimum range of the temperature in the past twenty-four hours are also given. These data, condensed by means of the cipher-code into ten or twelve words for each report, as soon as received in the telegraph-room of the Washington office, are translated from cipher and entered on the bulletin blanks, and also entered in their proper places on the weather-maps. This is done in the room where the predictions and storm-warnings are prepared after all the dispatches are in, and under the eye of the assistant engaged in shaping the weather-predictions for the public press. This was, for some years after the Signal Service was organized, pioneer work—the first attempt at weather forecasts based on simultaneous telegraphic reports ever set on foot.

Synoptic Weather-Map.—As a concomitant and indispensable aid in the analysis of the reports and in utilizing them for purposes of prediction, synoptic weather-maps, which would show the concurrent conditions of the weather as they simultaneously and actually exist over the country, for the first time became possible in 1870. The aim kept in view had been to secure a bird's-eye view of the atmosphere, and the data thrice daily supplied by the Signal Service reports sufficed for the construction daily of three maps, showing the weather-status and all the wind and storm movements in their connection and interdependence. By preparing a graphic weather-map embodying the telegraphic data furnished to the Chief Signal Officer every eight hours in the day, the officer charged with formulating the storm-predictions could gain and retain a clear idea and mental image of the aërial ocean. A great soldier has said, "There is nothing ideal in war"; and it may be said with equal force, there is no work which for its intelligent execution demands greater precision of method, more copious and circumstantial details, and closer attention to the developments of the hour, than weather-forecasting over a continent. The weather-map brings all these minutiæ within view, and makes the

meteorologist master of the whole mass of observations, as hours consumed in the study of the numerical data could not do. Every weather-map is, therefore, a *generalization* in itself, as well as a record of the data. A series of weather-maps is a history of the ebb and flow, the fluctuations and tossings of the aërial ocean, and of the more subtile yet influential processes concerned in producing the weather and determining the climate of the country.

These maps, offering in a synoptic view the results deduced or deducible from thousands of observations, enable the Chief Signal Officer to prepare statistics and reports for the use of individuals, institutions, and the public journals, upon special requests for such meteorological information as their business or publications demand. The calls for such consolidated data, and the elucidation of obscure climatic conditions, which these reports and maps alone can supply, have increased until compliance with them has become a work of magnitude, requiring a greater force than the office now has at command.

Military Organization.—An economic feature of the Weather Bureau is that it is a *military service*. All its observational work is done by enlisted men and officers of the army, and all its official publications are prepared under authority, and with the regularity and dispatch to be had only under military discipline. The military relations of the Signal Service have been found by experience to give it great advantages in extending its network of stations in the sparsely populated territories of the country, whence, for the development of its scientific research, it must draw many of the most indispensable meteorological reports. The observers of the Signal Corps are trained not only in the art and practice of miltary field-signaling, but in the ordinary army drill and rules and habits of discipline; so that in time of war they constitute a part of the regular fighting force of the nation, ready for active service in repressing internal disorder and repelling foreign invasion. Constituting, in fact, only a portion of the regular army, occupied in time of peace with scientific work, but available for duty in the ranks in the emergency of war, the cost of their maintenance is but a small additional burden upon the country, far more than requited by their meteorological services to it. Experience has fully shown in other countries that arduous meteorological labors such as they perform can not be secured from any civil corps. As the Signal Service observers must report several times a day to the Washington office, each regular general report serves in effect as a telegraphic roll-call of all the stations spread over the country from the Atlantic to the Pacific, and from the lakes to the Gulf of Mexico, insuring promptitude, vigilance, and steadiness in the entire Signal Corps.

In addition to this regular force of military observers, there was transferred to the Signal

Service on February 2, 1874, at the instance of Professor Joseph Henry of the Smithsonian Institution, the entire body of Smithsonian weather-observers in all parts of the United States. This volunteer civilian force continues to the present day to contribute its scientific labors in behalf of the Signal Service researches in the domain of continental meteorology and climatology. The volunteer observers thus co-operating with General Myer, with others who have embarked in the work since 1874, now number 240, and their observational data great-ly enrich the records of the Signal Office. Many of them have acquired great exactness and ex-perience in instrumental observation and not-ing and recording physical phenomena, so that their monthly reports to the Chief Signal Offi-cer alone make a rich repository of American climatology. This voluntary corps is under-going constant additions, and inducements are held out by the Service to competent civilians, especially in the sparsely settled and frontier districts, to join in its investigations.

Practical Uses of Weather-Reports.—With this brief notice of the organization of the Service and its methods of weather-observing and weather-forecasting, we hasten to the prac-tical applications of the work. In referring to the wide-spread interest in the weather-pre-dictions of the past few years, a recent writer in the "Quarterly Review" observes, "Some basis of solid value to the public must exist to account for such a general popularity of the weather-service." The fact is, that the public are just beginning to see some of its more ob-vious utilities.

The tri-daily "Indications" are designed to give timely notice of the general weather-changes to occur in the twenty-four hours fol-lowing their issue. As they are telegraphed from the Washington office, and adapted to the convenience of the daily press, they are greatly condensed, to bring the cost of tele-graphing within the restricted means of the Service; and yet they must be made sufficient-ly full to cover the whole country. These con-ditions are hindrances to their usefulness, and the brevity of the dispatches exposes them at times to popular misinterpretation. But, notwithstanding these drawbacks, the scope of their practical application to all classes of industry is large and continually increasing. When the first propositions of a weather bureau were advanced, the highest end thought attain-able, by the most sanguine, was to give warn-ings of the *great* storms that ravage the sea-coasts of the United States. This, however, is but a small part of the public interests it sub-serves. The number of persons who find that the reports and forecasts of the Service may be utilized for every-day life is constantly increas-ing. Signal observers are not unfrequently subpœnaed to bring the records of the weather into the courts, as legal evidence in cases upon which they bear. Grain and cotton merchants find the "Indications" of value in calculations

of the forthcoming crops. Emigrants and "prospectors" intending change of residence use them to determine the climate of new towns. Physicians, sanitarians, and boards of health employ their data to detect dangerous conditions of the atmosphere of the cities, and for investigating the origin and spread of dis-eases and epidemics, as in the case of the recent yellow-fever visitations of the South. The pork-packers, fruit-importers, and fish- and oyster-dealers keep an eye on them to secure themselves against exposure of perishable goods to weather too damp or too warm. They are of use to specialists in manufacturing and hy-gienic interests, and are consulted by thousands planning journeys or excursions for health or pleasure. River-boatmen, farmers, sugar-plant-ers, fruit-growers, and ice dealers find occasion to utilize them. Mechanics judge from the prognostics whether they can work outside on the morrow. The meteorological data supply engineers with information indispensable for planning economical and storm-proof archi-tecture. Railroad officials, during snow-block-ades, are kept advised by the reports, so that they are enabled to make provision for clearing the tracks; and railroad freight officers find them useful for facilitating transportation. These are some of the daily applications made of the Signal Service work in the interior and central, not less than in the seaboard sections of the country. In every branch of agriculture and trade the deductions that could be made from the published synopses and indications of the weather would have immensely enhanced value if the public could be instructed how to frame them. In military operations over the vast West, the intelligence of approaching storms is of no little value, in timing move-ments so as to avoid heavy roads and danger-ous delays. "Had we, a quarter of a century ago," says a British meteorologist, "known the rigor of the Crimean climate, who would have dared to send out an army unprepared to meet the hardships of a Black Sea winter? Ask the physician at what price he would value the power of giving timely warning of a 'cold snap' to his patients. Ask the builders of London what they have lost in the last ten years by sudden frosts or unexpected down-pours of rain. Above all things, go to the farmer and ask what he would freely pay to know at seed-time what weather he might really expect in harvest. The fact is, there is not a profession, not a handicraft, not a process in animal or vegetable life, which is not influ-enced by meteorological changes."

Wide Diffusion of the Weather-Reports.—The distribution of the tri-daily "Synopses and Indications" over the whole country may be understood from the following official facts: The total number of these forecasts — 1,095 issued every year—are telegraphed at the mo-ment of issue to the principal cities, and are published in some form in almost every news-paper in the country. In many public and conspicuous places, they are also bulletined for popular inspection. In order that they may reach the farming populations, an arrangement is effected with the Post-Office Department, by which special "Farmers' Bulletins" may be distributed at an early morning hour of each day, except Sunday, along the railroads radiating from the chief cities of the Union. These "Farmers' Bulletins" contain all the matter of the "midnight" report made up in the Washington office at 1 A. M. of each day, which, when it reaches the outlying stations by telegraph, is printed before daylight, and copies of it mailed to the rural postmasters for many miles around, and by them displayed in their offices. There are now nineteen cities at which the Signal Service observers reprint and circulate the telegraphic forecasts to 6,042 sub-centers among the agricultural communities while the reports are yet fresh and timely. Each postmaster has the order of the Postmaster-General to display the report as soon as received in a frame furnished for the purpose, and to report in writing to the Chief Signal Officer the time of its receipt and display. The intelligence of weather-changes, with predictions and other data useful to the farmer in securing his crops or in other ways, it has been found, on an average, reaches the different railway stations, hamlets, and villages throughout the United States in the forenoon. As the predictions cover twenty-four hours, and often hold good for twice that period, they therefore reach the denser rural populations twelve or fourteen hours before the period to which they apply expires, and not unfrequently a day and a half or more.

To make the reports still more widely useful to the agricultural interests, the Chief Signal Officer, by an arrangement between the War Department and different railways, has established a "Railway Weather Bulletin Service." In this work 103 railway companies, distributing daily 3,180 reports to as many railway stations, are now without charge coöperating. The midnight report, exhibiting the "Synopsis and Indications," is telegraphed to the railway companies, whose superintendents are charged with seeing that copies of it are bulletined and posted along their lines a few hours after it emanates from the Washington office. By this means large masses of the rural populations, and residents of districts which can not otherwise be reached in time, secure the benefits of the Government weather service. This system of distribution is in its incipiency, but is capable of indefinite extension, and of diffusing the desired weather-data to vast numbers of farmers in the interior centers. The immense demand which has ever existed among all classes for weather-forecasts is strikingly illustrated by the fact, mentioned by the "Penny Post" (an old English paper) in 1833, that up to that year the annual sale of "Moore's Almanack," the weather prognostics of which were proverbially without any basis of scientific observations, still amounted to "a quarter of a million copies."

As many farmers, however, reside too far from an railway station or post-office to obtain timely reports of storms and weather-changes, General Myer has for some time been preparing for distribution at cost-price among such a simple apparatus, which will serve even the uneducated as an indicator of coming changes. This is the "WEATHER-CASE, or FARMER'S WEATHER-INDICATOR." This automatically working instrument is of value in enabling agriculturists to interpret whatever official weather-intelligence reaches them, and to determine for themselves in advance the chief weather-changes, as well as to direct their thoughts and study to those atmospheric phenomena upon a knowledge of which their craft must so much depend. Instructions and rules for interpreting the instrumental variations will accompany the weather-case, and thus practically extend the already immense circle within which the reports are utilized.

Preparing the "Synopsis and Indications."— From reading in the morning newspapers the "Synopsis and Indications" for the day, no one not initiated in the method of preparing them would suspect the magnitude of the work involved in their preparation. The study prerequisite for each of the tri-daily press reports issued includes the draughting of eight graphic charts exhibiting the multiform data furnished by the simultaneous reports telegraphed from all the stations. These charts are: (a.) A chart of barometric pressures, temperatures, and winds (wind-direction and velocity) at the different stations, with the amount of clouds and the kind and amount of precipitation at each station. The isobars (or lines connecting stations where the barometric pressure is the same) are then drawn for every tenth of an inch, as also are isothermal lines for every 10° of temperature; while wind-directions are marked by arrows and their hourly velocities by numbers. (b.) A chart of relative humidities at all stations, with the character and amount of the upper and lower clouds, which have been well called "Nature's weather-guides." On this are traced lines of equal relative humidity over the country, showing the territorial areas over which precipitation is likely to ensue upon the reduction of temperature, or where the clouds are likely to be dissipated by a rise of temperature. As isothermal lines are drawn on this chart, such deductions are facilitated. (c.) A chart of the various cloud-conditions prevailing at the time over the United States, with the "weather" at each station depicted by symbols; also the minimum temperatures and the maximum wind-velocities. The cloud-areas—each form of cloud represented by a different symbol—are outlined, and each one is distinguished. The appearance of the western sky at each station as observed at sunset, which affords a strong indication of the weather to be anticipated for

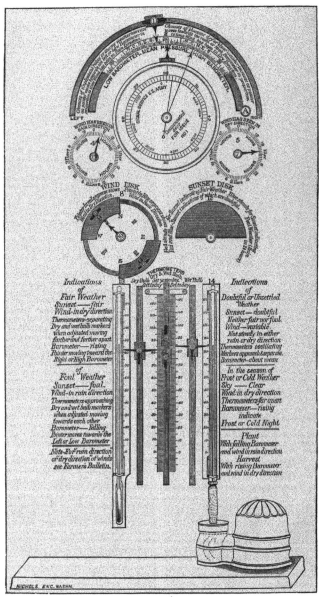

WEATHER-CASE, OR FARMER'S WEATHER-INDICATOR.

the next twenty-four hours, is also marked on this chart. (d.) A chart of the *normal* pressures—those which from a long series of observations should be expected—and of variations of the actual from the average pressures. The deviations or "departures" of the actual pressures from those which generally prevail are marked on the map by appropriate lines; as also, by the lines of "no variation," the districts in which the atmosphere is in a state of equilibrium are delineated. (e.) A chart of actual variations of pressure transpiring since the last report, showing the fluctuations of the atmosphere during the previous eight hours. (f.) A chart of dew-point variations which have taken place at the stations during the preceding eight and twenty-four hours. (g.) Lastly, a chart of dew-points, vapor-tensions, and the actual amounts of humidity in the air at the various points of observation. All these charts, each covering the whole of the country, must be made out, and the mass of data they embody sifted and analyzed, preliminary to the preparation of every one of the tri-daily bulletins issued from the central office. This system of mapping, symbolizing, grouping, and numerically notating the data enables the Signal Officer to picture to his eye the exact status of the aërial masses, and to catch the

"run" of the weather in the separate sections of the vast field of observation over which it is executing its manifold manœuvres. These charts have all to be draughted in about an hour or an hour and a half; but they are inter-corrective, each chart serving as a check on the others.

Armed with this charted material, the officer preparing the predictions proceeds first to make up the "Synopsis," showing the conditions of weather now existing, and then to deduce and write the "Indications," showing the changes to occur afterward. As soon as this is done, the deductions are telegraphed direct from the office of the Chief Signal Officer to all parts of the country, and are given to the newspapers. The average time elapsing between the simultaneous reading of the instruments at the 290 separate stations scattered over the United States, and the issue of the "Synopsis" and "Indications" based on these readings, has been calculated at one hour and forty minutes.

Verifications of Predictions.—An analysis of the predictions, made for the year ending June 30, 1879, and a comparison with the weather-conditions which actually occurred within the twenty-four hours next ensuing, give the following percentages of verifications:

PERCENTAGE OF VERIFICATIONS FOR EACH MONTH OF THE YEAR ENDING JUNE 30, 1879.

REGIONS.	1878.						1879.					
	July.	Aug.	Sept.	Oct.	Nov.	Dec.	Jan.	Feb.	March.	April.	May.	June.
New England..........................	80·6	84·4	83·5	87·6	89·1	88·6	55·5	93·8	89·8	81·8	84·3	84·0
Middle States	77·8	87·6	85·9	88·4	90·8	87·0	86·0	94·1	90·5	87·2	85·6	86·0
South Atlantic States	83·5	89·5	89·2	87·3	91·8	85·5	88·6	92·3	91·6	82·0	80·4	79·8
Eastern Gulf States.................	89·8	91·0	83·4	87·2	88·2	90·1	87·0	92·7	90·7	85·5	76·6	80·4
Western Gulf States.................	88·7	91·2	89·5	89·1	90·4	88·6	83·5	90·9	87·8	81·9	76·7	81·1
Lower Lakes........................	84·9	86·7	81·9	85·3	91·0	87·1	87·0	94·1	91·2	83·2	84·7	88·6
Upper Lakes........................	83·1	87·6	83·8	87·4	89·7	88·4	88·1	92·5	89·6	81·8	87·1	86·8
Tennessee and Ohio Valley...........	81·6	82·3	85·8	86·8	92·4	85·5	86·3	95·8	89·4	84·4	84·2	84·9
Upper Mississippi Valley.............	84·3	86·8	84·2	89·4	92·4	85·2	85·6	92·1	85·1	81·5	84·1	88·3
Lower Missouri Valley	82·9	83·2	82·8	86·8	91·5	84·6	84·6	91·4	89·1	80·1	84·0	81·2
Total percentage of verifications...	88·7	87·1	85·0	87·5	90·7	87·1	86·2	98·0	89·3	82·9	82·8	88·7

Percentage of verifications for the year (changes of barometric pressures, temperatures, wind-direction, and character of weather expected, comprised)........... .... 86·6
Percentage of verifications for the year (forecasts of the character of the weather only). .... 90·7

These percentages of accuracy refer to predictions of barometric, thermometric, wind-direction, and general weather changes, which are more difficult to make than those relating to future conditions of the weather alone. The percentage of accuracy of the forecasts of the weather alone (including the state of the skies, whether clear, fair, or cloudy, and whether with or without rain) in all of the different districts has been 90·7. The percentage for the Pacific coast region is 89·3. Out of a hundred preannouncements of the single element of the "weather" for all parts of the country (apart from barometric changes), ninety have been fulfilled by the event.

River Reports. — The important work of overseeing the fluctuations and floods of the great Western rivers, so sensitive to the meteorological changes occurring in their basins,

was at an early period of its history undertaken by the Signal Service. The interstate commerce being necessarily much affected by the oscillations of the rivers, timely warnings of their rise and fall, and daily reports of the exact depth of water at numerous points, were eagerly asked for. The observations of this kind were found of so much importance that they have been extended over the Western, Southern, and California rivers, and deductions made from them, indicating impending changes, are daily published in the Washington weather-reports. All measurements at each river-station are made from the "bench-mark," as known to the river-men of the vicinity, and the depth of water from the bed of the river to this mark is daily gauged and telegraphed to the central office. Knowing from such telegrams the height of the river at any station, and knowing the present and antecedent rainfall higher up the river-valley, the office is thus enabled to calculate and announce the time and degree of coming changes. Thus timely premonitions of the great flood-waves that pass down the Mississippi, and also its fluctuations, are issued from the office to the places which it reached on its southerly way.

The gauge used is very simple. It is a plank (A, Fig. 2) of pine or oak timber, two inches thick, ten inches wide, and long enough, when placed obliquely on the slope of the river-bank, to cover the extreme low-water and high-water marks. When firmly imbedded in

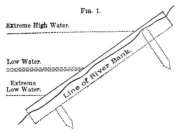

FIG. 1.

Extreme High Water.

Low Water.

Extreme
Low Water.

Line of River Bank.

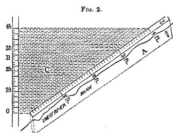

FIG. 2.

SIGNAL SERVICE RIVER-GAUGE.

the earth, the mean level of the river or "benchmark" is marked on it as zero, and it is carefully graduated in feet and inches by means of an upright measuring-rod (B), a straight-edge and spirit-level crosswise, as shown by the dotted lines (C) in the cut, each foot and its subdivisions exactly corresponding to the vertical foot and subdivisions of which they are intended to be indices. A "danger-line" is marked on the gauge, showing how far the water may rise, but no farther, without danger of a flood. The reports telegraphed to the press, stating how near each stream has risen to or fallen below the "danger-line," enable the public to predetermine dangerous inundations, and furnish steamboat-men and merchants the daily information requisite for intelligently directing the movements of their craft. During the flood-months the tele-

graphic river-reports are especially valuable to all river-shipping, and to all interested in the traveling and transportation facilities which depend upon it, as well as giving timely warnings of ice floods or sudden rises and falls. The levee systems of the Mississippi and other great rivers can thus be guarded, and the immense agricultural interests secured, as the flood-warning comes in time to summon the State force to strengthen the imperiled works. Daily bulletins of the river-reports are regularly displayed at Augusta (Ga.), Cairo, Chattanooga, Cincinnati, Davenport, Dubuque, and Keokuk (Iowa), La Crosse (Wis.), Leavenworth, Louisville, Memphis, Morgantown (W. Va.), Nashville, New Orleans, Omaha, Pittsburgh, Portland (Oregon), Red Bluff (Cal.), Shreveport, St. Louis, St. Paul, Umatilla (Oregon), Vicksburg, and Yankton (D. T.).

In connection with this service, surface and bottom water-temperatures at points upon the rivers, lakes, and seacoasts are observed and reported for the United States Commissioner of Fish and Fisheries, with a view to ascertain the proper waters in which to plant the various food-fishes and furnish statistics desired for the development of the national system of pisciculture.

There is also to be mentioned the oversight given by the office to the changes of temperature by which the canals are closed by freezing, or opened by thaws for transportation. During the months when the market-rates and freight-schedules are affected by the probabilities of the canals closing, and when these waterways are thronged with hundreds of laden barges, the daily predictions indicate the thermometric conditions likely to ensue along their lines of transit. Such information may often protect the public from the imposition of excessive railway-rates in the shipment of the grain-crops, especially in any autumn season of protracted mildness, and effect a large saving to the mercantile world.

The Cautionary Storm-Signals, which accompany the "Synopsis and Indications" issued to the press three times each day, constitute a very important part of the Signal Service work; and it was the possibility of preparing such storm-warnings for the benefit of navigation that originally gave the chief stimulus to the establishment of a Weather Bureau. The United States has a double front with over 7,000 miles of sea-beaten coast, exclusive of the shore-line of its great lakes, ravaged by terrific tempests; and this vast stretch of marginal territory needs to be environed with stations from which observations can be taken, and premonitory intelligence of cyclone and anticyclone signaled by day and by night to storm-menaced shipping. If no other duty devolved upon the Service, this alone would more than justify its whole cost, and warrant its extension. It is one of the most difficult and responsible tasks which can fall to the meteorologist, to put his science to its utmost stretch of accurate prevision (and often it must be done with a very few minutes for deliberation) to decide at what points on the coast the storm-wind will strike with dangerous effect. It is practically fatal to the value of his warnings if they are found to be superfluous, since in that case they cease to command the attention of seamen. Nor, for like reason, must they be displayed too late; nor yet too early, lest they should interfere with the movements of vessels which might run out of the dangerous vicinity before the storm can reach them. Thus the perplexing questions which spring up at every display of the signals lend to this part of the Service duty the intensest interest. No such work had ever been undertaken in this country when the Signal Service was organized; and though maritime storm-signaling on a small scale had been tentatively prosecuted in England by Admiral Fitzroy, his labors were held by his own Government of questionable success, and at his death in 1866 the experiment had been abandoned by it as premature, if not utterly hopeless.

On the organization of the United States Weather Service in 1870, the Chief Signal Officer began with great caution to prepare for this difficult and delicate part of his arduous task; and on the 24th of October, 1871, the display of signals on the seacoasts and lakes commenced. The order regulating this dis-

play contemplated that the warning should be sent only to stations at which a storm-wind having a velocity of twenty-five miles an hour would occur. As the anemometer at every station registers the wind's velocity for every hour, it is easy to ascertain whether any signal has been justified. Every such display is carefully followed up by the office, and the result—"justified" or "not justified"—is recorded, as reported by the observers hoisting the signals by telegraphic order from the Chief Signal Officer.

The cautionary signals are of two kinds: 1. Those premonishing dangerous winds to blow from any direction; 2. Those premonishing off-shore winds, likely to drive vessels out to sea. Both kinds are needed by mariners as the storm - centers approach or depart from a maritime station. The first, distinctively termed the "Cautionary Signal," consists of a *red flag* with a *black square* in the center, for warning in the daytime, and a *red light* by night. The second, or "Cautionary Off-Shore Signal," consists of a *white flag* with black square in the center shown above a red flag with square black center by day, or a *white light* shown above a red light by night, indicating that, while the storm has not yet passed the station, and dangerous winds may yet be felt there, they will probably be from a northerly or westerly direction. The display of

THE CAUTIONARY SIGNAL-FLAG, AS SEEN IN NEW YORK HARBOR.

either signal, however, is always intended to be *cautionary*, and calls for great vigilance on the part of vessels within sight of it.

The Chief Signal Officer's report for the year ending June 30, 1879, states that, in that year, 2,573 such signals had been displayed in anticipation of 96 dangerous storms assailing the lake and ocean coasts of the United States;

and that of the number of "cautionary" signals displayed, 79·8 per cent. have been afterward reported as justified by dangerous winds; while of the number of "cautionary off-shore" signals displayed, 93·9 per cent. have been afterward reported as justified. According to the rules of the office, a signal is set down as not justified unless it is shown after the display that storm-winds exceeding twenty-five miles an hour in velocity have occurred at the display-station or within a radius of one hundred miles.

The total number of seaports and points on the lakes and seacoasts where the storm-signals are hoisted now is *one hundred and eleven*. The points whence storm-signals are displayed, however, are only those of the maritime margins of the field of research. The network of the Signal Service stations now extends over the continent from the Atlantic to the Pacific coasts, and the intervening territory from the Gulf to the Canadian frontier, and is in receipt of daily telegraphic intelligence of the weather from the Canadian Dominion and its outlying posts. The office work is still hampered for want of more stations in the interior and Northwest; but it is thought provision will ere long be made for supplying them, as a new trans-continental telegraph-line is carried from Minnesota to the shores of the Northern Pacific.

Sunset Stations.—In this connection it may be as well to add that, besides the regular stations reporting by wire thrice daily to the office of the Chief Signal Officer, "sunset stations," as they have been called, have also been established. By careful study of the condition of the sky at sunset, especially on the interior plateau, it was believed an advance could be made toward a simple method of predicting the next day's weather, within the grasp of any unscientific but intelligent observer. The observers at the sunset stations note whether the western sky at the precise time of sunset is "fair," "foul," or "doubtful," and from these observations with others (instrumental) they make predictions for the ensuing day. Some of these observations are roughly spectroscopic, the sunset report being based in part on such different appearances of the sun and the effects produced by his rays as are caused by their passage through differently conditioned atmospheric media. The sergeants of the Signal Corps practiced in this kind of forecasting have acquired considerable skill and accuracy in predetermining the local weather-changes; their forecasts, as computed in the Chief Signal Office, having reached a percentage of 82·6 of correctness for trans-Mississippi districts, where the meteorological conditions are most constant, and 81·6 for the region east of the Mississippi Valley. "There can be no reason," says the Chief Signal Officer, "why any intelligent farmer, supplied with the necessary simple instruments, habituated to similar observations, and furnished with data, should fail to attain an equal accuracy."

Private Forecasts.—To facilitate such private forecasting, especially by the agriculturists of the great West and the interior plateau, the Chief Signal Officer has caused to be prepared the "Weather-Case," or "Farmer's Weather-Indicator," before mentioned. This instrument is very simple, and when thoroughly tested, and by aid of the accompanying rules

for using it, it is hoped agriculturists and persons of ordinary education will find it possible to determine for themselves in advance the character of the weather from local indications. At isolated places, where the official reports can not be had, the diligent practice of such forecasting would probably in a short time afford good results. · It is to call into play the intelligence of the popular mind and train it in the highly utilitarian work of private prognostications, as well as to explain its own forecasts, that the Signal Office issues a "Synopsis" of the weather-data with every bulletin of "Indications." That the farmer and seaman may know the changes going on each day, and acquire the habit of tracing the sequences of meteorological phenomena, the "Synopsis" is invaluable. Most of the newspapers print only the "Indications," and omit the "Synopsis"—a practice to be greatly regretted. The late Professor Smee, F. R. S., one of the most gifted and practical of modern scientists, was much interested in the storm-signals hoisted on the English coast by Admiral Fitzroy. After much personal intercourse with the English fishermen, and close inquiry into the use made of Fitzroy's "warnings" among the humble coasters, he recommended that "the reasons for hoisting the signal" should be communicated to the public, that those interested might study the official warning in its local applications. The Signal Service has always encouraged the private study and intelligent local application of its press reports, and expects those who use them to consult their own barometers and other instruments, and to examine the local signs of the weather, as clouds, etc., with the view of giving greater efficacy to its necessarily brief telegrams. Its plan is, not to deliver oracular and dogmatic statements to the people, but to guide them rather to meteorological knowledge as it is daily needed.

In the execution of the last-named plan, the "Daily Graphic" of New York publishes every twenty-four hours a reproduction of the Signal Service weather-map, showing the cyclonic, anti-cyclonic, thermometric, wind, rainfall, and other conditions prevailing over the country at the time of going to press. These charts, according to a plan devised by Lieutenant H. H. C. Dunwoody, Acting Signal Officer and Assistant, are transmitted from the Washington office by telegraph. By this ingenious device, it is not difficult to transmit to any city reached by telegraph—and by the common telegraphic instrument—such data prepared in the Chief Signal Office as will enable any newspaper to reproduce on its pages the official weather-map for the current period. Thus, the Signal Service weather-map for 1 A. M. of any day, precisely as charted then in the Washington office, can be telegraphed to Boston, Chicago, St. Louis, Indianapolis, or any other city, and published, in any size the editors may prefer, in the papers printed *that morning!*

The adoption of this method of popularizing and disseminating weather-knowledge, while the public interest in the data is fresh, will vastly extend the benefits of the Service in all sections of the country, and familiarize the popular eye with the behavior and march of atmospheric phenomena.

To an untutored eye, it may seem trivial to dwell upon apparently slight changes in barometric and other conditions which are curso-

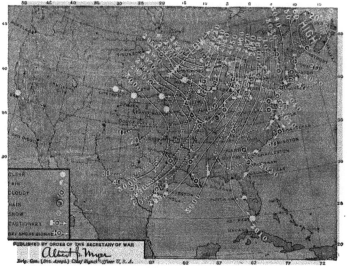

WAR DEPARTMENT WEATHER MAP—A DAILY METEOROLOGICAL CHART TRANSMITTED BY TELEGRAPH FROM WASHINGTON.

rily glanced at on the weather-map; but a moment's reflection shows the importance of accuracy. A fall of only *one tenth* of an inch in the barometer, trifling as it appears to be, indicates the presence of an enormous force. The normal atmospheric pressure, which is only 15 pounds upon a square inch, is 2,160 pounds upon a square foot, and this amounts to about 30,000,000 tons upon every square mile. With this pressure the column of mercury in the barometric tube is 30·00 inches high. When, therefore, it falls to 29·90 inches only, as any one may calculate, over 100,000 tons of pressure are lifted up and removed from every square mile over which the diminution of pressure extends. Conversely, if the barometer registers on its scale so small an increase of pressure as one tenth of an inch, it indicates the arrival of a new mechanical power exerting an additional force of 100,000 tons weight to the square mile. Such minute but common barometric changes, representing forces of great moment in the operation of the atmospheric machinery, must not be overlooked in the deductions of practical meteorology. But without the weather-map of simultaneous observations the presence and influence of such changes can not be detected and estimated.

Signal Service Instruments.—The necessity for accurate observations in a system of weather-telegraphy brings us to speak of the instruments employed by the Signal Service Corps. These have been selected from the best models known, and subjected to experimental tests to perfect their registrations. Every barometer, thermometer, or other instrument used at the stations undergoes thorough comparison with the highest standards before it is sent out from the office of the Chief Signal Officer, in which there is a large apartment devoted to the work of instrumental meteorology, known as "the instrument and model room."

The barometer is the great dependence of the meteorologist, and upon its faithful accuracy in registering the subtile yet momentous changes of atmospheric pressure he must chiefly rely. It measures the weight, at the spot where it is located, of a column of air having a diameter equal to that of its own tube. It has been in use since the beginning of the eighteenth century; but not until 1853, when Adie constructed a marine barometer, did it accomplish its work satisfactorily. Fortin's barometer, however, became the most satisfactory for *stations*, since it has the best cistern (having a flexible base with a glass cylinder), gets rid of some errors, and is compactly put together. This barometer, as afterward improved by the Kew Observatory, and brought to the highest standard of effectiveness by Mr. James Green of New York, is the one used by the Signal Office at all its stations for obtaining the telegraphic data. The instrument is kept in a room of as

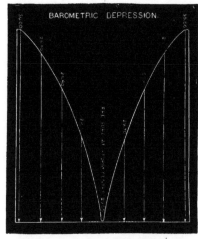

BAROMETRIC DEPRESSION.

DIAGRAM OF PRESSURES IN A SECTION OF A CYCLONE.

uniform a temperature as practicable, and in a vertically suspended wooden box which can be closed when the observer is not taking observations. For purposes of comparison and the detection of any error, as well as to have a substitute in case of accident, two barometers are supplied to each station. Each instrument after it comes from the maker's hands is subjected to the Signal Office tests, and the residual errors are determined by comparison with the great standard barometer kept at the office, when a certificate of corrections is made out and attached to the instrument; it now becomes a *standard* itself. Its readings may deviate to a very slight extent from those of the " regulator"; but such deviations being known to a thousandth part of an inch, allowance is made for them whenever the observer makes his barometric report. As the elevation of the barometer above sea-level is determined for each station, the proper correction for that is also applied at each reading.

Great care is taken in the location, correction, and reading of the Service thermometers, which are of the highest standard. The instrument is placed in the open air, so situated that it will be always in the shade and yet have a free circulation of air around, but exposed to no currents of air, and beyond the influence of

any artificial heat. Its surface is also carefully protected and freed from rain or moisture of any kind, and its bulb so placed as to have no contact with the metallic scale or back. Every thermometer sent out to a signal-station undergoes several previous crucial tests, and is brought up to the standard kept in the instrument-room of the central office, where every error is corrected and recorded, and the character of the instrument fully studied. The maximum and minimum thermometers are likewise tested, and the slightest variations from the standard instruments determined by protracted experimentation, to the satisfaction of the office, before they are issued to the observers. These instruments, by constant and minute inspection of an officer detailed to visit all the stations, as also by the rigid scrutiny of the observers themselves, are kept up to the highest point of accuracy and precision. In the instrument-room of the Washington office, 1,105 meteorological instruments were last year carefully compared with the " official standards," and 982 were issued to the stations.

The rain-gauge employed is also constructed with the utmost precision, to register the amount of precipitation to inches and tenths of an inch. This instrument is placed with the top at least twelve inches from the ground, and where it will not be affected by local peculiarities or obstructions from any object near by, so that the rain as it descends from the clouds may be fully caught and measured. It is fixed firmly in a vertical position, and beyond the risk of being tampered with by unauthorized hands. The rain-water collecting in it is measured by a measuring-rod, graduated to inches and tenths of inches; snow is melted and then measured in the same way.

The wind-velocity measurer or *anemometer*, which up to the present time has been found the most satisfactory, is that of Robinson. It consists of four hemispherical cups revolving in a horizontal plane and communicating their motion to a vertical shaft or axis. In whatever direction the wind blows, these cups will always be driven round with their convex sides foremost, since the air presses with more effect into the cups than on their exteriors. Experiments have shown that the velocity of the cups in all cases equals one third of that with which the wind blows, no matter from what point of the compass it comes; and that this relation between the velocity of the cups and that of the winds is independent of the size of the instrument. By an arrangement of beveled wheels every revolution of the cups is made, through the shaft, to revolve a horizontal cylinder carrying a pencil, which marks on prepared paper the total number of revolutions made by the cups. As the distance traveled by the cups is three times that traveled by the wind, the velocity of the latter can be easily deduced.

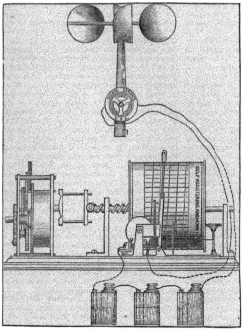

SIGNAL SERVICE ANEMOMETER, WITH SELF-REGISTERING ATTACHMENTS.

and printing barometer, Wild's barometer, and Gibbon's barograph—have been for years under careful testing by the office, with the view of securing forms adapted to general use on stations, and also to obtain an instrument so fitted with apparatus and electric wires attached that its action at a remote point may be automatically registered on paper in the Washington office. Although much has been done to settle this question, it is yet unsolved, and it awaits further experimentation.

The International Weather Service.—This novel and vast extension of the national work done by the United States weather service is perhaps the most remarkable practical result of the development of modern meteorology. Previous to the introduction of the system of "simultaneous" weather-reports by General Myer in 1870, no observations were taken in any country that could be strictly called synchronous, suitable for the preparation of synoptic weather-charts, or that could be regarded as strictly inter-comparable; but, in each country where weather-reports on a large scale were made, they were prepared from daily observations made at moments of time more or less widely separated. Under the old observational methods, concert among the nations in meteorological work was practically out of the question. Not until the new method of simultaneous observations had been put to the test, and a feasible system devised in which all nations could coöperate, was it possible to combine their investigations of the weather into one grand and uniform scheme, for the purpose of observing the aërial envelope of the globe as a unit. To do this required not only a uniformity in the instruments employed, but also a simultaneity in the hours for reading the instruments; that is, that weather-observers all round the globe should take their observations at *one and the same fixed moment of physical time.* The organization and successful working of a weather bureau upon such a simultaneous system in the United States prepared the way, however, for an international weather service. Accordingly, when in September, 1873, an International Meteorological Congress was convened at Vienna—an assemblage composed of the official heads of the meteorological bureaus of the different powers—an original proposition was made by General Myer, as the Chief

The importance of accurate anemometers was recently illustrated in the storm which overwhelmed the Tay Bridge in Scotland, carrying a passenger-train into the tempest-lashed Firth with instant and total destruction; an accident which, in the judgment of many, would never have occurred had the bridge-constructors and railway authorities possessed anemometric instruments showing the real velocity and force of the gale. In some American storms the wind has been found to blow with the tremendous velocity of from 100 to 138 miles per hour; and it is difficult to find or frame an anemometer which, while delicate enough to register small disturbances, will be strong enough to stand the force of such hurricanes. But the experiments of the Signal Service, it is hoped, will lead to some instrumental improvements in this direction.

But the great question, as respects instruments, with which the Signal Service has been concerned, is to obtain barometers, thermometers, etc., which will be self-recording, and give without manipulation continuous, exact, and graphic registers of the atmospheric fluctuations. Numerous ingenious contrivances of this kind—as Hough's electric meteorograph

Signal Officer of the United States Army, looking toward a world-wide scheme of weather-research. General Myer's proposition was to this effect: "That it is desirable, with a view to their exchange, that at least one uniform observation, of such character as to be suited for the preparation of synoptic charts, be taken and recorded daily at as many stations as practicable throughout the world." The author of this proposition had in his report to the United States Congress in 1872 expressed a desire for such a cosmopolitan work—" a grand chain of interchanged international reports, destined with a higher civilization to bind together the signal services of the world"; and the Vienna conference now responded to his overture with alacrity. As well might the United States or Great Britain seek to unravel the mysteries of the Gulf Stream by surveying only that portion of the great ocean-current which impinges on its own shores, leaving unobserved its sources in the equatorial Atlantic and its northeastward deflection from Newfoundland, as to expect to master the mysteries of the atmospheric ocean by studying only the winds and storms which sweep over its own national bounds. The atmosphere is a *unit*, and to be understood must be studied as a unit. The storms which pass over us all have their "polar" and "equatorial" air-currents; and, to comprehend the forces which conspire to make a single cyclone, we must extend our investigations far beyond our own territorial limits.

The adoption of General Myer's proposition by the Vienna Congress, and the courteous cooperation on the part of all the leading governments of Europe, soon enabled him to collect materials for laying the foundation of the international research. Rapidly expanding in 1874, the exchange of simultaneous reports became numerous enough to admit of making a daily "International Weather Bulletin and Chart"; and on July 1, 1875, the Signal Office at Washington commenced the daily publication of the "International Bulletin," presenting the tabulated results of simultaneous weather-observations from all the coöperating nations and from the oceans. These reports are intended to cover the combined territorial extent of Algiers, Australasia, Austria, Belgium, Central America, China, Denmark, France, Germany, Great Britain, Greece, Greenland, India, Ireland, Italy, Japan, Mexico, Morocco, the Netherlands, Norway, Portugal, Russia, Spain, Sweden, Switzerland, Tunis, Turkey, British North America, the United States, the Azores, Malta, Mauritius, the Sandwich Islands, South Africa, South America, and the West Indies, so far as they have been placed under meteorological surveillance; and also the great ocean - highways, from which the ships of all flags take observations while *en route* from port to port.

As early as July 1, 1878, in connection with the daily "International Bulletin" issued by the Washington Signal Office, General Myer began the daily publication of a graphic synoptic "International Weather-Map." This chart covers the whole international network of observations, and is the supplement and key to the daily bulletin, both being based on the same data, and both of the same date. The "International Weather-Map of Simultaneous Observations" (see map opposite) exhibits the aërial phenomena as they actually existed all around the earth at a fixed moment of time; it is, so to speak, a *photograph* of the atmospheric machinery, picturing its varied movements and delineating its component parts and elements, so as to represent it as a *whole*—the desideratum of science in all ages. In carrying out this international coöperative enterprise, the Signal Office, by an order of the Secretary of the Navy, receives the daily simultaneous reports from all vessels of the United States Navy, and has the coöperation of the Pacific Mail Steamship Company's vessels, as also that of the White Star Line, the Occidental and Oriental Steamship Company, the North German Lloyd, the American Steamship Company, the Red Star Line, the Allan Line of steamers, and others, whose contributions swell the daily international reports to over five hundred in number. The daily bulletins and charts prepared from the collective data are mailed to every coöperating seaman and civilian observer without charge, as an acknowledgment of his service to science, and constitute in themselves an invaluable meteorological library. In the cases of all maritime observers, the Signal Office bears all expenses for forms, postage, etc.; and when necessary it furnishes the shipmaster with the requisite instruments. The number of observations now made by separate vessels at sea is 122, and all ocean-going vessels are requested to embark in this system of research. As a striking illustration of the opportunities which a vessel at sea has for aiding in this meteorological work, it may be mentioned that the steamship Faraday, when laying the last Atlantic cable, encountered a severe cyclone in mid-ocean, which, without heaving to, she reported by her telegraphic wire to Europe, noting the successive changes of wind as the different quadrants of the storm passed over her; thus indicating to those on land the direction and progressive velocity of the gale, so that they could calculate the time and locality at which it would strike upon the European coasts. If, as General Myer holds, it is practicable to establish floating stations in mid-Atlantic, connected by cable with the continent, the reports from such posts would be of incalculable value to British and continental meteorologists in making out their daily weather-forecasts and ordering storm-warnings for their seaports.

The United States is the geographical theatre upon which cyclopean aërial forces of arctic, tropic, and Pacific origin play their mighty parts in the ceaseless conflict, the vicissitudes of which give us the alternations and extremes

of heat and cold, drought and precipitation. The issue from the Signal Office of the "International Map of the Northern Hemisphere" has widely extended the vield of view. Professor Loomis, Professor Henry, and many other scientists had pointed out the necessity for extending the scope of the Signal Service observations beyond the national territorial boundaries, if we are ever to learn the secrets of our national meteorology. The proposition of General Myer at Vienna, in 1873, having that end in view, was that observations be taken daily and simultaneously at as many stations as practicable "throughout the WORLD." A recent meteorological conference at Hamburg recommended a concert of all nations for

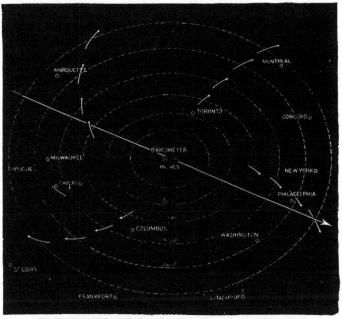

AN ANTICYCLONE, OR WAVE OF HIGH BAROMETRIC PRESSURE FROM THE NORTHWEST.
(Large arrow shows direction of its progress; small arrows show its winds.)

planting a cordon of weather observatories in high northern and southern latitudes around the poles. Indeed, there is scarcely a problem relating to the physical geography and meteorology of our own country which can be fully solved without recourse to more extended investigations outside of the United States. The international weather service, we may therefore say, is the great hope of the meteorology of the future.

In addition to the daily international charts published by the Chief Signal Officer, he has begun the issue of *monthly international charts* of the northern hemisphere, displaying the monthly ocean-storm tracks, the average lines of equal barometric pressure, the wind-zones, isothermals, etc. These charts are published in the "Monthly Weather Review," a journal sent to all observers, on land and sea, who co-

operate with the Signal Office in its international research. To aid shipmasters of every flag in keeping their instruments correct, the Chief Signal Officer has also placed standard barometers at the ports of New York, San Francisco, and elsewhere, for reference and comparison. Without pecuniary charge to for eign or American ships, their barometers, on application to the signal offices at these ports, are carefully tested, adjusted, and corrected for effective use at sea.

With the extension and collation of the international weather-reports, we may hope, as General Myer has said, that "the questions as to the translations of storms from continent to continent, and of the times and directions they may take in such movements; the movement of areas of high and low barometer; the conditions of temperature, pressure, etc., existing around the earth at a fixed instant of time; as well as questions of climatology and others bearing upon the prediction of weather-changes far in advance of the time at which these changes happen, or queries as to the character of coming seasons, may be settled." If the Signal Service undertook no other duty, but, discarding prognostications, limited its scope of researches to this international collection of materials for the construction of the sciences of meteorology and climatology, it is not too much to say that the harvest of observational data thus garnered would ultimately be worth all the labor and expense the Service has cost the Government. But, to secure such results, it can not be too widely or urgently insisted on that navigators, ship-owners, steamship companies, and all naval officers should use their earnest efforts and influence to obtain simultaneous weather-reports from all sea-going steamers and sailing vessels. The ablest scientific journal of Great Britain, "Nature," recently said that it "earnestly hopes that the navies and the mercantile vessels of all nations will soon join in carrying out this magnificent scheme of observations, originated by the Americans in 1873, and since then further developed and carried on by them with the greatest ability and success." Sentiments similar in effect were expressed at the International Meteorological Congress convened in Rome, Italy, in April, 1879.

The Coast Signal Service is another important arm of the organization. By act of Congress, the Secretary of War was authorized to establish signal stations at the lighthouses and life-saving stations on the lakes and seacoasts, and to connect these signal stations with telegraph-lines, to be constructed, maintained, and worked under the direction of the Chief Signal Officer of the Army; and the use made of the life-saving stations is subject to such regulations as are fixed upon by the Chief Signal Officer, the Secretary of War, and the Secretary of the Treasury. By this coöperative arrangement, the Signal Service has become a valuable if not an indispensable auxiliary to the sister services with which it connects, and shares very materially in the labors and responsibilities especially of the Life-Saving Service.

The coast signal stations aim to warn vessels within signaling distance of the approach of storms, and to give the life-saving stations quick notice of marine disasters calling for rescue, as also to furnish any intelligence to the latter, or to the lighthouses, which may insure their more efficient working. Connected by wire or submarine cable, as all the signal stations on the coast are, from Sandy Hook, N. J., to Smithville, N. C., and connected similarly with the office of the Chief Signal Officer at Washington, whence they are kept advised of any change in the meteorological status, they are thus enabled, from their full ocean view, to communicate directly any warnings from

the Chief Signal Officer to passing ships, or to convey to him any facts which may be of use to the Washington office. The telegraphic wires connect each station with the War Department. The weather reports and observations on the indications of the sea thus obtained are often of the greatest value to the Washington office in its work of preannouncing the force, direction, and velocity of the great hurricanes from the West Indies, which impinge upon our Atlantic seaboard and sweep the sail-whitened waters on the eastern side of the United States.

As an illustration of this, it may suffice to note the *ocean conditions* which the Coast Signal Service telegraphs to the Chief Signal Office thrice daily, and oftener if need be. It has long been known by meteorologists that marine cyclones foreannounce their movements by a storm-wave formed in the central part of the barometric depression, where, the attenuation of the atmosphere being much greater than on the outer circles, the circumferential pressure serves to head up the water of the sea. "When living on the Bermuda Islands," says General Reid, the eminent investigator of storm-phenomena, "I was frequently interested by observing the change of direction in the surf beating against their shores. A coming storm would roll its undulations so as to break upon the south and southwest side of these Atlantic islands; and, as gales proceeded northward, the sea was seen breaking on their northern reefs." The "cyclone-rollers," as Piddington observed, may be "felt at a great distance from storms"; and, as he shows, even a ship far out at sea, if her commander will carefully note the swell of the ocean, may be forewarned of an approaching gale. Both of these investigators give abundant evidence that the peculiar ocean-swell "is often felt at 10° or 15° (600 to 900 miles) of distance" from the tempest. In the summer of 1873, when the great August hurricane which so furiously assailed and wrecked several hundred sail, was still passing over the Bermudas, its long dead swell was outrunning its center by 600 miles, driving in the bathers at Long Branch and pouring into New York Bay. The steamer Albemarle encountered its forerunning wave on her voyage from Halifax to the Bermudas; and, though the morning was fair, suspecting danger, the vessel was hove to for a few hours to examine the swell. Concluding that the hurricane was advancing directly upon him, her captain changed his course from southerly to westerly, and by a slight *détour* eluded the gale. As one by one, yet all independently, the coast signal observers on any day telegraph to the central office the same significant tidings of the ocean-indications of an Atlantic gale—the intensity and direction of the swell—their concurrent observations often present unmistakable proofs of the presence, course, and progressive rate of these menacing meteors. The intelligence thus afforded is indispensable to the storm-warning and weather-prediction work of the Washington authorities.

But, apart from the meteorological value of such a Coast Signal Service, its incidental contributions to the life-saving stations have already proved of the greatest assistance. On the 22d of March, 1877, after a severe storm on the middle Atlantic coast, Sergeant William Stein of the Signal Service, in charge of the Cape Henry station, discovered before dawn a large vessel stranded on a shoal off that station, and summoned the wreckers at Norfolk to come to the rescue. With the earliest light the Sergeant displayed the "attention-flags" of the international code, with which every seacoast signal station is supplied; and, receiving answer that she was the Winchester of Liverpool, with request for two steam-tugs to be sent to the vessel, he telegraphed at once to Norfolk for wrecking-steamers. Before sundown active efforts were made to save the stranded vessel. She was gotten off the shoal

after some days' labor; but meantime three other vessels, in a second storm (of the 25th), were stranded within a mile of her. Sergeant Stein again telegraphed the wreckers at Norfolk for aid. He ascertained the name of the bark in greatest peril to be the Pantzer, a Norwegian vessel, and the crew of the Life-Saving Service a little later succeeded in bring a life-line over her deck. The Norwegians did not comprehend its use; but after some effort the Signal Service officer, by means of international signals, instructed her crew to "haul in on the line," and by nine o'clock all the crew of the Pantzer were safely landed. In the wrecks of the steamships L'Amérique, Rusland, and Huron (of the United States Navy), the first tidings were conveyed by the Signal Service wires, and through them succor was speedily summoned. In the case of the Huron, drifted ashore near Kittyhawk, a private of the Signal Service, A. T. Sherwood, stationed at that place, received the first intelligence November

23d, and, after telegraphing to Washington, hastened to the awful scene, walking sixteen miles through the sand, and brought full reports of the situation to his station, which were instantly telegraphed to the Chief Signal Officer. The War and Navy Departments and the Life-Saving Service were thus notified, and by them steamers of the navy and wrecking companies were started to the fatal point of the shore on which the Huron had gone to pieces. The Kittyhawk observer, immediately on receiving orders from the Chief Signal Officer, opened his a "wreck-station" abreast of the foundered vessel before daylight of the 25th, connecting it by a temporary telegraph-wire with his station, and, working this improvised station on the open beach, while the gale was yet raging, drew toward the spot the whole organized relief force of the Government. A similar service was performed on the

stormy night of January 31, 1878, by another private soldier of the Signal Corps, William Davis, when the steamship Metropolis, with 248 souls on board, became a total wreck twenty miles from Kittyhawk station. At 6.55 P. M. on that night intelligence of the disaster reached Kittyhawk, and in less than fifteen minutes private Davis, carrying telegraphic and signal apparatus, was riding through the night and storm to the scene. By 4 A. M. he had reached the vessel, established his telegraph station abreast of her, opened communication, and forwarded a report to the Chief Signal Office at Washington, and was putting in motion all the machinery of relief and succor which the country could command. The observers of the coast signal stations, whenever it is practicable, *board* vessels that have gone ashore, and open communication with the land. An instance of this may be cited from the action of private Harrison of the Signal Corps, at Cape Henry, when the bark Giuseppe Massonne was wrecked near that station, February 10, 1878. His presence prevented the crew from deserting their ship, which, by the aid of powerful wrecking steamers, was subsequently saved. Other instances of boarding vessels could be cited, as those of the Italian bark Francesco Bellagamba and the British steamship Antonio, both boarded by Signal Service men who afterward kept up signal conversation with the shore until the ships were saved. But these cases will suffice to show the immense share the Coast Signal Service has in the results announced by the Life-Saving Service. Without the Signal Service coöperation, the latter would often, in emergencies that arise, be powerless to command the needed help, as well as to communicate with stranded vessels. For the latter service, only men drilled in signaling can avail.

So arranged is the Coast Signal Service, that not only are its storm-flags and danger-warnings visible by vessels moving off the coast, but even a vessel *en voyage* (say one which is bound from the equator to New York), as she

passes Cape Henlopen, may inquire by signals whether any hurricane is impending; if so, whether she has time to reach Sandy Hook before its arrival, or must take shelter behind the Delaware Breakwater. Or, a vessel bound from New York or any northern port southward, on reaching the Capes of the Delaware, can make inquiry as to whether any storm is likely to strike her before she can pass Cape Hatteras, and receive full advice by telegraph from the Chief Signal Office at Washington, in a very brief time. With adequate appropriations, this Coast Signal Service could easily be made of far greater value to all the shipping and mercantile interests. As the Chief Signal Officer has said, " The time is not far distant when the possession of a coast not covered by seacoast storm-signal and Signal Service stations, watching as sentinels each its own beat of sea and shore, and ready to summon aid by electric wires, will be held as much an evidence of semi-barbarism, as is now among civilized nations the holding of any national coast without a system of lighthouse lights." In the event of war, with a completed chain of coast signal stations, no part of our exposed sea-front could be threatened without immediate intelligence of the fact being flashed to the Washington office and all along the coast. and the defensive power of the Government concentrated at the point endangered. The chain of telegraphic seacoast stations at present is 610 miles long, stretching from Sandy Hook to the mouth of Cape Fear River.

The Signal Service Telegraph System. constructed, owned, and operated by the Signal Service, covers, however, a much larger area than the seacoast mentioned. In pursuance of acts of Congress, this service has now completed in the interior and upon the frontier an extensive network of telegraphic lines for connecting military posts, with a view to the protection of the population from Indian depredations, and the rendition of meteorological, military, and other reports to the Government. A total length of 4,000 miles of frontier line is now operated and maintained by the Signal Corps. This connected system of telegraph-lines is one of the most effective safeguards against Indian raids and warlike movements, since it enables the scattered military forces of the United States to obtain timely notice of such movements, and to concentrate quickly at any threatened point to repel attack. The Indian strategy is to pass between the Government army posts unobserved, so that their plans may not be reported — a very difficult thing in a region traversed by electric wires. To break them is to announce their purpose and betray themselves. alarming the posts and settlements on

SIGNAL SERVICE SEACOAST TELEGRAPH LINES.

both sides of the break, and evoking spirited pursuit and severe punishment by the troops. As an engine of civilization the frontier telegraph rivals the railway, enabling the Government to throw an ægis of protection over the rapidly expanding wave of Western emigration, and thus facilitating no doubt the sale and settlement, as well as the material development, of the public lands. These Signal Service lines are in part self-supporting, as they transmit not only Government but private telegrams of the civilian population, and save the expense of telegraphing by other lines the meteorological reports necessary for the weather-work at Washington, besides serving to convey a great number of official dispatches and correspondence for various departments of the Government, that would otherwise have to be transmitted at considerable cost on non-governmental lines or sent by couriers.

But, apart from all the incidental benefits and economies wrought by this frontier telegraph system, its value in the scientific work of the Weather Bureau proper is felt to be the greatest. The lines in Texas have made it possible to furnish weather-reports daily on the coast of that State; and those in the Northwest permit a series of observations and reports not otherwise attainable, which are of the first importance for all purposes of weather-prediction throughout the United States. Meager as the data now obtainable from the Northwest are, they are indispensable for the processes of weather-telegraphy in the Mississippi Valley and lake region. To study these momentous meteorological agencies, and to receive timely notice of their arrival on the *extreme northwestern* frontier, is perhaps the most important task, so far as weather-prognostication goes, that the Signal Service could pursue. The extension of its telegraphic and observational stations in this direction would immensely enhance its general effectiveness, and give a fresh stimulus to almost every meteorological investigation which the Service is now pushing.

The length of Signal Service telegraph-lines in the interior and on the frontier at present is as follows: Arizona Division, 934 miles, with 17 stations, from 12 of which weather-reports are received at Washington; New Mexico Division, 486 miles, with 12 stations, from 6 of which reports are daily received; Texas Division, 1,590 miles, with 28 stations, 25 of which telegraph full meteorological reports; the Northwestern Division, 921 miles, with 18 stations; and the Washington Territory Division, 69 miles, with 2 stations; total, 4,000 miles, with 77 stations.

In concluding this necessarily much condensed sketch of the national weather service, its pressing wants should not be overlooked. No other service appeals so strongly to the interests which it daily subserves for intelligent coöperation. The public press can do much to advance its development by systematic republication and explanation of its observations and

deductions, and especially by reproducing the data furnished in its "Monthly Weather Review," and in the daily telegraphic "Synopsis." Time and toil are necessary to harvest the fruit of seeds sown; but, as the President of the American Geographical Society, Chief Justice Daly, has said, "Nothing in the nature of scientific investigation by the national Government has proved so acceptable to the people, or has been productive in so short a time of such important results, as the establishment of the Signal Service Bureau." Like a little army, however, which has fought its way to a commanding yet difficult position, its ranks must be recruited and its resources be augmented before it can push its conquests forward or reap what it has sown.

SOUTH CAROLINA. By a letter dated February 24, 1879, addressed to Lieutenant-Governor Simpson as acting Governor, Wade Hampton resigned his office of Governor of South Carolina. On the 26th W. D. Simpson was formally sworn in and installed as Governor of the State. On the same day Governor Simpson commissioned Mr. Hampton as United States Senator from South Carolina, to which office the two Houses of the Legislature at the November session of 1878 had elected him by a unanimous vote.

For the regular session of 1879, the Legislature met at Columbia on November 25th.

On December 10th the two Houses convened in joint assembly to elect an Associate Justice of the Supreme Court in the place of A. C. Haskell, who at the beginning of that month had resigned. The candidates were Samuel McGowan of Abbeville and W. D. Wallace of Union. Mr. McGowan was elected by a majority of three, the vote having stood 76 and 73 respectively. The joint convention then proceeded to ballot for the election of a Chief Justice of that Court for six years. Henry McIver, one of the two Associate Justices, was unanimously elected, having received all of the 146 votes then cast. On December 15th Judge McIver declined the office, and the two Houses met together again on the 18th. Governor Simpson received 131 votes, the whole number cast, and was elected. In regard to the vacancy of this seat as occurring in 1880, there is a decided disagreement between its present occupant, Chief Justice Willard, and the State Legislature. He was elected by the Legislature of 1877 upon the office becoming vacant by the death of Judge Moses; and while the Legislature of 1879 was formally electing his successor, he plainly declared, as he has also done since, that no vacancy of his office is to occur in 1880; that he was elected in 1877 for the full term of six years; that the Legislature, according to the State Constitution, has no legal power to elect his successor before the expiration of his sexennial term; and that he is determined to keep his seat after August 1, 1880, leaving to the now elected Chief Justice the task of dispossessing him of it on a writ of *quo warranto.* On the other side, it is stated that at the time of his election in 1877 "the understanding and intention of those who elected him was to elect him for only the three unexpired years of the term of Chief Justice Moses, ending August 1, 1880," and that be accepted the position on that understanding.

The Legislature of 1879 closed its session on December 24th, having passed about two hundred acts and joint resolutions, among which are the following:

"An act to extend the time for the redemption of forfeited lands."

" A joint resolution proposing an amendment to the Constitution of the State relating to the homestead, and providing for the benefits thereof to be shared equally by all classes of citizens." It provides for a homestead not exceeding one thousand dollars in value to every citizen in possession of land; and for an exemption of five hundred dollars' worth of personal property, and the crops and products of the said land; with an amendment extending the exemption of the said amendment to any married woman who is not the head of a family and owns a separate estate, while the head of the family does not.

" An act requiring railroads to furnish consignees an itemized statement of freight charges, and to settle according to the bills of lading."

" An act to prohibit the running of freight trains, and to regulate the running of passenger and mail trains, on Sundays."

" An act to prevent and punish the intermarrying of races."

" An act to enforce the use of a uniform series of text-books in the free public schools of this State."

" An act to provide artificial limbs for all soldiers of the State who lost their legs or arms during military service in the years 1861, 1862, 1863, 1864, and 1865."

" An act to raise supplies and make appropriations for the fiscal year commencing November 1, 1879." In the engrossment of this act two grave mistakes occurred, both in the second section, which were discovered when it was too late to correct them. As passed by the two Houses, the act orders the levy of a State tax of four and a half mills on the dollar; as ratified and published, it orders the levy of a tax of four and three quarters mills. It also makes provision for the Charleston military organization, which had not been agreed to by the House of Representatives.

" An act to continue in force an act extending the time for funding the unquestioned debt of the State."

The settlement of her questioned debt has been provided for by another act, which is considered the most important of the session of 1879, as it finally and for ever determines a matter which has long kept the creditors and citizens of South Carolina in great anxiety. In 1873 the State sifted all her outstanding obligations of every denomination, amounting in the aggregate to about eighteen million dollars, threw out six millions of them altogether, and proposed as a compromise to recognize one half of the remaining twelve millions, or fifty cents in the dollar, as valid, to be funded and bear interest payable at stated times thereafter, thus reducing her entire debt to about six millions. This was sanctioned on her part by a law enacted at that year's session, known as the funding or consolidation act, entitled " An act to reduce the public debt of the State, and to provide for the payment of the same. Approved December 22, 1873." This compromise was accepted by the State's creditors, was for the most part executed during the subsequent years, and was regarded generally as a final settlement. In 1877 the Legislature appointed a special committee " to investigate the public debt of the State." This committee presented to the Legislature of 1878 a detailed report of its labors, declaring about $1,800,000 of the said consolidated debt not valid, either totally or partially, as tainted with fraud, or resting on vouchers not issued in accordance with the law. This report was decidedly opposed by a large number of the members, who insisted on the inviolability of the consolidation act, and as decidedly favored by a larger number, who stood for rejecting the fraudulent or illegal portion of the funded debt. To prevent a split in the Democratic party, which seemed imminent, a compromise was finally agreed to by referring the whole matter to the decision of a special court consisting of three Circuit Judges, with the right of appeal from it to the Supreme Court of the State, and to the Supreme Court of the United States. This special court, commonly styled "the Bond Court," was then created, and its members designated by a law enacted for that purpose. Cases embracing all classes of State bonds were made up and duly argued before this Court, which decided some of them, as did also the State Supreme Court on appeal on September 27th, establishing rules for determining whether, how far, and for what reason any State obligation is null and void, according to the State Constitution. At the meeting of the Legislature in November, 1879, the previous year's disagreement concerning the rejection of a portion of the consolidated debt was renewed among its members, so that a proposition to abolish the Bond Court was introduced and barely defeated, the vote being 52 to 57 in the House of Representatives and 16 to 16 in the Senate. All contention was at last ended apparently for ever by the passage of the law before mentioned, entitled " An act to provide for the settlement of the public debt of the State in accordance with the decision of the Supreme Court of South Carolina." It creates the office of a Special Commissioner, and appoints James O. Colt as such. His duties are to examine the outstanding obligations of the State under denominations pointed out in the act, and ascertain the validity, total or partial, of each, in accordance with the principles laid down by the Supreme Court of the State in the decision of the cases referred to by the act, and, if any obligations are found partially invalid, to ascertain the exact amount of their valid portion, and compute the interest accrued on it up to July 1, 1878; to report monthly to the Treasurer the State obligations so investigated and ascertained, specifying their respective denominations and numbers, with the amounts of the valid and invalid portions of each, and the amount of interest accrued on the valid portion to July 1, 1878; and so continue until he shall have examined and reported on the entire consolidated debt. The act gives the holder of State obligations so investigated and reported upon the right to surrender them to the State Treasurer for cancellation, and authorizes the Treasurer to issue and hand to the holder a new bond or certificate of stock equal in amount to the valid portion of the bond, certificate of stock, coupon, or interest order so surrendered and canceled. The new bond so issued "is to have the same benefits and privileges as those provided for in the act approved December 22, 1873, entitled 'An act to reduce the volume of the public debt of the State, and provide for the payment of the same.'" The maturity of the first coupon or interest due on these new bonds is fixed by the act on January 1, 1879.

A bill to redistrict the State, increasing the number of her Congressional districts from four to five, was introduced in the Lower House, and, after debate, indefinitely postponed by a vote of 55 to 40. It is stated that the passage of this bill would have secured a Republican Congressman for Charleston for ever, as the election in that district would have been then controlled by the colored vote.

A registration bill requiring all voters to be able to write their names, and several bills prohibiting the carrying of concealed weapons, were voted down or indefinitely postponed.

A joint resolution calling for a Constitutional Convention was introduced in the Lower House, and, on motion, tabled unanimously without debate.

The State finances appear to be in a satisfactory condition, and the administration of the government commendably economical. The aggregate expenditures for the legislative, executive, and judicial departments during the fiscal year ended October 31, 1879, amounted to $124,895. For the year ending October 31, 1880, the State and ordinary county taxes to be levied are as follows: A general State tax of 4¼ mills on the dollar, with two mills additional for the public schools, and a county tax of 3 mills for ordinary purposes. The 4¼ mills of State tax, reckoning the aggregate value of taxable property in South Carolina at $135,-000,000, are expected to yield $100,000 each mill, in all $475,000. Of this amount, $344,-372 is appropriated to pay the interest on the consolidated debt for 1880, and $34,000 to pay the deficiency bonds of the State. To com-

plete the payment of the interest due on the consolidated debt for 1879, the sum of $144,-375 was appropriated out of the $175,000 collected in the two previous years for that purpose, and lying still in the Treasury. The remaining $117,000 out of the $475,000 of the State tax, and the royalty to be collected on phosphates, are considered sufficient to cover all the ordinary expenditures for the new year. The $200,000 yielded by the two additional mills of State tax, and the entire poll-tax, amounting to $100,000, are applied exclusively to the public schools.

The schools were attended in 1879 by 58,-368 white pupils and 64,095 colored—in all, 122,463, which is the largest number on record for any one year in South Carolina. The average number of colored children in the public schools in 1879 was about 45 per cent. greater than in any preceding year. The newly erected lyceum for colored students in Charleston was dedicated on September 2d.

From the reports made by circuit judges and solicitors, after due inquiries instituted in their respective sections, it appears that crime in South Carolina has decreased at least one third since 1877. The number of convicts committed to the State Prison from November 1, 1878, to the latter part of November, 1879, was 1,017. Nearly three fourths of that number had been leased out by the Board of Directors of the Penitentiary, as authorized by law, to nine different parties, among them four railway companies, to be kept at the places of their several works, and under their charge. The applicant for convict-labor, after his application has been approved, is required by the Board of Directors to sign a contract embodying the terms of the lease, and give a sufficient bond for its faithful execution; the terms usually being that the lessee shall feed, clothe, and guard the prisoners intrusted to him, provide them with medical attendance, and in addition pay to the State a stipulated monthly rate for each convict during the time he has worked. The prisoners thus leased out up to the close of November, 1879, numbered 727, of whom 157 had died, 77 had escaped, and some had been killed. Among the prisoners remaining in the penitentiary itself, their average monthly number being 290, there were from November 1, 1878, to the latter part of November, 1879, 33 deaths, 8 escapes, and 1 killed. Since January 1, 1879, ten months, the deaths of the convicts at the State Prison numbered 13, including 5 returned thither from the places of their work outside in a dying condition. The Greenwood and Augusta Railway Company, to whom the largest number of convicts have been leased, is charged with having violated the terms of its contract in all points respecting their treatment. Out of the 285 prisoners sent to this company, 128 had died, a rate of mortality exceeding 40 per cent., and 37 had escaped. On complaints made during the summer, the Board of Directors sent three physicians at different times to visit the convicts employed on that line, and report professionally as to their treatment and the cause of their mortality. The separate reports of these physicians all pointed out its cause by averring that the convicts leased to that road were most inhumanly treated in all respects, giving details of what they saw among the prisoners at the place of their work as well as among the sick at the stockades and the hospital, so called. The most unfit for duty among these convicts, 26 in number, were by order of the Board of Directors, under the care of two physicians, removed to the penitentiary on September 16th, two of them dying before reaching it, and one soon after his arrival. By a subsequent order the Board of Directors recalled almost all of the convicts leased to the Greenwood and Augusta Railroad; but the company refused to comply with the order, on the ground that the convicts had been granted them by the Legislature, and that only the Legislature could take them away. This matter was brought to the attention of the Legislature early in the session of 1879, and two sets of resolutions, very strongly worded, were introduced in the Lower House, to investigate the subject and bring the guilty parties to condign punishment; the one intrusting the investigation to a special committee appointed for that purpose, the other to the two Committees on the Penitentiary of the Senate and House of Representatives, working jointly, with power to send for persons and papers.

The general condition of South Carolina with regard to trade and other material interests appears to have considerably improved of late years. There was in 1879 a large increase in the quantity of bacon made in the State; besides, provisions in general were low, and the colored people employed worked well. The crops in 1879, with some exceptions, were good, and sold at remunerative prices. In consequence, the farmers as a body are in better circumstances and out of debt, or nearly so, for the first time in a long series of years. The advance in the selling price of cotton at the end of the year was equal to $12 a bale; which, on a crop of 300,000 bales raised in the State, makes a difference of over $3,000,000 in favor of planters and farmers. The value of land in South Carolina has increased, especially in the middle and upper districts. An Agricultural Department is now established in the State by a law entitled "An act to create a Department of Agriculture, defining its powers and duties, and charging it with the inspection of phosphates and the regulation and sale of commercial fertilizers."

The establishment and working of cotton-mills for the production of shirting, sheeting, drilling, and yarn, seem to be growing into great dimensions in South Carolina. The scarcity of competent operatives, which was before the chief difficulty encountered in the development of this industry, has been in a great mea-

sure supplied by the importation of some skilled hands from the Northern mills, who have taught a number of native young women and men how to feed and direct the machines. Nine such factories were in operation in different parts of the State in June, 1879, some of which were organized in 1855, but most of them since 1870. All were busy, with more orders than they could execute, and carrying on a very lucrative business. They employ in the aggregate above 55,000 spindles, with a proportionate number of looms, attended to by about 1,400 operatives at wages ranging from 25 cents to $3 a day, according to usefulness. A large proportion of these operatives are lodged in convenient cabins erected near the factories for that purpose. Their aggregate annual production is reckoned at above 55,000,000 yards of shirting, sheeting, and drilling, and many million pounds of yarn. One of the three largest among these establishments is the Piedmont Manufacturing Company's mill, incorporated three years ago, and situated on the Saluda River, about eleven miles from Greenville, on the Greenville and Columbia Railroad line. It has 12,300 spindles, employs 275 operatives, and produces daily about 16,000 yards of shirting, sheeting, and drilling, and 2,300 pounds of yarns. From the books of this company it appears that, for the year ended March 31, 1879, its surplus assets over all liabilities amounted to $36,889, and the gross profits on the sale of that year's manufactures to $56,684, classified as follows: Profits on local sales, $24,320.04; on sales to New York, $9,401.98; on sales to Boston (yarns), $10,619.64; on sales to Baltimore, $7,180.12; on sales to all other parts, $5,163.46.

L. F. Cardozo, ex-Treasurer of South Carolina, and Robert Smalls, a member of her Legislature in both Houses for a number of terms, and lastly a Representative in Congress, both colored, and since November 28, 1878, under sentence for high crimes and misdemeanors in office, with regard especially to money matters, were pardoned by Governor Simpson on April 23, 1879. He had previously pardoned L. Cass Carpenter, a white Republican Senator in the State Legislature, convicted on a like charge. In October, 1879, the Supreme Court of the United States, to whom Mr. Smalls had brought his case on appeal from the State Supreme Court, on a writ of error, dismissed it on motion of the Attorney-General of the State, the appellant's counsel concurring. Mr. Smalls is to pay the costs in the case. This is said to be the last one of the numerous criminal prosecutions, called political cases, instituted before the courts of South Carolina.

SPAIN, a kingdom of southern Europe. King, Alfonso XII., born November 28, 1857, proclaimed King December 30, 1874. He was married on January 23, 1878, to Maria de las Mercedes (born June 24, 1860, died June 26, 1878), and again on November 29, 1879, to Maria Christine (born July 21, 1858), daughter of Archduke Charles Ferdinand of Austria.

The area of Spain is 196,036 square miles; the population, according to the census of 1877, 16,623,384. Of the total population, 8,132,741 were males, and 8,490,643 females. There are also 2,476 inhabitants in the Spanish possessions of northern Africa, making in all 16,625,860. Of this number, 40,741 were foreigners.

The revenue was estimated in the budget of 1878–'79 at 750,630,202 pesetas (1 peseta = 19·3 cents), and the expenditures at 753,177,- 865 pesetas. The public debt on June 30, 1878, amounted to 12,875,007,428 pesetas.

According to a new plan of the Minister of War, the Spanish army is to consist in time of peace of 100,000 men, of whom 69,492 will belong to the infantry, 16,130 to the cavalry, 10,232 to the artillery, and 4,146 to the corps of engineers. The fleet in 1878 was composed as follows:

NAVY.	Guns.	Horse-power.
Vessels of the first class :		
5 ironclads	72	4,300
9 screw-frigates	249	5,020
2 paddle-steamers	15	1,000
Vessels of the second class :		
7 paddle-steamers	24	2,080
9 screw-steamers	83	1,895
2 transports	..	600
Vessels of the third class :		
1 iron-clad monitor	8	960
16 screw steamers	86	2,320
28 gunboats	23	935
7 paddle-steamers	13	787
8 screw transport-vessels	..	410
Vessels not classified :		
2 steamers	7	510
29 small steamers	88	1,134
190 Total	523	21,271

The commerce in 1878 was as follows (value in pesetas):

ARTICLES.	Imports.	Exports.
Grain	22,100,000	20,500,000
Beverages	10,600,000	138,900,000
Colonial goods	83,700,000	7,700,000
Seeds and fruits	1,600,000	54,900,000
Animals and animal provisions	19,600,000	18,800,000
1. Articles of food	92,600,000	235,800,000
Coal	21,900,000	....
Ores and minerals	....	52,200,000
Raw metals	7,800,000	58,400,000
Hides and leather	16,200,000	....
Spinning material	105,300,000	6,800,000
Esparto	....	7,100,000
Wood and cork	82,300,000	1,100,000
2. Raw materials	182,800,000	125,600,000
Glass and pottery ware	2,800,000	....
Metallic goods	10,700,000	2,800,000
Machines	17,100,000	....
Yarns	21,800,000	....
Woven goods	28,000,000	....
Furniture	2,500,000	....
Corks	....	84,000,000
Paper and playing cards	4,500,000	2,600,000
3. Manufactured goods	87,400,000	88,900,000
Drugs, etc	19,400,000	5,900,000
Resin, fats, and oils	18,300,000	25,600,000
Miscellaneous goods	2,300,000	....
4. Miscellaneous	35,000,000	31,500,000
Total	897,800,000	481,800,000

The area and population of the foreign colonies are as follows :

COLONIES.	Square miles.	Population.	Year.
1. AMERICA :			
Cuba	45,884	1,394,516	1877
Porto Rico	3,596	661,494	1877
Total	49,480	2,056,010	....
2. ASIA AND OCEANICA :			
Philippines	65,866	6,168,682	1878
Carolines	584	18,800	1874
Palaos	846	10,000	1862
Ladrones or Marianas	417	8,000	1878
Total	67,163	6,200,482	....
3. AFRICA :			
Guinea Islands	851	35,000	1858
Total colonies	117,494	8,291,442	....

Of the total population of Cuba, 764,164 are whites, 344,050 free colored persons, 227,- 902 slaves, and 58,400 coolies. In Porto Rico there are 363,434 whites and 298,060 free colored.

In the beginning of March a new Ministry was formed, under the presidency of Martinez Campos, who had shortly before returned from Cuba. The Chambers were dissolved, and the new Chambers were ordered to assemble on June 1st, the election to take place for deputies on April 20th, and for senators on May 3d. In these new Chambers Cuba was to be represented for the first time by 12 senators and 40 deputies. The elections on April 20th resulted in the return of 275 Ministerialists, 32 Constitutionalists, and 38 members of other parties. The Ministerial majority, however, was increased to over 300 with the deputies from the colonies. The Government candidates were returned in the majority of those districts which elect but one deputy, and were also at the head of the poll in the three-cornered constituencies owing to the systematic abstention of the Intransigente Federals. The coalition of the Progressists, the Constitutional party, and the friends of Castelar obtained for the three groups respectively 8, 34, and 9 seats. In the ranks of the majority more than 250 belonged to old followers of the last Cabinet devoted to Canovas del Castillo. The rest were chiefly Moderados, friends of Marshal Campos. More abstentions took place under the limited franchise bill than in 1876 with universal suffrage ; but the Liberals, who contested more than 140 seats, were often beaten by a narrow majority. In Madrid 7,000 out of 21,000 voted, and in Barcelona 2,300 out of 8,200. The senatorial elections also gave to the Ministry a large majority in the Upper Chamber.

The Cortes were opened on June 1st by the King in person. In his speech from the throne he said that the Government would continue in the exercise of liberal principles, abolish abuses in the administration, and be as economical as possible. The relations to the foreign powers were satisfactory. Proposals would be made to relieve the distress caused by the war in Cuba, and to abolish slavery in the Antilles, and with the assistance of the Cortes the Government would endeavor to assimilate the position of the colony to that of a province of Spain. On June 26th the Marquis of Orovio, Minister of Finance, presented the estimates for 1879–'80. The expenditure was put at 828,000,000 pesetas, and the probable revenue at 812,000,-000. The estimates showed an increase of expenditure, owing to the interest on the debt and the heavy military outlays. The Minister fixed the probable revenue at a higher sum than the returns for the current year, admitting a deficit on the estimates as well as on the floating debt of the Treasury. The address was voted on July 14th by 247 against 44. The Cortes were prorogued on July 26th, without having done any work of importance.

The Chambers reassembled on November 3d. The principal question before them in this session was the abolition of slavery in Cuba. On November 4th the Minister of the Colonies read in the Senate the Government bill providing for this measure. The bill commenced by declaring that slavery will cease from the date of the promulgation of the law in the "Official Gazette" of Havana. All slaves will be compelled to remain for a period of eight years in the service of their present masters, who will act as their protectors, tending them when sick, paying them wages, and instructing the most capable. After the lapse of five years one fourth of the freed men will be completely emancipated from the control of the masters, the choice in this case being determined by lot; and on the expiration of the eighth year the power of the masters over the freed men will entirely cease. Corporal punishment will then be no longer permitted, and any offenses committed by the negroes will be dealt with by the public prosecutors, any act of rebellion being, however, punished by court-martial. In explaining the object and intention of the bill, the Minister said that slavery was contrary to the laws of nature, and could no longer be maintained in the civilized world. Owing to the impoverished state of the Spanish Exchequer, it was impossible to pay an indemnity to the owners of slaves, and the Government deemed it indispensable that the freed negroes should remain for a certain period under the patronage of their former masters; for by adopting this course the dangers which might ensue from the immediate and simultaneous emancipation of all the slaves would be avoided. He added that the Government considered that the scheme for the gradual enfranchisement of the slaves was contrary to the laws of 1870. Bills were also introduced by the Government for assimilating Cuba to the provinces of the kingdom, for tariff legislation, and other reforms. As it seemed impossible to obtain a majority in favor of these measures, the Ministry resigned, and a new one was formed on December 8th, under Canovas del Castillo. As soon as this Ministry

had assumed office, it substituted in place of the abolition bill of the former Ministry a new one, which provided for the gradual emancipation of the slaves in Cuba after eight years of provisional servitude under their present masters, in 1886, 1887, and 1888. In this shape it passed the Senate on December 26th, although the West Indian deputies declared that it would satisfy neither the owners nor the slaves. Both Houses then adjourned.

On November 24th the King was married to the Archduchess Maria Christine of Austria. The new Queen of Spain, who is the second wife of Alfonso XII., was born July 21, 1858. She is a daughter of Archduke Charles Ferdinand of Austria, who died in 1874. Her relationship to the Emperor of Austria is shown by the genealogical table given in the article AUSTRO-HUNGARIAN MONARCHY.

Juan Oliva y Moncasi, who attempted to assassinate King Alfonso in 1878, was executed on January 4th, in spite of numerous petitions for his pardon. Another attempt on the life of the King was made on December 30th. As he was driving from the palace with the Queen for his usual evening ride, two shots were fired at him by a man named Gonzalez. The would-be assassin, who was a waiter by profession and but nineteen years of age, was seized by the attendants.

A new rebellion broke out in Cuba in August. On the 27th of that month two insurgent bands appeared in the districts of Holguin and Santiago. General Blanco at once dispatched 2,000 men from Havana, and ordered the most energetic pursuit of the disturbers. The rebels were afterward joined by slaves who had demanded their liberty, and failing to get it had run away. The negroes soon assumed the lead, and began waging an indiscriminate war upon the whites, both Spaniards and Cubans. In imitation of what the Cubans did during the last insurrection, they constituted a so-called government in almost impenetrable woods and mountains, having at their head three mulattoes, ex-chiefs of the former insurrection—Maceo, Grombet, and Guillermon. Immediately upon the beginning of the disorders, Captain-General Blanco issued a decree in which he declared the province of Santiago de Cuba in a state of war. Another decree was published which, after describing the miserable condition of the inhabitants of the provinces of Puerto Principe and Santiago de Cuba in consequence of the last insurrection, directed that $50,000 be appropriated for the assistance of the province of Puerto Principe and $100,000 for that of Santiago de Cuba. The insurrection continued during the remainder of the year, although the Government denied that any importance was attached to it.

A new treaty with China regarding the immigration of Chinese to the island of Cuba was published in the "Official Gazette" of Havana in the beginning of July. Its principal points were as follows:

The immigration of Chinamen by contract is entirely prohibited; the immigrants will come to Cuba by their own free will, and both countries, China and Spain, bind themselves to prosecute those persons and vessels bringing Chinamen to Cuba against their will. Spain promises to treat the Chinese in Cuba with the same consideration as foreigners of the most favored nation. To this end the Chinese Government will provide with a passport every emigrant, and officials of both nations will visit every emigrant vessel leaving Chinese ports, in order to insure a full observance of this law. The Chinese Government will interpose no obstacle to the free emigration of Chinamen. The Emperor of China may appoint a consul at Havana and all other places on the island where consuls of other nations are stationed, and these consuls will enjoy the same prerogatives as their colleagues of other nations. Any Chinaman may leave Cuba whenever it pleases him, unless he is subject to judicial proceedings. All Chinamen can apply to the courts of justice, like any other foreigners; and if any of them have been treated contrary to law before this treaty was signed, their complaints will be examined and their rights accorded to them.

The treaty stipulates that a notification of one year must be given of desire of either party for any alteration of its provisions.

SWEDEN AND NORWAY, two kingdoms of northern Europe, united under the same dynasty. The King, Oscar II., born January 21, 1829, succeeded to the throne at the death of his brother, Charles XV., September 18, 1872. He married on June 6, 1857, Sophia, daughter of the Duke of Nassau, born July 9, 1836. Their oldest son is Gustavus, heir apparent, Duke of Wermland, born June 16, 1858.

SWEDEN.—The executive authority is in the hands of the King, who acts under the advice of a Ministry, formerly called the Council of State. The composition of the Ministry at the close of 1879 was as follows: Baron L. de Geer, Minister of State and Justice; O. M. Björnstjerna, Foreign Affairs; J. H. Rosenswärd, War; Baron F. W. von Otter, Navy; H. L. Forsell, Finance; Dr. C. G. Malmstrom, Education and Ecclesiastical Affairs; Dr. L. T. Almqvist, Justice. Besides these there are two Ministers without portfolios: Dr. N. H. Vult von Steyern, and Dr. J. H. Lovén.

The area of Sweden, inclusive of inland lakes, is 170,741 square miles. The population of the several provinces or läns on December 31, 1878, was as follows:

LÄNS.	Population.	LÄNS.	Population.
Stockholm, City....	169,420	Elfsborg..........	290,766
Stockholm, Län....	143,768	Skaraborg........	258,901
Upsala...........	108,841	Wermland........	269,586
Södermanland.....	144,821	Orebro...........	181,473
Ostergötland.....	270,328	Westmanland.....	127,586
Jönköping........	195,328	Kopparberg.......	190,299
Kronoberg........	160,890	Gefleborg........	172,517
Calmar...........	243,600	Westernorrland...	162,514
Gottland..........	55,611	Jämtland........	79,764
Blekinge.........	135,689	Westerbotten.....	103,151
Christianstad.....	232,116	Norbotten........	87,681
Malmöhus........	345,927		
Halland..........	135,411	Total...........	4,531,863
Gothenburg and Bohus..............	257,466		

Of the total population, 2,205,292 were males and 2,326,571 females. In 1877 there were 30,674 marriages, 142,674 births, 87,373 deaths, and 4,198 still-births.

The budget for 1880 estimates the revenue and expenditure at 72,630,000 crowns each (1 crown = 26.8 cents). Besides the budget, the Riksdag of 1879 voted 7,000,000 crowns for the construction of new railroads, and 1,500,000 crowns to increase the rolling-stock and other material of the existing roads. The expenses of the army, Church, and certain civil offices are in part defrayed out of the revenue of landed estates belonging to the Crown, and the amounts do not appear in the budget estimates. The public debt of Sweden on December 31, 1878, amounted to 212,548,240 crowns. The Swedish army in 1878 numbered 183,603 men. The navy consisted of 43 steamers, of 20,271 horse-power and 155 guns; 10 sailing vessels, of 105 guns; and 87 smaller vessels, of 113 guns.

The imports in 1877 amounted to 303,420,000 crowns, the exports to 215,913,000 crowns. The movement of shipping in 1877 was as follows:

FLAG.	ENTERED.		CLEARED.	
	Loaded vessels.	Tons.	Loaded vessels.	Tons.
Swedish..........	4,525	727,138	7,423	957,753
Norwegian.......	673	132,169	2,224	675,485
Foreign.........	4,341	723,552	5,161	972,207
Total.........	9,539	1,582,859	14,813	2,605,395

NORWAY.—In Norway the executive is represented by the King, who exercises his authority through a Council of State, composed of two ministers of state and nine councilors. Two of the councilors, who are changed every year, together with one of the ministers, form a delegation of the Council of State residing at Stockholm near the King. The Council of State was composed as follows in 1878: F. Stang, Minister of State; J. Holmboe, Finances and Customs; Dr. O. A. Bachke, Justice and Police; J. L. Johansen, Navy; N. Vogt, Interior; R. T. Nissen, Education and Worship; C. A. Selmer, Army; C. Jensen, Revision of Public Accounts. The delegation of the Council at Stockholm consisted of O. R. Kjerulf, Minister of State, H. L. Helliesen, and Major-General H. A. Munthe.

The area of Norway is 122,280 square miles, and the population according to the census of 1875 was 1,806,900. (For an account of the area and population of each of the provinces of Norway, see "Annual Cyclopædia" for 1876.) The movement of population in 1878 was as follows: Marriages, 13,825; births, 58,019; deaths, 29,541.

The receipts for 1878 amounted to 50,441,700 crowns (1 crown=26·8 cents), the expenditures to 51,771,300 crowns. The public debt on June 30, 1878, amounted to 91,600,000 crowns. The imports in 1878 were valued at 140,348,000 crowns, and the exports at 91,630,000 crowns. The war navy in July, 1879, consisted of 30 steamers with 144 guns, and 92 sailing vessels with 149 guns. The commercial navy in 1877 consisted of 8,064 vessels, of 1,493,041 tons.

The railroads in operation in 1879 amounted to 1,059 kilometres. The number of government telegraph stations on December 31, 1878, was 127; length of lines, 7,617, and of wires, 13,711 kilometres. The number of inland dispatches sent was 466,766; of foreign dispatches sent, 115,254; of foreign dispatches received, 130,128; and of transit dispatches, 2,820; making a total of 714,968. The railroad telegraphs are not included in these figures. The number of post-offices in 1878 was 867; the number of inland letters sent, 9,137,754; of foreign letters sent and received, 3,410,936. The number of newspapers sent and received was 8,984,996.

The Swedish Riksdag was opened on January 18th. In his speech from the throne, the King stated that, owing to the depressed state of commerce, the revenue for 1880 was expected to fall below the usual estimates, and the Government therefore proposed to increase the duties on liquors and tobacco, and also on sugar and coffee. In the budget for 1880 the revenue and expenditures were each estimated at 74,-650,000 crowns. In April both Chambers voted an increase of 20 ores (1 ore = 0·100 crown) per kanna (1 kanna = 2·76 quarts) in the tax on spirituous liquors. In May the Riksdag, in accordance with a Government proposition, passed a bill providing for the retirement of the notes of private banks of 5 and 10 crowns, and replacing them by notes of the Royal Bank. It was stated in support of the motion that over three quarters of all paper money is issued by the private banks, and that, while they had about 48,000,000 crowns in circulation, only one sixth of this amount was secured by coin deposits. In this way they drew interest to the amount of 3,000,000 crowns from a capital which did not exist, and which ought to pass into the Treasury of the state.

The Swedish Government in January returned to the French Government the 80,000 francs paid by the latter for the island of St. Bartholomew, for the purpose of founding a charitable institution on that island.

The Storthing of Norway was opened on February 3d by the King in person. In his speech from the throne he stated that the depressed condition of commerce necessitated an increase of the direct taxes. Propositions to this effect would be submitted by the Government. Bills would also be submitted affecting the army organization and the city schools. The budget, as submitted by the Government, amounted to 46,000,000 crowns, but was reduced by 4,500,000 crowns by the Storthing, the reductions principally affecting the army and navy. In consequence, numerous works on fortifications which had been begun had to be stopped. The general elections for the Storthing, held in October, left its political complexion unchanged.

SWITZERLAND, a republic of central Europe, consisting of twenty-two cantons, three of which are divided into two independent half cantons each. The President of the Federal Council for 1879 was B. Hammer of Soleure, and the Vice-President Dr. E. Welti of Aargau.

The area and population (according to an official estimate of July 1, 1878) of the different cantons are as follows:

CANTONS.	Square miles.	Population.
Zürich	666	298,642
Bern	2,669	586,606
Lucerne	580	133,605
Uri	415	17,188
Schwyz	351	49,756
Unterwalden ob dem Wald	188	15,221
Unterwalden nid dem Wald	112	12,098
Glarus	267	36,546
Zug	92	22,055
Freiburg	644	115,067
Soleure	308	78,907
Basel City	14	52,865
Basel Country	168	56,055
Schaffhausen	114	39,855
Appenzell Outer Rhodes	101	48,984
Appenzell Inner Rhodes	61	11,906
St. Gall	780	196,905
Grisons	2,774	98,307
Aargau	542	202,599
Thurgau	381	95,707
Ticino	1,088	132,586
Vaud	1,244	246,278
Valais	2,026	101,776
Neufchâtel	312	104,826
Geneva	108	101,586
Total	15,981	2,792,264

The movement of population in 1878 was: 20,550 marriages, 91,426 births, 68,904 deaths, and 3,593 still-births.

The total revenue of the Confederation for 1878 amounted to 41,536,226 francs, and the expenditures to 41,469,641 francs. The budget for 1879 estimated the receipts at 40,565,000 francs, and the expenditures at 42,028,000 francs. The liabilities of the republic amounted at the close of 1878 to 35,036,976 francs, as a set-off against which there was Federal property amounting to 41,197,489 francs.

The Federal army consists of the Bundesauszug, comprising all male persons between the ages of twenty and thirty-two, and the Landwehr, comprising all those between thirty-three and forty-four. In 1879 there were 578 officers and 119,419 men in the Bundesauszug, and 135 officers and 95,338 men in the Landwehr.

In 1878 there were 799 post-offices; number of internal letters sent, 47,530,128, and of foreign letters 20,201,012; newspapers, parcels of foreign and domestic printed matter, etc., 72,-716,096. The length of the Government telegraph lines in 1878 was 6,523 kilometres, and of Government wire 15,960 kilometres; number of stations, 1,161; of dispatches sent, 2,476,-988. The length of railroads in 1877 was 2,590 kilometres.

The principal question before the Federal Assembly in 1879 was the restoration of capital punishment. In March a bill was introduced restoring to the several cantons their liberty of action in this question. It was passed by the Cantonal Council on March 19th. In the National Council it was at first rejected, but was finally passed on March 28th. The question was submitted to a popular vote on May 18th, when it was adopted by 196,197 to 177,-263 votes. The cantons of Zürich, Bern, Basel City, Basel Country, Thurgau, Neufchâtel, and Geneva voted against it.

In December the Federal Assembly elected Dr. Welti of Aargau as President, and M. Anderwelt of Thurgau as Vice-President of the Swiss Confederation for 1880.

An important decision was given by the Federal Council in an appealed case on July 26th. The government of the Canton of Zürich in 1878 combined the Reformed and Catholic primary schools in one of its villages. The Catholic school officers appealed to the Federal Council against this action as unconstitutional. The Council disallowed the appeal, as the Federal Constitution simply provides that the public schools shall be open to children of all religious denominations.

T

TAYLOR, General RICHARD, the only son of General Zachary Taylor, born January 27, 1826, died in New York, April 12th. His ancestor, James Taylor, emigrated from England in 1682, and settled in southern Virginia. From him were descended two Presidents of the United States, James Madison and Zachary Taylor. Another distinguished scion, Richard Taylor, was lieutenant-colonel of the 9th Virginia regiment during the Revolutionary war. He married into the Strother family, and in 1791 removed to Kentucky. It was at his homestead, Springfield, near Louisville, Kentucky, that his grandson Richard Taylor, the subject of this sketch, was born. In the following spring he was taken to New Orleans, and the childhood of Richard Taylor was passed there or in frontier forts. His introduction to school life was at Fort Snelling, where he was the only white child in a school of half-breeds taught by a missionary. Soon after he was installed in the family of a life-long friend of his father, William C. Bullitt, with whose sons he attended the school of Robert N. Smith in Jefferson County, Kentucky. To that able and rigid instructor he was indebted for the foundation of his education. At the age of fifteen he was sent to Lancaster, Massachusetts, to be prepared for admission to Yale College. He entered the junior class in 1843, and graduated in 1845.

At the opening of the Mexican war in 1846 he joined his father, who was in command of the forces on the American frontier. Appointed his private secretary and aide-de-camp, he accompanied him through the campaign. He took part in the battles of Monterey, Resaca de la Palma, Palo Alto, Buena Vista, and others, where his father earned that military prestige which bore him triumphantly into the Presidential chair. During this period Richard Taylor went abroad. He was received everywhere with the highest distinction, which honors he accepted as intended for his country. His elegance of manner and conversational talent would anywhere, without adventitious aid, have secured his social success.

He afterward resided for some time near Rodney, Mississippi, on a plantation belonging to his father. In 1849 he removed to a sugar estate, Fashion Plantation, St. Charles Parish, twenty miles above New Orleans, on the Mississippi River. In 1851 he married Miss Myrthé Bringier. The family of Bringier de Lacadière are of noble French blood. They emigrated to Louisiana, where they possessed the Houmas and other estates, more extensive and valuable than many European pricipalities. The lady whom Richard Taylor married shared with fortitude the fortunes of her husband during the civil war. Their property was confiscated after the fall of New Orleans in 1862. While a refugee, escaping before the advancing army with her little ones, they were stricken by scarlet fever. One of her boys died on the way, the other only lived to reach Shreveport. In 1875 she died in New Orleans, leaving three surviving daughters, her four sons having preceded her to the grave.

For many years Taylor lived the easy, hospitable life of a Southern planter. He was fond of society, a voracious reader, and singularly unambitious. Several minor offices he filled with credit to himself and the State, but he was indifferent to political preferment, which was clearly within his grasp. The events of 1860 roused him from his lethargy. He went as delegate to the National Democratic Convention held in Charleston in that year, and endeavored to bind together the discordant elements of the party. After the split in the Convention he was a delegate to Baltimore. In 1861 he was Senator from the parish of St. Charles in the State Legislature, and assisted in framing the act calling a State Convention, which met in March and passed the secession ordinance. Taylor was chairman of the Committee on Federal Relations and Defense, a difficult position under a Governor like Moore, economical of public money and wholly incredulous of the possibility of war.

After the investment of Fort Pickens, Taylor joined General Bragg at Pensacola. While there he was appointed colonel of the 9th Louisiana regiment. Hurried on to Richmond, the regiment arrived on the field the day after the first battle of Manassas. It was placed in the brigade of General Walker, who was soon after transferred to a Georgia brigade. Taylor was passed over the heads of the senior colonels and made brigadier-general. He unwillingly accepted this promotion, which was unpopular with the brigade. Camp exposure had brought on an illness from which he was slowly recovering, and he had seen no service. The promotion was attributed to the partiality of President Davis toward the brother of his first wife, who was a daughter of Zachary Taylor. At the instance of General Joseph E. Johnston, Taylor went to Richmond to urge the adoption of that General's plan of army organization. During the Valley campain of 1862 Taylor fought under Stonewall Jackson. The brigade hore its part well in many a fray, at Luray, Port Republic, Front Royal, and Winchester. On one occasion they captured a battery and turned it upon the enemy. General Jackson, in recompense of their gallantry, presented the battery to the brigade. When Jackson marched to the Peninsula, Taylor's command, still in Ewell's division, confronted McClellan, and was engaged in the seven days' fight around Richmond. Jackson recommended him for promotion. He received his grade of major-general while in Richmond, stricken with paralysis. Taylor was then assigned to command in Louisiana.

During the siege of Vicksburg, the Indianola, a heavily armed ironclad, passed the town and controlled the Mississippi River. The only boats at Taylor's disposal were the towboat Webb and an ordinary river-steamer, the Queen of the West, recently captured from the Northeners. The Indianola, with a coal-barge lashed on each side, was lying off a point sixty miles below Vicksburg. The attack was made at night. Both the vessels suffered severely, but the Indianola was struck four times, and then surrendered in a sinking condition. In a battle with General Banks at Mansfield, 2,500 prisoners, 200 wagons, and 20 pieces of artillery, besides side-arms and colors, were captured by Taylor. This success was speedily followed by the fight at Pleasant Hill, at which Banks and Taylor each claimed the victory. The report of Admiral Porter, hearing date April 14, 1864, says: "The army here has met a great defeat, no matter what the generals try to make of it. With the defeat has come demoralization, and it will take some time to reorganize and make up the deficiencies in killed and prisoners." General Grant from Virginia reported to Halleck in Washington: "You can see from General Brayman's dispatch to me something of General Banks's disaster."

At the close of the Red River campaign, General Taylor, believing that further operations in this quarter would accomplish nothing, asked to be relieved from duty. He was promoted to lieutenant-general and placed in command of Alabama and Mississippi. At Meridian Forrest reported to him, and was sent to impede Sherman's communications north of the Tennessee, and thus relieve Hood's army, then west of Atlanta. In December Taylor went to Tupelo to take command of the remnant of Hood's Army of Tennessee. The soldiers were moved as speedily as possible to re-

enforce Johnston in North Carolina. Taylor was left confronting Canby and hard pressed by Wilson's cavalry. On the 8th of May, 1865, he surrendered to Canby at Citronelle, and his military career terminated.

After four years' absence, he returned to New Orleans penniless. This lord of many acres now called nothing his own but his horses. These he sold for $350, with which he began life afresh. He took charge of some important public works, among others of the Carondelet Canal. In January, 1873, he again visited Washington in the interest of his State, then torn in two by two rival Governors and Legislatures, and with the military overriding the civil power. His intervention proved vain. In May he was sent to Europe in the interest of some Northern capitalists, and was again received with the same kindness as when in the heyday of his father's glory he visited England. After the death of his wife, convinced that Louisiana was permanently blighted, he removed his family to Winchester, Virginia, the residence of Mrs. Dandridge, his sole surviving sister. He turned his attention to literature, and became a frequent contributor to periodicals, both French and English. He spoke both tongues with equal facility, and was wont to boast that he acquired "French in Louisiana, English at Fort Snelling, and American in the Old Dominion." Unfortunately, his sparkling wit and fund of anecdote are without record. His work on the war, "Destruction and Reconstruction," was written when the hand of disease was already upon him. He was in New York supervising its publication, when fatal symptoms manifested themselves.

TENNESSEE. The General Assembly met January 9th. The first question considered was that of reducing the emoluments of many of the officers of the State and counties. Functionaries who were paid by fees and perquisites were required to pay over to the State Comptroller, or to the County Trustee if a county officer, the amount of these fees which was in excess of $2,000 per annum. Many opposed this measure on constitutional grounds, as embodying an unauthorized mode of taxation. Many officers receiving stated salaries had their stipends reduced. A bill requiring insurance companies to pay the full amount of insurance named in the policy in the case of the total destruction of property by fire, and to pay on the basis of the value named in the policy in the case of partial destruction, was vetoed by the Governor, on the grounds that in the first instance named it would prove an incentive to incendiarism, negligence, and fraud, and was thus opposed to public policy, and that in the second class of cases it would prove prejudicial to policy-holders, as they usually undervalue their property in insurance policies.

The question which engrossed the attention of the Legislature to the exclusion of all others for a great part of the session, and on which steps were taken for an adjustment for the first time, was that of the settlement of the State debt. The interest on the bonds of the State has been in default since 1870, when the tax tariff was reduced from 60 to 20 mills on a dollar. In 1877 the creditors of the State agreed to compromise the debt at the rate of 60 cents on a dollar, at 6 per cent. interest. This was not accepted. The question of the adjustment of the debt finally became a political issue. Party lines were not strictly drawn, though the Republicans generally favored payment in full, or acceptance of the bondholders' proposed compromise at first, and afterward the settlement proposed by the Legislature at 50 cents and 4 per cent. interest. When the Legislature met, it was expected that the matter would be adjusted in some way. One party favored the acceptance of the bondholders' proposition; another, a settlement on the basis of 50 cents on the dollar at 6 per cent. interest; another advocated the basis of 33⅓ cents; and a fourth party declared itself in favor of total repudiation. This was made the leading issue of the popular elections, and many members of the Assembly had been elected upon it. Soon after the Legislature met, the question was taken up. It was referred to the Committee on Finance, Ways, and Means. Mr. Savage, chairman of the committee, submitted the majority report on the proposition regarding the settlement of the State debt on the 11th of March. The report was in the form of a bill embodying the following provisions:

1. That the Capitol bonds, amounting to $493,000, the Hermitage bonds, amounting to $35,000, the Agricultural bonds, amounting to $18,000, the bonds held by Mrs. Polk, amounting to $29,000, and the bonds held by the educational institutions of the State, upon which interest has been paid under a resolution of the last General Assembly, be settled and funded, with the accrued interest, at the rate of 60 cents to the dollar, at 4 per cent. per annum interest.

2. That the Union Bank bonds, amounting to $125,000, the Bank of Tennessee bonds, amounting to $214,000, the turnpike bonds, amounting to $728,000, the Hiawassee Railroad bonds, amounting to $280,000, the East Tennessee and Georgia Railroad bonds, amounting to $144,000, the La Grange and Memphis Railroad bonds, amounting to $68,000—all the above bonds, except bonds belonging to educational institutions, being bonds of the State debt proper—and the bonds issued under the internal improvement act of 1852 and amendments thereto, known as the ante-war railroad bonds, amounting to $8,583,000, be settled and funded, with accrued interest, at 50 cents to the dollar, at 4 per cent. per annum interest.

3. That the bonds funded under the act of 1868, amounting to $569,000, and the bonds funded under the act of 1873, amounting to $4,867,000, be settled and funded with accrued interest at 33⅓ cents to the dollar, at 4 per cent. per annum interest.

4. That the Mineral Home bonds, amounting to $63,000, and the bonds funded under the act of 1866, supposed to cover the war interest, amounting to $2,246,000, be rejected and not paid.

5. That the railroad bonds issued since the war, amounting to $2,268,000 now outstanding with accrued interest, be settled at the rate of 33⅓ cents to the dollar, and paid in the non-interest-bearing Treasury warrants of the State, in the denominations $5, $10, $20, and $50, neatly printed on good paper, which shall be receivable for taxes and all other dues to and from the State.

The new issue of bonds was to run nineteen years and be redeemable at the end of five years, the interest to be payable once a year at Nashville. The act was to be submitted to the people, who should vote upon it in a special election the first Thursday in August, and then passed upon finally by the Legislature after having received the popular approval. The committee gave the amount and character of the debt and the acts under which the several classes of bonds were issued, making a distinction between what they called the State debt proper, amounting to $2,105,000, and the bonds issued under and subsequent to the act of 1852 and posterior acts, including the funding acts. As to the nature and extent of the State's obligation for the rest of the debt incurred by the State, they declared, if there was any obligation, it was secondary, as endorsers, as to $11,221,000. Of these the law required certain conditions precedent and subsequent, which, in nearly every instance, were not observed. The greater part of the present debt they declared to be the result of a vicious policy and corrupt legislation. They denounced the acts for the sale of the railways and the payment of the purchase-money in bonds of any series, as having been procured by interested combinations. Setting out the requirements of the act of 1852, they concluded that seven of these were conditions precedent, and legal notice to purchasers of the bonds, and, having been violated, that $11,221,000 of bonds issued in aid of railways under the act of 1852 were void, and any settlement thereof by the State rests not in a valid contract, but upon consideration of State policy.

Senator Clapp prepared a minority report, in which he contested the grounds advanced in favor of the rejection of any part of the bonded debt. The arguments put forward in favor of scaling down the debt included, besides, that of the inability of the State to raise the taxes necessary to discharge the obligations in full. The report assumes that the liability of the State upon bonds issued in her name rests for its decision on the law and facts of the case, as in a controversy between private persons. If the Legislature has not inherent power to make contracts, it can not communicate such power to its creatures, private and public corporations. The State is the primary and only party liable for its bonds. As a legal proposition, the report can not understand upon what ground the State expects to escape liability as surety or guarantor on its railroad bonds as the maker of a negotiable instrument. As to funding the war interest, the minority knows of no principle of international law that suspends interest on interest-bearing debt due by one of the belligerents to the other. As to the charge of voidness of post-war bonds because of corrupt legislation and illegality of the government, he showed that the vested rights acquired would not be invalidated were the charge proved; but he insisted that the proof fails to show more than presumptive bribery and undue means, or to trace them to any member of the Legislature.

The bill, as it was afterward modified by amendments, embraced the proposition of funding the greater part of the debt at the rate of 50 cents on the dollar, with 4 per cent. interest. This settlement was to be subject to the acceptance of the bondholders and the approval of the people. The bill as amended was finally passed by a close vote on the 28th of March. Before the vote was taken the Governor had transmitted a message to the Assembly announcing a proposition from the managers of the different railroads to waive the immunity from taxation extended to the railroads in their charters, and contribute to the State taxes from $80,000 to $100,000 annually for the extinction of the principal and interest of the State debt. In accordance with this the actual burden of the debt would be reduced to 40 cents on the dollar and 4 per cent. interest if the compromise at 50 cents should be effected.

Governor Marks appointed B. A. Euloe and Nathaniel Baxter, Jr., to communicate with the holders of the State bonds and procure their acceptance of the compromise voted by the Legislature. Ex-Governors Porter and Brown and others were deputed by a mass-meeting of citizens to present the case to the creditors and citizens of the East. At a dinner in New York in the middle of April they received the approval of many bondholders, merchants, and bankers of the proposed settlement. The provisions of the bill required that the Governor should secure the acceptance of bondholders possessing an equal amount of bonds with those who had agreed to the proposition of 60 cents with 6 per cent. interest, before calling for a popular vote on the question. After fulfilling this condition, Governor Marks ordered the popular vote to be taken. On the 7th of August, the day appointed for this purpose, the proposed settlement was rejected by a large majority, 30,920 voting against it and 19,669 in its favor. This action of the people left the question of the final settlement still unresolved. Although understood to have been an expression of a popular sentiment in favor of total repudiation, it had only the effect of postponing the decision of the question, which belongs to the State Legislature.

The following is a statement of the funded debt and registered debt of the State on December 21, 1878: Registered (act of 1873), $14,665,000, at 6 per cent. interest; $292,300, at 5 per cent.; $397,000, at 6 per cent., not required to be registered; and $4,867,000 at 6 per cent. in funding bonds (1873). On the same day the unpaid interest amounted to $4,-201,902.50. The bonded debt, including unpaid interest under the present laws, would amount to about $25,676,500 on January 1, 1880. This sum does not include the school-fund certificates ($2,512,000), the railroad debt

due to the United States ($671,045.45), the outstanding notes and debts of the Bank of Tennessee, or the debts due to laborers on delinquent railroads while the State government was running them. The last three items mentioned amount to about $2,700,000. Should these sums be added to the State debt proper, it would amount to about $31,560,000.

By the improvement act of 1852 bonds of the State, which constitute the greater portion of its present debt, were issued and loaned to the railroad companies on the condition of the completion of stipulated portions of their roads, as a credit to encourage improvements of public benefit. By the original act these bonds were made a primary lien on the railroad property. This lien was removed by subsequent action of the Legislature, and the railroads were permitted to redeem the bonds by delivering into the Treasury State bonds of equal amount of any series. At a time when the securities of the State were sold in the market at a discount of 60 per cent. and over, several of the railroads availed themselves of this permission and redeemed their obligations to the State by returning bonds of other series. Other roads were afterward foreclosed upon by the State authorities and resold to other parties. Many of the holders of the Tennessee internal improvement bonds, while the matter was awaiting the decision of the people and the Legislature, brought as a test case a suit of foreclosure against the railroads, upon the advice of Charles O'Conor of New York, upon the ground that the lien on the railroad property was a part of the original contract contained in the bonds, and could not constitutionally be revoked by any subsequent action of the Legislature. The following is the amount of bonds claimed to be secured by a lien on the railroads named under the act mentioned, and which are still outstanding against those roads: Roads operated under what is known as the Wilson system of railways—Cincinnati, Cumberland Gap, and Charleston, $377,000; East Tennessee and Georgia, $1,102,000; East Tennessee and Virginia, $1,237,000; Memphis and Charleston, $841,000; total, $3,557,000. Roads included under the name of the Louisville and Nashville and Great Southern Railroad—Louisville and Nashville, main stem, $308,000; Memphis, Clarksville, and Louisville, $819,000; Memphis and Ohio, $1,199,000; Tennessee and Alabama, $479,000; Central Southern, $364,-000; total, $3,169,000. Roads now embraced under the name of the Nashville, Chattanooga, and St. Louis Railway—Nashville and Chattanooga, $120,000; Nashville and Northwestern, $1,422,000; McMinnville and Manchester, $360,-000; Winchester and Alabama, $479,000; total, $2,381,000. Other roads—Mississippi Central, $488,000; Mississippi and Tennessee, $105,000; Mobile and Ohio, $960,000. The St. Louis and Southeastern Railroad is sued for bonds issued to the Edgefield and Kentucky road. The amount of bonds originally issued toward the construction of the above roads was $29,251,-250; of this amount there are outstanding $12,-453,000; amount of funded bonds now outstanding and claimed as a part of these secured by a lien, about $2,423,000. Upon this amount there is an accrued interest of 21 per cent. The total amount claimed by the bondholders is between $17,000,000 and $18,000,000.

The basis of taxation and the receipts and expenditures are estimated by the Comptroller as follows:

BASIS OF PROPERTY OR AD VALOREM TAX.

Tax aggregate...	$223,212,153
Less 13 per cent............................	29,017,579
Net.....................................	$104,194,574

PERMANENT PRIVILEGES AND OTHER FIXED REVENUES.

Circuit Court clerks, including redemptions.....	$40,000
Other clerks, not including County Court clerks.	20,000
Insurance companies..........................	20,000
Penitentiary................................	70,000
Express, telegraphs, banks, etc................	10,000
Railroads....................................	100,000
Treasurers, agents, delinquents, etc............	35,000
Total...................................	$295,000

ESTIMATED EXPENDITURES.

Current expenses...........................	$525,000
Interest on school fund......................	150,750
Interest on State debt—$12,000,000 @ 4 per cent.	500,000
Total for one year........	$1,175,750

He estimates the receipts at different tariffs as follows: At 10 mills on a dollar, $649,194; at 15 mills, $761,000; at 20 mills, $883,389; at 25 mills, $995,583; at 30 mills, $1,107,583; at 35 mills, $1,219,680; at 40 mills, $1,331,778.

The bankrupt condition of the finances of Memphis and several other towns and cities led to a number of special acts revoking or modifying the charters of these municipalities. At the request of the city of Memphis, which was laboring under the burden of a debt estimated at over one third of the taxable property, and had been depopulated and impoverished by the ravages of the yellow fever, the charter was taken away, and the administration assumed by the State government. By a subsequent act the Governor was authorized to appoint commissioners for the settlement of the debts of extinct municipal districts. At the instance of certain holders of the city's securities, an action was brought before Judge Baxter, of the United States Court at Memphis, calling for the appointment of a receiver. The Court delivered the opinion that the act of the Legislature repealing the charter was unconstitutional and void, as was also the act creating a taxing district. The Judge appointed Mr. Latham receiver, to take charge of the assets of the city, to the exclusion of receiver Meriwether appointed by the State authorities. The Supreme Court of the State afterward declared the laws repealing the municipal charter and constituting a taxing district valid and within the Constitution—Judges Cooper, McFarland, and Deaderick concurring, and Judges Freeman and Turney dissenting. The

debts of the city of Memphis amounted altogether to $4,403,454, including the funded debt, consisting of the compromise bonds for $1,104,-825 issued in lieu of the old funded debt of $2,209,650, and the unfunded debt amounting to $3,298,629. The nominal assets amounted to $2,265,245, valued by a special committee at $904,878. There were over two million dollars' worth of uncollected taxes due to the city.

Governor Marks called an extra session of the General Assembly for the purposes of granting Memphis the power to perfect and carry out completer methods of sanitation, of amending the charters of towns and cities so as to enforce sanitary regulations, framing a law for the prevention of the spoliation of graves and traffic in dead bodies, and extending the charter of the Memphis and Paducah Railroad. The Assembly met at the time appointed, the 16th of December, and proceeded to consider the questions proposed to it.

The apportionment of school-taxes requires $75,375, distributed among the counties in proportion to their scholastic population. The total number of scholars in the State is 448,-917. Recent amendments of the school laws extend the school age to twenty-one years, and include the subject of agriculture in the curriculum of studies.

The first enforcement of the law against carrying deadly weapons was made by Judge Thomas D. Eldridge of the Bartlett Circuit, who sentenced a prisoner to a fine and three months' imprisonment for this offense.

The question of the constitutionality of the new law equalizing and reducing the pay of clerks, by requiring them to pay their fees in excess of a certain amount into the public Treasury, was brought before the Supreme Court, but was not decided on its merits in the absence of a real cause of action.

The yellow fever appeared again in Memphis in July, and continued until cold weather. The city was immediately deserted by all its inhabitants except a part of the poor and colored population. There was fear at one time that the deserted houses would be sacked, and that an anarchic condition would prevail. Governor Marks intrusted the duty of preserving order to the resident companies of colored militia. There were several hundred deaths by yellow fever during the season. It was principally to provide for extraordinary sanitary measures lest the disease should become endemic in this locality that the Governor called the special session of the Legislature.

TEXAS. The Legislature opened its regular session at Austin on January 14th, when the new Governor, Oran M. Roberts, was formally installed in office, and closed by final adjournment on April 24th.

A constitutional amendment adopted by the Legislature, exempting from taxation all agricultural products while in the farmer's hands, and all necessary supplies for his use, was voted upon the first Tuesday in September. This measure was denounced by a large portion of the people and press in the State, because it discriminates in favor of the farmers to the prejudice of those engaged in other pursuits, who are allowed no similar exemption. In Harris County, which is divided into twenty-six election precincts, polls were opened in five precincts only on the election day, and all of the votes cast were for the amendment.

An act was passed endowing the Governor with power to remove officers and the superintendents of charitable or other State institutions at his discretion. A portion of the press in the State protested against this bill as despotic. It went into force on September 1st.

An act was passed authorizing the issue of State bonds to the amount of $3,373,000, classified as follows: Bonds of $1,000 each, $1,373,-000; of $100 each, $1,000,000; of $10 and $5 each, $1,000,000. The bonds of the first two classes are payable in United States gold coin within thirty years from July 1, 1879, bearing interest at the rate of 5 per cent., payable semi-annually. The ten- and five-dollar bonds are payable in twenty years from July 1, 1879, bearing interest at 4 per cent. The interest coupons attached to the bonds are receivable for all State taxes.

The Governor vetoed the items in the general appropriation bill appropriating money for the payment of interest on the State debt, for the sinking fund, and for the public free schools, amounting in the aggregate to about $1,000,-000; and the Legislature adjourned without taking further action on the subject. The Governor's veto created intense excitement in the State; the more so because he had in a manner approved these appropriations in advance, as he had previously signed the tax bill in which a levy of taxes was ordered for each of those purposes. Enthusiastic mass meetings were held, and resolutions adopted expressing resentment against Governor Roberts for the injury he had done to the good name of the State and to education by depriving the public schools of that necessary support which the organic law has provided for their maintenance. Of the one hundred and two newspapers published in Texas, not more than two or three sustained the veto in full. It also threatened injury to the State's credit in the New York money market, as the holders of Texas bonds became apprehensive of the non-payment of the interest due them on July 1st. To allay their fears the State Comptroller wrote to New York assuring them that the State had ample means, and that the money to pay the interest on their bonds was ready. As these matters could not be delayed without detriment to the most vital interests of the State, the Governor, by a proclamation issued a few weeks after the close of the regular session, convened an extraordinary one for June 10th, chiefly to make the appropriations he had before vetoed; his proclamation beginning with the following

preamble: "*Whereas*, the Legislature which convened on the 14th of January, 1879, adjourned *sine die* on the 24th of April, 1879, without passing any law that is now in force making annual appropriations for the support of the free common schools, for the payment of the interest and sinking fund of the bonded public debt of the State, and for other objects necessary for the successful operation of the State government." The called session was opened at the appointed time, and passed the necessary appropriations, reducing that for the schools from one fourth to one sixth of the State revenue. By various messages sent in during its continuance, the Governor laid before the Legislature for consideration a number of subjects besides those mentioned in his proclamation.

A Sunday law was also passed at this session, the first and second sections of which provide that "any person who conscientiously believes that the seventh or any other day of the week is the Sabbath, and who actually refrains from business and labor on that day," may attend to business and labor himself, and employ others, on Sunday. The fourth section provides as follows: "Any merchant, grocer, or dealer in wares or merchandise, or trader in any lawful business whatsoever, who shall barter or sell on Sunday, shall be fined not less than twenty nor more than fifty dollars: *Provided*, this article shall not apply to markets, or dealers in provisions, as to sales made by them before 9 o'clock A. M. The preceding article shall not apply to the sale of drugs and medicines on Sunday." This law was very unfavorably commented upon by the press in the State; and the people assembled in meetings to condemn it on several accounts.

The financial condition of Texas is satisfactory, the State debt being inconsiderable and her revenue sufficient to meet all the public expenditures. Deficiencies have occurred in previous years, especially in 1876 and 1877, from defaulting sheriffs and collectors of taxes. It is estimated that nearly $800,000 are now due to the State on this score; for much of which sum suits have been instituted and judgments obtained, though the recovery of the money is considered difficult. The defects in the laws which gave rise to these defaults were mostly cured by an act passed in 1876, which went into effect August 31, 1877.

Of the salable lands of Texas, in regard to quantities, location, price, and manner of purchase, accurate information is given by the following reply of the State Land Commissioner to a request of the Governor:

GENERAL LAND-OFFICE, AUSTIN, *September* 16, 1879.

Hon O. M. Roberts, Governor of Texas.

SIR: In compliance with your request of the 13th inst., I append a brief statement of Texas State lands now for sale, with location, price, and mode of purchase:

1. Common-school lands, 12,800,000 acres. These are situated in various amounts in 210 of the 225 counties of the State, and consequently embrace every va-

riety of soil, climate, and production of our extensive territory. These lands are for sale at a minimum price of one dollar per acre, payable in ten equal annual payments, with interest. Each individual may purchase not less than 160 nor more than 640 acres of farming lands, or three sections of pasture land. Application to purchase must be made to the county surveyor.

2. University lands, 219,906 acres, situated in Cooke, Fannin, Grayson, Hunt, Collin, Lamar, McLennan, Shackelford, and Callahan Counties. These lands are in the richest and most populous portions of the State, and are for sale in tracts of 80 or 160 acres at a minimum price of $1.50 per acre, on the same terms as the school lands. Application to purchase must be made to the county surveyor.

3. Asylum lands, 407,015 acres, situated in the counties of Callahan, Comanche, Eastland, Jones, Shackelford, Stephens, Taylor, and Tom Green. This section is settling up and improving more rapidly now than any other portion of the State. For sale in tracts of 160 acres, at same price and on same terms as university lands.

4. State Capitol lands, 3,050,000 acres, situated in Dallas, Deaf Smith, Castro, Cochran, Lamb, Bailey, Hockley, Hartley, Oldham, and Parker Counties. Three million acres of these lands are subdivided into tracts of one league (4,428 acres) each, and the field-notes returned to the General Land-Office. They are for sale at 50 cents per acre in such quantities as may be desired. The 50,000 acres are divided into surveys of 640 acres each, and are likewise for sale at 50 cents per acre in such quantities as may be desired, provided that no section shall be divided. Application to purchase must be made to the General Land-Office. No expense attaches to the purchase of these lands, other than the purchase money and patent fee. These lands will not be offered for sale before January 24, 1880.

5. Public debt reserve. Under the act of July 14, 1879, all the vacant and unappropriated public land within the territory bounded on the north by the Indian Territory, on the east by the 100th degree of longitude, on the south by the 32d degree of latitude, on the west by the 103d degree of longitude, all the unappropriated land within the Pacific reservation, and all tracts of 640 acres or less within the organized counties of the State, are offered for sale in tracts of 640 acres each, or less, at 50 cents per acre. Purchasers must apply to the surveyor of the county or district in which the desired land may be situated. He will survey the land and return field-notes to the General Land-Office, at the expense of the purchaser. Within sixty days from the filing of the field-notes in the Land-Office, the purchaser must pay into the State Treasury 50 cents per acre, or forfeit all right to the lands. I have the honor to be, very respectfully, etc.

W. C. WALSH, Commissioner.

Concerning these lands, forgeries and deceits of all kinds have been for a long time extensively practiced to the injury of purchasers, especially immigrants who intended to settle in Texas. The Legislature of 1879 appointed from its own members a Special Committee on Land Frauds, charged to investigate the matter thoroughly. The evil appears to be of such magnitude that, after having spent nearly every night for a month in hearing testimony and examining written evidence, the committee were made sensible that frauds without end had been practiced.

The aggregate number of teachers employed in the public schools of the State is reckoned at 6,000, chiefly home-born. Most of them are paid from the school fund for four months of tuition, the average school time in the year;

but a large number of them keep their schools open for six months more in communities that are able to support their schools by private contributions.

The State Hospital for the Insane, which had 300 inmates in March, 1879, has been conducted with good success in the professional treatment of its patients under the superintendence of Dr. D. R. Wallace, who has gained a national reputation in this position. The Governor has recently removed him, as well as Henry E. McCulloch, Superintendent of the Institution for Deaf Mutes, both of whom had filled their offices for many years with eminent satisfaction.

Crime in Texas has rapidly increased. The number of criminals committed to the State Prison is great; but much greater is the number of those at large, who have escaped from confinement or evaded arrest. Those committed to the penitentiary, as is the practice also in some of the other Southern States, are leased out in gangs as laborers. Each lessee keeps them under his charge in a camp at the place of his work; the guards also are in his employ, and the State has no immediate control over the convicts, and no means to check the lessee's possible abuse of his powers in overworking or otherwise maltreating them. A list compiled from the official records of the several counties on file at the Adjutant-General's office, and published under his name, shows the number of Texas criminals going at large to be 4,585, charged with the following offenses: Murder, 856; attempted murder, resulting in wounding or crippling, and not in death, 911; infanticide, 5; accessory to murder, 7; threatening human life, 30; arson, 20; perjury, 39; forgery, 55; embezzlement, 32; burglary, 81; cattle-stealing, 541; hog-stealing, 169; horse-stealing, 601; abduction, 9; swindling, 127. One of the first official acts of Governor Roberts was to revoke all offers of reward previously announced in the name of the State for the capture of criminals.

The sheriffs' annual convention, held at Austin on September 10th, and attended by about forty sheriffs, was addressed by ex-Governor Lubbock on the duties of executive officers, and by the tax-clerk in the State Comptroller's office on the laws governing the Tax Department. Resolutions were adopted to provide for the publication of a monthly register of criminals, giving the fullest description possible; and a committee of five, besides the ex-officio chairman, Sheriff Corwin of Travis, was appointed with power to devise ways and means for the arrest of criminals. A resolution was also adopted taxing sheriffs five dollars each, and deputies half that amount, to aid in the arrest of parties charged with killing sheriffs or their deputies while engaged in the lawful discharge of their duty.

In connection with this subject, the following facts seem worthy of record: In February Deputy Sheriff Llewellyn of Omaha, Nebraska, secured at North Platte David Melisky and Charles Reed, *alias* Dud Douglas, a noted Texas murderer, for whom a large reward had been offered. Both men were confined in jail in Omaha. Several dispatches passed between the chief police officers of Omaha and Austin, Texas, regarding the prisoners, establishing the identity of both beyond doubt. The first telegram from Texas stated that Melisky was under indictment for murder, and the second stated that no appropriation had been made for the officers' expenses, and consequently that they could not come for the prisoners. The third dispatch repeated this fact, and Melisky was finally released in the District Court on a writ of *habeas corpus*, even after having confessed to the murder of three individuals. Reed murdered three soldiers at Fort Griffin, Texas, two years ago, while they were attempting to arrest him. He is twenty-two years of age. He was also released after considerable telegraphic correspondence, ending with the following dispatch from Governor Roberts: "Sorry to say we have no money appropriated yet to pay expense, and no one to send after Reed. Have been trying to do so for a week." Great indignation was manifested against Governor Roberts for allowing these two murderers to be set free; and afterward, when he commuted to imprisonment the sentence of death which the courts had passed on two other notorious criminals, Ouard and Fields, the former convicted of murder in the first degree, and the latter of rape.

TURKEY, an empire in eastern Europe, western Asia, and northern Africa. The reigning sovereign is Sultan Abdul-Hamid II., born September 22, 1842. He succeeded his elder brother, Sultan Murad V., August 31, 1876. The heir presumptive to the throne is his brother, Mehemet Reshad Effendi, born November 3, 1844.

The area and population of the Turkish Empire, after the changes produced by the treaties of 1878, are as follows:

POSSESSIONS.	Square miles.	Population.
In Europe:		
Immediate possessions............	72,132	5,044,000
Province of Eastern Roumelia......	18,668	751,000
Bosnia and Herzegovina, administered by Austria...............	20,117	1,213,000
Tributary Principality of Bulgaria..	24,661	1,859,000
Total in Europe..............	130,573	8,867,000
In Asia:		
Immediate possessions............	729,484	17,500,000
Tributary Principality of Samos.....	212	87,080
Total in Asia.................	729,696	17,587,080
In Africa:		
Vilayet of Tripoli................	344,485	1,010,000
Dependencies. { Egypt...........	869,888	17,386,000
Tunis............	45,716	2,100,000
Total in Africa................	1,259,589	20,496,000
Grand total................	2,119,808	46,900,000

The receipts and expenditures in the budget for the financial year 1295 (March 13, 1879, to

March 12, 1880) were estimated as follows by the Financial Commission (in piasters—1 piaster = 4 cents):

EXPENDITURES.

1. Public debt......................	165,048,851
2. Dotations......................	205,757,243
3. Restitutions....................	575,000
4. Ministries.....................	716,188,777
5. Police and gendarmes..........	116,716,901
6. Customs and indirect taxes.......	45,000,000
7. Archives......................	6,000,000
8. Forests and mines..............	12,000,000
9. Posts and telegraphs..........	80,000,000
10. Public health..................	7,105,169
Total......................	1,804,886,441

RECEIPTS.

1. Customs......................	160,000,000
2. Egyptian tribute................	76,500,000
3. Other receipts..................	1,188,082,000
Total......................	1,424,582,000

These estimates apparently leave a surplus of 120,245,559 piasters. This result, however, was obtained only by crossing out, in addition to the interest of which payment was previously suspended to the amount of 1,338,840,622 piasters, the interest on the loan of 1855 to the amount of 11,998,460 piasters, payment of which has been guaranteed by France and England. But, notwithstanding this operation, the surplus is only an apparent one; for if the new loan which it has been intended to make should not be brought about, one fifth of the taxes and other receipts—i. e., 237,616,400 piasters—would have to be used for the retirement of the paper money. There will also be another loss, as the remaining four fifths of the taxes will be paid in a depreciated coin, making in all a loss of 10 per cent., or 95,046,560 piasters. Finally, the customs are paid in silver, which is also worth from 5 to 6 per cent. less than gold. The total deficit may therefore be estimated at 342,272,960 piasters. The entire liabilities at the close of 1877 were estimated at 6,130,000,000 piasters.

The army in 1879 comprised 150,000 men, of whom 18,000 were stationed in and around Constantinople, 10,000 at Tchatalja, 30,000 in Eastern Roumelia and the territory evacuated by the Russians, 25,000 at Salonica, 17,000 in Albania, 30,000 around Kossovo, and 30,000 in Asia.

Nothing definite is known of the total commerce of Turkey. The total annual value of the imports is estimated at 537,500,000 francs, of the exports at 496,250,000 francs.

There are 1,243 kilometres of railroad in operation in European Turkey, and 274 kilometres in Asia. There are 334 post-offices and 417 telegraph stations. The length of the telegraph lines is 27,497 kilometres, and of the wires 52,142 kilometres.

The depreciation of the *caimés* (paper money) had already in 1878 produced considerable trouble, and in December of that year the price of a gold lira of 100 piasters suddenly rose to 420 paper piasters, and a crisis seemed imminent. The bakers, who were forced to sell their bread at a certain fixed price—a measure which was adopted to satisfy the multitude—declared that they would rather close their shops. In this critical situation the Minister of Finance had some 10,000 lira worth of caimés bought on account of the Treasury on the Exchange, while the police kept a watch on the money-changers in the streets and bazaars, who by offering caimés for sale might disturb the operations on the Exchange. This measure had the desired effect, and in a single day the caimés went down from 420 piasters to 176. On January 27th Zuhdi Pasha, Minister of Finance, was dismissed, and his immediate predecessor, Kiani Pasha, was put in his place. Zuhdi had been appointed on the faith of his assurances that he would find ways and means for withdrawing the paper currency, or at least permanently raising its value; and as his efforts had been entirely unsuccessful he was dismissed. One more attempt was made to solve the paper-currency question without a foreign loan. For this purpose an imperial rescript was published about March 22d providing that henceforth four fifths of all sums due to the Government should be paid in coin, and one fifth in paper, calculated at one fourth of the nominal value. On the other hand, the Government would henceforth make all payments in gold and silver, except for debts previously contracted. The immediate effect of this measure was a new and very great depreciation of the paper money, the value of the gold lira rising from 480 to 600 piasters within a few days. In the latter part of April the Government ordered that henceforth caimés should be receivable for taxes at the rate of 400 paper piasters for one lira. On April 29th Kiani Pasha was dismissed from the Ministry of Finance, and his predecessor, Zuhdi Effendi, appointed in his place.

On July 28th an imperial *irade* was published suppressing the Grand Vizierate, and appointing Aarifi Pasha Prime Minister and Safvet Pasha Minister for Foreign Affairs.

The financial depression existing throughout the various branches of the Government led to an important step in October, when the Sultan ordered the disbandment of 90,000 regular troops, the Finance Minister threatening to resign unless the Sultan took this step.

A new Cabinet was formed on October 18th, composed as follows: Said Pasha, Grand Vizier; Sawas Pasha, Minister for Foreign Affairs; Mahmoud Nedim Pasha, Minister of the Interior; Aarifi Pasha, President of the Council of State; Safvet Pasha, Inspector-General of Administration; Jevdet Pasha, Minister of Justice; Cadri Pasha, Minister of Commerce; and Edif Effendi, Minister of Finance. Osman Pasha remained Minister of War.

In the beginning of November energetic measures were taken by the British Government to secure the introduction of reforms in Asia Minor, which had been promised by the Porte. Admiral Hornby, the commander of the British Mediterranean squadron, received orders to take his squadron into Turkish waters by November 8th. Great excitement prevailed at the Porte in consequence, and Sir Austen Layard, the British Ambassador, having been requested by the Porte to explain the object of the dispatch of Admiral Hornby's squadron, semi-officially replied that the squadron would remain for the present at Voulah, but eventually might proceed to some other Turkish port, as England would not tolerate the oppression of the Christians in Asiatic Turkey. Sir Austen Layard said in a dispatch referring to a movement for the formation of an autonomous state in Armenia: "I have warned the Porte over and over again that unless it speedily introduced the reforms to which it has pledged itself in the Asiatic dominions of the Sultan, and can assure the protection and the just and equal government of the populations, the question of an Armenian nationality, and even of other nationalities, may be raised, which will probably end in further diminishing the authority and territory of his Majesty." The Porte, receiving no official explanations regarding the British squadron, telegraphed to Musurus Pasha, the Turkish Ambassador in London, instructing him to ask Lord Salisbury for information. The interview between Musurus Pasha and Lord Salisbury was a very stormy one. The result was that the dispatch of the fleet to Voulah was countermanded, the British Government at the same time stipulating for the fulfillment of certain conditions by the Porte. In its attitude England was supported by Austria, and even Russia was generally thought to have advised the Turkish Government that it would be necessary to introduce the required reforms. In view of the pressure brought to bear upon him, the Sultan concluded to take the steps demanded of him. On November 17th Baker Pasha was appointed the Sultan's representative to superintend the introduction of reforms throughout Asia Minor; and on the 18th an official declaration was published on the proposed measures. The document declared that formal orders had now been given to prepare and execute the measures best fitted for assuring to all classes of the population the benefits of equal justice and for developing in general the prosperity of the country. The Council of Ministers had arranged the necessary reforms in two categories. The first included a project of statutes for the administrative reorganization of the European provinces —statutes which had to be sent into the vilayets and to be there submitted to a preliminary examination by the local commissions. This category likewise included immediate execution of the reforms necessary for the reorganization of the administrative system in Asia and other localities of the empire. The second category comprehended the reorganization of the Ministry and of all branches of the public administration, so as to insure the speedy execution of affairs, the proper distribution of work by the various administrations according to their respective competence, and the prompt execution of all reforms of a nature to develop the resources of the country. The result of the researches and labors of the Council of Ministers in each of these great categories, having been submitted to his Majesty, had received his supreme sanction. The reality and efficacy of these reforms would speedily be publicly proved by certain and brilliant facts.

In November the Sultan signed a decree providing that from January 13, 1880, 1,350,000 pounds Turkish will be annually appropriated to pay interest half-yearly on the home and foreign debt. This interest will be guaranteed by the revenues of Cyprus and Eastern Roumelia, as well as by the receipts from the duties on tobacco, spirits, stamps, fish, and silk, after a previous reduction from the receipts of 1,100,-000 pounds to meet the claims of the Ottoman Bank and other creditors secured by mortgages. In case of a deficit, the Porte will undertake to make it good. Besides the sum of 1,350,000 pounds referred to, the Turkish Government cedes irrevocably to the bondholders the Bulgarian tribute and the Servian and Montenegrin contributions toward the Turkish debt; also one third of the proceeds of any new taxes, especially in the event of increased duties, and the receipts from patents; the mode of payment to be arranged with the creditors. This engagement is to be valid for ten years, unless modified with the consent of all parties interested.

The negotiations for a definite treaty of peace between Russia and Turkey were begun in the first days of January. A sudden end was threatened by a clause proposed by Russia declaring that the two contracting parties guarantee to each other the exact fulfillment of the Treaty of Berlin. This clause was opposed by Turkey, and eventually dropped by Russia. The treaty was finally signed on February 8th. It fixes the indemnity to be paid by Turkey at 802,-500,000 francs, and provides for compensation to Russian subjects in Turkey for losses sustained during the war to an amount not exceeding 26,750,000 francs.

The evacuation of Turkish territory by the Russian troops began on March 5th. On that day General Todleben departed from Adrianople, and it was immediately occupied by Turkish troops.

The negotiations with Greece for a new boundary line continued during the year, without leading to a definite result. (See GREECE.)

On April 21st a convention was signed with Austria, relative to Bosnia, Herzegovina, and Novi-Bazar. (See AUSTRO-HUNGARIAN MONARCHY.)

The troubles in Crete were brought to a satisfactory close in June. Photiades Pasha, Governor-General of the island, explained to the Council of Ministers the modifications in the organic statute desired by the Assembly, and the Sultan, having found them reasonable, determined to sanction them.

U

UNITED STATES. The only change in the Cabinet of President Hayes during the year consisted in the retirement of the Secretary of War, George W. McCrary. The vacancy was filled by the appointment in December of Alexander Ramsey of Minnesota, who was unanimously confirmed by the Senate without a reference to a committee. Mr. Ramsey was born in Dauphin County, Pennsylvania, in 1815. At the age of thirteen years he became a clerk in the office of the county register. He advanced from one place to another until he became secretary of the Electoral College of the State, and carried its vote to Washington. Then he was for several years Clerk of the Lower House of the State Legislature, and was next sent to Congress for two terms, from 1848 to 1847. In 1849 President Taylor made him the first Governor of the Territory of Minnesota. From 1849 to 1853 he made several important treaties with the Sioux and Chippewa Indians. Next he was Mayor of St. Paul, then Governor of the State for two terms. In 1862 he was elected a Senator in Congress, and again in 1869. His term expired in 1875.

Some changes were made in foreign missions, the most important of which was the ap-

pointment in March of Andrew D. White, President of Cornell University, to the vacancy occasioned by the death of Bayard Taylor at Berlin.

The general course of the Administration was uneventful, and the assault upon it at the extra session of Congress resulted in successes for the Republicans at the fall elections. The success of resumption and the abundant crops increased the prosperity of the people, and diminished their anxiety on financial issues.

The result of the extra session of Congress consisted in the passage of the appropriation bills without any provision for the payment of marshals and deputy marshals. An application was therefore made to Attorney-General Devens by the marshal at Detroit, asking whether the latter should continue to serve warrants in criminal cases. The Attorney-General on July 3d replied as follows:

DEAR SIR: I advise you to perform the duties of your office, which you are in no way forbidden to do, to the extent of your power. The law prescribes those duties and affixes certain fees as compensation therefor. No provision for the payment of the fees of marshals and their deputies has been made, nor can I make any contract or promise that this provision shall hereafter be made; but your performance of your duties, so far as the law contemplates that they are to be compensated by fees, seems to me to constitute good ground of obligation against the United States. When the services of deputies are required, and the expenditures are to be recognize the difficulties you may have to encounter. In all this matter, however, you will have to rely upon your expectation of future legislation by Congress that shall be just to you. All other expenses, except fees of marshals and their deputies, have been provided for.

(Signed)   CHARLES DEVENS,
Attorney-General.

Under the instructions of this letter the marshals continued to serve as before the failure of the appropriation.

The conflict between the Democratic majority in Congress and the President on the Federal election laws, which necessitated the extra session, ended in the simple omission to vote appropriations for the pay of the United States marshals and their deputies. Having voted the appropriations for the army in a bill divested of the unusual and objectionable conditional legislative clause by which, with a simple constitutional majority, the Democratic members had sought to frustrate the veto power of the President, they embodied the same measure in a separate enactment, which was returned to them with the President's veto. The question in controversy was that of the right of supervision over Congressional elections given to the Federal Government by the statutes of Congress passed for the enforcement of the fifteenth amendment, particularly the act of 1870 entitled "An act to enforce the right of citizens of the United States to vote in the several States of the Union, and for other purposes." The repeal of these laws was made a prominent object of Congress. The vetoed bill, entitled "An act to prevent military interference with elections," provided that it should not be lawful to bring to or to employ at any place where a general or special election is being held in any State any part of the army or navy, unless such force should be necessary to repel the armed enemies of the United States or to enforce section 4, Article IV., of the Constitution, and the laws made in pursuance thereof, and repealing all provisions of law inconsistent with the purposes of the bill. Its object was to repeal the clauses in an act of 1865, and in sections 2,002 and 5,528 of the Revised Statutes, allowing the presence of troops or armed men at elections under the authority of Federal officers when necessary "to keep the peace at the polls." The veto of President Hayes was based principally on the grounds that the bill would prohibit the civil officers of the United States from employing adequate civil force to enable them to keep the peace and execute certain laws of Congress at national elections; and that as a measure to prevent military interference at the polls the bill was unnecessary, since the interference of the military or naval forces with elections was already forbidden by existing laws. The President also took the position that the bill would cripple the Executive in the enforcement of the

laws of the United States, and suspend on certain days and in certain places certain long-established laws, especially section 5,298 of the Revised Statutes. The majority of the Committee on the Judiciary, to which the President's veto was referred (of which Proctor Knott was chairman), held that these laws were no more affected by the proposed statute than by the above-mentioned act of 1865 making it a penal offense for officers of the United States to keep troops or armed men at the place where any general or special election is held, except to repel the armed enemies of the United States or to keep peace at the polls. The committee took the constitutional ground in their report that Congress has no power under the Constitution to confer any authority upon officers of the Federal Government to keep the peace at the polls, or to impose any such duty upon them, since the power to establish such police regulations as may be necessary for the preservation of domestic order and the prevention of violence and crime affecting life or property within their respective limits belongs exclusively to the several States, and the Federal Government can only intervene to protect the State in the execution of its own laws for that purpose upon application of the Legislature, or the Governor when the Legislature can not be convened. They protested against the distinction made by the President between State and national elections. The electoral privilege in all elections was declared to be derived from the governments of the individual States, and the mode of its exercise subject to their statutory provisions; all laws for the preservation of the public peace must also emanate exclusively from the States, and all police regulations and authority belong to the separate States by virtue of their general sovereignty.

The claims of the United States against the Southern States for the war levy of $20,000,000, to which all the States were called upon to contribute at the beginning of the war of secession, have been remitted on the ground, taken by W. O. Tuggle of Georgia, in an argument before the Treasury Department, that no taxes or assessments lie against a State in its sovereign capacity, but only against the individual tax-payers. The claims, which amounted to about half a million dollars each for the Southern States, with interest, were partly collected by special agents from the tax-payers, but since reconstruction the State authorities have been held liable.

The question of the legality of the issue of United States legal-tender notes in time of peace was brought before the courts in a test case by General B. F. Butler and Congressman S. B. Chittenden of Brooklyn. A test case based on an actual mercantile transaction was presented to Judge Blatchford of the United States Circuit Court. The case was entitled Augustus D. Julliard against Thomas S. Greenman. The plaintiff had sold defendant in New

York one hundred bales of cotton, and had received a small sum on account, the balance to be paid in cash on delivery. The defendant tendered the amount in two legal-tender notes of the series of 1878, which the defendant alleged had been redeemed at the Sub-Treasury and reissued and kept in circulation, in pursuance of an act of Congress, approved May 31, 1878, entitled "An act to forbid further retirement of United States legal-tender notes." He stated that he was willing and ready to pay plaintiff in said notes. Judge Blatchford dismissed the complaint in a *pro forma* decision, Messrs. Butler and Chittenden—the latter of whom had intrusted the management of the ease of the plaintiff to Senator Edmunds and William Allen Butler—intending to appeal the case to the United States Supreme Court.

The constitutionality of the Pacific Railroad act of May 7, 1878, known as the Thurman act, was confirmed in the decisions of the Supreme Court rendered in the cases of the Union Pacific Railroad Company, appellant, against the United States, and the Central Pacific Railroad *et al.*, appellants, against Albert Gallatin. The point to be decided was, in the opinion of the Court, "whether a statute which requires the company in the management of its affairs to set aside a portion of its income as a sinking fund, to meet its subsidy bonds and other mortgage debts when they mature, deprives the company of its property without due process of law, or in any other way improperly interferes with vested rights." In less than twenty years from the present time there will become due from the Union Pacific Company about $80,000,000, secured by first and subsidy mortgages, besides the capital stock, representing $6,000,000 more. With the exception of the land-grant, little if anything except the earnings of the company can be depended on to meet these obligations when they mature. These earnings the company, after paying the interest on its own bonds, has been dividing from time to time among its stockholders, without laying by anything to meet the enormous debt which is so soon to become due. Thus the stockholders of the present time are receiving in the shape of dividends that which those of the future may be compelled to lose. The United States occupy toward this corporation a twofold relation—that of sovereign and that of creditor. In their relation of sovereign it is their duty to see to it that the current stockholders do not appropriate to their own use that which in equity belongs to others. A legislative regulation which does no more than require them to submit to their just contribution toward the payment of a bonded debt can not in any sense be said to deprive them of their property without due process of law. The Court holds, therefore, that the legislation complained of may be sustained as a reasonable regulation of the affairs of the corporation, and promotive of the interests of the public and the corporators. It is also warranted under the authority, by way of amendment, to change or modify the rights, privileges, and immunities granted by the charter. Chief Justice Waite delivered the opinion of the Court. Associate Justices Bradley, Strong, and Field dissented. Justice Field, in the course of his dissenting opinion, refers to the invasion of the law upon the rights of the State of California, and says: "The Central Pacific Railroad Company is a State corporation, and in creating it the State reserved the same control over it which it possesses over other railroad and telegraph companies created by it. It undertakes to control and manage it in all particulars required for the public service, and can there be any doubt in the mind of any one who has the least respect for the reserved rights of the State that over its own creations the State has supreme authority? I confess that I am utterly at a loss to find where authority on the part of the United States to interfere with the State in this repect and take such control from it is to be found, except in the theories of those who regard the General Government as the all-controlling power of the nation, to which States, even in local matters, must bend."

In view of the excessive accumulation of cases on the docket of the Supreme Court, which is now fully two years in arrears, and would require that time to clear its docket were no new cases to be added, it is proposed to create an intermediate appellate court which would relieve the Supreme Court of all but the weightier cases. The increase in the number of cases docketed in the successive years since 1840 has been as follows: In 1840, 92 cases; in 1841, 106; 1842, 170; 1843, 128; 1844, 168; 1845, 177; 1846, 182; 1847, 216; 1848, 230; 1849, 295; 1850, 252; 1851, 237; 1852, 156; 1853, 195; 1854, 158; 1855, 161; 1856, 256; 1857, 279; 1858, 314; 1859, 368; 1860 and 1861, 310 each; 1862, 336; 1863, 381; 1864, 388; 1865, 389; 1866, 451; 1867, 438; 1868, 538; 1869, 536; 1870, 636; 1871, 757; 1872, 676; 1873, 756; 1874, 831; 1875, 974; 1876, 1,046; 1877, 1,093; 1878, 1,133.

During the fiscal year which closed with June, the receipts from the sales of postage-stamps, stamped envelopes, and postal cards amounted to $29,539,050, being an increase of $971,866 over the receipts of the year 1877–'78. According to recent changes made by Congress in the laws regulating the postal service, domestic mail matter is rated in four classes. First-class matter includes letters or matter containing any writing in the nature of personal correspondence, and matter which is sealed against inspection. It is subject to the rate of three cents postage on each half ounce and fraction thereof. Second-class matter embraces matter sent by purchasers and news-dealers. Third-class matter embraces books, printed and blank, transient newspapers and periodicals, circulars and other matter wholly in print, proof-sheets and corrected proof-sheets and manuscript copy accompanying the same, prices current with prices filled out in writing, papers of legal proceedings, deeds of all kinds, way-bills, bills of lading, invoices, insurance policies, handbills, posters, envelopes with printing thereon, engravings, lithographs, etc., printed blanks, printed cards, etc. There may be placed upon the cover or blank leaves of any book or of any printed matter of the third class a simple manuscript dedication or inscription that does not partake of the nature of a personal correspondence. All packages of third-class matter must be so wrapped with open sides or ends that their contents may be readily examined. The postage on third-class matter is one cent for each two ounces and fraction thereof. The limit of weight of packages is four pounds, except in cases of single volumes of books in excess of said weight. Fourth-class matter embraces blank cards, cardboard, flexible patterns, letter-envelopes and letter-paper without printing thereon, merchandise, models, ornamented paper, sample cards, ores, metals, minerals, seeds, cuttings, bulbs, roots, scions, drawings, plans, designs, original paintings in oil or water-colors, and other mailable matter not included in the first, second, and third classes. The postage rate is one cent for each ounce and fractional part thereof. Mailable matter of the first, third, and fourth classes can be registered. Unmailable matter embraces liquids, poisons, explosive and inflammable articles, putty, substances easily liquefiable, live or dead animals (not stuffed), insects and reptiles, fruits or vegetable matter, confectionery, and substances exhaling a bad odor; and every letter upon the envelope of which, or postal card upon which, indecent or obscene delineations, epithets, terms, or language may be written or printed; also matter which from its form or nature is calculated to injure the contents of the mail-bags or harm the persons of those employed in the postal service, unless securely wrapped to prevent such injury.

The Secretary of State addressed a circular to the United States ministers abroad instructing them to call the attention of the governments to which they were accredited to the laws of the United States against polygamy, and to whatever facts they might be informed of, through the consular agents or otherwise, concerning the emigration of Mormons from the respective country to the United States, and to prefer a request to the several governments to put in force what laws they have against the gaining of converts and the organization of emigration by the Mormon agents and missionaries. Some of the governments replied to the representations of the ministers that it was inconvenient for them to inquire into the religion of people leaving their shores, or their place of destination. Such letters were sent to the diplomatic agents in Great Britain, Germany, Norway, Sweden, and Denmark. It was intended to take active steps to prevent the landing of Mormon emigrants in United States ports. The circular letter expressed the determined purpose of the United States Government to enforce the law against polygamy contained in section 5,352 of the Revised Statutes, the constitutionality of which had been recently sustained by a decision of the Supreme Court, and to eradicate the institution of Mormonism.

The intercession of the State Department was required in the case of the brothers Berselier, natives of St. Louis, of German parentage, whose father had taken up his residence in Germany again while they were children. Before attaining their majority they returned to St. Louis, where they had since resided. When they attained the military age the German magistracy took steps to enforce penalties against the property of their father in Germany, after their failure to present themselves for enrollment. On a statement of the facts of the case by the Minister at Berlin, the German Government interfered to prevent the proceedings of the local magistrates against the property or heritage of the younger Berseliers.

The causes of the decay of the American ocean-carrying trade were discussed by Senator James G. Blaine in a letter to a number of business men of New York who had invited him to express his views on that subject in a public meeting. He attributes the decline to the combined causes of the civil war, the substitution of iron and steam for wood and sails, and the inflation of prices brought about by a paper currency. In 1857 the entire foreign trade of the United States, export and import, amounted to $723,000,000, and of this total $510,000,000 was carried in American bottoms and only $213,000,000 in the ships of other countries. When the country was precipitated into war in 1861 there followed a series of events the effect of which was utterly disastrous to the American carrying trade. Nearly 70,000 seamen were withdrawn from the merchant service and enlisted in the navy to maintain the blockade that stretched from Delaware Bay to the mouth of the Rio Grande. More than a million tons of American shipping were withdrawn from commerce to take part in the blockade and to supply the transportation needed for the maintenance of the armies that were called to the defense of the Union. Added to the direct loss, 800,000 tons of American shipping, to escape destruction at the hands of cruisers flying the Confederate ensign, but built in British yards and manned by British sailors, canceled their American registry and sailed under the flags of other nations, and when worn out their place was supplied by foreign-built ships. Just at this time the screw was generally substituted for the paddle, and the compound engine took the place of the simple one. Iron now became a general substitute for wood, and hulls were built that would last as long as the engines. A steamer of the old kind, capable of carrying 3,000 tons, might sail on a voyage so long that she would be compelled to carry 2,200 tons of coal, leaving room for only 800 tons of freight; whereas one of the new kind, of the same capacity, would make the same voyage and reverse the figures, requiring only 800 tons of coal and carrying 2,200 tons of freight.

Under the continued operation of these causes, the American carrying trade has steadily declined, until in 1878, with an aggregate foreign commerce, outgoing and incoming, of well-nigh $1,200,000,000, American ships carried but little over 300 millions and foreign ships carried nearly 900 millions; or, to be accurate and specific, American ships carried $313,050,-906, and foreign ships carried $876,991,129. In 1857 American ships carried five sevenths of all we exported and all we imported, and ships of all other countries carried but two sevenths. In 1878 American ships carried less than two sevenths, and ships of all other countries more than five sevenths. The cargoes transported in American ships, with an increase of 70 per cent. in the amount of the foreign commerce, was 200 millions less in value in 1878 than in 1857. The profits on the carrying trade of American commerce have amounted since 1869 to nearly 1,200 million dollars, three quarters of which vast sum have gone to enrich Great Britain. The remedy for the poverty of American shipping Mr. Blaine does not look for in the repeal of the navigation laws and the free registry of foreign-built steamers, as such a course would make the United States entirely dependent on England for iron steamships, which require as many men on land to build and repair them as they do on the water to navigate them, and would leave America unprovided with the skill and knowledge necessary for the construction of war-ships. He recommends the example given by the European governments in subsidizing the ocean mail service, Great Britain paying for the last year to the various steamship lines $3,700,000 besides ocean postage, France over $4,500,000, Italy $1,500,000, Austria $500,000, and Belgium $200,000. Wooden-ship building, he thinks, will always remain a valuable interest. "For wooden sailing ships no further aid is needed than these laws afford, if we will only seek in every way to lighten the burden of taxation on vessels. We can build wooden ships better than any other country, and we can build them as cheaply; but after they are launched and in trade they should not be worried and harried and burdened with every form of taxation, port-charge, and quarantine exaction at home, and maltreated and oppressed, as they too often are, by our consuls in foreign ports. They should have every facility for supply in our ports that England gives to her ships. Wooden ships will always be used so long as trees grow and winds blow, and they will form a large resource to our country. Indeed, it is almost the only resource we now have in foreign trade, and we should cherish the interest as one inwoven with our history

and prosperity as a people." For the encouragement and development of iron steamship construction, in which class of vessels the larger half of the world's commerce is now conducted, he proposes a general subsidy which he declares is less than the sums paid by the Government for transporting smaller mails equal distances on land. "I would prefer a general law that should ignore individuals and enforce a policy. For instance, enact that any man or company of men who will build in an American yard, with American material, by American mechanics, a steamship of 3,000 tons, and sail her from any port of the United States to any foreign port, he or they shall receive for a monthly line a mail allowance of $25 per mile per annum, for the sailing distance between the two ports; for a semi-monthly line, $45 per mile; for a weekly line, $75 per mile. Should the steamers exceed 3,000 tons, a small advance on these rates might be allowed; if less than 3,000, a corresponding reduction; keeping 3,000 tons as the average and the standard. Provide that the steamships shall be thoroughly inspected by a competent commission under the direction of the Secretary of the Treasury, the Secretary of the Navy, and the Postmaster-General, and thus insure the very first class of construction for safety and for speed both for passenger and cargo."

At the time of the organization of the Forty-sixth Congress the Executive Committee of the National Greenback-Labor party, presuming that the nearly equal strength of the Republican and Democratic parties in Congress would place the balance of power in their hands, determined to manifest their strength in the organization of the House of Representatives. A letter, signed by James B. Weaver for the committee, dated March 14th, was sent to the Democratic and Republican members of the House, giving the names of a number of members from whom they were willing to select the Speaker, and containing the following declarations:

The Representatives of the National Greenback-Labor party feel that grave responsibility rests upon them in the organization of the House of Representatives. The Republican party is fully committed to the financial policy which has brought disaster and ruin upon all the industrial interests of the country. It is opposed to an exclusive Government money, is in favor of the issue of national-bank currency, and is the champion of monopolies. The Democratic party in its last National Convention proposed no remedy for existing financial evils, but, on the contrary, rejected propositions looking to currency reform. Both the old parties in many of the States, by earnest advocacy of our principles, have been able to defeat our party candidates and elect their own. The time has now come when devotion to principle must be tested and a suffering people be informed who are in favor of relief for them. We hold the balance of power, not only in the present House of Representatives, but in the States of Maine, Connecticut, New York, New Jersey, Pennsylvania, Ohio, Indiana, Illinois, and Michigan. In other words, in scarcely one of the Northern States has either of the old parties a majority. We intend to follow out our principles, and place the responsibility of their temporary defeat upon those who shall organize the House against them. There must be no mistaking our single and resolute purpose by our action to bring relief to our suffering constituents by giving full employment and adequate reward to labor, impart new life and vigor to the prostrate business industries of the country, and give hope to the despairing debtor.

The extraordinary growth of the local public debts in the United States has been recently animadverted upon as imposing an unbearable burden upon the industry and business of the country, and as constituting one of the chief causes of the late protracted commercial depression. The municipal debts of 130 cities of the Union are found to have increased between 1866 and 1876 from an aggregate of $221,312,-009 to $644,378,663. The assessed value of the property of the same in 1876 was $6,175,-082,158, in 1866, $3,451,619,831; annual taxation of the same in 1876, $112,711,275, in 1866, $64,000,914; population of the same in 1876, 8,576,249, in 1866, 5,919,914; increase in debt, 200 per cent.; in taxation, 83 per cent.; in valuation, 75 per cent.; and in population, only 33 per cent. The municipal debt alone of 130 cities, representing a population of only 8,576,249, exceeded in 1876 by over $28,000,-000 the county, town, and city indebtedness of the entire country in 1870. In six years the indebtedness of these cities had exceeded by over $316,000,000 the bonded and floating indebtedness of all the towns and cities in the United States in 1870, which, according to the census, amounted to $515,810,000.

The municipal and county debts in eleven States of the Union in 1878 are computed and compared with the same in 1870 as follows:

STATES.	Total local debt, 1878.	Total local debt, 1870.
New York	$244,079,859	$127,399,090
Massachusetts	80,601,156	40,940,657
Illinois	51,811,691	37,300,982
Ohio	41,205,840	12,509,910
Wisconsin	9,981,158	8,651,475
Minnesota	5,272,280	2,436,795
Kansas	18,473,197	4,848,976
Missouri	85,343,155	29,043,865
Connecticut	17,151,827	9,812,006
Georgia	26,180,351	15,209,212
Rhode Island	12,289,564	8,025,142
Total	$546,289,528	$286,179,060

The following is the valuation of the property in the above-named States for the two periods:

STATES.	Total assessed valuation of property, 1878.	Total assessed valuation of property, 1870.
New York	$2,755,740,318	$1,967,001,188
Massachusetts	1,568,988,210	1,591,958,119
Illinois	1,201,123,110	482,899,515
Ohio	1,574,645,768	1,167,731,697
Wisconsin	428,596,290	338,209,683
Minnesota	220,980,629	84,185,232
Kansas	187,826,648	92,125,968
Missouri	614,726,225	506,129,969
Connecticut	344,406,977	425,438,237
Georgia	285,659,530	227,219,519
Rhode Island	256,052,818	244,278,854
Total	$9,338,096,515	$7,172,148,179

Incomplete returns from other States show the municipal debt of twenty cities in Pennsylvania to aggregate $87,329,180; nine cities in New Jersey, $36,502,722; two cities in Maryland, $34,000,000; five cities in Louisiana, $20,000,000; and five cities in Kentucky, $12,-000,000. According to this calculation, the total local debt of the country at the close of the year 1878 was $1,051,106,112, exclusive of State debts.

The estimates of the year's crops, made in December, compared with the returns of the foregoing year, show an increase of over 6 per cent. in quantities and 26 per cent. in values. There was an increase of 12 per cent. in the acreage sown to winter wheat; the Hessian fly injured some of the early-sown crops, and the later-sown suffered from drought; nevertheless, the general prospects were above the average. The tobacco-crop showed but a slight improvement in average quality over the crop of 1878, though a marked improvement was observed in some of the States. The oat-crop was 12 per cent. less than in 1878. The area sown to potatoes was 3 per cent. greater than the previous year; the yield per acre was 98 bushels, against 69 in 1878 and 94 in 1877. The acreage under winter rye was 3 per cent. less, but greater in New England, Texas, and the States north of the Ohio River; the condition of the crop was generally above the average. The hay-crop was 10 per cent. less, New England and the Gulf States only having increased their area; the crops of the Southern inland States and north of the Ohio were injured greatly by drought, and showed a falling off of 20 to 30 per cent.; the average price per ton was $9.24, against $7.21 in 1878. The total estimates are as follows:

CROPS.	HARVEST OF 1878.		HARVEST OF 1879.	
	Quantities.	Value.	Quantities.	Value.
Wheat	420,192,400 bush.	$325,846,424	448,755,000 bush.	$499,006,000
Corn	1,388,218,750 "	441,153,105	1,544,809,000 "	580,289,000
Oats	418,078,560 "	101,945,830	364,258,600 "	120,535,000
Rye	28,842,790 "	13,592,826	23,846,500 "	15,555,000
Barley	42,245,680 "	24,488,315	40,184,000 "	23,605,300
Buckwheat	12,246,820 "	6,451,120	13,145,550 "	7,560,488
Cotton	5,216,608 bales.	190,854,641	5,020,387 bales.	231,000,000
Tobacco	392,548,700 lbs.	22,187,478	384,089,659 lbs.	21,454,691
Hay	39,608,093 tons.	285,248,752	35,548,000 tons.	325,851,280
Potatoes	124,126,650 bush.	78,059,125	181,360,000 bush.	73,971,000
Total		$1,488,570,866		$1,904,480,659

V

VERMONT. The term of office of the Governor, Redfield R. Proctor, expires in 1880. The other State officers are as follows: Lieutenant-Governor, Eben P. Colton; State Treasurer, John A. Page; Secretary of State, George Nichols; Deputy Secretary of State, Charles W. Porter; Auditor of Accounts, E. H. Powell; Sergeant-at-Arms, T. C. Phinney; Inspector of Finance, William H. Dubois. All these officers were elected on the Republican ticket. The representatives of the State in the United States Senate are George F. Edmunds, whose term expires in 1881, and Justin S. Morrill, whose term expires in 1885. The Legislature is divided between the political parties in the following proportions: Senate—Republicans 29, Democrat 1; House—Republicans 175, Democrats 43, Nationals 9, Independents 5.

There was on hand in the State Treasury on the 1st of August the sum of $68,750.39, with liabilities of $206,136.95. Of the latter $135,-500 consisted of the Agricultural College fund, due in 1891. The ordinary expenses paid during the year were $451,841.33; and in addition a temporary loan of $125,000 was paid and bonds of the State to the amount of $36,-000. There remained outstanding, besides the Agricultural College fund, State bonds to the amount of $4,000, on which interest ceased December 1, 1876. Court expenses form $102,-446.73 of the sum expended, being less by about $10,000 than those of each of the two preceding years.

The decennial increase in the population of the State for eighty years has been as follows:

CENSUS.	Population.	Increase.	Percentage.
1790.........	85,416	......	.....
1800.........	154,465	69,049	80·84
1810.........	217,713	63,248	40·05
1820.........	235,764	18,051	8·29
1830.........	280,652	44,888	19·04
1840.........	291,948	11,.96	4·02
1850.........	314,120	22,172	07·59
1860.........	315,116	996	0·82
1870.........	331,000	15,884	....

In answer to questions asked him by farmers in the Dairymen's Association with regard to the effect on the freight-rates on their competition with Western produce, ex-Governor Smith stated that although Western butter comes at very low rates from Chicago eastward, it pays as heavy a freight before reaching that city as Vermont butter pays in going to Boston. He declared that local freights had not been advanced on the Eastern lines to make up for losses on through freights. Local freights on the roads passing through Vermont are nevertheless reported to have been raised in the course of several years, whatever the motive may have been. The number of different lines to which freight must be transferred in going to market is supposed to work unfavorably for Vermont producers; and the consolidation of the different main lines passing through the State under a single management is spoken of as a measure which would enable them to compete in fruits and other produce in the Boston market. Governor Smith has attempted to consolidate different roads by leasing, but without success.

Some statistics as to the relative cost and profits of farming in Vermont and· in the West have been collected by Professor Dale. In the Government report for 1877 the yield of Indian corn per acre, value per bushel, and value of the crop per acre were given for the below enumerated States as follows:

STATES.	Average No. of bushels per acre.	Price per bushel.	Value per acre.
Vermont..........	39	$0 77	$30 13
Michigan..........	31	0 39	12 09
Iowa..............	32·05	0 25	8 01
Kansas	36·05	0 21	7 87

The cost of cultivation in Vermont per acre is as follows: Plowing and harrowing, $2; manure, $10; planting, $1.50; cultivating and hoeing, $5; cutting and harvesting, $5; husking, $2.25; in all, $25.75, to which must be added $3 for interest on land, making $28.-75. To the value of the corn-crop $15 per acre is to be added for the value of the stalks for fodder, making the total value of the harvest $45.13 per acre. The profit per acre in Vermont is thus $16.38. In Kansas the cost of cultivation on stubble-land is as follows: Plowing, $1; planting, 20 cents; cultivating, $1.50; husking, $1.25; interest on the land, $1; total, $4.95. Deducting this from the value of the crop, $7.37, there remains a profit of $2.62. The value of the stalks in Kansas does not more than market the corn, if it does that. Land fenced and under cultivation is reckoned worth $12 an acre, a low estimate. What is true of Kansas is true of Iowa. In Michigan the cost of producing is nearly the same, except that the land is held at a much higher value, and manure is frequently used. The cost of cultivation is probably $9.25; value of crop, $12.09; profit, $2.84. If these estimates are correct, an acre of corn in Vermont will pay 20 per cent. profit, in Kansas 15, and in Michigan not quite 3 per cent. In the older of the Western States the average yield of corn has decreased 20 per cent. in the last fifteen years. In estimating the cost of manure in Vermont, the amount is taken at what it would cost to restore to the soil the phosphoric acid, potash, and nitrogen taken from it by the grain-crop alone, supposing the stalks to be fed or used upon the ground. Nitrogen is valued at

25, phosphoric acid 12, and potash 6 cents per pound. In the West the stalks are not taken from the ground, but are plowed under in the spring, much to the discomfort of the man holding the plow. Experiments show that only a small percentage of the nitrogen found in the crop is absorbed from the soil; and, as that is the highest-priced ingredient in all commercial manures, it would very much lessen the cost of raising corn if a considerable part of it could be omitted.

The following is the reported yield and value of the wheat-crop in the respective States for the same year:

STATES.	Bushels per acre.	Price per bushel.	Value per acre.
Vermont.............	17	$1 60	$27 40
Michigan............	17·5	1 22	21 35
Iowa................	14·5	87	11 75
Kansas..............	13·5	85	11 05

The cost of raising wheat in Michigan, where good land is held at $80 to $100 per acre, and where no manure is used and the crop is alternated with clover, is as follows: Plowing and harrowing, $2; seed, $2.44; harvesting, $2; threshing, $1.75; interest on land, $5. This makes a total cost of $13.15, leaving a profit of $8.20, which, however, is only to be counted once in two years, as the crops are only taken off the land every alternate year. In Iowa the cost of plowing, harrowing, harvesting, and threshing is $5.25, of seed $1.74, and the interest on the land $1, making the total cost of cultivation $8.99 and the profit $2.76. In Kansas nearly the same figures hold true. In Vermont the cost of growing and harvesting is estimated at $19.95, making the profit $7.45.

In an agricultural meeting at Montpelier, Professor Collier of Washington described some experiments he had made in raising sorghum. He tried five kinds—early amber, Chinese, white Liberian, Honduras, and pearl-millet. He made analyses of the cane at several stages of its growth. The pearl-millet yielded the best results, which were better than any published analysis of the sugar-beet, and equal to that of Louisiana sugar-cane. The juice analyzed between the 15th of August and the 1st of November showed 14·67 to 17 per cent. of crystallizable, and from 65 to 154 per cent. of non-crystallizable sugar. The Honduras variety yields the heaviest crop of cane, but will only grow in the Southern States. The early amber, which will grow wherever Indian corn can be raised, will produce with good cultivation two tons of sugar to the acre. Professor Collier has made many experiments also with corn-stalks. Stalks when ripe, after the corn has been harvested, yielded 10·90 per cent. of good sugar. From the results of forty-five experiments in making sugar from sorghum-cane, he believed that wherever Indian corn will grow the cane will yield an average of sugar per acre equal to or above that of the sugar-lands of Louisiana. The process of ex-

tracting the juice and making the sugar is not at all difficult. There should be a good strong mill to get out the juice, which as soon as got out should be heated nearly to the boiling-point, and slacked lime mixed to the consistence of thick whitewash should be added; after which it should be brought to boiling, and the scum taken off as is usual in maple-sugar making. After this it should be taken off and allowed to cool and settle, where the clear liquid could be drawn off and then boiled down in an ordinary pan or evaporator; and by this process nineteen twentieths of the sugar could be secured. He would not advise the farmers to make sugar, but sell the sirup to the refiners, who could do the work more cheaply and effectively. The refiners would now buy 100,-000 barrels of high-grade sirup at good prices. After the juice is pressed from the corn or sorghum stalks, he believes, analysis shows them to be worth ton for ton as much as before they were pressed, though of course the amount would be much less. The pressed stalks or "bagasse" were just in the condition for feeding or for putting up in "silos" used for preserving corn-fodder green. Professor Collier expressed the opinion that in ten years the United States, instead of importing 811,767 tons of sugar as in 1877, might export a million tons; the State of Illinois might yield an amount equal to the entire present import.

The State Grange, at a meeting in Montpelier, gave expression to the old grievance against the railways in the following memorial to be presented to Congress:

To the Honorable the Senate and House of Representatives of the United States of America, in Congress assembled:

We, the citizens of —— county, State of ——, do most earnestly and persistently insist that the Congress of the United States enact such laws as will alleviate the oppressions imposed upon us by the transportation monopolies that now control the interstate commerce of our country. Railroads, or railways, as they are severally styled, exact fluctuating and excessive rates of transportation both for freights and passengers, and in all such arbitrary exactions are a law unto themselves, being beyond the reach of State legislation, and heretofore unrestrained by Congressional enactments.

While general prosperity pervades the land, agriculture, the corner-stone of our national progress, is depressed. The surplus of our farms is wrenched from us to enrich these giant monopolies. A buoyant market instantly enhances the freight-rates of transportation, robbing the producer of well-earned profits, and levying upon the consumer unjust taxation. A depressed market maintains the previously enhanced freight-rates, and in neither case do these common carriers attempt to promote the public weal.

The patience of an industrious, law-abiding people is sorely tried, and with anxiety they look for relief to your honorable bodies, from whom alone relief can come. That it will come in the near future, we have every reason to hope. To hasten its coming, we respectfully urge upon your bodies the enactment of such laws as will prevent fluctuations in freights, and unjust discriminations in transportation charges.

And your petitioners would ever pray.

Merino-sheep breeding is again becoming profitable, and very high prices are paid for the finest animals. A new breeders' association, with E. S. Stowell for president, called the Vermont Atwood Merino-Sheep Breeders' Club, has been formed in opposition to the Vermont Merino-Sheep Breeders' Association, with which fault is found owing to the admission on its register of sheep outside of the State.

A contention arose in November between the students and the faculty of Middlebury College. A student in the second year received demerits for some trifling breach of the rules, and afterward an additional number of demerit marks given to the whole class alike in consequence of a disturbance. The total was sufficient to suspend the student. His classmates considered this an injustice, and refused to attend college unless he were received back. The faculty tried to assert their authority by suspending the whole class, whereat the other classes joined the rebellion and refused also to go on with their studies unless the faculty yielded. The affair finally ended in a compromise.

The Burdett-Estey organ suit, which has been for a long time before the courts, was ended by the award of about $150,000 to the plaintiff by ex-Governor Stewart, Master in Chancery. The suit was brought in the name of Riley Burdett, whose rights had been transferred to Silas M. Waite, against Jacob Estey, Julius J. Estey, and Levi K. Fuller, for infringement of a patent on an arrangement of extra reeds in organs, which by being tuned a little above or below the diapason produce the wavy effect called by the plaintiff the "harmonie céleste" and by the defendants the "vox jubilante." On this contrivance, used in the manufacture of the Estey organ at Brattleboro, it was claimed that the plaintiff possessed letters patent. The case was first brought in the United States Circuit Court of Vermont, December 30, 1871. It was heard successively by Judges Smalley (in 1874), Woodruff, and Johnson, all of whom died before rendering a decision. Early in 1878 it was argued before Judges Blatchford and Wheeler at New York by distinguished lawyers, including Senator Edmunds, William M. Evarts, and E. W. Stoughton. Judge Blatchford affirmed the validity of the patent in part, and an accounting to determine the profit made by the Esteys on the improved mechanism was ordered, the result of which inquiry was the report of the Master in Chancery awarding the sum named, subject to the approval of the Court.

The case of James R. Langdon et al. vs. the Vermont and Canada Railroad Company et al. came up before the Supreme Court. This was a bill in chancery brought to establish the priority of the liens upon the trust property, or, in other words, to have the Supreme Court determine which should be paid first out of the avails of the Central and Canada roads and their property, the accrued rent due the Vermont and Canada, or the receiver's indebted-

ness, so called, which, in the shape of floating debt, equipment bonds, Stanstead, Shefford, and Chambly bonds, guaranteed bonds, and income and extension bonds, amounts to about $6,000,000.

The Bennington village election was made the subject of a legal dispute. An action of quo warranto was carried before the Supreme Court. The State set forth in the complaint that, by reason of the mob capturing the village meeting in April, 1879, no legal election was held. The defense answers that the said noise and confusion was no greater than usual on such occasions, and that a legal election was held. The moderator whose election was contested was S. F. Harris.

A new State workhouse has been built at Rutland. It is a brick building with walls 20 inches thick, the walls between lines of cells being of the same thickness. A corridor runs between the outer tiers of cells and the wall of the building. The cells are 72 in number and disposed in three double tiers. The cells are 7 feet by 5, and are ventilated by tubes communicating with the outside air at the roof.

VIRGINIA. The question of the settlement of the State debt still engrosses the public mind. The citizens are divided into two parties on this issue, called the Debt-Payers and the Readjusters. In the early part of the year a funding bill passed the Legislature by a considerable majority and received the approval of the Governor. The proposed method of funding the debt was accepted by a syndicate, composed of a Council of Foreign Bondholders and the Funding Association of the United States, representing nearly all the holders of Virginia State securities. The bill, which is known as the McCulloch bill, aroused the liveliest dissatisfaction after it had become a law. A strong agitation was set on foot for its repeal by the Readjusters. This was made the main issue on which members were elected to the General Assembly in November. The plan for funding the debt embodied in the McCulloch bill is to issue registered and coupon bonds dated January 1, 1879, the principal payable in 1919, with interest at 3 per cent. for ten years, 4 per cent. for the next twenty years, and 5 per cent. for the last ten years, payable at Richmond, New York, or London on January and July 1st in each year until the principal is redeemed. The State has the option to redeem any or all of the bonds by paying the principal and accrued interest at any time after the expiration of ten years from January 1, 1879. The coupons will be receivable at maturity for all taxes, debts, dues, and demands of the State. The holders of registered bonds are entitled to receive a certificate for interest, and this certificate will be good for taxes or other demands due the State. The bonds, coupons, and certificates are non-taxable. The law was to be binding if, on or before May 1, 1879, the Council of Foreign Bondholders and the Funding Association filed their assent with the Governor; and they might present for funding at least $8,000,000 of the outstanding obligations of the State on or before January 1, 1860. Every six months thereafter they may fund $5,000,000 until the whole debt of $34,-000,000 is funded. In the year 1885, and annually thereafter until all the new bonds are issued, there will be collected a tax of 2 cents on the $100 of the assessed valuation of all property for a sinking fund.

The position of the Readjusters in their opposition to the funding scheme was defined in the following resolutions adopted at their convention held in Richmond, February 25th:

1. That Virginia fully recognizes her just liability for her fair proportion of the public debt contracted before her territory was divided.

2. That Virginia can never recognize liability for that portion of the debt which should attach to West Virginia.

3. That in any settlement with the State's creditors, the annual interest of the recognized indebtedness must be brought within her revenues under the present rate of taxation.

4. That the capacity of these revenues to meet such interest must be determined by deducting therefrom the necessary expenses of the government, the apportionment to schools, and reasonable appropriations for the support of the charitable institutions of the State.

5. That these limitations should be carefully ascertained and guarded so as in no event to allow the primary obligations of the government and people to be subordinated to any other demands whatever.

6. That a settlement within the limitation designated is the utmost stretch of the people's ability to pay, and should be satisfactory to the creditor as the furthest exaction he can fairly insist on.

7. That any settlement, to be final, must rest upon the sovereignty of the State, and find its best security in the good will, good faith, and honor of the people of Virginia.

8. That the sovereignty of the State can not be pledged nor delegated except for public service, and when so pledged or delegated is at any time revocable by the Legislature.

9. That any self-executing lien upon public revenues, such as is given by tax-receivable coupons, is against public policy and degrading to the State and people.

10. That no discrimination between creditors can be made or sanctioned by the State, in any readjustment that may be consummated.

11. That Virginia should deal directly and frankly with her creditors, and should never place either their claims or her revenues and obligations in the hands of intermediaries who are not completely under her control and direction.

12. That all exemptions from taxation not authorized by the Constitution are intolerable, and can not be afforded in the present condition of the State's finances.

13. That the rate of taxation is as high as can be borne, and, instead of entering into an undertaking that may necessitate an increase of taxation, a diminution in public burdens should be provided for.

14. That public free schools should be protected and sustained to the fullest extent.

15. That reform and economy should be energetically pressed in the administration of affairs of State and country.

16. That full recognition of these principles and declarations by the people of Virginia and her creditors is absolutely essential to any amicable readjustment, and no readjustment in which they or any of them shall have been neglected can be final, certain, and satisfactory.

The amount of the debt funded in accordance with the McCulloch bill was $8,491,961 at the time of the meeting of the Assembly on December 3d, the sum of $8,000,000 required to make the contract binding having been reached before the 1st of October. The total revenue of the State, based on the returns for 1878, is $2,762,519, derived from the following principal sources: Tax of 50 cents per $100 on total value of real estate (assessed as $244,563,717), $1,222,818; tax of 50 cents per $100 on personal property (assessed as $71,013,105), $355,065; tax of 1 per cent. on incomes exceeding $600 (aggregating $2,971,263), $29,712; capitation tax of $1 per head on male citizens over twenty-one years old (whites 175,970, colored 109,401), $285,371; licenses (regular merchants $332,-717, licenses and registered sales under Moffet liquor law, less expenses and rebates, $340,-766), $673,484; taxes derived from railroads, banks, insurance companies, etc., $120.000; revenue derived from other sources, $75,000. Deducting from the gross revenue the expenses of collection, errors in assessment, and defaults of insolvents and delinquents amounting to $237,951, a net revenue remains of $2,524,568, or, with the tax on coupons added, $2,586,078. The estimated expenses of government are $701,118, and the amount estimated to be due to the public free schools annually is $487,442, leaving an annual surplus applicable to the payment of interest on the debt, and to the extraordinary expenses of government (averaging for nine years $74,369 per annum), amounting to $1,397,517.

The state of the debt and interest charge stood on the 1st of October, 1879, as follows: Amount of bonds funded at 3 per cent. under the act of March 28, 1879 (dollar bonds $7,674,-449, sterling bonds $375,000—$8,049,449, less $105,134 bought in by the Commissioners of the Sinking Fund), $7,944,314, the annual interest on which amounts to $238,329; principal of sterling bonds outstanding, $1,472,805, the interest on which at 5 per cent. amounts to $73,-640; principal of dollar bonds issued under act of March 30, 1871, still outstanding, $20,250,184, the interest on which at 6 per cent. amounts to $1,215,011. The total principal under both acts amounted to $29,667,304, and the interest due annually thereupon to $1,526,980, which, deducted from the net revenue, stated above, applicable to the payment of interest, leaves a deficit of $129,463. Adding the interest at 5 and 6 per cent. on the debt held by the literary fund (principal $1,428,245), amounting to $84,349 per annum, the deficit increased to $213,813; if the interest on the literary fund is reduced to 3 per cent., the deficit is reduced to $172,310. Were the entire debt funded under the act of March 28, 1879, including one half of the interest in arrears on the bonded debt and full interest on the college and literary funds, the total principal would amount to $31,227,083; the interest on the refunded debt at 8 per cent. would amount to $936,812 per annum, the full interest payable under existing laws to colleges to $54,572, and the full interest due to the literary fund, as stated above, to $84,349, making a total interest charge of $1,075,735; this sum, deducted from the estimated net revenue stated above, minus the tax on consolidated bonds which would be lost on refunding (which amounts to $61,509 per annum, leaving a future net revenue of $1,336,007 applicable to interest payments), would leave an annual surplus revenue of $260,272. If the entire debt, including the consolidated bonds and the debt held by the literary fund and the colleges, were refunded, with half of the arrears of interest added, the bonded debt of the State would amount altogether to $32,881,695, on which the interest at 3 per cent. would amount annually to $986,450; this, deducted from the revenue available for interest, would leave an annual surplus in the Treasury at the present rates of taxation of $350,924.

Governor Frederick W. M. Holliday in his message expressed his views on the subject of funding the debt as follows:

I am not of those who believe that a heavier rate can not be borne to accomplish so grand an object as the fulfillment of the State's obligation and the preservation of her credit—objects which, in a republic like ours, far transcend every private consideration; indeed, which elevate private considerations, and make them partake of the strength and virtue of the Commonwealth itself. The investment of more taxes in such a cause would yield a far greater revenue than that invested in any war in which our ancestors ever engaged for the vindication of the right, both in the material development of our resources, and the hardy, robust, and honest growth of our people's character. That increase, however, need not be resorted to now. With the present laws properly enforced, the revenues will meet the requirements of the act, and leave a handsome surplus in the Treasury. . . . Whatever may be the views of some, I feel that should the present funding bill by any means be stopped in its execution, it would be a great misfortune. It has been regarded by the world as a fair and honorable settlement between the Commonwealth and her creditors; and though the funding under it has progressed with remarkable rapidity, considering the impediments that have been thrown in its way, we have every reason to believe that had no opposition been manifested, and its repeal not been mooted, the bonds by this time would have been well-nigh all brought in to be funded under its provisions.

The popular vote in the November election, which depended on the State issue of the settlement of the debt, was divided between the Debt-Payers and Readjusters into 69,763 of the former (62,074 Conservatives and 7,689 Republicans), and 77,070 of the latter (58,644 Conservatives and 18,426 Republicans). The total vote cast for members of the House of Delegates was 147,115. The composition of the new House of Delegates was as follows: Conservative Debt-Payers, 42; Conservative Readjusters, 40; Republicans (white), 6; Republicans (colored), 11; tie vote in Portsmouth, 1; total number of delegates, 100.

A convention of colored citizens, consisting in great part of inhabitants of Richmond and the vicinity, met in that city May 19th, and adopted the following resolution:

Resolved, That we recommend to our race throughout the State to organize themselves into emigration societies for the purpose of leaving the State; provided, our condition is not bettered by the authorities of the State.

A Citizens' Association was organized in Richmond, July 25th, for the object of obtaining modifications in the State and municipal Sunday laws which require the closing of all places where drinks are sold between midnight on Saturday and sunrise on Monday morning.

The James River and Kanawha Canal has been repaired by the labor of the convicts in the penitentiary, who have been employed also on the Clifton Forge and other railroads. There were 52 convicts less in the penitentiary at the close of the year, and a daily average of 32 less, than in the preceding year. The cost of their keeping per man was $62.47 for the year, or an average of 17 cents per diem. Of those who have been hired out under contract to railroad companies and other corporations, 42 have escaped. The mortality in the camps of convicts thus employed is twice as great as in the prison. The following are the statistics of the penitentiary: Maximum number of prisoners during the year, 1,070; minimum, 1,013; average, 1,041; average age of convicts now in prison, 26 years, 3 months, and 1 day; average sentence of convicts now in prison, 8 years, 2 months, and 10 days; per cent. of decrease from September 30, 1878, to September 30, 1879, 5¼ per cent. Number of prisoners for first conviction, 921; for second conviction, 91; for third conviction, 3; total, September 30, 1879, 1,015.

The following statement shows that the number of schools and attendance of pupils declined in 1878 to nearly one half of what they were in the preceding years: Number of schools (counting each grade in graded schools as a separate school) in 1879, 2,491; in 1878, 4,545; in 1877, 4,672. Pupils enrolled in 1879, 108,074; in 1878, 202,244; in 1877, 204,974. Average daily attendance in 1879, 65,771; in 1878, 116,464; in 1877, 117,843. The average number of months taught in the 2,491 schools (1,816 white and 675 colored) which were opened in 1879 was 5·36. The total school population was 483,701—280,849 white, 202,842 colored. Of the white schools 95 were graded, of the colored 33; together, 128. Of the 108,074 enrolled pupils, 72,306 were white, 35,768 colored; of the 65,771 in average daily attendance, 44,540 white, 21,231 colored. The falling off in schools and attendance was owing to the fact that in some districts the debts had been allowed to accumulate until the local boards determined to open no schools, but devote the income to paying off the debts; in others the supervisors had diminished the school levies. Under the bill passed by the General Assembly called the Henkel bill, the sum of $459,515 applicable to the support of public schools is obtained.

A writ of *habeas corpus* being applied for in

the United States Circuit Court in the case of a negro, Edward Kenney, and his wife, Mary Hall, a white woman—convicted under the law of March 14, 1878, prohibiting the intermarriage of races, and confined in the penitentiary—it was refused by Justice Hughes on the ground that the United States courts have no jurisdiction over questions of marriage, on which each State has sovereign and complete authority to make laws for its own citizens. The laws of Virginia make miscegenation a penal offense, and prohibit citizens from going outside the State for the purpose of contracting an unlawful marriage. The defendant was married to the white woman in the District of Columbia, and they returned and cohabited in Virginia.

The United States grand jury, under the instructions of Judge Rives, brought a bill of indictment against nine county court judges for violating the civil rights act in habitually refraining from placing colored citizens on the jury lists.

In answer to a petition from colored citizens requesting that colored men be selected for jurymen in cases where negroes were accused of crime, Judge Christian of the Hustings Court declared that he was enjoined by the law to select only such as he considered "well qualified to serve as jurors," and that to place colored men on juries on the ground of their race would be a violation of the fourteenth amendment.

W

WEST VIRGINIA. The composition of the Legislature of 1878-'79 according to parties was as follows: Senate—Democrats 21, Republicans 2, National 1; House—Democrats 40, Republicans 8, National 17. The Governor is H. M. Matthews, whose four years' term expires March 4, 1881. The names of the other State officers are as follows: Secretary of State, Sobieski Brady; Superintendent of Public Schools, W. K. Pendleton; Auditor, Joseph S. Miller; Treasurer, Thomas West; Attorney-General, Robert White. The election for the Legislature and all the State officers occurs October 12, 1880.

The Legislature assembled January 8th. George H. Moffett was elected President of the House, and D. D. Johnson President of the Senate. The session was marked by the passage of a large number of acts, some of them very important in their scope and bearings.

An act was passed making it a misdemeanor for a lawyer to receive moneys in trust for a client and fail to account for them within six months without good and sufficient reason. An accused lawyer may testify in his own behalf; on conviction he is to pay a fine and to be disbarred. Another act permits the Supreme Court to reopen in the regular term cases decided in the special term for the correction of clerical errors.

A law for the protection of farmers against spurious and adulterated fertilizers enables them to have samples analyzed free of charge by the Professor of Chemistry in the State University at Morgantown.

An act prohibits members of the county court, overseers of the poor, district-school officers, or any member of any other county or district boards, or any county or district officer, from being pecuniarily interested in any contract or service, in the award or letting of which he, as such member or officer, has any control.

An act imposes a penalty upon persons who transact the business of insurance without authority.

An act of 1875, providing for the inspection of tobacco, was repealed.

An act was passed prescribing regulations for the transportation of petroleum or other oils and liquids by railroad companies or transportation companies, or through pipes of iron or other material constructed for that purpose.

A usury bill, being a reënactment of the old Virginia interest law, fixing the rate at 6 per cent. per annum, and making a lender at usurious interest forfeit the entire interest, but not the principal of the debt, after much discussion, was defeated.

A bill was passed for the regulation of coal-mines and protection of persons employed in them.

A bill provided for the use of convict-labor on works of public improvement, including railroads.

A laborer's lien act was passed, giving mechanics and laborers a lien upon property for work performed in its construction or improvement. Every workman or laborer doing work for an incorporated company is given a prior lien for the amount of his wages on all the personal and real property of the company.

A resolution was adopted instructing the members of Congress to advocate the passage of the Texas Pacific Railroad subsidy bill. Earnest efforts were subsequently made to have it reconsidered, as several members who had voted in the affirmative desired to change their votes.

The extension of the normal schools by the preceding Legislature led to a reaction in the public mind, which manifested inself in a large reduction in the appropriations for these institutions. They were considered to have proved relatively of more advantage to the localities in which they were established than to the general common-school system of the State. By an amendment in the school laws, the selection of teachers is conferred upon the district boards of education, instead of being intrusted to the trustees of the sub-districts as formerly. The salary of the county superintendent is reduced to a mere nominal sum. The classification of teachers is altered, making three instead of five grades. Graduates of the normal schools may be required to undergo an examination. A school-book bill provides that the retail prices of school-books, not to exceed the present wholesale rates, shall be printed on the covers of the books and posted on the walls of the school-rooms, and requires the publishers to deal with the school authorities in the sale of their books.

A proposal for a constitutional amendment reforming the judiciary system was adopted. The amendment is to be submitted to the vote of the people in 1880. Its object is to transfer the functions of the county courts to the circuit courts. The number of the latter is to be increased. The jurisdiction of the county court, which will consist of three commissioners, is to be confined to police and fiscal matters. The amendment proposes also to increase the judicial functions of justices, revoking the right of a defendant in a case involving more than twenty dollars to remove it on his simple motion to the county court. The ability of justices to hear jury cases is extended. Their jurisdiction is extended to cases involving not above three hundred dollars. The amendment provides for the establishment of courts of limited jurisdiction in any incorporated town. The number of the circuits is to be increased from nine, each with one judge, to thirteen, with fourteen judges.

The committees of inquiry into the freight-rates of the Baltimore and Ohio Railroad made their reports to the Senate and House on January 15th. The reports accused the company of making unjust and unauthorized discriminations in its freight schedule in favor of through traffic and against way traffic. In view of the fact that the road had made material reductions in its charges for transportation within the State since the appointment of the committees of investigation, no action was taken on the reports by the Legislature. Johnson N. Camden was summoned before the bar of the Senate to answer charges of contempt in refusing to declare to the Committee on Railroad Freights the amount of the rebates allowed by the Baltimore and Ohio Railroad Company to the Camden Consolidated Oil Company in the transportation of oil. Projects of laws regulating the freight-rates on the Baltimore and Ohio Railroad were introduced by the committee and others, and discussed with much heat. By a joint resolution a new joint committee of five was appointed to confer with the managers of the road and ascertain what reductions of freight-charges should be carried out, and whether the company conformed to the provisions of its charter and the laws, and to report any contravention of the same to the At-

torney-General, who should institute proceedings against the railroad to compel the forfeiture of its charter, by means of a writ of *quo warranto* or otherwise.

The following account of the present condition of the State was communicated by Governor Matthews to a newspaper reporter:

The present population of the State is estimated at 500,000, a gain of about 60,000 since 1870, chiefly a natural increase, there having been very little immigration. The salt-works interest in the Kanawha Valley, which has been much depressed, is now picking up rapidly. The oil industry is not making much headway, and the business has lost its speculative character. The glass-works at Wheeling are prosperous, and new discoveries of valuable iron deposits are reported on New River, on the line between Virginia and West Virginia. The coal-fields are being worked to a much greater extent than formerly since the opening of the Chesapeake and Ohio Railroad, and West Virginia has more coal, and a much greater variety, too, in proportion to territorial extent, than any State in the Union. The State government is economically administered. The cost of feeding penitentiary convicts is only 6¼ cents per day, and the entire cost of food, clothing, guards, and salaries of officials is only 25 cents per day for each convict; while the cost of maintaining each inmate of the Insane Asylum, including all expenses, is only $2.33 per week. Governor Matthews says there is no State debt, and the people are willing to settle with Virginia by allowing West Virginia to be charged with all public improvements within her borders, and with her proportion of the current expenses of the State government since 1824, and to be credited with all taxes paid into the State Treasury by the counties of which she is composed since that date. Upon that basis, Governor Matthews says, it has been estimated that Virginia would be indebted to the new State about $500,000. The public schools are in good condition and improving, and the rate of State taxation is 20 cents on the $100 for State purposes, and 10 cents for the school fund. There are only 17,000 colored people in the State, not enough to form an important element of its population.

The railroad facilities are being so extended as to promise a speedy development of the natural resources of the State, which, though little exploited, are counted not inferior to those of scarcely any State in the Union. The Weston and Clarksburg Railroad has been completed. The Bellaire and Southwestern has also completed its track. The Pittsburgh Southern Railroad is being carried through the central part of the State. A company has been formed for the construction of a narrow-gauge road between Wheeling and Parkersburg, traversing one of the finest iron-ore fields on the continent.

A band of law-defying characters in Wetzel County, called the Red Men, who had terrorized the community for years by their arbitrary and violent deeds, taking vengeance upon all who refused to submit to their rule, and not shrinking from the most desperate and bloody acts, were proceeded against by the authorities. Seven of them, named John Ullom, George Ullom, Amos Hemeleck, John Steward, John Hostaller, Eloy Butcher, and John Lough, were arrested in the beginning of June. The organization originated in an act of Lynch justice perpetrated in 1870 on John Jennings, who had collected a band of desperate characters similar to that which the Red Men subsequently became. The lynchers who shot Jennings had stained their faces with red earth; hence the name. The prisoners were arrested on the charges of riot and house-breaking. Threats were uttered against any justice of the peace who would issue warrants for the arrest of the Red Men. About fifty of the band were still at large. They were all of the class of farmers and fairly educated. The organization extended into Marion County. A similar company of conspirators had formed also in Monongalia. The ringleaders of this gang were also arrested and brought to trial on the charge of conspiring against the liberty, property, and lives of citizens. The acts of these lawless bands were all prompted by some motive of supposed justice; thus they had lynched several persons on an accusation of adultery, and had driven two men off a farm on account of an alleged faulty title; they had also frightened a justice of the peace, one of whose decisions displeased them, out of the State.

An interesting decision was rendered by the Court of Appeals on the construction of the statutes relating to the separate estate of married women. The case was William Radford and Henry Light, appellants, against Martha A. and James Carwile, appellees. The appellant Radford had purchased of one Johnson a piece of land and sold it to the appellees, the deed being made out directly to Martha A. Carwile by Johnson to save the expense of a double transfer, and the appellees executing their joint and several bond to Radford for an unpaid balance. The lower Court held that the bond was no charge upon the separate estate, created by the deed, of the appellee Martha. The Court of Appeals sustained the decision, ruling that the separate personal estate of a married woman, including rents and produce of real estate, is liable for debts incurred during coverture, but that the common-law doctrine regarding the realty of married women, which exempts it from all liabilities incurred by debts or contracts made during coverture, is still in force.

The case of the United States against James M. Mason, in chancery, involving the privilege of operating a ferry across the Shenandoah at Harper's Ferry, was decided by J. J. Jackson of the United States District Court. The defendant claimed that the United States could not acquire a ferry because that species of property was not conducive to any of the objects for which the General Government was created. The Court ruled on this point as follows:

This proposition, if sound, virtually denies to the United States the power to furnish itself with means of transportation of any character whatever. They could not purchase and hold steamboats, railroads, wagons, or any other means of transportation. . . . It is a right incident to and inherent in all governments to purchase and hold what property they think is necessary for the due exercise of all powers belonging to them. No restriction is imposed upon the Government of the United States by the Constitution as to the character or kind of property it may purchase and hold.

The decision of the Court was delivered in the following terms:

The right of the United States in the ferry franchise purchased from Fairfax became forfeited by operation of law, and therefore she had no such right that she could sell or transfer; it also appears that the State had no power to establish a ferry for the defendant across the river Shenandoah, to and from the lands of the United States, and therefore, so far as the defendant Mason or his agents, or those claiming under him, attempt to operate a ferry from the 684-acre tract of land on the east side of said river, purchased by the United States from Fairfax, to the lands of the United States on the west side of said river, at Harper's Ferry, and to which the vendee of Neer & Co. hold an equitable title by purchase from the United States, the said Mason, his agents, or those claiming under him, are perpetually enjoined and inhibited from so doing until the assent of the United States is first obtained. But the defendant Mason is not inhibited or restrained from operating a ferry over the Shenandoah River, to and from any lands he may own, which ferry right he claims title to under the laws of this State.

In the case of Thomas Strander, plaintiff in error, against the State, the plaintiff, who had been convicted of murder in the Ohio County Circuit Court in 1874, and whose conviction had been confirmed by the Court of Appeals, was brought before the United States Circuit Court. The plaintiff appealed the case to the United States Court on the ground of the unconstitutionality of the jury law of West Virginia, under which the jury was impaneled which convicted him, as no colored person is eligible as a grand or petit juror in the State, in accordance with the following provision: "All *white* male persons who are twenty-one years of age and not over sixty, and who are citizens of this State, shall be liable to serve as jurors."

WHITTINGHAM, WILLIAM ROLLINSON, Bishop of the Protestant Episcopal Diocese of Maryland, born in New York, December 2, 1805, died at Orange, New Jersey, October 17th. At the early age of twenty he graduated from the General Theological Seminary in New York. In 1827 he was ordained a priest, and four years thereafter took charge of his first important parish, St. Luke's in New York. In 1835, after a trip to Europe taken for his health, he was chosen Professor of Ecclesiastical History in the General Theological Seminary. He was during this period quite active as a writer and editor of various publications. He edited the "Family Visitor" and "Children's Magazine," monthlies, "The Churchman," a weekly Church paper, "The Parish Library," Palmer's "Treatise on the Church," a translation of the Commentary of Vincent of Lérins, and Ratramn on the Lord's Supper. When a student he assisted Dr. Turner in the translation of "Jahn's Introduction." He was associated with Drs. Schroeder, Turner, and Eastburn in the authorship of "Essays and Dissertations in Biblical Literature." In 1840, after a sharp contest among the friends of several candidates, he was elected Bishop of Maryland, and consecrated at St. Paul's Church, in Baltimore, September 17th. Through the efforts of Bishop Whittingham several educational and charitable institutions were founded in the diocese, such as St. James College, Hagerstown; the Church Home and Infirmary, Baltimore; an order of deaconesses; and the Sisterhood of St. John, in Washington. In 1869 the Diocese of Easton was divided from that of Maryland. In 1870 the Rev. Dr. William Pinkney was appointed to relieve Bishop Whittingham of a part of his labors. Dr. Whittingham was a representative of the American Church at the Lambeth Conference in Great Britain, and also in 1872 at the meeting of Old Catholics at Bonn, Germany. He engaged in several controversies with the clergy on points of church government; among which were his presentation in 1876 for not bringing to trial the rector of Mount Calvary for reading prayers for the dead, and the earlier contest with the Rev. Dr. Trapnell of St. Andrews concerning the prior right of the Bishop to celebrate communion at confirmations. He was a pronounced High Churchman, but came to modify his ritualistic views somewhat in his later life. He took an interest in the Old Catholic movement, and gave a glowing account of its objects in his report of the Bonn Conference. During the war he adhered strongly to the cause of the Union, and rebuked his clergy for omitting the prayer for the President. Bishop Whittingham was an invalid for many years before his death. His last official act was performed November 7, 1878. At the time of his consecration he was the youngest bishop in the United States, and at the time of his death he was the senior bishop but one, having been thirty-nine years in the episcopal office.

WISCONSIN. The Legislature met at Madison January 8th, and adjourned March 5th. Coming together directly after the new Revised Statutes went into effect, there was a disposition to avoid changes in the general body of the statute law. Besides the election of a United States Senator and the levying of the State tax, there was little important business to attend to. Lieutenant-Governor James M. Bingham presided over the Senate the greater part of the time. Assemblyman Kelley was the Speaker of the House. About 400 bills were introduced in the Assembly, and about 200 in the Senate; and 256 of the whole number became laws.

A law was enacted providing that tramps should be either sentenced to six months' hard labor in the county jail where arrested, or be put in close confinement on bread and water for thirty days, in the discretion of the judge; or, in case of refusal to work, to be sent to State Prison for a term not exceeding two years. The Supreme Court declared unconstitutional those portions of the assessment law which regulated the reassessment of property

after litigation. This decision was confirmatory of one rendered by the lower Court. On February 4th Chief Justice Ryan delivered the decision to the Judiciary Committee of the Legislature, who immediately framed a new assessment law in conformity with the doctrine laid down by the Court, but not otherwise changing the general features of the law, which was passed without difficulty. Provision was made for regulating and to a certain degree restricting the adulteration of food, drugs, etc. A Board of Emigration was established, to consist of five persons, of whom the Governor and Secretary of State are *ex officio* members. Most of the acts are local in their character, and a large majority of these relate to the logging interests. Seymour and Ahuapee were incorporated as cities, and two new counties were erected, viz., Price and Marinette. The charters of some fifteen or twenty cities were amended. In the city charters of Fond du Lac, Oconomowoc, and Seymour, a departure from all previous legislation of doubtful constitutionality was injected, viz., the limitation of the right to hold office to freeholders. An important local measure was passed, to the effect that at municipal elections in Milwaukee, electors shall be registered as at general elections. Prominent Milwaukee lawyers regard this law as likewise unconstitutional.

The appropriations made amounted in all to $299,177, a saving of about $40,000 over those of 1878. The chief items were: State Hospital for the Insane, $80,747, including $22,100 for improvements; Northern Hospital for the Insane, $71,457; Industrial School for Boys, $52,000; Deaf and Dumb Institution, $30,000; Institution for the Education of the Blind, $18,500. The receipts into the State Treasury during the fiscal year ending September 30, 1879, from all sources, were $1,812,682.80; the balance on hand September 30, 1878, $403,288.29; making the total receipts $2,215,971.09. The disbursements during the same period for all purposes were $1,627,146.49; leaving a balance, September 30, 1879, of $588,824.60. The receipts into the general fund during the fiscal year were $1,249,338.02; balance from previous year, $79,055.98; total, $1,328,394. Of this sum there was derived from direct State tax, $682,388.99; railroad companies, license-taxes, $395,886.46; insurance companies, fees and license-taxes, $45,772.76; miscellaneous sources, $125,289.81. The disbursements from this fund were as follows:

Interest on the public debt...................	$157,560 00
School fund..................................	7,088 86
High schools.................................	25,000 00
State University.............................	41,810 30
Salaries and other permanent appropriations...	100,028 62
Legislative expenses	84,301 61
Benevolent and penal institutions............	378,815 72
Miscellaneous purposes......................	252,012 90
Total.........................	$1,055,112 51

The disbursements from this fund, which represent the actual expenses of the State, have been for several years past as follows: 1872, $1,076,442.96; 1873, $1,191,966.01; 1874, $1,038,703.34; 1875, $1,260,168.39; 1876, $1,-187,788.65; 1877, $1,204,900.40; 1878, $1,047,-796.23; 1879, $1,055,112.51.

The aggregate indebtedness of the State remained as at the close of the last fiscal year, and consists of

War bonds outstanding.......................	$11,000
Certificates of Indebtedness to trust funds........	2,241,000
Currency certificates.........................	57
Total...	$2,252,057

The indebtedness of the counties, cities, towns, villages, and school districts in the State amounts to $10,115,898, according to the returns made to the Secretary of State. More than usual efforts were made to secure accuracy in these returns. The total public indebtedness of the people of Wisconsin is therefore $12,367,955, or at the rate of about $8.50 per capita of estimated population, and 3¼ per cent. of the assessed valuation.

The value of all property in the State subject to taxation, as returned by the assessors for the past two years, is as follows:

PROPERTY.	1878.	1879.
Personal property.......	$96,077,208 00	$88,127,940 00
City and village lots.....	103,899,469 75	85,545,746 50
Other real estate........	255,863,904 57	232,629,498 50
Totals..............	$455,840,582 32	$406,303,185 00

This shows an apparent decrease in valuation of $49,037,397.32, but is an indication of the zeal with which communities seek to avoid the payment of their just proportion of the public expenditures.

The total taxes levied in the State for the year 1878 amounted to $7,969,859, which is $61,769 less than for the previous year, and was at the rate of $1.93 on each $100 of the State assessment for that year. The purposes for which these taxes were levied, and the respective amounts and rates, are as follows:

KIND OF TAX.	Amount.	Rate, mills.
State tax.....................	$681,589	1·65
County tax...................	1,770,481	4·30
Town tax.....................	2,428,997	5·87
School tax	1,998,742	4·84
Road tax.....................	1,090,050	2·64

These figures represent only the direct taxes levied upon property. Quite large amounts were collected by the State, and cities, villages, and towns, in addition, by way of licenses and otherwise. The total State tax, direct and indirect, is represented by the payments into the general fund, and these amounted to $1,-120,837.81 in the fiscal year ending September 30, 1878 and to $1,249,338.02 in the fiscal year ending September 30, 1879. The State tax for 1879 was $455,871.89, which is $226,517.10 less than was apportioned for collection in 1878, and more than 23 per cent. less than the least tax in many preceding years.

The Secretary of State estimated that the

expenditures for the calendar year 1880 would be $968,305.54, and the receipts under existing laws as follows: Taxes, $207,855.54; railway companies, $395,000; insurance companies, $45,000; miscellaneous sources, $29,600; total, $677,455.54. According to this estimate, a tax levy of $290,850 would be ample for all purposes.

The total amount of money expended for the support of the common schools during the year was $2,152,783.15, 74 per cent. of which was for teachers' wages. The number of pupils in attendance was 293,286; of teachers, 9,875; of schoolhouses, 5,626. The estimated value of the schoolhouses is $4,819,445.81; of sites, $738,520.95; of apparatus, $157,012.30; making an aggregate investment for common-school purposes of $5,214,979.06. The total number of children over four and under twenty years of age is reported at 484,353. The expenditures for the four normal schools were $72,-708.07, of which $57,498.40 were paid to instructors. The attendance during the year aggregated 1,803 pupils. The catalogue of the State University shows 481 different students in attendance during the year. The Board of Regents report $70,558.18 paid out during the year for current expenses, of which $40,206.77 were received by instructors.

The whole number of boys in attendance at the Industrial School for Boys, in Waukesha, during the fiscal year, was 435, and the average attendance 425. The number admitted was 125, as against 151 in the last year, and the number discharged 113. The current expenses were $42,866.72, or at the rate of $100.-86 per inmate, as against $114.52 in 1878. The amount paid for salaries and wages was $13,-810.36, and for subsistence $11,097.41. The sum of $13,800 has been paid toward the erection of new buildings. An epidemic of typho-malarial fever broke out in the institution in the summer, which elicited much discussion; the total number of cases was 30, of which 6 terminated fatally.

The number of convicts confined in the State Prison, September 30, 1879, was 309, 37 less than at the same date in 1878. The average number in confinement was 328, 9 less than the average for the preceding year. There were only 130 commitments during the year, as against 213 for the year ending September 30, 1878. It does not follow, however, that there has been a decrease in crime, as, under the change in the law relating to larceny, many are now sentenced to county jails who were formerly sent to State Prison. Of the 130 convicts committed during the year, only 20 had theretofore been in prison, and 17 were without the rudiments of an education. The total cost to feed, warm, clothe, guard, instruct, and discharge the prisoners was $40,270.08, or $2.36 each per week. The principal items of disbursements were: for salaries and wages, $15,535.75, and for subsistence, $14,367.02. The total receipts from all sources were $46,-

619.23; disbursements, $47,183.24; cash balance at the close of the year, $11,090.44. The expenses for the next fiscal year are estimated at $42,825, of which the prisoners' earnings are not expected to pay more than three fourths.

The whole number of children cared for in the Soldiers' Orphans' Home since March 31, 1866, when it was adopted by the State, has been 683, and the total cost to the State has been $342,300.

At the Northern Hospital for the Insane, 757 patients have received treatment, of whom 65 were discharged recovered and 68 improved. The daily average of patients was 553. The total expenditures were $132,452.62, of which $21,985.56 were for additions, repairs, and improvements, leaving as current expenses the sum of $110,467.06, or at the rate of $200 for each patient. The current expenses for the next hospital year are estimated at $122,991.96.

The Wisconsin State Hospital for the Insane has given treatment to 607 patients during the year, and reports 37 discharged cured and 85 discharged improved. The average number under treatment was 425, and the total expenditures were $135,555.82, of which $30,951.83 were for additions, repairs, and improvements, by which the capacity of the hospital has been increased to accommodate 180 additional patients. The current expenses were $104,603.99, an average of $246.12 for each patient. The current expenses for the next hospital year are estimated at $121,550.

At the Institution for the Education of the Blind, 90 pupils were in attendance, the average expense per scholar being $207.26.

At the Institution for the Education of the Deaf and Dumb, 187 names were upon the register at the close of the fiscal year. The total disbursements were $30,318. The articulate system of teaching was introduced with very satisfactory results. The main building of the institution was totally consumed by fire on September 16th.

There were completed 89.90 miles of new railroad in Wisconsin during the year, making the aggregate number of miles in operation 2,923, inclusive of 107 miles of narrow-gauge track. The total number of miles of road operated by the companies reporting to the Commissioner is 4,765. The cost of these roads and their equipments, as represented by capital stock and outstanding bonds, is $205,185,806.-88, and the net earnings are reported at $12,-691,006.90, being an average of 6.2 per cent. on the assumed cost. The total number of passengers carried on all the lines was 5,336,688, and the freight carried amounted to 7,997,399 tons. The number of personal casualties in Wisconsin was 133, as against 196 the previous year. On the entire lines of these roads, in all the States, there were 284 casualties. Two passengers were killed, neither of them in this State, and eight injured.

The condition of the trust funds and of the public lands, as revealed in a review of all the books by the Commissioners of Public Lands, is as follows: The number of acres of land held by the State September 30, 1878, was reported at 1,538,825·07. The increase by forfeiture during the year was 24,051.88; the increase by error in former reports, 27,550·50; the increase from school-land indemnity, 37,-089·09; making the total number of acres 1,627,516·54. The decrease by sales during the year was 52,827·21; leaving 1,574,689·33 acres held by the State, September 30, 1879. The productive trust fund was $4,166,866, an increase over the amount in 1878 of $67,204. The income of the trust funds was $353,241, which is $26,561 more than that of the preceding year.

The National party held their Convention at Watertown on July 15th. Reuben May of Vernon County was made temporary and permanent President. The following candidates for State officers were nominated: For Governor, Reuben May; for Lieutenant-Governor, W. L. Utley; for Secretary of State, George W. Lee; for Treasurer, Peter A. Griffiths; for Attorney-General, George B. Goodwin; for Superintendent of Public Instruction, W. H. Searles. The following resolutions were adopted:

Whereas, A money despotism has grown up which controls the law-making power of our country, dictates judicial decisions, wields an undue influence over the Executive of the nation, in consideration of laws passed for the benefit of the people, thus enabling the money power to carry on its schemes of public plunder, under and from which colossal fortunes have been gathered in the hands of the ambitious and unscrupulous men whose interests are at war with the interests of the people, hostile to popular government, and deaf to the demands of honest toil; therefore, we, the representatives of the Union Greenback-Labor party of Wisconsin, adopt the following as our platform of principles:

Resolved, That we demand the immediate calling in and payment of all United States bonds in full legal-tender money of the United States, gold and silver coin now in the Treasury for redemption purposes, and beyond such metal money in greenback full legal-tender money, to be created, issued, and protected as full legal-tender money of the United States; and that the United States Government never issue another bond of any kind or class.

Resolved, That we demand the abolition of the national banking system, and the prohibition of all banks of issue, either State or national.

Resolved, That the issue of greenback money be limited in value to the sum required to meet the just obligations of the Government, less the sum of coin money in the Treasury for resumption purposes.

Resolved, That we demand unlimited coinage of gold and silver as legal-tender money of the United States.

Resolved, That the rate of interest on money should not exceed the rate of profit derived from the productive industries of the country, and should be fixed by national law.

Resolved, That we denounce and condemn the efforts of both the old parties to create a solid North or a solid South, thereby sectionalizing the country, arraying one section against the other; that we know no North, no South, no East, no West; that we demand the government of our country be so administered as to secure equal rights to all our people, be they high or low, rich or poor, black or white.

Resolved, That convict-labor in our penal institutions be so arranged by law as not to interfere with free labor, and that prison-labor be utilized by the State, with no intermeddling of contractors.

Resolved, That we inflexibly oppose all fusion or coalition with either of the old parties, and invite honest men of all parties to unite with us in the interests of the wealth-producing, tax-paying classes of the United States. •

There were thirty counties represented in the Convention by 130 members.

The Republican State Convention assembled at Madison on July 23d. J. B. Cassidy of Rock County was chosen permanent President. The following State officers were nominated: For Governor, William E. Smith; for Lieutenant-Governor, James M. Bingham; for Secretary of State, Hans B. Warner; for Treasurer, Richard Guenther; for Attorney-General, Alexander Wilson; for Superintendent of Public Instruction, William C. Whitford. The following platform was adopted:

The Republicans of Wisconsin, by their representatives assembled in State Convention, declare their adhesion to the following propositions:

1. The Republic of the United States is a nation, not a confederacy of sovereign States, and its Government is clothed with permanent authority for the regulation of all subjects of national concern.

2. The elections of members of Congress are national elections, and as such the whole country is interested in having them fairly and peacefully conducted, so that every voter may be afforded an opportunity to exercise his right of suffrage freely and without fear of personal violence, to vote once, and only once, at a given election, and to have his vote honestly counted and returned. It is the duty of the national Government to enforce this right. The Republican party is opposed to any military interference with the elections, except when it is necessary to maintain the public peace and protect the constitutional rights of citizens. In no instance under a Republican administration have the United States troops interfered with the exercise of free suffrage on the part of the people. The Democratic party, by the votes of its Representatives in Congress against the proposition to prohibit the presence in the vicinity of the polls, not only of United States troops, but of all men armed with deadly weapons, have clearly shown the bad faith and hypocrisy of its affected horror of bayonets at the polls. It would permit an armed mob of its own partisans to surround the ballot-box, but would prohibit the employment of United States soldiers to protect peaceful citizens from intimidation and violence at the hands of the mob.

3. The refusal of a mere majority in Congress to make appropriations of money already collected by the tax from the people for the ordinary and legitimate expenses of the Government, for the purpose of compelling the President by such refusal to approve a measure which he regards as unwise and wrong, was revolutionary in principle, subversive of the Constitution, and deserving the condemnation of all good citizens.

4. The practice of attaching what are popularly termed political riders to appropriation bills is wicked legislation, and should be prohibited.

5. The thanks and grateful recognition of the people are due to President Hayes, and to the Republican members of Congress, for their firm and successful resistance to the attempts made by the Democratic party to disarm the national Government on election days, and to repeal all the laws for protecting the security of the ballot-box, and providing for the detection and punishment of fraudulent voting.

6. The successful resumption of specie payments has vindicated the wisdom of the Republican policy on that subject, and afforded a signal illustration of the lack of honesty of the statesmanship which led the Democratic party to oppose resumption, and to declare that it was impossible. It has already borne precious fruits in enabling the Government to fund its debt at four per cent. interest, or an economy of many millions per annum, and in promoting a feeling of confidence and security that is already giving a powerful impetus to business and industry and enterprise. The interests of all classes of people are best promoted by a currency possessing or representing intrinsic value, such as we have at present, and bearing a fixed relation to the world's money and that of commerce. All attempts to modify existing laws in a way to introduce a depreciation or fluctuation in the value of the money of the country should meet with a firm and determined resistance.

7. That it is the duty of Congress to enact laws to carry out the provisions of the Constitution with its amendments, and to secure to the people of the States the rights guaranteed by it; and that laws, when enacted, are supreme and must be obeyed and enforced, and the recent attempts of the Democratic Congress to repeal and strike from the statute-books such laws, some of which were placed there by our fathers and have been enforced nearly a century, has no parallel in the history of the country.

8. That our Governor and State officers are entitled to the thanks and approval of the people for their wise and faithful administration of the public trusts committed to them.

The Democratic State Convention met at Madison on September 9th. James R. Doolittle of Racine was chosen President. Alexander Mitchell was nominated for Governor, with the understanding that if he declined the nomination the nominee for Lieutenant-Governor, William J. Vilas, should be substituted in his stead. The latter declined the nomination, and was replaced upon the ticket by George H. King. The remainder of the ticket was made up as follows: For Secretary of State, Samuel Regan; for Treasurer, Andrew Haben; for Attorney-General, J. Montgomery Smith; for Superintendent of Public Instruction, Edward Searing. The platform adopted, besides other resolutions denouncing the rule of the Republicans in the South, condemning the inauguration of President Hayes, and deprecating the dangers of centralization, contained the following:

That the Democratic party adheres to the financial doctrine which it established when in power, that the constitutional currency of the country, and the basis of all other, should be gold and silver coin ; and so we maintain that all national Treasury notes and authorized currency should be convertible into the same on demand.

That the Democracy does not forget that to the promptness, valor, endurance, and noble devotion of the patriotic volunteers of the army and navy in the late war this country is indebted, under Providence, for the salvation of its form of government and the constitutional liberty and prosperity now enjoyed by all its citizens, and again thankfully acknowledges the debt of national and individual gratitude which is due to the living and dead heroes of the nation, an obligation which increases with years, and which entitles the survivors to receive all the marks of appreciation and honor which a grateful people can properly bestow.

That the administration of State affairs ought to be conducted with greater economy, and greater efforts be made to diminish the burden of taxes ; that all official salaries and fees and all expenditures for State charitable, educational, and penal institutions, raised to meet the necessities of high-priced times, must now be correspondingly reduced, and all useless boards and commissions abolished, and that the candidates of this Convention pledge their best endeavors to pursue a course of retrenchment in public expenditures.

We should protect our naturalized citizens as we do our native-born in every part of the civilized world, and we should resist all improper claims upon them by governments to which they no longer owe allegiance.

That as the Democratic party, being founded on those principles which best support the liberty and welfare of the citizen, has hitherto survived all former adversaries, so, by faithful adherence to its time-honored doctrines and the selection of honest and competent men for public offices, it looks forward with abiding confidence to its final and complete triumph over all who now oppose these principles.

The result of the November election was the continuance in office of the Governor, William E. Smith, and the Lieutenant-Governor, James M. Bingham, and the reëlection of the other State officers: Hans B. Warner, Secretary of State; Richard Guenther, Treasurer; Alexan-

der Wilson, Attorney-General; W. C. Whitford, Superintendent of Public Instruction; J. Turner, Railroad Commissioner; P. L. Spooner, Jr., Insurance Commissioner. Owing to the fact that the *ex-officio* State canvassers, the Secretary of State, Treasurer, and Attorney-General, were candidates for office, the Chief Justice, E. G. Ryan, appointed in their stead Judges David W. Small, Alva Stewart, and H. S. Conger. The votes cast for the different gubernatorial candidates were as follows: Smith, Republican, 100,535; Jenkins, Democrat, 75,-080; May, Greenback, 12,996; Bloomfield, Temperance, 387; electing Governor Smith by a plurality of 25,505 votes. The composition of the Legislature of 1879 was as follows: Senate—Republicans 25, Democrats 8; Assembly —Republicans 70, Democrats 27, Greenbackers 2, Independent 1. The next election takes place November 2, 1880.

Z

ZOOLOOS, a branch of the Caffres, residing in southeastern Africa. According to A. H. Keane, in his treatise appended to Keith Johnston's "Africa," the Caffres form a branch of the great "Bantu" family. To this family also belong the Matabele and other Betchuana populations of the interior, near the Zambesi, and in the regions visited by Dr. Livingstone in his earlier travels, and even the Suaheli and Wanyamwesi of the coast opposite Zanzibar and the Tanganyika region, and the nations inhabiting the shores of the Mozambique Channel. They are not negroes in the proper sense of the word, but East Africans. Their color is not black, but a dark brown; their eyes are black and brilliant; the hair is not so woolly as that of the negroes, and their features are of an Eastern type. The Caffres in southeastern Africa are divided into three distinct groups: the Amaxoso, located in British Caffraria or the Trans-Kei Territory, and including the Galekas and Gaikas, the Tembus, and the Pondos of St. John's River; the Basutos, who inhabit the country beyond the Drakenberg range; and the Zooloos, who are almost equal in number to all others put together. The Zooloos, numbering about 600,000, are almost equally divided between those living under British rule in the province of Natal and those forming the independent native kingdom to the north of Natal known as Zoolooland, of which Cetywayo or Ketchwayo was the ruler.

Zoolooland is bounded on the north by the country of the Amatongas, on the east by the Indian Ocean, on the southwest by Natal, and on the west by the Transvaal. Its area is about 15,000 square miles, and its population 300,000. The seacoast is low and flat, differing in this respect essentially from the shores of British Caffraria about the St. John's River, which abound with beautiful wooded hills and grassy

downs. The coast-line is indented by a series of lagoons and marshes, which tend to make the neighborhood decidedly unhealthy. About fifteen miles from the sea the land begins to rise in terraces, which are covered with rich grass, and are followed by two or three mountain-ranges successively, one above another. The principal river of Zoolooland is the Umvolosi, which empties into the Indian Ocean at St. Lucia Bay. It is formed by the confluence of two mountain-streams, the Black and White Umvolosi, near the center of Zoolooland. The border with Natal is formed by the Tugela River, and farther up by the Buffalo River, while in the north the most important is the Pongolo River. Between the Umvolosi and the Tugela are a number of smaller streams. The banks of the rivers are for the most part thickly wooded, or at least covered with thick bush, while the lower plains, where they are not swampy, are covered with scrub. The country is not subject to drought in any season. The rivers, which in summer are greatly swollen by the heavy rains in the highlands, dwindle away in the winter, from March to September, becoming insignificant streams, with here and there a deeper pool. There is no malaria in the hilly districts on the side toward Natal; but the lower parts are dangerous alike to man and beast, and the jungle is then infested by the tzetze fly, whose bite is fatal to horses and oxen.

The word Zooloo in the native language means heaven. The history of the Zooloo kingdom begins with Chaka, who was born in 1787. As his mother had fled with him from his father's kraal to the Umtetwas, a neighboring coast tribe, he was educated by the chieftain's orders, and here he learned all the Caffre accomplishments as a prince and a warrior. It was here that he met some English sailors who had been cast ashore in St. Lucia Bay, who told him of the deeds of Napoleon, then at the height of his power in Europe. Young Chaka listened attentively, and resolved to become the African Napoleon. Upon the death of his father he became ruling chief after turning out one of his half-brothers. A large portion of the Umtetwas, desiring a more warlike policy than that of their own ruler, joined the Zooloos. Chaka now entered upon an unchecked career of conquest. The whole male population of the Zooloo nation was subject to compulsory military service. He created an imperial guard of twelve or fifteen thousand prime warriors, who were kept ready at an hour's notice to march fifty miles in any direction without a halt, and to destroy a town, a chief, or a tribe in two or three days. He built numerous fortified kraals to be occupied as permanent camps by as many regiments of his army. The troops were drilled in a system of manœuvres not before practiced by African soldiers. By these means he succeeded in establishing the most formidable military power that has been wielded in modern times by any native African monarch. With this power he conquered all the surrounding countries, extending his sway from the Limpopo in the north to the St. John's River in the south. There were few or no Europeans in those parts. As for the natives, they were either entirely destroyed—the work of extermination being carried on so successfully that when the Dutch Boers came to Natal, in 1837, they found that country quite empty—or he obliged the conquered nations to take the name Zooloo, and to form part of the new compact and rigidly governed nation over which he ruled. The people of various tribes were divided up, and distributed here and there, in order to efface their original connections. Fifty or sixty tribes were thus dealt with in the course of Chaka's reign, and of these about forty have been resuscitated to a certain degree by collecting their survivors under British protection in Natal. His reign, as may be readily conceived, was marked by the most unheard-of cruelties, whole regiments with their wives and children being massacred in punishment for having suffered defeat. It was one of these outbursts of cruelty that cost Chaka his life. A regiment which he had sent out against one

of his neighbors having been unsuccessful, he determined to punish them by murdering some two thousand wives they had left at home. Among these were the wives of two of his brothers, Dingaan and Umhlangane, and they in revenge hired one of his attendants to murder Chaka. This deed was performed on September 23, 1828, and Dingaan, having murdered his other brother a few days after, ascended the throne. His reign from 1828 to 1840 was different from that of Chaka, inasmuch as he did not pretend to be a great warrior. But his government at home was cruelly tyrannical, and large numbers of his miserable subjects fled the kingdom to escape its merciless law, thousands going to Natal, where the British coast settlement at Durban had been founded in 1835. In 1838 the Boers came to the country, and a terrible massacre of them took place. For a time Dingaan was even successful against the Dutch and British in Natal and on the Orange and Vaal Rivers; but in February, 1840, he was disastrously defeated and killed. This defeat was mostly due to the defection of his brother Panda, who now ascended the throne and ruled until 1872. The rule of Panda was, according to Sir Theophilus Shepstone, "incomparably milder and more merciful" than that of Dingaan, which was principally due to the influence of the Dutch Boers. During his entire reign he regarded them with "feelings of grateful attachment and loyalty." His kingdom was tolerably quiet, as the systematic despotism established by his predecessors had effectually suppressed all internal disaffection, while the new European colonists on his borders were contented to let him alone. The history of Panda's relations with his neighbors is the same as that of the Boers and of the different British provinces of South Africa. Upon his death in 1872 he was succeeded by his son Cetywayo, who was installed by Sir Theophilus Shepstone, the Secretary for Native Affairs of Natal. King Cetywayo, upon whose accession great hopes had been built, early showed that he was animated by the same sanguinary and despotic spirit as his predecessors Chaka and Dingaan, and he soon came into conflict with his neighbors, which eventually resulted in war. (For an account of these difficulties and the war, see CAPE COLONY.)

INDEX OF SUBJECTS.

INDEX OF CONTENTS.

the discretion of investigating committees the question of public or secret sessions, 205 ; a second amendment requiring open sessions rejected, 206 ; the amended resolutions, 206 ; denunciation of roving investigating commissions, 206 ; the resolutions agreed to, 207.

In the Senate, text of the bill to regulate the counting of Presidential vote, 207, 208 ; the Constitution on the subject, 208 ; the right to appoint electors inheres in the individual States, 208, 209 ; after the electors are selected in the manner determined by the Legislature a State has no control over their action, 210 ; they are then officers of the United States, 210 ; the bill defines the mode of procedure in the legitimate action of Congress regarding the count, 210 ; the power of counting and determining the validity of electoral votes not a function of the President of the Senate, 211 ; every executive act implies an exercise of judgment, 211 ; the bill assumes that a power of authenticating the votes rests with the two Houses of Congress, but does not define its extent, 212 ; the procedure in the case of imperfect or conflicting returns, 213 ; action upon objections of members of both Houses to counting a vote, 213 ; it is competent to the States to settle election disputes in their own tribunals, 213 ; the language of the bill offers an opportunity to fraudulently disqualify a proper return, 213 ; evil of leaving the country in suspense as to the actual results of an election, 214, 215 ; two rules for returns according as they are or are not adjudicated upon in the States, 216 ; danger of allowing a Senator and a Representative to challenge returns, 216 ; legislation on the subject unconstitutional, 216 ; the language of the Constitution clear and conclusive, 217 ; a joint rule all that is called for, 217 ; improbable that the deciding power was delegated to the President of the Senate, 218 ; the motive of the bill to confirm the rights of States to legitimate electors, 218 ; the bill passed, 218.

In the House, text of a bill to restrict Chinese immigration, 218 ; Congressional legislation can rescind treaty obligations, 219 ; the courts upon the subject, 219, 224 ; previous efforts to prevent the influx of Chinamen, 219 ; defects of the Burlingame treaty, 220 ; hardship of Chinese competition, 220 ; memorial of Californian workingmen, 220, 221 ; case of special pledges not to legislate on a treaty, 222 ; the bill passed, 222 ; the Chinese bill in the Senate, 222 ; amendment providing for a new treaty with China, 222 ; only a question of expediency, 222 ; bad faith of abrogating the treaty, 223 ; amendment lost, 223 ; passage of the bill, 224 ; veto message of the President, 224–226 ; failure of the House to pass the Chinese bill over the veto, 226.

In the House, the army appropriation bill, 226 ; the question in previous Congress of attaching general measures to appropriation bills, 227 ; the action of the special sessions, 228 ; the question of reorganization and economy and the *posse comitatus* clause, 228 ; the latter should be revised, not repealed, 229 ; section 2002 of the Revised Statutes on "keeping the peace at the polls," 229 ; the British statute forbidding the presence of soldiers at elections, 229 ; provisions of British mutiny act, 230 ; amendments of sections 2002 and 5528 of the Revised Statutes attached to the appropriation bill, 230 ; struck out in the Senate, 230 ; the clause allowing troops at the polls a war measure dangerous to popular liberty, 231 ; previous conference negotiations on the measures in dispute, 232 ; time enough for the proposed legislation in the next Congress, 232 ; the obnoxious laws were directed against interference with elections, 233 ; they have not prevented free elections, 233 ; Republicans accused of legislative filibustering, 233 ; the bill fails to pass, 234.

In the House, the legislative, executive, and judicial

appropriation bill, 234 ; amendment abolishing and refusing pay to deputy marshals and supervisors of elections, 284 ; Democratic interests involved in the measure, 234 ; Republican arraignment of the Democratic party, 235 ; limited suffrage in Rhode Island, 285 ; Democratic counter-charges, 285 ; the colored vote not the property of the Republican party, 236 ; it is time that war measures were repealed, 236 ; Davenport's arrests of voters in New York, 236, 287 ; the act decided illegal in the case of a duly naturalized citizen, 287 ; dangers of similar arrests to defeat fair elections, 238 ; three propositions contained in the amendments, 238 ; removing the limitations on jury-panels, 238 ; making jury-trial political, 238 ; destroying the safeguards of the ballot-box, 238 ; demanded by the South, 238 ; the laws to be repealed obnoxious to the constitutional sovereignty of the States, 239 ; the statute conferring the powers of marshals and deputies at elections, 239 ; its tyranny, 239 ; the demanded repeal not a Southern measure, 240 ; Republican determination to uphold the laws, and Democratic responsibility for the emergency of an extra session, 240 ; arbitrary power and acts of marshals adduced, 241 ; Democratic declaration that appropriations shall be withheld until the grievances are redressed, 241 ; the amendment carried, 241 ; the second amendment appointing a commissioner of opposite politics from the clerk of a court to select half the names to be drawn for juries, 241 ; amendment carried, 242 ; the next amendment, abolishing supervisors and deputy marshals, carried, 242 ; the bill passed with the amendments, 242 ; the bill and amendments in the senate, 243 ; the clause requiring jurors to be drawn from both parties stricken out, 244 ; a conference committee, 244 ; no agreement on the repeal of the juror's test-oath, 244 ; nor on the repeal of the laws appointing marshals and deputies, 245 ; the evil effects of these laws, 245 ; impossible for the House majority to recede from their position, 246 ; the evils of an extra session, 246 ; a bill already passed by the Senate repealing the test-oath, 247 ; Democrats charged with the purpose of precipitating an extra session, 247 ; answer that a motion to suspend the rules and pass the repeal measures was defeated by a solid Republican vote, 247 ; the Speaker's adjournment speech, 247 ; review of the conference presented to the Senate, 248 ; Democratic agreement that if an extra session should be necessary separate bills embodying the repeal measures should be immediately brought forward, 248 ; the Senate refuse to withdraw from their position, 249.

Extra Session.—The President's proclamation calling an extra session, 249 ; his message defining its objects, 249 ; list of Senators and Representatives of the Forty-sixth Congress, 249–251.

In the House, bill making appropriations for the army presented, 251 ; the same bill that was considered in the regular session, 251 ; the clauses forbidding the presence of troops at the polls, 251 ; the calling out of troops to suppress insurrection different from keeping peace at the polls, 251 ; a marshal calls for troops as a *posse comitatus*, not as the army, 252 ; no such use of troops known until after the war, 252 ; the import of the repealing clauses, 252 ; let the vestiges of the war be effaced, 252 ; Congress may declare that the Executive shall not use the army for a particular purpose, 252 ; the law which it is desired to amend was originally introduced by a Democrat, 253 ; the words "to keep the peace at the polls" were added as an amendment, 253 ; the amendment was accepted by the Democrats, 253 ; not approved, as alleged, by eminent Democrats, 254 ; the custom of appending general measures to appropriation bills inaugurated by a Republican Congress, 254 ; Republican coercive measures in 1856

874; the votes canvassed by order of the Court, 375; the Supreme Court asserts its jurisdiction in the matter, and decides on alleged irregularities in returns, 375; a county return must not be thrown out because the vote of a single poll has not been received or included, 375; a mandamus to compel the Governor to issue a certificate of election, having already granted it to another candidate, 375; his official acts not subject to the control of the Court, 376; the law on requisitions for fugitives from justice, 376; the juror's test-oath decided to be void and unconstitutional by the United States Supreme Court, 876; another decision to the effect that the oath can be required only by the district attorney, 377; detailed crop returns of 1877, 877; the State Prison, 877; a ship-canal scheme, 877, 378; Indians, 378; education, 878.

FLOYD, SALLY BUCHANAN.—Biographical sketch, 379.

FOLEY, Bishop THOMAS.—Life and clerical services, 379.

Formation of Mountains.—Problems connected with mountain upheavals, 379; experiments on the compression of a plastic material, 880; various conditions of the earth's contraction reproduced, 881.

FOSTER, CHARLES.—Representative from Ohio, 198; on the army appropriation bill, 281, 282.

France.—Members of the Government, 881; movement of population, 881; marriage statistics, 881; area, population in 1872 and 1876, and vital statistics by departments, 883; vital statistics for a series of years, 884; revenue and expenditure, 384; the army under the new army law, 884; strength of the army in peace and on a war footing, 884; the navy, 884; commerce for a succession of years, 885; commerce by countries, 885; the classes of commodities for two years, 385; shipping, 835; railroads and telegraphs, 835; savings-banks, 885; area and population of colonies, 886; the new Cabinet, 886; biographical sketches of members, 886; elections for the Senate, 887; sessions of the Chambers, 387; official changes and the appointment of Republicans demanded, 887; MacMahon signs the dismissals in the departments, but refuses to remove army generals, 887; he resigns, 888; his letter of resignation, 888; Grévy elected President of the Republic by the Chambers, 888; the new President's message, 888; Gambetta's speech as President of the Chamber, 888; text of the amnesty bill, 889; passage of the same, 389; Marcère resigns the portfolio of the Interior, 389; debate on the impeachment of the De Broglie Ministry, 889; a vote of condemnation instead, 890; Ferry's bill on higher education, 890; the bill reorganizing the Supreme Council, 890; number of Jesuit colleges, 890; the question of Blanqui's pardon, 891; the Cassagnac episode, 891; the return of the Chambers to Paris debated and voted, 891; the Ferry bill passed, 892; increase of the Jesuits and the schools of unauthorized religious bodies, 892; the first meeting of the Chambers in Paris, 892; Gambetta's opening speech, 892; radicals charge the Government with slowness in amnestying the Communards, 893; the number of pardons and commutations granted and the number of political offenders still under sentence, 893; the Waddington Ministers resign, and Freycinet forms a Cabinet, 894; the question of the Napoleonic succession, 894; Legitimist banquets, 394.

FREYCINET, CHARLES LOUIS DE SAULCES DE.—French statesman, 894; life and career, 894.

FRIEDBERG, Dr. HEINRICH.—Prussian Minister of Justice, biographical notice, 740.

Friends.—A missionary society established, 395; the English Yearly Meeting, 395; English First-day schools, 395; missions, 396; Irish Friends, 396.

G.

GAMBETTA.—Elected President of the French Chamber, 888.

GARFIELD, JAMES A.—Representative from Ohio, 198, 251; on the army appropriation bill, 232, 233.

GARRISON, WILLIAM LLOYD.—Birth and education, 896; his antislavery agitation, 896; his extremism, 397; abolitionists mobbed, 897; the Liberty party, 897; end of the Antislavery Society, 398.

Geographical Progress and Discovery.—The field of exploration, 808; exploration of the Pamir, 899; the identity of the Sanpoo and Brahmapootra established, 899; the outlet of Lake Abistada, 400; western Thibet, 400; products and people, 400; the Hunias and Bhotias, 400; prospects of trans-Himalayan trade, 401; the French Ogowé expedition, 401, 402; new negro tribes encountered, 402; exploring a route to Nyassa, 402; discoveries in the Congo basin, 403; social and political conditions of the Matabeli, 403; civilized Bamangwato, 403; the kingdoms of South Central Africa described, 404; Serpa Pinto, 405; start of the Portuguese expedition, 405; the plain where the great rivers rise, 405; a white negro race, 406; other new tribes, 406; deserted in mid-Africa, 407; the fall of the Makololos, 407; the banks of the Zambesi, 407; the question of the Cubango, 407; a great salt-basin, 407; puzzling fluvial phenomenon, 408; Pinto emerges at Natal, 408; D'Albertis on New Guinea, 408-410; his first visit, 408; his sojourn on Yule Island, 409; his voyages of exploration up Fly River, 409; deserted and attacked by savages, 410; the products of New Guinea, 410; the Papuans, 411; Arctic explorations, 411-417; Nordenskjöld's search for the northeast passage, 411; the Vega's winter-quarters, 411; Arctic flora, 412; ice-locked, 412; Tchuktche villages, 412; thermometric table, 412; the aurora borealis, 412; tidal observations, 412; Arctic insects, birds, and mammals, 413; frost-proof garments, 414; meteorological and thermometrical observations, 414; conclusions regarding the value of the discovered route, 415; released from the icy prison, 415; character of the coast, 415; scientific observations at St. Lawrence Bay, 415; on the American shore, 416; on Behring Island, 416; arrival at Yokohama, 416; Dutch expedition to Franz-Josef Land, 417; Captain Markham's cruise in Barents Sea, 417; voyage of the Jeannette, 417; search for the Franklin relics, 417.

Geology, Experimental.—Artificial production of quartz, 417; conclusions obtained from Roman coins found in hot springs, 418; problem of the origin of limestone formations, 418; lithium in the ocean, 419; problem of the interior of the earth, 419.

Georgia.—Reopening of the Legislature, 420; railroad regulation bill, 420; local option, 421; reorganization of the militia, 421; the crime of lobbying, 421; frauds in the sale of wild lands for taxes, 421, 422; impeachment of the Comptroller-General, 422; indictment of the State Treasurer, 428; minority report in his favor, 424; the Treasurer offers his resignation, 425; he is impeached, 425; his acquittal, 425; legal proceedings against him, 425; charges against the keeper of the penitentiary, 425; the School Commissioner investigated, 426; finances of the State, 426; opinion of the Revenue Commissioner as to whether State bonds passed by banks in payment of checks are taxable as bills of credit, 426; tax valuation, 426; the colored university, 427; law of murder altered, 427; the system of hiring out convicts, 427; sheep-raising, 427, 428; the turpentine industry, 428; gold-mining, 428; ice-manufacture, 429; commerce of Savannah, 429; the question of State liability for the war levy, 429.

Germany.—Imperial family and ministry, 429; composition of the Federal Council, 429; area, population, and representation of the states, 430; rulers of the particular states, 430; the Brunswick ducal succession, 431; emigration from North Sea ports since 1832, 431; movement

Lightning Source UK Ltd.
Milton Keynes UK
UKHW012134180219
337529UK00012B/1377/P